Oxford Dictionary of
National Biography

Volume 57

Oxford Dictionary of National Biography

IN ASSOCIATION WITH
The British Academy

From the earliest times to the year 2000

Edited by
H. C. G. Matthew
and
Brian Harrison

Volume 57
Walliers–Welles

OXFORD
UNIVERSITY PRESS

OXFORD
UNIVERSITY PRESS

Great Clarendon Street, Oxford OX2 6DP

Oxford University Press is a department of the University of Oxford.
It furthers the University's objective of excellence in research, scholarship,
and education by publishing worldwide in

Oxford New York

Auckland Bangkok Buenos Aires Cape Town
Chennai Dar es Salaam Delhi Hong Kong Istanbul Karachi
Kolkata Kuala Lumpur Madrid Melbourne Mexico City Mumbai Nairobi
São Paulo Shanghai Taipei Tokyo Toronto

Oxford is a registered trade mark of Oxford University Press
in the UK and in certain other countries

Published in the United States
by Oxford University Press Inc., New York

British Library Cataloguing in Publication Data
Data available

Library of Congress Cataloging in Publication Data
Data available: for details see volume 1, p. iv

ISBN 0-19-861407-1 (this volume)
ISBN 0-19-861411-X (set of sixty volumes)

Text captured by Alliance Phototypesetters, Pondicherry
Illustrations reproduced and archived by
Alliance Graphics Ltd, UK
Typeset in OUP Swift by Interactive Sciences Limited, Gloucester
Printed in Great Britain on acid-free paper by
Butler and Tanner Ltd,
Frome, Somerset

LIST OF ABBREVIATIONS

1 *General abbreviations*

AB	bachelor of arts
ABC	Australian Broadcasting Corporation
ABC TV	ABC Television
act.	active
A$	Australian dollar
AD	*anno domini*
AFC	Air Force Cross
AIDS	acquired immune deficiency syndrome
AK	Alaska
AL	Alabama
A level	advanced level [examination]
ALS	associate of the Linnean Society
AM	master of arts
AMICE	associate member of the Institution of Civil Engineers
ANZAC	Australian and New Zealand Army Corps
appx *pl.* appxs	appendix(es)
AR	Arkansas
ARA	associate of the Royal Academy
ARCA	associate of the Royal College of Art
ARCM	associate of the Royal College of Music
ARCO	associate of the Royal College of Organists
ARIBA	associate of the Royal Institute of British Architects
ARP	air-raid precautions
ARRC	associate of the Royal Red Cross
ARSA	associate of the Royal Scottish Academy
art.	article / item
ASC	Army Service Corps
Asch	Austrian Schilling
ASDIC	Antisubmarine Detection Investigation Committee
ATS	Auxiliary Territorial Service
ATV	Associated Television
Aug	August
AZ	Arizona
b.	born
BA	bachelor of arts
BA (Admin.)	bachelor of arts (administration)
BAFTA	British Academy of Film and Television Arts
BAO	bachelor of arts in obstetrics
bap.	baptized
BBC	British Broadcasting Corporation / Company
BC	before Christ
BCE	before the common (*or* Christian) era
BCE	bachelor of civil engineering
BCG	bacillus of Calmette and Guérin [inoculation against tuberculosis]
BCh	bachelor of surgery
BChir	bachelor of surgery
BCL	bachelor of civil law

BCnL	bachelor of canon law
BCom	bachelor of commerce
BD	bachelor of divinity
BEd	bachelor of education
BEng	bachelor of engineering
bk *pl.* bks	book(s)
BL	bachelor of law / letters / literature
BLitt	bachelor of letters
BM	bachelor of medicine
BMus	bachelor of music
BP	before present
BP	British Petroleum
Bros.	Brothers
BS	(1) bachelor of science; (2) bachelor of surgery; (3) British standard
BSc	bachelor of science
BSc (Econ.)	bachelor of science (economics)
BSc (Eng.)	bachelor of science (engineering)
bt	baronet
BTh	bachelor of theology
bur.	buried
C.	command [identifier for published parliamentary papers]
c.	*circa*
c.	*capitulum pl. capitula*: chapter(s)
CA	California
Cantab.	Cantabrigiensis
cap.	*capitulum pl. capitula*: chapter(s)
CB	companion of the Bath
CBE	commander of the Order of the British Empire
CBS	Columbia Broadcasting System
cc	cubic centimetres
C$	Canadian dollar
CD	compact disc
Cd	command [identifier for published parliamentary papers]
CE	Common (*or* Christian) Era
cent.	century
cf.	compare
CH	Companion of Honour
chap.	chapter
ChB	bachelor of surgery
CI	Imperial Order of the Crown of India
CIA	Central Intelligence Agency
CID	Criminal Investigation Department
CIE	companion of the Order of the Indian Empire
Cie	Compagnie
CLit	companion of literature
CM	master of surgery
cm	centimetre(s)

Cmd	command [identifier for published parliamentary papers]		edn	edition
CMG	companion of the Order of St Michael and St George		EEC	European Economic Community
			EFTA	European Free Trade Association
Cmnd	command [identifier for published parliamentary papers]		EICS	East India Company Service
			EMI	Electrical and Musical Industries (Ltd)
CO	Colorado		Eng.	English
Co.	company		enl.	enlarged
co.	county		ENSA	Entertainments National Service Association
col. *pl.* cols.	column(s)		ep. *pl.* epp.	*epistola(e)*
Corp.	corporation		ESP	extra-sensory perception
CSE	certificate of secondary education		esp.	especially
CSI	companion of the Order of the Star of India		esq.	esquire
CT	Connecticut		est.	estimate / estimated
CVO	commander of the Royal Victorian Order		EU	European Union
cwt	hundredweight		ex	sold by (*lit.* out of)
$	(American) dollar		excl.	excludes / excluding
d.	(1) penny (pence); (2) died		exh.	exhibited
DBE	dame commander of the Order of the British Empire		exh. cat.	exhibition catalogue
			f. *pl.* ff.	following [pages]
DCH	diploma in child health		FA	Football Association
DCh	doctor of surgery		FACP	fellow of the American College of Physicians
DCL	doctor of civil law		facs.	facsimile
DCnL	doctor of canon law		FANY	First Aid Nursing Yeomanry
DCVO	dame commander of the Royal Victorian Order		FBA	fellow of the British Academy
			FBI	Federation of British Industries
DD	doctor of divinity		FCS	fellow of the Chemical Society
DE	Delaware		Feb	February
Dec	December		FEng	fellow of the Fellowship of Engineering
dem.	demolished		FFCM	fellow of the Faculty of Community Medicine
DEng	doctor of engineering		FGS	fellow of the Geological Society
des.	destroyed		fig.	figure
DFC	Distinguished Flying Cross		FIMechE	fellow of the Institution of Mechanical Engineers
DipEd	diploma in education			
DipPsych	diploma in psychiatry		FL	Florida
diss.	dissertation		*fl.*	*floruit*
DL	deputy lieutenant		FLS	fellow of the Linnean Society
DLitt	doctor of letters		FM	frequency modulation
DLittCelt	doctor of Celtic letters		fol. *pl.* fols.	folio(s)
DM	(1) Deutschmark; (2) doctor of medicine; (3) doctor of musical arts		Fr	French francs
			Fr.	French
DMus	doctor of music		FRAeS	fellow of the Royal Aeronautical Society
DNA	dioxyribonucleic acid		FRAI	fellow of the Royal Anthropological Institute
doc.	document		FRAM	fellow of the Royal Academy of Music
DOL	doctor of oriental learning		FRAS	(1) fellow of the Royal Asiatic Society; (2) fellow of the Royal Astronomical Society
DPH	diploma in public health			
DPhil	doctor of philosophy		FRCM	fellow of the Royal College of Music
DPM	diploma in psychological medicine		FRCO	fellow of the Royal College of Organists
DSC	Distinguished Service Cross		FRCOG	fellow of the Royal College of Obstetricians and Gynaecologists
DSc	doctor of science			
DSc (Econ.)	doctor of science (economics)		FRCP(C)	fellow of the Royal College of Physicians of Canada
DSc (Eng.)	doctor of science (engineering)			
DSM	Distinguished Service Medal		FRCP (Edin.)	fellow of the Royal College of Physicians of Edinburgh
DSO	companion of the Distinguished Service Order			
			FRCP (Lond.)	fellow of the Royal College of Physicians of London
DSocSc	doctor of social science			
DTech	doctor of technology		FRCPath	fellow of the Royal College of Pathologists
DTh	doctor of theology		FRCPsych	fellow of the Royal College of Psychiatrists
DTM	diploma in tropical medicine		FRCS	fellow of the Royal College of Surgeons
DTMH	diploma in tropical medicine and hygiene		FRGS	fellow of the Royal Geographical Society
DU	doctor of the university		FRIBA	fellow of the Royal Institute of British Architects
DUniv	doctor of the university		FRICS	fellow of the Royal Institute of Chartered Surveyors
dwt	pennyweight			
EC	European Community		FRS	fellow of the Royal Society
ed. *pl.* eds.	edited / edited by / editor(s)		FRSA	fellow of the Royal Society of Arts
Edin.	Edinburgh			

FRSCM	fellow of the Royal School of Church Music	ISO	companion of the Imperial Service Order
FRSE	fellow of the Royal Society of Edinburgh	It.	Italian
FRSL	fellow of the Royal Society of Literature	ITA	Independent Television Authority
FSA	fellow of the Society of Antiquaries	ITV	Independent Television
ft	foot *pl.* feet	Jan	January
FTCL	fellow of Trinity College of Music, London	JP	justice of the peace
ft-lb per min.	foot-pounds per minute [unit of horsepower]	jun.	junior
FZS	fellow of the Zoological Society	KB	knight of the Order of the Bath
GA	Georgia	KBE	knight commander of the Order of the British Empire
GBE	knight or dame grand cross of the Order of the British Empire	KC	king's counsel
GCB	knight grand cross of the Order of the Bath	kcal	kilocalorie
GCE	general certificate of education	KCB	knight commander of the Order of the Bath
GCH	knight grand cross of the Royal Guelphic Order	KCH	knight commander of the Royal Guelphic Order
GCHQ	government communications headquarters	KCIE	knight commander of the Order of the Indian Empire
GCIE	knight grand commander of the Order of the Indian Empire	KCMG	knight commander of the Order of St Michael and St George
GCMG	knight or dame grand cross of the Order of St Michael and St George	KCSI	knight commander of the Order of the Star of India
GCSE	general certificate of secondary education	KCVO	knight commander of the Royal Victorian Order
GCSI	knight grand commander of the Order of the Star of India	keV	kilo-electron-volt
GCStJ	bailiff or dame grand cross of the order of St John of Jerusalem	KG	knight of the Order of the Garter
		KGB	[Soviet committee of state security]
GCVO	knight or dame grand cross of the Royal Victorian Order	KH	knight of the Royal Guelphic Order
		KLM	Koninklijke Luchtvaart Maatschappij (Royal Dutch Air Lines)
GEC	General Electric Company	km	kilometre(s)
Ger.	German	KP	knight of the Order of St Patrick
GI	government (*or* general) issue	KS	Kansas
GMT	Greenwich mean time	KT	knight of the Order of the Thistle
GP	general practitioner	kt	knight
GPU	[Soviet special police unit]	KY	Kentucky
GSO	general staff officer	£	pound(s) sterling
Heb.	Hebrew	£E	Egyptian pound
HEICS	Honourable East India Company Service	L	lira *pl.* lire
HI	Hawaii	l. *pl.* ll.	line(s)
HIV	human immunodeficiency virus	LA	Lousiana
HK$	Hong Kong dollar	LAA	light anti-aircraft
HM	his / her majesty('s)	LAH	licentiate of the Apothecaries' Hall, Dublin
HMAS	his / her majesty's Australian ship	Lat.	Latin
HMNZS	his / her majesty's New Zealand ship	lb	pound(s), unit of weight
HMS	his / her majesty's ship	LDS	licence in dental surgery
HMSO	His / Her Majesty's Stationery Office	*lit.*	literally
HMV	His Master's Voice	LittB	bachelor of letters
Hon.	Honourable	LittD	doctor of letters
hp	horsepower	LKQCPI	licentiate of the King and Queen's College of Physicians, Ireland
hr	hour(s)	LLA	lady literate in arts
HRH	his / her royal highness	LLB	bachelor of laws
HTV	Harlech Television	LLD	doctor of laws
IA	Iowa	LLM	master of laws
ibid.	*ibidem*: in the same place	LM	licentiate in midwifery
ICI	Imperial Chemical Industries (Ltd)	LP	long-playing record
ID	Idaho	LRAM	licentiate of the Royal Academy of Music
IL	Illinois	LRCP	licentiate of the Royal College of Physicians
illus.	illustration	LRCPS (Glasgow)	licentiate of the Royal College of Physicians and Surgeons of Glasgow
illustr.	illustrated		
IN	Indiana	LRCS	licentiate of the Royal College of Surgeons
in.	inch(es)	LSA	licentiate of the Society of Apothecaries
Inc.	Incorporated	LSD	lysergic acid diethylamide
incl.	includes / including	LVO	lieutenant of the Royal Victorian Order
IOU	I owe you	M. *pl.* MM.	Monsieur *pl.* Messieurs
IQ	intelligence quotient	m	metre(s)
Ir£	Irish pound		
IRA	Irish Republican Army		

m. *pl.* mm.	membrane(s)
MA	(1) Massachusetts; (2) master of arts
MAI	master of engineering
MB	bachelor of medicine
MBA	master of business administration
MBE	member of the Order of the British Empire
MC	Military Cross
MCC	Marylebone Cricket Club
MCh	master of surgery
MChir	master of surgery
MCom	master of commerce
MD	(1) doctor of medicine; (2) Maryland
MDMA	methylenedioxymethamphetamine
ME	Maine
MEd	master of education
MEng	master of engineering
MEP	member of the European parliament
MG	Morris Garages
MGM	Metro-Goldwyn-Mayer
Mgr	Monsignor
MI	(1) Michigan; (2) military intelligence
MI1c	[secret intelligence department]
MI5	[military intelligence department]
MI6	[secret intelligence department]
MI9	[secret escape service]
MICE	member of the Institution of Civil Engineers
MIEE	member of the Institution of Electrical Engineers
min.	minute(s)
Mk	mark
ML	(1) licentiate of medicine; (2) master of laws
MLitt	master of letters
Mlle	Mademoiselle
mm	millimetre(s)
Mme	Madame
MN	Minnesota
MO	Missouri
MOH	medical officer of health
MP	member of parliament
m.p.h.	miles per hour
MPhil	master of philosophy
MRCP	member of the Royal College of Physicians
MRCS	member of the Royal College of Surgeons
MRCVS	member of the Royal College of Veterinary Surgeons
MRIA	member of the Royal Irish Academy
MS	(1) master of science; (2) Mississippi
MS *pl.* MSS	manuscript(s)
MSc	master of science
MSc (Econ.)	master of science (economics)
MT	Montana
MusB	bachelor of music
MusBac	bachelor of music
MusD	doctor of music
MV	motor vessel
MVO	member of the Royal Victorian Order
n. *pl.* nn.	note(s)
NAAFI	Navy, Army, and Air Force Institutes
NASA	National Aeronautics and Space Administration
NATO	North Atlantic Treaty Organization
NBC	National Broadcasting Corporation
NC	North Carolina
NCO	non-commissioned officer
ND	North Dakota
n.d.	no date
NE	Nebraska
nem. con.	*nemine contradicente*: unanimously
new ser.	new series
NH	New Hampshire
NHS	National Health Service
NJ	New Jersey
NKVD	[Soviet people's commissariat for internal affairs]
NM	New Mexico
nm	nanometre(s)
no. *pl.* nos.	number(s)
Nov	November
n.p.	no place [of publication]
NS	new style
NV	Nevada
NY	New York
NZBS	New Zealand Broadcasting Service
OBE	officer of the Order of the British Empire
obit.	obituary
Oct	October
OCTU	officer cadets training unit
OECD	Organization for Economic Co-operation and Development
OEEC	Organization for European Economic Co-operation
OFM	order of Friars Minor [Franciscans]
OFMCap	Ordine Frati Minori Cappucini: member of the Capuchin order
OH	Ohio
OK	Oklahoma
O level	ordinary level [examination]
OM	Order of Merit
OP	order of Preachers [Dominicans]
op. *pl.* opp.	opus *pl.* opera
OPEC	Organization of Petroleum Exporting Countries
OR	Oregon
orig.	original
OS	old style
OSB	Order of St Benedict
OTC	Officers' Training Corps
OWS	Old Watercolour Society
Oxon.	Oxoniensis
p. *pl.* pp.	page(s)
PA	Pennsylvania
p.a.	per annum
para.	paragraph
PAYE	pay as you earn
pbk *pl.* pbks	paperback(s)
per.	[during the] period
PhD	doctor of philosophy
pl.	(1) plate(s); (2) plural
priv. coll.	private collection
pt *pl.* pts	part(s)
pubd	published
PVC	polyvinyl chloride
q. *pl.* qq.	(1) question(s); (2) quire(s)
QC	queen's counsel
R	rand
R.	Rex / Regina
r	recto
r.	reigned / ruled
RA	Royal Academy / Royal Academician

RAC	Royal Automobile Club		Skr	Swedish krona
RAF	Royal Air Force		Span.	Spanish
RAFVR	Royal Air Force Volunteer Reserve		SPCK	Society for Promoting Christian Knowledge
RAM	[member of the] Royal Academy of Music		SS	(1) Santissimi; (2) Schutzstaffel; (3) steam ship
RAMC	Royal Army Medical Corps		STB	bachelor of theology
RCA	Royal College of Art		STD	doctor of theology
RCNC	Royal Corps of Naval Constructors		STM	master of theology
RCOG	Royal College of Obstetricians and Gynaecologists		STP	doctor of theology
RDI	royal designer for industry		*supp.*	supposedly
RE	Royal Engineers		suppl. *pl.* suppls.	supplement(s)
repr. *pl.* reprs.	reprint(s) / reprinted		s.v.	*sub verbo* / *sub voce*: under the word / heading
repro.	reproduced		SY	steam yacht
rev.	revised / revised by / reviser / revision		TA	Territorial Army
Revd	Reverend		TASS	[Soviet news agency]
RHA	Royal Hibernian Academy		TB	tuberculosis (*lit.* tubercle bacillus)
RI	(1) Rhode Island; (2) Royal Institute of Painters in Water-Colours		TD	(1) *teachtaí dála* (member of the Dáil); (2) territorial decoration
RIBA	Royal Institute of British Architects		TN	Tennessee
RIN	Royal Indian Navy		TNT	trinitrotoluene
RM	Reichsmark		trans.	translated / translated by / translation / translator
RMS	Royal Mail steamer		TT	tourist trophy
RN	Royal Navy		TUC	Trades Union Congress
RNA	ribonucleic acid		TX	Texas
RNAS	Royal Naval Air Service		U-boat	*Unterseeboot*: submarine
RNR	Royal Naval Reserve		Ufa	Universum-Film AG
RNVR	Royal Naval Volunteer Reserve		UMIST	University of Manchester Institute of Science and Technology
RO	Record Office		UN	United Nations
r.p.m.	revolutions per minute		UNESCO	United Nations Educational, Scientific, and Cultural Organization
RRS	royal research ship			
Rs	rupees		UNICEF	United Nations International Children's Emergency Fund
RSA	(1) Royal Scottish Academician; (2) Royal Society of Arts			
RSPCA	Royal Society for the Prevention of Cruelty to Animals		unpubd	unpublished
			USS	United States ship
Rt Hon.	Right Honourable		UT	Utah
Rt Revd	Right Reverend		*v*	verso
RUC	Royal Ulster Constabulary		v.	versus
Russ.	Russian		VA	Virginia
RWS	Royal Watercolour Society		VAD	Voluntary Aid Detachment
S4C	Sianel Pedwar Cymru		VC	Victoria Cross
s.	shilling(s)		VE-day	victory in Europe day
s.a.	*sub anno*: under the year		Ven.	Venerable
SABC	South African Broadcasting Corporation		VJ-day	victory over Japan day
SAS	Special Air Service		vol. *pl.* vols.	volume(s)
SC	South Carolina		VT	Vermont
ScD	doctor of science		WA	Washington [state]
S$	Singapore dollar		WAAC	Women's Auxiliary Army Corps
SD	South Dakota		WAAF	Women's Auxiliary Air Force
sec.	second(s)		WEA	Workers' Educational Association
sel.	selected		WHO	World Health Organization
sen.	senior		WI	Wisconsin
Sept	September		WRAF	Women's Royal Air Force
ser.	series		WRNS	Women's Royal Naval Service
SHAPE	supreme headquarters allied powers, Europe		WV	West Virginia
SIDRO	Société Internationale d'Énergie Hydro-Électrique		WVS	Women's Voluntary Service
			WY	Wyoming
sig. *pl.* sigs.	signature(s)		¥	yen
sing.	singular		YMCA	Young Men's Christian Association
SIS	Secret Intelligence Service		YWCA	Young Women's Christian Association
SJ	Society of Jesus			

2 Institution abbreviations

All Souls Oxf.	All Souls College, Oxford	Garr. Club	Garrick Club, London
AM Oxf.	Ashmolean Museum, Oxford	Girton Cam.	Girton College, Cambridge
Balliol Oxf.	Balliol College, Oxford	GL	Guildhall Library, London
BBC WAC	BBC Written Archives Centre, Reading	Glos. RO	Gloucestershire Record Office, Gloucester
Beds. & Luton ARS	Bedfordshire and Luton Archives and Record Service, Bedford	Gon. & Caius Cam.	Gonville and Caius College, Cambridge
		Gov. Art Coll.	Government Art Collection
Berks. RO	Berkshire Record Office, Reading	GS Lond.	Geological Society of London
BFI	British Film Institute, London	Hants. RO	Hampshire Record Office, Winchester
BFI NFTVA	British Film Institute, London, National Film and Television Archive	Harris Man. Oxf.	Harris Manchester College, Oxford
		Harvard TC	Harvard Theatre Collection, Harvard University, Cambridge, Massachusetts, Nathan Marsh Pusey Library
BGS	British Geological Survey, Keyworth, Nottingham		
Birm. CA	Birmingham Central Library, Birmingham City Archives	Harvard U.	Harvard University, Cambridge, Massachusetts
		Harvard U., Houghton L.	Harvard University, Cambridge, Massachusetts, Houghton Library
Birm. CL	Birmingham Central Library		
BL	British Library, London	Herefs. RO	Herefordshire Record Office, Hereford
BL NSA	British Library, London, National Sound Archive	Herts. ALS	Hertfordshire Archives and Local Studies, Hertford
BL OIOC	British Library, London, Oriental and India Office Collections	Hist. Soc. Penn.	Historical Society of Pennsylvania, Philadelphia
BLPES	London School of Economics and Political Science, British Library of Political and Economic Science	HLRO	House of Lords Record Office, London
		Hult. Arch.	Hulton Archive, London and New York
		Hunt. L.	Huntington Library, San Marino, California
BM	British Museum, London	ICL	Imperial College, London
Bodl. Oxf.	Bodleian Library, Oxford	Inst. CE	Institution of Civil Engineers, London
Bodl. RH	Bodleian Library of Commonwealth and African Studies at Rhodes House, Oxford	Inst. EE	Institution of Electrical Engineers, London
		IWM	Imperial War Museum, London
Borth. Inst.	Borthwick Institute of Historical Research, University of York	IWM FVA	Imperial War Museum, London, Film and Video Archive
Boston PL	Boston Public Library, Massachusetts	IWM SA	Imperial War Museum, London, Sound Archive
Bristol RO	Bristol Record Office		
Bucks. RLSS	Buckinghamshire Records and Local Studies Service, Aylesbury	JRL	John Rylands University Library of Manchester
		King's AC Cam.	King's College Archives Centre, Cambridge
CAC Cam.	Churchill College, Cambridge, Churchill Archives Centre	King's Cam.	King's College, Cambridge
		King's Lond.	King's College, London
Cambs. AS	Cambridgeshire Archive Service	King's Lond., Liddell Hart C.	King's College, London, Liddell Hart Centre for Military Archives
CCC Cam.	Corpus Christi College, Cambridge		
CCC Oxf.	Corpus Christi College, Oxford	Lancs. RO	Lancashire Record Office, Preston
Ches. & Chester ALSS	Cheshire and Chester Archives and Local Studies Service	L. Cong.	Library of Congress, Washington, DC
		Leics. RO	Leicestershire, Leicester, and Rutland Record Office, Leicester
Christ Church Oxf.	Christ Church, Oxford		
Christies	Christies, London	Lincs. Arch.	Lincolnshire Archives, Lincoln
City Westm. AC	City of Westminster Archives Centre, London	Linn. Soc.	Linnean Society of London
		LMA	London Metropolitan Archives
CKS	Centre for Kentish Studies, Maidstone	LPL	Lambeth Palace, London
CLRO	Corporation of London Records Office	Lpool RO	Liverpool Record Office and Local Studies Service
Coll. Arms	College of Arms, London		
Col. U.	Columbia University, New York	LUL	London University Library
Cornwall RO	Cornwall Record Office, Truro	Magd. Cam.	Magdalene College, Cambridge
Courtauld Inst.	Courtauld Institute of Art, London	Magd. Oxf.	Magdalen College, Oxford
CUL	Cambridge University Library	Man. City Gall.	Manchester City Galleries
Cumbria AS	Cumbria Archive Service	Man. CL	Manchester Central Library
Derbys. RO	Derbyshire Record Office, Matlock	Mass. Hist. Soc.	Massachusetts Historical Society, Boston
Devon RO	Devon Record Office, Exeter	Merton Oxf.	Merton College, Oxford
Dorset RO	Dorset Record Office, Dorchester	MHS Oxf.	Museum of the History of Science, Oxford
Duke U.	Duke University, Durham, North Carolina	Mitchell L., Glas.	Mitchell Library, Glasgow
Duke U., Perkins L.	Duke University, Durham, North Carolina, William R. Perkins Library	Mitchell L., NSW	State Library of New South Wales, Sydney, Mitchell Library
Durham Cath. CL	Durham Cathedral, chapter library	Morgan L.	Pierpont Morgan Library, New York
Durham RO	Durham Record Office	NA Canada	National Archives of Canada, Ottawa
DWL	Dr Williams's Library, London	NA Ire.	National Archives of Ireland, Dublin
Essex RO	Essex Record Office	NAM	National Army Museum, London
E. Sussex RO	East Sussex Record Office, Lewes	NA Scot.	National Archives of Scotland, Edinburgh
Eton	Eton College, Berkshire	News Int. RO	News International Record Office, London
FM Cam.	Fitzwilliam Museum, Cambridge	NG Ire.	National Gallery of Ireland, Dublin
Folger	Folger Shakespeare Library, Washington, DC		

NG Scot.	National Gallery of Scotland, Edinburgh
NHM	Natural History Museum, London
NL Aus.	National Library of Australia, Canberra
NL Ire.	National Library of Ireland, Dublin
NL NZ	National Library of New Zealand, Wellington
NL NZ, Turnbull L.	National Library of New Zealand, Wellington, Alexander Turnbull Library
NL Scot.	National Library of Scotland, Edinburgh
NL Wales	National Library of Wales, Aberystwyth
NMG Wales	National Museum and Gallery of Wales, Cardiff
NMM	National Maritime Museum, London
Norfolk RO	Norfolk Record Office, Norwich
Northants. RO	Northamptonshire Record Office, Northampton
Northumbd RO	Northumberland Record Office
Notts. Arch.	Nottinghamshire Archives, Nottingham
NPG	National Portrait Gallery, London
NRA	National Archives, London, Historical Manuscripts Commission, National Register of Archives
Nuffield Oxf.	Nuffield College, Oxford
N. Yorks. CRO	North Yorkshire County Record Office, Northallerton
NYPL	New York Public Library
Oxf. UA	Oxford University Archives
Oxf. U. Mus. NH	Oxford University Museum of Natural History
Oxon. RO	Oxfordshire Record Office, Oxford
Pembroke Cam.	Pembroke College, Cambridge
PRO	National Archives, London, Public Record Office
PRO NIre.	Public Record Office for Northern Ireland, Belfast
Pusey Oxf.	Pusey House, Oxford
RA	Royal Academy of Arts, London
Ransom HRC	Harry Ransom Humanities Research Center, University of Texas, Austin
RAS	Royal Astronomical Society, London
RBG Kew	Royal Botanic Gardens, Kew, London
RCP Lond.	Royal College of Physicians of London
RCS Eng.	Royal College of Surgeons of England, London
RGS	Royal Geographical Society, London
RIBA	Royal Institute of British Architects, London
RIBA BAL	Royal Institute of British Architects, London, British Architectural Library
Royal Arch.	Royal Archives, Windsor Castle, Berkshire [by gracious permission of her majesty the queen]
Royal Irish Acad.	Royal Irish Academy, Dublin
Royal Scot. Acad.	Royal Scottish Academy, Edinburgh
RS	Royal Society, London
RSA	Royal Society of Arts, London
RS Friends, Lond.	Religious Society of Friends, London
St Ant. Oxf.	St Antony's College, Oxford
St John Cam.	St John's College, Cambridge
S. Antiquaries, Lond.	Society of Antiquaries of London
Sci. Mus.	Science Museum, London
Scot. NPG	Scottish National Portrait Gallery, Edinburgh
Scott Polar RI	University of Cambridge, Scott Polar Research Institute
Sheff. Arch.	Sheffield Archives
Shrops. RRC	Shropshire Records and Research Centre, Shrewsbury
SOAS	School of Oriental and African Studies, London
Som. ARS	Somerset Archive and Record Service, Taunton
Staffs. RO	Staffordshire Record Office, Stafford
Suffolk RO	Suffolk Record Office
Surrey HC	Surrey History Centre, Woking
TCD	Trinity College, Dublin
Trinity Cam.	Trinity College, Cambridge
U. Aberdeen	University of Aberdeen
U. Birm.	University of Birmingham
U. Birm. L.	University of Birmingham Library
U. Cal.	University of California
U. Cam.	University of Cambridge
UCL	University College, London
U. Durham	University of Durham
U. Durham L.	University of Durham Library
U. Edin.	University of Edinburgh
U. Edin., New Coll.	University of Edinburgh, New College
U. Edin., New Coll. L.	University of Edinburgh, New College Library
U. Edin. L.	University of Edinburgh Library
U. Glas.	University of Glasgow
U. Glas. L.	University of Glasgow Library
U. Hull	University of Hull
U. Hull, Brynmor Jones L.	University of Hull, Brynmor Jones Library
U. Leeds	University of Leeds
U. Leeds, Brotherton L.	University of Leeds, Brotherton Library
U. Lond.	University of London
U. Lpool	University of Liverpool
U. Lpool L.	University of Liverpool Library
U. Mich.	University of Michigan, Ann Arbor
U. Mich., Clements L.	University of Michigan, Ann Arbor, William L. Clements Library
U. Newcastle	University of Newcastle upon Tyne
U. Newcastle, Robinson L.	University of Newcastle upon Tyne, Robinson Library
U. Nott.	University of Nottingham
U. Nott. L.	University of Nottingham Library
U. Oxf.	University of Oxford
U. Reading	University of Reading
U. Reading L.	University of Reading Library
U. St Andr.	University of St Andrews
U. St Andr. L.	University of St Andrews Library
U. Southampton	University of Southampton
U. Southampton L.	University of Southampton Library
U. Sussex	University of Sussex, Brighton
U. Texas	University of Texas, Austin
U. Wales	University of Wales
U. Warwick Mod. RC	University of Warwick, Coventry, Modern Records Centre
V&A	Victoria and Albert Museum, London
V&A NAL	Victoria and Albert Museum, London, National Art Library
Warks. CRO	Warwickshire County Record Office, Warwick
Wellcome L.	Wellcome Library for the History and Understanding of Medicine, London
Westm. DA	Westminster Diocesan Archives, London
Wilts. & Swindon RO	Wiltshire and Swindon Record Office, Trowbridge
Worcs. RO	Worcestershire Record Office, Worcester
W. Sussex RO	West Sussex Record Office, Chichester
W. Yorks. AS	West Yorkshire Archive Service
Yale U.	Yale University, New Haven, Connecticut
Yale U., Beinecke L.	Yale University, New Haven, Connecticut, Beinecke Rare Book and Manuscript Library
Yale U. CBA	Yale University, New Haven, Connecticut, Yale Center for British Art

3 Bibliographic abbreviations

Adams, *Drama* — W. D. Adams, *A dictionary of the drama*, 1: *A–G* (1904); 2: *H–Z* (1956) [vol. 2 microfilm only]

AFM — J O'Donovan, ed. and trans., *Annala rioghachta Eireann | Annals of the kingdom of Ireland by the four masters*, 7 vols. (1848–51); 2nd edn (1856); 3rd edn (1990)

Allibone, *Dict.* — S. A. Allibone, *A critical dictionary of English literature and British and American authors*, 3 vols. (1859–71); suppl. by J. F. Kirk, 2 vols. (1891)

ANB — J. A. Garraty and M. C. Carnes, eds., *American national biography*, 24 vols. (1999)

Anderson, *Scot. nat.* — W. Anderson, *The Scottish nation, or, The surnames, families, literature, honours, and biographical history of the people of Scotland*, 3 vols. (1859–63)

Ann. mon. — H. R. Luard, ed., *Annales monastici*, 5 vols., Rolls Series, 36 (1864–9)

Ann. Ulster — S. Mac Airt and G. Mac Niocaill, eds., *Annals of Ulster (to AD 1131)* (1983)

APC — *Acts of the privy council of England*, new ser., 46 vols. (1890–1964)

APS — *The acts of the parliaments of Scotland*, 12 vols. in 13 (1814–75)

Arber, *Regs. Stationers* — F. Arber, ed., *A transcript of the registers of the Company of Stationers of London, 1554–1640 AD*, 5 vols. (1875–94)

ArchR — *Architectural Review*

ASC — D. Whitelock, D. C. Douglas, and S. I. Tucker, ed. and trans., *The Anglo-Saxon Chronicle: a revised translation* (1961)

AS chart. — P. H. Sawyer, *Anglo-Saxon charters: an annotated list and bibliography*, Royal Historical Society Guides and Handbooks (1968)

AusDB — D. Pike and others, eds., *Australian dictionary of biography*, 16 vols. (1966–2002)

Baker, *Serjeants* — J. H. Baker, *The order of serjeants at law*, SeldS, suppl. ser., 5 (1984)

Bale, *Cat.* — J. Bale, *Scriptorum illustrium Maioris Brytannie, quam nunc Angliam et Scotiam vocant: catalogus*, 2 vols. in 1 (Basel, 1557–9); facs. edn (1971)

Bale, *Index* — J. Bale, *Index Britanniae scriptorum*, ed. R. L. Poole and M. Bateson (1902); facs. edn (1990)

BBCS — *Bulletin of the Board of Celtic Studies*

BDMBR — J. O. Baylen and N. J. Gossman, eds., *Biographical dictionary of modern British radicals*, 3 vols. in 4 (1979–88)

Bede, *Hist. eccl.* — *Bede's Ecclesiastical history of the English people*, ed. and trans. B. Colgrave and R. A. B. Mynors, OMT (1969); repr. (1991)

Bénézit, *Dict.* — E. Bénézit, *Dictionnaire critique et documentaire des peintres, sculpteurs, dessinateurs et graveurs*, 3 vols. (Paris, 1911–23); new edn, 8 vols. (1948–66), repr. (1966); 3rd edn, rev. and enl., 10 vols. (1976); 4th edn, 14 vols. (1999)

BIHR — *Bulletin of the Institute of Historical Research*

Birch, *Seals* — W. de Birch, *Catalogue of seals in the department of manuscripts in the British Museum*, 6 vols. (1887–1900)

Bishop Burnet's History — *Bishop Burnet's History of his own time*, ed. M. J. Routh, 2nd edn, 6 vols. (1833)

Blackwood — *Blackwood's [Edinburgh] Magazine*, 328 vols. (1817–1980)

Blain, Clements & Grundy, *Feminist comp.* — V. Blain, P. Clements, and I. Grundy, eds., *The feminist companion to literature in English* (1990)

BL cat. — *The British Library general catalogue of printed books* [in 360 vols. with suppls., also CD-ROM and online]

BMJ — *British Medical Journal*

Boase & Courtney, *Bibl. Corn.* — G. C. Boase and W. P. Courtney, *Bibliotheca Cornubiensis: a catalogue of the writings … of Cornishmen*, 3 vols. (1874–82)

Boase, *Mod. Eng. biog.* — F. Boase, *Modern English biography: containing many thousand concise memoirs of persons who have died since the year 1850*, 6 vols. (privately printed, Truro, 1892–1921); repr. (1965)

Boswell, *Life* — *Boswell's Life of Johnson: together with Journal of a tour to the Hebrides and Johnson's Diary of a journey into north Wales*, ed. G. B. Hill, enl. edn, rev. L. F. Powell, 6 vols. (1934–50); 2nd edn (1964); repr. (1971)

Brown & Stratton, *Brit. mus.* — J. D. Brown and S. S. Stratton, *British musical biography* (1897)

Bryan, *Painters* — M. Bryan, *A biographical and critical dictionary of painters and engravers*, 2 vols. (1816); new edn, ed. G. Stanley (1849); new edn, ed. R. E. Graves and W. Armstrong, 2 vols. (1886–9); [4th edn], ed. G. C. Williamson, 5 vols. (1903–5) [various reprs.]

Burke, *Gen. GB* — J. Burke, *A genealogical and heraldic history of the commoners of Great Britain and Ireland*, 4 vols. (1833–8); new edn as *A genealogical and heraldic dictionary of the landed gentry of Great Britain and Ireland*, 3 vols. [1843–9] [many later edns]

Burke, *Gen. Ire.* — J. B. Burke, *A genealogical and heraldic history of the landed gentry of Ireland* (1899); 2nd edn (1904); 3rd edn (1912); 4th edn (1958); 5th edn as *Burke's Irish family records* (1976)

Burke, *Peerage* — J. Burke, *A general [later edns A genealogical] and heraldic dictionary of the peerage and baronetage of the United Kingdom [later edns the British empire]* (1829–)

Burney, *Hist. mus.* — C. Burney, *A general history of music, from the earliest ages to the present period*, 4 vols. (1776–89)

Burtchaell & Sadleir, *Alum. Dubl.* — G. D. Burtchaell and T. U. Sadleir, *Alumni Dublinenses: a register of the students, graduates, and provosts of Trinity College* (1924); [2nd edn], with suppl., in 2 pts (1935)

Calamy rev. — A. G. Matthews, *Calamy revised* (1934); repr. (1988)

CCI — *Calendar of confirmations and inventories granted and given up in the several commissariots of Scotland* (1876–)

CClR — *Calendar of the close rolls preserved in the Public Record Office*, 47 vols. (1892–1963)

CDS — J. Bain, ed., *Calendar of documents relating to Scotland*, 4 vols., PRO (1881–8); suppl. vol. 5, ed. G. G. Simpson and J. D. Galbraith [1986]

CEPR letters — W. H. Bliss, C. Johnson, and J. Twemlow, eds., *Calendar of entries in the papal registers relating to Great Britain and Ireland: papal letters* (1893–)

CGPLA — *Calendars of the grants of probate and letters of administration [in 4 ser.: England & Wales, Northern Ireland, Ireland, and Éire]*

Chambers, *Scots.* — R. Chambers, ed., *A biographical dictionary of eminent Scotsmen*, 4 vols. (1832–5)

Chancery records — chancery records pubd by the PRO

Chancery records (RC) — chancery records pubd by the Record Commissions

CIPM	*Calendar of inquisitions post mortem*, [20 vols.], PRO (1904–); also Henry VII, 3 vols. (1898–1955)
Clarendon, *Hist. rebellion*	E. Hyde, earl of Clarendon, *The history of the rebellion and civil wars in England*, 6 vols. (1888); repr. (1958) and (1992)
Cobbett, *Parl. hist.*	W. Cobbett and J. Wright, eds., *Cobbett's Parliamentary history of England*, 36 vols. (1806–1820)
Colvin, *Archs.*	H. Colvin, *A biographical dictionary of British architects, 1600–1840*, 3rd edn (1995)
Cooper, *Ath. Cantab.*	C. H. Cooper and T. Cooper, *Athenae Cantabrigienses*, 3 vols. (1858–1913); repr. (1967)
CPR	*Calendar of the patent rolls preserved in the Public Record Office* (1891–)
Crockford	*Crockford's Clerical Directory*
CS	Camden Society
CSP	*Calendar of state papers* [in 11 ser.: domestic, Scotland, Scottish series, Ireland, colonial, Commonwealth, foreign, Spain [at Simancas], Rome, Milan, and Venice]
CYS	Canterbury and York Society
DAB	*Dictionary of American biography*, 21 vols. (1928–36), repr. in 11 vols. (1964); 10 suppls. (1944–96)
DBB	D. J. Jeremy, ed., *Dictionary of business biography*, 5 vols. (1984–6)
DCB	G. W. Brown and others, *Dictionary of Canadian biography*, [14 vols.] (1966–)
Debrett's Peerage	*Debrett's Peerage* (1803–) [sometimes *Debrett's Illustrated peerage*]
Desmond, *Botanists*	R. Desmond, *Dictionary of British and Irish botanists and horticulturists* (1977); rev. edn (1994)
Dir. Brit. archs.	A. Felstead, J. Franklin, and L. Pinfield, eds., *Directory of British architects, 1834–1900* (1993); 2nd edn, ed. A. Brodie and others, 2 vols. (2001)
DLB	J. M. Bellamy and J. Saville, eds., *Dictionary of labour biography*, [10 vols.] (1972–)
DLitB	Dictionary of Literary Biography
DNB	*Dictionary of national biography*, 63 vols. (1885–1900), suppl., 3 vols. (1901); repr. in 22 vols. (1908–9); 10 further suppls. (1912–96); *Missing persons* (1993)
DNZB	W. H. Oliver and C. Orange, eds., *The dictionary of New Zealand biography*, 5 vols. (1990–2000)
DSAB	W. J. de Kock and others, eds., *Dictionary of South African biography*, 5 vols. (1968–87)
DSB	C. C. Gillispie and F. L. Holmes, eds., *Dictionary of scientific biography*, 16 vols. (1970–80); repr. in 8 vols. (1981); 2 vol. suppl. (1990)
DSBB	A. Slaven and S. Checkland, eds., *Dictionary of Scottish business biography, 1860–1960*, 2 vols. (1986–90)
DSCHT	N. M. de S. Cameron and others, eds., *Dictionary of Scottish church history and theology* (1993)
Dugdale, *Monasticon*	W. Dugdale, *Monasticon Anglicanum*, 3 vols. (1655–72); 2nd edn, 3 vols. (1661–82); new edn, ed. J. Caley, J. Ellis, and B. Bandinel, 6 vols. in 8 pts (1817–30); repr. (1846) and (1970)
DWB	J. E. Lloyd and others, eds., *Dictionary of Welsh biography down to 1940* (1959) [Eng. trans. of *Y bywgraffiadur Cymreig hyd 1940*, 2nd edn (1954)]
EdinR	*Edinburgh Review, or, Critical Journal*
EETS	Early English Text Society
Emden, *Cam.*	A. B. Emden, *A biographical register of the University of Cambridge to 1500* (1963)
Emden, *Oxf.*	A. B. Emden, *A biographical register of the University of Oxford to AD 1500*, 3 vols. (1957–9); also *A biographical register of the University of Oxford, AD 1501 to 1540* (1974)
EngHR	*English Historical Review*
Engraved Brit. ports.	F. M. O'Donoghue and H. M. Hake, *Catalogue of engraved British portraits preserved in the department of prints and drawings in the British Museum*, 6 vols. (1908–25)
ER	The English Reports, 178 vols. (1900–32)
ESTC	*English short title catalogue, 1475–1800* [CD-ROM and online]
Evelyn, *Diary*	*The diary of John Evelyn*, ed. E. S. De Beer, 6 vols. (1955); repr. (2000)
Farington, *Diary*	*The diary of Joseph Farington*, ed. K. Garlick and others, 17 vols. (1978–98)
Fasti Angl. (Hardy)	J. Le Neve, *Fasti ecclesiae Anglicanae*, ed. T. D. Hardy, 3 vols. (1854)
Fasti Angl., 1066–1300	[J. Le Neve], *Fasti ecclesiae Anglicanae, 1066–1300*, ed. D. E. Greenway and J. S. Barrow, [8 vols.] (1968–)
Fasti Angl., 1300–1541	[J. Le Neve], *Fasti ecclesiae Anglicanae, 1300–1541*, 12 vols. (1962–7)
Fasti Angl., 1541–1857	[J. Le Neve], *Fasti ecclesiae Anglicanae, 1541–1857*, ed. J. M. Horn, D. M. Smith, and D. S. Bailey, [9 vols.] (1969–)
Fasti Scot.	H. Scott, *Fasti ecclesiae Scoticanae*, 3 vols. in 6 (1871); new edn, [11 vols.] (1915–)
FO List	*Foreign Office List*
Fortescue, *Brit. army*	J. W. Fortescue, *A history of the British army*, 13 vols. (1899–1930)
Foss, *Judges*	E. Foss, *The judges of England*, 9 vols. (1848–64); repr. (1966)
Foster, *Alum. Oxon.*	J. Foster, ed., *Alumni Oxonienses: the members of the University of Oxford, 1715–1886*, 4 vols. (1887–8); later edn (1891); also *Alumni Oxonienses … 1500–1714*, 4 vols. (1891–2); 8 vol. repr. (1968) and (2000)
Fuller, *Worthies*	T. Fuller, *The history of the worthies of England*, 4 pts (1662); new edn, 2 vols., ed. J. Nichols (1811); new edn, 3 vols., ed. P. A. Nuttall (1840); repr. (1965)
GEC, *Baronetage*	G. E. Cokayne, *Complete baronetage*, 6 vols. (1900–09); repr. (1983) [microprint]
GEC, *Peerage*	G. E. C. [G. E. Cokayne], *The complete peerage of England, Scotland, Ireland, Great Britain, and the United Kingdom*, 8 vols. (1887–98); new edn, ed. V. Gibbs and others, 14 vols. in 15 (1910–98); microprint repr. (1982) and (1987)
Genest, *Eng. stage*	J. Genest, *Some account of the English stage from the Restoration in 1660 to 1830*, 10 vols. (1832); repr. [New York, 1965]
Gillow, *Lit. biog. hist.*	J. Gillow, *A literary and biographical history or bibliographical dictionary of the English Catholics, from the breach with Rome, in 1534, to the present time*, 5 vols. [1885–1902]; repr. (1961); repr. with preface by C. Gillow (1999)
Gir. Camb. opera	*Giraldi Cambrensis opera*, ed. J. S. Brewer, J. F. Dimock, and G. F. Warner, 8 vols., Rolls Series, 21 (1861–91)
GJ	*Geographical Journal*

Gladstone, *Diaries* — *The Gladstone diaries: with cabinet minutes and prime-ministerial correspondence*, ed. M. R. D. Foot and H. C. G. Matthew, 14 vols. (1968–94)

GM — *Gentleman's Magazine*

Graves, *Artists* — A. Graves, ed., *A dictionary of artists who have exhibited works in the principal London exhibitions of oil paintings from 1760 to 1880* (1884); new edn (1895); 3rd edn (1901); facs. edn (1969); repr. [1970], (1973), and (1984)

Graves, *Brit. Inst.* — A. Graves, *The British Institution, 1806–1867: a complete dictionary of contributors and their work from the foundation of the institution* (1875); facs. edn (1908); repr. (1969)

Graves, *RA exhibitors* — A. Graves, *The Royal Academy of Arts: a complete dictionary of contributors and their work from its foundation in 1769 to 1904*, 8 vols. (1905–6); repr. in 4 vols. (1970) and (1972)

Graves, *Soc. Artists* — A. Graves, *The Society of Artists of Great Britain, 1760–1791, the Free Society of Artists, 1761–1783: a complete dictionary* (1907); facs. edn (1969)

Greaves & Zaller, *BDBR* — R. L. Greaves and R. Zaller, eds., *Biographical dictionary of British radicals in the seventeenth century*, 3 vols. (1982–4)

Grove, *Dict. mus.* — G. Grove, ed., *A dictionary of music and musicians*, 5 vols. (1878–90); 2nd edn, ed. J. A. Fuller Maitland (1904–10); 3rd edn, ed. H. C. Colles (1927); 4th edn with suppl. (1940); 5th edn, ed. E. Blom, 9 vols. (1954); suppl. (1961) [see also *New Grove*]

Hall, *Dramatic ports.* — L. A. Hall, *Catalogue of dramatic portraits in the theatre collection of the Harvard College library*, 4 vols. (1930–34)

Hansard — *Hansard's parliamentary debates*, ser. 1–5 (1803–)

Highfill, Burnim & Langhans, *BDA* — P. H. Highfill, K. A. Burnim, and E. A. Langhans, *A biographical dictionary of actors, actresses, musicians, dancers, managers, and other stage personnel in London, 1660–1800*, 16 vols. (1973–93)

Hist. U. Oxf. — T. H. Aston, ed., *The history of the University of Oxford*, 8 vols. (1984–2000) [1: *The early Oxford schools*, ed. J. I. Catto (1984); 2: *Late medieval Oxford*, ed. J. I. Catto and R. Evans (1992); 3: *The collegiate university*, ed. J. McConica (1986); 4: *Seventeenth-century Oxford*, ed. N. Tyacke (1997); 5: *The eighteenth century*, ed. L. S. Sutherland and L. G. Mitchell (1986); 6–7: *Nineteenth-century Oxford*, ed. M. G. Brock and M. C. Curthoys (1997–2000); 8: *The twentieth century*, ed. B. Harrison (2000)]

HJ — *Historical Journal*

HMC — Historical Manuscripts Commission

Holdsworth, *Eng. law* — W. S. Holdsworth, *A history of English law*, ed. A. L. Goodhart and H. L. Hanbury, 17 vols. (1903–72)

HoP, *Commons* — *The history of parliament: the House of Commons* [*1386–1421*, ed. J. S. Roskell, L. Clark, and C. Rawcliffe, 4 vols. (1992); *1509–1558*, ed. S. T. Bindoff, 3 vols. (1982); *1558–1603*, ed. P. W. Hasler, 3 vols. (1981); *1660–1690*, ed. B. D. Henning, 3 vols. (1983); *1690–1715*, ed. D. W. Hayton, E. Cruickshanks, and S. Handley, 5 vols. (2002); *1715–1754*, ed. R. Sedgwick, 2 vols. (1970); *1754–1790*, ed. L. Namier and J. Brooke, 3 vols. (1964), repr. (1985); *1790–1820*, ed. R. G. Thorne, 5 vols. (1986); in draft (used with permission): *1422–1504*, *1604–1629*, *1640–1660*, and *1820–1832*]

IGI — *International Genealogical Index*, Church of Jesus Christ of the Latterday Saints

ILN — *Illustrated London News*

IMC — Irish Manuscripts Commission

Irving, *Scots.* — J. Irving, ed., *The book of Scotsmen eminent for achievements in arms and arts, church and state, law, legislation and literature, commerce, science, travel and philanthropy* (1881)

JCS — *Journal of the Chemical Society*

JHC — *Journals of the House of Commons*

JHL — *Journals of the House of Lords*

John of Worcester, *Chron.* — *The chronicle of John of Worcester*, ed. R. R. Darlington and P. McGurk, trans. J. Bray and P. McGurk, 3 vols., OMT (1995–) [vol. 1 forthcoming]

Keeler, *Long Parliament* — M. F. Keeler, *The Long Parliament, 1640–1641: a biographical study of its members* (1954)

Kelly, *Handbk* — *The upper ten thousand: an alphabetical list of all members of noble families*, 3 vols. (1875–7); continued as *Kelly's handbook of the upper ten thousand for 1878* [1879], 2 vols. (1878–9); continued as *Kelly's handbook to the titled, landed and official classes*, 94 vols. (1880–1973)

LondG — *London Gazette*

LP Henry VIII — J. S. Brewer, J. Gairdner, and R. H. Brodie, eds., *Letters and papers, foreign and domestic, of the reign of Henry VIII*, 23 vols. in 38 (1862–1932); repr. (1965)

Mallalieu, *Watercolour artists* — H. L. Mallalieu, *The dictionary of British watercolour artists up to 1820*, 3 vols. (1976–90); vol. 1, 2nd edn (1986)

Memoirs FRS — *Biographical Memoirs of Fellows of the Royal Society*

MGH — Monumenta Germaniae Historica

MT — *Musical Times*

Munk, *Roll* — W. Munk, *The roll of the Royal College of Physicians of London*, 2 vols. (1861); 2nd edn, 3 vols. (1878)

N&Q — *Notes and Queries*

New Grove — S. Sadie, ed., *The new Grove dictionary of music and musicians*, 20 vols. (1980); 2nd edn, 29 vols. (2001) [also online edn; see also Grove, *Dict. mus.*]

Nichols, *Illustrations* — J. Nichols and J. B. Nichols, *Illustrations of the literary history of the eighteenth century*, 8 vols. (1817–58)

Nichols, *Lit. anecdotes* — J. Nichols, *Literary anecdotes of the eighteenth century*, 9 vols. (1812–16); facs. edn (1966)

Obits. FRS — *Obituary Notices of Fellows of the Royal Society*

O'Byrne, *Naval biog. dict.* — W. R. O'Byrne, *A naval biographical dictionary* (1849); repr. (1990); [2nd edn], 2 vols. (1861)

OHS — Oxford Historical Society

Old Westminsters — *The record of Old Westminsters*, 1–2, ed. G. F. R. Barker and A. H. Stenning (1928); suppl. 1, ed. J. B. Whitmore and G. R. Y. Radcliffe [1938]; 3, ed. J. B. Whitmore, G. R. Y. Radcliffe, and D. C. Simpson (1963); suppl. 2, ed. F. E. Pagan (1978); 4, ed. F. E. Pagan and H. E. Pagan (1992)

OMT — Oxford Medieval Texts

Ordericus Vitalis, *Eccl. hist.* — *The ecclesiastical history of Orderic Vitalis*, ed. and trans. M. Chibnall, 6 vols., OMT (1969–80); repr. (1990)

Paris, *Chron.* — *Matthaei Parisiensis, monachi sancti Albani, chronica majora*, ed. H. R. Luard, Rolls Series, 7 vols. (1872–83)

Parl. papers — *Parliamentary papers* (1801–)

PBA — *Proceedings of the British Academy*

Pepys, *Diary*	*The diary of Samuel Pepys*, ed. R. Latham and W. Matthews, 11 vols. (1970–83); repr. (1995) and (2000)
Pevsner	N. Pevsner and others, Buildings of England series
PICE	*Proceedings of the Institution of Civil Engineers*
Pipe rolls	*The great roll of the pipe for . . .*, PRSoc. (1884–)
PRO	Public Record Office
PRS	*Proceedings of the Royal Society of London*
PRSoc.	Pipe Roll Society
PTRS	*Philosophical Transactions of the Royal Society*
QR	*Quarterly Review*
RC	Record Commissions
Redgrave, *Artists*	S. Redgrave, *A dictionary of artists of the English school* (1874); rev. edn (1878); repr. (1970)
Reg. Oxf.	C. W. Boase and A. Clark, eds., *Register of the University of Oxford*, 5 vols., OHS, 1, 10–12, 14 (1885–9)
Reg. PCS	J. H. Burton and others, eds., *The register of the privy council of Scotland*, 1st ser., 14 vols. (1877–98); 2nd ser., 8 vols. (1899–1908); 3rd ser., [16 vols.] (1908–70)
Reg. RAN	H. W. C. Davis and others, eds., *Regesta regum Anglo-Normannorum, 1066–1154*, 4 vols. (1913–69)
RIBA Journal	*Journal of the Royal Institute of British Architects* [later *RIBA Journal*]
RotP	J. Strachey, ed., *Rotuli parliamentorum ut et petitiones, et placita in parliamento*, 6 vols. (1767–77)
RotS	D. Macpherson, J. Caley, and W. Illingworth, eds., *Rotuli Scotiae in Turri Londinensi et in domo capitulari Westmonasteriensi asservati*, 2 vols., RC, 14 (1814–19)
RS	Record(s) Society
Rymer, *Foedera*	T. Rymer and R. Sanderson, eds., *Foedera, conventiones, literae et cuiuscunque generis acta publica inter reges Angliae et alios quosvis imperatores, reges, pontifices, principes, vel communitates*, 20 vols. (1704–35); 2nd edn, 20 vols. (1726–35); 3rd edn, 10 vols. (1739–45); facs. edn (1967); new edn, ed. A. Clarke, J. Caley, and F. Holbrooke, 4 vols., RC, 50 (1816–30)
Sainty, *Judges*	J. Sainty, ed., *The judges of England, 1272–1990*, SeldS, suppl. ser., 10 (1993)
Sainty, *King's counsel*	J. Sainty, ed., *A list of English law officers and king's counsel*, SeldS, suppl. ser., 7 (1987)
SCH	Studies in Church History
Scots peerage	J. B. Paul, ed. *The Scots peerage, founded on Wood's edition of Sir Robert Douglas's Peerage of Scotland, containing an historical and genealogical account of the nobility of that kingdom*, 9 vols. (1904–14)
SeldS	Selden Society
SHR	*Scottish Historical Review*
State trials	T. B. Howell and T. J. Howell, eds., *Cobbett's Complete collection of state trials*, 34 vols. (1809–28)
STC, 1475–1640	A. W. Pollard, G. R. Redgrave, and others, eds., *A short-title catalogue of … English books … 1475–1640* (1926); 2nd edn, ed. W. A. Jackson, F. S. Ferguson, and K. F. Pantzer, 3 vols. (1976–91) [see also Wing, *STC*]
STS	Scottish Text Society
SurtS	Surtees Society
Symeon of Durham, *Opera*	*Symeonis monachi opera omnia*, ed. T. Arnold, 2 vols., Rolls Series, 75 (1882–5); repr. (1965)
Tanner, *Bibl. Brit.-Hib.*	T. Tanner, *Bibliotheca Britannico-Hibernica*, ed. D. Wilkins (1748); repr. (1963)
Thieme & Becker, *Allgemeines Lexikon*	U. Thieme, F. Becker, and H. Vollmer, eds., *Allgemeines Lexikon der bildenden Künstler von der Antike bis zur Gegenwart*, 37 vols. (Leipzig, 1907–50); repr. (1961–5), (1983), and (1992)
Thurloe, *State papers*	*A collection of the state papers of John Thurloe*, ed. T. Birch, 7 vols. (1742)
TLS	*Times Literary Supplement*
Tout, *Admin. hist.*	T. F. Tout, *Chapters in the administrative history of mediaeval England: the wardrobe, the chamber, and the small seals*, 6 vols. (1920–33); repr. (1967)
TRHS	*Transactions of the Royal Historical Society*
VCH	H. A. Doubleday and others, eds., *The Victoria history of the counties of England*, [88 vols.] (1900–)
Venn, *Alum. Cant.*	J. Venn and J. A. Venn, *Alumni Cantabrigienses: a biographical list of all known students, graduates, and holders of office at the University of Cambridge, from the earliest times to 1900*, 10 vols. (1922–54); repr. in 2 vols. (1974–8)
Vertue, *Note books*	[G. Vertue], *Note books*, ed. K. Esdaile, earl of Ilchester, and H. M. Hake, 6 vols., Walpole Society, 18, 20, 22, 24, 26, 30 (1930–55)
VF	*Vanity Fair*
Walford, *County families*	E. Walford, *The county families of the United Kingdom, or, Royal manual of the titled and untitled aristocracy of Great Britain and Ireland* (1860)
Walker rev.	A. G. Matthews, *Walker revised: being a revision of John Walker's Sufferings of the clergy during the grand rebellion, 1642–60* (1948); repr. (1988)
Walpole, *Corr.*	*The Yale edition of Horace Walpole's correspondence*, ed. W. S. Lewis, 48 vols. (1937–83)
Ward, *Men of the reign*	T. H. Ward, ed., *Men of the reign: a biographical dictionary of eminent persons of British and colonial birth who have died during the reign of Queen Victoria* (1885); repr. (Graz, 1968)
Waterhouse, *18c painters*	E. Waterhouse, *The dictionary of 18th century painters in oils and crayons* (1981); repr. as *British 18th century painters in oils and crayons* (1991), vol. 2 of *Dictionary of British art*
Watt, *Bibl. Brit.*	R. Watt, *Bibliotheca Britannica, or, A general index to British and foreign literature*, 4 vols. (1824) [many reprs.]
Wellesley index	W. E. Houghton, ed., *The Wellesley index to Victorian periodicals, 1824–1900*, 5 vols. (1966–89); new edn (1999) [CD-ROM]
Wing, *STC*	D. Wing, ed., *Short-title catalogue of … English books … 1641–1700*, 3 vols. (1945–51); 2nd edn (1972–88); rev. and enl. edn, ed. J. J. Morrison, C. W. Nelson, and M. Seccombe, 4 vols. (1994–8) [see also *STC, 1475–1640*]
Wisden	*John Wisden's Cricketer's Almanack*
Wood, *Ath. Oxon.*	A. Wood, *Athenae Oxonienses … to which are added the Fasti*, 2 vols. (1691–2); 2nd edn (1721); new edn, 4 vols., ed. P. Bliss (1813–20); repr. (1967) and (1969)
Wood, *Vic. painters*	C. Wood, *Dictionary of Victorian painters* (1971); 2nd edn (1978); 3rd edn as *Victorian painters*, 2 vols. (1995), vol. 4 of *Dictionary of British art*
WW	*Who's who* (1849–)
WWBMP	M. Stenton and S. Lees, eds., *Who's who of British members of parliament*, 4 vols. (1976–81)
WWW	*Who was who* (1929–)

Walliers, Euphemia de [Euphemia of Wherwell] (*d.* 1257), abbess of Wherwell, was the daughter of Margaret de Walliers and the niece of Matilda de Bailleul. Her father may have been Theodore de Walliers whose obit (13 September) appears in the same psalter (Cambridge, St John's College, MS C.18) as her mother's.

Wherwell Abbey was a Benedictine nunnery in Hampshire. Euphemia joined the community during the long rule of her aunt, Abbess Matilda, and on the latter's death, between 1207 and 1219, she was elected abbess. The rest of her long and exemplary life was devoted to the abbey and its affairs, both spiritual and temporal. The number of nuns doubled from forty to eighty, but it is as a builder that she is remembered.

Euphemia had a large infirmary constructed, away from the abbey buildings, with a watercourse running beneath it and an adjoining chapel and garden. On the decrepit demesne manor she replaced the old mill and created a new walled court with a large hall and gardens beyond. Later she renewed buildings on two of the abbey's other nearby manors, partly to reduce fire risks. Rebuilding at the abbey became essential after the sudden fall of the bell-tower. Euphemia had it replaced with a tall stone spire which can be seen in the portrait of a sixteenth-century abbess. Towards the end of her life, when the presbytery was in danger of collapsing, Euphemia had it all dismantled and ensured that there were dry foundations for its replacement. She laid the foundation stone herself and lived to see it completed.

Abbess Euphemia died on 26 April 1257 and would undoubtedly have been buried in the abbey church. In the following century her long obituary was copied into the cartulary of Wherwell Abbey.   DIANA K. COLDICOTT

Sources cartulary of Wherwell Abbey, BL, Egerton MS 2104a, ch. 59, fols. 43*v*–44*v* · *VCH Hampshire and the Isle of Wight*, 2.132–3 · calendar of Wherwell Abbey, Saltykov-Shchedrin Public Library, St Petersburg, Russia, MS Lat.Q.v.I.62 · feet of fines, Berkshire, PRO, CP25/1/7/7, no. 46 · R. M. Thomson, *Manuscripts from St Albans Abbey, 1066–1235*, 2 vols. (1982) · M. R. James, *A descriptive catalogue of the manuscripts in the library of St John's College, Cambridge* (1913) · D. K. Coldicott, *Hampshire nunneries* (1989)
Archives Saltykov-Shchedrin Public Library, St Petersburg, MS Lat.Q.v.I.62

Wallin, Benjamin (1711–1782), Particular Baptist minister, was born in London to Edward Wallin (1678–1733), minister of Maze Pond Particular Baptist Church. Lame due to an accident shortly after birth, he received medical attention in 1725 that enabled him to walk well enough.

Wallin received the rudiments of education under two Baptist pastors, John Needham of Hitchin, Hertfordshire, and Sayer Rudd, who was a pastor in London. Joseph Stennett, another well-known London Baptist minister, helped to prepare him for pastoral ministry. Initially, though, he entered into business and married, on 15 November 1733, Sarah Heathfield (*c.*1710–1752) at St Mildred Poultry, London. His wife predeceased him, dying on 29 February 1752. Although long hesitant to enter into pastoral ministry, he finally accepted the invitation of Maze Pond Church to become their pastor in 1741.

Through his ministry at Maze Pond over the next forty-one years Wallin became widely regarded as a pillar of his denomination. After John Gill, the doyen of mid-eighteenth-century Particular Baptist theology, Wallin was the most prolific author in this era of the Particular Baptist community's history. His numerous sermons and other religious works helped to create a distinct identity in terms of spirituality and churchmanship for the Particular Baptists in Great Britain. Given his deep-set Baptist convictions, it is not surprising that he was critical of the mid-eighteenth-century evangelical revival in England, whose leadership was largely Anglican. Nevertheless, he was a warm supporter of the Baptist movement in New England, itself a product of the revival. His support of the New England Baptists, channelled through such key individuals as Isaac Backus, helped to imbue them with deep confidence about their distinct denominational identity. In this way Wallin played a role in the strong advance of the American Baptists after the great awakening. He was granted an honorary MA by the College of Rhode Island (later Brown University) in 1771.

Rarely ill throughout his life, Wallin's death in London on 19 February 1782 followed a brief illness. He was buried in the Maze Pond Church burial-ground, and Samuel Stennett preached his funeral sermon.

MICHAEL A. G. HAYKIN

Sources S. Stennett, *The faithful minister rewarded* (1782) · J. Ivimey, *A history of the English Baptists*, 3 (1823), vol. 3, pp. 472–85 · W. Wilson, *The history and antiquities of the dissenting churches and meeting houses in London, Westminster and Southwark*, 4 vols. (1808–14), vol. 4, pp. 290–94 · *IGI* · R. Philip Roberts, *Continuity and change: London Calvinistic Baptists and the evangelical revival, 1760–1820* (1989), 69–70
Archives Regent's Park College, Oxford, Maze Pond Church minute books

Wallinger, Sir John Arnold (1869–1931), intelligence officer and literary prototype, was born on 25 October 1869 at Poona, India, the son of William H. Arnold Wallinger, deputy conservator of forests in the Indian forest service, and his wife, Anne Jane. He had two brothers and two sisters.

In 1896 Wallinger joined the Indian police in Ahmadabad as an inspector. Having been promoted assistant superintendent, in 1902 he was seconded to the Metropolitan Police in London as an instructor at a time of rising anxiety about Indian political activists and fears concerning the security of the coronation of Edward VII. He then stayed in England on 'special deputation' to Scotland Yard. In 1904 he returned to India and established a reputation as a brave officer with a talent for acquiring local native dialects and a flair for undercover criminal intelligence operations when he would 'black up'. On one occasion, while mounted, he saved a subordinate from a mob during a violent strike by charging a hostile crowd, and received a sword wound to the head that kept him in hospital for three months. Wallinger was transferred to London in 1910, with the rank of superintendent, to head the Indian political intelligence office, a new organization created to monitor the subversive activities in Britain of Indian nationalists.

In 1915 Wallinger acquired an assistant, Philip Vickery,

who was gazetted with the rank of major, and attached to general headquarters (GHQ) in France as a staff officer to assess discontent among Indian troops. His task was to identify and isolate malcontents while preventing enemy propaganda from undermining morale at the front and in India. While at GHQ he encountered his younger brother Ernest, a gunnery officer who had lost a foot at Le Cateau and had joined the Secret Intelligence Service (SIS). Based in offices in Basil Street, below his flat, Ernest Wallinger had organized an espionage network of train watchers, code-named WL, that stretched behind the German lines and into Belgium and neutral Holland. John Wallinger was appointed his controller in Geneva, supervising a network of British agents in Switzerland. According to the deputy director of military intelligence, Sir Walter Kirke, an attempt to expand into Holland and Scandinavia proved unsuccessful.

Wallinger is said to have been a keen reader of spy stories, but his initial agents—mostly waiters in restaurants—were easily spotted by the Swiss authorities. Instead, in autumn 1915 he persuaded an established writer, W. Somerset Maugham, to work for him, based in Geneva. The latter was subsequently very dismissive of his experiences, which he described as 'on the whole extremely monotonous' (Maugham, viii), and by summer 1916 he had returned to Britain. Nevertheless, he accumulated enough material for a book of short stories, *Ashenden, or, The British Agent*, published in 1928.

Interestingly, Maugham used Wallinger as the model for his spymaster in the Colonel R stories. This character had 'a yellow, deeply-lined face … [with] thin grey hair and a toothbrush moustache … a man that you could neither like nor trust at first sight' (Maugham, 2). Colonel R reminded the narrator that: 'If you do well you'll get no thanks and if you get into trouble you'll get no help' (ibid., 4). Alfred Hitchcock's film *The Secret Agent* (1936), starring Madeline Carroll and John Gielgud, was based on the stories. According to one authority, in his portrait of 'R', Maugham expressed a mood of disenchantment and hard-nosed realism that 'set the tone for an entirely new generation of espionage writing' (Stafford, 182).

In August 1916 Wallinger was posted back to India to suppress agitation there, and was busy with such intelligence operations until the end of the war. In 1919 he was seconded to Egypt. On his return to London in the following year he was appointed deputy inspector-general of the Indian police service. In 1925 he was knighted. Although offered the post of deputy commissioner of the Metropolitan Police, Wallinger chose to retire to Brighton in 1926. He died on 7 January 1931 at his home, Kingswood, Surrenden Road, Brighton. Wallinger never married, but Maugham later recalled dining with him and his attractive mistress. NIGEL WEST

Sources WWW · *The Times* (9 Jan 1931) · C. Andrew, *Secret service: the making of the British intelligence community* (1985) · d. cert. · *CGPLA Eng. & Wales* (1931) · M. Occleshaw, *Armour against fate: British military intelligence in the First World War* (1989) · R. Popplewell, *Intelligence and imperial defence: British intelligence and the defence of the Indian empire, 1904–1924* (1995) · W. S. Maugham, *Ashenden, or, The secret agent* (1928) · T. Morgan, *Somerset Maugham* (1980) · bap. reg., BL OIOC · D. Stafford, *The silent world: the real world of imaginary spies* (1988) · A. Masters, *Literary agents: the novelist as spy* (1987)
Wealth at death £1567 8s. 11d.: probate, 1931, *CGPLA Eng. & Wales*

Wallingford, John of (d. 1258). *See under* Paris, Matthew (c.1200–1259).

Wallingford, Richard (c.1292–1336), abbot of St Albans and astronomer, was born at Wallingford, near Oxford, the son of William, a blacksmith, and his wife, Isabella. On his father's death (c.1302) he was adopted by William Kirkeby, the prior of the Benedictine cell of St Albans in Wallingford, who about 1308 sent Richard to Oxford, where he determined in arts some time before 1316. He then assumed the monastic habit at St Albans, was ordained successively deacon (18 December 1316) and priest (28 May 1317), and was again sent to Oxford by his abbot—perhaps to Gloucester College, a Benedictine foundation. At Oxford he studied philosophy and theology for nine years (bachelor of theology, 1327), but on the evidence of his writings he gave most of his thought to astronomy and ancillary mathematics. To these studies his monastic biographer, writing in the *Gesta abbatum* of the abbey, adds music, and remarks that when Wallingford was abbot he was often heard to regret that he had allowed his mathematical and astronomical pursuits to direct his attention away from philosophy and theology.

Early scientific writings Two commentaries on the astronomical tables of John Maudith, the Merton College astronomer, were almost certainly written by Richard Wallingford, and were perhaps his first essay in this genre. He followed them with a lengthy four-part essay (*Quadripartitum*) on the fundamentals of trigonometry as required for the practice of astronomy. The first part provides trigonometrical identities, essentially as a basis for the calculation of sines and cosines. The later parts of the work give a systematic account of the theorem of Menelaus (*fl. c.*100 BC), in the 'eighteen modes' of Thabit ibn Qurra (d. 901), and the treatise ends with the application of these principles to advanced astronomical problems. The resulting book was the first comprehensive medieval treatise on the subject to have been written in the West, outside Muslim Spain. When Wallingford was abbot he wrote *De sectore*, a revision of this, his first substantial work, now taking into account some writings by a Spanish mathematician, Jabir ibn Aflah (*fl.* 1145).

Perhaps appreciably before leaving Oxford for the second time, in 1327, Richard Wallingford composed an astrological treatise, a six-part work on the 'prognostication of times', *Exafrenon pronosticacionum temporis*: that is, on astrological meteorology. The treatise *Exafrenon* is based in part on a short treatise by Robert Grosseteste (d. 1253), but ultimately draws most on classical Islamic writers, especially Abu Maʿshar (Albumasar; d. 886), and the pseudo-Ptolemaic *Centiloquium*. The Latin text of *Exafrenon* was translated into Middle English, on perhaps three occasions. *Exafrenon* was probably not Richard Wallingford's only astrological work, for it seems likely that after he became abbot he wrote another, above the ecclesiastical calendar of an unspecified queen. The work in question,

Richard Wallingford (*c.*1292–1336), manuscript illumination

similar to those simpler devices. It simulated rather the trigonometrical steps taken in a normal calculation done on the basis of tables, and with upward of seventy graduated scales, some of them spiral, some oval, it was by far the most sophisticated instrument of its kind in the middle ages. It had on its reverse a universal astrolabe—one for any geographical latitude—and a star map. The treatise was much copied and edited by later scholars. Simon Tunsted (*d.* 1369), provincial minister of the Franciscans a generation later, produced one version, and another was prepared by John of Gmunden (*d.* 1442), a famous Viennese master of the following century. A much inferior version was prepared by the great Renaissance scholar Regiomontanus (*d.* 1476). John of Gmunden's version included some new parameters and was much copied in southern Europe. The instrument continued in use until well into the sixteenth century and influenced the instruments produced by John Schöner (*d.* 1547) and Peter Apian (*d.* 1551). Despite all this, only two metal albions are known to survive from the middle ages, and they only in part.

Abbot of St Albans It is hard to avoid the feeling that of Richard Wallingford's various writings, his finest, the treatise on the albion, was given a name aimed at impressing the monks of his abbey. 'Albion' described his country, as well as his instrument, which was glossed as an 'all-by-one', and the name was also close to 'Alban', England's proto-martyr. His treatise was composed at a very opportune moment. His biographer in the *Gesta abbatum* does not mention it in this light, but seizes rather on his astrological reputation when telling a strange story of how Wallingford had 'foretold by means of the constellations the death of Abbot Hugh, and that he himself would be the future abbot' (*Gesta abbatum*, 2.183). The position as head of England's premier monastery—not as large or wealthy as Christ Church, Canterbury, but not inferior to it in power, art, or scholarship—was one to be coveted. His return to the abbey at the time of Hugh's death was ostensibly to ask for his inauguration expenses as a new bachelor in theology at Oxford in 1327. On the day of the election (29 October), one of the candidates, Richard Tring, spoke on the text 'Ye have not chosen me but I have chosen you'. Wallingford countered by addressing the chapter on the text 'Elect from among you the one who is most worthy', and was elected (*Gesta abbatum*, 2.183–4). While he was accused of feigning hesitation in accepting the office, he had good reason to do so, for his predecessors had been accumulating heavy debts for over half a century, and the fabric of the abbey was in serious disrepair. As in many other monastic towns in 1327, the villeins were on the point of revolt against the abbey's feudal privileges and had forced concessions from Abbot Hugh only a few months previously. The new abbot lived frugally, however, and took only a small retinue on his visits to the king at Nottingham and to the pope (John XXII) at Avignon, when obtaining confirmation in his post.

Sickness and opposition No sooner had Wallingford returned to St Albans from Avignon than he became aware that he was suffering from 'leprosy' (whether this

of which there are at least five copies, is ascribed only to an abbot of St Albans and is quite different in character from the more austerely 'scientific' *Exafrenon*, being now concerned with nativities and other aspects of astrology relating to personal fortunes. The queen might well have been Philippa, queen of Edward III, but this is a matter of speculation, especially in the absence of a calendar with the work included.

Treatise on the albion Probably in 1326, Wallingford composed a work describing a highly original astronomical instrument for observing and for calculating celestial co-ordinates (the so-called 'rectangulus'), and at much the same period he wrote his most important and influential *Tractatus albionis* ('Treatise on the albion'), which describes the construction and use of an equatorium he had designed. The rectangulus was an instrument made entirely of intricately jointed straight rods, by which the same astronomical problems could be solved as using an armillary sphere or a more expensive 'torquetum', which might in turn be described as a sort of equatorially mounted theodolite. It can be regarded as an instrument obviating the need for complex mathematics in transforming one set of celestial co-ordinates to another, and this was undoubtedly a problem to which its author gave much thought, as can be seen from four short tracts he sketched on that subject, probably after becoming abbot.

The albion was primarily an equatorium, a device allowing for the rapid calculation of planetary positions, and a substitute for slow and painful techniques that made use of such astronomical tables as the Toledan and Alfonsine. Equatoria were originally relatively simple assemblages of graduated discs of metal, wood, or parchment, that simulated the various circles (deferent circles, epicycles, and so forth) of Ptolemaic planetary theory. The albion used an arrangement of discs that was only superficially was one of the forms of disease now known by that name, or one of several diseases with similar symptoms, is not known). Beginning by causing partial blindness in the right eye, the disease progressed relentlessly thereafter. It did not cause him to be any more lenient with his monks, whose deportment had become extremely lax, and he launched a new rule of retrenchment and reform. This was much resented and a disgruntled Richard Tring led a rebellion by some of the younger monks. Punishments subsequently meted out by the abbot were so strong as to inspire 'a conspiracy by certain false brothers' (*Gesta abbatum*, 2.199) against him, and his leprosy was alleged as an argument for deposing him. He rode out the storm, nevertheless, by a series of ingenious manoeuvres, such as banishing the worst of the troublemakers to distant cells, while as regards excommunication he obtained some of the rights of a bishop by royal charter, due largely to his friendship with the powerful Richard Bury, the future bishop of Durham.

Wallingford's abbacy, which had begun by antagonizing the brethren, gradually changed to one in which he earned their respect. In part this was because he was victorious in a series of trials of strength with the villeins, especially from 1331 onwards. He successfully indicted the townsmen on charges concerning their misdeeds against Abbot Hugh, for example. He became expert in legal matters—more so, said the chronicler, than his own counsel. In one of his many appeals to the courts he exacted arrears of rent from Queen Isabella from a mill at Little Langley (court order of 22 March 1334). He kept the troublesome visiting mendicant friars in their place, humiliating them on points of canon law when they came to preach and hear confessions in the hope of poaching young monks. But in larger measure the abbot's rising popularity was undoubtedly due to a vast and extraordinary astronomical clock he was building for the abbey. This, the achievement for which he was best remembered in his monastery after his death, is discussed below.

By 1333 the infirmity of the abbot, who was old-fashioned in the extent to which he lived with his monks, had reached a point where 'he was unable to live the monastic life with others without causing offence' (*Gesta abbatum*, 2.286). This was the judgment of two of the bishop of Lincoln's commissioners, who were acting on a papal initiative—prompted in the first place by a missive from Richard Ildesle (or Ilsley), a Benedictine monk of Abingdon who is said to have aspired to the abbot's place. The monks received the commissioners with hostility. Abbot Richard stood firm, and took the precaution of complaining to the king, then at York, about the intervention of the Roman curia in the affairs of his monastery. The king's wrath fell on those who had prompted papal interference, and even on Richard Bury, who had sealed the letter—though he pleaded coercion. Letters from the prior and convent and from the king were sent to Rome, drawing attention to the undoubted benefits the abbey had drawn from its abbot's rule, and to the fact that he had appointed his able prior, Nicholas Flamstede, to look after the material affairs of the abbey. This prior, ten years his

senior, was perhaps his closest friend, although they quarrelled late in Wallingford's life. As for Richard Ildesle, the brethren, many 'of great stature and strength', threatened to cut him to pieces as an example to others. 'His conscience telling him this was not a sufficient reason for martyrdom' (*Gesta abbatum*, 2.292), he fled the town of St Albans.

The great astronomical clock It is not known when during his abbacy Richard Wallingford first began work on his astronomical clock, but since it came as a natural extension of his work at Oxford he probably began almost at once. His abilities in this direction might even explain why he was so desirable a candidate as abbot, for this was a time when several religious foundations were vying with one another in producing ever finer specimens of this relatively new technological marvel (the invention was about half a century old). The abbot's own father had been a smith, so that work in iron, the material of large monumental clocks, was not new to him; but he would in any case have been able to call on the services of professional clock builders, and indeed the employment at St Albans of two such men, Roger and Laurence Stoke, is known. Judging by the St Albans manuscript from which the evidence for the clock derives (now MS Ashmole 1796 in the Bodleian Library, Oxford), Wallingford began to write a thoroughly academic treatise on the subject, and he completed an opening section on the arithmetical techniques to be used in calculating trains of gears for general astronomical use. It is likely that he died before editing his several drafts of later chapters describing the actual construction, and what remains is an incomplete and misbound copy of a disordered set of originals, in which irrelevant material is interspersed. From reconstructed parallel drafts it can be seen how he improved his technique, until he had devised a train for the moon's monthly motion round the heavens that was accurate to seven parts in a million. At the same time the moon rotated to show its correct phases.

The dial was a large astrolabe-type plate more than two metres across, with the rete overlaying a plate of stars—the reverse of the more usual astrolabe arrangement. He had a device (an oval contrate wheel, without parallel before at least the sixteenth century) for driving the sun around the zodiac at a variable speed, and this, like many other of his mechanical ideas, is without known precedents. The clock had a dial showing the tides at London Bridge, a wheel of fortune, and a bell that struck the hours on a 24-hour system. What is historically of very great interest is that the escapement controlling both the weight-driven clock and the weight-driven strike was of a double pin-wheel type superior to what used to be thought the oldest mechanical escapement (the simple 'verge and foliot'). Even more surprising is that the St Albans escapement is found in use by Leonardo da Vinci, about 1495. The clock is the oldest mechanical clock of which there is detailed knowledge. Laurence Stoke made the final adjustments to it only after Richard's death and it survived in its position in the south transept of the abbey into the sixteenth century, when it was said to be without equal in Europe, but disappeared after the dissolution of the monasteries. A partial reconstruction of it was made for the Time Museum, Rockford, Illinois, but was subsequently sold.

Other writings, death, and reputation A few ecclesiastical writings by Richard Wallingford are known. He wrote a treatise on the general statutes of the Benedictine order, something for which his administrative experience made him well qualified. He also wrote on the prologue to the rule of St Benedict, and statutes for brethren staying at Redbourn, a place for recreation at which three monks at a time were privileged to spend at least a month in a retreat which amounted to a holiday. Apart from four prayers and a number of administrative documents, the only other possibly authentic work not mentioned above is a small fragment of a computus, a work for determining the moveable feasts in the church calendar. There are several literary ghosts. The tradition that he wrote a work on eclipses derives fairly surely from treating a section of his *Albion* as a separate work. The same goes for a work 'on diameters', *De diametris*. *De opimetris* (a meaningless phrase) was almost certainly an invention of C. L. Kingsford, Wallingford's biographer in the *Dictionary of National Biography*, who presumably misread his own notes on *De diametris*. Thomas Tanner mistakenly gave to Richard Wallingford an anonymous work on the saphea, thinking that the saphea (a universal astrolabe plate) was an instrument of Richard's invention since it is found on the albion.

Richard Wallingford died on 23 May 1336. His tomb is the second from the left, facing the altar in the abbey church (now St Albans Cathedral), the one with the longest and narrowest stone. Its inscription is now lost, but Richard Gough (1786) recorded these words of French from it: 'Richard gist ici Dieu de sa alme eit merci. Vous ke par ici passes Pater e Ave pur l'alme prierunt … jours de pardun averunt' (North, 3.125). The abbot's physical condition had been declining rapidly over his last four years. Even in April 1332, at a time when he forced the townsmen to surrender their charter, he was scarcely able to speak. In 1334 there was a great thunderstorm which set fire to his chamber, and from that day to the end of his life he was in constant pain. Some of his personal prayers, mentioning his leprosy, survive. The chronicler of the *Gesta* put down his severity to his infirmity and the laxity of his predecessor, but in many ways admired it, and by the time of Wallingford's death there was probably a consensus on this point within the abbey walls. The buildings were almost completely re-roofed, the mills were in repair, there was a new almonry school, and the foundations for a new cloister were laid. He had experimented with some success at fertilizing the fields with crushed acorns to increase yields of corn. These were only a few of the changes he had brought about, but of course the greatest marvel he had provided for his abbey, and the one that probably accounted more than anything else for his monks' loyalty, was his clock. Why, the king once asked him, did he spend so much on that, when the abbey was in

disrepair? He answered that when he was gone there would be nobody capable of doing the work; and in that, the chronicler added, he was right.   J. D. NORTH

Sources *Richard of Wallingford: an edition of his writings*, ed. and trans. J. D. North, 3 vols. (1976) [Lat. orig., with parallel Eng. trans.] · *Gesta abbatum monasterii Sancti Albani, a Thoma Walsingham*, ed. H. T. Riley, 3 vols., pt 4 of *Chronica monasterii S. Albani*, Rolls Series, 28 (1867–9) · Emden, *Oxf.*
Likenesses manuscript drawing, BL, Cotton MS Nero D.vii, fol. 20r; repro. in North, *Richard of Wallingford*, vol. 3, pl. 1 · manuscript illumination, BL, Cotton MS Claudius E.iv, pt 1, fol. 201r [*see illus.*]

Wallingford, William (d. 1492), abbot of St Albans, was almost certainly born at Wallingford, Berkshire, where the Benedictine priory was a dependent cell of St Albans. It was probably under Prior John Stoke's patronage that he entered St Albans as a novice, during the 1430s. Following his profession he was sent to Oxford to study at Gloucester College. It appears he was intended to study canon law—later he demonstrated considerable legal knowledge when defending himself against charges of embezzlement—but he remained at the university for no more than five years and left without taking a degree: Abbot John Whethamstede later observed that all Wallingford had acquired at Oxford was 'a taste for money' (Riley, 2.130). Wallingford returned to St Albans in the early 1440s and under John Stoke, newly elected abbot, was promoted to a succession of senior obedientiary posts: by 1445 he held five offices simultaneously, including archdeacon, cellarer, bursar, forester, and sub-cellarer, and before 1451 he had also been appointed official-general. Following Stoke's death in December 1451, Wallingford was one of three candidates proposed for the abbacy. However, when it became clear that the former abbot, John Whethamstede, was prepared to resume office he withdrew his candidacy.

During the vacancy following Stoke's death, Wallingford and his brother Thomas were investigated for their involvement in the embezzlement of 1000 marks from conventual funds, a crime to which Stoke himself had confessed shortly before his death. Stoke claimed he had entrusted the brothers with the money and that they had concealed it in a chest in the dormitory. The chest was recovered, but it was found to contain no more than 250 marks. Wallingford's suspected dishonesty was recalled in 1453, when he was required to render accounts for his various offices. These revealed significant losses, and suggested that Stoke and his officials had been guilty of widespread mismanagement. Wallingford withdrew in disgrace, and Whethamstede began an investigation into his predecessor's administration. His findings confirmed that so substantial a fall in income could have occurred only through maladministration or outright embezzlement. Wallingford responded with the scholarly but evasive argument that it was inevitable for a monk charged with such worldly responsibilities to fall in with the 'unrighteous followers of Mammon' (Riley, 2.111–12). He also secured the support of other senior monks, and the protection of some distinguished noble patrons, including Edmund Tudor, earl of Richmond, and Lord and Lady

Sudeley, who prevailed upon Whethamstede to judge him leniently. Presenting new accounts to Whethamstede, Wallingford appears to have made a partial admission of guilt, but claimed that the amount lost was considerably less than had been alleged. Whethamstede again seems to have been persuaded, and even commended Wallingford for his business skills. However, in 1454, when Whethamstede requested a contribution from Wallingford towards a clerical tenth, Wallingford now denied that he had any money at all, although in his own revised accounts he had claimed to hold over £160. Whethamstede accused him of perjury, but once again Wallingford seems to have been saved from any punitive actions by the intercession of others. Whethamstede was persuaded to maintain Wallingford in his offices, provided that he raised at least £200 or £300 from them within the next two years.

Despite these repeated allegations, Wallingford remained in office throughout the 1450s and 1460s. He was again proposed as a candidate for the abbacy following Whethamstede's death in 1465, but the prior, William Albon, was preferred. Under Albon, Wallingford himself became prior, an office he held for over eleven years. Then, following Albon's death in 1476, he again declared his candidacy and this time was elected abbot on 5 August.

Wallingford's rule as abbot has long been seen as indicative of the corruption and decadence into which English monasteries fell in the century before the dissolution. His register reveals that he misappropriated conventual resources, maintained his own liveried retainers at the community's expense, and granted offices and rents to friends, family, and members of the local nobility. His register also suggests he frequently abused his ecclesiastical authority in the local community, making fraudulent charges against testators, granting a licence for mass to be celebrated in an alehouse, and deposing the prioress of Sopwell on false grounds of heresy. Moreover Cardinal John Morton, in a monition issued on 5 July 1490, accused Wallingford of wide-ranging financial mismanagement, simony, usury, and wasting the goods of the monastery to the value of 8000 marks. He claimed Wallingford had misgoverned St Albans and its dependent communities, attacking those monks who wished to lead a religious life, and interfering in the elections of the nunneries and priories under his jurisdiction, and he made serious allegations concerning Wallingford's sexual corruption and his tolerance of moral laxity in others, accusing the abbot of soliciting the wife of a St Albans man, and tolerating the affair between a local woman and Thomas Sudbury, formerly a monk of St Albans who was now prior of St Andrew's, Northampton. Although it is difficult to substantiate many of these claims, a number of the documents in Wallingford's register give credence to the accusations surrounding his management of the dependent cells.

The evidence of Wallingford's misrule should not, however, be allowed to obscure his wider achievements as abbot. His relationship with his nunneries may have broken down, but he seems to have maintained a stable relationship with the other cells, and was credited with settling a long-standing dispute between the mother house and the priory at Tynemouth. He also made significant improvements to the abbey buildings, spending over £8000 in the completion of the new bakehouse, chapter house, and library which had been begun under Whethamstede; and adding costly new decorations to the interior of the abbey church. He also developed a considerable public reputation as spokesman for his order and even, surprisingly, as a reformer. A leading figure in the Benedictine general chapters, he presided at their meetings, and at least once, in 1480, served as visitor for all the Benedictine houses in the diocese of Lincoln. Wallingford also appears to have been a generous patron of education and scholarship. He increased the number of his own monks who studied at Oxford and Cambridge, and supported as many as a dozen local boys through school and university. He seems also to have encouraged the work of the so-called 'St Albans printer', who established a press—the earliest outside Westminster—perhaps within the abbey precincts, c.1480.

Perhaps most significant, however, were Wallingford's efforts to defend and extend St Albans' privileges and exemptions from episcopal and royal control. Although the independence of the religious orders was coming under increasing criticism, Wallingford successfully blocked all efforts to interfere in the management of his community or its endowments. Throughout the 1480s he had maintained representatives at the curia, and secured a number of significant new privileges, including the right to assume episcopal orders for himself and his successors. Between 1487 and 1492 he also successfully defended the abbey from the efforts of Henry VII and Morton to deprive it of its exempt status and subject it to archiepiscopal visitation. In 1487 the king had secured the bull *Quantas in Dei ecclesias* from Innocent VIII empowering Morton to visit all exempt communities. Wallingford immediately dispatched a representative to the curia to secure confirmation of the abbey's exemptions and privileges—on 6 February 1490 Morton received a bull warning him not to allow St Albans to suffer any further 'molestation'. The archbishop then sent his own delegation to Rome, which apparently presented the pope with allegations of Wallingford's corruption and misrule. Consequently on 6 March 1490 Innocent issued another bull, declaring that it had recently been brought to his attention that in 'certain houses' the monks 'are leading a wanton and most dissolute life' (Coulton, 4.515–16), and ordering that these houses be subject to immediate visitation, without recourse to earlier exemptions. Morton received this bull on 24 April and appears to have made preparations for a visitation. However, Wallingford also responded quickly, dispatching another delegation to the curia to renew his appeal for confirmation of the abbey's privileges. Innocent appears to have responded verbally to both parties between 30 June and 4 July, remarkably giving his assent to the claims of each. Despite his bull of 6 March, Innocent seems to have offered the St Albans monks full confirmation of their privileges, and at the same time offered Morton notional support for his planned visitation. Consequently on 5 July, Morton issued Wallingford with his *Monitio*, detailing the allegations of corruption made in the curia, and calling upon him to reform his own house and the nunneries within thirty days, and his other communities within sixty days, or face archiepiscopal visitation. It appears that Wallingford then made further appeals to the pope, for on 30 July, Morton received notification that the monks' claims to exemption were under consideration by a committee of papal chaplains. This seems to have been enough to halt an immediate visitation, and in spite of a further bull from Innocent issued on the same day, declaring his support for monastic reform, there is no evidence to suggest that a visitation took place. With Thomas Sudbury's death in 1490, and Wallingford's own death two years later, Morton perhaps considered the imperative for reform at St Albans had been removed.

Wallingford died at St Albans between 23 May and 5 June 1492, and was probably buried in St Albans Abbey church.

JAMES G. CLARK

Sources Emden, *Oxf.*, 3.1967–8 · H. T. Riley, ed., *Registra quorundam abbatum monasterii S. Albani*, 2, Rolls Series, 28/6 (1873), 140–291 · G. G. Coulton, *Five centuries of religion*, 4 (1950), 508–44 · D. Knowles [M. C. Knowles], *The religious orders in England*, 3 (1959), 8–9, 77–9 · D. Knowles, 'The case of St Albans Abbey in 1490', *Journal of Ecclesiastical History*, 3 (1952), 144–58 · C. L. Kingsford, ed., *The Stonor letters and papers, 1290–1483*, 2, CS, 3rd ser., 30 (1919); repr. as *Kingsford's Stonor letters and papers, 1290–1483*, ed. C. Carpenter (1996), 82–3 · E. F. Jacob, 'The Book of St Albans', *Bulletin of the John Rylands University Library*, 28 (1944), 99–118; repr. in *Essays in later medieval history* (1968), 194–213 · Wallingford's abbatial register, Bodl. Oxf., MS Rawl. B.332; edited in 'Registrum Iohannis Whethamstede', *Registra quorundam abbatum monasterii S. Albani*, ed. H. T. Riley, 2 vols., Rolls Series, 28/6 (1872–3) · W. A. Pantin, ed., *Documents illustrating the activities of … the English black monks, 1215–1540*, 3 vols., CS, 3rd ser., 45, 47, 54 (1931–7), esp. vol. 3, p. 233
Archives Bodl. Oxf., MS Rawl. B.332 | Stonor MSS, letter
Likenesses drawing, BL, Cotton MS Nero D.vii, fol. 42*v*

Wallington, Nehemiah (1598–1658), turner and diarist, was born on 12 May 1598 in the parish of St Leonard Eastcheap, London, the tenth of twelve children and the fourth son of John Wallington, citizen and turner (1552/3–1638), and his wife, Elizabeth (1562/3–1603), the daughter of Anthony Hall, citizen and skinner, and his wife, Jane. Following the death of Elizabeth, John Wallington married Joan Hinde, a widow with two children, and following her death in 1605 he married, as his third wife, Alice Harrison (*d.* 1634), also a widow with two children and the mother of Patience, Nehemiah's half-sister.

Wallington was never apprenticed but set up shop as a turner after admission to the Turners' Company, by patrimony, on 18 May 1620. Within a year he had married Grace Rampaigne; she was the sister of Livewell Rampaigne, a minister of Burton and then Broxholme, whose letters of comfort Nehemiah preserved and whose widow, Sarah, and her two children lived with the Wallingtons from 1635 until her death in 1654, and of Zachariah Rampaigne, a planter in Ireland killed during the rising of 1641, whose son Charles was taken in by the Wallingtons and served as Nehemiah's apprentice until his freedom in 1655.

Wallington's freedom as a turner and his marriage followed two years of mental breakdown, during which, doubting of his salvation, he had made a number of suicide attempts, complicated by his desire to protect his father and the puritan community from the disgrace of such an ungodly act, and had first begun to write. His work, initially a record of his sins and God's mercies, was abandoned in 1620 when he began 'A record of God's mercies, or, A thankful remembrance', part diary, part commonplace book, which he continued intermittently well into the 1630s. A combination of work and family responsibilities apparently prevented any further breakdown. Wallington was sustained by the friendship and counsel of Henry Roborough, the young curate and lecturer at St Leonard Eastcheap, by the steady common sense and strength of Grace, and perhaps by the discipline of writing. He also received a loan from the Turners' Company. However, the death of his first child, Elizabeth, in 1625 led to a fresh crisis, during which Wallington confessed that he forgot all his 'purposes, promises and covenants' with God and was inconsolable until reminded by Grace that their daughter had gone 'home to her husband Christ Jesus' ('A record of God's mercies', Guildhall Library, MS 204, p. 409). Their son John died six months after Elizabeth, their second son, Nehemiah, in 1627, and their last child, Samuel, born in 1630, died in October 1632. Only their daughter Sarah, born in 1627, survived to adulthood to marry, on 20 July 1647, a young godly turner, John Houghton.

Unlike his father and his elder brother John, both of whom were liverymen, serving their turn as masters, Wallington never left the yeomanry of the Turners' Company. Although he apparently worked steadily at his craft he had no head for business, as he confessed on more than one occasion, and struggled all his life to find some balance between the demands of his calling as a turner and the more compelling demands of his calling as a Christian. He regularly rose in the small hours of the morning to write before private prayer in his closet and further public prayers with his household. He admitted to spending too much on books, particularly on news-sheets during the 1640s, and had a library of more than 200 works, beginning with William Gouge's *Of Domestical Duties*, which he purchased soon after his marriage. By 1654, when he compiled a catalogue of his writings, he listed fifty notebooks, ranging from his diary to memorials of God's judgements against sabbath breakers, commonplaces from scripture, and various puritan guides to the godly life, sermon notes, a volume of collected letters, a number of volumes detailing the mercies he had received, and a number of volumes of political news collected during the 1640s. Aside from a book called *The Mighty Works of the Lord, which is a Prop to Faith*, which he gave to his wife, and a book on patience, which he left to his half-sister Patience, he bequeathed all his notebooks to his son-in-law, John Houghton. He had little else to leave and apparently made no will.

Wallington was in many respects the quintessential

puritan, introspective, bookish, sermon-going, scrupulous in his business relations, and constantly struggling for even-tempered acceptance of life and of himself, which he believed should accompany assurance of election. He followed the fortunes of protestantism during the Thirty Years' War and those of parliament during the civil war. Although he served conscientiously as a lay elder in the fourth London classis from 1646 until his last years his Presbyterianism was based on his desire for parish discipline, and his only quarrel with the protectorate was that it did not bring the godly reformation that he had long prayed for. As he wrote in 1655, it was the toleration of 'many strange, false forms of worship', of 'Sabbath profanation', of 'our cruel oppression of the poor', and of 'our impudent pride' that he found profoundly disillusioning and that made him fear in his last years a dreadful punishment of his 'rebellious City' ('A memorial of God's judgments upon sabbath breakers, drunkards and other vile livers', BL, Sloane MS 1457, fols. 99r–101v). Wallington died in Eastcheap in August 1658. P. S. SEAVER

Sources P. S. Seaver, *Wallington's world: a puritan artisan in seventeenth-century London* (1985) · N. Wallington, *Historical notices of events occurring chiefly in the reign of Charles I*, ed. R. Webb, 2 vols. (1869) · parish register, St Leonard Eastcheap, GL, MS 17607 · Turners' Company, book of apprentice bindings, GL, MS 3302/1 · Turners' Company, court minutes, 1605–33, GL, MS 3295/1
Archives BL, 'The growth of a Christian', Add. MS 40883 · BL, letter-book, Sloane MS 922 · BL, 'A memorial of God's judgements upon sabbath breakers, drunkards and other vile livers', Sloane MS 1457 · BL, untitled MS, partly published as *Historical notices*, Add. MS 21935 · Folger, 'Extract of the passages of my life', MS V.a.436 · GL, 'A record of God's mercies, or, A thankful remembrance', MS 204 · Tatton Park, Cheshire, 'A record of mercies continued', MS CR 4–7

Wallis, Sir Barnes Neville (1887–1979), aeronautical designer and engineer, was born on 26 September 1887 at Ripley, Derbyshire, the second child in the family of three sons and one daughter of Charles George Wallis, general practitioner, and his wife, Edith Eyre, daughter of the Revd John Ashby. In 1891 the family moved to New Cross, south London. After Charles Wallis was crippled by polio in 1893 they lived in straitened, genteel circumstances. Wallis first attended Haberdashers' Aske's School in nearby Hatcham. His mother, a strong influence on him, encouraged him to enter Christ's Hospital. He took the entrance examination in 1900. It was here that he first suffered the migraines by which he was plagued for the rest of his life. He excelled in mathematics, English, and sciences. He learned to think and to refer to basic principles, to use French and German, and was taught mechanical drawing. He left school in 1904 and was indentured to the Thames Engineering Works at Blackheath. In 1908 he transferred his articles to the J. S. White Company at Cowes, where at age twenty-one he soon moved into the drawing office. Urged by his mother, he also took, and passed, the London matriculation examinations.

Airship development, 1911–1928 In 1911 Wallis's mother died, and he was saddled with some responsibility for his father and the junior members of the family, but this was offset by the arrival at the next drafting table of his future

Sir Barnes Neville Wallis (1887–1979), by Alfred Egerton Cooper, 1942

collaborator H. B. Pratt, who had left Vickers when they cancelled the development of the first rigid airship, Mayfly, on which he worked. Pratt and Wallis became good friends and remained in touch until Pratt's suicide in 1940. In 1913 Pratt was recalled to Vickers as chief engineer, airships, to begin work on the new rigid airship, No. 9, and he picked Wallis as his chief designer with J. E. Temple as chief calculator. But No. 9, a copy of Zeppelin LZ IV of 1912, was well out of date when it first became airborne in 1916. Wallis next helped with No. 23 and with R 26 (the nomenclature had changed), both outdated designs.

All his life Wallis felt ashamed that he had not served in the armed forces during the First World War. He briefly joined the Artists' Rifles, but was recalled to Vickers at Barrow in Furness. There he did a short stint in the Royal Naval Volunteer Reserve, where he helped manage the air side of airship construction. Again he was forced to resign because he worked in a vital industry.

By 1916 Pratt had recognized that Wallis had design genius. Thus Wallis started working on the design of the radically different R 80, incorporating all that had been learned from the most recently shot down German Zeppelins. For not the last time in his life, Wallis disbelieved wind tunnel tests done at the National Physical Laboratory which he insisted were distorted by the small shape of the models unless extrapolated using Reynolds numbers. Of equal importance, he had to design a new airship which could be built in the existing shed on the Isle of Walney, Barrow, in which No. 23 and R 26 had been erected. The result was a fully streamlined ship which had drag of only 3 per cent of a flat plate of the same diameter, as against the 16 per cent of R 26. R 80 was always in Wallis, the artist–creator's, mind his best ship. Unfortunately, she was delayed in building and only flew in mid-July 1920, and was then dismantled in 1925. Nevertheless, Wallis used the knowledge gained in other works.

After a nervous breakdown in 1919 Wallis was offered a retainer and was then laid off in 1921. He crammed for the external degree in engineering at the University of London, succeeding in 1922 at the age of thirty-three. In the meantime he had fallen in love with Mary (Molly) Frances Bloxham (d. 1986) and taken a position as mathematics master at the Chillon School in Switzerland, where he stayed in the latter half of 1922. He was a lucid lecturer, and also coached his fiancée by mail in the intricacies of the subject. For the rest of their lives she was his sounding board. They married on 23 April 1925 at Hampstead, and had two sons and two daughters.

After the end of the war a member of the Vickers board, Commander C. Dennistoun Burney, had put forward a scheme for an imperial airship service at a time when the hydrogen-filled airship obviously had great long-distance advantages over the passenger aeroplanes of the day, as R 34 had demonstrated in 1919 by a round trip across the north Atlantic. Vickers accepted the idea contingent upon government support. Pratt declined to join the venture, and so Wallis, now back at Vickers, became the chief designer under Burney from 15 May 1923. This was not a happy arrangement and further strengthened Wallis's antipathy to both government bureaucrats and high company officers. This might be attributed to his professional arrogance and to his total immersion in the work, where he had to solve every problem himself working 16-hour days. Wallis had the virtues of self-reliance, independence, and pride, and was a strong Anglo-Catholic—he often prayed when searching for a solution. He was also a cross-country runner and loved other sports as well. All his life he took cold baths and was a semi-vegetarian. Moreover, he was always learning. In 1923 he joined the territorials and became an anti-aircraft gunner at Vickers, commissioned a second lieutenant in 1925.

In 1924 the new Labour government confirmed a contract with the Airship Guarantee Company (AGC) for a single ship, R 100, to compete with a government one, the ill-fated R 101. Wallis was now officially chief designer of the AGC with N. S. Norway (the novelist Nevil Shute) as his assistant. In the meantime, while in Germany on a visit with Burney to Friedrichshafen to negotiate for a Zeppelin, he had got the germ of the geodetic idea of standard parts prefabricated into triangles. Having had practical training, as so many of the designers and aircraft manufacturers of his day had, Wallis believed in simplicity. He had designed R 80 with a minimum number of fabricated pieces. He advanced R 100 by reducing this to nine while at the same time carefully thinking through every detail including the gasbag restraints, which transferred lift to the hull. Moreover, Wallis did not believe in using dynamic lift with its associated drag and danger of nosing over if the elevators broke. R 100 was designed always to move in perfect equilibrium. He started the design from first principles and ended with more than a hundred patents on the geodetic system. By 1928 he had been

awarded the silver star of the Royal Aeronautical Society for his design work, but Burney had become a burden. Wallis had a second breakdown and went to France for rest. At about the same time, from Howden, Yorkshire, where R 100 was being assembled, he visited neighbouring Brough, talked with Jack Rennie of Blackburn, and became enamoured of aeroplane design.

Aeroplane work, 1928–1945 Fortunately this new interest coincided with the desire of the new Vickers chairman, Sir Robert McLean, to add Wallis to the aeroplane team which included Supermarine's R. J. Mitchell and R. K. Pierson of Vickers at Weybridge. In November 1928 Wallis became chief designer, co-equal with Mitchell and Pierson. Though Wallis still loved R 100, relations with Burney worsened. On 1 January 1930 he signed the Vickers contract for a salary of £7000 p.a., moved to Weybridge, and bought White Hall House, Effingham, for his family. For a short time he was sent to help Mitchell, but since R. J. was not told that Wallis had full authority he returned to Weybridge. He immediately saved Pierson by redesigning the Jockey fighter (Type 151) to stop tail vibrations. From then on Pierson trusted his structures engineer and co-chief designer, and his experience with light alloys. Thus given a free hand, Wallis applied geodetics to aircraft fuselages with a great savings in weight and added strength. This revolution in aircraft structures gave him a new career.

In October 1930 Wallis started on the design of a geodetic bomber. While his too light first design, the M/130 torpedo bomber, broke up in the air, his Vickers private venture to specification G.4/31 became the Wellesley which proved itself as a record-breaking long-distance monoplane in the 1938 flight of 7158 miles non-stop from Egypt to Australia. The geodetic system left the interior of both wings and fuselage clear while allowing fabric to continue to be used for the outer cover at a time when the British aircraft industry had not yet mastered all metal stressed skin construction.

Simultaneously Wallis and Pierson were working on the Air Ministry's B.9/32 specification for a twin-engined heavy bomber, the geodetic Wellington, of which 11,461 were built, the aircraft staying in production throughout the Second World War. Even before the Wellington entered squadron service in October 1938, the Vickers team was working on B.1/35, a heavy bomber called the Warwick. In the course of these developments Wallis had been challenged on the grounds that his system was too complex and difficult to manufacture. Here his hands-on training paid off. He had designed R 100 to be built largely by semi-skilled labour and he applied the same principles to Wellington production, designing the necessary machine tools himself. Then on 1 May 1940 the air staff decided that British bombers needed to carry 4000 lb bombs, which were then being developed. By the time they were approved in March 1941 Wallis had the Wellington ready to receive them. A Warwick variant of this design became the four-engined, elliptical winged Windsor of 1943, of which only prototypes were built. A very large 68,000 lb aircraft designed to fly at 345 m.p.h. at

31,000 feet with 12,000 pounds of bombs, it was to have had remotely controlled rearward firing defensive armament mounted in the back of the engine nacelles. Wallis had the bad luck to lose the first prototype in an accident and the second in an enemy air raid. Yet the truly large aircraft could have demonstrated the efficiency of the geodetic system best, even if the early flights at high speeds revealed fabric wrinkling.

In the meantime Wallis, still at Weybridge, had decided that what the RAF needed were deep penetration bombs which the aborted Pierson–Wallis six-engined design of 1936 could have delivered. In 1939 his work was interrupted by the need to sweep magnetic mines in shallow waters such as the Thames estuary. His response was operational in six weeks, the degaussing-ring Wellington. Then in 1940 he began studying the German war economy, devised a scheme for preventing German gliders landing on English fields, and sang in the local choir. Of these accomplishments, the most important was, of course, his work on the German economy, which led to his realization that at the heart of German steel production was the water impounded in various Ruhr dams. This led to his most publicized development, the dam busting bombs carried by 617 squadron on 17 May 1943, known colloquially as the bouncing bombs. The raid was the outcome of a long bureaucratic campaign by Wallis to give priority to the destruction of the industrial capacity of the Ruhr, in the course of which he made many enemies and also gained some allies. His paranoia was such that when, in early 1943, his plan was finally accepted, he interpreted the short time that he was given for its implementation as a plot to sabotage his credibility. In putting his ideas into practice he had to make considerable compromises due to shortage of time and resources; in particular the original plan for a spherical bouncing bomb had to be modified to accommodate a cylindrical shape. In the final analysis the raid was partially successful, and gave the enemy a considerable shock.

Concurrently Wallis had been developing the Tallboy 12,000 lb deep penetration bomb and the 22,000 lb 'tenton' bomb (both based on R 100's shape). The latter was delayed because the RAF had no suitable bombsight—a matter of which Wallis was not apprised or, no doubt, he would have created one. In addition to certain senior RAF officers opposing the big bombs, Lord Cherwell, Prime Minister Churchill's right-hand man, opposed it. After the dams raid, Wallis was put forward for a knighthood, but it was quashed by both his own Vickers board and by Sir Stafford Cripps, who had never forgiven him for predicting the demise of R 101. This was the second time he was denied the honour; he had also been put forward early in 1941. He was appointed CBE. Later, the advent of the V 1 and V 2 brought a demand for the Tallboy to demolish the launching sites in France.

Post-war life and work, 1945–1979 At the end of the war which his designs had helped to win Wallis received the Ewing medal from the Royal Society of which he was elected a fellow. But there was no national recognition for him as a patriot until 1968 when at last he received the knighthood he so richly deserved. Nevertheless, in the post-war years he gained a public image as representing the Second World War boffin; his work on dam busting bombs was dramatically represented in the film *The Dam Busters* (1954), based on Paul Brickhill's 1951 book of the same title. The heroic and hagiographic aspects of Brickhill's book were carried over into the film, and Michael Redgrave's representation of Wallis as the much misunderstood genius, already quite similar to the way in which Wallis was accustomed to see himself, subsequently became ever more part of Wallis's public persona, continually redrawn in his many broadcast interviews.

In 1945 the new chairman of Vickers, Sir Hew Kilmer, offered Wallis the post of special director of an independent research department. This allowed him to work on his next advanced project, the variable geometry supersonic aircraft which used the wing to control flight. Already by 1946 his concepts were clearly set out in an unpublished paper on the application of aerodynamic properties (Wallis MSS, Sci. Mus.). His proposal was startling: abolish the tail empennage and ailerons so as to reduce profile drag and all up weight in order to be able to achieve the longest ranged flight possible, the basic goal of his professional life. Having worked on airships and conventional aircraft, Wallis was now in his third phase of development and once again he was too radical for the people controlling the British aircraft industry, no longer by 1952 his influential friends. Moreover, he himself, at sixty-eight, was less the dynamic creator than the philosopher–king of his team.

In 1951 Wallis was awarded a £10,000 gratuity from the Royal Commission on Awards to Inventors, which he invested in Christ's Hospital for children of RAF staff. In his professional work he stuck to models of his military and civil variable geometry aircraft, Wild Goose and Swallow. When in 1953 neither Vickers nor the air staff could come up with a successor to the V-bombers, Wallis's answer was the radical swept wing Swallow with its delta fuselage cross-section, engines mounted on swivels so that as the wings swept they remained parallel to the flight path, and a pop-up cockpit that gave 360° visibility for take-off and landing. Though a successful model was test fired from a gun, Vickers had withdrawn support in 1953 and the whole died by 1958 after the Duncan Sandys white paper on defence. Wallis's last professional venture came at the age of eighty when he designed nuclear cargo submarines. In the meantime he had been treasurer of the almoners of Christ's Hospital, had redesigned the West Horsham buildings, had fought for science education there, and won, and had raised nearly £1 million for the school.

Wallis was an ascetic, driven man with at times a furious temper against politicians and bureaucrats. He was unpopular at Vickers as a maverick. A charming person most of the time, he was driven by his self-assurance and his knowledge, which was deeper and better calculated than that of almost anyone with whom he came in contact. Yet he was naive, especially about human relations. He retired from Vickers in 1971 at the age of eighty-four and died at Leatherhead Hospital on 30 October 1979.

ROBIN HIGHAM

Sources J. E. Morpurgo, *Barnes Wallis* (1972) · C. F. Andrews, *Vickers aircraft since 1908* (1969) · R. D. S. Higham, *The British rigid airship, 1908–1931: a study in weapons policy* (1961) · D. Wood, *Project cancelled* (1975) · N. Shute, *Slide rule: the autobiography of an engineer* (1954) · personal knowledge (2004) · private information (2004) · *Journal of the Royal Aeronautical Society*, 70 (1966) · P. Brickhill, *The dam busters* (1951) · J. D. Scott, *Vickers: a history* (1962); repr. (1963) · *The aeroplane directory* (1961) · *DNB* · *WW*
Archives Brooklands Museum, Weybridge, films, photographs, and research papers · CAC Cam., aeronautical research papers · Royal Air Force Museum, Hendon, department of research and information services, personal and general corresp. files · Sci. Mus., corresp. and papers, incl. material relating to airships, bouncing bomb, etc. · Vickers, Weybridge | CAC Cam., corresp. with Sir E. C. Bullard · IWM, corresp. with Sir Henry Tizzard · Nuffield Oxf., corresp. with Lord Cherwell · Trinity Cam., corresp. with Sir Geoffrey Taylor · U. Leeds, Brotherton L., corresp. with Sir Harry Legge–Bourke and related papers · U. Leeds, Brotherton L., corresp. with Jack Morpurgo · University of Bristol, corresp. with R. R. Jamison relating to research projects
Likenesses A. E. Cooper, oils, 1942, NPG [*see illus.*] · W. Stoneman, photograph, 1945, NPG · photographs, 1945–77, Hult. Arch. · G. Argent, photograph, 1968, NPG · M. M. Kaye, bronze bust, 1970, RAF Club, London · D. Norris, bronze head, 1974, RAF Museum, Hendon, London · photographs, British Aerospace · portrait, repro. in Wood, *Project cancelled*, 187 · portrait, repro. in R. Higham, *Air power*, 2nd edn (1984), 100
Wealth at death £139,766: probate, 14 Jan 1980, *CGPLA Eng. & Wales*

Wallis, George (1740–1802), physician and writer, was born at York. Little is known of his early life, but he studied medicine, and, after graduating MD from Aberdeen, obtained a large practice at York. He was much attached to theatrical amusements, and, in addition to other pieces, such as the satirical *Perjury* (1774), he composed a mock tragedy entitled *Alexander and Statira*, which was acted at York, Leeds, and Edinburgh. In 1775 a dramatic satire by him, entitled *The Mercantile Lovers*, was acted at York. Despite its intrinsic merit, the play sketched too plainly the foibles of prominent citizens of the town, and as a result of their resentment, Wallis lost his entire medical practice. He was obliged to move to Buckingham Street, London, where an expurgated edition of the play appeared in the same year. In London he commenced as a lecturer on the theory and practice of physic, and in 1778 published an *Essay on the Evil Consequences Attending Injudicious Bleeding in Pregnancy* (1781). His other medical writings included: *Nosologia methodica oculorum, or, A Treatise on the Diseases of the Eyes, Translated and Selected from the Latin of Francis Bossier de Sauvages* (1785); *The Art of Preventing Diseases and Restoring Health* (1793; 2nd edn, 1796), which was translated into German in 1800; and *An Essay on the Gout* (1798). He also edited the *Works of Thomas Sydenham on Acute and Chronic Diseases* (2 vols., 1789) and the third edition of George Motherby's *Medical Dictionary* (1791). Wallis died on 29 January 1802 at Red Lion Square, London.

E. I. CARLYLE, *rev.* REBECCA MILLS

Sources *GM*, 1st ser., 72 (1802), 186 · T. Gilliland, *The dramatic mirror, containing the history of the stage from the earliest period, to the present time*, 1 (1808), 608 · D. E. Baker, *Biographia dramatica, or, A companion to the playhouse*, rev. I. Reed, new edn, rev. S. Jones, 1/2 (1812), 735 · Watt, *Bibl. Brit.* · T. K. Monro, *The physician as man of letters, science and action* (1951), 33 · S. Halkett and J. Laing, *A dictionary of the anonymous and pseudonymous literature of Great Britain*, 4 vols. (1882–8) · P. J. Wallis and R. V. Wallis, *Eighteenth century medics*, 2nd edn (1988)

Wallis, George (1811–1891), museum curator and art teacher, son of John Wallis (1783–1818) and Mary Price (1784–1864), was born at Wolverhampton on 8 June 1811 and educated at Wolverhampton grammar school from 1820 to 1827. He practised as a decorative artist at Manchester from 1832 to 1837, but he developed an interest in art education as it applied to design for manufactures, and joined the government School of Design at Somerset House, London, in 1841. He married, on 30 June 1842, Matilda, daughter of William Cundall of Camberwell. They had at least two sons. He became headmaster of the Spitalfields School in January 1843 and was promoted to the headmastership of the Manchester School of Design on 15 January 1844, which position he resigned in 1846, as he could not agree with administrative and educational changes at Somerset House. As part of a continued advocacy of industrial exhibitions of the sort held quinquennially in Paris, he organized what was probably the first exhibition of art manufactures ever held in England, at the Manchester Royal Institution in 1845. In the same year he delivered a systematic course of lectures on the principles of decorative art which led Lord Clarendon to ask him to draw up a chart of artistic and scientific instruction in relation to industrial art. Wallis's ideas on the subject were claimed as an important influence on the system of instruction later developed by the Department of Science and Art.

The royal commissioners for the Great Exhibition of 1851 appointed Wallis deputy commissioner for the eastern division of London, the northern counties of England, and the whole of Ireland, a position he exercised from 1850. During the Great Exhibition itself he was superintendent of the British textile division and a deputy commissioner of juries. After the close of the exhibition, he accepted the headmastership of the Birmingham School of Design. In 1853 he was again appointed as a commissioner sent by the government to the United States to report on the New York Industrial Exhibition, along with Charles Lyall, Wentworth Dilke, Joseph Whitworth, and John Wilson. Wallis's and Whitworth's reports were subsequently used to compile *The Industry of the United States in Machinery, Manufactures, and Useful and Ornamental Arts* (1854), which helped frame British attitudes to the threat of American economic competition. During the International Exhibition of 1862 Wallis acted in the same capacity as he had done in 1851 and was again actively engaged in the British sections for the Paris Exhibitions of 1855 and 1867.

In 1858 Wallis left Birmingham and joined the South Kensington Museum, where in 1863 he was appointed senior keeper of the art collections, a post he retained until just before his death; he thus presided over a period of marked expansion in the museum's collections and installations. He was succeeded by Caspar Purdon Clarke. Wallis was an early advocate of state aid for art and had a large share in promoting the system of circulating works of art in provincial museums. He exhibited a few paintings at the Academy, Suffolk Street, and elsewhere. On 7 March 1878 he was elected FSA. He wrote in most of the leading artistic periodicals, including the *Magazine of Art* and the *Art Journal*, to which he was one of the earliest contributors, and also delivered a vast number of lectures on design and kindred subjects. He published a number of books on decorative and industrial art, fine arts, and art education. He died at 21 St George's Road, Wimbledon, on 24 October 1891 and was buried in Highgate cemetery on 28 October.   G. C. BOASE, *rev.* R. C. DENIS

Sources *Art Journal*, new ser., 11 (1891), 384 · *The Athenaeum* (31 Oct 1891), 591 · *Magazine of Art*, 15 (1891–2), 69–72, esp. 69 · *ILN* (17 Oct 1891) · *CGPLA Eng. & Wales* (1892)
Likenesses A. Legros, oils, V&A · portrait, repro. in *Daily Graphic* (28 Oct 1891) · portrait, repro. in *Art Journal* · portrait, repro. in *ILN* · portrait, repro. in *London Figaro* (14 Oct 1891) · portrait, repro. in *Magazine of Art*
Wealth at death £1817 9s. 8d.: resworn probate, Oct 1892, *CGPLA Eng. & Wales* (1891)

Wallis, Helen Margaret (1924–1995), map librarian and historian of cartography, was born on 17 August 1924 at Dunkery, Park Road, Barnet, Hertfordshire, the daughter of Leonard Francis Wallis (1880–1965), a headmaster, and his wife, Mary McCulloch Jones (1884–1957), a teacher. She had a twin brother. After attending St Paul's Girls' School (1934–43), and following wartime teaching at her old prep school, she went to St Hugh's College, Oxford, in 1945 as a scholar, to read geography. Among the awards she gained was the Royal Geographical Society's university essay prize (1948), marking the start of a long and close association with that society. At that time the history of discoveries was one of the sub-disciplines of geography. This enabled Wallis to bridge the geography–history gap in her unpublished thesis 'The exploration of the South Sea, 1519 to 1644', assisted initially by a Mary Gray Allen senior scholarship from St Hugh's (1949). (She was awarded the degree of DPhil in 1954.) She was to remain devoted to St Hugh's and its association of senior members, of which she later became president.

Wallis was appointed assistant keeper in the map room of the British Museum in 1951. Unfortunately her relations with the then superintendent, R. A. Skelton (who had been her thesis supervisor since her arrival at the museum), became strained. Wallis worked hard to overcome a natural diffidence, even to the extent of radically changing her appearance, but she had to face a further setback when the time came to choose Skelton's successor. Although she was the obvious candidate, his unfavourable assessment of her caused a morale-sagging delay before she was appointed in 1967 as the first woman to hold that post.

Wallis's pent-up energies were then released and by the time she retired in 1986 she had established herself as the leading figure in the world of map librarianship in the country and, probably, internationally. At her death, nine years after retirement, she was certainly the best-known historian of cartography in the world. It may not be fanciful to see, in her relentless drive, a determination to overturn her predecessor's judgement on her. A bibliography produced to mark her retirement already contained 250 entries.

The thirty-five years that Wallis spent in the British Museum (from 1973 the British Library) provided the springboard for almost everything she did. She and the map room (latterly map library) were indivisible. In pursuing scholarship she was continuing a long museum tradition, if with exceptional brio and versatility. Much of her research was based on the library's cartographic collections, which she augmented, most significantly, with the only known copy of the woodcut wall map of the world by Giacomo Gastaldi (1561) and, in 1968, the map collection of the Royal United Services Institution—the largest map purchase in the museum's history.

Wallis's most splendid publication, and probably the one on which her long-term reputation will rest—although not necessarily for its elaboration of earlier claims for a sixteenth-century Portuguese discovery of Australia—was the facsimile of Jean Rotz's *Boke of Idrography* (1542), which she edited for Viscount Eccles to present to the Roxburghe Club in 1981. The original had been made for Henry VIII; when President Reagan of the USA visited Britain the queen presented him with Wallis's edition. She valued more than any other award her appointment as OBE which she received from the queen on her retirement.

Wallis realized that exhibitions could make the map room more visible both within the museum and outside. Illustrating topics as diverse as the voyages of Cook, the development of thematic mapping, and oriental cartography, Wallis's exhibitions set new standards of approachable scholarship, with maps interspersed among books and artefacts. Her approach was interdisciplinary before this became fashionable, and this is reflected in the terms of the research fellowship set up in her memory at the British Library. That the exhibitions entitled 'American War of Independence' (1975), 'The voyage of Francis Drake' (1977), and 'Raleigh and Roanoke' (1988) were able to travel to North America was largely the result of Wallis's numerous contacts among American librarians, historians, and collectors. The honorary degree of DLitt she received from Davidson College, North Carolina (1985), recognized her contributions to American history.

Whenever possible, Wallis brought people together. The museum staff restaurant was host to many impromptu seminars as she sought out and found unsuspected academic links between visiting scholars and her colleagues. On the more formal level she was a committed and energetic member of numerous societies and groups, several of which she helped to create and for many of which she was the driving force. Reflecting her enduring interest in the history of discoveries, she served on the council of the Hakluyt Society for almost fifty years and edited for them *Carteret's Voyage Round the World, 1766–1769* (1965). To the Society of Nautical Research she gave almost thirty years' continuous service, including a long spell as chairman. This was one of the many instances of her thriving in a man's world. She was the first woman to hold several of the positions she occupied, and these distinctions awarded merit, not assertiveness. She found it amusing to be classed as an honorary man in Japan.

Wallis also served on the councils of the Society of Antiquaries and the Royal Geographical Society, which posthumously awarded her its prestigious Victoria medal. Having held the presidency of the British Cartographic Society and co-founded its map curators' group, she was awarded its silver medal in 1988. Her fellow librarians had earlier honoured her with an honorary fellowship of the Library Association in 1985. With this range of experience she was a natural choice to represent a group of 230 societies on the council of the Foundation for Science and Technology.

On the wider front, Wallis was instrumental in establishing a history of cartography commission within the International Cartographic Association (ICA), whose honorary fellowship she was awarded in 1991. It was for the ICA that she and Arthur Robinson edited *Cartographical Innovations: an International Handbook of Mapping Terms to 1900* (1987).

Wallis was notably constant to friends and colleagues, and to research themes, and her first project, a study of British globes, was also the one she was working on at the very end. Her discovery at Petworth House of the earliest version of England's first globe, by Emery Molyneux, provided the subject of her first publication, in the year she joined the British Museum. Appropriately, the volume of tributes prepared by her friends and colleagues was entitled *The Globe my World* (1995), a reference too, perhaps, to her zest for travel.

Wallis had bubbling and urgent enthusiasm for the vast range of subjects on which she was knowledgeable. Her breathless lecturing style, with commentary and slides seemingly racing one another, was engagingly inimitable. She was equally encouraging to her own staff and to younger scholars. She was natural and friendly to all she met and found it impossible to refuse commissions. Unmarried, she devoted most of her free time to academic and society matters, as well as choral singing. At social gatherings she would invariably have a camera in hand.

Wallis's archive at the British Library contains notes on unfinished projects, such as the Rawlinson copperplates at the Bodleian Library and the related Innys atlas at Holkham Hall. The archive also includes a video interview taken close to the end of her life in which, though ill, she ranged fluently and amusingly over her career. Undoubtedly her deeply held Christian belief, stemming from the time of her adult baptism at Oxford, and the prayer circle maintained by friends around the world, helped to sustain her cheerfulness to the end. It was during those last months that she completed the first national inventory of cartographic resources, *Historian's Guide to Early Maps of the British Isles* (1994), edited, under her direction, for the Royal Historical Society by Anita McConnell.

Shortly before what proved to be her final illness, she accepted a fellowship at the Mitchell Library, Sydney. Wallis died of cancer on 7 February 1995 at the Hospital of St John and St Elizabeth in St John's Wood, London. A funeral service at St John's Wood Church on 10 February was followed by cremation at Golders Green crematorium.

TONY CAMPBELL

Sources S. Tyacke and T. Campbell, eds., *The globe my world: tributes to Dr. Helen Wallis OBE, 1924–1995* (1995) • *Imago Mundi*, 47 (1995), 185–92 [incl. sel. bibliography] • T. Kay, 'Helen M. Wallis: a bibliography of published works', *Map Collector*, 40 (1987), 30–38 • personal knowledge (2004) • private information (2004) [Peter Wallis] • St Hugh's College Oxford, Association of Senior Members, *Helen Margaret Wallis: a celebration, 12 April 1997* (privately printed, 1997) • 'Helen Margaret Wallis: a celebration, St Hugh's College, Oxford, 12th April, 1997', *Cartographiti: the newsletter of the Map Curators' Group of the British Cartographic Society*, 50 (1997), 5–11 • *The Guardian* (24 Feb 1995) • *The Independent* (14 Feb 1995) • *The Times* (17 Feb 1995) • [V. Scott and T. Campbell], *Map Collector*, 70 (1995), 43 • V. Scott, ed., '"Helen" to retire', *Map Collector*, 35 (1986), 40–41 • *GJ*, 161 (1995), 240–41 • *Kartographische Nachrichten*, 45 (1995), 159–60 • *ICA Newsletter* [International Cartographic Association], 25 (1995), 14–15 • *Transactions of the Institute of British Geographers*, new ser., 21 (1996), 299–301 • *The Globe: journal of the Australian Map Circle*, 42 (1995), 71–2 • *Library Association Record*, 97 (1995), 235 • *Geographical Magazine*, 67 (1995), 30–31 • 'Profiles of council members: Dr Helen Wallis OBE FSA', *Technology, Innovation and Society*, 9 (1993), 23 • A. Sutherland, ed., 'Dr. Helen Wallis, O.B.E.', *Cartographiti: the newsletter of the Map Curators' Group of the British Cartographic Society*, 42 (1995), 3–8
Archives BL, archives | SOUND BL NSA, oral history interview • BL NSA, performance recordings
Likenesses photographs, BL, Map Library, Wallis archive; repro. in *The Times*
Wealth at death £232,603: probate, 3 July 1995, *CGPLA Eng. & Wales*

Wallis, Henry (*bap.* 1806, *d.* 1890). *See under* Wallis, Robert William (1794–1878).

Wallis, Henry (1830–1916), painter and ceramics expert, was born in London on 21 February 1830. His father's name and occupation are unknown. When in 1845 his mother, Mary Anne Thomas, married Andrew Wallis, a prosperous London property owner, Henry took his stepfather's surname.

Wallis commenced his training at F. S. Cary's academy in Bloomsbury. He was admitted as a probationer in the Royal Academy on 7 January 1848 and enrolled in the painting school there on 31 March. He also studied in Paris in the atelier of M. G. C. Gleyre and at the Académie des Beaux-Arts, probably some time between 1849 and 1853. He first exhibited in England at the Royal Manchester Institution in 1853 and in London in February 1854 at the British Institution.

By early 1855 Wallis was acquainted with the novelist and poet George Meredith. This led to Meredith's posing for the face of the dead poet Thomas Chatterton in Wallis's painting *Chatterton* (Tate collection), which was exhibited at the Royal Academy in 1856. This picture made Wallis famous overnight: John Ruskin, for example, described it as 'faultless and wonderful' (Parris, 144). Its continuing fascination for the public owes much to the way in which it is inextricably linked with a real-life 'romance': in the summer of 1857, if not before, Wallis and Meredith's wife, Mary Ellen, daughter of Thomas Love Peacock, became lovers. Mary Meredith left her husband, and had a son with Wallis, Harold (Felix) Meredith (later Wallis) in April 1858. Mary Ellen died in October 1861.

Contact with the melancholy sensibility and radicalism of Gleyre, as well as with the work of French realist painters, led Wallis to paint his masterpiece, *The Stonebreaker* (1857; Birmingham Museum and Art Gallery), though his direct inspiration was Thomas Carlyle's *Sartor Resartus*. Wallis's sombre and realistic image of a dead labourer is both pioneering and unique in British art. *The Stonebreaker*, exhibited in 1858, consolidated Wallis's reputation as a true Pre-Raphaelite.

However, after his stepfather's death in 1859, when he came into a comfortable inheritance, Wallis never again made the same artistic impact, though he remained a Royal Academy exhibitor until 1877. He also exhibited with the Old Watercolour Society, of which he became a member in 1880. An interest in archaeology, ceramics, and Renaissance art took him increasingly abroad and he became a perceptive and quietly passionate writer on these subjects—notably for the *Art Journal* between 1882 and 1890. Always interested in contemporary artistic matters, he was also honorary secretary of the committee for the preservation of St Mark's, Venice, between 1882 and 1890. Wallis's most notable achievement between 1885 and 1899 was to publish in twenty slim volumes, most of them illustrated by himself, his researches into Persian, Egyptian, Greek, and Byzantine ceramics.

A discerning collector, Wallis made a small but highly original contribution to the art and connoisseurship of his time. For all this, he remains an elusive personality: according to W. M. Rossetti he was 'a very agreeable companion, of solid character and open mind'. Wallis never married. He died on 20 December 1916 at his home, 1 Walpole Road, Croydon, Surrey, and was buried in Highgate cemetery.   ROBIN HAMLYN, *rev.*

Sources will, 1859, PRO · A. Van de Put, 'Henry Wallis, 1830–1916', *Faenza*, 2 (1917), 33–4 · *Burlington Magazine*, 30 (1917), 123–4 · D. Johnson, *The true history of the first Mrs Meredith and other lesser lives* (1973) · [L. Parris], ed., *The Pre-Raphaelites* (1984) [exhibition catalogue, Tate Gallery, London, 7 March – 28 May 1984] · *CGPLA Eng. & Wales* (1917) · T. Wilson, 'A Victorian artist as ceramic-collector—the letters of Henry Wallis, part 1', *Journal of the History of Collections*, 14 (2002), 139–59
Archives Bodl. Oxf., letters to F. G. Stephens
Wealth at death £15,923 18s. 6d.: probate, 9 Feb 1917, *CGPLA Eng. & Wales*

Wallis [*née* McCall], **Janet Sophia** (1858–1928), philanthropist and founder of the Mission of Hope, was born in Wood Street, Walthamstow, on 13 June 1858, the only daughter of John McCall, a provision merchant, and his wife, Agnes Allen. Little is known of her early life, but spiritual matters seemed to have weighed heavily on her as a child. According to her daughter, she was saved at the age of twelve and teased by her brothers who called her 'Saint Janet' (Wallis, 15). She married Ransome Wallis (1849/50–

1927), a prosperous businessman and widower, on 22 November 1883. While not engaging in paid work herself, she spent the first years of her marriage conducting religious meetings for women and children in the Walthamstow area. Her life's work was to grow out of personal sorrow; in the period of one year her infant daughter Marjorie died and her son Allan became gravely ill. Janet Wallis promised to dedicate herself to the welfare of children should Allan recover. The Mission of Hope (continued as Christian Family Concern in Croydon, which opened in Walthamstow as the 'Haven for Homeless Little Ones', in 1893, was the result of her commitment to children and her concern for the plight of the unmarried mother.

Janet Wallis's original intention was to provide a form of orphanage, where the children of unmarried mothers would be received and cared for. Almost immediately, though, she began arranging informal adoptions; between 1893 and 1927 (when the practice was given legal status) over 1000 children were placed in this way. Emigration was sometimes arranged for older children. For those children who remained in the home or who were placed with foster parents, mothers were encouraged to contribute what they could to the care of their children and an affiliation department was set up to track down fathers and enforce on them their financial responsibilities. As the work grew, the mission sought larger premises first in Walthamstow, then Walton Heath, and finally in south Croydon. In its mature form, the Mission of Hope comprised several homes for boys, girls, toddlers, and babies clustered near the railway station in south Croydon; a maternity hospital was opened in 1910 in Camberwell, to be followed by five similar institutions by 1918. Unlike other philanthropic organizations, Janet Wallis did not restrict entry to those women who were having their first babies and could thus be termed the innocent victims of sin or male lust. Her daughter praised this strategy: 'experience throughout the years has proved again and again that a "second case" is as reachable and salvable … as the first' (Wallis, 24). Such a policy, coupled with Janet Wallis's evident desire to provide for every child and every woman who came to the doors of her homes, meant that the mission over-extended itself during the war years and was left with a large debt. Mrs Wallis's last years were spent clearing this debt and scaling down the mission, a task she accomplished with the help of her daughter Adeline who joined the mission in 1913.

Janet Wallis was evidently a woman of considerable energy and strong beliefs. She felt that religion was essential to the reformation of both mother and child and attacked the recommendation of the majority report of the royal commission on the poor law (1908) which allowed for the provision of state homes for unmarried mothers. After his retirement from business, Ransome Wallis assisted his wife with the mission, conducting Bible classes in the homes. Her husband's death on 17 March 1927 marked the beginning of Janet Wallis's retirement from active work in the mission. Her own health declined quickly and she suffered a stroke in January 1928; she died a few weeks later on 14 February 1928 at her home, 2 South Park Hill Road, Croydon, and was buried on 17 February in Croydon cemetery. L. E. LAUER

Sources *'What she could.' Being a brief sketch of the life and work of Mrs Ransome Wallis, by two of her daughters* (c.1928) · A. Wallis, *These three: the story of the Mission of Hope* (1937) · *Croydon Advertiser* (18 Feb 1928), 9 · b. cert. · m. cert. · d. cert.
Likenesses Elliott & Fry, photograph, repro. in Wallis, *These three*, frontispiece · photograph, repro. in *'What she could.'*, frontispiece · photograph (with her husband), repro. in A. Wallis, *What they found* (1940), frontispiece
Wealth at death £2217 13s. 1d.: probate, 17 April 1928, *CGPLA Eng. & Wales*

Wallis, John (1616–1703), mathematician and cryptographer, was born on 3 December 1616 at Ashford in Kent. He was the third of five children of the Revd John Wallis (1567–1622), son of Robert Wallis of Finedon, Northamptonshire, Cambridge BA and MA (Trinity College), and minister at Ashford from 1602 until his death on 30 November 1622, and his second wife, Joanna (d. 1643), daughter of Henry and Mary Chapman of Godmersham, Kent. She raised Wallis and his two brothers and two sisters after their father's death.

Education and early life Wallis's education was begun at Ashford. Following an outbreak of the plague in 1625 he studied Latin grammar at a private school in Tenterden in Kent. The school had been started by a Mr Finch who had enrolled a schoolmaster to instruct his children, and it closed in 1630 when the eldest child was sent to university and the other children were sent elsewhere. Although Wallis claimed to be already fit for university, in 1631 he was sent to another school, run by Martin Holbeach at Felsted in Essex, where he continued his studies of Latin and learned Greek and Hebrew, as well as some logic. Mathematics was not taught, but Wallis gained some knowledge in that field at home during the Christmas vacation of 1631, when his brother passed on to him the knowledge he had acquired 'in Order to a Trade' (Scriba, 'Autobiography of John Wallis', 26).

At Christmas 1632 Wallis was admitted as a pensioner to Emmanuel College, Cambridge, where he became noted as a dialectician. He studied natural philosophy, ethics, metaphysics, theology, anatomy, and medicine, and graduated BA in 1637 and MA in 1640. His tutors were Anthony Burgess, divine and later member of the Westminster assembly, Thomas Horton, later president of Queens' College and professor of divinity at Gresham College, and Benjamin Whichcote, later provost of King's College and vice-chancellor of the university, and to these three men Wallis addressed the dedicatory letter of his *De angulo contactus et semicirculo disquisitio geometrica* (1656). Wallis claimed that, as a student of the anatomist and physician Francis Glisson, he was the first to defend publicly at Cambridge Harvey's doctrine of the circulation of the blood. At the end of his life he maintained to have been self-taught, after the informal instruction by his brother, with regard to the study of mathematics:

> I did thenceforth prosecute it, (at school and in the University) not as a formal Study, but as a pleasing Diversion, at spare hours; as books of *Arithmetick*, or other *Mathematical*

John Wallis (1616–1703), by Sir Godfrey Kneller, 1701

> fell occasionally in my way. For I had none to direct me, what books to read, or what to seek, or in what method to proceed. For Mathematicks, (at that time, with us) were scarce looked upon as *Accademical* studies, but rather *Mechanical*; as the business of *Traders*, *Merchants*, *Seamen*, *Carpenters*, *Surveyors of Lands*, or the like; and perhaps some *Almanak-makers in London*. And amongst more than Two hundred students (at that time) in our College, I do not know of any Two (perhaps not any) who had more of *Mathematicks* than I, (if so much) which was then but little; And but very few, in that whole University. For the Study of *Mathematicks* was at that time more cultivated in *London* than in the Universities. (Scriba, 'Autobiography of John Wallis', 27)

In 1640 Wallis was ordained by the bishop of Winchester and became chaplain first to Sir Richard Darley at Buttercrambe, Yorkshire, then to the widow of Horatio, Lord Vere, alternately at Castle Hedingham in Essex and in London. One evening in late 1642, sitting at supper at Lady Vere's in London, he was able to decipher in about two hours a letter in code that was shown to him. Cryptography remained one of Wallis's activities during the civil war, when he exercised it on behalf of the parliamentary party, and later in his life, as he wrote in his autobiography:

> being encouraged by this success, beyond expectation; I afterwards ventured on many others (some of more, some of less difficulty) and scarce missed of any, that I undertook, for many years, during our civil Wars, and afterwards. But of

late years, *the French Methods of Cipher* are grown so intricate beyond what it was wont to be, that I failed of many; tho' I have master'd divers of them.   (Scriba, 'Autobiography of John Wallis', 38)

In 1643, following the death of his mother, Wallis was left a substantial estate in Kent. In the same year he published *Truth Tried, or, Animadversions on the Lord Brooke's Treatise on the Nature of Truth*. From 1644 he acted as secretary to the assembly of divines at Westminster, London, which was charged with proposing a new form of church government. In his autobiography he provided an interesting retrospective account of the activities and debates of the Westminster assembly. Also in 1644 he obtained a fellowship at Queens' College, Cambridge, but he resigned after about a year when, on 24 March 1645, he married Susanna (1622–1687), daughter of John and Rachel Glyde of Northiam, Sussex. In 1644 he gave evidence against Archbishop Laud, but in 1648 he signed the remonstrance against the execution of Charles I and in 1649 the 'Serious and Faithful Representation'.

Anticipating the Royal Society During this period in London Wallis became engaged in experimental philosophy, and his circle was one of those whence the Royal Society emerged after the Restoration. His account of those early events is of considerable interest:

> About the year 1645, while I lived in *London* (at a time, when, by our Civil Wars, Academical Studies were much interrupted in both our Universities:) beside the Conversation of divers eminent Divines, as to matters Theological; I had the opportunity of being acquainted with divers worthy Persons, inquisitive into Natural Philosophy, and other parts of Humane Learning; And particularly of what hath been called the *New Philosophy* or *Experimental Philosophy*. We did by agreement, divers of us, meet weekly in *London* on a certain day, to treat and discours of such affairs. Of which number were *Dr. John Wilkins* (afterward *Bishop of Chester*), *Dr. Jonathan Goddard*, *Dr. George Ent*, *Dr. Glisson*, *Dr. Merret* (*Drs. in Physick*) *Mr. Samuel Foster* then Professor of Astronomy at *Gresham College*, *Mr Theodore Haak* (a German of the *Palatinate* and then Resident in *London*, who, I think, gave the first occasion, and first suggested those meetings) and many others. These meetings we held sometimes at *Dr. Goddards* lodgings in *Woodstreet* (or some convenient place near) on occasion of his keeping an Operator in his house, for grinding Glasses for Telescopes and Microscopes; and sometime at a convenient place in *Cheap-side*; sometime at *Gresham College* or some place near adjoyning. Our business was (precluding matters of Theology and State Affairs) to discours and consider of *Philosophical Enquiries*, and such as related thereunto; as *Physick, Anatomy, Geometry, Astronomy, Navigation, Staticks, Magneticks, Chymicks, Mechanicks,* and *Natural Experiments*; with the State of these Studies, as then cultivated, at home and abroad. We there discoursed of the *Circulation of the Blood, the Valves in the Veins, the Venae Lacteae, the Lymphatick vessels, the Copernican Hypothesis, the Nature of Comets, and New Stars, the Satellites of Jupiter, the Oval Shape* (as it then appeared) *of Saturn, the spots in the Sun, and its Turning on its own Axis, the Inequalities and Selenography of the Moon, the several Phases of Venus and Mercury, the Improvement of Telescopes, and grinding of Glasses for that purpose, the Weight of Air, the Possibility or Impossibility of Vacuities, and Natures Abhorrence thereof; the Torricellian Experiment in Quicksilver, the Descent of heavy Bodies, and the degrees of Acceleration therein*; and divers other things of like nature. Some of which were then but New Discoveries, and others not so generally known and

imbraced, as now they are; With other things appertaining to what hath been called *The New Philosophy*; which, from the times of *Galileo* at *Florence*, and *Sir Francis Bacon* (*Lord Verulam*) in *England*, hath been much cultivated in *Italy, France, Germany,* and other Parts abroad, as well as with us in *England*. About the year 1648, 1649, some of our company being removed to *Oxford* (first *Dr. Wilkins*, then I, and soon after *Dr. Goddard*) our company divided. Those in *London* continued to meet there as before (and we with them, when we had occasion to be there;) and those of us at *Oxford*; with *Dr. Ward* (since *Bishop of Salisbury*), *Dr. Ralph Bathurst* (now *President of Trinity College in Oxford*) *Dr. Petty* (since *Sir William Petty*) *Dr. Willis* (then an eminent Physician in *Oxford*) and divers others, continued such meetings in *Oxford*; and brought those Studies into fashion there; meeting first at *Dr. Petties* Lodgings, (in an Apothecaries house) because of the convenience of inspecting Drugs, and the like, as there was occasion; and after his remove to *Ireland* (tho' not so constantly) at the Lodgings of *Dr. Wilkins*, then Warden of *Wadham Coll*. And after his removal to *Trinity College in Cambridge*, at the Lodgings of *the Honorable Mr. Robert Boyle*, then resident for divers years in *Oxford*. Those meetings in *London* continued, and (after the Kings return in 1660) were increased with the accession of divers worthy and Honorable Persons; and were afterwards incorporated by the name of *the Royal Society*, etc. and so continue to this day.   (Scriba, 'Autobiography of John Wallis', 39–40)

Wallis was a founding member of the Royal Society and one of its most active fellows. He contributed more than sixty papers on several subjects and reviews of mathematical books to the society's *Philosophical Transactions*.

Savilian professorship In June 1649 Wallis was appointed Savilian professor of geometry at Oxford, and was incorporated MA from Exeter College in the same year. He held his professorship for over half a century. His predecessor, Peter Turner, was a royalist and had been removed by parliament. Wallis's mathematical accomplishments were hitherto very limited. In 1648 he had composed a *Treatise of Angular Sections* (which remained unpublished until 1685), in which he developed results from William Oughtred's *Clavis mathematicae* (1631), a book he read about 1647 or 1648. In 1648 he provided an explanation of Descartes's treatment of fourth-degree equations to the Cambridge Platonist John Smith (1618–1652), lecturer of mathematics and fellow of Emmanuel College and later of Queens'. Within a few years Wallis was to become one of the leading mathematicians of his time.

In 1653 Wallis published *Grammatica linguae Anglicanae*, with a treatise *De loquela* and a *Praxis grammatica*. This work was often reprinted and has been praised by linguists for its deep insights and careful attention to sounds. *De loquela* served as a theoretical basis for Wallis's attempts to teach the profoundly deaf how to speak. He reported on his attempts to teach Alexander Popham in the *Philosophical Transactions*, though failure to mention Popham's previous instructor, William Holder, led to a bitter confrontation.

Wallis was admitted doctor of divinity in 1654. In 1658 he succeeded, by a somewhat doubtful procedure, Gerard Langbaine the elder as keeper of the university archives. His election elicited the protest of Henry Stubbe in *The Savilian Professor's Case Stated*. Despite such inauspicious beginnings, Wallis rendered valuable services to the university archives by putting the records and other papers under his care into such exact order, and managing its lawsuits with such success, that he apparently convinced even those opposed to his election that he had been an excellent choice for that post. His repertory of the entire collection was not replaced until the twentieth century.

Wallis was confirmed in his posts by Charles II in 1660, was made a royal chaplain, and in 1661 was appointed among the divines commissioned to revise the prayer book. He remained a loyal member of the official church throughout his life. Royal favour, together with his strenuous denials, are sufficient grounds for doubting the accusations that during the civil war he deciphered important letters relating to the royal family and public safety, making them available to the parliamentarians. In 1653 Wallis had deposited in the Bodleian Library a partial collection of the letters he had deciphered; these were later published by John Davys in his *Essay on the Art of Decyphering* (1737). Wallis continued to decipher intercepted letters on behalf of the government for many years. In old age he passed the art to his grandson William Blencowe, but refused to impart it to Leibniz, who had requested information on it on behalf of his rulers.

Publications As Savilian professor, Wallis had to lecture on the *Elements* by Euclid, *Conics* by Apollonius, the works by Archimedes, and teach introductory courses in arithmetic. The statutes suggested also lectures on subjects such as cosmography, trigonometry, applied geometry, mechanics, and the theory of music. In the mid-1650s Wallis published several mathematical treatises within a couple of years, under the headings *Operum mathematicorum pars prima* (1657) and *Operum mathematicorum pars altera* (1656). They include, in the first volume, his *Oratio inauguralis: mathesis universalis, seu opus arithmeticum*, and other minor works. The second volume was an outcome of his university lectures, and in it Wallis stressed the importance of a unified notation and was influenced by William Oughtred. It also contained *De angulo contactus et semicirculo disquisitio geometrica*, already mentioned, and *De sectionibus conicis*, which dealt with a classical subject in a new fashion, namely, following the treatment introduced by Descartes. In this work Wallis introduced the sign for infinity, ∞, and used $1/\infty$ to represent an infinitesimal height. Moreover, Wallis employed the method of indivisibles in the version developed by Evangelista Torricelli, the Italian mathematician and pupil of Galileo. The method was and still is attributed to another pupil of Galileo, Bonaventura Cavalieri, whose books Wallis repeatedly sought in vain in bookshops.

Wallis's main work, *Arithmetica infinitorum*, was also included in the second volume of *Opera mathematicorum*, though it had already been printed separately and distributed in 1655 with a dedication to William Oughtred. Newton was greatly influenced by this work when he studied it in the winter of 1664–5. Wallis was able to find an infinite series expressing the value of $4/\pi$ by an ingenious series of interpolations. Indeed, the very term for the method was given by Wallis, who relied in this work on techniques

that appear closely related to those he had devised for deciphering coded letters. As a result of his position and publications, Wallis was engaged in many mathematical challenges and disputes, notably with Pierre de Fermat, Blaise Pascal, and especially Thomas Hobbes, who in 1655 had claimed to possess an absolute quadrature of the circle. The virulent controversy, in which Hobbes also claimed erroneously to have duplicated the cube, thus solving another of the great mathematical problems, lasted for about a quarter-century, ending with Hobbes's death in 1679.

Following the discussion on the laws of impact at the Royal Society in 1668, Wallis, Christopher Wren, and Christiaan Huygens submitted papers. Wallis's was published in the *Philosophical Transactions* for that year and was followed by *Mechanica, sive, De motu tractatus geometricus* (1670–71), the major and most comprehensive work on a range of mechanical problems—such as statics, impact laws, and centres of gravity—published in England to that point. His last great mathematical work, *A Treatise of Algebra, both Historical and Practical* (1685) in 100 chapters, combined technical and historical exposition. An expanded Latin edition was included in the second volume of Wallis's *Opera mathematica* of 1693. The historical account was heavily biased towards English achievements and went as far as to claim that Descartes had gained knowledge in algebra from Thomas Harriot. The *Algebra* also included a discussion of the methods of exhaustion, of indivisibles, and of infinite series. Moreover, the work included the first printed account, expanded in the later edition, of some of Newton's achievements. Wallis's determination to defend English priority made him press his case with Newton, lest the glory of his inventions went to a foreigner. The third and last volume of Wallis's *Opera mathematica* (1693–9) contained a collection of letters on the priority dispute between Newton and Leibniz, the main items being Newton's so-called *epistola prior* and *epistola posterior* of 1676. In *Institutio logicae* (1687) Wallis put forward influential views concerning ways of treating singular terms as if they were general and conditional statements.

Wallis was also an active editor of works in the mathematical disciplines, including Archimedes' *Arenarius et dimensio circuli* (1676), Jeremiah Horrocks's *Opera posthuma* (1672–3 and 1678), Ptolemy's *Harmonicorum libri tres* (1682), Aristarchus's *De magnitudinibus et distantiis solis et lunae* (1688), and a fragment from Pappus (1688). His editorial work stimulated discussions at the Royal Society on musical theory, astronomy, and the theory of tides, and publications in the *Philosophical Transactions*.

Wallis's wife died on 27 March 1687, leaving him with one son and two daughters: John, Anne, and Elizabeth. John married Elizabeth Harris and had three children, Anne married Sir John Blencowe and had one child, while Elizabeth married William Benson and had no children.

Between 1690 and 1692 Wallis published eight letters and three sermons in defence of the Trinity against unitarian doctrines. He employed a mathematical analogy, arguing that the mystery of the Trinity could be grasped with the help of a cubical body with three dimensions: 'This *longum, latum, profundum,* (Long, Broad, and Tall), is but *One Cube;* of *Three Dimensions,* and yet but *One Body.* And this *Father, Son,* and *Holy-Ghost:* three persons, and yet but One God' (Archibald, 36). Wallis's theological works were often praised for their clarity and straightforward language. In 1692 he successfully opposed the introduction of the Gregorian calendar in Britain.

Throughout his life Wallis enjoyed excellent health and remarkable intellectual powers, with a prodigious memory for figures. Only in his eighties did he complain that his sight, hearing, and strength were not as they used to be. He died at Oxford on 8 November 1703, aged eighty-six, and was buried in St Mary's Church, Oxford, where his son placed a mural monument in his honour.

DOMENICO BERTOLONI MELI

Sources C. J. Scriba, 'The autobiography of John Wallis', *Notes and Records of the Royal Society,* 25 (1970), 17–46 · C. J. Scriba, *Studien zur Mathematik des John Wallis (1616–1703)* (1966) · J. F. Scott, *The mathematical work of John Wallis, D.D., F.R.S. (1616–1703)* (1938) · C. J. Scriba, 'A tentative index of the correspondence of John Wallis', *Notes and Records of the Royal Society,* 22 (1967), 58–93 · C. J. Scriba, 'Wallis, John', *DSB* · R. C. Archibald, 'Wallis on the Trinity', *American Mathematical Monthly,* 43 (1936), 35–7 · D. E. Smith, 'John Wallis as a cryptographer', *Bulletin of the American Mathematical Society,* 24 (1917), 82–96 · R. S. Westfall, *Force in Newton's physics* (1979), 231–44 · J. L. Subbiondo, 'John Wallis' *Grammatica linguae Anglicanae', Diversions of Galway,* ed. A. Ahlqvist and others (1992) · L. Maierù, *Fra Descartes e Newton: Isaac Barrow e John Wallis* (1994) · K. Hill, 'Neither ancient nor modern: Wallis and Barrow on the composition of continua', *Notes and Records of the Royal Society,* 50 (1996), 165–78 · A. R. Hall, *Philosophers at war: the quarrel between Newton and Leibniz* (1980)

Archives Archbishop Marsh's Library, Dublin, paper on theory of music · BL, corresp. and papers, Sloane MSS 2284, 4025; Add. MS 32499 · Bodl. Oxf., corresp. and papers · Bodl. Oxf., political corresp. in cipher [copies] · CKS, autobiography · RS, treatise on logic | Bibliotheek der Rijksuniversiteit Leiden, corresp. with Christiaan Huygens · BL, letters to Sir Hans Sloane, Sloane MS 4025 · Bodl. Oxf., corresp. with Sir Thomas Smith · Christ Church Oxf., MSS relating to the Paschal and Calendar · Leics. RO, corresp. with Lord Nottingham · NRA, priv. coll., letters to John Collins · RS, letters to Henry Oldenburg · RS, letters to Sir Hans Sloane

Likenesses D. Loggan, line engraving, 1678, BM, NPG · G. Soest, oils, before 1681, RS · W. Sonmans, portrait, 1698 · M. Burghers, line engraving, 1699 (after W. Sonmans), BM, NPG, V&A; repro. in M. Burghers, *Opera mathematica* (1699) · G. Kneller, oils, 1701, Bodl. Oxf. [*see illus.*] · W. Townesend, bust, 1703, St Mary's Church, Oxford · W. Faithorne, line engraving, BM, NPG; repro. in J. Wallis, *Mechanica* (1670) · G. Kneller, portrait · oils (after G. Kneller, 1701), NPG

Wallis, John (1714–1793), antiquary and natural historian, the son of John Wallis (or Wallace) of Croglin, Cumberland, was born at Castlenook in South Tynedale, Northumberland. He matriculated from Queen's College, Oxford, on 3 February 1733, graduated BA in 1737, and proceeded MA in 1740. Having taken orders, he held a curacy for a few years in Portsmouth, where he married; his wife, whose name was Elizabeth, died in 1801. The marriage proved to be an extremely happy one (Winch, 145). Wallis then became curate of Simonburn, Northumberland, where he remained until 1771. It was here that he began to

collect and record information relating to the history, archaeology, and natural history of his native county. Despite the remote nature of his parish, it is clear from his published work that Wallis travelled widely in Northumberland and had an extensive network of contacts, including other antiquarians, notably Thomas Pennant and George Allan.

In 1748 Wallis published, by subscription, *The Occasional Miscellany, in Prose and Verse* which contained several sermons and two poems. His chief work, however, was *The natural history and antiquities of Northumberland, and so much of the county of Durham as lies between the rivers Tyne and Tweed, commonly called North Bishoprick* (2 vols., 1769). The first volume deals with the minerals, fossils, plants, and animals of the county. The plants, including cryptogams, are listed using the nomenclature proposed by John Ray, and although Winch notes that 'two or three of the most remarkable plants which he supposed he had discovered growing with us were not the species he took them for' (Winch, 2.45), his list is reliable and must be considered as the first substantial account of the flora of Northumberland. Swan, while acknowledging Wallis's work, notes that 'he did not attempt to include more than just a selection of vascular plants, evidently mainly those which are considered useful (e.g. medicinally) ornamental, or otherwise striking; many large groups [are] completely missing' (Swan, 11). This criticism may equally be applied to his other lists (fishes, reptiles, and so on,) but none the less Wallis provided a benchmark for today's naturalists, as well as a source of eighteenth-century English and Northumbrian names for many common species of plants and animals. The second volume deals with the antiquities, arranged in three tours through the county and is also still considered a valuable point of reference.

On the death of the rector of Simonburn in 1771 the living was given to James Scott (1733–1813), and as a result Wallis was compelled to leave his curacy. His college friend Edward Wilson, vicar of the Northumberland village of Haltwhistle provided work until 1775 when Wallis was appointed temporary curate at Haughton-le-Skerne, co. Durham; later in the same year he moved to Billingham, near Stockton, where he remained until 1792, when increasing illness forced him to resign.

Wallis was never financially secure, his posts as curate never earning more than £30 a year. In 1779 Thomas Pennant made efforts to secure help from the bishop of Durham. About two years before his death Wallis acquired a small estate on the death of a brother, and Bishop Shute Barrington provided an annual pension when he resigned the curacy of Billingham. Wallis moved to the neighbouring village of Norton, where he died on 19 July 1793. According to one biographer, Wallis, 'though possessed of good natural abilities, and no small share of acquired knowledge, lived and died in an obscure station' (*GM*).

G. S. BOULGER, *rev.* PETER DAVIS

Sources *GM,* 1st ser., 2 (1732), 769–70 · Nichols, *Lit. anecdotes,* 7.704; 8.758–60 · N. J. Winch, *Transactions of the Natural History Society of Northumberland, Durham and Newcastle upon Tyne,* 2 (1832), 145 ·

J. G. Baker, *Transactions of the Natural History Society of Northumberland, Durham and Newcastle upon Tyne*, 14 (1903), 77 • Desmond, *Botanists*, 637 • G. A. Swan, *Flora of Northumberland* (1993), 11

Wallis, John (1789–1866), topographer and cartographer, born in Fore Street, Bodmin, on 11 April 1789, was the eldest child of John Wallis (1759–1842), attorney and town clerk of Bodmin, and his wife, Isabella Mary, daughter of Henry Slogget, purser in the Royal Navy. He had a twin brother, Henry, and a younger sister, Isabella Mary. He was educated at Tiverton grammar school, and afterwards articled to his father. After being admitted a solicitor and proctor about 1811 he practised as an attorney in Bodmin with his father and John Bennett until 1814. He matriculated from Exeter College, Oxford, on 17 December 1813, graduating BA on 7 July 1820, and MA on 20 March 1821. On completing his residence at Oxford he was ordained in 1817, curate at Blisland, and was then appointed vicar of Bodmin on 17 November of the same year. He was a capital burgess of the borough, and served as mayor in 1822. In 1840 he became deputy registrar of the archdeaconry of Cornwall, a post which he retained until his death. He was also vice-warden of the stannaries of Cornwall.

Wallis was a keen topographer and cartographer of Bodmin and the surrounding districts. His first publication was a reprint of the index to Thomas Martyn's 'Map of the county of Cornwall', to which he appended a short account of the archdeaconry of Cornwall (1816). In 1825 he published thirteen outline maps of the archdeaconry and county of Cornwall, at the scale of 4 miles to the inch. Between 1831 and 1834 he published several reports and tables about Bodmin, and between 1827 and 1838 he published in twenty parts *The Bodmin Register*, which contained much historical and geographical information about Bodmin and Cornwall in general. Of his projected *Exeter Register* only the first part was published (1831). His *Cornwall Register* (1847–8), in twelve parts, contained particulars of Cornish parishes, and was accompanied by a map of Cornwall at the scale of 4 miles to the inch. He also wrote a *Family Register* (1827) and several pamphlets, chiefly on topographical subjects.

Wallis died at Bodmin vicarage, unmarried, on 6 December 1866, and was buried at Berry cemetery, Bodmin, on the 11th. He was described as amiable and energetic, able to stay on friendly terms with the many nonconformists in his parish.   E. I. Carlyle, *rev.* Elizabeth Baigent

Sources *Royal Cornwall Gazette*, 13 (Dec 1866), 4 • *GM*, 4th ser., 3 (1867), 124 • Foster, *Alum. Oxon.* • Boase, *Mod. Eng. biog.* • *CGPLA Eng. & Wales* (1866) • J. Maclean, *The parochial and family history of the deanery of Trigg Minor in the county of Cornwall*, 3 vols. (1873–9) • private information (2004)
Wealth at death under £1500: probate, 20 Dec 1866, *CGPLA Eng. & Wales*

Wallis, Sir Provo William Parry (1791–1892), naval officer, only son of Provo Featherstone Wallis, chief clerk to the naval commissioner at Halifax, Nova Scotia, was born at Halifax on 12 April 1791. His mother was a daughter of William Lawlor, major in the 1st battalion of the Halifax regiment. It has been suggested that he was related to Captain Samuel *Wallis, which is not improbable. It is more certain that he was the grandson of Provo Wallis, a carpenter in the navy, who, after serving through the Seven Years' War, was in 1776 carpenter of the *Eagle*, flagship of Lord Howe in North America, and appointed by him on 3 March 1778 master shipwright of the naval yard at New York. After the peace he was transferred to Halifax.

At an early age Wallis was sent to England, and while there at school his name was on the books of several different ships on the Halifax station. He actually entered the navy in October 1804 on the frigate *Cleopatra* (32 guns), commanded by Sir Robert Laurie. On her way out to the West Indies on 16 February 1805 the *Cleopatra*, after a gallant action, was captured by the French frigate *Ville de Milan* (40 guns), which was herself so much damaged that a week later (23 February) she surrendered without resistance to the *Leander* (50 guns). The *Cleopatra* was recaptured at the same time, and Laurie was reinstated in the command. Shortly afterwards Laurie was appointed to the *Ville de Milan*, commissioned as the *Milan*, and Wallis went with him.

In November 1806 Wallis was appointed acting lieutenant of the *Triumph*, with Sir Thomas Masterman Hardy, and on 30 November 1808 was officially promoted lieutenant of the brig *Curieux*, which on 3 November 1809 was wrecked on the coast of Guadeloupe. After one or two changes he was appointed in January 1812 to the *Shannon*, commanded by Captain Philip Bowes Vere Broke. He was her second lieutenant in the brilliant capture of the *Chesapeake* on 1 June 1813, and, being left—by the death of the first lieutenant and Broke's dangerous wound—commanding officer, took the *Shannon* and her prize to Halifax. The prisoners, being considerably more numerous than the crew of the *Shannon*, were secured in handcuffs, which they themselves had provided. On 9 July Wallis was promoted commander, and, returning to England in the *Shannon* in October, was appointed in January 1814 to the sloop *Snipe*. On 19 October 1817, Wallis married Juliana, second daughter of Archdeacon Roger Massey; they had two daughters. On 12 August 1819 he was advanced to post rank.

From 1824 to 1826 Wallis commanded the *Niemen* on the Halifax station; in 1838–9 the *Madagascar* in the West Indies and off Vera Cruz; and from 1843 to 1846 the *Warspite* in the Mediterranean. He married, secondly, on 21 July 1849, Jemima Mary Gwyne, a daughter of General Sir Robert Thomas Wilson, governor of Gibraltar. On 27 August 1851 he was promoted rear-admiral, and in 1857 was appointed commander-in-chief on the south-east coast of South America, from where he was recalled on his promotion to vice-admiral on 10 September 1857. He had no further service, but was made a KCB on 18 May 1860 and promoted admiral on 2 March 1863, rear-admiral of the United Kingdom in 1869, and vice-admiral of the United Kingdom in 1870. He became GCB on 24 May 1873 and was made admiral of the fleet on 11 December 1877. By a special clause in Childers's retirement scheme of 1870 it was provided that the names of those old officers, who had commanded a ship during the French wars, should be retained on the active list, and the few days that Wallis was in command of the *Shannon* brought him within this rule. His name was thus retained on the active list until his death.

During the latter part of his life Wallis resided mainly at Funtington House, Funtington, near Chichester, in full enjoyment of his faculties, and reading or writing with ease until a few months before his death. On his 100th birthday (12 April 1891) he received congratulations from many, including the queen and the captain and officers of the *Shannon*. He died at home at Funtington House on 13 February 1892 and was buried with military honours at Funtington on 18 February. Wallis was an officer of great good fortune; he had no great merits but by the death of the *Shannon*'s first lieutenant and sheer longevity he became a celebrity.

J. K. LAUGHTON, *rev.* ANDREW LAMBERT

Sources J. G. Brighton, *Admiral of the fleet, Sir Provo W. P. Wallis* (1892) · P. Padfield, *Broke and the 'Shannon'* (1968) · Boase, *Mod. Eng. biog.* · Kelly, *Handbk* (1891)
Likenesses R. Taylor, wood-engraving (aged nineteen), BM; repro. in *ILN* (1890) · portrait, repro. in Brighton, *Admiral of the fleet*
Wealth at death £80,137 19s. 0d.: resworn probate, June 1894, *CGPLA Eng. & Wales* (1892)

Wallis, Ralph [*called* the Cobbler of Gloucester] (*d.* **1669**), pamphleteer, was born in a country village, probably in Gloucestershire. Wallis describes himself as 'of mean descent for parentage' (Wallis, *More News from Rome*, foreword). The date of his birth is unknown, but by the mid-1660s he considered himself old, and in the 1620s he was memorizing anti-popish verse. His own upbringing, in a poor family, was by no means a fiercely protestant one. His parents were Roman Catholics but 'church papists', who conformed enough to the demands of the Church of England to escape persecution. His father died when Wallis was nine, leaving to his son a collection of missals, beads, and crucifixes. He moved later to Gloucester to pursue the trade of cobbler, which, he explained, meant repairing boots and shoes, not making them.

Like many with radical protestant leanings, Wallis found that the civil wars provided him with opportunities. By October 1643, he was involved in sequestering the rents of Gloucestershire royalists on behalf of the parliamentarian garrison at Gloucester. On one of these forays, at Pamington, near Cheltenham, he was betrayed into the hands of scouts from the royalist garrison of Sudeley Castle, and was imprisoned at Sudeley and later in Oxford. His wife, Dorothy, petitioned Governor Edward Massie for relief, on behalf of her family of three children, and she was awarded 18s. Her expressed hope that Wallis would benefit in an exchange of prisoners may have been fulfilled. According to a hostile anonymous biographer, he subsequently served as an agent to sequestrators of royalists' property. On 8 June 1648 he was appointed by the Gloucester corporation to be schoolmaster at Holy Trinity Church. The corporation was dominated by puritans of

the stamp of Thomas Pury, the city's MP, and Wallis performed other duties for his masters, including acting as a messenger to London. He was regarded highly enough to be singled out for remuneration in August 1651, and on 24 September 1658 he was elected burgess and freeman in recognition of his services. He was sworn the following day, in what was the apotheosis of his public career. He is said to have begun writing pamphlets against the governments of the 1650s, but no trace of them has survived, and it seems a little unlikely in one who had benefited from republican regimes. On the other hand, the work *Harry Hangman's Honour* (1655), which is part apology for the Gloucestershire tobacco planters, part wry commentary on public life, foreshadows much of Wallis's later style as a writer, and probably marks his authorial début.

Wallis never held civic office in Gloucester, and it may be assumed that he had lost his teaching post before the arrival in the city of the commissioners for regulating corporations soon after the Restoration. He reverted to his trade, and was drawn to preaching as a possible calling. In the climate of extreme hostility to protestant dissenters he was nothing daunted, and began to travel, presumably as an itinerant preacher. It was alleged that he was a frequent visitor to Kidderminster, where Richard Baxter had nurtured a godly civic culture during the 1650s. About this time he married his wife, Elizabeth, who was much younger than him; he also considered taking up offers of remuneration as a minister. A potential alternative source of income was alehouse-keeping, of which he evidently had some experience. Elizabeth declared: 'I might have been more happy in the world than to have had you, yet upon condition you will neither sell ale nor preach, I will be contented with my position' (Wallis, *Rome for Good News*, sig. A2i). Wallis was assisted financially by James Forbes, in the 1650s an Independent minister in Gloucester but by the mid-1660s a shoemaker at Clapham. Both men had come to the attention of the authorities in Gloucester and London by January 1664, but it was not until September that they were arrested by the government censor Roger L'Estrange; they were examined by him on 1 October. In late November the government evidently thought to grant Wallis bail in order to allow him to publish his work, to uncover the centre of a ring of subversives, but no such network was unveiled. In his petition to Henry Bennet, Wallis begged not to be crushed like a worm, described his own work as 'drollery', and assured Bennet he only attacked the clergy 'to teach them better manners, and will scribble as much against fanatics when the worm gets into his cracked pate' (*CSP dom.*, 1663–4, 156–7).

Thereafter Wallis suffered persecution at the hands of civic authorities in Bristol and Gloucester, and appeared before Thomas Windsor, Lord Windsor, probably in Worcestershire, in the manner endured by Quakers. It did not prevent him publishing, however, and at least three titles of his appeared between 1665 and 1668: some may have been second editions of works published earlier. At the heart of *Rome for Good News* (1665) is the verse in ballad stanzas that he memorized forty years before: a dialogue between a Catholic priest and a supposed protestant, where the priest shows the protestant that he remains in thrall to popery. His real target is the Church of England, an 'old whore' (*Rome for Good News*, 19). *More News from Rome, or, Magna Charta, Discoursed of between a Poor Man & his Wife* (1666), written after his interrogation by L'Estrange, provides a catalogue of the scandalous and shameful conduct of Anglican clergymen, gathered mostly from the south-west midlands. Wallis returned to this theme in *Room for the Cobler of Gloucester and his Wife* (1668), described by L'Estrange as 'the damnedest thing [that] has come out yet' (*CSP dom.*, 1667–8, 357). In this grossly libellous work, Wallis adopted a prurient and scatological tone, providing outrageous if entertaining anecdotes about clergymen whose names and addresses he knew. His depiction of the rites and ceremonies of the Church of England as 'the parings of the devil's bum-hole' (Wallis, *Room for the Cobler*, 40) are among his milder observations.

In sharp contrast to the libels and anti-Anglican polemic of these works are the dedicatory epistles to Elizabeth that precede them. Her support for Wallis, and her care for their four young children during his sufferings, were acknowledged in affectionate and touching detail. By 1665 he evidently suffered a serious disability in his right arm, and walked only with crutches, raising the possibility that his venom against the church was fuelled by chronic physical pain. He returned to Gloucester after his wanderings and died there in 1669; he was buried at St Mary de Crypt, the parish where James Forbes had ministered, on 9 February. His hostile biographer provides a description: 'His complexion was of a sunburnt gipsy colour, and his skin was rough and tawny, like singed bacon; his hair was brown and bristly upon his head, but his locks were weather-turned, like a barber's show periwig' (*Life and Death of Ralph Wallis*, 20). His precise religious affiliation puzzled contemporaries, but he seems best described as an unaligned nonconformist, whose hatred of Anglicanism provided him with a driving energy. His memory lingered: 1704 saw the publication of *The Cobler of Gloucester Reviv'd; in a Letter to the Observator's Country-Man*.

STEPHEN K. ROBERTS

Sources [R. Wallis], *Rome for good news, or, Good news from Rome* (privately printed, London, [1642]) • [R. Wallis], *More news from Rome, or, Magna charta* (1666) • R. Wallis, *Room for the Cobler of Gloucester and his wife* (privately printed, London, 1668) • *The life and death of Ralph Wallis* (1670) • *CSP dom.*, 1663–4; 1667–8 • P. Ripley and J. Juřica, eds., *Calendar of the registers of the freemen of the city of Gloucester, 1641–1838* (1991) • corporation order books, Glos. RO, Gloucester borough records, GBR B3/2, 3 • parish register, St Mary de Crypt, 9 Feb 1669, Glos. RO [burial] • *Calamy rev.* • PRO, SP28/129/5, fols. 9v, 10v, 14v; SP28/228/299
Archives Glos. RO, Hyett Pamphlets, pamphlets and anonymous 1670 biography

Wallis, Robert William (1794–1878), line engraver, was born in London on 7 November 1794, the eldest son of Thomas Wallis (*d.* 1839), assistant to the topographical engraver Charles Theodosius Heath (1785–1848), and his wife, Sarah Newsome. Although he seems to have lived in the country until about 1818, he was taught engraving by his father. On his return to London he immediately found employment as a landscape engraver on steel, providing illustrations for the numerous travel books then reaching the market. James Baylis Allen (1803–1876) worked as his assistant. By the mid-century Wallis was judged one of the ablest landscape engravers, excelling in the interpretation of the work of Joseph Mallord William Turner. He was employed on Turner's illustrations to Cooke's *Southern Coast of England*; Turner's *England and Wales* and his *Rivers of France*; *Heath's Picturesque Annual*; *Jennings Landscape Annual*; and the illustrations to many fine editions of popular works. Fourteen of his engravings were published in the *Art Journal* between 1849 and 1880. His finest productions were the large plates after Turner's *Lake of Nemi* and *The Approach to Venice*, a proof of which was exhibited at the Royal Academy in 1859. Wallis then retired, and passed the remainder of his life in the Brighton area; he died at his home, 30 York Road, Hove, Sussex, on 23 November 1878. The name of his wife is unknown, but he was survived by a daughter, Frances Catherine Wallis (*b.* 1831).

Robert's brother **Henry Wallis** (*bap.* 1806, *d.* 1890), baptized at St Dunstan, Stepney, on 8 August 1806, practised for some years as an engraver of small topographical illustrations for books. Both Henry and Robert often signed their work simply 'Wallis', leading on occasion to problems of identification.

In the 1840s Henry suffered two attacks of paralysis which obliged him to find another occupation. He then turned to picture dealing, and in 1861 was offered the post of manager at the French Gallery at 120 Pall Mall. He bought out the owner, Ernest Gambart, in 1867 for £1000. In 1871 he retired in favour of his son Thomas. He died at home at 55 Effra Road, Brixton, on 15 October 1890.

Another brother, William Wallis (*b.* 1796), likewise an engraver on steel, produced illustrations of landscapes and indoor views in Britain and abroad for a range of travel books, besides contributing to *Jennings Landscape Annual*, *Heath's Picturesque Annual*, *Keepsake*, and other annuals.

ANITA MCCONNELL

Sources *The Athenaeum* (1878), ii, 695 • *Art Journal*, 41 (1879) • Redgrave, *Artists* • *The Times* (27 Nov 1878), 6e • *The Times* (24 Oct 1890), 7 • parish registers of St Luke's, Old Street, and St Dunstan, Stepney, LMA • census returns, 1881 • d. cert. • B. Hunnisett, *An illustrated dictionary of British steel engravers*, new edn (1989), 95–7 • d. cert. [Henry Wallis]

Wallis, Samuel (1728–1795), naval officer and Pacific explorer, the son of John Wallis (1680–1768) and Sarah Barrett (*d.* 1731), was born in April 1728 at Fentonwoon, Cornwall, and baptized on 23 April 1728 at Lanteglos. He served in the navy as midshipman and master's mate before receiving his lieutenant's commission in October 1748. After serving as lieutenant on several ships from 1753 onwards, he received his first command, the sloop *Swan*, in June 1756. In April 1757 he was appointed to the frigate *Port Mahon*, and in September 1758 to the *Prince of Orange* (60 guns). In 1759 he took part in the Quebec campaign under Vice-Admiral Charles Saunders before returning with his ship to home waters for the rest of the Seven Years' War.

Samuel Wallis (1728–1795), by unknown artist

In June 1766 Wallis took command of the frigate *Dolphin* (24 guns) just back from Commodore John Byron's circumnavigation. The choice of Wallis for the second voyage of Pacific exploration in the reign of George III was perhaps a sign of his meritorious service during the war, which would have been observed at first hand by Saunders, now second lord of the Admiralty. In a long naval career the voyage of 1766 to 1768 represents Wallis's claim to fame. It had different objectives from Byron's voyage, for his instructions from the Admiralty, headed by the earl of Egmont, ordered Wallis to search for the great continent 'Terra Australis Incognita' in the south Pacific. Byron seems to have played an important role in framing this new directive. When sailing through the Tuamotus in June 1765 he had become convinced that there was a land mass to the south; and it appears to have been his belief in the existence of this southern continent that persuaded Egmont to point Wallis towards its discovery.

Wallis sailed on 21 August 1767, accompanied by Philip Carteret in the old and decrepit sloop *Swallow*. There were few problems with the well-provisioned *Dolphin*, only the third naval vessel to be copper-sheathed. After a gruelling passage through the Strait of Magellan of record-breaking length (the *Dolphin* took 115 days, the *Swallow* 119), the two vessels became separated on 11 April 1767 as they struggled out of the strait and into the Pacific. Carteret suspected that Wallis had deliberately abandoned the slow-sailing *Swallow*; but it is more likely that the explanation lies in a combination of the hazardous sailing conditions off Cape Pillar at the western exit of the strait and the different sailing qualities of the two ships. While in the strait Wallis had taken the opportunity to measure the height of

a group of Patagonians, and his findings—the tallest person was 6 feet 7 inches, and most were under 6 feet—did something to dispel the notion of 'Patagonian giants' brought back by Byron.

Once clear of the Strait of Magellan Wallis followed his instructions to 'Stretch to the Westward … from Cape Horn, loosing as little Southing as possible' (Wallis, 2.303); but by the end of April contrary winds and scurvy among the crew forced him northwards into warmer waters. On 6 June he reached the Tuamotus, where he sighted five islands unknown to Europeans, and on 17 June the first of the Society Islands at Mehetia. The next day Tahiti was sighted, and there the *Dolphin* stayed for five weeks. During this time the sick among the crew recovered, but Wallis (and his first lieutenant) were struck down with with 'a Bilious Disorder' (Carrington, 116). For most of the stay Wallis was too weak to keep the deck, and much depended on George Robertson, the *Dolphin*'s experienced master, and Tobias Furneaux, second lieutenant. The captain's incapacity was the more worrying, given the outbreaks of violence that marked the first days after the *Dolphin*'s arrival and thwarted Wallis's hopes of avoiding the use of force. It took blasts of grape and ball from the ship's cannon, and many dead and wounded among the Tahitians, to quell the disturbances. Wallis's description of Tahiti (as printed in Hawkesworth's *Voyages* of 1773) as a lush and fertile land with garlanded women eager to trade sexual favours helped, along with the accounts of James Cook and Joseph Banks, to stamp an erotic imprint on Europe's image of the south seas. In practical ways, too, Tahiti was important, for it provided an ideal base for Cook and his successors. For Robertson, the island also seemed to be an outlier of the great southern continent, whose mountain-tops the master thought he had glimpsed only 60 miles to the south. Wallis's views on this are not known, but on 27 July 1767 he left Tahiti on a westerly course and made no attempt to explore to the south. Further uncharted islands were sighted as the *Dolphin* continued west and then northwest before heading into the north Pacific. The last part of the voyage brought Wallis home by way of Tinian, Batavia, and the Cape. The *Dolphin* reached the Downs on 28 May 1768, with Wallis still seriously ill.

Wallis's voyage is now seen as a more creditable undertaking than was once thought. On his own count, he had discovered and charted fifteen islands, some of them admittedly tiny atolls. Although in wretched health for months on end, he had achieved much that was to help shape Cook's *Endeavour* voyage. Tahiti provided the essential base for the astronomical observations of the transit of Venus in 1769, and rumours brought back by the *Dolphin* of mountain-tops sighted south of the island led to Cook's instructions to sail directly south from Tahiti in search of a continent. Whether there was direct contact between Wallis and Cook in the summer of 1768 is not known, but many of Cook's measures to keep his crews healthy had already been put into practice by Wallis. He made every effort to obtain greens and citrus fruits, he kept the crew's clothes and bedding dry and clean, and he introduced a three-watch system to give the men more rest. They in turn seem to have respected and liked their captain; in a petition at the end of the voyage they applauded his 'Humane and generous treatment', and signed themselves 'the Dolphins' (Wallis, 1.47). There were serious and debilitating outbreaks of scurvy on the *Dolphin*, but not a single man died from this disease, and the mortality rate on the voyage was remarkably low: two dead from accidents, and three from malaria and dysentery.

Wallis took a long time to recover from 'the uncommon fatigue and anxiety' of the voyage. During it he had been 'quite worn down', he told the Admiralty in February 1770, when he still suffered from bouts of ill health. He was awarded a gratuity of £525 before, in November 1770, he was given command of the *Torbay*, and later of the *Queen*. From 1782 to 1783, and from 1787 until his death, Wallis held the responsible position of extra commissioner of the navy. He died on 21 January 1795 in Devonshire Street, Portland Place, London, and was survived by his wife, Betty Hearle, who died on 13 November 1804.

GLYNDWR WILLIAMS

Sources J. Hawkesworth, ed., *An account of the voyages undertaken by the order of his present majesty … by Commodore Byron, Captain Wallis, Captain Carteret, and Captain Cook*, 3 vols. (1773) · *The discovery of Tahiti: a journal of the second voyage of HMS Dolphin round the world … written by her master George Robertson*, ed. H. Carrington, Hakluyt Society, 2nd ser., 98 (1948) · *Carteret's voyage around the world, 1766–1769*, ed. H. Wallis, 2 vols., Hakluyt Society, 2nd ser., 124–5 (1965) · R. Cock, 'Precursors of Cook: the voyages of the *Dolphin*, 1764–8', *Mariner's Mirror*, 85 (1999), 30–52 · G. Williams, 'The *Endeavour* voyage: a coincidence of motives', [forthcoming] · M. Lincoln, ed., *Science and exploration in the Pacific: European voyages to the southern oceans in the eighteenth century* (1998), 3–18

Archives Cornwall RO, letter-book · Mitchell L., NSW, private journal · NL NZ, Turnbull L., logbook · PRO, corresp. and official log of *Dolphin*, Adm 55/35

Likenesses portrait, NPG [*see illus.*]

Wallis [*married name* Campbell], **Tryphosa Jane** (1774–1848), actress, was the daughter of the provincial performers Jane Wallis (1750–1785) and Fielding Wallis (1754–1817), whose father, Revd Thomas Wallis, was rector of Boho and Templecarne, co. Fermanagh, Ireland. The eldest of eight children, she was born on 11 January 1774 at Richmond, Yorkshire, where her maternal grandmother was associated with the management of the theatre. She appeared as a child in Dublin at the Smock Alley and Crow Street theatres with her parents. The family returned to England, where she continued performing, and after her mother's death in 1785 she was essentially adopted by Lord and Lady Loughborough (later earl and countess of Rosslyn). Through their influence she made her début at Covent Garden on 10 January 1789, as Sigismunda in James Thomson's *Tancred and Sigismunda*. The *European Magazine* described her as exhibiting 'great marks of feeling and sensibility'. The following season she gained an engagement in Bath, and played Rosalind in *As You Like It* for her first appearance (17 October 1790).

Tryphosa Wallis was thereafter seen as Lucile in *False Appearances*, Indiana in Richard Steele's *The Conscious Lovers*, Calista in Nicholas Rowe's *The Fair Penitent*, Maria in *The Citizen*, and Beatrice in *Much Ado about Nothing*. She performed in both Bath and Bristol until 1794, and became a

Tryphosa Jane Wallis (1774–1848), by Joseph Grozer, pubd 1796 (after John Graham) [as Juliet in *Romeo and Juliet*]

great favourite. On 4 March 1794 she delivered an effusive speech at a farewell benefit and was presented with a medallion from the ladies and gentlemen of Bath, as a 'small tribute to her private virtue and public merit'.

On 7 October 1794, as 'Miss Wallis' from Bath, she reappeared at Covent Garden, where she was engaged for three years at £18 a week, and played Imogen in *Cymbeline*. She repeated many of the prominent characters in which she had been seen in Bath, including Juliet, Calista, Beatrice, and Cordelia, and played several original parts, of which the most considerable were Georgina in Hannah Cowley's *Town Before You*, Julia in Miles Peter Andrews's *Mysteries of the Castle*, Lady Danvers in Frederick Reynolds's *Fortune's Fool*, and Miss Dorillon in Elizabeth Inchbald's *Wives as they Were and Maids as they Are*. Although the critics were relatively complimentary, there are some hints that puffs advertising her performances were exaggerated in their praise. The *Secret History of the Green Rooms* (1795) noted that she could justly deliver 'deserted love, plaintive melancholy, and soft friendship … all beyond these nature has denied and art will scarcely supply them'. Roach's *Authentic Memoirs of the Green Room* (1796) was harsher: 'it is not the approbation of a *lerd* or *lady*, nor being engaged at an exorbitant salary, can make John Bull see more merit than there actually is'.

Tryphosa Wallis's final performance at Covent Garden was on 22 May 1797. She then appeared for a short time at Newcastle and Edinburgh before marrying James Elijah Campbell of the 3rd regiment of the foot guards, at Glads-muir, East Lothian, in June or July. On her marriage she left the stage for a time.

On 20 February 1813, as 'Mrs Campbell late Miss Wallis', she reappeared at Covent Garden, playing the title role in Garrick's *Isabella* but she lost her nerve and was a failure. The *Theatrical Inquisitor* (1813) noted her 'matronly appear-ance and deportment', commented that her face was expressive of the amiable and domestic passions, but acknowledged she was 'unequal to the successful person-ation of the higher characters of drama'. Despite this faint praise, she reappeared at Bath in April and was employed there for the following season, but she never recovered her lost ground. After this final engagement she retired permanently from the stage, aged thirty. Contemporary biographers mention her as a good daughter, a good sister, and a good wife.

Tryphosa Jane Campbell and her husband had at least seven children. One daughter, Charlotte Eliza Jane, died in 1826, and her will reveals the names of her brothers: James, John, Fielding, and Hugh. The deaths of two other daughters, Jane and Mary, aged twenty and seventeen, were reported in the *Gentleman's Magazine* of March 1833. The same announcement mentioned that their father was, by that time, a captain in the Royal Navy. He had evi-dently died by the time of his wife's death, on 29 Decem-ber 1848, as her tombstone at All Saints' in Edmonton, Middlesex, describes her as a widow.   K. A. CROUCH

Sources Highfill, Burnim & Langhans, *BDA* · C. B. Hogan, ed., *The London stage, 1660–1800*, pt 5: *1776–1800* (1968) · S. Rosenfeld, *Geor-gian theatre of Richmond, Yorkshire and its circuit: Beverly, Harrogate, Kendal, Northallerton, Ulverston, and Whitby* (1984) · Genest, *Eng. stage* · D. E. Baker, *Biographia dramatica, or, A companion to the play-house*, rev. I. Reed, new edn, rev. S. Jones, 3 vols. in 4 (1812) · *Theatri-cal Inquisitor* (1813) · *GM*, 1st ser., 67 (1797), 613 · *GM*, 1st ser., 103/1 (1833), 380 · *European Magazine and London Review*, 15 (1789), 45 · review, *European Magazine and London Review*, 26 (1794), 286 · *Monthly Mirror*, 4 (Sept 1797), 172–5 · J. Roach, *Roach's authentic mem-oirs of the green room* (1796) · [J. Haslewood], *The secret history of the green rooms: containing authentic and entertaining memoirs of the actors and actresses in the three Theatres Royal*, new edn, 2 vols. (1795) · B. S. Penley, *The Bath stage: a history of dramatic representations in Bath* (1892) · A. Pasquin [J. Williams], *The pin basket to the children of Thes-pis* (1796) · *The thespian dictionary, or, Dramatic biography of the present age*, 2nd edn (1805) · *Biographical and Imperial Magazine* (Jan 1789), 71

Likenesses G. Romney, oils, 1788, Petworth House, Sussex · F. Bartolozzi, engraving, 1795, BM · G. Dupont, oils, 1795, Norton Art Gallery, West Palm Beach, Florida · D. Gibson, engraving, 1795 (after miniature) · J. Graham, portrait, 1796 · J. Grozer, mezzotint, pubd 1796 (after J. Graham), BM, NPG [*see illus.*] · J. R. Smith, engrav-ing, 1797 · J. Jones, engraving, 1798 (after G. Romney) · G. Keating, engraving, 1799 (after G. Romney) · P. Audinet, engraving (as Aspasia in *Irene*), repro. in J. Bell, *Bell's British theatre* (1796) · prints, BM · three prints, Harvard TC

Wallis, William (*fl.* 1824–1830), silk weaver and radical leader, is a figure about whom little is known except his involvement in radical artisan politics in Spitalfields in London. He was not by origin from Spitalfields but by the mid-1820s was a leading figure in the campaigns and organizations of the silk weavers there.

The silk weavers were at that time the most distressed of the London artisan trades, mainly because of a glut of labour and provincial competition; but the situation was worsened by the repeal in 1824 of the Spitalfields Acts by which wages were legally fixed, and in 1826 by the ending of the prohibition on importing foreign silks. The weavers often experienced real destitution, and in the late 1820s were active in campaigns for parliamentary reform and legislation to protect labour.

The prominence of Wallis in the struggle of London artisans against the threatened reimposition of the com-bination laws in 1825 brought him into association with John *Gast, whom he helped in that year to establish and run the Mutual Improvement Society and the *Trades' News-paper*. In 1826 he organized the silk weavers into a General Protection Society, which unsuccessfully tried to restore wages to the 1824 levels. He led their campaign in 1829 to persuade the government to provide the means to settle unemployed weavers on uncultivated land so that they might become self-supporting. He also led weaver support for the General Association, founded by Gast in 1827, to unite the London artisan trades in favour of measures to check the spread of machinery and relieve those rendered unemployed by it, and to make locally agreed wage rates legally binding. While in favour of parliamentary reform to reduce corruption, privilege, and taxation, he favoured single-issue campaigns, but was displaced in the leader-ship of the weavers in 1829 by more radical figures.

When late in 1831 the group around Francis *Place formed the National Political Union in support of the Reform Bill, Place organized Wallis's election to its coun-cil as a steady and moderate reformer in opposition to extremists; and Wallis was a leading figure in organizing support for the bill in Spitalfields and Bethnal Green. With Place and his associates he seceded from the National Political Union in 1833 and founded the Radical Club, of which he was still a member in 1840. He remained a good friend of Place throughout the 1830s, but took part in the weavers' campaigns in favour of protection; he was also an administrator of the Queen Adelaide Fund estab-lished to relieve destitute weavers.

IORWERTH PROTHERO

Sources I. J. Prothero, *Artisans and politics in early nineteenth-century London: John Gast and his times* (1979)

Wallmoden, Amalie Sophie Marianne von [*née* Amalie Sophie Marianne von Wendt], *suo jure* **countess of Yar-mouth** (1704–1765), royal mistress, was born on 1 April 1704, the daughter of Johann Franz Dietrich von Wendt, a general in the Hanoverian army, and his wife, Friderike Charlotte, *née* von dem Bussche, the widow of another Hanoverian general named Welk. Her grandmother Maria Elisabeth von Meysenbug was probably the first mistress of George I in the late 1670s, and her father's intense cor-respondence with Ernest Augustus, duke of York and

Amalie Sophie Marianne von Wallmoden, *suo jure* countess of Yarmouth (1704-1765), by G. de Köning (after Peter Van Hoogh)

Albany, the brother of George I, has been interpreted as evidence of a homosexual relationship. In 1727 Amalie married Gottlieb Adam von Wallmoden (d. 1752), *Oberhauptmann* of Calenberg in the electorate of Hanover; they had a son, Franz Ernst, and a daughter, Friderike.

In 1735 Amalie von Wallmoden met *George II (1683–1760) on one of his visits to Hanover, and they began a love affair. According to John, Lord Hervey, the king sent a detailed account of the relationship's progress to Queen Caroline, who remained in London. Reports of Wallmoden, 'a young married woman of the first fashion' (Hervey, 2.457), alarmed the queen, who saw in her a royal mistress who could threaten the queen's influence with George II, and also Sir Robert Walpole, who saw in Wallmoden not only a rival to Queen Caroline but also an incentive for George II to remain in Germany and impede the effectiveness of the British government. During the king's stay in Hanover, Wallmoden conceived a child, Johann Ludwig von Wallmoden (1736–1811), who was widely believed to be the king's, although he was never recognized as such. George returned to Hanover to be with his mistress in 1736, but the queen was opposed to her following the king to Britain. The affair became public knowledge in London, where details, real or imagined, were seized upon by the opposition to Walpole. Wallmoden was said, without foundation, to be a Catholic, and on the king's return it was reported that he 'caused the picture of his mistress … to be hung up opposite to his bed's feet' (16 March 1737, *Egmont Diary*, 2.369–70).

Following Queen Caroline's death in November 1737, Walpole was convinced that only Wallmoden could maintain the king's well-being; he probably also preferred a Hanoverian mistress over a British one with her own family connections, who might influence George II against his ministers. The king's casual relationship with Mary Scott, countess of Deloraine, was put aside. Wallmoden arrived in London in June 1738, and moved into apartments at St James's Palace and Kensington Palace. According to one report she was accompanied by Gottlieb Adam von Wallmoden, but with George II requiring her to act as the king's hostess at court and as the royal sexual partner there was no room for her husband, who divorced her in Hanover in summer 1740. By then, on 8 February 1740, Wallmoden had been naturalized a British subject, and on 24 March 1740 she was created a British peeress, for life, as countess of Yarmouth. She was awarded a pension of £4000 a year from the Irish revenues.

Lady Yarmouth 'appears at the drawing-room like one that has been used to the courts of Princes' (A. Windham to [Charles, third Viscount Townshend], 22 June 1738, *Townshend MSS*, 356), but she was a newcomer to British politics. For the first few years of her period as mistress of George II it may have been true that she 'had the good sense to abstain as a rule from meddling in court intrigues' (*DNB*), but although she seems to have exhibited good sense she came to be relied upon by the king's ministers to introduce George II to people and ideas that the king might have resisted. She also took a role in the creation of peers; it was alleged that she had been allocated the fees for peerage creations in 1741, and in 1747 Horace Walpole wrote to George Montagu that she had 'touched twelve thousand for Sir Jacob Bouverie's coronet' (Walpole, *Corr.*, 9.51). These activities made her a more effective political mistress to George II than her predecessor Henrietta Howard, countess of Suffolk. Contrary to what some supposed or hoped, she did not rule the king. In the 1740s, Philip Stanhope, fourth earl of Chesterfield, thought that by cultivating her interest he could strengthen his position in Henry Pelham's cabinet, but Lady Yarmouth's approval on a personal level did not lead her to intercede in his favour, and he was eased out of office in February 1748. Lady Yarmouth was more supportive of Thomas Pelham-Holles, duke of Newcastle, when he sought the removal of John Russell, fourth duke of Bedford, as a secretary of state in 1750–51. She helped persuade George II that Bedford was a liability to the administration, contributing towards the latter's resignation in 1751. In the political turmoil of the 1750s Lady Yarmouth's word was useful even to members of the royal family; after William, duke of Cumberland, had capitulated to the French army at Kloster-Zeven in September 1757, he approached Lady Yarmouth to inform the king of his intention to resign his offices. Her alliance with Newcastle has been credited with persuading George II to remain faithful to the Pitt–Newcastle ministry formed in 1757, despite the king's antipathy to William Pitt.

Lady Yarmouth was credited by Horace Walpole with persuading George II to support a 'jubilee masquerade in the Venetian manner' (Walpole, *Corr.*, 20.46–7) at Ranelagh Gardens following the treaty of Aix-la-Chapelle in

1749, but in general she appeared content with the unexciting routine of the widowed king's court. Horace Walpole said that she was left 'A strong box containing about ten thousand pounds' (ibid., 21.450) by the king when he died on 25 October 1760, to which George III added the other contents of the bureau where the money was found. She remained in Britain at first, and spent summer 1761 with the duke and duchess of Newcastle, but afterwards returned to Hanover, where she died of 'a cancer in her breast' (J. Twells to the duke of Newcastle, 31 Oct 1765, BL, Add. MS 33069, fol. 295) on 19 October 1765. She was reported to have 'left her two sons a million of crowns' (*GM*, 1st ser., 35, 1765, 534), although this may express the financial rapacity conventionally ascribed to royal mistresses rather than a genuine estimate of her wealth. Her younger son, Johann Ludwig, was made a count in 1783, became a field marshal in the Hanoverian army during the French revolutionary war, and died in 1811.

MATTHEW KILBURN

Sources John, Lord Hervey, *Some materials towards memoirs of the reign of King George II*, ed. R. Sedgwick, 3 vols. (1931) · *Manuscripts of the earl of Egmont: diary of Viscount Percival, afterwards first earl of Egmont*, 3 vols., HMC, 63 (1920–23) · Walpole, *Corr.* · *GM*, 1st ser., 10 (1740), 90; 35 (1765), 534 · R. Browning, *The duke of Newcastle* (1975) · *The manuscripts of the Marquess Townshend*, HMC, 19 (1887) · GEC, *Peerage*, new edn, 12/2.893–4 · *Reminiscences written by Mr Horace Walpole in 1788*, ed. P. Toynbee (1924) · *DNB* · *The letters of Philip Dormer Stanhope, fourth earl of Chesterfield*, ed. B. Dobrée, 6 vols. (1932)
Archives BL, letters, Add. MSS 6856, 23814 | BL, corresp. with Count Bentinck, Egerton MS 1722, fols. 35, 128, 132, 205 · BL, corresp. with second earl of Egmont, Add. MS 47014B, fols. 107–10 · BL, corresp. with duke of Newcastle, Add. MSS 32710–32969, *passim* · NRA Scotland, priv. coll., letters to Lady Mary Coke
Likenesses G. de Köning, mezzotint (after P. Van Hoogh), NPG [*see illus.*]
Wealth at death 'a million of crowns': *GM*, 35 (1765), 534 · £4000 p.a. pension on Irish establishment

Wallop, Elizabeth. *See* Griffin, Elizabeth (*bap.* 1691, *d.* 1762).

Wallop, Gerald Vernon, ninth earl of Portsmouth (1898–1984), politician and environmentalist, was born on 16 May 1898 in Chicago, the eldest son of Oliver Henry Wallop, Viscount Lymington, later eighth earl of Portsmouth (1861–1943), and his American wife, Marguerite Walker (*d.* 1938). He spent his early years at his parents' ranch at Little Goose canyon, near Sheridan, Wyoming. Sent to England at eleven, he was educated at a preparatory school in Farnborough, then at Winchester College from 1911 and, after war service, at Balliol College, Oxford (1919–21). On 31 July 1920 he married Mary Lawrence Kintzing Post (*d.* 1964). From 1923 he began to take in hand the family's estate at Farleigh Wallop, Hampshire, where the reforms he instituted formed the basis of a career as an agricultural writer and occasional broadcaster. Initially advocating national self-sufficiency, Wallop went on to develop a bleak yet prescient view of the environmental impact of arable monoculture and indiscriminate use of chemicals in farming. His critiques of contemporary farming, *Famine in England* (1938) and *Alternative to Death* (1943), circulated widely within farming circles and

beyond. Indeed, although his publisher, Faber and Faber, published a number of environmentalists, its director, T. S. Eliot, took a particular interest in Wallop's work, reviewed him favourably in *Criterion*, and absorbed something of his distaste for inter-war society.

Succeeding to the courtesy title of Viscount Lymington in 1925 Wallop also pursued a political career as a county councillor and then as Conservative MP for Basingstoke (1929–34). Energetic in opposition, he grew restless as a National Conservative, his career advancing no further than the Milk Marketing Board. He resigned in 1934. Shortly beforehand he had visited India on behalf of the India Defence League, for which he wrote a report supporting imperial government through a princes' federation of states. Monarchy, and the feudal society he thought he saw in India, appealed to his romanticized concept of loyalty and service. In this he was powerfully influenced by the English Mistery, a secretive, quasi-military organization stressing 'back to the land', English nationalism, and monarchism. Lymington directed the Mistery from 1930, and from 1936 its successor the English Array. From the latter there emerged three further initiatives: a pro-German and antisemitic magazine *New Pioneer* (December 1938 – January 1940), which Lymington edited; the British Council Against European Commitments, which he founded in 1938 in response to the Czechoslovak crisis; and the Kinship in Husbandry. The latter, a self-appointed agricultural think tank, combined right-wing ruralism with agricultural science in criticism of industrialized farming and promotion of traditional husbandry and self-sufficiency. Lymington's marriage was dissolved in 1936, and on 14 August of that year he married Bridget Cory Crohan (*d.* 1979).

Lymington's rank, outspokenness, and German contacts (he had visited Berlin to lecture on soil erosion in April 1939) inevitably made him prominent in pro-German circles in the autumn of 1939. He attended several secret meetings of leading British 'fellow travellers of the right' in 1939–40, at which strategy co-ordination was inconclusively discussed along with proposals for a negotiated peace. Yet Lymington seems not to have been a serious candidate for internment. The innate shire tory in him was drawn back to fight on the home front in Hampshire, where he helped direct its war agricultural executive committee. After the war Portsmouth (he succeeded to the title in 1943) worked energetically for rural reconstruction, especially as president (1947–9) of the County Landowners' Association. He was a formative influence on the Soil Association and also took an active interest in bio-dynamic farming. As a platform speaker he was much in demand on issues ranging from dietary reform to anti-vaccination and anti-pasteurization. He was also a prominent member of the Land Resettlement Association and of the Ministry of Agriculture's advisory committee on agricultural smallholdings.

However, Portsmouth was temperamentally uneasy in post-war Britain. In 1948 he purchased the first of his three estates in Kenya, taking up permanent residency there in 1950. His interest in agricultural reform was unabated, even after the nationalization of his farms following independence. He represented agricultural interests in the Kenyan legislative council (1957–61), chaired the government's forestry advisory committee (1954–61), and was vice-chairman of the East African Natural Resources Research Council from 1963. He returned to Britain only in 1977 following a debilitating stroke from which he never recovered. He lived with his children before moving into a nursing home. Portsmouth died on 28 September 1984 and was buried in Farleigh Wallop churchyard.

A career mixing muck, mysticism, and the more esoteric reaches of British fascism might at best seem to qualify him for a place in the rich gallery of English eccentrics, but Wallop was nevertheless a seminal influence on the early environmentalist and organic farming movements.

MALCOLM CHASE

Sources Hants. RO, Wallop MSS · R. Griffiths, *Fellow travellers of the right: British enthusiasts for Nazi Germany, 1933–9*, pbk edn (1983) · Earl of Portsmouth [G. V. Wallop], *A knot of roots: an autobiography* (1965) · A. Bramwell, *Ecology in the 20th century* (1989) · M. Chase, 'This is no claptrap: this is our heritage', *The imagined past: history and nostalgia*, ed. C. Shaw and M. Chase (1989), 128–46 · A. W. B. Simpson, *'In the highest degree odious': detention without trial in wartime Britain* (1992) · private information (2004) · *The Field* (4 Jan 1941) · L. Menand, 'Eliot and the Jews', *New York Review of Books* (6 June 1996), 34–41 · C. Raine, 'T. S. Eliot is innocent', *The Observer* (8 Sept 1996) · T. S. Eliot, *Criterion* (Oct 1938), 59 · Burke, *Peerage* · P. Conford, *The origins of the organic movement* (2001)

Archives Hants. RO, corresp. and papers

Likenesses M. Cohen, oils, *c*.1935, priv. coll.; repro. in Wallop, *Knot of roots*

Wealth at death £2362—in England and Wales: probate, 28 May 1986, *CGPLA Eng. & Wales*

Wallop, Sir Henry (*c*.1531–1599), administrator and member of parliament, was born at Farleigh Wallop, Hampshire, the first son of Sir Oliver Wallop (*c*.1502–1566), landowner, and his first wife, Bridget Pigott of Beachampton, Buckinghamshire. His father, an early protestant, served Hampshire as a justice of the peace from 1554 to 1564 and as sheriff in 1558. In 1547 Protector Somerset knighted him in Scotland. Because his brother Sir John *Wallop (*d*. 1551), a prominent Henrician courtier and diplomat, failed to produce an heir Sir Oliver inherited his large estates which passed to Henry Wallop upon the death of his father on 28 February 1566.

Early career When Henry Wallop was a youth, Sir John Wallop and Oliver Wallop negotiated a marriage contract with Sir Thomas Wriothesley for a union between his daughter Anne and Henry. That agreement was cancelled on 29 August 1545 for unstated but possibly religious reasons. Henry later married Katherine (*d*. 1599), daughter of Richard Gifford of King's Somborne, Hampshire, a prominent early protestant in the county. Otherwise his early years were uneventful. It was not until Elizabeth I's reign began that he became active in local government. Appointed a JP in 1558, he continued to hold that office until at least 1594. Bishop Robert Horne of Winchester in 1564 listed both Henry and his father as favourers of the protestant religion.

When Sir Oliver Wallop died Henry became one of the largest landowners in Hampshire. Two months later Sir John Mason, Hampshire's senior knight of the shire, died on 21 April 1566, setting the stage for Wallop's first foray into politics. By September the government had decided to recall parliament, which necessitated a by-election for Mason's seat. The next few weeks were filled with convoluted manoeuvring by the rival factions associated with Bishop Horne and the lord treasurer, William Paulet. By election day on 4 November, Horne and a tightly knit group of protestants had picked Wallop as their candidate, while the Paulet faction had decided on the lord treasurer's grandson Sir John Berkeley. In a closely contested election Wallop lost, causing his friends to accuse the sheriff, Sir Richard Pexsall, of misusing his position. A series of fruitless suits and counter-suits followed in Star Chamber.

The defeat did not affect Wallop's developing career. In 1569 Queen Elizabeth knighted him at Basing, Hampshire. He had also established a residence in Southampton and became a freeman of the town in 1572. That same year the town elected him as one of their burgesses. While in parliament Wallop served on committees for legal matters, weapons, port bills, cloth bills, wine, church discipline, and wharves, all things of interest to a protestant member of the gentry and a resident of Southampton. His hard work gained him a reputation for usefulness. Other local government offices came his way: he was a commissioner for musters in Hampshire in 1573, an ecclesiastical commissioner in 1575, and a commissioner for piracy in 1577. He also worked as a commissioner concerning grain exports out of Surrey and in that capacity revealed himself as a supporter of free trade, an unsurprising stand for a person who maintained his wealth by selling grain on the open market. In religious matters he became recognized as a staunch protestant. He also appears to have gained the favourable notice of Sir Francis Walsingham, the principal secretary of state. Unfortunately for Wallop, his hard work and efficiency were rewarded by an assignment to that great quagmire, Tudor Ireland.

Arrival in Ireland and the second Desmond rebellion Walsingham approached Sir Henry in July 1579 about serving as under-treasurer of Ireland, a post that had just come open as a result of the death of Sir Edward Fitton. Wallop demurred, citing his lack of experience and money. He also requested time to settle his personal business before he could go to Ireland. While no time was especially auspicious for becoming an official in Tudor Ireland, the summer of 1579 was particularly bad as the second Desmond rebellion (1579–83) was just breaking out in Munster. Walsingham ignored Wallop's excuses and ordered him to London in early August where he received his instructions which included command of a company of troops. Adverse winds delayed his sailing from Bristol but on 10 September he was finally able to depart, arriving at Waterford two days later.

Wallop's arrival in Ireland was not a happy one as his reports to Walsingham and Lord Burghley show. The

£10,000 he carried into Ireland was consumed with alarming rapidity. Military operations against the Irish were also ineffective as the insurgents had lost their fear of English troops, having acquired up-to-date weapons and tactics. The Irish also hated the English while favouring the Spanish. By 29 December 1579 Wallop could remark to Burghley that 'It is easier to talk at home of Irish wars than to be in them' (*CSP Ire., 1574–85*, 201). He also began to develop a great dislike for the victuallers supplying the English army, all of whom he considered to be bad. Meanwhile Lord Justice William Drury had sickened and, after a long illness, died on 3 October 1579. Wallop feared for his own life when he too became ill. In an effort to take care of his family he requested that in the event of his death Sir Francis Walsingham be granted the wardship of his son Henry. His hope was that Walsingham would marry one of his daughters to Wallop's son. Wallop also started to complain about having to spend significant amounts of his own money to fulfil his Irish duties. At the same time he recognized the possibilities for economic gain in Ireland. He began to plan an increase of grain farming in Ireland in November 1579 and sought licences to export that grain. By February 1580 he had planted 1000 acres of grain.

The strain of serving in Ireland was beginning to tell on Wallop by early 1580. From his point of view the government provided too little money which arrived consistently too late for the Irish officials effectively to fight the insurgents. His letters and reports to Walsingham and Burghley were filled with complaints and demands. Soon Burghley took exception to Wallop's tone and chided him for it, going on to offer suggestions on how he might write more diplomatically. After that exchange relations between the two men remained soured for years. Burghley viewed Wallop as a sensationalizing complainer while Wallop consistently worried, and rightly so, that Burghley disliked him. Walsingham ended up acting as a protector for Wallop and provided a sympathetic listener for his complaints.

The Desmond rebellion was a grim time in Ireland for Wallop. Although he could report on 1 March 1581 that his troops had killed more rebels than all the other bands in Ireland, he remained deeply pessimistic. Only two weeks later he expressed his doubts to Walsingham about the government ever being able to develop policies that would bring peace to Ireland, and he also expressed his wish to return to England. Increasingly his letters included requests to be relieved of his office along with complaints about harsh treatment by Burghley and even the queen. By 25 June 1585 he was considering turning over his office to the son of the sometime lord deputy Sir William Fitzwilliam. Instead Queen Elizabeth appointed Wallop and Archbishop Loftus joint lords justices of Ireland on 25 August 1582. They held that office until 21 June 1584, an added responsibility about which Wallop complained bitterly to Walsingham. Meanwhile Wallop struggled to make his accounts satisfactory for the royal auditors. The capture and execution of Desmond on 9 November 1583 ended the rebellion and eased the pressures on Wallop and the Irish government.

Wallop and Ireland: attitudes and policies Wallop developed definite ideas on the proper way to pacify and govern Ireland. By January 1580 he was warning that the unsettled state of Ireland was consuming the queen's treasure and the lives of her soldiers with no end in sight. He also quickly became a firm opponent of co-opting Irish lords into the government as he did not feel that they could be trusted. The same observation applied to the practice of training and equipping native troops for use against rebels. By April 1581 he had come to think that such training should be forbidden because in every rebellion it was the Irish rebels possessed of English military training who always proved to be the most dangerous enemies. No admirer of Gaelic Irish people or culture, Wallop advocated the harsh expedient of putting rebels to the sword and planting better people in their stead. Such opinions reflected his typically protestant English world view and prejudices. Nothing that he experienced in Ireland during his almost twenty years of service caused him to alter his early opinions. He advocated a policy of assimilating—or as he would have put it civilizing—the Gaelic Irish and even the Old English settlers. For him, Ireland was a land of great economic promise. A strong economy would help to civilize the Irish, or rather it would turn them into Elizabethan English. Early on Wallop personally worked to increase Irish grain production. By 1585 he was suggesting the growing of woad as a way to develop an export commodity. If such development plans worked, everyone benefited, including Wallop.

The English government in Dublin was riven by animosities and factionalism. Resources were few while problems were myriad and the successful implementation of policies frequently proved elusive. Under such circumstances, recriminations and backbiting among government officials were inevitable. Wallop and Lord Deputy Sir John Perrot hated each other, but most people in the Irish government also hated Perrot. Wallop also disliked and distrusted Thomas Butler, tenth earl of Ormond, but that reflected his anti-Irish stance and he was not alone in his opinion. The royal auditor Thomas Jenyson was a particular *bête noire* of his, whom Wallop attempted to discredit by calling him a papist. In contrast Jenyson complained that Wallop kept sloppy accounts. There were occasional tiffs with other government officials such as Sir Edward Waterhouse, but overall Wallop worked well with his English colleagues and maintained relations of mutual respect.

Later years in Ireland and England Wallop happily participated in the plantation of Munster that followed the suppression of the Desmond rebellion, and established his own settlement at Enniscorthy, co. Wexford. Peace brought an end to his requests to be relieved of his office. But troubles with Lord Deputy Perrot, the auditing of Wallop's accounts, and petty outbreaks of violence among the Irish continued to keep Wallop busy. He also entered into long-drawn-out struggles to obtain possession of Athlone Castle and the lands of Adare Abbey in Ireland. Beginning in 1586 he sought permission to return to England so that he could handle his personal business there. Initially refused, he obtained such permission in 1587 but the treason of Sir William Stanley that year and the Armada threat of the following year kept him in Ireland. He personally interrogated a number of Armada survivors and showed himself to be both astute and compassionate. Finally, in April 1589, he sailed for England, where he stayed until July 1595 while a deputy performed his duties in Ireland. As early as August 1592 Wallop's long absence aroused the complaint of the royal auditor Christopher Peyton, who had to travel to Wallop's Hampshire home to clear his accounts. But it was not until 19 July 1595 that Wallop returned to Ireland to serve as treasurer-at-war just as the Nine Years' War (1594–1603) was starting to take an ominous turn. He was soon predicting that it would be a long and expensive war. Always an advocate of doing things properly, Wallop called upon the government to provide adequate resources to support the troops in Ireland. All that suggestion earned him was a scolding from Burghley on behalf of the parsimonious queen.

Wallop's final years in Ireland were unhappy as the English position deteriorated. During January 1596 he and Sir Robert Gardiner conducted negotiations with the earl of Tyrone. The earl drove a tough bargain but the agreement resulted in an extension of the peace for a much needed three months. Unfortunately Queen Elizabeth took exception to the obsequious and overly friendly tone that Wallop and Gardiner took with Tyrone. Her royal censure hurt Wallop deeply. In July 1597 Wallop proposed equipping the English army in Ireland with Irish-style clothing, a practical suggestion that was greeted with derision and cynicism. Lord Burghley accused Wallop of seeking his own personal enrichment. This setback came in the midst of Wallop's ongoing struggle to refute charges of peculation that had first surfaced in October 1596 and were still plaguing him a year later. Offended yet again, he attempted to resign but the government in London would not hear of it. They needed his experience and ability. By 22 February 1598 the ageing and ill Wallop was so desperate that he was threatening to leave his post and return to England without licence. It did no good. Meanwhile his son Oliver was brutally killed in a skirmish with some Irish rebels which added to Wallop's misery. Finally in March 1599 the queen agreed to replace Wallop as treasurer with Sir George Carey but ordered Wallop to stay on in Ireland and advise Carey for an unspecified period of time. Sadly Wallop died in Dublin on 14 April 1599, the day Carey reached Ireland. He was buried in St Patrick's, Dublin. His wife, Katherine, died soon after, on 16 July, and was buried alongside him with their son Oliver. He was succeeded by his only surviving son, Henry (1568–1642), who married Elizabeth Corbet of Shropshire and was elected to parliament many times.

The elder Sir Henry Wallop was a typical middle-ranking Tudor official, efficient and conscientious but also continually looking to his own personal advantage. His attitudes toward the Irish were also characteristic of protestant Elizabethan England—conquest followed by assimilation or extermination of the native population.

RONALD H. FRITZE

Sources DNB · HoP, *Commons, 1558–1603* · R. H. Fritze, 'Faith and faction: religious changes, national politics, and the development of local factionalism in Hampshire, 1485–1570', PhD diss., U. Cam., 1981 · C. Falls, *Elizabeth's Irish wars* (1950) · *CSP Ire.* · S. G. Ellis, *Ireland in the age of the Tudors* (1998) · N. Canny, *Kingdom and colony: Ireland in the Atlantic world, 1560–1800* (1988) · R. Bagwell, *Ireland under the Tudors*, 3 vols. (1885–90) · J. McGurk, *The Elizabethan conquest of Ireland: the 1590s crisis* (1997) · C. Brady, *The chief governors: the rise and fall of reform government in Tudor Ireland, 1536–1588* (1994) · R. Dudley Edwards, *Ireland in the age of the Tudors: the destruction of Hiberno-Norman civilization* (1977) · W. Palmer, *The problem of Ireland in Tudor foreign policy, 1485–1603* (1994) · will, PRO, PROB 11/95, fols. 1v–3r · W. A. Shaw, *The knights of England*, 2 (1906), 74

Archives Hants. RO, accounts and family papers

Likenesses portrait; in possession of the earl of Portsmouth in the 1890s

Wealth at death manors and bequests of land: will, PRO, PROB 11/95, fols. 1v–3r

Wallop, Sir John (*b.* before **1492**, *d.* **1551**), soldier and diplomat, was the eldest of three sons and a daughter of Stephen Wallop (*b.* in or after 1473, *d.* 1526/7), administrator, and his wife, Ashley (*d.* in or after 1515), only daughter of Hugh Ashley of Wimborne St Giles, Dorset, and his wife, Elizabeth. His younger brother Giles was born in 1491 or 1492. The Wallops were substantial members of the Hampshire gentry, having acquired the estate of Farleigh Wallop near Basingstoke through marriage early in the fifteenth century.

Early years and education, to 1524 Little is known about Wallop's education but it must have been reasonably thorough because throughout his life he displayed an aptitude for languages (including French and Spanish, and possibly German and Italian, though not Latin). The celebrated humanist Juan Luis Vives described how Wallop knew 'the customs and tongues of many men' (*LP Henry VIII*, 4/3, no. 6795). He had two brothers, Giles (*b.* 1491/2, *d.* in or after 1530), a priest and notable scholar, and Sir Oliver Wallop (*c.*1502–1566), and a sister, Margaret (*fl.* 1502–1542), who married Thomas Barnaby. His uncles Richard Wallop (1455/6–1503) and Sir Robert Wallop (1472/3–1535) were regularly appointed sheriff of Hampshire between 1501 and 1524.

Sir Robert Wallop may have provided Wallop with an income as feoffee of his manor in Basing, Hampshire, in the last years of Henry VII's reign but it was insufficient to provide for his needs and, with little expectation of inheriting, he pursued a military career and was constantly on the lookout for preferment. He began this career principally serving in Henry VIII's navy and reputedly participated in Sir Edward Poyning's successful expedition to the Low Countries in 1511, the year in which his father was included in the Hampshire commission of array with Sir Robert Wallop. His military proficiency must already have been evident and he was promoted captain by 1512 and knighted in 1512 or 1513. He was joint captain with Sir John Wyseman of the *Henry Grace à Dieu* from April 1513. Wallop went on the reckless but chivalrous expedition to Brest of Sir Edward Howard, the lord admiral. He led a series of harsh raids on French coastal communities while commanding a succession of mid-size vessels during Henry's campaign in France in 1513–14 and had joint command of a large squadron with Wyseman under Thomas Howard, earl of Surrey, in May 1514. He was also made one of the king's spears and continued to serve under Surrey during the summer. He revenged the French attack on the Sussex coast in autumn 1515 by retaliating effectively in a series of devastating raids on Normandy, despite inadequate manpower. At some point after September 1513 Wallop married Elizabeth (d. 1516), daughter of Sir Oliver St John of Lydiard Tregoze, Wiltshire, and his wife, Elizabeth, and widow of Gerald Fitzgerald, eighth earl of Kildare. She was a cousin of Henry VII and, although this made the match more prestigious, it is uncertain whether or not she regained control of her substantial dower lands or these passed to her son by her first marriage. She must have been considerably older than Wallop, suggesting he hoped her a rich widow. The marriage was short-lived and childless, with Lady Wallop dying on 28 June 1516. Wallop also participated in court life and his combination of martial skill, intelligence, learning, and prudence probably recommended him to the young Henry VIII, who began to employ him as a diplomat. His first mission, in August 1515, was to Margaret of Savoy, regent of the Low Countries.

Wallop led an itinerant life, spending the majority of his career serving abroad, and had an insatiable curiosity for foreign places. He served Manuel, king of Portugal, against the Muslims from 1516 to 1518, being sufficiently wealthy to fight at his own expense, an indication that he was not a mercenary but a volunteer. He probably lived off the booty he took, fighting near Tangier in Morocco, and was made a knight of the order of Christ. Wallop continued to favour the Portuguese on his return home. He was among the pensioners appointed in September 1518 to entertain the French embassy, meaning he was an active courtier rather than a supernumerary. He served in Ireland under Surrey, lord lieutenant between 1520 and 1522. Surrey had a high opinion of Wallop, appointing him vice-treasurer of Ireland, describing him to Cardinal Thomas Wolsey in August 1520 as a 'man right mete to do the kynges grace gode service in his warrys … diligent and with goode will woll take payne in … thynges as from tyme to tyme you commande hym to do', and using him to bring money and supplies and to convey important news (PRO, SP 60/1/14, fol. 43r). He was integral to Surrey's more aggressive policy as a negotiator in England on his behalf and asked the king in early 1521 for 300 cavalry and 500 infantry. He benefited from service and held the office of bailiff and receiver, then constable, of the lordship of Trim, co. Meath, from 1522 to 1524. He used this revenue to support Giles Wallop's education at the University of Louvain in the early 1520s and had an almost paternal relationship with his younger brother.

Service as a diplomat and at Calais, 1524–1535 Wallop was appointed marshal of the rearward during the war with France in 1522–3 because of his expertise at leading raids, recently honed in the desultory fighting in Ireland, and in conducting sieges. He participated in the raid on Brittany and was among the first to storm Morlaix in July 1522, after which he garrisoned St Omer with 1000 men. He was

then based in the Calais pale, from where he led devastating attacks on the French. He was vital to the taking of Montdidier and other French towns. Wallop was rewarded for his good service with appointment as high marshal of Calais on 31 March 1524. He defeated the French near St Omer in May but was subsequently forced to retire in the face of superior numbers. He lived at court or at one of his uncle's properties whenever he was in England and cultivated his Hampshire connections. For example, Sir John Paulet appointed him feoffee to uses on 2 January 1525.

Wallop was used increasingly as a diplomat from 1526, as were other men with military backgrounds, such as Poynings and Sir Richard Jerningham. The 'soldier diplomat' was useful because he was regarded as tough, methodical, and honourable (Potter, 104). Promotion to gentleman of the privy chamber in 1526 enhanced his status by giving Wallop additional prestige as an intimate of the king. He was sent with a large amount of money as special ambassador to Hungary in September 1526 in response to the Ottoman invasion. This mission was very important because of the prestige Henry could gain by saving Christendom from the Muslims and Wallop was chosen because of his military expertise. Wallop received an audience with Margaret of Savoy on 16 September. Then, after spending time in Cologne, Brussels, Mainz, and Augsburg, he received an audience with Ferdinand, king of the Romans, at Prague on 5 February 1527. Ferdinand discussed the situation in detail and, among other things, gave Wallop two large gilt cups, but subsequently proved unwilling to permit him to go to Hungary to speak with his rival Jan Zapolya, *voivode* of Transylvania. Wallop received an audience with Sigismund I, king of Poland, at Breslau in Silesia in early May at which they discussed the danger of Lutheranism. He was the first English ambassador to Poland. Wallop intended to return to Hungary in June and even considered going to Istanbul. He was at Vienna in July and probably returned to England the following month due to lack of funds.

Wallop continued to acquire offices and rewards. He was named, with Sir Richard Page, surveyor and receiver of the subsidies on kerseys in London and Southampton on 17 March 1528 with a joint salary of £100. He was special ambassador to France between February and May and received an audience with François I at Poissy on 28 February. The French were keen that Wallop should not discover their intentions regarding relations with Charles V and had a very high opinion of his abilities, despite regarding him as pro-imperialist. The French ambassador in England, Jean du Bellay, bishop of Bayonne, commented that Sir John Russell was likely to replace Wallop and would be 'better than any other whose name is not Wallop' (*LP Henry VIII*, 4/3, appendix, 190). Wallop returned to Calais in June. His father died at some point during 1526 or 1527 but he inherited little.

Wallop became keeper of the lordship and park of Ditton, Buckinghamshire, on 6 April 1529, making him responsible for running the estate and for raising tenants in time of war or insurrection. He married Elizabeth (d.

1552), daughter of Sir Clement Harleston of South Ockendon, Essex, at Windsor Castle on 8 June 1530. She must have been considerably younger than him and had been in service to Anne Boleyn, continuing as a member of her circle after the marriage. Wallop was promoted to lieutenant of Calais on 23 June at a salary of £56 10s. per annum. However, his pay was often in arrears and he got into debt. He had forty-nine soldiers under him but his charge, the castle overlooking the harbour, was woefully outdated and the weakest part in the Calais pale. Wallop was now the second most senior officer in the garrison after the deputy and was a member of the council, though he did not attend council meetings frequently. He was at Calais during the extensive repairs carried out in September and October 1531. Lady Wallop handled aspects of their finances, including receiving wages from the exchequer. Wallop was in an awkward position because he did not support Henry's attempts to divorce Katherine of Aragon. There were conflicting family loyalties over the divorce because Lady Wallop continued as a member of the Boleyn circle until at least 1532, but by December 1535 she was described as Katherine's 'creatura' (*LP Henry VIII*, vol. 9, no. 970). Despite this, Wallop was selected to be ambassador in France, although Surrey (now third duke of Norfolk) felt 'that such a charge was not altogether suitable for him, being more a man of war than of counsel' (*LP Henry VIII*, vol. 5, no. 1109). He was resident ambassador with a salary of £486 13s. 4d. from 11 September 1532 to mid-March 1537.

Wallop arrived at the French court by 1 January 1533 and immediately became involved in delicate but intense negotiations in an attempt to gain François's support for the divorce. He returned to Calais at some point before July and nearly drowned at Newneham Bridge, perhaps as a result of deficiencies in the maintenance of the network of sluices there. With Stephen Gardiner, bishop of Winchester, and Sir Francis Bryan he was present at the interview between François and Clement VII at Marseilles on 11 October. They were under strict instructions not to present themselves to the pope. Despite the tense circumstances, Bryan was convivial company. Wallop probably spent the first half of 1534 in England or at Calais but returned to the French court by October. He lived in a succession of inns and lodging houses. In 1534–5 he skilfully negotiated a defensive league with François against Charles, whose reaction to the Henrician Reformation was a source of great anxiety, and then changed tactics by re-establishing good relations with the emperor when the situation eased. Henry had become disillusioned with the French alliance. Wallop also tried to persuade Philip Melanchthon to go to England in July 1535, in the hope that the reformer would support the Henrician Reformation. Thomas Cromwell, the king's secretary, instructed him to justify the executions of John Fisher, bishop of Rochester, and Sir Thomas More, to François. Cromwell and he may have been at odds as a consequence of Wolsey's fall but they briefly settled their differences. Other delicate tasks Wallop carried out included renegotiating the French pension and informing François, not without delight, of

Anne's fall in May 1536. He spent time hawking during the summer. Wallop remained with the French court between October 1535 and March 1537. He was initially unimpressed by James V's reticent character when he met him in November 1536, telling the deputy of Calais, Arthur Plantagenet, sixth Viscount Lisle, that if it were not for the talkative nature of the Scottish king's prospective bride, Madeleine de Valois, 'the house should be very quiet' (*Lisle Letters*, 3.524). His reports are valuable as observations of general developments in France and he played one party off against the other with some dexterity and *élan*.

Hampshire gentleman and garrison commander, 1535–1547
Sir Robert Wallop died on 16 June 1535 and Sir John Wallop, his eldest nephew, inherited most of his property. Wallop lobbied hard for his recall from France because, as Henry put it, he had 'ever right honestly referred yourself as by your sundry lettres it apperethe to Returne hither into our Realme aswel to visyte and see us as to loke uppon suche youre inheritannce as sethens your departure hathe descended and fallen unto youe' (BL, Add. MS 25114, fol. 241r). Despite his frequent absences, Wallop tried to keep an eye on local developments. His client, John Coke, was registrar of Winchester and was involved in an ongoing and ultimately successful quarrel with the protestant John Palmes in the 1530s. Yet Thomas Cranmer, archbishop of Canterbury, could provide another protestant, Robert Vaws, with the living of Over Wallop, despite strong opposition from Wallop and the Hampshire clergy. Wallop was JP for Hampshire from 1538 to 1551. On 3 March 1539 he appointed his cousin John Cooke as one of his feoffees to uses. Cooke was receiver and surveyor of Wallop's lands by 1551. Before August 1545 Sir John and Oliver Wallop contracted with the lord chancellor, Thomas Wriothesley, Baron Wriothesley of Titchfield, for a marriage between Henry *Wallop (c.1531–1599) and Anne Wriothesley. Wallop was one of the six gentlemen of the privy chamber who supported the canopy at the christening of Edward, prince of Wales, on 15 October 1537 and his wife attended the funeral of Jane Seymour on 12 November. He was granted the extensive lands of the dissolved monastery of Barlinch, Somerset, on 29 May 1538, including the manors of Brompton Ralph, Bury, and Warleigh, all in Somerset, and Morebath in Devon. Consequently, he spent part of the autumn in Somerset and was considered as a potential candidate as sheriff of Devon for 1538–9. Wealth brought status. The schoolmaster Leonard Cox sought his literary patronage but Wallop was not supportive. Wallop did have one of his servants taught to play the viol, though. He returned to Calais in March 1539 because of renewed fears of war with France and from May was involved in the troubles there over religion through close association with William Sandys, first Baron Sandys and captain of Guînes, and with Lisle. They opposed the local protestants and used this against Cromwell. According to Sir George Carew, they 'shoyth them selwys unwyllyng that the word of god shold prosper & go forward amongst us' (PRO, SP 1/151, fol. 226r). This divided the council and the junior officers.

Wallop and his wife were close friends of Lord and Lady

Lisle, their relationship being reinforced by vicinage, both men being leading Hampshire landowners. He was on good terms with Sir Richard Grenville, high marshal, Sir Thomas Palmer, high porter, and the other senior officers at Calais. The letters between them provide a vivid picture of life in their circle at Calais and reveal Wallop's dry sense of humour. He wrote regularly to Lisle when away, even going into detail about the situation in France normally reserved for the king. On 18 December 1536 he wrote to congratulate Lisle on his impending fatherhood and expressed the hope that his own marriage would produce children, especially if his wife and he could 'return once quietly to the Castle'. He bought Lady Lisle some special water at Avignon for the later stages of her pregnancy that, among other things, he assured her husband 'when a woman's breasts be long, it raiseth them higher and rounder, which peradventure shall be good for some of your neighbours'. However, he hoped Lisle would not misconstrue his meaning by taking his comment to be derogatory towards his wife's appearance and pointed out that her figure was fine and she 'needeth not' such cosmetic aid (*Lisle Letters*, 3.571–2). Wallop had no children.

Wallop was resident ambassador in France again from 2 February 1540 to March 1541, with an annual salary of £730, and was instructed to sever ties between François and Charles and build close relations with Marguerite of Navarre. His secretary, Nicholas Alexander, was involved closely in these negotiations. Norfolk and Wallop received an audience with François in the king's bedchamber at Abbeville on 23 February 1540. The French king was on good terms with Wallop, who was uncertain about Franco-imperial relations. However, Wallop's work was done for him when Charles baulked at handing Milan over in April. He was appointed a commissioner of oyer and terminer, despite his absence, in June. Wallop was involved in the complex negotiations with the French over the Cowswade, within the Calais pale, between October 1540 and February 1541. Henry used tension over this to renegotiate his French pension.

Wallop was caught up in the religious faction of the early 1540s that was a consequence of Cromwell's fall. His Catholicism was well known and Henry became suspicious of him after hearing allegations of treason in June 1540. He was appointed captain of Guînes, the only modernized fortification in the Calais pale, in December but was recalled from France and examined in March 1541, as was Alexander. However, Henry handled the situation with care and despite seizing his papers and trying to elicit information through subterfuge, he permitted Wallop to speak openly in his defence to the privy council. Wallop was accused of conducting treasonable correspondence with Richard Pate and, realizing his safest course was to admit his guilt, he did so and submitted to the king's mercy. He was pardoned on 21 March and was restored as captain of Guînes in April, his appointment being confirmed on 7 July 1543, when he was also named commander of English forces in France. Wallop commanded a company of 100 cavalry and oversaw new engineering work at Calais in summer 1542. He frequently received instructions from the privy council on how to conduct his various duties, including provisioning the garrison and keeping 'a good eye unto the Pale, &c' and dealt carefully but effectively with numerous local matters that might impair the efficiency of his men, like the conduct of one soldier, Anthony Hutchinson, who spoke 'certeyne lewde and unsemely worddes' while drunk (*APC, 1542–7*, 54, 87). To try to prevent this behaviour from recurring he appointed Thomas Audley of St Ives, Huntingdon, provost marshal in August. Wallop used his diplomatic nature to good effect by coming to an accommodation in autumn 1542 with the local French commander, Oudart de Biez, marshal of France, that made their duties easier. This was part of a wider Anglo-French *rapprochement* in 1542–3. Biez and he became good friends. They hunted in Guînes Forest together, sent each other gifts of venison, and their families dined with one another when the opportunity arose. Biez used these meetings to try to learn more about the modernization taking place at Calais, but Wallop had 'to muche practised a brode for a Frencheman / to pike [pick] any thinge owte of me' (PRO, SP 1/171, fol. 8v). Wallop advanced the military careers of promising young gentlemen, including that of James Wilford of Hartridge, Kent, whose aptitude for siege engineering and with ordnance he found striking when they met in June 1542.

Henry allied with Charles in February 1543. Wallop provided a detailed plan on how to conduct the campaign and was made captain-general of an army of between 5000 and 6000 men and sent to Calais to assist in the defence of the Low Countries in June. He invaded the Boulonnais in July, destroying fortifications and harbours and devastating the countryside. He then participated in the siege of Landrecies from September to November, during which he became ill. The emperor praised him for his professionalism and he retired with his men as the campaigning season drew to a close in November. Henry was so satisfied with Wallop's performance of his duties that he agreed to his nomination to the Order of the Garter on 24 December 1543. Wallop was installed on 18 May 1544, with the king providing him with the ceremonial robes from his own wardrobe. He was busy during the invasion of France in 1544 and maintained a large force at Guînes. In January 1545 he argued with the lieutenant of Hammes Castle, William Grey, thirteenth Baron Grey of Wilton, and despite attempts at mediation, their disagreement rumbled on into the autumn. Grey of Wilton was a difficult man to get on with. The privy council thanked Wallop for his bravery in June. In June 1546 he was placed on the second commission to determine the boundaries of the Boulonnais and was appointed to the third commission in March 1547.

Last years, 1547–1551 Wallop promptly ingratiated himself with the new regime, writing to Edward Seymour, duke of Somerset and lord protector to Edward VI, from Calais on 23 February 1547 and asking to 'remayne in suche aucthorytie and permynence at guisnes as I and other captenes have done' (PRO, SP 68/13, fol. 94r). He continued as captain of Guînes, being placed in command of the defence of English territory in France, and was reappointed JP for Hampshire in May, although he was removed from the privy chamber. Wriothesley (now first earl of Southampton) retained him as keeper of his newly acquired manor and park of Dogmersfield, Hampshire, in July. This friendship with the disgraced former lord chancellor did Wallop no harm and reflected their shared Catholicism. Wallop was involved in the defence of the outlying forts of Boulogne and Calais against the French in 1548–9 and Russell (now Baron Russell), wrote to the lord admiral, Thomas Seymour, Baron Seymour of Sudeley, on 13 August 1548, describing how during one of the frequent skirmishes and, despite his age, Wallop 'findinge the lyke entertaynement abowte his parties [parts], made owte and slewe of those whiche came to seke playe, xij or xiiij: and put the rest to flight' (PRO, SP 10/4/44, M fol. 87v). Wallop was at court in early 1550 and retained the confidence of John Dudley, earl of Warwick, in the aftermath of the October coup against Somerset. Warwick wrote to the privy council on 1 February 1550 and, among others, asked them to commend him to 'myne olde acquayntance Sir John Wallop', to whom he intended to write on his return to court (BL, Cotton MS Caligula E. iv, fol. 206r). Wallop was considered a reliable military client and, oddly, identified as a member of Warwick's protestant party. This was a surprising but adroit shift in loyalties for the old soldier and was probably based on Warwick's genuine admiration for Wallop, whom he knew through his late stepfather, Lisle. Wallop was a commissioner for settling the boundary of English territory in France. He was rewarded too, receiving an annuity of £20 for life in June 1551.

Wallop made his last will on 22 May 1551. Even at the end he struck a neat balance between service and faith. The opening formula declared Edward to be 'supreme hed of the churche of England and Irelande', yet Wallop, using the traditional Catholic phrasing, commended his soul to God, while 'humbly desyring our Lady saynt Marie the virgyn mother of our lorde Jesus Christ / and all the holy company in heaven to be mediators and Intercessors for me'. Testament to the strength of his marriage was his decision to appoint Lady Wallop his sole executor; she was to receive the revenue from part of his estates and his household goods during her life, and he remembered fondly, when leaving a bequest to Sir Edward Wotton, that it was 'my gilt cupp with a cover whiche I and my wief dyd use to drynke caudels in'. Among others, he left bequests to Somerset, Warwick, his steward John Smale, and another cousin, Cooke, sergeant of the king's hart hounds. He left half a year's wages to his servants and provided an annuity for Alexander, now captain of Newneham Bridge, of £6 13s. 4d. He also petitioned the privy council 'to Remytt my said debt or parte therof' (which amounted to £138 9s. 1d. in 1546), since it had been accrued through royal service, and to pay his wages until 17 October (PRO, PROB 11/34, sig. 24). Sir Oliver Wallop was his heir male and stood to inherit one of the largest estates in Hampshire. Sir John Wallop died at Guînes on 13 July, of the sweating sickness, a particularly virulent disease to which, peculiarly, the fittest were most susceptible, and was buried there after a substantial funeral ceremony,

probably in the churchyard (having provided £5 towards the church's restoration). His body was subsequently removed and reburied in the parish church at Farleigh Wallop. Henry Machyn's assessment epitomized the opinion of many of his contemporaries: 'gentyll sir John … was a nobull captayne as ever was' (*The Diary of Henry Machyn, Citizen and Merchant-Taylor of London, from 1550–1563*, ed. J. G. Nichols, *Camden Miscellany*, 1st ser., 42, CS, 1848, 8). Wallop was the epitome of the Tudor gentleman, a brilliant naval officer and soldier (who kept abreast of changing tactics and military technology), long remembered for his skill as a commander, his professionalism, and his ferocity as a foe, a fine diplomat, and an able royal servant. His wife survived him and retired to South Ockendon but was in failing health by March 1552 and died shortly after. ALAN BRYSON

Sources APC, 1542–52 · E. Bapst, *Deux gentils hommes-poètes de la cour de Henri VIII* (Paris, 1891) · G. M. Bell, *A handlist of British diplomatic representatives, 1509–1688*, Royal Historical Society Guides and Handbooks, 16 (1990) · R. E. Brock, 'The courtier in early Tudor society: illustrated from select examples', PhD diss., U. Lond., 1964 · CPR, 1547–9; 1550–53 · A. Collins, *The peerage of England: containing a genealogical and historical account of all the peers of England* · R. H. Fritze, 'Faith and faction: religious changes, national politics, and the development of local factionalism in Hampshire, 1485–1570', PhD diss., U. Cam., 1981 · D. I. Grummitt, 'Calais, 1485–1547: a study in early Tudor politics and government', PhD diss., U. Lond., 1997 · J. A. Guy, 'Thomas Wolsey, Thomas Cromwell and the reform of Henrician government', *The reign of Henry VIII: politics, policy and piety*, ed. D. MacCulloch (1995), 35–57 · *Hall's chronicle*, ed. H. Ellis (1809) · H. M. Colvin and others, eds., *The history of the king's works*, 3–4 (1975–82) · HoP, *Commons, 1558–1603*, 3.567–8 · E. Ives, *Anne Boleyn* (1992) · R. J. Knecht, *The rise and fall of Renaissance France, 1483–1610* (1996) · LP Henry VIII · M. St C. Byrne, ed., *The Lisle letters*, 6 vols. (1981) · DNB · D. L. Potter, 'Foreign policy', *The reign of Henry VIII: politics, policy and piety*, ed. D. MacCulloch (1995), 101–33 · will, PRO, PROB 11/34, sig. 24 · PRO, PROB 11/18, sig. 7 · PRO, state papers foreign, Edward VI, SP 68/1, fols. 120r–123v · PRO, state papers foreign, Edward VI, SP 68/13, fols. 9r–10v, 34r–35v, 46r–47v, 93r–94v, 119r–120v, 167r–168v, 182r–183v, 191r–192v · PRO, state papers foreign, Edward VI, SP 68/14, fols. 39r–40v, 59r–60v, 71r–74v · PRO, state papers Ireland, Henry VIII, SP 60/1/14, fols. 43r–43v; SP 60/1/15, fols. 44r–45v; SP 60/1/37, fols. 86r–88v · *State papers published under … Henry VIII*, 11 vols. (1830–52) · V. J. Watney, *The Wallop family and their ancestry*, 4 vols. (1928)

Archives Hants. RO, MSS | BL, Cotton MSS Vespasian F. iv; Vitellius B. xxi · PRO, SP 1; SP 3; SP 68

Wallop, John, first earl of Portsmouth (1690–1762), politician, was born on 15 April 1690, the third son of John Wallop (d. 1694), of Farleigh Wallop, Hampshire, and his wife, Alicia (d. 1744), third daughter of William Borlace or Borlase, of Great Marlow, Buckinghamshire. The Wallop family had been landholders in Hampshire since at least the early fourteenth century, and in the eighteenth century claimed descent from the pre-conquest aristocracy. His great-grandfather was the parliamentarian and councillor of state under the Commonwealth, Robert Wallop. Following the death of his father in 1694 and of his elder brother Bluet Wallop from peripneumonia in 1707, he succeeded to the Wallop family estates in Hampshire. In 1708 he left Eton College to complete his education with an extended tour of Europe. On his way to Geneva he served as a volunteer at the battle of Oudenarde. Following a year at school in Geneva he travelled in Italy and Germany, where in Hanover he became acquainted with the elector, later to become George I.

Wallop's background and sympathies were firmly whig, and he inherited influence over the seats at Andover and Whitchurch. He failed to be elected for Hampshire in 1713, but in 1715 was returned for both Hampshire and Andover, choosing to sit for the county. On 20 May 1716 he married Lady Bridget Bennet (*bap.* 1696, *d.* 1738), eldest daughter of Charles Bennet, first earl of Tankerville. They had six sons and four daughters. He chose not to go into opposition with Robert Walpole and Charles, second Viscount Townshend, in 1717, and was rewarded with an appointment as a lord of the Treasury on 3 April. He was usually loyal to the Sunderland ministry, but voted against the repeal of the Occasional Conformity and Schism Acts in 1719. The return of Walpole and Townshend to the ministry in 1720 forced Wallop from office, but he was compensated on 11 June with elevation to the Lords as Baron Wallop and Viscount Lymington. He took little part in state affairs but quietly worked to establish his loyalty to Walpole. In 1731 he wrote to Charlotte Clayton suggesting that he would be a better manager of government patronage than Charles Powlett, third duke of Bolton. His appointment as chief justice in eyre north of Trent on 5 December 1732 acknowledged his loyalty. When Bolton was expelled from his offices after voting against the government on the excise in 1733, Lymington succeeded him as lord lieutenant of Hampshire (7 August 1733), vice-admiral of Hampshire, and lord warden of the New Forest (2 November 1733), and later became governor of the Isle of Wight (18 June 1734) although he then surrendered his chief justiceship. On 7 August 1739 he became a governor of the Foundling Hospital. During this period Lymington rebuilt Farleigh House, his ancestral home which had been burnt down in 1667. The south front, built in 1731, remains much as Lymington left it, but the north front was altered in 1935. His wife died of apoplexy on 12 October 1738 at Lyndhurst, Hampshire, and was buried at Farleigh Wallop. She was survived by four of her sons and a daughter. On 9 June 1741 Lymington married Elizabeth *Griffin (*bap.* 1691, *d.* 1762), daughter of James Griffin, second Baron Griffin, and widow of Henry Grey. They had no children.

In July 1742, following Walpole's resignation, all Lymington's appointments were terminated. On 11 April 1743 he was compensated with the earldom of Portsmouth. On 19 February 1746 he was reappointed governor of the Isle of Wight, a position he held until his death. He continued to correspond with the duke of Newcastle on political and patronage matters, but seems to have kept his independence; when Newcastle wrote to Portsmouth in 1760, asking him to support the ministerial candidate at Andover, Sir Francis Blake Delaval, alongside his wife's nephew Sir John Griffin Griffin, he replied that he would only intervene in Griffin's favour and not on behalf of another candidate.

Portsmouth died three months after his second wife on 22 November 1762 and was buried in St Andrew's Church,

Farleigh Wallop, Hampshire. A marble monument on the south wall bears a lengthy inscription of his life. His eldest son, John, Viscount Lymington (1718–1749), MP for Andover from 1741 until his death, had married Catherine, daughter of John Conduitt, Sir Isaac Newton's successor as master of the Royal Mint, and a close friend of Portsmouth. Catherine was Newton's niece and coheir, and his papers and scientific papers were inherited by her eldest son, John Wallop (1742–1797), who following the death of his grandfather became second earl of Portsmouth.

JOHN MARTIN

Sources GEC, *Peerage* • A. Valentine, *The British establishment, 1760–1784* (1970) • J. H. Round, *Peerage and pedigree: studies in peerage law and family history*, 2 vols. (1910) • N. W. Surrey and J. H. Thomas, *Portsmouth record series book of original entries, 1731–1751* (1976) • *Collectanea topographica ed genealogica*, 8 (1843), 380–87 • E. W. Brayleg and J. Britton, *The beauties of England*, 18 vols. in 21 (1801–15), 6.234 • P. Watson, 'Wallop, John', HoP, *Commons, 1715–54* • V. J. Watney, *The Wallop family and their ancestry*, 4 vols. (1925), 1.lv–lix • L. B. Namier, 'Andover', HoP, *Commons, 1754–90*, 1.293–4 • Burke, *Peerage* (1999) • 'Hampshire treasures', www.hants.gov.uk/hampshiretreasures/vol02, 120–21

Archives Hants. RO, papers | BL, letters to Lord Hardwicke, Add. MSS 35588–35604, 36269, *passim* • BL, corresp. with duke of Newcastle, Add. MSS 32689–32937, *passim*

Likenesses oils, 1700–25, Audley End House, Essex • marble monument, St Andrew's Church, Farleigh Wallop, Hampshire

Wallop, Richard (*bap.* 1616, *d.* 1697), lawyer, was baptized at Bugbrooke, Northamptonshire, on 10 June 1616, the son of Richard Wallop and his wife, Mary Spencer, sister and coheir of William Spencer of Everton, Northamptonshire. The Wallop family was originally from Hampshire. At eighteen Wallop matriculated at Pembroke College, Oxford, on 10 October 1634. He graduated BA on 2 June 1635, and was called to the bar by the Middle Temple in February 1646.

Of his career during the interregnum nothing can be said, although Wallop may have acquired in those years the anti-royalist sensibilities that some have discerned in his later life. His marriage to Mary produced at least one daughter; his wife outlived him. In 1666 he became a bencher, and in 1673 was appointed treasurer of the Middle Temple.

Wallop rose to prominence during the final years of Charles II's reign and throughout the reign of James II. Characterized by one contemporary as an 'eminent lawyer', he became one of the most visible of the whig lawyers, representing whig defendants in many of the great state trials of the era (*CSP dom.*, James II, 2.150). In 1682 he assisted in the defence of the City of London against Charles II's writ of *quo warranto*. He defended several whigs against charges of rioting during parliamentary elections, and represented Sir John Hampden in his trial for his part in the Rye House plot. When two men were arrested for charging the king with the murder of the earl of Essex, Wallop defended them and was himself charged with a 'zeal for faction and sedition' (Irving, 195). He also assisted the cause of the plantiff in *Godden v. Hales*, and even participated in the defence of Titus Oates on perjury charges, although on this occasion he appears to have acted as assigned counsel. Wallop's regular participation in the defence of the whigs earned him the truly remarkable hostility of Chief Justice George Jeffreys. When Wallop appeared before Jeffreys to defend Richard Baxter against sedition charges, Jeffreys said from the bench:

> Mr. Wallop, I observe you are in all these dirty causes; and were it not for you gentlemen of the long robe, who should have more wit and honesty to support and hold these factious knaves by the chin, we should not be at the pass we are at. (Foss, *Judges*, 7.697)

Jeffreys bitterly berated Wallop for his defence of Lord Grey on the charge of having 'debauched' Lady Henrietta Berkeley. During the trial of Thomas Rosewell for high treason, Jeffreys ejected Wallop from the court, refusing him even the right to observe the trial from the audience. It is doubtful whether these confrontations rendered Wallop 'eternally famous', as one nineteenth-century authority has asserted, but he is indeed mostly remembered for providing Jeffreys with opportunities for flaunting his vicious temper.

It should be noted that Wallop was capable of representing clients whose political views he probably found less than congenial. Most remarkably he represented the duke of York when indicted for recusancy in 1681. He served as counsel for the maligned 'popish Lords' Lord Petre and Viscount Stafford in 1679–80. On 4 February 1684 he appeared before king's bench as one of the earl of Danby's councillors. Indeed, in 1685 Lord Brandon felt it plausible to recommend Wallop as a king's councillor. Perhaps not surprisingly, the earl of Sunderland declined the advice on behalf of the king. Jeffreys's biographer Irving described Wallop as 'tactless' and unlearned, but even he (a virtual apologist for Jeffreys and a biased source) admits that nothing substantiates Jeffreys's charge that Wallop had a 'hectoring and swaggering manner' (Irving, 303). Mostly Wallop seems to have had a remarkable nose for publicity. He involved himself in a great many high-profile political trials. On 16 March 1696 he was made a baron of the exchequer, but did not live to enjoy the honour for long. He died on 22 August 1697 and was buried four days later in the church at the Middle Temple.

JEFFREY R. COLLINS

Sources Foss, *Judges* · *State trials* · H. B. Irving, *The life of Judge Jeffreys* (1898) · *DNB* · *CSP dom.*, 1685–9 · Foster, *Alum. Oxon.* · PRO, PROB 11/439, sig. 171

Wallop, Robert (1601–1667), politician, was born on 20 July 1601, the only son of Sir Henry Wallop (1568–1642) of Farleigh Wallop in Hampshire, and Elizabeth (*d.* 1624), daughter and heir of Robert Corbet of Morton Corbet in Shropshire. Sir Henry, one of the wealthiest members of the Hampshire gentry, and many times an MP, was heir to the substantial Irish estates acquired by his father, Sir Henry *Wallop, vice-treasurer and lord justice in Ireland. The family's status ensured that Robert, who matriculated from Hart Hall, Oxford, on 5 May 1615, was certain to assume an important role in his native county, and he did so even during his father's lifetime. He was returned to parliament for Andover in 1621, 1624, and 1628, and as a knight of the shire for Hampshire in 1625 and 1626, and, having been given permission to chose his bride, was able

to secure a prestigious match in the shape of Anne (*d.* 1662), daughter of Henry Wriothesley, third earl of Southampton.

By 1640 Wallop was probably identified with the opposition to Charles I, having offered resistance to certain government policies. He delayed paying the forced loan, refused to compound for his knighthood, and declined to contribute to the first bishops' war (1639). Returned to both the Short and Long parliaments for Andover, he made no immediate impression but became an important figure on committees relating to Ireland once the rebellion there threatened his estates in Wexford. Thereafter, Irish affairs became one of his abiding concerns, although his support for parliament rested on more than self-interest. After 1642 he also became a linchpin of the parliamentarian war effort and administration in Hampshire, and by February 1644 was sufficiently influential to secure nomination to the committee of both kingdoms, and became deeply involved in negotiations with the Scots, and in preparing for negotiations with the king at Uxbridge in early 1645. He supported those who sought a harsh settlement, and who masterminded the self-denying ordinance, and he was a stalwart of those committees on Irish affairs instigated by the Independents rather than the presbyterians. It was as an Independent that he was involved in the increasingly tense negotiations with the Scots in late 1646, culminating in the treaty whereby the king was handed over to parliament (January 1647).

Wallop became less prominent at Westminster after the presbyterian 'counter-revolution' in the summer of 1647, perhaps because of the growing need to oversee the security of Hampshire, although he was a member of the Derby House committee during 1648. He was willing to sit in the Rump after Pride's Purge, and was made a commissioner for the high court of justice to try the king. Although he attended two meetings of the commissioners and two days of the trial, he was absent at the sentencing on 27 January, and did not sign the death warrant. He remained willing to serve the republic, however, and was probably perceived to be a zealous advocate of the new regime. He was named to the first council of state (14 January 1649), and took the engagement (19 February). He claimed to have lost £50,000 through the war and his services to the parliamentarian cause were rewarded with the grant of £10,000 out of the estate of the marquess of Winchester. Although increasingly inactive, Wallop secured nomination to the second council of state (12 February 1650), and to its most important subcommittees. He was not elected again in February 1651, but was emphatically restored to the council in the poll held on 25 November, on the back of a tide of republican fervour after the army's success at Worcester. His attendance in council was becoming erratic, however, and his interests were apparently limited to the affairs of Ireland and Scotland. He was re-elected to the council of state in November 1652 but by then he was probably growing disillusioned with the drift of political events, and the growing influence of the army.

Wallop was prepared to accommodate the protectorate, although he probably opposed its establishment. He was able to secure election for Hampshire to both the 1654 and 1656 parliaments despite rumours of his involvement in a plot against Cromwell. His active participation in national affairs only resumed, however, as a 'commonwealthsman' during the elections for the protectoral parliament of Richard Cromwell, to which he was himself returned for Hampshire, and in which he sought to assert the power of the Commons over the protector and the 'other house'. During the restored Rump in the summer of 1659 he was chosen for the council of state, although he withdrew from Westminster in the face of growing pressure from the army, until he was able to help secure the Rump's second restoration in December 1659. Thereafter he returned to the Commons and council of state, until retiring once again with the readmission of the secluded members in February 1660.

Although he assisted the escape of some regicides, Wallop saw no reason to flee as the Restoration approached, and even secured election to the Convention Parliament, for Whitchurch, although he was quickly made incapable of sitting. He did not face trial in 1660, since he was neither a signatory of the king's death warrant, nor accounted a regicide for having been present when the sentence was read. Nevertheless, at some point before July 1661 he was imprisoned for his part in the proceedings, having failed to secure a pardon. He protested that he 'ever did and doth from his soul abhor and detest that most horrid and execrable murder' (*Seventh Report*, HMC, 151), and that he had attended the trial at the behest of prominent royalists, in order to help the king. His ill fortune may have been linked to his great wealth, and a concerted attempt was clearly made to take control of his estate. His property was eventually protected by his brother-in-law, the earl of Southampton, on behalf of the family, while he himself languished in prison, to be subjected to ritual punishment each January. Despite his illness and imprisonment, he was able to marry twice following the death of his first wife in 1662. On 16 February 1663 he married Mary, daughter of the parliamentarian general John Lambert, and on 16 May 1666 he married one Elizabeth Thompson, who was granted permission to remain with him in the Tower until his death on 16 November 1667; his body was released for burial at Farleigh Wallop, on 7 January 1668. Wallop's widow, who married one Robert Needham in May 1669, was eventually awarded portions of the Irish estate, while his son Henry Wallop sat for Whitchurch in the Cavalier Parliament. Wallop's great-grandson, John Wallop, was created earl of Portsmouth in 1743.

J. T. PEACEY

Sources JHC, 2–8 (1640–67) · HoP, *Commons, 1690–1715* [draft] · C. H. Firth and R. S. Rait, eds., *Acts and ordinances of the interregnum, 1642–1660*, 3 vols. (1911) · CSP dom., 1644–70 · CSP Ire., 1633–60 · Thurloe, *State papers* · *The memoirs of Edmund Ludlow*, ed. C. H. Firth, 2 vols. (1894) · *Seventh report*, HMC, 6 (1879) · V. J. Watney, *The Wallop family*, 4 vols. (1928) · BL, Add. MS 21922 · BL, Add. MS 26781 · *The manuscripts of his grace the duke of Portland*, 10 vols., HMC, 29 (1891–1931), vol. 1 · Keeler, *Long Parliament*

Walls, Tom Kirby (1883–1949), actor and theatre manager, was born on 18 February 1883 in 7 Moore Street, Kingsley Park, Kingsthorpe, a suburb of Northampton, the son of John William Walls, a plumber and builder, and his wife, Ellen (*née* Brewer). He was educated at Northampton county school. Following several false starts in work, Walls spent a year in Canada before returning to join the Metropolitan Police in London. Feeling a stronger pull from the stage, he joined a seafront pierrot troupe in Brighton. His first stage appearance was in pantomime (*Aladdin*) at Christmas 1905 in Glasgow. He joined a concert party, The Highwaymen, and then toured Britain and North America in *The Scarlet Mysteries* and other musical comedies.

Walls's first London appearance was at the Empire, Leicester Square, in August 1907 as Ensign Ruffler in *Sir Roger de Coverley*. In 1908–9 he played in a succession of comedies before touring in 1910–11 in Australia in *The Arcadians* (as Peter Doody), *Miss Hook of Holland*, and *The Belle of Brittany*. On 2 February 1910 he married Alice Hilda Edwards, also of the musical comedy stage. They had one son, Tom Walls junior. Between 1912 and 1921 Walls cemented his position in the West End through fourteen musical comedies at eight major theatres. His forte was the portrayal of amiable philanderers or eccentric older gentlemen, usually with a forceful, even hectoring manner.

In 1922, in partnership with Leslie Henson, Walls entered management of the Shaftesbury Theatre. Here they produced the farce *Tons of Money*, by Will Evans and Valentine (A. T. Pechey), in which Walls also appeared, as Henry; it was a huge success and ran for two years. With the profits Walls and Henson took over the Aldwych, where they produced an American farce, *It Pays to Advertise*, followed by a series (1925–31) of farces by Ben Travers, whose pieces quickly became an institution in London theatreland. Walls acted in all these, alongside Ralph Lynn, with Mary Brough and Robertson Hare in support. 'The Walls–Lynn partnership became as famous as any on the stage, the brusque, abrupt, decisive technique of Walls proving to be the ideal foil to the wilfully fatuous inanity of the monocled Mr Lynn' (*The Times*, 29 Nov 1949, 7). *A Cuckoo in the Nest* was followed by *Rookery Nook*, *Thark*, *Plunder*, *A Cup of Kindness*, *A Night Like This*, and *Turkey Time*. Over six years some £1,500,000 was taken at the box-office.

With his mounting prosperity Walls assumed in 1927 the management of the Fortune Theatre, where he put on Frederick Lonsdale's *On Approval*, which ran for over a year, followed by *Mischief*, another Travers farce, and *Aren't We All?*, again by Lonsdale. He followed these with the more serious productions *The Last Enemy* and *Cape Forlorn* (1929–30). Through these successful years Walls, in partnership with Henson or, separately, with Reginald Highley, also controlled several touring companies.

Many of Walls's successful shows proved profitable subjects to satisfy the great demand for British screen comedy across the empire, and Walls was now lost to the stage for seven years (1931–8). He made his film début with *Rookery*

Nook and made twenty-two films between 1930 and 1938. Seventeen of these were of Travers plays; nineteen of them Walls directed himself. He made nine films for the British and Dominion studio and ten for Gaumont-British, but for the last in this period, *Old Iron*, he formed his own company, TW Productions.

Late in 1938 Walls returned to the stage, touring variety theatres in *The Van Dyke*. In 1939 he took over the Alexandra in Stoke Newington, which he ran as a repertory theatre. He produced, and played in, *His Majesty's Guest* at the Shaftesbury (1939), toured in *Springtime for Henry* (1940) and *Canaries Sometimes Sing* (1941), the Lonsdale play he had filmed in 1930, and he was in his own production of *Why Not To-Night?* at the Ambassadors (1942). His last stage appearance was in 1948, as Edward Moulton-Barrett in a revival of *The Barretts of Wimpole Street*, but it was not well received. Deafness hampered his acting in his final years. He returned to the screen in 1943, now often in more serious character roles. His later films included *Love Story* and *The Halfway House* (1944), *Johnny Frenchman* (1945), *This Man is Mine* (1946), *Master of Bankdam* (1947), *Spring in Park Lane* (1948), and *Maytime in Mayfair* (1949). His last film was *The Interrupted Journey*.

Walls's wealth also enabled him to support his passion for horses, especially riding to hounds (he was sometime master of the Sussex draghounds), which he had first done before he was ten years old. He maintained a racing stable at his home in Ewell in Surrey, where he set up as a trainer in 1927, with sometimes as many as twenty-five horses in his string. Only five years later he trained his colt April the Fifth to victory in the Derby. Altogether his horses won about 150 races. Walls was also a keen golfer.

Walls could be disputatious, but was a generous man and a bon viveur. Ill-fated ventures, high living, and the cost of his establishment at Ewell eventually took their toll on his finances. In 1948 he gave up training and his few remaining horses were sold. He died, insolvent, at his home on 27 November 1949. His ashes were scattered on nearby Epsom racecourse. Within a few months his house and many of its effects and his stables had to be sold by his executors. His wife survived him.

SEAN FIELDING, rev. ROBERT SHARP

Sources *DNB* · *The Times* (29 Nov 1949) · *Who was who in the theatre, 1912–1976*, 4 vols. (1978) · P. Hartnoll and P. Found, eds., *The concise Oxford companion to the theatre*, 2nd edn (1992) · *CGPLA Eng. & Wales* (1950) · b. cert. · m. cert. · d. cert.
Archives Surrey HC, papers and photographs relating to horse racing · Theatre Museum, London, contract and administrative papers relating to shows | FILM BFI NFTVA, documentary footage · BFI NFTVA, performance footage | SOUND BL NSA, oral history interview
Likenesses A. Darnley, bronze head
Wealth at death £3283 18s. 2d.: probate, 22 March 1950, *CGPLA Eng. & Wales*

Walmesley, Charles (1722–1797), vicar apostolic of the western district and mathematician, born on 13 January 1722 at Westwood House, near Wigan, Lancashire, was the seventh son of John Walmesley of Westwood House, and his wife, Mary, daughter of William Greaves. He was educated in the English Benedictine college of St Gregory at

Charles Walmesley (1722–1797), by unknown artist

Douai, and in the English Benedictine monastery of St Edmund at Paris, where he was clothed in the habit on 28 September 1738 and made his profession as a monk of the Benedictine order on 29 September 1739. At the Sorbonne he took his master's degree in 1742, and his licentiate in theology in 1750 was followed by a DD. Such degrees allowed him to hold the benefice of St Marcel, near Châlons-sur-Marne. He held the office of prior from 1749 until 1753, founding a literary and scientific society for the community and its lay associates. He was criticized, however, for his undue preoccupation with his mathematical studies. In 1754 he went to Rome as the English Benedictine *procurator in curia*, his main task being the defence of the monks' privileges against the incursions of the secular clergy. It was during this time that he probably visited Mount Etna for purposes of scientific investigation.

Walmesley's election as coadjutor, to Bishop Laurence York, vicar apostolic of the western district of England, with the right to succeed, was made by the *propaganda fide* on 6 April 1756, and was approved by the pope on 2 May. He was consecrated at Rome with the title of bishop of Rama, *in partibus*, on 21 December 1756. He administered the vicariate from Bath after the retirement of Bishop York in 1763, and succeeded to the vicariate on the death of his predecessor in 1770.

While administering the vicariate Walmesley continued to be involved in directing Benedictine studies, and drew up a course of studies for junior monks which recommended the study of contemporary scientists and philosophers. His own passion for Newtonian science was reflected in his most popular work, *The General History of* the *Christian Church … by Sig. Pastorini* (1770), a commentary on the book of Revelation which secured his gloomy prophecies about the future on a foundation of Newtonian theory. His *Ezekiel's Vision Explained* (1778) contained a similar message. He believed his forebodings were confirmed in the destruction caused by the Gordon riots in 1780, when his property, papers, and the bulk of his library were destroyed at Bath. Among his possessions that were burned were his scientific papers. By 1747 he had become involved in the debate then being held among astronomers in Paris over 'the problem of the Three Bodies'. In December 1748 he attempted to persuade Alexis-Claude Clairaut (1713–1765), by means of Newtonian mathematics, about the source of the discrepancy in calculating the motion of the moon's apse. He followed this up with a book, *Théorie du mouvement des apsides en général, et en particulier des apsides de l'orbite de la lune* (1749; English trans., 1754), based on Isaac Newton's propositions and a theorem of John Machin. Although he showed some skill in integrating these, the book also included some questionable assumptions. In 1749 he published his translation of the *Harmonia mensurarum* of Roger Cotes under the title *Analyse des mesures, des rapports et des angles*, the importance of which lay in transmitting to Europe a set of rules for carrying out numerical integrations, and hence was cited by the astronomer Roger Boscovich SJ. His work on Newton's theory of fluxions brought Walmesley some fame, and in 1750 he became a fellow of the Royal Society of Berlin and the Royal Society of London. It was at this time that he seems to have been involved in the discussions on the adoption of the Gregorian calendar. Between 1756 and 1761 he published a series of papers on astronomy in the Royal Society of London's *Philosophical Transactions*. During the 1750s he was also attempting to derive the precession of the equinoxes and the nutation through the use of Newtonian geometry. In 1758 his book *De inaequalitatibus motuum lunarium* was published in Florence, and he presented a copy in 1761 to Thomas Birch, secretary of the Royal Society. Walmesley is reputed to have turned his back on scientific investigation when he found himself one day tracing geometric diagrams with the paten during mass.

Following his cautious acceptance of the 1778 Catholic Relief Act, Walmesley signed his name to the 'protestation' of the Catholic Committee, objecting to the term 'protesting Catholic dissenters' found in the oath which followed on from the 'protestation'. Henceforth, he became the principal episcopal champion of the party opposed to the Cisalpines, who sought further measures of relief from the English government in return for the loyalty of Catholics. He continued this struggle until his death at Bath on 25 November 1797. He was buried at St Joseph's Chapel, Trenchard Street, Bristol, where Charles Plowden inscribed an epitaph on his tomb. In 1906 his remains were transferred to Downside Abbey church, Bath, where a new monument carried a Latin epitaph by Bishop G. A. Burton, which translated runs: 'Proud Lancashire bore me, Rome consecrated me, and Bath, which I cared for, carried me off'. Through his consecration of John Carroll in the Weld Chapel at Lulworth on 15 August 1790, Walmesley became the father of the Roman Catholic hierarchy in the United States. GEOFFREY SCOTT

Sources G. Scott, 'The early career of Bishop Charles Walmesley', *Downside Review*, 115 (1997), 249–70 · G. Scott, '"The times are fast approaching": Bishop Charles Walmesley OSB (1722–1797) as prophet', *Journal of Ecclesiastical History*, 36 (1985), 590–604 · G. Scott, *Gothic rage undone: English monks in the age of Enlightenment* (1992) · B. Ward, *The dawn of the Catholic revival in England, 1781–1803*, 2 vols. (1909) · *Orthodox Journal* (Feb 1819), 65–6 [biographical account of Walmesley] · Gillow, *Lit. biog. hist.* · J. Kirk, *Biographies of English Catholics in the eighteenth century*, ed. J. H. Pollen and E. Burton (1909) · J. A. Williams, ed., *Post-Reformation Catholicism in Bath*, 2 vols., Catholic RS, 65–6 (1975–6) · E. Duffy, 'Ecclesiastical democracy detected [pt 2]', *Recusant History*, 10 (1969–70), 309–31 · A. Le Glay, *Notice sur Charles Walmesley* (1858) · A. Bellenger, '"An Anglo-American memorial": Bishop Walmesley's tomb at Downside', *Southwestern Catholic History*, 8 (1990), 40–46 · A. Bellenger, ed., *Fathers in faith: the western district, 1688–1988* (1991) · English Benedictine records

Archives Bristol RO, corresp. and papers · Clifton Roman Catholic diocese, Bristol, letters [copies] and prayers · Downside Abbey, near Bath, corresp. [transcripts] · Ushaw College, Durham, corresp. | Archives du Nord, Lille, 18 H 64 · Douai Abbey, Woolhampton, Berkshire, minute books of the Society of St Edmund · English College, Rome, 50 · Northumbd RO, Roman Catholic diocesan MSS · Westm. DA, main series, xliii

Likenesses Hudson, miniature, Downside Abbey, near Bath · Hudson, oils, Downside Abbey, near Bath · Keenan, oils, Lulworth Castle, Dorset · engraving, repro. in *Laity's directory* (1802) · oils, bishop's house, Clifton · oils, Douai Abbey · oils, English College, Rome · portrait, priv. coll. · portrait, priv. coll. · portrait, Downside Abbey, Bath [*see illus.*]

Walmesley, Sir Thomas. *See* Walmsley, Sir Thomas (1537–1612).

Walmisley, Gilbert (*bap.* 1682, *d.* 1751), friend of Samuel Johnson, was descended from an ancient family in Lancashire. He was baptized in Lichfield Cathedral on 4 October 1682, the son of William Walmisley (*d.* 1713), chancellor of Lichfield from 1698 to 1713, and MP for the city in 1701, who married in Lichfield Cathedral on 22 April 1675 Dorothy Gilbert, and was buried in the cathedral on 18 July 1713. Gilbert matriculated as a commoner from Trinity College, Oxford, on 14 April 1698, but did not take a degree. In 1707 he was called to the bar at the Inner Temple, and became registrar of the ecclesiastical court of Lichfield. He was probably a near relative of William Walmisley, prebendary of Lichfield from 1718 to 1720, and dean from 1720 to 1730.

Walmisley, 'the most able scholar and the finest gentleman' in the city according to Anna Seward (*Poetical Works*, 1.lxix), lived in the bishop's palace at Lichfield for thirty years; and Johnson, then a stripling at school, spent there, with David Garrick, 'many cheerful and instructive hours, with companions such as are not often found'. He was 'a whig with all the virulence and malevolence of his party', but polite and learned, so that Johnson could not name 'a man of equal knowledge', and the benefit of this intercourse remained to him throughout life (S. Johnson, *Lives of the English Poets*, ed. G. B. Hill, 1905, 2.20–21). He endeavoured in 1735 to procure for Johnson the mastership of a school at Solihull in Warwickshire, but without success.

An abiding tribute to his memory was paid by Johnson in his life of Edmund Smith.

On 30 March 1736 Walmisley, 'being tired since the death of my brother of living quite alone', married Magdalen, commonly called Margaret or Margery (*bap.* 1709, *d.* 1786), fourth of the eight daughters of Sir Thomas Aston, bt, of Aston, Cheshire. His marriage was said to have extinguished certain expectations entertained by Garrick of a settlement from his friend. Walmisley died at Lichfield on 3 August 1751, and his widow died on 11 November 1786, aged seventy-seven. Both are buried in a vault near the south side of the west door in Lichfield Cathedral. A poetical epitaph by Thomas Seward was inscribed on a temporary monument which stood over the grave during the year after his death; it is printed in the *Gentleman's Magazine* (55/1, 1785, 166). It is said that Johnson promised to write an epitaph for him, but procrastinated until it was too late; he may be acquitted of any share in the composition printed as his in the *Gentleman's Magazine* (67/2, 1797, 726). A prose inscription to Walmisley's memory is on the south side of the west door of Lichfield Cathedral. Johnson's eulogy from his 'Life' of Smith was also inscribed on an adjoining monument.

Walmisley's library was sold by Thomas Osborne of Gray's Inn in 1756. The Latin translation of Byrom's verses, beginning 'My time, O ye muses', printed in the *Gentleman's Magazine* (15, 1745, 102–3) as by G. Walmsley of 'Sid. Coll. Camb', and sometimes attributed to Gilbert Walmisley, is no doubt by Galfridus Walmsley, BA from that college in 1746. Some correspondence between Garrick and Johnson and Walmisley is printed in Garrick's *Private Correspondence* and in Johnson's *Letters*. Anna Seward commented that 'while Johnson and Garrick are remembered, their first patron will not be forgotten' (*Poetical Works*, 1.lxii): Walmisley 'sowed benevolence, and reaped immortality' (*Private Correspondence*, 1.1).

W. P. COURTNEY, *rev.* FREYA JOHNSTON

Sources *Boswell's Life of Johnson*, ed. G. B. Hill, 1–4 (1887) • *The letters of Samuel Johnson*, ed. B. Redford, 1–4 (1992–4) • Nichols, *Lit. anecdotes*, vols. 2–3, 8–9 • *Johnsonian miscellanies*, ed. G. B. Hill, 2 vols. (1897); repr. (1970) • T. Harwood, *The history and antiquities of the church and city of Lichfield* (1806) • *The private correspondence of David Garrick*, ed. J. Boaden, 2nd edn, 2 vols. (1835) • *The poetical works of Anna Seward*, ed. W. Scott, 1 (1810) • Foster, *Alum. Oxon.* • *GM*, 1st ser., 21 (1751), 380 • *GM*, 1st ser., 49 (1779), 456 • *GM*, 1st ser., 67 (1797), 811 • IGI
Archives Bodl. Oxf., letters to George Duckett
Likenesses monument, 1751, Lichfield Cathedral

Walmisley, Thomas Attwood (1814–1856), composer and organist, was born on 21 January 1814 at 18 Cowley Street, Westminster. He was the son of Thomas Forbes *Walmisley (1783–1866), composer and organist, and his wife, who was the eldest daughter of William Capon, draughtsman to the duke of York. Displaying musical ability at an early age, he was initially guided by his father and subsequently placed under his godfather Thomas *Attwood, organist of St Paul's Cathedral and composer to the Chapel Royal. In 1830 he was appointed organist of Croydon parish church,

where he made the acquaintance of Thomas Miller, a former fellow of Trinity College, Cambridge, an amateur musician and well-known tutor. Miller not only encouraged Walmisley's interest in literature and mathematics, but was also probably instrumental in his gaining election on 1 February 1833, as organist of Trinity and St John's colleges, and in his subsequent decision to read for an arts degree. An attempt the previous year by the impresario Monck Mason to persuade him to write an opera for his season at the King's Theatre in London had proved unsuccessful, and Walmisley spent virtually the rest of his life in Cambridge.

In 1832 Walmisley competed unsuccessfully for the Gresham prize, awarded annually for the best new anthem or service setting. On 1 July 1833 he graduated MusB from Trinity, his exercise being the orchestrally accompanied anthem 'Let God arise', and in Michaelmas 1834 he matriculated at Corpus Christi College. Later in the year he moved to Jesus College, and he subsequently took the mathematical tripos, graduating eighteenth junior optime in 1838 and proceeding MA (from Trinity) in 1841. The (non-resident) professor of music, John Clarke-Whitfeld—under whom music enjoyed a very low status within the university—was aged and infirm and it fell to Walmisley to compose the *Ode for the Installation of the Marquis of Camden as Chancellor of the University*, performed on 7 July 1835 under Sir George Smart and with Maria Malibran as principal soloist. After Clarke-Whitfeld's death in 1836 Walmisley, though still an undergraduate, was chosen to succeed him, and in 1848 he presented himself for the MusD. During his tenure he raised the standing of the faculty of music both through his own position and education (as the first professor to be a full member of the university) and through his institution of regular lectures. After fourteen years in office he could observe that although music was still not greatly cultivated by university members, a taste for it was rapidly increasing.

Professorial duties apart, the main focus of Walmisley's professional activity lay in his direction of the joint choir of Trinity and St John's. This involved playing for at least four services each Sunday, but the choir achieved a reputation as one of the best in England. He composed a number of important services and anthems for them in which, like his contemporary S. S. Wesley, he developed the concept of an independent organ accompaniment. Notable in this respect are 'If the Lord himself' and 'The Lord shall comfort Zion' (both 1840) and his best-known work, the evening service in D minor (1855). Other works of note are the evening service in B♭ for double choir (1845), which reflects his admiration for the music of J. S. Bach, and 'Remember, O Lord' (with orchestral accompaniment) which won the prize offered in 1838 by the Ancient Concerts Society in Dublin.

Although remembered today solely for his church music, in his youth Walmisley composed extensively for the orchestra and chamber ensembles. A piano trio, two string quartets, two organ concertos, and two overtures all predate his appointment to Cambridge, but thereafter his secular works were predominantly vocal, including some attractive songs and madrigals. Noteworthy exceptions are a fine third string quartet (1840) and two sonatinas for oboe and piano (c.1846). He also wrote a symphony (now unfortunately lost), which was played at the Philharmonic Society in 1840; however, he was disheartened by Mendelssohn's comment 'No. 1! Let us first see what no. 12 will be!' (an allusion to the twelve symphonies for string orchestra that Mendelssohn had completed before writing his first one for full orchestra), and never returned to orchestral writing. An early supporter of the Cambridge University Musical Society, Walmisley also established a madrigal society and was active as a conductor: at a concert in the Senate House on 5 July 1847 Jenny Lind, Marietta Alboni, and Luigi Lablache were among the soloists, while the young Joachim played Mendelssohn's violin concerto.

Although renowned locally as an organist and composer, Walmisley never sought—or earned—the national recognition enjoyed by S. S. Wesley. Few of his compositions were published in his lifetime and most of his church music remained in manuscript until his father edited an extensive selection in 1857. Walmisley's health was eventually affected by his fondness for wine, which probably reduced his creativity and contributed to his early death. In the autumn of 1855, by now seriously ill, he moved to the Sussex coast. He died from bronchitis at 4 Caroline Place, St Mary-in-the-Castle, Hastings, on 17 January 1856 and was buried in Fairlight churchyard.

PETER HORTON

Sources A. D. Coleridge, 'Walmisley, Thomas Attwood', Grove, *Dict. mus.* · N. Temperley, 'Walmisley, Thomas Attwood', *New Grove* · W. E. Dickson, *Fifty years of church music* (1894) · C. V. Stanford, *Pages from an unwritten diary* (1914) · J. S. Bumpus, *A history of English cathedral music, 1549–1889*, 2 vols. [1908]; repr. (1972) · J. T. Fowler, *Life and letters of John Bacchus Dykes* (1897) · N. Temperley, 'T. A. Walmisley's secular music', *MT*, 97 (1956), 636–9 · W. Shaw, 'Thomas Attwood Walmisley', *English Church Music*, 27 (1957), 2–8 · N. Temperley, 'A list of T. A. Walmisley's church music', *English Church Music*, 27 (1957), 8–11 · *DNB* · Venn, *Alum. Cant.* · *GM*, 2nd ser., 45 (1856), 322 · W. Glover, *Memoirs of a Cambridge chorister* (1885) · W. J. Gatens, *Victorian cathedral music in theory and practice* (1986)
Archives Royal College of Music, London · Royal School of Church Music, London, library · St John Cam., library · Trinity Cam., library
Likenesses Harraden, oils, repro. in *MT*, 44 (1903), 374–5; formerly in Royal Academy of Music, London [now lost] · engraving, BM · oils, repro. in N. Temperley, 'T. A. Walmisley's secular music'

Walmisley, Thomas Forbes (1783–1866), composer and organist, third son of William Walmisley, clerk of the papers to the House of Lords, was born in Union (later St Margaret's) Street, Westminster, on 22 May 1783. He, like all his brothers, was a chorister in Westminster Abbey, and he was a scholar at Westminster School from 1793 to 1798. He studied music under John Spencer and Thomas Attwood, a pupil of Mozart. He began his career as a teacher of the piano and singing in 1803 and as a composer of vocal music in 1805. From 1810 to 1814 he was assistant organist to the female orphan asylum in Lambeth. Also in 1810 he married the eldest daughter of William *Capon (1757–1827), draughtsman to the duke of York. They had twelve children, of whom ten survived beyond infancy.

Thomas Attwood *Walmisley, composer and organist, was the eldest. Another son, Henry (1830–1857), also became an organist, of Holy Trinity, Bessborough Gardens, Pimlico. Frederick Walmisley (1815–1875) became a moderately successful artist. A great-niece, Jessie Walmisley, married Samuel Coleridge-Taylor (1875–1912), composer. In 1814 Walmisley succeeded Robert Cooke (*fl.* 1793–1814) as organist of St Martin-in-the-Fields, which post he resigned, on a pension, in March 1854. From 1817 he was secretary of the re-established Concentores Sodales, which was dissolved in 1847, the society's stock of wine becoming his property; and in 1827 he was elected a professional member of the Catch Club.

Walmisley was principally a composer of glees; he wrote fifty-nine, four of which gained prizes and many of which were published in four separate collections. He also composed ten anthems, one short morning and evening service, and *Sacred Songs* (1841). He was well known as a teacher: perhaps his most distinguished pupil was Edward J. Hopkins. Walmisley died at 19 Earl's Court Gardens, Brompton, London, on 10 July 1866 and was buried in the family grave at Brompton cemetery.

F. G. EDWARDS, *rev.* NILANJANA BANERJI

Sources *New Grove* · Brown & Stratton, *Brit. mus.* · J. D. Brown, *Biographical dictionary of musicians: with a bibliography of English writings on music* (1886) · D. Baptie, *A handbook of musical biography* (1883) · D. Baptie, *Sketches of the English glee composers: historical, biographical and critical (from about 1735–1866)* [1896] · G. F. R. Barker and A. H. Stenning, eds., *The Westminster School register from 1764 to 1883* (1892) · *CGPLA Eng. & Wales* (1866) · d. cert.
Likenesses oils, NPG
Wealth at death under £1500: probate, 3 Aug 1866, *CGPLA Eng. & Wales*

Walmsley, Sir Joshua (1794–1871), politician, son of John Walmsley and his wife, Elizabeth Berry, was born at Concert Street, Liverpool, on 29 September 1794. His father, a builder, architect, and statuary mason, who owned marble and stone quarries, designed and constructed several notable buildings in Liverpool. Joshua was educated at Knowsley, Lancashire, and Eden Hall, Westmorland. On the death of his father in 1807 he became a teacher in Eden Hall School, and on returning to Liverpool in 1811 took a similar situation in Mr Knowles's school. He was then employed by a corn merchant in 1814, and at the end of his engagement went into the same business himself, and ultimately acquired a comfortable income. He married in 1815 Adeline, *née* Mulleneux.

Walmsley was an early advocate of the repeal of the duty on corn, and was afterwards an active member of the Anti-Corn Law League. In 1826 he became president of the Liverpool Mechanics' Institute, and about the same time began his close friendship and business partnership with George Stephenson. Elected a member of the Liverpool town council in 1835, he worked to improve the police, sanitary, and educational affairs of the borough; he was notable for promoting non-sectarian schools. He was appointed mayor in November 1838 and knighted in 1840 on presenting an address to Queen Victoria from the town council of Liverpool on the occasion of her marriage. In 1837 he founded the Tradesmen's Reform Association, which campaigned to secure the ballot, Liberal representation for Liverpool, and repeal of the corn laws. With Palmerston he unsuccessfully contested Liverpool in June 1841. He retired to Ranton Abbey, Staffordshire, in 1843, and at the general election of 1847 was elected MP for Leicester, but was unseated on petition.

Walmsley was the founder in 1848, president, and chief organizer of the National Reform Association and was a supporter of the forty-shilling freehold movement. In 1849 he was returned as MP for Bolton, Lancashire, but in 1852 exchanged that seat for Leicester, where his efforts on behalf of the framework knitters had made him popular. His parliamentary campaign for a reform bill was overshadowed by continental affairs. In his dealings with continental liberals—he was friendly with Louis Kossuth—he opposed all violent actions and, as proprietor of the *Daily News*, he adopted a non-interventionist stance during the Crimean War. He resisted attempts to limit extension of the Factory Acts and supported the protection and regulation of small workshop trades. He lost his seat in 1857, as a result of a sabbatarian coalition; from 1856 to 1869 he retained the presidency of Joseph Hume's Sunday Society, which campaigned for the opening of museums, galleries, and libraries on Sundays.

Walmsley died on 17 November 1871 at his residence at Hume Towers, Bournemouth. His wife survived him by two years.   C. W. SUTTON, *rev.* MATTHEW LEE

Sources H. M. Walmsley, *The life of Sir Joshua Walmsley* (1879) • *Free Sunday Advocate* (Dec 1871) • M. Taylor, *The decline of British radicalism, 1847–1860* (1995) • Walford, *County families* • *CGPLA Eng. & Wales* (1872) • Colvin, *Archs.*

Archives Dorset RO, papers | Bolton Archive and Local Studies Service, corresp. with Robert Heywood • W. Sussex RO, corresp. with Richard Cobden

Likenesses T. H. Illidge, portrait, 1839, Liverpool City Corporation • W. Daniels, oils, V&A • lithograph, NPG • portrait, repro. in Walmsley, *Life of Sir Joshua Walmsley*

Wealth at death under £140,000: probate, 3 Feb 1872, *CGPLA Eng. & Wales*

Walmsley [Walmesley], **Sir Thomas** (1537–1612), judge, was the eldest of the ten children of Thomas Walmsley (*d.* 1584) of Showley Hall, Clayton-le-Dale, Lancashire, and Margaret Livesey. Having entered Lincoln's Inn in 1559, he was called to the bar in 1567 and made a bencher of the inn in 1574. He was Lent reader in 1578 and autumn reader in 1580, when he was created serjeant-at-law. In 1589 he was made a judge of the court of common pleas, which place he continued to occupy until his death. Walmsley was undoubtedly a very capable lawyer—in 1603, the year he was knighted, Robert Cecil ranked him alongside the two chief justices for learning—though he was in a very conservative mould: he resisted to the end what he regarded as undesirable developments in the common law, sometimes continuing his grumbling opposition long after they had become settled law. He was not a man to succumb to pressure to conform to the opinions of others. In 1591, early in his judicial career, he earned a royal reprimand for allowing bail to a prisoner accused of murder, contrary to the express instructions of the queen.

Nowhere was his independence of mind more visible than in *Calvin's case* (1608), when the judges were required to determine whether a Scot born after the accession of James I was a naturalized Englishman. Alone among the judges giving advice to the House of Lords, Walmsley refused to accept this, maintaining his dissent in the court of exchequer chamber.

Walmsley retained strong Lancashire links throughout his life, representing the county in the parliament of 1589. His marriage *c.*1570 to Anne Shuttleworth (*d.* 1635) brought him an estate at Hacking, though not without litigation against her family; and in 1571 he bought the lands and mansion at Dunkenhalgh which were to be his principal home for the rest of his life. He continued to invest heavily in lands in Lancashire and in Yorkshire; according to the account of one of his descendants, Walmsley's expenditure on land in the course of his lifetime was in excess of £30,000. To the rentals from these estates and his earnings from legal practice, he added a steady stream of income from moneylending. Tradition has it that his dealings were not always fair; and his surviving account books suggest that he was, at the least, a tough dealer not given to magnanimous gestures where business was concerned. On the other hand, he was actively involved in charitable works, most notably as a governor of the grammar school at Blackburn.

Walmsley's wife, who survived him by many years, was an unashamed recusant, and although perhaps not a practising Catholic himself, Walmsley was generally thought to have been actively sympathetic to their cause. During his time as justice of assize on the northern circuit (1589–91) the anti-Catholic legislation was enforced with the gentlest of hands, though protestant nonconformists were treated with firmness. It was perhaps because of this that he was moved in quick succession to the home circuit, then to the midland, and then to the west (where he could be watched over by the orthodox chief justice Sir Edmund Anderson). He returned to the northern circuit to ride with John Savile in 1602, and once again brought comfort to the Catholics and consternation to their opponents.

In his later years Walmsley suffered from palsy and was plagued by gout. He died at Dunkenhalgh on 26 November 1612, at the age of seventy-five. His funeral was a lavish affair, with well over 2000 guests at the funeral feast, and many hundreds of pounds expended on mourning black. Buried at Blackburn beneath a handsome monument, which was largely destroyed in 1625, Walmsley was a local hero in northern Lancashire; the inn named in his memory at Whalley has survived to the present day.

DAVID IBBETSON

Sources M. Brigg, 'The Walmesleys of Dunkenhalgh', *Transactions of the Lancashire and Cheshire Antiquarian Society*, 75–6 (1965–6), 72–102 • T. D. Whitaker, *An history of the original parish of Whalley*, rev. J. G. Nichols and P. A. Lyons, 4th edn, 2 vols. (1872–6) • W. A. Abram, *A history of Blackburn* (1877) • *HoP, Commons, 1558–1603* • Lancs. RO, DDPt/46 • J. Foster, ed., *Pedigrees of the county families of England*, 1: *Lancashire* (1873) • *CSP dom., 1601–3*, 285 • Baker, *Serjeants*, 542 •

Sainty, *Judges*, 74 · W. P. Baildon, ed., *The records of the Honorable Society of Lincoln's Inn: the black books*, 1 (1897) · *State trials*, vol. 2
Archives Free Library of Philadelphia, commonplace book · Lancs. RO, commonplace book, DDPt/46
Likenesses oils (after Petre), Lincoln's Inn, London · oils, priv. coll. · oils, priv. coll.

Walmsley, Thomas (1763–1805/6), landscape painter, was descended from a family of good position at Rochdale, Lancashire. He is sometimes referred to as John Walmsley. He was born in Dublin, where his father, Thomas Walmsley, captain-lieutenant of the 18th dragoons, was stationed with his regiment. He quarrelled with his family, and went to London to earn his living. He studied scene-painting under Giovanni Battista Colombo at the opera-house, and was himself employed there and at Covent Garden Theatre and the King's Theatre; he also worked at Crow Street Theatre, Dublin, after it reopened in 1788. In 1790 he began to exhibit landscapes in London, where he lived until 1795, when he retired to Bath. He showed a Welsh landscape at the Incorporated Society of Arts in 1790 and sent many pictures to the Royal Academy, chiefly views in Wales; but in 1796, the last year in which he exhibited, three views of Killarney. He painted chiefly in body colour but also in oils in a small size and in watercolours. His trees were heavy and conventional, and he had no capacity for drawing figures, but he was skilful in painting skies, especially with a warm evening glow, which was well reproduced in the coloured aquatints by Francis Jukes and others, through which he is best known at the present day. Of these several series were published both before and after his death: *Views of the Dee and North Wales* (1792–4); *Larger Views of North Wales* (1800); *Views of Killarney and Kenmare* (1800–02); *Miscellaneous British Scenery* (1801); *Views in Bohemia* (1801); *Views of the Isle of Wight* (1802–3); *Miscellaneous Irish Scenery* (1806); *Views in Scotland* (1810). Walmsley died at Bath either in 1805 (Edwards gives his date of death as August 1805) or in 1806. Examples of his work in gouache are held in the Victoria and Albert Museum and the British Museum, London.

CAMPBELL DODGSON, rev. ANNETTE PEACH

Sources Redgrave, *Artists* · Bryan, *Painters* (1903–5) · Bénézit, *Dict.*, 4th edn · Graves, *RA exhibitors* · Waterhouse, *18c painters* · E. Edwards, *Anecdotes of painters* (1808); facs. edn (1970) · W. G. Strickland, *A dictionary of Irish artists*, 2 vols. (1913); repr. with introduction by T. J. Snoddy (1989) · M. Pilkington, *A general dictionary of painters: containing memoirs of the lives and works*, ed. A. Cunningham and R. A. Davenport, new edn (1857) · J. Gould, *Biographical dictionary of painters, sculptors, engravers and architects*, new edn, 2 vols. (1839)

Walpole, Charlotte. See Atkyns, Charlotte (c.1758–1836).

Walpole [*alias* Pauper], **Edward** (bap. 1560, d. 1637), Jesuit, was the son and heir of John Walpole (d. 1588) of Houghton, Norfolk, and Catherine Calibut (d. 1612) of Coxford in the same county, and was baptized on 28 January 1560 at Houghton. Educated at Norwich School between approximately 1571 and 1576 he matriculated as a fellow-commoner at Peterhouse, Cambridge, in May 1576, the year after his cousin Henry Walpole, also later a Jesuit, had entered the same college as a pensioner. In 1580 or 1581 Edward was admitted to Lincoln's Inn from Furnival's Inn.

Here, as at Cambridge, he was influenced by his older cousin, especially in religious matters. Edward, raised a strict protestant, was gradually won over to Roman Catholicism. According to Henry Foley, Edward's parents were so distressed by their son's increasingly popish sentiments and by his resolution to adhere to the Roman church that they complained to the privy council. As a result Henry fled to the continent, arriving in Rheims in July 1582. Edward's parents fought back: they engaged protestant ministers first in Norfolk and then in London to demonstrate popish errors through disputation. Failure to do so resulted in Edward's being disowned by his family and thrown out of Houghton in 1585. Assuming the name of Pauper to mark his new identity he 'gave proof of a nobler spirit than was implied in the splendour of any earthly descent' (Foley, 2.260).

Edward's plans to follow his cousin to the continent were frustrated, so he returned to Norfolk where another cousin, William Walpole, who shared his religious sentiments, offered him asylum at Tuddenham. Edward repaid his generosity by reconciling William to his wife, Mary Blackwell, from whom he had been for some years estranged. In October 1587 William died, leaving the great bulk of his large property to his cousin Edward, subject to the life interest of his widow.

In April of 1588 Edward's father died, leaving all to his second son, Calibut, and not even naming his elder son in the will. Five months later Robert, earl of Leicester, died. The earl had a life interest in the estates of his first wife, Amy Robsart, which lay contiguous to those of the Walpoles, and these now descended to Edward Walpole as heir-at-law to Sir John Robsart, Amy's father. Edward at once surrendered by deed all claim and title on the Robsart and the Houghton estates to his brother Calibut, and the estates accordingly descended through him to Sir Robert Walpole and the earls of Oxford. Similarly Edward sold the reversion of the manor of Tuddenham for 1000 marks.

In 1589 the Jesuit John Gerard began his successful missionary work among Norfolk recusant gentry and it was he who formally reconciled Edward Walpole to the Roman church. Under the Jesuit's direction Edward slipped away to the continent. Admitted to the English College, Rome, on 23 October 1590 he was ordained on the feast of the Ascension, 7 May 1592, in the college chapel. He departed for Flanders in May 1593 and entered the noviciate of the province on 4 July, pronouncing his first vows as a Jesuit on 25 December 1594. On 8 July 1595 he was sent to Louvain, where he studied humanities for two years before doing pastoral work in Brussels and Antwerp. By 1598 he was in England, where he remained until his death. On 21 May 1609 he was solemnly professed of the three vows in London.

In 1621 he was superior of the Jesuits in the Worcestershire district. In 1623 he was named superior of the residence of the Blessed Stanislaus (Devon). Upon completing his three-year term, he was transferred to the residence of St Dominic (Lincolnshire), where he was superior from at least 1628 until 1630. From 1631 until 1633 he was at the residence of St Thomas of Canterbury (Hampshire). In 1634–5 he worked from the house of probation of St Ignatius (London) and in 1636 at the College of the Holy Apostles, recently established by Lord Petre, in East Anglia. Some time in 1637 Walpole returned to London where he died on 3 November 1637.

Walpole translated Louis Richeome's *The Pilgrime of Loreto* (1629), a notable example of the Salesian spirituality then fashionable.   THOMAS M. McCOOG

Sources T. M. McCoog, *English and Welsh Jesuits, 1555–1650*, 2 vols., Catholic RS, 74–5 (1994–5) · T. M. McCoog, ed., *Monumenta Angliae*, 1–2 (1992) · H. Foley, ed., *Records of the English province of the Society of Jesus*, 7 vols. in 8 (1875–83) · Venn, *Alum. Cant.* · A. Jessopp, *One generation of a Norfolk house*, 3rd edn (1913) · W. Kelly, ed., *Liber ruber venerabilis collegii Anglorum de urbe*, 1, Catholic RS, 37 (1940) · *John Gerard: the autobiography of an Elizabethan*, trans. P. Caraman, 2nd edn (1956) · A. F. Allison and D. M. Rogers, eds., *The contemporary printed literature of the English Counter-Reformation between 1558 and 1640*, 2 vols. (1989–94) · T. H. Clancy, *A literary history of the English Jesuits: a century of books, 1615–1714* (1996) · *The Elizabethan Jesuits: Historia missionis Anglicanae Societatis Jesu* (1660) *of Henry More*, ed. and trans. F. Edwards (1981)
Archives Archives of the British Province of the Society of Jesus, London · Archivum Romanum Societatis Iesu, Rome | Stonyhurst College, Lancashire

Walpole, George (1758–1835), army officer, born on 20 June 1758 at Wickmere, Norfolk, was the third son of Horatio Walpole, second Lord Walpole of Wolterton (1723–1809), a politician, and his wife, Lady Rachel Cavendish (*d.* 1805), the third daughter of William, third duke of Devonshire. His father succeeded his cousin Horatio Walpole, fourth earl of Orford, as fourth Lord Walpole of Walpole in 1797, and was created earl of Orford in 1806. George Walpole was educated at Eton College between 1769 and 1776, was commissioned cornet in the 12th light dragoons on 12 May 1777, and became lieutenant in the 9th dragoons on 17 April 1780. He returned to the 12th light dragoons as captain lieutenant on 10 December 1781 and exchanged to the 8th light dragoons on 13 August 1782. On 25 June 1785 he was promoted major in the 13th light dragoons, and on 31 October 1792 he became lieutenant-colonel of that regiment.

In 1795 Walpole went with his regiment to Jamaica, and took a leading part in suppressing the insurrection of the Trelawny maroons. Descendants of fugitive slaves freed sixty years before, they numbered fewer than 700, but they had been joined by many runaway slaves, and the insurrection threatened to spread. Some feared the involvement of French revolutionaries. Jamaica's 'cockpit' country (that is, characterized by eroded basins) was extremely difficult for regular troops; two of the detachments sent against the maroons fell into ambushes and their commanders were killed. At the beginning of October, Walpole was charged with the general conduct of the operations, and the governor—Alexander Lindsay, sixth earl of Balcarres—gave him the local and temporary rank of major-general. By skilful dispositions he captured several of the maroon cockpits. On 24 October the governor wrote to the secretary of state: 'General Walpole is going on vastly well. His figure and talents are well adapted for the service he is upon, and he has got the confidence of the militia and the country' (A. Lindsay, *Lives of the Lindsays*, 1858, 3.80). By 22 December he had come to terms with the insurgents. They were to ask pardon, to leave their fastnesses and settle in any district assigned to them, and to give up the runaway slaves. On these conditions Walpole promised that they should not be sent out of the island, and the terms were ratified by the governor.

Only a few of the insurgents came in, and in the middle of January, Walpole moved against them with a strong column, accompanied by hunting dogs which had been brought at his suggestion from Cuba. The maroons then surrendered and were taken to Montego Bay. In March the assembly and the governor decided to deport them to Nova Scotia. Walpole strongly remonstrated against what he regarded as a breach of faith. He argued that the treaty might have been cancelled when the maroons failed to fulfil its terms, but that the governor had deliberately abstained from cancelling it. He declined a gift of 500 guineas which the assembly voted for the purchase of a sword and obtained leave to return to England. His intemperate letter declining the sword was expunged from the minutes of the house, and the assembly even contemplated arresting him.

Walpole was made colonel in the army on 3 May 1796, but he retired from the service in 1797. In January of that year the Cavendish family interest returned him to parliament for Derby, which he represented until 1806. A follower of Fox, he voted for reform, but when, in May 1798, he spoke on behalf of the maroons, his motion was defeated. The same month he was George Tierney's second in his duel with William Pitt. When Fox came into office as foreign secretary Walpole was appointed under-secretary (20 February 1806), but he did not retain this office long after Fox's death. He was MP for Dungarvan from 1807 until 1820, when, chronically endebted, he resigned his seat. In 1833 he was made comptroller of cash in the Excise Office for the rest of his life. He died, unmarried, in May 1835.   E. M. LLOYD, *rev.* DAVID P. GEGGUS

Sources R. G. Thorne, 'Walpole, George', HoP, *Commons, 1790–1820* · A. E. Furness, 'The maroon war of 1795', *Jamaican Historical Review*, 5/2 (1965), 30–49 · B. Edwards, *The proceedings of the governor and assembly of Jamaica in regard to the maroon negroes* (1796) · *GM*, 2nd ser., 4 (1835), 547–8 · Burke, *Peerage* (1959) · Burke, *Peerage* (1970) · R. Dallas, *The history of the maroons*, 2 vols. (1803) · official correspondence, Jamaica, PRO, CO 137/95–96, CO 140/85 · G. W. Bridges, *The annals of Jamaica*, 2 vols. (1827–8) · W. J. Gardner, *A history of Jamaica* (1873) · *Journals of the Assembly of Jamaica*, ed. Assembly of Jamaica, 14 vols. (1811–29), vol. 9 · IGI
Archives Rt Hon. Lord Walpole of Wolterton, bank passbook | NL Scot., corresp. with Lord Balcarres · U. Durham L., letters to Charles, second Earl Grey

Walpole, Henry [St Henry Walpole] (*bap.* 1558, *d.* 1595), Jesuit and martyr, was baptized in October 1558 in Docking, Norfolk, the eldest of the ten children of Christopher Walpole (*d.* 1596), gentleman, and his wife, Margery Warner, daughter of Richard and Alice Beckham of Narford. The Walpole family had lived in Norfolk for at least 600 years. At the end of Queen Mary's reign Henry's father settled at

Docking Hall. Upon the increase of the family he acquired Anmer Hall, with a large estate in Anmer and Dersingham, in 1575. This estate was contiguous to his cousin's estate at Houghton and his nephew's estate at Herpley. The three estates covered 50 square miles. His brother John Walpole of Herpley was a serjeant-at-law.

Christopher and John Walpole both sent their sons to the grammar school in Norwich which Edward Coke, the future chief justice of the common pleas, had also attended. Henry Walpole probably entered the school in 1566 or 1567, when his master was Stephen Limpert. In 1575 he matriculated at Cambridge and entered Peterhouse to study philosophy, and spent four years in learning languages. He took an interest in religious controversy, 'which piece of curiosity … ended in his conversion to the Catholick faith' (Dodd, 148). Henry More, however, says that Walpole was 'nurtured from childhood in Catholic tenets', and that when he was older, 'he gave such example of discretion and good sense that he could take the place of parents for his brothers' (Elizabethan Jesuits, 254). Meanwhile John Walpole had entrusted the education of his son William to Thomas Thirlby, bishop of Ely, who was sent to the Tower of London in 1560. At the time Henry Walpole entered Peterhouse another young man of similar background, Dudley Fenner, also entered. Jessopp says that Fenner was 'a rigid and fervent Puritan; Walpole, as earnest and devoted a Catholic' (Jessopp, 75). Both were driven into exile and to exercise their ministries in Belgium, one as a puritan preacher, the other as a Jesuit priest. In 1576 Henry's cousin Edward also matriculated at Peterhouse. Along with him came four recusant neighbours—Edward Yelverton of Rougham, John Cobbe of Sandringham, Philip Paris of Pudding Norton, and Bernard Gardiner of Coxford Abbey. Neither Henry nor Edward Walpole proceeded to a degree, presumably because of the oath required. Henry's name appears in the buttery books of Peterhouse for the last time on 17 April 1579. He was also a student at Gray's Inn in 1578, following in his father's and uncle's footsteps. Jessopp notes that 'Gray's Inn was at this time a favourite haunt of all who were "Catholicly" inclined' (ibid., 127).

It was not long after this that the course of Walpole's life was to change dramatically. It all began with a group of fourteen leaving Rome for England on 18 April 1580. This group was led initially by Thomas Goldwell, Marian bishop of St Asaph and the last surviving bishop of the old hierarchy, and Laurence Vaux, last warden of the collegiate church of Manchester. It was decided at St Omer that Goldwell, who was nearing eighty, and some other priests, were too old to withstand the dangers of going to England. In the end Robert Persons, Edmund Campion, and the others entered England in small groups. It was Henry Walpole's attendance at Campion's execution at Tyburn on 1 December 1581 that changed his life. Some blood from the martyr splashed onto Walpole, who had earlier attended Campion's disputation in the Tower of London, and also his trial. Walpole accepted this as a call to take up the work of Campion. He immediately wrote a poem entitled 'An Epitaph of the Life and Death of …

Edmund Campion'. There was a huge demand for the manuscript. Some extracts read:

our new apostle cumyng to restore
the faith, wich Austen planted here before …
they thought it best to take hys lyfe awaye,
because they sawe he wuld theire matter marre …
All Europe wonders at so rare a man.
(Jessopp, 133–7)

The government made successful efforts to track down and destroy copies of this poem. It was not long before Walpole was suspected of being the author: he was already under suspicion of converting over twenty young men to his faith. Valenger, one of Walpole's friends, on whose private press it was printed, was brought before the council, and was condemned to lose his ears. Walpole considered it expedient to slip away to Norfolk and was concealed in a hiding place at Anmer Hall. In this he must have had the support of his family. On leaving Anmer Hall en route for the continent he concealed himself in the woods by day and eventually arrived at Newcastle, where he took ship for France. He went to Rouen and Paris and arrived on 7 July 1582 at the English College, Rheims, where he was enrolled as a theological student. He remained about ten months, and was then accepted by the English College, Rome, on 28 April 1583. In 1584 he applied for admission to the Jesuit order and completed two years' probation at Verdun. He became prefect of the convictors at Pont-à-Mousson and was ordained priest in Paris on 17 December 1588. Later he served as a chaplain in Colonel William Stanley's regiment in the Netherlands. In the meantime his brother Richard *Walpole spent three years at Peterhouse, and then followed his elder brother to the English College, Rome, in 1584. Richard was ordained as a Jesuit priest in 1589. Likewise another two of Henry's brothers, Christopher and Michael *Walpole, and his cousin Edward *Walpole, became Jesuit priests.

To Walpole's five brothers sitting round their hearth at Anmer Hall in the winter of 1589 came the news that he had been arrested in Flushing when it was captured by English troops. One of the English officers, Captain Russels of West Rudham, a cousin of the Walpoles, got word back to Norfolk. Michael Walpole immediately set out for Flushing, paid the ransom, and procured Henry's release in January 1590. For most of the next two years Henry Walpole exercised his priestly functions on the continent. He met there many old friends and all his brothers, except Geoffrey, who had all left England during this unsettled period. At this time Walpole was at the Jesuit college at Tournai. Meanwhile the government was so concerned about the growth of the overseas seminaries and the activities of their alumni that in November 1591 the queen published her famous edict denouncing them. Persons immediately composed his Responsio ad edictum in reply in Latin, under the name of Philopater. An English version was considered advisable, and Henry Walpole was entrusted with the task. This reply was aimed at showing that it was not the queen who was responsible for the edict and repressive measures against the seminary priests, but her council, Cecil in particular. A spy forwarded a copy of Walpole's translation to the council, and his ultimate fate was then sealed. Walpole was working on the translation when he was summoned to join Persons in Spain. He attended the opening of the chapel of the new Jesuit college in Seville in December 1592, where he met his brother Richard for the first time in years. After two months in Seville, Henry was sent to Valladolid, where he held the post of minister at St Alban's College.

Persons told Walpole in June 1593 that it had been decided to send him on the English mission; Walpole had for some time wished to emulate the successful mission of the Jesuit John Gerard in East Anglia. Before leaving he was presented to Philip II at the Escorial. He sailed from Bilbao to Calais and then went to Douai. He joined his brother Thomas and Edward Lingen, both former officers of Sir William Stanley's English regiment. They had to wait some weeks at St Omer, awaiting a ship to England. At last arrangements were made for passage to Essex, Suffolk, or Norfolk. But the weather on the voyage in early December 1593 was so bad that Walpole's party had to land at Bridlington, Yorkshire. One of Walsingham's spies had previously disembarked from an accompanying vessel, and he went to warn the authorities in York. Ignorant of Yorkshire, and without a map, they committed the blunder of keeping together. At this time Yorkshire was under the iron grip of the president of the council of the north, Henry, earl of Huntingdon, and the party was soon apprehended at Kilham on 7 December and confined at York Castle.

Upon questioning Walpole admitted to being a Jesuit priest, but neither he nor Lingen would incriminate others. Thomas Walpole, however, admitted all he knew, even to revealing where his brother had buried a packet of letters on landing. On 25 January 1594 Richard Topcliffe wrote to Lord Keeper Puckering: 'Much more lies hidden in the Jesuit and Lingen, which cannot be digged out without further authority than his Lordship has ... They must be dealt with sharply, and more will burst out' (*CSP dom.*, *1591–4*, 417). Several conferences with protestant clergy were arranged, on which occasions Walpole 'discovered both his zeal and learning, which were far above the commonest'. The earl of Huntingdon wrote to Lord Burghley on 23 February 1594: 'the Jesuit Walpole and his brother shal be sent towards London ..., and before they goe I will examine them bothe again ... But I think Mr. Topcliffe had all with him' (Pollen, 240). On the day Walpole was sent to London, he was placed in Topcliffe's custody. It was then that his sufferings really began. He was committed to the Tower of London where there were a number of other notable recusant prisoners, including Philip Howard, earl of Arundel, and Robert Southwell. He was placed in solitary confinement for nearly two months, and on 27 April he underwent his first examination before Serjeant Drewe, Sir Edward Coke, and Topcliffe. Official records indicate the many questions and answers during the six examinations between then and 17 June 1594. So far Walpole had only disclosed facts the examiners already knew. In June he revealed a conversation with Persons on the lawfulness of assassinating the queen, when Persons had stated 'that

Catholics ... ought to suffer violence, but offer none, chiefly to princes' (Jessopp, 284). He was then put on the rack many times, and gradually gave more valuable information on the seminaries in Spain and the names of the students. One thing he did not do was to compromise anyone in England whose life would have been in peril as the result of revelations. But, as Jessopp points out, there were worse ordeals to come: in July 1594 he was able to write, but, after being left with Topcliffe for a further nine months, his writing had become an illegible scrawl.

By the spring of 1595 Walpole was sent to York for trial. One of his judges was Francis Beaumont, a fellow former commoner of Peterhouse. The indictment contained three counts: that Walpole had abjured the realm without licence; that he had received holy orders overseas; and that he had returned to England as a Jesuit priest to exercise his priestly functions. According to the relevant statute, to so return was to be guilty of high treason. Walpole's own confessions, extracted under torture, were read to the court, and the jury was asked to pronounce its verdict on this evidence. The judge refused to hear Walpole in his defence, apart from a brief statement. Despite this, Walpole acquitted himself with great ability, as befitted a one-time student of Gray's Inn. The judge ordered the jury to find him guilty. While awaiting sentence Walpole managed to write to his father and friends. One of these letters was addressed to a fellow Jesuit, Richard Holtby. Jessopp quotes a letter from Holtby, then in the archives of Stonyhurst College, giving an account of Walpole's final hours. Another conference with protestant clergy was arranged in the days before he died.

Walpole's execution in York occurred on 17 April 1595. When the day dawned, Walpole was dragged to the place of execution on a hurdle. Once again he testified his loyalty to the queen, so that some tried to persuade the magistrate to stop the execution. On the scaffold he was pushed and hanged before he could complete his prayers. He was immediately drawn and quartered.

His father died broken-hearted in 1596, fifteen months after Walpole's execution. The Norfolk property was divided between Geoffrey and Thomas Walpole. Thomas took Anmer Hall: both he and his wife, Thomasine, were listed as Norfolk recusants in 1615. His cousin Calibut Walpole died in 1646, just thirty years before his lineal descendant Sir Robert Walpole, England's first prime minister, was born, and the fortunes of the house of Walpole rose again. A portrait of Henry Walpole is one of sixteen martyr portraits at St Alban's College, Valladolid. A copy was made for Frederick Walpole of Mannington Hall, Norfolk. In 1970 Henry Walpole was canonized by Pope Paul VI as one of the forty martyrs of England and Wales. His feast day is observed on 25 October.

ANTONY CHARLES RYAN

Sources A. Jessopp, *One generation of a Norfolk house*, 3rd edn (1913) · J. H. Pollen, ed., *Unpublished documents relating to the English martyrs*, 1, Catholic RS, 5 (1908) · *The Elizabethan Jesuits: Historia missionis Anglicanae Societatis Jesu (1660) of Henry More*, ed. and trans. F. Edwards (1981), 254–82 · A. F. Allison and D. M. Rogers, eds., *The contemporary printed literature of the English Counter-Reformation between 1558 and 1640*, 2 (1994), 153, no. 776 · H. Foley, ed., *Records of the English province of the Society of Jesus, 2 (1875), 235 [pedigree] • M. E. Williams, St Alban's College, Valladolid: four centuries of English Catholic presence in Spain (1986), 9, 16, 64, 257 • D. A. Bellenger, ed., English and Welsh priests, 1558–1800 (1984) • Venn, Alum. Cant., 1/4 • C. Dodd [H. Tootell], The church history of England, from the year 1500, to the year 1688, 2 (1739), 148–9 • J. Foster, The register of admissions to Gray's Inn, 1521–1889, together with the register of marriages in Gray's Inn chapel, 1695–1754 (privately printed, London, 1889) • T. M. McCoog, English and Welsh Jesuits, 1555–1650, 2, Catholic RS, 75 (1995) • T. F. Knox and others, eds., The first and second diaries of the English College, Douay (1878) • Letters of Fa. Henry Walpole, S. J., ed. A. Jessopp (1873) • H. Foley, Letters and notices, 9 (1873), 46–63 • J. Cresswell, Histoire de la vie et ferme constance du Père Henri Walpole (1596) • CSP dom., 1591–4, 489–521

Archives Stonyhurst College, Lancashire, MSS, Anglia, i, n. 49, fol. 92 | ARSI, Anglia historia, ii, fol. 64 • BL, Harley MS 6996, fol. 72 • BL, Lansdowne MS 982, fol. 233

Likenesses oils, Cambridge University Catholic Chaplaincy, Fisher House, Cambridge • portrait, St Alban's College, Valladolid; repro. in Williams, St Alban's College

Walpole, Horatio [Horace], first Baron Walpole of Wolterton

(1678–1757), diplomatist and politician, was born at Houghton, Norfolk, on 8 December 1678, the fifth and second surviving son of Robert *Walpole (1650–1700) and his wife, Mary (1654/5–1711), the daughter and heir of Sir Jeffrey Burwell, of Rougham, Suffolk. Horatio, usually known as Horace, was the younger brother and close political collaborator of Robert *Walpole, first earl of Orford. Surviving letters between them when they were in their early twenties show a close and affectionate relationship, expressed in a frank obscenity characteristic of the time. Like his elder brother, Horace was educated at Eton College (1693–8) and at King's College, Cambridge (1698–1700), where he was elected fellow from 1702 to 1714. He was admitted to Lincoln's Inn in October 1700 but soon entered parliament in the whig interest, being first elected in July 1702 for the Castle Rising seat which his brother had just quitted. He sat in the Commons for the best part of fifty-four years, until his elevation to the peerage on 4 June 1756. In 1710 he briefly held the seat of Lostwithiel, and from December 1710 to 1715 was again member for Castle Rising. From 1715 to 1717 he held the seat of Bere Alston, Devon, and from 1718 to 1722 that of East Looe, Cornwall. He represented the borough of Great Yarmouth from 1722 to 1734 and the still more prestigious constituency of Norwich from 1734 to 1756.

Early diplomatic and political career Walpole owed his career almost entirely to Sir Robert, and never forgot his obligations to the man whom he still called, towards the end of his own life, 'my late, Dear, Good & Great Brother' (Sir Robert Walpole MSS, Lewis Walpole Library). He left the centre of politics when his brother resigned. Early in his public life he became involved in both foreign service and domestic politics, a combination which was to characterize the whole of his career. In 1706–7 he served as secretary to General James Stanhope, the envoy to Charles III, who ultimately failed to establish his claim to the Spanish throne. From 1707 he was secretary to Henry Boyle, Lord Carleton, who had been chancellor of the exchequer since 1701 and from 1708 to 1710 was secretary of state for the northern department. Walpole acted briefly as Carleton's

Horatio Walpole, first Baron Walpole of Wolterton (1678–1757), by Jean Baptiste van Loo, 1739

under-secretary, a valuable preparation for a diplomatic career and one which he undertook again in 1714–15 under Viscount Townshend. His knowledge of office routine and procedures was to be as valuable as his understanding of treaties and protocol. From May 1709 to March 1711 he was given his first taste of regular overseas diplomacy when he was posted as secretary to the embassy at The Hague, beginning a long association with the United Provinces. In 1715 and 1716 he acted as British minister at The Hague, in place of William, Lord Cadogan, and sought Dutch help both to protect shipping convoys in the Baltic against Swedish privateers and to furnish military aid against the Jacobite rising of 1715. Though his honest and burgher-like approach made him a success in the United Provinces, he was frustrated, not for the last time, by the decentralized and slow-moving Dutch decision-making process. In October 1716 he wrote to Stephen Poyntz: 'I must own I dread the sight of a Messenger from England lest he should bring with him a Black box containing the full Powers, Black indeed to me & more terrible than Pandora's' (Honest Diplomat, 359).

Walpole served as secretary to the Treasury under Sir Robert Walpole from October 1715 to April 1717, and in 1717 was made surveyor and auditor-general of the revenue in America (for life), a valuable sinecure. The salary was £250 per annum, but the post was made to yield several thousands and was the subject of a charge against him in 1742 when his brother fell, and the impeachment of both men was agitated in parliament. From 1721 to 1730 Walpole was once again secretary to the Treasury under his brother, giving up the post only to become cofferer of the royal household from 1730. He exchanged this lucrative place in 1741 for a more modest one, a life sinecure as teller of the exchequer, at £3000 per annum. Walpole's avarice was a frequent subject of contemporary comment, linked to his mean hospitality and the slovenly dress on which he rather prided himself. Queen Caroline, if Lord Hervey is to be believed, found Walpole grating, 'his silly laugh hurting her ears, and his dirty sweaty body offending her nose' (Hervey, 3.732). His familiar style of writing offended her too. In 1734 Walpole apologized to his brother:

> I am extreamly sorry to find that the dress of my letters to the Q—n are not liked altho' the matter is approved, I solemnly protest to you, I doe not affect that free stile but I can no more write otherwise than I can tell how to dress my person better than I doe. (H. Walpole to R. Walpole, 9 Nov 1734, Osborn MS 48)

His manner among his equals may be gauged from a story told by his nephew:

> One Day, when the Speaker [Arthur Onslow] had voted in the Committee, against the Army, Horace Walpole … reproved Him for it: The Speaker said why really Mr. Walpole in some Things a Man must *Feel Himself*. Feel himself! replied Mr. W. I'll tell you a Story: a Gentleman married a Girl with Forty Thous^d Pds. The Morning after the Wedding night, in which He had given his Bride no Reason to think herself married, He said, well, my Dear, how do you *Feel Yourself*? Feel Myself! replied She: did my Father give you Forty Thousand Pound for me to *Feel myself*? (Walpole, 'Robert Walpole miscellany', 107)

Yet in parliament Walpole was a strong and effective speaker, his judgement of political affairs and personalities was shrewd, and, despite his strong Norfolk accent and lack of the usual graces and deportment of the aristocratic diplomatic world, he was able to recommend himself to a wide range of ministers both abroad and at home. The disparaging accounts of both Hervey and Horace Walpole jun., in fact, are tinged both by personal malice and by a repugnance against his reputedly plain and slatternly wife, to whom Walpole was devoted. Hervey waspishly characterized her as having 'a form scarce human, as offensive to the nose and the ears as to the eye, and one to whom he was kind not from any principle of gratitude, but from the bestiality of his inclination' (Hervey, 1.284). Horace Walpole jun. coldly referred to 'Horace and his Dirty Wife … a French Staymaker's Daughter, whom he used to call Pug, & who brought him a great Fortune, & saved him a greater' (Walpole, 'Robert Walpole miscellany', 131, 132). He married, late in life (on 21 July 1720, at the age of forty-two) but happily, Mary Magdalen (1694/5–1783), the daughter of Peter Lombard, of Burnham Thorpe, Norfolk, and they had four sons and three daughters. The eldest son, another Horatio (1723–1809), succeeded his father as second Baron Walpole on 5 February 1757 and later inherited the estates of his cousin Horace, fourth earl of Orford, the youngest son of Sir Robert, taking the title of Baron Walpole of Walpole on 2 March 1797 and that of earl of Orford on 10 April 1806.

Paris embassy and the treaty of Seville The foundations of this dynastic success were laid with the return to power of

Sir Robert Walpole and Townshend in 1720, when Horace was made a privy councillor (Ireland) and secretary to the lord lieutenant of Ireland (1720–21). From May to July 1722 he was again at The Hague, negotiating military aid during the crisis of the Atterbury Jacobite plot. He had the confidence of his brother-in-law Townshend and of his brother as an adroit diplomat, and it was for 'his usual dexterity' that they sent him rather irregularly to Paris in October 1723 (Coxe, 2.270). His task was to displace the ambassador there, Sir Luke Schaub, and undermine the policies of their rival Lord Carteret. At first, Carteret and Schaub believed that Walpole could be confined to the specific task of bringing Portugal into the Quadruple Alliance. He swiftly dispelled that illusion, and bluntly compelled Schaub to act with him, relying on the credit of 'the persons concerned (as to myselfe I mean to whom I belong)' to gain him recognition as the principal (Stanhope to Carteret, 15 Nov 1723, BL, Add. MS 4204, fol. 328; H. Walpole to Newcastle, 12 Nov 1723, BL, Add. MS 32686, fols. 378–82). Within a month of his arrival Walpole was congratulated by the duke of Newcastle on his grasp of French policy, though this was 'the foreign court, with which you have been less conversant than any other in Europe' (Newcastle to H. Walpole, 6 Nov 1723, BL, Add. MS 32686, fol. 403). He pursued the Townshend–Walpole policy until Schaub was recalled, after Carteret's fall, in May 1724. Walpole succeeded him as ambassador-extraordinary until August 1727, then as ambassador-extraordinary and plenipotentiary until September 1730. From the beginning of his embassy his official correspondence shows that he was vigilant in employing informants and using every means to detect and forestall Jacobite manoeuvres, bringing frequent commendations from George II. Vital to his success in his Paris mission was the fact that he cultivated excellent personal relations with André Hercule de Fleury, bishop of Fréjus, who in June 1726 became France's leading minister. Walpole called upon Fleury at Issy in December 1725, when it was generally believed that the bishop was in disgrace at court, a mark of respect and confidence which Fleury never forgot.

Walpole's strength as a diplomat lay in his robust grasp of what was possible for ministers 'in a popular government as ours is' (H. Walpole to Newcastle, 24 July 1728, BL, Add. MS 32757, fol. 147). He never lost sight of domestic political realities amid the complexities of European rivalries and plans. His combative loyalty and closeness to his brother made him a senior member of Sir Robert's ministry, regularly informed and consulted about policy issues even when he was abroad. From Paris or The Hague, Walpole laid before the inner circle of ministers his drafts and proposals and was supplied by Newcastle with copies of correspondence in and out of the secretary of state's office. He, Newcastle, Lord Hardwicke, and later Henry Pelham made up the core of the ministry at least in its last ten years, a group among whom discussion was open and confidence was extensive, if not always quite complete. Walpole was therefore more than simply an ambassador, and he took it upon himself in his regular correspondence to inform, question, and sometimes harangue other leading envoys. When other diplomats worked alongside him, as at the Congress of Soissons, when he was joined with Stephen Poyntz and William Stanhope, they were expected to take a subordinate place. Walpole's most substantial achievement in these years was to negotiate, with Poyntz, the treaty of mutual defence between Britain, France, and Spain, signed at Seville on 9 November 1729. The treaty of Seville was attacked in opposition writings as a slavish subservience to the Catholic Bourbon powers; it was popularly supposed to contain secret clauses which forced the ministry to tolerate Spanish depredations upon British shipping. Seville was a name which recurred regularly in ballads and newspapers, almost always as a reproach to the Walpole brothers. Horace himself always referred to the treaty with satisfaction, though almost as soon as it was published Sir Robert felt impelled anonymously to publish a pamphlet, *Observations upon the Treaty*, to explain and justify its clauses.

Parliamentarian When Townshend resigned in May 1730 Walpole declined the offer to succeed him as secretary of state and accepted the appointment of cofferer of the household, which brought him into regular contact with the king. He returned from Paris at the end of July to take up his post, and in November 1730 became an English privy councillor. From this time he acted as Sir Robert's deputy in party and Commons affairs, organizing support and sometimes sponsoring legislation, most notably the 1733 Molasses Act. In October 1733 he went on a special mission to The Hague to escort the prince of Orange to England for his marriage to the princess royal, and in April 1734 he returned there as ambassador, a post which he held (with a number of absences, in parliament or in Hanover) until the outbreak of war with Spain, returning to Britain permanently on 19 November 1739. His most sustained period of political activity in Westminster was over by 1734, and had not been an unmixed success. Hervey, with a characteristic combination of shrewdness and malice, dismissed him at this period as:

> a very good treaty dictionary, to which his brother often referred for facts … He loved business, had great application, and was indefatigable, but from having a most unclear head, no genius, no method, and a most inconclusive manner of reasoning, he was absolutely useless to his brother in every [other] capacity. (Hervey, 1.285)

He may have been verbose in parliamentary speaking, yet his surviving papers show Walpole to have been an indefatigable drafter of projects, memorials, and memoranda characterized by strong logic and remorseless chronological completeness. He propounded this as the only sure method for evaluating political developments and for avoiding misrepresentation and partisan argument. 'I speak this from no small experience … by the Method abovementioned, which I have used for some years past, I have been able to form a judgement which has seldom err'd in matters of the greatest importance' ('Note of facts relating to the expeditions for America', BL, Wolterton (Walpole) MSS). His were in fact valuable contributions to decision making behind the scenes, and he

was often called upon to lay out papers of this kind. The same talent was exercised publicly in several closely reasoned pamphlets defending the ministry. Two of them, *The Grand Question, whether War, or No War, with Spain* and *The Convention Vindicated from the Misrepresentations of the Enemies of our Peace*, were distributed to the extent of 11,000 copies each in 1739.

Walpole's oratory was not of the polished or witty kind which Hervey preferred, but his strengths could be considerable, as in the important debate of March 1739 on the convention with Spain, when he led for the government in a robust two-hour speech. As a colleague Walpole was stubborn once he had taken an emotional stand and was prone to fancy his advice ignored. Though not slow to criticize others, he was himself sensitive to slights. He was inclined, too, to overreach himself, a trait which eventually seems to have lost him favour at court. In March 1737 he initially supported a bill brought in by Sir John Barnard to reduce the interest of the national debt from 4 to 3 per cent. This seemingly uncontentious step would harm the fortunes of the moneyed men behind the government, as Barnard meant it to. Walpole and the king and queen therefore worked hard to defeat it. Walpole, according to Hervey, did not trouble to conceal that he was acting against his conscience in helping to sink Barnard's bill, and wearied the queen with his complaints:

> She told him, because he had some practice in treaties and was employed in foreign affairs, that he began to think he understood everything better than anybody else; and that it was really quite new his setting himself up to understand the revenue, money-matters, and the House of Commons better than his brother. 'What are you', said the Queen, 'without your brother? Or what are you all but a rope of sand that would crumble away in little grains one after another, if it was not for him?' (Hervey, 3.732)

From 1738 onwards, and with increasing persistence from 1740, Walpole pressed for an alliance with Prussia, though he knew it ran counter to the king's 'little, low, partial, electoral notions' (Coxe, 3.535–7). This stand hastened the cooling of George II's affection for him, as he noted in his private manuscript 'Apology for the life of Mr. Walpole' (BL, Add. MS 9132). When Sir Robert resigned in February 1742, both brothers were threatened with impeachment, and Horace's notorious covetousness seems to have rankled as much in opponents' minds as Sir Robert's greater power but much freer spending. Walpole went home to Wolterton (his house designed by Thomas Ripley in the mid-1720s) and burnt large quantities of his personal papers to prevent their seizure by the secret committee set up to investigate Sir Robert. In 1743 he had a warm argument in the house, when the opposition member William Richard Chetwynd, a friend of Bolingbroke, told him that both the brothers deserved to be hanged. The two men stepped outside into Pipe's Ground and fought a duel, in which Chetwynd was wounded and Walpole was saved only by his opponent's sword striking a button. Arrested by Speaker Onslow to put an end to the affair, Walpole was pleased with his exploit: 'he thought it was a great and hard thing to fight a duel, because young fellows used to make such ado about it, but he says there is nothing at all in it now, he finds' (Francis, Lord Hastings, to earl of Huntington, 15 March 1743, *Hastings MSS*, 3.38).

Final years Walpole remained active in parliament, and defended the decision by his brother to take into government pay 16,000 Hanoverian troops, a measure extremely unpopular with the public. In early 1743 Lord Chesterfield's pamphlet *The Case of the Hanover Forces* drew loud support, and in April, Walpole produced a refutation of it, *The Interest of Great Britain Steadily Pursued*, which quickly went through three editions. Soon, however, he ceased to be part of the inner circle of leading politicians, though he remained an informed political commentator. In February 1746, on the eve of the notorious cabinet walkout which compelled George II to accept Pitt as a minister, Walpole urged the king in a letter to give way gracefully. In December 1747 he lobbied the duke of Cumberland, in person and by letter, to persuade the king to make an alliance with Prussia as the only means to a lasting peace.

Walpole continued to compile his analyses of international affairs, including 'A rhapsody of foreign politics', criticizing the 1748 peace of Aix-la-Chapelle. He actually presented to the king his 'Observations on the system of affairs in 1751', which gave tactlessly free rein to his own anti-Hanoverian views. In February 1752 he caused a roar of laughter in the Commons when he spoke against a subsidy to the elector of Saxony yet ended with a call to the 'old corps' of whigs to join him in voting for it (Walpole, *Corr.*, 20.299–300). In 1755, when Newcastle was first minister, Walpole was once again consulted, and characteristically read to the cabinet a paper urging against the king's going abroad. Such a span of influence justifies Coxe's summary:

> it would be difficult to point out another character, who, for so long a period, was more trusted with the secrets of government, more acquainted with the motives and springs of action, and possessed more influence in the direction of foreign and domestic affairs. (Coxe, xii)

His main concern at the end of his life, though, lay in securing the interests of his family. His eldest son, Horatio, had been married in May 1748 to Lady Rachel Cavendish, the third daughter of the duke of Devonshire, and with his friend Newcastle in power Walpole sought a hereditary peerage for his son's benefit. Meanwhile he persuaded Sir Robert's 26-year-old grandson, Lord Cholmondeley, to agree to a mutual entail of the Houghton and Wolterton estates in which the benefit lay on the Wolterton side. Though in the event not harmful to the family, the agreement, which only accidentally came to the attention of Sir Robert's surviving children, was bitterly opposed by Horace Walpole jun. and created serious bad feeling. On 1 June 1756 Walpole was created Baron Walpole of Wolterton. Soon afterwards he suffered a return of the stone, a complaint common in the family, and he died at Wolterton Hall on 5 February 1757.

PHILIP WOODFINE

Sources *Memoirs of Horatio, Lord Walpole*, ed. W. Coxe, 2 vols. (1802) · BL, Wolterton (Walpole) MSS · BL, Newcastle MSS, Add. MSS 32685–32865 · BL, Hardwicke MSS, Add. MSS 35586–35594 · CUL, Cholmondeley (Houghton) MSS · MSS of Sir Robert and Horace Walpole, BL, Add. MSS 63749–63750 · letters to Sir Robert Walpole, University of Chicago Library, MS 274 · H. Walpole jun., 'Robert Walpole miscellany', Yale U., Lewis Walpole Library, Walpole papers · Yale U., Beinecke L., Pelham papers, Osborn MS 48 · *An honest diplomat at The Hague: the private letters of Horatio Walpole, 1715–1716*, ed. J. J. Murray [1955] · Walpole, *Corr.* · John, Lord Hervey, *Some materials towards memoirs of the reign of King George II*, ed. R. Sedgwick, 3 vols. (1931) · D. B. Horn, ed., *British diplomatic representatives, 1689–1789*, CS, 3rd ser., 46 (1932) · R. R. Sedgwick, 'Walpole, Horace', HoP, *Commons, 1715–54* · GEC, *Peerage* · P. Woodfine, ed., 'Horace Walpole and British relations with Spain, 1738', *Camden miscellany, XXXII*, CS, 5th ser., 3 (1994), 289–328 · *Report on the manuscripts of the late Reginald Rawdon Hastings*, 4 vols., HMC, 78 (1928–47), vol. 3, p. 38

Archives BL, corresp. as secretary to second Viscount Townshend, Add. MSS 38500–38501 · BL, general corresp., Add. MS 63750 · BL, letters, political papers, speeches, Add. MSS 9131–9132 · BL, papers, deposit 9201 · BL, Wolterton (Walpole) MSS · Bodl. Oxf., corresp. as secretary to Lord Townshend · CUL, papers · Lincs. Arch., letter-book as secretary to lord-lieutenant of Ireland · Norfolk RO, estate and financial papers · Rt Hon. Lord Walpole of Wolterton, corresp. and papers · Yale U., Farmington, Lewis Walpole Library, letters | BL, letters to Lord Carteret, Add. MS 32738 · BL, corresp. with first and second earls of Hardwicke and C. Yorke, Add. MSS 35586–35635 · BL, letters to Lord Harrington, Add. MSS 32739–32801 · BL, corresp. with Benjamin Keene, Add. MSS 32751–32799, 43412, 43418–43422, *passim* · BL, corresp. with duke of Newcastle, Add. MSS 32685–32865 · BL, letters to Sir Thomas Robinson, Add. MSS 23780–23824 · BL, corresp. with Walter Titley, Egerton MSS 2683–2686 · BL, corresp. with second Viscount Townshend, Add. MSS 32739–32764, 37634, 38502–38504, 46856, 48981–48982, Egerton MS 3124 · BL, corresp. with Robert Walpole, Add. MS 63749A · BL, corresp. with Lord Whitworth, Add. MSS 37356–37397 · Bucks. RLSS, letters to R. Trevor · Chatsworth House, Derbyshire, letters to third and fourth dukes of Devonshire · CKS, letters to James Stanhope · CKS, letters to Robert Trevor · CUL, corresp. with Sir Robert Walpole · NA Scot., corresp. with Lord Polwarth · NRA, priv. coll., corresp. with first Earl Waldegrave · U. Cal., Berkeley, letters, mainly to Charles Holzendorf · U. Nott. L., letters, mainly to Henry Pelham · University of Chicago Library, letters from him and other members of the family to Sir Robert Walpole · Yale U., Farmington, Lewis Walpole Library, letters, mainly to Lord Harrington

Likenesses C. F. Zincke, enamel miniature, 1720–25, NPG · J. Richardson, oils, *c*.1722, Houghton Hall, Norfolk · J. B. van Loo, oils, *c*.1728, Yale U., Connecticut, Lewis Walpole Library · J. B. van Loo, oils, 1739, priv. coll. [*see illus.*] · D. Heins, oils, 1740, Blackfriars' Hall, Norwich · J. Simon, mezzotint, 1741 (after J. B. van Loo), BM, NPG · oils, 1747, St Mary's College, Twickenham · oils (after J. B. van Loo), Hardwick Hall, Derbyshire

Walpole, Horatio [Horace], **fourth earl of Orford (1717–1797)**, author, politician, and patron of the arts, was born on 24 September 1717 at his father's house in Arlington Street, Piccadilly, Westminster. The father was Robert *Walpole, first earl of Orford (1676–1745), already a leading whig politician and on his way to becoming Britain's longest-serving prime minister. Though not of noble lineage, the family was of long standing in Norfolk, with a squirearchical estate to match. Walpole's mother, Catherine, *née* Shorter (*d*. 1737), came of mercantile stock, and was the granddaughter of a lord mayor of London and the daughter of a dealer in the Baltic trade. The union of county and counting-house was appropriate for a whig dynasty in the making.

Horatio Walpole, fourth earl of Orford (1717–1797), by Sir
Joshua Reynolds, c.1756–7

Early years, 1717–1739 Horace, named after his father's
brother and close political associate 'Old Horace' [see Walpole, Horatio, first Baron Walpole of Wolterton], was the
late and last child of his parents' marriage. There is a story
that he was the product of a liaison between Catherine
Walpole and Carr, Lord Hervey, though no contemporary
evidence exists to substantiate it, let alone any suggestion
that Horace himself questioned his parentage. The innuendo originated with a recollection of Lady Louisa Stuart
in the 1830s, which apparently derived from her grandmother Lady Mary Wortley Montagu. Malice on either of
their parts might explain it. Lady Louisa remembered Walpole as 'my old ill-natured friend' (J. A. Home, ed., *Letters of
Lady Louisa Stuart to Miss Louisa Clinton*, 1901, 252).

The child was sickly and much cherished by his mother,
whose domestic life was narrowed by her husband's
absences with his mistress Maria Skerrett on his Norfolk
estate at Houghton and in his hunting-lodge in Richmond
Park. She dwelled mainly in Arlington Street, and during
the summer at the family villa in Chelsea, where much of
the young Horace's time was spent. Through his aunt
Dorothy Walpole the family was allied to another Norfolk
family, the Townshends of Rainham. Horace's early education was received among his Townshend cousins,
whose tutor was Edward Weston, son of the bishop of
Exeter.

In April 1727 the boy was sent to Eton College, his
father's school. There the rough and tumble of a boarding-
school apparently passed him by. Perhaps being the son of
the prime minister protected him. In any event, his own
experience contrasted with that of others at this time who

recalled their schooldays at Eton as being more bruising.
The mature Walpole's characteristic self-assurance was
already well developed during these years, owing something, no doubt, to his insulated, cosseted upbringing
under his mother's eye. He proved adept at forming protective affinities at school, mostly with boys of less
favoured families. Of these the most notable was the
so-called 'quadruple alliance', made up of Walpole,
Thomas Gray, Thomas Ashton, and Richard West. Walpole's three associates were all impecunious, all had literary inclinations, and all joined in their fashionable
friend's wistful musings and romantic evocations among
Etonian shades and springs.

Other friends were made during these years, some of
them long-lasting: Walpole's cousins Frances and Henry
Seymour Conway, George Selwyn, later MP and colourful
man about town, Charles Lyttelton, eventually bishop of
Carlisle, the genial and indolent George Montagu, and
William Cole, an enduring if unlikely friend as a tory clergyman and antiquarian.

Walpole left Eton in September 1734, and commenced
at King's College, Cambridge, in March 1735, Gray and
Ashton having preceded him by a few months. There he
proved a poor mathematician but seems to have done better at other subjects. Among senior members of the university he met Conyers Middleton, whose heterodox writings had made him notorious even in a time and place of
some theological latitude. It is often said that Walpole's
lifelong religious scepticism owed something to this connection. There is no evidence that he read widely enough
to ground it in his own studies.

The Cambridge years incidentally brought Walpole
somewhat closer to his father. In the summer of 1736 he
set foot in Sir Robert's palatial mansion recently completed at Houghton. Remarkably, this was Horace's first
encounter with his Norfolk roots. In August 1737 Lady
Walpole died, the severest personal loss that Horace had
suffered or would ever suffer. His father displayed little
emotion, and married his mistress Maria Skerrett soon
after. But within a year of the first wife's death, the second
died in childbirth, deeply afflicting Sir Robert and making
any attention bestowed by his youngest son all the more
welcome.

The young Walpole attained his majority in 1738, the
year in which he finally left Cambridge, after increasingly
erratic appearances there. A legal career had been talked
of, but his father saved him the trouble of acquiring a profession or finding a remunerated vocation. Three sinecure
revenue offices that he was granted at this time he held for
life: usher of the exchequer, comptroller of the pipe, and
clerk of the estreates.

For a young man of means and no duties the continental
tour beckoned. Walpole invited Gray to accompany him.
Despite its closeness, their friendship was ill-adapted to a
travelling companionship. Gray had no resources of his
own and could not but feel the inequality. Moreover, his
proneness to melancholy and propensity to criticize could
be hard to bear. On the other hand, Walpole's already
characteristic capacity to combine personal detachment

with emotional exploitation could inflict hurt. Later in life he generously recalled, 'We had not got to Calais before Gray was dissatisfied, for I was a boy, and he, though infinitely more a man, was not enough so to make allowances' (Walpole, *Corr.*, 28.114).

Grand tour, 1739–1741 Walpole and Gray left Dover at Easter 1739. Two months were spent in Paris, where they learned the first lesson of all grand tourists, that it was easier to pass time with other travellers than with the natives. Gray seems to have been the more adaptable, perhaps because he was more absorbed by what he observed than preoccupied with those he expected to meet. Even so, the variety of amusements and sights in Paris was such that neither could claim to be disappointed.

On retreating to Rheims to improve their French, Walpole and Gray found a quiet provincial city with little to detain them. They moved south in September, were charmed by the superior manners of Dijon and Lyons, and exhilarated by a foray into the Alps which included a visit to the Grande Chartreuse. 'We stayed there two hours, rode back through this charming picture, wished for a painter, wished to be poets!' Walpole reported to West (Walpole, *Corr.*, 13.182).

After Lyons they expected to winter in the south of France, but Walpole's father encouraged them to move on to Italy, perhaps with a view to the worsening diplomatic climate. The travellers accordingly pressed on, enduring a disagreeable crossing of the Alps, pausing briefly in Turin (where they met one of Walpole's Etonian contacts, the earl of Lincoln), and making for Florence, where they arrived shortly before Christmas 1739. As elsewhere on their journeying, Gray relished the exposure to the legacies of Rome and the Renaissance more than his companion did. Walpole threw himself into the social life of Florence.

It might not have been so if Walpole had not had an ideal master of ceremonies. The British minister to the court of Tuscany, Horace Mann, was doubtless polite to the son of the prime minister, but at the age of thirty-eight might not have expected to strike up a close friendship with his young charges. Yet the three became genuinely close friends. In due course Mann was to be prominent in that *tableau vivant* of personal correspondents that Walpole constructed around himself when he returned to Britain. No less significant was his meeting with John Chute, a younger son who unexpectedly succeeded to the family estate at The Vyne in Hampshire, and was in due course to bring his artistic ability and interest in classical design to his new friend's aid.

From February to July 1740 Gray and Walpole were in Rome, to observe the eternal city in the throes of a papal election. This proved less engrossing than expected, though Walpole dutifully inspected classical sites, collected medals, and observed the activities of James Stuart (the Pretender) and his court, at a time when Jacobite hopes had been raised by the gathering clouds of a great European war. After tiring of Rome (in Walpole's case if not Gray's) the travellers returned to the routine they had established in Florence. Their friendship did not survive the tour. They left Florence together but parted company at Reggio in May 1741. The precise cause is obscure. Attempts to repair the breach, aided from a distance by Mann, failed and Gray made his own way home, assisted by clandestine grants from Walpole so that the source of the funds remained unknown. By then Walpole himself had come close to death at Reggio. He went down with a severe 'quinsy' which would have gone uncured but for the arrival of Lincoln and his tutor Joseph Spence, and the medical intervention they arranged. Walpole accompanied Lincoln's party to Venice, and thence via Genoa, Antibes (by sea), and Paris, arriving in London on 14 September 1741.

The emotional significance of the tour in Walpole's life has been much discussed, and not only in relation to Gray. Before Italy, Walpole had expressed a passing tenderness for his cousin Anne Conway. At Florence, in tune with local manners, he became *cicisbeo* to the wife of the Marchese Grifoni, Elisabetta Capponi. If he ever slept with any woman, it was the Grifoni. Walpole was to have a number of close but ambiguous relationships with women. Not only did he tend to avoid genuine commitment; he left considerable pain in his wake when he retreated. This was certainly the case with the Grifoni, who wept for him long after he had pretended to spare a thought for her. Even so, their relationship must have affected his understanding of his own feelings. Visiting aristocrats were accustomed to take advantage of the sexual permissiveness of Italian society. If Walpole did not avail himself of the opportunity, he was a less than typical English tourist.

Some men had the power to hurt Walpole as women perhaps did not. Anne Conway's brother Henry Conway was one such, perhaps because he was a tangible link with his own mother (Conway's mother was her sister). Conway had been one of Walpole's circle after Eton, and was in France with him in 1740. Another young man whose Italian paths crossed Walpole's was the red-blooded young Lord Lincoln.

There is a temptation to suppose that men of more evident masculinity than Walpole figured in his sexual aspirations and perhaps activities. It has even been suggested that the whole of his purpose during his tour had been to engineer recurrent assignations with Lincoln as his lover (Mowl, chaps. 3–4). This theory requires much deception on behalf of a number of parties, not only Walpole but also Lincoln himself and his tutor Joseph Spence. It leaves unexplained why Walpole did not always linger where Lincoln was, for example in Turin in 1740. Above all it turns his sexual ambivalence, which must remain a matter for speculation, into a consummated passion for one highly heterosexual young man whose conduct did not suggest anything like a corresponding commitment. In these matters it is easy to be misled by Walpole's epistolary language, which was sometimes extravagant but not beyond the conventions of the day among the *jeunesse dorée*. Still less exceptional was the sexual banter common among aristocratic young men, especially those educated at public school.

Walpolian politics, 1741–1755 Walpole's return brought him close once more to his father. The two shared homes in Downing Street, Arlington Street, and the great mansion at Houghton. Horace spent three successive summers at Houghton, revelling in the grandeur that the scion of a family of squires had conjured into stone and plaster. He also tried out his analytical skills as a connoisseur on the collection of old masters that his father had assembled. In 1742 he composed a *Sermon on Painting* that was preached by his father's chaplain. A year later he completed his *Aedes Walpolianae*, a methodically constructed catalogue preceded by some extravagant and often dismissive judgements. It was later privately printed in 1747 and reissued in a revised edition in 1752.

In addition to making himself familiar with the contents of Houghton, Walpole seems to have enacted a passable imitation of a country gentleman, with expeditions to neighbouring establishments including, somewhat further afield, his uncle's home at Wolterton, and hare coursing in the country around. These last sojourns with his father brought him close to the manes Walpoliani and provided vivid memories to the end of his life. But he remained a town dweller whose rural retreats were never too far from St James's Square and carefully constructed to his own design.

In another of his father's ruling passions, politics, Horace did more than dabble. Even while making his way back to Britain in the summer of 1741 he had been elected MP for Callington in Cornwall. The seat was effectively owned by the Rolle family, into which his eldest brother had married, and though the new legislator sat for it until 1754, he never needed to pay his constituents a visit. Walpole's first session witnessed the last, tumultuous phase of his father's ministerial career, fought with characteristic tenacity against opponents who after many years of unavailing pursuit now smelled blood. Horace shared the strain of this struggle and helped provide solace when the premier retreated to Arlington Street. He also took pride in the latter's dignified retirement to the Lords, the continuing credit he enjoyed at court, and, especially after his death in 1745, a gathering public reaction in favour of a man whom his successors soon made it easy to recall with respect. These were turbulent years which witnessed growing discontent with the Hanoverian foreign policy of the new ministry, and in due course a revival of the Jacobite threat and the rising of 1745. Of all these things the son was a fascinated observer and astute narrator.

As a participant, Walpole was no more than moderately active. He appears to have spoken only once during his first two parliamentary sessions, on 23 March 1742, against a motion for a secret committee of inquiry into his father's administration. He spoke again on 18 January 1744 for government, seconding a motion on the employment of Hanoverian troops. It included a courtly Latin compliment on the valour of George II at Dettingen, and attracted 'deserved applause from everybody' (HoP, *Commons, 1715–54*, 2.511). But this was a set piece which he would have had ample time to prepare. The cut and thrust

of daily debate required qualities which he did not possess. He lacked the presence, the voice, and the combative instinct that made for success in the eighteenth-century House of Commons. Its roughness, familiarity, and practical business-mindedness were all rather alien to him.

Walpole's politics were shaped by what he took to be the opinions of his father and those of his father's followers who had not been implicated in his downfall in 1742. The leader of these was Henry Fox, around whom there congregated a group of young whigs that included several on close social as well as political terms with Horace: George Selwyn, George James ('Gilly') Williams, Sir Charles Hanbury Williams, Richard Edgcumbe, and Richard Rigby. Between 1742 and 1746 struggles at court established Henry Pelham and his brother the duke of Newcastle in power and quelled those who had opposed the Walpole regime in the 1730s and briefly triumphed in 1742. Pelham was the obvious heir to Sir Robert Walpole, but the whigs closest to Horace showed signs of restlessness under Pelhamite rule. They believed that Newcastle had treacherously intrigued against their leader in 1742. They also found Henry Pelham's cultivation of the moderate tories objectionable. Walpole fully shared these convictions.

On his re-election to parliament in 1747 Walpole was still considered a friend of government. In reality he secretly supported the new opposition launched by Frederick, prince of Wales. He wrote a number of anonymous articles for the press. Two of these, masquerading as 'speeches' delivered in the Commons, arose from a political dispute in Buckinghamshire, where the Grenville family sought to disable their principal opponent in the county, Lord Chief Justice Willes, by seeking an act of parliament moving the assizes and with them much political power from Aylesbury to the Grenville stronghold at Buckingham. Walpole seems to have been moved solely by sympathy with Willes on account of the latter's long-standing friendship with Sir Robert Walpole. One unfortunate result was an unseemly altercation with his father's old friend the speaker, Arthur Onslow, for which Walpole was compelled to apologize.

A further excursion into print found Walpole attacking the Pelhams more directly, though again without revealing his identity. *Delenda est Oxonia*, defending Oxford against ministerial plans to remove the university's independence of the crown, was intercepted at the printer's before publication. This clandestine warfare did not prevent the author also wooing the Pelhams. On several occasions between 1751 and 1758 he sought to improve his income from the sinecure places that he and his brother enjoyed, all in vain. Throughout this period he was nominally a supporter in government. Yet his secret intrigues did not cease and included, in December 1752, an easily discredited depiction of the arrangements made for the education of the future George III as part of a plot to restore the Stuart government. In the pattern of politics that he had settled into on his father's death it is hard to see anything more than inherited prejudices and personal interest, combined with a tendency to mischievous intrigue.

Home and friends, 1745–1760 Walpole's inheritance from his father was the lease of the town house in Arlington Street, cash to the value of £5000, and revenues of approximately £1400 from the collectorship of the customs held by his brother Edward. These sums were additional to the sinecures that he held in his own right. His overall income from public sources was not less than £3000 per annum and was to increase over the years through no effort of his own. He never thought these perquisites incompatible with self-consciously high-minded whiggism, even fancied republicanism.

During the summer of 1746 Walpole found a congenial substitute for his escapes to Houghton in a small house at Windsor, close enough to the metropolis to ensure that the *longueurs* of rural life were never more than half a day's ride from town. In the following spring a more permanent solution was found when he bought the leasehold of a somewhat unpromising house in Twickenham with 5 acres of Thameside scenery. In due course the leasehold became freehold and the 5 acres became 14.

Strawberry Hill gave its name to a whole genre of Gothic revival that has had a variable press since Walpole's 'committee of taste' transformed it into a 'little Gothic castle' (Walpole, *Corr.*, 20.111). The committee comprised, in addition to Walpole himself, his antiquarian friend John Chute and the dilettante Richard Bentley, son of Thomas, the classical scholar and master of Trinity College, Cambridge. Bentley was valued by Walpole not only because, as he observed, 'his drawings and architecture are admirable', but also because he 'to all the ornament of learning has the amiable turn of mind, disposition and wit' (ibid., 16.25). He proved an at times irritating colleague, but his creativity was critical to the realization of Walpole's vision. Between 1750 and 1753, when Bentley withdrew to Jersey to protect himself from his creditors, the appearance of the house at Twickenham was transformed, though much of the early work was superficial rather than structural. Battlements and arched windows altered the appearance without radically affecting the overall layout. The one major exception at this stage was the newly designed staircase and hall, the latter monastically 'decked with long saints in lean arched windows and with taper columns, which we call the Paraclete, in memory of Eloisa's cloister' (ibid., 20.372).

Thereafter, in 1754 new rooms were added, the refectory or great parlour, and Strawberry Hill's most remarkable chamber, its library. It was begun by Bentley (who supplied Walpole with a deputy, the German painter John Henry Müntz), but completed by Walpole and Chute, and triumphantly finished with bookcases and a chimney-piece derived from medieval tombs in the original St Paul's, Westminster Abbey, and Canterbury Cathedral. Walpole's pride in his ancestry was displayed in a variety of details in the house, but nowhere so exuberantly as in the library, where the ceiling displayed the arms of the families with which he was allied.

Strawberry Hill bears no resemblance to Houghton, but it was to Horace what Houghton had been to Sir Robert, with due allowance for their respective resources. It complemented an urban lifestyle, providing an outlet for energies that could not be released in town, and above all created a satisfying picture of the way Walpole wished to be perceived by others. In their different ways both Houghton and Strawberry Hill were daring and imaginative projects, designed to leave a permanent public monument to their owners.

This is not to say that Walpole lost his attachment to Houghton. In 1751, when his brother the second earl of Orford died, he did his best to engineer a marriage between the heir, his nephew George, and an heiress acquainted with his friend Chute, Margaret Nicoll. The plan was complicated by the intervention of Walpole's uncle 'Old Horace', who thought the match more appropriate for one of his own sons, and wrecked altogether when George himself rebelled on account of an unfavourable report of Miss Nicoll's looks and temper. The Horaces quarrelled bitterly and irretrievably, and the third earl of Orford retreated into a life of increasing eccentricity and, eventually, evident insanity.

Walpole's personal relationships gradually settled into a pattern during the years that followed his father's death. In November 1745 a lasting reconciliation with Gray took place, for reasons which remain obscure. West had died in June 1742. With Ashton, who plainly viewed their connection as a means of personal advancement, relations grew cooler until Horace irrevocably parted company in 1750. Some of the young politicians with whom he consorted became close associates as his 'out-of-town party' at Twickenham in the 1750s: Selwyn, Williams, and Edgcumbe.

As for women, the Grifoni was consigned to oblivion. There were hints in some verse that Walpole wrote in 1746—'The Beauties'—of another female attachment, Elizabeth Evelyn. It must have been at most a passing affectation of sexual ambition. Four years later she married into the Bathurst family. On the other hand, Walpole gradually acquired a reputation as a collector of ladies whose friendship nobody could mistake for sexual attraction, though with them he was prone to employ a gently ironic language of gallantry that became highly characteristic. In some cases he appreciated them as living memoirs for the historian of recent times. Lady Suffolk, at Marble Hill, had been the mistress of George II and somewhat ineffectual opponent of Sir Robert Walpole and Queen Caroline. Lady Hervey, once, as Molly Leppell, the toast of St James's and now widow of Robert Walpole's confidant Lord Hervey, was herself another repository of anecdote about an era that fascinated Walpole. Others were women of influence and wit in the high society of the day: such were Etheldreda, Lady Townshend, and Anne Pitt, sister of William Pitt the elder.

Other exhibits in Walpole's feminine gallery were less likely, among them Kitty Clive, the actress he encountered as a neighbour in Twickenham and installed in a small house near Strawberry Hill. Her infectious gaiety and direct manner made her a surprising social asset as well as an engaging neighbour. Another incongruous friend was Lady Mary Coke, relict of an unconsummated marriage, and ridiculed for her pursuit of the royal duke of York. With her Walpole adopted a flirtatious manner that made some suspect that he was smitten with her. A further female connection that was to strengthen over the years and continue until Walpole's death was Anne Liddell, successively duchess of Grafton and, after her divorce in 1769, countess of Upper Ossory. Almost all of these women not only helped people his private correspondence but themselves became correspondents of his at one time or another.

The rhythm of Walpole's life was predictable as well as agreeable: winters in town, summers for the most part at Strawberry Hill, each with its own cast of players, sometimes overlapping. By the mid-1750s the range of his activities provided him with all that suited him and made an admirable substitute for the political career to which he might once have aspired. Aside from the gout that began to afflict him in the mid-1750s there was little to disrupt his chosen mode of life. In these years at least, its centre of human interest was in Arlington Street. 'My jaunts to town will prevent my news from being quite provincial and marvellous', he had written to Mann during his Windsor sojourn in 1746 and the pattern was the same once he had acquired Strawberry Hill (Walpole, *Corr.*, 19.298). Balls and masquerades, opera and theatre, Ranelagh and Vauxhall, dinners, galas and routs, weddings and funerals, all appear with a vividness that could only come from the pen of an ironic spectator who also an enthusiastic participant. Anecdotes of 'politesse anglaise' abound, recording 'excellent vulgarisms', 'terrible disgrazie', and a vast diversity of social contretemps, all with malice enough to lend spice to the story but without sourness or more than a trace of detached superiority.

Historian, author, and publisher, 1746–1764 Walpole saw himself as the historian of his own times, though he insisted in characteristically self-deprecating fashion that what he wrote were 'casual memoirs' for use by 'my superiors the historians of Britain' (Walpole, *George II*, xxxi). The letters to Mann, addressed to one who had been 'absent long enough to read of your own country as history' provided the obvious foundations for his work (Walpole, *Corr.*, 21.403). Walpole later stated that he had begun his history in 1751 and certainly what is known to posterity as *Memoirs of the Last Ten Years of the Reign of George II* commenced in that year, but he had first asked Mann to return his letters in September 1748. Earlier still Gray was aware of a plan to compose 'Mémoires', assuring Walpole that 'posterity will ever be glad to know the absurdity of their ancestors' (ibid., 14.9, 13). A draft of this earlier attempt is extant, though unpublished.

Mann, who could be expected to take an interest in the doings of politicians but not necessarily in other matters, was not the only recipient of materials for the memoirs. George Montagu was regaled with London's social life, a role that was eventually taken over by the countess of Upper Ossory. Each was familiar with the class whose doings Walpole described but somewhat removed from immediate knowledge of them, the first because he rarely came to town, the second as a divorcee excluded from high society. Most of Walpole's major correspondents occupied a specialist niche in his personal gallery that provided a living and retrievable repository for his opinions, researches, and activities. Literary matters were discussed with Gray, and after his death, with William Mason. William Cole, whom Walpole had known at Eton, came to perform the same function for antiquarian topics. This pigeonholing of his friends and almost clinical replacing of them as they died or disappeared from his ken was essential to his personal project. As a contemporary historian, Walpole treated his own letters as his sourcebooks.

Walpole also engaged with the earlier history of his country. His grand tour did not give him a lasting interest in classical antiquity or indeed the Renaissance, notwithstanding the interest in high art that his father's collection had helped inculcate. By 1752 he could write, 'I have done with virtu, and deal only with the Goths and Vandals' (Walpole, *Corr.*, 9.144). His patriotic instincts combined with the accessibility of the English past to lead him into the architectural highways and byways of medieval culture. (Its literary inheritance he was less learned in, with unfortunate results when he encountered Thomas Chatterton.) Initially, with Chute he conducted 'Gothic pilgrimages' that brought much information and insight. For one source he acquired a particular veneration. In Oxford he found 'what remains of the true Gothic *un-Gibbs'd*' and delighted in 'the profusion of painted glass' (ibid., 35.155). This is not to say that he venerated the residents. As he later told Lady Upper Ossory, his regard was for 'the buildings, not the wretched oafs that inhabit it' (ibid., 33.483).

Of his social connections Walpole took maximum advantage. His 'Journals of country seats', not published until the twentieth century, provide a meticulous record of his visits, which combined congenial company with close inspection of buildings and monuments. From not a few he came away with ornaments to decorate his own home. His spoliation of stained glass was unashamed and not excused by the fact that it took the form of authorized gifts or unauthorized sales. On the other hand he strongly opposed the destruction that occurred sometimes when 'a spirit of restoration and decoration has taken place', as when Wyatt's work on Salisbury Cathedral resulted in the demolition of its Beauchamp and Hungerford chapels (Walpole, *Corr.*, 42.259).

In due course this antiquarian investment proved productive. In the meantime there were literary activities of various kinds. In 1748 some of Walpole's poems had been published in Dodsley's *Collection of Poems*. Two years later, having inadvertently permitted Gray's *Elegy in a Country Churchyard* to be pirated from a manuscript version that he had circulated among his friends, he undertook to see the authorized version through the press. He then persuaded Gray to allow publication of his remaining poems in an edition illustrated by Bentley. Managing the temperaments of author and illustrator was no small task, but in

March 1753 the elegant, rococo result was *Designs by Mr. R. Bentley, for Six Poems by Mr. T. Gray*.

At the same time Walpole began publishing on his own account in a new essay periodical, *The World*, contributing a small number of well-regarded papers on diverse cultural and contemporary themes. Not the least interesting to posterity is an ironic essay on old women as satisfactory objects for love. More explicitly drawing on personal experience was his piece on the politeness of highwaymen, resulting from a brush in November 1749 with the celebrated James Maclaine (Maclean). In June 1757 his literary ambitions impelled Walpole in a new direction with the establishment of a printing press at Strawberry Hill. The first production was of two odes from Gray's hand. Neither the publicity that attended its launch nor the critical reception of *The Progress of Poesy* and *The Bard* pleased the hypersensitive Gray. Other volumes soon followed: an account of England in 1598 by the German Paul Hentzner, and in April 1758 Walpole's own *A Catalogue of the Royal and Noble Authors of England, with Lists of their Works*, a work which displayed the characteristic strengths and weaknesses of his brand of amateur antiquarianism. The latter brought some discomfiture. His scholarly errors were discussed in public and private, and his markedly whig bias gave much offence.

The productions of the press included some notable coups. One was the first printing of *The Life of Edward Lord Herbert of Cherbury, Written by Himself* in 1764, achieved only after some persuasion had been required to convince its owner, Lord Powis, that his ancestor's exploits could be revealed without exposing the family to ridicule. Much else was to follow over the years, including a number of Walpole's own writings. *Fugitive Pieces in Verse and Prose*, dedicated to Conway, had appeared in 1758. By this time he was working on his *Anecdotes of Painting in England*: two volumes appeared in 1762 and a third, together with his *Catalogue of Engravers* in 1764. It had something in common with his *Royal and Noble Authors*, offering list and commentary in accessible and amusing dress. But it was to live longer, mainly because it was based on materials which Walpole had purchased from the widow of the engraver George Vertue in 1758. He had known Vertue himself since 1743 and perhaps owed something of his evolving interest in English portraiture to his knowledgeable encouragement. The 'forty volumes of his MS. Collection relating to English painters, sculptors, gravers, and architects' amply justified Walpole's claim that they contained 'an infinite quantity of new and curious things'. Later in life he described the *Anecdotes* as 'the only thing I ever published of any use' (Walpole, *Corr.*, 33.574).

Gothic extravagances, 1750–1768 Further work on Strawberry Hill had to take account of some personal awkwardnesses. Müntz was dismissed in 1759, having annoyed his employer by his 'airs and insolence' (Walpole, *Corr.*, 9.260) and his seduction of one of the maids. More distressing still, there came a breach with Bentley in 1761, ascribed partly to Bentley's unbusinesslike habits, partly to Mrs Bentley's presumptuous manners. On the credit side, Walpole gained a new assistant in the shape of the elder Pitt's

nephew Thomas Pitt, a new resident of Twickenham. There were major new projects in hand for Strawberry Hill which were to double the size of the house. His Holbein chamber, decorated with tracings of Holbeins in the Royal Collection, was finished in 1759. More ambitiously, there rose up a cloister with gallery above, the latter constituting Walpole's *chef d'œuvre*, a careful execution of variations on a perpendicular Gothic theme combined with sumptuous gold and crimson furnishings, and filled with the owner's most prized possessions. Later came the Round Tower, overlooking the road to Hampton, and a chapel or cabinet intended emphatically for the display of secular treasures rather than devotional purposes. These additions were largely complete by 1763.

Soon after, Walpole published (though not from his own press) *The Castle of Otranto: a Story*, advertised as the translation, by one 'William Marshal, Gent', of an Italian work discovered in the library of an old Roman Catholic family in the north of England. Considering its contents this disguise was understandable, though in the event the reception was so favourable that within six months of publication he was issuing a second edition in which his authorship was revealed.

Otranto, set in medieval Naples, in an imaginary castle of whose actual existence Walpole was unaware until long after publication, was a wholly unbelievable tale, but its atmospheric power easily made up for its thin characterization. Impressive theatrical effects included a gigantic heavenly helmet with magical powers, a bleeding statue, a sword that could only be borne by fifty men, an anchorite whose flesh had melted away to leave only an animated skeleton, and a portrait that strode out of its frame. The fascination with the fantastic was the same that created Strawberry Hill, but unrestrained by the requirements of bricks and mortar. It caught a tide of interest in exotic evocations of ancient and medieval cultures. Later Walpole observed, more self-deprecatingly than was necessary:

> It was fit for nothing but the age in which it was written, an age in which much was known; that required only to be amused, nor cared whether its amusements were conformable to truth and the models of good sense; that could not be spoiled; was in no danger of being too credulous; and rather wanted to be brought back to imagination, than to be led astray by it. (Walpole, *Corr.*, 31.221)

Medievalism had a firm grip on Walpole by this time. Three years after *Otranto* he published his *Historic Doubts on the Life and Reign of King Richard the Third*, another work not initially printed at Strawberry Hill. It enjoyed considerable success, re-igniting public interest in the ancient controversy surrounding the murder of the princes in the Tower. Walpole was an uncompromising Ricardian. There were several ripostes, the most damaging from Jeremiah Milles, the president of the Society of Antiquaries, who demolished the principal documentary evidence. Though Walpole did not reply in print, this hurt was sufficient for him to resign his membership of the society in due course.

While composing the *Historic Doubts*, Walpole was also working on a blank verse drama entitled *The Mysterious*

Mother. It was published at Strawberry Hill in a limited edition of fifty copies in 1768. The feeling of his friends was that, however well it might be done, it had better not have been done at all. The story, set in pre-Reformation Narbonne, was of the unintentional double incest of a young man who had been seduced by his mother masquerading as a servant and eventually married her daughter by him. What it revealed about Walpole's personal insecurities may be debated. It certainly allowed him to trail his anti-Romish prejudices by giving a repulsive friar the responsibility for malevolently arranging the marriage.

Politics, 1757–1765 The passion that sustained *Otranto*, the *Historic Doubts*, and *Mysterious Mother* perhaps had its origin in the emotional turmoil that Walpole experienced at this time. This grand climacteric was the result of a personal commitment to a political cause far beyond any that he had made before or was to make again. Since the mid-1750s Walpole had been adrift of his political moorings. It was inevitable that a man whose sole political principle was adherence to the memory, measures, and friends of his father would in time find the last of these increasingly difficult to comprehend. Clandestine opposition to Newcastle and Pelham had been justified on the grounds that both had supposedly helped to bring Sir Robert down. But when followers of his father cast their lot definitively with the Pelhams, as Fox did in 1755, it was less easy to reconcile past principles and present practice. Walpole's response was characteristically ambivalent. On the one hand he made it clear to Fox how deeply he resented his conduct. On the other he published in *The World* in 1757 a 'character' of Fox written some years before that was almost embarrassingly eulogistic. At the same time he turned increasingly to Henry Seymour Conway, who developed a political as well as military career when in 1754 he became chief secretary to the lord lieutenant of Ireland, conventionally a stepping-stone to a higher office.

Walpole himself took a step of some consequence when in 1757 the electors of King's Lynn, once represented by Sir Robert, more recently by 'Old Horace' and his son, sought his candidature. King's Lynn, with its still thriving trade and turbulent politics, was very different from Callington, which he represented from 1741 to 1754, and Castle Rising, another close borough for which he sat between 1754 and 1757. With some trepidation he accepted the call, presented himself in the constituency (a novel experience for him), and remained member without controversy until his retirement from parliament in 1768. He left a memorable account of his part in popular elections in a letter to Montagu about his 'new vocation':

> Think of me, the subject of a mob, who was scarce ever
> before in a mob! Addressing them in the town-hall, riding at
> the head of two thousand people through such a town as
> Lynn, dining with above two hundred of them amid
> bumpers, huzzas, songs and tobacco, and finishing with
> country dances at a ball and six-penny whisk! (Walpole,
> *Corr.*, 9.350)

Walpole's brief absence from the Commons, after his resignation of Castle Rising and before his re-election for King's Lynn, coincided with the loss of Minorca and what looked like the judicial murder of Admiral Byng as the scapegoat. Walpole became incensed by the case, helped postpone the final outcome, and deplored Byng's execution when it took place. His fury was unleashed in an icily ironic little tract, *A Letter from Xo Ho, a Chinese Philosopher at London, at his Friend Lien Chi, at Peking*, exposing the absurdity of a political system that condemned an admiral for decisions made by his political masters. The episode completed his disenchantment with Fox, who had been one of the most active of Byng's detractors.

The Seven Years' War brought Conway's military career once more to the fore, initially with unfortunate results as second in command of the disastrous Rochefort expedition of 1757. Eventually he more than regained his reputation with the British forces in Germany, watched from afar by Walpole with anxious admiration. At home Walpole admired Pitt, continued to detest Newcastle, and observed the accession of George III in 1760 and the elevation of his favourite Lord Bute, like a 'satisfied spectator', as he later admitted (Walpole, *George III*, 1.167). One of the instruments of the new regime was Henry Fox, whose irritation with his old friend culminated in the spiteful gesture of slowing down the payments due to Walpole for his exchequer office. Insult was added to injury when Bute awarded the reversion of the office to a supporter who had acted as Fox's agent in the transaction.

Bute's successor, George Grenville, was a whig of conventional mould who quickly ruined himself in Walpole's eyes by prosecuting John Wilkes for an alleged libel on the king through the use of a 'general warrant', considered by many whigs an arbitrary and potentially tyrannical procedure. By this time Conway was again pursuing his peacetime career as a loyal supporter of government, but rebelled at the persecution of Wilkes, voting repeatedly against the use of general warrants. The response of the ministry was firm. Conway was dismissed from both the command of his regiment and his place as groom of the bedchamber.

Walpole's behaviour at this time startled both friends and enemies. He blamed himself for Conway's downfall, and laboured frantically to have him and his friends restored to office. When the ministry commissioned a defence of its actions in the form of William Guthrie's *Address to the Public on the Late Dismissal of a General Officer*, Walpole replied with a *Counter Address* that in turn provoked a riposte, the *Reply to the Counter Address*. In it Guthrie resorted to brutal tactics, fastening on his antagonist's supposed effeminacy, likening him to a 'hermaphrodite horse' and attributing his animus to the 'unsuccessful passion during the course of twenty years' that he had nourished for Conway. To Conway, Walpole reacted robustly:

> They have nothing better to say than that I am in love with
> you, have been so these twenty years, and am no giant. I am a
> very constant old swain: they might have made the years
> above thirty; it is so long I have had the same unalterable
> friendship for you, independent of being near relations and
> bred up together. (Walpole, *Corr.*, 38.437)

The political crisis of 1764–5 was resolved by a palace

revolution that had nothing to do with Wilkes and general warrants. The upshot, however, was favourable to the whigs, displacing Grenville and putting in his place the old Newcastle party, led by Lord Rockingham and featuring Conway as secretary of state and leader of the House of Commons. This should have been the moment of triumph, but for Walpole it apparently became one of the most profound humiliation. No reward for his own activities was offered by the new government, nor any arrangement that might prevent any further political meddling with his official salary. The ingratitude on Conway's part appalled him. Privately he retreated into stoical resignation. 'His temper hurt me, but I forgave his virtue, of which I am confident, and know it was superior to my own' (Walpole, *George III*, 2.152). Publicly he announced his intention to recoup his health by spending a winter in Paris. Unfortunately Conway made matters worse by treating his withdrawal as desertion. Walpole fled.

Deffand and Chatterton, 1765–1777 In Paris, Walpole needed no tutoring to play the role of eccentric islander in a Francophile mode that would to his own countrymen have not seemed very English at all. He relished a reception that made him something of a celebrity, though there were features of life in Paris that disturbed him. A sceptic himself, he was none the less a little shocked by the irreligion that he found, and more irritated by the tedium of fashionable philosophical discourse. A city that welcomed not only Walpole but also David Hume, who was secretary to the embassy there, could not be considered an unalloyed blessing. He detested Hume's *History*, 'so falsified in many points, so partial in as many, so very unequal in its parts'. Of his conversation he was dismissive: 'he understood nothing till he had written upon it.' And as philosopher Hume was a 'superficial mountebank' (Walpole, *Corr.*, 10.176; 16.266; 42.78).

Hume's employer as British ambassador was Walpole's own cousin and Conway's brother Lord Hertford. If Walpole's relations with Hume were at best polite, it is unlikely that he intended actively to humiliate him. That, however, was what he proceeded to do. In the winter of 1765–6 a principal topic of conversation in Paris was the behaviour of Jean-Jacques Rousseau, who had left Switzerland after acrimonious public disputes, believed himself to be the victim of an elaborate conspiracy, and sought congenial refuge, which Hume intended to provide by taking him to Britain. In the midst of these transactions Walpole penned a letter from Frederick II to Rousseau inviting him to take shelter in Prussia. The letter satirized Rousseau's paranoia (not the most difficult of targets), made a considerable stir in Paris, and provoked a furious reaction from the latter, who came to suspect that Hume himself had been party to it. It was an extreme example of the unintended havoc that Walpole's mischief-making could cause, and one which Hume showed magnanimity in dismissing as 'a piece of levity'. His remark about its author—'it is a strange inclination we have to be wits, preferably to every thing else'—might provide a devastating commentary on much else in Walpole's life and character (E. C. Mossner, *The Life of David Hume*, 1954, 514).

Life in Paris absorbed Walpole to the full, but increasingly his interest came to focus on the outmoded but once powerful salon of Madame du Deffand, 'a blind old lady of wit', as he described her in his journal (Walpole, *Corr.*, 7.261). She initially acted as a kind of French Lady Suffolk, a repository of knowledge about a period fast disappearing from living memory. From her standpoint Walpole was a charming newcomer who took as much trouble to fascinate her as if she had been forty years younger. Thus began a relationship increasingly charged with emotion and, not for the first or last time, on his side highly ambiguous in its commitment.

All the evidence is that during these months Walpole confided in Madame du Deffand as much as she confided in him. When he left he can have been in no doubt of the extent to which she had become dependent on him, uncomfortable though it increasingly made him feel. One night out of Paris, on the road to Calais, he wrote in terms which can only be recovered from her reply. In it she reassured him that their correspondence would be kept secret, expressed her joy at what he had said of his feelings for her, declared 'I want to be at my ease and to say that it is impossible to love more tenderly than I love you', and urged him not to alter his relationship with her. 'Remember that you are my tutor, my director; do not abandon my education' (Craveri, 273–4). Once out of her presence, the intensity of this attachment caused him as much embarrassment as pleasure, though he never severed it.

The correspondence that began at this time eventually involved more than 800 exchanges over fourteen years. It is one of the most famous in the history of letter-writing and has provided much evidence for the prosecution when Walpole is charged with cynicism and duplicity. 'She loves me better than all France', he told Conway in 1774 (Walpole, *Corr.*, 39.189), but his apparently frequent pleas for her not to speak of love, his horror of ridicule concerning their relationship, and his promises to return to France repeatedly broken, all appear to condemn him with his own words. Remarkably, she bore this bizarre form of devotion, agreeing to be 'amis sans amitié'. She was a woman of the world, had been once the mistress of the regent of France, and enjoyed the regard of countless men of rank or wit or both. But twenty years older than Walpole and bereft of her sight, with time heavy on her hand, she considered him the lodestar of her existence.

Walpole journeyed again to see her in 1767, 1769, 1771, and 1775, on each occasion apparently restoring the relationship to something of the intensity that it had originally generated. He wrote to Lady Ailesbury in 1775, 'I have found my dear old woman so well, and looking so much better than she did four years ago, that I am transported with pleasure' (Walpole, *Corr.*, 39.255). Yet each time he left, the old reserve reasserted itself. These years coincided with worsening health for him, which genuinely rendered travel more uncomfortable and even threatened his life; at least, so Madame du Deffand feared. It was she who died first, none the less, in August 1780. She left him her papers, a gold box bearing a portrait in wax of her last little dog, Tonton, together with Tonton himself, whom he cherished for many years and even permitted 'to lie on every couch and chair' (ibid., 11.51).

Walpole's apparent heartlessness toward Madame du Deffand was a hostage to fortune that he entrusted to posterity by preserving her letters to him while destroying his own to her. But another supposed instance of it was brought to a contemporary public. In March 1769 he received from the young, and at that time unknown, Thomas Chatterton a copy of selections from the manuscript remains of one Thomas Rowley, who had supposedly in 1469 described the rise of painting in England and composed poems of which Chatterton provided examples. Walpole unwarily responded by asking for further examples and offering to publish specimens. Chatterton duly obliged and requested his new patron's support in obtaining employment. By this time Walpole had grown suspicious and sought independent information about his correspondent and advice from Mason and Gray about the manuscripts, with the predictable result. There followed an exchange in which he disengaged himself 'with as much kindness and tenderness as if I had been his guardian' (*Works*, 4.223). In April 1770 Chatterton made his way to London and engaged in various satirical activities that included attacks on Walpole's antiquarian researches under the pen of Baron Otranto. Walpole was probably unaware at this time that their author was Chatterton. Nor, when Chatterton committed suicide in August 1770, did he hear of it until the following April.

In subsequent years interest in Chatterton grew. In 1777, after the publication of the Rowley poems, the allegation that Walpole had driven their author to self-murder gained currency. Restless though he was under mounting attacks, Walpole did not issue a fully public rebuttal until 1782. It made little difference. The Chatterton smear, which had no origin in truth other than his initial gullibility, was to do his reputation enduring harm.

Politics, 1766–1790 One of the mainsprings of Walpole's existence had long been politics, even if his pleasure in it must have been largely vicarious, since he never showed a serious interest in obtaining public office himself. In his own words he lacked 'the least tincture of ambition' but possessed 'a propensity to faction' (Walpole, *George II*, xxix). His disillusionment with Henry Seymour Conway and his decision to retire from parliament in 1768 effectively shut down this aspect of his self-constructed identity, more conclusively perhaps than he himself anticipated. He did not discontinue his memoirs of the reign of George III, which he had commenced in 1766, and what were later to be known as his 'last journals' took the story on eventually to 1783. But it was the story increasingly of an outsider.

Walpole attended only occasionally to hear the debates of either house, recognized that the newspapers were beginning to provide accounts as accurate as anything he could offer, and in time came to feel remote from the politicians of the day. By 1785 he could confess to Mann, apropos of the leading satires of the day, 'as there are continually allusions to parliamentary speeches and events, they are often obscure to me till I get them explained; and besides, I do not know several of the satirized heroes even by sight' (Walpole, *Corr.*, 25.612).

Walpole's own last political tract was published after the Stamp Act crisis in 1766, two years before he resigned his seat. The *Account of the Giants Lately Discovered* ironically suggested that reports of a newly found race of giants in South America would soon be followed by a parliamentary attempt to tax them. He consistently opposed the measures that led to war with America as well as the war itself, and derived no consolation from the accuracy of his prophecies on the subject. 'My English or selfish pride is mortified at seeing the decadence of our empire' he wrote when American independence was conceded by treaty in 1783 (Walpole, *Corr.*, 33.420).

Despite his irritation with Conway, relations were repaired, though not restored to their earlier warmth, and Walpole's political sentiments remained those of whigs like him. Accordingly he was a moderate reformer at best. When economical reform threatened his sinecures in 1783, he gracefully promised the prime minister, Lord Shelburne, his co-operation, an undertaking carrying little risk since abolition without compensation was not proposed and Shelburne had political troubles that soon overwhelmed his reforming ambitions. Of parliamentary reform Walpole disapproved, characteristically offering a disarmingly casual argument. Fashion ruled all, he remarked:

> I carry this way of thinking still farther, and extend it to almost all reformations. Could one cure the world of being foolish, it were something—but to cure it of any one folly, is only making room for some other, which one is sure will succeed to the vacant place. (Walpole, *Corr.*, 25.642)

Walpole's sympathies in the 1780s remained with the Foxite whigs who inherited the Rockingham mantle and continued to command the allegiance of Conway. Of Pitt and his supporters, especially those whigs who threw in their lot with him in 1784, he was contemptuous. He quarrelled with a friend and correspondent of some years' standing, William Mason, in the process drawing up a concise statement of his political credo at this time:

> I have for five and forty years acted upon the principles of the constitution as it was settled at the Revolution, the best form of government that I know of in the world, and which made us a free people, a rich people, and a victorious people, by diffusing liberty, protecting property and encouraging commerce; and by the combination of all, empowering us to resist the ambition of the House of Bourbon, and to place ourselves on a level with that formidable neighbour. The narrow plan of royalty, which had so often preferred the aggrandizement of the Crown to the dignity of presiding over a great and puissant free kingdom, threw away one predominant source of our potency by aspiring to enslave America—and would now compensate for that blunder and its consequence by assuming a despotic tone at home. It has found a tool in the light and juvenile son of the great minister who carried our glory to its highest pitch—but it shall never have the insignificant approbation of an old and worn out son of another minister, who though less brilliant, maintained this country in the enjoyment of the twenty happiest years that England ever enjoyed. (Walpole, *Corr.*, 25.351)

Many new developments of the period found Walpole equally unsympathetic. The fashionable tolerance that was improving the lot of Catholics awoke misgivings, and not only because of the plebeian outrage and violence that it unleashed in the Gordon riots of 1780s. The horror of 'popery' as a political force never forsook him: 'You know I have ever been averse to toleration of an intolerant religion', he told Mann in 1784. The Irish reforming movement that inspired many liberal whiggish sympathizers left him cold, principally on this account. He warned of the 'impossibility of satisfying *Irish* Catholics, without restoring their estates. It was particularly silly to revive the subject in this age, when Popery was so rapidly declining' (Walpole, *Corr.*, 25.541). The rise of a new empire in the East did not comfort him. During the proceedings to impeach Warren Hastings he quipped about either 'black-washing' or 'white-washing' Hastings but entertained no doubt that India had been 'blood-washed by our country-men!' (ibid., 25.630). When Cornwallis crushed the princi-pal obstacle to British supremacy in India, Tippoo Sahib, in 1792, he rejoiced without rapture 'for we have usurped India till it is become part of our vitals' (ibid., 34.146).

No very great analysis or thought went into these judge-ments. They were the instinctive reactions of one taught to fear those who had corrupted other societies and sought thereby to corrupt their own. Walpole approved Edward Gibbon's analysis of the decline of Rome. Even the explorations of the wider world that excited much contemporary opinion merely evoked his distaste for bar-baric cultures. The famous prints of South Sea faces in James Cook's *Voyage* he dismissed as:

> a parcel of ugly faces with blubber lips and flat noses, dressed as unbecomingly as if both sexes were ladies of the first fashion; and rows of savages with backgrounds of palm-trees. Indeed, I shall not give five guineas and half—nay, they sell already for nine, for such uncouth lubbers: nor do I desire to know how unpolished the north or south poles have remained ever since Adam and Eve were just such mortals.   (Walpole, *Corr.*, 33.436)

Such insensitivity did not imply an absence of concern for the undertrodden. Walpole opposed slavery and the slave trade long before that became a fashionable humanitarian cause of the 1770s. He did so on robustly whiggish grounds. It is doubtful whether he ever thought in terms of what were coming to be called 'natural rights'. The cult of nature of the 1760s had never impressed him, though as in other matters the contradictions in his think-ing would require more pains to reconcile than he ever showed signs of taking. When, in 1780, he added a fourth volume to his *Anecdotes of Painting*, covering the reigns of the first two Hanoverian kings, he also included a neat lit-tle *Essay on Modern Gardening*, trumpeting the triumphs of English landscape gardening as pioneered by Kent and developed by Brown. His friend the former French ambas-sador the duc de Nivernais provided an elegant transla-tion of the *Essay*, which was printed at the Strawberry Hill press. Walpole's extravagant dismissal of the 'unnatural' French taste in gardening does not seem to have inhibited its success across the channel.

On the other hand, Walpole struck a modest literary blow at naturalism when he briefly figured as a dramatist on the London stage. In 1772 he had written his *Hieroglyphic Tales*, written with a child as reader in mind and later pub-lished in 1785. The fantastic incongruity of these little fairy stories was followed up with a 'moral entertainment' that he wrote in 1773, entitled *Nature will Prevail*. It was staged by George Colman in 1778 with some success. Its moral was that in a state of nature on a desert island human nature does indeed revert to ill will and unkind-ness.

If the French Revolution had a simple creed, it was that of natural rights. But the revolution appalled Walpole. He was never a Francophobe but he had always disliked the doctrinaire atheism of the professedly enlightened. His own scepticism perfectly reflected the modish theology that prevailed at court during his father's day. 'I have a real affection for Bishop Hoadley: he stands with me in lieu of what are called *the Fathers*' (Walpole, *Corr.*, 16.282–3). By the time he wrote this, in 1785, there were other forms of fashionable latitudinarianism that he might have cited, but he took care not to read anything that might have served such a purpose. Whatever he learned from his interest in the middle ages, it had nothing to do with the spiritual belief that had underpinned so much of the Gothic legacy. He relished the story of Henry V's diversion of funds from a hospital for war victims to Archbishop Chichele's foundation of All Souls College, Oxford. 'How history makes one shudder and laugh by turns!' (ibid., 35.387). The evangelical revival passed him by, except as matter for mockery. Among his more spectacu-larly faulty prophecies was that of the decline of Method-ism after the deaths of John Wesley and Lady Huntingdon in 1791 (ibid., 11.297).

In all this it was taste rather than very deep thought that guided Walpole. The manner of the French *philosophes* and indeed many others seems to have offended him more than what they said. To Lady Upper Ossory, who had ven-tured to praise Beaumarchais, he denounced 'the dictator-ial pertness of the modern French authors' with a passion which must have disconcerted her by its brutality (Wal-pole, *Corr.*, 33.543). For one of Walpole's temperament and prejudices the revolution was the supreme example of the French capacity to apply a frivolous mind to serious matters. He would not have denied his own supposedly English readiness to apply serious thought to frivolous matters. That is not to say that he did not take seriously the war of ideas that the revolution unleashed. He admired Edmund Burke's *Reflections on the Revolution*, and in terms that might have surprised some. 'Every page shows how sincerely he is in earnest—a wondrous merit in a political pamphlet—All other party writers *act* zeal for the public, but it never seems to flow from the heart' (ibid., 34.98). He even endorsed Burke's controversial purple passage in praise of Marie Antoinette, recalling the occasion when he himself had first set eyes on her and instantly worshipped at the same shrine.

Family and friends, 1768–1790 A younger son not expected to sustain the fortunes of his house by marriage or an active career, Walpole never lost his attachment to his family and viewed with mounting if somewhat fatalistic dismay its descent into ruin. For his beloved Houghton and its contents the prospects were bleak indeed. His father had died in debt. The second earl's fortunes were sustained by state sinecures which lapsed on his death. The third earl brought nothing but gross mismanagement and extravagance to the task of preserving his patrimony. By 1773 both the estate and his senses were in such disorder that his uncle intervened to set about restoring the former. It proved a short respite. Despite promises to reform, the third earl's folly continued. In 1779 he took the catastrophic step that his nephew had dreaded most, selling the Houghton picture collection to Catherine II of Russia. 'It is the most signal mortification to my idolatry for my father's memory, that it could receive', he wrote to Lady Upper Ossory. 'It is stripping the temple of his glory and of his affection. A madman excited by rascals has burnt his Ephesus. I must never cast a thought toward Norfolk more—nor will hear my nephew's name if I can avoid it' (Walpole, *Corr.*, 32.86).

Walpole's brother Sir Edward died in 1784, taking with him their mutually beneficial share of the collectorship of the customs. One of his natural daughters, Maria, to whom her uncle was particularly attached, married the much older Lord Waldegrave, whose politics were congenial. Waldegrave died only four years after the marriage, in 1763. To Walpole's embarrassment Maria became involved with one of the king's brothers, the duke of Gloucester, and contracted a secret marriage with him in 1766. When the marriage was revealed to the king in 1771, the couple and all who attended them were excluded from court, a challenge which Walpole eagerly confronted by publicly visiting the duke and duchess at the first available opportunity. Though the relationship had been cemented against his wishes, henceforward the Waldegrave family became in effect his own adopted family.

Walpole's own legacy, at Strawberry Hill, continued to be his main preoccupation. Work on it had not ceased when the major extensions of the 1760s were complete. There followed two large bedchambers, the 'Great North' and the 'State', a new tower designed by the architect James Essex, and the Beauclerk Tower, named after illustrations of *The Mysterious Mother* drawn by Lady Diana Beauclerk. A chapel was added in the garden mainly to house some of his ever expanding collection of painting, monuments, relics, and curios. His own catalogue of the collection was printed in 1774 as *Description of Strawberry Hill*; a revised edition appeared ten years later. By this time the house, close to London and in a charming locality, was well placed to attract the tourist as well as its owner's personal friends. The bizarre diversity of the contents added to the impact. Walpole never pretended that his was other than a highly idiosyncratic collection, and items such as Wolsey's red hat and Henry VIII's clock with obscene pendulum certainly provided confirmation. The first royal visit had been that of the duke of Cumberland in 1754; the last was that of Queen Charlotte with eight princesses in 1795. For less privileged visitors there was a carefully arranged set of rules governing the issue of tickets and orderly behaviour.

Walpole's circle of friends contracted during the decade following his disillusionment with Conway. Lady Suffolk died in 1767, Lady Hervey in 1768. A little later, in 1771, he lost Gray. More mysteriously, one of his earliest friends and correspondents, the country squire George Montagu, broke with him in 1770, but the most grievous deprivation was that of Chute, in 1776. 'My loss is most irreparable. To me he was the most faithful and secure of friends, and a delightful companion.' He added, most revealingly, 'I shall not seek to replace him' (Walpole, *Corr.*, 24.212).

All through his life, on the stage that he created for himself, Walpole had manipulated the other players, not always with complete success. But as the casualties mounted replacement became increasingly difficult. Cole, with whom his relations had remained so consistent and warm, despite their divergent politics, died in 1782. In 1785 he lost his nearest neighbour, Kitty Clive, and in 1786 his most distant, Horace Mann, on whom he had not set eyes since 1741 but with whom he had corresponded regularly and fully during the intervening forty-five years. There were new contacts and correspondents indeed, but not all of a calibre to match those they might be thought to replace. A partial exception was the antiquary John Pinkerton, though Walpole cannot have been unaware of his self-serving nature. Pinkerton was later to publish his recollections of the master in *Walpoliana*.

Increasingly Walpole recognized his own isolation. To Conway he wrote in June 1784: 'I am very well content to be a Strulbrug, and to *exist* after I have done *being*' (Walpole, *Corr.*, 39.415). To Mann, soon after, he added, 'I do worse than live out of the world, for I live with the old women of my neighbourbood' (ibid., 25.542). Women certainly predominated. Lady Diana Beauclerk, like Lady Upper Ossory, a divorcée whom Walpole cultivated both before and after her fall from social grace, became a frequent companion when she moved to Twickenham following her second husband's death in 1780. For Conway's daughter, married briefly and unhappily to John Damer, who took his own life to release himself from debt, Walpole had an enduring affection. Lady Diana was a draughtswoman, Anne Damer a sculptress. Of the talents of each Walpole was an unreserved admirer. Other women who figured among his acquaintance had to work harder to earn his approval. Hannah More took his teasing about her religious views ('My dear Saint Hannah') in good part and displayed her poetic more than her puritanical side, thereby permitting to flourish what might have been a somewhat fraught relationship.

Last years, 1790–1797 Among the women in Walpole's life, two sisters, 'two pearls that I found in my path' came to be his close friends (Walpole, *Corr.*, 34.26). The Misses Berry, Mary and Agnes, became neighbours of Walpole's in Twickenham when their impecunious father rented a house there in 1788. 'My two StrawBerries' (ibid.) were in their mid-twenties, had polite manners without the affectation of fashionable society, and were delighted, not merely dutiful, listeners. Some of the anecdotes that he deployed they published in his *Reminiscences, Written in 1788, for the Amusement of Miss Mary and Miss Agnes Berry*. Many of these he had originally received from that earlier neighbour in Twickenham, Lady Suffolk.

Now in his seventies, Walpole at last needed company more than it needed him. He also found himself dropping the emotional guard which had so long kept him free of attachments that he could not control for his own purposes. For Mary especially he acquired a particular affection. His letters pursued the sisters when they toured England with their father in 1789 and again when they resorted to the continent in 1790. The dangers they were courting in France increased his fury with the revolution. 'It remained for the enlightened eighteenth century to baffle language and invent horrors that can be found in no vocabulary', he wrote to Lady Upper Ossory after the execution of Louis XVI (Walpole, *Corr.*, 34.177). The resulting anxiety and agitation made his letters to his 'dear, dear wives' unlike any others, perhaps, that he ever composed (ibid., 11.326). Their return in November 1791 was a huge relief, not least because he settled them in Little Strawberry Hill, or Cliveden, the house formerly occupied by Kitty Clive.

For the remaining years of his life the Berrys and Mrs Damer were Walpole's principal props, though they cannot be said to have led a serene existence. Mary Berry was in love with a military friend of Conway, General Charles O'Hara, a passion interrupted by his spells abroad and terminated when she plucked up courage to leave her father and Walpole in order to marry him, only to quarrel with her fiancé before they married. Mrs Damer also took an interest in Mary Berry that was not without a sexual tinge. Walpole seems to have succeeded in ignoring this emotional turbulence. From his own hand, at least, there is no suggestion that he entertained the notion of marrying Mary himself, though his evident affection for her certainly led others to speculate, if only concerning any designs she might have on his fortune.

By this time Walpole was fourth earl of Orford, following the death of his nephew in December 1791. His inheritance was bleak indeed. The estate was heavily encumbered with debt. Houghton had been despoiled not only of its pictures but also of much else that the third earl had alienated. The new peer never appeared in the House of Lords. With the keenest sense of Sir Robert Walpole's grandeur and glory he had inherited only the ruins of the former and had no prospect of passing on the latter.

The deaths of the 1790s removed Walpole's oldest and closest connections: Selwyn in 1791, Lincoln in 1794, Conway in 1795. Berkeley Square (which had replaced Arlington Street in 1778, when its lease was about to fall in) in winter, Strawberry Hill in summer, and a contracting circle in each provided his final scenes. His health was not good. To his gout was added recurrent rheumatism. The end came after an illness first brought on by a cold spell at Strawberry Hill in November 1796. Removal to Berkeley Square did not mend matters and he died there on 2 March 1797. He was buried in Houghton church in the family tomb on 13 March.

The legacy In default of male heirs Houghton went to the Cholmondely family through Sir Robert's daughter Mary. It has remained there ever since. Strawberry Hill was destined for the Waldegraves, though Anne Damer was granted possession for life, a right which she ceded in 1811. The seventh earl, who succeeded to the title in 1835, demolished portions of the house and auctioned off its treasurers in 1842: the sale lasted thirty-two days and realized over £33,000. But his widow, Frances, gave it a new lease of life during her two subsequent marriages, to George Harcourt MP and Lord Carlingford. Some of the dispersed collections were restored and the house partly rebuilt. As a leading hostess she again made Strawberry Hill a place of social and political resort. After her death the house passed to Baron Stern and later into institutional hands. Having survived a German bomb in 1941, it remains remarkably well preserved to this day.

In 1784 Walpole had explicitly condemned 'all publication of private letters in which living persons are named', claiming to have postponed publication of the fourth volume of his *Anecdotes of Painters* on this account (Walpole, *Corr.*, 42.121). During his last years he was engaged on editing his correspondence with Mann, and the first letters from his own collection appeared soon after his death in 1798, as part of the five-volume edition of his *Works*, superintended by Mary Berry. During the following decades further instalments were issued, beginning with that of Madame du Deffand, in 1810. Few private correspondences would have withstood the resulting glare, but Walpole's moral ambiguity and malicious irony were particularly ill-calculated to appeal to a public audience. The attack from which his reputation was not to recover for almost a century was made by Macaulay when he reviewed the early letters to Mann, published with Waldegrave's support by the Conservative politician Lord Dover in 1833. Macaulay boasted that finishing his article on Walpole was 'one of the happy moments of my life: … I think that this article will be a hit. … I have laid it on Walpole so unsparingly that I shall not be surprised if Miss Berry should cut me' (Dover to Hannah Macaulay, G. O. Macaulay, ed., *The Life and Letters of Lord Macaulay*, 1886, 239). The most damaging charge was Walpole's supposedly phenomenal duplicity and hypocrisy: 'mask upon mask'.

It would be wrong, however, wholly to blame either Macaulay or the letters for the rapid decline of Walpole's reputation. The *Memoirs*, which are very different in tone and temper as well as literary structure and style, were not much better received. Although unquestionably written with posterity in mind, their publication had been delayed by Walpole himself. He left instructions drawing attention to 'a large wainscot chest marked on the outside with a great A' which was to remain securely locked until an Earl Waldegrave attained the age of thirty-five. In due course in 1810 the sixth earl, expecting 'silver, gold or precious jewels', opened the chest to find the manuscripts of Walpole's memoirs. On Lord Holland's advice the volumes covering the reign of George II were published in 1822, almost unexpurgated. Holland made no progress with the later memoirs of the reign of George III, which were entrusted to Sir Denis Le Marchant and published in 1845. The *Last Journals* appeared later, in 1859, edited by Alban Doran.

To many the *Memoirs* confirmed the impression left by the *Letters*. The belletrist Anne Grant of Laggan was shocked by a 'Pandora's box' that poured

> forth its pernicious and very malicious contents upon the devoted heads of the sons and successors of all the great characters, whose talents and whose virtues shed lustre over names that will be honoured and revered, while that of Horace lives with the French wits and philosophers of the last century, to show, like them, how worthless are wit and talents, when perverted to be the implements of mischief to mankind. (J. P. Grant, ed., *Memoir and Correspondence of Mrs. Grant of Laggan*, 3 vols., 1844, 2.325)

The politician and reviewer John Croker, who believed Walpole 'to have been as bad a man as ever lived', devoted his critical talents to 'exposing his errors and defeating his personal malevolence' (L. J. Jennings, ed., *The Croker Papers: the Correspondence and Diaries of the Late Right Honourable John Wilson Croker*, 2nd edn, 3 vols., 1885, 1.270–71). Even approving readers tended to be less than enthusiastic. The whig wit Joseph Jekyll compared the *Memoirs* to 'cold meat on the side table' (A. Bourke, ed., *Correspondence of Mr. Joseph Jekyll with his Sister-in-Law, Lady Gertrude Sloane Stanley, 1818–1838*, 1894, 134). The *Memoirs* were widely read and plundered, providing a crucial source for the history of the eighteenth century, yet the author's reputation benefited little.

It did not help Walpole's posthumous standing that he had carried to the grave personal manners that seemed to embody the least appealing features of eighteenth-century social life. The waspish wit and man about town of the 1740s was portrayed in the 1780s and 1790s by men and women whose verdict, even when well meant, damned him with subsequent audiences. James Boswell (no impartial judge considering Walpole's dislike of Samuel Johnson) called him 'genteel, fastidious, priggish' (I. S. Lustig and F. A. Pottle, eds., *Boswell: the English Experiment, 1785–1789*, 1986, 217). His physical appearance and demeanour tended to confirm the impression. He was slight and slender, reinforcing the effeminate manner that a less than strong voice, a somewhat mincing gait, and an affected mode of address conveyed. In later life the animation that all associated with him was lessened by his bowed frame and constricted movement, though to the end observers found his eyes strikingly bright. In his own generation there was nothing about his personal appearance that was not acceptable and agreeable, but changing models of masculinity tended to emphasize a more muscular, more robust, more reserved and less precious pattern of manly conduct, making him seem anachronistic and eccentric.

Walpole was never completely swamped by Victorian disapproval, and the revival of interest in the literary legacy of the eighteenth century at the end of the nineteenth promised something of a reassessment. Austin Dobson's contribution to the *Dictionary of National Biography* reflected this less grudging recognition of Walpole's talents. At the same time his manners and morals were coming to

seem less problematic especially to a generation in the early twentieth century that found Victorian high-mindedness and solemnity increasingly oppressive or even ridiculous. On the other hand, one of his securer achievements, the generally accurate information and clear, if often biased, interpretations of the *Memoirs*, came under some severe criticism from a new school of historians. The Namier assault on whig interpretations of eighteenth-century politics fastened on sources that supported the depiction of George III as a tyrannical opponent of the constitutional balance achieved in 1688. After Edmund Burke, Walpole offered the most telling testimony and suffered accordingly.

Even so, Walpole fared better with the twentieth century than the nineteenth. Partly this was a matter of changing intellectual fashions. Modern art history is less judgemental than it once was and his role in the Gothic revival attracts more tolerant scholarship than it formerly did. Similarly his literary and antiquarian works have gained from locating them in their cultural context rather than rating them for their canonical status. His political views are no longer central to historiographical warfare; his adherence to a mild version of whig republicanism looks less like gross hypocrisy than sentimental, if self-indulgent, antiquarianism and a logical part of the past that he constructed around himself. But above all the wealth of material that has now been published about him permits a more rounded and wholly humane picture than any selection could.

That this is so is largely due to one man, Wilmarth Sheldon Lewis (1897–1979). Lewis was a Yale scholar who in his early twenties developed an entirely amiable obsession with Walpole and his work. With the keen support of his wife he set about collecting whatever was purchasable that had to do with Walpole, his works, or his possessions. He also engaged on a massive edition of Walpole's correspondence, which ran to forty-eight volumes, published between 1937 and 1983. At Farmington, Connecticut, a large proportion of Walpole's library has been reassembled to sit alongside a considerable number of the furnishings, portraits, and curiosities once at Strawberry Hill. Evidence of Lewis's own fixation abounds, not without self-parody worthy of his subject. A commemoration in oils to mark the scholar's seventy-third birthday depicts birthday cake, champagne, and a volume entitled *Fifty Years of Lewis*, 'by Walpole'. The history of this remarkable act of reconstruction will itself provide a fertile field of inquiry.

Though his scholarship was immaculate, Lewis's own writings are not voluminous. He left no canonical biography nor any extended body of critical work on the subject, unless it be his charming collection of essays, *Rescuing Horace Walpole*, which provides the historical context for certain items at Farmington based on his fantasy of a divine injunction to select twenty-six objects of the many thousands that he had amassed, and an elegant collection of Mellon lectures delivered in 1960.

Towards the end of his life Lewis was evidently well aware that his lifelong mission would provoke debate. For himself he remarked that he had grown to like Walpole 'more and more as a person'. He also recorded his judgement that Walpole was to be placed third after Franklin and Jefferson among those English-speaking men who were 'most like the versatile men of the Renaissance' (Lewis, *Selected Letters of Horace Walpole*, 1973, xix). However others judge these matters, the legacy of Horace Walpole is now the legacy of Walpole and Lewis.

PAUL LANGFORD

Sources *The works of Horatio Walpole, earl of Orford*, 5 vols. (1798) · Walpole, *Corr.* · H. Walpole, *Memoirs of King George II*, ed. J. Brooke, 3 vols. (1985) · H. Walpole, *Memoirs of the reign of King George III*, ed. D. Jarrett, 4 vols. (2000) · *The last journals of Horace Walpole*, ed. Dr Doran, rev. A. F. Steuart, 2 vols. (1910) · *Reminiscences written by Mr. Horace Walpole in 1788*, ed. P. Toynbee (1924) · L. E. Troide, ed., *Horace Walpole's miscellany, 1786–1795* (1978) · H. Walpole, 'Horace Walpole's journals of visits to country seats', *Walpole Society*, 16 (1927–8), 9–80 · R. W. Ketton-Cremer, *Horace Walpole: a biography*, 3rd edn (1964) · W. S. Lewis, *Horace Walpole: the A. W. Mellon lectures in the fine arts, 1960* · W. S. Lewis, *Rescuing Horace Walpole* (1978) · W. S. Lewis, *Horace Walpole's library* (1958) · B. Fothergill, *The Strawberry Hill set: Horace Walpole and his circle* (1983) · W. H. Smith, ed., *Horace Walpole: writer, politician, and connoisseur* (1967) · P. Sabor, *Horace Walpole: a reference guide* (1984) · A. T. Hazen, *A bibliography of Horace Walpole* (1948) · I. W. Urban Chase, *Horace Walpole: gardenist* (1943) · R. A. Barrell, *Horace Walpole (1717–1797) and France* (1991) · T. Mowl, *Horace Walpole: the great outsider* (1996) · A. F. de Koven, *Horace Walpole and Madame du Deffand, an eighteenth-century friendship* (1929) · B. Craveri, *Madame du Deffand and her world* (1994) · G. H. Heggarty, 'Walpoliana', *Eighteenth-Century Studies*, 34 (2001), 227–49

Archives BL, corresp., literary MSS, and papers, Add. MSS 5810–5874, 5952–5953, 9828, 23078, 23098, 23218–23219, 23234, 28800, 32559–32563, 32569, 34523, 37728, 47568, 47593; King's MS 305 · BL, printed works with MS notes and additions · Bodl. Oxf., letters · Chetham's Library, Manchester, Strawberry Hill accounts, expenditure on furnishings, etc. · CUL, papers · Hunt. L., letters; miscellanea · King's School, Canterbury, heavily annotated copies of Colley Cibber's *Life* and Lord Hardwicke's *Walpoliana* · priv. coll., corresp., journal, memoirs of George II–III, etc. · U. Nott. L., letters · V&A NAL, letters · Yale U., Farmington, Lewis Walpole Library | BL, letters to Edward Gibbon, Add. MS 34886 · BL, corresp. with Lord Holland, Add. MS 51404 · BL, corresp. with G. Montagu, Add. MSS 70987–70989 · BL, letters to Lady Suffolk, Add. MS 22626 · Bodl. Oxf., corresp. with notes on portraits by Mme du Deffand · FM Cam., letters to Thomas Walpole · Lpool RO, corresp. with William Roscoe · Morgan L., letters to the Berry sisters · NA Scot., letters to Lady Mary Coke · Newport Central Library, letters to Sir C. H. Williams · V&A NAL, letters to George Montagu · Yale U., Farmington, Lewis Walpole Library, corresp. with Sir Horace Mann

Likenesses J. Richardson, c.1735, Chewton Mendip, Somerset · R. Carriera, pastel drawing, 1741, Houghton Hall, Norfolk · J. G. Eccardt, oils, 1754, NPG · J. Reynolds, oils, c.1756–1757, Art Gallery of Toronto, Canada; version, Ragley Hall, Warwickshire · J. Reynolds, oils, c.1756–1757, NPG [*see illus.*] · D. P. Pariset, stipple, 1768 (after P. Falconet), BM, NPG · three sketches, 1788, Hunt. L. · G. Dance, pencil drawing, 1793, NPG · T. Lawrence, pencil drawing, 1795, NPG · S. W. Reynolds, mezzotint, pubd 1820 (after J. Reynolds), BM, NPG · Dean, stipple and line engraving, pubd 1834 (after miniature by C. F. Zincke, 1745), NPG · W. Greatbach, line engraving, pubd 1842 (after G. P. Harding), NPG · W. Greatbach, stipple and line engraving, pubd 1857 (after J. G. Eccardt), NPG · W. Greatbach, stipple and line engraving, pubd 1858 (after Muntz), NPG · T. Evans, stipple (after pencil drawing by T. Lawrence, 1795), BM, NG Ire. · J. Macardell, engraving (after J. Reynolds), BM · pen and wash drawing (after J. G. Eccardt), Hunt. L. · photogravure (after J. Reynolds), NPG

Walpole, Sir Hugh Seymour (1884–1941), novelist, was born on 13 March 1884 in Auckland, New Zealand, the first of the three children of English parents, the Revd George Henry Somerset Walpole (1854–1929), canon of St Mary's Cathedral, Auckland, and later bishop of Edinburgh, and his wife, Mildred Helen Barham (1854–1925), daughter of Charles Barham, physician, of Truro. There was a noted author on each side of the family: Horace *Walpole (1717–1797), novelist and letter writer, and Richard Harris *Barham (1788–1845), author of *The Ingoldsby Legends*. When the Revd Dr Walpole assumed the chair of systematic theology in the General Theological Seminary of New York city, the remainder of the family in 1889 moved from Auckland to the Barham household in Truro, Cornwall, where Hugh learned to read and write at the nearby high school for girls. The following year the family was reunited at 412 West 20th Street in New York. Hugh was schooled by a governess, but because his relationship with American children proved difficult he was sent to England in 1892 to the first of a series of boarding-schools: Newham House in Truro, followed by Marlow in Buckinghamshire, and in 1896 King's School, Canterbury. In 1898 Walpole's father became principal at Bede College in Durham, at which time Hugh left Canterbury to become a day boy at Bede College for four years. In 1902 he matriculated from Emmanuel College, Cambridge, graduating BA in history in 1906.

Between 1898 and 1903 Hugh Walpole, already a voracious reader, edited a family magazine he called the *Social Weekly* (sometimes *Monthly*) containing poetry, short stories, and articles written mostly by himself under varied pen names. This periodical, complemented by several historical novels Walpole also wrote during this time, constitutes a solid body of juvenilia. In 1905 his essay 'Two Meredithian heroines' was published in the *Emmanuel College Magazine*.

To help satisfy his father's expectation that he would enter the ministry after going down from Cambridge, Hugh Walpole served for a year in 1906 as lay minister at the Mersey Mission to Seamen in Liverpool, but he and his parents soon realized their misjudgement. Instead, he became tutor in Germany to the children of the popular English novelist Elizabeth von Arnim, and then spent a year as a schoolmaster at Epsom College in Surrey.

In 1909, now living in London and writing book reviews for the London *Standard*, Walpole published his first novel, *The Wooden Horse*, to favourable reviews. He had found his true occupation and was by this time a practising homosexual. He formed close friendships with Arnold Bennett, Henry James, and later Joseph Conrad, who were glad to encourage this ebullient, attractive son of the new bishop of Edinburgh. He repaid their efforts not only with deference but with unceasing energy, coupled with modesty.

Five more novels—one per year—would emerge from Walpole's pen by 1914. *Mr. Perrin and Mr. Traill* (1911), set in a boys' school run by feuding schoolmasters, won public praise from Arnold Bennett, and *The Duchess of Wrexe* (1914)

brought an accolade from Henry James. *Fortitude* (1913) remained a favourite for many years among his admirers. The other novels of this period were *Maradick at Forty* (1910), something of a fantasy, and *The Prelude to Adventure* (1912), a murder mystery which attracted the interest of the psychologist Carl Jung.

During the First World War, rejected for military service because of poor eyesight, Walpole served in Russia as a Red Cross sanitar, for which he received the George Cross, followed by appointment as head of the Anglo-Russian Propaganda Bureau, Petrograd. He was in Russia before and during the first revolution of 1917, in March, and drew from the experience in two of his better novels, *The Dark Forest* (1915) and *The Secret City* (1919); the latter won the James Tait Black memorial prize. He was appointed CBE in 1918. Back in London, Walpole worked for a short period with the novelist John Buchan in the department of information. In 1919 Walpole published a series of popular children's stories about a young boy Jeremy which follows him to boarding-school in *Jeremy at Crale*, hailed as one of the best school stories since Rudyard Kipling's *Stalky and Co.* (It is suggested that these stories helped to popularize the name Jeremy in Britain.)

After the war Walpole settled in Piccadilly, London, and in the early 1920s bought a country house at Brackenburn, Manesty Park, Derwentwater, Cumberland. Walpole was Rede lecturer at Cambridge University in 1925. From 1926 until his death his companion was Harold Cheevers (*b.* 1893), a married policeman who also became his chauffeur.

In the 1920s and 1930s Walpole experimented generically with an ecclesiastical exposé, *The Cathedral* (1922), a very effective horror story, *Portrait of a Man with Red Hair* (1925), a homily, *Wintersmoon* (1928), and an artist-tale, *Hans Frost* (1929). Just as the depression was making long 'costume romances' popular again, he published his most noted work, *Rogue Herries* (1930), followed in 1931 by its only slightly less well received sequel *Judith Paris*. Four more Herries novels followed in subsequent years, all set in Cumberland. Stretching from Elizabeth I's reign to the mid-1930s, the six volumes were a *tour de force*, and contain much of his best work. During this period he averaged better than one work per year, writing even as he travelled by rail throughout the United States on five extensive lecture tours (1919–20, 1922–3, 1926–7, 1930, and 1936). He was a brilliant raconteur and made a considerable amount of money as a result of these talks. Combined with his income from his writing, this placed him in a comfortable financial position, and he was able to offer generous help to the arts and to friends. He became a major sponsor of the Danish baritone Lauritz Melchior, financing the lessons that helped create that notable *Heldentenor*.

Just as Walpole's talent and reputation were reaching their peak, however, his confidence was severely shaken by Somerset Maugham's lampoon of him as Alroy Kear, a literary opportunist, in *Cakes and Ale* (1930). Walpole continued to turn out novels, but his best writing was done by 1931. He served as president of the Book Society, and

wrote film scripts in Hollywood in 1934–5 for classics such as *David Copperfield* (MGM, 1935), in which he played a bit part, and *Little Lord Fauntleroy* (1936). He was knighted in 1937.

In the last three years of his life Walpole published four more novels, including *The Bright Pavilions* (1940), the first in a new series of Herries novels, and embarked on the unfinished *Katherine Christian*, published in 1944, another in the Herries series. During the Second World War, Walpole suffered from diabetes and heart congestion, and taking part in a war parade at nearby Keswick, Cumberland, may have aggravated his condition. Walpole died at his home at Brackenburn on 1 June 1941. He was buried in St John's churchyard, Keswick.

In all, Walpole published thirty-six novels, five volumes of short stories, including *All Souls' Night* (1933), two plays, three autobiographies, two literary studies, and numerous pamphlets and reviews. For a time his work was given serious attention by eminent writer–critics such as Arnold Bennett and Joseph Conrad, his contemporaries W. L. George and Joseph Hergesheimer, and younger critics like J. B. Priestley, Joseph Warren Beach, Clemence Dane, Marguerite Steen, and L. A. G. Strong. But time passed and Walpole lost credit with critics especially as modernism flourished. Surprisingly, his relationship with Virginia Woolf was close and friendly.

After his death and especially by the end of the Second World War, much of Walpole's work was seen as dated. His psychology was not deep enough for the polemicist, his diction not free enough for those returning from war, and his zest disastrous to a public wary of personal commitment. Nevertheless, in the 1980s the Herries chronicle was dramatized on British radio.   ELIZABETH STEELE

Sources R. Hart-Davis, *Hugh Walpole: a biography* (1952) • E. Steele, *Hugh Walpole* (1972) • *DNB* • P. Parker and F. Kermode, eds., *The reader's companion to twentieth-century writers* (1995)

Archives Keswick Museum and Art Gallery, literary MSS and corresp. • King's School, Canterbury, literary collection presented to King's School, Canterbury • L. Cong., corresp., literary MSS, and papers • NRA, corresp. and literary papers • Ransom HRC, corresp. and literary MSS • William Morris Gallery, MSS relating to appreciation of W. Morris | BL, corresp. with Macmillans, Add. MSS 54958–54961 • BL, corresp. with Society of Authors, Add. MS 63340 • Bodl. Oxf., letters mainly to A. Spemann and papers • CAC Cam., letters to Cecil Roberts • NL Scot., letters to Newman Flower • NL Scot., letters to William Roughead • NYPL, Berg collection, corresp. with Edward March • Queen's University, Kingston, Ontario, corresp. with John Buchan • Royal Society of Literature, London, letters to the Royal Society of Literature • U. Birm. L., corresp. with F. Brett Young • U. Durham L., letters to Mrs M. D. Darwin • U. Reading, corresp. with the Bodley Head Ltd • U. Sussex, corresp. with Virginia Woolf • W. Yorks. AS, Bradford, corresp. with Bradford English Society

Likenesses B. Schotz, bronze head, 1924, Scot. NPG • R. J. Swan, pencil drawing, 1925, U. Texas • A. John, oils, *c.*1926, King's School, Canterbury • A. John, red chalk drawing, 1926, FM Cam. • W. R. Sickert, oils, 1928, FM Cam. • D. Evans, bronze head, 1929, NPG • W. R. Sickert, oils, 1929, Art Gallery and Museum, Glasgow • print, *c.*1929, NPG • photographs, *c.*1930–1931, Hult. Arch. • H. Coster, photographs, 1931, NPG • W. Stoneman, photograph, 1939, NPG • R. G. Eves, oils, *c.*1940, National Book League, London • S. Bone, oils, NPG • J. Epstein, bronze, Fitz Park Museum, Keswick •

G. Kelly, oils · G. Kelly, oils · G. Kelly, oils; in possession of the artist, in 1959 · D. Low, two pencil caricatures, NPG
Wealth at death £43,116 12s. 8d.: probate, 30 July 1941, *CGPLA Eng. & Wales*

Walpole, Michael [*pseud.* Michael Christopherson] (*bap.* 1570, *d.* 1625), Jesuit, was baptized on 1 October 1570 at Docking, Norfolk, the son of Christopher Walpole (*d.* 1596) of Anmer Hall, near Docking, and Margery Beckham. He was the youngest of seven brothers, four of whom became Jesuits, including Henry *Walpole and Richard *Walpole. After being educated at Norwich School he met the Jesuit John Gerard on the latter's arrival in Norfolk in 1588, and became his constant companion for a year. On learning of his brother Henry's imprisonment at Flushing in December 1589, he crossed the sea with ransom money for his release. He then proceeded to Rome with his cousin Edward *Walpole and entered the English College on 12 May 1590. Following in the path of his brothers and of his cousin Edward he entered the Society of Jesus in September 1593. For the next ten years little is recorded of him, except that after his theological studies at Rome he appears at the English College, Valladolid, as prefect of studies in 1603.

From about this time Walpole's life became bound up with that of a noble lady and benefactor of the English mission, Luisa de Carvajal, who took up residence in London in 1606, bringing Walpole with her as confessor and spiritual adviser. James I's proclamation of 2 June 1610, issued in response to the assassination of Henri IV of France and urging the carrying out of all penal laws against the recusants and the ministering of the oath of allegiance, led Walpole to publish *A Briefe Admonition to All English Catholikes*, under the initials M. C. P. (Michael Christopherson Priest). It contained an appeal to Queen Anne, who was known to have Catholic sympathies, if not to be a Catholic, to act as Queen Esther and intercede for the deliverance of English Catholics. In the same year he was arrested at Doña Luisa's house and imprisoned, and released only on condition of his leaving the country.

Walpole then lived for a time at Douai, where he engaged in further controversy with George Downame, one of the royal chaplains, who had in 1603 published *A Treatise Concerning Antichrist*, against Cardinal Bellarmine. After consultation with Bellarmine, Walpole brought out an answering *Treatise Concerning Antichrist*, under the above pseudonym, in two parts (1613–14). Dedicating his book to James I, he drew the king's attention to the sufferings of English Catholics, remarking how 'many things lie hid which would astonish and amaze the world'. On 17 August 1613 Walpole was appointed superior of the English mission and returned to London in the retinue of the new Spanish ambassador, Count Gondomar. When Doña Luisa died in January 1614 he was by her side, and the following year he accompanied her body to its resting place in Spain. It was not until August 1615, on the death of the previous superior, Robert Jones, that he was able to assume fully the responsibilities of his new position.

About this time he also turned his pen from works of controversy to translations of saints' lives. Already for

Luisa de Carvajal he had translated the autobiography of St Teresa of Avila in 1611, and in 1616 he brought out his translation of Ribadeneira's popular biography of St Ignatius of Loyola. In 1619 Walpole retired to Spain, and held posts at the English College, Seville. He died in Seville on 11 November 1625 os.

AUGUSTUS JESSOPP, *rev.* PETER MILWARD

Sources A. Jessopp, *One generation of a Norfolk house* (1878) · *John Gerard: the autobiography of an Elizabethan*, trans. P. Caraman (1951), 17–23 · H. Foley, ed., *Records of the English province of the Society of Jesus*, 2 (1875), 235, 265–9; 6 (1880), 182, 528 · P. Milward, *Religious controversies of the Jacobean age* (1978), 120–21, 131–3 · T. M. McCoog, *English and Welsh Jesuits, 1555–1650*, 2 vols., Catholic RS, 74–5 (1994–5) · A. J. Loomie, *Spain and the early Stuarts, 1585–1655* (1996)

Walpole, Ralph of (*d.* 1302), bishop of Norwich and of Ely, was a Norfolk man, probably the son of Sir John of Walpole of Houghton and his wife, Lucy. He is first recorded in February 1272 when, with the degree of MA, he was admitted by Richard of Gravesend, bishop of Lincoln, to the living of Somersham, Huntingdonshire, at the presentation of Hugh of Balsham, bishop of Ely. No later than 12 July in the same year he became archdeacon of Ely, a preferment of unusual scope and responsibility. He was also a theologian, recorded as determining in a disputation in the Cambridge theology faculty in the early 1280s. By March 1287 he was doctor of theology, while in 1290 he gave his house in Cambridge to Balsham's new foundation of Peterhouse. With his intellectual interests and wide administrative experience, it is not surprising that, following the death of William Middleton, bishop of Norwich, on 1 September 1288, the electing committee of seven monks should on 11 November following have unanimously chosen Walpole to succeed him. Their decision, according to the chronicler Bartholomew Cotton, deeply offended local opinion in the diocese, but Walpole, who had travelled as far as Bonnegarde in the south of Gascony to obtain Edward I's consent to his election, was confirmed by Archbishop John Pecham on 1 February 1289. Before Pecham acted, he persuaded Walpole to renounce the right to first fruits—the first year's revenues from a living—which the bishops of Norwich had enjoyed since the time of Pandulf (*d.* 1226). The temporalities were restored on 7 February, and Walpole was consecrated by Pecham on 20 March.

As bishop of Norwich, Walpole was much engaged in local affairs, not least in what became a lengthy dispute with the townspeople of Bishop's Lynn over episcopal lordship, a dispute only settled by Walpole's successor, Bishop John Salmon, in 1309. In 1289 he conducted a visitation of his diocese. Although he did not entirely observe his undertaking to abandon his claim to first fruits (which continued to augment the income of his successors), he made only modest demands on new incumbents. His relations with his own cathedral priory seem to have been good; Walpole secured a licence from the crown enabling him to transfer three messuages in Norwich from himself to the priory, and resolved disputes between the monks and the rector of Great Cressingham and the archdeacon of Suffolk. More visibly, perhaps, he took the lead in the reconstruction of the cloister (and possibly also the chapter house), made necessary by damage inflicted in riots in 1272. Although he attended a provincial council in 1290, Walpole played little part in national affairs, secular or ecclesiastical, before 1296–7, when he gave steady support to Archbishop Robert Winchelsey in the latter's resistance to Edward I's increasingly heavy taxation of the English church. The papal decree *Clericis laicos* in February 1296 forbade the clergy to contribute to lay taxation without papal consent; in January 1297 Walpole was one of the ecclesiastical envoys who informed the king of the English church's resolve to obey the bull, and he is said to have been one of the bishops who held out longest against royal demands. Although Walpole was one of the lay and secular magnates who, as the king endeavoured to resolve the crisis, performed homage to Prince Edward on 14 July 1297, he was still apparently regarded as one of the king's opponents in September, appearing among a group of the latter summoned to parliament.

His position on the issue of clerical taxation did not, however, prevent Walpole's elevation to another see. Following the death of William of Louth, bishop of Ely, on 25 March 1298, the monks of the cathedral priory were divided in their preferences between their own prior, John Salmon, and the treasurer of the exchequer, John Langton, whose candidature was favoured by the king. The monks first approached Archbishop Winchelsey, and then appealed to the pope. Both candidates appeared before Boniface VIII (*r.* 1294–1303), and resigned their rights into the pope's hands. Boniface invited the monks to elect again, as a favour to their church licensing them to choose one of the abbots of an exempt Benedictine house; but their proctors could not agree, whereupon Boniface resolved the dispute on 5 June 1299 by translating Walpole to Ely, and providing Salmon to Norwich. Edward I acquiesced, the temporalities of Ely being restored on 10 October. The expenses of Walpole's proctor at Rome amounted to at least £1200.

Walpole was bishop of Ely for less than three years. In 1300, following a visitation, he issued ordinances for the cathedral priory. The thirty-nine statutes contain little out of the ordinary, dealing with such issues as the need to maintain the full complement of seventy monks, restrictions on pocket money and on dealings with women, and the proper application of the convent's revenues. But they may also reflect the bishop's academic training, since they are essentially a compilation from earlier legislation, mostly by former archbishops of Canterbury and bishops of Ely. Ralph of Walpole died on 20 March 1302, and was buried before the high altar of Ely Cathedral on 1 April following.   DOROTHY M. OWEN

Sources F. M. Powicke and C. R. Cheney, eds., *Councils and synods with other documents relating to the English church, 1205–1313*, 2 (1964), 1171–2 · *CEPR letters*, 1.582 · [H. Wharton], ed., *Anglia sacra*, 1 (1691), 412, 639–40 · J. Bentham, *The history and antiquities of the conventual and cathedral church of Ely*, ed. J. Bentham, 2nd edn (1812), 153–4 · *Chancery records* · H. R. Luard, ed., *Flores historiarum*, 3 vols., Rolls Series, 95 (1890), vol. 3 · Emden, *Cam.*, 612 · B. Dodwell, ed., *The charters of Norwich Cathedral priory*, 1, PRSoc., 40, new ser., 78 (1974), 137–43 · D. Wilkins, ed., *Concilia Magnae Britanniae et Hiberniae*, 2 (1737) · S. J. A. Evans, ed., 'Ely chapter ordinances and visitation records, 1241–1515', *Camden miscellany, XVII*, CS, 3rd ser., 64 (1940), v–xx, 1–74 · *Fasti Angl., 1066–1300*, [Monastic cathedrals], 47, 58 · A. G. Little and F. Pelster, *Oxford theology and theologians*, OHS, 96 (1934) · J. H. Denton, *Robert Winchelsey and the crown, 1294–1313: a study in the defence of ecclesiastical liberty*, Cambridge Studies in Medieval Life and Thought, 3rd ser., 14 (1980) · I. Atherton and others, eds., *Norwich Cathedral: church, city and diocese, 1096–1996* (1996) · *Willelmi Rishanger … chronica et annales*, ed. H. T. Riley, pt 2 of *Chronica monasterii S. Albani*, Rolls Series, 28 (1865), 475

Walpole, Richard (*bap.* 1564, *d.* 1607), Jesuit, was baptized at Docking, Norfolk, on 8 October 1564, the son of Christopher Walpole and Margery Beckham. His four brothers included the Jesuits Henry *Walpole (*bap.* 1558, *d.* 1595) and Michael *Walpole (*bap.* 1570, *d.* 1625). Richard Walpole entered Peterhouse, Cambridge, on 1 April 1579, a fortnight before his brother Henry left the university. He was elected to one of the scholarships lately founded at his college by Edward, Lord North, but took no degree. In summer 1584 he left England to become an alumnus of the seminary at Rheims. He left after a few months and on 25 April 1585 he entered the English College at Rome. His ability and scholarship were at once recognized and after remaining there for the next four years he was ordained priest at St John Lateran on 3 December 1589 and then sent to Spain. The intention was that he proceed from there to England but instead he gained admittance to St Alban's College, Valladolid, on 1 September 1591 and proceeded from there to St Gregory's, Seville, on 8 November 1592. In the following year he entered the Society of Jesus and spent his life assisting Robert Persons in his work for the English colleges abroad. It was in the course of his work in Seville that he met Edward Squire, who, in 1598, falsely accused him of plotting to assassinate Queen Elizabeth. Squire was hanged and Walpole was defended in writing in 'The discoverie and confutation of a tragical fiction' (1598) by Martin Aray, but remained in Spain. After the execution of his brother Henry at York in 1595 Joseph Creswell SJ had written a life of the martyr which had been translated into Spanish. The book produced a favourable impression on Luisa de Carvajal, a rich and pious lady who lived near the college at Valladolid, and she resolved to go as a missionary to England. Richard Walpole was her spiritual director and before leaving for England in 1606 she appointed him her executor. He was prefect of studies and lecturer in cases of conscience at St Gregory's College, Seville, in 1600, then confessor and consultor in Rome until 1604, when he took up residence at Valladolid. In 1603 he published a work of controversy, *A Brief and Cleere Confutation*, in response to Matthew Sutcliffe's attack on Persons. He died in Valladolid in September 1607.

His younger brother, Christopher Walpole (1569–1606), was born in October 1569 and was one of John Gerard's early converts when that busy proselytizer was at work in Norfolk. He was admitted as a Jesuit at Rome in September 1592, thus preceding Richard into the society. He obtained permission to join his brother at Seville in 1597 and was probably ordained there between 1600 and 1603. In 1693 he was confessor and lecturer in moral theology at St Alban's College, Valladolid, and predeceased his brother, dying at the college in 1606.

AUGUSTUS JESSOPP, *rev.* MICHAEL E. WILLIAMS

Sources A. Jessopp, *One generation of a Norfolk house* (1878) · M. Murphy, *St Gregory's College, Seville, 1592–1767*, Catholic RS, 73 (1992) · T. M. McCoog, *English and Welsh Jesuits, 1555–1650*, 2, Catholic RS, 75 (1995) · F. Edwards, 'The strange case of the poisoned pommel. Richard Walpole and the Squire plot: 1597–1598', *Archivum Historicum S.J.*, 56 (1987), 3–82 · M. E. Williams, *St Alban's College, Valladolid: four centuries of English Catholic presence in Spain* (1986), 64–6 · G. Anstruther, *The seminary priests*, 1 (1969), 369–70

Walpole, Robert (1650–1700), agricultural improver and politician, was born on 18 November 1650 at Houghton, Norfolk, the second but eldest surviving son of Sir Edward Walpole (1621–1668) and his wife, Susan Crane (*c*.1625–1667). From 1667 he studied briefly at Trinity College, Cambridge, but his formal education was ended by the death of his father on 18 March 1668. Walpole was only seventeen when he inherited his family's estates, from which he had to provide for seven younger siblings. About 22 February 1671 he married Mary Burwell (1654/5–1711), daughter of Sir Jeffrey Burwell of Rougham, Suffolk; the couple were subsequently the prodigious parents of seven daughters and ten sons. Of these the eldest surviving son was Sir Robert *Walpole (1676–1745), the celebrated whig politician and chief minister of George I and George II, and the second surviving son was Horatio *Walpole, first Baron Walpole of Wolterton. Although Robert Walpole's own achievements have largely been obscured by the brilliance of his famous son, they were significant in their own right. During his brief time at Cambridge he acquired a reputation for 'learning and study extraordinary' (North, 3.304), and his scholarly interests persisted throughout his life. He founded the great library at Houghton and regularly stocked it with good editions of the Latin classics, history, law, and theology. Fascinated by the new learning, he acquired nearly all the works of Sir Francis Bacon.

Walpole was equally serious in the management of his own estates, where his intelligence can best be seen. He was quick to realize the value of agricultural techniques pioneered in Flanders and Holland, and by the 1670s he and his Norfolk neighbours were introducing many of the practices hailed a century later by Arthur Young as an 'agricultural revolution'. He introduced crop rotation and devoted extensive acreage to turnips, clover, and grasses in order to enrich the light, sandy soil of his farms. Swift to seize his chances when he scented gain, he successfully experimented with growing wheat and made regular profits by fattening cattle for the voracious London market. Walpole's enterprise was matched by his frugality. Holding a tight rein on his own and his family's spending, he gradually increased the productivity of his holdings. He then invested the bulk of accumulated capital in additional land, thus transforming an inheritance worth little more than £800 a year into an estate which yielded in excess of £1300 per annum (Plumb, *Men and Places*, 123–7; Plumb, *Sir Robert Walpole*, 83–6).

Walpole also harboured political ambitions. He was appointed justice of the peace and deputy lieutenant for Norfolk in 1673 and was moderately active in those capacities. Yet in the 1670s and early 1680s he gave no overt sign of his later whiggish inclinations. He did not join his colleagues on the lieutenancy who resigned in 1676 over the ouster of the proto-whig lord lieutenant, Horatio, Lord Townshend. Furthermore, in March 1682 he surprised Townshend's tory and crypto-Catholic successor, Lord Yarmouth, by signing the loyal address abhorring the whig association. However, in 1688 he refused to consent to the repeal of the Test Acts and was removed from local office (Cruickshanks, 663). When the king offered to restore him in October 1688, Walpole declined to act 'in conjunction with persons unqualified or incapacitated by the law of the realm' (Cozens-Hardy, 89).

Restored to office by William III, in 1689 Walpole was elected MP for the pocket borough of Castle Rising on the duke of Norfolk's interest. From 1690 onwards he departed from his usual parsimony to buy up enough cottages (burgages) carrying a vote to gain control over one of the borough's seats (Ingleby, 33–4), and these investments assured his election in 1690, 1695, and 1698. However, Walpole's parliamentary career was to be curtailed by the deterioration of his health. He explained his irregular presence in the Commons after 1692 as due to his 'consumptive' condition (Hayton). Nevertheless, accounted a 'Court Whig' (Cruickshanks, 663), he was a dependable supporter of whig measures when able to attend parliament and was regarded a leader of the Norfolk whigs in the late 1690s. Walpole died at Houghton Hall on his fiftieth birthday, 18 November 1700, and was buried at Houghton.

RICHARD MINTA DUNN

Sources J. H. Plumb, *Sir Robert Walpole*, 1 (1956) · J. H. Plumb, *Men and places* (1963) · E. Cruickshanks, 'Walpole, Robert', HoP, *Commons, 1660–90* · D. W. Hayton, 'Walpole, Robert', HoP, *Commons, 1690–1715* [draft] · B. Cozens-Hardy, ed., *Norfolk lieutenancy journal, 1676–1701*, Norfolk RS, 30 (1961) · R. M. Dunn, ed., *Norfolk lieutenancy journal, 1660–1676*, Norfolk RS, 45 (1977) · C. Ingleby, ed., *A supplement to Blomefield's Norfolk* (1929) · R. North, *The lives of ... Francis North ... Dudley North ... and ... John North*, new edn, 3 vols. (1826), vol. 3

Archives Houghton Hall, King's Lynn, papers · NRA, priv. coll., papers | U. Cam., Cholmondeley (Houghton) MSS

Likenesses M. Beale, oils, 1660–99, Houghton Hall, King's Lynn; repro. in Plumb, *Sir Robert Walpole*, vol. 1 · stipple, pubd 1801, NPG; repro. in W. Cox, *Memoirs of Lord Walpole* (1802) · stipple, pubd 1801, BM

Wealth at death over £1300 p.a. but 'did not exceed £2000 a year': Plumb, *Sir Robert Walpole*; W. Rye, *The later history of the family of Walpole* (1920)

Walpole, Robert, first earl of Orford (1676–1745), prime minister, was born on 26 August 1676 in the old manor house at Houghton, Norfolk, the fifth of the seventeen children of Robert *Walpole (1650–1700), landowner and MP, and his wife, Mary (1654/5–1711), daughter of Sir Jeffrey Burwell, a Suffolk landowner. The Walpoles were a well-established and prominent gentry family in north Norfolk. Robert senior was an educated man who built up the library at Houghton. He also worked hard at improving the family estates, which were worth more than £2000

Robert Walpole, first earl of Orford (1676–1745), by Jean Baptiste van Loo, 1740 [replica]

by the time of his death. In the years after the revolution of 1688 he sat in parliament for Castle Rising—his father, Edward (1621–1668), had represented King's Lynn in the early years of the Restoration—and he established himself as a whig.

At the age of six Robert was sent to study at Great Dunham under the Revd Richard Ransome. On 4 September 1690 he was admitted to Eton College, where he developed a close friendship with Henry Bland, for whom he later secured the deanery of Durham. The Eton register falsely recorded his age as twelve in order to qualify him as a king's scholar. He was duly elected to King's College, Cambridge, on 5 August 1695 and admitted on 22 April of the following year. While at King's, where his tutor was Francis Hare, later bishop of Chichester, he fell seriously ill with smallpox and was attended by Robert Brady, the tory historian and physician. According to his early biographer, Coxe, Walpole was 'originally designed for the church' (Coxe, *Walpole*, 1.5), but these plans were cut short by the death of his eldest brother, Edward, in 1698. His second brother, Burwell, had already been killed at the battle of Beachy Head in 1690, and under pressure from his

father Walpole returned to Houghton to learn about the management of the estates to which he was now heir. He resigned his scholarship on 19 May 1698.

Marriage and private life Once Walpole was settled at Houghton, the search began to find him a wife. Walpole and his father, assisted in their negotiations by Sir John Mordaunt, settled on Catherine (c.1682–1737), daughter of John Shorter, a Baltic timber merchant from Bybrook in Kent, and granddaughter of a former lord mayor of London. Her mother, Elizabeth, was the daughter of Sir Erasmus Philipps of Picton Castle. Walpole at this time was short and stout, with a tendency towards corpulence which became very marked in later life; Catherine was described by Coxe as 'a woman of exquisite beauty and accomplished manners' (Coxe, *Walpole*, 1.5). They were married on 30 July 1700 at Knightsbridge Chapel in London, Catherine bringing with her a dowry of £7000. The transformation of Walpole's life was completed in November 1700 by the death of his father, who left his son an estate considerably richer and more secure than he had inherited. However, Walpole did face financial pressures. He had to support his mother, who lived until 1711, two sisters, and two young brothers. Catherine preferred London to Norfolk and shared the extravagance of her grandmother, Lady Philipps. Her inclinations were probably shared by Walpole himself, who was keen to play a more prominent role in both political and social life. Having been elected to parliament in 1701, he quickly became part of a young, aristocratic whig circle, to which he was introduced by Charles, second Viscount Townshend, his Norfolk neighbour to whom his father had acted as guardian, and Lady Philipps, who was related to the Stanhopes. During their early years in London, the Walpoles lived with Lady Philipps in Berkeley Street, and only as Walpole's ministerial career advanced did they move, first to Dover Street in 1705 and then to 17 Arlington Street in 1715. Even so, their extravagant lifestyle meant that they were living well beyond their means—debts accumulated, lands were mortgaged and sold, and on one occasion Walpole was saved from imprisonment for debt only by a loan from his scrivener, Thomas Gibson.

In the early years of their marriage the Walpoles' relationship appears to have been happy. In Robert's only surviving love letter, dating from July 1702, he told Catherine that he had 'that love, that tendernesse, for you, that are there any failings in you they are still perfections to me' (Plumb, *Sir Robert Walpole*, 1.90). Between 1701 and 1706 they had two sons and two daughters. The eldest son, Robert (1701–1751), succeeded his father as earl of Orford, and was himself survived by one son, George (1730–1791). The second son, Edward (1706–1784), never married, but had four illegitimate children with Maria Clements. Of these, Laura married Bishop Frederick Keppel; Maria married first James Waldegrave, second Earl Waldegrave, and second William Henry, duke of Gloucester; and Charlotte married Lionel Tollemache, earl of Dysart. Of Walpole's daughters, the elder, Catherine, died unmarried after a long and painful illness in 1722, while the younger, Mary (d. 1731), married George Cholmondeley, Viscount Malpas and later earl of Cholmondeley. From about the time of Edward's birth in 1706, however, the relationship between Robert and Catherine deteriorated. They continued to live together and publicly appearances were maintained. Catherine continued to play the role of the wife of a leading politician. When she was singled out at court by Queen Caroline in 1727 immediately after the accession of George II, it was seen as an early sign that Walpole had not fallen out of favour.

In private, however, the marriage had broken down, the couple living virtually separate lives. In April 1716 Robert fell seriously ill, but this did not deter Catherine from making her annual trip to Bath. Her affairs became the talk of the town. The earl of Egmont claimed that 'she was as gallant, if report be true, with the men as he with the women' (*Egmont Diary*, 2.431). Lady Cowper even alleged that Catherine, with the connivance of Walpole himself, had an affair with the prince of Wales. Walpole's modern biographer J. H. Plumb believed that Horatio (Horace) *Walpole (1717–1797), born on 24 September 1717, may well not have been Robert's son, though the allegation made in the early nineteenth century by Lady Louisa Stuart that he was the son of Carr, Lord Hervey, lacks any contemporary corroboration. Robert probably had numerous mistresses, including Carey Daye (*d*. in or after 1746), with whom he had a daughter, Catherine (*d*. 1775), about 1724. Little is known about either mother or daughter, though both were living in Chichester at the time of Walpole's death. It is likely that Carey Daye's successor was Maria (1702–1738), daughter of Thomas Skerrett, a London staymaker, and his first wife, Hester Stafford, widow of John Pleydell. According to contemporary gossip, Maria was procured for Walpole by Lady Mary Wortley Montagu, and it is possible that they first met at her house at Twickenham in summer 1724. Certainly their relationship was well established by the end of that year, as the first of their two daughters, Maria or Mary (*d*. 1801), was born in 1725. On his resignation in 1742 Walpole obtained for her a patent of precedence as the daughter of an earl, an act which, according to the ministerial whig William Hay, 'brought more Odium on him than perhaps any Act of Power' (Taylor and Jones, 176). In 1746 Lady Maria Walpole married Colonel Charles Churchill, the illegitimate son of General Charles Churchill. Their second daughter died before 1738.

In July 1725 Walpole's eldest son (then Lord Walpole) was appointed ranger of Richmond Park (PRO, E 403/2473, p. 44), but it was his father, as deputy ranger, who regularly retreated to the ranger's lodge at weekends to spend time with Maria Skerrett in what Hervey called 'his bower of bliss' (Hervey, 3.832). On 20 August 1737 Lady Walpole died at Chelsea, and she was buried at Houghton a week later. Within weeks rumours began to circulate that Walpole had married his mistress, but the ceremony probably did not take place until shortly before 3 March 1738. Scurrilous verses circulated on the subject of the minister's marriage to 'a public whore' (*Egmont Diary*, 2.471), though the scandal did not prevent the new Lady Walpole being presented at court. According to Bishop Hare, she brought with her a fortune of some £30,000, accumulated in large part by her father. The diplomatist Horatio *Walpole observed that his brother's happiness was 'wrapt up' in Maria, whom he described as 'a very sensible well-behaved modest woman'. Her death on 4 June 1738 following a miscarriage flung Walpole into a 'deplorable and comfortless condition' (*Buckinghamshire MSS*, 13, 17, 238), which continued for several weeks and from which he was diverted only by plunging himself into work.

Early political career The death of Walpole's father on 18 November 1700 vacated his parliamentary seat at Castle Rising. Even before the funeral Walpole had written to Thomas Howard to secure his support at the by-election, but parliament was dissolved before the writ could be issued. He took the opportunity of the general election to stand as a candidate for Norfolk, but was decisively defeated and was returned for Castle Rising. From the moment Walpole entered the Commons, he began to play an active role in its proceedings. In his first session he took over from his brother-in-law, Sir Charles Turner, the management of a bill to establish a workhouse at King's Lynn and successfully piloted it onto the statute book. At the elections of 1702 he moved to King's Lynn, the constituency which he then represented continuously, except for a short break in 1712, until his elevation to the Lords in February 1742. At Castle Rising he exerted the family interest to secure the return of his tory uncle, Horatio Walpole. This prompted fears among Norfolk whigs that he was 'turning with the wind'. The explanation, however, lay in Walpole's desperate need for cash—the consent of his uncle, as trustee to his mother and sisters, was necessary before he could raise money on property in Suffolk. In fact, there is no doubting his commitment to the whig cause in parliament. His closest connections at this time were with the Norfolk whigs, among whom his friend and neighbour the young Lord Townshend was emerging as a leading figure, and he developed a friendship with William Cavendish, earl of Hartington, who was for a while his fellow MP for Castle Rising. But he was also establishing a wider reputation as a rising politician, as revealed by his election as a member of the Kit-Cat Club in 1703, and he forged close relationships with other prominent young whigs, including James Stanhope and Spencer Compton.

By the time of the parliamentary session of 1704–5 Walpole was attracting attention as a leading whig performer in the Commons. His colleagues regarded his presence as essential for major debates, such as those on the address and the Occasional Conformity Bill, and even the Dutch agent in London noted that he was 'un de ceux qui se distinguoient le plus parmi les Whigs' (Hayton, 5.777). At the beginning of 1705 it was rumoured that he would be offered a place in government, and in June he was appointed to the Admiralty council 'at the particular recommendation of Marlborough' (ibid.). The office carried a salary of £1000 per annum, which did a little to ease Walpole's financial problems. But he was still desperately short of money, and in later years the duchess of Marlborough liked to recall 'the beggary she first knew him in' (F. Harris, 207). The Admiralty board offered Walpole the opportunity to impress Queen Anne's leading ministers, the earl of Godolphin and the duke of Marlborough, with his energy and efficiency, and over the next few years he became increasingly identified with the 'Lord Treasurer's whigs'. He was exasperated, however, by the failings of the board, and even considered resigning in May. Despite this, in December 1708 he defended the Admiralty board, and particularly Admiral George Churchill, against an attack by both whigs and tories, justifying himself by saying to his friends that 'he should be ashamed to sit at a board, and not be in a capacity to defend its proceedings' (*Bishop Burnet's History*, 5.343).

In the reconstruction of the ministry following the resignation of Robert Harley in February 1708, Walpole's competence and moderation made him a natural choice as secretary at war, and he was appointed on 25 February. Walpole's support for the 'duumvirs', Godolphin and Marlborough, however, continued to provoke whig criticism, and at a meeting of the Kit-Cat Club in June 1708 Jacob Tonson called him 'the greatest villain' in the world for 'forsaking his patrons and benefactors the juncto' (*Portland MSS*, 4.493). Even as late as the end of 1709 Godolphin still saw Walpole as a possible ally against the junto, who were trying to dominate the ministry, but by this time Walpole, like Townshend and Devonshire, had moved back into the junto camp. As secretary at war Walpole once again demonstrated his capacity for business and the detail of administration. The office brought him into close contact with the duke of Marlborough, who formed a high opinion of him as 'a very honest man' (Hayton, 5.778), and it was almost certainly through Marlborough's influence that he was made treasurer of the navy in January 1710 while still continuing as secretary at war.

A few weeks previously, on 13 December 1709, Walpole had been appointed to the Commons committee responsible for drawing up articles of impeachment against the high-flying tory preacher Henry Sacheverell, whose sermon *The Perils of False Brethren*, denying that resistance had taken place in 1688, was regarded by many whigs as seditious. Walpole played a leading role in the trial, justifying the right of resistance in a major speech on the first article. Defending whig constitutional principles, he claimed that 'To assert non-resistance in that boundless and unlimited sense, in which Dr. Sacheverell presumes to assert it, is to undermine the very foundations of our government' (Hayton, 5.779). In a speech which delighted his fellow whigs, he went on to suggest that Sacheverell's arguments were designed to pave the way for a Jacobite restoration. Sacheverell was found guilty, but the whig triumph was short-lived. In the 1710 elections the tory campaign, based on the cry of 'the Church in danger', was fuelled by the Sacheverell prosecution. Managers of the impeachment were singled out as particular targets. At Norwich, where Walpole was standing for the county for the first time since 1701, the mob pelted him 'with dirt and stones and drove him out of his tent, spoiling his fine laced coat which they told him came out of the Treasury' (Holmes, 252). Two tories were elected and Walpole was decisively defeated, coming bottom of the poll with almost 400 votes fewer than his whig partner. Once again, however, he was returned for King's Lynn, though he never contested the county again.

Even before the elections the ministry's position had been deteriorating. Walpole himself became embroiled in the worsening relationship between Queen Anne and the Marlboroughs. When he advised the duke to accede to the demand that Samuel Masham, the husband of the queen's favourite, Abigail, be made a brigadier, the duchess suspected him of double-dealing. The suspicions were probably unfounded, as there is little concrete evidence that Walpole was trimming. On the contrary, when the earl of Sunderland was dismissed in June 1710, the first major casualty of Robert Harley's remodelling of the ministry, Walpole was one of several junior whigs who advocated a mass resignation. But his earlier moderation encouraged Harley, who considered him to be 'worth half his party', to try to detach him from the whigs (Hayton). In September 1710 Walpole was dismissed as secretary at war, but was allowed to retain the treasurership of the navy. When parliament assembled in November 1710, however, it soon became apparent that Walpole had committed himself to opposition to Harley's ministry. On 2 January 1711 he received a letter dismissing him as treasurer of the navy and on the same day led the whig attack in the Commons on the government's policy towards the war in Spain. He continued to play a prominent role in Commons debates through the rest of the session, Swift describing him as 'one of the Whigs chief speakers' (Swift, *Journal to Stella*, 2.442).

His prominence as a speaker aside, Swift dismissed Walpole as 'one who is otherwise altogether obscure' (Swift, *History*, 65). This judgement, however, is hardly borne out by the behaviour of the tories. First, Harley tried again to win him over in the summer of 1711, but failed. Then, when parliament reassembled in late autumn, they resolved to put him 'out of the way of disturbing them in the house' (*Bishop Burnet's History*, 6.100), William Bromley, the speaker, declaring that this was 'the *unum necessarium*' (Coxe, *Walpole*, 1.36). By the beginning of December it was known that the commissioners of public accounts had charges to bring against Walpole. On 21 December their report alleged that, while secretary of war, he had reserved part of two forage contracts for the army in Scotland for his friend and banker, Robert Mann, and that the other contractors had then bought out Mann's share for 500 guineas. More seriously, the bills for Mann's payment had been made out to Walpole, and in one case the receipt bore his signature. The commissioners therefore alleged clear proof that Walpole had been bribed. Mann swore that the money had all been paid to him, but when the case was debated in the Commons on 17 January 1712 a majority of more than fifty found Walpole guilty of 'a high breach of trust and notorious corruption' (Hayton, 5.782). He was then expelled from the house and committed to the Tower, though declining majorities in these votes reflected the partisan nature of the proceedings. Walpole continued to assert his own innocence, writing to his sister that 'this barbarous injustice being only the effect of party malice, does not concern me at all and I heartily despise what I shall one day revenge' (Plumb, 1.181). Most biographers have accepted his professions, but he was under great obligations to Mann, who had been his financial adviser since his father's death, and, as David Hayton has pointed out, Mann was committed to custody by the Commons for refusing to answer further questions from the commissioners of public accounts (ibid.).

Imprisonment turned Walpole into a national political figure and a whig martyr. He was visited daily by the leading whigs, a ballad composed in his honour described him as 'the Jewel in the *Tower*' (Coxe, *Walpole*, 1.39–40), and at the King's Lynn by-election he was triumphantly returned, defeating a local tory. The Commons promptly declared his re-election void, so even after his release from imprisonment on 8 July 1712 he was left without a seat in parliament. During this period he turned to pamphleteering. He probably contributed to *Mr Walpole's Case* (1712), a refutation of the charges brought against him by the Commons. Then in 1713 he attacked the peace of Utrecht and the commercial treaty with France in *A Short History of the Parliament*, which rapidly went through at least three editions. Horace Walpole later attributed many more pamphlets to his father, including *Four Letters to a Friend in North Britain* (1710) on the Sacheverell affair and *The Debts of the Nation Stated and Considered* (1711). Recent research, however, has demonstrated conclusively that these were the work of Arthur Maynwaring, although Walpole may have assisted with comments.

At the 1713 elections the tories, benefiting from public support for the peace, increased their majority. Walpole, however, was returned unopposed as MP for King's Lynn. His election address, subsequently published, contained a fierce attack on the ministry's foreign policy and provoked new efforts to expel him from the Commons. In the next session of parliament, he played a leading role for the whigs in all the major debates. On 18 March 1714 he opened the defence of Richard Steele against tory attempts to expel him from the Commons, delivering what colleagues agreed was his best ever speech. He continued to attack the Utrecht settlement, developed the whig case that the protestant succession was in danger 'from the dubious conduct of some persons in high stations' (Hayton, 5.783), and spoke out strongly against the Schism Bill, arguing that papists and nonjurors posed more danger to church and state than dissenters.

The Hanoverian succession and whig schism The situation of the whig party was transformed by the accession of George I. The ministry constructed in late September and early October 1714 following the king's arrival in England was dominated by whigs: the only tory to receive major office was the earl of Nottingham as lord president of the council. There was considerable rivalry between the leading whigs for power and influence, but in the early months of the reign Townshend, secretary of state for the north, appears to have emerged as the English politician who most enjoyed the king's confidence. The relationship between Walpole and Townshend was now closer than ever, as Townshend had married Walpole's sister Dolly in July 1713. Walpole himself, however, was only appointed paymaster of the forces.

But in the House of Commons, Walpole quickly resumed the leading role in debates that he had played in Queen Anne's last parliament. The whigs enjoyed a comfortable majority, and they set about using it to consolidate their power and to attack the tory leadership. On 23 March, Walpole opened the first major debate of the new parliament by proposing the address to the king. It included a powerful denunciation of the former tory ministers and the treaty of Utrecht, and threatened those who had conspired to restore the Pretender with 'condign punishment' (Chandler, 6.13). Within a month Walpole had been elected chairman of the secret committee charged with investigating the peace negotiations and the conduct of the tory ministry. A serious illness prevented him from attending several meetings, but he was well enough to present the committee's report on 9 June and the next day impeached Viscount Bolingbroke of high treason. Similar charges were then laid against the earl of Oxford and the duke of Ormond, while the earl of Stafford was accused of high crimes and misdemeanours. The conduct of the trials was entrusted to the secret committee, which spent the next three months preparing the articles. The surviving reports suggest that Walpole was driving this process forward, and he reported the articles of impeachment against Oxford to the Commons on 7 July, followed by those against Bolingbroke, Ormond, and Stafford on 4, 5, and 31 August respectively.

By the time that parliament was adjourned on 21 September 1715 it was clear that Walpole had emerged as the leading spokesman for the ministry in the Commons, eclipsing his friend James Stanhope, the secretary of state for the south. Walpole's reward, and confirmation of Townshend's dominance within the ministry, came with his appointment in October as first lord of the Treasury and chancellor of the exchequer. This period, however, not only witnessed his rise to high ministerial office, but also saw a dramatic increase in his wealth. J. H. Plumb has calculated that between August 1714 and October 1717 over £100,000 passed through Walpole's hands, of which more than £60,000 was invested. The rest was spent, partly paying off old debts and mortgages and partly in lavish expenditure. A large part of the investments was probably Treasury and pay office surpluses; contemporary practice allowed Walpole to enjoy the interest on these sums. It is also clear that Walpole profited from intelligent investments. Even so, the source of his wealth—and he did suddenly become very rich—remains a mystery. What is more, the period from 1714 to 1717 merely laid the foundations for his aristocratic lifestyle. His vast spending on building, furniture, and pictures still lay in the future. It is unfortunate that so few of his financial papers have survived.

The dominance of Townshend and Walpole provoked suspicion and hostility among other whigs. First, there was a group of country whigs, such as Edward Wortley Montagu, for whom Walpole was tainted by corruption and consequently unfit to hold high ministerial office. Such men were clearly unconvinced that the charges made against him in 1711 were merely an expression of tory malice, but their concerns also prefigured the attacks made on him in the 1730s and perhaps reflect doubts about the sources of his new wealth. Second, various court whigs, notably the lord chancellor, Earl Cowper, believed that Townshend and Walpole were trying to dominate the ministry and monopolize the power of the crown. This belief was strengthened by the perception that Walpole was trying to fill the Treasury with his own creatures. Third, there was the earl of Sunderland, the youngest member of the junto, who felt slighted that he had received only the lord lieutenancy of Ireland on George I's accession and was little more content with his promotion to lord privy seal in September 1715. These discontents were to split the whig party and bring about the fall of Walpole and Townshend.

Matters came to a head during George I's visit to Hanover, for which he departed on 7 July, accompanied by Stanhope. They were followed in late summer by Sunderland, ostensibly to take the waters at Aix, but intent, as Walpole foresaw, on undermining the ministry. In the early summer Walpole was still recovering from a serious illness that had prevented him from participating in the debates on the Septennial Act, but it was foreign affairs, Townshend's province, that provided the focus for growing ministerial tensions. Sunderland exploited the reluctance of Townshend to support George I's desire for a more active policy in support of Hanoverian ambitions in the Baltic. He also worked on the king's suspicions of the prince of Wales, who had been appointed regent, insinuating that Walpole and Townshend were intriguing with him to undermine the king's authority. More surprisingly, Sunderland won support from Stanhope. Stanhope also came to favour more active British participation in the Great Northern War, and it is likely that he was particularly alienated from his old friends, as was George, by the delays in signing the Anglo-French alliance that he was largely responsible for negotiating. Finally, on 4 December, Stanhope sent a dispatch to London informing Townshend of the king's decision to dismiss him from the secretaryship of state and offering him the lord lieutenancy of Ireland. It was accompanied by a private letter to Walpole, urging him to persuade Townshend to accept the offer, but warning him that, if he did not, plans had been made to exclude the Townshend–Walpole faction from the ministry and reconstruct it around Stanhope and Sunderland.

Walpole was astonished, above all by Stanhope's conduct, which he found 'unaccountable' (Coxe, *Walpole*, 2.143). He and Townshend had been comprehensively outmanoeuvred. They had been totally ignorant of Stanhope's role in the intrigues at Hanover, and through the autumn they had continued to write frank letters to him confiding their fears about Sunderland and the Germans. After some initial hesitation, they decided to await the

king's return and Townshend accepted the lieutenancy. Soon after the opening of the new session of parliament in February 1717, however, it became apparent that the divisions within the ministry could not be papered over. In the Commons, Walpole gave only lukewarm support to proposals for measures against Sweden following the revelation of its ambassador's involvement in plotting with the Jacobites, and some of his supporters voted against the court, reducing its majority to just four. When Townshend voted against the Mutiny Bill in the Lords, he was immediately dismissed. On the following day, 10 April, Walpole resigned, followed by a number of his whig allies, including Lord Orford, William Pulteney, Paul Methuen, and the duke of Devonshire.

Initially, Walpole appeared to eschew formal opposition, declaring on 16 April that he did not intend 'to make the king uneasy, or to embarrass his affairs' (Cobbett, *Parl. hist.*, 7.449). He continued to support the proposals for reducing the interest on part of the national debt and establishing a sinking fund, though he did so as 'a Country Gentleman' (Chandler, 6.120). A clearer indication of his intentions was provided on 12 May, when Walpole supported the proposal of William Wyndham, a leading tory, that Andrew Snape, a prominent high-churchman, be invited to preach before the Commons on 29 May. The motion was carried by an alliance of tories and opposition whigs against the government by 141 votes to 131. The depth of the personal breach between Walpole and Stanhope became apparent to all on 20 May, when Stanhope launched a personal attack on Walpole, pointedly remarking that 'he would content himself with the Salary and lawful Perquisites of his Office' (ibid., 6.133). This provoked a violent quarrel and the house had to intervene to prevent the matter being taken further.

In so far as the origins of the whig schism lay in divisions over foreign policy, an element of political principle was involved. The same cannot be said about the behaviour of Walpole and Townshend over the next two years. To some extent whig opposition to the ministry was accorded legitimacy by the divisions within the royal family, which were formalized when the king ordered the prince of Wales to leave St James's in November 1717. The prince and princess set up an alternative court at Leicester House, where Walpole and Townshend were frequent visitors. But, in the Commons in particular, Walpole's efforts to harry the ministry led him to embrace the politics of faction to an extent that sometimes discomfited even his followers. Not only did he frequently co-operate with the tories, but he also abandoned positions which he had formerly held. In 1715 he had pressed vigorously for the impeachment of the earl of Oxford, claiming that it was essential that 'the Ax was laid to the Root' (Archbishop King papers, MS 1995–2008/2410). But in the 1717 session he stayed away from most of the meetings of the committee responsible for preparing the case, despite the fact that he was its chairman. His abandonment of whig principles was even more striking in January 1719, when he led the opposition in the Commons to the repeal of the Occasional Conformity and Schism Acts, two anti-dissenting measures that he had condemned in the previous reign. According to one observer, he 'bore harder upon the Court than any Tory durst attempt to do', comparing its measures to those of James II (Taylor and Jones, 214).

Walpole's efforts to defeat repeal failed. In the next session, however, he found the perfect opportunity to embarrass the government in the Peerage Bill, a measure designed to limit the size of the House of Lords. His behaviour again appeared to many to be pure faction—Arthur Onslow recalled that Walpole cajoled his allies into opposing the bill, despite their belief that they would be acting in contradiction to whig principles. However, Walpole had played a prominent role in a pamphlet debate in the spring of 1719 about an earlier attempt by the ministry to legislate on this issue. Given the sentiments he had expressed in his *Thoughts of a Member of the Lower House*, he was already committed to opposing the bill that was introduced into the House of Lords on 25 November 1719. Speaking towards the end of the Commons debate on 7 December, Walpole condemned it as a blatant attempt by the ministry to secure its power in the upper house, and he played effectively on the ambitions of country gentlemen that their families might one day be raised to the peerage. But his main argument was that it would 'subvert the whole constitution' by destroying the 'due balance between the three branches of the legislature' (Coxe, *Walpole*, 1.123). The speech was possibly the best he ever delivered, and helped to secure the defeat of the bill by 269 votes to 177. Even Onslow admitted that it 'had as much of natural eloquence and of genius in it as had been heard by any of the audience within those walls' (*Buckinghamshire MSS*, 459).

Return to government and the South Sea Bubble Six months after the defeat of the Peerage Bill, Walpole was back in the ministry. On 11 June 1720 he returned to office as paymaster-general of the forces, and on the same day his brother-in-law Lord Townshend was appointed lord president of the council. But it would be dangerous to draw the conclusion that these events were directly linked. While Walpole had demonstrated his ability to inflict a striking, if occasional, defeat on the Sunderland–Stanhope administration, he was far from controlling a majority in the Commons. What, then, led the two whig factions to sink their differences?

Unfortunately, little evidence survives to illuminate the motives of those who participated in the negotiations in spring 1720. Walpole and Townshend were probably motivated in large part by the recognition that their current tactics were leading nowhere. Their sense of weakness was doubtless increased by the scheme introduced into the House of Commons on 22 January 1720 for the South Sea Company to take over a large part of the national debt. If that scheme was a success—and in spring and early summer 1720 it appeared to be—then the burden of the national debt would be reduced and the position of the ministry strengthened. More puzzling, therefore, was the ministry's willingness to enter into negotiations, especially in the light of the animosity between Walpole and Sunderland. The desire to weaken the opposition in parliament surely played a part, especially in view of the king's desire to secure the payment of the civil-list debts, an issue which it would have been easy for Walpole to exploit. Also important was Walpole's ability to bring about a reconciliation in the royal family on terms acceptable to George I. As Lady Cowper observed, the prince of Wales was 'guided' by his wife, who had been 'engross'd & Monopolis'd' by Walpole 'to a degree of shutting every body out & making her deaf to every thing [that] did not come from him' (Cowper, diary, fols. 104*v*, 75*r*). The reconciliation was made public when the prince and princess were received at St James's on 23 April, and the whig schism was over.

Publicly, harmony had been restored among the leading figures of the whig party. There was 'great hugging & kissing between the two old & two new Ministers' and they were observed walking 'all four with their Arms round each other to show they are now all one' (Cowper, diary, fol. 99*r*). But the reality was that Walpole and Townshend were joining the Sunderland–Stanhope ministry as junior partners, and their public acknowledgement of this fact was crucial to their readmission to office. They had to wait another month before receiving their offices, Walpole was not a member of the cabinet, and they were unable to secure appointments for their allies. Of those who had left government with them in 1717, only Paul Methuen received a major office, as comptroller of the household. Even William Pulteney, one of Walpole's most loyal lieutenants in the Commons over the previous three years, was left out in the cold, creating a bitter resentment that contributed to his move into opposition in 1725.

Within weeks, however, the bursting of the South Sea Bubble had transformed British politics. Since the announcement of the scheme for the company to take over a large part of the national debt, there had been wild speculation in its stock. The price had risen from 170 at the beginning of March to a peak of 1050 on 24 June, accompanied by a more general stock market boom. In August the bubble burst. By 1 September the price of company stock had fallen to 775, and then to 290 by 1 October. The crash threatened the stability of public credit and also generated a clamour for revenge from those who had lost heavily in the fever of speculation.

The next year was a crucial period in Walpole's political career, as he played the leading role in formulating and implementing the ministry's response to the crisis. By the middle of 1721 he had re-established Townshend and himself as key members of the administration. However, the image of Walpole as the far-sighted statesman, remaining aloof until summoned by the public to rescue the country from disaster, is simply inaccurate. To understand his role it is necessary to examine his personal finances, the policies he pursued for the restoration of public credit, and his responses to the political reverberations of the bubble.

As J. H. Plumb has demonstrated through a study of Walpole's surviving accounts, it is simply untrue that he made a fortune by purchasing South Sea stock and selling out at the top of the market. At the beginning of 1720 Walpole held almost £10,000 of stock, but he had sold all of that by 18 March, denying himself the opportunity of profiting from the rapid rise in its value over the next three months. He did not invest again until the third subscription in June, at a time when the price was approaching its peak. Indeed, far from making a profit out of South Sea stock, it seems likely that Walpole suffered a significant loss on his June investments, and he certainly lost £27,000 in loans to Sir Cesar Child and Lord Hillsborough who were bankrupted in the crash. The losses were probably more than balanced by the 'small fortune' (Plumb, *Sir Robert Walpole*, 1.309) that he made from other investments in 1720, particularly in insurance and the Royal African Company. But Walpole had no special insight into the weaknesses of the South Sea scheme. In summer 1720 he was saved from making significant losses on insurance stocks only by the prudence of his banker, Robert Jacombe, and as late as the end of August he was willing to commit further substantial sums to the South Sea Company. Through this period Walpole was also investing heavily in land in Norfolk. This might appear a sensible response to the fever of stock market speculation, but the bubble was also pushing up land prices, and at no other time in his career would Walpole have paid as much for the estates he purchased.

It is easy to exaggerate Walpole's importance in restoring public finances: time was more important than government action in bringing stability back to the markets. None the less, as an acknowledged expert in financial matters and one of the few members of the administration not tainted by association with the original legislation, Walpole played a leading role in ministerial and parliamentary deliberations about the crisis in late 1720 and through 1721. As early as November 1720 newspapers were referring to him as 'the famous Mr. W—le' (Dickson, 159). He recognized that, despite the clamour, the scheme had actually succeeded in its aim of altering the structure of the national debt and significantly reducing the burden of interest payable by the government. In the Commons he strongly resisted efforts by public creditors to get out of their agreements to purchase South Sea stock, securing the endorsement of this 'Fundamental' position on 20 December (Chandler, 6.225). Other early initiatives achieved less. Walpole was probably largely responsible for the so-called bank contract, drawn up after a meeting on 19 September, but it never took effect. The first comprehensive scheme, known to contemporaries as the ingraftment, was developed by Walpole with the assistance of Robert Jacombe in the autumn and embodied in legislation which passed into law in March 1721, but it was permissive only and never put into effect. Not until August 1721 was an act 'to restore the publick Credit' finally passed. Walpole again appears to have been 'the main architect' of the provisions, which forced the South Sea Company to disgorge its surplus stock and abandon its claims to be paid in full for what it had sold, while investors had to reconcile themselves to substantial losses (Dickson, 176).

From the time when parliament reassembled in December 1720, however, public attention focused on the campaign to punish the men responsible for the disaster, particularly the directors of the South Sea Company and those ministers implicated in the affair. Walpole felt no temptation to lead the call for revenge. Elections were due in 1722 and the destruction of the ministry could not be risked. Besides, his position in the closet would not be strengthened by joining an investigation directed at the king's favourite ministers and which might implicate the court itself in the scandal. Walpole set about doing what he could to defend the ministry. His task was made easier by the deaths of Stanhope and the two James Craggs, father and son. Even so, the South Sea directors had to be sacrificed to the popular clamour, as did John Aislabie, the chancellor of the exchequer. During the debate on Aislabie the opposition were quick to notice that 'Walpole's corner satt mute as fishes' (Coxe, *Walpole*, 2.210), an act that Aislabie resented for the rest of his life. Crucially, however, on 15 March, Sunderland was acquitted by 233 votes to 172 with Walpole leading his defence.

Walpole was widely seen as the principal ministerial figure obstructing the investigation into the Bubble. Nicknamed 'the skreen' (Coxe, *Walpole*, 2.216–17), he attracted widespread opprobrium and abuse. But through his conduct he had done much to re-establish the power of the Townshend–Walpole faction within the ministry, demonstrating to the king that, for the time being at least, he was essential to the continuance of the government. The rewards of office soon followed. After the death of Stanhope, Townshend was again appointed secretary of state on 10 February 1721. Moreover, despite his acquittal, Sunderland was too tainted to continue as first lord of the Treasury, and he was replaced by Walpole on 3 April.

Some historians have dated the beginning of the Townshend–Walpole ministry from this point, but there are problems with this analysis. Sunderland remained a powerful figure at court and he retained the office of groom of the stole, which gave him easy access to the king. He had ensured that one of his allies, John, Lord Carteret, succeeded Craggs in the other secretaryship, and throughout the next year many commentators continued to regard him as the leading minister. Barely a façade of harmony was preserved within the ministry, and rumours were common in London about Christmas 1721 that Walpole was on the verge of dismissal. The tensions became deeper as the 1722 elections approached—in several constituencies Walpole and Sunderland supported rival candidates. Walpole was not in a strong position to win this battle. Sunderland still enjoyed the trust of the king, who had no love for Walpole and was resolved that he 'should not govern' (Plumb, *Sir Robert Walpole*, 1.366). However, after a short illness Sunderland died on 19 April 1722. This date is a far more convincing starting point for the Townshend–Walpole ministry, as George I had little option in the short term other than to place himself in their hands.

Consolidation of power and management of the Commons Walpole and Townshend had now established their dominance of the ministry, but their position was by no means secure. The king accepted them, but only *faute de mieux*. Indeed, a new rival for power was emerging in the person of Lord Carteret. As early as June 1722 gossip was circulating to the effect that he was now the favourite at court, one observer even remarking that he was 'looked on as Premier at present' (*Portland MSS*, 7.328). In this context Walpole can hardly have been reassured by the knowledge that he was widely distrusted among the whig party in parliament. In the House of Lords the ministry was faced by a small but vocal opposition, composed mainly of tories, but led by the former whig lord chancellor, Earl Cowper, which had been brought together in reaction to the extensive political corruption revealed by the South Sea Bubble. Similar sentiments were expressed by a small group of country whigs in the Commons, who condemned the abandonment of whig principles by Sunderland and Walpole. Their ideas were developed most effectively by John Trenchard and Thomas Gordon in the popular *Cato's Letters*, published initially in the *London Journal* in 1720–22. More generally, Walpole had damaged his whig credentials by co-operating with tories during the whig schism and screening men widely believed to be guilty during the South Sea crisis. Over the next year, however, he was able to exploit another political crisis to consolidate the position of the ministry.

On 21 April 1722, just two days after Sunderland's death, the ministry received intelligence from the French government about a Jacobite plot, better known as the Atterbury plot after one of its leaders, Francis Atterbury, bishop of Rochester. The plot had its origins in negotiations between Sunderland and some leading tories which had begun in early 1721 as part of his strategy to undermine Walpole. These contacts came to nothing and eventually the tories realized that they were being duped, but in their enthusiasm they had sent off an invitation to the Pretender. In November, Atterbury and a number of the other conspirators committed themselves to plans for a landing by the duke of Ormond, though by April 1722 it was increasingly clear that this scheme was impractical.

Walpole and Townshend acted immediately, and the opening of the posts produced a substantial amount of Jacobite correspondence. The ministers had a good idea who the leading Jacobites were, but as the conspirators went to ground and the letters dried up they lacked the proof needed for a prosecution or even to justify stationing troops in Hyde Park. Then, in the summer, Walpole had a great stroke of luck, as the intercepted letters of Christopher Layer, a minor plotter, revealed plans for a rebellion and the assassination of George I. This provided the justification for the arrest of Atterbury, Lord Orrery, and Lord North, as well as Layer. The evidence against Layer was clear and he was convicted of treason. His fantasies, however, were entirely unconnected with the plans of the Atterbury circle, and by the end of 1722 it was becoming clear to Walpole, as he carefully sifted the evidence, that there was not enough to prosecute Orrery and North and that even the case against Atterbury was too weak to risk a treason trial. Consequently, he decided to resort to the 'arbitrary procedure' (Bennett, 89) of a bill of pains and penalties, which simply required him to persuade parliament that it was expedient to punish a man dangerous to the state. Walpole managed to weave together the evidence from the two plots, Atterbury's and Layer's, into a continuous narrative, creating the impression that a dangerous rebellion had only just been averted. In May 1723 the bill was passed: Atterbury was deprived of his bishopric and banished. There is little doubt that he was guilty, but he was convicted on manufactured evidence.

The Atterbury plot strengthened Walpole's position enormously. Within the ministry the plot helped him to win the support of important figures such as the duke of Newcastle, who had previously been a supporter of Sunderland. In the Commons his playing of the Jacobite card rallied the whig party behind him and helped to re-establish his reputation as a defender of whig principles and the Hanoverian succession. Above all, his vigilance earned him more of the king's trust than he had ever enjoyed before. Moreover, the plot weakened the opposition to Walpole both within the ministry and in parliament. The trial left the tories cowed and dispirited and effectively brought to an end the activities of Cowper's opposition group in the Lords. The revelations of the Atterbury plot also contributed to the posthumous discrediting of Sunderland and, by association, his protégé Carteret, whose intrigues with the tories now appeared to have been very dangerous.

The plot also highlighted Walpole's skills as a parliamentary manager. It should be emphasized how important these were to his remaining one of the king's leading ministers for twenty years. A key element in Walpole's appeal to George I and George II was his ability to get the king's business through the Commons. Conversely, Walpole's prominence within the ministry was increased because, until the emergence of Henry Pelham in the 1730s, he was the only cabinet minister sitting in the Commons and therefore took the lead in defending government policy across the full range of its activities. He never underestimated the significance of the Lords and was at times personally involved in its management, but he recognized the Commons to be of greater importance for most regular government business, above all financial legislation. For this reason Walpole chose to eschew precedent and remain in the House of Commons. In June 1723 he refused a peerage, accepting one instead for his eldest son, Robert, though he did become a knight of the Bath on the restitution of that order in 1725 and then, the following year, a knight of the Garter. The latter honour was one of which he was particularly proud, as he was the first commoner to be instituted since the Restoration.

Many contemporaries and later historians have claimed that Walpole achieved his dominance over the Commons through the use of patronage. Places and pensions were distributed to MPs, making them dependent on the ministry and guaranteeing it a parliamentary majority. This analysis was propagated particularly effectively from 1726 in the pages of *The Craftsman*, which condemned Walpolean corruption and warned that the constitution was being undermined as parliament was reduced to little more than a rubber stamp for government policy. There is, indeed, no doubt that patronage did play a key role in Walpole's parliamentary management, or that he continued the development of the role of the first lord of the Treasury in its distribution and co-ordination. However, patronage was a blunt and limited tool of management, and there are two other reasons why he was so successful.

First, Walpole was a party leader as well as the king's minister. The reputation which he had acquired as a whig martyr in Anne's reign had been tarnished somewhat by events between 1717 and 1721, but through his exploitation of the Atterbury plot he had done much to re-establish himself as a politician committed to the defence of the revolution and the protestant monarchy. Some groups of whigs remained suspicious of Walpole's principles and motives, but he always retained the ability to appeal to party solidarity, especially by invoking the spectre of Jacobitism and portraying his administration as the only real defence for the Hanoverian succession. At moments of crisis, as, for example, in the immediate aftermath of the excise crisis in 1733, he exploited this appeal vigorously—some would say cynically—to rally support to the ministry. Second, the testimony of contemporaries makes it clear that Walpole possessed unrivalled abilities as a parliament man. The earl of Shelburne later recalled that Walpole was 'eminently qualified' for managing the Commons 'by the plainness and soundness of his understanding, his steadiness, experience, and country conviviality' (Fitzmaurice, 1.32). More revealingly, perhaps, a very similar assessment was made by one of the leaders of the opposition to Walpole, the earl of Chesterfield. He was:

> both the ablest parliament man, and the ablest manager of parliament, that I believe ever lived. An artful rather than an eloquent speaker, he saw as by intuition, the disposition of the House, and pressed or receded accordingly. So clear in stating the most intricate matters, especially in the finances, that while he was speaking the most ignorant thought that they understood what they really did not. (Franklin, 114)

In this context his very public decision to decline a peerage assumes added significance. It not only revealed Walpole's assessment of the importance of the Commons in managing the king's business, but it also enhanced his standing there. As one contemporary noted, 'Mr W. chooses to give nobility to others, rather than to accept it himself' (John Wainwright to Timothy Thomas, 17 Nov 1723, BL, Add. MS 70400).

Building and collecting Walpole's return to power in 1720 was reflected in his decision to rebuild the family home at Houghton. In 1700, 1716, and 1719 a certain amount of work had been undertaken modernizing the old house, and the decision to rebuild completely was taken no earlier than late summer 1720. The foundation-stone was laid on 24 May 1722 on a site a few yards to the east of the old house, and the exterior was completed in 1729, with the exception of William Kent's stables of 1733. The poverty of Walpole's heirs meant that Houghton Hall has survived remarkably intact through to the present. Unfortunately, however, relatively few sources survive to detail the building process, with the result that even the architect is not known with certainty. It is no more clear who was responsible for the design of the park, which included moving the village of Houghton and levelling the site, but it is likely that Charles Bridgeman played at least a major part.

There is little doubt that Walpole himself took a close interest in planning and building the new hall, which had to serve a variety of purposes. On the one hand, it 'was a place of parade', which could be used to receive and entertain state guests in suitable fashion. On the other hand, it was a country retreat for family and political allies. This dual purpose was, to some extent, reflected in the design of the house. The ground floor or, as Lord Hervey described it, 'rustic story' was 'dedicated to fox-hunters, hospitality, noise, dirt and business'. The first floor, by contrast, was 'the floor of taste, expense, state and parade' (Ilchester, 71). It contained the state rooms, decorated in rich, opulent fashion by Kent—the gold trimmings of the state bed alone cost £1219 3s. 11d.

Above all, Houghton Hall was a statement and celebration of Walpole's power and prestige as the king's minister. It was intended to rival, if not eclipse, the seats of both political allies and rivals, and there is little doubt that it served its purpose. Robinson not only wrote that 'it is the greatest house in the world for its size, capable of the greatest reception for company', but also claimed that the interior was 'a pattern for all great houses that may hereafter be built' (Carlisle MSS, 85). Indeed, such was the impression that the house made on contemporaries that it was the subject of 'the first monograph on a British country house', Isaac Ware's The Plans, Elevations and Sections of Houghton in Norfolk, published in 1735 (Moore, 24).

The impact of Houghton Hall was all the greater because it provided a setting for Walpole's magnificent art collection, which even the earl of Oxford was compelled to admire. His earliest recorded purchase was of two landscapes by Jan Griffier senior in April 1718; by 1736 he owned 421 pictures, of which at least 400 had been acquired by him. His taste mirrored that of the age, and the collection was particularly strong in Dutch, especially Flemish, works, while containing significant numbers of paintings from the French and Italian schools. Walpole also patronized contemporary artists, notably Charles Jervas, both as a portraitist and as a copyist, and the young William Hogarth, who painted a portrait of Horace Walpole aged ten. At Houghton, the old masters were concentrated in the salon and drawing room and included such masterpieces as Van Dyck's The Holy Family and Rembrandt's Abraham's Sacrifice. In 1739 George Vertue described Walpole's collection of 'Paintings statues Busts &c' as 'the most considerable now of any in England' (Moore, 48). Its importance was still recognized almost half a century later, when John Boydell published The Houghton Gallery, a collection of 162 prints after paintings at Houghton. It is hardly surprising that, when the third earl of Orford was considering selling the collection to raise money, it attracted the attention of Catherine the Great, who purchased about 180 pictures to add to her collection at the Hermitage for between £35,000 and £40,000.

For long periods, of course, Walpole resided not at Houghton, but in London. He continued to live at 17 Arlington Street until 1732, moving first to 32 St James's Square and then, in 1735, to 10 Downing Street, a residence accepted by Walpole from George II for the first lord of the Treasury. After his resignation in 1742 he returned to Arlington Street. It was, however, Orford House, which he occupied from 1715 as paymaster-general of Chelsea Hospital, that was his favourite London residence. Between 1715 and 1716 he employed Sir John Vanbrugh to enlarge the seventeenth-century house. He also extended the gardens at the expense of the hospital, adding a river embankment, orangery, and summer-house.

Minister of George I Between 1720 and 1723 English politics had been dominated by financial and domestic affairs, and by the end of the parliamentary session of 1722–3 the Townshend–Walpole ministry was firmly established. Much of the credit for this has to be given to Walpole. However, a major rival, Lord Carteret, still occupied high office. Walpole had tried, but failed, to persuade the king to remove him from office in January 1723, and Carteret had an influential ally in Earl Cadogan, who was hoping to succeed his former patron, the duke of Marlborough, as captain-general. Once parliament had been prorogued, attention shifted to foreign policy, the province of Townshend, and over the next few months the struggle within the ministry was conducted largely in Hanover, for which George I departed, accompanied by both Townshend and Carteret, at the beginning of June. Throughout the summer and autumn Walpole was in a state of high anxiety, recalling, no doubt, how he and Townshend had been outmanoeuvred in 1716. In his desperation to secure an unequivocal demonstration of George I's support and favour, Walpole risked provoking the king by becoming needlessly involved in a dispute over Cadogan's right to command the Horse Guards.

At Hanover, however, Townshend succeeded in outmanoeuvring Carteret over relations first with Russia and then with France, and in particular over the negotiations to marry the daughter of Countess von Platen, the king's Roman Catholic mistress, into the Vrillière family. The sign of royal confidence for which Walpole was so desperate finally came in April 1724, after the king's return from Hanover, when Sir Luke Schaub, the ambassador to France and friend of Carteret, was recalled, to be replaced in May by Robert Walpole's brother Horatio (Horace) *Walpole. Schaub's dismissal was followed two months later by that of Carteret, who was compensated with the lord lieutenancy of Ireland. London gossip had suggested that the new secretary of state would be William Pulteney; instead the duke of Newcastle was appointed. Pulteney's disappointment undoubtedly undermined further his relations with Walpole, but it is far from obvious that it is evidence, as is often claimed, of Walpole's dislike for men of talent as his colleagues. Newcastle may have been

fussy and a poor parliamentary speaker, but he was an energetic minister, and any man who can hold one of the highest government offices almost continuously for thirty-eight years hardly lacks ability. More revealing, therefore, might be Hervey's claim that Pulteney was also intriguing with Carteret in 1723 (Hervey, 1.9).

At the time of Carteret's appointment as lord lieutenant, Ireland was already deep in the crisis caused by the grant of a patent to mint copper halfpence to William Wood, a Birmingham ironmaster. Widely seen as a trick to ruin Ireland by draining it of bullion, the patent provoked strenuous opposition and prompted attacks on Ireland's constitutional dependence on Britain. Walpole later denied having any role in devising it, but late in 1723 he was determined to support it, partly because the opposition was challenging the king's right to issue such patents and partly because he believed it to be a sound measure that would benefit the Irish economy. In his view the problems stemmed from the shortcomings of the lord lieutenant, the duke of Grafton, the failings of Irish politicians, and the intrigues of Carteret with Lord Midleton, the Irish lord chancellor, in an attempt to undermine Walpole's credit with the king. The removal of Grafton in April 1724 and his replacement with a new viceroy apparently offered a solution. It says a lot about Walpole's attitude to Irish politics, therefore, that he did not believe that Carteret would succeed and instead saw his appointment as viceroy as a means of completing his disgrace. To Walpole's surprise, however, Carteret broke with Midleton and carried out the instructions of the ministers in London. But he warned them that, if they adhered to their policy, it would be impossible to persuade the Irish parliament to vote supply when it reassembled. With the same advice coming from more trusted sources in Dublin, such as the new primate, Hugh Boulter, Walpole finally capitulated and withdrew the patent in August 1725.

With Carteret sidelined in Dublin, the Walpole–Townshend faction was able further to consolidate itself in power. The major event in the session of 1725, however, was the resignation and subsequent impeachment of the lord chancellor, the earl of Macclesfield, who was found guilty of corruption for having sold masterships in chancery. Walpole's attitude towards the trial is difficult to discern. He ensured that some ministerialists were involved in its management, probably, as Onslow claimed, to prevent the inquiry being widened. But he showed little concern at Macclesfield's fall, doubtless glad that the removal of one of Sunderland's former allies had been accomplished so easily. That was certainly the interpretation placed on events by the French envoy, Chammorel. In March 1725 Lord Carleton, another member of the Sunderland faction, died and was replaced as lord president of the council by Walpole's old friend and former colleague as MP for Castle Rising, the duke of Devonshire. Then, in May, Walpole was finally able to persuade the king to dismiss Cadogan as master-general of the ordnance, appointing the duke of Argyll in his place.

Hitherto, in the government of Scotland, Walpole seems to have tried to maintain a balance between the two main whig factions, the Squadrone and the Argathelians, despite the fact that the duke of Roxburghe, the Scottish secretary of state and one of the leaders of the Squadrone, had been implicated in Carteret's intrigues. However, during summer 1725 serious rioting broke out in Glasgow in protest at the imposition of the malt tax. This incident was seized on by Walpole as an opportunity to undermine Roxburghe. Although there is little hard evidence to suggest that Roxburghe was behind the disturbances, Walpole's dispatches to Hanover accused him of supporting the protests against the tax and undermining the government's response to the crisis. He achieved his aim in August, when Roxburghe was dismissed and his office suppressed. Henceforth, the business of the Scottish secretary was undertaken by Newcastle and Townshend, but much of the responsibility for government policy and patronage in Scotland was handed over to the duke of Argyll and his brother, the earl of Ilay, who were to dominate Scottish politics for the rest of the Walpole ministry.

In the course of 1724 and 1725, therefore, the old Sunderland faction was effectively destroyed as a political force. But parliament's session of 1725 was also important for two events which did much to determine the nature of the opposition to Walpole over the next decade. First, on 8 April 1725 in a speech against a proposal for discharging the civil-list debts, Pulteney delivered a fierce personal attack on Walpole. He was dismissed from his office as cofferer of the household at the end of the session, and by the summer was 'reckoned the head of the discontented party in England' (Realey, 160). Second, a bill was passed for the restitution of Bolingbroke's estates—he had already been pardoned in 1723. Walpole supported the bill, but very reluctantly, and had to be 'forced to submit' (*Onslow MSS*, 515). Bolingbroke was well aware of Walpole's hostility, which he saw as the reason for his failure to obtain the full restitution of his rights that would have allowed him to resume his political career. For some months, however, Bolingbroke continued to hope for further concessions from the ministry, and it was not until summer 1726 that he began to work with Pulteney. The first major result of their collaboration was the publication on 5 December 1726 of the first issue of *The Craftsman*, the weekly newspaper that was to be the most effective organ of the opposition to Walpole through the next decade. In its pages Bolingbroke and Pulteney proclaimed an end to party divisions: 'let the very Names of *Whig* and *Tory* be for ever buried in Oblivion', called the issue of 24 April 1727 (*The Craftsman*, 1.252). Their aim was to create an opposition platform behind which both whigs and tories could unite in opposition to the corruption of Walpole and his allies.

The mid-1720s also saw the development of government policy along the lines which were to characterize the rest of Walpole's administration. As first lord of the Treasury and chancellor of the exchequer Walpole's first responsibility was financial policy. In particular, he was faced with the massive burden of debt incurred during the French wars of 1689–1713. He set out, therefore, to reduce that burden, both through redeeming part of the national debt

and by reducing the interest payable on the remainder. As has been seen, in 1717 he continued to support his proposals to establish a sinking fund, which would reduce the capital of the debt, even after he had gone into opposition, and he was quick to recognize that the South Sea scheme, by encouraging the holders of irredeemable annuities to exchange them for company stock, made a significant contribution to cutting interest payments. Between 1727 and 1730 the interest paid on government stock held by the three great financial companies—the Bank of England, the East India Company, and the South Sea Company—was further reduced from 5 to 4 per cent. Together, between 1721 and 1741, these measures contributed to the reduction of the national debt by £6.25 million net and the annual interest charge from £2.57 million to £1.89 million.

At the same time Walpole was keen to see the burden of taxation—or, more specifically, of the land tax—reduced. For most of his administration, he kept the land tax down to 2s. in the pound, even managing to reduce it to 1s. in 1731–2. In part, this was for political reasons. He was well aware of the way in which the high level of the land tax during the French wars had stimulated toryism among the country gentry, and thus keeping rates low was one means of underpinning the electoral position of his whig administration. But in part Walpole was acting out of principle. He objected to the land tax on the ground that it was paid by only one class, the landed gentry. The working out of these ideas in practice was seen most controversially in 1732, when the salt tax was reimposed in order to keep the land tax at 1s. More generally, Walpole's ministry saw the balance gradually shift from direct to indirect taxation. This trend can be seen as early as 1726 when higher current expenditure was funded not by increasing the land tax, as was normal in peacetime, but by raising a loan of £500,000 to be funded by a new tax on victuallers.

Another way of keeping taxes down was to improve the efficiency of the fiscal system. It was generally accepted that widespread smuggling reduced the yields from many customs duties. To combat this Walpole brought forward a proposal in 1723 to transfer the duties on tea, coffee, and chocolate from the customs to the excise. The scheme was successful, increasing revenue by £120,000 a year, and in 1733 Walpole tried to extend it to tobacco, a proposal that will be discussed later. Customs and excise duties, however, were not simply ways of raising revenue; they also offered mechanisms for the encouragement and regulation of trade. In keeping with contemporary 'mercantilist' theories Walpole acted in 1721 to remove many of the remaining export duties on manufactured goods and import duties on raw materials, and throughout his ministry he constantly emphasized his concern for overseas trade.

Walpole was also closely involved in developing the ministry's religious policy. Both the first lord of the Treasury and the senior secretary of state claimed the right to advise the king on the distribution of ecclesiastical patronage, and it was Walpole as much as Townshend who selected Edmund Gibson, bishop of London, as their

'Church minister' in 1723, saying 'He must be Pope' (BL, Add. MS 32686, fols. 326–7). The aim of whig policy through the next decade was, as summarized by Gibson, 'to bring the Body of the Clergy to a liking of a Whig-Administration, or at least to an acquiescence in it, and a disposition to be quiet and easy under it' (Hunt. L., Gibson papers, bound vol., no. 13). To this end the ministry pursued policies towards the church that led some to accuse it of adopting tory principles (Hervey, 1.3–4), and there is an element of truth in this. The memory of the Sacheverell affair was etched deeply on Walpole's mind and he feared the damage that a revival of the cry 'The Church in danger' could do to the stability of his administration. Consequently, he abandoned the religious liberalism of the Sunderland–Stanhope ministry and discountenanced the discussion in parliament of any question relating to the rights and privileges of the church or the extension of Toleration Act. However, to some extent the description of Gibson as 'Walpole's Pope', popularized by Horace Walpole, is misleading. Through the 1720s it was Townshend, rather than Walpole, who was apparently closer to the 'Church minister' and who was more involved in the day-to-day management of religious policy, helping Gibson to achieve the creation of the Whitehall preacherships and the regius professorships of history at Oxford and Cambridge.

Initially, too, Walpole was little involved in foreign affairs, though he was not as ignorant of them as is often made out. In 1723 he had been acting secretary of state in London; he could rely on the advice of his brother Horace, who was one of the leading diplomats of the period; and there is good evidence that he had a reading knowledge of French—the story that he conversed with George I in dog Latin is almost certainly apocryphal. But there is little doubt that the ministry's foreign policy was made by Townshend. In 1726 the Austrian envoy, Palm, commented that Walpole 'does not meddle with foreign affairs, but receives accounts of them in general, leaving for the rest the direction of them entirely to Ld. Townshend' (Cholmondeley (Houghton) correspondence, 1379). However, there are indications that from 1725 Walpole began to take more of an interest in European affairs. In that year, responding to the threat posed by the treaty of Vienna (1724) between Spain and the Habsburg emperor, Townshend concluded the alliance of Hanover with France and Prussia. For the next three years Europe organized itself into two great armed camps, and briefly war broke out between Britain and Spain in 1726–7. This caused problems for Walpole in the Commons. He not only had to find the money for military preparations, forcing him to increase the land tax from its normal peacetime rate of 2 s. to 4 s. in 1727 and 3 s. in 1728–9, but also had to defend a policy that was distrusted by many whigs, who had been brought up to believe in the necessity of allying with Austria to resist French aggression. Moreover, he clearly did not believe that the situation in Europe was as bad as it was portrayed, prompting rumours of tensions between Townshend and Walpole.

In the last years of George I's reign the Townshend–Walpole ministry stood high in the king's favour. The ministers' personal standing was revealed clearly by their appointment, in 1724 and 1726, as knights of the Garter. The evidence suggests that Townshend enjoyed the closer relationship with George, and some observers still saw him as the leading figure in the ministry. But even Walpole was honoured by the king in 1726 with two visits to his house at Richmond for dinner. The parliamentary opposition presented little threat to Walpole's position: its best parliamentary performance came in 1727 when it reduced the government's majority to 107. Court intrigues proved no more effective. Through the duchess of Kendal, Bolingbroke succeeded in presenting a memorial to the king and even obtained an audience, but his complaints against Walpole were dismissed as 'bagatelles' (Coxe, *Walpole*, 2.345). The only real threat to the supremacy of Townshend and Walpole came from the hostility of the prince of Wales.

The emergence of the 'great man' The beginning of the prince's dislike of Walpole probably stemmed from the terms negotiated by Walpole for the reconciliation in the royal family in 1720. Certainly by 1726 it was common knowledge that the prince 'treats him very distantly and coldly, to say the least of it, and shows his dislike to him on every possible occasion' (*Foreign View of England*, 175). The unexpected death of George I on 11 June 1727, while travelling to Hanover, suddenly made the opinions of the new king of the utmost political importance. Walpole himself took the news to the king and queen at Richmond on 14 June and received the curt instruction, 'Go to Chiswick and take your directions from Sir Spencer Compton' (Hervey, 1.22). This was no surprise: it was generally expected that Walpole would be dismissed and replaced by Compton, the speaker of the Commons and the prince's treasurer. Walpole was of the same opinion, confessing to Arthur Onslow that he would be content with any place at court, 'even with the Comptroller's staff' (*Buckinghamshire MSS*, 517). However, later that day Compton sought Walpole's assistance in drafting the new king's declaration to the privy council, and the following day George II was discussing the civil list with Walpole. Walpole exploited his opportunity. By 15 June the French ambassador was reporting that the old ministry would remain in office, and within three weeks Compton, recognizing that his credit was declining, 'left off the constancy of his attendance' on the king (King, 454).

Why had Walpole survived, despite the universal expectation that he would be replaced? Links with the prince of Wales's court had been kept open through the mid-1720s, notably through the duke of Devonshire, Walpole's friend and lord president of the council, who was welcome at Leicester House, and the prince's own friends were not excluded from preferment—the earl of Scarbrough, for example, received the Garter. Of much more significance, however, was Walpole's continuing friendship with Queen Caroline. Unlike many politicians, including Compton, he had never cultivated the new king's mistress, Henrietta Howard, recognizing that she exercised no political influence. As he said, in a phrase that illustrates his occasional coarseness of speech, Compton 'took the wrong sow by the ear … I the right' (Hardwicke, 6). Certainly, Walpole and a number of contemporary commentators saw his continuance in power as a demonstration of Caroline's influence at the beginning of the new reign. Lord Hervey also emphasized the importance of Walpole's undertaking to obtain parliamentary approval for a civil list of £800,000 a year for George II, £100,000 more than his father, plus £100,000 for the queen. This 'exorbitant augmentation' (Hervey, 1.34) was certainly pleasing for the king, but it is important not to place too much weight on it. The real significance of the new civil list was that it provided a timely demonstration for George of Walpole's unrivalled ability to secure the support of the Commons for the king's business, reiterating the message that he was receiving from his wife.

Walpole had retained his position, but in some respects it was weaker than in the last years of George I's reign. Individuals over whom he had little influence were rewarded with places. Scarbrough became master of the horse, while Augustus Schulz replaced Viscount Malpas, his own son-in-law, as master of the robes. Another of Walpole's loyal lieutenants, Sir William Yonge, was dismissed as a Treasury commissioner. Most significantly, Compton retained his office of paymaster and was raised to the peerage as Lord Wilmington, remaining a brooding presence in the ministry, his continued favour with the king demonstrated when he became lord president of the council in 1730. Even in the church Walpole's influence was curtailed by the queen's insistence on the appointment of the high-churchman and former tory Thomas Sherlock to the bishopric of Bangor. Walpole himself appears to have felt vulnerable, complaining in late 1727 that, while he enjoyed 'great credit' with the king, he was 'struck at' by those who had been disappointed at the beginning of the reign (King, 455–6).

Most contemporaries, however, interpreted Walpole's situation very differently. His survival as the king's minister appeared to be a remarkable demonstration of his political dominance, and it is from this point that it is possible to date a real shift in the popular perception of Walpole. The description of him as 'the great man' can be found as early as 1725 (Various Collections, 8.390), but it became a commonplace only after the accession of George II. In July 1727 The Craftsman coined the phrase 'the Robinocracy' to describe the Walpolean regime (The Craftsman, 2.78). Then, on 29 January 1728 John Gay's The Beggar's Opera opened in London and became an overnight success. The political satire of this work was much more pointed and personal than anything in Jonathan Swift's Gulliver's Travels (1726). Audiences found it easy to draw parallels between both the highwayman Macheath and the thief-taker Peachum on the one hand and Walpole on the other. Henceforth the link between the thief and the corrupt statesman became a familiar trope in opposition literature, drawing especially on the popular accounts of the life of Jonathan Wild, the notorious mastermind of the London underworld executed in 1725 and the model for Gay's Peachum.

Walpole's growing prominence was accompanied by a decline in Townshend's profile, and a rift began to develop between the two men. The death of Lady Townshend, Walpole's sister Dorothy, on 29 March 1726 had broken the closest personal connection between them. Matters deteriorated so far that, by the end of the decade, one quarrel led them to lay hands on each other and then on their swords before being parted by colleagues. In part, the sources of the breach lay in foreign policy, over which Walpole and Townshend quarrelled, if not over their shared aims—reconciliation with Austria and less dependence on France—then certainly over the approach and the cost.

Walpole's victory over Townshend was not inevitable. During the early years of the new reign various rumours circulated about the reconstruction of the ministry. Townshend wanted to replace Newcastle as secretary of state with his ally Chesterfield as a means of strengthening his hold over foreign policy and weakening Walpole's position. Conversely, Walpole saw Devonshire's death as an opportunity to oust Townshend by making him lord president. The major weakness in Townshend's position was his lack of influence at court. His relationship with George II gradually improved and the king was not prepared to dismiss him. But crucially the Caroline–Walpole axis held firm, giving Walpole an immense advantage over his rival. The prolonged period of ministerial instability finally ended with Townshend's resignation on 16 May 1730, a recognition of the fact that he had lost what Bishop Gibson described as the 'competition for power' between them (St Andrews University Library, Gibson MS 5315).

Arguably, it is not until this point that Walpole should be regarded as having established himself as prime minister. It was, indeed, only in the 1730s that this phrase began to be used commonly, not only by the opposition but also, albeit less frequently, by ministerial MPs and even the pro-government press. Only after Townshend's resignation can it be convincingly claimed that Walpole monopolized the counsels of the king or dominated the administration and its policies. A clear demonstration of his power came within weeks when he secured the dismissal of Carteret as lord lieutenant of Ireland. Even more revealing, in some ways, was his increasingly active role in foreign policy. During the summer of 1730 he was helping to draft instructions to British envoys, and when the second treaty of Vienna was signed in March the following year, concluding a new alliance between Britain and Austria, it was portrayed in the press very much as Walpole's achievement.

Paradoxically, the same session that saw Walpole emerge as George II's prime minister also witnessed a marked increase in the size and effectiveness of the parliamentary opposition. The position of the ministry after the 1727 elections was stronger than at the dissolution, and its critics in 1728 and 1729 were able to make little impression on the government's majority. At the beginning of 1730, however, it soon became clear that Walpole would face a reinvigorated opposition. The main force of the opposition attack came on 10 February, when Sir William Wyndham surprised the Commons with revelations that Dunkirk harbour had been repaired contrary to the provisions of the treaty of Utrecht. According to Hervey, this put the whole house 'in a flame' and the ministry was 'stronger pushed than they had ever been on any occasion before' (Hervey, 1.116). Walpole managed to have the debate put off until 27 February, by which time he was able to deflect criticism of the administration by producing an undertaking from the king of France that the works at Dunkirk would be demolished. However, in the midst of the crisis he failed by ten votes to secure the defeat of the Place Bill, an opposition proposal intended to limit the number of government office-holders sitting in the Commons.

The growing effectiveness of the opposition can be explained in part by better leadership and organization bringing together dissident whigs and tories, and in particular by the role of Bolingbroke, a fact that Walpole himself recognized and exploited in the Dunkirk debate. Other factors included the struggle within the ministry between Walpole and Townshend; the growing concern both inside parliament and outside, particularly in the City of London, about the ministry's foreign policy, especially the French alliance; and, most significantly, the prominence of political corruption as a critique of the ministry. As has been seen, this analysis of the Walpolean regime stretched back through the Macclesfield impeachment to the South Sea Bubble—indeed, opposition MPs were still fond of referring to Walpole's sojourn in the Tower during Anne's reign. But in the late 1720s and early 1730s it appeared to some that an ever more pervasive stink of corruption was hanging over the government. In 1729–30 a Commons committee uncovered a pattern of extensive abuse in the management of gaols, which was felt to reflect badly on the administration, especially when it came to be suspected that it was screening judges who might be implicated. In 1732 another Commons investigation revealed widespread fraud in the management of the charitable corporation, as a result of which Sir Robert Sutton was expelled from the house. Walpole again appeared tainted, seeking to 'skreen' Sutton and ensuring that no further punishment was inflicted on him (Hanham, 325). In the same session more frauds were revealed in the sale of the confiscated estates of the earl of Derwentwater. In the eyes of opposition writers, however, it was not only the Walpolean polity that was corrupt, but also Walpole himself. From around 1730 the personal attacks on Walpole became more pointed, and it is from this time that representations of him became common in the rapidly developing culture of satirical prints. A good example is a print of 1730, which drew an explicit parallel between Walpole and Colonel Francis Charteris, a notorious rake convicted of rape but controversially pardoned by the king (Langford, *Walpole*, 60–61).

The crises of 1733 and 1736 During the sessions of 1731 and 1732 the parliamentary opposition tried to maintain the pressure on Walpole—in both sessions place bills passed

the Commons, only to be defeated by the ministerial majority in the Lords. Walpole, however, was generally successful at containing the threat. First, the conclusion of the second treaty of Vienna between Britain and Austria in March 1731 undermined the opposition critique of the government's foreign policy by re-establishing the 'old system' and bringing to an end the Anglo-French alliance. Second, the alliance allowed Walpole to discharge the Hessian troops, whose employment had been a focus for criticism in earlier sessions. Third, the reduction of tension in Europe enabled him to appeal to the country gentry and the more independently minded backbenchers by reducing the land tax. That this strategy was not quite as straightforward as it seemed, however, was revealed in 1732, when Walpole proposed reimposing the salt tax in order to bring down the land tax to 1s. in the pound and even hinted at the possibility of abolishing it. This proposal provoked fierce opposition, and the government's majority fell to a mere twenty-nine. The salt duty had been abolished only two years earlier, and in part the Commons were antagonized by the attempt to reverse a measure enacted for the benefit of 'the poor Artificers and Manufacturers' (Chandler, 7.52). But, more significantly, MPs were alarmed by the re-establishment of a revenue department that provided significant ministerial patronage and by the hints of the abolition of the land tax, which was valued by the country gentlemen as a tax that was voted annually, administered, and collected by them, and thus outside direct government control. These concerns were particularly significant in the light of events in the following year.

The parliamentary session of 1733 witnessed the most serious crisis for the Walpole administration until his fall in 1741–2 in the defeat of the Tobacco Excise Bill, a major plank in his fiscal strategy. In outline, Walpole's proposals were simple and broadly similar to the legislation introduced for tea, coffee, and chocolate in 1723. First, all tobacco and wine (the legislation relating to wine was never introduced) were to be placed in the king's warehouse until all duties had been paid. Second, the existing customs duties, payable on import, were to be replaced for the most part by excise duties, payable when the goods were removed from the warehouse for consumption. There were sound commercial and colonial reasons for introducing the Tobacco Excise Bill. The Virginia tobacco planters were lobbying for precisely such a measure, and there were even hopes that the system of bonded warehouses would stimulate trade by encouraging the development of London as a 'free port'. There is little doubt, however, that fiscal and broader political concerns were more important in ministerial reasoning. Walpole clearly saw it as an essentially technical measure that would increase government revenue, perhaps by as much as £300,000 a year, by curbing fraud and smuggling. That was a significant sum and would assist Walpole in his aim of keeping the land tax low. With trade booming and agricultural prices subdued, it appeared equitable to shift part of the tax burden away from land. But in the year before a general election there was a clear political dimension to the legislation, and there is no doubt that Walpole believed it would be a vote winner among the landed gentry.

However, Walpole had blundered. His excise proposals provoked massive opposition. Some of this came from retailers and traders who were concerned that the legislation would subject them to inspection by excise officers. Far more important, however, was the hostility of the wine and tobacco merchants, both in London and in the major provincial ports. Many if not most of them were heavily implicated in fraud, and thus the legislation represented an attack on a powerful pressure group with a vested interest in the existing system. When the London tobacco merchants met in January, they succeeded in raising £300 to fund their campaign against the bill. More generally, the excise legislation revived issues which had been raised during the debates on the salt tax in the previous year. Opposition propaganda made much of fears that the Tobacco Bill was merely the first step towards a 'general excise', a charge denied by Walpole. But underlying this was a concern about the expansion of the excise service, whose 'arbitrary' powers of search were seen as a threat to English liberties. In this context Walpole's proposals, far from appealing to the country gentlemen by reducing their tax burden, appeared to be an attempt to concentrate power still further in the hands of an already over-mighty, and possibly corrupt, state.

Walpole's next miscalculation was to press ahead with his proposals. He had plenty of time to change tack: the drafting of the bill did not begin until January 1733. However, he did not do so, continuing to believe his scheme attractive. In March, when the proposals were introduced into the Commons against the background of large demonstrations in Westminster, it appeared likely that he would get away with it, securing relatively comfortable majorities of sixty-one and sixty in a full house. However, when parliament resumed in April after the Easter recess, his majority collapsed. On 10 April it fell to just seventeen on a motion to receive the City of London's petition against the bill. This was the occasion on which Walpole did so much to alienate City opinion by describing the petitioning merchants as 'sturdy beggars' (*Egmont Diary*, 1.363). But the decision to drop the bill had already been made, and on the following day Walpole proposed that further discussion should be postponed until 12 June, by when the house would be in recess. During the celebrations in the City that night Walpole was burnt in effigy by the mob.

If the origins of the excise crisis revealed Walpole's political failings, its aftermath highlighted his skills. On 11 April, Walpole was mobbed in the court of requests after the abandonment of the bill. The next day this riot was complained of in the Commons, Walpole himself recounting 'the design made upon his life' (*Egmont Diary*, 1.362). The episode was then effectively exploited to turn parliamentary opinion against the opposition, as members reacted against what was portrayed as an attempt to influence its liberty of speech. Later in the month the opposition tried to push home its advantage by launching

an inquiry into frauds in the customs service. On the evening before the vote to select members of the committee, Walpole summoned his supporters to a meeting in the Cockpit and delivered a speech in which he appealed to 'Whig principles' and raised the spectre of Jacobitism (Hervey, 1.182), implying that the revolution settlement itself was under threat. According to Hervey, his performance was so effective that 'for two or three days there seemed to be a resurrection of that party spirit which had so long been dormant' (ibid., 1.184), and the court list was carried by the comfortable majority of eighty-five.

The key to the collapse in the ministry's majority during the passage of the bill was its failure to ensure the attendance of its own supporters, and the main reason for this was the crisis at court. A number of influential figures, including lords Chesterfield, Stair, Bolton, Clinton, and Scarbrough, made clear their opposition to the bill. They intrigued in the closet and spread rumours outside it, encouraging the belief that the support of the king and queen was wavering. Despite the claims of Hervey (Hervey, 1.149), there are hints that George II's confidence in Walpole was shaken. In any event, it was perceptions that mattered, and in this context the dismissal of Clinton and Chesterfield from their court offices on 13 April provided the public reaffirmation of royal confidence in Walpole that was crucial to re-establishing his position in the Commons.

Walpole had demonstrated that he could not be brought down on a single issue like the excise, and despite opposition pressure in the 1734 session his majority remained solid. He even risked attempting to defeat Samuel Sandys's 'Place Bill' in the Commons, which he succeeded in doing, albeit by only thirty-nine votes. Outside parliament, however, the reverberations of the crisis continued to be felt. The flood of propaganda continued, with more being published in the year after the defeat of the bill than in the months before. In particular, there was an explosion in the production of satirical prints attacking ministerial corruption and arbitrary power, in which Walpole himself was a familiar figure, often easily identified by his Garter star. The issue of the excise, and continuing fears of a general excise, dominated the campaign leading to the elections of 1734, at which the opposition were determined to defeat 'the villain Walpole' (Hanham, 393). There was a massive movement of opinion against the government in the large, open constituencies; even the country gentry, who had most to gain from the reduction of the land tax, were roused by fears of a general excise. There is little doubt that, in what was one of the most contested elections of the century, most of the electorate voted against Walpole's ministry. In the counties and large towns the opposition did very well. But in the smaller boroughs the ministry made its influence felt, as it did in Scotland and Cornwall, with the result that Walpole was able to face the new parliament in 1735 with a majority of over ninety.

Reviewing the excise crisis, the earl of Egmont commented that 'it may be foretold that Sir Robert Walpole's influence in the House will never be again so great as it has been' (*Egmont Diary*, 1.361). This view has been shared by many historians, encouraging a tendency to portray his fall as a long process beginning in 1733. There is clearly an element of truth in this interpretation. From 1733 Walpole constantly had to work with a substantial opposition which knew that, given the right issue, it could defeat the minister. He was never again to enjoy the easy parliamentary dominance of the years before 1730. However, the contrast is relative. Walpole continued as prime minister for another eight years, and through most of that period he remained the dominating figure of politics, apparently unassailable in parliament, his power explicable to his critics only as the product of widespread corruption. Certainly, the opposition entered the new parliament divided and disillusioned. Despite their electoral success their strength in the Commons was no greater than in the previous parliament, while in the Lords they were weakened by the defeat of their supporters in the elections of the Scottish representative peers. William Pulteney made some half-hearted overtures to the ministry, Bolingbroke retired to France, and Walpole faced no significant problems in the first session of the new parliament.

The next major crisis faced by Walpole occurred in the 1736 session. In character it was very different from that of 1733: at no time was the ministry itself threatened, but it did severely disrupt Walpole's religious policy. The roots of the crisis lay in the rising tide of whig anti-clericalism through the early 1730s and in the growing pressure from the dissenters for the repeal of the Test Act. These pressures created problems for Walpole in his relations with the church, and in particular with his 'Church minister', Bishop Gibson. For Gibson, a crucial element in the church–whig alliance that he had been promoting since the early 1720s was ministerial support for the revolution settlement in the church, by which he meant a limited toleration for dissenters accompanied by a test act. In the early 1730s Gibson came to believe that Walpole was not doing enough to discourage the succession of anti-clerical initiatives which came before parliament in those years. In fact, in 1733 and 1734 Walpole was working hard to discourage the dissenters from applying to parliament for a repeal of the test. Even so, Gibson's complaints may not have been without foundation. Some of Walpole's favourite pamphleteers, including William Arnall and Thomas Gordon, were prominent in the anti-clerical campaigns, and Walpole may have been unwilling to rein in the attacks of some of his supporters on the church and clergy for fear of alienating anti-clerical whigs and strengthening further the parliamentary opposition.

Events came to a head with the introduction of three measures into parliament in 1736—a motion for the repeal of the test, the Mortmain Bill, and the Quaker Tithe Bill. There is little doubt that Walpole expected that debate on religious issues would emphasize divisions between whigs and tories, and this is certainly what happened in the Commons. During the debates about the test, Walpole adhered to the church–whig alliance by opposing repeal. But ministerial arguments on this occasion 'that this was not a proper time' (Taylor and Jones, 21) were

hardly reassuring to clerical opinion, especially in the light of Walpole's support for the repeal of the Irish Test Act in 1733. The other two proposals, however, left the tories isolated in opposition. The Mortmain Bill, an attack on high-church corporate philanthropy, passed into law despite considerable clerical disquiet. The Quaker Tithe Bill proved even more controversial. Walpole had given assurances to the Quakers that he would support this measure to provide limited relief for those Friends who suffered through their conscientious refusal to pay tithes. He saw the bill as a limited and relatively uncontroversial extension of the toleration, but, as in 1733, he had miscalculated. To Gibson and most of the bishops and parochial clergy it represented a serious assault on the legal rights and privileges of the church. Gibson co-ordinated a vigorous public campaign against the bill, which was eventually defeated on its second reading in the Lords, with all the bishops present voting against.

The Tithe Bill affair created serious problems for Walpole. First, it threatened to undermine a religious policy which had been remarkably successful during the previous thirteen years in persuading the clergy that the church was safe in whig hands. Second, the support of the bench of bishops was crucial for the maintenance of ministerial majorities in the upper house. As in 1733, however, Walpole, having done much to create the crisis, demonstrated his political skills in extricating himself from the consequences of it. Among the bishops Gibson was denounced as the 'Ringleader of Sedition' (St Andrews University Library, Gibson MS 5303) and singled out for attack, provoking his resignation as 'Church minister'. Meanwhile, Walpole worked hard to restore his links with other bishops, such as Thomas Sherlock and John Potter, who became archbishop of Canterbury the following year. Anti-clerical attacks on the church in parliament stopped, and in 1739 Walpole even took advantage of another motion by the dissenters for repeal of the Test Act to affirm unequivocally his support for the existing constitutional settlement. In retrospect the Tithe Bill appears merely as a blip in the story of whig rapprochement with the church, though at the end of the 1730s a small group of bishops could be found in regular opposition to Walpole, alienated at least in part by his religious policy.

Through this period, however, arguably the major issue facing Walpole and the ministry was the British response to the War of the Polish Succession that had broken out in 1733. The British government refused to intervene in support of Austria in her struggle with France, despite its obligations under the treaty of Vienna. Walpole's policy was determined in part by concerns of parliamentary management: he wished to avoid any continental entanglements that would involve expense. However, the policy of nonintervention was made much easier by the absence of any clearly perceived threat to British interests. What is much less clear is how far this policy was Walpole's. The traditional interpretation, drawn largely from Hervey's *Memoirs*, is that Walpole had to struggle hard to maintain the policy of neutrality against fierce opposition from the king and queen. More recent research, however, suggests that the views of Walpole and the king, though different in emphasis, were not that far apart, and that George was certainly not a strident advocate of intervention. It is, indeed, difficult to give much credit to the idea that Britain could have intervened, given the domestic political situation, though there is no doubt that this policy carried a price in the later 1730s, when she was left without any major ally on the continent.

Scotland, the court, and the 'new opposition' In 1737 the opposition once again attacked Walpole's financial policy. On 21 March Sir John Barnard, MP for the City of London, proposed a motion to reduce the interest on part of the national debt from 4 to 3 per cent. This was a subtle move, as the proposal appeared to be an extension of Walpole's own efforts to reduce the burden of the national debt. But if Walpole had supported it, he would have risked conceding the initiative in fiscal affairs to the opposition and at the same time alienating the financial interest in the City. Initially, therefore, he prevaricated, and Barnard's initiative opened up unexpected divisions among the supporters of the ministry. However, the opposition overplayed its hand, which allowed Walpole to oppose the second reading, securing its defeat by the comfortable majority of 115. Divisions within the opposition, partly a legacy of the previous year, were starkly revealed by this vote. However, the 1737 session also witnessed debates on two controversial issues that were to cause significant problems for Walpole in the longer term.

The first was the affair of Captain John Porteous. Porteous had been in command of the Edinburgh city guard in 1736 when it had fired on a crowd of demonstrators, killing six people. For this action he was tried and found guilty of murder. Following a royal reprieve ordering a stay of execution, however, a highly organized riot took place in the city, seizing Porteous from gaol and hanging him. In 1737 the opposition in the Lords, led by Carteret, exploited concern about the collapse of law and order in Edinburgh to call for a parliamentary inquiry into both Porteous's trial and the subsequent riot. There is no doubt that the opposition's motive was, as Edward Harley observed, 'to ruin Sir R. Walpole with the Scotch' (Taylor and Jones, 30). Walpole was certainly placed in a very difficult position. In the Lords, Newcastle and Hardwicke supported the introduction of a bill of pains and penalties to punish Edinburgh, but it was opposed by the duke of Argyll, the earl of Ilay, and all the Scottish peers. Walpole, fearful of losing the support of the Scots in the Commons, made it clear that he was prepared to see the bill emasculated, with the result that, when it passed into law, the only penal clause remaining was one debarring Andrew Wilson, the provost of Edinburgh, from holding public office.

The affair hinted at deeper tensions within the ministry. In part, Hardwicke and Newcastle were concerned with vindicating the rule of law in Scotland, but it was also widely suspected that they were pursuing a feud with Ilay. It is difficult to know whether there is any truth in these claims, but there is no doubt that the Porteous affair saw Newcastle and his allies within the ministry adopt a more

independent attitude than hitherto. More seriously, the opposition strategy to alienate the Scots from the ministry paid dividends. Ilay abstained when the Lords voted on the bill. His brother, Argyll, by contrast, denounced it and was not reconciled by the Commons amendments. From this point he moved steadily into outright opposition to Walpole, finally being dismissed from his colonelcy of the Horse Guards in 1740. Some Scottish MPs followed his lead, but in the longer term this was less of a problem for Walpole than the considerable influence which he was able to exert in the 1741 elections, preventing the ministry from securing its usual clean sweep in Scotland.

The second major event to disrupt the 1737 session of parliament was the debate over the prince of Wales's allowance. Relations between the prince and both his parents and the ministry had been deteriorating for some time. During the excise crisis he had talked 'violently and publicly against Sir Robert' (Stopford-Sackville MSS, 1.157), but he had been reluctant to go into opposition and had supported the administration in Cornwall during the 1734 elections. Matters finally came to a head following his marriage, when the whig opposition proposed a motion to increase his allowance from £50,000 to £100,000, the sum that George II had enjoyed as prince of Wales. This motion was well calculated to embarrass Walpole. Many of the more independent whigs were sympathetic to the prince, remembering that the settlement of the civil list in 1727 had notionally included £100,000 for the prince's household. Younger members of the ministry, including Newcastle and Hardwicke, were concerned about the consequences of a total breach at court and urged reconciliation. However, George II and Caroline were resolutely opposed to making any concessions to their son. Before the debate commentators were predicting that the opposition would secure a majority of up to forty, and Walpole himself believed that, if the motion passed, 'it was to be followed by another to send him to the Tower' (Egmont Diary, 2.356). With great difficulty he persuaded the king to offer to settle £50,000 a year absolutely on the prince together with a jointure for the princess. As Walpole expected the prince rejected this composition, but when the offer was revealed in the debate it helped to secure a majority of thirty against the motion, though even this narrow victory was only achieved thanks to the abstention of forty-five tories.

In September 1737 the breach in the royal family became irreparable. Frederick established his own court, first at Norfolk House and then at Leicester House, and from this point he became ever more closely identified with the opposition to the ministry and particularly to Walpole, whom they marked out as 'the chief object of their resentment' (Hervey, 3.839). The following year Pope referred to the 'New Opposition' (Correspondence of Alexander Pope, 4.143). In many respects the group that coalesced around the prince of Wales was different from the parliamentary opposition of the early 1730s. Pulteney and Carteret were never quite trusted at Leicester House. Instead, Chesterfield emerged as one of the leading figures, along with the group of young Cobhamite whigs, among whom

George Lyttelton and William Pitt were prominent. *Common Sense* replaced *The Craftsman* as the leading opposition journal, preaching a 'broad-bottomed' programme of party co-operation against the corruption and self-interest of Walpolean government that was subtly different from *The Craftsman*'s rhetoric about the end of party distinctions.

As in the late 1720s and early 1730s the opposition attracted a number of influential writers. Late in 1738 Bolingbroke, back in England again, wrote his exhortatory treatise, *The Idea of a Patriot King*, which appears to have circulated in manuscript among Frederick's circle. The ideas developed by Bolingbroke of a patriot prince who would heal party divisions, stamp out corruption, and reinvigorate the nation were common currency among opposition writers. In the late 1730s they appeared in a whole series of works, including David Mallet's *Mustapha*, Henry Brooke's *Gustavus Vasa*, James Thomson's *Edward and Eleanora*, and Richard Glover's *Leonidas*. Henry Fielding, who had already cruelly satirized Walpole as Quidam in his 1737 play *The Historical Register*, also became an active opposition propagandist, editing and writing for the influential newspaper *The Champion*, which was first published in November 1739.

The weakening of Walpole's position in 1737, however, should not be exaggerated. The defection of the prince of Wales had little immediate effect on his parliamentary position, and even the developing literary and newspaper campaign seems to have caused him scant concern: government subsidies to the press declined considerably in the years after 1735. The real significance of the prince's opposition to Walpole became apparent only in the 1741 elections, when he threw his influence in Cornwall against the ministry. Indeed, many contemporaries believed that the greatest threat to Walpole in 1737 was the death in November of Queen Caroline, widely seen as his most committed supporter at court and the key to his influence over the king. According to Hervey, even Walpole himself feared that his position would be undermined. As in 1727, however, those who predicted his fall were disappointed, as George appears to have become if anything even more committed to his minister.

Foreign policy and war, 1738–1741 The parliamentary session of 1738 saw the emergence of an issue which was to prove fruitful for the opposition over the next few years and which ultimately played an important role in the disintegration of the Walpole administration. A range of problems—British possession of Gibraltar, the establishment of the new colony of Georgia, and the depredations committed by Spanish coastguards against British merchants trading with South America and the Caribbean—combined to turn government policy towards Spain into a major subject of debate in both press and parliament. These issues could be exploited effectively by the opposition, uniting under the banner of an expansionist, imperial patriotism and standing up for British mercantile and commercial interests against a pusillanimous ministry that was only too ready to betray them. Once more, satirical prints provided a particularly vivid summary of the

opposition's case; in one, Walpole was portrayed standing by while a Spaniard removed the claws from the British lion. Allegations of Spanish depredations against British shipping proved particularly explosive, dominating debates in the Commons through March 1738. It was on this occasion that Captain Robert Jenkins helped to whip up anti-Spanish feeling by producing his pickled ear which, he claimed, had been cut off by Spanish coastguards. Walpole was anxious to deter the Commons from any action that would 'make a War unavoidable' (Chandler, 10.199), and ultimately persuaded it to reject Pulteney's aggressive resolutions by a comfortable majority. He was, however, obliged to commit the ministry to resolutions which denounced Spanish depredations and attempts to interrupt British commerce with the Americas.

Walpole was committed to securing a peaceful settlement of the disputes with Spain. When parliament reassembled in February 1739, however, the opposition immediately attacked what it saw as the unsatisfactory provisions of the convention of El Pardo signed in the previous year, and in particular the continued assertion by the Spanish of a right of search of British vessels. The ministry's majority collapsed, and on 8 March in the vote of thanks for the convention Walpole secured victory by only twenty-eight votes in a house of nearly 500. When the Lords had debated the convention eight days earlier the prince of Wales had voted against the administration for the first time, and the opposition had mustered seventy-four votes in the biggest Lords division of the Walpole period.

Walpole's position was not as weak as these votes might suggest, and the debates on the convention obscured deep divisions within the opposition. These differences were exacerbated when parliament reassembled in November 1739. By that time the convention had collapsed, largely as a result of the South Sea Company's refusal to pay its debts to the Spanish government, and Britain had declared war against Spain. Now that the clamour for war had been satisfied, Walpole and his ministry were clearly going to enjoy a breathing space. But Pulteney's enthusiastic support for the speech from the throne alienated many of the tories, who were 'heartily angry' with him (Colley, 226).

In the short term, therefore, the outbreak of war impeded the opposition's campaign against Walpole, but it also did little for the unity of the administration. Tensions had been growing for some time within the ministry between Walpole on the one hand and Newcastle and Hardwicke on the other. The latter were critical of Walpole's pacific attitude and favoured a more aggressive policy towards Spain, and by the summer of 1739 the split in the cabinet was common knowledge in London. The disagreements between ministers were exacerbated by the appointment of Lord Hervey as lord privy seal in April 1740. Newcastle, who detested Hervey, was infuriated by Walpole's 'indifference' and threatened to resign—an action from which he was dissuaded only by Hardwicke. The affair deepened the 'resentment' between Newcastle and Walpole, Newcastle complaining bitterly of 'the natural jealousy of his temper' (Yorke, *Life and Correspondence*, 1.231), while Walpole lamented 'how hard it was for him to serve with Newcastle' (BL, Add. MS 32692, fol. 450). After the collapse of the convention Walpole agreed only reluctantly to the declaration of war, and according to Henry Etough, his chaplain and the author of an early memoir, his policy having failed, he 'applied for leave to resign' and remained in office only at the insistence of the king (BL, Add. MS 9200, fol. 68v). However, Walpole appears effectively to have abdicated responsibility for the conduct of the war: in October 1740 he told Newcastle, 'This war is yours, you have had the conduct of it, I wish you joy of it' (Yorke, 1.251). His attitude may have had something to do with his poor health, but with Newcastle acting as *de facto* war minister it is clear that Walpole was increasingly marginalized from the major policy decisions of the ministry over which he presided.

Under the pressure of war, further divisions opened up within the government. By spring 1740 the earl of Egmont was reporting that there were three parties at court, the third consisting of 'Lord Wilmington [formerly Spencer Compton], Duke of Dorset and their friends' (*Egmont Diary*, 3.141). Wilmington, of course, having failed to displace Walpole in 1727, had never been an enthusiastic supporter of the ministry and owed his post as lord president of the council largely to the support of the king. However, his 'party' now began to flirt ever more openly with the opposition. In 1740 George Bubb Dodington, a former protégé of Walpole, threw in his lot with the opposition and was dismissed from the Treasury board. Even after this, however, relations between Wilmington and Dodington remained cordial. But the real significance of this group did not lie in the support that it could muster in the Commons, which was very limited. Rather, the fact that court politicians so close to the king were distancing themselves from Walpole communicated a powerful message about the prime minister's waning power to the wider political world.

The opposition were very conscious of the divisions within the ministry and tried to exploit them. By Christmas 1739 some of 'the Leaders of the Opposers' had overcome their suspicions of each other and agreed to concentrate their attacks on Walpole personally, by 'using the word Minister in the singular Number in both Houses; and making it as familiar to name him there, as in Print or in private conversation' (Taylor and Jones, 164). In the press this approach was very effective, particularly as the ministry's war policy appeared increasingly muddled and ineffective following the early success of the capture of Porto Bello. The production of satirical prints increased rapidly, many focusing on Walpole himself, depicting him unflatteringly as 'the English Colossus' and comparing him with Julius Caesar, Cardinal Wolsey, and Piers Gaveston. In parliament, however, the strategy was less successful. As so often in the past, place bills offered an effective line of attack; in January 1740 Walpole's majority was reduced to sixteen. The following month, however, when Pulteney tried to revive the issue of the convention as a

prelude to impeachment, Walpole was able to rally his supporters. He deliberately applied the question 'personally to Himself, Called upon those who were his Freinds to stand by Him. Said He was now upon his Tryal; and desired either Acquittal or Judgment' (ibid., 44). At the end of the debate, the opposition motion was comfortably defeated by 247 votes to 196.

Despite this failure, on 13 February 1741, in the final session of parliament before the general election, the opposition attempted again to isolate Walpole from his colleagues. In both the Commons and the Lords motions were introduced requesting the king to remove Walpole 'from his majesty's presence and counsels for ever' (Cobbett, *Parl. hist.*, 11.1242). Proposing the motion in the Commons, Samuel Sandys launched a wide-ranging attack on the whole conduct of the government's foreign policy since the 1720s. He further claimed that Walpole had 'usurped a regal power, ... possessed himself of a place of French extraction, the place of sole minister', and engrossed 'ev'ry branch of government into his own hands' (ibid., 11.1244–5). It is unlikely that Pulteney, Sandys, and their allies expected to be able to bring Walpole down; rather, they were hoping for a propaganda victory that could be exploited in the election campaign. However, the 'motion' proved to be a serious miscalculation, once more revealing deep divisions within the opposition. Seventy-eight tories and dissident whigs either voted against the motion or abstained, largely because they objected to an attempt to condemn a man without bringing specific charges against him. Consequently, the final weeks of the parliament were dominated by recriminations within the opposition. Moreover, the pro-Walpole press appeared to have been revived by recent events, and for the first time an effective series of pro-ministerial satirical prints was published, drawing attention to the failure of the motion.

The fall of Walpole, 1741–1742 While the parliamentary opposition was deeply divided, in retrospect it is the weakness, not the strength, of Walpole's position that is most apparent as the elections of 1741 approached. Between the opening of parliament in 1735 and its dissolution in 1741, the number of tories and dissident whigs had increased by thirty, reducing the ministry's nominal majority in the Commons to forty-two. The conduct of the war provided an issue which the opposition could exploit, but, unlike the Excise Bill in 1733, could not be defused by Walpole's own actions. Moreover, his position within the ministry was far more vulnerable than it had been at any time since Carteret's dismissal as secretary of state, and his vulnerability was increased by the fact that he was at best a reluctant supporter of his own administration's war policy.

In some respects the 1741 elections went better for the ministry than might have been expected. Through most of England and Wales it appears to have slightly improved its position. However, the gains were not enough to reverse the losses to the opposition between 1735 and 1741 and they were, moreover, more than counterbalanced by what happened in Cornwall and Scotland, where the consequences of the defections of the prince of Wales and duke of Argyll were finally made clear. Contemporaries found it difficult to calculate the balance of parties in the new parliament, partly because there were 148 new members. However, Newcastle estimated that Walpole had a majority of only fourteen in the Commons, a verdict endorsed by most modern historians, who place the majority at between sixteen and eighteen. By autumn 1741 it was obvious that, as the earl of Ilay remarked, he was facing 'a very warm session' (Jones, 'Fall of Walpole', 105).

Events before the opening of parliament on 1 December increased the pressure on Walpole and his colleagues. The war against Spain was going badly. In April 1741 a combined naval and military attack on Cartagena was a disastrous failure, a fact that Admiral Edward Vernon did not hesitate to blame on the ministry. Events in the West Indies, however, were now competing for public attention with the situation in Europe, where Frederick II's seizure of Silesia at the end of 1740 had precipitated an attempt by France to dismember the Austrian empire of Maria Theresa. Opinion in Britain was galvanized by the plight of the queen of Hungary, as Maria Theresa was known, but British efforts to rally support for Austria were undermined in October 1741 by the decision of George II, as elector of Hanover, to conclude a treaty of neutrality between the electorate and France. As Newcastle recognized, the king's actions brought the issue of Hanoverian influence over British policy to the forefront of political debate, and he believed that it would be 'impossible to prevent a parliamentary enquiry into this conduct' (Hill, 222). By the beginning of November the press was full of the issue, Horace Walpole, the prime minister's son, believing that it 'threatens to be an *Excise* or *Convention*' (Walpole, *Corr.*, 17.187).

The new parliament opened promisingly for the ministry when it secured a majority of forty-five in the Lords in a debate on the address. In the Commons, however, its position was much less secure. In December, Walpole's candidate for the chairmanship of the crucial Commons committee of privileges and elections, Giles Earle, was defeated by the opposition candidate, George Lee. There is no doubt that Walpole committed a serious tactical error: Earle had made himself unpopular, and many ministerialists had expected him to propose someone more impartial. On 18 December, Walpole did manage to rally his supporters to reject a series of opposition motions for correspondence relating to diplomatic negotiations, but the year ended badly in a string of narrow defeats on the Westminster election petition. One of the biggest problems facing Walpole at this time was the abstention of normally reliable MPs, including Dorset's son, Lord John Sackville, and Charles Hanbury Williams. As the earl of Hartington observed, 'some stay away to see how things will turn out' (Devonshire MS 260.10, 17 Dec 1741).

Walpole's own strategy at this time is difficult to determine. Some of his followers were unduly optimistic about the mood of parliament. The duke of Newcastle, by contrast, was exasperated by Walpole's inaction over Christmas, complaining of the 'fatal obstinacy of one single man, resolved to ruin, or rule the State' (Owen, 27).

Indeed, relations between the two men grew so bad that the king was obliged to intervene and instruct them to make up their quarrel. Newcastle, however, had a point. Walpole's only initiative was to try to heal the breach at court, but the prince of Wales rejected the offers made to him, informing his father that Walpole's removal from power was the precondition for any negotiations. Consequently, Walpole himself emerged ever more clearly as the key to resolving the crisis. When parliament reassembled, he did succeed in defeating Pulteney's motion for a secret committee to investigate the conduct of the war, Walpole himself making an impressive and memorable speech. But the margin of victory in what was essentially a motion of confidence was so small—253 votes to 250—that it was clear that normal government business could no longer be conducted in parliament. A week later, on 28 January, the ministry was again defeated by one vote on the Chippenham election petition, and Walpole was finally persuaded to resign by his family and 'some of his particular friends' (Walpole, *Corr.*, 17.319). On 2 February, following a second defeat on the Chippenham election, 'Sir R. Walpole went out of the House immediately … and never returned; plainly foreseeing he could never for the future carry any Question in that House' (Taylor and Jones, 176). He finally resigned the seals of office on 11 February, having been created earl of Orford on 6 February. He also obtained from the king a pension of £4000 per annum, though he did not apply for it for more than two years, and secured a warrant giving his illegitimate daughter by Maria Skerrett the precedence of an earl's daughter. These final acts of power not only 'disgusted the nobility' but were also viewed even by loyal ministerialists such as William Hay as 'an Abuse of the Kings favour' (ibid.).

Last years One factor influencing Walpole's decision to resign was his desire to maintain whig government. He recognized that his resignation would facilitate the reconstruction of the ministry around his former supporters, 'the old corps' (Coxe, *Pelham*, 1.92), and this was precisely what happened. It is likely that Newcastle, Pelham, and Hardwicke had maintained discreet contacts with Carteret and Pulteney at least since the outbreak of war, and these now developed into formal negotiations. Walpole's colleagues saw the possibility of detaching the Carteret–Pulteney group from the rest of the opposition, and especially from the tories. Carteret was made secretary of state in place of Harrington, Sandys became chancellor of the exchequer, while Wilmington succeeded Walpole as first lord of the Treasury. Pulteney, who had often proclaimed that he had no ambition for office, was rewarded with the earldom of Bath. Meanwhile, the prince of Wales was persuaded to endorse the new ministerial arrangements by agreeing to a reconciliation with his father, and he also gave assurances to Walpole that he would not 'be molested in any shape, or upon any account' (Coxe, *Walpole*, 3.594).

Parliament had been adjourned for two weeks to allow for the reconstruction of the government, and when it reassembled on 18 February feelings against the new earl of Orford were still running high. Part of the reason for this was that Orford was believed to be the minister 'behind the curtain' (*Egmont Diary*, 3.248), a perception that was industriously cultivated by the tories. On 9 March, Lord Limerick proposed a motion for a secret committee to inquire into the conduct of Walpole's administration during the previous twenty years. The old corps, however, stood firm behind their former leader, and in the absence of Pulteney, Sandys, and some of Frederick's servants the motion was narrowly defeated by two votes in a very full house. But the leaders of the opposition were determined not to let the issue rest, and two weeks later Limerick introduced another proposal for a committee of inquiry, restricted now to the last ten years of the ministry. Even so, Orford's opponents secured at best a limited triumph, winning the vote by only 252 votes against 245. When the house came to select the members of the committee on 26 March, Pelham adopted a moderate approach, including some of the less violent tories and opposition whigs on the court list. His policy was vindicated, when five old corps whigs were elected and all of Orford's most bitter opponents were defeated.

The results of the committee's proceedings were distinctly underwhelming. Its investigations focused on the granting of government contracts, corrupt influence in elections, and misappropriation of secret service money, but as William Coxe pointed out in 1798, hard evidence was confined to the appointment of customs officials in Weymouth and one contract for furnishing money to pay troops in Jamaica. This outcome was not, perhaps, surprising. Examination of the secret service accounts was difficult and made more so by the mixed composition of the committee. But its work was also hampered by what one leading opposition figure called efforts 'to Screen' the former minister (Taylor and Jones, 59). On 1 December 1742, at the beginning of the next session of parliament, Lyttelton attempted to revive the committee, but his efforts failed, with the earl of Bath now declaring openly that he was opposed to any further persecution of Orford.

There is no evidence to substantiate the opposition's claims that Orford continued to act as a minister 'behind the curtain', but he still retained his interest in politics, giving his advice and support freely to his former colleagues, and especially to his former protégé Henry Pelham. In August 1743, following the death of Wilmington, he urged Pelham to accept the offer of the Treasury 'however circumscrib'd, conditional or disagreeable' (Owen, 171), as it would provide a firm basis on which to consolidate his power. When Pelham's appointment was announced, he offered his hearty congratulations together with detailed advice on how to undermine the position of Carteret and Bath by drawing support from the Cobhamite, broad-bottom whigs. His suspicion of the tories, however, was as strong as ever, and he warned Pelham to 'Whig it with all opponents that will parly; but 'ware Tory!' (Coxe, *Pelham*, 1.93). Orford's interventions in debates in the Lords were infrequent and not always effective: in what may have been his last parliamentary speech on 16 April 1744, he failed miserably to secure the reversal of the lord chancellor's judgment in the case of *Le Neve v. Norris*. But he could still be an effective politician. Contemporaries were all agreed that it was his lobbying behind the scenes that secured the ministry's victory in the debates on the employment of Hanoverian troops at the end of January 1744.

At the beginning of November, as the struggle for power between Earl Granville (as Carteret had now become) and the Pelhams reached its crisis, George II sent a message to Orford to ask him to come to London to give his advice. Orford agreed to make the journey as soon as he could, but in his reply made it clear that he disapproved of Granville's foreign policy. When pressed further by another message, Orford explicitly declared his support for the Pelhams—he appears never to have shared the animosity of his son Horace for his former colleagues—and advised the king to accept the views of the majority of the cabinet. By the time that Orford arrived in London, the crisis had been resolved by the resignation of Granville. However, by this time his health was deteriorating rapidly. He had suffered from urinary gravel at least from 1718, and by 1744 he seems to have been almost constantly ill. After the painful journey from Houghton to London in November, his condition worsened. In mid-December he began to take large quantities of Dr Jurin's lixivium; this had the effect of dissolving the stone, which Orford passed on 4 February. By now, however, he was beyond recovery. For some weeks he continued in severe pain, relieved only by large doses of opium. In his last hours he showed no fear of death, but nor does his attitude appear to have been one of traditional Christian resignation. He finally died at his house at 5 Arlington Street on 18 March 1745, and was buried in the parish church at Houghton on 25 March. It is possible that Jurin's treatment had serious side effects, and a pamphlet war broke out after his death in which both his surgeon, John Ranby, and probably Jurin were involved, but a more recent medical assessment of his illness concludes that he died of 'kidney failure after impaction of a large stone in the bladder outlet' (Spriggs, 427). At his death, according to Horace Walpole, he was 'very poor: his debts, with his legacies which are trifling, amount to fifty thousand pounds. His estate, a nominal eight thousand a year, much mortgaged' (Walpole, *Corr.*, 19.32). In fact, the legacies amounted to considerably more than £10,000, and in a study of the Walpole family finances Plumb has argued that the debts were 'of no great significance in relation to Walpole's total estate' (Plumb, 'Walpoles', 204).

Assessment Viewed from one perspective, Walpole stands at the end of a long line of leading ministers—men like Wolsey, Burghley, and Buckingham—who made a personal fortune during their years of royal service. No first minister after Walpole was to build a country house like Houghton. From another perspective he stands at the beginning of a line of modern ministers of the crown: as every schoolboy was long taught, he was the country's first prime minister. Some nineteenth-century constitutional writers went further, arguing that Walpole established the system of 'parliamentary government' presided over by Peel and Russell (Kemp, 128). Such claims would gain little support from modern historians, all too aware of the enormous differences between the political systems of the early Hanoverian and Victorian periods. However, the idea that Walpole was the first prime minister remains one of the truisms of British constitutional history, and it has much to commend it. The phrase 'prime minister' can be found before the rise of Walpole, but it was only during his ministry, and particularly in the years after 1727, that its use became commonplace, not only by the minister's opponents but also by his supporters.

The development of the position of prime minister was an expression of the new conditions of the post-revolutionary political system, and one of the best definitions of the role in the early eighteenth century is provided by Clayton Roberts: 'He monopolized the counsels of the King, he closely superintended the administration, he ruthlessly controlled patronage, and he led the predominant party in Parliament' (Roberts, *Growth of Responsible Government*, 402). The emphasis on parliamentary management is important, as it highlights what distinguishes early eighteenth-century prime ministers from first ministers, like Danby, in the pre-revolutionary period. Of Walpole's predecessors, both Robert Harley and the earl of Sunderland might be thought to have a better claim than Walpole to be the first prime minister. Both were described as 'prime ministers' by contemporaries and it can be argued that they fulfil Roberts's criteria, though Harley probably never regarded himself as the leader of the tory party and Sunderland shared power with Stanhope for much of his ministry. What really made Walpole different was his longevity in office. He occupied the post of first lord of the Treasury, which by the nineteenth century had come to be associated with the office of prime minister, for twenty-one years, and he had no serious rival for dominance of the administration for eleven. Consequently, it was during Walpole's ministry that the phrase 'prime minister' passed into common usage.

In part, Walpole's political longevity had little to do with him. The decision of George I and George II that they could not trust the tories as a party forced those monarchs to restrict their choice of ministers to whigs. In part, his success can be attributed to good fortune, including the death of some of his most powerful whig rivals. But Walpole was also an outstanding politician. He was very much at home in the intimate world of the early Hanoverian court, a fact that is too often neglected. What has been much more readily recognized by historians is his pre-eminence as a parliamentarian. He was one of the first politicians to recognize the importance of the Commons in the early eighteenth-century constitution, and there is no doubt that his decision to remain in the lower house throughout his premiership was crucial to his success. It is hardly coincidental that all the most successful prime ministers of the eighteenth century—Walpole, Pelham, North, and Pitt—were members of the Commons. His real skill, however, lay in his ability to link court and Commons. As Romney Sedgwick observed, he performed the 'dual role of "minister with the King in the House of Commons" and "minister for the House of Commons in the Closet" his influence in each place being strengthened by his influence in the other' (Sedgwick, 1.41).

Walpole's contemporaries were very aware that he was different, even if they were not sure how. He dominated the public consciousness in a manner that no politician had ever done before. In part, this was simply a reflection of the extent and durability of Walpole's power. But it was also a consequence of the rapid development of the press during the early eighteenth century. The Walpole years saw not only the appearance of newspapers like *The Craftsman*, but also the emergence almost from nothing of an indigenous industry producing satirical prints, as a result of which visual representations of the prime minister became familiar to a large part of the population, if only from the windows of print shops. The effectiveness of the pro-ministerial press should not be underestimated. Pamphlets defending the prime minister and his policies poured from the press, and he attracted the support of some of the period's leading political pamphleteers, including Thomas Gordon, John, Lord Hervey, and Benjamin Hoadly. Even at the time, however, it often appeared that the opposition had the better of the argument. No ministerial newspaper could rival the circulation of *The Craftsman* in the late 1720s and early 1730s or of *Common Sense* at the end of the 1730s. In retrospect, moreover, Walpole's critics often appear to have been even more effective. One reason for this is because so many of the period's canonical authors—Swift, Gay, Pope, Fielding, Thomson—were critics either of Walpole or of Walpolean society.

It can be argued that Walpole attracted criticism both because of his role as an 'early modern' royal favourite and as a 'modern' prime minister. On the one hand, his enormous wealth, flaunted most visibly in the construction of Houghton, prompted attacks. To many it seemed obvious that he was abusing power and exploiting the state to enrich himself and his family, a perception which helped to underpin the common parallel between Walpole and Jonathan Wild. To some extent Walpole was the victim of a shift in perceptions of public morality; among the next generation of politicians both Henry Pelham and William Pitt were able to make political capital out of their refusal to benefit personally from government service. On the other hand, his political methods were denounced as corrupt by the opposition. He was portrayed as using the patronage available to the ministry, government offices and pensions, to buy support of members of both houses of parliament and of the electorate. In this way Walpole was not only corrupting individuals, but he was also destroying the balance of the constitution by securing for the crown an illegitimate and corrupt influence over the legislature.

Thus, opposition writers created an image of a regime, the Robinocracy, permeated by the stench of corruption, an image reinforced by Walpole's obvious love of power and his ruthless efforts to secure a monopoly of it for himself and his followers. This interpretation has informed a tradition of criticism that can be identified throughout the historiography of the two and a half centuries following Walpole's death, though for much of the nineteenth and twentieth centuries it was supplemented by disapproval of his private morality, his open liaison with Maria Skerrett, and the vulgarity, even lewdness, of his conversation. The most recent, and in many respects the most sophisticated, exposition of this tradition can be found in E. P. Thompson's *Whigs and Hunters*, which draws a dark picture of Walpole as a nasty little eighteenth-century mafioso presiding over a country that had 'something of the sick quality of a "banana republic"'. According to Thompson, Walpole's greatest achievement was 'his systematizing of the means of corruption, with unusual blatancy' (Thompson, 197, 214).

In his biography of Walpole, Archdeacon Coxe observed that 'While he was in power, he was reviled with unceasing obloquy, and his whole conduct arraigned as a mass of corruption and political depravity' (Coxe, *Walpole*, 1.753). But soon after his fall a more positive view began to emerge, helped by the tributes of former opponents like Pitt and Chesterfield. By the end of the eighteenth century he was being acclaimed by the economist and political writer Josiah Tucker as 'the best commercial Minister this Country ever had' (Tucker, 222), while Edmund Burke admitted him into the whig pantheon, proclaiming him 'an intelligent, prudent, and safe minister', who 'governed by party attachments' (*Works*, 3.50). This reappraisal of Walpole culminated in 1798 with the appearance of Coxe's massive biography—ever since the starting point for all serious study of its subject, and still the only full-scale treatment of his whole life. In an interpretation which continues to exert an enormous influence over our understanding of Walpole, Coxe emphasized his parliamentary skills, his pursuit of peace, and his financial administration. Through the nineteenth century the portrayal of Walpole as a sound manager of the nation's finances and the architect of the sinking fund allowed him to be seen as the precursor of the political tradition represented by the younger Pitt, Peel, and Gladstone.

In his influential survey of eighteenth-century England first published in 1878, William Lecky tried to present a balanced picture of Walpole, reflecting both his achievements and the corruption of his administration. But his overall appraisal was strikingly positive—Walpole stood in 'the foremost rank of politicians', and his achievement lay:

in establishing on an impregnable basis a dynasty which seemed to be tottering to its fall, in rendering ... the House of Commons the most powerful body in the State, in moderating permanently the ferocity of political factions and the intolerance of ecclesiastical legislation. (Lecky, 328)

Most twentieth-century commentators tend to agree with this judgement. Walpole may not have been a great reformer like the younger Pitt, an inspiring war leader like Chatham, or an original political thinker like Burke, but he was a supreme exponent of the art of politics. Thus, the dominant themes of J. H. Plumb's major unfinished

biography, political and financial management, are familiar to readers of Coxe and Lecky. Plumb plays down Walpole's failings—he excuses as necessary or legitimate by the standards of the day practices frequently denounced as corrupt—but his assessment of Walpole's achievement is remarkably similar to Lecky's. For Plumb, Walpole was the architect of the political stability that made the eighteenth century in England so different from the seventeenth:

aided both by events, and by the tidal sweep of history, a politician of genius, Robert Walpole, was able to create what had eluded kings and ministers since the days of Elizabeth I—a government and a policy acceptable to the Court, to the Commons, and to the majority of the political establishment in the nation at large. (Plumb, *Political Stability*, 158)

In the last quarter of the twentieth century historians began to cut Walpole down to size. Paul Langford's *Excise Crisis*, for example, raised important doubts about his political skills, demonstrating conclusively that the crisis developed from a serious miscalculation by Walpole himself. At the same time, growing scepticism is being expressed about Plumb's portrayal of Walpole as the architect of political stability. Instead, there is a tendency to see him as the beneficiary of a series of longer-term political, constitutional, and financial developments which he was able to exploit with some skill and a great deal of luck (Roberts, 'Political stability'). Inevitably, this makes Walpole's historical significance even more difficult to explain. He was not a great reformer or war leader. He has no claims to be an architect of empire. Nor, despite his pre-eminence in the Commons, was he a great orator. But if this appears a curiously negative assessment of Walpole, that impression perhaps stems from a preoccupation with measuring a politician's achievements. Walpole is a crucial figure in British history because, for twenty years, he dominated the political scene and the political consciousness of the nation in a way in which very few politicians have done before or since. Later historians have appropriated the opposition's description of his tenure of power, and he remains the only prime minister to have given his—or her—name to his period of office, the Robinocracy.

STEPHEN TAYLOR

Sources *Life of William, earl of Shelburne ... with extracts from his papers and correspondence*, ed. E. G. P. Fitzmaurice, 2nd edn, 2 vols. (1912) • R. W. Ketton-Cremer, *Horace Walpole: a biography* (1940) • F. Harris, *A passion for government: the life of Sarah, duchess of Marlborough* (1991) • G. Holmes, *The trial of Dr Sacheverell* (1973) • J. Swift, *Journal to Stella*, ed. H. Williams, 2 vols. (1948) • J. Swift, *The history of the four last years of the queen*, ed. H. Williams (1951) • P. Rogers, 'The authorship of *Four letters to a friend in north Britain* and other pamphlets attributed to Robert Walpole', *BIHR*, 44 (1971), 229–36 • H. L. Snyder, 'Daniel Defoe, Arthur Maynwaring, Robert Walpole, and Abel Boyer: some conversations of authorship', *Huntington Library Quarterly*, 33 (1969–70), 133–53 • H. Walpole, *A catalogue of the royal and noble authors of England, with lists of their works*, 2nd edn, 2 vols. (1759) • Second earl of Hardwicke [P. Yorke], *Walpoliana* (1781) • *The letters and works of Lady Mary Wortley Montagu*, ed. Lord Wharncliffe, 2 vols. (1893) • D. Lemmings, 'Lord Chancellor Cowper and the whigs, 1714–16', *Parliamentary History*, 9 (1990), 163–74 • B. Williams, *Stanhope: a study in eighteenth-century war and diplomacy* (1932) • N. A. Brisco, *The economic policy of Robert Walpole* (1907) • S. Taylor and C. Jones, eds., *Tory and whig: the parliamentary papers of*

Edward Harley, third earl of Oxford, and William Hay, MP for Seaford, 1716–1753 (1998) • C. Jones, '"Venice preserv'd; or A plot discovered": the political and social context of the Peerage Bill of 1719', *A pillar of the constitution: the House of Lords in British politics, 1640–1784*, ed. C. Jones (1989), 79–112 • Cobbett, *Parl. hist.* • *The manuscripts of the earl of Buckinghamshire, the earl of Lindsey … and James Round*, HMC, 38 (1895) • E. R. Turner, 'The Peerage Bill of 1719', *EngHR*, 28 (1913), 243–59 • P. G. M. Dickson, *The financial revolution in England: a study in the development of public credit, 1688–1756* (1967) • M. Cowper, diary, 1714–16, 1720, Herts. ALS, Panshanger MS, D/EP F205 • W. Coxe, *Memoirs of the life and administration of Sir Robert Walpole, earl of Orford*, 3 vols. (1798) • G. V. Bennett, 'Jacobitism and the rise of Walpole', *Historical perspectives*, ed. N. McKendrick (1974), 70–92 • C. Jones, 'The new opposition in the House of Lords, 1720–1723', *HJ*, 36 (1993), 309–29 • R. R. Sedgwick, 'Walpole, Robert', HoP, *Commons, 1715–54* • C. Franklin, *Lord Chesterfield: his character and 'Characters'* (1993) • BL, Add. MS 70400 • PRO, E 403/2473, p. 44 • Sir John Clerk's tour in England, 1733, NA Scot., GD 18/2110 • A. Moore, ed., *Houghton Hall: the prime minister, the empress and the Hermitage* (1996) [exhibition catalogue, Norwich Castle Museum and The Iveagh Bequest, Kenwood, 12 Oct 1996 – 20 April 1997] • D. Horn, *British diplomatic representatives, 1689–1789* (1932) • *The manuscripts of the earl of Carlisle*, HMC, 42 (1897) • *The manuscripts of his grace the duke of Portland*, 10 vols., HMC, 29 (1891–1931), vols. 1–4 • C. Hussey, *English country houses: early Georgian, 1715–1760* (1955) • *Lord Hervey and his friends, 1726–38*, ed. earl of Ilchester [G. S. Holland Fox-Strangways] (1950) • J. Cornforth, 'Houghton Hall, Norfolk — I', *Country Life* (30 April 1987), 124–9 • J. Cornforth, 'Houghton Hall, Norfolk — II', *Country Life* (7 May 1987), 104–8 • C. Downes, *The Royal Chelsea Hospital* (1950) • TCD, King MSS 1995–2008 • D. Hayton, 'Walpole and Ireland', *Britain in the age of Walpole*, ed. J. Black (1984), 95–119 • C. B. Realey, *The early opposition to Sir Robert Walpole, 1720–1727* (1931) • H. T. Dickinson, *Walpole and the whig supremacy* (1973) • F. G. James, *Ireland in the empire, 1688–1770: a history of Ireland from the Williamite wars to the eve of the American revolution* (Cambridge, Mass., 1973) • I. G. Doolittle, 'Walpole's City Elections Act (1725)', *EngHR*, 97 (1982), 504–29 • *The Craftsman*, 14 vols. (1731–7) • W. A. Speck, 'Whigs and tories dim their glories: English political parties under the first two Georges', *The whig ascendancy*, ed. J. Cannon (1981), 51–76 • BL, (Newcastle papers), Add. MSS 32686, 32692 • *A letter on a proposed alteration of the Thirty-Nine Articles by Lord Walpole written 1751* (1863) • Hunt. L., Gibson papers • John, Lord Hervey, *Some materials towards memoirs of the reign of King George II*, ed. R. Sedgwick, 3 vols. (1931) • CUL, Cholmondeley (Houghton) MSS • W. Kennedy, *English taxation, 1640–1799* (1913) • *A foreign view of England in the reigns of George I and George II: the letters of Monsieur César de Saussure to his family*, ed. Madame van Muyden (1902) • Lord King [P. King], 'Notes of foreign and domestic affairs', *The life and letters of John Locke* (1858) • W. R. Irwin, *The making of Jonathan Wild* (1941) • *Report on manuscripts in various collections*, 8 vols., HMC, 55 (1901–14) • J. Black, 'Fresh light on the fall of Townshend', *HJ*, 29 (1986), 41–64 • J. Black, *The collapse of the Anglo-French alliance, 1727–1731* (1987) • J. Black, 'Additional light on the fall of Townshend', *Yale University Library Gazette*, 63 (1989), 132–6 • U. St Andr. L., Gibson MSS • L. Colley, *In defiance of oligarchy: the tory party, 1714–60* (1982) • A. A. Hanham, 'Whig opposition to Sir Robert Walpole in the House of Commons, 1727–1734', PhD diss., University of Leicester, 1992 • P. Langford, *Walpole and the Robinocracy* (1986) • P. Langford, *The excise crisis: society and politics in the age of Walpole* (1975) • N. C. Hunt, *Two early political associations: the Quakers and the dissenting deputies in the age of Sir Robert Walpole* (1961) • S. Taylor, 'Sir Robert Walpole, the Church of England, and the Quakers Tithe Bill of 1736', *HJ*, 28 (1985), 51–77 • J. Black, 'An "ignoramus" in European affairs?', *British Journal for Eighteenth-Century Studies*, 6 (1983), 55–65 • H. T. Dickinson and K. Logue, 'The Porteous riot: a study of the breakdown of law and order in Edinburgh, 1736–1737', *Journal of Scottish Labour History*, 10 (1976), 21–40 • state box, Yale U., Beinecke L., Osborn shelves • *Report on the manuscripts of Mrs Stopford-Sackville*, 2 vols., HMC, 49 (1904–10) • C. Gerrard, *The patriot opposition to Walpole: politics, poetry, and national myth, 1725–1742* (1994) • T. R. Cleary, *Henry Fielding: political writer* (1984) • *The correspondence of Alexander Pope*, ed. G. Sherburn, 5 vols. (1956) • B. W. Hill, *The growth of parliamentary parties, 1689–1742* (1976) • J. B. Owen, *The rise of the Pelhams* (1957) • P. C. Yorke, *The life and correspondence of Philip Yorke, earl of Hardwicke*, 3 vols. (1913) • R. Browning, *The duke of Newcastle* (1975) • P. Woodfine, *Britannia's glories: the Walpole ministry and the 1739 war with Spain* (1998) • R. Harris, *A patriot press: national politics and the London press in the 1740s* (1993) • C. Jones, 'The House of Lords and the fall of Walpole', *Hanoverian Britain and empire: essays in memory of Philip Lawson*, ed. S. Taylor, R. Connors, and C. Jones (1998), 102–36 • collections of the Revd Henry Etough, part II, BL, Add. MS 9200 • I. G. Doolittle, 'A first-hand account of the Commons debate on the removal of Sir Robert Walpole, 13 February 1741', *BIHR*, 53 (1980), 125–40 • Walpole, *Corr.* • Chatsworth House, Derbyshire, Devonshire MSS • W. Coxe, *Memoirs of the administration of the Right Honourable Henry Pelham*, 2 vols. (1829) • J. H. Plumb, 'The Walpoles: father and son', ed. J. H. Plumb, *Studies in Social History* • E. A. Spriggs, 'The illnesses and death of Sir Robert Walpole', *Medical History*, 26 (1982), 421–8 • B. Kemp, *Sir Robert Walpole* (1976) • C. Roberts, *The growth of responsible government in Stuart England* (1966) • E. P. Thompson, *Whigs and hunters: the origin of the Black Act*, paperback edn (1977) • J. Tucker, *A treatise concerning civil government* (1781) • *Works*, 8 vols. (1889–91) • J. H. Plumb, *The growth of political stability in England, 1675–1725* (1967) • W. E. H. Lecky, *A history of England in the eighteenth century*, 8 vols. (1879–90) • C. Roberts, 'The growth of political stability reconsidered', *Albion*, 25 (1993), 237–55 • J. H. Plumb, *Sir Robert Walpole*, 2 vols. (1957–60) • D. Hayton, 'Walpole, Robert', HoP, *Commons, 1690–1715* • *Bishop Burnet's History* • R. Chandler, *The history and proceedings of the House of Commons, from the death of Queen Anne, to the present time* (1742) • *Manuscripts of the earl of Egmont: diary of Viscount Percival, afterwards first earl of Egmont*, 3 vols., HMC, 63 (1920–23), vol. 2

Archives BL, catalogue, Add. MS 23089, fol. 26 • BL, corresp. and papers, Add. MS 35335 • Bodl. Oxf., papers relating to committee to inquire into conduct • Castle Howard, North Yorkshire, misc. material • CUL, corresp. and papers • Houghton Hall, Norfolk, financial and other papers • University of Chicago, family papers, MS 274 • Yale U., Farmington, Lewis Walpole Library, corresp. | BL, Blenheim MSS • BL, corresp. with duke of Newcastle, etc., Add. MSS 32686–23793, *passim* • BL, corresp. with H. Walpole, Add. MS 63749A • BL, corresp. with C. Whitworth and Lord Polwarth, Add. MS 37391–37392 • BL, Coxe MSS, Add. MSS 9078–9283 • BL, Stowe MS 251 • CAC Cam., Erle MSS • Chatsworth House, Derbyshire, Devonshire MSS • Chatsworth House, Derbyshire, letters to second and third dukes of Devonshire • CKS, corresp. with Lord Stanhope, U1590/O138–45 • NA Scot., letters to duke of Argyll • NA Scot., letters to Lord Leven, GD26/9/444 • Norfolk RO, political corresp. with Lady D. Fielding and Thomas Howard • NRA, priv. coll., corresp. with first Earl Waldegrave • PRO, state papers, domestic, George I and George II, SP 35, 36 • Suffolk RO, Bury St Edmunds, corresp. with duke of Grafton • U. Nott., letters, Newcastle (Clumber) MSS • U. Nott. L., letters to Henry Pelham and Sir Robert Munro • Warks. CRO, letters to Sir John Mordaunt

Likenesses C. Jervas, oils, *c*.1708–1710, Houghton Hall, Norfolk • G. Kneller, oils, *c*.1710–1715, NPG; repro. in Moore, ed., *Houghton Hall*, 84 • C. Jervas, oils, *c*.1725, priv. coll.; repro. in *Cam: Cambridge Alumni Magazine*, 36 (2002), 2 • J. Wootton and J. Richardson, oils, *c*.1726, Houghton Hall, Norfolk; repro. in Moore, ed., *Houghton Hall*, 84 • J. Rysbrack, marble bust, *c*.1726–1730, Houghton Hall, Norfolk • J. Eccardt and J. Wootton, oils, *c*.1727, Yale U., Farmington, Lewis Walpole Library; repro. in Moore, ed., *Houghton Hall*, 83 • attrib. J. Wootton, oils, *c*.1727, Althorp House, Northamptonshire • satirical portraits, 1733–43, BM; repro. in Langford, *Walpole and the Robinocracy* • H. Hysing, oils, *c*.1734, King's Cam. • J. Goupy, gouache, *c*.1735, BM; repro. in Moore, ed., *Houghton Hall*, 18 • J. Rysbrack, terracotta bust, 1738, NPG; repro. in Dickinson, *Walpole and the whig supremacy* • studio of J. B. van Loo, oils, 1740, NPG; version,

Royal Collection · J. B. van Loo, oils, 1740 (replica), priv. coll. [*see illus.*] · S. Slaughter, oils, 1742, Wolterton Hall, Norfolk · J. Dassier, copper medal, 1744, FM Cam. · J. Houbraken, line engraving, 1746 (after A. Pond), BM, NPG · G. Vertue, line engraving, 1748 (after C. F. Zincke), NPG · J. Watson, mezzotint, 1788 (after J. van Loo, 1739), NG Ire. · stipple, pubd 1800 (after J. Richardson), BM, NPG · stipple, pubd 1806 (after J. Richardson), BM, NPG · W. Aikman, oils, Blickling Hall, Norfolk · G. Bockman, mezzotint (after T. Gibson), BM, NPG · J. Cooper, mezzotint, BM, NPG · J. Simon, mezzotint (after C. Jervas), NPG · J. Simon, mezzotint (after H. Hysing), BM, NPG · attrib. S. Slaughter, double portrait, oils (with H. Legge), Gov. Art Coll.

Wealth at death £40,000–£50,000 in debt; estate only worth £8000 p.a., and much mortgaged: Walpole, *Corr.*, 19.32, 42.18 · debts insignificant in relation to total estate: Plumb, 'Walpole', 204

Walpole, Robert (1781–1856), classical scholar, was born in Lisbon, Portugal, on 8 August 1781, the eldest son of Robert Walpole, clerk of the privy council and envoy to Portugal, and his first wife, Diana, daughter of Walter Grossett. Horatio *Walpole, first Baron Walpole, was his grandfather. He was educated at Charterhouse and matriculated at Merton College, Oxford, in 1797, but migrated to Cambridge, where he was admitted to Trinity College in 1800. He was made a scholar and won the Sir William Browne medal for a Greek ode in 1801. He graduated BA in 1803, MA in 1809, and BD in 1828. In 1805 he published *Comicorum Graecorum fragmenta*. In 1809 he became rector of Itteringham, Norfolk, in 1815 rector of Tivetshall, Norfolk, and in 1828 rector of Christ Church, Marylebone, Middlesex. He held Itteringham and Christ Church until his death.

Soon after going down from Trinity, Walpole travelled in Greece, and in 1817 he published his *Memoirs Relating to European and Asiatic Turkey* (2nd edn, 1818), and in 1820 *Travels in Various Countries of the East*, two interesting volumes consisting mainly of unpublished papers written by John Bacon Sawrey Morritt, John Sibthorp, Dr Hunt, and other travellers, with descriptions of antiquities and notes and excursuses by Walpole himself. He was also joint author with Sir William Drummond of *Herculanensia*, published in 1810, a work chiefly concerned with the explanation of a philosophical papyrus recently discovered at Herculaneum.

On 6 February 1811 Walpole married Caroline Frances, daughter of John Hyde; they had two sons and two daughters. Walpole died in Harewood Street, London, on 16 April 1856. He had estates at Carrow Abbey, near Norwich, and at Scole Lodge, Osmundeston, Norfolk.

W. W. WROTH, rev. RICHARD SMAIL

Sources *GM*, 2nd ser., 45 (1856), 659 · Venn, *Alum. Cant.* · [J. Chambers], *A general history of the county of Norfolk*, 2 vols. (1829), 129, 1314 · [J. Watkins and F. Shoberl], *A biographical dictionary of the living authors of Great Britain and Ireland* (1816) · Foster, *Alum. Oxon.* · J. Foster, ed., *Index ecclesiasticus, or, Alphabetical lists of all ecclesiastical dignitaries in England and Wales since the Reformation* (1890)

Walpole, Sir Robert (1808–1876), army officer, third son of Thomas Walpole (1755–1840) of Stagbury Park, Surrey, sometime British minister at Munich, and Lady Margaret (1769–1854), eighth daughter of John *Perceval, second earl of Egmont, was born on 1 December 1808. Spencer

Horatio *Walpole was his elder brother. Educated at Dr Goodenough's school at Ealing and at Eton College, Robert received a commission as ensign in the rifle brigade on 11 May 1825, and was promoted lieutenant on 26 September of the following year.

Walpole served during the earlier part of his career with his corps in Nova Scotia (1825–36), Ireland, Birmingham during the bread riots (1839), Jersey, and Malta (1841–3). He was promoted captain on 24 January 1834, major on 31 May 1844, and lieutenant-colonel on 2 July 1847, in which year he was appointed to the staff as deputy adjutant and quartermaster-general at Corfu, where he remained until 1856, having been promoted colonel in the army on 25 November 1854.

In 1857 Walpole went to India to take part in the suppression of the mutiny, for which he was mentioned in dispatches. He commanded the 6th brigade of the army under Sir Colin Campbell at the battle of Cawnpore on 6 December 1857, then assisted Campbell in preparations for the siege of Lucknow. During the siege, in 1858, Walpole commanded the 3rd division, comprising the 5th and 6th brigades, in a variety of skirmishes. After the capture of Lucknow he was sent in command of a division to march through Rohilkhand. He left Lucknow on 7 April, and on the 15th ineptly attacked Fort Ruiya, and was repulsed with considerable loss, although the enemy evacuated the fort the same night. Walpole's conduct of this operation was severely censured, and Malleson, in his *History of the Indian Mutiny*, not only asserted that the second in command, Brigadier Adrian Hope, who was killed in the attack, had no confidence in his chief, but that Walpole was altogether incompetent as a general in command. Walpole was not a great commander, but the strictures passed upon him were undeserved. On the occasion in question Walpole undervalued his enemy, and in consequence many valuable lives were lost; but the commander-in-chief was fully cognizant of all that took place, and, far from withdrawing from Walpole his confidence, he continued to employ him in positions of trust and in important commands during the remainder of the fighting in India. He commanded the troops under Lord Clyde at the battle of Bareilly on 5 May, when he was wounded by a sabre cut, and his horse was also wounded in three places. He commanded the Rohilkhand division from 1858 to 1860, and commanded in person at the fight of Maler Ghat on the River Sarda on 15 January 1859, when, with 360 men, 60 of whom were Europeans, he entirely defeated 2500 of the enemy and took two guns.

For his services in the Indian mutiny Walpole received the medal with clasp for Lucknow; he was made first a companion, and then in May 1859 a knight commander in the Order of the Bath, and he received the thanks of parliament. In 1861 he commanded the Lucknow division, but in the same year was transferred to the command of the infantry brigade at Gibraltar. He was promoted major-general on 30 May 1862, brought home in 1864 to command the Chatham military district, and selected to command at the volunteer review in 1865. He relinquished the

Chatham command in 1866, was promoted lieutenant-general on 25 October 1871, and was selected for command at the autumn manoeuvres of 1872.

Walpole married, on 29 January 1846, Gertrude, youngest daughter of General William Henry Ford of the Royal Engineers. They had nine children. Walpole died on 12 July 1876 at his house, The Grove, West Molesey, Surrey. His wife, two sons, and three daughters survived him.

R. H. VETCH, *rev.* H. C. G. MATTHEW

Sources J. W. Kaye, *A history of the Sepoy War in India, 1857–1858*, 3 vols. (1864–76) · G. B. Malleson, *History of the Indian mutiny, 1857–1858: commencing from the close of the second volume of Sir John Kaye's History of the Sepoy War*, 3 vols. (1878–80) · J. H. Grant, *Incidents in the Sepoy War, 1857–1858* (1873) · W. Cope, *The history of the rifle brigade* (1877) · W. Gordon-Alexander, *Recollections of a highland subaltern* (1898) · P. J. O. Taylor, ed., *A companion to the 'Indian mutiny' of 1857* (1996) · Boase, *Mod. Eng. biog.*

Likenesses A. E. Chalon, watercolour, 1826; formerly in possession of Lady Walpole of Hampden Court Palace · J. Phillip, oils, 1847; formerly in possession of Lady Walpole of Hampden Court Palace · portrait, repro. in *ILN*, 35 (1859), 135

Wealth at death under £35,000: administration, 28 July 1876, *CGPLA Eng. & Wales*

Walpole, Sir Spencer (1839–1907), historian and civil servant, born in Serle Street, Lincoln's Inn Fields, London, on 6 February 1839, was the elder son of Spencer Horatio *Walpole (1806–1898), the politician, and his wife, Isabella (1801–1886), fourth daughter of Spencer *Perceval, the prime minister. His younger brother, Sir Horatio George Walpole, was assistant under-secretary for India from 1883 to 1907.

Walpole's health in childhood was delicate, and it was chiefly on his account that his father, when the boy was six years old, moved with his family from London to Ealing for the sake of purer air. In the autumn of 1852 he was sent to Eton College, where he became a favourite pupil of the Revd William Gifford Cookesley. In 1854, when Cookesley left Eton, Walpole changed to the pupil-room of William Johnson (afterwards Cory). At Eton he gained health and strength through rowing: he became captain of a boat and later attributed the excellent constitution which he enjoyed through life after an ailing childhood to the effects of the sport. Acceptance of office as home secretary in the short-lived administration of 1852 involved for Walpole's father the loss of a good practice at the bar, and for this reason the son, instead of being sent to a university on leaving Eton in 1857, became at the age of nineteen a clerk in the War Office, where he won first place in the preliminary examination. Though Walpole always regretted that he missed a university career, the loss allowed him, when his father again became home secretary in 1858, to gain an early insight into public life as his private secretary. He continued to hold the same position under Sotheron Estcourt, home secretary after the elder Walpole resigned in January 1859. Estcourt on his retirement the following June wrote to the head of the War Office that almost his only regret in quitting office was that he lost Walpole as a companion of his work. Walpole resumed his

Sir Spencer Walpole (1839–1907), by Hugh Goldwin Riviere, *c*.1903

duties at the War Office until, on his father's return to the Home Office in 1866, he once more became his private secretary. As such, he was a good deal involved with the volunteer movement (he joined the Ealing division).

In March 1867 Walpole's father (reducing the usual salary to compensate for the nepotism) got him appointed as one of the two inspectors of fisheries in England and Wales, with a salary of £700 p.a. This required him to travel a good deal, often with his colleague F. T. Buckland, the naturalist; from this sprang his *Manual of the Law of Salmon Fisheries* (1877). The post also enabled him to marry, on 12 November 1867, Marion Jane, youngest daughter of Sir John Digby Murray, tenth bt. They had a son, who died at the age of two, and a daughter, Maud (who later married Francis C. Holland). Walpole lost money by bad investment and his income was insufficient; he began to supplement it by writing. Initially he wrote financial articles for the *Pall Mall Gazette*. He also began the task of writing the biography of his grandfather Spencer Perceval, published in two volumes (1874); a substantial and well-researched work written from the family papers, it held the field until 1963. So delighted with this work was the head of the Perceval family, the sixth earl of Egmont, that he bequeathed £10,000 to Walpole, and obligingly died almost immediately. This gave Walpole financial independence and freedom from inspecting and journalism. He quickly began work on his *History of England from the Conclusion of the Great War in 1815*, of which the first two volumes were published in 1878. This was an important work, which contributed to the settlement of the narrative of the history of nineteenth-century England. Walpole was, despite his family background, a strong free-trader and a believer that, on the whole, the history of the century showed a strong tendency to progress; this he itemized with elaborate statistics, showing an excellent knowledge of the parliamentary papers. He thought Peel the greatest statesman of the century. The work seems to have been conceived as a history of the century almost as a whole, but by 1890 Walpole had only reached the early 1860s, and the final volume of the 1890 edition concludes with the ten great gains (with sub-sections) of the century to that point. Walpole's lists of progressive achievements were not original, but they played an important part in codifying the progressive calendar. In 1904 he brought the story almost up to date with *A History of Twenty-Five Years, 1856–1880* and was working on further volumes until his death.

Walpole, who later became a member of the Cobden Club, strongly disapproved of Disraeli's foreign and imperial policy in the 1870s. He left the tory party and the Carlton Club, and wrote two volumes in the English Citizen series—*The Electorate and the Legislature* (1881) and *Foreign Relations* (1882)—which were in part a comment on recent tory rule. In 1882 he accepted Gladstone's invitation to govern the Isle of Man, a post he held for nearly twelve years. The burdens of the office left Walpole adequate time for further literary work, and in 1889 he published the official life of Lord John Russell, in two volumes, written with full access to the Russell papers. This was a more demanding assignment than the life of Spencer Perceval. Walpole saw the advantage to historians gained by his access to a wide range of political collections, including, most unusually for the time, some of the Royal Archives; he quoted extensively from original correspondence and memoranda, and his book has lasting value as a quarry. But the book was marred by its commissioner, Lady Russell, who banned mention of herself and consequently of her supposedly bad influence on her husband's judgement. Walpole accepted the limitation, complaining privately of 'the Influence' (Prest, xvi). While governor, Walpole also wrote *The Land of Home Rule: an Essay on the History and Constitution of the Isle of Man* (1893) and articles for the *Edinburgh Review*.

In 1893 Walpole became secretary to the Post Office, in which office he was an energetic reformer. In 1897 he was the British delegate to the postal congress held in Washington. In 1898 he was somewhat belatedly appointed KCB. He retired from the Post Office in February 1899, and the following year purchased Hartfield Grove, on the edge of the Ashdown Forest in Sussex. He remained active: in 1894 he became president of the Literary Society (an office held by his father for thirty years). In 1901 he became chairman of the Pacific cable board, and in 1902 a director of the London, Brighton, and South Coast Railway. In 1904 he was given an honorary DLitt by Goschen on his installation as chancellor of Oxford University, and he was elected a fellow of the British Academy. In Sussex he was a

magistrate and a golfer as well as continuing his writing. He died at Hartfield Grove of a cerebral haemorrhage on 7 July 1907. His wife survived him; she died on 9 May 1912. Sir Alfred Lyall finished for publication two further volumes of the *History of Twenty-Five Years* (1908). Walpole's *Essays Political and Biographical*, with a memoir by his daughter, Maud Holland, were also published posthumously (1908). Walpole was not a great historian, and was no stylist, but he was a very thorough writer and editor whose biographies and history of his own times held the field well into the twentieth century and represented the optimistic orthodoxy which historians between the wars so energetically sought to refute. H. C. G. MATTHEW

Sources DNB · A. C. Lyall, 'Sir Spencer Walpole, 1839–1907', *PBA*, [3] (1907–8), 373–8 · M. Holland, 'Memoir', in *Essays political and biographical*, ed. F. Holland (1908) · J. Prest, *Lord John Russell* (1972)
Archives NRA, priv. coll., corresp. and papers | BL, corresp. with Lord Stanmore, Add. MS 49272 · Bodl. Oxf., Harcourt MSS, corresp. with Sir William Harcourt · ICL, letters to Thomas Huxley and his wife · U. Durham L., corresp. with third earl Grey · Wellcome L., letters to Henry Lee
Likenesses H. C. Riviere, chalk drawing, *c.*1903, NPG [*see illus.*] · photographs, repro. in Holland, 'Memoir' · photographs (*Members of the Imperial Penny Postage Conference, 1898*), NPG
Wealth at death £17,452 9s. 9d.: resworn probate, 15 Aug 1907, CGPLA Eng. & Wales

Walpole, Spencer Horatio (1806–1898), politician, was born at Epsom, Surrey, on 11 September 1806, the second son of Thomas Walpole (1755–1840) of Stagbury Park, Epsom, British minister in Munich from 1784 to 1796, and his wife, Lady Margaret Perceval (1769–1854), eighth and youngest daughter of John *Perceval, second earl of Egmont, and his second wife, Catherine Compton, created Baroness Arden in 1770. His great-grandfather was Horatio *Walpole, first Lord Walpole of Wolterton, brother of the prime minister; one grandfather, Thomas Walpole (1727–1803), was a friend of Chatham; the other, Egmont, had led the parliamentary opposition to George II and the Pelhams; he owed his first name to his maternal uncle Spencer *Perceval, the prime minister, and his second name indirectly to the Walpoles, directly to Nelson, the cousin and friend of his father. His elder brother was Sir Robert *Walpole (1808–1876). At Ealing on 6 October 1835 he married his cousin, Spencer Perceval's fourth daughter, Isabella (1801–1886), one of the beneficiaries of parliament's grant of £50,000 to the family of the assassinated minister.

Education and early career Walpole went to Eton College where he was prominent in the debating society and became head of the school. At election in 1823 he gave the speech which Lord Strafford had delivered on the scaffold; Canning, who was present and who had recited the same speech in 1787, congratulated him on the fervour and feeling he had shown. He was admitted pensioner at Trinity College, Cambridge, on 22 March 1824, had Whewell for his tutor, won the first declamation prize and the prize for the best essay on the character of William III, became an 'Apostle', was president of the union in the Michaelmas

Spencer Horatio Walpole (1806–1898), by John Watkins

term of 1827, and graduated BA in 1828. But, from the published memoirs and correspondence of his notable contemporaries and fellow Apostles such as Maurice, Sterling, Monckton Milnes, Kemble, Donne, and Trench, it does not seem that he belonged to their inner circle of friends.

Walpole was admitted at Lincoln's Inn on 23 June 1827 and called to the bar on 10 June 1831. Like Spencer Perceval he practised in chancery, and with considerable success and profit. He was made QC on 2 July 1846 and bencher on 2 November. On 30 January 1846, at the height of the battle over repeal of the corn laws, he had been returned unopposed in a by-election as MP for Midhurst, where his cousin George James Perceval, sixth earl of Egmont, had the preponderant interest. In his acceptance speech he claimed that he would enter the Commons pledged to no party, while declaring his fixed opposition to reducing the taxes on corn 'by an atom' (*The Times*, 2 Feb 1846). When the Conservative Party split, he stayed with the protectionists. Since they were virtually without experienced leaders in the Commons, Walpole's ability as a speaker and capacity for business propelled him speedily into prominence and into the counsels of the party. He made a reactionary speech in the house on 8 February 1848 against removing Jewish disabilities, which was admired and published; in the following year he argued powerfully against the repeal of the Navigation Acts; and it seems that he was one of those regarded as possible alternatives to Disraeli as leader of the protectionists in the Commons in the confused period following Lord George Bentinck's

resignation (Vincent, 71). He did not aim so high, and continued to work and prosper at the bar, where he was 'a great power indeed' (*Law Magazine and Review*, 371).

Home secretary When Stanley tried to form a government in February 1851, Walpole was destined to be solicitor-general, though according to the *Stanley Journals* (Vincent, 71) he was asked and agreed to take on the Home Office just before the attempt was abandoned. He now advocated dropping the party's demand for a return to agricultural protectionism. But he remained an unbending defender of the claims and privileges of the Church of England, declaring in a strong speech against 'papal aggression' on 21 March 1851 that 'conscience is pleaded, but dominion is meant. Toleration is asked for, but empire is designed.' The speech was published and 'put him up very high, and would enable Stanley to make him secretary of State' (*Greville Memoirs*, 6.397). He went on to try to stiffen the Ecclesiastical Titles Bill, and on 2 June had many tory MPs whipped to support his amendments. On the day, however, he backed down, partly because of 'some legal difficulties, overlooked until that moment'. This 'instant and irretrievable' 'break-down', illustrating 'his self-acknowledged tendency to vacillation', infuriated his party (Vincent, 67; *Men of the time*). However, he was regarded as the obvious candidate for home secretary when Derby formed his first government in February 1852. It was generally understood that this meant the end of his active legal career and hence a great financial sacrifice. He made himself 'respected as an amiable and useful officer' and piloted the crucial militia bill through the Commons; but at one stage he had provoked derision by proposing in the house, without prior consultation, to give all militiamen the vote, a plan which had to be 'withdrawn as abruptly as it had been proposed' (Vincent, 71). On 15 June he issued a proclamation forbidding the wearing of Catholic vestments and ornaments in public. Intended to calm anti-papal feeling, it was held to have contributed to the Stockport riots at the end of the month. It certainly enhanced his lifelong reputation 'as a zealous protestant prone to detect Jesuitism and kindred dangers in unsuspected quarters' (*The Times*, 23 May 1898). As a speaker he was described by Disraeli to the queen as showing on one occasion 'great taste and moderation' (Monypenny & Buckle, 3.354), and on another as 'addressing the House with a spirit unusual with him' (*Letters of Queen Victoria*, 2.389), while Lord Henry Lennox called him 'the dear, the gentle Spencer' (Monypenny & Buckle, 3.382). By the end of this ministry in December 1852 his public character was established. *Men of the time* (1853) described him as:

> one of the most sincere, as well as one of the most individually unobnoxious members of his party … As a lawyer, an essayist, a scholar, and a gentleman, Mr Walpole is respectable; but as a party debater, a wary manoeuvrer, a dexterous master of the prejudices and passions of a popular assembly, he is very deficient.

He had acquired a reputation for integrity and lack of partisanship which, combined with his limited ambition and means, made it natural to think of him as a possible speaker from as early as June 1852, an idea which attracted him and which repeatedly surfaced both before and after Palmerston had John Evelyn Denison elected to the office in 1857.

Other interests While in opposition from the end of 1852 to early 1858 Walpole was a director of the Great Western Railway from 1853 and its chairman in 1855–6, when he established a committee to investigate its debts, and he resumed his directorship between 1859 and 1866, taking the chairmanship again in 1862–3. In 1853, at the instigation of the new chancellor of Oxford, Derby, he was awarded an honorary DCL at Oxford together with Disraeli, Malmesbury, and Stanley. He was active in the debates on the reform of the old universities. After a motion had been carried for admitting dissenters to them in June 1854, the Liberals, wrote Greville:

> imprudently pressed on another division in which they were beaten, though by a small majority, and this of course does away with a good deal of the effect of the first division. It seems it was Mr. Walpole who insisted on the second division, … and it was rather dexterously done. (*Greville Memoirs*, 7.167 and n.)

His desire to maintain Anglican exclusiveness endeared him to the conservative majority of Cambridge dons, who encouraged him after the death of Goulburn to move from his constituency of Midhurst to represent the university, where he was elected after a disorderly contest on 11 February 1856, defeating the Liberal Denman. This was the only one of his thirteen elections which went to a poll, a subscription reimbursed him for the costs of fighting a petition to unseat him, and he retained the seat until he retired in 1882. He was one of the leading tories who, as against Disraeli, argued that they should 'support the Executive Government, because it is the Executive Government, wherever they can' (in 1854) and 'give up … all mere struggles for place & power, & act on those Conservative principles of which we are or ought to be the exponents' (in 1857: Stewart, 290, 312). Before and during the Crimean War he was 'ultra-Peace' (Monypenny & Buckle, 4.19), and in the political crisis of February 1855 he agreed with Derby that a government consisting only of Conservatives was hopeless. He continued to uphold the rights of the established church, arguing in a speech of 17 June 1856, which was published, that the national system of education in Ireland was obsolete and unfair and that schools of the Church of Ireland ought to be allowed to receive state grants even if they made the whole Bible available to their pupils. In these years, as throughout his parliamentary career, he resisted dissenting and radical attacks on church rates and put forward measures intended to settle the issue in a manner advantageous to the Church of England.

Home secretary again, and party politics When in February 1858 Derby formed his second ministry, Walpole returned to the Home Office, but only after making difficulties, complaining that on major issues such as parliamentary reform there was no party agreement. The cabinet's debates about its Reform Bill were protracted. At one point Walpole and other dissidents sent Derby a 'Chancery brief, 87 folios' (Monypenny & Buckle, 4.193) objecting particularly to the lowering of one of the county franchises to the same level as the borough franchise, and to the abolition of existing constituencies. Finally, with J. W. Henley, Walpole resigned at the end of February 1859.

> The House listened [to his rather bitter resignation speech] with an attention worthy of the gravity of the character of him who addressed it. A most elaborate, and carefully prepared essay was given to us. No smile lighted the face of any Member. After an hour … Mr W. uttered these words … 'How will you define the terms "rotten" and "pocket" borough?' Quick as lightning Bernal Osborne said distinctly 'Midhurst' … The effect was an instant and deafening roar through the whole House. (Fraser, 264–5)

Greville wrote on Christmas day 1859 that Walpole and Henley were now 'null' (8.276). In fact Walpole's resignation enhanced his general reputation, because, though universally known to be a poor man by comparison with most ministers, he had given up £5000 a year as home secretary only a few weeks before he would have become eligible for a ministerial pension of £2000 p.a. for life. Hence 'no man in the house is held … in higher honour than Mr Walpole' (Gurowich, 144n.). He had resisted attempts to send him to govern a colony. The absence of any but the shortest account of his life and career has no doubt had much to do with the neglect of his role: references to him seldom even get into indexes (cf. Gladstone, *Diaries*). But it is clear that he played a crucial though unusual part in the politics of this parliament. In the spring of 1859 he and Henley 'would have followed Gladstone if he had not joined [Palmerston's] government' (Morley, 2.31). During this ministry, recorded Trelawny, 'they sit just above the gangway on the 3rd bench, from which I infer their wish to be unamenable to D'Israelite discipline' (*Parliamentary Diaries*, 1.105), and Walpole seems to have acted as the unofficial leader in the Commons of those tories—probably the majority of the party—who preferred to allow Palmerston to remain in power rather than risk joining with the radicals or the Irish Catholic MPs, as Disraeli was tempted to do, to bring down the government. In spite or because of this semi-independent stance, Walpole was frequently consulted about party tactics by Derby and Disraeli throughout the years of Palmerston's second government (June 1859 – October 1865). When Disraeli offered his resignation as leader in June 1860, declaring that 'the Tories … chalk the walls in the marketplace with my opprobrium' (Monypenny & Buckle, 4.291), Walpole was among those mobilized to dissuade him. However, in May–June 1861 he was only with difficulty induced to support Disraeli's line, which the party had adopted, against the repeal of the paper duties; Palmerston made him chairman of a Commons committee to consider the role of the Lords in financial matters, and Gladstone recalled that 'in the plan of uniting the financial proposals in one bill … Spencer Walpole gave honourable support' (*Gladstone*, ed. Brooke and Sorensen, 1.89) During this parliament Disraeli liked to boast that the Conservatives were now a church party for the first time since 1840. One reason for this was the determination of Walpole, a 'devoted' church commissioner (1856–8, 1862–6) at a salary of £1200 p.a. (Best, 431; Vincent, 193), to mobilize it against radical motions on such issues as church rate and clerical subscription. Early in 1862 he led the opposition to the government's revised code for primary education and secured numerous changes in it. At the end of the debates Lowe, the minister responsible, offered him:

> sincere acknowledgments of the manner in which he has conducted this controversy. He has had the good fortune … of having carried out substantially that which he proposed; and …, in the moment of triumph and victory, he has had the wisdom and moderation to stop short, and to leave to the enemy, almost lying under foot, the remainder to which he clung … It is a rare instance of candour, moderation, and good feeling.   (Walpole, *Twenty-Five Years*, 1.513n.)

Later in the same session, however, when on 3 June the Conservatives seemed poised to defeat the government on a motion demanding financial retrenchment, Palmerston made the issue a vote of confidence and, in Disraeli's words, 'my second in command [Walpole] lost his head and heart the moment the trumpets sounded for battle' and withdrew the amendment (Monypenny & Buckle, 4.288). According to Stanley, 'Walpole's conduct is blamed by all parties', but was not simply due to his 'infirmity of purpose'. The whigs had been courting him, making vague offers of the speakership.

> Personally, Walpole is poor, has a family, the pension is an object, and Mrs Walpole, … who with her father's narrowness of mind has much of his ambition, never ceases to urge him on. (This he has told me himself.) She is further stimulated by an extreme jealousy of Disraeli, as a Jew, and as having counselled the admission of Jews to parliament: a subject on which her feelings are fanatically strong.

Stanley believed that Mrs Walpole had persuaded her husband to back down and that he had privately told Palmerston he would do so if the issue were made one of confidence (Vincent, 186–7). The general importance of Mrs Walpole's influence is supported by the story of Walpole's resignation in 1867 and by his remark to Hardy of 19 June 1858: 'I have consulted my Prime Minister here at home' (Gathorne-Hardy, 1.123). But Hardy's view of the episode of 1862 was different from Stanley's:

> Walpole has been put in a most unfortunate position, and I fear will feel Disraeli's taunts greatly. Still I am not sure that for the party he has not done good in withdrawing the amendment; for after Pam's declaration there would have been a good many defaulters, and so division within exposed.   (ibid., 1.156)

Home secretary in 1867–1868 and political reform When planning a future cabinet, Derby agreed at the end of December 1863 'that Walpole had behaved so ill that he deserved nothing' (Vincent, 203) but a month later was ready to appoint him to the 'Home Office long enough to serve for his pension, which object it seems he puts forward openly' (ibid., 206). After the election of 1865 and the death of Palmerston, his successor Russell's Reform Bill provoked a split in the Liberal Party. On 8 March 1866 a meeting of Disraeli, Northcote, Cranborne, Heathcote, and Walpole agreed to work with the dissidents to defeat the bill. When this occurred in June and the government fell, Derby made overtures to some of them, but with almost no success, and so he formed his third Conservative cabinet at the beginning of July with Walpole again home secretary—though there is some evidence that Derby tried to find an alternative. In the more technical business of the office Walpole had previously shown himself 'the most timid of politicians' in the face of the opposition of vested interests to sanitary reform (Lambert, 387). But in 1867 he brought in two bills which extended the coverage of the Factory Acts to many more trades and to workshops, thus affecting, he claimed, 1.4 million women and children. One writer believed that this was in his own eyes his most important achievement (*VF*, 10 Feb 1872). By the time these measures had been passed, however, he had resigned office following 'the Capitulation of Hyde Park', the event for which alone he is generally remembered, especially because of its prominence in Carlyle's *Shooting Niagara* and Matthew Arnold's *Culture and Anarchy*.

The drama had two acts. The first took place just after the formation of the cabinet. Following the defeat of the Reform Bill the Reform League called a meeting to revive the issue in Trafalgar Square for 2 July, which was first forbidden by the police and then permitted. The league then called for processions from all over London to converge on Hyde Park for a massive meeting on Monday 23 July. The government possessed a legal opinion, written in 1856 after an earlier confrontation over meetings in the park, stating that there was power to close the gates and exclude all citizens, whether aristocrats riding or poor men protesting, but no power to forbid just the meeting; and further, that, if the meeting became obstreperous, the police could only remove individuals as trespassers, with minimal force. Walpole concluded that the meeting must be permitted. The cabinet, however, would not accept this apparently weak course and, in order to stop the meeting, closed the park. The demonstration took place notwithstanding, the gates were broken down by the force of numbers, and the protesters occupied the park. Police and military were standing by. The president of the Reform League, Edmond Beales, and its council called on Walpole on Thursday 26 July and offered, if they were promised no military or police interference, to enter the park and urge the demonstrators to withdraw. Walpole accepted this proposal, on behalf of the government, provided that no violence occurred, and also agreed to give every facility for testing the law on the matter. He was then asked by a smaller deputation to allow a meeting the next Monday, to which he replied that he needed notice of that question. It was rumoured that he had burst into tears during the discussion. The league, however, called such a meeting, advertising it as 'by arrangement with the Government'. Walpole denied that he had made any such arrangement, and Holyoake, one of the deputation, supported his denial, denying also that he had burst into tears. The discrepancy may be explained by Stanley's remark on 26 July: 'Walpole has acted sensibly enough throughout this matter: but his extraordinary manner, (when he spoke of the railings being broken, and a few police hurt, he was on the point of bursting into tears) creates an impression of weakness' (Vincent, 261). The meeting was held and, though it was orderly, Walpole was strongly criticized for having apparently confessed that the forces of law and order could not control the 'mob' and for having effectively conceded the right to meet in the park. Derby spoke of 'this fiasco of Walpole's' (Monypenny & Buckle, 4.452), but at the end of this act he survived in office.

In the session of 1867 the government proceeded in a zig-zag fashion towards drafting and passing a reform bill, Walpole showing greater flexibility than he had in 1858–9 and accepting household suffrage. During the debates the Reform League decided to assert what they now saw as their right to meet in the park at a great meeting on 6 May. As in the previous year, Walpole explained to the cabinet the weakness of the government's legal position and favoured letting the meeting take place. The cabinet insisted on making some sort of a stand, and caused Walpole to issue a notice asserting that the meeting was illegal and urging people not to attend it, although they had decided to take no action to stop it. Beales went ahead, the meeting was held, the government and its forces let it occur, and there was no violence. The ministry was felt to have been humiliated. Disraeli had been especially anxious to avoid a confrontation with the league, and he was at least as much to blame for the withdrawal of the government as Walpole. Further, Walpole believed, as his son tells us, that Disraeli had been behind the main attack on his conduct in *The Times* (Walpole, *Twenty-Five Years*, 2.199). But the matter was within the home secretary's province and he accepted responsibility. 'From his somewhat weak and vacillating manner there is a tendency to assume that it was his personal doing' (Vincent, 307). Derby did not want to drop him, recognizing that the cabinet was at fault and not wishing to make him a scapegoat. But Mrs Walpole made an apparently decisive intervention: she sent a letter to the prime minister saying that her husband was not fit to continue. Hardy, who liked and admired Walpole, recorded him saying 'he was so overdone that he really was not fit for his work, and would persist in going out' (Gathorne-Hardy, 1.215). He had by now qualified for a pension of £2000 p.a. Kimberley wrote of his 'imbecility' as 'almost beyond belief. The loss of a man so utterly incapable must be a gain to the Ministry' (*Journal of John Wodehouse*, 202). But he remained a member of the cabinet without portfolio until Derby was replaced by Disraeli as prime minister in February 1868.

Final years For the rest of the parliament Walpole played a diminished role in the Commons, chairing the committee on the redistribution of seats and managing the Public Schools Bill. Thereafter, his interventions in the house were chiefly concerned with matters affecting Cambridge University and the British Museum, of which he was a trustee. He can be seen through documents in the university archives acting conscientiously on its behalf, as for example in trying to defeat a devious manoeuvre of Gladstone to establish a parliamentary commission on university property in 1871. Walpole's attitude was: 'When shall we have any quiet? Real study will never flourish in troubled waters' (Walpole to vice-chancellor, 27 Oct 1871). He had been made honorary LLD in 1860 and was high steward from 1887. It is singular that, on grounds of cost, he did not send either of his sons to university. His last years were a long decline and 'a period of oblivion' (Gathorne-Hardy, 2.367), until he died at his house at Ealing on 22 May 1898. His estate was valued at over £38,000.

In one of the very rare descriptions we have of him, Ritchie declared that he must have been 'very good-looking' in his youth, 'with his light, fresh complexion, well-chiselled features and clear blue eyes'. 'He chiefly affects black, and might be taken for a country vicar of good family' (Ritchie, 46). More brutally, Bernal Osborne compared him to 'a high-stepping Undertaker's horse' (*Parliamentary Diaries*, 1.200). As a speaker he was described as weak, dull, prosy, pompous, solemn, but he was also lucid. 'His language is very musical and harmonious. When necessary, Mr. Walpole can make a good speech' (Ritchie, 46). 'Sir R. Peel is his model. Walpole is a good-natured person in debate, but legal training crops out too much' (*Parliamentary Diaries*, 1.196). He was known for his gentleness and his personal kindness. That he was easy company is attested by his membership of the Club and Grillion's and his election as president both of the Literary Society and of Nobody's Club. He was FRS and FGS. He appears to have been deeply religious: his poem *The Saviour of Mankind* was privately printed in 1891. His only publications other than speeches were two articles on reform in the *Quarterly Review* for October 1859 and January 1860.

His elder son became Sir Spencer *Walpole (1839–1907). The younger, Sir Horatio George Walpole KCB, was assistant under-secretary of state for India from 1883 to 1907. A memoir by his granddaughter, Frances Holland, describes his life at Ealing Manor, in part of which he lived with his family while letting his Perceval sisters-in-law occupy the wing now called Pitshanger Manor at a nominal rent. Bought as a country retreat in 1844 for the sake of his elder son's supposedly weak constitution, by the end of his life it and its 'totally uninteresting garden' (Walpole, *Essays*, ix) were surrounded by suburbia. Walpole had taken a considerable part in supplying Ealing with amenities, especially schools and churches, and his funeral on 26 May 1898 at Ealing parish church was attended by representatives of many local bodies. The borough bought the house and grounds for £40,000 from Sir Spencer after the death of the last Perceval, and the garden is now Walpole Park.   DEREK BEALES

Sources DNB · *The Times* (23 May 1898) · *The Times* (27 May 1898) · *Annual Register* (1898) · *Hansard* · W. F. Monypenny and G. E. Buckle, *The life of Benjamin Disraeli*, 3–4 (1912–14) · *Disraeli, Derby and the conservative party: journals and memoirs of Edward Henry, Lord Stanley, 1849–1869*, ed. J. R. Vincent (1978) · *The parliamentary diaries of Sir John Trelawny, 1858–1865*, ed. T. A. Jenkins, CS, 4th ser., 40 (1990) · *Men of the time* (1853) · *Dod's Parliamentary Companion* · *Law Magazine*, 4th ser., 23 (1897–8), 369–72 · VF (10 Feb 1872) · CUL, department of manuscripts and university archives · *The letters of Queen Victoria*, ed. A. C. Benson, Lord Esher [R. B. Brett], and G. E. Buckle, 9 vols. (1907–32), 1st ser., vols. 2–3; 2nd ser., vols. 1, 3 · *The Greville memoirs*,

1814–1860, ed. L. Strachey and R. Fulford, 8 vols. (1938), vols. 6–8 •
R. Stewart, *The foundation of the conservative party, 1830–1867* (1978) •
P. M. Gurowich, 'Party and independence in the early and mid-Victorian House of Commons', PhD diss., U. Cam., 1986 • *Gathorne Hardy, first earl of Cranbrook: a memoir, with extracts from his diary and correspondence*, ed. A. E. Gathorne-Hardy, 2 vols. (1910) • W. Fraser, *Disraeli and his day* (1891) • J. E. Ritchie, *British senators* (1869) • J. Morley, *The life of William Ewart Gladstone*, 3 vols. (1903) • *W. E. Gladstone*, ed. J. Brooke and M. Sorensen, 1: *Autobiographica* (1971) • S. Walpole, *The history of twenty-five years, 1856–80* (1904–8), vols. 1–2 • *Essays political and biographical*, ed. F. Holland (1908) • W. C. Lubenow, *The Cambridge Apostles, 1820–1914* (1998) • G. I. T. Machin, *Politics and the churches in Great Britain, 1832 to 1868* (1977) • G. F. A. Best, *Temporal pillars: Queen Anne's bounty, the ecclesiastical commissioners, and the Church of England* (1964) • R. Lambert, *Sir John Simon, 1816–1904, and English social administration* (1963) • P. Smith, *Disraelian Conservatism and social reform* (1967) • E. T. Macdermot and O. S. Nock, *History of the Great Western Railway*, rev. C. R. Clinker, 3 vols. (1964) • A. Hawkins, *Parliament, party and the art of politics in Britain, 1855–1859* (1987) • *The journal of John Wodehouse, first earl of Kimberley, for 1862–1902*, ed. A. Hawkins and J. Powell, CS, 5th ser., 9 (1997)
Archives NRA, priv. coll., corresp. and papers | BL, minutes and corresp. with W. E. Gladstone, Add. MSS 44369–44746, *passim* • Bodl. Oxf., letters to Benjamin Disraeli • CUL, corresp. with Sedgwick • CUL, letters to Sir George Stokes • Herts. ALS, letters to Lord Lytton • LPL, corresp. with Baroness Burdett-Coutts • Lpool RO, letters to fourteenth earl of Derby • PRO NIre., letters to Lord Belmore, D3007 • Som. ARS, letters to Sir William Jolliffe • Suffolk RO, Ipswich, letters to Lord Cranbrook
Likenesses C. Dressler, relief effigy, plaster, 1882, NPG • A. Cecioni, caricature, watercolour study, NPG; repro. in *VF* (10 Feb 1872) • G. Cook, stipple (after photograph by S. A. Walker), NPG • W. & D. Downey, carte-de-visite, NPG • H. Gales, group portrait, watercolour (*The Derby Cabinet of 1867*), NPG • W. Holl, stipple (after G. Richmond), BM • Lock & Whitfield, photograph, woodburytype, NPG; repro. in T. Cooper, *Men of mark: a gallery of contemporary portraits* (1876) • J. Phillip, group portrait, oils (*The House of Commons, 1860*), Palace of Westminster, London • Walker & Sons, carte-de-visite (seated), NPG • J. Watkins, carte-de-visite, NPG [*see illus.*] • bust, Pitshanger Manor, Middlesex
Wealth at death £38,664 13s. 4d.: probate, 24 June 1898, *CGPLA Eng. & Wales*

Walrond, Humphrey (*b.* 1602, *d.* in or after 1668), colonial official, was the eldest son of Humphrey Walrond (*d.* 1621) of Sea, in the parish of Ilminster, Somerset, and his wife, Elizabeth Colles. He had six siblings: Maurice, Edward, John, George, Katherine, and Elizabeth. No later than 1623 Humphrey Walrond married Grace, daughter of Dr John Seaman of Painswick, Gloucestershire, and his wife, Elizabeth. Grace and Humphrey Walrond had ten children. Four of their five sons—George (1624–1688), Henry, John (1634–1674), and Thomas—followed their father into prominent positions in the political life of Barbados.

Little is known of the first forty years of Walrond's life, other than his involvement in the west fen drainage scheme in Lincolnshire in the early 1630s. Richard Ligon, a friend of Walrond in Barbados, invested in a nearby fen drainage scheme, and it is possible that the two men met at this time.

In April 1643 Walrond appears in the records as having executed a deed intended to satisfy his debts and distribute the remainder of his estate to his family in the event of his death. He next appears in July 1645, when the defeated royalist garrison of Bridgwater handed him over to parliament as a hostage to guarantee the terms of its surrender.

Despite this fact, Walrond's actions during the civil wars remain unclear. In a petition provided to parliament in October 1645, while he was still a prisoner, he claimed that he had not accepted a commission from the king. Instead, he claimed that he protected supporters of parliament, in return for which he was robbed and forced to flee to Bridgwater. Apparently contradicting these claims, he received a grant of arms by Charles I for his services in the conflict, and may have served as deputy governor of Bridgwater, perhaps holding the rank of colonel. In addition, after the Restoration his wife and children claimed that his loyalty during the civil wars entitled them to compensation of various sorts. These claims could not, it seems, be verified. In any case, his petition to compound was granted in June 1646, and soon afterward he left England for Barbados, accompanied by his brother Edward and son George. He had arrived by early October 1646.

Humphrey Walrond and his brother were to become major figures in Barbados in the 1640s, but there is reason to doubt the long-standing portrayal of Humphrey as a staunch royalist and the history of Barbados in the 1640s as an extension of the civil war. From the mid-1640s, Barbados was transformed by sugar and plantation slavery. The island's major planters, supported by Governor Philip Bell, pursued profits and effective home rule by placing their interests as sugar planters above politics. Ligon's *True and Exact History of the Island of Barbados* (1657) is a valuable source for this transformation and the careful neutrality of the island's planters, who informally forbade use of the words 'cavalier' and 'roundhead'. But home rule depended on the distractions of war in England, and after the execution of Charles I parliament sought to re-establish control of the island. Humphrey Walrond responded by urging an alliance with the Bermuda colony to resist parliament. After this plan was rejected, he managed to stir up dissent among the planters by claiming that parliament was behind a thwarted 1650 uprising among the island's servants. In April that year he had become a central figure in the 'rebellion' on Barbados, playing on his fellow sugar planters' many fears: that title to their plantations was insecure, that the exploding population of servants and African slaves on the island threatened their safety, and that close oversight of their affairs would restrict the new and very profitable sugar trade.

Walrond had come very close to seizing control of the island when Francis Willoughby, fifth Baron Willoughby of Parham, arrived in possession of the proprietary rights to the island of James Hay, third earl of Carlisle, and an appointment as governor of Barbados from Charles II. Walrond was able to delay Willoughby's accession for three months, but no longer. Willoughby tried to placate parliament and retain the island's home rule by, among other things, dismissing Humphrey and Edward Walrond from their posts, but in October 1650 parliament cut off all trade with Barbados and began assembling a fleet to bring the island to heel. The fleet finally arrived in late 1651, and the island surrendered in January 1652. The settlement, known as the charter of Barbados, required Humphrey and Edward to leave the island for a year, and forbade them to return without the permission of parliament. Both returned to England.

Humphrey Walrond was back in Barbados in October 1656, and in 1660 Willoughby appointed him president of the council. His three-year tenure was eventful. As he had been in the 1640s, he was a strong proponent of home rule. He was outspoken in the struggle over revoking the proprietorship of Barbados (on the authority of which his own office depended) in favour of a royal governor. Some of his fellow planters proposed an export duty in exchange for secure title to their lands. He opposed the export duty and even argued for Barbados's exclusion from the Navigation Acts, which controlled imperial trade, on the questionable grounds that sugar was no longer a profitable commodity. Home rule was simply no longer an option in the 1660s, but with characteristic directness Walrond refused to moderate his views, and in 1661 he dissolved the Barbadian assembly for disagreeing with them.

Walrond's most controversial policy was to trade surplus African slaves to Spanish merchants in Martinique, in direct violation of both the Navigation Acts and the decision of the Barbados council. As a result of this decision, in 1663 Philip IV of Spain granted him several titles—marquess of Vallado, count of Valderonda, and count of Parama. It is uncertain whether Walrond ever received the patent for these titles, but there exists no better example of his willingness to march to his own tune. Although his decision was later approved by authorities in England, he refused to relinquish the commission paid to him by the Spanish, perhaps using the money to build the grand stone residence appropriated by Willoughby as the governor's mansion.

The decision to trade with Spain was one of Walrond's gravest miscalculations, and it was compounded by his order that planters on Barbados be freed of prosecution for debt. Not only was this order issued without consulting the colony's assembly, but it suspiciously eased his own financial problems. In 1663 Willoughby returned to the colony, now as the royal governor. He called on Walrond to account for the sums owed to the crown from the Spanish commission, as well as others he was said to have appropriated, and Walrond resisted. After a warrant was issued for his arrest, he was reported to be riding around the island with armed servants, inciting the planters to rebellion. Despite Willoughby's efforts to arrest him and threats to prosecute his allies for sedition and treason, Walrond demonstrated that he retained some support on the island by successfully evading the patrols and eventually escaping Barbados.

After his flight from Barbados, Walrond appeared in England, where the privy council ordered him to be imprisoned. Again he escaped, and little is known of his life after this point. In 1668 his wife, Grace, petitioned the king on his behalf, claiming that he had left England and asking that he be allowed to reappear and defend himself. There is no record of a reply, and given the many warrants for his arrest, this is hardly surprising. He does not resurface after this date, and it is assumed that he died soon afterwards.   MICHAEL A. LACOMBE

Sources P. F. Campbell, 'Two generations of Walronds', *Journal of the Barbados Museum and Historical Society*, 38 (1989), 253–85 · P. F. Campbell, 'Two generations of Walronds (continued)', *Journal of the Barbados Museum and Historical Society*, 39 (1991), 1–23 · P. F. Campbell, *Some early Barbadian history* (1993), chap. 11 · G. A. Puckrein, *Little England: plantation society and Anglo-Barbadian politics, 1627–1700* (1984), 109–13 · V. T. Harlow, *A history of Barbados, 1625–1685* (1926); repr. (1969), 132–51 · J. A. Williamson, *The Caribbee islands under the proprietary patents* (1926), 164–77, 206–11 · C. Bridenbaugh and R. Bridenbaugh, *No peace beyond the line: the English in the Caribbean, 1624–1690* (1972), 131–7, 146–8, 157–60 · H. McD. Beckles, *A history of Barbados: from Amerindian settlement to nation-state* (1990) · R. S. Dunn, *Sugar and slaves: the rise of the planter class in the English West Indies, 1624–1713* (1972) · *CSP col.*, 1.346, 391, 494; 5.45–6, 48, 128, 165, 166, 168, 170, 557

Walsh, Adela Constantia Mary Pankhurst (1885–1961), suffragette and pacifist, was born on 19 June 1885 at Chorlton upon Medlock, Manchester, Lancashire, the fourth of five children and the third and youngest daughter of Richard Marsden Pankhurst (1835/6–1898), barrister, and his wife, Emmeline *Pankhurst, *née* Goulden (1858–1928), suffragette leader. In 1888 Richard Pankhurst, seeking a parliamentary career, moved his family to 8 Russell Square, Bloomsbury, London, where Adela received her early education. The Pankhursts returned to Manchester in 1893, to 4 Buckingham Crescent, and Adela and her sisters, Christabel *Pankhurst and Sylvia *Pankhurst, were enrolled at Manchester Girls High School. After Richard Pankhurst's death in 1898, the family, in reduced circumstances, moved to 62 Nelson Street. Adela left school at sixteen after a severe illness, and helped in her mother's fancy goods shop. At seventeen she became a pupil-teacher in a working-class suburb of Manchester.

A child apart, fragile physically from birth, Adela Pankhurst developed a strong will and her own ideas, becoming secretly a believer in Jesus in spite of her father's rigid opposition to religion. At seventeen, after a traumatic visit to Chorlton workhouse, she was drawn to a vague but passionate Christian socialism, and began to help her mother in her work for women's suffrage and the Independent Labour Party.

At eighteen Adela became the youngest of the early members of the Women's Social and Political Union (WSPU) formed by her mother in October 1903, and her enthusiastic campaigning led to arrests and prison terms. After a month in Holloway gaol, following the riot at the House of Commons in October 1906, Adela left teaching to work full-time for the WSPU, mainly in the north of England or Scotland, speaking, writing, and organizing in testing conditions. She was prominent in the rowdy and successful suffragette by-election campaigns of 1907 and 1908. But by 1910 Adela's criticism of the increasingly militant tactics of Christabel's leadership of the WSPU led to conflict with her mother. Christabel, firmly concentrated on the women's vote issue, saw Adela 'as a very black sheep … because of the warmth of her Socialism', as the middle sister, Sylvia, artist and socialist, noted in her

Adela Constantia Mary Pankhurst Walsh (1885–1961), by unknown photographer, c.1908

memoir, *The Suffragette Movement* (E.S. Pankhurst, 367). 'One of Adela is too many', said Christabel (ibid., 384).

Following a severe breakdown in health in 1912 Adela Pankhurst agreed to withdraw from campaigning, to take a course, paid for by her mother, at Studley Horticultural College, Warwickshire. After graduating she escaped (from an arduous gardening job near Bath) to Switzerland, in the summer of 1913, as governess to the children of feminist Helen Archdale. But she was still seen as dangerously divisive and after a final painful interview with her mother in Paris in January, Adela agreed to sail for Australia on 2 February 1914. She never saw England or her family again.

Partly because of this sudden disappearance, Adela Pankhurst has received little attention in British suffragist history, though her many admirers included Rebecca West, and her memoirs, 'Looking backwards' (in *Stead's Review*, Melbourne, 1928–30) are illuminating. Always impetuous and restless, she managed in Australia to offend communists, socialists, trade unionists, patriots, feminists, nationalists, imperialists, and conservatives as she zigzagged from left to right, denigrated as a renegade by the left, an eccentric by the right. Yet, brimming with Pankhurst self-belief and a naïve, Joan of Arc sense of mission, she showed enormous energy and will, as well as flashes of insight and a talent for charismatic leadership, as for three decades she struggled to have her say on social, economic, and foreign policy, at a time when few women featured in public life in Australia.

After arriving in Melbourne on 27 March 1914, Adela Pankhurst worked for the women's movement with the prominent Australian feminist Vida Goldstein. An ardent pacifist since the Second South African War, she became a leading speaker for the Women's Peace Army when the First World War broke out, travelling widely in Australia and New Zealand.

Adela Pankhurst's journalism for the *Australian Woman Voter* and *The Socialist* and her popular anti-war polemic, *Put Up the Sword* (1915), brought her under the notice of military intelligence and into conflict with Prime Minister W. M. Hughes. Late in 1916 she left the Goldstein group unexpectedly to work for the Victorian Socialist Party. Only 4 feet 11 inches tall, the tiny, fair-haired, grey-eyed, 'Maid of Peace', became a courageous star speaker in the bitter campaigns against conscription of 1916 and 1917, and published an anti-war play, *Betrayed* (1917), and a pamphlet, *After the War, What?* (1917). Her mother disowned her, and Adela's leadership of demonstrations led to her arrest and imprisonment in Pentridge, Melbourne, from late 1917 to January 1918.

On 30 September 1917, between prison terms, Adela Pankhurst married Irish-born Thomas Walsh (1871–1943), militant unionist and socialist, a widower fourteen years her senior, in a Free Religious Fellowship service. In her happy marriage Adela bore a son and four daughters between 1918 and 1926, in chaotic and straitened conditions in Sydney and Melbourne, while also caring for three stepdaughters and pursuing her socialist interests. But her increasing advocacy of a family-centred feminism dismayed many feminists.

Adela Pankhurst Walsh campaigned with her husband (who was general secretary of the Seamen's Union), in the landmark seamen's strike of 1919, and wrote for and helped edit the *Seamen's Journal*. A foundation member of the Australian Communist Party in 1920, along with Walsh, she was an active communist until, disillusioned with revolution, she resigned in 1922. She also lost faith in militant unionism after the seamen's strike of 1925, when Walsh was imprisoned and threatened with deportation; and the death of her newborn baby in 1926 further sapped her confidence. When years of violent struggle in the union ended in 1928 with Walsh's expulsion over his ideas of industrial peace (that is, co-operation between employers and employees), she rejected unionism, socialism, and the Labor Party, and was reconciled with her mother just before Emmeline's death in 1928.

In 1929 Adela Pankhurst Walsh formed an Australian branch of the London-based Women's Guild of Empire, a conservative welfare group with a mainly middle-class following. During the 1930s, through this group and its organ, the *Empire Gazette*, Adela preached anti-communism, the benefits of industrial peace, the importance of the family, and the need for a strong British empire. In 1937 she received the Coronation Medal for community services. Savaged as a radical turncoat, Adela Pankhurst Walsh also lost many of her conservative followers when, as a pacifist, she opposed the Second World War in 1939. Forced to resign from the shocked guild, she advocated economic co-operation with Japan and distrust of American imperialism in the Pacific. A visit she and Walsh made to Japan as guests of the Japanese tourist bureau in late 1939 resulted in the pamphlets *Conditions in Japan* (1940) and *What we Should Know about the Orient* (1940). In 1940 she stood unsuccessfully for the Australian senate.

In a last attempt to influence history, Adela joined in late 1941 with an anti-British group to create the Australia First movement, a tiny, nationalistic, xenophobic, anti-communist, anti-war party. After Japan's entry into the war, leading members were interned. Adela, who had resigned from the group, was interned on 20 March 1942 but released on 13 October after a hunger strike. Her husband died from cancer on 5 April 1943. Hampered by myocardial degeneration, Adela withdrew from public life, living with her children in turn, taking occasional work as a companion and a nurse for retarded children until of pensionable age.

Adela Pankhurst Walsh was an enthusiast to the end; her final conversion was to the Roman Catholic church in December 1960. She died from a coronary arrest at the Home of Peace, Wahroonga, Sydney, on 23 May 1961, and was buried the following day in the Unitarian section of the Northern Suburbs cemetery, Sydney, beside her husband.   VERNA COLEMAN

Sources NL Aus., Adela Pankhurst Walsh–Tom Walsh MSS, MS 2123 · files on Adela Pankhurst and Adela Pankhurst Walsh, Australian Archives, Canberra · A. P. Walsh, 'Looking backwards', *Stead's Review* (Oct 1928–Oct 1930) [Melb.] · Museum of London, David Mitchell Collection · E. S. Pankhurst, *The suffragette movement: an intimate account of persons and ideals* (1931); repr. (1977) · University of Wollongong, Chamber of Manufacturers of NSW MSS, corresp. Australian Women's Guild of Empire, WVA D14-762, D14-763 · NL Aus., Lloyd Ross MS 3939 · Mitchell L., NSW, E. M. Capel MS 4942 · S. Hogan, 'Thomas Walsh and Adela Constantia Mary Pankhurst Walsh', *AusDB*, 12.372–4 · V. Coleman, *Adela Pankhurst: the wayward suffragette* (1996) · D. Mitchell, *The fighting Pankhursts* (1967) · 'Suffragettes in London', exhibition, 1992, Museum of London · Museum of London, Suffragette collection · d. cert.
Archives National Archives of Australia, Canberra · NL Aus., MSS | Museum of London, David Mitchell Collection · NL Aus., Lloyd Ross MS 3939 | SOUND NL Aus.
Likenesses photograph, *c.*1908, Women's Library, London [*see illus.*] · photographs, 1908–12, Museum of London, Suffragette collection · photographs, *c.*1930–1939, repro. in *Sydney Morning Herald* · photograph, 1931, Hult. Arch. · photograph, repro. in D. Atkinson, *The suffragettes in pictures* (1996) · photograph, repro. in *Labor Daily* (21 Nov 1925) [Sydney] · photograph, repro. in *Pioneers* (July 1929) [Sydney] · photograph, repro. in *Stead's Review* (Nov 1928) [Melbourne] · photographs, Museum of London, items 262, 496, 574; repro. in *Suffragettes in London, 1906–1914* [exhibition catalogue] · photographs, NL Aus. · photographs, repro. in *The Lone Hand* (July 1914) [Sydney]

Walsh, Antoine Vincent, Jacobite first Earl Walsh (*bap.* 1703, *d.* 1763), Jacobite naval officer, was baptized on 22 January 1703 NS at St Malo in France, the third son of Philip Walsh (*bap.* 1666, *d.* 1708), a Waterford merchant who settled at St Malo about 1685, and his wife, Anne Whyte (*d.* 1727). On 10 January 1741 NS he married Marie, daughter of Luke O'Shiell of Nantes, and they had two sons, including Antoine Jean Baptiste (1745–1798), and a

daughter, Marie. After serving in the French navy Walsh became a merchant and made a fortune from the Nantes slave trade. He took a leading role in the Irish émigré community's planning and financing of Charles Edward Stuart's expedition to Scotland, which resulted in the 1745 Jacobite rising, and was 'a key figure throughout the naval side of the '45' (Gibson, 11). In their correspondence Walsh adopted the pseudonym Monsieur Le Grand and the young prince was Mr Douglas; they also had face-to-face discussions at Navarre in April 1745.

Accompanied by Walsh, Charles Edward left St Nazaire on 3 July 1745 NS in one of Walsh's vessels, the *Du Teillay* (18 guns, Captain Claude Durbé). On 20 July NS the warship *Elisabeth* (64 guns), hired from the French navy as a privateer to accompany them, encountered the British *Lyon* (58 guns) off the Lizard; the *Elisabeth* was badly damaged and had to return to port, and the *Du Teillay* continued alone, without the arms and Irish volunteers on the warship, landing Charles Edward at Lochailort in Loch-nan-Uamh in South Morar on 5 August NS, and departing on 17 August NS.

On his return to France, Walsh urged Louis XV to send assistance to Charles Edward, and was put in charge of assembling coastal craft in the channel ports for an invasion of England. When the invasion plans were abandoned he sent two of his own Nantes privateers, the *Mars* (36 guns) and the *Bellone* (32 guns), loaded with arms and 852,000 livres, to bring the prince home if necessary; but they were attacked by three British ships in Loch-nan-Uamh after landing the supplies on 3 May 1746 NS, and nobody could stay to search for Charles Edward.

After the battle of Culloden, Walsh sent detailed proposals for rescuing the prince to Maurepas, the minister of marine, some of which advice was acted upon, but following the failure of the rising he had fallen out of favour with the French court. He was, however, ennobled by Louis XV in December 1753, having been created Earl Walsh by James III (James Francis Edward Stuart) in October 1745, and remained a trusted friend of Charles Edward, acting as his intermediary with Earl Marischal in their dispute in 1754. He died at Cap Français, San Domingo (Haiti), on 2 March 1763. On his death the Jacobite peerage passed to his second and only surviving son, Antoine Jean Baptiste.   RANDOLPH COCK

Sources GEC, *Peerage* · J. S. Gibson, *Ships of the '45. The rescue of the Young Pretender* (1967) · F. J. McLynn, *Charles Edward Stuart: a tragedy in many acts* (1988) · A. G. Murray MacGregor, *A royalist family, Irish and French (1689–1789) and Prince Charles Edward* (1904) · H. H. Brindley, 'The action between HMS *Lyon* and the *Elisabeth*, July 1745', *The naval miscellany*, ed. W. G. Perrin, 3, Navy RS, 63 (1928) · R. Forbes, *The lyon in mourning, or, A collection of speeches, letters, journals … relative to … Prince Charles Edward Stuart*, ed. H. Paton, 3 vols., Scottish History Society, 20–22 (1895–6) · H. Thomas, 'The slave trade', *The Observer* (17 Oct 1965) [colour suppl.]
Archives Archives Nationales, Paris, B458
Likenesses double portrait, *c.*1746 (with Charles Edward Stuart), Scot. NPG

Walsh, Edward (1756–1832), physician, was born in Waterford, Ireland, the eldest son of John Walsh (1720–1785), a merchant of Ballymountain House, co. Waterford. Robert

*Walsh (1772–1852) was his younger brother. After early education at Waterford, he studied medicine at Edinburgh and at Glasgow, where he graduated MD in 1791.

Before leaving Waterford, Walsh founded a literary society there, an account of which by him appeared anonymously in the *British Magazine* in 1830 (pp. 99–105). A poem by him won a silver medal offered by this society, and was also successful some years later after it had been appropriated by one of the competitors for the Dublin College Historical Society medal (ibid., 102). In 1792 Walsh published a poem, *The Progress of Despotism: a Poem on the French Revolution*, which was dedicated to Charles James Fox, and a year later a collection of his work entitled *Bagatelles* appeared. About the same time he published in the *Anthologia Hibernica* a proposal for a universal alphabet.

Walsh began his professional career as medical officer on a West Indian packet. He was afterwards physician to the forces in Ireland during the 1798 rising, and was present at the battles in Wexford in 1798, and at the surrender of Humbert at Ballinamuck. Walsh also served in the Holland expedition of 1799, of which he later wrote an account, and at the attack on Copenhagen (2 April 1801), where his hand was shattered. He was afterwards sent with the 49th regiment to Canada, where he spent some years studying Native American life. He collected a vast amount of information for a statistical history of Canada, but never published the work. He was present during most of the battles of the Peninsular War, and at Waterloo, and also served in the Walcheren expedition. He held for some time the post of president of the medical board at Ostend. He died on 7 February 1832 at Summerhill, Dublin.   D. J. O'DONOGHUE, *rev.* PATRICK WALLIS

Sources *British Magazine*, 2 (1830), 99–105 • *N&Q*, 3rd ser., 12 (1867), 415–16 • *Dublin University Magazine*, 3 (1834) • D. J. O'Donoghue, *The poets of Ireland: a biographical and bibliographical dictionary* (1912) • Allibone, *Dict.* • *GM*, 1st ser., 102/1 (1832), 185
Archives NA Canada, corresp. and papers
Likenesses J. Kirkwood, line engraving, 1834 (after J. Comerford), Wellcome L. • engraving (after J. Comerford), repro. in *Dublin University Magazine*

Walsh, Edward [Éadbhard Breathnach] (**1805–1850**), poet and translator, was born in Londonderry. His parents were natives of Millstreet, West Muskerry, co. Cork. His father had had a small-holding there but was dispossessed after eloping with a young woman, Edward's mother, who was of a higher social standing than he. Walsh senior joined the North Cork militia for want of better employment. He was a sergeant and stationed in Londonderry when Edward was born, returning to his native place some years later.

West Muskerry was almost entirely Irish speaking at the beginning of the nineteenth century, and Edward, who spent many years in the area, had complete mastery of the language. Indeed it is likely that he first learned Irish from his own parents. Muskerry, moreover, had a vigorous Irish scribal and literary tradition and as part of his education in local 'hedge schools' Walsh learned to read and write Irish, an ability unusual at the time in much of Ireland.

The Irish form of his name was Éadbhard Breathnach, although most of his later publications appeared under the Anglicized version. Walsh eventually became a schoolmaster and was tutor for a while to the children of a local member of parliament. Walsh took part in anti-tithe agitation, which was widespread in west Cork, and is said to have been imprisoned for a period. He was appointed teacher in the national school in Glantane, near Mallow. Having written an article entitled 'What is repeal, Papa?' in *The Nation* (founded 1842), he was dismissed from his post.

About this time Walsh began writing English versions of Irish folk tales in the *Dublin Penny Journal*. He was next employed as a teacher at Tourin, near Cappoquin, co. Waterford. Here he met Bridget O'Sullivan, daughter of a teacher from Aglish, co. Waterford, whom he married about 1843. They had several children. While at Tourin Walsh contributed original compositions in English and translations of Irish poetry to various magazines. Walsh moved to Dublin about 1843 in the hope of improving his position in life. He was sub-editor for a while on a weekly newspaper called *The Monitor*, a post he obtained through the influence of John O'Daly and Sir Charles Gavan Duffy, editor of *The Nation*. He was thereafter employed as clerk in the corn exchange, where the work was particularly arduous.

In 1844, in collaboration with John O'Daly, Walsh published *Reliques of Irish Jacobite Poetry*, a collection of his own verse translations of eighteenth-century Irish songs together with the Irish texts. A second edition appeared in 1866. In 1847 he published a collection of original works and translations under the title *Irish Popular Songs*. A second edition appeared in 1883. Irish folk songs are noted for their restrained simplicity; Walsh's translations are by comparison precious and effusive. Although interesting as examples of Victorian sentimentality, they are greatly inferior to the Irish originals. His verses were none the less much admired in the nineteenth century, not least because of their overtly nationalist tone.

In 1847 poverty obliged Walsh to accept the post of schoolteacher to the young convicts in the penal settlement of Spike Island in Cork harbour. On 30 May 1848 he obtained a clandestine interview with John Mitchel, the political convict, and was dismissed. Walsh was always of delicate health; Mitchel in his *Jail Journal* says of him, 'Poor Walsh! He has a family of young children. He seems broken in health and spirits … There are more contented galley-slaves moiling at Spike than the schoolmaster' (Mitchel, 12). On 24 August 1848 Walsh was appointed resident teacher to the Cork union workhouse at a salary of £40 per annum. His health deteriorated further and he was compelled to take private lodgings at 13 Prince's Street, where he died on 6 August 1850. Walsh was buried in the Cork Botanical Gardens. A monument was erected to his memory by the trades of Cork city in 1857. His widow and children were befriended by Sir Charles Gavan Duffy and subsequently emigrated to Australia.

N. J. A. WILLIAMS

Sources T. Gleeson, 'Edward Walsh, the Irish poet and translator', *Poetry and legendary ballads of the south of Ireland* (Cork, 1894), 145–214 · J. Mitchel, *Jail journal* (1854) [repr. 1913]
Archives NL Ire., letters to John Daly

Walsh, John (1665/6–1736), music publisher and musical instrument maker, was probably of Irish ancestry. He appears to have been established in London in the early 1690s, and on 24 June 1692 was made musical instrument-maker-in-ordinary to William III, succeeding John Shaw in that post. He married Mary Allen on 28 January 1692 at St James Duke's Place, London; they had fifteen children, of which three survived infancy. His first child was baptized at St Mary-le-Strand on 26 January 1693. His son **John Walsh** (1709–1766), born in London on 23 December 1709, eventually assumed control of the family businesses. Although the elder John Walsh's address in 1692 seems to be unknown, from 1695 to 1736 his residence is noted as being the Golden Harp and Hautboy, Catherine Street, Strand. Works published at this address from 1730 onwards generally carry the imprint 'Printed for and sold by John Walsh Musick Printer and Instrument maker to his Majesty at the Harp and Hoboy in Catherine-street in the Strand'. Later this was shortened slightly, and by the time his son took over the business the usual form was 'Printed for J. Walsh in Catherine Street in the Strand'.

John Walsh senior began publishing in 1695, and his business soon flourished owing to the vacuum created in the market by the demise of John Playford's business. Walsh's earliest publications often come with highly ornamental engraved titles and frontispieces, some of which were reused for different works. From the 1710s, after apparently establishing a link with Étienne Roger of Amsterdam, Walsh's publications occasionally utilize Roger's original plates along with his own imprints. His own publications eventually saw the replacement of copper plates by cheaper pewter plates, and the replacement of engraving by the use of punches. Up to 1730 most of Walsh's publications include the name of John Hare of Cornhill, who provided city premises for his business. In addition to this association, Walsh appears, in October 1708, to have become a partner of Peter Randall, who presumably married Walsh's sister. Randall evidently gave up his own shop in 1709 and apparently remained with him until 1710. The Randalls' involvement in the Walsh family business continued through William Randall (*c.*1728–1776), who was either Peter Randall's son or his grandson. Upon the death of his cousin John Walsh junior in 1766, William, along with John Abell, eventually took over Walsh's business, in which they had presumably already been employed.

As a businessman Walsh was unquestionably progressive. He advertised extensively and often used subscription issues and free copies to entice prospective purchasers. His innovations as an advertiser included sponsoring the first publication of music by a periodical, in the *British Apollo*'s quarterly supplements in August and November 1709. His generally uncontested pre-eminence in Italian and English opera, as well as in songs and instrumental music, was obviously noticed by Handel, who on his first visit to England in 1710 sought to engage Walsh as the publisher of *Rinaldo*. In the event Walsh published the work in 1711 and is said (erroneously) to have made £1500 from the deal. When Handel received a fourteen-year monopoly for the publication of his own works in 1720, Walsh was one of the publishers allowed to issue Handel's music on his behalf, and by the early 1730s was handling the greater proportion of the composer's printed music. Despite apparent discrepancies in his estate's true value, Walsh's finances were obviously in good order at the end of his life. He is reported in the *London Daily Post and General Advertiser* as having left £20,000 and in the *Gentleman's Magazine* as having left £30,000. His finances did not extend, it would seem, to paying what he believed to be inappropriate taxes. In 1726 he was gaoled for non-payment of the government stamp duty, and he was released the following year. This same recalcitrance was observed by Sir John Hawkins, who claims that Walsh and his partner John Hare were illiterate men, 'unable to compose a title-page according to the rules of grammar and too penurious to employ others for the purpose' (Kidson, 443). Hawkins also writes of their publications as 'being, in numberless instances, a disgrace to the science [of music] and its professors' (ibid.), a statement which is surely unfair, but perhaps reflects the resentment some composers felt towards unscrupulous publishers in the early eighteenth century. Walsh died in London on 12 or 13 March 1736. According to an obituary notice for John Walsh the younger in the *Gazetteer and New Daily Advertiser* for 23 January 1766, Walsh was buried originally in St Mary-le-Strand in March 1736, only to be moved along with his wife (who had evidently predeceased him) to a new vault prepared in the churchyard.

John Walsh the younger took over the business about 1730, upon the demise of the Walshes' relationship with the Hare family. On 8 May 1731 he became instrument maker to George II, and around this time also began to number his firm's publications. In May 1736 he began publishing Handel's operas by subscription. Walsh excelled in promoting the works of Handel to such an extent that in 1739 he was given a monopoly of his music for fourteen years. Handel's op. 4 concertos are supposedly dedicated to Walsh. Walsh's commercial acumen extended to his role as Handel's editor: he sometimes added extra movements to Handel's work before publication in order to meet the expectations of a fashionable mid-century audience. In 1748 he was elected a governor of the Foundling Hospital, a connection which may have brought about Handel's first benefit concert for the hospital the next year. Walsh consolidated the business by selling the works of other publishers as well as snapping up smaller businesses that had ceased publishing. The excellence of Walsh's engravings of this period is evidenced in the fact that many of the company's apprentice engravers continued in business on their own, including John Caulfield, Thomas Straight, and Thomas Skillern. Walsh died in London on 15 January 1766, and was buried in St Mary-le-

Strand. According to Kidson there is no evidence of a memorial there. The business was valued upon his death at £40,000.   BENNETT MITCHELL ZON

Sources W. C. Smith, 'John Walsh, music publisher: the first twenty years', *The Library*, 5th ser., 1 (1946–7), 1–5 • W. C. Smith, *A bibliography of the musical works published by John Walsh … 1695–1720* (1948) • W. C. Smith, 'John Walsh and his successors', *The Library*, 5th ser., 3 (1948–9), 291–5 • W. C. Smith, ed., *A catalogue of music published by John Walsh and his successors* (1953) • C. Humphries and W. C. Smith, *Music publishing in the British Isles, from the earliest times to the middle of the nineteenth century: a dictionary of engravers, printers, publishers, and music sellers* (1954) • W. C. Smith, *A bibliography of the musical works published by John Walsh … 1695–1720* (1948); repr. (1968) • F. Kidson, 'Handel's publisher, John Walsh, his successors and contemporaries', *Musical Quarterly*, 6 (1920), 430–50 • F. Kidson, W. C. Smith, and P. W. Jones, 'Walsh, John (i)', *New Grove* • F. Kidson, W. C. Smith, and P. W. Jones, 'Walsh, John (ii)', *New Grove* • D. Burrows, *Handel* (1994) • R. McGuinness, 'Musical provocation in eighteenth-century London: the "British Apollo"', *Music and Letters*, 68 (1987), 333–42 • IGI
Wealth at death £30,000—John Walsh the elder: *GM* (1736–1737?) • £20,000—John Walsh the elder: *London Daily Post and General Advertiser* (1736?) • £40,000—John Walsh the younger: *Gazetteer and New Daily Advertiser* (23 Jan 1766)

Walsh, John (1709–1766). *See under* Walsh, John (1665/6–1736).

Walsh, John (1726–1795), natural philosopher and politician, was born on 21 May 1726 in Madras, the second son of the three children of Joseph Walsh (*d.* 1731), senior merchant in the East India Company, and his wife, Elizabeth (1697–1734), daughter of Nevil Maskelyne (1663–1711) of Purton, Wiltshire. Nevil Maskelyne (1732–1811), astronomer royal from 1765, and his sister, Margaret, wife of Robert, first Baron Clive (1725–1774), were his first cousins. Walsh's father conducted his mercantile business in partnership with his brother John Walsh of Hatton Garden, London, and, finding himself in financial difficulties in 1728, he went to London to seek his brother's help, accompanied by his elder son, Joseph (*b.* 1722), who died of smallpox there. He returned alone to India in 1729, where he died in 1731.

Walsh was sent to England immediately after his father's death, and was raised by his uncle John. His mother went into a decline and died in 1734. In 1742 Walsh joined the East India Company as a writer, and was sent to Madras. He was in England in 1747–9, and rose to the grade of senior merchant; in 1757 he was appointed secretary to Clive, and two years later he returned to England as his agent. He corresponded regularly with Clive and, after the latter's death in 1774, with his widow, Walsh's cousin. Clive's daughter Charlotte became his ward.

Walsh's mission in 1759 was to report Clive's military successes to the East India Company directors, and to give Prime Minister Pitt a copy of Clive's plan to reorganize the administration of Bengal. By now Walsh was a wealthy man, thanks to the booty distributed when Siraj-ud-Dawla, governor of Bengal, surrendered to Clive at Plassey. He settled in England and in 1761 purchased the manor of Hockenhull, Cheshire, which in 1771 he exchanged for Warfield Park, Bracknell, Berkshire. When his sister, Elizabeth Fowkes, was widowed and left penniless, he accommodated and educated her three children. Clive supported Walsh's election to the House of Commons to represent Worcester in 1761, claiming that he would energetically represent the whig interest. Walsh did speak occasionally on matters connected with the East India Company, but otherwise showed an independent spirit. In fact he had little taste for politics, preferring science: he was not a candidate in the elections of 1780 and 1790, and was defeated when he stood in 1784 and in the by-election of 1791.

Elected to the Royal Society in 1770, Walsh soon became absorbed in the subject for which he became briefly famous: the electric fish. The numbing shocks felt by anyone who touched the electric ray, *Torpedo marmorata*, which inhabited the Mediterranean and other shores of Europe, had been known since classical times. In 1769 Edward Banfield reported on the more powerful electric eel, *Gymnotus* (now *Silurus*) *electricus*, from tropical South America. Banfield proved that the eel emitted electric shocks, and Walsh set out to confirm that the ray had a similar power. In this he was encouraged by Benjamin Franklin, whose American colleagues were undertaking similar investigations. With his nephew Arthur Fowkes he spent the summer of 1772 at La Rochelle, where the ray was often captured. The fish could survive many hours out of water, and Walsh was able to conduct experiments ashore. He wired up the fish to a series of bowls of water, which were interlinked by people with a hand in each adjacent bowl. A shock was felt by all when the wire was led back to the fish and the circuit completed, proving that the ray's shocks were caused by electricity and could be transmitted through conducting substances. His letter to Franklin announcing these findings was published in the Royal Society's *Philosophical Transactions* (63, 1773, 461–77). The surgeon John Hunter dissected the ray and identified the organs concerned; the question of how recharge occurred remained for later scientists to discover.

The Royal Society awarded Walsh the Copley medal for his achievement, though some physicists still challenged his findings, as the ray's charge did not show the attraction and repulsion or sparks that they associated with electricity generated by the Leyden jar. Walsh and Hunter continued their experiments on the gymnotus, and Walsh endeavoured to obtain information on electric rays in Indian seas, though this work was not published; in later years Cavendish, Humboldt, and Faraday continued to investigate this animal electricity. Walsh died on 9 March 1795 at his town residence in Chesterfield Street, London. He was unmarried, and left his property to Sir John Benn, who in 1778 had married his niece Margaret. In accordance with the provisions of the will, Benn assumed the additional name of Walsh, and was the father of John Benn Walsh, first Baron Ormathwaite (1798–1881).

E. I. CARLYLE, *rev.* ANITA McCONNELL

Sources W. C. Walker, 'Animal electricity before Galvani', *Annals of Science*, 2 (1937), 84–113 • W. B. Willcox, 'From John Walsh: two notes', in *The papers of Benjamin Franklin*, 19, ed. W. B. Willcox (1975), 160–63 • *The papers of Benjamin Franklin*, 19, ed. W. B. Willcox (1975),

204–6, 285–9 • *The papers of Benjamin Franklin*, 20, ed. W. B. Willcox (1976), 258–67 • *Encyclopaedia Britannica*, 8th edn (1853–60), vol. 1, p. 737; vol. 8, pp. 572–3 • M. M. Drummond, 'Walsh, John', HoP, *Commons, 1754–90* • H. Dodwell, *Calendar of the Madras records, 1740–44* (1917), 379, 417 • BL OIOC, MSS Eur. D 546/1, D 546/4

Archives BL OIOC, corresp. and family papers, MSS Eur. D 546 • JRL, travel journal and notes • NL Wales, corresp. and papers • RS, papers • TCD, deeds and estate papers | BL OIOC, letters to Lord Clive, MSS Eur. G 37 • NL Wales, corresp. with Lord Clive

Walsh, John (1830–1898), Roman Catholic archbishop of Toronto, the son of James Walsh and his wife, Ellen Macdonald, was born at Mooncoin, co. Kilkenny, on 23 or 24 May 1830. After education at St John's College, Waterford, he emigrated to Canada in April 1852, entered the grand seminary at Montreal, and received the tonsure. His Irish years made him a convinced nationalist in the style of Daniel O'Connell and a strong ultramontanist. Soon after reaching Canada he was struck down by cholera and his health never fully recovered.

In 1854 Walsh served on the Brock mission on Lake Simcoe; shortly after the consecration of Dr Lynch as bishop of Toronto in 1859, he became rector of St Michael's Cathedral in that city, and in 1862 was nominated vicar-general of the diocese. In 1864 he visited Rome and was nominated by Pius IX bishop-elect of Sandwich. Four years later he controversially removed the episcopal residence from Sandwich to London, Ontario, to which city the see was transferred by a decree from the *propaganda fide* dated 15 November 1869. Great scope was now afforded to Walsh's administrative ability. Within three years he paid off a large debt. Ill health prevented his attendance at the 1869–70 Vatican Council, but he replied sturdily to W. E. Gladstone's campaign against 'Vaticanism' in 1874–5. In 1876, when he again visited Rome, he reported twenty-eight new churches and seventeen presbyteries built within his diocese, in addition to a college, an orphanage, and the episcopal residence at Mount Hope. In May 1881 the cornerstone of the new cathedral in London was laid, and St Peter's was dedicated by Walsh on 28 June 1885. In 1882 he visited Ireland. By a brief dated 27 August 1889 he was appointed archbishop of Toronto, and he died in that city on 27 July 1898. As a pulpit orator and a prudent organizer he enjoyed a great reputation in Canada. He was also very popular in Ireland, and took a leading part during the summer of 1896 in organizing the Irish race convention in Dublin, by which it was hoped to reconcile the various sections of the nationalist party, though he was unable to attend it personally.

THOMAS SECCOMBE, *rev.* H. C. G. MATTHEW

Sources M. Power, 'Walsh, John', DCB, vol. 12 • W. Perkins Bull, *From Macdonell to McGuigan: the history of the growth of the Roman Catholic church in Upper Canada* [1939] • *The Tablet* (6 Aug 1898) • *The Globe* [Toronto] (1 Aug 1898)

Walsh, John (1835–1881), poet and schoolmaster, was born on 1 April 1835 at Belville Park, Cappoquin, co. Waterford, of which estate his father, William Walsh, was steward. He was educated at Cappoquin national school, where he became a monitor and then an assistant teacher. In January 1853 he entered the Marlborough Street Training School, Dublin, and in October 1854 was put in charge of

the Cappoquin national school where he remained until early 1869, when he held a similar position at Whitechurch, co. Waterford. He married a Tipperary woman, Julia Kavanagh (not to be confused with the Tipperary novelist and biographer of that name, 1824–1877). They had six children, including the minor poet Paul Walsh (*d.* 1891).

During his time in Dublin, Walsh came under the influence of the poet Robert Dwyer Joyce, who probably encouraged an interest in Irish legend and song. (Walsh is to be distinguished from the barrister John Walsh, who wrote verse for the same journal under the pseudonym Montanus. He was also unrelated to Edward Walsh (1805–1850) poet and translator.) A national schoolmaster 'could not safely parade the authorship' of poems of national sentiment (*Irish Monthly*, 1892, 433) and thus Walsh had many *noms de plume*: in the *Irish Harp* (1863) he signed himself Lyrista; in *The Irishman*, Shamrock (and later Lismore); in *The Celt* (Kilkenny), Corner Stone; in the *Waterford Citizen*, A Cappoquin Girl; and in the *Irish People*, Kilmartin. In *The Nation* he wrote as J. J. W., J. W., and Boz. He also wrote for *The Emerald* in 1868, a journal edited by his brother-in-law Michael Kavanagh who had emigrated in 1848 to Washington, USA.

Walsh's poems have occasionally been anthologized, but as they are by turns sentimental and banal, most scarcely justify collection. His 'Lament of the Ejected Irish Peasant', however, printed in *Dublin University Magazine* (35/205, January 1850, 134–5), was republished as a broadside, and his 'Drimin donn dilis' ('Dear brown cow') found its way into the edition of Stopford A. Brooke and T. W. Rolleston, *A Treasury of Irish Poetry in the English Tongue* (1900):

> Oh! *drimin donn dîlis!* the landlord has come,
> Like a foul blast of death has he swept o'er our home;
> He has withered our roof-tree—beneath the cold sky,
> Poor, houseless, and homeless, to-night we must lie.
> …
> But they racked and they ground me with tax and with rent,
> Till my heart it was sore and my life blood was spent;
> Today they have finished, and on the wide world
> With the mocking of fiends from my home I was hurled.

Both poems have more recently been anthologized in *The Hungry Voice: the Poetry of the Irish Famine* (1989, 77–8).

In 1872 Walsh took charge of the national school in Cashel, co. Tipperary, where he died on 27 February 1881. He was buried in the graveyard attached to the ruins on the Rock of Cashel.   WARWICK GOULD

Sources M. P. Hickey, 'Our poets: no. 28—John Walsh', *Irish Monthly*, 20 (1892), 430–36 • D. J. O'Donoghue, *The poets of Ireland: a biographical dictionary with biographical particulars*, 1 vol. in 3 pts (1892–3) [articles in *Waterford Star* (1891–2)] • C. Morash, ed., *The hungry voice: the poetry of the Irish famine* (1989)

Walsh, John Benn-, first Baron Ormathwaite (1798–1881), politician, born at Warfield Park, Berkshire, on 9 December 1798, was the only son of Sir John Benn-Walsh, baronet, of Warfield Park, Berkshire, and Ormathwaite, Cumberland. His father was the son of William Benn of Moor Row, Cumberland, a member of an old north-country family; he married, in 1778, Margaret [*see* Walsh,

Margaret Benn-, *under* Fowke, Joseph (1716–1800)], daughter of Joseph *Fowke of Bexley, Kent, and his wife, Elizabeth, daughter of Joseph Walsh, governor of Fort St George. On 4 April 1795 he assumed the surname and arms of Walsh by royal licence, in compliance with the will of his wife's uncle, John Walsh (1726–1795), son of Joseph Walsh. He was created a baronet on 14 June 1804, sat for Bletchingly in 1802–6, and died on 7 June 1825.

Walsh was educated at Eton College, and matriculated from Christ Church, Oxford, on 3 December 1816. He entered parliament for the borough of Sudbury in 1830, and represented that constituency as a tory until December 1834. An energetic politician and an able writer, he published several pamphlets on parliamentary reform, the second of which, *Observations on the Ministerial Plan of Reform* (1831), Lord Ellenborough thought would secure him 'a good efficient place' (Aspinall, 77); but he had no seat when Peel regained office in 1834. In January 1835 he contested the county of Radnor, but was defeated by a small majority. After defeat at Poole in the general election of 1837, he was elected for Salisbury at a by-election in March 1838. He then moved, unopposed, to Radnorshire at a by-election in June 1840, holding the seat unopposed (except in 1841) until 1868. Despite his ability, he did not hold office, even in the three Derby–Disraeli tory governments.

Walsh was JP and deputy lieutenant for Berkshire, and served as high sheriff of that county in 1823. Being lord of the manor of Trewerne in Radnorshire and the owner of over 12,000 acres there (his seat was Newcastle Court), he was also JP for that county and high sheriff in 1825; he was lord lieutenant and *custos rotulorum* of Radnorshire from 1842 to 1875. He was a staunch defender of Anglicanism in Wales. He married, on 8 November 1825, Jane (1803–1877), youngest daughter of George Harry Grey, sixth earl of Stamford and Warrington. With her he had two sons and two daughters.

In addition to his political pamphlets, Walsh wrote *Chapters of Contemporary History* (1836), *Political Back-Games* (1871), *Astronomy and Geology Compared* (1872), and *Lessons of the French Revolution, 1789–1872* (1873). On 16 April 1868 Disraeli had him created Baron Ormathwaite of Ormathwaite. He died at his Berkshire seat, Warfield Park, on 3 February 1881 and was buried at Warfield.

W. R. WILLIAMS, *rev.* H. C. G. MATTHEW

Sources GEC, *Peerage* • A. Aspinall, ed., *Three early nineteenth-century diaries* (1952) [extracts from Le Marchant, E. J. Littleton, Baron Hatherton, and E. Law, earl of Ellenborough] • Boase, *Mod. Eng. biog.* • Gladstone, *Diaries*
Archives NL Wales | BL, Add. MSS 40491–40538; Peel MSS

Walsh, John Edward (1816–1869), judge and writer, was born in Tolka, co. Dublin, on 12 November 1816, the son of Robert Walsh (1772–1852) a cleric, and his wife, Ann Eliza Ellen (*d.* 1879), daughter of John Bayly. He received his early education at Bective School, co. Dublin, and matriculated at Trinity College, Dublin, on 5 July 1832; he became a scholar in 1835 and graduated BA in 1837 with the first gold medal in both classics and ethics. In 1845 he was

granted the honorary degree of LLD. He entered the Middle Temple, London, in 1838 and was called to the Irish bar in the Michaelmas term of 1839, upon which he joined the Leinster circuit. On 1 October 1841 he married Blair Belinda, the daughter of Captain Gordon MacNeill. They had five sons and one daughter.

During his early years at the bar Walsh contributed frequently to the *Dublin University Magazine*. He also edited several law books; one, which he published jointly with Richard Nun, *The Powers and Duties of Justices of the Peace in Ireland* (1844), became a standard textbook on the subject. In 1847 he also published, anonymously, *Ireland Sixty Years Ago*, a well-known book in its day, which offered a portrait of life and manners in Ireland during the Grattan parliament. Walsh was a reporter in the court of chancery from 1843 to 1852 and was elected a member of the Royal Irish Academy in 1855.

In 1857 Walsh became a queen's counsel, and, two years later, crown prosecutor at Green Street. A lifelong Conservative, he was in 1866 appointed attorney-general for Ireland in Lord Derby's third administration, and in the same year he was elected to represent the University of Dublin in parliament. Again in the same year he was raised to the Irish bench as master of the rolls, in succession to Thomas Barry Cusack-Smith. His most famous judgment was that in *MacCormac* v. *The Queen's University*, which invalidated the charter granted to the university in 1866 by Lord Russell's government. It was also during his tenure of office as master of the rolls that the Irish Public Record Office was reorganized under Sir Samuel Ferguson.

After the disestablishment of the Church of Ireland, Walsh became an active member of the provisional convention for settling the new constitution of the church. His normal place of residence was Merrion Square, Dublin, but he died after a very short illness, in Paris, on 20 October 1869; he was survived by his wife.

C. L. FALKINER, *rev.* SINÉAD AGNEW

Sources Boase, *Mod. Eng. biog.* • F. E. Ball, *The judges in Ireland, 1221–1921*, 2 (1926), 302, 304, 327, 366 • Burtchaell & Sadleir, *Alum. Dubl.*, 2nd edn • Allibone, *Dict.* • *Irish Law Times and Solicitors' Journal* (22 Oct 1870) • *The Times* (21 Oct 1869), 9 • *The Times* (22 Oct 1869), 7 • *CGPLA Ire.* (1869)
Likenesses C. Smith, portrait, priv. coll.
Wealth at death under £14,000: administration, 22 Nov 1869, *CGPLA Ire.*

Walsh, John Henry [*pseud.* Stonehenge] (1810–1888), writer on sport, son of Benjamin Walsh, was born at Hackney, Middlesex, on 21 October 1810, baptized at St John's, Hackney, on 22 February 1811, and educated at a private school. In 1832 he passed as a member of the Royal College of Surgeons, and in 1844 he became a fellow of the college by examination. For some time he was surgeon to the Ophthalmic Institution, and lectured on surgery and descriptive anatomy at the Aldersgate school of medicine. He married, first, on 21 July 1835, Margaret Nash Stevenson, daughter of Thomas Stevenson of Claines, Worcestershire, who died nine months later; second Susan Emily, daughter of Dr Malden of Worcester, who died eight months later.

By 1837 Walsh was in practice at Worcester with Thomas W. Walsh in Foregate Street and The Tything. With William Harcourt Ranking, a Norwich physician, he edited *The Provincial Medical and Surgical Journal* from 1849 to 1852. He left Worcester for London in 1852. He always had an intense love of sport, he rode well to hounds, kept greyhounds and entered them at coursing meetings, broke his own pointers and setters, and also trained hawks. He was also fond of shooting, and, owing to the bursting of his gun, lost a portion of his left hand. On 1 January 1852 he married his third wife, Louisa, eldest daughter of the Revd William Parker.

In 1853, under the pseudonym of Stonehenge, Walsh brought out his book *The greyhound, on the art of breeding, rearing, and training greyhounds for public running, their diseases and treatment* (3rd edn, 1875), based on articles he had written in *Bell's Life*. Three years later, in 1856, appeared *Manual of British Rural Sports*, which covers the whole cycle of field sports, and, among other things, deals in a scientific manner with the breeding of horses. It was frequently reprinted, as were *The Horse in the Stable and in the Field* (1861) and *A Manual of Domestic Economy Suited to Families Spending from £100 to £1000 a Year* (1857). He wrote many other books, mostly on sports but a few of them on cookery. In 1856 he originated the *Coursing Calendar*, which he conducted through fifty half-yearly volumes. About 1856 he began to write for *The Field*, and at the end of 1857 accepted the editorship.

Between 1858 and 1875, Walsh organized the *Field* trials of guns and rifles, which wound up the controversy as to the merits of breech-loaders and muzzle-loaders. Again, in 1878, he endeavoured to make clear what were the respective merits of Schultze and black powder, discovering that light pressure with Schultze produced better shooting than tight ramming. Other experiments led to his invention of the *Field* force gauge, which gave results more reliable than the paper pads previously in use. In 1879 another gun trial was carried out to determine the merits of 12-bores, 16-bores, and 20-bores. In 1883 he instituted the rifle trial at Putney to demonstrate and measure the accuracy of shooting of Express rifles at the target, and subsequently organized trials to ascertain the cause of so many breakages in guns, the testing of powders by the lead cylinder method, the various effects of nitro compounds, and the strain on the barrels of small bores. His comments on proof powder in *The Field*, when he stated that the powder used in testing gun barrels was 50 per cent below the proof required, led to an action, *Birmingham Proof House Guardians* v. *Walsh*, in which a verdict was given against him of 40s. damages. However, the guardians' reluctance to provide powder for independent experts to test made a bad impression, and ultimately Walsh succeeded in obtaining some useful changes.

Walsh was one of the founders of the National Coursing Club and of the All England Lawn Tennis and Croquet Club, and he was on the committee of the Kennel Club. He was a good chess player, and on the managing committees of several clubs. He died at his home, 7 Montserrat Road, Putney, London, on 12 February 1888, owing to sudden complications from kidney stones, and was buried on 16 February in the old cemetery at Putney Common. He was survived by his third wife and two daughters.

G. C. BOASE, rev. JULIAN LOCK

Sources *The Field* (18 Feb 1888), 205–6 · *The Times* (14 Feb 1888) · Boase, *Mod. Eng. biog.* · *In memoriam J. H. Walsh* (1888) · *The Times* (3 July 1885) [law reports] · *The Times* (10 Aug 1885) [law reports] · private information (1899) · *CGPLA Eng. & Wales* (1888) · T. Stratford, *Guide and directory for the city and suburbs of Worcester* (1837) · *Pigot and Co.'s Royal national and commercial directory and topography of the counties of Warwick, Leicester, Rutland, Lincoln, Northampton, Nottingham, Stafford, Worcester, York* (c.1843) · *Slater's Directory of Worcester* [1849] · www.familysearch.org, Jan 2003

Likenesses portrait, repro. in *Stonehenge's British rural sport* (1875) · portrait, repro. in *London Figaro* (18 Feb 1888), 12 · woodengraving, NPG; repro. in *ILN* (25 Feb 1888)

Wealth at death £2126 11s. 11d.: probate, 28 Feb 1888, *CGPLA Eng. & Wales*

Walsh, Louis Joseph (1880–1942), Irish nationalist, was born at Magherafelt, co. Londonderry, on 11 September 1880, son of Louis Walsh (d. 1917), a Maghera hotelier who belonged to the Irish Republican Brotherhood as a teenager in the 1860s and was the principal Land League and Irish party activist in Londonderry South in the 1880s, and his wife, Elizabeth Donnelly. A sister, Helena Walsh Concannon, became a popular writer on religious and historical subjects and served as Fianna Fáil member of the Dáil (1933–7) and senator (1937–48) for the National University of Ireland.

Walsh was educated at St Columb's College, Derry city, and the Carmelite-run Terenure College, Dublin, then became a contemporary of James Joyce at the Jesuit-run University College in Dublin. Walsh denounced Joyce's irreligion and lack of conventional patriotism, while Joyce mocked his artistic pretensions. (Walsh's verse 'Art thou real, my ideal' appears in *Ulysses* as a favourite of the sentimental and frustrated Gerty MacDowell, who finds it in a newspaper used as toilet paper. Hughes in *Stephen Hero* is a composite of Walsh and another northern student, Hugh Kennedy—later chief justice of the Irish Free State.) During this period Walsh joined the Gaelic League; P. H. Pearse taught him Irish.

On graduation in 1902 Walsh trained as a solicitor, and after qualifying in 1905 set up practice in Maghera and Draperstown in co. Londonderry, and in Ballycastle, co. Antrim. He married Mary McKenna of Maghera on 26 September 1907; they had two sons and five daughters. He achieved national prominence in 1910 after leading a protest campaign against the appointment of an allegedly unqualified candidate, Signora Degani, to a lectureship in Spanish and Italian in University College, Dublin, under circumstances suggesting political favouritism. (Helena Concannon was one of the unsuccessful candidates.)

Walsh was an active supporter of the Irish Parliamentary Party (with some reservations), but broke with them over their acceptance of partition in 1916 and helped to found the Irish Nation League, subsequently absorbed into Sinn Féin. Walsh went along with this, though he was privately critical of the failure of the national Sinn Féin leadership's ignorance of Ulster conditions. In 1918 he contested the Westminster constituency of Londonderry South on behalf of Sinn Féin. In 1920 he was elected to Antrim county council for the Ballymoney area and stood unsuccessfully for Antrim in the first election to the Northern Ireland parliament. After presiding over an unofficial Sinn Féin court in his area Walsh had to spend some time on the run in the Sperrin mountains. He was later imprisoned in Derry gaol for sedition, then interned in Ballykinlar camp, co. Down, in 1920–21. He described these experiences in *On My Keeping—and In Theirs* (1921). Walsh supported the Anglo-Irish treaty of 1921, and moved to the new Free State. He was the first district justice appointed by the new regime (for north co. Donegal). He also served on the rules committee which regulated the new district courts, and advised Kennedy on the Gaelicization of the legal system. Walsh, who recalled official hostility to the Irish language under the old regime, did much to make legal services in Irish available to the Donegal Gaeltacht. His judicial *obiter dicta* denouncing the decline of public morals and occasional grumblings by Donegal protestants at the ethos of the new state frequently attracted national attention.

Throughout his life Walsh contributed stories and articles to local newspapers (notably the *Derry Journal*) and Catholic periodicals such as *The Leader*, the *Irish Rosary*, and the *Catholic Bulletin*. His sketches of small-town Ulster life (notable for sentimentality and political propaganda) were collected in *The Yarns of a Country Attorney* (1917), *Twilight Reveries* (1924)—the most autobiographical of the three, consisting of recollections of his childhood and youth in 'Gortnanan' (Maghera), and *Our Own Wee Town* (1928). He was well known as an amateur dramatist. His best-known play, *The Pope in Killybuck* (1913), popular with amateur groups for decades, was performed twice in Ballykinlar camp—for the 36th Ulster division in 1914 and by Sinn Féin internees in 1920. (Its Dublin première was disrupted by Sinn Féiners who assumed the author was an Orangeman.) He also published a novel about the Young Ireland rising of 1848, *The Next Time* (1920); *John Mitchel* (1934), a popular life of the nineteenth-century Ulster protestant nationalist; and a collection of articles about notable people he had met, *Old Friends* (1929)—mostly local celebrities, but including Pearse. For some years he contributed a weekly column to the Belfast *Irish News* under the pseudonym Cormac Mac Airt.

Walsh's attitudes were conventional among the provincial Irish Catholic middle class of his day, and unusual only for the openness with which he articulated them. He saw the new nationalist ruling class as a Catholic aristocracy replacing the failed protestant ascendancy. He was personally generous and charitable, possessing the common touch, and proud of his judicial role as defender of the poor; but his sentimental paternalism took for granted the social distinctions of provincial society, and he never thought poverty might be alleviated by social and economic modernization. He believed small farmers could solve their problems by becoming self-sufficient instead of producing for the market. He lobbied to exempt Donegal craft industries from health and safety legislation on the grounds that household production was morally preferable to factory work. He opposed raising the school leaving age to fifteen, alleging this would make young people dissatisfied and encourage rural depopulation. He complained that Irish speakers like himself who were sent to official posts in the Gaeltacht faced extra expense in educating their children and sending them to university. Like his sister he denounced feminist critics of the 1937 Irish constitution as cranks. Walsh disliked the cinema as a demoralizing influence, and outspokenly supported literary censorship. His criticism of an English Jesuit who praised a novel by Kate O'Brien banned in Ireland as a work of Catholic literature, and his view that literature should be judged by the standards which would be applied by 'a wise old mountainy mother', were criticized by the liberal intellectual monthly *The Bell* and put into the mouth of a medieval censor in Mervyn Wall's satirical novel *The Return of Fursey*.

Walsh died at Letterkenny, co. Donegal, on 26 December 1942 of a duodenal ulcer, leaving an autobiography unfinished; the manuscript's present whereabouts are unknown, but it may still exist in private ownership. He was buried at Conwal cemetery, Letterkenny, on 28 December. His son Brian later served as Fianna Fáil leader in the Irish senate.   PATRICK MAUME

Sources L. J. Walsh, *On my keeping — and in theirs* (1921) · L. J. Walsh, *Our own wee town* (1928) · S. Joyce, *My brother's keeper* (1958) · C. P. Curran, *James Joyce remembered* (1968) · L. J. Walsh, *Old friends* (1929) · L. J. Walsh, *Twilight reveries* (1924) · *Irish News and Belfast Morning News* (28 Dec 1942), 2 · *Irish News and Belfast Morning News* (29 Dec 1942) · L. O'Carroll, *Derry Journal* (30 Dec 1942) · *Irish Independent* (25 Dec 1942), 2 · *Irish Independent* (26 Dec 1942), 2 · *Irish Independent* (28 Dec 1942), 2 · M. J. Macmanus, *Irish Press* (25–8 Dec 1942), 3 · *Irish Times* (28 Dec 1942), 3 · L. J. Walsh, *Yarns of a country attorney* (1917) · d. cert.
Archives PRO NIre., business papers | University College, Dublin, Hugh Kennedy MSS, corresp.
Likenesses photograph, repro. in *Irish Press*

Walsh, Margaret Benn-, Lady Benn-Walsh (1758–1836). *See under* Fowke, Joseph (1716–1800).

Walsh, Nicholas (*d.* 1585), Church of Ireland bishop of Ossory, was the son of Patrick Walsh (*d.* 1577), Church of Ireland bishop of Waterford and Lismore; Patrick became bishop in 1551 and resigned his see in 1566. His son Nicholas was born in the city of Waterford. He spent time in the universities of Paris, Oxford, and Cambridge and was granted the degree of BA by the senate of the University of Cambridge in 1562/3 on the grounds of his having kept twelve terms of residence at these universities. He was granted an MA in 1567. In 1571 he was made chancellor of St Patrick's Cathedral, Dublin.

There is evidence that Walsh was recommended for the bishopric of Kilmacduagh in 1572, but that he declined the appointment. In February 1578 he became bishop of Ossory. He was a conscientious bishop; he attempted to enforce the law against recusants and his contemporary, Sir Henry Wallop, said that he 'was the only man of his coat, that I ever knew born in [Ireland], that did most sincerely know and teach the Gospel'.

Walsh was probably tall and thin for he refers to himself

as 'Nicholas the Scar[e]crowe'. He was the author of a collection of sermons in Latin and was also involved in the translation of the New Testament into Irish. This was a collaborative effort, initially involving Walsh, Nehemiah Donellan, and John Kearney, an associate of Walsh since their days in Cambridge together. Walsh's contribution to the translation began about 1573 while he and Kearney were both in St Patrick's Cathedral. While in Dublin Walsh and Kearney were instrumental in introducing Gaelic type into Ireland. The Irish New Testament was finally published by William Daniel in 1602 or 1603.

Bishop Walsh seems always to have been short of funds. In April 1581 he begged that he be allowed to hold *in commendam* any benefices in his diocese that might become vacant. Otherwise, he claimed, he would have to vacate the bishopric for lack of money. On 14 December 1585 Walsh was stabbed to death in his own house in Kilkenny by James Dullard, 'a profligate wretch' whom he had cited in his consistory court for adultery; it was said that Dullard killed the bishop in order to prevent the case going any further. At the time Walsh was also engaged in proceedings to recover the properties of his see. Walsh was buried on the south side of the great aisle of Kilkenny Cathedral, where a monument was erected to him. Dullard was hanged.   N. J. A. WILLIAMS

Sources N. J. A. Williams, *I bprionta i leabhar* (1987) · W. A. Phillips, ed., *History of the Church of Ireland*, 2 (1934) · *DNB* · *The whole works of Sir James Ware concerning Ireland*, ed. and trans. W. Harris, 1 (1739)

Walsh, Octavia (*bap.* 1677, *d.* 1706), poet, was baptized at Abberley, Worcestershire, on 1 January 1677, the youngest of eight children of Joseph Walsh (1618/19–1682) of Abberley, and Elizabeth (*bap.* 1637, *d.* 1719), daughter of Sir Bryan Palmes of Lindley, Yorkshire. Octavia wrote her earliest surviving poems at the age of fifteen, by which time her brother, William *Walsh (*bap.* 1662, *d.* 1708), was a published poet and friend of Dryden, but she did not show her verses to any of her close family.

The original manuscript of Walsh's verse (Bodl. Oxf., MS Eng. poet. e. 31) is a notebook containing 150 pages of drafts and copies of poems, some recipes, a note dated 22 January 1705, and a pen and wash portrait of her. Another manuscript, probably prepared by Octavia's family after her death, was listed in a bookseller's catalogue of 1962 but has not been located. It was said to contain prose discourses on religious subjects as well as poems and a pen and wash portrait of the author. The surviving poems include a few comic narratives and burlesques which sometimes hover on the brink of indelicacy; there are some pastorals; but death, solitude, contempt of the world, and the goodness of providence are more common subjects. There are some apparent references to an unhappy love affair.

Walsh never married. She died of smallpox on 10 October 1706 and was buried in Worcester Cathedral; a long monumental inscription to her was erected on the south wall of the nave. Seven of her poems were published in *Poems upon Divine and Moral Subjects* by Simon Patrick (1626–1707) 'and other eminent hands' (1719). The anonymous dedication of this volume claims that the authors in it were 'once dear to' the dedicatee, William Talbot (1659?–1730), bishop of Salisbury. Talbot was dean of Worcester from 1691 to 1715. One of Octavia's poems appears, with an informative headnote, in Roger Lonsdale's *Eighteenth-Century Women Poets: an Oxford Anthology* (1989).

JAMES SAMBROOK

Sources R. Lonsdale, ed., *Eighteenth-century women poets: an Oxford anthology* (1989), 52–3 · P. M. Hill, *Rare books catalogue*, 82 (1962), 33 · Bodl. Oxf., MS Eng. poet. e. 31 · T. Nash, *Collections for the history of Worcestershire*, 1 (1781), 2–3 · parish register (baptism), Abberley, 1 Jan 1677 · IGI
Archives Bodl. Oxf., MSS
Likenesses ink and wash drawing, Bodl. Oxf.
Wealth at death approx. £500—est. value of property, cash legacies, and annuities: will

Walsh, Patrick (*b.* 1813x24). *See under* Knock, visionaries of (*act.* 1879).

Walsh, Peter (*c.*1618–1688), Roman Catholic priest, also known as Petrus Valesius, was born at Mooretown, co. Kildare, Ireland. His father was a chandler in Naas, and his mother, whose maiden name was Goodie, was alleged to have been an English protestant.

Education Walsh, like many sons of the Old English Catholic gentry, was educated in Europe. About 1630 he joined the Franciscan college of St Anthony, Louvain, founded by Florence Conry in 1606. He excelled in his studies, and became a member of the order and a doctor, and later professor of divinity. His doctoral thesis was dedicated to his friend and mentor Cornelius Jansen, then bishop-elect of Ypres. Although Walsh did not share Jansen's doctrine of grace on the controversial contemporary issue of papal supremacy, his views were certainly Jansenist and Gallican. The struggle for supremacy between spiritual and temporal authority, papal and monarchical power, divided Catholic Europe at this time and would be manifested in Ireland in these decades with decisive results. It was Walsh's stance on this crucial issue, together with his future association with James Butler, first duke of Ormond, which would fundamentally affect the rest of his life and determine his place in Irish history.

Walsh in Ireland, 1646–1652 Walsh returned to Ireland in 1646, at the height of the confederate war, to Kilkenny, headquarters of the Catholic confederacy. He joined the Franciscan house, and was appointed public lecturer in divinity and later chaplain to the army in Munster. He was immediately embroiled in the political controversy surrounding the peace treaty proclaimed on 30 July 1646 and agreed between the confederate supreme council and Ormond, the king's representative. The majority of the council and the Old English Catholic nobility supported the treaty, but most of the clergy, under the authority of the papal nuncio, Giovanni Battista Rinuccini, archbishop of Fermo, rejected its terms. Rinuccini argued that the Catholic majority in Ireland should not compromise with a heretic protestant king whose current crisis presented the opportunity to insist upon the establishment of the Catholic church in Ireland. At a meeting of the clergy in Waterford, Walsh was among a minority who opposed the nuncio and the so-called unanimous decree of 12 August which declared perjured any Catholics who adhered to the peace treaty, said to have violated the previous oath of association. Walsh's defiance of the nuncio and the principle of papal supremacy in Ireland resulted in his excommunication on 1 September. Rinuccini blamed him for misleading the nobility with his heretical ideas.

With the supreme council in prison and Rinuccini apparently dominant, Walsh continued the verbal offensive. In 1647, in nine successive sermons in St Canice's Cathedral, Kilkenny, he preached against the teaching of Cornelius Mahony, a Jesuit from Cork then living in Lisbon. In 1645 Mahony had published *Disputatio apologetica*, which argued that the English crown had forfeited the right to govern Ireland, having broken the terms of Pope Adrian's grant. Walsh was subsequently deprived of his house and appointment at Kilkenny and forbidden access to a library. However, with the support of David Rothe, bishop of Ossory, and most of the supreme council, he continued to speak out against Rinuccini's stance. Walsh argued that loyalty to a protestant king was not only consistent with Catholic faith and moral duty but also the best option for the future of the Catholic church in Ireland.

A cessation of arms agreed between the supreme council and Inchiquin on 20 May 1648 was also condemned by Rinuccini, who proclaimed all its adherents excommunicated. The guardian of the Franciscans, Paul King, who enforced the nuncio's censure, was arrested by the council and replaced by Walsh. The council, with Walsh's assistance and the support of fourteen prelates, appealed directly to Rome against the censure. Despite the agency of Luke Wadding, another product of Louvain, the pope rejected their appeal, and unconditional absolution was only officially granted in 1688. Walsh was charged by Rothe and the supporting clergy with drafting a defence of their position. In 1648, with Owen Roe O'Neill, a supporter of Rinuccini, and the Ulster army encamped around Kilkenny, Walsh took three days and nights to write *Queries Concerning the Lawfulness of the Present Cessation*, his first publication. Thomas Dease, bishop of Meath, gave the paper his approval, and no one at the time attempted a response. Although Dease was the only bishop to support Walsh, he had significant support among the Old English Jesuits, lawyers, and gentry.

Walsh's articulate opposition to Rinuccini brought him to the attention of Ormond, whom he met in Kilkenny for the first time in September 1648. Walsh's background and education, together with the support of many of Ormond's Old English friends and relatives, would also have recommended him. The conclusion of the second peace treaty between Ormond and the confederate council, approved by nine bishops on 17 January 1649, signalled the defeat of the nuncio and his departure from Ireland. Rinuccini's supporters were not all from a Gaelic Irish background, but the vast majority of Walsh's clerical support would have been considered Old English. It was the clergy of 'English extraction' who were later blamed for betraying the cause in Ireland in the 1640s (R. O'Ferrall and R. O'Connell, *Commentarius Rinuccinianus de sedis*

apostolicae legatione ad foederatos Hiberniae catholicos per annos 1645–9, ed. S. Kavanagh, 6 vols., 1932–49, vol. 4, pp. 212–14).

In June 1649 Walsh was disciplined by Thomas McKiernan, provincial of the friars minor in Ireland, and sent to the convent at Castle Dermott 'for *domo diciplinae*, or prison' (Gilbert, 1.272), and there he remained until rescued by James Tuchet, earl of Castlehaven. Cromwell's victory at Kilkenny in March 1650 left Walsh without shelter and exposed to the persecution of his clerical opponents. Despite assistance from Castlehaven, who made Walsh his personal chaplain, conflict and opposition continued to plague him. The strength of feeling was such that Terence Albert O'Brien, bishop of Emly, threatened to undermine Castlehaven's forces at Limerick unless he abandoned Walsh. When the earl left for France in the autumn of 1651, Walsh was forced into hiding.

Years in exile and hiding, 1652–1660 In September 1652 Walsh was granted a passport by the parliamentary commissioners in Dublin, travelled to London, where he managed to remain until September 1654, and then went voluntarily to Madrid. On arrival in Spain he was imprisoned for several months before journeying to the Netherlands. Walsh suffered at this time from a lack of friends and supporters in the church, where the Roman hierarchy continued to censure him, and in Ireland, where his royalist connections to Ormond precluded favour. He was, however, able to live in hiding in England, only briefly venturing to Paris on one occasion. Apart from the Portuguese embassy in London, he received shelter in the homes of other Catholics or royalist associates of Ormond, with whom he maintained contact. In April 1660 he corresponded, in cipher, with the earl under the alias of Mr Weston, and was able to report positive developments in London preceding the king's restoration (MS Carte 214, fols. 71, 147).

Restoration After the restoration of Charles II in May 1660 there were few Irish Catholic clerics better placed than Walsh or with greater potential to influence Irish politics. He was resident in London and had maintained contact with Ormond, one of the king's closest advisers. In the declaration of Breda, 4 April 1660, the basis for restoration, Charles had promised liberty of conscience, and Walsh must have been hopeful for the future. Like Sir Nicholas Plunkett and other agents for the Irish Catholic laity, he expected the terms of the peace treaty of 1649 to be honoured in respect of those that had, at great personal cost, remained loyal to the king in Ireland and served him in exile. In August, however, despite the king's personal plea, Irish Catholics were excluded from general pardon in the Act of Indemnity passed by the English parliament. By October 1660 Walsh expressed his concerns in a letter to Ormond 'desiring a just and merciful regard of the Roman Catholics of Ireland' (Walsh to Ormond, Oct 1660, MS Carte 59, fols. 421–87). He urged Ormond to allay the fears and criticisms of even his 'fastest friends' (ibid., fol. 487) by acting promptly to ensure justice for the innocent and mercy for the guilty who had already suffered significantly for their crimes. The letter, later published, provoked a response from Roger Boyle, earl of Orrery. In *Irish Colours Displayed* Boyle highlighted Catholic treachery in 1641. In his response, *Irish Colours Folded* (1662), Walsh stated that casualty figures in the war were greatly exaggerated, and any atrocities were committed by the 'rascal multitude'.

The king's declaration for the settlement of Ireland, issued on 30 November 1660, reflected Orrery's views and confirmed Walsh's fears. The Cromwellian settlement of former Catholic lands would be maintained except where the old proprietors could prove their 'innocence' in respect of events from 1641. It was apparent to Walsh that the recent past remained a stumbling block for future favour. Ormond had not forgotten what he considered the treachery of the Catholic prelates. Walsh therefore urged the church hierarchy to make a positive representation to the king so that their silence could not be misinterpreted as dissension.

At the Restoration there were only three Catholic bishops in Ireland. Eugene Sweeney, bishop of Kilmore (1630–69), who was bedridden; the Franciscan Anthony MacGeoghegan, bishop of Clonmacnoise (1648–57) and Meath (1657–61), a fierce opponent of Walsh; and the primate, Edmund O'Reilly, archbishop of Armagh (1658–69). Given Walsh's position and the political context, and despite previous conflict, O'Reilly had little option but to appoint him as agent for the Catholic clergy at Whitehall. A procuration or power of attorney, dated 1 January 1661, was forwarded to Walsh by Anthony Gearnon, the queen mother's chaplain, and signed by the available members of the hierarchy including Patrick Plunkett, bishop of Dromore and Ardagh, and, by proxy, Nicholas French, bishop of Ferns. Walsh was delegated to 'obtain what favours his Majesty should think fit by connivance or otherwise, for the exercise of their religion, and to save them from persecution' (Walsh, *History*, 4–5). He was 'soundly checked' by Ormond for receiving such a document from those previously 'very obnoxious to the laws and disaffected' to the king's interest (ibid., 6), but despite initial hostility Walsh did receive his assistance in securing the release of 120 priests from prison without distinction or qualification.

Fear and uncertainty mounted in Ireland throughout 1661. The king's declaration proved practically unworkable and, as Patrick Darcy argued, legally deficient as a basis for the settlement of Ireland. The Irish parliament, convened on 8 May 1661, with an entirely protestant House of Commons, only served to heighten political tensions. Stories of the alleged activities of Jesuits and rumours of priests collecting funds for another rebellion were widespread. The king's response to the crisis only served to enhance Walsh's political influence. On 4 November he announced that Ormond would return to Ireland as viceroy; Walsh's experience and influence were now indispensable.

Although Walsh did not draft the Catholic remonstrance of December 1661, its author, Richard Bellings,

was familiar enough with Ormond and the political context to recognize the need to offer reassurance regarding the allegiance of the Irish clergy. They were not only the focus of protestant fears but also Ormond's resentment, and Walsh was convinced that the laity would suffer in the forthcoming Act of Settlement as a result. The remonstrance or loyal formulary was drafted at a small gathering in Dublin. The document was sent to England and given to Walsh by Luke Plunkett, third earl of Fingall, with the request that Ormond present it to the king. The duke dismissed the remonstrance as only a useful paper without signatures, but Walsh, acting as agent, defended their actions and pointed out that a large gathering of Catholics in Dublin at that time would have been impossible. He subsequently called together the Irish Catholic clergy then in London, and on 11 and 15 January 1662 Oliver Darcy, bishop of Dromore, and thirty other Catholic clerics met to discuss subscription. Twenty-four of their number signed the document, which was, with Ormond's approval, presented to the king on 3 February and was well received. At the time Walsh accepted plausible excuses from those who failed to subscribe, but their outright opposition later became apparent. Ninety-eight members of the Irish nobility and gentry in London signed their own copy of the remonstrance, which was an unequivocal declaration of allegiance to the king regardless of any other power or opinion either princely or papal.

Three weeks after the remonstrance was accepted by the king, Walsh again expressed his fears to Ormond about the Irish settlement. The two men had clearly exchanged views on the subject. Walsh admitted that his conscience was troubled ever since because he had remained silent regarding what he believed to be the 'great inequality in the intended distribution of justice' (Walsh to Ormond, 24 Feb [1662], MS Carte 45, fols. 274–5) to Irish Catholics. He informed Ormond that he was morally bound to honour the peace treaty of 1649 and warned of the judgment of God on both himself and the king if they neglected their obligation.

Walsh in Ireland, 1662–1669 In an effort to explain and promote the remonstrance, Walsh published a 'little book' in 1662 entitled *A More Ample Account*, but this only seemed to galvanize opposition. By the time he reached Ireland that summer, despite the additional signatures of forty-five clerics and thirty-two members of the laity, opponents of the remonstrance were dominant, particularly among the church hierarchy. With the benefit of Ormond's patronage Walsh evidently lived quite comfortably in Kennedy's Court, near Christ Church, but by the end of that year Sir Nicholas Plunkett observed that the oath had actually added to the troubles facing the Catholic interest. They now faced not only their enemies within the protestant interest but also the united opposition of the Catholic church both at home and abroad (MS Carte 32, fol. 146).

The oath was condemned by Walsh's own faculty at Louvain, the Brussels internuncio de Vechiis, and Cardinal Francesco Barberini in Rome. Walsh's aim had been to acknowledge and draw a line under the mistakes of the past and begin to build trust and confidence, which he believed would lead to liberty for their religion in the future. However, the division created by the oath had the opposite effect and suggested that nothing had changed in Ireland since the 1640s. Given the European controversy on this very issue, Walsh must surely have anticipated this outcome. Political and religious tensions in Ireland were such that by 1663 the king's earlier private instructions to Ormond to promote the remonstrance were rescinded. Promotion of the oath thereafter was almost negligible, and by 1665 of approximately 2000 Catholic clerics in Ireland (1200 secular, 800 regular) only 69 were remonstrants (Brenan, 481). Walsh later stated that 70 clerics and 124 members of the laity had subscribed (P. Walsh, *Four Letters*, 1686, 3).

Walsh, like Ormond, refused to countenance other versions of the oath offered by Jesuits, Dominicans, and Franciscans, and argued that their refusal to subscribe to the 1661 remonstrance was in itself conclusive. He recalled a secret meeting in September 1664, in the backyard of Somerset House, with Peter Talbot, later archbishop of Dublin, Patrick Maginn, Redmond Caron, and the Brussels internuncio de Vechiis, who had come to England incognito. An alternate oath suggested by Talbot was dismissed by Walsh at the time and later by Ormond (Walsh, *History*, 511–12).

In 1666, described by Walsh as a 'wonderful year' (Walsh, *History*, 664), he convinced Ormond to allow a national synod of the Catholic church because he apparently still believed that the prelates could be persuaded by debate and by observing the desperate plight of the Irish Catholic people. The theological faculty of the Sorbonne, Paris, had produced six propositions in 1663 which affirmed the supremacy of the king, and Walsh may have thought that this development would add weight to his argument. The synod met for fifteen days from 11 June in the parish house of St Audoen's, Dublin. Primate O'Reilly brought with him letters of condemnation from Giacomo Rospigliosi, Brussels internuncio, against the remonstrance and the meeting itself. The oath and the Sorbonne propositions, which denied papal supremacy, were rejected, and an alternative declaration of loyalty to the king, which they produced, proved unacceptable to Ormond. The clergy refused to acknowledge any guilt or responsibility for the events of the 1640s. Nicholas French later told Walsh that his assertion that the hostilities in the 1640s had been a 'rebellion' rather than a 'just war' had offended him more than the remonstrance itself (Walsh, *Four Letters*, 32). Walsh's opponents alleged that the synod, like the oath, was used by Ormond not only to cause division but also to justify the iniquitous settlement of Ireland by suggesting that little had changed since 1641.

Walsh enjoyed a degree of influence in Ireland while Ormond remained in the viceroyalty, but this may well have been the case without the remonstrance. For Walsh and his supporters a fundamental problem remained. The oath, despite its unprecedented declaration of allegiance and the support of Louis XIV and the Gallican church, had secured no tangible benefits for its adherents. The whole affair proved irrelevant to the Restoration land settlement in Ireland, and, contrary to Walsh's request, existing royal chaplains and new appointees were not required to subscribe. Ormond himself had recommended Patrick Maginn (a non-subscriber) for promotion at court to the post of grand almoner to the queen (Ormond to the king, 9 Dec 1665, MS Carte 219, fol. 58). Father Thomas Talbot, brother of Peter and Richard, complained to Walsh that unless the world changed the remonstrance would prove useless (Talbot to Walsh, 19 May 1662, MS Carte 31, fols. 373–4). By the time Ormond was removed from the lieutenancy on 24 February 1669 Walsh had failed to achieve his objectives, and the few remaining remonstrant clergy in Ireland were left at a considerable disadvantage.

Years in opposition, 1669–1673 The Roman authorities were determined to retain control of the church in Ireland, and Walsh observed that while Rome governed appointments to the Irish hierarchy they held real power in the country. Walsh was informed in 1669 that the papal internuncio was not interested in doctrine or debate but in obedience. Opposition to Walsh and the remonstrance had become a prerequisite for high office in the Irish Catholic church at this time. In 1669 the newly appointed archbishops of Armagh and Dublin, Oliver Plunkett and Peter Talbot respectively, were avowed enemies of Walsh. Plunkett, a stout proponent of papal authority, described him as 'a lost soul, another Luther' (*Letters of Saint Oliver Plunkett*, 42). Talbot, a sworn enemy of Ormond and Walsh, referred to the latter as 'that wrangling friar' (Talbot's vindication from Walsh's opinion, MS Carte 45, fol. 283). He branded him 'Peter pence' (ibid., fol. 287) and made much of the fact that Walsh had received £300 per year from Ormond throughout these years. Walsh also had £100 per year for the seneschalship of Winchester from 1667, with Bishop Morley's approval (Burke, 12).

Archbishop Talbot in particular relentlessly pursued the remonstrant clergy in a determined effort to force them to recant. Walsh, who was resident in England during the period of the cabal and the secret treaty of Dover, endeavoured to highlight their plight by petitioning the king, Ormond, and Lord Berkeley, the Irish lord lieutenant, on their behalf. Berkeley, however, had little time for Ormond and grew to hate Walsh because of his repeated references to his patron's superior government of Ireland. The remonstrant clergy therefore found themselves isolated, with Walsh or Ormond virtually powerless to influence events. Walsh himself was excommunicated for the second time on 24 May 1670 by the chapter-general of the Franciscans at Valladolid for publishing material without official sanction—insubordination rather than heresy. In a petition to the king, Thomas Harold referred to the 'daring prosecution' of Walsh in London in 1669, 1670, and 1671 by the church court (petition of Thomas Harold to the king, MS Carte 45, fols. 244–8). Walsh, however, continued to publish material to support his arguments and defend his actions. In 1672 his *Epistola prima ad Thomam Haroldum*, was printed (Harold was a remonstrant and a prisoner in Brussels) and in 1673 a series of twelve letters purportedly between a Catholic and protestant gentleman, *The controversial letters, or, Grand controversy concerning the temporal authority of the popes over the whole earth, &c.*, was published.

Reaction and resurgence, 1673–1677 It was not the new administration of Arthur Capel, earl of Essex and Irish lord lieutenant (1672–7), which produced a political change but the address of the English House of Commons to the king in March 1673. Charles II was forced to cancel the second declaration of indulgence and curtail the activities in Ireland of Peter Talbot in particular, something that Walsh had been requesting for years. Essex was certainly more willing to receive petitions from Walsh and advice from Ormond regarding the Catholic clergy. However, as Walsh reflected on events since 1660 he was clearly entertaining doubts, not least about Ormond's motives in the whole remonstrance affair. In a letter to his patron he suggested that the opposition and persecution might have been prevented if his advice had been followed regarding the subscription of royal chaplains and Ormond had not stopped a circular letter from the Catholic nobility in 1663. He added that Edward Hyde, earl of Clarendon, should have published the remonstrance rather than returning it to the clergy. Walsh was also deeply troubled by stories that Ormond had deliberately divided the Catholic clergy and, in fact, used him to that purpose. He concluded by saying that he would no longer be surprised by anything because, since the restoration, he had seen so many 'strange things done, quite contrary' to equity and policy and, 'which is worst of all, to honesty and justice' ([Walsh to Ormond], 30 July [1673], MS Carte 45, fols. 407–12). By 1674 Walsh blamed himself for opening a 'spring' which turned into a 'bitter fountain' (Walsh to Essex, 4 Aug 1674, MS Carte 45, fols. 252–5).

Walsh's major work, *The History and Vindication of the Loyal Formulary, or Irish Remonstrance*, was published in 1674. His *Letter to the Catholics of England, Ireland and Scotland, &c.*, written in 1673 and printed earlier in 1674, constituted the preface. The book, a significant account of Irish Catholic political and religious history since the 1640s, contains copies of many important contemporary documents. Walsh draws on European and Irish church history, secular history, theology, law, and philosophy to explain and defend the remonstrance. His arguments were not only Gallican but also logical and pragmatic within the Irish context, and he was convinced that they did not contradict Catholic faith and teaching. Walsh believed that, apart from addressing the practical difficulties facing Catholics in Ireland, the oath would lay a foundation of trust which could bring about a reunion of the churches of England and Rome. However, with the benefit of hindsight, Walsh was ironically philosophical regarding the whole affair. Acknowledging the failure of the remonstrance Walsh encouraged his readers to take the 'comfort of a good conscience' before any earthly gain, and look for a reward in a 'better place' (Walsh, *History*, 37).

Ormond's viceroyalty and Walsh's later years, 1677–1688 Throughout the remainder of the 1670s Walsh enjoyed the patronage and protection of Ormond, particularly after the duke's return to the lord lieutenancy of Ireland in 1677. Walsh was again in a position to solicit favour for his family in Ireland, albeit discreetly. Any toleration of Catholicism, however, proved difficult after 1673, but during the alleged Popish Plot and exclusion crisis it was almost impossible, and certainly politically too dangerous.

In 1682, on the advice of Castlehaven, Walsh published the first part of *A Prospect of the State of Ireland from 1556–1652*, a rather poor historical account. His *Causa Valesiana*, written in Latin in his usual verbose style, was published in 1684. Addressed to a wider European audience, it again defended his stance and that of Caron against the church hierarchy. The details included in this work, however, caused great offence among some of Walsh's most valuable friends. The bishop of Winchester was alarmed that Walsh had publicly acknowledged his part in ensuring his payment for the seneschalship of Winchester. Morley resolved never again to communicate with Walsh (Walsh to Ormond, 21 Sept 1684, *Ormonde MSS*, 7.273). Ormond was also offended by Walsh's reference to a conversation in 1661 with an unnamed 'illustrious person' who informed him of an intention to repeal the penal laws against Catholics. The duke was most concerned that either Clarendon or himself were implicated, and Walsh was equally anxious to publish a denial (Walsh to Ormond, 10 Jan 1685, *Ormonde MSS*, 306–9).

On the succession of James II in February 1685 the remonstrance controversy and the whole issue of oaths of allegiance was revived. The new king had not required the oaths of supremacy or allegiance from his army officers in Ireland, but was content with a simple promise of fidelity. Walsh's opponents saw this as proof that the English authorities had never demanded the remonstrance in the first place. In 1686 Walsh published his *Four Letters on Several Subjects to Persons of Quality*, who included the earl of Essex and Nicholas French, bishop of Ferns. The correspondence between Walsh and French was mostly a retrospective discussion of controversial events in Ireland and Ormond's actions regarding the Catholic interest.

In almost forty years of association with Ormond, Walsh had never spoken of religion until 1686. He informed the duke that while the Catholic church had many faults it was still the 'mother' and the 'safest for salvation to die therein'. Ormond replied that he could not embrace what he condemned and wondered why, if he stood in such eternal danger, Walsh had not spoken to his 'good friend' sooner (MS Carte 69, fol. 78). In a letter to Sir Robert Southwell in 1687, who was himself writing a history of these years, Walsh indicated his agreement that there had been as much rebellion in the oath of association as in the covenant. He declared, however, that religion had not been the true cause of the 1641 rebellion but 'liberty and property and the shaking off of the English yoke'. He had actually substituted the word 'liberty' for 'religion' in

Castlehaven's history of the time (Walsh to Southwell, 19 March 1687, MS Carte 70, fol. 564).

On 13 March 1688, just before his death, Walsh agreed and signed a retraction of the remonstrance and submitted his 'private judgement to that of the church' (Brenan, 486). The declaration was witnessed by Genetti, the nuncio Adda's chaplain, and three Irish Franciscans, including John Everard, himself a subscriber to the remonstrance. On the same day he dictated a final letter to Ormond which contained two last requests. Walsh asked that the Franciscans be given the convent in Kilkenny which they had formerly occupied, and that Ormond would help his nephew Andrew Laborne, who had eleven children and little support (Walsh to Ormond, 13 March 1688, MS Carte 118, fol. 357). Walsh died two days later on 15 March having received absolution from Genetti. He was later buried in London, in St Dunstan-in-the-West.

Contemporary comment on Walsh's life and historical contribution has depended not only on the author's relationship to Walsh but also to Ormond, his patron. Rinuccini described Walsh as a 'sacrilegious profaner' who 'vomited forth in one hour more filth (*sordes*) and blasphemy than Luther and Calvin together in three years' (Moran, 3.72). The writer of the *Aphorismical Discovery* branded him a 'protestant English slut's son', a 'Judas', a 'Lutheran dogmatist', and a 'hireling wolf in sheep's clothing' (Gilbert, 1.238, 273–6), among other things. Even his friend Castlehaven referred to him as the 'earl's [Ormond's] ghostly father' (*Memoirs of … Castlehaven*, 117). Burnet, however, described him as the 'honestest and learnedest' member of the Catholic clergy he had ever met (*Bishop Burnet's History*, 1.355). There is no doubt that Walsh enjoyed the mutual respect of several members of the Anglican hierarchy, such as Archbishop Dolben of York and Bishop Barlow of Winchester. He was also, surprisingly, on friendly terms with Arthur Annesley, earl of Anglesey. In terms of Irish nationalist historiography, Walsh has been tried and found guilty by association with Ormond, the 'unkind deserter of loyal men and true friends' and the 'avowed' enemy of Irish Catholics, according to Brenan (Brenan, 478). Although dismissed as the 'giddy friar' in the *Unkinde Deserter of Loyal Men and True Friends*, (Brussels; see Barnard and Fenlon, 181), his scholarship has been acknowledged by Corish, Millett, and Brenan. The latter described Walsh as 'naturally bold, impetuous and enterprising' (Brenan, 478), while Millett referred to him as a 'stormy petrel but a very able controversialist' (Millett, 'Irish literature in Latin', 578). Corish has also acknowledged him to be a 'man of some learning in canon law' (Corish, 'Ormond, Rinuccini and the confederates', 330).

There is little doubt that Walsh's views represented sincerely held convictions rather than political expedients, although he reminded readers of his history that while the poor Catholics of Ireland suffered for their principles the Roman hierarchy enjoyed the comfort of that 'city of fortune' (Walsh, *History*, 27–8, 30). His attempt to address and resolve the problem of Irish Catholic civil allegiance and break the dominance of Rome over the Irish Catholic church was his most significant historical contribution. If he had succeeded, the consequences could have been far reaching not least for the Stuarts and the events which followed his death in 1688.   M. A. CREIGHTON

Sources Bodl. Oxf., MSS Carte 31, 45, 59, 69, 70, 118, 214 · A. Creighton, 'The Catholic interest in Irish politics in the reign of Charles II, 1660–85', PhD diss., Queen's University, Belfast, 2000 · P. Walsh, *The history and vindication of the loyal formulary, or Irish remonstrance* (1674) · P. Walsh, *Letter to the Catholics of England, Ireland and Scotland, &c.* (1674) · *The letters of Saint Oliver Plunkett, 1625–1681, archbishop of Armagh and primate of all Ireland*, ed. J. Hanly (Dublin, 1979) · J. T. Gilbert, ed., *A contemporary history of affairs in Ireland from 1641 to 1652*, 3 vols. (1879–80), vols. 1–2 · P. F. Moran, ed., *Spicilegium Ossoriense, being a collection of original letters and papers illustrative of the history of the Irish church from the Reformation to the year 1800*, 3 vols. (1874–84) · M. J. Brenan, *An ecclesiastical history of Ireland, from the introduction of Christianity into that country to the year MDCCCXXIX*, 1 (1864) · W. D. Killen, *The ecclesiastical history of Ireland from the earliest period to the present time*, 2 vols. (1875), vol. 2 · P. J. Corish, *The Catholic community in the seventeenth and eighteenth centuries* (Dublin, 1981) · P. J. Corish, 'Ormond, Rinuccini, and the confederates, 1645–9', *A new history of Ireland*, ed. T. W. Moody and others, 3: *Early modern Ireland, 1534–1691* (1976), 317–35 · B. Millett, *The Irish Franciscans, 1651–1665* (Rome, 1964) · B. Millett, *Survival and reorganization, 1650–1695* (1968), vol. 3/7 of *A history of Irish Catholicism* · B. Millett, 'Irish literature in Latin, 1550–1700', *A new history of Ireland*, ed. T. W. Moody and others, 3: *Early modern Ireland, 1534–1691* (1976), 561–86; repr. with corrections (1991) · *Calendar of the manuscripts of the marquess of Ormonde*, new ser., 8 vols., HMC, 36 (1902–20), vols. 5, 7 · *CSP Ire., 1660–70* · T. Carte, *An history of the life of James, duke of Ormond*, 3 vols. (1735–6), vol. 2 · J. G. Simms, 'The Restoration, 1660–1685', *A new history of Ireland*, ed. T. W. Moody and others, 3: *Early modern Ireland, 1534–1691* (1976), 420–53; repr. with corrections (1991) · W. P. Burke, *The Irish priests in the penal times, 1660–1760* (1914) · C. Butler, *Historical memoirs respecting the English, Irish and Scottish Catholics, from the Reformation to the present time*, 2nd edn, 2 (1819) · R. Bagwell, *Ireland under the Stuarts*, 3 vols. (1909–16); repr. (1963), vols. 2–3 · *Bishop Burnet's History* · T. Barnard and J. Fenlon, *The dukes of Ormonde, 1610–1745* (2000) · *The memoirs of James, Lord Audley, earl of Castlehaven, his engagement and carriage in the wars of Ireland from the year 1642 to the year 1651* (1680)

Archives Bodl. Oxf., MSS Carte, letters to Ormond

Wealth at death almost non-existent: Walsh to Ormond, 13 Mar 1688, Bodl. Oxf., MS Carte 118, fol. 357

Walsh, Richard Hussey (1825–1862), economist, born at Kilduff, Tyrrellspass, King's county, and baptized at Philipstown (now Daingean) Roman Catholic Church in King's county on 3 August 1825, was the fifth son of John Hussey Walsh of Kilduff and his wife, Maria, daughter of Michael Henley of La Mancha, co. Dublin. His grandmother Margaret was the daughter and heir of John Hussey of Mull Hussey, Roscommon. After being educated by private tutors, in 1842 Walsh entered Trinity College, Dublin, where he graduated BA in 1847, taking the highest honours in mathematics and physics. In the next year he obtained the senior mathematical prize founded by John Law, bishop of Elphin. On 5 May 1848 he was admitted a student of Lincoln's Inn, but he soon abandoned the study of law.

As a Roman Catholic, Walsh was precluded from reading for a fellowship at Trinity College, and in consequence turned his attention to the study of political economy, with the intention of competing for the Whately professorship. At the prize examination in the subject in 1850 he obtained the first place and in the same year was appointed to one of the Barrington lectureships in political economy administered by the Dublin Statistical Society (later renamed the Statistical and Social Inquiry Society of Ireland). In 1851 he was elected one of the honorary secretaries of this society and was also appointed Whately professor on the results of the examination held in that year.

In 1853 Walsh published one of the courses of lectures he gave as professor, under the title *An Elementary Treatise on Metallic Currency*. The book was unusual for its time in attempting to set out fully the state of knowledge in this branch of political economy. It contained some perceptive comments on the likely effect of recent gold discoveries on price levels when monometallic or bimetallic standards were in use and was favourably received by Nassau Senior and J. S. Mill but was more notable for its lucidity and completeness than for its originality. Walsh also contributed papers to the *Proceedings of the Dublin Statistical Society*, the statistical section of the British Association, and *The Economist*. Between 1848 and 1855 he also wrote elementary school books on political and domestic economy for the series of Education Lessons edited by Edward Hughes.

In the winter of 1853 Walsh acted temporarily as deputy for the professor of jurisprudence and political economy at Queen's College, Belfast, but when his term of office in the Whately chair ended in 1856, he took up a government post, under W. Neilson Hancock, as assistant secretary to the endowed schools (Ireland) commission. Because of the ability he displayed in this capacity, he was recommended for appointment as superintendent of the government schools in Mauritius, and entered on his duties in May 1857. These combined the responsibilities that in England were divided between commissioners, secretaries, and inspectors. He established new schools, and before he had been in office twenty months he increased their number from twenty to forty-four. His energy attracted the notice of the governor, William Stevenson, who placed him on a civil service commission nominated to inquire into the organization of the twenty-two civil service departments into which the island was divided. The work occupied nearly two years, and the results were highly approved by the duke of Newcastle, the colonial secretary (*Mauritius Gazette*, 5 Oct 1861). Walsh was also entrusted with the conduct of the census of the island taken in 1861 and had just completed it when he suffered a brain haemorrhage. Four days later he died, unmarried, at Port Louis on 30 January 1862.   R. D. COLLISON BLACK

Sources W. N. Hancock, *Journal of the Statistical and Social Inquiry Society of Ireland*, 3 (June 1862), 181 · R. D. C. Black, *The Statistical and Social Inquiry Society of Ireland centenary volume, 1847–1947* (1947), 74–5 · Burke, *Gen. GB* · W. P. Baildon, ed., *The records of the Honorable Society of Lincoln's Inn: admissions*, 2 (1896), 238 · Burtchaell & Sadleir, *Alum. Dubl.* · parish register (baptism), King's county, Philipstown, Killederry, Kill and Ballycommon, 1825 · *Thom's directory* (1848)
Wealth at death under £1500: administration, 26 June 1862, *CGPLA Ire.*

Walsh, Robert (1772–1852), author, born in Waterford, was the brother of Edward *Walsh (1756–1832) and the younger son of John Walsh (1720–1785), merchant, of Ballymountain House, co. Waterford. He was educated at Waterford and then entered Trinity College, Dublin, on 2 November 1789 as a pensioner, his tutor being Thomas Elrington (1760–1835). He graduated BA in 1796. He was elected scholar in 1794 and was ordained in 1802, and, after being for a short time a curate in Dublin under Walter Blake Kirwan, was appointed in 1806 to the curacy of Finglas, co. Dublin, where he remained until 1820. While he held this curacy he discovered the 'cross of Nethercross', supposedly buried during Oliver Cromwell's victorious march through the country by the alarmed inhabitants. On digging in the place pointed out by some of the older people, who had been told of it by their parents, Walsh discovered a Celtic cross in good preservation. It was erected in the churchyard of Finglas.

In 1813 Walsh married Ann Eliza Ellen (*d.* 1879), daughter of John Bayly of Tolka. They had two children, a daughter and a son, John Edward *Walsh, who became a judge and MP.

Walsh spent several years of his earlier life as a curate preparing a *History of the City of Dublin* (2 vols., 1815), a well-received work, in which he drew on the research of James Whitelaw and John Warburton.

In 1820—during which year he received a certificate of diploma of MD from the Royal College, Aberdeen, as well as a grace for the degree of LLD from Trinity College, Dublin—Walsh accepted the offer of the chaplaincy to the British embassy of Lord Strangford at Constantinople. He remained in that post for some years, during which time he made many extensive expeditions through Turkey and other parts of Asia, on occasion using his medical skills while in remote areas. From Constantinople he went to the embassy at St Petersburg, to which he had been appointed chaplain, but in 1828 went to Rio de Janeiro. He published the well-reviewed *Notices of Brazil* (1830) and his investigations into the slave trade in Brazil led to his appointment to the committee of the Society for the Abolition of Slavery.

After returning to Britain in 1831 Walsh was again sent to Constantinople. He finally settled in Ireland about 1835, and was given the living of Kilbride, co. Wicklow, which he exchanged in 1839 for that of Finglas, co. Dublin. He died at Finglas on 30 June 1852.

Walsh wrote much for periodicals, but his main works stem from his knowledge of Turkey and include *An Essay on Ancient Coins, Medals, and Gems* (1828), *Narrative of a Journey from Constantinople to England* (1828), *Residence at Constantinople during the Greek and Turkish Revolutions* (2 vols., 1836), and *Constantinople and the Scenery of the Seven Churches of Asia Minor* (2 vols., n.d. [1839?]). Many of his publications were favourably reviewed at the time.

D. J. O'DONOGHUE, *rev.* ELIZABETH BAIGENT

Sources 'Our portrait gallery, no. V: Rev. Robert Walsh', *Dublin University Magazine*, 15 (1840), 172–5 · J. Britten and G. S. Boulger, eds., *A biographical index of British and Irish botanists* (1893) · Allibone, *Dict.* · R. Walsh, *Fingal and its churches* (1888) · Burke, *Gen. Ire.*

Walsh, Stephen (1859–1929), trade unionist and politician, was born at Kirkdale, Liverpool, on 26 August 1859. His parents were of Irish descent. His father, John Walsh, died before his son's birth. His mother died while he was still an infant. Walsh was admitted as a foundling to the Kirkdale Industrial School and Orphanage, near Liverpool. There he received an elementary education, and acquired a proficiency in mathematics and a love of reading.

At the age of thirteen Walsh went to live with his brother, and became a working miner at Ashton in Makerfield, near Wigan. He became active in trade union affairs and his articulacy gave him influence among his fellow workers. He was elected district officer and secretary of the local union organization in 1890, and in 1901 he was appointed agent of the Lancashire and Cheshire Miners' Federation. He rose to become president of that federation, and in 1922 vice-president of the Miners' Federation of Great Britain. He became expert in wage negotiations, being skilled in dealing with intricate calculations, and from 1914 to 1920 he was chairman of the miners' section of the English conciliation board.

In 1906 Walsh was sponsored by the Miners' Federation to contest the Ince division of Lancashire as a Labour candidate. He won the seat, and retained it for the remainder of his life. He was also a justice of the peace and deputy lieutenant for the county of Lancaster. Although he was a man of small stature and homely presence, Walsh made an impact in parliament. He spoke with effect on industrial questions, and he made valuable contributions to debates on the Mines Act of 1911 and on the Minimum Wage Act of 1912. He was elected a vice-chairman of the Parliamentary Labour Party in 1922.

During the First World War, Walsh strongly supported recruiting campaigns and was an advocate of compulsory military service, consistently maintaining during the war, as he had maintained during the coal mining crisis in 1912, that the claims of citizenship were superior to those of trade unionism. He was parliamentary secretary to the Ministry of National Service in 1917, and to the Local Government Board during 1917–18.

In January 1924, on the formation of the first Labour government, Walsh was appointed secretary of state for war and president of the army council; when the government resigned in November of the same year he had achieved recognition as a capable and popular minister. Among the Conservatives there was praise for his support of military matters, and this caused him continuing difficulties with sections of his own party.

Walsh met his wife, Anne, daughter of John Adamson, an Ashton miner, when she was working on a colliery pitbank. They were married on 16 August 1885 and had four sons and six daughters. The eldest son, Arthur, was killed in action in 1918.

In November 1927 Walsh was appointed a member of the (Simon) statutory commission set up under the provisions of the Government of India Act of 1919, but owing to failing health he was unable to serve. He died at his home at 8 Swinley Road, Wigan, on 16 March 1929, and was buried on 20 March at Holy Trinity Church in Ashton in Makerfield. He was survived by his wife.

A. E. WATKIN, *rev.* MARC BRODIE

Sources *The Times* (18 March 1929), 19b · S. Walsh, 'How I got on', *Pearson's Weekly* (29 March 1906), 691 · *DLB* · *CGPLA Eng. & Wales* (1929)
Archives PRO, corresp. with Ramsay Macdonald, PRO 30/69/1/209
Wealth at death £8157 9s. 8d.: probate, 22 June 1929, *CGPLA Eng. & Wales*

Walsh, Thomas (1776–1849), vicar apostolic of the London district, was born in London on 3 October 1776, son of Charles and Mary Walsh, *née* Brittle. His father, a Catholic merchant, apparently died while his son was still an infant, perhaps even before his birth, since Thomas did not receive a Catholic baptism as a child. His mother, a protestant, sent him to St Albans grammar school. His father's brother, a London priest, then persuaded her to send him to the continent where, in 1792, he was enrolled at St Omers College at Liège. In August 1793, however, the college was confiscated by the French revolutionaries, as was the English College at Douai soon afterwards. Students and staff of both colleges were imprisoned at Doullens.

Following his release and return to England, Walsh was enrolled at St Edmund's College, near Ware, in August 1795. There he was confirmed on 19 December 1795, having received 'conditional' baptism on 27 September. He was ordained deacon on 20 December 1800. In March 1801 Dr Gregory Stapleton, president of St Edmund's, as he had been of St Omers, was made bishop and vicar apostolic of the midland district, one of four missionary vicariates into which Rome had divided England in 1688. Walsh, though still a deacon, accompanied him to Wolverhampton as private secretary, and was ordained priest on the following 19 September. Upon Stapleton's premature death in May 1802, Walsh remained as secretary to his successor, John Milner, while also serving the mission of Longbirch. In 1804 the bishop appointed him spiritual director and vice-president at Sedgley Park School. In 1808 he was assigned a similar position at Oscott College where, in 1818, he became president, an office he held until 1825. In 1824 Milner appealed to Rome for a coadjutor bishop to assist him. Walsh was appointed, and on 1 May 1825 was consecrated titular bishop of Cambysopolis. Upon Milner's death on 19 April 1826, Walsh succeeded him as vicar apostolic of the midland district.

Walsh's episcopate coincided with a period of great importance for Roman Catholics in the midland district. It was, in fact, due largely to his efforts that the so-called Catholic revival flourished there. As a result of the relentless efforts of Daniel O'Connell, whom Walsh had known since they were students at Liège, Catholic emancipation became law in 1829, allowing Roman Catholics to serve in parliament. John Talbot, sixteenth earl of Shrewsbury (1791–1852), resident and benefactor of the midland district, took his seat in the House of Lords along with other members of the Catholic aristocracy. Walsh depended upon Shrewsbury's generosity and influence as he pursued an ambitious building programme within the district. Under Walsh's direction twenty-nine new missions were established and approximately fifty churches constructed. Walsh recognized the genius of Augustus Welby Pugin and commissioned him to design churches in Birmingham, Nottingham, Derby, and elsewhere, and to complete, as well, the chapel of the new Oscott College, near Birmingham. The debts incurred by so extensive a programme were enormous and led Walsh's successor into bankruptcy court and even brief imprisonment, but the value of Walsh's personal achievement was considered remarkable.

An older generation of Catholics was critical of Walsh, rejecting the Gothic style embraced and promoted by Pugin, not only in his buildings but also in the flowing liturgical vestments which he designed. Similarly there were those who blamed Walsh for encouraging foreign devotional practices, such as Gregorian chant. Some resented his support for the Oeuvre pour la Propagation de la Foi, a French foundation for supporting missionary endeavours which, it was felt, deprived the English church of much-needed support. Walsh even accepted the presidency of the English branch of the Oeuvre in September 1838 and in addition encouraged public prayers for the conversion of England, considered by some as an ostentatious practice that would undermine the advance of Catholics in public life.

Walsh recognized his own limitations especially in relating to the Oxford Movement, launched in the summer of 1833. The presence of Oxford and Cambridge in the midland district tended to highlight the comparative lack of scholarly institutions and personnel to serve the Catholic community just at a time when the Catholic revival appeared to provide common ground with a significant number of Anglicans. Walsh had been persistent in urging Nicholas Wiseman, rector of the English College in Rome and a brilliant young scholar, to serve as his coadjutor bishop in the midland district. In 1840 the number of mission districts was doubled from four to eight, and the former midland district was renamed the central district, with the number of its counties reduced by half. Wiseman was at last named coadjutor bishop to Walsh, who immediately appointed him president of Oscott College, where he welcomed a number of influential converts. These included John Henry Newman, who was confirmed in the Oscott Chapel. Walsh turned the administrative work of the district over to Wiseman, under whom the Catholic revival continued to blossom, always with Walsh's support. Both men encouraged religious orders to work in the district, for example. If Wiseman's literary efforts, and the attention that he brought to Oscott College in his own right and through the distinguished visitors whom he welcomed there, soon received more attention than Walsh's activities, it was the older man who had the wisdom and foresight to support consistently the numerous works—literary, artistic, and pastoral—that were so much a part of the Catholic revival.

As Catholic numbers and influence grew, there was increasing pressure upon Rome to establish a proper ecclesiastical hierarchy in England. In 1847 Wiseman was commissioned by the other bishops to visit Rome and work out details. While he was there, the London vicar apostolic died and Wiseman returned as pro-vicar apostolic of that district. In 1848 the Holy See determined that a hierarchy would be restored immediately, but the revolutionary activities of 1848 and exile of the pope postponed the step. On 28 July 1848, however, in spite of his own protests based upon his age and ill health, Walsh was transferred to London, in anticipation of his later becoming Roman Catholic archbishop of a restored hierarchy. His position as senior vicar apostolic and his tireless zeal in promoting Catholicism were major factors in Rome's decision. Wiseman was named his coadjutor with right of succession. Physically unable to bear the administrative duties of an office which he had neither sought nor wanted, Walsh died at 35 Golden Square, London, on 18 February 1849. Following services both in London and Birmingham, he was buried on 2 March in the crypt of St Chad's Cathedral, Birmingham, designed by Pugin, which Walsh had himself consecrated in 1841.

RICHARD J. SCHIEFEN

Sources G. Anstruther, *The seminary priests*, 4 (1977) · J. L. Whitfield, 'Walsh, Thomas', *The Catholic encyclopedia*, ed. C. G. Herbermann and others, 15 (1912) · R. J. Schiefen, *Nicholas Wiseman and the transformation of English Catholicism* (1984) · B. N. Ward, *The eve of Catholic emancipation*, 3 vols. (1911–12) · B. Ward, *The sequel to Catholic emancipation*, 2 vols. (1915)
Archives Birmingham Archdiocesan Archives, corresp. and papers · Oscott College, Birmingham, papers relating to Oscott · Ushaw College, Durham, corresp. | Ushaw College, Durham, letters to Lord Shrewsbury
Likenesses J. R. Herbert, oils, Oscott College, Birmingham
Wealth at death under £600: Anstruther, *Seminary priests*

Walsh, Walter (d. 1538). *See under* Henry VIII, privy chamber of (*act.* 1509–1547).

Walsh, Walter (1847–1912), religious controversialist and author, was born on 23 January 1847 at Folkestone, the second son of Thomas Walsh, a hotel porter, and his wife, Sarah. He had at least one brother and two sisters. The extent of his formal education is unknown. Walsh experienced conversion in childhood and became involved in full-time protestant work early in adult life. In the 1860s and 1870s he was engaged in a number of spheres. Two years spent in Dublin with the Irish Church Missions were followed by five in Oxford with the Protestant Reformation Society. Thus his early career concentrated on anti-Catholic activity. It was at Oxford that he first became seriously involved in anti-ritualism, helping to found a branch of the Church Association. In 1874 Walsh married Elizabeth, daughter of George Adams. They had three sons (one of whom died in a cycling accident in 1902) and a daughter.

After Oxford, Walsh became the political agent of Charles Newdegate (1816–1887), Conservative MP for Nuneaton and a fanatical protestant. During this time Walsh began to produce his 'Protestant notes' for the *Press and St James Chronicle* newspaper. When the latter amalgamated with the *English Churchman* in 1884 Walsh moved to London as a sub-editor. By 1888 Walsh was also editing the *Protestant Observer*. Nevertheless Walsh's significance lies largely in one book, *The Secret History of the Oxford Movement*, published in London by Swan Sonnenschein in 1897. It ran to many editions and was a runaway success with the protestant public. This was due to a fortuitous conjunction of literary style, Anglo-Catholic predilection for clandestine organization, and the first stirrings of renewed anti-ritualist agitation. Walsh did not invent his material, but marshalled it adroitly for the purposes of protestant propaganda. Though an unwavering Anglican himself Walsh was an ardent believer in pan-evangelical co-operation across both national and denominational boundaries. He was thus a founder member of the Imperial Protestant Federation, a body created in 1896 to embody just such principles. Walsh resigned as sub-editor of the *English Churchman* in 1900, but continued to write its inimitable 'Protestant notes'. He became founding editor of the magazine *Grievances from Ireland* in 1905, an enterprise which marked his continuing interest in Irish religion and politics.

Walsh was an example of a distinctive type of Victorian protestant: from humble origins he undertook protestant apologetics in a professional capacity, and success in his work enabled him to enjoy a certain measure of upward social mobility. He was a tall, strongly built man, and was well-known for his caution and sound judgement, qualities not often associated with the militant protestants of his time. Though in demand as a speaker he possessed few oratorical skills. He wrote numerous pamphlets and articles, and a number of other books, including: *The History of the Romeward Movement in the Church of England, 1833–1864* (1900), a work on similar lines to *The Secret History of the Oxford Movement*, though perhaps rather less prone to populist sensationalism; *The Religious Life and Influence of Queen Victoria* (1902), which presents the recently deceased monarch as a protestant heroine; *The Jesuits in Great Britain: an Historical Inquiry into their Political Influence* (1903), a poor book, of no credit to Walsh, which sought to attribute most of Britain's troubles to the Society of Jesus; *The Women Martyrs of the Reformation* (1905); and *England's Fight with the Papacy: a Political History* (1912), an interesting account from the militant protestant point of view of English hostility to Rome since the Reformation. Walsh died on 25 February 1912 at St Mary's Church, Spring Grove, Isleworth, and was buried in Brookwood cemetery, Woking. His wife survived him.   I. T. FOSTER

Sources *The Times* (27 Feb 1912), 11 • *Record* (1 March 1912), 205 • *English Churchman* (29 Feb 1912), 139 • *Protestant Alliance Magazine* (April 1912), 47 • *Protestant Observer* (April 1912), 57–62 • census returns, 1851, PRO, HO 107/1633 • WWW
Likenesses photograph, repro. in *English Churchman*
Wealth at death £987 0s. 7d.: probate, 25 Nov 1912, CGPLA Eng. & Wales

Walsh, William (1511/12?–1577), Roman Catholic bishop of Meath, is better documented than many other Irish martyrs, although parts of his career are shrouded in mystery. According to a letter he wrote towards the end of his life, he was probably born in 1511 or 1512; otherwise little is certain regarding his early years. His parentage is unrecorded, though it is known that he was conceived within wedlock. Some sources, composed in the early to mid-seventeenth century, claim he was born in Meath, at Dunboyne; others, written at about the same time, make Waterford his birthplace. The case for his being a native of Meath is supported by a papal document of the 1550s that refers to him as a priest of Meath, 'sacerdotis Midensis' (Moran, 131).

Confusion also surrounds Walsh's early career in the church. Although it is indisputable that as a young man he joined the Cistercian order, it is not certain which Cistercian monastery he entered. It is often claimed that he joined the community at Bective Abbey, Meath, and stayed there until the abbey was dissolved by officials of Henry VIII. However, this is contradicted by the fact that his name does not appear among the documents of the dissolution pertaining to Bective. Instead, government records mention a 'William Walsh' as resident at another Cistercian house, St Mary's Abbey in Dublin, when it was dissolved in October 1539. If this is the same William as the future bishop, then he was granted a pension of £10 by the Henrician government in recompense for his loss of position.

The sequence of Walsh's subsequent movements is difficult to disentangle. All that is certain is that in the fifteen or so years before his nomination to the bishopric of Meath in 1554 he refused to reach an accommodation with the royal government while it remained in schism. He visited Rome, studied at a European university (possibly Rome, but certainly not Oxford, as is sometimes claimed) and became a doctor of divinity, and received a papal appointment as guardian of Duleek Priory and rector of Loughseedy in the diocese of Meath. While in Italy he is reputed to have been a chaplain or follower of Cardinal Reginald Pole. In order to attain his position at Duleek, an Augustinian house, he obtained a special dispensation from Rome to become an Augustinian canon, a record of which survives in the papal archives; curiously, no Cistercian writer of the sixteenth or seventeenth century acknowledges that Walsh changed orders. Most likely he was granted Duleek in order to minister to the Meath Catholic community as the Church of Ireland moved from schism to open protestant heresy.

Soon after the accession of Mary I in 1553 Walsh emerged to play a leading role in church and state in Ireland. In April 1554 he agreed to serve, at his own cost, as one of three commissioners chosen to proceed against protestant clergymen—significantly, not on the grounds of their being heretics, but because they were married, 'cohabiting' contrary to canon law. It was a strategy that conformed with Pole's policy of restoring papal control by concentrating on clerical behaviour instead of belief. By 29 June the commission had had its desired effect, facilitating the deprivation of the Church of Ireland bishop of Meath, Edward Staples. Immediately, Walsh was nominated as Staples's replacement. He was elected to the vacant see in accordance with a *congé d'élire* directed to the archdeacon and chapter of Meath by the crown, and by August he had received royal letters patent authorizing his consecration. Before he could be consecrated, however, Walsh needed to have his position confirmed by Rome 'like other bishops', and in a petition to Philip and Mary he explained that he had been too busy with other church business to attend to this. Papal recognition of his appointment arrived in September in the form of an official *relatio*, a document which also noted his ongoing association with the Augustinians. Some historians have contended that Walsh held his bishopric by royal authority only, not papal, but the *relatio* contradicts this view. Although it was July 1555 before Cardinal Pole was made papal legate to Ireland, he had power to appoint Walsh in 1554. The bishopric of Meath, the *relatio* states, 'though situated in Ireland is looked on as an English see'; accordingly it fell within Pole's English legatine jurisdiction (Moran, 412–13). Late in the autumn of 1554, acting at the request of Queen Mary, who recognized his superior authority in the matter, Pole issued a licence for the consecration of William Walsh, bishop-elect of Meath. The consecration occurred some time after 18 October, on which date Walsh was also granted the temporalities of his see by the royal government.

As bishop of Meath, Walsh assumed a major role in secular affairs as a member of the Irish privy council. On occasions this necessitated his involvement in military business, despite his being a cleric: in June 1556 he undertook personally to prepare eight archers on horseback for a hosting against the Scots in Ulster; and as a matter of course he put his signature to proclamations imposing martial law and the death penalty on idlemen, vagabonds, and other offenders. Only in February 1557 did he exhibit any discomfort with this situation. A declaration of war having been drafted against a midlands chieftain, Walsh and the archbishop of Dublin together felt compelled to add a postscript in the council minutes expressing their general consent 'to all thinges' contained in the proclamation, 'saving what toucheth the lief of man, whiche we forbeare to do lest we shulde incurre the daunger of irregularitie' (*Haliday MSS*, 29–30).

Involvement in government did not prevent Walsh from performing his episcopal duties successfully. Even before he assumed the bishopric the gentry of Meath had signalled their aversion to protestant doctrine, angrily rejecting his predecessor, Staples, for denying them the sacrificial mass. Walsh built on this foundation, and the continuing attachment of the diocese to Catholicism became his most lasting achievement. All his other triumphs were overthrown, however, following the death of Queen Mary in November 1558 and the succession of her protestant half-sister, Elizabeth I. Walsh vigorously opposed the return of protestantism. Within weeks of Elizabeth's accession he was reported as railing against the schismatic doctrines of Henry VIII, a dangerous instance of *lèse-majesté* under the new order; and early in 1559 he was identified by Lord Deputy Sussex as one of two prelates most likely to oppose new ecclesiastical legislation in parliament. For a time he was allowed to remain

as bishop and a council member, but his continued defence of the Marian religious settlement soon brought about his deprivation and imprisonment. On 4 February 1560, having struggled in vain to obstruct the passage of the Act of Uniformity, he was asked to take the oath of supremacy. He refused, and by May he had been deprived of his see.

Following his deprivation Walsh disappears from extant records for long stretches of time, probably because he was under restraint. It is impossible to ascertain the amount of time he spent in prison. In later life, having escaped to France, he claimed he had been thirteen years a prisoner, but this comment cannot be taken at face value; a letter written in 1563 reported that Walsh had spent a year in prison for the sake of his faith during 1560–61, but had recently been restored to his freedom. Unlike other Marian clergy he refused to embrace a quiet life under Elizabeth. A habitual offender against the royal supremacy, he was constantly in and out of gaol. A letter by the Church of Ireland archbishop responsible for his punishment gives a sense of the government's frustration with him:

> Ever since the parliament he hath manifestly contemned and openly showed himself to be a misliker of all the queen's proceedings: he openly protested before all the people … that he would never communicate or be present where the Protestant service should be ministered; for it was against his conscience and against God's word. (Loftus to Cecil, 16 July 1564, PRO, SP 63/14/22)

Worse, his stance brought him 'great credit amongst his countrymen' (ibid.) and prevented his protestant replacement in Meath, Hugh Brady, from making converts; the only way to silence him was to lock him up.

Walsh's arrest on 13 July 1565 seems to have instigated a lengthier period in prison than before, for when he next appears in documents, in 1567, he was still in Dublin Castle, smuggling letters to clergy in Lord Slane's household in the pale and to Pole's old friend, Cardinal Morone, on the continent. Some time thereafter he was released again, perhaps as early as the spring of 1569, when he is known to have signed an Irish petition to Philip II seeking Spanish military assistance against 'the accursed and contagious heresy' of the English (Binchy, 365–6). He was definitely at liberty before Michaelmas 1570, when, at a time of political crisis, the commissioners for ecclesiastical causes moved to restrict his movements, confining him to certain counties and towns in the pale and ordering him not to speak or write against the established church. Evidently he paid as much attention to these conditions as to earlier ones: by 21 March 1572 he had been returned to the cells of Dublin Castle where, his health declining, he was given a servant to attend him.

At Christmas 1572 Walsh escaped, through the efforts of his friends—unfortunately unnamed—slipping out of Dublin Castle and taking a ship to France. Sailing in rough seas in the middle of winter the voyage took sixteen days, finally ending, he later claimed, when the ship was wrecked off the Brittany coast. At some stage he wrote to the pope from Flanders, and he stayed in Nantes for several months before the papal nuncio helped him to reach Paris in July 1573. From there he penned a letter that was destined to form the basis of subsequent efforts of the Irish Catholic church to have him recognized as a martyr for the faith. In it he gave an exaggerated account of his sufferings while in prison: as well as claiming he had been thirteen years in gaol, confined to 'a subterraneous dungeon, damp and noisome', he described his treatment as cruel, and blamed it for his growing infirmities (Moran, 131; Brady, 2.337). Roman Catholic writers from the seventeenth century onwards have contended that his prison experience precipitated his death, yet he was strong enough to travel to Spain in 1574, to serve as suffragan to the archbishop of Toledo, and to return briefly to Ireland to oversee the provinces of Armagh and Dublin during the absence of the Roman Catholic primate, Richard Creagh. A more satisfactory explanation for his death is suggested by his last letter, written from Alcalá in Spain in 1576, in which he begged the cardinal of Como to procure him a position in Brittany as, owing to his advanced years, he could no longer endure the severe temperatures of central Spain. He died at Alcalá on 2 January 1577 and was buried there at the Cistercian collegiate church of St Secundinus three days later.   DAVID EDWARDS

Sources Irish Jesuit Archives, Leeson Street, Dublin, MacErlean MSS, MACE/MTYR/17 · P. F. Moran, *History of the Catholic archbishops of Dublin since the Reformation* (1864) · *CSP Rome, 1572–8* · Cardinal Pole: register, Douai Public Library, tome 1, fol. 18 · TCD, MS 1087 · J. Morrin, ed., *Calendar of the patent and close rolls of chancery in Ireland, of the reigns of Henry VIII, Edward VI, Mary, and Elizabeth*, 1 (1861) · E. P. Shirley, ed., *Original letters and papers in illustration of the history of the church in Ireland during the reigns of Edward VI, Mary and Elizabeth* (1851) · J. Linchaeo [J. Lynch], *De praesulibus Hiberniae*, ed. J. F. O'Doherty, 2 vols., IMC (1944) · *CPR, 1553–8* · *Correspondence of Matthew Parker*, ed. J. Bruce and T. T. Perowne, Parker Society, 42 (1853) · F. Hogan, 'William Walsh, bishop of Meath, 1554–1577', *Riocht na Midhe*, 6/3 (1977), 3–18 · W. M. Brady, *The episcopal succession in England, Scotland, and Ireland, AD 1400 to 1875*, 3 vols. (1876–7) · 'The see of Leighlin', *Irish Ecclesiastical Record*, [new ser.], 2 (1865–6), 544–51 · R. D. Edwards, *Church and state in Tudor Ireland* (1935) · H. A. Jefferies, 'The Irish parliament of 1560: the Anglican reforms authorized', *Irish Historical Studies*, 26 (1988–9), 128–41 · D. A. Binchy, 'An Irish ambassador at the Spanish court, 1569–74', *Studies: an Irish Quarterly Review*, 10 (1921), 353–74 · C. Ó. Conbhuidhe, *Studies in Irish Cistercian history* (1998) · R. Bagwell, *Ireland under the Tudors*, 3 vols. (1885–90) · *The manuscripts of Charles Haliday ... Acts of the privy council in Ireland, 1556–1571*, HMC, 40 (1897)
Archives Douai public library, Cardinal Pole: register, tome 1, fol. 18

Walsh, William (*bap.* 1662, *d.* 1708), poet, baptized at Abberley, Worcestershire, on 6 October 1662, was the second of eight children (two boys, six girls) born to Joseph Walsh (1618/19–1682) of Abberley, and Elizabeth (*bap.* 1637, *d.* 1719), daughter of Sir Bryan Palmes of Lindley, Yorkshire. Both Joseph and his father-in-law were of old county families and fought in the civil war on the royalist side. William Walsh became a gentleman-commoner of Wadham College, Oxford, on 14 May 1678 and a student of the Middle Temple on 6 December 1679. He did not take a degree, but, after the death of his father in 1682, divided his time between the pursuits of a country gentleman at Abberley and those of a conspicuously well-dressed, amorous beau in London. It was said, perhaps with exaggeration, that his wig cost £80 and required more than 3 pounds of powder.

Walsh joined the wits at Will's Coffee House in Covent Garden, presided over by Dryden, who corrected his verse and wrote a eulogistic preface to his prose *Dialogue Concerning Women, being a Defence of the Sex* (1691), which, despite its subtitle, is as much an attack as a defence. The *Dialogue* was addressed to 'Eugenia', believed to be the countess of Kingston, one of Walsh's mistresses. His next publication was *Letters and Poems, Amorous and Gallant* (1692, reprinted in *Dryden's Miscellany*, pt 4, 1716), a collection of light and pretty love poems, pastorals, epigrams, and prose love letters, with a shrewd and amusing preface. Even so, Dryden's often-quoted judgement in the postscript to his translation of Virgil (1697) that Walsh was 'without flattery, the best Critick of our Nation' was probably based more upon conversation, letters, and unpublished writings than upon this brief preface.

A few more poems found their way into print during Walsh's lifetime: he mourned Queen Mary in an elegy (1695), he praised William III in an imitation of Horace, *Odes*, iii.3 (1706), and he celebrated the victory at Ramillies in a thanksgiving ode (1706). He probably wrote *The Confederates*, a lampoon on Peter Anthony Motteux, published in *Poems on Affairs of State* (vol. 2, 1703), and he contributed to *Commendatory Verses* (1700) a collective satire on Sir Richard Blackmore. In another collective work Walsh wrote the third act of *Squire Trelooby*, a comedy adapted from Molière's *Monsieur de Pourceaugnac*, the other two acts being written by his friends William Congreve and Sir John Vanbrugh. Their play was performed three times in 1704 and, with a new third act by Vanbrugh, another four times in 1706, but was never printed. It seems that Walsh had a gentlemanly negligence about publication: most of his verse appeared in miscellanies and journals after his death, or remains unpublished.

Walsh was a low-church whig, devoted to the revolution settlement, and war against France. In August 1698, with the support of the lord chancellor, John Somers, he became MP for Worcestershire. He was re-elected in January 1701 after a contest which prompted his unpublished ballad, *The Worcester Cabal* to the tune of 'Pakington's Pound': one of his opponents being the tory Sir John Pakington (1671–1727). In November 1701 he lost the seat to another tory, but, with the active help of William Lloyd (1627–1717), bishop of Worcester, he regained it in August 1702. He now obtained a court appointment as gentleman of the horse under the new master of the horse, Charles Seymour, duke of Somerset (1662–1748). Responding to an anonymous tory Messianic poem on the accession of Queen Anne, Walsh wrote a polished, insolently urbane parody of Virgil's fourth eclogue, *The Golden Age Restor'd*, published in *Poems on Affairs of State* (1703). He escaped from the exciting politics of Worcester when he was returned to parliament unopposed at a by-election for Richmond, Yorkshire, in June 1705. He was a member of the Kit-Cat Club.

Walsh never married. He wrote of love: 'there is not one folly of that kind (excepting marriage) which I have not already committed' (W. Walsh, *Letters Amorous and Gallant*, 1692, letter 20). Political and literary enemies called him a fop; in an anonymous squib he is also called 'Master Eat-Finger' (*Poems on Affairs of State*, 5.10), but no other evidence has been found of this infantile trait. He died intestate (so perhaps suddenly?) at Marlborough, Wiltshire, on 15 March 1708 and was buried at Abberley on 18 March. He was survived by his mother, who was granted letters of administration, and several sisters: his younger siblings Octavia *Walsh and Walter had predeceased him. Abberley was inherited by his sister Ann, wife of Francis Bromley.

Walsh left unfinished at his death a mock epic fragment, 'Abigail's Lamentation for the Loss of Mr Harley', satirizing Robert Harley and Abigail Masham. This and other poems appeared posthumously in various miscellanies, as did Walsh's prose satire 'Aesculapius, or, The Hospital of Fools' in *Poems and Translations by Several Hands* (1714). Nevertheless his still unpublished poems are at least as numerous as the printed ones.

Walsh's main literary importance is as Alexander Pope's mentor. He saw manuscripts of some of Pope's pastorals, forwarded by their common friend Wycherley, perhaps as early as 1705; certainly he wrote very encouragingly to Pope in the following year; and in August 1707, when Pope visited him at Abberley, he famously advised the young poet to make correctness his study and aim. Walsh commented upon and corrected Pope's pastorals, and Pope appropriated some of his critical ideas for his 'Discourse on pastoral poetry'. Walsh may also have seen an early draft of the *Essay on Criticism*, a poem that seems to have been conceived under his influence and concludes with high praise of Walsh as 'the Muse's Judge and Friend'.

JAMES SAMBROOK

Sources *The correspondence of Alexander Pope*, ed. G. Sherburn, 1 (1956) • J. Spence, *Observations, anecdotes, and characters, of books and men*, ed. J. M. Osborn, new edn, 1 (1966) • *The letters of John Dryden*, ed. C. E. Ward (1942) • *William Congreve: letters and documents*, ed. J. C. Hodges (1964) • *VCH Worcestershire*, vol. 4 • T. Nash, *Collections for the history of Worcestershire*, 1 (1781), 2–4 • J. Chambers, *Biographical illustrations of Worcestershire* (1820), 317–22 • G. de F. Lord and others, eds., *Poems on affairs of state: Augustan satirical verse, 1660–1714*, 7 vols. (1963–75), vols. 5–7 • Foster, *Alum. Oxon.* • S. Johnson, *Lives of the English poets*, ed. G. B. Hill, [new edn], 1 (1905) • R. Shiels, *The lives of the poets of Great Britain and Ireland*, ed. T. Cibber, 3 (1753), 151–5 • P. Freeman, 'William Walsh and Dryden: recently recovered letters', *Review of English Studies*, 24 (1948), 195–202 • P. Freeman, 'Two fragments of Walsh manuscripts', *Review of English Studies*, new ser., 8 (1957), 390–401 • P. Freeman, 'William Walsh's letters and poems in MS Malone 9', *Bodleian Library Quarterly Review*, 7 (1934), 503–7 • *The critical works of John Dennis*, ed. E. N. Hooker, 1 (1939), 416, 530–31 • G. D. Harley, '*Squire Trelooby* and *The Cornish squire*: a reconsideration', *Philological Quarterly*, 49 (1970), 520–29 • D. B. Vetter, 'William Walsh's "In defence of painting"', *Modern Language Notes*, 66 (1951), 518–23 • monuments, Abberley church, Worcestershire
Archives BL, MSS, Add. MSS 10434, 38001 • Worcs. RO, papers | BL, Harley MS 7001, fols. 211, 214–17 • BL, Sloane MSS 4039, fol. 133, and 4061, fol. 262 • Surrey HC, letters to Lord Somers • Worcs. RO, Foley scrapbook
Likenesses G. Kneller, oils, *c.*1708, NPG • J. Faber, engraving, 1735 (after Kneller) • engraving, repro. in Nash, *Collections for the history of Worcestershire*
Wealth at death substantial property at Abberley, Worcestershire

Walsh, William Henry (1913–1986), philosopher, was born on 10 December 1913 at 505 Harehills Lane, Leeds, the only son and the eldest of the three children of Fred Walsh (1895–1979), master baker and confectioner, and his wife, Mary, *née* Stephens (1897–1965). After attending Baildon national school, Bradford grammar school, and Quarrie Mount council school he completed the major part of his secondary education at Leeds grammar school (1923–32). There, as a result of acting in Shakespeare's *Richard II*, he acquired the nickname Richard by which he was always widely known (though among his family he was known as Harry). In 1932 he was awarded a classical exhibition at Merton College, Oxford, where he took firsts in classical moderations (1934) and Greats (1936), going on immediately to become a junior research fellow. On 29 July 1938 he married Frances Beatrix Ruth Pearson (*b.* 1912), daughter of Francis Gates Pearson, journalist. Trixie, as she was known, was a schoolteacher, and their happy and enduring marriage produced two daughters and one son.

During the Second World War, Walsh served first in the signals corps and then in the Foreign Office at Bletchley Park, where he worked in code-breaking and analysis. After the war he resumed his academic career as lecturer in philosophy at Dundee (1946–7), then part of St Andrews University, before he returned to Merton as fellow and tutor in philosophy (1947–60). Although he published two books in this period, he nevertheless found the increasing dominance of linguistic philosophy in Oxford narrow and dispiriting. A year as visiting professor at the University of Ohio (1957–8), where he was able to develop the metaphysical issues in philosophy that most interested him, played a decisive part in his future career, encouraging him to apply for the chair of logic and metaphysics at Edinburgh, which he held from 1960 until his retirement in 1979.

In Edinburgh, although his administrative abilities led to a number of onerous duties, including becoming dean of the faculty of arts (1966–8) and one of three vice-principals (1975–9), Walsh wrote many articles and three more books. Among many honours, he became the Dawes Hicks lecturer in the British Academy (1963), president of the Aristotelian Society (1964–5), fellow of the British Academy (1969), and fellow of the Royal Society of Edinburgh (1978). He received honorary degrees from the University of Rochester (1978) and, after his retirement, the University of Edinburgh (1985). He was also a visiting professor in America twice more, at Dartmouth College (1965) and the University of Maryland (1969).

Upon his retirement Walsh returned to Oxford, renewing his fond connection with Merton as a fellow emeritus of the college. Continuing to teach and publish, he was a founding member of the Hegel Society of Great Britain

(1979), of which he later became president (1985), and a visiting professor at the University of Kansas (1979–80) and Carleton University, Ottawa (1983). For some years, however, his health had been deteriorating, particularly with the onset of Parkinson's disease, and on 7 April 1986 he died from a combination of that and cancer at his home, 352 Banbury Road, Oxford. He was cremated and buried on 16 April 1986 at St Cross Church, Oxford. A memorial service, attended by many distinguished philosophers and former pupils, was held at Merton on 21 June.

Of Walsh's five books two are pre-eminent. The first, *An Introduction to Philosophy of History* (1951; 3rd edn, revised and enlarged, 1967), addressed what was then a relatively neglected subject. In the larger part of the book he argued that though history resembled the natural sciences in constituting a defensible body of knowledge, it differed from them with respect to its aims and the nature of the knowledge produced, leading to particular philosophical problems concerning the kinds of explanation it offered, the conception of the relation between truth and fact it presupposed, the degree of objectivity which it could reach, and (in the enlarged edition of 1967) the conception of causation utilized. His identification and discussion of these problems set the agenda for 'analytic' philosophy of history for the next thirty years. In the second part of the work he examined metaphysical theories of history, such as those of Kant, Hegel, Comte, and Marx, and though, given the nature of Anglo-Saxon philosophy at the time, this was less immediately influential, interest in these theories came strongly to the fore in the late 1970s. It is noteworthy that a Festschrift in his honour, *Substance and Form in History* (ed. L. Pompa and W. H. Dray, 1981, which includes a comprehensive bibliography of his published writings up to 1977), was devoted entirely to these two subjects. Walsh's other most important single book was *Kant's Criticism of Metaphysics* (1975), a masterly exposition and evaluation of the doctrines of Kant's *Critique of Pure Reason*, outstanding for its subtle thought and clarification of complex issues, always among Walsh's most impressive characteristics. For these works alone he would count among the most distinguished philosophers of his generation.

Of equal importance, however, in Walsh's contribution to the thought of this period, was his defence of the traditional concerns of philosophy, especially metaphysics and substantive ethics, at a time when, in England at least, these subjects were almost completely neglected. The character of his defence was strongly influenced by two convictions: first, that philosophy should be concerned with how to view and act in the world and, second, that it could not be appreciated independently of its historical past and present context. The combination of these beliefs led him in his first book, *Reason and Experience* (1947), to claim that Kant was correct in arguing that a set of categories was necessary for any coherent conception of the world, but wrong in thinking that they must be rational and therefore derivable a priori. This sensitivity

to history emerged in *Metaphysics* (1963), in which, via an analysis of various philosophers from Plato to Wittgenstein, he presented metaphysicians as advocating the adoption of different sets of rules for thinking about the world rather than trying to prove them once and for all, either deductively or inductively. Similarly, in *Hegelian Ethics* (1969) he argued that Kant's conception of the role of the a priori in philosophy led to an unacceptably narrow conception of the self as a basis for ethics and that Hegel's conception of the self as a necessarily social and historical entity offered a more adequate account of the factors which ought to influence moral decisions. Through these works, supported by many other essays, his second enduring achievement was to help keep a pre-analytic conception of philosophy alive in a period in which analytic philosophy was the dominant trend. By the start of the 1980s substantive ethics and political and legal philosophy were again flourishing, and interests in metaphysics were reviving.

Despite his devotion to philosophy as a subject, Walsh was no narrow academic, his interests including travel, current affairs, reading history and literature, and following sport. He greatly enjoyed good company, to which he contributed with a quizzical, often self-deprecating, sense of humour, and was a most welcoming host. Fundamentally, however, he had a deeply sincere and sympathetic nature, which led to many lasting friendships and expressed itself in two most striking general characteristics: his endless willingness to sacrifice his time in advising and helping others with their writings and careers; and the quite exceptional modesty with which he regarded his own achievements.   LEON POMPA

Sources L. Pompa, preface, *Substance and form in history: a collection of essays in philosophy of history*, ed. L. Pompa and W. H. Dray (1981) [incl. bibliography] · L. Pompa, *PBA*, 72 (1986), 511–24 · b. cert. · m. cert. · d. cert. · personal knowledge (2004) · private information (2004) [Mrs F. B. R. Walsh, widow; Mrs M. Ainsley, sister]
Archives Merton Oxf., notes · U. Edin., lectures and MSS
Likenesses photograph, repro. in Pompa, *PBA*, pl. 32
Wealth at death £32,528: administration, 23 Oct 1986, *CGPLA Eng. & Wales*

Walsh, William Joseph (1841–1921), Roman Catholic archbishop of Dublin, was born at 11 Essex Quay, Dublin, on 30 January 1841, the only child of Ralph Walsh, a watchmaker and jeweller, of co. Kerry, and his wife, Mary Pierce, of a Galway family. He was educated at St Laurence O'Toole's Seminary School, Dublin, and entered the Catholic University of Ireland (then under the rectorship of John Henry Newman) in 1855. He entered St Patrick's College, Maynooth, in 1858, and after an outstanding academic career was ordained to the priesthood in 1866. In 1867 he was appointed professor of dogmatic and moral theology at Maynooth, in 1878 vice-president, and in 1880 president. He gave evidence in support of the claims of the tenantry before the Bessborough commission (1880) but he had already come to prominence when he performed brilliantly as an expert witness on canon law in the celebrated O'Keefe law case in 1875.

William Joseph Walsh (1841–1921), by James Russell & Sons, pubd 1902

Following the death of Cardinal Edward McCabe in February 1885, Walsh was elected vicar-capitular of the Dublin archdiocese. On 23 June 1885 he was appointed archbishop of Dublin by Pope Leo XIII. That this was done despite government intrigue in Rome—Walsh's nationalist sympathies being well known—was hailed as a triumph by Irish nationalists. For the next quarter of a century Walsh was the dominating personality in the Irish Catholic church. He built or renovated churches and schools, conducted a busy schedule of pastoral visitations, and promoted initiatives in the areas of sacred music, catechetics, and temperance. A champion of Catholic educational interests, through his service on a number of public bodies he contributed significantly to the development of the modern Irish education system. He served on the senate of the Royal University of Ireland (1883–4), the national education board (1895–1901), the intermediate education board (1892–1909), and the senate of the National University of Ireland of which, in 1908, he became the first chancellor.

Walsh's life spanned the flood-tide of modern Irish nationalism. At the tender age of nine months he was enrolled by his father, a prominent nationalist, as a member of the Repeal Association, and while still a young boy he was introduced to Daniel O'Connell; in 1921 Eamon de Valera expressed gratitude for his 'ripe counsel … in any hour of need'. A constitutional nationalist like his father before him, Walsh was an advocate of home rule and agrarian reform. His support for the controversial Plan of Campaign earned him the displeasure of Rome and cost him the cardinal's hat. During the commission set up in 1888 to inquire into charges made by *The Times* against Charles Stewart Parnell he provided crucial assistance to Parnell in exposing Richard Pigott as a forger. When the Parnell divorce crisis broke in 1890, he resisted pressure from both nationalist politicians and ecclesiastics, such as Cardinal H. E. Manning and Archbishop T. W. Croke of Cashel, to come out against Parnell. It was only when

secret negotiations between Parnell and himself, conducted through an intermediary, failed to produce a compromise that he led the clerical attack on Parnell's leadership. In later life Walsh became disenchanted with the Irish Parliamentary Party, and in 1917 signalled his shift of allegiance to Sinn Féin. Though afflicted with poor health in his last years he continued to make an important contribution to political developments and served as a mentor to some Sinn Féin leaders.

Walsh had a progressive mind, favoured women's rights to the vote and to university education, and advocated bimetallism. He was an early advocate of the use of arbitration to settle labour disputes, and for his successful mediation which brought to an end a protracted strike on the Great Southern and Western Railway in 1890 he was made an honorary freeman of the city of Cork. Aloof in temperament, in private life he was pious, charitable, and of a simple way of living. Aside from law and music he had many interests which reflected his modern outlook. He mastered the Pitman script, became an enthusiastic cyclist and amateur photographer, and was one of the earliest patrons of the motor car. He died on 9 April 1921 at 32 Eccles Street, Dublin, and was buried in Glasnevin cemetery on 14 April.

D. A. KERR and DAVID C. SHEEHY, *rev.* DAVID C. SHEEHY

Sources P. J. Walsh, *William J. Walsh, archbishop of Dublin* (1928) · M. V. Ronan, *The most reverend W. J. Walsh D.D.* (1927) · M. Curran, 'The late archbishop of Dublin', *Dublin Review*, 169 (1921), 93–107 · E. Larkin, *The Roman Catholic church in Ireland and the fall of Parnell, 1888–1891* (1979) · D. Keogh, *The Vatican, the bishops and Irish politics, 1919–1939* (1986) · D. Miller, *Church, state and nation in Ireland, 1898–1921* (1973) · CGPLA Eng. & Wales (1922) · T. J. Morrissey, *William J. Walsh, archbishop of Dublin, 1841–1921* (2000)

Archives Dublin Roman Catholic Archives, corresp. and papers | Archives of the Church of St Mary of the Angels, London, Manning MSS · BL, corresp. with W. E. Gladstone, Add. MSS 44499–44512, *passim* · Bodl. Oxf., letters to W. R. Moss relating to bimetallism · Cashel Diocesan Archives, Croke MSS · Irish College, Rome, Kirby MSS · TCD, corresp. with John Dillon | FILM British Pathe Library

Likenesses J. Russell & Sons, photograph, pubd 1902, NPG [*see illus.*] · Lafayette, photograph, 1910, Dublin Diocesan Archives

Wealth at death £607 2s. 3d.—in England: Irish probate sealed in England, 1922, CGPLA Ire.

Walsh, William Pakenham (1820–1902), bishop of Ossory, Ferns, and Leighlin, was born at Mote Park, co. Roscommon, on 4 May 1820, the eldest son of Thomas Walsh of St Helena Lodge, co. Roscommon, and Mary, daughter of Robert Pakenham of Athlone. After being educated privately he entered Trinity College, Dublin, on 14 October 1836, where he won the vice-chancellor's, the Biblical Greek, and the divinity prizes, as well as the Theological Society's gold medal. He graduated BA in 1841, proceeding MA in 1853, and BD and DD in 1873. Ordained deacon in 1843, he was licensed to the curacy of Avoca, co. Wicklow, and ordained priest the following year. From 1845 to 1858 he was curate of Rathdrum, co. Wicklow, where in the famine years 1846–7 he worked hard to relieve the distress in his parish. From 1858 to 1873 he was chaplain of Sandford church, Ranelagh, co. Dublin, and in

1861 he married Clara, daughter of Samuel Ridley of Muswell Hill, Middlesex. She died in 1875. They had four sons and three daughters who survived Walsh.

Walsh had served the Church Missionary Society as association secretary for Ireland from 1848 to 1858. And in 1860, as Donnellan lecturer of Trinity College, he chose Christian missions as his theme. These lectures were published in 1862. From 1873 to 1878, when Walsh was dean of Cashel, he wrote and published several works. These included *The Forty Days of the Bible* (1874), *Daily Readings for Holy Seasons* (1876), and *Heroes of the Mission Fields* (1879). In 1878 he was elected to the united sees of Ossory, Ferns, and Leighlin, his consecration as bishop taking place in Christ Church, Dublin, in September 1878. On 8 May 1879 he married Annie Frances, *née* Hackett (*d.* 1930), the daughter of the incumbent of St James's, Bray, co. Dublin. They had two sons who survived Walsh, and two daughters who died in infancy.

As a bishop Walsh was known for his continued interest in and support of foreign missions. He preached the annual sermon of the Church Missionary Society in 1882, which resulted in a new plan to increase the society's funds. One of his sons went to work as a missionary in China and another served in India. Walsh continued the tradition of evangelicalism in the Church of Ireland, and he played a significant part in building up the church after disestablishment. However, ill health led to his resignation in October 1897. He died at his home, Crinken House, Shankill, co. Dublin, on 30 July 1902. A stained-glass window was placed in St Canice's Cathedral, Kilkenny, to commemorate his life.

A. R. BUCKLAND, *rev.* DAVID HUDDLESTON

Sources J. B. Leslie, *Ossory clergy and parishes* (1933), 43–4 · *WW* (1901) · *Men and women of the time* (1891), 923 · E. Stock, *History of the CMS* (1899), 2.37, 3.265 · Crockford (1901) · H. E. Patton, *Fifty years of disestablishment* (1922) · D. Bowen, *The protestant crusade in Ireland, 1800–70* (1978) · *CGPLA Ire.* (1902)
Archives TCD
Likenesses photograph, NPG
Wealth at death £4815 9s. 3d.: probate, 31 Oct 1902, *CGPLA Ire.* · £1960 8s. 7d. (in England): Irish probate sealed in England, 19 Nov 1902, *CGPLA Eng. & Wales*

Walsham, Sir John, second baronet (1830–1905), diplomatist, born at Cheltenham on 29 October 1830, was the eldest of four sons of Sir John James Walsham, first baronet, of Knill Court, Herefordshire, and his wife, Sarah Frances, second daughter of Matthew Bell of Woolsington House, Northumberland. The father's family, of Norfolk origin, migrated to Radnorshire in the sixteenth century, and acquired by marriage the estates of the Knill family. The baronetcy conferred on a direct ancestor, General Sir Thomas Morgan, on 1 February 1661, became extinct in 1768 and was revived in 1831 in favour of Sir John's father, who became high sheriff of Radnorshire in 1870.

After education at Bury St Edmunds grammar school and at Trinity College, Cambridge, where he graduated BA in 1854 and MA in 1857, Walsham entered the Audit Office in March 1854. In October of the same year he was appointed a clerk in the Foreign Office, and was temporarily attached to the British legation at Mexico from 30 December 1857. He was appointed paid attaché in 1860, and remained there until 1866, when he was transferred as second secretary to Madrid. The British legation was at that time engaged in correspondence arising out of the practice persisted in by the Spanish authorities of firing upon merchant vessels passing by the Spanish forts in the Strait of Gibraltar if they failed to display their national flags. Walsham was a commissioner dealing with the arbitration of claims under an agreement of 1865. On 5 March 1867 Walsham married Florence, only daughter of Peter Campbell *Scarlett, with whom he had two sons.

In 1870, after working for some time at the Foreign Office during the pressure of business occasioned by the outbreak of the Franco-Prussian War, Walsham proceeded to The Hague, and in 1873 was nominated as secretary of legation at Peking (Beijing). He did not take up the appointment, however, withdrawing from the service shortly before his father's death on 10 August 1874, when he succeeded as second baronet. In January 1875 he rejoined the service, being appointed secretary of legation at Madrid and remaining there until May 1878, when he was promoted to be secretary of embassy at Berlin. He was transferred to Paris in 1883, receiving promotion to the titular rank of minister-plenipotentiary, and on 24 November 1885 was made British envoy at Peking. This onerous post he held for seven years, until his health was seriously affected by the combined strain of work and climate. On 31 March 1890 he obtained from the Chinese government the signature of an additional article to the Chefoo (Yantai) agreement of 1875, formally declaring Chungking (Chongqing) on the Yangtze (Yangzi) River to be open to trade on the same footing as other treaty ports. In 1891 a succession of outbreaks occurred in different parts of China, in which missionary establishments were plundered and destroyed and several British subjects lost their lives. Walsham pressed with vigour for adequate measures to ensure punishment of those responsible and better protection in the future, and his efforts, supported by the home government, were attended with considerable success. He was transferred to Bucharest in April 1892, and retired on a pension in September 1894. He was made KCMG in February 1895.

Walsham was a hard-working and meritorious public servant, whose unselfishness and kindness of heart earned for him great popularity, but whose work, partly on account of his naturally retiring disposition, partly in consequence of physical breakdown from over-exertion, scarcely received full public recognition. He died at his home, Ryelands, at Randwick, near Stroud, on 10 December 1905, and was buried at the ancestral home of the family, Knill Court.

T. H. SANDERSON, *rev.* H. C. G. MATTHEW

Sources *The Times* (12 Dec 1905) · *FO List* (1906)
Archives BL, letters to Sir Austen Layard, Add. MSS 39008–39017, 39107–39109 · Lpool RO, letters to Lord Derby
Wealth at death £11,550 2s. 3d.: probate, 22 Feb 1906, *CGPLA Eng. & Wales*

Walsham, William Johnson (1847–1903), surgeon, born in London on 27 June 1847, was the elder son of William Walker Walsham, farmer, and his wife, Louisa Johnson. Educated privately at Highbury, he showed a mechanical bent, and became apprenticed to the engineering firm of Messrs Maudslay. He soon turned to chemistry and then to medicine, and in May 1867 he entered St Bartholomew's Hospital, where he obtained the chief school prizes in his first and second years of studentship. In 1869 he gained the gold medal given by the Society of Apothecaries for proficiency in materia medica and pharmaceutical chemistry, and in 1870 he was admitted a licentiate of the Society of Apothecaries. He then proceeded to Aberdeen, where he graduated MB and CM in 1871 with the highest honours. After returning to London he was admitted MRCS, on 17 November 1871.

Walsham worked as house physician and house surgeon at St Bartholomew's Hospital; in 1872–3 he was assistant demonstrator of anatomy in the medical school; he was full demonstrator between 1873 and 1880 and demonstrator of practical surgery from 1880 to 1889; he was lecturer on anatomy from 1889 to 1897; and he was lecturer on surgery from 1897. Walsham was also appointed assistant surgeon at St Bartholomew's on 10 March 1881, and he took charge of the orthopaedic department. He became full surgeon in 1897. In 1876 he had married Edith Maria Huntley Spencer, daughter of Joseph Huntley Spencer; they had no children.

At the Metropolitan Hospital, Walsham had been elected surgeon in 1876, taking charge of the department for diseases of the nose and throat. He became consulting surgeon there in 1896. He also served as surgeon to the Hospital for Diseases of the Chest from 1876 to 1884 and as consultant surgeon to the Bromley Cottage Hospital and the Hospital for Children with Hip and Spine Diseases at Sevenoaks, Kent. At the Royal College of Surgeons, Walsham was elected a fellow on 10 June 1875; he served as an examiner in anatomy, on the conjoint board in 1892, and in surgery, from 1897 to 1902.

Walsham was a first-rate teacher of medical students. As a pupil of Sir John Struthers at Aberdeen he showed interest in dissection, and many of his preparations are still preserved at St Bartholomew's Hospital. As surgical dresser to Sir James Paget he soon learned that pathology was the foundation of modern surgery. Physically delicate, he was said to be unequal to the major operations in surgery, but he excelled in those which required delicacy of touch, perfect anatomical knowledge, and perseverance, such as the plastic operations of harelip and cleft palate and the manipulations of orthopaedic surgery.

Walsham was an active freemason and a past grand deacon in the United Grand Lodge in England. He was a co-founder of the Rahere Lodge and the William Harvey chapter. He was also a member of the Savage Club. Walsham died at his London residence, 77 Harley Street, on 5 October 1903, of arteriosclerosis; he was buried at Highgate cemetery on the 9th. His wife survived him. His best-known published work was *Surgery: its Theory and Practice*

(1887), which had reached its 8th edition by 1903. Walsham contributed articles to other medical textbooks of his day and to the *Lancet*, the *Journal of Anatomy and Physiology*, and *St Bartholomew's Hospital Reports*, of which he was the editor from 1887 to 1897.

D'A. POWER, *rev.* KAYE BAGSHAW

Sources *BMJ* (10 Oct 1903), 945–6 · *The Lancet* (17 Oct 1903), 1122–5 · *St Bartholomew's Hospital Reports*, 39 (1903), xxxiii–xlii · *St Bartholomew's Hospital Journal*, 40 (1903), 17 · *Medico-Chirurgical Transactions*, 87 (1904), cxxxv–cxliii · V. G. Plarr, *Plarr's Lives of the fellows of the Royal College of Surgeons of England*, rev. D'A. Power, 2 vols. (1930) · private information (1912) · personal knowledge (1912) · *CGPLA Eng. & Wales* (1903)

Likenesses portrait, repro. in *BMJ* · portrait, repro. in *The Lancet* · portrait, repro. in *St Bartholomew's Hospital Reports* · portrait, repro. in *St Bartholomew's Hospital Journal*

Wealth at death £36,145 10s. 5d.: probate, 31 Oct 1903, *CGPLA Eng. & Wales*

Walshe, Sir Francis Martin Rouse (1885–1973), neurologist, was born in London on 19 September 1885, the elder child and only son (a first son had died as a baby) of Michael Charles Walshe, a pioneer of agency nursing, originally from co. Mayo in Ireland, and his wife, Rose, daughter of Samuel Light, a yeoman farmer from Brixham. They claimed kinship with the hymn writer H. F. Lyte. Walshe was educated at Prior Park College, near Bath (1898–1901), and University College School, London (1901–3). The celebrated physicians John Hughlings Jackson and Sir William Gowers lived near to the Walshe family and were both familiar figures of his youth. Walshe took first-class honours in the London BSc (1908) and in the MB, BS (1910) at University College Hospital. During training at the National Hospital, Queen Square, he added the MD in 1912 and MRCP in 1913.

In 1915 Walshe joined the Royal Army Medical Corps and became consulting neurologist to the British forces in Egypt and the Middle East, where he worked with Sir Victor Horsley. In 1916 he married Bertha Marie (d. 1950), daughter of Charles Dennehy, surgeon, of St Lucia, West Indies, and Lismore, co. Cork. They had two sons, the elder of whom became a solicitor, and the younger a physician, an international authority on the nervous disease named after S. A. Kinnier Wilson, with whom Walshe had written his first paper in *Brain* in 1914. He was appointed OBE (1919) and mentioned in dispatches. He was elected FRCP in 1920, and appointed to the staff of the National Hospital in 1921. In 1924 the department of neurology was founded for him at University College Hospital and in the same year he obtained the London DSc.

Between 1920 and 1930 Walshe produced work of the first importance in the pioneering description and analysis of human reflexes in physiological terms. In 1931 and 1932 he was associated, with Gordon Holmes and James Taylor, in the publication of *Selected Writings of John Hughlings Jackson*, a part of his lifelong championship of Jacksonian principles. Between 1940 and 1960 he published, mainly in the journal *Brain*, an important series of critical papers on the function of the cerebral cortex in relation to movements, and on neural physiology in relation to the awareness of pain. He wrote *Critical Studies in*

Neurology (1948) and *Further Critical Studies in Neurology* (1965). Himself a Roman Catholic, he advised caution about some 'miraculous' cures at Lourdes (*Catholic Medical Guardian*, 1938 and 1939). From 1937 to 1953 Walshe was editor of *Brain*, a post which provided lasting satisfaction; and on his eightieth birthday, in a special issue of the journal, he provided a summary of his own thoughts and experience during fifty years as a neurologist.

Walshe established a reputation in medical education both as a teacher of clinical neurology and as a prolific author. He was responsible for the neurological sections of J. J. Conybeare's *Textbook of Medicine* (1936) and F. W. Price's *Textbook of the Practice of Medicine* (1937), and in 1940 produced his highly individual *Diseases of the Nervous System*, which reached its eleventh edition in 1970 and was translated into many languages. Between 1910 and 1973 he amassed 181 publications.

From 1953 onwards Walshe became more and more absorbed in the philosophical problems of the mind–brain relationship, and his last paper (1972) was on the neurophysiological approach to consciousness. He was critical of those who maintained that psychology and biology are 'nothing but' physics and chemistry, and his criticisms could be wounding. Though his work had been based on Sherringtonian physiology, later in life he came to believe that patients with nervous disease must benefit more from advances in biochemistry and pharmacology than from physiological elaborations. He maintained an extensive correspondence with those in his own field and in allied subjects, and his critical writings did not impair many friendships at home and abroad.

Walshe continued in consulting practice until his late seventies. He disapproved of the National Health Service and never accepted any salary for his extensive hospital work. He disliked a merit award system based on secret negotiations. He needed 'a freedom of life and action that are essential to me. I was born to be a free-lance and not a power-seeker' (*Memoirs FRS*, 473).

Walshe was elected FRS in 1946 and knighted in 1953. He received many other honours. He was a fellow of University College, London, and held honorary doctorates from the National University of Ireland (1941) and the University of Cincinnati (1959). He was an honorary member of the neurological societies of America, Canada, Denmark, France, Germany, Spain, and Uruguay, and of the New York and American academies of neurology. He particularly enjoyed his presidency of the Association of British Neurologists (1950–51) and of the Royal Society of Medicine (1952–4). He was president of the Royal Institute of Public Health and Hygiene (1962–4). He delivered the Oliver Sharpey lecture (1929) and the Harveian oration (1948) at the Royal College of Physicians; the Ferrier lecture (1953) at the Royal Society; and the Hughlings Jackson, Gowers, and Victor Horsley lectures among many other named lectures. He received five gold medals. Walshe died at Brampton, near Huntingdon, on 21 February 1973.

WILLIAM GOODDY, *rev.*

Sources C. G. Phillips, *Memoirs FRS*, 20 (1974), 457–81 • personal knowledge (1986) • private information (1986)

Archives RCP Lond., anatomical notebook • UCL, corresp. and papers
Likenesses V. Horsley, photograph, 1915, repro. in Phillips, *Memoirs FRS*, facing p. 459 • W. Stoneman, photograph, *c*.1946, repro. in Phillips, *Memoirs FRS*
Wealth at death £16,326: probate, 15 May 1973, *CGPLA Eng. & Wales*

Walshe, Walter Hayle (1812–1892), physician, son of William Walshe, a barrister, was born in Dublin on 19 March 1812. He studied at Trinity College, Dublin, entering in 1827, but did not take a degree. In 1830 he went to live in Paris, and at first he studied oriental languages. However, in 1832 he turned his attention to medicine. He became acquainted in 1834 with the great morbid anatomist Pierre Charles Alexandre Louis, whose *Recherches sur la phthisie* he translated into English in 1844. Oliver Wendell Holmes and F. L. I. Valleix, the distinguished French physician, were his fellow students, and they became lifelong friends. Walshe moved to Edinburgh in 1835, graduated MD there in 1836, and in 1838 began practice in north London.

In 1839 and 1840 Walshe wrote many articles on pathology in William Birmingham Costello's *Cyclopaedia of Practical Surgery*. These contributions led to his election as professor of morbid anatomy at University College, London, in 1841. He lectured on morbid anatomy until 1846, when he was elected Holme professor of clinical medicine. In the same year he published a large volume, *On the Nature and Treatment of Cancer*, a collection of the then existing knowledge of new growths and hypotheses as to their origin. In 1848 he was appointed professor of the principles and practice of medicine, an office which he held until 1862. In his lectures he discussed points upon his fingers in the manner of schoolteachers, and he was fond of numerical statements of fact and of reaching a definite conclusion as a result of the denial of a series of alternative hypotheses. Sir William Jenner said that he had never heard a more able or clearer lecturer. Walshe was appointed physician at University College Hospital in 1844 and consulting physician in 1877. His clinical investigations were exhaustive, but his diagnoses were not always proportionately exact.

In 1843 Walshe published *The Physical Diagnosis of Diseases of the Lungs*, a complete and useful treatise, which was superseded before his death by Samuel Gee's *Auscultation and Percussion*. In 1851 Walshe published *A Practical Treatise on Diseases of the Lungs and Heart*, of which several editions appeared, and part of which was enlarged into *A Practical Treatise on the Diseases of the Heart and Great Vessels*. In 1852 he was elected a fellow of the Royal College of Physicians. He first lived in Upper Charlotte Street and afterwards in Queen Anne Street, and he had for some years a considerable practice as a physician. On 16 December 1869 he married Caroline Ellen (*b.* 1838/9), daughter of John Durand Baker, a clergyman; they had one son.

Walshe's pupils maintained that his was the first accurate description of the anatomy of movable kidney and of haemorrhage into the *dura mater*, known as haematoma;

he was also the first to teach that patients with regurgitation through the aortic valves are likely to die suddenly. However, Sir Andrew Clark considered that he had little ability in the treatment of disease. Besides his books Walsh wrote many contributions to medical journals and transactions, and in 1885 he published *The Colloquial Linguistic Faculty and its Physiological Groundwork*. He was well read in acoustics, had a taste for music, especially Italian opera, and published in 1881 a short treatise, *Dramatic Singing Physiologically Estimated*. Walshe died at his home, 41 Hyde Park Square, London, on 14 December 1892. His wife survived him. NORMAN MOORE, *rev.* MICHAEL BEVAN

Sources *BMJ* (31 Dec 1892), 1455–6 · *The Lancet* (31 Dec 1892) · *Medico-Chirurgical Transactions*, 76 (1893), 4–10 · Munk, *Roll* · W. R. Merrington, *University College Hospital and its medical school: a history* (1976) · m. cert. · d. cert.
Likenesses Benson & Co., lithograph, Wellcome L.
Wealth at death £81,634 2s.: probate, 18 Jan 1893, *CGPLA Eng. & Wales*

Walsingham. For this title name *see* Stanhope, Petronilla Melusina, *suo jure* countess of Walsingham, and countess of Chesterfield (1693–1778) [*see under* Stanhope, Philip Dormer, fourth earl of Chesterfield (1694–1773)]; Grey, William de, first Baron Walsingham (1719–1781); Grey, Thomas de, second Baron Walsingham (1748–1818); Grey, Thomas de, sixth Baron Walsingham (1843–1919).

Walsingham, Alan (*d.* 1363), prior of Ely, presumably came from Walsingham in Norfolk, perhaps from a family of goldsmiths: he was described as skilled in goldsmith's work when, already a monk of the Benedictine cathedral priory at Ely, he assisted at the opening of the putative shrine of St Alban in 1314. His continuing interest in the craft is indicated by his provision of a workshop for the goldsmith of the monastery; by the purchase of the manor of Brame in 1336, to provide an income for the goldsmith; and by his latest surviving deed, which is partly concerned with the same subject. In 1318 he was keeper of the lady chapel (then in the south choir aisle); on 25 March 1321 he laid the foundation stone of the new lady chapel north of the choir, but the work was supervised by another monk, John Wisbech. In February 1321, as a protégé of Bishop John Hotham (*d.* 1337), he was appointed sub-prior, on the removal from office of Prior Freshingfield. In December 1321 he was elected sacrist, an office he held for twenty years.

From 1322 onwards Walsingham built a sacristy range on the north edge of the precinct: the two-storey stone building (walls survive) included an exchequer, with a squared calculating table, a kitchen with ancillary offices, and the goldsmith's workshop. Walsingham also built the 'bougre', perhaps the monastic latrine. In 1334–5 a building was in progress off the infirmary, where monks could receive their female relatives; but it was otherwise reserved for Walsingham's sole use during his lifetime. This has been identified with the 'painted chamber' recorded in 1541, a two-storey hall projecting at right angles from the north side of the infirmary ruins; but, while it may stand on the site of Walsingham's building,

the existing structure must, on stylistic grounds, be dated after his death.

The building with which Alan Walsingham's name is most famously associated is the Ely octagon, with its wooden lantern, which was built to replace the Anglo-Norman tower of the cathedral which collapsed on 13 February 1322. According to a brief chronicle published in Wharton's *Anglia sacra*, Walsingham, after initial dismay and uncertainty how to proceed, cleared the fallen masonry and personally marked the positions of the eight new piers, ensuring that they would be built on firm ground. Yet, despite the tradition that he was the architect of the octagon, there is no evidence that he was a trained mason, with the skills in geometry required for setting out building plans, elevations, and masonry details. If the idea of the octagon was Walsingham's, he must still have needed the services of a professional architect and carpenter. His work as sacrist, which also included protecting the monastery's influence in the outside world, was presumably full-time; all the evidence indicates that he was primarily a highly skilled, energetic, and wide-ranging administrator. Nevertheless, he took a close interest in building at Ely, in 1323–4 accompanying a carpenter to select timber at Chicksands, Bedfordshire; and, although the sacristy was financially responsible only for the octagon, he may have had general supervision of the other cathedral works, namely the lady chapel and choir bays. In 1324/5 the sacristy paid for sharpening the axes of the masons building the choir for the bishop; and similar decorative details throughout these works and Prior Crauden's chapel suggest co-operation between the building teams. The octagon was a major expense for the monastery, and Walsingham differentiated the 'new work' in the sacrist's accounts. Another responsibility he undertook in the cathedral was to hang the bells in the west tower.

In October 1341 Walsingham was elected prior in succession to Crauden. On the death of Bishop Simon Montagu in 1345, he was the monks' choice as bishop; but he was set aside by a papal provision in favour of the Dominican Thomas Lisle (*d.* 1361). After 1348 Walsingham was among those appointed vicars-general to deputize during Lisle's absence. In 1361 he and twenty-nine monks bought the manor of Mepal for the monastery, while in 1363 he issued a deed concerning the disposal of the income from the Brame estate, partly for the goldsmith and partly for an obit for Prior Crauden, Walsingham himself, and his parents. This anniversary was later kept in May: Walsingham died at Ely, probably not long after July 1363.

Alan Walsingham was buried in the octagon, just outside the monks' choir. His epitaph described him as *flos operatorum*; but, as it then mentioned his purchases of Brame and Mepal as well as his rebuilding of the tower, it was clearly praising his administrative and wealth-creating, rather than architectural, skills. All the same, it may be to his vision and organizing abilities that one of the glories of the English Decorated style owes its existence. NICOLA COLDSTREAM

Sources [H. Wharton], ed., *Anglia sacra*, 2 vols. (1691), 643–63 · Dugdale, *Monasticon*, new edn, 1.464–8 · F. R. Chapman, ed., *Sacrist*

rolls of Ely, 2 vols. (1907) · *Thomae Walsingham, quondam monachi S. Albani, historia Anglicana*, ed. H. T. Riley, 2 vols., pt 1 of *Chronica monasterii S. Albani*, Rolls Series, 28 (1863–4), vol. 1, pp. 138–9 · P. G. Lindley, 'The monastic cathedral of Ely, *circa* 1320 to *circa* 1350: art and patronage in medieval East Anglia', PhD diss., U. Cam., 1985 · T. D. Atkinson, *An architectural history of the Benedictine monastery of St Etheldreda at Ely* (1933) · *VCH Cambridgeshire and the Isle of Ely*, 4.62 · S. J. A. Evans, 'The purchase and mortification of Mepal by the prior and convent of Ely, 1361', *EngHR*, 51 (1936), 113–20 · Ely muniments
Archives CUL, Ely diocesan records

Walsingham, Sir Edmund (*b.* in or before **1480**, *d.* **1550**), soldier, was the eldest son of James Walsingham (1462–1540), landowner, of Scadbury, in Chislehurst, Kent, and his wife, Eleanor (*b.* before 1465, *d.* after 1540), daughter of Walter Writtle of Bobbingworth, Essex. His pedigree traces family ancestors to thirteenth-century Walsingham, Norfolk, but his earliest documented forebears were London citizens: Alan Walsingham (*fl.* 1415), a cordwainer; Thomas Walsingham (*d.* 1457), a vintner, who bought Scadbury in 1424; and Thomas Walsingham (1436–1467), his grandfather. Edmund Walsingham's brother William (*d.* 1534), was the father of Sir Francis *Walsingham (*c.*1532–1590).

Walsingham inherited Scadbury only in 1541 and was not a JP in Kent until 1547. Earlier he became involved in Surrey politics, marrying Katherine (*b.* before 1495, *d. c.*1526), daughter of John Gunter of Chilworth, and widow of Henry Morgan of Pen-coed, Monmouthshire, by 1510, and entering service with Thomas Howard, earl of Surrey, by 1513. The couple had four sons, including Sir Thomas Walsingham (1526–1584), father of Sir Thomas *Walsingham (1560/61–1630), and four daughters. In 1513, outside Guildford, Walsingham, John Westbroke, and John Shirley (all Howard men) 'mayhaymed' Nicholas Eliot of Shalford, cut off his ears, and so abused his wife that 'what with fear and with the hurt she had than she was seke [sick] many a daye' (PRO, STAC 2/26/355). Cardinal Thomas Wolsey's investigation of Surrey corruption in 1519 revealed that when Sir William Fitzwilliam informed the earl of Surrey, the three assailants agreed to pay Eliot 20 nobles but probably reneged. Walsingham fought at Flodden on 9 September 1513, and Surrey knighted him four days later. After Henry VIII created Surrey second duke of Norfolk in 1514, Walsingham became a Surrey JP, but only briefly (perhaps owing to fluctuating Howard fortunes locally). He was frequently a subsidy commissioner for Surrey from 1523 until 1545, when he was elected knight of the shire with Sir Anthony Browne, and a muster commissioner in 1544. He also served on other commissions in Essex, Kent, London, and Surrey.

Walsingham accompanied Henry to meetings with François I at the Field of Cloth of Gold and Charles V at Gravelines in 1520, and when the emperor visited England in 1522. In 1521 he served on the jury at the treason trial of Henry Stafford, third duke of Buckingham, became a sewer in the royal household, was made a freeman of the London Mercers' Company, and gained appointment as lieutenant of the Tower of London. Though the constable held higher rank, the lieutenant was actually in charge of

prisoners. Walsingham resided there with an annual salary of £100 and collected lucrative fees from inmates, for example £14 10s. 0d. a month for Arthur Plantagenet, sixth Viscount Lisle. The king rebuilt his house in 1539 at a cost of £66 and prisoners exited the Belfry through it.

Walsingham had many famous prisoners, including Anne Boleyn and Katherine Howard. Some complained of their treatment, including John Fisher, bishop of Rochester, Margaret Pole, countess of Salisbury, and Agnes Howard, duchess of Norfolk. However, Walsingham allowed Anne Tankerfelde such liberty that she escaped temporarily. He was kind to Curtoyse, the chaplain of Sir Thomas Cromwell, the principal secretary; to the protestant John Frith, of whom he wrote, 'it were a pity to lose him if he may be reconciled' (Webb, Miller, and Beckwith, 123); and to Sir Thomas More, who joked upon ascending the executioner's scaffold, 'I pray you, Master Lieutenant, see me safe up and, for my coming down, let me shift for myself' (Roper, 254). Besides executions, Walsingham supervised torture, but the story that he refused the command of Thomas Wriothesley, Lord Wriothesley, the lord chancellor, to continue racking Anne Askew is erroneous (it was his successor, Sir Anthony Knyvet). Walsingham relinquished his position in 1543 and became vice-chamberlain of Katherine Parr's household in 1544. She perhaps helped him win election to parliament as MP for Surrey in 1545.

Walsingham acquired a substantial estate including St Paul's Cray, Swanton Court, West Peckham, and Yokes in Kent; Gomshall Towerhill in Surrey, which he sold in 1549 for £600; nine houses in London (in 1539); and various leases. Katherine Walsingham died about 1526. Between 1535 and 1543 Walsingham married Anne Drury (*d.* 1559), daughter of Edward Jerningham of Somerleyton, Suffolk, and his wife, Mary. She had been widowed four times. The couple had no children. Walsingham died on 10 February 1550. His will was dated 7 February and requested burial at Chislehurst 'within the chapell there, where myself have usually sitten' (Webb, Miller, and Beckwith, 378). Most of his estate went to his heir, Thomas. His widow received £40, property at Blackfriars and Yokes, and much jewellery and plate. Walsingham left a further £29 13s. 8d. in bequests, £12 18s. 8d. in annuities, and additional leases and goods. In 1581 Thomas erected a monument, above which hang Walsingham's helmet and sword.

WILLIAM B. ROBISON

Sources HoP, *Commons, 1509–58*, 3.539–40 · E. A. Webb, G. W. Miller, and J. Beckwith, eds., *The history of Chislehurst: its church, manors, and parish* (1899) · W. B. Robison, 'The justices of the peace of Surrey in national and county politics, 1483–1570', PhD diss., Louisiana State University, 1983 · *DNB* · M. St C. Byrne, ed., *The Lisle letters*, 6 vols. (1981) · W. Roper, 'The life of Sir Thomas More', *Two early Tudor lives*, ed. R. S. Sylvester and D. P. Harding (1962) · W. Hepworth Dixon, *Her majesty's Tower* (1884) · C. Read, *Mr Secretary Walsingham and the policy of Queen Elizabeth*, 3 vols. (1925) · *VCH Kent* · *VCH Surrey* · *LP Henry VIII*, vols. 3/1, 4/1, 20/1 · will, PRO, PROB 11/35/25 · PRO, C 142/91/30 · PRO, WARD 7/5/60
Wealth at death numerous lands, some property, and leases; a quantity of jewellery, plate, and possessions; bequests in money totalling £69 13s. 8d., excluding other unspecified sums; annuities totalling £12 18s. 8d.: will, PRO, PROB 11/35/25

Walsingham, Edward (*d.* 1663), royalist author, possibly came from the 'genteel' (Wood, *Ath. Oxon.: Fasti*, 2.60) family of Exhall, Warwickshire, distantly related to Elizabeth's secretary of state, Francis Walsingham. He came under the patronage of the Digby family of the earls of Bristol, a dominant aristocratic force in Warwickshire, and following the outbreak of the civil war became secretary to the secretary of state, George, Lord Digby, under whose favour, as high steward of Oxford, he was made MA (or possibly LLB) of the university in 1643. He went on to compose a series of elegiac tributes to cavalier commanding officers fallen in the civil war, writings which etched out royalist propaganda themes. One of the messages of these works was the equation between royalism and rank—as in his tribute to Sir Henry Gage, *Alter Britanniae heros* (1645)—and the obverse equation of parliamentarianism and base birth. As a royalist military obituarist, in his panegyric on Sir John Smith, *Britannicae virtutis imago* (1645), he was celebrating the disappearing chivalric world of a man said to have been the last banneret, knighted on the field, 'That noble, valiant, gallant knight renowned Smith' (Carlton, 193). The same hero, though, was the victim of some of Walsingham's less felicitous versifying:

> His name was Smith, who for his king fighting
> Unto his foes seem'd a flash of Lightning.
> (Walsingham, 143)

However, the primary purpose of these elegies was not to make a social point about royalism but a religious one, and specifically a distinctively Catholic one: that Catholicism and self-sacrificial loyalty to the crown were entirely compatible, and that the Catholic faith formed the foundations for royalist martyrdoms. It was in his memorial to Sir John Digby, *Hector Britannicus*, unpublished until 1910, that Walsingham achieved the fullest 'subsuming of the Catholic gentleman with the Royalist cause' (Newman, 210). While all his heroic subjects in this series were Catholics by faith, Walsingham's Digby was the very perfect gentle Catholic knight, whose defiance of the Scots in the bishops' war—'Sr I am a Roman Catholique and so am resolved to live and dy' (Walsingham, 77)—he lovingly recalled. Already by the mid-1640s, then, when his own sympathies were so clearly Catholic, he was showing that tendency that was to haunt the remainder of his life, that of subjugating the interests of political royalism to those of religious Catholicism.

Even so, Walsingham was deeply involved in royalist espionage work in the mid-1640s. From the personal tone of the intelligence-gathering correspondence that he sent to Digby from Oxford—'Sir John Digby's death affect me greatly' (*CSP dom.*, 1645–7, 51–3)—we may assume that the letters were his own. They provided broad, informed, and sharply written surveys of current affairs in Britain and the rest of Europe and, on the basis of these briefings alone, it would be possible to agree with the description of him as the 'young Catholic intellectual … brilliantly gifted' (Roy, 85) who served George Digby, feeding in particular his rivalry with Prince Rupert and his ambitions as a Catholic royalist leader: 'Now is the time for your Lordship to make this poor kingdom happy' (*CSP dom.*, 1645–7, 140).

Malice and meddling were the darker sides of Walsingham's high gifts. In February 1648 he could still be described, by the Anglican royalist secretary of state, Sir Edward Nicholas (whose protestant royalist circle detested Walsingham), as a 'pragmatical knave' (Roy, 86), 'busy instrument of the Jesuits' (Warner, 2.142), and 'great babbler of his most secret employments' in the character of 'Lord Digby's intimate servant' (Walsingham, 63, 94 n. a). However, by late August, Digby was reported 'discarding Walsingham for giving offence' (ibid., 94).

Walsingham's capacity for disruptive conduct in the most delicate affairs was shown at its worst in 1648 in Ireland, where his busy aim of obtaining maximum religious gains for Irish Catholics ran counter to the marquess of Ormond's patient negotiations between September 1648 and January 1649 to achieve accord between protestant royalists and Catholic confederates based on Ormond's assent to 'the repeal of the penalties in any statutes which affected the free exercise of the *Roman* Catholick Religion' (Carte, 2.48). Part of Walsingham's fault line was, clearly, his tendency to present—and distort—material in line with his own passionately partisan commitment, so that, for example, when it was reported in March 1651 that he was to have charge of editing Ormond's papers, it was claimed (by Nicholas) that 'all honest men' would disvalue the edition that had come 'through his hands' (Warner, 1.225). In the early 1650s he was a focus of the Catholic factionalism that threatened to disrupt the already divisive life of the English court in Paris (where he had already spent some time between 1646 and 1648). In April 1651 it was reported that the queen's favourite Lord Jermyn, in his bid to become 'first Minister of State' (*CSP dom.*, 1651, 127) in the government in exile, had picked Walsingham for a secretary. More dangerously, in terms of a realistic Stuart hope of the family's return to a devotedly protestant country, between June and November 1655 he was hard at work attempting to convert Charles II's youngest brother Henry, duke of Gloucester, to Rome: Parisian *curés* were said to be offering prayers of gratitude for that outcome and rooms in the Jesuits' college were being prepared for the duke. Key features of Walsingham's character—hero worship, especially for Lord Digby, combined with malice and innuendo, exaggeration of his own role in the world, excess religious partisanship, and hyperbole, are seen in the reports of his Paris conversation with Gloucester in November 1654: he

> spared none of you [the Nicholas cavalier circle] there or any loyall person elsewhere, [and] told *the Duke of Gloucester* that he was a confident of his blessed father even above his *Councell*, and that *Lo. Digby* was soe much the ablest *Councell* to the *King* … and that this *Lo. Digby*, as he had allwayes told him [Walsingham] he preferred the Romish before the English church, had now put himselfe into a *Jesuites'* colledge, where he had declared himselfe a *Papist*. (Warner, 2.134)

Understandably, in December, Nicholas was hoping that Walsingham would soon be forbidden Gloucester's company.

In the following year, though, Walsingham did not devise but instead scotched, by disclosing it, a conspiracy—one, or rather two, mooted by Catholic and presbyterian royalists to remove the indispensable Edward Hyde (later earl of Clarendon) from Charles II's counsels. Whatever Walsingham's motives were in this disclosure, Hyde seems to have been grateful to him for it, and in July 1659 had confidential correspondence entrusted to him, identifying him as a relative of the earl of Bristol. Yet Walsingham did not return with the royalist exiles in 1660; he was ordained a Catholic priest in the year of the Restoration and stayed in France as secretary to the confessor of an English *émigré* convent. He returned to England in 1663 and died there on 9 October of that year. He was ardent, hyperactive, passionately sincere, and gifted, a victim and archetype of the sterility of Stuart royalism for much of the 1640s and 50s.   MICHAEL MULLETT

Sources *The Nicholas papers*, ed. G. F. Warner, 2, CS, new ser., 50 (1892) · [E. Walsingham], 'Life of Sir John Digby, 1605–1645', ed. G. Bernard, *Camden miscellany, XII*, CS, 3rd ser., 18 (1910) · *CSP dom., 1644–7; 1651; 1658–9* · E. Hyde, earl of Clarendon, *The history of the rebellion and civil wars in England*, new edn (1843) · I. Roy, 'George Digby, royalist intrigue and the collapse of the cause', *Soldiers, writers and statesmen of the English revolution*, ed. I. Gentles and others (1998), 68–90 · Wood, *Ath. Oxon.: Fasti* (1820) · P. R. Newman, *The old service: royalist regimental colonels and the civil war, 1642–1646* (1993) · T. Carte, *An history of the life of James, duke of Ormonde*, 3 vols. (1735–6), vol. 2 · C. Carlton, *Going to the wars: the experience of the British wars, 1638–1651* (1992) · G. Anstruther, *The seminary priests*, 3 (1976) · *VCH Warwickshire*

Archives Bodl. Oxf., Carte MSS · Bodl. Oxf., Rawlinson MSS · Bodl. Oxf., Tanner MSS

Walsingham, Sir Francis (*c*.1532–1590), principal secretary, was born either in London or at Foots Cray, Kent, the only son of William Walsingham (*b*. after 1480, *d*. 1534), lawyer and landowner, of Scadbury in Chislehurst, Kent, and his wife, Joyce (1506/7–1560), daughter of Sir Edmund Denny of Cheshunt, Hertfordshire, and his second wife, Mary. He had five sisters, including Mary (1527/8–1577), who married Sir Walter *Mildmay (1520/21–1589) on 25 May 1546, Elizabeth (*d*. 1596), who married Peter *Wentworth (1524–1597), and Christiana, who married John Tamworth (*c*.1524–1569), keeper of the privy purse from 1559 to 1569, in 1562. His uncle was Sir Edmund *Walsingham (*b*. in or before 1480, *d*. 1550), lieutenant of the Tower of London from 1521 until his death. Like so many of Elizabeth I's servants he came from a family with existing court connections.

Education and early career, *c*.1532–1568 William Walsingham was a member of Gray's Inn and autumn reader in 1530. He was also involved in local administration in Kent and purchased Foots Cray in 1529. His last will was written on 1 March and proved on 23 March 1534 and left Foots Cray to his son, Francis Walsingham. About 1536 his widow married Sir John Carey of Plashy in Hertfordshire, the younger brother of William Carey, who married Mary Boleyn (*c*.1499–1543) [*see* Stafford, Mary], and with whom she had two sons. Francis Walsingham probably first went up to King's College, Cambridge, as a fellow-commoner in

Sir Francis Walsingham (*c*.1532–1590), attrib. John de Critz the elder, *c*.1585

spring 1548. He was certainly there by 2 June and matriculated as a pensioner of the college on 29 September. Thanks to its provost, Sir John Cheke, the ethos of the college was strongly reformist after 1547, with emphasis on study of scripture to justify one's argument, and on learning rhetoric and dialectic through the works of Aristotle, Plato, and Cicero. As befitted his status Walsingham left on 29 September 1550 without taking a degree. According to the inscription on his tomb, after leaving Cambridge he apparently travelled on the continent, though where and in what capacity is unknown, but he had returned by 1552, when his stepfather died, and he was admitted to Gray's Inn.

Walsingham returned to the continent in the reign of Mary I, but under circumstances that pose a number of questions. He is first encountered in Basel in autumn 1555 escorting his cousins, the three sons of his mother's brother Sir Anthony *Denny (1501–1549), of Cheshunt. However, by the end of the year he had moved to Padua, where he enrolled as a student in civil law at the university and on 29 December 1555 was appointed *consilarius* or spokesman for the English students there, a position he retained until 8 April 1556. Thereafter his movements are unknown. The Dennys had in fact been in Padua in autumn 1554, together with Walsingham's future brother-in-law Tamworth, and there is no reason why he could not have been with them then.

In December 1555 Padua was the centre of much activity. Francis Russell, second earl of Bedford, had been living in Venice since June, and Edward Courtenay, earl of Devon, arrived in Padua in January 1556 *en route* for Venice. The assembly of Englishmen there has been associated with the conspiracy known as the Dudley plot, which was halted first by the French, who signed the truce of Vaucelles with Charles V on 5 February, and then by the exposure of the plot in England in March. Devon died in Padua on 18 September. During 1556 many of the Englishmen there dispersed and it is possible that Walsingham returned to Basel. In moments of stress in later life he recalled his time in Switzerland almost with longing. On 28 March 1586 he complained to Robert Dudley, earl of Leicester, 'the opynion of my partyalytie contynewethe [continueth] noryshed by factyon, which makethe me weerye of the place I serve in, and to wysshe myself emongst the trewe harted Swy[ss]', and he expressed similar sentiments on 22 June 1588: 'I would … we were … in Basil [Basel] to pray for Princes' (*Correspondence of Robert Dudley, Earl of Leycester*, ed. J. Bruce, CS, old ser., 27, 1844, 192; *Salisbury MSS*, 3.332).

Although it is not known precisely why he went into exile, or how far he was involved in the conspiracies of 1555–6, several of Walsingham's later associates were companions abroad. Three works of John Foxe, Basel's most famous English resident, were later dedicated to him. More immediately significant may have been the connection to Bedford, for Walsingham is next detected as an MP for Bossiney, Cornwall, in the parliament that assembled on 23 January 1559 to enact the settlement of religion. Bedford (who was lord warden of the stannaries) is the obvious patron, though it is also clear that his westcountry seats were used as a form of reserve for men the privy council wished to see returned as MPs. In 1563 Walsingham was returned for Lyme Regis, Dorset; there is a reference by Sir William Cecil, the principal secretary, to wishing to see him in the parliament. However, Walsingham made little impression on the House of Commons in the 1560s, and even when he was principal secretary his parliamentary performances as knight of the shire for Surrey (1572, 1584, 1586, and 1589) were perfunctory. P. W. Hasler has observed that 'it is clear that the House of Commons held little appeal for him' (HoP, *Commons, 1558–1603*, 3.573).

No less mysterious is the apparent absence of any public employment before 1568, given Walsingham's sudden rise to international prominence after 1570, or of much information about him at all during the 1560s. One reason is the disappearance of his personal papers. As secretary, Walsingham organized his official papers very carefully. A pocket index compiled by his secretary Thomas Lake about 1588 survives, now entitled 'Walsingham's table book' (BL, Stowe MS 162). As well as the standard bundles of correspondence, Walsingham's papers contained 'books of matters' (effectively reference books), and 'Diaria' or repertories, either indices to bundles of correspondence or letter-books. Their fate after his death was complicated. According to his brother-in-law Robert *Beale (1541–1601), writing about 1592, 'all his papers and bookes both publicke and private were seazed on and carried away' (Read, *Walsingham*, 1.431). Other evidence shows them kept as a collection, though whether they remained as such or were taken into the Cecil papers later in the

1590s is less clear. Only a few of the books survive, but the correspondence now forms a large part of the Elizabethan state papers. In the process all private material was weeded out and has disappeared with the exception of two semi-official diaries or 'leigerbooks', one covering the years 1570 to 1583 (Martin, ed., 'Journal of Sir Francis Walsingham'), and the other 1583 to 1584 (BL, Harley MS 6035). Like that of his protégé William Davison—but unlike Leicester's—Walsingham's official career can be reconstructed in detail, but his private life remains largely a blank.

Walsingham's mother died in 1560 and was buried beside his father in St Mary Aldermanbury, London. In 1562 Walsingham married Anne (d. 1564), daughter of Sir George Barne of London, and his wife, Alice, and widow of Alexander Carleill. They had no children. She was a wealthy woman when she died in summer or autumn 1564 (her will dated 28 July and proved 22 November), leaving her children in Walsingham's care. These included the future soldier and naval commander Christopher *Carleill (1551?–1593), for whom he had a particular affection and whose career he promoted assiduously. It was probably to his marriage that he owed his association with the Muscovy Company. Sir George Barne was one of the founders of the company and Alexander Carleill had been one of the original stockholders. Walsingham was involved heavily in the company's activities by summer 1568 and became an assistant the following year.

In autumn 1566 he married Ursula (d. 1602), daughter of Henry St Barbe of Somerset and widow of Sir Richard Worseley of the Isle of Wight. His courtship was probably the reason for his earliest surviving letter, a ponderously jocular request to Sir William More of Loseley, Surrey, on 23 October 1565 for his help in persuading 'the gentlewoman from her resolution of sole lyfe' (Surrey RO, Guildford, Loseley corresp., 3/56). The couple had two daughters, Frances (c.1568–1632), who married Sir Philip *Sidney (1554–1586) on 21 September 1583, and Mary, who died as a child in 1580. After 1566 Walsingham established his household at his new wife's house, Appuldurcomb, in Wiltshire, and then at her late husband's house, Carisbrooke Castle on the Isle of Wight. On 6 September 1567 an accidental explosion of gunpowder at the gatehouse at Appuldurcomb killed his two stepsons from his second marriage. Consequently legal action began over Ursula Walsingham's rights in the Worseley estate at Carisbrooke Priory which continued until July 1571. Ursula Walsingham features little in the surviving record but she was regarded with genuine affection by her husband's friends, including Leicester, whose distant cousin she was.

Royal service and embassy to France, 1568–1573 Walsingham's residence in Wiltshire and the Isle of Wight in the late 1560s may explain his escape from public employment. On the other hand, by 1568 he was an established protégé of Sir Nicholas Throckmorton, an association that probably began through their connection with Bedford during the Marian exile. Walsingham may have served in an unrecorded capacity with Throckmorton on one of his Scottish embassies in the late 1560s. His earliest surviving letter to Cecil was written on Throckmorton's behalf in August 1568 and dealt with a subject of major importance. This was the mission of Robert Stewart, who brought from Louis de Bourbon-Vendôme, prince de Condé, and Gaspard de Coligny, admiral of France, the first proposal that Elizabeth should marry Henri, duc d'Anjou.

On 20 December 1568 Walsingham wrote to Cecil that 'there is lesse daynger in fearinge to myche then to lyttle', and 'ther is nothinge more dayngerowse then [than] securyte' (PRO, SP 12/48/61, fol. 165r). In this case by 'securyte' he meant carelessness or a culpable absence of anxiety. These statements became his credo. In autumn 1569 Cecil used Walsingham as the guardian of Roberto di Ridolfi. However, Walsingham's handling of Ridolfi was not assured and his reports to Cecil about him appear naïve in retrospect. Conyers Read thought that Walsingham might have been the anonymous author of a tract produced at this time attacking the prospective marriage between Mary, queen of Scots, and Thomas Howard, fourth duke of Norfolk (BL, Harley MS 290), but the attribution has since been challenged.

In February 1570 Walsingham and Henry Killigrew were nominated as successors to Sir Henry Norris as resident ambassador in Paris. The embassy to the French court was the only permanent English residency (it had been agreed by treaty in 1518), but it was notoriously considered very expensive. Norris (for example) was married to the heir of a baron. Although Killigrew was the more experienced, Cecil appears to have considered him 'in livelihood much inferior' to Walsingham, and by summer 1570 Walsingham was the main candidate (Read, *Walsingham*, 1.94). If he lacked diplomatic experience, he possessed the requisite linguistic skills. He was fluent in both French and Italian, though not (on his own admission) Spanish.

Walsingham was initially appointed special ambassador to France on 11 August 1570 (with a diet of £2 per day), to assist Norris in persuading Charles IX to bring the third War of Religion to an end—but even before he left England the peace of St Germain was signed (8 August). He had an audience with Charles on or about 29 August, which consisted largely of congratulations on the settlement. Shortly afterwards he was informed that he would be Norris's successor, but he was allowed to return to England to organize his private affairs first, and left Paris on 29 September. His letters of instruction for the resident embassy were dated 19 December. He had protested that he could not afford the embassy, and as a result his diets were increased to £3 6s. 8d. per day, slightly more than Norris had received. Walsingham took with him as secretary his brother-in-law Beale (married to his wife's sister Edith), who served with him until his own appointment as clerk of the privy council in July 1572. Walsingham presented his credentials at a formal audience with Charles on 25 January 1571.

Cecil and Leicester had backed Walsingham's appointment, and he was clearly on very close terms with both. Leicester addressed him throughout his embassy as 'my good Francis'. Paris was the cockpit of Europe during the two and a half years of Walsingham's residence (which

lasted until 10 May 1573), and as a result he became an international figure, forming a range of friendships and contacts that he sustained throughout his future career. His correspondence files for the embassy were later obtained by Sir Robert Cotton (probably purloined from the state paper office), and numerous copies of them were made. One was published in 1655 as *The compleat ambassador*, the first printed collection of diplomatic papers in English.

Initially Walsingham had a much easier task than his predecessors. After the peace of St Germain the Huguenots were prominent at court, the Guise had withdrawn, and Catherine de' Medici was eager for good relations with Elizabeth. This marked a major turning point in Elizabethan foreign policy, for since the beginning of the reign relations with France had been tense at best. However, the trade war with Spain that began in 1569 and suspected Spanish intrigues in Ireland suggested that Philip II now posed the greater danger. This was confirmed during the first year of Walsingham's embassy by the exposure of the Ridolfi plot (summer 1571), which revealed that Philip was prepared to support the deposition of Elizabeth in favour of Mary.

Walsingham's contribution to the formulation of policy was to argue along these lines, and certain themes that became central to his future approach to foreign affairs can be detected in his correspondence from France. Like many protestants he remained convinced that a Catholic league had been made at Bayonne, where Charles IX and Catherine met Fernando Alvarez de Toledo, duke of Alva, between 15 June and 2 July 1565, but he was now convinced that Spain represented the greater threat. If not entirely persuaded by the expressions of goodwill from the French royal family he considered that so long as the Huguenots remained powerful France could not harm England. The most immediate danger to Elizabeth was the queen of Scots, and he never ceased to regret publicly that she was not executed in 1572. On the other hand he felt that Elizabeth could be assured of Scotland if she subsidized the protestant and Anglophile king's party.

Two major issues came to dominate Walsingham's embassy: the proposed marriage to Anjou and the Netherlands enterprise. The Huguenots, who had first proposed the Anjou marriage in 1568, revived it in autumn 1570 as a means of making a close alliance between England and France which would sustain their newly won security. The suggestion was well received by Catherine, though for her own motives: Anjou was her favourite son, and she was convinced by a prophecy that all her sons would wear crowns. At the same time alliances with both England and the Holy Roman empire (Charles IX married Maximilian II's daughter Elizabeth in 1570) would neutralize the Huguenots' main foreign allies. Elizabeth was less enthusiastic, particularly over the age difference (she was thirty-seven and Anjou nineteen). Moreover, as had been the case with Archduke Karl between 1565 and 1567, she expected to be wooed, and thus the negotiations tended to be conducted either through the French ambassador in London, Bertrand de Salignac de la Motte-Fénélon, or by special envoys. Walsingham's contribution to the negotiations was to keep her informed of the attitude of Catherine and Charles.

Early in 1571 a draft set of the French terms was sent to England. The English response was that overall Anjou would be offered the terms granted to Philip when he had married Mary I in 1554, but Elizabeth would not (as she had previously refused the Archduke Karl) grant him public exercise of Catholicism. For his part Anjou had no desire for the marriage. At the beginning of 1571 he had openly described Elizabeth as a woman of immoral character (which his mother anxiously denied), and by the summer he made it clear he would accept nothing less than public exercise of his religion.

By then Walsingham had become involved heavily in the Netherlands enterprise. This was the plan devised by the supporters of William of Orange and the Huguenots for an alliance of England, France, and the German protestant princes to support a revolt in the Netherlands against Philip's governor-general, Alva. Once the Spaniards had been driven out the Netherlands would be partitioned, France obtaining Artois and Flanders, and Elizabeth Holland and Zealand, while the remaining provinces under the immediate government of Orange would rejoin the Holy Roman empire. On 19 July 1571 Louis of Nassau, Orange's brother, presented the plan to Charles IX at an interview arranged by Coligny. On 6 August Louis had a similar meeting with Walsingham.

The Netherlands enterprise set the tone for Walsingham's future approach to foreign affairs. It was a bold stroke, and risks would have to be run, but the advantages success offered outweighed the risks. Together with his detailed reports on his conversations with Louis of Nassau and others he drafted a short memorandum on the subject: 'Whether it may stand in good policy for her majesty to join with France in the enterprise of Burgundy'. A number of manuscript copies (including BL, Harley MS 168, fols. 154r–157v) of the memorandum survive, but Read curiously overlooked it. Some of the copies attribute the memorandum to Cecil (Baron Burghley from 1571), but similarities in phraseology between the memorandum and Walsingham's reports to London in August 1571 establishes him as the author. Walsingham used the memorandum to answer the main objections to the plan: that it would engage Elizabeth in a major war, that it would break the old alliance with Burgundy, and that the French motive for participating was simply to annex the Netherlands. He justified the enterprise on the grounds that recent events had revealed Spain to be Elizabeth's main enemy, that under Philip's rule the Netherlands were no longer an ally, and that partition would prevent French expansion. Moreover, Charles's reception of Louis of Nassau suggested that the French crown was sincerely committed to the enterprise.

Thanks to the enterprise it was vital that even if the marriage failed a formal alliance should still be made with France. Leicester may have suggested the alliance as an alternative to the marriage at the beginning of July, but Walsingham gave it his support early in August, and

Charles at roughly the same time. Elizabeth and Burghley were more sceptical, but in early September they came round and the queen agreed to send a special envoy to join Walsingham in negotiating the treaty. At this point Walsingham was forced to take to his bed for nearly four months (3 November 1571 to 28 February 1572). The cause was a urinary complaint—a 'certaine difficulté de uryne qui le travaille fort', as la Motte-Fénélon described it—that dogged him for the rest of his life (*Correspondence*, ed. Teulet, 4.247). Killigrew was sent to Paris to substitute for him, followed by Sir Thomas Smith, who was to join him in making the treaty.

As soon as he had recovered Walsingham and Smith negotiated what became the treaty of Blois, signed on 19 April 1572. On instructions from London the Anglo-French alliance was kept strictly defensive and the Netherlands enterprise was not mentioned, although it was implied in the agreement to shift the English cloth staple from the Netherlands (actually based in Hamburg since the embargo of 1569) to France. The most debated items were the English demand that the defensive arrangements should override religious considerations (*etiamsi causa religionis*), so that France was committed to aid England in the event of an attack by Spain, and the French demand for the inclusion of the queen of Scots. In the event a compromise was struck and neither was included. Walsingham was prepared to accept an assurance of assistance in a private letter from Charles, while the French effectively conceded to the ascendancy of the king's party over the Marians in Scotland.

The negotiation of the treaty of Blois was accompanied by Catherine's revival of the marriage proposal, now on the part of her youngest son, François, duc d'Alençon. Against the obvious objections to the even wider difference in age (Elizabeth was almost thirty-nine, Alençon only seventeen) and his facial deformities, Catherine offered the assurance that he would be more flexible in religion than his brother. Elizabeth was even less happy with the Alençon proposal, but it initiated a major revolution in her 'courtships'. Alençon displayed an enthusiasm for the marriage and sent his current favourite, Joseph de Boniface, seigneur de La Molle, to England to begin the wooing in summer 1572. However, the cautious Anglo-French negotiations had already been overtaken by the revolt in the Netherlands that followed the landing of the Sea Beggars at Den Briel on 1 April. While various Huguenot forces attempted to come to the rebels' assistance, neither Charles nor Elizabeth (for their various reasons) were prepared to fulfil the role planned for them in the enterprise. Walsingham was left in the position of exhorting London not to let the opportunity slip. He wrote to Leicester on 28 May:

> I hope it shall manifestly appear unto you, that upon the good success or evil success of this [enterprise depends the] common cause of religion. And besides, the same not well proceeding, her Majestie cannot promise to herself any great safety, having so dangerous a neighbour, whose greatness shall receive no small increase, if he overcome this brunt. I pray God therefore that her Majestie may incline to do that

which may be for her safety. (*Compleat Ambassador*, ed. Digges, 216)

The Netherlands enterprise was one of the many casualties of the massacre of St Bartholomew's eve (23–4 August). Walsingham has left no account of his experiences, and the extent of his personal danger is unclear. His residence was in the Faubourg St Germain on the left bank, at a distance from the main riots, and he was able to provide a refuge for Sidney and other Englishmen in Paris, and possibly some Huguenots as well. He carried himself with considerable dignity and restraint in his first audience with Catherine after the massacre (14 September), but the experience scarred him and shaped his future attitude to France.

At the audience Catherine emphasized that the massacre was purely an internal affair, that the treaty of Blois remained in force, and that she was still keen for the marriage of Elizabeth and Alençon, even proposing that she and Elizabeth meet. Both Walsingham and Elizabeth regarded these professions of goodwill with scepticism, and Elizabeth was ready to recall him immediately. However, in view of the confused situation it was decided that he should remain for the meantime as a gesture of her goodwill, while a successor was chosen. But as Walsingham admitted candidly to the privy council a month afterwards, he had been wrong about the French royal family and his whole Netherlands strategy was in ruins: 'I may seem to have dealt over-confidently; but I know your honours do consider that my error in that behalf was common with a great many wiser than myself, and therefore I hope you do hold me excused' (*Compleat Ambassador*, ed. Digges, 257). Like his colleagues in London he considered that the assurance of Scotland through an effective alliance with the king's party was now the most immediate concern and entered into a direct correspondence with the Scottish regents to that effect. The remainder of his embassy in France was something of an anticlimax. Apart from reporting the course of the fourth War of Religion, which broke out after the massacre, his main activity was to help London evaluate the bona fides of Jerôme de l'Huillier, seigneur de Maisonfleur, whom Alençon sent to Elizabeth in November to persuade her that he had opposed the massacre and wished to seek refuge in England. At last in May 1573 Dr Valentine Dale was dispatched to relieve him and Walsingham was able to return.

Principal secretary and privy councillor, 1573–1578 On 20 December 1573 Walsingham was appointed a principal secretary, and on the following day a privy councillor. This was the final stage of the first major reshaping of Elizabeth's privy council since the beginning of the reign. After the appointments of Leicester and Norfolk in 1562 the privy council had remained effectively static, except for the deaths of older members (six, all peers, died between 1570 and 1573) and their replacement. There was an established inner ring of Cecil, Leicester, and Sir Nicholas Bacon, whom Elizabeth showed no desire to change. What initiated the reshaping was Cecil's creation as Baron Burghley on 25 February 1571. At the time Leicester informed Walsingham that Burghley would be appointed

lord privy seal as well. This did not happen, and instead in March, Smith, who had been principal secretary from 1548 to 1549 as well as ambassador to France from 1563 to 1565, was sworn of the privy council, perhaps to assist Burghley in the secretaryship. A possible alternative, Throckmorton, was eliminated by his death on 12 February 1571. The death of the lord treasurer, William Paulet, first marquess of Winchester, on 10 March 1572 triggered a more complicated reshuffle. On 13 July (after his return from France) Smith was appointed principal secretary and William Howard, first Baron Howard of Effingham, surrendered the lord chamberlaincy to Thomas Radcliffe, third earl of Sussex (who had been sworn of the privy council in December 1570). On 15 July Burghley was appointed lord treasurer, and Howard, lord privy seal, but he died only six months later on 12 January 1573.

This reshuffle brought little new blood into the privy council. Apart from Sussex, Smith, and George Talbot, sixth earl of Shrewsbury (also in 1571), the only other new privy councillor since 1569 was Leicester's brother Ambrose Dudley, earl of Warwick (5 September 1573). Walsingham may have expected appointment as principal secretary on his return, for Leicester had informed him on 8 January 1573, 'you know what opinion is here of you, and to what place all men would have you unto … besides that, the place you alreadie hold is a Counsellours place' (*Compleat Ambassador*, ed. Digges, 322). However, Elizabeth may have baulked initially at the appointment of a second principal secretary—a novelty for her reign. Retrospectively, Walsingham's appointment was seen as the consequence of his diplomatic achievements, creating a widespread belief that the secretaryship would be the culmination of a successful diplomatic career, but in practice this rarely occurred.

A few surviving privy council memoranda in his hand from early January 1574 reveal Walsingham already at work, but tracing a specific influence thereafter is less easy. Read noted that 'the actual information which we possess about his life' during Walsingham's first four years as secretary, from 1574 to 1578, is 'lamentably little' (Read, *Walsingham*, 1.372). The secretaryship was perhaps the most onerous of the major offices, involving almost constant attendance on the queen as well as the privy council. As the handler of routine correspondence the secretary was the primary point of contact for a range of diplomats and officials, as well as the multitude of suitors to the crown. In the absence of a lord privy seal the secretary also had charge of that seal. However, the loss of privy seal records in the Whitehall Palace fire of 1619 has made it almost impossible to assess that side of his duties. Walsingham's urinary complaint (which may have been a kidney stone) forced him to take frequent sick leave. He was absent from the court for nearly four months between 24 December 1574 and 17 April 1575 (though writing letters furiously from his bed), and further absences were noted at the beginning of 1576, 1577, and 1578. In the autumn of 1576 he informed Burghley that he was exhausted and wished to resign.

The reshuffle had made little difference to the size of

the privy council, which numbered sixteen in 1574 as against fifteen in 1568. Moreover, the principal figures, Leicester, Burghley, Bacon, and, after 1571, Sussex, retained their dominant influence with Elizabeth. Walsingham only slowly obtained a position similar to theirs. Smith was the senior secretary in 1574, but he was elderly, his health was deteriorating, and he retired sick in April 1576, dying on 12 August 1577. Sir Thomas Wilson quickly replaced him on 12 November 1577, the day on which Sir Christopher Hatton was appointed vice-chamberlain and sworn of the privy council. Walsingham's observations on the pressure of business at the time of Wilson's appointment make it clear that an assistant was considered necessary. Although Wilson was considerably older than Walsingham and had recent diplomatic experience in the Netherlands, Walsingham was now clearly the senior secretary, as was reflected in his knighting on 1 December 1577.

Walsingham's entry into high politics was very much as subordinate to Burghley and Leicester. He acted as their agent in executing the abortive plan to free Alençon on the eve of Charles's death on 30 May 1574 and then in sending a subsidy to Friedrich III, the elector palatine, to aid Alençon and the Huguenots during the fifth War of Religion in autumn 1575. The triumvirate of Burghley, Leicester, and Sussex dominated Irish affairs, and it was only in 1575 that Walsingham began to join them. Walsingham's own hand is clearest in French policy, not least because his agents (like the Italian Jacomo Manucci) continued to serve his successors. He also took a particular interest in Scotland, cultivating close contacts with the regent, James Douglas, fourth earl of Morton, whom he openly admired, and who in turn relied on him for news and information.

The Netherlands proved the most difficult area. There is some evidence that Burghley (with Elizabeth's backing) had hoped to use the treaty of Blois and her refusal to execute Mary as a means of persuading Spain into a peaceful settlement of the trade war. In the months after St Bartholomew's eve Burghley moved swiftly to restore trade with the Netherlands and Spain (the convention of Nijmegen, March 1573). Thereafter he retained a close control over negotiations with the Netherlands, seeking to mediate a settlement between Philip and the rebels, rather than give open support to Orange. On the other hand Walsingham had had close Orangeist connections since 1571 and they clearly saw him as a sympathetic figure. When in December 1575 a delegation from the states of Holland and Zealand offered Elizabeth the sovereignty of the provinces, Walsingham apparently warned them they were wasting their time. However, several months later, when a crisis developed over the Dutch attempt to prevent the English trading with Antwerp, he was instrumental in arranging a settlement between Orange and the queen. A major transformation occurred in autumn 1576, when the success of the revolt, coupled with the arrival of the new governor-general, Don John of Austria, widely believed to be planning the liberation of the queen of Scots, converted Elizabeth to a policy of defending the status quo.

This time, however, there was no trusting the French crown: indeed the outbreak of the sixth War of Religion in spring 1577 revived suspicions (shared by Walsingham) that there was indeed a Catholic league. This assessment contained a fatal flaw that would cause Walsingham major problems in formulating policy towards France. Despite his flamboyant Catholic devotion Henri III (the former duc d'Anjou), once firmly on the throne, had no interest in foreign adventures and was a great admirer of Elizabeth. Walsingham never fully appreciated this, and, being fed appraisals of French politics by his Huguenot friends such as Philippe Duplessis-Mornay, who were obsessed by the supposed ambitions of Henri Guise, third duc de Guise, constantly overrated his influence on the king.

The events of 1577 also showed that there would not be much help from the German princes either. By the end of the year, as relations between the states general of the United Provinces and Don John deteriorated, the issue became one of unilateral intervention. This caused an important division of opinion between Burghley and Walsingham, especially after the defeat of the states' army by Don John at Gembloux on 31 January 1578. Burghley was doubtful of Dutch political coherence and considered a mediated settlement the best way out, while Walsingham, supported by William Davison, then agent in the Netherlands, as well as by Bacon, argued that the strength of the Dutch cities would, with adequate assistance, make a reconquest impossible. However, the risks of full-scale war with Spain were heightened when Morton was dismissed as regent of Scotland on 12 March, while Sir Thomas Stukeley was preparing an expedition for Ireland in Italy and Spain. In these circumstances Elizabeth decided to send only limited military and financial assistance to the Netherlands to stabilize the situation and encourage a mediated settlement, while keeping a larger expedition in reserve.

It was at this point (February and March 1578) that Alençon, now duc d'Anjou, launched his own eccentric version of Coligny's 1571 Netherlands enterprise. Although he had shown recurrent interest in a Netherlands enterprise since 1576 his behaviour in the sixth War of Religion had discredited him and he was notoriously at odds with his brother. The latter aspect of the Anjou enterprise was crucial, as Walsingham noted immediately, writing to Davison on 28 March that: '[I] cannot tell what to make of his dealings with the States being divided as he is from the French king without whose aid he shall not perform anything' (BL, Add. MS 19398, fol. 88r). On the other hand Henri's ultimate intentions proved almost impossible to penetrate, and Walsingham's deep suspicion of the French crown led him to assume the worst: 'it will behove the Prince [Orange], therefore, to look substantially into the matter and not to forget the late accident on St Batholomew's Day' (Read, *Walsingham*, 1.377).

Elizabeth's initial response was to try to keep Anjou out of the Netherlands by threatening to withdraw all assistance if the Dutch negotiated with him, but he bullied his way into discussions in April. In May she adopted a dangerous two-pronged approach. A special embassy was to be sent to the Netherlands to assess the situation, while she sought to divert Anjou by dangling marriage before him—this was communicated to the French ambassador, Castelnau de Mauvissière, through Sussex. Leicester wanted to head the embassy, but instead Elizabeth chose Walsingham, despite his objections (possibly on grounds of health), together with William Brooke, tenth Baron Cobham. Their instructions were drafted on 12 June and they arrived at Dunkirk on the 23rd.

The Anjou episode, 1578–1581 At the beginning of June the Holy Roman emperor, Rudolph II, suddenly offered to mediate a settlement in the Netherlands. As a result the Walsingham–Cobham embassy was instructed first to persuade Don John to agree to the imperial mediation. If unsuccessful, they were to co-ordinate the defence against him, including Anjou if he was prepared to co-operate. Last, if necessary, Elizabeth would send major English assistance, particularly if Anjou allied with Don John, a recurrent fear during spring and summer, for it was widely known that Catherine had tried to marry him to one of Philip's daughters. Including Anjou in the defence of the Netherlands, rather than diverting him, was a recent and major concession.

Walsingham and Cobham arrived in grand style, Walsingham's own expenses for the embassy coming to £1298 4s. 6d. They were lavishly entertained by the Dutch when they reached Antwerp on 1 July, not entirely to Walsingham's taste, but much to the chagrin of Anjou's penniless agents. Their ambassadorial train also included a number of military officers, whose role was to assess the strength of the Dutch towns. Walsingham found his earlier assumptions justified, as he wrote to Leicester on 14 July 1578: 'the more I consider of the state of this country the harder I find it for the King of Spain ever to recover the full possession thereof, unless God should take away the Prince [of Orange], whose advice they cannot well spare, though their towns by the new fortifications be made impregnable' (Kervijn de Lettenhove, 10.588). Otherwise the embassy was difficult and awkward, exacerbated by the plague epidemic that killed Don John on 1 October. The military situation did stabilize when, on 1 August, Don John attacked the states' camp at Rijmenamt and was fought off, the English contingent playing a distinguished role. However, in mid-July Anjou himself arrived secretly at Mons, demanding a conclusion to his treaty with the states general. At the same time he sent agents to Elizabeth offering to place himself at her disposal and confirming his desire to marry her.

Walsingham had found the states unwilling to treat with Don John and equally unwilling to abandon the treaty with Anjou. This was signed on 28 August, though in practice it meant little. He and Cobham entered a formal protest, but it was difficult to sustain given Elizabeth's reception of Anjou's envoys. However, they finally persuaded the states to send an embassy to Don John, which they and Pomponne de Bellièvre, whom Henri had sent to impede the Anjou enterprise, accompanied. On 26 August Walsingham had a personal interview with Don John at his headquarters in the village of Perwez near Louvain. Don John refused to negotiate on the terms the states offered, but then several days later (1 September) announced that Philip had accepted Rudolph's mediation. On receipt of this news Elizabeth gave Walsingham and Cobham leave to retire, which they did on 27 September, arriving at Richmond Palace on 7 October.

Walsingham returned deeply frustrated by what he regarded as Elizabeth's failure to seize the opportunity. His own assessment of the situation, which he had argued since the spring, was that the queen should pre-empt Anjou by making a firmer financial and military commitment. When taken with his praise for Orange—he described him to Leicester on 6 July as 'the rarest man in Christendom'—it made him the target of criticism (possibly from the French) that he and Orange were conspiring to bounce Elizabeth into taking on the protectorate of the Netherlands. She in turn had made things more difficult for him by negotiating with Anjou directly. How much Walsingham knew about her revival of the marriage before he left for the Netherlands is unclear, but he was certainly informed of it by Leicester at the end of July. Leicester also warned him not to let himself be identified as an open opponent of the marriage. He answered with his often quoted observation that he understood why Anjou would wish to marry Elizabeth, 'being as she is the best marriage in her parish', but he also found the marriage difficult to square with Anjou's place in the French succession, for Henri had publicly admitted earlier in the year that he and his wife would have no children (BL, Cotton MS Galba C. vi, fol. 94r).

The acceptance by the states general of the imperial mediation, which resulted in the Cologne conference in summer 1579, brought Anjou's enterprise to a halt, much to his frustration. Before Walsingham left the Netherlands, Elizabeth had returned Anjou's agents with a reiteration of her long-established requirement that a personal and informal interview—so that they could assess their mutual compatibility—was essential if the marriage negotiations were to proceed. During the summer there had been much perplexity in England about both Anjou's motives in proposing marriage and Elizabeth's seriousness in entertaining his offers. Leicester assumed her motive was to divert him from the Netherlands, but did not see why he would surrender his ambitions there for something so uncertain. Burghley was worried that a rebuff over the marriage would simply drive Anjou into the arms of Spain. Sussex was the only privy councillor to see the marriage in a positive light, arguing that Henri would not abandon his brother and therefore Anjou was a force to be reckoned with—and that consequently the marriage would make Elizabeth the arbiter of Europe. Walsingham stuck to his assessment that the marriage was ultimately impossible and therefore Elizabeth should not waste her time on it. He wrote to Hatton on 9 October 1578, 'I would to God her Majesty would forbear the entertaining any longer the marriage matter. No one thing has procured her so much hatred abroad as these wooing matters, for that it is conceived she dallieth therein' (H. Nicolas, *Memoirs of the Life and Times of Sir Christopher Hatton*, 1847, 94).

Anjou did not accept Elizabeth's invitation. Instead he sent his *maître d'hôtel*, Jean de Simier, baron de St Marc, to negotiate a marriage treaty, despite warnings relayed by Walsingham in November that Elizabeth would not discuss a treaty before the interview. Nevertheless Simier arrived on 6 January 1579 and Elizabeth commissioned Walsingham, together with Burghley, Leicester, and Sussex to treat with him. Simier demanded to negotiate on the basis of the French articles of 1571, only to be told again that the interview must come first. At the end of March Anjou informed Simier that he would come in advance of a treaty, and in turn Elizabeth ordered the English commissioners to discuss the terms. It soon became clear that the English were not prepared to accept the 1571 articles, while the all important religious conditions were held over for discussion at the interview. At the end of April, according to the Spanish ambassador, Bernardino de Mendoza (who was well informed if obviously hostile to Anjou's Netherlands ambitions), Elizabeth asked her privy councillors for an individual written assessment of the marriage. This is the best explanation (as Read, alone of those who have written on the subject, has observed) for the large number of personal memoranda. They survive from Burghley, Sussex, Mildmay, and Wilson, as well as Walsingham (printed in Read, *Walsingham*, 2.14–18). Only Hatton and Leicester are missing, though Sidney's famous letter to the queen may have been written on his uncle's behalf.

Once again the most outspoken supporter of the marriage was Sussex, who saw it as a diplomatic masterstroke. This provoked a violent reaction from Mildmay. By contrast the difference between the views of Burghley and Walsingham was much narrower. They surveyed many of the same points, both positive and negative, and expressed concern (as did Wilson) that if Anjou were rebuffed over the marriage he would turn to Spain. What tipped Burghley into support was his concern that the marriage was the final chance for an heir of Elizabeth's body, while Walsingham (along with Davison in private correspondence) was both sceptical that she would conceive (she was then forty-six) and worried that she might damage her health as a result. More fundamentally Walsingham continued to argue that Anjou's place in the French succession made the marriage impossible, and his residual suspicion of the Valois caused him to doubt Anjou's sincerity: he considered the wooing of Elizabeth simply a ploy to encourage a counter-offer from Spain.

Whatever their individual opinions the English still had no intention of agreeing a treaty in advance of the interview, which was never certain until Anjou actually arrived on 17 August 1579. His visit coincided with two of a series of external events that reshaped the context of the marriage negotiations over the following years. The first was the landing of James fitz Maurice Fitzgerald in Ireland on

18 July, the second the arrival of Esmé Stewart, sixth seigneur d'Aubigny, at Leith on 8 September. Although fitz Maurice was killed shortly afterwards, his very arrival was evidence of Spanish hostility and made good relations with France all the more important. It also inspired the rebellion of Gerald fitz James Fitzgerald, fourteenth earl of Desmond, in October, which crippled Elizabeth financially until 1583. Aubigny's motive for venturing to Scotland was actually the private one of securing his rights to the Lennox inheritance, but he was seen (not least by Walsingham) as an agent of the house of Guise, and this strengthened English suspicion of France.

Anjou's interview lasted almost a fortnight (17 to 28 August 1579). He spent the whole time privately with Elizabeth at Greenwich Palace, and what transpired there remains as much a mystery as it was to contemporaries, except that they both expressed public satisfaction with each other's company. In late September Elizabeth took a short progress into Essex, making much of Simier and Mauvissière, but in no hurry to proceed to a treaty. Only after hectoring from Simier did she summon the privy council to discuss the terms. On 6 October twelve privy councillors met: the majority rejected the marriage outright, and the four in favour (Sussex, Burghley, Wilson, and Henry Carey, first Baron Hunsdon) were not enthusiastic. It took further badgering from Simier for Elizabeth to commission a group of privy councillors to provide him with draft articles in late November. The religious conditions remained unresolved, and the final treaty was to be concluded by a formal embassy from France when Elizabeth summoned it.

Although Walsingham was in attendance during the Essex progress, 4 October was the date of his last recorded presence on the privy council until 24 December, with the exception of 9 November. He thus missed the October debates, and there is conflicting evidence as to whether he was included in the commission that drafted the articles for Simier. The precise cause of his absence remains unclear. There are references in correspondence of late November to improvements in his health, which would suggest that it was another urinary attack. Mendoza, however, reported on 16 October that Elizabeth, greatly irritated with those who opposed the marriage, had told Walsingham 'begone and that the only thing he was good for was a protector of heretics', although he was not sure whether this was all artifice (Hume, 1568–79, art. 607). On 30 December, just after his return, Walsingham informed the new ambassador in France, Sir Henry Brooke (known as Cobham), that he had 'no access of speech to her majesty since my repair to court, being still entertained as a man not thoroughly restored to her favour' (*CSP for.*, 1579–80, art. 112). Yet, when reporting Walsingham's return and the queen's moderating her 'très mauvayse chère' against him and Leicester to Henri on 16 January 1580, Mauvissière referred to his having been 'absent y mallade' (PRO, PRO 31/3/28, fols. 9v, 10v).

Walsingham's absence has inspired speculation about his involvement in John Stubbe's pamphlet *The discoverie of a gaping gulf*, which appeared in September 1579. However, no direct connection has ever been discovered. Although many of Stubbe's arguments against the marriage were little different than those advanced by Walsingham earlier, he stridently demanded that the privy council prevent a silly woman making a fool of herself. Elizabeth's hostility to controversy in print was well established, and it is difficult to believe that someone in Walsingham's position did not appreciate that it would only make things worse.

From the end of December 1579 Walsingham was again in regular attendance at court, but it is not known what influence he may have had on Elizabeth's informing Anjou in January 1580 that no religious concessions would be granted. However, the spring of 1580 saw the marriage negotiations transformed by yet further events. The interview had coincided with the failure of the Cologne conference and subsequently Anjou's Netherlands ambitions had revived. By the beginning of 1580 Orange had made clear his intention of repudiating Philip's sovereignty and nominating Anjou instead. The Dutch debate over Anjou had strong similarities to the English one, and Orange deployed the marriage to Elizabeth as evidence of Anjou's bona fides. It was now vital for Anjou to avoid a rebuff in England, even if the continued negotiations were only a pretence. On 31 January the cardinal–king Enriques of Portugal died and Catherine's bizarre yet obsessive interest in the Portuguese succession raised the possibility of a Franco-Spanish contest over Portugal. Lastly, the spring of 1580 saw the outbreak of the seventh War of Religion. Anjou acted as mediator, while simultaneously negotiating with the Dutch, on the assumption that Henri would reward his efforts by supporting his enterprise. The treaty of Plessis-lès-Tours (19 September 1580), in which the states recognized Anjou as their *seigneur*, was contingent on Henri's commitment, but despite Anjou's lies about having the support of his brother, this was not forthcoming. Nevertheless, in spring 1581 Anjou proceeded with his Netherlands enterprise, focusing in the summer on the relief of Cambrai.

For all Anjou's protestations of allegiance Elizabeth had little control over his actions, except to refuse to proceed with the marriage treaty until peace was made in France. However, in September 1580 the simultaneous return of Francis Drake from the circumnavigation voyage and the landing of the Italian–Spanish relief force in Ireland threatened a new confrontation with Spain. During autumn 1580 Henry Cobham was instructed to hint discreetly at an alliance over Portugal. Henri responded on 28 February 1581 by commissioning a large embassy to conclude the marriage treaty. Henri's motives are still debated: whether he deliberately made marriage to Elizabeth the price of assistance to his brother, counting on her refusal; whether he believed the marriage was necessary to tie the queen into an alliance against Spain; whether the revival of the marriage was yet another attempt to divert his brother from the Netherlands; or (on Catherine de' Medici's part) whether it was intended to divert Anjou from a marriage to Catherine of Bourbon, which she opposed. The spring of 1581 also saw the final session of

the parliament of 1572, which tightened substantially the laws against recusancy, possibly as a signal to France that no concessions would be made on religion. Walsingham played his usual minor role, relaying his jaundiced view of parliament to Henry Hastings, third earl of Huntingdon: 'otherwise there hath no past any matter of importance, so careful have men been to prefer their private causes before the common benefits of the state' (Hunt. L., Hastings MS 13062).

The French commissioners arrived on 16 May, Anjou seeking to cross as well but being driven back by bad weather. Walsingham was sceptical about their chances: 'the issue of great causes is uncertain … yet if I can judge anything and others that have some cause to know her majesty inwards, I see no reason to fear the matter' (Hunt. L., Hastings MS 13066). He was ill at the time of their initial reception, but at a meeting on the 30th he informed the French commission that parliament had expressed considerable opposition to the match and that as a result Elizabeth intended to settle the controversial aspects directly with Anjou. He then hinted that she would be prepared to consider an alliance, only to find that the commissioners were not empowered to negotiate anything other than the marriage. On 11 June a marriage treaty was signed, but the religious clauses and other contentious issues were reserved for settlement between Elizabeth and Anjou.

The embassy of 1581 Elizabeth had kept Walsingham at a remove from her communications with Anjou during 1580. He in turn became increasingly fixated by the rise of Aubigny in Scotland. He was convinced from the start that Aubigny was a Guise agent, and by spring 1580 was growing frustrated at the failure to find evidence. For this Cobham was blamed, the source of some hostility to Walsingham thereafter. Walsingham was also certain that Aubigny (first earl of Lennox from March 1580) was intending the overthrow of Morton. However, here he and Burghley made a mistake by seeing Lennox as the sole issue, which could be countered by his removal or (on Morton's advice) by buying James VI with a large subsidy. What they failed to appreciate was the depth of hostility to Morton among James's protestant councillors, the treasurer, William Ruthven, fourth Baron Ruthven, in particular. Morton was arrested on 5 December 1580 on trumped-up charges of complicity in the murder of Henry Stewart, Lord Darnley.

The issue was now what could be done to save him. Walsingham, whose loyalty to Morton was unquestioned, argued for military intervention, if necessary. However, his cousin Thomas *Randolph (1525/6–1590) (whom he always referred to as uncle), who was sent to Scotland in early 1581 to assess the situation, undermined the case for intervention by reporting that there was no internal support for Morton's restoration. Elizabeth backed away from formal intervention on an apparent verbal promise from James that he would spare Morton's life. To this Walsingham gave a typical response in a letter to Huntingdon of 5 April: 'by which account I see that Scotland is clean lost, and a great gate opened thereby for the loss of Ireland' (Hunt. L., Hastings MS 13067). James's promise was broken by Morton's execution on 2 June 1581, and it opened a new chapter in Anglo-Scots relations, dominated by Elizabeth's distrust of the adolescent king. Although Mendoza is the source for her denunciation of James as 'that false Scots urchin', Walsingham recalled during his 1583 embassy to Scotland 'the impression I have always found that your majesty had of the disposition of this young king … as your majesty has always doubted, so I think you shall find him most ungrateful' (Hume, 1580–86, 207; *CSP Scot.*, 1581–3, 611).

On 22 July, however, Walsingham was sent on an embassy to France that lasted until 21 September. Just after the marriage treaty was signed Henri had informed Elizabeth that he was prepared to consider a full alliance after the marriage was concluded, yet at the same time it was obvious that he was trying to obstruct his brother's Netherlands plans. The basic purpose of the embassy was to discover what he was up to and to keep Anjou's enterprise alive. The complex instructions Walsingham was given reflect the genuine English puzzlement over Henri's intentions. Walsingham tried to escape the embassy, fearing a repetition of 1578, but without success. There was, however, a challenge for him. During the spring he had become increasingly interested in plans for a naval expedition to aid the Portuguese pretender, Dom Antonio, and invested in it himself. In May Dom Antonio had sent an envoy to Elizabeth, who claimed that Henri had promised him assistance. When Elizabeth offered to share the costs the French king replied that he would do so only after the marriage. Walsingham observed to Huntingdon on 29 June, 'yt is to be gathered by this could [cold] answer that yf the mariadge take not place, the portugalls can look for no relefe out of France and that the French King will come some other coorse' (Hunt. L., Hastings MS 13070).

Once in France, Walsingham went first to see Anjou at his crowded headquarters at La Fère-en-Tardenois on 3 August 1581, where they had to retire to the latter's bedchamber to escape the noise of the courtiers in the adjoining apartment. Here he expressed Elizabeth's concern that the marriage would commit her to an open war with Spain, though she was willing to ally with France and would aid him discreetly. Anjou replied that his brother would do nothing until the marriage was concluded. However, he responded to her promise of assistance by requesting a loan to keep his forces in the field. Walsingham thought this a good way of retaining control of him. Shortly afterwards Walsingham encountered Catherine, who had come to dissuade Anjou from the enterprise and to agree to a Spanish marriage, but he apparently managed to persuade her to support an English alliance. He then went to Paris, where he had his first audience with Henri on 10 August. He found him difficult to pin down, but concluded that without the marriage Henri would not agree to an alliance. On 24 August Elizabeth followed Walsingham's advice by agreeing quickly to the loan

Anjou had requested. However, at the same time Walsingham discovered that his negotiations with Henri were being sabotaged by reports from Mauvissière and Anjou's agent Pierre Clausse, sieur de Marchaumont, that Elizabeth would ultimately proceed with the marriage. With this stalemate his embassy came to an end.

Walsingham's expenses had come to £625 19s. 7d., and he returned frustrated that yet another opportunity had been let slip. He blamed Elizabeth for failing to clarify her position over the marriage, for had she been amenable to it the alliance posed no problem. Instead she had given the impression that her only concern was to avoid expenditure, which, using one of the medical metaphors he regularly employed, he argued was impossible: 'common experience teacheth that it is hard in a politique body to prevent any mischief without charges as in a natural body diseased to cure the same without pain' (Read, *Walsingham*, 2.87). On his return he revised his old memorandum of 1571 under a new title, 'Whether it be good for her majesty to assist the duke of Anjou in his enterprise of the Low Countries'. Many of the arguments of the earlier memorandum reappeared. Spain was clearly the chief enemy and the Netherlands should not be allowed to return to Philip's allegiance. France was less of a threat, thanks to the Huguenots, and the danger of French annexation of the Netherlands was a hypothetical risk that could be run. With regard to Anjou himself, the old fear that if rebuffed he might turn to Spain remained and therefore his enterprise had to be encouraged and supported. However, the most radical section was a new one that dealt with finance. Walsingham considered that parliament should be acquainted with the reasons for aiding Anjou to pre-empt criticism, and if an open war with Spain followed then 'some portion of the Bishops' temporalities may by sale be converted into fee farms' (BL, Harley MS 1582, fols. 38r–41r; Read, *Walsingham*, 2.94). The discreet subsidizing of Anjou was in fact the policy Elizabeth followed in 1582.

Principal secretary, 1581–1583 On 30 July 1581, just after Walsingham arrived in France, Leicester relayed a message from the queen: 'she willed me to say thus unto you that as she doth know her Moor cannot change his colour, no more shall it be found that she will alter her old wont, which is always to hold both eyes and ears open for her good servants' (Read, *Walsingham*, 2.60). In the letter he wrote to Elizabeth on 2 September, criticizing her for failing to clarify her position, Walsingham replied with laboured jocularity: 'the lawes of Ethiopia my native soyle are verie severe against those that condemne a person unheard … I should then be worthie to receave the most sharpe punishment that either the Ethiopian severitie or Dracus lawes can yeilde' (BL, Harley MS 6265, fols. 71v–72r). Although—as with all the nicknames that Elizabeth used—the precise origin of 'the Moor' is unknown, it marks Walsingham's admission into what was the true élite of Elizabethan England, the queen's intimates.

Owing to the loss of his private papers Walsingham's personal life at this point is difficult to detail. He certainly maintained a substantial establishment. From the 1560s his London residence was in Seething Lane, a house that survived the great fire of 1666. The Victorian office block on the site still bears his name. In February 1579 Elizabeth granted him the lease of the manor of Barn Elms in Surrey, close to Richmond Palace, his brother-in-law Beale's house at Barnes, and Dr John Dee's at Mortlake. This became his principal suburban residence. He also had a country house at Odiham in Hampshire. It was to Odiham that he invited Leicester and Warwick for 'a Friday night's drinking after the ancient and catholic order' on their return from a journey to Wilton in Wiltshire in November 1578 (Cottrell Dormer MS, MSS letters, 1570–1630, art. 25).

None of Walsingham's houses appears to have been architecturally prepossessing, and nothing remains of any of them. Of all the Elizabethan grandees he seems to have been least interested in creating or leaving behind him a major architectural monument. He was, however, a notable patron of learning, upwards of forty books being dedicated to him, chiefly on religion, philosophy, and exploration. Edmund Spenser wrote a dedicatory sonnet to him in his *The Faerie Queene* (1590), calling him

the great Mecenas of this age,
As wel to al the civil artes professe
As those that are inspird with Martial rage.
(*The Faerie Queene*, ed. A. C. Hamilton, 1989, 742)

Walsingham's clearest personal tastes were for gardening (an interest that he shared with Leicester and Burghley), falconry, and music. The composer John Cosyn dedicated his work *Musike of six, and five partes* to him in 1585. Walsingham also employed the young lutenist and composer Daniel Bacheler, whose apprenticeship was signed over to him in June 1586 and who composed various works for mixed instruments for him.

The most famous of all the books dedicated to Walsingham was the first (1589) edition of Richard Hakluyt's *The principall navigations*. His interest in exploration may have been a product of his early association with the Russia Company. He supported Martin Frobisher's three attempts to unlock the north-west passage (1576, 1577, 1578) but became more cautious with each venture. If he remained fascinated with the north-west passage it was for strategic rather than commercial reasons, for he hoped it would be a way into the Pacific free from the Spanish. Dee's journal records a conference in 1583 with Adrian Gilbert, John Davis, and Walsingham over the significance of the north-west passage. Walsingham later sponsored Davis's heroic series of voyages deep into the Arctic in 1585, 1586, and 1587.

Walsingham's main rewards from the queen were a series of export licences for cloth (and occasionally wool), beginning in 1574. He received one other office in these years, the honorific dignity of the chancellorship of the Order of the Garter (22 April 1578). At the same time, his stature was also reflected in expanding local influence. He was named of the quorum of the peace for Hampshire about 1573, added to the quorum for Hertfordshire about 1574, promoted *custos rotulorum* for Hampshire in 1577,

and was of the quorum for Surrey by 1579. More significant was the fact that boroughs felt it important to gain his goodwill. Colchester appointed him recorder in 1578, and he was high steward of Salisbury (1581), Ipswich (1581), Winchester (1582), Kingston upon Hull (1583), and King's Lynn (1588).

After the death of Sir Thomas Wilson on 20 May 1581 no second secretary was appointed until 1586, possibly for financial reasons. As a result Walsingham's own informal secretariat expanded dramatically and was at the centre of many of his subsequent activities. He relied heavily on Beale, who, although clerk of the privy council, deputized for him during his embassy in Scotland in 1583. His immediate team of secretaries included Francis Mylles, who had been in his service since 1566, Laurence Thomson, who entered his service about 1575 and served as his secretary in the Netherlands embassy of 1578, and lastly Nicholas Faunt, who was in his service from 1578. They were later joined by Lake and possibly Thomas Edmondes. When Walsingham became secretary there was an established coterie of diplomatic agents, including Killigrew and Randolph, but however personally close, they were of an older generation. The first of his own protégés to follow a diplomatic career was Davison, who may have been with him in the French embassy of 1571–3. In the 1580s he relied increasingly heavily on more shadowy figures: Edward Burnham, Francis Needham, and Walter Williams. Burnham, Williams, and his Italian agent, Manucci, were all with him in the Netherlands in 1578. It was this rather loose organization that Beale later criticized (Read, *Walsingham*, 1.427).

On 21 September 1583, while Walsingham was in Scotland, his surviving daughter Frances married Sidney, and as part of the marriage arrangement they lived in Walsingham's home. Walsingham had known Sidney since 1572, and in political terms the marriage appeared to reflect the ties between him and Sidney's uncle Leicester. Yet Sidney's father, Sir Henry Sidney, had been unhappy, relating in a famous prolix account of his life that he lacked the estate to endow his son sufficiently, while Elizabeth was annoyed at not being consulted first. However, Walsingham cherished Sidney's intelligence, and Sidney's steady emergence as a political figure in 1584–5 took place under his tutelage as well as Leicester's. By spring 1585 he too was deputizing for Walsingham during his repeated illnesses.

Walsingham's religious allegiances, on the other hand, are puzzling. As early as 1574 la Motte-Fénélon labelled him a puritan, by which he meant an ally of the Huguenots; the term was also used by the queen of Scots to identify her enemies and by Spanish agents to identify Orange's sympathizers. There is evidence of Walsingham's assistance to individual puritan divines, and he left £100 in his will for a lectureship for John Reynolds at Oxford. However, John Foxe is the only prominent author found in the twenty or so books on religious subjects dedicated to him. The only other noteworthy feature is the dedication to him of a number of polemics against the

Jesuits during the early 1580s, which may reflect active encouragement on his part.

Read was struck 'by the almost complete absence of any evidence revealing a disposition on his part to support the puritan movement in his conduct of office' (Read, *Walsingham*, 2.262). While Davison, Beale, Tomson, and Faunt, and others close to him, were famously outspoken on the subject, his own caution and discretion are summed up by his warning to Davison: 'I would have all reformations done by public authority. It were very dangerous that every private man's zeal should carry sufficient authority of reforming things amiss' (ibid., 265). On the other hand his proposals for the sale of temporalities in 1581 and his disparaging description of the bishops as 'assez refroidis' to a Genevan envoy seeking a loan in 1582–3 are revealing. This hostile attitude to the episcopate helped to shape the defence of the church that John Whitgift mounted after his appointment as archbishop of Canterbury in 1583.

The queen of Scots, 1581–1584 Walsingham's embassy of 1581 had an unexpected side effect. In Paris he had learned of 'the association' from Archibald Douglas, a Church of Scotland minister accused of involvement in Darnley's murder who had fled to France after Morton's fall. This was the response of the queen of Scots to the new situation in Scotland, a plan for restoring relations with her son, in which she would recognize him as king if he revoked her demission (abdication) of 1566 and ruled jointly with her. Walsingham also learned of the mission of the Jesuit William Crichton (or Creighton) to Scotland, though not its full import. It was this conjuncture that inaugurated his career as a spymaster.

Various English attempts to persuade Mary to clarify her relations to her son met with hints that she knew more than she was prepared to let on and that she had extensive contacts in Scotland. Her attitude confirmed Elizabeth's and Walsingham's suspicions of James and underlined the pressing need to separate him from Lennox. Lennox was finally excluded from James's presence on 23 August 1582, by what is known as the Ruthven raid, in which supporters of Ruthven (now first earl of Gowrie) kidnapped the king. After Morton's execution his nephew Archibald Douglas, eighth earl of Angus and later sixth earl of Morton, and a few supporters had gone into exile in England, and Walsingham has been widely suspected of instigating this conspiracy through them. However, the lack of control the English had over subsequent events in Scotland suggests the opposite. The cause lay in Lennox's attempts to revive the episcopate, which had alarmed both the kirk and the protestant nobility.

The Ruthven raid provided Walsingham with two key pieces of intelligence: evidence of discussions about the Association between agents of Mary and James in Paris in autumn 1581 (with Henri's apparent approval), and evidence that Mauvissière had been informing Lennox about English contacts with Angus and with Lennox's enemies in Scotland. The latter Mauvissière had obtained from Archibald Douglas, who had followed Walsingham to England and cultivated Angus. Mauvissière had managed to turn Douglas by offering Mary's help in obtaining a pardon for him for his role in Darnley's murder. The full details are difficult to establish because there are large gaps in Mauvissière's surviving correspondence after June 1581.

This evidence of French duplicity, despite Elizabeth's assistance to Anjou, led Walsingham to treat Mauvissière as a legitimate target. He was able to turn Douglas into a double agent (apparently by threats to send him back to Scotland to stand trial) and in spring 1583 gained the services of the mysterious Henry Fagot, a member of Mauvissière's household. By the end of 1583 he had also suborned one of Mauvissière's secretaries, who provided him with drafts of much of the French ambassador's correspondence. In 1991 and 1999 John Bossy published two detailed accounts of this intelligence operation in which he argued that Fagot was none other than Giordano Bruno, and showed how much can be reconstructed from Walsingham's intelligence work from the elliptical, unsigned, and encrypted records that remain. There were further ramifications. Because Mauvissière acted as agent for the French crown with the imprisoned Mary, Walsingham was able to tap into her correspondence as well. From Fagot, and possibly others, he also learned in early 1583 that Lord Henry Howard was an informant of Mendoza. This is confirmed by Mendoza's own reports. Following a row with Elizabeth in September 1580 over Drake's circumnavigation voyage Mendoza visited the court on only one further occasion, and all his information on English court politics came from Howard.

Although this intelligence operation was to yield major rewards over time, the immediate situation in Scotland deteriorated. Lennox was forced to retire to France at the end of 1582 (he died there shortly afterwards), but James openly resented the Ruthvenites and the question of his understanding with his mother remained. To solidify their position the Ruthvenites turned to England for help, not simply for money, but to pacify James by granting him the English lands of his grandfather Matthew Stewart, thirteenth earl of Lennox. There was, however, a rival claimant, his cousin Lady Arabella Stuart, whose interests Elizabeth was not prepared to sacrifice. Elizabeth's attitude alienated Colonel William Stewart, who engineered James's escape from the Ruthvenites on 29 June 1583.

The dismissal of Gowrie and the restoration of Lennox's former ally, James Stewart, earl of Arran, soon followed James's escape. The resurrection of Arran was the cause of what became Walsingham's final embassy, his mission to James from 13 August to 21 October 1583. Because of his poor health he travelled slowly. Prior to his audience with the king at Perth on 8 September, he decided to take a high line: 'the best way to make them seek her majesty is make little account of them' (Read, *Walsingham*, 2.211). He lectured James on his choice of privy councillors, and when James responded that he was an absolute king, he told him he was too young to make serious political decisions. At a second interview he returned to the theme, criticizing James for the destruction of 'so well-deserving a servant' as Morton, and refusing to meet Arran (ibid., 2.217).

Although he considered James's hostile response proof that he was operating on his mother's advice Walsingham very quickly appreciated that he had perhaps overreached himself, for he had only exacerbated the king's resentment. He had also miscalculated about Arran, who, if mercenary, was a committed protestant. Arran's response was what Walsingham soon dubbed the 'by-course'. This was a complaint to Elizabeth through Hunsdon, the governor of Berwick, that Walsingham had slandered James. James was not in league with his mother and wished friendship with Elizabeth, but he also intended to discipline the protestant nobles and the kirk. Walsingham considered the by-course a device of Mary's that Hunsdon was too naïve and ambitious to appreciate, and Elizabeth remained too suspicious of James to be convinced by it.

About the time that Walsingham left for Scotland, the privy council caught the first glimpses of what became known as the Throckmorton plot, in particular the visit to England of the Roman Catholic exile Charles Paget in August and September to canvass support among the nobility for a landing by the duc de Guise on the south coast. This was a revision of an earlier plan to free Mary discussed between Crichton and Lennox at Dalkeith in March 1582. The plot was broken on 4 November 1583 with the arrest of Francis Throckmorton, who had acted as a confidential messenger between Mary, Mauvissière, and Mendoza. Papers found in Throckmorton's possession and his own confession (possibly under torture) in December incriminated Lord Henry Howard, Philip Howard, thirteenth earl of Arundel, and Henry Percy, eighth earl of Northumberland, all of whom were arrested, while Thomas Paget, third Baron Paget, and Charles Arundell fled to France.

There are still several unexplained aspects to this affair. Throckmorton, who was the crown's only witness, was tried on 20 May 1584 and executed on 10 July, yet no proceedings were undertaken against the peers, who simply remained in prison. Mendoza was expelled in January 1584 for refusing to hand over papers Throckmorton had left with him, and diplomatic contact between England and Spain came to an end. Yet no action was taken against Mauvissière, who was far more deeply involved. John Bossy has supplied the reason here. Walsingham was tapping Mauvissière's correspondence through his suborned secretary and had no desire to see him depart. Lastly, there was Walsingham's own role. His agents, Fagot among them, provided the information on the comings and goings in Mauvissière's residence, yet Walsingham did not return from Scotland until a fortnight before Throckmorton's arrest. Burghley in fact supervised much of the investigation.

The most important consequence of the plot was its apparent confirmation of an 'enterprise of England' to replace Elizabeth with the queen of Scots, in which Spain, the papacy, the Jesuits, the Guise, some Scots, and possibly Mary herself were involved. The enterprise provides the leitmotif for English policy in 1584–5. In the immediate term it caused an invasion panic in January 1584, which a month later inspired a naval treaty with Orange, the first of the many steps that drew England and the United Provinces closer together and lay behind the Dutch participation in the defeat of the Spanish Armada. Walsingham, who was ill in bed between 8 February and 10 March 1584, drafted the treaty.

France, Scotland, and the Netherlands, 1584–1585 The wider diplomatic response to the Throckmorton plot dogged Walsingham for the next four years. This was his awkward relationship to the most controversial of Elizabethan ambassadors, Sir Edward Stafford, who was appointed to succeed Cobham as resident at the French court on 15 September 1583. Stafford's French was fluent, he was socially at ease in the French court, and he had been Elizabeth's preferred confidential agent with Anjou since 1578. He was also married to Leicester's former mistress, Douglas Sheffield, dowager Baroness Sheffield. He was not Walsingham's first choice, but as so often happened the others on the shortlist were not available. Walsingham considered his doubts about the new ambassador confirmed when in December Stafford and his wife entertained her cousin Arundell at the Paris embassy, claiming to be ignorant of his reasons for leaving England. During 1584 relations between the two rapidly descended into mutual bickering, Walsingham accusing Stafford of wasting money and laziness, Stafford complaining at Walsingham's constant carping and criticism. There was also an issue of substance. Walsingham never lost his residual suspicion of the French royal family, while Stafford appreciated that however bizarrely Henri behaved he was determined to maintain his independence of action and was no pawn of the Guise.

The situation in 1584 has supplied considerable evidence for students of Elizabethan faction. Even before he left for France, Stafford had ostentatiously sought Burghley's protection, and thereafter sent him copies of his reports to Walsingham. At the same time Hunsdon turned to Burghley for support for the by-course in Scotland. Yet for all Burghley's encouragement of their confidence, there is no evidence that the lord treasurer was actively pursuing different policies from Walsingham's. It is dangerous to argue from archival survival, but a secret correspondence between Stafford and Burghley does not survive, and apart from complaints about Walsingham, the copies of his reports that Stafford sent to Burghley contain no additional material. By the same token, Walsingham was fully aware of Hunsdon's progress with the by-course. The explanation may be that Burghley, aware of Walsingham's temper, was simply keeping the options open.

At the beginning of 1584 Scotland posed the more immediate problems. In spite of Walsingham's warnings, at the end of 1583 James had the Ruthven raid condemned as treason by a convention of estates, and those involved were ordered into exile. In response Andrew Melville denounced James as a tyrant and Gowrie and his allies mounted a hasty rebellion in spring 1584. Gowrie was captured immediately and executed on 3 May. Angus and John Erskine, second earl of Mar, briefly occupied Stirling Castle (17 to 23 April) and then fled to England followed by a substantial body of ministers. All later acknowledged the generous treatment they received from Walsingham. At the time James claimed that the English had instigated the rebellion, but there is no reliable evidence for more than vague foreknowledge. There was, however, a rapid response in which Davison was sent to aid the lords in their effort to remove Arran, with instructions drafted by both Walsingham and Burghley. However, they had abandoned Stirling before he reached Berwick. It is revealing of the depth of Elizabeth's distrust of James that unusually for her she defended the exiled lords against his accusations of treason.

Given this stalemate the by-course revived, with Arran now offering to restore amity between Elizabeth and James. Elizabeth responded with charges that James had wronged her by making the Association with his mother and demanded that to prove his bona fides he should reveal all he knew of the plots against her. This Arran agreed to do in a personal meeting with Hunsdon, but Walsingham confided to the exiled Scottish minister James Carmichael that 'he lukit that his [Hunsdon's] injunctions being so strait, and not satisfied fullie, sould compt himself to haif bin trompit with fair words in tyme bypast' ('Letters and papers of Mr. James Carmichael', 415). The meeting took place at Foulden church near Berwick on 13 August, and was reported by Hunsdon to Walsingham the next day. Arran promised that Patrick Gray, master of Gray, whom he intended to send to England, would reveal all to Elizabeth. The queen was underwhelmed.

Concerning Mary herself there was the practical issue that she had to be removed from Shrewsbury's custody after he had been compromised by his wife's denunciations of his relations with her. At the beginning of the year Elizabeth had intimated that in view of the revelations of the Throckmorton plot and events in Scotland she was unwilling to discuss Mary's release any longer. Mary had responded by claiming that she still wished to negotiate, and in May she was asked to demonstrate her goodwill by mediating the return of the exiled lords to Scotland. Mary, however, demanded her release first. It was in these circumstances that she was moved from Sheffield in September, still claiming that James had agreed to be ordered by her in all things.

In summer 1584 greater matters intruded with the death of Anjou on 10 June, and then the assassination of Orange on 10 July. Their deaths initiated both the crisis over the fate of the Dutch revolt and the even greater crisis over the French succession. In the face of the bold exploitation of Dutch political disunion by Alessandro Farnese, duke of Parma, in 1583, during the spring of 1584 Elizabeth had been encouraging Henri to back his brother more effectively. What he would do after his brother's death was now the question, but Henri was more than usually elusive and more concerned with reaching an agreement with Henri of Navarre that would pre-empt Catholic opposition to a protestant succession. Yet at the same time he sent mixed signals to the Dutch over whether he would support them in the crisis surrounding the siege of Antwerp. Finally in August he sent Roch de Sorbies, seigneur de Pruneaux, Anjou's former agent, to The Hague to announce that he would accept an offer of sovereignty. Stafford had great difficulty in supplying solid information during these months, which merely increased Walsingham's doubts about him, especially as he himself was reading Mauvissière's mail.

Walsingham was convinced that Elizabeth could not abandon the Dutch whatever happened, a case he argued in a memorandum on 14 July: 'Points to be considered touching the peril that may grow by Spain when he shall have full possession of Holland and Zealand' (BL, Cotton MS Galba C. viii, fols. 94r–95r). In August the states of Holland and Zealand, who were unhappy about accepting the French king, appealed to Elizabeth to take them under protection, but her preference was for a joint intervention with Henri. Her response encouraged a majority of the provinces to accept the French offer, a process concluded by early October.

At the same time Walsingham scored another major intelligence coup. On 23 August Crichton was caught by a routine Dutch naval patrol on a voyage to Scotland, carrying various papers in English and Italian about a great enterprise against England. The local Dutch commander sent these to Walsingham, and he immediately responded by sending a warship to bring Crichton to England. By 14 September he was lodged in Walsingham's house. What Crichton possessed was a copy of the old Lennox invasion plan of 1582, which Walsingham immediately recognized lay behind the Charles Paget–Throckmorton scheme of 1583. Walsingham also learned that 'the Scottish Queen was made privy', but that 'the French king hath no way been a party in them, which ought to move the queen the rather to accompt of his friendship'. Last, and most important, according to Crichton, the enterprise was merely suspended, and would be put in execution 'when the king of Spain shalbe ridde of his low cuntryes trowbles' (State Papers and Letters of Sir Ralph Sadler, 2.400–01; PRO, SP 12/173/13; BL, Cotton MS Caligula C. ix, fol. 133r).

Crichton's revelations lay behind two major decisions taken in mid-October. A full-scale meeting of the privy council was held on the 10th, which agreed that Elizabeth could not afford to let the Netherlands collapse, and would need to intervene unilaterally if the French did not. This would involve making a settlement with Scotland. The other was the bond of association, signed by the privy council on 19 October. In contrast with the records of the discussion over the Netherlands, no memoranda concerning the bond have survived, nor was it mentioned in the privy council discussions of the 10th. The bond committed its signatories to defend Elizabeth's life and 'pursue, aswell by force of armes, as by all other meanes of revenge, all maner of persons, of what estate soever they shalbe … that shall attempt … the harme of Her Majesties Royall Personne'. Members swore 'to prosecute such person or persons to the death, with joint or particular forces;

and to take the uttermost revenge on them … for their utter overthrowe and extirpation', and no pretended successor by whom or for whom the queen's assassination was attempted or committed would be accepted (PRO, SP 12/174/1, fols. 4v–5r). Its origins can be found in various proposals by Burghley, some dating back to the 1560s, and in an advice to Elizabeth written by Leicester earlier in 1584. Burghley and Walsingham were responsible for drafting it, and Burghley, Walsingham, and Leicester took responsibility for its circulation.

The targets of the bond were Mary and James; ironically Mary was allowed to sign it at her own request. Its title was an equally ironic—not necessarily conscious—reference to Mary's and James's Association. Yet it quickly became superfluous, thanks to the arrival of Gray early in November. Gray was expected to conclude the by-course by revealing the plots, which he did not in fact do. But he did dissociate James from his mother, and also offered to overthrow Arran, apparently out of revenge for the execution of Gowrie, who was a relative of his. In the course of his embassy he forged social links with Leicester, Sidney (who became a personal friend), and Walsingham. Thanks to Gray a new Scottish policy was formulated in winter 1584. Once James abandoned his mother, negotiations with her ceased, and in January 1585 she was moved to Tutbury, Staffordshire, with her communications severely restricted. After John St John, second Baron St John of Bletso, escaped appointment as her governor, Sir Amias Paulet was named in April. The new relationship with James was initially more difficult. Gray brought with him his allies Sir Lewis Bellenden of Auchnoll and Sir John Maitland of Thirlestane. However, the Scottish exiles distrusted Gray, and getting James to accept their return would not be easy.

Overshadowing the Scottish situation was the Netherlands. English policy was in suspension until Henri had decided whether to accept the offer of sovereignty, and Davison was sent to The Hague in November as an observer. Walsingham, who was ill again in December 1584 and January 1585, had been sceptical all along that the French king would ever accept, but Elizabeth, now aware that Henri had no interest in joint intervention, wished to prevent the French from acting independently. The tension boiled over in a spat with Burghley, in which Walsingham initially accused him of opposing his suit for the customs farm of the outports, though later accepted his 'playne manner of proceeding' (PRO, SP 12/176/19, fol. 34r). The news that Henri had in the end rejected the Dutch offer reached England on 6 March 1585, and the response was swift. A privy council meeting was held on the 8th, and on the following day Burnham was sent to Davison with an offer of English assistance.

This offer was presented formally to the states general on 30 March, and the provinces were then consulted. By the beginning of May all except Zealand had agreed. Zealand delayed the embassy for nearly a month, and when it finally departed it had a difficult voyage and did not reach England until 23 June. The negotiation of the two treaties of Nonsuch took place over the next month and a half, conducted largely by Burghley and Walsingham on Elizabeth's behalf. The contract, as the treaties became known, was hastily drafted, and this was one cause of the Anglo-Dutch tensions of the following two years. Not the least of the reasons was that it was not the only major diplomatic issue of those months. In May Walsingham's cousin Edward *Wotton, later first Baron Wotton (1548–1628), was sent to James to negotiate a new relationship, and Walsingham's correspondence with him provides a valuable running commentary on the Nonsuch treaty.

What complicated the Scottish negotiations was Gray's decision in June to arrange Arran's assassination. This Walsingham and Leicester thought a course unduly 'bluddy … wherunto that nation is overmiche bent' (Bain, 2.648). They felt that English complicity, or even the appearance of it, would compromise Elizabeth's position with James. Instead Walsingham was prepared to accept a settlement in Scotland in which Arran was permitted to remain but watched closely by Gray and his allies, with either a tacit or an overt alliance with England. However, Gray was not so easy to control. On 22 June it was reported that there was great 'disdaining' between Arran and Gray, who was attempting to draw the king from the earl's influence while creating a league against him (CSP Scot., 1584–5, 498). Walsingham, seeing a personal victory many months in preparation now slipping away, was privately angry: 'I have bestowed a great deale of care and cost in vayne; and therefor I am now fully resolved [not] to have any further dealyng therein than as the rest of my colleags' (Bain, 2.694).

In the event, the fortuitous death in a border fracas of Francis Russell, Lord Russell, on 27 July during a day of truce attended by Arran led to the toppling of the earl's regime. Russell's death was exploited adeptly by Gray and Wotton, who claimed that Arran planned it to disrupt the amity between Elizabeth and James. By early November Angus, Mar, and the exiles were at Stirling, and Arran panicked and fled west. In spring 1586 Randolph returned to Scotland to negotiate the league with England, which was signed by Roger Manners, fourth earl of Rutland, on behalf of Elizabeth at Berwick on 2 July 1586. James was now formally allied in return for a pension of £4000, and at least a façade of a friendly government in Scotland was restored.

Henri's rejection of the Dutch offer of sovereignty was in part a response to a Guise-led revolt in France in spring 1585. In the summer, partly under pressure from his mother, he reached an agreement with the Guise, but at the price of revoking the edicts of toleration and thereby provoking Huguenot resistance, the eighth War of Religion. Navarre sought assistance from Elizabeth in June and July 1585. Much to the anger of the Huguenots the queen would provide only limited aid, given her commitments in the Netherlands, and they were encouraged to seek further help from the German protestants. At this point a significant disagreement broke out between Walsingham and Stafford. Walsingham was convinced that

Henri had finally showed his true colours and that there was now an active international Catholic league. Stafford, acutely enough, reported to Burghley on 5 July that, whatever the appearances, 'there is great heartburning and mistrust between the King and them [the Guise] which wille never be quenched' (PRO, SP 78/14/30). Walsingham was furious, insinuating, 'I should be abused and by thatt meanes abuse her majestie concerning theire procedynges', not least because it gave Elizabeth a counter to his case that Navarre needed full-scale assistance (PRO, SP 78/14/15).

The outbreak of war with Spain and final years, 1585–1590 The eighteen months from summer 1585 were probably the most dramatic of Walsingham's life, but the strains undoubtedly caused a serious deterioration of his health and helped to bring on his death. After the Nonsuch treaty was concluded Leicester departed for a holiday at Kenilworth. Walsingham was intending to join him, but cried off at the last minute owing to the bad weather, much to Leicester's disappointment: 'I am persuaded that nothing in the world would have done you more good, nor any man in England should be more welcome than yourself' (Adams, *Household Accounts*, 285, 290). He was thus in post when the news of the surrender of Antwerp was received and was able to respond quickly by sending Davison back to the Netherlands with Elizabeth's offer of increased assistance, including Leicester as commander of the English forces. However, this placed Walsingham in the middle of the tensions between Elizabeth and Leicester over the Netherlands. They continued throughout 1586, as Leicester's political and military difficulties increased. At the same time Walsingham knew Elizabeth was following another by-course, by entertaining peace feelers from Parma through Burghley.

However, what dominated 1586 was the destruction of Mary. In September 1585 the replacement of Mauvissière by Guillaume de l'Aubespeine, baron de Châteauneuf, caused Walsingham further to restrict Mary's communications by ordering that all correspondence formerly sent through the French embassy (which he had been reading since 1583) should now be sent through him. At the end of the year Mary was moved from Tutbury (which she hated) to the house of Robert Devereux, second earl of Essex, at Chartley in Staffordshire. It was at this point that Walsingham devised a scheme to encourage her to re-establish her secret correspondence, probably modelled on his treatment of Mauvissière. A plausible double agent, Gilbert Gifford, presented himself to Mary and the French embassy, claiming to be able to provide a vehicle for communication with the outside world. In a complex intelligence operation, from January 1586 Mary, through letters apparently smuggled in and out of Chartley in beer barrels, was able to read and reply to over a year's backlog of correspondence. All these letters, both incoming and outgoing, passed through Walsingham's office, where they were deciphered by Thomas Phelippes. Through this lethal mechanism Mary replied to Anthony Babington, a

gentleman who sought her blessing on 6 July for a genuine, if imprecise, plot on Elizabeth's life. Mary, for whatever reason, perhaps as a result of her many years' imprisonment, compromised herself by conveying assent in a ciphered commission to Babington on 17 July.

On 2 August Phelippes asked Walsingham whether Babington should be arrested, 'or otherwise played with' (Pollen, cl). Walsingham replied the following day, telling Phelippes that 'you wyll not beleve howe much I am greved with the event of this cause [an]d feare the addytyon of the postscrypt hathe bread the jealousie' (BL, Cotton MS, appx L, fol. 144r). By 'jealousie' he meant suspicion. Walsingham had added a postscript to Mary's letter to Babington of 31 July, asking him to name the six gentlemen who would assassinate Elizabeth. He now feared that this had made Babington suspicious and risked the entire operation. It shows how carefully he manipulated the situation to entrap Mary. Luckily for Walsingham, in mid-August Babington and his fellow conspirators were arrested. Walsingham balanced the need to use men he trusted with a clear desire not to be associated with the arrests, and wherever possible warrants were issued by other privy councillors. It is not clear that Walsingham expected to uncover an assassination plot of this type, but he had been convinced for years that Mary was at the centre of the enterprise of England, and her apparent willingness to countenance an assassination justified all his suspicions. Walsingham was certain that now was the time to deal with her once and for all. Mary saw through his ploys, and at her trial at Fotheringhay Castle in Northamptonshire on 14 and 15 October she formally accused him of engineering her destruction by falsifying evidence. He rose to his feet and denied this:

> I call God to witness that as a private person I have done nothing unbeseeming an honest man, nor, as I bear the place of a public man, have I done anything unworthy of my place. I confess that being very careful for the safety of the queen and the realm, I have curiously searched out all the practices against the same.   (Read, *Walsingham*, 3.53)

He could have been speaking his credo.

The trial was moved to Westminster Palace on 25 October, where the 42-man commission, including Walsingham, found Mary guilty of plotting Elizabeth's assassination. As Walsingham had expected, Elizabeth proved reluctant to execute her rival and prevented a public verdict being decided after the trial. At this point various personal matters intruded. Elizabeth had been generous to him in August 1585 by granting the farm of the customs of the outports, which he had been seeking since the beginning of the year. In September she had eased the secretarial burden by appointing Davison a principal secretary, as well as the Latin secretary, Sir John Woolley, to the privy council. However, during the course of Mary's trial Walsingham learned of the death of Sidney on 17 October 1586 as a result of a wound received at the battle of Zutphen. This brought with it the burden of Sidney's financial affairs, complicated by the recent death of his father, Sir Henry Sidney. Walsingham was faced with honouring £6000 of debts.

Walsingham's request to Elizabeth for further financial assistance to deal with the Sidney debts met a hostile response. Davison said that the queen should aid Walsingham 'as one to whom under God she ought to acknowledge the preservacion of her life … alleaging unto her the hard estate you stand in and the dishonour must fall uppon herself if such a servaunt shuld be suffered to quaile' (PRO, SP 12/195/54, fol. 99r). Burghley and Leicester ('I confess I see what you find and find like you have found') added their support, but without success (BL, Harley MS 285, fol. 266r). With this something snapped and Walsingham retired to Barn Elms in mid-December, transferring the signet and the privy seal to Davison's custody. He did not return to court until 14 February 1587. The combination of personal and political grievance led to a physical collapse: 'the grief of my mynd hath brought me into a dangerous dysease' (PRO, SP 12/197, fol. 6v).

As a result Walsingham was absent from Greenwich when Elizabeth signed Mary's death warrant in Davison's presence on 1 February. Her famous sardonic joke that Davison should inform Walsingham, 'the grief thereof will go near to kill him outright', mirrors his own humour (Read, *Walsingham*, 3.63). Yet Walsingham's role was more than passive. By February he had moved to Seething Lane, and when Davison saw him there on the night of the 1st Walsingham arranged for him and Beale to meet the following morning. There they made the arrangements for Beale to convey the warrant to Fotheringhay and for sending the executioner (whom Walsingham had in readiness) in secret (BL, Add. MS 48027, fol. 636r–v). After the privy council signed the order for dispatching the warrant under Burghley's leadership on the 3rd it was sent to Walsingham for his own signature. Although Beale readily undertook the mission, in later years when he was singled out as one of Mary's enemies, he never forgave Walsingham, which helps to account for his tart comments about his brother-in-law.

Mary was executed on 8 February. Walsingham was recalled to court on the 14th and resumed sitting on the privy council on the 15th. Ironically, for all his laments over Sidney, unlike Leicester he did not take part in his funeral at St Paul's Cathedral on the following day. Elizabeth had no doubt of his role in Mary's execution, but she was angrier with Burghley and Davison. Walsingham was in constant attendance until August, when he was 'taken with the stopping of my water, as I dispaired … of recovery', followed by a fever in September that kept him in bed until mid-December (BL, Cotton MS Galba D. i, fol. 248r). Ironically, for all his complaints the previous December, Elizabeth gave him several manors in fee farm in April 1587. He also received the chancellorship of the duchy of Lancaster, vacant following Sir Ralph Sadler's death, on 15 June 1587, although he had to surrender his chancellorship of the Garter to his main competitor, Sir Amias Paulet.

Walsingham's immediate task in February 1587 was to deal with the Scottish and French reactions to Mary's execution. These, as he had half predicted, were muted, although he continued to fret at Elizabeth's refusal to agree to James's demands for the Lennox lands. France proved more complex, owing not least to Walsingham's continued suspicions of Stafford. However, German assistance for Navarre proved difficult to raise, and Elizabeth refused to bear the full burden. As a result the German army under John Casimir of the Palatinate that finally entered France to campaign for Navarre in summer 1587 was both too little and too late. Although Walsingham initially doubted Stafford's claims that Henri had no desire to see Navarre eliminated and was seeking a compromise settlement, during the course of 1587 he slowly came to see some truth in it, although he found the king's inability to take action frustrating. On the other hand he appears to have been ignorant of Stafford's contacts with Mendoza in January 1587.

The most difficult issue was the Netherlands, and here Walsingham engaged in manoeuvres that have puzzled many. The stalemate of the Leicester intervention had caused Elizabeth to take more seriously the peace feelers Parma was sending forth. Walsingham never saw them as more than a smokescreen for the Spanish invasion preparations and a tactic for causing dissension between Elizabeth and the Dutch. On the other hand he was also aware of the collapse in relations between Leicester and the states general and tensions within the English army. On 3 December 1586 he invited Thomas Wilkes, the resident English agent, to write to him confidentially and sent him a cipher, in which Leicester was identified as Themistocles. From Wilkes came a stream of criticisms against Leicester's administration (*CSP for.*, 1586–7; BL, Add. MS 48127; Brigham Young University, Salt Lake City, Beale–Walsingham state papers). In January 1587 a Dutch delegation arrived both to complain against Leicester and to demand a further increase of Elizabeth's assistance. Her solution was to send Thomas Sackville, first Baron Buckhurst, in March to attempt reconciliation, and from Buckhurst too came a stream of complaints against Themistocles.

In the face of the criticisms and the crippling debts he had incurred in going to the Netherlands in 1585, Leicester wished to resign. Yet in April 1587 the decision was taken to send him back, with the almost paradoxical mission of stabilizing the military situation (in particular the threat to Ostend and Sluys) and persuading the Dutch to co-operate in Elizabeth's peace negotiations. On his arrival at the end of June, Wilkes, Buckhurst, and Sir John Norreys returned to England rather than meet him. For this contempt, Leicester demanded and obtained their imprisonment. In July Walsingham sent his agent Needham to accompany Leicester, and he too sent a stream of criticism using the Themistocles cipher.

There has been much speculation about a cooling of relations between Walsingham and Leicester in 1587. Read, relying on the gossip of Catholic exiles, attributed this not just to Walsingham's doubts about Leicester's competence, but also to personal matters, especially Leicester's refusal to help him over Sidney's debts and opposition to his appointment as chancellor of the duchy of Lancaster. Yet of the latter there is no other proof. The one clear sign of the former was Leicester's distress on learning in July that Walsingham, 'one whom the world accompted & he esteemed his dearest friend', had eased the terms of Wilkes's imprisonment (BL, Harley MS 287, fol. 37r). It may be significant that Leicester, who had named Walsingham an overseer of his will of 1582, omitted him from the will he was drafting in July 1587. Walsingham clearly regretted the dissensions surrounding Leicester, and may have felt an obligation to Wilkes—for he had observed in 1585 that Leicester was 'a shrewde ennemye where he taketh'—but he may have been doing no more than keeping the lines open as Burghley had done with Stafford (Bain, 2.666).

In autumn 1587 the overwhelming evidence of Spanish invasion preparations heightened the tension over Elizabeth's continued desire to pursue peace negotiations. Walsingham was grateful that his illness prevented her from including him in the delegation. On 12 November he wrote to Leicester:

> the manner of our cold and carelesse proceeding here in this time of perill and daunger maketh mee to take no comfort of my recoverie of health, for that I see apparently, unlesse it shall please God in mercie and miraculously to preserve us, we cannot long stand. (BL, Cotton MS Galba D. ii, fol. 192v)

However, Elizabeth did agree to larger sums being spent on secret intelligence than before; these amounted to £3300 between March 1587 and June 1588.

Walsingham's return to attendance in December 1587 was broken by 'a defluctyon into one of my eyes', which kept him in bed during January 1588, but thereafter he was in constant attendance during the year, except for another illness in October (CSP Scot., 1586–8, 535). He was at the centre of the preparations against the Armada. Although, like everyone else, he was uncertain whether the Armada would ever depart, he was confident that without it there was no threat from Parma's army. Once it arrived in the channel, he informed Henry Radcliffe, fourth earl of Sussex, on 24 July that 'we have certainlie discovered that their whole Plott and Desseigne is against the Cittie of London' (Adams, 'Armada correspondence'). His correspondence with Leicester at Tilbury provides one of the best sources for the assessment of the situation at court. He supported Leicester's plan for Elizabeth to visit the army at Tilbury, despite the danger of assassination, and intended himself 'to steale to the campe, when her majestie shall be there', joining the queen on her visit on 8 and 9 August (BL, Cotton MS Galba D. iii, fol. 227r). Like many others he was frustrated by the failure to achieve a more conclusive victory against the Spanish, lamenting on 8 August 'our halfe doings doth breed dishonour, and leaveth the disease uncured' (T. Wright, Queen Elizabeth and her Times, 2 vols., 1838, 2.385).

In the eighteen months after the Armada, Walsingham's health deteriorated sharply. He was absent from the privy council for almost the entire period from 15 February to 5 June 1589, although he rallied in the latter half of the year and attended until a week before his death. As a result his influence over the shaping of policy diminished. Although he supported the expedition planned by

Drake and Norreys in autumn 1588 (afterwards known as the Portugal voyage), he had little to do with its final departure in spring 1589. Perhaps his last important intervention came after Henri's assassination on 1 August 1589, when he urged Elizabeth to support Navarre, now the new protestant king Henri IV. She responded rapidly with a loan of £35,000 and an army of 4000 men under Peregrine Bertie, thirteenth Baron Willoughby de Eresby.

Walsingham wrote his last will on 12 December 1589, and it was proved on 27 May 1590. It was found in a secret cabinet on the day after his death. The tone is somewhat pessimistic; Walsingham could not resist commenting on the need for God's 'mercyfull protection especiallye in this tyme wherein Synne and iniquitie doth so muche abounde'. He stipulated that he should 'be buryed without any such extraordinarie ceremonyes as usuallye apperteyne to a man servinge in my place in respect of the greatnes of my debtes and the mean state I shall leave my wife and heire in'. His 'moste kynde and lovinge wife' was appointed sole executor and residuary legatee, with Edward Carey, Beale, and William Dodington as overseers (PRO, PROB 11/75, sig. 33). Their daughter was granted £100 per annum from Walsingham's lands in Lincolnshire in lieu of the dower portion she should have expected from her first husband and on top of the £200 per annum already settled on her. Presumably she would enjoy more land when her mother died. Surprisingly Walsingham had already cleared most of his debts and left his remaining goods, chattels, plate, and jewels to his wife. Yet for all his care with his own estate Walsingham died owing the queen about £42,000, largely from expenditure on the crown's business without obtaining privy seal warrants, or so Beale later claimed. This debt appears to have been waived in James I's reign.

Walsingham died at his house in Seething Lane on 6 April 1590 and was buried in St Paul's in the same tomb as Sidney at 10 o'clock the following evening in a simple ceremony. The tomb was destroyed during the great fire of 1666, and a plaque now commemorates Sidney but not Walsingham. Ursula Walsingham died suddenly at Barn Elms on 18 June 1602 and was buried near her husband after a simple ceremony the next evening.

Posthumous reputation Walsingham's stock has fluctuated among historians over the centuries. To the historians of the seventeenth century, including William Camden and Sir Robert Naunton, Burghley and he were the twin pillars of the Elizabethan state. Camden described Walsingham as wise, hard-working, devout, and cunning, with the interests of the realm at heart. Historiography since the nineteenth century has valued Walsingham in terms of its contemporary attitudes to the causes in which he believed: protestantism, a vigorous foreign policy, exploration and empire, suppression of Catholicism in England, destruction of Mary, queen of Scots, union of Scotland and England, and the necessity of espionage. James Anthony Froude's History of England from the fall of Wolsey to the defeat of the Spanish Armada (1856–70) provided the classic study of Burghley and Walsingham holding together the government despite Elizabeth's incompetence, and created Walsingham's lasting image as her spymaster. In 1899 Sidney Lee wrote in his approving article on Walsingham: 'his methods of espionage were worked at the expense of some modern considerations of morality, but his detective weapons were those of England's enemies, and were employed solely in the public interest' (*DNB*).

Between 1902 and 1908 Karl Stählin produced a series of detailed studies of Walsingham, although his planned biography did not go beyond 1573. In 1925 the American historian Conyers Read produced his monumental three-volume study, *Mr Secretary Walsingham and the Policy of Queen Elizabeth*, running to nearly 1400 pages. He too approved of his subject's motives and methods. His work was more than just a biographical treatment, and sought to analyse and assess all aspects of Walsingham's role in policy making. Thanks to its scale and the depth of Read's research it has dominated the subject since and discouraged a new substantial biography. Interestingly Read helped to set up, under William J. Donovan, the research and analysis branch of the office of strategic services (the precursor of the Central Intelligence Agency).

Walsingham is now best remembered in the popular imagination for his role as a spymaster, which continues to generate a certain notoriety. His casual and brief employment of Christopher Marlowe as an agent in 1587 still gives rise to implausible conspiracy theories. Above all the Babington plot lives on in the popular memory. The film *Elizabeth* (1998), in which Geoffrey Rush memorably portrayed him, put a new spin on the popular image of Walsingham. It was a dazzling, romantic concoction, playing fast and loose with chronology and fact. Walsingham was shown as godless and Machiavellian, as well as homosexual, but the performance did capture his intensity and obsession with the queen's security.

Readers of Walsingham's extensive correspondence gain a sharply critical impression of Elizabethan government, full of complaints about Elizabeth's prevarications and half measures. Despite his conspiratorial reputation he was notoriously indiscreet with those whom he trusted—Davison or Wotton for example. Leicester had to warn him of this habit during his first French embassy in early 1573. One effect of these indiscretions was his constant portrayal of malign and factious forces at work, as he admitted to Burghley during their spat in January 1585, 'when I sawe somme cawse to sospect that the grownde therof grewe of factyon (that reyghnethe ordynarylie in coortes)' (PRO, SP 12/176/19, fol. 34*r*). As a result he has been a major source for students of Elizabethan faction, especially Read, who concluded that during the period from 1578 to 1587 it dominated Elizabeth's government.

When Read came to his life of Burghley thirty years later he modified his conclusions on faction considerably. Several general observations are worth making. Walsingham had an impulsive streak and never ceased to complain when he felt opportunities were lost. Second, Read focused on the Netherlands and Anjou debates of 1578 to 1585; these were issues of considerable disagreement, but this was not necessarily the case with other areas of policy. Third, the malign forces Walsingham suspected during his embassies of 1578 and 1581 may have been French envoys rather than his colleagues. Last, as sophisticated students of Tudor politics have observed, factions were powerful only when the monarch was weak.

In this respect the most important relationship of Walsingham's career was with Elizabeth. It lacked the long acquaintance of the queen's relationships with Burghley and Leicester and the emotional dependence she placed on Leicester and Hatton. Her tolerance of his constant nagging and complaining has puzzled generations of historians. On the other hand like Burghley, Walsingham was a workaholic, whose efficiency was undoubted and whose sardonic humour mirrored her own. If they disagreed over the Netherlands or Anjou, they were in close agreement over James and Mary. It is possible that Elizabeth accepted retrospectively that she had blundered in accepting James's promise over Morton in 1581, and that Walsingham had been right.

Walsingham's absences during the crucial months in 1579 and 1586 are to some extent the keys to their relationship. The genuine weakness of Walsingham's health has not been fully appreciated, although he had no compunction in using ill health as an excuse for a certain 'je m'en foutisme'. Yet, however irritated Elizabeth may have been with him, she made no effort to replace him. This certain distance from the court is also reflected in Walsingham's quite precocious employment of the vocabulary of the state, something not shared by his colleagues.

On the surface Walsingham's views on foreign affairs appear ideological. He never lost his residual suspicion of a Catholic league, the ambitions of the queen of Scots, and (after 1572) the French royal family. His loyalties to foreign protestants were open and sincere. Yet he was no fanatic and his assessments of situations were always balanced. He was right about Anjou, less on ideological grounds than in his appreciation that the duc's motives and behaviour did not make sense.

Perhaps the best way to conclude is with two contemporary comments on Walsingham's death. On 8 April 1590 a Spanish spy in London wrote to Philip with the news, telling him, 'Secretary Walsingham has just expired, at which there is much sorrow'. On receiving the letter, the king scribbled in the margin 'There, yes! But it is good news here' (Hume, 1587–1603, 578). On 30 June, when considering the impact of Walsingham's death, Burghley began a letter to a friend, 'I am fully perswaded … the Queen's Majesty, and hir realm, and I and others his particular frendes have had a great loss, both for the publyck use of his good and paynfull long services, and for the privat comfort I had by his mutuall frendship' (BL, Lansdowne MS 103, fol. 194*r*).

SIMON ADAMS, ALAN BRYSON, and MITCHELL LEIMON

Sources S. Adams, ed., *Household accounts and disbursement books of Robert Dudley, earl of Leicester, 1558–1561, 1584–1586*, CS, 6 (1995) · S. Adams, 'The decision to intervene: England and the United Provinces, 1584–1585', *Felipe II (1527–1598): Europa y la monarquía Católica*, ed. J. Martínez Millan, 5 vols. (Madrid, 1999), 1.19–31 · S. Adams,

Leicester and the court: essays on Elizabethan politics (2002) • S. Adams, ed., 'The Armada correspondence in Cotton MSS Otho E VII and E IX', *The naval miscellany*, Navy RS, 6 [forthcoming] • S. Adams and M. Greengrass, eds., 'Mémoires et procédure de ma negotiation en Angleterre (8 October 1582–8 October 1583) by Jean Malliet, councillor of Geneva', *Religion, politics and society in sixteenth-century England*, ed. I. Archer and others, CS [forthcoming] • *APC*, 1558–90 • I. Backus, 'Laurence Tomson (1539–1608) and Elizabethan puritanism', *Journal of Ecclesiastical History*, 28 (1977), 17–27 • J. Bain, ed., *The Hamilton papers, letters and papers illustrating the political relations of England and Scotland in the XVIth century*, 2 vols. (1890–92) • P. Basing, 'Robert Beale and the queen of Scots', *British Library Journal*, 20 (1994), 65–82 • Yale U., Beinecke L., Osborn shelves, MS Fa 9; Osborn files: Walsingham • registre Mauvissière dispatches, 1578–81, Bibliothèque Nationale de France, Paris, MS français 15973 • Beale–Walsingham state papers, Brigham Young University, Salt Lake City • J. Bossy, *Giordano Bruno and the embassy affair* (1991) • J. Bossy, *Under the molehill: an Elizabethan spy story* (2001) • *CSP dom.*, *1547–90; 1601–3, with addenda, 1547–79* • *CSP for.*, 1558–90 • *CSP Ire.*, *1509–92* • *CSP Scot.*, *1547–93* • *The state papers and letters of Sir Ralph Sadler*, ed. A. Clifford, 2 vols. (1809) • P. Collinson, 'The monarchical republic of Queen Elizabeth I', *The Tudor monarchy*, ed. J. A. Guy (1997), 110–34 • P. Collinson, 'De republica Anglorum, or, History with the politics put back', in P. Collinson, *Elizabethan essays* (1994), 1–27 • MSS letters, chiefly Elizabethan, 1570–1630, Rousham House, Oxfordshire, Cottrell Dormer MSS • S. Doran, *Monarchy and matrimony: the courtships of Elizabeth I* (1996) • F. Duquenne, *L'entreprise du duc d'Anjou aux Pays-Bas de 1580 à 1584: les responsabilités d'un échec à partager* (Lille, 1998) • H. Ellis, ed., *Original letters, illustrative of English history … from autographs in the British Museum and … other collections*, 3 vols., 1st ser. (1824) • F. M. G. Evans, *The principal secretary of state: a survey of the office from 1558 to 1680* (1923) • S. D'Ewes, *The journals of the parliaments during the reign of Queen Elizabeth, both of the House of Lords and House of Commons, collected by Sir S. D'Ewes …*, rev. P. Bowes (1682) • C. H. Garrett, *The Marian exiles: a study in the origins of Elizabethan puritanism* (1938) • S. Haynes, ed., *A collection of state papers … left by William Cecill Lord Burghley* (1740) • Hastings papers, Hunt. L. • *Calendar of the manuscripts of the most hon. the marquis of Salisbury*, 24 vols., HMC, 9 (1883–1976) • *Calendar of the manuscripts of the marquis of Bath preserved at Longleat, Wiltshire*, 5 vols., HMC, 58 (1904–80) • *The manuscripts of his grace the duke of Rutland*, 4 vols., HMC, 24 (1888–1905) • *HoP, Commons, 1558–1603*, 3.571–6 • M. A. S. Hume, ed., *Letters and papers relating to English affairs, preserved principally in the archives of Simancas*, 4 vols. (1892–9) • J. Hogan and N. McNeill, eds., *The Walsingham letter-book or register of Ireland, May 1578 to December 1579* (1959) • C. Jenkins, 'Sir Francis Walsingham', *Church Quarterly Review*, 101 (1926), 278–318 • *JHL* • E. P. Kuhl, 'Walsingham and the Elizabethan stage', *Modern Language Notes*, 46 (1931), 39–40 • 'Letters and papers of Mr. James Carmichael, minister of Haddington, 1584–1586', *The miscellany of the Wodrow Society*, ed. D. Laing, Wodrow Society, [9] (1844), 410–52 • M. Leimon, 'Sir Francis Walsingham and the Anjou marriage plan, 1574–1581', PhD diss., U. Cam., 1989 • M. Leimon and G. Parker, 'Treason and plot in Elizabethan diplomacy: the "fame of Sir Edward Stafford" reconsidered', *EngHR*, 111 (1996), 1134–58 • Baron Kervyn de Lettenhove [J. M. B. C. Kervyn de Lettenhove] and L. Gilliodts-van Severen, eds., *Relations politiques des Pays-Bas et de l'Angleterre sous le règne de Philippe II*, 11 vols. (Brussels, 1882–1900) • E. Lodge, ed., *Illustrations of British history, biography, and manners, in the reigns of Henry VIII, Edward VI, Mary, Elizabeth, and James I, exhibited in a series of original papers*, 3 vols. (1838) • W. T. MacCaffrey, *The shaping of the Elizabethan regime: Elizabethan politics, 1558–1572* (1968) • W. T. MacCaffrey, *Queen Elizabeth and the making of policy, 1572–1588* (Princeton, NJ, 1981) • W. T. MacCaffrey, *Elizabeth I: war and politics, 1588–1603* (Princeton, NJ, 1992) • N. Mears, 'The "personal rule" of Elizabeth I: marriage, succession and Catholic conspiracy, c.1578–c.1582', PhD diss., U. St Andr., 1999 • *Correspondance diplomatique de Bertrand de Salignac de la Mothe Fénélon*, ed. A. Teulet, 7 vols., Bannatyne Club, 67 (1838–40) • W. Murdin, *Collection of state papers, relating to affairs in the reign of Queen Elizabeth from the year 1571 to 1596* (1759) • *DNB* • J. H. Pollen, ed., *Mary queen of Scots and the Babington plot*, Scottish History Society, 3rd ser., 3 (1922) • will, PRO, PROB 11/75, sig. 33 • Baschet transcripts, 1575–85, PRO, PRO 31/3/27–28 • state papers domestic, Elizabeth I, PRO, SP 12 • state papers Scotland, Elizabeth I, PRO, SP 52 • state papers Ireland, Elizabeth I, PRO, SP 63 • state papers foreign, Flanders, PRO, SP 77 • state papers foreign, France, PRO, SP 78 • state papers foreign, Holland and Flanders, PRO, SP 83 • state papers foreign, Holland, PRO, SP 84 • signet office docquet book, 1585–March 1597, PRO, SO 3/1 • M. B. Pulman, *The Elizabethan privy council in the 1570s* (1971) • C. Read, 'Walsingham and Burghley in Queen Elizabeth's privy council', *EngHR*, 28 (1913), 34–58 • C. Read, *Mr Secretary Walsingham and the policy of Queen Elizabeth*, 3 vols. (1925) • C. Read, *Mr Secretary Cecil and Queen Elizabeth* (1955) • C. Read, *Lord Burghley and Queen Elizabeth* (1960) • K. Stählin, *Der Kampf um Schottland und die Gesandtschafts-Reise Sir Francis Walsinghams im Jahre 1583* (Leipzig, 1902) • K. Stählin, *Sir Francis Walsingham und seine Zeit* (Heidelberg, 1908) • More-Molyneux of Loseley MSS, Surrey RO, Guildford Muniment Room • M. Taviner, 'Robert Beale and the Elizabethan polity', PhD diss., U. St Andr., 2000 • *The compleat ambassador, or, Two treatises of the intended marriage of qu: Elizabeth; comprised in letters of negotiation of sir F. Walsingham, with the answers of the lord Burleigh, and others*, ed. D. Digges (1655) • C. T. Martin, ed., 'Journal of Sir Francis Walsingham, from December 1570 to April 1583', *Camden miscellany*, VI, CS, 104 (1871) • Middelburg Rijksarchief in Zeeland, Zeeuws Archief, 1198 1–II stukken ingekomen bij de gecomitteerde rade 1584

Archives BL, corresp. and papers, Add. MSS 5752–5754, 30156, 33531, 33594, 35841; Egerton MSS 1693–1694 • BL, Cotton MSS, corresp. and papers • BL, Harley MSS, corresp. and papers • BL, expense account kept as ambassador to the Low Countries, M 488 [microfilm] • BL, 'table-book', Stowe MS 162 • Blackburn Central Library, letter-book • CUL, letter-book • CUL, letters • Folger, corresp. • Hatfield House, Hertfordshire, letters and papers • Hunt. L., letter-book relating to France • Inner Temple, London, instructions for, and letters written as ambassador to the French king • NRA, priv. coll., diplomatic letter-book • PRO, diary and letter-book, PRO 30/5 | BL, letters to William Ashby, Egerton MS 2598 • BL, letters to Edward Wotton, Add. MS 32657 • BL, Yelverton MSS • CKS, corresp. with Sir Henry Sidney • Hunt. L., letters to Lord Chancellor Ellesmere and Sir John Popham • Hunt. L., corresp. with third earl of Huntingdon about the Scottish situation • Lincs. Arch., corresp. with Lord Willoughby • NL Scot., corresp. relating to Mary, queen of Scots • NRA, priv. coll., corresp. with Lord(s) Paget • PRO, SP 12, SP 15, SP 46, SP 52, SP 70 • Sheff. Arch., Wentworth Woodhouse MSS, copies of corresp. between the archbishop of Canterbury and Burghley, Walsingham, and the council, etc.

Likenesses attrib. J. de Critz the elder, oils, c.1585, NPG [*see illus.*] • attrib. J. de Critz the elder, oils, second version, 1587, King's Cam. • J. Houbraken, line engraving, pubd 1738 (after F. Zuccaro), BM, NPG • Passe, line engraving, BM, NPG; repro. in H. Holland, *Herōologia* (1620) • oils (after J. de Critz the elder?, 1587), NPG

Walsingham, Francis [*alias* John Fennell] (*bap.* 1577, *d.* 1647), Jesuit, was born in Berwick and was baptized on 7 February 1577, the son of Edward Walsingham (*d.* 1576) of Exhall, near Alcester, Warwickshire, a kinsman to the secretary of state, Sir Francis Walsingham. His father having died before his birth, his mother, who was a Catholic, brought him to London and entrusted his education to his guardian, Humphrey Walsingham, a citizen of London, who sent him to St Paul's School. He appears to have studied theology at All Souls College, Oxford, and then spent some time as a soldier in the Low Countries under Sir Robert Sidney, governor of Flushing. Then, after returning to London, he took up the study of civil and common law. He also taught for a time at Kingsbury in Middlesex and was ordained deacon by the bishop of Ely in 1603.

About this time he began to have misgivings about his position in the Church of England, after reading Robert Persons's book *A Defence of the Censure* (1585). So deep were his misgivings that he decided to set them forth in a memorial which he presented to James I at Greenwich on 6 April 1604; he was told by the king to discuss the matter with his new archbishop of Canterbury, Richard Bancroft. Under the latter's direction he had further discussions with two Anglican divines, William Covell and George Downame, as well as the former Jesuit diplomat Christopher Perkins—but to no avail. Finally, on meeting an imprisoned priest, Edward Tempest, he made a spiritual retreat and was reconciled to the Roman Catholic church.

In 1606 Walsingham was one of forty-seven priests banished from England after the Gunpowder Plot. Entering the English College, Rome, on 27 October 1606 he was ordained priest on 12 April 1608 and was sent back to England the following April. However, on reaching Douai in June 1609 he retraced his steps to Rome and entered the Society of Jesus there. Now with the assistance and encouragement of Robert Persons, rector of the English College, he set forth an account of his spiritual pilgrimage in *A Search Made into Matters of Religion* (1609), with a dedication to James I. This work, by which he is said to have 'immortalized his name' (Foley, 6.241), went into a second edition in 1615 and was reprinted in 1843. He went on in 1618 to publish *Reasons for Embracing the Catholick Faith*, but no copy of it seems to have survived.

Walsingham was sent on the English mission in 1616 under the alias of John Fennell, and there he laboured, as Foley says, 'with indefatigable zeal and abundant fruit' (Foley, 2.382), first in the Leicestershire district until 1633, then in the Derbyshire district until his death on 1 July 1647 there at the age of seventy-one. It is said of him that he engaged in 'many conferences with Protestant ministers, in which he displayed great learning and talent', but that for the most part 'his mission lay amongst the poor, for it was his delight to instruct the ignorant and needy', especially the children (ibid., 2.382). All the time he was never far from danger, especially from pursuivants; but he eluded their searches in ways that often seemed miraculous. He is praised as a man of prayer, 'possessed of the sweetest manners and a dovelike simplicity' and 'athirst for the glory of God' (ibid., 2.383).   PETER MILWARD

Sources F. Walsingham, *A search made into matters of religion* (1615) · H. Foley, ed., *Records of the English province of the Society of Jesus*, 2 (1875), 318–89; 6 (1880), 241; 7 (1882–3), 811 · C. Dodd [H. Tootell], *The church history of England, from the year 1500, to the year 1688*, 2 (1739), 408–9 · G. Anstruther, *The seminary priests*, 2 (1975), 334–5 · P. Milward, *Religious controversies of the Jacobean age* (1978), 168–9 · *Menology S. J.* (1902), 2.1–2 · T. M. McCoog, *English and Welsh Jesuits, 1555–1650*, 2 vols., Catholic RS, 74–5 (1994–5), 324

Walsingham, John (*supp. fl.* **1326**), supposed Carmelite friar and theologian, is first recorded in Johann Tritheim's *Catalogus scriptorum ecclesiasticorum sive illustrium virorum* of 1531. Bale's *Scriptorum illustrium maioris Brytanniae, quam* *nunc Angliam et Scotiam vocant, Catalogus* (published in Basel in 1559), Pits's *Relationum historicarum de rebus Anglicis tomus primus* (published at Paris in 1619), Casanate's *Paradisus Carmelici decoris* (published at Leiden in 1639), and Leland's *Commentarii de scriptoribus Britannicis* (published at Oxford in 1709) all add details. They tell of his education at Norwich and Oxford, his growing fame as a theologian, his election in 1326 to be provincial of the English Carmelites, and his services to the papacy in the cause of doctrinal orthodoxy. The information provided by these authors, as the article on John Walsingham in the *Dictionary of National Biography* cautiously indicates, is often uncorroborated. The detail given for his life could easily have been inferred from general information about the Carmelite order, student life at Oxford and Paris, and from theological discussions of papal authority in the relevant era. As the *Dictionary of National Biography* article and its sources wisely indicate, moreover, there are great inconsistencies in the various accounts of John Walsingham's life and works. The *Dictionary of National Biography*, while not going so far as to question John's existence, nevertheless concluded that 'the silence of his contemporaries attests that Walsingham's writings exercised no influence on his age'.

B. M. Xiberta, in his *De scriptoribus scholasticis saeculi XIV ex ordine Carmelitarum*, after diligently examining the manuscript evidence given by John Bale on page 378 of his *Catalogus*, concluded emphatically that John Walsingham never existed. He found that many of the details of the life of John were details that also fit the life of Robert *Walsingham. Other items belonged in reality to John Baconthorpe or John Walsham. Even the seemingly more solid manuscript evidence lost its strength before Xiberta's careful eye. Joannes W. had wrongly been inferred to be Joannes Walsingham. MS Digby 41 in the Bodleian Library, Oxford, mentions a Joannes Walssinbham, but the work is a treatise against the Lollards and belongs to a much later time than that of the supposed early fourteenth-century Carmelite. William Bintre (d. 1493) is said to have named a John Walsingham among the defenders of transubstantiation, but since this work is now lost and it is Bale who provides the reference, this information, like all the rest, lacks a guarantee.   S. F. BROWN

Sources B. M. Xiberta, *De scriptoribus scholasticis saeculi XIV ex ordine Carmelitarum* (Louvain, 1931), 111–36 · Emden, *Oxf.*, 3.1970 · *DNB*

Walsingham, Robert (*d.* in or after **1313**), theologian and Carmelite friar, probably came from Norfolk. He studied at Oxford, where he is recorded as a disciple of William Pagan *c.*1280, and was later listed as a supporter of the provincial, William Lidlyngton, when the latter protested against the division of the English Carmelite province ordered by the general chapter of the Carmelites held at Narbonne in 1303. At his vesperies held in 1312 (part of the process whereby he was made a master) Walsingham's opponent was Walter Heyham. A report of Walsingham's death at Norwich in 1310 is clearly false, since he is known to have become master in 1312 and he determined two quodlibets about 1312–13.

The scriptural treatises attributed to Walsingham

include a *Determinationes scripturae* and commentaries on Proverbs and Ecclesiasticus. Excerpts from his *Elucidationes sententiarum Petri Lombardi* and his *Quaestiones ordinariae* survive in Bodl. Oxf., MS Bodley 73, and also in BL, Harley MS 3838. The quodlibets were determined after the *Quaestiones ordinariae*, since the latter are cited in *Quodlibet I*, question 1, and in *Quodlibet II*, question 1. The quodlibets are the source for most of what is known regarding Walsingham's teaching. He cites Aristotle with great frequency and uses the Islamic commentators, Avicenna and Averroes (Ibn Rushd), equally. In *Quodlibet I*, question 14, he wrongly assumes that the commentator on Aristotle's *Ethics* is also Averroes. Among medieval Latin writers, he refers to Godefroi de Fontaines and Pierre d'Auvergne as 'moderns', but gives a special status to Godefroi, Thomas Aquinas, and Henri de Gand, whom he describes as 'magni'. He at times opposes Alexander of Hales, his fellow Carmelite Gerardo da Bologna, Henri de Gand, Giles of Rome (Egidio Romano), John Duns Scotus, Simon of Faversham, Robert Cowton, Henry Harclay, and Richard Conington. However, despite his occasional disagreements with Henri de Gand, Walsingham should generally be listed, along with the Franciscan Conington, as one of Henri's strong followers.

With Henri, Walsingham admits that the possibles themselves have a type of existence, and that there must be some form of a real distinction between essence and existence, since if existence were included in the concept of essence, creatures would exist necessarily. It is thus important to note that in interpreting Henri's intentional distinction, Walsingham claims that it is more in the class of a real distinction than a distinction of reason. In treating of causality, Walsingham argues that something is totally the effect of God according to its existence, and is also totally the effect of secondary causes in regard to its specific kind of existence. Like Henri de Gand, therefore, he stresses the role of the uncreated cause in all productions in order to affirm true creation, whereas secondary causes effect nothing as far as their creation as such is concerned, but only channel the specific kind of existence they have through the creative action of God as he works through creatures. Once again, like Henri, Walsingham contends that neither form nor matter are principles of individuation; yet, in regard to matter and form, he also shows an allegiance to Giles of Rome by admitting a certain pre-existence of the form in the potency of the matter.

Even though Robert Walsingham and Richard Conington are the leading followers of Henri de Gand, they do not always agree. Conington, for example, teaches that the human intellect, when it elicits the proper idea of any creature, at the same time (in fact, even by a priority of nature) conceives a proper idea of God in an actual and formal way, although imperceptibly. Walsingham denies that we have such a simple positive concept of God in an actual and formal way. He also manifests a certain independence from his fellow Carmelites, since at times he disagrees with Gerardo da Bologna and Guido Terreni. Yet he sides with Guido in regard to the number of personal relations in the Trinity, and joins both Gerardo and Guido, against both Henri and Thomas Aquinas, by arguing that the Holy Spirit would be distinct from the Son, even if it did not proceed from the Son. In short, he follows Henri de Gand, but with some independence.   S. F. BROWN

Sources B. M. Xiberta, *De scriptoribus scholasticis saeculi XIV ex ordine Carmelitarum* (Louvain, 1931), 111–13 · F. Stegmüller, ed., *Repertorium biblicum medii aevi*, 5 (Madrid, 1955), nn. 7491–3 · F. Stegmüller, ed., *Repertorium commentariorum in sententias Petri Lombardi*, 1 (Würzburg, 1947), n. 749 · R. Schönberger and B. Kible, *Repertorium edierter Texte des Mittelalters* (Berlin, 1994), n. 17576 · W. J. Courtenay, *Schools and scholars in fourteenth-century England* (1987), 72 · J. Beumer, 'Erleuchteter Glaube: die Theorie Heinrichs von Gent und ihr Fortleben in der Spätscholastik', *Franziskanische Studien*, 37 (1955), 156 · S. D. Dumont, 'Theology as a science and Duns Scotus's distinction between intuitive and abstractive cognition', *Speculum*, 64 (1989), 579–99, esp. 588 · T. A. Graf, ed., *De subjecto psychico gratiae et virtutum secundum doctrinam scholasticam usque ad medium saeculi XIV* (1934–55) [105*–10*, question 14] · Emden, *Oxf.*, 3.1970–71
Archives BL, Harley MS 3838 · Bodl. Oxf., MS Bodley 73

Walsingham, Thomas (*c*.1340–*c*.1422), historian and prior of Wymondham, probably came from Walsingham in Norfolk. An entry in the register of Simon Sudbury (*d*. 1381), bishop of London between 1362 and 1375, mentions that Thomas Walsingham, a monk of St Albans from the diocese of Norwich, was ordained priest on 21 September 1364. That entry suggests he was born *c*.1340. It is probable, although not entirely certain, that some time before 1376 Walsingham studied at Oxford, for in criticizing the university in his *Chronica majora* on account of its association with Lollardy, he disclaimed any disloyalty on his own part. The one piece of evidence to determine his position within St Albans before the 1390s is an entry in the *Liber benefactorum* (BL, Cotton MS Nero D.vii) which he himself compiled in 1380. There he is described as precentor and *scriptorarius* of St Albans Abbey, and appears twenty-second in a list of fifty-four monks. In September 1394 he became prior of the cell at Wymondham, Norfolk, and this is the only time when he is known to have been absent from St Albans. In 1396 he was recalled to St Albans at his own request after the death of abbot Thomas de la Mare in that year. The abbot's death appears to coincide with a change in Walsingham's position. After 1396 he was no longer termed *scriptorarius*, and he never again held a senior post within the abbey. None the less he continued work on his chronicles for a further twenty years. The last historical work with which his name is undoubtedly associated is the *Ypodigma Neustriae*, which he dedicated to Henry V about 1420. He almost certainly died shortly after this, about 1422, probably at St Albans.

Walsingham has been described as the last of the great medieval chroniclers. But although he was pre-eminently a writer of history, his interests were by no means confined to historical writing. Apart from the *Liber benefactorum*, a work of St Albans piety, Walsingham wrote a treatise on monasticism which follows the *Gesta abbatum* in BL, Cotton MS Claudius E.iv, and also a treatise on mensural music. This latter work (BL, Lansdowne MS 763, fols. 97v–104v) arose out of his duties as precentor. In this treatise Walsingham discussed such matters as the note shapes, the durational values of various note forms, and concluded with a consideration of rhythmic modes. Walsingham's treatise is one of a handful surviving in England from this period, and the knowledge of continental treatises that it reveals lends weight to the possibility of an Oxford background to his writing. Walsingham also displayed an interest in the literature of antiquity. This interest is seen in a number of works, including the *Archana deorum*, which was a commentary on Ovid's *Metamorphoses*, dedicated by Walsingham to Simon Southerey, prior of St Albans (1396/7–1405). Walsingham also wrote the *Dites ditatus*, which was a version of Dictys of Crete's history of the Trojan War, a history of Alexander, and the *Prohemia poetarum*, which contained an account of classical and medieval authors.

Walsingham's historical writing was cast in a traditional mould. If he is the last true representative of the great St Albans school of history that is partly because of the influence of Matthew Paris (*d*. 1259). That influence is seen not only in the form of Walsingham's history, but also in his attempt to make his *Chronica majora* a continuation of the work of Matthew Paris. Although it was once thought that there were at the end of the fourteenth century a number of chroniclers writing at St Albans, the work of V. H. Galbraith has shown that during the late fourteenth and early fifteenth centuries there was one author only, namely Thomas Walsingham, who in addition to a *Chronica majora*, which he began in 1376, wrote a number of other historical works. The most authoritative text of the *Chronica majora* itself is found in two manuscripts, BL, Royal MS 13 E.ix, which contains a text to 1392, and Bodl. Oxf., MS Bodley 462, a later manuscript, which continues the narrative to 1420. Internal references indicate that Walsingham was the author of the Royal manuscript, which was written at St Albans during the late 1390s, and of the early part of the 'short chronicle', which was an abbreviation of the *Chronica majora* extending to 1419. Although there are no personal references to Walsingham in the later part of the *Chronica majora*, or in the 'short chronicle', he is the most probable author of these parts of the narrative also. It seems likely that both the *Chronica majora* and the 'short chronicle' were initially composed in stages during the 1380s and 1390s, and that drafts of both versions were in circulation before Walsingham went to Wymondham in 1394. At some point Walsingham added a retrospective section to the *Chronica majora*, beginning in 1272, in order to link the history of his own times to those of Matthew Paris.

One problem relating to the *Chronica majora* concerns the opening section of the contemporary chronicle in 1376. This opening section is notable for its criticism of John of Gaunt, duke of Lancaster, and its sympathetic account of the Good Parliament of that year. Because of the outspoken references to Gaunt it appears that this section was removed from the Royal manuscript by the monks at St Albans during the 1390s, and possibly as late as 1399. The opening is now to be found in three manuscripts: Bodl. Oxf., MS Bodley 316 (a *Polychronicon* in which only one leaf of this early history remains); BL, Harley MS 3634 (a section of which once formed part of Bodley 316); and BL, Cotton MS Otho C.ii, which survives in a fragmentary and mutilated form. These three manuscripts contain the so-called 'scandalous chronicle', a narrative of the years 1376–7, and a comparison of their texts reveals that the process of revision had begun before the removal of this section of the chronicle from the Royal manuscript.

If Walsingham is traditionally the chronicler of the Lancastrian revolution, his history is also a major source for the history of Richard II's reign. It describes in detail events such as the peasants' revolt, the emergence of John Wyclif (*d*. 1384), and the political struggles of the reign. Walsingham's account of the early Lancastrian kings, although valuable, was composed on a smaller scale, and after 1399 he never again quite recaptured the zest of his earlier writing. His work, considered as a whole, is significant for several reasons. It preserves firstly a valuable record of political events. St Albans was an important centre, and Walsingham was well placed to receive information concerning events in London and elsewhere. His history gives some indication also of the change in attitude of the St Albans community towards the leading personalities of the day. Although Walsingham began his chronicle in 1376 in a manner bitterly hostile to John of Gaunt, during the 1380s his opinion of Gaunt changed, and he came to praise the duke for his patience and moderation. Yet as Gaunt's star rose so that of Richard declined in Walsingham's narrative, and he viewed more critically a king whom he felt did not adequately fulfil the role of kingship. Walsingham's work is again of the greatest interest because of the manner in which it reveals a medieval history in the process of being revised.

Although Walsingham was for a time the official chronicler of his house, and many of the opinions expressed in the *Chronica majora* were undoubtedly those of the St Albans community, he brought to his work a viewpoint and qualities of his own. Thus Walsingham was more of a scholar than Matthew Paris if less of a literary artist. In outlook he was thoroughly conservative, resisting change, and particularly hostile to the ideas of John Wyclif. His interests were mainly if not entirely insular. Although he dealt with events such as the conciliar movement, it was England and the political struggle at home that concerned him most. Throughout the *Chronica majora* his prejudices inform his writing. Thus he disliked foreigners, had little sympathy with the lower sections of society, and disapproved of the mendicants.

In addition to the *Chronica majora* and the 'short chronicle', Walsingham's other historical writings are of some importance. In the *Gesta abbatum* he once more continued the work of Matthew Paris. He recast Matthew Paris's account of the abbots of St Albans which had been continued to 1308, and wrote a further continuation from 1308 to 1393 dealing at length with the abbacy of Thomas de la Mare. It seems probable that the *Gesta abbatum*, written in the early 1390s, was never put into a final shape because of Walsingham's move to Wymondham and Abbot Thomas's death. A continuation which extends to 1411, found in Cambridge, Corpus Christi College, MS 7, is unlikely to be the work of Walsingham himself. Walsingham's last piece of historical writing was the *Ypodigma Neustriae*, an epitome of English history from 911 to 1419. From 1377 to 1419 this was little more than a recapitulation of the 'short chronicle'. With Walsingham's death the *Chronica majora* itself came to an end, and with it a form of historical writing that went back to the days of Wendover and Paris.

In its own day Walsingham's narrative attracted an audience outside St Albans. It was used by the first author of the *Historia vitae et regni Ricardi secundi*, and parts of its text were incorporated in certain of the *Polychronicon* continuations. In more recent times the *Chronica majora* has suffered from the disadvantage of not having been printed as a continuous whole. A form of the text of the *Chronica majora* to 1406 is found in three separate publications in the Rolls Series, in the first two of which it is combined with sections from the 'short chronicle'. The years 1376–7 are found in the *Chronicon Angliae* (pp. 68–147); 1377–92 in the *Historia Anglicana* (1.329–484; 2.1–211); and 1393–1406 in the *Annales Ricardi II et Henrici IV* (pp. 155–420). The *Chronicon Angliae*, edited by E. Maunde Thompson, was taken from an early and partially revised manuscript of the *Chronica majora* found in BL, Harley MS 3634, which concludes in 1382. This edition contains the valuable opening to Walsingham's contemporary history beginning in 1376, which Thompson skilfully reconstructed from the Harley manuscript itself and from two other sources (BL, Cotton MS Otho. C.ii, and Bodl. Oxf., MS Bodley 316). The *Historia Anglicana*, edited by H. T. Riley, contains the best available printed text of the *Chronica majora* from 1377 to 1392. Although printed not from BL, Royal MS 13 E.ix, but from a late transcript (Coll. Arms, Arundel MS 7), it preserves for the years 1377–82 a more fully revised text than that found in the Harley manuscript. Despite his reliance on the Arundel transcript, Riley was fully aware of the value of the Royal manuscript, and in an appendix to volume 2 of the *Historia Anglicana* (pp. 360–410) printed passages from the Royal manuscript that had been omitted in the Arundel text. The concluding section of Walsingham's *Chronica majora*, which was not included in the Rolls Series publications, was printed in 1937 by V. H. Galbraith as the *St Albans Chronicle, 1406–1420*. Work on a new edition of the *Chronica majora*, to be published in the Oxford Medieval Texts series, is now in progress.

JOHN TAYLOR

Sources [T. Walsingham], *Chronicon Angliae, ab anno Domini 1328 usque ad annum 1388*, ed. E. M. Thompson, Rolls Series, 64 (1874) • *Thomae Walsingham, quondam monachi S. Albani, historia Anglicana*, ed. H. T. Riley, 2 vols., pt 1 of *Chronica monasterii S. Albani*, Rolls Series, 28 (1863–4) • 'Annales Ricardi secundi et Henrici quarti, regum Angliae', *Johannis de Trokelowe et Henrici de Blaneforde … chronica et annales*, ed. H. T. Riley, pt 3 of *Chronica monasterii S. Albani*, Rolls Series, 28 (1866), 155–420 • 'Annales Ricardi secundi et Henrici quarti, regum Angliae', *Johannis de Trokelowe et Henrici de Blaneforde … chronica et annales*, ed. H. T. Riley, pt 3 of *Chronica monasterii S. Albani*, Rolls Series, 28 (1866), 155–420 • *Gesta abbatum monasterii Sancti Albani, a Thoma Walsingham*, ed. H. T. Riley, 3 vols., pt 4 of *Chronica monasterii S. Albani*, Rolls Series, 28 (1867–9) • T. Walsingham, *The St Albans chronicle, 1406–1420*, ed. V. H. Galbraith (1937) • G. B. Stow, ed., *Historia vitae et regni Ricardi Secundi* (1977) • V. H. Galbraith, 'Thomas Walsingham and the St Albans Chronicle', *EngHR*, 47 (1932), 12–29 • V. H. Galbraith, 'The *Historia aurea* of John, vicar of Tynemouth, and the sources of the St Albans Chronicle (1327–1377)', *Essays in history presented to Reginald Lane Poole*, ed. H. W. C. Davis (1927), 379–98; repr. (1969) • A. Gransden, *Historical writing in England*, 2 (1982), 118–56 • J. Taylor, *English historical literature in the fourteenth century* (1987), 60–77 • G. B. Stow, 'Thomas Walsingham, John Malvern, and the *Vita Ricardi secundi*, 1377–1381: a reassessment', *Mediaeval Studies*, 39 (1977), 490–97 • G. B. Stow, 'Bodleian Library MS Bodley 316 and the dating of Thomas Walsingham's literary career', *Manuscripta*, 25 (1981), 67–76 • G. B. Stow, 'Richard II in Thomas Walsingham's chronicles', *Speculum*, 59 (1984), 68–103 • *Registrum Simonis de Sudbiria, diocesis Londoniensis, AD 1362–1375*, ed. R. C. Fowler, 2, CYS, 38 (1938) • Emden, *Oxf.*, vol. 3

Archives BL, Cotton MS Claudius E.iv • BL, Cotton MS Nero D.vii • BL, Cotton MS Otho C.ii • BL, Harley MS 3634 • BL, Lansdowne MS 763, fols. 97v–104v • BL, Royal MS 13 E.ix • Bodl. Oxf., MS Bodley 316 • Bodl. Oxf., MS Bodley 462 • Coll. Arms, Arundel MS 7

Walsingham, Sir Thomas (1560/61–1630), literary patron, was the third son of Sir Thomas Walsingham (1526–1584) and Dorothy, daughter of Sir John Guildford of Benenden, and grandson of Sir Edmund *Walsingham (*b*. in or before 1480, *d*. 1550), lieutenant of the Tower. In his youth Thomas was probably employed by his uncle Sir Francis *Walsingham to gather intelligence of Catholic plots against the crown. In 1589 he inherited the manor of Scadbury, Chislehurst, Kent, from his elder brother Edmund.

In 1590 Thomas Watson dedicated a Latin eclogue, *Meliboeus*, on the death of Sir Francis Walsingham, to Thomas Walsingham where he is figured as Tityrus and the author, Corydon, speaks of him as 'sweet friend'. At this time, Thomas had already become a close friend of Christopher Marlowe, for on 18 May 1593 the privy council instructed:

> Henry Maunder, one of the messengers of H. M. chamber to repair to the house of Mr. Thomas Walsingham in Kent, or to any other place where he shall understand Christopher Marlowe to be remaining, and to bring him to the court. (*APC*, 1592–3, 244)

On 1 June 1593 Marlowe was killed in a tavern at Deptford; Ingram Frizer, who was responsible for Marlowe's death, was ironically a servant of Thomas Walsingham. In 1598, when Edward Blunt published his edition of Marlowe's *Hero and Leander*, he dedicated it to Sir Thomas and the 'Preface' speaks of Walsingham's close association with Marlowe:

> wee thinke not ourselves discharged of the duty we owe to our friend, when wee have brought the brethlesse bodie to the earth … the impression … of the man, that hath beene deare unto us, living an after life in our memory, there putteth us in mind of further obsequies due unto the deceased … knowing that in his life time you bestowed many kind favors.

Walsingham was, apparently, one of the mourners present at Marlowe's funeral.

In 1596 Walsingham was appointed justice of the peace for the hundred of Rokesley and in the same year, when a second armada threatened, he, with others, was directed to take 1080 men to protect the chain strung across the River Medway for the defence of Rochester. By this time he had been knighted, and in the following year Elizabeth visited Scadbury, where she planted an oak. In the same year he was allowed to extend his estates to include the manor of Dartford. It was also in 1597 that Sir Thomas first became MP for Rochester; he served again in 1601 and 1603. His wife, Audrey Shelton (*d*. 1624), daughter of Sir Ralph Shelton of Shelton, Norfolk, was a favourite of the queen; both husband and wife gave and received many gifts to and from Elizabeth. In 1599 Thomas was granted the reversion of the keepership of the Great Park at Eltham. After the death of Elizabeth, Audrey Walsingham was one of the ladies sent to accompany James's queen, Anne of Denmark, to London. Initially the queen took a dislike to Audrey but James appointed Sir Thomas and his wife as keepers of the queen's wardrobe and, in 1604, granted Audrey a pension of £200 per annum for life. The Walsinghams remained royal favourites and Audrey took part in the queen's many masques including Ben Jonson's *Masque of Blackness* (1604/5).

In the early 1600s Walsingham had become a close friend of George Chapman, who in 1605 dedicated *All Fooles* to 'my long lov'd and Honourable friend Sir Thomas Walsingham' and dedicated a sonnet to him in affectionate terms. Again the 1608 edition of *The Conspiracie and Tragedy of Charles Duke of Byron* is dedicated 'To My Honourable and Constant Friend ... And to my much loved from his birth ... his sonne'. Since this son, also Thomas, was only eight in 1608 Chapman appears to have been on terms of intimate friendship with the whole family. Thomas died on 11 August 1630 at Chislehurst and was buried in the Scadbury chapel in St Nicholas's Church, Chislehurst; his wife, Audrey, predeceased him in 1624.

REAVLEY GAIR

Sources E. A. Webb, G. W. Miller, and J. Beckwith, eds., *The history of Chislehurst: its church, manors, and parish* (1899) · F. S. Boas, *Christopher Marlowe* (1940)

Walston [*formerly* Waldstein], **Sir Charles** (1856–1927), classical archaeologist, was born on 30 March 1856 in New York, the third son of Henry Waldstein, a merchant, and his wife, Sophie Srisheim. The family name was Anglicized in the spring of 1918. Educated at Columbia College, New York, and thereafter at Heidelberg University, Walston was one of the principal founders and promoters of the study of classical archaeology at the University of Cambridge. He began his Cambridge career as a lecturer in the classics faculty in 1880, and was appointed to the first readership in classical archaeology in 1883, a post which he held until 1907. Classical sculpture, painting, and topography were the subjects he pioneered: his first book, in 1885, was an enthusiastic study of the presumed works of the Greek sculptor Phidias of the fifth century BC. The flavour of Walston's lecturing style is easily gained from this and successive publications, up to his last monograph (*Alcamenes*, 1926); more importantly, it is clear from his admiration of the aesthetics of classical form why he became such a passionate advocate of assembling a collection of casts of ancient sculpture at Cambridge.

Walston's interests extended much further than classical sculpture, however. He was knowledgeable about art generally. He wrote a monograph on John Ruskin in 1894, and twice held the Slade professorship of art at Cambridge (1895–1901, then again 1904–11). He was also a competent field archaeologist, excavating at Plataea in 1889–90, then the tomb of Aristotle at Eretria in 1891, followed by the temple of Hera outside Argos in 1892–5. He served as director of the American School at Athens from 1889–93. However, his most ambitious project was launched in Italy. This involved the creation of an international body for the preservation and further exploration of the site of Herculaneum (the plan is outlined in a book written with L. Shoobridge: *Herculaneum Past, Present and Future*, 1908). A testament to Walston's enormous powers of organization, and in many respects ahead of its time, the project was only blocked by a backbench revolt in the Italian parliament (though Mussolini himself was supportive).

It was not Walston's sympathy with the ancient world so much as his belief in international co-operation and amateur athleticism that inspired his support for the renewed Olympic movement. A member of Baron de Coubertin's founding Olympic committee, Walston won a silver medal for shooting at the games in Athens in 1896 (on behalf of the United States team). In 1909 he married Florence Seligman of New York; they had two children: a daughter, Evelyn, and a son, Harry (Henry), who later became a Labour peer. Walston took British citizenship in 1899. Knighted in 1912, he staged a colourful libel action in 1919 when Viscount Galway accused him of being a German sympathizer. Although he was to be critical of the eventual constitution of the League of Nations, he maintained his faith in the international ideal, a faith expressed in speeches and publications (*Aristodemocracy*, 1916; *Eugenics, Civics, Ethics*, 1920). He also served as high sheriff for Cambridgeshire and Huntingdonshire in 1922–3.

Walston's studies of Greek art show an approach now generally regarded as whimsical, and are hardly ever referred to. The Museum of Classical Archaeology at Cambridge, however, represents an enduring monument. One of the finest collections of sculpture casts in the world, its original nucleus was assembled in 1884 by Sidney Colvin, the first director of the Fitzwilliam Museum in Cambridge. It was Walston who used the collection for his lectures, and Walston who succeeded Colvin as director of the Fitzwilliam in 1883 (a post he occupied until 1889). Walston saw the casts as integral museum objects. Characteristically grandiose, he dreamed of setting up a comprehensive didactic 'museum of the plastic arts' as a part of the Fitzwilliam. Against his wish, the cast collection was eventually divorced from the Fitzwilliam in 1910. But it retains the function which Walston cherished, as a 'laboratory' of sculpture for the instruction of students. And a great many of its contents are there as the permanent fruits of Walston's initiative.

Walston died in Naples on 21 March 1927. He was survived by his wife. There are further memorials to him at Cambridge in the shape of a studentship which enables undergraduates to travel to Greece, and the back gates of his college, King's, which he donated in 1924.

NIGEL SPIVEY

Sources private information (2004) · U. Cam., Museum of Classical Archaeology, archives · *WWW* · *The Times* (29 March 1919) [libel case] · *Cambridge University Reporter* (29 Nov 1927) · *Harpers Weekly* (18 April 1896) [Olympic movement] · King's Cam. [Walston's lecture notes] · Venn, *Alum. Cant.* · *CGPLA Eng. & Wales* (1927)

Archives King's AC Cam., modern archives, corresp., and papers | King's AC Cam., letters to Oscar Browning; letters to Nathaniel Wedd · U. Cam., Museum of Classical Archaeology

Likenesses photograph, U. Cam., Museum of Classical Archaeology

Wealth at death £15,432 15s. 4d.: probate, 20 Aug 1927, *CGPLA Eng. & Wales*

Walter [Walter of Lorraine] (d. **1079**?), bishop of Hereford, was of Lotharingian origin, according to John of Worcester. He evidently must have been one of the fairly numerous group of Lotharingian clerics invited into England by Edward the Confessor to serve the royal court. The life of King Edward refers to Walter as a man of learning. He became chaplain to Edith, Edward's queen, before 1060. Domesday Book records that he held from King Edward the church of the manor of Basingstoke, Hampshire, in 1066. This church had no connection with the endowments of the see of Hereford and may have been remuneration for his position as chaplain. At Christmas 1060 Ealdred, bishop of Worcester, who had been supervising the see of Hereford in the vacancy following the death of Bishop Leofgar in July 1056, was made archbishop of York, and Edward appointed Walter bishop of Hereford. To avoid being consecrated by Archbishop Stigand, Walter and a fellow bishop-elect, Giso of Wells, were commanded by Edward to travel to Rome so that they could be consecrated by Pope Nicholas II. They probably formed part of the band of English travellers to Rome headed by Earl Tostig and Ealdred, the newly appointed archbishop of York. The consecration took place during the Easter Synod of 1061 (15 April). On the first day of the return journey, the group of English travellers was ambushed and had to return to Rome, and the date of Walter's return to England is uncertain, although if he accompanied Giso he would have reached England in June.

Walter seems to have played, as bishop, little part in public life either before or after the conquest, although after Hastings he was one of the bishops who submitted to William the Conqueror at Berkhamsted. He also attended the ecclesiastical councils held at Windsor, on 27 May 1072, and London, between Christmas 1074 and Michaelmas 1075. Walter's activities within his diocese are hard to trace. No charter issued by him survives. He seems to have allowed some of his church's holdings to depreciate and, in exchange for less valuable land, granted to William fitz Osbern, earl of Hereford, a site which William promptly used to set up a huge new market place, outrivalling the previous market, which had been in the part of the city belonging to the bishop.

Walter's death is not recorded in any narrative source save William of Malmesbury's *Gesta pontificum*, where it is said that the bishop, consumed with lust for a seamstress in Hereford, lured her into his palace on the pretext of requiring clothes to be made for his attendants, that when

he tried to rape her she stabbed him with a pair of scissors, and that William the Conqueror suppressed news of this story for fear of scandal (Malmesbury, *De gestis pontificum*, 300). Since Malmesbury introduces the story with the phrase 'unless rumour lies' it is possible that it was merely gossip, though the silence of other sources on Walter's death may perhaps suggest that his decease was not wholly respectable. Certainly Hereford Cathedral made no attempt to record his death in its obit book nor to include Walter in the series of elaborate tombs constructed in the late thirteenth century to commemorate most of the post-conquest bishops. Walter died before 29 December 1079, when his successor, Robert the Lotharingian, was consecrated. His place of burial is unknown.

JULIA BARROW

Sources John of Worcester, *Chron.*, 2.586–9, 606–7 · F. Barlow, ed. and trans., *The life of King Edward who rests at Westminster*, 2nd edn, OMT (1992), 35 · A. Farley, ed., *Domesday Book*, 2 vols. (1783), 1.43a, 181c · F. Barlow, *The English church, 1000–1066: a history of the later Anglo-Saxon church*, 2nd edn (1979), 25, 76, 83, 88, 109n, 114, 119, 157, 218, 238n, 303n · J. Barrow, ed., *Hereford, 1079–1234*, English Episcopal Acta, 7 (1993), xxxi–xxxiii · J. Barrow, 'A Lotharingian in Hereford: Bishop Robert's reorganisation of the church of Hereford, 1079–1095', *Medieval art, architecture and archaeology at Hereford*, ed. D. Whitehead, British Archaeological Association Conference Transactions, 15 (1995), 29–49, esp. 30–31 · *Willelmi Malmesbiriensis monachi de gestis pontificum Anglorum libri quinque*, ed. N. E. S. A. Hamilton, Rolls Series, 52 (1870), 300 · Symeon of Durham, *Opera*, 2.173–4 · *Reg. RAN*, 1.148 · D. Whitelock, M. Brett, and C. N. L. Brooke, eds., *Councils and synods with other documents relating to the English church, 871–1204*, 2 (1981), 585n, 592, 604 · *Fasti Angl., 1066–1300*, [Hereford]

Walter (d. **1182**), bishop of Rochester, was the son of Norman parents who had settled near Le Bec-Hellouin, and the brother of *Theobald, archbishop of Canterbury (d. 1161). He joined Theobald's household and was shortly appointed archdeacon of Canterbury. Walter seems to have been an active administrator. He appears as addressee or witness to more than a dozen archiepiscopal charters, and he was responsible for imposing a tax called 'second aids' on the churches of the diocese. This supplement, however, was later thought to have been excessive and was abolished by Theobald.

Bishop Ascelin of Rochester died on 24 January 1148, and Walter was elected *ex more* by the cathedral priory monks in the chapter house at Canterbury three days later. He owed his position to his brother, and Theobald later named him an executor of his will. Once elected Walter did homage and fealty to Theobald and swore to defend the rights of Canterbury in the diocese of Rochester. On 14 March 1148 he was consecrated bishop of Rochester by Theobald, and made his profession of obedience. In his household can be found the usual chaplains and chamberlains, clerks, and stewards, as well as a group of men educated in the schools. From 1148 to 1176 he assisted with the consecration of twelve bishops and archbishops, and in April 1161, when the primate was ill, Walter himself consecrated Richard Peche to Coventry. After Theobald's death in the same year, Walter took charge of the spiritual affairs at Canterbury and consecrated Bartholomew to Exeter. His name appears fairly often among the witnesses to Theobald's charters, and he also confirmed grants to a number of religious houses, and acted with the archbishop in the settlement of judicial cases. A dispute with his own archdeacon, Paris, over the share of income from ecclesiastical pleas, was decided in favour of the bishop. A quarrel with his monks over a church that Walter had given to Roger, his kinsman (*nepos*), involved appeals to Rome by both sides before a satisfactory agreement was reached. In the end the bishop increased his donations to the poor and obit payments to the convent, and presented the monks with a gold cup and cloth, and a silk pall.

Throughout his career Walter appears to have been a faithful royal servant. In obedience to Stephen he did not attend the papal council at Rheims in 1148 and was suspended by Eugenius III. In 1153 he was among the bishops who witnessed the treaty between Stephen and Duke Henry, and he was present at the latter's coronation in December 1154. He was again in London in October 1163 for the translation of Edward the Confessor, and he can be found at several other royal councils, including Henry II's settlement of the Castile–Navarre controversy in 1177. In the Becket conflict Walter had only a modest role. He has been described in this context as 'a colourless personality' (Knowles, *Thomas Becket*, 66), an assessment that may reveal ignorance of his character rather than facts about it, though it probably reflects his caution with regard to the king. In June 1162 Walter, who had been acting as *vicarius* of Canterbury since Theobald's death, ordained Becket to the priesthood. The right of consecration, however, he was forced to cede to Henry of Winchester. Gervase obscures the reasons, but emphasizes Walter's noble character and piety.

Previously Walter had befriended Becket on two occasions when he was briefly forced out of Theobald's household; he acted on his behalf to demand a safe conduct after the Council of Northampton; he excused himself from the London council in 1169 called by Henry to resist the archbishop; and he was ready to welcome him to Rochester upon his return to England in 1170. On the other hand, Gilbert Foliot, in his defence of the bishops at Clarendon, says that Walter did not join them to oppose the king. Perhaps fearful of the consequences of Foliot's excommunication, Walter remained away from Rochester in the spring of 1169. In the greater crisis of June 1170, against a papal injunction, Walter joined his colleagues at the coronation of the Young King, Henry, and was suspended by Alexander III. John of Salisbury had earlier written to reproach Walter for failing to act decisively on Becket's behalf and scolded him for personal extravagance but public parsimony. Rather later Peter of Blois chided him for his love of hunting, which did not suit a bishop, especially one who was eighty years old. He was accused of neglecting his pastoral duties and a complaint had been made in Rome. Walter, it seems, like most bishops, carried the burden of the ecclesiastical order without complaint, but aspired neither to reform nor to sainthood. He died on 26 July 1182.

EVERETT U. CROSBY

Sources J. Thorpe, ed., *Registrum Roffense, or, A collection of antient records, charters and instruments … illustrating the ecclesiastical history and antiquities of the diocese and cathedral church of Rochester* (1769) • *The historical works of Gervase of Canterbury*, ed. W. Stubbs, 2 vols., Rolls Series, 73 (1879–80) • *The letters of John of Salisbury*, ed. and trans. H. E. Butler and W. J. Millor, rev. C. N. L. Brooke, 2 vols., OMT (1979–86) [Lat. orig. with parallel Eng. text] • *Patrologia Latina*, 207 (1855) • Dugdale, *Monasticon*, vol. 1 • A. Saltman, *Theobald, archbishop of Canterbury* (1956) • M. Richter, ed., *Canterbury professions*, CYS, 67 (1973) • *Fasti Angl., 1066–1300*, [Monastic cathedrals] • *Materials for the history of Thomas Becket, archbishop of Canterbury*, 3, ed. J. C. Robertson, Rolls Series, 67 (1877) • C. R. Cheney and B. E. A. Jones, eds., *Canterbury, 1162–1190*, English Episcopal Acta, 2 (1986) • D. Knowles, *Thomas Becket* (1970) • D. Knowles, *The episcopal colleagues of Archbishop Thomas Becket* (1951) • 'Ernulfi episcopi Rossensis', *Anglia sacra*, ed. [H. Wharton], 1 (1691), 329–77
Archives BL, MS Cotton Domitian A.x

Walter [*called* Walter Offamil] (*d.* 1190), archbishop of Palermo, was assumed by earlier authorities to have been English from his nickname Offamil, which they rendered 'Of the Mill', but this is now interpreted as meaning chief counsellor, from the Latin *protofamiliaris*. When he became archbishop of Palermo in 1168, Peter of Blois's letter of congratulations to him referred to Walter's humble birth, although his mother Bona was a patron of Cluny, and was described by the king in 1172 as 'devota et fidelis nostra'; his father's name is unknown.

Walter is first recorded in court circles in 1160, when he was Latin tutor to the sons of William I (*r.* 1151–66). From 1169 he was prominent in government, one of a small group of royal familiars who managed the administration of the kingdom. After William II died childless in 1189, it was Walter who crowned as his successor William's cousin Tancredi di Lecce, at the behest of Pope Clement III (*r.* 1187–91). A conscientious bishop, he rebuilt Palermo Cathedral, where he was eventually buried. John Bale, writing in the late 1550s in the belief that Walter was English, attributed various works to him, including a book on the rudiments of the Latin tongue. On account of this attribution, Hervieux saw in Walter the likely author of twelfth-century adaptations into rhythmic Latin of Aesop's fables, even suggesting that they were intended to provide the young William II with appropriately instructive and attractive reading matter.   D. J. A. MATTHEW

Sources H. Falcandus, *La Historia, o, Liber de Regno Sicilie*, ed. G. B. Siragusa, 2 vols. (Rome, 1897–1904) • *Romualdi Salernitani chronicon*, ed. C. A. Garufi, 1 (Città di Castello, 1914), 258 • 'Petri Blesensis epistolae', *Patrologia Latina*, 207 (1855), 195, no. 66 • R. Pirri, *Sicilia sacra disquisitionibus et notitiis illustrata*, ed. A. Mongitore, 3rd edn, 1 (Palermo, 1733), 103–13 • L. Hervieux, *Les fabulistes latins*, 5 vols. (Paris, 1893–9), vol. 1, p. 494 • L. J. A. Loewenthal, 'For the biography of Walter Ophamil, archbishop of Palermo', *EngHR*, 87 (1972), 75–82

Walter (*b.* early 1820s, *d.* in or after 1894), anonymous autobiographer, wrote the pornographic *My Secret Life*, published from the late 1880s at Amsterdam in eleven volumes. Among the subjects of the *Oxford Dictionary of National Biography* he is unusual in possibly duplicating an existing entry—for Henry Spencer *Ashbee, who is often alleged to have based the work on his own experiences. Yet *My Secret Life*'s most recent and thorough investigator, while arguing strongly for Ashbee's authorship, admits that his case rests on 'entirely circumstantial' evidence (Gibson, 229). Whether Walter existed independently of Ashbee or not, his impact deserves to be recorded separately, for it was considerable at more than one level and in more than one period. Furthermore, in compiling an autobiography devoted solely to the sexual dimension of his life, if that is what Walter did, he produced a work which throws into relief the silences of conventional autobiography, where this important dimension of life is played down. Whereas sexual episodes constitute only regretted and semi-concealed one-line episodes in Gladstone's huge diary, for example, Walter's superabundant sexuality is so central to his diary that outside events impinge rarely and only momentarily.

A remarkable amount is known about Walter, and at the same time almost nothing, for pornography combines anonymity with unusual abundance in a very limited area of the subject's life. According to the sole source, Walter's diary, he seems to have been born in the early 1820s and was still compiling *My Secret Life* sixty years later. Brought up within a well-to-do family, with several siblings and servants, he was educated at home and then became a day boy at a public school. During his teenage years the family came down in the world, and his father died when Walter was sixteen. Walter prepared at first for the army, but his circumstances improved when his godfather, by leaving him a fortune, enabled him to buy himself out at twenty-one. At this time he began keeping his diary.

Extravagance rapidly consumed Walter's fortune and led him to depend on hand-outs from his mother, and five years later to marry (unhappily) for money. Further legacies and wealthy relatives then again eased his path, a legacy eventually freeing him to walk out of his marriage for further adventures in Europe. When he heard that his wife had died, he remarried. Monogamy, however, was beyond him, and he spent the rest of his life in promiscuity, moving confidently between the worlds where Victorian puritans located their enemy: London clubland, the country house, and adventurous travel abroad, especially in Paris. Not until the 1860s did Walter think of printing his autobiography privately, and he did not take action until about 1882, when he summoned Auguste Brancart, a printer of erotica from Amsterdam. Printing—in eleven volumes totalling 4200 pages, with a remarkably detailed index—was not complete until 1894. Walter paid 1100 guineas for the work, but did not publish for sale. He wanted only six copies printed, though there may have been more; certainly by the 1960s six had survived, including one each in the British Museum Library and the Kinsey Institute of Sex Research.

Walter initially seems to have kept his diary in an entirely conventional Victorian way; not until his mid-twenties did it become erotic. He kept it going for several years, allowed it to lapse, then resumed it in his mid-thirties as his sexual experience broadened. His practice was to make notes soon after the event, then fill out the account, usually after a few days. Two serious illnesses in his early forties gave him the leisure to sort through his memoirs, complete them, censor them as needed, and

incorporate reflections upon them. All this was done, however, with little attempt to impose internal consistency, let alone overall coherence; the text includes passages at different levels of composition. The style is unpretentious, and he often quotes vernacular conversations whose authentic ring brings Henry Mayhew's *London Labour and the London Poor* to mind. His failures, ignorance, and puzzlements are not concealed, and the tone even of the didactic passages is practical and down-to-earth, but the diary neglects the emotions for an obsessive preoccupation with physical detail.

Walter in some respects anticipates the sexual attitudes which the twentieth-century spread of birth control diffused more widely, with all its potential for a disjunction not only between sexuality and reproduction but between sexual relations and lasting all-round commitment between partners. But there are important contrasts, for in Walter's world feminism and sexual permissiveness were not allied causes: for him the role of the condom was not to protect the women from pregnancy but to protect himself from venereal disease. His sexual adventures made several women pregnant; as he put it, 'women have all the after trouble, we none' (*My Secret Life*, 8.1725). Yet in its yearning to understand rather than merely to condemn, Walter's diary faintly echoes the earnestness of the pioneer late Victorian sexologists such as Havelock Ellis and Edward Carpenter who are now seen as pioneers of the 'permissive society'. The worlds of sex research and pornography have never been clearly distinct, nor have those in authority ever been keen to sharpen the distinction. *My Secret Life* records experiences which constitute the author's lifelong quest both to understand himself and to secure complete identification with others, male or female. It diverges from pornographic works—Frank Harris, Fanny Hill—in not boasting or exaggerating, and in frequently describing conduct systematically in a semi-sociological way in so far as that was possible through one man generalizing from his own experience.

My Secret Life's record of its author's steadily broadening experience even at times almost parodies, through inversion, the reticence of the Victorian self-help autobiography. The milestones in Walter's life are secret sexual, not publicly conventional, climacterics: sexuality is for Walter central to human existence, and as he gradually progressed towards hedonistically glorifying the natural, he saw sexual inventiveness as the mark of mankind's supremacy within the natural world. For him the sexual organs are 'emblems of the Creator' (*My Secret Life*, 8.1622), and at times his paeans to sexuality take on an almost religious tone, crediting 'the Creator' with sponsoring enjoyment rather than repression. The diary was, he said, 'written … with absolute truth and without any regard whatever for what the world calls decency' (ibid., 1.7). Accepted attitudes are frequently pilloried as absurd. The prostitute was not inevitably doomed to the gutter, for example, and 'to their class I owe a debt of gratitude … I shall never throw stones at them, nor speak harshly to them, nor of them' (ibid., 5.902). Public and private virtue should not be equated: 'it seems to me, that both men and women may be straight, and fair in all they do, be as good and useful members of society as others, yet take their chief delight in carnal pleasures' (ibid., 6.1250).

Yet Walter did not shed all Victorian values; indeed, like the selection from Arthur Munby's memoirs published by Derek Hudson as *Munby: Man of Two Worlds* (1972), *My Secret Life* reveals a Walter who may have cumulatively abandoned inhibitions, but who by no means lost them all. He felt the need to justify each new breach of convention to a potentially disapproving reader. Furthermore, although *My Secret Life* sometimes records an almost egalitarian delight at sexuality's dissolution of class barriers, it also retains what later came to seem callous and prejudiced attitudes to gender, ethnic, economic, and social-class relations. A major contrast with the sexuality of the 1960s lay in the enormous power that Victorian discrepancies in wealth could wield: according to Walter, recurrently wielding his sovereigns, 'money will open every female's legs' (*My Secret Life*, 8.1599). Even on sexual matters he retained some conventional attitudes: in his emphasis on the debilitating effects of male masturbation, for example, and in his abhorrence of homosexuality.

Walter has a second role in British history: *My Secret Life* played a modest part in relaxing censorship in Britain. Sections of the book were reprinted by various inter-war publishers, and during the 1960s Drs Eberhard and Phyllis Kronhausen brought out a heavily edited selection, *Walter: the English Casanova*, in the United States. It was republished in Britain in two paperback volumes by Polybooks, supplemented in 1970 by a third paperback volume with minimal editorial comment, *More Walter*, published by Morntide Ltd, and subtitled 'The unique memoirs of England's most uninhibited lover'. By 1970, said the Kronhausens, Walter had become 'as well known … as his illustrious predecessors Casanova and … Don Juan' (*More Walter*, 5). It was Steven Marcus's *The Other Victorians* (1966), however, that drew *My Secret Life* to serious academic attention. With access to the Victoriana collected at the Kinsey Institute, and with the institute's full encouragement, Marcus included in this study of nineteenth-century pornography a detailed analysis of Walter's memoirs, complete with unbowdlerized quotations. Marcus, like the Kronhausens, viewed Walter as a pioneer of modern sexuality. Libertarian in his approach to private enjoyment, rationalistic in his down-to-earth approach to the facts of sexuality and to sex education, Walter declared that 'your body is your own, and you may use it as you like. Its usage concerns no one else but its owner' (*My Secret Life*, 5.1043). For Marcus, Walter was 'a representative figure of cultural subversion in his own time, he representatively anticipates what is about to become the conformity of ours' (*The Other Victorians*, 155).

In 1966 Grove Press of New York published the full text as a single volume. The firm's United Kingdom agent was Arthur Dobson, a 31-year-old Bradford bookseller, who sold about 250 copies. When Grove revoked the agreement, Dobson republished the first two volumes, but in 1969 he was prosecuted for doing so before Mr Justice Veale and a jury at Leeds assizes. Dobson pleaded not guilty to all charges. He was defended in court by Stephen Marcus, John Mortimer, and others on the ground that publication was justified under the Obscene Publications Act (1959) as being 'in the interests of science, literature, art or learning, or of other objects of general concern'. For the prosecution, however, the book was 'utterly and totally obscene', and had been written by a man who 'from a very early stage in his life gave himself over to a life of unremitting fornication and diverse and perverted sexual malpractices' (Watkins, 210). For Veale, passing judgment on 3 February 1969, Dobson's motive was not scholarly: 'I have no doubt at all that you are a professional purveyor of filth.' For this and for publishing two other pornographic volumes Dobson was required to destroy the books and was sentenced to two years' imprisonment and a fine of £1000 plus £2000 towards the cost of the prosecution. On 28 November this was reduced on appeal to fifteen months in prison and a fine of £510.

How justified were the claims made during Dobson's trial about *My Secret Life*'s historical value? The recollections are observant, says Marcus, and show 'a larger measure of disinterested sympathy than Mayhew and the early descriptive sociologists' (*The Other Victorians*, 100). They reflect an obsessive and lifelong inquisitiveness about sexual conduct which led Walter even to confront his sexual partners with memorized questionnaires. They provide a striking reminder that the 'official' and dominant culture of Victorian Britain faced continuous challenge from a male-dominated sexually libertarian counter-culture. This is the amoral counterpart of the moralistic and feminist Victorian code promoted in the careers of Josephine Butler and W. T. Stead; it offers a sociology and a geography of London prostitution which have for once been compiled by the consumer. Whatever their value for the majority of their readers, Walter's diaries, like Joe Orton's for the 1960s, offer to the student of Victoriana the insights that spring from contrast: from the sudden illumination of the familiar when viewed from a new angle, from the uncompromising exposure of the concealments and self-deceptions that buttress social convention, and from the bizarre juxtapositions that reveal how thin is the membrane that separates day-to-day normality from a hidden world beneath.   BRIAN HARRISON

Sources *My secret life*, vols. 1–11 (New York, 1966) [introduction by G. Legman] • I. Gibson, *The erotomaniac: the secret life of Henry Spencer Ashbee* (2001) • B. Harrison, 'Underneath the Victorians', *Victorian Studies*, 11 (1967–8), 239–62 • M. Mason, *The making of Victorian sexuality* (1994) • J. Sutherland, *Offensive literature: decensorship in Britain, 1960–1982* (c.1982) • A. Watkins, 'A slight case of obscenity', *New Statesman* (14 Feb 1969), 210

Walter de Hopton. *See* Hopton, Sir Walter of (c.1235–1295/6).

Walter, Sir, fitz Gilbert (d. in or before 1346). *See under* Hamilton family (per. 1295–1479).

Walter son of Alan (c.1198–1241). *See under* Stewart family (per. c.1110–c.1350).

Walter, Arthur Fraser (1846–1910), newspaper proprietor, was born on 12 September 1846 at Waterloo House, near Wokingham, Berkshire, the second of the two sons of John *Walter (1818–1894), grandson of the founder of *The Times*, and of his first wife, Emily Frances (*d.* 1858), eldest daughter of Henry Court of Castlemans, Berkshire. It was Arthur Walter's misfortune to be head of the family at the moment when circumstances forced the sale of the paper. It was in a different sense a personal misfortune. His elder brother, John, groomed for a dynastic role as John Walter the fourth, was drowned on Christmas eve 1870, while rescuing one of his half-brothers and a cousin from the frozen lake at the family home, Bear Wood in Newland, Berkshire. Arthur thus found himself thrust into a position for which he was prepared neither by upbringing nor by temperament.

At Eton College, Arthur Walter, though less sociable than his elder brother, was a painstaking scholar and an excellent games player. He completed his education at Christ Church, Oxford, where he took a first in classical moderations and a third in finals. The latter may have been due to the competing appeal of cricket, which he played for the university against Cambridge. He made no great mark in his college, except that he was active in a campaign against poor college food, which became known as 'the bread-and-butter row' and attracted (not surprisingly, the campaign's opponents remarked) the friendly support of *The Times*. Shortly after graduating Walter started helping his father with the paper. He also entered Lincoln's Inn and was called to the bar in 1875, but he never practised. On 15 October 1872 he married Henrietta Maria (*b.* 1846/7), eldest daughter of the Revd Thomas Anchitel Anson, of Longford rectory, Derbyshire. They had two sons and two daughters. In 1885 his father, by now sixty-seven, made him joint manager of *The Times*, and in 1894, on his father's death, he became chief proprietor. He conducted the paper along its traditional gentlemanly and politically independent lines. He did not seek to impose his views on the editor, G. E. Buckle, with whom he got on well and who was in the chair throughout his proprietorship. The printing side was left entirely to his younger half-brother Godfrey. None of this took him away from Bear Wood for more than three or four days a week.

This apparently stable regime was deceptive. The structure of *The Times* had grown cumbersome. Two-thirds of the buildings and printing business now belonged to Arthur Walter, and one-third to Godfrey. The printing business had a longstanding contract with the paper (which had been founded to provide it with work). *The Times* itself was owned as a co-partnership, in which the shares, divided into sixteenths, were often subdivided. Arthur Walter owned two sixteenths. There were about 100 other partners. These arrangements sufficed, so long as the paper made a profit. If it did not, the partners would be bound to object, since their liabilities at law were unlimited. This was precisely the problem developing at about the time of Arthur Walter's succession. His single most important action in response, and arguably the most important decision of his career, was the appointment in 1890 of C. F. Moberly Bell as his assistant manager. The choice was all the more remarkable because Bell had spent most of his working life in business in Egypt, where latterly he was the *Times* correspondent, and Walter did not know him well. The appointment had profound consequences. Bell's formidable personality and absorption in the job enabled him to dominate his nominal superior and, eventually, to defeat the Walters' own plans for *The Times* and to sell it to Alfred Harmsworth. Bell found a paper with steadily declining circulation and advertising, archaic design, and outdated printing services for which it was overcharged. He sought relief in such money-making initiatives as a reprint of the ninth edition of *Encyclopaedia Britannica* and the *Times* book club. At length legal action by some of the partners led to a dissolution of the partnership, and in July 1907 *The Times* went up for sale. Arthur Walter, on Godfrey's initiative, sought a limited liability company in which the main injection of capital would come from the newspaper entrepreneur C. Arthur Pearson. Neither Bell nor Buckle was privy to this scheme. When it was disclosed precipitately after a mischievous paragraph in Harmsworth's *Observer*, Bell immediately determined to defeat it. Pearson, who founded the *Daily Express*, was known as a 'hustler'. Harmsworth too ran papers that were the antithesis of *The Times* in looks and content. But his record was stronger and he was prepared to give Bell assurances about maintaining the paper's character and independence. Arthur Walter abandoned Pearson and threw in his lot with Bell. During the negotiations Harmsworth's identity remained secret—even from Walter and his son John *Walter (1873–1968), who joined the business in 1898. Walter's influence helped to bring round the partners and nullify alternative schemes. In March 1908 the court approved the sale, chiefly to Harmsworth nominees, of whom Bell was the principal. Arthur Walter was the second largest single shareholder and became chairman of the new Times Publishing Company Limited. Had he worked with Bell from the beginning, the problems of the old structure might well have been resolved without the Walter proprietorship coming to an end.

Quite apart from the traditions of *The Times*, which meant that the proprietor, though instantly deferred to, was never obtrusive, Arthur Walter was by nature reserved and aloof, and he lacked imagination. A portrait by H. Riviere shows him in middle age, balding and with flowing moustaches typical of his generation. His education completely failed to equip him for business in a rapidly changing newspaper world. The Bear Wood estate, amounting to 7000 acres, always engaged his interest—for instance in landscape gardening. Locally he was known as a country gentleman whom private affairs frequently called to London. He served as a county councillor, a railway company director, and a Territorial Army colonel. Arthur Walter died at Bear Wood on 22 February 1910 after an attack of influenza.   COLIN SEYMOUR-URE

Sources [S. Morison and others], *The history of The Times*, 3 (1947) • *The Times* (23 Feb 1910) • J. H. Kitchin, *Moberly Bell and his times* (1925) • *The Times: past, present, future* (1932) • K. Jones, *Fleet Street and Downing Street* (1920) • W. D. Bowman, *The story of 'The Times'* (1931) • R. Pound and G. Harmsworth, *Northcliffe* (1959) • S. E. Koss, *The rise*

and fall of the political press in Britain, 2 (1984) • W. Steed, *The press* (1938) • *CGPLA Eng. & Wales* (1910) • b. cert. • m. cert. • d. cert.
Archives News Int. RO, papers
Likenesses H. Riviere, oils?, repro. in [Morison and others], *History of The Times*, 3
Wealth at death £287,403 8s. 1d.: probate, 29 April 1910, *CGPLA Eng. & Wales*

Walter, Sir Edward (1823–1904), founder of the Corps of Commissionaires, was born in London on 9 December 1823, the third son of John *Walter (1776–1847), proprietor of *The Times*, and his wife, Mary, the daughter of Henry Smithe of Eastling, Kent. Like his brothers, he was educated at Eton College and at Exeter College, Oxford, where he matriculated on 6 May 1841. He entered the army in 1843 as ensign of the 44th regiment, transferred to the 8th hussars as captain in 1848, and retired from the army in 1853, the same year in which he married, on 5 April, Mary Anne Eliza Athorpe (1831/2–1912), the daughter of John Carver Athorpe of Dinnington Hall, Rotherham, Yorkshire. They had three daughters and two sons, one of whom later joined the 7th hussars.

After his retirement from the army Walter grew increasingly frustrated by the spectacle of soldiers, seriously wounded in the Crimean War and the Indian mutiny, who had been honorably discharged but were unable to find work. His idea was that a niche could be found for these disabled men of good character to be employed as porters and messengers in big cities to deliver parcels and urgent letters. In order to provide an organization which would be able to match the needs of potential employers with the wounded, and which would be able to provide character references, in February 1859 he set up the Corps of Commissionaires. At first confining his efforts to wounded men only, through his army and family contacts he found situations in London for eight men, each of whom had lost a limb, who were first accepted by Messrs Hunt and Roskell of Bond Street and Mr Poole, a tailor. On 13 February 1859 Walter took seven disabled men to Westminster Abbey to give thanks for having found employment. Two days later he organized twenty-seven veterans of the army and navy into a society set up to be self-supporting and entirely dependent on the earnings of its members. He provided the men with uniforms and took offices in Exchange Court, where he carried on his work with only his family to help him. A number of the men were unable to keep their jobs, but Walter refused to despair of the project, and was sustained in his work by his family for the first five difficult years. In 1864, by which time the corps had risen to 250 men, he appealed to the public for donations, creating an officers' endowment fund to enable him to engage a staff of officers to assist.

The appeal met with a generous response, and new branches of the corps were opened in Dublin and Edinburgh. By 1874 numbers had reached just under 500, and, by 1886, 1200. In 1884 Walter received a testimonial from officers of the navy and army, and in 1885 he was knighted, being nominated KCB (civil) in 1887. By 1911 the corps employed 4152 men, about half of whom were based in London, the remainder being scattered in Belfast, Birmingham, Bristol, Edinburgh, Glasgow, Leeds, Liverpool, Manchester, Newcastle, and Nottingham.

Walter spent his last years at Perran Lodge, Branksome, near Bournemouth, where he died after a long illness on 26 February 1904. He was buried on 2 March at Bear Wood, Wokingham, and a granite obelisk was erected by the corps to his memory in Brookwood cemetery. He was succeeded in the command of the corps by his nephew, Major Frederick Edward Walter (second son of John Walter of Bear Wood).

The Corps of Commissionaires was still in existence at the time of writing. Its aim remained that of finding employment for former service personnel. In 1969 its scope was widened to include former members of other uniformed services, such as the police, fire brigade, and coastguard. It was controlled by the Walter family until the retirement of Lieutenant-Colonel Reginald Walter in 1975, and its turnover in 1994 was £16 million.

H. M. VIBART, *rev.* MARK CLEMENT

Sources WWW, 1897–1915 • Burke, *Gen. GB* (1965) • Foster, *Alum. Oxon.* • private information (2004) • *The Times* (29 Feb 1904), 8 • d. cert. [Mary Walter] • *CGPLA Eng. & Wales* (1904)
Likenesses Mrs Wey, oils, priv. coll.
Wealth at death £19,546 10s. 10d.: probate, 30 March 1904, *CGPLA Eng. & Wales*

Walter, (William) Grey (1910–1977), neurophysiologist, was born in Kansas City, Missouri, on 19 February 1910, the only child of Karl Wilhelm Walter (1880–1965), a British journalist then working on the Kansas City *Star*, and his wife, Minerva Lucrezia (Margaret) Hardy (1879–1953), an American journalist. His parents had met and married in Italy, where they spent much of their lives. During the First World War they moved from the United States to Britain, where Grey Walter spent the rest of his life. He was educated at Westminster School (1922–8), where he specialized in classics and then in science, which he continued at King's College, Cambridge, from 1928. He took a third class in part one (1930) and a first class in physiology in part two of the natural sciences tripos (1931), and went on to do postgraduate research on nerve physiology and conditioned reflexes. His MA dissertation on 'Conduction in nerve and muscle' was accepted in 1935.

Walter then joined Professor F. L. Golla, an eminent neurologist who was director of the central pathological laboratories at the Maudsley Hospital. Golla wanted to apply the new method of investigating the brain by recording its electrical activity (electroencephalogram or EEG) to clinical problems and was able to provide various types of patients for Walter to study. In 1936 a patient thought to be suffering from schizophrenia was found to have abnormal activity in the EEG and then discovered to have a cerebral tumour. Recordings done in the operating theatre confirmed that the activity was associated with the tumour. Between 1936 and 1939 many hundreds of patients were investigated; those with epilepsy were shown to have abnormal activity in the EEG between attacks.

In 1939 Golla and Walter moved to Bristol to open the Burden Neurological Institute as a research centre in

(William) Grey Walter (1910–1977), by unknown photographer [detail]

neuropsychiatry. There Walter made many novel instruments to analyse the EEG. On-line frequency analysis was developed in 1943, sensory stimuli used to provoke abnormal activity in the EEG in 1947, and the toposcope to analyse the frequency and phase structure of the EEG in 1950. The work on conditioning went on and in the early 1960s led to the discovery of the contingent negative variation, which became a subject of study throughout the world.

Walter also developed models that mimicked brain systems and this involved him with Norbert Wiener and others in early work on cybernetics. His 'tortoises', displayed at the Festival of Britain in 1951, were designed to show the interaction of two sensory systems: light-sensitive and touch-sensitive control mechanisms (in effect, two nerve cells with visual and tactile inputs). These systems interacted with the motor drive in such a way that the 'animals' exhibited 'behaviour', finding their way round obstacles, for example.

Walter was a fluent speaker and writer, on general as well as technical subjects. He was fluent in French, Italian, and German. He was the author of 170 scientific publications and gave a number of important lectures. He relished making broadcasts and giving talks; he was a frequent guest on BBC television's *The Brains Trust*. He wrote two books: *The Living Brain* (1953), which was popular science and was the first introduction that many people had to the brain, and a science fiction novel, *Further Outlook* (1956), which was not very successful. He was awarded an ScD by Cambridge in 1947, and in 1949 was made a professor of the University of Aix-Marseilles. In 1974 he was awarded the Oliver–Sharpey prize of the Royal College of Physicians. In 1975, the Electroencephalographic Society, of which he was a founder member, commemorated his achievements by striking a Grey Walter medal, 'to be presented … in recognition of outstanding services to clinical neurophysiology'. He was the first recipient of the medal.

A member of the Cambridge Apostles from 1933, he was a communist supporter before and during the war but later became more sympathetic, first to anarchism, and then to syndicalism. He was an active member of the Association of Scientific Workers. He was involved in the peace movement, being a member of the Peace Pledge Union in the 1930s and the Bristol committee of 100 in the 1960s; but was never a pacifist, and he served in the Home Guard during the Second World War. A firm atheist, he was interested in, though unconvinced by, the paranormal, and also did research on hypnosis.

In 1934 Walter married Katharine Monica (*b*. 1911), younger daughter of Samuel Kerkham Ratcliffe, a British journalist and lecturer; they separated in 1945 and divorced in 1946. They had two sons, Nicolas, who became a journalist and lecturer, and Jeremy, who became a physicist. In 1947 he married Vivian Joan (1915–1980), daughter of John Dovey, colour manufacturer. She was a colleague for many years. They separated in 1960; they had one son, Timothy (1949–1976). From 1960 to 1972 he lived with Lorraine Josephine, daughter of Mr Donn, property developer, and former wife of Keith Aldridge. In 1970 he suffered severe brain damage in a road accident which effectively ended his career. For forty years he had been at the forefront of research on the living brain, using its electrical activity to chart normal and abnormal function. He died of a heart attack at his home at Flat 2, 20 Richmond Park Road, Clifton, Bristol, on 6 May 1977 and was cremated on 12 May.   RAY COOPER

Sources personal knowledge (1993) · private information (1993) [Nicolas Walter, son] · R. Cooper and J. Bird, *The Burden: fifty years of clinical and experimental neuroscience at the Burden Neurological Institute* (1989) · m. certs. · d. cert.
Archives Burden Neurological Institute, Bristol
Likenesses J. Codner, oils, 1975, Burden Neurological Institute, Bristol · photograph, Burden Neurological Institute, Bristol [*see illus.*] · photographs, repro. in Cooper and Bird, *The Burden* (1989)
Wealth at death £21,450: probate, 4 July 1977, *CGPLA Eng. & Wales*

Walter, Henry (1611–1678?), clergyman and ejected minister, was born at Piercefield, St Arvans parish, Monmouthshire. He was probably the third son of a family of eight children. His parents, John and Bridget Walter, were of minor gentry status: his brother Edmund lived at the substantial farmhouse of Cophill, near Piercefield, and the family enjoyed the tithes of the extra-parochial liberty of Howick, which contained Cophill. The tithes were in the hands of Henry Walter when he made his will in 1675: his mother had left them to him in reversion in her will, proved in 1625. He matriculated at Jesus College, Oxford, on 12 April 1633 and graduated BCL later that year.

Henry Walter's brother John secured him the curacy of the small parish of Mounton, next to St Arvans, early in 1639. Despite this appointment, and despite the frequency with which members of the Walter family demonstrated loyalty to the Church of England by leaving small bequests to Llandaff Cathedral in their wills, he revealed his sympathies to be with those who sought a purer form of worship in gathered congregations. He was one of those ministers who assisted the Independent cause at Broadmead, Bristol, and was greatly influenced by William Wroth, a main force behind the Independent congregation at Llanfaches, Monmouthshire. Walter was principal executor of Wroth's will, made in September 1638. With the advent of civil war Walter joined the puritan ministerial diaspora from south-east Wales, and is likely to have made for London, where another founder of the Llanfaches church, Walter Cradock, was able to acquire a ministerial appointment and thus provide a springboard for a regrouping of Welsh puritan activity. By leaving Monmouthshire, Henry Walter was able to avoid the fate of his brother Edmund, forced against his will by the royalist colonel Charles Gerard in October 1644 to journey with him to Worcester.

On 28 October 1646 Walter, Cradock, and Richard Symonds were ordered by the House of Commons to hasten to Wales to preach in Welsh there, and when the Rump Parliament approved the Act for the Propagation of the Gospel on 22 February 1650 Walter's name headed the list of clerical commissioners to approve ministerial appointments in Wales. He was an active itinerant preacher in Monmouthshire and Glamorgan, but was evidently based in the county of his birth. After the non-renewal of the Propagation Act in 1653 Walter was settled as vicar of St Woolloos, Newport, where his stipend was augmented to nearly £100 by grants of the tithes of other parishes in the county, formerly property of the dean and chapter of Llandaff. In his ministry he was not as strident in tone as Vavasor Powell nor as sympathetic to 'new lights' as Morgan Llwyd. Indeed, although he was the recipient of fraternal letters from the radical preacher William Erbury, Walter showed scant sympathy for the leading south Wales Quaker Francis Gawler, who had been a member of his congregation before Walter expelled him, believing him to be bewitched. In 1655 Walter subscribed to the *Humble Representation and Address* to Oliver Cromwell, which supported the protectorate against the hostile denunciations of it contained in *A Word for God*, the work of Vavasor Powell.

Walter remained at Newport until he was ejected from the living in 1662, and removed to Parc-y-Pîl, in Llanfihangel Llantarnam parish. Even before that he had been made uncomfortable by the Restoration; in July 1660 he and other puritan preachers were roughed up at Llantarnam, a centre for Catholicism and home of the Morgan family, long sympathetic to that faith. In 1672, during the indulgence, he was licensed to minister at Llantarnam, and in that year was involved in a legal dispute with Henry Somerset, third marquess of Worcester, the leading promoter of Roman Catholicism in Monmouthshire. By 1675 he was reported to be the inspiration behind the Independent congregation at Mynyddislwyn. He made his will on 13 January 1675, and left a modest bequest to 'poor Christians' at Mynyddislwyn. That his will mentioned a loan of books on canon and civil law he had made to Thomas Aubrey, 'called chancellor' (in his words) of Llandaff Cathedral, suggests that towards the end of his life he had made some partial rapprochement with the Anglican church (N L Wal., will of Henry Walter, LL/1678/62). Henry Walter died at Parc-y-Pîl before 8 August 1678; at least four sons and two daughters of his were living at his death.

STEPHEN K. ROBERTS

Sources DWB · T. Richards, *A history of the puritan movement in Wales* (1920) · T. Richards, *Religious developments in Wales, 1654–1662*

(1923) · T. Rees, *History of protestant nonconformity in Wales*, 2nd edn (1883) · will and inventory, NL Wales, LL/1678/62 · wills, NL Wales, MS 7618D [Walter family, copies] · Glamorgan Archive Service, CL/MS 4.266 [letter book of John Byrd] · F. Gawler, *A record of some persecutions … in south Wales* (1659) · J. A. Bradney, *A history of Monmouthshire*, 3/2 (1923) · J. A. Bradney, *A history of Monmouthshire*, 4/1–2 (1932–3) · G. Williams, ed., *Glamorgan county history*, 4: *Early modern Glamorgan* (1974)
Wealth at death £58 3s. 8d.: will and inventory, NL Wales, LL/1678/62

Walter, Henry (1785–1859), Church of England clergyman, natural philosopher and historian, born at Louth in Lincolnshire on 28 January 1785, was the eldest of the eighteen children of James Walter (*d.* 8 Feb 1845), master of the grammar school at Louth and afterwards rector of Market Rasen in Lincolnshire, and his wife, Frances Maria Walter. After education at Brigg he was admitted to St John's College, Cambridge, on 1 March 1802, and graduated BA in 1806, being classed as second wrangler in the mathematical tripos. In the same year he was elected to a fellowship at St John's, a position which he held until his marriage on 3 June 1824 to Emily Anne, daughter of William Baker, of Bayfordbury, Hertfordshire. In January 1813 his kinswoman Jane Austen wrote of her satisfaction at hearing him described by a St John's man as 'the best classick in the university' (Faye, 199). He was ordained priest on 23 March 1810. On the foundation of the East India College, Haileybury, in 1806, he was appointed professor of natural philosophy and mathematics, and he was elected a fellow of the Royal Society in November 1819. In 1830 he took up residence at the rectory of Hazelbury Bryan, Dorset, to which he had been instituted in May 1821 on the presentation of the duke of Northumberland, who had been one of his pupils at Cambridge.

Walter was a notable scholar of the English Reformation, and edited three volumes of works by William Tyndale for the Parker Society (1848–50). In 1825 he published an edition of Edward VI's primer. His other publications included a seven-volume school book, *History of England* (1840), 'intended to consider Man and Events on Christian Principles', and minor works of an evangelical or didactic nature. Walter died at Hazelbury Bryan on 25 January 1859, and was buried in the parish churchyard.

G. MARTIN MURPHY

Sources Venn, *Alum. Cant.* · *Jane Austen's letters*, ed. D. Le Faye, 3rd edn (1995), 180, 183–4, 199 · *GM*, 3rd ser., 6 (1859), 326 · *CGPLA Eng. & Wales* (1859)
Likenesses G. Richmond, black lead drawing, 1821, BM
Wealth at death under £1000: probate, 17 Feb 1859, *CGPLA Eng. & Wales*

Walter, Hubert (*d.* 1205), justiciar and archbishop of Canterbury, was born during Stephen's reign, probably at West Dereham, Norfolk, and retained his East Anglian connections throughout his life.

Origins and early career Hubert was the son of Sir Hervey Walter, a Norfolk knight of middling status, and Matilda de Valognes, daughter of Theobald de Valognes, lord of Parham, Suffolk, and Hickling, Norfolk. Hubert Walter's most important relationship, however, was with his

Hubert Walter (*d.* 1205), seal [obverse]

mother's sister Bertha de Valognes and her husband Ranulf de *Glanville, sheriff of Yorkshire and, after 1178, justiciar for Henry II. Hubert and his brother Theobald *Butler were brought up in Glanville's household, acquiring there a set of connections that in Hubert's case would influence the rest of his career.

Hubert Walter is not known to have spent any time in the schools, and in later life his lack of formal education was sometimes an embarrassment to him. He received a wealth of administrative and legal training in Glanville's household, however, and it was in his uncle's service that he rose to prominence around the royal court during the 1180s. As Ranulf de Glanville's chief deputy in England, Walter was involved in the full range of administrative business for which the justiciar was responsible, serving as one of the barons of the exchequer during the 1180s, and sitting regularly with Glanville and others as a justice of the exchequer court. He developed considerable expertise as a justice during these years, and several of his legal opinions are cited respectfully in the contemporary law book known as *Glanvill* (1187–9). During the last few years of Henry II's reign, the king employed him in chancery and diplomatic work also. Walter carried money to south Wales for the king's troops, and conveyed messages between England and the king in France. On Henry II's orders, he also tried to mediate the dispute between Archbishop Baldwin of Canterbury and the monks of Christ Church over Baldwin's proposal to establish a house of canons at Lambeth.

In 1186, during a vacancy at York, the king appointed Hubert Walter dean of York Cathedral. A few months later the chapter named him as one of five candidates to be the new archbishop, but the king refused to accept any of the nominations and the see remained vacant. In 1188, in a fitting acknowledgement of the debts he owed his patron, Walter founded a Premonstratensian monastery at West Dereham to pray for himself, his family, and his aunt and uncle, Bertha and Ranulf de Glanville.

When Richard I came to the throne in 1189, Ranulf de Glanville was compelled to resign as justiciar. Many of Glanville's followers also lost their offices at this time. Hubert Walter, however, survived the purge, and although disappointed yet again of the archbishopric of York, which went to the new king's half-brother Geoffrey, on 15 September 1189 he was elected bishop of Salisbury at King Richard's command. Consecrated in St Katherine's Chapel, Westminster, on 22 October 1189 by his longtime friend, Archbishop Baldwin of Canterbury, Walter quickly found himself embroiled yet again in attempts to settle the dispute between the archbishop and the monks of Christ Church.

Crusader The new bishop of Salisbury spent little time in his see. Like others of the Glanville faction, including Ranulf himself, Hubert Walter had vowed to go on the crusade that King Richard was now gathering in earnest. Until Richard's departure in December 1189, Walter was almost constantly at court. Thereafter he may have visited Salisbury briefly, but by March 1190 he was in Normandy with the king. After a brief visit to England, he was back on the continent from 3 July until 5 August, when he set sail from Marseilles for the Holy Land.

Hubert Walter arrived in Tyre on 16 September 1190, in a party that included Ranulf de Glanville and Archbishop Baldwin. In early October they joined the crusader army besieging Acre. Conditions in the crusader camp were terrible, and the leaders of the English contingent, including Glanville, Baldwin, and the earl of Derby, were all dead by the end of November. As bishop of Salisbury, Walter thus became the leader of the English contingent at Acre, and quickly began to reorganize the camp; an executor of Baldwin's will, he used the archbishop's possessions to pay wages to the sentries and buy food for the starving common soldiers. He led sorties against Saladin's camp, and also ministered to the religious needs of the army. Morale rose; and when King Richard at last arrived at Acre in June 1191, having spent the winter in Messina, he found the army in far better shape than it had been six months before.

Hubert Walter's stature in the crusading army continued to grow after Richard's arrival. He distinguished himself in several battles, and handled a variety of sensitive negotiations between the competing crusade leaders. In August 1192, when Richard fell ill, it was Walter who arranged a truce in the fighting. Soon afterwards he negotiated a more permanent peace treaty with the Muslim leader Saladin that guaranteed free access for Western Christians to Jerusalem and restored Latin services in Bethlehem, Nazareth, and the church of the Holy Sepulchre in Jerusalem. Walter then fulfilled his crusader's vow by leading one of the first contingents of Western pilgrims to visit Jerusalem under the terms of the new peace treaty.

Archbishop and justiciar Hubert Walter and King Richard both left the Holy Land in October 1192. Walter's route home took him to Sicily and then to Rome, where he met with Pope Celestine III in January 1193. It was probably in Rome that rumours of Richard's captivity first reached him. By March 1193 Walter, accompanied by the exchequer clerk William de Ste Mère-Église, had found the king at Ochsenfurt, on the River Main. They were the first of his subjects to reach him. Walter immediately began negotiating terms for Richard's release. In late March he and Ste Mère-Église left for England carrying letters from the captive king concerning his ransom. Among these letters was the king's command to Queen Eleanor, the justiciars, and the monks of Christ Church to have Hubert Walter elected archbishop of Canterbury. The monks of Christ Church complied, electing Walter on 28 May at Canterbury, one day in advance of the council summoned to London for this purpose. On 29 May the monks went up to London to announce their election to the royal council, where the suffragan bishops of Canterbury, too, voted to elect him. Papal permission to translate him from Salisbury to Canterbury was received, and on 7 November 1193 a papal nuncio invested Hubert Walter with the archiepiscopal pallium at Canterbury. At Christmas 1193 the captive king appointed him his justiciar also.

Hubert Walter had returned to England in April 1193 as King Richard's representative, to restore peace to a country disturbed by the rebellion of Prince John, the king's brother, and to raise money for the king's ransom. His appointment as justiciar regularized his position, but did not substantially alter the sweeping nature of the governmental responsibilities he had already undertaken. His formal appointment as justiciar may, however, have given him the immediate authority he needed to begin military operations against John's castellans. After summoning a council to condemn John and his followers, in February 1194 Walter himself led the successful siege of Marlborough Castle. A few weeks later he personally accepted the peaceful surrender of Lancaster Castle by its constable, his brother Theobald Walter, John's butler since 1185, whom Hubert now reconciled with the king. By 13 March 1194, when King Richard returned to the country, John's rebellion was over. As archbishop of Canterbury, Walter took part in Richard's solemn crown-wearing at Winchester on 17 April. A few weeks later Richard returned to Normandy to take charge of the war with Philip Augustus, king of France. For the next four years both the temporal and the spiritual government of England would rest in the hands of Hubert Walter.

The beginnings of administrative reform A series of remarkable administrative developments followed. The four and a half years of Hubert Walter's justiciarship were characterized by the systematization of existing procedures and the creation of new ones. None of the changes was in itself revolutionary; most built upon developments that went back to the days of Glanville's justiciarship. Nor were they the product of disinterested administrative reflection. Behind the reforms lay the relentless demand for money to support King Richard's war in France. The full measure of Hubert Walter's administrative genius is therefore to be found less in the efficiency of his governance, although that was considerable, than in his ability, as justiciar, to raise the enormous sums needed for war, while retaining, and even enhancing, the confidence of the king's subjects

in the fairness of royal justice. It was an achievement his successors as justiciar might envy, but could not repeat.

The first clear sign of the new justiciar's plans came in September 1194, when Hubert sent teams of itinerant justices throughout the country on a general eyre. Within two months, royal justices had visited every shire in England, with the justiciar himself heading up the eastern circuit. The remarkable speed with which this eyre was carried through testifies to the urgency of the situation facing the justiciar. Hubert Walter wanted a quick restoration of royal justice after the disorders that had marked John's rebellion. But as the articles of the eyre made clear, he also wanted a full accounting of the lands and goods forfeited by the rebels, and of the crown's other financial resources in the shires, including the profits of justice. To this end, local knights were now to be elected as coroners in every shire, to record crown pleas and present them to the justices on eyre. Beyond the hearing of crown and civil pleas, the eyre justices in 1194 were also ordered to inquire into the royal demesne manors, recording their fixed rents, present stocking levels, and economic potential if fully and properly stocked. More such inquiries followed in 1195, when a number of demesne manors were removed from the sheriffs and transferred into the hands of specially appointed custodians. In 1194 the eyre justices also inquired into escheats, custodies, and wardships that either were or should have been in the king's hands. All such lands were now to be handed over to local men for exploitation and restocking. In turn, these local escheators were to answer either to Hugh Bardolf (in the north) or William de Ste Mère-Église (in the south), exchequer officials whom Hubert Walter had appointed earlier in the year to supervise the management of the crown's escheats. Such reliance on local knights as administrators was one of the hallmarks of Angevin government, but it was a particular feature of Hubert Walter's reforms.

Jewish debts The eyre of 1194 also initiated a new system for the administration of debts owed by Christians to Jewish moneylenders. After first making a record of all Jewish property the justices were ordered to establish special chests in six or seven different towns. These chests were to be supervised by two Christians, two Jews, two scribes, and a royal official. Henceforward, all lending by Jews was to be done by two-part chirograph. One part of each document was deposited in the chest; the other, sealed by the debtor, was to be given to the Jewish lender. All transactions concerning Jewish debts were to take place only before the supervisory officials, who would keep a written record of payments, debits, or other alterations to the original loan. These local officials were in turn placed under the supervision of William de Ste Mère-Église and his clerk, William de Chemillé, who would now exercise a general oversight over all exchequer business involving Jews.

These measures must have provided the king with a better sense than he had had before of the wealth of his Jewish subjects. The main purpose of the new arrangements was not, however, exploitative. In fact, under Hubert Walter the government of England taxed its Jewish subjects very moderately. The new system was principally intended to control fraud in connection with moneylending. Once a debt had been deposited in the chests, the receipt rolls would prevent a dishonest borrower from claiming falsely to have paid it. At the same time debtors who had paid off their debts would have verifiable evidence of the payments they had made, even if their charters of indebtedness were not returned to them. And this, in turn, helped to ensure that paid-up debts would not pass into the king's hands as if they were unpaid, and be summoned again for collection by the exchequer. The new system offered advantages to everyone, and that must be one of the reasons why it endured.

Taxation and justice Further administrative and financial measures were also speedily undertaken. A new forest eyre was launched in 1194. Scutages were imposed in 1194, 1195, and 1196; the tallages begun by the justices on eyre in 1194 were continued and extended in 1195 and 1196; carucages were imposed in 1194 and again in 1198; and a new assize of measures was pronounced in 1196. In 1195 Hubert Walter also issued an important edict on peacekeeping, the first significant such measure since the assize of Clarendon in 1166. Itinerant justices continued to visit individual shires, and Walter himself took an active role in negotiating fines and offerings from individuals seeking the king's favour. The wording of judicial writs continued to evolve, and in 1195 Walter personally introduced a new three-part form of chirograph. He may also have begun the systematic retention of plea rolls from the royal court. The earliest such rolls to survive date from 1195. Walter also began the practice of recording private conveyances and agreements on the royal judicial rolls. Files of these 'feet of fines' begin in 1195, and were particularly valued by the small landowners of East Anglia and Lincolnshire, whose interests Hubert Walter understood especially well, having grown up among them. Finally, in 1198 he laid the groundwork for a new kingdom-wide inquiry into serjeanties and another general eyre, both of which would be carried through by his successor as justiciar, Geoffrey fitz Peter.

Perhaps the most lasting administrative development of Walter's justiciarship was, however, the increasing judicial specialization of the king's court. In 1194 jurisdiction over legal cases involving Jews was removed from the justices on eyre and transferred to the exchequer court. By 1196 a clear differentiation of judicial from exchequer business was beginning to develop within the exchequer court itself, a development that would lead by 1198 to the emergence of the common bench as a body of legal experts distinct from the barons of the exchequer. In the autumn of 1198, just a few months after Hubert Walter's resignation as justiciar, there emerged yet another separate body of justices, the exchequer of the Jews, before whom legal cases between Jews and Christians would hereafter be heard and determined. As justiciar, Walter himself linked these increasingly specialized curial groups together. As justiciar, he presided over the exchequer, he served as chief justice in legal proceedings, and he was responsible for crown policy toward the Jews. But beneath him, the king's court was becoming an increasingly professionalized and specialized set of institutions.

Last years as justiciar As justiciar Hubert Walter ruled England as the king's vicegerent. To be effective, he had to have the support both of the king and of the English magnates. Walter's relationship with Richard came briefly under stress in 1196, when Richard dispatched the abbot of Caen to England to audit the justiciar's accounts. The abbot died before his accounting could proceed too far, however, and the matter was not raised again. Whether this incident lay behind Hubert Walter's reported request in 1196 to resign as justiciar can only be a matter of speculation. Richard rejected the request, however, declaring that 'there was no one else upon whom he could rely to rule the country' (Young, 115). Thereafter Richard's support for his justiciar remained steadfast. Between June and October 1197 Walter represented Richard in diplomatic negotiations with the king of France, the count of Flanders, and with the archbishop of Rouen over Richard's decision to build Château Gaillard on archiepiscopal property.

By 1198, however, support for the justiciar among the ecclesiastical magnates of England may have been wearing thin. Hubert Walter's reputation among churchmen had already been compromised in 1196, when the church of St Mary-le-Bow in London was set on fire in order to drive from sanctuary William fitz Osbert, who had led a popular rising against the city's oligarchy. In December 1197, when Walter confronted a council of churchmen with King Richard's request that they supply him with an additional force of 300 knights for a year's service in Normandy, the bishops of Lincoln and Salisbury refused to comply, and the council broke up in confusion. The saintly Bishop Hugh of Lincoln, a long-time critic of Hubert Walter, escaped unscathed; but the bishop of Salisbury paid heavily for his temerity, and Hubert Walter seems finally to have succeeded in raising the force the king required. At the same time Walter's reputation as a guardian of ecclesiastical liberties was being further blackened by the furious resistance of the monks of Christ Church to his attempts to revive Archbishop Baldwin's plans to build a collegiate church at Lambeth staffed by canons holding prebends. The accession of a new pope, Innocent III, a man unsympathetic to churchmen holding secular office, may have been the final straw. In July 1198 Hubert Walter resigned as justiciar. This time King Richard accepted the resignation, citing the burden of the work and his justiciar's ill health as grounds for the resignation.

Chancellor of England Hubert Walter's resignation as justiciar did not, however, mean that he was retiring from governmental affairs. In September 1198 he returned to Normandy at Richard's request to negotiate peace with France. Walter was still on the continent in April 1199, when news of Richard's death reached him in Normandy.

He had known Prince John since at least 1182–3, when John was being educated in the household of Ranulf de Glanville. Despite Walter's role in suppressing John's rebellion in 1194, there was probably never any serious prospect that he would support any other claimant to the English throne after Richard's death. Stories that he did so, told independently by the St Albans chronicler and by the biographer of William (I) Marshal, are almost certainly projections of authors writing many years after the event. Contemporary chroniclers, by contrast, report that Walter, together with William Marshal, quickly organized the Norman magnates in support of John. The English magnates were in John's camp already; and on 27 May 1199 Hubert Walter crowned him king of England in Westminster Abbey. On the same day John appointed Walter his chancellor.

Walter brought to the chancery the same systematizing and reforming spirit he had exhibited as justiciar. Immediately upon taking office he instituted a new, fixed schedule of chancery fees. Within two weeks he had begun to insist that outgoing chancery writs and charters be enrolled in chronological order on special rolls. Copies of some royal charters were being kept on rolls before 1199, but as C. R. Cheney has remarked, 'there was nothing comparable to the comprehensive and continuous series which began within a few weeks of John's accession' (Cheney, 108). Nor are there any exact parallels for such chronological enrolments in the known procedures of other contemporary chanceries. Whatever precisely the inspiration, the innovation seems to have been Walter's.

Even as chancellor, Hubert Walter continued to play an active role both at the exchequer and in judicial proceedings. The justiciar, Geoffrey fitz Peter, was an old friend who had also begun his career in Glanville's household, and he frequently sought Walter's advice on difficult cases. The two men co-operated in collecting taxation, particularly the seventh of 1203; and in 1203 they led a joint diplomatic mission to the Welsh marches. Walter also remained active in negotiations with France, first in the spring of 1202, and again in the spring of 1204. As an elder statesman, he also played a crucial role in mediating between the impetuous king and the unfortunate victims of his wrath, as he did, for example, in negotiating a settlement between the king and the Cistercians in 1200. He also acted as a stabilizing influence on policy. In June 1205, only a few weeks before his death, Hubert Walter and William Marshal are reported to have persuaded King John to abandon his plans to lead a new expedition to France.

Archbishop of Canterbury Remarkable as it was, Hubert Walter's political career is but one aspect of his public life. While serving as justiciar and chancellor he was also archbishop of Canterbury and, from 1195 until 1198, resident papal legate in England. As archbishop, Hubert Walter reorganized the archiepiscopal estates and increased their revenues. He acquired new lands and erected new buildings. Although he was often personally absent from Canterbury, his officials administered the spiritual affairs of the diocese with conscientious efficiency. As metropolitan, Walter was an energetic visitor of monasteries and

vacant bishoprics, a task made easier by his simultaneous position as papal legate. At papal request, he also headed commissions of inquiry for the canonizations of Gilbert of Sempringham and Wulfstan of Worcester, and served frequently as a papal judge-delegate. Walter was also an active legislator, issuing canons for the archdiocese of York in 1195, and for Canterbury in 1200. The Canterbury canons were particularly ambitious, and formed the basis upon which Archbishop Langton would erect his own more famous canons of 1213. His quarrel of 1197–1200 with the monks of Christ Church notwithstanding, Walter was also generally regarded as a friend and supporter of monks. He took the habit of the Augustinian canons upon becoming archbishop, and remained on warm terms with the Cistercian order, which accepted him into confraternity in 1195. A generous man, he was particularly noted for his gifts of elaborate vestments to monastic houses, including the Carthusian house at Witham.

Death and significance Hubert Walter died on 13 July 1205 at the manor of Teynham, Kent, of a high fever resulting from an untreated carbuncle on his lower back. He was buried the following day in Canterbury Cathedral, in the south ambulatory of the Trinity chapel. His tomb was opened in 1890, and the vestments and ornaments removed. They are now displayed in the cathedral library. In his will, which he updated annually, the archbishop left the monks of Christ Church a much more splendid set of vestments, but King John took these, and presented them to Peter des Roches for the latter's enthronement as bishop of Winchester in 1206. Hubert Walter's executors, James Savage and Master Elias of Dereham, accounted for debts of £913 1s. on the pipe rolls. The total value of Walter's estate is unknown, but it must have been considerably greater than his debts.

Hubert Walter had at least five brothers. Osbert Walter, a royal justice under King John, died in 1206; Roger, Hamo, and Bartholomew Walter are occasionally mentioned in charters, but are otherwise unknown. Hubert's heir was his brother Theobald, the ancestor of the Butlers of Ormond, who died before Michaelmas 1205, and whose interests Hubert was particularly assiduous in promoting. Concerned though he was to advance his family's interests, Hubert Walter was also undoubtedly a pious man. Piety, however, did not in his eyes require poverty. He was an ambitious man who enjoyed the trappings of power, including wealth. Nevertheless, he was not a hoarder. He was famous for keeping a lavish household, rivalling even the king himself, and his hospitality was unfailing. He was a generous and effective patron to his followers, his family, and his supporters, just as Glanville had been for him. But also like Glanville, he chose men of real ability to staff his household, and many of them went on to make famous careers of their own in the service of church or crown. Walter's reputation as a just and compassionate judge was deserved, but he was at the same time one of the most active purchasers of wardships and custodies in England, both for himself and his relatives. Inevitably there was an occasional clash of interests. When this happened, the conflict usually turned out to Hubert's advantage. Few men can have worn so many hats with such success, both for himself and for those he served, as did Hubert Walter.

ROBERT C. STACEY

Sources C. R. Cheney, *Hubert Walter* (1967) · R. Mortimer, 'The family of Rannulf de Glanville', *BIHR*, 54 (1981), 1–16 · C. R. Young, *Hubert Walter, lord of Canterbury and lord of England* (1968) · Pipe rolls · Pipe rolls, 1 John [memoranda roll] · Chancery records (RC) · *Radulphi de Coggeshall chronicon Anglicanum*, ed. J. Stevenson, Rolls Series, 66 (1875) · F. J. West, *The justiciarship in England, 1066–1232* (1966) · C. R. Cheney and E. John, eds., *Canterbury, 1193–1205*, English Episcopal Acta, 3 (1986) · *The chronicle of Jocelin of Brakelond: concerning the acts of Samson, abbot of the monastery of St Edmund*, ed. H. E. Butler (1949)
Archives BM · Canterbury Cathedral, dean and chapter muniments · LPL | PRO
Likenesses seal, BL; Birch, *Seals*, 1187 [see illus.] · tomb effigy, Canterbury Cathedral
Wealth at death estate must have been 'considerably greater than … debts' of £913 1s. od.: Young, *Hubert Walter*, p. 166 n. 20

Walter, John (d. 1412?), astronomer, probably came from south-west England. It has often been claimed that he was educated at Winchester College. This cannot be strictly true, since he was at Oxford well before 1383, that is, before the school's foundation (1387), but it is possible that he was at the school it superseded. Walter's name first occurs in Oxford records in connection with his renting a school from Exeter College in 1383 and 1384, by which time he was master of arts. By 1386 he was a fellow of Winchester's sister foundation in Oxford, the newly founded college of St Mary (commonly known as New College, founded in 1379). Ordained successively subdeacon (1387) and deacon (1388), he was made subwarden of the college in 1389, finally vacating his fellowship in 1393. He became rector of Shere in Surrey in 1390, a position he had vacated by May 1407.

Two surviving astronomical works are ascribed to Walter, both of them chiefly concerned with a single narrow problem, that of casting the houses for an astrological figure (that is, calculating a horoscope). The first, apart from some standard astrological and astronomical material drawn largely from elsewhere, is a table of houses of a straightforward kind, prepared for the latitude of Oxford and provided with canons explaining its use. The canons in one manuscript (Bodl. Oxf., MS Laud misc. 674) that has strong associations with William Worcester (d. 1482) end with a statement associating Walter with Winchester and New College and saying that they were copied by William Worcester in 1438. While there was much work in calculating the original tables—much more than in the simple canons for their use—they were done according to a standard method and could have drawn on earlier Oxford work.

The second work ascribed to Walter is of a higher level of mathematical originality, although in certain respects somewhat muddled. The disadvantage of standard tables of astrological houses was that they held good only for a particular geographical latitude. The astronomer calculating them made use of tables of ascensional differences, likewise generally done for one latitude; but the Oxford astronomer John Maudith earlier in the century had made

use of Toledan tables of the latter type that applied to any latitude. It seems likely that some English astronomer of the fourteenth, or possibly early fifteenth, century, familiar with this work, was trying to make use of the same idea when he drafted the universally applicable tables for the houses in what is now Cambridge University Library, MS Ee.3.61. Lewis Caerleon (d. in or after 1495) makes it clear in this, his own copy of the work, that he is sceptical about John Walter's authorship and about the exactness of the method. The work is certainly ascribed to Walter in an earlier copy (in Bodl. Oxf., MS Rawl. D.238), but he can at best have been responsible for only a part of it.

John Walter's name is often mentioned in later astrological writing, simply because he was the author of tables of the astrological houses which were much in demand as they could lighten the burden of calculation. He seems not to have been responsible for anything more profound. In his lifetime he presented a book to New College, an exposition of the Apocalypse. It is not known when he died. John Leland provides information that might not have been as purely speculative as some of his other comments: he claims that Walter returned to Winchester and died and was buried there in 1412.

J. D. NORTH

Sources J. D. North, *Horoscopes and history* (1986), 84, 126–31, 158 · Emden, *Oxf.*, 3.1972 · *Commentarii de scriptoribus Britannicis, auctore Joanne Lelando*, ed. A. Hall, 2 vols. (1918–21)
Archives Bodl. Oxf., MS Laud misc. 674 · Bodl. Oxf., MS Rawl. D.238 · CUL, MS Ee.3.61

Walter, Sir John (bap. 1565, d. 1630), judge and politician, was baptized at Ludlow, Shropshire, on 1 May 1565, the second son of the common lawyer and Welsh judge Edmund Walter (d. 1592), of Ludlow, and his wife, Mary Hackluit (d. 1583). After matriculating from Brasenose College, Oxford, in 1579, John followed his elder brother, James, to the Inner Temple, where he was admitted gratis as a bencher's son on 21 April 1583. Called to the bar by the Inner Temple parliament on 22 November 1590, Walter took his place at the bar table on 6 June next year, and served as reader of Lyon's Inn in 1595.

The details of Walter's immediate professional ascent are scanty, but by 1600 he was pleading in Star Chamber, admittedly as the junior of three counsel (Baildon, 116). On 24 February 1601 he married Margaret Offley (d. c.1620) of London, with whom he would rear a family of four sons and four daughters. By 1604 Walter had entered Queen Anne's service as a fee'd counsellor at law. His call to join the bench of the Inner Temple in 1605 came a good five years earlier than strict seniority and the average continuance of those so promoted over the previous decade would predict, while his reading in the summer of 1607 on the statute 43 Eliz. I c.1 (confirmations of patents) was sufficiently well received for a fellow practitioner on the Oxford circuit to characterize him as 'a reader of great reputation' (*Liber famelicus*, 31). As 'worthy Counsellor' to the University of Oxford Walter advised Sir Thomas Bodley on his founding endowment of the university's library, and in 1609 refused a fee for drafting the deed of grant (Wood, 2.912); the following year he was retained by the crown to defend the royal title to aulnage before the House of Lords. In 1613 Walter became attorney-general to the prince of Wales, and received an honorary MA from the University of Oxford. By 1615, when he bought the widowed Lady Cope's substantial house in the Strand (*Letters of John Chamberlain*, 1.594), Walter was among the leaders of the Westminster bar, even in chancery, where his closeness to Sir Edward Coke may not have facilitated his practice. Having previously acquired a house and lands in the north Oxfordshire parish of Sarsden, Walter next year bought the former abbey of Godstow and the manor of Wolvercote outside Oxford, which became his main residence. At this time 'in regard of his good deserts and experience in the government of the house' (*Inner Temple Records*, 2.100), Walter's Inner Temple colleagues agreed to seat him at the head of the bench table in hall.

Yet high professional standing was in itself insufficient to guarantee further preferment. Although 'all the world had destinated' Walter to succeed Henry Yelverton as solicitor-general in 1617 (*Liber famelicus*, 54) the office went instead to his Inner Temple junior Thomas Coventry, a mere 'green reader' (ibid., 53). Next year's closely fought election for the recordership of London saw Walter nominated in place of his 'verye good friend' Whitelocke (ibid., 31), once the king himself had declared the latter unacceptable. In these circumstances his narrow defeat was no disgrace, and the knighthood conferred on Walter in May 1619 can hardly have been a consolation prize, especially since two more of the prince's legal officers received the same honour. His notably forceful stance against monopolists and projectors in the parliament of 1621, where he sat as member for the Cornish borough of East Looe, may however reflect Walter's continuing distance from court power and patronage. If so, when he was next returned for the same constituency on Prince Charles's nomination in 1624, that gap had much narrowed, as Walter now urged his fellow members to send military support to their distressed protestant brethren abroad by voting the crown at least four subsidies.

During the vacation after Hilary term 1625, in the last month of James I's life, Walter and Sir Thomas Trevor, the prince's solicitor-general, both received writs to be called serjeant immediately, along with patents as king's serjeants. This irregular procedure of swearing in serjeants during vacation was possibly part of a plan to make Walter the fifth justice of king's bench, a promotion he apparently did not welcome, since it would reduce the fee income of all puisne justices. That potential difficulty was resolved in April by Sir Robert Tanfield's death, enabling Walter to be made chief baron of the exchequer. Meanwhile a judicial conference reinstated the traditional process for calling serjeants, with writs returnable on the first day of Easter term; in Walter's case his patrons were Lord Keeper Williams, Buckingham, Pembroke, and Baron Ley (Baker, *Serjeants*, 358–9, 438). On 12 May the lord keeper finally administered Walter's oath as chief baron, 'and his response was good, grave, and full of honesty' (*Diary of Sir Richard Hutton*, 58).

The gravity contemporaries deemed particularly fitting to his office epitomized Walter's judicial demeanour; when a colleague on the western circuit remarked 'My Lord, you are not merry', Walter supposedly replied 'Merry enough, for a judge' (Fuller, *Worthies*, new edn, 1840, 3.62). Yet despite a rumour in January 1626 that Walter would succeed the recently deceased Sir Henry Hobart as chief justice of common pleas, the position remained unfilled until late November, when it went to the more pliant Thomas Richardson. Whatever the truth of that rumour, Walter's chances of further promotion were irretrievably damaged by his prominent role in the judges' resistance to government attempts from mid-October to secure their collective endorsement of the forced loan. Walter was one of the trio who represented the judiciary in negotiations with Lord Keeper Coventry. These culminated in Chief Justice Crewe's dismissal after a personal interview with Charles I, who then summoned Walter: 'and much passed between them and again the Chief Baron was constant and would not change' (*Diary of Sir Richard Hutton*, 66).

On this and later occasions Walter was protected by his patent, which gave him tenure during good behaviour, and he continued to discharge his duties, including attendance on Lords' committees during the 1628 parliament. The illness which excused him from judicial consultations on the king's questions in May of that year was possibly genuine, since in January sickness also prevented his sitting in Westminster Hall. The same reason was given for his absence in May 1629, when the judges faced further royal enquiries touching the habeas corpus applications of the imprisoned MPs. But while the crown could hardly complain at the handling of Richard Chambers's suits against tonnage and poundage by Walter's court that June, at the beginning of Michaelmas term he was pressed to resign his place. Walter now apparently constituted the main individual obstacle to Charles's preferred handling of sensitive politico-legal issues and, according to Bulstrode Whitelocke, 'His Opinion was contrary to all the rest of the Judges' (Whitelocke, *Memorials*, 16). His refusal to step aside, since, 'as he often affirmed, he had never given any cause of offence to the king in any matter that he knew of' (*Diary of Sir Richard Hutton*, 83). led the king on 22 October to suspend him from exercising his office.

Walter's continued insistence on knowing the cause of royal displeasure ensured that disablement continued throughout the final year of his life. He died well prepared at Serjeant's Inn, Fleet Street, on 18 November 1630 and was buried at Wolvercote. This 'grave, religious man, of great learning, sound judgment and good conscience' (*Diary of Sir Richard Hutton*, 83) left large benefactions to Jesus College, Oxford, to his second wife, Anne Biggs (*née* Wytham), whom he had married on 18 July 1622, and to the surviving children of his first marriage. Several manuscript collections of his law reports and notes taken at his Inner Temple reading survive; his name is also attached to a printed abridgement of Plowden's *Commentaries* (1659).

WILFRID PREST

Sources DNB · *The diary of Sir Richard Hutton, 1614–1639*, ed. W. R. Prest, SeldS, suppl. ser., 9 (1991) · Baker, *Serjeants* · J. P. Ferris, HoP,

Commons, 1604–29; HoP, Commons, 1640–60 [drafts] • W. R. Prest, The rise of the barristers: a social history of the English bar, 1590–1640, 2nd edn (1991) • F. A. Inderwick and R. A. Roberts, eds., A calendar of the Inner Temple records, 1 (1896); 2 (1898) • Liber famelicus of Sir James Whitelocke, a judge of the court of king's bench in the reigns of James I and Charles I, ed. J. Bruce, CS, old ser., 70 (1858) • Les reportes del cases in camera stellata, 1593 to 1609, from the original ms. of John Hawarde, ed. W. P. Baildon (privately printed, London, 1894) • A. Wood, The history and antiquities of the University of Oxford, ed. J. Gutch, 2 (1796) • PRO, PROB 11/158, fols. 220–21 • Foss, Judges, vol. 6 • VCH Oxfordshire, vol. 12 • L. J. Reeve, Charles I and the road to personal rule (1989) • IGI • [B. Whitelocke], Memorials of the English affairs (1682) • The letters of John Chamberlain, ed. N. E. McClure, 2 vols. (1939)

Archives BL, reports, Hargrave MSS 5, 8; Lansdowne MS 1060 • Bodl. Oxf., MS Rawl. C 341

Likenesses effigy, St Peter's, Wolvercote, Oxfordshire • oils, Inner Temple, London

Wealth at death substantial: bequests incl. portions of £3000 each for two daughters; £140 to the poor of Sarsden, Churchill, Lyneham, Wolvercote, Twickenham, and the Savoy; £2000 to Jesus College (reduced by codicil to £1000): will, PRO, PROB 11/158, fols. 220–21

Walter, John (1739?–1812), printer and newspaper proprietor, was born in London, the third son of Richard Walter (1704?–1755?), coal merchant, and his wife, Esther. The couple had two other sons: Robert (1731?–1785) and Richard (1733–1773). John Walter began in the coal business at about the age of sixteen, immediately after the death of his father. He married Frances Landen (d. 1798) on 31 May 1759, with whom he had four daughters and two sons, including John *Walter (1776–1847), later proprietor of The Times. He also had an illegitimate child, Walter *Wilson (1781–1847), with Catherine Wilson. He traded as a coal merchant for twelve years and became head of the firm of Walter, Bradley, and Sage and chairman of the coal market. Although he was initially successful and made a great deal of money, in later years Walter began to find the business less profitable, and decided instead to concentrate on insurance underwriting; he joined Lloyds in 1781. However, a combination of American privateers, French men-of-war, and a hurricane off Jamaica forced him into bankruptcy the following year. Walter had to leave a house in Battersea Rise, Clapham, which he had owned for ten years, but was allowed to keep most of the contents of his residence in Queen Square, Bloomsbury, except for his valuable library, which was sold. He appears to have been determined to clear his debts, and this he seems to have managed by 1790.

After this financial disaster, Walter relied on his friends to secure him a government post, but the dismissal of North's administration in 1782 ruined his chances. He then decided to turn his attention to another type of career altogether, and specifically to developing a new method of typographical composition. This had been invented by the London printer Henry Johnson for use in the making of lottery blanks, which Walter hoped to extend to the general letterpress. This method used 'logotypes' or founts composed of complete words instead of separate letters, which was supposed to speed up composition and cut down on printing errors. In 1782 Walter bought the patent to the logographic system and worked with Johnson on developing it further. Two years later,

John Walter (1739?–1812), by unknown artist, c.1783–4

and supposedly with money given to him by his creditors on the settlement of his bankruptcy, he purchased the former King's Printing House in Blackfriars and reopened it as the Logographic Press on 1 June 1784. From the start, Walter appears to have obtained the job of printing 'Lloyd's list', the daily shipping news, presumably because of his earlier connections. In the following year Walter began to print a newspaper, the Daily Universal Register, using his logographic method. In 1789 he changed the title of the paper to The Times. Although the paper was to become relatively successful in Walter's lifetime, it was not until the early nineteenth century, under the leadership of his son John, that it became the best-selling and most influential newspaper in the country. Walter's own input to the content of The Times before then appears to have been limited. The paper's politics were almost certainly decided by an editor, and were not particularly distinctive. Under Walter, The Times was overshadowed by more opinionated and successful newspapers such as the Morning Chronicle and the Morning Herald.

In addition to his newspaper, Walter also published books and pamphlets at his Logographic Press, as well as undertaking some official printing work for the government. He failed in his attempt to become printer to the Stationery Office, but in 1787 he secured the position of printer to the customs office. A connection with John Trusler of the Literary Society also ensured a steady supply of new works, which included the infamous Apology for the Life of George Anne Bellamy. Despite Walter's attempts to improve the quality of printing, his publications were often attacked for their frequent typographical errors.

Undeterred, in 1789 he opened a bookshop in the West End. However, the book publishing side of his business does not appear to have flourished. The word 'logographic' disappeared from the heading of *The Times* in 1792 and the whole experiment seems to have come to an end. Walter later wrote somewhat disingenuously that the failure was due to a lack of patronage and resistance from journeymen printers:

> I was advised to get a number of nobility and men of letters … to patronise the plan, to which his majesty was to have been the patron. But happening unfortunately, as it turned out, to correspond with Dr. Franklin, then ambassador at Paris, whose opinion I wished for, his name was among my list of subscribers … Thus ended royal patronage; and when it [the invention] was used by me in business, the journeymen cabaled and refused to work at the invention without I paid the prices as paid in the common way. Thus all the expense and labour I had been at for some years fell to the ground. (Walter to Lord Kenyon, 6 July 1799, *Kenyon MSS*, 552)

With the failure of the logographic method, the newspaper side of his business increasingly predominated, and was the source of most of his profits. From 1788 *The Times* was edited by William Finey, and the paper appears to have enjoyed a period of success, claiming sales of almost 3000 per day in 1792 and 4000 in the following year. In 1790 Walter also began an evening paper, the *Evening Mail*. However, his success was not without its problems. On 15 March 1786, for example, Walter was fined £50 for a libel in *The Times* on Lord Loughborough. Much greater trouble was to come. Like other newspaper proprietors of the period, Walter received money from the Treasury to ensure a degree of favourable coverage. During the later 1780s and 1790s this amounted to £300 a year. Part of the agreement required Walter to publish certain paragraphs approved by the government. However, this turned out to be a disastrous bargain for Walter, since on 21 February 1789 he printed articles from Thomas Steele, the joint secretary of the Treasury, which accused the royal dukes of insincerity in celebrating the king's recovery from illness and of conducting an opposition party. Steele's articles were declared by the courts to be libels on the royal dukes. Walter was sentenced in November to a £50 fine and a year's imprisonment for his attack on the duke of York. While still in prison, Walter was further tried for libels on the prince of Wales and the duke of Clarence, and sentenced to an additional £200 in fines and a further year in prison.

Walter complained bitterly of his sentence. In a letter written from Newgate to Bland Burges he railed:

> Little did I ever expect ever to be an inhabitant of this vile receptacle or that any political sin would doom me to so severe a sentence. I am the more astonished when I daily read in the Opposition prints the most atrocious libels and treasonable paragraphs against those who gave birth to my prosecutors and yet without notice. (*Letters and Correspondence*, 157)

Some years later, Walter noted that 'Had I disclosed the authors and their employers, I might have escaped prosecution myself, and proved it on others' (*Kenyon MSS*, 552),

but instead he remained silent. One of Walter's daughters, Mary Knox, appealed to the prince of Wales. This, in addition to Walter's letters of complaint to various politicians, appears to have had some effect; he was released on 9 March 1791 and £250 was given to him from the Treasury, apparently as a form of compensation.

In 1795 Walter retired from active involvement in his printing business and moved to a house in Teddington. He claimed in 1799 that his earlier imprisonment had 'produced a corpulence of habit, and I was frequently attacked by fits of the gout' (*Kenyon MSS*, 552). His wife, Frances, died at Printing House Square on 30 January 1798. His elder son, William Walter, took over from his father for a time, although he was not a success and two years later was joined by his brother, John Walter, who took over completely in 1802. Walter's government subsidy was stopped abruptly in 1799 following the publication in July of a paragraph criticizing the administration, and his position of printer to the customs board was also ended. The same year also saw him convicted of a libel on Lord Cowper. In 1800 Grenville declared *The Times* to be 'a paper which, under cover of a pretended support of Government, is in decided hostility to it' (Lord Grenville to the earl of Carysfort, 16 Dec 1800, *Fortescue MSS*, 6.409).

Walter died on 16 November 1812 at Teddington. It has been suggested that he may have fallen out with his son John at some point, since his will failed to leave him a majority share in *The Times*, which the son had effectively saved from failure after 1795. Instead John Walter's daughters, Anna, Catherine, Fanny, and Mary, were left one-sixteenth share each, as was his illegitimate son, Walter Wilson, and his nephew, also John Walter, who had already been given three shares in 1801, 1806, and 1810. The pattern of ownership that resulted from Walter's will produced lengthy and costly litigation which continued for many years.   HANNAH BARKER

Sources [S. Morison and others], *The history of The Times*, 1 (1935) · I. Maxted, *The London book trades, 1775–1800: a topographical guide* (privately printed, Exeter, 1980) · *The manuscripts of Lord Kenyon*, HMC, 35 (1894) · *Selections from the letters and correspondence of Sir James Bland Burges*, ed. J. Hutton (1885) · *The manuscripts of J. B. Fortescue*, 10 vols., HMC, 30 (1892–1927) · H. R. F. Bourne, *English newspapers*, 2 vols. (1887) · J. Grant, *The newspaper press: its origin, progress, and present position*, 3 vols. (1871–2) · A. Andrews, *The history of British journalism*, 2 vols. (1859) · C. Pebody, *English journalism and the men who have made it* (1882) · F. K. Hunt, *The fourth estate*, 2 vols. (1850)
Likenesses oils, *c*.1783–1784, News International Syndication, London [*see illus.*]
Wealth at death approx. £30,000 from 11/16 share in *The Times*

Walter, John (1776–1847), newspaper proprietor and politician, was born at Battersea on 23 February 1776, the second son of John *Walter (1739?–1812), printer and founder of *The Times*, and Frances Landen. He was educated at the Merchant Taylors' School, and at fourteen was apprenticed to Thomas Longman, the publisher and bookseller, and later to his father. In 1794 he matriculated at Trinity College, Oxford, where he stayed for a year. In 1797 he became a master printer and assumed a half interest in his father's printing business. In 1803, on the retirement of

John Walter (1776–1847), by unknown artist

his elder brother, William, he became sole manager of both the printing business and the two newspapers published at Printing House Square, *The Times* and the *Evening Mail*. Although he engaged in a number of civic and political activities throughout his life, his contemporaries always identified him with *The Times*. At his death in 1847 he was still directing the future course of the paper; indeed, he died at Printing House Square a few days after settling who would succeed him as editor and proprietor.

Walter and the success of *The Times* In the spring of 1801 Walter's father gave him a one-sixteenth share in *The Times*, signalling his intention for his son's future. By the time he took over the sole direction of *The Times* in 1803, the newspaper had gone through several years in which it had made very little profit, mainly because William Walter had been both an ineffective editor and an indifferent businessman. In addition, John Walter sen. had lost money on the printing business through some poor publishing decisions and a disastrous attempt to modernize his printing processes with an experimental logographic press. Even the family's branch bookshop in Piccadilly had lost money. Walter began his new career by focusing his attention on expanding *The Times*, reasoning quite rightly that the success of the newspaper would also mean success for the print shop. His plan was simplicity itself: he would concentrate on gathering and publishing news, both foreign and domestic, and publish it before rival newspapers could. To do so, he established his own corps of foreign correspondents on the continent, whose job it was to read and translate articles of importance in the foreign press and send summaries to the London office.

Unfortunately, this practice brought *The Times* into conflict with the Post Office, which had years before established the foreign newspaper post to supply continental newspapers and summary translations to the London press for a fee that varied from about 60 to 100 guineas per annum. The system was open to abuse: some journals managed to obtain priority treatment by bribing postal clerks. Walter continued to pay his annual 60 guineas to the foreign post office, but dispensed with their 'services' by having his correspondents send reports to him privately. Because he did not have to depend on the vagaries of government clerks or observe the foreign post office courtesy of allowing government officials and diplomats the first opportunity of perusing dispatches from the continent, he made few friends either among other journalists or in the government. The foreign post office's reaction was to hold up foreign mail addressed to *The Times*. In response, Walter arranged with several businesses in the City to have his mail delivered to them, since the foreign post office had no control over mail delivered to commercial houses. Walter devised a code, which he varied regularly, so that the businesses could identify the mail intended for *The Times*. Unfortunately, while this complicated plan worked well for the delivery of letters, postal officials could easily identify and confiscate foreign newspapers.

Walter protested regularly to friends in the government, but to no effect. When he complained to Francis Freeling, secretary to the Post Office, that some rival journals received their foreign newspapers undisturbed while his were regularly 'lost', Freeling replied that newspapers supporting the administration received certain favours, and that *The Times* might be similarly honoured were it to pledge a similar support. Walter refused to accept the offer, and in 1807 began to attack the Post Office generally and Freeling specifically for corruption. As a result, Walter was charged with libel and stood trial (with his father as co-defendant) on 3 July 1807. The government won the case, and father and son were required to print an apology and pay costs and a £200 fine.

This temporary set-back did not, however, slow Walter in his attempts to gather continental news independently. As the Napoleonic wars dragged on and the blockade of the continent ended normal ship traffic, Walter, with the tacit approval of John Wilson Croker, the secretary to the Admiralty, employed blockade runners to deliver French newspapers. Walter's success in publishing news that was, in many cases, weeks ahead of even the diplomatic channels made *The Times* one of the most powerful, most profitable, and most widely read newspapers in England.

The war with the theatres Walter also boosted the preeminence of *The Times* by establishing a professional, independent theatre review department. At the beginning of the nineteenth century, stage reviews were usually little more than puff pieces, often written by the theatre owners and playwrights themselves. Influential theatre reviewers were regularly bribed to write good reviews.

Walter, taking his cue from Leigh Hunt, insisted that plays be reviewed honestly; in 1805 he hired Barron Field, a twenty-year-old friend of Hunt's, as theatre critic. Field was not allowed to accept free tickets, nor did he mix socially with theatre managers on a regular basis. His candid reviews drew the ire of the theatrical establishment; indeed, Richard Sheridan, who had been friendly with Walter's father, threatened him with a libel suit or worse after a particularly biting review. In addition to insisting on honest criticism, Walter also insisted that the theatres pay full price for inserting advertisements in *The Times*, in contravention to the common practice of requiring payment only of the stamp duty. Drury Lane at first refused to pay, and attacked Walter through newspapers heavily under the influence of the theatre interests. However, the growing power and circulation of *The Times* made it imperative that play notices be published in it, and eventually all of the theatres bowed to *The Times*'s policy.

Technological advances While he increased the circulation of *The Times* substantially in the first decade of the nineteenth century, Walter was frustrated by the slow process and significant costs of manual printing. As early as 1804 he had invested in the development of a steam press, an investment which was opposed by his father, and which eventually yielded nothing. In 1812 the German inventor Frederick Koenig demonstrated his newly designed steam press; Walter immediately contracted for two of the machines, and Koenig began to build them in a house in Whitecross Street, next to *The Times*'s offices. Walter instinctively knew that the new machines would revolutionize the newspaper industry, both by increasing exponentially the number of newspapers that could be printed and by decreasing labour costs. In anticipation of the first issue, his contract with Koenig required that the inventor not sell any of his machines to a rival newspaper for less than the price Walter was paying for them. In anticipation of the second issue, which would clearly cause labour difficulties among the printers, Walter bound Koenig and his workers to secrecy during the construction stage. And to protect himself in case the machines did not work to their specifications, Walter contracted to sell them back to Koenig if they would not print a minimum of 1100 sheets per hour. Finally, Walter contracted to buy any future machines that might print more efficiently than the ones Koenig was building for him.

Walter had reason to be concerned about the reaction of his pressmen. All his life he had fought the formation of 'combinations', or unions, in the printing business. In 1810, when his compositors struck for a wage equivalent to that being paid on other newspapers, Walter prosecuted them for combination, and nineteen were convicted and jailed. In addition, the promise (or threat, depending on the point of view) of mechanized printing had been around for years, and pressmen all over London had vowed to smash any machines that might take their jobs from them. Finally, on 28 November 1814, Walter personally supervised the printing of the next day's edition of *The Times* on the new presses, then announced to the pressmen waiting for copy that the newspaper had already been printed. He did show his humanity on that occasion, however, by announcing that he would continue the wages of his suddenly redundant compositors until they could find suitable work elsewhere. Eventually, the Koenig machines were able to print 1800 sheets per hour; the new press reduced the time required to print an issue of 3000–4000 copies from ten hours to three. In five years, Walter more than doubled his circulation, and revenue from sales and advertising made *The Times* the leading daily in England. Interestingly, he did not stop tinkering with printing machinery; in 1827 he contracted with Cowper and Applegarth to build a machine with four cylinders capable of printing 4000 sheets per hour.

Political independence From the day in 1803 that he assumed editorial control of *The Times*, Walter reserved the right to offer criticism as well as support to the sitting government. His policy toward the administration was something like his policy toward the theatres: if he accepted nothing from them, he owed them nothing. In a leader published on 10 February 1810 he explained that he strove to conduct the paper with an 'independent spirit' that could support 'the men in power, but without suffering them to repay [*The Times*'s] partiality by contributions calculated to produce any reduction whatsoever in the expense of managing the concern'. He went on to say that the

> [Addington] Administration, therefore, had, as he before states, his disinterested support, because he believed it then, as he believes it now, to have been a virtuous, and an upright Administration; but not knowing how long it might continue so, he did not chuse to surrender his right of free-judgment, by accepting of obligations, though offered in the most unexceptionable manner.

That independence was bound to lead to trouble at a time when most newspapers were allied to a political faction. In 1804 Walter allowed *The Times* to take sides against Pitt in a cabinet squabble. In retaliation, the secretary of the Custom House informed Walter on 26 April 1805 that he was cancelling a lucrative Custom House printing contract with the family firm. Walter sen. was furious with his son, but nothing could be done until Pitt lost power. In February 1806, with a new coalition government in place, Walter asked to resume the Custom House contract. Even though he supported the new government editorially, his request went unanswered. When it was suggested to him that he make a formal petition for reinstatement, he refused on the grounds that such a move might encourage some in the government to believe that, by granting him a favour, they might have influence over him. When his friends presented a petition on his behalf, he refused to support it, causing the rift with his father to widen.

Walter's political independence did not, of course, protect him from charges of corruption. Twice he was accused of being in the pay of the French, once for supposedly accepting payments for inserting letters in support of the French monarchy but written by the French secret police, and another time for taking a large bribe from the duc de Blacas, again for supporting the Bourbons. The first charge was rather vague, and had been made against a number of the leading London journals; in some cases, it may have been true, although it was never proven. The second charge was decidedly untrue, and led to some spectacular developments. Barry O'Meara, a surgeon and former British soldier, had served for a brief time as medical adviser to Napoleon. In 1822 he published his reminiscences, *Napoleon in Exile, or, A Voice from St. Helena*, in which he charged that in 1816 Blacas had paid Walter £3000 for editorial influence on behalf of the Bourbons. A *Times* leader called the charge a lie, and O'Meara determined to horsewhip Walter publicly. He waited outside the Stratford Club, and when the man he was told was Walter emerged, O'Meara began thrashing him. The man turned out to be William, John Walter's older brother, who had O'Meara arrested for assault. The matter was finally concluded on 12 November 1822, when Walter published a letter from Blacas in which the duke stated unequivocally 'nothing was ever given or offered to you by my intervention' (*History of 'The Times'*, 225). Although O'Meara continued to insist on the truth of his accusation through the rival *Morning Chronicle*, Walter appears to have been generally vindicated by Blacas's letter.

Sole director of *The Times* John Walter sen. died on 16 November 1812. Although he had apparently been on good terms with his son for several years, his will reflected his anger over the loss of the Custom House contract and probably the fine for libel, as well as some pettiness over his son's printing decisions. Instead of leaving his shares in the newspaper to Walter jun., he merely left him the opportunity to buy two of the shares at an inflated price, and directed that Walter Wilson's share should revert to Walter jun. at Wilson's death. On the positive side, the will required that Walter jun. be sole manager of *The Times* and be paid an annual salary of £1000, with provisions for a sliding-scale reduction if profits were to slip below £5000 per annum.

Even though the will made him a minority stockholder, the legal recognition of his position as chief proprietor gave Walter the chance to build *The Times* both as a business venture and a journalistic force. Sole control was an important issue; Walter did not get on well with his sisters and his older brother, who were all stockholders. As early as 1808 he had worried, during a serious bout of illness, that the family might interfere disastrously in the conduct of *The Times*. Apparently they felt that his independence diminished their profits. However, he soon recognized that he could not manage the printing business, the business affairs of the paper, and the routine editorial affairs involved in publishing a daily. As early as 1805 he had cast about for young talent and, in addition to hiring Field as theatre critic, he had hired John Dyer Collier to report from the court of king's bench; Collier's sons William and John Payne Collier, James Murray, and John and Charles Ross as reporters; and Henry Crabb Robinson as

correspondent for the north of Europe and later as occasional editor. After his father's death he hired Peter Lovett Fraser, who acted as managing editor in Walter's absence; Edward Sterling; John Stoddart, who held the formal title of editor for three disastrous years; and Thomas Barnes, the first in a series of long-serving, influential editors, who took over from Stoddart in 1817 and served until his death in 1841. And he paid his staff well: John Dyer Collier received £200 p.a. to report the court of king's bench from 1804 to 1808; John Payne Collier earned up to 210 guineas p.a. as parliamentary reporter; while his brother William Collier began as a reporter at 3 guineas a week. Walter's first formal editor, John Stoddart, received £1400 annually, plus an additional £100 for an insurance premium. In fact, he was known to have 'treated his staff so liberally, that in the days of the Regency, a position on the staff of *The Times* was regarded as one of the "plums" of the journalistic profession' (Bowman, *The Story of 'The Times'*, 111). The core of that staff—Crabb Robinson, Walter, Peter Fraser, and Thomas Barnes—were professional colleagues and personal friends, and remained so for almost forty years.

Personal life and parliament In 1814 Walter appointed Stoddart as editor so that he might pursue some personal interests, not least of which was a love affair with the daughter of Dr George Gregory, vicar of West Ham. Unfortunately, Miss Gregory's brothers, who were negotiating the marriage settlement on her behalf, apparently could not agree with Walter on several of the articles, and in later 1814, to Walter's distress, the marriage appeared to be off. Adding to his personal distress, he acquired a new home for his bride-to-be and himself in Brompton Row, London, and was devoting a considerable amount of time and money preparing it. Walter finally settled his issues with the Gregory family and the marriage took place on 6 May 1815; sadly, the new Mrs Walter almost immediately 'fell into a consumption' (*History of 'The Times'*, 1.159) and died later in the year. Walter gave up the house in Brompton Row and returned to his old apartments at Printing House Square. He also threw himself back into the management of the newspaper, which had declined somewhat under Stoddart. Eventually, in 1817, he removed Stoddart from the editor's chair and replaced him with the more whiggish Thomas Barnes.

With Barnes's appointment, Walter could turn his attention to another private pursuit: the construction of a country estate. Bear Wood, near Reading, took over three years and thousands of pounds to build—and thousands of pounds to maintain. Walter remarried in January 1818, and he and his new wife, Mary Smithe, daughter of Henry Smithe of Eastling, Kent, were finally settled in the new estate in 1822, where they lived off and on for the rest of his life. He enjoyed the role of country gentleman, keeping a rather large staff and entertaining lavishly. He also kept a house in town, first in Brompton Row, later at Charing Cross, and continued to lease the apartments at Printing House Square, all at considerable cost. His first son, also John Walter, was born in 1818.

In 1819 Walter determined to sell off most of his interest in The Times, although he would continue in his position as chief proprietor until his death. He apparently was motivated in part by the need for money to maintain his several homes. He had also decided on a parliamentary career, and he knew that the editor of a newspaper, even one as respectable as The Times, would not be an acceptable MP. By 1831 he had retired completely from all responsibilities for the newspaper, and was elected on a reforming ticket for Berkshire in 1832. It should be noted, however, that although Walter refrained from any direct management of the newspaper, he still owned a one-thirty-second share; he still owned the premises and, more importantly, the printing business at Printing House Square; and he still received rent from the newspaper for the space that it occupied at the square. In 1827, for example, his total annual income from the various pieces of the business amounted to over £13,000.

Although Walter represented Berkshire as a whig, he continued the political independence that he had established at The Times. His parliamentary career was not particularly distinguished. He was not an effective public speaker, and the only cause he took leadership in was the opposition to the Poor Law Bill of 1834. However, his constituents appear to have felt that he was a conscientious representative, and he worked tirelessly for them, especially in projects for poor relief. Despite his independence, he worked well with his colleagues in parliament; his only enemy was Daniel O'Connell, a favourite target of Times leading articles. As the whig party factionalized in the 1830s, Walter broke away to join Peel's nascent Conservatives, and resigned his Berkshire constituency in 1837. He stood unsuccessfully for Southwark in 1840, and was finally returned for Nottingham as a Conservative at a by-election on 27 April 1841. He lost the seat at the general election in June the same year, but won the seat back at another by-election in August 1842, only to lose it again on petition. Still, he maintained his political independence: his Nottingham supporters comprised both Conservatives and Chartists, and he opposed Peel's poor-law policies. Walter believed that Peel was ultimately responsible for the loss of his Nottingham seat, and as a result Peel never again received support from Walter or The Times.

The last years Walter never returned to parliament. Barnes died shortly before Walter lost his Nottingham seat, and the paper once again claimed his attention. He appointed the 23-year-old J. T. Delane as editor, but took back much of the authority of managing the paper. During his last six years he took on the increasingly powerful railroad speculators, and his investigations into fraud and conspiracy resulted in the erection of commemorative tablets in his name by the lord mayor of London. He also insisted that the newspaper maintain an independent, if somewhat conservative, establishment-oriented political position.

Walter had hoped that his eldest son, John *Walter (1818–1894), would succeed him as sole proprietor, but

young Walter showed little inclination to become involved in either the paper or the printing business. In addition, Walter was an old-line evangelical, and his son's involvement with the Oxford Tractarians very nearly caused the two to break off relations in 1845. However, they reconciled in 1846 and Walter jun. took a position at The Times in the business office. Later that year, Walter sen. began suffering from what later would be diagnosed as throat cancer. Feeling his mortality, and knowing how important to the future of the newspaper a clear line of succession would be, he appointed his eldest son joint manager on 5 November 1846.

The last six months of his life were difficult for Walter and those around him. As the cancer grew, he became understandably more temperamental toward his family and his staff. He lived at Printing House Square, which put him in the closest possible contact with the business. He insisted on actively directing the business affairs and even the editorial policies of The Times. He had undertaken a bitter battle with his old friend and partner William Delane, father of the current editor, over the future control of the paper. He grew querulous, and at times was completely unreasonable. Although it was clear to him and those around him that his cancer was terminal, in January 1847 he met with representatives from Reading to discuss his candidacy for parliament in the next election. However, he finally accepted the inevitability of his imminent death and announced his retirement from politics in February. The uncertainty over the future direction of the paper and J. T. Delane's part in it caused serious dissension among the staff. Finally, on 1 July John Walter jun. was appointed sole manager. On 20 July an agreement was reached between the elder Delane and Walter on the disputed proprietorship, leaving John Walter jun. in complete control of The Times. J. T. Delane was to continue as editor. Walter jun. would, like his father, enter parliament as member for Nottingham and assume the role of businessman, politician, head of a family, and country gentleman.

Walter died on 28 July 1847 in the apartments at Printing House Square. He was survived by his wife and three sons, John, to whom he left his entire interest in The Times, Henry, and Edward *Walter. He was once described by Crabb Robinson as 'slow at conversation, caring only for "real things", a man great in reserve' (History of 'The Times', 1.80). Although he entertained on a large scale, he was said to be somewhat quiet, indeed 'bashful'. He was an ardent fisherman and landscape gardener. 'He enjoyed the country. He rode well. He wrote a supremely good letter; he had a remarkably good head for figures' (ibid., 1.8). He was a loyal friend and, obviously, a sound businessman. His establishment of The Times as one of the most influential newspapers in the world makes him one of the genuinely remarkable men of the nineteenth century.

RICHARD D. FULTON

Sources [S. Morison and others], The history of The Times, 1 (1935) • [S. Morison and others], The history of The Times, 2 (1939) • O. Woods and J. Bishop, The story of 'The Times' (1983) • W. D. Bowman, The story of 'The Times' (1931) • E. Cook, Delane of The Times (1916) • GM, 2nd ser., 28 (1847), 318–22, 660 [details of will]

Archives Berks. RO, estate and family MSS • News Int. RO, corresp. • NRA, priv. coll., corresp. | DWL, Henry Crabb Robinson MSS
Likenesses G. Hayter, group portrait, oils, 1833–43 (The House of Commons, 1833), NPG • oils, News International Syndication, London [see illus.] • watercolour miniature, News International Syndication, London
Wealth at death £90,000: GM, 660

Walter, John (1818–1894), newspaper proprietor and politician, was born on 8 October 1818 at Printing House Square, London, the eldest son of John *Walter (1776–1847) of Printing House Square and his second wife, Mary, née Smithe, of Eastling, Kent. Sir Edward *Walter was his brother. He was educated at Eton College and at Exeter College, Oxford, where he graduated in 1840 with second-class honours in classics. After taking his MA in 1843 he became a member of Lincoln's Inn, and was called to the bar in 1847, by which time he had become actively connected with The Times. He served first as manager in the difficult circumstances which attended the end of the Delane–Alsager joint managership in 1846. He continued in this capacity until he became chief proprietor on the death of his father in July 1847.

It was noted later that Walter had been 'trained from birth to exercise a potent and controlling influence in the counsels of a newspaper which his father had raised to the first place in the world' (The Times, 5 Nov 1894). His stately progress to this position, however, was not entirely untroubled. The Puseyite sympathies which he had acquired at Oxford led to a disagreement with his father over the editorial line pursued by The Times on church issues. This rift was sufficiently serious to prompt his temporary withdrawal from managerial duties, but appears to have been short-lived. After he returned The Times adopted a more open attitude to the Tractarians, though his earnest Anglicanism, growing more robust as he aged, precluded any danger of a drift to Rome. 'Popery', in his view, was 'not a fit religion for an Englishman' (History of The Times, 2.46). But he retained throughout his life a high regard for J. H. Newman, whose brother-in-law, Thomas Mozley, was a valued contributor and the Times correspondent at the First Vatican Council.

Walter's parliamentary career began at the same time as his proprietorship of The Times. He was returned, along with Feargus O'Connor, the Chartist agitator, as member for Nottingham on 28 July 1847, the day of his father's death. Though he was not unknown to the electors, having sought their favour unsuccessfully in 1843, his victory was remarkable in that it was achieved without the benefit of a personal appearance prior to the polls. A triumphant visit to his constituency after the result had been declared prompted the remark, attributed by Walter to Tyas, a Times reporter, that he had achieved 'more than Caesar … for he "came, saw and conquered" whilst I never came, nor saw, yet conquered!' (Walter to Delane, 29 July 1847; Delane–Dasent Correspondence, 2/77). He continued to represent Nottingham until 1859, adopting a 'Liberal-

John Walter (1818–1894), by Sir Hubert von Herkomer, 1889

Conservative' label and sitting with the Liberals at Westminster. He retired from Nottingham undefeated to seek the Liberal nomination in Berkshire, his home county, which he represented in parliament from 1859 to 1865, and again from 1868 to his retirement in 1885. Over this period he remained attached to free trade and moderate parliamentary reform while retaining a conservative instinct which, at an earlier juncture, would have allowed him to sit comfortably among the Portland whigs. 'I am one of those', he confided, 'who are old-fashioned enough to think that the Devil was let loose at the French Revolution … and that Waterloo was a great act of retributive justice, which was richly deserved' (Walter to Delane, 6 Dec 1859; Walter MSS, 383).

The Times, under Walter's aegis, retained and developed its unique influence. With an average daily circulation of 38,141 in 1850, more than double the combined total of its five metropolitan rivals, it was 'unequalled in the breadth and depth of its reporting, the gravity of its tone, the grandeur of its pretensions and its sheer physical bulk' (Morley, 11). Walter's contribution to its success should not be underestimated, for—the influence of its editors and contributors notwithstanding—he was 'in the last resort a deciding voice in the policy and conduct of this journal' (The Times, 5 Nov 1894). His editors, notably John Delane, who served from 1847 to 1877, exercised a relatively free hand, but within well-understood parameters reinforced by Walter's close scrutiny of the paper's content and style. For Walter an independent 'fourth estate' was a benign and restraining influence in politics and society. Mediating directly between the government and the governed The Times, in his view, was helping to supply any deficiencies in the representative system and was 'therefore more conservative in its effects than any machinery that constitution-mongers can devise' (Walter to Dasent, 6 Oct 1858; Delane–Dasent correspondence, 9/64).

For most of the half-century in which *The Times* was under Walter's control its political influence was underpinned by solid prosperity, and his contribution was especially important in ensuring that this was the case. Innovations in printing technology, in which he took a particular interest, kept *The Times* ahead of the field, allowing him to reduce the cover price to 3*d.* in 1869, increasing average daily circulation by 20,000 at a stroke. The famous Walter press, installed at *The Times* in 1866, was the outcome of years of patient experimentation begun under Walter's father. From 1848 *The Times* was printed on a vertical cylinder press devised by Augustus Applegarth, the chief printer, to meet the demand for a machine that would print 10,000 sheets an hour, but by 1856 Walter had become convinced of the advantages of horizontal cylinders and introduced American-designed Hoe presses at Printing House Square. His correspondence with John Cameron MacDonald, the printing office manager, testifies to Walter's keen interest in this aspect of the business. The most important breakthrough, however, occurred when James Dellagana, an Italian typefounder brought to *The Times* by Walter, cast metal stereotypes into papier mâché moulds. This development, combined with a continuous feeding mechanism, made the press 'the wonder of its day', for it allowed a continuous roll of paper to be printed on both sides from curved stereos as it passed through a series of rotating horizontal cylinders. It was possible, using this revolutionary process, to print 12,000 eight-page papers in an hour. Even so, *The Times* from the mid-1860s was eclipsed in circulation by the *Daily Telegraph*.

The pre-eminence of *The Times* among newspapers and the elevated political status which it gained as a consequence attracted significant criticism. In these circumstances Walter sought to establish a distinction between his dual roles as chief proprietor of *The Times* and member of parliament. When confronted in 1860 by Edward Horsman, the member for Stroud, who had been offended by published comments about the venality of certain MPs, Walter protested that his connection with *The Times* was strictly proprietorial, denying 'any responsibility on my part for any opinion or statement which it contained' (*Hansard 3*, 158, 1860, col. 761). This was less than convincing, and the question of Walter's potentially conflicting interests surfaced again in 1864 when he supplied information to Lord Robert Cecil which was then used to harass Robert Lowe from office. Although Walter claimed that he had acted, in this instance, solely in his capacity as member for Berkshire, his subsequent private apology to Lowe suggests an uneasy conscience (Winter, 193). On such occasions his capacity for delicate judgement on matters relating to the interests of *The Times* was tested. As he aged, his touch became less certain in this respect. This was most evident in the decision to purchase and then publish letters, subsequently proved to have been forged, which appeared to link Charles Stewart Parnell, the Irish nationalist leader, with the Phoenix Park murders. The notorious 'Parnellism and crime' articles, published in 1887, proved an expensive embarrassment for *The Times*, which had to meet the full cost (£200,000) of the ensuing judicial commission. As a result the healthy financial position which had been established over the years since 1847 was much weakened. As chief proprietor Walter could not escape censure for the fateful decision, though in mitigation it might be noted that the most recent account of this episode is more critical of the editor, George Buckle, and the manager, John Cameron MacDonald (Woods and Bishop, 157).

John Walter was married twice, first, on 27 September 1842, to Emily Frances Court of Castlemans, Berkshire, with whom he had six sons and one daughter. Widowed in 1858, Walter married again on 1 January 1861; his second wife was Flora MacNabb of Highfield Park, Hampshire, with whom he had a further three sons. 'The Griff', as Walter was known at *The Times* since, like a griffin, he was considered both grim and vigilant, retreated to his palatial home on the family estate at Bear Wood, near Wokingham, where he died after a short illness, diagnosed as purpura, on 3 November 1894. He was buried at St Catherine's, Bear Wood. On his death he was succeeded as chief proprietor of *The Times* by Arthur Fraser *Walter (1846–1910), second son of his first marriage.

DILWYN PORTER

Sources News Int. RO, *The Times* archive, Walter MSS · News Int. RO, *The Times* archive, Delane–Dasent correspondence · *The Times* (5 Nov 1894) · *Hansard 3* (1860), 158.757-75 · [S. Morison and others], *The history of The Times*, 2 (1939) · [S. Morison and others], *The history of The Times*, 3 (1947) · T. Morley, 'The Times and the concept of the fourth estate: theory and practice in mid-nineteenth century Britain', *Journal of Newspaper and Periodical History*, 1 (summer 1985), 11–23 · C. Claire, *A history of printing in England* (1965), 212–17 · S. E. Koss, *The rise and fall of the political press in Britain*, 1 (1981) · J. Winter, *Robert Lowe* (1976) · O. Woods and J. Bishop, *The story of 'The Times'* (1983) · *Some men of 'The Times' from the first John Walter to Thadeus Delane* · M. Girouard, 'Bear Wood, Berkshire: the home of Bearwood College [pt 1]', *Country Life*, 144 (1968), 964–7 · M. Girouard, 'Bear Wood, Berkshire: the home of Bearwood College [pt 2]', *Country Life*, 144 (1968), 1060–63 · Burke, *Gen. GB*
Archives News Int. RO, papers · NRA, priv. coll., papers | Bodl. Oxf., letters to Benjamin Disraeli; corresp. with Lord Kimberley
Likenesses S. Bellin, mezzotint, pubd 1853 (after J. Lucas), BM · H. von Herkomer, oils, 1889, Times Newspapers Ltd, London [*see illus.*] · Barraud, photograph, NPG; repro. in *Men and Women of the Day*, 4 (1891) · D. J. Pound, stipple and line engraving (after photograph by Mayall), NPG; repro. in D. J. Pound, *Drawing room gallery of eminent personages* · Spy [L. Ward], chromolithograph caricature, NPG; repro. in *VF* (10 Sept 1881) · portrait (*John Walter III, chief proprietor, 1847–94*; after oil painting), priv. coll.; repro. in Morison and others, *History of The Times*, 2, frontispiece · portrait (*John Walter III in 1847*; after wood-engraving), repro. in Morison and others, *History of The Times*, 2, facing p. 46
Wealth at death £310,228 14*s.* 3*d.*: resworn probate, July 1896, *CGPLA Eng. & Wales*

Walter, John (1873–1968), newspaper proprietor, was born in London on 8 August 1873, the elder son of Arthur Fraser *Walter (1846–1910), newspaper proprietor, and his wife, Henrietta Maria, eldest daughter of the Revd Thomas Anchitel Anson, of Longford rectory, Derbyshire. *The*

Times newspaper had been founded by his great-great-grandfather in 1785. His father was the second son of John *Walter the third (1818–1894) but succeeded to the control of *The Times* because his elder brother, John, had been drowned while life saving at the family estate, Bear Wood, Wokingham, Berkshire, in 1870. Walter strove throughout his life to be known as John Walter the fifth. His father, Arthur Walter, became chief proprietor of *The Times* in 1894 and died in 1910; so John Walter had a long warning of, and schooling in, the responsibilities of Printing House Square.

Walter's heritage was, however, no longer a controlling interest. The complicated financial quarrels in the Walter family which led to loss of control began in 1898, the year John Walter started work on *The Times*. For nearly a decade he had little interest in them. Educated at Eton College and Christ Church, Oxford, where he obtained a third class in *literae humaniores* (1897), he served nominally as assistant to C. F. Moberly Bell, manager of *The Times*. Bell straddled, particularly on the foreign side, both managerial and editorial departments in a way none of his successors did. John Walter's interests were all editorial. He visited the paper's correspondents in Vienna, St Petersburg, and Berlin, and was often in Paris. He knew de Blowitz, the famous Paris correspondent of *The Times*, well, and wrote his obituary in 1903. Some years later he refused the Paris post. He was present as a representative of his paper at the first Hague conference in 1899. The same year he attended the retrial of Henri Dreyfus at Rennes. He visited Canada and the United States in 1902. He was based in Madrid as *The Times*'s correspondent for the Iberian peninsula at the time his father died. He had a lifelong affection for Spain. He spent the years 1916–18 as publicity attaché at the British embassy in Madrid, countering German propaganda; his elder son, John, was to serve in the embassy's press section in the Second World War.

Nevertheless, in view of his eventual succession, Walter took some part in abortive negotiations with C. Arthur Pearson and when the ensuing ones with Alfred *Harmsworth, Viscount Northcliffe, succeeded in 1908 it was agreed he should become chairman of *The Times* on his father's death. By 1910 the two-year 'honeymoon period' of the new partnership was nearing its end. Walter stepped into twelve agitated and occasionally stormy years, which broke even his patience at the last. Walter's relations with Northcliffe were never simple. The picture of him as an ineffectual man, continually overridden, obscures the better lights of his character. He was determined not to be an absentee figurehead like his father, who had never had any close working association with *The Times*. John Walter, shortly after he had become chairman, went back to Portugal to report the revolution there.

Walter was convinced that *The Times* needed new blood. But he soon realized that with a man such as Northcliffe, at heart far more a journalist than a newspaper owner, any hope of editorial independence was frail. In 1913, at personal financial sacrifice, he obtained an option to buy back Northcliffe's shares on the latter's death. Meanwhile he soldiered on in his quiet way for the traditions of the paper. Northcliffe at times became impatient with Walter, as he did with everyone else. Yet the two men kept a liking for each other. At last in 1922 Walter's staying power was exhausted. In June he cancelled the 1913 agreement and with it the option. Northcliffe asked him to continue as chairman. Walter, regaining his nerve, agreed, provided the option was maintained. In August Northcliffe died.

In the ensuing battle for *The Times*, involving Lloyd George, the first Lord Rothermere, and others, Walter wisely chose the best ally. When, on 23 October 1922, he and John *Astor (1886–1971) became joint chief proprietors of *The Times*, Walter had achieved his aim of ensuring the paper's complete editorial independence. He stayed much the junior partner in a stable relationship, and his chief proprietorship, involving by that time only responsibility for the appointment and dismissal of the editor, lasted until *The Times* and the *Sunday Times* were merged under Lord Thomson of Fleet on 1 January 1967, when his family's long connection with *The Times* came to an end.

Combining great courtesy and an austere manner, Walter was essentially an uncombative man. He married in 1903 Charlotte Hilda (Phyllis), youngest daughter of Colonel Charles Edward Foster, of Buckby Hall, Northamptonshire. They had two sons and two daughters. She died in 1937. His second wife, Rosemary, only daughter of James Adair Crawford of the Indian Civil Service, whom he married in 1939, survived him.

To hear Walter describe earlier crises in the history of *The Times* was to realize the generations he spanned. Yet in his ninetieth birthday luncheon speech in Printing House Square he spoke only of the future. He did not feel his position precluded him from letting the editor know his views on public affairs. (He was against *The Times*'s appeasement policy.) He always emphasized that he did so as an ordinary reader, and meant it. His loyalty to his editor's authority was absolute. If he was less forceful than his predecessors as head of *The Times*, he was more versatile. He painted and drew extremely well. He wrote clear prose. In his nineties he still read *The Times* closely, his dry comments making him an engaging companion. In 1961 he was received into the Roman Catholic church, as his mother had been. He had known the splendours of Bear Wood, had lived in the Private House at Printing House Square, and had seen it demolished; he died in a modest flat at 69 The Drive, Hove, Sussex, on 11 August 1968.

WILLIAM HALEY, *rev.*

Sources News Int. RO, *The Times* archive · personal knowledge (1981) · *WWW* · *The Times* (12 Aug 1968) · *CGPLA Eng. & Wales* (1968) · O. Woods and J. Bishop, *The story of 'The Times'* (1983) · R. Pound and G. Harmsworth, *Northcliffe* (1959) · D. Wilson, *The Astors, 1763–1992: landscape with millionaires* (1993) · [S. Morison and others], *The history of The Times*, 3 (1947) · [S. Morison and others], *The history of The Times*, 4 (1952) · I. McDonald, *The history of The Times*, 5 (1984)

Archives BL, corresp. with Lord Northcliffe, Add. MSS 62238–62239 · Bodl. Oxf., corresp. with Geoffrey Dawson · News Int. RO, papers

Likenesses P. A. de Laszlo, oils, c.1924, Times Newspapers, London

Wealth at death £189,497: probate, 1 Oct 1968, *CGPLA Eng. & Wales*

Walter, Lucy (1630?–1658), mother of James, duke of Monmouth, was the daughter of William Walter (d. 1650) of Roch Castle, near Haverfordwest, Pembrokeshire, and Elizabeth Prothero (d. 1652), daughter of John Prothero and niece of John Vaughan, first earl of Carbery. For about a year in 1648–9 Lucy was the mistress of the heir to the throne, Prince Charles, subsequently *Charles II, and Charles was the acknowledged father of the boy born to Lucy on 9 April 1649. Christened James [see Scott, James], the child was the first of Charles II's many bastards, and was created duke of Monmouth in 1663. He became important politically in the 1670s and 1680s because of suggestions not only that he was the son of Charles II, but that he was also the legitimate son. During the exclusion crisis of 1679–82, and during the rebellion which Monmouth subsequently led against James II in 1685, a central political question was whether or not his mother had gone through a form of marriage with his father, Charles, in the course of their relationship in 1648–9. While most of the political nation was rightly sceptical (and Charles himself maintained absolutely that there had been no marriage), Lucy was by then dead, and there was just sufficient confusion over exactly what had taken place over thirty years earlier, and sufficient people with an interest in asserting that Monmouth was legitimate, for the story of a marriage to enjoy a scrap of credibility. The supposed marriage was critical, because if it had taken place, Monmouth was legitimate and thus, as the king's eldest son, was the heir to the throne. During the exclusion crisis this offered the whigs the easiest way of excluding the duke of York from the throne, while in 1685 it legitimized those who took up arms for Monmouth against James II. For these reasons Lucy Walter's short life is important as it explains why most of the political nation considered that a marriage between her and Charles was highly unlikely, but shows too that there were some straws available for the pro-marriage party to make use of.

Lucy Walter was born at Roch Castle, Pembrokeshire. Her parents were middling Welsh gentry (her mother brought a dowry of £600 to her marriage), and though formally uneducated Lucy received the social manners which enabled her to mix with good society. This became important when, in 1640, her parents separated, her father remaining at Roch Castle while Lucy went with her mother to grow up in the cosmopolitan society of civil war London. By the end of the war she was the mistress of the parliamentarian officer Algernon Sidney, who, according to James II, bought her services for 40 gold pieces. When, however, he was ordered away with his regiment to Ireland, Lucy decided to seek a new lover where young aristocrats were thickest to be found, and took ship to join the exiled royalist camp in the Netherlands. Here she made herself known to the younger and royalist brother of her former lover, Robert Sidney, later second earl of Leicester. His time with her was brief, however, for in May 1648 part of the parliamentarian fleet mutinied and sailed to the royalists in Holland. This brought Prince Charles hurrying from France to inspect his new prize, and in a hectic week Lucy used her connections to meet, charm, and seduce the heir to the throne. She was then just eighteen, Charles a year older. She remained with him until September 1649, when he left for Jersey and thence to Scotland the following year. During this time John Evelyn remembered her as a 'browne, beautiful bold but insipid creature' (Evelyn, 2.561–2), and even James II conceded that she was 'very handsome, [though] of little wit, and some cunning' (MacPherson, 1.76).

While Charles pursued his expedition to Scotland and England in 1650–1, Lucy Walter supported herself and her young son in the only way she could, taking as her protector Theobald, second Viscount Taafe, with whom she had a daughter, Mary (b. 1651). When Charles returned to exile in 1652, he made it clear that their relationship was finished, but Lucy refused to accept this, and for the next four years created so many scandalous scenes that in 1656 she was given some money and a pearl necklace and shipped with her children back to England. Incapable of living quietly, she soon attracted the attention of the government, and was imprisoned in the Tower. Deciding that not even the royalists could be using her as a spy, the republic sent her back to Flanders, while its propaganda sheet made capital out of this woman 'who passed for Charles Stuart's wife' (*Mercurius Politicus*). Back in Brussels Lucy resumed her stormy ways, now using her growing son as a means of leverage against Charles and his advisers. After an attempt to kidnap the boy had resulted in a public fiasco, she was persuaded in March 1658 to give him up to a tutor named by Charles. By then she had contracted venereal disease, and after making a general confession to John Cosin (later bishop of Durham), she died in Paris towards the end of 1658 at the age of twenty-eight and was buried there.

Although the details of Lucy Walter's short relationship with Charles in 1648–9, together with the whole tenor of her life, made the notion of a marriage between the two highly implausible, Lucy's general confession of her life to Cosin became the basis for the most circumstantial of the marriage stories. It was suggested that, in this confession, Lucy not only swore that a marriage had taken place, but entrusted Cosin with documentary proof, which was kept in a 'black box'. Cosin's death in 1671 then left no direct witnesses when, in the 1670s, the enemies of James, duke of York, resurrected the Cosin story, and began a fruitless search for the 'black box'. Supporting evidence they uncovered amounted to nothing more than memories that in the 1650s Lucy had insisted that she was no mere mistress but a wife. The political nation remained unconvinced of Monmouth's legitimacy, although in 1679 Charles went to the length of formally denying, at the privy council, that he had ever been married to Lucy Walter. Lucy Walter's name is sometimes misspelt as Mrs Walters or Waters and during her life abroad she adopted the alias of Mrs Barlow or Barlo.   ROBIN CLIFTON

Sources J. MacPherson, ed., *Original papers … and life of James II*, 3 vols. (1749) · *The life of Edward, earl of Clarendon … written by himself*, 3 vols. (1759) · Evelyn, *Diary* · R. Clifton, *The last popular rebellion: the western rising of 1685* (1984) · G. Scott, *Lucy Walter, wife or mistress* (1947) · *DNB* · Thurloe, *State papers* · *The Nicholas papers*, ed. G. F.

Warner, 2, CS, new ser., 50 (1892) · *Mercurius Politicus* (10–17 July 1656) · *CSP dom.*, 1655–8 · *The life of Edward, earl of Clarendon … written by himself*, new edn, 3 vols. (1827)

Likenesses double portrait (with the infant duke of Monmouth), priv. coll. · portrait, priv. coll. · portrait, priv. coll. · portrait, priv. coll.

Walter, Richard (1717–1785), Church of England clergyman and naval chaplain, was born on 21 October 1717 in the parish of St Martin Ludgate, London, and was baptized on 29 October there. He was the son of Arthur Walter, silk mercer and resident of St Martin, and his wife, Mary. Richard went to Okenham school, in Berkshire. He is mentioned in the records of the Fishmongers' Company as having applied to the company for a scholarship. He was admitted pensioner of Sidney Sussex College, Cambridge, on 3 July 1735, matriculated in 1736, and graduated BA in 1739. He was elected to a fellowship in 1740.

Walter was ordained deacon by the bishop of Norwich in June 1740 and in that year was appointed chaplain of the *Centurion* (60 guns), then fitting out for her voyage against the Spanish under the command of Commodore George Anson (afterwards Baron Anson of Soberton). The *Centurion* sailed on 18 September 1740 with a crew which included both pensioners and raw recruits so that though 'a puny, weakly, and sickly man, pale, and of a low stature' (Walter and Robins, xxiii), Walter often had to help with the actual working of the ship, until her arrival in Macaõ in November 1742. In December he obtained Anson's permission to return to England in one of the East India Company's ships.

Back in England, Walter graduated MA in 1744 and in March 1745 was appointed chaplain of Portsmouth Dockyard. On 5 May 1748 he married, in Gray's Inn Chapel, Jane Sabbarton of St Margaret's, Lothbury: they had four surviving children: Sophie, Arthur, Mary, and Jane. Jane married Isaac Prescott and their son was Henry *Prescott (1783–1874). In 1748 Walter published *A Voyage Round the World in the Years MDCCXL, I, II, III, IV by George Anson*. The book had been eagerly awaited. The main result of Anson's voyage was the capture in June 1743 of a treasure-laden galleon sailing from Acapulco to Manila. Anson had arrived home with treasure worth more than £400,000, and the event had captured public imagination and excitement.

The book became something of a best-seller, running through numerous editions in its full or abridged form and being translated into several European languages. Walter's authorship of the work was, however, disputed in 1761: James Wilson, who edited the *Mathematical Tracts* of Benjamin Robins, claimed that Robins was the real author of the book, Walter having simply supplied notes. Walter did not contest this account at the time, perhaps because by then he was seriously ill, but after his death his widow wrote to John Walter, printer and proprietor of *The Times* and a relation of Richard Walter, rebutting the suggestion that Walter had simply supplied the raw material for publication. According to her account he had been actively engaged at all stages of editing.

The matter was largely resolved by G. Williams in his *Documents Relating to Anson's Voyage* (1967), in which documents 141–59 concern the authorship of the work. It seems clear that the initiative for publishing an authorized account of the voyage was taken by Walter, but that he was unable, unwilling, or both to bring the project to fruition and Robins was called upon to complete the task. Walter does seem to have had a hand in publishing, as distinct from editing, the work. He gathered names of subscribers and profited handsomely therefrom. It is also clear that Anson himself took a very close interest in the work, which is as a result very complimentary of his actions but provides an interesting insight into his thinking. Walter's and Robins's contributions to the work can probably never be completely disentangled, but this should not obscure its continued popularity (a full electronic edition was published in 2001 and there has been a steady stream of paper editions since its publication). It provided the inspiration and the basis for Patrick O'Brian's popular novel *The Golden Ocean* (1956), his first sea novel.

Walter remained chaplain to the Portsmouth Dockyard until his death on 10 March 1785. He was buried at Great Staughton, Huntingdonshire, where he owned some property, though it seems that he never lived there.

ELIZABETH BAIGENT

Sources Venn, *Alum. Cant.* · private information (2004) [J. W. Devonshire] · G. Williams, ed., *Documents relating to Anson's voyage round the world, 1740–1744*, Navy RS, 109 (1967) · R. J. Walter and B. Robins, *A voyage round the world in the years MDCCXL, I, II, III, IV by George Anson*, ed. G. Williams (1974) · will, PRO, PROB 11/1129/255, fols. 137v–139v · *DNB* · 'Walter, John (1739–1812)', *DNB*

Walter, Theobald. *See* Butler, Theobald (*d.* 1205).

Walter, William (*fl. c.*1525–1533), poet and translator, is a man about whose life little is known. He describes himself on the title-page of *Tytus and Gesyppus* (*c.*1525) as 'somtyme servaunte to syr Henry Marney knyght chaunceler of the duchy of Lancastre'. The title-pages of *Guystarde and Sygysmonde* (1532) and *The Spectacle of Lovers* (1533?) repeat this claim. All of Walter's known writings postdate Marney's death in 1523.

Tytus and Gesyppus (812 lines) is a narrative of two friends who were 'confederate in amyte' (456) to the extent that Gesyppus ceded his wife to Titus; subsequently both take the blame for a murder neither committed but of which each suspected the other to be guilty. The narrative's conclusion leaves the two in 'love & parfyte amyte' (805).

Guystarde and Sygysmonde (642 lines) recounts the murder of Guystarde by Tancred, the father of his love Sygysmonde, whose heart he subsequently gives to his grieving daughter 'in a cuppe of golde' (477), whereupon she dies. The relative brevity of the narrative is expanded in various interpolations ascribed to Wynkyn de Worde's associate, Robert Copland, who provides a prologue, envoy, and several interjections amounting to about a fifth of the entire work (lines 1–28, 239–59, 442–62, 505–25, 610–44).

Both of these narratives are based on parts of Boccaccio's *Decameron* and are the earliest printed English translations of parts of that work. They do not, however, appear to be direct translations but to be based on Latin versions by Leonardo Bruni and Philip Beroaldo respectively. Both are in rhyme-royal stanzas.

Walter's other surviving work, *The Spectacle of Lovers*, again is in rhyme royal. It is subtitled 'a lytell contravers dyalogue bytwene love and councell', a characterization that gives some indication of its anti-feminist cast. After a *chanson d'aventure* opening it consists of a dialogue between Consultator (the narrator) and Amator (a complaining lover) in which the former rebuts the arguments in favour of love advanced by the latter. The following passage is representative:

> Ye lovers delyte in slouthe and sadnesse
> In stede of myrthe ye syghe contynually
> Despare dothe ofte encrese your hevynesse
> Ye be also troubled by Jalousy
> By such meanes ye be brought in fransy.
> (*Spectacle of Lovers*, Biii)

Copland again provides an envoy.

All of Walter's works survive only in editions by Wynkyn de Worde, who valued the Boccaccio translations sufficiently to commission woodcuts specifically for them. Some stanzas from the *Spectacle of Lovers* also appear in the Bodleian Library's MS Rawlinson C. 813, possibly copied from a printed edition.   A. S. G. EDWARDS

Sources H. G. Wright, ed., *Early English versions of the tales of Guiscardo and Ghismonda and Titus and Gisippus from 'The Decameron'*, EETS, old ser., 205 (1937) · M. Brackman, 'A new source for the pains of love in Rawlinson MS C 813', *Neophilologus*, 77 (1993), 127–34 · *Poems: Robert Copland*, ed. M. C. Erler (1993), 64–5 [incl. Copland's envoy to the *Spectacle of lovers*]

Walters, Catherine [*nicknamed* Skittles; *known as* Mrs Baillie] (1839–1920), courtesan, was born on 13 June 1839 at 1 Henderson Street, Toxteth, Liverpool, the third of the five children of Edward Walters (*d.* 1864), a customs employee, and his wife, Mary Ann Fowler. She was baptized as a Roman Catholic. Three attributes saved Catherine from the fate of most girls growing up in dockside Liverpool: her exceptional beauty, her practical nature, and her riding skills, acquired while working in a livery stable. Cheerfully amoral, she became, at the age of sixteen, the mistress of George, Lord Fitzwilliam, master of the Fitzwilliam hounds. He set her up in London and, on finally parting from her, made her a generous settlement. It was perhaps under his guidance that she developed her passion for hunting: in later years she was to ride regularly with the Quorn.

Small and slender, with grey-blue eyes and chestnut-coloured hair, Catherine Walters never looked like a whore; she dressed with an unexpected decorousness. But there was nothing decorous about her talk: she was effervescent, outspoken, bawdy. Her naturalness was one of her chief attractions. Unlike so many prostitutes, she remained affectionate and sympathetic. 'She was the only whore in history to retain her heart intact,' wrote the journalist Henry Labouchere (Blyth, xii).

It was as one of the celebrated 'horse-breakers' who paraded in Hyde Park that Catherine Walters first attracted wide public attention. She particularly drew the young Spencer *Cavendish, Lord Hartington, eldest son of the

Catherine Walters [Skittles] (1839–1920), by unknown photographer

seventh duke of Devonshire. By 1859 she had become his mistress and was installed in a house in Mayfair, with an annual allowance. By that time she was known as Skittles, possibly a reference to the fact that in youth she had earned a few pence by setting up the skittles in some local bowling alley. Once, when Lord Hartington was accompanying that tireless practical joker the prince of Wales on an official visit to Coventry, the mayor drew Hartington's attention to the town's bowling alley, explaining that the prince had asked especially for its inclusion in their tour in tribute to Hartington's love of skittles.

When her relationship with Lord Hartington cooled, Catherine Walters moved to France. Here she quickly established herself as one of that select band of *grandes cocottes* who were such a feature of Second Empire Paris. Among her many admirers was the young poet Wilfrid Scawen *Blunt (1840–1922), who fell deeply in love with her and with whom she remained on good terms for the rest of her life. She was the inspiration for his narrative poem 'Esther'.

By the fall of the Second Empire in 1870, Catherine Walters was back in England, dividing her time between hunting and entertaining a varied circle of men. Her Sunday afternoon tea parties were famous. Among her guests were W. E. Gladstone (though there is nothing in Gladstone's diaries to substantiate this) who was fascinated by prostitutes but with whom her relationship seems to have been platonic; and *Edward, prince of Wales, with whom it apparently was not. Even after their liaison had ended, the prince paid her an allowance and, whenever she was ill, sent his own doctor to attend to her. His letters to her were so confidential that once, when she was thought to be dying, he had his private secretary collect and destroy over three hundred of them.

In 1872 Catherine Walters moved to 15 South Street, Park Lane, London, where she lived for the rest of her life. By the mid-1880s she was calling herself Mrs Baillie, but it seems unlikely that she actually married Alexander Horatio Baillie. Close friends of her sunset years were the faithful Blunt and the Hon. Gerald de Saumarez, whom she had first met when he was a schoolboy and to whom she bequeathed the bulk of her estate. Crippled by arthritis, she died at 15 South Street, of a cerebral haemorrhage, on 5 August 1920. Blunt arranged for her to be buried in the churchyard of the Franciscan monastery in Crawley, Sussex. THEO ARONSON

Sources H. Blyth, *Skittles: the last Victorian courtesan* (1970) · E. Longford [E. H. Pakenham, countess of Longford], *A pilgrimage of passion: the life of Wilfrid Scawen Blunt* (1979) · W. S. Blunt, diary, FM Cam. · P. Jackson, 'Skittles and the marquis: a Victorian love affair', *History Today*, 45/12 (1995), 47–52 · d. cert. · *CGPLA Eng. & Wales* (1920)
Archives Chatsworth House, Derbyshire, Devonshire MSS
Likenesses photograph, NPG [*see illus.*] · photographs, repro. in Blyth, *Skittles*
Wealth at death £2764 19s. 6d.: probate, 25 Sept 1920, *CGPLA Eng. & Wales*

Walters, Edward (1808–1872), architect, was born in December 1808 at 11 Fenchurch Buildings, London, the residence and office of his father, John Walters (1782–1821), architect. His mother was a sister of the architect Edward I'Anson the elder (with whom John Walters had studied under Daniel Alexander). Walters was educated at Brighton, and shortly after his father's early death in 1821 he entered, without articles, the office of Isaac Clarke, one of his father's pupils. Three years' training with Clarke was followed successively by engagements under the renowned builder Thomas Cubitt, the architect Lewis Vulliamy (with whom Owen Jones was a student at the time), the surveyor and architect John Wallen, and finally the civil engineer Sir John Rennie.

In March 1832 Walters was sent by Rennie to Constantinople to superintend construction of a small-arms factory and other works for the Turkish government. While there he made the acquaintance of W. H. Barlow, engineer to the Midland Railway, with whom he subsequently collaborated in various works in England. In Turkey Walters made plans for a palace for the sultan (unbuilt) and at the same time became a friend of Richard Cobden, who was then staying in Constantinople.

Walters left Turkey in 1837, and made a journey through Italy, Sicily, and France with Barlow, before returning to England in January 1838. In 1839, on Cobden's advice, he established an architectural practice at 20 (later 24) Cooper Street in Manchester. One of his earliest works was a warehouse for Cobden at 16 Mosley Street. Other early works included schools, suburban residences, and chapels in a modest Gothic style, for example, in 1842, Granby Row Church. He gained attention with Oakwood Hall, near Stockport, a Tudor-style mansion, for Ormerod Heyworth, and St Andrew's Free Church at the corner of Grosvenor Square and Oxford Street in 1840. In 1851 Walters was brought prominence by his design for the warehouse at the angle of Aytoun Street and Portland Street for Messrs Brown & Co., which initiated the fashion of building Manchester warehouses in the style of the Italian Renaissance. *The Builder* considered the palazzo style appropriate as warehouses were not merely store-places for heavy goods but also commodity 'emporia' (*The Builder*, 16, 1858, 97). Until 1860 he was the pre-eminent architect of the town, with a prolific practice that included warehouses, residences, banks, and chapels (listed in *The Builder*, 30, 1872 201).

Walters's most renowned works were the Free Trade Hall (1853–6) and the Manchester and Salford Bank in Mosley Street (1860). His design for the Free Trade Hall was chosen in a limited competition, and is a fine example of the palazzo type, much praised and illustrated at the time (see *The Builder*, 14, 1856, 526; and 71, 1896, 380). Its cost (£25,000) was raised by subscription, and the contemporary author T. R. Smith praised its acoustic properties in *A Rudimentary Treatise on the Acoustics of Public Buildings* (1861). It was partly reconstructed by L. C. Howitt (1896–1964) in 1950–51, following war damage but suffered more damage by an IRA bomb in 1996.

In 1860 Walters unsuccessfully submitted a design in the Manchester assize courts competition, and between 1860 and 1865 he reduced his practice. In the 1860s he joined Barlow in laying out the railway between Ambergate and Manchester, and designed many of the stations, the most successful being those at Bakewell and Miller's Dale; he also worked with his former pupils Barker and Ellis, by whom his practice was continued after his retirement in 1865.

Though Walters worked in Gothic at the opening of his career, his most successful works were in a Renaissance style. Contemporaries and later commentators (Pevsner, *Lancashire*, 282) praised his original and careful adaptation of the Renaissance palazzo to large-scale buildings and the dull Manchester climate. *The Builder* praised his buildings for 'the grouping of principal and subordinate features, for the manner of overcoming difficulties of numerous stories and closely set windows, … for the … mouldings, and the invention in details' (*The Builder*, 16, 1858, 97).

After Walters's retirement in 1865 he travelled in England and Italy. He died at 11 Oriental Place, Brighton, on 22 January 1872. He was remembered as 'a singularly modest' man 'with social qualities of the highest order' (*The Builder*, 30, 1872, 200). He never married.

PAUL WATERHOUSE, *rev.* M. A. GOODALL

Sources *The Builder*, 30 (1872), 69, 199-201 · E. I'Anson, 'The late Edward Walters, architect, of Manchester', *Sessional Papers of the Royal Institute of British Architects* (1871–2), 113–14 · 'Art, and buildings at Manchester', *The Builder*, 16 (1858), 97 · [W. Papworth], ed., *The dictionary of architecture*, 11 vols. (1853–92) · C. Knight, ed., *The English cyclopaedia: biography*, 6 vols. (1856–8) [suppl. (1872)] · 'The new free-trade hall, Manchester', *The Builder*, 14 (1856), 526–7 · *Civil Engineer and Architect's Journal*, 5 (1842), 27 · Boase, *Mod. Eng. biog.* · Graves, *RA exhibitors* · A. K. Placzek, ed., *Macmillan encyclopedia of architects*, 4 vols. (1982) · R. Dixon and S. Muthesius, *Victorian architecture* (1978), 121, 127–8, 149–50, 230, 268c · J. H. G. Archer, ed., *Art and architecture in Victorian Manchester* (1985), 12, 16, 19–20, 24 · *Lancashire*, Pevsner · biography file, RIBA BAL · *Dir. Brit. archs.* · d. cert. · *CGPLA Eng. & Wales* (1872)

Archives RIBA BAL

Wealth at death under £25,000: probate, 8 March 1872, *CGPLA Eng. & Wales*

Walters, John (*bap.* 1721, *d.* 1797), Church of England clergyman and lexicographer, was baptized on 22 August 1721 in Llanedi, Carmarthenshire, the son of John Walters (*d. c.*1734), timber merchant. Local tradition claims that he was born in a small house in the hamlet of Fforest, near Llanedi (Rowlands, 528). His parents died during his adolescence. He kept a school in Basaleg, Monmouthshire, and then went to Cowbridge School to improve his Greek and Latin. This enabled him to obtain a post as a schoolmaster at Margam, Glamorgan, and there he won the support of the Mansel Talbot family. He was ordained priest in 1750, obtained the curacy of Baglan, Glamorgan, and was appointed perpetual curate in Michaelston, Glamorgan, in 1754.

Walters married Hannah Clark, housekeeper to the Talbot family, on 14 September 1758, and they had five sons: John (1760–1789), Daniel (1762–1787), Henry (1766–1829), William (1770–1789), Lewis (1772–1844). The Welsh bard Edward Williams (Iolo Morganwg; 1747–1826) admired Walters's scholarship but described him as being 'a severe Father' and claimed that he 'kept his Children at too great a distance'. He was 'fastidious, Extremely formal, punctilious, squeamish rather than [having] fine Taste, had an eye more microscopic than Telescopic, very much afraid of going to law' (Williams, 146).

On 1 March 1759 Walters obtained the rectory of Llandough and on 10 August the same year the vicarage of St Hilary, near Cowbridge, Glamorgan. He also served in the adjacent parish of St Mary, was made chaplain to the high sheriff of Glamorgan in 1783 and prebendary to Llandaff Cathedral in 1795, and served as domestic chaplain to the Mansel family (*Archaeologia Cambrensis*, 238).

Walters's earliest literary work appears to be the unpublished 'The history of the noble family of the Mansels' (1752), now in the National Library of Wales. His 'Dissertation on the Welsh language', first published in 1771, was appended to each edition of his dictionary. He was also the author of *Dwy bregeth ar Ezec. xxxiii. – 11, etc.* ('Two sermons on Ezek. xxxiii. – 11, etc.') (1772) and 'An Ode to Humanity', which was appended to *An Ode on the Immortality of the Soul* (1786) by his eldest son, John Walters [*see below*].

Walters's most important work was *An English–Welsh Dictionary*, which was published in fifteen parts between 1770 and 1794. From 1770 to 1776 the parts came out regularly, but by 1776 progress had slowed down owing to financial difficulties. Walters complained that many of the subscribers (who included Samuel Johnson, William Seward, and Mrs Thrale) did not pay for the parts as they were published. Moreover Rhys Thomas, the printer, who had moved from Llandovery to print the dictionary and thereby establish the first printing press in Glamorgan, was also in deep financial trouble. Only four parts were published between 1778 and 1783, and the final parts were published in London in 1794 by Owen Jones (Owain Myfyr; 1741–1814).

Walters had obtained the manuscript of William Gambold's unpublished English–Welsh dictionary and used it in compiling his own work. Walters's dictionary, like Gambold's, not only gives translations for individual words but also translates English idioms. Its aim was to enable Welsh writers to discuss all branches of knowledge and the arts in Welsh, and Walters accomplished this by drawing on the resources of the literary language and the spoken language, as well as coining many new words, many of which gained currency and are still used today. Two other editions of the dictionary were published, one in 1815 and the other by Walters's granddaughter Hannah, in 1828. Walters died on 1 June 1797 at Cowbridge, leaving a widow and two sons, and was buried at Llandough on 4 June 1797.

His eldest son, **John Walters** (1760–1789), Church of England clergyman and scholar, was born on 11 June 1760 at Llandough parsonage, Glamorgan. He was educated at Cowbridge School, where he later became headmaster (1783), and at Jesus College, Oxford, which he entered on 17 December 1777. He served for a time as sub-librarian in the Bodleian Library, and proceeded BA on 21 June 1781 and MA on 10 July 1784. He became headmaster of Ruthin School in 1784, and subsequently rector of Efenechdid, Denbighshire. He married Jane Davies (*b.* 1766) on 23 February 1785.

The younger John Walters is chiefly remembered as a poet, and in his day was regarded as a promising young scholar. He published his volume of poems, *Poems with Notes* (1780), while at Jesus College and a volume of metrical translations of old Welsh poems, *Translated Specimens of Welsh Poetry* (1782). His edition of Llywarch Hen's poems with a literal English translation were included in the Revd W. Warrington's *The History of Wales* (1788) and he also supplied notes for Edward Jones's *Musical and Poetical Relicks of the Welsh Bards* (1784). He published several other works, including a reprint of Roger Ascham's *Toxophilus* (1778), as well as a number of sermons. Walters died on 28 June 1789 in Ruthin, possibly of tuberculosis, leaving a widow and two daughters. He was buried on 1 July at Efenechdid, where a monument, with a long Latin inscription by his father, was erected to his memory.

RICHARD CROWE

Sources G. J. Williams, *Iolo Morganwg* (1956), 135–50, 391–411 · NL Wales, MS 6515B, fols. 1, 39, 48, 49 · W. Rowlands, *Cambrian bibliography / Llyfryddiaeth y Cymry*, ed. D. S. Evans (1869), 528 · letter from

John Montgomery Traherne to the editors, 10 June 1851, *Archaeologia Cambrensis*, 2nd ser., 2 (1851), 238 · bishop's transcripts, Llandaff, Llandough-juxta-Cowbridge, 1760, NL Wales · bishop's transcripts, St David's, Llanelli, 1679–1820, NL Wales · bishop's transcripts, St Asaph, Wrexham, NL Wales

Archives NL Wales, family letters and papers | BL, letters to Owen Jones, Add. MSS 15024–15031 · Cardiff Central Library, letters to Edward Davies · NL Wales, MSS 4731C, 6514E, 6515B, 6516A, 6517E, 6563B, 15415–15416E, 21280–21286E, 22362B

Wealth at death under £100

Walters, John (1760–1789). *See under* Walters, John (*bap.* 1721, *d.* 1797).

Waltham, John (*d.* 1395), administrator and bishop of Salisbury, was born at Waltham near Grimsby, Lincolnshire, where his parents, John (an esquire) and Margaret, owned the principal manor. He was a younger son. Among many identifiable kin (for he was born into a tight clan) were two uncles, Richard *Ravenser (*d.* 1386) and John Ravenser, both prominent clerks in the royal chancery, while John *Thoresby (*d.* 1373), archbishop of York (1352–73), was a great-uncle. A favourite nephew and namesake was still alive in 1416.

Early career Waltham's career was predetermined by his family and he is said to have served in the royal chancery from boyhood, where his uncles were not his only kinsmen. He had his first preferment, by gift of the crown, in 1371 and was a clerk by 28 June 1375 when appointed to take custody of Welhowe Abbey near Grimsby, which was deep in debt. Likewise, on 28 November 1375 he was one of those appointed to amend the state of the important St Leonard's Hospital, York. He advanced to inclusion as a professional administrator in high-ranking embassies: to investigate breaches of the truce with Scotland (1 January 1378); to treat with France (22 October 1378); to receive money owed to the crown by the king of Scots (28 May 1380).

On 8 September 1381 Waltham was appointed keeper of the rolls of chancery, the senior position in the chancellor's department. As a corollary he acted as a receiver of petitions for England in every parliament between November 1381 and November 1386, and was frequently appointed as proctor there by many ecclesiastical corporations and absent prelates. He received attorneys in Ireland for principals staying in England on 24 June and 1 September 1382, and had custody of the great seal from 10 to 13 March 1383 after the discredited Bishop Reginald Braybrooke's abrupt resignation. He was included in several major commissions: to investigate Walsingham Priory (1 March 1384); to inspect, under John of Gaunt, duke of Lancaster, and a galaxy of great names, the Foss Dyke from the Trent to Lincoln (15 July 1384); to hear, with another battery of leading magnates, an unpleasant, long-running case in the court of chivalry between William Montagu, earl of Salisbury, and his brother John (12 February 1385). It is probable, of course, that his specialist contribution to all of these tasks was made among his rolls in Chancery Lane, rather than, for example, by conversing knowledgeably on site about the fauna of ditches or the finer points of drainage. Closer to home, on 28 March 1385

John Waltham (*d.* 1395), memorial brass

he was asked to act as deputy for the chancellor to inspect the king's hospital of St Giles beyond Holborn. He was given custody of the temporalities of the see of Bath and Wells before their restitution to the new bishop, Walter Skirlawe, on 3 November 1386; there is no evidence that he himself had been a candidate. He had, none the less, enjoyed a very profitable accretion of ecclesiastical preferment, as senior chancery clerks always did, and with his great-uncle helping too, culminating in his obtaining the powerful and lucrative archdeaconry of Richmond, in the York diocese, by exchange on 29 December 1384. He took a period of official leave from the chancery at once, no doubt to establish himself there.

Role in government Waltham's career had not been political, but his reputation as an impeccable senior member of what would today be termed the civil service now led him into dangerous waters. On 24 October 1386 he was promoted to be keeper of the privy seal. This was not in itself an unusual progression, but his predecessor, Bishop Skirlawe, resigned on the same day that the chancellor, the earl of Suffolk, was dismissed to face impeachment, and the treasurer, Bishop John Fordham of Durham, went out of office too. Whatever veneer was attempted, this was all done as a direct assault on the personal authority of the king, who even had to face a threat to his own position. Waltham's promotion was certainly intended by the king's opponents to indicate a serious and mature policy towards the government of the realm, and he was, of course, placed on the broad-based commission to 'advise' the king's reordering of his rule. Waltham may be credited with an important and contentious extension of the use of the writ, *sub poena*. His uncle, John Thoresby, had developed this while chancellor (1349–56) as issued under the great seal and returnable to answer suits in chancery; Waltham deployed it under the privy seal to bring cases before the council. The king took himself off to the midlands in 1387 to organize legal and military opposition to this restraint. Waltham remained in Westminster at his desk. On 14 November 1387 he was at Waltham Cross, north of London, to witness formally the appeal of the lords appellant against the king's adherents.

When the crisis came to a head in 1388, Alexander Neville, archbishop of York, a detested associate of the king, lost his see and a complicated sequence of translations followed. Waltham was papally provided to the bishopric of Salisbury on 3 April 1388, received his temporalities on 13 September, and was consecrated at Barnwell, Cambridgeshire, on 20 September (during the time of a parliament at Cambridge). He was enthroned at Salisbury on 8 December. On 4 May 1389 Waltham left office as keeper of the privy seal, as did the chancellor, Archbishop Thomas Arundel, and the treasurer, Bishop John Gilbert. Richard II had declared his resumption of personal authority the previous day and, as a matter of principle, could not work with the three chief officers imposed on him so unwelcomely thirty months before.

An important perspective on that defining crisis of 1386–8 comes from the relationship of Waltham and the king hereafter. The bishop naturally took to his diocese, but he attended a meeting of the king's council on 28 April 1390, and was then appointed as a supervisor of the recent parliamentary subsidy, and this duty, or perhaps a generally renewed involvement with the government, kept him in London over the following business year. On 2 May 1391 he was recalled to high office by Richard as treasurer, in succession, indeed, to Gilbert, whom the king had reappointed after the briefest of symbolic intervals and who even now remained on the council. Arundel was to return as chancellor on 27 September. This might indeed suggest that the king, now firmly in control, was willing to do anything to disarm, confuse, or divide his many recent critics. In Waltham's case, however, the king was to show a warmth that it is difficult to reduce to posturing. Obviously, Richard's use of a riot in London involving the bishop's servants as reason to estrange himself from the city and attack its privileges in 1392–3 was opportunistic. On the other hand, his intervention on the bishop's death to apprehend the body from its destined tomb in Salisbury and have it buried not simply in Westminster Abbey, but in Edward the Confessor's chapel itself, which the king was building up for his personal mausoleum, was a very personal sign, given to only a few royal servants. The bishop reciprocated their special relationship in his will.

Bishop of Salisbury Before then, Waltham had supervised the exchequer with excellent apolitical competence, which was entirely what the king wanted. Richard placed the utmost priority in these years on securing domestic respect alongside financial stability through a peaceful foreign policy, as the premise for why his opponents had been able to bring him low in the past, and the platform for wreaking violent justice on them in the future. As early as July 1389 Waltham had ordered his own diocesan clergy to lead their parishioners in twice-weekly processions in praise of recent peace agreements and in hopes of better weather, fewer earthquakes, better harvests, no more internal dissension, and the repentance of heretics and schismatics. It was a newsletter on English and world affairs that the king could have written himself. As even

Henry IV had to admit, Richard's choice of administrators, as opposed to intimates, in his last decade was flawless. Waltham in these years also headed the attorneys for Henry Bolingbroke when he went on crusade to eastern Europe in 1393, and—a diocesan gesture—was supervisor of the will of Sir John Golafre in January 1393.

Waltham returned each summer to his diocese and moved about it actively. He took up the bitter long-standing dispute with the cathedral chapter about episcopal authority over them, locally, nationally, and in Rome. In 1392, largely through Richard II's unqualified support, a hand-picked committee of arbitration came down entirely in the bishop's favour. Waltham used the victory generously to turn the chapter into allies, and it became the most distinguished in the land under his successors, Richard Medford and Robert Hallum. Like other bishops, he opposed the attempt by Archbishop William Courtenay to conduct a vigorous programme of archiepiscopal visitations, indeed to the point of appealing to Rome and obliging the king himself to warn both parties against violence between their men. He was by career a conservative in principle but a constructive pragmatist. He freely tolerated exchanges of benefices by his clergy, a practice against which Courtenay promoted the other great campaign of his rule as archbishop. Likewise, he fully supported the value of indulgences in support of good causes. He dealt firmly with the several early Lollards brought to his notice, but also responded supportively to those parishioners who brought suits against their clergy for failing to fulfil their liturgical roles. He was, indeed, notably severe in punishing priests who fell short in any way. His triennial visitations of his diocese in 1391 and 1394 were demanding, and brought the authority of a bishop home to the least parishioner. Predictably, he brought old northern friends with him as his household familiars.

Death and burial Waltham did not see death coming. It has been suggested, reasonably, that he was still not much over fifty. He had been travelling and working as hard as ever, and was in London in mid-August 1395. But he then made a long and detailed will at Sonning, Berkshire, an episcopal manor, on 2 September 1395, declaring the Blessed Virgin and both St Johns as his special patrons. There are many signs that, unlike most other senior churchmen, he had not prepared a draft. He requested burial in Salisbury Cathedral in 'a fitting and convenient place' which his executors should agree with the chapter; evidently he had not made the usual prearrangements, and likewise he had to leave it to his executors to decide his funeral rites. The cathedral was left a miscellany of vestments and artefacts, to pray for him and, interestingly, for Sir William Scrope, perhaps already Richard II's most detested adviser. The king was to have 1000 marks and some richly jewelled ornaments. Archbishops William Courtenay and Arundel were to have some valuable artefacts too. Indicative of the haste of it all, his executors were to use his manors for a major scheme of memorial to the king and himself which he sketched out only roughly. A torrent of bequests to his former benefices, to monasteries and friaries, to his servants, and to many other people and places followed, often backtracking and supplementing. Late on, 'If my father's bones can be found, they are to be taken to join my mother's bones, with a marble stone' (PRO, PROB 11/1/5). Why had he never done this before? There is enormous and anxious detail in the will, but no structure. William Scrope headed the executors. It is fascinating as a study of deathbed religion, but most uncharacteristic of the testator's own professional life. Perhaps it sheds more light on his private personality. In the event, Waltham lingered on at Sonning until 18 September. As has been said, he was buried at the king's behest in the chapel of St Edward the Confessor in Westminster Abbey, where a perpetual anniversary came to be observed. The monks' initial dismay was assuaged by Richard's magnificent gift of a vestment worth 1000 marks—but, as has also been said, the bishop had left him enough money to buy it.   R. G. DAVIES

Sources R. G. Davies, 'The episcopate in England and Wales, 1375–1443', PhD diss., University of Manchester, 1974, 3.ccciv–vi · A. H. Thompson, 'The registers of the archdeaconry of Richmond', *Yorkshire Archaeological Journal*, 25 (1918–20), 129–268, esp. 257–60 · *The register of John Waltham, bishop of Salisbury, 1388–1395*, ed. T. C. B. Timmins, CYS, 80 (1994) · will, PRO, PROB 11/1, sig. 5 · W. M. Ormrod, 'The origins of the *sub poena* writ', *Historical Research*, 61 (1988), 11–20 · S. K. Walker, 'Richard II's views on kingship', *Rulers and ruled in later medieval England: essays presented to Gerald Harriss*, ed. R. E. Archer and S. Walker (1995), 49–64 · B. Harvey, *Westminster Abbey and its estates in the middle ages* (1977), 372–80
Archives Salisbury diocesan RO, episcopal register
Likenesses memorial brass, Westminster Abbey, St Edward's chapel [*see illus.*]
Wealth at death wealthy: will, PRO, PROB 11/1, sig. 5

Waltham, Roger (*d.* 1332×41), administrator, first occurs in 1300 as a clerk in the household of Antony (I) Bek, bishop of Durham. Here, together with the future chancellor Robert Baldock, he received the training that would later fit him for royal service. By June 1303 he had obtained a canonry and prebend in the collegiate church of Darlington. He was rector of Long Newton by March 1304, when he obtained a papal dispensation to hold a further benefice worth 30 marks. Bishop Bek singled him out for his patronage in July 1306 when he authorized him to acquire benefices to the value of 200 marks. By 1309 Waltham was a canon of St Paul's, London. In the same year he was appointed chancellor to Bishop Bek. By 1314 he had amassed four prebends in collegiate churches in the diocese of Durham and exchanged Long Newton for the neighbouring parish of Eaglescliffe.

From 1 May 1322 to 19 October 1323 Waltham was keeper of the wardrobe. It is probably significant that his period in royal service began shortly after the royal victory at Boroughbridge and during the ascendancy of Robert Baldock. (Until 8 July 1323 Baldock was keeper of the privy seal and exercised the office of comptroller of the wardrobe by deputy.) He is probably to be identified with the Roger Waltham who was keeper of contrariant lands in Staffordshire from March 1322 to July 1323 and of Tutbury Castle in March 1323. His keepership of the wardrobe coincided with the unsuccessful Scottish campaign of 1322, and was followed by a period of stringency in the auditing of accounts. It is therefore not surprising that he had difficulty in presenting his accounts, for which he received an impatient royal summons in September 1324. His final account was not made until 22 May 1329. His account book survives as BL, Stowe MS 553; and BL, Add. MS 36763, is a roll of expenses of the royal household from July to 19 October 1323 which was presented on that day.

During his period of office Waltham was granted the archdeaconry of Buckingham on 28 June 1322, although the grant was revoked the following October, as the former holder was discovered still to be alive. On Baldock's recommendation he obtained the rectory of Hatfield in Yorkshire in April 1323; by the following August he was a prebendary of the collegiate church of Howden. In December 1323 he obtained a licence to endow a chantry in St Paul's, to which he subsequently granted property and rich vestments in return for prayers for the souls of his family and benefactors, including Antony Bek. He last occurs as a canon of St Paul's in 1332, and was dead by October 1341 at the latest, probably on 12 October, the date of his obit.

Waltham's principal significance lies in his *Compendium morale*. Together with works by Thomas Aquinas and Giles of Rome, the *Compendium* is cited in the opening chapter of John Fortescue's *The Governance of England*, written in the reign of Edward IV, as a source for Fortescue's distinction between a *dominium regale* and a *dominium politicum et regale*. The *Compendium* survives in a number of manuscripts: Bodl. Oxf., MSS Laud misc. 616, Fairfax 4, and Bodley 805; BL, Royal MSS 7 E.vii and 8 G.vi, and Cotton MS Vespasian B.xxi; and Cambridge, Gonville and Caius College, MS 294/688. Three of these contain an extensive index compiled by Thomas Graunt, an Oxford scholar who died in 1474, suggesting that it was widely used in the fifteenth century. The *Compendium* is a treatise on princely virtues rather than a work of political theory in its own right. It shows some concern about clerical immunity; one of the thirteen chapters discusses King John's conflict with the church in some detail. Above all, it is a quarry for quotations from biblical and classical sources, reflecting the author's own wide reading. Besides the *Compendium*, a list of pittances of St Paul's Cathedral drawn up by Waltham survives. John Leland attributes to him a work which has not survived, entitled *Imagines oratorum*.

M. C. BUCK

Sources BL, Add. MS 36763 · BL, Stowe MS 553 · BL, Cotton MS Vespasian B.xxi · BL, Royal MS 7 E.vii · BL, Royal MS 8 G.vi · Bodl. Oxf., MS Laud misc. 616 · Bodl. Oxf., MS Fairfax 4 · Bodl. Oxf., MS Bodley 805 · Gon. & Caius Cam., MS 294/688 · *Chancery records* · PRO, exchequer, memoranda roll of king's remembrancer, E.159/97, mm.30, 146d, 296–7; 101, m.78d; 107, m.94 · PRO, special collections, ancient correspondence, SC.1/63/160 · [R. E. Latham], ed., *Calendar of memoranda rolls (exchequer) …: Michaelmas 1326 – Michaelmas 1327*, PRO (1968), no. 293 · Emden, *Oxf.* · *Fasti Angl., 1300–1541*, [St Paul's, London] · *Fasti Angl., 1300–1541*, [York] · 'Registrum palatinum Dunelmense': the register of Richard de Kellawe, lord palatine and bishop of Durham, ed. T. D. Hardy, 4 vols., Rolls Series, 62 (1873–8) · C. M. Fraser, *A history of Antony Bek, bishop of Durham, 1283–1311* (1957) · J. Fortescue, *The governance of England*, ed. C. Plummer (1885), 109, 173–5 · *Ninth report*, 1, HMC, 8 (1883) · W. Dugdale, *The history of St Paul's Cathedral in London*, new edn, ed. H. Ellis (1818) ·

C. L. Kingsford, ed., *The Song of Lewes* (1890) • W. S. Simpson, ed., *Documents illustrating the history of St Paul's Cathedral*, CS, new ser., 26 (1880)
Archives BL, Add. MS 36763 • BL, Cotton MS Vespasian B.xxi • BL, Royal MSS 7 E.vii, 8 G.vi • BL, Stowe MS 553 • Bodl. Oxf., MS Bodley 805 • Bodl. Oxf., MS Fairfax 4 • Bodl. Oxf., MS Laud misc. 616 • Gon. & Caius Cam., MS 294/688

Waltheof, earl of Northumbria (*c*.1050–1076), magnate, was the second son of the Danish interloper *Siward, earl of Northumbria (*d.* 1055), and his first wife, Ælfflæd, daughter of Earl Ealdred, son of Earl *Uhtred. His mother was a member of the house of Bamburgh, which had ruled Northumbria until Cnut's reign.

Early life and promotion Waltheof may have been born about 1050, and it was later believed that Siward intended him to rule north of the Tees. The death in battle in 1054 of a much older brother, Osbearn, made Waltheof his father's heir, but too young to succeed as earl of Northumbria when Siward himself died in 1055. King Edward instead appointed an outsider, Tostig.

The next ten years are a blank in Waltheof's life. Given his parentage it is likely that he spent part of his childhood at court, and he may have received some of the estates in southern England which he was holding by 1066. Later traditions recorded only that he learned the psalms by heart, which was perhaps normal for a boy of his rank. The earliest opportunity which the king had to promote him came when he was perhaps fourteen or fifteen, after the Northumbrian revolt against Tostig in 1065. Waltheof again failed to gain preferment in the north, but his father had also been earl in the south-east midlands, and there is indirect evidence that Waltheof was made earl over the shires of Huntingdon and Northampton, and possibly others (though the title 'earl of Huntingdon' accorded him by many historians is an anachronism).

By 1066 Waltheof owned manors in eight counties, mostly in the east midlands (Huntingdonshire, Northamptonshire, Leicestershire, Rutland, and Lincolnshire), but also two big manors near London (Tottenham and Walthamstow) and the large soke of Hallamshire in the West Riding of Yorkshire. It was a modest estate, but many smaller landowners throughout the east midlands had already put themselves under his protection. His influence thus extended into Buckinghamshire and Bedfordshire and was most striking in Cambridgeshire, where, however, Waltheof had no manors of his own.

Anglo-Norman earl Waltheof's appointment as earl inaugurated an eventful public career. He submitted peacefully to William the Conqueror in 1066, and was among the young English aristocrats whom the new king kept at court in Normandy and England throughout 1067 and until Whitsun 1068 or later. Afterwards, however, he left court for rebellion in the north, and in the company of other Northumbrian leaders joined forces with an invading Danish fleet in 1069 to attack the king's castles in York. When William arrived in late 1069, Waltheof and his cousin *Gospatric, earl of Northumbria, retreated from York, and in early 1070 submitted to the king on the banks of the Tees. Both were pardoned, and Waltheof not only resumed authority in his southern earldom, but married the king's niece Judith.

The marriage was intended to cement Waltheof into the new ruling group around William. Judith was the daughter of the king's sister Adelaide and the second of her three husbands, Count Lambert of Lens, who died in 1054, at about the time Judith was born. She had probably been brought up partly in her mother's dower county of Aumale, partly at the Norman court. She and Waltheof had two daughters, Maud and Alice (also known as Judith). Long after their father's death, Maud married first Simon (I) de *Senlis, earl of Northampton and of Huntingdon, and then *David, later king of Scots; Alice's husband was Ralph de Tosny.

Waltheof continued to acquire lands in the south of England under William I, for instance manors which the rebel Thorkell of Harringworth forfeited probably in 1069. At their full extent they may have corresponded closely to the estate which Judith still owned in 1086: some 200 rural manors mainly scattered between Lincoln, Leicester, Northampton, Bedford, and Cambridge, with houses in several east midland towns. Even so, Waltheof was nothing like as rich as the dozen or so most powerful Norman barons in England.

Waltheof's dealings with the great Benedictine monasteries of the fens were double-edged. Ely, Thorney, and especially Crowland all remembered him as a brother, but he bargained or stole manors from both Thorney and Peterborough, while Crowland's tradition that when Abbot Wulfketel was rebuilding the abbey church Waltheof donated the vill of Barnack, which included quarries of fine building stone, appears to have been wishful thinking. Waltheof was more generous to churches outside his immediate area of influence, especially the new cathedral church of Lincoln, on which he bestowed the valuable Huntingdonshire manor of Leighton Bromswold some time about 1072. Another beneficiary was Bury St Edmunds.

Waltheof also apparently played an active part in the affairs of London, demonstrated by his involvement in the transfer of the Surrey manor of Tooting from its pre-conquest owners to Westminster Abbey. The family concerned was that of Swein and his nephew Æthelnoth, rich Londoners. Swein gave the manor to Waltheof; Waltheof mortgaged it to Æthelnoth; Æthelnoth donated it to the abbey when he became a monk, along with three houses in London and a small estate adjoining Waltheof's at Walthamstow.

The earl's power and standing were immeasurably enhanced in 1072, when William I expelled Gospatric from the earldom of Northumbria and gave it to Waltheof, probably by then in his early twenties. The earldom came with very large estates both north of the Tees and in Yorkshire, but was almost ungovernable in the aftermath of the king's brutality in 1069–70. Waltheof had many enemies in Northumbria, not least other members of the house of Bamburgh excluded from power, and he certainly involved himself in the darker side of the region's politics, notably in a bold move in 1074 against a Yorkshire family of four brothers, the sons of Karl, which had long been the enemy of his own. Over two generations the brothers' grandfather and father had killed Waltheof's maternal great-grandfather and grandfather. Waltheof now sent his retainers to ambush them, and succeeded in murdering the two oldest brothers. The raid has long been seen as the final act in a long feud, but even at the time it must have been difficult to distinguish notions of family honour from the violence of ordinary politics. It might equally be claimed that Waltheof was acting for King William in destroying enemies who had refused to come to terms.

Revolt and execution A year later, in 1075, Waltheof himself was broken over his part in the revolt of earls Ralph of East Anglia and Roger of Hereford. His motives, even his actions, were uncertain at the time and have been contentious ever since. Waltheof certainly did not rebel openly. It may have been simply (as one later version had it) that he knew about a conspiracy against the king and was slow in reporting it, or (following another account) that he went along with the plot when it was first put to him, only to have immediate reservations and throw himself on the king's mercy, using Archbishop Lanfranc as an intermediary. Whatever the truth of the matter, the king regarded him as deeply implicated. After a trial whose decision was repeatedly postponed, and almost a year under confinement, Waltheof was hurriedly executed by beheading on St Giles's Hill outside Winchester on 31 May 1076.

Why the king ordered Waltheof's death is unclear. The modern view has been that he was applying to an Englishman the English penalty for treason, but that ignores the lifetime imprisonment served on Earl Morcar a few years earlier. Perhaps the king drew the line at Waltheof's second rebellion, or had simply had enough of Englishmen whose obedience was not absolute and unquestioning. Waltheof's body was thrown in a ditch, but a fortnight later, at his widow's request, Abbot Wulfketel of Crowland retrieved it for more honourable burial in the chapter house of his monastery.

Waltheof's dramatic end made a deep and unexpected impact upon the popular imagination. The earl was said to have spent his months of captivity as a penitent in prayer and fasting, his innocence supported by Archbishop Lanfranc. He was executed almost in secret, and the few people present evidently believed that when the sword fell during Waltheof's recitation of the Lord's prayer, his severed head voiced the final 'but deliver us from evil, Amen'. His guilt must have been vigorously debated in the months before, with English and Normans taking opposite sides, and a widespread expectation that he would be spared. The event itself was a potent brew of treason and piety, involving an angry king, summary justice, and the frightening beheading—itself unprecedented since 1066—of one of the foremost living Englishmen.

The beginnings of the cult The febrile atmosphere in Winchester nourished the idea that Waltheof was a martyr, even a saint. Such views were cultivated especially at Crowland, which had a financial stake in his reputation.

After a disastrous fire Abbot Ingulf moved the body in 1092 from the ruined chapter house to a prominent place in the abbey church. On opening the coffin the corpse was found intact, the head rejoined to the trunk with only a fine crimson line showing where it had been cut off. The miracle was publicized by Crowland and began to draw pilgrims to the tomb.

Elsewhere a second centre of interest in Waltheof was apparently developing at a shrine in the nunnery of Romsey in Hampshire, not far from Winchester. Popular support there for the idea that Waltheof was a saint was stirred up by the mysterious presence in the village of a man claiming to be his son. The cult had the tacit approval of the nuns, but no consent from the bishop of Winchester. It may, for one thing, have had an unwelcome anti-Norman flavour, since in the 1090s Romsey still had close ties with the remnants of the English nobility. In 1102, having tried persuasion and failed, Archbishop Anselm of Canterbury threatened the nuns with an interdict, and sent an archdeacon to suppress the cult and drive away Waltheof's 'son'. No more was heard of it or him.

The field was thus clear for Crowland to shape its own sanitized version of the cult of St Waltheof. Healing miracles began around 1111, but they were confined to the abbey precinct and largely to pilgrims from the abbey's own manors, suggesting that interest was not widespread. The author of the Hyde chronicle, writing about 1130, knew something of the story of a man whom he termed Waltheof the Gentle, still working miracles at a tomb which the chronicler could not locate. Many of the cures which Crowland recorded took place at dawn, the time of Waltheof's execution, and three-quarters of them involved the restoration of sight. The Crowland cult may at first have had undercurrents similar to those at Romsey: a visiting Norman monk denigrated Waltheof as a traitor, and was immediately struck down with an illness that proved fatal. Probably by then, however, the cult was being depoliticized by abbots anxious to play down any element of hostility to Norman rule. One sign of Waltheof's rehabilitation among the Normans is that about 1105 it was possible for his daughter Maud to give his name to her second child, whose father was a Norman baron, Simon de Senlis, and indeed whose cousin was Henry I.

Elaborations and variations Crowland's documentation of the cult was taken a step further perhaps in 1119, when Abbot Geoffrey, once a monk at St Evroult in Normandy, invited its historian Orderic Vitalis to come and improve the written record of the abbey's traditions. Orderic spent five weeks at Crowland and wrote an account of Waltheof and the 1075 rebellion which he later elaborated in his ecclesiastical history and which became the basis at Crowland for a thirteenth-century life and passion of Waltheof. Orderic clearly tried to make sense of Crowland's traditions about Waltheof in the light of what he already knew about the early years of Norman rule in England. As a historian and a monk with deep-rooted English sympathies, he was much taken by Waltheof's story and the monks' devotion to his memory. In his hands the 1075 rebellion took on a moral dimension, as an illustration of how earthly glory fades, albeit one interwoven with some of Orderic's characteristic prejudices. There were legitimate objections (he thought) to William I's violent and arbitrary rule, but a stronger case for fidelity to a king. Orderic gave the former side of the argument to earls Roger and Ralph, and the latter to Waltheof, whom he presented as faultless except in taking a foolish oath not to reveal the conspiracy. He pointedly contrasted a brave and contrite Waltheof with his Norman enemies and faithless wife, who between them brought about his condemnation.

Other historians of the early twelfth century fashioned their own versions of the fall of Earl Waltheof. Henry of Huntingdon and John of Worcester added only snippets to the bare account which they found in the Anglo-Saxon Chronicle, but William of Malmesbury went to the trouble of consulting the prior of Crowland, and finally decided that he agreed with the English who thought Waltheof innocent. In both his and Orderic's accounts, however, it is difficult to separate eleventh-century fact from Crowland tradition, or indeed from their own personal views. Significantly, other near-contemporaries without direct access to the Crowland tradition were much less clear about Waltheof. The Hyde chronicler's treatment of the rebellion was vague and strewn with errors, while the Norman genealogist Robert de Torigni, often precise with details of families, was badly confused about Waltheof's. Clearly by the 1130s authentic independent information about Waltheof was difficult to come by. Nor did the Crowland tradition penetrate Northumbria. Durham historians of the early twelfth century took little interest in him.

Meanwhile quite different stories of Waltheof's deeds, in a wholly different genre, were circulating as skaldic poetry. A single verse about Waltheof's heroic exploits during the attack on York in 1069 was known at Crowland in the twelfth century, and three more surfaced in the thirteenth in the Icelander Snorri Sturluson's masterpiece, *Heimskringla*. Since, however, the tendency in skaldic verse was for the poet to praise famous men irrespective of the facts, they cannot necessarily be regarded as containing authentic details. In any case Snorri's account of Waltheof was utterly unhistorical, making him a brother of Earl Harold, and successively leader of the English army at Gate Fulford in 1066 and hero of an improbable episode on the evening of the battle of Hastings.

Historical significance Neither the warrior hero of the skaldic tradition nor the saint of Crowland's cult can be read as an accurate representation of the young earl who was active in politics during the decade 1065–75. From an early date Waltheof's life-story was made to carry the weight of different and widely divergent views on the course of late Anglo-Saxon history. A century later he passed into fiction proper when his name was selected by an educated East Anglian poet of about 1200 for the hero of the Anglo-Norman *Roman de Waldef*. Meanwhile the greatest importance of the real Waltheof, so often seen by historians as archetypally English, was perhaps that he

was the ancestor, through his daughters, of three notable 'Norman' families: the Senlis, the Tosnys, and the kings of Scots descended from David I.   C. P. LEWIS

Sources Ordericus Vitalis, *Eccl. hist.* · 'Vita et passio Waldevi comitis', *Vita quorundum Anglo-Saxonum: original lives of Anglo-Saxons and others who lived before the conquest*, ed. J. A. Giles, Caxton Society, 16 (1854), 1–30; repr. (1967) · Ingulf, 'Descriptio … abbatem monasterii Croyland', *Rerum Anglicarum scriptorum veterum*, ed. [W. Fulman], 1 (1684), 1–107 · A. Farley, ed., *Domesday Book*, 2 vols. (1783) · H. S. Offler, ed., *Durham episcopal charters, 1071–1152*, SurtS, 179 (1968) · Symeon of Durham, *Opera* · Snorri Sturluson and B. Aðalbjarnarson, *Heimskringla*, 3 vols. (Reykjavik, 1941–51) · *S. Anselmi Cantuariensis archiepiscopi opera omnia*, ed. F. S. Schmitt, 6 vols. (1938–61) · F. S. Scott, 'Earl Waltheof of Northumbria', *Archaeologia Aeliana*, 4th ser., 30 (1952), 149–215 · A. Williams, *The English and the Norman conquest* (1995) · GEC, *Peerage*, new edn, 6.637–47; 9.662–4 · F. E. Harmer, ed., *Anglo-Saxon writs* (1952), no. 92 and 311–13, 573 · *VCH Essex*, 6.89, 184 · C. R. Hart, *The early charters of eastern England* (1966), no. 160 · W. E. Kapelle, *The Norman conquest of the north: the region and its transformation, 1000–1135* (1979) · C. J. Morris, *Marriage and murder in eleventh-century Northumbria: a study of De obsessione Dunelmi*, Borthwick Papers, 82 (1992) · C. Watkins, 'The cult of Earl Waltheof at Crowland', *Hagiographica*, 3 (1996), 95–111 · A. J. Holden, ed., *Le roman de Waldef (cod. Bodmer 168)* (Geneva, 1984) · Henry, archdeacon of Huntingdon, *Historia Anglorum*, ed. D. E. Greenway, OMT (1996) · *Willelmi Malmesbiriensis monachi de gestis pontificum Anglorum libri quinque*, ed. N. E. S. A. Hamilton, Rolls Series, 52 (1870) · John of Worcester, *Chron.* · R. Howlett, ed., *Chronicles of the reigns of Stephen, Henry II, and Richard I*, 4, Rolls Series, 82 (1889) · E. Edwards, ed., *Liber monasterii de Hyda*, Rolls Series, 45 (1866) · ASC

Waltheof. *See* Waldef (c.1095–1159).

Waltheof, third earl of Lothian (d. 1182), magnate, was the eldest son of *Gospatric, second earl of Lothian (d. 1166), and his wife, Derder (Deirdre). His first appearance on the political scene took place within a year of the death of his grandfather *Gospatric, probably at the battle of the Standard in 1138. Richard of Hexham recorded that among the Scottish hostages given to King Stephen to ensure the loyalty and good behaviour of David I was 'the son of earl Gospatrick' (Anderson, *Scottish Annals*, 214). This is generally taken to be a reference to Waltheof, who must have been only a youth at this time.

Under the year 1166, the chronicle of Melrose tersely records the death of Earl Gospatric and the succession of his son. The sequence of events surrounding Waltheof's succession is complicated by the possibility that he witnessed a charter of 1165 as earl, so that he may have received the earldom before his father's death. This would accord well with evidence that Gospatric had retired as a monk to Durham late in life. Whatever the case may have been, Waltheof inherited both the earldom of Lothian in Scotland and the lordship of Beanley in Northumbria, making him a third generation cross-border landholder. Despite this, little is known of his activities in Northumbria, although some evidence survives for litigation over his English lands.

Waltheof's involvement in one of the crucial episodes of the reign of King William the Lion illustrates both his primarily Scottish allegiance and his prominent position among the Scottish nobility. In 1173 William, angered by his failure to receive the earldom of Northumbria from

Henry II of England, decided to make war on the English king. Jordan Fantosme describes how Waltheof and Duncan of Fife strove, unsuccessfully, to restrain the Scottish king from going to war. After William's ensuing capture at Alnwick in 1174, Waltheof acted as one of the hostages for the king under the terms of the treaty of Falaise of 1174. The hostages swore that if the king of Scots broke the agreement, they would side with the English king in order to force him to comply with the terms of the agreement. That Waltheof enjoyed a prominent place among the nobility of Scotland is attested not only by his role in the events of the 1170s, but also by his presence in the king's court when important disputes were settled, for instance that between Melrose Abbey and Richard de Moreville in 1180, and by his frequent attestations of King William's charters, suggesting that he was often in close attendance upon the king. This evidence makes it difficult to agree with those historians who argue that he preferred to remain aloof from political matters.

Unlike his father, Waltheof does not appear to have been a particularly active benefactor of the church. He did, however, confirm some of the grants made by his ancestors, as well as bestow several grants upon the abbeys of Kelso and Melrose. These included a gift of some neifs (serfs) to Kelso and a common pasture to Melrose. Waltheof married a woman named Alina, of whom nothing more is known except that she predeceased her husband, dying in 1179. Waltheof and Alina had two sons and one daughter: *Patrick, who succeeded Waltheof as earl; Constantine; and Alice or Helen. On his death, in 1182, Waltheof was called by the chronicle of Melrose 'earl of Dunbar', while the same source referred to Alina as 'countess of Dunbar' on her death (Anderson, *Early Sources*, 2.306, 301). These are the first occasions when the earldom was referred to as being of 'Dunbar' rather than 'Lothian', but in both his charters and on his seal Waltheof always referred to himself simply as 'Earl Waltheof'.

ANDREW MCDONALD

Sources A. O. Anderson, ed. and trans., *Early sources of Scottish history, AD 500 to 1286*, 2 vols. (1922); repr. with corrections (1990) • A. O. Anderson, ed., *Scottish annals from English chroniclers, AD 500 to 1286* (1908) • *Jordan Fantosme's chronicle*, ed. R. C. Johnston (1981) • G. W. S. Barrow, ed., *Regesta regum Scottorum*, 2 (1971) • [C. Innes], ed., *Liber sancte Marie de Melros*, 2 vols., Bannatyne Club, 56 (1837) • *Scots peerage* • *A history of Northumberland*, Northumberland County History Committee, 15 vols. (1893–1940), vol. 7 • W. P. Hedley, *Northumberland families*, 1, Society of Antiquaries of Newcastle upon Tyne, Record Series (1968)
Archives University of Guelph, Ontario, Sir A. H. Dunbar, 'Autotypes etc., collected by Sir Archibald Hamilton Dunbar'
Likenesses seal, Durham

Walton [*née* Deck], **Amy Catherine** [*known as* Mrs O. F. Walton] (**1849–1939**), children's writer, daughter of the Revd John Deck (1815–1882), vicar of St Stephen's, Hull, and Mary Ann Sanderson Gibson (1813–1903), hymn writer, was born on 7 August 1849 at 5 Belgrave Terrace, Hull. She has been confused in the British Library catalogue, the Bodleian catalogue, and elsewhere with Mrs Catherine Augusta Walton (*d.* 1906), wife of Oriel Farnell Walton (1846–1886), a barrister, and eldest daughter of Lord Cecil

James Gordon-Moore (1806–1878) and his wife, Emily Moore (*d.* 1902).

The Deck family's Anglican evangelical credentials were proved by the father's fiercely anti-Puseyite publications, the collaborative hymn writing of mother and daughter, and the middle names of Amy's younger brother, Henry Legh Richmond (*b.* 1853). Her best-known work, *Christie's Old Organ, or, 'Home Sweet Home'* (1874), was written to illustrate her mother's hymn 'There is a city bright', to which Amy had contributed the first verse. One of her first works for children, *My Mates and I* (1873), had been sold under her father's name to the Religious Tract Society for £24. The Religious Tract Society's payments were low (she received £15 for *Christie's Old Organ* with a bonus of more than £6), yet by 1919 she had received a further £492 from their profits on her early works. Another of her piously sentimental best-sellers for children, *Little Dot* (1873), had also been written before her marriage, on 16 February 1875, at St Stephen's, Hull, to the Revd Octavius Frank Walton (1844–1933), who had served as her father's curate for the previous three years. Her work had been published anonymously before her marriage; post-1875 works and reprints were printed under her married name.

Immediately after their marriage Octavius Walton took up the ecclesiastically contentious post of incumbent of Christ Church, Mount Zion, Jerusalem, but returned in 1876 to a chaplaincy established for English textile workers in the Scottish borders at Cally, Kirkcudbright. Here they stayed until 1883. Subsequent moves took Octavius Walton to the tradesmen's church of St Thomas, York (1883–93); St Jude's, Wolverhampton, Staffordshire (1893–1906), where Amy's widowed mother joined them; and Leigh, Tonbridge, Kent (1906–17). After a period of retirement in Shamley Green, near Guildford, Surrey, the couple returned to live at Great Barnetts, Leigh.

By the time Octavius became vicar of Leigh, Amy had immersed herself in parish work, such as the Sunday school, the mothers' union, and sewing classes for teenage girls, leaving little time for her writing: only two of her thirty titles appeared after this move. A photograph of this period shows a woman of kindly if slightly masculine appearance, her hair scraped back and presenting a strange contrast with the rather fussily feminine clothes she is wearing.

Although Walton's tales sometimes espoused topical philanthropic causes, such as the outcry against the moral and physical risks suffered by child actors in cheap theatres and travelling fairs, featured in *A Peep Behind the Scenes* (1877), or the campaign for safer seafaring conditions, alluded to in *Saved at Sea* (1879) and *Launch the Lifeboat* (1886), their chief purpose was always the evangelical work of conversion. The effect of their sentimental piety was unmarred by sectarian prejudice: the labours of devout parochial clergymen were rated no more highly than those of mission chapels or scripture readers, or the timely words of a Christian neighbour, in achieving the great work of salvation. Despite asserting that earthly pilgrimage is but a prelude to reward or punishment in the afterlife, her tales rarely refrained from offering shorter-term proof of the fates awaiting the redeemed and the unredeemed. Both structurally and morally her stories leaned heavily upon a fairy-tale inheritance that made them palatable to children, and their sanitized pictures of virtuous orphaned waifs, whose innate cleanliness and gentility was often confirmed by the satisfying revelation of a genetic entitlement to middle-class status, made them safe presents for children of every class. Tales that had initially appeared in cheap tract format were often republished as more sumptuous illustrated gift-books. She and her publishers were to approve a film version of *A Peep Behind the Scenes*, shown by the Studio of Portsmouth Road, Thames Ditton, Surrey, on 11 December 1918.

Walton also wrote simple retellings of biblical stories, such as *The King's Cup-Bearer: the Story of Nehemiah* (1891), and *Dr Forester* (1906), a romantic Christian mystery tale aimed at an adolescent readership. Walton died on 5 July 1939 at Dry Bank House, Dry Hill, Park Road, Tonbridge, Kent. The cause of death was heart failure following a fall in her home.   ELISABETH JAY

Sources M. N. Cutt, *Ministering angels: a study of nineteenth-century evangelical writing for children* (1979), 155–70 · D. M. Lewis, ed., *The Blackwell dictionary of evangelical biography, 1730–1860*, 2 vols. (1995) · b. cert. · m. cert. · d. cert. · Burke, *Peerage* [Catherine Augusta Walton] · J. Foster, *Men-at-the-bar: a biographical hand-list of the members of the various inns of court*, 2nd edn (1885) [Catherine Augusta Walton]
Likenesses photograph, repro. in *The Quiver* (1906), 676
Wealth at death £500 2s. 2d.: probate, 31 Aug 1939, *CGPLA Eng. & Wales*

Walton, Arthur (1897–1959), physiologist, was born in London on 16 March 1897, the second son of Edward Arthur *Walton (1860–1922), one of the Glasgow school of artists, and his wife, Helen, *née* Henderson (1859–1945), of Renfrewshire, widow of Thomas Law. His elder brother, John, became professor of botany at Glasgow (1930–62); an elder sister, Cecile *Walton, was a painter and illustrator; and another sister married Sir W. O. Hutchison, president of the Royal Scottish Academy. Walton was educated at Daniel Stewart College, Edinburgh, and at Edinburgh University, where he obtained a degree in agriculture in 1923. His training in biological research began under F. A. E. Crew in the newly established animal breeding research department, and his interest in the physiology of sperm led to his first scientific paper, 'The flocculation of sperm suspensions in relation to surface charge' (1924). This interest took him to Cambridge to study under F. H. A. Marshall and John Hammond and in 1927 he was awarded his PhD for his work on the preservation of mammalian spermatozoa. Walton remained in Cambridge for the rest of his life, on the staff of the school of agriculture and as a scientific member of staff of the Agricultural Research Council in its Animal Research Station. On 16 September 1939 he married Elsie Ann (b. 1907/8), daughter of William Henry Sheldon, representative for a textile manufacturer.

Walton's contribution to the field of reproductive physiology, especially the physiology of fertility, was sustained and fundamental. He demonstrated that the metabolic activity of ram and bull spermatozoa, particularly their respiration, is directly correlated with motility and that, under certain conditions, respiring spermatozoa produce hydrogen peroxide which, in turn, is responsible for a gradually inhibitory effect on respiration and decline in motility. He then developed an ingenious apparatus to maintain spermatozoa alive for long periods by allowing both continuous feeding and removal of toxic metabolites. This was crucial to the development of artificial insemination, which he first tested just before the Second World War by transporting ram semen to Poland, where it was used successfully to inseminate ewes. In 1941 Walton and J. Edwards proposed to the Agricultural Improvement Council the organization of a system for the artificial insemination of the British dairy herd. The proposal was opposed at the time, partly due to its commercial orientation, Walton being closely associated with the Cambridge Cattle Breeding Society (a farmers' co-operative which he had helped to organize to take advantage of the new technology). However, after suitable revisions it won acceptance, and the following year two national centres for artificial insemination were established in Reading and Cambridge.

By 1957 artificial insemination was widely practised and the Royal Agricultural Society of England celebrated the achievement by bestowing on Walton its medal for outstanding research in agriculture. Yet Walton was not concerned solely with the agricultural applications of his scientific results. Perhaps for quite personal reasons—he and his wife had adopted a son and a daughter—he was also very interested in human reproduction and fertility. He lectured widely on sex, and in 1944 he was involved in a small meeting on infertility which had been organized by the Family Planning Association. He later described this meeting as drawing together all those agricultural, medical, and biological researchers sharing 'a common interest in problems connected with reproductive physiology and the diagnosis, prevention, and cure of impaired infertility' (Parkes, 328). A second meeting was agreed for 1945, and they then became an annual affair. In 1951, after some disagreements over their nature and orientation, these meetings gave way to annual gatherings of a newly established Society for the Study of Fertility. Walton, who was centrally involved in these developments, was elected chairman of the society for 1956–9. Walton's contributions were recognized in Cambridge by the posthumous naming of a new chair in reproductive physiology after him. Walton died at Addenbrooke's Hospital, Cambridge, on 6 April 1959. He was survived by his wife.

JOSEPH EDWARDS, *rev.* PAOLO PALLADINO

Sources DNB · A. S. Parkes, *Off-beat biologist* (1985) · *The Times* (9 April 1959) · *CGPLA Eng. & Wales* (1959) · m. cert.
Likenesses E. A. Walton, oils (as a child), Scot. NPG · E. A. Walton, portrait, priv. coll.
Wealth at death £8757 2s. 9d.: probate, 1 July 1959, *CGPLA Eng. & Wales*

Walton, Brian (1600–1661), bishop of Chester and biblicist, was born in the district of Cleveland in the North

Brian Walton (1600–1661), by Pierre Lombart, 1657

Riding of Yorkshire, either at Hilton or the adjoining parish of Seamer or Seymour; he had at least one brother, William, who survived him. He matriculated sizar from Magdalene College, Cambridge, in 1616. Two years later, on 4 December 1618, aged eighteen, he migrated to Peterhouse, from where he graduated BA in 1620 and proceeded MA in 1623.

Early career Following his ordination that year Walton exercised a clerical and teaching ministry in Suffolk. Here he met his first wife, Anne Claxton (d. 1640), whose family name occurs at Chedeston and Livermere. Shortly after his marriage he went to London, where some time before 1 April 1625 he became assistant to Richard Stock, the puritan rector of All Hallows, Bread Street. It is not clear what Walton's position was in the months following Stock's death in April 1626. On 1 October 1628 he was presented by the dean and chapter of St Paul's to the rectory of St Martin Orgar, Cannon Street.

Walton was an active and controversial clerical figure during the 1630s, clashing with civic leaders as well as with his own parishioners, among whom puritanism was strong. He organized much of the campaign by London clergy to address the perceived problem of significant underpayment of tithes by many citizens, who could not then be prosecuted in the ecclesiastical courts. Following the failure of earlier efforts to achieve legislative redress, in 1634 Walton and others presented a petition on the subject to Charles I. By December referral to a committee for

arbitration had failed to resolve the issue and the king took it up himself. Walton delivered to him a lengthy work on the history of tithes and a valuation of all the livings in the capital that he had laboriously compiled, eventually published first as *An Abstract of a Treatise* [1641] and then in full as *A Treatise Concerning the Payment of Tythes and Obligations in London* in Samuel Brewster's *Collectanea ecclesiastica* (1752). Surviving manuscripts in Lambeth Palace Library written by, or annotated by, Walton demonstrate the lengths to which he went to compose this work. Since some of the documents he consulted were destroyed in the great fire of London it remains a valuable source for clerical perspectives and parish finances before the civil war, but immediate impact was limited. After an ineffectual order that meetings of arrangement should be held in each parish, towards the end of 1638 Charles gave leave to the clergy to sue individually in the ecclesiastical courts.

Meanwhile Walton, having gained notice, was presented by the king on 15 January 1636 to the two livings of St Giles-in-the-Fields and Sandon, Essex, the former of which he swiftly resigned. He is said to have served as a royal chaplain, although there is no independent evidence for this. In 1639 he proceeded DD. On 25 May 1640 his wife died and was buried at Sandon.

Conflict and sequestration Walton's enthusiastic support for the policies of Archbishop William Laud and staunch opposition to puritanism had led in the 1630s to a protracted feud with a number of his puritan parishioners at St Martin Orgar, played out in the court of high commission. In 1641 a section of his parishioners took advantage of favourable political conditions to present a petition to parliament seeking the deprivation of their minister. In the same year they published it as *The articles and charges prov'd in parliament against Dr Walton, minister of St Martin's Orgars in Cannon Street*. Walton was accused of being disruptive, appropriating to his own use church income intended for other purposes, maliciously seeking to excommunicate parishioners, and refusing to preach on Sunday afternoons or allow members of the parish to hire a preacher. In response he claimed that a malicious minority had instigated the petition, and most of these had been persuaded or pressured into signing up to the charges. He depicted his opponents as unrepresentative of the general opinion in the parish, of lowly position, and pursuing a hidden agenda, but whatever the motives of the parishioners many were of considerable standing and wealth: five had served on the vestry during the 1630s and two were among the wealthiest in the parish.

In January 1642 the House of Commons referred the petition to committee and the following December Walton was summoned as a delinquent. By 20 June 1643 he had been sequestrated from his benefices. At some point he went to the royalist headquarters at Oxford, where he was appointed to wait on the duke of York and where, in 1645, he was incorporated DD. Following the surrender of the city in June 1646, on 17 October he petitioned to compound on the Oxford articles for the 'remainder of his estate, his library and other goods to the value of £1,000 having been sold' (*DNB*). This was granted on 7 January 1647, and he was fined a tenth of his estate, some £35 10s., but by July he was in trouble for encouraging his former parishioners at Sandon not to pay tithes to the minister who had replaced him. On 27 September the committee for plundered ministers ordered that he be sent for in custody; according to John Walker he suffered at the hands of the soldiers at Sandon. Subsequently he moved to London, where he lodged with the ejected rector of St Giles Cripplegate, William *Fuller (1579/80–1659), who had also been in the royalist garrison at Oxford. Some time before 28 October 1657, when his son Bryan was baptized, Walton married Fuller's daughter Jane.

The London polyglot Bible In Oxford oriental studies had been flourishing at least since the time of Laud's ascendancy. Here Walton had taken the opportunity of enforced leisure to acquire some knowledge of the ancient biblical languages, and had developed the project of producing a polyglot Bible. Three such Bibles had been produced at Alcalá, Antwerp, and Paris between 1500 and 1650, all massive works compiled over some time by consortia of scholars at considerable expense. Walton acknowledged that the prohibitive cost of the Paris version, published a few years earlier, had resulted in very poor sales, but argued that the advanced state of oriental learning in England rendered an improved edition possible within the terms of his scheme.

On 11 July 1652 the council of state passed a resolution to inform Walton that they found the project worthy, but thought it more suitable for the consideration of parliament. He possessed no influence with the regime and it is possible that John Milton was responsible for the positive reception of a work already being spoken of with great expectation. The council lent Walton books which had come into its possession to facilitate his work, but neither it nor the protectorate government gave the editor any pecuniary support beyond allowing him to import paper duty free. However, on a work the size of the polyglot Bible, this represented a considerable financial saving. Walton thanked Oliver Cromwell in the preface of early editions, but after the Restoration a reprinted preface was substituted alluding to an endeavour on Cromwell's part to suppress the work unless it was dedicated to him and asserting, on the other hand, that the king, consulted in exile, had expressed himself willing to bear its costs were it not for his banishment.

Walton's project received the approbation of Archbishop James Ussher and the distinguished parliamentarian, jurist, and oriental scholar John Selden. The services of many eminent scholars at both universities were retained. Most of those who made their services available were royalists, though a few had conformed to the change of regime. Expertise, rather than political or religious allegiance, was the key criterion for involvement. *A Brief Description of an Edition of the Bible* (1653) and *Propositions Concerning the Printing of the Bible* (1653) contained a number of errors and the quality of printing was poor. Critics, including Arnold Boate, were quick to express their criticisms. Walton, however, promised that these defects

would be remedied. A committee of reputable persons was formed to receive the subscriptions that were solicited in the prospectus, with the promise of a complete copy of the work for every £10 subscribed. A strategic campaign to encourage subscribers was highly successful, bringing in, from abroad as well as at home, some £8000 in just a few months. Colleges of both universities made sacrifices to support the work. This enabled Walton to commission the founding of new types to significantly improve the print quality of the publication.

The printing of the work began in 1653, two presses being kept employed, and between 1654 and 1657 all six volumes appeared. Volumes 1–4 contained the Old Testament and Apocrypha, volume 5 the New Testament, and volume 6 various critical appendices. Nine languages are represented in the work, although no single book of the Bible appears in more than eight versions. The correcting committee consisted of David Stokes, Abraham Wheelocke, Herbert Thorndike, Edward Pococke, Thomas Greaves, John Vicars, and Thomas Smith; on the death of Wheelocke in 1653 Thomas Hyde was substituted for him. Much of the work was done by Edmund Castell, whose *Heptaglot Lexicon* afterwards formed a valuable supplement to the polyglot Bible. Castell had a fractious relationship with Walton and later complained that his services had been inadequately recognized. Many other scholars contributed, but Walton claimed responsibility for the whole, and provided it with prolegomena giving a critical history of the texts and some account of the languages that they represented. The prolegomena were reprinted in Germany in 1777, and England in 1828, testament to the lasting importance of Walton's scholarly expositions. Walton also published in 1655 a brief *Introductio in lectionem linguarum orientalium*, containing the alphabets and grammatical paradigms of all the languages printed in the polyglot Bible as well as of some others. Intended as an advertisement, it also provided those interested in studying the polyglot Bible with the necessary apparatus to develop the required linguistic skills. The work demonstrates the breadth of Walton's knowledge of ancient languages.

The polyglot Bible was regarded at the time of its appearance as a monument to the intellectual capacity of an English nation previously eclipsed by some of its European brethren. It was also a successful commercial speculation. Though not the first book printed by subscription in England it was one of the earliest and most ambitious. The work commanded a high price on the continent; in a letter to John Buxtorf the younger, at Basel, Walton puts the price at £50. In the latter half of the seventeenth century secondhand copies in England invariably fetched in excess of £10. The London polyglot Bible often constituted the single most expensive item in the libraries of scholars and gentlemen.

The polyglot Bible was put on the *Index librorum prohibitorum* at Rome, and in England was attacked by John Owen in *Of the Divine Original of Scripture*. He rejected a number of academic positions postulated by Walton in the prolegomena to the polyglot Bible, but his chief fear was that the publication would provide ammunition to those who wished to undermine the status of scripture. Walton responded immediately in a work called *The Considerator Considered* (1659), which never mentioned Owen by name, but dismissed his arguments out of hand and defended the validity and necessity of responsible biblical scholarship.

Later years In 1657 Walton was consulted by members of the grand committee of religion appointed to consider the desirability of a revision of the English Bible. In 1658 Walton contributed to a work by the Laudian propagandist Thomas Pierce, *Heauton timoroumenos, or, The Self-Revenger Exemplified*, which sought to claim that Archbishop James Ussher had abandoned Calvinism and embraced the Arminian creed shortly before his death. Walton testified to conversations he had held with the primate in which Ussher had espoused such beliefs. However, Ussher's former chaplain, Nicholas Bernard, and others rejected the claims, and since Ussher was ever willing to mediate between protestant factions, the likelihood that he abandoned a lifelong commitment to Calvinism is remote.

At the Restoration, Walton was reinstated in his benefices and made chaplain-in-ordinary to the king. On 14 August 1660 he received the prebend of Wenlakesbarn in St Paul's Cathedral. Later that year he was made bishop of Chester and was consecrated in Westminster Abbey on 2 December. In March 1661 he became a member of the Savoy conference. He also petitioned for and received other livings to hold *in commendam* with his bishopric. He visited his diocese in September 1661 and was well received, but after returning to London he died in his house in Aldersgate Street on 29 November. On 5 December he was buried at St Paul's, following a public funeral. In his will, dated 2 August 1658, he had declared his firm adherence to the liturgy of the Church of England, 'as itt was constituted before this Rebellion of the Puritanes'. He was, he declared, 'in Communion with the Catholique Church of Christ, both for doctrine, discipline, government and publique worshipp, rejecting as schismaticks, heretiques, and sacralegious persons marked in these latter ages under the vizerr of Protestants and Reformers'. Since presbyterians, Independents, and sectaries had 'broken the Communion of the Church, no fellowshipp in worshipp or discipline cann bee lawfully maintained with them' (PRO, PROB 11/306, sig. 207). The principal portion of his estate was divided between his son Bryan and wife, Jane, the former receiving £500, the latter £1000. He left a copy of the great Bible, in imperial paper, to Bryan to pass on through the family. Twenty clergymen who 'have suffered in these tymes for theire loyaltie and constancy in the Truth' (ibid.) were each to receive £5. In 1683 Walton's library was auctioned by the London bookseller Samuel Carr. The sale comprised 1840 lots. Latin books included bibles, patristic publications, and works on early church history. There were fifty-three manuscripts, including Hebrew, Arabic, Persian, and Syriac texts. English works included a large number of pamphlets from the civil war and Commonwealth times.

The London polyglot Bible represented the apogee of Renaissance biblical productions. The work was highly regarded in Europe in intellectual theological circles throughout the seventeenth and eighteenth centuries. Walton's pivotal role in its production was recognized and praised by his contemporaries, while his learned prolegomena to the work drew compliments into the nineteenth century. The *Dictionary of National Biography* regarded him as having only a tolerable knowledge of biblical and oriental languages. It would be more accurate to describe him as a considerable scholar wise enough to draw on the very considerable expertise of his contemporaries.

D. S. MARGOLIOUTH, *rev.* NICHOLAS KEENE

Sources DNB · H. J. Todd, *Memoirs of the life and writings of the Right Rev. Brian Walton, D. D.*, 2 vols. (1821) · Venn, *Alum. Cant.* · *Walker rev.* · G. J. Tooner, *Eastern wisedom and learning* (1996) · L. Twells, *The theological works of the learned Dr. Pocock*, 2 vols. (1740) · B. Hall, *The great polyglot Bibles* (1966) · *The works of John Owen*, ed. W. H. Goold (1968), vol. 16 · R. Simon, *Histoire critique du Vieux Testament* (Paris, 1678) · Emery, *Dissertations sur les prolegomenes de Walton* (1699) · *Hist. U. Oxf.* 4: *17th-cent. Oxf.* · Tai Liu, *Puritan London: a study of religion and society in the City parishes* (1986) · K. Lindley, *Popular politics and religion in civil war London* (1997) · D. Como and P. Lake, 'Puritans, Antinomians and Laudians in Caroline London: the strange case of Peter Shaw and its contexts', *Journal of Ecclesiastical History*, 50 (1999), 684–715 · will, PRO, PROB 11/306, sig. 207 · IGI [parish register of St Giles, Cripplegate] · G. Hennessy, *Novum repertorium ecclesiasticum parochiale Londinense, or, London diocesan clergy succession from the earliest time to the year 1898* (1898), 31 · *Bibliotheca Waltoniana* (1683) · J. Lawler, *Book auctions in England in the seventeenth century (1676–1700)* (1898), 144–5
Likenesses P. Lombart, line engraving, BM, NPG; repro. in B. Waltonus [B. Walton], ed., *Biblia sacra polyglotta*, 1 (1657) [*see illus.*] · oils, Peterhouse, Cambridge
Wealth at death over £1500: will, PRO, PROB 11/306, sig. 207

Walton, Cecile (1891–1956), painter and illustrator, was born on 29 March 1891 at 203 Bath Street, Glasgow, the eldest child of Edward Arthur *Walton (1860–1922) and his wife, Helen, *née* Henderson (1859–1945), who previously had been married to Thomas Law. The physiologist Arthur *Walton was a younger brother. E. A. Walton was a landscape and portrait painter and was one of the so-called Glasgow Boys; Helen Walton had trained as an artist in Paris prior to her first marriage. Cecile was a child prodigy; she was able to draw at an early age and the artistic environment in which she grew up was remarkable. Her father moved to London in the 1890s and it was in his studio that Cecile met James Guthrie, John Lavery, James Pryde, and, not least, Whistler, who asked her to make a drawing of him. It was during these formative years that Cecile found the work of Holman Hunt and the Pre-Raphaelites more to her taste than the work of her father and his friends; she was beginning to drift into a world of fairy tale, poetry, and romance. After the turn of the century E. A. Walton moved to Edinburgh where Cecile was encouraged to work in watercolours and where Jessie M. King taught her to draw with pen and ink. But the most significant influence in her development as an artist came through her introduction to the Scottish symbolist painter John Duncan (1866–1945), whose Thursday afternoon 'at home' attracted many young artists as well as a fascinating cross-section of intellectuals and academics including the botanist and sociologist Patrick Geddes. It was Duncan who taught Cecile how to etch and no doubt Duncan introduced her to another aspect of Edinburgh society that revolved around André Raffalovitch and Father John Gray.

When she was seventeen, Cecile Walton was sent to Paris to study at the atelier La Grande Chaumière, but she considered its teaching methods old-fashioned and later moved to La Palette where Jacques-Emile Blanche was a visiting professor. After a year in Paris she returned to Edinburgh where she attended a limited number of classes at the Edinburgh College of Art, and she was commissioned by T. C. and E. C. Jack to illustrate *Hans Andersen's Fairy Tales*, which was published in 1911. She also met the young Scottish artist Eric Harald Macbeth Robertson [*see below*], whose rather flamboyant lifestyle raised a few eyebrows in certain Edinburgh circles. The Waltons, alarmed by this turn of events, promptly sent Cecile to Florence to stay with an uncle with the hope that she might forget Robertson. Her enforced exile was fortuitous, as she recognized in the work of the early Italian painters the path she would take as an artist. The year she spent apart from Robertson did not dampen her desire to know him better, and on her return to Edinburgh her close friend Mary Newbery and Robertson became the subjects of her first major painting in oils (on loan to the Scottish National Portrait Gallery, Edinburgh).

Eric Harald Macbeth Robertson (1887–1941) was one of the most brilliant art students of his period and often scandalized Edinburgh society with his drawings of the female nude. But he was a fine landscape and portrait painter and was well aware of developments in English art, particularly vorticism which he tentatively adopted in a modified form, calling it expressionism. He was also influenced by Gustave Moreau, the Pre-Raphaelite painters, and their followers, and not least John Duncan. But Duncan saw a clearly defined element of decadence in Robertson's work and kept his distance from him, much to Robertson's dismay. During the years leading up to the First World War, Robertson carried out designs and decorative work for Professor Patrick Geddes, and at the same time he painted landscape, portraits, and Celtic myth and legend in a symbolist style.

Cecile Walton and Robertson were married in Edinburgh on 21 February 1914 and their first child, Gavril, was born the following year. In 1916 Robertson joined the Friends' Ambulance Unit and he spent the rest of the war in France. Cecile was engaged with a major work in oils, *The Walking Tour* (1916), and she painted in watercolours more than twenty illustrations to a number of Polish fairy tales in translations by Maude Ashurst Biggs. These were published as *Polish Fairy Tales* by the Bodley Head (1920). But during the years apart there were infidelities on both sides and their marriage was no longer as sound as it had once been, though their second child, Edward, was born in 1919. With the re-formation of the Edinburgh Group of artists, of which Cecile and Robertson were prominent members, Cecile produced her finest work. Major works in oils are *Grass of Parnassus* (1919), *And These Also* (1919), *The Back of Beyond* (1920), *Romance* (1920; Scottish National Portrait Gallery, Edinburgh), and *To Nobody Knows Where* (1921), which received the Royal Scottish Academy Guthrie award. But it is her painting *Romance* that will be looked upon as her masterpiece; it is a self-portrait shortly after the birth of her second child, the midwife in attendance while her first child stands at the foot of the bed. The artist sees herself as woman and mother in the form of two iconographic traditions, the nude and mother and child. In terms of its subject matter the painting is unique in

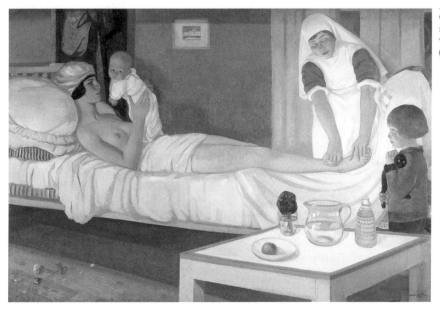

Cecile Walton (1891–1956), self-portrait, 1920 [*Romance*; with her children, Edward (right) and Gavril]

Scottish art and when it was first shown at the Edinburgh Group exhibition in 1920 it caused a furore.

On his return to Scotland, Robertson painted a number of war subjects, the most interesting of these being *Shellburst* (1919; City of Edinburgh Art Collection), painted in his expressionist style. Other works in the same style, though not war subjects, are *Despair* (1921; Glasgow Art Gallery and Museum) and *Cartwheels* (c.1920; on loan to the Scottish National Gallery of Modern Art, Edinburgh). In the early 1920s Robertson and Cecile Walton created a stir in Edinburgh with the paintings they exhibited with the Edinburgh Group at the New Gallery, and it was said that 'Half Edinburgh goes to Shandwick Place secretly desiring to be righteously shocked, and the other half goes feeling deliciously uncertain it may be disappointed not finding anything sufficiently shocking' (F. Quinton, *National Outlook*, November 1920, 102–3). Typical of the works exhibited is Robertson's *Loves Invading* (1919; City of Edinburgh Art Collection).

The achievements of Cecile Walton and Robertson lasted but a few years, as their individual lifestyles became untenable and in 1923 Robertson left Edinburgh for Liverpool. With the failure of their marriage they lost their way as artists, and for the remainder of the 1920s Cecile produced very little: some mural paintings, principally *Suffer the Little Children to Come unto Me* (Wolfsonian-FIU Museum, Florida), and a series of black and white illustrations to a collection of poems by Dorothy Una Ratcliffe, published as *Nightlights* by the Bodley Head (1929).

In Liverpool, Robertson shared a studio with the artist Sydney Merrills and tried to establish himself as a portrait painter. He married again in 1927: his second wife was a nurse, (Agnes Catherine) Wynne Walker. By the early 1930s his efforts to maintain a wife and daughter (b. 1932) failed through lack of commissions, and though he turned briefly to commercial art his career as an artist was finished. He died on the Wirral, Cheshire, in 1941.

Cecile Walton's career took a new turn towards the end of the 1920s, when Tyrone Guthrie was appointed to manage the Festival Theatre in Cambridge and engaged Cecile as décor artist for four seasons. Her work in the theatre led to her being invited by the BBC Scottish regional director, David Gleghorn Thompson, to apply for the position of organizer of the BBC Scottish *Children's Hour* in Edinburgh. She was interviewed by Lord Reith and, following a three-week period working with the *Children's Hour* team in London, she took over from Kathleen Garscadden who had been running both the Glasgow and Edinburgh *Children's Hour*. But on 27 November 1936 she married the BBC producer (Robert) Gordon Thomson Gildard (b. 1899/1900), who was about to be transferred to Glasgow, and this move required her to give up her position at the BBC.

With the commencement of the Second World War, Cecile Walton returned to Edinburgh (probably unaware that Robertson was dying of tuberculosis in a sanatorium near Liverpool) to work for the British Council in connection with Czechoslovakian refugees. In 1948, having divorced her second husband in 1945, she moved to Kirkcudbright and started to paint again; and though she did

not regain the earlier stature she had achieved during the years she was married to Robertson, she did produce some interesting paintings during a number of visits to Algeria. In 1949 she published *The Children's Theatre Book* (Adam and Charles Black, London) with illustrations by herself and her son Edward. A few years later she completed a number of illustrations for *Jingling Lane* (Lund Humphries, 1954), an idyll set in a Yorkshire dale.

Cecile Walton was admitted to Mortonhall House, an Edinburgh hospital, in 1956 where she died on 23 April of cancer. Her work is also represented in Perth Art Gallery and Museum, Aberdeen Art Gallery, and the Walker Art Gallery, Liverpool. JOHN KEMPLAY

Sources J. Kemplay, *The two companions* (1991) · C. Walton, *Atalanta in Caledonia* (1926) · b. cert. · m. cert. [1914] · m. cert. [1936] · d. cert.
Archives NL Scot., memoirs, Acc. 10425 | NL Scot., corresp. with Eric Robertson, deposit 285, Acc. 11858/1/2
Likenesses C. Walton, self-portrait, oils, 1920, Scot. NPG [*see illus.*] · E. H. M. Robertson, oils, 1922, Aberdeen Art Gallery · C. Walton, oils (Eric Harald Macbeth Robertson, with Mary Newbery); on loan to Scot. NPG

Walton, Christopher (1809–1877), collector of theosophical works, was born in June 1809 at Worsley, Lancashire, the son of John Walton (c.1781–1844) and his wife, Hannah (d. 1855). He was educated by the Revd Jonathan Crowther (1794–1856), and while at school joined the Methodist Society at Frodsham in March 1823. His father and grandfather were fervent supporters of Methodism. After serving an apprenticeship in a Manchester warehouse Walton spent some time on the continent. In July 1829, while in Paris, he advertised English lessons after the Hamiltonian system [*see* Hamilton, James (1769–1829)]. He came to London in 1830, and to the alarm of his father, because 'the Rent & Expenses in London are so terrible' (DWL, MS 189.6 (23) J. W., 12 Oct 1831), began business first as a silk-mercer and then as a goldsmith on Ludgate Hill, a business in which he remained until 1875. He made a fortune as a jeweller and goldsmith, enabling him to pursue his interest in theosophy. He became particularly interested in the mystical works of William Law.

Walton was introduced to the writings of Law by Wesley's *Extracts from the Rev. Mr Law's Later Works* (1768), and through Law he discovered the early seventeenth-century Silesian mystic Jakob Boehme. As a result he became an indefatigable collector of the works of Law and Boehme. Walton devoted 'time, means, and untiring energy to the collection, elucidation, and, as far as possible, the geometrical demonstration of the system' contained in Boehme's writings (*Christian Life*, 535), believing he had discovered the key to Boehme in the diagrams of Dionysius Andrew Freher. About 1845 he advertised for an assistant to help prepare a biography of Law, for which he acquired a great collection of antiquarian works in addition to his existing library. He began to print an *Outline of the Qualifications ... for the Biography of ... Law* in November 1847, finally completing it at Christmas 1853, but he circulated copies of the incomplete text before it was finished. To the completed work he added *To the Christianity, the philosophy, the erudition, science and noble intelligence of the age. Notes and materials for … biography of … Law. Comprising an elucidation of … the writings of … Böhme, and of his great commentator … Freher; with a notice of the mystical divinity … of all ages of the world* (1854). The 700-page work is disorderly beyond description, 'a chaotic mixture of the relevant and the irrelevant' (Hobhouse, 196), yet it contains much bibliographical and biographical information of value. He also printed *Introduction to Theosophy, or, The Science of the 'Mystery of Christ'* (1854), projected to be completed in 30 volumes, but only fragmentary pieces by Law gathered by Walton were issued in a second volume. Walton donated copies to every major public library in the world. Some other anonymous works relating to theosophy were probably written at Walton's suggestion and printed at his expense. He kept his 'Theosophian Library' at 8 Ludgate Hill, and made it freely available to those who shared his interests. In August 1876, at the suggestion of his friend Keningale Cook, Walton offered the books he had collected to Dr Williams's Library, stipulating that they should be kept apart as the 'Walton Theosophical Library', and always be available to those interested in the subject. His manuscripts relating to Law were included in the gift. Alexander Gordon was paid £20 to catalogue the books. The Walton collection now forms the best collection of books on seventeenth- and eighteenth-century mysticism in Britain.

Walton's interest in Law, Boehme, and Freher was religious, and, though he could criticize Wesley, his lifelong attachment to Methodism was the expression of a deep personal conviction. On his settlement in London in 1830 he joined the City Road Chapel. From 1839 he was one of the secretaries to the Strangers' Friend Society, and about 1843 he wrote its history. The new Methodist chapel built at Benfleet, Essex, in 1877 was a gift of Walton. He married twice. With his first wife, Anna Maria Pickford, whom he had married on 1 January 1841, he had two sons and three daughters; she died on 29 December 1863 after a lengthy illness. On 2 October 1876 he married Sarah Ann Tyler; they had one daughter.

Walton died on 11 October 1877 at 16 Cambridge Terrace, Southend-on-Sea, Essex, and was buried in Highgate cemetery on 15 October. His second wife survived him. Alexander Gordon, a personal acquaintance, described him as physically 'of large build and in character sententious but kindly, and absolutely destitute of humour' (*DNB*). From family correspondence it is clear that he quarrelled bitterly with some of the closest members of his family. A demanding husband and parent, he spent long periods estranged from his elder son, John, who in 1868 had him committed to Newgate for libel. They were eventually reconciled, but Walton's sister and his daughter Mary Elizabeth also began actions against him for libel. On the death of his son Christopher he adopted a boy (said to be his natural son), to whom he gave his own name.

DAVID L. WYKES

Sources *DNB* · 'In memoriam: the late Christopher Walton', *Watchman and Wesleyan Advertiser* (17 Oct 1877) · *Christian Life* (3 Nov

1877), 535 · G. J. Stevenson, *City Road Chapel, London, and its associations, historical, biographical and memorial* (1872) · DWL, Walton family letters and papers, MS 189.6 · Dr Williams's Trust, minute book, 1874–84, DWL, Dr Williams's Trust MSS · S. Hobhouse, *Forty years and an epilogue: an autobiography (1881–1951)* (1951) · IGI · m. cert., 1841 · m. cert., 1876 · d. cert.
Archives DWL, corresp. and MSS
Likenesses Marsh Bros., photograph, *c.*1870–1879, DWL
Wealth at death under £18,000: administration with will, 19 Feb 1878, CGPLA Eng. & Wales

Walton, Edward Arthur (1860–1922), painter, was born at Glanderston House, Neilston, Renfrewshire, on 15 April 1860, the sixth son and ninth child of Jackson Walton (*c.*1808–1873), variously merchant, commission agent, engineer, and amateur artist, and his second wife, Eliza Anne (1826–1902), daughter of Thomas Balfour Nicholson. Walton was brought up in Glasgow from 1862; nothing is known of his early education but in 1876–7 he studied at the Staatliche Kunstakademie, Düsseldorf. From 1877 to 1879 he also studied at Glasgow School of Art. In 1879 his brother Richard married Judith Crawhall of Morpeth and at the wedding Walton met her brother Joseph Crawhall and his friend James Guthrie. For the next ten years these three men spent much of their spare time in each other's company, at first taking summer holidays together painting (Crawhall and Guthrie being apprenticed to John Pettie until 1881) but from 1882 making longer and more sustained contact in Lincolnshire, Glasgow, Berwickshire, and Kirkcudbrightshire. Like Guthrie, Walton fell under the influence of Jules Bastien-Lepage, a French naturalist painter, and Walton also adopted his manner of *plein-air* painting with an emphasis on scenes from rural life. Together, Walton, Crawhall, and Guthrie formed the most important of the various coteries of artists who made up the *Glasgow Boys in the 1880s. His work, alongside that of Guthrie, George Henry, and John Lavery, defined this particular branch of naturalist painting and identified him with the Glasgow school of painting in its many international exhibitions between 1885 and 1914.

From 1880 Walton had a studio in Glasgow, first at 134 Bath Street. Walton and Guthrie began to exhibit at the Glasgow (later Royal Glasgow) Institute of the Fine Arts, where their reputation grew, and also, in Walton's case, at the Royal Scottish Society of Painters in Watercolour. Walton was a fine watercolourist, as were several of his siblings, and his earliest important works of this period, including *Winchelsea* (priv. coll.), *At Rosneath* (Glasgow Museums), *Grandfather's Garden* (priv. coll.), and *The Herd Boy* (priv. coll.), are often watercolours. Although all of these were painted in a naturalist manner, Walton was not committed just to painting working-class rural life; several of his best works of the period, again in watercolour, depict the daily lives of the ladies of middle-class society in Helensburgh, such as *Victoria Road, Helensburgh* (priv. coll.) and *En plein air* (priv. coll.).

Walton also painted in oils and produced a striking portrait of Joseph Crawhall (1884; NG Scot.) and several paintings at Cockburnspath, where he worked with Guthrie in the summers of 1883–5. *A Daydream* (1885; NG Scot.) is his masterpiece of this period, first shown at the Glasgow

Institute in 1887 and later that year at the New English Art Club, London, when Walton was elected a member. It stands alongside key works by Guthrie in defining the particular qualities of the success of the Glasgow Boys in the 1880s. In 1889 he was elected associate of the Royal Scottish Academy and a full academician in 1905. Walton also took part in an exhibition of Glasgow school painting at the Grosvenor Gallery, London, in 1890, which received much press attention, and which led to the Glasgow Boys being shown in the major cities of Europe and the eastern United States of America.

On 2 June 1890 Walton married Helen Law (1859–1945), widow of Thomas Law and daughter of James Henderson. Their eldest child was the painter and illustrator Cecile *Walton, and their second son was the physiologist Arthur *Walton. Also in 1890 Walton took a leading part in the initiative organized by the Glasgow Art Club to persuade Glasgow corporation to purchase James McNeill Whistler's portrait of Thomas Carlyle. Having secured Whistler's agreement to the sale, the Art Club then petitioned Glasgow corporation to acquire the painting for its civic collection. The corporation agreed and the painting was purchased, not without some typical bluster by Whistler, in April 1891, the first painting by Whistler to enter any public collection, predating the purchase of the portrait of Whistler's mother by the Musée du Luxembourg. Walton was instrumental in the negotiations with Whistler and the contacts he made were no doubt a factor in Walton's decision to leave Glasgow in 1893 and settle in London. Several of the leading members of the Glasgow Boys had already left, or were considering it, all of them spurred on by the opportunities for new portrait commissions in London, and by the waning market for paintings in Glasgow.

Walton moved first to 22 Cromwell Road, London, later commissioning a house from C. R. Ashbee at 73 Cheyne Walk. His immediate neighbours there were Whistler and Philip Wilson Steer. Walton's career was thriving and he continued to receive portrait commissions and to sell his paintings to collectors and museums in Europe and America. He was also at work on a large mural panel, *15th Century Glasgow Fair*, commissioned in 1889 by Glasgow corporation for the Banqueting Hall of the new City Chambers, which he delivered in 1901. Through his friendship with Whistler, Walton was instrumental in persuading him to accept the role of president of the newly formed International Society of Sculptors, Painters, and Gravers, founded in London in 1897. On Whistler's death in 1903, Walton was one of the pallbearers at his funeral.

In 1902 James Guthrie became president of the Royal Scottish Academy. After years of rivalry between Scottish painters of the east and west coasts a Glasgow artist had finally become president, but Guthrie felt exposed and insecure. He asked Walton to return to Scotland to give him practical and spiritual support and in July 1904 Walton moved to Edinburgh, settling at 7 Belford Park. Walton and Guthrie resumed their close friendship and Guthrie diverted to his old friend many of the portrait commissions that academy business prevented him from accepting. His list of sitters began to rival Guthrie's, including Andrew Carnegie (1911; University of St Andrews) and J. G. Bartholomew (NG Scot.). At the same time he resumed his painting of landscape, particularly of Galloway, and he held several exhibitions of these paintings, usually at Alexander Reid's gallery in Glasgow. These later paintings, although usually made *en plein air*, have little of the realist brushwork or palette of the paintings of the 1880s and show a move towards a more impressionist manner.

In 1922 Walton contracted influenza and, although seeming to make a good recovery, died suddenly of heart failure at his home in Edinburgh on 18 March 1922. Guthrie was a pallbearer at his funeral and two years later organized a memorial exhibition, shown in both Glasgow and Edinburgh.   ROGER BILLCLIFFE

Sources F. McSporran, *Edward Arthur Walton, 1860–1922* (1987) · R. Billcliffe, *The Glasgow Boys: the Glasgow school of painting, 1875–1895* (1985) · *E. A. Walton, 1860–1922* (1981) [exhibition catalogue, Bourne Fine Art, Edinburgh] · E. A. Taylor, 'E. A. Walton PRSW RSA: memorial exhibition', *The Studio*, 87 (1924), 10–16 · J. L. Caw, 'A Scottish painter', *The Studio*, 26 (1902), 161–70

Archives NL Scot., corresp. and papers

Likenesses E. A. Walton, self-portrait, 1921–2, FM Cam. · photographs

Wealth at death £2619 18s. 5d.: confirmation, 4 Aug 1922, *CCI*

Walton, Elijah (1832–1880), landscape painter, was born on 22 November 1832 in Birmingham, the son of Elijah Samuel Walton and his wife, Mary Ann Lees. Walton's father was a tailor and his mother a straw bonnet maker, and money was scarce. However, he showed an early talent for art, and, aided most probably by a local benefactress, he studied at the School of Art in Birmingham. In 1851 he exhibited his first picture, a study of fruit, at the Royal Academy, and in July 1855 he became a student at the Royal Academy Schools. Although he exhibited genre paintings at the academy until 1859, he became interested in mountain scenery through copying pictures. About 1856 he went to Australia, where his elder brother had settled at Geelong, and he exhibited six works at the Mechanics' Institute there in 1857.

On 13 July 1860 Walton married Mary, the daughter of John Neale; their honeymoon was spent in Switzerland and Egypt, where Mary died. Walton travelled and painted in the Middle East until returning to London in spring 1862. Later in 1862 William Mathews, of Edgbaston, the founder of the Alpine Club, offered Walton a commission to travel to the Tarentaise Alps, and for the next five years he journeyed and painted in the Alps or in Egypt. In 1864 he exhibited at the Royal Academy *The Pyramids* and in 1865 *Tombs of the Sultans Near Cairo—Sunset*, a huge oil painting now at the Fitzwilliam Museum, Cambridge. Walton also exhibited at the British Institution and the Suffolk Street Galleries. The Victoria and Albert Museum has a collection of his watercolours of the Middle East, and the British Museum has six watercolours of mountain views. In some of these alpine watercolours there is a sharpness of outline delineating mountain peaks combined with a brilliancy of colour which has great vitality and freshness.

On 20 June 1867 Walton married Fanny Heyes Phipson, the daughter of John Phipson, a manufacturer. Walton's sketching tours became less frequent, although he visited Norway (with T. G. Bonney) in 1869, and continued to travel to the Alps. In 1870 he visited Greece. Like many Victorian artists, he became passionately interested in the nature he painted and how it was formed. He became a fellow of the Geological Society in March 1867 and of the Royal Historical Society in November 1872. In 1874 Walton exhibited at the Burlington Gallery, Piccadilly, London. He wrote and illustrated three books: *The Camel: its Anatomy, Proportion and Paces* (1865), *Clouds: their Forms and Combinations* (1868), and *Peaks in Pen and Pencil for Students of Alpine Scenery* (1872). The thoroughness of Walton's observation of the camel could, perhaps, compare with George Stubbs's on the horse in the previous century; his line drawings of the camel are in the Victoria and Albert Museum and Birmingham Museum and Art Gallery. He also illustrated seven books by his friend T. G. Bonney, including *The Peaks and Valleys of the Alps* (1867), *The Coast of Norway* (1871), and *Welsh Scenery* (1875).

From 1856 to 1865 Walton lived at various addresses in London, and after his second marriage he lived at Staines and then Bromsgrove. He was said to have 'affected peculiar dress and ways, wearing his hair in little curls all over his head and a tunic of black velvet, with the sleeves slashed at the shoulders with some very bright colour' (Howard, 20). Fanny died on 7 December 1872 and Elijah Walton's health declined; he died at his home, Beacon Farm, Lickey, Bromsgrove, on 25 August 1880, leaving three sons. He was buried at Bromsgrove cemetery. Further collections of his watercolours are at Smith Art Gallery, Stirling, the Alpine Club, London, the Birmingham Museums and Art Gallery, and the Frenchay Museum, Bristol.   SARAH WIMBUSH

Sources *DNB* · private information (2004) [Pat Tansell] · T. G. Bonney, *Alpine Journal*, 10 (1880–82), 74 · A. L. Mumm, *The Alpine Club register, 1857–1863* (1923) · Wood, *Vic. painters*, 3rd edn · Graves, *RA exhibitors* · Walton file, Courtauld Inst., Witt Library · *The Times* (31 Aug 1880) · *Catalogue of the collection of drawings by Elijah Walton of the late Rev T. G. Bonney* [sale catalogue, Christies, 1924] · m. certs. · d. cert. · C. Howard, *Recollections of Victorian Frenchay* (1994)
Archives V&A NAL, drawings and notes
Likenesses E. Walton, self-portrait, ink drawing, 1864, V&A

Walton, Ernest Thomas Sinton (1903–1995), physicist, was born on 6 October 1903 at Dungarvon, co. Waterford, Ireland, the son of the Revd John Arthur Walton, Methodist minister, and his wife, Anna, *née* Sinton. His father's calling led to frequent moves within Ireland; he rose to be president of the Methodist church in Ireland. His mother was of Quaker stock. Walton himself remained a lifelong Methodist. He was educated at schools in Banbridge, co. Down, and Cookstown, co. Tyrone, before entering the Methodist college in Belfast. From there he won a scholarship in mathematics to Trinity College, Dublin, which he entered in 1922. He graduated with first-class honours, winning the Brooke prize and the gold medal for experimental science, and began research under Professor J. L. Synge, for which he was awarded the degree of MSc in

1927. The account of his first experimental investigation, which concerned the formation of vortices behind a moving cylinder and was published in the *Proceedings of the Royal Dublin Society*, showed the careful attention to detail and manipulative skill which earned him a research scholarship. The professor of geology, John Joly, who had worked with Sir Ernest Rutherford, Cavendish professor at Cambridge, gave him such support as to secure his acceptance as a research student in the Cavendish Laboratory.

Walton arrived in Cambridge with embryonic schemes for accelerating charged particles to high energies, in the hope of extending Rutherford's disintegration of light nuclei by naturally occurring alpha particles. Encouraged by Rutherford, he began with electrons in circular orbits, confined in an evacuated chamber by a magnetic field and accelerated by an induced electric field. The Cavendish tradition of simple experiments with cheap apparatus (partly by choice, but mainly in response to chronic penury) must take some blame for Walton's lack of success, since the basic ideas were good. He was aware of the need to control the electron motion, but lacked the knowledge to solve all the problems. More experienced, and more generously supported, D. W. Kerst in 1940 realized Walton's ambition when he built his betatron at the University of Illinois. Having abandoned this first venture, Walton turned to his next idea, but that too came to nothing. Instead of electrons, heavy positive ions were to be projected through a succession of metal tubes which were connected alternately to the two sides of an oscillatory circuit. The frequency was chosen to change the potential of each tube so that as the ion passed from one to the next it always received an accelerating impulse. This is essentially the mode of operation of a modern linear accelerator, but once again the technical means available were inadequate.

Working next to Walton in the Cavendish was John *Cockcroft, six years older although for various reasons not so far ahead in research experience; he was inspired in 1929 by George Gamow's quantum theory of alpha-particle emission from radioactive nuclei to see that a positively charged particle might tunnel into a nucleus even though it had insufficient energy to ride over the Coulomb barrier. He estimated that acceleration of a proton through a few hundred thousand volts would allow it a good chance of entering a light nucleus. The opportunity overcame Rutherford's reluctance to ask for money; he obtained £1000 for a high-voltage transformer and other electrical equipment, and encouraged Cockcroft and Walton to join forces in the new enterprise, which involved in the first stages scrounging glass tubing, vacuum pumps, and all the necessary bits and pieces. Walton's practical skill and Cockcroft's technical and entrepreneurial experience enjoyed full scope as they built a particle accelerator in conformity with the Cavendish ideal—looking as if thrown together, while giving satisfactory performance. It took two years, and in early March 1932 Walton bombarded a beryllium target with protons. Nothing of interest was observed, but on 14 April, working alone, he inserted a target of metallic lithium and switched on the proton beam; a myriad of flashes appeared on the scintillation screen beside the target. Next day Rutherford came to see for himself and was convinced of the truth of Walton's conjecture that a proton entering a lithium nucleus was splitting it into two alpha particles. This was the first nuclear transformation by artificially accelerated particles, the forerunner of advances by a host of ever more ambitious machines, as exemplified by the enormous accelerators at the Conseil Européen de Recherches Nucléaires and elsewhere. Cockcroft and Walton lost no time in writing a letter to *Nature*; it was published on 30 April 1932 and aroused worldwide excitement. Characteristically neither man was deflected by sudden fame from the now obvious extension of the programme to the disintegration of other elements by protons and the recently discovered deuterons (or diplons, as they called them). One item in the full account of their success, in the *Proceedings of the Royal Society* for 1 July 1932, revealed something both of their personalities and of the prevailing scientific ethos. Knowing the energy of the incident protons and of the alpha particles produced, and from mass spectrometry the masses of all the nuclei involved, they could report satisfactory agreement, in accordance with Einstein's $E=mc^2$, between the energy produced and the mass lost. They made no parade of their success and claimed no credit, as well they might have done, for the first direct verification of a fundamental law.

At the height of their triumph, after little more than two years and a handful of published papers, Walton and Cockcroft turned their backs on the life of research. Cockcroft became a distinguished scientific administrator and Walton, who would have been welcome in many a leading research group, preferred to return to Trinity College, Dublin, as a fellow. In 1947 he succeeded to Erasmus Smith's chair of natural and experimental philosophy, and held it until retirement in 1974. Having experienced life in the front line of science, he had no urgent desire to indulge in minor investigations, the only sort that Ireland could afford. Without resentment, indeed with enthusiasm, he turned to lecturing and demonstrating to Trinity students with a skill that they long remembered. As a citizen of Éire he was not called to war service, but he was pressed by James Chadwick to join in the Manhattan project, the allied project to develop the atomic bomb. The moral scruples of a deeply peaceable nature would probably have held him back, but the decision was taken over his head when the provost of Trinity decreed that he could not be spared. He never regretted it; a humble and high-principled man of great gifts, he enjoyed his years of fame and was content with what he had achieved.

In 1938 Cockcroft and Walton shared the Hughes medal of the Royal Society, and in 1951 the Nobel prize for physics. The accelerator used for the first artificial disintegration of a nucleus is now in the Science Museum, London. Walton was never elected a fellow of the Royal Society. He married in 1934 Winifred Isabel Wilson, who died in 1983; they had two sons and two daughters who all followed him into science, as also did several grandchildren. In 1994 he was visited by the president of the Republic of Ireland in the Belfast nursing home at 37 Deramore Park South to which he had retired, and where he died on 25 June 1995. He was buried in Dean's Grange cemetery, Dublin.   BRIAN PIPPARD

Sources E. T. S. Walton, 'Personal recollections', *Cambridge physics in the thirties*, ed. J. Hendry (1984), 49 • E. T. S. Walton, 'Recollections of nuclear physics', *Europhysics News*, 13/1 (1982) • R. H. Stuewer, ed., *Nuclear physics in retrospect* (1979) • *WWW*, 1991–5 • *The Times* (29 June 1995) • *The Independent* (29 June 1995) • private information (2004) [A. J. Walton]

Archives CAC Cam., corresp. and papers, incl. Cavendish Laboratory notebooks, WLTN • TCD, papers, MS 10657 | Sci. Mus., Cockcroft Walton accelerator

Likenesses photograph, 1951, repro. in *The Independent* • photograph, 1951, Hult. Arch. • T. Ryan, oils, TCD • photograph, repro. in *The Times*

Walton, Frederick Edward (*bap.* 1834, *d.* 1928), inventor of linoleum, was baptized on 19 May 1834 in Sowerby Bridge, near Halifax, Yorkshire, the second son and second child in the family of James *Walton (1802/3–1883), engineer, and his wife, Ann Kenworthy. He was educated in Bradford and Wakefield, and spent some time in France and Belgium before entering into partnership with his father and elder brother in Haughton Dale, near Manchester, manufacturing India rubber wire cards for carding cotton. On 19 March 1867 he married Alice Ann (*d. c.*1886), daughter of Thomas Scruby, veterinary surgeon; they had one son and three daughters.

For five years Walton was involved in many experiments, and it was while trying to make a quick-drying paint for use in oilcloth manufacture that he discovered oxidized linseed oil, a new elastic mass with a rubbery consistency, when he realized that an open tin of paint had developed a skin similar to rubber. He patented a process for exposing linseed oil to air, enabling it to absorb oxygen and solidify, in 1860.

In 1860 Walton sold his partnership to his father, moved to London, and established his own works in Chiswick, where he continued his experiments. Many people had been trying to produce a durable floorcloth, and patents had been taken out for floor coverings containing India rubber, including Kamptulicon, patented in 1844, a thick floor covering made of rubber and cork. Walton worked on substituting oxidized oil for the rubber, and in 1863 he made the first piece of what he called linoleum (from the Latin *linum*, linen thread, and *oleum*, oil), from a mixture of oxidized linseed oil, gum, resin, and ground cork, rolled out on the back of a piece of hessian. This was patented in 1864. He moved to a larger factory in Staines, setting up a company which became the Linoleum Manufacturing Company. Although sales were slow at first, once he began advertising in London railway stations that linoleum was 'warm, soft, and durable', and opened a showroom at 67 Newgate Street, sales increased, and linoleum became a popular floor covering in the home, while its use gradually spread to offices and public buildings such as hospitals, because it was easy to clean and hard-wearing. In 1872 Walton went to New York to set up the American Linoleum Company on Staten Island, and he ran it for two years. His patents expired in 1877, but despite his attempt to retain the exclusive right to use the name linoleum, the High Court ruled in 1878 that linoleum was the name of a material, and not the name of the product of one company. This meant that leading floorcloth manufacturers such as Nairns of Kirkcaldy and Williamsons of Lancaster were able to use the name, and they contributed to the rapid growth of the British linoleum industry.

Walton retired from active management of the company in 1878, although he remained the largest shareholder. In 1877 he patented a method for embossing fabrics suitable for wall and ceiling decoration. Production of Lincrusta-Walton began in Sunbury-on-Thames in 1878, and he also set up companies in Paris and Hanover. Inlaid or mosaic linoleum, patented in 1888 and 1890, was Walton's other major invention. The Greenwich Inlaid Linoleum Company, formed in 1894, was very profitable until 1914, but was taken over by Nairns in 1922.

Walton was an inventor rather than a businessman. He took out eighty-eight British patents, the last in 1914, two-thirds of which concerned oxidized linseed oil. The others ranged from meat extracts and artificial ebonite to wheels for motor vehicles and aircraft components. His development of flexible metallic tubing proved important in oil extraction. About 1922 Walton moved to Nice, where he wrote *The Infancy and Development of Linoleum Floorcloth* (1925), and pursued his hobbies of watercolour painting and reading poetry. He was killed in a car accident in Nice on 16 May 1928, and buried there at La Caucada cemetery in August. Picasso became interested in working in linoleum and admired Walton's invention.

ANNE PIMLOTT BAKER

Sources R. Parsons, *From floor to ceiling* (1997) · W. Coleman, 'Frederick Walton', *Industrial and Engineering Chemistry*, 12 (1934), 119 · F. Walton, *The infancy and development of linoleum floorcloth* (1925) · P. J. Gooderson, *Lord Linoleum: Lord Ashton, Lancaster, and the rise of the British oilcloth and linoleum industry* (1996) · C. Edwards, 'Floorcloth and linoleum: aspects of the history of oil-coated materials for floors', *Textile History*, 27 (1996), 148–71 · L. Day and I. McNeil, eds., *Biographical dictionary of the history of technology* (1996), 736 · IGI · m. cert. · *The Times* (3 Aug 1928) · DNB
Likenesses photograph, repro. in Walton, *Infancy and development of linoleum floorcloth*, frontispiece · photograph, repro. in Coleman, 'Frederick Walton'
Wealth at death £60,262 2s. 8d.: resworn probate, 28 July 1928, CGPLA Eng. & Wales

Walton, Frederick Parker (1858–1948), jurist, was born in Nottingham on 28 November 1858, the only son of Isaac Walton of Buxton, banker's clerk, and his wife, Mary Ann Parker. He was educated at Lincoln College, Oxford, where he matriculated in October 1879 and gained a first class in classical moderations (1881) and a second class in *literae humaniores* (1883). From Oxford he went to Edinburgh where he took the LLB degree in 1886 with distinction, and in the same year was called to the Scottish bar. In 1892 he married Mary Victoria Hamilton, daughter of Duncan Taylor of Edinburgh, a minister of the established Church of Scotland. There were no children of the marriage. From 1894 to 1895 Walton lectured in Roman law at Glasgow University. He also acquired some practical experience as

legal secretary to the lord advocate, J. B. Balfour, in 1895. In 1897 he became dean of the law faculty of McGill University in Montreal, Quebec. His wife became a noted supporter of the movement aimed at providing playgrounds for children in Montreal. He resigned from McGill to become director of the Khedival School of Law at Cairo in 1915. He returned to England in 1923 and settled in Oxford where Lincoln College elected him an honorary fellow in 1933. He continued to study and to write, and acted for some years as secretary of the Law Club. He was an active proponent of the study of comparative law, versed in the legal systems of England and of Scotland, and of many other countries. The breadth of his learning was considerable and extended far beyond the confines of law. His *Historical Introduction to the Roman Law* (1903; 4th edn, 1920) contains a vast amount of information on the archaeological origins of Rome and the ethnographical background of its people. He insisted always on the vital importance of historical treatment of legal surveys. Law, shepherded into isolation from history, was to him meaningless, and he placed considerable emphasis on the importance of the continuity of Roman law.

Walton was also a profound canonist. He wrote two works on the Scottish laws of marriage, one academic and one for the general public. His longest work was his exhaustive treatise *The Egyptian Law of Obligations* (1920), a commentary on the Egyptian code and hence, in effect, also a commentary on the French code.

Walton followed this work with several articles on the law of torts, focusing on a comparative analysis of duties in common and civil law. His comparativist approach was exemplified in his concern with the civil-law doctrine of abuse of rights and its parallels (or lack thereof) in English law. He started to write a treatise on French law, but finding that his old friend Sir Maurice Amos was engaged on the same enterprise, arranged to collaborate with him, and the valuable *Introduction to French Law* (1935) was the result.

Walton was a KC of the Quebec bar, and an honorary LLD of the universities of Aberdeen (1906), McGill (1911), and Marburg. On the death of his wife in 1932 he left Oxford and went to live in Edinburgh, where he died on 21 March 1948.   H. G. HANBURY, *rev.* ERIC METCALFE

Sources private information (1959) · personal knowledge (1959) · Foster, *Alum. Oxon.* · H. J. Morgan, ed., *The Canadian men and women of the time*, 2nd edn (1912)
Wealth at death £61,261 10s. 10d.: confirmation, 2 June 1948, CCI

Walton, Sir George (1664/5–1739), naval officer, was born into a family from Little Burstead, Essex, although details of his parentage and early life are unknown. He was commissioned lieutenant on 22 February 1690 and assigned to the *Anne* (Captain John Tyrell). In May the ship was dismasted in the battle of Beachy Head. Unable to sail under a jury rig she was run ashore to the west of Rye, and burnt to the waterline to prevent her capture. Following Tyrell to his new command, Walton moved to the *Ossory*, in which he saw action at the battle of Barfleur. In 1693 he became first lieutenant of the *Devonshire* (Captain Henry Haughton), serving in the channel, and in 1696 he moved to the *Restoration* (Captain Thomas Fowlis) with the main fleet. On 19 January 1697 he was promoted captain and ordered to command the *Seaford* (24 guns). He was in command of her when the French captured and burnt the vessel off the Isles of Scilly. After returning to England he was assigned to the *Seahorse*, which he commanded for the following two years, seeing service in the North Sea and off the coast of Holland, before joining Vice-Admiral Matthew Aylmer in the Mediterranean in 1699. For ten months between 1701 and 1702 he commanded the *Carcass*; he went in her to the West Indies, with the squadron under Vice-Admiral John Benbow, by whom, in March 1702, he was appointed to the *Ruby* (48 guns), one of the squadron with Benbow in the actions with Admiral Jean-Baptiste Du Casse on 19–24 August 1702 off Cape Santa Marta on the coast of what was later Colombia. Of all those engaged Walton was the only captain whose conduct was above reproach; the *Ruby* closely supported the flag until disabled and ordered to make her way to Port Royal, Jamaica, with a prize. In June 1703 Walton was moved to the *Canterbury* by Vice-Admiral John Graydon with whom he returned to England in the following October. Continuing in the *Canterbury* for a total of six years and nine months, he was employed in the Mediterranean during 1705 and 1706. In 1707 he accompanied Sir Thomas Hardy in the voyage to Lisbon; at the subsequent court martial Walton gave evidence strongly in favour of Hardy, whose conduct was called in question. In September 1710 he took command of the *Montagu*, one of the fleet sent to attack Quebec under Sir Hovenden Walker; Walton captured two prizes during the passage. On his return in December 1712 he was ordered to act as commander-in-chief at Portsmouth.

Early in January 1718 he was appointed to the *Defiance*, and shortly afterwards he moved to the *Canterbury*; in her he went out to the Mediterranean with Sir George Byng (afterwards Viscount Torrington), and had a singular share in the action off Cape Passaro on 31 July 1718, having been sent in command of a detached five-ship squadron in pursuit of a division of the Spanish fleet. Walton took six ships and destroyed a further six in the Strait of Messina. His letter of 5 August informing Byng of his success was, according to *Gentleman's Magazine*, 'remarkable for naval Eloquence': 'Sir, we have taken and destroyed all the Spanish ships which were upon the coast: the number as per margin' (*GM*, 606). Walton's laconic style was the source of some humour. Thomas Corbett pronounced him fitter to achieve a 'gallant action' than to describe one, although in fact the extract from *Gentleman's Magazine* forms only the final section of Walton's letter.

In 1720 Walton was appointed to the guardship *Nassau* at Sheerness and on 15 January 1721 he was knighted for his exploits off the coast of Sicily in 1718. On 16 February 1723 he was promoted rear-admiral of the blue, and in 1726 he was second in command of the fleet in the Baltic under Sir Charles Wager, wearing his flag in the *Cumberland*. Recalled from that service, he was again under Wager off Cadiz and Gibraltar in late 1726. In April 1727 he returned

to the Baltic approaches with his flag in the *Captain*, second in command to Admiral Sir John Norris, and in the following year he was promoted vice-admiral of the white. In 1729 he was again with Wager in the channel and in the Mediterranean, flying his flag in the *Princess Amelia*. Commander-in-chief at Spithead in 1731, and vice-admiral of the red in January 1732, he was promoted admiral of the blue on 26 February 1734. In 1734–5 he was commander-in-chief at the Nore, with his flag in the *Revenge* and then the *Newark*. In 1736 Walton retired on a pension of £600 a year. He died, apparently unmarried, on 21 November 1739, aged seventy-four, and was buried at the parish church of St Mary the Virgin in Little Burstead, Essex, where his ancestors were also interred. Among the total of £9600 he left in specific legacies, Walton gave £3000 to his niece, Pooley Onslow, wife of Richard Onslow (who was his executor and to whom he also left the residue of his estate); £2000 to their son; £2000 to Charles Duran, the son of his natural daughter, Sarah, the wife of Jonas Duran, a Middlesex pewterer; and £500 to his god-daughter, Anne, the youngest daughter of Sir John Tyrell, bt.

J. K. LAUGHTON, *rev.* JOHN B. HATTENDORF

Sources J. Charnock, ed., *Biographia navalis*, 3 (1795), 177–82 · J. Campbell, *Lives of the admirals*, 4 vols. (1748) · commissions and warrants, PRO, ADM 6 · captain's letters, PRO, ADM 1 · J. B. Hattendorf, 'Benbow's last fight', *The naval miscellany*, ed. N. A. M. Rodger, 5, Navy RS, 125 (1984), 143–206 · list of captains, NMM, Sergison MSS, Ser/136 · *Pattee Byng's journal, 1718–1720*, ed. J. L. Cranmer-Byng, Navy RS, 88 (1950) · J. B. Hattendorf, 'Byng: Passaro, 1718', *Great battles of the Royal Navy*, ed. E. Grove (1994), 63–70 · PRO, PROB 11/699, fols. 208–9 · *GM*, 1st ser., 9 (1739), 606
Archives Hunt. L., letters to George Pocock · PRO, ADM MSS
Likenesses B. Dandridge, oils, *c*.1734–1739, NMM
Wealth at death £9600: will, PRO, PROB 11/699, fols. 208–9

Walton, George (1749/50–1804), revolutionary politician in America, was born in Cumberland county, Virginia, the fourth child of Robert Walton (*d.* 1749/50), farmer, and his wife, Mary Hughes (*d.* 1749/50). He was born between 5 September 1749 when his father made a will and 25 June 1750 when the will was proved. His mother died soon after his birth and George was reared by his uncle George Walton, a planter of Prince Edward county, Virginia. George's older brothers John and Robert moved to Augusta in the Georgia backcountry and George followed them in 1769. A quick learner, he began a successful law practice in Savannah after two years of study as a clerk.

The revolutionary movement offered new opportunities for advancement and Walton was an early defender of American rights. His name appeared on the announcement calling for a Georgia provincial congress in 1775, and when the congress met the delegates elected Walton secretary. He was named to the executive agency of the congress, the council of safety, and in December 1775 became its president. In January 1776 Georgia's second provincial congress elected Walton to the continental congress. Blockading British vessels delayed his departure, but after the warships sailed away with their prizes Walton joined Lyman Hall and Button Gwinnett in Philadelphia. He arrived on 1 July 1776, in time to affix his name to the Declaration of Independence.

In the face of a British threat congress adjourned to Baltimore, leaving its business to be conducted by a committee composed of Robert Morris, George Clymer, and George Walton. Walton concluded a treaty with the Iroquois on behalf of the United States, but congress disavowed the treaty when it returned to Philadelphia on 12 March 1777. Walton was instrumental in arranging the transfer of General Lachlan McIntosh out of Georgia after McIntosh killed Button Gwinnett in a duel. In October 1777 Walton returned to Georgia to serve as colonel of militia and to take part in an abortive invasion of British-controlled Florida in 1778. In September of that year he married fifteen-year-old Dorothy Camber (1762/3–1832). Walton was severely wounded in the unsuccessful defence of Savannah on 28 December 1778. As royal government returned to the Georgia low country Walton recuperated at Sunbury, a prisoner of war. Exchanged a year later, after the failure of the Franco-American effort to recapture Savannah, he was ordered by General Benjamin Lincoln to go to Augusta and organize a constitutional government. Elections were held; an assembly met on 23 November 1779 and elected Walton governor. Although the assembly did other business, its most noteworthy action was the dispatch of a letter to congress asking for the removal from the state of General Lachlan McIntosh, who had returned to Georgia in July. In January 1780 Walton was elected again to the continental congress, and although he failed to win re-election in 1781 he remained in Philadelphia with his family until the war was over. When he returned to Georgia in 1783 he faced bitter recriminations from McIntosh and his friends who claimed that the assembly's letter calling for McIntosh's removal had been a forgery. Walton admitted as much, but said it represented the sense of the assembly. The assembly vindicated McIntosh, and proceeded to elect Walton chief justice.

Walton moved to Augusta and devoted his efforts to building up that town, the capital of the state from 1785 until 1795. He served again as governor of the state in 1789, and under the new constitution held the office of superior court judge. He served on the commission that established Richmond Academy in 1783, the first public academy in Georgia, and attempted to have the new state university located on his land west of town called College Hill. Walton was plagued by debt during his last years. He died at Meadow Garden, his residence in Augusta, on 2 February 1804 and was buried the same day at Rosney, Richmond county, Georgia, the home of his nephew Robert Watkins. Dorothy Camber Walton died in 1832 at the home of her son George Walton junior in Pensacola, Florida. In 1848 Walton's body was reinterred beneath the Signers Monument in Augusta along with that of Lyman Hall.   EDWARD J. CASHIN

Sources E. C. Bridges, 'George Walton: a political biography', PhD diss., University of Chicago, 1981 • E. J. Cashin, 'George Walton and the forged letter', *Georgia Historical Quarterly*, 62 (1978), 133–45 • K. Coleman and C. S. Gurr, eds., *Dictionary of Georgia biography*, 2 vols. (Athens, GA, 1983) • J. F. Cook, *The governors of Georgia* (Huntsville, AL, 1979), 43–6 • A. D. Candler, *The revolutionary records of the state of Georgia*, 3 vols. (1908)
Archives Duke U., papers
Likenesses C. W. Peale, watercolour on ivory, *c*.1781, Yale U. Art Gallery
Wealth at death in debt: probate court records, Richmond county courthouse, Augusta, Georgia

Walton, George Henry (1867–1933), designer and architect, was born on 3 June 1867 at 58 Buccleuch Street, Glasgow, the youngest of the twelve children of Jackson Walton (*c*.1808–1873) and his second wife, Eliza Anne Nicholson (1826–1902), daughter of Thomas Balfour Nicholson and his wife, Hughina. His parents were both Scottish. Son of a wealthy cotton importer, Walton's father inherited a flourishing commission agency in 1838, which subsequently foundered. Later, he made a number of unsuccessful excursions into manufacturing while his fortune dwindled. At home he was a keen amateur painter and photographer. He died in 1873, when George was six, leaving the family with limited means. The family was close, however, and Walton's childhood was not unhappy.

Walton was educated at Sutherlands School, Hillhead, from 1874 to 1876 and at Partick Academy from about 1876 to 1881. At fourteen he was obliged to start work, and found employment at the British linen bank, Glasgow. At home he was surrounded by artists: his sisters Helen and Hannah taught painting and decorated china and glass, while Constance excelled in watercolours. His brother Edward Arthur *Walton (1860–1922) was a leading member of the painting group the Glasgow Boys, and a friend of the artist James McNeill Whistler; George often accompanied him on painting trips. Before 1888, when he abandoned finance to start his career as a decorator, he had attended classes at the Glasgow Atelier Fine Arts (1887–9) and the Glasgow School of Art. Walton launched his new company, George Walton & Co., ecclesiastical and house decorators, of 152 Wellington Street, Glasgow, on the strength of a commission from Catherine Cranston. His work at her 114 Argyle Street tea-room included stencil designs in a style influenced by William Morris. Over the next few years Walton's workshops took on glass staining, picture-frame making, cabinet-making, and metalwork. Commissions included the decoration of a church, several residential and shop interiors, and a large stained-glass window for the shipowner William Burrell. Walton married Kate Gall on 3 June 1891; their only daughter, Marguerite, was born the following year.

By the mid-1890s the reputation of Walton's company was spreading further afield. A large redecoration job was completed at Drumalis, Larne, Northern Ireland (1893), and the company's first Yorkshire job was carried out in Scarborough for the Rowntree family in 1896. An office was opened in York in 1898. Elm Bank, York, now a hotel, has the largest collection of surviving decorative work in the area. In Glasgow, Walton decorated and furnished 91–3 Buchanan Street (1896–7) for Miss Cranston. This and the

George Henry Walton (1867–1933), by James Craig Annan, c.1897

refurbishment of the 114 Argyle Street tea-room (1899), on which he had worked at the outset of his career, were shared with the young architect Charles Rennie Mackintosh. Walton's style of work was distinctive: his simplification of form and pattern parallels the work of the English designer C. F. A. Voysey—a lifelong friend—while the decorative details and colour schemes show the influence of Whistler and the Glasgow Boys. Elongation of uprights, extension of cornice mouldings, and the inclusion of beaten copper and leaded glass panels characterize his work, which was an early influence on the development of the Glasgow style—a Scottish response to the English arts and crafts movement.

In 1896 George Walton & Co. became a limited company. Continuing as managing director, Walton moved to London the following year. Through the Glaswegian photographer James Craig Annan he met J. B. B. Wellington and George Davison, members of the Linked Ring photographic society. Davison, working for the Eastman Photographic Company (later Kodak Ltd), commissioned Walton to design a series of shops, including sites in Brussels, Milan, Vienna, and Moscow, which contributed to a growing interest in his work on the continent. Walton had gained credibility as an architect and Wellington commissioned him to design a house in 1901: The Leys, Elstree, a very individual building in the arts and crafts tradition, was decorated and furnished throughout by Walton.

Living from 1901 at 44 Holland Street, Walton concentrated on his London-based practice. In 1903 he resigned the directorship of George Walton & Co., which closed in 1905. Davison became Walton's major client, commissioning a houseboat (1902–3), two completely furnished residences—the White House, Shiplake (1908), and Wern Fawr, Harlech (c.1908–11)—and the St David's Hotel, Harlech (1909–10). These buildings show the inspiration of Georgian architecture. Other notable projects of this period were St John's, Ryde, Isle of Wight, and the interiors of Alma House, Cheltenham. Walton was elected a licentiate member of the RIBA in 1911. During the First World War he worked with Harry Redfern and C. F. A. Voysey for the central control board (liquor traffic). His first wife having died, he met his second wife, Dorothy Anne Jeram (b. 1889/90), at the board; they were married on 20 August 1918 and a son, Edward, was born in 1920.

After the war, when building work was scarce, Walton was supported by commissions from old friends—Wellington, Davison, and James Morton, a Scottish textile manufacturer; he nevertheless suffered increasing financial difficulty. His later work included an addition to The Leys, the chapel of St George, Cap d'Antibes, stained glass, and textile designs. Walton was reserved in his manner but warm and loyal in his friendships. He died on 10 December 1933 at home at 70 Seabrook Road, Hythe, and was buried on 13 December at Marylebone cemetery, East Finchley. His second wife survived him. In 1933, when the *Architectural Review* was planning an exhibition on architects of Walton's generation, Nikolaus Pevsner and John Betjeman hailed Walton as a pioneer of the Modern Movement. Thomas Howarth's 1952 monograph on Mackintosh also drew attention to Walton and in 1993 Glasgow museums mounted a major exhibition of his work. His designs and other works are held by the George Walton archive, a private collection, the Glasgow museums and art galleries, and the RIBA drawings collection; photographs of his work for Kodak are to be found in the National Museum of Photography, Film, and Television, at Bradford.   KAREN MOON

Sources K. Moon, *George Walton: designer and architect* (1993) • priv. coll., George Walton archive • RIBA BAL, Walton MSS and drawings • RIBA BAL, Walton MSS and photographs • letters between George Walton and James Morton, V&A NAL • N. Pevsner, 'George Walton, his life and work', *RIBA Journal*, 46 (1938–9), 537–48 • private information (2004) • T. Howarth, *Charles Rennie Mackintosh and the modern movement* (1952) • *The Times* (1933)
Archives priv. coll. • RIBA • RIBA BAL | V&A NAL, Morton MSS
Likenesses J. C. Annan, photograph, 1892, priv. coll. • J. C. Annan, photograph, c.1897, Scot. NPG [*see illus.*] • W. D. Hutchison, oils, 1923, Scot. NPG

Walton, Henry (*bap.* 1746, *d.* 1813), painter and picture dealer, was baptized on 5 January 1746 at Dickleburgh, Norfolk. Walton was the second of three children of Samuel Walton (1710–1797), yeoman farmer, and his wife, Ann Newstead (1711–1797). His father was also a churchwarden and overseer of the poor. Walton's early education is unknown, although the contents of his library, sold after his wife's death, indicate that he was able to read Greek, Latin, and French. In 1765, aged nineteen, Walton moved to London, although not apparently with the intention of becoming an artist. Walton's earliest recorded portraits— of Mr and Mrs John Frere—date from 1768 (priv. coll.). In

1770 he began studying art at the Maiden Lane Academy, in Covent Garden, London. It was about this time that he became a pupil of Johan Zoffany, to whom he was probably introduced by his friend Ambrose Humphreys, who featured in one of Walton's early group portraits, *William Mason and John Mason with Mr Humphreys Playing Cricket at Harrow* (1772; priv. coll.). While with Zoffany, Walton copied his *Beggars on the Road to Stanmore* of 1769–70 (priv. coll.). In 1771 Walton was living at Great Chandos Street, Covent Garden, painting portraits in oil and miniatures, and often featuring close friends and family. At this time he took on an apprentice, the miniature painter Edward Miles (1752–1828), of Great Yarmouth. Miles, who made a number of copies after Walton, remained with him until 1794. In 1771 Walton was elected a fellow of the Society of Artists, where he exhibited two portraits. In 1772 he was elected a director of the society, showing four works at that year's exhibition. He exhibited there again in 1773 and 1776.

On 10 September 1771 Walton married Elizabeth Rust (1746–1828) of Wortham, Suffolk, the daughter of a wool draper, and herself a miniature painter. They did not have children. Shortly after the marriage Walton purchased Oak Tree Farm, in the village of Burgate, near Wortham, where he converted one of the cottages into a house and studio. There Walton apparently painted landscapes, although these remain unidentified. During the early to mid-1770s Walton seems to have worked principally as a portrait painter, among his most celebrated sitters being Edward Gibbon, whom he painted on no fewer than six occasions (including NPG). Other prominent sitters included the Revd William Gilpin, Horatio Walpole, first earl of Orford, and Lord Cornwallis. All these portraits were engraved during the artist's lifetime, the print after Lord Cornwallis reputedly hanging in virtually every household in Suffolk (Farrer, 146). At some time during 1773 to 1774 it has been supposed that Walton travelled to Paris, making the acquaintance of the French artist Jean-Baptiste Siméon Chardin. According to his friend Dawson Turner, Walton frequently went there 'with a view of studying or of buying pictures' (Turner, 22). In 1776 Walton exhibited his first genre subject, *A Girl Plucking a Turkey* (Tate collection), at the Society of Artists. This was followed by other genre subjects, notably *The Silver Age* (Yale U. CBA), *A Girl Buying a Ballad* (Tate collection), and *A Group of Figures with a Fruit Barrow* (priv. coll.), exhibited at the Royal Academy respectively in 1777, 1778, and 1779.

In November 1778 Walton was turned down for membership of the Royal Academy, allegedly because of his prior affiliation to the rival Society of Artists. Feeling snubbed, he showed only two more works there in 1779 after which he ceased to exhibit altogether. During the 1780s Walton devoted himself increasingly to his farm in Burgate. He also travelled to Yorkshire, where he painted portraits of important local families. Among his more significant portraits and conversation pieces of this later period are *William Crowfoot and the Burroughes Brothers Boating on the River Waveney* (c.1780; priv. coll.), *Sir Bellingham Graham, 5th Bt. and his Children* (c.1785; priv. coll.), and *Sir*

Robert Buxton and Lady Buxton with their Daughter Anne (1786; Norfolk Museum Services). Walton also painted the figures in several sporting pictures by Sawrey Gilpin and George Barratt. By the early 1790s he was established as a picture dealer and adviser to some major private collectors, notably Lord Lansdowne, Lord Fitzwilliam, and Sir Thomas Beauchamp-Proctor, to whom he sold a Poussin from the collection of Sir Joshua Reynolds. Walton's expertise was apparently such that 'there was scarcely a picture of note in this country, with the history of which he was unacquainted' (Turner, 22). Walton continued to paint local Norfolk and Suffolk families well into the early 1800s, among his last works being an unfinished portrait of John Trew (priv. coll.), an old servant of his friends the Frere family, painted in 1810. By now Walton was in poor health, having contracted a fever 'which caused a great alteration in his appearance' (Farington, *Diary*, 12.4362). One evening in May 1813, on returning from a party to his London lodgings in New Bond Street, Walton complained of feeling ill. He was found dead in bed the next morning, the immediate cause of death being described as hydrothorax and pleurisy. His obituary appeared in the *Gentleman's Magazine* on 13 May 1813. Walton was buried near his parents in the churchyard at Brome, Suffolk. His will, dated 29 March 1812, was proved on 4 September 1813 and on 6 December 1828, following his wife's death.

MARTIN POSTLE

Sources E. Bell, 'The life and work of Henry Walton', *Gainsborough's House Review* (1998–9), 39–104 · E. Farrer, *The Connoisseur*, 25 (1909), 139–47 · M. Rajnai, *Paintings by Henry Walton (1746–1813)* (1963) [exhibition catalogue, Castle Museum, Norwich] · *Henry Walton, 1746–1813* (1950) [exhibition catalogue, H. Blairman and Sons Ltd, London, 1950] · D. Turner, *Outline of lithography* (1840) · *GM*, 1st ser., 83/1 (1813), 591
Archives NRA, priv. coll., letters to Lord Lansdowne
Likenesses H. Walton, self-portrait, watercolour miniature (as young man), priv. coll.

Walton, Izaak (1593–1683), author and biographer, was born in September 1593 and baptized on 21 September at St Mary's Church, Stafford, the only surviving son of Gervase Walton (d. 1597) of Yoxall, Staffordshire, and his wife, Anne (c.1554–1623). His father was a tippler (he kept an inn but provided neither meals nor rooms) and had moved to Stafford in 1591 after at least fifteen years of marriage. Izaak's elder brother Ambrose was buried in the town on 3 March 1596; there may have been other siblings, but only Izaak and his sister Anne survived to adulthood. Their father died on 11 February 1597, and on 8 August 1598 their mother married Humphrey Burne, baker and inn-holder. She continued to live in Stafford until her death, and was buried at St Mary's on 23 May 1623. Burne was buried on 16 March 1639.

Early life Izaak Walton was educated at the Edward VI Grammar School, Stafford, then situated in St Bertelin's Church at the west end of St Mary's parish and likely to have been run by a single schoolmaster. This was all the formal education he received: once he became known as an author, friendly and unfriendly critics alike were inclined to note that he was rather literate than learned. It

Izaak Walton (1593–1683), by Jacob Huysmans, c.1672

is true that, as a non-university figure who spent much of his adult life with poets and divines, he was vulnerable to patronizing judgements. But while books he is known to have owned later in life are almost all written in English, they demonstrate breadth and some intellectual curiosity, as well as a bias towards sacramentalist devotional literature. Anthony Wood, for example, remarked of his biographies that they were 'well done, considering the education of the author' (Wood, *Ath. Oxon.*, 1.698), in a very similar spirit to the one in which Leslie Stephen, over two centuries later, was to call him a 'worthy tradesman' (Beeching, 60).

About 1608, his fifteenth year, Walton left school and followed his sister Anne's new husband, Thomas Grinsell, a well-to-do linen draper, to the parish of St Dunstan-in-the-West, London, and in 1611 became his apprentice. In London, some time between 1608 and 1613, he discovered poets and poetry. Curiosity, and perhaps the 'genius for friendship' (Keynes, 614) which served him so well throughout his life, helped Walton to find his way in his late teens into a literary circle which included Ben Jonson (he later wrote an uncharacteristically concise—not to say sharp—character sketch of Jonson, in 1680, in a letter to John Aubrey, intended for the latter's *Brief Lives*). His initial introduction may have been through Samuel Page, vicar of St Nicholas, Deptford, who contributed prefatory verses to Thomas Coryat's *Crudities* (1611), a volume which included work by such writers as Michael Drayton, John Donne, and Thomas Campion. In 1613 Page brought out his book *The Loves of Amos and Laura*: printed by Grinsell's neighbour Richard Hawkins, the volume is dedicated to the twenty-year-old 'Iz[aak] Wa[lton]'. On 12 November

1618 Walton, recommended by Grinsell, became a freeman of the Ironmongers' Company, the guild under which his own trade fell. He was a linen draper and sempster (that is, he sold cloth and made it up into garments, probably including hats), and by then he owned 'half a shop' in Chancery Lane. His rise to prominence in the guild was marked in November 1629, when he was made a 'batchelor in foins': the honour conferred was signified by an official fur-trimmed costume.

Friend of John Donne In spring 1624 John Donne became vicar of Walton's parish of St Dunstan-in-the-West. Walton was impressed by Donne, describing himself as his 'convert', and his friendship was returned. Through Donne, Walton met and grew friendly with a number of his circle, including Sir Henry Wotton and the poet Henry King, later bishop of Chichester. On 27 December 1626 Walton married Rachel, daughter of William Floud and his wife, Susannah Cranmer, niece of Archbishop Thomas Cranmer; Walton had the following verse inscribed on his marriage-chest:

> We once were two, we two made one
> We no more two, through life bee one.
> (*Selected Writings of Izaak Walton*, ed. J. Martin, 1997, 158)

Their first child, Izaak, was born on 19 December 1627; a second son, John, followed on 23 July 1629. John died some time that year, the first of the infant deaths which punctuated his parents' marriage: in 1631 Thomas, born on 21 January, died at six weeks on 6 March; and three-year-old Izaak was dead too by 28 March. Henry, born on 12 October 1632, lived only five days; a namesake born on 21 March 1634 lived only until 4 December 1634; and their last son, William, died in August 1637. A daughter, Anne (1640–1642), was born on 10 July 1640, but Rachel herself then died on 22 August.

By the end of March 1631 John Donne had also died. Walton's later account in his *Life of Donne* (1640) strongly implies that he was present for Donne's last sermon on 25 February 1631; if so, then Donne 'preach[ed] … mortality by a decayed body and dying face' (*Lives*, ed. Saintsbury, 75) to a father whose three children were dead or dying. Perhaps Walton was at Donne's deathbed, three days after the death of small Izaak, witnessing at first hand the extraordinary self-possession of Donne's last performance all the way to his final breath when he 'closed his own eyes; and then disposed his hands and body into such a posture as required not the least alteration by those that came to shroud him' (ibid., 82). Walton's presence is suggested, if rather tentatively, in Henry King's letter to Walton, printed with the revisions of the *Life of Donne* after 1670 and first published with the *Life of Hooker* of 1665. Walton's intimacy with Donne is definitely, though problematically, implied in his involvement with the posthumous sorting and publication of Donne's work. The issue was complicated by growing difficulties between Donne's son John and his initial literary executor, Henry King, over who had authority to publish Donne's texts; but in the publications of the 1630s the employment of Walton's friend John Marriot as publisher is a reasonably stable indication of Walton's closeness to the early projects. In

Poems, by JD (1633), one of the appended elegies, rough but attractive, is by Walton himself; in the 1635 edition further verses by Walton appear to accompany an engraving of Donne by William Marshall, and look towards the publication of the sermons. After 1637 the right of John Marriot and his son Richard to the copyrights of Donne's works was disputed by Donne the younger. Since Walton continued to use the Marriots as publishers for his own works it may be assumed that he on the whole distanced himself from the editorial claims of Donne's son, siding instead with King and the Marriots.

Walton was made junior warden of the yeomanry in 1637, and in 1638 was promoted to senior warden, an administrative post: he collected fines and advised members of coming meetings. That year also saw the publication of his complimentary verses before Lewis Roberts's *Merchants Mappe of Commerce*. In February 1640 Walton became verger at St Dunstan-in-the-West. The final year of the decade also saw the preparation and publication of Walton's first, and perhaps most considerable, biography: that of Donne. It initially appeared as a preface to Donne's *LXXX Sermons* (1640), though it was revised and expanded three times more in Walton's lifetime, in 1658, 1670, and 1675. Marriot was the printer; but some inconclusive evidence suggests that Walton may have tried to deal with both sides of the now hopelessly fractured editorial team: an ambiguous allusion in one of King's letters refers to Walton as the 'Messenger' who had 'lost both to me and your self' the collected manuscripts to Donne's son (*Lives*, ed. Saintsbury, 15). Walton's own version, given in his introduction, of his involvement in the production of the 1640 volume was that he had researched a life projected by Sir Henry Wotton, but that Wotton's death and the spectre of a volume 'publisht without the Authors Life' (Walton, *Life and Death of Dr Donne*, A3) had galvanized Walton, albeit unworthily, into authorship.

Whatever the accuracy of this modest account of its inception (Wotton's death, in December 1639, would have left little time for Walton to write his *Life of Donne* from scratch), the result was remarkable. As a layman, Walton had a real problem of authorial voice in constructing a preface to a clerical biography, where an exemplary intention would have gained firepower from clerical authorship. Whence came Walton's power to edify? Walton adopted a modest position, stressing the condescension involved in Donne's intimacy with him (a condescension implicit also to a lesser degree on the part of other clerical members of his coterie) and promising a life which was necessarily honest in lacking 'skill to deceive' (*Lives*, ed. Saintsbury, 21). The emphasis on author–subject intimacy not only formed a pattern for Walton's later biographies, but also influenced the modern stress on particularity and intimacy in the genre. Walton also made so extensive a use of Donne's own written work that it is hardly an exaggeration to describe the *Life* as a patchwork sewn almost entirely from Donne's words, artfully juxtaposed and paraphrased to highlight the side of Donne most apparent after his ordination in 1615. This selectivity reflected both the context of religious controversy in which the 1640 volume was conceived and Walton's sense of the clerical Donne's exemplary importance; the slant this gave to his portrait took insufficient account of his early career and was unfair to Donne's secular interests. Yet the Donne that Walton paints is both passionate and changeable, figured in the prominent use of St Augustine in its typology; the portrait is of a performer in pulpit and deathbed, given to mood swings which Walton's creative editing of his letters rather deepens than smoothes. The 'Character' with which Walton concludes the *Life* is perhaps his finest piece of writing; and made finer in its sensitive counterpoint with sources in Donne's own work.

Civil war, interregnum, and *The Compleat Angler* Walton's sympathy for the Laudian ecclesiastical programme was translated from 1642 into support for the king; he proved an unwavering royalist. He was one of several linen drapers, and several parishioners of St Dunstan-in-the-West, who signed the London petitions for peace of 14 and 22 December 1642. Since his last child, Anne, had died on 11 May 1642, his house in Chancery Lane was empty and he probably left in 1643, though he may not at this point have left London altogether. Wood thinks he spent the 1640s and 1650s travelling, staying with 'eminent Clergymen' (Wood, *Ath. Oxon.*, 1.264–5), but Walton's own attestation in his *Life of Sanderson* (1678) is that he was at least part of the time in London, and he says that he was there for Laud's execution in January 1645. Other evidence bears this out. Walton is likely to have written the preface for Francis Quarles's *Shepheards Oracles* (1646), signed by John Marriot on 9 November 1645 and issued by the Marriots from their shop in St Dunstan's churchyard. It was at St James's, Clerkenwell, that on 23 April 1647 Walton married, second, Anne (1610–1662), daughter of Thomas Ken (d. 1651), an attorney of Furnivall's Inn, London, and half-sister of Thomas *Ken (1637–1711), who lived with the couple after Thomas senior's death. Izaak and Anne had three children: Anne, born on 11 March 1648; Izaak, born on 10 February 1650, who died in infancy; and another **Izaak Walton** (1651–1719), later Church of England clergyman, born in Clerkenwell on 7 September 1651. At the beginning of 1651 Walton had left London briefly for the one adventure of his life—to fetch the garter jewel, the 'lesser George' lost at the battle of Worcester, and deliver it to Colonel Thomas Blagge, imprisoned in the City of London. The Waltons are likely to have lived in Clerkenwell until about 1655.

Walton's complimentary verses prefaced another Marriot publication, Edward Sparke's *Scintillula altaris*, in 1652, and, in spite of the handicap which his political sympathies might have been expected to impose upon his publications, his writing career was beginning, in his sixties, to take off. In 1651 the second of his biographies, *The Life of Sir Henry Wotton*, appeared, again as a preface, this time to *Reliquiae Wottonianae* (though the entry of the *Reliquiae* in the Stationers' register in 1648 suggests that it was written some years earlier). This is a genial memorial which stresses their shared love for Donne and for angling; more secular in its subject than any of Walton's other biographies, it nevertheless uses Wotton's ordination as deacon (on becoming provost of Eton College) as a conversion point not unlike Donne's ordination, and depicts an orderly life whose 'Circumference' was 'closed up' by a serene and exemplary death (*Lives*, ed. Saintsbury, 150–51). Four more editions of his *Life of Sir Henry Wotton* appeared in Walton's lifetime: in 1654, 1670, 1672, and 1675; as was Walton's invariable practice, it too was considerably expanded and revised in the process of reissue.

Walton's lives of Wotton and of Donne were rather differently refracted in his third and most enduring (though not, in his lifetime, his most esteemed) work: *The Compleat Angler* (1653). The fishing manual, which has gone through more than 400 editions since its publication in that difficult year, is suggestively but not sufficiently characterized by its epigraph from I Thessalonians: 'Study to be quiet.' Like the pastoral tradition of which it was a part, Walton's *Angler* reflected on a fractured world by celebrating (and recommending) an order characterized as both 'natural' and vulnerable. In a manner reminiscent of other poets of the Commonwealth, such as Robert Herrick in his *Hesperides* (1648) or Andrew Marvell in his 'Upon Appleton House' of the early 1650s, the disorder of the present times received muted comment in the work's scenes of harmony. Similarly, Donne's love of church music was to receive, in Walton's revised *Life of Donne* in 1658, the gloss (dated 1656) 'but now, O Lord, how is that place become desolate'; and Wotton's 'surplice', in 1651 a forbidden item, was in Walton's *Life of Wotton* offered as a potent sign of holy employments. The abolition in 1649 of regular Wednesday fast-days, on which one might eat exclusively fish and 'sallets', is deplored in the *Angler* as bad for the health both of soul and body (though they were replaced by frequent occasional fast-days). Walton used an abundance of sources, ancient and modern, for the 'facts' of fish and fishing, from Pliny and Gesner to Topsel and Bacon; and he quoted from George Herbert, Donne, and Michael Drayton, who all died in the early 1630s but might have been expected to support his political views, and from Herbert's imitator Christopher Harvey, still very much alive, who did.

The Compleat Angler was conceived as dialogue between men travelling on foot who each represented a different recreation. In the first edition there were two, Piscator (fisherman) and Viator (traveller); in the second and much expanded edition of 1655 the two had become three: Viator was now Venator (hunter), and Auceps (falconer) was added. By this means the art of fishing was introduced, defended, and expounded: its strong precedent in the fishermen apostles of the New Testament was established, the detail of baiting for, catching, and cooking different kinds of fish was catalogued, and the whole was accompanied by aphorisms which would show the reader what it might mean to live well. Walton's conservative message was not lost on one reader, Richard Franck, who in his own book *Northern Memoirs* (1694) attacked Walton for historical and technical inaccuracy. Franck fished for Scottish salmon, not Staffordshire trout, and had served

under Cromwell, so it is hardly surprising that in their only meeting Walton 'huffed away' (Franck, 1821, 10.175). Walton revised the *Compleat Angler* four times in his lifetime: in 1655, 1661 (with a second issue in 1664), 1668, and 1676. Its last edition was so much expanded from the first as to constitute almost a different text.

Alongside his larger projects, Walton also wrote smaller pieces. From this period comes his manuscript commemorative couplet for the puritan conformist preacher Richard Sibbes, written in the 1650 edition of the latter's *Returning Backslider*, and his preface for *Heroe of Lorenzo* (1652), Sir John Skeffington's translation of Baltasar Gracian y Morales's exemplary study of aristocratic (and monarchical) virtue. As well as this, Walton's *Life of Donne* (1658) was published alone (perhaps only because he no longer had access to the copyrights of the sermons) and was revised accordingly. At the same time he began to take notes for a projected life of Richard Hooker at the back of his copy of Eusebius.

Restoration and *Life of Hooker* Walton celebrated the Restoration (and his own return to London) with a celebratory eclogue, 'Daman and Dorus', a conventional pastoral dialogue in praise of Charles II, printed in Alexander Brome's *Songs and Other Poems* (1661). In the same year he provided verses for Christopher Harvey's *The Synagogue* and joined, belatedly, the flurry of elegists for the conservative William Cartwright (*d.* 1643). Much later, in 1676, he wrote dedicatory verses for Cartwright's nephew Jeremiah Rich, promoter of Cartwright's shorthand system.

Walton received a Restoration reward of his own, indirectly, through the translation of his friend George Morley, then bishop of Worcester, to the see of Winchester in 1661. Walton seems to have had some connection (how much is not clear) with several former members of the Great Tew circle, and most intimately with Morley, who made Walton his steward. Walton accordingly moved with Morley; his wife, Anne, died in Winchester in April 1662, and was touchingly commemorated by her husband (*Selected Writings of Izaak Walton*, ed. J. Martin, 1997, 163–4); and in 1665 their daughter, Anne, married one of the cathedral prebendaries, William Hawkins, also rector of Droxford in Hampshire. The same year Thomas Ken moved to Winchester as Morley's chaplain. Morley, together with the then bishop of London, Gilbert Sheldon, was also the instigator of Walton's next project. This was his *Life of Mr. R. Hooker*, which appeared first alone in 1665, and then in 1666 as a biographical preface to Hooker's *Works*. Morley and Sheldon more or less commissioned Walton, as a known loyalist, to provide a suitably conservative biographical gloss on Hooker's work which would undo the damage (as they saw it) done by the Restoration edition of Hooker prefaced by the moderate bishop of Exeter, John Gauden. Gauden had edited a copy of Hooker's *Works* in 1661/2 which issued all eight books of the latter's *Lawes of Ecclesiastical Politie*: that is to say, it added books 6 and 8 (first published in 1648 by James Ussher) and book 7, which had never yet been published. These last three were unrevised and contentious texts, and book 8 put the cat firmly among the pigeons by discussing the rights of the monarch in terms which were by no means exclusively predicated on divine right. To make things worse, Gauden's prolix biography (which also, incidentally, made Hooker sound extraordinarily dreary) had made his own moderate views rather too plain. Walton's brief was to discredit Gauden's version and the provenance of the disputed Hookerian books; he was offered the lease of a house in Paternoster Row at the same time.

Walton had an indirect connection with Hooker through his first wife. George Cranmer, Rachel Walton's maternal uncle, had been Hooker's friend, and her maternal aunt Dorothy Cranmer married Hooker's executor, John Spenser, president of Corpus Christi College, Oxford. Walton took on the task (and the lease) as offered, and wrote a biography which characterized Hooker as a figure like John the Baptist who prophesied the 'unity' of the Restoration from his vantage point in the 1590s. Walton chose not to 'engage' himself in the episcopal squabbles directly and put all his evidence about the 'doubtfull Books' into appendices signed by senior clergymen (*Lives*, ed. Saintsbury, 236). The backdrop against which this was drawn was a highly biased parallel picture of the squabbles of the 1580s and 1590s, seen through a filter defined by the civil wars, and characterized by the debates on conformity between Archbishop John Whitgift and Thomas Cartwright. Notwithstanding, in writing on Hooker, whom he had never known, Walton reached for authoritative narration by making extensive use of his family connection with the Cranmers, which forced him to treat the oral information he received from them somewhat trustingly. In the circumstances this was a pity, not least for the memory of Mistress Hooker; the estate was in litigation, and the information Walton received, and famously recorded, on Joan Hooker's shrewishness was given by witnesses who had every reason for prejudice. However, it formed an essential part of another pastoral scene, where Hooker read Horace's *Odes* while he minded the sheep in his benefice or was forced to 'rock the Cradle' of his firstborn. This, and the picture Walton drew of Hooker's obscure and peaceable round of pastoral duty while writing the *Lawes of Ecclesiastical Politie* in his last parish of Bishopsborne, drew for the first time the 'heat-pimpled' face of the Church of England rural parson in what was to become a highly recognizable clerical mixture of personal asceticism, distrust for emotional extremes, a love of hierarchical order, and passionless masculinity. In this book one critic claims Walton 'invented Anglicanism' (Lake, 229–30); certainly it did more than any of Hooker's own works to establish Hooker as the primary representative of the 'Anglican' *via media*.

Later Lives   This commissioned biography by Walton was followed in 1670 by a 'free-will offering' (*Lives*, ed. Saintsbury, 6), the *Life of Mr George Herbert*. It appeared first as a flyer, not for an edition of Herbert's works but for a collected edition in the same year of the four lives Walton had so far written, which sufficiently indicates, perhaps, not only the extent to which Walton had become established as a biographer but also the new dignity which was being accorded to the genre. His life of Herbert again dealt with someone Walton had not known but 'only seen' (ibid., 259), but their mutual intimacy with Wotton and Donne, and Walton's readiness to 'know' his subjects through their writings, made him less troubled by the task than he had been in his life of Hooker. The *Life of Herbert*, too, is a tissue of paraphrase and quotation, more Herbert than Walton—except that every word is deployed to insist upon the essential nobility of the priesthood (particularly the country priesthood) as a vocation, and the events are transformed and marked by edifices (the churches Herbert is narrated as restoring, for example) which underscore Walton's belief in the beauty of holiness and transform Herbert's own book of precept, *The Country Parson*, into 'factual' example, and his poetry into an untroubled version of a spiritual autobiography.

Walton's *Lives*—of Donne, Wotton, Hooker, and Herbert—was reissued in 1675 with further revisions and expansions: Donne's vision of the death of his wife, for instance, was added at this time. In 1676 Walton published his fifth and final edition of the *Angler*, under the title *The Universal Angler*. This included a section by Charles Cotton on trout fishing which paid touching tribute to their relationship: 'he gives me leave', wrote Cotton, 'to call him Father, and I hope is not yet ashamed to own me for his adopted Son' (I. Walton, *Universal Angler*, pt 2, [x]). Walton also made some notes for a life of John Hales, another of the Great Tew circle—not, apparently, intending to write them up himself (he was, after all, over eighty by this time) but collecting them for another writer; and he produced an anonymous piece of polemic, *Love and Truth* (1680), which in its anxious insistence on lay obedience echoed with some precision the concerns of his life of Hooker.

Finally, somewhat against his will, Walton was persuaded by Morley into his last considerable work, *The Life of Dr Sanderson*. A fascinating figure, Robert Sanderson was a stern Calvinist yet an eminent casuist. He had been chaplain to Charles I, yet was also in 1627 the last preacher on predestination at Paul's Cross before the subject was proscribed, and had been invited to join the Westminster assembly (an honour he declined). He was made bishop of Lincoln at the Restoration, in the first flurry of moderate appointments; yet he found it extraordinarily difficult to come to terms with the predominantly Arminian temper of his Restoration colleagues. Walton had known Sanderson personally, and this *Life* is the only one in which Walton appears in the narrative. However, the Sanderson presented by Walton shows no trace of Sanderson's distinguishing Calvinism; instead Walton concentrates on the preservation of ceremonies and liturgy, to which the bishop was also committed. As *Hooker* prefigured the 'unity' of 1660, so arguably *Sanderson*, which narrated the events of the civil wars and Commonwealth, was intended as a warning against potential religious and political dissent. The most involved of the biographies, and showing some small signs of age (for instance, Walton began to get his scriptural allusions a little muddled), it nevertheless made particularly sensitive and ingenious use of its subject's prose. It appeared in 1678, the year that the exclusion crisis erupted and that Walton's son Izaak (who had matriculated from Christ Church, Oxford, in 1668, graduated BA in 1672, and proceeded MA in 1676) was made domestic chaplain to the bishop of Salisbury, Seth Ward. Walton's biography supposedly prefaced works by Sanderson; but in fact the main 'work' it headed was a digest of different fragments, and the *Life* emerged as the central point of the edition. A revised version was published in 1681 (one of Walton's last pieces of work), prefacing the 'eighth edition' of Sanderson's *Thirty Five Sermons*.

Last years and reputation By this time Walton was probably living with his daughter and son-in-law in Droxford. Approaching ninety, he was still writing. His letter to John Aubrey on Ben Jonson was composed in 1680, and in 1683, the year of his death, he wrote the preface to a verse pastoral, *Thealma and Clearchus*, attributed to John Chalkhill. His will, a humane and readable document, is dated 9 August of that year, but it was on 24 October that Walton signed and sealed it with the bloodstone seal left to him by John Donne. Walton died in Winchester, on 15 December 1683, when the weather was exceptionally cold, and was buried in the cathedral's Silkstede Chapel. He was survived by his daughter, who died in 1715, and son Izaak, who after a successful clerical career in the diocese of Salisbury died unmarried in London on 29 December 1719 and was buried in Salisbury Cathedral.

In the course of his long life (he was born, after all, before Shakespeare had really got into his stride) Walton produced a work—*The Compleat Angler*—which has commanded huge popularity: it has been reprinted almost as many times as *A Pilgrim's Progress*. Yet for biography, arguably, he performed a yet greater service. His unique combination of intimacy and edification formed a model highly influential on James Boswell and Samuel Johnson; and this makes him, perhaps, modern biography's father. Though he has been censured for his inaccuracy (and he was inaccurate) and for his bias (for which Dr Johnson's own judgement of him as a 'great panegyrist' is perhaps a fairer characterization), and though he was regarded by many as a naïve and thus, in a sense, accidentally effective writer, nevertheless his skill is at last receiving the recognition it deserves.   JESSICA MARTIN

Sources Wood, *Ath. Oxon.*, new edn, 1.698 • T. Fuller, *The church-history of Britain*, 11 pts in 1 (1655), pt 10, p. 112 • R. Franck, *Northern memoirs* (1694); 10 (1821), 175 • H. C. Beeching, *Religio laici* (1902) • D. Novarr, *The making of Walton's Lives* (1958) • P. G. Stanwood, *Izaak Walton* (New York, 1998) • J. Carey, *John Donne: life, mind, and art* (1981) • R. C. Bald, *John Donne: a life*, ed. W. Milgate (1970) • R. C. Bald, 'Dr Donne and the booksellers', *Studies in Bibliography*, 18 (1965), 69–80 • J. Bevan, 'Izaak Walton and his publisher', *The Library*, 5th ser., 32 (1977), 344–59 • J. Bevan, 'Henry Valentine, John Donne, and Izaak Walton', *Review of English Studies*, 40 (1989), 179–201 • J. M. French, 'Bowman v Donne', *TLS* (12 Dec 1936), 1035 • R. Krueger, 'The publication of John Donne's sermons', *Review of English Studies*, new ser., 15 (1964), 151–60 • J. Butt, 'Izaak Walton's methods in biography', *Essays and Studies by Members of the English Association*, 19 (1933), 67–84 • J. Martin, *Walton's Lives: conformist commemorations and the rise of biography* (2001) • J. Bevan, 'Some books from Walton's library', *The Library*, 6th ser., 2/3 (1980) • R. E. Bennett, 'Walton's use

of Donne's letters', *Philological Quarterly*, 16 (1937), 30–34 • G. Keynes, ed., *The compleat Walton* (1929) • H. J. Oliver, 'The composition and revision of *The compleat angler*', *Modern Language Review*, 42 (1947), 295–313 • N. Smith, 'Oliver Cromwell's angler', *The Seventeenth Century*, 8 (1993), 55–6 • E. Ashmole, *The institution, laws and ceremonies of the most noble order of the Garter* (1672) • D. H. Radcliffe, '"Study to be quiet": genre and politics in Izaak Walton's *Compleat angler*', *English Literary History*, 22 (1992), 24–37 • P. Lake, *Anglicans and puritans? Presbyterianism and English conformist thought from Whitgift to Hooker* (1988) • C. D. Lein, 'Art and structure in Walton's life of Mr. George Herbert', *University of Toronto Quarterly*, 46 (1976–7), 162–76 • J. Butt, 'Izaak Walton's collections for Fulman's life of John Hales', *Modern Language Review*, 29 (1934), 267–73 • J. Bevan, 'Izaak Walton's collections for Fulman's life of John Hales: the Walker part', *Bodleian Library Record*, 13 (1988–91), 160–71 • A. M. Coon, 'The life of Izaak Walton', unpublished diss., Cornell University, 1938 • J. Anderson, *Biographical truth: the representation of historical persons in Tudor–Stuart writing* (New Haven, 1984) • R. Wendorf, *The elements of life: biography and portrait-painting in Stuart and Georgian England* (1990) • K. Lindley, *Popular politics and religion in civil war London* (1997) • I. Walton, *Lives*, ed. G. Saintsbury (1927) • I. Walton, *The life and death of Dr Donne*, in *LXXX sermons preached by that learned and reverend divine, John Donne*, ed. J. Donne the younger (1640) • I. Walton, *The compleat angler, 1653–1676*, ed. J. Bevan (1983) • I. Walton, *The life of John Donne, dr. in divinity*, 2nd edn (1658) • I. Walton, *Life of Dr Sanderson, late bishop of Lincoln … to which is added, some short tracts* (1678) • *Waltoniana: inedited remains in verse and prose of Izaak Walton*, ed. R. H. Shepherd (1878)

Likenesses J. Huysmans, oils, *c*.1672, NPG [*see illus.*] • stained-glass window, 1918, Winchester Cathedral • G. Maile, mezzotint (after J. Huysmans), BM, NPG • engravings (after J. Huysmans)

Wealth at death see PRO, inventory of goods and chattels, PROB 4/8265

Walton, Izaak (1651–1719). *See under* Walton, Izaak (1593–1683).

Walton, Jacob (*d.* 1743), mathematical controversialist, was a Dubliner whose antecedents are unknown. A gentleman of the same name and place whose will (now lost) was proved in 1719 could have been his father. From 1719 to 1740 Walton's name appears in lists of subscribers to a dozen books, all but two published in Dublin. In 1731 'Mr. Walton' attended the first meeting of the Dublin Society, and two years later his full name appeared in the list of members. He came to public notice in England in 1735 as J. Walton, author of *A vindication of Sir Isaac Newton's principles of fluxions against the objections contained in 'The analyst'*. The latter book had been published anonymously in London and Dublin in 1734 by George Berkeley (1685–1753), bishop of Cloyne.

Berkeley's objections to fluxions (calculus) as expounded by Newton and Leibniz had centred around the logical absurdity of conceiving the ratio of two infinitely reducing quantities when both vanished; to believe in this fundamental construct of fluxions required an act of faith as great as that demanded by religion. Berkeley answered Walton, 'this Dublin Professor', in *A Defence of Free Thinking in Mathematics* (1735), accusing him of evading many of the issues and with the parting shot 'I leave him to be tried by his Scholars' (p. 71). Walton's rejoinder was *The Catechism of the Author [Berkeley] of 'The Minute Philosopher' Fully Answer'd*. Still anonymous, Berkeley issued *Reasons for not Replying to Mr. Walton's Full Answer* (1735), in fact a sarcastic reply ('a facetious man … an opponent who writes on my side of the Question'; p. 4). Walton responded with an appendix to his *Catechism* (added also to a second edition of Berkeley's *Reasons*). All the tracts following Berkeley's first were published in Dublin in 1735, and all except *Reasons* in London also.

Walton based his counter-argument on Newton's *Principia* and *Quadratura curvarum*; while showing 'a good intuitive grasp of fluxions', he 'lacked deep philosophic insight' (Cajori, 93), and can be faulted on some explanations in his *Catechism*. Berkeley had shrewdly pinpointed weaknesses in the formulation of the theory that Walton failed to address. The argument was taken up by British mathematicians, including James Jurin (1684–1750), Benjamin Robins (1707–1751), and Colin Maclaurin (1698–1746). The foundations of calculus still remained unsatisfactory, bedevilled by loyalty to Newton, shifting definitions, reliance on geometrical intuition, and lack of appropriate mathematical symbolism. The resolution emerged only in the early nineteenth century, through the work of A. L. Cauchy (1789–1857) and others.

Since he did not use a forename on his tracts, Walton's identity became obscured. Influenced by Berkeley's reference and by Cajori (p. 69), the entry in the British Museum catalogue (1964) reads 'WALTON (JOHN) Professor of Mathematics in Dublin University'. There was none such: Jacob Walton was probably a private teacher of mathematics.

'Jacob Walton, a very eminent Mathematician', died on 12 July 1743 (*Dublin Journal*) in Peter Street, Dublin; he was buried on 15 July in the city's parish of St Peter and St Kevin. The *Gentleman's Magazine* added that he had 'left upwards of £4,000 to his two Maid-servants' (*GM*, 443), perhaps indicating that he had no close relative. Such a large sum was unlikely to have come from teaching alone.

Walton was one of those lesser mathematicians who, without original contribution, assimilated and disseminated Newton's ideas and techniques. For an Irish mathematician he was exceptional in having his writings noticed and reprinted in England.   RUTH WALLIS

Sources F. Cajori, *A history of the conceptions of limits and fluxions in Great Britain: from Newton to Woodhouse* (1919) • *GM*, 1st ser., 13 (1743), 443 • *Dublin Journal* (16 July 1743) • A. F. Berry, *The history of the Royal Society of Dublin* (1915), 6, 27 • R. V. Wallis and P. J. Wallis, eds., *Biobibliography of British mathematics and its applications*, 2 (1986), 28, 54, 58, 161–2, 225 • R. Wallis, 'Who was J. Walton?', *Annals of Science*, 51 (1994), 539–40 • parish register (burial), 15 July 1743, St Peter and St Kevin, Dublin
Wealth at death over £4000: *GM*

Walton, James (1802/3–1883), card clothing manufacturer and innovator, was born at Stubbin, Sowerby, in the West Riding of Yorkshire, the son of Isaac Walton, a merchant. On 27 July 1830 he married Ann Kenworthy, of Millbank, Sowerby, at St John's Church, Halifax. As a young man he was in business as a cloth dresser, or friezer, and developed a new method of friezing petersham, a type of heavy woollen cloth. He then turned his attention to the manufacture of card clothing, a brush-like material consisting of wire staples set in a flexible backing which is used to cover the rollers on carding and cloth finishing machines.

Employing a mechanic from January 1834 to help in his experiments, Walton first produced a synthetic backing for his card clothing which combined india rubber with a woven fabric. Patented in March 1834, it was to prove the effective substitute for leather for which the card-making trade had long been searching. Walton's next achievement was to build an improved card-setting machine, patented in 1838, which set 300 teeth per minute, five times the rate of earlier machines. His task had been considerably eased by the adoption of his rubberized material, which proved much easier than leather to work in a machine. The machine was first shown in public at an industrial exhibition organized by the Sowerby Bridge Mechanics' Institute, of which Walton was chairman, in 1839. It revolutionized the trade, quickly replacing thousands of hand-setters previously employed around Halifax.

In order to profit from his innovations, Walton left Yorkshire, for the patented machine worked best with the rubber backing which was not then suitable for carding wool. He joined the existing partnership of Curtis and Parr, card makers, in Store Street, Manchester, about 1839. Curtis and Parr were also machine makers, having succeeded to the business of Joseph Chessborough Dyer, whose machine had provided the basis for Walton's improvements. Walton seems to have become sole proprietor of the firm by about 1846, when he built a large new factory in Chapel Street, Ancoats. This was followed by a move in 1853 to yet larger premises at Haughton Dale, Denton, near Manchester, where he worked in partnership with his two surviving sons, William (b. 1831) and Frederick Edward *Walton, the inventor of linoleum. His sons received some of the credit for later innovations, including the 'endless sheet machine', which made card setting a continuous process, and developments in wire-drawing. Walton's machine-made card clothing was of a superior quality to hand-made cards, at about a third of the price.

Although Walton did not formally retire until he was in his late seventies, he spent increasing periods away at his various country estates, at Compstall in Derbyshire, at Cwmllygodig in Merioneth, and then at Dolforgan Hall, Kerry, near Newtown, Montgomeryshire, an estate of 4250 acres which he had bought for £5000 in 1870. He served as sheriff of that county in 1877. Walton maintained an interest in social and moral issues, and built a school for his child employees. He founded and endowed the church of St Mary the Virgin in Haughton in 1876, at a cost of £4000, and also gave generously to an ancient church near his estate in Kerry. He died at Dolforgan Hall on 5 November 1883, at the age of eighty. He had survived an operation for cancer two years earlier, but died of the disease after a short illness.   GILLIAN COOKSON

Sources *Halifax Guardian* (10 Nov 1883) • *The Times* (8 Nov 1883) • *Manchester Guardian* (8 Nov 1883) • *Textile Manufacturer* (Nov 1883) • *DNB* • 'Card clothing and how it is made', *Textile Manufacturer* (Dec 1878); (Jan 1879); (Feb 1879) • 'Evenings at the exhibition', *Halifax Guardian* (19 Oct 1839) • 'Select committee on … laws affecting exportation of machinery: first report', *Parl. papers* (1841), session 1, 7.110–24, no. 201 • G. Cookson, 'The mechanization of Yorkshire card-making', *Textile History*, 29 (1998), 41–61

Archives W. Yorks. AS, Calderdale, affidavits etc. relating to patent infringements, NOR:12, NOR:13

Wealth at death £186,576 15s. 5d.: probate, 3 Dec 1883, *CGPLA Eng. & Wales*

Walton, John (*fl.* 1410), translator and Augustinian canon, of Osney Abbey, Oxford, translated the *De consolatione philosophiae* of Boethius into English verse. Very little is known of his life (he was previously confused with John Walton, abbot of Osney (*d. c.*1490), and John Waltham, subdean of York). He is presumably the John Walton, Augustinian canon of Osney, who was given the dignity of papal chaplain on 1 April 1399, and who, on 13 April of the same year, was granted papal dispensation to hold his canonry with another benefice. A number of the manuscripts of the work call him capellanus ('chaplain') and 'canon of Osney', or 'formerly canon of Osney'. Several give the date 1410. The translator's preface makes it clear that Walton is translating the book at the request of a patron, whose name is given, in the final prayer which appears in the printed edition, as Elizabeth Berkeley (*d.* 1422), probably the daughter of Thomas, Lord Berkeley (*d.* 1417), who subsequently became the wife of Richard Beauchamp, earl of Warwick. Walton may also have translated the *De re militari* of Vegetius (into prose) for Sir Thomas Berkeley in 1408. The translation of Boethius was evidently popular: it survives in over twenty manuscripts as well as in the printed edition (*The Boke of Comfort called in Laten Boetius De Consolatione Philosophiae*, 1523) by T. Rychard in the monastery at Tavistock. Walton's choice of verse for his translation is not surprising in this period, when verse was a common vehicle for didactic and instructional writing. He does not imitate Boethius's alternation of prose and verse:

> in prose and metre enterchaungyngly
> Wiþ wordes set in colour wonder wele
> Of rethoryk endited craftily.
> (bk 1, prologue, stanza 20)

Nor, indeed, did Chaucer, whose prose translation Walton uses. He writes the first three books in eight-line stanzas, the last two in rhyme-royal. The whole poem is preceded by a 'Preface of the translator', in which he apologetically draws attention to the difficulty of his task, and speaks admiringly of Chaucer and Gower. The prologue to the *Boke* gives an account of Boethius and his death, and of the terrible punishment of the emperor Theodoric. Books 4 and 5 are also preceded by a 'Preface of the translator'. In the form of a prayer he dedicates the 'labour' to God, 'þe welle of sapience', the mysteries of whose wisdom are inscrutable. No earthly creature can comprehend divine providence. The preface signals the importance of this subject in the final books, and it may be that Walton shifted to the rhyme-royal stanza because he thought it might be a better vehicle for high philosophical matter. His translation is in general workmanlike, clear, and readable, and his versions of some of the lyrics have a genuine eloquence. DOUGLAS GRAY

Sources *Boethius: De consolatione philosophiae*, ed. M. Science, trans. J. Walton, EETS, orig. ser., 170 (1927) · Emden, *Oxf.*, 3.1975 · D. C. Fowler, 'New light on John Trevisa', *Traditio*, 18 (1962), 289–317

Walton, John (*b.* before 1415, *d.* 1489?), archbishop of Dublin, was born before 1415 in the diocese of Lincoln. He was educated at Oxford, being dispensed in connection with qualifications for a doctorate on 6 June 1450, and was made a BCnL before 1472, probably long before that date. He was a canon of the Augustinian abbey of Osney, near Oxford, by 1433 and was ordained deacon in Worcester Cathedral on 20 February 1434. In 1452 he became abbot of Osney; the temporalities were restored on 1 November 1452. After twenty years as abbot, during which the *English Register* of the abbey was compiled, he was promoted by Edward IV to the archbishopric of Dublin in 1472. On 19 March 1472 he was granted custody of temporalities of the see; the papal provision was dated 4 May 1472 and he was consecrated archbishop in England by August of that year. Subsequently he was enthroned in Holy Trinity Cathedral in Dublin.

Within his diocese Walton was active in pastoral and diocesan affairs if not in politics. He defended the rights of his see; he controversially attempted to exercise his jurisdiction over the dean and chapter of St Patrick's Cathedral; he asserted his rights of visitation of religious houses. In 1478 he procured from the Irish parliament the restitution of several manors alienated by his predecessors earlier in the century. A letter was addressed to him by the University of Oxford about its *degenerate alumni* preaching heresy in his diocese in 1483. He retained connections with Osney Abbey and clearly travelled between Ireland and England since letters of protection were granted to him crossing to England on business in 1474 and 1477. On 14 June 1484, being then blind and infirm, Walton resigned the archbishopric and retired to his manor of Swords with an annual pension of £100 drawn from the revenues of the archiepiscopal mensa of Dublin. The manor of Swords was also reserved to him for his maintenance for life, the possession of which was assured to him by an act of parliament in the following year. According to the antiquarian James Ware, the register of Swords commented favourably on Walton's generous hospitality and cheerful, innocent disposition.

Despite his infirmity Walton continued to preach on occasion. On St Patrick's day (17 March) 1489 he preached a sermon before the lord deputy and nobility in St Patrick's Cathedral in Dublin. He died soon afterwards. His will is undated but was made, before his resignation as archbishop, on an occasion when he was about to cross from Ireland to England. In it he requested that should he die in England his body should be buried among the abbots in Osney Abbey. He wished his copy of John de Burgh's *Pupilla oculi* to be restored to the abbey, along with numerous vestments and mass requisites and other books. It is unknown, however, where and when he died or where he was buried; but it is most probable that he died at his castle of Swords and that he was buried in the vicinity.

A. F. POLLARD, *rev.* VIRGINIA DAVIS

Sources Emden, *Oxf.* · H. F. Berry, ed., *Register of wills and inventories of the diocese of Dublin … 1457–1483* (1898) · M. V. Ronan, 'Anglo-Norman Dublin and diocese', *Irish Ecclesiastical Record*, 5th ser., 48 (1936), 170–93, 378–96 · H. E. Salter, 'The annals of the abbots of

Oseney', *EngHR*, 33 (1918), 498–500 • *CPR* • H. Anstey, ed., *Epistolae academicae Oxon.*, 2 vols., OHS, 35–6 (1898) • H. E. Salter, ed., *Cartulary of Oseney Abbey*, 1, OHS, 89 (1929) • A. Clark, ed., *The English register of Oseney Abbey*, EETS, 1st ser., 133–4 (1907–13) • J. W. Willis-Bund, ed., *Worcester sede vacante register* (1897) • *CEPR letters*

Walton, Sir John Lawson (1852–1908), barrister and politician, was born on 4 August 1852, the son of John Walton, Wesleyan minister in Ceylon and at Grahamstown, Cape Colony, who became president of the Wesleyan conference in 1887 and died on 5 June 1904, aged eighty. His mother was Emma Walton, daughter of the Revd Thomas Harris. After receiving his early education at Merchant Taylors' School, Great Crosby, in Lancashire, John Walton matriculated in 1872 at London University, but did not graduate, and entering the Inner Temple as a student on 2 November 1874, he was called to the bar on 13 June 1877. On 21 August 1882 he married Joanna M'Neilage, only daughter of Robert Hedderwick, of the *Glasgow Citizen* newspaper; they had one daughter and two sons.

Joining the north-eastern circuit, Walton rose rapidly in the profession, taking silk in 1890, only thirteen years after his call. He was helped at the start by a strong connection among the Wesleyans, especially in the West Riding towns. A born advocate, persuasive, tactful, and adroit, Walton acquired as large a practice in London as on circuit. He first came into public notice in March 1896 with his victory over Sir Frank Lockwood in the action brought against Dr William Smoult Playfair for libel and slander; the damages, £12,000, were the largest that had been awarded by an English jury up to that date. His services were much in request on behalf of the trade unions, and he appeared for the respondents in the House of Lords in the case of *Allen v. Flood* (1898).

Walton was from his earliest years a keen politician, and in 1891 was chosen as the Liberal candidate for Battersea; but rather than divide the party he withdrew his candidature in deference to the strong local claims of John Burns. At the general election of 1892 he contested Central Leeds unsuccessfully; at the by-election, however, which followed the elevation of Sir Lyon Playfair to the peerage in the same year, he was returned for South Leeds, a seat which he held against all comers down to his death. During the ten years of Unionist administration between 1895 and 1905 he played a prominent part in opposition; and though he carried his forensic style with him into parliament, his pleasant voice and carefully chosen language always procured him a ready hearing. A strong radical in domestic politics, especially where the House of Lords and the established church were concerned, he was a member of the Liberal Imperialist group associated with Lord Rosebery during the Second South African War of 1899–1902. Though not himself a member of the Church of England, he took a lively interest in its affairs, and was a witness before the royal commission appointed in 1904 to inquire into ecclesiastical disorders; there he advocated a more effective procedure against clergy charged with breaking the law.

On the formation of Sir Henry Campbell-Bannerman's government in December 1905 Walton was made attorney-general, and was knighted. The appointment was a result of R. B. Haldane's choice of the War Office in preference to legal preferment. Though personally popular on all sides, Walton seemed never quite at home in his office. His attainments as a lawyer were neither deep nor varied, and ill health interfered with his regular attendance in the House of Commons. One of his first duties as law officer was on 28 March 1906 to introduce the Trade Disputes Bill, which, as then drafted, made trade unions or their executive committees responsible for breaches of the law committed by their members. He attacked trade union proposals for immunity as 'class privileges' and the bill provoked a major row with the Labour Party, the cabinet quickly changing its position to permit immunity. On the second reading on 25 April, the solicitor-general, Sir William Robson, announced that the clause would be abandoned in committee. This surrender on the part of the government did not tend to strengthen the attorney-general's position.

Walton died after a short illness at his house, 42 Great Cumberland Place, London, on 18 January 1908. He was buried at Ellesborough, near Wendover in Buckinghamshire.   J. B. ATLAY, *rev.* H. C. G. MATTHEW

Sources *The Times* (20 Jan 1908) • *Dod's Parliamentary Companion* • H. A. Clegg, A. Fox, and A. F. Thompson, *A history of British trade unions since 1889*, 1 (1964) • H. C. G. Matthew, *The liberal imperialists: the ideas and politics of a post-Gladstonian élite* (1973) • *CGPLA Eng. & Wales* (1908)

Archives BL, letters to Lord H. J. Gladstone, Add. MSS 46054–46064

Likenesses Spy [L. Ward], chromolithograph cartoon, NPG; repro. in *VF* (6 March 1902)

Wealth at death £56,949 9s. 1d.: probate, 20 Feb 1908, *CGPLA Eng. & Wales*

Walton, Sir Joseph (1845–1910), judge, was born in Liverpool on 25 September 1845, the eldest son of Joseph Walton, merchant, of Fazakerley Hall, Lancashire, and his wife, Winifred Cowley. His parents were Roman Catholics. Educated at St Francis Xavier's College, Salisbury Street, and at Stonyhurst College, he graduated from the University of London in 1865 with first-class honours in mental and moral science. He entered Lincoln's Inn in November of the same year, and was called to the bar on 17 November 1868. On 12 September 1871 he married Teresa, fourth daughter of Nicholas D'Arcy of Ballyforan, co. Roscommon; they had eight sons and a daughter.

Joining the northern circuit, Walton entered the chambers of Charles Russell, then one of the leading juniors, and practised for several years as a 'local' at Liverpool. His chief work was in commercial and shipping cases. As a Roman Catholic and a distinguished advocate, Walton was retained in successful *habeas corpus* actions brought against Thomas John Barnardo on the behalf of Roman Catholic children, including *Barnardo v. Ford* (1891) and *Barnardo v. McHugh* (1892), which reached the House of Lords.

Walton's advancement in the profession was slow. He took silk in 1892, and became recorder of Wigan in 1895 and a bencher of Lincoln's Inn in 1896; but the general esteem in which he was held was shown by his election in

1899 as chairman of the general council of the bar. He succeeded Sir Charles Russell as leading counsel to the Jockey Club, and appeared as such in *Powell* v. *The Kempton Park Racecourse Company Ltd* (1899), in which the House of Lords considered the interpretation of the Betting Act of 1853. He also appeared in the copyright case of *Walter* v. *Lane* (1900), which arose out of the republication of reports from *The Times* of speeches by Lord Rosebery.

On the appointment of Sir James Mathew as lord justice of appeal, Walton was appointed a justice of the King's Bench Division of the High Court on 22 October 1901 and subsequently knighted, though Lord Salisbury had thought 'of making Walton Lord Justice at once over Mathew's head' (letter of 30 Sept 1901) in the light of the Liberal Mathew's conduct as chairman of the royal commission on evicted tenants of 1892. Walton's wide experience of commercial matters was of service to the commercial court, and his decisions in commercial cases came to be cited with respect, though his over-conscientiousness and a lack of confidence prevented a complete fulfilment of expectation.

Outside the judicial sphere Walton was interested in the work of the Medico-Legal Society, becoming its second president in 1905. He took an active part in the social and educational movements of his church, and was for a time a member of the Liverpool school board. Much of his leisure time was spent yachting, and he was a frequent prizewinner at the Orford and Aldeburgh regattas. He wrote a small work on the practice and procedure of the court of common pleas at Lancaster (1870), and was among the editors of the *Annual Practice of the Supreme Court* for 1884–5 and 1885–6.

Walton died, probably of heart failure, at his home at Shinglestreet, near Woodbridge, Suffolk, on 12 August 1910, having only in the previous week taken an active part in the proceedings of the International Law Association in London. He was buried on 17 August 1910 in the Roman Catholic cemetery, Kensal Green. His wife survived him.   N. G. JONES

Sources *The Times* (15 Aug 1910) · *The Times* (18 Aug 1910) · *Law Journal* (20 Aug 1910), 549 · *Transactions of the Medico-Legal Society*, 7 (1910), 180–82 · R. F. V. Heuston, *Lives of the lord chancellors, 1885–1940* (1964), 60 · J. Foster, *Men-at-the-bar: a biographical hand-list of the members of the various inns of court*, 2nd edn (1885) · d. cert.
Likenesses Hudson, portrait; in possession of Lady Walton, 1912 · Spy [L. Ward], chromolithograph caricature, NPG; repro. in *VF* (24 July 1902) · charcoal drawing, Trinity Cam.
Wealth at death £46,037 13*s*. 11*d*.: administration, 5 Sept 1910, *CGPLA Eng. & Wales*

Walton [*née* Bourchier], **Philippa** (1674/5–1749), gunpowder manufacturer, was the fourth of five daughters and the coheir of John Bourchier of Ipswich, MD. She married William Walton, a London merchant, who in 1702 set up as a gunpowder manufacturer at Waltham Abbey in Essex, and at Balham in Surrey where they lived. Her husband became one of the largest suppliers of gunpowder to the government's Ordnance board, and when William died intestate in 1711 Philippa became the sole administrator of

his estate. She was then thirty-six and the mother of ten young children, nine of whom were to survive her.

Philippa Walton took over the management of the gunpowder business, initially on her own; then in 1723 she brought in her second eldest son, John, as a partner with a quarter share. In 1730 they formed an equal partnership, a partnership valued in 1732 at £10,000. The evidence suggests that Philippa Walton retained a close interest in the business thereafter, and that she did not immediately become a sleeping partner. It was not until the mid-1740s that she retired to Ongar in Essex to live with her sister, Jane Bourchier. The period when she took control was a difficult one for the gunpowder industry. The end of the War of Spanish Succession in 1714 and the long period of peace until the 1740s meant a drop in demand from the largest customer, the Ordnance board. There was a private market to be exploited, but this could never compensate for the drop in demand. Under such circumstances the industry contracted: some producers reduced their capacity, others withdrew. Philippa Walton chose the former course. She ceased production at Balham and concentrated on the site at Waltham Abbey, purchasing it outright in 1718 for £1100, her own family acting as trustees.

During the first decade of her management Philippa Walton was one of the few producers to obtain the scarcer ordnance contracts, and she entered into partnership with three other producers to build a gunpowder magazine at Barking in Essex and exploit the private markets. The business continued unchanged after her son became involved, and in the 1740s it was sufficiently robust to emerge as the second largest supplier to the Ordnance during the War of Austrian Succession. Other producers who had continued after 1714 were not so successful in maintaining their businesses intact.

Philippa Walton was not the only widow to produce gunpowder in the early eighteenth century, but she was the most successful and the only one to continue so long. Nothing is known about the problems she faced as a woman in business but it can be noted that the *Commons Journals* entered her name as Philip not Philippa in 1718 (*Commons Journals*, 19, 1718, 85). She died on 7 December 1749, probably at Ongar in Essex, and was buried in the churchyard at Mickleham, Surrey, where her son Philip was vicar. Her memorial at Mickleham records that she died 'in calm and Christian serenity' after having improved her property and formed the minds of her children by her instruction and example. In her will she emphasized that her six sons had already received sufficient assistance to satisfy any claim on their father's estate, and so left her share of the partnership to her three surviving daughters, all of whom remained spinsters. Soon afterwards her son John purchased this share.

Philippa Walton's eldest son, William, was to be one of only two sons not involved in the family business, and he was the only child to have children. After John's death in 1757, the business passed to a succession of three of Philippa's other male children until 1782, when Philippa's grandchild, John Walton, inherited. It was he who sold the

Waltham Abbey site to the Ordnance board in 1789, after which it remained in government hands as an important explosives production site until the Second World War.

K. R. FAIRCLOUGH

Sources J. West, *Gunpowder government in the mid-eighteenth century* (1991) · K. R. Fairclough, 'Early gunpowder production at Waltham', *Essex Journal*, 20 (1985), 11–16 · K. R. Fairclough, 'Gunpowder production at Balham House', *London's Industrial Archaeology*, 4 (1989), 32–4 · K. R. Fairclough, 'Philippa Walton, gunpowder manufacturer at Waltham Abbey', *Essex Journal*, 31 (1996), 18–22, 55–9 · O. Manning and W. Bray, *The history and antiquities of the county of Surrey*, 2 (1809), 663 · Ordnance Office records, PRO · Treasury solicitor's office, Taunton, TS 1136/50 · will, PRO, PROB 11/775, sig. 391

Wealth at death   see will, PRO, PROB 11/775, sig. 391

Walton [Wauton], **Simon of** (d. 1265/6), justice and bishop of Norwich, was probably a native of Walton d'Eiville, Warwickshire. In 1235–6 Master Simon of Walton appears as a plaintiff concerning lands in nearby Tysoe. A trained canon lawyer, his services brought him a pension from Osney Abbey, and he was also employed by the king, from whom he began to receive gifts. In 1242 he was made keeper of the vacant see of Lichfield, and in 1245 he was involved in much administrative work in connection with Henry III's Welsh campaign.

Walton began a career as an itinerant justice in the midlands and west of England in January 1246, the year in which he received the farm of the royal manor of Feckenham, Worcestershire. Later the king gave him deer for his park of Stock Bradley in the royal forest near Feckenham. From the prior and convent of Worcester, where a Robert of Walton, possibly his brother, was chamberlain, he received in 1253 the rectory of Stoke Prior, Herefordshire, and in 1254 the lease of the manor of Harvington, Worcestershire. The acquisition of property accompanied his rise as a justice. He was the effective leader on one of the two circuits of the eyre in 1254–6, at the end of which he returned as chief justice to the bench of common pleas, on which he had sat for the first time in Michaelmas term 1251. In March 1254 he was allowed the temporary use of the bishop of Carlisle's London house. Finally, in June 1257 he was elected to the bishopric of Norwich, receiving the temporalities of the see on favourable terms.

Walton remained conspicuously loyal to the king throughout the years of baronial reform and rebellion. In 1259 he was employed in negotiations with the king of France and to adjudicate upon breaches of the truce with the Welsh; and in 1260 he was one of the commission of bishops proposed to settle the private disputes between Simon de Montfort and the king. His ultimate offence in the eyes of the baronial party was his appointment in 1261, along with Boniface, archbishop of Canterbury, and John Mansel, to execute the papal bulls which Henry had procured, enjoining the barons to obey the king and absolving them from their oaths of allegiance to the provisions of Oxford. In 1263 he was forced to flee from his cathedral to the abbey of Bury St Edmunds, a secure refuge since its liberty 'was exceedingly precious in the eyes of the barons' (*Chronicle of Bury St Edmunds*, 27). The 'Song of the Barons' called Walton 'the good shepherd of Norwich,

who devours the sheep', and cursed anyone 'who left a mite to him, for he knew much about shame' (Aspin, 19–20). The baronial *custos pacis* for Norfolk was ordered to confiscate his lands, but these were restored to him when he took an oath to support the provisions. He was one of the prelates summoned to London for Simon de Montfort's parliament in January 1265. He did not long enjoy the king's triumph over his enemies in August of that year, for he died 'about the feast of the Circumcision' (1 January), 1266, 'in good old age' (*Ann. mon.*, 4. 183). He was buried in Norwich Cathedral; on 18 January the king granted the guardians of the vacant diocese of Norwich the administration of his will. A John of Walton held lands at Bradley, Worcestershire, in 1274–5.

ALAN HARDING

Sources Chancery records · E. Stokes and F. C. Wellstood, eds., *Warwickshire feet of fines*, 1, Dugdale Society, 11 (1932), 106 · *VCH Worcestershire*, 3.114, 359, 389 · D. Crook, *Records of the general eyre*, Public Record Office Handbooks, 20 (1982) · A. Gransden, ed. and trans., *The chronicle of Bury St Edmunds, 1212–1301* [1964] · I. S. T. Aspin, ed., *Anglo-Norman political songs*, Anglo-Norman Texts, 11 (1953) · *Ann. mon.*, vol. 4 · P. A. Brand, *The origins of the English legal profession* (1992)

Walton, Thomas. *See* Waweton, Sir Thomas (d. in or after 1450).

Walton, Valentine (1593/4–1661), parliamentarian army officer and regicide, was the son of Nicholas Walton. His father, a member of a younger branch of an old gentry family in Huntingdonshire, died when he was young, certainly by 1606 when Valentine at the age of twelve inherited the manor of Great Staughton in that county from his grandfather's cousin. His inheritance, estimated in 1640 as about £400 per annum, did not go uncontested: a kinsman unsuccessfully challenged it in 1624 before both the privy council and the House of Commons and by illegally occupying the manor house of Great Staughton. Walton was for a time a ward of Sir Oliver Cromwell of Hinchinbrook, the leading figure in the county until the 1620s. On 20 June 1617 Walton married Sir Oliver's niece, Margaret Cromwell (bap. 1601), daughter of Robert Cromwell of Huntingdon and sister of Oliver *Cromwell, the future lord protector. She had evidently died by July 1644, when her brother wrote a letter to Walton which did not mention her among the kin he asked to be remembered to. Walton's second wife, the daughter of one Pym of Brill, Buckinghamshire, and widow of one Austen of the same place, died on 14 November 1662 and was buried in St Mary's Church, Oxford.

During the 1630s Walton consistently opposed attempts to levy non-parliamentary taxation, though he appears to have met demands for knighthood and ship money at least half-way. He was imprisoned for defaulting 2s. 6d. on payment of the latter, for example. However, his stance evidently won him a sufficient number of admirers for him to be returned MP for Huntingdonshire in the election to the Long Parliament in October 1640. Despite his own relatively modest place within the ranks of county society (an observer described him as 'a private obscure gentleman') he was able to overcome the nominee of the powerful Henry Cromwell, the son of his former guardian (Keeler, *Long Parliament*, 379). In parliament he sat on a number of important committees. His puritan commitment is indicated by his inclusion on a subcommittee of the grand committee on religion and on another committee to consider 'An Act for the Abolishing of Superstition and Idolatry and for the Better Advancing of the True Worship and Service of God'—on both committees alongside his brother-in-law. In 1642 he helped Cromwell prevent Cambridge University sending its plate to the king at Nottingham, raised a troop of horse to serve under the earl of Essex, and was taken prisoner by the royalists at the battle of Edgehill. During his confinement he was treated kindly by Thomas Laurence, the master of Balliol College and the Lady Margaret professor of divinity. Walton later reciprocated this generosity in obtaining for Laurence the chapelry of Colne in the parish of Somersham, Huntingdonshire, endowing the living with its tithes before installing Laurence after his ejection from Oxford.

In July 1643 Walton was exchanged for Sir Thomas Lunsford and became colonel of a regiment of foot in the army of the eastern association and governor of King's Lynn. Under his government Lynn, which had recently been seized and briefly held by the royalists, was strongly fortified and, according to the gossip of the royalists, reserved as a city of refuge for the Independents should the need arise. By May 1644 he was commanding a regiment of dragoons. In July his eldest son, Valentine, was killed at Marston Moor. Cromwell's letter to Walton combined condolence—'a precious young man, fit for God'—with exultation in the victory; young Valentine had died in a state of spiritual comfort, regretting only 'that God had not suffered him to be no more the executioner of His enemies' (*Writings and Speeches*, 1.288). Although he had a hand in his brother-in-law's quarrel with the earl of Manchester Walton was ruled out from military command with the passage subsequently of the self-denying ordinance. He held no commission in the New Model Army.

In 1649 Walton was appointed one of the king's judges, in which capacity he attended most of the sittings of the court, and signed the warrant for the execution of Charles I [*see also* Regicides]. Under the Commonwealth he was a member of all the five councils of state appointed by parliament and acted as an admiralty commissioner, but he did not sit either in the parliaments or councils of the protectorate. When Richard Cromwell became protector and called a parliament, Walton, who thought of being a candidate, was obliged to vindicate himself from the charge of being opposed to the government. Nevertheless he was not elected; but when Richard Cromwell was overthrown he returned to his seat in the Long Parliament, and was elected by it a member of the council of state and one of the commissioners of the navy. On 12 October 1659, when the parliament annulled Charles Fleetwood's commission as commander-in-chief, Walton was one of the seven persons in whom the control of the army was vested. Acting in that capacity, Walton, aided by Sir Arthur Hesilrige, occupied Portsmouth, declared against the army leaders, and entered into communication with George Monck.

When the troops in London restored the Long Parliament for the second time, Walton was given command of the regiment lately Colonel Disbrowe's, and he was continued as one of the commissioners for the government of the army until 21 February 1660, when Monck was appointed commander-in-chief. His temporary importance then ended, and he was deprived of his regiment by Monck, who gave it to Colonel Charles Howard.

At the Restoration Walton was excepted from the Act of Indemnity, and lost Somersham, Huntingdonshire, and other estates forming part of the dowry of Queen Henrietta Maria, which he had purchased during the period of republic. He escaped to Germany, and became a burgess of Hanau in order to obtain the protection of that town. His later history is uncertain. According to Anthony Wood he lived for some time in Flanders or the Low Countries, under a borrowed name, maintaining himself as a gardener, and died there soon after the Restoration. Mark Noble, the eighteenth-century historian of the Cromwell family, states that he died in 1661. Walton is said to have written a history of the civil wars, containing many original letters of Cromwell, the manuscript of which was still extant in 1733.　　C. H. FIRTH, *rev.* SEAN KELSEY

Sources M. Noble, *Memoires of the protectoral-house of Cromwell*, 2nd edn, 2 vols. (1787), 1.221–8 • Keeler, *Long Parliament* • C. Holmes, *The eastern association in the English civil war* (1974) • *VCH Huntingdonshire*, 2.357 • C. Polizzotto, 'Walton (or Wauton), Valentine', Greaves & Zaller, *BDBR*, 3.285–6 • I. Gentles, *The New Model Army in England, Ireland, and Scotland, 1645–1653* (1992) • *The writings and speeches of Oliver Cromwell*, ed. W. C. Abbott and C. D. Crane, 4 vols. (1937–47), vols. 1–2 • E. Peacock, *The army lists of the roundheads and cavaliers* (1863) • *The memoirs of Edmund Ludlow*, ed. C. H. Firth, 2 vols. (1894) • *JHC* • C. Walker, *The compleat history of Independency* (1661), bk 1, 148 • Thurloe, *State papers*, 7.587 • *Reliquiae Hearnianae: the remains of Thomas Hearne*, ed. P. Bliss, 2nd edn, 3 (1869), 108 • *The life and times of Anthony Wood*, ed. A. Clark, 5 vols., OHS, 19, 21, 26, 30, 40 (1891–1900), vol. 1, p. 461; vol. 2, p. 462 • R. W. Ketton-Cremer, *Norfolk in the civil war: a portrait of a society in conflict* (1969)

Walton, William (1783/4–1857), writer on Spain, was the son of William Walton, the consul for Spain in Liverpool. At an early age he was sent to Spain and Portugal to learn the languages and to fit himself for a commercial career before going to South America. He acted as a junior secretary to the British expedition which captured the town of Santo Domingo from the French in 1802, and remained there as British agent. In 1809 he returned to England, living in Bristol before moving to London, where he devoted himself to political journalism, writing pamphlets against current ministerial policies towards Spain and Portugal, including open letters to the marquess of Lansdowne, Viscount Palmerston, and Earl Grey.

Walton contemplated compiling a history of the Spanish colonies, and in spite of losing the material he had collected, he wrote *The Present State of the Spanish Colonies* (1810) and *An Exposé on the Dissentions of Spanish America* (1814). In 1811 appeared *An Historical and Descriptive Account of the Peruvian Sheep* (vicuña), in which he recommended their naturalization in Britain, a project which interested him and which he reverted to in *The Alpaca* (1844). He also promoted the importation of guano, to be used as a fertilizer, although the idea originally met with incredulity on the part of British merchants.

Walton translated several works from the Spanish, including Antonio Puigblanch's *The Inquisition Unmasked* (1816) and Tomás de Comyn's *State of the Philippine Islands* (1821). Among his longer journalistic publications, on subjects of concern to his contemporaries, but which have proved to be of slight permanent value, were *Spain! or, Who is the Lawful Successor to the Throne?* (1834), *A Reply to the Anglo-Christino Pamphlet Entitled 'The Policy of England towards Spain'* (by the earl of Carnarvon), and *The Revolutions of Spain, from 1808 to the End of 1836* (both 1837). He died at his home in Longwall, Oxford, on 5 May 1857.

C. A. HARRIS, rev. IAN CAMPBELL ROBERTSON

Sources J. Alberich, *Bibliografía Anglo-Hispánica, 1801–1850* (1978) · *GM*, 3rd ser., 3 (1857), 96

Archives NRA, letters to first earl of Sheffield relating to South America

Walton, Sir William Turner (1902–1983), composer, was born at 93 Werneth Hall Road, Oldham, Lancashire, on 29 March 1902, the second son among the four children (three sons and a daughter) born to Charles Alexander Walton (1867–1924?) and his wife, Louisa Maria Turner (1866–1954). His siblings were Noel (*b.* 1899), Nora (*b.* 1908), and Alexander (*b.* 1910). Charles Walton was born in Hale, Cheshire, the son of an Inland Revenue official. He met Louisa Turner, an amateur contralto who was born in Stretford in 1866, at a recital in Chorlton-cum-Hardy, Manchester. They were married in Chorlton on 10 August 1898 and set up home in Oldham, where Charles worked in an ironworks, although he described himself on his marriage certificate as a singing teacher. He had been (at the age of twenty-six) one of the first intake of pupils when the Royal Manchester College of Music opened in 1893 with Sir Charles Hallé as its principal. After his marriage Charles Walton taught music at Hulme grammar school, Oldham, and for twenty-one years was organist and choirmaster of St John's Church, Werneth, in addition to teaching elsewhere. According to his son William he was a very good baritone. His sons Noel and William were among his choristers; he had a violent temper, and if one of them made a mistake he rapped him on the knuckles with his ring ('it hurt'; Sitwell, 174).

Chorister at Oxford According to his mother, William could sing 'bits of *Messiah*' before he could talk. He remembered 'making a scene' when he was six because he was not allowed to sing a solo in the choir. He learned to play the piano and organ ('very badly') and had some violin lessons, which were stopped because he would not practise. His early general education was at a board school, but in 1912 his father saw in a local newspaper an advertisement for a voice trial for probationer choristers at Christ Church Cathedral choir school, Oxford. The application was accepted, and William and his mother travelled by train from Manchester to Oxford. They missed the first train because the money for the tickets had been spent by Charles Walton the previous evening in a public house and Mrs Walton had to borrow the fares from a greengrocer. William was sick on his first long journey, and when they arrived the trials were over. Mrs Walton pleaded for her son to be heard, and the organist, Dr Henry G. Ley, heard him in Marcello's 'O Lord, our governor' and asked him to sing the middle note of a five-note chord. He was accepted and remained at the choir school for the next six years.

Walton described his first term as 'odious' until he learned how to disguise his Lancashire accent. There were two choir practices and two services a day, and Walton said that the rest of his education was 'pretty poor'. But he was good at sports, playing football, running the 100 yards, and coxing the college boat. He was fortunate that the dean of Christ Church was Dr Thomas Strong (later bishop of Oxford), who was extremely musical and saw

Sir William Turner Walton (1902–1983), by Michael Ayrton, 1948

Walton's potential. Strong thought Walton should train as an organist, but the boy's lack of aptitude for musical instruments thwarted this ambition. The outbreak of war in August 1914 had an immediate effect on Charles Walton's finances because it meant fewer pupils. There was a danger that William would have to leave Oxford, but Strong paid the balance of fees not met by the scholarship.

Walton was already composing pieces for his fellow choristers, including *A Litany* ('Drop, drop, slow tears'), to a text by Phineas Fletcher, which he revised in 1916 and, for publication, in 1930; and two four-part songs, 'Tell me where is fancy bred' and 'Where the bee sucks'. His attitude as he approached puberty was characteristically expressed in later life: 'I thought "I must make myself interesting somehow or when my voice breaks I'll be sent back to Oldham. What can I do? Write music." So I did' (television documentary, *At the Haunted End of the Day*). About 1917 he gave Strong a bundle of his compositions for the dean to scrutinize. Sir Hubert Parry was staying in Christ Church at the time and also looked at them. He said to Strong: 'There's a lot in this chap. You must keep your eyes on him' (Kennedy, 7). Walton's instruction was supervised by Hugh P. Allen, then organist of New College. Allen played him Stravinsky's *Petrushka* on the piano and, Walton recounted, gave him insights 'into the mysteries of the orchestra as he could bring scores vividly to life by playing them on the organ' (Schafer, 74). Strong invited the senior choristers to his house after the Sunday morning service and sometimes played them contemporary music on his piano. In this way Walton first heard Schoenberg's *Six Little Pieces*, op. 19, which he found 'very funny' (private information), and music by Bartók and Prokofiev. He also spent many hours in the Radcliffe Camera in the Ellis Library of Music, which possessed scores by Debussy, Ravel, Prokofiev, and Stravinsky. Among Walton's other teachers were H. G. Ley, Basil Allchin, and Ernest Walker.

In the vacations Walton was taken by his father to Hallé concerts in Manchester. He also attended some of the operas conducted by Sir Thomas Beecham, with the Hallé in the pit, in Manchester in 1916 and 1917. The colour and spectacle of Mussorgsky's *Boris Godunov* and Rimsky-Korsakov's *The Golden Cockerel* left a deep impression on him. Walton's voice broke in 1916, but he remained at the choir school, subsidized by Strong and others, for two more years. He passed the first half of his BMus examination in June 1918, after which Strong suggested to Charles Walton that William should join the college as an undergraduate in October 1918 and continue his studies under Allen. His fees would be met by a fund controlled by the dean which helped needy undergraduates.

With the Sitwells At sixteen years and seven months, Walton arrived at Oxford at what was then a very young age. But he did not survive there for long. He admitted that he had neglected general academic subjects, such as Greek or Latin, French, German, and mathematics, for music. He failed the examination known as responsions at three attempts—in June, September, and December 1919. He passed the second part of his BMus in June 1920 but did not submit a music exercise as third part. He was not in residence for the Hilary and Trinity terms of 1920 but returned for Michaelmas, although he did not live in college.

Luck, however, came Walton's way again during his brief period as an undergraduate when he met Sacheverell *Sitwell, of Balliol College, youngest of the three children of Sir George Sitwell who were already making a stir in artistic circles, and the poet Roy Campbell. During 1918 Walton had begun to compose his first large-scale work, the piano quartet, and he played some of it to Sitwell, who was convinced that it was the creation of a genius. The latter sent for his brother (Francis) Osbert *Sitwell to go to Oxford to hear it in February 1919. After the first of Walton's exam failures the Sitwells invited him to stay with them in Swan Walk, Chelsea.

Within weeks Walton's life was transformed and his cultural outlook and experience broadened beyond anything he could have foreseen. He and Sacheverell planned a recital of Walton's songs (cancelled because of the singer's illness) and attended recitals by Alfred Cortot and Busoni. He was invited to Lady Ottoline Morrell's house and taken to the new ballet *Parade*. Shy, taciturn, and looking as if he had not had enough to eat, the young Walton was taken under the wing of the Sitwells' cook. In the spring of 1920 and with a gift of £50 from Dr Strong, he went with the Sitwells to Italy. This, he said, 'changed my whole attitude about life and music' (Anson, 117). During the train journey it rained all the time in France ('Oldham again!'), but when they arrived in Italy it was 'ablaze with sunlight, a new world' (Kennedy, 16). They stayed at Amalfi in a former monastery converted into a hotel. Walton had a 'cell' in which he composed.

On their return to London Walton moved into Osbert's house, 2 Carlyle Square, where he lived in the attic 'eating bags of black cherries and throwing the stones out of the window on to unsuspecting passers-by' (Sitwell, 174). The Sitwells combined with Dr Strong, Lord Berners the composer, and Siegfried Sassoon the poet to guarantee Walton an income of £250 a year so that he could devote himself to composition. They vetoed any suggestion that he should enter either the Royal Academy or Royal College of Music, and arranged for him to meet Edward J. Dent and Ernest Ansermet. Walton sent some of his music to Busoni, who was not impressed. From the pianist Angus Morrison we get the strongest portrait of Walton in the early 1920s. Morrison was struck 'even then by a sense of latent power, an inner fire, still hidden below the surface but which one felt would inevitably declare itself in the fulness of time' (Kennedy, 32). This complements the impression that Walton made at Oxford on Roy Campbell: 'a sense of vocation and how a man can live for his art … William was already equipped for greatness' (Campbell, 181).

Few of Walton's works from this period survive except for some songs. Among discarded works were a setting for tenor and chamber orchestra of Christopher Marlowe's

The Passionate Shepherd and a 'pedagogic overture', *Dr Syntax*. He had written two movements of a string quartet at Oxford in 1919, and these were performed in London in March 1921. He then revised them, inserted a scherzo, and submitted it to the International Society for Contemporary Music, which selected it for its second festival in Salzburg in August 1923, when it was admired by Alban Berg. Walton then withdrew but did not destroy it. When it was recorded after his death, it was found to be a complex, dense structure, not atonal in Schoenberg's style, but harmonically advanced and unlike most of Walton's music in its intellectual rigour.

Façade and Portsmouth Point In November and December 1921 Walton composed the work that made his name known, the 'entertainment' *Façade*, in which poems by Edith *Sitwell were recited through a megaphone to an accompaniment for four instrumentalists. The poems were written as studies in word-rhythms and onomatopoeia, and although they may appear superficially to be nonsensical, a thread runs through them of allusions to events and people in Edith's unhappy childhood. Walton's music is witty and also contains parodies of Rossini and quotations from music-hall songs as well as employing jazz rhythms.

But the work performed in Osbert Sitwell's drawing-room for about twenty people on 24 January 1922 would scarcely be recognized today. Of its eighteen items, only six survived into the definitive version. For the first public performance in June 1923 ten more items were added. The twenty-eight were reduced to twenty-six for the next performance in 1926. When *Façade* was performed at the International Society for Contemporary Music festival in Siena in September 1928, it consisted of twenty-two items including, for the first time, what is now the most popular movement, 'Popular Song'. By now the work had also acquired its best reciter, Constant Lambert, who became Walton's closest friend. When the definitive 21-item version of *Façade* was published in 1951, it was dedicated to Lambert. For the 1979 Aldeburgh Festival eight of the discarded numbers were re-worked as *Façade 2* and recorded. In 1926 Walton had orchestrated five numbers as a suite, and he followed this with six others as the suite no. 2 in 1938. The first suite formed the basis of the ballet with choreography by Frederick Ashton which was first performed in 1931, with items added in 1935 and 1940.

'Drivel they paid to hear' was a headline which typified press and public response to the 1923 performance of *Façade*. It led to a rather effective revue parody by Noël Coward three months later for which the Sitwells never forgave him (Walton enjoyed it). But in 1926 *Façade* was rapturously received and the critic Ernest Newman praised Walton's musical wit. Despite the annual allowance, Walton still needed money and earned some by arranging foxtrots for Debroy Somers's Savoy Orpheans. He wanted to involve them in a large-scale *Fantasia concertante* for two pianos, jazz band, and orchestra in 1925 but scrapped it. This was the year, too, in which he met George Gershwin in London (Kennedy, 40). It was the London of the 'bright young things' and 'flappers' and of visits to

London by Duke Ellington's band and by the black singer Florence Mills. Walton's circle of friends included not only the hard-drinking Lambert and Philip Heseltine (known as Peter Warlock professionally from 1916) but also Siegfried Sassoon, Rex Whistler, Peter Quennell, Spike (Patrick) Hughes, Beryl de Zoete, Christabel McLaren (later Lady Aberconway), and Stephen Tennant (the original of Sebastian Flyte in Evelyn Waugh's *Brideshead Revisited*). Lambert maintained that Gershwin's influence could be detected in incidental music that Walton wrote in 1925 for Lytton Strachey's unsuccessful play *A Son of Heaven*.

More important was the overture *Portsmouth Point*, inspired by a Rowlandson etching, which made hay with Stravinskyan and jazzy rhythms to give a twentieth-century musical slant on the artist's boisterous eighteenth-century scene. It was first performed at the International Society for Contemporary Music festival in Zürich in June 1926 and was the first work by Walton to be accepted and published by the newly formed (1923) music department of Oxford University Press, headed by Hubert Foss. Walton's contract gave him a royalty on every copy sold and half of the Performing Right Society's fee. Throughout his life Walton was keenly interested in the commercial value of his works and the state of his royalties. He had a horror of poverty, the legacy of his Oldham childhood. He regularly sent cheques to his mother in Oldham, while he himself for much of the 1920s was financially assisted by Sassoon.

Portsmouth Point typifies the spiky, brittle, rhythmical side of Walton. His next work—the short *Siesta* for small orchestra—is in his lazier, relaxed, lyrical mode. Both these aspects of his musical personality are to be found in his next work, the *Sinfonia concertante* for piano and orchestra of 1927, which Walton recast from a ballet score Diaghilev had rejected. Each of the three movements is a portrait of, and was dedicated to, one of the Sitwells, in the order Osbert, Edith, and Sacheverell. It was first performed at a Royal Philharmonic Society concert in January 1928, with York Bowen as soloist and Ernest Ansermet conducting.

This was Walton's first major London concert appearance as a composer, and it was a success. (In 1943 he revised it, although since his death the tendency has been to revert to the first version. When the full score was published in 1953 the Sitwell dedications were removed.) But it was eclipsed by his next work, the viola concerto, which Beecham had suggested he should write for the celebrated English violist Lionel Tertis. He wrote it at Amalfi in the winter of 1928–9 and sent it to Tertis, who promptly rejected it because of its modernity, although he soon regretted his action and took it into his repertory. The first performance, conducted by Walton at a Promenade Concert in October 1929, was given by Paul Hindemith. It was at once hailed as a masterpiece, and some would still regard it as his finest work.

Belshazzar's Feast Although the concerto is dedicated to Christabel Aberconway, Walton was at this time involved with Imma, widow of Baron Hans-Karl Doernberg and daughter of Prince and Princess Alexander of Erbach-Schoenberg. He was living with her in Switzerland for some of the time he was composing *Belshazzar's Feast*. This originated as *Nebuchadnezzar: the Writing on the Wall*, a BBC commission for soloist, small chorus, and orchestra not exceeding fifteen players. The libretto was compiled from biblical sources by Osbert Sitwell. The work soon outgrew its BBC restrictions and was offered to the 1931 Leeds festival, where it was conducted by Malcolm Sargent on 8 October.

It had a tumultuous reception. Lasting barely thirty-five minutes, it made a tremendous impact. The choral and orchestral depiction of Babylonian excess and depravity was bolstered by barbaric jazzy outbursts and the use of two extra brass sections and was contrasted with the extraordinarily beautiful lamentation of the Jewish captives. Many critics judged this oratorio, or cantata, to be the most important English choral work since Elgar's *The Dream of Gerontius* in 1900, and it established Walton firmly as the foremost English composer of his generation. Early in 1932 Sir Hamilton Harty, then conductor of the Hallé Orchestra in Manchester, asked him for a symphony, and he accepted, hoping he might be 'able to knock Bax off the map' (Kennedy, 65). He was stimulated by rivalling other composers: *Belshazzar's Feast*, for example, was a response to the success of Lambert's *The Rio Grande*. Harty's request coincided with the news that the musical patron Mrs Samuel Courtauld, wife of the financier and textile manufacturer, had left Walton £500 a year for life because, as her widower told Sassoon, 'we both thought that what he has already done is far ahead of anything written in this country for a very long time—and in the front rank anywhere' (Kennedy, 67). Walton later told his wife that the money was given by Samuel Courtauld at Christabel Aberconway's behest.

The symphony was long in gestation, and a scheduled first performance in March 1934 in London was postponed; Harty had left the Hallé to become conductor of the London Symphony Orchestra. The music's turbulent character, with a scherzo marked to be played 'with malice', undoubtedly owed something to the breakup of his relationship with Imma, who left him for a Hungarian doctor. When a second postponement seemed probable, because the finale, although partly written, was incomplete, the orchestra (governed by a committee drawn from its members) persuaded Walton to allow the first three movements to be performed at Queen's Hall on 3 December 1934. By then Walton had formed a relationship with Alice Katherine Sibell Wimborne (née Grosvenor) (1880–1948), wife of the second Viscount Wimborne, and the exuberance of the finale, which was finished in August 1935, was attributed to his domestic happiness. The complete symphony was performed on 6 November 1935 and impelled another composer, John Ireland, to describe it as 'the work of a true master ... colossal, grand, original and moving ...' (Kennedy, 85).

A further alleviation of Walton's financial worries came with his first commission for music for a film, Paul Czinner's *Escape me Never*, in 1934, followed by *As You Like It*

in 1936. He was the obvious choice to write a march, *Crown Imperial*, for the coronation of George VI in May 1937. For the Leeds festival that year he composed a short cantata, *In Honour of the City of London*. In July of this year he first met Benjamin Britten, eleven years his junior, who recorded the meeting in his diary: 'He is charming, but ... he is so obviously the head-prefect of English music whereas I'm the promising new boy ... I am patronised in a very friendly manner' (entry in Britten's diary, 28 July 1937, quoted in Carpenter, 110). Incidentally, Britten in his diary had described Walton's symphony as 'dull & depressing' (ibid., 70).

Walton was now immersed in composition of a violin concerto commissioned by Jascha Heifetz. He composed it at the Villa Cimbrone, above Amalfi, where Alice Wimborne had taken him. She was good at making him work and prising him away from Lambert's and Alan Rawsthorne's circle of drinking companions. The concerto, one of his most beautiful and melodic works, was completed in June 1939 and was first performed by Heifetz with the Cleveland Orchestra on 7 December 1939. Because war on Germany had been declared on 3 September, Walton was unable to travel to the United States for the occasion. He conducted the first London performance, with Henry Holst as soloist, on 1 November 1941.

Walton's first wartime task was the composition of a ballet for Sadler's Wells, where Constant Lambert was conductor, with choreography by Frederick Ashton, décor by Rex Whistler, and Margot Fonteyn and Michael Somes as principal dancers. *The Wise Virgins* was a transcription of music from J. S. Bach's cantatas. It was first performed in April 1940, and Walton later recorded an orchestral suite from it. He fulfilled a commission from the Chicago Symphony Orchestra for its fiftieth anniversary, composing *Scapino*, an exuberantly virtuosic comedy overture, like an English *Till Eulenspiegel*. This was followed by music for John Gielgud's new production of *Macbeth* (1942) and for two propaganda films, *The Foreman Went to France* and *The First of the Few*, the latter about the design and building of the Spitfire fighter aircraft. He also composed an elaborate score for a radio production of Louis MacNeice's play *Christopher Columbus*. Another Ashton ballet, *The Quest* (1943), followed, but Walton's most significant wartime contribution was his music for Laurence Olivier's film of Shakespeare's *Henry V*, a score that ranks with the best in film music.

Opera and marriage When Walton was interviewed in New York in June 1939, he said: 'I seriously advise all sensitive composers to die at the age of 37 [his age at the time]. I know: I've gone through the first halcyon periods and am just about ripe for critical damnation' (*New York Times*). These were prophetic words. A month after the end of the war in Europe, in June 1945, Britten's opera *Peter Grimes* was produced at Sadler's Wells to general acclaim and Walton, the pre-war 'white hope', found himself displaced. His first post-war work, the string quartet, performed in May 1947, was coolly received. But when in 1947 the BBC commissioned an opera from him, the success of *Peter Grimes* provided the old stimulus of rivalry. He selected the subject of *Troilus and Cressida* and invited Christopher Hassall to be his librettist, a choice resented by the Sitwells: his friendship with the Sitwells had cooled since his association with Alice Wimborne, of whom they disapproved. Work on the libretto and music occupied him for the next seven years. He diverted from it only to compose music for another Olivier Shakespeare film, *Hamlet*, a violin sonata, and the march *Orb and Sceptre* for Queen Elizabeth II's coronation in 1953, for which he also wrote a Te Deum.

Alice Wimborne died in April 1948, leaving Walton a London home and £10,000, and in the autumn, while a delegate to an international conference of the Performing Right Society in Buenos Aires, he met and, on 13 December 1948, married the 22-year-old Susana Valeria Rose Gil Passo (*b*. 1926), daughter of a lawyer. He decreed that they would spend at least six months of each year in Italy; because no houses were available near Amalfi, he rented one at Forio on the island of Ischia in the Bay of Naples. Eventually they made their permanent home there, building a villa, La Mortella, and creating a magnificent garden.

Troilus and Cressida was performed at Covent Garden on 3 December 1954 and later in San Francisco, New York, and Milan. Its reception was respectful rather than enthusiastic. Romanticism was out of fashion in the mid-1950s, and the music of Britten and Tippett was regarded as nearer to the spirit of the time. The opera's relative failure wounded Walton, who for the next twenty years campaigned relentlessly for its revival. It returned to Covent Garden in 1963 and 1976. For the latter date he revised it and transposed the role of Cressida from soprano to mezzo-soprano to accommodate Janet Baker. Even then, despite full houses, the critics' reaction was lukewarm. The opera contains a wealth of beautiful music, but the treatment of the two protagonists, especially of Troilus, lacks dramatic flair.

Walton's next large-scale compositions were the luscious cello concerto (1955–6), written for Gregor Piatigorsky, the brilliant *Partita*, for the fortieth anniversary of the Cleveland Orchestra, and the second symphony (1957–60), commissioned by Liverpool Philharmonic Society. The symphony was regarded as inferior to its predecessor and was generally damned by the critics, although it is a very different kind of work from the first symphony, somewhat enigmatic in mood, and a superb example of Walton's more mature, concise, and mellow post-1945 style. That he suffered no creative block as a result of being out of critical favour is shown by the number of works he produced in this period. In addition to those mentioned above, he composed two delightful song-cycles, *Anon. in Love* (1959) and *A Song for the Lord Mayor's Table* (1962), and a Gloria (1960) for the 125th anniversary of Huddersfield Choral Society. In 1963 came one of his best and most elegant compositions, the *Variations on a Theme of Hindemith*. Again, its initial reception was tepid.

Last two decades In 1963 Walton travelled to Israel, the United States, Australia, and New Zealand to conduct his own works. His next new compositions were both choral,

The Twelve (to a text by W. H. Auden) for his alma mater Christ Church Cathedral choir, and a *Missa brevis* for Coventry Cathedral: 'as brevissima as possible', Walton commented to his publisher, 'remembering the boredom I suffered as a dear little choirboy' (Kennedy, 228). Then Peter Pears suggested he should write a one-act opera based on Chekhov's *The Bear* for the Aldeburgh Festival. Walton asked Paul Dehn to write the libretto but work was interrupted in January 1966 when Walton underwent an operation for lung cancer. Later in the year he had eleven weeks of cobalt radiation. He completed *The Bear* at the end of April 1967, and it was performed at Aldeburgh in June, when it was well received. It is Walton at his wittiest. The same vein was continued in his *Capriccio burlesco* (1968), written for the New York Philharmonic's 125th anniversary.

Invited next to compose music for the film *The Battle of Britain*, Walton was outraged to discover, after the soundtrack had been recorded, that another composer had been asked to supply a new score. Only one sequence by Walton was retained when the film was shown. A happier experience was the success of his San Francisco Symphony commission, *Improvisations on an Impromptu by Benjamin Britten* (1968–9), a hauntingly beautiful and prophetically elegiac composition. In 1970–71 he wrote *Five Bagatelles* for solo guitar for Julian Bream.

For his seventieth birthday Walton was honoured by a dinner party at 10 Downing Street, hosted by the prime minister, Edward Heath, with Queen Elizabeth the queen mother as chief guest, and by concerts throughout Britain. He began a third symphony, wrote a short choral work, and made alternative versions of some of his existing works, but infirmity was slowing him down and he made his last appearance as a conductor in June 1973 for the fiftieth anniversary of *Façade*. He devoted his energies to revising *Troilus and Cressida* for the revival at Covent Garden in 1976, but was taken ill after the last performance. On recovery he wrote some short works and arranged for brass band *The First Shoot*, a ballet he had written for a C. B. Cochran revue in 1935. Work on the symphony defeated him, but he wrote a passacaglia for solo cello for Rostropovich and a *Prologo e fantasia* for Mstislav Rostropovich's Washington orchestra. His eightieth birthday in March 1982 was marked by a London performance of *Belshazzar's Feast*, which he attended. A few days later he was again taken seriously ill. He returned to Ischia in April and died there on 8 March 1983, at La Mortella. After cremation in Florence on 11 March, his ashes were interred in a rock in the garden of La Mortella. He was survived by his wife.

Distinctive style Walton's progress from being a kind of *enfant terrible* to an old age when he seemed to have been left behind by musical fashion is a pattern familiar for many a creative artist. But Walton's music has survived its decline from fashion, and has come to be regarded as among the finest composed by Englishmen in the twentieth century. His style is distinctive and individual—a few notes are enough for his hallmark to be recognized. He was, for all his diffidence and the appearance he liked to give of laziness, a hard-working professional and a superb craftsman. He composed something every day to the last day of his life even if he then scrapped it; he claimed that an indiarubber was the most important instrument at his disposal. He was always self-critical and grew more so with age.

The idea that Walton's music after 1945 was not as good as the pre-war works dies hard, but it is now clear that the later works were, if emotionally less direct, more profound—and often more difficult to play. As a conductor of his own music, he was unsurpassed. Although never tempted to follow the serialist path, he maintained a lively interest in the latest developments in music. Requests for avant-garde scores to be sent to him in Ischia were regular. He was a prey to insecurity and depression, acutely sensitive to adverse criticism, and often jealous of other composers' success and achievements. 'I think I could have done better', he said in a radio interview at the end of his life. 'I'm a disappointment to myself' (*Kaleidoscope*, BBC Radio 4, transmitted 8 March 1983). His personal charm and sardonic humour masked a steely determination. He made many friends, of whom Lambert and Malcolm Arnold were perhaps closest to him, but he could ruthlessly discard them too. He had a long estrangement from the Sitwells, and when Stephen Tennant quarrelled with Siegfried Sassoon, Walton took Tennant's part and dropped Sassoon, who had been so generous to him financially. He had a roving eye for women. Alice Wimborne was the love of his life, but there is no doubt that his marriage brought him great happiness.

Walton was knighted in 1951 and appointed to the Order of Merit in 1967. He was made a freeman of the borough of Oldham in 1961. His honorary university doctorates were at Durham (DMus, 1937), Oxford (DMus, 1942), Dublin (DMus, 1948), Manchester (DMus, 1952), Cambridge (DMus, 1955), London (DMus, 1955), and Sussex (DLitt, 1968). Honorary fellowships were awarded to him by the Royal College of Music (1937) and the Royal Academy of Music (1938) among others. He was made an honorary member of the Royal Swedish Academy of Music (1945), the Accademia de Santa Cecilia, Rome (1962), and the Royal Manchester College of Music (1971), and was awarded the Benjamin Franklin medal (1972), the gold medal of the Royal Philharmonic Society (1947), and the medal of the Worshipful Company of Musicians (1947).

MICHAEL KENNEDY

Sources M. Kennedy, *Portrait of Walton* (1989) • S. Walton, *William Walton: behind the façade* (1988) • N. Tierney, *William Walton: his life and music* (1984) • S. Craggs, *William Walton: a catalogue* (1990) • J. Lehmann, *A nest of tigers: Edith, Osbert and Sacheverell Sitwell in their times* (1968) • R. Campbell, *Light on a dark horse* (1951) • J. Pearson, *Façades: Edith, Osbert and Sacheverell Sitwell* (1978) • S. Craggs, *William Walton: a source book* (1993) • T. Palmer, *At the haunted end of the day*, ITV television film, 1981 • H. Carpenter, *Benjamin Britten: a biography* (1992) • *New York Times* (4 June 1939) • interview, 8 March 1983 [*Kaleidoscope*, BBC Radio 4] • O. Sitwell, *Laughter in the next room* (1950), vol. 4 of *Left hand, right hand! An autobiography* • private information (2004) [Lady Walton, widow] • R. M. Schafer, *British composers in interview* (1963), 74 • H. Anson, *T. B. Strong: bishop, musician, dean, vice-chancellor* (1949), 117 • Burke, *Peerage* (2000)

Archives La Mortella, Forio d'Ischia, Italy • priv. coll., MSS | BL, letters to Sir Henry Wood, Add. MS 56422 • King's AC Cam., letters to E. J. Dent • Tate collection, corresp. with Lord Clark | FILM BFI NFTVA, *The South Bank show*, 19 April 1981 • BFI NFTVA, documentary footage | SOUND BL NSA, documentary recordings • BL NSA, 'Drivel they paid to hear', H4096/2 • BL NSA, 'Walton's "Troilus and Cressida"', 1995, H4615/4 • BL NSA, 'An extraordinary relationship', B5928/6 • BL NSA, *Richard Baker compares notes*, B7555/03 • BL NSA, *Talking about music*, 208, 1LP0202106 S2 BD3 BBC TRANSC • BL NSA, *Talking about music*, 325, 1LP0205903 S1 BD2 BBC TRANSC • BL NSA, 'Walton as conductor', H2978/02 • BL NSA, 'Willie: the young Walton and his masterpieces', 31 Jan 1984, T8850 C1

Likenesses M. Lambert, bronze head, *c*.1925, NPG • C. Wood, drawing, 1929? • R. Whistler, drawing, 1934? • M. Ayrton, portrait, 1948, NPG [*see illus.*] • photograph, 1963, Hult. Arch. • A. Newman, bromide print, 1978?, NPG • C. Beaton, photograph • E. Frink, bronze bust; copy, La Mortella, Ischia • A. McBean, photograph

Walworth, Sir William (*d.* 1386?), merchant and mayor of London, was one of twin sons, possibly of the William Walworth who was granted land in 1314 in Darlington, co. Durham. Evidently both boys were well educated, possibly at Durham: Thomas gained a master's degree and became a canon of York, while William himself acquired numerous books of theology, devotion, and law, which he carefully distributed in his will. Among his bequests was one remitting a debt of 100 marks owed to him by the monastery at Durham, where his arms were displayed in the cloisters. They were borne also by the family that succeeded him in the manor of Middleton St George, near Darlington. His will, though, does not mention either parent, and his bequests for masses and the foundation of a chantry were for the soul of his former master, the rich fishmonger and four-times mayor of London, John Lovekyn, who was the founder of his fortune.

Lovekyn's will of 1368, which appointed Walworth as one of his executors, refers to him still as his servant. Walworth's social origins and education were not uncommon among apprentices in the greater livery companies, which offered prospects of wealth in the wool trade. Fishmongers were prominent in the trade because they owned ships, and Lovekyn was one of London's biggest wool exporters in the 1360s. Walworth also dealt in corn as well as fish. In 1369 he was licensed to send £200 to Sweden to buy herring, and similarly to buy 1000 quarters of wheat and malt in the ports between Newcastle and Orwell to ship to London. His bequests for the repair of the highway between Southwark and Newenton, and to local churches, as well as his property at Walworth, suggest that this area was important in his business.

Before Lovekyn's death Walworth must have been acting as his partner because he succeeded him as alderman of the fishmongers' ward of Bridge, and he quickly became prominent in London's politics. In 1369 he was one of the four Londoners experienced in naval and mercantile matters who were elected to advise the king after the war against France was renewed in that year. He was one of the merchants who complained in 1370 that the ships they had loaded at Sluys had been plundered at Calais. He was also one of the foremost defenders of the overseas wool staple, which was the principal means by which the English merchants defeated alien competition in the export trade.

Walworth was elected mayor of the Westminster staple

in 1369. This position, which he held to his death, meant that he acquired an expert knowledge of the credit operations of the London wool merchants, and also of the chief money market of the kingdom. His financial abilities and legal interests equipped him well for this and for later appointments of a judicial or financial nature. In 1370 he was chosen to hear cases of usury in London. He also had extensive financial resources of his own. In 1370 he was the third highest contributor to the city's loan to the king, and he continued thereafter, with other leading London merchants, to be a crucial source of loans for the crown.

Walworth's election as sheriff in 1370 came at a time when the renewal of the French war had inaugurated a period of exceptional strain in the political life of the kingdom and also within the city of London. The war necessitated repeated taxation, which culminated in the levying of the unpopular poll taxes. The export of coin, and its shortage at home, brought about depression and unemployment in the towns. Merchant ships were impressed to carry troops, and suffered losses from naval warfare. Royal policy, which favoured alien merchants for financial reasons, threatened not only the London wool merchants but also importers and craftsmen. They sought to protect their businesses by recovering the old commercial privileges of the city, which had allowed them to exclude aliens and non-citizens from its retail and distributive trade. In 1370 the draper John Northampton, a skilled agitator, and some disaffected mercers began to stir up protests and disorder in the streets of London.

The chief anxiety of Walworth and his fellow staplers was the crown's policy, begun in 1371, of raising money by selling licences for wool exporters to evade the Calais staple. His election as an MP for London that year, and then as mayor for the first time in 1374–5, undoubtedly reflected the staplers' hopes that he would defend their interests against those aldermen who were profiting from the sale of the licences and from raising expensive loans for the crown. Walworth failed in his attempt to outbid them by offering cheaper loans in return for the enforcement of the overseas staple.

The discontents of the kingdom at large were vented against the royal government in the Good Parliament of 1376. The London staplers made common cause with Northampton's rebellious group to elect Walworth and one of Northampton's supporters as MPs. But whereas the staplers were successful in their demands, Northampton failed to win the restoration of London's commercial privileges and undoubtedly believed he had been betrayed by the staplers. Under the threat of creating disorders which would invite the crown's intervention, Northampton forced the staplers to agree to constitutional changes that he hoped would increase the power of his following in London. These included the annual election of aldermen, and of common councillors by the mysteries instead of the wards. Walworth was one of the two aldermen chosen to assure the king that these changes would ensure the good government of the city.

One reason for the choice of Walworth was that he was friendly with influential courtiers, probably through lending them money. He first acted as a feoffee that year for William Wykeham, bishop of Winchester and chancellor of England. Their friendship proved to be lasting. They shared a love of books and art, something that once led Walworth to take as security from a Flemish merchant not the usual plate but a book of romance and a tapestry of Arras work. Wykeham later chose Walworth to assist in the endowment of his college at Winchester and Walworth bequeathed money to Wykeham and two of his books to the bishop's foundation of New College, Oxford. They also both experienced the enmity of John of Gaunt, duke of Lancaster, who in 1377 secured the disgrace of Wykeham, while at the same time threatening the independence of the city.

Walworth was again elected an MP for London in October 1377, and was chosen by the Commons as one of two treasurers to receive and disburse the taxes granted for the war to ensure that they were spent only for that purpose. Lancaster caused both treasurers to be removed at the parliament held in 1378 at Gloucester, but Walworth testified to the stout opposition put up by the city's representatives against the court's attacks on them. The same year he was appointed with three other staplers to attend a royal council to advise on protection at sea. Once Lancaster's influence had waned, Walworth was appointed to other royal inquiries, for instance that of March 1380 into the destitution of the people. Another testimony to his judgement and his fairness was his election in January 1381 by the German merchants resident in London as their alderman to represent their interests.

By then Walworth was serving as mayor for a second time. Disturbances in November 1380 indicated that many Londoners shared the discontents of the kingdom for which the poll tax of 1381 provided the spark of revolt. Londoners may have helped to co-ordinate the marches on the city of the rebel peasants from Kent and Essex. Indeed, two aldermen–fishmongers, John Sibyl and Walter Horn, were later alleged to have opened the gates to admit the rebels. These accusations originated among enemies of Walworth's, and should probably be discounted—the opening of the gates may simply have been the result of the prevailing confusion. But there are grounds for believing that Horn, who was sent by Walworth to negotiate with the peasants at Blackheath, gave them some encouragement. Whether Walworth connived with him it is impossible to say; certainly he had reason to doubt whether he could count on the city's militia to defeat the rebels. But after the murder of royal ministers only the city's government stood between the kingdom and revolution. The militia was obviously in readiness, but within the city, when the king met the rebels at Smithfield on 15 June. Probably Walworth did not plan to kill Wat Tyler. However, in previous personal confrontations he had shown an impetuous streak, and Tyler's insolence roused him to lunge at him with his sword, either killing him outright or inflicting a mortal wound, before he rode off to fetch the militia. Walworth was knighted by Richard

II with three other aldermen on the field, and he subsequently helped to restore order in London, Kent, and Middlesex.

Walworth's successor as mayor in October 1381 was John Northampton, who seems to have been chosen by the aldermen to appease his powerful patron, Lancaster. When the staplers refused to raise loans for Lancaster's military plans, Northampton brought pressure on them by attacking the fishmongers who held six aldermanries. In a succession of measures he deprived them of their trade and of all political offices. Uncharacteristically, it seems that Walworth did nothing to defend his mystery. A fellow fishmonger claimed that Northampton was attacking them to avenge his arrest by Walworth when he was sheriff in 1371, and after what had happened to Northampton's other prominent victims Walworth may have feared for his own safety. However, in March 1383 he did stand surety for the four former aldermen whom Northampton had imprisoned in the Tower of London. When Sir Nicholas Brembre defeated Northampton in that year's mayoral election, the statutes against the fishmongers were repealed. Subsequently Walworth tried without success to conciliate Northampton, and to persuade him to end his violent pursuit of power.

Walworth acquired extensive property in London which he bequeathed for her lifetime to his wife, Margaret. They had no surviving children, and she died in 1394. He was obviously close to his brother, Thomas, to whom he bequeathed most of his books, plate, and other personal possessions. Walworth died, probably in January 1386, at his house in Thames Street; his will, dated 20 December 1385, was enrolled on 13 January 1386. He was buried in St Michael, Crooked Lane, which he had greatly enlarged by adding a new choir and chapel, and where he had established a small college of chantry chaplains. His sister, Cecilia, predeceased him, leaving five daughters, and his sister, Agnes, was married to a London chandler. He bequeathed £20 to each of his two apprentices, one of whom, William Askham, succeeded him as the occupier of his house in Thames Street, where Lovekyn had once lived. It was to become the site of the Fishmongers' Hall where a larger than life, and still surviving, wooden statute of Walworth was set up in 1685.

PAMELA NIGHTINGALE

Sources will, PRO, PROB 11/1, sig. 1 · R. R. Sharpe, ed., *Calendar of letter-books preserved in the archives of the corporation of the City of London*, [12 vols.] (1899–1912), vols. G–H · A. H. Thomas and P. E. Jones, eds., *Calendar of plea and memoranda rolls preserved among the archives of the corporation of the City of London at the Guildhall*, 2–3 (1929–32) · R. R. Sharpe, ed., *Calendar of wills proved and enrolled in the court of husting, London, AD 1258 – AD 1688*, 2 (1890) · H. T. Riley, ed., *Memorials of London and London life in the XIIIth, XIVth, and XVth centuries* (1868) · P. Nightingale, *A medieval mercantile community: the Grocers' Company and the politics and trade of London, 1000–1485* (1995) · P. Metcalf, *The halls of the Fishmongers' Company* (1977)
Likenesses Pierce, wooden effigy, 1685, Fishmongers' Hall, London · drawing (for the mayoral pageant of 1616), Fishmongers' Hall, London · prints, GL
Wealth at death over £750 in cash legacies; plus extensive property in London and elsewhere; also books and plate: will, 1385, PRO, PROB 11/1, sig. 1

Walwyn, Fulke Thomas Tyndall (1910–1991), racehorse trainer, was born on 8 November 1910 at The Gables, Wrexham, Denbighshire, the son of Fulke James Walwyn, a captain (later lieutenant-colonel) in the Royal Welch Fusiliers, and his wife, Louisa Norah Lockhart, *née* Greenshields. He was educated at Malvern College and the Royal Military College, Sandhurst, before being commissioned into the 9th lancers. He resigned in 1935 following adverse publicity from a court case involving a Soho night-club fracas in which he appeared as a prosecution witness. At the outbreak of the Second World War he was ruled unfit for active service and became a military policeman at Tidworth for two years before securing a medical upgrade and serving with his old regiment in France. His first marriage was on 28 September 1937 to Diana Carlos Clarke (1916/17–1949), daughter of Major Charles Loraine Carlos Clarke, army officer. There were no children of the marriage. On 24 June 1952 he married Catherine (*b.* 1928), fourth and youngest daughter of Sir Humphrey Edmund de Trafford, fourth baronet. They had one daughter, Jane (*b.* 1957).

Walwyn's father had been an outstanding showjumper and master of the Monmouthshire hounds, and Walwyn and his twin sister, Helen, learned to ride and hunt at an early age. His first racing win was on Ciren in a point-to-point in April 1930 and his first under National Hunt rules on Alpine Hut at Cardiff the same month. He became a successful gentleman rider, winning the amateur championship three times and piloting Reynoldstown to victory in the 1936 Grand National despite losing both his whip and an iron. After resigning from the army he turned professional and won several races before a near-fatal fall at Ludlow in 1939 fractured his skull and rendered him unconscious for a month. He then turned to training, operating a small establishment at Delamere House in Lambourn and winning eighteen races before the outbreak of war.

In 1944 Walwyn purchased Saxon House Stables in Upper Lambourn and in 1946–7 he took the first of three successive National Hunt trainers' titles. For a number of years he was also a successful flat race trainer. Much of his early success over jumps and hurdles was with Dorothy Paget's horses. Although she had a reputation for dismissing her trainers at whim, Walwyn lasted nearly ten years and even curbed her habit of late-night phone calls and nocturnal visits to the stables. On one memorable occasion on 29 September 1948 Walwyn and jockey Bryan Marshall almost took her horses through the card at Folkestone, winning five and coming second in the last race. Ultimately he broke with Miss Paget in 1954, after having 'had enough' of her difficult behaviour (Munting, 122). His boxes did not remain empty for long. He attracted some outstanding animals, including Mill House, who in 1963 won the Cheltenham Gold Cup, the Hennessy, and the King George, and Diamond Edge, twice a Whitbread winner, in 1979 and 1981. His favourite, however, was the diminutive Mandarin who arrived in 1954 with a reputation as a poor jumper but under Walwyn's tuition won the Hennessy and King George in 1957, the King George again in blast even before they dismounted. Yet he was also quick to praise. If a jockey had ridden a good race he would be the first to say so. He rode out every day until he was sixty-six, only then choosing to accompany his horses to morning exercise in a Land Rover.

Walwyn died of bronchopneumonia and ischaemic heart disease at Saxon House on 18 February 1991, a year after retiring and handing over the running of the stables to his wife, who, with his daughter, survived him. He was appointed CVO in 1983 but probably would have been more honoured by the posthumous renaming of the Kim Muir memorial chase—the three-mile race for amateur riders on the opening day of the Cheltenham National Hunt festival—as the Fulke Walwyn challenge cup chase. A memorial service, attended by Queen Elizabeth, the queen mother, was held at the church of St Michael and All Angels, Lambourn, Berkshire, on 11 March 1991.

WRAY VAMPLEW

Sources B. Fuller, *Fulke Walwyn: a pictorial tribute* (1990) · *The Independent* (20 Feb 1991) · *The Times* (20 Feb 1991) · R. Munting, *Hedges and hurdles* (1987) · A. Lee, *Lambourn, village of racing* (1982) · P. Smyly, ed., *Encyclopaedia of steeplechasing* (1979) · *WWW*, 1991–5 · b. cert. · m. certs. · d. cert.

Likenesses photograph, 1974, Empics Sports Photo Agency, Nottingham [*see illus.*] · photograph, repro. in *The Times* · photograph, repro. in *The Independent* · photographs, repro. in Fuller, *Fulke Walwyn*

Wealth at death £393,229: probate, 24 Dec 1991, *CGPLA Eng. & Wales*

Fulke Thomas Tyndall Walwyn (1910–1991), by unknown photographer, 1974

1959, the Hennessy again in 1961, and the Cheltenham Gold Cup the following year. In 1973, following the death of Peter Cazalet, the queen mother transferred her horses to Saxon House and Walwyn went on to win 150 races for her.

Walwyn had a remarkable career. In addition to his five training titles (he won again in 1957–8 and 1963–4) his horses brought him the prestigious Hennessy and Whitbread chases seven times each, the Grand Military gold cup also seven times, the King George VI five times, the Cheltenham Gold Cup four times, the Champion Hurdle and the Scottish Grand National twice, and the Aintree Grand National once. Ironically for a man brought up near Chepstow racecourse he never won the Welsh Grand National. Overall he trained the winners of 2188 races over jumps and hurdles. To celebrate his 2000th winner Warwick racecourse held a Fulke Walwyn Day.

Walwyn lived for his horses. He understood them and treated each one of his string as an individual animal. He was a wizard with doubtful legs, had unswerving patience, and never hurried an injured horse back into serious training. His was an intuitive art, and when asked the secret of his success he always acknowledged the contributions of his staff, many of whom stayed with him for decades. The lads, he explained, were closest to the horses, and a good one could tell a trainer much about the animals for which he was responsible. Nevertheless he disliked delegation. He had infinite patience with horses, less with people, and jockeys who failed to ride to orders or who were too hard on his horses could expect a fierce

Walwyn, William (*bap.* 1600, *d.* 1681), Leveller and medical practitioner, was baptized on 17 August 1600 at Newland, Worcestershire. He was the second son of Robert Walwyn (*d.* in or before 1616) of Newland, a landed gentleman, and his second wife, Elizabeth (*d.* in or before 1659), daughter of Herbert Westphaling, bishop of Hereford, and Anne, daughter of William Barlow, bishop of Chichester. Robert Walwyn was a man of 'Repute in his Country, and of between three and four hundred pounds Annual Estate' (H. Brooke, *Charity of Church-Men*, 1649, 10).

Education and marriage William's formal education was entrusted to tutors of whom he had a poor opinion. He knew no language other than English and declared that he would have learned Latin 'but for the tediousnesse, and impertinancy of my teachers' (W. Walwyn, *Walwyns Just Defence*, 1649, 9). Although Walwyn regretted his lack of Latin he deplored learning 'which puffeth up, and makes men scornfull pedants' (ibid., 9). For his own moral breeding Walwyn honoured his parents, 'to whose exemplary virtue I owe more, then for my being' (W. Walwyn, *Fountain of Slaunder*, 1649, 1).

In 1619 Walwyn was bound apprentice to a London silk merchant. For seven years he lived with his master in Paternoster Row, during which he was trained as a weaver. Released from his articles, on 17 April 1627 he married Anne, daughter of William Gundell, a chandler in the London parish of St James Garlickhythe. The Walwyns lived in the parish until 1643, remaining in the Thames Street house of Anne's father for at least six years. The parish register records many baptisms and burials of sons and daughters. In separated and revealing statements Walwyn

William Walwyn (*bap.* 1600, *d.* 1681), by Robert White

wrote: 'I have been married 21 years and have had almost 20 Children'; nine pages later he states that in all the years he and his wife have lived together, 'I cannot say she enjoyed a week together in good health' (W. Walwyn, *Fountain of Slaunder*, 2, 11). The parish register records that soon after his marriage Walwyn became a master weaver, that he was a vestryman in the church, and that by August 1632 he was a merchant and member of the Merchant Adventurers' Company. In 1643 the Walwyns moved to Moorfields, north of the City wall, where Walwyn maintained his family 'in a middle and moderate but contentful condition' (Brooke, *Charity of Church-Men*, 11). Humphrey Brooke, Walwyn's son-in-law, who lived with the family for eight years, wrote with admiration of Walwyn's gentle kindness, describing a loving marriage and family. 'The most of my recreation', said Walwyn, 'being a good Book, or an honest and discursing Friend' (Walwyn, *Fountain of Slaunder*, 22).

Wide reading enlarged Walwyn's concerns and convictions. He studied theologians, classical works, and humane writers, particularly Montaigne, whose inclusive tolerance enduringly attracted Walwyn. He considered the Bible 'the Book of Books' (Brooke, *Charity of Church-Men*, 5), and his principal guide was the New Testament. Walwyn acknowledged that his critical judgement developed slowly. In his first signed tract he recalled his long inability to judge without the approbation of authors and teachers he admired. The scriptures, 'taken in singly, and void of glosse' came to his assistance (W. Walwyn, *Whisper in the Eare*, 1646, 3), and liberated by 'that pearle in the field, free justification by Christ alone; I became master of what I heard, or read' (Walwyn, *Walwyns Just Defence*, 10).

Religious and political liberty Walwyn's conversion from the predestinarian doctrine of Calvinism to belief in free grace, accepting love, and inner peace led to his commitment to unlimited religious freedom. He observed the beliefs and practices of various sectaries and concluded that religious diversity was inevitable: as long as knowledge was imperfect, 'men must differ' (W. Walwyn, *A Parable*, 1646, 4).

Religious conviction, Walwyn believed, was reached in two ways: reason and divine revelation. Jesus and his apostles used 'no meanes but argument and perswasion to alter or controle' the views of the Sadducees (W. Walwyn, *Good Counsell to All*, 1644, 86). At the same time Walwyn recognized the limits of reason. That there was a God or that the scriptures were the word of God, 'I have not believed them so to be, by force of any argument I have either heard or read' (W. Walwyn, *A Still and Soft Voice*, 1647, 12). These truths were disclosed by God's revelation. Whether attained by revelation or reason, religious convictions were to be respected and accepted. It was the greatest of sins, Walwyn contended, to compel a man to profess beliefs of which he was not persuaded: to 'beleive as the Synod would have us … [is to] become, as said an honest man, not the Disciples of Christ, but of the Synod' (W. Walwyn, *The Compassionate Samaritane*, 2nd edn, 1644, 42–3).

Walwyn's advocacy of religious liberty was rooted in his belief that it was the way of Jesus. No injunction was ever 'given by Christ or his Apostles for the extirpation of the Romans or any others that denyed our God' (W. Walwyn, *A Demurre to the Bill*, 1646, 4). Between 1641 and January 1646 Walwyn published seven anonymous tracts that contended for inclusive liberty of conscience and particularly urged toleration of sectaries. The tracts indicate that the writer was not a sectary but spoke on behalf of 'harmlesse people' whose proponent he became 'after much inquiry and examination of their Tenets, and practice' (W. Walwyn, *The Compassionate Samaritane*, 2nd edn, 64–5). No bounds could be set to toleration, not even to one 'whose mind is so mis-informed as to deny a Deity' (W. Walwyn, *Toleration Justified*, 1646, 9). Walwyn's early appeals for unrestricted toleration were 'very hazardable' (Brooke, *Charity of Church-Men*, 11), provoking widespread fear and opposition. It is understandable that they were published anonymously.

Walwyn's political convictions, like his commitment to religious liberty, were inspired by his belief that love was the heart of true religion and that it was possible to serve God only by loving and serving our neighbours. 'I am one', he wrote, 'that do truly and heartily love all mankind … it is from this disposition in me, that I have engaged my self in publick affairs, and from no other' (Walwyn, *Whisper in the Eare*, 2, 3). With the outbreak of civil war Walwyn found his political cause. In November 1642, three months after the war began, he was appointed the Vintry ward member of a committee to collect assessments to support the war. His second tract, published the same month, carried a political message as well as a plea for toleration. Avowedly written to expose 'cunning adversaries' who wished to divide good men religiously, with equal vigour the tract assailed those who would 'take away our courages and dull our resolutions by commending peace' which was of no value if unaccompanied by 'liberty which we may now if we will our selves obtaine' (W. Walwyn, *Some Considerations*, 1642, 4, 13–14).

Throughout the first civil war Walwyn was involved with sectaries and political radicals at Salters' Hall, in London, and he encountered John Lilburne on 19 July 1645 when Walwyn and a deputation came from the hall to accuse Speaker Lenthall of correspondence with royalists and the king. Lilburne, as often, was at Westminster to answer charges about illicit tracts. He promptly joined Walwyn's group and was taken into custody the same day. Walwyn came to Lilburne's defence in a tract which conjoined the biblical roots of his political beliefs with his understanding of natural law: 'the common Law of equitie and justice' (W. Walwyn, *Englands Lamentable Slaverie*, 1645, 5). Addressing Lilburne, Walwyn stated that the difference between them in religion (Lilburne was a separatist and Calvinist) in no way diminished Walwyn's respect for Lilburne's 'undaunted resolution' in defence of liberty, but he chided Lilburne for his reliance on Magna Carta. Magna Carta wrested abusive laws 'out of the pawes' of kings, but 'that messe of pottage' should not be extolled as the birthright of the people. The liberty that Lilburne claimed was 'as due you as the ayre you breathe'; it was as unnatural for a man to testify against himself 'as to urge a man to kill himselfe' (ibid., 1, 4, 5). Walwyn's concepts were more advanced than Lilburne's and his intellect was more profound, but he was captivated by the younger man's purpose and courage, and with Richard Overton they led those who would be called Levellers.

Religious freedom was a cornerstone of the birthrights that became the heart of the Leveller programme. Walwyn's *Toleration Justified* was the first of many tracts that he published during the religious controversy that flooded the presses in 1646. Walwyn recalled the year as a time when, while parliament's army was victorious,

> there brake forth here about London a spirit of persecution; whereby private meetings were molested, & divers pastors of congregations imprisoned, & all threatned; Mr. Edwards, and others, fell foule upon them, with his Gangreen after Gangreen, slander upon slander. (Walwyn, *Walwyns Just Defence*, 2)

Walwyn's five replies to Thomas Edwards are among his most attractive pamphlets. Edwards's relentless censure of proponents of toleration—which included direct attacks on Walwyn as 'a desperate dangerous man, a

Seeker and Libertine' (T. Edwards, *The Second Part of Gangraena*, 1646, 26)—were countered by Walwyn's steady appeals to reason, flashes of wit and irony, and ultimate reliance on love. The first reply, with the softly subtle title *A Whisper in the Eare of Mr. Thomas Edwards*, is the first tract that Walwyn published over his own name.

Leveller leader The Levellers were the only proponents of representative democracy in revolutionary England and until 1647 they invariably appealed to the House of Commons for implementation of their proposals. In February 1645, replying to William Prynne's proposal for a national religion, Walwyn wrote that liberty of conscience was beyond the regulation of any elected body: 'the people of a Nation in chusing of a Parliament cannot confer more than that power which was justly in themselves … therefore no man can refer matters of Religion to any others regulation' (W. Walwyn, *A Helpe to the Right Understanding*, 1645, 4). In October *England's Lamentable Slaverie*'s defence of birthrights added secular rights beyond the power of parliament. Seven months later, in May 1646, *A Word in Season* praised parliament as the guardian of the people's interests and in June *The Just Man in Bonds* reiterated faith in the Commons as Walwyn urged them to free Lilburne from his imprisonment by the Lords. Lilburne was not released, and in the first week of July, Overton, with some assistance from Walwyn, released a wider appeal: *A Remonstrance of Many Thousand Citizens*.

A Remonstrance was the first of the great Leveller petitions—and the first comprehensive statement of Leveller goals. Addressed 'to their owne House of Commons', the manifesto reminds members that they hold their trust as representatives of the sovereign people. Amid harsh denunciations of kingship and the Lords, demands emerge: absolute religious freedom; a press free to all; an end to monopolies and discriminatory taxes; unjust laws reformed in 'agreement with common equity, and right reason'; kings—'the continuall Oppressours of the Nation'—and the House of Lords abolished (R. Overton and W. Walwyn, *A Remonstrance*, 1646, title, 5, 15).

A Remonstrance fractured an alliance between the Levellers and Independents. In May, John Goodwin's congregation had contributed 50s. toward the second printing of Walwyn's *Word in Season*, which Lilburne distributed in Westminster Hall. After *A Remonstrance* was published, two petitions were suppressed because 'Goodwins people, and some other of the Independent Churches' contended that it was 'against the season'. At the same time a 'most shamefull aspertion' was dispersed about Walwyn, who believed that a committee of Goodwin's people was formed to discover 'whatsoever I had said, that might tend to my disparagement' (Walwyn, *Walwyns Just Defence*, 2–3). Independents concluded that the most dangerous Leveller was 'Mr William Walwyn, who (as the Serpent that deceived our first Parents was more subtle then any beast of the field which the Lord God made) is much more crafty then the rest of his brethren' (J. Price, *Walwins Wiles*, 2nd edn, 1649, 2).

From August 1646 until November 1647 Walwyn played

the leading role in the co-ordination of the Levellers as a distinct party with a programme and an organization to advance it. Overton had been arrested five weeks after the publication of *A Remonstrance*; like Lilburne he remained in custody until autumn of 1647. Neither Lilburne nor Overton was silenced while in gaol, but the organization and promotion of petitions were the work of Walwyn. The petitions were primarily manifestoes designed to publicize demands and bring dissidents together. Walwyn later denied 'that I, or any that I ever knew, petitioned for such things as we did hope the Parliament would not grant', although he conceded that 'we had cause to doubt' that the parliament would agree (Walwyn, *Walwyns Just Defence*, 5).

Between March and early June 1647 Walwyn advanced four petitions addressed to the Commons. The first, the 'large petition' (W. Walwyn, *Gold Tried in the Fire*, 1647, A1), which Walwyn subsequently implied was his work, was a response to rising harassment by high presbyterians in the city. Walwyn's principal allies were General Baptists who gave a lead to other sectaries who provided steady support for the four appeals. The large petition (March 1647) presented a programme for the reforms demanded in the 1646 *Remonstrance*: an end to any negative voice for the Commons; comprehensive law reform published in English; speedy justice and humane treatment of prisoners; dissolution of all monopolies; unlimited religious freedom, and abolition of tithes. Printed copies of the petition were circulated and on 15 March two advocates of the appeal were imprisoned. On the 20th a second petition was presented that asserted the right of petition and demanded that the prisoners be released and the first petition received. On 20 May a third petition again protested the arbitrary arrests and again asked for the right to present the large petition. The house ordered the three petitions burnt.

Meetings with Oliver Cromwell and City Independents alarmed by the growing power of the high presbyterians were followed by a fourth petition 'of many thousands' (Walwyn, *Gold Tried in the Fire*, 11)—'the last and most sharp of any' (Walwyn, *Walwyns Just Defence*, 5)—that conjoined grievances of Levellers, Independents, and opponents of summary disbandment of the New Model Army. On 2 June the petition was laid aside by the Commons. Within a fortnight Walwyn reprinted all the petitions with a preface that recounted their history and concluded that there was no good 'at all to be expected from those that burn such Petitions as these' (Walwyn, *Gold Tried in the Fire*, A2v).

The final petition included a demand for a response 'unto all the just and reasonable desires of your Commanders, Officers, & Souldiers' (Walwyn, *Gold Tried in the Fire*, 12), and the publication of *Gold Tried in the Fire* exposed Walwyn's disillusionment with parliament and his move toward the army as the rising political power. Walwyn subsequently wrote that he 'perswaded' Cromwell to join the regiments at Newmarket in early June and that when army headquarters moved to Reading a month later he 'was by very eminent persons of the Army, sent for to

Reading, to be advised withall touching the good of the people' (Walwyn, *Walwyns Just Defence*, 6). In addition to 'eminent persons' (ibid.) it is probable that Walwyn met with regimental agitators who, on 6 July, presented Lord-General Fairfax with a paper protesting the imprisonments of Lilburne and Overton. Walwyn's influence was also discernible when the army's general council assembled on 16 July. Agitators immediately submitted a 'Representation' that called for a march on London unless parliament responded to demands that included the release and indemnification of all 'illegally committed' prisoners (Firth, 1.171).

Walwyn's accord with senior officers and Independents collapsed in August. The army entered London and Walwyn and his allies journeyed to headquarters to urge Fairfax to put the Tower, City, and borough under the control of citizens rather than regiments. Fairfax decided otherwise, siding with the City Independents. Harsh attacks on Walwyn again circulated and the 'great falling out amongst our Friends and theirs in London' (Walwyn, *Walwyns Just Defence*, 7) extended to grandee officers who, 'notwithstanding their glorious March through London', had utterly neglected 'the prerogative Prisoners in the Tower, New-gate, and elsewhere' (J. Lilburne and others, *The Second Part of Englands New-Chaines*, 1649, 4).

The concurrence of Levellers and army radicals that was indicated at Reading played a major role in the general council that began at Putney on 28 October. The meeting was prompted by *The Case of the Army Truly Stated*, which was presented to Fairfax on 18 October. It is unlikely that Walwyn had any part in the drafting of the patchy text, but shortly after the general council convened Walwyn's hand can be detected in the *Agreement of the People* that all but replaced the prolix *Case* during the debates. Under 1000 words overall, the substance of the *Agreement* was common to all Leveller penmen but the lucid phrasing of four concise articles and the eloquence of the preamble and conclusion leave little doubt that the final draft was Walwyn's work. Inflammatory demands were avoided and the first three articles concerned the redistribution of parliamentary seats, dissolution of the present parliament, and biennial elections. The heart of the Leveller programme was the final article, which enumerated five rights beyond the power of parliament: freedom of religion; freedom from conscription; freedom from questions about conduct during the war unless excepted by parliament; equality before the law; just laws, not destructive to the people's well-being. 'These things', stated the conclusion, 'we declare to be our native Rights, and therefore are agreed and resolved to maintain them' (*An Agreement of the People*, 1647, 5).

Walwyn took no part in the debates at Putney and no known part in the failed November mutiny to establish *An Agreement* by force. It is probable, however, that he participated in the November campaign to secure signatures in support of *An Agreement*, which became a propaganda device. After the turn of the year the party structure evinced during his petitioning campaign the previous spring was revealed, but Walwyn escaped notice in contemporary accounts of Leveller activities and he apparently published nothing during the first seven months of 1648.

The violence of the second civil war roused Walwyn to ill-considered anger against parliament and senior officers. *The Bloody Project* of August 1648 advanced from the (unfair) premise that the war was the 'causelesse' design of 'Grandee Factions' to a denunciation of the deaths of thousands who had never been told the goals for which they were fighting. How Walwyn would have dealt with royalist forces that initiated the war to defeat parliament and its army was not revealed. Walwyn's desire for an exposition of purpose was not unreasonable, and his harsh criticism of erstwhile allies was followed by reiteration of the Leveller programme. In the postscript Walwyn's appeal for reconciliation advanced sensible compromises including one solution that would be instituted in 1689: 'If the Peace of the Nation cannot be secured without the Restauration of the King, let it be done … and provide against his mis-government for the future; let his power be declared and limited by Law' (W. P. Gent [W. Walwyn], *The Bloody Project*, 1648, title-page, 16).

With the return of peace the Levellers led the way for a new settlement. In November, Walwyn was one of four Levellers on the committee of sixteen established to draw up a constitution. At Windsor the Levellers and Henry Marten prepared a working draft while the army marched to London to 'breake up the Parliament'—which, wrote Lilburne, 'was very much opposed by M. Walwyn, and many reasons he gave against their march to London at all' (J. Lilburne, *The Legall Fundamentall Liberties*, 1649, 34). The 'many reasons' (ibid.) may have included fear of further violence; there is no indication of how Walwyn would have managed a parliamentary majority poised to surrender to the king. In London, the committee of sixteen completed a draft agreement that prescribed biennial parliaments and a council of state, extended the franchise and reapportioned house seats. Eight explicit rights were reserved to the people, including equal justice under law and the free practice of religion for anyone professing Christianity. The text was presented to the council of officers at Whitehall on 11 December.

Walwyn and John Wildman attended at least one council debate after Lilburne withdrew and published his version of the second *Agreement*, and their absence from Leveller activities thereafter suggests a division within the Leveller leadership. Walwyn's withdrawal is explicable. With the end of the second war his innate optimism reappeared as he worked for an acceptable settlement. In April he concluded that the officers' *Agreement*:

> although in many things short … of what is necessary for the good of the Commonwealth, … yet, had it been put in execution, we should scarcely have interrupted the proceedings thereof, since therein is contained many things of great and important concernment to the Commonwealth. (W. Walwyn, *A Manifestation*, 1649, 7)

The Levellers were silent during the trial and execution of the king and the establishment of the republican Commonwealth, but on 28 March, four days after the appearance of *The Second Part of Englands New-Chaines Discovered*, the new government arrested Lilburne, Overton, Thomas Prince, and Walwyn. Lilburne was astonished that Walwyn was included, 'he having for some moneths by past … never bin at any of our meetings, where such things were managed' (J. Lilburne and others, *The Picture of the Councel of State*, 1649, 2). Walwyn ultimately concluded that his arrest had been incited by adversaries in John Goodwin's congregation. Less than three weeks before his seizure Walwyn had published harsh attacks on the Independents, questioning their lack of 'true piety or reall Christian vertue' (W. Walwyn, *The Vanitie of the Present Churches*, 1649, 23). Three weeks after he was imprisoned a vicious attack, principally if not solely authored by John Price, a lay preacher in Goodwin's church, described Walwyn as skilled in 'deluding, cozening and deceiving a plain and honest generation', a man of 'Atheisticall and blasphemous opprobries' who contended that 'it would never be well untill all things were common' (J. Price, *Walwins Wiles*, 1649, 3, 9, 13).

Walwyn's decency and charity belie the monster described in *Walwins Wiles*. At the same time Walwyn's portrayal of himself as an artless innocent is unsupported by his writings or activities. He was, as he contended, a believer in absolute religious freedom and the power of reason. He was, as his son-in-law Brooke stated, a good and gentle man who treasured his quiet family life yet felt compelled to work for the liberties of all men. He was also a shrewd politician. Independents were right about his skilful use of petitions. Conclusions about his economic beliefs are risky. Walwyn insisted that 'turning the world upside down' was 'not a work I ever intended' (Walwyn, *Walwyns Just Defence*, 24), but he never denied that his ideal state included economic as well as political and legal justice. As early as 1643 Walwyn praised the sharing practices of early Christians when 'the multitude of beleevers had all things common' (W. Walwyn, *The Power of Love*, 1643, A4v). In 1649 he drafted *A Manifestation*, which, even as it denies any intent of 'equalling mens estates', adds that it would be injurious 'unlesse there did precede an universall assent thereunto' (W. Walwyn, *A Manifestation*, 1649, 4). Walwyn did not, like Lilburne, repudiate the communism of Gerrard Winstanley and his 'true Levellers' (J. Lilburne, *Legall Fundamentall Liberties*, 1649, 75), but there is no evidence that he supported Winstanley and in 1652 Walwyn delineated the essence of capitalism in contending for competition in a free market. He may have assisted a communal plan projected by Peter Cornelius Plockhoy in 1659, but the evidence is tenuous, and Walwyn made no known statement about economic equality after 1649.

Interregnum and Restoration By the time the four Leveller prisoners were released on 8 November 1649 the party they had created was shattered. Walwyn took the engagement of loyalty to the Commonwealth the day he left the Tower and resumed his quiet life in Moorfields. Nothing suggests that he again associated with dissidents and the only political pamphlet that he published includes an expression of confidence in the Commonwealth. *Juries Justified* was provoked by Henry Robinson's proposal to replace juries in small jurisdictions with judges named by parliament. The plan was contrary to the Leveller belief in judgment 'by twelve sworn men of the Neighbor-hood' (J. Lilburne, and others, *An Agreement of the People of England*, 1649, art. 25). In a masterful defence of a 'fundamental essential liberty' Walwyn refuted Robinson point by point as he upheld the willingness of freeborn Englishmen to serve and their ability to judge fairly, concluding that his defence probably is not necessary 'for certainly Juries cannot in time of Parliament be in any danger' (Walwyn, *Juries Justified*, 1651, 1, 14).

Five months later Walwyn presented the council of state's committee for trade and foreign affairs with a paper supporting free-traders in dispute with the Levant Company. Free trade was a basic Leveller tenet and despite his years of prosperity as a member of the Merchant Adventurers' Company, Walwyn had denounced 'the oppressive Monopoly of Merchant-adventurers' in the large petition of March 1647 (Walwyn, *Gold Tried in the Fire*, 2). His 1652 argument began with a characteristic equation of 'a publique good' with 'Common Right'—which had 'ever proved to include what hath been most proper and commodious for the Common-wealth'. From 'the ancient and continuall Claime of Right unto a generall freedome of Trade' Walwyn proceeded to an enumeration of the practical economic benefits of competition. Free trade might not immediately 'produce so many wealthy men, as have been in the same time by Companies, … yet it will produce Thousands more of able men to beare publique Charges or what other publique occasions they may be called unto'. Trade should not, *Conceptions* concluded, be restricted to companies that secured monopolies by 'a Purchase from prerogative, … the Common Enemy', but returned to the people, whose claim 'hath its foundation in Common Right' (*Writings*, 447, 451–2). Reasonable and clearly stated, Walwyn's plea did not prevail.

The summer of 1653 was filled with reports of conspiracies, and on 29 August the council of state issued an order to commit Walwyn to the Tower. No record has been found of his imprisonment or release and it is unlikely that the order was executed. There is no hint that Walwyn had any subsequent brush with officials. His name is last known in a political context during the chaos that preceded the Restoration. A Leveller tract by William Bray included Walwyn among those listed as champions of free parliaments bound to comply with 'the Fundamental Lawes and Liberties of the Nation' (W. Bray, *A Plea for the Peoples Fundamental Liberties*, 1660, 9).

Medical practitioner Some years before the Restoration, Walwyn became a medical practitioner. Precisely when this occurred is not known, but he was dispensing medications by 1654 when he wrote that he had been studying things appertaining to health for many years. Abandonment of trade as a merchant may not have been Walwyn's

decision. He had broken his oath of loyalty to the Merchant Adventurers in 1647 and it is unlikely that the company would have overlooked the attack. Whatever the reason for his move Walwyn continued to prosper and his first medical treatise stated that 'next the things of everlasting concernment' nothing had given him 'so much satisfaction in minde' as the practice of medicine (W. W. [W. Walwyn], *Spirits Moderated*, 1654, 25–6).

Walwyn was singularly qualified for the profession of lay physician. His medical judgement was grounded in his philosophy of love and his natural humanity assisted the thoughtful intelligence with which he considered the needs of the sick. Nothing, he wrote, should be given to the sick that might not safely and profitably be taken by those in health, and such 'molesters of the sick' as bleeding, purging, vomiting, sweating, and blistering ought to be 'laid asleep for ever' (W. W. Healths Student [W. Walwyn], *Physick for Families*, 1669, 6, 20). The sick should at all times be treated with kindness, quietness, and hopefulness, and be protected from 'busie talkers' and 'dejected visitants' (ibid., 1674 edn, 11). Case histories and testimonials recorded from *Healths New Store-House Opened* (1661) through four editions of *Physick for Families* suggest that Walwyn's 'Milde and pleasant' potions (Walwyn, *Spirits Moderated*, 14) were harmless and consequently achieved the customary success that follows inert treatment.

Walwyn did not immediately disparage professional physicians. His medicines were first dispensed from the Aldgate house of his physician son-in-law, Dr Humphrey Brooke, who doubtless gave Walwyn some guidance. Both men were concerned with prevention as well as cure, and Walwyn advises a sensible diet and recourse 'to the judicious and conscionable Physitian, in times of Sickess' (Walwyn, *Spirits Moderated*, 4). Fifteen years later, before vivid descriptions of 'molesters of the sick', Walwyn questioned 'the Worth or Ability of Physitians' compared with 'the Reality and Excellency of Medicines'. One practice he most harshly condemned was repeated bleeding, 'a hazard of a strange nature for Patients … upon which Death so often follows' (W. W. Healths Student, *Physick for Families*, 9–10). The title page of Walwyn's second medical tract describes him as 'Health's Student' (*Healths New Store-House Opened*, 1661, title-page), and the two editions of *Physick for Families* published in his lifetime are by 'W. W. Healths Student' (1669, A3v; 1674 edn, title-page). There is no known evidence that Walwyn used a different title for any publications.

By 1661 Walwyn's medicines were being sold at The Star in Postern Street joining Little Moorfields, the area where Walwyn had lived since 1643. Presumably the potions continued to be available at The Star through Walwyn's lifetime, including during the plague of 1665 when Walwyn moved his family to Surrey but took care that his preparations were obtainable while he was away. The 1681 posthumous edition of *Physick for Families*, 'By William Walwyn Physician', advertised the medicines for sale at the house of Richard Halford, Walwyn's son-in-law, of Finsbury, Little Moorfields, who stated that he had assisted Walwyn 'for many years' and possessed 'all his Secrets and Receipts' (*Physick for Families*, 1681 edn, title-page, last page verso of unpaged index).

Walwyn died in January 1681 and was buried on the 16th of that month at St Giles Cripplegate, London. Halford was executor of his will, which indicated that Walwyn outlived his wife and all his children. The will named two sons-in-law and four grandchildren, and bequests of £200 each to a son-in-law and three granddaughters suggest that Walwyn had no financial difficulties. The will also revealed Walwyn's inherent optimism and joyous expectation that bodily death would be followed by a life of the spirit in the presence of a loving God.

Summary Walwyn is an attractive revolutionary. Principled and perceptive, he was a clear thinker, a talented writer, and a respected adversary. Opponents who considered him the ablest of the Leveller leaders were openly dismayed by his proficiency in framing and managing petitions promoting the Leveller programme. More enduring than his work with petitions are Walwyn's many pamphlets. Love of mankind was the source of his commitment to the rights of all people and his bold proposals were unsurpassed. Unqualified freedom of religion; equal justice; representative governments elected by the sovereign people; an end to harsh and futile treatments for the sick—all these Walwyn advocated in readable prose distinguished by the probity of the writing as well as the humanity of the proposals. Walwyn believed everything he wrote, which gives his works an integrity illuminated by his ability to present radical solutions with civility and conviction.

Walwyn's writings are as revealing of his character as of his intellectual depth and literary skill. Sometimes subtle, often optimistic, and always purposeful, he was as concerned with the individuals whose rights he defended as with their abstract liberties. The gentle goodness and loving family life described by his son-in-law are compatible with Walwyn's avoidance of public notice, rejection of destructive tactics of any kind, and belief that men should follow the golden rule—'whatsoever ye would that men should do unto you, that do you unto them'—the 'rule of reason and pure nature' (W. Walwyn, *Toleration Justified*, 1646, 14). As long as men were imperfect, contended Walwyn, they would differ, and all differences should be considered by rules of reason: 'There being nothing that maintaines love, unity and friendship in families, Societies, Cities, Countries, Authorities, Nations; so much as a condescension to the giving, and hearing, and debating of reason' (Walwyn, *Fountain of Slaunder*, 18).

BARBARA TAFT

Sources *The writings of William Walwyn*, ed. J. R. McMichael and B. Taft (1989) • T. Habington, *A survey of Worcestershire*, ed. J. Amphlett, 2 vols., Worcestershire Historical Society (1895–9), vol. 2 • W. Schenk, *The concern for social justice in the puritan revolution* (1948), chap. 3 • L. Harder and M. Harder, *Plockhoy from Zurik-zee* (1952) • L. Mulligan, 'The religious roots of William Walwyn's radicalism', *Journal of Religious History*, 12 (1982–3), 162–79 • W. Haller, ed., *Tracts on liberty in the puritan revolution*, 3 vols. (1933–4), vol. 1 • W. Haller and G. Davies, eds., *The Leveller tracts, 1647–1653* (1944) • D. M. Wolfe, ed., *Leveller manifestoes of the puritan revolution* (1944) • G. E. Aylmer,

ed., *The Levellers in the English revolution* (1975) • A. L. Morton, ed., *Freedom in arms* (1975) • T. C. Pease, *The Leveller movement* (1916) • J. Frank, *The Levellers* (1955) • A. L. Morton, *The world of the Ranters: religious radicalism in the English revolution* (1970), chap. 6 • P. Gregg, *Free-born John: a biography of John Lilburne* (1961) • *CSP dom.*, 1649–54 • *The Clarke papers*, ed. C. H. Firth, 4 vols., CS, new ser., 49, 54, 61–2 (1891–1901), vols. 1 and 2 • *IGI* • parish register and vestry minutes, St James Garlickhythe, GL • parish register, Newland, Worcester, 17 Aug 1600, Worcs. RO [baptism] • parish register, St Giles Cripplegate, 16 Jan 1681, GL [burial]

Likenesses R. White, engraving, NPG [*see illus.*] • engraving, repro. in W. Walwyn, *Physick for families*, new edn (1681), frontispiece

Wealth at death moderate: *Writings of William Walwyn*, ed. McMichael and Taft

Walzer, Richard Rudolf (1900–1975), classical scholar and orientalist, was born on 14 July 1900 in Berlin, son of Max Walzer, a Jewish businessman of modest means, and his wife, Elfriede, *née* Mannheim. On leaving the Werner Siemens Realgymnasium in 1918, he began to study medicine and Hebrew, but very soon upon attending a series of lectures by Ulrich von Wilamowitz-Moellendorff in the summer of 1919, he decided to learn Greek and devote himself to classical studies. He would later recall how Wilamowitz used to describe the classical scholar as someone who 'must try to acquire an absolute mastery of the language on all its levels', and that there was 'no escaping from this rule and no short-cut. But apart from this, there should be no limits to his interest' ('S. M. Stern: In Memoriam', *Israel Oriental Studies*, 2, 1972, 14). This is a characterization of which Walzer himself was a distinguished illustration.

The subject of Walzer's doctoral dissertation, *Magna moralia und Aristotelische Ethik* (1927; published in an expanded version in 1929) was however determined by Werner Jaeger's *Aristoteles* (1923) and his *privatissima* on the *Nicomachean Ethics*, given in 1924–5. Against the then prevalent thesis of Hans von Arnim that the *Magna moralia* was the oldest of the three Aristotelian works on ethics, Walzer endeavoured to show that it was not by Aristotle at all but had originated in the school of Theophrastus. Subsequent scholarship almost unanimously followed him in this conclusion.

Walzer's *Habilitationsschrift* of 1932, *Studien zur Einheit des Herodoteischen Geschichtswerkes*, remained unpublished. By then, he had already taken up Arabic studies and was collaborating with such leading German orientalists as G. Bergsträsser (then in Munich) and H. Ritter (then in Istanbul). The title of Walzer's *Antrittsvorlesung* of the same year, *Klassische Altertumswissenschaft und Orientalistik* (published in *Zeitschrift der Deutschen Morgenländischen Gesellschaft*, 86, 1933, 153–69) outlined the programme which would remain at the core of his scholarly work for the rest of his life: the tradition of Greek thought in Arabic, and the recovery from Arabic translations of works lost in the original Greek.

Walzer taught as a *privatdozent* in Berlin for a year before being dismissed from his post in 1933 while on a visit to Italy with his wife, Sofie, daughter of Bruno Cassirer, whom he had married in 1927. She was a fine connoisseur of impressionist painting. Warned by friends that it was not safe to return home, they remained in Rome until 1938, when the situation in Italy, too, became dangerous for Jews. During that period Walzer published a collection of the fragments of Aristotle's lost dialogues (1934) and prepared an edition of the fragments of Heraclitus (published in 1939). His Arabic and Islamic studies were pursued in close collaboration with C. A. Nallino and G. Levi della Vida.

Upon leaving Italy for England, Walzer found a permanent home at Oxford where, with the help of Sir David Ross, he became a member of Oriel College in 1942. By then he had come to devote himself almost exclusively to medieval Islamic philosophy, though he stood in on various occasions for the regius professor of Greek, E. R. Dodds, lecturing on Plato and related subjects in ancient Greek philosophy. Before the end of the war, he was appointed lecturer in medieval philosophy (Arabic and Hebrew), and in 1950, the post of senior lecturer in late Greek and medieval Arabic philosophy was created for him in the faculty of oriental studies. He was made a reader in 1960; and in 1962 he moved from Oriel College to St Catherine's, where he became a professorial fellow.

Walzer's publications during those years broke much new ground. Especially noteworthy are his contributions to *Plato Arabus* (al-Farabi, *De Platonis philosophia*, 1943, and Galen, *Compendium Timaei Platonis*, 1951) and his studies on Galen, above all his *Galen on Jews and Christians* (1949), which has remained a model of how to interpret fragments of Greek philosophy transmitted in the world of Islam, and how to unravel the various transformations they had undergone before being assimilated by a different culture.

In Walzer's later years, his interests focused on the Arabic tradition's own contributions to Greek thought translated and assimilated in the world of Islam. His last great work (published posthumously in 1985), which showed his ambidextrous skills at their best, was a critical edition with extensive commentary of al-Farabi's *Views of the Citizens of the Perfect State*. While allowing for lost models in some form of late Greek Platonism, he set out to show in detail how the Muslim philosopher, in assimilating his Greek sources, created something strikingly new.

Walzer was a scholar in the best tradition of European humanism. Throughout the vicissitudes of his career, he was loyal to the ideal of a universal encyclopaedia of knowledge contributing to which he deemed a privilege rather than a duty. He died at his home, 2 Bladon Close, Oxford, on 16 April 1975. His edition of Aristotle's *Eudemian Ethics*, completed by J. M. Mingay, was published in 1991.   LUC DEITZ

Sources F. W. Zimmerman, 'Richard Walzer, 1900–1975', *Der Islam*, 53 (1976), 1–3 • D. A. Russell, 'Richard Rudolf Walzer (1902–1975)', *PBA*, 73 (1987), 705–10 • F. Wehrli, 'Richard Walzer', *Gnomon*, 48 (1976), 221–2 • S. M. Stern, A. Hourani, and V. Brown, eds., *Islamic philosophy and the classical tradition: essays presented [...] to Richard Walzer on his seventieth birthday* (1972) [incl. nearly complete work list] • Promotions-Urkunde of 14 May 1929, Humboldt-Universität, Berlin, archives • d. cert.

Archives Hebrew University, Jerusalem, working copies of his books and MSS

Likenesses photograph, *c.*1970, repro. in Stern, Hourani, and Brown, eds., *Islamic philosophy* • W. Stoneman, photograph, repro. in D. A. Russell, 'Richard Rudolf Walzer'

Wealth at death £13,024: probate, 11 July 1975, *CGPLA Eng. & Wales*

Wanamaker [*formerly* Watenmaker], **Samuel** [Sam] (1919–1993), actor and director, was born Samuel Watenmaker on 14 June 1919 in Chicago, USA, the second son of Morris Watenmaker, later Wanamaker, and his wife, Molly, *née* Bobele. His parents were first generation Russian-Jewish immigrants. It is quite possible that his stage début as a teenager in a plywood and paper replica of the Globe at the Chicago World Fair in 1934 was the cathartic experience which inspired his lifelong devotion to the Bard and brought into being the Shakespeare Globe Theatre on London's South Bank.

Like many young actors in the 1930s, Wanamaker honed his talents in summer stock (1936–9) and was fortunate to be accepted into the celebrated Goodman Theatre School in Chicago. There he was first introduced to the tenets of Stanislavsky, acquiring the realistic acting skills which stood him in good stead throughout his career. He also studied at Drake University, Iowa. In 1940 he married Charlotte Holland. They had three daughters, one of whom, Zoë, inherited the unmistakable Wanamaker 'chutzpah' and became a leading actress in England.

Wanamaker's Broadway début was as Lester Freed in the play *Cafe Crown* (1941), which was also Elia Kazan's first Broadway production. That was followed in 1942 with an appearance in *Counter-Attack*. In 1943 he joined the war effort, serving in the Pacific with the US marine battalions which captured Iwo Jima in the spring of 1945. After demobilization, his career sprang immediately back into gear. In rapid succession he appeared in *This, Too, Shall Pass* at the Belasco (1946), *Joan of Lorraine* opposite Ingrid Bergman at the Alvin (1946), and *Goodbye My Fancy* at the Morosco (1948), which he also directed. He also appeared in *Give Us This Day* (1949), an independent film which, at the time, was considered to be remorselessly left-wing, if not explicitly communist.

By this time the House Un-American Activities Committee (HUAC) was in full swing and the McCarthy era was about to trample upon many of the socially conscious, left-wing zealots in the entertainment industry. Although Wanamaker never made an appearance before the HUAC, he was radical by temperament and always politically outspoken, and was scheduled to be subpoenaed shortly before flying to England to appear in Clifford Odets's *The Country Girl* (which in its London incarnation was entitled *Winter Journey*) in 1952. Michael Redgrave and Googie Withers were also in the cast and despite the fact that both Wanamaker and Redgrave espoused the Stanislavsky system there were sizzling tensions between them which soon became hot gossip in the West End. Fully aware of the ravages the blacklist was wreaking in the United States, Wanamaker opted to remain in England and within five years had established himself both as a formidable American actor and a gifted stage director, mounting plays such as *The Shrike* (1953), *The Big Knife* (1954), *The Rainmaker* (1956), and *A Hatful of Rain* (1957), all highly charged American dramas which exemplified the 'method' style of acting which had recently gained prominence in both America and the UK. Wanamaker's presence in England provided a dynamic model of the gritty, hard-hitting acting style which was proving triumphant in both New York and Hollywood with method-trained actors such as Marlon Brando, James Dean, Rod Steiger, Julie Harris, and Kim Stanley.

Nevertheless, Wanamaker's stage productions tended to be tame revivals of American commercial successes. When he took over the New Shakespeare Theatre in Liverpool, and presumably could dictate his own repertory, his seasons included predictable items such as *Tea and Sympathy* (1957), *Cat on a Hot Tin Roof* (1957), *The Rose Tattoo* (1958), *Finian's Rainbow* (1958), and *Bus Stop* (1958). But in 1956 he staged a rollicking production of Bertolt Brecht's *The Threepenny Opera* at the Royal Court Theatre. It was as if, having been chastened by the personal calamities perpetrated by McCarthyism in his own country, Wanamaker was determined to demonstrate a guarded catholicism in his adopted country.

Wanamaker's film career, *Give Us This Day* apart, bore virtually no relation to either his personal tastes or his political convictions. It included such uncharacteristic items as *Those Magnificent Men in their Flying Machines* (1964), *Private Benjamin* (1980), *The Competition* (1980), *Irreconcilable Differences* (1983), *Raw Deal* (1985), and *Superman IV* (1986). His stage work, on the other hand, was truly illustrious, even when the play itself lacked substance. His most notable stage performance may well have been in 1959 when he played Iago to Paul Robeson's Othello at the Shakespeare Memorial Theatre in Stratford. Although his strident, dentalized diction was considered very un-Shakespearian by the critics, the performance had a savage, Chicago-gangsterish quality which was startlingly unorthodox for the period. A brief ten years later it might well have been lauded for being very 'mod' and innovative.

Once the more immediate dangers of the blacklist had subsided, Wanamaker was back in the United States involving himself both in perishable films and serial television (including *Hawaii 5-0* and *Columbo*) and appeared to be little more than a jobbing actor. But, paradoxically, during this period he gained new distinction as an opera director, mounting Michael Tippett's *King Priam* at the Coventry Theatre and the Royal Opera House, Covent Garden (1962, 1967, and 1972), followed by a spectacular *La forza del destino* (1962) at Covent Garden, and Prokofiev's *War and Peace*, which in 1973 opened in the new Sydney Opera House to great acclaim.

Whatever his qualities as an actor and a director (and they were considerable), Wanamaker's most durable and outstanding achievement was the creation of the Globe Playhouse Trust (later the Shakespeare Globe Trust) in 1971, which, after some twenty-five years, succeeded in replicating the Globe Theatre in Southwark. Actively opposed by the local council, who wished to develop the land for low-income housing, and disparaged by members of his own profession who viewed the American bardolator as 'an upstart crow' (very much as Robert Greene had Shakespeare himself), Wanamaker, despite two decades of crippling setbacks and petty antagonisms, persevered with architects, scholars, artists, and backers who shared his vision. These eventually included the duke of Edinburgh and a bevy of distinguished supporters such as Sir John Gielgud, Dame Judi Dench, and Sir Anthony Hopkins. Opened for 'Workshop' and 'Prologue' seasons in 1995 and 1996, and finally formally opened in 1997 by the queen, 'Wanamaker's Folly' quickly established itself as one of London's most irresistible attractions. It is an irony worthy of Shakespeare's own tragedies that Wanamaker died on 18 December 1993, at his home, 7 Bentinck Close, Prince Albert Road, Westminster, of prostate cancer, shortly before he could see his dream fulfilled. He was

Samuel Wanamaker (1919–1993), by Robin Mayes, 1993

survived by his wife and three daughters. A memorial service was held at Southwark Cathedral on 2 March 1994.

In 1952, when he first arrived in London as a jobbing actor, Wanamaker sought out the site of Shakespeare's Globe, expecting to see it grandiloquently memorialized. Instead, he found only a dirty plaque rammed into the wall of a Courage brewery bottling plant on a back street in Southwark. It will remain one of history's abiding ironies that the most visible tribute to England's greatest poet and playwright was created, not by a magnanimous British philanthropist, but by a Jewish player from a lowly ghetto in Chicago. He was appointed honorary CBE in 1993.   CHARLES MAROWITZ

Sources *The Times* (20 Dec 1993) · *The Times* (3 March 1994) · *The Independent* (20 Dec 1993) · *WWW*, 1991–5 · *Who's who in the theatre* · personal knowledge (2004) · private information (2004) · d. cert.
Likenesses G. Lewis, photograph, 1991, repro. in *The Independent* · R. Mayes, photograph, 1993, News International Syndication, London [*see illus.*] · photograph, repro. in *The Times* (20 Dec 1993)

Wanchese (*fl.* **1584–1586**). *See under* American Indians in England (*act. c.*1500–1609).

Wand, (John) William Charles (1885–1977), bishop of London, was born in Grantham, Lincolnshire, on 25 January 1885, the eldest of the family of three sons of Arthur James Henry Wand, a shopkeeper, at first a butcher and later a grocer, and his wife, Elizabeth Ann Ovelin Turner. His parents had both been confirmed in the Church of England, but on Sunday mornings the father played the harmonium at the Calvinist chapel, taking his sons with him. The future bishop was always to remember that he had known undiluted Calvinism from the inside.

Wand was educated at King's School, Grantham, during which period he was himself confirmed, and (with a scholarship) at St Edmund Hall, Oxford, where he graduated with a first class in theology in 1907. After a further year as a theological student at Bishop Jacob Hostel, Newcastle upon Tyne, he was ordained in 1908, and served curacies at Benwell, Northumberland (1908–11), and Lancaster (1911–14). Wand married in 1911 Amy Agnes (d. 1966), the youngest daughter of William Wiggins JP, a farmer at Watlington, Oxfordshire. They had one son and one daughter.

Wand's scholarly interests were part of the attraction which led to his appointment in 1914 as a vicar choral of Salisbury Cathedral, a post which also opened to him the opportunity of lecturing at the local theological college; but the outbreak of the First World War came soon after his arrival, and in 1915 he became an army chaplain, serving first in Gallipoli and then in France. His post at Salisbury had been kept open, but on his return in 1919 he was appointed vicar of St Mark's, Salisbury, and also resumed his lecturing at the theological college.

In 1925 Wand became fellow, dean, and tutor of Oriel College, Oxford, a post for which his capacity for business and his approachability were an ideal combination, and which had for him the great attraction of bringing him into touch with a wider world of scholarship. He published his first scholarly books at this time, notably his commentary on the epistles of Peter and Jude (1934).

In 1934, through the recommendation of St Clair G. A.

Donaldson, bishop of Salisbury, who had held the same office, he was elected archbishop of Brisbane. His arrival there was almost immediately clouded by a personal tragedy, the death when mountaineering in the Alps of his undergraduate son, for whom he had the deepest affection. To the diocese of Brisbane, and to the province of Queensland of which he was metropolitan, he brought outstanding qualities of leadership and administration, and he did much to raise the standard of the clergy. He made full use of the opportunities provided by broadcasting and journalism to address the widest possible public. When after the fall of France in the Second World War there was widespread anxiety in Australia about British policy, Wand tried to allay this by publishing a pamphlet entitled *Has Britain Let Us Down?* It was to have a wide sale, and incidentally, through the approval it received in British government circles, to influence the decision to recall him in 1943 to be bishop of Bath and Wells.

Wand's period of office there was marked by fresh energy for the reorganization which the war had made necessary, and, as a new Education Act was passed in 1944, by vigorous support for church schools. Their maintenance was dear to Wand's heart, for he had been educated in one himself. His stay in the diocese was, however, to be short; in 1945 he was nominated by Winston Churchill to succeed G. F. Fisher as bishop of London.

Wand saw it as his task in London to achieve recovery from the effects of the war. Many churches and schools had been damaged or destroyed, the clergy were fewer and beset by many problems. The diocese, with the largest population of any in England, needed considerable reorganization. Wand set out to achieve this. Some protestant groups were at first hostile to him as an acknowledged Anglo-Catholic, but his tolerance and understanding soon brought this hostility to an end.

As the new bishop, Wand began with the organization of a teaching mission throughout the diocese, and followed this up with a more directly evangelistic mission to London. As he realized, this was to be more effective in the encouragement of church people than in bringing in new members, but this was a necessary stage in the process of recovery. In the City of London, with its many redundant parish churches, a scheme for guild churches, with specialized tasks, set a new pattern. And by greater delegation of responsibility to suffragan bishops, Wand began a process that was to develop further after his episcopate. In the wider affairs of the church he took a full part, notably in the ecumenical movement, and he was chairman of commissions on artificial insemination and on nullity.

As Wand had planned, he retired from his bishopric at the age of seventy, but to his delight he was appointed as a canon of St Paul's, where he became cathedral treasurer. He was appointed KCVO in the same year (1955). His canonry gave him sufficient leisure for reading and writing, and an opportunity, which he valued highly, to preach and take part in the services of the cathedral.

Sturdy in appearance and genial in manner, Wand always combined friendliness with dignity. He was a man of wide, rather than specialized, scholarship. He spoke of reading and writing as his 'favourite hobbies', and published a number of books, these often being based on courses of lectures he had given, especially in Lent. His wide-ranging theological and historical interests made him a suitable appointment as editor, from 1956 to 1968, of the *Church Quarterly Review*.

Wand was admitted to the privy council in 1945. He had travelled widely, and received doctorates on both sides of the Atlantic: from Oxford (1934); Columbia (STP, 1947); Toronto (STD, 1947); Ripon, USA (DLitt, 1949); King's College, London (DD and honorary fellow, 1955; fellow, 1956); and Western Ontario (DD, 1957). He was also an honorary fellow of St Edmund Hall and Oriel College. He was dean of the chapels royal (1945–55), prelate of the Order of the British Empire (1946–55), and prelate emeritus from 1957 to his death. In 1969 he retired to a cottage at Maplehurst, Sussex; he died at the College of St Barnabas, Lingfield, Surrey, on 16 August 1977.   HAROLD RILEY, *rev.*

Sources *The Times* (17 Aug 1977) · W. Wand, *Changeful page: the autobiography of William Wand* (1955) · personal knowledge (1986) · A. Hastings, *A history of English Christianity, 1920–1990*, 3rd edn (1991) · *CGPLA Eng. & Wales* (1977)
Archives LPL, papers | FILM BFI NFTVA, documentary footage · BFI NFTVA, news footage · BFI NFTVA, record footage
Wealth at death £16,197: probate, 11 Nov 1977, *CGPLA Eng. & Wales*

Wandesford, Christopher (1592–1640), politician and administrator, was born at Bishop Burton, near Beverley, Yorkshire, on 24 September 1592 and baptized there on 18 October. He was the son of Sir George Wandesford (1573–1612), landowner, of Kirklington, Yorkshire, and Catherine, daughter of Ralph Hansby of Gray's Inn. He attended school at Well, together with his kinsman Thomas Wentworth, later earl of Strafford, and matriculated from Clare College, Cambridge, in Michaelmas 1610. He was admitted to Gray's Inn on 1 November 1612, but the death of his father that year forced him to attend to an estate much of which was leased out at uneconomic rents and burdened with debts. Prudent management of his financial resources enabled him to free the estate from wardship, provide for his brothers and sisters, and, by 1630, to spend at least £1600 in improvements to his seat at Kirklington. Wandesford is said by Lodge to have married, as his first wife, a daughter of William Ramsden of Byrom, Yorkshire, but this seems highly unlikely. On 22 September 1614 he married Alice (1592–1659), only daughter of Sir Hewett Osborne. She was sister to Sir Edward Osborne, vice-president, under Wentworth, of the council of the north. They had seven children, five of whom survived to adulthood, including Alice [see Thornton, Alice], whose autobiography presents the marriage as a very happy one.

MP for Yorkshire Wandesford sat for Aldborough, Yorkshire, in the parliaments of 1621 and 1624, and probably gained a seat at Richmond in 1625 and 1626 through his friendship with Wentworth; in 1626 he appears to have considered challenging Sir John Savile and his son Thomas for a county seat. In July 1625 he was placed on the commission of the peace for the North Riding. Wandesford was particularly active in the 1626 parliament, taking a leading role in the Commons' attack on the duke of Buckingham, handling the especially dangerous charge of administering medicine to James I. In consequence he was removed from the commission of the peace and issued with a privy seal loan demand of £100. He remarked to Wentworth that 'when the privy seals cum, I think itt will be the proportion only that shall trouble me' (Strafford papers, 16/242), but his willingness to accept that the king might be entitled to some form of non-parliamentary revenue did not extend to the forced loan. His refusal to pay did not result in imprisonment, in contrast to his kinsmen Wentworth and Sir George Radcliffe, although he kept them company in London for part of the summer of 1627. By the autumn he was anticipating the calling of another parliament, making preparations to keep Wentworth's 'syde warme by the bar agayne' (Strafford papers, 20/262), and asking his friend to use his influence with Coryton and Seymour to secure him a west country seat in case he should fail in his native county. His letters to Wentworth from the autumn and winter of 1627–8 reveal his hopes for a more moderate stance by the Commons: 'if the howse doe mete, I pray God send them the discrete mixture of patience and curradge to apply the proper cure to thess bleeding wounds'. What was needed was a more circumspect approach:

> The miseryes, or injuryes (call them as you please) fallen upon perticuler persons will not possess them so totally as to make them neglect the prosecution of the whole; save the ship first and then punish the neglect of thoss mariners that brought her into hazard. (Strafford papers, 16/261; 20/262)

Wandesford sat for Thirsk in 1628, through Wentworth's influence with the Bellasis family. On 5 June, following the king's demand that the Commons avoid any business that might lay scandal upon the state, he supported the remonstrance with the complaint that 'we are taxed with puritanism, faction, popularity' (Johnson, Keeler, and others, 4.124). Throughout the session he played a less prominent role than in 1626, when Wentworth had been absent, but Wentworth's removal to the Lords before the next session placed Wandesford once again in an important position. On 2 March 1629 he spoke against Holles's proposal that no merchant be permitted to pay tonnage and poundage, having argued, together with John Pym, for a more moderate approach to the problem.

Wentworth's appointment as president of the council of the north brought benefits for Wandesford, the first being his restoration to the commission of the peace in December 1628. The following year he was added to the commission of the peace for the West Riding and the northern commission for compounding with recusants, and he was successful in his efforts to replace Sir Thomas Hoby as chief seneschal of the manor of Ripon. In 1630 he was granted further northern offices, including the posts of deputy bailiff of Richmondshire and deputy constable of Richmond and Middleham castles. He was rumoured to have been offered the ambassadorship to Spain in 1630, and to be a candidate for the post of master of the wardrobe in March 1632, but he took up office in Ireland in 1633 following Wentworth's appointment as lord deputy. Wandesford explained why he had rejected the 'private and countrey life' which he recommended to his son:

> my Affection to the Person of my Lord Deputy, purposing to attend upon his Lordship as near as I could in all Fortunes, carryed me along with him whithersoever he went ... no Hopes, no Promises, indeed, no Assurance of a greater Fortune, could have tempted me from the security of my own Retiredness, but the Comfort I took in his Friendship and Conversation.   (Wandesford, 62–3)

Irish official Wandesford had assisted Wentworth with his personal and political affairs since at least 1620. While living in London during the early 1620s, Wandesford had acted as Wentworth's 'ambassadour' (Wentworth to Wandesford, 30 July 1623, Strafford papers, 2.105), sending him court news and handling his business with Sir Arthur Ingram. Their surviving correspondence reveals the closeness of their friendship: during Wentworth's imprisonment in 1627 they maintained a 'wekely discourse' (Wandesford to Wentworth, 9 Sept 1627, ibid., 16.261) in which they shared their views on political developments. Wandesford was prepared to offer Wentworth frank advice and in July 1628 he informed Wentworth of the generally unfavourable response in the West Riding to his elevation to the peerage. By the early 1630s he regularly conveyed messages to Wentworth from the lord treasurer, Weston, and waited on Wentworth's other political contacts at court. Wandesford and Radcliffe formed the core of the team that Wentworth assembled in Dublin, and their devoted and capable service was emphasized by Wentworth in his reports to his political allies and colleagues.

Wandesford was sworn of the Irish privy council on 25 July 1633. He had already been granted the mastership of the rolls in Ireland on 17 May, initially for the duration of Wentworth's deputyship, a restriction that might suggest that the king initially harboured doubts about a man who had been instrumental in the attempted impeachment of Buckingham. In March 1634, however, the post was granted to him for life. Also in 1634 Wandesford was appointed to a small committee established to examine alleged exactions by Irish office-holders, and his seat on the court of castle chamber assisted Wentworth in his efforts to control all organs of government. In the 1634–5 parliament Wandesford was MP for Kildare, after Richard Boyle, earl of Cork, declined to secure him one of the seats that he controlled. Wandesford accompanied Wentworth to Connaught in 1635 during the lord deputy's preparations for plantation, and he served as one of the lords justices during Wentworth's two visits to England: in 1636, with Viscount Loftus, and in 1639, with Lord Dillon. He assisted the earl of Ormond in his land dispute with Sir Thomas Butler, and enjoyed good relations with John Bramhall, bishop of Derry, whose living of Elvington lay close to Kirklington. His letters to Bramhall of the late 1630s show him to have become apprehensive about the growing crisis in Scotland and its impact on the other Stuart kingdoms.

It would seem likely that Wandesford, as well as Radcliffe, was offered a knighthood in 1633, and his refusal might, as Comber suggested, have been prompted by consideration of his financial situation. Unlike Radcliffe, he did not buy into the Irish customs farm, and he seems to have relied on the profitable mastership of the rolls to purchase and invest an Irish estate. Following his death, the king issued instructions that fees payable to Irish officers be reduced and the mastership was given particular emphasis. In 1635 Wandesford bought an estate in the Naas, co. Kildare, where, during the autumn of 1636, he completed his *Book of Instructions* for his son, not published until 1777. In 1637, having sold the land to Wentworth, Wandesford acquired Castlecomer and 20,000 acres of largely undeveloped land in Idough, co. Kilkenny, known as 'Brennan's country', where he rebuilt the house, built a market town, planted woods, and founded collieries and a forge. The expulsion of the Brennans appears to have troubled Wandesford, as his will included an offer of compensation. Their claim was, however, quashed by decree in 1695 following their support for the Jacobite cause.

Lord deputy, death, and descendants Wandesford was elected MP for Kildare again in 1640. He was then appointed lord deputy on 1 April 1640, following Wentworth's elevation to the lieutenancy in January and an apparently successful parliamentary session in March during which four subsidies were voted. According to Comber, Wandesford was granted the titles Baron Mowbray and Musters and Viscount Castlecomer on his appointment as lord deputy, a mark of honour that he rejected with the remark 'Is it a fit Time for a faithful Subject to appear higher than usual when the King, the Fountain of Honours, is likely to be reduced lower than ever?' (Comber, 121–2). Wandesford's term in office was short and unpleasant. Parliament reassembled in June and he was forced to allow writs to be sent to the seven boroughs deprived of representation by Wentworth in 1635, leading to increased Old English representation in the Commons. His attempts to secure legislation confirming the plantation of Connaught failed when the bill was apparently dropped. On 13 June he was not able to prevent the Commons from rejecting the new method by which the subsidies were to be levied. In these actions Old English representatives evidently received a measure of support from protestant members. Wandesford's letter to Radcliffe, dated 12 June, expressed his anxiety at the combination of 'the Irish' with 'those of our owne partye (as we call them)' (Whitaker, *Life*, 249–50): the willingness of protestant members to entrust matters to committees on which Catholics were in the majority suggests a degree of co-operation against the administration. The lord deputy could not count on the assistance of the whole council: the absence of some on military duties was not helpful, but the remaining councillors failed to support the government wholeheartedly. Wandesford could find few to praise in his report to Radcliffe.

Parliament reassembled on 1 October and proved no less

difficult to manage than it had been in June. Wandesford's need to finance the Irish army left him with little choice but to hold parliament. He attempted to recover some of the ground lost in June in his refusal to send writs to the disputed boroughs, but the Commons put in place a new method of assessment for the three subsidies yet to be collected that would reduce their yield from an anticipated £45,000 to about £12,000 each. The orders of 20 October and 11 November on this matter were torn out of the Commons' journal by the lord deputy on the instructions of the king. Wandesford failed to prevent the house from passing the petition of remonstrance against Wentworth's administration and naming a committee to present it to the king. He prorogued parliament on 12 November and ordered the committee to remain in Ireland, but the privy council's removal of travel restrictions between the two countries enabled the committee to take the remonstrance to England. Wandesford appears to have had a very pleasant personality, lacking the abrasive, intimidatory characteristics possessed by Wentworth. In November 1640 Wentworth thought it necessary to insist, through Radcliffe, that Wandesford's 'old rule of moderate counsells will not serve his turne in cases of this extremity; to be a fine, well-natured gentleman will not doe it' (Whitaker, *Life*, 221). The same month Wandesford learned of Wentworth's imprisonment, and before the end of November he was seriously ill of a fever. He died at Dublin on 3 December 1640 and was buried there, in Christ Church, seven days later. His funeral sermon was preached by Bramhall, one of the executors of his will. According to his daughter, the Irish 'did sett up their lamentable hone, as they call it, for him in the church, which was never knowne before for any Englishman don' (*Autobiography of Mrs Alice Thornton*, 26).

Wandesford was survived by his wife who died on 10 December 1659. Their third son, Christopher (*b*. 1628), was created a baronet on 5 August 1662. He married Eleanor, daughter of Sir John Lowther, and was father of Christopher (1656–1707), politician, the second baronet, later created Viscount Castlecomer, who married Elizabeth (*d*. 1731), daughter of the Hon. George Montagu of Horton, Northamptonshire.

Their eldest son, **Christopher Wandesford**, second Viscount Castlecomer (*bap*. 1684, *d*. 1719), politician and government official, was baptized at St Margaret's, Westminster, on 2 March 1684. He was MP for St Canice in the Irish parliament in 1707 before succeeding to the peerage on the death of his father on 15 September 1707. He was appointed an Irish privy councillor in 1710 but then pursued a political career in England, sitting for Morpeth as a whig in 1710–13, and for Ripon from 1715 until his death. In 1713, with his brother-in-law Lord Newcastle and others, he founded the Hanover Club, and in May that year he spoke in parliament against a commercial clause of the treaty of Utrecht. In October 1714 George I appointed him a privy councillor and gave him the governorship of Kilkenny in September 1715. On 31 May 1715 he married the Hon. Frances, daughter of Thomas *Pelham, first Baron Pelham, and their only child, Christopher, third Viscount

Castlecomer, was born in 1717. He died at Newport Street, London, on 23 June 1719. His wife survived him, dying on 27 June 1756.   FIONA POGSON

Sources *DNB* • C. Wandesford, *A book of instructions* (1777) • T. Comber, *Memoirs of the life and death of the lord deputy Wandesford* (1778) • *The autobiography of Mrs Alice Thornton*, ed. [C. Jackson], SurtS, 62 (1875) • Strafford papers, Sheff. Arch., Wentworth Woodhouse muniments, vols. 2, 12, 16 • J. P. Cooper, ed., *Wentworth papers, 1597–1628*, CS, 4th ser., 12 (1973) • H. B. McCall, *The story of the family of Kirklington and Castlecomer* (1904) • T. D. Whitaker, ed., *The life and original correspondence of Sir George Radcliffe* (1810) • T. D. Whitaker, *A history of Richmondshire*, 2 vols. (1823), vol. 2 • J. K. Gruenfelder, 'The electoral patronage of Sir Thomas Wentworth, earl of Strafford, 1614–1640', *Journal of Modern History*, 49 (1977), 557–74 • M. Jansson and W. B. Bidwell, eds., *Proceedings in parliament, 1625* (1987) • W. B. Bidwell and M. Jansson, eds., *Proceedings in parliament, 1626*, 2–3: *House of Commons* (1992), vols. 2–3 • R. C. Johnson and others, eds., *Commons debates, 1628*, 6 vols. (1977–83), vols. 2–4 • C. Thompson, 'The divided leadership of the House of Commons in 1629', *Faction and parliament*, ed. K. Sharpe (1985), 245–84 • R. P. Cust, *The forced loan and English politics, 1626–1628* (1987) • R. Cust, 'Wentworth's "change of sides" in the 1620s', *The political world of Thomas Wentworth, earl of Strafford, 1621–1641*, ed. J. F. Merritt (1996), 63–80 • C. Russell, *Parliaments and English politics, 1621–1629* (1979) • GEC, *Peerage*, new edn • E. Cruickshanks and R. D. Harrison, 'Wandesford, Christopher', HoP, *Commons, 1690–1715*, 5.790–91 • PRO, C 231/4; C 231/5 • J. Foster, *The register of admissions to Gray's Inn, 1521–1889, together with the register of marriages in Gray's Inn chapel, 1695–1754* (privately printed, London, 1889) • Venn, *Alum. Cant.* • Rymer, *Foedera*, 3rd edn, vol. 8 • H. Kearney, *Strafford in Ireland*, 2nd edn (1989) • J. T. Cliffe, *The Yorkshire gentry from the Reformation to the civil war* (1969) • *CSP dom., 1631–3* • *CSP Ire., 1633–47* • J. Lodge, *The peerage of Ireland*, 4 vols. (1754), vol. 3 • PRO, SP 16/214/64 • *The journals of the House of Commons of the kingdom of Ireland* (1796), vol. 1 • P. Roebuck, *Yorkshire baronets, 1640–1760* (1980) • G. E. Aylmer, *The king's servants: the civil service of Charles I, 1625–1642* (1961) • *Report on manuscripts in various collections*, 8 vols., HMC, 55 (1901–14), vol. 3 • *Calendar of the manuscripts of the marquess of Ormonde*, new ser., 8 vols., HMC, 36 (1902–20), vols. 1–2 • [T. Carte], *The life of James, duke of Ormond*, new edn, 6 vols. (1851), vol. 5 • E. Rawdon, ed., *The Rawdon papers* (1819) • B. Williams, *Carteret and Newcastle* (1966) • *The Wentworth papers, 1705–1739*, ed. J. J. Cartwright (1883)

Archives Bodl. Oxf., letters to Sir George Radcliffe, MS Add. C. 286 [copies] • NL Ire., corresp. with Ormonde • Sheff. Arch., Wentworth Woodhouse Muniments, Strafford papers, corresp. with Thomas Wentworth

Likenesses portrait, exh. 1868; in possession of Alice Comber, 1904 • G. P. Harding, watercolour drawing (after portrait, 1630), NPG • portrait; in possession of Christopher, first Viscount Castlecomer, 1904

Wealth at death Yorkshire estate rent roll £1060 p.a. by 1640; Irish estate worth several thousand pounds p.a.; Wandesford's steward claimed that between Nov 1641 and April 1642 estate lost £4000 in rents and rent arrears, plus £3000 in goods and debts: Cliffe, *Yorkshire gentry*, 44; Lodge, *Peerage of Ireland*, 198

Wandesford, Christopher, second Viscount Castlecomer (*bap*. 1684, *d*. 1719). *See under* Wandesford, Christopher (1592–1640).

Wandsworth. For this title name *see* Stern, Sydney James, Baron Wandsworth (1844–1912) [*see under* Stern family (*per*. *c*.1830–1964)].

Wanklyn, (Malcolm) David (1911–1942), naval officer, was born on 28 June 1911 at The Hermitage, Alipore, India, the third of the six children of William Lumb Wanklyn (1872–

1932), engineer, and his wife, Marjorie Josephine Rawson (*b.* 1885). At Parkfield preparatory school in Haywards Heath, Sussex, he was a solemn child, and he seldom laughed in later life. He showed no enthusiasm for team games; and on expeditions when his brothers raced adventurously ahead up mountain slopes, he held back. He much preferred bird-watching, stamp collecting, and photography. Wanklyn entered the Royal Naval College, Dartmouth, in 1925 as a thirteen-year-old, having learned for his medical to conceal colour-blindness. The family dubbed him Admiral but he did not impress fellow cadets. As a fully-fledged officer he tried, dutifully, to be 'one of the boys' when the occasion demanded: on wardroom guest nights he was known to sit on his hands and, double jointedly, wrap both long legs around his neck; and he could also sing dubiously worded comic songs. He was at his ease with ratings and famously tolerant towards sailors who had over-indulged ashore. Wanklyn married Elspeth Kinloch (*b.* 1912) on 5 May 1938.

In August 1940 Wanklyn was appointed in command of the small submarine HMS *Upholder*, still building at Barrow, with a crew of three other officers and twenty-nine ratings. She had four torpedo tubes, with space for four reloads, and a 12-pounder gun. In common with other British submarines (but unlike American and German boats) the straight-running torpedoes could not be continuously pre-angled before discharge. Instead, the whole submarine had to be pointed ahead of the target, like a cumbersome four-barrelled rifle. Slipping through a screen of escorts to the right range, at the right time, on the right course for firing at a zigging target demanded skill, nerve, and a fair measure of luck.

HMS *Upholder* joined the submarine flotilla at beleaguered Malta on 14 January 1941. The prime task was to prevent supplies and reinforcements from Italy reaching Rommel's Afrika Korps. Targets were abundant—so were axis anti-submarine forces and minefields—but torpedoes had to be husbanded because nobody knew when more might reach the island. By the middle of April Wanklyn had fired thirty torpedoes for only one sure hit. His command was in jeopardy until, suddenly, he got the knack—greatly assisted by being made privy to ULTRA special intelligence of enemy movements.

From the end of April *Upholder* scored steadily, and sometimes spectacularly; but Wanklyn was aware of increasing odds against him—especially on 20 May off Sicily when the ASDIC underwater listening-set packed up, making it impossible to judge what was happening on the surface when *Upholder* was below periscope depth. Wanklyn did not consider returning to Malta for repair: important convoys were expected to emerge from the Messina Strait.

Upholder's torpedoes duly damaged a tanker at very long range on 20 May and sank another three days later. Stealing away from the ensuing mêlée with only two torpedoes remaining, Wanklyn found himself in the path of three large, fast liner-troopships surrounded by energetic destroyers. He chose the 18,000 ton *Conte Rosso*, packed with troops bound for north Africa, as his prize; but with limited ammunition remaining he needed to fire from close range to be sure of a hit. Time did not permit evasive deviations from the optimum attacking course, so he decided to act as if the enemy destroyers did not exist.

Both torpedoes struck *Conte Rosso*: 2729 soldiers and crew died with her when she sank. None of thirty-seven retaliatory depth charges exploded within the lethal 30 feet of *Upholder's* hull, but one man's nerve broke: he dashed to the lower conning-tower hatch and started to ease back the clips—a futile gesture because 20 tons of sea-pressure was keeping the upper hatch shut. Wanklyn quietly continued giving helm orders to take the boat out of trouble. The only virtue he acknowledged, reluctantly, was imperturbability; but determination was his hallmark.

In twenty-four strenuous patrols, after a disappointing début, Wanklyn sent two Italian U-boats and a destroyer to the bottom, damaged a cruiser and a destroyer, and sank or seriously damaged nineteen axis transports and supply vessels. *Upholder* failed to return from her twenty-fifth patrol: an aircraft sighted her submerged off Tripoli on 14 April 1942, and the Italian chaser *Pegaso* dropped a random but evidently fatal pattern of charges without even claiming a kill—an ironically inconsequential end for Wanklyn and his gallant company.

An unlikely hero, Wanklyn was awarded the Victoria Cross for the *Conte Rosso* action. Reserved and introspective, he did not flaunt his unusual qualities of leadership; and, even while sinking a record number of enemy vessels during the brief brilliance of his Malta-based wartime submarine command, he remained a byword for modesty.

RICHARD COMPTON-HALL

Sources J. M. Allaway, 'The hero of the Upholder': the story of Lieutenant Commander M. D. Wanklyn VC, DSO (1991) • Submarine and personnel (officers) records, Royal Naval Submarine Museum, Gosport • private information (2004) • S. Hart, Submarine Upholder (1960) • G. W. G. Simpson, Periscope view: a professional autobiography (1972) • W. S. Jameson, Submariners VC (1962) • CGPLA Eng. & Wales (1943)

Archives SOUND IWM SA, oral history interview

Likenesses H. Morley, oils, 1943 (after photographs), HMS *Dolphin*, Gosport, Hampshire

Wealth at death £1736 3s. 7d.: probate, 18 Jan 1943, CGPLA Eng. & Wales

Wanklyn, James Alfred (1834–1906), chemist, was born at Ashton under Lyne on 18 February 1834, son of Thomas Wanklyn and his wife, Ann (*née* Dakeyne), members of the Moravian Brethren. He was educated at the Moravian school of Fairfield, served an apprenticeship to Dr John Boutflower in Manchester, and became MRCS in 1856. During his apprenticeship Wanklyn began the study of chemistry at Owens College, under Edward Frankland (1825–1899). In 1857 he went to study with Frankland's mentor, Robert Bunsen, in Heidelberg; he gained his PhD in 1859. For the next three years Wanklyn was demonstrator in chemistry at Edinburgh, under Lyon Playfair. From 1862 to 1869 he held the chair of chemistry at the London Institution, and from 1877 to 1880 was lecturer in chemistry at St George's Hospital.

Wanklyn held appointments as public analyst to Buckingham, Peterborough, High Wycombe, and Shrewsbury. In 1869 he was, through the influence of Liebig, elected a corresponding member of the Royal Bavarian Academy. He was at one time a fellow of the Royal Society of Edinburgh, and a member of the Chemical Society and the Society of Public Analysts. He never married.

Wanklyn's scientific career had two phases. From 1856 until about 1868 he was viewed as one of the most promising young chemists in Britain. At Manchester and Heidelberg, Wanklyn extended Frankland's research on organometallic compounds, obtaining ethyl and methyl halides—work with significance for the then new concept of valency. He also synthesized propionic (propanoic) and acetic (ethanoic) acids. At Edinburgh he worked with Playfair on methods of determining vapour density. With other co-authors he published on aniline dyes, derivatives of mannitol, and on atomic theory. By 1870 Wanklyn had published fifty-seven papers in the *Philosophical Magazine*, the *Journal of the Chemical Society*, and the *Proceedings of the Royal Society*, many reprinted in the German journals.

From about 1868 Wanklyn worked mainly as a consulting analyst on commercial and public health matters, based first in London, and then, after 1886, in New Malden, Surrey. In June 1867 he developed the controversial 'ammonia process' of water analysis, in which water samples were treated with alkaline potassium permanganate and distilled, yielding products which Wanklyn labelled 'free' and 'albuminoid' ammonia. Though suspect both in terms of chemical theory and hygienic relevance, the process was easy to use and became the standard form of water analysis in Britain and the United States until displaced by bacteriological methods in the 1890s. It was also the basis on which Kjeldahl developed his process for the determination of organic nitrogen. Wanklyn's manual *Water Analysis* (with Ernest Chapman, co-inventor of the ammonia process) appeared in eleven editions between 1868 and 1906, and he produced manuals entitled *A Gas Engineer's Chemical Manual* (1886), *Milk Analysis* (1873, 1886), *Tea, Coffee and Cocoa* (1874), and *Arsenic* (1901). Together with his long-time associate W. J. Cooper he wrote *Bread Analysis* (1881, 1886), *Air Analysis, with an Appendix on Illuminating Gas* (1890), and *Sewage Analysis* (1899, 1905). None of these latter works was particularly successful; several of them digressed into irrelevant polemics.

Wanklyn's polemicism was indeed the bane of his later career. His main target was Frankland, who had introduced the rival 'combustion' process of water analysis in January 1868 and had criticized Wanklyn's claims for his own process. From then on, Wanklyn increasingly isolated himself from the profession, claiming that Frankland and other leaders of the Chemical Society had sabotaged his career, even hinting that they had stolen his ideas. He left the Chemical Society in 1871 and the Society of Public Analysts (of which he had been vice-president) in 1876, only two years after its foundation. While the main sources of Wanklyn's difficulties were his tactlessness and unwillingness to accept criticism, his habits of research also contributed. Even Wanklyn's early papers, though

sometimes innovative, had been criticized for speculation and a lack of completeness. He had a tendency to make assertions, insisting, for example, that albuminoid ammonia was, or bore a constant relationship to, whatever it was that was harmful in water. In later years Wanklyn devoted much time to defending his analytical processes rather than adapting them to new knowledge. Thus he refused to accept the utility of microbiology or bacteriology for assessing water. He also took the unusual step of patenting some of his analytical processes in order to control their use, and thereby, he hoped, better defend their credibility. He died on 19 July 1906 of heart failure at New Malden, Surrey, and was buried in New Malden cemetery.

CHRISTOPHER HAMLIN

Sources W. H. Brock, 'Wanklyn, James Alfred', *DSB* · C. Hamlin, *A science of impurity: water analysis in nineteenth century Britain* (1990) · 'Memoir', J. A. Wanklyn, *Water analysis*, 11th edn (1907) · C. A. Russell, *Edward Frankland: chemistry, controversy and conspiracy in Victorian England* (1996) · *BMJ* (4 Aug 1906), 278–9 · *Chemical News* [index to vols. 1–100 (1859–1910)] · A. J. Rocke, *The quiet revolution: Herman Kolbe and the science of organic chemistry* (1993) · R. C. Chirnside and J. H. Hamence, *The 'practising chemists': a history of the Society for Analytical Chemistry, 1874–1974* (1974) · F. Szabadvary, 'Kjeldahl, Johann Gustav Christoffer', *DSB* · J. R. Partington, *A history of chemistry*, 4 (1964)
Likenesses portrait, repro. in Wanklyn, *Water analysis*, frontispiece

Wanley, Humfrey (1672–1726), Old English scholar and librarian, was born on 21 March 1672 at the Vicarage House adjoining Jesus Hall, Coventry, the youngest of five children of Nathaniel *Wanley (1632/3–1680), vicar of Holy Trinity, Coventry (1662), and his wife, Ellen Burton (1632–1719), daughter of Humfrey Burton, clerk to Coventry council (1636–85). He was educated at Coventry Free School and, on leaving school, was bound apprentice to a Coventry linen draper. The life of a provincial draper did not suit Wanley and did not detain him long. At least as early as June 1691 he was transcribing local Warwick records; later the same year he made for himself a copy of the Old English grammar from G. Hickes's *Institutiones grammaticae Anglo-Saxonicae* (1689) and of the catalogue of Anglo-Saxon manuscripts in the Bodleian Library from the same work.

By October 1694, a draper no more, Wanley was employed seeking out collections of manuscripts for inclusion in the *Catalogi librorum manuscriptorum Angliae et Hiberniae*, commonly known as Bernard's Catalogue, then being compiled at Oxford. Bernard's Catalogue was published in 1697 and Wanley was author of four catalogues in it. But by then he had long been established at Oxford. The traditional account, which there seems no reason to disbelieve, is that Wanley moved to Oxford in 1695 under the patronage of William Lloyd, bishop of Coventry and Lichfield since 1692. His official subscription and oath taken on his admission to the university is dated 7 May 1695. He was briefly in residence at St Edmund Hall before moving to University College at the invitation of the master, Arthur Charlett.

Wanley arrived at Oxford with the interests that were the foundation of his later achievements already fixed.

Humfrey Wanley (1672–1726), by Thomas Hill, 1722

Oxford was to transform a young man's appetite for copying old manuscripts and for northern languages into the mature scholar's mastery of palaeography and of Old English, and the letters of these years present a striking picture of Wanley's rapidly developing and formidable talents—the growth of his knowledge, the refining of his skills, and the maturing of his judgement. The evidence for Old English is to be found in Wanley's great catalogue of Anglo-Saxon manuscripts, *Librorum veterum septentrionalium, qui in Angliae bibliothecis extant … catalogus historico-criticus*, largely completed in Oxford between 1695 and 1701 but not published until 1705—as volume 2 of George Hickes's *Linguarum veterum septentrionalium thesaurus*. It is in his letters of the 1690s to Hickes, Thomas Smith, and others that the discipline of palaeography can be seen being formulated for English scholarship and from English materials.

Wanley's appointment as assistant at the Bodleian Library in November 1695, six months after his arrival in Oxford, gave him the freedom of the greatest treasure house of manuscripts in public or private hands in England. As his experience was enriched by daily contact with the Bodleian collections, he was defining for himself the whole range of questions that exercise palaeographers, and turning his powerful mind and methodical genius to their explanation and, as often as not, their solution. Hickes was his only competitor, and Hickes, as he himself confessed, was Wanley's pupil: 'I have learnt more from you', he wrote in 1698, 'than ever I did from any other man' (*Letters*, xv, n. 8). At the time of writing Hickes was fifty-five, Wanley twenty-five—and not four years out of the draper's shop.

Throughout the Oxford years Wanley was full of plans for great enterprises. As early as 1695 he urged the collecting of all fragments of scripture remaining in Old English. In 1698 he proposed to undertake what is in effect a comprehensive work on English diplomatic. Probably in 1698 he submitted to the curators of the Bodleian a request to be allowed to remove all manuscript leaves used as pastedowns in printed books in the library, so that they could be arranged to illustrate the development of handwriting. In the summer of 1700 he put forward the grandest scheme of all, proposing to visit the libraries of France, Germany, and Italy to examine manuscripts, collate important texts, take specimens of handwriting, and search for works bearing on English history. These are ambitiously conceived schemes and they are a young man's schemes; most were never begun, none was completed. There is no doubt Wanley would have been wiser to attempt something more manageable. But for Wanley modest ambitions held only moderate attractions.

It is important to remember how far ahead of their time were Wanley's proposals. Anglo-Saxon biblical pieces were first collected by A. S. Cooke in 1898. The comprehensive study of early English charters had to wait for Kemble and Earle in the nineteenth century and Sawyer and others in the twentieth. Bodleian pastedowns remained unlisted until N. R. Ker's *Pastedowns in Oxford Bindings* (1954). Of schemes subsequently put forward by Wanley during his early years in Harley's service, the publication of the acts of the privy council was undertaken by Sir Nicholas Harris Nicholas (1834–7), while the plan to publish the original sources of English history, taken up by Thomas Hearne, is really the forerunner of that monumental Victorian enterprise, the Rolls Series. The only major work Wanley carried to completion, his catalogue of Anglo-Saxon manuscripts, held the field until N. R. Ker published his *Catalogue of Manuscripts Containing Anglo-Saxon* in 1957.

In December 1700, amid much rancour and bitterness, Wanley left Oxford for good and moved to London. The precise occasion of his departure is not known. Institutional indifference, social prejudice, and the ill will of those less talented than himself—Hearne, alluding to the favour shown Wanley by Arthur Charlett, called him 'the Master's pimp' (*Remarks*, 1.212)—all played their part in persuading Wanley that his advancement at Oxford was blocked and that he would do well to seek a future elsewhere.

There followed years of drudgery for Wanley in London, as assistant secretary (later secretary) of the recently founded SPCK, where in the course of duty he published J. F. Ostervald's *The Grounds and Principles of the Christian Religion* (1704), in an English translation from the French, and as assistant to Hans Sloane, secretary of the Royal Society. Wanley was elected FRS in 1706. They are also years of ill health and unhappiness, and of desperate attempts to find a post more congenial to his interests and his talents than the SPCK or the Royal Society afforded, and a post sufficiently well paid to enable him to support a wife and family. On 1 May 1705 he married his landlady, Ann Berenclow (*d.* 1722), daughter of Thomas Bourchier of Newcastle upon Tyne, and widow of Bernard Martin Berenclow, whose family Wanley had lodged with at 3 Duke Street, York Buildings, Westminster, since 1704. Already the mother of several children by Berenclow, she and Wanley had three children, none of whom survived infancy.

The settled station in life that Wanley so earnestly sought was long delayed. His formal introduction to Robert Harley, then speaker of the House of Commons, which was the encounter that decided the course of Wanley's subsequent career, took place in April 1701. Already in the preface to his catalogue of Anglo-Saxon manuscripts, signed off in August 1704, he extols Harley as his Maecenas. Harley employed him regularly, though not consistently, until Wanley's resignation from the secretaryship of the SPCK in June 1708. Thereafter his future lay in the service of the Harleys, as library-keeper to Robert Harley and to his son Edward Harley.

From 1708 the tale of Wanley's life is largely the story of the Harleian Library and of his official relationship with his employers, chiefly from 1711 with Edward Harley. That story is, in a single word, the story of accumulation. The Harleys, especially Edward, bought books and manuscripts on a scale that challenges understanding, and Wanley's diary is the stolid record of Wanley's brilliance as the agent of an appetite that, after Wanley's death, brought Edward Harley to despair and to financial ruin. Wanley's diary, buttressed by the catalogue of the Harleys' manuscript collections, completed by Wanley as far as the middle of Harley MS 2408 at the time of his death, and by the evidence of the sale catalogue of the Harley printed books sold off after Edward Harley's death in 1741, allows those who assert Wanley's pre-eminence as a librarian to rest their case.

There is no doubt that Wanley's career can be seen as a happy variation of Stubbs's principle that if you put the worst man in the best place you have all the good ones striving to show how much better they are, and so benefiting the world. He had hopes, more or less well founded, of becoming, at different times, Bodley's librarian, a fellow of Worcester College, Oxford, keeper of the Cotton Library, commissioner of Hackney coaches, and historiographer royal. He also had thoughts, not nearly so well founded—though he prosecuted his candidacy no less vigorously for that—of becoming library-keeper to the lord chancellor, and of succeeding Richard Bentley as keeper of the royal libraries, William Petyt as keeper of the records in the Tower, and John Chamberlayne in his post at the state paper office. In all these he failed, and he was obliged to squander his energies on developing the talents that made him the greatest Anglo-Saxonist of his generation, and one of the greatest palaeographers and librarians of his age.

Wanley's years in the service of the Harleys were satisfying and secure; in his later years he seems to have achieved a moderate prosperity, owning in 1719 a parcel of land valued at £400 and a second parcel at Leicester. He had from the first the confidence of Edward Harley and the freedom of his houses in Westminster and at Wimpole, near Cambridge. He had the respect of scholars and, through Harley, the amused affection of poets. Alexander Pope consulted him about the purchase of port wine. John Gay assigned him a stanza, beginning

O Wanley, whence com'st thou with shortned hair
And visage from thy Shelves with dust besprent?

in his poem 'Mr Popes Welcome from Greece' (*Poetry and Prose*, 1.259). Matthew Prior, tongue in cheek, places him in the exalted company of Socrates and Cicero in his *Alma, or, The Progress of the Mind* (*Literary Works*, 1.516). There are four portraits of him from these years, three by Thomas Hill, and the fourth showing a countenance, says Dibdin, 'absolutely peppered with variolous indentations' (Dibdin, 346), evidence of the smallpox that afflicted him in childhood.

The Harley years were, Wanley's indefatigable prosecution of library business apart, unremarkable. In 1717 he was active in the refounding of the Society of Antiquaries, which he had originally helped found in 1707. His wife, Ann, died on 3 January 1722 and was buried at St Paul's, Covent Garden, on 5 January. In 1726 he married again (his second wife was also called Ann) shortly before his death of dropsy at Clarges Street, Hanover Square, Piccadilly, London, on 6 July 1726. He was buried at St Marylebone Church. He died intestate; letters of administration granted to his widow are dated 3 November 1726.

PETER HEYWORTH

Sources *Letters of Humfrey Wanley: palaeographer, Anglo-Saxonist, librarian, 1672–1726*, ed. P. L. Heyworth (1989) · *The diary of Humfrey Wanley, 1715–1726*, ed. C. E. Wright and R. C. Wright, 2 vols. (1966) · J. Crossley, 'Humphrey Wanley: autograph notices of his family', *N&Q*, 4th ser., 5 (1870), 142–3 · *DNB* · C. E. Wright, 'Humfrey Wanley: Saxonist and library keeper', *PBA*, 46 (1960), 99–129 · K. Sisam, 'Humfrey Wanley', *Studies in the history of Old English literature* (1953), 259–77 · D. C. Douglas, *English scholars, 1660–1730*, 2nd edn (1951), 98–118 · J. A. W. Bennett, 'Hickes's *Thesaurus*: a study in Oxford book-production', *Essays and Studies by Members of the English Association*, new ser., 1 (1948), 28–45 · J. Evans, *A history of the Society of Antiquaries* (1956), chaps. 3–4 · C. E. Wright, 'Portrait of a bibliophile VIII: Edward Harley, 2nd earl of Oxford, 1689–1741', *Book Collector*, 11 (1962), 158–74 · *Remarks and collections of Thomas Hearne*, ed. C. E. Doble and others, 11 vols., OHS, 2, 7, 13, 34, 42–3, 48, 50, 65, 67, 72 (1885–1921) · *John Gay: poetry and prose*, ed. V. A. Dearing and C. A. Beckwith, 1 (1974), 259 · *The literary works of Matthew Prior*, ed. H. B. Wright and M. K. Spears, 2nd edn, 1 (1971), 516 · T. F. Dibdin, *Bibliomania, or, Book madness: a bibliographical romance*, 2nd edn, [2 vols.] (1811)

Archives BL, catalogues of MSS and charters, Add. MSS 45699–45711 · BL, collections of Italian madrigals and papers, Harley MSS 1272–1273, 7578 · BL, corresp. and papers, Add. MSS 70469–70492 · BL, diary, Lansdowne MSS 771–772 | BL, Harley MSS, letters to John Bagford · BL, letters to John Covell, Add. MSS 28877–28894 · BL, letters to Edward Harley, Add. MSS · BL, Sloane MSS, letters to Sir Hans Sloane · BL, letters to Ann Wanley, Add. MSS · Bodl. Oxf., letters to Arthur Charlett · Bodl. Oxf., letters to George Hickes · Bodl. Oxf., letters to Thomas Smith · Bodl. Oxf., letters to Giovanni Zamboni · CUL, letters to John Strype · Essex RO, Chelmsford, corresp. with William Holman

Likenesses T. Hill, oils, 1711, S. Antiquaries, Lond.; repro. in Heyworth, ed., *Letters of Humphrey Wanley* · oils, 1716 (after T. Hill), Bodl. Oxf. · T. Hill, oils, 1717, NPG; repro. in K. K. Young and M. Pettmon, eds., *National Portrait Gallery complete illustrated catalogue, 1856–1979*

(1981), 593 · T. Hill, oils, 1717, Bodl. Oxf. · J. Smith, mezzotint, 1718 (after T. Hill, 1717), BM, NPG · T. Hill, portrait, 1722, BM [see illus.] · A. Wivell, engraving (after T. Hill), BM, NPG

Wanley, Nathaniel (1632/3–1680), Church of England clergyman and poet, was baptized on 27 March 1633 in St Martin's parish, Leicester, second of the five children of Samuel Wanley (1605–1658), mercer and briefly mayor of Leicester, and his wife, Elizabeth (b. 1610), daughter of Richard Benskin of Wanlip and his wife, Mary. Samuel died suddenly in November 1658, shortly after his appointment as mayor of Leicester. He had earlier apprenticed all four of his sons as mercers, and it fell to Nathaniel to pay off the principal for his own apprenticeship and that of his elder brother, Samuel, a debt that afflicted him 'above twenty years after' (Nichols, 4, pt 2.1048).

During his childhood Wanley attended the sermons of moderate godly preachers such as John Angell, town lecturer at St Martin's from 1628 to 1651. On Angell's death in 1655 Wanley wrote that the preacher had overcome the divisiveness of the times and drawn 'crowds from all sides' with his 'sweet becoming gravitye' (Poems, 77–8). Another such figure was John Bryan, vicar of Holy Trinity, Coventry, from 1644 to 1662 and afterwards a gifted trainer of nonconformist ministers. His house in St Martin's was leased to the church for the use of its vicar from about 1648. Wanley was later to describe Bryan, probably his closest friend, as 'a Person of such Real Worth, as is as hard almost to express as imitate' (N. Wanley, Peace and Rest for the Upright, 1681, 27).

Unlike his brothers, Wanley did not follow the family trade but matriculated at Peterhouse, Cambridge, as a pensioner on 21 December 1649. His entry to the college, like that of John Bryan's four sons, was no doubt assisted by the connection between Bryan and the then master of Peterhouse, Lazarus Seaman. The two men had been contemporaries at Emmanuel in the 1620s, and together attended Francis Higginson's godly seminary at Leicester after graduating. On 27 January 1652 Wanley moved to Trinity College, Cambridge, possibly as a result of internal disputes between Seaman and the Peterhouse fellowship. He graduated BA in 1653 and MA in 1657. On 24 July 1655 he was married by John Bryan to Ellenor Burton (1632–1719), daughter of Humphrey, the long-standing coroner and town clerk of Coventry. Of their five children four survived infancy: Ellen, Nathaniel, Elizabeth, and the future librarian and palaeographer Humfrey *Wanley. In his will Wanley asked to be buried alongside the first-born child, Samuel, who died in 1665.

Wanley's first publication, Vox Dei (1658), is dedicated to Dorothy Spencer, countess of Sunderland, who in 1657 preferred Wanley to the living of Beby, near Leicester. Most of his extant poetry was written by about 1660 or shortly afterwards. His Scintillulae sacrae, an accomplished body of about forty devotional lyrics, shows the uncommon influence of Henry Vaughan's Silex scintillans (1650; 2nd edn 1655) as well as that of Herbert, Donne, and Quarles. Like his poetry, Wanley's extant prose (which includes letters from 1667–74) blends the homiletic with the delightful, often citing morally improving passages from Vaughan, Suckling, or Donne. Wanley's advice on spiritual perseverance in Vox Dei, for instance, is illustrated by what is clearly a moralized paraphrase of lines 7–10 of Donne's 'Loves Alchymie' (46). Also surviving are two narrative poems, Lazarus and The Witch of Endor (the latter written in the early 1660s), and an Englishing of Latin verses by John Bryan's friend Thomas Dugard, vicar of Barford in Warwickshire.

Before the Restoration, Wanley seems to have been one of the large number of ministers Richard Baxter called 'dis-engaged faithful men': moderate puritans without particular sect or party (Reliquiae Baxterianae, 148). In Vox Dei Wanley places Archbishop James Ussher first in a list of recently dead 'lights of the church', following him with such moderate presbyterians as Richard Vines and Thomas Hill (master of Trinity until his death in 1653). Wanley's list strongly suggests that in 1658 his religious views were far closer to those of John Bryan and Richard Baxter (both shortly to dissent) than the Restoration terminology of 'conformist' and 'dissenter' might suggest.

In March 1661 Wanley petitioned Charles II for the living of Lutterworth, Leicestershire, then held by the elderly poet and royalist Thomas Pestell, 'whose desire is it that your petitioner should succeed him' (PRO, SP 29/33/71). Wanley signed the subscription book as curate at Lutterworth in September 1662, but on 20 October of that year became vicar of Holy Trinity, Coventry, after John Bryan found he could not, in conscience, remain within the church. Wanley seems to have conformed without difficulty, despite an enduring sympathy with presbyterians. His petition for the Lutterworth rectory describes him as 'a true Sonne of the Church of England both to the Discipline and Doctrine of it', and he was similarly styled in An Ingenious Contention (1668), a rhymed broadside debate conducted with the dissenting minister and poet Robert Wilde, in which Wanley does his best to encourage Wilde to conform (PRO, SP 29/33/71).

A love of religious harmony, nostalgically expressed in his elegy on John Angell (c.1655), was no doubt nurtured in Wanley by his college tutors, James Clarke (Peterhouse) and John Templer (Trinity), both associates of Cambridge Platonists Henry More and Ralph Cudworth. Liberal and adaptable religious views were far from unusual in those educated during the civil war and Commonwealth. The second wave of latitudinarians, including John Tillotson (b. 1630), Edward Fowler (b. 1632), and Isaac Barrow (b. 1630), belonged to Wanley's generation; coinciding with Wanley's time there, Barrow was a fellow of Trinity from 1649 and Fowler during 1653–5. Wanley's religious temper is nicely characterized by his donation to Coventry grammar school (it is not known when) of a manuscript of The Imitation of Christ: the choice of gift reflects not only Wanley's antiquarian interests and the enduring popularity of the Imitation, but also the moral emphasis of the Restoration church to which Wanley became a 'true Sonne'.

A great deal of Wanley's time at Coventry went into restoring the fabric of Holy Trinity. As well as replacing the old font and eagle lectern removed during Bryan's incumbency, he organized a campaign of fund-raising and church repairs, intensifying efforts after lightning destroyed the steeple in January 1666. Contributors to further repairs in 1673 included Basil Fielding, earl of Denbigh, whose family history Wanley wrote in the early 1670s (printed by Nichols, 4, pt 1). A love of the ministerial calling and its duties emerges in several of Wanley's poems, including verses from the 1660s written 'Upon his forced absence from the church, and sight of others going thither' and an earlier poem, 'Sunday', in which a minister imagines angels 'bear[ing] a part' in his congregation's 'Harmonie' (*Poems*, 50, 25).

Despite such job satisfactions, it is clear from his letters that Wanley found Coventry rather dull, and clear from his publications that he found consolation in omnivorous reading. The fruits of his frustration include a translation from Lipsius, *A Discourse of Constancy* (1670; repr., 1672) and his work best known to posterity, *The Wonders of the Little World, or, A General History of Man* (1678), an exhaustive and carefully documented compendium of human prodigies, which ran to at least six editions in the eighteenth and early nineteenth centuries. In an agreement with his publisher Bassett, Wanley received thirteen copies of the book: six plain bound, six in marble, and one with a blank leaf bound between each printed one to create space for further entries. He died two years later, aged forty-seven, and was buried in Holy Trinity churchyard on 2 December 1680. In his will he endowed an annual Christmas sermon at Trinity, with a fee of 10 s. charged on a house in Bishop Street. *Peace and Rest for the Upright*, his funeral sermon for John Bryan, was published posthumously in Coventry in 1681.   PHILIP WEST

Sources J. Nichols, *The history and antiquities of the county of Leicester*, 4 vols. (1795–1815) · Wanley family Bible, BL, Add. MS 70491 · *The poems of Nathaniel Wanley*, ed. L. C. Martin (1928) · N. Wanley, *Vox Dei, or, The great duty of self-reflection upon a mans own wayes* (1658) · L. C. Martin, 'A forgotten poet of the seventeenth century', *Essays and Studies by Members of the English Association*, 11 (1925), 5–31 · T. A. Walker, ed., *Admissions to Peterhouse or St Peter's College in the University of Cambridge* (1912) · W. W. Rouse Ball and J. A. Venn, eds., *Admissions to Trinity College, Cambridge*, 2 (1913) · diocese subscription book, 1662–96, Leics. RO, ID41/34/MM2 · probate inventories, Leics. RO, PR/I/56/2; PR/I/87/186; PR/I/53/6; PR/I/69/80 [Samuel Wanley, sen., Samuel Wanley, Edward Wanley, and Jonathan Wanley] · T. A. Walker, *Peterhouse* (1906) · C. H. Cooper, *Annals of Cambridge*, 3 (1845) · T. Webster, *Godly clergy in early Stuart England: the Caroline puritan movement, c.1620–1643* (1997) · J. Simon, 'The two John Angels', *Leicestershire Archaeological and Historical Society Transactions*, 31 (1955), 32–50 · *Calamy rev.* · D. Lloyd, *Memoires of the lives … of those … personages that suffered … for the protestant religion* (1668) · genealogical notes on the Benkin family, Leics. RO, DE 3748 · Holy Trinity, Coventry: churchwardens' accounts, 1620–1726, Warks. CRO, DR 581/46 · Holy Trinity, Coventry: vestry book, 1603–94, Warks. CRO, DR 581/64 · PRO, SP 29/33/71 · 'Catalogus impressorum librorum bibliothecæ publicæ in civitate Coventriensis', CUL, Add. MS 4468 (BB) · *Reliquiae Baxterianae, or, Mr Richard Baxter's narrative of the most memorable passages of his life and times*, ed. M. Sylvester, 1 vol. in 3 pts (1696) · T. Sharp, *Illustrative papers on the history and antiquities of the city of Coventry* (1871) · church records, St Martin, Leics. RO

Archives BL, Add. MSS 22472, 70492 · BL, Harley MSS 6430, 6646, 6922 · U. Cal., Los Angeles, William Andrews Clark Memorial Library, IW2485M3/5486/[1675]
Likenesses oils, Bodl. Oxf.

Wanostrocht, Nicholas [*pseud.* Nicholas Felix] (1804–1876), cricketer and schoolmaster, was born on 5 October 1804 at Alfred House Academy, Peckham Road, Camberwell, the eldest son of Vincent Wanostrocht (1783–1824). He was educated (*c.*1809–*c.*1820) at the academy, which had been founded by his great-uncle.

The family, of Flemish origin, had come to England in the 1770s, when **Nicolas Wanostrocht** (1745–1812), uncle of Vincent, was appointed tutor to the children of Henry Bathurst, second Earl Bathurst, at Cirencester Park. By 1795 he was financially able to found a school known as the Alfred House Academy in Camberwell, a location, according to the prospectus, 'very convenient on account of the coaches going to and from London every hour'. He wrote a number of textbooks on French language, grammar, and syntax, mostly for children's use. With his wife, Sarah (*d.* 1820), he compiled *Le livre des enfans* (4th edn, 1808). The school itself was ahead of its time in encouraging the teaching of French rather than the classics and in its civilized approach to both discipline and leisure. Nicolas Wanostrocht, who printed the letters LLD after his name, died, probably at Alfred House, on 19 November 1812, aged sixty-three. He was buried at St Giles, Camberwell. After his death the school was continued by his nephew Vincent Wanostrocht, who as a child in 1789 had been allowed to leave France for England because of a pass signed by Robespierre. Besides revising his uncle's editions of the French classics, Vincent published in 1823 *The British Constitution, or, An Epitome of Blackstone's Commentaries on the Laws of England*, which, although intended for school use, ran to 845 pages. Vincent Wanostrocht died in Camberwell on 25 January 1824.

Although only nineteen, Nicholas succeeded his father as headmaster of Alfred House. He was 'facetious, jostling, merry, lively and amusing', a character far removed from the notion of a schoolmaster of the time. This perhaps explains why 'the notch-making Felix' played his cricket under a happy pseudonym with which he concealed his cricketing activities from the parents of his pupils. He gradually developed into a brilliant left-handed bat, with an effective cut to the off side from the shoulder. His slow 'lobs' were described as fatal to batsmen. His first match at Lord's was suitably marked by the fact that he, a classical scholar, and one Pontifex took thirteen wickets between them. In 1831 he first played for the Gentlemen against the Players, and he continued to appear spasmodically in that fixture down to 1851. In 1832 Wanostrocht moved his school to Blackheath in Kent, and between 1831 and 1852 he made fifty-five appearances for the county, for which Alfred Mynn also played. The two 'chimed in together' in friendship, although twice, in 1846, Mynn defeated Felix in single-wicket matches. In June 1846 he received the first benefit ever awarded to an amateur in a game 'in his honour' at Lord's. Although he was not a member, the MCC initiated the game in the knowledge that he had not made much money as a schoolmaster but had given much pleasure as a player. Before 'an immense assemblage' (*Bell's Life*, 7 June 1846), including the prince consort, twenty-two of the best players available played a match hailed for its brilliance, although no record survives of how much money Felix received. His own eleven lost to that of Fuller Pilch, who admired Wanostrocht's left-handed batting as 'a beautiful thing to see'.

The grace and fluency of Felix's batting were mirrored in his skill as an artist. Of some 200 works in pencil, pastel, or watercolour, many show his cricketing contemporaries, while his group portraiture created a harmonic unity in which each individual was allowed to be a solo performer in his own right. Thus the *All-England Eleven* of 1847 shows the elegance and authority of Mynn and Pilch, as pillars on either side of the picture, with Felix himself modestly in the second row. He also commissioned the rising young artist George Frederick Watts, who attended evening classes at his school, to produce a series of lithographs to illustrate batting techniques. Felix himself was the model and knew that, as a left-hander, the printed image in reverse would be particularly useful in instruction. They are the finest examples of cricketing art in the age before photography.

In 1845 Wanostrocht published *Felix on the bat; being a scientific enquiry into the use of the cricket bat, together with the history and use of the Catapulta*, which forms one of the classics of cricket. Although not the first instructional book, it was the first to give practical and illustrated advice. Felix's sense of humour was expressed in drawings showing what to do and what *not* to do. The lithographs illustrating particular strokes are attributed to Watts but it would be more correct to say that they are in his style and based on the work that he had done for Felix eight years earlier. It seems probable that those used in 1845 were modelled on drawings by Felix himself and John Gilbert. The Catapulta was the first bowling machine ever devised. The original idea for such a machine was Felix's, and once it had been developed a demonstration took place at Gravesend in 1845, with Pilch participating. It was intended both for practice and for coaching: Harrow School and the newly formed Surrey county club were the first purchasers. Felix was also responsible for some other important cricketing innovations. To protect batsmen in a time of uncertainty in bowling actions, as well as roughness in pitches, he designed batting gloves and leg-guards placed inside a player's trousers. He also devised a cap that was more suitable than the conventional top hat. None of his inventions, however, brought him much money as he was content to sell his patents modestly to others.

Wanostrocht began to suffer from rheumatism in the 1850s and gave up his school in 1854. He moved to Brighton and subsequently, in 1871, to Wimborne in Dorset. His first wife, Elizabeth Heale (*b.* 1806), whom he had married in 1825, died in 1863 and in the same year he married a widow, Catherine Bolls (1816–1900). The last years of his life were marred by ill health, but consoled by a happy marriage, encouraged by occasional painting commissions, and supported by an annuity of £50 from a capital sum raised through the endeavours of the Revd James Pycroft and Frederick Lillywhite. Wanostrocht died at his home, 1 Julian Villas, Wimborne, on 3 September 1876 and was buried in Wimborne parish church cemetery.

THOMAS SECCOMBE, *rev.* GERALD M. D. HOWAT

Sources G. Brodribb, *Felix on the bat: a memoir* (1962) · A. Haygarth, *Arthur Haygarth's cricket scores and biographies*, 15 vols. (1862–1925), vols. 2–3 · F. Gale, 'The late Mr Felix', *Baily's Magazine*, 29 (1876), 188–91 · N. Wanostrocht, scrapbooks (2 vols.), Marylebone Cricket Club, Lord's, London, MCC collection · F. Gale, *Cricket* (10 May 1888) · G. Brodribb, *Felix and the Eleven of England* (2002)

Archives Lord's, London, Marylebone Cricket Club, scrapbooks | Lord's, London, Marylebone Cricket Club, A. L. Ford scrapbooks

Likenesses C. Cousens, double portrait, 1846 (with Alfred Mynn), Lord's, London, Marylebone Cricket Club collection · N. Felix, watercolour, 1847 (All England), Lord's, London, Marylebone Cricket Club collection · N. Wanostrocht, self-portrait, pencil, 1853, Lord's, London, Marylebone Cricket Club collection · N. Wanostrocht, self-portrait, watercolour, *c*.1860, Lord's, London, Marylebone Cricket Club collection · G. H. Phillips, group portrait, lithograph (*A cricket match between Sussex and Kent*; after W. Drummond and C. J. Basebe), Lord's, London, Marylebone Cricket Club collection · N. Ploszczynsky, lithograph (*The eleven of England selected to contend in the great cricket matches of the north for the year 1847*; after N. Felix), Lord's, London, Marylebone Cricket Club collection · N. Wanostrocht, self-portrait, lithograph, Lord's, London, Marylebone Cricket Club collection · G. F. Watts and others, pencil, Lord's, London, Marylebone Cricket Club collection

Wealth at death under £450: probate, 27 Oct 1876, *CGPLA Eng. & Wales*

Wanostrocht, Nicolas (1745–1812). *See under* Wanostrocht, Nicholas (1804–1876).

Wansey, Henry (1751–1827), woollen manufacturer and traveller, was born on 10 August 1751 at Warminster, Wiltshire, the sixth son among at least ten children of George Wansey (1713–1762), clothier, and his wife, Esther Greene (1713–1795). For two years he attended the Lord Weymouth Grammar School in Church Street, Warminster, simultaneously learning writing from an independent Warminster schoolmaster. Then from the age of eight until the age of fifteen he, like his three surviving elder brothers, was sent to the boarding-school at Frenchay, near Bristol, kept by the Revd Joshua Griffith, minister of the Presbyterian chapel there. He was prevented by his father's death in 1762 from attending one of the dissenting academies whose rationalist theology attracted both his father and later himself.

Wansey served a traditional clothier's apprenticeship, possibly in Salisbury, where he was an established clothier by 1773. He remained in Salisbury for over thirty years, becoming a prosperous and influential, if at times contentious, gentleman capitalist. Controversially, he was associated with the introduction of the spinning jenny into the city, apparently in 1791. He shared the woollen lobby's protectionist views and vigorously defended the old prohibition on the export of wool in his *Wool Encouraged without Exportation* (1791). Towards the end of his career and in retirement he joined the Bath and West of England Society and advocated various means of improving the quality of British wools: urging free- and wide-range shepherding techniques and campaigning for the improved Ryeland breed of sheep. As a Salisbury householder he joined the chorus of complaints against the rising costs of poor relief, publishing *Thoughts on Poor Houses* (1801).

On 14 June 1779 Wansey married Alice Abigail Gwynn (*d.* 1793), third child and second daughter of Captain Richard Gwynn RN (*d.* 1766), and his first wife, Elizabeth, of Upham, Hampshire. They had one daughter, Jane (1781–1805). Beyond work and family, Wansey vented his convictions and passions in three directions: travel, the defence of religious liberty, and antiquarianism.

Wansey began indulging his taste for long-distance travel in 1794, the year after his wife died. He travelled to America in order to survey the American market for textiles and to discover the state of woollen manufacturing in the newly independent nation, possibly with a view to setting up a business himself. A prudent investment in American land likewise motivated him. He therefore bought two shares in the English settlement established on the Loyalsoc in western Pennsylvania by his co-religionist the Unitarian and scientist Dr Joseph Priestley. At the same time he purchased 1200 acres at Chest Creek on the west branch of the Susquehanna. In the new fashion of the day, he published an account of his American experiences, *The Journal of an Excursion to the United States of North America in the Summer of 1794* (1796), which was published in a German translation in 1797.

As an English Presbyterian, Wansey followed the denomination's dominant theological shifts, from Arianism to Socinianism. Privately he believed that a new translation of the Bible would resolve denominational differences. Although a Unitarian, he sprang to the defence of orthodox, and therefore Trinitarian, dissenters during the 1790s. His *Letter to the Bishop of Salisbury* (1798) stoutly upheld the right of dissenters to preach in the villages and, more widely, defended a universal right to freedom of private religious belief. In the 1820s he was embroiled in a controversy among Unitarians about missionary preaching.

After retiring to Warminster about 1805, Wansey's summers were spent either on his travels or riding over the Wiltshire downs on antiquarian pursuits, and his winters were passed in the pleasant society of Bath. In 1806 he made a tour of the eastern counties, indulging his passion for family and local history. In 1814 he travelled to Paris with his nephew George Wansey to see and record the condition of France after Napoleon's confinement to Elba, of which he published an account, *A Visit to Paris in June 1814* (1814).

From early adulthood Wansey was interested in medieval and Roman remains, particularly Farleigh Hungerford Castle. He was elected a fellow of the Society of Antiquaries in 1789, having made drawings of monuments in Salisbury Cathedral which were either rearranged or demolished during the restoration scheme of Bishop Shute Barrington and the architect James Wyatt. He also publicly speculated on the origins of Stonehenge. In retirement he joined the circle of antiquaries who helped Sir Richard Colt Hoare at Stourhead in compiling a history of Wiltshire. His contribution was posthumously published, jointly with Hoare, as *The Hundred of Warminister* in volume 3 (1831) of *The History of Modern Wiltshire* (1822–44), edited by Sir Colt Hoare.

Wansey died of a paralytic seizure at his home, Byne House, Church Street, Warminster, on 19 July 1827 and was buried in the town's Boreham Road nonconformist cemetery, a burial-ground which he had largely financed. He left an estate which included liquid assets of over £10,000.   DAVID J. JEREMY

Sources *Henry Wansey and his American journal, 1794*, ed. D. J. Jeremy (1970) • J. de L. Mann, *The cloth industry in the west of England from 1660 to 1880* (1971) • *GM*, 1st ser., 97/2 (1827), 373–4 • *DNB*
Archives priv. coll. • Wilts. & Swindon RO, letters
Likenesses W. Artaud, oils, priv. coll.; repro. in Jeremy, ed., *Henry Wansey and his American Journal* • S. Woodforde, oils, Stourhead, Wiltshire; repro. in Jeremy, ed., *Henry Wansey and his American Journal*
Wealth at death £10,000 value of moveables and liquid assets

Wantage. For this title name *see* Lindsay, Robert James Loyd-, Baron Wantage (1832–1901); Lindsay, Harriet Sarah Loyd-, Lady Wantage (1837–1920).

Wanton, Gideon (1693–1767), merchant and colonial governor, was born on 20 October 1693 in Tiverton, Massachusetts, the third of the six children of Joseph Wanton (1664–1754), shipbuilder and farmer, and his wife, Sarah (1667–1737), daughter of Gideon Freeborn of Tiverton and his wife, Sarah. Born into a family of Quaker shipbuilders and seafarers, on 6 February 1718 Wanton married Mary Codman (1693–1780) of Tiverton, with whom he had five children. He worked in his father's shipyard until moving to Newport in 1733 where he was elected treasurer of the colony with the backing of his two remarkable uncles, William Wanton (1670–1733), governor of Rhode Island, and John *Wanton (1672–1740), deputy governor. He served as treasurer for twelve consecutive years and also opened a merchant business during this time.

On William Wanton's death in December 1733, John Wanton succeeded him as governor until his death in July 1740, and five years later Gideon was elected governor for a term and then elected again for another single term in 1747. Thus, between 1730 and 1748, the three Wantons were elected to twelve of the eighteen gubernatorial terms. Gideon Wanton's governorship was distinguished primarily by his enthusiastic support of Britain's war with France. 'Although a Quaker, he was a belligerent one', one biographer wrote of this militaristic politician who faithfully attended the Friends' Meeting all his life (Mohr, 106).

Under Wanton's leadership in his first term Rhode Island played a pivotal role in the great siege of Louisbourg, one of the most celebrated victories in the epic wars between Britain and France for control of North America. Wanton's predecessor, Governor William Greene, had received but ignored entreaties from the duke of Marlborough and Governor William Shirley of Massachusetts to furnish men, supplies, and ships for an expedition to the north to attack the French at Cape Breton. Governor Shirley renewed his pleading in letters to Wanton that also complained that Rhode Island harboured seamen who fled there illegally after being legally pressed into his majesty's service.

Encouraged by Shirley's belief that Wanton could be persuaded to help, Sir Peter Warren, the admiral commanding the British fleet, wrote to the new governor personally begging him for assistance. Warren also promised Wanton that the people of Rhode Island would benefit greatly from trade with Louisbourg if it fell and that a rich booty would be available to British privateers who seized French ships. Whether patriotism or greed provided the greater motive will never be known, but Governor Wanton used his authority and influence to prod the Rhode Island general assembly into supplying gunpowder, letters of marque to five ships, provisions, several hundred soldiers, and a warship. After Louisbourg's fall on 16 June 1745, Wanton received a string of letters of thanks from Admiral Warren, General Sir William Pepperell, commander of the land forces, Governor Shirley, and his successor, William Phipps. The gratitude of these gentlemen, however, did not prevent them from pressing Governor Wanton to maintain his support now that the fruits of victory had to be defended.

Propelled into high office by his family's political connections, Wanton also had his career destroyed by partisan forces. William Greene, the incumbent governor whom Wanton defeated in 1745 and 1747, roared back into power with a vengeance in 1748 and won a string of seven consecutive elections. Greene formed an alliance with the Ward family of Westerly, whose members had long opposed the Wantons. Gideon proved inept as a partisan combatant and retired from public life after his defeat in 1748. The Wanton family turned to his younger cousins, Edward, George, Joseph, and Joseph II, for leadership. After his withdrawal, the aged governor suffered a final indignity in 1754 when the general assembly, under the domination of the Greene–Ward faction, ordered him to appear before a magistrate in Newport to answer charges that he 'grossly abused the General Assembly of this colony' in a public speech. Only in Rhode Island did colonial politics descend into such acts of petty reprisal.

Wanton lived thirteen more years after this humiliation and pursued his career as a merchant in relative peace. He died on 12 September 1767 and was buried at the Friends' burial-ground, Newport. Had he lived two more years until 1769, he would have been gratified to see once again a family member, his second cousin, Joseph *Wanton, in the governor's chair. Although Gideon left a voluminous correspondence over military matters, it reveals little of his personality, which remains obscure.

BRUCE C. DANIELS

Sources J. R. Bartlett, *History of the Wanton family of Newport, R.I.* (1878) • S. V. James, *Colonial Rhode Island: a history* (1975) • D. Lovejoy, *Rhode Island politics and the American Revolution, 1760–1776* (1958) • B. Lippencott, 'The Wanton family of Jamestown, Rhode Island', *Newport History*, 58 (summer 1985), 73–8 • E. C. Forman, *A dependent people: Newport, Rhode Island, in the revolutionary era* (1985) • R. Mohr, *Governors for three hundred years: Rhode Island and Providence plantations* (1954) • G. S. Kimball, ed., *Correspondence of the colonial governors of Rhode Island* (1902)
Archives Newport Historical Society, Rhode Island, papers • Rhode Island Archives, Providence, official corresp. • Rhode Island Historical Society Library, Providence, letters

Wanton, John (1672–1740), merchant and colonial governor, was born on 24 December 1672 in Scituate, Massachusetts, the fifth of the seven children of Edward Wanton (1631–1716), farmer and shipbuilder, and his second wife, Elizabeth Phillips (*d.* 1716?). In 1691 Wanton followed his elder brother William (1670–1733) to Newport, Rhode Island, and the two brothers became heroes for their swashbuckling adventures as privateers in the wars of King William and Queen Anne. They also became rich, powerful, and the progenitors of 'the most aristocratic and wealthy family [of which] the colony could boast' (Lovejoy, 11). John Wanton served intermittently as one of Newport's deputies to the general assembly (1706–14), speaker of the assembly (1710–12 and 1713–14), a member of the governor's council (1715–21 and 1723–4), deputy governor (1720–22), and then deputy governor again, for five years (1729–34), during the last four of which his brother William was governor. In 1734, shortly after his brother's death, he succeeded to the governor's chair and remained in office until his death.

Having retired from the sea in 1706 Wanton carried into his political life the habits of ruthlessness, daring, and aggressiveness that had made him so successful as a privateer. Throughout his lengthy career in government he championed economic policies that expanded the supply of currency and credit and favoured his own business interests. Early in his terms as a Newport deputy he and his brother fought the efforts of Governor Samuel Cranston (1659–1727) to stabilize Rhode Island's emissions of paper money. To undercut the governor, who was a fellow Newport merchant, the Wanton brothers entered into alliances in 1714 with like-minded supporters of inflationary measures in Providence and Warwick. Wanton's support of a shaky venture to create a bank that would emit currency based on mortgaged land, and his intemperate verbal attacks on British customs officers, made him infamous with imperial officials and highly popular with Rhode Island's freemen. After Cranston's death he served for two years as deputy governor under Governor Joseph Jenkes (1656–1740) but then failed to be re-elected after drifting into enmity with Jenkes and also with the other major figure in Rhode Island's government, Richard Ward (1689–1763), the colony secretary. In 1729, with Jenkes still in office, Wanton was again elected deputy governor. When Jenkes, with Ward's encouragement, refused to give his assent to a bill that emitted land-backed bank notes Wanton audaciously appealed to the crown on the grounds that the Rhode Island charter of 1663 did not give the governor a veto power. Amazingly, even though imperial officials despised both Wanton and the bill, they agreed with his constitutional argument and set aside the governor's pocket veto. Humiliated, angry, and confused the ageing governor retired, to be succeeded by Wanton's brother William in the next election. For the only time in American history brothers served simultaneously as governor and deputy governor of a colony.

Wanton's success at creating an abundant supply of specie infuriated merchants and officials in Britain and in colonial ports outside Rhode Island; to them the colony seemed shockingly irresponsible. In the 1730s Rhode Island currency exchanged at a ratio of twenty to one with sterling. Conservative Rhode Islanders such as governors Cranston and Jenkes thought the policies endangered the island's charter by providing Britain with cause for abrogating it. Responsible or not Rhode Island—and particularly Newport—prospered under the loose money policy promoted by Wanton and his brother.

Despite the militaristic origins of his career and his ruthless political behaviour Wanton—unlike his brother William, who became an Anglican—remained committed to the Quaker religion. He faithfully attended the Newport monthly meeting and several times represented New England Friends at meetings in such distant places as Philadelphia and the West Indies. Thus it must have been a sorrow to him when Newport's Quakers expelled him in 1734, after he had signed military commissions in his capacity as governor.

Wanton had no formal education but surprisingly managed to become a cultivated, refined man whose Newport home was known as a centre of intellectual activity. On 1 June 1689 he married Ann Freeborn, who died childless at an early age; he then married Mary Stafford, who survived him, as did four of their six children. No further details are known of these marriages. Wanton died on 5 July 1740 in Newport, where he had lived all his adult life, and was buried two days later in Coddington burial-grounds. Though an enigmatic and immensely capable man his historical identity is linked forever with that of his brother William. He embodied the free-spiritedness for which colonial Rhode Island was legendary. His nephews Gideon *Wanton, son of Joseph Wanton (1664–1754), and Joseph *Wanton, son of William Wanton, also served as Rhode Island's governor, from 1745 and 1769 respectively.

BRUCE C. DANIELS

Sources S. V. James, *Colonial Rhode Island: a history* (1975) • D. S. Lovejoy, *Rhode Island politics and the American revolution, 1760–1776* (1958) • A. J. Worrall, 'Wanton, John', *ANB* • E. C. Forman, *A dependent people: Newport, Rhode Island, in the revolutionary era* (1985) • J. R. Bartlett, *History of the Wanton family of Newport, Rhode Island* (1878) • B. Lippencott, 'The Wanton family of Jamestown, Rhode Island', *Newport History*, 58 (1985), 73–8 • G. S. Kimball, ed., *The correspondence of the colonial governors of Rhode Island, 1723–1775*, 2 vols. (1902–3) • J. R. Bartlett, ed., *Records of the colony of Rhode Island and Providence plantations, in New England*, 10 vols. (1856–65), vol. 4

Archives Newport Historical Society, Newport, Rhode Island, papers • Rhode Island Colony Archives, State Capitol Building, Providence, corresp. • Rhode Island Historical Society, Providence, corresp.

Likenesses oils, Rhode Island State Capitol, Providence; repro. in R. S. Mohr, *Governors for three hundred years: Rhode Island and Providence plantations* (Providence, RI, 1954), 101

Wanton, Joseph (1705–1780), merchant and colonial governor, was born on 15 August 1705 in Newport, Rhode Island, the seventh of the nine children of William Wanton (1670–1733), merchant and colonial governor, and his wife, Ruth (c.1672–1715), daughter of John and Mary Bryant of Scituate, Massachusetts. Born into one of eighteenth-century Rhode Island's wealthiest families Wanton was to witness his family rising to unprecedented political heights—his father, uncle, and cousin also served Rhode Island as governors—only to plummet to disaster during the American War of Independence. Wanton, elected governor in 1769, forcibly defended patriotic interests in the pre-war agitation but refused to make war on his king. Deposed from office and his estate confiscated he became Rhode Island's most famous loyalist, and his family lost its fortune, power, and exalted status.

The Wanton family made its money from the sea, first in a relatively modest way as shipbuilders in Scituate, Massachusetts, and Tiverton, Rhode Island, in the late seventeenth century and then as privateers and merchants in Newport. Joseph's father and his uncle John *Wanton became wealthy men by seizing French ships during the wars of King William and Queen Anne. Having amassed their fortunes as legal buccaneers the Wanton brothers moved into the more respectable coastal trade between New England and the West Indies. At an early age Joseph joined his father in business; after his father's death he brought his own sons into the firm of Joseph and William Wanton. Less involved in the slave trade than many of Newport's merchants, Wanton became one of the pioneer investors in whaling expeditions and spermaceti candle manufacturing. A well-liked man, he might easily have lived his life in historical obscurity had he not been dragged into government service by his family's prominence and by the swirling vortex of Rhode Island's political battles.

Unrivalled for its internecine bitterness mid-century Rhode Island developed the nearest proxy to political parties in the American colonies. Contending factions from Rhode Island's co-capitals and two major ports, Newport and Providence, fought yearly for control of the colony government, which, unlike all other colonies with the exception of Connecticut, elected all the major officers of the colony, including the governor and his council. As the imperial quarrel with Britain quickened in the 1760s many Rhode Islanders thought that the local bickering should cease in light of the more momentous struggle. Both factions opposed British changes in policy and they tried to bury the local hatchet by uniting on compromise candidates. Joseph Wanton fitted the political bill perfectly. He was an Anglican, as was his father, but most of his extended family were Quakers. He was on good terms with merchants in both co-capitals and with the other major families of both sides: the Browns, the Hopkinses, and the Wards. And of course he had his family's name and tradition of service.

Immediately after Wanton's election events plunged Rhode Island into turmoil when an angry mob boarded a customs ship, *Liberty*, renowned for abusive treatment of shippers, and set it adrift by cutting its rigging. Wanton incurred the wrath of British officials by not vigorously pursuing the alleged offenders. He also dismissed the beating of a Rhode Island customs officer as a mere case of 'drunken sailors' (James, 37) getting out of control. By his willingness to tolerate vigilantes on Narragansett Bay he inadvertently helped to set the political stage for the Gaspee affair, one of the most celebrated events of the pre-revolutionary era. Lieutenant Dudington, captain of the Gaspee (the ship that replaced the Liberty), may have been even more high-handed than his predecessor. As governor Wanton wrote Dudington two letters rebuking his conduct and touched off a firestorm of reaction. Admiral John Montagu, commander of the royal fleet in American waters, informed Wanton that imperial officials were 'ashamed to find that they [the letters to Dudington] came from one of his majesty's governors' (Bartlett, 87). Moreover Montagu promised to report 'your insolence to his majesty's secretaries' (ibid., 88). The Gaspee's seizure and burning by a mob in 1772 provoked a crisis in the Anglo-Atlantic world. The culmination of the affair cemented Wanton's reputation as one of the colony's staunchest patriots when he released confidential information to the general assembly about investigations into the affair being conducted by a special board of inquiry.

Despite his willingness to do political battle on behalf of principle and local interests Wanton was not willing to become a revolutionary. Still in office and still immensely popular when war broke out at Lexington and Concord in April 1775 he declined to take the oath of office as required by his re-election three weeks later in May. Shortly afterwards the general assembly enquired 'whether your Honour will sign, as Commander-in-Chief of this colony' (Bartlett, 103) the commissions of the officers whom Rhode Island was sending to join the continental army forming on the outskirts of Boston. When he refused to sign the assembly replied that his conduct was 'inimical to the rights and liberties of America' and that he 'is heretofore rendered totally unfit … and hath forfeited the office of governor of this colony' (ibid., 112).

Although deposed from office and publicly branded a traitor Wanton's favourable pre-war reputation spared him the personal indignities visited on most high-ranking loyalists. He lived out the remaining five years of his life in Newport and was treated courteously by the townspeople, the British army who occupied it, and the Americans who had reoccupied it by the time of his death, which occurred in Newport on 19 July 1780.

This modicum of normality, familiarity, and civility must have provided some comfort to a lonely old man who had suffered much for answering the call of duty. During all his tumultuous political life he was a widower. His wife, Mary Winthrop (1708–1767), whom he had married on 24 August 1729, died while he still lived a life of relative tranquillity as a private citizen in Newport. His eldest son, Joseph (1730–1780)—who had served two terms as Rhode Island's deputy governor (1764–5 and 1767–8)— was arrested and imprisoned after refusing General Charles Lee's command to take an oath of fidelity to the patriotic cause; he died thirty days before his father. The revolution scattered the Wanton family, which was never again a major force in Rhode Island's politics or economy. Wanton was buried in a family vault at Clifton burial-grounds, Newport. BRUCE C. DANIELS

Sources J. R. Bartlett, *History of the Wanton family of Newport, Rhode Island* (1878) • S. V. James, *Colonial Rhode Island: a history* (1975) • A. J. Worrall, 'Wanton, Joseph', *ANB* • D. S. Lovejoy, *Rhode Island politics and the American revolution, 1760–1776* (1958) • B. Lippencott, 'The Wanton family of Jamestown, Rhode Island', *Newport History*, 58 (1985), 73–8 • E. C. Forman, *A dependant people: Newport, Rhode Island in the revolutionary era* (1985)
Archives Newport Historical Society, Newport, papers • Rhode Island Colony Archives, State Capitol Building, Providence, corresp. • Rhode Island Historical Society, Providence, corresp.
Likenesses oils, Redwood Library, Newport, Rhode Island; repro. in L. Dexter and A. Pryce-Jones, eds., *Redwood papers: a bicentennial collection* (Newport, RI, 1976), 66 • oils, Rhode Island State Capitol; repro. in R. S. Mohr, *Governors for three hundred years: Rhode Island and Providence plantations* (Providence, RI, 1954), 115

Warbeck, Perkin [Pierrechon de Werbecque; *alias* Richard Plantagenet, duke of York] (*c.*1474–1499), impostor and claimant to the English throne, was, according to the confession he made in 1497, born at Tournai in France, the son of John Osbek, comptroller of the town of Tournai, and Kataryn de Faro. His parents can be identified as Jehan de Werbecque and Nicaise Farou, members of Tournai's prosperous class of leading artisans, small merchants, and civic officials. Warbeck's early experiences were cosmopolitan. In 1484–7 he was in Antwerp, Bergen op Zoom, and Middelburg, completing his education by learning Flemish and working for merchants, probably in the cloth trade. In April–May 1487 he moved on to the Portuguese court in the company of Lady Margaret Beaumont, wife of the Anglo-Portuguese Jewish convert courtier and international trader Sir Edward Brampton. At Lisbon he took service with the royal councillor and explorer Pero Vaz de Cunha, then in 1488 with a Breton merchant, Pregent Meno. With Meno he sailed to Cork in December 1491 to sell silks. There he was prevailed upon by Yorkists, led by the former mayor John Atwater and the English exile John Taylor, to impersonate *Richard, duke of York, second son of Edward IV, who had disappeared in 1483 together with his elder brother, Edward V.

Warbeck's promoters, seeking patrons for their pretender, rapidly gained the support of the earl of Desmond; but it was Charles VIII, king of France (*r.* 1483–98), the man who had funded Taylor's trip to Ireland in the hope of distracting Henry VII from the defence of Brittany against French annexation, whose fleet brought Warbeck from Cork to Harfleur in March 1492, and so firmly onto the European stage. Charles's use for him ended when he made peace with Henry in November, but Warbeck and his adherents escaped to Malines. There he was welcomed by Margaret of York, dowager duchess of Burgundy, as her miraculously preserved nephew. Early in 1493, if trial evidence is to be believed, senior figures at the English court began to be drawn into plotting on Warbeck's behalf: John, Lord Fitzwalter, Sir Robert Clifford, William Worsley, dean of St Paul's, and even the chamberlain of the king's household, Sir William Stanley. Old loyalties to the house of York in general, and to young Duke Richard in particular, sustained the conspiracy across a wide geographical and social range. A long and earnest struggle of espionage and counter-espionage, propaganda and counter-propaganda began in the summer. Ireland was temporarily pacified, some plotters captured and others driven into sanctuary, and the invasion planned by the growing circle of exiles in the Netherlands failed to come to fruition. Yet Henry's attempt to force the Netherlanders to disown Warbeck by suspending English trade proved counter-productive, and Warbeck was sent on to Vienna to meet Maximilian, king of the Romans (r. 1493–1519), and secure his support.

Maximilian was won over, and Warbeck accompanied him as an honoured guest on his return to the Low Countries in August 1494 for the ceremonial reception of his son Philip the Fair as ruler of the various Netherlandish principalities. At the turn of the year, however, the conspiracy suffered a blow as Clifford defected from Malines, taking Henry clear evidence of the treason of Stanley, Fitzwalter, and others. Arrests, trials, and executions followed. Yet Warbeck's partisans managed to co-ordinate renewed rebellion in Ireland with an attempted invasion of England, backed by Maximilian with ships and experienced soldiers. A landing at Deal on 3 July misfired: while Warbeck and most of his force were still on their ships, an advance party was overwhelmed by local levies, with 163 men captured and perhaps 150 killed. Warbeck's flotilla sailed on to Youghall and Waterford, joining Desmond in his siege of the city. The siege failed, but Warbeck soon found yet another patron in James IV of Scots. On 20 November he was welcomed to Stirling Castle.

Not all Scots were convinced by Warbeck's claims, but James demonstrated his commitment to the pretender in a number of ways. On or about 13 January 1496 he married him to Lady Katherine Gordon, daughter of George, earl of Huntly, and a distant royal relative by marriage. Soon afterwards he provided Falkland Palace as a base for Warbeck's 1400 adherents, whom he was supporting at considerable expense, and began to plan an invasion of England. On 21 September James and Warbeck, who had promised him Berwick as reward for his help, crossed the border. Warbeck almost immediately withdrew, discouraged by the failure of his manifesto denouncing Henry's misgovernment to elicit any visible English support for his cause. James was left to demolish a few towers and follow the pretender home. His involvement with Warbeck soon threatened to cost him more than this frustration, as Henry prepared a huge army to invade Scotland.

Suddenly events turned in Warbeck's favour. In May 1497 Henry's heavy taxation sparked rebellion in Cornwall. Disaffection soon spread to Somerset and beyond, and as the rebels prepared to march on London they apparently called on Warbeck to lead them. Henry's victory at Blackheath on 17 June drove the remnants of the rebel army back to Cornwall, but there they were able to welcome Warbeck, who had come from Scotland by way of Ireland to land at Whitesand Bay on 7 September. In Ireland he had found little support, thanks to Henry's pacification of the country under the government of the earl of

Kildare. In Cornwall, by contrast, his force of 300 or so companions multiplied rapidly; by the time they laid siege to Exeter on 17 September they were reportedly 8000 strong. Yet the earl of Devon and his garrison bloodily rebuffed their attacks, and they withdrew to Taunton, arriving there on 19 September. There, as Henry's armies marched towards them, the rebels began to melt away until, in the early hours of 21 September, the pretender and his closest followers made their escape.

John Taylor, one of Warbeck's first promoters, escaped to France, others to sanctuary in London. Warbeck and three companions took sanctuary at Beaulieu Abbey, Hampshire, but were recognized and surrendered on promise of pardon. Brought before Henry and his nobles at Taunton Castle on 5 October, Warbeck confessed his imposture. His wife, whom he had left in sanctuary at St Buryan, was entrusted to the care of Queen Elizabeth. Meanwhile Warbeck was repeatedly paraded through the city on Henry's return to London, and then accompanied the king on his progresses until 9 June 1498, when he escaped, perhaps with the king's connivance. He was soon found, in the Charterhouse at Sheen, twice displayed in the stocks atop a scaffold of empty wine barrels, and on 18 June locked up in shackles in the Tower of London for life. There, in the summer of 1499, he became entangled in his last plot, an attempt by sympathizers in London to free his fellow prisoner Edward, earl of Warwick, and himself, and to place one of them on the throne. Exactly what part he played in the conspiracy, and in its betrayal to the king on 3 August, is hard to establish, but Henry and his council resolved to punish all the principal participants. Warbeck was tried on 16 November in the White Hall of the Palace of Westminster together with Taylor and Atwater, who had been recovered from France and Ireland; all were condemned. On 23 November 1499, after one final confession that he was no Plantagenet, Warbeck was hanged at Tyburn. The king and queen treated his widow generously and she remarried three times in the following reign; she died late in 1537 and was buried in the church at Fyfield, Berkshire. Warbeck's career was portrayed, not unsympathetically, in John Ford's play *Perkin Warbeck*, published in 1634.

S. J. GUNN

Sources I. Arthurson, *The Perkin Warbeck conspiracy, 1491–1499* (1994) · D. Dunlop, 'The masked comedian: Perkin Warbeck's adventures in Scotland and England from 1495 to 1497', *SHR*, 70 (1991), 97–128
Likenesses J. Le Boucq, drawing, 1530–70, Bibliothèque d'Arras, MS 266

Warburg, Edmund Frederic (1908–1966), botanist, was born in London on 22 March 1908, the eldest of the four sons of Sir Oscar Emanuel Warburg, a businessman and later chairman of the London county council, and his wife, Catherine Widdrington, daughter of Sir Edmund W. *Byrne, judge. His family was of German–Jewish origin, and his German relatives included Otto Warburg the systematist, and Otto Warburg the eminent plant physiologist, widely remembered as the inventor of the Warburg manometer.

For many years Warburg's family home was Boidier at

Headley, near Epsom in Surrey, where his father, a keen horticulturist and amateur botanist, assembled a large collection of hardy plants, notably *Cistus*, *Berberis*, and oaks. His father's zeal no doubt channelled Warburg's interest in botany, for, after being educated at Marlborough College (1921–7) and going up to Trinity College, Cambridge, as an entrance scholar in mathematics in 1927, he transferred to natural sciences. He was subsequently elected a senior scholar. He obtained a second class in part one of the natural sciences tripos in 1929. Taking botany as his part two subject in the same tripos, he obtained a first class in 1930.

While an undergraduate, Warburg made a botanical expedition with T. G. Tutin to the Azores, some results of which they published in the *Journal of Botany* in 1932. Warburg was responsible for the introduction to cultivation of *Daboecia cantabrica* ssp. *azorica*, a plant new to science. Before graduating, Warburg wrote an account of the genus *Cistus* with his father as co-author, and shortly afterwards they wrote a useful paper on oaks in cultivation. Meanwhile Warburg prepared a PhD thesis on the cytotaxonomy of the Geraniales, under the supervision of Edith Saunders. On the strength of this work he was elected a research fellow of Trinity College in 1933 and was awarded his PhD in 1937.

In 1938 Warburg was appointed an assistant lecturer at Bedford College, London, and in 1941 joined the RAF. Attached to the photographic interpretation unit at Medmenham, Buckinghamshire, Warburg found his botanical pursuits restricted. This encouraged him to turn to the humble Bryophyta, a collection of which he had made in the Azores and a group which was to absorb much of his efforts for the rest of his life. After the war, Warburg returned to Bedford College and in 1948 went to the department of botany at Oxford as university demonstrator in botany and curator of the Druce herbarium. In the same year he married Primrose Churchman, of Melton (the home of her grandfather, Sir William Churchman, bt, where she was brought up) in Suffolk, daughter of Gilbert Barrett, sometime of the RAF; they had met on a botanical excursion in a Cambridge fen. They had two sons and a daughter.

At Oxford, Warburg's first task was the putting in order of the herbarium, then still at the house of George Claridge Druce (1850–1932) in Crick Road, and the supervision of its transfer to the newly built botany school. At Oxford Warburg's gifts of patient pedagogy, particularly appreciated by the unsure and the amateur, with whom he took immense trouble, his good taxonomic 'eye' and his unexcelled skill as a tireless field botanist endeared him to his pupils and his colleagues. He is remembered for his sound common sense concerning university matters and for his unfashionably wide approach to botany. In 1964 he was made reader in plant taxonomy and elected a fellow of New College.

Warburg was elected fellow of the Linnean Society in 1934 and joined the Botanical Society of the British Isles in 1946. For the rest of his life he served on its committees, including the distribution maps committee, whose work

resulted in *The Atlas of the British Flora*, and was a member of its council, while from 1949 to 1960 he was editor of its journal, *Watsonia*. Like Druce before him, he was a key figure in the society. In 1960 he was elected an honorary member and was its president from 1965 until his death. From 1946 Warburg had been a recorder of mosses for the British Bryological Society and was its president from 1962 to 1963. At the time of his death he was engaged in writing a new British moss flora with A. C. Crundwell. This was one of several incomplete projects, for Warburg lacked the drive to carry through major works such as an extension of his study of oaks, or of *Sorbus*, on the British species of which he was an authority. In consequence most of Warburg's accumulated knowledge has been lost, for with so many distracting interests he published relatively little beyond short bryological papers, though in 1963 he edited, in a most scholarly way, the third edition of *A Census Catalogue of British Mosses*.

Heff, as Warburg was universally known in botanical circles (he was nicknamed Heffalump, for he was well over 6 feet tall, yet a surprisingly good wicket-keeper), was the leading field botanist of his day and his knowledge of the British flora was remarkable in any age. He is most widely known as one of the joint authors of the *Flora of the British Isles* (by A. R. Clapham, T. G. Tutin, and E. F. Warburg, 1952, 1962), the first comprehensive scientific flora to be produced for seventy years. Here, particularly in sections of Rosaceae, and on those families with many familiar cultivated plants, on which he was also very knowledgeable, Warburg will be remembered.

Warburg's leisure activities also centred on plants. At his house, South Hayes, Yarnell's Hill, near Oxford, he built up a fine collection of hardy plants, notably crocuses, on which he was an authority. He was a founder member of the Berkshire, Buckinghamshire and Oxfordshire Naturalists' Trust and later a vice-president; one of their properties, rich in interesting flora, was named the Warburg Reserve in 1967 as a memorial to him. He advised the Oxford Preservation Trust and Oxford city on trees and shrubs; the city council named Warburg Crescent after him in 1969. His name is also commemorated in a moss, *Anoectangium warburgii*, a species that he recognized as new in the Outer Hebrides in 1946. He died from heart disease in the Radcliffe Infirmary, Oxford, on 9 June 1966.

D. J. MABBERLEY

Sources *The Times* (11 June 1966) · *Nature*, 212 (1966), 240 · *Proceedings of the Botanical Society of the British Isles*, 7 (1967), 67–9 [with bibliography] · Desmond, *Botanists*, rev. edn, 716 · private information (1981) · private information (2004) · CGPLA Eng. & Wales (1967)
Archives NHM · U. Cam., department of plant sciences · U. Cam. Botanic Garden · U. Oxf., Fielding-Druce Herbarium
Likenesses photograph, repro. in *Proceedings of the Botanical Society of the British Isles*, 6 (1966), 207–8
Wealth at death £72,789: probate, 3 Feb 1967, CGPLA Eng. & Wales

Warburg, Frederic John (1898–1981), publisher, was born at 117 Gloucester Terrace, Paddington, London, on 27 November 1898, the only son of the three children of Jewish parents, John Cimon Warburg (1865/6–1931), amateur photographer, and his wife, Violet Amalia, *née* Sichel

(1866/7–c.1930). Educated first at home by Miss Coolie, a governess, Frederic John was sent at the age of nine to Wilkinson's preparatory school for boys, St Petersburg Place, Bayswater. At thirteen he won a scholarship to Westminster School. While he excelled academically, he described his years there, particularly the first two, as 'among the most hateful … of my life' (Warburg, *Occupation*, 30). As a Jew he felt an outsider and he often took refuge in books.

In July 1917 Warburg enlisted in the Royal Garrison Artillery and received his commission as second lieutenant in October. Just after his nineteenth birthday he was posted to the 184th siege battery and sent to France, where he served in the Ypres salient until the end of the war. After being demobilized in 1919 he took up his exhibition at Christ Church, Oxford, where he initially read chemistry. Believing that 'words for me … were the stuff out of which I had to manufacture the fabric of my life', he switched to *literae humaniores* in spring 1920 (Warburg, *Occupation*, 70). He took a second and proceeded MA in 1922. That year, with the recommendation of his brother-in-law, he became an apprentice at the publishing firm of George Routledge & Sons Ltd under the tutelage of the head of Routledge, William Swan Stallybrass, whom Warburg referred to as 'my Master' and the 'greatest scholar–publisher of his day' (ibid., 121). Warburg 'became a publisher by osmotic absorption, sucking in the wisdom of my elders through the sceptical filter of a mind trained in the metaphysical hair-splitting of an Oxford course in Greats' (ibid., 89).

On 5 July 1922 Warburg married May Nellie Holt (*b.* 1902/3), daughter of Hellier Holt. They had three sons but were divorced in 1932. On 21 January 1933 he married the painter and designer Pamela Bryer, *née* de Bayou (1904/5–1978), a widow with whom he had a son who died of a cerebral haemorrhage only twenty-four hours after his birth. After Stallybrass's death in 1931 Warburg became increasingly dissatisfied with his job at Routledge. He attempted innovations, but in 1935 he was dismissed from the company. That year he and Roger Senhouse purchased the publishing firm of Martin Secker, which was in receivership, for £3100. With Senhouse looking after the finances and Warburg concerned with 'practically everything else' (Warburg, *Occupation*, 175), Secker and Warburg, as it was renamed, published the works of Thomas Mann, H. G. Wells, André Gide, Louis Mumford, and George Orwell. The firm quickly became known for its radical stance, but while it was anti-fascist, it was also anti-communist and thus in direct opposition to the ethos of many intellectuals of the day, especially those published by Victor Gollancz. When Orwell and Gollancz parted company over *The Road to Wigan Pier*—Gollancz was unhappy with Orwell's equivocal socialist beliefs—it was to Warburg that Orwell took *Homage to Catalonia*. Thereafter the firm published all of Orwell's work, and the author and the publisher became trusted friends. During the Second World War, Warburg served as a corporal in the St John's Wood company Home Guard; his sergeant was Blair (Orwell).

In 1951, with its fortunes in difficulty, Secker and Warburg joined the Heinemann Group of publishers. In 1952 Warburg helped to found the magazine *Encounter* and persuaded Stephen Spender to be its British editor. Intended as an English version of the French *Preuves*, a cultural magazine arising out of the Society for Cultural Freedom (of which Warburg was treasurer), *Encounter* was first published in October 1953. It later came under fire from Spender and others when it was made public that much of the money to produce the magazine came from the CIA. Warburg defended this by saying that 'in the early fifties the C.I.A. was not by any means the hated organization it is today. Then the Russians appeared hostile … while the Bay of Pigs and the brutalities of the Vietnam involvement lay in the future' (Warburg, *Occupation*, 156).

Warburg's ability to stand up to the establishment was tested in 1954 when he faced prosecution for publishing a supposedly obscene book, *The Philanderer* by Stanley Kaufmann. He related his version of events in 'A slight case of obscenity', in the *New Yorker Magazine* in April 1957. Although he was offered the chance to plead guilty and therefore incur a relatively modest fine with the injunction to destroy all copies of the book, Warburg opted for a much riskier—and more public—trial at the Old Bailey. The gamble paid off, and he was acquitted by a unanimous jury of all charges. The presiding justice's summing up became 'famous throughout legal and literary circles' (Warburg, *All Authors are Equal*, 188) for its common-sense approach to a difficult subject. It was printed as an appendix in later editions of *The Philanderer*. The case opened the way for the changes to the Obscene Publications Act, long before the famous *Lady Chatterley* trial in 1960.

During the 1950s Secker and Warbug published the works of Simone de Beauvoir, Colette, Alberto Moravia, Günter Grass, and Angus Wilson, as well as the translation of Pierre Boulle's *La pont de la rivière Kwai*. William Shirer's *The Rise and Fall of the Third Reich* (1960) marked the firm's entry into the new decade, which saw the publication of the novels of Melvyn Bragg and Julian Gloag. In 1961 Warburg was elected director of the Heinemann Group, a post he held until his retirement in 1971.

Warburg published two volumes of autobiography: *An Occupation for a Gentleman* (1959) and *All Authors are Equal* (1973). His wife, Pamela, was a sustaining force in his life until her death in 1978. Frederic Warburg died of heart failure at University College Hospital, London, on 25 May 1981. JANE POTTER

Sources F. Warburg, *An occupation for a gentleman* (1959) · F. Warburg, *All authors are equal* (1973) · *WWW*, 1981–90 · obit. · b. cert. · m. certs. · d. cert.
Archives U. Reading L., George Routledge & Sons Ltd archive, corresp. · U. Reading L., Secker and Warburg Ltd archive, corresp.
Likenesses photograph, *c.*1906, repro. in Warburg, *An occupation for a gentleman* · photograph, *c.*1917, repro. in Warburg, *An occupation for a gentleman* · P. de Bayou, oils, *c.*1950, repro. in Warburg, *An occupation for a gentleman* · A. McBean, photograph, 1959, repro. in Warburg, *An occupation for a gentleman* · photograph, *c.*1970, repro. in Warburg, *All authors are equal*

Warburg, Sir Siegmund George (1902–1982), banker, was born on 30 September 1902 at Tübingen, Germany,

Sir Siegmund George Warburg (1902–1982), by unknown photographer, c.1950

the only child of Georges Siegmund Warburg (1871–1923), landowner and farmer, of Hamburg and Urach, and his wife, Lucie (1866–1955), daughter of Max Kaulla, a lawyer in Stuttgart and descendant of a distinguished German-Jewish banking family. Warburg was educated in the Altes Gymnasium in Reutlingen, and subsequently in Urach at the Evangelisches Seminar, established in 1479 and maintaining well into Warburg's time a strong tradition in classical studies.

Apprentice banker Living on the isolated estate in the hills outside Urach, with relatively few physical comforts and those further reduced throughout the First World War, Siegmund Warburg grew up in an environment of some austerity, certainly compared with his wealthier Hamburg cousins, though with no sense of personal deprivation. Without companions of his own age and sheltered from the wider world, he read widely, and under the influence of his mother acquired a formidable sense of duty and lofty standards for himself and others. Although in his school years he had developed a strong interest in history and philosophy, subjects he hoped to study at university before embarking on a political career, he was instead persuaded at the age of seventeen, on the invitation of his father's first cousin Max Warburg, to enter M. M. Warburg & Co. in Hamburg, the family bank established in 1798. A major factor in his decision to join the bank was the knowledge that his parents' fortune, patriotically invested almost entirely in German war loan, had been largely dissipated by the post-war inflation. After three years as a trainee in Hamburg, Warburg undertook the traditional

private banker's apprenticeship, spending prolonged periods with leading banks and trading houses with which M. M. Warburg & Co. had connections, including N. M. Rothschild & Sons in London and Kuhn, Loeb & Co. in New York. After returning to Hamburg in 1928, Warburg found his progress within the family firm gallingly slow, despite his obvious gifts for both banking and diplomacy and his growing acquaintance in the worlds of politics and business. He was named a partner in M. M. Warburg & Co. in 1930, a year after his cousin Eric, Max's only son and the heir apparent, and he opened an office for the firm in Berlin, where he established valuable connections in banking, industry, and government. He was also involved in the delicate international negotiations that enabled M. M. Warburg & Co. to survive the banking crisis of 1931 with the help of the American branch of the Warburg family, Max Warburg's brothers Paul and Felix, who were backed by the substantial resources of Kuhn, Loeb & Co., the first-rank investment-banking house in New York, in which Felix was a partner.

Establishment of S. G. Warburg & Co. Correctly perceiving in Hitler's assumption of power the grave personal and collective threat that his more sanguine cousins continued until much later to deny, Warburg withdrew what small capital he could and left Germany for England early in 1933. He established a modest company in the City of London, the New Trading Company, attracting a small staff that with help from the Rothschild family and other English friends slowly built up a clientele for the firm's financial and investment services. Established with a capital of £125,000 subscribed by an investor group including Dutch International Corporation, an affiliate of M. M. Warburg & Co., the New Trading Company began by financing small and medium-sized businesses, arranging commercial credits for exports and imports, accepting bills, and gradually expanding into other merchant-banking activities such as dealings in securities and foreign exchange. Initially there were no salaries for the senior staff, and the first year's profits amounted to about £850. Warburg himself became a British subject in 1939, but several of his associates had to endure the stigma of 'enemy alien' status until well into the war. His principal colleague was a former German industrialist, Henry Grunfeld, to whom in later years Warburg unfailingly ascribed co-responsibility for his firm's extraordinary success. In its beginnings, however, limited by its small capital, meagre contacts, and later the paucity of opportunity in wartime London, the firm laboured in relative obscurity; it adopted the name S. G. Warburg & Co. only in 1946, when it had capital and reserves of some £290,000, which included a profit that year of about £12,000.

Driven by shared ambitions to recoup the standing and fortunes they had lost in their flight from the Third Reich, the senior directors of Warburgs, as the firm came to be known, brought to even the smallest transaction an intense concentration and attention to detail that were rare enough in the City, and the company came to be valued by a growing list of industrial and other clients. S. G. Warburg differed decisively from other banks in the City, in both methods and atmosphere: hard work and long hours were taken for granted, not considered a lapse from gentlemanly behaviour. The internal information system within Warburgs was unique, based on circulation each afternoon of a daily précis of every important communication received or sent, including telephone calls and internal memoranda; moreover, all significant current business was thoroughly discussed by the entire executive cadre at the celebrated 9.15 a.m. meetings, chaired each week by a different director, no matter how junior. Clients were a collective responsibility; teams of associates and seniors were assigned to individual transactions, but every executive was responsible for knowing details of all business being conducted in the house. Punctilious in keeping to his schedule, Siegmund Warburg none the less always had time for his young colleagues, who rarely realized how quickly their written work came to his attention. Accurate and literate writing could propel a young executive rapidly upward, while no sloppiness or inelegance escaped notice, with the perpetrator being invited pointedly to improve.

The puritanical work ethic within the bank, with its legendary long days and relatively austere, briskly paced and purposeful business lunches, was initially a source of condescending City amusement, but it ultimately attracted a wide admiration not untinged with envy. That ethic reflected Warburg's personal dedication to perfectionism in every detail, and his concentration on important—as opposed to merely urgent—matters. The relentlessly high standard he set himself and his colleagues was influenced by the early work habits inculcated by his mother, whose example he often cited, and to whom he remained profoundly devoted until her death in London in 1955.

Widening international connections In the mid-1950s, the expanding S. G. Warburg & Co. acquired a stock-exchange listing by merging into a listed corporate shell, which then changed its name to Mercury Securities. Mercury was in due course to create substantial wealth for its shareholders, and to serve as the vehicle for further acquisitions. With the purchase of Seligman Brothers in 1957, S. G. Warburg & Co., then with a staff of eighty, gained entry to the Accepting Houses Committee, and thus the top rank of City merchant banks, which materially facilitated access to larger corporate clients, both British and foreign. The firm's widening international connections were based to no small degree on Siegmund Warburg's indefatigable cultivation of potential clients, often met in the course of meticulously planned and documented trips which he used to cement old friendships and to explore new global business possibilities.

When in late 1958 Warburgs advised an Anglo-American group in its successful takeover of British Aluminium, overcoming bitter opposition from a phalanx of the City establishment, Siegmund Warburg achieved a personal triumph that captured much political and press attention and revealed a mastery of public relations and a flair for bold but carefully prepared strategy that were to be repeatedly deployed by the firm in subsequent take-over bids and defences on behalf of major British and foreign companies. The British Aluminium struggle was acknowledged even at the time as a defining moment for the City of London: by appealing for the first time directly to the shareholders of a target company, despite the opposition and indeed over the heads of its board of directors, Warburgs pioneered the modern take-over bid in London; such techniques were afterwards widely emulated, acting as a catalyst for industrial change and corporate expansion, and transforming relations among shareholders, corporate executives, and the wider investing public. Grand Metropolitan's acquisition of Watneys, a pillar of the old-established brewing companies, was another example of Warburg's willingness to confront venerable companies and their bankers on behalf of clients. Acting sometimes for controversial figures such as Cecil King or Roy Thomson, Warburg chose and prepared all his moves with the detailed precision associated with military operations. He was not a speculator, but was willing to take reasoned risks based on feelings and intuition as well as on a cool assessment of likely outcomes; he became as celebrated in the City for the clients he avoided, such as Bernie Cornfeld and Charles Clore, as for those for whom he chose to act. He would take on an assignment only if convinced that it was in the client's best interest, and consistently maintained that the firm should immediately withdraw if a client did not accept the firm's advice.

As S. G. Warburg & Co. prospered on an increasing volume of investment and financing advice undertaken for government agencies as well as corporate clients, it moved to larger premises. The firm trebled in size and by the late 1960s was regarded as one of the leading merchant banks in London, no longer the striving outsider but the very embodiment of the City's post-war success and international prestige. The firm and Siegmund Warburg personally were increasingly sought for advice on a whole range of corporate matters, sometimes going far beyond finance to delicate issues of corporate governance, psychology, and even ethics. Siegmund Warburg observed the achievements of his firm with some misgivings, cautioning constantly against complacency, self-congratulation, and the sclerosis inherent in establishment conventionality and in sheer size. Always indifferent to the trappings of personal wealth, he continued to live in an elegant but understated London flat, eschewing the traditional City banker's pursuits of country life, clubs and social functions, or sport of any kind. Although he was surrounded by carefully chosen objects reflecting a cultivated taste in furniture and art, Warburg was not interested in collecting *per se*: aside from the books he bought and read he accumulated no collections. He never drove a car; his recreations throughout his life remained those of his youth: reading widely, listening to music, and, above all, conversation. He often enjoyed a convivial game of cards, most usually within his family.

The Eurobond market Perceiving opportunities in the large pool of United States dollars that had accumulated in Europe after the Second World War, Warburg was the individual most influential in establishing the Eurobond market (which ultimately became the main source of international finance for business and government borrowing), with the pioneer underwriting in 1963 of a $15 million loan for Autostrade Italiane, an Italian government agency. The Autostrade underwriting, which had the strong support of the Banca d'Italia, represented an innovative transaction that compelled wide admiration. The success of that issue and a subsequent stream of Eurocurrency issues of increasing complexity spurred the polyglot Warburgs' team to develop a special expertise in Eurobond financing, leading a group of international underwriters that enabled issuers to place their bonds simultaneously in major world markets. Borrowers turning to the firm for assistance included governments, international agencies such as the European Coal and Steel Community, the European Investment Bank, and public agencies, notably the Cassa per il Mezzogiorno, and corporate clients from all over the world, including Mobil, ITT, Hoechst, Chrysler, Imperial Chemical Industries, and many others. S. G. Warburg & Co. also played a major role in opening up the Japanese market, following Siegmund Warburg's visit to Tokyo in 1963 with a merchant-banking delegation from London; additionally the firm was active elsewhere in Asia, including Australia and New Zealand.

Siegmund Warburg's ambition to establish a truly global investment bank was, however, frustrated by successive disappointments in the American market, where first the link with his Schiff and Warburg cousins in Kuhn, Loeb & Co., and then a number of other banking alliances, failed to cohere and to generate the momentum necessary to compete with the American investment banks, which had vastly greater capitalization and substantial domestic placing power. A major failure was Siegmund Warburg's inability to find the appropriate chief executive who could realize his ambition of establishing an important presence in North America. A complicated partnership between Warburgs, Paribas, and then the American firm A. G. Becker, from 1974 to its dissolution in 1982 produced more controversy than profits and threatened to embroil Warburgs in the clash that arose over the French socialist regime's intention to nationalize Paribas. The concept of the Warburg–Paribas alliance was none the less a significant expression of Siegmund Warburg's abiding interest in establishing an élite international investment-banking group, focusing on corporate and government business without offering retail banking services. The investment management side of Warburgs, a part of the firm in which Siegmund Warburg took relatively little personal interest, continued however to prosper impressively, as did European investment banking, which had always engaged a larger share of his energies and involvement.

In all his efforts as a banker, Warburg was animated by a large-scale vision of strategic alliances among leading banks in the world's major financial centres, in which he saw the City of London, with its expertise and peerless infrastructure, as the leader, fulfilling its traditional role in mobilizing investment capital on a global scale. Warburg resigned from the chairmanship of Mercury Securities in 1964, and a few years later from its board, but retained the title of president. Whatever his title or however others might choose to define his frequent retirements, he kept in the closest touch with the firm, spending hours each day on its affairs, which he knew in the minutest detail thanks to frequent telephone contact and the ceaseless stream of correspondence that followed him wherever he was. To the end of his life he retained a veto over decision making at the bank, and he took a keen interest in strategies, individual transactions, and personnel matters.

Management style A complex personality of enormous charm and intelligence, with an abundant share of aristocratic pride and a sometimes touchy sensitivity, Siegmund Warburg both fascinated and intimidated his associates, many of whom monitored his moods with anxious attention. They competed with each other for preferment—like so many courtiers of a sovereign who could be extremely generous, avuncular, even affectionate, but who might also withdraw his favour abruptly, casting the object of displeasure into a painful internal exile that was often the prelude to departure from the firm. Sometimes profoundly pessimistic, even despondent when brooding over disappointments and losses, Warburg could also feel unrestrained enthusiasms for ideas, books, or individuals, whom he would on occasion pursue with a warmth few could resist.

Employing graphological analysis, which he found an indispensable aid in assessing personality, Warburg recruited and nurtured several generations of young men, often with backgrounds in the liberal arts, who were given large responsibilities and were well compensated at much earlier ages than their contemporaries elsewhere in the City. Solicitous of their welfare, at times almost paternal, he took considerable pleasure in their advancement within the firm. He demanded of them in return unswerving loyalty, work days that often lasted far into the night and weekends, and a willingness to travel on short notice as the firm's ambassadors to anywhere its business might demand. Not all his bright young men stayed the course; many indeed departed, some with relief, to occupy executive positions in other leading investment banks in London and elsewhere, an élite cohort who for the most part maintained their relationships with Warburgs and with one another. Despite the time and attention Warburg lavished on personnel matters, on occasion he made serious errors of judgement in choosing new colleagues. These failures, though rare, resulted from over-generous assessments based on sometimes euphoric first impressions. Disappointments in people rather than circumstances could plunge Warburg into moods of bleak dejection, from which he would emerge chastened but unembittered, prepared again to trust that others might be found to share his demanding criteria for effort and achievement.

Ever the schoolmaster upholding the highest standards, Warburg orchestrated his celebrated, frightening rages for maximum didactic effect, requiring that mistakes and failures be minutely investigated with a view to gleaning from them valuable lessons for the future. 'There is every use crying over spilt milk!' he would insist, and no English locution infuriated him more than 'let's cross that bridge when we come to it': he always maintained that bridge-crossing had to be meticulously prepared long in advance. Mere correctness, moreover, was insufficient for him: communications were drafted and redrafted for elegance and succinctness, and Warburg shared with several of his originally continental colleagues a sharp editorial eye for niceties of English usage, though he and they never lost their German accents. He was consistently offended by shoddiness and superficiality of any kind, intellectual dishonesty, and cheerful self-congratulation, qualities he found abundant in certain establishment circles; and he was forever worried that the firm's success would lead to hubris, or its growing size to a falling-off in that concentrated enthusiasm that he referred to as *feu sacré*.

Cosmopolitan and profoundly European in culture, at home in several languages, Warburg detested chauvinism and parochialism of all kinds, and was not partisan in politics, which he followed both domestically and internationally with keen interest. In later years he used occasionally to remark that if he had not been compelled to flee his native land he might well have gone into politics or diplomacy instead of banking. Despite his minor conceit that he never read the newspapers, Warburg was in fact remarkably well informed on all issues of the day, except for sports, to which he remained consistently indifferent, if not scornful. He was always immensely demanding, not least of himself, and was icily dismissive of time-wasting, mere affability, and easy answers. Above all he prized what he termed *élan vital*, the life-affirming energy with which he himself was abundantly endowed, and which he was happy to acknowledge in those he might meet from any walk of life. Despite his unmistakably aristocratic bearing, he was able to establish rapport easily with individuals of all social origins, and often took pleasure in learning about their lives and quietly helping those who turned to him for advice or assistance. Warburg's benefactions were generous, discriminating, and often anonymous, reflecting his lifelong aversion to ostentation in any form.

Personal life Warburg had an ambivalent relationship with his Jewish origins: intensely aware and proud of his German-Jewish ancestry, he had imbibed from his mother Jewish ethical teachings, but no actual observance. Having shared the collective Jewish fate of persecution and exile, he remained none the less far from any Jewish ritual, avoiding even pro forma synagogue attendance at high holy days, and working as usual on sabbaths and festivals. He expressed considerable admiration and support for Israeli achievements until his favourable opinion of Israel was soured by a dislike of Menahem Begin's Likud government and its policies, which he regarded as dangerously misguided and morally dubious. Warburg objected in particular to the Likud's aggressive encouragement of Jewish settlement in occupied Arab territories, and the strident tone of its nationalism. He was, however, a fierce defender of his firm when it was threatened by the Arab anti-Israel boycott. Throughout the entire boycott affair, the names of houses which had resisted and those that had not were meticulously recorded, and in due course Warburgs was in a position to reward its friends. By the late 1970s the Warburg name was lifted from the boycott list, enabling the firm to participate in international underwriting syndicates that included Arab firms.

Siegmund Warburg had an imposing physical presence, distinguished by his dark and exceptionally penetrating eyes. Somewhat bowed in later life, he dressed invariably with impeccable English taste and a certain formality. He had married on 8 November 1926 Eva Maria, the beautiful daughter of a leading Swedish banker, Mauritz Philipson. With the unobtrusive devotion in which she was schooled, Lady Warburg was an indispensable, constant source of strength for her husband, tempering both his enthusiasms and his lapses into despair with calm realism, and presiding discreetly over the small-scale entertaining he preferred. She survived him by one year. They had a son, George Siegmund, and a daughter, Anna Maria Biegun, who became residents respectively of the United States and of Israel.

Final years After handing over the chairmanship of Mercury Securities to Henry Grunfeld in 1964, Warburg retained his various directorships of companies within the group until 1969, though he retired officially from his firm shortly after being knighted in 1966. In the mid-1960s Warburg built a holiday home at Roccamare on the Italian coast, hoping to retire there and to put some distance between himself and the quotidian pressures of the City. Frustrated, however, by its remoteness and poor telephone links, he sold the house at Roccamare and in 1972 took up residence in Switzerland, at Blonay near Vevey, a location that facilitated his frequent travel to the main European financial centres in efforts to develop his firm's business. He was chairman of the advisory council of the Warburg group from 1978 until his death, and he continued to travel and negotiate on behalf of the firm until the end, in constant telephone contact with London and consulted by his colleagues on matters great and small. In Tokyo in 1978 he received personally from the Japanese prime minister the first-class order of the Sacred Treasure, analogous to a knighthood in Japanese terms, in recognition of his many years of effort to foster Anglo-Japanese financial and trade relations. He died at 20 Devonshire Place, Westminster, London, on 18 October 1982, from complications following a stroke. His body was cremated.

Obituaries referred to Warburg as perhaps the most influential financier of his time in the City of London, the post-war wonder of merchant banking, who played a pivotal role in fostering the concept of the international investment bank and in helping to maintain the leading position of the City in international finance. He was described as not only an outstanding figure in finance but also an extraordinary personality—an exemplar of non-conformism, intensity, and truly impressive self-discipline. He was without doubt the most creative and distinguished investment banker of his generation. Warburg's perspective on those human constants greed and fear, and his rigorous judgements on the banking enterprise itself, have if anything gained lustre since his death, and are frequently cited in commentaries on subsequent developments within his own firm (acquired by the Swiss Bank Corporation in 1994) and in the wider financial world of the City and beyond. A. J. SHERMAN

Sources R. Chernow, *The Warburgs* (1994) · E. Rosenbaum and A. J. Sherman, *M. M. Warburg & Co., 1798–1938* (1978) · J. Wechsberg, *The merchant bankers* (1966) · *The way it was: an oral history of finance, 1967–1987*, ed. Institutional Investor (1988) · personal knowledge (2004) · d. cert.
Archives S. G. Warburg & Co. Ltd, London, archive | M. M. Warburg & Co., Hamburg, Familienarchiv
Likenesses photograph, *c.*1950, Hult. Arch. [*see illus.*] · S. Meagher, photograph, 1968, Hult. Arch. · R. Skipp, portrait, 1970, S. G. Warburg & Co. Ltd, London

Warburton, Adrian (1918–1944), air force officer, was born at Middlesbrough on 10 March 1918, the younger child of Commander Geoffrey Warburton RN DSO OBE and his wife, Muriel, daughter of Barnard Hankey Davidson, of the Burmese police force. His father, a submarine commander, was laid off by the navy as a result of cuts in defence expenditure and became manager of the Empire cinema, Shepherd's Bush. He was educated at Sangeen School, Bournemouth, and then at St Edward's School, Oxford, where he was remembered as a loner who avoided team games and the other corporate activities in which the school prided itself. In 1936 he was articled to a chartered accountant in London. Living at home at Enfield, in 1937 he joined an armoured territorial unit which he left after little more than a year when he began to learn to fly. In October 1938 he joined the Royal Air Force Volunteer Reserve with a short-service commission. His ability as a pilot was below the average and his early service career was undistinguished. He was posted to 22 squadron, Coastal Command, based in Britain, flying Vickers Vildebeeste biplanes, but spent much of the first year of the war undergoing courses. On 28 October 1939, shortly after the outbreak of war, he married Eileen Adelaide Mary (Betty), barmaid in The Bush public house, Portsmouth, and daughter of William Mitchell, chargehand of the shipwrights, HM Dockyard, Portsmouth. The marriage soon foundered, though they never divorced. Warburton's marriage troubles were compounded by debts, and his commanding officer wanted him out of the country for his own good.

In September 1940 Warburton was posted to Malta with 431 flight (then operating with Martin Marylands) and while still a pilot officer he made his first operational photographic reconnaissance work over the bases used by the Italian navy. Initially he was a navigator, but sickness among crews soon gave him the opportunity to become a pilot. Although 'ham-fisted'—his landings and take-offs were notoriously clumsy and never improved—once in the air he was 'completely at one with the aircraft' (Spooner, 99). His flying career was one of spectacular success. A great individualist, with an exceptional talent for both high-altitude and low-level photography, 'nothing could keep him on the ground'. He was especially notable for his aggressive persistence in the face of danger and for

his resourcefulness, as well as for his brilliant flying and accurate photography. In November 1940 he first became famous as 'the man who had photographed the Italian fleet at Taranto from fifty feet'. As a result of his observations, the Fleet Air Arm was able to launch a devastating night attack on the Italian ships. Although it was no part of his duties, he often attacked the enemy when flying types of aircraft equipped with guns for defence.

In December 1940 Warburton was awarded the DFC for his steady record of daring and successful sorties, and during 1941 and 1942, at six-monthly intervals, he was appointed to the DSO and awarded two bars to his DFC. For eight months of this time he was attached to no. 2 photographic reconnaissance unit at Heliopolis, Cairo, but most of his photographic flights were made from Malta, which was ideally placed for tracking the axis convoys between Naples and north Africa. He thrived during the siege of Malta, when conditions forced convention to be set aside and much was left to individual initiative; he adopted an unusual garb of an army battledress blouse, which he wore with a cravat, and a pair of Oxford bags, his only uniform being his threadbare RAF cap. With a revolver at his waist and a knife in his army desert boots, his appearance was likened to a brigand. During the siege he formed a glamorous partnership with a cabaret singer, Christina.

In August 1942 Warburton attained the acting rank of squadron leader and was put in command of 69 squadron, which had succeeded 431 flight at Malta. Before the end of the year he was given the acting rank of wing commander. This promotion coincided with one of his most remarkable adventures: on 15 November 1942 he set off from Malta to photograph Bizerte, but did not return and was reported missing. Several days later he reported back to base, when it proved that during the reconnaissance his Spitfire had been hit, but after crash-landing at the allied-held airfield at Bône he had managed to make his way back to Malta, via Algiers and Gibraltar, flying in three different kinds of aircraft.

From February 1943 Warburton commanded 683 squadron, mainly comprising Spitfires. He got on well with the Americans of the United States Air Force's 3rd reconnaissance group, which began to operate from Malta; they liked his informal, unstuffy manner. Fair, slight, and good-looking, he had an impish, inquisitive, and friendly personality, but his normal manner was almost shy—in marked contrast to the ruthless daring in the air which had made him a legendary figure. He was awarded the American DFC for a particularly daring low-level reconnaissance of the heavily defended coastline of Pantelleria in June 1943. This was his sixth decoration—he had already received a bar to his DSO—hence the legend of 'six-medal Warburton', although he was more usually known as Warby.

In October 1943 Warburton was attached to the allied headquarters of photographic reconnaissance in the Mediterranean area (the north-west African photographic reconnaissance wing) commanded by Colonel Elliott Roosevelt, and then based at Tunis; Warburton was given command of the British photographic reconnaissance wing (336 wing). However, as the result of a serious motor accident near Tunis in November 1943, he was grounded. While he was recovering in hospital 336 wing was moved to Italy, and at the end of December he was relieved of his command. Early in 1944 he returned to England and was posted to the special duties list. On 12 April 1944 he took off from Mount Farm, the American photographic reconnaissance base in Oxfordshire, in a USAAF Lightning, allegedly to fly to San Severo in Italy. He never arrived, and the circumstances of his disappearance long remained a mystery. In 2002 his remains were found in the cockpit of his Lightning in a field near Egling an der Paar, southern Germany. He was buried in the Commonwealth War Graves Commission cemetery at Durnbach on 14 May 2003.

CONSTANCE BABINGTON SMITH, rev. M. C. CURTHOYS

Sources air ministry and US Air Force records · private information (1959) · C. B. Smith, *Evidence in camera: the story of photographic intelligence in World War II* (1958) · A. Spooner, *Warburton's war: the life of Wing Commander Adrian Warburton* (1987) · *The Times* (30 Nov 2002), 21 · *The Independent* (17 Dec 2002), 5 · *Daily Telegraph* (15 May 2003), 11
Likenesses photographs, repro. in Spooner, *Warburton's war*

Warburton, Bartholomew Elliott George [*pseud.* Eliot Warburton] (1810–1852), writer, eldest son of George Warburton of Aughrim, co. Galway, formerly inspector-general of constabulary in Ireland, who married, on 6 July 1806, Anna, daughter of Thomas Acton of Westaston, co. Wicklow, was born near Tullamore, King's county. After being educated by a private tutor at Wakefield, Yorkshire, he was admitted pensioner at Queens' College, Cambridge, on 8 December 1828, but migrated to Trinity College on 23 February 1830. He graduated BA on 22 May 1834 and proceeded MA in 1837. He was admitted to the Inner Temple in 1832 and to the King's Inn, Dublin, in 1833, and was called to the Irish bar in 1837, but abandoned the law to superintend his Irish estates, travel, and write, always under the name Eliot Warburton.

In 1843 Warburton made an extended tour through Syria, Palestine, and Egypt, describing his travels in the *Dublin University Magazine* (1843 and 1844) and in *The Crescent and the Cross, or, Romance and Realities of Eastern Travel* (2 vols., 1845), which reached seventeen editions. He married at St James's, Piccadilly, London, on 11 January 1848, Matilda Jane (1819/20–1861), second daughter of the late Edward Grove of Shenstone Park, Staffordshire. The Warburtons led a roving life. Their eldest son was born on 20 October 1848, when they were at Lynmouth, Devon. In January 1849 Warburton was dwelling at a château in Switzerland. The summer of 1851 was passed on the Tweed and Yarrow. He was popular and enjoyed adventure.

After publishing *Zoe: an Episode in the Greek War* (1847), Warburton produced the *Memoirs of Prince Rupert and the Cavaliers* (3 vols., 1849; French trans., 1851), which was sympathetically treated, and a lifeless novel, *Reginald Hastings* (1850). In 1851 he edited the *Memoirs of Horace Walpole and his Contemporaries*, a compilation by Robert Folkestone Williams, and in 1852 published *Darien, or, The Merchant*

Prince (3 vols.). Warburton could find no publisher and so abandoned a projected 'impartial' history of Ireland. He collected the materials for a 'History of the poor', and his last visit to Ireland was to examine poverty in Dublin.

At the close of 1851 Warburton was deputed by the Atlantic and Pacific Junction Company to negotiate with the Indian peoples on the Isthmus of Darien on the northern coast of South America, and he embarked from Southampton on 2 January 1852, on board the West India mail steamer *Amazon*, with that object, and with the intention of exploring the district. The ship caught fire and Warburton was among those that perished off Land's End on 4 January. A window was erected to his memory in Iffley church, near Oxford. His widow in 1855 chiefly lived with her two little boys at Oxford or at Iffley. She married, on 6 August 1857, Henry Salusbury Milman, fellow of All Souls College, Oxford, and barrister, and died at Bevere Firs, near Worcester, on 23 October 1861, aged forty-one, having had three daughters with her second husband. Warburton's eldest sister, Sidney, was author of *Letters to my Unknown Friends* (1846). She died at Clifton, Bristol, on 18 June 1858.

One brother was George Drought *Warburton. Another brother, **Thomas Acton Warburton** (*c.*1813–1894), Church of England clergyman and writer, was educated at Trinity College, Dublin (BA 1835, LLB and LLD 1852), and was called to the bar in 1840. He was ordained deacon in 1851 and priest in 1852. He was curate of Horspath, Oxford (1851–3), and vicar of Iffley (1853–76) and of St John the Evangelist, East Dulwich (1876–88). His chief works were the poorly reviewed *Rollo and his Race, or, Footsteps of the Normans* (2 vols., 1848) and *The Equity Pleader's Manual* (1850). He died at Hastings Lodge, Dulwich Wood Park, Dulwich, London, on 22 August 1894, and was buried in Iffley churchyard. He left a widow, Emily Alicia.

W. P. COURTNEY, rev. ELIZABETH BAIGENT

Sources C. Knight, ed., *The English cyclopaedia: biography*, 1 (1856) · Venn, *Alum. Cant.* · *The Times* (7 Jan 1852) · Burke, *Peerage* · Burke, *Gen. GB* · W. R. Dawson and E. P. Uphill, *Who was who in Egyptology*, 3rd edn, rev. M. L. Bierbrier (1995) · GM, 2nd ser., 29 (1848), 421 · GM, 2nd ser., 30 (1848), 645 · GM, 3rd ser., 3 (1857), 330 · GM, 3rd ser., 5 (1858), 202 · GM, 3rd ser., 11 (1861), 693 · private information (1899) · CGPLA Eng. & Wales (1894) [Thomas Acton Warburton] · 'Warburton, T. A.', Allibone, *Dict.* · Boase, *Mod. Eng. biog.* [Thomas Acton Warburton]
Wealth at death £306 8s. 0d.—Thomas Acton Warburton: probate, 5 Nov 1894, CGPLA Eng. & Wales

Warburton, George Drought (1816–1857), army officer and writer on Canada, the third son of George Warburton, of Aughrim, Galway, formerly inspector-general of constabulary in Ireland, and his wife, Anna, the daughter of Thomas Acton of Westaston, co. Wicklow, was born at Wicklow on 2 June 1816. He was educated at the Royal Military Academy, Woolwich, and served in the Royal Artillery from June 1833. From 1837 to 1838 he was with a detachment of the Royal Artillery serving in the Carlist War in Spain, where he was badly wounded in action. For his services he was made knight of the first class of San Fernando. In July 1844 he was sent to Canada, where he was stationed at Montreal. His anonymous description of the

George Drought Warburton (1816–1857), by Herbert Watkins, late 1850s

country under the title *Hochelaga, or, England in the New World* (2 vols., 1846) was published as 'edited by Eliot Warburton', that is, his elder brother Bartholomew Elliott George *Warburton, who had already established himself as a travel writer. George Drought's work quickly ran to several editions in England and the USA and soon became staple reading for travellers.

Warburton returned from Canada in 1846 and was in 1848 promoted captain and served briefly in Corfu; he returned to Woolwich in 1849. The success of his first book encouraged him to write another anonymous work, *The Conquest of Canada* (2 vols., 1849), which like the first passed through several editions and was widely read for its mixture of careful research, exotic descriptions, and lively style. In 1850 he was stationed at Harwich, from where he made frequent visits to London and joined Lady Morgan's literary circle with his brother Eliot.

On 1 June 1853 Warburton married at St George's, Hanover Square, Elizabeth Augusta Bateman-Hanbury, the third daughter of the first Lord Bateman (1780–1845) and his wife, Elizabeth (d. 1882), the daughter of Lord Spencer Stanley Chichester. Their only daughter married Lord Edward Spencer-Churchill. For his next book Warburton followed his brother by turning to biography in his *Memoir of Charles Mordaunt* (2 vols., 1853). He retired from the army as a major on full pay in November 1854 to live at Henley House, Frant, Sussex. On 28 March 1857 he became independent Liberal MP for Harwich, having unsuccessfully contested the seat in 1852. He was in favour of extending the franchise, but opposed to the endowment of Maynooth.

Warburton was subject to severe attacks of what has been described as 'indigestion' and, gripped by one such attack, shot himself through the head at Henley House on 23 October 1857. He was buried at Iffley, near Oxford, where his brother Thomas Acton was vicar and where there is a monument to his brother Eliot, who also died prematurely in tragic circumstances. Although his work is overshadowed by that of his brother, it was much read in its time.

On 15 April 1869 Warburton's widow married George Rushout, third Lord Northwick, and in 1886 they received the Dunmow Flitch, a side of bacon presented each year at Dunmow, Essex, to a married couple who had lived in harmony for a year and a day.

W. P. COURTNEY, rev. ELIZABETH BAIGENT

Sources DCB, vol. 8 · *Essex Standard* (30 Oct 1857), 4 · *The Athenaeum* (31 Oct 1857), 1359 · Burke, *Peerage* · GM, 2nd ser., 40 (1853), 305 · private information (1899) · GEC, *Peerage* · J. H. Leslie, *Landguard fort* (1898) · WWBMP
Archives Essex RO, Chelmsford, corresp. and papers
Likenesses H. Watkins, photograph, albumen print, 1856–9, NPG [*see illus.*]

Warburton, Henry (1784–1858), politician, son of John Warburton of Eltham, Kent, a timber merchant, was born on 12 November 1784. He was educated at Eton College (he was in the fifth form, upper division, in 1799) and at Trinity College, Cambridge, where he was admitted on 24 June 1802. He was in the first class of the college examinations as freshman in 1803, and as junior soph in 1804. He was admitted scholar on 13 April 1804, graduated BA (being twelfth wrangler and placed next to Ralph Bernal) in 1806, and proceeded MA in 1812. George Pryme knew him in his undergraduate days, and both Bernal and Pryme were later his colleagues in political action. While at Cambridge he obtained distinction as a 'scholar and man of science' (Grote, 76).

For some years after leaving the university Warburton was engaged in the timber trade at Lambeth. He took over his father's business in 1808 and gained great experience of the Baltic timber trade, but his interest in science and politics ultimately led to his abandoning commercial life, and in 1831 he ceased trading. He led a long and eventually successful campaign against the timber duties. He was elected FRS on 16 February 1809. Dr William Hyde Wollaston was his closest friend, and in the autumn of 1818 they made a tour together on the continent. When Michael Faraday desired to become FRS, Warburton had objections to his election, on the ground that Faraday had on one occasion treated Wollaston unfairly. Correspondence ensued, and these objections were dispelled (H. B. Jones, *The Life and Letters of Faraday*, 2 vols., 1870, 1.347–53). Warburton was also a member of the Political Economy Club from its foundation in 1821 to his death, and introduced its discussion on tithes, rents, and profits on 13 January 1823. He became a close friend of David Ricardo, who often mentions him in his *Letters to Malthus*. 'Philosopher Warburton', as he was nicknamed, was one of the leading supporters of Brougham in founding London University, and was a member of its first council in 1827.

At the general election of 1826 Warburton was returned to parliament for the borough of Bridport in Dorset as a radical. He made his first long speech on 30 November, on foreign goods, and was re-elected in 1830, 1831, 1833, 1835, 1837, and 1841, all of the elections after the Reform Bill of 1832 being severely contested. Even after the 1832 act, Bridport only had 500 voters; it was notoriously corrupt, as well as being dominated by the naval interest. Here Warburton's lumber experience assisted him and he topped the poll. On 8 September 1841 Warburton resigned his seat on the ground that a petition would have 'proved gross bribery against his colleague [John Romilly]' in which his own agent would have been implicated (Grote, 144). It subsequently came out that before the passing of the Reform Bill he himself had paid large sums of money improperly to certain of the electors. A select committee was appointed to inquire into 'corrupt compromises' alleged to have been made in certain constituencies, so as to avoid investigation into past transactions, and the question whether bribery had been practised at Bridport was referred to the same committee, but nothing resulted from its investigations. Warburton was out of the Commons until 9 November 1843, when he was elected for Kendal. At the dissolution of 1847 he retired from political life, letting it be known that the reforms which he had at heart had been effected.

Warburton's constituency difficulties were similar to those of a number of radicals in the 1830s: they were reformers returned by what were really pre-reform constituencies. Warburton was in some respects an 'avowed Benthamite' (Richardson, 108), but he did not always act with the philosophic radical group, and indeed in 1837 was the subject of severe personal ridicule from Sir William Molesworth in the Commons (Thomas, 239). He was, however, more associated with the group around Molesworth, George Grote, and Charles Buller than any other. In January 1835 Warburton, who was already in contact with Daniel O'Connell on electoral matters, developed a plan for three 'brigades' to enable a progressive government to gain a majority in the Commons. He secured O'Connell's support for a united opposition front to Peel's tory government. Warburton himself sent off individual circulars summoning the Irish MPs to the important meeting in Lichfield House on 18 February 1836, which produced the Lichfield House compact, described as 'one of the most decisive events in British political history between 1832 and 1847' (Macintyre, 144). It would be wrong to say that Warburton made the compact, but it would be fair to say that he enabled it.

Warburton was an indefatigable MP, who often spent twelve hours a day in the house. He was active in a variety of causes, such as bankruptcy, the repeal of the stamp duty on newspapers, the Anti-Corn Law League, and the introduction of penny postage (he was secretary of the select committee on postal reform). He was also noted for his success in achieving the reduction and then abolition of the timber duties; he was a member of the select committee on them in 1835–6. In the course of this he was in March 1836 the subject of a censure motion by G. F. Young, who claimed that Warburton had fiddled his evidence to

the committee to suit his case (Young withdrew his motion when Warburton gained whiggish support).

It was, however, as the spokesman in the Commons for the medical reformers that Warburton's chief impact was made. Following an exchange with Peel in 1827 and the lectures given by George Birkbeck that year, Warburton persuaded the Commons to establish the select committee on anatomy in 1828 (dealing with the supply of corpses for dissection and 'bodysnatching'), wrote its report, and played a central role in the passing of the Anatomy Act (after several attempts) in 1832. Warburton hoped the measure would deal not only with corpses but also with the domestic conditions of the poor. His intention was 'to bring science to the poor man's door' (Richardson, chap. 8) but in this wider hope he was largely disappointed (ibid., 210–15). Warburton's reform acted as a focus for medical reformers generally and for the Benthamites, and sometimes took a curious direction: Richard Carlile gave a gross speech in 1829 announcing that his corpse would be left for dissection, with his skin to be used to cover an armchair for Warburton (ibid., 168). Warburton was later attacked by William Roberts for being himself a shareholder in the London University anatomy school and for applying the act 'to advance the pecuniary interests of himself and his friends … by a traffic in the bodies of the poor' (ibid., 248). The accusation rested on the failure of the act to prohibit the sale of corpses; despite the serious character of the charges, Warburton did not sue for libel though he attacked Roberts in the Commons. He tried to improve the act by a commission in 1840, which failed to report. In 1834 Warburton was chairman of a select committee on the medical profession and in 1840 he, Thomas Wakley (with whom he had disagreed on the anatomy question), and Benjamin Hawes introduced a bill to register medical practitioners and establish a college of medicine, a proposal which the vested interests of the medical profession quickly saw off.

Warburton, who was apparently unmarried, died at his home, 45 Cadogan Place, Chelsea, London, on 16 September 1858. He frequently sailed near the wind, and sometimes almost capsized; but his significance in early Victorian parliamentary radicalism was considerable.

H. C. G. MATTHEW

Sources DNB · Venn, *Alum. Cant.* · R. Richardson, *Death, dissection and the destitute*, pbk edn (1988) · Boase, *Mod. Eng. biog.* · D. M. Williams, 'Henry Warburton and the free trade movement', *Proceedings of the Dorset Natural History and Archaeological Society*, 90 (1968), 285–94 · C. Newman, *The evolution of medical education in the nineteenth century* (1957) · M. J. Peterson, *The medical profession in mid-Victorian London* (1978) · A. D. Macintyre, *The Liberator: Daniel O'Connell and the Irish party, 1830–1847* (1965) · W. Thomas, *The philosophic radicals: nine studies in theory and practice, 1817–1841* (1979) · H. Grote, *The personal life of George Grote* (1873) · C. R. Dod, *Electoral facts, from 1832 to 1853* (1853) · *GM*, 3rd ser., 5 (1858), 531 · *PRS*, 9 (1857–9), 555

Archives BL, corresp. with Francis Place, Add. MSS 35149–35151 · RS, corresp. with Sir John Herschel

Likenesses W. H. Mote, stipple and line engraving, pubd 1840 (after G. Hayter), BM, NPG · G. Hayter, group portrait, oils (*The House of Commons, 1833*), NPG · W. H. Mote, stipple (after J. Holmes),

BM, NPG; repro. in J. Saunders, *Portraits and memoirs of eminent living political reformers* (1840)
Wealth at death under £45,000: probate, 15 Oct 1858, *CGPLA Eng. & Wales*

Warburton, John (1682–1759), herald and antiquary, was born on 26 February 1682 at Bury, Lancashire, the eldest of four sons and eight children, apart from an unnamed infant burial, of Benjamin Warburton (1653–1710) of Elton, in the parish of Bury, and his wife, Mary (d. in or before 1732), daughter of Michael Buxton of Manchester, woollen draper. His father was a yeoman and tenant of Lord Derby, on whose recommendation Warburton was admitted as a recruit to the Inland Revenue on 8 February 1706. In August 1708, while a customs officer at Raven-glass, Cumberland, he effected an exchange to Cocker-mouth. Three weeks later he was reduced to the grade of assistant and sent to Newcastle upon Tyne for entering in his diaries details of surveys that he had not made. In November 1708 he was appointed officer of Darlington Ride Station; he was at Hartlepool when he married, on 1 October 1710 at Whitbeck, Cumberland, Dorothy (b. 1664), daughter of Andrew Hudleston of Hutton John, and his wife, Katherine, daughter of Sir Wilfred Lawson, baronet. She was twice widowed; her former husbands were John Parke (d. 1699), of Whitbeck Hall, with whom she had at least one child, and Edmund Gibson (d. 1708/9) of Town-end, Whitbeck.

In 1712 Warburton was promoted supervisor at Hexham, where he acted as a government informer during the Jacobite rising of 1715 and afterwards assisted the commissioners appointed to inquire into forfeited estates, for which he was advanced to the rank of collector at Richmond, Yorkshire, in 1716. In the same year he separated from his wife and published a map of Northumberland. He remained at Richmond until August 1718, when he was reduced, for drunkenness, to the position of supervisor at Wakefield. Shortly afterwards he resigned from the Inland Revenue and began work on a map of Yorkshire, published about 1720, undertaking two journeys through Yorkshire, in 1718 and 1719, for which the journals survive (BL, Lansdowne MS 911, fols. 346–351b, and 378–99). While at Leeds he stayed with the antiquary Ralph Thoresby. He was admitted a fellow of the Royal Society in March 1719 and of the Society of Antiquaries on 13 January 1720 but was eventually ejected from both bodies, the former in 1757 and the latter before 1752. By 1720 he was already of note as a collector of manuscripts and antiquities. The diary of Humfrey Wanley, Lord Oxford's librarian, reveals, on 6 July 1720, Warburton's 'resolution to part with his Roman Altars' and that on 13 July he sold manuscripts for 100 guineas to Lord Oxford, many of which came from the library of Lord William Howard (1563–1640) at Naworth, Cumberland (pp. 56–7).

Warburton was appointed Somerset herald by patent dated 18 June 1720 because, according to Stephen Martin Leake, Garter king of arms, he had 'made himself service-able to the government in convicting some of the rebels'

John Warburton Esq. Somerset Herald of Arms. Fellow of the Royal Society and of the Antiquarian Society of London 1740.

John Warburton (1682–1759), by Andrew Miller, 1740 (after Gerard Vandergucht)

(Coll. Arms, MS SML 65, 252). From the time of his appointment his relations with the other heralds were bad, initially because he sought subscribers to his maps in return for publishing their arms in the margins without establishing their entitlement to arms. He denied knowledge of the advertisements that appeared in three newspapers in December 1722 stating that the contest between him and the provincial kings of arms about this matter had been determined in his favour. A map of Middlesex, Essex, and Hertfordshire, engraved by Samuel Parker on the scale of two-thirds of an inch to the mile, was published about 1724 under the names of Warburton, Joseph Bland, and Paylor Smyth. Warburton regularly failed to attend chapter meetings at the college, and at the coronation of George II, on 11 October 1727, though he was senior herald by length of appointment the deputy earl marshal ordered that he should officiate as junior herald, and Edward Stibbs, Chester herald, became acting senior herald and proclaimed the challenge.

Warburton's second wife was Mary (1697/8–1778), widow of William Bury of Blankney, Lincolnshire, and daughter of Robert Morrison of London, a merchant. They married at some time between 15 April 1731, when Mary's first husband made his will, which was proved in June 1731, and 3 August 1732, when their son, John, was born. From her first marriage Mary had eight children, and with Warburton she had two; John married Anne Catherine, sister of the antiquary Edward Rowe Mores, and Amelia (1735–1786) became the wife of John Elphinston, a captain in the Royal Navy.

In 1749 Warburton published a map of London and Middlesex engraved by Nathaniel Hill. His colleagues complained that it contained false arms. Warburton justified the arms in *London and Middlesex Illustrated* (1749). He attempted to sell his office for £500 but failed. His *Vallum Romanum* (1753) is largely a reprint of extracts from the *Britannia Romana* of John Horsley (1685–1732); in the preface he stated not only that he suggested in 1715 that the Roman road from Newcastle upon Tyne to Carlisle should be repaired—which after the 1745 Jacobite rising resulted in the 1751 act of parliament for making the road—but also made the unfounded claim of his having been instrumental in the revival of Roman learning and the foundation of the Society of Antiquaries in 1717 by publication of his 1716 map of Northumberland.

Warburton bore a marked physical resemblance to George II, who was one year his junior, as can be seen in the portrait of him in a tabard by Vandergucht, engraved in mezzotint by Andrew Miller in 1740. Contemporaries did not speak well of him; Thomas Pennant, the eminent traveller, wrote:

> I knew Warburton well. He was the most illiterate man I ever met with. Ignorant not only of the learned and foreign languages, but even of his own. As to drawing he had not the humblest rudiments of it. Nor was his knowledge greater in surveying … And yet this man had the Art or rather Cunning to pass through life with credit and to be spoken of after his death as a man of learning and ingenuity. (*N&Q*, 149, 292)

According to Francis Grose 'All the publications under his name both books and maps were done by others hired by him' (Grose, 158).

Stephen Martin Leake states that Warburton remained for many years a prisoner for debt in the Fleet prison. Latterly he lived in the College of Arms, where he died on 11 May 1759; he was survived by his wife, who died, aged eighty, in 1778. He was buried on 17 May at St Benet Paul's Wharf, following his testamentary wish to lie 'as near as possible to the remains of my old friend Gregory King, Esq. York Herald in the parish church of St. Benet's Paul's Wharf'. King, who was Lancaster (not York) herald, had died in 1712, eight years before Warburton became Somerset herald. A codicil, dated 25 April 1759, to Warburton's undated will, proved on 18 May 1759, refers to his being very feeble in his legs and hips. He is said to have made over £2000 by the sale of his maps, but spent more, partly on forming the magnificent manuscript and other collections that were largely dispersed at his death and are his most lasting monument. His collection of Elizabethan and Jacobean plays, several of which were unique, was destroyed through his own carelessness and the ignorance of Betsy Baker, his cook, by whom they were 'unluckily burnd or put under pye bottoms' (*DNB*). A list of the fifty-five plays destroyed is in the British Library (BL, Lansdowne MS 807). Warburton's library of printed books and manuscripts was sold at auction in 764 lots by Samuel Paterson at Essex House, Strand, in six evening sales commencing on Monday 19 November 1759. Edward Howard, ninth duke of Norfolk, purchased sixty-three lots and presented them to the College of Arms, where they form the EDN collection. The three-volume *Baronagium genealogicum*, for which the sale catalogue states that Warburton had been offered £500 by the late earl of Oxford, was purchased by Joseph Edmondson, who based his 1764 six-volume peerage of the same name on it. There was a subsequent sale on 7 and 8 March 1766. Thirty-eight volumes of Warburton's manuscript collections are in the Lansdowne collection in the British Library, of which twenty-one relate to Yorkshire.   THOMAS WOODCOCK

Sources A. Wagner, *Heralds of England: a history of the office and College of Arms* (1967), 317, 341, 346n., 350–51, 383–4, 389–90, 395, 399, 404, 419–20, 493 · *Archaeologia Aeliana*, 4th ser., 10 (1933), 1–57 · *N&Q*, 149 (1925), 292; 165 (1933), 42–4, 105 · W. H. Godfrey, A. Wagner, and H. Stanford London, *The College of Arms, Queen Victoria Street* (1963), 160–61 · *The diary of Humfrey Wanley, 1715–1726*, ed. C. E. Wright and R. C. Wright, 2 vols. (1966), 39, 47, 54–8, 61–2, 65–6, 69–71, 84, 130, 197, 404, 406, 408, 410, 413 · M. Noble, *A history of the College of Arms* (1804), 388–93 · S. M. Leake, *Heraldo memoriale*, ed. A. R. Wagner (1981), 5–6, 43, 46, 103, 108 · A. R. Wagner, *The records and collections of the College of Arms* (1952), 25, 40 · C. E. Wright, *Fontes Harleiani* (1972), 346–7 · F. Grose, *The Olio* (1792), 158–60 · T. Moule, *Bibliotheca heraldica Magnae Britanniae* (privately printed, London, 1822), 313–14, 374–5 · *DNB* · A. Sparke, ed., *The registers of the parish church of Bury, 1647–1698*, Lancashire Parish Register Society, 24 (1905), 79 · 'Alphabetical list of Scottish arms, A–C', Lyon Office Library, Edinburgh, MS 63

Archives BL, MS list of lost plays formerly in his possession, Lansdowne MS 807 · Bodl. Oxf., additions to John Tilston's MS catalogue of the English nobility and officers of the state, MS Add. C77 · Bodl. Oxf., collections of Irish arms, MS Eng misc C25 · CKS, ordinary of Kentish arms, U1706 · Coll. Arms | Alnwick Castle, Northumberland, collections for the history of Northumberland · BL, Harley MSS 2188, 2195, 2311, 2320, 2377, 2880, 2885, 2965, 3013, 3097, 3490, 3639, 3723, 3724, 3766, 3775, 3776, 3826, 3846, 3897, 3908, 3911, 3935, 4219, 4344 · BL, Lansdowne MSS, 886–923 · BL, memorandum book, collections and papers, incl. sketches, and an account of Kingston upon Hull, Add. MSS 1046, 5151, 5480, 21977, 23703–23708, 25352, 35336 · Coll. Arms, EDN Collection · Coll. Arms, Segar's Baronagium · Lyon Office Library, Edinburgh, 'Alphabetical list of Scottish arms, A–C', MS 63 · priv. coll., papers and collections relating to Norfolk · S. Antiquaries, Lond., MSS 233–235 · S. Antiquaries, Lond., Berkshire, Cornwall, and Hampshire collections · Syon House, two vols. on Northumberland, formerly belonging to duke of Northumberland

Likenesses A. Miller, mezzotint, 1740 (after G. Vandergucht), BM, NPG [*see illus.*]

Wealth at death will, PRO · 'clearly proved truth of proverb which says, Honesty is the best policy … by dying a beggar': Grose, *The Olio*, 160

Warburton, John Paul (1840–1919), police officer in India, was born on 28 August 1840 in Kabul, Afghanistan. His mother was Shah Jahan Begum (*d.* in or after 1866), a member of an Afghan noble family and relative of Shah Shuja, king of Kabul. His adoptive father was Lieutenant-Colonel Robert Warburton (*d.* 1864) of the Bengal army. The identity of Warburton's natural father is not certain. Warburton was born Jahan Dad Khan, and it is most likely that his father was Shah Jahan Begum's first husband, Sirdar Faiz Talab Khan, a high official in the service of the emir of Kabul. Warburton embraced the culture of his adopted father and typically dressed in English rather than Indian fashion. According to his biographer, G. D. Martineau, 'He never saw England, but anyone glancing at him or meeting him casually at a party would have taken him for an Englishman wearing an immaculate suit, of fashionable cut, and often a topi' (Martineau, 73). Warburton had one younger half-brother, Sir Robert *Warburton (1842–1899), Royal Artillery officer and author of *Eighteen Years in the Khyber*. There was a marked difference in the treatment of the two sons. While Robert Warburton was educated in England and secured a commission in the Royal Artillery, John Paul was educated at a Roman Catholic school in Agra. In 1864, possibly through his father's influence, he received a much less prestigious appointment as an assistant superintendent in the Punjab police. A year earlier he had married Mary Whayman (1842–1889), the widow of a British army ensign. They had six children. In 1872 Warburton became superintendent of police in Ludhiana district in the Punjab, where he served for thirteen years.

Warburton gained a reputation as the greatest detective of nineteenth-century India. He was aided in police work by his fluency in several Indian languages, and, according to British observers, his Afghan background was believed to give him an important 'native' insight into the workings of the Indian criminal mind. Among Punjabis, Warburton earned the nickname of Button Sahib, and a reputation as 'a controller of many devils' that allowed him to gain information about criminal activities. Warburton also had a reputation of being a master of disguise, and popular stories attributed to him the power to change his shape into that of a tiger. In reality, Warburton's success was based on patient and painstaking detective work. According to Percival Griffiths, 'It can safely be said that few men have possessed his power of unravelling criminal problems. ... He achieved his results by a remarkable understanding of criminal psychology and by a capacity for relentless, logical deduction from ascertained clues' (Griffiths, 405).

Much of Warburton's work involved the investigation of 'criminal tribes', such as the Sansiahs, which the colonial state considered to be one of the greatest threats to public order in late nineteenth-century India. He was particularly successful at a common method for dealing with collective crime in British India: persuading gang members to turn approver (or king's witness) in exchange for pardon or reduced sentences. In two of his most famous cases, Warburton broke up a gang of dacoits (gang robbers) who were believed to be responsible for over 600 robberies in the Punjab, and a gang of poisoners who had been active for over two decades. On several occasions he was selected by the government of India for special duties in the investigation of important criminal cases in other provinces. Rudyard Kipling interviewed Warburton about the nature of Indian police work while he was writing the stories that became *Plain Tales from the Hills* (1888), and Warburton provided the model for Rudyard Kipling's police character Strickland. In 'Miss Youghal's Sais', the story that introduces Strickland, the narrator writes that Strickland took for his model the one man 'in the whole of

upper India ... who can pass for Hindu or Mahommedan, hide-dresser or priest, as he pleases. He is feared and respected by the natives from the Ghor Kathri to the Jamma Musjid; and he is supposed to have the gift of invisibility and executive control over many Devils' (Kipling, 24).

Warburton retired from the Punjab police in 1900, after reaching the rank of assistant inspector-general. After his retirement he served as inspector-general of the Patiala police under Maharaja Rajinder Singh. At George V's 1911 coronation durbar in Delhi, Warburton was made a CIE for his rescue of a British doctor during riots against plague measures in Patiala in 1902. He also received a grant of land in the Punjab for his services, and a village and railway station there were named for him. Warburton died in October 1919 at Kasauli, in the Punjab, following a riding accident.   MICHAEL SILVESTRI

Sources G. D. Martineau, *Controller of devils: a life of John Paul Warburton, C. I. E., of the Punjab police* (1965) · E. Candler, *The Times* (29 Dec 1919) · P. Griffiths, *To guard my people: the history of the Indian police* (1971), 404–5 · R. Kipling, 'Miss Youghal's sais', *Plain tales from the hills* (1888); new edn (1987)
Archives BL OIOC, government of the Punjab, police annual administration and police proceedings reports
Likenesses photographs, repro. in Martineau, *Controller of Devils*

Warburton, Katharine Anne Egerton- [*known as* Mother Kate] (1840–1923), Anglican nun, was born at Warburton, Cheshire, on 24 March 1840, the eldest child of James Francis Egerton-Warburton (1807–1849), a Church of England priest from an ancient Cheshire family, and his wife, Anne (*d.* 1886), second daughter of George Stone of Blisworth, Northamptonshire. A lively girl, she loved the outdoor life and the company of horses and dogs. She was also sensitive and intelligent, with a keen eye for colour and a gift for drawing and writing. Her father was influenced by the Oxford Movement but died when she was only nine; her religious formation therefore owed more to her cousin at Arley Hall, Rowland Egerton-Warburton, and his chaplain, Charles Gutch, who prepared her for confirmation and her first confession.

At the age of eighteen, inspired by Henry Collins's missionary and social work in London docks, Katharine wanted to join Elizabeth Neale's sisterhood of the Holy Cross in Wapping, but was persuaded by Gutch to join the Society of St Margaret at East Grinstead founded by Elizabeth's brother J. M. Neale. This was an active order, devoted mainly to nursing and caring for orphans and the poor. She took life vows the day after her twenty-first birthday. Almost immediately after being received into the community she was sent to work among the poor in the slums of Soho, in the parish of St Mary's, Crown Street, where J. C. Chambers was incumbent. Nursing the sick and dying, and teaching in both day and night schools, she proved to have an extraordinary affinity with people, especially with the rough diamonds among the boys. She vividly describes the scenes and incidents of her seven years there in some of her occasional writings, which were collected into two books, *Memories of a Sister of S Saviour's Priory* (1903) and *Old Soho Days and other Memories* (1906). The work in Soho was disbanded in 1865, but in

April 1866 she went with a small group of sisters to Haggerston in the East End to establish an autonomous daughter house. The secession of most of the sisters to the Roman Catholic church in 1868 led to her election as mother, and she embarked on her life's work, encouraged and advised by the chaplain, Father Machonochie, vicar of St Alban the Martyr, Holborn, and aided in practical ways by, among others, Robert Brett.

Haggerston was an area 'of unparalleled dreariness', 'of crushed down desolate poverty', but Mother Kate—as she was popularly known—had an indomitable spirit. The sisters had only just moved on to the site in Great Cambridge Street (now Queensbridge Road) where St Saviour's Priory was to be built when there was an outbreak of smallpox. Their heroic work in nursing, and their distribution of food, clothing, and bedding, provided by an appeal through *The Times*, gained them much support and goodwill. Mother Kate's great concern was to serve Christ in the poor, the sick, and the neglected. The needs of the area were almost overwhelming, but she did what seemed most practical and realistic. This led to many experiments; some were short-lived, but others lasted until they were taken over by the welfare state, such as the day nursery (the first of its kind in London, set up in 1879 to care for the children of working mothers) and the dispensary (opened in 1888 in the new purpose-built priory). Another project in which she took particular interest was the establishment of a series of holiday homes. All this was in addition to a vast amount of welfare and social work.

Mother Kate had a natural courtesy, and respected the dignity of the poor. 'Her power of listening amounted to genius', as one of the sisters said (*Memories of Mother Kate*, 41). Her interests were wide, including books, art, politics, and sport: the prince of Wales, when visiting the priory, was amused to see a photograph of a well-known jockey in her sitting room. She involved many lay helpers in the priory's work, as well as inspiring the other sisters, and made the idea of sisterhoods much more widely accepted. She resigned as mother only a few days before her death on 18 October 1923 at St Saviour's Priory. She was buried in City of London cemetery, Ilford, on 22 October.

PETER G. COBB

Sources [Mother Cicely and Sister D. Beerbohm SSM], *Memories of Mother Kate* (1925) [probable authors] · [K. A. Egerton-Warburton SSM], *Memories of a sister of S. Saviour's Priory*, new edn (1912) · Mother Kate [K. A. Egerton-Warburton SSM], *Old Soho days and other memories* (1906) · *A hundred years in Haggerston: the story of St Saviour's Priory*, St Saviour's Priory (1966) · C. Booth, *Life and labour of the people in London*, 3rd ser., in C. Booth, 2 (1902), 89–92 · P. F. Anson, *The call of the cloister: religious communities and kindred bodies in the Anglican communion*, rev. edn (1964), 347–50 · Burke, *Gen. GB* · M. Hall, 'Arley Hall, Cheshire', *Country Life* (7 June 1990), 140–45 · parish register (baptism), Warburton, Cheshire
Archives St Saviour's Priory archive, London
Likenesses F. Egerton-Warburton, crayon, *c.*1848, St Saviour's Priory, London · N. Taylor, photograph, *c.*1874, St Saviour's Priory, London · Law, photograph, St Saviour's Priory, London · photographs, St Saviour's Priory, London
Wealth at death £6004 16s. 2d.: probate, 20 Dec 1923, *CGPLA Eng. & Wales*

Warburton, Mabel Clarisse (1879–1961), missionary and educationist, was born on 22 June 1879 at Kings Langley, Hemel Hempstead, Hertfordshire, the second of two children of Thomas Frederick Warburton and his wife, Mabel Catherine Harries (*d.* 1879). Her father was already deceased, and her mother did not survive the birth, so Warburton was raised by her grandmother Mrs Harries, at Bradwell House near Wolverton, Buckinghamshire. Her brother was declared insane and died at an institution.

Mabel Warburton attended Cheltenham Ladies' College from 1895 to 1897, and was greatly inspired by its famous principal and pioneer of women's education, Dorothea Beale. Like Beale, Warburton was profoundly religious in the moderate Church of England mould. A combination of religious conviction, sense of service, and pioneering role for women's education led Warburton, who never married, to join the British Syrian Mission. At the age of twenty-two, after a period in Egypt, Warburton was appointed headmistress of the British Syrian Training College at Beirut, a position she held until the First World War broke out in 1914.

In January 1918, after the British occupation of Jerusalem, Mabel Warburton was one of the first British women to be allowed into Palestine to engage in rescue work. In co-operation with several Anglican mission organizations Warburton founded and partly financed a high school and college for girls, the Jerusalem Girls' College, where she was principal from 1919 to 1926. The institution, which was open to both Arab and Jewish pupils, offered a liberal, English education and high academic standards, including a teacher's training course, for girls from the middle and upper class.

The Anglican schools in Palestine were known as centres of ethnic and religious reconciliation, and the Jerusalem Girls' College stressed tolerance and peaceful co-existence between the Christian, Muslim, and Jewish pupils. The institution was a success not only academically, but also as non-nationalistic alternative in a society characterized by increasingly nationalistic antagonism. Warburton continued to support the college financially until it was forced to close down in 1948, when the British mandate came to an end.

Mabel Warburton, who modernized the traditional missionary role, insisting on academically trained teachers as well as equal treatment of Arab and European staff members, was described by a colleague as:

a very cheerful, extrovert woman, deeply religious, friendly to everybody, She had a fat and rather ugly fox terrier called Jim, who always accompanied her on long country walks around Jerusalem. She spoke Arabic well, and never seemed to be conscious of difference in race or national outlook. (Emery MSS, 2/4, 122)

While the Middle East and especially the Holy Land had a long tradition of educated, middle-class British women engaging in missionary and educational work, Mabel Warburton played a much more pioneering role. According to the Anglican bishop in Jerusalem, W. H. Stewart, Warburton had the qualifications, the vision, and the gifts of 'a missionary and educational statesman' (*Bible Lands*, January 1962). Her talents as organizer and educationist within the Anglican church were given a wide range in the period from 1926 until the 1950s.

From 1926 until 1935 Warburton was active in social work in St Hilda's Settlement, Bethnal Green, London, where she was 'one of the most inspiring and beloved workers' (Beauman, 91). At the same time she held the post as assistant secretary to the missionary council of the church assembly. This work was to give her a unique insight into the policy of the church as a whole—travelling extensively in Egypt, Sudan, Uganda, Palestine, and Persia—and also of the missionary societies whose headquarters were in London.

In 1934 Warburton became educational adviser for the Anglican church in the Middle East, and as secretary of a new diocesan board of education she was given a key role in reviewing and planning Christian education in the Middle East. In her survey of education in Palestine, published in 1937, Warburton's vision of Christian schools was explicitly stated as:

> to implant in the pupils, the future leaders of the country, Moslem, Jew and Christian, that width of outlook, balance of mind, and sensibility to the claims of others, which will help to build up a better understanding between the peoples of the Holy Land. (Jerusalem and East Mission archives, XXXVII/5)

After the Second World War Warburton established the Ahliyyah School for Girls in Amman. However, her base continued to be the home she had built for herself in the 1920s, Welcome Cottage in Waltham Abbey, Essex, which was not only a private retreat, but open for parties from Bethnal Green. During this period Warburton was educational and political counsellor of missionary societies and overseas bishops, a role that led to much travel. In recognition of her work she was appointed MBE. She resigned the last of her church-related advisory posts in 1957. Mabel Warburton died of cancer on 16 November 1961 at the War Memorial Hospital, Waltham Abbey.

INGER MARIE OKKENHAUG

Sources St Ant. Oxf., Middle East Centre, Jerusalem and the East Mission, XXXI, XXXVII, XXXVIII, XLI · *Bible Lands*, 5 (1919) · *Bible Lands*, 10 (1939) · *Bible Lands* (Jan 1962) · St Ant. Oxf., Middle East Centre, Emery MSS, box 2/4 · I. M. Okkenhaug, 'A study of Anglican [the Jerusalem and East Mission] women missionaries and female education in Palestine, 1888–1948', PhD diss., Institute of History, University of Bergen, Norway, 1999 · K. B. Beauman, *Women and the settlement movement* (1996) · *CGPLA Eng. & Wales* (1962) · b. cert. · d. cert.
Archives St Ant. Oxf., Middle East Centre, Jerusalem and East Mission
Likenesses group photograph, 1920–24, St Ant. Oxf., Middle East Centre
Wealth at death £33,548 7s. 7d.: probate, 1962, *CGPLA Eng. & Wales*

Warburton, Sir Peter (*c.*1540–1621), judge, was the elder son of Thomas Warburton, of Nantwich, Cheshire, and his wife, Anne, daughter of Richard Maisterson of Nantwich, 'a gentlewoman of good discent' (BL, Lansdowne MS 85, fol. 118). After attending Staple Inn, Warburton entered Lincoln's Inn on 2 May 1562, and was called to the bar in February 1572, together with Thomas Egerton. Two years later a former fellow student jokingly lamented his abandonment of bachelorhood to marry (on 4 October 1574) Margaret Barlow, of Dransfield, Derbyshire, with whom he would have two daughters. Promoted bencher in 1582, he delivered the Lent reading of 1584 on the statute 21 Henry VIII c. 15 (falsifying recoveries).

Already JP for the county and legal counsel to the town of Chester, where he had possibly owned a house since 1579, Warburton was recommended by the earl of Leicester, chamberlain of the palatinate of Chester, for one of the borough's seats in the parliament of 1584. Rebuffed on this occasion, he was still returned for Newcastle under Lyme, thanks to his own duchy of Lancaster connections. Warburton became an alderman of Chester in 1585 (as proposed the previous year by both Leicester and the earl of Derby), and represented the city in the parliaments of 1586, 1589, and 1597, declining nomination in 1593 on grounds of pressure of work. He had been appointed queen's attorney in the palatine courts of Chester and Lancaster in 1592, and vice-chamberlain of Chester the following year, when he also received a serjeant's writ. At the creation ceremony in Easter term 1594 Warburton invoked the names of two noble 'patrons' (the earl of Derby and Lord Dudley), linking them with three common lawyers, the late master of the rolls, Sir Gilbert Gerard, his successor, Thomas Egerton, and another Lincoln's Inn man, the judge Thomas Walmsley.

Whether brought in to advise a fellow Lancaster lawyer on a complex conveyance, or earning 'credit and countenance' (*Salisbury MSS*, 4.522) from a jury not initially predisposed in his favour, Warburton's abilities and legal learning gained respect from both laymen and professional colleagues. Several surviving copies of his reports of cases in the court of common pleas run from the year of his serjeantcy. Warburton was raised to the common pleas bench on 24 November 1600. The displeasure of the formidable Dowager Lady Russell, whom he had the misfortune to cross shortly afterwards, did not damage his relationship with her nephew Robert Cecil. Confirmed as judge following James I's accession, when he was also knighted, Warburton served on a succession of important state trials, besides following the Oxford, midland, and Norfolk assize circuits. He also continued to accumulate property in and around Chester, including the manor of Grafton where he built an elaborate red brick house. Such conspicuous worldly success doubtless helped assuage anxieties underlying his ultimately successful claims to a version of the heraldic arms of the Warburtons of Arley, into which family he married after the death of his second wife, Elizabeth, daughter of Sir Thomas Butler of Warrington, Lancashire. Alice Warburton also predeceased him.

Warburton died at Grafton Hall, Tilston, on 7 September 1621, and was buried in Tilston church, 'an ancient, reverend and learned judge … [who] made a good end of this life' (*Diary of Sir Richard Hutton*, 40). After an orthodox Calvinist preamble his holograph will left his surviving daughter, Elizabeth Stanley, to supervise cash bequests totalling nearly £1800, and gifts of books by Bellarmine, Calvin, Camden, Foxe, Luther, and Speed, plus 'all my manuscripts and written bookes of the Lawes of England' (Ches. & Chester ALSS, MF 164/2).　　　WILFRID PREST

Sources DNB · A. Harding, 'Warburton, Peter', HoP, *Commons, 1558–1603*, 3.577–8 · will, Ches. & Chester ALSS, EDA 2/2 (MF 164/2) · Baker, *Serjeants* · BL, Lansdowne MS 85, fols. 116–20 · W. P. Baildon, ed., *The records of the Honorable Society of Lincoln's Inn: admissions*, 1 (1896) · W. P. Baildon, ed., *The records of the Honorable Society of Lincoln's Inn: the black books*, 1–2 (1897–8) · G. Ormerod, *The history of the county palatine and city of Chester*, 2nd edn, ed. T. Helsby, 2 (1882), 704–5 · *Calendar of the manuscripts of the most hon. the marquis of Salisbury*, 4–5, HMC, 9 (1892–4); 14 (1923); 18 (1940) · *The diary of Sir Richard Hutton, 1614–1639*, ed. W. R. Prest, SeldS, suppl. ser., 9 (1991) · Foss, *Judges*, 6.195–6 · *The letters of John Chamberlain*, ed. N. E. McClure, 2 vols. (1939)
Archives BL, law reports, Harley 4817 · CUL, law reports, MS Ii.525 · Harvard U., law school, law reports, MS 5070 · Lincoln's Inn, London, notes on reading, MS Misc. 367 | BL, corresp. with Michael Hicks, MS Lansdowne 85, fols. 116–20 · Hunt. L., Warburton's associates at Lincoln's Inn, Ellesmere 482
Wealth at death manor of Grafton; parts of manors of Stretton and Thorneton; other lands in Northwich, Barneton, Weverham, Sandyway, Geldon Sutton, Leith, Saltney, Flintshire, Denbighshire, and Chester; bequests of approx. £1800 in cash, plus plate, bedding, and books: Ormerod, *History of the county palatine*, 2.704–5; will, Ches. & Chester ALSS, EDA 2/2 (MF 164/2)

Warburton, Peter (1588–1666), lawyer, was born on 27 March 1588, the eldest son of Peter Warburton of Hefferston Grange, Cheshire, and Magdalen, daughter of Robert Moulton of St Alban, Wood Street, London, auditor of the exchequer during the reign of Elizabeth I. He matriculated at Brasenose College, Oxford, on 11 May 1604 and graduated BA on 22 November 1606. He entered Lincoln's Inn on 27 January 1607, possibly after a period at Staple Inn, and was called to the bar in 1612. At an unknown date he married Alice, daughter of John Gardener of Worcester. This may not have been his only marriage: his will of 1664 implies that not all his children were the offspring of his then wife.

On 1 February 1641, Warburton was part of a commission in Cheshire for the levying of the first of the Long Parliament's two subsidies. In June 1649 the Rump created him serjeant and raised him to the bench of the common pleas as part of a larger move to replace the seven of the fifteen common-law judges who had declined to continue under the Commonwealth. He was a member of the commission that tried the Leveller leader John Lilburne at the London Guildhall in October 1649. Over the course of the interregnum Warburton served on all circuits. He was 'a strong adherent of the Rump' and Oliver Cromwell did not renew his appointment upon his accession as lord protector at the end of 1653 (Black, 'Coram protectore', 59). He seems to have played little role in public life over the next two years although it appears that he served on the militia commission for Cheshire on 14 March 1655 along with Sir George Booth and Sir William Brereton. Warburton re-emerged from obscurity with Cromwell's raising of him to the upper bench in February 1656, and on 9 February the next year he presided with Lord Chief Justice Glynne at the trial of Miles Sindercombe. On succeeding as protector, Richard Cromwell re-appointed Warburton on 29 September 1658 but in May 1660 the Convention Parliament declined to continue his appointment. Although Warburton was pardoned at the Restoration, Charles II did not confirm him as serjeant. By the time Warburton came to draw up his will in February 1664 he was living in Wood Street, London. He bequeathed land in Staffordshire, Middlesex, and London to his son Peter, and other legacies to his son Robert, daughters Esther, Lady Goodricke, Elizabeth, Anne, and Abigail, and to his wife and her daughters, Sara and Anne. He died on either 26 or (more probably) 28 February 1666, and was buried at Fetcham church, Surrey.　　　D. A. ORR

Sources Baker, *Serjeants*, 189, 543 · Sainty, *Judges* · PRO, PROB 11/320, fols. 54r–55v · DNB · E. Foss, *Biographia juridica: a biographical dictionary of the judges of England … 1066–1870* (1870) · S. F. Black, 'The courts and judges of Westminster Hall during the great rebellion, 1640–1660', *Journal of Legal History*, 7 (1986), 23–52 · S. F. Black, 'Coram protectore: the judges of Westminster Hall under the protectorate of Oliver Cromwell', *American Journal of Legal History*, 20 (1976), 33–64 · J. S. Cockburn, *A history of English assizes, 1558–1714* (1972), 219–45, 262–93 · A. Cromartie, *Sir Matthew Hale, 1609–1676* (1995), 58–88

Warburton, Peter Egerton (1813–1889), explorer in Australia, was the fourth son of the Revd Rowland Egerton Warburton (1778–1846) of Arley Hall, Northwich, Cheshire, and his wife, Emma (1782–1881), the daughter of John Croxton and the granddaughter and sole heir of Sir Peter Warburton of Warburton and Arley, Cheshire. Peter was the younger brother of Rowland Eyles Egerton *Warburton and was born at Arley Hall on 16 August 1813. After being educated at Orléans and Paris, he enlisted in the navy in 1825. Having served over three years, he entered the Royal Indian Military College, Addiscombe, in 1829; he became an ensign in the 13th native infantry battalion of the Bombay army on 9 June 1831, and after service in India was promoted lieutenant on 18 July 1837. On 8 October 1838 he married Alicia (d. 1892), the daughter of Henry Mant of Bath. They had three sons and three daughters. One of their sons was his second in command in his later journey of exploration. Warburton was promoted captain on 24 January 1845 and served as deputy adjutant-general for some time. In 1853 he retired with the brevet rank of major, intending to settle in New Zealand. Ultimately he chose South Australia instead, and arrived in Adelaide in September of that year. Almost at once he was appointed commissioner of police for South Australia. This office gave him the opportunity to explore little-known districts in the arid centre of South Australia and lakes Eyre and Torrens. In 1866 he discovered a large river, since named after him, which he traced from Lake Eyre north to near the Queensland border. In 1867, after a secret court of inquiry, the government suggested Warburton resign his position. When he refused he was dismissed. A later board could find no justification for his dismissal, but he was not reinstated despite its recommendation, and had to be content with the less well paid post of chief staff officer and the rank of colonel of the volunteer force of South Australia, which he accepted in 1869.

In 1872 Warburton was selected by the government of

South Australia to command an expedition to open up overland communication between that colony and Western Australia. When the project was abandoned by the government and taken up by two colonists, Thomas Elder and Walter Hughes, Warburton remained in command. He left Adelaide on 21 September 1872, and Beltana station on the 26th, travelling northward with sixteen camels and supplies. After he arrived at Alice Springs on 21 December 1872 he found the country suffering from drought, and decided to wait there for the rains; but he was disappointed. He started westward for the serious work of his expedition on 15 April 1873, but was in trouble for want of water on the 20th, which, with the extreme heat, caused constant anxiety. Making for the rivers Hugh and Finke in the direction of their supposed courses, he found that they were wrongly mapped. He reached Central Mount Wedge on 8 May, and soon afterwards Table Mountain. About 20 August he had attained Augustus Gregory's farthest point. The expedition continued across the arid terrain, short of food and water, losing their camels, until on 11 December they struck the Oakover River, about 200 miles from the Western Australian coast. On 30 December they were relieved by settlers from Roeborne, which they reached on 26 January 1874. They were the first explorers to cross the continent from the centre to the west and to survive a crossing of the Great Sandy Desert and nearly 1000 miles of country hitherto unknown to Europeans. On their return to Adelaide they were entertained at a public banquet, at which Warburton, who had lost the sight of one eye, attributed his survival to his Aborigine companion Charlie. The legislative assembly voted him £1000, and the Royal Geographical Society awarded him their gold medal for 1874.

In 1875 Warburton was created CMG, elected a fellow of the Royal Geographical Society, and published his *Journey across the Western Interior of Australia* (with introduction and additions by C. M. Eden and edited by H. W. Bates). He retired from the post of colonel commandant of volunteers in 1877 and took charge of the imperial pensions establishment. He lived at Norley Bank, Beaumont, near Adelaide, where he died on 5 November 1889, survived by his widow and two sons and a daughter. He was buried in the churchyard of St Matthew's, Kensington.

C. A. HARRIS, *rev.* ELIZABETH BAIGENT

Sources J. B. Hirst, 'Warburton, Peter Egerton (1813–1889)', *AusDB*, vol. 6 · Burke, *Gen. GB* · 'Warburton, Rowland Eyles Egerton-', *DNB* · BL OIOC · C. R. Markham, *The fifty years' work of the Royal Geographical Society* (1881) · *South Australian Register* (6 Nov 1889)
Wealth at death £5000: probate, *AusDB*

Warburton, Sir Robert (1842–1899), army officer, born in a Ghilzai fort between Jagdalak and Gandamak on 11 July 1842, was the only son of Robert Warburton (*d.* 10 Nov 1864), lieutenant-colonel in the Royal Artillery, and his wife, Shah Jahan Begum (*d.* in or after 1866), a noble Afghan lady, niece of the Amir Dost Muhammad. His half-brother was John Paul *Warburton (1840–1919). At the

Sir Robert Warburton (1842–1899), by W. & D. Downey

time of his birth his mother was fleeing from the troops of Sardar Muhammad Akbar Khan, who pursued her for months after the massacre of the British at Kabul on 1 November 1841. She was sheltered by her relatives, and rejoined her husband on 20 September 1842. At the close of the First Anglo-Afghan War Robert and his mother accompanied his father's battery to Sipri, and then to Morar in Gwalior. In 1850 he was placed at school at Mussooree under Robert North Maddock, where he remained until 1 December 1856. He was then sent to England, and was placed at Kensington grammar school under the Revd George Frost. Thence he obtained a military cadetship, and after one term at Addiscombe College and two at the Royal Military Academy at Woolwich he was commissioned into the Royal Artillery on 18 December 1861.

In 1862 Warburton was sent to India and stationed with the 1st battery of the 24th brigade at Fort Govindghar, the fortress of Amritsar. In August 1864 he exchanged into F battery of the 18th brigade and was stationed at Mian Mir. In 1866 the failure of the Agra and Masterman's Bank left him with only his pay to support himself and his mother. To increase his resources he exchanged into the 21st Punjab infantry. They were under orders for Abyssinia, and disembarked at Zoula on 1 February 1868. While serving with the transport train he showed great tact in conciliating local feeling, and he received the thanks of Sir Robert Napier. When he was invalided to England Napier wrote to the lieutenant-governor of the Punjab recommending

Warburton for employment on the frontier. In 1868 Warburton married Mary, eldest daughter of William Cecil of Dyffryn, Monmouthshire. On his return to India in April 1869 he was attached to the 15th Ludhiana Sikhs, and in July 1870 he was appointed to the Punjab commission as an assistant commissioner to the Peshawar division. At the end of September 1872 he was removed temporarily to the sub-district of Yusufzai and stationed at Hoti-mardan, and in February 1876 he was permanently appointed to the post. Under Sir Pierre Louis Napoleon Cavagnari he took part in several campaigns against the hill peoples who raided British territory, particularly against the Utman Khel in 1878, and was repeatedly complimented by the government of the Punjab and by the secretary of state for India. In 1879, during the Afghan campaign, Cavagnari made repeated applications for Warburton's services, but the Punjab government refused to spare him. In July, however, he was appointed political officer of the Khyber, a post he held for eighteen years.

On the news of the murder of Cavagnari at Kabul, Warburton was nominated chief political officer with General Sir R. O. Bright, commanding the Jalalabad field force. He joined the force on 10 October 1879 and proceeded to Jalalabad to ascertain the revenues of the district. In April 1880 he was invalided to England, and he did not return to the Khyber until 16 February 1882. From that time he remained on the frontier almost continuously until his retirement. Stern and implacable when necessary, he acquired a remarkable influence over the hill peoples, due in part to his Afghan ancestry. He raised the Khyber Rifles from among these peoples, and for many years kept the pass tranquil. His camp became the rendezvous of mutually hostile tribesmen. He was accustomed to travel with no weapon but a walking-stick, and everywhere met with demonstrations of affection. Able to converse fluently with the learned in Persian and with the common folk in the vernacular Pashto, he succeeded, by his acquaintance with tribal life and character, in gaining an unequalled influence over the border Afghans.

In 1881 Warburton was promoted major, and in 1887 lieutenant-colonel. On 1 January 1890 he was created CSI. In 1893 he was promoted brevet colonel. He resigned his post on 11 July 1897 and received the thanks of the Punjab government. He had frequently requested the government to appoint an assistant who might continue his policy and succeed to his post after his retirement. This request was never granted, and the appointment of a successor without local experience was immediately followed by unrest. On the outbreak of unrest among the Afridis in August 1897 Warburton was asked by the Indian government on 13 August whether he would resume his service in connection with the Khyber Pass and the Afridis. He declared himself willing, but on 23 August, before definite orders had been given, open hostilities broke out. He served with the Tirah expedition of 1897-8, and in May 1898 he was created KCIE. The hardships of the rapid campaign wore out his constitution, and the loss of the Khyber posts caused him great heart-ache. He returned to England in poor health. He died at his home, 3 Russell Road, Kensington, on 22 April 1899, and was buried at Brompton cemetery on 27 April. Warburton's reminiscences were published posthumously as *Eighteen Years in the Khyber* (1900).

E. I. CARLYLE, *rev.* JAMES FALKNER

Sources Army List · R. Warburton, *Eighteen years in the Khyber* (1900) · *The Times* (24–8 April 1899) · Boase, *Mod. Eng. biog.* · M. Barthorp, *The frontier ablaze: north-west frontier rising, 1897–1898* (1996)
Likenesses W. & D. Downey, photograph, repro. in Warburton, *Eighteen years in the Khyber* [*see illus.*] · photograph, repro. in *Black and White Magazine* (25 Sept 1897)
Wealth at death £4517 13s. 4d.: probate, 2 June 1899, *CGPLA Eng. & Wales*

Warburton, Rowland Eyles Egerton (1804–1891), foxhunter and poet, was born on 14 September 1804 at Norley Bank, Cheshire, the eldest son of the Revd Rowland Egerton (1778–1846), who added the name Warburton by royal licence on 10 August 1813, and his wife, Emma (1782–1881), daughter of John Croxton of Norley Bank, Cheshire, and his wife, Emma (*née* Warburton). Rowland Egerton Warburton's mother was heir to the estates of Sir Peter Warburton, fifth baronet, and on the baronet's death in 1813 Rowland succeeded to the Arley and Warburton estates. His younger brother Peter Egerton *Warburton was an explorer in Australia.

Rowland Egerton Warburton was educated at Eton College and was admitted to Corpus Christi College, Oxford, in February 1823, though there is no evidence that he proceeded to a degree. On leaving Oxford he did the grand tour, returning to an active life as squire of Arley Hall, which he substantially rebuilt at a cost exceeding £10,000. Egerton Warburton was born into a county steeped in hunting lore and tradition and rode to hounds from an early age, riding with the oldest surviving hunt club in England, the Tarporley Hunt Club (founded 1762), of which he was elected a member in 1825 and president in 1838. He also hunted with the Cheshire hounds. On retiring from active fox-hunting in 1873 he was elected an honorary member of the Tarporley Club, an honour of which he was most proud.

As squire of Arley, Egerton Warburton was very active in local life, being an ardent high-churchman and tory. Throughout his life he attended choral matins in the chapel at Arley Hall, wearing his hunting red on hunt days. He was, to quote his friend Samuel Wilberforce (1805–1873), bishop of Oxford and later Winchester, equally at home in the hunting field and the parish church. His politics were passive, though his long friendship with his neighbour W. E. Gladstone nearly foundered on the latter's disestablishment of the Irish church in 1869. He served as a JP and as high sheriff of Cheshire in 1833.

On 7 May 1831 Egerton Warburton married Mary Brooke (1810?–1881), eldest daughter of Sir Richard Brooke, sixth baronet, of Norton Priory. The marriage produced three children, a son and heir, Piers (1839–1914), and two daughters, Mary Alice (*d.* 1901) and Mary (*d.* 1923). After the death of his wife in 1881, his younger daughter, Mary, and her family lived with him. Egerton Warburton's social background and education provided the perfect basis for his reputation as a poet of the hunting field, and he was known as the poet laureate of the Tarporley Hunt Club. He wrote verses for pleasure and for the enjoyment of his fellow huntsmen, and his *Hunting Songs*, first published in 1834, ran to eight editions in his lifetime. His style was humorous and jolly, reflecting the close social companionship of the hunt. Titles such as 'A Good Merry Gallop for Me!', 'Hard-riding Dick', 'Tarporley Hunting Song, 1870', and 'Farmer Dobbin' give an idea as to subject matter. His 'Quaesitum meritis', a nine-stanza poem, encapsulates the hunting man and his calling and shows Egerton Warburton at his best. His poetical output was not extensive, however, and was limited to hunting and archery. Apart from his verse he published documents on the cattle plague of 1747–9.

Egerton Warburton suffered from glaucoma in 1874 and within a year was blind. This was a severe blow to a man of the countryside, but he still walked, being led by his gardener Peter Burgess on a leather strap. This was not enough, so he had a Furlong Walk constructed from wire along the terrace at Arley. From 1888 his health failed and he died on 6 December 1891. He was buried in the family vault at St Mary and All Saints Church, Great Budworth, Cheshire, on 10 December 1891.   DAMIAN ATKINSON

Sources G. Fergusson, *The green collars: the Tarporley Hunt Club and Cheshire hunting history* (1993) · private information (2004) · *DNB* · H. Maxwell, 'Memoir', *Hunting songs* (1912) · Burke, *Peerage* · Burke, *Gen. GB* · Foster, *Alum. Oxon.* · *The Times* (9 Dec 1891) · *Northwich Chronicle and Mid Cheshire Advertiser* (12 Dec 1891) · J. Shattock, ed., *The Cambridge bibliography of English literature*, 3rd edn, 4 (1999)
Archives JRL, corresp. · priv. coll., various corresp. | BL, letters to W. E. Gladstone, Add. MSS 44367–44485 · Ches. & Chester ALSS, letters to Thomas Hughes · Ches. & Chester ALSS, letters, verses, etc. to Lord and Lady de Tabley
Likenesses C. A. Duval, portrait, priv. coll. · photographs, priv. coll. · photographs, repro. in Fergusson, *Green collars*
Wealth at death £51,670 3s. 11d.: probate, 10 Feb 1892, *CGPLA Eng. & Wales*

Warburton, Thomas Acton (*c.*1813–1894). *See under* Warburton, Bartholomew Elliott George (1810–1852).

Warburton, William (1698–1779), bishop of Gloucester and religious controversialist, was born in Newark, Nottinghamshire, on 24 December 1698, the second and only surviving son of George Warburton (*d.* 1706), attorney and town clerk of Newark, and his wife, Elizabeth (*d.* 1749), daughter of William Holman, an alderman of the town. The Warburton family originated in Cheshire, and Warburton's grandfather had been involved in Booth's attempted royalist rising at Chester in 1659. He himself wrote out some biographical and genealogical memoranda, which can be found in the British Library (Add. MS 4320, fols. 206–9). He attended school at Newark; one of his masters there was later rather surprised by the appearance of Warburton's major work, *The Divine Legation of Moses*, because 'when at school, he had always considered young Warburton to be the dullest of all dull scholars' (*GM*, 1st ser., 50, 1780, 474). He briefly moved to Oakham School before returning to Newark, where he was taught

William Warburton (1698–1779), attrib. William Hoare, *c.*1750–55

by a cousin, also named William Warburton. His father died in 1706, so it was important that the young Warburton, who was responsible for his sisters and his mother (to whom he was devoted), should secure a career relatively early in life, and he was therefore articled for five years to an attorney, John Kirke, at East Markham, Nottinghamshire, on 23 April 1714. On completion of his articles he practised law in Newark from 1719 to 1723.

Literary-cum-ecclesiastic vocation Warburton had a pronounced appetite for reading, in which he was encouraged by his schoolmaster cousin, and it was this literary bent that led him to consider a change in vocation: he decided to take orders in the church. He was ordained deacon on 23 December 1723 by Archbishop William Dawes, of York. In that year his first publication appeared: *Miscellaneous Translations in Prose and Verse*, a small volume which he addressed to his patron, Sir Robert Sutton, MP for Nottinghamshire, who in 1727 presented him to his first small living, Greaseley, in Nottinghamshire. He was ordained priest by Edmund Gibson, bishop of London, at St Paul's on 1 March 1727, and in June 1728 Sutton presented him to the rich living of Brant Broughton, in Lincolnshire, which he continued to hold until 1746. In taking the living of Brant Broughton he resigned Greaseley, but in 1730 he was given the additional living of Firsby, in Leicestershire, by the duke of Newcastle (with whom he corresponded), which he held as a non-resident, with Steeping Magna, until 1756.

Warburton became close to William Stukeley, the antiquary, who lived nearby at Stamford, and from 1722 until the eve of Stukeley's death in 1765 they exchanged letters, many of which were published in the second volume of J. Nichols's *Illustrations of the Literary History of the Eighteenth Century*. Francis Peck and John Towne, both antiquaries, were also close to Warburton at this time, as was the philosopher David Hartley, then practising as a physician at Newark. Warburton was granted an MA at Cambridge, at the recommendation of Sutton, on the occasion of the king's visit in 1728. His literary ambitions had been further encouraged by a meeting in London at Christmas 1726 with Lewis Theobald, which had been organized by Matthew Concanen. Theobald used some of his new acquaintance's notes in his edition of Shakespeare; he corresponded with Warburton, chiefly about variant readings, for seven years. Warburton concurred with Concanen and Theobald in their severe criticisms of Pope, remarking in a letter to Concanen of 2 January 1727 that 'Dryden borrowed for want of leisure, and Pope for want of genius' (Nichols, *Illustrations*, 2.195). It was fortunate for Warburton that Pope remained unaware of this letter, which was first published by Mark Akenside in a note to his 'Ode to Thomas Edwards' in 1751.

Concanen also arranged the publication of Warburton's first substantial work, *A critical and philosophical enquiry into the causes of prodigies and miracles, as related by historians* (1727), in which the fledgeling author attacked, *inter alia*, Hobbes, Shaftesbury, and Mandeville (for their antipathy to religion), as well as a whole mass of ancient and medieval historians and chroniclers (for their credulousness). Aside from Ralegh and Clarendon, Warburton was equally critical of modern historians as supposedly lacking any real knowledge of human nature, and he was especially censorious when condemning the antiquarian tastes promoted by the followers of Stow and Holinshed, which he denounced as 'a deprav'd Appetite for *Trash* and *Cinders*' (W. Warburton, *A Critical and Philosophical Enquiry*, 65). He was concerned to demonstrate the role of providence in human affairs, particularly as evinced through the miracles of the Old and New testaments, in contradistinction to a superstitious reverence for portents and signs, which he associated with heathenism. The assured tone of this work would prove typical of his later writings, although this was a text that he quickly decided to suppress. When his disciple Richard Hurd came to edit Warburton's works he too chose not to republish it. Though the work appeared anonymously Warburton sent out presentation copies. He also published a less contentious work in 1727, *The Legal Judicature in Chancery Stated*, which drew on his legal training in stating the relationship between the chancery and the rolls court. This was an early instance of his marked interest in the law and the English constitution, subjects which retained his attention for the rest of his career. He would also long prove all too happy either to praise or defame prominent characters in print, and an early instance of this occurred just before he himself acquired a public reputation in the 1730s. Sir Robert Sutton was expelled from the House of Commons in 1732 as a result of corruption relating to the Charitable Corporation for the Relief of the Industrious Poor, of which he

was a director; the following year Warburton provided *An Apology for Sir Robert Sutton*, in which he absolved him of the charges laid against him, concluding that his patron was a victim of malice, cavil, and hearsay. He later requested that Pope remove slighting references to Sutton in this connection from both *Of the Use of Riches* and his *Epilogue to the Satires*.

Warburton's years at Brant Broughton were productive ones, and he spent a great deal of his time there in retired study. As Hurd wrote in his introduction to his edition of Warburton's works:

> living by himself, and not having the fashionable opinions of a great society to bias his own, he might acquire an enlarged turn of mind, and strike out for himself, as he clearly did, an original cast both of thought and composition. (Hurd, *Discourse*, 6)

The first major result of this independence of mind was his controversial defence of the established church and the Test Acts, *The Alliance between Church and State* (1736). Warburton argued that religion alone can supply the rewards necessary to ensure that individual virtue continues to underpin the proper function of civil government. The magistrate was to oversee the government of the body, the church that of the soul. Fundamental to the alliance so formed was the influence that the church could give to the service of the state, and the support and protection that the state could in turn give to the church. Above all the church was to oversee that popular measure of the early and mid-eighteenth-century Church of England, the 'reformation of manners'. Warburton argued that an established denomination provided moral security for the state, and that it should therefore be composed by the majority confession of the nation, thereby standing clear of any multiplication and fragmentation into sectarianism. Sectarianism he identified as the source of contention and internal wars. Reflection on the legacy of the civil war, a subject on which he had planned to write a history, comprised a major part of his thinking on such matters. He read most of the political pamphlets produced between 1640 and 1660, and his very full annotations to Clarendon's *History* were finally published by the Clarendon Press in 1826. While he argued that the civil magistrate could not coerce opinions he also declared that such opinions should always give way to civil peace. Utility was absolutely central to his argument, but it was a utility that led to knowledge of divine truth through the proper, tolerant practice of Christianity as a revealed religion. Hobbes and Roman Catholicism represented the two extremes to be avoided; Hooker and Locke were lauded as the defenders of a tolerant church. Neither high- nor low-church apologists were ready to accept what seemed to many to be an overly legalistic and compromisingly Erastian understanding of the church. Warburton's Erastianism was decidedly atypical of established apologetic in the eighteenth century, as was his explicit appeal to Lockean contract theory. None the less the work won him the admiration of Bishop Francis Hare of Chichester, who had been more critical of an edition of Velleius Paterculus that Warburton had addressed to him and which he published in the *Bibliothèque Britannique* in 1736. Hare recommended Warburton, on the altogether securer strength of the *Alliance*, to the theologically sophisticated Queen Caroline, long noted for taking a close personal interest in church affairs. Unfortunately for Warburton the queen died in November 1737, and the preferment that he might otherwise have expected did not come his way.

Friendship with Pope Bishop Hare died in 1740, leaving Warburton without an important supporter, but a friendship which was to prove extremely beneficial to him began in the same year. Although he had attacked Pope when a member of the Theobald circle, even contributing anonymous articles against him in the *Daily Journal* in March and April 1728, he defended the theology of Pope's *Essay on Man* in a series of letters in *The History of the Works of the Learned* in December 1738. These letters were a reply to a work by a Swiss divine, Jean Pierre de Crousaz, who, in his *Examen de l'essai de Monsieur Pope sur l'homme* (1737), had identified the argument of the poem with Leibnizianism; Warburton's able, if suitably combative, defence appeared as *Vindication*, in 1740. As a result of this unexpected defence, in which Pope's essay was read as an exercise in Newtonian natural theology, Warburton spent a week with him at Twickenham in 1740, having been introduced to him through the good offices of William Murray, later Lord Mansfield. Pope thus gained an increasingly influential theologian as his philosophical apologist, and Warburton gained the friendship of an extremely well-connected writer. Warburton seems to have brought Pope back to Christian orthodoxy, gradually supplanting the religiously suspect Bolingbroke in his affections. Pope attributed to Warburton the creation of the fourth book of the *Dunciad*, in its 1743 version; Warburton's notes to the poem are as concerned with theology as they are with literary questions, as are his detailed and expansive annotations to the *Essay on Criticism* and the *Essay on Man*. Such was the close nature of the friendship that when in 1741 an offer of an Oxford DD was made to Warburton, only to be rapidly withdrawn, Pope declined the simultaneous offer of an LLD that the university had made to him. At the poet's death Warburton became his executor, from which position he made rather a lot of money, and an interesting exchange of letters between him and his publisher Knapton on this and allied matters has been published as *Pope's Literary Legacy*.

It was through Pope that Warburton met Ralph Allen, the postal entrepreneur and Bath philanthropist, who had invited both men to his home, Prior Park, in November 1741. This was to prove Warburton's fortune, since he married Allen's favourite niece, Gertrude Tucker (*d.* 1796), on 5 September 1745. When Allen died in 1764 Warburton was the beneficiary of a generous bequest, and it had also been arranged that Mrs Warburton was to be left Prior Park at the death of her uncle's widow. Warburton spent the greater part of the year at Prior Park from the date of his marriage, and it was largely for this reason that he resigned the living of Brant Broughton in 1746, the year in

which Murray, as solicitor-general, secured him the lucrative and influential preachership at Lincoln's Inn. His lectures on religion at Lincoln's Inn were published in two volumes in 1753 as *The Principles of Natural and Revealed Religion Occasionally Opened and Explained*. His links with Lincoln's Inn were affirmed in 1769, when he founded the Warburtonian lectures on the proof of Christianity through prophecies (a favoured proof in eighteenth-century Christian apologetics).

Warburton had long been deeply interested in literature, and his friendship with Pope consolidated this interest. He was also close to Samuel Richardson, for whom he wrote a preface to *Clarissa*, and he likewise provided a dissertation on chivalry for Thomas Jarvis's translation of *Don Quixote* (1742). Henry Fielding knew him through a mutual friendship with Allen, and a mock encomium to his learning is to be found in *Tom Jones* (bk 3, chap. 1). Laurence Sterne, whom he met through a friendship with David Garrick, had offered to make him Tristram's tutor in *The Life and Opinions of Tristram Shandy, Gentleman* but Warburton allegedly prevented this by presenting Sterne with a small present of a bag of gold. Warburton had long been fascinated by Shakespeare, contributing much to Sir Thomas Hanmer's edition of the works. The question of how much he actually contributed to this edition later provoked a furious quarrel, as can be seen in Philip Nichols's pamphlet *The Castrated Letter of Sir T. Hanmer* (1763). Warburton had produced his own edition of Shakespeare in 1747. This quickly proved controversial, not least as many of his emendations are nothing if not absurd, and he was attacked by Thomas Edwards of Lincoln's Inn (where Warburton was the recently installed preacher) in his *Canons of Criticism* (1748). Edwards's criticisms were reaffirmed by John Upton in *Critical Observations on Shakespeare* (1748) and by Benjamin Heath in *Revisal of Shakespeare's Text* (1766). Warburton's contributions to the developing art of the editor were, however, considerable, if markedly uneven in quality. Much attention to these matters is apparent in Warburton's lengthy correspondence with Thomas Birch, to whom he had declared on 24 November 1737 that 'the most agreeable subject in the world … is literary history' (BL, Add. MS 4320, fol. 119*r*). In a much later letter to Birch, of 25 October 1763, Warburton characteristically emphasized an allied commitment in a manner otherwise surprising in a bishop: 'You must know I am a great Antiquarian, tho' I make no word of it; as half-ashamed of my taste; like a man who has taken an odd fancy to an ugly mistress' (ibid., fol. 199*r*). It was this union of assumed piety and frank worldliness that gave Warburton so ambiguous a contemporary reputation. This applied to all his public dealings, and especially in regard to his literary labours, where he acquired a reputation for graceless irascibility. Edwards's well-received, deeply humorous critique of Warburton's Shakespeare edition had delighted Akenside, a declared enemy of Warburton, who similarly lampooned Warburton's work on editions of Milton and of Pope's poetry in his 'Ode to Thomas Edwards' (1751), declaring that no poet required the assistance of 'such a militant divine':

[a] sophist vain,
Who durst approach his hallow'd strain
With unwash'd hands and lips profane.
(ll. 40–42)

Nevertheless whatever their actual opinions of Warburton all writers owed him a debt for his work on literary property. His *Letter from an Author to a Member of Parliament Concerning Literary Property* (1747) was the first theoretical examination of the subject, a treatment not unrelated to his own interest in his role as Pope's literary executor. His edition of Pope's works appeared in 1751; he wrote a large part of the life of Pope—attributed to Owen Ruffhead—that appeared in the 1769 edition of the works.

Pope had been concerned to introduce his new friend to his old confidant Bolingbroke. He wrote to Allen on 6 March 1744 how he wished to introduce Warburton to 'the One Great Man in Europe, who knows as much as He' (*Correspondence of Alexander Pope*, 4.504–5). The introduction heralded a poisonous rivalry, and Warburton responded testily, in *A Letter to the Lord Viscount B—* (1749), to Bolingbroke's equivocal remarks concerning Pope in his *Idea of a Patriot King*, which led to a war of words in which Bolingbroke made some telling points in his *Familiar Letter to the most Impudent Man Living* (1749). This was an encounter which led to the most tedious and unnecessary of Warburton's writings, *A View of Lord Bolingbroke's Philosophy* (1754–5), a work which Montesquieu admired. Pope himself had seen a dark side of Warburton's character, which he noted in a letter of August 1743 to Martha Blount, who had felt slighted by Warburton and the Allens: 'W. is a sneaking Parson, & I told him he flattered' (*Correspondence of Alexander Pope*, 4.463–4).

Theological and literary controversies: *The Divine Legation of Moses Demonstrated* Warburton's friendship with Pope had begun in the short interval between the appearance of the first and second volumes of his major work, *The Divine Legation of Moses Demonstrated* (1738–41), an audacious demonstration of sometimes prodigious and always combative learning that guaranteed him his reputation as the would-be literary dictator of mid-eighteenth-century England, a role which his work as Pope's executor only served to emphasize. Pope's reading of the first volume left him rhapsodic, as he wrote to Warburton on 24 June 1740:

> I am not really Learned enough to be a judge in Works of the nature & Depth of yours, but I travel thro your book, as thro an Amazing Scene of ancient Egypt or Greece, struck with Veneration & Wonder, but at every step wanting an Instructor to tell me all I wish to know. Such you prove to me in the Walks of Antiquity & such you will prove to all Mankind. (*Correspondence of Alexander Pope*, 4.251)

Hurd's comparable praise for the work is not without foundation, especially his claim that 'in the whole compass of modern or antient theology, there is nothing equal or similar to this extraordinary performance' (Hurd, *Discourse*, 36). The central argument of this work is built on a daring paradox, the pivotal need for which is apparent in the subtitle to the *Divine Legation*, in which the truth of Christianity is to be shown on the principles of a 'religious deist'. Deists had dismissed all priestly religions as providing false comfort to humanity through the fallacious doctrines of a future life, which were merely an 'engine' of 'priestcraft' by which the clergy gained false authority and illegitimate status in society. According to Warburton, however, Moses did not even mention such a doctrine, thereby proving that his was the true revealed faith, since God chose not to reveal such a doctrine immediately but hid it until the time was right for its proper promulgation. In defence of this paradox Warburton argued that God had intervened directly in the ancient world of the Hebrews through extraordinary providences, and there was thus no need for comforting doctrines of futurity; not one of the characters in the Old Testament acted according to the doctrine of a future state, living only with respect to the present life. This proved a contentious proposition, and it was one which Warburton had quickly to defend from a host of critics, both freethinkers and Christians. Replies to the central paradox of the work appeared in rapid succession throughout the 1740s and 1750s; enmity to Warburton's ideas frequently united otherwise disparate groups of clergy. His arguments were challenged by Cambridge Newtonians such as Arthur Ashley Sykes and John Jackson, in 1744 and 1745 respectively; by Hutchinsonians such as Julius Bate, in a tract of 1741; by William Law, the nonjuror and mystical Behmenist, as late as 1756; and, very effectively, by the ultra-latitudinarian Francis Blackburne, in 1757. It is a tribute to the polemical ire of Warburton's writings that opposition to them could encompass such an unprecedentedly wide arc of clerical opinion. Benjamin Newton, writing in 1758, suggested that the work actually provided ammunition for the very freethinkers that it was designed to refute, while John Tillard, in a tract published in 1742, defended the ancient religions against Warburton's criticisms. Bishop Potter of London, who distrusted Warburton, encouraged the clergy of his diocese to publish critiques of *The Divine Legation*. Most controversially Warburton subsequently became embroiled in a very public dispute in 1756 over the nature of the book of Job with Robert Lowth, professor of Hebrew at Oxford, an encounter in which he came out much worse than the learned Lowth, who had originally been offended by a slighting remark that Warburton had made regarding his father (Warburton was both envious and suspicious of clerical dynasties). As a result of this encounter Warburton once more argued, in a 1765 addition to the work, that Job had had no knowledge of futurity and that the work was a political allegory; Lowth again contested this, in *Letter to the Author of 'The Divine Legation'*, and he was not above pointing to Warburton's poor command of Hebrew in making his case.

Quite aside from its paradoxical kernel *The Divine Legation* proved controversial because, in Hurd's words, it 'took in all that was most curious in Gentile, Jewish, and Christian antiquity' (Hurd, *Discourse*, 20). His theories regarding the origins of writing were to prove particularly influential: Condillac translated sections of the work on the nature of hieroglyphs, guaranteeing Warburton a high status in linguistic speculation throughout late eighteenth-century Europe. This standing was questioned by others in France: Voltaire wrote a short refutation of the bishop's work, *A Warburton*, and Rousseau criticized his notions of church and state relations in his *Contrat Social*. A German translation of *The Divine Legation* was produced at Leipzig and Frankfurt between 1751 and 1753; it was to influence a number of German theologians and classical scholars. Praise for the work was also received from Virginia, where the book was much discussed. Warburton's readings of classical sources were, however, often as unhappily received as were his readings of sacred literature. A long-standing friendship with Conyers Middleton, with whom he shared marked hatreds of more consciously orthodox divines, was brought to an abrupt end when Middleton, the biographer of Cicero, questioned Warburton's interpretation of Cicero's religion in the fifth edition of his *Letter from Rome* (1742). Warburton distanced himself from Middleton when writing against other critics of his work; his notes to later editions of *The Divine Legation* further allowed him to finish off his critics in a brutal manner, a characteristic that his contemporaries found increasingly distasteful. Nevertheless this public distancing from an erstwhile friend also served to reinforce Warburton's otherwise contentious reputation for orthodoxy, as Middleton's reputation for heterodoxy had grown markedly over the preceding decade and a half. Similarly Warburton's friendship with John Jortin, who, like Middleton, was a Cambridge divine of advanced theological opinions, ended when Jortin mildly censured his reading of the sixth book of the *Aeneid* in *Six Dissertations* (1755). Jortin was savagely attacked by Richard Hurd, Warburton's young acolyte, who was to prove a long-standing epistolary confidant, in a vituperative pamphlet, *The Delicacy of Friendship*. Edward Gibbon's first venture into print in English, *Critical Observations on the Sixth Book of the Aeneid* (1770), was also largely concerned with Warburton's alleged misreading of the text, and his engagements with Warburton were of great significance for him at the outset of his intellectual life, as is clear in his account in the *Autobiographies*.

Middleton had produced a critique of the miracles of the early church which appeared posthumously in 1749; it initiated a major debate among churchmen and other interested parties. Warburton seized the opportunity to affirm his orthodoxy by arguing for the truth of what was one of the latest possible miracles, according to the standards of protestantism: that which faced the emperor Julian at the rebuilding of the temple at Jerusalem. His *Julian* (1751) proved a controversial work; Montesquieu greatly admired it, while Voltaire loathed it. The nonconformist divine Philip Doddridge, a friend and frequent correspondent of Warburton, was also impressed by the work. The Doddridge–Warburton correspondence—eighteen letters from Warburton are reproduced in G. F. Nuttall's *Calendar* of Doddridge's correspondence (1979)—reveals Warburton's more professedly pious commitments; he was also a great admirer of Doddridge's expositions of the New Testament and a manifest follower of his recommendations for family prayer and devotions.

Doddridge was interested too in Warburton's feelings on being attacked by John Byrom in *Enthusiasm: a Poetical Essay*. Warburton's relations with 'enthusiasm' were not happy. His dislike of Methodism was deep, and he condemned both the soteriology and the practical enthusiasm of John Wesley and George Whitefield in *The Doctrine of Grace* (1763), a work which drew hurt replies from both men. Both Wesley and Whitefield believed that his notion of grace revealed Warburton to be less than orthodox, leading Whitefield to expostulate, 'Alas! What could a Middleton say more?' (G. Whitefield, *Observations on some Fatal Mistakes, in a Book Lately Published, and Intitled, 'The Doctrine of Grace'*, 1764, 7). The work also drew eloquent criticisms from John Andrews, a clergyman of Warburton's diocese, and Thomas Leland, of Trinity College, Dublin, both of whom felt it too vituperative a work and one which potentially exposed the Church of England to doctrinal assault concerning the nature of grace from more orthodox protestants. Thomas Hartley condemned Warburton's views in an appendix to his *Paradise Restored* (1764). Samuel Chandler defended Warburton against Wesley but there was otherwise little support for *The Doctrine of Grace*. Warburton's work on the doctrine of the sacraments, *A Rational Account of the Nature and End of the Lord's Supper* (1761), was, surprisingly perhaps, quietly received. The 1760s proved the zenith of Warburton's controversial career, climaxing in the quarrel with Lowth, and this was at least as much a consequence of his political as of his theological opinions. Lowth's words in his 1765 *Letter* to Warburton had done their work: 'I am a staunch Republican and a zealous Protestant in Literature, nor will ever bear with a Perpetual Dictator, or an Infallible Pope, whose Decrees are to be submitted to without appeal, and to be received with implicit assent' (p. 133).

Warburton the whig Warburton had always profited from his strict adherence to the interests of the whig party. His dedication of the second volume of *The Divine Legation* to Lord Chesterfield had resulted in the offer of an Irish chaplaincy in 1745, when Chesterfield was made lord lieutenant, an offer which subsequently fell through when family duties made it impossible for Warburton to leave England, a decision which Chesterfield much respected. A new edition of *The Alliance* was also dedicated to Chesterfield, in 1747. Warburton was, however, no mere place-seeker: he was a staunchly loyal whig and he published two strongly anti-Jacobite sermons when Charles Edward Stuart's forces were in England. The politico-theology of these sermons was challenged as extreme by Henry Stebbing, a critic of *The Divine Legation*, and Warburton replied to him in equally strong terms in *An Apologetical Dedication to the Reverend Dr Henry Stebbing* (1746), virtually accusing him of crypto-Jacobitism. Warburton's dual standing as Pope's editor and whig churchman was satirized in an anonymous work, *Proposals for printing, by subscription, in one volume in quarto, a commentary critical and theological upon the learned Mr William Warburton's apologetical dedication to the Reverend Dr Henry Stebbing* (1746), the tone of which reveals just how unpopular Warburton had become with many of his critics. This is also apparent in William Dodd's satire, *A New Dunciad*. Warburton's denunciations of free-thinkers also gained him enemies in the sceptical camp, most notably David Hume. Warburton had originally thought Hume too low a specimen of the sceptical breed to notice but he felt obliged to respond to Hume's *Natural History of Religion* with *Remarks* (1757). Even then he felt it proper to publish the *Remarks* anonymously, completing the work with Hurd's assistance. Hume was unimpressed by the performance. In a letter to William Strahan of 25 June 1771 he made an observation that would have been shared by many other writers:

> It is petulance, and Insolence and abuse, that distinguish the Warburtonian School, even above all other Parsons and Theologians … I remember Lord Mansfield said to me that Warburton was a very opposite man in company to what he was in his Books; then, replyd I, he must be the most agreeable Companion in Europe, for surely he is the most odious Writer. (*Letters*, 2.244)

A consistent whig in his politics, Warburton had been notably loyal to Newcastle and then to Lord Chancellor Hardwicke, who rewarded him with a prebend at Gloucester in 1754. Warburton profitably exchanged this for one at Durham, in whose chapter library he read widely. It was at Durham that he critically annotated a copy of Daniel Neal's *History of the Puritans* in preparation for his assault on Methodism, an early manuscript preparation of which, 'The true Methodist, or, Christian in earnest', revised in July 1755, is in the John Rylands Library at Manchester (MS 253 AB). In 1754 he became a chaplain to the king and was granted a Canterbury DD by Archbishop Herring. He regularly exchanged letters with Charles Yorke, the future attorney-general, a correspondence (published in 1812) in which his wife occasionally joined in successfully seeking a naval command for her brother (BL, Egerton 1952, fols. 223–4, 226, 228, 230). In 1757 Warburton was made dean of Bristol, and through the local interest of Allen and of William Pitt, an admirer and frequent correspondent, he was made bishop of Gloucester in 1760 (holding his Durham prebend *in commendam*). This did not win universal approval and Horace Walpole later observed that Pitt had promoted him 'to the opposition of the whole episcopal bench', as Warburton's 'doubtful Christianity … writings and turbulent arrogance made him generally obnoxious' (Walpole, 85). Warburton's principled whiggery was expressed in his sermon to the House of Lords on 31 January 1760 and in a sermon condemning slavery which he delivered in 1766 to the Society for the Propagation of the Gospel in Foreign Parts.

Warburton's political associations, combined with his monopoly on Pope's writings, served to expose him to the ire of John Wilkes, who grotesquely parodied the bishop's minute and pugnacious style of annotation in the notes to his notorious *Essay on Woman* (1763), a clandestine work that Warburton, the earl of Sandwich, and Lord Mansfield sought out and suppressed. The notes, attributed to Warburton, were as obscene as the poem itself. This attack on Wilkes, widely perceived as a 'patriot', gained Warburton further notoriety, and he was condemned for it at some length by the clerical poet Charles Churchill, in *The Duellist*

(1764) and in the dedication to his posthumously published *Sermons* (1765). In *The Duellist* Warburton's pride, meanness, ambition, gracelessness, and hypocrisy were blended with allusions to his writings, leading Churchill to a curt dismissal with which many contemporaries would have concurred:

> A great Divine, as Lords agree,
> Without the least Divinity;
> To crown all, in a declining age,
> Enflam'd with Church and Party-rage,
> Behold him, full and perfect quite,
> A false Saint, and true Hypocrite.
> (bk 3, ll. 806–10)

Churchill also libelled Warburton and his wife in this poem, claiming that their only child (who was to predecease both) was not Warburton's at all; he was rumoured by some to be the son of his chaplain, Martin Stafford Smith, whom his widow subsequently married in 1781. Walpole greatly enjoyed Warburton's apparent discomfiture during the Lords' debate on Wilkes in 1763, and he claimed that Warburton had subsequently used his connections to try to gain the bishopric of London for himself as a recompense for the abuse that he had suffered from Wilkes and his allies. Warburton certainly believed that he deserved better than the see of Gloucester, and his letters to Hurd reveal the suspicions and envies of a disappointed man.

Decline, death, and posthumous reputation Warburton fell into a rapid decline in the wake of the controversies of the 1760s. He left Prior Park to reside in Gloucester in 1769, where he had a serious fall in his library in 1770, from the effects of which he never recovered. The loss of his young son (*b.* 1756) in 1775 exacerbated his illness, and he fell into senility, dying in the bishop's palace at Gloucester on 7 June 1779. He was buried in the cathedral, where his widow erected a monument to him bearing an inscription by Hurd. Hurd continued to correspond with her after she remarried, especially regarding the edition of Warburton's works, about which Hurd was very careful. He wrote to her on 23 March 1784, noting:

> We have reduced the expense as low as possible by printing only 200 copies, & by agreeing for a Head to be engraved from the picture at Gloucester at 20£, & for examining the Greek & Latin quotations, which must be done with care, 20£ more. (BL, Egerton 1958, fol. 98*v*)

Hurd and Mrs Stafford Smith were Warburton's closest posthumous allies. The Warburtonian party had never been large, encompassing John Towne, Thomas Balguy, Jonathan Toup, and (though they later fell out) John Brown, whose *Estimate* Warburton had much enjoyed. He especially favoured Brown's critique of Shaftesbury's moral doctrine in his *Essays on the Characteristics*; Warburton had always detested Shaftesbury and frequently bemoaned his influence on what he derided as fashionable opinion. Warburton had written a preface to Catharine Cockburn's *Remarks*, on Thomas Rutherforth, in 1747 but otherwise wrote sparingly on moral theory. He had neither the aptitude nor the inclination to write in a philosophical manner, devoting himself instead to historical and literary defences of Christianity. His reputation in the mid-eighteenth century was high but the changing nature of apologetic, which would favour such divines as Joseph Butler, meant that it fell into obsolescence with remarkable speed.

As early as 1785 John Disney observed that 'Few learned theological books have been more universally read in their day, than Mr. Warburton's Divine legation, and still fewer of those which have been so much noticed, have been so soon neglected, disregarded and forgotten' (Disney, 269). Disney believed that the engagement with Lowth had proved decisive in Warburton's decline. When in conversation with 'three very learned and respectable dignitaries of the established church' Disney noted that all wondered whether Warburton's writings had better served the cause of infidelity than they had Christianity (ibid., 270). The seven-volume edition of his works financed by his widow under the editorship of Hurd, which appeared in 1788, signally failed to make an impact; it contained some hitherto unpublished material, notably parts of the uncompleted ninth book of *The Divine Legation*, *Directions for the Study of Theology*, and Warburton's notes on Neal's *History of the Puritans*. His reputation was further harmed when Samuel Parr, an opponent of what he identified as the small Warburtonian party in the church, published the long-disowned *Enquiry into the Causes of Prodigies and Miracles* in *Tracts by Warburton and a Warburtonian* (1789). Not all of his readers were so dismissive, however: George Grote, in making manuscript notes from his writings, had been convinced by the argument of Warburton's *Julian* (BL, Add. MS 29524, fols. 80–86), an admiration in which the secular historian had been unpredictably joined by Joseph Milner, the pre-eminent evangelical church historian. The publication in 1809 of the letters between Hurd and Warburton added to this sense of a re-evaluation of the bishop and his works. In 1828 a prominent evangelical, James Garbett, published an Oxford fellowship dissertation, *An Essay on Warburton's 'Divine Legation'* (1828), which contained judicious praise as well as a level of predictable censure. Gladstone strongly condemned the teaching of the *Alliance* in *The State in its Relations with the Church* (1838), although Macaulay was a little more accommodating of the Warburtonian thesis in his *Edinburgh Review* account of Gladstone's book. Francis Kilvert published an edition of the previously unpublished papers in 1841 and John Selby Watson produced a notably unsympathetic biography in 1863. Mark Pattison wrote excellently about Warburton, both as a subject in himself and as an editor of Pope's poetry, while essays concerning him by both Leslie and James Fitzjames Stephen appeared in the 1870s; he is also interestingly examined in Leslie Stephen's *History of English Thought in the Eighteenth Century* (1878). A. W. Evans produced a well-balanced and sympathetic biography in 1932. Warburton's significance has been increasingly recognized by literary historians and by such intellectual historians as J. G. A. Pocock, as well as by Jacques Derrida, in *Of Grammatology*, an instance of his continuing relevance to European, as much as to British, intellectual history. B. W. YOUNG

Sources A. W. Evans, *Warburton and the Warburtonians: a study in some eighteenth-century controversies* (1932) · Nichols, *Lit. anecdotes* · J. Selby Watson, *William Warburton* (1863) · R. Hurd, *A discourse, by way of general preface to the quarto edition of Bishop Warburton's works* (1794) · R. Hurd, *Letters from a late eminent prelate* (1809) · *The correspondence of Alexander Pope*, ed. G. Sherburn, 5 vols. (1956) · W. Warburton, *Letter to Charles Yorke* (1822) · J. Disney, *Memoirs of the life and writings of Arthur Ashley Sykes* (1785) · L. Sturnow, *History of English thought in the 18th century* (1878) · *The letters of David Hume*, ed. J. Y. T. Greig, 2 vols. (1932) · H. Walpole, *Memoirs of King George II*, ed. J. Brooke, 3 vols. (1985) · D. W. Nichol, ed., *Pope's literary legacy* (1992) · S. Jarvis, *Scholars and gentlemen* (1991) · M. Walsh, *Shakespeare, Milton, and 18th-century editing* (1997) · N. Hudson, *Writing and European thought* (1994) · B. W. Young, *Religion and Enlightenment in eighteenth-century England: theological debate from Locke to Burke* (1998)

Archives BL, corresp., sermons, notes, and MSS, Add. MSS 46184, 47663, Egerton MSS 1952–1960 | BL, corresp. with T. Birch, Add. MS 4320 · BL, letters to P. Desmaizeaux, Add. MS 4288 · BL, letters to N. Foster, Add. MS 11275 · BL, letters to W. Mason, Add. MS 32563 · BL, corresp. with duke of Newcastle, Add. MSS 32687, 32731, 32939 · BL, letters to T. Warton, Add. MSS 42560–42561 · BL, letters to C. Yorke, Add. MS 35404 · Bodl. Oxf., corresp. with R. Lowth; letters to W. Stukeley · Glos. RO, letters mainly to his sister Frances · NL Scot., letters to D. Dalrymple; letters to Lord Hailes · V&A NAL, letters to D. Garrick · Westminster Abbey, letters to Z. Pearce

Likenesses C. Philips, oils, *c*.1737, NPG · attrib. W. Hoare, oils, *c*.1750–1755, bishop's palace, Gloucester [*see illus.*] · W. Hoare, drawing, 1765, Hartlebury Castle, Worcestershire · W. Hoare, oils, 1765, Hurd Episcopal Library, Hartlebury Castle, Worcestershire · attrib. T. King, medallion, 1779, Gloucester Cathedral · T. Burford, mezzotint (after C. Philips), BM, NPG · H. Gravelot, medallion, etching, BM, NPG · J. Houbraken, line engraving, BM, NPG · J. Lodge, caricature, etching (after T. Worlidge), NPG

Warcup, Sir Edmund (1627–1712), magistrate, was born on 4 July 1627, one of twenty-one children of Samuel Warcup of English, near Henley, Oxfordshire, later bailiff of Southwark, and Anne Lenthall, sister of William *Lenthall, speaker of the Long Parliament. Warcup himself was to have a large family after his marriage to Anne Hudson (1623–1713). It was Speaker Lenthall that (after Warcup's short stay at St Alban Hall, Oxford, and a sojourn aboard) used his influence to make him secretary to the parliamentary commissioners in the Isle of Wight in 1648.

In 1651 Warcup was at Lincoln's Inn, where a number of memoranda show him engaged in litigation, trusts, and Welsh land deals. However in spring 1660 he vainly produced papers to George Monck, first duke of Albemarle, and others to form the basis of a bill setting out terms for the restoration of Charles II. In January 1660 he became a captain in the regiment (formerly Fleetwood's) of Sir Anthony Ashley Cooper (later first earl of Shaftesbury), and the connection continued after the Restoration, when Shaftesbury was chancellor of the exchequer and Warcup, among other financial concessions, was a farmer of the excise in Wiltshire and Dorset, as well as justice of the peace in London. Warcup also availed himself further of his relationship to Monck. In February 1664 he succeeded to his father's office as bailiff of Southwark. In the following years he was active in combating the effects of the plague alongside his fellow justice Sir Edmund Godfrey. Unfortunately, Warcup presumed too much on his use of the name of Henry Bennet, earl of Arlington, to cover his own corrupt financial transactions and in July 1666 he was committed to the Fleet prison. He was eventually released about August 1666. Nevertheless Warcup was soon climbing into office again. Once more on the fringes of the court, he was involved in fruitless attempts to reconcile first John Maitland, first duke of Lauderdale, and then Thomas Osborne, first earl of Danby, with Shaftesbury in 1676 and 1677.

It was in the Popish Plot of 1678 that Warcup found most notoriety. A JP of Middlesex and Westminster for many years, he searched for papists and for popish books. He was noted as having a great zeal for the protestant religion, and his stated political views included a dislike of France and the activities of the duchess of Portsmouth in particular. In the aftermath of Oates's revelations, Warcup was employed by the committee of the House of Lords for the examination of witnesses, dominated by Shaftesbury. He subsequently claimed to have taken the information of over 100 witnesses, both English and Irish. Many of his activities are detailed in his private journal of 1676–84, and he was in contact with most of the major informers of the day. As long as Shaftesbury was lord president of the council, Warcup found no difficulty in reconciling his loyalties, and even after Shaftesbury's dismissal in October 1679 he was used, following an hour's private conversation with the king alone in the royal bedchamber, in trying to bring Charles II and the earl together again. But in February 1681 many witnesses began to see more advantage in making themselves acceptable to the government than to the whigs, and in stating that attempts had been made to suborn them to give evidence. In that same month Warcup had several meetings with the king and his ministers Laurence Hyde, later first earl of Rochester, and Sir Leoline Jenkins; and on 4 March the council ordered him £1500 by privy seal for his expenses. His dealing with the witnesses now had a different purpose, and he was employed to sift their information as they related to the alleged treason of Shaftesbury, sitting alongside the government solicitor Richard Graham.

After Shaftesbury's acquittal it was Warcup's turn to face counter-accusations of conspiracy to suborn witnesses, as well as (he said) being burnt in effigy with the pope, libelled in pamphlets, and assaulted in the streets. Reaction against Warcup's part in such affairs had already led him to make a strategic withdrawal to Oxfordshire in 1682. Indeed he spent most of that year there on his estate, Northmoor, near Eynsham. As compensation for his troubles he was knighted on 15 December 1684. Thereafter he spent most of his time peacefully employed with the expansion of his estates and his family (whose female members often proved quarrelsome), and in supporting the military careers of his two sons, Edmund and Lenthall, both of whom were killed in action at the battle of Steenkerke in 1692. Warcup had welcomed the accession of James II, but given his former politics he applauded the revolution of 1688, emerging politically in the 1690s as a

church tory. Edmund Warcup died at Gaunt House, Northmoor, on 1 May 1712, and was buried in the family vault in the church of St Denys, Northmoor, leaving his wealth and estate to his wife, daughters, and grandchildren.

Warcup was typical of the many minor figures of his day in that he all too easily became involved in the Popish Plot and its politics. While he undoubtedly played fast and loose with the plot witnesses during his association with Shaftesbury, he soon switched sides when he thought it prudent. In his youth, about which little is known, Warcup had suffered from scrofula, until he was cured during the 1640s. According to Pepys, the affliction was said to have left Warcup allergic to roses, and for sport he could prove this to companions by touching his nose with the flower and bringing up a number of welts on his skin. In other respects, politics especially, Warcup was to prove equally as sensitive to the ebbs and flows of his age.

K. H. D. HALEY, *rev.* ALAN MARSHALL

Sources memorial tablet and family memorial, Church of St Denys, Northmoor, Oxfordshire · 'The journals of Edmund Warcup, 1676–84', ed. K. G. Feiling and F. R. D. Needham, *EngHR*, 40 (1925), 235–60 · *CSP dom.*, 1660–85 · will, PRO, PROB 11/530/253 · Foster, *Alum. Oxon.*

Archives Bodl. Oxf., corresp. and papers; corresp. · Bodl. Oxf., treaty in the Isle of Wight

Wealth at death legacies of £7407 1s. 0d., estate at Northmoor and elsewhere to be divided among wife, children, and grandchildren: will, PRO, PROB 11/530/253

Ward, Sir Adolphus William (1837–1924), historian, born at Hampstead, Middlesex, on 2 December 1837, was the second son of John *Ward (1805–1890), diplomatist, and his wife, Caroline (d. 1905), daughter of the Revd John Bullock, rector of Radwinter, Essex. In 1841 Ward's father was sent to Germany on the first of a series of missions and appointments which kept him there until his retirement in 1870. This transplantation exerted a profound influence on Adolphus, whose education began at Leipzig, where his father was then consul-general; his early interest in Germany never waned. At the age of sixteen he was moved to King Edward VI School, Bury St Edmunds, of which John William Donaldson was then headmaster, and in 1855 he entered Peterhouse, Cambridge, as a pensioner. He graduated in 1859 with a first class in the classical tripos, and was elected a fellow of his college in 1862. He entered the Inner Temple in 1860, and was called to the bar in 1866, but never practised. After brief periods as classical lecturer at Peterhouse, examiner at the education office, and assistant to George Gilbert Ramsay, professor of humanity in the University of Glasgow, he was appointed professor of history and English language and literature at Owens College, Manchester, in 1866.

For the next thirty-one years Ward laboured with unflagging enthusiasm as a teacher and an administrator. His commanding presence and impressive lectures combined with his wide-ranging knowledge to make him one of the leading teachers of his time. He was the founder of the history school, which placed Manchester with Oxford and Cambridge universities in the professionalization of the discipline. The appointment of T. N. Toller as professor

Sir Adolphus William Ward (1837–1924), by Hugh Goldwin Riviere, 1911

of English philology in 1880 relieved him of part of his duties; but until he became principal in 1889, Ward remained responsible both for English literature and for the whole range of history, and he continued to lecture on history until he left Manchester in 1897.

No member of the staff played a more active part than Ward in raising the academic status of Owens College. In 1875, with three of his colleagues, he began to advocate its transformation into an independent university. Instead, the federal Victoria University was created in 1880, with its seat in Manchester, and Owens College as its first constituent member; the colleges of Liverpool and Leeds were added later. Ward was vice-chancellor of the new university from 1886 to 1890 and again from 1894 to 1896. In recognition of his services to the community, Ward received the freedom of the city in 1897, the year in which he left Manchester. He remained in close touch with his old friends, and rejoiced at the establishment of an independent University of Manchester in 1903.

Ward's publications during the Manchester years were mainly in the field of English literature, although his translation, published in five volumes as the *History of Greece* (1868–73), of the work by Ernst Curtius reflected his interest in ancient history and his admiration for German scholarship. His *History of English Dramatic Literature to the Death of Queen Anne* (2 vols., 1875; rev. and enlarged edn in 3 vols., 1899), the first systematic attempt to cover this immense field, put him among the leading British scholars of the period. His editions of works by Christopher Marlowe, Robert Greene, and Thomas Heywood, his

article 'Drama' written for the ninth edition of the *Encyclopaedia Britannica*, and his contributions to the *Manchester Guardian*, of which he was for many years drama critic, bear witness to his interest in drama from the sixteenth century to the nineteenth. The volumes *Chaucer* (1879) and *Dickens* (1882), his editions of the works of Alexander Pope, of John Byrom, the Manchester Jacobite, and, in later years, of George Crabbe and of Elizabeth Gaskell, showed his continuing interest in poetry and fiction. In fact, his only substantial historical work in these years was *The Counter-Reformation* (1889), a terse but thorough Europe-wide survey, with good insights and balanced judgement. He contributed a considerable number of articles to the *Dictionary of National Biography* and he was one of the leading supporters of the *English Historical Review* from its foundation in 1886: he supplied 184 separate items for it over the next forty years, mainly book reviews.

On leaving Manchester at the age of sixty, Ward settled in London. A little volume, combining historical and literary analysis, on *Sir Henry Wotton* (1898) was followed by the Ford lectures at Oxford University on *Great Britain and Hanover* (1899; German translation, 1906). He had begun work on *The Electress Sophia and the Hanoverian Succession* (1903; rev. and enlarged edn, 1909) when, in 1900, his old college called him back as its master. He played a full part in the lives of both Peterhouse and of the university, of which he was vice-chancellor in 1901. He was also chairman of the press syndicate from 1905 to 1919, and he was active on the library syndicate.

The death of Lord Acton in 1902 deprived the editors of the *Cambridge Modern History* of his guiding hand. As editor-in-chief, with the aid of George Walter Prothero and Stanley Leathes, Ward carried through this immense undertaking in eleven years (1901–12). Of his own contributions, which appeared in seven of the twelve volumes, the most important are the six chapters on the Thirty Years' War. The success of the enterprise encouraged him to suggest, and the university press to undertake, the *Cambridge History of English Literature*, edited by Ward and Alfred Rayney Waller, and published in 1907–16 (reissued 1932 and 1949–53). Here Ward's contributions appear in nine of the fourteen volumes; these chapters are generally shorter and less impressive than those which he wrote for the *Cambridge Modern History*.

The outbreak of the First World War in 1914 grieved the Germanophile Ward. His dislike of Teutonic militarism in no way disturbed the balance of his major historical work, *Germany, 1815–1890* (1916–18), in which he was able to draw on his youthful experiences. The third volume, with an epilogue extending to 1907, is shorter and slighter; the octogenarian Ward was anxious not to leave an unfinished work. Ward's *Collected Papers* (1921) were also a substantial publication, but his selection was not impeccable: some important material was omitted, and a few ephemeral reviews were included.

Though now over eighty and rather deaf, Ward was still full of energy. With G. P. Gooch he edited *The Cambridge History of British Foreign Policy, 1783–1919*, published in three volumes in 1922–3. His chapter on the Schleswig-Holstein question, for which he used the unpublished papers of his father, was of more use than his lengthy introduction sketching the evolution of diplomacy up to 1783. A briefer survey of British policy in Greece and the Ionian Islands from 1832 to 1864 incorporated personal reminiscences of an early visit to Athens, where he had conversed in modern Greek with veterans of the war of independence. After the meticulous completion of this last editorial enterprise, Ward restricted himself to the writing of articles and reviews.

Ward received many honours in Britain and abroad. He was knighted in 1913, the year in which he presided over the international historical congress in London, and he was created a knight of the Prussian order of the crown in 1911. He received honorary degrees from the universities of Manchester, Glasgow, St Andrews, and Leipzig. He was president of the British Academy (of which he was an original member) from 1911 to 1913; he also served in the same capacity for several other historical, literary, and antiquarian societies.

On 8 February 1879 Ward married his cousin Adelaide Laura, daughter of the Revd Thomas Burne Lancaster, rector of Grittleton, Wiltshire. This marriage brought him enduring happiness; the marriage in 1916 of their only surviving child, Adelaide, to E. W. *Barnes (1874–1953), at the time master of the Temple, afterwards a controversial bishop of Birmingham, added to the interest of his later life. Ward was conspicuous in every gathering he attended, and his hospitality made him an ideal host. He took special pleasure in entertaining foreign scholars. Despite his stately courtesy, he was fundamentally simple and kind-hearted. In politics he was a Liberal, and he disliked imperialism both at home and abroad. He died in Cambridge on 19 June 1924 and was buried in the churchyard at Cherry Hinton. His wife survived him.

Ward was one of the outstanding scholars of his age, contributing original work over a remarkable range. As a literary critic, his *œuvre* is now largely superseded, and even his historical writings are little consulted. Yet a number of them retain their authority, in particular his studies of Hanover and its impact on British policy. On the history of the German lands as a whole, from the sixteenth century to the nineteenth, Ward was at his best. With Acton, but much more productively, he made available, and built upon, the results of central European scholarship in that field. He owed most to Leopold Ranke and to disciples of Ranke such as Anton Gindely. Like them, he concentrated on the policy of states, which he aimed to describe with complete objectivity; events and institutions were of more interest to him than social and economic factors or religious and political ideas. Though his style was at times 'a little lacking in simplicity, directness, and charm' (Tout, 434), he always wrote carefully and efficiently, and could rise to passages of restrained eloquence.

Ward left a substantial collection of his books to Peterhouse, where the undergraduate library now bears his name. They form an important resource, especially for the history of Germany. The college also possesses some of his working papers, most of them in a series of seventy-nine notebooks, containing drafts of lectures and extensive source compilations.   G. P. GOOCH, *rev.* R. J. W. EVANS

Sources T. F. Tout, 'Sir Adolphus William Ward, 1837–1924', *PBA*, 11 (1924–5), 427–40 · A. T. Bartholomew, *A bibliography of Sir A. W. Ward* (1926) · *In memoriam A. W. Ward* (1924) · S. Leathes and G. P. Gooch, 'Notes and communications', *Cambridge Historical Journal*, 1 (1923–5), 219–24 · P. J. Hartog, ed., *The Owens College, Manchester* (1900) · T. F. Tout and J. Tait, eds., *Historical essays by members of the Owens College, Manchester* (1902) · P. R. H. Slee, *Learning and a liberal education: the study of modern history in the universities of Oxford, Cambridge and Manchester, 1800–1914* (1986) · personal knowledge (1937) · m. cert. · *CGPLA Eng. & Wales* (1924)
Archives CUL, corresp. relating to Cambridge Modern History · Peterhouse, Cambridge, papers | BL, letters to Michael Field, Add. MSS 45851–45852 · BL, corresp. with Macmillans, Add. MS 55073 · CUL, letters to Lord Acton · CUL, corresp. with Lord Kelvin Stokes · JRL, letters to E. A. Freeman · JRL, letters to C. P. Scott · JRL, letters to Thomas Tout · King's Cam., letters to Oscar Browning · NAM, letters to Professor Spenser Wilkinson on University and literary affairs
Likenesses H. von Herkomer, oils, 1898, University of Manchester · H. G. Riviere, oils, 1911, Peterhouse, Cambridge [*see illus.*] · W. Stoneman, photograph, 1918, NPG
Wealth at death £10,792 6s. 7d.: probate, 1 Aug 1924, *CGPLA Eng. & Wales*

Ward, Ann (1715/16–1789), printer, married a York printer, Caesar *Ward (*bap.* 1710, *d.* 1759), about 1738, but little else is known about her early life. She is best known for her role in the publication of the first edition of Laurence Sterne's *Tristram Shandy* (1760).

Women had always been active in the York newspaper trade. Its first newspaper, the *York Mercury*, was printed and published by Grace White and John Hammond from 1719 to 1721; later it was printed by Alice Bourne. The *York Courant*, established by John White in 1725, was for a time printed by another woman—Sarah Coke. It changed ownership several times before 1739, when it was bought by Caesar Ward and his brother-in-law Richard Chandler. Chandler's over-ambitious publishing ventures led to his suicide and Ward's bankruptcy in 1744, but Ward recovered his interest in the *Courant*, and the proprietorship passed to Ann Ward when her husband died in 1759.

Kenneth Monkman has shown beyond any bibliographical doubt that Ann Ward was the printer of the first two volumes of *Tristram Shandy*. It is true that Sterne turned first to the literary publisher Robert Dodsley to oversee the printing and publishing of his book in London, but when Dodsley questioned the author's conditions, Sterne took his manuscript to a York printer whose work he already knew: Caesar Ward had printed several of Sterne's sermons, and his widow, Ann Ward, had recently taken over the Coney Street business. 'The Book shall be printed here', Sterne wrote to Dodsley in October 1759,

> & the Impression sent up to You; for as I live at York & shall correct every Proof myself, it shall go perfect into the World—& be printed in so creditable a way as to Paper Type etc—as to do no Dishonour to You, who I know never chuse to print a Book meanly. (*Correspondence*, 421)

This first instalment of *Tristram Shandy* convinced readers and the trade alike: the book sold well, Dodsley bought up the copyright (at a far higher price than Sterne had originally asked), and Ann Ward attracted more business.

Like most provincial printers, Ann Ward printed primarily local material: sermons preached at York, trials, official publications, poll books, guidebooks, and regional history, including editions of Francis Drake's *Eboracum*. Other favourite authors were John Evelyn and William Mason. Horace Walpole called Mason's York-printed translation of Dufresnoy's *De arte graphica* 'a very handsome book' (*Letters*, 403). The *Eighteenth-Century Short-Title Catalogue* records almost a hundred different titles printed by Ann Ward, many of them in association with the Dodsleys or other important London booksellers.

For much of her career, Ann Ward was assisted by the printer David Russell, formerly employed by her husband. Russell became part-owner of the business, although his name did not appear in their imprints. About 1787 Ann Ward bought back Russell's share, so that the whole of her printing business could be passed on to her son-in-law George Peacock.

Ann and Caesar Ward had at least eight children, among them Caesar Ward (baptized 4 December 1741), who became free of the Stationers' Company in 1763 and set up a printing house in London, and Mary (baptized 27 June 1740), who married George Peacock, her mother's successor in business. Ann Ward was said to be seventy-three years old when she died on 10 April 1789.

C. Y. FERDINAND

Sources R. Davies, *A memoir of the York press: with notices of authors, printers, and stationers, in the sixteenth, seventeenth, and eighteenth centuries* (1868) • K. Monkman, 'The bibliography of the early editions of *Tristram Shandy*', *The Library*, 5th ser., 25 (1970), 11–39 • ESTC • *The correspondence of Robert Dodsley, 1733–1764*, ed. J. E. Tierney (1988) • parish register, York, St Martin Coney Street, Borth. Inst., PR Y/MCS.3 [see also J. Malden, ed., *Register of York freemen, 1680 to 1986* (1989); IGI; York city marriage bond index, 1701–1750; Boyd's marriage index] • I. Maxted, ed., *The British book trades, 1710–1777: an index of the masters and their apprentices* (1983) • I. Maxted, *The British book trades, 1775–1787: an index to insurance policies* (1992) • *The letters of Horace Walpole, fourth earl of Orford*, ed. P. Toynbee, 12 (1904), 403
Wealth at death two properties in York: will

Ward, Arthur Henry [Arthur Sarsfield Ward; *pseud*. Sax Rohmer] (**1883–1959**), writer, was born in Ladywood, Birmingham, on 15 February 1883, the only child of Irish immigrant parents, a clerk, William Ward (1847x51–1932), and Margaret Mary, *née* Furey (1849x52–1901). A lifetime spent in autobiographical embroidering means that little reliable information is known about his early life, or his schooling, but we do know that the family moved to London about 1886, and from a young age Ward appears to have devoured thrillers and historical novels, and to have written imaginative stories.

After various false starts, including a stint in a bank, another as a gas company clerk, and a third as a reporter, Ward—who replaced his middle name Henry with the more unusual Sarsfield at the time of his mother's death—began to have success as a music-hall sketch and song writer. He also turned out copy as a hack journalist, and he sold his first piece of fiction in 1903 to *Chambers's Journal*, earning his living from this parcel of activities

between 1906 and 1909. In 1905 Ward met a variety-act juggler, Rose Elisabeth Knox (1886–1979), sister of the Crazy Gang comedian Teddy Knox, and they were married in London on 14 January 1909. In 1910 Ward published *Pause!*, a collection of stories in collaboration with George Robey, and in 1911 ghost-wrote an autobiography of Harry Relph (Little Tich). Encouraged by Elisabeth, Ward published his first serial in *Cassell's Magazine* in 1912, using his Sax Rohmer pseudonym which first appeared with one of his songs in 1908. 'The Sins of Severac Babylon' (published in book form in 1914) was an antisemitic fantasy starring a 'Jewish Robin Hood'.

But it was Ward's 'Chinese' creation, the villainous Fu Manchu, leader of the secret society the Si-Fan, with whom he remains most strongly identified. Although Chinese themes had always had a niche in collections of mysteries and thriller novels, Ward's were to prove by far the most successful. His inspiration lay squarely in the unapologetic opportunism of a professional hack writer: 'Conditions for launching a Chinese villain on the market', he is reputed to have said, 'were ideal' (Van Ash and Rohmer, 75). The first Fu Manchu story was serialized in 1912–13 in the wake of the 1911 revolution in China. *The Mystery of Dr Fu Manchu* (1913) launched the career of a villain with all the 'cruel cunning of the entire Eastern race, accumulated in one giant intellect, with all the resources of a wealthy government ... Dr Fu Manchu, the yellow peril incarnate in one man' (p. 23). Incarnate in one woman, too, as Fu Manchu's mysterious slave-girl, or later his daughter, supplied somewhat hazily suggestive sex-interest for the works. Ward's villain was regularly killed off over the years, but revived (as late as 1957) by popular demand or at the insistence of Ward's publishers or wallet. The books partly developed with their times: having once aimed to rule the Edwardian world, by 1948 (in *Shadow of Fu Manchu*) the Devil Doctor was trying to save the planet from communism.

Some fifteen Fu Manchu books appeared in all, and their popularity was exploited and reinforced in turn by film adaptations (serials and single films) and radio series, and also by a legion of copyists. Most of the stories were initially set in London's Limehouse district, then entering a period when the tiny Chinese community was the focus of sensationalist newspaper reportage and literary 'exposés'. These concentrated on relationships between British women and Chinese men, on illegal immigration, and, somewhat relentlessly, on opium. The criminalization of opium and cocaine possession in the wake of the First World War focused the minds of jobbing hacks on the possibilities of Limehouse, which was presented to the popular reading public as an opium-addled 'Orient' in London's East End. Later Fu Manchu tales were located in the United States, and their narrators and heroes were American too, reflecting Ward's appreciation of the power of market forces.

Limehouse developed as a literary sub-genre in itself and Ward took advantage of its notoriety—and thereby greatly boosted it—writing more particular, and equally influential, works in which drug smuggling, 'white slavery', and opium dens played major roles. *Dope: a Story of Chinatown and the Drug Traffic* (1919), for example, was a speedy, factional retelling of the cocaine-related death of the actress Billie Carleton and the sensational exposure of a Mayfair opium-smoking set which followed. Ward's Chinatown fiction intentionally had the appearance of reportage, while his savvy marketing of things allegedly Chinese further extended to his music-hall songs and monologues, and even to the creation of a perfume, styled Honan, which was produced by a Chinese workforce in Limehouse, and launched with opium-redolent packaging and publicity in 1919.

A brief period of war service (1915–16) in the Artists' Rifles (from which he was invalided), and some work for MI7 (b), which dealt with press propaganda questions, hardly put Ward off his writing stride. But after 1919 he made concerted efforts to achieve success in a different field, the theatre. His activities began moderately well with *Round in Fifty* (1922), a reworking of Jules Verne's *Around the World in 80 Days*, but his mystery plays *The Eye of Siva* (1923) and *Secret Egypt* (1928) were unsuccessful, and other projects came to nothing, so he returned to fiction writing. Ward had fallen victim to more than one dishonest agent, but still earned enough to build his own house near Reigate in Surrey, travel widely, and indulge in roulette 'systems'. Nevertheless, it seemed that he was always having to write one more book to earn his living.

As the magazine serial form died out after the Second World War, so Ward's popularity waned, but he was adept at reinventing himself. His biggest market was in the United States, to which the Wards moved in 1947, having been frequent visitors since 1919. Film, radio, and latterly television royalties there became his main source of income. The Fu Manchu character was recycled, initially for a BBC radio serial, as a female criminal, Sumuru. This led to a series of luridly titled books, including *Nude in Mink* (1950) and *Virgin in Flames* (1953); Ward's style was fundamentally innocent, and of a different era, but he still made the shift in emphasis from poison in Fu Manchu to sex in the Sumuru series.

For all of Ward's pretensions as a composer of well-written popular fiction, he was never considered to be more than a writer of lurid lowbrow shockers by his contemporaries. His reputation today rests on his creation of Fu Manchu, but largely because it has become a byword for racist stereotyping of Chinese people. The pervasiveness of the figure of the Chinese villain gave rise to contemporary complaints, and even to efforts by the Chinese nationalist government in the 1930s to thwart Hollywood adaptations of such works. Such moves ultimately had little impact on a widely disseminated stereotype, and the Fu Manchu idea easily survived the death of its creator on 1 June 1959 from pneumonia and a cerebral haemorrhage at University College Hospital, London. Ward was buried in Kensal Green Roman Catholic cemetery, London.

As a thriller writer Ward is of little importance. His prose is pompous and ponderous, and his plotting thin, predictable, and repetitive. However, Ward was an entrepreneur with an instinctive knowledge of his market, in the face of rapid developments in popular fiction in the twentieth century. ROBERT BICKERS

Sources C. Van Ash and E. S. Rohmer, *Master of villainy: a biography of Sax Rohmer*, ed. R. E. Briney (1972) • R. E. Briney, 'Sax Rohmer revisited', *Views and Reviews*, 3 (1971–2), 2 (52–7), 3 (56–62), 4 (64–71) • R. Bickers, *Britain in China: community, culture and colonialism, 1900–49* (1999) • CGPLA Eng. & Wales (1960) • J. L. Biggers, 'A walking tour of Sax Rohmer's London', *The Rohmer Review*, 18 (1981), 14 • private information (2004) [R. E. Briney]
Archives BBC WAC, corresp. with BBC staff • BL, corresp. with League of Dramatists, Add. MS 63433 • BL, corresp. with Society of Authors, Add. MS 56791
Likenesses photographs, repro. in Van Ash and Rohmer, *Master of villainy*, ed. Briney
Wealth at death £1047 16s. 10d.: probate, 22 Feb 1960, CGPLA Eng. & Wales

Ward [*married name* Jackson], **Barbara Mary**, Baroness Jackson of Lodsworth (1914–1981), journalist and economist, was born on 23 May 1914 in Malton Road, Heworth, Yorkshire, the second child and only daughter of Walter Ward, a solicitor, and his wife, Teresa Mary Burge. Soon after her birth the family moved to Felixstowe, where her father worked as solicitor to the Port of Ipswich. He had a house built for the family, Picketts, in Picketts Road, then on the edge of the town. Walter Ward was a non-practising Christian with Quaker leanings; his wife, Teresa, came from a devout Roman Catholic family and brought up Barbara similarly; her faith remained an important element throughout her life. Barbara was sent to school at the Convent of Jesus and Mary in Felixstowe. In September 1929 she went to Paris to study at the Lycée Molière, and later for just under a year at the Sorbonne. In August 1931 she went on to Germany. Her original intention had been to study modern languages, but while staying near Darmstadt she encountered a recent Oxford graduate who suggested that if she wished to be a political secretary she should consider studying politics, philosophy, and economics, then a relatively new degree. She took his advice and sat the entrance examination for Somerville College, going up in autumn 1932. She graduated with first-class honours in 1935.

On leaving Oxford Ward began a doctorate on the political and economic situation of Austria, under the auspices of the Royal Institute of International Affairs, and supported herself by lecturing and by some freelance journalism. As a lecturer she had enormous success. Partly through this, and partly through her family contacts, she became well known, especially in Roman Catholic circles in London. Aided by a scholarship she was able to spend summers studying conditions on the continent of Europe. Like many of her co-religionists in the 1930s she was at first sympathetic to Hitler, but her attitude changed after experiencing at first hand antisemitism in Germany and Austria. She began to work for Jewish refugees and, with the historian (Henry) Christopher Dawson, to whom she had been introduced by the Dominican Thomas Gilbey, started to plan how to mobilize the Catholic church behind the war effort should war break out. These ideas

Barbara Mary Ward, Baroness Jackson of Lodsworth (1914–1981), by Rodrigo Moynihan

eventually took shape as the Sword of the Spirit, a name inspired by a broadcast by Cardinal Hinsley, archbishop of Westminster, on 10 December 1939. The cardinal's enthusiasm for what was originally intended to be a joint Catholic and Anglican body to promote Christian values was not shared by many of his fellow bishops, and it became a wholly Catholic organization, presided over by Dawson with Barbara Ward as secretary. Dawson also took over for a time at the beginning of the war the editorship of the Catholic quarterly, the *Dublin Review*. Both he and Ward wrote regularly for this journal, using it to promote the policies of Sword.

At the outbreak of war Ward was sent to Oxford—where she shared lodgings with the novelist Charles Williams—to work for the Ministry of Information. She had already met Geoffrey Crowther, the editor of *The Economist*, to which she had occasionally contributed, and when her post in the Ministry of Information was abruptly terminated after only a few weeks he offered her a post on the paper. Ward remained there, first as assistant, and then as foreign editor until 1950, continuing to write major pieces for it throughout her life. During the war she travelled widely on behalf of the Ministry of Information, especially in the USA. At home she served for a time as president of the Catholic Women's League, and she also became a regular, and extremely popular, contributor to the BBC's *The Brains Trust*, brought to the programme by A. F. C. Beales, a fellow member of the Sword executive,

who had been drafted into the BBC from King's College, London. At the end of the war she was made a governor of the BBC—by mistake, she always claimed. An interest in opera—she had an excellent singing voice, and had at one time in the 1930s considered becoming a professional singer—led to her appointment from 1944 to 1953 to the boards of Sadler's Wells and the Old Vic.

Barbara Ward was already a prolific author. Her first book, *The International Share-out* (1938), was a study of the colonial powers, and it was this which first attracted Crowther. A visit to her brother John, then an engineer in Turkey, resulted in *Turkey*, published in 1941 by Oxford University Press, which went on to commission pamphlets on Russian and Italian foreign policy. Her commitment to upholding Christian values in the war led to *The Defence of the West*, a series of five broadcasts first published in *The Listener*. After the war she was a fervent supporter of the Marshall plan for the reconstruction of Europe, commending it in the pages of *The Economist* and in *The West at Bay* (1948), in which she advocated a European free trade area. The theme of a strong Europe, both economically and ideologically, was also a central theme of *Policy for the West* (1951).

Barbara Ward's marriage to Commander Robert Gillman Alan *Jackson (1911–1991) took place in St Felix's Church, Felixstowe, on 16 November 1950; the ceremony was performed by John Carmel Heenan, the future cardinal-archbishop of Westminster. Jackson was an Australian by birth, a former government official working by this time for the United Nations, and for the first year of their marriage they lived in Australia, a country to which Barbara Ward was not attracted. Jackson was appointed to head the development commission in the Gold Coast, and to oversee the construction of the Volta Dam. While preparing himself for this he travelled in the Far East, particularly in India, and it was the experience of India, to which she returned several times, combined with nearly a decade of living in west Africa, that formed Ward's ideas about economic development. She expressed her convictions in *Faith and Freedom* (1954) in which she urged the need for the Western nations to share their wealth with developing countries.

Ward's son Robert was born on 25 February 1956, the year that her husband was knighted and she became Lady Jackson, though she continued to use her maiden name. By this time she was much in demand as a lecturer in the United States as elsewhere. A series of lectures in Montreal in 1955 was published two years later as *Interplay of East and West*, while lectures at the University of Ghana appeared in 1959 as *Five Ideas that Change the World*. Both of these discussed the forces which dominate modern civilization, seen largely from a Christian standpoint. In *India and the West* (1961) Ward discussed the particular economic problems of the subcontinent and the need to create international bodies to channel both aid and trade to India—a theme to which she returned on a broader canvas in *The Rich Nations and the Poor Nations* (1961), originally a series of lectures for the Canadian Broadcasting Corporation. She again addressed the topic of India in *The Plan under Pressure* (1963), another series of lectures, on this occasion delivered in Bombay.

Ward's frequent visits to North America had brought her into contact with the political establishment in the United States. She was close to Adlai Stevenson and friendly with John F. Kennedy long before he became president. Her feelings towards Kennedy cooled over the Cuban missile crisis, largely because she felt he had abandoned Stevenson, then his ambassador to the UN. Though openly critical of American strategy in Vietnam, she regularly visited the White House during the administration of Lyndon Johnson. These contacts Ward used to further her pleas for economic aid to the developing countries, and especially to India and to the Volta River project in Ghana. She served as an adviser to Robert McNamara when he became president of the World Bank.

Much of Ward's work in the late 1950s and into the 1960s was funded by the Carnegie Foundation. From 1957 to 1968 she was Carnegie fellow at Harvard, where she spent the winters, living at 6 Ash Street, Cambridge, Massachusetts—the family home, after they left Ghana in 1961, was for tax reasons established in Jersey, Channel Islands. During the early 1960s Ward tried to persuade the Roman Catholic bishops, gathered in Rome for the Second Vatican Council, to put development issues on her church's agenda: she was part of the group which helped to create the pontifical commission for justice and peace. In 1971 she became the first woman to address a synod of Roman Catholic bishops. All this travelling put too much of a strain on her marriage and she and her husband drifted apart. Though never divorced, they separated formally in 1973. After the separation she thought she ought to resign from the pontifical commission, but her offer was rejected by Archbishop Benelli.

Growing out of the campaign on development issues were *Nationalism and Ideology* (1966), a series of lectures delivered at Carleton University, Ottawa, *Spaceship Earth* (1966) and *The Lopsided World* (1968), lectures delivered at Johns Hopkins University. Common themes were the growing interdependence of peoples and the urgency of assistance to developing countries to maintain stability. As Albert Schweitzer professor of international economic development at Columbia University from 1968 to 1973—an appointment greeted with hostility by some members of the faculty—Ward was able to address these problems at an academic level, and as someone committed to international organizations and the author of *Spaceship Earth* she was a natural choice with René Dubois to write the key text for the UN's 1972 Stockholm conference on the Human Environment. *Only One Earth* is described as an unofficial report on the title page, though it appeared before the conference opened. *The Home of Man* was similarly produced for the 1976 UN's Habitat Conference on Human Settlements, held in Vancouver.

After retiring from the Schweitzer chair Ward took up permanent residence in England, in the village of Lodsworth, near Petworth, Sussex. She was created a DBE in 1974, and a life peer, with the title of Baroness Jackson of Lodsworth, in 1976. She was awarded many honorary degrees, and was made an honorary fellow of the Royal Institute of British Architects in 1975 and of the London School of Economics in 1976. Awarded the Jawaharlal Nehru prize in 1974 she gave the money to a leper colony. She was given the Albert medal of the Royal Society of Arts in 1980.

Ward's concern in the 1970s was less with economic development, more with problems of the environment: this was the theme of her keynote address to the bishops of the Anglican communion, gathered for the 1978 Lambeth conference. In 1973 Barbara Ward became president, and in 1980, chairman, of the International Institute for Environment and Development—she herself insisted on adding the last two words to the institute's title. *Progress for a Small Planet* (1979), her last book, still argued the case for the world's poor, but in a broader context of the exploitation by the rich countries of the world's resources, to the detriment of what she called the planetary community. She wrote the book despite ill health. In the late 1940s she had been diagnosed with cancer but was cured, she believed, through the prayers of the Italian stigmatist Padre Pio. In gratitude she gave considerable amounts of money to his hospital at San Giovanni Rotondo. But in the late 1960s the disease recurred. She underwent two operations, but they were unsuccessful in halting the spread of the cancer. She died at her home, the Pound House, Lodsworth, on 31 May 1981. Her requiem was said in the local Roman Catholic church, in the presence of Cardinal Bernardin Gantin, a Benin-born member of the papal curia, sent by Pope Paul VI as his personal representative. At her request, however, she was buried in the local, Anglican, graveyard at Lodsworth.

MICHAEL J. WALSH

Sources Georgetown University, Washington, DC, Barbara Ward (Lady Jackson) papers · E. Usherwood, *Women first* (1989), 114–24 · R. Bird, 'Barbara Ward', *The Economist* (6 June 1981), 21–5 · R. D. Edwards, *The pursuit of reason: The Economist, 1843–1993* (1993) · private information (2004) · b. cert. · d. cert. · *CGPLA Eng. & Wales* (1981) · *WW*
Archives Georgetown University, Washington, DC, corresp. and papers | CAC Cam., corresp. with Sir W. J. Haley | FILM BFI NFTVA, documentary footage
Likenesses photograph, *c*.1945, BBC WAC · D. Lowe, drawings, *c*.1952, NPG · R. Moynihan, painting, priv. coll. [*see illus.*] · photograph (after R. Moynihan), NPG
Wealth at death £82,145—in England and Wales: probate, 9 Sept 1981, *CGPLA Eng. & Wales*

Ward, Bernard Nicholas (1857–1920), headmaster and historian, was born on 4 February 1857, the youngest of three sons and seventh of eight children of William George *Ward (1812–1882) and his wife, Frances Mary (*d.* 1898), daughter of John Wingfield, prebendary of Worcester. The Ward family lived in a house, designed by Augustus Welby Pugin, at St Edmund's College, Old Hall Green, near Ware in Hertfordshire. Ward's father had taught moral philosophy and dogmatic theology there since 1846, the year following his conversion.

The year after Ward's birth his father moved the family to the Isle of Wight where he had come into an inheritance, but within three years he returned to Ware and remained there for another ten years. Bernard's earliest instruction was at home under the care of tutors, but he entered St Edmund's in August 1868 and remained there as a lay student until 1875. He planned to enter upon a business career, but first, accompanied by his sister Emily, he toured Canada and the United States. He had developed a taste for travel when, in 1873, he joined a pilgrimage to Paray-le-Monial. A year later he visited the shrine of St Edmund at Pontigny. His first visit to Rome was in 1877, and he returned in 1879 when he included Switzerland and Lourdes in his itinerary. Shortly afterwards he determined to become a priest.

In January 1880 Ward began his theological studies at Oscott College, Birmingham, where he was ordained deacon on Holy Saturday 1882. He then returned to St Edmund's as prefect of discipline and on 8 October 1882 was ordained to the priesthood by Cardinal Manning in the chapel of the Archbishop's House. In 1885 he was assigned the task of founding a mission at Willesden, where he worked until January 1888, when he accepted a position at Oscott as professor of science. In the summer of 1890, however, he returned to St Edmund's as vice-president and prefect of studies. He remained there until 1916.

When Herbert Vaughan became archbishop of Westminster in 1892, St Edmund's was in precarious financial straits, with a declining number of students. Vaughan considered closing the college, but first appointed Ward as president to see what might be done to save it. Ward proved to be a far-sighted and astute administrator. He was also generous in sharing his personal resources to benefit the college.

In 1893, to mark the centenary of St Edmund's, Ward founded *The Edmundian*, the college magazine, for which, until 1915, he wrote most of the editorial notes. Also in 1893 he published his *History of St Edmund's College*, thus launching his historical career. In April 1895 he was elevated to the rank of domestic prelate by Pope Leo XIII. In that year, in response to a request by Cardinal Vaughan, the Holy See gave permission for Catholics to attend English universities. Ward, hopeful that at least some students at St Edmund's would receive university degrees, began negotiations which led to the affiliation of the college with the University of Cambridge, 'on the understanding that a hostel subject to the ordinary laws of the University should be opened there' (*The Edmundian*, 12, 1920, 331). With the financial assistance of the duke of Norfolk, St Edmund's House was founded, and in 1897 studies were arranged at St Edmund's College for the Cambridge local examinations.

Ward was instrumental in founding an organization of Catholic headmasters which he served as secretary. On three occasions (1898, 1906, 1911), he hosted meetings of the group at St Edmund's. He was also a member of the education committee of the Hertfordshire county council. In May 1903, to mark the golden jubilee of the college chapel, he published his *Life of St Edmund*, as well as *Catholic London a Hundred Years Ago*.

In 1905 Ward was named a canon of the archdiocese of Westminster. In October 1907 a rumour circulated to the effect that he was to be the new bishop of Northampton. The appointment was never made, but he seems to have been unable to settle down again at the college. During the subsequent six years he nevertheless made his most significant historical contribution with *The Dawn of the Catholic Revival in England, 1781–1803* (2 vols., 1909), *The eve of Catholic emancipation, being the history of the English Catholics during the first thirty years of the nineteenth century* (3 vols., 1911), and *The Sequel to Catholic Emancipation, 1830–1850* (2 vols., 1915). These seven volumes have remained the most comprehensive study of Roman Catholic institutional life in the last quarter of the eighteenth and first half of the nineteenth centuries. Ward was inspired, at least in part, by the work of Canon Edwin Burton, vice-president of St Edmund's, whose *Life and Times of Bishop Challoner* (2 vols., 1909) he had read in manuscript form. His own research was carried out in England and also in Rome where he consulted documents at the English College as well as those which he was permitted to use at the Congregation for the Propagation of the Faith. In 1909 he was elected a member of the Old Brotherhood of the Secular Clergy, an honour which he deeply appreciated.

In November 1915 Ward's health clearly began to fail. He formally resigned his office on 19 July 1916 and was appointed to the mission at Brook Green, Hammersmith. In 1917 he was named bishop of the new diocese of Essex. He was to serve initially as apostolic administrator of the designated territory until the new diocese could be organized. He was elevated to the episcopate, therefore, as titular bishop of Lydda. Within a few months it was determined that Brentwood would be the cathedral town of the diocese, and in October of 1917 Ward was enthroned there.

In spite of poor health, Ward proved to be an energetic bishop, visiting every church of the diocese as well as undertaking the annual visitation of all convents. New missions were opened, the cathedral chapter was formed, and churches were consecrated. In 1918 he published a volume on *The Priestly Vocation*, composed of lectures that he had given as president of St Edmund's. In March of 1919 he made his *ad limina* visit to Rome and later in the year, his last pilgrimage to Lourdes. He died during the night of 20 January 1920 and was buried, as he had requested, in the chapel of St Edmund's College on the 26th.

RICHARD J. SCHIEFEN

Sources *The Edmundian* [St Edmund's College, Hertfordshire], 12/78 (1920) [Bishop Ward memorial number] · R. J. Schiefen, 'Bishop Bernard Ward, 1857–1920', *The Edmundian* [St Edmund's College, Hertfordshire], 33 (1993–4), 153–64 [centenary issue] · S. Foster, 'A bishop for Essex: Bernard Ward and the diocese of Brentwood', *Recusant History*, 21 (1992–3), 556–71 · *CGPLA Eng. & Wales* (1920)

Archives Brentwood diocesan archives · Southwark archdiocesan archives · Westm. DA, corresp. and papers | Westm. DA, St Edmund's College MSS

Likenesses photograph, 1917–20, repro. in *The Edmundian*, 12/78 (April 1920), facing title page · photograph, repro. in *The Edmundian*, 12/78 (April 1920), 328 · photograph, repro. in *The Edmundian*, 33/2 (215) (1993–4), 159

Wealth at death £6395 10s.: probate, 10 April 1920, *CGPLA Eng. & Wales*

Ward, Caesar (*bap.* **1710**, *d.* **1759**), bookseller and historian, was baptized on 2 June 1710 in the parish of St Sepulchre, Holborn, London, the son of Caesar Ward (1675–1712), apothecary, and his wife, Ann. He married first Mary Kilsha (*b. c.*1715) of Clothall, Hertfordshire, on 29 February 1736, but she evidently died within the year. His second marriage, in or before 1738, was to Ann *Ward (1715/16–1789), about whose early life little is known.

Ward was apprenticed in 1725 to Robert Gosling, bookseller and father of the bookseller–banker Sir Francis Gosling. About the time of his freedom of the Stationers' Company in September 1732, Ward set up business at the sign of the Ship between the Temple Gates, Fleet Street, in a shop formerly occupied by the bookseller James Lacy. His brother-in-law and partner Richard Chandler joined him soon after this, and by 1734 the partnership had a second shop in Scarborough, at the corner of Long Room Street.

Ward was admitted to the freedom of the city of York by purchase in 1736, and by 1737 he and Chandler had added a third shop to their business, one formerly occupied by Mr Mancklin in Coney Street, York. At about the same time they moved their London shop to the Strand, at the Ship without Temple Bar. Parish accounts suggest that Richard Chandler was the main tenant at this address until 1742, when he was replaced by the bookseller William Sandby, probably elder brother to Edward Sandby, apprenticed to Ward in York in 1744. William Sandby acted as Ward's London agent until Ward's death.

The partnership seemed to prosper in this unusually enterprising arrangement. Ward and Chandler maintained valuable connections with the London trade, regularly buying and selling books and copies (that is, shares) in books at numerous London trade sales in the 1730s and early 1740s. They published a wide range of books, including *Popery Confuted by Papists* (1736), Thomas Cox's *Magna Britannica* (1738), Defoe's *Colonel Jack* (1739), and Cervantes' *Persiles and Sigismunda* (1741). The proximity of their London shops to the inns of court and Chancery Lane probably lay behind the preponderance of law books in their list, including the *Attorney's Compleat Pocket-Book* and the *Law for and Against Bankrupts* (both 1743). The wording of the imprint of one of their books—James Anderson's *New Book of Constitutions of the Antient and Honourable Fraternity of Free and Accepted Masons*, 'printed for Brothers Cæsar Ward and Richard Chandler' (1738)—suggests that both were freemasons. In January 1739 the partners took over the proprietorship of the *York Courant* (established in 1725) from Alexander Staples, as well as his printing house in the former Bagnio, Coney Street.

The downfall of the partnership lay in Richard Chandler's over-investment in the multi-volume *History and Proceedings of the House of Commons from the Restoration to the Present Time* (1742–4). While the venture initially seemed successful—Frederick, prince of Wales, gave the *History* some encouragement—the financial burden evidently became too much for Chandler and he killed himself in 1744. As Thomas Gent describes it, this was

> an action that for awhile seemed to obumbrate the glory of Cæsar, who found such a deficiency in his partner's accounts, so great a want of money, and such a woful sight of flowing creditors, that made him succumb under the obligation to a statute of bankruptcy.   (*Life*, 192)

To make matters worse, Ward was called before the bar of the House of Commons on 5 April 1745, accused of illegally publishing the proceedings of the house in the *York Courant*. The accusations were undeniably true, and Ward was reprimanded by the speaker and fined. Printing parliamentary proceedings was a common offence among the newspaper trade of the day, but the timing of this case was particularly damaging for Ward. His bankruptcy notice appeared in the *London Gazette* in June 1745.

Although Ward had the help of friends, including the York historian Francis Drake, his recovery had much to do with his own determination: he announced in the *York Courant* of 25 June 1745 that he had been obliged to sell his printing house to meet his debts; Richard Bucktrout, a former employee, made a further announcement in the same paper that the newspaper and printing business would continue as usual. That was followed early the next year (27 February 1746) by a London sale where Ward's remaining book stock—bound and in quires—as well as his shares were auctioned to his book-trade colleagues for the benefit of his creditors. Somewhat unusually for one of these events, a selection of Ward's silver plate was also offered. Ward was still concerned to repay the partnership's outstanding debts when he wrote his will in October 1756: he directed that his executor should, within three years of his decease, divide £200 among the remaining creditors.

Although Ward took up business again, his book-trade career had changed. Before the bankruptcy he had bookshops in three locations, he was running a successful newspaper, and most of the books in which his name appeared were ones in which he had a financial share. The London shop was in William Sandby's possession before the bankruptcy and Ward spent most of his time in York. The proprietorship of the *York Courant* now passed out of his hands, at least for some years. He was listed as the paper's printer again in mid-1747, and he continued to print books for others, even though he no longer held many shares. He printed minor verse, such as Thomas Comber's *Ode to Frugality* (1758), and documents for local institutions, but most of his surviving works are sermons. In 1750 he printed Laurence Sterne's *Abuses of Conscience, Set Forth in a Sermon*. (Sterne was to turn to Caesar Ward's widow, Ann, when he needed a printer for *Tristram Shandy* in 1759.) A further typical example was a two-volume collection of sermons preached by another local, Richard Warneford, vicar of St Martin's, Coney Street, which Ward printed for Warneford's subscribers in 1757.

But one printing job led to the major achievement of Ward's career, the secret co-editorship with Francis Drake of the *Parliamentary or Constitutional History of England* in twenty-four volumes (1751–61). As Ward describes the evolution of the *History* to Charles Lyttleton, then dean of Exeter,

> The first 8 Vols. I did little more than soften some Expressions; but the last ten was such a Skeleton of a History, that I can say, with great Truth, I have bestow'd as many Hours, at least, upon it as Mr. D. himself. I do not mean hereby to claim any Share of Honor as an Author—Profit is more suitable to the Circumstance of a Man who has a Wife & 6 Children; and You will please to observe that, *by Agreement*, I am to disburse the whole Charge of Paper & Print &c. And (this paid) we are to divide the Profits.   (Ward to Lyttleton, 13 Jan 1755, BL, Stowe MSS)

These claims to motivation notwithstanding, Ward writes with the pleasure of a gifted historian about the work that took up much of his last ten years, tracking down and borrowing manuscript material from collectors such as Horace Walpole, collating originals with printed sources, and including a profitable 'three Days Confinement in a Garret of Old Pamphlets' (Ward to Lyttleton, 18 Sept 1754, BL, Stowe MSS). Drake readily acknowledged Ward as his 'Fellow-Labourer' (Drake to Lyttleton, 25 Aug 1755, BL, Stowe MSS), whose work on the project continued until its near completion at Ward's death on 24 April 1759 of 'a violent fever which carried him off in a few Days; to which his over-great Attachment to Business did not a little contribute' (Drake to Lyttleton, 28 April 1759, BL, Stowe MSS). He was buried at St Martin's, Coney Street, York, on 27 April 1759. The *History* was successful enough to go into a second edition in 1762, but, by design, neither editor's name ever appeared on the title-page.

When Ann Ward took over the business after her husband's death, she reassured readers of the *York Courant* that the paper would

> be carried on with the same Diligence and Impartiality as before; under the Conduct of the same Person, who, for some Years last past, has had the principal Management of it; Mr. Ward's own Time being mostly taken up in carrying on a large Work of another Nature.   (*York Courant*, 1 May 1759)

Of the seven children who survived their father, the younger Caesar (*b.* 1741) also followed the printing trade in London, but the relationship between father and son seems to have been uneasy. In his will Caesar Ward notes that his son should receive 'Five Pounds and no more he having already by his Extravagance cost me his proportion'. His daughter Mary married George Peacock, who was to carry on the York printing and bookselling business after the death of Ann Ward on 10 April 1789.

C. Y. FERDINAND

Sources R. Davies, *A memoir of the York press: with notices of authors, printers, and stationers, in the sixteenth, seventeenth, and eighteenth centuries* (1868) · *The life of Mr Thomas Gent … written by himself*, ed. J. Hunter (1832) · C. Ward to Dr C. Lyttleton, 1749–58, BL, Stowe MSS 753–754 · will, Borth. Inst. · 'A catalogue of the remaining bound stock … of Mr Caesar Ward, bookseller, which will be sold … February 27, 1745-6', Bodl. Oxf., John Johnson collection · A. H. Cash, *Laurence Sterne: the early and middle years* (1975) · *JHC*, 24 (1741–5), 798, 854 · *ESTC* · D. F. McKenzie, ed., *Stationers' Company apprentices*, [3]: *1701–1800* (1978) · *IGI* · marriage allegations, GL, MS 10091/76

Ward [*other married name* Mason], **Catherine George** (*b.* **1787**), actress and writer, published various literary works, including poetry, novels, and children's fiction over a period of twenty-eight years. George Virtue, publisher of seven of her novels, noted that these had 'all succeeded better than any others I have published' (Virtue to Ward, 1832, Royal Literary Fund archives). None the less very little information is available about her early life. She was born in Scotland, but spent her childhood partly in the Isle of Wight, and she had family connections in Norfolk. She seems to have acted briefly on the stage in Edinburgh, but by the 1810s she had settled in London. Ward's significance is as an author, however, a pursuit entered into after her first marriage. Applying in 1816 to the Royal Literary Fund, she claimed that 'for twelve succeeding years, the labours of my Literary Occupation have wholly supported an Infant Family'.

Ward's first work, a small collection of *Poems* (mainly ballads and lyrics), was published by subscription in Edinburgh in 1805; however, her professional literary career began in earnest five years later with her first novel, *The Daughter of St Omar*. The work combines a typical depiction of the country heroine encountering the fashionable world, together with a full narrative account of her marriage to an unprincipled seducer, terminating in reunion with a supposedly dead lover. During the four decades in which she published, Ward's output included six collections of poetry and twenty-one novels; she also claimed as unpublished two operas and a farce. Containing stock figures of the period and stereotypical plot devices, her fiction is written in verbose, often convoluted sentences, and is characterized by an intrusive authorial presence. Some titles, such as *The Eve of St Agnes* (1831), however, were better than her usual populist standard. Many of Ward's novels published from the mid-1820s were originally serialized, and then republished in collected volumes with new title-pages. From the late 1810s Ward was releasing two or three titles a year, and some of her novels were popular enough to warrant sequels: *The Mysterious Marriage* (1820) was followed two years later by *Family Portraits*; *The Fisher's Daughter* (1824) notes in its title-page that it is 'the sequel to that so greatly admired and popular work', *The Cottage on the Cliff* (1823).

Ward claimed to have received financial support during her literary career from a number of notable contemporaries, including Princess Elizabeth (seventh daughter of George III), Earl Spencer, the countess of Craven, and the duchess of York. In 1817 she published *A Tributary Poem on the Death of the Princess Charlotte of Saxe-Coburg*, commemorating the death, in childbirth, of the prince regent's only legitimate child, Charlotte-Augusta (1796–1817), and she later fictionalized Charlotte's life in *The Rose of Claremont* (1820?). She also enjoyed financial support from the earl of Sussex, and claimed patronage from the duke of Buccleuch in Scotland.

Ward's family life seems hardly less sensational than her novels, involving the tragedies of early death, ill health, and penury. She requested financial aid from the

Royal Literary Fund on five separate occasions from 1816 to 1832, receiving a total of £35 in grants. Most of these applications were made in order to defray the costs of burying her two husbands and an only child. In May 1816 Ward thanked the fund for money aiding her in the funeral expenses of her 'beloved child', as well as enabling her to pay for medical aid she needed at this time. William Molineux, who printed two of her works, informed the fund that Ward's financial difficulties were partly 'occasioned by the indiscretions of her husband, as well as want of employment for a considerable time'. Ward's first husband, suffering from insolvency and tuberculosis, was bedridden for eight months in 1822, and finally died on 12 January 1824. Ward received £5 assistance from the Royal Literary Fund, after stating that she was left 'with the remains of a dear Husband, now lying near me, without the means of providing him a decent burial'. In August 1824 Ward once more appealed (this time, unsuccessfully) to the fund for aid, stating that she had been detained at the king's bench prison for her husband's debts, which amounted to £70. Ward wrote of finding herself 'suddenly accosted for the sum of Ten Pounds which I had not the means of immediately discharging', and of being confined since 18 June 1824.

Despite her imprisonment, Ward managed to publish three novels in 1824, and by 1826–7 had married her second husband, James M. Mason, after which she published as 'Mrs Mason'. By late 1832, Mason himself had succumbed to tuberculosis and bankruptcy: in her last appeal to the Royal Literary Fund, Catherine Mason noted that she was suffering from 'ill health occasion'd by the fearful anxious Watching over the bed of a dying Husband whose failure in business progressively induc'd Consumption'. She added that owing to 'the pressures of the times' her usual publishers could print no further titles of hers, and that as a consequence she had been forced to auction her furniture to meet the demands of creditors and daily living expenses. Her desperate hope in these last appeals was that she might be able to meet the costs of a journey to her 'native mountains' of Scotland. Over a month after receiving a grant of £10 she apologized for her tardiness in thanking the fund, attributing this to 'an inflammation of the chest', which might indicate that she too was suffering from consumption like her family before her.

By the late 1820s Catherine Mason's career was on the wane (between 1828 and 1833 she only published three novels), and her last work, *Alice Gray*, was published in 1833. Writing to her on 8 November 1832, her most frequent publisher, the successful George Virtue, apologetically explained that 'it is the depressive state of Business alone that prevents me from Employing you at present'. Finally defeated by her troubles of 1832, Catherine Mason faded quietly from the literary market place; whether she ultimately reached her native Scotland or died a silent death in London is now a matter for conjecture.

A. A. MANDAL

Sources N. Cross, ed., *Archives of the Royal Literary Fund, 1790–1918* (1982–3), file 344 [microfilm] • Blain, Clements & Grundy, *Feminist comp.* • P. Garside, 'Catherine George Ward', *The Cambridge bibliography of English literature*, ed. J. Shattock, 3rd edn, 4 (1999) • J. R. de J. Jackson, *Romantic poetry by women: a bibliography* (1993)
Likenesses portrait, repro. in C. G. Ward, *The first child, or, The heiress of Monteith* (1824), frontispiece

Ward, Sir (Alfred) Dudley (1905–1991), army officer, was born on 27 January 1905 in Avenue Road, Wimborne, Dorset, the son of Lionel Howell Ward, accountant in poor law, and his wife, Lillie Maud (*née* Morgan). He was educated at Wimborne grammar school, was a chorister in Wimborne Minster, and began his career as an apprentice of the Eastern Telegraph Company in Gibraltar. In 1924 he enlisted in the Bedfordshire and Hertfordshire regiment and, after being selected from the ranks as a potential officer, was sent to the Royal Military College, Sandhurst, from which he was commissioned into the Dorset regiment in 1929. On 29 April 1933 he married Beatrice Constance Griffith (*d.* 1962), daughter of the Revd Thomas Francis Griffith, of The Bourne, Farnham, Surrey. There was one daughter of the marriage, Jill Beatrice (*b.* 1935). Meanwhile Ward served in India and on the north-west frontier before attending the Staff College, Quetta, where he was taught by the future Field Marshal Montgomery. After graduation he transferred to the King's (Liverpool) regiment in 1937, served on the staff in military intelligence, returned to the Staff College as an instructor, served on the staff again, and then was appointed to command 43rd reconnaissance regiment.

In 1943 Ward was promoted to command the 17th infantry brigade, which advanced from Sicily through Italy during 1943–4. The skill he demonstrated in various river crossings and pitched battles on rugged terrain led to command of the 4th (British) division. In the May 1944 offensive at Cassino he displayed outstanding leadership, for the division had the task of crossing the strongly fortified Rapido River, close to the bombed ruins of the monastery. Although at times it seemed that the task might be too difficult Ward's determination and initiative ensured that it was a success. Similar skills and determination were displayed in subsequent battles for Lake Trasimene, Florence, and the penetration of the Gothic and Rimini lines (as the German fortifications across the peninsula were called). At the end of a gruelling campaign, when his division was expecting a lengthy rest and rehabilitation in Egypt, it was switched to Greece, where the communists were rebelling against Papandreou's pro-allied government with a view to installing their own regime. Although initially it seemed that his resources were insufficient for the task, and his own headquarters was attacked by ELAS (the communist National People's Liberation Army), he eventually outfought his opponents and cleared Athens.

After the end of the Second World War Ward was director of military operations at the War Office from 1947 to 1948, and commandant of the Staff College, Camberley, from 1948 to 1951, before becoming commander of 1st corps in Germany—a position he held from 1951 to 1952. In 1953 he returned to England to become deputy chief of the Imperial General Staff, but he was back in Germany as commander, northern army group, and commander-in-chief of the British army of the Rhine from 1957 to 1959. His next appointment was that of commander-in-chief, British forces, Near East, where he set up the sovereign base in Cyprus. From 1962 to 1965 he was governor of Gibraltar, a vital point in NATO strategy, where he had to keep a wary eye on General Franco, who was conducting a campaign to have the Rock returned to Spain, and might have tried a military coup. Ward's combination of tact and firmness were very reassuring to the Gibraltarians. On a personal level, Ward's time in Gibraltar was marked both by tragedy and happiness. On 17 October 1962, shortly after arriving in Gibraltar, his first wife, Beatrice, died. On 28 September 1963 Ward married Joan Elspeth de Pechell Scott (b. 1920/21), head of the Red Cross in Gibraltar, and daughter of Colonel Donald Charles Scott, of the Royal Army Medical Corps. There were no children of this second marriage.

One of Ward's particular skills was assessing risks. During his time as director of military operations, the Soviet Union had been testing allied resolve by interfering with road and rail access to Berlin, activities which culminated in the 1948 blockade. When subsequently commanding NATO forces in Germany, Ward had to decide what, if any, response should be made to provocative gestures by the Russians: he was only too well aware that overreaction might trigger a third world war. Ward was a soldier who thought and planned ahead realistically, and trained his men accordingly. However, he knew when to delegate. He also believed that life should be enjoyed. As a young man he had been an excellent athlete (army champion at 100 and 220 yards); later he took up sailing and golf. He was appointed DSO in 1944, and made CBE and CB in 1945, KBE in 1953, KCB in 1957, and GCB in 1959.

Ward died of bronchopneumonia and cancer of the colon at his home, Wynneys Farmhouse, Dennington, Woodbridge, Suffolk, on 28 December 1991. He was survived by his second wife, and by the daughter of his first marriage. A memorial service was held at the Royal Hospital, Chelsea, on 25 March 1992.   PHILIP WARNER

Sources WWW, 1991–5 · The Times (31 Dec 1991) · The Times (30 Jan 1992) · The Independent (4 Jan 1992) · b. cert. · m. cert. (1963) · d. cert. · Burke, Peerage
Likenesses photograph, 1923, Hult. Arch. · photograph, repro. in The Times (31 Dec 1991); (30 Jan 1992); The Independent
Wealth at death £125,000: probate, 20 March 1992, CGPLA Eng. & Wales

Ward, Sir Edward (1638–1714), lawyer and judge, was born in Northamptonshire, the second son of William Ward of Preston, Rutland. He was educated under Francis Meres at the free school at Uppingham, Leicestershire. Ward then studied at Clifford's Inn and in June 1664 entered the Inner Temple. He was called to the bar on 27 November 1670. On 30 March 1676 he married Elizabeth (1658–1723), daughter of Thomas *Papillon MP, a London merchant. They had four sons and five daughters. Ward soon gained an extensive practice, particularly in the exchequer, where he was the leading pleader on the equity side of the court in 1680.

In July 1683 Ward was counsel for Lord William Russell during his trial for treason. In November 1684 he was counsel for his father-in-law in the action for false imprisonment brought against him by Sir William Pritchard. Also in November 1684 Ward appeared for the earl of Macclesfield in the action of scandalum magnatum brought against John Starkey, a member of the Cheshire grand jury which had presented the peer as disaffected. From these cases it can be discerned that Ward's political sympathies lay with the whigs.

On 20 November 1687 Ward was called to the bench of the Inner Temple. Following the revolution of 1688 Ward was chosen by William III in April 1689 as a judge, but he was allowed to refuse the place probably because of the financial penalties involved in giving up his lucrative practice. In July 1689 Ward was assigned as counsel to Dr Elliott and others accused of dispersing James II's declaration. In April it was rumoured that Ward would be made a serjeant-at-law, but he did not receive a writ. In March 1693 he was sounded out about the possibility of becoming solicitor-general by the new lord keeper, Sir John Somers. In the event, on 30 March Ward kissed the king's hand for the post of attorney-general, his patent being dated 4 April 1693. William III had been influenced by some of his tory ministers to appoint Ward to the higher office, much to the chagrin of the solicitor-general, Sir Thomas Trevor, who was the junto whig candidate for the post. Ward was knighted on 30 October 1693. In November 1694 it was reported that Ward would be made lord chief baron of the exchequer, but that the appointment would be delayed to allow Ward to be made a serjeant-at-law. He was informed by the king of his impending appointment to the bench on 5 May 1695, and he was made a serjeant on the morning of 8 June, his patrons being lords Godolphin and Somers; in the afternoon he was sworn in as lord chief baron. It appears that the king offered him £500 p.a. as compensation for quitting his practice (but this remained unpaid until 1700, when it was raised to £600 p.a. and paid). After sitting as a judge on the home circuit, on 29 July 1695 Ward received a summons as an assistant to the House of Lords. This was a necessary step in view of the fact that he had a commission to sit as speaker of the Lords on the following day, when parliament was prorogued. He acted as speaker at two further prorogations before parliament was dissolved in October 1695. In March 1696 he tried Robert Charnock and his associates for treason. In January 1700 he excused himself from giving an opinion on the bankers' case. Following the dismissal of Somers from the lord chancellorship, in May 1700 Ward was named a commissioner of the great seal. In May 1701 he presided over the trials of Captain Kidd for murder and piracy. Ward was reappointed lord chief baron following the accession of Queen Anne in 1702.

Ward was taken ill just before going on circuit in July 1714, and died on 16 July at his house in Essex Street on the Strand. He was buried at Stoke Doyle, Northamptonshire, which he had purchased in the mid-1690s. He was survived by his wife, four sons, including his heir, Edward, another lawyer, and five daughters, only one of whom had married when Ward's will was drawn up in 1712. As one newsletter writer put it, 'the world will miss him, not only for his great ability in the law, but for his politeness in politics' (*Portland MSS*, 5.472). This was certainly an improvement on the earl of Ailesbury's assessment when Ward was attorney-general that he and the recorder of London were 'the two greatest blockheads of the robe' (Bruce, 1.305). Ward also had the distinction of being the only law officer between 1680 and 1819 never to have sat in the House of Commons. Ward left five case notebooks (1673–97), nine volumes of exchequer cases (1696–1713), and twenty-one volumes of causes (1674–1714), all now in Lincoln's Inn library, London. His eldest son, Edward, rebuilt Stoke Doyle church and erected in it a monument to his father.

SAMUEL PYEATT MENEFEE and STUART HANDLEY

Sources E. Foss, *Biographia juridica: a biographical dictionary of the judges of England … 1066–1870* (1870) · G. Brooks, *Trial of Captain Kidd* (1930) · Sainty, *Judges* · Sainty, *King's counsel* · Baker, *Serjeants* · *Memoirs of Thomas, earl of Ailesbury*, ed. W. E. Buckley, 1, Roxburghe Club, 122 (1890), 305 · *The manuscripts of his grace the duke of Portland*, 10 vols., HMC, 29 (1891–1931), vol. 5, p. 472 · N. Luttrell, *A brief historical relation of state affairs from September 1678 to April 1714*, 6 vols. (1857) · *State trials*, vols. 10, 12, 14 · will, PRO, PROB 11/541/168, fols. 297r–305r · Lincoln's Inn, London, MS 582 · *CSP dom.*, 1689–90, 59, 65 · D. Lemmings, *Gentlemen and barristers: the inns of court and the English bar, 1680–1730* (1990) · D. Lemmings, *Professors of the law: barristers and English legal culture in the 18th century* (2000)
Archives Georgetown University, Law Center, notebooks incl. law reports [transcripts] · Lincoln's Inn Library, legal papers, notebooks, and reports, MSS 582, 510–540, 555–559 · PRO, private papers, E192
Likenesses R. White, line engraving, 1702 (after G. Kneller), NPG · J. M. Rysbrack, marble tomb effigy, c.1720, St Rumbold's Church, Stoke Doyle, Northamptonshire · G. Kneller, portrait

Ward, Edward [Ned] (**1667–1731**), satirist, was born of unknown parentage, probably in the English midlands. According to Shiels, he was 'of low extraction and irregular education' (Cibber, 4.293), but Ward himself spoke of his ancestors in Leicestershire as men of property (dedicatory epistle, *Nuptial Dialogues and Debates*), and his writings display some knowledge of Latin and French. In 1706 he expressed his 'indissoluble Obligations' to some unspecified noble family 'for the best and greatest share' of his youthful education (dedicatory epistle, *Writings*).

Ward was in London by 1691, the date of his first traced publication, *The Poet's Ramble after Riches*, in which he laments his poverty in Hudibrastic verse. It is likely that he wrote a good deal more in the next seven years, but the only identifiable works of his are the prose satires *Female Policy Detected, or, The Arts of a Designing Woman Laid Open* (1695) and *A Trip to Jamaica* (1698). The latter tells how Ward sailed for Jamaica in January 1697 to seek his fortune, but returned disappointed to London before the end of the year: it may well be based on first-hand experience, unlike its sequel, *A Trip to New-England* (1699). He now adapted the 'trip' format to a satirical portrait of London. *The London Spy* (its title doubtless modelled on the French work translated as *The Turkish Spy*, 1687–94) was published in eighteen monthly parts, beginning in November 1698. In lively prose, with occasional songs and verses, it graphically

Whilst Butler in Immortal Glory sits Enthrond, as King of Poets and of Wits; Ward seeks not to usurp his Endless Fame, But Courts his Genius to revive his Name

Edward [Ned] **Ward (1667–1731)**, by Michael Vandergucht, pubd 1710

described the seamy side of London life, with racy anecdotes and character sketches, and established Ward's name and style. It was followed by over 100 identifiable satires in prose and verse, many of them reissued singly, sometimes in revised form, as well as appearing in at least a dozen partial collections of Ward's writings between 1700 and 1718. *The London Spy* itself was reprinted complete five times in Ward's lifetime.

Ward's typical targets included cheating vintners and ale house keepers in *Sot's Paradise* (1698), astrologers in *The World Bewitched* (1699), and dissenting ministers, apothecaries, physicians, lawyers, parish poor officers, pirate booksellers, and cheating vintners again in *A Journey to Hell* (3 parts, 1700–05). In 1699 and 1700 he extended the 'trip' formula to Islington, Sadler's Wells, Bath, and 'Stir-Bitch' (Stourbridge) fair near Cambridge. He expanded some satires into periodicals, such as *The Weekly Comedy, as it is Dayly Acted at most Coffee-Houses in London* (10 numbers, May to July 1699), rehashed as *The Humours of a Coffee-House* (7 numbers, June to August 1707), after which Ward relinquished it to William Oldisworth, perhaps because, from July 1707, Ward was simultaneously producing two other short-lived satirical periodicals: *The Diverting Muse* (6 numbers) and *The London Terraefilius* (6 numbers). In *Honesty in Distress but Relieved by No Party* (1705) he tried his hand at a droll of the type presented at Bartholomew fair, but there is no record of its being performed. (All the other dramas attributed to Ward in *Biographia dramatica* are either not dramas or probably not by Ward.)

Ward developed seventeenth-century 'character writing' in prose and verse by placing character in locale and bringing it to life through dialogue. Each of his fifty-four *Nuptial Dialogues and Debates* (1710), for instance, dramatizes a conflict between some prickly pair, such as 'a nice affected gentleman and his careless slatternly wife', and concludes with 'moral reflexions' of a paternalist kind. Other characters are humorously displayed in their professional or social groupings: for instance the two armed services in *The Wooden World Dissected* (1706) and *Mars Stript of his Armour* (1708), or the thirty-two societies in *The Secret History of Clubs* (1709). Most clubs satirized in this collection were fictitious, but one exception was the Kit-Cat, the resort of whig statesmen and men of letters. Ward probably also had a hand in *The Secret History of the Calves-Head Club, or, The Republicans Unmask'd*, first issued in January 1703 and reissued, with revisions and additions, annually for ten years. The club, whether real or legendary, was alleged to be a profane whig society which met on 30 January to honour regicides and deride Charles I.

Ward was a high-church tory who involved himself in political controversy from at least as early as 1698 with *Ecclesia et factio*, the first of his several attacks on low-church moderation and occasional conformity. That attack was broadened in *The Dissenting Hypocrite* (1704) to include dissenters in general and the leading whig journalists Tutchin and Defoe. Both those works were in Hudibrastic verse, as was Ward's best-known political publication, *Hudibras Redivivus*, issued in twenty-four monthly parts between August 1705 and June 1707. This open-ended burlesque at first drew topical material, month by month, from the political struggle, but became less controversial after Ward was taken into custody in February and again in June 1706, charged with seditious libel. He had accused the queen of being faint-hearted in failing to support the tories in parliament (*Hudibras Redivivus*, pt 5); he pleaded guilty, and on 14 November 1706, was fined 40 marks (£26 13s. 4d.) and condemned to stand twice for one hour in the pillory. He was not silenced, for, in the closing numbers of *Hudibras Redivivus*, he hit on a safe, indirect vehicle of political satire by versifying passages from Clarendon's *History of the Grand Rebellion*. He returned to outspoken politics with *Vulgus Britannicus, or, The British Hudibras* (5 parts, 1710), which described in verse the riots accompanying the Sacheverell trial. Soon afterwards the newly triumphant tories passed their act to outlaw occasional conformity and Ward's outpouring of political satire slackened a little. He now completed versifications of *Don Quixote* (2 vols., 1711–12) and Clarendon's *History* (3 vols., 1713–15). Each work ran to 900 pages; the Clarendon also had eighty-five plates and cost £500 to print: Ward lost money by it.

From 1702 or earlier Ward had lived in Gray's Inn, but in the autumn of 1712 he made a career move and opened an ale house near Clerkenwell Green. He had published over 100 separate works in fourteen years and achieved popular success but was perhaps aware that writing provided only precarious subsistence. In *The Hudibrastick Brewer* (1714), a mild satire against himself, he wrote that it is better 'To *live* by *Malt*, than *starve* by *Meter*'. Between 1714 and 1717 he fired a few parting shots against the whigs in satires on Marlborough, Wharton, and bishops Burnet and Hoadly, but under George I his pen was far less active than under Anne. From about 1717 to about 1730 Ward kept the Bacchus tavern in Moorfields, where 'with his Wit, Humour, and good Liquor [he] has afforded his Guests a pleasurable Entertainment; especially the High-Church Party, which is compos'd of Men of his Principles, and to whom he is very much oblig'd for their constant Resort' (Jacob, 2.295). His scattering of new Hudibrastic poems in this period included *The Delights of the Bottle* (1720), describing the amenities and customers of his tavern, *The Merry Travellers* (1721), about a trip from Moorfields to Bromley, and *The Parish Guttlers* (1722), a biting satire on his local parish vestry. Reprints of his most popular earlier works sold well not only at home but in America: so much so that Cotton Mather in 1726 warned his readers against 'such Pestilences, and indeed all those worse than Egyptian Toads (the Spawns of a Butler, and a Brown, and a Ward …)' (Troyer, 227–8).

Moorfields was geographically only a step away from Grub Street and Ward was a popular author whose subjects and readership were vulgar, so he was a natural target for Pope, though it seems that his only personal offence was to print Pope's epigram about the lady who pissed at a performance of Addison's *Cato* in his periodical the *Poetical Entertainer* in February 1714, when Pope was trying to interest Addison in his Homer translation. Whatever the cause, Pope attacked Ward twice in 1728. In *Peri Bathous* Ward is one of the frogs who 'live generally in the bottom of a ditch, and make a great noise whenever they thrust their heads above water' (Pope, *Prose Works*, 2.197), and there are two more contemptuous references to him in *The Dunciad*, one of which (l. 200) is a sneer at Ward's popularity in America. In the following year Ward responded with a weak verse satire *Durgen* (that is, 'dwarf'); Pope responded in the apparatus to *The Dunciad Variorum*, where, among other charges, he repeatedly called Ward an ale house keeper; and Ward replied in his scurrilous *Apollo's Maggot in his Cups*, in verse with a prose postscript refuting Pope's falsehoods. Stung by the ale house taunt, Ward insisted that he sold no malt liquor at the Bacchus, which was a tavern, not a public house, and that Pope himself had drunk wine there. Ward was evidently more sensitive about his social than his literary rank.

At some time between August 1729 and October 1730 Ward gave up the Bacchus tavern and established himself in the British Coffee House in Fullwood's Rents near Gray's Inn. He died there on 20 June 1731 and was buried on 27 June in St Pancras churchyard, Middlesex, with one mourning coach for his wife and daughter, as he had directed in his poetical will, dated 24 June 1725 and printed in *Appleby's Journal* on 28 September 1731. The names of his wife and children and the date of his marriage have not been traced. Ward's writings remained popular to the end of his life but sank without trace soon afterwards, except for *The London Spy*, which was serialized in several London and provincial newspapers in the 1730s. Later it was quarried by historians from Macaulay to the present day, even though Macaulay ungratefully called it 'nauseous balderdash' (Macaulay, 1.340n).   JAMES SAMBROOK

Sources H. W. Troyer, *Ned Ward of Grubstreet: a study of sub-literary London in the eighteenth century* (1946) · [G. Jacob], *The poetical register, or, The lives and characters of all the English poets*, 2 (1723), 295 · D. E. Baker, *Biographia dramatica, or, A companion to the playhouse*, rev. I. Reed, new edn, rev. S. Jones, 1 (1812), 736–7 · E. Ward, dedicatory epistle, *Nuptial dialogues and debates* (1710) · E. Ward, dedicatory epistle, *Writings*, 3 (1706) · E. Ward, preface, *Miscellanies*, 5 (1717) · E. Ward, *To the right honourable Sir Humphrey Parsons* (1730) · *Appleby's Journal* (28 Sept 1731) · E. Ward, *Apollo's maggot in his cups* (1729), 30–45 · *The prose works of Alexander Pope*, ed. R. Cowler, 2 (1986), 197 · A. Pope, *The Dunciad*, ed. J. Sutherland (1943), vol. 5 of *The Twickenham edition of the poems of Alexander Pope*, ed. J. Butt (1939–61); 3rd edn [in 1 vol.] (1963); repr. (1965) · R. Shiels, *The lives of the poets of Great Britain and Ireland*, ed. T. Cibber, 4 (1753), 293–4 · *The life and errors of John Dunton*, [rev. edn], ed. J. B. Nichols, 2 vols. (1818) · N. Luttrell, *A brief historical relation of state affairs from September 1678 to April 1714*, 6 vols. (1857) · R. M. Wiles, *Serial publication in England before 1750* (1957) · *Remarks and collections of Thomas Hearne*, ed. C. E. Doble and others, 1, OHS, 2 (1885), 179–80, 308 · D. F. Foxon, ed., *English verse, 1701–1750: a catalogue of separately printed poems with notes on contemporary collected editions*, 2 vols. (1975) · *GM*, 1st ser., 1 (1731), 266 · T. B. Macaulay, *The history of England from the accession of James II*, new edn, ed. C. H. Firth, 6 vols. (1913–15)

Archives NMM, workbook

Likenesses mezzotint, 1714 · W. Sherwin, line engraving, 1715, BM; repro. in E. Ward, *Hudibras redivivus*, 4th edn (1722) · T. Johnson, mezzotint, *c*.1721, BM · Sympson, engraving · M. Vandergucht, line engraving, BM, NPG; repro. in Ward, *Nuptial dialogues* [see illus.]

Wealth at death see verse will, repr. in *Appleby's Journal*

Ward, Edward Matthew (1816–1879), historical genre painter, was born on 14 July 1816 in Belgrave Place, Pimlico, London, the younger son of Charles James Ward (1781–1858), an employee of Coutts's Bank in London, and his wife, Mary Ford, sister-in-law of the novelist Horace Smith. Ward won a silver medal from the Society of Arts in 1830 for a drawing, and he studied painting for a year in the studio of John Cawse in Henrietta Street, Covent Garden. On the advice of Francis Chantrey and with the sponsorship of David Wilkie, he entered the Royal Academy Schools in 1834. He had already exhibited that year at the Royal Academy a portrait of O. Smith in the role of Don Quixote. His painting *The Dead Ass*, from Laurence Sterne's *Sentimental Journey*, was accepted but not hung at the Royal Academy in 1835, and he left London in July 1836 to study in Rome. After visiting Paris and Venice, he stayed in Rome two and a half years, studying with Filippo Agricola at the Accademia di San Luca, and in 1838 won a silver medal for historical composition from the academy.

Ward returned to London in 1839 after learning fresco

Edward Matthew Ward (1816–1879), by George Richmond, 1859

technique in Munich from Peter von Cornelius, a prominent Nazarene painter in Germany and Rome. That year he exhibited at the Royal Academy *Cimabue and Giotto*, which had been painted in Rome. In the 1840s he became a renowned painter of English and French history and the lives of writers. He exhibited in London every year from 1839 to 1877 and showed works at the Paris Universal Exhibition in 1855 and the Manchester Art Treasures Exhibition in 1857. He was elected an ARA in 1846 and an RA in 1855. *Napoleon in the Prison of Nice*, exhibited at the British Institution in 1841 and bought by the duke of Wellington, is one of many scenes of prisons, trials, arrests, and executions produced throughout his career. His first such picture was *Reminiscences of a Scene in the Prisoner's Lock of the Tribunal of Naples in 1838* (exh. RA, 1840). He also exhibited *Cornet Joyce Seizes the King at Holmby, 1647* (exh. 1841) and *The Disgrace of Lord Clarendon* (exh. 1846) at the Royal Academy, and established himself as a painter of seventeenth-century political history.

Ward also succeeded with eighteenth-century subjects such as *Dr Johnson Perusing the Manuscript of 'The Vicar of Wakefield'* (exh. RA, 1843) and *Dr Johnson in Lord Chesterfield's Ante-Room in 1748* (exh. RA, 1845; Tate collection). These two paintings depict drawbacks of private patronage and the difficulty of making a living in the arts, themes which also appear in *The Early Life of Oliver Goldsmith* (exh. RA, 1844) and *Daniel Defoe with the Manuscript of 'Robinson Crusoe'* (exh. RA, 1849). Such issues were widely discussed in the 1840s, especially in regard to painters, when the British government began to commission artists to decorate the new houses of parliament with frescos. Ward entered the first parliament fresco competition in 1843, but his cartoon of Boudicca did not win any prize. In 1851, nevertheless, he was commissioned to execute eight pictures in the corridor of the House of Commons: *The Execution of Montrose*, *The Last Sleep of Argyll*, *Alice Lisle Concealing Fugitives*, *Monk Declaring for a Free Parliament*, *The Escape of Charles II with Jane Lane*, *The Landing of Charles II*, *The Acquittal of the Seven Bishops*, and *William and Mary Receiving the Lords and Commons*. He visited Scotland in 1853 to gather material for *Montrose*, and completed and exhibited it at the Royal Academy that year; this and *Argyll*, which was completed and exhibited in 1854, were painted in oil. The lighting of the corridor made the canvases virtually impossible to see, and he was commissioned to repaint these first two subjects and execute the remaining subjects in fresco on framed sheets of slate, a task which was completed in the later 1860s. Ward painted oil replicas of the parliament frescoes and exhibited them individually at the Royal Academy over many years until 1875. The frescoes, like his oils, present a sweetened seventeenth-century style based on the popular art of David Wilkie; his smaller oils sometimes exhibit bolder brushwork and brighter colours. Despite his links to Cornelius, he did not embrace the medievalizing style of the German Nazarenes, who influenced other of the parliament artists; he remained a conservative figure, in contrast to the Pre-Raphaelite Brotherhood at mid-century.

On 4 May 1848 Ward married Henrietta Mary Ada *Ward (1832–1924), daughter of George Raphael *Ward [see under Ward, James (1769–1859)] and Mary Webb Ward. She was the granddaughter of the artist James Ward and became herself a noted painter, producing—within a narrower range—many works similar to those of her husband. She and Ward had eight children: Alice, Leslie, Eva, Flora, Wriothesley, Beatrice, Enid, and Stanhope. By 1852 the family had settled at 11 Upton Park Villas, Slough, and then at 3 Queens Villas, Windsor. For several years Ward also retained a studio in London at 1 Kent Villas, Lansdowne Road, Notting Hill.

Ward's successes in the 1850s included *James II Receiving News of the Landing of the Prince of Orange* (exh. RA, 1850; Tate collection) and *The Royal Family of France in the Prison of the Temple* (exh. RA, 1851; Harris Museum and Art Gallery, Preston). Queen Victoria commissioned him to paint *Napoleon III Receiving the Order of the Garter* and *The Visit of Queen Victoria to the Tomb of Napoleon* (both exh. RA, 1858; Royal Collection). He also produced literary paintings: *Byron's Early Love: a Dream of Annesley Hall* (exh. RA, 1856; Manchester City Galleries) and *John Gilpin Delayed by his Customers* (exh. RA, 1851).

Ward's style and subjects remained largely unchanged in the 1860s and 1870s. He painted *The Death of Charles II* (exh. RA, 1861), *Hogarth in his Studio* (exh. RA, 1863; York City Art Gallery), *Amy Robsart and Leicester* (exh. RA, 1866), *The Eve of St Bartholomew* (exh. RA, 1873), and *William III at Windsor* (exh. RA, 1877), and numerous canvases memorializing Marie Antoinette and other figures of the *ancien*

régime. About 1875, however, he visited Brittany and Normandy and enlarged his range by painting French street scenes and a modern historical genre painting, *A Year after the Battle: the Memento Scene at Dinan* (exh. RA, 1876; Forbes Magazine collection, New York).

Ward was a large man, with black hair, reportedly rough in manner and appearance. On 10 January 1879 he was found raving on the floor of his dressing-room, his throat cut with a razor; he was shouting, 'I was mad when I did it; the devil prompted me' (*The Times*, 18 Jan 1879, 11). Medical help arrived, but he died on 15 January at his home, 3 Queens Villas, in Windsor. The inquest in Windsor on 17 January found that he committed suicide while temporarily insane. Ward was buried at Upton Old Church on 21 January and the contents of his studio were sold at Christies, London, on 29 March. Of his children, Leslie *Ward (1851–1922) was Spy, the caricaturist for *Vanity Fair*, and Eva and Flora were miniature painters.

KENNETH BENDINER

Sources 'British artists, their style and character: no. II, Edward Matthew Ward', *Art Journal*, 17 (1855), 45–8 • H. W. Sweny, 'Our living artists: Edward Matthew Ward', *Magazine of Art*, 1 (1877–8), 14–19 • *Art Journal*, 41 (1879), 72 • *The Times* (18 Jan 1879) • D. Robertson, *Sir Charles Eastlake and the Victorian art world* (1978), 199–200, 333–4 • K. Bendiner, *An introduction to Victorian painting* (1985), 27–45 • Graves, *RA exhibitors*, 8 (1906), 127–36 • H. M. A. Ward, *Memories of ninety years*, ed. I. G. McAllister [1924] • P. G. Nunn, *Victorian women artists* (1987), 132–47 • R. Treble, ed., *Great Victorian pictures: their paths to fame* (1978), 84 [exhibition catalogue, Leeds, Leicester, Bristol, and London, 28 Jan – Sept 1978] • *DNB* • P. G. Nunn, *Problem pictures: women and men in Victorian painting* (1995) • d. cert. • *CGPLA Eng. & Wales* (1879)

Likenesses J. Smyth, line engraving, 1847 (after T. Brigstocke), BM, NPG; repro. in *Art Union Journal* (1847) • G. Richmond, chalk drawing, 1859, NPG [see illus.] • G. Richmond, portrait, exh. RA 1861 • C. W. Cope, drawing, c.1862, NPG • Elliott & Fry, carte-de-visite, NPG • W. Hall, engraving (after G. Richmond), repro. in *Art Journal* (1879), 84 • Lock & Whitfield, photograph, woodburytype, NPG; repro. in T. Cooper, *Men of mark: a gallery of contemporary portraits* (1878) • Maull & Polyblank, carte-de-visite, NPG • D. J. Pound, stipple and line engraving (after photograph by Mayall), BM, NPG; repro. in *Illustrated News of the World* • Spy [L. Ward], caricature, watercolour study, NPG; repro. in *VF* (20 Dec 1873) • J. Watkins and C. Watkins, carte-de-visite, NPG • Window & Bridge, carte-de-visite, NPG • woodcuts, BM

Wealth at death under £3000: probate, 20 March 1879, *CGPLA Eng. & Wales*

Ward, Sir Edward Willis Duncan, first baronet (1853–1928), army officer, was born on 17 December 1853 at Oban, the only son of Captain John Ward RN (d. 1868), of Oban, and his wife, Mary Hope (d. 1890), daughter of John Bowie. Educated at a private school, he entered in 1874 the commissariat branch of the control department, an organization of military officials outside the army. He married on 5 February 1880 Florence Caroline (d. 1934), daughter of Henry Minchin Simons, merchant, of 72 Courtfield Gardens, London, and Singapore, and had two sons, the elder of whom, Edward Simons (1882–1930), succeeded him as second baronet.

Ward was promoted assistant commissary-general for active service in the Sudan (1885), and when the Army Service Corps was established (1888) as part of the army he was commissioned in it as major and promoted lieutenant-colonel in 1890. Having been noticed by Wolseley in the Sudan in 1885, and in Ireland, where he served from 1888 to 1892, Ward held staff appointments in Dublin (1892–5), on the Asante expedition (1895–6, when he was made CB), and as deputy assistant adjutant-general home district staff in London (1895–9), where, given official charge, as secretary, of the originally unofficial military tournament at Islington (which later became the Royal Tournament), his energy and business ability prepared its later success at Olympia and promoted its substantial contributions to service charities. He published *Handbook of Army Service Corps Duties in Peace and War* (1897).

In 1899, war in South Africa appearing imminent, Ward was among the officers sent out in advance and, as chief supply officer (assistant adjutant-general) in Natal, collected large stocks at Ladysmith, which was besieged on 2 November. Commandeering all traders' supplies, he took responsibility for feeding troops and inhabitants until relief came on 28 February 1900. He had only two and a half months' rations, eked out with horseflesh; but they were administered so ably that Sir George White praised Ward as the best commissariat officer since Moses. After the relief Ward was director of supplies to Roberts, and returned to England with him late in 1900, being promoted full colonel and created KCB. He was assistant quartermaster-general headquarters from February to April 1901.

In April 1901 the secretary of state for war, W. St J. Brodrick, wanting to deal directly with the military heads of departments without a civilian interposed as permanent under-secretary of state, tried to turn the position by giving that post to Ward, who held it from 1901 to 1914. But to the military heads Ward's commissariat record, however successful, made him more official than soldier; however, to H. O. Arnold-Forster, who succeeded Brodrick in 1903, he was more soldier than official, lacking the civil servant's special knowledge and experience. In 1904 the War Office reconstitution committee under Viscount Esher established direct contact between the secretary of state and soldiers as colleagues on the army council, while the permanent under-secretary, no longer interposed, was reduced to the position of secretary of the army council, retaining the (civil) headship of the department. Loyal in disappointment, Ward tried to make the new machinery work smoothly.

Ill-yoked with R. B. Haldane, Ward contributed to the latter's reforms as chairman of the committee on the Officers' Training Corps. With his drive, knowledge of men, and tact, he was at his best chairing a committee with a definite task; other instances of such success were the substitution of former military clerks for civilians in the military departments of the War Office, the Brodrick reorganization of the army medical department, and the compilation of the original war book detailing War Office action on mobilization. By organizing the War Office Sports Club, comprising officers, other ranks, and civilians, he gave the office personnel more camaraderie.

Devoted to the welfare of soldiers past and present, Ward involved himself in schemes for civil employment of discharged men and reservists, and took the lead in founding the Union Jack Club for soldiers and sailors passing through London, of which, after presiding over the originating committee (1902), he was president for twenty-two years.

Ward was created KCVO in 1907 and a baronet on retiring from the civil service in January 1914, when he became chairman and director of substantial companies. In the war he was again immersed in public duties, notably as: organizer and commandant-in-chief of the Metropolitan special constabulary, Lord Kitchener's deputy in superintending the personal welfare of all overseas troops, organizer of the war camps library, and director-general of the voluntary organizations of helpers in war hospitals and munition workers' canteens. He was also chairman of the Royal Society for the Prevention of Cruelty to Animals. He was created GBE in 1919.

Strong but genial, imperturbable, and somewhat taciturn, Ward's forte was in execution rather than in counsel. He died on 11 September 1928 in Paris, of ptomaine poisoning, and was buried at Brompton cemetery.

C. HARRIS, *rev.* JAMES LUNT

Sources O. Wheeler, *The war office past and present* (1914) • E. M. Spiers, *Haldane: an army reformer* (1980) • L. S. Amery, *The problem of an army* (1903) • L. S. Amery, ed., *The Times history of the war in South Africa*, 7 vols. (1900–09) • Burke, *Peerage* • *WWW* • private information (1937) • personal knowledge (1937) • PRO, War office records

Likenesses W. Stoneman, photograph, 1918, NPG • Spy [L. Ward], chromolithograph caricature, cartoon, NPG; repro. in *VF* (30 May 1901) • photograph, Gov. Art Coll.

Wealth at death £12,281 19s. 3d.: probate, 21 Dec 1928, *CGPLA Eng. & Wales*

Ward [*née* Lord], **Emily Mary Jane** (1850–1930), headmistress and founder of the Norland Institute for nursery-nursing, was born at Parkfield, St Alkmund, Derby, on 13 August 1850, the daughter of James Lord, barrister, and his wife, Elizabeth Mary, formerly Coy. Early in her life her parents moved to south London, first to Lavender Hill, Battersea, and later to Falcon Road, Clapham Junction. Her early education was provided by a governess and she was later educated at a boarding-school in central London. Little is known of her childhood, but in her early twenties she became an infant teacher at Notting Hill high school and was attracted to the progressive theories of Friedrich Froebel. She based most of her teaching and later work on the philosophy of this eminent German educationist.

Lord's ambition was to open her own school, and this was achieved in 1876 when she established Norland Place School, specifically to educate children aged three to eight years. In 1874 Lord was enrolled as a member of the Froebel Society of Great Britain. In 1879, after spending the summer in Geneva under Madame du Portugal, one of Froebel's most prominent disciples, she implemented his teaching within her own classrooms. The morning was dedicated to formal class lessons and the afternoons were spent in creative work, exercise, and nature study. Lord was described by Madame Michael and Mr Kestley Moore as a 'bright young form-mistress who took a profound interest in the new teachings of Froebel'. Norland Place School was awarded a first-class commendation from the Froebel Society in 1879. By 1882 Lord was a lecturer of the Froebel Society itself.

Lord's marriage to Walter Cyril Ward (1843–1924), a retired tea merchant, on 17 October 1891 surprised many of her friends and colleagues. It was a match bound more by mutual respect than passion. There were no children of the marriage but they adopted three from the Plumer family: one died in 1900, Claude went into the Royal Navy from Osborne College, and Adelaide was married from the Norland Institute in 1919.

The fitness of nursemaids to rear the children in well-to-do families had been questioned by Ward since before her marriage; she considered that it would be more appropriate for such children to be nurtured and tutored from birth by an educated woman versed in principles such as those she herself had adopted. She strongly disagreed with the Victorian sentiment that children were miniature defective adults who should be seen and not heard, and felt they should be brought up by those who understood what it felt like to be a child and who knew that children thrive on love and harmony. It was her ambition to set up a suitable training course for gentlewomen as children's nurses. The idea of such an institute was ridiculed by many of her colleagues and friends. Who would wish to train for such a menial task and who would want to employ an educated gentlewoman to care for their children? However, when she moved out of her suite at the Norland Place School after her marriage the vacated rooms provided convenient accommodation for a fledgeling Norland Institute. In association with her protégée Isabel Sharman the Norland Institute opened its doors for the first time on 25 September 1892 with five students. Six more arrived in the new year—some of them older than Mrs Ward—and by the summer of 1893 it was clear that Norland would need new premises. It moved to Holland Park Terrace (later Holland Park Avenue), then, in 1900, to Pembridge Square. From its inception Norland never recognized the need to hurt children either physically or emotionally, and Norland nurses were forbidden to use any such form of punishment in the care and discipline of young children. Ward was an affectionate, motherly principal: she would kiss her students goodnight and trim all their uniform bonnets by hand. She was a committed Christian and it was she who adopted the college motto from 1 Corinthians 13: 11, 'Love never faileth'.

In 1919 the Wards moved to Bognor, but Emily retained her contact with Norland—she had built a Norland holiday home called Fieldhouse in the town, and it seldom lacked bookings from both Norlanders in private employment and Norland nurseries. In 1924 Ward erected a beautiful stained-glass window in memory of her late husband in the town's St John's Church; the church was demolished in 1971. The window was re-erected in the restored chapel of the Norland College in Denford House, Berkshire, and was rededicated with the chapel in 1996.

Under Ward's leadership the Norland Institute grew and flourished. It became the model on which all future nursery-nurse training was based. Ward died peacefully at her home, Sudley Lodge, Upper Bognor Road, Bognor Regis, Sussex, on 15 June 1930, after a series of several strokes. Her funeral was held at St John's Church, Bognor Regis, on 18 June, and her remains were cremated at Woking crematorium. A Norland nurse said of her: 'She has always been so marvellously abreast with the times and wonderful in the way she always saw the difficulties of youth from youth's point of view, which is a great gift accorded only to a few.'   LOUISE E. DAVIS

Sources Emily M. J. Ward, 13th Aug 1850 – 15th June 1930 (privately printed) · Norland Quarterly, Christmas (1930) · private notebook of Mrs Emily Ward, Norland College Archives, Hungerford · P. Stokes, Norland, 1892–1992: the story of the first one hundred years (1992) · b. cert. · m. cert. · d. cert. · CGPLA Eng. & Wales (1930) **Archives** Norland College, Hungerford, Berkshire, archives **Wealth at death** £46,047 5s. 3d.: resworn probate, 25 July 1930, CGPLA Eng. & Wales

Ward, Francis [Frank] **Kingdon-** (1885–1958), plant collector and explorer, was born in Manchester on 6 November 1885, younger surviving child and only son of Harry Marshall *Ward (1854–1906), lecturer in botany, and Selina Mary (d. 1922), daughter of Francis Kingdon of Exeter. Winifred Mary Kingdon-*Ward was his elder sister. Strictly brought up under a father who disapproved of ordinary childhood indulgences, Frank (as he always preferred to be called) was sent, in 1889, to a convent school in France, where he stayed for a year. In 1894, aged nine, he went to Colet Court, the preparatory school for St Paul's, Hammersmith, from which, in turn, he went up to Christ's College, Cambridge, on a science exhibition in 1904. After taking part one of the natural sciences tripos, the brilliant academic career predicted for him was abruptly put paid to by the early death of his father, which left the family impoverished and forced him to leave university after only two years.

Through the professor of Chinese at Cambridge, Kingdon-Ward was put on to a teaching vacancy at the replica of an English public school in Shanghai. But school-mastering quickly palled, and in 1909 he jumped at an invitation, through another family friend, to join an American zoological expedition sponsored by the duke of Bedford. Granted leave of absence, he went with this up the Yangtze (Yangzi) River to the borders of Tibet, found three small vertebrates new to science and returned with a passion for exploring the interior of Asia which was thenceforth to govern his life.

Almost at once a further family contact enabled Kingdon-Ward to start realizing this ambition by becoming a professional plant collector. Arthur Bulley, a wealthy Liverpool cotton broker who had founded Bees of Chester, a leading firm of nurserymen, had just lost George Forrest to a rival patron and was looking for a replacement exclusive to himself. Kingdon-Ward immediately accepted the commission and, breaking his contract with the school, set off in January 1911 on a year-long return to the mountains of south-west China. The expedition yielded a haul of horticultural novelties rich enough to launch him on the precarious career of plant collector. A second commission

Francis Kingdon-Ward (1885–1958), by E. M. Gregson, 1952

from Bulley saw him back in the eastern Himalayas in 1913–14, but this time he fell foul of the Chinese authorities and was forced to move further west. This proved providential. The peoples of Burma, Assam, and Tibet were much more to his liking and the region, being more difficult of access, was even less well known and its flora more splendid still. Thereafter he was content to leave Yunnan to the jealously territorial George Forrest.

The First World War came as an unwelcome interruption to Kingdon-Ward's botanizing. Service as a junior officer in the Indian army proved frustratingly inactive and, despite being posted to Mesopotamia, he never saw combat. After the war, sponsors fortunately continued to materialize and his fifth expedition, in 1924–5, was probably his most successful of all. Besides penetrating to the hitherto mysterious gorges and waterfalls of the Tsangpo River (the upper section of the Brahmaputra), he collected ninety-seven different rhododendrons as well as the first viable seed of the elusive and spectacular blue poppy, *Meconopsis betonicifolia*, which became one of the most prized of garden plants after it had flowered back in England.

As a botanist, Kingdon-Ward had an excellent working knowledge of several plant groups and in the intervals between expeditions he identified his specimens and, alone or in collaboration with specialists, described a number of new species especially of rhododendron and primula. His fully documented material, in the national herbaria of Britain and also in institutions overseas, reveals a keen observation of botanical detail and grasp of plant ecology. His published contributions to the study of plant geography were also noteworthy. Observations

made over many years in the region convinced him that the rain screen formed by the main Himalayan range was traceable into north-west Yunnan, acting as a barrier for northward or southward plant dispersal but allowing lateral spreading to the west or east. This provided a plausible explanation for the striking similarities between the flora and fauna of the Himalayas and those of south-west China.

Perhaps more deeply, though, Kingdon-Ward was a plantsman, a horticultural connoisseur. The keen aesthetic sense which made him a vivid describer of scenery and an excellent photographer also gave him a sure eye for flowers of garden potential. Plants hardy enough to grow out of doors in Britain tended to occur in temperate forest and mountain meadows, and financial necessity largely limited him to those zones and to the more conspicuous elements in their vegetation, constricting him botanically.

But it was as an explorer first and foremost that Kingdon-Ward preferred to see himself: the founder's medal (1930) and honorary fellowship bestowed on him by the Royal Geographical Society meant more to him than their equivalents from its horticultural counterpart—the Victoria medal of honour (1932) and the Veitch memorial medal (1936). Working in country still undermapped, he was fortunate to possess qualities that fitted him outstandingly for this role: ability to blend into the local way of life, sinewy toughness, a superb visual memory, imperturbability, and enduring patience. Offsetting these were a fear of heights and an over-ascetic approach to provisioning. Despite the risks associated with working in largely uncharted country over the years, he also had to contend with arthritis, bouts of deep depression, porters who were surly or drunk or absconded, the loss of his spectacles, impalement on a bamboo spike (in 1937), and (in 1950) one of the worst earthquakes on record. Although much of the time the local political situation was unsettled, he travelled for preference alone, dispensing even with collecting assistants. Solitary and withdrawn by nature, he made an uncomfortable companion in any case, liable to push himself to his physical limits and to lapse into day-long silences. Of the few who ever accompanied him (some tolerated for the funds they could provide) only two proved wholly amenable—and one of those was his second wife.

On 11 April 1923 Kingdon-Ward married Florinda Norman-Thompson, from an Irish landed family. They had very different interests and she opted out of his expeditions. As a result, the fourteen years that the marriage lasted saw them together for scarcely four; they divorced in 1937. The couple had two daughters and Kingdon-Ward remembered his wife in *Primula florindae*, a giant cowslip he came across in Tibet in 1924, considered by many the best of his numerous gifts to horticulture. By contrast, Jean Macklin, the daughter of an Indian high court judge, was attracted to Kingdon-Ward precisely because the life of an explorer was one she was keen and well suited to share. Though the marriage, on 12 November 1947, was opposed by her parents on account of the great age difference and Kingdon-Ward's lack of money, it proved an ideal partnership, to be commemorated in turn in *Lilium mackliniae*, which they found on a mountain in Manipur, on one of the five expeditions they made together.

Money was a worry for Kingdon-Ward throughout his career, and, despite his growing reputation, securing financial backing became progressively harder. At the same time, his mother and sister and, later, a home and children, made calls on his own slender purse. As an investment he bought a partnership in a Torquay market garden in 1920, but this quickly foundered. The running of an Assam tea estate for a few months represented his only venture into regular employment after 1911. Although he wrote easily and prolifically, making first drafts in the field, his twenty-five books, mostly on his travels, had only a limited appeal and earned depressingly little. Instead, he had to be content with honours (culminating in the OBE in 1952) and a renown that bestrode several continents.

Still planning yet another Asian trip at seventy-three, despite waning robustness and spinal arthritis resulting from a wartime accident in India, Kingdon-Ward died of a stroke in hospital at 31 Copse Hill, Wimbledon, on 8 April 1958. He was buried in the churchyard at Grantchester, not far from the Cambridge home of his adolescent years. He is commemorated in numerous species, of animals as well as plants, and in the genus *Kingdon-Wardia*, a member of the Gentian family.   D. E. ALLEN

Sources C. Lyte, *Frank Kingdon-Ward: the last of the great plant hunters* (1989) · A. M. Coats, *The quest for plants* (1969), 128–31, 172–98 · T. Schilling, 'Frank Kingdon Ward (1885–1958)', *The Garden*, 110 (1985), 264–9 · *The Times* (10 April 1958) · *Nature*, 181 (1958), 1505–6 · *Journal of the Royal Horticultural Society*, 84 (1959), 206–12 · *CGPLA Eng. & Wales* (1958) · E. H. M. Cox, *Plant hunting in China* (1945)
Archives NHM · RBG Kew, diaries; letters and notes of expeditions; papers · Royal Botanic Garden, Edinburgh, corresp. on primula | NL Scot., letters to Sir George Taylor · RBG Kew, corresp. with Sir Frederick Stern
Likenesses E. M. Gregson, oils, 1952, RGS [*see illus.*] · Popperfoto, photograph, repro. in Lyte, *Frank Kingdon-Ward*, facing p. 113 · photograph, repro. in *Country Life*, 188 (21 Nov 1985), 1654 · photograph, repro. in *The Times* · photograph, repro. in *Gardeners' Chronicle*, 1 (1932), 322 · photograph, repro. in *Lily yearbook* (1958), 9 · photograph, repro. in *Journal of the Royal Horticultural Society*, 206 · photograph, RGS
Wealth at death £9021 13s. 2d.: probate, 21 Oct 1958, *CGPLA Eng. & Wales*

Ward, Dame (**Lucy**) **Genevieve Teresa** (1837–1922), singer and actress, the only daughter of Samuel Ward, a diplomatist, and his wife, Lucy, *née* Leigh, was born in New York on 27 March 1837. She accompanied her parents in 1840 to Europe, where she later showed early promise as a singer and was introduced to Rossini, who arranged for her tuition in Florence. At the age of seventeen she met a Russian nobleman, Count Constantine de Guerbel, whom she married at a civil ceremony in Nice on 10 November 1855. Although this was to have been followed by a religious service in Paris, de Guerbel defaulted. Only after considerable diplomatic intervention was he compelled to meet

Dame (Lucy) Genevieve Teresa Ward (1837–1922), by Hugh Goldwin Riviere, 1906

his obligations at a ceremony in Warsaw. Ward and he separated immediately afterwards and she returned to Italy to resume her studies.

Ward began her operatic career as a soprano, at La Scala, Milan, under the stage name Madame Ginevra Guerrabella in 1857, playing in Donizetti's *Lucrezia Borgia*. After appearing in Italy and in Paris, where she performed as Elvira in Mozart's *Don Giovanni* (Théâtre des Italiens, 1859), she and her mother travelled to England, where Ward began oratorio lessons and made herself known through a series of concerts. She was offered by the Pyne-Harrison Opera Company the role of Maid Marian in George Macfarren's *Robin Hood*, which opened at Covent Garden on 8 November 1861, and a further role in Vincent Wallace's *Maritana* (29 November 1861). With her appearance as Elvira in Bellini's *I puritani* at Her Majesty's Theatre on 10 May 1862, her future as an operatic singer seemed assured. She returned to New York and made her American début at the Academy of Music, performing Violetta in Verdi's *La traviata* (10 November 1862). A strenuous tour with an opera company in the south of the United States, however, followed by a season in Cuba, resulted in vocal strain which, with the complication of diphtheria, brought her operatic career to an end.

From 1862 to 1873 Ward recuperated and readjusted her sights on a dramatic career. She taught singing while herself taking lessons from Fanny Morant in New York. She saw Charlotte Cushman and corresponded with her during the latter's last years as a performer, while developing the basis of a future repertory of roles, including Lady

Macbeth, Queen Katharine in *Henry VIII*, Adrienne Lecouvreur, and Medea.

Ward left America having reassumed her maiden name, and with the recommendations of Lewis Wingfield and George Augustus Sala appeared in Manchester at the Theatre Royal as Lady Macbeth (1 October 1873). After touring to Dublin, she made her dramatic début in London at the Adelphi Theatre, as Alexina in *Elizabeth, or, The Exiles of Siberia*, but it was her dual roles as Blanche de Valois and Unarita at the same theatre in Benjamin Webster's *The Prayer in the Storm* that really attracted attention to her abilities: 'our stage has received a valuable addition' (*The Times*, 30 March 1874). Ward consolidated her position in the years up to 1878 by extensive tours in Ireland and Scotland, then returned to Manchester, where she played Queen Katharine in Charles Calvert's production of *Henry VIII* and Beatrice in *Much Ado about Nothing*. Quite consciously she positioned herself within a tradition which stretched back into the eighteenth century by assuming roles which had been identified with Mrs Siddons: Mrs Haller in Kotzebue's *The Stranger* and Belvidera in Otway's *Venice Preserv'd*, which Ward played at the Gaiety in 1876 on 18 March and 19 April respectively. During this period she also came into contact with Adelaide Ristori, whom she helped with her English version of Lady Macbeth. It initiated a friendship which lasted until Ristori's death in 1906 and a histrionic indebtedness which critics would increasingly notice.

In 1878 Ward revisited America for the first time as a dramatic actress, and opened in New York at Booth's Theatre (2 September 1878) in W. G. Wills's version of Nicholas Rowe's *Jane Shore*. The *New York Times* admired her conception and technique but found her imagination wanting (3 September 1878). After performing her Shakespearian roles she returned to London in April 1879 and took over the management of the Lyceum during Irving's summer recess. Although she was less than successful in J. Palgrave Simpson and Claude Templar's *Zillah*, it was her performance as Stephanie de Mohrivart in Herman Merivale and F. C. Grove's *Forget-me-Not* (21 August 1879) which brought her critical acclaim and a role which she would adopt as her own for the remainder of her career; she played it for the last time in September 1914.

The roles of the badly treated 'adventuress' willing to challenge social and personal modes of conduct or the passionate woman who seeks retribution for past wrongs particularly attracted Ward, as her performances of Medea, Antigone, and Meg Merrilies in *Guy Mannering* showed. She took *Forget-me-Not* on her second visit to the United States in 1881–2. William Winter saw her and, although he was troubled by the morality of the play and that of her character, her performance 'was an image of imperial will, made radiant with beauty and electric with flashes of passion' (*The Wallet of Time*, 2.410).

Ward returned to England in late 1882 and leased the Olympic Theatre for a season, which lasted from January to June 1883. She repeated her round of characters, adding to them the role of Sarah Churchill in Sydney Grundy's *The Queen's Favourite*, an adaptation of Scribe's *Le verre d'eau*

(2 June 1883). Restless and adventurous by temperament, she gathered together a company, expanded her repertory again, and began a tour in December 1883 to include North America, Australia, and New Zealand which lasted until the beginning of 1887. Accompanied by W. H. Vernon as her leading man, she toured the east coast of Australia extensively from Brisbane to Adelaide, with lengthy stays in Sydney and Melbourne, as well as crossing to New Zealand, playing in *Forget-me-Not*, *The Queen's Favourite*, *Macbeth*, *Henry VIII*, *Lucrezia Borgia*, and another Grundy play adapted for her, *Rachel*. She left Australia on 1 December 1885 and returned to England in May 1886 via San Francisco and New York. This, however, was only a brief hiatus, as she continued her demanding tour of North America from September 1886 to April 1887. After opening in New York (24 September 1886) in *Forget-me-Not*, she and Vernon visited Ottawa and Montreal before embarking on a series of short engagements throughout the southern and Midwestern states of America, then Toronto, Hamilton, and London, Ontario.

The period after her return to England until 1891 was taken up with provincial tours with occasional appearances in London. Ward also began a career as an acting teacher in 1890. She was joined by Vernon, and continued to teach until his death in 1905. In 1889 Ward played Lona Hessel in Ibsen's *Pillars of Society* (Opera Comique, 17 July), the first of two attempts she made to come to terms with the 'new drama'. On 25 November 1891, together with Vernon, she began a tour of South Africa, supported by a company under the management of Luscombe Searelle. She opened in Cape Town with *Forget-me-Not* (10 December) before continuing on to Pretoria, Johannesburg, Bloemfontein, and East London. In addition to her established repertory, she added new plays: *Hamlet*, *The Merchant of Venice*, *Othello*, J. P. Simpson's adaptation of Sardou's *Les pattes de mouche* called *A Scrap of Paper*, Boucicault's *London Assurance*, Oxenford's *The Two Orphans*, and J. B. Buckstone's comedy *Married Life*. Though Ward did not perform in all the plays, she and Vernon were responsible for their productions. She claimed to have mounted twenty-six plays in nine months before returning to England in October 1892.

Ward never again embarked on tours outside England, but continued her provincial touring virtually until her death. The period to 1899, however, was marked by her appearances for Irving at the Lyceum. She played Eleanor of Aquitaine in the original production of Tennyson's *Becket* (6 February 1893), her old role of Queen Katharine in *Henry VIII* (10 July 1893), Morgan le Fay in Comyns Carr's *King Arthur* (12 January 1895), the Queen in *Cymbeline* (22 September 1896), and Margaret of Anjou in *Richard III*, a role she continued to revive. Her second essay into Ibsen took place on 3 May 1897 under the auspices of the New Century Theatre, when she played Mrs Borkman in a production of *John Gabriel Borkman*, with Vernon as Borkman and Elizabeth Robins as Ella Rentheim. She found the experience a tedious one. 'The truth is, her tragic style, derived from Ristori, was not made for Ibsen', wrote Shaw

(*Saturday Review*, 8 May 1897), although he had appreciated her performance in the earlier production.

During the remainder of her career Ward appeared infrequently on the London stage. She did, however, join F. R. Benson's company from time to time and added one last great role to her repertory when she played Volumnia in *Coriolanus* at the Comedy Theatre (13 February 1901). A. B. Walkley in *The Times* compared her performance directly with that of Sarah Siddons (14 February 1901). She repeated this on tours with Benson at Stratford and at the Old Vic. From that time Ward appeared occasionally at benefit concerts. Her last role in London was that of the duchess of Autevielle in L. N. Parker's *The Aristocrat* at the invitation of George Alexander (St James's Theatre, 25 January 1917): 'an aged *grande dame*, aged but not vulnerable, caustic of speech, regretting that she has outlived her sins' (*The Times*, 26 Jan 1917). Ward was created a dame commander in the Order of the British Empire (27 March 1921) 'in recognition of the distinguished position which she has occupied for so long in her profession, and of the services rendered by her to dramatic art' (*The Times*, 19 Aug 1922). She died on 18 August 1922 at 22 Avenue Road, London, and was cremated at Golders Green crematorium on the 21st.

Genevieve Ward saw herself primarily as a tragic actress embodying a tradition which stretched back to Mrs Barry and Sarah Siddons. She was also much influenced in her style and choice of material by Fanny Kemble and Charlotte Cushman. Her cosmopolitan early life and her involvement with Italian opera also brought her into contact with European performers whose overt emotionalism she absorbed: she became particularly noted in roles which demanded violent emotional oscillations. Bram Stoker in his reminiscences of Irving remarked on the blazing eyes of 'a particularly *strong* actress, good at invective' (Stoker, 2.175). She was drawn towards resolute and individualistic female characters outside tragedy, ones which pitted her against ruthless men in a clash of wills. In this she was fortunate to secure an excellent foil in W. H. Vernon and in Sydney Grundy, who adapted and wrote plays to suit their partnership. Drawn to the 'new drama' and its expansion of the thematic boundaries especially for women, she found herself repelled by Ibsen's suburban drabness and the fact that the plays offered no clear-cut dramatic intentions which audiences could understand (Ward and Whiteing, 196–202). Her indefatigable touring reflected both her interest in people and her understanding of the role of theatre as a cultural bond.   VICTOR EMELJANOW

Sources G. Ward and R. Whiteing, *Both sides of the curtain* (1918) · d. cert. · *The Times* (19 Aug 1922) · *The Era* (23 Aug 1922) · *New York Times* (19 Aug 1922) · *DAB* · W. Winter, *The wallet of time: containing personal, biographical, and critical reminiscence of the American theatre*, 2 vols. (1913) · Z. B. Gustafson, *Genevieve Ward: a biographical sketch* (1882) · B. Stoker, *Personal reminiscences of Henry Irving*, 2 vols. (1906) · 'Wills and bequests', *The Times* (16 Nov 1922) · C. E. Pascoe, ed., *The dramatic list*, 2nd edn (1880)
Archives Harvard TC | New York University, Elmer Holmes Bobst Library, Elizabeth Robins MSS

Likenesses H. Riviere, oils, 1906, Royal Shakespeare Theatre Picture Gallery, Stratford upon Avon [*see illus.*] · Ellis and Walery, photographs, repro. in Ward and Whiteing, *Both sides of the curtain* · London Stereoscopic Co., photographs (in character), repro. in Ward and Whiteing, *Both sides of the curtain* · C. Smith, photographs, repro. in Ward and Whiteing, *Both sides of the curtain* · photograph, repro. in *The Times*
Wealth at death £9354 4s. 2d.: probate, 11 Nov 1922, *CGPLA Eng. & Wales*

Ward, George Raphael (1799–1878). *See under* Ward, James (1769–1859).

Ward, Harry Marshall (1854–1906), botanist, was born on 21 March 1854 in Victoria Street, Hereford, the eldest son of Francis Marshall Ward, professor of music, and his wife, Mary Hannah East. Ward was educated at the cathedral school at Lincoln, and at a private school at Nottingham. In 1874 and 1875 he attended lectures by T. H. Huxley and W. T. Thiselton-Dyer at the Royal College of Science, South Kensington. In 1875 he went to Owens College, Manchester. The following year he was awarded an open science scholarship at Christ's College, Cambridge. At Cambridge he attended lectures on physiology, embryology, and botany, before graduating with first-class honours in the natural sciences tripos in 1879.

In 1880 Ward travelled to the continent, working for several months at the laboratories of Julius Sachs at the University of Würzburg and of Anton de Bary at the University of Strasbourg. He then went to Ceylon, where his expertise as a cryptogamic botanist was urgently needed by the Colonial Office. Ward spent two years in Ceylon investigating the coffee-leaf disease that was ravaging the island. Although he successfully analysed the life history of the fungus, he was unable to find any effective method of preventing the disease it caused. His experience in Ceylon was formative for Ward's views on parasitism and largely influenced much of his later work.

On his return to England, in 1882, Ward was elected Berkeley fellow at Owens College and became assistant lecturer at Manchester for the next three years. In 1883 he was elected to a fellowship at Christ's College and obtained the MA degree in Cambridge. In the same year, on 25 July, he married Selina Mary Kingdon (d. 1922), daughter of Francis Kingdon, a lecturer at Owens College. The couple later had a daughter, Winifred Mary Kingdon-*Ward, and a son, Francis Kingdon-*Ward, who became a plant collector and explorer. Ward's application for the chair of botany at Glasgow in 1885 was unsuccessful, but in the same year he became professor of botany in the Royal Indian Engineering College, Coopers Hill. After the death of the professor of botany at Cambridge, Charles Babington, in 1895, Ward succeeded him and became professorial fellow of Sidney Sussex College. In Cambridge Ward found a more congenial atmosphere and, working with great energy, he gave a fresh impulse to the botanical school. Under his care the school acquired such importance that the university erected a new and well-equipped botanical institute, opened in 1904.

During his career Ward published more than fifty

reports, papers, and books. They included an English edition of Sachs's *Vorlesungen über Pflanzenphysiologie* (1887), *Timber and Some of its Diseases* (1889), *Diseases of Plants* (1889), *The Oak* (1892), a second edition of Thomas Laslett's *Timber and Timber-Trees* (1894), *Grasses* (1901), and *Trees: a Handbook of Forest Botany* (3 vols., 1904–5).

Ward's earliest scientific papers date back to 1880, when he was interested in the development of the embryo sac. His investigations in Ceylon resulted in a series of reports and papers on the morphology and development of fungi, especially with regards to diseases in plants. His paper 'On the tubercular swellings on the roots of *Vicia faba*' (1887) deserves special attention. Ward discovered that the tubercular swellings were of parasitic origin. His views on parasitism were further developed in the Croonian lecture of 1890, which was entitled 'On some relations between host and parasite in certain epidemic diseases of plants'.

In 1892–9 Ward, in collaboration with Percy Frankland, carried out a series of laborious investigations on the bacteriology of water at the request of the Royal Society. Ward identified eighty species of bacteria in the water of the Thames. His conclusions about the destructive effects of light upon bacteria attracted public attention because of their hygienic implications. His last important line of research was the investigation of rusts that affect the brome grasses (oat-like grasses). In connection with these investigations he became involved in a controversy on the mycoplasm theory.

Ward received many honours for his contributions to science. He was made ScD at the Royal Indian Engineering College in 1892 and was awarded an honorary DSc of Victoria University in 1902. He became fellow of the Linnean Society in 1886 and served on its council in 1887–9. He was elected to the Royal Society in 1888 and received the royal medal in 1893. Ward died at Babbacombe, Torquay, on 26 August 1906. He was buried on 3 September in the Huntingdon Road cemetery in Cambridge. His wife survived him.   THOMAS JUNKER

Sources S. H. Vines, *Annals of Botany*, 21 (1907), ix–xiii • S. H. Vines, *Nature*, 74 (1906), 493–5 • *DNB* • F. O. Bower, *Journal of Botany, British and Foreign*, 44 (1906), 422–5 • F. O. Bower, 'H. Marshall Ward', *Sixty years of botany in Britain, 1875–1935* (1938), 54–6 • B. D. J. [B. D. Jackson], *Proceedings of the Linnean Society of London*, 119th session (1906–7), 54–7 • T. Johnson, *Berichte der Deutschen Botanischen Gesellschaft*, 26a (1908) • m. cert. • b. cert. • *CGPLA Eng. & Wales* (1906)
Archives Oxf. U. Mus. NH, letters to Sir E. B. Poulton
Likenesses chalk drawing, Christ's College, Cambridge • photograph, repro. in Vines, *Annals of Botany* • photograph, RS; repro. in Bower, 'H. Marshall Ward'
Wealth at death £7548 11s. 5d.: probate, 22 Dec 1906, *CGPLA Eng. & Wales*

Ward, Henrietta Mary Ada (1832–1924), historical genre painter, was born on 1 June 1832 at 6 Newman Street, London, the only child of artists George Raphael *Ward (1799–1878) [*see under* Ward, James] and his wife Mary Webb, and granddaughter of the painter James *Ward (1769–1859). She was taught by her mother and, from 1843, by the history painter Edward Matthew *Ward (1816–1879). She also attended Sass's drawing academy and, though women

were not officially invited, attended Royal Academy lectures. On 4 May 1848 in Marylebone, Middlesex, Ward married her teacher E. M. Ward, sixteen years her senior, despite her parents' vigorous opposition, and from 1850 on bore eight children, five daughters and three sons. Of these, Leslie *Ward, Flora, and Eva became practising artists. From 1850, with the exhibition of *Rowena* at the Royal Academy, Ward pursued historical genre painting. Although critics often implied that her work owed too much to that of her husband, who was among the leading painters of this genre of his generation, Ward brought a feminine slant to her choice of sources, subjects, and narrative emphasis, often selecting child protagonists (*Scene from the Childhood of Joan of Arc*, 1867), dramas of family separation and maternal suffering (*Queen Mary Quitting Stirling Castle*, 1863), and instances of female heroism (*Newgate, 1818*, 1876; Wellcome Institute, London). She interspersed these set pieces with domestic scenes drawn from her own family life (*The Morning Lesson*, 1855) and literary fancy pictures (*The May Queen*, 1856). Many of Ward's works were engraved including *Newgate, 1818* (1879), the artist's favourite work and her greatest popular success. She benefited from the lifelong support of S. C. and Maria Hall, who promoted her (and her husband) in their monthly magazine, the *Art Journal*, the leading art periodical of the day.

From 1854 Ward taught several of Queen Victoria's children. The royal commissions she received from this date on, for copies and originals such as portraits and landscapes, furthered her reputation with the general public. Her work commanded high prices for a female artist (*The Tower, ay the Tower* was sold from exhibition in 1864 for 200 guineas) and was acquired in her lifetime by several notable collectors of contemporary art including A. Holtz, Sir William Call, Edwin Bullock, Henry Wallis, George Fox, and Viscount Burnham. Ward exhibited at the Royal Academy from 1846 until 1904 (virtually annually until 1882) and irregularly at the Society of Female Artists from its inception in 1857 until 1881 (honorary member, 1877–86). Through the fifties and sixties she showed frequently at other London venues including the Crystal Palace, where she won a gold medal in 1873, and Wallis's winter exhibitions (from 1859). She also exhibited at the leading provincial exhibitions: Liverpool (1854–79), Birmingham (1855–69), Manchester (1851–1904), Leeds, Bristol, and Glasgow (1868–73). Her work was represented at a number of international exhibitions, including the Great Exhibition, London (1851; gold and silver medals), the International Exhibition, London (1867), the International exhibition, Vienna (1873; bronze medal), the world fair, Philadelphia (1876), and the Universal Exhibition, Paris (1878). She was proposed for membership of the Royal Academy in 1875 and 1876, although women were not officially eligible—a sign of the esteem in which she was held by many of her male contemporaries.

On her husband's death in 1879, financial necessity prompted Henrietta Ward to open a private art school where, from 1880, she successfully taught young women, including the children of royalty and the aristocracy. Henrietta Ward died on 12 July 1924 at her home, 59 Sydney Street, Chelsea, London.

Ward was one of the most prominent if not the best-known of female artists of the mid-Victorian period, viewed as a pioneer of the inevitable acceptance of female artists within the British art scene. Her paintings are to be found in the public collections of Rochdale, Liverpool (Walker Gallery), Bristol, and Leicester, as well as that of the Society of Friends, London.

PAMELA GERRISH NUNN

Sources J. Dafforne, 'British artists, their style and character, no. LXXVII: Henrietta Ward', *Art Journal*, 26 (1864), 357–9 · *Mrs E. M. Ward's reminiscences*, ed. E. O'Donnell (1911) · I. G. McAllister, ed., *Memories of ninety years* (1924) · P. G. Nunn, 'The case history of a woman artist: Henrietta Ward', *Art History*, 1 (1978), 293–308 · P. G. Nunn, ed., *Canvassing: recollections by six Victorian women artists* (1986) · d. cert.
Likenesses E. Edwards, photograph, 1866, repro. in *Portraits of men of eminence*, 4 (1866) · photograph, c.1880, repro. in McAllister, ed., *Memories of ninety years*
Wealth at death £5536 13s. 9d.: probate, 5 Nov 1924, CGPLA Eng. & Wales

Ward, Sir Henry George (1797–1860), politician and colonial governor, was born on 27 February 1797 in London, the only son of Robert Plumer *Ward (1765–1846), novelist and politician, afterwards of Gilston Park, Hertfordshire, and his first wife, Catherine Julia (1772–1821), daughter of Christopher Thompson Maling of West Herrington, co. Durham. Educated at Harrow School and sent abroad to learn languages, Ward entered the diplomatic service in 1816 as attaché in Sweden. Transferred to The Hague in 1818 and to Spain in 1819, he was joint commissioner in Mexico, 1823–4, and chargé d'affaires, 1825–7. He resigned in 1827 and returned to England with his wife, Emily Elizabeth (1798–1882), second daughter of Sir John Swinburne, bt (1762–1860), of Capheaton, whom he had married in 1824. In 1828 he published *Mexico in 1827*, a vivid and acutely observed account of the country.

Ward entered parliament as an advanced Liberal in January 1833, sitting first for the notoriously corrupt borough of St Albans and then from July 1837 until 1849 for Sheffield. After an unpromising beginning (cf. *The Times*, 30 March, 3 and 5 April 1833), he became one of the acknowledged radical leaders. An able speaker, with a terse, vigorous style, he first came to notice by his motion, the first of many, on appropriating the surplus revenues of the Irish church (*Speech of H. G. Ward, esq., M.P. on moving certain resolutions respecting the Irish Church in the House of Commons ... May 27, 1834*, published in 1834), which resulted, whether intentionally, as was widely assumed, or not, in completing the breach in the reform ministry. He was also prominent in such issues as free trade, the ballot, and franchise extension, and the establishment of the Reform Club and the Central Reform Association, using the *Weekly Chronicle*, of which he became political editor early in 1836 and proprietor in November 1838, to promote his views and combat Chartism. Keenly interested in colonial questions, he was a founder member of the Colonial Society of 1837, was active in the affairs of the South

Australia Association and the New Zealand Company, and assiduous in promoting the colonization methods associated with Edward Gibbon Wakefield as a means for relieving social distress (as shown in *The debate of Mr. Ward's resolutions on colonization in the House of Commons, June 27, 1839, containing the speeches of H. G. Ward ... Sir W. Molesworth, etc.*, 1839). In August 1839 he was offered, and refused, the secretaryship of the Board of Control by Lord Melbourne, although he now joined the ranks of the whig supporters, free trade and the ballot having been left as open questions. He accepted office in June 1846 as secretary to the Admiralty under Lord Auckland, whose defects in debate he ably supplied.

Ward's pecuniary embarrassments, meantime, exacerbated by feckless extravagance, were coming to an issue. His financial arrangements in Mexico had drawn forth several magisterial rebukes from the Foreign Office; he spent £12,000 on his two elections for St Albans, the interest and insurance on which caused a considerable drain on family resources. His difficulties became the subject of unfavourable comment in the press (among others the *Sheffield Mercury*, 15 April 1843), and serious doubt of his being able to retain his seat. After severe retrenchment in his Hertfordshire estates, the management of which he had had since August 1838, his immediate problems were resolved by December 1843. Nevertheless, ill-judged railway speculation resulted in considerable losses during the panic of 1846, while his growing unpopularity in Sheffield in consequence of his identification with Russell's administration made offers of colonial governorships all the more attractive. His financial distress and the illness of his much loved wife thus obliged him to accept the proffered appointment of lord high commissioner in the Ionian Islands in April 1849.

Ward arrived at Corfu in June, to find himself in a difficult position. His predecessor, Lord Seaton, had proposed considerable reforms of the hitherto restrictive constitution, which Ward, after modifications, effected. But his suppression with no unsparing hand of an agrarian–nationalist revolt in Cephalonia that autumn earned him the unenviable sobriquet of 'Dead or Alive Ward', and damned his reputation with his erstwhile radical associates, most notably Joseph Hume, who were vociferous in their attacks upon his proceedings. Meanwhile reform had aroused extravagant expectations of further concessions leading to the ultimate union of the islands with Greece. Ward at first tried conciliation and, that failing, governing by prorogations of the assembly and the use of administrative exile for the more intractable government opponents. Beyond this he was a markedly able governor, a considerable personality in the tortuous political and diplomatic affairs of the Levant during the early stages of the Crimean War, and active in checking Greek irredentist designs in Thessaly and Epirus.

In March 1855 Ward was appointed to the senior governorship of Ceylon, arriving in May. He toured the island extensively and, fortunate that his administration coincided with a period of economic growth, soon made his mark in developing communications, restoring and extending irrigation works, and encouraging the unofficial element in the legislative council. Identifying himself wholly with the interests of the island, he was active in the consolidation of the civil service, the amelioration of the conditions of seasonal migrants, and the abolition of polygamy. In June 1860 he was promoted to the governorship of Madras in succession to Sir Charles Trevelyan. He arrived there in July, succumbed to cholera and died at Government House on 2 August 1860. He was buried in the Anglican church of Fort St George, survived by his wife and ten children.

A tall, powerful man, with light brown hair, full round face and good-natured countenance, Ward was an expert swordsman and shot, and devoted to hunting. Possessed of considerable administrative talents, firmness of purpose, and a high sense of duty, he was an undeniably able man. As a politician, he earned the respect of men of all parties; and while events in the Ionian Islands afforded him little scope in the exercise of his talents beyond rebuffing the more extreme claims of Hellenic nationalism, his administration of Ceylon was adjudged as highly successful. He was appointed GCMG in June 1849. A statue commemorating his work in Ceylon was erected at Kandy by public subscription.   A. A. D. SEYMOUR

Sources H. M. Johnston, *Missions to Mexico: a tale of British diplomacy in the 1820s* (1992) · R. E. Leader, *Chapters in the political history of Sheffield, 1832–1849: consisting of letters from Mr John Parker, MP and Mr Henry George Ward, MP* (1884) · *Selections from the correspondence of Sir Henry George Ward while Lord High Commissioner of the Ionian Islands, 1849–55*, ed. A. A. D. Seymour [in preparation with a biographical sketch and a survey of his Ionian administration] · *Speeches and minutes of the late Sir Henry George Ward, KGCMG, governor and commander-in-chief in and over the island of Ceylon with the dependencies thereof; with other papers connected with his administration of the government of Ceylon, 1855–60* (1864) · S. V. Balasingham, *The administration of Sir Henry Ward, governor of Ceylon, 1855–60* (1968) · H. A. J. Hulugalle, *British governors of Ceylon* (1963) · *Annual Register* (1860) · *Sheffield Daily Telegraph* (5 Sept 1860) · *Sheffield and Rotherham Independent* (15 Sept 1860) · *The Times* (3 Sept 1860)
Archives Mulgrave Castle archive, North Yorkshire, letters on colonial, personal, and political affairs | All Souls Oxf., letters to Charles Richard Vaughan · BL, corresp. with Admiral Sir Charles Napier, Add. MSS 40028–40041 · BL, corresp. with Lord Westmorland, M/509/3 [microfilm copy] · BL, corresp. with Charles Wood, Add. MS 49551, *passim* · Bodl. RH, letters to Henry Labouchere · Borth. Inst., letters to Sir Charles Wood · Herts. ALS, letters to Lord Lytton · Herts. ALS, corresp. · NL Scot., corresp. with G. R. Gleig, MSS 3870–3871 · Northumbd RO, Newcastle upon Tyne, letters to Sir John Swinburne, ZSW 536, ZSW 542 · priv. coll., Seaton MSS · PRO, corresp. with Lord John Russell, PRO 30/22 · Sheff. Arch., R. E. Leader collection · U. Cal., Los Angeles, letters to Sir John Bowring · U. Durham, letters to third Earl Grey, Sir Benjamin Hawes, and others · U. Nott. L., letters to fifth duke of Newcastle · U. Southampton L., corresp. with Lord Palmerston
Likenesses W. H. Mote, stipple, pubd 1842 (after J. Holmes, *c.*1838), BM, NPG; repro. in Johnston, *Missions to Mexico* · engraving, repro. in Hulugalle, *British governors of Ceylon*, facing p. 98 · oils, repro. in Balasingham, *Administration of Sir Henry Ward*, frontispiece; former Government House, Colombo, Sri Lanka · statue, Kandy; repro. in Balasingham, *Administration of Sir Henry Ward*, jacket
Wealth at death under £20: resworn administration, May 1864, *CGPLA Eng. & Wales* (1860)

Ward, Henry Leigh Douglas [Harry] (1825–1906), literary historian, was born on 18 February 1825 at Chelmsford, Essex, the fourth son of John Giffard Ward (1779–1860) and his wife, Amelia (*b. c.*1780, *d.* after 1860). John Ward, then rector of Chelmsford, became rector of St James's, Piccadilly, London, in 1825, and in 1846 dean of Lincoln, where he died in office.

Ward became a pupil at Winchester College in 1838 and matriculated at University College, Oxford, in 1844, taking a pass degree in 1847. Two years later he joined the department of manuscripts in the British Museum, then under the direction of Sir Frederick Madden, and remained there until he retired in 1893. Madden was an exceptionally gifted palaeographer, but an unpredictable director of a department. He could readily appreciate scholarly ability, however, and Ward was able to do the work to which he was best suited, and which he continued under the very different regimes of Edward Augustus Bond and Edward Maunde Thompson. He had a wider linguistic competence than Madden, and arguably more intellectual depth. On 28 April 1866 Ward married Mary Elizabeth (*b. c.*1821), daughter of Samuel George Fox.

Ward's first official task was a catalogue of the Icelandic manuscripts in the museum, a comprehensive description which was never published but which was kept as a work of reference for students. Instead of pursuing the sagas, which he was well equipped to do, he then turned from them to the richer and formidably broad field of medieval romance, which occupied him for the rest of his life. It was a theme of the widest significance, linking courtly and popular literature, Christian imagery, as in the legends of the holy grail, and remnants of classical myth and epic. The tale of chivalry at the heart of the genre was one of the defining features of medieval culture, and its afterlife, from Cervantes to Sir Walter Scott, proved equally vigorous.

Ward displayed his intuitive grasp of the subject, and an early familiarity with the sources, in an article on medieval romance which he contributed in 1873 to the *English Cyclopaedia* edited by Charles Knight. The contents of his *Catalogue of Romances in the British Museum* (1883–1910), however, went far beyond a survey of the manuscript sources. Ward took careful account of the work of continental scholars, but his particular contribution was to combine detailed knowledge of the material, and of the manifold traditions of the romance, with a clear view of the whole subject over several centuries.

The first and largest volume of Ward's authoritative catalogue was published in 1883. It identifies and discusses the Arthurian cycles and the legends of Charlemagne, the stories of Troy, and the extraordinary variety of tales of Alexander, together with the other major cycles in verse and prose. The second volume, published in 1893, deals with the northern legends from *Beowulf* and the *Niebelungenlied* to the Icelandic sagas, with the medieval derivatives of Aesop's fables, and the miracles of the Virgin. The third volume, prepared for the press by his colleagues and published posthumously in 1910, marshals the *exempla* used by medieval preachers and moralists. It is again a work of remarkable learning, and like its predecessors is still a starting point for further study of that prolific field. Ward's other published work, beyond reviews, was quite slight, but he was sought out by many scholars, from home and abroad, to whom he rendered prompt and generous assistance from his own stores of knowledge. He was awarded an honorary PhD by the University of Halle in recognition of his work on the romances.

There was nothing reclusive about Ward, despite his intense commitment to scholarship. He entered the circle of Dante Gabriel Rossetti, Sir Edward Burne-Jones, and other members of the Pre-Raphaelite Brotherhood, probably through his friendship with his colleague Coventry Patmore. Other close friends included T. W. Robertson, actor and dramatist, and W. H. Brookfield, a royal chaplain, who had been his father's curate at St James's, Piccadilly. Ward died at his home, 96 South Hill Park, Hampstead, London, on 28 January 1906, survived by his wife, their four sons, and two of their three daughters.

G. H. MARTIN

Sources *The Times* (1 Feb 1906) · census returns for Lincoln, 1851 · census returns for London, 1891 · Foster, *Alum. Oxon.* · PO Directory, Hampstead, 1890 · J. B. Wainewright, ed., *Winchester College, 1836–1906: a register* (1907) · *DNB*
Likenesses photograph, St John's College, Oxford
Wealth at death £8894 9s. 3d.: probate, 23 March 1906, *CGPLA Eng. & Wales*

Ward, Henry Snowden (1865–1911), photographer and author, was born at Great Horton, Bradford, on 27 February 1865, the eldest of five sons of William Ward, stuff manufacturer, and his wife, Mary, the only daughter of Henry Snowden, manufacturer. He was educated at Great Horton national school, Bradford grammar school (1876–9), and Bradford Technical College.

Ward entered his father's business in 1880, at which time he met and collaborated with Herbert James Riley to establish the periodical the *Practical Naturalist* (later amalgamated with the *Naturalist's World*), and founded the Practical Naturalists' Society. In 1885 he joined the printing and publishing firm of Percy Lund & Co. of Bradford, for whom he founded and edited the monthly periodical *Practical Photographer* in 1890. He soon became a recognized authority on photography and the printing arts.

Ward left Bradford for London in 1891, where he would remain for most of his life. In 1892 he made his first visit to America and it was there he met, and in 1893 married, his American wife, Catharine Weed Barnes of Albany, New York, the daughter of William Barnes and granddaughter of the prominent New York journalist and politician Thurlow Weed, and a respected photographic expert in her own right. Together they edited such London photographic periodicals as *The Photogram* (1894–1905), continued from 1906 as the *Photographic Monthly*; the *Process Photogram* (1895–1905), continued from 1906 as the *Process Engravers Monthly*; as well as *Photograms of the Year* (from 1896) and the *Photographic Annual* (from 1908). Henry Ward also compiled many technical handbooks, chiefly the first English handbook on the röntgen, or X-rays, *Practical Radiography* (with A. W. Isenthal, 1896; new edns 1897, 1898,

and 1901); *The Figures, Facts, and Formulæ of Photography* (3 edns, 1903); *Photography for the Press* (1905; 3rd edn 1909); and *Finishing the Negative* (1907).

As the joint director of the photographic firm of Dawbarn and Ward (1894–1911), Ward edited the Useful Arts Series (1899), the Home Worker's Series, and Rural Handbooks (1902). During this time he combined his photographic publications with a treatise on theosophy, his other interest. He contributed to the photographic world through lectures in Canada, the United States, and Britain as a member of both the Royal Photographic Society (made a fellow in 1895) and the Röntgen Society (1897). He presided over the 1909 meeting in Canterbury of the photographic convention founded in 1886 to promote photographic research.

Literature and topography also attracted Ward, and he and his wife wrote and copiously illustrated with their own photographs *Shakespeare's Town and Times* (1896; 3rd enlarged edn 1908), *The Shakespearean Guide to Stratford-on-Avon* (1897), *The Real Dickens Land* (1903), and *The Canterbury Pilgrimages* (1904). Ward also edited, with notes and introduction, an edition, elaborately illustrated by his wife, of R. D. Blackmore's *Lorna Doone* in 1908.

Ward was an ardent traveller, and made many lecturing tours on topics both technical and literary. An enthusiastic admirer of Dickens, he was an original member of the Dickens Fellowship, was chairman of council (1907–8), and was mainly responsible for the acquisition for the Guildhall Library of Frederick George Kitton's collection of Dickensiana in 1908. As commissioner of the Dickens Fellowship he travelled in October 1911 to America on a six months' lecture tour to stimulate American interest in the Dickens centenary. This tour was cut short by his sudden death at 26 West 61st Street, Manhattan, New York, from mastoiditis-meningitis on 7 December 1911. He was buried in Albany, New York state, and was survived by his wife.

W. B. OWEN, rev. KELLEY WILDER

Sources *WW* (1911) · *The Photogram*, 1/1 (1894) · *The Times* (8 Dec 1911) · *The Dickensian*, 8 (1912) · private information (1912) [Catharine Ward] · *Photographic Journal*, new ser. 35 (1911), 427–8 · *CGPLA Eng. & Wales* (1912)
Likenesses portrait, repro. in *The Photogram* · portrait, repro. in *The Dickensian*
Wealth at death £857 3s. 1d.: administration with will, 22 March 1912, *CGPLA Eng. & Wales*

Ward, Hugh [Hugo Vardeus, Aodh Buidhe Mac an Bhaird] (1592–1635), Franciscan friar and historian, a native of co. Donegal, was a member of the *Mac an Bhaird family, hereditary poets to the O'Donnells of Tirconaill. His parents were Eugenius Wardeus (possibly to be identified as Eoghan Ruadh *Mac an Bhaird [see under Mac an Bhaird family]) and Maria Ní Chlery. His early education was obtained within his own family circle. He left Ireland in 1612 to study at the Irish College in Salamanca, Spain, and joined the Franciscan order there in 1616—a career not untypical of his learned contemporaries for whom traditional sources of patronage had significantly diminished after 1603. On 22 March 1622 Ward was appointed to teach philosophy at the Irish Franciscan college of St Anthony in

Louvain and travelled from Salamanca to Louvain, via Paris, Rouen, and Nantes, early in 1623. He never returned to Ireland.

Ward was in Paris in March 1623 serving as companion to Francis de Arriba, confessor of the queen of France. There he came into contact with fellow Franciscans Patrick Fleming and Hugh MacCaughwell and the secular priest Thomas Messingham. The group discussed their shared interest in researching the lives of Irish saints and agreed to collaborate on publishing their findings. The association with Messingham was not long-lived, but Fleming and Ward continued to work together until Fleming's death in 1631. Ward subsequently collaborated with John Colgan and other Louvain-based Irish Franciscans. One of the first hagiographical publications to emerge from Louvain was Robert Rochford's *Life of the glorious bishop St Patrick … together with the lives of the holy Virgin, St Brigid, and of the glorious Abbot St Columb, patrons of Ireland*, published at St Omer in 1625. It provides evidence that Ward's interest in Irish saints' lives was shared by others in his community also. In Louvain, Ward's fellow Franciscans included Thomas Fleming, Florence Conry, Robert Chamberlain, John Colgan, Micheál Ó Cléirigh, and his own brother, Ferdinand Ward. He also received encouragement in his historical researches from Luke Wadding in Rome.

Ward was elected guardian of St Anthony's three years after his arrival there, the appointment being confirmed on 22 April 1626. The following day he was authorized to conduct research in German and French libraries on the lives of Irish saints, but was probably away for a relatively short time. In addition to his administrative duties at the college he also taught theology. Ward became a prominent figure in the Catholic church in the diocese of Malines and his work on behalf of the Franciscan order was not confined to the world of the college of St Anthony. A proposal that he be transferred to the new Irish Franciscan college at Prague in 1630 was not implemented.

From his Louvain base Ward directed Micheál Ó Cléirigh's researches in Ireland on the early history of Ireland and her saints and kings. He particularly welcomed the compilation of the martyrology of Donegal, completed in 1630. In 1631, at the request of the archbishop of Malines, Ward was himself researching the life of St Romuald, patron of the diocese of Malines, drawing on the earlier lives already in circulation. This work, *Sancti Rumoldi … acta*, completed in 1631, was published posthumously, edited by Thomas Sirinus (Sheeran) in 1662, 'least he should be forgotten who had begun these studies, or least it should be supposed that nothing had been achieved by all his toil' (Jennings, *Michael O Cleirigh*, 105, citing preface to *Sancti Rumoldi … acta*). Ward co-operated with the Bollandists in their hagiographical researches, contributing lives of saints Mochua, Maedóc, and Fechin to their *Acta sanctorum*, and preparing material for subsequent volumes.

Although Ward worked indefatigably on researching Irish saints' lives, administrative responsibilities and poor health prevented his research being published in his lifetime. John Colgan's *Acta sanctorum … Hiberniae* (1645) owed much to his efforts. Colgan's preface reveals that Ward would have seen the project through to publication but for his early death. He died on 8 November 1635, of dropsy, at the early age of forty-three. Throughout his life he had devoted much time to the study of the works of the philosopher John Duns Scotus and rejoiced at dying on his feast day. He was buried in Louvain.

BERNADETTE CUNNINGHAM

Sources B. Jennings, *Michael O Cleirigh, chief of the four masters, and his associates* (1936) · R. Sharpe, *Medieval Irish saints' lives: an introduction to Vitae sanctorum Hiberniae* (1991) · H. Vardaeus, *Sancti Rumoldi … acta*, ed. T. Sirinus (1662) · J. Colgan, *Acta sanctorum veteris et majoris Scotiae seu Hiberniae* (1645), preface · B. Jennings, ed., 'Documents from the archives of St Isidore's College, Rome', *Analecta Hibernica*, 6 (1934), 203–47 · B. Jennings and C. Giblin, eds., *Louvain papers, 1606–1827*, IMC (1968) · P. F. Moran, ed., *Spicilegium Ossoriense*, 3 (1884), 52 · D. J. O'Doherty, 'Students of the Irish College, Salamanca (1595–1619) [pt 1]', *Archivium Hibernicum*, 2 (1913), 1–36, esp. 29 · P. A. Breatnach, 'An Irish Bollandus: Fr Hugh Ward and the Louvain hagiographical enterprise', *Éigse*, 31 (1999), 1–30 · *Report on Franciscan manuscripts preserved at the convent, Merchants' Quay, Dublin*, HMC, 65 (1906) · B. Jennings, ed., *Wadding papers, 1614–38*, IMC (1953) · Franciscan House of Studies, Killiney, co. Dublin

Archives Franciscan House of Studies, Killiney, co. Dublin, Franciscan archives · St. Isidore's College, Rome, archives

Ward, Mrs Humphry. *See* Ward, Mary Augusta (1851–1920).

Ward, Ida Caroline (1880–1949), phonetician and scholar of west African languages, was born at Bradford, Yorkshire, on 4 October 1880, the eighth child of Samson Ward, a wool merchant, and his wife, Hannah, daughter of Charles Tempest, also of Bradford. She went to school in Bradford and then to Darlington Training College and Durham University, where she graduated BLitt in 1902.

After sixteen years of secondary schoolteaching Ida Ward joined the phonetics department of University College, London, in 1919, and became an authority on the phonetics of the main European languages, and on speech defects. During this period she collaborated with Lillian E. Armstrong in *A Handbook of English Intonation*, and also wrote *The Phonetics of English*. Her interest turned to African languages and in 1932 she joined the staff of what later became the School of Oriental and African Studies of London University, and in 1933 was awarded the degree DLitt for her *Phonetic and Tonal Structure of Efik*, which opened a new chapter in the study of African languages by analysing scientifically the element of tone which plays a vital part in them. There followed her important *Introduction to the Ibo Language* (1936) with its elucidation of Igbo vowel harmony as well as of tone.

In 1937 Ward became head of the new department of African languages and cultures at the school and in 1944 was made professor of west African languages. She gradually built up the department from small beginnings into an institution of international standing for research, teaching, and consultation. Missionary and educational bodies sought her help, and after the Second World War the Colonial Office called for courses in eleven African languages for some hundred colonial officials annually. She also trained Africans in the scientific study of their own mother tongues. The importance of this contribution became increasingly evident with the development of the various African universities. Working at a crucial time in African history she matched her opportunity by her achievement which received official recognition in 1948 when she was appointed CBE, and after her death when the secretary of state for the colonies paid tribute to the immense amount of time and work which she had devoted to the interests of colonial peoples.

After her third visit to west Africa Ward published her report on Gold Coast language problems (1945); her *Introduction to the Yoruba Language* appeared posthumously in 1952. In 1948 she visited universities and learned societies in the United States under a Rockefeller grant, and in that year retired from her chair, although continuing as adviser in African studies. She also gave unstinted help to the International African Institute and was closely involved in the production of its 1952 *Handbook of African Languages*. Her own *Practical Phonetics for Students of African Languages* (with Professor D. H. Westermann, 1933) was widely influential.

Ida Ward's achievements were due not only to scholarship but to her warm human qualities. Her Christianity was a living force and her large-hearted generosity, her zest, wisdom, and courage made working with her a continuous and fruitful adventure. Her genial common sense, sound judgement, and adaptability helped her in dealing with official bodies and difficult situations. Friendly, unpretentious, understanding, and accessible, but with natural dignity, she was regarded with affectionate respect by all and conveyed to all her own enjoyment of life. She was unmarried, but the happy home life which she shared with her widowed sister and the keen interest she took in her great-nephews and nieces were as real to her as her work. She died at the Royal Surrey County Hospital, Guildford, Surrey, on 10 October 1949, and was cremated four days later at Woking.

M. M. GREEN, rev. D. W. ARNOTT

Sources *Bulletin of the School of Oriental and African Studies*, 13 (1950), 542–7 · D. Westermann and M. A. Bryan, *Handbook of African languages*, 2nd edn, 2: *The languages of West Africa* (1970) · SOAS, archives · private information (1959) · *CGPLA Eng. & Wales* (1950)
Archives SOAS
Likenesses group portrait, photograph, 1948 (with African department members), SOAS · portrait (with members of the department of Africa at SOAS), SOAS; repro. in *Bulletin of the School of Oriental and African Studies*
Wealth at death £12,027 3s. 3d.: probate, 8 Feb 1950, *CGPLA Eng. & Wales*

Ward, Irene Mary Bewick, Baroness Ward of North Tyneside (1895–1980), politician, was born at 28 St Stephen's Mansions, Westminster, London, on 23 February 1895, the only child of (Alfred) John Bewick Ward (1855/6–1901), an architect who designed some of the mosaics in Westminster Cathedral, and his wife, Elvina Mary Ellis (d.

Irene Mary Bewick Ward, Baroness Ward of North Tyneside (1895–1980), by Elliott & Fry

1944). After the death of her husband, who left his family in straitened circumstances, Elvina moved with Irene to Newcastle upon Tyne, and eventually settled in Gosforth, where an uncle paid for their lodgings and Irene's education at Newcastle Church High School. Elvina ensured that her daughter grew up aware of the wider world, including women's suffrage—an issue which interested mother more than daughter. Despite the lack of money, Irene had elocution and dancing lessons, acted in amateur dramatics, and was taken by her mother to the theatre. At sixteen she wanted to be a writer—some of her stories were published in the local press—but she earned her living as a secretary, her work for the coalowner and Liberal MP Sir Cecil Cochrane being the most significant of her various posts. He gave her financial support in the early stages of her career. During the First World War she delivered her first public speech, deputizing for the head of the voluntary aid detachment unit of the St John Ambulance Brigade to address stretcher-bearers leaving for the front.

Acting as a poll clerk in the 1919 general election probably marked the beginning of Ward's political activity. Her friendship with Sir George Renwick MP and Lady Renwick led in 1920 to an invitation to be the central Newcastle Conservative association's honorary secretary. At the 1923 Conservative Party conference at Plymouth her public-speaking skills brought her to the attention of the party leadership. She was invited to contest Morpeth in the 1924 general election (despite being too young to vote) after she had failed to be selected for Wansbeck. The party's chief organizer, Sir T. J. Leigh Maclachlan, was impressed by the manner in which she took the Wansbeck rejection and advised the Morpeth constituency association that the party would pay her election expenses. The seat was unwinnable in 1924 but Irene put up a spirited fight, and came second to the Labour candidate. Her bravery in dealing with the unorthodox tactics of some of her opponent's supporters won her electorate's regard and instilled in her a lifelong respect for miners.

Undeterred by another unsuccessful contest at Morpeth in 1929, Ward was one of the sixty-two women candidates to stand at the 1931 general election. In one of the two all-women contests at that election she defeated her Labour opponent, Margaret Bondfield, at Wallsend. On the night of her victory she vowed never to forget her obligation to maintain the trust of those constituents who were not natural Conservative voters. Despite her later description of herself as a progressive Conservative and membership of the Tory Reform Group, her own brand of Conservatism was essentially pragmatic and too personal to lead to ministerial office. But she thrived as a back-bencher. Before the war she was one of the two most frequent women speakers from the 1931 intake.

Ward's maiden speech in May 1932 during the debate on the Coal Mines Bill criticized the government for failing to guarantee miners' wages. She was not the only woman MP to master 'masculine' topics such as shipbuilding, engineering, and mining, but this mastery, and her tenacity and zest, contributed to her re-election for Wallsend in 1935. That result was very much a personal triumph, for several of her male colleagues in the north-east lost their seats and the number of Conservative women MPs was cut from twelve to six.

Ward's lifelong campaign against injustice and in defence of the individual stemmed from her belief that though she had known 'hard luck', many others had known harder luck and she had a duty to them. The first of the four private members' bills which she successfully introduced (still an unbroken record at the end of the century) was an amendment in 1937 to the Poor Law Act, allocating 2s. weekly pocket money to elderly inhabitants in poor-law institutions. She championed international as well as national and constituency causes. Between 1933 and 1935 she campaigned to ensure that Indian women's suffrage was incorporated into the Government of India Bill. In 1937 and 1938 she was a member of a committee of MPs concerned with the evacuation of women and children during the Spanish Civil War; and she represented Britain at the League of Nations. During the Second World War she was concerned with issues of women's employment and equal pay; she chaired the women's power committee, which advised the Ministry of Labour, and visited factories and Auxiliary Territorial Service bases. From August 1943 to February 1944 she travelled through China, India, and the Middle East on behalf of the Ministry of Information, explaining the British war effort; later she visited newly liberated France.

After losing her Wallsend seat in the 1945 general election Ward embarked on more official speaking tours overseas; she also toured camps for displaced persons in Palestine and Germany and attended the Nuremberg trials with her friend Thelma Cazalet-Keir. This work and her appointment as a Newcastle JP absorbed some of her prodigious energy until she was adopted by the Conservatives as prospective parliamentary candidate for Tynemouth in 1946. She was returned to parliament in 1950. The 1950s and early 1960s saw Ward actively campaigning for women's economic rights, mainly through the Equal Pay Campaign Committee. She published an account of the Women's Transport Service, *F.A.N.Y. Invicta* (1955), and lobbied for an official history of the Special Operations Executive, an organization in which she had had many friends. She promoted the interests of nurses, service widows, pensioners, and others living on small incomes. Her 1954 private member's bill Right of Entry (Gas and Electricity Boards) protected householders' rights. She was also active on behalf of the Carl Rosa touring opera. She became the longest serving woman MP, holding the Tynemouth seat until the February 1974 general election, when she stood down. Her contribution to political life was acknowledged in a series of awards: CBE (1929), DBE (1955), CH (1973), and a life peerage (1974).

Irene Ward lacked the personal ambition of many of her contemporaries. Her manner had always been direct and she never lacked courage, but in later life her understanding of the complexities of an issue was sometimes imperfect and her political judgement questionable. Her political style and willingness to harry governments, even to the extent of being excluded from the house for five days by the speaker in 1968, made her a popular but also, in the eyes of some commentators, a slightly odd national figure. The large hats, capacious handbags, and bold jewellery she favoured might appear to mirror her personality but her character was more complex. Some found her difficult to know but her kindness was remembered fondly by many. Although several men were attracted to her, she does not appear to have had any intimate relationships. She once remarked enigmatically (Sleight, 107) that she would have liked to marry, though only if she could have married the man she wanted. An undated note in her papers records her belief that work and charity could compensate for the absence of love. The pivotal figures in her life were her mother and Sir Cecil Cochrane. Outside politics her great interest was travelling. Domestic bases were a flat in Gosforth, shared with her mother until the latter's death in 1944, Thelma Cazalet-Keir's house in Eaton Place, the Ladies' Carlton Club, and the Sloane Club in London, but her natural habitat was the houses of parliament. She died on 26 April 1980 in the Knaresborough Nursing Home, 7 Knaresborough Place, Kensington, London, following a fall. She was cremated and her ashes were transported by a fishing boat from her old constituency and scattered in the North Sea.   HELEN LANGLEY

Sources Bodl. Oxf., MSS Irene Ward · B. Harrison, interview with Irene Ward, 1977, Women's Library, London, British women's history in the 20th century series, tape 59 · P. Brookes, *Women at Westminster: an account of women in the British parliament, 1918–1966* (1967) · M. Pugh, *Women and the women's movement in Britain, 1914–1959* (1992) · J. Sleight, *Woman on the march* (1980) · Women's Library, London, Equal Pay Campaign Committee MSS · Irene Ward press cuttings, Women's Library, London · press cuttings relating to Irene Ward, Newcastle upon Tyne City Library · Tynemouth conservative party files, Newcastle City Archives · T. Cazalet-Keir, *From the wings* (1967) · U. Reading L., Lady Astor MSS · J. Mann, *Woman in parliament* (1962) · E. Summerskill, *A woman's world* (1967) · b. cert. · d. cert. · private information (2004) [D. Greenslade, B. Wright, E. Standing, H. Balfour, Lord Walker, Baroness Castle, Baroness Thatcher, D. Butler, M. R. D. Foot] · *WWW*

Archives Bodl. Oxf., corresp. and papers · Newcastle upon Tyne Central Library, press cuttings · Women's Library, London, press cuttings | Tyne and Wear Archives Service, Newcastle upon Tyne, Tynemouth conservative party files · Women's Library, London, equal pay campaign committee MSS | SOUND BL NSA, Bow dialogues, 18 June 1968, C 812/20 C2 · BL NSA, documentary recordings

Likenesses Turnbridge, photograph, *c*.1940, Hult. Arch. · Elliott & Fry, photograph, NPG [*see illus.*] · photograph, NPG · photographs, North of England Open Air Museum, Beamish, co. Durham

Wealth at death £44,691: probate, 9 Sept 1980, *CGPLA Eng. & Wales*

Ward, James (1769–1859), painter and printmaker, was born on 23 October 1769 in Thames Street, London, the middle of five children of James Ward, fruit merchant, and his wife, Rachael (1736/7–1835). He was baptized at All Hallows-the-Great, Upper Thames Street, on 12 November, that same year.

Early life and training Ward's father was intemperate in his habits, and, as a result, at the time of James's birth the family's fortunes had declined. Although his elder brother, William *Ward, attended school, Ward did not, and in later years he was self-conscious about his lack of formal education. When he was twelve he was apprenticed, like his brother William, to the engraver John Raphael Smith, although Ward subsequently claimed that he had little encouragement from his master, and his apprenticeship was terminated after fewer than two years because of problems between them. He completed his indenture with his brother. It was during his apprenticeship to Smith that James demonstrated his artistic ability, reportedly reproducing from memory a drawing by Henry Fuseli. The few extant drawings from this period attest to his youthful skills.

From the outset of his career Ward was a successful and highly respected mezzotint engraver of works by other artists. However, engravers were not eligible for election to the Royal Academy, and Ward therefore decided to abandon his lucrative career as an interpreter of the works of others and to dedicate himself to painting. The artists who employed Ward tried to persuade him to remain a printmaker, and he continued to create prints, especially after his own compositions; in the 1820s he also became a very accomplished lithographer. Ward donated a large collection of his prints in various states to the British Museum. In 1794 he was appointed painter and

engraver in mezzotint to the prince of Wales. On 4 December he married Mary Ann Ward (*d.* 1819; no relation) at the parish church of St Marylebone, London.

Of the several children of James and Mary Ann Ward, **George Raphael Ward** (1799–1878) became a painter and engraver. He was born on 17 July 1799 and was baptized on 8 November that year at St Mary's, St Marylebone Road. After studying under his father in 1822 he entered the Royal Academy Schools, when his age was given as twenty-one. The following year he won a silver medal at the Society of Arts and continued to exhibit, particularly at the Royal Academy and New Water Colour Society until 1864. On 30 December 1827 he married Mary Webb, with whom he had a daughter, Henrietta Mary Ada *Ward (1832–1924), also an artist, who became the wife of Edward Matthew *Ward (1816–1879), historical genre painter. George Ward became a miniaturist and engraver, and made copies in miniature after portraits by Sir Thomas Lawrence. He signed these G. R. Ward and on some gave his address as 7 Newman Street, Oxford Street. Foskett commented of that 'at its best [his work] is good', his 'colours pleasant with blue-grey shadows'; some works, she noted, were executed 'in a continental style of painting' (Foskett, 671). Walter Armstrong noted that Ward was 'better known, however, by his engraved portraits, which show considerable skill' (*DNB*). Examples of his mezzotint engravings are in the National Portrait Gallery's collection. George Ward died on 18 December 1878.

Early painting career Ward's painting career is traditionally divided into two phases, the first dominated by the influence of George Morland, his brother-in-law, the second by Peter Paul Rubens, the great seventeenth-century Flemish master. However, such a division oversimplifies Ward's artistic development. When the young Ward began painting about 1790 both his subject matter and painting style were indebted to Morland. An early work such as *Old Grey Horse and Ass* (*c*.1791–3; V&A) demonstrates, in both its rustic subject matter and its style with loose brushwork, soft forms, and limited palette, how strong this influence was. Ward resented being labelled a student of Morland since he claimed that his brother-in-law, fearing competition, had taught him nothing. His so-called Rubensian phase was ushered in by his seeing in 1803 Rubens's *Château de Steen* (National Gallery, London). The picture had recently been acquired by the connoisseur Sir George Beaumont, and was in the studio of Ward's neighbour in Newman Street, Benjamin West, president of the Royal Academy. In response to this work Ward painted *Bulls Fighting with a View of St Donat's Castle in the Background* (1803; V&A).

There is no doubt that Ward was much influenced by the loosely painted rustic genre scenes of Morland and the richly colored baroque compositions of Rubens. However, the sources of Ward's mature style were numerous and diverse; they ranged from the Elgin marbles and other classical sculpture to old masters including Titian, Van Dyck, Paulus Potter, and Rembrandt as well as Rubens. He also studied animal and human anatomy and sketched constantly from nature. In the mid-1790s Ward had access to the Orléans collection that had come to England from revolutionary France to be sold; he engraved a number of the works for the art dealer Michael Bryan. Ward subsequently painted Bryan's family group portrait (*c*.1797–8; Laing Art Gallery, Newcastle upon Tyne), which shows the impact of Titian's palette on his early style. He was also familiar with the work of his British predecessors and contemporaries such as George Stubbs and P. J. de Loutherbourg, and occasionally looked to them for compositional and technical ideas. Ward's animal portraits are particularly indebted to Stubbs's compositions in which a horse or a dog is silhouetted against an expansive landscape, while a heightening of his colour reveals an admiration for the dramatic intensity of de Loutherbourg's palette.

At the turn of the century Ward created a series of paintings for the board of agriculture which set out to record the various breeds of livestock in Britain; the compositions were then engraved by Boydell. This undertaking clearly had nationalistic overtones during a period of ongoing hostilities with France. Championed by Lord Somerville, one of Ward's earliest patrons, the project was never completed. The paintings, for example *A Durham Bull* (*c*.1802; Nottingham Castle Museum), often incorporated landscape vignettes that are reminiscent of the compositions of Thomas Bewick, and their composition, fluidity of brushwork, rich coloration, and meticulous rendering of detail suggest Ward's many sources. Tireless in his efforts to gather information on British livestock, Ward travelled extensively throughout England. In the process he executed a large body of drawings that he utilized throughout his long life.

Ward hoped to establish his reputation with *Bulls Fighting* and *Liboya Serpent Seizing its Prey* (lost). The latter, painted on a monumental scale, depicted a serpent wrapping itself around an African seated on a white horse. Both these paintings may have had allegorical meanings with the former perhaps alluding to the current struggle between France and England and the latter to the evils of the slave trade. Ward was sympathetic to the anti-slavery movement and counted among his associates some of its leaders. *Bulls Fighting* is one of the earliest examples of Ward's use of parallel emotions in humans and animals, a common artistic conceit of the time, to underscore the drama taking place. Instead of gaining the approval of the artistic establishment, *Bulls Fighting* and *Liboya Serpent* brought on a temporary rupture with the Royal Academy. In part owing to its size, *Liboya Serpent* was rejected for exhibition and *Bulls Fighting* was relegated to an undesirable position. In a pique, Ward requested that he be allowed to withdraw the latter, and his petition was reluctantly granted. The rift was soon healed, however, as Ward recognized the importance of the academy to his professional future, and successfully sought amends through the diarist and painter Joseph Farington, as well as through other academicians. Ward was elected an associate of the Royal Academy in 1807, and was made a full

academician in 1811. By this time he had established himself as an animal painter of the first order and his accomplishments could not be ignored by the art establishment, although some of his fellow artists found him vulgar.

Middle period Ward's portrait of a celebrated stallion, *Eagle* (1809; Yale U. CBA) was critical in establishing his reputation. The *Sporting Magazine*'s opinion was that the painting established Ward as 'the first of English animal painters now living' (1811, 265). *Eagle* exudes the power and force typical of Ward's finest animal portraits and with its anatomical detail and rich colouring also reveals some of the influences that shaped Ward's mature style. Shown in profile, the horse dominates a vast Rubensian landscape that seems to stretch to infinity beneath a brilliant Venetian-coloured sky.

Works such as *Eagle* brought Ward numerous patrons from the merchant class, landed gentry, and aristocracy. His one surviving account book, now on deposit at the Royal Academy, covers the period 1804 to 1827, when Ward became one of Britain's greatest animal painters. The majority of the commissions were for horse portraits, but the book also details paintings of other animals as well as landscapes and genre subjects. Ward also produced several major religious and history pictures at this time, such as *The Waterloo Allegory*, *Pool of Bethesda*, and *Battle near Boston*. The records of both the Royal Academy and the British Institution from these decades also suggest the artist's activity and ambition through the number of works exhibited and the subjects treated.

Despite receiving recognition as an outstanding animal painter Ward told Farington that he did not 'wish to be admitted to the Academy as a Horse-Painter', which he considered a lower form of art (Farington, *Diary*, 20 June 1811). The painting Ward submitted as his diploma piece, *A Bacchanalian* (1811; RA), underscores his aspirations. Although such works can be appreciated for their technical facility, they do not today occupy a high place in his *œuvre* nor were they generally admired at the time. On the other hand, Ward's animal paintings remain among the finest works he created and justify his being considered a major artist of the early nineteenth century.

Throughout the 1810s and 1820s Ward remained in great demand as a horse painter. Among the most important of his works are the portraits he made of horses in the early 1820s, especially those related to the combatants of the Napoleonic wars: Napoleon's charger Marengo (1824; priv. coll.); the duke of Wellington's Copenhagen (priv. coll.); and George IV's Nonpareil (Royal Collection). Although portraits of specific animals, the horses and landscapes also symbolized their owners. When exhibited at the Royal Academy in 1826, the landscape in the painting of Marengo (Napoleon's charger) was said to be emblematic of Napoleon's downfall. The setting sun and the horse's agitated appearance as it stares across a dark sea underscore the painting's message. When seen with *Copenhagen* (1824), it is clear that the two pictures were intended as companion pieces with Napoleon's steed looking to the right with fear across the channel at the horse of the duke of Wellington. *Copenhagen* is posed in a rolling English landscape, calm but wary, clearly prepared for what might happen. *Nonpareil* (1824) is placed in a landscape with Windsor in the background. The horse in proud majesty stands sentinel over its domain. These three portraits belong to a series of pictures of celebrated horses published as lithographs by Ackermann in 1823–4.

Gordale Scar* and *The Waterloo Allegory In the two decades following his election as academician Ward produced some of his finest works. The subject matter varied enormously. In addition to animal paintings such as *Eagle* and portraits of men and animals hunting in a landscape, for example *Theophilus Levett and a Favourite Hunter* (1817; Yale U. CBA), Ward also attempted some of his most ambitious and monumental canvases, including *Gordale Scar* (1812–14; Tate collection), *The Waterloo Allegory* (1815–21), for which now only a large finished study exists (1815; Royal Hospital, Chelsea), and *Group of Cattle* (1822; Tate collection).

Commissioned by Lord Ribblesdale, whose son, Thomas Lister, studied with Ward, *Gordale Scar* depicts a dramatic site in Yorkshire. It is Ward's masterpiece. Guarded over by an aboriginal white bull and populated with a host of animals that could not fit within the topographical limitations of the actual scar, the dark and towering scene is a fine example of the sublime in British art. Other landscapes by Ward from the same period reflect the aesthetic ideas of the beautiful (*Tabley Lake and Tower*, 1814; Tate collection) and picturesque (*A Cow-Layer: Evening after Rain*, also called *Cattle-Piece? Marylebone Park*, 1807; Tate collection) that were also current at the time.

The Waterloo Allegory was commissioned by the British Institution after a competition to commemorate the victory of Wellington over Napoleon at Waterloo. Reportedly cut up when it was returned to Ward's descendants about 1880, it was a gigantic canvas that measured 21 x 35 feet. Its complex iconography, which includes a portrait of the duke of Wellington, representations of Britannia, and the visualizations of abstract concepts such as religion, charity, and envy, was adapted from a variety of sources, and the overall composition is indebted to Rubens's *The Sacrament Triumphant over Ignorance and Blindness*. The painting's apocalyptic imagery as well as the elaborate explanation reflect to some extent the ideas of the German mystic Jacob Böhme. Exhibited in London with an admission fee at the Egyptian Hall in Piccadilly, *The Waterloo Allegory* was a failure, financially and critically. Angered by the response, Ward set out to prove his detractors wrong by painting *Group of Cattle* (1822; Tate collection), a life-size canvas conceived to compete with Paulus Potter's *Young Bull* (Mauritshuis, The Hague). This monumental painting (129½ x 191 inches) was purchased by the National Gallery in 1862; it has not been on view for decades. As in many of Ward's paintings, the animals take on an almost anthropomorphic quality, and in subsequent works such as *The Deer-Stealer* (1822; Tate collection), *Day's Sport* (1826; Yale U. CBA), and *L'amour du cheval* (1827; Tate collection), he explored even further than he had in the past parallel emotions between man and beast.

Retirement and death When Ward was working on *The Waterloo Allegory* his wife and two of his children died. With personal tragedy and professional problems, the artist turned increasingly to religion for solace and subjects. However, he still sought and executed animal portraits. In the late 1820s and 1830s he travelled to Newmarket and other parts of East Anglia in search of commissions. Letters and notebooks dealing with these trips are in the Research Library at the Getty Research Institute, Los Angeles. On 27 October 1827 Ward married Charlotte Fritche (*b.* before 1778), a family friend. Three years later the couple retired to Cheshunt, Hertfordshire.

Prior to the departure for Cheshunt, Ward sold at Christies many works from his studio and rented out his house in Newman Street. Now aged sixty, the artist was clearly putting his life in order. There were many reasons for the move from London, not least of which were his wife's preference for country life and financial problems involving his children. But Ward also had an apocalyptic view of the future, and he expressed these sentiments in letters to friends and in the treatise *New Trial of the Spirits* (1835), which was a defence of Edward Irving, whose Catholic Apostolic Church was near Ward's house in Newman Street. Convinced that he was one of the elect and with strong millenarian beliefs, Ward saw in contemporary events signs of the second coming and warnings about the approaching end of the world.

Ward considered painting his religious duty. Although he continued to portray animals and regularly sent works to exhibition, he became increasingly divorced from the art world and his non-commissioned works were often religious. *Intercession* (1837), which depicted Christ at the last few moments on the cross, was so criticized when it was exhibited at the Royal Academy that Ward was stung into response. The next year eight works, all somehow dealing with this slight, were exhibited. The most pertinent was *Tickling the Ear* (1838), in which a monkey (critic) sitting on the back of a bull (British public) tickles the animal's ear with a peacock feather (flattery). *Ignorance, Envy and Jealousy*, formerly *Miranda and Caliban* (1837; Royal Shakespeare Theatre, Stratford upon Avon), dealt with the critic's calumny concerning Ward's religious beliefs; the iconography is indebted to Böhme.

Not infrequently Ward's exhibition pictures had lengthy explanations or poems, written by the artist, in the catalogue. He also wrote pamphlets that dealt with such things as cruelty to animals in the docking of a horse's tail and a defence of a beard (his was long and white). Even when, about 1840, he painted a series of pictures devoted to the life of the horse, the works had strong moralistic overtones. Although ostensibly about horses, these paintings were actually conceived as a means of exploring man's spiritual and moral state by comparing human and animal conditions, as is evident from the descriptions in the catalogue for the exhibition at Newman Street in 1841.

For the next twelve years Ward continued to exhibit

regularly at both the Royal Academy and the British Institution. Although he still occasionally produced a significant work, both his technical and his mental powers were on the decline. His painting became increasingly mannered and his compositions could be awkward. *The Council of Horses* (exh. RA, 1848) was one of his last major works to sell to an important collector, Robert Vernon. At the time Ward's financial situation was so bad that he had petitioned the Royal Academy the previous year for a pension of £100 annually, and received the grant. He continued to paint, and two landscapes dealing with the cruelty of deer-hunting, exhibited at the academy in 1852, served as a coda to his long career. A few years later he suffered a stroke and his career was at an end. He died on 16 November 1859 at his home, Round Croft Cottage, Cheshunt, Hertfordshire, and was buried in Kensal Green, London. He was survived by his wife.

James Ward was considered by his contemporaries to be the greatest animal painter of his generation; however, his *œuvre* covered a wide range of subject matter from landscape to portraiture (human as well as animal), from genre to history painting (allegorical, religious, literary, and mythological subjects), and even an occasional still life. Extraordinarily prolific, Ward produced hundreds of paintings and thousands of drawings during his long life. But his output was also extremely uneven. His greatest works were executed in the first quarter of the nineteenth century. The large quantity and varying quality of his work make a balanced evaluation of him as an artist difficult. Nevertheless, he ranks among the leading artists of the British Romantic movement, particularly in his depiction of horses and in his rendering of dramatic landscapes. Examples of his work are held by many public collections, including the Tate collection, Victoria and Albert Museum, and National Portrait Gallery in London, the Ashmolean Museum, Oxford, the Walker Art Gallery, Liverpool, and the Yale Center for British Art, New Haven, Connecticut.   EDWARD J. NYGREN

Sources E. Nygren, *The art of James Ward* (1980) • E. Nygren, 'James Ward's exhibition pictures of 1838', *Art Bulletin*, 61/3 (Sept 1979), 448–59 • E. Nygren, *James Ward's 'Gordale Scar'* (1982) • O. Beckett, *The life and works of James Ward* (1995) • G. E. Fussell, *James Ward, RA, animal painter* (1974) • J. Munro, *James Ward, R.A., 1769–1859* (1991) • C. R. Grundy, *James Ward, R.A.* (1909) • Farington, *Diary* • D. Foskett, *Miniatures: dictionary and guide* (1987) • d. cert. • *CGPLA Eng. & Wales* (1860) • IGI • www.npg.org.uk, 10 Jan 2003 • S. C. Hutchison, 'The Royal Academy Schools, 1768–1830', *Walpole Society*, 38 (1960–62), 123–91, esp. 175

Archives Getty Research Institute, Research Library, papers • RA, papers | V&A NAL, letters to Mr and Mrs Garle and miscellanea, 86.00.7

Likenesses stipple, pubd 1826, BM, NPG • J. Ward, self-portrait, oils, 1830, Yale U. CBA • J. Ward, self-portrait, 1834, NPG • J. Ward, self-portrait, oils, 1848, NPG

Wealth at death under £1000: probate, 16 April 1860, *CGPLA Eng. & Wales*

Ward, James [Jem] (**1800–1884**), pugilist and artist, was born near Ratcliffe Highway (now the Highway), London, the eldest son of a butcher, later a ballast-heaver, stated as being either Nathaniel or Nicholas Ward. His date of birth has been variously given as 14, 25, or 26 December 1800.

From an early age he displayed talent as a boxer and he later recalled his first fight as being against George Robinson when seven months short of sixteen years of age (*Daily Telegraph*, 11 Nov 1881). He soon became a leading light in a sparring club at Bromley New Town to which all budding East End of London aspirants to 'milling' fame repaired. At the time he was pursuing the occupation of coal-whipper, 'unloading sea-borne coals in the Pool [of London]', hence his cognomen of the Black Diamond (*Morning Advertiser*, 4 April 1884). His formal introduction to the Fives Court, St Martin's Street, then the haunt of the fancy, took place on 22 January 1822 and, in sparring with Joe Spencer, he showed great promise.

Ward's first appearance in the field was at Moulsey Hurst, Surrey, on 12 June of the same year, when he beat Dick Acton in six rounds. On 10 September following he easily overcame Young Burke of Woolwich and next met Bill Abbott on 22 October. To please his backer, Ward allowed his opponent to win but, having confessed his duplicity, all bets were declared off. On 4 February 1823, at Wimbledon Common, he defeated Ned Baldwin, known as Whiteheaded Bob, in twenty rounds lasting nineteen minutes. During a sparring tour of the provinces he was involved in a further act of dishonesty. At the conclusion of Bath races on 4 July he beat Rickens, a native of the city, who was tricked into the match, being unaware of Ward's true identity. Ward then travelled to Southampton, where, on 20 August, after the races, he comfortably defeated the much inferior Johnson. Back in London he was matched to fight Josh Hudson for £100 a side at Moulsey Hurst on 11 November 1823 but was forced to concede to his resolute opponent. At Colnbrook, near Slough, on 21 June 1824, he conquered the Birmingham Youth, Phil Sampson, in fifty minutes. The two met again at Perry Lodge, 4 miles from Stony Stratford, on 28 December 1824. From the first Sampson never had much chance of victory and was vanquished in twenty-seven rounds.

Ward was now at the height of his fame and, disputing Tom Cannon's self-elected right to the title of champion of England, accepted the latter's open challenge for £1000 (*Pierce Egan's Life in London*, 20 Feb 1825). The encounter took place near Warwick on 19 July 1825 in the presence of an immense number of persons of varying character and class. Cannon fell insensible in the tenth round, his bustling style not being suited to the excessive heat of the day. Ward was proclaimed the winner and on 22 July, at the Fives Court, was presented with a belt bearing the inscription 'British Champion'. He remained without a match until 2 January 1827, when he fought Peter Crawley at Royston Heath, near Cambridge, and was beaten in a manly battle occupying eleven rounds. Crawley retired two days later and Ward immediately laid claim to the title. His next encounter was with Jack Carter, on 27 May 1828, at Shepperton Range, Middlesex. Youth and science triumphed over age and Carter was defeated in thirty-two minutes.

On 10 March 1829 Ward was due to meet the Irishman Simon Byrne for the championship at Leicester but at the last minute declined to enter the ring. His conduct was greatly condemned, his backers and friends abandoned him, and the Fair Play Club refused to allow him to fight under their jurisdiction. For two years he stayed inactive before meeting Byrne on 12 July 1831 at Willeycott, near Stratford upon Avon. The contest, for £200 a side, lasted one hour and seventeen minutes and, with the defeat of the Irishman, Ward's final battle for the championship of England ended. On the following Thursday he was presented with a second champion's belt at Reuben Marten's Tennis and Fives Court, Peter Street, Soho. When the stake money was given up the next day, Ward offered to make a match with any man in England for a sum from £100 to £500, but the challenge was not accepted.

In a letter to the editor of *Bell's Life in London*, written on 24 January 1832 (printed on 29 January), Ward stated that he was retiring from the ring and had commenced trading as a publican at The Belt, Whitechapel, Liverpool. On 8 September 1831 he had married Eliza, daughter of former pugilist George Cooper; their only child, Eleanor, was born on 1 September 1832. A pupil of the composer and conductor Sir Julius Benedict, Eleanor Ward subsequently earned public acclaim as an accomplished pianist. Ward himself later carried on business at The Star inn and then the York Hotel, both in Williamson Square, before moving to London in 1853. There he was host of various hostelries including The Rose, 96 Jermyn Street; the Three Tuns (renamed the Champion Stores), 429 Oxford Street; the King's Arms, Whitechapel Road; The George, Ratcliffe Highway; the Sir John Falstaff, Brydges Street (now Catherine Street); and the Harlequin tavern, 69 Drury Lane.

In conjunction with his profession as a publican, Ward also became an artist, creating numerous landscapes and other pieces of unquestionable merit. His paintings were displayed at more than one of the Liverpool exhibitions and earned praise from the press of the time. Perhaps his best-known work was *The Sayers and Heenan Fight*, a very large picture containing 270 portraits, produced in 1860. He was also a talented musician, playing the violin, flute, flageolet, piano, and guitar, besides being a competent pigeon-shooter and quoits player. His manners were mild and unassuming, and in his fighting prime he was described by a friend as 'a man only in the ring, a child out of it' (*Weekly Dispatch*, 4 July 1824). This may account for his occasionally being led astray during his pugilistic career, something that he greatly regretted in later life.

Ward's interest in painting and music did little to encourage his success as a sporting publican and, at length, after several failures in business, he retired to the Licensed Victuallers' Asylum in the Old Kent Road. There, well past his eightieth birthday, he could still be found actively producing saleable landscapes in both watercolour and oils. He died at the asylum on 2 April 1884 and was buried six days later at Nunhead cemetery in the same grave where already reposed his wife and grandson.

Nicholas Ward (1813–1850), younger brother of James, also aspired to fistic glory but, despite being a scientific boxer, did not have the commitment required to become a first-rate pugilist. Although he followed in the title-winning footsteps of his more illustrious sibling, his ring performances were generally uninspired. Nicholas Ward's championship victory over Ben Caunt on 2 February 1841 was entirely due to the latter's impetuosity, and three months later, having yielded submissively to the same fighter, he ended his 'milling' career.

G. C. BOASE, *rev.* TONY GEE

Sources H. D. Miles, *Pugilistica*, 2 (1880), 199–232 · *Morning Advertiser* (4 April 1884) · *The Sportsman* (4 April 1884) · *Reynolds's Newspaper* (6 April 1884) · *Liverpool Echo* (5 April 1884) · *Bell's Life in London* (5 April 1884) · *Sporting Chronicle* [Manchester] (10 April 1884) · fight reports, etc., *Bell's Life in London*; *Weekly Dispatch*; *Star Daily Evening Advertiser*; *Pierce Egan's Life in London*; *Pierce Egan's Weekly Courier*; *Trades' Newspaper and Mechanics' Weekly Journal*; *Morning Chronicle*; *The Times* · J. Ward, letter, *Pierce Egan's Life in London* (20 Feb 1825) · J. Ward, letter, *Bell's Life in London* (29 Jan 1832) · One of the crowd, 'How the poor live', *Daily Telegraph* (11 Nov 1881) · *Weekly Dispatch* (4 July 1824) · *Illustrated Sporting News* (14 Feb 1863) · *Licensed Victuallers' Gazette and Hotel Courier* (8 June 1888) [profile] · *Famous fights in the prize ring* (1877), 245–7, 254–6, 258–9, 263–4, 269–72 · E. Mingaud, *The life and adventures of James Ward* (1882) · Pendragon, 'Sporting notions', *Referee* (24 Feb 1884) · Pendragon, 'Sporting notions', *Referee* (2 March 1884) · Pendragon, 'Sporting notions', *Referee* (16 March 1884) · Pendragon, 'Sporting notions', *Referee* (24 March 1884) · [F. Dowling], *Fights for the championship; and celebrated prize battles* (1855), 83–8, 93–122 · [F. L. Dowling], *Fistiana, or, The oracle of the ring* (1866), 120–21 · d. cert.

Likenesses McInnes, engraving, 1835 (after W. Daniels) · Woolnoth, engraving, 1835 (after Fingel) · H. Adlard, stipple (after T. Wageman), BM, NPG · Robert, engraving (after Cruikshank) · W. Thomas, engraving (after Patten, 1826), repro. in Miles, *Pugilistica* · portrait (after a photograph), repro. in *Illustrated Sporting News*; priv. coll.

Ward, James (1843–1925), philosopher and psychologist, was born at Hull on 27 January 1843, the eldest of the nine children of James Ward and his wife, Hannah Aston. His father was a clever and ambitious, but extremely unsuccessful, merchant, whose frequent business failures were a burden to the family. James Ward was educated briefly at the Liverpool Institute. At the age of eleven, during a brief period of family prosperity, he was sent to Mostyn House, a preparatory school for Rugby School at Parkgate on the Wirral peninsula. Two years later, when his father went bankrupt, his formal schooling ended. The family settled in a small house at Waterloo, a village near Liverpool, and James was left free to roam the neighbouring sandhills. For the first time he became aware of the pleasures of the natural world. Later he said, 'it was here that the optimism began, in those wild wastes absolutely untouched by the hand of man; ... all was beautiful, all was good, and I was one with it all' (Campbell, 8).

Ward's father arranged for his apprenticeship to a firm of architects in Liverpool before Ward turned sixteen. The father had noticed James's talent for draughtsmanship when he asked him to sketch an invention—one of the father's many failed business schemes. Ward's architectural experiences did not make much of an impression on his later life, except that he retained enough knowledge to torment the architects whom he later hired. In this period Ward studied Greek and logic, and he was also an enthusiastic Sunday school teacher. After four years of office work he decided, to his family's delight, to become a minister.

Ward, like his family, was a Congregationalist, biblical and Calvinist in his theology. In 1863 he managed to enter Spring Hill College, near Birmingham (later absorbed in Mansfield College, Oxford). He remained there until 1869, taking the London BA degree examinations, along with his theological course. His time there was not unhappy, although he was harassed by the bad health which was to bedevil him his entire life, by his insufficient means, and possibly already by religious doubt.

Funded by a scholarship Ward went to Germany, where he encountered a new theological environment and became immersed in speculations on fundamental problems. Living at the Dom Candidatenstift in Berlin, a college for German ministers, he attended the lectures of Isaac August Dorner. In the spring of 1870 he moved to Göttingen to study under Rudolf Hermann Lotze, who exerted a permanent influence on his thought; he left at the outbreak of the Franco-Prussian War. Unsettled and unsettling as his speculations were, Ward still saw himself as a Christian.

After returning to Britain Ward went to Cambridge, where he preached for a month at Emmanuel Congregational Chapel. He accepted a call to be its minister in January 1871, and although never ordained, remained until March 1872. His preaching was controversial. Never very charismatic, his liberal tone offended some of the congregation, in particular many of those involved in fundraising for a new chapel. At the same time, in what he later recalled as the most unhappy period of his life, a struggle was going on in his own mind which led Ward to conclude that his teaching was not appropriate to the Christian pulpit.

The Cambridge philosopher Henry Sidgwick persuaded Ward that there were other possibilities for him, and at twenty-nine Ward entered Cambridge University as a non-collegiate student. Although not estranged from his family—he made payments to his father's creditors for the entirety of his father's long life—Ward was never again as close to them. His university entry was the first step away from his past life. In 1873 he gained an open scholarship at Trinity College, a year later he was placed alone in the first class in the moral science tripos, and in 1875 he was elected to a fellowship at Trinity which he held for the remainder of his life. The break with his former career was complete: he always held himself aloof from institutional religion, but he did not tend towards secularism or even agnosticism. His early belief in spiritual values and his respect for all sincere religion never left him: 'he buried the past, he burned his boats; but he remained for all that a native of other shores' (Campbell, 47).

Ward's academic career then followed a normal course, but rather slowly. He began lecturing for the moral sciences tripos in 1878, through Sidgwick's influence became a college lecturer in 1881, and in 1897 was appointed to the newly founded professorship of mental philosophy and logic.

Like many who moved away from evangelical religion, as Ward's religious fervour faded his interest in nature revived. One day, on a walk, 'the old feeling of the would-be naturalist of ten years ago rose up and confronted the self-excommunicated sceptic' (Campbell, 47). It is worth noting that the first publications of this new period were two short communications, 'Animal locomotion', in *Nature* (1874).

Ward's fellowship dissertation, 'The relation of physiology to psychology', was printed but not published, although a portion of it, 'An attempt to interpret Fechner's law', appeared in the first volume of *Mind* (1876). After election to a fellowship he worked for the greater part of a year (1876–7) in Carl Ludwig's physiological institute at Leipzig. In light of Ward's later shift to the field of psychology it is somewhat ironic that there he apparently did not encounter Wilhelm Wundt, regarded as the founder of modern psychology. Wundt was already the holder of a philosophy chair at Leipzig, although his famous psychological institute was not set up until 1879. Back in Cambridge, Ward worked in Michael Foster's physiological laboratory. Ward's was now the career path of a promising young physiologist. Indeed, when he turned towards the domain of the mind and away from experimentalism, which he found frustrating, Michael Foster lamented that Ward was a 'physiologist spoiled' (Campbell, 72).

Ward published two physiological papers: 'Ueber die Auslösung von Reflexbewegungen durch eine Summe schwacher Reize' (*Archiv für Physiologie*, 1880)—actually written by Ludwig—and 'The physiology of the nervous system of the freshwater crayfish' (*Journal of Physiology*, 1879; abstract in *PRS*, 1879). But attracted as he was, and always remained, to research in natural science, Ward turned now to the study of psychology.

In 1880 Ward contributed the article on Johann Friedrich Herbart to the ninth edition of the *Encyclopaedia Britannica*; in 1880–81 he printed (without publishing) four papers on general analysis of mind and other fundamental problems in psychology, and in 1883 he began a series of articles in *Mind*, 'Psychological principles'. Ward planned a book, but first agreed to write the article 'Psychology' in the ninth edition of the *Encyclopaedia Britannica*. This article had an immediate and profound effect upon the teaching of psychology, and it is almost entirely due to the influence of the article that when *Psychological Principles* finally appeared in 1918, the *Times* reviewer dubbed Ward 'the Father of Modern British Psychology' (Turner, 209).

The most controversial of Ward's psychological doctrines concerned the standpoint of the science and what he called the 'general analysis' of mind. He disputed the contending contemporary approaches of physiologists and associationists: 'The standpoint of psychology is individualistic; by whatever method, from whatever sources its facts are ascertained, they must—to have a psychological import—be regarded as having place in, or as being part of, *some one's consciousness*.' By 'consciousness' Ward meant that where and only where there is an object presented to a subject are we in the domain of mind. The other sciences could disregard this fact of presentation as irrelevant for their purposes; but Ward contended that it was fundamental for psychology. Ward's 'subject', however, is not to be identified either with the 'soul' of rational psychology or with a nondescript 'mindstuff'. It is not a mere passive recipient of presentations; it feels and it acts (or attends). The feeling and the activity characterize the 'subject' only. From this position Ward worked out a system of psychology which contained many points of novelty—as in the account of space and time, the clear distinction between the perception and the conception of each, the bold extension of the doctrine of secondary automatism, the emphasis on the importance of subjective as well as natural selection in mental development, and the stress laid on the function of inter-subjective intercourse in leading to knowledge of the external world and of self.

In 1880 and for a few years afterwards Ward also lectured on education, and these lectures form the basis of his *Psychology Applied to Education* (1926). He was Gifford lecturer at Aberdeen University, 1895–8, and again at St Andrews University, 1907–10. In each case the result was an important philosophical treatise—*Naturalism and Agnosticism* (1899) and *The Realm of Ends, or, Pluralism and Theism* (1911). In 1912 he gave the Henry Sidgwick memorial lecture *Heredity and Memory* (published 1913) at Newnham College, Cambridge, where his wife, Mary, was a lecturer. Ward, like Sidgwick had been, was a strong supporter of the 'woman's cause'. He was among the first at Cambridge to open his lectures to women, and his wife, then Mary Martin, the daughter of a Congregationalist minister, was one of his most promising students. They married in 1884 and they had one son and two daughters.

Ward's politics were liberal and progressive, and he moved eventually from the Liberal to the Labour Party. The idealist philosopher and close colleague W. R. Sorley wrote: 'Not liberalism only but Nonconformity was in his blood, and he was always inclined to sympathize with the individual who appeared to be oppressed by the institution—whether church or state or trade-union' (Sorley, *Mind*, 275). Characteristically, during the First World War, Ward protested at the dismissal of Bertrand Russell—who later called Ward 'my chief teacher'—from his Trinity lectureship (Turner, 210).

After his first physiological articles Ward's early published work was almost entirely psychological, although his writings demonstrated a philosophical bent; after 1894 his work was mainly philosophical. Ward allied himself with prominent idealist philosophers, and flirted with personal idealism—he wrote on 6 December 1922 to F. H. Bradley: 'Your outlook on things and also Bosanquet's is that with which I am most anxious to orientate myself'. But he continued, 'But I must do it in my own way' (Bradley MSS, Merton College, Oxford). Ward, like many of his generation, retained the anti-dogmatism of his nonconformist childhood, and throughout his career resisted subscribing fully to any set of beliefs.

In the two Gifford lecture series Ward's philosophy was fully worked out. In both cases construction was preceded by an elaborate, and ultimately more convincing, criticism. In *Naturalism and Agnosticism* (1899) he began with the distinction between science and the philosophical theory to which it had been supposed to lead and with which it was often confused, and this opened the way for his refutation of naturalism with its satellite doctrines such as the mechanical theory of reality and psychophysical parallelism. Not all his points were new, but Ward's criticism gave the final blow to scientific naturalism and to its alliance with agnosticism as promulgated by Herbert Spencer and others. Ward contrasted the real world of history with the sterile, detached, and abstract world of science. In philosophy, he argued, we must proceed from an experience which implies a subject–object. In the argument which followed the subjective element was given a position of primacy, and the result was a theory of 'spiritualistic monadism' which interpreted the whole of reality from the side of the subject and whose objects were themselves always monads or arrangements of monads. This view was extended in *The Realm of Ends* (1911) after criticism of other forms of pluralism. Ward held, with Spinoza and Leibniz, that 'all individual things are animated, although in diverse degrees'. According to this form of pluralism reality consists of active subjects of experience interacting with an environment which consists of other spiritual monads; and these active beings have all a nisus towards goodness. It was chiefly this that led Ward to see the unity of the whole from the theistic standpoint. This essential optimism of Ward—almost 'an existentialist without angst' (Turner, 227)—divided his thought from the post-First World War world, and contributed to its perceived irrelevance. Ward did not think that theism could be proved, but he held that the idea of God alone enables us to co-ordinate our experience, and the concluding chapters of this book are a series of reflections on the cosmology of theism.

One of a number of late Victorian thinkers who turned against positivism and scientific reductionism, Ward was influential as both a psychologist and a philosopher in his own lifetime, but soon after his death in 1925 almost entirely forgotten. This was due somewhat to the eclecticism of his work, but the reputation of William James, the American psychologist and philosopher, who also began as a physiologist, did not suffer the same fate. In part the similarity of James's and Ward's own thought contributed to James's overshadowing Ward. Ward's contributions to psychology were further diminished because of his criticisms of the new experimental, physiological psychology associated with Wundt's laboratory. Although Ward may have fathered British psychology, in the end his child joined the move to experimentalism. James made similar criticisms of modern psychology, but still was credited with introducing the new German methods to America. As a philosopher Ward's most enduring contribution was his attack on the scientific naturalism of the late nineteenth century, but he dismantled it so effectively that his criticisms seemed quaint and redundant to the next generation of philosophers.

Much honoured in his lifetime, Ward received the honorary degree of LLD from Edinburgh University in 1889 and from his own university in 1920; he was a founding fellow of the British Academy, and was elected a *correspondant* of the Institut de France. He spent the summer and early autumn of 1904 in America, lecturing for a term at Berkeley in California, reading a paper at the Congress of Arts and Sciences held in connection with the St Louis Exhibition, and visiting friends in several universities.

Ward's last book was *A Study of Kant* (1922), and several shorter writings appeared in the three years that followed. He died at Cambridge on 4 March 1925. He was cremated, a memorial service being held for him at Trinity College on 8 March. His wife survived him.

W. R. SORLEY, *rev.* TERRIE M. ROMANO

Sources O. W. Campbell, 'Memoir', in J. Ward, *Essays in philosophy* (1927) · A. H. Murray, *The philosophy of James Ward* (1937) · F. M. Turner, 'James Ward: psychologist of faith and freedom', *Between science and religion: the reaction to scientific naturalism in late Victorian England* (1974), 201–45 · G. F. Stout and others, *The Monist* [Ward commemoration number], 36/1 (1926) [includes bibliography] · W. R. Sorley, *Mind*, new ser., 34 (1925), 273–9 · W. R. Sorley, 'James Ward, 1843–1925', *PBA*, 12 (1926), 306–16 · G. D. Hicks, 'The philosophy of James Ward', *Mind*, new ser., 34 (1925), 280–99 · G. S. Brett, *Modern psychology* (1921), vol. 3 of *A history of psychology* · G. L. Geison, *Michael Foster and the Cambridge school of physiology: the scientific enterprise in late Victorian society* (1978) · T. H. Leahy, *A history of psychology: main currents in psychological thought* (1997) · M. Wertheimer, *A brief history of psychology*, rev. edn (1979) · M. J. Walsh, *A history of philosophy* (1985) · *CGPLA Eng. & Wales* (1925)
Archives U. St Andr. L., corresp. | CUL, letters to G. E. Moore · King's Cam., letters to Oscar Browning · McMaster University, Hamilton, Ontario, letters to Bertrand Russell · Merton Oxf., MSS Bradley, letters to F. H. Bradley
Likenesses V. H. Mottram, portrait, 1911, repro. in J. Ward, *Essays in philosophy* (1927), between pp. 54 and 55 · A. McEvoy, oils, 1913, FM Cam. · P. Clarke (after photograph by Mottram, 1911), repro. in J. Ward, *Essays in philosophy* (1927), frontispiece · photograph (aged twenty-one), repro. in J. Ward, *Essays in philosophy* (1927), 3 · photograph (with Mary Ward, during the First World War), repro. in J. Ward, *Essays in philosophy* (1927), following pp. 90 and 91
Wealth at death £7066 5s. 3d.: probate, 6 May 1925, *CGPLA Eng. & Wales*

Ward, James Clifton (1843–1880), geologist, was born at Clapham Common, Surrey, on 13 April 1843, son of James Ward, schoolmaster, and his wife, Mary Ann (*née* Morris). After schooling at Hastings, Ward entered the Royal School of Mines in 1861 and gained the Edward Forbes medal in 1864. In 1865 he was appointed to the geological survey and worked for three years in the West Riding. In 1869 Ward was transferred to the Lake District where he worked for eight years, notably in the Keswick district. His important *Geology of the Northern Part of the Lake District* was published in 1876. On 11 January 1877 he married Elizabeth Ann Benson, daughter of Cockermouth solicitor Robert Benson. In 1878 he was ordained, and became assistant curate at St John's, Keswick.

Ward was one of the first survey geologists to deploy Henry Sorby's method of examining rock sections with a microscope, and applied it to the Lakeland lavas and ash beds. He adopted Andrew Ramsay's views on the glacial origins of lake basins and wrote several papers on glacial theory and glacial phenomena, giving support to the 'glacial submergence' theory.

Studying the Skiddaw Slates of northern Lakeland, Ward regarded them as rather gently folded with a thickness of about 12,000 feet. He examined the metamorphic aureole round the underlying Skiddaw Granite and figured this prominently in the survey's published sections. He sought to establish the depth and pressure under which the granite had formed, linking the stratigraphic evidence to that provided by microscopic examination of the liquid cavities of the granite's quartz crystals. The Slates were correlated with the Arenig (then regarded as Cambrian) rocks of north Wales, and the slates of the Isle of Man, both places where Ward worked for a time. Considering estimated rates of erosion, he suggested that the time elapsed since the Skiddaw Slates period was about 62 million years, in keeping with estimates of geological time favoured in his day. Ward contemplated the idea that granites might be of metamorphic origin, being associated with water in their formation.

Ward also worked on the difficult problems and terrain of what are now called the Borrowdale Volcanics, subdividing them into nine units, assigning the lower ones to the 'Cambrian', again by correlation with Welsh formations. He supposed that the central Lakeland massif had existed since the Palaeozoic era.

Ward was important in Lakeland intellectual life, helping to establish the Cumberland Association for the Advancement of Literature and Science and lecturing in the Keswick district. He collected information on archaeological sites in the region and displayed this, as well as the results of his geological researches, in maps and models in the Keswick Museum.

By all accounts, Ward was a man of most attractive character, cultured, a nature lover, serious-minded, and deeply religious. His field notes contain poems indicative of his romantic temperament and religious zeal. In 1880 he was appointed perpetual curate at Rydal, Westmorland, but taken ill with a chill he died on 16 April that year, survived by his wife and two daughters. He was only thirty-seven. He was buried in the churchyard of St John's, Keswick, on 20 April 1880.

DAVID OLDROYD

Sources R. Etheridge, 'Rev. James Clifton Ward', *Proceedings of the Geological Society of London*, 37 (1880–81), 41–3 · F. H. Day, 'The Rev. J. Clifton Ward', *Proceedings of the Cumberland Geological Society*, 1 (1964), 5–7 · T. V. H. [T. V. Holmes], 'Rev. James Clifton Ward', *Geological Magazine*, new ser., 2nd decade, 7 (1880), 334–6 · J. C. Ward, *The geology of the northern part of the Lake District* (1876) · private information (2004) [David M. Bowcock, Cumbria Archive Service; Keswick Museum] · personal knowledge (2004) · M. Reeks, *Register of the associates and old students of the Royal School of Mines* (1920), 200 · *CGPLA Eng. & Wales* (1880)
Likenesses photograph, Keswick Museum, Cumbria · photograph, BGS
Wealth at death under £2000: probate, 31 May 1880, *CGPLA Eng. & Wales*

Ward, John [*called* Issouf Reis, Captain Wardiyya] (c.1553–1623?), pirate, was said to have been a fisherman at Faversham, Kent, perhaps (from an informant's estimate of his age as fifty-five in 1608) born about 1553. He was later at

Plymouth, where he joined the Royal Navy, and may have been on privateering voyages to the West Indies. Apparently he served as a petty officer on the *Lion's Whelp*, built in 1601. His career of piracy seems to have begun in 1603 with an abortive attempt to seize the considerable wealth a recusant was reported to be carrying over to France. More successfully, he captured a large French ship (renamed the *Little John*). During 1604 Ward succeeded Edward Fall as leader of this pirate band, and after putting into Cawsand Bay on the coast of Cornwall to recruit more crew, he sailed for the Mediterranean, plundering as he went.

Arriving off Algiers, Ward received a hostile reception and so continued east, in December taking prizes at the mouth of the Adriatic. In 1605 he was at Salé, a nest of corsairs on Morocco's Atlantic shore, but by mid-1606 he had adopted Tunis as his base, commanding a 28-gun ship and other vessels with crews numbering 500. He was thus one of those European renegades who introduced the Barbary corsairs to the advantages for piracy of the berton or heavily armed square-rigged ship from northern waters. Later in 1606, accompanied by a pinnace of 50 tons, he cruised the eastern Mediterranean in a Flemish flyboat of 200 tons aptly named the *Gift*, manned not only by English, Dutch, and Spanish Christians but also by Turks. On this cruise he made his fortune by the capture of the *Rubin*, a Venetian argosy of 300 tons from Alexandria with a cargo of pepper, indigo, flax, and 3000 pieces of gold. Ward then fitted her out as a man-of-war, used some of his new wealth to redeem and recruit seamen from the prisons of Tunis, and put to sea again. In April 1607 he captured a second Venetian argosy, the *Reniera e Soderina*, ship and cargo being reputedly worth 'one hundred times a thousand pounds' (Ewen, 5–6) and then in June took a third. Ward sold the cargoes to Osman Bey, commander of the janizaries and *de facto* ruler of Tunis, turned the *Soderina* into a berton mounting sixty guns, and with a crew of 250 Turks and 150 Englishmen joined at least five other Dutch corsairs. Overgunned, top-heavy, slow, and with rotting timbers, the *Soderina* proved impractical as a warship. Ward transferred to a captured prize, leaving the *Soderina* to founder and her crew to drown off Cerigo early in 1608. Despite other reverses Ward was in both the eastern and western basins of the Mediterranean that year, capturing a Venetian galleon off the Peloponnese in March and bringing prizes into Algiers later in the year.

A description of Ward at this time records that he was:

> very short, with little hair, and that quite white, bald in front; swarthy face and beard. Speaks little, and almost always swearing. Drunk from morn till night. Most prodigal and plucky. Sleeps a great deal, and often on board when in port. The habits of a thorough 'salt'. A fool and an idiot out of his trade. (Ewen, 8)

Nevertheless about this time he was negotiating to retire to Tuscany with a fortune of 150,000 crowns.

In 1609 Ward continued his depredations: he was said to be off Sardinia in May with nine bertons, and his subordinate Bishop was off Ireland with ten or eleven ships and 1000 men in August. An English attempt to negotiate Ward's return to England failed, as did an attempt on his life, and despite a joint Spanish and French attack on Tunis which fired some thirty vessels, some apparently Ward's, he was said to be about to leave for Ireland with a squadron of fourteen vessels at the end of the year. By now his reputation in England was such that his exploits were celebrated not only by three ballads but by two pamphlets, neither factually reliable: *Newes from sea, of two notorious pyrats Ward the Englishman and Danseker the Dutchman, with a true relation of all or the most piraces by them committed unto the sixt of Aprill 1609* and *A true and certaine report of the beginning, proceedings, overthrowes, and now present estate of Captaine Ward and Dansker, the two late famous pirates; from their first setting foorth to this present time, as also with the death of divers of Wards chiefe captaines*.

The years 1610–12 repeated the pattern of previous years: during sweeps through the eastern Mediterranean at least two of Ward's vessels were shipwrecked in late 1610 but his fleet still had fifteen vessels and 1500 men; in June 1611 he was said to have left Tunis for either Calabria or the Adriatic; and in March 1612 he captured the *Valnegrina*, bound for Alexandria. In late 1610 he had converted to Islam, his apostasy being made the subject of Robert Daborne's play, *A Christian Turn'd Turke* (1612), in which the fictionalized Ward met his just deserts by being torn to pieces and his remains thrown into the sea. In the same year both he and Dansiker were named and discussed in Thomas Dekker's *If this be not a Good Play the Devil is in it*. According to the Venetians he took the name of Issouf Reis; to a Tunisian source of the late seventeenth century, itself a testimony to the longevity of his fame, he was Captain Wardiyya.

Clearly by 1612 he had given up any idea of leaving Tunis. In or before 1615 the Scottish traveller William Lithgow dined with him in Tunis at his 'faire Palace, beautified with rich Marble and Alabaster stones' (Ewen, 12) and in 1616 reported that Ward in his retirement had taken to rearing chicks by incubating eggs in camel dung. Ward may have gone to sea one last time in 1622. Apparently he died in Tunis during an outbreak of plague in the summer of 1623; his body was thrown into the sea. Besides a wife in England, there was another in Tunis: Jessimina, a Palermitan renegade.   DAVID R. RANSOME

Sources C. L'E. Ewen, *Captain John Ward, 'Arch-Pirate'* (1939) · C. M. Senior, *A nation of pirates* (1976) · C. Lloyd, *English corsairs on the Barbary coast* (1981) · N. Matar, *Turks, Moors, and Englishmen in the age of discovery* (New York, 1999) · *CSP Venice, 1607–23* · N. Matar, *Islam in Britain, 1558–1685* (1998)
Wealth at death unknown, but probably considerable

Ward, John (*bap.* 1590, *d.* 1638), composer and administrator, was baptized on 15 February 1590 at St Mary Bredman, Canterbury. His parents are not named in the baptismal record, but a visitation pedigree dated 1634 names his father as John Ward of Canterbury, son of William Ward of Yorkshire. His mother was Susan, daughter of Thomas Dunkin of Canterbury (Metcalfe, 518). This document, when checked against local baptismal records, may imply that John Ward senior was a singing man at Canterbury Cathedral, most probably the minor canon of that name who died in 1617. Another theory, however, is that the composer's father was a domestic servant of Elizabeth Smyth of Ashford and Westhanger who married, about 1594, Sir Henry Fanshawe of Ware Park, Hertfordshire, remembrancer of the exchequer and a patron of the arts. According to this theory, two John Wards served the Fanshawes, father (from before about 1594 until his death probably between February and August 1630), and son (the composer, from about 1607 until his death in 1638); but if the composer's father was indeed the cathedral singing man, then all references to the domestic servant must be taken to apply to the composer.

Ward the composer was a chorister at the cathedral from 1597 to 1604 and a king's scholar at the grammar school in Canterbury from 1604 to 1607. He subsequently joined Sir Henry Fanshawe's flourishing musical establishment; in his *First Set of English Madrigals* (1613) he addresses Sir Henry as 'my very good Maister' and claims that the contents are 'the primitiae of my Muse, planted in your pleasure, and cherisht by … your favour' (p. xv).

This work has until recently been the chief foundation of Ward's fame. Its contents proclaim him to be a very important figure among the English school of madrigalists who drew inspiration from contemporaries such as John Wilbye, George Kirbye, and Thomas Weelkes; his six-part works in particular have been praised for their musical quality. Other works of this type, unpublished in his lifetime, include elegies on the deaths of Henry, prince of Wales (1612) and of Fanshawe (1616), while the gap between sacred and secular, and vocal and instrumental music is filled by a small number of attractive consort songs (for voices and viols in parts ranging from three to six) set to colourful sacred texts and intended for domestic use. As a composer with important contacts at court (through his patron) Ward was widely respected by his contemporaries. This is reflected in the number of his works that occur in contemporary manuscripts and prints; these include two short contributions to Sir William Leighton's *Tears or Lamentations of a Sorrowful Soul* (1614) and an evening service setting and two anthems of outstanding quality included in John Barnard's *First Book of Selected Church Music* (1641).

When Fanshawe drew up his will in 1613 it was witnessed by John Ward, probably the composer's father but possibly the composer himself. Following Sir Henry's death in 1616 his son and successor in the remembrancership, Sir Thomas Fanshawe, gave less support to the family's musical establishment and it was probably about this time (and certainly by April 1621) that Ward obtained a modest post in the remembrancer's office. As an attorney or subordinate substitute for Sir Thomas in minor exchequer business he was thereafter desk-bound in London for much of his time. In 1619 Sir Thomas arranged for John Ward, gentleman (more likely the composer's father), to receive a grant from the king of the arrears owing to the crown on a yearly sum of £8 6s. 8d. out of the Fanshawes' manor of Bengeo, Hertfordshire. Two years later a Mr John Ward, 'servant of Sir Thomas Fanshawe', authorized to collect his patron's salary on the latter's behalf (BL, Add. MS 41578, fol. 101r) was probably the composer. However, the John Ward named as a trustee in a settlement by Elizabeth Fanshawe on 21 May 1629 of her manor of Dengey, Essex, was more likely to have been her servant, Ward senior; her will of 20 February 1630 was witnessed by John Ward, gentleman, referred to as the testatrix's 'auncient servant'.

Ward the composer married Thomasine, daughter of Thomas Clee of London, 'dwelling nere the Tower dock' (*Visitations of Essex*, 518), about 1625 and they at first probably lived in the Fanshawes' Warwick Lane mansion. However, it was at Barking, Essex, that their fifth child, Mary, apparently was baptized in August 1630 and buried on 2 January 1633. This suggests that John Ward senior, who had built up a modest estate at Great Ilford, a village in Barking parish, had recently died and that the composer and his wife had moved their household from Warwick Lane to Ilford. According to the terms of the Dengey trust deed of 1629 the place of each trustee would be taken at his death by his heir, and 'Johannes Ward generous' (presumably the composer) appears as a 'farmer' of the manor in surviving court rolls dated 1632, 1634, and 1636. Ward was still at his post in the remembrancer's office in May 1638 but died that summer; his will, made on 1 April 1634, was proved on 31 August 1638.   IAN PAYNE

Sources I. Payne, 'John Ward (c. 1589–1638): the case for one composer of the madrigals, sacred music and five- and six-part consorts', *Chelys*, 23 (1994), 1–16 • I. Payne, 'The handwriting of John Ward', *Music and Letters*, 65 (1984), 176–88 • R. Ford, 'John Ward of Canterbury', *Journal of the Viola da Gamba Society of America*, 23 (1986), 51–63 • private information (2004) [Roger Bowers] • J. Ward, *First set of English madrigals, 1613*, rev. edn (1968), vol. 19 of *The English madrigalists*, ed. E. H. Fellowes, rev. T. Dart • J. Ward, *Consort music of five and six parts*, ed. I. Payne, Musica Britannica, 67 (1995) • W. C. Metcalfe, ed., *The visitations of Essex*, 1, Harleian Society, 13 (1878) • BL, Add. MS 41578 • A. Ashbee, *The harmonious musick of John Jenkins*, 1 (1992), 119–29, 230–31 • parish register, Canterbury, St Mary Bredman, 15 Feb 1590 [baptism]

Ward, John (1599?–1658?), parliamentarian officer and poet, was a native of Tewkesbury, Gloucestershire. Both his date of birth and parentage are unknown, though the baptism of a John Ward, son of Thomas, at Tewkesbury Abbey on 10 June 1599 may refer to the poet (Glos. RO, bishop's transcripts). Ward was a puritan, and at the outbreak of the civil war he became 'commissary generall of the provisions' to the troops of horse under William Russell, fifth earl of Bedford. On 13 October 1642 Ward printed *An encouragement to warre, or, Bellum parliamentale, shewing the unlawfulnesse of the late Bellum episcopale*, in which he vents his spleen against the moral and theological shortcomings of the cavaliers. The poem was reissued on 4 July 1643 as *The Christians incouragement earnestly to contend for Christ his gospell & for all our Christian liberties in thrall which who refuseth let him be for aye accursed*. It was printed along with an anonymous tract entitled *The humble petition of the protestant inhabitants of the counties of Antrim, Downe, Tyrone, &c*, first published in 1641. On 12 December 1642 Ward participated in the storming of Winchester and the capture of Lord Grandison under the command of Sir William Waller. He celebrated the event in the poem *The Taking of*

Winchester by the Parliaments Forces. Ward gives a detailed account of the whole skirmish. He laments over Grandison's subsequent escape from captivity, and marshals Gloucestershire and Tewkesbury in particular, to stand against the royalists. Ward may also be the author of the militantly republican poem 'The changes, or, A vicissitude of change of government' (Bodl. Oxf., MS Ashmole 49), written shortly after the dissolution of the Long Parliament on 20 April 1653. He calls upon the people 'to strip away the veils of custom and to see more deeply into the age's political possibilities' (Norbrook, 13.185).

The remainder of Ward's military career is shrouded in mystery. It is impossible to be certain that the details of two (or three) John Wards are not being conflated, but he may have been the John Ward who was made captain of a troop of foot soldiers in Yorkshire on 10 April 1650. Three and a half years later the treasurers of Ely House, the hospital for soldiers and sailors, granted a pension to one John Ward, 'in respect of his poverty and wounds in the service' (PRO, SP 25/72, p. 28). According to his widow, Anne, Captain Ward had served from the beginning of the wars, and during the early part of the protectorate he was a member of Cromwell's household guard under Walter Strickland. Thereafter he joined Colonel Henry Lillingston's regiment at Dunkirk and was killed at the battle of the Dunes on 4 June 1658. Ward died intestate. Sir William Lockhart, colonel of the Flanders horse, appealed to John Thurloe in respect of his widow, 'to move something in her behalf, that may be an encouragement to other married officers amongst us' (Thurloe, 7.224). Anne and her two young children were granted a solatium of £100.

LYNN HULSE

Sources J. Ward, *An encouragement to warre, or, Bellum parliamentale* [1642] [Thomason tract E 122(2)]; repr. as *The Christians incouragement* (1643) [E 59(3)] • J. W. [J. Ward], *The taking of Winchester by the parliaments forces* (1642–3) [Thomason tract E 245(14)] • D. Norbrook, 'A republican verse manifesto, 1653: John Ward's "The Changes"', *The seventeenth century*, 13 (1998), 185–211 • J. Ward, 'The changes, or, A vicissitude of change of Government', Bodl. Oxf., MS Ashmole 49 • bishop's transcripts, Glos. RO • *A catalogue of the names of the dukes, marquesses ... with the names of the troops of horse under the command of William earle of Bedford* (1642) [Thomason tracts E 83(9), E 64(4)] • pay warrants and orders for supply, PRO, SP 28, vols. 1–5 • petition of John Ward, 8 Nov 1653, PRO, SP 25/72, p. 28 • petition of Anne Ward, 10 July 1658, PRO, SP 18/182/68 • *CSP dom., 1650*, p. 506 • Thurloe, *State papers*, vol. 7 • T. Corser, *Collectanea Anglo-poetica, or, A ... catalogue of a ... collection of early English poetry*, 10, ed. J. Crossley, Chetham Society, 108 (1880), 338–42 • C. H. Firth and G. Davies, *The regimental history of Cromwell's army*, 2 (1940), 689–90 • R. Sherwood, *The court of Oliver Cromwell* (1977)
Archives PRO, SP 18, SP 28, SP 25

Ward, John (1678/9–1758), antiquary and biographer, was born in London, one of the fourteen children of John Ward (1635–1717), a Baptist minister originally from Tysoe, Warwickshire, and his wife, Constancy Rayner (*d.* 1697), a lady of acknowledged piety. John and his sister Abigail (*d.* 1745) were their only surviving children. For some years Ward toiled as a clerk in the Navy Office, feeding his appetite for literature by dint of study in his leisure hours with the assistance of John Ker, a physician who kept an academy in Bethnal Green. Ward left the Navy Office in 1710 and opened his own school for the children of his acquaintances, in Tenter Alley, Moorfields, which he kept for many years. Clearly a sociable man, he was throughout his life a member of various societies, both formal and informal; in 1712 he became one of the earliest members of a society composed principally of divines and lawyers who met periodically to discuss notable texts of civil law or politics in classical times.

Ward's reputation for a knowledge of polite literature, together with some minor publications of his own, led to his appointment in September 1720 as professor of rhetoric in Gresham College. He lived in the college thereafter, possibly with his sister, since she died in his apartments in 1745. Ward was elected a fellow of the Royal Society in November 1723, contributed several articles on aspects of Roman archaeology and numismatics to the society's *Philosophical Transactions*, served on its council, and in 1752 was elected one of its vice-presidents. He was one of several who engaged in published dispute with Conyers Middleton—in Ward's case on the status of physicians in classical Rome. More profitably he contributed to a range of publications, by checking text, writing introductions, and providing translations. Among these works were J. A. De Thou's *History of his Own Age* (1728, from the French of 1604–8); Robert Ainsworth's *Latin Dictionary* (1736 and later editions); the works of the dissenting minister George Benson; and the second edition of Martin Folkes's *Tables of English Silver and Gold Coins* (1763). He translated into Latin the eighth edition of Richard Mead's *Discourse of the Plague* (1723), and for the 1732 edition of William Lily's *A Short Introduction of Latin Grammar* (first published in 1652) he restored the defective text and provided a history of that grammar. He contributed an essay on the Peutinger table, so far as it related to Britain, to John Horsley's *Britannia Romana* (3 vols., 1732) and his own copy of that work, with manuscript corrections, is in the British Library. Assistance to a member of the University of Edinburgh brought him the degree of LLD in 1751.

In August 1733 Ward set off on a tour of the Low Countries, Flanders, and France, from which he returned home in October. He assiduously visited the tourist sites and of course the better known bookshops, and called on acquaintances, among them Abraham Gronovius, whom he was assisting with an edition of Aelianus's *De natura animalium*. In February 1736 he was elected a fellow of the Society of Antiquaries, of which he became director in January 1747 and vice-president in April 1753. Also in 1736 he joined another society, formed by various gentlemen and noblemen for the encouragement of learning (probably the 'Societas ad literas promovendi', which published *De natura animalium* in 1744) and he later became a member of the Spalding Gentlemen's Society.

Ward's major work is undoubtedly his *Lives of the professors of Gresham College, to which is prefaced the life of the founder, Sir Thomas Gresham* (1740), which dealt with all those who had been appointed since 1597, when the first inaugural lectures were delivered. An interleaved copy with Ward's corrections and additions, now in the British Library, was presumably intended for a second edition. His own lectures were published in two volumes as *A system of oratory, delivered in a course of lectures publickly read at Gresham College, London* (1759).

When the British Museum was founded in 1753 Ward was elected one of its trustees. He regularly attended meetings and advised on various aspects of cataloguing until November 1757, when illness kept him at home. He died in his apartments in Gresham College in the early hours of 18 October 1758. He was buried in the dissenters' burial-ground at Bunhill Fields, where his sister had previously been interred, having written his own obituary in 1752, when he gave his age as seventy-three. In his will Ward left his globes, coin collection, and certain early printed books to specific friends, directing his executors to arrange a public sale of his library and other effects.

ANITA McCONNELL

Sources A. Chalmers, ed., *The general biographical dictionary*, new edn, 32 vols. (1812–17) · T. Birch, *An account of the life of John Ward, LLD, professor of rhetoric in Gresham College, FRS and FSA* (1766) · *GM*, 1st ser., 28 (1758), 504 · will, PRO, PROB 11/841, sig. 316 · D. Laing, ed., *A catalogue of the graduates … of the University of Edinburgh*, Bannatyne Club, 106 (1858), 256 · W. P. Bowyer, *Miscellaneous tracts, by the late William Bowyer … on literary subjects* (1785) · *DNB* · H. McLachlan, *English education under the Test Acts: being the history of the nonconformist academies, 1662–1820* (1931), 85–6
Archives BL, corresp. and papers, Add. MSS 6231–6233, 6195–6204, 6181 · BL, papers relating to Royal Society, Add. MS 6180 | BL, letters to Thomas Birch, Add. MSS 4320, 4326b
Likenesses A. Ramsay, oils, 1749, County Museum, Warwick · oils, NPG

Ward, John, second Viscount Dudley and Ward (1725–1788), industrialist and politician, was born on 22 February 1725 at Sedgley Park, Wolverhampton, the eldest son of John, sixth Baron Ward of Birmingham (1700–1774), who was created Viscount Dudley and Ward in 1763, and his first wife, Anna Maria Bourchier (*c*.1700–1725), daughter of Charles Bourchier of Clontarf, co. Dublin. His mother died when he was a baby and his father married a Jamaican heiress with whom he had another son, William. The first viscount inherited in 1740 potentially the nation's most valuable mineral estate per acre in Staffordshire and Worcestershire, most of it being underlain by a 10 yard seam of coal as well as other strata of coal, brick clay, and ironstone. There were also reserves of high quality limestone and fireclay. Unfortunately the estate was isolated by its elevation and its distance from navigable rivers. Even the opening of the Birmingham Canal in 1772 did little to assist as its line ran to the north-east of a ridge which transects the Black Country while much of the viscount's estate lay to the south-west. Moreover, his father's main object was to use his wealth to reconstruct the mansion in ornamental grounds at Himley rather than develop the mineral estate. John matriculated at Oriel College, Oxford, in February 1742 and graduated MA in 1745; he also graduated LLB from Cambridge University in 1769. He went on the grand tour in 1751 and in 1754 was elected

John Ward, second Viscount Dudley and Ward (1725–1788), by John Singleton Copley, 1781–1804

MP for Marlborough, on the interest of the family of a fellow student of Oriel College, Richard Brudenell. In 1761 John became MP for Worcestershire and spoke with growing frequency in the Commons, largely in support of tory administrations, but promoting local interests wherever possible. He remained an MP until he succeeded his father in 1774 as second viscount and as recorder of Kidderminster.

Dudley had always wanted to increase his income. In 1760 he had tried but failed to find a suitable wealthy heiress perhaps because he lacked the requisite charm; he was later described as 'the butcherly soaker … from Himley … our graceless Lord' (Pakington and Pakington, 101–2). Therefore he had to await his inheritance to fulfil his financial ambitions through becoming one of the leading aristocratic entrepreneurs of his time. Dudley used his parliamentary, proprietorial, and masonic influence to place himself at the head of a local interest group and to secure beneficial legislation to develop his estate by means of canals, turnpikes, and eventually enclosure acts. This was assisted by his membership of the House of Lords committee on private bills, his active support of local interests and institutions, and his skill in playing off rival canal lobbies against each other and in forging alliances with interest groups from distant areas. Almost immediately the Dudley and Stourbridge canals were cut largely across his property following the outcrops of coal, giving access via the Staffordshire and Worcestershire Canal to the River Severn. He then obtained access to the valuable Birmingham market by constructing a tunnel through the ridge to the Birmingham Canal, although he failed to secure an independent outlet for his mines to the Severn in 1786. Meanwhile large-scale pits and ironworks were developed using the latest technology including coking furnaces and blowing engines. The timing of this accelerated development strongly suggests that Dudley furnished the necessary entrepreneurial spirit. His contribution to the region's industrialization generally is reflected both in the correspondence of local manufacturers and by the thanks of local bodies for his efforts.

T. J. Raybould calls the enclosure acts for the extensive commons on Dudley's estate the 'cornerstone' of its development (Raybould, 35). Although the second viscount as lord of the manor owned all the minerals under these commons, there were problems in providing the infrastructure for development. By two enclosure acts he secured the surface above the most valuable mines, obtaining a generous compensation for his ancient rights, but avoided any costly claims for surface damage by a clause throwing the cost on to all of the new proprietors by a rate. Whether intentional or not, this proved impossible to arrange and served to prevent any claims for subsidence against the estate even when houses built on former common land started to collapse. The enclosures also addressed his concern about recent local bread riots because they increased food production; to help remedy this problem he also took an active role in establishing a large and profitable inn with a corn market at Dudley.

Dudley was content to live for many years with a young widow, Mary Baker (d. 1810), and fathered an illegitimate daughter, Anna Maria Ward, in 1778. However in 1788 he fell out with William, his brother and heir, who used a chancery action to prevent the felling of ornamental trees around Himley Hall. Dudley then married Mrs Baker, in the hope of producing a legitimate direct heir. His efforts proved unfruitful during the three months before his death at Himley Hall on 9 October 1788. He was buried at Himley church on 20 October. William's assumption of the title was delayed by unfounded rumours of the viscountess's pregnancy. Dudley left all his personalty and unsettled estates to his daughter, the settled estates having been entailed upon his brother. This produced a series of legal disputes between his brother and his daughter's trustees.

DAVID BROWN

Sources T. J. Raybould, *The economic emergence of the Black Country: a study of the Dudley estate* (1973) · GEC, *Peerage* · C. Hadfield, *The canals of the west midlands*, 2nd edn (1969) · M. W. McCahill, *Order and equipoise: the peerage and the House of Lords, 1783–1806* (1978) · J. Money, *Experience and identity: Birmingham and the west midlands, 1760–1800* (1977) · *GM*, 1st ser., 58 (1788), 937 · M. M. Drummond, 'Ward, John', HoP, *Commons, 1754–90*, 3.606 · J. Ingamells, ed., *A dictionary of British and Irish travellers in Italy, 1701–1800* (1997) · C. L. Shadwell, *Registrum Orielense*, 2 (1902) · H. Pakington and R. Pakington, *The Pakingtons of Westwood* (1975) · *Aris's Birmingham Gazette* (1774–88) · *Hansard 1* (1812–13), vols. 18–25

Archives Birm. CL, Boulton and Watt MSS, Assay Office box, and Muirhead collection · Dudley Estate archive, Dudley · PRO, Dudley canal records, Rail 824/2 and 10 · PRO, Home Office letters, HO42.3 · Raynham Hall, Norfolk, Raynham MSS

Likenesses P. L. Ghezzi, caricature, *c.*1751; Sothebys, 23 March 1972 · J. Reynolds, two caricatures, *c.*1751, NG Ire. · J. S. Copley, oils, *c.*1778, HLRO · J. S. Copley, portrait, 1781–1804; Sothebys, 14 March 1984, lot 58 [*see illus.*] · oils, Hammersons, Dudley House, Park Lane, London

Ward, John [*called* Zion Ward] (1781–1837), founder of the Shilohites, was born at the Cove of Cork in Ireland on 25 December 1781. Taken by his parents, who were strict Calvinists, to Bristol in July 1790, he was for three years apprenticed to a shipwright and fell into bad company. Following his father to London, where he learned shoemaking with his brother, he then entered the navy, serving as a shipwright on board the *Blanche*, a man-of-war, seeing action at the battle of Copenhagen on 2 April 1801. The sense of guilt and fear of death and judgment which he had known as a child now increased, and in 1803 he secured his discharge at Sheerness. He married a pious girl and worked as a shoemaker, the family moving to Carmarthen for three years, where he became disillusioned with Methodism and religion generally. On his return to London he chanced to hear Jeremiah Garrett in Southwark and became a Baptist, though on Garrett's death in 1806 he joined the Independents and later, in 1813, the Sandemanians, for whom he became a preacher.

In 1814 Ward was thrilled to discover what he considered to be an example of inspired prophecy, when he read *The Fifth Book of Wonders* by Joanna Southcott, who had just died, and for a while he rejoined and preached for the Methodists, but they rejected his enthusiasm for 'the pure Word of Joanna'. He then, in turn, was associated with two claimants to Joanna's mantle, first George Turner (who died in 1821) and then in 1825 the illiterate Mary Boon of Staverton, Devon, becoming the reader of her letters to her London followers and later acting as her secretary. However, in 1826, the year from which his followers came to reckon their beginning of time, Ward started to see himself as a prophetic leader. A series of dreams and visions convinced him that he himself was Shiloh, the Promised One, he, indeed, was Jesus Christ, and the biblical prophecies referred to him. His mother's name being Mary and his birthday being on 25 December seemed to confirm this realization. When in 1828 he gave up his work as a shoemaker and began to proclaim his messiahship, his wife decided that he was mad and the local magistrate committed him to the Newington workhouse for six months.

In November 1828 Ward escaped and, with help from Charles William Twort of Walworth—a loyal henchman from then until his death in 1878—Ward began to gather a following, claiming to be 'a new man, having a new name'. Sometimes he called himself Shiloh, the name which Joanna Southcott had given to her expected child, but more often he was now known as Zion. His first book, *The Vision of Judgment, or, The Return of Joanna from her Trance* (1829), was not well received by the Southcottians, but a series of visits to Nottingham, Chesterfield, Birmingham, Sheffield, and other northern towns produced an encouraging response. It is not clear at what stage he encountered the writings of the radical freethinker Richard Carlile, but when Ward taught that biblical events and characters were not historical but figurative, and that he (Ward) was not just Jesus Christ but also Satan and God as well, there are manifest echoes of some of Carlile's ideas. In addition to such daring suggestions Ward had also adopted a politically radical programme, ferociously castigating the government, landlords, and clergy. 'The Archbishop was "His Grease", the Bishops "canting tricksters", the clergy "scurvy nincompoops"' (Balleine, 99). In the context of the Reform Bill disturbances, this sort of oratory was bound to polarize reactions to his addresses at Borough Chapel, Southwark, and at the Rotunda in Blackfriars Road during 1831. By and large his message appealed to the poorer classes, though he was supported financially by some wealthier patrons, such as the Birmingham manufacturers of tobacco and snuff, Bradley and Holinsworth.

In Derby, on 4 August 1832, Ward and Twort were found guilty of blasphemy (Twort being convicted also of assault) and they were imprisoned for eighteen months in Derby gaol. When, on 15 August, Henry Hunt presented a petition to the House of Commons asking for the release of Ward and Twort, he seized the occasion for a fierce attack on the government. The almost incoherent denunciation of the petition by Spencer Perceval (a pious son of the assassinated prime minister) was probably provoked, at least partially, by Ward having ostentatiously feasted on a leg of mutton on the day appointed by parliament for repentant fasting in the face of the cholera epidemic. Ward's sentence was not mitigated, but the conditions of confinement were comparatively mild.

Released on 3 February 1834, Ward returned briefly to London and then tried to revive the support which he had previously found in many midland and northern chapels, but with little success. The destructive and individualistic elements in his preaching, which had been so topical during the reform crisis, were hardly calculated to nurture or edify congregational life. In January 1835 he moved to Bristol where he gathered a following which included for a while J. P. Greaves and Sophia Chichester, but in October a stroke deprived him of the use of his hands. In spite of a second stroke he could still speak, and began another tour. Lifted onto the platform at meetings, he could still gather a crowd. 'The man in the street was impressed by the sight of a preacher, obviously earnest and religious, proclaiming that the Bible was a fiction, that prayer was useless, that clergymen were liars, and that God did not care whether men did good or evil' (Balleine, 104). In November 1836 Ward finally settled at Leeds, but suffered a third stroke and died at 91 Park Lane on 12 March 1837. His devoted follower C. B. Holinsworth perpetuated his master's memory in a collection of Ward's writings in seventeen volumes (1899–1904).

TIMOTHY C. F. STUNT

Sources C. B. H. [C. B. Holinsworth], *Memoir of John Ward* (1881) · G. R. Balleine, 'Zion Ward, iconoclast', *Past finding out: the tragic story of Joanna Southcott and her successors* (1956), 94–105 · W. H. Oliver, 'John Ward – the messiah as agitator', *Prophets and millennialists: the uses of biblical prophecy in England from the 1790s to the 1840s* (1978), 151–69 · J. F. C. Harrison, *The second coming: popular millenarianism, 1780–1850* (1979), 152–60 · DNB · J. E. M. Latham, *Search for a new Eden, James Pierrepont Greaves (1777–1842): the sacred socialist and his followers* (1999)
Archives BL, letters and papers, Add. MSS 43509

Ward, John (1805–1890), diplomatist, was born on 28 August 1805 at East Cowes, Isle of Wight, where his father, John Ward, was collector of customs. His mother, Martha (also known as Patty), was one of the four sisters of Thomas *Arnold (1795–1842); his grandfather William Arnold had been his father's predecessor in the customs post. Ward was much influenced by the Arnoldian context in which he was reared and by his uncle's friends, such as Richard Whately. In 1831 he jointly edited with his uncle the short-lived weekly journal the *Englishman's Register*, of which Arnold was the proprietor. He abandoned the law, for which he had been trained, on his appointment in 1837 to an inspectorship of prisons. The following year, after acting for some months as private secretary to the first earl of Durham, he became through the earl's influence secretary to the New Zealand Colonization Company, for which he wrote *The British Colonization of New Zealand* (1834), with E. J. Wakefield, and *Information Relative to New Zealand* (1839; 2nd enlarged edn, 1840). He had for many years previously taken a keen interest in the politics, and more especially in the commercial and industrial progress, of France, Belgium, and Germany, and had published articles on both home and foreign affairs in the *Edinburgh Review* and the *British and Foreign Review*. Early in 1841 he was appointed British commissioner for the revision of the state tolls. In 1844 he was sent to Berlin as British commissioner for the settlement, through the arbitration of the king of Prussia, of the so-called Portendic claims on France, arising out of a blockade by French ships of part of the African coast. In the summer of 1845 Lord Aberdeen appointed him consul-general at Leipzig, with the further commission to visit periodically those places in Germany where the conferences of the Zollverein should be held. At the close of 1850 Lord Palmerston instructed him to act as secretary of legation at Dresden during the diplomatic conferences held in that capital, where he was a close witness of the notable victory achieved by the policy of Austria, represented by Schwarzenberg. In 1854 he attended the Munich exhibition of arts and manufactures, and wrote a report on the state of technical instruction in Bavaria. In 1857 he was charged with an inquiry into the political condition of the duchies of Schleswig and Holstein, their relations with the Danish crown, and the best remedies for grievances which the promulgation of the joint constitution of 1855 had notoriously augmented. His report, though praised by the prince consort and Lord Stratford de Redcliffe, was left unpublished by Lord Clarendon, and the subsequent course of events prevented any possibility of acting on his recommendation to reorganize the Danish monarchy upon federal principles.

In 1860 Ward, after being made a CB, had been nominated chargé d'affaires and consul-general for the Hanse towns and the surrounding parts of Germany, and after in 1865 negotiating, together with Lord Napier and Ettrick, a commercial treaty with the Zollverein, he was in the following year raised to the rank of minister-resident. In 1870, owing to the abolition of direct diplomatic relations with the Hanse towns on their joining the North German federation, he left Hamburg. The remainder of his life he spent in retirement at Dover and in Essex (where his home was Gaston House, near Bishop's Stortford), writing his reminiscences. Ward was married to Caroline (d. 1905), daughter of John Bullock, rector of Radwinter, Essex. The second of their sons was the historian Sir Adolphus *Ward. Ward died at his home in Kent, 11 Waterloo Crescent, Dover, on 1 September 1890.

A. W. WARD, rev. H. C. G. MATTHEW

Sources J. Ward, *Experiences of a diplomatist* (1872) · *FO List* (1889) · *CGPLA Eng. & Wales* (1890)
Archives Peterhouse, Cambridge, papers | BL, corresp. with Sir Austen Layard, Add. MSS 39101–39113, *passim* · W. Yorks. AS, Leeds, corresp. with Lord Canning
Wealth at death £2466 0s. 7d.: probate, 15 Oct 1890, *CGPLA Eng. & Wales*

Ward, John (1825–1896), naval officer and surveyor, was the son of Lieutenant Edward Willis Ward RN (d. 1855). He entered the navy in 1840 on the brig *Spey*, packet-boat to the West Indies and the Gulf of Mexico. In November 1840 the *Spey* was wrecked on the Bahama bank, and young Ward was sent to the *Thunder*, then surveying the Bahamas. He passed his examination in December 1848, and was promoted lieutenant on 2 October 1850. He married, in 1852, Mary Hope, daughter of John Bowie of Edinburgh; they had at least one child. During 1851–3 Ward was borne on the books of the *Fisgard* for surveying duties, and in March 1854 was appointed to the steamer *Alban*, then commanded by Captain Henry Charles Otter, and attached to the fleet in the Baltic, where she served usefully in destroying telegraphs and in reconnoitring in the neighbourhood of Sveaborg and at Bomarsund. In 1855–6 he was with Otter in the *Firefly*, surveying on the coast of Scotland, and in February 1857 was appointed to command the *Emperor*, a steam yacht going out as a present to the emperor of Japan. In her he went with Lord Elgin to Yeddo, in August 1858, and, when the vessel had been handed over to the Japanese, returned to Shanghai in the *Retribution*.

On 24 September Ward was promoted to command the surveying ship *Actaeon*, and in her tender, the gunboat *Dove*, he accompanied Lord Elgin in his remarkable voyage up the Yang-tse, rendering important assistance in examining the navigable channels of the river. For the next three years he commanded the *Actaeon*, and in her surveyed the coast of the Gulf of Pecheli (Beizhili), including the harbours of Weihaiwei and Ta-lien-wan (Dalianwan), until then unknown, as also the Yang-tse for 200 miles above Han-kow (Hankou). For two years after paying off the *Actaeon* at the end of 1861, he was employed at the hydrographic office in printing the work of the survey, and in March 1864 he was appointed to the *Rifleman* to continue the survey of the China seas. In 1866 his health gave way, and he was obliged to return to England. He had no further service, and in 1870 accepted the new retirement

scheme. On 24 September 1873 he was promoted captain on the retired list, and he died at London on 20 January 1896, at the age of seventy.

J. K. LAUGHTON, rev. ANDREW LAMBERT

Sources D. Bonner-Smith and E. W. R. Lumby, eds., *The Second China War, 1856–1860*, Navy RS, 95 (1954) · *The Times* (22 Jan 1896) · *Annual Register* (1896) · *Navy List* · L. Oliphant, *Narrative of the earl of Elgin's mission to China and Japan, 1857–9*, 2 vols. (1859) · L. S. Dawson, *Memoirs of hydrography*, 2 vols. (1885), vol. 2

Ward, John (1866–1934), trade unionist and politician, was born at Oatlands Park, Surrey, on 21 November 1866, the son of Robert Ward, plasterer, and his wife, Caroline Edmonds. His father died when he was three, and he grew up in his mother's home town of Appleshaw, near Andover, in Hampshire. With little formal education, Ward worked at a variety of jobs from the age of seven. At twelve he lodged with a man in Weyhill village and began work as a navvy on the Andover and Weyhill Railway, after which he was employed on many public works, including the Manchester Ship Canal. Volunteering for the Sudan campaign in 1885, he was engaged in the construction of the abortive military railway from Suakin to Berber, and received the queen's silver medal and the khedive's bronze star, with medal and clasp.

As a teenager Ward took classes to learn to read, and his later political development was considerably influenced, he said, by his reading of Kropotkin's *Appeal to the Young* and Henry George's *Progress and Poverty* (1881). In 1886 he joined the Social Democratic Federation (SDF) and was selected to test the legality of the proclamation of the chief commissioner of the London Metropolitan Police, Sir Charles Warren, prohibiting demonstrations of the unemployed in Trafalgar Square. The meeting was held on lord mayor's day, 9 November 1886, and Ward was arrested, but the defence made much of his war record and he escaped with a fine. He founded the Navvies' Union in 1889, and also helped to establish the short-lived National Federation of Labour Union the same year. On the foundation of the General Federation of Trade Unions in 1901, Ward was elected to the management committee and served until 1929, for the last sixteen years as treasurer.

Ward stood for local elections as an SDF candidate in 1888 and 1892. After being defeated in these attempts, he began to move increasingly towards radical Liberal politics, and was an important figure in the National Democratic League formed in 1900. Ward was one of the Labour candidates who refused to sign the Labour Representation Committee constitution in 1903, and was elected without their endorsement in Stoke-on-Trent in the 1906 general election. He stood as a coalition, or National, Liberal in elections after the war, and in 1924 won as a constitutionalist, backed by Liberals and Conservatives. He held his seat until 1929 when he was defeated by the Labour Party candidate, Lady Cynthia Mosley.

When war broke out in 1914 Ward was gazetted lieutenant-colonel of the 21st Middlesex regiment, for which he recruited five labour battalions, and served with them for a time in France. He and his men survived the mining of the troopship *Tyndareus* off South Africa in February 1917. During the allied intervention after the Russian revolution, Ward's battalion was attached to the forces of Admiral Kolchak, who instigated an anti-Bolshevik rising in Vladivostok. Ward wrote of these experiences in *With the Diehards in Siberia*, published in 1920.

Ward was appointed CMG in 1918 and CB in 1919; he received the French, Italian, and Czechoslovakian Croix de Guerre, and was created a Cossack ataman.

In 1892 Ward married Lilian Elizabeth (*d*. 1926), daughter of George Gibbs. She shared actively in his political work. They had three sons, one of whom died in 1928, and one daughter. Exceptionally tall, Ward retained a soldierly bearing throughout his life. An effective speaker, he was always very active in Liberal Party campaigns. The Navvies' Union gradually passed out of existence, as mechanical methods replaced some of the manual labour of the navvy, and as the larger general labourers' unions recruited in this area. After his election defeat in 1929, Ward retired to Hampshire where he was active in local affairs, becoming a magistrate and president of the Andover branch of the British Legion. Ward died at his home, Omsk, Weyhill, near Andover, on 19 December 1934, and was buried on 22 December at Appleshaw.

MARC BRODIE

Sources 'How I got on', *Pearson's Weekly* (15 March 1906), 655 · *The Times* (20 Dec 1934) · *The Times* (24 Dec 1934) · *DLB*
Archives Labour History Archive and Study Centre, Manchester, papers
Likenesses W. Stoneman, photograph, 1921, NPG · Spy [L. Ward], chromolithograph (after an engraving), NPG · Spy [L. Ward], mechanically reproduced cartoon (with Ben Tillett), NPG; repro. in *VF* (29 July 1908) · photograph, repro. in *The Times* (20 Dec 1934), 17
Wealth at death £5234 5*s*.: administration with will, 4 July 1935, *CGPLA Eng. & Wales*

Ward, John William, earl of Dudley (1781–1833), politician, was born on 9 August 1781, only child of William Ward (1750–1823), later third Viscount Dudley and Ward, and his wife, Julia (1754–1833), daughter of Godfrey Bosvile of Gunthwaite, Yorkshire. He was descended from Humble Ward (*c*.1614–1670), who married Frances (1611–1697), granddaughter of Edward Sutton, fifth Baron Dudley, and was created Baron Ward in 1644. His son Edward (1631–1701) succeeded to both baronies, and Edward's great-nephew John Ward (*c*.1704–1774) became sixth Baron Ward in 1740. He was created Viscount Dudley and Ward in 1763, and his second son, William, the father of this subject, succeeded as third viscount on the death of his elder half-brother, John, in 1788.

William was a harsh and neglectful parent to John William, who later blamed the 'malady' of depression and self-loathing which blighted his adult life on 'the brutal neglect and unkindness with which I was treated in my early years … I was bred under a task-master and the sound of the lash is never quite out of my ears' (Ward to Lord Aberdeen, 17 Dec 1822, BL, Add. MS 43231, fol. 36). After his education by a succession of private tutors and at the universities of Edinburgh (where he found in Mrs Dugald Stewart a surrogate mother) and Oxford, his father bought him a seat in parliament for the second earl

John William Ward, earl of Dudley (1781–1833), by Frederick Christian Lewis senior (after Joseph Slater)

of Radnor's borough of Downton at the general election of 1802, just before he came of age. In August 1803 he was returned unopposed for Worcestershire, where his family had a leading interest. Initially he adhered, like his father, to Pitt, but he became disillusioned with him and joined the Foxite and Grenvillite opposition to his second ministry in 1804. He supported them in office, 1806–7, having abandoned the county and come in as a paying guest, at his father's expense, for Petersfield on the interest of the Jolliffe family at the general election of 1806. He was at first loyal to the whigs in opposition from 1807 when, now politically estranged from his father, he found a seat for Wareham, where the Calcraft family were the patrons. He made a few impressive speeches, which gave him the look of a rising star, but he was never a frequent, and seldom an influential, debater. He was made chairman of the Commons select committee on sinecures in 1810. By then he had become disenchanted with the divisions and incompetence of the whigs. His drift towards a personal attachment to Canning was confirmed by their mutual support for Catholic claims and hostility to parliamentary reform. He declined to be considered for office when the whigs were cabinet-making at the start of the regency in 1811; and in June 1812, when they refused to assume power on a point of punctilio, he washed his hands of them and enlisted with Canning. He thereby lost some whig friends and gained a reputation as a place-seeker.

At the general election of 1812 Ward bought a seat for Ilchester from Sir William Manners. To his mortification, which he tried unsuccessfully to conceal with wry jokes against himself, he was left stranded by Canning's disbandment of his parliamentary squad in July 1813. On

Canning's rapprochement with the Liverpool ministry the following year Ward refused the offer of a privy councillorship and an unpaid place at the India board. He spent much time on the continent until May 1816, when he resumed his seat and, with Canning back in the cabinet, supported the government *faute de mieux*. Abroad at the time of the 1818 general election, he lost his seat for Ilchester, but in April 1819 he was returned by Canning's friend James Stuart Wortley for Bossiney, where he sat for the remainder of his Commons career, turning down an opportunity to stand for Worcestershire in 1820. In deference to Canning he stayed neutral in the parliamentary struggle over Queen Caroline in 1821. On 12 February during that session his speech in support of the transfer of Grampound's seats to Leeds as a safe and practical reform was reckoned to have been instrumental in carrying the question against ministers (Grenville, *Memoirs of the Court of George IV*, 1.123). He was abroad for most of the 1822 session and returned to England in the summer in a state verging on nervous collapse. In September Canning, having been made foreign secretary after Lord Londonderry's suicide, offered him the under-secretaryship. He did so merely to raise Ward's self-esteem, and neither expected nor wished him to accept; but Ward took him seriously and agonized for three weeks, during which he overcame his father's objections, before declining. Within two months he was torturing himself with remorse over what he now considered a fatally wrong decision. He supported the government silently and without hope of recognition until his father's death removed him from the Commons on 25 April 1823, when he succeeded to the viscountcy and to extensive estates in Staffordshire and Worcestershire, which contained lucrative coal and mineral deposits and brought him £120,000 a year.

In April 1827 Dudley belatedly attained the public eminence which he craved by accepting Canning's invitation to become foreign secretary in his new administration, in the first instance until the end of the session. He was sworn of the privy council on 30 April. After Canning's death he was persuaded to stay in office under Lord Goderich, who had him created earl of Dudley on 5 October 1827. The duke of Wellington retained him in January 1828, but he resigned with Huskisson and the other former Canningites in May. His performance at the Foreign Office, where he was initially Canning's cipher, was adequate but undistinguished. His tenure coincided with the British naval victory at Navarino. At home his notorious liaison with Lady Lyndhurst, the wife of the lord chancellor, prompted the jest that he had become 'a ward in Chancery' (*Creevey Papers*, 2.141). Lady Lyndhurst later claimed that one of her daughters was his child and seems to have blackmailed Dudley, who never married, and whose journals, which were destroyed by his executors along with all his other papers, contained pornographic descriptions of his remorseless but joyless sexual exploits with women 'both in high and low life' (*Greville Memoirs*, 5.438).

Dudley made his last speech in the Lords, a vehement denunciation of the Reform Bill, on 5 October 1831. His later years were marked by increasing absences of mind and eccentricities of behaviour, particularly his habit of conducting tormented dialogues with himself in different voices. In the spring of 1832 he exhibited 'every mark of harmless derangement' and was placed under restraint at Norwood, Surrey (*Croker Papers*, 2.171). Raikes commented: 'Here is a man with high rank, character, very cultivated talents, and a colossal fortune, courted in society, surrounded with every means of receiving and conferring happiness,—the most enviable position perhaps in life that could be pictured,—and what is the result? One single dispensation annihilates the whole!' (*Portion of the Journal*, 1.20). Dudley never appeared in society again and died at Norwood, after suffering a series of strokes, on 6 March 1833. His earldom and viscountcy became extinct, but the barony passed to his second cousin, William Humble Ward (1781–1835), on whom he had settled £4000 a year. The bulk of his great fortune went to his heir's son, William Ward (1817–1885), who was created earl of Dudley on 17 February 1860. By a codicil to his will, which was proved under £350,000, Dudley left annuities of £2000 to Lady Lyndhurst and £800 to Susan, the wife of the poet William Spencer, and a legacy of £25,000 to one of her sons, 'whom he always tacitly acknowledged' (*GM*, 2nd ser., 103, 1833; PRO, PROB 11/1821/566). His letters (1814–23) to Edward Copleston, bishop of Llandaff, and to Mrs Stewart (1803–32) were subsequently published.

Lord Holland recalled Dudley as 'a man of highly cultivated mind and of exquisite and refined though somewhat elaborate wit' given to 'bitter hatreds and unwarrantable resentments', but 'not entirely devoid of benevolence and even generosity' (Fox, 165). Five years after his death Brougham paid him a fulsome and perhaps inflated tribute as 'one of the most remarkable men that have appeared in this country', who 'possessed one of the most acute and vigorous understandings that any man ever was armed with', but was undermined by 'an oversensitiveness, an exquisitely fastidious taste, a nervous temperament', so that 'unsteadiness of purpose ... greatly chequered his existence as a public man during the latter years of his brilliant, but unhappy life' (*EdinR*, 67, 1838, 77–9). Creevey wasted no words on his epitaph: 'Poor Ward, with all his acquirements and talents, made little of it, went mad and died' (*Creevey Papers*, 2.255).

D. R. Fisher

Sources 'Ward, John William', HoP, *Commons* · *Letters of the earl of Dudley to the bishop of Llandaff* (1840) · S. H. Romilly, *Letters to 'Ivy' from the first earl of Dudley* (1905) · *EdinR*, 67 (1838), 1–80, esp. 77–9 · *The Creevey papers*, ed. H. Maxwell, 2 (1903), 141, 255 · Lord Holland [H. R. V. Fox] and J. Allen, *The Holland House diaries, 1831–1840*, ed. A. D. Kriegel (1977), 165 · *The Croker papers: the correspondence and diaries of ... John Wilson Croker*, ed. L. J. Jennings, 2 (1884), 171 · *A portion of the journal kept by Thomas Raikes from 1831–1847: comprising reminiscences of social and political life in London and Paris during that period*, 1 (1856), 19–20 · *GM*, 1st ser., 103/1 (1833), 367–9 · Duke of Buckingham and Chandos [R. Grenville], *Memoirs of the court of England during the regency, 1811–1820*, 2 vols. (1856) · GEC, *Peerage* · Duke of Buckingham and Chandos [R. Grenville], *Memoirs of the court of*

George IV, 2 vols. (1859) · letter to Lord Aberdeen, BL · *The Greville memoirs, 1814–1860*, ed. L. Strachey and R. Fulford, 8 vols. (1938), vol. 2, p. 360; vol. 5, p. 438

Archives BL, corresp. with Lord Aberdeen, Add. MSS 43230–43231 · BL, corresp. with Sir William A'Court, Add. MSS 41555–41556 · BL, corresp. with Sir Robert Gordon, Add. MS 43214 · BL, corresp. with William Huskisson, Add. MSS 38737–38756 · BL, letters to Prince Lieven, Add. MSS 47262 · BL, corresp. with Lord Melbourne, Add. MSS 60424–60447 · Bodl. Oxf., letters to Edward Copleston, MS Eng. lett. d.309 · Derbys. RO, letters to Sir R. J. Wilmot-Horton · Devon RO, letters to Edward Copleston · Durham RO, letters to Lord Londonderry, D/Lo · LPL, letters to Edward Copleston · PRO, corresp. with Stratford Canning, FO 352 · PRO, book of dispatches from Lord Cowley, FO 519 · PRO, corresp. with Lord Granville, PRO 30/29 [copies] · Staffs. RO, letters to Lord Hatherden

Likenesses E. Berens, lithograph, *c.*1800, BM, NPG; repro. in *Letters of the earl of Dudley* · J. Slater, drawing, *c.*1828, repro. in Romilly, *Letters to 'Ivy'* · F. C. Lewis senior, stipple (after J. Slater), BM, NPG [see illus.]

Wealth at death under £350,000: PRO, death duty registers, IR 26/1317/615

Ward, Sir Joseph George, first baronet (1856–1930), entrepreneur and prime minister of New Zealand, was born in Hawke Street, north Melbourne, Australia, on 26 April 1856, the third and last surviving of the ten children born to Irish immigrants William Thomas Ward, a merchant, and his wife, Hannah, *née* Dorney, who became a hotel keeper after her husband's death in 1860. In September 1863, following a second and unsuccessful marriage to John Barron, Ward's mother took her three children to Bluff, at the southern tip of New Zealand's South Island, where Joseph grew up, attending the local school and helping his devoutly Catholic mother run the Club Hotel.

Ward's formal education ended in 1869, when he joined the Bluff post office as a telegraph messenger. He learned Morse code and then worked as a clerk at Samuel Nichol's general store on the Bluff waterfront. In 1876 he briefly joined the railways department as chief clerk in charge of the loading and unloading of ships. The following year he built storage sheds and became a merchant on his own account. Ultimately he acquired shipping agencies and bought wool, grain, and skins from local farmers, to whom he sold grass seed, fertilizer, and stockfeed. All his life a merchant company carrying his name traded from Bluff and the nearby town of Invercargill.

Ward was elected to the local borough council in 1878 and to the Bluff harbour board and the mayoralty three years later. In February 1883 he became chairman of the harbour board, and at the age of twenty-seven was the most influential citizen in the small port. Handsome, of medium height, with an expansive moustache that was later trimmed back then waxed, he married on 4 December 1883 Theresa Dorothea, the daughter of Henry J. de Smidt, a licensed victualler of Bluff. She was tall, graceful, and ten years younger than he; they had five children, and their most successful marriage lasted until Theresa's relatively early death in February 1927. She was Ward's chief admirer and dressed elegantly with extravagant hats.

In 1887 Ward entered parliament for the seat of Awarua.

He supported the mildly expansionary Stout–Vogel ministry. The ministry was defeated by conservatives and Ward soon allied himself with those calling for tariff protection and closer settlement of the land. Courteous, well dressed, with a 'bright and happy' style of debating, Ward revealed himself a technocrat with a passion for getting maximum value from government expenditure. When John Ballance's Liberal Party took office in 1891 he became postmaster-general, while continuing to expand his private business. Ballance died in April 1893, and Ward was appointed colonial treasurer in Richard John Seddon's ministry. He was now obliged to spend longer periods away from home, and his business, which had moved somewhat recklessly into the frozen meat trade, suffered. His greatest early achievement, the Government Advances to Settlers Act 1894, which saw the government raise money in London at 3 per cent and lend it to New Zealand farmers at 4½ per cent, thus undercutting the trading banks, was designed in part to inject money into farming, particularly in the province of Southland, where Ward's own business needed stimulation. While many thousands of farmers benefited nationally, the cash injection was not enough to save Ward. By 1895 the J. G. Ward Farmers' Association owed £100,000 to the Colonial Bank, which itself was on the verge of collapse. As colonial treasurer Ward was responsible for an act that merged the Colonial Bank with the larger Bank of New Zealand, but the new structure refused to accept liability for the Ward Farmers' Association account. The business went into receivership. Ward's friends sought to buy it, but the supreme court refused to sanction the sale in a decision that many Southlanders regarded as an act of political persecution by the judge.

Ward resigned from the cabinet in June 1896 and in July 1897 he surrendered his public offices and became a bankrupt. The law at that time did not prevent bankrupts being elected to parliament, and Ward won the by-election for Awarua with an increased majority. With the assistance of friends and family, he was discharged from bankruptcy on 5 November 1897. Over the next two years, while helping Seddon's government from the back bench in parliament, Ward devoted most of his time to rehabilitating his finances. He spent the summer of 1899 in London, where he managed to sell for a good price a parcel of shipping company shares earlier deemed worthless by the official assignee. This windfall enabled Ward to repay all his creditors, and in time he became a wealthy man. After the 1899 election, with encouragement from Ward's friends in the ministry, Seddon made Ward his deputy as colonial secretary, postmaster-general, minister of railways, and, later in the year, minister of health. In 1901 Ward was created KCMG for arranging a royal visit. He shifted his family to Wellington, where they occupied Awarua House, later known as Premier House. His rehabilitation was complete, although stories, many of them inaccurate, lingered for many years about his bankruptcy.

Ward devoted himself to the rapid expansion of post offices and telephones and the completion of the North

Island Main Trunk Railway. He reduced postal, telephone, and rail charges, causing a huge expansion in patronage. He established the department of health and introduced superannuation schemes for government employees. Business acumen and a talent for figures made him indispensable to Seddon.

When Seddon died in June 1906 Ward was in London. He hastened back to New Zealand and was sworn as prime minister on 6 August 1906. He restructured the cabinet, but divisions among the Liberals caused him problems. Worried by a dwindling supply of land and constant demands for access to it, Ward's ministry advanced the concept of leasehold tenure in a series of bills, only one of which was enacted. Friends and foes alike became disconcerted by vacillations in policy. Growing union unrest and strikes—unknown since 1894—also bedevilled Ward's government, but he held on to office in the election of 1908—his only outright victory as Liberal leader.

However, Ward was soon in trouble. The economy turned down temporarily, and, with little success, Ward endeavoured to fasten attention on imperial matters by a gift to the Royal Navy of a dreadnought, HMS *New Zealand*. His posturing at the naval conference of 1909 and the Imperial Conference in 1911 made him the object of ridicule among left-wing elements at home; a baronetcy for the portly premier in the coronation honours list drew special attention from cartoonists. The general election of December 1911 produced deadlock, but in February 1912, on the speaker's casting vote, Ward survived. He resigned from the prime ministership in March, and in July his party limped into opposition. He spent many months in Europe in 1913, but returned late that year to assume the position of leader of the opposition. The election of 1914 produced stalemate again. Ward failed to staunch the flow of former Liberal voters to various Labour groupings. His old foe, William Ferguson Massey of the Reform Party, held the top position in a national ministry that took office on 12 August 1915. Ward managed at the same time to hold the positions of deputy prime minister, minister of finance, and leader of the opposition.

Ward was obliged to accept responsibility for wartime inflation and wage controls. He attended two imperial conferences in London with Massey as well as the Paris peace conference in 1919. Hoping that he could topple Massey's government, he withdrew from the national ministry in August 1919 and attempted to relaunch the Liberals as a radical party. They were humiliated in the election of December 1919, and Ward lost his seat.

Aged sixty-three, Ward was for the first time in forty-two years without elected office. Most assumed that his overlong career was nearing its end: yet he sought to return to parliament in a by-election in 1923, and did become MP for Invercargill in 1925. With speeches that rambled down memory lane, he seemed a political irrelevance. But the uncertain economy of the 1920s nurtured nostalgia. The new United Party invited the frail 72-year-old to lead it into the election of 1928. Suffering from diabetes and poor eyesight, Ward inadvertently promised to borrow £70 million

in one year to revive New Zealand's economy. He was the winner in the November election, although his party lacked a majority. With Labour Party support in parliament, Ward defeated the Reform government of Gordon Coates, and on 10 December 1928, although frail, he took office again as prime minister. Farce followed. Little money was borrowed, unemployment rose rapidly, and Ward fell ill; he nearly died in November 1929. He clung to office and accepted a GCMG in the new year's honours, but he was scarcely in touch with affairs for many months as he sought a cure in the thermal waters of Rotorua. His life flickered. In May 1930 his children and fellow ministers obliged him to resign the prime ministership, though he remained a minister until his death, at his home, 47 Molesworth Street, Wellington, on 8 July 1930. He was buried on 13 July in Bluff cemetery, overlooking the small town that had nurtured him, and which he had represented for most of his political life. With his death went the former Liberal Party's principal entrepreneur, a poor strategist, yet a major contributor to the infrastructure of New Zealand. MICHAEL BASSETT

Sources M. Bassett, *Sir Joseph Ward* (1993) · M. Bassett, 'Ward, Sir Joseph', *DNZB*, vol. 2 · b. cert. · m. cert. · d. cert.
Archives NL NZ, Turnbull L. | Archives New Zealand, Wellington, Seddon MSS · NL NZ, Turnbull L., Fisher MSS · NL NZ, Turnbull L., Hogg MSS · NL NZ, Turnbull L., Pember Reeves MSS | FILM Archives New Zealand, Wellington, footage
Likenesses B. Stone, photograph, 1909, Birm. CL · S. Orpen, oils, 1919, NPG
Wealth at death £337,000: *New Zealand Herald*, 27 Aug 1930

Ward, Joshua (1684/5–1761), medical practitioner and inventor of medicines, was the son of William Ward, owner of an alum works, of Guisborough, Cleveland. He had at least two brothers, one being the wealthy and dishonest businessman and MP John Ward of Hackney (d. 1755), and two sisters. According to John Ayrton Paris he was originally a footman who, while serving on the continent, obtained the recipes of his nostrums from some monks. The only certainty however, is that he worked with his brother William as a drysalter in Thames Street, London, where he presumably gained some useful experience in the properties of drugs.

Ward is claimed to have fled to France in 1715 on account of a 'particular affair', apparently involving sympathy with the Jacobite cause (*Annual Register*, 1761, 185). Yet in the same year he became a member of parliament for Marlborough, after one of two rival mayors got hold of the election writ and inserted Ward's name. Ward was returned even though no one had voted for him. Nominally a whig he voted against the Septennial Act of 1716, but in May 1717 he was unseated on petition.

Ward remained in France for about sixteen years, spending time near Paris and among the English colony at Dunkirk. In 1725 he was co-defendant with his brother John in an action brought in England by the widow of John Sheffield, first duke of Buckingham and Normanby, over some alum works the duke had earlier leased to them. It emerged that John Ward had cheated the duke out of

Joshua Ward (1684/5–1761), by John Faber junior (after E. Loving)

£70,000, only £10,000 being recovered, and he was convicted of fraud and forgery; being abroad, Joshua Ward escaped blame.

While in France, Ward invented the medicines known as Ward's Pill and Ward's Drop. The composition of these and other nostrums, such as sweating drops and paste for fistula, varied greatly over the years, but essentially the pills contained antimony and a vegetable substance—dragon's blood—mixed with wine, whereas the drops comprised a fearsome brew of nitric acid, ammonium chloride, and mercury. Those taking such remedies, in an age when cupping and blistering were regular treatments, thought that the resulting heavy perspiration, vomiting, or purging had beneficial effects. After receiving a pardon from George II, Ward returned to England in 1734, settled in London, and overnight became the talk of the town.

Ward's reputation was greatly enhanced by royal patronage. He spotted that the king's painful thumb was not gouty but dislocated, and cured it with a violent wrench. For this he was rewarded with the use of an apartment in the almonry office, Whitehall, and the privilege of driving through St James's Park. Ward was also adept at puffing himself, asserting in press advertisements his ability to cure gout, rheumatism, scurvy, palsy, syphilis, scrofula, and cancer. He converted three houses near St James's Park into a hospital for the poor, and set up a further treatment centre in Threadneedle Street, in the City of London. He subsidized these activities by charging the rich what they could afford.

Not unexpectedly, Ward's spectacular success evoked harsh criticism, not merely from reputable doctors. He

was widely accused of hiring 'patients' at half a crown a week and instructing them on how to simulate the symptoms of diseases; better-dressed impostors were said to arrive in their coaches and throng his consulting-rooms for 5s. a day. The large sums he contributed to charity—put at over £3000 a year—and the coins he regularly threw from his carriage only fanned hostility towards him. The *Grub Street Journal*, in articles from 1734 onwards, repeated verbatim in the *Gentleman's Magazine*, at first reasonably attacked the public's indiscriminate use of the medicines, but later castigated him openly as the friend of undertakers, coffin makers, and sextons by poisoning the sick. Ward responded by taking the journal to court on charges of libel—inadvisedly, as it turned out, as his scant medical knowledge was revealed and his case was thrown out, the defendants gleefully commemorating their victory in prose and doggerel.

Among men of letters, reactions to Ward and his activities were decidedly mixed. Henry Fielding commended his powers of curing the poor with no expectation of reward, in his *Voyage to Lisbon* (1755), and Horace Walpole approved of the way in which Ward relieved headaches with a dab of ointment on the forehead. Edward Gibbon as a sickly twelve-year-old was successfully treated by Ward during a life-threatening illness. On the other hand Alexander Pope satirized Ward as a despicable quack at least four times in his verses. In William Hogarth's 'The Company of Undertakers', Ward is depicted with the surgeon and oculist John Taylor (1703–1772) and the notorious bone-setter Mrs Mapp as an impudent fraud.

Notwithstanding these mixed reactions, Ward seems to have maintained the confidence of the élite. George II cautiously permitted his daughter Princess Caroline—egged on by John Hervey, Baron Hervey of Ickworth (1696–1743)—to take Ward's pills for her rheumatism. In 1748, when the House of Commons debated a bill to control apothecaries and others who were dispensing adulterated drugs, Ward petitioned the house, alleging that over the past fifteen years he had had no fewer than 2000 patients under his care, 300 being soldiers; he was duly exempted in the bill, which was rejected in the House of Lords.

Ward's notoriety for his pills and his treatment of the sick overshadowed his scientific experiments. He had two trained assistants, John White and F. J. D'Osterman, with whose help in 1736 he began to make sulphuric acid at Twickenham, in what were known as the 'Great Vitriol Works'. This acid was produced by igniting nitre (or saltpetre) and sulphur in round-bottomed flasks set in sand. While the chemistry of the process was by then tolerably well known, for the first time manufacture was on a large enough scale to permit continuous production, one operative being able successively to attend the large number of flasks in the works. The price of sulphuric acid was consequently reduced to about one-sixteenth of its former cost. Later Ward removed operations to Richmond, and he patented his process in 1749. In both localities the fumes from the chimneys and the general stench aroused much irritation among the neighbours.

Ward was a large and ungainly man, his double chin and

rotund figure indicating his taste for the good things of life. His nickname of Spot Ward arose from the claret-coloured birthmark on the right side of his face, shown in some (but not all) portraits of him. He showed no undue respect to those above him, even making impertinent remarks to the king, but was kindly and condescending to those he deemed his inferiors.

There is no evidence that Ward ever married. The 'affair' which drove him abroad was undoubtedly political rather than of the heart. Perhaps he had too many secrets to risk marriage. The last word on a contemporary must go to Dr Johnson: he judged Ward to have been the dullest man he had ever known.

Ward died at his home in Whitehall, London, on 21 December 1761, his fortune being estimated at £16,000, with £5000 earmarked in bequests, mainly to relatives. He asked for his body to be buried in Westminster Abbey, if possible close to the high altar; he did after all reside within the parish. He was duly interred on 26 December with great pomp in Poets' Corner, not inappropriately for one so versified against. A bust in his possession was to have been placed next to that of John Dryden; however, the only lapidary likeness available was a full-length statue by Agostino Carlini, which was too ostentatious for the abbey. Presented to the Royal Society of Arts by a great-nephew in 1792, it is now in the Victoria and Albert Museum, London. Ward's grave remains unmarked and his nostrums were likewise soon virtually forgotten. His friend John Page, an MP and one-time deputy paymaster-general, inherited the recipes, and published them in 1763. White and D'Osterman continued production helped by pensions from George III, and the proceeds were to be divided between the Asylum for Female Orphans and the Magdalen Home for Fallen Women. These revenues, at first plentiful, soon declined sharply. Unlike the fever powders of Robert James, the pill and drop did not long survive their self-important creator.

T. A. B. CORLEY

Sources HoP, *Commons, 1715–54*, 2.320, 519–21 · M. H. Nicolson, 'Ward's "pill and drop" and men of letters', *Journal of the History of Ideas*, 29 (1968), 177–96 · *Ward v. duke of Buckingham* [1725], 3 Brown PC 581, 1 ER 1511 · B. Hill, 'Scavenger of the faculty, Joshua Ward (1685–1761)', *The Practitioner*, 203 (1969), 820–25 · W. A. Campbell, 'Portrait of a quack, Joshua Ward (1685–1761)', *University of Newcastle Medical Gazette* (1964), 118–22 · J. T. Smith, *Nollekens and his times*, ed. W. Whitten, new edn, 2 (1920), 132–5 · Boswell, *Life*, 3.389–90 · *Annual Register* (1761), 185 · *Annual Register* (1763), 109–20 · *GM*, 1st ser., 4 (1734) · *GM*, 1st ser., 5 (1735) · *GM*, 1st ser., 6 (1736) · *GM*, 1st ser., 10 (1740) · *GM*, 1st ser., 29 (1759) · *GM*, 1st ser., 30 (1760) · *GM*, 1st ser., 32 (1762), 208–9 · *GM*, 1st ser., 36 (1766), 100 · *London Chronicle* (19–22 Dec 1761), 606; (22–4 Dec 1761), 615; (24–31 Dec 1761), 634; (25–7 Feb 1762), 197; (2–4 March 1762), 210 · *London Magazine*, 4 (1735), 11–2 · *London Magazine*, 17 (1748), 225 · J. A. Paris, *Pharmacologia*, 5th edn (1822), 2.335 · A. Macaulay, *A dictionary of medicine*, 5th edn (1837), 611 · J. L. Chester, ed., *The marriage, baptismal, and burial registers of the collegiate church or abbey of St Peter, Westminster*, Harleian Society, 10 (1876), 399 · *An inventory of the historical monuments in London*, Royal Commission on Historical Monuments (England), 1 (1924), 109

Likenesses W. Hogarth, cartoon, 1736 (*The Company of undertakers*), BM · W. Hogarth, etching, 1736 (after his *Various doctors and quacks* by W. Hogarth), Wellcome L. · group portrait, line engraving, pubd 1749 (after T. Bardwell, 1749), BM, Wellcome L. · T. Bardwell, portrait, *c*.1760, repro. in Campbell, 'Portrait of a quack', 118 · A. Carlini, statue, *c*.1760, V&A · E. Loving, portrait, *c*.1760, repro. in Campbell, 'Portrait of a quack', 118 · line engraving, 1820 (after T. Bardwell), Wellcome L. · J. Faber junior, mezzotint (after E. Loving), BM [*see illus.*]

Wealth at death £16,000: *London Chronicle*, 10 (1761), 634

Ward, Sir Lancelot Edward Barrington- (1884–1953), surgeon, was born at Worcester on 4 July 1884, the second son of Mark James Barrington-Ward (*d.* 1924) and his wife, Caroline Pearson; the father was an inspector of schools, and later became rector of Duloe in Cornwall and an honorary canon of Truro Cathedral. Barrington-Ward's four brothers all distinguished themselves in their various professions, one of them, R. M. Barrington-*Ward, becoming editor of *The Times*. Barrington-Ward entered Westminster School as a classical scholar, but became unwell and was transferred to Bromsgrove in his native county, where he was restored to health. He gained a classical exhibition at Worcester College, Oxford, but decided on medicine as a career and entered Edinburgh University, where he qualified in 1908. Also captain of the university rugby fifteen, he was awarded four English international caps and played against Wales in the first international match played on the new ground at Twickenham.

Barrington-Ward passed the Edinburgh fellowship examination in 1910 and the English fellowship two years later, after studying at the Middlesex Hospital in London. In 1913 he returned to Edinburgh to obtain the degree of ChM and was awarded the Chiene medal for outstanding ability. His London career in surgery began with his appointment in 1910 as a resident at the Great Ormond Street Hospital for Sick Children, where he assisted two of the leading children's surgeons of the day—George E. Waugh and Thomas Fairbank. He continued his work at this hospital as medical superintendent, and was appointed to the consulting staff in 1914. Immediately after the outbreak of war later that year he volunteered to go to the Balkans as surgeon-in-chief of no. 2 Serbian Relief Fund Hospital, with the honorary rank of lieutenant-colonel. He was awarded the grand cross of the order of St Olave and St Sava.

While still a young man Barrington-Ward's skill as a surgeon was widely recognized. He was much sought after by private patients and operated on several members of the royal family. In 1935 he was appointed KCVO and two years later he was made surgeon to the king's household. In 1952 he was invited to become an extra-surgeon to the queen.

Barrington-Ward's experience in children's surgery is recorded in numerous articles which he published in various journals, and in a standard textbook entitled *Abdominal Surgery of Children* (1928). In addition to his work at Great Ormond Street, he was also on the staff of the Wood Green and Royal Northern hospitals. At the last of these he eventually became senior surgeon. He suggested to his colleagues there that they produce a textbook of operative surgery in which the various members of staff dealt with their own specialities; under his editorship *Royal*

Northern Operative Surgery was published in 1939. As a surgeon, his success was not only due to his clinical judgement and technical skill; he was also gentle and sympathetic and had the enviable knack of obtaining the confidence of children who were his patients. In the operating theatre he showed punctilious courtesy to all the staff including the most junior nurse.

Barrington-Ward was twice married: first in 1917 to Dorothy Anne, second daughter of T. W. Miles, of Caragh, co. Kerry; she did much charitable work for the hospitals with which her husband was connected and also for the Peter Pan League. She died in 1935, leaving three daughters. In 1941 Barrington-Ward married Catherine Wilhelmina, only daughter of E. G. Reuter, of Harrogate; they had one son.

Barrington-Ward enjoyed welcoming his friends to his country home, Hawkedon House, Hawkedon, near Bury St Edmunds. He was knowledgeable enough about agriculture to be elected president of the Suffolk Agricultural Association. Unfortunately he did not have the chance to enjoy retirement, for despite undergoing drastic surgery he died at his home on 17 November 1953.

MN. LOVE, *rev.*

Sources *The Times* (18 Nov 1953) • *BMJ* (28 Nov 1953), 1221 • *BMJ* (12 Dec 1953), 1327–8 • *The Lancet* (28 Nov 1953) • private information (1971) • personal knowledge (1971)
Likenesses J. Barrington-Ward, bust; exh. Society of Portrait Sculptors, 1959
Wealth at death £26,130 16s. 10d.: probate, 3 April 1954, *CGPLA Eng. & Wales*

Ward, Sir Leslie [*pseud.* Spy] (**1851–1922**), caricaturist and portrait painter, was born on 21 November 1851 in Harewood Square, London, one of the eight children of the history painter Edward Matthew *Ward (1816–1879) and his wife, Henrietta Mary Ada *Ward (1832–1924), a fashionable portrait painter, art teacher, and hostess. Although they had the same surname before marriage, his parents were not related. Both were history painters of some note. His mother came from a line of painters and engravers, including her father, the engraver and miniature painter George Raphael *Ward [see under Ward, James (1769–1859)], and her grandfather, the celebrated animal painter James Ward. She was niece and great-niece respectively of the portrait painter John Jackson and the painter George Morland. Both parents had studios in their homes, Upton Park, Slough, Buckinghamshire, and Kent Villa, Kensington, London, where they entertained the London artistic and literary *haute monde*. His father was an exceptional mimic who delighted Charles Dickens and other eminent guests, and it may be inferred that Ward's eye for caricature was awakened in response to the lively atmosphere of his parents' home. Although they never gave their son formal training, they and their artistic friends encouraged the young Ward to draw, paint, and sculpt.

After preparatory instruction at Chase's School at Salt Hill, near Slough, Ward was sent to Eton College where he drew caricatures of his schoolfellows and masters. In 1867

Sir Leslie Ward [Spy] (1851–1922), by Pal (Jean de Paleologu), pubd 1889

his bust of his brother was exhibited at the Royal Academy, London. An undistinguished student, he left Eton in 1869 when his father attempted to deflect him into architecture. After an unhappy year in the office of the architect Sydney Smirke, who was a family friend, the artist W. P. Frith intervened on his behalf and Ward's father agreed to support his training as an artist. He thus entered the Royal Academy Schools in 1871.

Some artists rebelled against what they perceived as the stultifying influence of the Royal Academy; but not Ward, who found what he called the 'back to land' movement 'blatant realism that becomes nauseous' (L. Ward, 49). He might have made a living painting portraits and pictures which satisfied the tastes of prosperous Victorians, but his métier was polite caricature. In the winter of 1873 the painter John Everett Millais, another family friend, recommended that he bring his caricature of the comparative zoologist 'Old Bones' (Professor Richard Owen) to the founder owner and editor of *Vanity Fair*, Thomas Gibson Bowles. Having temporarily fallen out with Ape (Carlo Pellegrini), Bowles noted Ward's ability to capture the likenesses of prominent public figures and invited him to join the staff of *Vanity Fair*. As his *nom de crayon*, Ward suggested to Bowles that he use 'Spy ... "to observe secretly, or to discover at a distance or in concealment". "Just the thing", said Bowles' (ibid., 94).

Between 1873 and 1889, the year of Pellegrini's death, both he and Ward dominated the weekly coloured cartoon featured in *Vanity Fair*. The bohemian Pellegrini—witty, volatile, and gregarious—had developed the *portrait chargé* in *Vanity Fair*. He claimed that he taught Ward all he knew, a charge Ward later wished he had denied (L. Ward, 95–6). Ward was an observant caricaturist, especially effective in his treatment of judges, preachers, and literary figures. His witty caricature of the portly, myopic Anthony Trollope for *Vanity Fair* in 1873 (National Portrait Gallery, London), infuriated the novelist. Among the 1325 cartoons he drew for *Vanity Fair* between 1873 and 1911 are a significant number of revealing caricatures which captured the public persona of the victim. His portrayals, however, of royalty, nobility, and women were oversympathetic, if not sycophantic. Later in his career he became even more of a complimentary portraitist, a charge he acknowledged in *Forty Years of Spy* (1915), his genial, rambling memoir. Nevertheless, in 1900 he produced a penetrating and clever picture of Field Marshal Lord Roberts, and his 1907 sketch of the Conservative politician F. E. Smith (Lord Birkenhead) was a devastating indictment of an ambitious and unpleasant man.

Ward worked methodically, often from memory, after observing his 'victims' in their element at the racecourse, in the law courts, in church, in the university lecture theatre, or in the lobby of the houses of parliament. Sometimes they came to his studio. A caricaturist, he believed, was born, not made. As he observed, 'A good memory, an eye for detail, and a mind to appreciate and grasp the whole atmosphere and peculiarity of the "subject" are of course essentials' (L. Ward, 109). A caricature should never depend on a physical defect, nor should it be forced. 'If I could sum up the art in a sentence it would be that caricature should be a comic impression with a kindly touch, and always devoid of vulgarity' (Matthews, 57).

Ward was droll, gentle, and something of a snob. He lived a comfortable, pleasant, upper-class bachelor life in London. His family connections, education, and personal acquaintances meant that he was a member of society. His clubs included the Arts, the Orleans, the Fielding, the Lotus, the Punch Bowl, and the Beefsteak (where he was one of the original members). There he sketched many of his victims. In 1899, years after her father had refused Ward permission to marry her, Ward married the society hostess Judith Mary Topham-Watney, the only daughter of Major Richard Topham, 4th hussars. They had one daughter, Sidney.

Ward's last cartoon for *Vanity Fair* appeared in June 1911; he had recently begun to contribute 'character' portraits to *The World* and *Mayfair*. He supplemented his income and fulfilled his artistic yearnings by painting portraits, some of which are still extant. In 1918 he was knighted. Eileen Harris observed that '*Spy* spent forty years being a tamed

Ape' (Harris, 56), a not inconsiderable accomplishment. Ward prophesied that 'when the history of the Victorian Era comes to be written in true perspective, the most faithful mirror and record of representative men and spirit of their times will be sought and found in *Vanity Fair*' (L. Ward, 331). *Vanity Fair* portraits are still referred to by many as 'Spy Cartoons'. After a nervous breakdown Ward died suddenly of heart failure at 4 Dorset Square, Marylebone, London, on 15 May 1922 and was buried on 18 May at Kensal Green cemetery, London. About 300 of his original drawings for *Vanity Fair* are in the National Portrait Gallery, London.   PETER MELLINI

Sources DNB · L. Ward, *Forty years of Spy* (1915) · *Vanity Fair* albums, 1873–1911 · R. T. Matthews and P. Mellini, *In 'Vanity Fair'* (1982) · R. T. Matthews, 'Spy', *British History Illustrated*, 2 (June–July 1976), 50–57 · *The Times* (16 May 1922) · *The Times* (19 May 1922) · E. Harris, 'Carlo Pellegrini: man and "Ape"', *Apollo*, 103 (1976), 53–7 · *CGPLA Eng. & Wales* (1922) · *Mrs E. M. Ward's reminiscences*, ed. E. O'Donnell (1911) · J. J. Savory and others, *The 'Vanity Fair' gallery* (1979) · W. Feaver, *Masters of caricature: from Hogarth and Gillray to Scarfe and Levine*, ed. A. Green (1981) · M. Bryant and S. Heneage, eds., *Dictionary of British cartoonists and caricaturists, 1730–1980* (1994)

Likenesses B. Stone, photograph, 1901, NPG · Vandyk, photograph, c.1915, repro. in Ward, *Forty years of Spy*, frontispiece · Pal [J. de Paleologu], caricature, watercolour, NPG; repro. in VF (23 Nov 1889) [*see illus.*] · Pal [J. de Paleologu], caricature, chromolithograph, repro. in VF (29 Nov 1889)

Wealth at death £397 5s. 8d.: administration, 23 June 1922, *CGPLA Eng. & Wales*

Ward, Martin Theodore (*c*.1799–1874). *See under* Ward, William (1766–1826).

Ward, Mary (1585–1645), Roman Catholic nun and founder of the Institute of the Blessed Virgin Mary, was born on 23 January 1585 at Mulwith Manor, near Ripon in Yorkshire. She was the eldest of the six children of Marmaduke Ward (*b. c*.1552), gentleman and bailiff to Henry Percy, ninth earl of Northumberland, and Ursula Wright (*b. c*.1565), the widow of John Constable; both her parents belonged to close-knit families of minor east Yorkshire gentry. They and their relatives were Roman Catholics who persisted in their faith after the Elizabethan settlement, many of them experiencing a loss of wealth and periods of imprisonment as convicted recusants. From the age of five Mary Ward was cared for mostly in the households of relatives and, through close female relatives, gained practical knowledge of the vital part played by women in the preservation and practice of Catholicism in England. She was educated at home, learning Latin from an early age and later becoming proficient in the major European modern languages.

Becoming a nun Between the ages of five and ten Mary Ward lived with her grandparents Robert and Ursula Wright on their estate, Ploughland, near Welwick in Holderness, returning to her parents when her grandfather died in 1594. But the following year Mulwith Manor was completely destroyed by fire and the rest of the family moved, in 1597, to the Percy estate at Alnwick in Northumberland. Mary Ward herself went first to live with her widowed relative Katherine Ardington at Harewell House near Ripon and then, from 1600 to 1606, with Sir Ralph

Mary Ward (1585–1645), by unknown artist, 1621

and Lady Grace Bapthorpe of Osgodby and Babthorpe near York. In this highly religious household, with its Jesuit priest and daily regime of devotions and instruction, Mary Ward began to order her life around prayer and spiritual reading. According to her autobiographical notes, made largely in 1617 and 1627, she was about fifteen when she first expressed the hope of becoming a nun. Her family, however, wished her to marry and encouraged the three or four suitors who made offers of marriage. Contemporaries commented on her beauty and attractiveness of personality while the visual sources, in the form of contemporary and posthumous portraits along with the unusual fifty narrative paintings from the seventeenth and eighteenth centuries which comprise the painted life of Mary Ward, convey these same qualities.

By 1605 Mary Ward was sufficiently sure of her religious calling to refuse the hand of Edmund Neville, the Catholic claimant to the forfeited earldom of Westmorland, despite the views of her father and her confessor, Father Richard Holtby, that it was her duty to accept. In that same year her father was arrested as an alleged conspirator in the Gunpowder Plot. He was not charged and, according to Peters, was unlikely even to have known of the plans. But two of her uncles, Christopher and John Wright, and Thomas Percy, the husband of her aunt Martha Wright, were deeply involved and were killed in the courtyard of Holbeach House while resisting arrest. In May 1606, soon after this significant series of personal and political events, Mary Ward left England for St Omer in Flanders to

seek admission to one of the enclosed contemplative orders.

Through her contacts, particularly with the Jesuits who had their English College in St Omer, Mary Ward was admitted as a novice external sister with the Walloon Poor Clares. Becoming convinced, however, that her call was to help found a Poor Clare convent for Englishwomen she left the Walloon community in April 1607 to undertake the necessary negotiations with the ecclesiastical and civil authorities. Although she was young and unknown her initiative succeeded and the new convent was established in Gravelines by the end of 1608 with an endowment from the governor and the transfer of professed English nuns from the St Omer Poor Clares. Attracting applicants immediately from England it grew rapidly and Mary Ward, who was one of the novices, recorded her total contentment there. However, according to these same autobiographical notes, in May 1609 she received the first of a series of visions that changed the course of her life and led her to play a significant part in a debate about the role of women religious in the Catholic church that continued beyond her lifetime.

Founding the institute These mystical illuminations, which she described as intellectual rather than visual or aural revelations, were central to Mary Ward's subsequent actions. From the first occasion in May 1609 she understood only that she was to leave the newly founded Poor Clares and undertake an unspecified work that would bring her opprobrium. She therefore left and returned to London, where she used her social networks to undertake domestic evangelization and religious instruction of former Catholics. While in London she experienced a second illumination (the gloria vision) in November, which made clear that her unspecified mission would be wholly good and for the glory of God. During this period she gathered a group of seven young women from similar backgrounds, several of them related to one another and to her, who were prepared to follow her leadership and to live together in St Omer. There, close to the Jesuit college, they set up a quasi-religious house in early 1610 and gave religious instruction and teaching, first to the adult English émigrés living locally and then to their children and boarders sent from England. Known as the 'English Ladies' this small community had ten members by 1611 and was supported by the Jesuits and Bishop Blaes of St Omer. In 1611 Mary Ward's third and crucial vision led her to understand that her community, which had a conventual style of life, a Jesuit confessor, and private vows but as yet no rule, habit, or perpetual vows, should 'take the same of the Society' (Peters, 114), adapted where necessary for women. Peters argues from documentary evidence that Mary Ward interpreted her vision to mean that the fledgeling institute should adopt the *Formula Instituti* of the Society of Jesus, a position confirmed and reinforced by the final illumination, known as the vision of the 'just soul', of November 1615 (Peters, 116). The vision also revealed that the Jesuits would never permit this, as indeed they could not, since Ignatius of Loyola had expressly forbidden the society to take on the work of directing orders of nuns. The constitution of Ward's institute became, therefore, the critical issue. Between the first vision of 1611 and the last in 1615 individual Jesuits (including her confessor, Father Roger Lee) and other ecclesiastical friends drew up rules for a teaching institute, Schola Beatae Mariae, which Mary Ward ultimately rejected as only approximating to a Jesuit way of life. Simultaneously her proposals and activities prompted controversy within the society and there began a hostile campaign against the institute involving Jesuits, secular clergy, and leading members of the English laity.

Mary Ward's attempts to realize her revelations through the establishment of a new canonical institute challenged the *status quo* in three ways: first, it required a recognition that women living under vows could undertake educational and other work, including missionary activity, outside the cloister; second, that an institute of women could be organized across diocesan and state boundaries and therefore needed to be accountable to Rome under the delegated authority of a female chief superior, rather than more locally under a bishop; and third, that in adopting the constitutions of the Society of Jesus women religious would be permitted to develop the same kind of liberty as Jesuits to determine, under obedience to the pope by their fourth vow, what ministries would best achieve the 'greater glory of God and, in any place further the propagation of our Holy Mother, the Catholic Church', even to the point of working individually rather than in community (Byrne, 34). Hers was not the only initiative in this vein, but taken together these three proposals went beyond others and even beyond what the church would accept for women by the early twentieth century.

Expansion Not much is known about Mary Ward between 1609 to 1615, although what is certain is that she led the English Ladies in the development of two distinct ministries: missionary and catechetical work with adults, usually women, in England, and teaching girls in their own schools in St Omer. The first activity was necessarily clandestine, undertaken by a smaller number of highly trained women who worked individually and, like priests, were protected by Catholic families. The second was public, highly regarded by some clerics and involving at least thirty teachers by 1615. Valued though this was by her for its evangelical potential, because through it future wives and mothers would acquire the necessary education to sustain the faith of their households, Mary Ward nevertheless continued to attach considerable importance to the more hidden work in England as the institute expanded across Europe.

Between 1616 and 1628 the experience of Mary Ward's institute was characterized on the one hand by expansion, new foundations, and support from monarchs and churchmen and on the other by virulent hostility, poverty, and failure to achieve official approval. New houses and schools were opened across the continent: Liège (1616), Cologne and Trier (1620–21), Rome (1622), Naples (1623), Perugia (1624), Munich (1627), Vienna (1627), and Pressburg (1628). Mary Ward travelled considerable distances throughout this time, raised financial resources, and organized the network of her senior and most trusted members to run the new houses. The schools flourished and received hundreds of pupils, impressing Maximilian I, duke of Bavaria, who became a major proponent of their educational work, and Pope Urban VIII, who admired Mary Ward as an individual. As important was her redrafting of the constitution and her attempt to gain papal approbation of the institute from Paul V, Gregory XV, and Urban VIII. She and several companions travelled thousands of miles on foot across Europe to present the document personally to Pope Gregory XV in Rome in 1621 and later to Pope Urban VIII. Mary Ward found the normal Vatican bureaucratic procedures and caution difficult to understand and, despite her optimism about approbation, she received none. Alongside letters of support for the institute the Roman authorities received highly critical documents and petitions from England and elsewhere calling the English Ladies 'Jesuitesses', 'galloping girls', 'chattering hussies' (Peters, 341), and accusing them of moral laxity, usurpation of priestly roles, and even heresy. The controversy became increasingly damaging to the institute. Action was taken by the Inquisition to warn and then to suppress houses of the institute from 1628 onwards, culminating in the promulgation of the papal bull *Pastoralis Romani pontificis* in January 1631. Described by one source as the 'harshest Bull ever to emanate from Rome', it suppressed the institute itself and denounced its members (Littlehales, 213).

Mary Ward herself was imprisoned for nine weeks. Throughout these events she remained unswervingly loyal both to her own mission and to the church. In turn many members of the institute stayed loyal to her and she continued to be seen as an exceptional and holy woman by many she encountered personally. On her release she went directly to Rome for an audience with Pope Urban who cleared her of the charge of heresy and allowed her, in 1632, to establish a group of women and a school in Rome under protection of the Holy See. The pope himself paid her a pension and supplied medicines and wine. Former members, working as lay teachers, also reopened the school in Munich in 1635, under the protection of Maximilian of Bavaria.

Final years and legacy These modest restorations of the institute's work were important for future developments, but her own life was now dominated by the ill health she had long experienced from a chronic gallstone condition. In 1637 she made her way slowly across Europe from Rome, visiting Paris and Liège before arriving in London in May 1639. There she remained until the civil war forced her to travel north home to Yorkshire in 1642. She died at Heworth Manor near York on 20 January 1645, attended by members of the institute, including two of her first companions, Mary Poyntz and Winifred Wigmore, and she was buried in the parish church of St Thomas in the village of Osbaldwick just outside Heworth. Her simple gravestone reads 'To love the poore, persever in the same, live dy and rise with them was all the ayme of Mary Ward'.

Mary Ward remained a controversial figure in the church long after her death. The institute survived and slowly expanded from the core that remained in Italy, England (York and Hammersmith), and Bavaria but the houses in different countries developed independently and did not sustain the unity across boundaries that had been integral to her vision. Moreover, the tradition of Mary Ward as founder became suppressed within them because the bull of 1631—and a subsequent bull concerning women's religious institutes, *Quamvis justo*, issued by Benedict XIV in 1749, which repeated many of the earlier accusations—had such force. During the eighteenth and early nineteenth centuries much archival material on her life was destroyed or was, like the Painted Life series, hidden. Mary Ward's eventual rehabilitation was the work of individual nuns in the English houses, with support from a learned Jesuit writer, and formed part of a more general impulse among nineteenth-century Catholics in England to recover an English Catholic past and create a public identity with a history. As a result of their researches and efforts the different houses joined forces temporarily to petition for papal approbation, which was finally granted in 1877. Detailed research into Mary Ward's life, using archives across Europe, led to the publication of Catherine Chambers's two-volume life in 1882–5. In the context of changing female roles Mary Ward became of interest and her ideas were no longer seen as dangerously radical. By 1909 Pope Pius X was ready to rehabilitate her as founder of the institute, now called Institute of the Blessed Virgin Mary, leading the way to the unification of all the branches in England, Ireland, Germany, Austria, Italy, and Canada in 1911. Interest in Mary Ward from a variety of quarters outside her own institute continued to develop during the twentieth century with Pope John Paul II choosing the first papal visit to Britain in 1982 to single her out as 'an extraordinary Yorkshire woman … a pioneer of the active unenclosed congregations for women' (*The Pope Teaches* (1982) pt5, 143).   SUSAN O'BRIEN

Sources H. Peters, *Mary Ward: a world in contemplation*, trans. H. Butterworth (1994) · M. M. W. Littlehales, *Mary Ward: pilgrim and mystic* (1998) · M. C. Chambers, *The life of Mary Ward*, 2 vols. (1882–5) · L. Byrne, *Mary Ward: a pilgrim finds her way* (Dublin, 1984) · M. G. Kirkus, '"Yes, my lord": some eighteenth and nineteenth century bishops and the Institute of the Blessed Virgin Mary', *Recusant History*, 24/2 (1998), 171–92 · I. Wetter, 'Mary Ward's apostolic vision', *The Way*, supplement 17 (1972), 69–91
Archives Institute of the Blessed Virgin Mary, Rome, archives of the Generalate · Institute of the Blessed Virgin Mary, Munich, archives · State Archives of Belgium, Liège, MSS | Sacra Congregazione di Propaganda Fide, Rome, MSS · Society of Jesus, Brussels, archives
Likenesses fifty oils, 17th cent.–18th cent. (*The painted life of Mary Ward*), provincial house of the Institute of the Blessed Virgin Mary, Augsburg, Germany; facsimile copy, Bar convent, York · oils, 1621, provincial house of the Institute of the Blessed Virgin Mary, Augsburg, Germany [*see illus.*] · oils, 1733 (*Pilgrim to Rome in 1621*), provincial house of the Institute of the Blessed Virgin Mary, Augsburg, Germany · J. Moerl, line engraving, BM · postcards (from *Painted life*), repro. in Littlehales, *Mary Ward*

Ward [*née* King], **Mary** [*pseud.* the Hon. Mrs Ward] (1827–1869), microscopist and author, was born on 27 April 1827, at Ballylin, near Ferbane, King's county, Ireland, the daughter of the Revd Henry King, landowner, and his wife, Harriett Lloyd, whose sister was the mother of the third earl of Rosse. Mary was the youngest of four children, three of them girls, who were educated at home and encouraged by their parents to interest themselves in astronomy and natural history, as well as to practise drawing and painting. Ballylin was a cultured home, and Mary also frequently visited her cousin, William, earl of Rosse, at Birr Castle, only a few miles away. Mary's childhood enthusiasm developed into a serious study of the natural world, using the microscope made by Andrew Ross, one of the three leading instrument makers of London, that her father bought her when she was eighteen. She presented microscopical shows to family, friends, and the estate workers, and received much encouragement in her work both at home and from scientific friends of Lord Rosse, whom she met at Birr, and on visits to London. Her drawings and paintings of animals, birds, and insects, and of specimens seen through the microscope, were skilled and accurate.

In 1854, when she was twenty-seven, Mary married Henry William Crosbie Ward (1828–1911), second son of the third Viscount Bangor of Castle Ward, co. Down, whose elder brother, Edward, had succeeded to the title and estates. Henry resigned his army commission shortly after his marriage and took no regular employment, despite the fact that Mary's considerable dowry, in shares, did not maintain its value, so that they were unable to live on the income. Eight children were born to the couple between 1855 and 1867, and for much of this time they had no permanent home and were in constant financial difficulties.

Mary Ward continued to pursue the scientific interests that had been so much encouraged during her girlhood. Her close friendship with her cousin, Lord Rosse, and his wife meant that she was often at Birr during the building of the great telescope with its 6 foot diameter mirror, completed in 1845; she was one of the first to make observations with it. Among the distinguished visitors to her parents' home was Sir David Brewster, who became a friend; he sent her specimens to mount for microscopical examination and used her illustrations to accompany some of his publications. He also obtained books for her and sent her copies of his own works. The result of her microscopical research and reading was that by the time of her marriage Mary had the capacity to write for publication; the difficulty was that, at that period, it was not easy for a woman to become a contributor to scientific journals, nor to find a publisher for a book.

In 1856 Mary embarked on her literary career, writing and hand printing a booklet on specimens of insect eggs and larvae that had been sent to her, and which she examined under the microscope. *A Windfall for the Microscope* was intended for distribution to friends, and was formally published only much later. The original microscope slides and other material were discovered during 1982–4 by Dr

Owen Harry among the archives at Castle Ward. This was the family home of Henry Ward, who inherited the title of fifth Viscount Bangor in 1874, and moved there with his children five years after Mary's death. This first venture was followed a year later by *Sketches with the Microscope*, a collection of letters on common objects suitable for examination under the microscope. The plates Mary lithographed herself and had hand coloured by a Dublin engraver. Then a local printer in Parsonstown was commissioned to print 250 copies. One was shown by a relative of Mary to a London publisher, Groombridge & Sons, of Paternoster Row, who bought the copyright and republished it in 1858 under the title *A World of Wonders Revealed by the Microscope*.

This book, and its companion volume on the telescope, proved highly successful, and went through several editions, with revisions, first under the titles *Telescope Teachings* (first published 1859) and *Microscope Teachings* (published with this title in 1864), and later simply as *The Microscope* and *The Telescope*, by 'The Hon. Mrs Ward' (a title to which she had no right). They were favourably reviewed for their easy style and especially for the quality of Mary's illustrations. Mary Ward also published, in 1859, *Entomology in Sport and Entomology in Earnest* in collaboration with her sister, Lady Jane Mahon, as well as a number of articles in monthly journals such as *Recreative Science*, under the imprint of Groombridge & Sons.

What had clearly become a successful, if minor, literary career was cut short on 31 August 1869 when Mary Ward was killed in an accidental fall when riding in a steam road locomotive at Birr Castle. She takes her place among the popularizers of science who, during the eighteenth and nineteenth centuries, did much to encourage a knowledge of, and interest in, the natural world among the general public, and thus to stimulate the advances in science and technology that marked the industrial revolution.

G. L'E. TURNER

Sources O. G. Harry, 'The Hon. Mrs Ward and "A windfall for the microscope", of 1856 and 1864', *Annals of Science*, 41 (1984), 471–82 · O. Harry, 'Mary Ward', *Some people and places in Irish science and technology*, ed. C. Mollan, W. Davis, and B. Finucane (1985), 52–3 · O. Harry, 'The Hon. Mrs Ward (1827–1869)', ed. J. R. Nudds, N. D. McMillan, D. L. Weaire, and S. M. P. McKenna Lawlor, *Science in Ireland, 1800–1930: tradition and reform* [Proceedings of an International Symposium held at Trinity College, Dublin, 3/1986] (1988), 187–97 · Desmond, *Botanists*, rev. edn, 717

Likenesses countess of Rosse, photograph, Birr Castle, co. Offaly · portrait, repro. in Harry, 'The Hon. Mrs Ward (1827–1869)'

Ward [*née* Arnold], **Mary Augusta** [*known as* Mrs Humphry Ward] **(1851–1920)**, novelist, philanthropist, and political lobbyist, born on 11 June 1851 in Hobart Town, Van Diemen's Land, was the eldest child of Thomas *Arnold (1823–1900), inspector of schools in Hobart Town, and his wife, Julia Sorell (1826–1888), daughter of William Sorell, of Hobart Town. Her father was the second son of Dr Thomas *Arnold of Rugby and her uncle was the poet Matthew Arnold. Following her father's reception into the Roman Catholic church in January 1856 his position in Tasmania became untenable and the family returned to England. Julia and the three children were temporarily

Mary Augusta Ward [Mrs Humphry Ward] **(1851–1920)**, by Barraud, pubd 1889

installed at Fox How, the Arnolds' family home in the Lake District, and Thomas went to Dublin to take up a tutorship secured for him by J. H. Newman at the Catholic University. While her mother and her younger siblings were united with Thomas Arnold in Ireland, Mary remained at Fox How. From 1858 to 1860 she was a boarder at Anne Jemima Clough's school at Eller How, Ambleside. Thereafter she boarded at a succession of schools.

In 1865, when Thomas Arnold converted back to Anglicanism, he was able to take up a university teaching post at Oxford. In July 1867 Mary was finally reunited with her family at Laleham, the large house which Arnold had built for his family in the Banbury Road. Possessed of striking looks (which she attributed to Spanish ancestry on her mother's side) and a powerful, if as yet unformed, mind, she was taken on as a protégée by Mark Pattison (whom she was later to use as the model for Wendover in *Robert Elsmere*). It was at Pattison's instigation that she began her research into early Spanish history, and she was also writing tales and novels which found no favour with publishers. At this period of her life she was strongly influenced by the philosopher T. H. Green.

In July 1871 Mary Arnold met a young fellow of Brasenose College, (Thomas) Humphry Ward (1845–1926), son of the Revd Henry Ward and Jane Sandwith; they were married on 6 April 1872. Through her husband she acquired other influential friends, notably Mandell Creighton and his wife, Louise, Walter Pater, and John

Richard Green. She was by now publishing some of the fruits of her Spanish research. In 1873 she was instrumental with Louise Creighton and Mrs T. H. Green (Charlotte Green) in setting up the Lectures for Women Committee, an initiative which led to the establishment of Somerville Hall (later Somerville College) in 1879. The Wards had three children: Dorothy Mary Ward (1874–1964), Arnold Sandwith Ward (1876–1950), and Janet Penrose Ward (1879–1956).

Following the success of his anthology *The English Poets* in 1879, Humphry Ward resolved to give up academic life. He took a position on *The Times* in January 1881, and a year later became the newspaper's principal art critic and occasional leader writer. In November 1881 the family moved to London. Over the next few years Mary Ward established herself as a leading journalist and literary hostess. In 1881 she published her first book, *Milly and Olly*, a tale for children. Her translation of Henri Amiel's *Journal intime* was published in 1885. She met Henry James in November 1882, and it was a trip with James to the theatre to see the American actress Mary Anderson in January 1884 which led to Ward's first published novel, *Miss Bretherton*. Macmillans published the novel, which was well received but sold poorly.

None the less Mary Ward was encouraged to embark on a more ambitious work—*Robert Elsmere*. Macmillans turned the new project down, but it was accepted by the prescient George Smith, of Smith Elder. After much revision, Mrs Ward's drama of religious faith and doubt was finally published on 24 April 1888. It was critically reviewed at length by W. F. Gladstone in the May 1888 issue of *Nineteenth Century*. *Robert Elsmere* was amazingly successful, in Britain and in the United States (where it was not, however, protected by international copyright). On the strength of her sales, Mrs Ward secured a record-breaking £7000 for the American rights of her third novel, *David Grieve*. This work, which marked the author's growing concern with social problems, was published in 1892, having been held back until the passing of the international copyright agreement in the USA. It was another best-seller. On the strength of her sales success Mrs Ward bought a large country house, Stocks, near Aldbury in Hertfordshire—a costly establishment which was to absorb much of her income. Despite alarming collapses in her health she produced a series of highly successful novels over the next few years in partnership with Smith Elder. *Marcella* (1894) was her first attempt at a literary heroine, a line continued with *Helbeck of Bannisdale* (1898) which contains a sensitive evocation of her early relationship with her father.

Mrs Ward's philanthropy, and her practicality, were expressed in the establishment of a 'Settlement' for the working classes in the St Pancras area of London. Initially founded on Unitarian principles, 'University Hall' in Gordon Square eventually led to the building of the secular Passmore Edwards Settlement (named after its principal donor, J. Passmore Edwards) on the corner of Tavistock Square. The centre (which pioneered the children's play movement in England) opened in 1897. Mrs Ward's uneasy relationship with Anglicanism was given expression in a campaign conducted in *The Times* in September 1899, arguing that the sacraments should not be denied to those who could not bring themselves to believe in the biblical accounts of miracles. Meanwhile her output of best-selling fiction continued unabated, though poor health and the increasing need to write for money were taking their toll. *Eleanor* (1900) reflected the author's love of Italy, where she now habitually spent holidays. *Lady Rose's Daughter* (1903) and *The Marriage of William Ashe* (1905) marked a growing penchant for melodrama. A distinct decline in the quality of her writing is detectable in *Fenwick's Career* (1905) and *The Testing of Diana Mallory* (1908).

In 1904 Mrs Ward's daughter Janet married the historian G. M. Trevelyan, and her first grandchild, Mary Trevelyan was born in 1905. Her son Arnold had embarked on a career in politics and was elected Liberal Unionist member for West Hertfordshire in 1910, a seat he held until 1918. 1908 was a pinnacle in Mrs Ward's career, for it was in this year that she made a triumphant tour of North America (where, among other powerful contacts, she formed a friendship with Theodore Roosevelt).

Less happily it was in June 1908 that Mrs Ward consented to head the Women's Anti-Suffrage Association. The anti-suffrage fiction which followed (*Daphne*, 1909; *Delia Blanchflower*, 1915) triggered a downturn in her popularity, particularly in the United States. Members of her own family, friends such as Louise Creighton, Somerville College (which she had helped found), and the bulk of those associated with the Passmore Edwards centre were opposed to her political views on women's rights. *The Case of Richard Meynell* (1911), a sequel to *Robert Elsmere*, was also something of a failure. Poor health and an exhausting round of speech-making and article-writing for the anti-suffrage cause conduced to a deterioration in her fiction. She was now writing principally for money, a situation exacerbated by financial losses in 1913 in the form of Arnold's massive gambling debts, which his mother undertook to pay.

During the years 1914–18 Mrs Ward's authorial fortunes mended somewhat. At the request of Roosevelt she wrote a work of propaganda for the American market, *England's Effort* (1916), a book which is credited with helping to bring the United States into the First World War. It was followed by the similarly journalistic *Towards the Goal* (1917) and the post-war *Fields of Victory* (1919). She was assisted in the writing of these works and in the running of the Passmore Edwards centre by her unmarried daughter, Dorothy. The war novel *Missing* (1917) and the evocation of the Oxford of her girlhood, *Lady Connie* (1916), are the best fiction she produced in the last phase of her career. Also of interest is the autobiographical *A Writer's Recollections* (1918). Tax demands and Arnold Ward's continued gaming losses led to her finding herself virtually bankrupt in 1919. She was made a CBE in March 1919 and in February 1920 was invited by the lord chancellor to be one of the country's first women magistrates. In the same month she was awarded an honorary degree by Edinburgh University. By now she was totally disabled by bronchitis, neuritis, and heart disease. She died on 24 March at 4 Connaught Square, London, and three days later was buried near Stocks at the church of St John the Baptist, Aldbury, Hertfordshire. She was survived by her husband.

JOHN SUTHERLAND

Sources J. P. Trevelyan, *The life of Mrs Humphry Ward* (1923?) · E. Huws Jones, *Mrs Humphry Ward* (1973) · J. Sutherland, *Mrs Humphry Ward: eminent Victorian, pre-eminent Edwardian* (1990) · *The letters of Thomas Arnold the younger, 1850–1900*, ed. J. Bertram (1980) · *The New Zealand letters of Thomas Arnold the younger, 1847–1851*, ed. J. Bertram (1966) · d. cert.
Archives BL, Add. MS 43505 · Bodl. Oxf., notebook, incl. Oxford Lectures for Ladies minutes · Claremont Colleges, California, Honnold/Mudd Library, corresp., literary MSS, and papers · Col. U., Library, corresp., literary MSS, and papers · Hunt. L., letters · Mary Ward Centre, Queen's Square, London, corresp. and papers · NYPL · Pusey Oxf., corresp. and literary papers · UCL, family diaries · Washington University, St Louis, Missouri, notes and literary papers | BL, corresp. with Thomas Anstey Guthrie (F. Anstey) · BL, corresp. with Macmillans, Add. MS 54928 · BL, corresp. with Society of Authors, Add. MS 56840 · BLPES, letters to Frederic Harrison · Bodl. Oxf., corresp. with Viscount Addison · Castle Howard, North Yorkshire, letters to ninth earl of Carlisle · NL Scot., corresp. with Lord Haldane · NL Scot., corresp., mainly with Lord Rosebery · Richmond Local Studies Library, London, Sladen MSS · U. Leeds, Brotherton L., letters to Edmund Gosse · Wellcome L., letters to the Barlow family
Likenesses C. L. Dodgson, photograph, 1872, NPG · Barraud, photograph, pubd 1889, NPG [*see illus.*] · L. Graham Smith, pastel drawing, 1889, Somerville College, Oxford · J. R. Story, oils, 1889, NPG · R. Lehmann, chalk drawing, 1890, BM · E. Arnold, photograph, 1898?, Somerville College, Oxford · W. & D. Downey, photograph, woodburytype, NPG; repro. in W. Downey and D. Downey, *The cabinet portrait gallery*, 1 (1890) · Elliott & Fry, photograph, NPG · Loud, photogravure (after Elliott & Fry), NPG · A. Steiner, crayon drawing, Mary Ward Centre, London · photographs, repro. in Sutherland, *Mrs Humphry Ward*
Wealth at death £11,306 3s.: administration, 8 May 1920, CGPLA Eng. & Wales

Ward [*married name* Sheed], **Mary Josephine** [Maisie] (1889–1975), writer and publisher, was born on 4 January 1889 at Snowdon House, Shanklin, Isle of Wight, the first of the five children of Wilfrid Philip *Ward (1856–1916), biographer and editor of the *Dublin Review*, and his wife, Josephine Mary Hope-Scott (1864–1932), Catholic novelist and daughter of James Robert Hope-*Scott and Victoria Howard. Her parents were both English. On her maternal side she was related to the duke of Norfolk, the highest ranking Catholic peer, and on her paternal side to William George *Ward, Oxford don, colleague of John Henry Newman, and the first of the Oxford Movement to 'go over to Rome'. All four of her grandparents were converts to Roman Catholicism.

Maisie, as she was always known, lived initially on the Isle of Wight, where the Ward family had considerable influence, and later in Eastbourne and then Dorking. After her father's death she lived with her mother in London. One brother died in youth, another lived on the Isle of Wight, and the youngest became a priest and died young. Her only sister married and became a writer, but like the youngest brother she was psychologically fragile. Maisie was educated at home, at a convent school in Dorking, and at St Mary's Convent School, a boarding-

school in Cambridge (1905–6), where she displayed a good command of Latin. She was influenced there by the preaching of Robert Hugh Benson and the inspiration of the seventeenth-century Mary Ward, whose nuns ran the school.

The atmosphere of the Ward home was Catholic and intellectual. Both parents were prolific writers who included among their friends Catholic intellectuals of the day—G. K. Chesterton, Hilaire Belloc, Friedrich and Anatole von Hügel, and William Basil Maturin. Her father's difficult confrontation with the modernist movement left its mark on Maisie. After finishing her schooling she worked as his secretary and during the First World War volunteered for the Red Cross. Although her younger brothers attended Oxford, she did not, even though she was encouraged to do so by her teachers. By her own account, for almost fifteen years she dithered away her life.

In 1919 Maisie Ward's life changed when she became a founding member of the Catholic Evidence Guild (CEG); she remained active in this movement for almost fifty years. Through it she met her future husband, an Australian law student, Francis Joseph *Sheed (1897–1981), whom she married on 27 April 1926. The CEG played a major role in their professional and personal lives. They devoted many hours each week to training and speaking. In the year of their marriage they co-founded the publishing firm of Sheed and Ward with money given by Josephine Ward. Many CEG friends joined them in working at Sheed and Ward, which Tom Burns in *The Use of Memory: Publishing and Further Pursuits* (1993) called a cross between 'a sweat-shop and a university'. Seven years later an American office of Sheed and Ward was opened in New York. It was only in 1973 that the Sheeds sold the American company.

Through her twenty-seven books and her work in the firm Ward influenced several generations of educated Anglo-American Catholics. Beginning in the late 1920s Sheed and Ward took the continental Catholic intellectual revival first to England and then to the United States. Sheed and Ward authors included the French authors Leon Bloy, François Mauriac, and Paul Claudel, and the English Christopher Dawson, E. I. Watkin, C. C. Martindale, Martin D'Arcy, and Ronald Knox, as well as Frank Sheed. Maisie first translated and edited volumes for Sheed and Ward. An early contribution was *The English Way* (1933), edited essays about English spiritual writers from Bede to Newman. Her first major publication was *The Wilfrid Wards and the Transition* (1934, 1937), a two-volume study of the Ward family which established her as heir of William George Ward and hence the 'granddaughter of the Oxford Movement'.

In 1927 Maisie gave birth to Rosemary; three years later Wilfrid was born. The latter became a noted American writer and essayist. The Sheeds' domestic life was managed by Frank's Australian mother, who lived with the family. For many years the Sheeds lived at Horley in Surrey, where they opened a chapel which served the rural Catholic community. Frank and Maisie educated the community in the faith, in music, and in liturgical practice.

During the Second World War Maisie and their children moved to Torresdale, near Philadelphia, while Frank continued to travel back and forth to London to maintain the publishing business. During these war years Maisie wrote *This Burning Heat: Gilbert Keith Chesterton* (1943), her most popular book, and *The Splendor of the Rosary* (1945). She returned to England after the war and published her favourite book, *Young Mr. Newman* (1948), and *Return to Chesterton* (1952). Her interest in the priest-worker movement led to *France Pagan?* (1949), and efforts to bolster family life produced *Be not Solicitous* (1953). In the 1950s she turned to religious topics and wrote *They Saw His Glory: an Introduction to the Gospels and Acts* (1956) and *Saints who Made History* (1959). She commemorated the life of her friend Caryll Houselander in *The Divine Eccentric* (1962) and *The Letters of Caryll Houselander* (1965). Her final major work was a two-volume study, *Robert Browning and his World* (1967–9), which celebrated her favourite poet. She wrote two autobiographies: *Unfinished Business* (1964) and *To and fro on the Earth* (1973). Almost all of her books were published by Sheed and Ward. Although her prose was never brilliant, her research was extensive, and she wrote with an obvious and contagious sympathy and enthusiasm.

After 1940 Ward travelled extensively between England, the continent, and America, and later to Australia and Asia. The purpose of this travel was often research and lecturing. This did not deter her writing, which she did in hotels, on planes and trains, and in waiting-rooms.

Ward's prodigious writing life was paralleled by a commitment to social concerns. She was a great friend of Dorothy Day, the American who founded the Catholic Worker Movement, although they differed on the issue of pacifism. She also worked with the Russian Baroness Catherine de Hueck, founder of Friendship House. During her early married life she was influenced by distributism and operated several unsuccessful farms. Her love of community led her to support the Marycrest community in New York, the Taena community in England, the Canadian maritime co-operatives, priest-worker groups in France, and the land reform movement in India. She was co-founder of the Catholic Housing Aid Society in England, which worked to ameliorate the housing crisis created by the war.

Ward's literary, religious, and social interests became the subjects of the lecturing on street corners, at Catholic colleges and universities, and at church gatherings, particularly in the United States. She was usually the only woman on the speakers' platform, appearing with prelates, priests, and laymen. Although not considered a handsome woman, she was charming and attentive and won others over through her evident dedication and erudition. In America her success as a speaker was in part attributable to her English breeding and manner of speech. In private she was reserved and retiring except when engaged with ideas. She was immensely forthright and, by her own definition, not a feminine woman; she was too steely, demanding, and unwilling to ingratiate.

She was blindly loyal to family and friends and she and her husband always presented a unified stance in public.

Maisie Ward's life was framed by her Catholicism and her Ward family history. Through these family connections and her writing and work she reflected in microcosm the history of the Roman Catholic church in the Anglo-American world for a century and a half. Her visibility and influence were greater in the United States than in England. With her husband she helped to prepare Catholic laity for the changes of the Second Vatican Council. Sheed and Ward published work by many of the leading theologians of the council, including Hans Kung, F. X. Durrwell, Hans Urs von Balthasar, Karl Rahner, and Edward Schillebeeckx. Ironically, Maisie, and Frank even more so, interpreted the realization of some of the council's changes as injurious to the church. While her second autobiography, written two years before her death, described the confusion she saw in the church after the Vatican Council, it continued to affirm the need to heal suffering in the world.

The contribution of Maisie Ward is not based on any one of her multiple activities—her writing, social commitments, publishing, lecturing, or street preaching—but rather on the totality of these efforts which refer back to an inner dynamism and dedication to the principles of her Catholic faith. In the global reach of these activities and in her ability to sustain them into the last years of her life she was remarkable. In the world of publishing and Catholic intellectual life she was as a woman *sui generis*. For the last decade of her life she lived permanently in the United States in New Jersey. She died in City Hospital, New York, on 28 January 1975 after a short illness and was buried on 30 January in Jersey City, New Jersey. She predeceased Frank Sheed, who was eight years her junior.

DANA GREENE

Sources D. Greene, *The living of Maisie Ward* (1997) • M. Ward, *Unfinished business* (1964) • M. Ward, *To and fro on the earth* (1973) • M. Ward, *The Wilfrid Wards and the transition*, 2 vols. (1934–7) • M. Ward, 'Maisie Ward', *Born Catholics*, ed. F. J. Sheed (1954), 123–44 • W. Sheed, *Frank and Maisie: a memoir with parents* (1986) • F. Sheed, *The instructed heart* (1979) • F. Sheed, *The church and I* (Garden City, NY, 1974) • D. Campbell, 'The gleanings of a laywoman's ministry: Maisie Ward as preacher, publisher and social activist', *American Catholic Historical Society of Philadelphia*, 98 (1987), 21–8 • M. Coulter, '"A Terrific Bond": the spiritual friendship of Caryll Houselander and Maisie Ward', *Downside Review*, 107 (1989), 106–18 • T. Burns, *The use of memory: publishing and further pursuits* (1993) • K. L. Riley, 'Ward, Maisie', *ANB* • b. cert. • m. cert. • tombstone, Jersey City, New Jersey, USA

Archives University of Notre Dame, Indiana, corresp. and papers | BL, corresp. and papers relating to G. K. Chesterton, Add. MSS 73193, 73195, 73197, 73231, 73236, 73400, 73455, 73481

Likenesses photograph, priv. coll.; repro. in Greene, *Living of Maisie Ward* • photograph, University of Notre Dame, university archives, Sheed and Ward family MSS; repro. in Greene, *Living of Maisie Ward* • photographs, repro. in Greene, *Living of Maisie Ward*

Ward, Michael (1683–1759), judge, was the second but eldest surviving son of Bernard Ward (1654–1690), landowner, of Castle Ward, co. Down, and of Anne, daughter of Richard Ward of Newcastle under Lyme and sister of Michael Ward, bishop of Derry. A child when his father was killed in a duel at Downpatrick, Ward attended the school of a Mr Jones in Dublin before matriculation at Trinity College in 1699. Entered as a student in the Inner Temple the next year, he was called to the Irish bar in 1705. Four years later he married Anne Catherine (1690/91–1760), daughter and coheir of James Hamilton of Bangor, co. Down. While the match was initially opposed, seemingly by both families, it added considerably to Ward's wealth. Ward was returned as an MP for County Down in 1715 and again in 1727. During his parliamentary career he complained twice over intrusion of his proprietorial rights during 'a time of privilege': trespass at his manor in Bangor and interference with rights of tithe. Ward was named a judge of the Irish king's bench in October 1727, though his patent was not sealed until two years later. His long judicial tenure won Ward a reputation for probity and assiduity, but criticism was voiced too, over his conduct during the Munster assizes in 1733 and over his rebuke of counsel at Monaghan in 1740 when counsel opposed Ward's insistence that an Irish interpreter be present at the hearing of a malicious injuries claim.

Ward also acquired a reputation as an agriculturist. The layout of the grounds at Castle Ward is his legacy. He oversaw the excavation of the ornamental lake (Temple water), and chose the various trees and shrubs for planting. His wife planned the walled garden. Marl was found on the estate in 1707 and was immediately put to use as a fertilizer. Crop rotation, too, was introduced, and Ward found an unusual source of power to drive his new cornmill:

> On the bay that opens to the garden is a singular contrivance for supplying a mill with water. A dead wall is carried across the gut in which are two arches, and in them two flood-gates fixed, the one to admit the tide, and the other to keep it in or out, as occasion serves. (Harris, *The Ancient and Present State*, 41)

Ward supported the burgeoning linen trade and, to facilitate the export of grain, constructed a harbour at Killough. Killough was where Ward also started a charter school. Ward served on the committee assembling in Dublin in 1731 that led to the establishment of the Dublin society 'for improving husbandry, manufactures and other useful arts'. Ward can thus be counted among what H. F. Berry in his *A History of the Royal Dublin Society* (1915) calls that 'small band of patriotic reformers, actuated by the purest and noblest motives' (p. 5).

Ward and his wife had three children. Bernard, Ward's only son and heir, built the house that now stands at Castle Ward; he was subsequently created Viscount Bangor. Ward's correspondence provides great insight into the management of a large eighteenth-century estate; it also reveals the judge handling the problem of impecunious relatives and aligning himself with his tenants in disputes over tithe and 'trade money' with the established church. Illness prevented Ward travelling circuit in his last years. He died at Castle Ward on 19 February 1759.　　　　　　W. N. OSBOROUGH

Sources Burtchaell & Sadleir, *Alum. Dubl.* · E. Keane, P. Beryl Phair, and T. U. Sadleir, eds., *King's Inns admission papers, 1607–1867*, IMC (1982) · T. K. Lowry, ed., *The Hamilton MSS* (1867) · J. Stevenson,

Two centuries of life in Down (1920) · F. E. Ball, *The judges in Ireland, 1221–1921*, 2 vols. (1926) · W. Harris, *The ancient and present state of co. Down* (1744) · [W. Harris], *The topographical and chorographical survey of co. Down* (1740) · National Trust, *Castle Ward co. Down* (1982) · C. E. B. Brett, *Long shadows cast before: nine lives in Ulster, 1625–1977* (1978) · K. Milne, *The Irish charter schools, 1730–1830* (1988) · R. H. Buchanan, 'The Lecale peninsula, county Down', *Atlas of the Irish rural landscape*, ed. F. H. A. Aalen, K. Whelan, and M. Stout (1997), 277, 282 · *Dublin directory*, various edns
Archives PRO NIre., family MSS | PRO NIre., T1123 and T1128
Likenesses Jervas?, oils, Castle Ward, co. Down
Wealth at death see will, 1759, A. Vicars, ed., *Index to Irish prerogative wills*

Ward, Nathaniel (1578–1652), clergyman and compiler of a law code for Massachusetts, was born in Haverhill, Suffolk, the second of five children of John Ward (*d.* 1598), lecturer successively of Haverhill, Writtle in Essex, and Bury St Edmunds, Suffolk, and his wife, Susan (*d.* in or after 1639). His brothers, Samuel *Ward (1577–1640) and John (*d.* 1661), both followed their father in careers as clergymen. Ward's mother married Richard *Rogers, lecturer at Wethersfield, Essex, some time after his father's death in 1598, thereby uniting two puritan clerical families. His stepbrothers by this marriage were the ministers Daniel *Rogers and Ezekiel *Rogers. He was admitted to Emmanuel College, Cambridge, in 1596, and graduated BA in 1600 and proceeded MA in 1603. His wife, Elizabeth, remains a shadowy figure; they were married before 1606, when their first child was born. Ward decided to pursue a legal career and was admitted to Lincoln's Inn in 1607. After completing his legal training, he travelled throughout northern Europe, studying under David Pareus, professor of theology at the University of Heidelberg, who probably persuaded him to change his career. Ward was ordained in 1618 and in the same year he edited his brother Samuel's sermon *Jethro's Justice of Peace*. From 1620 to 1624 he served as chaplain to the British merchants at Elbing, Prussia, but was back in England by 1626, when he was curate of St James's, Piccadilly. While in London Ward met Sir Nathaniel Rich, a landowner with strong puritan sympathies, who inspired his interest in the Massachusetts Bay Colony and who became his patron when he gave him the living as rector of Stondon Massey, Essex, in 1628. Ward became part of Thomas Hooker's Essex circle of puritan opposition to Archbishop Laud's attempts to standardize the Church of England. His willingness to conform to the church was questioned as early as 1628, and he supported William Sandcroft for the mastership of Emmanuel College in the same year. Sandcroft's successful election meant the college would continue to produce suitable candidates to occupy puritan pulpits. In 1629 Ward was one of forty-eight Essex ministers who signed a petition to Laud in support of Hooker. The petition was unsuccessful, and Hooker fled to Holland before settling in New England. Ward was offered a position as pastor to the Massachusetts Company, but he declined. However, he maintained an interest in the New England colony and corresponded with Governor John Winthrop to reserve space on an emigrant ship for two families in his congregation.

Ward's position in Essex came under threat during

Laud's visitation of the county in 1631. He was accused of not wearing his surplice, of rejecting the ceremonies of the Book of Common Prayer, and of refusing to promote the Book of Sports. Using his legal background to good effect, he talked himself out of trouble on condition that he repaired his surplice and agreed to conform. He turned to his friend John Cotton for emotional support; Cotton, a central figure for puritans in the south-east of England, fled to Massachusetts in 1632. Despite being deeply involved in the project of puritan emigration to Massachusetts, Ward tried to save his position at Stondon when he was again called to account by Laud. However, on this occasion he failed, and was excommunicated and deprived in 1632. He emigrated to Massachusetts in 1634 and took up the pastorship of the church at Ipswich, which he held until 1636 when ill health forced him to retire. Ward's two sons John and James, his daughter Susan, and her husband, Giles Firmin joined him in Massachusetts in 1639; presumably his wife had died by this date. In the same year Ward and Cotton, now living in Boston, were each requested to draft a code of laws for Massachusetts. It was Ward's model which was accepted after a complicated procedure (though portions of Cotton's contribution were added in the final version) and the Massachusetts 'body of liberties' was adopted as law in 1641. Ward's code was based on a combination of English common law and biblical law, and was made up of 100 specific liberties which were accepted as the rights of the freemen of the colony. His concern for authority, especially in the limitation of the power of the magistrate and proper legal procedure, is evident throughout the code. His experiences and those of his puritan colleagues in England also had an influence, with freedom of assembly and movement, the right to bail, and an intolerant attitude to religious matters as characteristic. Ward's influence with the colonial government was considerable. In 1641 he preached the sermon for the general election and received a grant for 600 acres of land near Pentucket, afterwards Haverhill. Two years later he joined with other ministers, including his stepbrother Ezekiel on behalf of Essex county to protest at Winthrop's involvement in the affairs of Massachusetts's French neighbours. He also supported the persecution of religious radicals, most notably in the case of Anne Hutchinson. Ward continued to be a favourite of the freemen of Massachusetts, who often requested a sermon to commemorate events. He maintained his position despite his son James being arrested for theft while a student at Harvard; it was then realized that the 'body of liberties' had no punishment recommended for burglary. Ward served on the committee to revise the laws in 1645 and also began work on *The Simple Cobbler of Agawam in America*, which offers a statement of his beliefs.

By 1646, perhaps inspired by his success in Massachusetts, Ward decided to return to England with the hope of helping to resolve the crisis in his homeland. He sent *The Simple Cobbler* ahead to his brother John, a member of the Westminster assembly, for publication, and gave his land to Harvard College before leaving Massachusetts. His son

John stayed in the colony as minister at Haverhill; Ward's other children returned to England with him. *The Simple Cobbler of Agawam* proved to be a huge success. Published in 1647 under the pseudonym Theodore de la Guard, it quickly went through four editions. Ward's fame from his wittily written and many-layered rant against religious toleration and immoral women's fashions imported from France, together with a plea to the king to compromise with his people and end the civil war, resulted in his invitation to preach the monthly fast sermon before the House of Commons in June 1647. The sermon focused on the need for authority in the state and the importance of moderation and consideration in reform. He also censured the army for its control of parliament. The sermon was not well received and Ward was not voted thanks, nor did parliament order it to be printed. It was eventually printed with a covering letter by Ward, which identified the reasons for its unpopularity as 'My perswading so much to lament the King' and 'some passages concerning the Army' (Ward, *Sermon*, sig. A3v). Ward continued his conservative approach and attacks on the army with another sermon of 1647, *A Religious Retreat Sounded to a Religious Army*, which advocated state control of the army so that it was 'neither a terror nor a burthen to the Country' (Ward, *Religious Retreat*, 5). Early in 1648 Ward took the living at Shenfield, Essex. In that year he continued his protest at the army's control of the kingdom in a petition presented to parliament on behalf of the eastern association. Deploring religious toleration and the lack of religious union promoted by parliament and the army, he also advised against deposing the king and supported the idea of the kingdom as a mercy of continuity granted by God. The eastern association's concerns also included the practical matters of resolving the quartering and payment of soldiers. Ward continued to be an able preacher until the end of his life. He condemned the execution of Charles I along with his stepbrother Daniel and his son-in-law Firmin. He continued to write, and in 1650 he provided a prefatory poem for Anne Bradstreet's *The Tenth Muse Lately Sprung up in America*. Ward died sometime before November 1652, when his successor at Shenfield started to keep the parish records.

K. GRUDZIEN BASTON

Sources J. W. Dean, *A memoir of the Rev. Nathaniel Ward* (1868) · E. H. L. Reeve, *Stondon Massey, Essex*, new edn (1906) · T. de la Guard [N. Ward], *The simple cobbler of Agawam in America*, ed. D. Pulsifer (1843) · T. Webster, *Godly clergy in early Stuart England: the Caroline puritan movement, c.1620–1643* (1997) · *VCH Essex*, vols. 2, 4 · *The correspondence of John Cotton*, ed. S. Bush (2001) · *The journal of John Winthrop, 1630–1649*, ed. R. S. Dunn, J. Savage, and L. Yeandle (1996) · J. Béranger, *Nathaniel Ward* (1969) · M. R. McCarl, 'Ward, Nathaniel', *ANB* · N. Ward, *A sermon preached before the honourable House of Commons*, 1647, BL, MS Thomason E.394/20 · [N. Ward], *A religious retreat sounded to a religious army*, 1647, BL, MS Thomason E.404/34 · [N. Ward], *To the high and honourable parliament … the humble petitions … of some … gentlemen, yeomen, and freeholders of the eastern association*, 1648, BL, MS Thomason E.438/15 · J. B. Felt, *History of Ipswich, Essex, and Hamilton* (1834) · J. Beardsley, ed., 'The liberties of New Englishmen', www.winthropsociety.org/liberty.htm [online version of 'The Massachusetts body of liberties'], 27 Feb 2002 · *DNB* · Venn, *Alum. Cant.*

Archives BL, Burney MSS, corresp. with M. Casaubon · BL, Stowe MSS, letters to E. Dering · Bodl. Oxf., Candler MSS · Bodl. Oxf., MSS Harley, 6071 · Bodl. Oxf., Tanner MSS, 180 and 257

Ward, Nathaniel Bagshaw (1791–1868), botanist, was born in London, the son of Stephen Smith Ward, general practitioner, of Whitechapel. Everyday contact with the nearby docks stimulated a longing for a sailor's life and he was sent on a voyage to Jamaica at the age of thirteen, which, while it succeeded in curing him of that ambition, developed instead a lifelong appetite for luxuriant vegetation. He decided on a medical career and attended lectures at the London Hospital and those given at the Chelsea Physic Garden by the demonstrator to the Society of Apothecaries, Thomas Wheeler, who was a charismatic leader of its plant-hunting excursions into the countryside. Ward was one of many captivated by these: after he qualified in 1812 and joined his father's practice, he kept up a taste for rising before dawn in summer and snatching a few hours in the fields for botanizing before morning surgery. About 1817 he married Charlotte Witte. The couple had nine children.

A dedicated gardener, Ward at first found the polluted atmosphere of London's East End repeatedly frustrated his efforts. In 1830, however, the chance sprouting of some seedlings in a bottle in which he had placed a chrysalis suggested a solution: if protected with an almost airtight casing of glass, plants could be kept alive indefinitely by the interacting effects of sunlight, soil, and their own transpiration. Though anticipated in this discovery by a professor of law at Glasgow University, Alexander Maconochie (1806–1885), Ward was the first to provide practical demonstration of the principle on an extensive scale and make it widely known. Three years of successful experimenting in collaboration with Loddiges' nursery culminated in the dispatch in 1833 of two of the resulting small cases to Australia. When opened three months later, the plants inside were found to be still growing sturdily; the cases were then refilled and on the return journey their contents again passed unharmed through snow and equatorial heat alike. Meanwhile John Claudius Loudon (1783–1843) had visited Ward's house, seen with astonishment its profusion of greenery, and dashed off an excited report in his widely read *Gardener's Magazine*. In the next issue Ward was induced to provide the first exposition in print of the underlying principle and the method of constructing what were thenceforward known as Wardian cases. Through shortage of time (or diffidence) that was a mere brief note, as were further communications of his in 1836 in the *Transactions of the Society of Arts* and the *Companion to the Botanical Magazine*, the latter run off for private circulation among his friends. Lectures and demonstrations to various learned bodies increasingly followed, but only in 1842 did he eventually come forward with a properly detailed account, *On the Growth of Plants in Closely Glazed Cases*; by then the décor of many a gas-lit home had already acquired through this means a permanent accession of foliage, particularly of ferns.

The aesthetic impact of Wardian cases was far outweighed, however, by the possibilities they opened up for colonial agriculture. Early adopted by Kew, they substantially changed the world economy by enabling plantation crops to be transferred to novel regions: tea from China to the Himalayas, cinchona from the Andes to India and Java, rubber from the Amazon to Ceylon and Malaya. Rarely has an observation so simple had such far-reaching results.

Nor was the impact solely botanical. In 1836 Ward pointed out that animals could be kept alive on just the same principle. The parallel invention by him of the vivarium followed and, in 1841, of what he termed the 'aquavivarium', though the later fashion for aquariums was mainly due to the writings of Philip Henry Gosse (1810–1888), and the working out of the oxygenating principle that made them possible was the achievement of Robert Warington.

Ward's allegiance to the Society of Apothecaries proved enduring. For many years he managed its Chelsea garden, initiating numerous improvements, and acted as the examiner in botany. This led to his election as master in 1854. As a botanical investigator, though, he was content with a largely passive role and published almost nothing: his election as FRS in 1852 was for forwarding science in other ways, notably by the pivotal part he played in it socially. Through his often weekly *soirées*—his 'stitching parties', as he dubbed them dismissively—his successive houses were, in J. D. Hooker's words, 'the most frequent metropolitan resort of naturalists from all quarters of the globe of any since Sir Joseph Banks' day' (*Gardeners' Chronicle*, 20 June 1868). Displays of microscopy were a particular feature at these occasions and led to the founding in 1839 of what became the Royal Microscopical Society.

Cheerful and genial, an excellent raconteur with a large store of anecdotes, Ward was at the same time self-effacing almost to a fault, leaving it to others to speak up on his behalf when he failed to receive recognition he was felt to deserve and to agitate for the repeal of the onerous excise duties on glass; the latter was a cause especially dear to him, in his wish to see hospitals and the inner areas of cities benefit from what he believed to be the therapeutic ambience of living plants. Foremost among these champions was his eldest son, Stephen Henry Ward MD, one of two sons who carried on the family's medical tradition.

On retiring from practice Ward moved to Clapham Rise, in the more salubrious southern environs of London, where he named his house The Ferns. He died at St Leonards, Sussex, on 4 June 1868 and was buried in Norwood cemetery on 10 June. His herbarium of 25,000 specimens was divided between the British Museum and Oxford University. A genus of South African mosses, *Wardia*, was named after him.   D. E. ALLEN

Sources S. H. W., 'Nathaniel Bagshaw Ward', *Gardeners' Chronicle* (20 June 1868), 655–6 · D. E. Allen, *The Victorian fern craze* (1969), 8–16 · S. H. Ward, 'On the growth of plants in closely glazed cases', *Notices of the Proceedings at the Meetings of the Members of the Royal Institution*, 1 (1854), 407–12 · D. E. Allen, 'Dr Ward's case', *BMJ* (10 May 1975), 324–6 · J. H. Balfour, *Transactions of the Botanical Society* [Edinburgh], 9 (1868), 426–30 · S. Hibberd, *Rustic adornments for homes of taste* (1856)

Archives Linn. Soc., corresp. | Harvard U., letters to Asa Gray

Likenesses J. P. Knight, oils, 1856, Society of Apothecaries, Apothecaries' Hall, London · R. J. Lane, lithograph, 1859 (after J. P. Knight), NPG · A. A. Hunt, oils, 1867, Linn. Soc. · Maull & Polyblank, photograph, RS

Wealth at death under £5000: probate, 13 July 1868, *CGPLA Eng. & Wales*

Ward, Sir Patience (1629–1696), merchant and politician, was born on 7 December 1629 at the manor of Tanshelf, near Pontefract, Yorkshire, the seventh son of Thomas Ward (*d.* 1635) and his wife, Elizabeth (*d.* after 1651). Hoping for a daughter, Ward's puritan father had vowed to name his next child Patience, should he again be disappointed. After his father's death, Ward's mother intended him for the ministry. He was sent up to Cambridge in 1643, but he claimed to have found little edification there. He would instead find his vocation in commerce. He served an apprenticeship, beginning in 1646, to Launcelot Tolson, a London merchant who traded to France. In 1654–5 he entered the French trade himself, becoming free of the Merchant Taylors' Company, and setting up a large establishment in the parish of St Laurence Pountney. He married Elizabeth Hobson (*d.* 1685) of Hackney on 8 June 1653. His wife's religious and political heritage matched his own puritan background, and his father-in-law, haberdasher William Hobson, was a leading London Independent and a supporter of the root and branch petition. Ward himself was both a reformed protestant with dissenting sympathies and an occasional conformist. (One of Ward's brothers, an Independent, was removed as a Pontefract alderman under the Corporation Act of 1662.)

As a young merchant in the 1650s and 1660s Ward focused on business rather than politics, eventually becoming a major exporter of cloth to France. However, his future as a political opponent of Charles II was anticipated as early as 1664, when he was briefly imprisoned for a 'seditious' petition about the customs. In 1670 he was elected alderman for the ward of Farringdon Within and was accepted by the full court of aldermen after first being rejected. He was also chosen, with a dissenting colleague, as sheriff of London and Middlesex for 1670–71. These elections were intended by urban dissenters to block the local enforcement of the 1670 Conventicle Act. He was also chosen as master of the Merchant Taylors' Company in 1671.

Ward soon became a spokesman for London dissenters who desired liberty of conscience and for merchants with concerns about the growing commercial rivalry with France. His extensive connections to Huguenot traders reinforced his own reformed protestant perspectives: the threat from Louis XIV was, for him, also a threat to English protestantism. In 1673 he was among four aldermen who 'hung an asse' and refused to act as stewards for a London Artillery Company feast in honour of the duke of York, a recent convert to Roman Catholicism. He also promoted a 1673 London petition to the crown about the city's trade, and he was one of the authors and signers of the anti-French *Scheme of the Trade as it is at Present Carried on between England and France* (1674). Although knighted by Charles in October 1675, he was by then associated with the urban opposition to the Anglican loyalist agenda of the earl of Danby. In 1678 his evidence before the committee of trade of the House of Lords contributed to the adoption of a three-year ban on many French imports. In September 1679 he was one of several London aldermen who refused to acknowledge the king's brother on a visit to Windsor. By 1680 his next-door neighbour was Dr Gilbert Burnet, who may also have been his friend.

Ward was deeply involved in the movement to exclude the duke of York from the succession during the three parliaments of 1679–81. He was a member of each, serving for Pontefract. He was also elected lord mayor of London in September 1680. He marked that occasion with a speech recommending protestant accommodation or a 'Union in Affection of all those who profess the same Faith', published as *The Speech of … Sir Patience Warde … the Day of his Election* (1680) (p. 3). Charles II indicated his displeasure with Ward's election by refusing to attend his mayoral installation. Several leading parliamentary advocates of exclusion did attend, however, and some Londoners celebrated his installation in the streets as a prelude to the anticipated recognition of the duke of Monmouth's claim to the throne. During Ward's mayoralty the strengthening alliance between parliamentary, county, and civic advocates of a protestant succession became known as the whigs. For their part, Anglican loyalists (or tories as they became known) charged that 1200 or 1300 dissenters were admitted to the London electorate during his mayoralty without taking the required oaths.

When the House of Commons adopted an exclusion bill on 11 November 1680 Ward immediately summoned a meeting of the London common council. The king regarded him as responsible for the ensuing unwelcome civic petition that he 'hearken and Incline to the Humble Advice' of his parliament (*To the Kings most Excellent Majesty*, 1680). Ward was also among the MPs who promoted an address to the crown for the removal of the London recorder, Sir George Jeffreys. He claimed that Jeffreys had sought to undercut an earlier London petition by falsely suggesting that 'Such Petitioning was bordering upon Treason, and the beginning of Rebellion' (A. Grey, *Debates of the House of Commons*, 10 vols., 1763, 7.463).

Ward's own commitment to the right of petitioning was further demonstrated when the London whigs reacted to Charles's prorogation of parliament on 10 January 1681. Amid mutterings that the MPs might resume their session in the city, Ward summoned another common council that requested Charles to recall parliament. Charles responded both by dissolving parliament and by warning Ward against meddling 'with those things that do not Concern you' (Library of Congress, London Newsletters, 7.148).

Ward's subsequent lengthy illness prevented him from taking any part in the events surrounding the third Exclusion Parliament. On 11 May 1681, however, he defied a royal order against summoning a common council, claiming that the 'terrors and amazements' of the time made one necessary (*CSP dom.*, 1680–81, 269). When common council adopted another petition for a parliament, Ward and other leading civic whigs were deprived of their places on the London lieutenancy commission. His encouragement of the whig movement in the city hastened Charles's decision to intervene in the corporation on behalf of the tories. Ward's mayoralty was also notable for the decision taken, in part at his behest, to inscribe on the fire monument the famous attribution of the great fire of 1666 to a Catholic conspiracy. Shortly after his mayoralty he was elected a fellow of the Royal Society.

Ward remained a critical whig player in the 1681–3 political contest for the city. He also continued to advocate accommodation between the Church of England and the dissenters. He invited Burnet to preach in favour of protestant union at the election of his mayoral successor. He presented Charles with a petition against the persecution of protestants and, as a city magistrate, refused to act on several informations against conventicles. Angered by the government's efforts of 1681 to convict the earl of Shaftesbury and other whigs of treason, Ward was rumoured in December 1681 to be collecting depositions for the impeachment of the king's chief ministers, should another parliament be called. In January 1682 he was chosen in common council as a member of the committee to defend the London charter against the crown's *quo warranto*. In April 1682 he was one of the organizers of a whig banquet in honour of the duke of Monmouth that was objected to by the crown. He was frequently in the company of both Monmouth and Shaftesbury during the next months, and his home was an occasional meeting-place for the whig grandees. Indeed, Shaftesbury may have been at Ward's house as late as 17 October 1682, by which time the earl may have been plotting resistance to the regime.

Shortly after Shaftesbury's disappearance Ward offered evidence in the trial of his whig friend, Alderman Thomas Pilkington. Pilkington faced the charge of *scandalum magnatum*, at the suit of the duke of York, for allegedly suggesting in public that York had burnt London and intended death to its leading citizens. When Pilkington was convicted of the words, Ward was charged with perjury. His trial in May 1683 provided Sir George Jeffreys, who urged his conviction, with an opportunity for revenge. When found guilty Ward had already gone underground. He was discovered in June in the Barbican house of surgeon Charles Bateman, who was involved in whig resistance plans, but succeeded in fleeing to the Netherlands.

By this time Ward's unusual given name had become a byword in the tory prints for whig impatience and disloyalty. Indeed, Aphra Behn had employed his name and his fear of 'French papishes' as early as 1678 in the first of her dramatic political satires. Nevertheless, the extent of Ward's knowledge about whig conspiracy in 1682–3 is unclear. The circle of conspirators around Robert West actually marked him for punishment as a 'trimmer' who had insufficiently advanced the whig cause during his mayoralty (*State trials*, 9.420).

Exiled in the Netherlands for the next five years, Ward moved within various circles of English refugees and rebels, keeping his distance from some but consorting with others. Transferring part of his wealth abroad, he contributed £500 to Monmouth's failed rebellion of 1685. He also associated with John Locke, Slingsby Bethel, Robert Ferguson, Thomas Papillon, Sir John Thompson, Lord Wharton, John Wildman, and Benjamin Furley, the Quaker merchant and book collector. He was a financial backer of the English cloth manufactory at Leeuwarden, the profits of which were intended to support resistance to the regime of James II. Sobered by the death of his wife in 1685, and surprised by James's turn towards toleration, he sought and received pardon for his political past in 1687.

Ward returned to civic and national prominence in the wake of the revolution of 1688. In London he resumed his aldermanic place, was added to the lieutenancy commission, assumed command of a militia regiment, and was elected one of the City MPs for the Convention. The new government also rewarded him with appointments to the customs commission, the commission for discouraging the export of wool, and the assessments commissions for London and the West Riding of Yorkshire. His activity in the Convention demonstrated his continuing commitments to electoral rights, to reformed protestantism in England and abroad, and to advancing English against French trade. In the city he supported a whig effort to release the electorate and the common council from most magisterial restraints. In the Convention he favoured an investigation of the royal intrusion upon civic rights after the Oxford parliament. He also favoured repealing the sacramental test for office-holding, a position that prompted tory talk about expelling him for nonconformity.

Although Ward promoted corporation loans to the new regime, he and William III were uneasy with one another by September 1689. When the king moved towards the tories in early 1690 Ward lost his militia colonelcy. Like the other whig City MPs in the Convention, he was defeated by the London church candidates who stood for the new parliament. Still an active merchant, he remained a commissioner for the customs and for the London lieutenancy. In 1694 he acquired £4000 of the original stock of the Bank of England. A contributor to funds for the support of dissenting ministry, he also became a member of the largely nonconformist New England Company, which sponsored missionaries to Native Americans.

Ward died, childless, on 10 July 1696 at St Laurence Pountney and was buried in his parish church of St Mary Abchurch. Still committed to reformed protestantism within the Church of England, he left money to support impoverished Anglican clergy. Complaining of losses amounting to £40,000, he left few other legacies but offered forgiveness to all those who had 'trespassed against and persecuted' him in the late 'evil times' (PRO, PROB 11/433/167). He had already advanced his London nephew, Sir John Ward (1650–1726), who followed him in civic, parliamentary, and commercial affairs.

GARY S. DE KREY

Sources C. E. Whiting, 'Sir Patience Ward of Tanshelf', *Yorkshire Archaeological Journal*, 34 (1938–9), 245–72 • HoP, *Commons, 1660–90*,

1.481–2 • E. Cruickshanks, 'Ward, Sir Patience', HoP, *Commons, 1660–90,* 3.667–70 • BL, Add. MS 4224, fols. 33–4; Add. MS 41812 (Middleton MSS, 10), fols. 17, 34, 77, 210, 222; Add. MS 41818 (Middleton MSS, 16), fols. 17, 106–8, 185, 238, 256–7; Add. MS 41819 (Middleton MSS, 17), fols. 59–61. Harleian MS 6845, fol. 272 • *CSP dom.,* 1673, 594–5; *1680–81,* 33, 52, 131–2, 265–9, 272–4, 276–80, 440, 484–5, 615; *1682,* 8, 104–6, 328–9, 475, 560–61, 573, 584; *Jan–June 1683,* 67, 196, 356 • M. Priestley, 'London merchants and opposition politics in Charles II's reign', *BIHR,* 29 (1956), 205–19 • R. Zaller, 'Ward, Patience', Greaves & Zaller, *BDBR,* 3.289–91 • J. R. Woodhead, *The rulers of London, 1660–1689* (1965), 170–71 • L. Cong., manuscript division, London newsletters collection • CLRO, Journal 47, fols. 262–3, 264–5; Journal 49, fols. 155–7, 170–74, 204–11, 221–5; Repertory 86, fol. 128 • *State trials,* 9.299–352, 420 • will, PRO, PROB 11/433, sig. 167 • *DNB* • A. Behn, *Sir Patient Fancy, The works of Aphra Behn,* ed. J. Todd, 6 (1992–6), 1–81

Likenesses G. Kneller?, oils, 1690, Merchant Taylors' Company, London; repro. in F. M. Fry, *A historical catalogue of the pictures … at Merchant Taylors' Hall* (1907) • T. Athow, wash drawing, AM Oxf. • J. Riley, oils, Squerryes Court, Kent • funeral monument, repro. in F. M. Fry, *A historical catalogue of the pictures … at Merchant Taylors' Hall* (1907), facing p. 85 • oils, Squerryes Court, Kent • watercolour drawing, NPG

Wealth at death complained of losses of £40,000; 'which prevented my intentions to my relations and other public uses'; left third nephew house at St Laurence Pountney, valued at £5000; other legacies amounted to only £300: H. B. Wilson, *A history of the parish of St Laurence Pountney* (1831), 243–4

Ward, Richard (1689–1763), merchant and colonial governor, was born on 15 April 1689 in Newport, Rhode Island, the youngest of the three children of Thomas Ward (1641–1689), merchant and colonial official of Rhode Island, and his second wife, Amy (1658–1732), daughter of Samuel Billings of Newport and his wife, Seaborn. Educated at home by his mother and step-father, Arnold Collins of Newport, also a merchant, Ward became the eldest son in this prominent trading family after his brother, Thomas (1683–1695), died. Ward expanded the Ward–Collins family business, which shipped food, lumber, and slaves from New England to the West Indies in exchange for molasses, and had an exceptionally prosperous career. He also made considerable money through land speculation in the Narragansett country of western Rhode Island and eastern Connecticut. His marriage to Mary Tillinghast (1690–1767) of Newport, which took place on 2 November 1709, produced fourteen children, of whom several were prominent, including Samuel *Ward (1725–1776), governor of Rhode Island and a leading figure in the early sessions of the continental congress.

Ward's political career followed a curious path. Despite having no training or experience in the practice of law, he was named Rhode Island's attorney-general for two years, beginning in 1712 at the remarkably young age of twenty-three. From 1714 to 1730 he served as secretary of the colony, and from 1731 to 1740 as a deputy to the general assembly. Having been elected deputy governor of Rhode Island in 1740, after two months he succeeded to the governorship on the death of Governor John Wanton. Ward was elected governor in his own right in 1741 and then easily re-elected a year on; he voluntarily did not seek re-election in the following year. Rhode Island politics, famed for their factional ferocity, were at their stormiest during Ward's three terms in the governor's office, and he

did not have the stomach to continue to fight. Battles over paper money, over the Rhode Island boundary with the old Plymouth colony, and with Britain over the meaning of the Rhode Island charter of 1663 soured Ward's desire to stay in office, though he did not withdraw entirely from public life. Rather, he threw his support behind William Greene (1696–1758) of Warwick, who succeeded him as governor in 1743; he remained a behind-the-scenes adviser to Greene and to his son, Samuel Ward, who was elected governor in 1762, a year before his father's death.

Richard Ward's political career was distinguished more by his continual involvement and by his vigorous championing of Newport's mercantile interests than by any specific accomplishments. He steadfastly defended the integrity of Rhode Island's currency emissions in the face of strong opposition from Boston merchants, who felt the depreciated notes gave Newport an unfair advantage in the coasting trade. His efforts bore results and Newport prospered relative to its rivals until the 1760s, when Providence began to overtake it. Ward lived his entire life in Newport, died there on 21 August 1763 after a sudden illness, and was buried in the Newport common ground cemetery. He was survived by his wife, who died on 19 October 1767. Successful as both a politician and merchant, Ward left few clues to his personality in his political and business correspondence.   BRUCE C. DANIELS

Sources S. V. James, *Colonial Rhode Island: a history* (1975) • D. S. Lovejoy, *Rhode Island politics and the American revolution, 1760–1776* (1958) • B. C. Daniels, *Dissent and conformity on Narragansett Bay: the colonial Rhode Island town* (1983) • J. Ward, *A memoir of Lieutenant-Colonel Samuel Ward* (1875) • C. P. Monahon, *Genealogy of the Ward family* (1952) • *Correspondence of Governor Samuel Ward,* ed. B. Knollenberg (1952) • B. C. Daniels, *The fragmentation of New England: comparative perspectives on economic, political, and social divisions in the eighteenth century* (1988) • J. Bartlett, ed., *Rhode Island colony records,* 5 (1860)

Archives Newport Historical Society and the Rhode Island Historical Society Library, letters and documents

Likenesses oils, Rhode Island State House, Providence; repro. in R. S. Mohr, *Rhode Island colonial governors for three hundred years, 1638–1954* (Providence, RI, 1954)

Ward, Robert McGowan Barrington- (1891–1948), journalist, was born in Worcester on 23 February 1891, the fourth son of Mark James Barrington-Ward (d. 1924), an inspector of schools and later rector of Duloe, Cornwall, and his wife, Caroline Pearson. The surgeon Lancelot Edward Barrington-*Ward was an elder brother. He was educated at Westminster School, where he gained distinction in the classics and was captain of the school, and Balliol College, Oxford, where he held a scholarship (1909–13). At Oxford he wrote light verse for university magazines, and became president of the union in 1912. Having obtained a second in classical moderations (1911) and a third in Greats (1913), and been awarded the Tancred scholarship at Lincoln's Inn in 1911, he had intended to embark upon a legal career. However, a parallel interest in journalism resulted in a fortunate introduction to Geoffrey Robinson (later Geoffrey Dawson), then editor of *The Times.* Barrington-Ward joined the staff of the newspaper in 1913, and showed sufficient promise to be made editorial secretary in February 1914. He contributed the chapter 'The foreign office and its agencies' to the *Oxford Survey of the British Empire* (1914).

On the outbreak of war in August 1914, Barrington-Ward was commissioned in the 6th battalion of the Duke of Cornwall's light infantry, and he became battalion adjutant in 1916. Wounded at Bellacourt in 1917, he became a staff officer attached to the 58th division, and in 1918 he wrote *Platoon Fighting*, an attempt to apply the tactical lessons of the fighting on the western front. He was a brave soldier who was awarded both the MC (1917) and the DSO (1918).

Like many young men of his generation, Barrington-Ward was 'marked by the trenches' (Cowling, 128) and fearful of another war, and was a strong supporter of the League of Nations. He covered the peace negotiations for his newspaper in Paris and sympathized with German grievances, a sentiment which was shared by many in Britain. 'As to British opinion generally,' he wrote, 'our difficulty has been to find enough letters stating what might crudely be called the anti-German view to balance the correspondence' (Lentin, 149). He epitomized the unease felt by many about the treatment of Germany in 1919, dragging the 'nation's self-forged fetters around with him and raised his voice in grief-stricken means of self reproach' (ibid., 150).

Although called to the bar in 1919, Barrington-Ward decided to follow a career in journalism, and spent eight years as assistant editor to *The Observer* under J. L. Garvin before returning to *The Times* in October 1927, as assistant editor under Geoffrey Dawson. In 1926 he married Margaret Adele, daughter of Evasio Radice of the Indian Civil Service; they had two sons and a daughter.

As the position of foreign editor was abolished in 1928, Barrington-Ward and Geoffrey Dawson were responsible for *The Times*'s coverage of foreign affairs. Barrington-Ward was also chief leader writer. A particular interest was Anglo-German affairs, and he remained convinced that the treaty of Versailles had been misconceived. Although no admirer of Nazism, he hoped for an accommodation with the Hitler government. Thus, when the Germans illegally re-entered the demilitarized Rhineland on 7 March 1936, the *Times* leader was headed 'A chance to rebuild'. The previous day, Barrington-Ward had lamented that Britain was '"tied and bound by the chain of our sins", stretching all the way back to the General Election of 1918' (*The Times*, 6 March 1936).

The pro-appeasement line of Dawson and Barrington-Ward caused tensions in the *Times* office, as the latter admitted—writing in his diary during the 1938 Czech crisis that 'most of the office is against me' (MacDonald, 65). Outside it, Barrington-Ward's leaders could also arouse fierce opposition, so that when the paper urged concessions on the Czech government before Godesberg, Harold Nicolson denounced the deputy editor's work (to his face), as 'a masterpiece of unctuous ambiguity' (Nicolson, 362).

In later years Barrington-Ward, like Dawson, had to live with the opprobrium directed towards the policy of appeasement advocated by *The Times*, and as a result his wider record was largely forgotten. His leaders on unemployment, for example, resulted in the appointment of a government commission in 1934. After his appointment as editor on 1 October 1941, when Dawson retired, he was a strong supporter of Sir William Beveridge and of the need for wholesale social reform. During his editorship, *The Times* moved to the left, and he himself came to agree with Beveridge that 'sooner or later, and probably very soon, the whole British economy … must become a planned economy' (Beveridge paper, 'Co-ordination in war', 17 Sept 1939, Layton MSS). The condemnation by *The Times* of British intervention in Greece in 1944 provoked a stinging response by Winston Churchill in the House of Commons on 18 January 1945. The paper had not been forgiven for its association with appeasement, and Barrington-Ward noted that the parliamentary cheer which followed Churchill's attack was the 'loudest, largest and most vicious—even savage—that I have ever heard in the House' (Barrington-Ward, diary, 18 Jan 1945). He also went on the record to say that he did not regard *The Times* as a Tory newspaper.

Unlike Dawson, Barrington-Ward delegated the writing of editorials to others, notably to E. H. Carr, later a distinguished left-orientated historian. Such consistent radicalism in his later years, in the direction of the post-war corporatist consensus, hardly substantiates suggestions that Barrington-Ward's later poor health undermined his judgement. He came to see himself as a tory radical but as one who liked to keep in touch with his old roots: he was, for example, involved in the discussions about the succession to his old mentor Garvin at *The Observer*.

Barrington-Ward was a governor of Westminster School and wrote a memoir (1924) of his headmaster, James Gow. In 1947 he was made an honorary fellow of Balliol College. His health weakened at a relatively early age, and he died on 29 February 1948 while on a cruise to South Africa designed to help recovery. He was buried in the Kiriondoni cemetery, Dar es Salaam.   PETER NEVILLE

Sources D. McLachlan, *In the chair: Barrington-Ward of The Times, 1927–1948* (1971) • *The Times* (1 March 1948) • DNB • Barrington-Ward papers, News Int. RO, *The Times* archive, Barrington-Ward papers • R. Cockett, *Twilight of truth: Chamberlain, appeasement, and the manipulation of the press* (1989) • J. E. Wrench, *Geoffrey Dawson and our Times* (1955) • M. Cowling, *The impact of Hitler: British politics and British policy, 1933–1940* (1975) • A. Lentin, *Guilt at Versailles: Lloyd George and the pre-history of appeasement* (1985) • I. MacDonald, *A man of The Times: talks and travels in a disrupted world* (1976) • H. Nicolson, *Diaries and letters*, ed. N. Nicolson, 1 (1966) • Trinity Cam., Layton MSS, box 5 • D. Ayerst, *Garvin of The Observer* (1985) • F. R. Gannon, *The British press and Germany, 1936–1939* (1971) • [S. Morison and others], *The history of The Times*, 4 (1952) • CGPLA Eng. & Wales (1948) • *The Times* (29 Nov 2000), section 2, p. 6

Archives News Int. RO, *The Times* archive, papers • NRA, corresp. and diaries | Bodl. Oxf., corresp. with Sir Henry Burdett • Bodl. Oxf., corresp. with L. G. Curtis • Bodl. Oxf., corresp. with Geoffrey Dawson • HLRO, corresp. with J. C. C. Davidson • Nuffield Oxf., corresp. with Lord Cherwell • Cambridge, Trinity College, Layton MSS

Wealth at death £24,179 8s. 8d.: probate, 27 May 1948, CGPLA Eng. & Wales

Ward, Robert Plumer (1765–1846), politician and writer, was born in Mount Street, Mayfair, on 19 March 1765, the sixth son and eighth child of John Ward (*d.* 1791), a merchant resident in Gibraltar and chief clerk of the civil department in the garrison, and his wife, Rebecca Raphael (1732–1768), who was descended from a Genoese Jewish family settled in Spain. She died when Robert was three years old. Ward was educated at Macfarlane's academy, Walthamstow, and afterwards at Christ Church, Oxford, which he entered in January 1783. He remained at Oxford until 1787 and, after leaving, travelled in France while pursuing studies in law. During his time in France he witnessed the early stages of the French Revolution. He returned to London and was called to the bar by the Inner Temple on 18 June 1790.

Ward initially practised law on the western circuit, as well as conducting business in London where he undertook appeals before the privy council. In 1794 he came to the attention of William Pitt when he provided details of a republican plot. This incident occurred on the eve of the government's decision to prosecute members of the London reform societies. Even so, it seems unlikely that the evidence that Ward presented had any influence on the subsequent course of events (Veitch, 304). Nevertheless this meeting just prior to the treason trials led to a suggestion from the brother of Lord Elton that he write a book on international law. *An inquiry into the foundation and history of the law of nations in Europe from the time of the Greeks and Romans to the age of Grotius* (2 vols.) duly appeared in 1795. Shortly after this, on 2 April 1796 Ward married Catherine Julia Maling (1772–1821) of West Herrington, co. Durham, thereby becoming closely connected with Henry Phipps, first earl of Mulgrave, who had recently married her eldest sister, Sophia. They had one son, Sir Henry George *Ward.

Ward now moved his legal practice to the northern circuit. The rise of the League of Armed Neutrality brought a request from the foreign secretary, Lord Grenville, for a defence of the rights of belligerents, and Ward produced *A treatise of the relative rights and duties of belligerents and neutral powers in maritime affairs, in which the principles of the armed neutralities and the opinions of Hübner and Schlegel are fully discussed* (1801). These political services were rewarded when on the personal recommendation of William Pitt he was offered a seat in the House of Commons for the Lowther pocket borough of Cockermouth in June 1802. Both Viscount Lowther and Ward's brother-in-law the future earl of Mulgrave had been Pittite MPs before inheriting peerages. Ward's maiden speech in December 1802 had supported the Addington administration but by the following year Pitt's friends, especially after the resumption of the war against France, moved to restore the former minister. On his own initiative Ward published a pamphlet favourable to Pitt in response to Patten's criticism of Addington's dealings with Bonaparte. When Pitt did return to power in 1804 Ward supported the government's position following the seizure of four Spanish frigates prior to the declaration of war on Spain on 16 October 1804 by publishing *An enquiry into the manner in which the different wars of Europe have commenced during the past two centuries* (1804).

In January 1805 Lord Mulgrave was appointed foreign secretary and Ward was offered the post of undersecretary. He decided to accept, turning his back on a lucrative legal career and the offer of a Welsh judicial post. Ward did not speak in parliament on foreign affairs, though a little earlier he had attempted to bolster the government's position by informing the press that French claims of a Russian capitulation at what proved to be Austerlitz were fabrications (*Creevey Papers*, 45). The death of Pitt in February 1806 and the advent of the 'ministry of all the talents' led to Ward's resignation and move into opposition. He was not a candidate at the election of 1806 but was returned for Haslemere as Lord Lowther's nominee in January 1807. When later that year the duke of Portland took office, Lord Mulgrave was made first lord of the Admiralty and Ward appointed a junior lord with a place on the Admiralty board. Until 1811 Ward moved the naval estimates in the house and undertook to defend the interest of the Admiralty on other questions.

Ward worked quite closely with Spencer Perceval, then chancellor of the exchequer, and came to admire his abilities and character. When Perceval became prime minister, Ward continued a firm supporter of the ministry and kept a political diary. The portions published by Phipps cover the period 1809–May 1812 and October 1819–November 1820. Croker declared the journals 'trustworthy and authentic' but cautioned that apart from his undersecretaryship 'Ward … was not in what is considered confidential office—and had little or no personal share in what we may call the interior working of the higher parts of the political machine' (Croker, 241–2). Perceval offered him a place on the Treasury board but Ward preferred to remain at the Admiralty. However, when Lord Mulgrave became master-general of the ordnance he willingly transferred and was appointed clerk from June 1811. From 1812 he moved the ordnance estimates in the house and by 1816, with the establishment of peace he was able to announce a reduction of £3 million. The earl of Mulgrave made way at the Ordnance for the duke of Wellington in 1818. After initial doubt about his position Ward remained in the post until April 1823. He was then granted the post of auditor of the civil list until its abolition as a sinecure by the whig government in 1831.

Ward's wife had died on 28 December 1821 and with his political career now over, he produced his first novel, *Tremaine, or, The Man of Refinement* (1825), published anonymously by Colburn. The work had been edited by Colburn's reader P. S. Patmore, who some two years later, their mutual identities now disclosed, became Ward's literary adviser and close friend. *Tremaine* was in essence a didactic work, in parts resembling a theological tract. Charles Tremaine is a dandy who flees fashionable society and a short-lived parliamentary career for his country estate. This life too he finds unsatisfactory. Protracted exchanges follow between Tremaine and a neighbouring clergyman, Dr

Evelyn, on such themes as deism, free will, and the problem of evil. Tremaine, whose ideas contain many of the assumptions of eighteenth-century *philosophes*, is gradually won over to orthodox Christianity and the hand of Evelyn's daughter Georgina. The novel had drawn a flattering portrait of fashionable society and was an immediate success, selling 1500 copies in three weeks. It was a pioneer of the silver fork genre, Michael Sadleir calling it 'the chief impulse to *Vivian Grey*' and 'the inspiration of the two most influential novelists of the 'thirties and 'forties' (Sadleir, 117).

Ward's second novel, *De Vere, or, The Man of Independence*, appeared in four volumes in 1827, and may have prompted Canning's quip that Ward's law books were as interesting as novels and his novels as dull as law books. *De Vere* took ambition as its main subject, and Ward considered it as didactic as *Tremaine* but more dramatic. Sharply contrasted with the world-weary Tremaine, Mortimer De Vere is the unworldly idealist whose subsequent enlightenment comes when he enters parliament. He finds himself unwilling to be the tool of his uncle Lord Mowbray and instead gives his support to the opposition leader Wentworth. De Vere declares he will put his trust in 'measures not men', and for this his uncle disowns him. Some of the characters were portraits of actual political figures, Wentworth apparently a composite of Pitt, Canning, and Bolingbroke, and Mowbray in part modelled on the duke of Newcastle. *De Vere* was a detailed study of the political ethos and politics the motivation behind the action. Its main weakness was a lack of imaginative power (Rosa, 67–8).

On 16 July 1828 Ward married the wealthy widow Jane Lewin, *née* Hamilton (1768–1831), a granddaughter of the seventh earl of Abercorn. Her first husband had been William Plumer (*d.* 1822), and her second husband Richard John Lewin RN (*d.* 1827). Subsequent to the marriage settlement, Ward assumed the additional name and arms of Plumer. Robert Plumer Ward at once took up residence at his wife's estate, Gilston Park, Hertfordshire, and served as sheriff of Hertfordshire in 1832. Mrs Plumer Ward seems to have been on bad terms with her husband's children (Disraeli, *Letters*, 235–6). She died on 26 March 1831 at Gilston shortly after the deaths within days of each other of Ward's two older daughters Catherine and Julia. His youngest daughter Anne died of the same consumptive illness as her sisters in 1835.

On 14 February 1833 Ward married his third wife, Mary-Anne Okeover (1803–1875), daughter of the Hon. Sir George Anson GCB, and widow of the Revd Charles Gregory Okeover. She was the mother of a young son and daughter. Ward and she now spent long periods on the continent. *Illustrations of Human Life* (1837) appeared at this time. After his wife became the trustee of her son's estate at Okeover, Staffordshire, Ward and his new family left Gilston to Henry George Ward and his eight children. Ward wrote to Patmore in November 1838 saying 'my son is very welcome to all the cockneys and radicals of Herts. I never felt a real country gentleman before' (Patmore, 97).

At this time he published *An historical essay on the real character and amount of the precedent of the Revolution of 1688* (2 vols., 1838). This was followed by *Pictures of the World at Home and Abroad* (3 vols., 1839) and at length his last novel, *De Clifford, or, The Constant Man* (4 vols., 1841).

In appearance Ward showed no trace of his Spanish ancestry 'his cast of countenance was essentially Saxon; and the bright blue eye, even flow of spirits, and indefatigable energy of his mind and body, proclaimed him a nature-born Englishman' (Phipps, 1.2). Croker said of him:

> he had abundance of small talk and lively conversation, with a prodigious untaught musical talent; and all through life, and even to the last—though reduced to an ear trumpet—he had a jaunty air, and appeared, both in countenance and figure, very much younger than he really was. (Croker, 274)

Early in 1846, Ward, now in his eighty-first year, and his wife joined her father Lieutenant-General Sir George Anson at his official residence in Chelsea Hospital. Ward died there on 13 August 1846, after a sudden attack of angina pectoris. CLIVE TOWSE

Sources E. Phipps, *Memoirs of the political and literary life of Robert Plumer Ward*, 2 vols. (1850) • HoP, *Commons, 1790–1820* • [J. W. Croker], review, *QR*, 87 (1850), 239–76 • M. W. Rosa, *The silver-fork school: novels of fashion preceding Vanity Fair* (1936), 63–8 • Burke, *Gen. GB* (1834) • P. G. Patmore, *My friends and acquaintance*, 2 (1854), 1–202 • *The Creevey papers*, ed. H. Maxwell, 3rd edn (1905); repr. (1923), 45 • M. Sadleir, *Bulwer: a panorama*, 1: *Edward and Rosina, 1803–1836* (1931), 115–18 • G. S. Veitch, *The genesis of parliamentary reform* (1913), 304 • *GM*, 2nd ser., 26 (1846), 650–52 • *GM*, 2nd ser., 28 (1847), 653 • *Benjamin Disraeli letters*, ed. J. A. W. Gunn and others (1982–), vol. 1, p. 235–6 • Foster, *Alum. Oxon.*

Archives Wellcome L., extracts, medical receipts, and notes | BL, corresp. with Lord Liverpool, Add. MSS 38245–38272 • BL, corresp. with Sir Robert Peel, Add. MSS 40233–40494, *passim* • Bodl. Oxf., corresp. with Isaac D'Israeli • Cumbria AS, Carlisle, letters to Lord Lonsdale • Hunt. L., letters to Grenville family

Likenesses J. Thomson, stipple, 1831 (after drawing by F. R. Say), BM, NPG; repro. in *New Monthly Magazine* (1831) • H. Briggs, portrait, 1839 • C. Turner, mezzotint, 1850 (after H. Briggs), repro. in Phipps, *Memoirs*, vol. 1, frontispiece • T. Lawrence, chalk and wash drawing, Royal Collection

Wealth at death over £9000: PRO, death duty registers, IR 26/1759

Ward, Samuel (1572–1643), theologian and college head, was born at Bishop Middleham, co. Durham, the son of John Ward, a man of 'more ancientry than estate' (BL, Harleian MS 7038, p. 355), and baptized on 13 January 1572. He matriculated pensioner of Christ's College, Cambridge, in 1589, graduated BA in 1593, and proceeded MA in 1596. His financial condition while a student was precarious: James Montagu and William Perkins helped him with his college debts. The diary and sermon notebook he kept from 1592 to 1601, along with other notebooks collected in the Sidney Sussex archives, reveal that he was in his youth a vigorous and outspoken puritan, devoted to biblical studies and to intense introspection and self-castigation for his most trivial sins. An ardent admirer of Perkins and of Laurence Chaderton, he was like them much troubled by the introduction of popish 'ceremonies' into the Church of England, by clergy 'too pontifical and papistical', and generally by the 'sins of the land', especially 'want of zeal' and 'coldness in our holy profession' (Sidney Sussex College, Ward MS B, fols. 30*v*–31; MS 45, fol. 62*v*). He was thus a natural choice for election to a fellowship of Emmanuel College in 1596 and in 1610 to the mastership of the newest puritan foundation, Sidney Sussex College, where he remained until his death. He proceeded BD from Emmanuel in 1603 and DD from Sidney Sussex in 1610.

Two major projects occupied Ward during the first decade of the seventeenth century. First, Perkins entrusted to him posthumous publication of his treatise, *Problema de Romanae fidei ementito Catholicismo*, which duly appeared in 1611. Second, from 1604 until 1611 he worked on translation of the Apocrypha for the Authorized Version of the Bible. He was rewarded with multiple ecclesiastical offices, becoming prebend of Yatton in Wells Cathedral (1610), a royal chaplain (1611), archdeacon of Taunton and *ex officio* prebend of Milverton I in Wells (1615), rector of Great Munden in Hertfordshire (1616), and canon of York (1618). In 1638 the rectory of Terrington, Norfolk, was added to the list.

Evidence of Ward's activities outside Cambridge is sparse. As archdeacon, he apparently did visit Taunton on occasion, and he maintained a house in Wells. His designated surrogates in the archidiaconal court can be identified with puritan colleges in Cambridge and in one case—Walter Vesey, Ward's vicar as prebendary of Milverton—with outright nonconformity. A collection of English sermons in Ward's hand (Sidney Sussex College, Ward MS O.8) may have been intended for visitations to Taunton or to one of his rectories. Apart from one on the Gunpowder Plot, their concern is with the state of the heart, and the language is designed to stir the emotions. The style and tone of his vernacular preaching are strikingly different from his Latin academic sermons, which are restrained in tone, rigorously logical, and tightly focused on specific theological questions. His extant sermons are few in number. While committed to the principle that 'Christ frameth men by the word preached', as he wrote in his diary, Ward suffered from a speech impediment that had almost caused him to choose mathematics rather than divinity as his field (Sidney Sussex College, MS 45, fols. 51, 46*v*); it was Perkins who had persuaded him to study theology.

Ward's principal commitments were always to his college, to biblical and theological scholarship, and especially to the maintenance of Calvinist orthodoxy. His notebooks reveal that administration of the college and its properties occupied much of his time, and also that he devoted attention to areas of scholarship rather new to early modern universities, purchasing globes, maps, and scientific instruments for the college and participating in scholarly exchanges with historians and antiquaries as well as divines. Highly regarded by the other college heads for meticulous scholarship and integrity of life, he was elected vice-chancellor of the university for 1620–21, increasing his administrative burden but not diminishing his theological efforts. The preponderance of both his writing and his use of time was always for theological ends. The virulent anti-Catholicism visible in his edition

of Perkins's work is also evident in his actions from 1610 to 1643 as a member of the university vice-chancellor's court, where he actively prosecuted those who articulated 'popish' notions in university sermons. In the 1636 case against John Normanton of Gonville and Caius College, for instance, he added his own detailed list of complaints to the official charges against this obviously Catholic fellow (Sidney Sussex College, Ward MS F, fol. 28).

Ward also addressed what he regarded as the enemy within protestantism. An outspoken Calvinist, he was one of the five British delegates sent by the king in 1618 to the Synod of Dort, where Episcopius found him 'the most learned member' (J. Hacket, *Sermons*, 1675, xxvi). Historians of the synod have associated Ward with John Davenant against the other three delegates in lending support to the remonstrant doctrine of universalism; however, a debate he recorded with the synod's president, Johannes Bogerman, indicates that the rift was more apparent than real. Ward argued that Christ's death won only the possibility of salvation for all and remained merely potential for the reprobate, God having selected some persons but not others 'liberare efficaciter ex massa damnata' ('to free efficaciously from the mass of the reprobate'; Sidney Sussex College, Ward MS L.4, fol. 3*v*). Ward joined the other delegates in full support of all five articles of the synod against the remonstrants in *The Collegiate Suffrage of the Divines of Great Britain* (1619, tr. 1629). A few years after his return to England he was made Lady Margaret professor of divinity (1623), from which position he continued to affirm his commitment to strict predestinarianism. His university sermon, *Gratia discriminans: concio ad clerum habita Cantabrigiae* (preached 1625, published 1626) labels the doctrine of resistible grace a 'perversa notione' and the idea of free will 'radix non paucorum errorum' ('root of many errors'; pp. 18–19).

In the changed theological atmosphere following the accession of Charles I, Ward found this orthodoxy increasingly threatened by new Arminian heads, supporters of 'novelties in both rites and doctrines', advanced to power in the university by the court (*Whole Works of ... Ussher*, 15.581, 500–1, 405). In 1629 he was among those censured by the vice-chancellor, Matthew Wren, for purchasing William Prynne's *Anti-Arminianisme*; later in the year he departed from his reputation for eirenicism by engaging in a name-calling match with Jerome Beale in the consistory over his own *Gratia discriminans*. He continued actively to defend Calvinists and puritans and oppose Arminians and ceremonialists along with Catholics before the vice-chancellor's court, but with less success than he had enjoyed in the previous reign. Puritans like Thomas Edwards (1628), Nathaniel Bernard and Richard Spynke (1632), William Strong (1634), Christopher Goad (1635), and Thomas Riley (1636) were forced to recant or leave the university for objecting to altars, ceremonies, and Arminian doctrine; anti-Calvinists and ceremonialists like John Tourney and Peter Hausted (1634) and Sylvester Adams and Anthony Sparrow (1637) were exonerated over the vociferous protest of Ward and other Calvinist heads. By 1634 Ward had begun to fear for his own position. He complained to archbishop James Ussher that he had never found university affairs 'in a worse condition since I was a member thereof', with Calvinists 'disgraced and checked, … as myself was … for favoring puritans in consistory'—a reference to his recent defence of the Sidney Sussex puritan John Barcroft in the vice-chancellor's court (*Whole Works of … Ussher*, 15.579–81, 16.521).

Placing Ward along the spectrum of puritans and conformists is none the less a challenge. Clearly in his twenties he identified himself with the Cambridge puritan circle of Perkins and Chaderton, and the spiritual anxieties expressed in his diary are classic puritan fare. But his mature vernacular sermons show a continuity in his experimental spirituality, and his complaints about corruption and 'novelties' in the church and about popular irreligion continued throughout his life. He was one of the licensers of George Carleton's book attacking Richard Mountague. His actions on the vice-chancellor's court, including his opposition to Laudian metropolitical visitation of the university in 1635, all identify him with a puritan opposition and won him approbation by William Prynne (*Canterburies Doome*, 159–92). Puritans regularly consulted him about matters of conscience, judging him 'a man famous for learning and of high estimation … for his soundness of faith and integrity of conversation', as Nicholas Estwick remarked in 1634 (Bodl. Oxf., MS Tanner 71, fols. 186–7). Sidney Sussex College under his leadership continued its tradition of attracting puritans and their sons (including the presbyterian Thomas Edwards, Oliver Cromwell, and the sons of Samuel Ward of Ipswich, John Rogers, and Thomas Gataker) as well as Calvinist refugees from Heidelberg. As master he maintained strict discipline, even ordering surprise raids by tutors on their students' rooms to ensure godly behaviour (Sidney Sussex College, *Acta collegii*, p. 39, fol. 3 from the back). When in 1643 the iconoclast William Dowsing visited Cambridge for parliament he had few complaints about Ward's college: the chapel remained unconsecrated and communion was celebrated at a table rather than an altar, without rail or cross. Ward was invited to be a member of the Westminster assembly of divines as one of two representatives of the university, suggesting that he was perceived by presbyterian puritans as an ally. On the other hand, he supported episcopacy, he was clearly a pluralist, as archdeacon he would have had a seat in convocation, and despite his own strict sabbatarianism he argued in 1634 that the Book of Sports ought to be read for the sake of obedience and order. He maintained close friendships and produced a voluminous lifelong correspondence with Calvinist bishops like William Bedell, Ussher, John Davenant, and Arthur Lake. The puritanism of his youth seems at least to have moderated as he matured. Correspondence with Bedell suggests that he came to realize that if he were to maintain a position from which he could teach true doctrine and preach the gospel, he would have to keep his complaints about the present state of the church muted and compromise on issues he deemed of less importance than the evangelical mandate. His student Thomas Fuller noted that he 'turned with the times', but found him 'a true protestant at all times' (Fuller, *Worthies*, 1.488).

It is almost as difficult to place Ward along the political spectrum. His writings suggest a traditional devotion to monarchy, as to episcopacy, but he befriended and sheltered the Dutch republican Isaac Dorislaus when in 1627 the latter fell into disfavour for lectures construed as advocating republicanism and the legitimacy of regicide. In the 1620s he privately criticized the king for sabbath breach and 'indulging papists' and the queen for 'want of religion' (Sidney Sussex College, Ward MS B, fol. 31). In 1642 he declined personally to offer financial assistance for the royalist war effort, and he failed to make good on his college's promise of £100 for the king. On the other hand, in March 1643 Ward also refused on behalf of his college to give financial aid to parliament, despite a personal plea from Cromwell. With parliamentarian troops then occupying Cambridge, Ward was imprisoned in St John's College, accompanied voluntarily by his faithful servitor Seth Ward (unrelated, later bishop of Salisbury). Released early in August because of illness contracted in the dank conditions of his imprisonment, Samuel Ward died in the master's lodge at Sidney Sussex on 7 September 1643 and was buried in his college chapel; he was survived by his wife, Martha, about whom nothing further is known. A funeral oration was given in Great St Mary's by Henry Molle, the public orator, on 30 November, and a sermon was preached by Ralph Brownrigg, but the most eloquent tribute to Ward's saintly life, his scholarship, and his strict enforcement of discipline in his college is Seth Ward's prefatory eulogy to the posthumous collection of his theological works, *Opera nonnulla: determinationes theologicae, tractatus de justificatione, praelectiones de peccato originali* (1658); he called his former master Errorum Malleus (sig. A3v), a title that Ward would doubtless have embraced. Another treatise, *De baptismatis infantilis vi et efficacia disceptatio*, also posthumously published (1653) as part of a debate among nonconformists about the nature of baptism, stands testimony to Ward's enduring importance to puritan theology.   MARGO TODD

Sources M. Todd, 'The Samuel Ward papers at Sidney Sussex College, Cambridge', *Transactions of the Cambridge Bibliographical Society*, 8 (1981–5), 582–92 • M. Todd, 'Puritan self-fashioning: the diary of Samuel Ward', *Journal of British Studies*, 31 (1992), 236–64 • M. Todd, 'An act of discretion: evangelical conformity and the puritan dons', *Albion*, 18 (1986), 581–99 • M. Todd, 'Providence, chance and the new science in early Stuart Cambridge', *HJ*, 29 (1986), 697–711 • *The whole works of … James Ussher*, ed. C. R. Elrington and J. H. Todd, 17 vols. (1847–64), vols. 15–16 • letters to and from Ward, Bodl. Oxf., MSS Tanner 65–76, 279, 303 • Sidney Sussex College, Cambridge, MSS Ward A–S • Ward's commonplace book, Sidney Sussex College, Cambridge, MS 44 • Ward's diary, Sidney Sussex College, Cambridge, MS 45 • account book, 1598–, Sidney Sussex College, Cambridge • *Acta collegii*, 1604, Sidney Sussex College, Cambridge [1604–] • CUL, Mm 2.23, fols. 198–211; Mm 2.25, fols. 159–66; Com. Ct. 1 18, fols. 69–82, 110, 129–47v, 188; CUR 6.1, 18.6 • CUL, VC Ct MSS 1.8–9, 12, 42, 49, 51, 53–8; 3.27, 33, 36 • BL, Harleian MSS, 7019, 7038 • Fuller, *Worthies* (1840), 1.173, 487–8; 3.287 • Venn, *Alum. Cant.* • will, PRO, PROB 10, Box 642
Archives Sidney Sussex College, Cambridge, diary, College MSS 44–45 | Bodl. Oxf., Tanner MSS, corresp. and papers, 63–76, 279, 303

Likenesses oils, Sidney Sussex College, Cambridge

Wealth at death exact sum unknown; bequeathed in money £260; also lease of lands belonging to his archdeaconry, a collection of Roman coins, and books: PRO, PROB 10, Box 642; CUL, University Probate Records, trans. III, fols. 271v–272v; CUL MS Mm 1.37, pp. 197–8; Sidney Sussex MR.103

Ward, Samuel (1577–1640), preacher, was born in Haverhill, Suffolk, the eldest of three sons of John Ward (*d.* 1598), lecturer successively of Haverhill, Writtle, and Bury St Edmunds, and Susan (*d.* in or after 1639), his wife; his younger brothers were Nathaniel *Ward (1578–1652) and John (*d.* 1661). After her husband's death in October 1598 Susan Ward married Richard *Rogers (1551–1618), lecturer at Wethersfield near Sudbury, taking on two older stepsons Daniel *Rogers (1573–1652) and Ezekiel *Rogers (1588–1660); she was still living there in 1639. In November 1594 Samuel was admitted to St John's College, Cambridge, a scholar on Lord Burghley's nomination. He graduated BA in 1597, was a founder fellow at Sidney Sussex College in 1599, and proceeded MA the next year. Like his brothers and stepbrothers, he entered the ministry. Ordained in June 1601, he was for a time lecturer at Haverhill, where his sermon on the calling of Zaccheus converted the eight-year-old Samuel Fairclough. Ward vacated his fellowship on marrying a clergyman's widow, Deborah Bolton (*née* Leech) (*d.* 1652), at Isleham, Cambridgeshire, on 2 January 1604, taking on two stepsons, John and Robert Bolton.

On 1 November 1605 Ward was appointed town preacher of Ipswich, preaching up to three times a week to the assembled corporation in St Mary-le-Tower Church while business in the town was suspended. His generous stipend, which over five years increased from £67 to £100 a year, and the house provided for him (19–21 Lower Brook Street today), are two measures of his standing in the town. In 1607 he took a BD. As Thomas Fuller says, 'he was preferred minister in, or rather, of, Ipswich, having a care over and a love from all the parishes in that populous place' (Fuller, *Worthies*, 70–71). He believed, and was not afraid to state from the pulpit, that those who held office in church and state should be puritans, which led to complaints that he interfered in parliamentary elections. He quickly took control of the grammar school, hiring and firing schoolmasters, and planning to divert the endowments to a charity school. From 1612 Ward was given funds and the former dorter of the Blackfriars for a library for his own and other preachers' use, the schoolmasters acting as librarians. More than 100 donors, knights, gentlemen, corporation members, ministers, and townsmen, gave money or books, and the collection survives into the twenty-first century substantially complete, in which Ward's hand effacing crosses and references to historical characters as saints may still be seen.

Following what was to be the first of many publications, *A Coal from the Altar to Kindle the Holy Fire of Zeal* (1615), and his first sermon at Paul's Cross, issued as *Balm from Gilead to Recover Conscience* (1617), Ward began to exert more than local influence. Consciousness of the importance of a minister's public role is evident in his *Jethro's Justice of Peace*

Samuel Ward (1577–1640), by unknown artist, 1620

(1618), preached at Bury St Edmunds assizes, in which he emphasized the mutuality of magistracy and ministry—'the principal lights', 'these two opticke pieces', 'guardians and tutors' of the people. In the preface to his *The Happiness of Practice* (1621) he explained that, in expounding half the scriptures to his hearers, he had 'endeavoured to acquaint you with the whole counsel of God; and what is now the top of all my ambition, but to make you doers of what you have been hearers'. In 1621 he rashly allowed an engraving to be published from Amsterdam inscribed 'Invented by Samuell Ward, Preacher of Ipswich' (BM, Prints and Drawings, DG41, formerly Satires 41). It shows, on the left, the Armada in the grip of a storm, on the right, Gunpowder Plot discovered, and in a central pavilion the pope and his cardinals conferring with the king of Spain, the devil presiding. The Spanish ambassador Gondomar, at the time negotiating a match between Charles, prince of Wales and the Spanish infanta, claimed that this insulted his royal master. After examination by the privy council, Ward was committed to the Fleet. His petition to the king in April 1621 claimed that the 'embleme was … composed … five yeeres since' (probably during earlier overtures from Spain), and that he sent it to the printer 'nigh a yeere since', 'coupling the two grand blessings of God to this nation … without anie sinister intencion … of meddling in any of your Majesties secrett affaires' (Bruce, 1–2). He promised to be more cautious in future and only designed title-pages for his published sermons, most notably that of his anecdotal *Woe to Drunkards* (1622).

In 1622 Ward again pleaded for his liberty so that he

could maintain his wife and eight children by continuing to preach in Ipswich. He was successful in this, but that August the bailiffs received a letter from the king, demanding that they 'inhibit Mr Ward from preaching the lecture' (Suffolk RO, Ipswich, great court book, 6 Aug 1622). Bishop Samuel Harsnett of Norwich took up the charges of nonconformity against him in his own consistory court, but Ward again appealed to the king, who referred the matter to Lord Keeper John Williams. Williams decided that Ward, though not altogether blameless, was easily won over by fair dealing, and persuaded Harsnett to accept Ward's submission and not to suspend him. Ward was loyal to the church, providing that it resisted what he regarded as corruption; allegations at the time that he stirred up feelings against the king's favourite, Buckingham, were never substantiated, and his general loyalty to the crown is evident in *A Peace Offering to God for the Blessings we Enjoy under his Majesties Reign* (1624). He reluctantly allowed nine of his sermons to be printed and sold, and the first collected edition appeared in 1627.

For two periods Ward was incumbent at the Tower church in Ipswich, as well as preacher, but between 1627 and 1630 a conformist minister, Jonathan Skinner, held the cure, and was well placed to collect Ward's public indiscretions for later use. Once William Laud became archbishop of Canterbury in 1633, there was less scope for compromise. His commissary and agent in the town, Dr Henry Dade, soon found an ally in Skinner, and in February 1634 reported to Laud that two ships with 160 emigrants were ready to leave Ipswich for New England, and that, 'Of the breeders of these persons Mr Ward is chief of those parts has caused this giddiness'. However, because Ward was 'very potent in London and about Ipswich', it was recommended that Timothy Dalton, parson of Woolverstone (4 miles down the Orwell), 'a great stickler for transporting these people', be examined instead (*CSP dom.*, 1633–4, 450). None the less, that November Ward faced forty-three articles requiring answers in the court of high commission; they were eventually reduced to eleven. He had to make many journeys to London over the next year, and sometimes failed to appear. His preaching against set prayers, devotional attitudes, bowing at the name of Jesus, the real presence, and the like, for stating that religion and the gospel 'stood on tiptoes ready to be gone', were some of the grounds for complaint (ibid., 1635–6, lii). On 26 November 1635 he was ordered to be removed from office and suspended from all ministry, to pay £50 costs (his delay was contempt), and to admit his offences in writing. This he was prepared to do only in his own words, and he was committed temporarily to the Gatehouse prison at Westminster.

Ward's reputation in Ipswich was greatly enhanced, and the townsmen refused to replace him, hoping in vain that the authorities would eventually relent. Matthew Wren, newly appointed bishop of Norwich, was intent on cleansing the town of puritan dissent, but underestimated the risk of public disorder. When other ministers (including Ward's son-in-law John *Ashburne at the Tower Church) were ejected, there were riots on the streets and Wren's agents were driven from the town. On their next visit to Ipswich, Wren and his wife felt intimidated and left hurriedly. For ignoring these commotions, the bailiffs and portmen were summoned to the Star Chamber. Suggestions that Samuel Ward joined William Bridge in the Netherlands on his release can be firmly refuted, as the Ward concerned was John, ordained at Norwich in 1614 and rector of St Michael-at-Plea there from 1617 to his suspension in 1636.

Over his thirty-five years in Ipswich, Ward was executor to many of the leading townspeople, usually a beneficiary, and became increasingly wealthy. In 1631 he was offered and 'thankfully accepted' (Suffolk RO, Ipswich C/4/3/1/5, assembly book, 196) the interest on the town's £100 stake in the Virginia plantation by a grateful corporation. In the following year he offered land worth £1000 to one Jeffery Kirbye, who would have bequeathed it to the Grocers' Company had they chosen Ipswich rather than Oundle for their foundation. In April 1638 he bought his tied house from the borough for £140. Following his death at his home in March 1640, he was buried on 8 March in the centre nave aisle at St Mary-le-Tower under a stone with the inscription 'Watch Ward and yet a little while and he that shall come will come' (monumental inscription). He was remembered in the anonymous tract *Wrens Anatomy, Discovering his Notorious Pranks and Shamefull Wickednesse* (1641) as that 'ancient famous, good and painfull Master Ward'. His widow, Deborah, and eldest son, Samuel, continued to enjoy his stipend for their lives. Samuel, a Cambridge graduate, showed symptoms of schizophrenia, for in August 1661 he murdered his brother-in-law John Ashburne by stabbing. Two other sons were in orders. Nathaniel was rector of Stapleford, Cambridgeshire, and Joseph was rector of Badingham, where his mother spent her last days and was buried on 22 October 1652.

J. M. BLATCHLY

Sources *CSP dom.*, 1635–6, xxxi–lx · F. R. Grace, 'Schismaticall and factious humour', *Religious dissent in East Anglia* [Norwich 1996], ed. D. Chadd (1996), 97–119 · J. M. Blatchly, *Ipswich town library: a history and catalogue* (1989) · assembly and great court books, Suffolk RO, Ipswich, Ipswich borough archives · J. Bruce, *N&Q*, 4th ser., 1 (1868), 1–2 · Fuller, *Worthies* (1662), 3.70–71 · S. Ward, *Sermons and treatises*, ed. J. C. Ryle (1862), preface · parish register, St Mary-le-Tower, Suffolk RO, Ipswich · will, 16 Oct 1639, proved 24 Oct 1640, PRO, PROB 11/182, sig. 47 · tombstone, Suffolk, Ipswich, St Mary-le-Tower
Archives PRO, State Papers, domestic
Likenesses oils, 1620, Ipswich Museums [*see illus.*]
Wealth at death house in Ipswich; lands and house at Brightlingsea: will, PRO, PROB 11/182, sig. 47

Ward, Samuel (1725–1776), merchant and revolutionary politician in America, was born on 27 May 1725 in Newport, Rhode Island, the ninth of fourteen children of Richard *Ward (1689–1763), farmer, merchant, and secretary (1714–30) and governor (1740–43) of the colony of Rhode Island, and Mary (1690–1767), the daughter of John and Isabel Sayles Tillinghast and the granddaughter of the colony's founder, Roger Williams. According to one student of the period, the Ward family had 'a Hapsburgian flair for marriage', finding mates from 'other prolific and intelligent families' (James, 297). Samuel was no exception to this rule, marrying on 20 December 1745 Anna Ray (1728–1770), the daughter of Simon and Deborah Greene Ray of New Shoreham, Block Island, with whom he had eleven children. After their marriage Ward acquired property near the present town of Westerly, Rhode Island, from his father-in-law, where he and Anna lived for the rest of their lives. A successful farmer, Ward also operated a country store, and acted as a merchant in arranging to have local products sent to bigger urban markets. He quickly established himself as a leading citizen of the community.

Ward first entered politics in 1756, when he was elected to the Rhode Island assembly. He was re-elected in 1757. That same year Ward became involved in a political rivalry with Stephen Hopkins. This rivalry, which was more personal and sectional than ideological, became known as the Ward–Hopkins controversy and defined Rhode Island politics throughout the 1760s. Ward's involvement started as the author of a pamphlet attacking Hopkins, who was standing for election as governor against William Greene. Hopkins was so angered by Ward's pamphlet that he unsuccessfully sued Ward for libel. Greene won the election, but died in office. Hopkins became the governor and Ward his chief opponent. For the next four years Ward stood against Hopkins and was defeated each time. After his defeat in 1761 Ward was elected chief justice of the superior court by the Rhode Island assembly, despite the fact that he had no legal training. During his one year term Ward delivered a decision against Jewish naturalization in Rhode Island that challenged the authority of the British parliament and went further than any previous decision towards declaring a law of parliament void.

In May 1762 Ward again stood for governor and this time defeated Hopkins, though Hopkins won back the governorship the following year. Ward again won the governorship in 1765. During that term he enthusiastically led the colony's opposition to the Stamp Act. His conduct during that crisis was obviously approved of, for he won re-election. His second administration was less eventful, however, and the insolvency and resultant discrediting of his chief political supporter in the northern part of the colony, Deputy Governor Elisha Brown, left Ward politically vulnerable. He was defeated by Hopkins's forces in the gubernatorial election of 1767. Thereupon Ward withdrew from politics. The death of his wife in 1770 strengthened his resolve to eschew electoral office. He did, however, remain an active supporter of colonial rights. He was among the first to hold a public meeting—at his home—to protest against British punishment of Boston for its Tea Party, and he drew up a series of resolutions that set forth colonial grievances. When relations between America and Britain reached a crisis with British passage of the Coercive Acts in 1774, Ward decided once more to return to representative politics and that year he and his bitter rival Hopkins were chosen as Rhode Island's representatives to the first continental congress. The next year both men returned as the state's delegates to the second continental congress.

As delegate from Rhode Island, Ward was a firmer proponent of colonial rights and colonial resistance to British measures than Hopkins. After fighting broke out Ward voted against compromise and for independence, while Hopkins still held out hope of a *rapprochement* with Britain. It was Ward who proposed and helped secure the appointment of George Washington as commander-in-chief, and he would have undoubtedly been an important advocate for the Declaration of Independence had he not contracted smallpox and died on 26 March 1776 (less than four months before its signing) while congress was in session. He was buried two days later at the Baptist burial-ground in Philadelphia.

Remembered primarily for his political activities, Ward was a successful businessman, building up considerable wealth. An active Seventh Day Baptist, he was one of the original trustees of the Baptist Rhode Island College (later Brown University).   DENNIS M. CONRAD

Sources B. Knollenberg, ed., *Correspondence of Governor Samuel Ward, May 1775–March 1776, and genealogy of the Ward family*, Providence, Rhode Island Historical Society (1952) • M. R. McCarl, 'Ward, Samuel', *ANB* • D. S. Lovejoy, *Rhode Island politics and the American Revolution* (1958) • S. V. James, *Colonial Rhode Island: a history* (1975) • M. E. Thompson, 'The Ward–Hopkins controversy and the American Revolution', *William and Mary Quarterly*, 3rd ser., 16 (1959), 363–75 • J. R. Bartlett, ed., *Records of the colony of Rhode Island and Providence plantations*, 6–7 (1861–2) • M. Appleton, 'Ward, Samuel', *DAB*
Archives Rhode Island Historical Society, papers

Ward [*née* Achurch], **Sarah** (1726/7–1771), actress and theatre manager, was born in 1726 or early 1727, the daughter of the York-based actor Thomas Achurch (1707?–1771). The identity of her mother is unknown, but she is likely to have been the Mrs Achurch named on a London playbill for 31 May 1734. Sarah had at least three sisters: Henrietta Achurch, who was acting in York in 1763 and who, along with a Miss Anne Achurch, was a subscriber to Henry Ward's *Works* (1746), and a third, whose first name is unknown but who married Robert Mahon.

Sarah Achurch began her theatrical career in the mid-1740s at York. About 1744 she married her fellow actor and a minor playwright Henry Ward (d. 1758). Around 1745 she and her husband transferred to Thomas Este's Taylor's Hall company in Edinburgh. Following internal disputes the company split into two groups, one led by Sarah Ward. Ward's company, expanded to include Lacy Ryan and West *Digges (1725?–1786), was thwarted in its attempt to perform in Aberdeen, but opened the new Canongate Theatre in Edinburgh on 16 November 1747.

Ward made her London début at Covent Garden on 3 October 1748, as Cordelia to James Quin's Lear. Susannah Cibber having fallen ill while recovering from the birth of a son, David Garrick was keen to secure the services of Ward, who made her Drury Lane début on 13 October 1749, playing Cordelia to his Lear. Although her beauty was admitted by all, she was deemed to have a poor figure. Garrick found her intractable and unteachable, and

Spranger Barry took such a dislike to her that he refused to appear with her in the same play.

Ward's career continued to combine regular contracts at Drury Lane with provincial appearances, including the summer season of 1750 with Linnett's company at Bath and Bristol. In 1752 she returned to Edinburgh with John Lee, who, having finally escaped his contract with Garrick, had quit London to assume management in Edinburgh. Among Lee's company were James Love, Stampier, Digges, and Ward, and it was around this time that the latter two began their affair. In September 1752 Ward joined Thomas Sheridan's Smock Alley company, and made her Dublin début on 24 November 1752, as Monimia in Thomas Otway's *The Orphan*. She was a favourite with Dublin audiences and spent three years there. 1755 saw her return to Edinburgh, where she appeared as Mrs Sullen in George Farquhar's *The Beaux' Stratagem* on 25 November.

In a complicated financial dispute, Lee lost control of the Edinburgh theatre. While James Callender was briefly appointed business manager, 'artistic policy' was controlled by Digges, who rejoined the Edinburgh company in September 1756. It was during this season, on 14 December, that Ward appeared as Lady Barnet (the original name given to the character of Lady Randolph) to Digges's Norval in the première of John Home's *Douglas*. It was to prove one of her most popular and celebrated roles.

Ward remained in Edinburgh until May 1758, when she left to appear in Newcastle (where she briefly used the name of Mrs Digges) and Liverpool. She travelled on to Dublin, where she and Digges played the 1758–9 season at Smock Alley. During the summer of 1759 her relationship with Digges finally ended. Ward returned to Covent Garden and remained there for the next twelve seasons.

It is uncertain just how many children Ward had: certainly at least three with Henry Ward, of whom at least two became actors; Thomas Achurch Ward (1747–1835) appeared in London, married the actress Sarah Hoare (1756–1838), and became actor–manager at Manchester; Margaretta Priscilla Ward (1752–1793) was seen regularly at Covent Garden, married the actor Thomas Kniveton, and appeared as Mrs Kniveton and later Mrs John Banks; there was also a son (*b.* 24 January 1751). Ward had at least six more children with Digges, although how many survived to maturity is not known.

Ward died on 9 March 1771 at the age of forty-four. In her career she had displayed great tenacity, managing a company at a time when women managers were almost unheard of and then becoming the partner of West Digges in a personal as well as a professional sense. Her independent career shows that she was not overshadowed by Digges, although her strength of character was clearly of a kind that made her a difficult member of companies led by the likes of Garrick and Barry. While she has not been especially celebrated by later eras, Ward was clearly one of the more remarkable performers of her day.

ADRIENNE SCULLION

Sources Highfill, Burnim & Langhans, *BDA* • G. H. Bushnell, 'The original Lady Randolph', *Theatre Notebook*, 13 (1958–9), 119–23 • J. C. Dibdin, *The annals of the Edinburgh stage* (1888) • G. A. Bellamy, *An apology for the life of George Anne Bellamy*, ed. [A. Bicknell], 3rd edn, 6 vols. (1785) • F. Gaye, ed., *Who's who in the theatre*, 14th edn (1967) • Genest, *Eng. stage* • J. K. Angus, *A Scotch play-house: being the historical records of the old Theatre Royal, Marischal Street, Aberdeen* (1878) • W. Baynham, *The Glasgow stage* (1892) • *The autobiography of Dr Alexander Carlyle of Inveresk, 1722–1805*, ed. J. H. Burton (1910) • R. Lawson, *The story of the Scots stage* (1917) • H. Mackenzie, *An account of the life and writings of John Home* (1822) • M. Nash, *The provoked wife: the life and times of Susannah Cibber* (1977) • *Memoirs of Charles Lee Lewes, containing anecdotes, historical and biographical, of the English and Scottish stages during a period of forty years*, 2 vols. (1805) • H. P. Brougham, *The life and times of Henry, Lord Brougham*, ed. W. Brougham, 2nd edn, 3 vols. (1871)

Ward [*née* Ainsworth], **Sarah Adelaide** (1895–1969), politician, was born on 26 December 1895 at Meaford Farm, Stone, Staffordshire, the daughter of John Ainsworth of Meaford, a farmer, and his wife, Harriet, *née* Thorley. She was educated at Orme Girls' School, Newcastle under Lyme, and served during the First World War as a nurse with the 9th Staffordshire voluntary aid detachment. On 9 August 1921 she married William John Ward (*b.* 1893/4), a farmer, of Blackwall Heath, the son of William Charles Ward, also a farmer; they had one daughter.

Ward's long involvement in Conservative local politics led to her adoption as the candidate for Cannock, Staffordshire, at the general election of 1931. At first sight she had little chance of success. The seat had been held by the Labour member William Adamson since 1922 and he was defending a majority of over 11,000 in 1931. Ward's position, though, was strengthened by the absence of a Liberal candidate, and by the atmosphere of national crisis in which the election took place. Voters across the country sought stability in the National Government, and the trend was reflected at Cannock, where Ward won by 4665 votes.

As a predominantly agricultural and mining constituency Cannock was hard hit by the economic crises of the day and Ward took it upon herself in parliament to defend 'the British miner and the British agriculturist … the worst paid workers in the country' (*Hansard 5C*, vol. 260, col. 815). In her maiden speech in November 1931 she welcomed emergency import duties on agricultural products as 'the first step on the road to prosperity for the countryside' (ibid.). The importance of this objective went far beyond economics and had to be seen 'from the point of view of preserving the physical wellbeing of the nation' (*The Times*, 1 Dec 1931). It was essential 'to breed a race of Englishmen strong and sturdy in body and in limb, and healthy in mind. Those men can only be bred in the countryside, amid green fields, clear waters and fresh air' (*Hansard 5C*, vol. 260, col. 813). Import duties, she believed, would create jobs and help to reverse the tide of rural depopulation. The flight from the countryside was of special concern to her, and in February 1933 she moved the second reading of the Home and Empire Settlement Bill. This aimed to encourage the settlement of rural areas in Britain, as well as the dominions, and Ward hoped that it would begin the process of 'getting our people back to the land' (*The Times*, 25 Feb 1933).

Ward's faith in the regenerative powers of import

duties led her naturally to support the Ottawa trade agreements in 1932. In October of that year she informed the Commons that the benefits of protection were already being seen in her own constituency, where blast furnaces had restarted after years of disuse, burning coal from Cannock collieries. In spite of this optimism Ward was realistic enough to recognize the underlying unprofitability of the mines in her region. She nevertheless rejected pit closures as a solution, urging instead 'a bold Cromwellian outlook' to explore alternative markets for coal (*Hansard 5C*, vol. 265, col. 1021).

Ward's instinctive sympathy for the industrial worker caused her to welcome the extension of unemployment insurance in May 1934, and to criticize the application, though not the principle, of the means test. She also drew attention to a class of woman seldom mentioned in the Commons debates:

> As a woman, I would like to pay my tribute to them. … The wives of the unemployed have to bear the biggest brunt of the burden of unemployment; they have to eke out the meagre money and to cheer up the despondent husbands and sons who are unemployed. (*Hansard 5C*, vol. 289, col. 1520)

As the wife of a tenant farmer herself the realities of household finances were never far away. In June 1934 she welcomed a bill to improve the quality of milk, while expressing concern over the likely cost, and recognized the thrift of the housewife in rural and industrial areas: 'It is amazing to see the way in which she allocates her threepences and sixpences to this, that, and the other thing, and if she wants more of one thing, she must go short of something else' (*Hansard 5C*, vol. 290, col. 1165). Ward's perspective as a woman and a mother also informed her contribution to the debate on whipping, during consideration of the Children and Young Persons Bill in June 1932. She supported this punishment, provided that the person administering it had a real understanding of the child's temperament and could thus judge the likely effect:

> I believe that a good sound whipping occasionally does every child good, and that we ought not to be too namby-pamby about this. We can be too lenient with a naughty child and I think whipping occasionally a very good thing. (*Hansard 5C*, col. 2085)

In her short time in parliament Ward had worked hard to defend beleaguered industries in Cannock and had shown herself to be an able and a committed parliamentarian. She could not, though, prevent Labour from reclaiming the seat at the November 1935 general election. A creditable performance kept William Adamson's winning majority down to just over a thousand votes.

Ward remained active in politics after losing her seat, and at the Conservative conference at Scarborough in October 1937 attacked the inconsistency and irresponsibility of Labour policy on defence and foreign affairs. She served as a junior commander in the Auxiliary Territorial Service from 1940 to 1943, and twice stood again for parliament—at Lichfield and Tamworth, Staffordshire, in February 1950, and at Perry Barr, Birmingham, in October 1951. On both occasions she was decisively beaten by the Labour candidate. After this she concentrated on local politics: she was a member of Staffordshire county council from 1950, and chaired its welfare services committee from 1956 to 1964. In 1961 she was appointed CBE, having been appointed OBE in 1952. She died on 9 April 1969, at The Limes, Linley Road, Rushall. She was survived by her husband.

MARK POTTLE

Sources WWW · WWBMP · *The Times* (1 Dec 1931) · *The Times* (25 Feb 1932) · *The Times* (29 April 1932) · *The Times* (1 July 1932) · *The Times* (21 Oct 1932) · *The Times* (25 Feb 1933) · *The Times* (25 May 1933) · *The Times* (30 June 1933) · *The Times* (1 Feb 1934) · *The Times* (15 May 1934) · *The Times* (8 June 1934) · *The Times* (6 Feb 1935) · *The Times* (8 Oct 1937) · *The Times* (14 April 1969) · *Hansard 5C* (1931), vol. 260; (1932), vols. 265, 267, 269; (1934), vols. 289–90 · F. W. S. Craig, *British parliamentary election results, 1918–1949*, rev. edn (1977) · F. W. S. Craig, *British parliamentary election results, 1950–1970* (1971) · P. Brookes, *Women at Westminster: an account of women in the British parliament, 1918–1966* (1967) · C. Rallings and M. Thrasher, *British electoral facts, 1832–1999* (2000) · b. cert. · m. cert. · d. cert.

Ward, Seth (1617–1689), astronomer and bishop of Exeter and Salisbury, was born in Buntingford, Hertfordshire, and was baptized at St Mary's Church in nearby Aspenden on 5 April 1617. He was the second son of John Ward (*d.* 1656), an attorney in Buntingford, and his wife, Martha Dalton (*d.* 1646). His friend and first biographer, Walter Pope (*c.*1630–1714), said that he had never heard Ward speak of his father, but that he often spoke fondly and admiringly of his mother, and believed that his character was due to her (Pope, 4–5). John and Martha produced two other sons, John and Clement, and three daughters. Seth never married, but Clement left three sons and a number of daughters to his care while he was Savilian professor at Oxford, and he also provided throughout his life for his sisters and a number of their sons and daughters. In fact he was so dutiful in looking after his extended family that in later life his enemies found it easy to accuse him of nepotism.

Cambridge years From the grammar school in Buntingford, Ward entered Sidney Sussex College, Cambridge, on 1 December 1632; he graduated BA in 1637 and MA on 27 July 1640. There he quickly became the favourite of the master, Samuel Ward (*d.* 1643). He lodged in the latter's apartments and had the use of the college library, where he spent much time, being shy of going into the town. He showed great promise, and may have been tutored by Samuel Ward, who had a keen interest in the mathematical sciences. In his third year a disputation of his in mathematics impressed John Bainbridge, first Savilian professor of astronomy, and when taking his BA he disputed on the differences between the Julian and Gregorian calendars. Pope's suggestion that Ward was effectively an autodidact in mathematics is almost certainly incorrect (Pope, 10). Having been chosen in July 1640 by the vice-chancellor, John Cosin (1594–1672), as *praevaricator*, or official jester, Ward inadvertently offended Cosin and was suspended from his degree, but reinstated the following day. In 1643 he was made the university's mathematical lecturer.

In the same year Samuel Ward, with other leading members of the university, was imprisoned in St John's College

Seth Ward (1617–1689), by John Greenhill, 1673

for refusing the covenant. Seth Ward voluntarily remained in confinement with his mentor, and upon his release accompanied him home to care for him during his final illness. At that time Ward, together with Peter Gunning (1614–1684), John Barwick (1612–1664), and Isaac Barrow (d. 1680), published *Certain Disquisitions and Considerations Representing to the Conscience the Unlawfulness of the … Solemn League and Covenant*. In the spring of 1644 Ward refused to swear to the covenant, though at least in part this refusal was prompted by the visitors' practice of implying that those who would not take the oath were guilty of various immoralities. Deprived of his fellowship in August, Ward stayed for a time with relatives of Samuel Ward, in or near London, and then went to stay with the mathematician William Oughtred in Albury, Surrey.

Ward used this unsettled period to improve his mathematics. He had made the acquaintance of Oughtred in 1643 when, together with Charles Scarburgh (1615–1694), he visited Albury to clarify some obscurities in Oughtred's *Clavis mathematicae* (1631). Ward subsequently introduced the *Clavis* into his lectures at Cambridge. After studying with Oughtred for a while he went as tutor to the sons of his friend Ralph Freeman to Aspenden, where he remained until 1649. He then served for some months as chaplain to Lord Wenman (1596–1665) at Thame. From there Ward went to Oxford as Savilian professor of astronomy, a post he secured with the help of John Greaves (1602–1652), the ejected professor, and Sir John Trevor (d. 1673), who was able to arrange that Ward did not have to take the covenant or the engagement.

Astronomer at Oxford From 29 April 1650 Ward lived as a fellow-commoner at Wadham College, Oxford, where he

became a close friend of the much admired warden, John Wilkins, and a leading member of the group of natural philosophers who met in the city at this time. He reinstated the university's astronomy lectures, which had been discontinued for some time, and was the first Savilian professor to teach the Copernican theory. In spite of being exempted from the pulpit as a Savilian professor, he also preached frequently. His first publication as Savilian professor was a work of natural theology, *A philosophical essay towards an eviction of the being and attributes of God, the immortality of the souls of men, and the truth and authority of scripture* (1652). This exercise in theology shows the influence of John Wilkins, who was a vigorous proponent of rationalist approaches to theology.

In 1653 Ward produced a study of the nature of comets, *De cometis, ubi de cometarum natura disseritur*, and an examination of the paths of the planets, *In Ismaelis Bullialdi astronomiae philolaicae fundamenta inquisitio brevis*, which was to prove much more influential. Ward's refinement of Johann Kepler's second law of planetary motion, presented as a response to Ismael Boulliau's *Astronomia philolaica* (Paris, 1645), was developed more completely in his *Astronomia geometrica; ubi methodus proponitur qua primariorum planetarum astronomia sive elliptica sive circularis possit geometrice absolvi* (1656). Kepler's second law proved unsatisfactory to astronomers because it did not provide an easy way of determining planetary movements. In trying to solve these difficulties Boulliau developed a complex scheme which Ward was able to simplify dramatically. While Boulliau defined planetary movements by reference to the axis of imaginary cones, Ward pointed out that this was equivalent to supposing that planets move in their elliptical orbits with uniform angular velocity about the empty focus of the ellipse (the sun being at the other focus). Neither Boulliau's nor Ward's innovations were a real improvement on Kepler's second law, being only approximately true, but they proved influential among astronomers who would otherwise have to struggle with trial and error or successive approximation methods if they adhered to Kepler's original formulation.

Ward also wrote, in collaboration with John Wilkins, *Vindiciae academiarum* (1654). This was a defence of the English universities against John Webster, an illuminist and antinomian sectarian who had just published *Academiarum examen*; Thomas Hobbes, who had criticized the universities in his *Leviathan* (1651); and William Dell, master of Gonville and Caius College, Cambridge, who suggested that there should be universities in all large towns. Ward returned to criticism of Hobbes in 1656 with *In Thomae Hobbii philosophiam exercitatio epistolica*, an examination of the philosophy and theology of Hobbes occasioned by the appearance of the latter's *De corpore* in 1655, but ranging over his other works. This represented a marked change of attitude towards Hobbes, since Ward had written (though it was signed by the printer, Francis Bowman) the adulatory preface to Hobbes's *Humane Nature* of 1650. Hobbes replied to Ward's criticisms in the last of his *Six Lessons to the Savilian Professors of the Mathematics* (1656), the other five being aimed at the more damaging mathematical critique of John Wallis (1618–1673). According to Pope, this exchange so soured things between Hobbes and his erstwhile admirer that whenever their mutual friend Charles Scarburgh entertained leading intellectuals at his home, Hobbes would always check first that Ward was not present before deigning to enter the room (Pope, 125–6).

Universal language The *Vindiciae academiarum* also made public Ward's interest in continental schemes to provide a universal language that could be understood by all. Through Samuel Hartlib, Ward learned of the efforts of Cyprian Kinner (*fl.* 1650), a Silesian disciple of the intellectual reformer Jan Amos Comenius, to develop a philosophical language in which the words themselves, by their form and structure, reveal all the attributes of the things they signify. By 1650 Ward, one of the first English thinkers to engage with the subject, was trying to develop his own scheme, and he directly inspired Wilkins and George Dalgarno (*c.*1619–1687) in their own universal language schemes. Ward's projected scheme was rather different from that developed by Wilkins in his *Essay towards a Real Character and a Philosophical Language* (1668). Wilkins's scheme depended upon more orderly and clearer classifications of knowledge, and the assumption that the elements of ensuing classificatory tables could then be given a distinctive oral and visual form. Ward, even in 1654, realized that such a scheme would require an 'almost infinite' number of characters. His own scheme sought to discover supposed 'simple notions', perhaps fewer than a hundred in number, into which all discourse could be analysed and which would form the basis for a more austere and exact discourse capable of revealing the very nature of things. Ward acknowledged the influence of Ramon Lull's *Ars magna* (1517) and George Ritschel's *Contemplationes metaphysicae* (1648) upon his thinking. Ward was a member of the unproductive committee established by the Royal Society after the publication of Wilkins's *Essay* to further universal language schemes, and he also corresponded in 1676 with friends (including Robert Hooke, Andrew Paschall, Francis Lodwyck, and John Ray) who wished to complete Wilkins's project. Their awareness of the fundamental differences between Ward's and Wilkins's approaches added to the already considerable difficulties involved in producing a universal language.

Bishop of Exeter and Salisbury In 1656 Ward had become chaplain to Dr Ralph Brownrig, the ejected bishop of Exeter, and not only accepted from him the precentorship of Exeter but also paid the full fees for this to Brownrig's secretary, even though there was then little hope that the Anglican church would be restored. The following year the fellows elected him principal of Jesus College, Oxford, but Cromwell put in Francis Howell (1625–1679), a fellow of Exeter College. Ward must have impressed Cromwell, however, since the latter compensated him with an extra stipend of £80 per annum. After Cromwell's death Ward petitioned for its continuation, and from January 1659 it was paid out of a revenue managed by the governors of Windsor.

Meanwhile, Ward was elected president of Trinity College, Oxford, on 14 September 1659, and immediately began to settle the troubled affairs of the college. At the Restoration, however, he properly resigned his place to Hannibal Potter (1592–1664), who had been ejected in 1649. In August 1660 Ward also resigned the Savilian professorship and settled in London as vicar of St Lawrence Jewry, a benefice in the king's gift. Now Ward's investment gamble with Brownrig paid off. He was confirmed as precentor of Exeter Cathedral on 25 July 1660 and as prebendary in September, elected dean on 26 December 1661, and consecrated bishop on 20 July 1662.

Ward proved to be an extremely able administrator and immediately began to fill vacant ecclesiastical preferments in his diocese, restore church buildings to their proper use (including the bishop's palace), recover church property, and reform various abuses. He managed to augment the value of the poorer benefices and increase the revenues of the prebendaries, while spending over £25,000 on restoring the cathedral. It is small wonder that Ward declared himself to be £2000 the worse for being bishop of Exeter. He also began to earn a reputation as a prosecutor, even a persecutor, of dissenters, though it is not clear how justified this reputation was. He seems to have approved of and used the Clarendon code, and he certainly supported the Five Mile Act. Nevertheless, Pope records a number of Ward's acts of kindness to individual dissenters.

Ward's success at Exeter was rewarded by translation to the wealthier see of Salisbury on 5 September 1667. He had buildings repaired, including the bishop's palace and the Guildhall; the cathedral itself had been well preserved during the interregnum, but Ward had the floor of the choir laid with marble and the cloister paved. He tried to exert conformity, and it was said that he was so vigorous in suppressing conventicles that the local cloth trade—conducted largely by nonconformists—began to suffer, but there is no independent evidence of this (Pope, 71; Whiteman, 437). During his episcopacy he divided his time between his diocese and London, where he assiduously attended the House of Lords. He used various addresses in London until 1673, when he bought, or possibly had built, a grand house in Knightsbridge, apparently attracted by the opportunities it provided for horse-riding. Always a good horseman, he was encouraged to ride regularly by his physician, Thomas Sydenham (1624–1689), who regarded it as the perfect form of healthy exercise. (Ward had been prone to bouts of ill health after a bad fever which he suffered in 1660.)

In 1674 Ward was offered translation to Durham, but he refused it, he told Pope, because he 'did not like the conditions' (Pope, 96). It is not clear what these conditions were, but they might refer to suggestions that Charles II had promised Nell Gwynne an allowance out of Durham's bishopric funds (Whiteman, 36–7). Pope also claimed to have heard Gilbert Sheldon (1598–1677) speak of Ward as his preferred successor to the see of Canterbury (Pope, 97), but by the time Sheldon died Ward was out of favour at court.

While at Salisbury, Ward engaged in a number of charitable schemes. He gave £100 for the building of Chelsea College in 1668 and promised another £100 in 1678. In 1681 he donated £100 to Wadham College, Oxford, and subsequently endowed Christ's College, Cambridge, with four scholarships. In 1682 he established a so-called College of Matrons (to avoid the stigma of the designation 'hospital') in the cathedral close at Salisbury for the maintenance of ten widows of orthodox clergymen. Two years later he established a hospital for ten poor men at Buntingford, his birthplace. In his will he left money to his native parish of Aspenden for apprenticing poor boys, and £1000 for the upkeep of the fabric of Salisbury Cathedral.

In 1669 Ward successfully petitioned for the return of the chancellorship of the Order of the Garter to the bishops of Salisbury, a right that had originally been granted in the fifteenth century, and he became the new chancellor in 1671 after the death of the lay holder of the office. Ward's administration of Garter funds brought him into trouble, however. He retained money left over from various expenses for himself, and a commission investigating charges of malversation in 1684 ordered him to refund all of this money to the crown. By then he was also busy defending himself against charges of usurping special powers and prerogatives of the king's. In 1682 Cornelius Yeate, vicar of St Mary's, Marlborough, and Thomas Pierce, dean of Salisbury, argued falsely that Salisbury was one of the king's chapels royal, like Windsor and Westminster, and that all its prebends were in the king's gift. Yeate and Pierce's son had been denied preferments by Ward and this was evidently a major cause of their animosity towards him, since charges of nepotism were prominent in their attacks upon him. He was undoubtedly guilty of favouritism, but perhaps no more so than many contemporaries in similar positions, and he arranged preferments for various protégés, including Isaac Barrow, William Lloyd (1627–1717), and Izaac Walton (1593–1683) (Whiteman, 460–64). He was vindicated from the more serious charges laid against him in 1686, when the dean submitted to an archiepiscopal visitation that found in Ward's favour.

By then, however, Ward had declined into an incapable senility. In his last five years memory failed him, even to the extent that he forgot what he was talking about in the very moment of speaking, and he was hardly aware of what was going on around him. Pope was so affected by his friend's sad decline that he alluded to it in his famous poem, 'Wish':

To outlive my senses may it not be my Fate,
To be blind, to be deaf, to know nothing at all,
But rather let Death come before 'tis so late.
(Pope, 195)

Death came to Ward, overdue, on 6 January 1689, at his home in Knightsbridge, and he was buried in the choir of Salisbury Cathedral.

Reputation and influence John Aubrey (1626–1697) described Ward as 'a handsome man, pleasant and sanguine' with 'a most magnificent and munificent mind', but Robert Hooke (1635–1703) simply called him 'fals' and 'a courtier' (Whiteman, 50–51). Gilbert Burnet (1643–1715) said that his 'sincerity was much questioned' (*Of the Final Twelve Years of the Reign of King Charles II*, 1823, 332); Anthony Wood assessed him as a 'Politician' and remarked on 'his cowardly wavering for lucre and honour sake' (*Athenae Oxonienses*, 1721, 2, cols. 827, 1172). Ward's strength was as an ecclesiastical administrator. It is impossible to determine the precise nature of his theological or religious beliefs, but he was a great success in restoring the cathedrals of Exeter and Salisbury, and in reforming the administration of those dioceses after the rigours of the interregnum. During his tenure as Savilian professor he developed an international reputation as a mathematical astronomer, but after leaving Oxford he did not maintain his interest. He did not entirely repudiate natural philosophy, being a fairly active member of the Royal Society from its foundation in 1660 until about 1675, but he made no significant contribution to the development of the natural sciences, nor to that of the universal language schemes.

JOHN HENRY

Sources E. A. O. Whiteman, 'The episcopate of Dr Seth Ward, bishop of Exeter (1662–1667) and Salisbury (1667–1688/9), with special reference to the ecclesiastical problems of his time', DPhil diss., U. Oxf., 1951 • W. Pope, *The life of the right reverend father in God, Seth, lord bishop of Salisbury* (1697); repr. as *The life of Seth, Lord Bishop of Salisbury*, ed. J. B. Bamborough (1961) • C. A. Wilson, 'From Kepler's laws, so-called, to universal gravitation: empirical factors', *Archive for History of Exact Sciences*, 6 (1969–70), 89–170 • J. Knowlson, *Universal language schemes in England and France, 1600–1800* (1975) • M. M. Slaughter, *Universal languages and scientific taxonomy in the seventeenth century* (1982) • J. L. Subbiondo, ed., *John Wilkins and 17th-century British linguistics* (1992) • N. Malcolm, 'Hobbes and the Royal Society', *Perspectives on Thomas Hobbes*, ed. G. A. J. Rogers and A. Ryan (1988), 43–66 • M. Feingold, *The mathematicians' apprenticeship: science, universities and society in England, 1560–1640* (1984) • B. J. Shapiro, *John Wilkins, 1614–1672: an intellectual biography* (1969) • A. G. Debus, *Science and education in the seventeenth century: the Webster–Ward debate* (1970) • J. E. B. Mayor, 'Seth Ward', *N&Q*, 2nd ser., 7 (1859), 269–70 • *DNB*

Archives Bodl. Oxf., MSS • Devon RO, papers • Salisbury Cathedral, papers | Bodl. Oxf., corresp. with Sancroft and papers • diocesan registry, Exeter, MSS of the bishop of Exeter • Exeter Cathedral, MSS of the dean and chapter of Exeter

Likenesses J. Greenhill, oils, 1673, Salisbury, Guildhall, Wiltshire [*see illus.*] • D. Loggan, engraving, 1678, BM, NPG • J. Greenhill, oils, second version, Trinity College, Oxford • bust, Salisbury Cathedral, Wiltshire

Wealth at death left money for apprenticeships and £1000 for upkeep of Salisbury Cathedral: will

Ward, Stephen Thomas (1912–1963), osteopath and scapegoat, was born on 19 October 1912 at Lemsford vicarage, Hatfield, Hertfordshire, second of three sons of Arthur Evelyn Ward (1877–1944), clergyman, and his wife, Eileen Esmée (1881–1955), daughter of Thomas Mercer Cliffe Vigors, Anglo-Irish landowner. He was a descendant of the second Baron Castlemaine and first cousin of the traveller Wilfred Thesiger. After schooling at Canford, he worked as a translator in Hamburg (1929–30) and as a

Parisian tourist guide while studying at the Sorbonne (*c.*1930–1932). Next he qualified in osteopathy at Kirksville, Missouri (1934–9), which entitled him to practise as a physician in the USA; he henceforth used the prefix of doctor, but had no British medical qualifications.

After briefly practising osteopathy in Torquay, Ward entered the Royal Armoured Corps as a private, reaching the rank of captain in the Royal Army Medical Corps. Settling in London after the war, his first important patient was the US ambassador Averell Harriman. In 1947 he set up an osteopathic practice in Cavendish Square. Although Lady Gladwyn 'disliked his jaunty conceited manner' (*Diaries of Cynthia Gladwyn*, 288), she acknowledged the efficacy of his techniques; her fellow patients (including Sir Winston Churchill, Elizabeth Taylor, Paul Getty, King Peter of Yugoslavia) were more appreciative of Ward's fluent, ingratiating, well-informed conversation. Uninhibited, indiscreet, carefree, kind, plausible, and charming, his voice was rich and resonant. He was an inveterate name-dropper who delighted in crossing social barriers. From early manhood he was fascinated by prostitution and relished the company of beautiful women, but he had a low libido. On 27 July 1949 he married an actress, Patricia Mary (*b.* 1928), daughter of Eric Clifford Kingsley Baines, textiles company director. The marriage failed after six weeks and was ended by divorce three years later. He became more dissolute with age, although his preference was for talking about other people's sexual activity rather than for acting himself.

Ward attended classes at the Slade School of Art, and a new phase of his career opened with an exhibition of his sketches of patients (12 July 1960). He supplied the *Illustrated London News* with further celebrity sketches and the *Daily Telegraph* with drawings of Adolph Eichmann's trial (1961). He hoped to sketch the Politburo, and was introduced by his patient Colin Coote, editor of the *Daily Telegraph*, to Yevgeny Ivanov, the Russian naval attaché. Ward was soon enlisted by MI5 in an attempt to entrap Ivanov (June 1961), became a messenger between British and Soviet intelligence, and was an unofficial intermediary during the Cuban missile crisis (1962). Briefly Ward had real utility, but overrated his influence.

In 1956 the third Viscount Astor, who had been Ward's friend and patient since 1950, allowed him to lease for a peppercorn rent Spring Cottage in his grounds at Cliveden. In July 1961 Astor held a house party attended by John Profumo, minister for war. Ward's guests that weekend included Ivanov and Christine Keeler, with whom Ward had intermittently lived on a non-sexual basis since 1959. For some months until December 1961 Keeler and Profumo had an affair. This need not have caused a public convulsion, but after an interval was exploited by George Wigg MP, whose mischief-making resulted in Profumo making a formal denial in the House of Commons of 'impropriety … with Miss Keeler' (22 March 1963). This was the first public sensation of the Profumo affair, a moral panic in which fears of foreign espionage were muddled together with political opportunism, prurience,

and malice under the cover of cant phrases about maintaining standards in public life. Ward and Keeler both confirmed Profumo's statement, but on 26 March Ward spoke with naïve candour to Wigg in an effort to minimize the scandal. Perhaps he was shadowed to his meeting with the Labour MP, for the next day the Conservative home secretary, Henry *Brooke (1903–1984), who wanted Ward discredited or silenced, asked the commissioner of police if there was police interest in Ward. A wide investigation was launched on 1 April to see if Ward could be caught for a crime. Up to 140 of his friends and patients were repeatedly interviewed in a campaign of harassment (Keeler was interviewed twenty-four times). The police pressurized and intimidated witnesses in a fishing operation which destroyed Ward's osteopathic practice. Initially Ward was co-operative, believing that his intelligence work would secure his immunity from this persecution, but when he realized that he was being set up as a scapegoat he contacted journalists, and at a meeting with the prime minister's private secretary and a representative of the Security Service declared that Profumo's Commons denial had been untrue. Profumo resigned on 4 June.

On 8 June, in an act of political revenge, Ward was arrested and charged under the Sexual Offences Act of 1956 with living on immoral earnings. He had introduced men and women who had subsequently slept together, but the allegation that he was a pimp would have been impossible to sustain in a less politically hysterical atmosphere. Ward's trial, which was hurriedly opened at the Old Bailey on 22 July, was one of historic injustice. It established him as the British Dreyfus. The charges were dubious; the testimony of prostitutes dredged up by the police was never reliable. But the prosecuting counsel, Mervyn Griffith-Jones (who in 1960 had been the senior prosecuting counsel in the unsuccessful prosecution of Penguin Books for publishing an unexpurgated version of D. H. Lawrence's *Lady Chatterley's Lover*), blackened Ward's character with a closing speech which presented verdicts of guilty as the jury's patriotic duty. In the early morning of 31 July, before the last day of the trial, Ward took thirty-five grains of Nembutal barbiturate. 'It is really more than I can stand—the horror day after day at the court and in the streets', he wrote in his suicide note. 'I am sorry to disappoint the vultures. … Delay resuscitation as long as possible' (Knightley and Kennedy, 245; Crawford, 170). The judge having refused to halt the trial, Ward was found guilty, but no sentence was announced before his death, after eighty hours in a coma, on 3 August 1963 at St Stephen's Hospital, Fulham Road, London. He was cremated at Mortlake (9 August). Ward was in fact incidental to the Profumo episode: he was a sacrificial offering. The exorcism of scandal in high places required the façade of his conviction on vice charges.

John Hurt acted the part of Ward in the film *Scandal* (1989).   RICHARD DAVENPORT-HINES

Sources P. Knightley and C. Kennedy, *An affair of state: the Profumo case and the framing of Stephen Ward* (1987) · L. Kennedy, *The trial of Stephen Ward* (1964) · N. West, *A matter of trust: MI5, 1945–72* (1982) · C. Irving, R. Hall, and J. Wallington, *Scandal 63* (1963) · I. Crawford,

The Profumo affair (1963) • W. Young, *The Profumo affair* (1964) • G. Playfair, *Six studies in hypocrisy* (1969), 198–245 • *The diaries of Cynthia Gladwyn*, ed. M. Jebb (1995) • 'Lord Denning's report', *Parl. papers* (1962–3), 24.349, Cmnd 2152 • M. Collis, *Diaries, 1949–1969* (1978) • b. cert. • m. cert. • *The Times* (4 April 1963)
Archives FILM BFI NFTVA, *This week*, Rediffusion, 8 Aug 1963 • BFI NFTVA, current affairs footage | SOUND priv. coll., tapes
Wealth at death £14,620: administration, 21 Aug 1963, *CGPLA Eng. & Wales*

Ward, Thomas (1652–1708), Roman Catholic controversialist, was born on 13 April 1652 at Danby Castle, near Guisborough, Yorkshire, the eldest son of a farmer, and was educated at Pickering School, becoming proficient in arithmetic, geometry, and astronomy. He declined his father's advice to enter one of the professions and became tutor to the children of a gentleman of fortune, in which post he became interested in religious controversy, church history, the fathers, and scripture. His 'lively eccentric fancy strongly inclined him' (Ward, *Reformation*, xxiv) to a love of burlesque poetry. He had been brought up as a Presbyterian or Calvinist, but his studies in theological controversy induced him to join the Roman Catholic church, against the wishes of his father, who cut him out of his will. He married a Catholic wife soon after his conversion. After his father's death he brought about the conversion of his mother and the rest of his family. With his wife's and mother's consent he travelled in France and Italy, and at Rome he accepted a commission in the pope's guards, remaining in the service for five or six years, during which time he served in the maritime war against the Turks. Before this he may have served as a trooper in the Horse Guards in England. In Rome he frequented monuments and libraries, especially that of the Vatican, where he researched key documents relating to the religious history of England.

In 1685, following the demands of his wife and family, Ward returned to England, where lords Derwentwater and Lumley, Colonel Thomas Radcliffe, and Mr Thornton, who were impressed by his learning and wit, became his patrons. His *Errata to the Protestant Bible* (1688), which saw many editions, showed him to be 'a man of genious, judgment, and erudition' (Ward, *Reformation*, xxvii). Based on Gregory Martin's *Discoverie of the Manifold Corruptions of the Holy Scriptures by the Heretiques of our Daies* (1582), it sought to demonstrate that errors found in protestant translations of the scriptures were deliberate. From this time he engaged in a polemical war with protestants. His translation of *Some Queries to the Protestants* (1687), by the convert dean of Derry, Peter Manby, was answered by Dr William Clagett, and his posthumous *The Controversy of Ordination Truly Stated* (1719), an attack on Gilbert Burnet's *Vindication* (1677), was responded to by David Williams and Thomas Elrington. A local disputation of 1697–8 is recorded in *An Interesting Controversy with Mr. Ritschel, Vicar of Hexham* (1819). He was one of the few Catholics who used the broadsheet as a medium, as in his *Roman Catholick Souldier's Letter to Dr. Tho. Tenison* (1688), and his 'Speculum ecclesiasticum' (1687), which was an epitome of church history, and probably identical to 'The tree of life, or, The

church of Christ represented' (1688). He defended the argument of the 'Speculum' in his *Monomachia, or, A Duel between Dr Tho. Tenison … and a Roman Catholick Souldier* (1687), though Tenison believed its author was really a Jesuit in disguise, and Henry Wharton assured the public that this soldier was originally a Cambridge scholar who had exchanged his black coat for a red one. *England's Reformation from the Time K. Henry VIII to the End of Oates's Plot* (1710), his most popular, though unfinished work, was modelled on Samuel Butler's *Hudibras* and written as a burlesque, a 'ludicrous channel for conveying the history of the Reformation to the public, because he saw it most adapted to the state of the times' (Ward, *Reformation*, xxvii). Its later editions with engravings are a unique example from this period of English Catholic graphic satire.

Ward's flight to the continent at the revolution prevented publication of his 'History of England'. He had one son, the secular priest Lawrence Ward, alias Green, and three daughters, one of whom was a nun in Brussels. He is said to have died and been buried at St Germain in 1708, though there is no reference to his burial in the registers of St Germain-en-Laye. 'His disposition was generous and mild, though not incapable of being provoked to resentment; he even fought two duels in his youth … He was, in fine, a valiant soldier, a penetrating naturalist, an accurate writer, an agreeable companion, and a charitable Christian' (Ward, *Reformation*, xxvii).

GEOFFREY SCOTT

Sources T. Ward, *England's Reformation* (1815) [incl. 'The life of the author'] • T. Ward, *Errata to the protestant Bible* (1807) [incl. 'The life of the author'] • C. Dodd [H. Tootell], *The church history of England, from the year 1500, to the year 1688*, 3 (1742) • T. H. Clancy, *English Catholic books, 1641–1700: a bibliography*, rev. edn (1996) • F. Blom and others, *English Catholic books, 1701–1800: a bibliography* (1996) • W. T. Lowndes, *The bibliographer's manual of English literature*, ed. H. G. Bohn, [new edn], 4 (1864) • T. Ward, *An interesting controversy with Mr. Ritschel, vicar of Hexham* (1819) • T. Ward, 'The speculum ecclesiasticum', [n.d.] • Wing, *STC* • G. Anstruther, *The seminary priests*, 3 (1976) • Gillow, *Lit. biog. hist.*, vol. 5 • H. Pope, *English versions of the Bible* (1952) • G. Scott, 'Thomas Ward (1652–1708) and Hexhamshire: Catholic apologetics in the Tyne Valley', *Northern Catholic History* [forthcoming]

Ward, Thomas, Baron Ward in the nobility of the Austrian empire (1810–1858), jockey and finance minister, was born on 9 October 1810, the elder son of William Ward of Howden in Yorkshire and his wife, Margaret Marvil of York. He was educated at the national school in York until the age of nine, when he was sent to work in the stables of Robert Ridsdale, possibly at Merton. He was sent to Vienna, where he was jockey to Prince Wenzel zu Liechtenstein from 1826 to 1828, and head groom to Count Francis Hunyady from 1829 to 1831. He was recommended to Charles Louis of Bourbon, duke of Lucca, a great lover of horses, who made him his personal valet. He became the duke's confidential adviser, and in this position suggested that the political independence of Lucca be relinquished to Austria in exchange for relief of the duke's personal financial embarrassment. This end was achieved in 1843 in a meeting between Ward and Archduke Ferdinand. In 1846 he was promoted to be master of the horse and to be director-general of finance, with the title of baron. He is said to have sought popularity by arbitrarily lowering the price of corn, and the partial repudiation or 'reduction' of the debt of Lucca is also attributed to his counsels. In 1847, on the death of the Archduchess Marie Louise, duchess of Parma, and former empress of the French, Ward was sent on a mission to Florence to superintend the details of the transfer of Lucca to Tuscany in accordance with the convention of 1818, by which Charles Louis also succeeded to the duchy of Parma.

At Parma Ward remained chief minister to the duke, and continued his subservience to the Austrian government, acting as an Austrian agent during the revolutions of 1848 and negotiating the abdication of his old patron in May 1849 and the placing of Charles Louis's son, Duke Charles III, on the throne of Parma. He remained in Vienna as minister-plenipotentiary representing the duchy, and the emperor made him a baron of the Austrian empire. He had married in 1838 Louise Genthner, who came from a Viennese family of housekeepers and domestic servants, and had three sons and a daughter. In 1850 he acquired an estate, Urschendorff, near Vienna, from which he was periodically summoned by Charles III to attend to the chaotic finances of the ducal household. He was regarded with deep suspicion by many at the Parmesan court, particularly by the ultra-legitimist and anti-Austrian Duchess Marie Louise. On 21 July 1853 he received a patent of concession of all the mining rights over iron and copper in the duchy of Parma.

In 1854 Duke Charles III was assassinated, reputedly by Mazzinians, and Ward was dismissed from all his offices, with some ignominy, and his mining concessions were withdrawn, the duchess regent suspecting him of designs on the sovereignty of Parma. He retired completely from public life, devoting himself to farming, his family, and litigation for the restoration of his mining concessions, in which he had made considerable capital investments. Shortly before his death his suit succeeded. He patented a steam reaping machine, which won the gold medal at the Vienna Exhibition of 1857. He died at Urschendorff on 5 October 1858.

Dedicated to maintaining the absolutist dukes on their thrones, Ward was constantly hampered by the weakness and indecision of his masters. Despite his meteoric career, he remained 'simple, sometimes even uncouth' in manner (Lamington, 60), and, with little formal education, spoke and wrote in French, German, and Italian, conducting the affairs of state with 'considerable cleverness, if not with remarkable straightforwardness' (GM, 535).

C. A. HARRIS, rev. K. D. REYNOLDS

Sources J. Myers, *Baron Ward and the dukes of Parma* (1938) · *GM*, 3rd ser., 5 (1858), 535 · Lord Lamington, 'In the days of the dandies', *Blackwood*, 147 (1890), 1–16, 169–84, 313–30; pubd separately (1890), esp. 56–61 · G. Ferrata and E. Vittorini, *La tragica vicenda di Carlo III* (1939)

Archives Bodl. Oxf., corresp. | Österreichisches Staatsarchiv, Vienna, Haus-, Hof-, und Staatsarchiv, corresp. with Austrian government · Österreichisches Staatsarchiv, Vienna, Haus-, Hof-, und Staatsarchiv, corresp. with Metternich · Archivio di Stato, Florence, corresp. with Tuscan government · Archivio di Stato, Lucca, Italy, household/finance ministerial MSS · Archivio di Stato, Parma, household/finance ministerial MSS · PRO, Foreign Office MSS (Tuscan)
Likenesses portrait, repro. in Myers, *Baron Ward and the dukes of Parma*

Ward, Wilfrid Philip (1856–1916), biographer and ecclesiastical historian, was born on 2 January 1856, the sixth surviving child and second son of the philosopher William George *Ward (1812–1882) and his wife, Frances, *née* Wingfield (1816/17–1898), the daughter of an Anglican clergyman, John Wingfield (1760–1825), who was successively vicar of Bromsgrove, Worcestershire, prebendary of Worcester, and canon of York. Ward was born in Old Hall House, a Gothic building designed by Pugin and set in the grounds of the seminary of St Edmund's, Ware (where his father was a lecturer), and was raised in an uncompromisingly Catholic atmosphere. Three of his sisters became nuns, one of them, Agnes, the Benedictine abbess of Oulton (d. 1921), while his younger brother Bernard Nicholas *Ward (1857–1920) became a distinguished historian and bishop of Brentwood. He was named by his ultramontane parents after St Wilfrid, the champion of Roman rule in the Anglo-Saxon church and patron of Frederick William Faber's original order of Wilfridians, and after St Philip Neri, the Apostle of Rome and founder of the Roman Oratory. Minna, duchess of Norfolk, who, like her husband, the fourteenth duke, was a warm supporter of Faber's Brompton Oratory in London, was chosen as his godmother.

The three great Victorian archbishops of Westminster, Nicholas Wiseman, Henry Edward Manning, and Herbert Vaughan, loomed large in Ward's childhood. According to family legend, Wiseman placed his biretta on the boy's head and told him 'You will be a Cardinal' (Ward, *The Wilfrid Wards*, 1.20), but the great unseen influence upon him, the ghost at this cardinalitial banquet, was that of John Henry Newman, whose *University Sermons* had formed his father's philosophy, but who had become a lost leader to the Wards by distancing himself from the new nineteenth-century trend towards ultramontanism.

Ward was sent to school at Downside Abbey, near Bath, in 1868–9, and then returned to St Edmund's, near Ware. His father encouraged his interest in Newman's philosophy of religion, and he took the external University of London BA (matriculated 1872, graduated 1876). He was enrolled in 1874 as a student at Manning's ill-fated Catholic University in Kensington, where he profited from the expert philosophical instruction of Father Robert Francis Clarke, though he later regretted his father's refusal, on religious grounds, to send him to his own alma mater, the University of Oxford. In 1877, on Vaughan's advice, he tried his vocation to the priesthood at the English College, Rome. He was touched there by *romanità*, the spirit of

Wilfrid Philip Ward (1856–1916), by unknown photographer, *c*.1913

Roman Christianity, and enjoyed being organist in the college chapel, but was dissatisfied by his Roman philosophical teaching as simply relying on past authority. In 1878 ill health forced him to leave Rome for the seminary of Ushaw College in co. Durham, where he was choirmaster and wrote the music for an operetta, *The Gambler of Metz*. Bishops Vaughan and Ullathorne confirmed his growing sense that he had no clerical vocation, so he abandoned the idea of ordination and left Ushaw in 1881.

Ward half-heartedly entered at the Inner Temple, London, to become a barrister, while the contempt of one of his sisters (he did not record which one) and fear of his father's anger strangled at birth his fleeting impulse to become an opera singer. He began to see his vocation as one to advance English Catholic intellectual life, but recognized that there was no official encouragement or structure for such a career outside the priesthood. His only academic positions were to be as examiner in mental and moral philosophy for the Royal University of Ireland (1890) and a member of the royal commission on Irish university education in 1902. Otherwise his influence was as a freelance scholar and journalist, albeit one with a private income from the sale of the family living. His first essays, inspired by Newman's theory of belief, appeared in *The Nineteenth Century* (1882–3) and the *National Review* (1884), and were republished as *The Wish to Believe* (1885) and *The*

Clothes of Religion (1886). The latter attacked the *laissez-faire* apologist Herbert Spencer and the positivist Frederic Harrison. His works were praised by William George Ward and by another of Newman's disciples, Richard Holt Hutton, editor of *The Spectator*, and were commended by Newman himself.

Newman's writings, especially his *University Sermons* (1843) and *Grammar of Assent* (1870), helped Ward to absorb and transcend the overwhelming and overbearing legacy of his father. He discharged his filial and intellectual obligations first by editing Ward senior's *Essays on the Philosophy of Theism* (2 vols., 1884) and then by writing his two-part biography, *William George Ward and the Oxford Movement* (1889) and *William George Ward and the Catholic Revival* (1893). These volumes, which reconstructed the Tractarian and Roman Catholic controversies of the early and high Victorian eras, included two essays of particular historical merit: 'The Oxford school and modern religious thought' (in the first biography) and 'The Catholic revival and the new ultramontanism', written with the help of Friedrich von Hügel (in its sequel). His vivid, penetrating, and affectionate evocation of the formidable, lovable, infuriating, and dogmatic personality of his father has left the elder Ward with a reputation as one of the most colourful characters of the high Victorian era. In addition to applying personal knowledge to historical analysis, Ward's work on his father's biography strengthened or created his ties with his father's friend and neighbour on the Isle of Wight, Lord Tennyson, and with other former members of his father's Metaphysical Society such as Thomas Henry Huxley, Henry Sidgwick, and Frederic Myers. This encouraged him, with the help of A. J. Balfour, Charles Gore, and Edward Talbot, to found in 1896 the Synthetic Society for the learned discussion of religious belief, with a few former surviving Metaphysicals (James Martineau, Hutton, Sidgwick, Myers) as well as some new members (Lord Hugh Cecil, George Wyndham, A. V. Dicey). The membership embraced nonconformists, an Irvingite (Henry Percy, Lord Warkworth), high- and broad-church Anglicans (including Henry Scott Holland and Hastings Rashdall), G. K. Chesterton (before his conversion to Catholicism), and some Catholics, notably the modernists George Tyrrell and von Hügel. The society was dissolved in 1908.

These contacts encouraged Ward in his role as a 'liaison officer' (M. Ward, *The Wilfrid Wards and the Transition*, 1.96) between Catholicism and other religious traditions, and in gathering first-hand historical material on the last generation of eminent Victorians. Ward's marriage on 24 November 1887 to Josephine Mary (1864–1932), the second daughter of James Robert Hope-*Scott of Abbotsford (1812–1873) and his second wife, Victoria Howard (1840–1870), herself daughter of the fourteenth duke of Norfolk, brought Ward closer to the fifteenth duke, to whom he became an adviser on theological and ecclesiastical affairs, as over the admission of Catholics to Oxford in 1895, the validity of Anglican orders in 1896, and later the modernist controversy (1907–10). The Wards had five children, one of whom, the precocious Wilfrid Hope Ward (1890–1902), died young; the eldest, Mary Josephine *Ward (1889–1975), known as Maisie, was to be a considerable influence on the golden age of English Catholic intellectual life between the wars, and her books about her father remain the best sources for his life.

Ward's interest in ecclesiastical biography was confirmed by his unsuccessful attempt with the duke of Norfolk, Vaughan, and Baron von Hügel to censor or prevent the publication of Edmund Sheridan Purcell's scandalous biography of Henry Edward Manning which appeared in 1895. Yet Purcell's indiscretions had the advantage of leaving no hiding place for ecclesiastical secrets. The truth looked so much more edifying than Purcell's account of Manning's alleged unscrupulous ambition that Ward could be frank when his mentor Herbert Vaughan, by then a cardinal, asked him to write *The Life of Cardinal Wiseman* (2 vols., 1897). This careful documentary history combined a lively critical narrative of high religious politics with a warm portrait of the most exuberant of the great English ecclesiastics of his generation. It also led to Ward's most ambitious undertaking, a life of his intellectual patron, Cardinal Newman.

Ward's projected biography of Newman had the support of the latter's successor as superior of the Birmingham Oratory, Ignatius Ryder, who had, however, been excluded by Newman from any use of his papers, which were jealously guarded by the cardinal's executor, William Neville. After Neville's death the work began to reach proof stage in 1907, when the fathers of the Birmingham Oratory, who had custody of Newman's correspondence, were appalled to find that Ward thought Newman's philosophy to have been incidentally condemned by Pius X's anti-modernist encyclical *Pascendi* (1907). Ward was known to be a friend of the Jesuit George Tyrrell, who had appealed to Newman's work to defend himself against accusations of modernist errors. As editor of the *Dublin Review* from 1906, Ward was vulnerable to criticism from hyper-orthodox Catholics. His friendship with von Hügel, who was equally tarnished with a reputation for modernism, hardly helped him; indeed, the baron's correspondence with other radical scholars was the nearest that Catholic modernism ever came to being a movement, and compromised all his associates. It was at Cardinal Rampolla's insistence that in 1911 Ward withdrew his wholly orthodox epilogue to the Wiseman biography, 'The exclusive church and the Zeitgeist', after it had been denounced to Rome. The biography which Ward eventually completed was almost wholly devoted to Newman's life as a Catholic, his forty-four years as an Anglican being dispatched in one chapter of fifty-two pages. In this respect Ward was writing a Roman Catholic 'Tract for the Times' on the need for orthodoxy to be self-critical, though this preoccupation hardly appears on the smooth surface of the narrative. Yet Ward was a 'prodigious blab' (*The Letters and Diaries of John Henry Newman*, ed. C. S. Dessain and others, 31 vols., 11–31, 1961–77, 11.xix), 'vehement, rash and excitable' (M. Ward, *The Wilfrid Wards and the Transition*, 1.103), and given to

writing angry letters which his wife and daughter tried to stop him from posting. His temperament was not one conducive to mental peace, and in the anti-modernist climate in the church Ward's theological view of a careful, critical, and discriminating, if not a 'liberal', Catholicism obscured to hyper-orthodox Catholics the great gulf which lay between him and a modernist like Tyrrell, who denied fundamental credal doctrines. The Oratorians also disliked Ward's stress on the suffering side of Newman's personality, as if he were 'hyper-sensitive, a *souffre-douleur*' in Abbot Butler's phrase (*The Letters and Diaries of John Henry Newman*, ed. C. S. Dessain and others, 31 vols., 11–31, 1961–77, 11.xx). They also mistrusted the intellectual dialectic of the work, which argued that Newman's Catholicism had dissented strongly from both the liberal Catholicism of Richard Simpson and Sir John Acton and the new ultramontanism of William George Ward and Manning, trying instead to hold the balance between the two schools by combining the critical sense of the one with the orthodoxy of the other. This was, at least in part, a backward projection of Ward's own difficult mediating position between modernists and integralists and, in part, his own final resolution of his father's great battle with Newman, in Newman's favour. After extensive revision, *The Life of John Henry Cardinal Newman* (2 vols.) appeared in 1912 to critical acclaim, but the Oratorians declined to publish a third volume of letters on the grounds that 'it would make the letters subordinate to Mr Ward's presentation of Newman' (*The Letters and Diaries of John Henry Newman*, ed. C. S. Dessain and others, 31 vols., 11–31, 1961–77, 11.xix).

Ward also edited the 1864 and 1865 editions of Newman's *Apologia* (1913). According to the later editor of Newman's diaries and correspondence, Charles Stephen Dessain, Ward's 'best work on Newman' appeared in his Lowell lectures in America in 1914 (*The Letters and Diaries of John Henry Newman*, ed. C. S. Dessain and others, 31 vols., 11–31, 1961–77, 31.328). These were edited with his lectures on biography at the Royal Institution (1914–15) as *Last Lectures* (1918) by his wife, who wrote a long introductory study for them. She also wrote eight novels with religious themes, including *One Poor Scruple* (1899) and *Great Possessions* (1909). Ward himself also wrote a study of the Irish Catholic convert poet Aubrey de Vere (1904) and about 250 articles and reviews, some of which were collected and published as books (*Witnesses to the Unseen*, 1893; *Problems and Persons*, 1903; *Ten Personal Studies*, 1908; *Men and Matters*, 1914). Still valuable as primary sources, mingling personal reminiscence and private knowledge and anecdote with wide reading, their main theme was the enduring value of the great Victorians' contribution to the perception of religious truth.

Ward was a strong conservative who opposed home rule for Ireland, and after 1914 campaigned among Catholic circles for the allied cause. In 1915 he inherited the Isle of Wight family fortune from his eccentric elder brother, Edmund Granville (1853–1915), who had died during the war when property was in the doldrums, and had left several times the value of the estate to the Catholic Church and Catholic education. Ward's humiliation in trying to reach a financial settlement with the church after the long dark night of the modernist controversy made him ill, and he contracted cancer. He died at The Nook, Holford Road, Hampstead Heath, London, on 9 April 1916, and was buried on the family estate at Freshwater on the Isle of Wight. The family estates passed to his elder surviving son, Herbert Joseph Ward (b. 1896).

SHERIDAN GILLEY

Sources M. Ward, *The Wilfrid Wards and the transition*, 1 (1934) · M. Ward, *The Wilfrid Wards and the transition*, 2 (1937) · M. Ward, *Unfinished business* (1964) · M. J. Weaver, *Letters from a 'modernist': the letters of George Tyrrell to Wilfrid Ward, 1893–1908* (1981) · M. J. Weaver, 'A bibliography of the published works of Wilfrid Ward', *Heythrop Journal*, 20 (1979), 399–420 · E. Kelly, 'Newman, Wilfrid Ward, and the modernist crisis', *Thought*, 43 (1973), 508–19 · W. J. Schoenl, *The intellectual crisis in English Catholicism* (1982) · W. Sheed, *Frank and Maisie: a memoir with parents* (1986) · S. Gilley, 'Wilfrid Ward and his life of Newman', *Journal of Ecclesiastical History*, 29 (1978), 177–93 · S. Gilley, 'An intellectual discipleship: Newman and the making of Wilfrid Ward', *Louvain Studies*, 15 (1990), 318–45 · S. Gilley, 'New light on an old scandal: Purcell's *Life of Cardinal Manning*', *Opening the scrolls: essays in Catholic history in honour of Godfrey Anstruther*, ed. D. A. Bellenger (1987), 166–98 · W. Ward, *William George Ward and the Oxford Movement* (1889) · W. Ward, *William George Ward and the Catholic revival* (1893) · *CGPLA Eng. & Wales* (1916)
Archives priv. coll., family MSS · U. St Andr. L., corresp. and papers · Westm. DA, letters | Birmingham Oratory, corresp., mainly relating to his biography of J. H. Newman · Borth. Inst., corresp. with second Viscount Halifax · Herefs. RO, letters to earl of Lytton · NL Ire., letters to first and second barons Emly · U. Hull, Brynmor Jones L., letters to Ruskin · U. St Andr. L., von Hügel MSS
Likenesses J. Cameron, photograph, 1871, repro. in Ward, *The Wilfrid Wards*, vol. 1, frontispiece · photograph, c.1913, repro. in Ward, *The Wilfrid Wards*, vol. 2, frontispiece [*see illus.*]
Wealth at death £10,658 16s. 4d.: probate, 21 June 1916, *CGPLA Eng. & Wales*

Ward [Warde], **William** (1534–1609), physician and translator, was born at Landbeach, Cambridgeshire, in 1534. He was educated at Eton College, and then was elected a scholar at King's College, Cambridge, on 13 August 1550. On 14 August 1553 he became a fellow. He graduated BA in 1555 and proceeded MA in 1558. On 27 February 1552 the provost of his college requested him to take up the study of medicine, and he became MD in 1567. In 1568 he left his fellowship. His name is attached to the petition signed in 1572 against the new statutes of the university which allowed students to begin their medical training without first undertaking preliminary training in the arts. Ward became regius professor of physic at Cambridge in succession to Thomas Lorkin, who died in 1591. It is probably through his official post at Cambridge that Ward is spoken of as physician to Elizabeth I and James I. Ward was married twice: first, on 26 January 1568, to Margaret Fletcher; second, on 10 February 1584, to Jane Bosom, both times at Great St Mary's Church, Cambridge. He had at least three sons, William, Thomas, and Roger.

Ward was translator of *The Secretes of the Reverende Maister Alexis Piemont: Containing Excellent Remedies Against Divers Diseases and other Accidents*. The first edition was published in 1558 containing only the first part, and consisting of six

books. Another two editions were printed in 1559 and contain a dedicatory letter by Ward to the earl of Bedford, notable for its protest against the folly of 'some curious Christians among us nowadays … which most impudently despise all manner of medicines', and for its defence of the 'heavenly science' of physic. Ward mentions Christopher Plantin's edition of a French translation (Antwerp, 1557) as his original. The work became very popular as a treasury of medical and other knowledge in all the countries of Europe. The identity of Alessio of Piedmont has not been satisfactorily settled. Of this first part numerous editions were published in England. It occurs usually bound up with *The Seconde Parte of the Secrets of Maister Alexis of Piemont*, again translated by Ward and published in 1560 and 1563. *The Thyrde and Last Parte of the Secretes of the Reverende Maister Alexis of Piemont* translated by Ward appeared first in 1562. It contains six books, like the first part. Here his work seems to have ended but in many copies of the book a fourth and fifth part are added, translated by R. Androse.

Ward was the translator of other works from French into English: *Thre notable sermones made by the godly and famous clerke, Maister John Calvyn, on thre severall Sondayes in Maye, the yere 1561, upon the Psalm 46. … Englished by William Warde* was published in 1562, while *The most excellent, profitable, and pleasaunt booke of the famous doctor and expert astrologian Arcandam or Aleandrin* appeared in 1578 and was sufficiently popular to be reprinted another four times by 1670. Based on an elaborate calculation of the numerical value of letters in a person's name, it was derived from the 'spheres of life and death', and was of a type that went back to the ancient world. It was a work translated into Latin from 'a confused and indistinct' original by Richard Roussat, *canonicus Lingoniensis*, and published at Paris in 1542. There is also a copy of Latin verses by Ward before James Robothum's *Pleasaunt and Wittie Playe of the Cheastes* (chess), published in 1562, which Ward may have translated from the French.

William Ward died in 1609 and was buried at Great St Mary's, Cambridge, on 8 August. In 1590 he had given to the same parish 7½ acres of arable land in Howsfield and 2 acres of meadowland in Chesterton.

RONALD BAYNE, *rev.* PATRICK WALLIS

Sources Venn, *Alum. Cant.* · W. Sterry, ed., *The Eton College register, 1441–1698* (1943) · J. Ames, T. F. Dibdin, and W. Herbert, eds., *Typographical antiquities, or, The history of printing in England, Scotland and Ireland*, 4 vols. (1810–19) · Cooper, *Ath. Cantab.*, vols. 1–2 · P. Bayle, *An historical and critical dictionary*, 4 vols. (1710) · *CSP dom.*, 1601–3 · 'Codex Chartaceus', Bodl. Oxf., MS Rawl. B. 265, fol. 140 · A. Rook, ed., *Cambridge and its contribution to medicine* [Cambridge 1969] (1971) · K. Thomas, *Religion and the decline of magic* (1971) · will, PRO, PROB 11/114, sig. 82
Wealth at death property in Cambridgeshire

Ward, William (1708/9–1772), grammarian and headmaster, was born some time between 5 November 1708 and 5 May 1709 in Thornton-le-Dale, in Yorkshire, and baptized there on 17 January 1710, the son of William Ward, gentleman. He was educated at Thornton Free School and, later, at Sidney Sussex College, Cambridge, where he was admitted sizar on 5 May 1727; he graduated BA in 1730 and MA in

1740. On 4 June 1732 he was ordained deacon at Lincoln, and at Chester on 6 October 1734 he was ordained priest. In 1734, too, he was instituted curate of Normanby, where he had been licensed assistant curate the previous year. In 1736 he was licensed master of the Thornton School.

In 1737, probably in August, Ward married Elizabeth (1709?–1798), daughter of John Watson of New Malton. The marriage was by bishop's licence, dated 1 August 1737, for solemnization either at Thornton parish church or St Leonard's Malton. Ten children—three sons and seven daughters (one of whom died in infancy)—were born to the couple. The family moved to Beverley in 1751, when Ward was appointed master of Beverley grammar school. At the same date he was licensed to perform the office of 'lecturer', or assistant curate, in the united churches of St Mary and St Nicholas in Beverley. He was something of a pluralist; besides his appointment at Beverley he was vicar of Scalby, near Scarborough, from 1737 until his death in 1772 and perpetual curate of Yedingham from 1740 to 1767. Earlier, at Thornton, he officiated at the parish church and may also have been curate of Cloughton. He does not appear to have been replaced as curate at Normanby until 1767.

As master of Beverley grammar school Ward introduced performances by the scholars of Latin plays. One was the *Heauton-timoroumenos* of Terence, with interlinking speeches in English that Ward composed himself. He is best known, however, for his two grammars: *An essay on grammar, as it may be applied to the English language, in two treatises: the one speculative, being an attempt to investigate proper principles, the other practical, containing definitions and rules deduced from the principles, and illustrated by a variety of examples from the most approved writers* (1765) and *A Grammar of the English Language in Two Treatises* (1767). The later grammar is essentially an abridgement of the *Essay*, with the practical section placed first. Although Ward intended it for use in teaching the boys at his school the *Essay* goes far beyond a school textbook, especially in the speculative part. In a facsimile edition of the *Essay* Robin Alston notes that it was 'by far the most comprehensive of the many grammars of English produced during the Eighteenth Century' (Ward, *Essay*, note). Ward was a strenuous and often original thinker; he did not simply repeat the grammatical theories of his day, as many grammarians did. He frequently disagreed with the accepted ideas and definitions of grammatical categories to pursue a new line of thought. Unfortunately his style is long-winded and his arguments, which are not easy to follow, are inclined to stop short, just when he appears to be reaching some new perception. His influence on later grammarians, therefore, is marginal. In 1768 Ward resigned his position as master of Beverley grammar school because of poor health. He died on 5 November 1772 aged sixty-three and was buried in St Mary's Church, Beverley, two days later. His widow died on 4 November 1798.

FRANCES AUSTIN

Sources J. R. Witty, *A history of Beverley grammar school* (1986) · R. W. Jeffery, *Thornton-le-Dale* (1931) · clergy card index, Borth. Inst. · institution act books, Borth. Inst., AB.11A, AB12, AB13, AB14 · I. Michael, *English grammatical categories and the tradition to 1800* (1970) · I. Michael, *The teaching of English from the sixteenth century to 1870* (1987) · W. Ward, *An essay on grammar*, ed. R. Alston, English Language Series 1500–1800, no. 15 (1967) · W. Ward, prologue, interlude, and epilogue, *Heauton-timoroumenos of Terence, acted by the young gentlemen of Beverley School, at Christmas 1756* (1757) [Hull Central Library] · Venn, *Alum. Cant.* · *IGI* · parish register, Thornton-le-Dale, 17 Jan 1710 [baptism] · parish register, Beverley, St Mary's, 7 Nov 1772 [burial] · tombstone, St Mary's Church, Beverley [Elizabeth Ward]

Ward, William (1766–1826), printmaker, was born in London, probably in Thames Street, near Southwark Bridge, the son of James Ward, a manager for a wholesale fruit and cider merchant, and his wife, Rachel (1736/7–1835), and the elder brother of the painter James *Ward (1769–1859). He was educated at the Merchant Taylors' School in London before being apprenticed to the printmaker John Raphael Smith. In 1781–2 his brother James was also apprenticed to Smith, although William took over his brother's indentures when he left Smith in 1783. James worked as William's apprentice until 1791, and it has been suggested that some of the plates James engraved during his apprenticeship years were issued under William's name. About 1785 William and his brother moved with their parents and two unmarried sisters (a third sister had already married) to a house in the Harrow Road, near to J. R. Smith's establishment; by then William's printmaking work was sufficiently well established for him to take on another apprentice, Thomas Gosse. In August 1786 he married the artist Maria Morland, the sister of the painter George *Morland, and a month later Morland married William's sister Anne; the two couples set up house together for a short time.

In 1792 William Ward bought two of his brother's paintings, *Compassionate Children* and *The Haymakers*, and the following year engraved and published prints after them. In 1799 the two brothers, with 50 per cent funding from a third partner, Dr Daw, formed a short-lived print publishing business, known as Messrs Ward & Co. In 1804 William was appointed mezzotint engraver to the duke of York and in 1813 engraver to the prince of Wales; in 1814 he became an associate engraver of the Royal Academy. Ward engraved both in stipple and in mezzotint; during the 1780s he produced stipple and crayon manner prints, many printed in colours, after drawings by John Hoppner, J. R. Smith, George Morland, and others, as well as some of his own drawings, with titles such as *Thoughts on Matrimony* (1786) and *The Musing Charmer* (1787). Among his mezzotint works are plates after paintings by Morland, such as *A Visit to the Child at Nurse* (1788) and *A Visit to the Boarding School* (1789), as well as portraits and fancy pictures after contemporary painters such as Joshua Reynolds and Hoppner, notably such impressive pieces as *The Daughters of Sir Thomas Strickland* (1797) and *Mrs Michelangelo Tayler as 'Miranda'* (1798), both after Hoppner. He also reproduced historical paintings, including work by Correggio and Murillo and plates after seventeenth-century Dutch and Flemish artists such as Ferdinand Bol, Gerrit van Honthorst, and Rubens. Ward died on 1 or 21 December 1826 at his home in Warren Street, Fitzroy Square, London. The print rooms of the British Museum and the Victoria and Albert Museum both hold collections of his prints. **Martin Theodore Ward** (*c*.1799–1874), painter, was William Ward's eldest son. He was trained as a painter under Edwin Landseer, and specialized in portraits of animals commissioned by members of the gentry and lesser aristocracy, showing their favourite hunting dogs, such as terriers, spaniels, and pointers, and horses. He exhibited at the Royal Academy from 1820 to 1825 and at the British Institution from 1819 to 1829, where he showed animal portraits as well as a few animal genre pieces with titles such as *The Painful Bite* (1821) and *The Intrusion* (1829). About 1840 he settled in Yorkshire, where he became noted for his eccentricity; he exhibited only once more, at the British Institution in 1858, and died in poverty in York on 13 February 1874.

William James Ward (*c*.1800–1840), printmaker, the second son of William Ward, was trained by his father and showed precocious talent, winning medals for drawing from the Society of Arts between 1813 and 1815. His work as a printmaker consists mostly of mezzotint prints after contemporary portrait painters such as Sir Thomas Lawrence, William Owen, and H. W. Pickersgill, although he also engraved the work of earlier artists, such as Van Dyck. He was made engraver to the duke of Clarence, but became insane some time before his death, on 1 March 1840. SARAH HYDE

William Ward (1769–1823), by Henry Hoppner Meyer, pubd 1821 (after John Jackson) [baptizing a Hindu in the Ganges at Serampore]

Sources J. Frankau, *Eighteenth century artists and engravers: William Ward, ARA, James Ward, RA, their lives and works* (1904) • C. R. Grundy, *James Ward, RA: his life and works* (1909) • O. Beckett, *The life and work of James Ward, RA* (1995) • H. M. A. Ward, *Memories of ninety years*, ed. I. G. McAllister [1924] • Graves, *RA exhibitors* • Bryan, *Painters* (1903–5) • Graves, *Brit. Inst.* • index of prints, V&A, department of prints and drawings [William Ward jun.]
Archives BM, James Ward's book of letters • RA, account book, commonplace book, daybook, Ward-Jackson MSS, as well as individual letters
Likenesses G. Morland?, oils, priv. coll. • G. Morland?, oils, priv. coll.

Ward, William (1769–1823), missionary in India and journalist, born at Derby on 20 October 1769, was the son of John Ward, a carpenter and builder of that town, and grandson of Thomas Ward, a farmer at Stretton, near Burton in Staffordshire. His father died while William was a child, and the care of his upbringing devolved on his mother, a woman of great energy of character and of exemplary Methodist piety. He was placed with a schoolmaster named Congreve, near Derby, and afterwards with another named Breary. On leaving school he was bound apprentice to a printer and bookseller of Derby named John Drewry, with whom he continued two years after the expiry of his indentures, assisting him to edit the *Derby Mercury* and in due course editing the paper himself. In 1794 or 1795 he moved to Stafford, where he assisted Joshua Drewry, a relative of his former master, to edit the *Staffordshire Advertiser*. At the end of 1795 he proceeded to

Hull, where he followed his business as a printer, and was for nine months in 1796 editor of the *Hull Advertiser and Exchange Gazette*.

Ward began to attend a Baptist church, probably between 1791 and 1793, and on 28 August 1796, after many troubles of heart—'fierce volcano fires not to be quenched by a mere sprinkling of words'—he was baptized at Hull. Preaching constantly in the neighbouring villages, he became known as a man of promise, and, with the assistance of a member of the Baptist community named Fishwick, he proceeded in August 1797 to Ewood Hall, near Halifax in Yorkshire, the theological academy of John Fawcett (1740–1817), where he studied for a year and a half. In the autumn of 1798 a member of the committee of the newly founded Baptist Missionary Society visited Ewood, and Ward offered himself as a missionary, influenced perhaps by a remark made to him in 1793 by William Carey (1761–1834) concerning the need of a printer in the Indian mission field. He sailed from England in the *Criterion* in May 1799, in company with Joshua Marshman, Daniel Brunsdon, William Grant, and their families. On arriving at Calcutta the party was prevented from joining Carey by an order from the East India Company government, and was obliged to proceed to the Danish settlement of Serampore, where they were joined by Carey. On 10 May 1802 Ward was married at Serampore to Mary, *née* Tidd, widow of John Fountain, a Baptist missionary. They had two sons and two daughters, but only two of the children survived.

In India Ward's time was chiefly occupied in superintending the printing press, by means of which the Bible, translated into Bengali, Marathi, Hindi, and more than twenty other languages, was disseminated throughout India. Numerous philological works were also issued. Ward found time, however, to keep a copious journal and to preach the gospel to the Hindus. Until 1806 he made frequent tours among the towns and villages of the province, but after that year the increasing claims of the press on his time, and the extension of the missionary labours in Serampore and Calcutta, prevented him quitting headquarters. In 1812 the printing office was destroyed by fire. It contained the types of all the scriptures that had been printed, to the value of at least £10,000. The moulds for casting fresh type, however, were recovered from the debris, and by the liberality of friends in Great Britain the loss was soon repaired.

In 1819 Ward, having been for some time in bad health, revisited England. He was entrusted with the task of pleading for funds with which to endow a college at Serampore for the purpose of instructing Bengalis in European literature and science. He undertook a series of journeys through England and Scotland, and also visited Holland and north Germany. In October 1820 he embarked for New York and travelled through the United States, returning to England in April 1821. On 28 May he sailed for India in the *Abberton* bearing £3000 for the new college, which had been founded during his absence and which still survives.

Ward was the author of a number of publications, of which much the most important was his *Account of the Writings, Religion, and Manners of the Hindoos*, the first volume of which was published by the Serampore mission press in 1806. The complete four-volume edition first appeared in 1811. A one-volume abridged version edited by W. O. Simpson was published as late as 1863. In the later editions the title was changed to *View of the History, Literature, and Religion of the Hindoos*. Although Ward did not mince his words in his condemnation of 'Hindoo idolatry', he did comment favourably on the literary and philological achievements of Hindu scholars, and in later versions modified somewhat the harshness of his strictures on Hinduism. Despite some serious inaccuracies, Ward's work remains without parallel as a detailed account by a European observer of Hindu society and religion in early nineteenth-century Bengal. Ward died of cholera at Serampore on 7 March 1823, and was interred in the mission burial-ground there.

E. I. CARLYLE, *rev.* BRIAN STANLEY

Sources S. Stennett, *Memoirs of the life of the Rev. William Ward* (1825) • A. C. Smith, 'William Ward, radical reform, and missions in the 1790s', *American Baptist Quarterly*, 10 (1991), 218–44 • J. C. Marshman, *The life and times of Carey, Marshman and Ward*, 2 vols. (1859) • B. Stanley, *The history of the Baptist Missionary Society, 1792–1992* (1992) • W. O. Simpson, 'Introduction', in W. Ward, *A view of the history, literature, and religion of the Hindoos*, 5th edn (1863), 1–12
Archives Regent's Park College, Oxford, Angus Library, corresp., journal, and papers, incl. those of his son, Nathaniel Ward | Fuller Baptist Church, Kettering, Northamptonshire

Likenesses stipple, pubd 1817, NPG • H. H. Meyer, stipple, pubd 1821 (after J. Jackson), Scot. NPG [*see illus.*] • E. Scriven, stipple, pubd 1823 (after T. Overton), BM • R. Baker, engraving (after Overton), repro. in W. Ward, *Brief memoir of Krishna-pal*, 2nd edn (1823) • portrait, Regent's Park College, Oxford

Ward, William (1787–1849), cricketer and banker, was born at Highbury Place, Highbury, Middlesex, in July 1787, the second son of George Ward (*d.* 1829), of Northwood Park, Cowes, a London merchant and large-scale landowner in the Isle of Wight and Hampshire, and his wife, Mary (*d.* 1813), daughter of Henry Sampson Woodfall. Robert Plumer Ward was William's uncle.

Ward was educated at Winchester College. He was destined for commerce, and spent some time at Antwerp in a banking house. On his return, his father took him into partnership in 1810. On 26 April 1811 he married Emily (*d.* 1848), fifth daughter of Alderman Harvey Christian Combe, a prosperous brewer and radical London politician. They had two daughters and four sons, one of whom was William George *Ward, a prominent Roman Catholic theologian and philosopher.

In 1817 Ward was elected a director of the Bank of England, and distinguished himself by his accurate knowledge of foreign exchanges. In 1819 he gave evidence before the parliamentary committees on the restrictions on payments in cash by the Bank of England. However, from his early days as a director Ward was critical of the bank's singular lack of general plans. And on 6 December 1827 he moved and carried a measure rescinding its policy of reducing its issues so as to obtain a favourable return in the exchanges. Telling the story in 1832, Ward noted that when the bank had been most at fault it had also been 'most in accordance with the Government and the Parliament and the Public at large' (Clapham, 117).

On 9 June 1826 Ward was elected for the City of London as a conservative MP, and in 1830 at the request of the duke of Wellington, he acted as chairman of the committee appointed to investigate the affairs of the East India Company preparatory to the opening of the China trade. In 1831, discontented at the spirit of reform, he declined to stand for parliament. In 1835 he presented himself as a candidate, and was defeated by the whigs. From about that period he retired from public life. In 1847 he published *Remarks on the Monetary Legislation of Great Britain*, in which he condemned the act of 1816 establishing an exclusive gold standard, and called for a bimetallic currency.

In addition to his career in the City of London, Ward was a prominent cricketer, and a patron of the sport. Probably the most powerful batsman of his day, he made a record 278 at Lord's on 24 July 1820 for the Marylebone Cricket Club (MCC) against Norfolk. A 'gentleman' rather than a 'player', he was one of those described by Mary Russell Mitford in 1823 in *Our Village* as playing 'dressed in tight white jackets with neck cloths primly tied around their throats, fine japanned shoes, silk stockings and gloves' (Lewis, 59).

Ward's greatest contribution to the sport, however, was to save the Lord's ground from the building speculation planned by Thomas Lord. In return for £5000, Ward acquired the lease in 1825. Together with its honorary secretary Benjamin Aislabie, he was one of the dominant figures in the club during the subsequent decade.

In 1835, around the time of his parliamentary defeat, Ward appears to have suffered 'a reversal of fortune', during which he was assisted by his brother Matthew (Harris and Ashley-Cooper, 49). For whatever reason, in that year Ward transferred the lease to J. H. Dark for £2000. The latter also undertook to pay an annuity of £425 to the Ward family during the remaining fifty-nine years of the lease. Despite ceasing to be proprietor, Ward continued to play occasionally until 1845.

Ward died on 30 June 1849 at 14 Wyndham Place, London. In his will he left a number of cricketing memorabilia to his children, including his 'only remaining cricket bat and balls' to his daughter Georgiana Mary (Harris and Ashley-Cooper, 49).

E. I. CARLYLE, rev. ROBERT BROWN

Sources T. Lewis, *Double century: the story of MCC and cricket* (1987) · J. Clapham, *The Bank of England: a history*, 2 (1944) · P. Warner, *Lord's, 1787–1945* (1946) · Lord Harris and F. S. Ashley-Cooper, *Lord's and the MCC* (1914) · *GM*, 2nd ser., 32 (1849), 206 · Ward, *Men of the reign* · d. cert.

Likenesses engraving, repro. in Lewis, *Double century*, 67 · engraving, repro. in Harris and Ashley-Cooper, *Lord's and the MCC*, 47

William George Ward (1812–1882), by George J. Stodart, pubd 1889 (after Emily Combe, c.1832)

Ward, William George (1812–1882), theologian and philosopher, was born in London on 21 March 1812, the eldest son of the four sons and four daughters of William *Ward (1787–1849), MP, director of the Bank of England, and proprietor of Lord's cricket ground, and his wife, Emily, *née* Combe (d. 1848), the fifth daughter of Harvey Christian Combe (1752–1818) of Cobham Park, Surrey, MP and brewer.

Early life From 1820 to 1823 Ward attended a private school, Eagle House, Brook Green, Hammersmith, and in 1823 went to Winchester College, where he won the gold medal for Latin prose composition in 1829, although his verses were deliberately grotesque. In 1830 he matriculated from Christ Church, Oxford, and was president of the university's undergraduate debating society, the Union, in the Michaelmas term of 1832. In 1833 he won a scholarship to Lincoln College, Oxford, but in spite of his first-rate abilities as a mathematician and Latinist he took only a second-class degree because he refused to answer questions on applied mathematics and literary history. In 1834 he was elected a fellow of Balliol College, Oxford, at the same time as the future archbishop of Canterbury Archibald Campbell Tait, and was made college lecturer in both logic and mathematics. Being fat and thick-skinned, he claimed to have 'the intellect of an archangel, and the habits of an eating, walking and sleeping rhinoceros' (Chadwick, 130). His liveliness as a debater, lecturer, and conversationalist went with acute depression, which he treated by indulging his love for burlesque, drama, opera, and music; his sensibility oscillated between the dramatic and the dogmatic. Many years later, however, his second son, Wilfrid Philip *Ward, would give up an ambition to become an opera singer, out of fear that he would be

angry. His deepest friendship was with his pupil Arthur Hugh Clough, although a platonic interpretation must be placed on Ward's request to Clough for the 'unnatural demonstrations' which Clough recorded in his diary (*Oxford Diaries*, 85).

The Oxford Movement and *Ideal of a Christian Church* Ward's intellectual development was spurred by his sometimes brutal impatience with what he saw as insincerity and shams. He was first influenced by the logical clarity of the utilitarians Bentham and James Mill, then by the proto-liberalism of Whately and Thomas Arnold, from whom he also derived an intense moral earnestness and sympathy for the poor. He was ordained a deacon in 1836, when still an advocate of Arnold's liberal theology, but soon concluded that this led straight to scepticism. Arnold's moralism, however, prepared Ward to receive J. H. Newman's argument that conscience is the foundation of religion. He attended Newman's lectures defending the Church of England as a *via media* between popery and popular protestantism at St Mary's in 1836, and after the publication of the first two volumes of Froude's *Remains* in 1838, when he was ordained a priest, he proclaimed himself a follower of Newman and of the high-church movement, taken in its ultra-Catholic sense.

Ward still held that Rome was corrupt, but, lacking historical sympathy, he had no affection for the Church of England as a complicated institution created by historic compromise. His love of logic and pure mathematics left him unsatisfied with any position that was less than wholly self-coherent, and made him a restless Anglican. Newman told Wilfrid Ward that his father 'was never a High Churchman, never a Tractarian, never a Puseyite, never a Newmanite' (W. Ward, *Ward and the Oxford Movement*, 136). This was not quite true; Ward was a Newmanite in his absolute trust and regard for Newman, who was embarrassed by his daring logical deductions from his own premisses. From 1838 Ward was the chief of a Romanizing party among the Tractarians, containing another fellow of Balliol, Frederick Oakeley, as well as F. W. Faber, J. D. Dalgairns, J. A. Froude, and J. B. Morris, all of whom (except Froude) were to become Roman Catholics.

When Newman's Tract 90 (1841) was attacked by four Oxford tutors, one of them Ward's Balliol friend Tait, Ward wrote two pamphlets, *A Few Words in Defence of Tract 90* and *A Few Words More*, in which he incautiously translated Newman's view that the seemingly protestant Thirty-Nine Articles should be read in their 'literal and grammatical sense' into the idea that they might be subscribed in their 'non-natural' sense, that is, in the opposite sense to that intended by their framers. In the resulting furore, Ward readily gave up his college lectureships. 'What *heresy* may he not insinuate under the form of a syllogism!' worried the master of Balliol, Richard Jenkyns (W. Ward, *Ward and the Oxford Movement*, 175), though Ward was allowed to become junior bursar in 1841 and senior bursar in 1842. His friendships included the Catholic converts and Gothic enthusiasts Augustus Welby Pugin and Ambrose Phillipps, afterwards Phillipps De Lisle. Once Newman had retreated from Oxford to Littlemore, Ward took on the role of a leader of the Oxford Movement, and between 1841 and 1843 contributed eight articles to the *British Critic*, then under the editorship of Tom Mozley, in which he frankly presented the Roman Catholic church as the model of the one true church. William Palmer of Worcester College wrote in reply his anti-Roman *Narrative of Events Connected with the Publication of the Tracts for the Times* (1843). Ward responded to Palmer in his most celebrated work, *The Ideal of a Christian Church Considered in Comparison with Existing Practice* (1844), in which he argued that neither evangelical emotion nor the liberal intellect but conscience was the foundation for religion, but that the only proper discipline for conscience was the Roman Catholic church. According to this Newmanesque position, the Catholic church alone trained up conscience into the holiness necessary to eternal salvation, as defined by her moral, ascetic, and mystical theology, and as inculcated practically and pastorally by her religious orders sanctified by vows of chastity, poverty, and obedience.

Ward's title earned him notoriety under the sobriquet of 'Ideal' Ward. His obvious offence to protestant opinion lay in passages like 'oh most joyful, most wonderful, most unexpected sight, we find the whole cycle of Roman doctrine gradually possessing numbers of English Churchmen' (*The Ideal of a Christian Church*, 565) and 'Three years have passed since I said plainly that in subscribing the Articles I renounce no one Roman doctrine' (ibid., 567). These and five other passages were cited by the vice-chancellor of Oxford, Benjamin Parsons Symons, on 13 December 1844 as cause for a motion to the university convocation to condemn the *Ideal* as inconsistent with the Thirty-Nine Articles and to strip Ward of his degrees (literally to

'degrade' him). A third proposal, to require subscription to the articles in the sense intended by their sixteenth-century framers, raised a storm among liberals like Ward's great friend Arthur Penrhyn Stanley. Like Stanley, Ward argued that the Church of England could not censure any position, not even liberalism, and so could not condemn him, but must be consistent in its inconsistency. The proposal for a test on the articles was abandoned, but was replaced by a censure on Newman's Tract 90. In one of the most celebrated incidents in the history of the Victorian church, in a snow-bound Oxford, with Ward falling head over heels on the steps of the Sheldonian, convocation voted by 777 votes to 386 to condemn the *Ideal* and by 569 votes to 511 to degrade him (to remove his MA). The two proctors, one of them Newman's disciple Richard Church, vetoed a vote on the condemnation of Tract 90. The size of the minorities that voted for Ward was astonishing, given the charges, while the undergraduates showed their sympathy for him by snowballing the vice-chancellor.

Marriage and conversion On 31 March 1845 Ward married Frances Mary Wingfield (1816/17–1898), youngest daughter of John Wingfield (1760–1825), vicar of Bromsgrove, Worcestershire, prebendary of Worcester, and canon of York. Having publicly stated his belief in the virtue of clerical celibacy, Ward was an easy target for the press, and had already provoked ridicule though a letter to *The Times* in which he declared himself too gross for the celibate priesthood. 'How', he wrote, 'any one can imagine that I have ever professed any vocation to a high and ascetic life, I am utterly at a loss to conceive' (*The Times*, 3 March 1845). His son, who wrote his biography, could not bring himself to publish this self-accusation, but it seems to confirm the poet laureate Tennyson's assessment that Ward was 'the most truthful man I ever knew …. He was grotesquely truthful' (W. Ward, *Ward and the Catholic Revival*, 399). On 5 September 1845 Ward and his wife, Frances, were received into the Roman Catholic church at Farm Street by the Jesuit Father Brownbill. In 1846, Ward employed Pugin to design him a Gothic house near the seminary of St Edmund's, Old Hall, near Ware, in Hertfordshire. In 1849 he inherited a fortune on the Isle of Wight from his childless uncle, George Henry Ward, which was entailed on him from his grandfather George Ward (1751–1829). The birth of four daughters preceded that of the first of his three sons, Edmund Granville, in 1853, which elicited a storm of congratulations from fellow Catholics, provoking Ward's indignant remark that fatherhood, unlike theology or philosophy, was 'a thing any man may do' (ibid., 43). Characteristically rigorous, he argued from a syllogism that he must lack affection for his children while they were under the age of reason since: '1. "I can have no affection for persons with whose character I am unacquainted;" 2. "I know nothing of the character of my younger children; *ergo*, I can have no affection for them."' Once they had become 'reasonable beings', however, he showed them an attention which won their undying loyalty (ibid., 67). His youngest son, Bernard Nicholas *Ward (b. 1857), later became a headmaster and historian.

Moral philosopher and dogmatic theologian In 1851 Nicholas Wiseman, then cardinal archbishop of Westminster, appointed Ward lecturer in moral philosophy at St Edmund's Hall, near Ware, and then, in 1852, lecturer in dogmatic theology. In order to defer to Catholic opposition to his position as a layman in a seminary, he declined to accept the title of professor. Pope Pius IX conferred on him a doctorate of philosophy in 1854, and is supposed to have defended his status as a seminary teacher by declaring that it was 'a novel objection to anyone who is engaged in the work of God' that Ward should have received a sacrament, marriage, which no pope or priest could receive (M. Ward, *The Wilfrid Wards and the Transition*, 1.12). Ward also had the backing of a new friend, the vice-president of St Edmund's, Herbert (later Cardinal) Vaughan.

Ward resigned his position at St Edmund's in 1858, but so disliked his life as 'Squire Ward' at Northwood House, Cowes, on the Isle of Wight, that he returned to the seminary in 1861, coming back to Wight in 1871 to live in a new house, Weston Manor, on his estate at Freshwater at the western end of the island.

Ward's sympathies in the 1860s in the conflict between the liberal Catholic school of John Acton and Richard Simpson and the 'new ultramontanes' like Henry Edward Manning and Ward's own confessor, Father Faber, were entirely with the latter group, as the liberal Catholics seemed to him to exalt the scientific intellect over conscience and the need for holiness. For the same reasons he repudiated his old master, Newman, fearing that he might be a crypto-liberal, although he remained deeply fascinated by him. In a dream, he was once dining with a veiled lady, to whom he exclaimed, '"I have never felt such charm in any conversation since I used to talk with John Henry Newman, at Oxford." "I am John Henry Newman", the lady replied', raising her veil (W. Ward, *Life of John Henry Cardinal Newman*, 2 vols., 1912, 2.349).

The *Dublin Review* and Metaphysical Society In 1863 Ward became editor of the Catholic journal the *Dublin Review*, of which Manning was the proprietor. Leaving politics, literature, and secular history to his sub-editors, Edward Healy Thompson and John Cashel Hoey, he made the *Dublin Review* 'a kind of theological battering ram' (M. Ward, 'W. G. Ward and Wilfrid Ward', *Dublin Review*, 198, 1936, 237) for his unbending ultramontanism; he warned Hoey he would be '*very* narrow and *very* strong' (W. Ward, *Ward and the Catholic Revival*, 223). There is no exact date given for the celebrated story that, during the First Vatican Council of 1869–70, he said that he 'should like a new papal Bull every morning with my *Times* at breakfast' (ibid., 14), but he had defended the infallibility of the anti-liberal encyclical 'Quanta cura' and the accompanying Syllabus of Errors of 1864 as if the pope could hardly open his mouth without making an infallible pronouncement. His critic the Oratorian Ignatius Ryder compared such an extreme view of papal infallibility with the Midas touch of gold, as very inconvenient if very wonderful; Ward was said to have enunciated his startling conclusions with the 'serenity of a philosopher' but defended them with 'the vehemence of a fanatic' (*DNB*). His uncompromising teaching

on the papacy was summed up in *De infallibilitatis extensione* (1869), and he had written about 125 essays and reviews for the *Dublin Review* by the time of his retirement as its editor in 1878. When, in 1865, the notoriously pro-papal Manning became archbishop of Westminster he jumped with joy once, or according to another account, thrice, over a chair. In 1865 he supported the parliamentary candidature of an anti-Catholic Conservative against Sir John Simeon on the Isle of Wight because he counted Simeon, a Catholic convert like himself, as a liberal Catholic. Pope Pius IX recognized Ward's services to theology in a special brief addressed to him in 1870.

Ward's connections with philosophers extended far beyond the circle of his fellow Catholics. In his friendly correspondence with John Stuart Mill, which began with his two articles in *The Tablet* in 1848 on Mill's *Political Economy* and was resumed in 1865, he denied Mill's empiricism, that knowledge could be derived wholly from reason and experience, on the intuitionist grounds that knowledge depended on the reliability of memory, which could only be assumed. The two joined forces in 1866 to condemn Governor Eyre's brutal repression of the Jamaican rising. In 1871 in the *Dublin Review* Ward attacked Mill's 'anti-theistic philosophy', arguing against scientific determinism, for the possibility of miracles, and for the freedom of the will. Mill described Ward's writings as 'the best that is likely to be said by any future champion' (W. Ward, *Ward and the Catholic Revival*, 320), while Ward returned the compliment by describing Mill's death in 1873 as a 'severe controversial disappointment' (ibid., 295). With Manning and his neighbour at Freshwater, Tennyson, Ward was a founder member of the Metaphysical Society, created in 1869 by the editor James Knowles. He read three papers to the society in 1869–70, and was its chairman during 1870; his intuitionism, theism, and moralism aligned him with the Unitarian James Martineau against the agnostic T. H. Huxley. Knowles told Huxley's biographer son Leonard Huxley that the 'wonderfully genial and kindly tone' of the society's meetings 'was very largely owing to your father & to Dr Ward—who habitually hit each other at the hardest—but never with a touch of lost temper or lost courtesy' (P. Metcalf, *James Knowles: Victorian Editor and Architect*, 1980, 224).

Death and final assessment Mill and Huxley's affectionate portraits of Ward confirm the otherwise inexplicable description of him by the most moderate of men, Richard Church, as 'the most amusing, the most tolerant man in Oxford' (W. Ward, *Ward and the Oxford Movement*, 214), and may account for the request from his old Balliol friend and foe, Archibald Campbell Tait, then archbishop of Canterbury, who was near the grave himself, for news of Ward's condition as he lay dying. Ward died at Netherhall House, Fitzjohn Avenue, Hampstead, London, on 6 July 1882, and was buried in the Catholic churchyard of Weston Manor after a panegyric by Herbert Vaughan, then bishop of Salford. Tennyson recited James Shirley's 'The Glories of our Blood and State' at his graveside, beginning with the last lines,

Only the laurels of the just
Smell sweet, and blossom in their dust.

He also composed an elegy on Ward; the second, revised, version ran:

Farewell, whose living like I shall not find,
—Whose faith and work were bells of full accord,—
My friend, the most unworldly of mankind,
Most generous of all Ultramontanes, Ward.
How subtle at tierce and quart of mind with mind,
How loyal in the following of thy Lord!

SHERIDAN GILLEY

Sources W. Ward, *William George Ward and the Oxford Movement* (1889) · W. Ward, *William George Ward and the Catholic revival* (1893) · M. Ward, *The Wilfrid Wards and the transition*, 1 (1934) · K. T. Hoppen, 'W. G. Ward and liberal Catholicism', *Journal of Ecclesiastical History*, 23 (1972), 323–44 · K. T. Hoppen, 'Church, state and ultramontanism in mid-Victorian England: the case of William George Ward', *Journal of Church and State*, 18 (1976), 289–309 · K. T. Hoppen, 'William George Ward and nineteenth-century Catholicism', PhD diss., U. Cam., 1966 · *Wellesley index* · O. Chadwick, *From Bossuet to Newman*, 2nd edn (1987) · *The Oxford diaries of Arthur Hugh Clough*, ed. A. Kenny (1990), 85
Archives U. St Andr. L., corresp. and papers · Westm. DA, corresp., MSS, and lecture notes | Birmingham Oratory, letters to J. H. Newman · BL, corresp. with W. E. Gladstone, Add. MSS 44360–44527 · LPL, letters to A. C. Tait · LUL, corresp. with G. C. Robertson · Westm. DA, corresp. with E. H. Thompson, etc.
Likenesses G. J. Stodart, engraving (after miniature by E. Combe, c.1832), repro. in Ward, *William George Ward and the Oxford Movement*, frontispiece [*see illus.*] · G. W. Wilson, photograph, priv. coll. · portrait (after bust by M. Raggi), repro. in Ward, *William George Ward and the Catholic revival*, frontispiece · wood-engraving, NPG; repro. in *ILN* (29 July 1882)
Wealth at death £40,262 18s. 2d.: probate, 2 Nov 1882, *CGPLA Eng. & Wales*

Ward, William Humble, second earl of Dudley (1867–1932), lord lieutenant of Ireland and governor-general of Australia, was born on 25 May 1867 at Dudley House, Park Lane, London, the eldest of the seven children of William Ward, first earl of Dudley (1817–1885), and his second wife, Georgiana Elizabeth Moncreiffe (1846–1929). A celebrated beauty, portrayed by J. E. Millais in his *Apple Blossoms*, Georgiana was a favourite of the prince of Wales, later Edward VII. Young Ward—styled Lord Ednam and known to friends as Eddie—was educated at Eton College from 1881 to 1884; while at school he broke his leg and as a result he was lame for life. On his father's death he inherited, at the age of seventeen, some 25,000 acres, mainly in Worcestershire—including profitable ironworks and collieries—and he later bought sugar plantations in Jamaica. In 1885–7 he cruised around the world in his steam yacht, *Marchesa*. He soon sold his father's fine porcelain and art collections—Cornelius Vanderbilt of New York bought J. M. W. Turner's *Grand Canal of Venice*. An admirable horseman, and master of the Worcestershire hunt, Dudley failed in costly attempts to breed racehorses. He was, however, a winning yachtsman and a fine golfer, with a reported handicap of three.

On 14 September 1891, at Trinity Church, Chelsea, Dudley married Rachel Gurney (c.1867–1920). The younger daughter of Charles Gurney, a Quaker banker from Norfolk, following her father's business failure she had been

adopted, in effect, by her cousin Adeline, the wife of the tenth duke of Bedford. Young and wealthy, the earl of Dudley turned to politics as a Conservative, being elected to the London county council to represent Finsbury (Holborn) in March 1895, and mayor of Dudley in 1895 and 1896. In Lord Salisbury's ministry from July 1895 to 1902 he was parliamentary secretary to the Board of Trade. During the Second South African War he served as major in the Worcestershire yeomanry and in 1900 saw action in the Orange Free State and the Transvaal.

In August 1902 Dudley was appointed lord lieutenant of Ireland and sworn of the privy council; in 1903 he was appointed GCVO. He entertained lavishly, travelled widely, and hosted two successful royal visits, but was criticized by Ulster loyalists and his own party for supporting Lord Dunraven's devolution policy. Lady Dudley took an interest in health care and established a system of district nurses. The viceroy and his consort were immortalized in James Joyce's *Ulysses*, in a fictional cavalcade through Dublin on 16 June 1904, 'Bloomsday'. Dudley left office on the defeat of the Balfour ministry in December 1905. Although he was reproached by *The Times* for his 'mistakes', he was praised by the Irish nationalist *Freeman's Journal*.

Partly at the urging of the king, the Campbell-Bannerman government, which had appointed Dudley chairman of the royal commission on congestion in Ireland, selected him to be fourth governor-general of Australia. Having been appointed GCMG, and after travelling via Canada, the earl was sworn in at Sydney in September 1908. He was 6 feet tall, broad shouldered, and dark haired, with a thick, black military moustache; Melbourne *Punch* credited him with a 'charming speaking voice—soft, liquid, but penetrating' (24 Sept 1908). His term in Australia was not successful, either publicly or privately. A political crisis in May 1909 led to his refusing the request of the Labor prime minister, Andrew Fisher, for a dissolution of parliament and Alfred Deakin formed a government. Relations with the second Fisher administration, which took office in April 1910, were strained. His excellency's request to visit distant regions in a steam yacht was refused. The breakdown in the governor-general's marriage also became public knowledge, some newspapers accusing him of amorous intrigues with Australian married ladies.

Lady Dudley, though possessed of a reserved and absent manner, took an unusually prominent public role for the wife of a governor-general. Her ambitious attempt to establish a national order for district nursing failed, but she set up state-based bush-nursing associations which operated in outback Australia for more than sixty years. The countess of Dudley challenge cup, presented by her husband for a polo competition, was still being contested in New South Wales ninety years later. Dudley left Australia in July 1911, his public career curtailed and his ambition of becoming viceroy of India shattered. He was appointed GCB.

In August 1912 the Dudleys' marriage ended with a final,

formal separation. The earl commanded the Worcestershire hussars in Egypt and at Gallipoli in 1915 and was promoted lieutenant-colonel but then invalided home; in 1916 he was attached to the headquarters staff of the 40th division. His wife was also active in the war, establishing in France the Australian Volunteer (later no. 32 British Stationary) Hospital in August 1914 and clubs for officers. She was appointed CBE in 1918 and awarded the Royal Red Cross, second class, in 1919. Lady Dudley died while bathing in the sea on the Connemara coast of Ireland on 26 June 1920. Portraits of her were painted by John Singer Sargent and John Longstaff.

In Paris, on 30 April 1924, Dudley married the actress Gertie *Millar (1879–1952). Survived by her, and by the four sons and three daughters of his first marriage, he died at 17 Park Lane, London, of cancer on 29 June 1932 and was buried on 2 July in the gardens of his home at Himley Hall, Wolverhampton.

CHRISTOPHER CUNNEEN

Sources C. Cunneen, *Kings' men* (1983) · C. Cunneen, 'Dudley, William Humble Ward', *AusDB*, vol. 8 · *The Times* (14–15 Dec 1905) · *The Times* (7 Nov 1918) · *The Times* (28 June 1920) · *The Times* (30 June 1932) · *The Bulletin* [Sydney, NSW] (26 March 1908), 20 · *The Bulletin* [Sydney, NSW] (8 Oct 1908), 22 · *The Sun* [Sydney] (5 Sept 1910), 1 · *Sydney Morning Herald* (7 Sept 1908), 7 · *Truth* [Sydney] (18 Sept 1910), 1–2 · GEC, *Peerage*, new edn, vol. 4 · Burke, *Peerage* (1999) · *Punch* [Melbourne] (24 Sept 1908) · *The Times* (15 Sept 1891), 7 · *The Times* (4 March 1895), 7 · *The Times* (5 July 1895) · *The Times* (18 Aug 1902), 8 · *The Times* (19 March 1906), 4 · *The Times* (20 March 1908), 7 · *The Times* (25 Nov 1913), 15 · *The Times* (6 Aug 1914), 3 · *The Times* (22 Sept 1915), 5 · *The Times* (1 May 1924), 19 · *The Times* (4 Feb 1929), 17 · *The Times* (4 July 1932), 15 · *Manchester Guardian Weekly* (1 July 1932) · *Sydney Mail* (5 July 1911), 27 · *Sydney Morning Herald* (16 April 1927), 6 · *Sydney Morning Herald* (18 April 1974), 14 · *Sydney Morning Herald* (1 March 1977), 75 · *The Argus* [Melbourne] (21 March 1908), 17 · *The Argus* [Melbourne] (21 July 1910), 9 · *The Argus* [Melbourne] (7 Sept 1910), 12 · *Punch* [Melbourne] (22 Dec 1910), 933 · *The Eton register*, 5 (privately printed, Eton, 1908) · *Army List* (1908) · S. Weedon, *The countess of Dudley cup* (1985) · C. E. W. Bean, *The Australian imperial force in France 1916* (1935), vol. 3 of *The official history of Australia in the war of 1914–1918*, 161 · D. Gifford, *Ulysses annotated* (Berkeley, California, c.1988) · b. cert. · m. cert. · d. cert. · *CGPLA Eng. & Wales* (1932)
Archives BL, corresp. with Arthur James Balfour, Add. MS 49802, *passim* · Bodl. Oxf., corresp. with L. Harcourt · NL Aus., corresp. with Alfred Deakin | FILM BFI NFTVA, documentary footage
Likenesses P. A. de Laszlo, charcoal drawing, 1914; in possession of his widow, 1949 · Graphic Photo Union, photograph, c.1924 (with Gertie Millar), NPG · Graphic Photo Union, photograph, c.1924 (with Major Dudley Gilroy), NPG · A. Ellis, portrait (as a young man); known to be at Himley Hall, in 1949 · J. Longstaff, oils, Parliament House, Canberra
Wealth at death £400,000: probate, 18 Aug 1932, *CGPLA Eng. & Wales*

Ward, William James (c.1800–1840). *See under* Ward, William (1766–1826).

Ward, Winifred Mary Kingdon- (1884–1979), speech therapist, was born at 30 Victoria Road, Old Charlton, Kent, on 12 October 1884, the daughter of Harry Marshall *Ward (1854–1906), botanist, and his wife, Selina Mary, née Kingdon (d. 1922), daughter of Francis Kingdon, of Exeter. Her younger brother, Francis (Frank) Kingdon-*Ward, became a renowned plant collector and author. Winifred

studied speech and singing, and during the First World War was involved in working with wounded soldiers returning from the front. Many had suffered head injuries which led to disorders of speech and language, while others presented with stammering related to shell-shock. She was one of the first British speech therapists appointed to work with patients in a hospital setting and held posts at the West End Hospital for Nervous Diseases, Maida Vale Hospital, the West London Hospital, and Pembury Hospital in Kent.

After the war Kingdon-Ward saw the need for an academically and medically orientated form of training and began to offer aspiring speech therapists at the West End Hospital opportunities for observation and guidance. The West End Hospital school was founded under her direction in 1929. She also played a major part in the development of the British Society of Speech Therapists, which was formed in 1934. She left the West End Hospital school in 1935 in order to spend time in South Africa. When she returned to London shortly before the outbreak of the Second World War she was unable to resume her old post and took steps to set up a second course in conjunction with a former student, Amy Swallow. The London Hospitals School of Speech Therapy was founded in 1942 in Cavendish Square. The previous year she had published *Stammering: Problems and Theories*. This represented the first major text on the subject in the British literature and was one of the earliest works on any topic in the field. She was one of the first authorities to recognize that there are different types and causes of stammering and she maintained that therapists should adapt their approach accordingly. The German, French, and American authorities tended to talk of a single cause.

Kingdon-Ward retired from her post as principal of the London Hospitals School in 1948, and it was renamed the Kingdon-Ward School of Speech Therapy. She continued to work in the National Health Service for many years after normal retirement age. In 1954 she published *A Book of Rhymes and Jingles for Children* for the use of speech therapists. She had already produced a volume of poetry, *The Flaming Fountains*, published in 1927.

Kingdon-Ward was an enthusiastic and gifted therapist, and though somewhat shy had such a strong presence that a patient with whom she was working would hardly be aware of the group of students who were observing the session. She always insisted that students should develop their powers of observation. She had considerable foresight and strength of character, and always warmly supported the drive of the profession towards greater academic rigour. She died in the St Charles Hospital, Kensington, London, on 26 January 1979.

ROBERT FAWCUS

Sources S. Robertson, M. Kersner, and S. Davies, *A history of the college, 1945–1995* (1995) [history of Royal College of Speech and Language Therapists] · C. Lyte, *Frank Kingdon-Ward: the last of the great plant hunters* (1989) · personal knowledge (2004) · b. cert. · d. cert.
Likenesses photograph, repro. in Robertson, Kersner, and Davies, *History of the college* · photograph, repro. in Lyte, *Frank Kingdon-Ward*
Wealth at death £34,037: probate, 26 June 1979, *CGPLA Eng. & Wales*

Wardale, Edith Elizabeth (1863–1943), philologist and literary scholar, was born on 6 March 1863 at the rectory, Orcheston St Mary, Wiltshire, the daughter of the Revd John Wardale (1824–1903), rector of Orcheston St Mary and sometime fellow of Clare College, Cambridge, and his wife, Susannah Jennings Gay. After attending Miss Bidwell's school, Devizes, she entered Lady Margaret Hall, Oxford, in 1887, where her sister was also a student, and moved to St Hugh's Hall, Oxford, in January 1888. She achieved a first class in modern languages in 1889 and—remarkably early for a woman of her generation—was awarded the degree of PhD of Zürich University in August 1892 for a study of the phonology of Notker's psalter. She was a pupil of Joseph Wright, who thought very highly of her: she was 'the only woman in the whole history of Higher Education of Women in Oxford who has taken a decent degree', he wrote in 1895 (Wright, 1.221). He entrusted her with teaching responsibility in a wide range of philological subjects, including Old English, the history of Old German literature, and Middle and Old High German.

In 1891 Edith Wardale was appointed lecturer in Old English for the Oxford Association for the Education of Women and became tutor in English at St Hugh's. She was soon teaching all women reading English at that time, as well as lecturing at Royal Holloway College, London. In 1921 she became the first woman member of the medieval and modern languages and literature faculty board, and was the first woman examiner in English at Oxford (1925).

Wardale was a passionate enthusiast for the study of Old English as part of the undergraduate honours degree course in English; in 1921 she gave evidence to the Newbolt committee on the position of English in the educational system of England, with a defence of Old English of the kind periodically called for in the face of criticism from its detractors. 'English Literature was visibly based upon Old English though enormously modified by the influences that had come in since,' she argued. 'Anglo-Saxon literature gave the English outlook on life, and this had at all times been the same' (Board of Education, *The Teaching of English in England*, 1921, 224).

In 1923 Edith Wardale was one of the five tutors who resigned their posts at St Hugh's as a result of the notorious 'row' concerning the decision of the principal of the day, Eleanor Jourdain, not to propose the reappointment of Cecilia Ady, a popular history tutor. The 'row' was something of a *cause célèbre* in Oxford, and Jourdain's death from a heart attack in 1924, just before the chancellor's verdict on the matter, was directly attributed to it. Edith Wardale showed great courage in her support of Ady, reading a protest on behalf of those who had resigned which saw the principal's actions as 'a menace to the security, and an affront to the dignity, of the whole Tutorial body' (letter, 6 Dec 1923, Bodl. Oxf., Deneke 1956 deposit, box 9). She remained a member of the council of St Hugh's and became an honorary fellow in 1929. The 'row' was not openly spoken of for many years, but later tributes to her reflected the moral strength she had shown

during what was a very sorry chapter in the history of the college (*The Times*, 5 March 1943).

Edith Wardale's small stature belied this strength of personality:

[She] was a tiny, frail, neat, timid-seeming, quiet-voiced, unobtrusive little lady, as unlike an Oxford (woman) don as it is possible to imagine, in appearance. She had, however, a powerful and piercing intellect, unshakeable standards of justice, and moral courage.   (Iremonger, 108)

A fine and witty portrait (of 1936) of the principal and four fellows of St Hugh's by Henry Lamb RA depicts Miss Wardale, looking as frail and timid as ever, with the more imposing figure of Cecilia Ady in the foreground.

Edith Wardale published two very popular introductions to the study of Old and Middle English, *An Old English Grammar* (1922) and *An Introduction to Middle English* (1937), together with a scholarly and admirably lucid and readable study of Old English texts, *Chapters on Old English Literature* (1935), praised at the time for its freshness and originality and for its fine translations. She died on 27 February 1943 at her home, 12 St Margaret's Road, Oxford, from heart failure brought on by bronchitis.   D. PHILLIPS

Sources P. Griffin, ed., *St Hugh's: one hundred years of women's education in Oxford* (1986) • L. Iremonger, *The ghosts of Versailles: Miss Moberley and Miss Jourdain and their adventure, a critical study* (1957) • *The Times* (5 March 1943) • *WWW, 1941–50* • C. M. Ady, *Oxford Magazine* (27 May 1943) • E. M. Wright, *The life of Joseph Wright* (1932) • Bodl. Oxf., Deneke 1956 deposit, box 9 • b. cert. • d. cert.

Likenesses H. Lamb, group portrait, 1936, St Hugh's College, Oxford

Wealth at death £7305 6s. 11d.: resworn probate, 6 April 1943, *CGPLA Eng. & Wales*

Warde, Sir Edward Charles (1810–1884). *See under* Warde, Sir Henry (1766–1834).

Warde, Sir Henry (1766–1834), army officer and colonial governor, born on 7 January 1766, was the fourth son of John Warde (1721–1775) of Squerryes, near Westerham, Kent, and his second wife, Kitty Anne (d. 1767), daughter and sole heir of Charles Hoskins of Croydon, Surrey. The family was descended from a younger branch of that established at Hooton Pagnell in Yorkshire.

Warde entered the army as an ensign in the 1st foot guards in 1783, and on 6 July 1790 was promoted lieutenant and brevet captain. In 1791 he accompanied his regiment to the Netherlands, but was so severely wounded at the siege of Valenciennes that he had to return to England. He rejoined his regiment in June 1794, and continued to serve with it, acting as adjutant to the 3rd battalion, until his promotion to a company, with the brevet rank of lieutenant-colonel, on 15 October 1794, when he was sent home. Warde served in the expeditions to Ostend and The Helder, and received the brevet rank of colonel on 1 January 1801. In 1804 he was promoted brigadier-general, and in 1807 took part in the expedition to Copenhagen. In 1808 he became major-general. On 28 May 1808 he married Molina (1776–1835), daughter of John Thomas of Hereford. They had five sons including Henry John Warde, and a daughter, Harriett (d. 1874), who on 4 May 1826 married Francis North, sixth earl of Guilford.

Warde commanded the 1st brigade of foot guards sent to

Spain in 1808 with the force under Sir David Baird, and returned to England in 1809 after the battle of Corunna. In 1809 he was sent to India, and served under Lieutenant-General (afterwards Sir John) Abercromby (1772–1817) at the capture of Mauritius in 1810. He remained there for some time in command of the troops, and acted as governor from 9 April to 12 July 1811. In 1813 he was appointed colonel of the 68th foot, and promoted lieutenant-general. On the enlargement of the Order of the Bath on 2 January 1815 he was made KCB. On 8 February 1821 he was appointed governor of Barbados, in succession to Lord Combermere. He arrived at the island on 25 June, and continued in office until 21 June 1827. His administration was reportedly popular, although differences between the two branches of the legislature, the council and the house of assembly, at times made the governor's course difficult. The restlessness of the slaves, who were disturbed by rumours of emancipation, also occasioned him anxiety. In 1830 he became general, and in 1831 was appointed colonel of the 31st foot. On 13 September 1831 he was made GCB. He died at his residence, Dean House, near Alresford in Hampshire, on 1 October 1834, and was buried that month.

Sir Edward Charles Warde (1810–1884), army officer, born at Government House, Bangalore, India, on 13 November 1810, was Sir Henry Warde's second son. On 19 May 1828 he was gazetted second lieutenant, Royal Artillery, and on 30 June 1830 was promoted first lieutenant, Royal Horse Artillery. He obtained a company on 5 June 1841, and was promoted lieutenant-colonel on 17 February 1854. He commanded the siege train before Sevastopol until incapacitated by fever three weeks before the fall of the fortress; and on the conclusion of the war received, on 29 August 1857, the rank of colonel, taking command of the artillery at Aldershot. In 1859, when war with France seemed imminent, he was ordered to superintend the rearmament of Malta. In 1861 he was appointed to command the artillery in the south-west district, and in 1864 was selected to command the Woolwich district. An explosion at Erith destroyed the river wall and threatened to flood the country to Camberwell, and burst the great sewers just completed. In less than an hour Warde had taken measures which averted the catastrophe. He received the thanks of the government, and, on resigning the command in 1869, was made KCB (2 June 1869). He became major-general on 27 February 1866, colonel commandant on 29 March 1873, lieutenant-general on 17 November 1878, and general on 1 October 1877. On 24 August 1843 he married Jane (d. 1895), eldest daughter of Charles Lane, rector of Wrotham and rural dean of Shoreham, Kent; they had four sons and three daughters. He died at Brighton on 10 June 1884 and was buried at Wrotham, Kent. E. I. CARLYLE, *rev.* ROGER T. STEARN

Sources GM, 2nd ser., 4 (1835), 207 • Burke, *Gen. GB* (1914) • R. H. Schomburgk, *The history of Barbados* (1848) • T. C. W. Blanning, *The French revolutionary wars, 1787–1802* (1996) • R. Muir, *Britain and the defeat of Napoleon, 1807–1815* (1996) • Boase, *Mod. Eng. biog.*
Archives Barbados Museum and Historical Society, Bridgetown, Barbados, letters to Sir William Clinton • NL Scot., letters to Lord Minto

Warde, James Prescott (1792–1840), actor, the son of J. Prescott, was born in the west of England on 27 September 1792, and brought up in wealthy circumstances. Beginning with a grammar school education, including instruction in Latin and Greek, he went on to become a cadet first at the Royal Military College, Great Marlow, in 1806, and then at the Royal Military Academy at Woolwich in 1807. He became a second lieutenant in the Royal Artillery in 1809 and the following year was sent to the Cape of Good Hope, where he remained for three years. Ill health made him return to England in 1813 and resign from the army. He took to the stage, adopting the name of Warde, which was his mother's maiden name.

Warde's first appearance was at the Liverpool theatre as Lord Towneley in Colley Cibber's *The Provoked Husband*, followed by the Duke in John Tobin's *The Honeymoon*. To gain more experience he toured Derbyshire, Lancashire, and other provincial theatres. In Bath in December 1813 he was Achmet in Browne's tragedy *Barbarossa*, and the following year he played Faulkland in Sheridan's *The Rivals*, Harry Dornton in Thomas Holcroft's *The Road to Ruin*, and Aladdin in a pantomime at Christmas. In 1815 he was Laertes to W. C. Macready's Hamlet, and in the ensuing years he played a variety of other Shakespearian characters, such as Orlando in *As You Like It*, Macduff in *Macbeth*, Shylock in *The Merchant of Venice*, Edgar in *King Lear*, Posthumus in *Cymbeline*, and Florizel in *The Winter's Tale*. He was given the original role of Fitz-James in *The Lady of the Lake*, but found greater opportunities in the numerous revivals staged in Bath. He was seen as Jaffier in *Venice Preserv'd*, Joseph Surface in *The School for Scandal*, Doricourt in *The Belle's Stratagem*, Standard in *The Constant Couple*, Alonzo in *Pizarro*, and Bevil in Richard Steele's *The Conscious Lovers*. In April 1818 he appeared as Rob Roy when the play of that name was performed in Bath for the first time. In the meantime, during the vacations he widened his horizons by making successful and profitable visits to Cheltenham, Weymouth, and other provincial towns.

Warde made his début in London at the Haymarket on 17 July 1818, as Leon in Beaumont and Fletcher's *Rule a Wife and have a Wife*. His choice of part was judicious and he was well received. He was less successful as Shylock a few days later, but gradually established his reputation with the roles of Faulkland in *The Rivals*, Don Felix in Susannah Centlivre's *The Wonder*, Valmont in William Dimond's *The Foundling of the Forest*, and Inkle in *Inkle and Yarico*. At the close of this engagement Warde received an offer to play leading roles in Dublin, and appeared there for the first time in June 1820 as Leon. He remained in Dublin until a long and severe illness forced him to retire and set up as a teacher of elocution. After his wife nursed him back to health he was able to return to the stage, and made a strong impression in Birmingham. He became the manager of the Birmingham theatre for a while, but sustained heavy financial losses and had to retire in a state of insolvency.

Warde reappeared on the London stage in the autumn of 1825, when he was engaged at Covent Garden as second lead to Charles Kemble, and was seen as Brutus, Rob Roy,

Iago, and the original Kruitzner in Harriet Lee's *The Three Strangers*. He continued to act in many of his old parts, but occasionally tried new roles, such as Rolla in *Pizarro*, Macbeth, Cassius in *Julius Caesar*, Richmond in *Richard III*, Bolingbroke in *Richard II*, and Sir Brian de Boisgilbert in *Ivanhoe*. He played the title role in *Henri Quatre* for his own benefit in June 1830. Soon, however, the quality of the plays produced at Covent Garden began to decline and the finances of the house fell into a state of hopeless confusion. This reached a climax in 1833, when inability to obtain his salary drove Warde to seek refuge at the Olympic and afterwards at the Victoria Theatre, under the management of Abbott and Egerton. The decay of the old 'legitimate' drama to which he was accustomed combined with the decay of his own acting powers to reduce his opportunities to a minimum. He was engaged at Covent Garden during Macready's brief lesseeship of 1837–8, but was entrusted only with second-rate parts, such as Williams in *Henry V*. His personal life degenerated and he was constantly in debt and under arrest. He died in penury, without friends, in a lodging in Manchester Street, London, on 9 July 1840, at the age of forty-eight.

According to contemporary opinion, Warde was a seldom great but eminently pleasing actor. He was full of promise at the time of his first appearance in London; latterly, however, he developed 'an unfortunate whining drawl' which prevented him from ever emerging completely from the ranks of 'utility' actors.

THOMAS SECCOMBE, rev. NILANJANA BANERJI

Sources *Oxberry's Dramatic Biography*, 5/79 (1826), 253–62 • *The Era* (12 July 1840) • *Actors by Daylight*, 1 (1838) • Hall, *Dramatic ports.* • *GM*, 2nd ser., 15 (1841), 439 • Genest, *Eng. stage* • *Macready's reminiscences, and selections from his diaries and letters*, ed. F. Pollock, 2 vols. (1875)
Likenesses W. T. Fry, stipple, pubd 1819 (after T. Langdon), NPG • R. J. Lane, lithograph, pubd 1839 (as Cassius), NPG • lithograph, pubd 1839, NPG • Thurston, drawing (as Cassius); Charles Mathews collection, Garr. Club, 1899 • portrait, repro. in *Oxberry's Dramatic Biography* • prints, Harvard TC

Warde, Luke (*fl.* 1576–1590), sea captain, sailed with Martin Frobisher in his three north-west voyages (1576–8). In 1578 he was admitted, gratis, as a £25 shareholder in the enterprise. In the early part of that year he was employed briefly in home waters against privateers; in May he sailed in Frobisher's third voyage as the vice-admiral of a 100-man colony, commanded by Edward Fenton, that was intended to winter upon Baffin Island. The scheme was abandoned due to loss of vital supplies. On 20 June 1578 he was one of a small party of Englishmen, led by Frobisher, which landed upon the southern coast of Greenland (mistakenly believed to be the mythical island of Friesland). Their landing place, possibly first descried by Warde, was named Luke's Sound. Three weeks later he was the first known Englishman to set foot on the northern shore of Hudson Strait; there he briefly parleyed and exchanged gifts with some Inuit.

In 1581 Warde was involved in preparations for the 'first enterprise', promoted by the earl of Leicester, Francis Drake, and others, to set out a fleet to fortify the Azores Island of Terceira in support of the Portuguese pretender,

Don Antonio, and thereafter to seize the Spanish plate fleets and sack the towns of New Spain. When the scheme was abandoned as too provocative, Warde was partly responsible for selling off its supplies. By 1582 he was the owner of a small barque, the *Elizabeth*, which he sold to Sir Humphrey Gilbert for £40. In that year he was appointed to serve as vice-admiral commanding the ship *Edward Bonaventure* in the intended Moluccas expedition under Edward Fenton (who superseded Martin Frobisher as its commander); he also invested £200 in the project. During the voyage he quarrelled with Fenton regarding their objectives, and the *Edward Bonaventure* abandoned the expedition following a sea fight against three Spanish ships at São Vicente. Warde later provided his account of the voyage to Richard Hakluyt for inclusion in the 1589 edition of *Principall Navigations*. He was named in a list of 5 January 1586 as one of seventy-six men 'fit to command ships'. In 1588 he served in the Armada battle as captain of the queen's ship *Tramontana* and, immediately after the campaign, of the *Foresight*. In 1589 he captained the *Tramontana* once more as part of Frobisher's Atlantic squadron, which tried and failed to intercept the Spanish plate fleets. On 2 January 1590 Warde was appointed to lead the small channel fleet that was to disembark Willoughby's diseased expeditionary force from Rouen; however, his old commander Frobisher assumed this command a few days later. Warde commanded the ship *Swallow* in the narrow seas during 1590; the declared accounts of the navy which record this are the final extant reference to his career.

Richard Madox, chaplain in the *Galleon Leicester* during Fenton's 1582 expedition, regarded Warde as 'a most villainous man' (Donno, 239). Conversely, his long relationship with Frobisher indicates that he remained a trusted colleague of that notoriously difficult personality. He was undoubtedly a competent sea captain, though possibly not entirely comfortable with the responsibilities his talents conferred. He appears not to have married; the only extant reference to his family is in Madox's diary, which reported that his mother came to the *Edward Bonaventure* to bid him farewell upon the 1582 voyage.

JAMES MCDERMOTT

Sources R. Hakluyt, *The principall navigations, voiages and discoveries of the English nation* (1589), 648–72 • *An Elizabethan in 1582: the diary of Richard Madox, fellow of All Souls*, ed. E. S. Donno, Hakluyt Society, 2nd ser., 147 (1976) • E. G. R. Taylor, ed., *The troublesome voyage of Captain Edward Fenton, 1582–1583*, Hakluyt Society, 2nd ser., 113 (1959) • declared accounts of the Navy, PRO, E351/2224–6 • state papers domestic, PRO, SP/12/123, 50; 12/186, 8; 12/215, 76; 12/216, 64 • E. Selman, account of the 1578 north-west voyage, BL, Harleian MS 167/40, fols. 166–180 • G. Best, *A true discourse of the late voyages of discoverie, for the finding of a passage to Cathaya, by the northwest, The three voyages of Martin Frobisher*, ed. R. Collinson (1867) • J. McDermott, 'The account books of Michael Lok, relating to the north-west voyages of Martin Frobisher, 1576–8: text and analysis', MPhil diss., U. Hull, 1984

Wardell, William Wilkinson (1823–1899), architect and engineer, was born on 27 September 1823 at 60 Cotton Street, Poplar, London, the second of the four children of Thomas Wardell (*c*.1800–1864), baker, and his wife, Mary

Dalton (*b. c.*1800). His parents subsequently became master and matron of Poplar union workhouse. Following a spell at sea, he served in the offices of Mr Morris, surveyor to the commissioners of London sewers, and W. F. East, an architect. While surveying land for new railways, he began measuring and drawing medieval buildings. Simultaneously the influence of A. W. N. Pugin drew him to the Roman Catholic church, into which he was received in 1846. On 5 October 1847 he married Lucy Anne (*c.*1820–1888), daughter of William Henry Butler, wine merchant, of Headington, near Oxford. They had five sons and six daughters.

Wardell designed about thirty Catholic churches, principally in London and the south-east, in a Gothic revival style almost indistinguishable from Pugin's, as well as presbyteries, convents, and schools. His town churches at Clapham (1851), Greenwich (1851), Commercial Road (1856), and Brook Green (1853) rank among the finest work of the 1850s. During these years he was elected FRIBA (1850), freeman of the City of London (1851), member of the Company of Fishmongers (1852), and associate of the Institution of Civil Engineers (1858).

Owing to the state of his health, Wardell sold his practice to Messrs Hadfield and Goldie of Sheffield, and emigrated to Australia with his family in 1858. As inspector-general of public works in Victoria from 1861, he was responsible for such undertakings as docks and harbours, as well as government buildings. Holding also the right of private practice, he designed churches and schools in and around Melbourne, principally St Patrick's Cathedral, finally consecrated in 1897. His career in Melbourne ended abruptly when all principal officers were dismissed on 'black Wednesday' 1878 in a government upheaval. He then moved to Sydney, where he confined himself to private practice, designing churches, houses, clubs, and banks in a variety of styles—renaissance, Gothic, and vernacular—and becoming thereby a significant figure.

Wardell's principal contribution to his age lay in his church work. His article in the *Weekly Register* (1849–50) demonstrates his concern for building within reasonable financial limits, his care for responsible historicism, and above all a strong commitment to the revived Gothic style. Never as fanatical as Pugin, however, Wardell compromised his commitment to Gothic with Italianate designs at St Mary in Hampstead, Sts Peter and Edward in Westminster, and Government House in Melbourne. His drawings of his English work, which survive in the Mitchell Library, Sydney, demonstrate also his competence in designing such furnishings as altars, screens, fonts, and stained glass.

Despite suffering from tuberculosis, Wardell worked energetically and efficiently. The advice of A. S. Hamilton in 1869 'to rest your exhausted brain' (de Jong, 9) suggests a busy lifestyle of endless examinations, commissions, reports, surveys, and designs. With hindsight, his dismissal in 1878 was a blessing. Throughout those stormy years, however, he had refuted criticisms of his work with patience and gentle good manners. Formative influences here were his happy marriage and his staunch commitment to his Catholic faith. Wardell died at his home, Upton Grange, Sydney, on 19 November 1899 and was buried at Gore Hill cemetery, Sydney. DENIS EVINSON

Sources D. I. M. McDonald, 'William Wilkinson Wardell: architect and engineer', *Victorian Historical Magazine*, 41/2 (1970) • biography file, RIBA BAL • *The Tablet* (6 Jan 1900), 27–8 • U. de Jong, *William Wilkinson Wardell: his life and work, 1823–1899* (1983) • *Weekly Register* (12 Jan 1850), 389–93 • Family History Centre • census returns, 1841 • *Catholic Annual Register* (1850), 114–16 • private information (2004) • m. cert.

Likenesses photograph, 1870, RIBA

Wealth at death £12,919—estate valued for probate: RIBA. biography file

Warden, William (1777–1849), naval surgeon and author, was born at Alyth in Forfarshire on 1 May 1777. From the parish school, he was sent to Montrose, where he served some years with a surgeon, being a fellow-pupil of William Burnett and Joseph Hume. He studied also for some time at Edinburgh University, and in 1795 entered the navy as surgeon's mate on board the frigate *Melpomene*, one of the ships implicated in the mutiny at the Nore. The story is told that the men demanded that the surgeon should be sent on shore and Warden appointed in his stead, but that Warden, on the advice of his captain, refused the promotion. He was, however, promoted in the following year; he was surgeon of the *Alcmène* at Copenhagen on 2 April 1801, and of the *Phoenix*, when she captured the *Didon* on 10 August 1805. In the latter engagement Warden was severely wounded, and he was for some time a pensioner of the Royal Naval Hospital, Greenwich. He also received a grant from the Patriotic Fund. In December 1811 the degrees of MA and MD *honoris causa* were conferred on him by the University of St Andrews. He afterwards served under Sir George Cockburn (1772–1853) during the Anglo-American War of 1812–14, and in 1815 was appointed to the *Northumberland*, Cockburn's flagship in the channel, ordered to take Napoleon to St Helena.

During the voyage, and afterwards for some months at St Helena, Warden was in frequent attendance on Napoleon, who probably talked frankly to him as to a non-combatant. Warden's knowledge of French, however, was limited, and the conversations seem to have been carried on principally, if not entirely, through the intermediary of Count de Las Cases, who acted as interpreter, sometimes, it may be supposed, not in good faith, and always with a very imperfect knowledge of English. The conversations, as Warden understood them, he noted down in his journal, and from them largely filled his letters to the lady whom he afterwards married. His friends' interest in these letters suggested that the subject matter of them— as far as they related to Napoleon—should be published; and Warden, having no experience as an author, and expecting to be called away on active service, put them into the hands of 'a literary gentleman' to prepare for publication and to see through the press.

The book was published under the title *Letters Written on Board His Majesty's Ship the 'Northumberland' and at St. Helena* (1816), and, owing to the intrinsic interest of the subject, ran through five editions in as many months. The favourable representation of Napoleon excited bitter criticism from the supporters of the government. In October 1816, in a savage article in the *Quarterly Review*, the author pointed out several passages and expressions which could not have been written by Warden at the time and under the circumstances stated, and plainly suggested that:

> Warden brought to England a few sheets of notes gleaned for the most part from the conversation of his better informed fellow-officers, and that he applied to some manufacturer of correspondence in London to spin them out into the 'Letters from St. Helena'.

There is no reason to doubt Warden's good faith, but his work has small historical value, for it is merely the 'literary gentleman's' version of Warden's recollection of what an ignorant and dishonest interpreter described Bonaparte as saying. Bonaparte—whether truthfully cannot be established—afterwards assured Sir Hudson Lowe that his conversation as reported by Warden was different from anything he had said. Lowe mentioned this in a letter to Lord Bathurst, then secretary for war, and represented that Warden, who had been permitted to visit Longwood only as a medical officer in the exercise of his functions, had committed a breach of discipline in publishing the conversations and in publicly commenting on the conduct and character of individuals. A copy of this letter was forwarded to the Admiralty, and they, recognizing the breach of discipline, struck Warden's name off the list of surgeons. It was, however, shortly afterwards replaced at the instance of Sir George Cockburn, and Warden was appointed surgeon of the hospital ship *Argonaut* at Chatham.

Warden married, in 1817, Elizabeth, daughter of Richard Hutt of Appleby, Isle of Wight, sister of Sir William Hutt and niece of Captain John Hutt. They had one son, George Cockburn Warden, and two daughters. In 1824 Warden took his MD at Edinburgh, and in 1825 he was appointed surgeon of the dockyard at Sheerness, whence he was moved in 1842 to the dockyard at Chatham, and there he died on 23 April 1849.

J. K. LAUGHTON, rev. ANDREW LAMBERT

Sources private information (1899) · review, *QR*, 17 (1817), 506–30
Likenesses mezzotint (as a young man), priv. coll.; in possession of his grandson, Charles John Warden, 1899

Warder, Joseph (1654/5–1724), writer on bee-keeping, of unknown parentage, was living at Croydon, Surrey, about 1688. He married, on 9 April 1702, Rachel Hammon of Croydon. For over thirty years Warder practised as a physician, being an extra licentiate of the Royal College of Physicians. He was a leading member and something of a controversialist in the local independent congregation, whose pastor was Richard Conder, his son-in-law.

Warder made a study of the habits of bees and their external anatomy using a light microscope, and embodied the results of many years of observation in his only book, *The True Amazons, or, The Monarchy of Bees* (1st edn, 1712). In it he described the use of a hand lens to confirm by simple dissection the sex of the then mysterious drones as male

bees. He explained why the drones were, contrary to popular opinion, important to the summer economy of the colony. In discussing the practical management of colonies he also advocated the provision of a nearby source of drinking water.

Working at a time when straw skeps were the normal accommodation for honeybee colonies Warder explained the advantages of octagonal wooden hives with glass windows. These he had made up on a template to give standard units that could be built up and subdivided as required. He thus laid the foundations of modern apicultural practice.

The True Amazons went through nine editions, all published in London, and after the first edition Warder obtained permission for a dedication to Queen Anne. The editions vary, with additional material not always carried into later versions, the last appearing in 1765. The book was translated into German (1718) and abridged into Italian (1748). Warder died at Croydon between 29 June and 1 July 1724, survived by his wife and two married daughters, to whom he left his several properties.

KARL SHOWLER

Sources J. Warder, *The true Amazons*, 2nd edn (1713) · H. M. Fraser, *History of beekeeping in Britain* (1958) · J. P. Harding and others, *British bee books: a bibliography, 1500–1976* (1979) · will, PRO, PROB 11/598, sig. 181 · *DNB*
Likenesses H. Hulsbergh, line engraving, 1712, NPG
Wealth at death several properties in Croydon: will, PRO, PROB 11/598, sig. 181

Wardington. For this title name *see* Pease, John William Beaumont, first Baron Wardington (1869–1950).

Wardlaw [*née* Halket], **Elizabeth**, Lady Wardlaw (1677–1727), poet, was born on 15 April 1677, the daughter of Sir Charles Halket, baronet, of Pitfirran, Fife, and Janet, daughter of Sir Patrick Murray. She married Sir Henry Wardlaw, baronet, of Pitreavie in 1696 and subsequently bore three daughters and a son.

Wardlaw was said to have been 'a woman of elegant accomplishments, *who wrote other poems*, and practiced drawing, and cutting paper with her scissors, and *who had much wit and humour*' (Chambers, 14). She died in 1727, and posthumously became a topic of much antiquarian discourse.

Wardlaw was the author of the ballad imitation 'Hardyknute'. The poem describes a battle between Haco, king of Norway, and Alexander III of Scotland—the battle of Largs, 2 October 1263; by the victory, largely due to the lord high steward of Scotland, Hardyknute, Scotland gained the Hebrides and the Isle of Man. Published in 1719 on folio sheets, the poem was not attributed. Somewhat later, it was republished, in extended form, in Allan Ramsay's *Ever Green* (1724) and in a variety of other antiquarian publications, reaching its apogee when it appeared in Thomas Percy's *Reliques of Ancient English Poetry* in 1765, courtesy of David Dalrymple, Lord Hailes, who had also sent Percy such 'canonical' exemplars of balladry as 'Sir Patrick Spense', 'Gil Morrice', 'Edward, Edward', 'Jew's Daughter', 'Young Waters', 'Edom o' Gordon', and 'Bonny

Earl of Murray'. In the second edition of the *Reliques*, dated 1767, Lady Wardlaw is named as author.

This set the stage for what became, in the words of Norval Clyne, the Lady Wardlaw heresy. It may have begun with David Laing and/or C. K. Sharpe, and subsequently other antiquaries, seeing a similarity between 'Hardyknute' and the other ballads sent from Scotland to Percy; a logical extension of this surmise was the attribution of the works to Lady Wardlaw. The 'heresy', however, came in the mid-nineteenth century in a publication by Robert Chambers, *The Romantic Scottish Ballads: their Epoch and Authorship* (1849). Chambers asserts that there is no evidence for similar compositions before the eighteenth century—that is, these are not old or minstrel productions; that structurally and stylistically these, and an array of other romantic ballads, are similar, sharing incidents and phrases and locales. And that, undoubtedly, the author or reviser is Lady Wardlaw, recognized already for the very similar 'Hardyknute'. Norval Clyne took great exception to Chambers's heavily comparative, stylistic analyses, asserting that if Chambers is right:

> a number of Scottish Ballads, hitherto supposed to be the production of various unknown rhymers living at different periods and in different parts of the country, will have to be assigned to one Scottish lady who amused herself with verse-making, 'and cutting paper with her scissors'.   (Clyne, 5)

This somewhat condescending put-down of Chambers, and of Lady Wardlaw who after all did successfully imitate structural and narrative aspects of traditional balladry, marked the end to extensive claims of authorship; but it did not obliterate the influence of 'Hardyknute' on Sir Walter Scott, who claimed that it was the first poem he learned by heart and would be the last he'd forget, making Lady Wardlaw his literary foremother and muse.

MARY ELLEN BROWN

Sources R. Chambers, *The romantic Scottish ballads: their epoch and authorship* (1849) • N. Clyne, *The romantic Scottish ballads and the Lady Wardlaw heresy* (1859) • T. Percy, ed., *Reliques of ancient English poetry*, rev. H. B. Wheatley, 3 vols. (1886); facs. edn (1966) • A. B. Friedman, *The ballad revival: studies in the influence of popular on sophisticated poetry* (1961) • M. E. Brown, 'Old singing women and the canons of Scottish balladry and song', *A history of Scottish women's writing*, ed. D. Gifford and D. McMillan (1997), 44–57 • Burke, *Peerage* (1851)
Archives NL Scot., papers

Wardlaw, Henry (*c.*1365–1440), bishop of St Andrews and founder of its university, was the nephew of the influential Cardinal Walter *Wardlaw; he came of a branch of the Wardlaw family established in the diocese of Aberdeen. A career in the church must have been decided for him at an early stage, as his uncle petitioned the pope on his behalf in 1378 for a canonry of Glasgow. On 7 December 1380 he was granted a safe conduct to enable him and his kinsman Alexander Wardlaw to attend either Oxford or Cambridge university, but there is no evidence for their presence there, and by 1383 both men had taken a BA degree at Paris, where Henry became licentiate of arts by 1385. By October 1387 he had been studying civil law at Orléans for at least two years, after which he continued his studies at the University of Avignon. He was styled scholar of canon law by 1394, bachelor of canon law by 1399, and doctor of canon law by September 1403.

Wardlaw came to hold canonries and prebends in Glasgow, Moray, and Aberdeen, in addition to the precentorship of Glasgow and the church of Cavers. Initially he secured patronage for his ecclesiastical career from his uncle, the cardinal, but following the latter's death in 1387 it was almost certainly royal patronage which secured the Glasgow precentorship for him and service at the papal court, Scotland having espoused the cause of Avignon during the schism, which brought him subsequent rewards. Wardlaw was provided to the bishopric of St Andrews, left vacant by the death of Walter Trail in 1401, by Benedict XIII on 10 September 1403, although his appointment was opposed by Chancellor Gilbert Greenlaw, bishop of Aberdeen, who was the candidate preferred by the duke of Albany, then governor of Scotland, and by the St Andrews Cathedral chapter. He was consecrated between 21 September and 4 October and returned to Scotland in the following year.

Robert III seems to have placed considerable trust in Wardlaw, as it was to him that he sent his son, the young Prince James, for safe keeping some time between 1404 and 1406. Albany's hostility caused Wardlaw to seek other political allies, and he made common cause with Sir David Fleming of Biggar and Cumbernauld and with Henry Sinclair, earl of Orkney. Orkney's sphere of influence was the south-east of Scotland; consequently relations with England were a matter of particular concern to all three men. When Henry Percy, earl of Northumberland, rebelled against Henry IV, Wardlaw, with Fleming and Orkney, provided Scottish support for the rebel earl, and Wardlaw received him in St Andrews Castle following his flight from England. So far was Wardlaw in his confidence that Northumberland left his grandson and heir, another Henry Percy, in the bishop's care, where he was educated alongside Prince James. This period was one of political ascendancy for Wardlaw, Orkney, and Fleming, as the king's closest councillors, but after the death of Robert III on 4 April 1406 and the subsequent appointment of Albany as governor of the realm Wardlaw of necessity turned his attention to ecclesiastical affairs.

St Andrews became the focus of Wardlaw's activities, and he seldom seems to have travelled far from the diocese. Walter Bower, a contemporary of Wardlaw, describes him as a gentle man, but censures him for entertaining on a lavish scale, spending far beyond his means. He certainly devoted considerable effort to restoring St Andrews Cathedral following a serious fire, sending ships to Prussia to fetch timber for the rebuilding, and he improved the route for pilgrims travelling to St Andrews by erecting the Guard Bridge over the mouth of the River Eden. That he concerned himself with trade is shown by the protests which Wardlaw lodged with Henry IV of England over a trading vessel returning to St Andrews from Flanders which was captured by the English in 1404; restitution had been secured by March 1405. In 1405 he received from Robert III a grant of the whole of the customs of St Andrews for himself and his episcopal successors, a significant advance on the one-third enjoyed by his predecessors.

Wardlaw's particular claim to fame is his establishment of St Andrews as the first university in Scotland, the first lectures being delivered, according to Bower, after Whitsunday 1410. On 28 February 1411 Wardlaw issued a charter referring to his foundation as a university, so taking advantage of his influence with Benedict XIII to anticipate papal acceptance; this duly followed in the form of a bull on 28 August 1413 which granted apostolic confirmation and authorized the university to teach theology, canon and civil law, arts, and medicine, and to confer degrees. Wardlaw was nominated chancellor of the new university, and his active interest in its affairs sometimes led to clashes with Laurence Lindores, the principal master of the arts faculty's pedagogy. In 1417 the election of Martin V brought the schism to an end, and by August 1418 the University of St Andrews had made its submission to him.

Wardlaw's influence with the papacy later waned somewhat. As a result of a dispute between Wardlaw and the abbey of Arbroath concerning procurations in 1420 Martin V exempted the abbey from the bishop's jurisdiction for a short time, showing that Wardlaw could no longer depend on papal support. He officiated at the coronation of James I, which took place at Scone on 21 May 1424, but he was not so closely identified with royal policy that St Andrews could not be regarded as appropriately neutral ground for the detention of the Albany Stewarts following their arrest in 1425, and he later failed to support James I in his stand against the papacy. For this defiance the king intervened in university politics, siding with Laurence Lindores against Wardlaw and attempting, unsuccessfully, to transfer the university from St Andrews to Perth. On 15 October 1431 it was to Wardlaw that the three estates entrusted the chest of money raised for the king's northern campaign, in preference to allowing James I direct access to the money for fear he would squander it. Wardlaw died in the castle of St Andrews on 6 April 1440 and was buried in the cathedral.   C. A. McGLADDERY

Sources D. E. R. Watt, *A biographical dictionary of Scottish graduates to AD 1410* (1977), 564–9 • E. R. Lindsay and A. I. Cameron, eds., *Calendar of Scottish supplications to Rome*, 1: 1418–1422, Scottish History Society, 3rd ser., 23 (1934) • W. Bower, *Scotichronicon*, ed. D. E. R. Watt and others, new edn, 9 vols. (1987–98), vol. 8 • *APS*, 1424–1567 • *CEPR letters*, vol. 7 • J. Raine, ed., *The correspondence, inventories, account rolls and law proceedings of Coldingham Priory*, SurtS, 12 (1841) • *The 'Original chronicle' of Andrew of Wyntoun*, ed. F. J. Amours, 2, STS, 1st ser., 50 (1903) • H. Boece, *The history and chronicles of Scotland*, trans. J. Bellenden, 2 vols. (1821)

Wardlaw, Ralph (1779–1853), Congregational minister and theologian, was born on 22 December 1779 in Dalkeith, near Edinburgh. He was the fourth of eight children of William Wardlaw (1741–1821), merchant and later a bailie of Glasgow, and his second wife, Anne Fisher (*d.* 1784), daughter of James Fisher, professor of divinity in the Associate Synod (popularly known as the Burgher church), a nonconformist Presbyterian denomination. The family moved to Glasgow six months after Ralph's birth, and his mother died in childbirth when he was only five. After attending the Glasgow grammar school (1787–91) Ralph matriculated at the University of Glasgow in October 1791, while not yet twelve years of age. From 1795 to 1800 he prepared for the ministry of the Associate Synod. The Associate Synod was at that time being split by a bitter dispute over the nature of the relationship between church and state. Alienated by the controversy, young Wardlaw was drawn to the Congregational church, which was then being revitalized in Scotland through the evangelistic work of the brothers Robert and James Haldane. Wardlaw joined the Congregational church in 1800, and soon gained recognition as a forceful evangelical preacher at meetings sponsored by the Haldanes. He had developed into a handsome, vigorous man of medium height and slim build, with a love for literature and poetry, and a gift for expressive language. The Congregationalists in Glasgow built a church for him on North Albion Street, and Wardlaw was ordained as its minister on 16 February 1803. Several months later, on 23 August 1803, he married his cousin, Jane Smith, the daughter of a Secession minister in Dunfermline. They would eventually have eleven children together, nine of whom survived to adulthood.

In 1808 the Congregational church in Scotland experienced a disruption when the Haldanes and their followers rejected the doctrine of infant baptism and seceded from the Congregational church, entering the Baptist church. It was a bitter break. Wardlaw, who had published a pamphlet in support of infant baptism the previous year, remained within the Congregational church. When in 1811 the Congregational church formed the Glasgow Theological Academy for the training of its ministers, Wardlaw was appointed professor of systematic theology, serving alongside his friend Greville Ewing, who taught biblical literature. Combining his professorship with his busy urban pastorate, he developed a reputation as both a forceful champion of orthodox reformed theology and an evangelical activist. In 1812 he took a leading role in the formation of the Glasgow auxiliary of the British and Foreign Bible Society, serving as its secretary for twenty-seven years. He worked to establish schools for the children of the labouring poor of Glasgow. His treatise on the doctrine of the atonement, published in 1814 in response to the Unitarian teaching, presented a lucid exposition of the care of the poor, rejecting compulsory assessments on property for poor relief and insisting that the care of the poor should be left to voluntary charitable societies. In May 1818 he travelled to London to preach one of the annual sermons on behalf of the London Missionary Society, which brought him acclaim from the English nonconformist community, and in September of that year he was granted a doctorate in divinity by Yale College in the United States. His growing Glasgow congregation erected a large new chapel, with an imposing Grecian front and accommodation for 1600, which was opened late in 1819.

A long-standing opponent of slavery, Wardlaw was one of the founders of the Glasgow Anti-Slavery Society in 1823. He came to reject the moderate anti-slavery position that the abolition of slavery should be a gradual process. In November 1830 he delivered a powerful speech before the Glasgow Anti-Slavery Society, in which he demanded the immediate abolition of slavery. This was a courageous position to take in Glasgow, which had long-standing trading connections with the West Indies. The speech led to the break-up of old friendships, a decline in attendance at his church, and personal attacks upon him in the press. Although his health collapsed under the strain in the spring of 1831, he would not relent in his advocacy of immediate abolition.

The following year saw the beginning of the voluntary movement in Scotland, with a number of leading nonconformists calling for the disestablishment and disendowment of the Church of Scotland. Religion, the voluntaries argued, should be placed on a purely voluntary basis, with all denominations enjoying equal status before the law and none having a connection with the state. Wardlaw became active in the voluntary movement from the autumn of 1832, speaking at public meetings, and in 1833 he was elected president of the Voluntary Church Association. For him voluntarism was a matter of religious principle, and he refused to engage in invective against the established church. In 1838 he was a member of a deputation from the Scottish central board of dissenters sent to London to lobby politicians against the proposal to grant public money for building new churches in connection with the establishment. The following year, at the invitation of representatives of the main English nonconformist denominations, Wardlaw presented a series of lectures on voluntarism in London—in response to the lectures given in support of establishments by his fellow Scot, the celebrated Thomas Chalmers, in 1838. His fellow nonconformists heralded Wardlaw's lectures as a triumph, and some 14,000 copies of the lectures were sold within a few months.

In the mid-1840s Wardlaw turned his attention from disestablishment to protestant church union, taking an active part in the Evangelical Alliance, formed in 1845, and contributing (alongside his former opponent Chalmers) to the influential collection *Essays on Christian Union* published that same year. His last years were troubled by controversy, as in 1849 a faction within his congregation charged him with having misused his pastoral connection with an elderly widow thirty years before to obtain a gift of money. He successfully defended his reputation, but the attack had pained him deeply. Wardlaw died in his home in Easterhouse, Glasgow, on 17 December 1853, and received a public funeral. He was buried at the Glasgow necropolis on 23 December. A figure of courage, eloquence, and learning, Wardlaw contributed significantly to the growth of religious and political liberalism in Britain.   STEWART J. BROWN

Sources R. Wardlaw, *Posthumous works*, 8 vols. (1861–2) • W. L. Alexander, *Memoirs of the life and writings of Ralph Wardlaw, D.D.* (1856) • R. Wardlaw, *Systematic theology*, ed. J. R. Campbell, 3 vols. (1856) • R. Wardlaw, *Discourses on the principal points of the Socinian controversy* (1814) • R. Wardlaw, *National church establishments examined* (1839) • *DNB*

Archives U. Edin. L., corresp. | DWL, corresp. relating to Dublin Theological Academy
Likenesses D. Macnee, oils, 1851, Corporation Art Gallery, Glasgow • J. Andrews, stipple, NPG • J. Faed, engraving (after portrait by by D. Macnee), Scot. NPG • H. Haig, engraving (after portrait by by W. Bonner), Scot. NPG • D. Macnee, ink and wash drawing, Scot. NPG • G. B. Shaw, engraving (after drawing by H. Anelay), Scot. NPG
Wealth at death £1732 16s.: inventory, 1854, NA Scot., SC 36/48/40, fols. 187–8

Wardlaw, Walter (*c.*1320–1387), bishop of Glasgow and cardinal, was possibly the son of Henry Wardlaw, who possessed half of the barony of Wilton, Roxburghshire; his mother, according to later tradition, was the daughter of Sir James Stewart of Durrisdeer, a cousin of King Robert II. He was also related to Gilbert Wardlaw, an Edinburgh burgess. From the later 1330s until the mid-1350s Wardlaw attended Paris University. He obtained several degrees including a doctorate of theology by 1358. In addition to his studies and teaching responsibilities, Wardlaw served periodically as regent in arts and as proctor of the English nation, and in 1345 as university rector. He has been credited with authorship of works which no longer survive, including a history of his family and others entitled *De fallacia astrologorum* and *De inani divinationum vititarum scientia*.

Academic prestige did little to augment Wardlaw's financial resources. Among the poorest class of student in 1341, his ecclesiastical advancement was initially limited. He held a canonry of Glasgow by 1344 and, together with this, successively the parishes of Dunino, Fife, by 1349 and Errol, Perthshire, by 1351. It was not until after the conclusion of his university career that more lucrative benefices followed. By 1359 he had been appointed archdeacon of Lothian (the southern part of the diocese of St Andrews), and in 1366 he won Edward III's approval to exercise his office in the English-controlled parts of the archdeaconry. He also obtained canonries in Aberdeen, Moray, and Ross. In part this advancement reflected the patronage of William Landel, bishop of St Andrews, whose family were Roxburghshire neighbours of the Wardlaws of Wilton. Wardlaw presided at Landel's funeral at St Andrews in 1385, which was delayed until his arrival. It was perhaps also Landel's influence which led to Wardlaw's appointment as royal secretary. He held this position from at least May 1363 and probably until 1367. From 1359, but especially when secretary, he regularly witnessed royal charters and served on embassies to England, often with Landel. It was probably with David II's support that Wardlaw was elected bishop of Glasgow, his consecration taking place at Avignon in 1367, probably in April.

Wardlaw's domestic political prominence declined following Robert II's accession in 1371. He assisted in the negotiation of the Franco-Scottish alliance of 1371 but spent the ensuing five years at the papal court, returning to Avignon periodically afterwards, notably in the immediate aftermath of the schism of 1378. It is possible that having been a leading agent of David II, he deliberately chose to distance himself thus from the new king, with whom his relations may have been uneasy. So rarely was he seen in Scotland that rumours of his death in 1374 prompted the seizure of his moveable goods. On 23 December 1383, while Wardlaw was briefly home, Pope Clement VII appointed him a cardinal, the first ever from Scotland. He continued to act as bishop of Glasgow *in commendam*, but also resumed his diplomatic career, visiting Berwick in 1380 to conclude an Anglo-Scottish truce; Vincennes in 1383 to conclude another Franco-Scottish alliance; and Leulinghen in 1384 to represent Scottish interests at the international conference there. The exact date and place of Wardlaw's death are unknown. He witnessed a charter at Edinburgh on 22 May 1387 and was dead by 20 September following. Sixteenth-century sources place his death on 21 or 23 August.

DAVID DITCHBURN

Sources D. E. R. Watt, *A biographical dictionary of Scottish graduates to AD 1410* (1977), 569–75 · C. Burns, ed., *Papal letters to Scotland of Clement VII of Avignon*, Scottish History Society, 4th ser., 12 (1976) · *RotS*, vols. 1–2 · G. Burnett and others, eds., *The exchequer rolls of Scotland*, 2 (1878) · *CDS*, vols. 4–5 · W. Bower, *Scotichronicon*, ed. D. E. R. Watt and others, new edn, 9 vols. (1987–98), vols. 6–9 · J. C. Gibson, *The Wardlaws in Scotland* (1912) · G. W. S. Barrow and others, eds., *Regesta regum Scottorum*, 6, ed. B. Webster (1982) · J. M. Thomson and others, eds., *Registrum magni sigilli regum Scotorum / The register of the great seal of Scotland*, 2nd edn, 1, ed. T. Thomson (1912) · Andrew of Wyntoun, *The orygynale cronykil of Scotland*, [rev. edn], ed. D. Laing, 3 vols. (1872–9) · C. Innes, ed., *Registrum episcopatus Glasguensis*, 2 vols., Bannatyne Club, 75 (1843); also pubd as 2 vols., Maitland Club, 61 (1843) · A. D. M. Barrell, *The papacy, Scotland and northern England, 1342–1378* (1995) · S. I. Boardman, *The early Stewart kings: Robert II and Robert III, 1371–1406* (1996) · W. H. Bliss, ed., *Calendar of entries in the papal registers relating to Great Britain and Ireland: petitions to the pope* (1896) · *CEPR letters*, vol. 4

Wardlaw, William (1892–1958), chemist, was born on 29 March 1892 at Newcastle upon Tyne, the elder son of William Wardlaw, a journeyman joiner, and his wife, Margaret Kirkup. He was educated at Rutherford College (1904–10) and then Armstrong (later King's) College, University of Durham (1910–15). He obtained his BSc in 1913. His early research interest was in inorganic chemistry, for which he was awarded a special prize and an honourable mention (as a result of his submission for the Friere-Marecco prize and medal in 1913); he obtained an 1851 Exhibition scholarship in 1915. His first major series of papers dealt with the oxidizing properties of sulphur dioxide, for which he was awarded the DSc.

Although he volunteered for military service during the First World War, Wardlaw was transferred to the army reserve and employed as a chemist by the Ministry of Munitions. He started his academic career in 1918 when he was employed as an assistant lecturer and demonstrator in chemistry at the University of Birmingham. He was promoted to lecturer in 1921, and senior lecturer eight years later. His career at Birmingham was interrupted by a bout of tuberculosis, but treatment led to a complete recovery. During his time in the city he was married twice, first, on 16 August 1921, to Margaret Emily Griffin from Knaresborough, who died in 1930, and second, in 1932, to Doris Whitfield, a former student of his who had first-class honours in chemistry. There were no children from the first marriage, a daughter from the second.

In 1937 Wardlaw was appointed to the chair in physical chemistry tenable at Birkbeck College in the University of London, where he remained until his retirement in 1957, when he was honoured with the title of professor emeritus. During the Second World War he served on the staff of the central register of the Ministry of Labour and in 1941–5 as a member, on behalf of the Ministry of Production, of the scientific advisory committee of the war cabinet. From 1944 until his death Wardlaw held a part-time appointment as scientific adviser to the technical and scientific register. He was created CBE in 1949.

Wardlaw's contributions to chemistry came as a researcher, teacher, administrator, and active member of professional organizations, through which he sought to promote the importance of chemistry as a discipline which extended well beyond the university laboratory. After initial investigations into inorganic oxidation processes and contributions to the chemistry of molybdenum he became interested in the stereochemistry of metal complexes. He later combined this interest with research into the esters of transition metals, building up an active research school at Birkbeck. This research influenced the development of ideas on the relationship between physical properties and molecular structure.

Colleagues regarded Wardlaw as a sympathetic teacher, who directed considerable energy to the production of the next generation of scientists, and was ready to offer enthusiastic encouragement to deserving students. A reflection of this interest was his willingness to act as external examiner to eleven different universities during the latter years of his career, and his involvement with the national certificates in chemistry in 1940–57. As an administrator he had first to overcome the difficulties of working in cramped conditions before overseeing the move of his department to new quarters in Bloomsbury, where he was able to plan and equip new laboratories, to increase the number of staff and expand research activities.

Involvement with professional organizations started early, and Wardlaw's membership of the Society of Chemical Industry dated from 1917. He was actively involved with the Royal Institute of Chemistry, serving on the council twice (1929–32 and 1933–6), as an examiner for the associateship in 1936–51, and as president from 1957 until his death. He was honorary secretary of the Chemical Society in 1940–48, and president in 1954–6. In 1952 he presided over the meetings of Section B (chemistry) of the British Association, and from 1955 served as its general secretary. Wardlaw died at his home, 13 Hillersdon Avenue, Edgware, on 19 December 1958, survived by his wife. His remains were cremated on 23 December 1958 at Golders Green crematorium.

SALLY M. HORROCKS

Sources *DNB* · *Nature*, 183 (1959), 505 · *The Times* (20 Dec 1958) · *Chemistry and Industry* (10 Jan 1959) · *Journal of the Royal Institute of Chemistry*, 83 (1959), 1–2 · 'Our new president', *Journal of the Royal Institute of Chemistry*, 81 (1957), 258 · *WWW, 1951–60* · m. cert. [Margaret Emily Griffin]

Likenesses photograph, repro. in *Proceedings of the Chemical Society* (Nov 1961), 398 · photograph, repro. in *Royal Institute of Chemistry Journal* · photograph, Royal Society of Chemistry, London

Wealth at death £24,806 15s. 5d.: probate, 2 March 1959, *CGPLA Eng. & Wales*

Wardle, Gwyllym Lloyd (1761?–1833), soldier and politician, born at Chester, was the only son of Francis Wardle JP, of Hartsheath, near Mold in Flintshire, and his wife, Catherine, daughter and heir of Richard Lloyd Gwyllym of Hartsheath. He was at Harrow School in 1775, but left through ill health. He was afterwards educated in the school of George Henry Glasse at Greenford, near Ealing, Middlesex, and was admitted pensioner at St John's College, Cambridge, on 12 February 1780, but did not take a degree. After travelling on the continent, he settled at Hartsheath. In November 1792 he married Ellen Elizabeth Parry, daughter of Love Parry of Madryn, Caernarvonshire, who brought him considerable estates in that county, and to whom he was frequently unfaithful, especially in London; they had seven children. Wardle became a partner of W. A. Madocks in the development of Porthmadog.

When Sir Watkin Williams Wynn raised a troop of dragoons, officially called 'the ancient British light dragoons', and popularly known as 'Wynn's lambs', Wardle served in the troop, accompanied it to Ireland, and is said to have fought at Vinegar Hill. At the Peace of Amiens the troop was disbanded, and Wardle, who desired in vain to be incorporated with the regular forces, retired with the rank of lieutenant-colonel.

About 1804 Wardle rented Green Park Place, Bath, and is said by William Farquharson, in a pamphlet on him, to have been concerned in a gin distillery in Jersey. He was resident at Bath when he was elected for Okehampton in 1807; he was at the head of the poll with 113 votes, and is said to have been returned without the support of the borough's patron. He voted against the government in most of the divisions in 1808, and developed an interest in corruption in army contracts, naming Frederick, duke of York. The next year he took this further, introducing the name of the duke's former mistress, Mary Anne *Clarke. His motion led to an investigation by the whole house on 1 February 1809, which lasted until 20 March, with huge public interest focused on the saucy and resourceful Mrs Clarke. With whig support, and despite initial setbacks, Wardle pressed his case and secured the duke's resignation as commander-in-chief, a remarkable achievement for a recently elected back-bencher. He followed up his triumph with a programme of retrenchment, presented in a three-hour speech on 19 June 1809; his resolutions were accepted by ministers who knew they were impractical.

This was the crowning point in Wardle's popularity. The freedom of the City of London was voted to him on 6 April 1809, and congratulatory addresses were presented to him by many corporations throughout the kingdom. A medallion with a striking likeness of him was published by Bisset of Birmingham, and portraits and engravings of him were widely sold. By the following summer his popularity was gone. An upholsterer, Francis Wright, brought an action against him on 3 July for alleged non-payment of a bill for furnishing Mrs Clarke's house. The attorney-general led the prosecution, making clear the government's intention to destroy Wardle. It emerged that he had had negotiations with Mrs Clarke about the duke before launching his parliamentary attack. She alleged he had bought her testimony with a promise to furnish her house. The jury found against him. Wardle brought, on 11 December, an action against the Wrights and Mrs Clarke for conspiracy, but it failed. In 1810 Mrs Clarke's *The Rival Princes* portrayed the whole affair as a conspiracy organized by the duke of Kent, with Wardle in his confidence. Charles Williams Wynn gave this assessment of Wardle in August 1810:

> until last year I had no doubt of his honour or integrity. He had lived certainly rather a debauched life but not more so than many others … Wardle may be a rogue but I am sure he is also an enthusiast and blinds himself to his own misconduct. (HoP, *Commons*)

Wardle voted against the duke of York's reinstatement on 11 June 1811, but was not re-elected at the dissolution in 1812 (a Westminster politician named Brooks is said to have raised a subscription of £4000 for him). He withdrew to a farm between Tunbridge Wells and Rochester, taking, as Mrs Clarke said, 'to selling milk about Tunbridge'. About 1815, in severe financial difficulties, he went abroad, and settled in Florence. An address, *Colonel Wardle to his Countrymen*, arguing for Catholic emancipation, was circulated in 1828; it was dated 'Florence, 3 Nov 1827', and referred to the happy conditions of life in Catholic Tuscany. He died in Florence on 30 November 1833, aged seventy-one. W. P. COURTNEY, rev. H. C. G. MATTHEW

Sources HoP, *Commons* · M. A. Clarke, *Authentic memoirs* (c.1809) · W. H. Reid, *Memoirs of the life of Colonel Wardle* (1809) · M. A. Clarke, *The rival princes* (1810) · F. Wright, *The trial at large between Francis Wright … and G. L. Wardle* (1809) · G. L. Wardle, *The trial of Colonel Wardle* (1809) · J. Drakard, *Public and private life of Col. Wardle* (1810?) · T. Farquharson, *Truth in pursuit of Wardle* (1810) · I. McCalman, *Radical underworld: prophets, revolutionaries, and pornographers in London, 1795–1840* (1988); pbk edn (1993)
Archives Clwyd RO · Flintshire RO, Hawarden, legal papers · NL Wales · U. Wales, Bangor, papers | Berks. RO, letters among papers relating to the trafficking in commissions scandal · NRA, Hartsheath MSS
Likenesses J. Bisset, medallion, 1809 · A. W. Devis, oils, 1809, NPG · J. Hopwood, stipple, pubd 1809 (after Armstrong), BM, NPG; for a report of the trial of the duke of York · T. Rowlandson, sketch, 1809? · C. Turner, mezzotint, pubd 1809 (after bust by P. Tunerelli), BM, NPG · stipple, BM, NPG

Wardle, Sir Thomas (1831–1909), silk dyer and printer, was born on 26 January 1831 in Macclesfield, Cheshire, the eldest son of Joshua and Mary Wardle. He received his early education in Macclesfield before attending Leek grammar school, and later went to work in the dyeworks at Leekbrook which his father had established in 1831. On 14 April 1857 he married Elizabeth (d. 1902), the daughter of Hugh Wardle, a chemist, of Overton Bank, Leek. They originally lived at Cheddleton Heath, but in 1866 moved to Leek, first to 62 and later to 54 St Edward's Street, a dignified Georgian house. They had fourteen children, nine of whom survived their father.

In 1872 Wardle acquired the Hencroft dyeworks in the town of Leek, and later established the Churnet works close by. These dyeworks benefited from the waters of the River Churnet, which were particularly clean and soft and possessed exceptional dyeing properties, particularly for the raven black dye, on account of the presence of unique chemical constituents which reacted to produce a deep blue-black when treated with tannic acid and iron salts. Wardle also helped found the Leek Spun Silk Company in 1882, which produced yarn and sewing thread from silk waste for the recently invented sewing machine. Leek was then the only town in England producing such silk sewing thread.

William Morris sought Wardle's advice on working with vegetable dyes such as madder, woad, and indigo, which had fallen into disuse following the invention of aniline dyes in 1856. Wardle employed dyers who had direct experience of them, and in the years 1875 to 1877 Morris came to experiment at the Hencroft dyeworks frequently, lodging at Wardle's house. By 1878 Wardle was printing fourteen of Morris's designs on silk and cotton. He also printed designs by other well-known designers, such as Walter Crane. Later Wardle and his son Thomas designed printed fabrics themselves, notably 'Ajunta', 'Primula', and 'Tomato'. Between 1883 and 1888 he had his own fabric shop at 71 New Bond Street, London, while his wife ran the Leek Embroidery Society shop in Leek which she had established in 1879.

By 1872 Wardle had succeeded in first bleaching and then dyeing the wild, or tussore, silk of India, previously of limited use because of its brown colour. His success with tussore stemmed from his microscopic analysis of the structure of silk, which revealed the differences between the coarser, flatter tussore fibre and the rounder, thinner one produced by the domesticated silkworm (*Bombyx mori*). He exhibited hanks of dyed tussore and woven samples at the Paris Exhibition of 1878, and it was soon widely used in the west Yorkshire waste silk industry for the manufacture of sealcloth and plush, both of which were short-pile fabrics. Tussore made good embroidery thread with a glassy sheen, which was extensively used by the Leek Embroidery Society. It was also cheaper than many other silks.

Wardle was keen to promote Indian silks, principally to avoid dependence on raw silks from Italy, France, China, and Japan. Asked by the secretary of state for India to report on the condition of Indian sericulture and the commercial possibilities of tussore silk, he visited Bengal in 1885. There he found that 60 per cent of silkworms died from pebrine disease and that most of the silk reeling was of uneven quality. He collected Indian silk fabrics for display in the silk culture court of the Indian and Colonial Exhibition of 1886 and in the Manchester Jubilee Exhibition of 1887, where he was chairman of the silk section. In that year he was a founder of the Silk Association of Great Britain and Ireland and served as president. The following year he also helped to form the Ladies' National Silk Association.

Wardle worked constantly to improve the Indian silk industry, particularly in Bengal and Kashmir, and was authorized by the India Office to visit Italy and France in 1897 to compare their silk-reeling equipment. He arranged for both the Italian Tavelette Keller and the French Chambon reeling machines, which produced a smoother and more even thread, to be sent to India, and he ensured that silkworm eggs guaranteed free of disease were sent from France to India annually. In 1904 he visited Kashmir, where he saw for himself the newly erected sericulture houses and filatures that he had recommended. As a result of these measures the quality of the Indian raw silk improved considerably and greater amounts were exported to England.

In recognition of his contribution to the Paris Exhibition of 1878, Wardle was made a knight of the Légion d'honneur and an officer of the Académie Royale des Sciences, and in 1897 he received a knighthood for his services to the English and Indian silk industries.

In 1884 Wardle provided an extensive report on the English silk industry. Having visited the continental silk centres, he recognized the need to raise the standard of British silk manufacture by the establishment of technical schools in order to withstand foreign competition. The report contained comparative statistical data relating to the English silk towns and also to countries such as France, Italy, India, China, and Japan.

Wardle firmly believed in trade protection and, to prove his point, compared the success of the silk industry in America with its depressed condition in Britain, noting in 1908 that the American industry was protected by a 50 per cent import duty, whereas the last vestiges of British protection had gone in 1860.

A keen geologist, Wardle wrote on the geology of the Leek district, the Roaches, Shutlingslow, in Cheshire, Cromer, in Norfolk and Kashmir. A fossil fern bears his name. He was a member of many societies, including the Geological Society, the Chemical Society, the Statistical Society, and the North Staffordshire Field Club, and gave numerous lectures on silk dyeing, sericulture, arts and crafts, bacteriology, and his own method of sewage disposal, to various technical colleges and associations.

Wardle was an active member of the Church of England, and composed music for the canticles and hymns for his daughter's marriage service. Shortly before his death he donated a new chancel to Warslow church, near to his country home at Swainsley Hall, some 8 miles from Leek. Here he spent weekends fishing on the River Manifold and shooting. Politically Wardle was a Conservative. He served as a justice of the peace, a member of the North Staffordshire Railway Company, and a president of the Leek United Benefit Building Society.

Four of Wardle's sons became dyers and printers employed by their father: Gilbert Charles worked at Leekbrook with his cousin Horace; Arthur Henry was employed at the Churnet works; and Bernard and Thomas were at Hencroft. The fifth son, Frederick Darlington, became the town clerk of Bath. After her mother's death the eldest daughter, Lydia, took over the Leek Embroidery Society.

Wardle died at his house in Leek on 3 January 1909, aged seventy-seven, and was buried in Cheddleton churchyard on 7 January. The *Leek Post* described him as 'a man endowed with an indomitable perseverance ... who pursued the ideals he had set before himself with a pertinacity which no obstacles could quench' (*Leek Post*, 9 Jan 1909).

SARAH BUSH

Sources T. Wardle, *Kashmir: its new silk industry* (1904) • F. Warner, *The silk industry of the United Kingdom: its origin and development* (1921) • T. Wardle, *On the history and growing utilisations of tussur silk* (1891) • *The Field* (9 Jan 1909) • *Textile Recorder* (15 Jan 1909) • *The Times* (8 Jan 1909) • *Leek Post* (9 Jan 1909) • *Staffordshire Sentinel* (9 Jan 1909) • T. Wardle, correspondence with William Morris, 1875–7, Staffs. RO, D618 [copy of typescript of 61 letters] • 'Royal commission on technical instruction: second report', *Parl. papers* (1884), 31.xxix-cvi, C. 3981-II [Eng. silk industry] • T. Wardle, *Royal Jubilee Exhibition, Manchester, 1887: descriptive catalogue of the silk section* (1887) [exhibition catalogue, Manchester, 1887] • T. Wardle, *Royal commission and government of India silk culture court: descriptive catalogue* (1886) [exhibition catalogue, Colonial and Indian Exhibition, 1886] • priv. coll. • A. Jacques, *The Wardle story* (1996) • L. Parry, *William Morris textiles* (1983) • A. Jacques, 'Thomas Wardle and the Kashmir silk industry', *Staffordshire Studies*, 6 (1994) • *Leek Post* (July 1976) • C. Woods, 'Wardle, Sir Thomas', *DBB* • G. C. Wardle, 'Memoir of Sir Thomas Wardle', *Journal of Indian Art and Industry*, 13 (Oct 1909), 5 • *Leek Post* (28 Nov 1908) • *Royal commission on tariff reform* (1904) • *Art Journal*, new ser., 11 (1891) • m. cert. • d. cert. • baptismal record, Sutton, near Macclesfield, St George's chapel, 1831

Archives Duke U., Perkins L., corresp. • Leek Library, Leek, Staffordshire • NRA, priv. coll., Sir Thomas Wardle and Arthur Wardle MSS • Staffs. RO, Joshua Wardle MSS • V&A • Whitworth Art Gallery, Manchester, Wardle collection of printed fabrics

Likenesses W. H. Horne, photograph, repro. in *Leek Post* (Jan 1909) • attrib. Sandeman of Leek, photograph, repro. in *The Field* • photograph, repro. in *Textile Recorder* • photograph, repro. in Wardle, *Kashmir and the new silk industry*, frontispiece

Wealth at death £50,376 19s. 6d.: resworn probate, 26 March 1909, *CGPLA Eng. & Wales*

Wardley, Jane (*fl.* 1747–1770), a founder of the Shakers, is an elusive figure, as the dates of her birth, marriage, and death, and the names of her parents are unknown. She was a tailor who lived with her husband, James Wardley, also a tailor, in Bolton in the 1740s. In 1747 the Wardleys founded a group of religious enthusiasts influenced by Quakerism, Methodism, and the French prophets. The sect combined fervent millennial theology with bodily manifestations of spiritual ecstasy described by an observer in 1769 as gradually accelerated 'trembling, shaking and screeching ... at the same time their features are not distinguishable by reason of the quick motion of their heads' (Morse, 3). According to members of the group they might meditate silently until 'they were seized with a mighty trembling' or 'singing, shouting, and leaping for joy', sometimes 'swiftly passing and repassing each other, like clouds agitated with a mighty wind' (Green and Wells, 5). Outsiders derisively termed them 'Shaking Quakers' or 'Shakers'. Jane Wardley, or 'Mother Jane', was acknowledged as the more spiritually gifted of the couple. She encouraged her followers to practise public confession of sin, and celibacy, or at least celibacy within marriage.

The Wardleys devoted themselves to the nurture of their band of believers, frequently worshipping several times a day. The sect met first in Bolton and later in Manchester, Maretown, and other locations in Lancashire and Cheshire. At the invitation of one of their followers, a bricklayer named John Townley, the Wardleys moved into his spacious home on Cannon Street in Manchester. In 1758 the thirty-member Shaker group was joined by a 22-year-old woman, Ann Lee (1736–1784). At some time in 1766 Ann Lee approached Mother Jane with a problem: the deaths of her four children bore out her conviction that sexual intercourse was always sinful. Jane Wardley reportedly told Ann Lee 'James and I lodge together: but we do not touch each other any more than two babes. You may return home and do likewise' (*Testimonies*, 38).

Jane Wardley saw the doctrinal ground of Shakerism shift after Ann Lee was released from a prison stay in 1770. While imprisoned Ann Lee had experienced a vision outlining the centrality of celibacy to Shaker theology. After that time the Wardleys deferred to the spiritual leadership of Ann Lee and saw their adherents drift away, discouraged by Lee's more rigorous insistence on public confession and celibacy. Ann Lee and eight followers emigrated to America in 1774, and most remaining English Shakers abandoned the faith, including the Wardleys' patron, John Townley. According to the nineteenth-century historian William Axon the Wardleys moved into an almshouse and died there, at unknown dates. Jane Wardley certainly died before Ann Lee's own death in 1784 because Ann Lee told her American followers 'I have seen Jane in the world of spirits, praising God in the dance' (Evans, 154). By the time the Shaker apostate Thomas Brown published a history of the Shakers in 1812 Jane Wardley was viewed by the Shakers as a female John the Baptist, whose role was 'to prepare the way for the second appearing of Christ, in the order of the female [Ann Lee]' (Brown, 312).

TERRIE DOPP AAMODT

Sources W. E. A. Axon, *Lancashire gleanings* (1883), 79–107 • T. Brown, *An account of the people called Shakers* (1812) • *Testimonies of the life, character, revelations and doctrines of Mother Ann Lee and the elders with her*, ed. R. Bishop and S. Y. Wells, 2nd edn (New York, 1888) • F. W. Evans, *Shakers: compendium of the origin, history, principles, rules and regulations, government, and doctrines of the United Society of Believers in Christ's second appearing* (New York, 1859) • C. Green and S. Wells, eds., *A summary view of the Millennial Church, or United Society of Believers (commonly called Shakers)* (1823) • F. Morse, *The Shakers and the world's people* (1980) • C. Garrett, *Spirit possession and popular religion* (1987)

Wealth at death died in an almshouse: Axon, *Lancashire gleanings*

Wardrop, James (1782–1869), surgeon, the youngest child of James Wardrop (1738–1830) and his wife, Marjory, daughter of Andrew Marjoribanks, of Marjoriebanks, Dumfriesshire, was born on 14 August 1782 at Torbane Hill, Linlithgow, a small property which had been in the family for generations. Wardrop was educated first under a Mr Stalker and then at Edinburgh high school from the age of seven. In 1797 he was apprenticed to his uncle, Andrew Wardrop (1752–1823), a surgeon in Edinburgh. He also assisted John Barclay, the anatomist, and he was appointed house surgeon at the Royal Infirmary, Edinburgh, at the age of nineteen.

Wardrop went to London in 1801 to attend the lectures of John Abernethy, Henry Cline, and Astley Cooper, and to see work at St Thomas's, Guy's, and St George's hospitals.

In May 1803 he went to Paris, and though English residents in France were treated at the time as prisoners of war, he evaded the police and, after a few months, escaped to Vienna, where Georg Joseph Beer's teaching first interested him in ophthalmic surgery. He returned to Edinburgh, and was admitted FRCS (Edinburgh) in 1804. He practised surgery there for a time, studying especially pathology and diseases of the eye, and was active in the formation of the museum of the Royal College of Surgeons.

As there was no immediate opening for Wardrop in Edinburgh, he went to London in April 1808; he first took rooms in York Street, and then rented 2 Charles Street, St James's Square, where he lived until his death. He married, in 1813, Margaret, a daughter of Colonel George Dalrymple, a lineal descendant of the earl of Stair, and they had four sons and a daughter.

In London Wardrop was admitted MRCS without examination in 1814, the master, Sir Everard Home, saying that Wardrop's published works were quite sufficient to entitle him to the diploma. He became FRCS (England) in 1843; the honorary degree of MD had been conferred upon him by the University of St Andrews in 1834. In September 1818 he was appointed surgeon-extraordinary to the prince regent, and in 1823, when the latter visited Scotland as George IV, he attended him on the journey.

Wardrop had practised for many years among the poor by giving advice chiefly at his own house. In 1826, with William Willocks Sleigh, he founded a hospital in Nutford Place, Edgware Road, called the West London Hospital of Surgery. It was not only a charitable institution, but it was free to every member of the medical profession. On one day each week operations of importance were done and a clinical discussion followed. The hospital's expenses were met mainly by Wardrop, who reluctantly had to close it at the end of ten years.

In 1826 Wardrop and William Lawrence gave a course of lectures on surgery at the Aldersgate Street school of medicine, and after Lawrence went to St Bartholomew's Hospital, Wardrop for a few seasons gave these lectures alone. He joined the Great Windmill Street School as a lecturer on surgery about 1835.

Wardrop took a leading part in the discussions on the state of the medical profession, and he was an active supporter of the liberal policy advocated by Thomas Wakley. In 1825-6 *The Lancet* published a series of letters from Wardrop, written under the pen name of Brutus, which attacked the way the College of Surgeons was organized. Wardrop also quarrelled with Robert Liston over bloodletting, Liston saying that patients should lose as little blood as possible, Wardrop the opposite.

Wardrop succeeded Astley Cooper as surgeon-in-ordinary to the king in 1828, and he declined a baronetcy shortly afterwards. Circumstances which occurred during the last illness of George IV convinced Wardrop that he was unfairly treated by several of his medical colleagues who were attached to the court, and after the king's death in 1830 he avoided their circles. Indeed, he took the matter much to heart, and exacted revenge by writing a series of anonymous 'Intercepted letters' for *The Lancet*. They claimed to contain confidential details of events communicated by Henry Halford, Benjamin Collins Brodie, and William MacMichael, librarian of the Royal College of Physicians. Scurrilous though they are, they are well written and amusing. However, when it leaked out that Wardrop was the author he was 'regarded as a "pariah" by men who could do much either to benefit or ruin him' (Clarke, 338), and he lost much of his practice.

Wardrop was celebrated not as an operator but as a diagnostician and a medical writer, and it is both as a surgeon cardiologist and as an ophthalmologist that he is remembered. He was, however, the first surgeon in England to remove a tumour of the lower jaw by total vertical section of the bone, and he carried out and modified Pierre Brasdor's operation for peripheral aneurysm (blood-filled sac) by distal ligature—that is, by tying the artery on the side of the aneurysm farthest from the heart (*On Aneurysm*, 1828). His treatise *On the Nature and Treatment of Diseases of the Heart* (1837, 1851) was never regarded as authoritative, but his ophthalmic works show 'shrewdness and enthusiasm … and testify to the brilliance of their author' (Albert and Robinson, 907). In sympathetic ophthalmitis, the germ of the idea of prophylactic enucleation of the eye to prevent the spread to the unaffected eye came from Wardrop, who had veterinary experience of the disease in horses and had treated the prince regent's horse. Wardrop himself had an exotropic left eye (wall eye). He coined the term 'keratitis' for inflammation of the cornea, and had a partial understanding of glaucoma. His publications in ophthalmology included his two-volume *Essays on the Morbid Anatomy of the Human Eye* (3 edns, 1808–34), a work on eye diseases of the horse (1819), and two papers. Wardrop also edited the works of Matthew Baillie in 1825, and prefixed to it a biographical sketch of the author.

A tall, thin man, Wardrop was vain and self-opinionated, and fond of scandal and gossip. However, his social gifts, family connections, knowledge of horses, and love of field sports brought him both friendly acquaintance and patients from the aristocracy. He collected art, though much of his collection was sold later in his life. He died at his house, 2 Charles Street, St James's Square, on 13 February 1869.   D'A. POWER, *rev.* JEAN LOUDON

Sources *Medical Times and Gazette* (20 Feb 1869), 207–8 • J. F. Clarke, *Autobiographical recollections of the medical profession* (1874) • 'Intercepted letters', *The Lancet* (5 Oct 1833) • 'Intercepted letters', *The Lancet* (28 Nov 1835) • 'Intercepted letters', *The Lancet* (5 Dec 1835) • *The Lancet* (20 Feb 1869), 280–81 • D. M. Albert and N. Robinson, 'James Wardrop: a brief review …', *Transactions of the Ophthalmological Societies of the United Kingdom*, 94 (1974), 892–908 • R. K. Blach, 'Prophylactic enucleation in sympathetic ophthalmitis', *Medical History*, 15 (1971), 190–92 • T. J. Pettigrew, *Medical portrait gallery: biographical memoirs of the most celebrated physicians, surgeons … who have contributed to the advancement of medical science*, 4 vols. in 2 [1838–40], vol. 2 • V. G. Plarr, *Plarr's Lives of the fellows of the Royal College of Surgeons of England*, rev. D'A. Power, 2 vols. (1930) • private information (1899) • B. Hill, 'A pioneer in surgery: James Wardrop, MD, FRCS, 1782–1869', *The Practitioner*, 202 (1969), 302–6 • I. Aird, *A companion in surgical studies*, 2nd edn (1956), 186 • F. H. Garrison, *An introduction to the history of medicine*, 4th edn (1929), 342 • P. J. Wallis

and R. V. Wallis, *Eighteenth century medics*, 2nd edn (1988) · I. Waddington, *The medical profession in the industrial revolution* (1984)
Likenesses R. Frain, oils; formerly in possession of son, H. D. H. Wardrop · A. Geddes, oils, Royal College of Surgeons of Edinburgh · T. M. Joy, oils, Scot. NPG · J. Thompson, stipple (after A. Geddes), BM, NPG; repro. in Pettigrew, *Medical portrait gallery*
Wealth at death under £1500: resworn probate, Feb 1870, *CGPLA Eng. & Wales* (1869)

Wardrop, Marjory Scott (1869–1909), Georgian scholar and translator, was born on 26 November 1869 at 41 Canton Street, Poplar, London, the only daughter and youngest of the three children of Thomas Caldwell Wardrop (1836–1903), a joiner and partner in a building firm, and his wife, Marjory Cameron Scott (1837–1918); both parents were Scottish. The family moved to Chislehurst, and she was educated there and at Eastbourne in private schools, where she learned French, German, and Latin. She later became fluent in Russian and Romanian; it is, however, for her mastery of Georgian that she was distinguished.

The Kingdom of Georgia (1888) by Marjory's brother (John) Oliver *Wardrop first excited Marjory Wardrop's interest in the Caucasus. She longed to travel there herself, rather than, as she wrote, 'stay at home, just doing nothing when I might be living, learning and working' (N. Wardrop, 511). At the age of twenty she began her study of Georgian with an alphabet and a gospel. Working at home with books sent by her brother, she embarked on the challenging task of translating the long twelfth-century poem *The Man in the Panther's Skin* by Shotʿa Rustʿaveli, a courtly epic from the classical period of Georgian literature. In this she was encouraged by the Georgian man of letters Prince Ilia Chadchadadze, whose permission she had sought to translate his poem *The Hermit*. Her letter so impressed him that he published it in his newspaper as a model of literary style. She worked on the epic throughout her life, modestly denying that it was perfect enough for publication, and it appeared only after her death, prepared for the press by her brother in 1912. Meanwhile she published *Georgian Folktales* (1894), the first translation into English of secular Georgian literature.

Marjory's parents were persuaded that she might join her brother, then in the Caucasus, and the pleasure that she took in her first visit is vividly described in her unpublished 'Notes on a journey into Georgia in 1894–5'. Georgians rate hospitality highly, and she and her brother were entertained by friends in literary circles with open-air banquets, dancing, and singing. It was known and appreciated that Marjory was translating their national epic, and in espousing the Georgian language the Wardrops were supporting the nationalist cause. Soon after this visit Marjory Wardrop's rendering of *The Hermit* (1895) was published. Her flowing verse makes it the best of her translations, and it was well received in Georgia. On her second visit to the Caucasus in 1896 she was fêted everywhere. Such was her gentle charm and warmth of character that she made many friends and kept up a close correspondence with them.

After her brother joined the consular service in 1895 Marjory Wardrop accompanied him on all his postings. For ten years she lived in Russia—at Kertch (1895–1902),

Sevastopol (1899), and St Petersburg (1903–5)—and she was briefly in Tunis, Haiti, and Poland. Using her collection of Georgian books, she continued her work on Rustʿaveli's epic and, with her brother, published from medieval texts the *Life of St Nino* (1900), on the fourth-century female evangelist of Georgia.

The contemporary problems of the country were also of great concern to Marjory Wardrop. While in St Petersburg during the Russian Revolution of 1905 she translated for the British embassy accounts of Cossack repression in Georgia. She was active on the Georgia Relief Committee and made a personal plea to the bishop of Gibraltar to intercede with the Russian holy synod on behalf of the Georgian church. The last three years of her life were spent in Romania (1906–9). After a brief illness she died, unmarried, on 7 December 1909 at the British consul-general's home in Bucharest, and on 21 December was buried in St Nicholas's parish churchyard, Sevenoaks, Kent.

Marjory Wardrop's translations were made at a time when Georgians were emphasizing their distinctive culture in the face of increasing Russification. Her work led to a wider appreciation not only of Georgian literature but of the country itself, and for this she was held in the highest regard and affection throughout Georgia. In his sister's memory Oliver Wardrop established in Oxford the Marjory Wardrop Fund with the aim of encouraging Georgian studies; her extensive library and papers are in the Wardrop collection of the Bodleian Library.

JENNIFER DONKIN

Sources N. Wardrop, 'Oliver, Marjory and Georgia', *Bodleian Library Record*, 14 (1994), 501–23 · D. M. Lang, 'Georgian studies in Oxford', *Oxford Slavonic Papers*, 6 (1955), 120–35 · D. Barrett, *Catalogue of the Wardrop collection* (1973) · M. Wardrop, 'Notes on a journey into Georgia in 1894–5', Bodl. Oxf., MS Wardr. d. 40/I · O. Wardrop, ed., preface, in Rustʿaveli, *The man in the panther's skin* (1912) · private information (2004) [Nino Wardrop, niece] · Bodl. Oxf., Wardrop collection · b. cert. · *CGPLA Eng. & Wales* (1910) · parish register, Sevenoaks, Kent, St Nicholas, 21 Dec 1909 [burial]
Archives Bodl. Oxf.
Likenesses double portrait, photograph, 1889 (with her brother), repro. in Wardrop, 'Oliver, Marjory and Georgia', 502; priv. coll. · photograph, c.1894–1895, Bodl. Oxf., Wardrop collection; repro. in Wardrop, 'Oliver, Marjory and Georgia', 519 · photograph, c.1900, repro. in Lang, *Modern history of Georgia*, pl. 20, following p. 114; priv. coll.
Wealth at death £1918 15s. 9d.: resworn administration, 1910, *CGPLA Eng. & Wales*

Wardrop, Sir (John) Oliver (1864–1948), diplomatist and Georgian scholar, was born on 10 October 1864 at 3 Wolsingham Place, Lambeth, Surrey, the first child and elder son of the three children of Thomas Caldwell Wardrop (1836–1903), a joiner and partner in a building firm, and his wife, Marjory Cameron Scott (1837–1918); both parents were Scottish. A delicate child, he was sent at the age of five to his grandparents' farm in West Calder, Midlothian, where he attended the village school. His education continued at the Coopers' Company grammar school, Stepney (1873–80), and then at schools in Paris and Dissen, Germany (1880–81). He later studied at the Sorbonne (1885–6) and in Rome, where he spent three months before embarking in 1886 on an extensive tour of Egypt, the Middle East, and Georgia.

Georgia immediately aroused Wardrop's enthusiasm. This is clearly apparent in his first book, *The Kingdom of Georgia: Notes of Travel in a Land of Women, Wine and Song* (1888), the subtitle of which belies its author's perception and erudition. W. R. Morfill, later his Russian tutor at Oxford, read the manuscript and recommended publication. Encouraged by James Bryce, the professor of civil law, who had recently made a tour of the Caucasus, Wardrop entered Balliol College, Oxford, in 1888, was thrice awarded the Taylorian exhibition, each time for a different language (Spanish, French, and Italian), and took a first in modern history in 1891.

Wardrop held a commission in the 19th Middlesex rifle volunteers and qualified as an army interpreter in Russian, which led to his appointment as private secretary (1892–3) to the British ambassador in St Petersburg, Sir Robert Morier. He kept in touch with his many friends in the Caucasus and continued his studies in both medieval and modern Georgian, sometimes collaborating with his sister, Marjory *Wardrop, who shared his admiration for the country. His annotated edition of Sulkhan-Saba Orbeliani's *Book of Wisdom and Lies* (1894), a seventeenth-century collection which enjoys in Georgia the same prestige as the fables of La Fontaine in France, was printed by William Morris at the Kelmscott Press. On his second visit to Georgia in 1894 he was joined by his mother and sister, and the English party was delighted by the warmth of their welcome. This was a testing time for the Georgians in the face of advancing Russification, and it was appreciated that the Wardrops' sympathies were with the nationalist cause. By their translations they were bringing Georgia to the notice of a wider public in the West.

Wardrop now determined to pursue a career in Russia and the Caucasus. In 1895 he entered the consular service, and he was thereafter accompanied on his postings by his sister. They worked together on *The Life of St Nino* (1900), a biography of the fourth-century female evangelist of Georgia translated from medieval texts. Wardrop was vice-consul in Kertch for seven years (1895–1902), was briefly in Sevastopol, and was, intermittently, acting consul-general in Poland, Romania, Tunis, and Haiti. When consul in St Petersburg (1903–6) during the Revolution of 1905, he was distressed at Cossack repression in Georgia and made great efforts on behalf of the Georgian nation, supporting public appeals and setting up a Georgian relief committee. He served as consul in Romania (1906–10), during which time his sister died and his own ill health led to his resignation from the service.

Wardrop married a Norwegian, Margrethe Collett (1877–1960), on 15 October 1912; it was a happy marriage, and there were two sons and a daughter. In retirement he devoted himself to Caucasian studies, making accessible two great poems of twelfth-century Georgia, akin to the lays of the minnesingers and troubadours. Rustʿaveli's *The Man in the Panther's Skin* (1912) was Marjory Wardrop's translation, which he prepared for publication. His own translation *Visramiani—the Story of the Loves of Vis and Ramin*

(1914), originally written in Persian and recast in Georgian, Wardrop described as one of the oldest novels in the world. His *English–Svanetian Vocabulary* appeared in 1911, followed by a *Catalogue of the Georgian Manuscripts in the British Museum* (1913), a translation of the liturgy of St James (1913), in collaboration with F. C. Conybeare, and *Laws of King George V of Georgia* (1914).

On the outbreak of the First World War Wardrop rejoined the Foreign Office, becoming consul-general in Bergen, then the chief channel of trade between Britain and northern Europe. He was created CMG in 1917 and appointed consul-general in Moscow, a hazardous posting in which he served throughout the revolution; on one occasion he was burning consular papers while his officials delayed armed police at the door. In 1919 he returned to the Foreign Office (political intelligence department).

After the Bolshevik Revolution the Caucasian states broke away from Russia, and in 1919 the British government took the imaginative step of appointing Wardrop, now the pre-eminent scholar of Georgian history and literature, as British chief commissioner to the newly independent republics of Georgia, Armenia, and Azerbaijan. This was the most interesting and appropriate appointment of his career; he was returning to the countries where he had travelled widely as a young man, whose languages he understood, and where he was known and highly regarded. He set up his headquarters in Tiblisi, where life was described by his assistant Harry Luke as a 'fascinating blend of the polished and the barbaric' (Luke, 118). Against the background of the advancing Bolshevik forces, Wardrop attempted to reconcile the interests of his beloved Georgia with those of Great Britain and the Western powers. It was an extremely tense time; the Caucasus was a focus for Russian émigrés, and the financial and social instability of the new republics caused much hardship; it was on Wardrop's generosity that the Georgian patriarch depended for his daily bread. When ill health again obliged Wardrop to retire, shortly before the British withdrawal in July 1920, Luke observed that for both his chief and the Georgians, Wardrop's departure was a moving event. He returned briefly to the Foreign Office (department of overseas trade) until appointed a British delegate to the inter-allied commission for the relief of Russia in Paris in 1921. He was created KBE in 1922 while in his final posting as consul-general in Strasbourg (1920–27).

Wardrop corresponded with Georgian scholars and had a fine collection of books and manuscripts; he bequeathed them to the Bodleian Library, where they form the basis of the Wardrop collection. He served on the council of the Royal Asiatic Society from 1928 (acting as vice-president in 1944) and was a governor of the School of Oriental and African Studies (1939–45). He was active on the board of management of the Marjory Wardrop Fund, which he established in Oxford in memory of his sister with the aim of encouraging Georgian studies.

Oliver Wardrop stands in the long line of scholar–public servants. The languages, history, and traditions of the Caucasus were his lifelong interests and determined the course of his career and achievements. The plight of Georgians under both tsarist and Soviet rule concerned him greatly, and he played a decisive role in making Georgia's distinctive culture better known to the British public.

For many years Wardrop lived at the Home Farm, Chipstead, Sevenoaks, Kent. He died on 19 October 1948 at his home, 49 Downshire Hill, Hampstead, London, and was buried in the family grave in St Nicholas's parish churchyard at Sevenoaks. JENNIFER DONKIN

Sources N. Wardrop, 'Oliver, Marjory and Georgia', *Bodleian Library Record*, 14 (1994), 501–23 · D. M. Lang, 'Georgian studies in Oxford', *Oxford Slavonic Papers*, 6 (1955), 120–35 · D. Barrett, *Catalogue of the Wardrop collection* (1973) · H. Luke, *Cities and men*, 2 (1953) · D. M. Lang, *A modern history of Georgia* (1962) · *The Times* (21 Oct 1948) · W. Foster, *Journal of the Royal Asiatic Society* (1949), 115–16 · Bodl. Oxf., Wardrop collection · O. Wardrop, *The kingdom of Georgia* (1888) · private information (2004) [Nino Wardrop, daughter] · *WWW, 1941–50* · b. cert. · d. cert. · gravestone, St Nicholas's parish churchyard, Sevenoaks, Kent · *Morning Post* (30 Dec 1918)

Archives Bodl. Oxf.

Likenesses photograph, 1889, repro. in Wardrop, 'Oliver, Marjory and Georgia', 502 · photograph, 1919, repro. in Lang, *Modern history of Georgia*; priv. coll.

Wealth at death £4928 2s. 2d.: probate, 8 Feb 1949, *CGPLA Eng. & Wales*

Wardwell, Samuel (*d.* 1692). *See under* Salem witches and their accusers (*act.* 1692).

Ware, Sir Fabian Arthur Goulstone (1869–1949), newspaper editor and the founder of the Imperial War Graves Commission, was born at Clifton, Bristol, on 17 June 1869. He was the only son of Charles Ware, a chartered accountant, and Amy Carew, *née* Goulstone. He was educated privately and at the universities of London and Paris. For ten years Ware earned his living as a schoolmaster, with occasional work as an examiner for the civil service and as an inspector of schools for the Board of Education. In 1895 he married Anna Margaret, *née* Phibbs (*b.* 1868). They had a son and daughter. From 1899 to 1901 he contributed articles to the *Morning Post*. He was thirty-two when he was chosen by Alfred Milner as assistant director of education for the Transvaal, one of the two Boer states annexed to the South African Union after the Second South African War. By 1903 Ware had been promoted director of education and elected a member of the Transvaal legislature. Like all members of Milner's 'kindergarten' he rewarded the pro-consul with a lifetime's devotion.

In April 1905 Ware was invited to succeed J. N. Dunn as editor of the *Morning Post*. This newspaper, high tory and ultra-imperialist in its political sympathies, had become hidebound by impractical, unbusinesslike traditions. The proprietor, Lord Glenesk, had hired Ware to be the much needed new broom. Inevitably not all editorial initiatives were welcomed by the staff. Spenser Wilkinson, the most distinguished of that number, who had served as editor for the short interregnum before Ware's arrival, questioned the new editor's authority to dictate a line upon matters of opinion. The two men's prolonged, acrimonious struggle was resolved in Ware's favour only when Lady Bathurst succeeded her father as proprietor in 1908.

A social imperialist, Ware was genuinely interested in

Sir Fabian Arthur Goulstone Ware (1869–1949), by Lafayette, 1932

social reform. He encouraged young, talented writers and thinkers, such as William Beveridge and R. H. Tawney, to contribute to the *Post*, despite their notorious radical sympathies. He was, however, not so happy that Hilaire Belloc, then the ultra-radical MP for Salford, had been given charge of the newspaper's literary pages. Ware's disapproval was unavailing because Belloc had been appointed by Glenesk. Ware's attitude on social reforms became markedly less generous after the 1909 Lloyd George budget. He supposed the Liberals' proposed welfare measures would lead inevitably to tyranny and revolution.

Ware was an intransigent tariff reformer. He fawned upon Joseph Chamberlain, then transferred the same devotion to Austen. Politician and journalist differed over one substantive issue only: Ware supported Charlie Beresford's cause while Chamberlain was an ally of Jacky Fisher in the debilitating quarrel between the two vain, opinionated admirals that divided the Edwardian navy. Ware demonstrated nothing like the same loyalty to Balfour that he gave to the Chamberlains. Balfour he considered too hopelessly pusillanimous to serve as tory leader. Increasingly Ware became associated with other intemperate tariff reform publicists, like L. J. Maxse. Early in 1908 Glenesk demanded that his editor cease his belligerent campaigning. Ware despaired. How in conscience could he remain editor and turn his back upon those political ideals to which he was so passionately attached? He was rescued from this dilemma by Glenesk's unexpected death.

The new proprietor, Lady Bathurst, shared Ware's adherence to aggressive, right-wing politics. Yet even she eventually perceived that Ware's pugnacious proselytizing was costing her newspaper readers and revenue. Events reached their climax when Ware unavailingly supported Richard Jebb as an independent candidate for the Marylebone parliamentary constituency. This challenge to Robert Cecil, a tory grandee, was offensive to every section of the tory party. The consequent loss in the *Morning Post*'s circulation demonstrated that the editor's political enthusiasm had become a commercial liability. Even so, Ware, as in the past, might have escaped with a warning had he not been careless in drawing some contracts which cost Lady Bathurst a considerable sum of money. This time there was to be no proprietorial forgiveness and, in 1911, Ware's association with the *Morning Post* was finally severed. Ware's fortunes during his comparatively brief editorial career clearly demonstrate how power had switched from editor to proprietor and how commercial considerations would increasingly dictate a newspaper's political allegiance.

In 1912 Ware was appointed to act as a special commissioner to negotiate with the French government on behalf of the Rio Tinto Company. Milner had only recently become chairman of that company's board. Ware's business career was interrupted by the outbreak of the First World War. He took command of a mobile unit of the British Red Cross serving with the French army. Ware early recognized the need both to locate and record the graves of soldiers killed in action. These endeavours were encouraged by General Sir Nevil Macready. In 1915 the War Office gave official recognition to Ware's registration commission. In 1917, by royal charter, what had begun as an essentially amateur enterprise became the Imperial War Graves Commission. The commission's charge was to undertake the reburial of the fallen soldiers of Britain and her empire in permanent cemeteries. Ware inspired the whole organization, and by his tact and persistence overcame all obstacles. Not least of Ware's problems was the reluctance of the Treasury, under Winston Churchill as chancellor, permanently to endow the War Graves Commission. Ware finally succeeded in overcoming Treasury intransigence. Throughout the 1920s and 1930s he devoted his time exclusively to the commission. With the outbreak of war in 1939, until 1944, as in the previous war, Ware combined his commission duties with those of director-general of grave registration and inquiries. He relinquished his burden in 1948, and then only when failing health obliged him to give up. The outstanding contribution he made was recognized by the governments of France and Belgium. He was appointed CMG in 1917, CB in 1919, KBE in 1920, and in 1922 KCVO.

Despite the often extreme demands made upon his time by his work for the commission Ware also concerned himself with rural affairs in Gloucestershire, his home county; he was chairman of the National Education Union; an honorary associate of the Royal Institute of British Architects; and a director of the journal *Nineteenth Century and After*. Ware died at Barnwood House Hospital, Gloucester, on 28 April 1949; his ashes were interred in the churchyard at Holy Trinity Church, Amberley, Gloucestershire, on 2 May. His tombstone is of the Imperial War Graves Commission design. His name is additionally commemorated in St George's Chapel in Westminster Abbey.

It was Ware's inspiration, imagination, dedication, and determination combined with considerable diplomatic skill and political finesse that ensured that throughout the world there are war cemeteries, quiet, dignified, immaculately maintained, welcomingly familiar in the guise of English gardens, providing a permanent and fitting reminder of the individual sacrifice made by British and dominion service personnel in two world wars.

A. J. A. MORRIS

Sources F. Ware, *The immortal heritage* (1937) · Lord Beveridge, *Power and influence* (1953) · J. Harris, *William Beveridge* (1977) · S. E. Koss, *The rise and fall of the political press in Britain*, 2 (1984) · DNB · WWW · A. Wilkinson, *The Church of England and the First World War* (1978) · A. Sykes, *Tariff reform in British politics, 1903–1913* (1979) · C. Carrington, *Rudyard Kipling and his work* (1955) · A. M. Gollin, *Proconsul in politics* (1964) · T. O'Brien, *Milner* (1979) · K. M. Wilson, *A study in the history and politics of the Morning Post, 1905–1926* (1990) · R. Lucas, *Lord Glenesk and the Morning Post* (1910) · *The Leo Amery diaries*, ed. J. Barnes and D. Nicholson, 1 (1980) · *A good innings: the private papers of Viscount Lee of Fareham*, ed. A. Clark (1974) · K. M. Wilson, *The Morning Post, 1905–26* (1998) · CGPLA Eng. & Wales (1949)
Archives Commonwealth Graves Commission, Maidenhead, corresp. and papers relating to work for Commonwealth war graves commission · U. Leeds, Brotherton L., corresp. | BLPES, corresp. with E. D. Morel · HLRO, corresp. with Andrew Bonar Law · JRL, letters to the *Manchester Guardian* · U. Birm., Austin Chamberlain and Joseph Chamberlain MSS · U. Leeds, Brotherton L., letters to Lilias, Countess Bathurst (*née* Borthwick) · U. Leeds, Brotherton L., letters to Algernon Borthwick, Baron Glenesk · U. Lond., Institute of Commonwealth Studies, corresp. with Richard Jebb
Likenesses W. Stoneman, photograph, 1919, NPG · Lafayette, photograph, 1932, NPG [*see illus.*] · W. Stoneman, photograph, 1942, NPG
Wealth at death £12,916 17s. 6d.: probate, 10 Aug 1949, CGPLA Eng. & Wales

Ware, Henry (*d.* 1420), administrator and bishop of Chichester, was from Wales, almost certainly from Glamorgan, where he had his earliest preferment (as a canon of Llandaff by May 1394 and as rector of Marcross by 1398) and other personal contacts. Even in his will he asked for an 'old bible' to be returned to Margam Abbey, and left vestments to St Buruoc's, Barry. He referred there also to a brother and 'poor kinsfolk', and to his sister, Margaret, who married one John Hayward; the latter may be the man of that name who, like Ware, sought patronage from Lady Despenser, a leading influence in south Wales. Despite this apparent relative lack of advantage in life, Ware was an MA of Oxford by 1399, in fact necessarily some while before, because he was a licentiate in both laws by late 1401; he never took a doctorate.

Ware's career was twofold. He was a notary public by 30 July 1398 and still on 28 February 1402, when witnessing an *actum* by Archbishop Arundel at Lambeth. In June 1402 he received preferment from the archbishop, for whom he was evidently working by now, being identified as the scribe of his *acta* in 1405, and was soon sitting over legal disputes in the diocese on Arundel's behalf. By July 1408 he was official of the court of Canterbury, and announced on behalf of a committee of the Canterbury convocation that the English church would promote the ending of the papal schism more urgently. He was still official on 25 September 1413 when he was on the tribunal which would try the heretic Sir John Oldcastle, was retained during the vacancy in the see in 1414, and was still in office under Archbishop Chichele in November 1415 and February 1416. From 20 August 1414 Bishop Philip Repingdon appointed him to supervise probate of all wills in the Lincoln diocese and used him in a heresy case in May 1415 and to confirm a hospital election in August 1416.

Meanwhile he had been included in embassies to France as early as 2 February–2 May 1400 and 11 July–2 October 1401, but this sort of work did not continue. From 3 November 1407, however, he was appointed several times to hear appeals from the court of admiralty or military courts. On 1 July 1412 he was living in the parish of St James Garlickhythe in London, and on 20 December 1413 he was exempted from the king's order to Welsh people to go home. On 10 and 28 November 1414 he was appointed to the crucial, large-scale embassy to France, no doubt in some expert capacity, and served on this from 2 February to 2 May. From 11 July to 2 October 1414 he was in France again to develop aspects of these ultimately fruitless peace talks. On 24 July 1415 he was appointed an executor of Henry V's will.

On 11 September 1416 Ware became keeper of the privy seal, a prominent example of Henry V's use of Canterbury men to staff his embryonic parallel administrations in England and France. He was something of a surprise choice, his not being among the names that had been bandied around, but the author of the *Gesta Henrici quinti* thought the king had done well to identify 'a man held in high respect' and 'of considerable repute' in the court of Canterbury (p. 159). Among all the many customary duties Ware received the oaths of John, duke of Burgundy, and his son, Philip, before their interview with Henry V on 2 October 1416; was a delegate from the council to the convocation of Canterbury to seek a subsidy on 18 November 1416; and was appointed to treat for peace with France on 12 March 1417 and for truces with Burgundy on 24 April and 23 July that year, proroguing this truce on 5 December. Some reversion to his original trade came with his service, unheard of by such a high officer of state, as vicar-general for Bishop Richard Clifford in the London diocese between 17 November 1417 and late April 1418; the administration had become badly unhorsed during the bishop's unpredictably delayed return from the continent and perhaps Ware, as the most experienced administrator in the southern province, felt obliged to seize the reins. Likewise he had found time to help arbitrate a dispute between the bishop and cathedral of Ely.

Ware had always been unusually underendowed with preferment and held no dignities at all. The crown had given him just the rectory of Tring, Hertfordshire, on 14 May 1414. On 28 February 1418 royal consent was given to his election to the see of Chichester, to which he was papally provided on 6 April. Even this was only moderate reward for a keeper of the privy seal. He secured the temporalities on 13 May, and was consecrated at Pont de l'Arche in Normandy on 17 July. His episcopal register has not survived, but it is known that John Blunham, precentor of the cathedral, was his vicar-general during his absences. The bishop had been preparing since 12 April 1418 to go abroad, being appointed to supervise the muster of various retinues on 16 April, a familiar role for any senior administrator treading the same path. Thus he joined the royal expedition in Normandy, being appointed to array retinues before Louviers on 9 June and to serve in the major embassy under Chichele and the earls of Warwick and Salisbury to treat with the dauphin on 26 October. He had resigned the privy seal on 21 September, presumably because he would be preoccupied in France. Ware was appointed to join in further important talks on 22 January (at Vienne) and 8 March 1419, and to muster the duke of Clarence's force on the 27th. He evidently returned to England shortly afterwards. He attended convocation in October, and he is known to have been in Chichester on 10 December 1419. However, apart from being appointed on 13 April 1420 to supervise the muster of the duke of Bedford's force before it left, he had undertaken no more formal business for either the crown or the Canterbury province since his return to England. It is likely that such an abrupt retirement at this time of intense royal administrative activity denotes a failure of health. He made his will on 7 July 1420 as a very sick man, and had died, probably in England, by the 23rd. He was buried, as requested, in the cathedral.   R. G. DAVIES

Sources Emden, *Oxf.* · R. G. Davies, 'The episcopate in England and Wales, 1375–1443', PhD diss., University of Manchester, 1974, 3.cccvii–x · E. F. Jacob, ed., *The register of Henry Chichele, archbishop of Canterbury, 1414–1443*, 2, CYS, 42 (1937), 195–7 · F. Taylor and J. S. Roskell, eds. and trans., *Gesta Henrici quinti / The deeds of Henry the Fifth*, OMT (1975)

Ware, Hugh (1771/2–1846), officer in the French service, born near Rathcoffey, co. Kildare, was descended from the same family, of English origin, as Sir James Ware the historian. Hugh supported the Irish national movement, and was a member of the United Irishmen. On the outbreak of the 1798 uprising he raised a body of insurgents and maintained a desultory warfare in co. Kildare. After the battle of Vinegar Hill (21 June), he joined a detachment of defeated insurgents and retreated towards co. Meath. They were dispersed by government troops, but Ware and some of the other leaders were imprisoned, he at Dublin, then at Kilmainham until the peace of Amiens in 1802, when he was released on condition of voluntary banishment for life.

On his release, Ware went to France, and in 1803, on the rupture of the peace of Amiens, obtained a lieutenancy in the new Irish legion in the French army. In 1804 he was appointed captain of grenadiers. After the breaking up of the camp at Boulogne, the legion served in the Netherlands, Spain, and Germany. Ware displayed undaunted courage on every occasion, and gained the respect of his superiors by his military talent. In 1810 the Irish regiment was sent into Spain, and it took part in the siege of Astorga. In June, at the siege of Ciudad Rodrigo by Ney, Ware was appointed by Junot to the command of an élite battalion selected from his own regiment. He took part at the head of 900 men in a successful attack by General St Croix on the British outposts, and was promoted *chef de bataillon* (lieutenant-colonel).

After the Russian campaign of 1812, the Irish legion was transferred to Germany to reinforce the French army. Ware served successfully in the 1813 campaign. On 28 March he drove a party of cossacks out of Celle, inflicting heavy losses. Under General Puthod he took part in the French victories at Bautzen and Gros Warschen, which gained for Napoleon the truce of 4 June. During the armistice Ware received the cross of the Légion d'honneur. In the battle of Löwenberg on 19 August, the Irish regiment bore the brunt of the engagement, and Ware received three grapeshot wounds and had his horse killed under him. In the second battle of Löwenberg, two days later, the colonel of the regiment, William Lawless, had his leg taken off by a cannon shot, and command devolved upon Ware, who led the regiment over the Bobr in the face of the enemy. At the battle of Goldberg on 23 August, he carried with the bayonet the hill of Goldberg, the key of the enemy's position, and had a second horse killed under him. At the conclusion of the action the French commander, General Lauriston, wrote from the field requesting for Ware the rank of colonel. On 29 August he saved the eagle of the regiment from capture. After the retreat from Leipzig, Ware took his regiment (reduced to ninety men) to the Netherlands, where the reserve battalion was stationed at Bois-le-Duc. He took part in the defence of Antwerp, and on 14 January 1814, at the head of 1000 men made a successful sortie against the British troops.

Napoleon, on his return from Elba, promoted Ware colonel. During the Belgian campaign, the Irish regiment was in garrison at Montreuil, and after Waterloo it was disbanded. Ware retired to Tours, where he died on 5 March 1846. Ware was tall, 'of gigantic proportions' and great strength (*GM*, 541), and was noted for his hospitality to English prisoners, whom he eagerly sought out during the Spanish campaigns.   E. I. CARLYLE, *rev.* JAMES LUNT

Sources *The Times* (27 March 1846) · D. Chandler, *The campaigns of Napoleon* (1966) · W. F. P. Napier, *History of the war in the Peninsula and in the south of France*, 3 vols. (1878) · *GM*, 2nd ser., 25 (1846), 540–41

Ware, Isaac (*bap.* **1704**, *d.* **1766**), architect, was born in London, where he was baptized in the church of St Giles Cripplegate on 6 March 1704; his father, also Isaac, was a cordwainer (or shoemaker). Ware himself is said to have told the sculptor Roubiliac that he began life as a chimney sweep's boy, and that he was launched on his architectural career when a benevolent gentleman spotted him sketching the Banqueting House in Whitehall with a piece of chalk; the anonymous gentleman, later putatively identified as the third earl of Burlington, had him educated, sent him to Italy, and on his return furthered his career. What is certain is that in 1721, aged seventeen, Ware was apprenticed in the Carpenters' Company to the

architect Thomas Ripley, who was shortly afterwards appointed master carpenter to the office of works. Ripley's intervention is likely to have secured for Ware the posts of clerk itinerant, draughtsman, and purveyor at the end of his apprenticeship in 1728. His rise in the office of works continued with clerkships of the works at Windsor Castle (1729–33) and Greenwich (1733–6), and finally the secretaryship of the board of works (1736–66).

Although Ware was thus a senior architectural civil servant of long standing, little or nothing can be attributed to him in this capacity, and his reputation rests on his activities outside the office of works. Whatever the truth of the story supposedly told to Roubiliac, he seems in the earlier years of his career to have been part of Lord Burlington's circle. Having in 1727 subscribed to William Kent's *Designs of Inigo Jones* (a volume sponsored by Burlington), in 1731 he published his own *Designs of Inigo Jones and Others*, which contained designs by the earl. Ware's translation of Palladio's *Quattro libri dell'architettura* (generally considered the best and most reliable English edition), published in 1738, was dedicated to Burlington, and acknowledges his assistance. Another project, reliant on his help, which Ware contemplated but never brought to completion, was a new edition of the Palladio drawings of Roman baths then in Burlington's collection. Other publications were, in 1735, *The Plans, Elevations and Sections of Houghton in Norfolk* (on whose construction he had probably worked as assistant to Ripley), and a translation of Lorenzo Sirigatti's *La prattica di prospettiva*, brought out serially in 1756–7. The same years also saw the serial publication of Ware's most important book, the massive and compendious *Complete Body of Architecture*.

Ware's known output as an architect is relatively small, and much of it has been demolished or drastically altered. It includes the conversion of Lanesborough House, Hyde Park Corner, into St George's Hospital (1733; rebuilt 1828–9), Oxford town hall (1751–2; dem. 1893), Wrotham Park, Hertfordshire (1754; altered 1811 and damaged by fire 1883), and Amisfield House, Haddingtonshire (1756–9; dem. *c*.1928). His most complete surviving building is Clifton Hill House in Bristol (1746–50), which can be said to have introduced Palladian restraint to the domestic architecture of that city. Other well-preserved Palladian interiors are at Leinster House, Dublin, remodelled about 1759 for the twentieth earl of Kildare; Ware's unexecuted designs for remodelling the earl's seat at Carton are dated 1762. Ware was also involved in speculative developments in London, particularly in Mayfair, and illustrated interior features from a number of the houses in the *Complete Body*.

Most of Ware's designs were as Palladian in character as might be expected from an architect of his background and credentials. However, as a prominent member of the St Martin's Lane Academy he was also a colleague of such rococo artists as Hogarth, Roubiliac, and Francis Hayman: this is reflected not only in the surprisingly latitudinarian views occasionally found in the pages of the *Complete Body* but also in the dazzling interiors of his most important work, Chesterfield House, Mayfair (1748–9; dem. 1934), designed in a full-blooded French rococo idiom for the francophile fourth earl of Chesterfield.

Ware was married twice; his first wife, Elizabeth, daughter of James Richards, master carver in the office of works, whom he married on 22 September 1729, bore a son, Walter James Ware. With his second wife, Mary Bolton (who predeceased him), he had two daughters, Mary and Charlotte, one of whom is depicted with him in the portrait by Andrea Soldi now in the RIBA drawings collection. In 1742 Ware bought a small estate at Westbourne Grove, Paddington, and subsequently built himself a new house there. In 1764 he moved to Frognall Hall, Hampstead, where he died on 6 January 1766; he was buried in Paddington Old Church. His skin was said to have retained the stain of the chimney sweep's soot until his dying day.

ROGER WHITE

Sources Colvin, *Archs.* • will, PRO, PROB 11/915, sig. 41 • GL, Carpenters' Company MSS • PRO, records of the office of works • R. White, 'Isaac Ware and Chesterfield House', *The rococo in England*, ed. C. Hind (1986), 175–92 • D. Griffin, 'Leinster House and Isaac Ware', *Decantations: a tribute to Maurice Craig*, ed. A. Bernelle (1992), 60–70 • D. Griffin, 'Carton and Isaac Ware', *Journal of the County Kildare Archaeological Society*, 18/11 (1994–5), 163–75
Archives BL, king's maps • Irish Architectural Archive, Dublin • RIBA BAL, designs for Westminster Bridge • Sir John Soane's Museum, London
Likenesses A. Soldi, double portrait, oils, c.1754 (with his daughter), RIBA • L.-F. Roubiliac, marble bust, NPG • L.-F. Roubiliac, marble bust, Detroit Institute of Arts
Wealth at death see will, PRO, PROB 11/915, sig. 41

Ware, Sir James (1594–1666), antiquary and historian, was born on 26 November 1594 in Castle Street, Dublin, the eldest son of Sir James Ware (d. 1632), and his wife, Mary Briden. His father had gone to Ireland as secretary to Sir William FitzWilliam, the lord deputy, in 1588; he became auditor-general, was knighted by James I, and was elected MP for Mallow in the Irish parliament of 1613. James Ware entered the recently founded Trinity College, Dublin, in 1610, graduating MA in 1616. While there, he encountered James Ussher, who encouraged him to take an interest in antiquarian matters. Shortly after leaving the university, about 1617, he married Mary, the daughter of John Newman of Dublin. Ware began to collect manuscripts and charters that had a bearing on Irish history, and developed an acquaintance with Irish scholars, one of whom, Duald MacFirbis (Dubhaltach Mac Fhirbhisig), proved particularly helpful to him. His first publication was *Archiepiscoporum Casseliensem et Tuamensium vitae* (1628), the lives of the archbishops of Cashel and Tuam. He went to England for the first time in 1629, and undertook research in several libraries.

In 1629 Ware was knighted, and in 1632, after the death of his father, he succeeded to the office of auditor-general. His political life developed rapidly thereafter: he was elected MP for the University of Dublin in the Irish parliaments of 1634 and 1637, and became a member of the privy council in Ireland in 1639; he also joined the staff of Thomas Wentworth, earl of Strafford, the lord deputy. In 1633 he made a major contribution to Irish scholarship by

publishing three important Elizabethan accounts of Ireland, by Edmund Campion, Meredith Hanmer, and Edmund Spenser. (This was the first printing of Spenser's *View of the Present State of Ireland*.) Ware entitled this collection *The History of Ireland* and dedicated it to Wentworth. Also dedicated to Wentworth was his *De scriptoribus Hiberniae*, published in Dublin, 1639, a biographical register of Irish writers which contains an impressive number of names and titles that give an impression of great scholarly achievement in the early Christian centuries. Unfortunately, in most cases only the names and titles have survived, and the texts have disappeared. The register is heavily dependent on the compilations of John Bale, the mid-sixteenth-century bishop of Ossory.

In 1643 Ware assisted the marquess of Ormond in the treaty with the Irish rebels after their defeat, and in 1644 he was sent by Ormond, along with Lord Edward Brabazon and Sir Henry Tichborne, to inform King Charles about the situation in Ireland. Charles was then based in Oxford, and Ware spent much time in the libraries there; he was created DCL during his visit. On the voyage back his ship was captured by a parliamentarian vessel, but Ware was able to throw overboard a packet of letters to Ormond from the king. For eleven months he was a prisoner in the Tower: on his release he returned to Dublin, only to be expelled from that city in 1649 by Colonel Michael Jones, the parliamentarian governor. Ware then went to France, where he spent time at Caen and Paris. At this time he formed a friendship with the French pastor and controversialist Samuel Bochart, who was based in Caen. Bochart had a lively antiquarian curiosity, and was the author of *Geographia sacra* (1646), which offered imaginative views of Old Testament history and described the settlements of the Phoenicians around the shore of Europe. Ware moved to London in 1651; his friends during this period in England included John Selden, Sir Roger Twysden, William Dugdale, Elias Ashmole, Sir John Marsham, and Edward Bysshe. In 1654 he published in London his major work *De Hibernia et antiquitatibus eius disquisitiones* (2nd edn, 1658), the most comprehensive account of Ireland, from its legendary origins to the conquest by the Normans, that had yet appeared.

De Hibernia remains a work of impressive scholarship in which Ware proves himself a worthy successor to his early patron James Ussher in the matter of Irish antiquities. The sections on the origins of the Irish people exhibit the characteristic preoccupations of his time with etymology and honourable lines of national descent: he derives the Scoti, who occupied Ireland in Roman times, from Scythii, and imputes a Scythian origin to the Irish, as had been the conventional opinion in the sixteenth century. He shows an unusual interest in the field monuments of ancient Ireland, with intelligent discussion of their significance. He painstakingly puts together all references to Ireland in the classical writers, to produce a valuable anthropological picture. As he moves into the early Christian period his sources multiply, so that he is able to construct a serious and credible account of the development of Irish society, with its particular manners and customs, up to the coming of the Normans. He explains at length the origins of the leading Irish families, and the meaning of Irish names, reports the superstitions of the country and the natural phenomena, and gives a knowledgeable description of Irish costume and the Irish ways of fighting. Particularly valuable are Ware's accounts of the forms of government, the codes of law, and the systems of land tenure that prevailed up to the Norman invasion. With its copious detail and trustworthy description of the antiquities and traditions of Ireland, *De Hibernia* finally brought the country out of the shadow of Britain and characterized it fully to a scholarly European audience.

Ware returned to Ireland at the Restoration in 1660, and resumed his position as auditor-general. He was made one of the commissioners for lands but managed to devote much time to antiquarian researches, publishing *Venerabilies Bedae epistolae duae* (1664), *Rerum Hibernicarum annales, 1485–1558* (1665), and *De praesulibus Hiberniae commentarius* (1665). He died at his family house in Castle Street, Dublin, on 1 December 1666, and was buried in St Werburgh's Church. His manuscripts, of which catalogues were published in Dublin in 1688 and in London in 1690, were purchased by Henry Hyde, second earl of Clarendon, in 1686 when he was lord lieutenant of Ireland. They subsequently passed to the British Library (Clarendon Collection) and the Bodleian Library (Rawlinson Collection).   GRAHAM PARRY

Sources *The antiquities and history of Ireland, by … Sir James Ware*, 1 vol. in 5 (1705) ['life'] • *The whole works of Sir James Ware concerning Ireland*, ed. and trans. W. Harris, 2 vols. in 3 (1739); rev. edn (1764) • Wood, *Ath. Oxon.: Fasti* (1820), 74 • *DNB*
Archives Armagh Public Library, papers relating to Irish history • BL, commonplace book, historical collections, and notes, Add. MSS 4783–4801, 4821–4822 • TCD, notebook relating to Irish history, incl. contemporary annals | Bodl. Oxf., Rawlinson collection
Likenesses G. Vertue, line engraving, 1738, BM, NPG; repro. in Harris, ed., *Works* (1739) • G. Vertue, line engraving, NG Ire.; repro. in Harris, ed., *Works*, frontispiece

Ware, James (1756–1815), surgeon and oculist, born at Portsmouth on 11 February 1756, was son of Elizabeth Dale (1716–1795) and Martin Ware (1717–1801), who was successively the master shipbuilder of the royal dockyards of Sheerness, Plymouth, and Deptford. James Ware was educated at the Portsmouth grammar school, and went on trial to Ramsay Karr, surgeon of the King's Yard in Portsmouth on 3 July 1770. He was bound apprentice to Karr on 2 March 1771, to serve for five years from the previous July. During his apprenticeship he attended the practice of the surgeons at the Haslar naval hospital, and, as he had served a part of his time, his master allowed him, as was then usual, to go to London for the purpose of attending the medical and surgical practice of one of the general hospitals. Ware selected St Thomas's, and entered himself as a student on 25 September 1773. He remained there for three years, during the course of which he kept a diary (now in the Guildford Muniment Room, Guildford, Surrey).

Ware made such progress that Joseph Else appointed him in 1776 his demonstrator of anatomy. On 1 January

1777 he began to act as assistant to Jonathan Wathen, a surgeon who devoted himself principally to diseases of the eye; and on 25 March 1778 he entered into partnership with Wathen, taking a fourth share. The partnership was dissolved in 1791, after which Ware began to practise on his own account, chiefly but not entirely in ophthalmic surgery. In 1788 he became one of the founders of the Society for the Relief of the Widows and Orphans of Medical Men in London and its vicinity, a society of which he was chosen president in 1809. In 1800 he founded the school for the indigent blind, in imitation of a similar institution which had been established at Liverpool ten years earlier. He was elected a fellow of the Society of Antiquaries of London on 18 January 1798, and on 11 March 1802 he was admitted a fellow of the Royal Society, where his proposers included the eminent surgeons Everard Home and John Abernethy. He married in 1787 Ursula, the widow of N. Polhill, and daughter of Robert Maitland; they had a large family of sons and daughters.

Wathen and his pupil Ware did much to raise the status of eye surgery. Specialism in this field was long associated with quackery and regarded with suspicion in many quarters, but the efforts of men like Ware promoted its acceptance as a respected branch of the profession. Ware had a receptive and enquiring mind, and was ready to learn from any source that satisfied his critical judgement. In his day he was the best-read man in his subject, and he greatly influenced his colleagues by his practice. He was the first English surgeon to arouse any enthusiasm for Dominique Anel's syringe in the treatment of diseases of the lacrimal duct, previously much disparaged by English surgeons. After Ware's visit to Paris in 1791, the method became widely adopted. In the same year he translated Baron de Wenzel's *Traité de la cataracte*. He freely acknowledged (although not without reservations) that he had learned more from the baron than from anyone else, even though Wenzel was often regarded as a quack. Ware himself was noted for his skill in the extraction of the lens in cataract, which was to supersede the traditional procedure of couching.

Ware was modest and self-critical. He did not like to talk about his philanthropic activities and, unusually for his time, he could write about his failures. *An Enquiry into the Causes which have Most Commonly Prevented Success in the Operation of Extracting the Cataract* was published in 1795. He was a prolific writer and some of his works were translated into several languages. His first book, *Remarks on the Ophthalmy, Psorophthalmy and Purulent Eye* (1780), first drew attention to the contagious nature of ophthalmia of the new-born, and its venereal origin. This work and his books on the treatment of lacrimal fistulae, as well as the translation of Wenzel, were collected and republished in 1805 in two volumes as *Chirurgical Observations Relative to the Eye*. Ware published several papers of professional importance in the *Transactions of the Medical Society of London* and the *Transactions of the Medical and Chirurgical Society*, of which the most interesting describe cases of recovery of sight after long periods of blindness. His contribution to the *Philosophical Transactions of the Royal Society* made some important observations on refractive errors.

Ware practised in New Bridge Street, Blackfriars, and his contemporaries regarded him as one of the leaders of the profession. He died at his country house at Turnham Green, Middlesex, on 13 April 1815, and was buried on 21 April in the family tomb in the Bunhill Fields burial-ground, London. D'A. POWER, *rev.* A. L. WYMAN

Sources T. J. Pettigrew, *Medical portrait gallery: biographical memoirs of the most celebrated physicians, surgeons … who have contributed to the advancement of medical science*, 4 vols. in 2 [1838–40] · R. R. James, ed., *Studies in the history of ophthalmology in England prior to the year 1800* (1933) · P. Dunn, 'James Ware', *British Journal of Ophthalmology*, 1 (1917), 401–10 · H. P. Hawkins, 'A student at St Thomas's in the years 1773–6', *St Thomas's Hospital Gazette*, 14 (1904), 57–62 · J. J. Abraham, *Lettsom, his life, times, friends and descendants* (1933) · R. Burgess, 'A satire on the influenza of 1803', *Medical History*, 23 (1979), 469–73 · J. Price, 'Dominique Anel and the small lachrymal syringe', *Medical History*, 13 (1969), 340–54 · private information (1899, 2004)
Archives RSH · Surrey HC · Wellcome L., exercise books and papers
Likenesses S. Medley, oils, 1800, Medical Society of London; repro. in Abraham, *Lettsom* · N. Branwhite, group portrait, stipple, pubd 1801 (*Institutors of the Medical Society of London*; after S. Medley), BM · silhouette, aquatint, 1801, Wellcome L. · T. West, print, 1803, Wellcome L. · W. Ridley, stipple, 1804 (after M. Brown), NPG; repro. in *European Magazine* (1804) · H. Cook, stipple, 1839 (after portrait by M. Brown), NPG, Wellcome L. · M. Brown, oils; formerly in possession of James T. Ware, Surrey, 1899 · J. Russell, pastels, priv. coll. · engraving, RS
Wealth at death £10,000 in annuities to wife; £24,000 in securities for children; plus property in freeholds and copyholds: abstract of will, James, *Studies* · will, PRO, PROB 11/1567/216

Ware, Lancelot Lionel (1915–2000), founder of Mensa, was born on 5 June 1915 at 44 Vectis Road, Mitcham, Surrey, the only son and elder child of Frederick Richard Ware (*d.* 1940), merchant's export clerk, and his wife, Eleanor Gwynne Emslie (*d.* 1952). His father invented a type of artificial leather, but lost out financially when his firm was taken over. After Steyning grammar school and Sutton grammar school, Ware took a BSc in mathematics and a PhD in chemistry at the Royal College of Science, Imperial College, London. He went to work at the National Institute for Medical Research in 1938 and at the chemical weapons research establishment at Porton Down in 1939. Then he tested products on animals for Boots, the chemists, in Nottingham (which he afterwards regretted) and lectured on biochemistry at St Thomas's Hospital Medical School, London (1941–6) before deciding on a change of career. He became a law student in 1945 at Lincoln College, Oxford.

While travelling home to Godalming by train in December 1945 Ware let himself be drawn into conversation by a middle-aged Australian named Roland Berrill, who disclosed that he had once applied to Oxford University too, only to be rejected. This led them to discuss cleverness and how to assess it. Phrenology was Berrill's suggestion; Ware put more faith in intelligence tests, having tried some on his gifted sister, Elaine. Mention was made of psychologist Cyril Burt, who in a radio broadcast had recently proposed asking a pool of people with high IQs to devise solutions to post-war problems. When the two men met again in Oxford Ware administered an IQ test to Berrill, who scored very highly. They considered a scheme to identify the 600 most intelligent people in the country so that the government might use them as a survey panel. Berrill, a wealthy enthusiast, paid for some pamphlets and advertisements, and the High IQ Club was launched from 12 St John Street, Oxford, where both of them lodged, on 1 October 1946. Its name was quickly changed to Mens (Latin for 'mind'), but, fearing misunderstandings that might put off women, they finally called the club Mensa ('table'), alluding to a notional round table at which no one presided. In fact Berrill dominated the society and, after recruiting about 400 members, soon drove most of them away with his fads for eugenics, astrology, and brighter clothing for men. Among those who dropped out about 1950 was Lance Ware.

Called to the bar in 1949, Dr Ware—who always used his title—specialized in patents and intellectual property, setting up his own chambers at 11 Old Square, Lincoln's Inn, in 1969. An active Conservative, he was a Surrey county councillor (1949–55) and an alderman of London county council (1955–61). He was appointed to the governing bodies of the London School of Economics, Imperial College, and St Thomas's Hospital.

Meanwhile, under the leadership of Victor Serebriakoff (1913–2000) since 1955, Mensa had transformed itself from a moribund dining club with under 100 members into an international body that promoted research into intelligence and, above all, provided social opportunities for participants, who all had to possess an IQ of 148 or over. Its growth was financed by charging aspiring entrants for their IQ tests. Ware rejoined in 1961 yet stayed on the sidelines until *Mensa Magazine*, in the late 1960s, hailed him as the long-lost founding father. The importance of his contribution was hotly disputed—not least by admirers of Serebriakoff—but, once the cranky Berrill and discredited Burt were dead, many Mensans welcomed a less embarrassing originator, who fervently denied that Mensa had ever been intended for any but social purposes. An uneasy *modus vivendi* eventually emerged: Serebriakoff, styled the builder of Mensa, became international president in 1982, while Ware was given the title *fons et origo Mensae*.

On 14 June 1980 Ware married (Joan) Francesca Rae Quint, *née* Gomez, fellow barrister and Mensan. Following his retirement in 1987, when he was appointed OBE for chairing the Institute of Patentees and Inventors, he had time to attend many Mensa gatherings around the world. Trim, dignified, and sprightly, with white hair and small eyes, he appeared supremely confident of his intellectual eminence. Real tennis, field sports, and do-it-yourself were among his pastimes. As chairman of the Shakespeare Authorship Trust he argued the case for the earl of Oxford.

By its fiftieth anniversary in 1996, Mensa comprised over 100,000 members. Ware, disappointed that so much time was wasted on games and puzzles, hoped that Mensans would one day play a greater role in society. He died of a pulmonary embolism at Brownscombe House, a nursing home at Haslemere, Surrey, on 15 August 2000, and was cremated at Guildford on 23 August. He was survived by his wife. JASON TOMES

Sources *Daily Telegraph* (18 Aug 2000) · *The Guardian* (18 Aug 2000) · *The Times* (18 Aug 2000) · *The Independent* (25 Aug 2000) · *The Economist* (2 Sept 2000) · 'Dr Lancelot L. Ware', www.mensa.org.uk [press release, 16 August 2000] · *Mensa International Journal*, 438 (Oct 2000), 1, 3 · V. Serebriakoff, *IQ: a Mensa analysis and history* (1966) · b. cert. · m. cert. · d. cert.

Ware, Samuel Hibbert- (1782–1848), antiquary and geologist, eldest son of Samuel Hibbert, linen yarn merchant, of Manchester, and Sarah, daughter of Robert Ware of Dublin, was born in St Ann's Square, Manchester, on 21 April 1782. He was educated at a private school (*c*.1792) and at the Manchester Academy (*c*.1795) under Dr Thomas Barnes. He had little taste for his father's business, and turned to literary pursuits, writing prologues for the Manchester theatres, election squibs for his friend Colonel Hanson, a pamphlet on commercial credit, and some doggerel verse. On 23 July 1803 he married Sarah, daughter of Thomas Crompton of Bridge Hall, Bury, Lancashire; they had three children before she died in 1822.

From 1809 to 1813 Hibbert held a lieutenant's commission in the 1st Royal Lancashire militia. After his father's death in 1815 he went to Edinburgh, and took the degree of MD in 1817 at the university with a dissertation entitled 'De vita humana', but he never practised. He lived in Edinburgh many years, and enjoyed the friendship there of Sir Walter Scott, Sir David Brewster, and others, as well as taking part in the work of the learned societies there. He had in 1805 been elected a member of the Manchester Literary and Philosophical Society, and contributed papers to its meetings.

In 1817 Hibbert visited Shetland, where he discovered 'chromate of iron' and undertook a geological survey of the country. For this discovery the Society of Arts awarded him in 1820 the Iris gold medal. In Shetland he also discovered what he described as 'native hydrate of magnesia'. In 1822 he published his *Description of the Shetland Islands*, in which he described the local geology and antiquities.

Hibbert contributed various papers to the Society of Antiquaries of Scotland, of which he was secretary from 1823 to 1827, with responsibility for obtaining contributions for meetings and preparing them for publication. He remained an active member of the society, editing volumes and helping run the museum, under what were sometimes difficult conditions. A paper on 'Spectral illusions', read by Hibbert before the Royal Society of Edinburgh, led to his *Sketches of the philosophy of apparitions, or, An attempt to trace such illusions to their physical causes* (1824), which ran to a second edition (1825). This provoked an anonymous reply in *Past Feelings Renovated* (1828), which aimed to 'counteract … any sentiments approaching materialism' aroused by Hibbert's essay. In 1824, at the request of the Manchester Literary and Philosophical

Society, Hibbert delivered at Manchester a course of lectures on geology, and in 1827 a further course for the Manchester Royal Institution.

On 8 January 1825 Hibbert married Charlotte Wilhelmina (*d*. 1835), widow of William Scott, receiver of customs in the Isle of Man, and daughter of Lord Henry Murray. They had three children. She accompanied him on many of his tours of Scotland and the continent, and executed drawings for his papers. He and his family also spent two or three years abroad, chiefly visiting the volcanic districts of France, Italy, and northern Germany, and he published a *History of the Extinct Volcanoes of the Basin of Neuwied on the Lower Rhine* (1832) on his return to Edinburgh.

In 1833–4 Hibbert published his chief antiquarian work, *The History of the Foundations in Manchester* (3 vols., vol. 3 being in two parts). He described Christ's Hospital, Chetham's Hospital, and the free grammar school, using in part material compiled by the Revd J. Creswell. The architect John Palmer and the biographer William Robert Whatton also contributed to the work.

Hibbert left Edinburgh in 1835, and, after living for a time at York, settled on a small paternal estate at Hale Barns, near Altrincham, Cheshire. In 1837 he assumed by royal licence the surname and arms of Ware, as representative of Sir James Ware, the historian of Ireland. In 1842 he married his third wife, Elizabeth Lefroy, daughter of Captain Anthony Lefroy. He was a member of the first council of the Chetham Society, and edited one of its early volumes, *Lancashire Memorials of the Rebellion in 1715* (1845). His last work was *The Ancient Parish Church of Manchester and why it was Collegiated* (1848), the manuscript of the final part of which was lost after his death. This work is often referred to as the final volume of his earlier *History*.

Hibbert-Ware died at Hale Barns on 30 December 1848 of bronchitis, from which he had suffered for several years. He was buried at Ardwick cemetery, Manchester. Hibbert-Ware's eldest son, Titus Herbert (1810–1890), was called to the bar in 1844, and published *Precedents of Conveyances* (1846). His second son, Dr William Hibbert, an army surgeon, died in Afghanistan in 1839.

C. W. SUTTON, *rev.* ELIZABETH BAIGENT

Sources M. C. H. Hibbert Ware, *The life and correspondence of the late Samuel Hibbert Ware* (1882) · *Manchester Guardian* (3 Jan 1849), 6 · C. R. J. Currie and C. P. Lewis, eds., *English county histories: a guide* (1994) · A. S. Bell, ed., *The Scottish antiquarian tradition* (1981) · D. Brewster, *Account of the native hydrate of magnesia, discovered by Dr Hibbert in Shetland* (1821)
Archives JRL, family and personal corresp. and papers · Man. CL, Manchester Archives and Local Studies, corresp. · NHM | U. Edin. L., letters to David Laing · U. Newcastle, Robinson L., letters to Sir Walter Trevelyan · U. St Andr. L., corresp. with James David Forbes

Ware, William of [*called* the Doctor Fundatus] (*fl.* **1290–1305**), Franciscan friar and theologian, was born at Ware in Hertfordshire. He entered the Franciscan order as a child oblate, according to the testimony of William Woodford, writing less than a century later. Almost certainly William of Ware studied at Oxford and lectured on the

Sentences there, but he is not listed among the Oxford masters and so he probably never incepted as a master of theology there. There is some evidence, but no certainty, that he also taught at Paris, perhaps lecturing there too on the *Sentences*. He was known as the Doctor Fundatus and less commonly the Doctor Praeclarus or the Doctor Profundus.

Only one work can reliably be attributed to him, a commentary on the *Sentences* which survives in many manuscripts: only small parts have been edited, by the Franciscans of Quaracchi (1904), and by A. Daniels (1909, 1913), P. Muscat (1927), J.-M. Bissen (1927), and L. Hödl (1990). William does not try to discuss every distinction, but concentrates on the topics he finds most important, devoting over 100 *quaestiones* to book 1 and just 129 to the remaining three books. Among the theologians whose views William discusses are Henri de Gand, Godefroi de Fontaines, Giles of Rome, and Richard of Middleton—a choice that indicates 1290–1305 as the time of composition. Since there exist three, or perhaps even four, recensions of the work, its composition and revision may well have been spread over these years.

Traditionally William of Ware has been considered the master of Duns Scotus. This view can be supported by some early evidence: in his treatise on the immaculate conception (*c*.1373) the Franciscan Thomas Rossy refers to William as the *magister Scoti*, as does Bartolomeo da Pisa in his *De conformitate vitae beati Francisci ad vitam domini Jesu* of the late 1380s. Perhaps *magister* here is not meant in the strict sense, since William does not seem ever to have become a master. Certainly, there is little doubt that William influenced Scotus, who definitely refers to his views on the nature of theology. Other aspects of his theology, which develops the Franciscan tradition in the context of the debates of the 1290s, are also close to Scotus. Most strikingly, both in discussing the attributes of God and elsewhere, he invokes a type of distinction which neither involves a real difference nor is merely a matter of the understanding. This is very close to Scotus's formal distinction, although William does not clearly give it this label.   JOHN MARENBON

Sources L. Hödl, *Recherches de Théologie Ancienne et Médiévale*, 57 (1990), 122–41 · E. Longpré, 'Maîtres franciscains de Paris: Guillaume de Ware OFM', *La France Franciscaine*, 5 (1922), 71–82 · A. G. Little, 'The Franciscan school at Oxford in the thirteenth century', *Archivum Franciscanum Historicum*, 19 (1926), 803–74 · G. Gál, 'Gulielmi de Ware, O. F. M. doctrina philosophica per summa capita proposita', *Franciscan Studies*, new ser., 14 (1954), 155–80, 265–92 · C. Balic, *Les commentaires de Jean Duns Scot sur les quatre livres des 'Sentences'* (1927), 50–51, 59–62 · F. Stegmüller, ed., *Repertorium commentariorum in sententias Petri Lombardi*, 1 (Würzburg, 1947), 142–3 · Emden, *Oxf.* · V. Doucet, 'Commentaires sur les *Sentences*: supplément au répertoire de M. Frédéric Stegmueller', *Archivum Franciscanum Historicum*, 47 (1954), 88–170 · *Hist. U. Oxf.* 1: *Early Oxf. schools*, 508, 510–11 · P. Glorieux, *Répertoire des maîtres en théologie de Paris au XIIIe siècle*, 2 (Paris, 1934), 144–5 · A. G. Little, *The Grey friars in Oxford*, OHS, 20 (1892), 213 · *Quaestiones disputatae de immaculata conceptione*, Bibliotheca Franciscana Scholastica Medii Aevi, 3 (1904) · A. Daniels, *Quellenbeiträge und Untersuchungen zur Geschichte der Gottesbeweise im dreizehnten Jahrhundert* (Münster, 1909), 89–104 · A. Daniels, 'Wilhelm von Ware über das menschliche Erkenntnis',

Studien zur Geschichte der Philosophie: Festgabe zum 60 Geburtstag Clemens Baeumker (Münster, 1913), 309–18 · P. Muscat, 'Guillelmi de Ware quaestio inedita de unitate Dei', *Antonianum*, 2 (1927), 335–50 · J.-M. Bissen, 'Question inédite de Guillaume de Ware, OFM, sur le motif de l'incarnation', *Études Franciscaines*, 46 (1934), 218–22 · Bartolommeo di Pisa, *De conformitate vitae Beati Francisci ad vitam Domini Jesu* (1542) · T. de Rossy, 'De conceptione Virginis immaculatae', ed. C. Piana, *Tractatus quatuor de immaculata in conceptione b. Maria Virginis* (Florence, 1954), 1–99

Wareham, Matilda of (*fl.* 1155), anchoress, figures in John of Forde's life of the hermit Wulfric of Haselbury (*d.* 1154/5) as an example of a devout woman whose life was changed by her meeting with Wulfric. Matilda's original plans, to go on a pilgrimage overseas, were forestalled by Wulfric's prophecy that she was to become an anchoress nearby. First, however, she was enjoined by Wulfric to become a cushion maker at Wareham, Dorset, for two and a half years before taking up residency in the cell which by then would be ready for her. Matilda complied with all Wulfric's wishes, living for fifteen years as a recluse, a model of virtue, not least to her servant Gertrude, who on Matilda's death took over her mistress's place as Wareham's hermit. Such a succession was quite usual in eremitical circles, as was the working of women hermits at some form of needlework.   HENRIETTA LEYSER

Sources *Wulfric of Haselbury, by John, abbot of Ford*, ed. M. Bell, Somerset RS, 47 (1933) · S. Elkins, *Holy women of twelfth-century England* (1988) · H. Mayr-Harting, 'Functions of a twelfth-century recluse', *History*, new ser., 60 (1975), 337–52

Warelwast, William de (*d.* 1137), administrator and bishop of Exeter, was a Norman who took his name from Ver-à-Val, some 5 kilometres north-west of Yvetot (Seine-Maritime), then on the demesne of the abbey of St Wandrille. His family, education, and career before 1087 are unknown. Although Hugh the Chanter, a hostile chronicler, claimed that he was no scholar (*scholasticus*), this, except possibly in the narrowest sense, is clearly wrong. His career in diplomacy at the highest ecclesiastical levels shows that he was a rhetorician and could speak, as well as read and write, Latin. And the subjects of his diplomacy and his work as a royal justice prove that he was well versed in law, probably of various kinds. As he sent his nephew, Robert, to school at Laon and, when bishop, was a great patron of Augustinian canons, Laon could have been his own alma mater.

Warelwast appears first at the very beginning of William Rufus's reign as a royal clerk, and he served Rufus as a specialist in diplomacy at the papal curia until the king's untimely death. He may well have been in the royal hunting party, also attended by the king's brother Count Henry, in the New Forest on 2 August 1100, when Rufus was killed. Certainly he transferred immediately to Henry's side, thus disregarding the claim to the throne of the eldest brother, Robert Curthose, for he attested the new king's letter, sent shortly after the hasty coronation on 5 August, to the exiled Archbishop Anselm of Canterbury, inviting him to return. That he witnessed third, after a bishop and a bishop-elect and before two important barons, one an earl, is proof that Henry was glad, despite his general dislike of Rufus's servants, to recruit the clerk;

and Warelwast served him for the whole of his reign, although after 1120 blindness began to restrict his activities.

As a trusted ambassador to the pope, Warelwast handled first Rufus's standing difficulties with his archbishop of Canterbury, Anselm, over the 'ancestral' royal customs in the English church, travelling to Rome in 1095, perhaps 1096, and 1098. Although he could not secure Anselm's deposition, he did manage to neutralize Urban II (r. 1088–99). He then took care of Henry I's dispute with Anselm over the investiture of bishops and abbots, with visits to the curia in 1101, 1103, 1105–6, and 1107. He must be regarded as one of the architects of the compromise of Bec (1106) which settled the English investiture dispute. Finally, he pursued the king's interests in the Canterbury–York quarrel over primacy, with embassies in 1116 (perhaps), 1119, and 1120. Eadmer, Anselm's companion and biographer, reports Warelwast's actions on a few of these occasions in some detail. His tone softens from his outrage at the clerk's examination of the archbishop's baggage, piece by piece, 'as though he was a fugitive and criminal' (Life, ed. and trans. Southern, 98) on the beach at Dover in 1097 as he prepared to leave for exile, to his eventual acceptance that in 1105–6 he was working for peace and was genuinely concerned over Anselm's weak health. In the meantime he marvels at the ambassador's fearless, indeed audacious, bearing at the papal curia and his skilful conduct of his business. In 1103 Warelwast used 'threatening words' to Pope Paschal II (r. 1099–1118) at the hearing of the case concerning investitures. He declared that all present should clearly understand that, whatever might be said there on this subject, 'my lord, the king, would rather lose his realm than suffer the loss of the investiture of churches'. To which the pope replied, 'And let me tell you before God, Pope Paschal would rather lose his head than allow him freely to retain them' (De gestis pontificum, 112)—intemperate words in open court, but a deal was done behind the scenes. Eadmer believed that the distribution of money and the threat of cutting off English subsidies were important weapons in Warelwast's armoury. The ambassador had no qualms about exploiting the insecure Urban's need for Henry's support or the weaker character of his successor.

Henry I rewarded his clerk by earmarking Warelwast for the bishopric of Exeter, vacant since Osbern's death in 1103, and put him in the archdeaconry until the settlement of the quarrel over investitures allowed his consecration by Anselm on 11 August 1107. These ecclesiastical offices seem hardly to have weakened Warelwast's closeness to the king. He appears to have been with him in Normandy from August 1111 to July 1115, in 1118, and from June 1123 to September 1126; and these may not have been the only occasions. The many absences from his diocese determined his style of government and required him to create a subordinate structure. Exeter, under the quasi-monastic rule of St Chrodegang, and presided over from 1050 until 1103 by two former clerks of Edward the Confessor, had become old-fashioned. The new bishop brought it into the new age. He replaced the single, personal archdeacon with four territorial archdeaconries; he probably enlarged the cathedral chapter to twenty-four canons and established two dignitaries, a treasurer and a precentor; he reformed Crediton Minster, the earlier see of the Devon bishops, as a satellite community; and c.1114 he started the rebuilding of the cathedral church. By 1133, four years before his death, when the church was dedicated, it extended to a west front flanked by the two great Norman towers that still survive in the transepts.

In the diocese at large Warelwast reformed in the 1120s the secular colleges at Plympton, Bodmin, and St Stephen's, Launceston as convents of Augustinian canons regular. Plympton, his favourite foundation, repaid by remembering him as a prelate intent on eradicating married priests and starting his reforms at the top. However that may be, he was, in a lawful way, a good family man. He made one nephew, Robert, his archdeacon and another, William, his steward, in effect his deputies in spiritualities and temporalities. He seems also to have burdened his church by enfeoffing an excessive number of knights on the episcopal demesne. Although it can hardly be thought that he fulfilled the prognosticon at his consecration, 'When thou makest a dinner or a supper, call not thy friends, nor thy brethren, neither thy kinsmen nor thy rich neighbours … but the poor, the maimed, the lame, the blind' (Luke 14: 12–13), he was clearly a man of many virtues. Not only did he enjoy the trust of both his royal masters, but he also earned the respect of the two popes with whom he negotiated. And even Anselm, the victim of much of his diplomacy, bore him no lasting grudge. He was a progressive and reforming diocesan bishop, a religious and probably good man. He and his nephew Robert were members of the Exeter Kalendar guild; and just before his death he retired to Plympton, where he was presumably admitted as a canon ad succurrendum, and where, after his death on 27 September 1137, he was buried in the chapter house of the priory. He was succeeded as bishop by his nephew, Robert de Warelwast, archdeacon of Exeter; and the two were remembered as great benefactors of the cathedral church.   FRANK BARLOW

Sources Willelmi Malmesbiriensis monachi de gestis pontificum Anglorum libri quinque, ed. N. E. S. A. Hamilton, Rolls Series, 52 (1870) · Hugh the Chanter: the history of the church of York, 1066–1127, ed. and trans. C. Johnson (1961) · Eadmeri Historia novorum in Anglia, ed. M. Rule, Rolls Series, 81 (1884) · Eadmer, The life of St Anselm, Archbishop of Canterbury, ed. and trans. R. W. Southern (1962) · F. Barlow, ed., Exeter, 1046–1184, English Episcopal Acta, 11 (1995) · 'Annales Plympton', Ungedruckte anglo-normannische Geschichtsquellen, ed. F. Liebermann (1879) · F. Barlow, The English church, 1066–1154: a history of the Anglo-Norman church (1979) · F. Barlow, William Rufus, new edn (1990) · D. W. Blake, 'Bishop William Warelwast', Report and Transactions of the Devonshire Society, 104 (1972), 15–33

Warenne. For this title name see individual entries under Warenne; see also William, earl of Surrey [Earl Warenne] (c.1135–1159).

Warenne, Ada de. See Ada, countess of Northumberland (c.1123–1178).

Warenne, Gundrada de (*d.* 1085), noblewoman, was the daughter of Gerbod, head of a noble Flemish family who was hereditary advocate of the important monastery of St Bertin. She had brothers called Gerbod and Frederic, and the family were players in the politics of the marcher counties between Flanders and Normandy. In 1067, for example, Frederic, alongside the count of Flanders, witnessed a charter of Count Guy of Ponthieu in favour of the abbey of St Riquier in the Somme valley. They may also have been involved in England before 1066, when, intriguingly a Frederic and a Gundrada between them held four manors fairly close to one another in Sussex and Kent. The names Frederic and Gundrada were certainly not English. Since Sussex was where Gundrada's husband was later given his most important lands in England, their presence before the conquest is plausibly explained as the result of Anglo-Flemish ties predating 1066.

Gundrada married the Norman baron William (I) de *Warenne (*d.* 1088), whose lands lay towards Flanders; their eldest son was William (II) de *Warenne; a second son was old enough to command troops in 1090, so the marriage probably lay within a few years either side of 1066. Warenne, already an important figure in Normandy, was a major beneficiary of the conquest and both his brothers-in-law also joined the expedition to England.

Frederic seems to have been rewarded with the lands of a rich Englishman called Toki in Norfolk, Suffolk, and Cambridgeshire, worth over £100 a year, but was killed in 1070 during the rebellion of Hereward the Wake in the Fens. His estates were assigned to Gundrada and her husband, and the fact that they were still known in 1086 as 'Frederic's fief' suggests that Gundrada retained control of them during her lifetime. One small manor among them belonged in 1086 to the abbey of St Riquier, perhaps Gundrada's gift in memory of her brother.

The other brother, Gerbod, was appointed by King William to a difficult military command in Chester, and may even have been given the title of earl. Probably in late 1070 he gave up his position in England and returned to Flanders to safeguard his interests there, rendered uncertain by the civil war which broke out on the death of the count. Reports of his fate in Flanders are contradictory. Fifty years after the event, one opinion was that he was killed, another that he fell into the hands of his enemies and was imprisoned. More attractive than either is the possibility that he was the Gerbod who accidentally killed his lord, young Count Arnulf, at the battle of Kassel in February 1071, travelled in penance to Rome, and ended as a monk of Cluny. A family connection with Cluny would provide a clear context for Gundrada and William de Warenne's later visit to the monastery and their foundation of a Cluniac priory at Lewes, probably in the early 1080s. The priory's valuable endowments in Norfolk came from what had been Frederic's lands. Gerbod's property in Flanders evidently passed to Gundrada, and her interest in the abbey of St Bertin was inherited by her younger son Reynold de Warenne.

Gundrada died in childbirth at Castle Acre on 27 May 1085 and was buried in the chapter house of Lewes Priory.

On the consecration of new monastic buildings *c.*1145, her bones were placed in a leaden chest under a magnificent tombstone of black Tournai marble, richly carved in the Romanesque style, with foliage and lions' heads, by a sculptor who later worked for Henry de Blois, bishop of Winchester and himself trained at Cluny. The tombstone was moved after the dissolution of Lewes Priory to Ifield church in Sussex, and in 1774 to the parish church of St John, Southover, in Lewes, where it still survives. Two leaden chests containing the remains of Gundrada and William were rediscovered in 1845 and placed in Southover church in 1847. C. P. LEWIS

Sources W. Farrer and others, eds., *Early Yorkshire charters*, 12 vols. (1914–65), vol. 8 · GEC, *Peerage*, new edn, 12/1.494 · G. Zarnecki, J. Holt, and T. Holland, eds., *English romanesque art, 1066–1200* (1984), 181–2 [exhibition catalogue, Hayward Gallery, London, 5 April–8 July 1984] · C. P. Lewis, 'The formation of the honor of Chester, 1066–1100', *Journal of the Chester Archaeological Society*, 71 (1991), 37–68, esp. 38–9 [G. Barraclough issue, *The earldom of Chester and its charters*, ed. A. T. Thacker] · E. Warlop, *The Flemish nobility before 1300*, 4 vols. (1975–6), 2/2.1024 · B. Golding, 'The coming of the Cluniacs', *Anglo-Norman Studies*, 3 (1980), 65–77, 208–12 · A. Farley, ed., *Domesday Book*, 2 vols. (1783) · Ordericus Vitalis, *Eccl. hist.* · E. A. Freeman, 'The parentage of Gundrada, wife of William of Warren', *EngHR*, 3 (1888), 680–701

Warenne, Hamelin de, earl of Surrey [Earl Warenne] (*d.* 1202), magnate, was the natural son of Geoffrey, count of Anjou (*d.* 1151), and half-brother of *Henry II, from whom he received the Warenne Anglo-Norman honours with the title earl of Surrey in April 1164 on his marriage to Isabel de *Warenne, countess of Surrey (*d.* 1203), widow of *William of Blois, Earl Warenne (*d.* 1159). Although Hamelin readily adopted the Warenne family name, he proudly acknowledged in his charters both his Angevin paternal heritage and his debt to his royal brother. Hamelin's first reported political act, a vociferous denunciation of Thomas Becket at the Council of Northampton in October 1164, was motivated by the archbishop's perceived injury to the royal family in blocking the marriage of William FitzEmpress to the Countess Isabel on grounds of consanguinity. William had died shortly thereafter while seeking the intervention of his mother, the Empress Matilda, in the matter. Many of his friends believed that the disappointment had helped to cause his death. Few at court could have missed the connection, psychological or otherwise, of Hamelin's good fortune in gaining his title and high-born wife with the equally great misfortune of the death of the king's (and Hamelin's) younger brother. It is within this context that Hamelin's early confrontational attitude towards Thomas Becket is best explained. Years later the earl became, as did Henry II himself, an active participant in the then sainted archbishop's cult, having been healed, miraculously it was thought, of a cataract in one eye by the covering which lay on Becket's tomb.

In England in 1166, and again in Normandy in 1172, Hamelin was one of a handful of élite Anglo-Norman courtiers who were not obligated to report their knights' fees and their royal or ducal knight service. Consequently the Warenne fiefs are missing from the great surveys of Henry II's reign: the *Cartae baronum* and the *Infeudationes militum*. None the less, other near-contemporary sources indicate something of the magnitude and importance of the Warenne honours. The Domesday evaluation of the family's lands in England amounted to some £1140, which placed them among the four or five wealthiest secular holdings below the king. By the second half of the twelfth century over 140 knights' fees had been subinfeudated by the Warennes, making Hamelin in 1173 the ninth greatest lord in England as reckoned by enfeoffments. What his ranking may have been in Normandy is difficult to say, except that his wife's ancestral lands, centred on the strategic castles of Mortemer and Bellencombre, would have made the earl a major force in Upper Normandy. Indeed castles are as good a measure as any other of power, prestige, and wealth. On the English side of the channel Hamelin inherited castles at Lewes, Castle Acre, Reigate, and Sandal. For his part he built (*c.*1180) the magnificent keep at Conisbrough, which was later to serve as an inspiration for Sir Walter Scott's *Ivanhoe*.

Hamelin was well connected politically outside the royal family. His brother-in-law, Reginald de Warenne, worked frequently as a baron of the English exchequer. Hugh de Cressy, a Warenne under-tenant and sometime seneschal, rose to become Henry II's constable for Rouen and constant companion. Like so many of his peers Hamelin enjoyed prestige and wealth without much interference from royal government. According to the English pipe rolls the earl was assessed a total of £276 over a period of thirty-eight years, against which he paid the sum of £74, mostly on scutages taken from his under-tenants. It would be wrong to conclude from this, however, that Hamelin lived the pampered life of a detached aristocrat. His wealth and connections did obligate him to an active participation in state affairs, an obligation he took seriously. Throughout his tenure as earl, Hamelin remained steadfastly loyal to his brother the king, to his nephew Richard I, and, when challenged, to Angevin royal interests.

Judging from the relatively low number of royal charters attested by Hamelin (ten), the earl apparently never entered the intimate, inner circle at Henry II's court, as did other family members like Reginald, earl of Cornwall. And yet, at critical moments in the reign, he is found at his brother's side. When Henry met Raymond de St Gilles, count of Toulouse, in February 1173 at Fontevrault to settle long-standing differences, Hamelin was there attesting charters as 'vicomte of the Touraine'. That Henry chose the earl to act as vicomte in this sensitive border region between the houses of Anjou and Blois displays great trust. Perhaps Hamelin took up this office during the king's stay in Ireland (1171–2), when the hostility of the French court, particularly the Blois family, was directed against the Angevin monarchy for Henry's perceived complicity in the murder of Thomas Becket. If so, Hamelin acted as one of the chief protectors of his brother's dominions during the time of Henry's self-imposed Irish exile. Equally important, the political manoeuvrings of February 1173 saw the king negotiating a marriage for

John to the daughter of the count of Maurienne and fending off the demand of Henry, the Young King, to be put in control of some part of his inheritance. Henry's announced intention of the conveyance of the Tourangeaux castles of Chinon and Loudun to the five-year-old John as a marriage portion precipitated the premature launching by Henry, the Young King, of the rebellion he had been planning against his father. Lost in subsequent events is the fact that Hamelin would have been the local overseer of John's properties had the original plan been carried out. Hamelin held fast with his brother against his nephews and their French and Scottish allies in the ensuing civil war and next appears in the chronicles in 1176 as a member of Joan's escort through central and southern France as his niece, the princess, journeyed to Sicily for her marriage with King William. In the 1180s Hamelin focused much of his energy on his estates in Yorkshire, building the wondrous castle and keep at Conisbrough. He undoubtedly spent more time in Yorkshire than any of the other Warenne earls and may have been attracted to the region as much by the opportunity to leave his own fresh mark in a family of prodigious builders as by the thriving northern economy. Years of experience at the Angevin court, coupled with private success in the management of the diverse Warenne properties, earned Hamelin a respect which would serve him well in the troubled years following Henry II's death in 1189.

Although Hamelin played no ceremonial role in Richard I's first coronation, as did other earls, he travelled widely with the new king, attesting thirteen charters, at Geddington (three), Bury St Edmunds (three), Canterbury (three), Rouen (three), and Montrichard (one), all before July 1190, when the main Angevin armies departed on crusade. With Richard gone Hamelin quickly attached himself to the king's chancellor, William de Longchamp, bishop of Ely. Their friendship was born of necessity: Longchamp was attempting to whittle down the power in the north of Hugh du Puiset, bishop of Durham, while fending off the intrigues of the king's brother, Count John; and Hamelin was equally disturbed by Hugh and John, holding true to the monarchy and his nephew, the king, as he had to his brother. Hamelin felt most comfortable adhering to the law (the legend on his seal reads 'pro lege, per lege') and, with Richard gone, William de Longchamp represented the law. When Geoffrey, archbishop of York (yet another nephew), was taken into custody at Dover in September 1191, when he attempted to enter England contrary to royal order, it was Earl Hamelin who was dispatched by the chancellor to bring the archbishop to London to face judgment by the 'barons of the realm'. When the outrage over the archbishop's treatment, combined with a growing sense of Longchamp's unrestrained ambition, allowed Count John to galvanize baronial discontent for a showdown with the chancellor at Loddon Bridge near Windsor in October, Hamelin again was conspicuous in his support of Longchamp. And after the chancellor's exile, when news of Richard's captivity in Germany reached England, Hamelin acted as one of only two magnates (William d'Aubigny, earl of Arundel, being the other) who were entrusted with the collection and safe keeping of the king's ransom. After Richard's return in 1194 the earl took a place of honour at a second coronation, carrying one of the three swords of state with William, king of Scots, and Ranulf (III), earl of Chester. A northern orientation again is apparent in these pairings. At the Council of Nottingham that same year Hamelin sat with Richard as sentences were handed out to John's followers and other disturbers of the king's peace. With this, Hamelin's long involvement in national politics slowed to an end. Present at John's coronation in May 1199, the earl attested no royal charters from the reign, though he is reported by Roger of Howden to have witnessed an oath given by William, king of Scots in November 1200.

Absorbed by private matters, most notably a dispute with Cluny over the right to appoint the prior of Lewes, Earl Hamelin died on 7 May 1202 and was buried in the chapter house at St Pancras Priory, Lewes, Sussex. The Countess Isabel died shortly thereafter and was interred with her husband. The earl and countess were survived by four children: William (IV) de *Warenne, who succeeded to the earldom; Isabel, who married first Robert de Lacy of Pontefract and second Gilbert de l'Aigle of Pevensey; Maud, who married first Henry, count of Eu, and second Henry de Stuteville, lord of Valmont in Normandy; and Ela, who married first Robert of Naburn and second William fitz William of Sprotborough. If many of the personal details of Earl Hamelin's life are unknown, something of his mind comes through in these words taken from a grant to Lewes: 'grounds for forgetfulness and dispute are wont to be removed by the good effect of a written deed' (*Cartulary of the Priory of St Pancras of Lewes*, 1932–3, 38.45). In his heart, then, the earl was both lawyer and historian.   THOMAS K. KEEFE

Sources R. Howlett, ed., *Chronicles of the reigns of Stephen, Henry II, and Richard I*, 4, Rolls Series, 82 (1889) • J. C. Robertson and J. B. Sheppard, eds., *Materials for the history of Thomas Becket, archbishop of Canterbury*, 7 vols., Rolls Series, 67 (1875–85) • W. Stubbs, ed., *Gesta regis Henrici secundi Benedicti abbatis: the chronicle of the reigns of Henry II and Richard I, AD 1169–1192*, 2 vols., Rolls Series, 49 (1867) • Ralph de Diceto, 'Ymagines historiarum', *Radulfi de Diceto … opera historica*, ed. W. Stubbs, 2 vols., Rolls Series, 68 (1876) • *Chronica magistri Rogeri de Hovedene*, ed. W. Stubbs, 4 vols., Rolls Series, 51 (1868–71) • W. Stubbs, ed., *Chronicles and memorials of the reign of Richard I*, 2: *Epistolae Cantuarienses*, Rolls Series, 38 (1865) • *Gir. Camb. opera* • *Chronicon Richardi Divisensis / The Chronicle of Richard of Devizes*, ed. J. T. Appleby (1963) • C. T. Clay, ed., *The honour of Warenne* (1949), vol. 8 of *Early Yorkshire charters*, ed. W. Farrer and others (1914–65) • W. Farrer, *Honors and knights' fees … from the eleventh to the fourteenth century*, 3 (1925) • T. K. Keefe, *Feudal assessments and the political community under Henry II and his sons* (1983) • H. M. Thomas, *Vassals, heiresses, crusaders, and thugs: the gentry of Angevin Yorkshire, 1154–1216* (1993) • J. T. Appleby, *England without Richard, 1189–1199* (1965)

Warenne, Isabel de, *suo jure* **countess of Surrey** (*d.* 1203), magnate, was the daughter and only surviving heir of William (III) de *Warenne, earl of Surrey (*c.*1119–1148), and Ela (*d.* 1174), daughter of Guillaume Talvas, count of Ponthieu. This position ensured her matches of considerable importance. In 1148, the year of her father's death, and at a critical moment in the civil war, she married *William of Blois (*d.* 1159), the younger son of King *Stephen, as part of

the king's attempt to ensure control of the Warenne estates. About 1162–3, in what may have been a love match, William FitzEmpress, the brother of Henry II, sought her hand in marriage. However, Thomas Becket, archbishop of Canterbury, objected on grounds of consanguinity, earning the lasting enmity of the allegedly heart-broken William. Isabel's reaction is, unfortunately, not recorded. In April 1164, with a valuable trousseau worth £41. 10s. 8d., she married Hamelin of Anjou (*d.* 1202), the half-brother of *Henry II, who by this marriage came to be known as Hamelin de *Warenne. Isabel had one son, William (IV) de *Warenne, who succeeded to the earldom and married Matilda, daughter of William *Marshal (*d.* 1219) and widow of Hugh Bigod (*d.* 1225). Her three daughters with Hamelin all married twice: Ela married Robert of Naburn and William fitz William (*d.* 1219); Isabel married Robert de Lacy and Gilbert de l'Aigle, lord of Pevensey; Matilda married Henry, count of Eu (*d.* 1190/91) and Henry de Stuteville: by the former marriage Isabel became grandmother of the powerful *Alice, countess of Eu (*d.* 1246).

As a countess and great heiress Isabel was involved in the secular and religious patronage of the Warenne estates. Of particular interest is her patronage during both marriages, and as a widow, of the chief English Cluniac house, Lewes Priory, Sussex, founded by her grandparents. She was present at Lambeth when a long-standing dispute between the great abbey of Cluny and her husband was resolved on 10 June 1201. She and Earl Hamelin also patronized St Mary's Abbey and West Dereham Abbey, Norfolk; St Katherine's Priory, Lincoln (*c.*1198–1202); and the chapel of St Philip and St James in their castle at Conisbrough (1180–89). In 1202–3, as a widow, she confirmed various grants to these houses, and was involved in pleas in her Yorkshire estates. Isabel died on 12 July 1203 and was buried alongside Earl Hamelin in the chapter house at Lewes, the traditional Warenne resting place. She was commemorated by the monks of Beauchief Abbey on 12 July.   SUSAN M. JOHNS

Sources W. Farrer and others, eds., *Early Yorkshire charters*, 12 vols. (1914–65) • R. Howlett, ed., *Chronicles of the reigns of Stephen, Henry II, and Richard I*, 4, Rolls Series, 82 (1889) • Stephen of Rouen, 'Draco Normannicus', ed. R. Howlett, *Chronicles of the reigns of Stephen, Henry II, and Richard I*, 2, 589–781, Rolls Series, 82 (1885) • *Pipe rolls, 10 Henry II* • GEC, *Peerage*, new edn • *Curia regis rolls preserved in the Public Record Office* (1922–)

Warenne, Isabel de [*married name* Isabel d'Aubigny], **countess of Arundel** (1226x30–1282), founder of Marham Abbey, Norfolk, and religious patron, was the daughter of William (IV) de *Warenne, earl of Surrey (*d.* 1240), and his second wife, Matilda (or Maud), coheir and daughter of William (I) *Marshal, earl of Pembroke. Matilda's first husband, Hugh Bigod, earl of Norfolk, died in February 1225, and she married Isabel's father on or before 13 October in the same year. They also had a son, John de *Warenne, later earl of Surrey (1231–1304). Isabel was almost certainly the elder of the two children, having been born probably between mid-1226 and early 1230. In

1234 she was married to the twenty-year-old Hugh d'Aubigny, earl of Arundel. The only details of the marriage come from a charter of Isabel's father, in which he granted to the couple a manor at Marham, Norfolk, worth £40 p.a. in rent.

Between 1231 and 1241 Isabel's father, three of her maternal uncles, and a maternal aunt died. The death of her husband on 7 May 1243 left her a childless teenage widow in possession of a considerable estate. Although on 29 May her marriage was granted to the king's Savoyard favourite Pierre de Genevre, provision was also made for her to remain unmarried: the entry on the patent roll provides that Pierre should be the recipient of any money that she might pay to retain her freedom of choice. Her dower consisted of the hundred and manor of Bourne, Lincolnshire, together with the manors of Wymondham and Kenninghall, Norfolk, and Stansted, Essex, and various other properties in Norfolk and Buckinghamshire. She continued to be styled countess of Arundel, even after Hugh's four sisters had divided the remainder of the Arundel estates. It was not until after Isabel's death that the male heirs of her husband's family again styled themselves earls of Arundel.

In 1249, less than a year after her mother's death and in the same year as that of her guardian, Isabel founded the convent of Marham on the land she had been granted by her father. Uniquely among English nunneries it was created as an abbey of the Cistercian order (rather than being incorporated in that order later): in its foundation charter, preserved in its cartulary, Isabel specifically refers to Marham as an abbey of the Cistercian order, and by 1250 it had been inspected by two Cistercian abbots. In 1252 she gained papal permission to enter the Cistercian house of Waverley to consult with the abbot there, and the Waverley annals record her grant of 4 marks and a cask of wine to the monks, presumably in gratitude for their help. Charters confirming the foundation were obtained from her brother, from the bishop of Norwich, and from Henry III. Marham acquired its most valuable endowments in these early years, among them eleven individual grants from its foundress, which in themselves provided it with a viable economic base.

Isabel's keen protection of her property rights, which so benefited Marham, also led to a quarrel with Henry III, recorded in some detail by Matthew Paris. In 1252 the king took custody of the estate of a recently deceased tenant, which included a quarter of a knight's fee whose wardship was legally held by Isabel. After the king had refused her request for the reversal of this appropriation, Isabel denounced Henry to his face. Paris, sympathetic to her cause, gives her a speech berating the king for his untrustworthiness, and hence for the frailty of the rules laid out in Magna Carta: 'Where are the liberties of England, so often recorded, so often granted, and so often ransomed?' (Waugh, 254). Although Paris depicted Isabel leaving the court empty-handed, Henry in fact surrendered her part of the wardship a year later, and pardoned the countess the 35 marks fine she had incurred in appealing her case.

Isabel was a notable patron of the hagiography then in vogue among lay noblewomen. Matthew Paris translated into Anglo-Norman verse his own life of St Edmund of Abingdon for her, and arranged for the loan to her of his vernacular lives of St Edward the Confessor and St Thomas of Canterbury. It was also at her request that Ralph Bocking wrote his Latin life of St Richard of Wyche (d. 1253) between 1268 and 1272. Bocking acknowledged the countess as a generous widow, who had declined to marry despite the entreaties of kings and princes. While he also states that she provided an example for nuns to follow, there is no evidence that she ever took the veil. Isabel died shortly before 23 November 1282 and was buried at Marham.

JOHN A. NICHOLS

Sources J. A. Nichols, 'Why found a medieval Cistercian nunnery?', *Medieval Prosopography*, 12 (1991), 1–28 • J. A. Nichols, 'The history and cartulary of the Cistercian nuns of Marham Abbey, 1249 to 1536', PhD diss., Kent State University, Ohio, 1974 • Paris, *Chron.*, vol. 5 • S. Thompson, *Women religious* (1991) • S. L. Waugh, *The lordship of England: royal wardships and marriages in English society and politics, 1217–1327* (1988) • D. Jones, *St Richard of Chichester: sources for his life*, Sussex RS, 79 (1995) [incl. Ralph Bocking's life] • A. Gransden, *Historical writing in England*, 1 (1974) • GEC, *Peerage*, new edn • *Ann. mon.*, vol. 2 • Dugdale, *Monasticon*, new edn, vol. 5 • J. M. Canivez, ed., *Statuta capitulorum generalium ordinis Cisterciensis*, 2 (1934) • F. Blomefield and C. Parkin, *An essay towards a topographical history of the county of Norfolk*, [2nd edn], 11 vols. (1805–10), 3.486–92 • A. Gransden, ed. and trans., *The chronicle of Bury St Edmunds, 1212–1301* [1964] • J. Burton, *Monastic and religious orders in Britain, 1000–1300* (1994) • CIPM, vol. 2 • J. Nichols, 'Heated conversation: the spoken words of Isabel de Aubigny, countess of Arundel', *Annual of Medieval Studies* (2001), 117–27

Archives Norfolk RO, Hare 1/232x

Wealth at death vast estates in Northamptonshire, Norfolk, Sussex, and Derbyshire; owed more than ten knight's fees to the king: CIPM, 2

Warenne, John de, sixth earl of Surrey [earl of Surrey and Sussex, Earl Warenne] (1231–1304), magnate, was the only son of William (IV) de *Warenne, earl of Surrey (d. 1240), and Maud, one of five daughters and eventual coheirs of William (I) *Marshal, earl of Pembroke (d. 1219), and widow of Hugh Bigod, earl of Norfolk (d. 1225). Isabel de *Warenne, founder of Marham Abbey, was his elder sister.

Inheritance, early career, and marriage Through his father, Warenne eventually inherited an estate that stretched across England. Centred on the barony of Lewes in Sussex, it included Stamford and Grantham in Lincolnshire; Castle Acre in Norfolk; Conisbrough, Sandal, and Wakefield in Yorkshire; and Reigate in Surrey. Through his mother, he was related to some of the most illustrious families in England and France.

Aged only nine on his father's death in 1240, John de Warenne became a ward of *Henry III, who gave Peter of Savoy custody of the family lands, but raised the boy at court. In 1246 Henry promised to marry his ward to one of Amadeus of Savoy's daughters, but the match was never made. Instead, in August of the following year Henry arranged for Warenne to marry Henry's own uterine sister, Alice, the daughter of Hugues de Lusignan, count of La Marche and lord of Lusignan and Valence, and of Isabella, daughter of Audemar, count of Angoulême and widow of

Henry's father, King *John. The marriage was part of Henry's policy of enriching his Lusignan relatives, and was accordingly denounced by Matthew Paris, claiming that it was beyond the bride's station. After marrying, Warenne received two extra robes at Christmas, and in 1248 received some of his father's lands.

In the early 1250s Warenne was drawn into the court circle that revolved around the Lusignans and the Lord Edward, eight years younger than Warenne. Brother-in-law of both William de *Valence and Aymer de *Lusignan, Warenne took part, along with William, in the dispute between Aymer, bishop-elect of Winchester, and the archbishop of Canterbury in 1252–3. In 1252 he came of age, and obtained the emoluments of his earldom. In 1254 he was knighted along with the Lord Edward and was with the king in Gascony, where he stood surety for Henry's debts in Bordeaux. The following year Warenne went overseas with William de Valence and the earl of Gloucester. He was also one of the English barons who escorted the young king of Scots, Alexander III, and his wife, Margaret, Henry's daughter, from Edinburgh to Wark-on-Tweed, where they met with Henry, and was present when a new regency council was instituted for Alexander. He accompanied Richard of Cornwall for his coronation as king of the Romans at Aachen in 1257. Warenne's first daughter, Alice, was born in 1251, followed by Isabel in 1253, and his only son, William, in January 1256. Yet his wife died less than a month later, and, perhaps surprisingly, Warenne never remarried.

Political vacillations Like many barons, Warenne changed allegiance several times during the turbulent period of reform that began in 1258, though, doubtless because of his background and upbringing, he most often supported the crown. In 1255 he had been among those barons who protested against the large number of foreigners Henry was bringing into England, but by 1257 he was a member of Edward's retinue, and was also often in the company of his own brother-in-law, William de Valence. When the reform movement coalesced at the Oxford parliament in July 1258, Warenne was one of the twelve chosen from Henry's side (who also included William and Aymer de Lusignan) to help elect a council of fifteen which was to direct the government of the realm. Though he swore to uphold the reforms, he baulked at the order to resume the lands and castles that Henry had given to his Lusignan favourites, and fled with the latter to Aymer's castle of Wolvesey. But Warenne was persuaded to abandon his resistance, and after the Lusignans had surrendered and were banished from the realm, he was one of the barons who escorted them to Dover.

Warenne was in the political affinity that Edward gathered in late 1258 and 1259 to assert his political independence. He stood by Edward when he allied with the earl of Gloucester in March 1259, and later in October witnessed Edward's letter giving support to Gloucester's opponent, Simon de Montfort. The following spring, however, Warenne's loyalty to Edward wavered, and he seems to have been induced to return to Henry's side. At the end of March 1260, Henry authorized payment of a yearly fee to

Warenne. When Edward appeared to be preparing to oppose his father in April 1260, Warenne was one of those magnates whom Henry summoned to come armed to London, where he was given lodgings inside the city while Edward was forbidden entry. Any rift between the earl and Edward was soon patched, however. After his reconciliation with his father, Edward travelled overseas to participate in tournaments, taking Warenne and other knights with him. Warenne had probably returned to England by 17 February 1261, when Henry summoned him and twenty-six other magnates to come armed to London.

Yet, with Henry's assertion of personal power that spring, Warenne once again sided with Simon de Montfort, along with Warenne's half-brothers, Roger (III) and Hugh Bigod. They insisted on adherence to the provisions of Oxford, and appealed to Louis IX of France to arbitrate in the dispute. In December, after the resistance had collapsed, Warenne like other opponents was pardoned for his actions. He then went overseas, and returned on 10 March 1263 in the company of Henry of Almain and Henry, son of Simon de Montfort. Simon himself returned from France in April, and assembled a group of young councillors including Warenne, Henry of Almain, and Gilbert de Clare. They met at Oxford, and again insisted on the enforcement of the provisions of Oxford. Warenne was then part of Montfort's army that attacked royalists and occupied the Welsh marches, and was among those summoned in May to come to Worcester armed for war. In August, after Henry III had capitulated to the barons, Warenne was named custodian of Pevensey Castle on the advice of the nobles. As a member of the royal council he was appointed, along with Simon de Montfort, Henry of Almain, and others, to negotiate for peace with Llywelyn ab Iorwerth. At about this time, however, he again changed sides and, with Henry of Almain, Roger and Hugh Bigod, and others, once more joined Edward. On 18 September Warenne received his reward, a heritable grant of all of the Norman lands that he held or that would fall to him within his estate. On 23 September Warenne and Henry of Almain sailed to France in the company of Henry III, Edward, and the queen to meet with King Louis. During December Warenne strengthened his ties to the king and Edward. He served on the royal council, witnessed charters, and received various favours. He was with the royal army that marched on Dover Castle on 3 December, and was listed among the royalists in the letter in which Henry agreed to submit the quarrel over the provisions to Louis's judgment. On 24 December the king appointed him military warden of the counties of Surrey and Sussex.

The barons' wars and their aftermath Warenne fought on the king's side throughout the civil war in 1264–5. Along with Roger of Leybourne he commanded Rochester Castle, which Simon de Montfort and his army besieged on 19–26 April. He fought under Edward at the battle of Lewes on 14 May but, when the tide of battle shifted and he saw the ferocity of the baronial attack, he and William de Valence, Gui de Lusignan, and Hugh Bigod fled to

Pevensey Castle, and thence overseas. Chroniclers condemned him for his flight, one of them blaming Edward's capture on him. While in France the exiles implored the king of France to aid their cause, and counselled the exiled Queen Eleanor to collect an invasion force. In England the seizure of Warenne's lands was ordered, and on 20 June they were committed to Gloucester's custody, except for the castles of Reigate and Lewes. Warenne's lands in Sussex were given to the younger Simon de Montfort.

Warenne did not return to England until the spring of 1265, as the country moved toward another military showdown. In early May Warenne landed in Pembroke with William de Valence and a force of 120 men, both cavalry and infantry, and they soon joined forces with the earl of Gloucester, who had deserted Montfort. A few weeks later Warenne and Valence sent the prior of Monmouth to meet with the king, who was then with Montfort at Hereford, and to sue for the restoration of their lands, claiming they had been seized unjustly. Henry replied that he was prepared to do justice to anyone and would give them a safe conduct, but added that they would also have to answer for certain trespasses. On 28 May Edward escaped from his captors, and soon linked up with Warenne and Valence. Under Edward's leadership they quickly captured several towns in the marches. On the night of 1–2 August Warenne and Valence accompanied Edward in his surprise attack on Kenilworth, which resulted in the capture of a considerable number of Montfort's noble commanders. Presumably, Warenne was with Edward at the battle of Evesham on 4 August, though the chronicles do not note his role.

Several features of Warenne's formative years stand out. He plunged into the thick of political conflict, but never became a prominent leader for either side. He was most often in the company of a group of coevals related by blood or marriage—the Lord Edward, Henry of Almain, William de Valence, and the Bigods—whose friendship may have been more meaningful to him than political idealism. He seems to have looked to one of his kinsmen—Edward, Henry, or William—for political cues for changes in allegiance. Yet despite his fickle loyalties, he forged a close bond to Edward that lasted throughout his life.

In the aftermath of the barons' wars Warenne was called upon to help restore order. He was dispatched to subdue Kent and the Cinque Ports, and brought 200 archers from the weald of Sussex to intimidate London. Warenne and Henry of Almain routed northern rebels led by the earl of Derby. He and William de Valence attacked Bury St Edmunds in an effort to reduce the turmoil and disobedience in East Anglia. In 1267 the king deputed the two men to urge Gloucester to attend parliament, which he had refused to do. In 1268 the king pardoned Warenne for any rebellion against the king and for the actions of his followers. His rewards were not particularly lavish. He received an important wardship, London houses forfeited by Hugh Neville, a promise of £100 of land out of royal escheats, 200 marks in cash, and several Jewish debts. The crown also made some gifts and pardons at his request.

At the parliament of Northampton in June 1268 Warenne, along with Edward, Henry of Almain, William de Valence, and other magnates, vowed to go on crusade. In the end, however, Warenne remained in England. Henry III died on 20 November 1272, and at his funeral four days later Warenne, together with other magnates and prelates, swore loyalty to Edward, who was still on his way back from Palestine. Warenne acted as one of the custodians of the realm, making a new seal, appointing officials, and protecting the king's treasure and peace in Edward's name.

Acts of violence Warenne was active and aggressive in asserting his privileges and property rights. In 1253 a royal court convicted him of unjustly enclosing much of the commons around Wakefield, and ordered him to tear down fences he had recently erected. In 1269 he collided with the earl of Lincoln over some pastureland. They mustered private armies, but royal justices determined that the land belonged to Lacy and averted war. A little later Warenne feared he would likewise lose another legal battle, with Alan de la Zouche. Appearing in court at Westminster, the two men exchanged increasingly insulting words until Warenne's followers drew their swords, set on the Zouches, and wounded Alan mortally. Warenne fled to his castle of Reigate, and only agreed to submit to the king's judgment after the earl of Gloucester and Henry of Almain guaranteed his safety. Warenne swore that he attacked Zouche not out of premeditated malice but out of uncontrollable anger. He was pardoned for a fine of 10,000 marks, which was initially to be paid off in instalments of 700 marks a year. The king reduced the annual payments to only 200 marks, but even then Warenne paid very little of the fine, to the consternation of some.

In 1270 the archbishop of York scolded Warenne for levying unheard-of exactions on account of the recent civil war. In 1274 archers and other men of the earl roamed about the lands of Robert d'Aguillon harassing his men and causing general disquiet in the neighbourhood. The inquests of 1274–6 recorded in the hundred rolls reveal 'diabolical, innumerable oppressions' by his stewards and bailiffs on manors throughout England (*Rotuli hundredorum*, 1.108). They prevented royal ministers from executing their duties; they levied arbitrary taxes, fines, and tolls; and they imprisoned persons who stood up to the earl or violated his rights. The earl high-handedly exercised liberties without royal warrant and illegally enclosed vast acres. The animals in his well-stocked parks posed a danger to crops in nearby fields, a complaint that Archbishop Pecham echoed in a letter to Warenne asking him to correct the situation. It is little wonder that the chancery rolls are peppered with commissions appointed to hear and determine claims of trespass against the earl's warrens, parks, lands, and animals.

When Edward I undertook a survey of military fees in 1284, Warenne's bailiffs refused to allow the commissioners to enter the earl's liberty, and his tenants refused to respond or appear before them. This background makes understandable the legend of Warenne's defiance of the king's justices in 1279. The story relates that when he was challenged to show by what warrant he held his lands, Warenne held up a rusty sword and declared

> Here my lords, here is my warrant! My ancestors came with William the Bastard and conquered their lands with the sword, and I shall defend them with the sword against anyone who tries to usurp them. The king did not conquer and subject the land by himself, but our forefathers were partners and co-workers with him. (*Chronicle of Walter of Guisborough*, 216)

Reynold de Grey of Ruthin, the justice of Chester, discovered that Warenne meant what he said about defending his lands with the sword, when in 1286–8 Warenne summoned military forces to combat Grey's alleged encroachment in his Welsh lordship.

Campaigns in Wales and Scotland Warenne was a prominent military commander in Edward I's wars in Wales and Scotland. He sat on the court that rendered judgment against Llywelyn ap Gruffudd in 1276. He served in Wales in 1276–7 and again in 1282–3, when he captured the castle of Dinas Brân. Edward rewarded him with Bromfield and Yale, one of several new lordships carved out of Welsh lands. During the uprising of Rhys ap Maredudd in 1287 he led a contingent to Wales, and was summoned again in 1294 to help reduce the rebellion in north Wales led by Madog ap Llywelyn. True to his character, in 1294 he strenuously, though unsuccessfully, asserted his right to the custody of the temporalities of the bishopric of St Asaph within his Welsh territories during vacancies.

Even during the Welsh wars Warenne was active in Scotland. In 1278 he accompanied Alexander III, king of Scots, to London and sat in parliament when Alexander swore fealty to Edward. Warenne travelled to Scotland with Edward in 1285, and in 1289–90 he served as a royal envoy in the sensitive negotiations for a marriage between Prince Edward and Margaret (the Maid of Norway), designated queen of Scots. He helped negotiate the treaty of Salisbury in the autumn of 1289, and the treaty of Birgham, which set the final terms of the marriage and of future relations between England and Scotland, in July 1290. Warenne was also one of the prince's proctors, and was one of the ambassadors sent to Margaret's father, Erik of Norway. In the discussions that followed Margaret's sudden death in September 1290, Warenne strongly supported the candidacy of his son-in-law, John *Balliol, to the throne of Scotland.

When Balliol and the Scots rebelled in 1295, Edward entrusted Warenne with the defence of English interests in Scotland, but the earl failed to live up to the confidence placed in him. He performed well at first. In 1295 Edward named Warenne keeper of the sea-coasts, one of the keepers of the northern part of England, and then keeper of Bamburgh Castle. Warenne captured Dunbar Castle on 27 April 1296, a minor battle but one proclaimed as a great victory, so demoralizing to the Scots. He then accompanied Edward on his victorious march through Scotland that summer, and on 3 September was appointed custodian of Scotland. Warenne, however, returned to the north of England, and refused to go back to Scotland when William Wallace's revolt erupted in May 1297, claiming that the weather there was bad for his health. The revolt raged out of control, and Edward ordered Warenne to return and fight. The earl slowly made his way northward and only reached Berwick in July. His grandson, Henry Percy (d. 1314), whom he had sent ahead, met with some success. In August Edward tried to replace Warenne as keeper of Scotland with Brian fitz Count, but Brian claimed that he was too poor to undertake such an expensive responsibility. At the beginning of September Edward firmly enjoined Warenne to stay in Scotland to subdue the rebellion. Warenne marched to Stirling, where a narrow bridge crossed the Forth, with the Scots camped on the opposite side. Warenne tried to negotiate, but Wallace would have nothing of it. Though warned of the danger, Warenne (who was being urged on by the Scottish treasurer, Hugh of Cressingham) decided to push ahead. On the morning of 11 September he overslept, and the advance made a late start. As predicted, the Scots attacked just after a substantial portion of the English and Welsh forces had crossed the bridge and cut them down. Warenne, who had stayed on the other side, ordered that the bridge be destroyed and fled the field, leaving behind a small force to hold the castle. He raced to Berwick, and then to Prince Edward. He was in York by 27 September.

Last years and death Notwithstanding the ineptitude Warenne had shown, and although one tradition had Edward speak derisively of his character, Edward still placed his trust in the old warrior, now in his mid-sixties, and in December 1297 appointed him captain of an expedition against the Scots. Warenne had not been directly involved in the crisis of 1297, but as a royalist he swore to uphold the *Confirmatio cartarum* in November and in January 1298 presided in Edward's name over a parliament at York which confirmed Magna Carta. He then led a quick campaign in Scotland and reoccupied Berwick. When Edward returned to England from Flanders, he warmly thanked Warenne for his service in Scotland and ordered him to come to England to discuss the Scottish situation. During the summer of 1298 Warenne served in Scotland, and he fought at Falkirk on 22 July. In November Edward appointed him one of the justices inquiring into the oppressions and misdeeds of forest officials throughout the realm. He was summoned for military service in Scotland once again the following year, and in September attended the banquet celebrating Edward's second marriage. In November the king entrusted Warenne with the custody of the latter's own grandson Edward Balliol, a potential claimant to the throne of Scotland. During the Scottish campaign in 1300, Warenne was given command of the 2nd battalion and was present at the siege of Caerlaverock, and he was summoned to Scotland again in 1301, 1302, and 1303. He died on about 29 September 1304 at Kennington, Kent, where his body lay until 1 December. After Christmas he was buried before the altar of Lewes Priory church. The archbishop of Canterbury conducted the funeral ceremony, with many nobles attending.

Warenne's children had married well, so that he left

behind highly ranked grandchildren. His daughter Alice had married Henry de *Percy (d. 1272) in 1268, and her son Henry fought along with Warenne in Scotland. Isabel was married in 1279 to John Balliol, who later became king of Scotland. Warenne's only son, William (V), married Joan (d. 1293), daughter of Robert de Vere, earl of Oxford (d. 1296). Their son John de *Warenne, was born on 30 June 1286 and baptized on 7 November just weeks before William was accidentally killed in a tournament (according to one chronicler he was murdered by envious rivals). Foreshadowing his role at the elder John's funeral, the archbishop of Canterbury presided at William's entombment before the altar at Lewes. The younger John de Warenne was thus his grandfather's heir.

High-handed and impudent in his dealings with tenants and subjects, John de Warenne seems to have been hesitant and perhaps even pusillanimous on the battlefield and in politics. A man who regularly missed the chances to take a lead in national life to which his high ancestry might appear to have entitled him, he became rather a symbol of a crude conservatism, given apt expression in the story of his defiance of the king's justices.

SCOTT L. WAUGH

Sources GEC, *Peerage*, new edn, 12/1.503–7 · F. Palgrave, ed., *The parliamentary writs and writs of military summons*, 2 vols. in 4 (1827–34) · *RotP*, vol. 1 · *Chancery records* · Rymer, *Foedera*, new edn · J. G. Edwards, *Calendar of ancient correspondence concerning Wales* (1935) · W. Rees, ed., *Calendar of ancient petitions relating to Wales* (1975) · W. Stubbs, ed., 'Annales Londonienses', *Chronicles of the reigns of Edward I and Edward II*, 1, Rolls Series, 76 (1882), 1–251 · W. H. Blaauw, 'On the early history of Lewes Priory', *Sussex Archaeological Collections*, 2 (1849), 7–37, esp. 24–37 [extracts from Lewes chronicle] · *Ann. mon.*, vols. 1–4 · H. R. Luard, ed., *Flores historiarum*, 3 vols., Rolls Series, 95 (1890) · *Willelmi Rishanger … chronica et annales*, ed. H. T. Riley, pt 2 of *Chronica monasterii S. Albani*, Rolls Series, 28 (1865) · Rishanger, *Chron.*, old ser., 15 (1840) · *The historical works of Gervase of Canterbury*, ed. W. Stubbs, 2 vols., Rolls Series, 73 (1879–80) · *The chronicle of Walter of Guisborough*, ed. H. Rothwell, CS, 3rd ser., 89 (1957) · I. J. Sanders, *English baronies: a study of their origin and descent, 1086–1327* (1960) · M. Prestwich, *Edward I* (1988) · R. F. Treharne, *The baronial plan of reform, 1258–1263* (1932) · J. R. Maddicott, *Simon de Montfort* (1994) · F. M. Powicke, *King Henry III and the Lord Edward: the community of the realm in the thirteenth century* (1966) · L. F. Salzman, ed., *The chartulary of the Priory of St Pancras of Lewes*, 2 vols., Sussex RS, 38, 40 (1932–4) · [W. Illingworth], ed., *Rotuli hundredorum temp. Hen. III et Edw. I*, RC, 1 (1812), 108

Warenne, John de, seventh earl of Surrey [earl of Surrey and Sussex, Earl Warenne] (**1286–1347**), magnate, was the son of William (V) de Warenne (d. 1286) and his wife, Joan (d. 1293), daughter of Robert de Vere, earl of Oxford (d. 1296), and the grandson and heir of John de *Warenne, earl of Surrey and Sussex (d. 1304).

Inheritance and marriage Born on 30 June 1286, John was less than a year old when his father died, and only seven when his mother, Joan, died in 1293. At the time of Joan's marriage to William de Warenne, it had been arranged that if William and Joan died leaving a minor, the custody of land and heir would fall to Joan's parents, Robert de Vere and his wife, Alice. Robert died in 1296, and it is not known where John de Warenne spent his childhood. He emerges from obscurity after his grandfather died in 1304.

Through his grandfather Warenne inherited the earldom of Surrey and Sussex, as well as lands and manors in Sussex, Surrey, Lincolnshire, Yorkshire, Wiltshire, and Norfolk. Since Warenne was still a minor, his grandfather's lands were taken into royal custody and held on his behalf until he came of age, which would have been in 1307. In February 1305 Edward I sent Warenne to attend a tournament at Guildford, part of his family estate, and provided considerable funds for his upkeep. Though the Warenne property remained in the hands of royal custodians, John de Warenne lived on the estate, and for that summer Edward commanded him to provide him with forty salted and dried deer, packed in barrels.

The parliament that met at Westminster in May 1306 marked Warenne's coming of age. On 7 April, just before parliament opened, Edward granted him his grandfather's lands, even though Warenne was not yet twenty-one, and had not performed homage. It is also likely that Warenne obtained the custody of his first cousin Edward *Balliol, son of John de Balliol, sometime king of Scots, and of Isabella, daughter of John's grandfather and so John's aunt. Edward had been entrusted to John de Warenne senior in November 1299, and remained with the younger John until King Edward ordered him to deliver the boy back into royal custody in 1310. On 15 May 1306, while parliament was in session, the king brought Warenne to the royal chamber at Westminster and offered him the marriage of his granddaughter, Joan, daughter of Henri, count of Bar, and *Edward II's daughter Eleanor. Warenne readily accepted, though the girl was less than half his age. Joan had arrived in England on 13 April and was escorted to Westminster with great pomp. A week after their betrothal Edward conducted a magnificent ceremony for the knighting of his eldest son, at which nearly 300 men were also knighted, including John de Warenne. The celebrations also involved the marriages of a number of barons and nobles. Warenne and Joan were married on 25 May, and about the same time Edmund *Fitzalan, who had been a ward in the custody of the elder John de Warenne, was married to the younger John's sister, Alice. John and Edmund would be closely linked over the next few years.

Early relations with Edward II A new phase of Warenne's career began with the death of Edward I on 7 July 1307. He was among those earls who witnessed Edward II's charter granting the earldom of Cornwall to Piers Gaveston on 6 August. On 26 August Warenne was summoned to parliament for the first time and was summoned continually thereafter. Early in 1308 he travelled with the king to France for Edward's marriage and performance of homage to the king of France. He was also summoned to attend Edward's coronation on 25 February.

Despite appearances of unity among the king and barons, relations were deteriorating rapidly, ushering in a lengthy period of political turmoil. John de Warenne's loyalties changed several times during the course of this conflict. However close he may have been to Edward at the very beginning of his reign, he soon opposed Gaveston. He fought, along with the earls of Arundel and Hereford, against Gaveston and his followers in a tournament at Wallingford in December 1307. Though the earls bested the favourite's side, Gaveston was declared the winner. Warenne was so annoyed that he showed Gaveston no favour thereafter. In January 1308, while he was with the king in France, he was one of the four earls who were party to an agreement at Boulogne that sought to ensure the redress of wrongs against the crown and oppressions against the people. This agreement is regarded as the first formal step in opposition to Gaveston. This opposition coalesced at the parliament in April when the nobility, including Warenne and Arundel, demanded that the king's favourite be exiled. At some point in these years Warenne became a retainer of Thomas, earl of Lancaster, the most powerful nobleman in England, and the staunchest opponent of Gaveston and Edward II. Warenne agreed to serve Lancaster with eighty men-at-arms and another earl. Perhaps this relationship had been sealed by the time of the tournament at Dunstable in late March and early April 1309, which Warenne attended in Lancaster's company along with Arundel, who may have been the other earl specified in the agreement. In June Edward forbade Lancaster, Warenne, Arundel, and three other earls to participate in any tournaments or adventures.

Shortly afterwards, however, Gaveston returned from exile, and Warenne moved over to the king. The earl of Lincoln, Henry de Lacy, was instrumental in persuading Warenne to accept Gaveston's return, and according to one chronicler Warenne became the latter's friend and helper. Warenne was with Edward and Gaveston in October at York, when all the other earls refused to attend a secret parliament that Edward summoned. In February 1310 Edward appointed him to help keep the peace in London during a parliament that other nobles would only attend in arms because of their fears about Gaveston. So close was he to Edward that he was the only earl besides the earl of Oxford who was not an ordainer in the following year. In response to a summons in August 1310 to fight against the Scots, Warenne travelled north with Edward, but he and Gloucester were the only earls willing to serve with Edward in Gaveston's company. In February 1311 the two earls rode through the forest of Selkirk, and received the foresters and others there into the king's peace. Warenne remained in Scotland through the spring and summer with a force of knights and men-at-arms. Warenne thus maintained his ties to Edward and Gaveston throughout 1310 and 1311.

Edward generously repaid Warenne's steadfastness. He granted favours to individuals at Warenne's request and a number of gifts to Warenne himself, including life grants of two Northamptonshire manors. In June 1310, moreover, Warenne received a life grant of the castle, forest, and honour of High Peak for an annual rent of just over 437 marks. The rent was to be paid in two instalments, but in 1310 Edward remitted the bulk of the rent, and the following year remitted payment for life. Although the honour and lands were subsequently resumed on several occasions, Warenne always recovered them.

The murder of Gaveston in 1312 strained Warenne's relationship with the king. Archbishop Winchelsey persuaded Warenne to join in the pursuit of Gaveston, who had returned to England unauthorized after parliament banished him from the realm in 1311. With the earl of Pembroke, Warenne besieged Gaveston in Scarborough Castle, forcing him to surrender on 19 May. The earls of Warwick and Lancaster captured Gaveston as Pembroke was escorting him to London, and he was summarily executed on 19 June. Gaveston's slaying enraged Edward and divided the baronage. Pembroke and Warenne stayed loyal to Edward. In August the king appointed Warenne keeper of the peace in Sussex. The following year, in both January and September, Edward issued orders forbidding Warenne to participate in tournaments, the latter involving Lancaster, Arundel, and three other earls. Then in June 1314, along with Lancaster, Arundel, and others, Warenne declined to participate in the ill-fated campaign in Scotland that ended at Bannockburn.

Marital difficulties Warenne may have wavered in support of Edward at this point because his domestic difficulties put an intense strain on all of his relationships. By 1313 it was clear that Warenne's marriage had proved unhappy and childless. The earliest official indication of problems came in 1309, when Edward gave the earl permission to make whomsoever he pleased his heir, as long as he did not disinherit any children he might have with Joan. Then, in the spring of 1313, Edward dispatched his yeoman William Aune to take Joan from Warenne's castle of Conisbrough and bring her to the king, and by June she was living in the Tower of London, supported by the king. Warenne was now living with his mistress, Maud Nereford, and as a result was threatened with excommunication in May. Though Edward initially stepped in to prevent it, the bishop of Chichester finally issued the sentence. There ensued a lengthy legal battle involving Warenne, the church, the king, and some of the nobility. Warenne wanted to dissolve his marriage to Joan so that he could marry Maud and make their two boys his legitimate heirs. He claimed that he had been pressured into marrying Joan against his will, and that they were within the prohibited degrees of kinship. Maud brought her own suit claiming that he had first contracted to marry her. Further disapproval of their relations was registered by a church council as well as by a council of nobles, who included Thomas of Lancaster. The case dragged on for another two years, as Warenne sought to find a friendly ecclesiastical forum, but he could not get satisfaction. In 1316 he promised to pay Joan £200 a year while the suit was in progress. In addition, he bound himself to provide Joan with lands worth 740 marks once their marriage was dissolved.

As the likelihood that Warenne would obtain an annulment faded, he set out on a different course. In a series of transactions in the summer of 1316, he surrendered the bulk of his family lands to the king, who then regranted them to Warenne for life. The regrants also specified that some of his lands would descend after his death first to John, son of Maud Nereford, then to his brother Thomas if this John died without heirs, and finally to the heirs general of Warenne if both sons died without heirs. Warenne stipulated that after his death, two of his more valuable properties, Stanford and Grantham, were to revert to the king, a clear benefit to the crown for engineering Warenne's settlement. In this manner, Warenne provided a legacy for his children but at great cost to the family patrimony. He did not give up hope for a dissolution of his marriage, and seems to have enlisted the assistance of the earl of Pembroke in presenting a petition to the pope seeking an annulment. In the meantime, in August 1316, Joan had departed England for France.

Supporter of Edward II Warenne soon incurred even greater costs. He steadfastly stuck to his support for Edward throughout the political crises of the middle years of Edward's reign. In February 1317 Edward summoned a small group of noblemen, including Warenne, to a colloquium at Clarendon. The topic was not specified, but they may have discussed the problems in Scotland as well as an attack on Lancaster. Warenne hesitated to carry out a direct assault, but on 9 May abducted Alice de Lacy, Lancaster's wife, from Canford Castle and took her to his own castle of Reigate. He did so, it was claimed, not for purposes of adultery but in order to humiliate Lancaster. Warenne may have acted in retaliation for Lancaster's opposition to his plan to dissolve his marriage, or for their long-standing political rivalry, or at the behest of Edward and the courtiers. Whatever the reason, Warenne soon discovered that he had bitten off more than he could chew. Lancaster was enraged, and in October and November launched a series of raids on those of Warenne's lands in Yorkshire that bordered his own estates. Edward tried to halt the fighting, but Lancaster persisted. He even ejected Maud Nereford from her property. In 1318 Edward, Lancaster, and other nobles tried to patch up their quarrels through a series of negotiations that culminated in the treaty of Leake on 9 August. Lancaster's war with Warenne, however, was regarded as a private matter and was specifically excluded from the negotiations, and in June 1318 Lancaster attacked Warenne's lordship of Bromfield and Yale in north Wales. Warenne was forced to come to terms with Lancaster on his own, and appears to have been coerced into a punishing settlement. He agreed to a disadvantageous exchange of lands, in which he gave up the Yorkshire and Welsh portions of his estate as well as lands in Norfolk for his life, in return for lands in Somerset, Dorset, and Wiltshire. In addition, he acknowledged that he owed Lancaster £50,000, though none of it was ever collected.

Not surprisingly, Warenne adhered to the king through most of the troubles that ensued over the next few years, though his loyalty sometimes wavered. He was ordered to attend a muster in 1319 at Newcastle and went to Scotland, but the campaign achieved little. In 1321 the barons, led by the lords of the Welsh marches, once again united in opposition to royal favourites, this time the Despensers, father and son. The baronial coalition pressured Warenne, Arundel, and Pembroke into joining them to banish the Despensers at a parliament in August. Edward later pardoned Warenne for his actions against the Despensers

between March and August. In October, however, Edward took the offensive, beginning with the siege of Leeds Castle in Kent, at which Warenne was present. He also marched west with Edward's army pursuing the marchers early in 1322. Warenne, Arundel, Pembroke, and Richmond were appointed to negotiate with Roger Mortimer of Wigmore on 17 January, an action that resulted in Mortimer's capture. Edward then turned northward to attack Lancaster. In March a council of magnates, including Warenne and Arundel, declared the rebels to be traitors and commissioned Warenne and Edmund, earl of Kent, to arrest Lancaster. Once Lancaster had been captured, Edward named Warenne as one of the judges at the trial that condemned him to death. Afterwards Warenne sat in the parliament at York that revoked the ordinances of 1311, participated in the campaign in Scotland that summer, and was in Scotland again in February 1323.

In 1325 Warenne was named captain of the expedition to Aquitaine. Abroad for a year, he returned in 1326 and was appointed as a captain of the array in the north in May and again in July. That May, Edward restored some of the lands that Lancaster had coerced from him. Yet, despite his support of Edward II, Warenne surrendered one of his manors to the elder Despenser to save himself from destruction. Time was now running out for the Despensers and Edward. Warenne adroitly shifted his allegiance to Queen Isabella after she landed in England in September 1326, and thereby avoided the fate of his brother-in-law, Edmund Fitzalan, who was executed in the fury that accompanied the downfall of Edward II. Warenne, in fact, was a member of the delegation that approached Edward in captivity in January 1327 and implored him to abdicate. He attended Edward III's coronation, and was a member of the regency council named to counsel and oversee the young king.

Warenne's domestic troubles seem to have subsided temporarily in these years. It was said that when he returned from Aquitaine in 1326, his wife, Joan, accompanied him, and in February 1327 he received protection to travel abroad with her. She had spent much of her time with Queen Isabella, and was in France with her and the young Prince Edward before their invasion. Furthermore, the upheaval in landholding that attended the rebellions in 1322 and 1326 led to the revision of the terms of Warenne's property settlement, in which he abandoned his effort to make his sons with Maud Nereford his heirs. Instead they entered the order of the hospital of St John of Jerusalem. Warenne's brother-in-law, Edmund Fitzalan, supported this change in his plans. Edward III settled some lands on Joan for her life in recognition of her service to his mother, Isabella, and granted her some of the goods forfeited by Fitzalan. Warenne finally recovered possession of his Yorkshire castles and lands from Henry of Lancaster in 1328, in return for a payment of 2000 marks.

Elder statesman Warenne had survived personal and political turmoil and remained an important figure at the royal court. Although chroniclers condemned the fickleness of the barons throughout Edward II's reign, Warenne's career shows why most nobles were uncertain in their loyalties and unwilling to cling unwaveringly to a particular position. The rampant factionalism that beset the court and country made steadfastness dangerous and trimming a rational act. Warenne never became a political figure as imposing as Lancaster, but he was consistently at the centre of political action.

For Edward III, Warenne proved to be a faithful servant in a variety of capacities. Edward named him an overseer of the keepers of the peace in Oxfordshire in 1327, and between 1327 and 1332 appointed him to several judicial commissions. In the spring of 1327 Edward summoned him to perform military service in Scotland, and appointed him to negotiate with the Scots in November. Like most of the baronage Warenne was actively engaged in the Scottish wars for the next few years. He thus served in Scotland in 1330, and in 1333 was present at the siege of Berwick and battle of Halidon Hill. When rumours of unrest in the Welsh marches reached the king that year, he ordered Warenne and others to take steps to keep order. For the campaign of 1334–5 in Scotland, Warenne sent a sizeable contingent but did not personally attend, though he was present at Newcastle on 12 June 1334 when his cousin Edward Balliol granted much of Scotland south of Forth to Edward III. He was with Balliol in the campaign of 1335. In 1336 he was named one of the defenders of the realm while the king was in Scotland. Warenne served Edward in the next few years by sitting on commissions, laying before the people of Surrey the decisions of the council (1337), and overseeing the array in some southern counties (1338). In 1339 he was acting sheriff of Surrey and Sussex. When Edward went overseas in 1338, and again in 1340, he named his eldest son, Edward, and Warenne as keepers of the realm in his absence. In 1345 Warenne was one of the councillors appointed to advise the regent, Edward's second son, Lionel.

Edward III rewarded Warenne amply for his service, especially at Halidon Hill. In 1333 he pardoned all debts owed by Warenne or his ancestors, and granted that his executors would have free administration of his goods after he died. In addition, Warenne's cousin and former ward, Edward Balliol, granted Warenne the earldom of Strathearn after Earl Malise had forfeited it. Thereafter, Warenne styled himself earl of Surrey and Sussex and earl of Strathearn. Edward III also promised to provide Warenne with 2000 marks out of the proceeds of wardships and escheats.

Perhaps as a result of his experiences under Edward II, Warenne managed to steer his way through the political undercurrents of the early years of Edward III's reign without getting deeply involved in the intrigue. He witnessed royal charters fairly consistently until his death, and played a role in government as a royal councillor. In 1330 the king granted him a manor and more than £230 in rents out of the properties forfeited by the earl of Kent, in return for his agreement to remain with the king. This agreement might indicate that he had the blessing of Roger Mortimer, who then controlled the government,

but he was unscathed by Mortimer's fall later in the year. In the financial and political crisis of 1340 he stood up in parliament to challenge the presence of royal officials, on the grounds that it was the peers of the realm who should give him aid and counsel. The only other possible indication of political resistance came in 1342, when Edward summoned Warenne to his campaign in Brittany. Warenne did not participate. Whether this was out of rebelliousness, or age—Warenne was now fifty-six—cannot be determined, but there were no repercussions. The same year he was excused from attending a tournament at Dunstable because of age and infirmity.

Last years and death Warenne's political steadfastness did not spill over into his private life, and domestic problems again haunted the last years of his life. Joan was in his company and regarded as his wife in 1331 and 1337, but went overseas in 1337 with her entire household. By this time Warenne may have been thinking once again of having his marriage dissolved. The bishop of Winchester wrote to him in 1344 charging him to hold Joan in marital affection, and to honour the dispensation that had been granted for his marriage. Joan went abroad yet again the following year, and the king acted at that time to guarantee her right to her lands in the face of any attempt by Warenne to regain them for himself. By 1345 Warenne was confessing that he had had an affair with Joan's aunt *Mary of Woodstock (1278–c.1332), daughter of Edward I, before he married Joan. Whatever the truth of the claim, it did not result in a dissolution of his marriage to Joan. What probably drove him to these lengths was the prospect of another marriage. Despite his age, he was living with another mistress, Isabella Holland, the daughter of Sir Robert Holland, long Thomas of Lancaster's leading retainer, and subsequently notorious for betraying his lord in 1322; in his will Warenne refers to Isabel as 'my companion'. He undertook a series of land transactions designed to undo his previous settlements and to make provision for Isabella and any potential heirs he might have with her. Initially the king acquiesced, until Richard (II) *Fitzalan, earl of Arundel, son of Warenne's brother-in-law Edmund Fitzalan, and thus Warenne's nephew, pointed out that the settlement would disinherit him since he was the heir general to Warenne's lands. The king agreed and nullified the new settlements. How disappointed Warenne might have been cannot be gauged, but in his will, dated 24 June 1347, just before his death, he left various gifts to Isabella and to various of his bastard children, and nothing to Joan. Despite his personal behaviour, Warenne demonstrated a reasonable degree of piety. He endowed a chantry, gave lands to monastic houses, entered the confraternity of Durham Priory, and possessed a Bible in French.

Warenne was becoming quite feeble, and in July 1346 Edward excused him from attending parliament or performing other services because of his frailty. He died without a legitimate heir between 28 and 30 June 1347 at his castle of Conisbrough, and was subsequently buried in Lewes Priory church. He was sixty-one. Joan was abroad when he died and lived for another fourteen years. Warenne left behind several illegitimate children, including at least three boys and three girls. His heir was Richard (II) Fitzalan, who obtained Warenne's estate but did not adopt the title of earl of Surrey until Joan died in 1361.

John de Warenne did not leave behind an impressive political or personal legacy. He was directly involved in most of the important political activity that occurred in England during his lifetime, but he was never a leader. Though he did not seem to act on high moral or political principles, he did display important chivalric qualities such as steadfastness, loyalty, and prowess. Yet his desire to provide for the descent of his lands, and his failure to sustain his marriage, undermined his actions and cost him dearly.   SCOTT L. WAUGH

Sources GEC, *Peerage*, new edn, 12/1.508–11 · F. Palgrave, ed., *The parliamentary writs and writs of military summons*, 2 vols. in 4 (1827–34) · *RotP*, vols. 1–2 · *Chancery records* · Rymer, *Foedera*, new edn · *Chronica monasterii de Melsa, a fundatione usque ad annum 1396, auctore Thoma de Burton*, ed. E. A. Bond, 3 vols., Rolls Series, 43 (1866–8) · W. Stubbs, ed., *Chronicles of the reigns of Edward I and Edward II*, 2 vols., Rolls Series, 76 (1882–3) [esp. *Annales Londonienses, Annales Paulini, Gesta Edwardi de Carnarvan, Vita et mors Edwardi II*] · H. R. Luard, ed., *Flores historiarum*, 3 vols., Rolls Series, 95 (1890), vol. 3 · N. Denholm-Young, ed. and trans., *Vita Edwardi secundi* (1957) · J. Stevenson, ed., *Chronicon de Lanercost, 1201–1346*, Bannatyne Club, 65 (1839) · W. H. Blaauw, 'On the early history of Lewes Priory', *Sussex Archaeological Collections*, 2 (1849), 7–37, esp. 23–7 · F. R. Fairbank, 'The last earl of Warenne and Surrey, and the distribution of his possessions', *Yorkshire Archaeological Journal*, 19 (1906–7), 193–264 · J. R. Maddicott, *Thomas of Lancaster, 1307–1322: a study in the reign of Edward II* (1970) · R. Somerville, *History of the duchy of Lancaster, 1265–1603* (1953) · J. R. S. Phillips, *Aymer de Valence, earl of Pembroke, 1307–1324: baronial politics in the reign of Edward II* (1972) · N. Fryde, *The tyranny and fall of Edward II, 1321–1326* (1979) · J. C. Davies, *The baronial opposition to Edward II* (1918) · W. M. Ormrod, *The reign of Edward III* (1990) · R. Nicholson, *Edward III and the Scots: the formative years of a military career, 1327–1335* (1965) · J. W. Walker, *Wakefield and its history and people*, 2nd edn (1939) · *CIPM*, 9, no. 54 · [J. Raine], ed., *Testamenta Eboracensia*, 1, SurtS, 4 (1836), 41–5
Wealth at death see *CIPM*

Warenne, Reginald [Rainald] de

Warenne, Reginald [Rainald] **de** (1121×6–1178/9), nobleman, was the third son among the five children of William (II) de *Warenne (d. 1138) and Isabel de Vermandois (d. 1147). He was thus the younger brother of William (III) de *Warenne, earl of Surrey, and brother of *Ada, later countess of Huntingdon and Northumberland. His half-brothers were *Waleran, count of Meulan, and *Robert, earl of Leicester, two of Isabel's children by her first husband, Robert de Beaumont, count of Meulan (he should not be confused with another Rainald de Warenne, possibly an illegitimate half-brother). Early in his career he married Alice, daughter and heir of William of Wormegay, whose Norfolk barony came to her on his death, *c.*1166. Warenne was shown in the pipe rolls to have owed a fine of over £466 for the inheritance, a large sum of which was still owed at his death. His heir was his only son, William. His daughters' names are not known with certainty, but they were very likely Gundreda, who married Peter de Valognes, William de Curcy, and Geoffrey Hose; Alice, who married Peter the Constable; Muriel, a

nun at Carrow Priory; and perhaps Ada or Ela, who married Duncan, earl of Fife.

Warenne's first public appearance was as early as 1138, as a witness to several of the charters of William (III) de Warenne. He became involved in the administration of some of the Norfolk estates of the honour of Warenne by 1146–7, and held lands of the honour in Sussex and Norfolk. He was certainly of age by 1147, when William (III) left him in charge of the Warenne lands upon his departure for the second crusade, from which he did not return, much to his brother's sadness. After William's death early in 1148 the Warenne inheritance went to his daughter Isabel, whom King Stephen promptly married to his son William, later count of Boulogne and Mortain. Warenne continued to administer the honour for the new earl and became his principal adviser. At this time he also began his long career of royal service, and witnessed several of Stephen's charters.

Warenne made a smooth transition between the reigns of Stephen and Henry II. He was specifically mentioned in the treaty of Winchester (November–December 1153) as having been given the option of having the custody of the Warenne castles at Bellencombre and Mortemer in Normandy, and he witnessed Stephen's notification of this treaty. He continued as a courtier; he witnessed charters under the new reign and also appeared with Henry II on several important occasions. He was present with the king at Battle Abbey in 1157, when the king judged a dispute between Archbishop Theobald and Abbot Silvester of St Augustine's, Canterbury, and a case regarding the abbot of Battle (a brother of royal favourite Richard de Lucy). He attended the Council of Clarendon (1164) and was among those chosen to accompany Henry's daughter Matilda to Saxony for her marriage in early 1168 to Duke Henry. His loyalty to the king and hostility to Thomas Becket when the archbishop landed in England in December 1170 earned him an unfavourable comparison to his crusader brother from a monastic writer. Warenne also worked as a government official during the reign and served as an itinerant justice in numerous southern and midlands counties (1168–76), as a baron of the exchequer (Michaelmas 1169), and as sheriff of Sussex (from Easter 1170 to Michaelmas 1176).

In addition to his public career Warenne also attended to the private business of religious benefaction with donations to the Warenne foundations of Lewes and Castle Acre priories, as well as gifts to St Mary Overie in Southwark, Carrow, Clerkenwell, and Binham priories, and a notification of a quitclaim to Battle Abbey. He retired from the worldly life to become a monk at the Warenne family foundation of Lewes Priory some time between Michaelmas 1178 and 1179, during which year he died.

VICTORIA CHANDLER

Sources W. Farrer and others, eds., *Early Yorkshire charters*, 12 vols. (1914–65), vol. 8 · W. Farrer, *Honors and knights' fees … from the eleventh to the fourteenth century*, 3 (1925) · *Pipe rolls* · R. V. Turner, *The English judiciary in the age of Glanvill and Bracton, c.1176–1239* (1985) · *Reg. RAN*, vol. 3 · R. W. Eyton, *Court, household, and itinerary of King Henry II* (1878) · E. Searle, ed., *The chronicle of Battle Abbey*, OMT (1980) · I. J.

Sanders, *English baronies: a study of their origin and descent, 1086–1327* (1960) • *Materials for the history of Thomas Becket, archbishop of Canterbury*, 1, ed. J. C. Robertson, Rolls Series, 67 (1875) • W. O. Hassall, ed., *Cartulary of St Mary Clerkenwell*, CS, 3rd ser., 71 (1949) • U. Rees, ed., *The cartulary of Shrewsbury Abbey*, 2 vols. (1975) • Dugdale, *Monasticon*, new edn • Binham Priory cartulary, BL, MS Cotton Claudius D.xiii, fol. 20 • Battle Abbey cartulary, Lincoln's Inn, London, MS 87, fols. 71b, 121 • D. M. Stenton, ed., *Pleas before the king or his justices, 1198–1212*, 3, SeldS, 83 (1967) • J. C. Holt and R. Mortimer, eds., *Acta of Henry II and Richard I* (1986) • G. W. S. Barrow, ed., *Regesta regum Scottorum*, 1 (1960)

Warenne, William (I) de, first earl of Surrey [Earl Warenne] (*d.* **1088**), magnate, was among the inner circle of Norman lords of Duke William's generation whose campaigns over some forty years consolidated the duchy and conquered England.

Background and early career William's father, Rodulf or Ralph de Warenne (*d.* in or after 1074), was a minor Norman magnate with lands near Rouen and in the Pays de Caux, and William's earlier ancestry has long been debated. In the twelfth century the Warennes were believed to be descended from a niece of Gunnor, the wife of Duke Richard (I) of Normandy (*d.* 996) and the person seen as the linchpin of the wider ducal kin. He was certainly related in some way to them, since Anselm, archbishop of Canterbury, later prohibited the proposed marriage of his son William (II) de *Warenne to a bastard daughter of Henry I on the grounds of their blood relationship. The most likely interpretation of the fragmentary evidence is that either William (I)'s mother or his paternal grandmother was Duchess Gunnor's niece Beatrice. Probably in his father's time the family adopted a surname from the village of Varenne, on the river of that name inland from Dieppe.

William owed his eventual standing more to his own capabilities than to family connections or inherited wealth. By the mid 1050s, though still young, he was capable and experienced enough to be given joint command of a Norman army. His first recorded military action, during a period in which the Normans were constantly at war, was in the Mortemer campaign of 1054, as one of the leaders of the army which defeated the French. His reward was a swathe of lands which had belonged to his disgraced kinsman Roger (I) de *Mortimer. Although some of the lands were soon restored to the Mortimers, William kept the important castles at Mortemer and Bellencombre. The latter, less than a day's ride from Varenne, became the capital of the Warenne estates in Normandy. At almost the same time he was further rewarded with lands confiscated in 1053 from William, count of Arques. The continuing confidence with which the duke regarded him kept William at the forefront of Norman affairs over the next two decades, and he was among those consulted when the expedition to England in 1066 was planned.

Service and rewards in England William de Warenne is among the handful of Normans known for certain to have fought at Hastings, and in 1067 was one of four men left in charge in England when the king returned to Normandy.

His role as a military commander continued to be important for another twenty years, suggesting a physical constitution as robust as the king's. In 1075 he and Richard de Clare were delegated to deal with the rebellion of Earl Ralph de Gael of East Anglia. The two first summoned the earl to attend the king's court to answer for an act of defiance, then mustered an army which defeated the rebels at Fawdon in south Cambridgeshire, mutilating their prisoners after the battle. Ralph retreated to Norwich, where Warenne and Clare began a siege which lasted three months but failed to prevent the earl's escape by boat. In the early 1080s William campaigned with the king's forces in Maine.

William de Warenne's rewards in England were very large, elevating him into the first rank of the magnates. By 1086 he was the fourth richest tenant-in-chief, surpassed only by the king's half-brothers and his long-standing comrade and kinsman Roger de *Montgomery. Such riches were accumulated over the course of the reign. The earliest acquisitions were presumably in Sussex, where he held the rape of Lewes, one of the five territories into which the shire was divided. The town of Lewes, a flourishing port on a tidal estuary, was divided between William and the king. One or the other built a castle there which became the capital of the Warenne lands in England. The original castle may have lain south of the town, where William is known to have reconstructed the church of St Pancras, and where a large mound may represent the motte. If that was the first site, it was abandoned in the 1070s when Warenne founded a priory there around the existing church. He would then have built the present castle north of the town, remarkable for having two mottes, one at each end of the bailey.

The rape of Lewes as first created for William de Warenne may have stretched from the River Adur on the west to the River Ouse on the east, and indeed beyond the Ouse at its northern extremity. Before 1073, however, the rapes were reorganized. A new rape west of Lewes was created for William (I) de Briouze, to whom Warenne surrendered seventeen manors. On the east, twenty-eight manors in four hundreds beyond the Ouse were transferred to the count of Mortain's rape of Pevensey. In compensation for those losses Warenne received lands in East Anglia.

William's second acquisition may have been the large estate of Conisbrough in Yorkshire, an important manor which occupied the gap between the marshes at the head of the Humber estuary and the Pennine foothills, and commanded the fords where the main road north crossed the River Don. Conisbrough was an old royal manor which had belonged to Earl Harold, and it seems likely that it was transferred to Warenne during the campaign against the English rebels at York in 1068.

Far more important than Conisbrough, and overshadowing even the rape of Lewes in 1086, were William's lands in eastern England. In Norfolk, especially the west of the county, he was the largest landowner in a large and wealthy shire, and his manors there were complemented by others which spilled over the county boundary and through the western side of Suffolk and Essex as far as the

Thames estuary and reached into south-east Cambridge-shire. The centre was at Castle Acre, where Warenne built not a castle but a large stone manor house (it was fortified only in the twelfth century). The estates in those four eastern shires were clearly acquired in stages. Some had belonged to Earl Harold and might have been handed over soon after 1066. Another group, before the conquest the possessions of a thegn called Toki, had fallen first to Warenne's Flemish brother-in-law Frederic, and after Frederic's death in 1070 came to William through his wife. He may not have controlled them directly until she died in 1085. Others seem to have been given to him in the aftermath of the 1075 rebellion, while the series of exchanges for parts of the original rape of Lewes may still have been going on in the 1080s.

Estates and their management In 1086 the eastern shires accounted for half the value of Warenne's estate (more than half of that being in Norfolk), and Sussex two fifths. The other tenth, which included Conisbrough, was scattered about the country in little parcels: a single manor in Hampshire, another in Buckinghamshire, Kimbolton and its outliers in Huntingdonshire and Bedfordshire, a couple of estates on the Thames near Wallingford, two small manors in south Lincolnshire, some fishermen in Wisbech. The rationale for their dispersal is not easy to discern, and it may be wrong to look for any single all-inclusive purpose. Several besides Conisbrough had belonged to Earl Harold, including Kimbolton and the Lincolnshire manors; indeed outside Wessex only Warenne and Hugh d'Avranches, earl of Chester, were given Harold's property. At least one of the manors furthest from William's bases in Sussex and Norfolk had strategic importance: his Hampshire property was Fratton on Portsea Island, watching the entrance to Portsmouth harbour.

William's dispositions of his landed estate suggest that he was a good organizer greedy for further spoils. Almost everywhere except Sussex he pushed at the limits of what he had been given, testing what more he could either claim legitimately, or simply take without opposition. Some of his extra acquisitions were peaceful enough, like the large manor of Whitchurch in Shropshire, which his distant cousin Roger de Montgomery gave him. But others were not. In Norfolk especially he asserted his lordship over freemen who might or might not have been assigned to him, leading to the many counterclaims and disputes recorded in Domesday Book. He was active even in shires where he was far less powerful. In Essex he stole land from the bishop of Durham and the abbot of Ely, and in Sussex from the nuns of Wilton; in Yorkshire he was at loggerheads with several of his neighbours about what properties were sokelands of Conisbrough; in Bedfordshire he won over the English thegn Augi from the Norman lord to whom the king had assigned him, and when Augi died took control of land which ought perhaps have gone to Augi's lord's successor; in Huntingdonshire in 1086 he staked some sort of a claim to a manor held by Hugh de Bolbec.

Warenne was wealthy enough not to need to concentrate his resources in just one or two parts of the country, and the pattern of demesne estates which he created after granting others to his men had the deliberate effect of accentuating its dispersal and shifting the balance towards Sussex rather than Norfolk. Whereas the ratios of manorial values in 1086 over the honour as a whole, between eastern England, Sussex, and the rest, were 49:41:10, what William chose to retain in his own hands was balanced 33:48:20. In Sussex he kept only four manors, but far and away the four largest, whereas in Norfolk he was not so choosy. Elsewhere he retained under his direct control one manor in each of Buckinghamshire and Oxfordshire, the core of Kimbolton, and all of Conisbrough.

William's options may have been constrained by a lack of close lieutenants to whom he was willing to give a great deal of land and authority. Despite his gains in Normandy in the 1050s his lands there were not very extensive, and he did not succeed to any part of his paternal inheritance until at least the mid-1070s. His father was still alive in 1074 and there was an older brother, Rodulf or Ralph, who inherited probably the greater part of their father's estates. Some of William's tenants in England, including the ancestors of the families of Cailly, Chesney, Grandcourt, Pierrepont, Rosay, and Wancy, can be traced back to fiefs around his Norman capital of Bellencombre, but they were only a small minority of the fifty or more men to whom William gave lands. Some others were perhaps his Norman kinsmen: Tezelin and Lambert, for instance, had unusual forenames which are known to have been used in other branches of Beatrice's family. Only a handful of his leading men held in both the eastern counties and the rape of Lewes, and the wealth which William had at his disposal was widely distributed.

Warenne's vigour in running his estates is evident from improvements in their economic condition. It seems that he took an interest in running his manors not just efficiently but aggressively, and that he was good at choosing capable reeves and bailiffs. Conisbrough was well stocked with ploughteams and intensively cultivated by Yorkshire standards, and, almost uniquely in a county devastated by warfare, more than doubled in value between 1066 and 1086. Values on the four demesne manors in Sussex also went up sharply after William acquired them, and at Castle Acre he more than tripled the size of his sheep flock.

Foundation of Lewes Priory Despite an evil reputation at Ely, where it was later believed, or at any rate hoped, that Warenne's departing soul had been claimed by demons, William was at least conventionally pious. The story of the foundation of Lewes Priory by William and his wife, Gundrada de *Warenne (d. 1085), was preserved there only in much later traditions, but in essence it is believable. Probably at an early stage William consulted Archbishop Lanfranc of Canterbury. Later, William and Gundrada went on pilgrimage to Rome, but reached no further than the great Burgundian abbey of Cluny because of the war in Italy between the pope and the emperor. Their journey probably took place within the period 1081–3 rather than at the date of 1077 assigned to it elsewhere. At Cluny the couple were received into the fellowship of the monks and resolved to found an English priory following the rule of Cluny. After difficulties and one false start, it was accomplished under a prior and three monks sent from Cluny. The monastery was established around the existing church of St Pancras in the suburbs of Lewes, it was well endowed, and an ambitious building programme was put in train. Lewes was the first house of Cluniac monks in England and the precursor of several others, and the importance of the Warennes' role in their arrival needs to be stressed.

William clearly regarded Lewes Priory as his spiritual home, and had both Gundrada and himself buried there. It was also a focus for the spiritual aspirations of his men, at least one of whom entered the priory as a monk and donated the manor which he had held as William's tenant. When he died, William was planning to establish a second priory at Castle Acre, a project brought to fruition by his son William (II).

Earldom, death, and family In the turmoil which enveloped England after the death of William the Conqueror in September 1087, William de Warenne stood firm by William Rufus. His reward, some time between Christmas 1087 and the end of March 1088, was the titular earldom of Surrey and very probably three valuable Surrey manors, Reigate, Dorking, and Shere. Warenne fought for the king during the invasion of England by supporters of Robert Curthose and was wounded by an arrow during the siege of Pevensey Castle in spring 1088. He was carried to Lewes and died there of his wounds on 24 June.

William's first wife was the Flemish noblewoman Gundrada, whom he married c.1066. They had at least three children and she died in childbirth in 1085. He then married a sister, name unknown, of Richard Gouet, a landowner in the Perche region. Her attempt to make restitution for the damage which he had inflicted upon Ely Abbey by a gift of 100 shillings a few days after his death was refused by the monks. William's elder son, William (II), succeeded him in England and Normandy; his younger son Reynold inherited Gundrada's Flemish lands. A nephew, Roger, son of Erneis, was first a knight in the household of Earl Hugh of Chester and later a monk of St Evroult, where he told the historian Orderic Vitalis much about the family.

William's remains were reburied in a leaden chest at Lewes Priory during rebuilding there c.1145, from where they were disinterred during railway construction in 1845. In 1847 they were placed alongside Gundrada's remains in the parish church of St John, Southover, in Lewes, where they still rest.   C. P. LEWIS

Sources W. Farrer and others, eds., *Early Yorkshire charters*, 12 vols. (1914–65), vol. 8 · GEC, *Peerage*, new edn, 12/1.492–5 · L. C. Loyd, 'The origin of the family of Warenne', *Yorkshire Archaeological Journal*, 31 (1932–4), 97–113 · K. S. B. Keats-Rohan, 'Aspects of Robert of Torigny's genealogies revisited', *Nottingham Medieval Studies*, 37 (1993), 21–7 · A. Farley, ed., *Domesday Book*, 2 vols. (1783) · J. F. A. Mason, *William the first and the Sussex rapes* (1966) · P. Dalton, *Conquest, anarchy, and lordship: Yorkshire, 1066–1154*, Cambridge Studies in Medieval Life and Thought, 4th ser., 27 (1994), 33–4, 64–5 · B. Golding, 'The coming of the Cluniacs', *Anglo-Norman Studies*, 3 (1980), 65–77, 208–12 · D. J. C. King, *Castellarium Anglicanum: an index and bibliography of the castles in England, Wales, and the islands*, 2 (1983), 306, 472 · C. P. Lewis, 'The earldom of Surrey and the date of Domesday Book', *Historical Research*, 63 (1990), 329–36 · L. C. Loyd, *The origins of some Anglo-Norman families*, ed. C. T. Clay and D. C. Douglas, Harleian Society, 103 (1951) · Ordericus Vitalis, *Eccl. hist.* · E. Edwards, ed., *Liber monasterii de Hyda*, Rolls Series, 45 (1866), 283–321 · B. Dickins, 'Fagaduna in Orderic (AD 1075)', *Otium et negotium: studies in onomatology and library science presented to Olof von Feilitzen*, ed. F. Sandgren (1973), 44–5

Warenne, William (II) de, second earl of Surrey [Earl Warenne] (d. 1138), magnate, the eldest son of William (I) de *Warenne (d. 1088) and Gundrada de *Warenne (d. 1085), sister of Gerbod the Fleming, earl of Chester, succeeded to the newly created earldom of Surrey on his father's death on 24 June 1088. He usually styled himself 'Willelmus comes de Warenna' and less often 'Willelmus de Warenna comes Sudreie' (or 'Surregie', 'Suthreie', or 'Sudreie'). He was a great-great-nephew of the Duchess Gunnor and thus a kinsman of the Norman kings. From his father he inherited one of the largest of all Domesday estates, with lands worth about £1165 a year spread across thirteen counties, concentrated in Sussex (the rape of Lewes), Norfolk (including Castle Acre), and Yorkshire (Conisbrough). He was a benefactor of the great Cluniac priory of St Pancras, Lewes, which his parents had founded about 1077, and also patronized the abbeys of St Evroult and St Amand and the priories of Castle Acre, Longueville, Wymondham, Pontefract, and Bellencombre. The Hyde chronicler reports that whereas William (II) de Warenne received his father's lands in England, his younger brother, Reginald, received the maternal lands in Flanders. The chronicler says nothing of the paternal lands in Upper Normandy, centring on the castles of Mortemer-sur-Eaulne and Bellencombre in the Pays de Caux, but they probably went to Reginald as well, and when Reginald died after 1106 passed to Earl William.

In 1118 or 1119 Earl William, probably in his later forties, married Isabel de Vermandois (d. 1147), granddaughter of Henri I of France and widow of the Beaumont magnate Robert, count of Meulan (d. 1118); the offspring of that marriage were the twins Waleran, count of Meulan, and Robert, earl of Leicester, and five or six other children. She and Earl William had five children, including William (III) de *Warenne, earl of Surrey (c.1119–1148), and Reginald de *Warenne (1121x6–1178/9). Through their daughter *Ada, countess of Northumberland (c.1123–1178), Isabel and Earl William were the grandparents of *Malcolm IV and *William the Lion, kings of Scotland. Henry of Huntingdon reports that Isabel's first husband, Robert, count of Meulan, had suffered the humiliation of having his wife carried off by 'a certain earl'. The circumstances and details of this scandalous event cannot be discerned, but it was not long after Count Robert's death in June 1118 that Isabel married Earl William.

Unlike his father William (I) de Warenne, a veteran of Hastings and a staunch royalist, Earl William was seldom at the court of William Rufus (he attested only one or possibly two of the king's surviving charters) and showed little respect for Henry I during his initial years. The trouble may have begun when, some time in the 1090s, Earl William tried unsuccessfully to win the hand of Matilda, the eldest daughter of King Malcolm and Queen Margaret of Scotland, who was later to marry Henry I. According to the late testimony of Master Wace, Earl William ridiculed the young Henry for his pedantic approach to the joyous aristocratic pastime of hunting, mocking him with the nickname 'Stagfoot' for having examined the sport so studiously that he could tell the number of tines in a stag's antlers simply by examining his footprint. At some point after his accession in 1100 Henry tried to win Earl William's support by offering him one of his bastard daughters in marriage, but Archbishop Anselm blocked the project on grounds of consanguinity. When Robert Curthose, duke of Normandy, invaded England on 20 July 1101, Earl William and many other barons joined the ducal side, but Henry bought off Duke Robert with an annuity of 3000 marks, and Earl William was left stranded. For the violation of his homage to the king, and perhaps as a punishment for acts of violence by his men in Norfolk, he was disseised of his English estates and forced into exile.

Earl William complained to Robert Curthose in Normandy of being deprived of his vast English estates, and recovered them when the duke crossed impulsively to England in 1103, interceded with Henry on the earl's behalf, and agreed to relinquish the annuity. Thenceforth Earl William gradually regained the king's confidence and became a trusted member of his *familia*. At the climactic battle of Tinchebrai in September 1106 he commanded a division of the victorious royal army, and from then until Henry's death in 1135 he is known to have been in the king's company on each of the royal sojourns in Normandy and England. He attended the royal council at Nottingham on 17 October 1109 and was a surety for the king in his treaty of Dover with Robert, count of Flanders, on 17 May 1110. In 1111 he served as a judge in the Norman ducal court. In 1119, on the eve of Henry's crucial battle against Louis VI at Brémule, with many Norman lords in rebellion, Earl William is said to have told the king, 'There is nobody who can persuade me to treason … I and my kinsmen here and now place ourselves in mortal opposition to the king of France and are totally faithful to you.' (*Liber monasterii de Hyda*, 316–7). With Earl William's force in the vanguard, Henry's army won a decisive victory.

Henry had taken steps to cement (or reward) Earl William's loyalty by adding to his holdings in England and Normandy. William received (*c*.1106–21) the great royal manor of Wakefield in Yorkshire, possibly relinquishing lands in Huntingdonshire, Bedfordshire, and Cambridgeshire in partial exchange for it. Henry also ceded to Earl William the castlery of St Saëns shortly after its lord, Elias de St Saëns, fled Normandy, *c*.1110, with Henry's nephew and adversary, William Clito. St Saëns, three miles up the River Varenne from Bellencombre, constituted a valuable addition to Earl William's estates in Upper Normandy and bound him even more closely to the royal cause. Should

Clito ever regain Normandy from Henry I, Clito's friend and guardian Elias would surely recover St Saëns. (His family had recovered the castlery by 1150.)

Thus, after his initial false step, William de Warenne became the most ardent of royalists. He attested no fewer than sixty-nine of Henry's charters, and in the reign's one surviving pipe roll (1130) he is recorded as receiving the third highest geld exemption of any English magnate (£104 8s. 11d.)—reflecting both the extent of his landed wealth and the warmth of the king's favour. He was at Henry's deathbed at Lyons-la-Forêt in 1135 and was one of five *comites* who escorted his corpse to Rouen for embalming. Afterwards the Norman magnates appointed Earl William governor of Rouen and the Pays de Caux. He was back in England in the spring of 1136 at Stephen's Easter court at Westminster (22 March) and at Oxford shortly afterwards, where he attested Stephen's charter of liberties for the church. His last attestations of royal charters occurred on Stephen's expedition against Exeter in mid-1136, but there is good reason to believe that he was alive in 1137. He probably died on 11 May 1138, and was buried with his parents in Lewes Priory.

C. WARREN HOLLISTER

Sources W. Farrer and others, eds., *Early Yorkshire charters*, 12 vols. (1914–65), vol. 8 · GEC, *Peerage*, new edn, vol. 12/1 · W. Farrer, *Honors and knights' fees … from the eleventh to the fourteenth century*, 3 (1925) · L. C. Loyd, 'The origin of the family of Warenne', *Yorkshire Archaeological Journal*, 31 (1932–4), 97–113 · C. W. Hollister, *Monarchy, magnates, and institutions in the Anglo-Norman world* (1986) · J. O. Prestwich, 'The military household of the Norman kings', *EngHR*, 96 (1981), 1–35, esp. 14–15 · I. J. Sanders, *English baronies: a study of their origin and descent, 1086–1327* (1960), 128–9 · William of Jumièges, *Gesta Normannorum ducum*, ed. J. Marx (Rouen and Paris, 1914) · *S. Anselmi Cantuariensis archiepiscopi opera omnia*, ed. F. S. Schmitt, 6 vols. (1938–61) · E. Edwards, ed., *Liber monasterii de Hyda*, Rolls Series, 45 (1866) · Ordericus Vitalis, *Eccl. hist.*, 4.180–82, 222, 272 · J. le Patousel, *The Norman empire* (1976) · *Reg. RAN*, vols. 2–3 · Lewes cartulary, BL, Cotton MS, Vespasian F15 [reproduced in *Sussex Record Society*, ed. L. F. Salzman, 2.15], fol.105ᵛ

Warenne, William (III) de, third earl of Surrey [Earl Warenne] (*c*.1119–1148), magnate and crusader, was the eldest of the five children of William (II) de *Warenne (*d*. 1138) and Isabel de Vermandois (*d*. 1147). His younger siblings included *Ada, later countess of Huntingdon and Northumberland, and Reginald de *Warenne. It was through his mother that he made the two most important family connections in his life: his eldest half-brother, Waleran, count of Meulan, the elder of the well-known Beaumont twins, and his distant cousin, Louis VII of France. Warenne married Ela, the daughter of Guillaume Talvas, count of Ponthieu, and Ela, daughter of Odo Borel, duke of Burgundy. She died on 4 October 1174. Their only child and Warenne's heir was a daughter, Isabel de *Warenne (*d*. 1203), who married William, son of King Stephen, and after his death, Hamelin, half-brother of King Henry II.

Between 1130 and 1138 Warenne appeared with his brother Ralph as co-grantor or witness in several of their father's charters, but his first known independent action was one which presaged a life of military misfortune. He was among those 'hot-headed youths' (as Orderic Vitalis called them) who deserted King Stephen during his unsuccessful attempt to take Normandy in 1137. Probably in 1138 Warenne's father died, and he succeeded as earl of Surrey, though he consistently styled himself as Earl Warenne. In the summer of 1138 he or his father witnessed and possibly acted as guarantor for Roger, earl of Warwick, in an important charter in which Roger, husband of William (III)'s sister Gundreda, settled marriage arrangements between Roger's daughter and the chamberlain Geoffrey of Clinton. By the end of the year he had joined Waleran in Normandy and acted along with him as a witness to an agreement made in Rouen on 18 December. The brothers proceeded to their kinsman King Louis's court on an embassy from Stephen. By no later than 1139 Warenne had returned to England, probably with Waleran, most likely to attend his sister Ada's marriage to Henry, son of King David of Scotland. At that time he began his attendance at Stephen's court, where he became a regular witness to royal charters (at least a dozen between then and 1147) and began a career of unbroken, if not always distinguished, service to that troubled monarch.

The low point in Warenne's service to Stephen was at the battle of Lincoln on 2 February 1141, at which he and Waleran were among those who panicked and ran when they faced the first charge of Earl Robert of Gloucester's army, leaving the king to be captured. That it was panic rather than treachery that caused the flight could be seen by their support of Queen Matilda during Stephen's captivity and Warenne's appearance at the king's court after his release. Warenne redeemed himself on 14 September of that year and achieved the brightest moment of his military career when he led the Flemish mercenaries (usually under the command of William of Ypres) in taking Robert of Gloucester prisoner at Stockbridge. His activities in the following years included an appearance at Stephen's Christmas court, held at Canterbury, and an expedition against the town of St Albans, which he and three of the king's other captains were kept from burning by the payment of a rich bribe by Abbot Geoffrey of St Albans.

The next word of Warenne's military activity came in January 1144, during the king's last effort to win Normandy from Geoffrey of Anjou. When the city of Rouen surrendered to Geoffrey's forces, Stephen's men refused to give up the royal castle, and, led by Warenne's mercenaries, they held out for another three months before surrendering the castle of Neufchâtel-en-Bray. A double irony of this event is that Earl William was not identified specifically as having been present at this exercise in gallant futility, and that one of the leaders to whom his men surrendered was Count Waleran, that half-brother who had most guided his early career and who had been forced by then to take the Angevin side to defend his Norman holdings. If Warenne was indeed in Normandy at some time during the year, he left for England, where he was present on two occasions at the royal court during 1144 and 1145.

On 24 March, Palm Sunday of 1146, motivated perhaps by the example of his royal cousin and of Count Waleran, or by the rhetoric of an emotionally moving occasion, or by the desire to leave behind bad memories of the Anglo-Norman war, Warenne took the cross near Vézelay. After making some confirmatory grants to Lewes Priory and making his brother Reginald administrator of the honour of Warenne in his absence, he departed in June 1147, and met up with the French king, Louis, at Worms on the Rhine. He served in the king's personal guard, in which capacity he suffered loss of men and materials in an early encounter with the enemy. On 19 January 1148 he was among those in Louis's rearguard who were butchered in the defiles of Laodicea, and neither the wishful thinking of his brother Reginald nor the rumours of his survival that reached the northern chronicler John of Hexham would bring Warenne home again.

Although his short life meant that Warenne could not compete with his comital contemporaries in the field of religious benefactions, he did fulfil his obligations with donations to the family foundations of Lewes Priory and, to a lesser extent, Castle Acre Priory. He also made grants to the abbey of St Mary, York, and the templars at Saddlescombe, and he founded the priory of the Holy Sepulchre, Thetford, and possibly Thetford Hospital as well. He issued confirmations to Battle Abbey and Coxford and Nostell priories.   VICTORIA CHANDLER

Sources W. Farrer and others, eds., *Early Yorkshire charters*, 12 vols. (1914–65), vol. 8 · GEC, *Peerage* · Ordericus Vitalis, *Eccl. hist.* · Henry, archdeacon of Huntingdon, *Historia Anglorum*, ed. D. E. Greenway, OMT (1996) · *Reg. RAN*, vol. 3 · D. Crouch, *The Beaumont twins: the roots and branches of power in the twelfth century*, Cambridge Studies in Medieval Life and Thought, 4th ser., 1 (1986) · *Chronique de Robert de Torigni*, ed. L. Delisle, 2 vols. (Rouen, 1872–3) · Odo of Deuil, *De profectione Ludovici VII in orientem*, ed. and trans. V. G. Berry (1948) · G. W. Watson, 'William de Warenne, earl of Surrey', *The Genealogist*, new ser., 11 (1894–5), 132 · John of Hexham, 'Historia regum continuata', Symeon of Durham, *Opera*, vol. 2 · D. Crouch, 'Geoffrey de Clinton and Roger, earl of Warwick: new men and magnates in the reign of Henry I', *BIHR*, 55 (1982), 113–24
Wealth at death significant landholder in several counties

Warenne, William (IV) de, fifth earl of Surrey [Earl Warenne] (*d.* 1240), magnate, was the only son and heir of Hamelin de *Warenne, earl of Surrey (*d.* 1202), an illegitimate son of Geoffrey, count of Anjou, and hence half-brother to *Henry II. William's mother, Isabel de *Warenne (*d.* 1203), daughter of William (III) de *Warenne (*d.* 1148), inherited a claim to the earldom of Surrey together with sixty knights' fees in England, the honour of Lewes in Sussex, the castles of Reigate in Surrey, Castle Acre in Norfolk, Conisbrough and Sandal near Wakefield in Yorkshire, and extensive estates in Normandy at Mortemer and Bellencombre close to Varenne, the original Warenne stronghold.

Warenne was probably raised in Normandy. He witnessed a charter of Richard I issued at Rouen in September 1197, and for several years before 1202 witnessed and confirmed charters of his father, Earl Hamelin. Hamelin died on 7 May 1202, and on 12 May, in Normandy, Warenne was allowed to do homage for his father's estates. Over the next eighteen months he played a leading part in the defence of Normandy against the French. With the collapse of Plantagenet power in 1204 he sought permission to do homage to the French king, Philip Augustus, for his Norman lands, while promising King John that his heart would remain loyal to the king of England. John refused this offer, and instead, in April 1205, Warenne was awarded the major estates of Stamford and Grantham in Lincolnshire as compensation for his Norman lands which were seized by the French. He none the less maintained his contacts with Normandy via his sisters, Isabel, married to Gilbert, lord of l'Aigle, and Matilda, married first to Henri, count of Eu, and later to Henry de Stuteville or Etoutteville, lord of Valmont. When Gilbert de l'Aigle defected to the French after 1204, Earl William fined £2000 with the crown to have possession of Gilbert's English estates on behalf of his sister, Gilbert's wife. The fine was paid in full between 1207 and 1212, and eventually, after 1217, Gilbert was able to recover his lands in England. Likewise in 1217 Warenne acquired custody of lands in Yorkshire, Nottinghamshire, and elsewhere, seized at the death of Leonia, mother of Henry de Stuteville, Warenne's brother-in-law. No doubt in the hope of regaining his French estates, in 1206 he served on the king's expedition to Poitou. In the following year he was engaged in peace negotiations with Scotland. He sent knights to the king's army in Ireland in 1210, and in 1212 was briefly appointed sheriff of Northumberland with custody of several castles seized from northern barons suspected of plotting against the king. Over the next two years he took charge of various baronial hostages surrendered to the king, and in 1213 acted as one of the king's guarantors for the terms of peace with the church, intended to put an end to the papal interdict on England and to encourage the exiled English bishops to return. In 1214 he sent knights to the king's army in Poitou.

With the outbreak of civil war Warenne sided with the crown: he carried out negotiations with the rebel barons at Northampton, and in June 1215 was named as one of the royalists present at the issue of Magna Carta. He attended the siege of Rochester in November 1215 and, once again, was involved in a parley with the rebel barons. Thereafter he served as royalist commander in Sussex and on 26 May 1216 was sent to take charge of the Cinque Ports. However, on 6 June 1216 the rebel army commanded by Louis of France was allowed to enter Warenne's castle at Reigate unopposed, and later that month, at Winchester, Warenne himself came to the French prince and offered him his support. Possibly he hoped that Louis would restore his estates in Normandy. Like the earls of Salisbury and Arundel, and the count of Aumale who defected at the same time, he may have believed the Plantagenet cause to be doomed. Alternatively it has been suggested that he had a more personal grievance against King John, who many years before had conducted an adulterous affair with one of Warenne's sisters, mother of the royal bastard Richard fitz Roy (or de Warenne); but this seems an improbable motive for rebellion given that the affair had taken place twenty years before and that Warenne was himself the son of Earl Hamelin, another royal bastard. Warenne remained in rebellion for less than a year. As early as March 1217 he was in receipt of instructions from King Henry III over land at Stamford, and at Chichester on about 17 April he entered into a truce with the royalists, negotiated by the papal legate Guala. Probably to safeguard his interests in France he was scrupulous in his approach to his former French allies, and in June 1217 sent formal letters to Louis notifying him of his decision to abandon the rebel camp. Although he himself took no part in the naval battle off Sandwich on 24 August 1217, he equipped a ship of knights which was one of the first to engage the French fleet, and which took many prisoners. In the aftermath Warenne was prominent in the negotiations which put an end to the war. His own interests were at stake here, since after the battle of Sandwich he had paid more than 1000 marks to the men of the Cinque Ports to take possession of various French prisoners, from whom he clearly hoped to extract heavy ransoms. The treaty arranged in September forbade any such ransom payments, so that Warenne was forced to accept an undertaking from his fellow royalists that he would be refunded the 1000 marks from the royal exchequer. The problems involved in obtaining this money ensured that for much of the next decade Warenne was dependent upon loans and occasional payments from the crown. He also borrowed heavily from his kinsman the justiciar Hubert de Burgh, who had married the daughter and heir of William de Warenne of Wormegay in Norfolk, a cousin of Earl William.

His kinship to Hubert de Burgh was to prove very useful to Warenne after 1217 in enabling him to obtain favours from the royal court. In 1218 he successfully pursued a claim to the sheriffdom of Surrey, disputed during the civil war by the alien royalist Engelard de Cigogné. He remained sheriff of Surrey until November 1226. In 1219 he was one of those who attended the funeral procession of William (I) Marshal, earl of Pembroke, from Caversham to the Temple Church in London, and in the same year he obtained the restoration of her estates to Alice, countess of Eu, his niece, who through negotiation had succeeded in recovering her lands both in Normandy and in England. Acting as custodian on Alice's behalf, Warenne henceforth enjoyed custody of the honours and castles of Tickhill in Yorkshire and Hastings in Sussex. His possession of Tickhill was vigorously resisted by a local magnate, Robert de Vieuxpont, leading for a time to the threat of violent unrest. In 1220 he was prominent in negotiations with the French and with the king of Scots, Alexander II, and in 1221 he sent knights to the army dispatched to recover Bytham Castle on behalf of Henry III. In the spring of 1223 he made a pilgrimage to Santiago de Compostela, but returned in time to serve on the king's campaign against Montgomery, providing the king with twenty knights, and witnessing the eventual terms of truce with the Welsh. During the winter of 1223–4 he supported Hubert de Burgh against his rivals at court. He joined the army besieging Bedford Castle in 1224 and afterwards was appointed to conduct the disgraced alien constable, Falkes de Bréauté, into exile. Probably in reward for his loyalty he was granted custody of the royal castle of Bramber, and the castle of Hornby in Lancashire. However, in November 1226 he was replaced as sheriff of Surrey and in February 1227 was forced to surrender Hornby to its rightful heir.

These disappointments may help to explain Warenne's involvement in a brief confederation against the crown, led between July and October 1227 by the king's brother Richard of Cornwall and the earls of Pembroke and Chester, confirmed at Warenne's manor of Stamford. In the aftermath Warenne was forced to surrender his custody of Tickhill, but his disgrace was short-lived. In 1228 he was confirmed in possession of the manors of Stamford and Grantham for life, and for the first time received the third penny of the county of Surrey, an honorary payment due to the earl of any particular county, but which seems previously to have been denied to Warenne and his father, despite their claim to be recognized as earls of Surrey by right of Warenne's mother. In 1230, during the king's expedition to Brittany, Warenne was appointed keeper of the ports of the English east coast, and in the following year he served with the king's army in Wales. In 1232 he was involved, albeit incidentally, in the disgrace of his former protector, Hubert de Burgh, being one of the four earls appointed to keep de Burgh prisoner at Devizes Castle. However, he seems to have remained sympathetic to de Burgh, and after the fall of Hubert's persecutors in 1234, returned to government, accepting the surrender of the castles of Bramber and Knepp from de Burgh's enemies. He served as a ceremonial cup-bearer at the coronation of Queen Eleanor in 1236, and in 1237 witnessed the reissue of Magna Carta as one of the few surviving barons who had witnessed the charter of 1215. In the same year he was admitted to the king's council, and in 1238 was sent to defend the papal legate Otto against violent attacks at Oxford.

Warenne married twice: first, before 1207, Matilda, daughter of William d'Aubigny, earl of Arundel (d. 1223). She is said to have died, childless, on 6 February 1215, and was buried at Lewes. His second wife, another Matilda, was the eldest daughter of William (I) Marshal, earl of Pembroke, and widow of Hugh Bigod, earl of Norfolk (d. 1225). Warenne purchased her marriage and her dower in Norfolk before July 1225. She outlived him by several years, and died in April 1248. Her body was buried at Tintern Abbey and her heart at Lewes. Warenne died in London on 27 or 28 May 1240, and was buried before the high altar of his family's foundation at Lewes in Sussex. The king ordered that a wayside cross be erected in his memory, on the road between Merton and Carshalton in Surrey. With Matilda Marshal Warenne had two children: a son and heir, John de *Warenne, who succeeded to his father's estates in 1248, and a daughter, Isabel de *Warenne (1226x30–1282), married to Hugh d'Aubigny, earl of Arundel (d. 1243). During his lifetime Warenne had been a regular patron of religious foundations. He granted or confirmed lands to the priories of Lewes, St Michael Stamford, and the Holy Sepulchre at Thetford, and at some time between 1219 and 1222 founded a Cluniac cell at Sleves Holm near Methwold, dependent upon Castle Acre Priory. In Normandy, before December 1203, he made gifts to the monks of Bonne-Nouvelle, and in 1223 he confirmed land at Little Palgrave in Norfolk to the monks of St Riquier in Picardy. He also supported the foundation by his subtenant, Hugh de Pleiz, of an Augustinian priory at Broomhill in Norfolk, and is credited, not entirely convincingly, with the foundation of priories or hospitals at Reigate and Stamford. His daughter, Isabel, widow of Hugh d'Aubigny, earl of Arundel, founded a Cistercian nunnery at Marham in Norfolk, on land that she had received from Warenne in dower. Warenne was the last survivor of the Anglo-Norman aristocracy who had held land in both France and England before 1204. It is clear that throughout his life he endeavoured to maintain the links between England and Normandy, in the hope that the old Anglo-Norman realm might one day be re-established.   NICHOLAS VINCENT

Sources Pipe rolls · Paris, Chron. · GEC, Peerage · F. Michel, ed., Histoire des ducs de Normandie et des rois d'Angleterre (Paris, 1840) · L. F. Salzman, ed., The chartulary of the Priory of St Pancras of Lewes, 2 vols., Sussex RS, 38, 40 (1932–4) · Sir Christopher Hatton's Book of seals, ed. L. C. Loyd and D. M. Stenton, Northamptonshire RS, 15 (1950) · Dugdale, Monasticon, new edn, 4.263, 478; 5.71–2, 729–30, 744 · St Ricquier inventory, Archives Départementales de la Somme, Amiens, MS 25H1, fol. 180v · Methwold charter, Cambridge, Christ's College muniments, A35 · Archives Départementales de la Seine-Maritime, Rouen, 20HP5 · W. Farrer and others, eds., Early Yorkshire charters, 12 vols. (1914–65), vol. 8 · W. Farrer, Honors and knights' fees … from the eleventh to the fourteenth century, 3 vols. (1923–5) · F. M. Powicke, The loss of Normandy, 1189–1204: studies in the history of the Angevin empire, 2nd edn (1961) · S. Painter, The reign of King John (1966) · D. A. Carpenter, The minority of Henry III (1990)

Warford, William (c.1560–1608), Jesuit, was born at Bristol. Little is known of his parents save that his mother was called Jane. He was admitted a scholar of Trinity College, Oxford, on 13 June 1574, graduated BA on 12 March 1578, was elected a fellow of his college in 1578, and graduated MA on 30 March 1582. He was reconciled to the Roman Catholic church at the English College, Rheims, on 7 November 1582 and remained there until sent to the English College at Rome on 13 August 1583. He took with him a glowing recommendation from Dr Barret, the president of Douai. He was ordained priest in the college chapel in Rome on 16 December 1584 and he remained there in the household of Cardinal Allen until 1588. After a visit to Spain he was sent to England on the mission in April 1591 and worked in Kent. He entered the Society of Jesus in Rome on 23 May 1594 and was penitentiary at St Peter's for some time. During his time in Rome between 1594 and 1599 he wrote his relation about the English martyrs, later collected by Christopher Grene and deposited among his transcripts at Stonyhurst. He left Rome in late 1599 for Lisbon, where he was confessor to the English College. He was in Cadiz until 1608 when, owing to ill health, he returned to Valladolid, which he had visited in 1594. He was the author of A Briefe Instruction by Way of Dialogue Concerning the Principall Poyntes of Christian Religion, Gathered out of the Holy Scriptures, Fathers, and Councels, published under the name George Doulye at Seville in 1600, and of *A Briefe Manner of Examination of Conscience for a Generall Confession*, published under the same pseudonym (Louvain, 1604). Both works saw a number of later editions. He died at the English College, Valladolid, on 6 November 1608, and was buried at Valladolid.

THOMPSON COOPER, *rev.* G. BRADLEY

Sources G. Anstruther, *The seminary priests*, 1 (1969), 370 · T. M. McCoog, *English and Welsh Jesuits, 1555–1650*, 2, Catholic RS, 75 (1995), 325, 353 · A. F. Allison and D. M. Rogers, eds., *A catalogue of Catholic books in English printed abroad or secretly in England, 1558–1640*, 1 (1956), 166 · Foster, *Alum. Oxon.* · T. F. Knox and others, eds., *The first and second diaries of the English College, Douay* (1878), 192, 196–7, 330 · W. Kelly, ed., *Liber ruber venerabilis collegii Anglorum de urbe*, 1, Catholic RS, 37 (1940), 47 · M. E. Williams, *St Alban's College, Valladolid: four centuries of English Catholic presence in Spain* (1986), 10, 20 · 'Father Warford's recollections', *Acts of English martyrs*, ed. J. H. Pollen (1891), 249–78
Archives Stonyhurst College, Lancashire, Fr. Christopher Grene SJ MSS, M, fols. 131–43

Wargrave. For this title name *see* Goulding, Edward Alfred, Baron Wargrave (1862–1936).

Warham, William (1450?–1532), administrator and archbishop of Canterbury, was born in Church Oakley, Hampshire. A later archbishop of Canterbury, Matthew Parker (*d.* 1575), said that this predecessor was of gentle birth, but Warham's origins were not distinguished. An uncle, Thomas, was a carpenter (but also a citizen of London) at one time professionally employed in the archiepiscopal residence in Croydon, which his nephew would later occupy; another relation was a 'taloughchaundeler' of London; William's parents, Robert and Elizabeth, are commemorated by a brass in their parish church of Church Oakley (presumably set up at their son's expense) which carries none of the emblems of social distinction. The Warhams eventually held considerable estates in north-west Hampshire thanks to William's promotion to the primacy of all England and subsequent purchases by his nephew and heir, Sir William Warham. By then the Warhams had arrived among the local élite.

Education and early career The future archbishop was educated at Winchester College and New College, Oxford, where he became a fellow in 1475 and acquired a doctorate in canon law. Eventually, in 1488, Warham went to London to a post in the court of arches, the first sign that he might fly high in public life. Two years later he probably went to Rome as a proctor of John Alcock (*d.* 1500), bishop of Ely, and was soon acquiring a variety of profitable sinecures, including (in 1496) the archdeaconry of Huntingdon, one of a number of archdeaconries that were regular stepping-stones to bishoprics, and the precentorship of Wells. In April 1491 he performed his first secular duty when he was appointed to the English party sent to Antwerp to settle disputes with Hanseatic merchants. Two years later he joined Sir Edward Poynings (*d.* 1521) on an embassy to Margaret, duchess of Burgundy, to halt Burgundian support for the pretender to the English

William Warham (1450?–1532), after Hans Holbein the younger, 1527

throne, Perkin Warbeck, and is reported to have made a powerful, though fruitless, speech on behalf of Henry VII. On 13 February 1494 he received his first royal preferment—to the mastership of the rolls. This in turn produced numerous assignments: in 1496 to negotiate with the Spanish ambassador details of the marriage of Prince Arthur to Katherine of Aragon, for instance; between 1496 and 1499 to deal with commercial disputes with the Netherlands and even the city of Riga; in September 1501 to conclude a deal with the emperor Maximilian I (*r.* 1493–1519) for the handing over to Henry of the chief surviving 'white rose' threat to his throne, Edmund de la Pole.

Warham had still not achieved major office in either church or state, despite all this activity. Quite suddenly, however, preferment was showered on him. On 20 October 1501 he was papally provided to the vacant see of London, though not consecrated until 25 September 1502. On the previous 11 August he was appointed keeper of the great seal and gained the full dignity of the lord chancellorship on 21 January 1504. At royal request Pope Julius II (*r.* 1503–13) had translated him on 29 November 1503 from London to Canterbury, where he was enthroned as archbishop on 9 March 1504, having sworn fealty to the pope and, on 2 February, received at Lambeth the symbol of his primatial authority, the pallium from Rome. After a distinctly slow start, therefore, he had suddenly soared to the highest office in the royal government and the supreme ecclesiastical dignity of archbishop of Canterbury, *legatus natus*, and primate of all England. Since he was by then well over fifty, neither he nor others could have expected that he would have a further claim to fame, that of almost being Canterbury's longest-serving archbishop. His primacy lasted 28 years and 7 months, second only to Thomas Bourchier's 31 years and 7 months (1454–86).

Affairs of state As chancellor Warham was presumably concerned with the day-to-day legal and formal administration business of his court, but there is no evidence that he had much impact on chancery's evolution. Initially, however, he was conspicuous on major state occasions. Thus he crowned the new king, Henry VIII, and his wife, Katherine of Aragon, at Westminster on 24 June 1509, and presented the golden rose sent to Henry in the following year by Pope Julius. He delivered the customary—but well received—speeches at the opening of four parliaments (those of 1504, 1510, 1512, and 1515), and on two occasions led a formidable delegation to the lower house to demand assent to heavy taxation. As well as being prominent in parliament, he presided *ex officio* over the upper house of southern convocation, which regularly met at the same time as the secular assembly. Indeed, the church's affairs brought him as much into the limelight as did those of the prince.

Warham's first convocation, that of 1504, had spoken firmly in defence of the 'liberties' of the church in England, by which was meant essentially the legal privileges of churchmen against a crown and its lawyers who were intent on clipping them. In 1512, despite strong opposition from convocation and in the Lords, and in the wake of an unsuccessful attempt two years before to secure a bill confirming the church's liberties, an act was passed that denied clergy in minor orders their 'benefit', that is, immunity from the king's courts when accused of serious crimes. As a compromise the act was to run for an initial trial period of three years. When it fell due for renewal in 1515, however, there quickly developed a dangerously heated confrontation between church and state—a conflict exacerbated by the famous case of Richard Hunne, allegedly murdered in 1514 by the bishop of London's officers, following a dispute over mortuaries—which split the episcopate and brought Warham into open opposition to the king. The climax to this crisis was a conference at Baynard's Castle, presided over by Henry, at which the archbishop dared to remind the assembly that a predecessor had died a martyr in defence of clerical liberties, whereupon Henry replied with a trumpet blast about kings of England never having had any superior 'but God only'. Warham's final attempt to stave off defeat by suggesting that the whole issue be referred to Rome for adjudication was brushed aside. His courage and loyalty to the church cost him a bruising.

Three years before there had been a sharp dispute between Warham and his suffragans concerning Canterbury's right to prove wills (and received fees therefrom) of persons who had had possessions in more than one diocese. Wrangles of this kind are the stuff of much medieval ecclesiastical history; but thanks particularly to the fact that the archbishop's opponents were led by Richard Fox (d. 1528), bishop of Winchester and keeper of the privy seal, this clash was especially sharp. A compromise

eventually emerged, but the whole episode was decidedly discomfiting.

Relations with Wolsey Shortly after that tense encounter at Baynard's Castle Warham was solemnly handing over a red hat to Thomas Wolsey, archbishop of York (d. 1530). On 22 December of that year (1515) he resigned the lord chancellorship, which passed to the same Thomas Wolsey. Some have supposed he was dismissed by the king. Edward Hall and Polydore Vergil believed he was thrust aside by the ambitious new cardinal. Thomas More (d. 1535), however, writing soon after the event, assured Erasmus that Warham was glad to quit. After eleven years as chancellor the archbishop may have resolved to devote himself entirely to his spiritual duties. Possibly the whole truth contains all these views. Warham had probably never been cordial with the young king, who had inherited him from his father, and could never have competed with the dashing, self-confident, and much younger Wolsey. The recent contretemps probably settled the matter for Henry. As for Warham himself, he could reasonably have supposed that he was nearing his end and that the time had come to escape the hurly-burly of public life. More was surely right when he reported that Warham had been wanting to go for some years in order to enjoy quietude and his books.

Wolsey probably always hoped thereafter that Warham would die and thus allow him to exchange York for Canterbury, the ultimate prize. But it was Wolsey who died. Warham probably disliked Wolsey, initially at least, as the latter bullied Rome into granting him both a red hat and a legateship *a latere*, eventually for life, which in theory brought the whole English church under his sway. So, when Wolsey summoned all the bishops of England and Wales to a legatine council in March 1519, Warham counter-attacked by calling his own southern convocation to meet the month before. An indignant Wolsey (called a 'great tyrant' by one of Warham's chaplains) summoned the archbishop to his presence. The same chaplain reported that a *praemunire* charge against Warham was being threatened. In the event Warham retreated. Whether Wolsey succeeded in holding a national legatine council in 1523 is uncertain; what is known is that in the meantime he and Warham had had a collision over testamentary jurisdiction that mirrored the earlier conflict between Warham and the bishops of his province, with Wolsey claiming that, as legate, he was entitled to override Canterbury's prerogative court and receive all the fees. Once again good sense prevailed. A remarkable compromise allowed Canterbury a half share of both testamentary administration and income.

Much of all this may have been formal ecclesiastical manoeuvring rather than genuine conflict. Certainly relations between cardinal and archbishop eventually became respectful, even warm. In 1522 Wolsey sent Warham a jewel for Becket's shrine, and the following year, when the archbishop fell ill, invited him to convalesce at Hampton Court. When, two years later, a dispute over the will of John Roper, father of More's son-in-law, apparently bypassed the recently established joint court, which dealt with business arising from both the legate's and the archbishop's jurisdictions, Wolsey handled a ruffled archbishop so tactfully that Warham could gratefully explain how it was only his 'very singular trust and confidence' in the cardinal's 'undoubted favour and benignity' towards him that had allowed him to undertake such 'plain writing' to him (*LP Henry VIII*, 4, no. 1157). Shortly after this episode the so-called 'amicable grant' (1525), an emergency war levy, caused much consternation and brought protesters to Warham's gate. But the latter could write to Wolsey that, while some called him an 'old fool' for co-operating with the government, much worse awaited the cardinal, for anyone 'in most favour and most in counsel with a great prince shall be maligned and ill-spoken of do he never so well' (ibid., 4, appendix no. 39).

Primate and patron An archbishop of Canterbury who can record that he is being called an old fool and write perceptively about a statesman's lot is endearing. It is no less noteworthy that Warham, trained in canon and civil law, and given to what many contemporary reformers would have regarded as a typical preoccupation with clerical rights and privileges, should nevertheless have also been an ally of John Colet and patron of Erasmus—both of them critics of the very system that Warham seemingly personified. In his famous address to convocation, traditionally assigned to 1512 but now thought to have been made in 1510, Colet had proclaimed the special dignity of the clerical estate, as well as denouncing war and clerical sins. He could not have been the leading speaker without the archbishop's approval. And then he was appointed to a committee to discuss clerical reform. It is not clear what, if anything, this body achieved, not least because Wolsey was soon on the scene, charged to use his legatine authority to carry forward a wide-ranging renewal of the church. After Wolsey's departure Warham returned to the cause of reform, so that what emerged from convocation in his last months represented a continuation rather than a new initiative.

In the meantime Warham had been one of Erasmus's most generous patrons. He showered him with gifts of cash and even a horse, and was eager to secure his return to England. 'No brother, or father even, could be more loving', declared Erasmus (*Correspondence*, no. 286), and gratefully dedicated to him his Latin translation of two plays of Euripides (1506–7) and Lucian's *Dialogi* (1514), and his multi-volumed edition of St Jerome's works. Warham also shared the dedication of Erasmus's celebrated New Testament of 1516.

Thanks to Hans Holbein the younger Warham's likeness has been preserved. He is the first archbishop of Canterbury of whom that can be said with complete confidence. His watery, melancholic eyes, thick nose, and heavy jowl are memorably depicted. He comes alive also, as do many of his contemporaries, in his correspondence with Erasmus, for whom he clearly had affection. Thus when Erasmus complained, as he often did, of 'stones', the archbishop could ask what was to be built 'super hanc petram', and continued, 'You are not, I imagine, building fancy houses … instead spend money to have those stones taken away; unlike me, who am spending money every day to have stones brought to my buildings' (*Correspondence*, no. 1504)—a reference in particular to the massive reconstruction of his palace at Otford.

In 1511, like other bishops in the southern province, Warham launched a sudden and fierce campaign against Lollardy in his diocese—the first major assault for over seventy years on a sect that was well rooted and organized in several towns, notably Maidstone, Staplehurst, and Tenterden. Of thirty-nine accused, thirty-four abjured, but five suffered death for obstinate heresy. The victims included William Carder of Tenterden, zealous leader of Kentish Lollardy, and one woman. Only Coventry produced a higher total of burnings. By the early 1520s Warham, like others, was beginning to be alarmed by the first signs of protestantism, and was eventually much concerned with the activities of Hugh Latimer (*d.* 1555). By 1527, however, a different crisis had broken, namely, the king's Great Matter. As primate of all England Warham was inevitably involved; and since he had allegedly had doubts about the validity of the papal dispensation that had enabled Henry to marry his dead brother's wife in 1509, he was someone from whom the king could expect support in his quest, nearly two decades later, to have his marriage declared null.

The king's divorce In May 1527 Warham agreed to examine the case secretly with Wolsey. However, it was soon apparent that this collusive action could not provide the definitive verdict that Henry required, and that it was therefore necessary to invoke the aid of Rome. After intense diplomatic activity Henry eventually persuaded Pope Clement VII (*r.* 1523–34) to send to England Cardinal Lorenzo Campeggi to preside with Wolsey over a legatine court at Blackfriars, London, and to try the case. In the meantime Warham had been appointed one of Katherine's counsel. Perhaps the appointment was a formality: Warham was scarcely a suitable nominee and does not seem to have exerted himself on her behalf. Indeed, Katherine reported that he had merely remarked unhelpfully 'ira principis mors est' ('the anger of the prince is death').

Katherine outwitted her husband. By late July 1529 she had appealed to the pope against her judges and the case had been 'advoked' to Rome. This humiliating setback for Henry was a crucial moment of his reign. Arguably, much that was done and said on the national stage during the next two or even three years, including the dismissal of Wolsey and the summoning of the Reformation Parliament, was intended to force the pope to hand the case back to England, where Henry was confident he would get his way. Even the episode known as the 'pardon of the clergy' in early 1531, which began with a *praemunire* charge against the whole clergy of the land, may similarly have been designed to intimidate Rome. And so also (probably) was the next royal move, which resulted in Warham's delivering to convocation the king's demand to be recognized as head of the church and possessed of the spiritual cure of his subjects. John Fisher of Rochester (*d.* 1535), Warham's episcopal neighbour, rallied his colleagues, including Warham, to reject the latter claim and accept the former only after the words 'as far as the law of Christ allows' had been added.

During the long and unsuccessful struggle to recover the case from Rome Henry frequently named Warham as the person most fit to be appointed judge, praising him for his integrity and independence. In fact he was confident that the archbishop could be trusted to deliver the right verdict. Further proof of this was that, as its chancellor (since 1506), he had encouraged Oxford to come down on the king's side when the well-known consultation of the universities was set in train, and in December 1530 even called Fisher to his house to urge him to retract what he had written on the queen's behalf. Fisher refused.

Manoeuvring between Westminster and Rome However, in the months that followed Warham shifted his ground, less perhaps because he had changed his mind about the intrinsic merits of the case, than because of the aggressive tactics of the king. Moreover, Rome had forbidden public discussion of the case while it was *sub judice*, and explicitly prohibited the archbishop of Canterbury from taking cognizance of it. On 13 January 1531 Clement VII's nuncio in England visited Warham to show him the latest papal brief and to bid him 'have regard to God, his conscience and the pope' (*LP Henry VIII*, 5, no. 45). Warham was reported to have replied that he would never disobey Rome.

It was later suggested that two other people helped to make the archbishop 'harder and less to favour the king's cause': one was John Fisher, who allegedly did all he could to 'embolden' him; the other was Elizabeth Barton, reputed 'the Holy Maid of Kent', whom Warham had treated with circumspection when she first claimed to have visions, but who may have impressed him when she later denounced the royal divorce and warned him, and Wolsey, not to 'meddle' further in the matter, else they would be 'utterly destroyed' (Whatmore, 467). That, at any rate, is what was claimed at her execution in November 1533.

Whatever the truth of this, on 24 February 1532, in an upper room in Lambeth Palace, Warham swore to a public instrument repudiating anything done or henceforth done since November 1529 that violated the rights of Rome, ecclesiastical authority, or the privileges of his metropolitical see. All were publicly condemned. That was provocative enough, but, according to the Venetian ambassador in London, on the following 15 March Warham went further. He stood up in the Lords and openly upbraided the king for his conduct.

It can reasonably be assumed that it was now, in response to such defiance, that the archbishop was charged with a *praemunire* offence. The charge was manifestly trumped up. Warham was accused of misprision of treason on the ground that fourteen years previously he had consecrated the new bishop of St Asaph before full royal assent had been given. The only record of this extraordinary episode is a draft of a heroic speech to be made in self-defence which has survived. There is no record of any formal proceedings, and no evidence that the speech was ever delivered, presumably because on 22 August 1532, in

Hackington, Kent, a natural death carried off the archbishop.

Yet that same apparently courageous and defiant Warham had on the previous 15 May presided over the convocation which surrendered its legislative independence to the crown, and was one of only three bishops who gave apparently unqualified assent to what is known as the 'submission of the clergy', after weeks of wrangling and cajoling. It is not easy to explain his conduct. Was he intimidated? Did he believe that his protest of 24 February had exonerated him of responsibility for betrayal seven weeks later of a fundamental liberty of the *Ecclesia Anglicana*? Was he acting merely *ex officio* when he delivered convocation's surrender document to the crown?

There is another possibility. Although modern historians have insisted that the events culminating in the humiliating submission of May 1532 had nothing to do with the royal divorce, it could be that this sudden assault on the clerical estate, like that of early 1531 and like so much else said and done after the débâcle at Blackfriars in July 1529, was another—the last—desperate attempt to bully Rome into handing back the case to England. If Warham had believed that much that was happening was not to be taken at its face value, but was sabre-rattling aimed at frightening a pope into compliance, his conduct becomes less unworthy and inconsistent. Fisher took royal words and deeds seriously. Some who were close to the king probably had exactly the agenda that Fisher perceived. But Warham (and maybe other bishops), while protesting at the extravagances, could have believed that the root problem was the king's Great Matter. This would surely be resolved. It was not something to die for. Once the crisis had blown over, all would be well again. The 'pardon', the 'submission', all the wild talk about the king's imperial status, and so on, would be forgotten. If this is a correct interpretation, Warham was guilty of naïvety and wishful thinking rather than anything more serious.

The archbishop and the man Warham was a respected, conscientious prelate but not a pastoral one. There is little evidence of preaching or concern for the instruction of his flock. But his large register survives in two volumes, containing 638 folios, to suggest that he attended carefully to the administration of his diocese. He was seriously dedicated to his books—which he bequeathed to Winchester, and to New College and All Souls at Oxford—and, as has been said, was a steadfast supporter of Erasmus. But since he could embarrass the latter by offering him the rectory of Aldington, Kent, and then, to avoid a flagrant example of non-residence, commute the gift to an annual pension, it is questionable how well he understood his client. In his will Warham recalls that he spent a prodigious £30,000 on buildings, especially his palace at Otford, which boasted a courtyard bigger than Hampton Court's. This was a distinctly un-Erasmian activity. On the other hand Erasmus tells us that, though he entertained sumptuously, Warham himself ate frugally and drank little wine. He neither hunted nor played dice. He died, More said, a poor man. There is no firm evidence that his 'nephew' William, upon whom he conferred the archdeaconry of Canterbury and other benefices, was really an illegitimate son, the offspring of some youthful liaison, and no source hints at sexual impropriety in later life. Warham seriously promoted clerical reform at the beginning and end of his episcopate, as well as defending clerical liberties and privileges throughout his career. But it must be added that 'reform' for him did not cut deeper than concern for clerical dress and conduct, and minor improvements in ecclesiastical procedures. But perhaps this was not so much because he was unperceptive, as because the English church was not in need of radical new legislation.

Although no believer in ostentation for its own sake, Warham remained mindful to the end of his days of the need to maintain the dignity of his primatial office. An account of his exequies written by a herald tells how the archbishop's coffin, with his effigy upon it, was placed in the sanctuary of the cathedral, on a hearse surmounted by huge candelabra bearing 1000 lights, before being interred in a small chantry chapel, which Warham had had built for himself as long ago as 1507. The chantry was situated in the Martyrdom, in the cathedral's north transept, and Warham was clearly devoted to Canterbury and St Thomas. He referred regularly to Becket in his correspondence, and seems always to have tried to be in the diocese for the saint's major feasts. He had fought hard for a bull to celebrate the 350th anniversary of Becket's death in 1520, and carefully chose to be buried as close as possible to the spot where Becket fell. He quoted Becket at Henry in 1515. When he faced the king again in 1532 the identification with his predecessor was complete.

The speech in which Warham had prepared to defend himself against the *praemunire* charge is, by any standards, magnificent. 'The case that I am put to trouble for is one of the articles that Saint Thomas of Canterbury died for', he declared, quoting from a contemporary life and the martyr's letters. He, Warham, had done no wrong. Rather, he had acted in obedience to Rome, and in accordance with his duty as primate. He had acted as all his predecessors had done. Let his assailants 'hew me to small pieces', he continued, but remember that whoever lays a violent hand on an archbishop shall be accursed and can be 'assoiled but by the pope', and the place where he is taken, together with the two neighbouring dioceses, put under an interdict; and so on (PRO, SP 1/70, fol. 236).

It was a long time since an archbishop had been ready to speak thus. Apparently the octogenarian Warham was seriously bracing himself for martyrdom. Had he lived a little longer and indeed chosen the path that John Fisher took, it would be much easier to pass a final verdict on him. Furthermore, the religious history of sixteenth-century England might be markedly different from the one we know.   J. J. SCARISBRICK

Sources *LP Henry VIII*, vols. 1–5 · J. Gairdner, ed., *Letters and papers illustrative of the reigns of Richard III and Henry VII*, 2 vols., Rolls Series, 24 (1861–3) · *The correspondence of Erasmus*, ed. and trans. R. A. B. Mynors and others, 22 vols. (1974–94), vols. 2–9 · *The correspondence of Sir Thomas More*, ed. E. F. Rogers (1947) · D. Wilkins, ed., *Concilia Magnae Britanniae et Hiberniae*, 4 vols. (1737) · *The Anglica historia of Polydore Vergil, AD 1485–1537*, ed. and trans. D. Hay, CS, 3rd ser., 74 (1950) · P. Gwyn, *The king's cardinal: the rise and fall of Thomas Wolsey* (1990) · M. J. Kelly, 'The submission of the clergy', *TRHS*, 5th ser., 15 (1965), 97–119 · M. J. Kelly, 'Canterbury jurisdiction and influence during the episcopate of William Warham, 1503–1532', PhD diss., U. Cam., 1965 · G. W. Bernard, *War, taxation, and rebellion in early Tudor England* (1986) · J. A. F. Thomson, *The later Lollards, 1414–1520* (1965) · L. E. Whatmore, ed., 'The sermon against the Holy Maid of Kent and her adherents … 1533', *EngHR*, 58 (1943), 463–75 · Emden, *Oxf.* · C. Wilson, 'The medieval monuments', *A history of Canterbury Cathedral, 598–1982*, ed. P. Collinson and others (1995), 451–510, esp. 487–8 · Reg. William Warham, LPL [2 vols.] · PRO, SP 1/70

Archives BL, letters · LPL, papers · LPL, register | PRO, letters · PRO, SP 1/70

Likenesses portrait, 1512 (*Parliament Roll*), Trinity Cam. · H. Holbein the younger, chalk drawing, *c.*1527, Royal Collection · H. Holbein the younger, oils, *c.*1527, Louvre, Paris · oils, 1527 (after H. Holbein the younger), NPG [*see illus.*] · H. Holbein the younger, portrait · tomb effigy, Canterbury Cathedral; repro. in P. Collinson and others, eds., *History of Canterbury Cathedral* (1995), pl. 116

Waring, Anna Letitia (1823–1910), poet, was born at Plas-y-felin, Neath, Glamorgan, on 19 April 1823, third of the seven children of Elijah Waring (1787–1857), merchant, and his wife, Deborah (1785–1867), daughter of Peter Price and his wife, Anna. The Warings were members of the Society of Friends, but Anna Letitia, like her uncle and father, eventually left the society: she was baptized into the Church of England on 15 May 1842 at St Martin Church, Winnall, Winchester. Her uncle was Samuel Miller Waring, who published a hymn collection, *Sacred Melodies* (1826). Elijah Waring wrote and published verse and a literary memoir, *Recollections and Anecdotes of Edward Williams, the Bard of Glamorgan* (1850), dedicated to his six surviving children. By this date the family was established in Bristol.

That year also marked the start of Anna Letitia Waring's literary career, with the publication of *Hymns and Meditations*. This popular collection was reprinted and extended many times, and several American reprints testify to her wide readership. *Additional Hymns* (1858) was integrated with the text of *Hymns and Meditations* in later editions, and Mary S. Talbot's memoir 'In Remembrance of Anna Letitia Waring' appeared with the final edition of *Hymns and Meditations* in 1911. This posthumous work collected previously unpublished pieces, both secular and religious. Domestic topics, especially animals, are in evidence in Waring's poems, which included a light-hearted piece on her cat. Many poems arise from the deaths of family members, demonstrating the consolation she found in her faith. This element of reassurance was valued by her readers, as comments from letters quoted in Talbot testify. This last collection projects a compassionate, reflective personality, with a sense of humour. Waring's writing offers the poetry of consolation and affirmation of the Christian faith. It is typical of one Victorian reaction to a world increasingly encompassed by doubt, a reaction also reflected in works of writers such as Charlotte Elliott (1789–1871) and Marianne Farningham (1834–1909).

What is known of her life suggests that Anna Letitia Waring typified a conventional Victorian view of womanhood, pious, reserved, and given to 'good works': she was a prison visitor in Bristol and worked for the Discharged

Prisoners' Aid Society. Her writing was largely devoted to her religion. A number of her poems were adapted as hymns, including her most often reprinted poem, 'Father I know that all my life is portion'd out for me'. This was sung at her own funeral. Her work was also disseminated widely through its reprinting in hymnbooks and anthologies, most notably in Robert H. Baynes's *Lyra Anglicana* (1862–79), Roundell Palmer's *The Book of Praise* (1862–1906), C. F. Alexander's *The Sunday Book of Poetry* (1864), *Wesley's Hymns* (1877) (later *The Methodist Hymn Book*), and *The Church Hymnary* (1898). Alfred H. Miles concluded his first volume of the Sacred Poets of the Nineteenth Century, *James Montgomery to Anna Letitia Waring* (1897), with a group of Waring's poems, introduced by a biographical note by W. Garrett Horder. This gave Waring's date of birth as 1820, an error which was perpetuated in T. Mardy Rees, *A History of the Quakers in Wales* (1925). (Horder also mistakes the number of poems in the first issue of *Hymns and Meditations*: it was twenty, not nineteen.) In 1886 Anna Letitia Waring also published a calendar of Bible texts, *Days of Remembrance*. Her familiarity with the scriptures is evident throughout her verse. (Waring taught herself Hebrew in order to read the Old Testament in the original language.)

Waring's verse maintains a quietly reflective mood that seems to owe something to her Quaker upbringing. The Unitarian James Martineau, who included five of her poems in his *Hymns of Praise and Prayer* (1874), commented in his preface that 'the new hymns admitted belong chiefly to the poetry of the inner life'. It is for such poetry that Anna Letitia Waring is remembered. She died of senile debility, with hepatic and pulmonary congestion, at her home, 3 Pembroke Road, Clifton, Bristol, on 10 May 1910, the last survivor of her four sisters, with whom she had lived on independent means. Her burial service, at Arnos Vale cemetery, on 14 May 1910, was taken by Canon Talbot, husband of one of her nieces.

ROSEMARY SCOTT

Sources 'Dictionary of Quaker biography', RS Friends, Lond. [card index] · M. S. Talbot, 'In remembrance of Anna Letitia Waring', in A. L. Waring, *Hymns and meditations* (1911) · *The Times* (24 May 1910) · J. Smith, ed., *A descriptive catalogue of Friends' books*, 2 (1867) · Hereford, Worcester and Wales QM digest of births and deaths, 1823–41, RS Friends, Lond. · *Clifton Chronicle and Directory* (18 May 1910) · *DNB* · J. Julian, ed., *A dictionary of hymnology*, rev. edn (1907); repr. in 2 vols. (1915) · census returns for Clifton, 1851, 1881, 1891 · directories, Bristol, 1848–1905 · E. Waring, sworn affidavit concerning inheritance of family property, 1844, Bristol RO, 26745/9 · d. cert. · parish register (baptism), Winnall, St Martin, 15/5/1842

Likenesses photograph, 1894, repro. in A. L. Waring, *Hymns and meditations* (1911)

Wealth at death £14,262 2s. 6d.: resworn probate, 10 June 1910, CGPLA Eng. & Wales

Waring [*married name* Harnett], **Dorothy Grace** [*pseud.* D. Gainsborough Waring] (1891–1977), fascist campaigner and author, was born on 8 June 1891 at Hill Top, Shrewsbury Lane, Plumstead, London, the only child of Colonel Henry Waring (*c*.1863–1940), officer in the Royal Artillery and later a farmer, and his wife, Florence Atthill (*d*. 1959). Educated in schools for children of military personnel in Malta and Gibraltar, she served in the Red Cross during the First World War and married army officer and barrister Edward St Clair Harnett (1881–1964) on 15 April 1916. They had one son, Denis Henry Waring (1917–1964). The marriage ended some years later, after public bitterness, and in 1927 St Clair Harnett remarried.

In the years following the First World War Dorothy Harnett became embroiled in the events of the troubles. Her father was the local B Special commander, and in September 1920 their home, Lisnacree House near Kilkeel (which also served as a B Special post), was raided by IRA members looking for guns and the family kept under 'arrest' for several hours. Harnett and her father pursued the IRA men who fired on, but failed to hit them.

From mid-1922 there were complaints about Harnett's activities as a female searcher at Lisnacree House, where, it was alleged, she strip-searched women suspected of carrying weapons or messages for the IRA. These allegations were strongly rejected by Colonel Henry Waring and Dorothy Harnett. Although initially defended by the Northern Ireland minister of home affairs, fears that her activities would cause rioting in the area led the RUC to dispense with her services in March 1923.

In the late 1920s Harnett joined the British Fascists (BF). As a close friend of the BF's founder, Rotha Lintorn-Orman, she became a senior member of the party. While staying at Lisnacree House Lintorn-Orman used the opportunity to hold fascist meetings in Northern Ireland. Although the organization was practically defunct by 1934, a number of its adherents continued to stay at Lisnacree House. In December 1933 an address by one such visitor, at the time of a Northern Ireland general election, provided the spark which led to a sectarian riot in Kilkeel.

In 1927 Harnett was Northern Ireland district officer, women's unit, of the BF, but by the following year was working in London. With Lintorn-Orman in increasingly poor health, Harnett became an influential figure in the organization and, after the BF split on the issue of joining Oswald Mosley in May 1932, was editor of the party newspaper. As late as May 1934 she remained the BF's propaganda officer. Her influence in the BF came to an end when it fell into financial difficulties and was effectively bought over.

After the death of Lintorn-Orman in March 1935 and the winding up of the BF in September, Harnett dropped out of party politics. She did, however, join the pro-German and often antisemitic organization the Link. By 1934 she had become involved with the Ulster Protestant League (UPL), which she attempted to sway towards some of her fascist ideas. With growing sectarian tensions in Belfast, though, she found herself out of touch with most UPL members—not least because of her sympathy for Catholic Irishmen who had fought for the British empire. In May 1934 she spoke at a UPL protest against the proposed renting of Belfast's Ulster Hall to the evangelical Catholic Truth Society, calling on those attending to band together and carry out military drills and adding: 'You will be told that you are stirring up feeling. ... Well, my reply is, for God's sake let us stir up feeling' (*Irish News*, 25 May 1934). In the wake of this meeting there were attacks on several Catholics and Catholic homes and premises. As a consequence of this speech Harnett was fined £20 and bound over to keep the peace for twelve months.

With the publication in 1936 of *Nothing Irredeemable*, the first of twelve novels, Harnett reinvented herself as the novelist D. Gainsborough Waring. Many of her novels were set in a barely fictionalized south Down and centred on the lives of the fast disappearing 'old gentry'; others dealt with the adventures of British intelligence officers, the occult, or both. Though no longer directly involved with fascism in a party-political forum, many of her early books made clear her continued admiration for Hitler. Following the advent of the Second World War, however, the pro-Nazi sympathies disappeared from her novels, though her anti-socialism remained.

During the war Harnett wrote a number of short thrillers and broadcast talks for the BBC. In the post-war era, as a regular member of the Northern Ireland Home Service's radio quiz *Up Against It*, she became a minor celebrity. The programme began in October 1946 and ran until 1960, when it transferred briefly to television. The reality behind her public celebrity was rather more grim. In September 1964 her son, Denis, died and during the rest of the decade her financial and physical condition continued to deteriorate. In 1971 she became a patient at Mourne House in Newcastle. In the following year her home, the 150-year-old Lisnacree House, was burnt down by arsonists. In the last months of her life Harnett was admitted to Mourne Hospital, Kilkeel, Down, where she died on the night of Monday 25 April 1977. At her request her body was donated for medical research and her ashes scattered in the Causeway River.   GORDON GILLESPIE

Sources G. Gillespie, *The secret life of D. G. Waring* (1998) · J. V. Gottlieb, *Feminine fascism* (2000) · investigation of complaints against Mrs Harnett, PRO NIre., HA 5/988 · reports on activities of fascist organisations, PRO NIre., HA 32/1/509 · R. Griffiths, *Fellow travellers of the right: British enthusiasts for Nazi Germany, 1933–9* (1980) · G. Walker, 'Protestantism before party: the Ulster Protestant League in the 1930s', *HJ*, 28 (1985), 961–7 · *Irish News and Belfast Morning News* (25 May 1934) · b. cert. · m. cert. · d. cert. · d. cert. [Henry Waring, father] · d. cert. [Florence Atthill, mother] · 'Old families of the Mourne country, no. 6: the Warings of Lisnacree', *Mourne Observer* (6 July 1956), 3 [interview] · *WWW* · will, PRO NIre.

Archives SOUND Ulster Folk and Transport Museum, 'Twenty-five years back', (28 Oct 1960) · Ulster Folk and Transport Museum, 'Up against it', (12 Feb 1957)

Likenesses photograph, repro. in *Mourne Observer* · photograph, repro. in *Belfast Telegraph* (26 April 1977)

Wealth at death £52,837: probate, 9 Feb 1978

Waring, Edward (*c*.**1735–1798**), mathematician, was born in Shrewsbury, the eldest son of John and Elizabeth Waring, a prosperous farming couple. He received his early education in Shrewsbury Free School under a Mr Hotchkin and was admitted as a sizar at Magdalene College, Cambridge, on 24 March 1753, being also Millington exhibitioner. His extraordinary talent for mathematics was recognized from his early years in Cambridge. In 1757 he graduated BA as senior wrangler and on 24 April 1758

Edward Waring (*c*.1735–1798), by Thomas Kerrich, 1794

was elected to a fellowship at Magdalene. He belonged to the Hyson Club, whose members included William Paley.

At the end of 1759 Waring published the first chapter of *Miscellanea analytica*. On 28 January the next year he was appointed Lucasian professor of mathematics, one of the highest positions in Cambridge. William Samuel Powell, then tutor in St John's College, opposed Waring's election and instead supported the candidacy of William Ludlam. In the polemic with Powell, Waring was backed by John Wilson (1741–1793). In fact Waring was very young and did not hold the MA, necessary for qualifying for the Lucasian chair, but this was granted him in 1760 by royal mandate. In 1762 he published the full *Miscellanea analytica*, mainly devoted to the theory of numbers and algebraic equations. In 1763 he was elected to the Royal Society. He was awarded its Copley medal in 1784 but withdrew from the society in 1795, after he had reached sixty, 'on account of [his] age' (Waring to Gilpin, 22 Aug 1794, RS). Waring was also a member of the academies of sciences of Göttingen and Bologna. In 1767 he took a degree of MD, but his activity in medicine was quite limited. He carried out dissections with Richard Watson, professor of chemistry and later bishop of Llandaff. From about 1770 he was physician at Addenbrooke's Hospital at Cambridge, and he also practised at St Ives, Huntingdonshire, where he lived for some years after 1767. His career as a physician was not very successful since he was seriously short-sighted and a very shy man.

Waring had a younger brother, Humphrey, who obtained a fellowship at Magdalene in 1775. In 1776

Waring married Mary Oswell, sister of a draper in Shrewsbury; they moved to Shrewsbury and then retired to Plealey, 8 miles out of the town, where Waring owned an estate. During his last years he sank into a deep religious melancholy, and a violent cold caused his death, in Plealey, on 15 August 1798. He was buried in the churchyard at Fitz, Shropshire.

Waring wrote a number of papers in the *Philosophical Transactions of the Royal Society*, dealing with the resolution of algebraic equations, number theory, series, approximation of roots, interpolation, the geometry of conic sections, and dynamics. The *Meditationes algebraicae* (1770), where many of the results published in *Miscellanea analytica* were reworked and expanded, was described by J. L. Lagrange as 'a work full of excellent researches' (Lagrange, 3.370). In this work Waring published many theorems concerning the solution of algebraical equations which attracted the attention of continental mathematicians, but his best results are in number theory. Included in this work was the so-called Goldbach conjecture (every even integer is the sum of two primes), and also the following conjecture: every odd integer is a prime or the sum of three primes. Euler had proved that every positive integer is the sum of not more than four squares; Waring suggested that every positive integer is either a cube or the sum of not more than nine cubes. He also advanced the hypothesis that every positive integer is either a biquadrate or the sum of not more than nineteen biquadrates. These hypotheses form what is known as 'Waring's problem'. He also published a theorem, due to his friend John Wilson, concerning prime numbers; it was later proved rigorously by Lagrange.

In *Proprietates algebraicarum curvarum* (1772) Waring reissued in a much revised form the first four chapters of the second part of *Miscellanea analytica*. He devoted himself to the classification of higher plane curves, improving results obtained by Newton, Stirling, Euler, and Cramer. In 1794 he published a few copies of a philosophical work entitled *An Essay on the Principles of Human Knowledge*, which were circulated among his friends.

Waring's mathematical style is highly analytical. In fact he criticized those British mathematicians who adhered too strictly to geometry. It is indicative that he was one of the subscribers of John Landen's *Residual Analysis* (1764), one of the works in which the tradition of the Newtonian fluxional calculus was more severely criticized. In the preface of *Meditationes analyticae* Waring showed a good knowledge of continental mathematicians such as Clairaut, d'Alembert, and Euler. He lamented the fact that in Great Britain mathematics was cultivated with less interest than on the continent, and clearly desired to be considered as highly as the great names in continental mathematics—there is no doubt that he was reading their work at a level never reached by any other eighteenth-century British mathematician. Most notably, at the end of chapter three of *Meditationes analyticae* Waring presents some partial fluxional equations (partial differential equations in Leibnizian terminology); such equations are a mathematical instrument of great importance in the study of continuous bodies which was almost completely neglected in Britain before Waring's researches. One of the most interesting results in *Meditationes analyticae* is a test for the convergence of series generally attributed to d'Alembert (the 'ratio test'). The theory of convergence of series (the object of which is to establish when the summation of an infinite number of terms can be said to have a finite 'sum') was not much advanced in the eighteenth century.

Waring's work was known both in Britain and on the continent, but it is difficult to evaluate his impact on the development of mathematics. His work on algebraical equations contained in *Miscellanea analytica* was translated into Italian by Vincenzo Riccati in 1770. Waring's style is not systematic and his exposition is often obscure. It seems that he never lectured and did not habitually correspond with other mathematicians. After J. J. Lalande in 1796 observed, in 'Notice sur la vie de Condorcet', that in 1764 there was not a single first-rate analyst in England, Waring's reply, published after his death as 'Original letter of the late Dr Waring' in the *Monthly Magazine*, stated that he had given 'somewhere between three and four hundred new propositions of one kind or another'. Waring's proud statement gives an idea of the lack of structure of his mathematical output, a study of which is still awaited.

NICCOLÒ GUICCIARDINI

Sources R. V. Wallis and P. J. Wallis, eds., *Biobibliography of British mathematics and its applications*, 2 (1986) • J. F. Scott, 'Waring, Edward', *DSB* • *DNB* • *GM*, 1st ser., 68 (1798), 730, 807 • *GM*, 1st ser., 71 (1801), 1165 • M. Cantor, ed., *Vorlesungen über Geschichte der Mathematik*, 4 (1908), 92–5 • C. Hutton, *A philosophical and mathematical dictionary*, new edn, 2 (1815), 584–5 • Venn, *Alum. Cant.* • W. Bulloch, 'Roll of the fellows of the Royal Society', RS • L. E. Dickson, *History of the theory of numbers* (1919–27) • *Collected works of Dugald Stewart*, ed. W. Hamilton, 11 vols. (1854–60) • J. L. Lagrange, *Œuvres*, 14 vols. (Paris, 1867–92) • V. Riccati, *Nuova raccolta di opuscoli scientifici* (1770) • J. J. Lalande, 'Notice sur la vie de Condorcet', *Mercure de France* (20 Jan 1796), 143 • 'Original letter of the late Dr. Waring', *Monthly Magazine*, 7 (1799), 306–10
Archives RS
Likenesses T. Kerrich, drawing, 1794; Christies, 21 March 1989, lot 86 [*see illus.*] • engraving, RS • portrait, Magd. Cam.

Waring, Edward Marsden [Eddie] (1910–1986), journalist and broadcaster, was born on 21 February 1910 at South View, Hollinroyd Road, Soothill Nether, near Dewsbury, the younger son of Arthur Waring, insurance agent, and his wife, Florence Harriet, *née* Marsden. He was educated at Eastborough School in Dewsbury and spent his teenage days between secretarial college, singing in Congregational chapel, and being active on the sports field. It was his love of sport that took him first into local journalism in Dewsbury and later he combined this with coaching. Aged twenty-four, he became the youngest manager of a rugby league club. Because of deafness in one ear, the result of a childhood illness, he was not accepted in the armed forces during the Second World War. He made his name by recruiting well-known players stationed in Yorkshire during the war, and thereby turned Dewsbury into a championship side (1941–2) and challenge cup winner (1942–3).

After the war Waring concentrated on journalism and

Edward Marsden [Eddie] **Waring** (1910–1986), by Green, 1969

he was assigned by the *Yorkshire Evening News* to report the British rugby league tour of Australia. Demonstrating his enterprise, Waring secured a passage on the aircraft-carrier HMS *Indomitable*, for which the Royal Navy charged him £11 11s. 2d. On returning to Britain he set out to become a commentator and contacted the BBC. Rugby league football, which had broken away from rugby union in 1895, was the professional thirteen-a-side game restricted to the north of England. Waring's enthusiasm persuaded BBC television that rugby league would be a success if televised regularly on Saturday afternoons. Deprived of other sports by contractual difficulties, the BBC were converted and took him on. So began a thirty-year career in television which saw Waring first as a commentator and later as a performer. It turned him into a national figure but he continued to live at Bramhope, on the outskirts of Leeds.

Waring made his début as a commentator in 1951. To much of the country he was unknown, and he felt that an unorthodox approach would help him. He had the ability to say what the man on the terraces was thinking. He introduced some polished one-liners: when a player was sent off the field, 'he is going for an early bath'; on the Humberside weather, 'It's a coat colder on the east coast'. One of his regular comments, 'up and under', delivered in a cheerful Yorkshire voice, became a national catch-phrase. But he was also compassionate. When a player missed a golden chance in the cup final at Wembley, his only comment was 'poor lad'. Waring had his detractors, mostly in the north. Some felt that he made fun of the game, but his inimitable style of commentary and his love for the sport made rugby league entertaining for many millions who knew it only from television.

From being the unseen man behind the microphone, Waring graduated in 1967 to being the referee in vision for a televised entertainment programme called *It's a Knock-Out*, a fairground frolic between various British seaside towns. It proved so popular in the 1970s that it became a successful European television programme, *Jeux sans frontières*, seen by millions across Europe. Now that he was a performer, albeit too much of a clown for some, he became famous and enjoyed it. But he restricted himself

to two luxuries: a Jaguar car and good hotels. He protected his private life; he was married to Mary Wolff, with whom he had a son.

Waring retired in 1981, the year in which he was appointed MBE. The final years were difficult: dementia meant long stays in hospital in Leeds. He died of pneumonia at High Royds Hospital, Menston, Yorkshire, on 28 October 1986.   PAUL FOX

Sources *The Times* (29 Oct 1986) · *The official history of Dewsbury rugby league football club* (1989) · *Official Rugby League Centenary Magazine* (1995) · L. Thompson, 'Leeds born and bred', *Dalesman* (1982) · personal knowledge (2004) · b. cert. · d. cert.
Archives FILM BBC Television archives | SOUND BBC Radio archives
Likenesses Green, photograph, 1969, Hult. Arch. [*see illus.*] · photographs, 1969, Hult. Arch.
Wealth at death £76,843: probate, 13 Jan 1987, *CGPLA Eng. & Wales*

Waring, Sir Holburt Jacob, first baronet (1866–1953), surgeon, was born at Heskin, Chorley, Lancashire, on 3 October 1866, the eldest son of Isaac Waring, schoolmaster, and his wife, Catherine Holburt. He was educated at Owens College, Manchester, and entered St Bartholomew's Hospital, London, as a scholar. He qualified MRCS, LRCP in 1890 and obtained his FRCS in 1891. He graduated BSc, London, in 1888, with second-class honours in physiology, MB in 1890, BS in 1891, and MS in 1893. In 1900 Waring married Annie Cassandra (*d.* 1948), daughter of Charles Johnston Hill.

Waring's whole career was centred on three institutions: St Bartholomew's Hospital, the Royal College of Surgeons, and the University of London. At the hospital he held several teaching appointments and was appointed assistant surgeon to W. Harrison Cripps in 1902, becoming full surgeon in 1909. He ultimately became consulting surgeon and governor of the hospital, and had the distinction of having a ward named after him during his lifetime. He was also consultant surgeon to the Metropolitan Hospital, the Royal Dental Hospital, and the Ministry of Pensions. He was very interested in the subject of cancer and for many years was treasurer of the Imperial Cancer Research Fund (1933–52). In 1928 he published a book entitled *Surgical Treatment of Malignant Disease*. His best-known work was *A Manual of Operative Surgery* (1898), which went through several editions and was an examination classic.

To the College of Surgeons Waring devoted a great deal of his time and energy. He was Jacksonian prizeman in 1894 for his essay 'The diagnosis and surgical treatment of diseases of the liver, gall-bladder and biliary ducts'. He was Erasmus Wilson lecturer (1898), Bradshaw lecturer (1921), and Hunterian orator (1928) on the bicentenary of the birth of John Hunter. He served as college vice-president (1923–5) and president (1932–5). While on the college council he represented that body on the General Medical Council, and was also its treasurer (1917–32). He served on the court of examiners (1911–20); he was a Hunterian trustee; and he received the first past president's badge in 1951.

In the University of London, Waring was dean of the faculty of medicine (1920) and vice-chancellor (1922–4). He was governor of the Imperial College of Science (1930–47), and governor and almoner of Christ's Hospital for a number of years. He was president of the Medical Society of London (1925–6) and president of the section of surgery of the Royal Society of Medicine (1928–30). He served as chairman and treasurer to the London School of Hygiene. He promoted the connection of the medical schools with the University of London and was the first to develop postgraduate training and research at the Royal College of Surgeons. He paid several visits to Cairo and did much to encourage Egyptian medical education. In 1935 he opened the new Royal Australasian College of Surgeons (of which he was an honorary fellow) at Melbourne and was presented with a ceremonial gold key.

During the war of 1914–18 Waring served as colonel in the Royal Army Medical Corps and was consulting surgeon to the London command in addition to his hospital work. He was appointed CBE in 1919, knighted in 1925, and created a baronet in 1935. He was an officer of the Légion d'honneur and received honorary degrees from Bristol, Durham, and Cairo.

Waring was a man of few words, inclined to be rude to his juniors, and he always liked to have his own way. Of stern appearance, he seldom smiled. During the last ten years of his life he became interested in printing and this interest made him a very rich man. He did not get on well with his only son, Alfred Harold (1902–1981), a research engineer in the Imperial Chemical Industries, and arranged his will so as to exclude him. Nevertheless, his son succeeded as second baronet when Waring died at Pen-Moel, Tidenham, Chepstow, Gloucestershire, on 10 February 1953.   CECIL WAKELEY, *rev.*

Sources *The Times* (11 Feb 1953) · *The Times* (19 Feb 1953) · annals, RCP Lond., vol. 12 · *A record of the years 1901–1950*, Royal College of Surgeons of England (1951) · *St Bartholomew's Hospital Journal*, 57 (1953), 116–17 · *BMJ* (21 Feb 1953), 456–7 · private information (1971) · personal knowledge (1971)
Likenesses M. Ayoub, oils, 1927–9 (*Council of the Royal College of Surgeons, 1926–27*), RCS Eng.
Wealth at death £310,148 16s. 0d.: probate, 20 July 1953, CGPLA Eng. & Wales

Waring [*alias* Ellis], **Humphrey** (*bap.* 1605, *d.* 1676), Roman Catholic priest, was baptized at Solihull, Warwickshire, on 19 November 1605. A member of 'a family of great antiquity and good account' (Gillow, *Lit. biog. hist.*), he was a son of Charles Waring of Berry Hall, Solihull, and his wife, Laetitia or Lettice Hugford (*d.* 1610). He entered the English College, Douai, with his brother William on 20 July 1622 and both lived at the college at their own expense. They studied humanities and philosophy and Humphrey publicly defended in philosophy on 16 August 1627. After one year's theology he and his brother were sent, on 25 August 1628 with seven other students and three professors, to assist the first president, Joseph Haynes, in opening the new English seminary in Lisbon, where they arrived on 22 November 1628. After completing the theology course under Thomas White, Humphrey stayed on for two years assisting as an apprentice teacher. He was then ordained priest on 24 August 1635 and

became professor of philosophy for two and a half years. In 1638 he began to teach theology and in March 1641 he was made interpreter for the Inquisition in the inspection of foreign ships. He became vice-president to Edward Daniel on 25 June 1642 and succeeded him as president of the college on 8 August 1648. After three years he resigned and received the doctorate in theology, on 23 June 1652. In September the death occurred of his brother William, who since his ordination in 1633 had been working on the mission in the English midlands. The same year Humphrey left Lisbon for England.

In 1658 Humphrey Ellis, as he was known, was elected to succeed Edward Daniel as dean of the English chapter, the effective governing body for secular clergy in England. He took up permanent residence in London in 1660. These were particularly difficult times for the administration of the Roman Catholic church in England. Nobody had been appointed to take the place of Richard Smith as bishop when he died in 1655. Ellis was anxious that Rome would appoint a person with full episcopal powers but there was resistance to this, especially from the Jesuits and other religious orders. The chapter strove to convince the king and the protestants of their loyalty in the hopes that some of the penalties against the Catholics would be relaxed. It was in the belief that episcopal jurisdiction had in the interim devolved on them that in 1662 the dean and chapter granted faculties to the queen's chaplain, D'Aubigny, enabling him to conduct a Catholic marriage between Charles II and his Catholic bride, Catherine of Braganza. Thanks to Ellis there was a private Catholic ceremony before witnesses preceding the public ceremony conducted by the bishop of London. In 1669 Claude Agretti, a canon of Bruges, was instructed by the pope to go to England to examine the condition of ecclesiastical affairs and in his report he noted that Ellis was extremely anxious that the powers of the chapter should be confirmed even if it meant the resignation and replacement of those who held office at present. Agretti described Ellis as 'noble, esteemed, learned and modest but withall tinged with Blackloism' (Brady, 3.110). Thomas White's, or Blacklo's, views on matters relating to the papacy were regarded with suspicion. Another visitor from Flanders in 1670, the internuncio, Airoldi, found Ellis and other leading chapter men more moderate than he had expected. Ellis died in London on 9 August 1676 'Beloved and honoured generally by all who knew him' (Guiney).

MICHAEL E. WILLIAMS

Sources E. H. Burton and T. L. Williams, eds., *The Douay College diaries, third, fourth and fifth, 1598–1654*, 1, Catholic RS, 10 (1911), 192, 270, 418; 2, Catholic RS, 11 (1911), 533, 546 · M. Sharratt, ed., *Lisbon College register, 1628–1813*, Catholic RS, 72 (1991), 210–11 · L. F. Guiney, 'A Chapter necrology, Oct 1670–Feb 1678', ed. J. Gillow, *Miscellanea, III*, Catholic RS, 3 (1906), 98–104, esp. 103 · W. M. Brady, *The episcopal succession in England, Scotland, and Ireland, AD 1400 to 1875*, 3 (1877), 108–10 · J. Sergeant, *An account of the chapter erected by William, titular bishop of Chalcedon*, ed. W. Turnbull (1853), 81–98 · Gillow, *Lit. biog. hist.*, 2.160–61 · C. Dodd [H. Tootell], *The church history of England, from the year 1500, to the year 1688*, 3 (1742), 295 · VCH *Warwickshire*, 4.217, 6.243 · G. Anstruther, *The seminary priests*, 2 (1975), 337–8 · J. Miller, *Popery and politics in England, 1660–1688*

(1973) • T. A. Birrell, 'English Catholics without a bishop, 1655–1672', *Recusant History*, 4 (1957–8), 142–78
Archives Lisbon College archives, MSS • Westm. DA, Old Brotherhood archives, MSS
Wealth at death individual bequests: Anstruther, *Seminary priests* • £100 to chapter; £50 to English College, Douai; £50 to English College, Lisbon: Old Brotherhood Archives, MSS

Waring, John Burley (1823–1875), architect, was born on 29 June 1823 at Lyme Regis, Dorset. Of his parents little is known except that his mother's maiden name seems to have been Franks. From 1836 he was educated at the Bristol branch of University College, London, where he was also taught watercolour drawing by Samuel Jackson. In 1840 he was apprenticed to his second cousin Henry E. Kendall, a London-based architect. Then in 1842 he became a student at the Royal Academy, and obtained a silver medal at the Society of Arts for designs in architectural adornments in 1843. His health was never robust and he spent the winter of 1843–4 in Italy 'to improve himself in art and to become a painter' (Waring, 9). On returning to England he was elected an associate of the RIBA in 1845 and became a draughtsman successively in the offices of A. Poynter, Laing of Birkenhead, Sir Robert Smirke (1846), and D. Mocatta (1847).

With Thomas R. Macquoid, Waring went to Italy and Spain in 1847 and studied architecture, measuring and drawing the public buildings. The result was an illustrated work entitled *Architectural Art in Italy and Spain*, which was published in 1850. For this all he received was a small payment for lithographing the sixty fine folio plates. He also produced *Designs for Civic Architecture*. From 1850 to 1852 he studied under Thomas Couture in Paris and afterwards lived at Burgos, where he studied the monuments at the Cartuja de Miraflores. In conjunction with Sir Matthew Digby Wyatt he wrote four architectural guidebooks to the courts of the Crystal Palace at Sydenham in 1854. While again in Italy in 1855 he made a further series of drawings, which were purchased for the South Kensington Museum, and published in 1858 as *The Arts Connected with Architecture in Central Italy*.

Waring was appointed superintendent of the works of ornamental art and sculpture in the Manchester exhibition of 1857, and edited *Art Treasures of the United Kingdom from the Art Treasures Exhibition, Manchester* (1858). He was elected FRIBA in 1860. In the International Exhibition at Kensington in 1862 he was the superintendent of the architectural gallery and of the classes for furniture, earthenware, and glass, goldsmiths' work and jewellery, and objects used in architecture. In connection with this exhibition he published *Masterpieces of Industrial Art and Sculpture* (3 vols., 1862), consisting of 300 coloured plates and descriptions, which were in English and French. He was chief commissioner of the exhibition of works of art held at Leeds in 1868. An extract from his exhibition report was published as *The National Exhibition of Works of Art at Leeds* (1867). He was interested in ancient glass paintings and wrote an introduction to C. Winston's *Catalogue of Drawings from Ancient Glass Paintings* (1865); he also wrote on *Ceramic Art in Remote Ages* (1874) and *Stone Monuments,*

Tumuli and Ornament of Remote Ages (1870). During a further tour in Italy he sent a series of notes to *The Architect*. In February 1871 the American Institute of Architects elected him an honorary member, but he obtained little practice.

Waring wrote several books on the subject of the church, faith, and doctrine, and was also the author of a volume of *Poems: by an Architect* (1858). At the age of twenty he had been an enthusiastic follower of Swedenborg's doctrines; later he somewhat changed his opinions, and in his *A Record of Thoughts on Religious, Political, Social, and Personal Subjects* (2 vols., 1873), he advanced an eccentric claim to write under 'special divine inspiration' and the power of making prophecies concerning political events. He died, apparently unmarried, at the Castle Hotel, Hastings, on 23 March 1875.   G. C. BOASE, *rev.* JOHN ELLIOTT

Sources *The Builder*, 33 (1875), 290 • *Journal of Proceedings of the Royal Institute of British Architects* (1874–5), 37 • *ILN* (27 June 1868), 633 • *CGPLA Eng. & Wales* (1875) • *Dir. Brit. archs.* • J. B. Waring, *My artistic life* (1873)
Likenesses lithograph, BM • portrait, repro. in *ILN*, 633 • portraits, repro. in *The Graphic* (10 April 1875), 342 and 356
Wealth at death under £3000: probate, 7 April 1875, *CGPLA Eng. & Wales*

Waring, John Scott- (1747–1819), agent of Warren Hastings, was born on 24 October 1747 in Shrewsbury, the eldest son of Jonathan Scott (*d.* August 1778) and Mary, daughter of Humphrey Sandford of the Isle of Rossall, Shropshire. The couple had three other sons: Richard, who went on to serve as a lieutenant-colonel in India, Jonathan *Scott, who made his name as an oriental scholar, and Henry, who became a commissioner of police in Bombay. Like his brothers, John Scott also had strong connections with India. In 1766 he became a cadet in the East India Company forces in Bombay, and in the following year transferred to the Bengal army. On 22 June 1772 he married Elizabeth (1745–1796), daughter of Alexander *Blackrie, surgeon-general. With Elizabeth, Scott had two sons—Edward, who became a civil servant in Bengal, and Charles, who died when young—and two daughters—Anna Maria (*d.* 1862), mother of the novelist Charles *Reade, and Eliza Sophia. Scott continued to rise up the ranks of the Bengal army and by 1778, when he first met Warren Hastings, he had reached captain. Scott became Hastings's aide-de-camp in September of that year, beginning an association which was to dominate the next twenty years of his life.

In response to growing controversy over his role in India, Hastings sent Scott to England to act as his political agent and defend his reputation. Scott arrived in London on 17 December 1781 and began to work with great zeal on behalf of his patron, whom he kept minutely informed of events. With financial backing provided by Hastings's considerable personal fortune, Scott bombarded the newspapers with letters and articles and wrote numerous pamphlets, in the hope of persuading the country that Hastings had been wrongly accused by Edmund Burke and Philip Francis. To this end he published *A Short Review of the Transactions in Bengal during the Last Ten Years* (1782), *A Letter to … Edmund Burke* (1783), and *The Conduct of his Majesty's*

Late Ministers Considered (1784), in addition to many other pamphlets in a similar vein. In 1784, with Pitt's rise to power, Scott became convinced that he could best serve Hastings from inside parliament. Accordingly he spent £4000 on securing for himself the seat of West Looe, Cornwall.

Unfortunately for Hastings, he had probably been misguided in his choice of agent, for although Scott was indefatigable in his cause, he proved himself to be somewhat inept. Indeed, Macaulay commented of Hastings that 'of all his errors the most serious was perhaps the choice of a champion' (Macaulay, 77). Scott proved to be neither a skilled political writer nor an accomplished parliamentarian. He became famous for the unremitting frequency of his speeches in the Commons, for the predictability of his subject matter, and for being something of a bore. More seriously, he was accused of forcing Burke to proceed with his threatened inquiry on 24 January 1786. General Grant wrote to Lord Cornwallis on 6 April that Hastings 'certainly in a great measure owes his misfortunes to the mistaken zeal of his friend Major Scott, who bullied Burke into persecution' (*Correspondence of … Cornwallis*, 1.364). However, Mrs Hastings claimed that Scott was acting upon the instructions of her husband who 'desired that he might be impeached that he might clear his character of various calumnies which had been thrown out against him' (Weitzman, 175).

After Hastings's return to England, Scott ceased to act as his paid agent, but continued as his spokesman in the Commons, and almost all of the numerous speeches he made there were connected with Indian affairs. On 28 May 1790 he was reprimanded by the speaker for publishing an article attacking Burke which was said to be disrespectful of the Commons. In the same year Scott paid another £4000 to become MP for Stockbridge, Hampshire. He had hoped this would be a 'quiet seat', but it proved troublesome and he was ousted on 11 February 1793. When Hastings was finally acquitted in 1795 Scott presented him with a bill of £21,840 for expenses incurred in his defence; these included payment for authors, printers, and newspapers, the costs of his elections, and his living expenses. Hastings appears to have been taken aback by the sums involved, but paid up nevertheless. Scott then argued that since he had been prepared to share in Hastings's ruin, he should expect to profit from his vindication and subsequent rewards from the East India Company. It is not known what financial arrangements followed, but the two remained on good terms.

With the trial over, Scott largely retired from political life, although he was sheriff of Cheshire from 1801 to 1802, and continued to publish the occasional pamphlet on Indian affairs. In particular, he was strongly opposed to sending missionaries to India. On 26 October 1796 his wife Elizabeth died. He married an Irish actress, Mary Hughes, that same year, and with her had another son and another daughter. In 1798, on the death of his cousin Richard Hill Waring, Scott inherited the Waring estates in Cheshire. As part of the terms of the bequest he took the additional surname Waring. In 1800 he sold the estate for £80,000 and a

year or two later bought Peterborough House, Parson's Green, Fulham. Here he was reputed to have gathered around him a varied company of actresses, wits, politicians, and royal princes. On 15 October 1812 he was married for the third time; his new wife was another actress, Harriet Pye *Esten *née* Bennett (1761?–1865), with whom he had a son and a daughter. He died seven years later on 5 May 1819 at Half Moon Street, Piccadilly.

HANNAH BARKER

Sources HoP, *Commons*, vols. 3, 5 • T. B. Macaulay, *Warren Hastings* (1841) • *Correspondence of Charles, first Marquis Cornwallis*, ed. C. Ross, 3 vols. (1859) • G. Cornall and C. Nicholson, eds., *Impeachment of Warren Hastings* (1989) • E. A. Bond, ed., *Speeches of the managers and counsel at the trial of Warren Hastings* (1860) • L. Werkmeister, *The London daily press, 1772–1792* (1963) • Charles L. Reade and Compton Reade, *Charles Reade, dramatist, novelist, journalist: a memoir compiled chiefly from his literary remains*, 2 vols. (1887) • S. Weitzman, *Warren Hastings and Philip Francis* (1929) • M. Kelly, *Reminiscences*, 2 vols. (1826)
Archives BL, letters to Warren Hastings, etc., Add. MSS 29133–29194, *passim* • NL Scot., letters to Scott family
Likenesses C. Turner, print, 1802 (after J. Masquerier), BM

Waring, Robert (1614?–1658), writer, was born to a family long settled at the Ley, Staffordshire. His father was Edmund Waring; his mother was the daughter of Richard Broughton of Owlbury in the parish of Bishops Castle, Shropshire, and a niece of the rabbinical scholar Hugh Broughton. He had at least one older brother, Walter Waring, and at least one sister, Anne, later Staunton.

Waring attended Westminster School and entered Christ Church, Oxford, in 1630. He matriculated in 1632, graduated with a BA on 20 June 1634, and received his MA on 26 April 1637. During the civil war he bore arms for Charles I at Oxford but his loyalty cost him dearly: no sooner had he been elected senior proctor and Camden professor of ancient history (on 29 April and 2 August 1647 respectively) than he was ordered to give up both posts by the parliamentary visitors sent that year to purge the colleges of royalists. Waring's election had been contested by Charles Wheare, son of the previous professor, Degory Wheare, whom the parliamentary visitors favoured (Burrows, 236). The prelude to the clash between the visitors and Christ Church is documented in *A Publike Conference Betwixt the Six Presbyterian Ministers, and Some Independent Commanders … a Satire* (1646), attributed to Waring, while an account of the heated dispute that ensued is given in *The University of Oxfords Plea Refuted* (1647). The latter was written jointly by several afflicted royalists, including Waring and John Fell, son of the dean of Christ Church, Samuel Fell; the latter had also been ousted by the visitors unceremoniously. Waring defended his position staunchly: he defied the visitors' order that he be removed from his posts and on 14 December 1647 was 'adjudged guilty of high contempt and denyall of authority of Parliament' (ibid., 185). Selden's intervention saved him from being entirely banished from the university, but on 7 April 1648 he was summoned to London and ordered into custody. Yet again Waring defied the order and escaped to Oxford; on 14 September 1648, however, he was among those ordered to leave the university within a fortnight (ibid., 19, 185–6).

In the end Waring was stripped of his proctorship, professorship, and student's place, and forced to hand in his books and other personal belongings to the visitors. Defeated, he retired to Apley, Shropshire, at the invitation of Sir William Whitmore, that 'great patron of distressed cavaliers' with whom he later travelled to France.

As an author Waring is probably best known for his *Amoris effigies, sive, Quid sit amor?* [1657], written in Latin and translated into English by John Norris in 1682 as *Effigies amoris in English, or, The Picture of Love Unveil'd*. Norris was clearly enraptured by Waring's treatise on love: having mastered 'this novel', he writes in the preface (Norris, *Effigies amoris in English*, 2nd edn, 1701, 5), 'the judicious reader … will discern new thoughts like little stars glimmering out of the rich Galaxy' (ibid., 8). Waring also published *A Sermon Preached at St. Margarets in Westminster, at the Funeral of Mrs Susanna Gray* (1657) and contributed to John Fell's *The Life of the most Learned, Reverend and Pious Dr H. Hammond* (1661). Some of his verse in Latin is included in various editions of *Amoris effigies*. In Wood he is described as a Latin and English poet 'but a better orator, … reckoned among the great wits of his time in the University' (Wood, *Ath. Oxon.*, 3rd edn, 3.453–4).

Back in England, Waring fell gravely ill and died in Lincoln's Inn Fields on 9 May 1658. On 10 May he was buried at St Michael's Church, College Hill. His eldest brother, Walter, was buried in the same grave only ten days after Robert's funeral (Wood, *Ath. Oxon.*, 3rd edn, 3.453–4). Robert never married; his will was proved by his sister and sole executor, Anne Staunton.

ARTEMIS GAUSE-STAMBOULOPOULOU

Sources [R. Waring], *A publike conference betwixt the six presbyterian ministers, and some Independent commanders … a satire* (1646) • [W. Prynne, R. Allestree, J. Fell, and R. Waring], *The University of Oxfords plea refuted* (1647) • [R. Waring], *Effigies amoris in English*, trans. J. Norris, 2nd rev. edn (1701) [preface is not paginated and is signed 'Phil-icon-erus'] • J. Norris, 'A brief account of the author and translator', in [R. Waring], *The picture of love unveil'd*, 4th edn (1744) • Wood, *Ath. Oxon.*, new edn, 3.453–4 • M. Burrows, ed., *The register of the visitors of the University of Oxford, from AD 1647 to AD 1658*, CS, new ser., 29 (1881), lxxxii, 19, 185–6, 236, 491 • Allibone, *Dict.* • DNB • Foster, *Alum. Oxon.* • *Thoroton's history of Nottinghamshire*, ed. J. Throsby, 1 (1790), 306, 309 • Watt, *Bibl. Brit.*, 2.950

Waring, William. *See* Barrow, William (c.1609–1679).

Warington, Robert (1807–1867), chemist, was born on 7 September 1807 at Sheerness, the third son of Thomas Warington, a provisioner of ships. His early childhood was spent in, among other places, Portsmouth and Boulogne. In 1818 he entered the Merchant Taylors' School and in November 1822 he was apprenticed for five years to the practical and manufacturing chemist John Thomas Cooper. There he became familiar with the rapidly evolving opportunities for a metropolitan chemist, such as the electrolytic manufacture of the recently discovered halogens and alkalis and the teaching of chemistry to medical students, required by the Apothecaries Act of 1815. In 1828

he was appointed an assistant to Edward Turner, first professor of chemistry in the new University of London. From 1831 until 1839 his principal employment was as a brewery chemist to the firm of Truman, Hanbury, and Buxton; he was among the first professional chemists to hold such a position. From 1842 to 1866 he was chemical operator and resident director to the Society of Apothecaries, giving up the position because of illness shortly before his death. From 1854 to 1861 he also served as a referee to several of the metropolitan gas companies. In 1835 he married Elizabeth, daughter of George Jackson, surgeon and microscopist; they had three children.

Recognizing the need for a professional association among the numerous young metropolitan chemists, Warington was instrumental in organizing the Chemical Society of London (later the Chemical Society) in early 1841. In large part it was initially to be a self-help institution, housing a laboratory, a library, and reagent resources that would have been beyond the means of most of its members. For the society's first decade Warington was honorary secretary, and he served as vice-president of the Chemical Society in 1851–4 and 1862–5. Warington was also involved in the establishment of the Cavendish Society (1846), formed to facilitate the translation and publication of important works in chemistry, and served as co-secretary of the society from 1846 to 1849. In 1845 he was a member of the provisional committee that established the Royal College of Chemistry. In June 1864 he was elected fellow of the Royal Society.

Most of Warington's scientific papers, of which there were about forty, dealt with the analysis of materials of commerce, such as tea, glass, distilled water, and guano, or the balanced aquarium, which he invented in 1850 as a device to illustrate complementary chemical activities of plants and animals that sustain life on earth, and which he presented initially to the Chemical Society; ownership of such an aquarium quickly became a popular hobby, providing a conversation piece for the mid-Victorian parlour. For Warington, however, the aquarium was an instrument for tentative explorations in what would now be called aquatic ecology. In this work he anticipated the popular naturalist P. H. Gosse, who would refocus the attention of aquarium enthusiasts on marine creatures. These interests were followed by his son Robert *Warington, who became an agricultural chemist and bacteriologist of note, and served as professor of rural economy at Oxford from 1894 to 1897.

In his post at the Society of Apothecaries Warington was concerned with modernizing the pharmacopoeia. In 1851 he took over revision of the pharmacopoeia of the Royal College of Physicians after the death of Richard Phillips, and after the 1858 reform of the medical profession he was centrally engaged in preparation of a national compendium. He was joint editor, with Boverton Redwood, of the second edition of the *British Pharmacopoeia* (1867), though by that time he was too ill to take an active role. This work chiefly entailed discovering chemical protocols by which practitioners could estimate the quality of raw materials and produce medicaments of known strength.

Warington was author of *A Series of Chemical Tables, Arranged for the Use of the Chemical Student* (1833), and assisted F. J. Farre and R. Bentley in preparation of a *Manual of Materia Medica and Therapeutics: being an Abridgement of … Dr. [Jonathan] Pereira's Elements of materia medica …* (1865). His most important contributions were not published articles and books, however, but his efforts in organizing metropolitan chemists and in standardizing pharmaceutical manufacture. He died at Poplar Cottage, Budleigh Salterton, Devon, on 12 November 1867. He was survived by his wife and sons.

CHRISTOPHER HAMLIN

Sources JCS, 21 (1868), xxxi · PRS, 16 (1867–8), xlix · C. Hamlin, 'Robert Warington and the moral economy of the aquarium', *Journal of the History of Biology*, 19 (1986), 131–53 · T. Redwood and J. Bell, *The progress of pharmacy* (1880) · R. F. Bud and G. K. Roberts, *Science versus practice: chemistry in Victorian Britain* (1984) · E. W. Stieb and G. Sonnedecker, *Drug adulteration: detection and control in nineteenth-century Britain* (1966) · W. H. Brock, 'The society for the perpetuation of Gmelin: the Cavendish Society, 1846–1872', *Annals of Science*, 35 (1978), 599–617 · *Catalogue of scientific papers*, Royal Society · R. Warington and B. Redwood, eds., *British pharmacopoeia*, 2nd edn (1867) · *Chemical News* (20 Dec 1867), 316 · *The Times* (14 Nov 1867) · *The Times* (15 Nov 1867) · *CGPLA Eng. & Wales* (1867) · G. K. Roberts, 'The establishment of the Royal College of Chemistry: an investigation of the social context of early Victorian chemistry', *Historical Studies in the Physical Sciences*, 7 (1976), 437–85
Archives Rothamsted Experimental Station Library, Harpenden, corresp. and papers · RS · RSA
Likenesses portraits, Chemical Society · portraits, RS
Wealth at death under £16,000: probate, 7 Dec 1867, *CGPLA Eng. & Wales*

Warington, Robert (1838–1907), agricultural chemist, was born at 22 Princes Street, Spitalfields, London, on 22 August 1838, eldest son and second child of Robert *Warington (1807–1867), one of the founders of the Chemical Society, and Elizabeth Jackson. Four years later his father was appointed chemical operator and resident director to the Society of Apothecaries and the family then moved residence to Apothecaries' Hall. Robert Warington's early education was restricted because of poor health and he did not undertake formal university or college study. However, as a youth he was introduced to chemistry in his father's laboratory and attended lectures by such leading scientific figures as Faraday, Brande, and Hofmann.

In 1859 Warington became an unpaid assistant to John Lawes at Rothamsted agricultural experimental station. The position was obtained for him by his father who had earlier advised Lawes in lawsuits brought to protect his patent on the manufacture of superphosphate. It was felt that a rural situation would benefit the young Warington's delicate constitution. After a year at Rothamsted, where he was chiefly engaged upon the analysis of the ash of wheat and grass, Warington returned to London where he worked as a research assistant to Edward Frankland at the Royal College of Chemistry. However, in October 1862 health problems again caused him to seek an appointment in the country and he went as teaching chemical assistant to the Royal Agricultural College at Cirencester, first under Augustus Voelcker (1822–1884) and, after 1863, to Professor Church.

It was at Cirencester that Warington's research led to the publication of his first scientific papers in the Chemical Society's *Journal*. Following Voelcker, this early work was on the quantitative determination of phosphoric acid, work which led to investigations into the role of ferric oxide and alumina in decomposing soluble phosphates and other salts, and retaining them in the soil. Warington was able to demonstrate that hydrated oxides of iron and aluminium took up phosphoric acid from a solution of any of its salts. He maintained that this was a chemical process—in contrast to Liebig who asserted that the action was physical.

While still at Cirencester, Warington offered to assist Lawes with a series of animal nutrition experiments at Rothamsted, and he lectured on the range of work which was being done there. He also prepared a book on the research, but it was never published because of the objection of Lawes's co-worker J. H. Gilbert, who believed that Warington was attempting to gain recognition on the basis of his investigations. This episode brought about a lifelong estrangement between the two men and had a deleterious impact on Warington's subsequent career.

On leaving Cirencester in 1867 Warington was appointed to the post of chemist at Lawes's manure and acid works at Barking and Millwall. While at the factory he dealt with various agricultural subjects for *Watts' Dictionary of Chemistry*; his work on citric and tartaric acid was published in the *Journal of the Chemical Society*. In 1876 Lawes invited Warington back to Rothamsted to investigate soil processes. This arrangement was strongly objected to by Gilbert and, after external attempts at mediation had failed, Warington worked as Lawes's personal assistant. In 1877 the role of micro-organisms in the process of nitrification was determined by Schloesing and Müntz in France: Warington was among the first to recognize the significance of their findings and he devoted much effort to an attempt to isolate the organisms involved by culture methods. He studied bacteriology at the Brown Institution in London under Klein in order to further his understanding of the subject, but his investigations were only partially successful. Although Warington produced cultures which converted ammonia into nitrites, and others which produced the further conversion of nitrites into nitrates, he was unable to isolate the specific micro-organisms involved. (This was done by Percy Frankland in 1890 and independently, using a superior technique, by Sergei Winogradsky who presented his results in a paper to the Académie Royale des Sciences in Paris in 1891.)

Warington had settled at Harpenden in 1876, but the establishment of the Lawes Agricultural Trust in 1889 meant that the management of Rothamsted passed to a trust committee, and as by this time relations between Gilbert and Warington had deteriorated still further, the trust determined that Warington's connection with the experimental station would have to be terminated at the end of 1890. This severance ended Warington's original work in agricultural science, but the trust did appoint him to lecture in America the following year. His addresses on the bacteriology of soil nitrogen to the Association of American Agricultural Experimental Stations were subsequently published by the United States department of agriculture. On his return to England Warington undertook further work on tartaric and citric acid at Lawes's Millwall factory, and in 1894 he was appointed for three years to the Sibthorpian professorship of agriculture at the University of Oxford. Several of his lectures there were published in 1900 as *Lectures on some of the Physical Properties of Soils.*

During the latter years of his life Warington's activities were curtailed by indifferent health and he devoted himself to charitable, educational, and religious work in Harpenden. E. John Russell (1872–1965), later the director of Rothamsted, found that on his first and only meeting with Warington in 1906 he appeared to have lost all interest in agricultural science (Russell, 160–66). It was a great disappointment to Warington that his fourteen-year period of research into nitrification had not been wholly successful, and his continual clashes with Gilbert had also taken their toll.

Warington was nevertheless a significant figure in agricultural science and chemistry during the second half of the nineteenth century. His extensive writing was marked by precision and clarity and he was highly industrious; his detailed notebooks indicated a number of avenues for later research. Apart from chemical articles, his output included writing the larger part of 'Rain and drainage waters at Rothamsted', which was published in the *Journal of the Royal Agricultural Society of England* between 1881 and 1883 (with Lawes and Gilbert), and entries to Thorpe's *Dictionary of Applied Chemistry* in 1895. His greatest success was with *The Chemistry of the Farm* (1881) which was the best-received of J. C. Morton's nine-volume Book of the Farm series. Warington's contribution passed through fourteen editions and four revisions within twenty years. His professional work was recognized by his election in 1863 as a fellow of the Chemical Society, of which he was later a vice-president, and his admission as a fellow to the Royal Society in 1886.

Warington's first wife, Helen Louisa Makins, whom he had married in 1884, died in 1898. In 1902 he married Rosa Jane Spackman. He died at his home, High Back, Harpenden, on 20 March 1907 and was buried at Harpenden. His connection with Rothamsted was continued by the appointment of Katherine Warington—one of five daughters from his first marriage—as a botanist there in 1921; she worked there for thirty-six years.

NICHOLAS GODDARD

Sources S. U. Pickering, *JCS*, 92 (1908), 2258–69 · E. J. Russell, *A history of agricultural science in Great Britain, 1620–1954* (1966), 160–66 · *CGPLA Eng. & Wales* (1907)
Archives Rothamsted Experimental Station Library, Harpenden, corresp. and papers
Wealth at death £6141 4s. 11d.: resworn probate, 18 April 1907, *CGPLA Eng. & Wales*

Wariston. For this title name *see* Johnston, Sir Archibald, Lord Wariston (*bap.* 1611, *d.* 1663).

Warkworth, John (*c.*1425–1500), ecclesiastic, college head, and supposed chronicler, is thought to have been a native of the diocese of Durham, named from the Northumberland village of Warkworth. He was elected bachelor of Merton College, Oxford in 1446, admitted as bachelor fellow *c.*1447 and was a fellow by *c.*1448. He still held that position in 1456. He was also second bursar there in 1451–3 and 1455–6. He graduated MA at Oxford in 1449, and at about that time was one of the fellows of Merton admitted to the confraternity of the English Hospital of the Holy Trinity and St Thomas the Martyr at Rome. He was appointed an auditor of university library accounts in 1449 and of the proctor's accounts in 1455. He was ordained acolyte at St Frideswide's Priory, Oxford, in 1450. The next year he became principal of Bull Hall, and in 1453 of Neville's Inn, both belonging to Merton College. He was appointed keeper of the Turville chest in December 1455. Some time after 1454 he became domestic chaplain to William Grey, bishop of Ely (*d.* 1478), after which he received various livings in Cambridgeshire: he was rector of Cottenham (1458–72); vicar of Wisbech St Peter (1472–3); and rector of Leverington (1473–90). He was also vicar of Latton, Essex (1460), and canon of Southwell and prebendary of Sacrista (1475–98). Cambridge permitted him to incept as doctor of theology in 1462–3. He was appointed in 1471 one of thirteen feoffees of whom Elizabeth Howard, dowager countess of Oxford, entrusted her lands; with six of his colleagues he later opposed turning the property over to Richard, duke of Gloucester, until Richard in 1474 successfully brought suit against them. In 1473 Bishop Grey appointed him master of Peterhouse, Cambridge.

Warkworth donated an astrolabe and fifty-five books to the library of Peterhouse in 1481, not 1483 as some have written. He also contributed 100 s. for the erection of Grove Wall on the west side of Peterhouse. About 1485 Cambridge granted Warkworth a grace, presumably on the grounds of ill health, so that he was not required to attend funeral rites of graduates, or meetings of congregations or convocations, unless he was specifically named. His first will was dated 31 December 1485, and a second was written on 28 May 1498. In the latter he requested burial in the chantry chapel that he had built and endowed in 1487 on the south side of the nave of St Mary-the-Less, Cambridge. He bequeathed a Bible to Merton College and made bequests to Peterhouse, the churches of St Mary-the-Less, Leverington, and Cottenham, and the monasteries of Ely, Crowland, and Barnwell. He also made bequests for masses for his own soul and for those of his parents and Bishop Grey. Peterhouse has a portrait of him as a cleric holding an open book. The date 1498 on the picture was added by a later hand. He remained master of Peterhouse until his death in October or November 1500. His will was proved on 17 November 1500. He is not to be confused with another John Warkworth of Durham, who was ordained acolyte by William Grey in 1468 and was a fellow of Peterhouse from 1468 to 1479.

One of Warkworth's books, a manuscript written in

English, *Liber cronicorum in Anglicis* (Cambridge, Peterhouse, MS 190), contains one of the two known texts of Warkworth's chronicle, which covers the first thirteen years (1461–74) of Edward IV's reign. This work's emphasis on events in northern England has led some to believe that Warkworth was the author of it, but there is no proof of this. A Latin note records that the book was given to Peterhouse by Warkworth, who may simply have commissioned its transcription. According to Lister Matheson, earlier scholars were incorrect in assuming that the first part of Peterhouse 190 is a copy of Caxton's 1482 edition of the *Chronicles of England*; it is instead a different *Brut* text, to which a second hand has added a continuation from 1419 to 1461 based upon one of Caxton's two editions of the *Chronicles of England* and his 1482 edition of Trevisa's translation of the *Polychronicon*. Warkworth's chronicle, covering the years 1461–74, was added to this continuation in the Peterhouse manuscript. The Peterhouse manuscript refers to another copy of Warkworth's continuation, the location of which was for many years unknown. Matheson, however, found a copy in University of Glasgow Library, Hunterian MS 83, and has argued that this is the text from which the Peterhouse version of Warkworth's chronicle was copied. Since the continuation of the *Brut* to 1461 in the Peterhouse manuscript could not have been written until after the publication of Caxton's *Polychronicon* in 1482, and since part of the Hunterian manuscript was copied from the St Albans edition of the *Chronicles of England* (c.1483), the two manuscripts of Warkworth's chronicle could not have been copied before c.1484, after Warkworth had donated his books to the library. Matheson believes that another fellow of Peterhouse, either Roger Lancaster or Thomas Metcalf, probably wrote the chronicle attributed to Warkworth.

The chronicle has some pro-Lancastrian bias, such as sympathy for the deposed Henry VI, and criticism of Edward IV for failing to establish peace and end the hardships caused by war. Nevertheless, the tone is generally moderate and reasonably objective. Scholars have valued it for the information it gives about events in the north, such as Edward IV's subjugation of Northumberland, Henry VI's capture of Lancaster (1465), the rebellion in Lincolnshire (1470), and the battle of Tewkesbury (1471). Written in 1484, after Richard III had become king, it does not include charges against Richard found in Tudor works, such as his being involved with the murder of Henry VI. At some points it confirms statements found in less objective accounts like the Yorkist *Chronicle of the Rebellion in Lincolnshire*. Known to Leland in the sixteenth century, Warkworth's chronicle was first published by the Camden Society in 1839, in an edition by J. O. Halliwell, and by the Boydell Press in 1999, in an edition by L. Matheson. EDWARD DONALD KENNEDY

Sources Emden, *Oxf.*, 3.1992–3 · Emden, *Cam.*, 618–19 · L. M. Matheson, 'Historical prose', *Middle English prose: a critical guide to major authors and genres*, ed. A. S. G. Edwards (1984), 224–5 · E. D. Kennedy, *A manual of the writings in Middle English, 1050–1500*, 8: *Chronicles and other historical writings*, ed. A. E. Hartung (1967), 2642–4, 2834–6 · A. Gransden, *Historical writing in England*, 2 (1982), 257–61 · E. A. B. Barnard, 'John Warkworth (c.1425–1500) and his chapel in St Mary's-the-Less, Cambridge', *Proceedings of the Cambridge Antiquarian Society*, 35 (1933–4), 131–5 · L. M. Matheson, 'Printer and scribe: Caxton, the *Polychronicon*, and the *Brut*', *Speculum*, 60 (1985), 593–614, esp. 609–10 · *DNB* · J. Warkworth, *A chronicle of the first thirteen years of the reign of King Edward the Fourth*, ed. J. O. Halliwell, CS, old ser., 10 (1839), ix–xxvii · C. L. Kingsford, *English historical literature in the fifteenth century* (1913), 171–3, 270 · L. M. Matheson, ed., *Death and dissent: 'The dethe of the kynge of Scotis' and Warkworth's chronicle* (1999), 61–92 · M. A. Hicks, 'The last days of Elizabeth, countess of Oxford', *EngHR*, 103 (1988), 76–95, esp. 81–5
Archives Peterhouse, Cambridge, MS 190 · U. Glas. L., Hunterian MS 83
Likenesses oils, Peterhouse, Cambridge
Wealth at death bequeathed a Bible to Merton College, Oxford; made bequests for masses for the souls of Bishop Grey, himself, and his parents, and for the churches of Leverington and Cottenham, the monasteries of Ely, Crowland, and Barnwell, and for Peterhouse

Warlock, Peter. *See* Heseltine, Philip Arnold (1894–1930).

Warltire, John (1725/6–1810), public lecturer, was born in Switzerland of unknown parentage. Nothing is known of his early life, but he probably spent an extended period at Palmyra in Syria. Indeed, M. H. Miller later recorded that Palmyra was among Warltire's 'favourite subjects, [owing to his] having lived many years among the Arabs' (Miller, 217). Warltire arrived in England, possibly to escape religious persecution, in the 1750s. He began work as a valet at Ashover, Derbyshire, but at Michaelmas 1760 started teaching at Ashover Hill School at £9 a year. He left in August 1762, having there 'improved himself in his studies' (White Watson). In November 1762 he married, at Wolverhampton, Mary Stringer (c.1743–1790), apparently a housekeeper in the residence where he had been valet. His age was recorded as twenty-three, probably incorrectly.

Warltire started his new career as an itinerant science lecturer in 1763. Over eighty advertisements for his courses have been located throughout the English provinces, in an area bounded by Plymouth, Chester, Manchester, Leeds, and Norwich. His first lecture course was at Lutterworth, where his eldest son was born in October 1763. He then lectured in many towns in that area, already giving special courses for women, demonstrating with orrery, air-pump, and solar microscope. His first emphasis was astronomy and he issued a *Short Account of the Solar System* in 1764 (seven editions with changing titles and emphases to post-1769). He later issued many other equally ephemeral publications, chiefly to accompany his lectures. By 1766, when he gave a course of lectures at Salisbury, his teaching covered the whole range of experimental philosophy and included 'new experiments in electricity' (*Salisbury Journal*, 14 April 1766). In 1769 Warltire added a new course in chemistry, recording in his lecture notes that 'the Atmosphere is composed of two distinct Sorts of fluid Matter'.

In 1771 Warltire was emphasizing the utility of his scientific lectures. In that year his course at Ashbourne was attended by Samuel Johnson (1709–1784), who was much stimulated by its metallurgical and mineralogical content. At Shifnal in 1772 Warltire carried out experiments on air in the blood of a live sheep. These were soon followed by other frigorific experiments, involving a thermometer placed in an air-pump, all for Erasmus Darwin (1731–1802). In 1773 Warltire gave lectures at Warrington and from 1774 assisted Joseph Priestley (1733–1804) with experiments and chemicals at Calne on dephlogisticated air (oxygen). By 1775 his 'Apparatus was equal to any in the Possession of a private Person in Britain' (*Exeter Flying Post*, 21 April 1775) and his charges had increased to a half-guinea for ten lectures.

In 1776 Warltire advertised courses of 'New Experiments upon Air' (*Bristol Journal*, 7 Sept 1776), in which he had been helped by William Withering (1741–1799); the price was now 1 guinea for twelve lectures. Between 1777 and 1781 Priestley printed descriptions of some of Warltire's experiments, including one of 1776 when Warltire also noticed the deposit of moisture produced on the inside of a tube after the explosion of a mixture of air and inflammable gas (hydrogen). This contributed to the intense debate on the composition of water, and who had discovered it.

In 1777 Warltire first delivered lectures about Stonehenge at Salisbury, having observed the local source for sarsen stones and how the Friar's Heelstone marked where the sun rose on the longest day. Probably in the same year, Warltire's Bristol lectures stimulated William Gregor (1761–1817), the discoverer of titanium, to take a first interest in chemistry. In 1778 Warltire subscribed to a book by fellow lecturer Thomas Malton. He gave a Wolverhampton address, suggesting that his long-suffering wife, at least, continued to live there. The following year, Warltire gave a new course on agricultural chemistry at Tamworth and he was now employed as personal chemistry tutor to John Wedgwood (1766–1844) and Robert Waring Darwin (1766–1848) at Etruria. In 1780 Warltire started another new course on metallurgy and mineralogy at Birmingham and was soon performing chemical analyses for friends. He was elected an early honorary member of the Manchester Literary and Philosophical Society in 1782.

In 1783 Warltire performed a vital piece of industrial espionage for James Watt (1736–1819), when he obtained a drawing of Jonathan Hornblower's new compound steam engine at Radstock while lecturing nearby. His observation that Exeter was built on an extinct volcano seems the first properly geological observation to be reported to the Chapter House Philosophical Society in London, in 1785. In 1786 Warltire gave lectures at Salisbury with his travelling mineral collection. In 1791 these led to renewed, if abortive, attempts to find coal at Shaftesbury in Dorset.

Warltire took a long interest in Stonehenge, which he thought 'a vast Theodolite for observing the motions of the heavens' (J. Britton, *Beauties of Wiltshire*, 2, 1801, 121). By 1786 he and his son William had made accurate cork models, as it then was and as it had first been. Warltire brought Roman pavements near Warminster to public attention in 1786. In 1790 Warltire's wife died at Wolverhampton, and no lecture notices have been traced from then until 1797, when his health was reported in decline.

His silence may have arisen from the danger of his association with Priestley, whose laboratory—when destroyed in 1791—included equipment constructed by Warltire.

Warltire returned to lecturing from 1798; his last known course was given at Ashbourne in 1809. He died at Bonehill, Tamworth, in August 1810 at 'a very advanced age' (*Derby Mercury*) and 'in great poverty' (Miller); burial records gave his age as eighty-four. The *Derby Mercury* unavailingly hoped for 'Memoirs of this distinguished and very useful character … and the publication of his very curious and original papers' (which John Farey (1766–1826) quoted with approval in 1813). Warltire was the itinerant science lecturer most closely associated with, and who reported the work of, the Lunar Society. His claimed Scottish degree has not been confirmed, but his MSS and fine apparatus passed into the hands of Richard Dalton of York, another itinerant lecturer of the next generation, who had lost many by 1827. Warltire was buried at Tamworth church on 23 August 1810.   H. S. TORRENS

Sources White Watson, 'Commonplace book', Duke of Northumberland archives, Alnwick Castle, Northumberland · D. McKie, 'Mr Warltire, a good chymist', *Endeavour*, 10 (1951), 46–9 · N. G. Coley, 'John Warltire, 1738/9–1810, itinerant lecturer and chemist', *West Midlands Studies*, 3 (1969), 31–44 · M. H. Miller, ed., *Olde Leeke*, 2nd ser. (1900), 217–20 · A. E. Musson and E. Robinson, *Science and technology in the industrial revolution* (1969) · R. E. Schofield, *The Lunar Society of Birmingham* (1963) · T. W. Peck and K. D. Wilkinson, *William Withering of Birmingham* (1950), 155–66 · G. Higgins, *The Celtic druids* (1827), i–xviii; 239–40 · L. J. Jordanova and R. S. Porter, *Images of the earth* (1979), 229–31 · H. S. Torrens, 'Winwoods of Bristol, engineers', *Bristol Industrial Archaeology Society Journal*, 13 (1980), 11 · J. Money, *Experience and identity: Birmingham and the west midlands, 1760–1800* (1977) · J. Golinski, *Science as public culture: chemistry and enlightenment in Britain, 1760–1820* (1992) · *Derby Mercury* (20 Dec 1810) · parish register (burial), 1790, Wolverhampton · parish register (burial), 23 Aug 1810, Tamworth

Archives Linn. Soc., Pulteney archive · Sheffield Central Library, W. Watson MSS · University of Keele, Wedgwood archives

Wealth at death "in great poverty": Miller, *Olde Leeke*, 217

Warmestry, Gervase (1604–1641), poet, was the second son of William Warmestry (d. 1640), principal registrar of the diocese of Worcester, and of his wife, Cicell (d. 1650), daughter of Thomas Smith of Cuerdley in Lancashire. Thomas *Warmestry was his younger brother. The Warmestrys were an ancient Worcester family who gave their name to the Warmestry Slip, a narrow street leading down from the city to the Severn, where their house formerly stood. The post of registrar of the diocese of Worcester had been held by a Warmestry since 1544 and Gervase was born and brought up in the city believing he would follow in this family tradition. He was educated first at Worcester grammar school, then moved on to Westminster School, and in 1621 was elected a scholar of Christ Church, Oxford. He matriculated on 24 July 1624 and graduated BA on 5 May 1625 and MA on 27 June 1628; in November 1628 he became a student of the Middle Temple.

Warmestry contributed a Latin poem to *Camdeni insignia: a Collection of Panegyrics on William Camden* (1624), but is more notable for a poetical tract entitled *Virescit vulnere virtus: England's Wound and Cure* (1628). It is a characteristic appeal to patriotism, couched in a poem dedicated to Endimion Porter, esquire, and written following the duke of Buckingham's disastrous expedition to the Île de Ré in 1627. This military humiliation, and its loss of men, had left king and parliament very much divided. A copy of the work, which is scarce, is in the Bodleian Library; it bears no name of place of publication nor of printer and was probably privately printed. The poem was reprinted in 1875 in the second series of *Fugitive Tracts, written in Verse, which Illustrate the Condition of Religious and Political Feeling in England, and the State of Society there during Two Centuries* (ed. W. C. Hazlitt). Warmestry's work was chosen as one of the few to throw light on the condition of England in the year leading up to the assassination of the duke of Buckingham, when crisis seemed close at hand.

Warmestry succeeded his father as registrar of the diocese of Worcester, having been appointed in reversion on 20 November 1630. He died on 28 May 1641 and was buried in Worcester Cathedral. He left a widow, Isabella, to whom letters of administration were granted in London on 31 August 1641.   BERTHA PORTER, *rev.* JOANNA MOODY

Sources Watt, *Bibl. Brit.*, 2.950 · W. T. Lowndes, *The bibliographer's manual of English literature*, ed. H. G. Bohn, [new edn], 4 (1864), 2843 · STC, 1475–1640 · Foster, *Alum. Oxon.* · *Old Westminsters* · H. A. C. Sturgess, ed., *Register of admissions to the Honourable Society of the Middle Temple, from the fifteenth century to the year 1944*, 3 vols. (1949)
Archives Bodl. Oxf.

Warmestry, Thomas (1609/10–1665), dean of Worcester, was born in Worcester, the son of William Warmestry (*d.* 1640) and his wife, Cicell Smith (*d.* 1650). The Warmestry family was prominent in the town: William, as registrar of the diocese, occupied a position which members of the family had held since 1544. Thomas's elder brother was the minor poet Gervase *Warmestry. Thomas was educated at the King's School, Worcester, and at Oxford. He graduated BA from Brasenose College on 3 July 1628, matriculated from Christ Church, aged eighteen, the following day, and proceeded MA on 30 April 1631. In April 1635 he was instituted rector of Whitchurch, Warwickshire. In 1640 he was clerk for Worcester diocese in both of the convocations of the clergy. At the second convocation he delivered a speech against 'Images, Altars, Crosses, the New Canons, the Oaths', which was edited for publication by his friend Thomas Dugard in 1641. It is highly significant that a man who on his subsequent record may be called a moderate Anglican should be driven by dislike of Laudian ceremonialism to take up such a position.

In the crisis of 1641–2 Warmestry, like many other moderates, turned increasingly to the idea of reconciliation, in both church and state, as in his *Pax vobis, or, A Charme for Tumultuous Spirits* and *Ramus olivae, or, An Humble Motion for Peace*. The former was published in London in 1641: its subtitle included 'an earnest and Christian advice to the people of London, to forbeare their disorderly meetings at Westminster'. 'Though he had always been accounted a Puritan' (Wood, *Ath. Oxon.*, 3.713), Warmestry joined the king at Oxford in 1642. There the same year he published *Ramus olivae* and was created DD. In 1643 he resigned the living of Whitchurch and became rector of Minchinhampton, Gloucestershire, but, as he stated in a petition to the House of Lords in 1660, he was 'hindered by the warre then on foot in that County' (*Walker rev.*, 178).

By 1644 Warmestry was back in the royalist city of Worcester. On 17 June 1646, during a lull in the siege of the city, he challenged Richard Baxter, chaplain to one of the besieging regiments, to a disputation about the nature of a church. 'The result', according to the account that Warmestry gave to the Worcestershire gentleman and diarist Henry Townshend, 'was a confession of Mr Baxter's that he differed from me but in Terms. To which I replied that "I would never quarrel with terms so they agreed in sense"' (*Diary*, 1.124). Warmestry was also one of those chosen to negotiate about the surrender of the city.

In 1648 Warmestry published *Suspiria ecclesiae et reipublicae Anglicanae*, dedicated to Prince Charles; he describes it as 'An Exhortation to Humiliation'. In the same year he wrote urging peace with the king (*The Preparative for London … An Hearty and Friendly Premonition to the City of London*) and a defence of the observance of Christmas. He may have been the author in 1649 of *A Handkirchife for Loyall Mourners, or, A Cordiall for Drooping Spirits, Groaning for the Bloody Murther, and Heavy Losse of our Gracious King*. For his failure to compound by 1650, his estate at Paxford, Worcestershire, was sold in 1653. By the latter year he seems to have acquired a church living in Shropshire (it is not clear which one). At any rate, in September 1653 Warmestry and another Shropshire conformist, Thomas Good, met Richard Baxter at Cleobury Mortimer in that county. They expressed their 'very good liking' of the new Worcestershire association. Baxter was delighted that 'some Men of great Learning and Piety that are of the Episcopal Way' were in favour of the association and were prepared to promote it in Shropshire (Keeble and Nuttall, 1.109; *Reliquiae Baxterianae*, pt 2, 164–6). However, Warmestry, after consulting his 'London Brethren' (notably, Peter Gunning), changed his mind about the association, and sent Baxter a series of objections to his views (they were, in fact, written by Gunning). This does not mean that Warmestry's initial interest had been insincere: as in 1640–42, his moderation and his Anglican loyalism pulled him in opposite directions.

In the interregnum Warmestry acted as confessor to ex-royalists and as an almoner to distressed cavaliers, living in London in the later 1650s. He waited, like other Anglicans, for the political and ecclesiastical climate to change; he regarded, for instance, the conversion of a Muslim effected by Gunning as a propitious sign to the Church of England 'in these evil times' (N. Matar, *Islam in Britain, 1558–1685*, 1998, 145). That change came about with the Restoration of 1660. In June Warmestry became master of the Savoy; in July a prebendary of Gloucester Cathedral; and on 27 November 1661 he was installed as dean of Worcester Cathedral, where he remained until his death. As dean he had to steer the cathedral through a difficult period of recovery and refurbishment after the damage suffered in the civil wars. One difficulty concerned the installation of a new choir organ. The dean interfered with the work of the organ-builder. In a letter of 5 August 1665 to Archbishop Sheldon (Bodl. Oxf., MS Tanner 45, fol. 19), Bishop Skinner commented on Warmestry's 'utter ignorance' of music.

Having supported Bishop Morley in his opposition to Baxter in 1661, Dean Warmestry went at least twice to Kidderminster after Baxter's departure from the town and preached 'vehement, tedious Invectives' (*Reliquiae Baxterianae*, bk 1, pt 2, 149) from the pulpit against Baxter and his former flock 'to cure them of the Admiration of my Person' (ibid., bk 1, pt 2, 376). He was being forced by the polarities of the time to relinquish his former moderation. At an unknown date, Warmestry married Anne or Anna Wright (d. 1671), daughter of Richard Wright, clerk, but they had no children. He died at Worcester on 30 October 1665, and was buried in Worcester Cathedral two days later.   C. D. GILBERT

Sources *Reliquiae Baxterianae, or, Mr Richard Baxter's narrative of the most memorable passages of his life and times*, ed. M. Sylvester, 1 vol. in 3 pts (1696) • A. Hughes, *Politics, society and civil war in Warwickshire, 1620–1660* (1987) • *Walker rev.*, 178 • *Calendar of the correspondence of Richard Baxter*, ed. N. H. Keeble and G. F. Nuttall, 2 vols. (1991) • Wood, *Ath. Oxon.*, new edn, 3.713 • M. Craze, *King's School, Worcester* (1972) • B. S. Smith, 'Two early sketches of the Worcester porcelain works', *Transactions of the Worcestershire Archaeological Society*, 3rd ser., 16 (1998), 221–5 • J. Noake, *The monastery and cathedral of Worcester* (1866) • *Diary of Henry Townshend of Elmley Lovett*, ed. J. W. Willis Bund, 4 pts in 2 vols., Worcestershire Historical Society (1915–20) • W. M. Ede, *The cathedral church of Christ and the Blessed Virgin Mary of Worcester: its monuments and their stories* [1925], 270 • *CSP dom.*, 1660–61, 16, 106–7 • M. A. E. Green, ed., *Calendar of the proceedings of the committee for compounding … 1643–1660*, 4, PRO (1892), 2661–2 • *Fasti Angl., 1541–1857*, [Ely] • W. R. Buchanan-Dunlop, ed., *The parish registers of St Michael's in Bedwardine, 1546–1812*, Worcestershire Archaeological Society, parish registers, 2nd ser., 2 (1954)
Archives HLRO, papers • Worcester Cathedral Library • Worcs. RO | BL, E 282/14 • Bodl. Oxf., Tanner papers
Wealth at death estate to his wife; £50 each to his nieces: will, Worcs. RO

Warmington, William (b. c.1556, d. after 1627), Roman Catholic priest, who used the alias Peters, was born in Dorset. His father, whose forename is unknown (d. before 1594), was a recusant and died in Ilchester gaol where he was imprisoned for his faith. His mother was named Eve (d. after 1594) and lived at Wimborne Minster. William matriculated on 20 December 1577 at Hart Hall, Oxford. He left England for the English College at Rheims to be trained as a Catholic missionary priest, arriving there on 7 December 1579. He was ordained at Soissons on 28 May 1580 and was sent to England on 31 January 1581. Arrested in England, he was committed to the Marshalsea prison on 10 December 1582 and was sentenced to death on the false charge of plotting the death of the queen. He was reprieved, however, and banished to France along with a number of other convicted priests. He made for his old college at Rheims, which he reached on 3 March 1585, and then left for Rome on 10 April 1586. Here he became chaplain to Cardinal William Allen. On the death of Allen in 1594 he became an oblate of St Charles.

Warmington decided to return to England to resume his work, and was certainly there in 1603. In 1608 he was arrested and committed to the Clink. In 1612 he gained instant notoriety by publishing a pamphlet entitled *A Moderate Defence of the Oath of Allegiance*. The oath of allegiance had been devised by James in the aftermath of the Gunpowder Plot as a test of Catholic loyalty. Catholics found it objectionable because it contained a clause denying the papal power in temporals. By accepting the oath Warmington was placing himself in opposition to many English Catholics, but not to all. For the government of James it was something of a public relations coup to have a former chaplain of the cardinal of England on their side. It is reported that Warmington was now cold-shouldered by some of his Catholic colleagues. He was given preferential treatment by the government, and in 1612 he was let out of prison and was placed for a time in the household of the Church of England bishop of Winchester. However, it is clear that he continued a Catholic, and between 1626 and 1627 was again imprisoned in the Clink. He ended his life in obscurity, and there seems to be no record of the date or circumstances of his death.   PETER HOLMES

Sources G. Anstruther, *The seminary priests*, 1 (1969) • *DNB* • Wood, *Ath. Oxon.*, new edn, 2.128 • *Calendar of the manuscripts of the most hon. the marquis of Salisbury*, 4, HMC, 9 (1892), 473, 477, 598 • *Miscellanea, II*, Catholic RS, 2 (1906), 233, 236 • J. H. Pollen, ed., *Unpublished documents relating to the English martyrs*, 1, Catholic RS, 5 (1908), 54 • *The letters and memorials of William, Cardinal Allen (1532–1594)*, ed. T. F. Knox (1882), vol. 2 of *Records of the English Catholics under the penal laws* (1878–82), 375 • W. Warmington, *A moderate defence of the oath of allegiance* (1612) • A. F. Allison and D. M. Rogers, eds., *The contemporary printed literature of the English Counter-Reformation between 1558 and 1640*, 2 vols. (1989–94) • *Miscellanea, IV*, Catholic RS, 4 (1907), 129 • A. G. Petti, ed., *Recusant documents from the Ellesmere manuscripts, 1577–1715*, Catholic RS, 60 (1968), 19–23 • 'The confession of John Hambly', ed. J. L. Whitfield, *Miscellanea, VII*, Catholic RS, 9 (1911), 167–73, esp. 169 • M. C. Questier, *Newsletters from the archpresbyterate of George Birkhead*, CS, 5th ser., 12 (1998)

Warne, Charles (1801–1887), archaeologist, was born in Moreton, Dorset, on 6 July 1801, the youngest son of Joseph Kingston Warne (d. 1823) and Leah Kingston Warne (d. 1838). Shortly after his birth the family moved to the manor house at Pokeswell, near Warmwell. Charles Warne was educated in schools in Weymouth and Wimborne, and after his mother's death in 1838 settled in Milborne St Andrew, Dorset. In 1844 he became a member of the British Archaeological Association, and in 1856 a fellow of the Society of Antiquaries. On 15 May 1847 he married Anne Holland of Upper Chelsea, London. Shortly after the birth of Alexander Bradley, one of their sons, in August 1850, they moved to London, and subsequently lived at Ewell, Surrey. On 15 April 1859 Anne died. Her wedding ring, late medieval and engraved with figures of saints, was sold at Sothebys in June 1959. Charles Warne, for the sake of his health, settled in Brighton, where he died at his home, 45 Brunswick Road, on 11 April 1887. He was buried in Brookwood cemetery, Woking.

Although Warne made archaeological tours in France in 1853 and 1854, in company with Charles Roach Smith and Frederick William Fairholt, the focus of his work was Dorset. After two years of travelling through Dorset, accompanied by Charles Hillier, he published an *Illustrated map of*

Dorsetshire giving the sites of its numerous Celtic, Roman, Saxon and Danish vestiges (1865). His studies also led to the *Celtic Tumuli of Dorset* (1866), and 'Observations and details of Vespasian's first campaign' (*Archaeologia*, 41, 1867). In *Ancient Dorset* (1872) he gave an account of the minting of Saxon, Danish, and Norman coinage in Dorset, and this 'exhaustive treatise' (Hutchins, 1.lxxii) was used for the third edition of Hutchins's *History of Dorset*. Charles Warne was a keen collector of coins and relics. Many of his coins were sold in 1899, but the museum at Dorchester received his splendid collection of relics and sepulchral urns in 1885, and these included over forty items of Bronze Age pottery. GLANVILLE J. DAVIES

Sources H. J. Moule, 'In memoriam', *Proceedings of the Dorset Natural History and Antiquarian Field Club*, 9 (1888), xiv–xxi · J. B. Calkin, 'Some records of barrow excavations re-examined', *Proceedings of the Dorset Natural History and Archaeological Society*, 88 (1966), 128–48 · J. Hutchins, *The history and antiquities of the county of Dorset*, 3rd edn, ed. W. Shipp and J. W. Hodson, 1 (1861), v, xiii, lxxii, 407; 3 (1868), 614; facs. edn (1973) · J. Ackland, 'Catalogue of sepulchral pottery in the Dorset County Museum', *Proceedings of the Dorset Natural History and Antiquarian Field Club*, 29 (1908), 126–42 · C. Blair, 'An iconographic ring connected with Charles Warne', *Proceedings of the Dorset Natural History and Archaeological Society*, 85 (1963), 110–11 · C. H. Mayo, 'Warne's collection of Dorset coins', *Notes and Queries for Somerset and Dorset*, 1 (1889), 225–6 · christenings, Moreton, 1741–1812, Dorset RO, PE/MTN RE 1/2 · christenings, Milborne St Andrew, 1813–64, Dorset RO, PE/MIA RE 2/1 [baptism of Alexander Bradley Warne, 27 Aug 1850] · census returns for Milborne St Andrew, 1851, PRO, HO 107/1853 · *DNB*

Wealth at death £17,427 0s. 9d.: resworn probate, Sept 1887, *CGPLA Eng. & Wales*

Warne, Frederick (1825–1901), bookseller and publisher, was born on 13 October 1825 in Westminster, London, the sixth and youngest son of the twelve children of Edmund Warne, builder, and Matilda, daughter of R. A. Stannard. Privately educated in Soho, Frederick, at the age of fourteen, joined his elder brother William Henry (d. 1859) and brother-in-law George *Routledge (1812–1888) in the retail bookselling business of George Routledge, located at 11 Ryders Court, Leicester Square, London. Founded in 1836, Routledge expanded from bookselling into publishing, and both William (in 1848) and Frederick (in 1851) became partners in the twice renamed firm: Routledge & Co. (1851); Routledge, Warne, and Routledge (1858). From 1851 until 1865 Frederick Warne was a vital member of the successful publishing firm. When a long-time friend, the publisher George Smith of Smith, Elder & Co., advised him to begin his own firm, Warne and his partners amicably dissolved their partnership, divided their holdings, and formed two independent publishing houses—George Routledge & Sons and Frederick Warne & Co. Edward James Dodd (from Routledge's) and A. W. Duret (from the Dalziel Brothers) helped Warne launch the new company, which he guided from 1865 to 1894.

Warne had sixteen years of publishing and bookselling experience when he opened his new offices on 1 July 1865 at 15 Bedford Street, Covent Garden. From the start he offered literature series, dictionaries, and semi-religious

Frederick Warne (1825–1901), by unknown photographer

novels to suit the middle-class Victorian family. His editorial policy had two key elements: wholesome entertainment and reasonable prices. In 1868, emulating Routledge's aim to popularize time-honoured literature, he inaugurated the Chandos Classics, an enormously well-liked series of ultimately 154 titles. Total sales exceeded 5 million copies, the Shakespeare edition alone selling more than 340,000 copies. Peter Austin Nuttall's *Standard Dictionary* also proved very successful when reissued under the Warne label (1867, 1886); nearly 1 million copies of the revised 1886 edition sold by 1911. Warne also published didactic self-improvement books (for example *Popular Tracts for Working and Cottage Homes*) and natural history books (for example *The Royal Natural History*, ed. Richard Lydekker, 1894–6). In the field of literature the firm published Disraeli's novels until 1870 (when Longman took over) and nearly all of Frances Hodgson Burnett's novels.

In the 1870s and 1880s Warne became one of the pioneers of the expanding trade in coloured picture books for children. The firm introduced several series of children's books including Aunt Louisa's Toy Books (a series named after Warne's wife, Louisa) and published works by prominent children's authors and illustrators: Edward Lear (*Book of Nonsense*), Randolph Caldecott, Kate Greenaway, and Walter Crane. Warne employed Edmund Evans to ensure effective colour printing of the work of Caldecott,

Crane, and Greenaway. The firm gained distinction for its skilful interweaving of text and colour illustration.

Under Warne's leadership the firm expanded, particularly in the 1880s. In 1881 Frederick Warne, accompanied by P. C. Leadbetter, founded an American branch in New York city. In the 1880s Warne's became the British agents for, and introduced to the British reading public, several American magazines: *Scribner's Magazine*, *Century Magazine*, and *St Nicholas' Magazine* (in which Frances Hodgson Burnett's *Little Lord Fauntleroy*, 1886, first appeared in serial form).

A dedicated and lifelong publisher, recognized for his limitless energy, Warne was also a family man. He was known to boast that he had married on the profits of *Uncle Tom's Cabin*, whose right to print he bought for Routledge from the USA in 1852, issuing the first 'cheap' British edition of the work in that same year. He had married Louisa Jane, daughter of William Fruing of Jersey, on 6 July 1852. Six of their children survived infancy, although Fred, the eldest, died in childhood. The others were Edith, Harold, Fruing, Amelia (Milly), and Norman. Moving his family from Doughty Street to 8 Bedford Square, Warne entertained relatives, friends, and business acquaintances. He also enjoyed playing whist and cribbage with his children and grandchildren, taking country carriage rides, and fishing.

As the Warne family grew, Frederick Warne & Co. grew into a family-run publishing house; Harold, Fruing, and Norman joined the business following their schooling and took over the company when Warne and Dodd retired in 1894. (Fittingly, the company's device, a wing and horseshoe motif, is believed to be derived from the coat of arms of a branch of the Warne family.) Harold, the eldest, oversaw the company's finances while Fruing and Norman concentrated on book production. At the turn of the century the firm continued its association with leading children's authors and illustrators, including Leslie Brooke, Edward Lear, Andrew Lang, and Beatrix Potter, whose self-illustrated books, with their distinctive small format, are for ever associated with the Warne label. Frederick Warne died at his home on 7 November 1901. He was buried in Highgate cemetery, Middlesex.

CATHERINE J. GOLDEN

Sources A. King and A. F. Stuart, *The house of Warne* (1957) · C. Golden, 'Frederick Warne and Company', *British literary publishing houses, 1820–1880*, ed. P. J. Anderson and J. Rose, DLitB, 106 (1991), 327–33 · *The Times* (15 Nov 1901), 4

Likenesses H. Stannard, oils, priv. coll. · photograph, Penguin Books, Harmondsworth, Middlesex [see illus.]

Wealth at death £45,502 8s. 8d.: probate, 28 Dec 1901, CGPLA Eng. & Wales

Warneford, Reginald Alexander John (1891–1915), airman, was born at Darjeeling, India, on 15 October 1891, the eldest child and only son of Reginald William Henry Warneford, civil engineer, of Piddletrenthide, Dorset, and his wife, Dora Alexandra Campbell. He was educated at the English College, Simla, and at King Edward VI Grammar School, Stratford upon Avon. In 1905 he joined the British India Steam Navigation Company, with which he

remained until 1914, when at the outbreak of the First World War he returned from Canada to Britain.

Turned down for Submarine Service, Warneford joined the second sportsman's battalion, Royal Fusiliers, but found uncongenial what he later described as 'a sort of Boy Scouts Jamboree for old gentlemen', and transferred to the Royal Navy; on 12 February 1915 he was granted a commission as a probationary flight sub-lieutenant in the Royal Naval Air Service. A naturally gifted pilot, he gained his certificate at Hendon on 25 February, and was posted first to the service's 2 squadron at Eastchurch. There his ill-disciplined behaviour led to a recommendation that he be dismissed from the service. Instead, he was posted to 1 squadron, at Dunkirk, France, where his commanding officer, who noted his 'remarkable keenness and ability', succeeded in reining in Warneford's indiscipline. On the night of 16 May 1915 he tackled and damaged the German army Zeppelin LZ39 which was returning from a raid on Calais.

Early on 7 June (the night of a heavy German raid on Hull), Warneford, who was flying a Morane monoplane, attacked near Ghent a Zeppelin, LZ37, on which he dropped six 20 lb bombs from close range. The airship exploded, throwing the Morane onto its back, its engine stopped. Warneford was forced to land in enemy territory, where after repairing a broken fuel line he was able to restart his engine and return to his aerodrome. For his achievement in destroying the first Zeppelin in air-to-air combat and thus revealing the airship's vulnerability to attack, he was on 11 June awarded the Victoria Cross—the first officer of the Royal Naval Air Service to be so honoured. His success, however, had the unfortunate result of confirming the tactic of bombing airships from above; its adoption proved an error, because airships could gain height faster than aeroplanes. Fifteen months elapsed before another airship was brought down (by William Leefe Robinson).

Warneford, who never married, did not long survive his fame. On 17 June 1915 he took off from Buc, near Paris, to test a Farman F27 which he was to fly to Dunkirk. The aircraft spun, Warneford was thrown out, and the aircraft broke up in the air. Both Warneford and his American journalist passenger were killed. His body was returned to England for burial on 22 June in Brompton cemetery, London, amid great ceremony and before a crowd estimated at 50,000.

DAVID GUNBY

Sources P. G. Cooksley, *VCs of the First World War: the air VCs* (1996), 12–22 · C. Bowyer, *For valour: the air VCs* (1978), 29–36 · R. L. Rimell, *Zeppelin!* (1984), 62–74 · C. Cole and E. F. Cheesman, *The air defence of Britain, 1914–1918* (1984) · DNB · CGPLA Eng. & Wales (1916)

Archives FILM BFI NFTVA, news footage · IWM FVA, news footage |SOUND IWM SA, oral history interview

Likenesses W. R. Flint, lithograph, 1915, IWM · photograph, repro. in Cole and Cheesman, *Air defence of Britain, 1914–1918*, 61 · photographs, repro. in Cooksley, *VCs of the First World War* · photographs, repro. in Rimell, *Zeppelin!*

Wealth at death £39 14s. 11d.: administration, 10 April 1916, CGPLA Eng. & Wales

Warneford, Samuel Wilson (1763–1855), philanthropist, was perhaps born at Warneford Place, in the hamlet of

Samuel Wilson Warneford (1763–1855), by J. Fisher (after Thomas Phillips)

Sevenhampton, attached to Highworth vicarage, north Wiltshire. His family, one of the most ancient in that district, owned the manor and all the land in Sevenhampton. Samuel Wilson was the younger son of the Revd Francis Warneford (1732–1784) of Warneford Place, who married Catherine (d. 1757), daughter of Samuel Calverley, a wealthy drug merchant of Southwark, and his third wife, Catherine, residing at Ewell, Surrey. Money from the Calverleys greatly enriched the Warnefords. He matriculated from University College, Oxford, on 14 December 1779, and graduated BA (18 June 1783), MA (23 May 1786), BCL (10 July 1790), and DCL (17 May 1810). He was ordained priest in 1787, becoming curate of Norton Broyne (later Brize Norton).

Warneford married, at Colney Hatch, Middlesex, on 27 September 1796, when he was described as 'of Broughton, Oxfordshire', Margaret (1775–1840), eldest daughter of Margaret and Edward Loveden Loveden (afterwards Edward Pryse Pryse, MP) of Buscot, Berkshire, and his own property was augmented by his wife's fortune. His wife, previously a ward of court, was sickly but rich. In due course, and in the face of strong hostility from Edward Loveden, a marriage settlement was reached linking the two fortunes. Deaths in both families subsequently further augmented Warneford's capital, his wife being left £34,000 by her grandfather. In 1809 Warneford purchased the advowson of the rectory of Lydiard Millicent, Wiltshire; he held the rectorship until his death, but sold the advowson to Pembroke College, Oxford, in 1828. In 1810 he also bought the advowson of the vicarage of Bourton

on the Hill, Gloucestershire. On the creation of honorary canonries in the cathedral of Gloucester in June 1844 his name was placed first on the list, and he remained an honorary canon until his death.

Warneford was an energetic and sharp manager of his and his wife's money and soon became known as an able man of business who expected high standards of his colleagues. He gave his donations gradually, so as to expose and be able to correct errors and deficiencies in the bodies to which he gave them. He did not sermonize, and, beyond his general intention to be a philanthropist, his priorities are chiefly to be inferred from his charitable actions, which were considerable. He became one of the governors of the Radcliffe Infirmary, Oxford, which in 1812 appointed a committee to establish a lunatic asylum for persons 'who though poor were not Paupers' (Beckwith, 25). Warneford was one of the subscribers. He was a member of the hospital and of the building committee, becoming impatient in 1831 at the slow progress in building the Radcliffe Asylum, as it was initially known. He particularly worked with Vaughan *Thomas on the asylum's development. Warneford's donations (over £70,000 in money and property over his lifetime) and his active involvement led to its being renamed the Warneford Lunatic Asylum in 1843.

The churches of Bourton and Moreton in Marsh were refitted and improved by Warneford at a cost of £1000 each. He built and endowed at Bourton a 'retreat for the aged', and at Moreton he erected school buildings for children and an infants' school with house for its mistress. He provided also means for securing medical aid for the poor of these districts. The whole diocese of Gloucester received large sums from him for similar purposes, and he gave numerous benefactions to the colonial sees of Sydney and Nova Scotia.

Warneford founded in 1832 the Warneford, Leamington, and South Warwickshire Hospital at Leamington, and left it at his death the sum of £10,000. His benefactions towards the cost of new buildings at the Queen's Hospital at Birmingham, and for endowments including chaplaincies, a professorship of pastoral theology, and scholarships at the Queen's College, represented a total of £25,000. He there became 'the real ruler of the college' (Beckwith, 43), but became discouraged at its lack of progress and did not leave it the large benefaction for which it hoped. On King's College, London, he bestowed large sums for the foundation of medical scholarships and for establishing prizes for the encouragement of theology among the matriculated medical students. He gave the site of a new boys' school to the Clergy Orphan School near Canterbury, and at his death he left that institution the sum of £13,000. He also contributed large sums, during his life and at his death, to the Society for the Propagation of the Gospel, the Society for Promoting Christian Knowledge, and the Corporation for the Sons of the Clergy. The total of such gifts is said to have equalled £200,000; in fulfilment of his intentions his niece, Lady Wetherell-Warneford, bequeathed £30,000, the income of which was to be applied in building churches and parsonage-houses in poor districts within the ancient diocese of Gloucester, and £45,000, the accruing interest of which was to be expended for the benefit of the widows and orphans of the poor clergy in the same district. His sister Philadelphia, a wealthy woman in her own right, contributed to many of the charities he supported. Warneford's correspondence with Joshua Watson on charities began in 1837 (Churton, 2.59, 313).

Warneford died at the rectory, Bourton, on 11 January 1855, in his ninety-second year, preserving his faculties to the last. On 17 January he was buried under a tomb in the church. Warneford, though strict, was not ostentatious. After his death it was noted in Leamington Spa: 'Little is now remembered of the good man except his yearly visits to partake of the Waters, and of the extent of his benefactions, few, besides the Committee of the period, were aware' (Beckwith, 52).

W. P. COURTNEY, rev. H. C. G. MATTHEW

Sources E. G. C. Beckwith, *Samuel Wilson Warneford, LL.D.* (1974) · V. Thomas, *Christian philanthropy exemplified in a memoir of the Rev. Samuel Warneford, illustrated by extracts from his letters* (1856) · V. Thomas, *The late Rev. Dr Warneford* (1855) · B. Parry-Jones, *The Warneford hospital, Oxford* (1976) · *Guardian* (24 Jan 1855), 71 · E. Churton, ed., *Memoir of Joshua Watson*, 2 vols. (1861) · J. Powrie, 'In search of Samuel Warneford LL.D.', *BM Insight*, 1 (2000), 24–7
Archives Bodl. Oxf., corresp. and papers · Glos. RO, papers · Warneford Hospital, Oxford, corresp. and papers relating to Asylum | Bodl. Oxf., corresp. with Sir Thomas Phillipps
Likenesses T. Phillips, portrait, 1835, Warneford Hospital, Oxford · P. Hollins, statue, 1840, Warneford Hospital, Oxford · J. Fisher, engraving (after statue), repro. in Thomas, *Christian philanthropy* · J. Fisher, stipple (after T. Phillips), NPG [*see illus.*] · portrait, Church House, Gloucester · portrait, Birmingham and Midland Institute, Birmingham · portrait, Warwick Hospital, Warwick

Warner [Garnier] (*fl.* 1106), Benedictine monk and homilist, may have come to England from Bec. He became a monk of Westminster, where he was present when the relics of St Wihtburh were translated in 1106. He was known as *homeliarius* on the strength of the book of homilies that he dedicated to Gilbert Crispin (*d.* 1117), then his abbot. Both the creation and the loss of this collection are significant in an age when original homilies are not common, and even the most modest addition to the surviving corpus would have been welcome. Gilbert Crispin may have provided him with a model through his own preaching, or perhaps even encouraged him directly in the work.   G. R. EVANS

Sources D. J. Stewart, ed., *Liber Eliensis* (1848) · *The works of Gilbert Crispin, abbot of Westminster*, ed. A. S. Abulafia and G. R. Evans (1986)

Warner, Charles [*real name* Charles John Lickfold] (1846–1909), actor, was born in Kensington, London, on 10 October 1846, the son of James Lickfold, an actor, and his wife, Hannah. He was educated at Westbury College, Highgate, and was intended to follow a paternal uncle into a career as an architect. His father was a member of Samuel Phelps's company at Sadler's Wells, and Charles made his

Charles Warner (1846–1909), by Walery, pubd 1891

first appearance on the stage on 24 January 1861 at Windsor Castle, as a page in Bulwer-Lytton's *Richelieu*, at a command performance by Phelps's company. He entered his uncle's office, but within a few months, despite his parents' objections, he ran away and obtained an engagement under James Rodgers at the Theatre Royal, Hanley. There he made his first appearance, in February 1862, as Bras Rouge in Charles Dillon's *The Mysteries of Paris* and, on the same evening, as Muley Sahib in M. G. Lewis's tragedy *The Castle Spectre*. He spent a short period with Rodgers at Hanley, Lichfield, and Worcester, and the following year joined H. Nye Chart's company at the Theatre Royal, Brighton.

Warner's London début was under George Vining's management at the Princess's Theatre on 25 April 1864, when he played Benvolio in *Romeo and Juliet* with Stella Colas. After a short season at Liverpool he was engaged by Edmund Falconer and F. B. Chatterton for three autumn and winter seasons at Drury Lane Theatre. He first appeared with Phelps there in September 1865 in a minor part in *Macbeth*, and from September 1866 to March 1868 he supported Phelps and others in a round of Shakespearian and other plays. In the summer of 1866 he acted at the Sadler's Wells and Haymarket theatres; his parts included Ned Plummer in *Dot*, Careless in *The School for Scandal*, and Modus in *The Hunchback*.

Warner opened at the Olympic Theatre in October 1869

as Steerforth in *Little Em'ly*, Andrew Halliday's adaptation of *David Copperfield*, and subsequently played there a series of parts, in one of which, Charley Burridge in H. J. Byron's *Daisy Farm*, he made his first pronounced success in London (May 1871). From the Olympic he went to the Lyceum Theatre, where, in December 1871, he succeeded Henry Irving as Alfred Jingle in James Albery's play *Pickwick*. In September 1872, at the Prince's Theatre, Manchester, he supported Adelaide Neilson as Romeo, Claude Melnotte, and Orlando, and in the following year he appeared with her in Paris at the Théâtre Athénée. Also in 1872 Warner married Frances Elizabeth Hards, who was unconnected with the stage.

On his return to London, Warner was engaged by David James and Thomas Thorne for the Vaudeville, and opened there in September 1873 as Charles Surface in *The School for Scandal*. On the first performance there of Byron's comedy *Our Boys* (16 January 1875) he created the part of Charles Middlewick. From the Vaudeville he passed to the Haymarket Theatre, where his roles included Claudio in *Measure for Measure* in support of Adelaide Neilson (April 1876). He was seen at the St James's Theatre under Mrs John Wood, and in January 1877 he made a great impression as Vladimir in *The Danischeffs*.

Later, at the Princess's Theatre, Warner achieved his chief reputation in melodrama. His performance of Tom Robinson in a revival of Charles Reade's drama *It's Never too Late to Mend* (December 1878) proved a popular triumph. In June 1879 his rendering at the same theatre of Coupeau in Reade's version of Emile Zola's *L'assommoir* entitled *Drink* placed him among the most popular actors of his day. His presentation of the drunkard, who dies of delirium tremens, was judged realistic and intense. The French critic Francisque Sarcey declared it to be infinitely superior to that of the French actor, Gil Naza, who had created the part in Paris.

In September 1880 Warner began performing at Sadler's Wells Theatre. A five years' engagement with the Gatti brothers at the Adelphi began in March 1881, where Warner confined himself chiefly to melodrama. He appeared as Michael Strogoff in Byron's adaptation from the French of a drama of that name, a performance at which he illustrated his strength of passion and will. In a grim duel between himself as hero and James Fernandez as the villain, he impulsively caught at his antagonist's unblunted dagger, and dangerously wounded his hand; he ended the play and took his call, but fainted as soon as the curtain fell, and for several hours his life seemed in jeopardy. The joint of his middle finger was permanently stiffened.

In December 1887 Warner was given a great complimentary benefit performance at Drury Lane before his departure on a tour of Australia. His daughter Grace then made her first appearance on the stage, playing Juliet to her father's Romeo in the balcony scene. Originally intended to last a few weeks, his Australian tour proved so successful that he remained in the country for two and a half years. His repertory included many of his old parts, notably those in *Drink*, *The Road to Ruin*, *The School for Scandal*, *It's Never too Late to Mend*, and *Dora*, also by Charles Reade.

In addition he played many new parts, among them Hamlet, and Pygmalion in *Pygmalion and Galatea*, and amassed a fortune from the production of Henry Pettitt's highly successful drama *Hands across the Sea*. On his return to England he acted for Augustus Harris at Drury Lane (September 1890). At the end of 1894 he toured, playing D'Artagnan in *The Three Musketeers* and performing in many ephemeral melodramas. At Wyndham's Theatre, on 1 March 1902, he gave another remarkable performance, as André Marex in *Heard at the Telephone*, and in 1904 he went to America, where he played in *Drink* and *The Two Orphans*.

After returning to London, Warner was at the Savoy Theatre with Mrs Brown-Potter in December 1904, as Canio in Charles Brookfield's dramatic version of the opera *Pagliacci*. At the New Theatre in May 1905 he gave a powerful performance of the part of Kleschna in C. M. S. McLellan's *Leah Kleschna*, and at His Majesty's Theatre in September 1906 he appeared as Leontes in Sir Herbert Beerbohm Tree's revival of *The Winter's Tale*, with Ellen Terry as Hermione. This was his last appearance on the regular stage in England. In 1907 he returned to America, and played at the leading vaudeville theatres in *At the Telephone*, *Devil Montague*, and a condensed version of *Drink*. He committed suicide by hanging himself at the Hotel Seymour, West 45th Street, New York, on 11 February 1909, and was buried at Woodlawn cemetery, New York, on 13 February 1909.

Warner was an effective actor in melodramatic parts which admitted of great nervous tension, but his highstrung nerves often found vent in a violence which was alarming to his colleagues on the stage and impaired his artistic control of voice and gesture. In old comedy he checked his emotional impulses with good results, and was a sound and sympathetic interpreter. In private life he was warm-hearted, generous, and buoyant, though towards the end of his life he was given to fits of deep depression. Of his two surviving children, both his son, H. B. Warner, and his daughter, Grace, adopted the stage as a profession. The latter married a promising actor, Franklin McLeay, a Canadian by birth, who died prematurely in 1900 at the age of thirty-three.

J. PARKER, *rev.* NILANJANA BANERJI

Sources *The Times* (13 Feb 1909) · *The Era* (13 Feb 1909) · *Daily Telegraph* (13 Feb 1909) · B. Hunt and J. Parker, eds., *The green room book, or, Who's who on the stage* (1906–9) · E. Reid and H. Compton, eds., *The dramatic peerage* [1891]; rev. edn [1892] · P. Hartnoll, ed., *The Oxford companion to the theatre* (1951); 2nd edn (1957); 3rd edn (1967) · P. Hartnoll, ed., *The concise Oxford companion to the theatre* (1972) · Hall, *Dramatic ports.* · review, *The Theatre*, 3rd ser., 3 (1881), 240–43 · *The Theatre*, 4th ser., 17 (1891), 88 · C. Scott, *The drama of yesterday and today*, 2 vols. (1899)

Likenesses Barraud, photograph, NPG; repro. in *Theatre* · Lock & Whitfield, photograph, woodburytype, NPG; repro. in *Theatre* · Lock & Whitfield, woodburytype, carte-de-visite, NPG · Walery, photograph, NPG; repro. in *Theatre* (Feb 1891) [*see illus.*] · caricature, repro. in *Entr'acte* (25 Sept 1880), plate · plate, repro. in *Illustrated Sporting and Dramatic News* (9 July 1887) · portrait, repro. in *Daily Telegraph* · portrait, repro. in *The Era*

Wealth at death £5018 19s. 7d.: resworn probate, 22 May 1909, *CGPLA Eng. & Wales*

Warner, Sir Edward (1511–1565), soldier, was the eldest son of Henry Warner (*d.* 1519), soldier, of Besthorpe, Norfolk, and Mary Blennerhasset. In 1542 Edward married Elizabeth, a daughter of Thomas Brooke, eighth Baron Cobham, and widow of Sir Thomas Wyatt (*d.* 1542); they had three sons, all of whom died in infancy. After Elizabeth's death Warner married in 1560 Audrey Hobart (*d.* 1580), daughter and heir of William Hare, of Beeston, Norfolk.

By 1537 Warner held a position in the household of Henry VIII, for which he was awarded tithes in Leicestershire. In 1543 he led six footmen in the army for Flanders and was then sent to Scotland, where he was knighted (18 May 1544) by the earl of Hertford for his service in the burning of Edinburgh. In Scotland he was the captain of 100 men. 1546 saw him brought before the privy council, with Lord Haward, to explain his 'indiscreet' talk about the scriptures, although the two were dismissed. Later in 1546 he was involved in an inquiry into the arms of Henry Howard, earl of Surrey, which were held to demonstrate some threat to King Henry. In 1549 he was involved in the defence of Norwich against Ket's rebellion. He was appointed lieutenant of the Tower in October 1552. In April 1553 he was appointed (with others) to audit the king's ordnance. During Henry's and Edward's reigns he received many grants of ecclesiastical lands. In May 1540 he and Lord Cobham were granted the lands of a former Carmelite priory in Norfolk, and in 1549 chantry lands in Norwich and Yorkshire followed. In 1545 and 1547 he was MP for Grantham.

When Mary acceded to the throne, Warner was removed from his position in the Tower. He was hostile to the new regime, and sympathetic to the cause of Lady Jane Grey; indeed he held the Tower for Northumberland during the attempted coup. He was MP for Grantham in Mary's first parliament, where he stood for the protestant religion. When Wyatt's rebellion unfolded, the government monitored his activities; he may have been involved in discussions about the rebellion at an early stage. In January 1554 Simon Renard (Charles V's ambassador in England) gave the chancellor information that Warner intended to surprise the Tower. He was arrested on 25 January 1554 with the marquess of Northampton, and taken to the Tower. On 10 November 1554 he was indicted. However, the privy council allowed his wife to receive his revenues while he was in prison. On 18 January 1555 he was released on a surety of 300 crowns, and on 2 July 1555 granted a pardon. He was subsequently employed by the crown: in early 1558 he was sent on a mission to the Isle of Wight under Sir Thomas Tresham.

In November 1558, after Elizabeth's accession, Warner was reappointed lieutenant of the Tower. In September 1559 he was an assistant to the mourners at the obsequies of Henri II in London. He was MP for Great Grimsby in 1559. In his duties as lieutenant of the Tower he dealt with suspected spies and counterfeiters. Among his most important prisoners were the deprived Marian bishops; Lord Wentworth, late lord deputy of Calais, suspected of treason; and, in 1562, John Kele and James Golbourne. The latter were suspected of selling information about the English court to the king of Sweden. The most important prisoner he had to deal with was Katherine Seymour, countess of Hertford. She had clandestinely married Edward Seymour, a union that Elizabeth viewed with suspicion as an attempt to establish their claim for her throne. Warner was instructed to examine her in August 1561. Other duties included his appointment in November 1561 to survey all lands within 2 miles of London that had been formerly used for archery practice, but were now enclosed. He was to see that these were to be reinstated because archery practice was declining. However, he was dismissed from his post at the Tower, and spent a short time in prison, because he treated his prisoners with too much leniency. In 1563 he was MP for the county of Norfolk, and at the opening of the first session of that parliament he was one of the nobles who held a canopy over Elizabeth in her procession. He was sent to the Low Countries in 1565 to examine the state of English trade. Finally in November of that year he was nominated as a commissioner to examine measures for dealing with piracy. He died in Norfolk on 7 November 1565 and was buried in the church at Little Plumstead in Norfolk, his will ordering that his funeral should be conducted with little pomp. In the church there is a monument and inscription to his memory. In 1566 his brother Robert, his heir, was granted licence to enter upon his lands.

It is clear that Warner was a committed protestant. The first sign of his radicalism was in 1546, and his Calvinism is apparent in the manner of his funeral. Moreover his parliamentary patron in the earlier years was the second earl of Rutland, a committed protestant. It is thus surprising that he escaped any severe punishment in Mary's reign. However, although he was suspected of involvement with Wyatt, this was never proved. He was also a very competent military commander; this may have helped save him in Mary's reign, as Philip did not wish to alienate the nobility and gentry, especially if they could prove useful in a military capacity.   C. P. Croly

Sources HoP, *Commons, 1509–58* · HoP, *Commons, 1558–1603* · *LP Henry VIII*, vols. 4–5, 11, 13, 16, 18–19 · APC, *1554–70* · CPR, *1554–66* · CSP Spain, *Jan–July 1554* · CSP for., *1558–63* · CSP dom., *1547–80* · D. Loades, *Two Tudor conspiracies*, 2nd edn (1992) · BL, Harley MS 6063 · PRO, SP 12/1 · BL, Cotton MS Caligula, E.v · J. Strype, *Ecclesiastical memorials*, 3/1 (1822)
Likenesses brass effigy, *c.*1565, St Protase and St Gervase Church, Little Plumstead, Norfolk

Warner, Edward (*b.* 1609/10). *See under* Warner, Sir Thomas (*c.*1580–1649).

Warner, Ferdinando (1703–1768), Church of England clergyman and writer, was born at Tewkesbury, possibly the son of James Warner, minister at Tewkesbury. He took holy orders, and was ordained deacon by the bishop of Salisbury in August 1727. On 15 December 1730 he was instituted to the vicarage of Rowde, Wiltshire, where he remained for two years. For the next decade his career is hard to trace, although he was married by 1736 when his son was born. He was admitted as a fellow commoner at

Clare College, Cambridge, on 19 January 1742. On 13 February 1747 he was appointed to the united rectories of St Michael and Holy Trinity, Queenhithe, London. In that capacity, he preached before the lord mayor on 30 January 1748 and again on 2 September 1749. He attracted some notice from Archbishop Thomas Herring who awarded him a Lambeth LLD in 1754. Herring's death obliged Warner to endear himself to Lord Chancellor Hardwicke and, to a lesser extent, to the duke of Newcastle. These contacts yielded little in practical results, though Warner depicted himself to Newcastle as 'having done more notwithstanding in support of Your Grace's administration than any man in England of my Rank—even those whom Your Grace has preferred not excepted' (BL, Add. MS 32947, fol. 218 11 March 1763). Warner welcomed the duke's return to office in 1765–6 but had no more success in extracting preferment from his patron, though his son, John *Warner (1736–1800), was a beneficiary. He had meanwhile received the rectory of Barnes in Surrey in June 1758 from the dean and chapter of St Paul's Cathedral.

Warner had an eclectic range of interests and published on them all. He began in the field of controversial divinity, editing compendia. The first was *A System of Divinity and Morality* (5 vols., 1750), a series of discourses on natural and revealed religion drawn from the writings of Anglican divines, mainly the moderate whigs who were installed in the 1690s, such as Tillotson and Stillingfleet; *A Rational Defence of the English Reformation and Protestant Religion* (1752) (dedicated to Archbishop Herring) had extracts from Anglican authors on points of Roman Catholic belief. In 1754 were published *An Illustration of the Book of Common Prayer and Administration of the Sacraments* and *A free and necessary enquiry whether the Church of England, in her liturgy … have not … given so great an advantage to papists and deists as may prove fatal to true religion*, his concern being with some ambiguous expressions in the liturgy too apparently suggestive of transubstantiation and the real presence. He was also the anonymous author of *Advice from a Bishop* (1759), intended to be of service to his son, who was on the point of entering the ministry. It was a manifesto for further moderate reformation in the established church. Warner bewailed the 'ignorance and sloth' prevalent in the church and used in evidence the failure to obtain subscriptions to his own history of England (*Advice from a Bishop*, 4–6). He was a constant advocate of improved clerical charities, as in *A Scheme of a Fund for the Better Maintenance of the Widows and Children of the Clergy* (1752), and *An address to the clergy; with some proposals for raising and establishing a fund … to make a provision for their widows and children* (1755). His later *Letter to the fellows of Sion College … proposing their forming themselves into a society for the maintenance of the widows and orphans of such clergymen* (1765) contained a proposal that was duly accepted.

Warner also tried his hand as a historian, showing some modest success. His *Ecclesiastical History to the Eighteenth Century* (1756–7) is the work for which he is best known, with the second volume dedicated to Hardwicke. The latter offered some material help with *The History of Ireland to the Year 1171* (1763), only one volume of which was published.

Warner worked on original manuscripts in Dublin during 1761. Despite backing from the Dublin Society, the Irish House of Commons extended no financial assistance and he abandoned the project. He made use of the material he collected for *The History of the Rebellion and Civil War in Ireland* (1767), a volume which expressed the hope that it would encourage greater religious tolerance in contemporary Ireland. Other miscellaneous writings by Warner were: three sermons; *An imaginary dialogue between Robert Boyle and Lord Bolingbroke, or, A dialogue on the origin and authority of revelation* (1755), the piece Warner himself most valued; *Memoirs of the Life of Sir Thomas More* (1758), dedicated to Sir Robert Henley, L.K., who helped him secure the living of Barnes; *Remarks on the History of Fingal and other Poems of Ossian* (1762); and *A full and plain account of the gout … with some new and important instructions for its relief, which the author's experience in the gout above thirty years hath induced him to impart* (1768). The irony was that Warner died of the disorder on 3 October 1768, within weeks of publication.

NIGEL ASTON

Sources Venn, *Alum. Cant.* · *VCH Wiltshire*, 7.218 · Nichols, *Lit. anecdotes* · bishops' registers, Wilts. & Swindon RO, D1/2/25 and 26 · Clare College archives, Clare College, Cambridge · parish register (burial), Barnes, Surrey RO, P6/1/2 · vestry minute book, Barnes, Surrey RO · *DNB* · private information (2004) [G. Nuttall] · BL, Newcastle MSS, Add. MS 32947, fol. 218
Archives BL, Hardwicke MSS, Add. MSS. 35637, fol. 106; 35595, fols. 61, 152, 377–8; 35596, fols. 211–12; 35638, fols. 66, 276 · BL, corresp. with duke of Newcastle and others, Add. MSS 32947, fol. 218; 32970, fols. 27, 46, 67

Warner, Sir Frank (1862–1930), silk manufacturer, was born at 5 Punderson's Place, Bethnal Green, London, on 13 September 1862, the son of Benjamin Warner (1828–1908), a silk designer, and his wife, Emma, née Branscomb. When he left school in 1878, Frank and his elder brother Alfred went to Lyons to study silk manufacture and political economy. The family had been connected with the silk industry for several generations, and in 1870 his father had established the silk weaving firm of Warner, Sillett, and Ramm, which produced high quality fabrics. The firm was renamed Warner and Ramm in 1874. Frank joined the firm in 1881, serving his apprenticeship at its Hollybush Gardens factory; when in 1891 he and Alfred were made partners, the firm became known as Warner & Sons. Under Benjamin Warner the business had developed through a series of take-overs of old-established weaving firms: Burnier in 1857, Norris & Co. in 1885, and Daniel Walters of Braintree in 1894. Many of the Hollybush Gardens staff moved to Braintree, and eventually all the weaving took place at New Mills, where it was directed by Frank Warner. These take-overs led to the acquisition of a magnificent collection of silk designs which was one of the main strengths of the firm, which aimed to maintain the quality of the richly woven silk fabrics made in the eighteenth and nineteenth centuries. Unfortunately the market for such goods was not large owing to their cost, but the firm was fortunate in receiving royal patronage and was commissioned to weave the coronation robes of both King Edward and Queen Alexandra and King George and

Sir Frank Warner (1862–1930), by Walter Stoneman, 1920

Queen Mary. At the same time Warners also began to produce modern designs provided by freelance designers, who included Crane, Butterfield, and Silver.

Following the death of Benjamin Warner in 1908, Frank Warner and his brother Alfred continued in partnership, and in 1922 Frank's son, Cloudesley Warner, who had supervised the installation of power-looms in 1919, also became a partner. On Cloudesley Warner's advice a Paris showroom was opened in the rue Edward VII, but this had to close in 1926. Further expansion took place in 1926, when the firm acquired the silk printing works of Newman, Smith, and Newman, of Dartford, Kent. The original staff remained, and until 1932 all printing was carried out by hand using the traditional woodblocks. Three months after the early death of Cloudesley Warner in September 1928, Warner & Sons became a private limited company, with the board consisting of Frank Warner, W. Bayford Stone, W. Vizard, and Warner's son-in-law Ernest Goodale.

Warner greatly contributed to the development of the English silk industry. In 1905, as a witness for the royal commission on tariff reform, he advocated a return to import duties on woven silks (which had been removed in 1860) in order to halt the decline of the industry. However, he realized that French designs were often superior and believed that designers should also receive a technical training in weaving. He gave lectures to the Society of Arts and numerous art and technical colleges, emphasizing the importance of the relationship between art and industry, and served as an examiner for the City and Guilds of London Institute from 1898 to 1905. He also played a part in organizing textile exhibitions both at home and abroad, notably those at Brussels in 1910, Turin in 1911, and Paris in 1925, when he served as chairman of the textile committee of the British section, for which he was made an officer of the Légion d'honneur. At home he organized the silk exhibition of 1912 and assisted with the Empire Exhibition at Wembley in 1924.

Warner served as president of the Silk Association of Great Britain and Ireland from 1910 to 1917 and of the Textile Institute from 1918 to 1920. He was chairman of the British Silk Research Association, the silk section of the London chamber of commerce, the silk advisory committee of the Imperial Institute (1917–21), and the Board of Trade committee for the British Industries Fair (1920). In addition he had been adviser on textiles to the Board of Trade during the First World War. He became a member of the council of the Royal Society of Arts and of the Victoria and Albert Museum. In 1918 he was created KBE for services to the textile industry.

Warner's invention of a velvet fabric with three different heights of pile, which was patented in the UK in 1914, demonstrated his technical ability. His literary ability and very extensive knowledge of silk manufacturing is revealed in his book *The Silk Industry of the United Kingdom: its Origin and Development* (1921).

Warner married Kate Dennis, the daughter of Edmund Strange Parsons of Shernbourne Hall, near Kings Lynn, Norfolk, on 3 September 1890 at the parish church of Ingoldisthorpe. They had three children, Frank Cloudesley Folliott, who married Louise Gouet of Paris; Evelyn Sandford, who married Leonard Tibbitts; and Gwendolen Branscombe, who married Ernest Goodale, a solicitor. The death of his wife in March 1928, followed by that of Cloudesley in France the following September, was a severe blow to Warner. He retired in the summer of 1929, and died of pneumonia on 23 January 1930, aged sixty-seven, at his home, Woodcroft, Mottingham, Kent. He was buried on 27 January in Chislehurst cemetery, where his tombstone bears the inscription 'He wove truth with trust'.   SARAH BUSH

Sources Milton Keynes, Warner Archive · E. Goodale, *Weaving and the Warners, 1870–1970* (1971) · F. Warner, *The silk industry of the United Kingdom: its origin and development* (1921) · *Textile Recorder* (15 Feb 1930) · *Textile Manufacturer* (Feb 1930) · *The Times* (24 Jan 1930) · *Silk Journal and Rayon World* (Feb 1930) · H. Bury, *A choice of design* (1981) · *Royal Commission on Tariff Reform* (1905) · F. Warner, 'Technical education: its relation to the textile industries', *Journal of the Textile Institute*, 1 (1910), 48–61 · *The cabinet maker and complete house furnisher* (1946) · F. Warner, 'Some business views on education', *Journal of the Textile Institute*, 9/3 (1919) · *Journal of the Royal Society of Arts*, 66 (1917–18), 764–6 · L. Parry, *Textiles of the arts and crafts movement* (1990), 152 · b. cert. · IGI · d. cert. · m. cert.

Archives V&A · Warner Archive, Milton Keynes

Likenesses photograph, 1908, repro. in Bury, *A choice of design*, 40 · W. Stoneman, photograph, 1920, NPG [*see illus.*] · photograph, repro. in *Journal of Textile Science* (1925) · photograph, repro. in *Silk Journal and Rayon World*

Wealth at death £58,450 16s. 6d.: probate, 29 March 1930, *CGPLA Eng. & Wales*

Warner, Sir Frederick Archibald [Fred] (1918–1995), diplomatist and politician, was born on 2 May 1918 at Blagdon, McKinley Road, Bournemouth, the son of Lieutenant-Commander Frederick Archibald Warner (*d.* 1918), a British naval officer who was born in Trinidad and killed on active service a few weeks before his son's birth, and his widow, Marjorie Miller, *née* Winants, of New Jersey, USA, who had become a naturalized British subject in 1917. His mother subsequently remarried, and Warner acquired two younger half-brothers. Fred Warner (as he was invariably known) was educated at the Royal Naval College, Dartmouth (1932–5), and after brief periods at sea as a midshipman between 1935 and 1937 he went up to Magdalen College, Oxford, and read politics, philosophy, and economics for two years before the outbreak of the Second World War caused his recall to the navy as a sub-lieutenant in the Royal Naval Volunteer Reserve. He rose to the temporary acting rank of lieutenant-commander and spent the last years of the war commanding gunboats and working with British and Italian small boat missions in the Mediterranean.

In February 1946, at the age of twenty-eight, Warner entered the diplomatic service and served in the southern department of the Foreign Office, where he was quickly identified as an officer of great promise. He was transferred to be private secretary to the minister of state, Hector McNeal, and consequently had the misfortune to work alongside Guy Burgess. Before the latter's defection to the Soviet Union, Warner was himself posted to Moscow as a first secretary between March 1950 and November 1951, and he did well there in the difficult cold war years. The news of Burgess's defection (with Donald Maclean) was a serious set-back to Warner's career. He was known to have been a friend as well as a close colleague of Burgess, and when the latter's louche lifestyle was disclosed after his defection Warner was among those who were thought either to have been tainted by it or—at the least—to have been dilatory in not drawing it to the attention of higher authority. Warner's own lifestyle was somewhat flamboyant: a bachelor of private means, he lived elegantly in chambers in the Albany and moved in exotic as well as distinguished social circles. He was subjected to intensive scrutiny not only by the security services but also by the press. While a question mark appeared to hover over his future, he was posted in June 1956 as head of Chancery in a distant and less than mainstream country—Burma.

It was much to Warner's credit that he put his heart and energies into his new job: he was reported by his superiors to have 'taken the embassy by the scruff of the neck' (private information) and he displayed efficiency, decision, and leadership. It was for him the beginning of a long affection for the Far East, and after a short spell in Athens, from September 1958 to November 1959, he was appointed head of the south-east Asia department of the Foreign Office at the time of confrontation between Malaysia and Indonesia. He continued to burn the candle at both ends, being seen on occasion coming into the Foreign Office in the early morning, straight from a night-club and still in a dinner-jacket, to draft a lucid and forceful submission to

ministers. But, possibly because he still felt insecure in the diplomatic service, he applied for adoption as a Conservative parliamentary candidate in 1963, the year in which he was appointed CMG. Since his candidature failed he remained in the service and was sent on a year's course to the Imperial Defence College, where he upset some of his military classmates by his obvious air of superiority.

Warner's first ambassadorial appointment was to Laos in May 1965, where his handling of the increasing instability of the region won him further praise. By now the shadow over his career had been finally dispelled and—as if to prove it—he was appointed to the sensitive job of minister at the UK delegation to NATO in October 1967. This in turn was followed by an appointment as the UK deputy permanent representative to the United Nations in New York in September 1969. Warner took naturally and happily to the lively social scene in New York, and it was while he was there that on 29 March 1971 he astonished his friends by marrying at the age of fifty-two. His bride was Simone Georgina, daughter of Colonel Hubert Jocelyn Nangle, and divorcee of Boz de Ferranti of the armaments firm. She had a daughter from her previous marriage, and she and Warner quickly consolidated their happy marriage with the birth of two sons, in 1972 and 1974.

Warner's last post in the diplomatic service was as ambassador to Japan from July 1972 to June 1975. He and his wife had previously spent some months at Sheffield University acquiring a very useful knowledge of the language, and Warner brought great zest to the job. He was notably successful in encouraging trade relations, and he made the embassy a cosmopolitan meeting-place for peoples of different cultures and backgrounds. If the Japanese were sometimes bewildered by his unconventional approach, they none the less admired his energy and style. His mission was crowned by a successful state visit by the queen, after which Warner was made a GCVO in 1975. He had already been knighted (KCMG) on his appointment to Tokyo.

Warner had hoped to end his diplomatic career as ambassador in Paris, and when this was denied him he took early retirement, despite a last-minute offer of the job as UK representative to the EC. One reason for this was a genuine desire—possibly prompted by his own fatherless childhood—to play an active role in bringing up his young children. Warner also threw himself into a wide variety of new activities: he had for many years owned a farm in Dorset which he now took in hand; he was elected as a Conservative member of the European parliament representing Somerset; and he played an active role in Strasbourg, particularly in Far Eastern affairs, from 1979 to 1984. He later took on the chairmanship of the Wessex region of the National Trust. He also served as a non-executive director on the boards of a number of large companies with international interests, as well as being chairman of the overseas committee of the Confederation of British Industry. Warner lived latterly at Inkpen House, near Newbury, Berkshire, and in London. He died at his London home, 13A Portobello Road, Kensington, of lung cancer, on 30 September 1995. He was survived by his wife, two sons, and stepdaughter. Tall, striking, and immensely persuasive in conversation, Warner was a larger-than-life figure in the establishment worlds in which he had made his career. There was a raffishness in his manner which concealed a deeply serious character: he would have been at home in the eighteenth-century world of Charles James Fox. Warner could be a daunting figure on first acquaintance, but he won affection as well as admiration from a diverse and powerful circle of friends.   JOHN URE

Sources personal knowledge (2004) · private information (2004) · foreign and commonwealth office records · *The Times* (2 Oct 1995) · *The Independent* (3 Oct 1995) · *WWW, 1991–5* · foreign office lists · b. cert. · d. cert.
Archives Bodl. Oxf., MSS relating to time as MEP
Likenesses photograph, repro. in *The Times* · photograph, repro. in *The Independent*

Warner, Sir George Frederic (1845–1936), archivist, was born at Winchester on 7 April 1845, the fourth son of Isaac Warner, solicitor, and his wife, Susanna, daughter of John Witt, who held a senior position in a shipping business at Southampton. Warner was educated at Christ's Hospital and at Pembroke College, Cambridge, where he became a scholar and obtained a second class in the classical tripos of 1868. In 1871 he entered the department of manuscripts in the British Museum, where he served for forty years: he became assistant keeper in 1888 and keeper and Egerton librarian in 1904. He acquired an exceptionally thorough knowledge of all branches of the department, and from the time of his becoming assistant keeper he in effect directed most of its general administration. He married in 1884 Marian Amelia Painter, the daughter of Richard Budd Painter MD of Brompton.

Warner's special interests were in palaeography and illuminated manuscripts. He was associated with his senior colleague and friend Sir Edward Maunde Thompson in the publications of the Palaeographical Society (1873–94) and in 1903 founded the New Palaeographical Society, of which he remained an editor until 1915. For many years he revised and edited the quinquennial volumes of the *Catalogue of Additions to the Department of Manuscripts* and himself superintended the volume for 1900–05 (1907). In 1894 he initiated *A Catalogue of Western Manuscripts in the Old Royal and King's Collections*. His successor in the keepership, Julius Parnell Gilson, continued to work on this project and it was published in 1921. In the sphere of illuminated manuscripts Warner's principal official publications were the facsimile of the Sforza Book of Hours (1894), two admirable series of facsimiles of the best manuscripts in the museum (the first comprising four series in colour, 1899–1903, and the second three series in black and white, 1907–8), and *Queen Mary's Psalter* (1912). Unofficial publications included the *Miracles de Nostre Dame* (1885), *The Benedictional of St Æthelwold* (1910), *The Gospels of Matilda, Countess of Salisbury* (1917), and *The Guthlac Roll* (1928), all for the Roxburghe Club, of which he became a member in 1911. His contributions extended to other societies too. For the Scottish History Society he edited *The Library of James VI* (1893); for the Henry Bradshaw Society *The Stowe Missal* (1893); and for the Hakluyt Society *The Voyage of Robert Dudley to the West Indies, 1594* (1899).

Warner's most important works of scholarship were his edition of the travels of Sir John Mandeville (*The Buke of John Maundeuill*, 1889), in which he identified the author and traced the sources from which he derived his romance, and *The Libelle of Englyshe Polycye* (1926), in which he elucidated the authorship of this plea for English sea power. Warner was an accurate and unpretending scholar and a good administrator. A stammer deterred him from public appearances. He was liked and respected by his colleagues, who were surprised that he did not become keeper until 1904, by which time the appointment only formalized a position that he had effectively occupied for years. It was also a matter of surprise that he did not succeed Maunde Thompson as principal librarian in 1909. Warner was a fellow of the Society of Antiquaries and a trustee of Shakespeare's birthplace. He was elected a fellow of the British Academy in 1906, and an honorary fellow of Pembroke College in 1911, and received the honorary degree of DLitt. from the University of Oxford on the occasion of the tercentenary of the Bodleian Library in 1902.

After retiring from the British Museum in 1911, in which year he was knighted, Warner lived successively at Beaconsfield, Ealing, and at Rowanhurst, Mayfield Road, Weybridge, Surrey, where he died on 17 January 1936. He was survived by his wife and his daughter Marjorie, his son having died young.

F. G. KENYON, *rev.* NILANJANA BANERJI

Sources *The Times* (18 Jan 1936) · Venn, *Alum. Cant.* · F. G. Kenyon, 'Sir George Warner, 1845–1936', *PBA*, 22 (1936), 345–57 · E. Miller, *That noble cabinet: a history of the British Museum* (1974) · *CGPLA Eng. & Wales* (1936)
Archives BL, corresp. as editor, New Palaeographical Society; letters to J. P. Gilson, Add. MSS 47686–47687 · NL Wales, letters to J. G. Evans
Likenesses W. Stoneman, photograph, 1917, NPG · photograph, repro. in *Miniatures and borders from a Flemish horae* (1911), frontispiece · photogravure, BM
Wealth at death £10,991 16s. 11d.: probate, 19 March 1936, *CGPLA Eng. & Wales*

Warner, Jack [*real name* Horace John Waters] (1895–1981), actor, was born on 24 October 1895 at 1 Rounton Road, Bromley, Poplar, London, the third child and second of four sons among the children of Edward William Waters, master fulling maker and undertaker's warehouseman, and his wife, Maud Mary Best. His two sisters Doris and Elsie *Waters became the successful radio and variety comedians Gert and Daisy in the 1930s and 1940s. He was educated at the Coopers' Company School, Mile End Road, and studied automobile engineering for one year at the Northampton Institute, later part of the City University, London. Warner was essentially a practical man, more at home with pistons and people than with books, and left to work in the garage of a firm of undertakers in Balham. In August 1913 he went to work as a mechanic in Paris, where, unusually for a boy of his background, he acquired

Jack Warner (1895–1981), by unknown photographer

a working knowledge of French which stood him in good stead throughout his life socially and as an entertainer. An imitation of Maurice Chevalier, in some ways his Parisian opposite number, became a standard part of his repertoire.

During the First World War Warner served in France as a driver with the Royal Flying Corps, and was awarded the meritorious service medal in 1918. He returned to England and the motor trade in 1919, graduating from hearses to occasional car racing at Brooklands. He was over thirty before he became a professional entertainer, having progressed from choirboy and wartime concert party performer through the Sutton Amateur Dramatic Club to cabaret work, and making his West End début in 1935 in the two-man act of Warner and Darnell. He changed his name to Warner at this point because he did not wish to appear to be resting on the reputation of his sisters. In December 1939 with BBC radio's *Garrison Theatre* he made the transition from cabaret singer to cockney comedian. He epitomized the patient, good hearted, cheeky Tommy of the First World War, reborn in 1939 and transferred from the music-hall to the broadcasting studio, and later matured into the reliable London bobby as Dixon of Dock Green on television. During the war he was a regular performer in radio and stage variety shows. In 1942 he made his first film, *Dummy Talks*.

The Jack Warner father figure emerged in his fourth film, *Holiday Camp* (1947). He played Mr Huggett, with Kathleen Harrison as his wife; they were typical, if romanticized, cockney parents, coping with adversity, often in the shape of their own children. The Huggetts featured in three more films and in a radio show from 1953 to 1962, an everyday story of urban folk. Warner's acting talent and ambitions were limited but although he never aspired to play Hamlet he did hope occasionally to break away from his stereotyped roles. He succeeded in this with more serious films such as *The Captive Heart* (1946), *It always Rains on Sunday* (1947), and *Against the Wind* (1947). In *The Final Test* (1953) he played a professional cricketer in his last great outing, exchanging his senior NCO role with that of a figure modelled on Jack Hobbs. But after a comparatively small part in *The Blue Lamp* (1949), as a fatherly London policeman shot by a young criminal, Jack Warner was enrolled as the regular screen parental police officer Dixon in a television series created by E. H. (Ted) Willis that ran from July 1955 until 1976. He was a reassuring traditional officer of the law adapting his pre-war standards and wisdom to the different world of the 1960s: his regular, opening 'Evening all' became embedded in the national vocabulary. The series altered its style as English society changed. Dixon became a less cosy sergeant, but the advent of a harsher view of police life in *Z Cars* brought an end to *Dixon of Dock Green* in 1976.

The series brought Jack Warner fame and financial security, which he enjoyed with Muriel Winifred (Mollie) Peters (*b.* 1898/9), a company secretary whom he married on 23 November 1933. The Warners had no children. Warner carried on with some stage work until 1980 and died of pneumonia in the Royal Masonic Hospital, Ravenscourt Park, London, on 24 May 1981.

Jack Warner was a tall, handsome man who possessed the solid virtues which he portrayed throughout his career. He had no formal training as an actor and performed rather than acted in a style that was ideal for radio, film, and television but was not suited to theatrical work. The character that he developed, a dependable soldier, family man, and policeman, growing from cockney irreverence to maturity, will be interesting for social historians as a picture of the working-class hero of the first half of the twentieth century, romanticized but not unreal. He was appointed OBE in 1965 and was made an honorary DLitt by City University in 1975. In 1972 he became a freeman of the City of London.   D. J. WENDEN, *rev.*

Sources J. Warner, *Jack of all trades* (1975) · *The Times* (26 May 1981) · b. cert. · m. cert. · *CGPLA Eng. & Wales* (1981)
Archives FILM BFI NFTVA, performance footage | SOUND BL NSA, *It's a funny business*, 1977, B7404/16 · BL NSA, documentary recordings
Likenesses photograph, NPG [*see illus.*]
Wealth at death £14,208: probate, 7 Oct 1981, *CGPLA Eng. & Wales*

Warner, John (*d.* 1565), dean of Winchester and physician, was born in Great Stanmore, Middlesex. He graduated BA at Oxford University in 1520, and was elected a fellow of All Souls College in the same year. He proceeded MA in 1525, and was admitted BM in 1529. At about the same time he was licensed to practise by the university. He acted as proctor in 1529 and 1530, proceeded DM in 1535, and was elected warden of All Souls on 26 May 1536, a position which he retained until 1560 (with an intermission under Mary). In 1540 Henry VIII appointed him first regius professor of medicine at Oxford University. He resigned the chair in 1554, when he became vice-chancellor, a post he also held in 1559–60.

Warner had taken holy orders in 1537 and became rector of Northmoor, Oxfordshire (1538), of Great Houghton, Northamptonshire (1539), Lower Heyford, Oxfordshire (1544), and Elmley Chapel, Kent (1545). On 30 April 1547 he was appointed to the prebend of Ealdstreet in the diocese of London, and in July of the same year he was nominated archdeacon of Cleveland, an appointment which he resigned about a year before his death. In 1550 he was installed a prebendary of Winchester. He was also archdeacon of Ely and of Cleveland, canon of St Paul's and of Lincoln, and royal chaplain, resigning before 1560. On account of his pro-Reformation sympathies, he was in disgrace during the reign of Mary, but received in 1557 the rectory of Hayes, together with the chapel of Norwood, in Middlesex. He was restored to All Souls in 1559, after the death of Mary, and then received a prebend at Salisbury; and on 15 October of the same year he was nominated dean of Winchester. He was also archdeacon of Ely in 1560, but resigned in the same year. On 17 October 1561 he was admitted a fellow of the College of Physicians.

Warner was clearly an ambitious man. Wood said that 'He was a learned man of his time, but published nothing, and was a great intruder into ecclesiastical benefices and dignities'. Warner died at his house in Warwick Lane, London, on 21 March 1565, and was buried in the chancel of the church of Great Stanmore, Middlesex. He bequeathed a small number of books to the library of All Souls.

E. I. CARLYLE, rev. SARAH BAKEWELL

Sources Munk, *Roll* · Foster, *Alum. Oxon.* · Wood, *Ath. Oxon.* · G. Lewis, 'The faculty of medicine', *Hist. U. Oxf.* 3: *Colleg. univ.*, 213–56, esp. 229–32, 343–5, 449 · Emden, *Oxf.*
Wealth at death bequeathed £20 to master and fellows of Balliol College, Oxford; £10 to All Souls College, Oxford; manor of Cassington, Oxford; site and buildings of Greyfriars, Oxford: Emden, *Oxf.*

Warner, John (*bap.* **1581**, *d.* **1666**), bishop of Rochester, was baptized on 17 September 1581 at St Clement Danes, London, the son of Harman Warner, a merchant tailor. He matriculated from Magdalen Hall, Oxford, on 13 October 1598, was a demy at Magdalen College from 1599, graduated BA on 13 December 1602, and proceeded MA on 12 June 1605. Already 'esteemed a witty man, a good logician and philosopher' (Wood, *Ath. Oxon.*, 4.731), Warner was elected perpetual fellow of Magdalen in 1604 but resigned in 1610, perhaps because of the £16,000 he was bequeathed by his godmother or the wealth inherited from his father. In 1613 he proceeded BD and was licensed to preach, and in 1616 he became DD. His first appointments came from Archbishop George Abbot: the rectory of St Michael's, Crooked Lane, London, in 1614, and the first prebend in the chapter of Canterbury in 1616. He resigned the former when he was instituted rector of Bishopsbourne with Barham, Kent, in 1619, but was allowed to retain the latter when Abbot appointed him rector of St Dionis Backchurch, London, in 1625. He also served as proctor for Canterbury diocese in the early 1620s.

After 1625 Warner may have been detaching himself from Abbot's influence, for he is said to have incurred the wrath of parliament for a sermon, highly critical of its opposition to royal policies, that he preached during Easter week 1626 or 1627 before Charles I at Whitehall on the text Matthew 11: 38 ('This is the heir; come, let us kill him, and seize on his inheritance'). He escaped punishment, but not before securing a royal pardon for any offence given. He became an active Laudian in London in the 1630s, without ever penetrating the inner circle of Caroline ecclesiastical power. In 1633 he was made dean of Lichfield; as a royal chaplain he accompanied Charles I to Scotland for his coronation in Edinburgh; and in 1635 he became rector of Hollingbourne with Hucking, Kent. He may have been the John Warner who on 4 May 1634 at St Michael at Plea, Norwich, married Bridget Bloye: it is certainly possible that his wife's name was Bridget, and becoming through inheritance and investment a rich man, Warner acquired land in Norfolk (where he bought Walsingham Abbey) as well as in Lincolnshire. Perhaps because of his personal wealth, in 1637, at the relatively advanced age of fifty-six or fifty-seven, he was nominated to the poorly endowed bishopric of Rochester. Having been forced to resign his deanery and other benefices, in 1638 he became rector of Bromley, Kent, which was often appropriated to that bishopric; here, although personally frugal, he is said to have been very hospitable. As bishop, Warner acted to enforce the railing of the communion table at the east end of the church; he was also the donor of the magnificent font erected in Canterbury Cathedral in 1639.

In March 1640 Warner preached in Rochester Cathedral another sermon against Charles's opponents, on Psalm 74: 23 ('Forget not the voice of thy enemies'), which was later denounced as self-serving in *The Scots Scouts Discoveries* (1642). He also gave £1500 to swell the royal coffers in the campaign against the Scots. He kept a brief diary during the Short Parliament of 1640, supported the decision to permit convocation to continue sitting after its dissolution, and played a part in drafting the new set of canons, which he subscribed. In September 1640 he was one of only two bishops who attended the great council of peers at York, and on 14 May 1641 he signed the protestation against threatened changes to the constitution of church and state. He was one of the thirteen bishops impeached on 4 August 1641 for passing the canons of 1640 and granting the king a benevolence, but was chosen by joint consent of the accused to organize their defence. His stubborn defence of the legality of their actions and of the canons themselves, together with pressure of other business in parliament, contributed to the impeachment's being dropped. On 13 February 1642 'dying episcopacy gave its last groan in the House of Lords' (Fuller, 6.237) when Warner and two other bishops defended the right of bishops to sit in the upper house.

In 1643 all Warner's lands and goods were sequestered, his books seized, and debts owed him were cancelled. Writing to Gilbert Sheldon in 1660, he recalled that he was also regularly harassed by parliamentarian forces, had to escape to Oxford in disguise, and then moved further west, living on the Welsh border for three years; he spent some time with his wife's relatives in Bromfield, Shropshire. By the late 1640s he was back in Kent, and was consulted by Henry Hammond about the legality of the toleration then being forced on the king; Warner clearly had reservations. At the king's command he also published *Church-Lands Not to be Sold*—a long pamphlet painstakingly rebutting parliament's case for the right to sell episcopal and capitular lands. Wood knew of an edition in 1646, but the only extant copies have '1648' on the title-page, amended on Thomason's copy to October 1647. Two years later Warner published *The Devilish Conspiracy*—a sermon on Luke 18: 31–3 (foretelling Christ's death) which Warner delivered on 4 February 1649, just days after Charles I's execution. In it he used the Jews' 'hellish treason, heathenish condemnation, and damnable murder' of Jesus Christ, their king (title-page), as the basis for a detailed comparison of the trials and executions of Christ and Charles.

Warner had already decided to pay fines of about £5000 to have the sequestration on his personal property discharged, and was finally forced out of Bromley Palace on Christmas eve 1648. In the 1650s he lived quietly, but read prayer book services twice daily, preached weekly, celebrated communion monthly, and confirmed the children of the supporters of the old church. In addition he kept in contact with other episcopalians, giving (he later claimed) up to £600 a year to sequestered clergy and their widows. Jeremy Taylor dedicated two books to him, but Warner wrote to Taylor criticizing his account of original sin in the second, *Unum necessarium*. Taylor printed this and responded to it in *An Answer to a Letter Written by the R. R. the Lord Bishop of Rochester* (1656). Although extensive sermon notes and many of Warner's other papers, including his notes on political matters in the 1640s and some of his financial records, survive (Bodl. Oxf., MS Eng th.b.4–8 and Norfolk RO, LEEW), the only publications correctly associated with Warner (apart from those cited above) are the three sets of visitation articles for Rochester diocese published in 1638, 1662, and 1666. However, he is said to have been generous in helping others prepare works for the press, such as William Somner's *Dictionarum Saxonico-Latino-Anglicum* (1659) and Matthew Poole's *Synopsis criticorum* (1669–76).

Warner appears to have played little part in 'the business of the Church'—the campaign to ensure the continuity of the episcopal succession—and at the Restoration, although he clearly expected promotion to a more important or richer see, and was at one stage allocated Norwich, he was passed over and soon felt 'utterly forgotten' (Bodl. Oxf., MS Tanner 49, fol. 23*r*). He was one of four surviving bishops, dressed in episcopal habits, to greet Charles II publicly on his return to London on 29 May 1660, and one of the five survivors who consecrated five new bishops in

Westminster Abbey on 28 October, and was placed on the list of court preachers in February 1661. In November he took his seat again in the House of Lords, but thereafter his public role was increasingly confined to his diocese. He addressed his clergy in Rochester Cathedral on 14 October 1662, telling them that he still had 'work enough to set all in order that is left undone or done amiss' (J. Lee-Warner, 47). Having drawn up his will in September 1666, on 21 or 22 October he died; he was buried in Merton's chapel in Rochester Cathedral, where a fine monument by Joseph Marshall was raised to him.

Warner died childless and his considerable estates descended to his sister's son John Lee, archdeacon of Rochester, who assumed the additional name of Warner as the bishop had stipulated in his will, proved on 7 February 1667. Warner was a great philanthropist, and a member of his family estimated that he gave the equivalent of over £40,000 to good causes during his lifetime and in his will. For example, in addition to the gifts already mentioned, Warner claimed to have given over £1000 to young scholars at Magdalen, a further £1000 to the repair of St Paul's, and over £2500 to redeem Christians held captive in north Africa in the 1660s. The font in Canterbury Cathedral cost him £3000, including repairs undertaken in 1660, and he bought books for the libraries of the college and cathedrals with which he had been associated; £2000 went to buy in impropriations to raise the value of poor vicarages in Rochester diocese, £8500 to build Bromley College, Kent, to house twenty impoverished widows of clergymen, plus £450 a year for its support, and £80 a year in perpetuity to Balliol College, Oxford, for scholarships to support four young Scottish ordinands each year. Warner's learning and wealth had been reflected in his book-collecting over several decades. In 1685 a collection of books said to consist 'principally' of Warner's library was auctioned: the accompanying catalogue, *Bibliotheca Warneriana*, listed well over 2400 titles, over half of which were 'valuable and scarce books in divinity'—editions of the fathers and councils, church histories, and biblical commentaries (many in Greek and Latin), and many treatises and sermons in English—together with works on history, philology, and mathematics. His manuscript sermons and political papers, together with this library, confirm what one near-contemporary affirmed, that he was 'a good scholar, an able linguist, a deep divine, and one well read in the Fathers' (BL, Add. MS 4224, fol. 76*r*).

IAN GREEN

Sources BL, Add. MSS 4224, fol. 76; 2800, fols. 111, 115, 142, 211, 223, 246 · BL, Lansdowne MS 986, fols. 50–53 · Bodl. Oxf., MSS Tanner 49, fol. 23; 58, fol. 484 · Bodl. Oxf., MSS Eng. th. b. 4–8, e. 62, e. 176–7 · Norfolk RO, Lee Warner family papers · *CSP dom.*, 1641–3, 421 · *The articles and charge proved in parliament against Dr Walton* (1641), 3 · Wood, *Ath. Oxon.*, new edn, 4.731–2 · T. Fuller, *The church history of Britain*, ed. J. S. Brewer, new edn, 6 vols. (1845) · *Biographia Britannica, or, The lives of the most eminent persons who have flourished in Great Britain and Ireland*, 7 vols. (1747–66), vol. 6, pt. 2, pp. 4159–61 · *N&Q*, 9th ser., 2 (1898) · Foster, *Alum. Oxon.* · J. Lee-Warner, 'A hitherto unpublished passage in the life of John Warner, bishop of Rochester', *Archaeological Journal*, 21 (1864), 42–7 · E. Lee-Warner, *The life of John Warner, bishop of Rochester, 1637–1666* (1901) · *Fasti Angl.*, 1541–1857, [Canterbury], 18, 52 · J. Davies, *The Caroline captivity of the* *church: Charles I and the remoulding of Anglicanism, 1625–1641* (1992), 99, 130, 218, 232–3, 273–4, 282–4 • P. King, 'The episcopate during the civil wars, 1642–1649', *EngHR*, 83 (1968), 525–31 • R. S. Bosher, *The making of the Restoration settlement: the influence of the Laudians, 1649–1662* (1951), 22, 123, 143, 181, 235 • I. M. Green, *The re-establishment of the Church of England, 1660–1663* (1978), 82–3, 88, 91 • *IGI*

Archives Bodl. Oxf., corresp. and papers • Bodl. Oxf., sermon notes and family papers • Norfolk RO, diary, corresp., and papers | BL, letters to Henry Oxenden, Add. MSS 28000–28004
Likenesses J. Marshall, effigy on monument, 1666, Rochester Cathedral • J. Taylor, oils, *c.*1670, Magd. Oxf.

Warner, John (1628–1692), Jesuit, was born in 1628 in Warwickshire, the third son of Robert Warner of Ratcliffe, Warwickshire. After his education and ordination in Spain in 1653 he lectured in philosophy and divinity at the English College at Douai from 1657 until 1661–2. During these years he wrote *Vindiciae censurae duacenae, seu, Confutatio scripti cujusdam Thomae Albii*, which was published in Douai in 1661 and which upheld the University of Douai's censures upon the work of Thomas White (alias Blacklo). Warner became a Jesuit in 1662 and from 1665 he lectured in divinity at the English Jesuit college at Liège. While there he wrote *Conclusiones ex universa theologia propugnandae in collegio Anglicano Soc. Jesu*, published in Liège in 1670. From 1671 until 1676 he was stationed at Paris as procurator responsible for the property of the English Jesuits there. He published a number of works of controversy, notably *Anti-Haman* (1678), entitled *A defence of the doctrin and holy rites of the Roman Catholic church from the calumnies and cavils of Dr Burnet's mystery of iniquity unveiled*, in its second edition (1688); he is sometimes accredited with authorship of *Dr. Stillingfleet Still Against Dr. Stillingfleet* (1675), more often attributed to John Keynes. From 1678 until 1679 he was rector of the college at Liège. In 1679 he was appointed provincial superior of the English Jesuits in succession to Thomas Whitbread, whose arrest Titus Oates had secured, and he held this appointment until 1683. Later he wrote of this period in a Latin manuscript history, later published under the title *The History of English Persecution of Catholics and the Presbyterian Plot* (1953). Of this work it has been said that his aim was to present a history of the plot for general European consumption in the light of the contemporary political scene (Warner, 1.xvii). Dodd considered Warner a man of profound learning and especially esteemed his controversial abilities. In 1682 Warner attended the twelfth general congregation of the Jesuits in Rome which elected Charles de Noyelle as superior-general and from 1683 to 1687 he was rector of St Omer College. In 1686 James II appointed him royal confessor. At the revolution he escaped to the continent but only after being arrested twice and imprisoned for a month in Maidstone gaol. It was at this time, probably, that he lost his letter-book covering the years 1678–85, a manuscript now in Cambridge University Library. After making his way to St Germain he followed James to Ireland as a chaplain. Soon after the king's return to France, Warner died at St Germain on 2 November 1692.

J. M. RIGG, *rev.* GEOFFREY HOLT

Sources H. Foley, ed., *Records of the English province of the Society of Jesus*, 5 (1879), 288; 7 (1882–3), 816 • J. Warner, *The history of English persecution of Catholics and the presbyterian plot*, ed. T. A. Birrell, trans. J. Bligh, 2 vols., Catholic RS, 47–8 (1953) • G. Holt, *The English Jesuits, 1650–1829: a biographical dictionary*, Catholic RS, 70 (1984), 258 • P. R. Harris, ed., *Douai College documents, 1639–1794*, Catholic RS, 63 (1972), 19 • G. Holt, 'The letter book of Fr John Warner', *Archivum Historicum Societatis Jesu*, 53 (1984), 443–68 • C. Dodd [H. Tootell], *The church history of England, from the year 1500, to the year 1688*, 3 (1742), 491 • [J. Keynes and T. Stapleton], *Florus Anglo-Bavaricus* (Liège, 1685), 108 • G. Oliver, *Collections towards illustrating the biography of the Scotch, English and Irish members, SJ* (1838), 200 • A. de Backer and others, *Bibliothèque de la Compagnie de Jésus*, new edn, 8, ed. C. Sommervogel (Brussels, 1898), 992 • *Third report*, HMC, 2 (1872), appx, p. 334 • *The manuscripts of the House of Lords*, 4 vols., HMC, 17 (1887–94), vol. 2, p. 61 • Evelyn, *Diary* • N. Luttrell, *A brief historical relation of state affairs from September 1678 to April 1714*, 2 (1857), 606 • Archives of the British Province of the Society of Jesus, London
Archives BM, holograph rough copy of his *History* • CUL, *History* and letter-book | Archives of the British Province of the Society of Jesus, London, Stonyhurst MSS, letters

Warner, John (*bap.* **1673**, *d.* **1760**), horticulturist, was baptized on 11 January 1673 at St Giles Cripplegate in the City of London, the son of James and Mary Warner. He was eminent for his skill in growing fruit. In business as a merchant, he lived in Rotherhithe, on the east side of East Lane, where he constructed a garden which became celebrated for its products. He paid special attention to cultivating vines, and, in 1720, was the first to introduce the Burgundy grape into England. Finding that this variety, when planted against a wall, ripened earlier than others, he conjectured that the vines might ripen as standards; on trial they succeeded beyond his expectation. He considerably enlarged his vineyard, until it afforded him more than 100 gallons of wine annually, and gave cuttings from his vines to all who would plant them. When he started his experiments the only other vineyards in the country, one at Dorking and the other at Bath, were planted with grapes less suited to the English climate.

Warner's garden comprised several acres. A broad canal ran through the length, on either side of which were planted, besides vines, a treble row of dwarf pears and apples. He raised pineapples, then a rare fruit in Britain, on stoves, and grew other exotic plants.

The name of Warner's wife, who predeceased him, is unknown. He was survived by a son, Simeon, a daughter, Ann, and their children, and by a daughter Mehitabel, who had married against his wish. Warner died at Rotherhithe on 24 February 1760 and was buried in the Quakers' burial-ground in Long Lane, Bermondsey, as requested in his will, where he speaks of 'the Quakers, with whom I have walked in communion since my youth' (PROB 11/854, sig 129).

E. I. CARLYLE, *rev.* ANITA MCCONNELL

Sources *GM*, 1st ser., 30 (1760), 153 • will, PRO, PROB 11/854 sig. 129 • W. Roberts, 'Some 17th and 18th century gardeners', *Gardeners' Chronicle*, 3rd ser., 62 (1917), 235–6

Warner, John (1736–1800), classical scholar and Church of England clergyman, was born in London, the son of Ferdinando Warner (1703–1768), a clergyman. After initial schooling in Greenwich, he was admitted to St Paul's School, London, on 30 March 1747. On leaving, he spent a few months in Lisbon, but his family felt him to be unsuited to the commercial life. Instead, on 2 July 1754, he was admitted as a sizar at Magdalene College, Cambridge, but moved to Trinity College on 6 November. After matriculating in the Lent term 1755, he became Pauline exhibitioner and Perry exhibitioner the same year. He graduated BA from Trinity College in 1758, and proceeded MA in 1761 and DD in 1773.

Warner was ordained priest in London on 21 September 1760, and on the 30th was elected lecturer of St Andrew by the Wardrobe and St Ann Blackfriars. That same month he was nominated as morning preacher of his own propriety chapel in Long Acre (later sold to Dr King, formerly chaplain of the British factory at St Petersburg) by the vicar of St Martin-in-the-Fields, so beginning a ministry which brought him some celebrity as an eloquent preacher at London. He looked to his father's connections with the old corps whigs for patronage. On 20 December 1763 he was licensed to perform the office of assistant preacher and reader at Tavistock Chapel in the parish of St Martin-in-the-Fields (leased from the Bedford estates) and on 30 November 1765 he was licensed as a general preacher throughout the London diocese. He also gained his first living, the vicarage of West Ham, Essex, which he held for ten years until resignation in March 1775, when he was admitted to the rectory of North Benfleet, Essex. West Ham was a crown living bestowed by the duke of Newcastle (newly returned to office) as a means of silencing Ferdinando Warner's complaints of official neglect.

John Warner also advanced his career outside the capital. In 1777 he was presented to the rectory of Scrivelsby-cum-Dalderby, Lincolnshire. Having been instituted on 4 August, he promptly resigned the living within two months, and was appointed instead to the united rectories of Hockcliffe and Chalgrave in Bedfordshire on 19 December 1777, suddenly vacant after the execution of the previous incumbent, the unfortunate Dr William Dodd, for forgery. The precise reasons for ceding the Lincolnshire parishes so quickly are unclear. Hockcliffe, at £200 p.a., was slightly more profitable than Scrivelsby, valued at £160 p.a. in 1777. It may be that Warner was attracted by the greater proximity to his metropolitan friends. Whatever the explanation, he was largely non-resident and continued to hunt for more comfortable preferment. It was his ambition, he told George Selwyn, 'to be a tight Trulliber, to feed pigs, and grow fat with them' (Jesse, 4.343). His search for the right living finally ended in 1790, when he resigned Hockcliffe and was presented by his friend Sir Richard Colt Hoare to the rectory of Stourton, Wiltshire (instituted 8 October), which he held until his death. In June 1790, on the recommendation of Frederick, fifth earl of Carlisle, and George Selwyn, Warner served as chaplain to the new British ambassador in Paris, Earl Gower. Warner knew the city well. His sister, a Roman Catholic convert, had become a nun there, while Warner himself had lived there previously in the winter of 1778–9, staying with the Abbé Raynal, a sure token of his progressive sympathies.

Once in France, Warner exhibited an enthusiasm for the revolution deemed excessive for an Anglican clergyman, and he stayed in France for the next three years beyond the closure of the embassy. With other radical whigs (including fellow cleric Horne Tooke) Warner's name was put forward in the Convention in September 1792 for citizenship as one 'known for his energetic speeches, in which he deploys his love of liberty and hatred for kings', as one French newspaper reported, with embarrassing exaggeration (Erdman, 188). There is no evidence to suggest it was granted. In October 1793 the Convention decreed the arrest of all British subjects. The decree came into force just as Warner had reached Boulogne, and he was obliged by the authorities to live outside the town until some time after the overthrow of Robespierre in July 1794. He remained sympathetic to the ideals of the revolution, despite the excesses of the terror, opining that he did not 'think it an advantage to this country [Britain], that Bourbon politics should grow in fashion, and that, because the French run mad, the sound principles of English liberty should be trodden under foot' (Monthly Magazine, 171).

Warner was a committed whig, an advocate of parliamentary reform, and a friend of his fellow radical parson Horne Tooke; he subscribed to the Diversions of Purley and left Tooke a silver goblet in his will. Warner was an excellent scholar with a reputation for wit that made him, in later life, a close friend of George Selwyn (by whom he was nicknamed The Snail) and a member of the circle of the fourth duke of Queensberry (whom he attended to both Drumlanrigg and Amesbury). As one obituarist recorded: 'His attachment to literature was unbounded; he was moderate to an extreme at the table, and equally abstemious at the bottle: a book, a pipe, and cheerful conversation, in which he eminently excelled, were his supreme delight' (GM, 70/1, 1800, 92). His humanitarian concerns were well known. He personally relieved distress among his parishioners in the 1790s and was an ardent admirer of his Bedfordshire neighbour the philanthropist John Howard: Warner was a moving spirit in the erection of the statue to Howard's memory in St Paul's Cathedral.

Warner died in St John's Square, Clerkenwell, on 22 January 1800, and was buried in a vault in St John's Church on the 30th. His genial, sociable temperament limited his literary productivity. He published anonymously, Metronariston, or, A new pleasure recommended, in a dissertation upon a part of Greek and Latin prosody (1797) and a memoir of Major Cartwright in Public Characters (1798). He never married.   NIGEL ASTON

Sources R. B. Gardiner, ed., *The admission registers of St Paul's School, from 1748 to 1876* (1884) • Venn, *Alum. Cant.* • *GM*, 1st ser., 67 (1797), 232 • *GM*, 1st ser., 70 (1800), 92 • *Monthly Magazine*, 9 (1800), 170–72 • *N&Q*, 2nd ser., 12 (1861), 474 • Nichols, *Illustrations*, 2.673, 682–3 • J. Johnson, *Memoirs of the life and writings of William Hayley* (1823), 1.351, 388, 410 • S. Lodge, *Scrivelsby: the home of the champions* (1893), 186 • J. G. Alger, *Englishmen in the French Revolution* (1889), 31–2 • J. H. Jesse, *George Selwyn and his contemporaries, with memoirs and notes*, 4 vols. (1843–4), vols. 3–4 • D. V. Erdman, *Commerce des lumières: John Oswald and the British in Paris, 1790–1793* (1986) • Lincs. Arch., E/BER/CG/L32/1 • diocese book, Lincs. Arch., Lincoln diocesan archives, SPE7, 252 • 'Speculum', 1663–1784, Lincs. Arch., SPE2, 215 • Lincs.

Arch., BEN 11/52 · bishops' registers, Lincs. Arch., Lincoln diocesan archives, fols. 295, 298, 525 · Wilts. & Swindon RO, WROD1/2/29 · BL, Newcastle MSS, Add. MS 32947, fols. 218, 220 · BL, Newcastle MSS, Add. MS 32970, fols. 46, 67 · *VCH Essex*, 6.116
Archives GL, ordination MSS, MS 10326/91 · GL, ordination register, MS 9535/3 · LMA | GL, bishop's act book, MS 9548
Wealth at death possessed of a considerable fortune

Warner, Joseph (1717–1801), surgeon, was the eldest son of Ashton Warner (1691–1752), politician, of Antigua in the West Indies. Joseph Warner later inherited the estate in Antigua, together with a ring, said to be the one given by Elizabeth I to the earl of Essex. Warner was sent to England when young and was educated for six or seven years at Westminster School. He was apprenticed for seven years to Samuel Sharp, surgeon to Guy's Hospital, on 3 December 1734. Warner passed his examination for the great diploma of the Company of Barber–Surgeons on 1 December 1741, and on 2 March following he paid the usual fee of £10 and took the livery of the company. At this time he was acting with his master, Sharp, as joint lecturer on anatomy at Guy's.

Warner volunteered to accompany the expedition in 1745, under the duke of Cumberland, to suppress the rebellion in Scotland, and he was elected surgeon to Guy's Hospital, in succession to James Pierce, on 22 February 1746, an office he resigned on 30 June 1780. He was elected a fellow of the Royal Society on 6 December 1750, and on 5 April 1764 he was chosen as a member of the court of assistants of the Company of Surgeons. He became a member of its court of examiners on 6 August 1771, and he served as its master in 1780 and in 1784. When the Royal College of Surgeons was created in 1800 Warner became its first member, so that he was one of the very few surgeons who belonged to the three corporate bodies of surgeons which have existed in England. He was a member of the college's court of assistants from 1800–01. Warner shared with William Bromfield, Sir Caesar Hawkins, and Sharp the civil surgical practice of London. He was one of those surgeons who 'from midcentury on … began to insist ever more vehemently that a good surgeon avoided operating if possible, and cured, instead, by regimen and medicines' (Lawrence, 305).

Warner contributed little to the literature of surgery, but what he wrote provides an insight into the opinions of contemporary surgeons. He was the first surgeon to tie the common carotid artery, an operation he performed in 1775. Warner's reputation rests on his *Cases on surgery … to which is added an account of the preparation and effects of the agaric of the oak in stopping of bleedings after some of the most capital operations* (1754), translated into French (Paris, 1757). The cases extend over the whole domain of surgery and are related with brevity, skill, and judgement. A dispute with John Hunter over surgical teaching at Guy's led Warner to write a memorandum in which he describes the nature of surgical training at the hospital. It is printed in Wilks and Bettany's *A Biographical History of Guy's Hospital* (1892). Warner died at his house in Hatton Street, London, on 24 July 1801. D'A. POWER, *rev.* MICHAEL BEVAN

Joseph Warner (1717–1801), by Samuel Medley

Sources S. Wilks and G. T. Bettany, *A biographical history of Guy's Hospital* (1892) · *GM*, 1st ser., 71 (1801), 956–7 · private information (1899) · W. Hill, 'Wills Library Humanities: Joseph Warner', *Guy's Hospital Gazette*, [3rd ser.], 81 (1967), 381–2 · S. C. Lawrence, *Charitable knowledge: hospital pupils and practitioners in eighteenth-century London* (1996) · Z. Cope, *The Royal College of Surgeons of England: a history* (1959)
Likenesses W. Branwhite, stipple, pubd 1801 (after S. Medley), BM, NPG · S. Medley, oils, RCS Eng. [*see illus.*]

Warner [*née* Huddart], **Mary Amelia** (1804–1854), actress and theatre manager, was born in Manchester, the daughter of Thomas Huddart (*d.* 1831), a Dublin chemist turned actor, and his wife, Ann, *née* Gough, of Limerick. Huddart had acted briefly at the Crow Street Theatre, Dublin, before appearing in London at the Theatre Royal, Covent Garden, in October 1798 as Othello and enjoying some success later in provincial theatres. After playing at Greenwich for her father's benefit, Mary Huddart joined John Brunton's company at the reputed age of fifteen, appearing at Plymouth, Exeter, Bristol, and Birmingham. She is said to have played also at the Surrey and Tottenham Street theatres in London. In 1829 she joined the company at the Theatre Royal, Dublin, and on 22 November 1830, as Miss Huddart from Dublin, appeared at the Theatre Royal, Drury Lane, as Belvidera in Thomas Otway's *Venice Preserv'd*, having been recommended to the managers, Captain Polhill and Alexander Lee, by W. C. Macready, who took the part of Pierre. Macready's diaries suggest that there was for a time a strong mutual attraction, and, despite his growing criticisms of her, both professional and personal, their friendship lasted until her death.

Among the parts played by Huddart in her first season

Mary Amelia Warner (1804–1854), by unknown engraver, pubd 1851 (after Paine) [as Hermione in *The Winter's Tale*]

were Emma in Sheridan Knowles's *William Tell*, Alicia in Nicholas Rowe's *Jane Shore*, and Constance in *King John*. She was also the original Queen Elswith in Knowles's *Alfred the Great*. She then returned to Dublin and played leading roles under Granby Calcraft. In 1836, under Alfred Bunn's management, she was again at Drury Lane, where she supported the American actor Edwin Forrest in John Galt's *Lady Macbeth* and was the original Marian in Knowles's *Daughter*, then called *The Wrecker's Daughter*. This led to her engagement at the Haymarket Theatre for the first production in London of *The Bridal*, on 26 June 1837. The play was an adaptation by Macready and Knowles of *The Maid's Tragedy*, in which Huddart appeared as Evadne with Macready as Melantius. She also played Portia to Samuel Phelps's Shylock and Helen McGregor to his Rob Roy. On 6 July 1837, at St George's, Bloomsbury, she married Robert William Warner, formerly the landlord of The Wrekin tavern, Broad Court, Bow Street, a haunt of actors and journalists, who had become bankrupt four months earlier. Warner described his subsequent role as making engagements for his wife and escorting her to and from rehearsals and performances.

In the autumn of 1837 Mrs Warner joined Macready's company at Covent Garden, where she stayed for two years, supporting him in many Shakespearian parts and gaining in reputation. She was the original Joan of Arc in T. J. Serle's play of that name. Premature labour prevented her from playing at Covent Garden the heroine of Thomas Talfourd's *The Athenian Captive*, but she took the part at the Haymarket on 4 August 1838. She was again in Macready's company when he took the Theatre Royal, Drury Lane, in the autumn of 1841, and played the Queen in *Hamlet* (29 April 1842), and the original Lady Lydia Lynterne in Westland Marston's *The Patrician's Daughter* (10 December 1842). In 1843 she acted with Phelps in Bath, and on 27 May 1844, with him and T. L. Greenwood, began the memorable management of Sadler's Wells Theatre, London, in which they sought to make the theatre 'a place for justly representing the works of our great dramatic poets' (*The Era*, 1 Oct 1854). She spoke the address, by Serle, on the opening night, when she played Lady Macbeth.

During the first season Mrs Warner appeared in many roles, including those of Mrs Oakley in Colman's *The Jealous Wife*, Gertrude in *Hamlet*, Lady Allworth in Kemble's *A New Way to Pay Old Debts*, Queen Margaret in *Richard III*, Portia in *The Merchant of Venice*, Evadne in *The Bridal*, Lady Frugal in Massinger's *City Madam*, Queen Katharine in *Henry VIII*, and Madeline in Serle's *The Priest's Daughter*. On 21 May 1845 she played Madame Chateaupres in Sullivan's *The King's Friend*. During the 1845–6 season she again took many parts, including Julie in Bulwer Lytton's *Richelieu*, Belvidera in *Venice Preserv'd*, Elvira in Sheridan's *Pizarro*, Hermione in *The Winter's Tale*, Clara Douglas in Bulwer Lytton's *Money*, and Alicia in *Jane Shore*. She then retired from the management of Sadler's Wells, and, in a spirit of apparent rivalry, undertook that of the Marylebone Theatre off the Edgware Road, then described as 'one of the prettiest minor theatres in London' (*The Times*, 31 Aug 1847). She opened on 30 August 1847 with *The Winter's Tale* and a farce, *The Windmill*, by Thomas Morton junior. She aimed, as at Sadler's Wells, to provide productions of Shakespeare based on the authentic text. She also sought historical accuracy in costume and set. Perhaps unwisely, she took parts better suited to a younger actress, such as Julia in Knowles's *The Hunchback*, Lady Teazle in Sheridan's *The School for Scandal*, and Lady Townly in Cibber and Vanbrugh's *The Provoked Husband*. In November she revived *The Scornful Lady* of Beaumont and Fletcher, altered by Serle, in which she played the Lady; and in April 1848 she put on Serle's *The Double Marriage*, playing Juliana. Macready starred with the company that month, but the theatre closed on 9 May with a reputed loss of £5000. Mrs Warner then returned to the Haymarket, where she supported Macready during his farewell performances before his departure for America. On 28 July 1851 Sadler's Wells was opened for a few nights before the beginning of the regular season to give Mrs Warner an opportunity of playing her best-known characters before also starting for America. What proved to be her last appearance in England was made in August, as Mrs Oakley in *The Jealous Wife*. She met with great success in America, but after developing cancer she travelled to England in 1852 for an operation, and then revisited New York. There she became too ill to fulfil her engagements, and she returned to London in June 1853, gravely ill. On 10 December 1853, through her husband, she applied for protection to the insolvent debtors' court, where it was reported that a fund had been established on her behalf by a group of friends, among them Dickens and Macready. Subscribers to this included the queen and Angela Burdett-Coutts. A benefit at Sadler's Wells brought her £150. Miss Burdett-Coutts undertook the charge of a daughter and Macready of her son, John Lawrence Warner, who later tried but failed to make a career as an actor. Mrs Warner died on 24 September 1854 at her home, 16 Euston Place, Euston Square, and was buried on 2 October at Highgate cemetery. Despite child bearing and a perennial burden of debt, Mrs Warner sustained leading roles in the principal London theatres for some fifteen years, most notably in tragedies, and was ranked second only to Helen Faucit (Lady Martin) and Mrs Charles Kean (Ellen Kean). She was equally good in pathos and in tragic emotion. Her chief success was obtained as Evadne, in which role Dickens described her as a 'defiant splendid Sin'. Both energy and intensity were at her disposal, though she was open to the charge of ranting. In management she followed Macready and Phelps in insisting on the original text of Shakespeare's plays, although she was happy to accept contemporary versions of other stage classics. Macready spoke of 'a sympathy in her friendship, a strong good sense in her observations and an acuteness of penetration that makes her society soothing and pleasing' (*Diaries*, 1.196), but later referred to her mind 'never very elevated, undergoing a process of vulgarization' (ibid., 2.357).

JOSEPH KNIGHT, *rev.* C. M. P. TAYLOR

Sources *Macready's reminiscences, and selections from his diaries and letters*, ed. F. Pollock, 2 vols. (1875) · *The Era* (1 Oct 1854) · *The Times* (30 Sept 1854) · *ILN* (30 Sept 1854) · *The diaries of William Charles Macready, 1833–1851*, ed. W. Toynbee, 2 vols. (1912) · *The history of the Theatre Royal, Dublin, from its foundation in 1821 to the present time* (1870) · *The Times* (5 Dec 1853) · *The Times* (1 Jan 1854) · *The life and reminiscences of E. L. Blanchard, with notes from the diary of Wm. Blanchard*, ed. C. W. Scott and C. Howard, 2 vols. (1891) · H. Morley, *The journal of a London playgoer from 1851 to 1866* (1866) · *The Times* (1 March 1837) · *The Era* (5 Sept 1847–14 May 1848) · *Actors by Daylight*, 2/19 (1839) · W. C. Russell, *Representative actors* [1888] · E. Sherson, *London's lost theatres of the nineteenth century: with notes on plays and players seen there* (1925) · J. E. Cunningham, *Theatre Royal, Birmingham* (1950) · W. J. Macqueen Pope, *Theatre Royal, Drury Lane* (1945) · B. S. Penley, *The Bath stage: a history of dramatic representations in Bath* (1892) · d. cert. · *The Era* (8 Oct 1854)

Likenesses R. J. Lane, lithograph, 1837, BM, NPG · lithograph, pubd 1839 (after unknown artist), NPG · eight prints, Harvard TC · portrait, BM, NPG; repro. in J. Tallis, ed., *Tallis's Dramatic Magazine and General Theatrical and Musical Review* (1850–53) · portrait, repro. in *Actors by Daylight* · stipple and line engraving (as Hermione in *The winter's tale*; after Paine), BM, NPG; repro. in J. Tallis, ed., *A drawing-room table book* (1851) [*see illus.*]

Warner, Sir Pelham Francis (1873–1963), cricketer and writer on cricket, was born on 2 October 1873 at The Hall, Port of Spain, Trinidad, the youngest of the eighteen children of Charles William Warner (1805–1887) and his second wife, Ellen Rosa (1830–1913), daughter of Juan José Cadiz. The Warner family had associations with the West Indies which went back three centuries to Sir Thomas Warner (*c*.1575–1649). His father was attorney-general of Trinidad, and his Spanish grandfather a barrister there. His early education (1883–7) was at Harrison College, Barbados, where, at the age of thirteen, he played cricket in

Sir Pelham Francis Warner (1873–1963), by Vandyk

the first eleven with those several years his senior. On his father's death in 1887, his mother went to live in England and sent her son to Rugby School. He was small, delicate, and not fit enough to play football, but in his first summer term he quickly made his mark as a cricketer. While still only sixteen, he made 177 not out against the Free Foresters, batting throughout the Rugby innings and much influenced by the coaching of the former Yorkshire player Tom Emmett. Cricket apart, he benefited from the naval and military history he was taught, which laid the basis of his lifelong devotion to the concept of the British empire. In 1912 he would edit and contribute to *Imperial Cricket*. It was at Rugby he acquired his cognomen, Plum. He went up to Oriel College, Oxford, in 1893. The duodenal ulcer which would plague him for so many years meant that he did not gain his blue until 1895, though he made his début for Middlesex in the preceding year. He was awarded a third-class degree in jurisprudence in 1896, passed his bar examinations in the same year, and was called to the Inner Temple in 1900.

Rugby, and especially Oxford, had introduced Warner to the men who would be his friends and associates for a lifetime. With some of them he would participate in seven overseas cricket tours (1897–1904) as a young bachelor to whom cricket made more appeal than the law. His first tour brought a return to the West Indies, and much local adulation, while in 1903–4 he captained the first MCC side to tour Australia overseas in pursuit of the Ashes. The appointment had been controversial since he was not the first choice, but he came back with the Ashes and was at once a public celebrity. In Australia the Melbourne *Truth* had devoted a whole column to his qualities of leadership.

Warner, on his return from Australia, married (7 June 1904) Agnes Blyth (1877–1955), daughter of a wealthy businessman, Henry Blyth. She lived with her widowed mother in Portland Place, London. In the circles in which she moved, Warner was no great 'catch'—a young man without money or career. They had two sons and a daughter, while her financial resources buttressed his modest earnings from journalism and authorship. Warner had reported the 1897 tour of the West Indies for *The Sportsman* and later wrote for the *Westminster Gazette* and *The Times*. As an anonymous special correspondent, he frequently reported on Middlesex's performances, including his own, and did so impartially and with balanced judgement. He had been a regular member of the county side from 1895 onwards and became captain in 1908. Six times he finished in the top twelve in the national averages. As a batsman he was correct without being flamboyant and was particularly reliable on sticky wickets. His frailty concealed a thoroughness and determination. His first appearance for England had been in South Africa in 1899, when he made 132 not out, carrying his bat throughout the innings. He won selection at home in 1909 and was again appointed captain of the MCC in Australia in 1911–12. But a breakdown in health, after making 151 in the opening match, meant that he played in no more games in the tour though leading from behind in another successful Ashes series.

To his interest in military history, Warner added practical experience when he was commissioned in 1908 in the Inns of Court regiment, within the newly formed Territorial Army. He believed the experience helped him as a cricket captain. Much of his writing throughout his life contained military analogies and he saw success in cricket in the context of a campaign. With the outbreak of war in 1914 his regiment became the Inns of Court Officers' Training Corps and he was involved in the selection of officers for eighteen months before illness struck again. He served (1917–18) in the department of information in the Foreign Office under John Buchan before being invalided out of the army. Gradually the climate of public opinion had accepted that it was not unpatriotic to play sport in wartime, despite the standpoint taken by W. G. Grace just before his death. In 1917 and 1918 Warner organized charity matches, while his final contribution to the 'war effort' was to serve on a Ministry of Labour committee for the resettlement of ex-servicemen.

Warner played for Middlesex for two seasons after the war, and that of 1920 provided a fitting climax to his career. Middlesex needed to defeat Surrey at Lord's in their last match to win the county championship. They did so with ten minutes to spare. Warner, an emotional figure and a romantic, was cheered by 30,000 spectators. *Wisden* called it 'the match of the season ... never to be forgotten' (*Wisden*, 1921, 50), and paid tribute to his skilful captaincy. With an occasional game to come, his career (1894–1929)

had brought him 29,028 runs (average 36.28) with sixty centuries and fifteen appearances for England (average 23.92). His highest score was 244 for the Rest of England v. Warwickshire in 1911.

Warner had first been an England selector in 1905—while still a player in contention himself—and was chairman on several occasions between the wars: crucially in 1926, when England regained the Ashes, and in 1932, when he selected D. R. Jardine as captain for the MCC tour to Australia. Warner, as a journalist, had publicly deplored in the English season of 1932 the short-pitched bowling which Jardine would later employ in Australia and came to be known as 'bodyline'. Warner was appointed manager of the tour. Wearing too many hats, he was forced to remain publicly silent throughout the bitter controversies which arose. He was privately desolate and only in his letters to his wife could he find an outlet for his feelings. 'Nothing can compensate me for the moral and intellectual damage which I have suffered on this tour. ... DRJ has almost made me hate cricket' (Warner to Agnes Warner, 8 Feb 1933, Warner MSS). Warner, who had gone bald very young, returned to Britain with his smooth, almost epicene face visibly aged. Outwardly he had been loyal to the MCC and to its captain, although there were those who said that his silence mutilated the virtue of his standpoint.

The Cricketer magazine, which he had founded in 1921 and of which he was editor (1921–62), remained a vehicle for Warner's opinions, often expressed anonymously, while his day-to-day reporting, after he retired from playing, was for the *Morning Post* (1921–32) and, briefly, for the *Daily Telegraph*. He was a persistent, if rather pedestrian, broadcaster. He had hoped for a role as a commentator after taking part in the initial BBC broadcasts on cricket in 1927 but he failed to impress his employers. It took the courage of a much younger man, Seymour de Lothbiniere, to tell him that the BBC were disappointed with his performances. In the last years of his life, though, the BBC again employed him, age giving distinction to what he said. In 1958 the BBC involved him in a tribute to what an internal memorandum called 'the most respected and best loved cricketer of all time' (Howat, 205).

The outbreak of war in 1939 led to Warner becoming deputy secretary of the MCC for the duration—effectively, the secretary acting for a younger man away on military service. The salary of £700 was welcome to one who had always depended on his wife for his standard of living. He was responsible for the administration of Lord's and for the organization of a large number of charity matches. He represented a frequently absent president and he served as secretary to the select committee on post-war cricket. In 1945, at the age of seventy-two, he relinquished his responsibilities, with a sense that his efforts were unrecognized.

The young Warner can be seen as a hedonist, pursuing pleasure rather than duty. The old one was a stoic, especially in his application to writing. Altogether, eighteen books came from his pen, three of them when he was in his seventies. In 1943 his *Cricket between Two Wars* became a best-seller. His *Lord's* immediately sold 15,000 copies and reviewers saw it as the outstanding publication on the 1946 Christmas list. His final book, his autobiographical *Long Innings* (1951), won accolades from writers such as Neville Cardus and sold 'almost like a Churchill' (Howat, 189). Such accolades mattered to him. He had been appointed MBE in 1919, knighted in 1937, and was president of Middlesex (1937–46). But the one which eluded him until he was nearly eighty was the presidency of the MCC. In the years immediately preceding he had sometimes not dared to go to the MCC annual general meeting, knowing his name would not be proposed. In 1950 the duke of Edinburgh nominated him as his successor. Eight years later a stand was built in his name at Lord's, and in 1961 he became the first life vice-president of the MCC.

The public and private Warner could be at variance. The man in public faced the enemy but in private disliked some of the consequences of the fray and was essentially a man of peace. Attrition and appeasement, as the events of 1932–3 had shown, made strange bedfellows. There was sometimes a reluctance to accept public responsibility for things which went wrong (notably, as a test selector) which he had privately urged. The public Warner delighted in the company of great men: the private one would be friendly with the humblest and most obscure of folk. There was not an iota of racialism in his outlook; it was Warner who appointed Learie Constantine to captain an eleven drawn entirely from the dominions to play against England in 1945.

The frail Warner survived the years to die, at the age of eighty-nine, on 30 January 1963 at West Lavington, near Midhurst, in Sussex. After cremation, his ashes were scattered at Lord's. A memorial service was held at Holy Trinity, Brompton, on 8 March 1963. He had brought to the game of cricket a commitment in time, knowledge, judgement, affection, and dedication which the circumstances of his life and generation permitted and which are unlikely ever to be paralleled. GERALD M. D. HOWAT

Sources G. Howat, *Plum Warner* (1987) • P. F. Warner, *Long innings* (1951) • P. F. Warner, *My cricketing life* (1921) • P. F. Warner, *Cricket in many climes* (1900) • P. F. Warner, *Cricket across the seas* (1903) • P. F. Warner, ed., *Imperial cricket* (1912) • R. Mason, *Plum Warner's last season* (1970) • *Wisden* • W. A. Bettesworth, 'P. F. Warner', *Cricket*, 22 (1903), 337 • *The Times* (31 Jan 1964) • *Daily Telegraph* (31 Jan 1964) • *The Cricketer*, 44 (1963), 9 • *CGPLA Eng. & Wales* (1963) • priv. coll., Warner MSS

Archives BBC WAC, files • Marylebone Cricket Club Museum, scrapbooks • priv. coll., MSS | NL Aus., Gowrie MSS, MS 2852 series 2 • NL Aus., Menzies MSS, MS 4936 | FILM BFI NFTVA, home footage • BFI NFTVA, news footage • BFI NFTVA, sports footage | SOUND BL NSA, recorded talk

Likenesses Elliott & Fry, photograph, 1897, Lord's, London • Spy [L. Ward], caricature, 1903, Lord's, London • A. Chevallier Tayler, lithograph, 1905 (after photograph by G. W. Bedlam), NPG • E. Hawkins, photograph, 1913, repro. in *Cricket*, new ser., 2 (31 May 1913), 237 • W. Stoneman, two photographs, 1940–53, NPG • A. R. Thompson, oils, 1945, Lord's, London • K. Lloyd, oils, 1949, Lord's, London • Vandyk, photograph, NPG [*see illus.*]

Wealth at death £3720 5*s*.: probate, 17 April 1963, *CGPLA Eng. & Wales*

Warner, Philip (*d.* 1689), army officer in Antigua, was born in the Leeward Islands, the third son of Sir Thomas *Warner (*c.*1580–1649), founder of English settlements there, whose family was from Suffolk. His mother, the second wife of Sir Thomas Warner, was Rebecca, daughter of Thomas Paine of Surrey. Warner reached his maturity during a period when island society, comprised largely of impoverished time-expired indentured servants, was crude in the extreme and dangerously exposed to destructive raids by Carib natives from the island of Dominica. In the disastrous war of 1666–7, in which all of the English Leewards except Nevis were captured and despoiled by the French and their Carib accomplices, he accompanied Deputy Governor Daniel Fitch in an undistinguished and unsuccessful mission to relieve the beleaguered island of Antigua. Thereafter, in 1667, he commanded a regiment of 500 men in successful assaults upon the French settlement at Cayenne and the Dutch fort at Surinam. After resettlement of the English Leeward colonies Warner returned to planting, taking part in the transition from tobacco to sugar culture. He was a member of the Antigua council and from 1672 to 1675 served as deputy governor of Antigua and commander of the militia, a force numbering 1052 foot soldiers and 100 horse. After a particularly destructive Carib raid in late 1674, he was dispatched by Colonel Stapleton, governor-general of the Leeward Islands, to avenge the English colonists. With 300 men he routed the Caribs of Dominica, killing many, including Indian Warner [see Warner, Thomas (*c.*1630–1674)], who was widely believed to be his half-brother, a natural son of Sir Thomas Warner and a female Carib slave. The crown was displeased. It considered Indian Warner a useful, if unreliable, ally in the colonial struggle against France and an asset in restraining hostile Caribs. On a visit to England in 1675 Warner was arrested for Indian Warner's murder and held for months in the Tower. He was tried in a Barbados court and acquitted. Events surrounding the death of Indian Warner remain disputed. Although abundant testimony by colonists affirmed the good character and proper conduct of Warner, he was forbidden to hold further office under the crown. He was elected to the Antigua assembly and became speaker in 1679. He died on 23 October 1689 of injuries sustained when his horse stumbled and fell on him, and was buried at St Paul's, Antigua. He and his wife, Henrietta (*d.* 1697), the daughter of Henry Ashton, a former governor of Antigua, had six children, two sons and four daughters. WILLIAM A. GREEN

Sources V. L. Oliver, *The history of the island of Antigua*, 3 vols. (1894–9) • A. Warner, *Sir Thomas Warner, pioneer of the West Indies: a chronicle of his family* (1973) • [Mrs Flanders], *Antigua and the Antiguans*, 2 vols. (1844) • V. T. Harlow, ed., *Colonizing expeditions to the West Indies and Guiana, 1623–1667*, Hakluyt Society, 2nd ser., 106 (1925) • 'The case of "Indian Warner" (1654–1676)', *Wild majesty: encounters with Caribs from Columbus to the present day, an anthology*, ed. P. Hulme and N. L. Whitehead (1992), 89–106 • R. S. Dunn, *Sugar and slaves: the rise of the planter class in the English West Indies, 1624–1713* (1972)

Archives PRO, C.O.1/22–37

Warner, Reginald Ernest [Rex] (1905–1986), novelist, classicist, and translator, was born on 9 March 1905 in Amberley, Gloucestershire, the only child of the Revd

Frederic Ernest Warner, vicar ('of the modernist persuasion') of Amberley, and his schoolteacher wife Kathleen, daughter of the Revd John James Luce of St Nicholas's Church, Gloucester. He was educated first at St George's School, Harpenden, and then at Wadham College, Oxford, which he entered with an open scholarship in classics in 1923, in spite of having been, according to his tutor, Maurice Bowra, ill taught at school, so that he 'found in Greek and Latin all the charms of novelty'. No doubt better taught at Wadham, he took a first class in classical honour moderations in 1925, but suffered a nervous breakdown in the following year and, after leaving Oxford for a time, returned to take a third class in English in 1928.

Among his Oxford contemporaries and friends were the poets W. H. Auden and Stephen Spender, and particularly Cecil Day-Lewis, who was at the same college and willing to share in some degree his athletic as well as his literary enthusiasms. Warner—tall, strongly built, and vigorous—captained a Wadham rugby team of which Day-Lewis was a member, and always retained his interest in and taste for energetic sporting pursuits. Day-Lewis, in his autobiography *The Buried Day* (1960), recalls his friend's 'Homeric boisterousness', which did not fade with the passing years.

Warner's entry on the literary scene was not immediate. On leaving Oxford he took teaching appointments in various schools, including at one stage, from 1932 to 1934, two posts in Egypt. His début, when it came in 1937, was auspicious. His *Poems*, published in that year, made no great mark, and in later years verse was only a small part of his prolific output. But it was also in 1937 that there appeared his novel *The Wild Goose Chase*, written mainly in England before he left for Egypt, and this strikingly original work made an immediate impression. His tale of three brothers and their quest in an unnamed country for the wild goose, symbol of hope and personal regeneration, was rightly seen as akin to the work of Franz Kafka; but it drew also on elements of classical mythology, and even of fairy tale, in a manner genuinely new in English fiction. *The Professor* (1938) was a very different work, a touching and almost purely naturalistic apology for traditional liberalism confronted, disastrously, with totalitarian amoralism. In *The Aerodrome* (1941) he reverted in part to a non-realistic, expressionist technique. Generally regarded as his best novel, this deeply gloomy work also sees human values collapsing before a rising tide of nihilistic materialism. Warner shared the Marxist enthusiasms of his student contemporaries but never joined the Communist Party. After the Molotov–Ribbentrop pact he saw communist dictatorship as scarcely preferable to the fascist variety. His own position is vigorously stated in his book of essays *The Cult of Power* (1946).

After a brief spell of service with the Allied Control Commission in Berlin, Warner became director (1945–7) of the British Institute in Athens. Later he held academic appointments in America, chairs at Bowdoin College in 1962–3 and at the University of Connecticut from 1964 to 1974. He was appointed to the Greek royal order of the Phoenix (1963), and awarded an honorary DLitt degree by Rider College (1968) and an honorary fellowship of his Oxford college, Wadham (1973).

From 1945 Warner's output of fiction, criticism, translations, and particularly retellings of classical legend and history, was unceasing—some thirty publications in as many years. But, after his rather slight novel *Escapade* (1953), it mostly took the form of what he himself called 'uncreative writing'—writing based rather on classical and historical scholarship than on imaginative invention. The quality of the work, however, was unfailingly high. *Imperial Caesar* (1960) won the Tait memorial prize, and special mention should be made of his version of the *Confessions* of St Augustine (1963), and of his translations of Aeschylus, Euripides, Thucydides, and Plutarch.

Warner was married three times, in unusual circumstances. In 1929 he married Frances Chamier, daughter of Frank Grove, civil engineer, who was much employed, before the First World War, in railway construction in China. They had two sons and a daughter. This marriage was dissolved in 1949 and in the same year he married Barbara Judith, divorced wife of Victor *Rothschild, third Baron Rothschild, and daughter of St John Hutchinson, barrister and recorder of Hastings; they had a daughter. The marriage was dissolved in 1962 and in 1966 he remarried Frances Chamier Warner, his former wife. He died at his home, Anchor House, St Leonard's Lane, Wallingford, on 24 June 1986.   G. J. WARNOCK, *rev.*

Sources M. Bowra, *Memories* (1966) · C. Day-Lewis, *The buried day* (1960) · personal knowledge (1996) · private information (1996) **Archives** BBC WAC · Connecticut University Library, notebooks and transcripts · Ransom HRC, corresp. and literary papers · U. Warwick Mod. RC · University of Bristol | King's Cam., Tillyard MSS · U. Leeds, Brotherton L., London Magazine MSS · U. Reading, British Council MSS, George Bell & Sons, Bodley Head 'adult editorial' and 'adult publicity' MSS · U. Reading L., Hogarth Press MSS | SOUND BL NSA **Likenesses** photograph, King's Cam. **Wealth at death** £132,058: probate, 24 Nov 1986, *CGPLA Eng. & Wales*

Warner, Richard (1713?–1775), botanist and literary scholar, was born in London, the third son of John Warner (1663–1721), goldsmith and banker, in business in the Strand, near Temple Bar. John Warner, sheriff of London in 1640, and lord mayor in 1648, in which year he was knighted, was probably his great-grandfather. His father was a friend of Bishop Burnet and with his brother Robert, a barrister, purchased property in Clerkenwell, comprising what was afterwards Little Warner Street, Cold Bath Square, Great and Little Bath streets, and the surrounding area. In 1722 after his father's death, Richard Warner's mother bought Harts, an estate at Woodford, Essex, which, at her death in 1743, she left to him. On the death of his brother Robert about 1765 he also inherited the Clerkenwell property.

Warner entered Wadham College, Oxford, in July 1730 and graduated BA in 1734. He was

> bred to the law, and for some time had chambers in Lincoln's Inn; but, being possessed of an ample fortune, resided chiefly at a good old house [built 1617 by Sir Humphrey Handforth, master of the wardrobe to James I; demolished

1815] at Woodford Green, where he maintained a botanical garden, and was very successful in the cultivation of rare exotics.   (Nichols, 75)

Little, except a few trees and the remains of a mock ruin, survives. He was 'also in his youth, as is related of the great Linnaeus … remarkably fond of dancing; nor, till his passion for that diversion subsided, did he convert the largest room in his house into a library' (R. Pulteney, *Historical and Biographical Sketches of the Progress of Botany in England*, 1790, 2.283).

In 1748 Pehr Kalm, a pupil of Linnaeus, then on his way to collect plants in North America, visited Warner at Harts. Warner took him to London, to Peter Collinson's garden at Peckham, to visit Philip Miller at Chelsea, and to see the aged Sir Hans Sloane. In 1754 Warner received from the Cape of Good Hope the so-called Cape jasmine, actually the gardenia, a double-flowered form of a Chinese species, which flowered for the first time in his hot-house four years later. In a letter to Linnaeus, John Ellis (1710?–1776) proposed that it should be called *Warneria*. Warner, however, objected because his friend Miller believed it to be a true jasmine, and Ellis named it *Gardenia*, now correctly *G. augusta* (Rubiaceae). Miller dedicated a genus based on the North American goldenseal to him in 1760, but that had been given the name *Hydrastis* by Linnaeus in the previous year, and so is known by that name.

Up until 1766 Warner, who had copies of all four early folio printings, had 'been long making collections for a new edition of Shakespeare; but on Mr [George] Steevens's advertisement of his design … he desisted' (Nichols, 75). In 1768 he published *A letter to David Garrick, esq., concerning a glossary to the plays of Shakespeare … to which is annexed a specimen*. Although turning aside to other studies, Warner was employed 'to the last hour of his life' on this glossary, and bequeathed all papers relating to it to his 'friend David Garrick, esq. of Adelphi Buildings', that they might be published, and the profits, if any, applied to a fund for decayed actors. In a codicil, however, he left the papers absolutely at Garrick's disposal, and gave £40 to the fund. Two manuscripts of this glossary, one in fifty-one quarto volumes, and the other in twenty octavo volumes, with an interleaved copy of Tonson's edition of Shakespeare (1734), with numerous manuscript notes by Warner, the original manuscript of the *Letter to Garrick*, and an alphabetical index of words requiring explanation in the plays of Beaumont and Fletcher, are now in the British Library (Add. MSS 10464–10543).

Warner also translated several plays of Plautus into prose, and the *Captives* into verse, before the announcement of Bonnell Thornton's version. In the preface to the two volumes published in 1766 Thornton writes that Warner,

to whom I was then a stranger, was pleased to decline all thoughts which he had before conceived of prosecuting the same intention … communicating to me whatever he thought might be of service. … The same gentleman also took upon himself the trouble of translating the life of our author from Petrus Crinitus.

On Thornton's death in May 1768 Warner issued a revised

edition of the two volumes (1769), and then continued the work, translating fourteen plays and issuing them in three additional volumes, two published in 1772, and the last in 1774, the continuation being dedicated to Garrick.

Meanwhile Warner had, in 1771, printed his best-known work, *Plantae Woodfordienses: Catalogue of … Plants Growing Spontaneously about Woodford*. This little book had its origin in the 'herborisations' of the Apothecaries' Company, to the master, wardens, and court of assistants of which it is dedicated. An index of Linnaean names is added. Though by no means free of errors, the *Plantae Woodfordienses* served as a model for Edward Jacob's *Plantae Favershamienses* (1777), and in 1784 Thomas Furly Forster thought it worthwhile to print some thirteen pages of 'Additions'. In one of his own copies of the book, now at Wadham College, Warner had made several additions for an intended reissue.

Warner died, unmarried, on 11 April 1775, at Harts, and was buried on the 20th in the churchyard of St Mary's, Woodford Green, being probably, as stated in the register, 'aged 62', and not, as stated on his tomb, sixty-four. He bequeathed the bulk of his property to Jervoise Clarke-Jervoise, the widower of his niece Katherine (Kitty), second child of his brother Robert. Having been elected a director of the East India Company in 1760, he left 'as is customary', £100 to its hospital at Poplar, £50 to Garrick, and all books and drawings relating to botany and natural history to Wadham College, with £300 to found a botanical exhibition at the college. Warner's books (over 4000 volumes), now at Wadham, comprise, besides several valuable botanical works, including presentation copies of Miller's works and other items from Miller's library, interleaved copies of Shakespeare, the works of Spenser, Milton, and Beaumont and Fletcher, and some small collections of dried plants of little intrinsic value. A collection of mosses and lichens made by him was presented by Sir Jervoise Clarke-Jervoise to the Essex Field Club.

G. S. BOULGER, rev. D. J. MABBERLEY

Sources G. S. Boulger, 'Richard Warner, 1711–1775', *Essex Naturalist*, 20 (1923–4), 206–17, 245–8 · S. Eames, *Harts and flowers* (1989) · G. D. R. Bridson, V. C. Phillips, and A. P. Harvey, *Natural history manuscript resources in the British Isles* (1980) · B. Henrey, *No ordinary gardener: Thomas Knowlton, 1691–1781*, ed. A. O. Chater (1986) · O. Pointer, 'The library', *Wadham College*, ed. C. S. L. Davies and J. Garnett (1994), 92–9 · will, Wadham College, Oxford · Nichols, *Lit. anecdotes*, vol. 3
Archives BL · Hants. RO, corresp. and papers relating to Hampshire history · Wadham College, Oxford, drawings and papers
Likenesses oils, priv. coll.
Wealth at death see will, Wadham College, Oxford

Warner, Richard (1763–1857), antiquary, was born on 18 October 1763 at St Marylebone, Middlesex, the only son of Richard Warner, a tradesman prosperous enough to retire about 1776 to Lymington in Hampshire as a gentleman with a substantial house. Lymington was dominated by the family of the younger Richard's friend Sir Henry Burrard Neale (1765–1840). Warner attended Christchurch grammar school and familiarized himself with the New Forest and its antiquities: he even excavated some barrows. He intended to enter the church, but his chosen route—from Winchester College to New College, Oxford, and a fellowship—proved unattainable. Only in 1787, after a period spent in an attorney's office, did he enter St Mary's Hall, Oxford; he left after eight terms without a degree, apparently to take up a curacy at Boldre, Hampshire. Here he served under the Revd William Gilpin (1724–1804), an enthusiastic walker and admirer of New Forest scenery, who could no longer minister to his parishioners himself. Gilpin became a close friend, a fatherly patron, and a formative literary influence. Since the bishop of Winchester, Brownlow North, would not ordain a non-graduate, Warner was ordained instead by Archbishop William Markham of York. He served three months as curate of Wales, near Doncaster, before returning to Boldre. About 1793 he became curate of Fawley, the valuable living of the Revd Henry Drummond of Cadland.

Warner's early publications were prodigious, if ephemeral. Unlike his mentor, Gilpin, his interests were antiquarian rather than picturesque. He wanted fame, but also wrote for money. Although his *Companion in a Tour Round Lymington* (1789) lost him £22 5s., he followed it immediately with a translation of the Hampshire Domesday, published in the same year. His *Southampton Guide* (1790) made a profit of £5, but his *Antiquitates culinariae* (1791) involved him in costs and damages of £70 for pirating a print. His scholarly *Attempt to Ascertain the Site of the Ancient Clausentum* (1792) was followed by his two-volume *Topographical Remarks on the South-Western Parts of Hampshire* (1793), his brief 'General view of the agriculture of the Isle of Wight' in the larger Hampshire volume (1794), and, in 1795, *A History of the Isle of Wight*. In the same year, he published a Gothic novel about Netley Abbey, which was well received (as were the four preceding publications). He also proposed a full-scale three-volume history of Hampshire, but although there were enough subscribers by 1793, he abandoned the project on grounds of expense. Warner's so-called *History of Hampshire* of 1795 was in fact the worthless compilation of another anonymous author.

In 1794 Warner became the first minister of All Saints, Bath, a curacy of Walcot, before moving next year to the officiating ministership of St James's, Bath, a curacy of Bath Abbey, where he remained until 1817. At once he immersed himself in the history, environs, and literary society of Bath, where he became a prominent figure and a frequent correspondent in the *Bath Journal*. The town's neglected Roman past stimulated his *Illustrations of the Roman Antiquities at Bath* (1797) and his full-scale *History of Bath* in 1801.

Warner's vacation in August 1796 was spent in Wales, walking from Bath to Caernarfon and back; he covered 36 miles on the first day and 462 miles in all, at an average of 26 miles a day. Naturally his tour included visits to antiquities, which he described in a series of eighteen letters, published as *A Walk through Wales* in 1797. Emboldened by the popularity of this work, he published works based on walks in Wales, the south-west, and the borders in 1798–1802; these reached further and even foreign editions.

Warner's marriage to Ann (*née* Pearson) in 1801 and fatherhood in 1802 may henceforth have focused his attention once again on Bath: in 1807–9 he published three satirical volumes on local society, under the pseudonyms of Peter Paul Pallet and Thomas Goosequill.

Warner 'distinguished himself by his worthy endeavour to inculcate rational piety' (*GM*, 1st ser., 100/1, 1830, 612): St James's Church was always crowded, and his sermons were 'models of pulpit eloquence'. Starting with a *Chronological History of our Lord and Saviour: an English Diatessaron* (1803), his religious publications included practical discourses, sermons, companions, and introductions. He was a political reformer, a supporter of Fox and the 1832 Reform Act. As an opponent of the younger Pitt, in 1804 he gave the sermon 'War inconsistent with Christianity' to volunteers destined for service abroad. Warner objected to evangelicalism for encouraging disrespect to the church:

> I conceive the *Evangelical Clergy* as a body of the established priesthood, separating themselves from their brethren of the ministry, by the arrogant claim of an exclusive *knowledge of the Gospel*, and as a sole right to be considered as *evangelical* preachers.   (*Letter to the Hon. and Rt Rev. Henry Ryder*, 15)

He also opposed Catholic emancipation, belittling the supposed ills of Catholics under Britain's constitution. From 1824 he found a sympathetic patron in Dr George Law (*d*. 1845), bishop of Bath and Wells.

According to the Revd Joseph Hunter, the Unitarian minister of Bath and a fellow antiquary, Warner's 'liberality of sentiment … stood in the way of his advancement' (BL, Add. MS 26527 fol. 134). He remained at Bath on presentation in 1809 by Burrard Neale to Great Chalfield rectory, worth only £62 a year, but resigned his curacy on presentation to Norton St Philip with Hinton Charterhouse in 1817. After remaining there only a year, he lived at Widcombe Cottage, Bath, from 1818 to 1822, when he let it to reside briefly at Great Chalfield. He moved subsequently to Newton St Loe (1822–7), Coltard, near Pensford (1827), and Castle Cary (1830). Surviving letters to Hunter illuminate his work on his *History of…Glaston: and…Town of Glastonbury* (1826), which he dedicated to Bishop Law. Law collated him in 1825–7 in turn to Timberscombe (worth £222), Croscombe (£170), and Chelwood by Bath (£200), where he apparently resided from 1833 to 1847. Though retaining Great Chalfield and Chelwood rectories until his death, Warner had retired by 1848 and died on 27 July 1857 at his home, Widcombe Cottage, Chelwood, where his long-blind widow died in 1865. He was buried on 11 August 1857 in Chelwood church. Of the Warners' two daughters, Ellen Rebecca died in 1833 and Elizabeth Sophia outlived them both.

Warner wrote with great facility and parade of learning, but his works were commercial rather than scholarly, and as such were often derivative and inaccurate. Hunter observed that 'he was deep in no subject. He had read little, made no particular preparations for publication, and began to read in a subject only when he had previously determined to publish upon it' (BL, Add. MS 26527, fol.

134). His histories of Bath and Glastonbury were useful compilations, but they left their subjects as Warner had found them.   MICHAEL HICKS

Sources DNB · R. Warner, *Literary recollections*, 2 vols. (1830) · W. F. Perkins, 'Parson Warner and Parsons Gilpin and Woodforde', Hants. RO, 14M86/1 · review of 'Literary recollections by Rev. Richard Warner', *GM*, 1st ser., 100/1 (1830), 612–15 · *GM*, 3rd ser., 4 (1858), 101–4 · M. A. Hicks, 'Hampshire and the Isle of Wight', *English county histories: a guide*, ed. C. Currie and C. Lewis (1994), 165–75 · R. Warner, *A walk through Wales in August 1797* (1797) · R. Warner, preface, *An history of the abbey of Glaston: and of the town of Glastonbury* (1826), i–xvi · R. Warner, preface, *The history of Bath* (1801), v–vi · *Original letters from Richard Baxter*, ed. R. Warner (1817) · R. Warner, *A letter to the Hon. and Rt Rev. Henry Ryder, D.D., lord bishop of Gloucester* (1818) · will of Richard Warner, PRO, PROB 11 · will of Ann Warner, Principal Registry of the Family Division, London · d. cert.
Archives Bath Central Library, diary and letters incl. to Sir George Burnard · BL, corresp. and papers, Add. MSS 24876, 33836, 34585, 42780A · Bodl. Oxf., corresp. · Hants. RO | Bodl. Oxf., corresp. with Sir Thomas Phillipps
Likenesses S. Harding, stipple, 1801 (after J. Williams), BM, NPG; repro. in R. Warner, *History of Bath* · Condé, engraving (after miniature by Engleheart) · L. Haghe, lithograph (after S. C. Smith), BM · J. Hibbert, engraving (after portrait by Bell)
Wealth at death under £7000: will, Ann Warner, Principal Registry of the Family Division, London

Warner, Samuel Alfred (1793/4–1853), charlatan, was born at Heathfield, Sussex, the son of William Warner, a carpenter. His own fanciful account of his early years was contradicted by information later confided to Sir Robert Peel when Peel was becoming convinced of Warner's deceit (BL, Add. MS 40555, fol. 160): this revealed that Warner's family resided at Faversham, but that he and his father were often away for long periods and were known locally as smugglers; and that Samuel Warner became friendly with a chemist in Holborn named Garrald whom he persuaded to move to Camberwell, where, perhaps, they devised around 1819 an explosive other than gunpowder for the so-called 'invisible shell'. This appears to have been a submerged mine which detonated when a passing ship entangled and dragged on a line attached to the charge.

Warner then entered the service of Emperor Dom Pedro of Portugal, taking part in 1832–3 in the defence of Oporto (from which time he styled himself 'Captain'). This episode was confirmed by two British officers who had also been there and who asserted that Warner had tried unsuccessfully to sell Dom Pedro his invisible shell. On his return Warner determined on selling his invention to the British government. News of the invisible shell reached a Mr Lufkin of the War Office and ultimately came to the ear of William IV. The 'sailor king' invited Warner to discussions and encouraged his ministers and sea lords to investigate the whole affair. Demonstrations were arranged and assorted experts gave evidence to several parliamentary select committees. Warner's own testimony involved a rambling account of an expedition on board his father's ship *Nautilus* during the late war, when it had been hired by the British government for undercover operations against the French; he claimed to have devised the shell

around 1819, and with it to have sunk two French privateers, leaving no survivors. However, the most diligent government enquiries failed to find trace of any such vessel or its logbook, or of the Warners' being hired for any such operations, or indeed of any prize money being claimed for sinking enemy ships.

As the experts failed to agree on the value of Warner's supposed invention, and one committee followed another, Warner became more truculent. He refused to demonstrate the shell before those whom he suspected of opposing him and he wrote boasting or defiant letters to various influential men and to the editor of *The Times*. The government found itself in a predicament: should Warner be ignored as just another impostor, or did he really have a secret of immense military value which must on no account fall into enemy hands? Warner refused to disclose the nature of his invention without a promise of £200,000 should the device be found acceptable; the government refused to make any such promise ahead of disclosure. Warner threatened and wheedled, ministers declared their wish to see him treated fairly, but neither party was willing to budge from its entrenched position. More demonstrations were arranged; in February 1841 a party including Sir Robert Peel, Sir George Murray, Sir Henry Hardinge, Sir Francis Burdett, Viscount Ingestre, and Colonel Goodwood gathered by a lake in Essex where Warner blew up a small boat, without allowing the onlookers to see how it was done.

In 1844 Warner advertised in the newspapers his intention to demonstrate his shell off Brighton. On 17 July a huge crowd, swelled by many MPs and Londoners brought there by excursion train, lined the cliffs to watch a tug steam into view, towing the target vessel which, at a signal from shore, blew up and sank in full view of the spectators. The event was colourfully described and pictured in the *Illustrated London News*. Members of parliament could not, however, agree on the value of what they had seen, for there was no clue as to where the charge had been laid or how it had been fired. Their doubts were fuelled by rumours from Shoreham harbour that the tug and target vessel had been connected by many underwater ropes, and moreover that timbers washed ashore from the wreck were found to have been sawn through as if to weaken the target's structure.

Warner's principal supporter at this time was Viscount Ingestre, who on 31 July delivered a long speech to the House of Commons arguing that the government had a duty to reach an agreement with the inventor. In the other camp was an equally vocal opponent, Lord Howard Douglas (author of the standard treatise on naval gunnery) who thought that Warner's invisible shell sounded remarkably like that described in print in 1821 by Montgéry, a French naval officer.

Warner then claimed to have invented in 1835 what he termed his 'long-range', which could deliver a shell onto a target such as an enemy fortress several miles distant. His price for disclosing the secret of this useful device was also £200,000. Eventually the government conceded a sum of under £2000 towards his expenses in preparing a demonstration. Peel and his advisers assumed that the long-range was a fired missile but when ordnance experts attended the demonstration they found that the shell was to be delivered by balloon. It later emerged that Warner, under an assumed name, had arranged with the noted balloonist Charles Green to provide and launch a balloon for trial. This balloon had risen to a great height and burst, but when the wreckage was examined, the gunpowder was still unexploded. Not surprisingly, Green was never paid for his contribution. When the government-funded demonstration took place in August 1846 before the appointed observers, the balloon was seen to trace an erratic path aloft, dropping shot from time to time, a delivery clearly so inaccurate and beyond control as to have no military value whatsoever. By May 1847 Peel and Douglas were describing Warner as a charlatan and impostor and most of the house agreed with them. Warner then found a new supporter in Lord Talbot, who, as the editor of the *United Service Magazine* remarked in the course of a blistering attack on Warner, his fabulous early life and his absurd demands that he 'like Frankenstein—has breathed life into this invisible shell. After the judgements of the Duke of Wellington, Sir Howard Douglas, Sir Byam Martin, Colonel Chalmer, and Captain Chads how could anyone be so credulous of Warner's claims' (Lord Talbot, 276–83).

The last committee to be appointed never reported. On 5 December 1853 Warner, resilient to the last, died suddenly of apoplexy at 1 Bloomfield Place, Pimlico, London, leaving a 'widow' and seven children destitute. He was buried in Brompton cemetery on 10 December, the cost of his funeral being met by a George Smith, and the local curate did his best to raise money for the support of his family. Even this family was not what it appeared to be, for Warner's real wife was found to be living on parish relief in Ashford, Kent, and one of his daughters was married to a clerk in the Stationery Office. The author of his obituary in the *Gentleman's Magazine* described him as 'one of those monomaniacs who after repeated attempts to deceive others, are at length supremely successful in deceiving themselves ... [He] maintained to the last that he was possessed of the secret of an explosive compound much more powerful than any in known use'. Few such impostors have, however, succeeded in playing successive governments on such a slender line for more than twenty years.

ANITA MCCONNELL

Sources *Hansard 3* (1844), 76.1578–623; (1847), 93.921–46 · 'Copy of correspondence between her majesty's government and Captain Warner', *Parl. papers* (1844), 33.419–88, no. 620 · 'Correspondence with her majesty's government on Mr Warner's inventions', *Parl. papers* (1846), 26.499–517, no. 351 · 'Copy of report of officers appointed to make a trial of Mr Warner's long-range', *Parl. papers* (1847), 36.473, no. 165 · *GM*, 2nd ser., 41 (1854), 549–51 · corresp. with Warner, BL, Peel MSS, Add. MS 40473 · BL, Peel MSS, Add. MS 40555, fol. 160 · Abstract of corresp. on Warner, BL, Byam Martin MSS, Add. MS 41369 · [Lord Talbot], 'Captain Warner's inventions', *Colburn's United Service Magazine*, 2 (1852) · *The Times* (10 Aug 1844), 6e · *The Times* (21 Aug 1844), 7c · *The Times* (29 Aug 1844), 6f · *The Times* (22 May 1852), 7c · *The Times* (9 Dec 1853), 7e · *The Times* (21 Dec 1853), 8d · d. cert.

Archives BL, corresp. with Sir Robert Peel, Add. MSS 40473–40579

Warner, (Nora) Sylvia Townsend (1893–1978), writer, was born on 6 December 1893 at Dame Armstrong's House, Church Hill, Harrow on the Hill, Middlesex, the only child of George Townsend Warner (1865–1916), a history master and head of the 'modern side' at Harrow School, and his wife, Eleanor Mary (1866–1950), *née* Hudleston. She received no formal education after kindergarten age, but was tutored by various masters at Harrow, including her own father, who developed her intellectual gifts to a high level, and the distinguished musician Percy *Buck (1871–1947), with whom she had a long-term, though secret, love affair for seventeen years. Warner's early career as a musicologist, a member of the editorial board (chaired by R. R. Terry) which published the first scholarly editions of *Tudor Church Music* (Clarendon Press, 1923–9), was gradually overtaken by the success she found as a writer. She began writing poetry in the early 1920s, at the same period as she made pivotal friendships with the writers David Garnett and T. F. Powys, the latter of whom she helped to get published. Warner's own first book, a collection of poems called *The Espalier*, appeared in 1925, and her first novel, *Lolly Willowes*, came out in the following year. The mixture of fantasy and acerbic wit in this story of a disregarded woman who turns to witchcraft as the only practical way of asserting herself had a wide appeal and the book was a considerable success. Her next novel, *Mr Fortune's Maggot* (1927), told the story of a missionary who manages to lose his own faith rather than make converts among a group of south sea islanders.

Warner's friendship with T. F. Powys made her a frequent visitor to his home in East Chaldon, Dorset, and she moved to the village in 1930 when she fell in love with the poet Valentine Ackland [see Ackland, Mary Kathleen Macrory-]. Their connection with the county—where they spent the rest of their lives, with the exception of a sixteen-month residence in Norfolk—has been recognized in a permanent exhibition at Dorset County Museum, where the archives of both women are kept. In 1937 Warner and Ackland moved to a small riverside house in Frome Vauchurch (where Warner was able to cultivate her passion for gardening). The domestic life of the two writers, in essence a thirty-eight year marriage, is documented in hundreds of letters they wrote to each other which, put in order by Warner after Valentine's death from cancer in 1969, and finally published in 1998 under the title *I'll Stand By You*, constitute an extraordinary lesbian love story.

Besides *Lolly Willowes*, *Mr Fortune's Maggot*, and *The True Heart* (1929), a romance based on the myth of Cupid and Psyche, Warner wrote four novels on historical themes, including a *tour de force*, *The Corner that Held them*, about life in a medieval Norfolk nunnery (1948) and *The Flint Anchor* (1954), a complex family saga set in a Norfolk fishing town in the 1840s. *Summer will Show*, a novel set in the 1848 revolution in Paris, had personal resonances. The story of the heroine's gradual involvement in revolutionary politics

(Nora) **Sylvia Townsend Warner** (1893–1978), by Sir Cecil Beaton, 1930

White's journals and letters (1946), and a highly praised life of T. H. White (1967). In the mid-1950s she was involved in the project to translate the last volume of Proust's *A la recherche du temps perdu* which led to her making the first English translation of the same author's essays, *Contre Sainte-Beuve* (1958). She was a fellow of the Royal Society of Literature, an honorary member of the American Academy of Arts and Letters, and won the prix Menton in 1969 for her story 'A Love Match'.

Warner's originality and her detachment from any literary school have tended to an undervaluing of her achievement in general, but posterity may well regard her as one of the great belletrists of the century. Since her death in 1978, her *Selected Stories* (1988), *Collected Poems* (1982), *Diaries* (1994), and perhaps most of all, her *Letters* (edited by William Maxwell, 1982) have impressed readers with their intelligence and precision. As an English prose stylist she has few rivals, and as a humane and unsentimental observer of life she can always be trusted to produce, in Maxwell's words, 'everything exactly as it is'.

She died at her home, Riverside, Lower Frome Vauchurch, Maiden Newton, Dorset, on 1 May 1978, and her ashes were buried at St Nicholas's Church, East Chaldon, three days later.   CLAIRE HARMAN

Sources C. Harman, *Sylvia Townsend Warner: a biography* (1989) · *The letters of Sylvia Townsend Warner*, ed. W. Maxwell (1982) · *The diaries of Sylvia Townsend Warner*, ed. C. Harman (1994) · W. Mulford, *This narrow place: Sylvia Townsend Warner and Valentine Ackland, life, letters and politics 1930–1951* (1988) · *The Guardian* (5 Jan 1977) · *DNB* · Dorset County Museum, S. T. Warner and V. Ackland MSS · b. cert. · d. cert.

Archives Dorset County Museum, Dorchester, S. T. Warner and V. Ackland collection, corresp. and papers incl. diaries and notebooks · Ransom HRC, corresp. and literary papers · Yale U., Beinecke L. | U. Leeds, Brotherton L., letters to Norah Smallwood · U. Reading, Chatto & Windus Archive, letters to Helen Thomas · U. Sussex Library, corresp. with Leonard Woolf

Likenesses C. Beaton, three photographs, 1930, NPG [*see illus.*] · H. Coster, photograph, 1934, NPG · J. Finzi, pencil drawing, 1960, U. Reading L. · C. Beaton, photograph, Sothebys archive, London

Wealth at death £171,239: probate, 12 Sept 1978, *CGPLA Eng. & Wales*

in some part mirrors Warner's own espousal of communism in 1935, to which she was actively and enthusiastically committed for many years. She and Ackland went to Barcelona during the Spanish Civil War in 1936 to work with the Red Cross and in 1937 were delegates at the International Writers' Conference in Madrid. Though Ackland later renounced communism, Warner's political sympathies remained strongly left-wing, and she was for some years a member of the executive committee of the Association of Writers for Intellectual Liberty. *After the Death of Don Juan* (1938), an allegory of the rise of fascism in Spain derived from the opera by Mozart and Da Ponte, also reflects Warner's politics.

Warner wrote poetry all her life, publishing *Time Importuned* in 1928, *Opus 7* in 1931, *Whether a Dove or Seagull* (with Valentine Ackland) in 1933, and *Boxwood* (with engravings by Reynolds Stone, 1957), but became most widely known from the 1930s onwards for her short stories. A long-lasting association with the *New Yorker* magazine ensured a wide readership for her fiction, by means of which she was able to explore many aspects of contemporary life, especially civilian life in wartime and the years following. Her short stories reached a level of great stylistic and interpretive power, culminating in the collection *The Innocent and the Guilty* (1971) and her highly unconventional moral fables *Kingdoms of Elfin* (1977). 'I hope some of it will annoy people', she said, 'because that is the surest way of being attended to.'

Warner was a perceptive critic and editor, producing a short study of Jane Austen (1951), a selection from Gilbert

Warner, Sir Thomas (*c*.1580–1649), colonial governor, was a younger son of William Warner, landowner, and Margaret, daughter of George Gernigan or Jerningham of Belsted, Suffolk. It is likely that Thomas Warner was born at Parham, in Suffolk, where his father owned land.

Very little is known of Thomas Warner's early life. By 1610 he had married Sarah, daughter of Walter Snelling of Dorchester. They had two children: Mary and Edward [*see below*]. Warner served as a captain in James I's bodyguard and as lieutenant of the Tower of London before embarking for Guiana on 30 April 1620 with Captain Roger North. The charter of North's Amazon Company was revoked by James I after Spanish protests and North was recalled and gaoled in the Tower. His colonists were left to fend for themselves. By this point Warner had met Thomas Painton, who impressed on him the advantages of a colony on one of the smaller Caribbean islands, principally St Kitts. The chief advantage was that small islands were less likely than a mainland colony to attract Spanish attention. In

1622 Warner left Guiana for England. On the way he visited several Caribbean islands including St Kitts, where he made the acquaintance of the Carib 'King Tegreman [or Tegramond], king of St Christophers', and settled on that island as a likely spot for a plantation (Hilton, 2).

Settlement of St Kitts, 1623–1626 After returning to Suffolk, Warner enlisted the support of Charles Jeaffreson, a neighbour and friend, and Ralph Merifield (or Merrifield), a merchant of London. In 1623 Warner, his wife (presumably Sarah), son Edward (aged thirteen), and about fourteen others, mostly from Suffolk, sailed for Virginia and from there to St Kitts, where they landed on 28 January 1624. The colonists set to work planting tobacco but their first crop was destroyed by a hurricane in September, which also carried away most of their houses. Their second crop was ready by February of the following year, and on 18 March 1625 Jeaffreson arrived in the *Hopewell* with men and provisions sent by Merifield. In September 1625 (either in the *Hopewell* or the *Black Bess* of Flushing) Warner returned to England with a cargo of tobacco. It may have been while in England that he married his second wife, Rebecca, daughter of Thomas Payne of Surrey; they had two sons, Thomas and Philip *Warner, an army officer.

While Warner was absent a French privateer commanded by Pierre Belan, sieur d'Esnambuc, stopped at St Kitts badly damaged and in need of refitting. The French were welcomed to the island, and their desire to establish a colony there was seconded by the English, most likely because of fear of the island's Carib population. It is also possible that the English recognized some French claim to prior possession: when Warner's first party arrived on St Kitts there was at least one Frenchman already living on the island and perhaps more. After the French colony was begun the combined French and English forces (who in Thomas's absence were under the command of his son Edward) fought off two concerted attacks by Caribs from St Kitts and neighbouring islands, in November and December 1625.

While in England, Warner secured royal recognition and protection for his colony, receiving on 13 September 1625 the first letters patent for a West Indian colony and the title of lieutenant of St Kitts, Nevis, Barbados, and Montserrat. In the grant St Kitts is also referred to as 'Merwar's Hope', a name derived from the first letters of Merifield and Warner, but the name never caught on. After securing his patent, title, more investment, and letters of marque, Warner left England for St Kitts. With him were the London merchant Maurice Thompson, about 100 colonists, and sixty slaves. Along the way Warner's small fleet of three ships took some Spanish prizes in the North Sea and the channel before unsuccessfully attacking the Spanish in Trinidad.

Treaty with the French and war with the Caribs, 1626–1629 Warner reached St Kitts in August 1626. Soon afterward an Indian woman (some sources suggest this may have been the same with whom Warner had an illegitimate son, Thomas *Warner, known as Indian Warner), warned him of another impending attack by the Caribs. In a pre-

emptive strike French and English forces surprised the island's original inhabitants at night, killing Tegreman and expelling all survivors from the island except an unknown number of women retained as slaves. After killing or driving off the Caribs, St Kitts's French and English settlers concluded a formal treaty on 13 May 1627 that divided the island and defined the relationship between the two groups. The treaty awarded each end of the island to the French and the middle portion to the English. The treaty also provided for mutual defence against Spanish or Carib attack and dictated neutrality in a European war unless expressly forbidden by each government, and only then after a warning had been given.

In June 1627 Warner's patent was replaced by a proprietary charter granted to James Hay, first earl of Carlisle, which offered the island's planters secure title to their lands and assistance in defending the island in exchange for a substantial rent. Although Warner's own patent was voided, as *de facto* governor he was diligent in furthering the earl's interests. During the late 1620s the population of St Kitts grew steadily in number, wealth, and importance, bolstered by a steady supply of migrants. Captain John Smith relates the arrival of Warner's wife in 1627, presumably his second wife, Rebecca; it is not known when she died, but at some point Warner married Anne, whose background is unknown. They had no children. As St Kitts became more populous and prosperous Warner oversaw the expansion of English settlements in the Leeward Islands: to Nevis in 1628 and Montserrat and Antigua about 1632. Montserrat was settled largely by the numerous Irish migrants to the Caribbean, and Antigua was first governed by Warner's son Edward.

Conflict with French and Spanish, 1630–1636 By 1629 the demands of the increasing English population for land had begun to sour relations with the French of St Kitts, who complained of encroachments on their territory. Relief arrived in August of that year, when Esnambuc returned to St Kitts accompanied by six ships of the line and 300 colonists. Esnambuc demanded that the English abandon French lands they had settled and, after seizing some English merchant ships, compelled the acting governor, Edward Warner (Warner had left for England in September or November 1628), to submit.

Unfortunately for the planters of St Kitts, the French fleet did not linger long, and in September 1629 an overwhelming Spanish force under Don Fadrique de Toledo attacked and laid waste to the island. After a brief fight many of the French colonists managed to escape to St Martin, and Edward Warner surrendered the English forces to the Spanish. Under the generous terms of surrender most of the island's settlers were allowed to return to England, but many retreated inland instead. After the Spanish withdrew, these colonists elected a governor and set about rebuilding. They were soon joined by returning French settlers and later by Warner, who had been knighted in England on 21 September, no doubt in recognition of his services since the void of his patent; a week later, on 29 September, Carlisle named him as governor of St Kitts for life. Since the island had been surrendered to the Spanish,

Warner was forced to renegotiate the rents owed to the earl (who had provided little or no protection from the Spanish). But despite his strained relationship with the planters, Warner resumed control.

Dissent, 1636–1639 After the death of the first earl of Carlisle in 1636 loyalties among the English settlements in the Caribbean became tangled and strained. St Kitts and the rest of the Carlisle patent (which included the Leewards, St Vincent, St Lucia, and Barbados) were caught up in the disputes between the second earl of Carlisle and his father's creditors. Warner, ever loyal to the first earl, was appointed lieutenant-general of all colonies under the Carlisle patent, but his authority was openly challenged by Henry Hawley, governor of Barbados, who refused to supply men from Barbados for Warner's plans to expand settlement in the Antilles.

In May 1639, acting in keeping with royal policy, Warner entered an agreement with Chevalier Phillippe de Longvilliers de Poincy, governor-general of all French island possessions, to ban tobacco cultivation in the islands for eighteen months. The policy was intended to prop up tobacco prices and force planters to diversify their crops. Although the French planters resumed tobacco cultivation after the term expired, tobacco planting in the English islands was banned for an additional twelve months, until 1 October 1641. During this period planters' debts increased, their servants' terms expired, and their plantations yielded them no marketable commodity. After they were allowed to resume planting, landholders faced the prospect of paying back-rent to the proprietor in addition to managing their increased debt burden and the need to pay for new servants. Since he re-established control in 1630 Warner had managed to rule St Kitts with an appointed council and without consulting the island's planters. But given the financial pressures on planters and Warner's staunch support for the proprietor's demand for rents, the situation soon became explosive.

Civil war in St Kitts, 1641–1649 In late 1641 the island's planters rebelled and in early 1642 Warner and his council declared martial law and imprisoned some of the leaders of the rising, succeeding briefly in regaining control. Rebellion flared again after Warner's council executed a man named Short for defaming John Jeaffreson, an old ally and a member of the council. On 8 February 1642, facing some 1500 armed rebels to his 100 supporters, Warner was presented with the landholders' grievances. Among other things the island's planters refused to pay rent to the proprietor and refused to acknowledge laws passed without their consent. Warner issued a general pardon on 11 February and soon afterwards the island elected its first assembly of burgesses, which began drafting new laws regarding the payment of rents and debt relief.

But Warner refused to share power with a representative assembly and by the end of 1642 he was back in complete control of the island. How he managed this is unclear, but Bennett suggests he may have had help from the French. The burgesses were dispersed: some were executed, some imprisoned, and some banished. Others had fled. Once the Antilles came under parliamentary control, Warner was rewarded with an appointment (on 4 November 1643) as governor and lieutenant-general of the Caribbee Islands under Robert Rich, earl of Warwick. This grant would be confirmed when the patent passed to Lord Willoughby of Parham, and Warner's position as the chief official in the British West Indies and the unquestioned ruler of St Kitts would continue until his death.

As a colonial governor and investor Warner was remarkably successful. Compared with other islands, St Kitts under his leadership was relatively stable and quickly profitable. In 1639 Warner estimated that the island generated £12,000 in fees and duties. Further, he survived many political changes, remaining virtually synonymous with the government of St Kitts from its founding until his death. His inflexible rule and powerful connections spared his colony the turmoil experienced by Barbados, but he also unwittingly contributed to the declining importance of the island among the British West Indian colonies. By the time the sugar revolution had come to Barbados, St Kitts's small landholdings, depleted soil, lack of credit, and high population density made it unsuitable for sugar plantation, and it forever faded in importance in comparison. Warner died on 10 March 1649 and was buried in the churchyard of St Thomas, Middle Island, St Kitts. His wife Anne outlived him by over forty years and died between 16 July 1692 and 27 February 1693.

Edward Warner (*b.* 1609/10), colonial governor, Sir Thomas's eldest son, travelled with his father on the initial voyage to St Kitts and acted as deputy governor of that colony during his father's frequent absences. Hilton describes him as 'young in yeares, & as yett not ensighted in government' but innocent of the plottings of his advisers (which in one case included murder): he was 'always of a loving, affable, tender disposicion' (Hilton, 6–7). In 1632 he was appointed by Sir Thomas the first governor of Antigua. Very little else is known of his life except that his wife and child are said to have been carried away from Antigua by Caribs in 1640. This tragedy is said to have contributed to his early death, the date of which is unknown.   MICHAEL A. LaCOMBE

Sources A. Warner, *Sir Thomas Warner: pioneer of the West Indies* (1933) • J. A. Williamson, *The Caribbee Islands under the proprietary patents* (1926) • V. T. Harlow, ed., *Colonising expeditions to the West Indies and Guiana, 1623–1667* (1925) • J. Hilton, 'Relation', *Colonising expeditions to the West Indies and Guiana, 1623–1667*, ed. V. T. Harlow (1925) • A. C. Burns, *History of the British West Indies*, 2nd edn (1965), 187–95, 768–80 • J. H. Bennett, 'The English Caribbees in the period of the civil war, 1642–1646', *William and Mary Quarterly*, 3rd ser., 24 (1967), 359–77 • *Complete works of Captain John Smith*, ed. P. Barbour (1986), vol. 3, pp. 224–33 • J.-B. du Tertre, *Histoire generale des Antilles* (Paris, 1667–71), vol. 1 • V. L. Oliver, *More monumental inscriptions* (San Bernardino, 1993), 184–5 • J. H. Lawrence-Archer, *Monumental inscriptions … West Indies* (1875), 409 • *CSP dom.*, 1625–6, 156, 322, 328; 1628–9, 286 • *CSP col.*, 1.75, 80, 101, 240, 294–5, 324; 9.321 • J. Featley, *A sermon preached to … Sir Thomas Warner … Septemb. 6, 1629* (1629) • Suckling, 2.215
Archives NA Scot., corresp. with Sir James Hay and Archibald Hay

Warner, Thomas [*called* Indian Warner] (*c.*1630–1674), colonial governor, was the son of Sir Thomas *Warner (c.1580–1649), colonial governor, and a Carib woman whose name is unknown but who lived from about 1600 to 1700. Warner was raised in his father's household until Sir Thomas's death in 1649, when his stepmother began treating him as a slave. Warner fled St Christopher for Dominica and soon assumed a leading role among that island's Carib settlements. Warner's ability to act as a mediator made him an important figure in England's Caribbean policy. In 1664 he was made governor of Dominica by Francis, Lord Willoughby of Parham. In this position Warner was able to soothe French fears of an English settlement on the island even as he held the title of British governor. During the Second Anglo-Dutch War, however, Warner was imprisoned by the French for two years and freed only after the personal intervention of William, Lord Willoughby, in 1668. Soon after gaining his freedom, Warner negotiated a peace between the English and the Caribs of Dominica, St Vincent, and St Lucia, and was reappointed governor of Dominica by Willoughby.

In retrospect it is impossible to say whether Warner's primary loyalty lay with the English or the Caribs, but English colonists on Antigua were certain that Warner was behind repeated Carib attacks. In December 1674 Antigua's governor, Colonel Philip *Warner (another son of Sir Thomas and therefore Thomas Warner's half-brother), led a controversial expedition against the Indians in Dominica, in the course of which Thomas Warner was killed under mysterious circumstances. An eyewitness accused Philip of luring his brother and many of his Indian allies on board his sloop and massacring them. Other contemporaries defended Philip by claiming that Thomas died in combat, but the circumstances of this battle are itself unclear. Philip's case was a *cause célèbre*: he was accused of murder, taken to England and imprisoned in the Tower, then sent to Barbados, where he was tried and finally cleared of all charges.

MICHAEL A. LACOMBE

Sources P. Hulme and N. Whitehead, eds., *Wild majesty: encounters with Caribs from Columbus to the present day* (1992) · C. S. S. Higham, *The development of the Leeward Islands under the Restoration, 1660–1688: a study of the foundations of the old colonial system* (1921) · A. Warner, *Sir Thomas Warner: pioneer of the West Indies* (1933) · CSP col., 5.535–6, 546, 547–8; 7.330–31, 395–6, 493–5, 495–7, 624–5; 9.154–63, 171, 175–6, 228, 248, 319–21, 333, 336–7, 382–5; 12.638

Warner, Walter (c.1558–1643), mathematician and natural philosopher, was born in Leicestershire. He had at least one brother. He was educated at Oxford, where he graduated BA in 1579. Originally a protégé of Robert Dudley, earl of Leicester, Warner entered the household of Henry Percy, ninth earl of Northumberland, as a gentleman servitor in 1590, and became a pensioner in 1617. Although he was a servant, Warner dined with the earl and his friends, and was a constant companion. While at Syon House, Warner's duties largely concerned the purchase and care of the earl's books and scientific instruments. He accompanied the earl on his military mission to the Low Countries in 1600–01, travelling back and forth across the channel as his confidential messenger.

While Northumberland was imprisoned in the Tower of London (1605–21), Warner brought his books from Syon, and joined in with the learned discussions of the earl and his other mathematical and scientific clients—Thomas Harriot, Robert Hues, and Nathaniel Torporley. Warner's unpublished natural philosophical writings date mainly from this period, and deal with such diverse topics as logic, psychology, animal locomotion, atomism, time and space, the nature of heat and light, bullion and exchange, hydrostatics, chemistry, and the circulation of the blood (which Warner claimed to have discovered before William Harvey). Warner was best known for his work on optics and mathematics. His tract on the sine law was published posthumously as part of Marin Mersenne's *Universae geometriae synopsis* (1644), and his unpublished logarithmical tables were widely held to be a great advance on those of Henry Briggs.

After 1620 Warner lived at the Woolstable in Charing Cross, London, and at Cranborne Lodge, near Windsor, with Sir Thomas Aylesbury, who sponsored his continued work on optics and mathematics. In 1631 Aylesbury encouraged Warner to edit and publish Harriot's treatise on algebra, the *Artis analyticae praxis*, and wrote on his behalf to Northumberland for a reimbursal of expenses. The earl died shortly afterwards, and the tenth earl, his son Algernon Percy (1602–1668), discontinued Warner's pension. From 1632 until his death, Warner continued to work over Harriot's papers, and collaborated with the young mathematician John Pell, on his logarithmical calculations.

In 1635 Warner sought the patronage of William Cavendish, first duke of Newcastle, and his brother Sir Charles Cavendish, to whom he sent tracts on telescope construction and concave and convex glasses, for which he received a reward of £20. Warner corresponded with other members of the Welbeck circle, including Robert Payne and Thomas Hobbes, whom Seth Ward accused of plagiarizing Warner's ideas. Hobbes ousted Warner as a Cavendish client by writing to the earl of Northumberland and belittling his abilities. Despite the assistance of Aylesbury, Warner was impoverished when he died, unmarried, on 28 March 1643. Some of his papers fell into the hands of Seth Ward, Sir Justinian Isham, John Collins, and Herbert Thorndike, but in 1646 Pell lamented that most of his papers had been 'unmathematically divided between sequestrators and creditors'.

STEPHEN CLUCAS, rev.

Sources Wood, *Ath. Oxon.* · *Brief lives, chiefly of contemporaries, set down by John Aubrey, between the years 1669 and 1696*, ed. A. Clark, 2 vols. (1898) · J. P. Schobinger, ed., *Die Philosophie des 17. Jahrhunderts*, 3 (Basel, 1988) · J. W. Shirley, ed., *Thomas Harriot: Renaissance scientist* (1974) · J. W. Shirley, *Thomas Harriot: a biography* (1983)
Archives BL, mathematical and philosophical papers, Add. MSS 4391, 4394–4396
Wealth at death in poverty

Warner, William (1558/9–1609), poet and lawyer, was born in London. His verse history, *Albion's England* (1586), confirms his father was a voyager who accompanied Richard Chancellor to Russia in 1553, and died on the way to Guiana under William Towerson in 1577 (book 11, chap.

62, ll. 1–2; book 12, chap. 70, l. 30). There are no records to support Anthony Wood's claim that Warner studied at Magdalen Hall, Oxford, and he certainly did not take a degree there. Nevertheless, *Albion's England* includes a panegyric on the 'Primer-schooling' university, which could be either Oxford or Cambridge (book 15, chap. 99, ll. 1–6). Having settled in London, Warner practised as an attorney in the court of common pleas. On 3 October 1599 he married the widow Anne Dale in Great Amwell, Hertfordshire; a son, William, was born at Ware in Hertfordshire on 18 February 1604 (Mahon, 8).

Warner's earliest publication was an episodic prose romance, *Pan his Syrinx, or Pipe, Compact of Seven Reedes* (1584); a second edition appeared in 1597. A translation of Plautus by 'W. W.', *Menaecmi: a Pleasant and Fine Conceited Comædie* (1595), has been attributed, probably mistakenly, to Warner. The author is more likely the committed innovator of English versification William Webbe, whose *Discourse of English Poetrie* (1586) includes a defence of Plautus.

Warner is best remembered for *Albion's England, or, Historicall Map of the same Island*, licensed to Thomas Cadman on 7 November 1586. A pirate edition had already been printed by Roger Ward; the sheets were seized on 17 October 1586. The long episodic poem narrates the history of Britain from the time of Noah until the Norman conquest, and contains a prose 'Breviat of the true Historie of ÆNEAS'. In the editions which followed in the next twenty-six years, *Albion's England* expanded from four to sixteen books. A second edition in six books appeared in 1589, complete with a folding woodcut detailing the lineages of the houses of Lancaster and York. The third and fourth editions of 1592 and 1596/7, in nine and twelve books respectively, continued the history of England up to the reign of Elizabeth I. In the fifth edition of 1602, enlarged to thirteen books, Warner added a prose 'Epitome of the whole historie of England'. Warner praised the new reign of James I in *A Continuance of Albion's England* (1606), and *Albion's England* appeared for the final time in 1612, after Warner's death.

Albion's England records in fourteen-syllable couplets 'the gests of *Brutons* stout, and acts of English men' (book 1, chap. 1, l. 4). The text is an eclectic mixture of classical mythology and Christian legend, together with episodes from the English chronicles and theological debate. *Albion's England* was dedicated to the lord chamberlain, Sir Henry Carey, first Lord Hunsdon; the 1606 *Continuance*, however, was dedicated to Sir Edward Coke. After Henry Carey's death in 1596, Warner added a second dedication in the fourth edition to Henry's son Sir George Carey, second Lord Hunsdon.

Warner was a well-respected poet in his time. Many quotations from *Albion's England* appeared in Robert Allott's *England's Parnassus* (1600) and Warner's story of Henry II and Rosamund probably influenced Samuel Daniel's *Complaint of Rosamond* (1592). Michael Drayton drew on Warner for *Matilda* (1594), *Englands Heroicall Epistles* (1597), and *Poly-Olbion* (1612), acknowledging the debt in 'To my most Dearly Loved Friend Henry Reynolds' (*The Works of*

Michael Drayton, 1931–41, 3.228). Francis Meres called Warner 'our English *Homer*' in *Palladis tamia* (1598, 281), while Gabriel Harvey found in *Albion's England* 'many things … commendable, divers things notable, somethings excellent' (*Pierces Supererogation*, 1593, 191). John Weever included an epigram on Warner, the 'prince of Poets', in his *Epigrammes in the Oldest Cut, and Newest Fashion* (1599, sig. G1r). Thomas Nashe is perhaps more lukewarm in his preface to Robert Greene's *Menaphon* (1589), concluding that poetry 'hath not beene any whit disparaged by *William Warners* absolute *Albions*' (1610 edn, sig. B3v).

Warner died on 9 March 1609 in the parish of Great Amwell, Hertfordshire, where he had 'dwelt awhile' according to John Scott's poem *Amwell* (1776). He was buried at the church of St John the Baptist on 11 March 1609. His sudden death is recorded in the parish register by Thomas Hassel, vicar of Great Amwell:

> Mr William Warner a man of good yeares and of honest reputation; by his profession an Atturnye at the common plese: author of *Albions England*, diynge suddanly in the night in his bedde without any former complaynt or sicknesse on Thursday night, beeinge the 9th daye of March; was buried the Saturday following, and lyeth in the church at the upper end under the stone of Gwallter Fader.

KATHARINE A. CRAIK

Sources W. A. Bacon, *William Warner's Syrinx, or, A sevenfold history* (1950) · J. W. Mahon, 'A study of William Warner's *Albion's England*', PhD diss., Columbia University, 1980 · R. Birley, *Sunk without trace: some forgotten masterpieces reconsidered: the Clark lectures, 1960–61* (1962) · *DNB* · Wood, *Ath. Oxon.*, new edn, 1.765 · Arber, *Regs. Stationers*, vols. 2–3 · H. G. Aldis and others, *A dictionary of printers and booksellers in England, Scotland and Ireland, and of foreign printers of English books, 1557–1640*, ed. R. B. McKerrow (1910) · W. J. Harvey, *Great Amwell: past and present* (1896) · J. Scott, *The poetical works of John Scott* (1782)

Warner, Sir William Lee- (1846–1914), administrator in India and author, was born at Little Walsingham vicarage on 18 April 1846, the fifth son of Henry James Lee-Warner (1802–1885), of Thorpland Hall, Norfolk, canon of Norwich, and his wife, Anne (d. 1878), daughter of Henry Nicholas Astley, rector of East Barsham, Norfolk. In 1859 he went to Rugby School and in 1865 was elected a scholar of St John's College, Cambridge, taking honours in the moral science tripos in 1869. Cambridge later awarded him the honorary degree of LLD. Both at school and university he was a keen sportsman and throughout his official career retained his love of outdoor activity. In 1867 he passed the open competition for the Indian Civil Service and in 1869 arrived in Bombay, initially to take up an appointment as assistant collector and magistrate of Poona. In 1872, and again in 1876, he was private secretary to the governor, Sir Philip Wodehouse, a fellow Norfolk man. On 2 August 1876 he married Ellen (Nellie) Paulina, eldest daughter of Major-General J. W. Holland, with whom he had four sons.

From the mid-1870s Lee-Warner's district appointments were punctuated by temporary postings in the Bombay secretariat. He also served on the education commission in 1882, officiated as junior under-secretary to the government of India in the foreign department in 1884, and officiated as political agent at Kolhapur in 1886. Regardless of his postings, however, he was never content to function in a purely local environment, and from his earliest days in India bombarded the press with anonymous commentaries on the performance of India's imperial and provincial governments. From 1881 to 1889 he contributed lengthy articles to *The Economist* on topics such as local self-government, direct taxation, and the relief of agrarian distress.

In August 1887 Lee-Warner was confirmed as political and judicial secretary to the Bombay government, in which position he forged a radical interpretation of Britain's power over the princely states. He had limited experience of the messy realities of political administration and this, coupled with his all-India outlook, made him ideally suited to impose order on the miscellany of treaties which constituted Indian political law. He redefined paramountcy on the basis of usage and sufferance, rather than existing contracts, arguing that the usage applied to one state was, by the law of precedence, equally applicable to another state, thereby reducing to the lowest common denominator of rights the complexities of the numerous treaties that Britain had signed with individual states over the previous two centuries. He promoted these views in his 1886 manuscript 'Elementary treatise on ... the conduct of political relations with native states', but was disappointed in not being asked to compile a textbook for the political service, a job which went to an equally influential colleague, Charles Tupper of the Punjab. He therefore published the work as a private individual, under the title *Protected Princes of India* (1894), a revised and enlarged edition of which appeared in 1910 as *The Native States of India*.

In 1893–4, and again in 1895, Lee-Warner represented Bombay in the central legislative council. In 1895 he was appointed resident in Mysore and chief commissioner of Coorg, but resigned after only six months when offered the post of political and secret secretary at the India Office. In England too, both in this capacity and later as a member of the secretary of state's council, to which he was appointed in November 1902 for ten years, he was influential in the formation of Indian policy. In 1898 he was created KCSI.

In his economic writings Lee-Warner espoused the laws of political economy, but in other respects his politics were conservative. Convinced that the lower levels of the executive were dominated by intriguing and disloyal Brahmans, he spearheaded the campaign to curtail the recruitment of Brahmans to government employ. He railed against the increasing centralization of the Indian bureaucracy under Lord Curzon, complaining that district officers were losing power to both the imperial centre above and the high-caste cliques below. He had no time for the political aspirations of educated Indians, believing that they sought only to exploit the peasantry, and throughout the council discussions over electoral reform in 1906–9 consistently opposed John Morley's liberal

intentions. That he did so, however, with skill and independence of judgement is apparent from Morley's recommendation in 1911, which was accepted, that he be promoted to GCSI.

In addition to his works on the princely states, Lee-Warner also published *The Citizen of India* (1897), designed to inculcate in Indian schoolboys notions of civic duty. A reviewer in *The Spectator* (13 August 1898), summed up the tone of this and others of his works when commenting that 'Mr. Lee-Warner's book, while thoroughly judicial in temper, is a great defence of British rule in India'. Other publications included the *Life of the Marquis of Dalhousie* (1904), *Memoirs of Field-Marshall Sir Henry Wylie Norman* (1908), and articles for the *Dictionary of National Biography*, the *Cambridge Modern History*, and the *Encyclopaedia Britannica*.

Lee-Warner was a devout churchman, with many charitable interests, among them the Civil Service Prayer Union and the Indian Church Aid Association. He founded the Bombay branch of the Society for the Prevention of Cruelty to Animals, and at the time of his death was chairman of the Indian section of the Royal Society of Arts. He retired from the India Office in 1912, but did not substantially reduce his workload. He died at Heigham Hall, Norwich, of heart failure, on 18 January 1914, and was buried three days later in Little Walsingham churchyard. He was survived by his wife and three of their sons; the fourth had drowned at Nanaimo, Vancouver Island, in 1906.

F. H. BROWN, *rev.* KATHERINE PRIOR

Sources I. Copland, *The British raj and the Indian princes* (1982) · BL OIOC, Lee-Warner MSS · *The Spectator* (13 Aug 1898) · *The Times* (19 Jan 1914) · *The Times* (20 Jan 1914) · *History of services of gazetted officers ... in the Bombay presidency* (1895) · Burke, *Gen. GB* (1914) · *CGPLA Eng. & Wales* (1914) · *Debrett's Peerage* (1924)
Archives BL OIOC, corresp. and papers, MS Eur. F 92 · BL OIOC, notebook, MS Eur. D 727 · BL OIOC, notes on reforms in India, MS Eur. D 573 | Castle Howard, North Yorkshire, letters to Lord Carlisle · CUL, corresp. with Lord Hardinge · Norfolk RO, letters to his brother, James Lee-Warner
Likenesses three photographs, *c*.1900, BL OIOC · photograph, repro. in *Black and White* (28 May 1898), 734
Wealth at death £11,836 1*s*.: probate, 14 Feb 1914, *CGPLA Eng. & Wales*

Warnock, Sir Geoffrey James (1923–1995), philosopher and college head, was born on 16 August 1923 at Nerike House, Chapel Allerton, Leeds, the only son of James Warnock (1880–1953), a general practitioner originally from northern Ireland, and his wife, Kathleen, *née* Hall (1890–1979). He was educated at Winchester College and New College, Oxford, being a scholar on both foundations. Between school and university he served in the Irish Guards (1942–5), took part in the advance into Germany, and attained the rank of captain. In 1948 he gained a first in philosophy, politics, and economics. He was elected to a fellowship by examination in philosophy at Magdalen College, Oxford, in 1949, and was subsequently fellow and tutor, first at Brasenose (1950–53) and then at Magdalen (1953–71). During his tutorial years he made several visits to the United States and taught and lectured at a number of American universities. In 1971 he became principal of which also possessed a particular interest as marking a moment of transition from the mainly critical work of the immediate post-war period to the renewal of more systematic endeavours in the later part of the century. He next turned to a subject which probably engages the interest of the majority of people more than any other philosophical topic—namely the nature of morality; and after subjecting some current views to a devastating critique in *Contemporary Moral Philosophy* (1967) he produced his own positive account in *The Object of Morality* (1971). The very title was contentious, like the subject itself; yet the author may be held to have come as close in this book to the truth of the matter as any other writer of his age—or perhaps of any age. It was marked throughout with the coolness and balance, sensitivity and humanity, which were typical of the man.

It was not only in the sphere of morality that Warnock showed his philosophical venturesomeness. Of all the philosophers of his time the one he admired more than any other was J. L. Austin; and Warnock undertook, and published as his last book, a critical study of Austin's work, *J. L. Austin* (1989). This was much earlier preceded by his brilliant reconstruction, from very fragmentary notes, of Austin's famous lectures on perception, delivered under the characteristic title *Sense and Sensibilia* (1962). In this he captured not only the substance of the lectures, but the personal style, the very note, of the man—the mordant wit, the total originality, the devastating force, the extreme sensitivity to the nuances of language. The reconstruction was a wonderful revelation of these qualities. It was also a tribute. So too, in its way, was his final study of Austin's entire œuvre. But this was not merely a tribute; for here Warnock gave his own critical, as well as expository, powers their full scope. His concern for accuracy, precision, and literal truth were brought to bear, and most tellingly brought to bear, on his subject. The necessary corrections and qualifications were duly and decisively made; but this without any abatement of recognition of the power and enduring value and influence of Austin's work. The book, in fact, was a demonstration that a sincere and discriminating admirer of a great and original philosopher need not be, and should not be, a mere disciple.

In the other strand of his career, as college and university administrator, Warnock showed equal distinction. As principal of Hertford College from 1971 to 1988 he presided over the transformation of what was once one of the smallest, poorest, and least regarded of Oxford's men's colleges into a mixed middle-sized college with sound finances and impressive academic results. Although some of the measures that benefited Hertford were in place before his arrival, notably the new and progressive admissions policy, their fruition owed much to his calm, clear-sighted, and good-humoured government. The qualities and leadership he there displayed led to his choice as vice-chancellor of the university in 1981, an office he held until 1985 during a difficult period of government retrenchment on higher education funding. He conducted the

Sir Geoffrey James Warnock (1923–1995), by David Hockney, 1978

Hertford College, Oxford, a post he retained until he retired in 1988; and from 1981 to 1985 he served as vice-chancellor of the university. On 2 July 1949 he married (Helen) Mary Wilson (*b.* 1924), daughter of Archibald Edward Wilson and his wife, Ethel Mary, eldest daughter of Sir Felix Otto Schuster, first baronet. Mary Warnock was herself a professional philosopher who became mistress of Girton College, Cambridge (1985–91), headed a number of public inquiries, and was made a life peer as Baroness Warnock of Weeke in 1985. They had three daughters and two sons.

Both to academic philosophy and to academic administration Warnock brought a rare and valuable combination of qualities. He wrote, of another philosopher, George Berkeley, the following words: 'He was the most acute of critics, a writer of perfect grace and lucidity, and by temperament an enemy to all dullness, pedantry, and needless sophistication' (G. J. Warnock, *Berkeley*, 1953, 12). The words can be applied, with even greater justice, to their author. While Berkeley was led, in the end, to embrace a fantastical metaphysics, Warnock never deviated from the clear and literal truth, and the difficult exercise of cleaving to that path he conducted, in his writings on perception and the philosophy of language, with such an absence of fussiness, with such coolness, urbanity, and elegance, that the result gave (and can still give) not only deep intellectual satisfaction but great aesthetic pleasure.

Warnock's *Berkeley* (1953), which exhibited the qualities he praised in its subject, was followed in 1958 by his second book, *English Philosophy since 1900*, an excellent survey, business of Oxford's hebdomadal council with such fairness and reasonableness, and such lucidity of presentation, that debate was minimized. He made no secret of the fact that he deplored the erosion of university funding—a theme he returned to in his last speech, made on the occasion of the opening of Hertford's new student residence, named Warnock House, on the Isis near Folly Bridge. Twelve days later he died of a disabling illness which he had borne with stoicism: it was typical of his courage and courtesy that he held off its advances long enough to come to the opening and to delight his friends and colleagues with a witty and eloquent valedictory speech. He was knighted in 1986 and had been previously elected to honorary fellowships at New College and Magdalen. His was an exemplary Oxford career.

The bare record of Warnock's professional and public achievement might give an impression of austerity. But he was far from austere. He had a great capacity for enjoyment, and a lively sense of the ridiculous, being vastly and delightfully amused by the absurdities which so often cropped up in human speech and behaviour. He was a games player, a keen cricketer and golfer; and all his friends and colleagues found him a charming companion, invariably courteous and considerate, indeed chivalrous, in personal relations. In the old phrase, he was 'a man of feeling'. He responded with equal warmth to the charm and beauty of Italy, its opera and architecture, and to the prose and poetry of England. He himself wrote and published distinguished verses (*Poems*, 1955), in which his characteristic combination of sensibility, realism, and restraint found happy expression in polished and elegant form. He died of fibrosing alveolitis on 8 October 1995 at his home, Brick House, Axford, near Marlborough, Wiltshire, and was buried on 13 October at Axford church. He was survived by his wife and five children.

P. F. STRAWSON

Sources *The Guardian* (11 Oct 1995) · *The Times* (12 Oct 1995) · *The Independent* · *WWW*, 1991–5 · personal knowledge (2004) · private information (2004) [Baroness Warnock]
Archives priv. coll.
Likenesses D. Hockney, chalk drawing, 1978, Hertford College, Oxford [*see illus.*] · H. Ocean, oils, 1984, Hertford College, Oxford · photograph, repro. in *The Guardian* · photograph, repro. in *The Times* · photograph, repro. in *The Independent*
Wealth at death £29,540: probate, 28 May 1996, *CGPLA Eng. & Wales*

Warr, Charles Laing (1892–1969), Church of Scotland minister and royal chaplain, was born at the manse, Rosneath, Dunbartonshire, on 20 May 1892, the younger son of the minister, the Revd Alfred Warr, himself a distinguished minister of the Church of Scotland, and his wife, Christian Grey, fifth daughter of Adam Laing. Warr grew up in the west of Scotland. He was educated at Glasgow Academy and the universities of Edinburgh and Glasgow. He received his Edinburgh MA in 1914, and was commissioned to the 9th Argyll and Sutherland Highlanders on 5 August of the same year. As he lay dangerously wounded at Ypres in May 1915 he underwent a spiritual experience, the result of which was that he took divinity classes at Glasgow and became assistant minister of the cathedral

there (1917–18). He was ordained before the end of the war and became minister of St Paul's, Greenock (1918–26). Warr married, in 1918, Christian Lawson Aitken (Ruby), the only daughter of Robert Rattray Tatlock. There were no children from the marriage.

To the surprise and consternation of several more senior churchmen, in 1926 Warr was appointed minister of St Giles's, Edinburgh. Moreover, to his own astonishment, and initially to the open hostility of the Scottish royal chaplains, he was also appointed both dean of the Chapel Royal and of the Order of the Thistle in the same year. Being only thirty-four years old at the time he was called 'my boy dean' by George V. Warr held both offices until his death. In 1926, although there was no vacancy on the list of royal chaplains in Scotland, he was made an extra chaplain to George V and in 1936 became his chaplain. His friendship with the royal family had begun when Princess Louise, duchess of Argyll, a daughter of Queen Victoria, had worshipped during the summer months at his father's church in Rosneath and had become interested in the minister's family. He became a close personal friend of George V. He was also chaplain to Edward VIII, George VI, and Elizabeth II. He declined the unanimous nomination for the moderatorship of the Church of Scotland in 1953.

Among Warr's many other chaplaincies were those to HM body guard for Scotland (the Royal Company of Archers), the order of St John of Jerusalem, the Royal Scottish Academy, the Convention of Royal Burghs of Scotland, the Royal College of Surgeons of Edinburgh, and the Merchant Company of Edinburgh. Among the directorships he held were those of the Royal Edinburgh Hospital for Sick Children and the Princess Margaret Rose Hospital for Crippled Children. As convener of the Church of Scotland committee on huts and canteens for HM forces throughout the Second World War he gave most distinguished service in helping the effort for the troops. For the church he was convener of the home mission committee and joint convener of the national church extension committee. He was a trustee of the National Library of Scotland and of Iona Cathedral.

Although Warr's public duties outnumbered those of any other minister he never allowed them to interfere with his work as a parish minister. 'The best way to run a parish is simply to love your people', he used to say, and he was a great believer in visiting his people, both in their homes and in hospital, and expected the same high standard from his assistants. Although not robust in health, he worked hard himself and expected the same dedication from those around him. Some outsiders knew him more for his participation in the many dignified occasions of church and state, and it is true that here he did more for the Church of Scotland than any other minister of his time. When performing these duties Warr's punctilious devotion to ceremonial sometimes aroused criticism. As a parish minister he gave quiet and peaceful evening services when the lights were lowered and he spoke from the pulpit in a way which comforted and helped people of all ages for the rest of the week ahead. Those who knew him most intimately will remember him as a man round his own fireside, with a love of people, a sense of fun, a deeply sincere and humble faith, and an almost jealous regard for the vocation of the ministry and the dignity and position of the church. Among his achievements were the lead he gave to the ecumenical movement in Scotland and his part in restoring St Margaret's Chapel, on the rock of Edinburgh Castle, the oldest ecclesiastical building in Scotland still in use as a place of worship.

Warr wrote *The Unseen Host* in February 1916 after being invalided out of the army at the early age of twenty-three. It soon became a best-seller, going into ten editions. In 1917 he published a biography of his father. Among his other books were *Echoes of Flanders* (1916), *Principal Caird* (1926), *The Call of the Island* (1929), *Scottish Sermons and Addresses* (1930), *The Presbyterian Tradition* (1933), and *The Glimmering Landscape* (autobiography, 1960).

Among Warr's many honours was that of being the only minister of the Church of Scotland to be created GCVO (1967), having previously been CVO (1937) and KCVO (1950). He was made a deputy lieutenant of the county of the city of Edinburgh (1953), honorary DD of Edinburgh (1931), honorary LLD of St Andrews (1937) and of Edinburgh (1953), honorary RSA (1927), FRSE from 1936, honorary FRCS of Edinburgh (1955), and honorary FRIBA (1967).

Warr received a colleague and successor in 1954—an arrangement which turned out neither as happily nor as successfully as he had hoped, and on his retirement from St Giles's in 1962 he joined the Canongate Kirk. In 1954 the queen gave him a grace-and-favour house in Moray Place, Edinburgh, where he spent his last years. Warr's wife died in 1961, and he died in Edinburgh on 14 June 1969.

RONALD SELBY WRIGHT, *rev.*

Sources C. L. Warr, *The glimmering landscape* (1960) · *Year Book of the Royal Society of Edinburgh* (1968–9) · personal knowledge (1981) · *The Times* (16 June 1969) · *WWW* · *DSCHT* · b. cert.
Archives NL Scot., corresp. with publishers · NL Scot., diaries and corresp.
Likenesses A. E. Borthwick, portrait, 1951, St Giles's Church, Edinburgh · D. Murray, bust, Canongate Kirk, Edinburgh

Warr, de la [De La Warr]. For this title name *see under* Warr, de la, family (*per. c.*1250–1427) [Warr, John de la, second Lord de la Warr (1276/7–1347); Warr, Roger de la, third Lord de la Warr (1326–1370); Warr, John de la, fourth Baron de la Warr (*c.*1345–1398); Warr, Thomas de la, fifth Baron de la Warr (*d.* 1427)]. *See also* West, Thomas, eighth Baron West and ninth Baron de la Warr (1472–1554); West, William, first Baron De La Warr (*c.*1519–1595) [*see under* West, Thomas, eighth Baron West and ninth Baron de la Warr (1472–1554)]; West, Thomas, third Baron De La Warr (1577–1618); West, John, first Earl De La Warr (1693–1766); West, John, second Earl De La Warr (1729–1777) [*see under* West, John, first Earl De La Warr (1693–1766)]; West, George John Sackville-, fifth Earl De La Warr (1791–1869) [*see under* West, John, first Earl De La Warr (1693–1766)]; West, Charles Richard Sackville-, sixth Earl De La Warr (1815–1873); Sackville, Herbrand Edward Dundonald Brassey, ninth Earl De La Warr (1900–1976).

Warr [Warre], **de la, family** (*per. c.*1250–1427), nobility, held lands in Gloucestershire, Somerset, and Sussex, and rose to prominence through profitable marriages and royal service, particularly in the retinue of Edward, prince of Wales (the Black Prince) in France. The family was first represented among the peerage by **Roger de la Warr**, first Lord La Warre (*d.* 1320), son and heir of Sir John de la Warr (*d. c.*1279) of Wickwar, Gloucestershire, and Brislington, Somerset, founder of St Bartholomew's Hospital in Bristol, and his wife, Olimpia, daughter of Sir Hugh of Folkington, of Folkington and Isfield, Sussex. In 1276 Roger married Clarice (*d.* 1289x1300), daughter and coheir of Sir John Tregoz, whose castle of Ewyas Harold, Herefordshire, and manors of Allington, Wiltshire, and Albrighton, Shropshire, would be inherited by Roger's son and heir, **John de la Warr**, second Lord de la Warr (1276/7–1347), after Sir John Tregoz's death in 1300. Roger was distrained to take up knighthood in 1278, and campaigned in Wales in 1282, Gascony in 1294–7, and Scotland in 1300. He was also a valued royal adviser, being summoned to councils or to attend the king between 1287 and 1307. In 1308 he attended Edward II's coronation. He also served as a Sussex keeper of the peace. His elevation to the peerage, as Lord La Warre, resulted from summonses to parliament issued between 1299 and 1311. In 1304 he was appointed to an embassy to the pope. He died on 20 June 1320, holding the manors of Milton, Sussex, Isfield, Folkington, Brislington, and Wickwar, as well as lands in Worcestershire and Berkshire.

John de la Warr married, in 1294 or 1295, Joan (*d.* 1353), daughter of Sir Robert Grelle of Manchester, and sister and heir of Sir Thomas Grelle, whose manors of Swineshead, Sixhills, Bloxham in Lincolnshire, and Woodhead in Rutland, passed to the de la Warrs through this marriage, together with Joan's own manor of Wakerley, Northamptonshire. The marriage also brought the barony of Manchester to the de la Warrs. Between 1300 and 1306 John unsuccessfully claimed all the knights' fees and advowsons pertaining to his maternal grandfather's castle of Ewyas Harold. John accompanied his father at the siege of Caerlaverock in July 1300, but in 1306 he was also one of those who, without permission, abandoned the Scottish campaign in order to attend a tournament, for which his lands were briefly confiscated. He may have been an adherent of Piers Gaveston at this time. He was certainly back in royal favour by May 1306, when he was knighted by the prince of Wales. He was summoned for military service on numerous occasions between 1308 and 1333, and also to Edward II's coronation, and to councils from 1308 to 1342, although illness temporarily removed him from public life in 1322, when his place was taken by his son, **John de la Warr** (*d.* in or before 1336). In August 1307 the elder John was summoned to parliament, thereby becoming Lord de la Warr during his father's lifetime: it is possible that Roger was suffering poor health, and thereby becoming increasingly inactive, during the last thirteen years of his life. John the elder may have had another bout of illness in 1336, when on a false report of his death his grandson's marriage and wardship were bought by Thomas Berkeley, but he survived until 9 May 1347.

Roger de la Warr, third Lord de la Warr (1326–1370), was the son of John de la Warr the younger and his wife, Margaret (d. 1349), daughter of Sir Robert *Holland of Lancashire and Staffordshire. By October 1338 he had married his first wife, Elizabeth (d. 1345x53), daughter of Sir Adam Welle and his wife, Margaret, of Lincolnshire. With his younger brother, Sir John (d. 1358), he served in the Black Prince's retinue for the Crécy and Calais campaigns (1346–7). After the deaths of his grandparents, Roger inherited Allington, Wickwar, Brislington, Wakerley, and Swineshead. By February 1354 he married his second wife, another Elizabeth (d. in or before 1358), and by July 1358 he had married his third and final wife, Eleanor (d. in or before 1387), daughter of Sir John (II) *Mowbray, lord of Axholme, Bramber, and Gower, and his wife, Joan, daughter of Henry, earl of Lancaster (d. 1345). Roger accompanied the Black Prince on the Poitiers campaign, and may have been among the captors of King John of France. He was himself captured during the 1359–60 invasion of France, but was back in England by 1362, when he was summoned to parliament as third Lord de la Warr. He returned to France in 1364, in the prince's service in Gascony, where he died in 1370. By his will of 1368 (which records his ownership of French books) he had requested burial in the abbey of Swineshead, where his grandfather had also been buried. His widow married Sir Lewis *Clifford, the 'Lollard knight', who in 1373 gave up his wife's jointure, which included the lordship of Manchester, in return for the grant to himself and his wife jointly of Ewyas Harold and other lands. Following Eleanor's death Clifford bought John de la Warr out of Ewyas Harold completely. Roger's surviving children were his eldest son, John [see below], and Thomas [see below], born of his first marriage; the identity of the mother of a daughter, Katherine, and younger sons Edward and John, is uncertain. Joan, daughter of Roger and Eleanor, appears not to have outlived her father; she married Thomas West.

John de la Warr, fourth Baron de la Warr (c.1345–1398), eldest son and heir of Roger, like his father and uncle served in the Black Prince's retinue, being one of his knights in Gascony in 1368–9. By this time he had married his first wife, Elizabeth, whose surname is unknown. He was back on campaign in France in 1372, and played a prominent part in the earl of Buckingham's Brittany raid in 1380–81, and was summoned for military service again in 1385. However, by this time he had been granted an exemption from attending parliament (he was first summoned in 1371) on account of his poor eyesight, and he seems to have taken little part in public life in his last decade. Between 1387 and 1389 he married Elizabeth (c.1343–1393), daughter and heir of Sir Gilbert Neville and his wife, Katherine (from whom were inherited properties in Lincolnshire, Wiltshire, Northamptonshire, and Hampshire), and widow of Simon Simeon of Lincolnshire. Elizabeth requested burial in the de la Warr family mausoleum at Swineshead. John died in 1398 without surviving children, leaving his brother Thomas, a priest, as heir.

By the time of his brother's death **Thomas de la Warr**, fifth Baron de la Warr (d. 1427), already had behind him a considerable ecclesiastical career: a graduate of Oxford, he was rector of Ashton under Lyne in 1372–3; of Swineshead in 1378–82 and 1394–1400; and of Manchester, another de la Warr possession, in 1382–1427; he also held prebends at Lincoln, York, and Southwell. He was summoned to parliament from August 1399 to 1426, but he continued to pursue his ecclesiastical career: he received a licence from Henry IV to absent himself from parliaments and councils, and he acquired further prebends at York and Lincoln, as well as transforming Manchester parish church into a college in 1421. The following year he was once again instituted to the rectory of Swineshead, which he held until his death, on 7 May 1427, and where he was probably buried. With his death the de la Warrs became extinct in the male line. Reginald West, son of Thomas's half-sister Joan, and John Griffon, descendant of Katherine, Thomas's aunt, were named as heirs.

Peter Fleming

Sources GEC, *Peerage*, 4.139–51 · *Chancery records* · *Calendar of chancery warrants*, 1: 1244–1326 (1927) · J. S. Hamilton, *Piers Gaveston, earl of Cornwall* (1988) · R. Barber, *Edward, prince of Wales and Aquitaine: a biography of the Black Prince* (1978) · Emden, *Oxf.*, 2.1111 · K. B. McFarlane, *Lancastrian kings and Lollard knights* (1972), 173–4

Warr, John (*fl.* 1648–1649), legal writer, is of unknown background and parentage. From his pamphlets it would seem that he had received a classical education and had some experience of litigation. For this reason he might be identified with the son and heir of the armigerous Somerset gentleman Edward Warre of Chipley, who was educated at Exeter College, Oxford, and Gray's Inn. However, this particular John Warre was never called to the bar, which may at least qualify him as a candidate for elimination. Very little is known about Warr the pamphleteer, though his measured disregard for the greed and professional self-interest of those lawyers whom Oliver Cromwell would style 'the sons of Zeruiah' suggests that he was probably not of that profession. In the 1650s a John Warre bought a number of sequestrated royalist estates in Somerset, but it is impossible to say whether it is the same man.

Warr is prominent as an advocate of fundamental reform of the law in a number of vividly written pamphlets. 'Even truth itself', he wrote, 'will jostle its adversary in a narrow pass' (J. Warr, *The Priviledges of the People*, 1649, 3). He is not easily pigeon-holed as a member of any particular faction. Those aspects of his thought which might appear to align him closely with Gerrard Winstanley and the Diggers (such as his dislike of the 'slavish ties and badges upon men' entailed by landed property) articulate a perfectly mainstream radical abhorrence of 'the Norman Yoke' chafing the necks of freeborn Englishmen. For this reason he has been called a Leveller. Less specifically, though conceivably more accurately, he belongs within the broad strain of thought characterized as antiformalist, rejecting the traditional, institutional arbiters of truth and justice, remarking for example that 'There are some sparks of freedom in the minds of most which ordinarily lie deep and are covered in the dark as a spark in the ashes' (*DNB*). Warr's first work, *Administrations Civil and Spiritual* (1648), published, like all his tracts, by the radical bookseller Giles Calvert, contrasts the dead hand of formal religion and the established social order with that personal revelation referred to frequently in this and after ages as the 'inner light'.

In *The Priviledges of the People*, seemingly published in the week after the execution of Charles I, Warr made an exceptionally strong case for the full establishment of that notion of popular sovereignty on which the constitutional revolution of 1649 was predicated. He advocated the absolute subjection of kings and parliaments to the rule of law. Under the existing arrangements he perceived 'an irreconcilable contest' between rulers and ruled 'which will never cease till either prerogative and privilege be swallowed up in freedom or liberty itself be led captive by prerogative' (J. Warr, *The Priviledges of the People*, 1649, 5). The foundation of the Commonwealth would prove his point amply. Later in 1649 Warr published a third pamphlet, *The Corruption and Deficiency of the Lawes of England*, in which he narrowed his focus to an attack on the chronic expense and delay encountered in any tangle with the English legal system. 'When the poor and oppressed want right, they meet with law … Many times the very law is the badge of our oppression, its proper intention being to enslave the people' (Hill, 272). He advocated reforms as fundamental, and as simple, as the keeping of legal records in the English language, rather than law French. Yet he went even beyond the Levellers and other disputants of the Norman yoke, having no truck with the notion of fundamental law, so central to the case made by John Lilburne, as yet another false idol. The rational spirit of justice must be freed from the restraint of all legal forms whatever. An agreement of the people might be as great an inhibition to the reign of truth as the court of chancery. All men must look within, and conquer the weakness of their own flesh, for 'such men are likely to be the hopeful fire of freedom who have the image of it engrafted in their own minds' (J. Warr, *The Corruption and Deficiency of the Lawes of England*, 1649, 15). Warr is not known to have published any further pamphlets and his date of death is unknown.   SEAN KELSEY

Sources DNB · A. J. Busch and R. Zaller, 'Warr, John', *Biographical dictionary of British radicals in the seventeenth century*, 3 (1984), 292–3 · D. Veall, *The popular movement for law reform, 1640–1660* (1970), 98, 101–2 · C. Hill, *The world turned upside down* (1972) · S. Sedley and L. Kaplan, eds., *A spark in the ashes: the pamphlets of John Warr* (1992)

Warr, John de la, second Lord de la Warr (1276/7–1347). *See under* Warr, de la, family (*per. c.*1250–1427).

Warr, John de la (d. in or before 1336). *See under* Warr, de la, family (*per. c.*1250–1427).

Warr, John de la, fourth Baron de la Warr (*c.*1345–1398). *See under* Warr, de la, family (*per. c.*1250–1427).

Warr, Roger de la, first Lord La Warre (d. 1320). *See under* Warr, de la, family (*per. c.*1250–1427).

Warr, Roger de la, third Lord de la Warr (1326–1370). *See under* Warr, de la, family (*per. c.*1250–1427).

Warr, Thomas de la, fifth Baron de la Warr (d. 1427). *See under* Warr, de la, family (*per. c.*1250–1427).

Warrack, Harriet (*bap.* 1825, *d.* 1910), headmistress, was baptized on 14 December 1825, at Old Machar, Aberdeen. Her father, James Warrack (*d.* 1863), an Aberdeen tea dealer and grocer, later a commission agent, was well known in Aberdeen business circles. Her mother, Harriet (*d.* 1857), was the daughter of George Morren, an Aberdeen stocking manufacturer. Harriet was the fifth child in a family of four brothers and two sisters. Three brothers were educated at the Aberdeen grammar school, but nothing definite is known of her education, though her obituarist referred to it as 'sound'. She may have attended the female Lancasterian school in Aberdeen, where one of her aunts was a teacher. Miss Warrack's father suffered financial difficulties and moved house a number of times, but even so the family lived on fashionable streets and were probably all brought up in reasonably comfortable middle-class surroundings. The two eldest brothers, John and James, went on to found shipping companies in Leith and Montrose; the youngest, Alexander, became a minister. Shortly after the death of her father in 1863 Harriet Warrack also found it necessary to support herself.

Accordingly, about 1867, when she was over forty, Miss Warrack opened in Aberdeen a private school for upper-middle-class girls, later to be known as Albyn School. Two years later the school moved to Union Place. An able woman, Miss Warrack ran her school with success, attracting boarders from the country as well as day girls from the town. She was in the vanguard in promoting better academic standards for upper-middle-class girls in Aberdeen, a cause advanced by the Aberdeen Ladies' Educational Association. She organized a private class for more advanced courses at the school and in the 1870s was the first Aberdeen school proprietor to persuade girls to sit the university local examinations. She also organized correspondence tutorial classes and not only held quarterly examinations of the pupils but published examples of them. By the time Miss Warrack retired in 1886 Albyn Place School was by far the largest and most academic private girls' school in Aberdeen, and the foundations had been laid for it to continue for more than another hundred years. In no small part this was owing to her wise selection of staff and, in particular, of her successor, Alexander Mackie, a brilliant teacher, to whom she gave full management and control after he had been at the school for six years.

Harriet Warrack was good-looking in a somewhat severe fashion, an admirable organizer, and a woman of strong character. She was a member of the Free Church of Scotland, attending the Free West Church while Revd Laidlaw was minister there and later the Queen's Cross Free Church. She died on 23 April 1910 at her home, 2 Queen's Gate, Aberdeen, and was buried at Allenvale cemetery, Aberdeen.   LINDY MOORE

Harriet Warrack (*bap.* 1825, *d.* 1910), by George Washington Wilson

Sources G. I. Duthie and H. M. E. Duncan, *Albyn School centenary* (1967) · M. Carson, 'Albyn School', *Scottish Field*, 112 (Oct 1965), 36–7 · H. Warrack, letter, 15 Feb 1876, U. Edin. L., special collections division, MS General 1877/23 · Aberdeen Ladies' Educational Association minute book, 1877, Aberdeen Public Library, MS LO 376 Ab3 · V. Forrest, 'The story of Albyn School for Girls', *Aberdeen Leopard* (April 1989), 10–11 · *In Memoriam: an Obituary of Aberdeen and Vicinity* (1910), 115–16 · *Aberdeen Daily Journal* (25 April 1910) · parish register (birth and baptism), 14 Dec 1825, Old Machar, Aberdeen **Likenesses** G. W. Wilson, photograph, priv. coll. [*see illus.*] · photographs, repro. in Duthie and Duncan, *Albyn School centenary* **Wealth at death** £12,607 5*s.* 9*d.*: confirmation, 30 June 1910, CCI

Warre, Edmond (1837–1920), headmaster, was born in Beaumont Street, Cavendish Square, London, on 12 February 1837, second son of Henry Warre of Bindon, Somerset, a member of the port wine family, and his wife, Mary, daughter of Nicholson Calvert MP, of Hunsdon House, Hertfordshire. He was at Eagle House preparatory school, in Hammersmith, a nursery of distinguished headmasters, before going on to Eton College in 1849. He was blessed with great energy and concentration of purpose, together with a remarkable memory, and this enabled him to become Newcastle scholar in 1854. Richmond's drawing shows a strikingly handsome and alert boy. He went up to Oxford in 1855 as a scholar of Balliol, obtained first classes in moderations and Greats, and in 1859 a fellowship at All Souls. He had already been an enthusiastic 'wetbob' at Eton, and at Oxford his distinction as an oarsman became evident; he was president of the university boat club in 1858. He also played a leading part in the foundation of the Oxford University rifle volunteer corps in 1859 in response to the war scare of that year, and he helped to launch the National Rifle Association.

The next year his Eton tutor, W. B. Marriott, fell ill and persuaded Warre to help with his boys. Warre had been hesitating between the bar and the army, but he now realized that schoolmastering was his vocation. He seems immediately to have influenced the Etonians to found a volunteer corps. He was offered an appointment by Dr C. O. Goodford, accepted, and, on the strength of the high income then available to Eton masters, married Florence Dora, daughter of Colonel C. Malet, of Fontmell Parva, Dorset, in August 1861. In the decentralized Eton of those days Warre was able to build himself a boys' house, Penn House, and this he quickly filled. Boys who came to him from Dr Edward Balston's house, when the latter became a fellow (and then headmaster), noticed immediately his bracing impact. Sir William Anson wrote: 'We all began to think it creditable to work … and when I left Eton I formed a strong determination to do something to the credit of Warre's house and my old school' (Fletcher, 47). Throughout his years at Eton, Warre was to imbue a sense of purpose into a large number of the boys in his care.

Warre took on other responsibilities: when the corps languished without adult leadership, he reorganized and commanded it; he became river master in charge of the watermen and of bathing; and at the request of successive captains of boats, he trained the eight (but he preserved the tradition that boys ran the boating). He had not much natural gift for teaching, and his schoolwork therefore depended on conscientious preparation. The result was a very long day—rising at 6.30 a.m. for early school and on the go until 2.30 a.m. the next morning with only two periods of short rest, after lunch and when the boys had been put to bed at 10 p.m.

In 1867 Warre was ordained, and was regarded as a possible successor to Dr Balston as headmaster when the latter resigned out of dislike for the reforms that the public schools commission had set in motion. Warre was only thirty, and the fellows preferred an older candidate, Dr J. J. Hornby. Warre gave Hornby loyal support despite his disappointment: 'He takes it heroically and is a Vesuvius of zeal, throwing out a new core of project and fervour every day', William Johnson, a master, commented in his journal (16 January 1868). Most of the good initiatives of Hornby's time owed much to Warre. They included the setting up of a school of mechanics at his own expense and the foundation of the Eton mission at Hackney Wick.

In 1884 Hornby became provost and Warre was chosen as his successor, despite some opposition, notably in *The Times*, where one correspondent alleged:

[Mr Warre] has made no mark as a scholar, a preacher, or a man of letters. His name is associated with no questions of

Edmond Warre (1837–1920), by John Singer Sargent, 1906

educational reform; on the other hand, he is well known as the best rowing coach in England and as an able field-officer of Volunteers. He is an oppidan of the oppidans. The ordinary Etonian character, for good or bad, has received a strong impression from his energy and strength of will.   (25 July 1884)

Yet Dr Warre (he at once acquired a DD) confounded his critics. His first letter to the governing body in October 1884 set out a comprehensive programme of reform to raise academic standards and improve discipline. The hours of schoolwork were extended, the curriculum was revised, and terminal examinations introduced; the head-master visited schoolrooms to check masters' teaching. A school office transformed the administration, and Warre could reduce the amount of punishment because boys' behaviour was more effectively controlled and sanctions more efficiently administered. Some of his schemes for rebuilding Eton were thwarted, fortunately sparing a number of the college's cherished older buildings. Never-theless, during his headmastership Eton was physically transformed—first a lower chapel and new schoolrooms, and finally the school library and school hall in memory of Etonians who fell in the Second South African War. With the expansion that also took place in the staff, the result

was a serious depletion of the college's assets. Yet the school's reputation and numbers rose.

The first half of Warre's headmastership was an impres-sive period, but the second half was less successful, partly no doubt because his health began to fail. A rift in the staff over the privileged position of classical tutors divided the community; and in 1903 there occurred a fatal fire started by a boy arsonist in a boarding-house. Warre had indeed previously attempted to improve fire precautions, but he did not assume responsibility, and some suspected that his tears freely shed arose at least partly from self-pity. Pressure on him to resign grew, and in the summer of 1905 he retired to a home at Finchampstead which he had recently rented to replace a substantial property on Exmoor.

Warre was to return as provost in 1909, but by then he was too handicapped by Parkinson's disease to play an effective role. In the difficult war years, leadership of the college passed to M. R. James, provost of King's College, Cambridge. In 1918 Warre retired to Colenorton, a house he had built in Eton, and there he died on 22 January 1920. He was buried in Eton cemetery on the 26th. Despite the substantial income he had earned, he had always spent generously and he left under £27,000.

Warre's headmastership caused an intermediate but lasting shift from the extreme liberty of the old Eton towards the achievement-driven, master-controlled Eton that has developed since the 1960s. Although he fits loosely into the age of muscular Christianity, the value he placed on the independence and authority of the boys ensured that Eton retained its individual character. He is more notable for his personality, however, than for his educational ideas. A typical Englishman of his time, he loved gardens (particularly rhododendrons) and animals. He was happy in his family life, with five sons and two daughters. He was a practical man, who modelled tri-remes and designed boats, a lover of classical quotation but not a true scholar, and in some ways philistine. He lacked eloquence, but impressed the boys with his simple homilies and his appeals to their goodness. His magna-nimity, fairness, and friendliness were characteristics that all could appreciate. A. C. Benson, an increasingly critical housemaster, nevertheless confided to his diary (11 May 1902): 'The more one thinks of him, the more *his great-ness* emerges—when I am in his presence I am entirely dominated by him.' With his towering figure he personi-fied Eton to the boys.   TIM CARD

Sources C. R. L. Fletcher, *Edmond Warre* (1922) · minutes and agenda papers of the provost and fellows, Eton · A. C. Benson, diary, Magd. Cam. · *Extracts from the letters and journals of William Cory*, ed. F. W. Cornish (privately printed, Oxford, 1897) · L. S. R. Byrne and E. L. Churchill, *Changing Eton* (1937) · M. D. Hill, *Eton and elsewhere* (1928) · P. Lubbock, *Shades of Eton* (1929) · L. E. Jones, *A Victorian boyhood* (1955) · D. Newsome, *Godliness and good learning* (1961) · *CGPLA Eng. & Wales* (1920)
Archives Eton | All Souls Oxf., letters to Sir William Anson · BL, letters to T. H. S. Escott, Add. MS 58795 · BL, letters to W. E. Glad-stone, Add. MSS 44509–44522 · King's AC Cam., letters to Oscar Browning

Likenesses G. Richmond, crayon drawing, 1854, Eton · J. S. Sargent, oils, 1906, Eton College [see illus.] · Barraud, photograph, NPG; repro. in *Men and Women of the Day*, 1 (1888) · W. & D. Downey, photograph, woodburytype, NPG; repro. in W. Downey and D. Downey, *The cabinet portrait gallery*, 1 (1890) · Spy [L. Ward], caricature, chromolithograph, NPG; repro. in *VF* (20 June 1885) · carte-de-visite, All Souls Oxf.

Wealth at death £26,724 19s. 7d.: probate, 19 March 1920, *CGPLA Eng. & Wales*

Warre, Sir William (1784–1853), army officer, was born at Oporto, Portugal, on 15 April 1784, the eldest son of James Warre and his wife, Eleanor, daughter of Thomas Greg of Coles Park, Hertfordshire. He was educated at Harrow School and on 5 November 1803 commissioned ensign in the 52nd foot, which he joined at Hythe. Promoted lieutenant by purchase on 2 June 1804, he purchased his company in the 98th foot on 25 April 1806. On 7 August he exchanged into the 23rd light dragoons, and joined them at Clonmel, co. Tipperary, in October 1806.

In the following summer Warre attended the recently established Royal Military College at High Wycombe. In May 1808 he became aide-de-camp to Major-General Sir Ronald Crauford Ferguson, who was serving in an expedition assembled at Cork to attack the Spanish colonies in America. However, the expedition sailed instead for Portugal under the command of Sir Arthur Wellesley. Warre took part in the battles of Roliça (17 August) and Vimeiro (21 August), after which he fell ill with dysentery. He was sent to Lisbon, where Major-General William Carr Beresford took him into his house, and on his recovery attached him to his staff. Warre served with Beresford throughout Sir John Moore's campaign, ending with the battle of Corunna on 16 January 1809. Warre remained with his division to cover the overnight evacuation of the army, embarking himself the following afternoon, along with Beresford and the rear guard.

Beresford accepted the chief command of the Portuguese army in March 1809 and took Warre with him, making him a major in the Portuguese service and his senior aide-de-camp. Warre was with Beresford at Lamego and the passage of the Douro on 12 May. After the capture of Oporto, Warre destroyed the bridges in the rear of the retreating French army, despite inadequate means and violent opposition from local peasants. As a consequence of Warre's work Wellington was able to overtake Marshal Soult at Salamonde, from where on 16 May Soult managed to escape only by abandoning his guns and baggage. Warre took part in all the operations of Beresford's division 1809–10, but during the withdrawal to the lines of Torres Vedras in September 1810 he fell ill with rheumatic fever and had eventually to return to England.

Warre rejoined Beresford in May 1811 after the battle of Albuera, and took part in the second siege of Badajoz in May and June. He was promoted brevet major in the British army on 30 May 1811, and lieutenant-colonel in the Portuguese service on 3 July. He was at the siege and capture of Ciudad Rodrigo on 19 January 1812, at the third siege and capture of Badajoz on 6 April, where with Lord FitzRoy Somerset he played a prominent part in Wellington's success, and at the battle of Salamanca, where Beresford was wounded, on 22 July. Warre accompanied him to Lisbon and then returned to England.

For his services Warre was made a knight of the Portuguese order of the Tower and Sword, and a commander of the Portuguese order of St Bento d'Avis (1816). He was promoted brevet lieutenant-colonel in the British army on 13 May 1813. His *Letters from the Peninsula, 1808–1812* was edited by his nephew the Revd Edmond Warre in 1909.

Warre married on 19 November 1812 Selina Anna (d. 3 Feb 1821), youngest daughter of Christopher Thomson Maling of West Herrington, Durham, and sister of the first countess of Mulgrave. They had seven children, three of whom died in South Africa. The third son, General Sir Henry James Warre (1819–1898), colonel of the Wiltshire regiment, served in the Crimean and New Zealand wars.

On Beresford's advice Warre accepted the appointment of deputy quartermaster-general at the Cape in 1813, returning from there in 1821. Two years later he was appointed one of the permanent assistant quartermasters-general, and for the following fourteen years served in middle-ranking staff appointments, mostly in England and Ireland. In December 1826 he was appointed assistant quartermaster-general of the force hastily assembled under Lieutenant General Sir William Henry Clinton to aid the Portuguese who were threatened by Spain. The troops did not have to fight, and Warre returned to England in 1828. In 1837 he was made commander of Chatham garrison. He was made CB on 19 July 1838 and knighted in 1839. On promotion to major-general on 23 November 1841 he relinquished the command in Chatham and became colonel of the 94th foot (Connaught Rangers). He was promoted lieutenant-general in November 1851 when he retired. He died at York on 26 July 1853 and was buried at Bishopthorpe.

R. H. VETCH, *rev.* JAMES LUNT

Sources War Office records · dispatches, *LondG* · *GM*, 2nd ser. (1853) · J. Philippart, ed., *The royal military calendar*, 3rd edn, 5 vols. (1820) · *Army List* · Burke, *Peerage* · E. Warre, ed., *Letters from the Peninsula* (1909)

Archives BL, corresp., diaries, etc., RP729 [microfilm] · Brenthurst Library, Johannesburg, South Africa, papers · NAM, corresp. and papers; papers incl. letters from Spain

Likenesses portrait (in the uniform of the 23rd light dragoons), priv. coll.

Warrell, Charles Watson (1889–1995), headmaster and writer, was born on 23 April 1889 at Farmborough, near Bath, Somerset, the son of Sidney Watson Warrell, headmaster of Farmborough village school, and his wife, Annie, *née* Stubbs. Charles Warrell was educated at Newfoundland Road School, Bristol, and from 1907 to 1909 attended his father's old college, Culham College, near Oxford, an Anglican teacher-training foundation. His first teaching appointment was at Frome council school in Somerset in 1909, followed by a post in Shropshire.

In 1913 Warrell was appointed headmaster to the village school in Higher Wych, Malpas, Cheshire, a rural farming community. He had married a fellow teacher, Elizabeth

Gill (*d.* 1952), about 1907; they had one son and two daughters. The Higher Wych school logbook reveals a respected, creative, and innovative head, whose enthusiasm for hands-on activities was already apparent. In 1914 a visiting inspector recorded that his 'work is marked by commendable skill and by unusual enthusiasm and enterprise. I cannot speak too highly of the practical character of his work, which is full of promise for the future'. Warrell joined the army in 1916 and served in Salonika, his wife acting as temporary headteacher in his absence. After the war he continued to teach at Higher Wych until 1923, when he went as headmaster to a school in Bridgnorth, Shropshire.

From 1926 to 1944 Warrell was headmaster of Pleasley Hill secondary school, Mansfield, Nottinghamshire. During these years he also developed his skills as a writer, producing articles for educational journals, plus textbooks including the I'll Teach You series, a set of self-improvement books for ex-servicemen. He is best known, however, as the originator in the late 1940s of the I-Spy series of children's books. At first called the I-Spy Spotterbooks, these were initially rejected by several publishers, so Warrell took the risk of publishing them himself, and sold them via a friendly contact in his local Woolworths. Their instant success enabled Warrell to become a full-time writer from 1948, producing a weekly 'I-spy' column first for the *Daily Mail* and then for the *News Chronicle* who 'poached' him in 1950. A long I-Spy series evolved under various publishers, with Warrell's role that of editor-in-chief, or 'Big Chief I-Spy' as he became known to children. The pocket-size sixpenny booklets covered subjects such as birds, trees, insects, farms, history, cars, the seaside, aircraft, and musical instruments. There were items to spot for points and boxes to tick for achieving each challenge. Small prizes were awarded for completed books and a Redskins club, costing 1s. to join, featured secret codes, badges, passwords and the occasional organized gathering. Warrell obviously enjoyed the ritual and regalia side of his creation and was 'always happy to appear in his giant head-dress on special, I-Spy pow-wows' (*The Independent*). For thousands of children in the 1950s and 1960s, the I-Spy books were an affordable and attractive purchase, and Warrell's coded catchphrase ODHU/NTINGGO (good hunting) in his weekly column epitomized the books' spirit of adventurous enquiry.

In 1946 Warrell moved to London with his secretary Marian Tucker (*d.* 1994), whom he later married after his first wife died in 1952. Marian was an enthusiastic supporter of I-Spy activities and was herself known as Running Deer. Warrell retired from his I-Spy writing in 1959, though the books continued under another editor and the series remained in print until 1986. Michelin relaunched it in 1991, replacing the line drawings with photographs and updating the items. In retirement Warrell lived for many years in Budleigh Salterton, Devon, enjoying gardening and walking. He continued to write articles, and was an enthusiastic supporter of the Culham College Association magazine, contributing short pieces and reminiscences into his nineties and beyond, and for some years enjoying the distinction of being the oldest surviving Culhamite. A man of small stature, he had a booming voice and abundant white hair. He remained sharp-witted and enthusiastic until the very end of his life, with only his failing eyesight curtailing his activities. The *Daily Telegraph* erroneously reported his death in 1991, but made amends by sending him a case of champagne which, as a teetotaller, he was unable to appreciate. Charles Warrell died on 26 November 1995 at the advanced age of 106, at the Valley Lodge Nursing Home, Bakewell Road, Matlock, Derbyshire.   BELINDA COPSON

Sources Culham Educational Foundation, Abingdon, archive · *The Independent* (30 Nov 1995) · *The Times* (1 Dec 1995) · log book, Higher Wych School, Malpas, Cheshire [now known as Borderbrook School, Talwrn Green, Malpas, Cheshire] · log book, Pleasley Hill secondary school, Mansfield, 1925–58, Notts. Arch., SL 109/7/2, book A · T. Wragg, 'Year of the twerp and Big Chief I-Spy', *Times Educational Supplement* (5 Jan 1996) · b. cert. · d. cert. · W. Whitewood, 'Big Chief I-Spy', MA diss., U. Nott., 2000 · private information (2004) [R. Whitewood, daughter; W. Whitewood, family]
Likenesses Ape [T. Cuff], photograph (aged one hundred and one), repro. in *The Times*
Wealth at death £288,929: probate, 29 Feb 1996, *CGPLA Eng. & Wales*

Warren, Ambrose William (*bap.* 1780, *d.* 1856). See under Warren, Charles (1766/7–1823).

Warren, Arthur (*fl.* 1605), poet, is known only through his authorship of a volume of poetry published in 1605, *The Poore Man's Passions, and Povertie's Patience*. Entered in the Stationers' register on 14 January 1605, it was published in London in 1605 and printed by I[ames] R[oberts]. Warren dedicated the volume to 'his kindest Favourer Maister Robert Quarme' (possibly the Robert Quarme of Woodhouse, Devon, father of Walter Quarme, BA 1615–16, Lincoln College, Oxford). Nothing else is known of Warren, but several nineteenth-century scholars have suggested that he was the 'A. W.' to whom were attributed a variety of poems in the last decades of the sixteenth century, but primarily the eighty-one in Francis Davison's miscellany, *A Poetical Rhapsody, 1602–1621*. If these poems were written by one person, 'then', as Hyder Rollins said in his edition (1932) of the miscellany, 'one of the greatest poets of the Elizabethan period is still unknown' (Davison, 2.65). However, thanks to Rollins's rigorous analysis it seems most likely that the 'A. W.' poems were by several writers, that Arthur Warren was not one of them, and that 'A. W.' probably stands for 'anonymous writer'.

It has been claimed that Warren composed his poems while he was imprisoned for debt. While there is no evidence for this, clearly the author is a man of some education living in extreme penury. In any case the two poems confirm that he was not 'one of the greatest poets of the Elizabethan period'. Both poems are as awkwardly phrased as they are monotonous, each obsessively concerned with a single topic. 'The Poore Man's Passions' describes the vast gulf between the heartless rich and hopelessly poor people like himself. 'Povertie's Patience' preaches to the poor that 'patience' produces 'content' and can only be gained by those ascetic enough to renounce all worldly goods. Yet despite their artistic ineptitude these poems merit attention as a literate outcry by someone rarely heard from at first hand in the Jacobean period, one of the 'poor naked wretches' of Shakespeare's *King Lear*. Warren's poems are not merely a complaint. They have a political agenda: that it is the toil of the poor that makes possible the extravagant, selfish lives of the Jacobean conspicuous consumers:

> Diggers, and Dikers, Drudges, Carters, Swaines,
> … The poorest persons worke thy richest gaines.
> … Coblers, and Curriers, Tinkers, Tanners all
> Support thy state, else would thy fortress fall;

and that the rulers should:

> Summon a Parliament …
> To extirpate the roots of misery.
> (*Poore Man's Passion*, sigs. [B4], [B5v])

Warren's words were eerily prophetic of various idealistic programmes like that of Gerrard Winstanley, the mid-century communitarian 'Digger', who argued that 'Rich men receive all they have from labourer's hand' (*The Law of Freedom*, 1652). But with the collapse of revolutionary fervour and the restoration of the monarchy those who had naïvely hoped to level the playing field soon discovered, as Warren foresaw, that like Tantalus:

> what they [the poor] stoop to take, too low doth lie;
> And what they reach to catch, ascends too hie.
> (*Poore Man's Passion*, sig. [E2])

P. J. FINKELPEARL

Sources *DNB* • F. Davison, *A poetical rhapsody, 1602–1621*, ed. H. E. Rollins, 2 vols. (1932) • Foster, *Alum. Oxon.* • C. Hill, *Society and puritanism in pre-revolutionary England* (1964)

Warren, Charles (1766/7–1823), engraver, was the eldest son of Bartholomew and Hannah Warren. The family appears to have moved to London before the baptism of David Bartholomew, a younger brother of Charles, on 15 October 1769 at St Martin-in-the-Fields. The name Bartholomew Warren occurs most frequently in Cornwall, which may be Warren's native county. Little is known of his early life, although his obituary in the *Gentleman's Magazine* mentions engraving on copper calico printing rollers as his earliest employment; he is also thought to have worked for gunsmiths. He married Elizabeth about 1787 (since their daughter Elizabeth was born on 20 March 1788).

Soon afterwards Warren began a long association with London booksellers, notably Charles Cooke, by engraving plates for popular works; the earliest were portraits of Fox, Pitt, and Thurlow, produced for *The Senator, or, Clarendon's Parliamentary Chronicle*, the first volume of which was issued in 1790. Many editions of literary works carried Warren's engravings in the last decade of the eighteenth century, and from 1803 he engraved for John Sharpe's series of classics. Later he engraved the plates for William Ottley's *Engravings of the … Marquis of Stafford's Collection of Pictures* (1814–18) and after Robert Smirke for a celebrated edition of Cervantes' *Don Quixote* (1818). His reputation was made by two plates engraved for John Boydell's edition of his *Shakspeare* (1803), which probably led to Warren's election—on the proposal of the mezzotint

engraver Valentine Green—to the Society of Arts on 31 October 1804; he engraved nine frontispiece portraits for the society's *Transactions* in 1805 and between 1813 and 1821. He was elected a member of the Committee of Polite Arts on 22 March 1805 and served until his death, being one of its two chairmen in 1805–7 and 1822–3. He was also elected a governor of the short-lived Society of Engravers (founded in 1802); it was succeeded by the Artists' Annuity Fund, established in 1810, of which Warren was president from 1812 to 1815. He was also a director and exhibitor of twenty plates at W. B. Cooke's exhibition of engravings in 1821. His style of copper-engraving was well adapted to his subjects and his execution was meticulous.

After the Plymouth Stock Bank had suffered losses from forgery, Warren was asked to design and execute a vignette for their notes. This resulted in his being requested to give evidence to the committee on forgery, set up by the Society of Arts: here, on 15 April 1818, he supported J. T. Barber Beaumont's campaign to persuade the Bank of England to use steel plates for printing their notes. To demonstrate his views, Warren engraved a head of Minerva on a decarbonized saw blade in May 1818, maintaining that the process of case hardening blocks of steel was unnecessary and potentially damaging. He devoted the next four years to further experiments and, with the aid of his platemaker Richard Hughes, finally produced a satisfactory technique, which was first demonstrated publicly in the frontispiece and engraved title-page for an edition of Philip Doddridge's *Rise and Progress of Religion* (May 1822). He thus made steel plates acceptable to engravers in general, for which the Society of Arts awarded him their gold medal in 1823. He died before he could receive it, and it was presented to his brother Ambrose by the duke of Sussex in May 1823. Warren was assisted by Samuel Davenport, Thomas Fairland, Joseph Phelps, and Henry Chawner Shenton, who married Warren's daughter Mary Ann on 9 March 1824 at St Pancras Old Church.

Warren died suddenly of heart disease in the middle of a conversation at East Hill, Wandsworth, on 21 April 1823; he was buried in St Sepulchre Church, Newgate Street, on 1 May. His many friends found him sociable, generous, and of a cheerful disposition, although he was inclined to be improvident. His will, dated 8 September 1816, is a key document which establishes his relationship as brother to both Ambrose William and William Warren. It makes no mention of his wife, who must have predeceased him, but names two daughters, Elizabeth, who married the engraver Luke Clennell in 1809 and died in 1819, and Mary Ann, who alone survived him and inherited most of his property. His brothers were left engravings, a complete set being bequeathed to Ambrose.

Ambrose William Warren (*bap.* 1780, *d.* 1856), engraver, the third son of Bartholomew and Hannah Warren, was baptized on 27 October 1780 at St Andrew's, Holborn. It is likely that he worked and was trained by his brother Charles (who is wrongly described as his father in the *Dictionary of National Biography*); their plates appear in the same publications. Among his earliest work was a portrait of Sir Roger Curtis, after C. M. Metz, published on 26

June 1802, and plates for Alexander Pope's *Essay on Man* (1819). Cervantes' *Don Quixote* (1818), Horace Walpole's *Castle of Otranto* (with Clara Reeves's *The Old English Baron*, 1817), Lord Byron's *Poems* (1816), William Ottley's *Engravings of the Marquis of Stafford's Pictures* (1814–18) and Edward Young's *Night Thoughts* (1811) are representative and were shown at W. B. Cooke's exhibition of engravings in 1821. He also engraved plates for the Society of Arts *Transactions* (1816–19) and for the *Description of the Collection of Ancient Marbles in the British Museum* (1812–45), by T. Combe and others. He married Elizabeth Rebecca Callow on 12 May 1810 at St Pancras Old Church; their daughter Mary Ann was baptized on 13 May 1816 at St Andrew's, Holborn. An Edmund Warren, possibly a son, was present at Ambrose's death. Ambrose Warren's steel plates included two for Walpole's *Anecdotes of Painting* (1827), many for various editions of Walter Scott's works, the annual *The Gem* (1830–31), several editions of David Hume and Tobias Smollett's *History of England* from 1834–6 onwards, and a series of royal portraits from Alfred the Great to George II. His most important single plates are *The Beggar's Petition*, after W. F. Witherington (1827), and *The New Coat*, after David Wilkie (1832). His plates, mostly well engraved, were signed variously 'A. W. Warren', 'A. Warren', or 'Warren'. He died of apoplexy at Orchard Cottage, Enfield Highway, on 24 April 1856, and was described on his death certificate as 'historical engraver'. Engravings by both Warrens are held in the prints and drawings department of the British Museum, London.   B. HUNNISETT

Sources *GM*, 1st ser., 93/2 (1823), 187 · J. Pye, *Patronage of British art: an historical sketch* (1845), 312–74; facs. edn [1970] · Redgrave, *Artists · Engraved Brit. ports.*, 6.710 · [W. B. Cooke], *Exhibition of engravings* (1822) [exhibition catalogue, 9 Soho Square, London, 1822] · H. Hammelmann, *Book illustrators in eighteenth-century England*, ed. T. S. R. Boase (1975), 10–102 · J. L. Roget, *A history of the 'Old Water-Colour' Society*, 1 (1891), 162–4 · IGI [Ambrose Warren] · [Society of Arts], *Report … relative to … preventing the forgery of bank notes* (1819), 1–39 · Society of Arts, minutes of committees, 1822/3, RSA, 78–82; 99–107 · T. Warren, *A history and genealogy of the Warren family* (1902); repr. (1982) · B. Hunnisett, 'Charles Warren engraver (1762–1823) … and the society [pts 1–2]', *Journal of the Royal Society of Arts*, 125 (1976–7), 488–91, 590–93 · B. Hunnisett, *Steel engraved book illustration in England* (1980), 18–32 · PRO, PROB 11/1671, fols. 249v–250 · d. cert. [Ambrose Warren] · *Annual Register* (1823), 195 · parish register, St Sepulchre, Newgate Street, London, 1 May 1823, entry 369 [burial]

Likenesses W. Mulready, portrait, c.1815, repro. in Pye, *Patronage of British art*, 329 · S. W. Reynolds, mezzotint, pubd 1824 (after marble bust by W. Behnes), BM, NPG · W. Behnes, marble bust, BM · J. Bromley, pencil drawing (after W. Behnes), BM

Warren, Sir Charles (1798–1866), army officer, born at Bangor on 27 October 1798, was the third son of John Warren (1766–1838), dean of Bangor, who was nephew of John Warren, bishop of Bangor. His mother was Elizabeth, daughter of Thomas Crooke MD, of Preston, Lancashire. He entered the Royal Military Academy at Woolwich but, being offered by the duke of York a commission in the infantry, he was gazetted ensign in the 30th foot on 24 November 1814, and joined the depot at Colchester on 24 January 1815. He commanded a detachment from Ostend

in the march of the duke of Wellington's army to Paris after Waterloo, and entered Paris with the allied army.

In January 1816 Warren embarked for India, and served at Fort St George, Madras, until his return to England in the summer of 1819. He was promoted lieutenant on 13 November 1818. On 17 August 1820 he transferred to the 55th foot. In December 1821 he embarked with his regiment for the Cape of Good Hope, was promoted captain by purchase on 1 August 1822, commanded a detachment of two companies on the Cape frontier from November 1824 to the end of 1825, and returned to England in 1827. During his service at the Cape he rode from Cape Town to Grahamstown, and, among other expeditions into the interior, he journeyed across the Orange and Vaal rivers to Sitlahoo with Mr Glegg of the Madras civil service, who published an account of it at the time. Warren visited the Griqua and BaRolong chiefs and Robert Moffat's mission station near Kuruman. Extracts from his journals were printed in the *Royal Engineers Journal* in June and July 1884. His notes and sketches were made use of by his son, Lieutenant-Colonel Charles *Warren of the Royal Engineers, when reporting on the Bechuana and the Griqua territories fifty years later, in 1876.

Warren married on 17 April 1830, and, with his wife, Mary Anne (d. 20 Jan 1846), daughter of William Hughes of Dublin and his wife, Margaret, embarked for India. He served at Fort St George, Madras, until the end of 1831, when he marched to Tunamalli and Bellary in command of a wing of the regiment. He commanded the 55th in the expedition against the raja of Coorg in April 1834 and was severely wounded. He was promoted major on 21 November 1834, sent to Vellore in 1835 and to Sikandarabad in 1836, and returned to England with his family in 1838.

On 26 June 1841 Warren sailed for China in command of a detachment; he arrived at Hong Kong in November, fought in the war of 1842, and was mentioned in dispatches. He was promoted brevet lieutenant-colonel on 23 December 1842, and the following day was made a companion in the Order of the Bath. He also received the war medal. After his return to England in August 1844, Warren was promoted regimental lieutenant-colonel to command the 55th regiment on 25 November 1845, and served with it in Ireland during the famine in 1846–7. In March 1851 he accompanied it to Gibraltar, where he served until May 1854, when he took it to Turkey and the Crimea. He commanded the regiment (which formed part of the 1st brigade, 2nd division), was wounded at the battle of the Alma, and was mentioned in dispatches. He commanded his brigade at Inkerman in November 1854, and was again wounded and mentioned in dispatches. He by now had a considerable reputation for bravery, publicly recognized by Lord Raglan, the commander-in-chief in the Crimea.

Warren was sent to Scutari and then on sick leave, until he was sufficiently recovered to return to the Crimea on 12 July 1855; on the 30th he resumed command of the 1st brigade, 2nd division, and served continuously in the trenches until the fall of Sevastopol, again being wounded. In February 1856 he was given the command of an independent brigade, composed of the 11th hussars, the siege-train, and four battalions of infantry, which he held until June, and in July he returned to England. For his Crimean services he received the medal with clasps for Alma, Inkerman, and Sevastopol, the reward for distinguished military service, the fourth class of the Légion d'honneur, the third class of the Mejidiye, and the Turkish and Sardinian medals.

On 8 August 1856 Warren was appointed to command a brigade at Malta with the temporary rank of major-general. On 26 October 1858 he was promoted major-general on the establishment of the army. He remained at Malta for five years, and, in the absence of the governor, acted for some time as governor and commander of the forces. He was made a knight commander in the Order of the Bath, military division, on 19 April 1865.

Charles and Mary Warren had six children, two of whom died young. Warren got married again on 4 October 1859, this time to Mary (d. 22 Dec 1860), daughter of George Bethell, rector of Worplesden and vice-provost of Eton College. There were no children from the second marriage. Warren's eldest son, John, served with him in the Crimea, dying of wounds at Scutari. His second son, Charles (aforementioned), had a varied and distinguished military career. Warren died at Monkstown, near Dublin, on 27 October 1866.

Warren had a natural ability for science and mathematics. His memory was so good that he could retain in his mind all the figures of a long calculation, and could correct and alter those figures at will. He was also a good draughtsman. He occupied his leisure time during the later years of his life in perfecting an instrument which he had invented for the graphic solution of astronomical problems for nautical purposes, and which he had brought to the notice of the Admiralty in 1845. The instrument was for the purpose of approximately determining the latitude from two observations taken before 9 a.m. and at noon, and also of finding the latitude by a south altitude, from the time of day, and of finding the amplitude and azimuth. The invention was considered ingenious, and its principle correct; but its adoption was not recommended for the Royal Navy, in case this induced neglect of even the slight acquaintance with nautical astronomy which officers were then required to possess.

R. H. Vetch, rev. H. C. G. Matthew

Sources Hart's Army List · A. W. Kinglake, The invasion of the Crimea, 8 vols. (1863–87) · J. Ouchterlony, The Chinese War (1844) · A. Murray, Doings in China (1842) · K. S. Mackenzie, Narrative of the second campaign in China (1842) · private information (1899)

Wealth at death under £1500: probate, 10 Nov 1866, CGPLA Eng. & Wales

Warren, Sir Charles (1840–1927), army officer, police commissioner, and archaeologist, was born on 7 February 1840 at Fairview House, Bangor, Caernarvonshire, the second son of Major-General Sir Charles *Warren (1798–1866) and his first wife, Mary Anne (d. 1846), daughter of William Hughes of Dublin and Carlow. Until the age of eight Warren was educated at home, then spent six years at Bridgnorth School, Shropshire, and Wem grammar school, Shropshire. He attended Cheltenham College for one

Sir Charles Warren (1840–1927), by Barraud, pubd 1888

term, from January to June 1854 (he was later a life member of the council of Cheltenham College, and in 1886–7 was president of the Cheltonian Society). He attended the Royal Military College, Sandhurst (1854), and the Royal Military Academy, Woolwich (1855–7). He was commissioned into the Royal Engineers on 27 December 1857. On 1 September 1864 he married Fanny Margaretta (d. 24 May 1919), daughter of Samuel Haydon of Guildford: they had two sons and two daughters. Throughout his life Warren was a staunch, devoted member of the Church of England. He was also a keen freemason, becoming the first master of the lodge of masonic research, Quatuor Coronati 2076, in 1886, and district grand master of the eastern archipelago in 1891.

In 1859 Warren was sent to work on the immense Gibraltar survey project. From 1865 to 1867 he was an assistant instructor in surveying at the School of Military engineering, Chatham. From 1867 to 1870 he worked for the Palestine Exploration Fund, and surveyed much of the region and excavated in Jerusalem, where he helped recover the Moabite Stone. He published his findings in The Recovery of Jerusalem (with Charles Wilson, 1871), Underground Jerusalem (1874), and The Temple or the Tomb (1880).

Ill health forced Warren to return to Britain in 1870, where he served at Dover (1871–2) and at the School of Gunnery at Shoeburyness (1872–6). He was rescued from obscurity by the Colonial Office, which appointed him special commissioner to delimit the boundary between

Griqualand West and the Orange Free State, for which he was created CMG (1877). He remained in the region, settling land problems in Griqualand and taking part in the Transkei War of 1877–8, when he commanded the Diamond Fields horse. He saw action in several engagements and was severely wounded at Perie Bush. He was mentioned in dispatches and promoted brevet lieutenant-colonel. After the war he was appointed special commissioner to investigate 'native questions' in Bechuanaland, where he became friendly with, and was influenced by, the pro-Tswana Scottish London Missionary Society missionary John Mackenzie, and so advocated further British intervention. In 1879 he became administrator of Griqualand West.

From 1880 to 1884 Warren was chief instructor of surveying at Chatham. In 1882 he was sent to discover the fate of Professor Edward Henry Palmer's archaeological expedition in Sinai. Warren found that Palmer and his colleagues had been robbed and murdered. After recovering their remains, Warren located the criminals and brought them to justice. He was created KCMG (24 May 1883) and the third class Mejidiye from the Egyptian government. In 1883 he was made knight of justice of the order of St John of Jerusalem, and in June 1884 was elected FRS.

Bechuanaland was considered crucial by British imperialists as the route to the north—the 'Missionaries' Road'—potentially enabling further British expansion. In 1884 it was threatened by German and Transvaal expansion. Transvaal-backed Boer freebooters from the self-styled republics of Stellaland and Goshen, exploiting local African rivalries, had taken African land and were raiding African cattle. Tswana chiefs had repeatedly requested British protection against the Boers, but the British government preferred saving pennies to saving Africans. Under pressure from missionaries and humanitarians—especially John Mackenzie—imperialists, and Cape colonists, belatedly the Gladstone cabinet—despite Gladstone himself, a Cobdenite relic in a Bismarckian world—decided in November 1884 to send a military expedition to assert British sovereignty and end the 'republics'. Warren was to command. He requested and was given a force of some 4000 troops, and landed at Cape Town in December 1884. In January 1885 the British government by an order in council gave the Bechuanaland protectorate a solid legal basis and stated its boundaries. Warren led north his force (the Warren expedition) of imperial troops and locally recruited volunteers, with artillery and three observation balloons (the first British use on active service): Warren made an ascent at Mafeking. He himself approved of the expedition's purpose, and insisted on taking with him John Mackenzie. Warren negotiated separately with Cecil Rhodes and Paul Kruger, but their goals were incompatible—Rhodes wanted Cape-settler control of Bechuanaland, Kruger wanted Boer control—and they did not agree. The Warren expedition was essentially successful: welcomed by the Tswana—Warren made treaties with Kgama of the Ngwato and other African rulers, ending the 'republics' without bloodshed, and asserting British sovereignty. Warren wanted a crown colony form

of government, separate from Cape Colony, but the British government (from June 1885 Salisbury's first ministry), wanting minimal involvement and cost, refused, and in September recalled Warren. He was made GCMG (4 October 1885). In September southern Bechuanaland was annexed as a colony, British Bechuanaland (in 1895 incorporated into Cape Colony), while northern Bechuanaland, north of the Malopo River, remained a protectorate (later Botswana).

In 1886 Warren stood for election as an independent Liberal in the Hallam division of Sheffield. Lord Wolseley, the adjutant-general, told Warren he needed special permission to stand because he was on half pay and refused to grant it. Warren stood, and was told that his career was effectively ended. Despite the radicalism of his manifesto, including free elementary schooling, House of Lords reform, and Irish home rule, he lost by 609 votes. However, Wolseley appointed Warren to the command at Suakin. He was there only a few weeks before he was appointed in 1886 chief commissioner of the Metropolitan Police.

Warren's main task was to restore public confidence in a force lacking leadership and discipline. However, his efforts were complicated by several difficulties: first, poor economic conditions continued to provoke large demonstrations by socialists and unemployed, one of which in February had led to the downfall of his predecessor, Sir Edmund Henderson, which caused propertied alarm and fear of insurrection; second, the new Conservative home secretary, Henry Matthews, with whom Warren did not get on; and third, the Jack the Ripper murders. Not all these challenges were overcome satisfactorily, but by the time Warren resigned in 1888 he had left a profound impression on the force.

Warren accomplished his primary task by bringing in former soldiers and appointing more inspectors and sergeants. His concern for police welfare made him popular. Although Warren's policing of the 1887 jubilee celebrations was considered successful, other actions earned him criticism and ridicule which long persisted. In 1886 he responded to a rabies outbreak by ordering all dogs to be muzzled and led; stray dogs were taken to the dogs' home or killed if rabid. Such peremptory action was derided by the press. His policing of the London demonstration by unemployed and socialists on 13 November 1887 ('bloody Sunday') was by some considered severe, but by others necessary. Initially he forbade the meeting, but when this was ignored he denied the demonstrators access to Trafalgar Square by using 4000 police, 300 soldiers, and 600 mounted police and Life Guards. A bayonet charge by the troops was narrowly averted, but they and the police eventually cleared the area, with 150 persons taken to hospital. Warren was criticized by the radical press and received death threats.

Some critics believed his treatment of the unemployed subsequently jeopardized police operations in Whitechapel during the summer and autumn of 1888, when searching for Jack the Ripper. However, Warren's methods, including a week-long, house-to-house search in

October 1888, were accepted by the local population. His actions also ensured that local Jews were not blamed for the murders. His supposed support for the use of bloodhounds, two of which apparently got lost during trials in fog on Tooting Common, was not true. He remained sceptical, and had the animals imposed on him by the Home Office reacting to public pressure. In the end the dogs were not used because Warren refused to buy them.

Warren's relations with Matthews deteriorated over two major issues: control of police finances, which Warren questioned; and the independence of the Criminal Investigation Department (CID), which Warren felt undermined good practice and discipline. Warren wrote an article in *Murray's Magazine* touching on the problems over the CID. Forbidden to write any more, he felt this infringed his right to reply to criticism and resigned. He was created KCB, civil division (7 January 1888).

From 1889 to 1894 Warren commanded at Singapore, where he organized a defence scheme and experimented with wireless telegraphy. From 1895 to 1897 he commanded the Thames district, working on completing the defence scheme, and in 1897 was promoted lieutenant-general. When the Second South African War began in October 1899 he was on the retired list, but in November he took the 5th division to the Cape.

In South Africa, Warren held the dormant commission (so that if anything happened to the commander-in-chief, Sir Redvers Buller, he would assume command): apparently this affected Buller's attitude to Warren. Warren joined Buller—who found personal relations with him painful—in Natal, and in January 1900 had a leading role in the second attempt to relieve White's besieged garrison in Ladysmith. Buller planned to outflank the Boer positions by crossing the Tugela River at Trichardt's Drift and by capturing the hills opposite, then to move onto the road leading to Ladysmith. Buller gave Warren control of the operation despite his never having commanded so large a force and not having been on active service for fifteen years. On 18 January Warren's 15,000 men crossed the river and between 20 and 23 January engaged the Boers in unsuccessful attempts to break through. Warren's approach was ponderous, slow, and indecisive, and he refused to support the enterprising Dundonald, whose cavalry had turned the Boers' right flank. Warren would not move until he felt his men had enough supplies. He wrote subsequently that he wanted to first blood his troops: 'it was my mission to introduce Mr Thomas Atkins to Mr Boer face to face, and bid them come together' (Williams, 288). Buller remained close by watching the action unfold and eventually intervened. It was decided to attack Spion Kop ('spy hill') which overlooked the road Warren favoured for his advance.

The hill was taken on the night of 23–4 January 1900 and in the morning was attacked by the Boers, who bombarded the British with guns on adjacent hills overlooking Spion Kop. Warren's handling of the battle was inept, although he was not helped by Buller's sporadic interference. Warren reacted slowly and failed to improve communications with the summit. Despite ordering his forces

on the right to attack and relieve the pressure on Spion Kop, he failed to do the same with his forces on the left; and he muddled the command on the summit itself, a situation made worse by Buller's intervention. By nightfall, the British position was considered hopeless and Spion Kop was evacuated, not by Warren's order but by the decision of Colonel Andrew W. Thorneycroft (of Thorneycroft's mounted infantry), made on the spot, leaving trenches full of British dead: 'that acre of massacre' (Pakenham, 297). Finally, Buller went to Warren's headquarters and ordered a retreat back across the Tugela.

Buller blamed Warren, and himself for not superseding Warren six days earlier. He wrote to his wife 'old Warren is a duffer and lost me a good chance' (Pakenham, 307), and in his dispatch criticized Warren for the failure to hold Spion Kop. Warren was unaware of this until the government published Buller's Spion Kop dispatch in April 1900. Warren felt betrayed by Buller, but Lord Roberts, commander-in-chief in South Africa from January 1900, forbade Warren to defend himself in print. Despite taking part in the eventual relief of Ladysmith and successfully crushing a Boer rebellion—which began in April 1900—in north-western Cape Colony, Warren returned to Britain in August 1900. The government considered him incompetent, and he never again commanded troops in the field. He was promoted general in 1904 and colonel-commandant, Royal Engineers, in 1905.

In retirement Warren was involved from 1908 in the Boy Scout movement, in scientific matters, on which he published several books and articles, and in freemasonry. He also published his memoirs, *On the Veldt in the Seventies*, in 1902. He died of pneumonia, following influenza, at his home, 3 Trinity Mansions, Weston-super-Mare, Somerset, on 21 January 1927, and after a military funeral at Canterbury was buried on 27 January in Westbere churchyard, Kent, close to the grave of his wife.

Warren's career was varied and controversial. He enjoyed high civil and military office, and helped reform the Metropolitan Police and extend British rule in southern Africa. However, his irascible, quarrelsome, eccentric character harmed his career, and he never received the full trust and confidence of colleagues and superiors. Historians of the Second South African War have agreed with contemporary condemnation of his generalship.

KEITH SURRIDGE

Sources W. W. Williams, *The life of General Sir Charles Warren* (1941) · T. Warren, *A history and genealogy of the Warren family* (1902) · P. Sugden, *The complete history of Jack the Ripper* (1995) · J. Symons, *Buller's campaign* (1963) · D. M. Schreuder, *Gladstone and Kruger: liberal government and colonial 'home rule', 1880–85* (1969) · T. Pakenham, *The Boer War*, another edn (1982) · *The diary of Gathorne Hardy, later Lord Cranbrook, 1866–1892: political selections*, ed. N. E. Johnson (1981) · A. Sillery, *Botswana: a short political history* (1974) · H. C. G. Matthew, *Gladstone, 1875–1898* (1995) · R. Robinson, J. Gallagher, and A. Denny, *Africa and the Victorians* (1961); repr. (1967) · A. Keppel-Jones, *Rhodes and Rhodesia: the white conquest of Zimbabwe, 1884–1902* (1983) · J. Haydn, *The book of dignities: containing lists of the official personages of the British empire*, ed. H. Ockerby, [new edn] (1890) · Boase, *Mod. Eng. biog.* · *WWW* · Burke, *Peerage* (1907) · E. S. Skirving, ed., *Cheltenham College register, 1841–1927* (1928) · G. S. Jones, *Outcast London: a study in the relationship between classes in Victorian society* (1971) ·

A. C. F. Jackson, 'Sir Charles Warren: founding master of Quatuor Coronati', *Ars Quatuor Coronatorum*, 99 (1986), 167–88 • W. Porter, *History of the corps of royal engineers*, 2 (1889)
Archives Palestine Exploration Fund, London, papers relating to exploration of Palestine | UCL, corresp. with Edwin Chadwick
Likenesses Ape [C. Pellegrini], caricature, chromolithograph, NPG; repro. in *VF* (6 Feb 1886) • Barraud, photograph, NPG; repro. in *Men and Women of the Day*, 1 (1888) [*see illus.*] • W. Stoneman, photograph, NPG
Wealth at death £4589 19*s*. 8*d*.: resworn probate, 30 March 1927, *CGPLA Eng. & Wales*

Warren, Edward Perry (1860–1928), art collector, was born at Waltham, Massachusetts, on 8 June 1860. He was one of five children of Samuel Dennis Warren (1817–1888) and his wife, Susan Cornelia, *née* Clarke (1825–1901). Samuel Warren, a descendant of modest farmers who came from England in the seventeenth century, worked his way from office boy to partner in a Boston paper making firm. Later he acquired his own company, and by the time Edward Perry Warren was born he was well on his way to becoming a millionaire.

After attending Phillips grammar school and Hopkinson School, both in Boston, Warren, known to friends as Ned, followed his oldest brother, Sam, to Harvard but was not happy there. From childhood he was introverted and his mother maintained that he was 'more nervous than the other children' (Sox, 3). On receiving his AB from Harvard (1883), he determined to spend the rest of his life abroad. In 1883 he matriculated at New College, Oxford, where he obtained a first class in classical moderations in 1885 but was prevented by ill health from taking the final honour school. However, he graduated BA with a pass degree in 1888.

Warren thrived in the environment of Oxford, where unlike Harvard he 'found people who did not damn my ideas as incorrect, but, on the contrary, found them interesting' (Sox, 15). At New College he met his lifelong partner, John Marshall (1862–1928), who was from Liverpool. He also met a number of like-minded young men who became friends and associates in collecting antiquities. Among them was Bernard Berenson, who was visiting Europe; Warren gave him financial assistance, making it possible for Berenson to begin his long career as an art connoisseur. Later, in 1911, Warren was made an honorary fellow of Corpus Christi College, Oxford, in recognition of his intention to bequeath to the college an endowment to revive its praelectorship of Greek. As a result, the college's first E. P. Warren praelectorship in classics, with a specific commitment to teaching Greek, was appointed in 1954, and has strengthened the college's classical resources ever since.

In 1890, two years after the death of his father, Warren was able to lease Lewes House, a large Georgian residence in the Sussex market town of Lewes which became the focal point of his enterprises. There with Warren lived Marshall and six other young men. It was described by William Rothenstein, a frequent visitor, as 'a monkish establishment where women were not welcomed. But Warren, who believed that scholars should live nobly, kept an ample table and a well-stocked wine-cellar …'

(W. Rothenstein, *Men and Memories: Recollections, 1872–1900*, 1931, 1.343, quoted in Sox, 45). Rothenstein also added that a 'secrecy seemed to permeate the rooms and corridors, to exhaust the air of the house. The social relations, too, were often strained …'.

Everything at Lewes House was shared, be it a walking stick, or the tub, where guests bathed *à l'antique* after an afternoon on horseback. Warren managed the establishment like a tiny German court: he took upon himself all the concerns of both his companions and his household staff. Matthew Stewart Prichard, the most able—and eccentric—of his friends, said that Warren was 'a sort of Buddha to consult upon everything' (Sox, 47). There was little interest in the outside world: newspapers were rarely read; neighbours never called—not even the vicar. Prichard's brother-in-law, T. H. Lyon, commented that it was 'an attempt to live again under a paganism long since dead … charged with something very like make-believe' (ibid., 172).

The great collecting centred at Lewes House was at its height in the 1890s. It was so successful that Alexander Murray of the British Museum complained that there was 'nothing to be got nowadays' as the Lewes House collectors were 'always on the spot first' (Burdett and Goddard, 79). The Boston Museum of Fine Arts received the lion's share of treasures, including the celebrated Chios head which Rodin coveted. Rodin was to create a version of *The Kiss* to suit Warren's specific requirements. It came later to the Tate. At the Ashmolean in Oxford is a treasure of Warren's, what has been described as one of the most perfect fifth-century BC bronze heads. An *Adam and Eve* by Cranach and a large tondo by Filippino Lippi, both of which used to grace the dining-room of Lewes House, are now respectively at the Courtauld Institute in London and the Cleveland Museum. In 1999 one of his most prized—and unusual—treasures surfaced from a private collection: a first-century AD Roman silver cup displaying homosexual love-making. It was purchased by the British Museum for £1.8 million.

After twelve years the Lewes House brotherhood started to break up. As John Fothergill, one of the companions—later famous as an innkeeping diarist—wrote:

> The whole thing was too comfortable and all-providing … When any of us went to London which we never did save on business, there was the petty cash box in an open drawer in the bureau. We had only to dip into a heap of sovereigns … I confess I thought this proceeding too horribly heavenly … Yet … we never felt secure at home against sudden departures to Italy and Greece.   (Sox, 153)

Prichard was the first to leave; in 1901 he went to Boston to work at the museum. The most devastating blow came in November 1907 when Marshall married Warren's spinster cousin, Mary Bliss, and they moved to Rome. For long Marshall had been stationed there alone and the marriage was more an act of spite than of romance. Warren was left alone in Lewes with a boy he had mysteriously adopted.

Despite the rejection, Warren made it possible for the Marshalls to live in a sumptuous flat overlooking the Spanish Steps. Marshall became associated with the

Metropolitan Museum in New York and purchased a number of antiquities for them. However, among the treasures were some spectacular fakes; most notably three 'Etruscan' warriors which were not formally recognized as fakes until 1961.

Mary Marshall died in 1925, and for the remaining three years of their lives Warren and Marshall were re-united. Marshall exhausted himself trying to track down the creator of several archaic Greek forgeries. In Frankfurt he became seriously ill and he died within two days of returning to Rome. Warren, who was with him, willed himself to die. His death, later in the same year, on 28 December 1928, at the Cambridge House Nursing Home, 4 Dorset Square, London, followed an abdominal operation in London.

Warren was cremated on 1 January 1929 and his ashes were taken to Bagni di Lucca in Italy where they were placed with Marshall's remains. At the English cemetery a simple monument was created topped appropriately with a Grecian urn.

Under the *nom de plume* Arthur Lyon Raile, Warren wrote a number of works, most notably *The Defence of Uranian Love* (3 vols., 1928–30), and a collection of poems, *The Wild Rose* (1910). But his most lasting achievements were the extraordinary antiquities and works of art which today can be seen as far afield as London, Oxford, Leipzig, Boston, and Bowdoin College in Maine.   DAVID SOX

Sources D. Sox, *Bachelors of art: Edward Perry Warren and the Lewes House Brotherhood* (1991) · O. Burdett and E. H. Goddard, *Edward Perry Warren: the biography of a connoisseur* (1941) · M. Green, *The Warrens of Mount Vernon Street: a Boston story, 1860–1910* (New York, 1989) · *Bowdoin* [Bowdoin College, Brunswick, ME], 61/1 (Sept 1987) · J. Fothergill, *My three inns* (1949), 231–40 · private papers owned by D. Sox · F. R. Symonds, 'Greece, women, and the tunnel: E. P. Warren and his Corpus connection', *Pelican Record*, 39/2 (1994–6), 12–21 · b. cert. · d. cert.
Likenesses photographs, priv. coll.
Wealth at death $1,204,000—listed 28 Dec 1928 in Boston newspapers · £626 11s. 2d. effects in England: probate, 20 July 1931, CGPLA Eng. & Wales

Warren, Elizabeth (*bap.* 1617), religious writer, was baptized at Woodbridge in Suffolk on 19 December 1617, the daughter of John and Elizabeth Warren; Warrens had been recorded in Woodbridge since 1568. The remarkable education displayed in her published works suggests she came from a clerical family, and it is possible that she was related to Thomas *Warren (*c.*1617–1694), a nonconformist divine from Suffolk. She is probably the Elizabeth Warren who married John Mace at Woodbridge on 27 October 1641, although she retained her unmarried name in her writings. In his preface to Warren's *Spiritual Thrift* (1647), Robert Cade, Woodbridge's vicar, observed that he had lived in the same town as the author for twenty-six years.

Warren's output consists of three learned theological treatises, the first of which appeared in 1646 entitled *The Old and Good Way Vindicated*. It is a defence of the clergy against extreme nonconformist doctrine. In 1929 E. M. Williams suggested that it was 'obviously' also a defence of the notoriously persecuted puritan clergyman Henry Burton (Williams, 561). However, Williams brought no supportive arguments and it is possible to read the work rather as a defence of the need for a highly educated, specialist élite who preach and interpret the gospel. Such a doctrine was within Anglican bounds, but the pamphlet did not defend episcopacy nor denounce unconventional religious assemblies. It went into a second edition, claiming to be much enlarged, but was in fact identical to the first. Warren's second work, *Spiritual Thrift*, is a book of devotional character, with only occasional allusions to the errors or vices of the time. The short treatise *A Warning-Peece from Heaven*, which appeared in 1649, was her final publication, and speaks in strong terms of the divine vengeance which England would incur because of its immorality. It deplores 'schismaticks' and 'Regicides', the latter now being 'stiled meritorious'. The church of St Mary's at Woodbridge was ravaged by the Cromwellian army at some point in the civil war, and perhaps their behaviour influenced Warren's opinions. The political position of the pamphlet is not obvious and interpretation is difficult: it refers to biblical examples of bad kings such as Ahab alongside examples of schismatics such as Korah who were smitten by God. Ahab was killed in battle, but most of Warren's readers would have known the story of how Jehovah sent a 'lying spirit' into the mouth of all his prophets in order to persuade Ahab to go into battle: the line between providence and outright regicide for his suffering subjects was unclear.

Cade, a signatory of the petition of Suffolk presbyterian ministers in 1646, evidently endorsed Warren's writings, and she has been classified as presbyterian or a moderate puritan. However, Warren's works operate on multiple levels, and it is not merely what she wrote but the fact that she was writing and actually publishing that is transgressive since she was intervening in debates restricted by law and custom to men. Warren displayed an extraordinary amount of classical and theological learning, quoting Latin authors in the original. Moreover, by sermonizing she behaves as if she herself were a minister—a profession from which women would be excluded for another three centuries. Although married, Warren published all her books under her maiden name and made no allusion to any need for a husband's authority. It is possible that she was a widow, but altogether her practice was more radical than her theory.

The prefaces to *The Old and Good Way* and to *Spiritual Thrift* reveal awareness of tension and sexist intolerance by labouring to justify or glorify a female writer. Cade stresses that Warren's abilities are gifts from God, while she herself writes: 'And if any suppose me, *Proteus*-like, to change the shape of my silent modesty, let their Christian moderation embrace this Maxime, That Grace devests Nature of no due ornament' (*The Old and Good Way*, 'To the Christian Reader'). While not taking issue with men's doctrine of woman's inferior and subordinate nature, she finds a way of by-passing it: grace (that is, divine blessing) has bestowed these gifts upon her.

Warren would surely have used her married name on any will, so she is probably not the Elizabeth Warren who wrote a will in 1656, the testator then being described as 'late of Chatham in the County of Kent, widdow', leaving her property to her son Hamlett (PRO, PROB 6/32, fol. 80v).   JULIA GASPER

Sources IGI • private information (2004) [R. Merrett, Woodbridge Museum, Suffolk; A. Hubbard, St Mary's Church, Woodbridge] • DNB • K. V. Thomas, 'Women and the civil war sects', Past and Present, 13 (1958), 42–62 • E. M. Williams, 'Women preachers in the civil war', Journal of Modern History, 1 (1929), 561–9 • Greaves & Zaller, BDBR, 293 • M. Bell, G. Parfitt, and S. Shepherd, A biographical dictionary of English women writers, 1580–1720 (1990), 207–8 • A. Fraser, The weaker vessel: woman's lot in seventeenth-century England (1984) • administration, PRO, PROB 6/32, fol. 80v

Warren, Emily Mary Bibbens (1869–1956). *See under* Women artists in Ruskin's circle (*act.* 1850s–1900s).

Warren, Enid Charis (1903–1980), medical social worker, was born on 22 May 1903 at 15 Lincoln Road, Finchley, London, the third of five daughters of Walter Richard Warren (d. 1930), barrister, and his wife, Annie, née Dixon. While she was still an infant her family moved to Belhaven, the house in Shepherds Hill, Highgate, which remained their home until 1931. Of many happy early memories, she once recalled how her father would hold her at the window so that she could see the sheep being driven from King's Cross to pasture overnight between their road and Alexandra Palace. The distinctive and strong character that impressed all who knew her was evident from a young age. Her sisters considered her 'formidable', 'like a resident governess'; 'a fighter for what she thought was right' (*A Portrait of a Social Worker*, 3), as did many of her colleagues in later years.

Enid Warren's secure, rational, and highly principled background and the ethos of the North London Collegiate School for Girls, which she and all her sisters attended, helped to develop her concern for less fortunate people and their social conditions, and to determine her choice of a career. In 1922 she went to the London School of Economics and took the two-year social science course. She decided to become a hospital almoner, no doubt partly influenced by her older sister, Marjory Winsome *Warren, who trained as a doctor and was to become a renowned geriatrician. On applying to the Institute of Hospital Almoners, she was advised first to get some experience. After a year at a settlement in Bermondsey she was accepted for training in 1925 and qualified in 1926. By this time she had grown into a woman of above average height. 'Tall, erect and angular in build, she moved with an air of dignity and freedom. The direct and searching gaze of her blue eyes could—and usually did—express a steadiness and calm that was immediately reassuring' (*Portrait of a Social Worker*, 5).

Warren's first post was at St Mary's Hospital, Paddington, one of London's voluntary hospitals, quickly followed by a locum post at the Royal Free Hospital, where she had been a student. In 1928 she took up a permanent appointment at the Miller Hospital in Greenwich. On the death of her father in 1930 she returned to the Royal Free Hospital, where she stayed until 1935. By this time the London county council had begun to appoint almoners to the twenty-eight municipal hospitals, developed from the

poor-law infirmaries. Miss Warren, as she was generally addressed throughout her long and distinguished career, realized and valued the potential the public hospital offered for developing social-work services. She worked in various LCC hospitals until 1942.

In 1942 Warren was appointed head almoner at the Hammersmith Hospital, the first municipal hospital with a postgraduate medical school, where she remained until her retirement in 1969. She was the unfailing champion of patients. Her absolute integrity, her capacity to engender good working relationships with colleagues of all disciplines and levels of experience, her insistence on the highest standards of work with patients, and her concern to develop the professional potential of staff all made her an outstanding departmental head and leader of the profession. An administrator rather than an academic, she applied her social-work skills to encouraging innovation and accountability. She developed a system to keep track of patients and the caseloads of each almoner. Her department was the first to provide a student unit for those undertaking the applied social studies course at the London School of Economics in 1954. Almost more significant was her decision in the early 1960s to experiment with staff supervision. She promoted a research project— 'medical social work in action', undertaken by Zofia Butrym—which showed that the social work department with nine medical social workers and six clerical staff received 607 referrals in the two-month period of study in 1964. The number of patients and relatives who referred themselves was almost as large as the number referred by doctors and nurses, perhaps reflecting the approachability of the department. Two-thirds of those referred required skilled social-work help, while the remainder needed help in obtaining medical care and in integrating with the community.

Warren's active role in the development of the social-work profession began early in her career, first as honorary secretary to the Hospital Almoners' Association. She later became vice-chairman and from 1937 to 1940 she was chairman. Maintaining an active and leading role, she saw the HAA amalgamate with the Institute of Hospital Almoners (the training body) in 1945 to form the Institute of Almoners, of which she became chairman in 1961. By the time she relinquished that office in 1966 the institute had been renamed the Institute of Medical Social Workers. She was appointed OBE in 1966. In 1968, on the retirement of Professor Sir Alan Moncrieff, she became the institute's president, the only social worker to do so. Her belief in the essential unity of social work was confirmed by the active part she played from 1962 to 1970 as vice-chairman of the Standing Conference of Organizations of Social Work, which led to the formation of the British Association of Social Workers in 1970, with Warren as its first chairman. The unified association of social workers came into being in the same year as legislation was passed to implement the Seebohm committee's proposals for the unification of personal social services in England and Wales.

In the early years of her retirement Warren devoted

much energy to helping the BASW become established. Her willingness to do any task, however menial, with integrity and reliability, did much to help reconcile the differing perspectives among members from different areas of social work. As a chairman she excelled. Always a good ambassador for social work, she enjoyed travels to Canada and Australia and made and renewed many life-long friendships. Warmth, wisdom, compassion, and integrity were combined with a great capacity to listen and always to put the patient at the centre of things. As the BASW became established, she became involved with other bodies, such as the Elfrida Rathbone Society, the League of Friends of University College Hospital, the Marshall Hall Trust, the Royal College of Midwives Benevolent Fund, and the Family Welfare Association (FWA) grants committee. She also served as a trustee of the Social Workers' Benevolent Trust and the Social Workers' Educational Trust.

Shortly after contributing to the tenth annual general meeting of the British Association of Social Workers, Warren became ill and was admitted to the Royal Free Hospital, now in Hampstead not Gray's Inn Road, where she began her career. She died there of cancer and hypernephroma of the kidney on 17 September 1980 and was buried at Golders Green cemetery. A service of thanksgiving for her life and work was held on 6 December 1980 at the City Temple, where, unbeknown to most of her friends, she worshipped regularly—a social-work giant, much loved and respected. JOAN BARACLOUGH

Sources *A portrait of a social worker*, [British Association of Social Workers] (1981) · J. Baraclough and others, *One hundred years of health related social work* (1996) · *Yearbook of Hospital Almoners' Association* (1927–48) · Z. Butrym, *Medical social work in action* (1968) · *The Almoner*, 1–17 (1948–65); continued by *Medical Social Work*, 18–22 (1965–70) · personal knowledge (2004) · b. cert. · d. cert.
Archives FILM BFI NFTVA, '100 years of health related social work', video, Kay Richards (producer), for the British Association of Social Workers, 1995 [contains photographs of Miss Warren]
Likenesses photographs (as a young woman and in the 1970s), repro. in *Portrait of a social worker* · photographs (as first chair of BASW and as a signatory to its articles of association), repro. in Baraclough and others, *One hundred years*, 50–51

Warren, Frederick (1775–1848), naval officer, was born in London in March 1775, the son of Dr Richard *Warren (1731–1797), physician to George III, and his wife, Elizabeth, only daughter of Dr Peter *Shaw; he was the elder brother of Pelham *Warren. He was admitted to Westminster School on 15 January 1783, and entered the navy in March 1789, on board the *Adamant*, flagship of Sir Richard Hughes on the Halifax station. When the *Adamant* was paid off in 1792, Warren was sent to the *Lion* (Captain Erasmus Gower), going out to China. Shortly after his return, on 24 October 1794, he was confirmed lieutenant and appointed to the *Prince George*. He afterwards served in the *Jason* on the home station, and in the *Latona* at Newfoundland, where he was promoted on 10 August 1797 to command the sloop *Shark*. In 1800 he commanded the *Fairy* (18 guns) in the West Indies, and on 12 May 1801 was promoted captain. On the renewal of the war in 1803 he commanded the sea fencibles of the Dundee district for

three years. He married, in 1804, Mary, only daughter of Rear-Admiral David Laird of Strathmartine House, Dundee; they had children, among whom the eldest son, Richard Laird Warren, died an admiral in 1875.

In November 1806 Warren was appointed to the frigate *Daedalus* (32 guns) and took her to the West Indies, where in April 1808 he was moved to the *Meleager* (36 guns), which was wrecked on Barebush Key, near Port Royal on 30 July 1808. Warren was acquitted of blame, and officially complimented on his exertions after the ship struck. In 1809 he commanded the *Melpomene* (38 guns) in the Baltic for a few months, attacking Russian shipping off the Finnish coast, and in the fortified port of Reval. On the night of 29–30 May the *Melpomene* fought in the Belt against about twenty Danish gunboats, which in a calm or light wind were formidable antagonists. At daybreak the wind freshened and the gunboats retired; the *Melpomene* had lost thirty-four men, killed and wounded, and her hull, masts, and rigging had suffered much damage, but she had saved a valuable convoy. She was shortly afterwards sent to England and sold out of the service as beyond economic repair.

In December 1809 Warren was appointed to the *Argo* (44 guns), which he commanded on the Lisbon station and in the Mediterranean for nearly three years. In 1814 he commanded the *Clarence* (74 guns) in the channel, and from 1825 to 1830 the *Spartiate* (76 guns). He was promoted rear-admiral on 22 July 1830; from 1831 to 1834 he was commander-in-chief at the Cape of Good Hope, and from 1837 to 1841 admiral-superintendent at Devonport Dockyard, Plymouth. There, according to the *Gentleman's Magazine*,

> Amidst the rival political interests which raged in the borough to the injury of the public service, and which placed the superintendent of the dockyard very often in a difficult position, the gallant admiral, with his masterly tact, was seldom unsuccessful in defeating party intrigues, and seldom failed in having the man selected who was adapted for the place, instead of having the place adapted for the man. (*GM*, 546)

He was made vice-admiral on 23 November 1841, and died at his seat, East Court, Cosham, near Portsmouth, on 22 March 1848. J. K. LAUGHTON, *rev.* ANDREW LAMBERT

Sources D. Syrett and R. L. DiNardo, *The commissioned sea officers of the Royal Navy, 1660–1815*, rev. edn, Occasional Publications of the Navy RS, 1 (1994) · *Annual Register* (1848), pt 2, p. 222 · O'Byrne, *Naval biog. dict.* · *GM*, 2nd ser., 29 (1848), 546
Archives NMM, letter-book | NL Scot., corresp. with Robert Liston
Likenesses R. J. Lane, lithograph, NPG

Warren [*formerly* Venables-Vernon], **George John**, **fifth Baron Vernon** (1803–1866), literary editor, was born George John Venables Vernon at Stapleford Hall, Nottinghamshire, on 22 June 1803. He was the only son of George Charles Venables Vernon, fourth Baron Vernon (1779–1835), of Sudbury, Derbyshire, and Frances Maria (*d.* 1837), only daughter of Admiral Sir John Borlase *Warren (1753–1822). Sir Richard Vernon, speaker of the House of Commons in 1426, was an ancestor. He was educated at Eton College and, from 1822 to 1824, at Christ Church, Oxford.

George John Warren, fifth Baron Vernon (1803–1866), by G. B. Black, 1861

As a youth he was taken to Italy, and afterwards lived in Florence, where he studied the Italian language and history. On 30 October 1824 he married Isabella Caroline (1805–1853), daughter of Cuthbert Ellison of Hebburn, Durham; they had five children.

Vernon entered public life in 1831 as MP for Derby. After the passing of the 1832 Reform Bill, which he warmly supported, the county had two divisions, and he became member for the southern part. He continued in the House of Commons until 1835, when he was called to the House of Lords on the death of his father. In 1837 he exchanged his birth name, Venables Vernon, for that of Warren, in compliance with the will of Lady Warren Bulkeley, which bequeathed the estates of Poynton and Stockport to her niece Frances Maria, Vernon's mother, in 1826. His children born before 1837, however, retained their own name.

Vernon was an expert rifle-shot, an energetic supporter of the volunteer movement, and in 1859 raised a company at Sudbury, where he erected a firing-range. His whole life, however, was devoted to Dante. With the advice and help of such friends and collaborators as Luigi Passerini, Sir Anthony Panizzi, and Pietro Fraticelli, he printed numerous texts, including *L'Inferno, secondo il testo di B. Lombardi con ordine e schiarimento per uso dei forestieri di L. V.* (1841); *Petri Allegherii super Dantis ipsius genitoris comœdiam commentarium*, edited by Vincenzio Nannucci (1845); *Chiose sopra Dante, testo inedito, ora per la prima volta pubblicato* (1846), commonly known as *Il falso Boccaccio*; *Il Febusso e Breusso, poema ora per la prima volta pubblicato* (1847); *Chiose alla Cantica dell' Inferno di Dante Allighieri attribuite a Jacopo suo figlio* (1848); and *Comento alla cantica di Dante Allighieri di*

autore anonimo (1848), reputedly the oldest commentary on the *Inferno* in existence, probably written about 1328.

Vernon's two most important works, however, were *Le prime quattro edizioni della 'Divina commedia' letteralmente ristampate* (1858) and *'L'Inferno' di Dante Alighieri disposto in ordine grammaticale e corredato di brevi dichiarazioni da G. G. Warren, Lord Vernon* (1858–65). Only a limited number of copies were issued for private circulation, as neither was intended for sale. *L'Inferno* was described by Henry Clark Barlow as a work 'which, for utility of purpose, comprehensiveness of design, and costly execution, has never been equalled in any country' (Barlow, 1). Some of the most distinguished artists and men of letters in Italy were occupied for twenty years in its preparation. It includes the text of the *Inferno* with a grammatical *ordo* and many notes and tables; the second volume is an encyclopaedia of history, geography, topography, and heraldry relating to Dante and Florence, with many unpublished documents; the third or album volume, which appeared after Lord Vernon's death, contains 112 original engravings of incidents in the *Inferno*, views of towns, castles, and other localities mentioned therein, and portraits, paintings, plans, and historical monuments illustrating the history of the fourteenth century.

Warren Vernon was a *socio corrispondente* of the Academia della Crusca from 1847 and a member of many other literary societies. His wife having died on 14 October 1853 he married, second, on 14 December 1859, his cousin Frances Maria Emma, only daughter of the Revd Brooke Boothby. Their only child, a son, died in infancy. In May 1865 Vernon was created cavaliere di San Maurizio e Lazzaro, in recognition of his labours on behalf of the national poet. The following year, after a long illness, he died at Sudbury Hall, Derbyshire, on 31 May; he was buried at Sudbury on 6 June. He had intended to print the famous Latin commentary Benvenuto da Imola delivered as public lectures at Bologna about 1375, but this was carried out by his second son, William Warren Vernon, in 1887, under the editorship of Sir J. P. Lacaita. A considerable Dante scholar in his own right, William Warren Vernon published a series of 'Readings of the "Commedia"' from 1888 to 1900.

Vernon's eldest son, **Augustus Henry Vernon**, sixth Baron Vernon (1829–1883), was born at Rome on 1 February 1829. He was lieutenant and captain in the Scots Fusilier Guards but retired in 1851. On 7 June of that year he married Harriet Frances Maria (1827–1898), third daughter of Thomas William Anson, first earl of Lichfield, who bore him four sons and six daughters. On the death of his father in 1866 he succeeded to the title. He was a president of the Royal Agricultural Society and, as chairman of the French farmers' seed fund in 1871, took an active part in the relief of the French agriculturists who had suffered during the time of war. Though not an Italian scholar he shared in the family devotion to Dante, and the third, or album, volume of his father's edition of *The Inferno* was issued under his care. He died at 17 Dover Street, London, on 1 May 1883, in his fifty-fifth year, and was buried at Sudbury four days later. He was succeeded by his son, George

William Henry Venables Vernon, seventh Baron Vernon (1854–1898).

The Vernon family's Dantesque endeavour was the last of the great whig politico-cultural projects typical of the Regency period. The fifth baron combined an eighteenth-century collector's interest in Dante with a nineteenth-century devotion to textual and historical scholarship. He also passed on a tradition of social responsibility; the sixth baron's work to relieve French farmers imitated his father's assistance to Lancashire and Cheshire during the cotton famine of 1862.

H. R. TEDDER, *rev.* ALISON MILBANK

Sources J. P. Lacaita, memoir, in G. G. Warren, *L'Inferno di Dante Alighieri disposto … da G. G. Warren, Lord Vernon*, 3 vols. (1858–65), vol. 3 · H. C. Barlow, *The Vernon Dante and other dissertations* (1870) · *The Times* (1 June 1866) · *The Times* (3 May 1883) · *The Times* (9 May 1883) · GEC, *Peerage*, new edn · Burke, *Peerage* (1975) · BL cat. · National Union Catalogue · John Rylands Special Collection Catalogue · *DNB* · Foster, *Alum. Oxon., 1715–1886* · Venn, *Alum. Cant.*
Archives BM, letters · Ches. & Chester ALSS, family MSS · L. Cong., MSS · Royal Holloway College, Egham, Surrey, letters relating to his edition of Dante | Balliol Oxf., letters to J. Conroy [Augustus Vernon] · BL, letters to Antonio Panizzi, Add. MSS 36715–36718, *passim* · CUL, letters to G. Stokes [Augustus Vernon] · JRL, Dante collection · UCL, letters to H. C. Barlow
Likenesses mezzotint, pubd 1839, BM · G. B. Black, engraving, 1861, NPG [*see illus.*] · G. Richmond, chalk drawing, 1866 (Augustus Vernon), Sudbury Hall, Derbyshire · A. Romagnoli, oils, 1884 (Augustus Vernon), Sudbury Hall, Derbyshire · J. Collier, oils, Sudbury Hall, Derbyshire · G. Hayter, group portrait, oils (*The House of Commons, 1833*), NPG · G. Hayter, pencil and ink drawing, BM · engraving, repro. in Lacaita, memoir
Wealth at death under £30,000: resworn probate, 1868, *CGPLA Eng. & Wales* (1866) · £65,436 12s. 8d.—Augustus Vernon: probate, 1883, *CGPLA Eng. & Wales*

Warren, Hardick (*fl.* **1650**), hermetic philosopher, is known only from what may be gleaned from a single printed pamphlet. Inspired by reading the work of William Lilly (p. 16), Warren wrote this work when a young man—'my tender years, which indeed are not many' (sig. A3)—in his 'private chamber' in London, on 9 November 1650. Entitled *Magick and Astrology Vindicated*, and carrying two recommendatory verses by 'W. A.' and 'J. R.', it was published in 1651 by Nathaniel Brook at the Angel in Cornhill, and was Warren's first, and seemingly his only, published work. His text was part of the pamphlet debates characteristic of the literature produced during the civil war period in England. Written in direct response and reply to an earlier pamphlet entitled *A Brief Declaration Against Judicial Astrology* (1650) by John Raunce, to whom Warren refers as the 'Priests Champion' (p. 1), it is part of the upsurge in interest in the occult arts and sciences, alternative religions and Paracelsian medicine in England and Europe in the 1650s and 1660s. Warren claimed he was trying to unite being a natural philosopher, a Platonist, an astrologer, a stoic, a 'Hermet', and a Christian (pp. 30–31). He offered a passionate, Neoplatonic defence of natural magic and natural astrology, explicitly distinguishing them from various 'diabolical practises' (sig. A2v) with which they had become associated, such as 'Necromancy, Witchcraft and the rest' (p. 3).

Warren's Neoplatonic conceptual prism refracts his specific religious, scientific, and political understanding. He cites Plato as his authority for saying that magic 'is an Art of Worshipping God'. Warren's magical religion is a form of antisemitic (p. 6), mystical, Christianity; an ancient theology (prisca theologia) in which Christianity was articulated through its Egyptian, Hebrew, Persian, Babylonian, and Greek Platonic influences. He sees this magical religion as scientific, the 'practical part of natural philosophy' involving: 'the investigation of those admirable Vertues, and occult Properties, which that infinite Wisdom hath bestowed and given to his Creatures; and how fitly to apply those things that are to work, to those things that are to suffer' (p. 5). Its investigative light is diffused from the 'first and true Light' from the divine mind, God, through the angels, the intelligences, the celestials, finally into man's mind where 'it is made a bright discourse of Reason, and the knowledge of divine things, and wholly rational' (pp. 11–12). Although the actual causal mechanism between the zodiac and its effect/signification is not discernible by reason, this does not lead Warren to question its scientific status. In his thinking it is comparable to the 'hidden Qualities' in the magnet or digestion, which we experience, but of which we do not know the 'secret Cause'.

This rational religion of natural magic is also a Paracelsian-influenced, physical medicine. 'Magick is the Connexion of Natural Agents and Patients', and:

> doth contain the whole Philosophy of Nature, which is that which bringeth to light the hidden Vertues, and drawing them out of Natures Bosom, and converting them to humane uses, by applying those things that work to those that suffer … it is nothing else but a mutual application of Natural Vertues, Agent and Suffering reciprocally. (p. 4)

It is linked implicitly with the doctrine of signatures through the ability it gives its practitioner to perceive the 'shewing forth of virtue' that God in his wisdom has infused into all inferior matter, the knowledge of which in turn, citing Ficino, 'may in some measure bring us to the true knowledge of the Divinity of Christ' (p. 5).

With regard to politics, Warren's pamphlet bears traces of the language of republicanism when he writes of the established churches and how their 'Sisypus Robberies of us the Commonalty (under specious pretence of a divine Right) with endless toyl'. There are also Hartlibian overtones when he writes of the 'Public Good' of making true natural magic available 'in thy own Dialect, not tyed in a Gardian knot of impossibilities'.

Yet at the same time there is an élitism in Warren's thinking. For true understanding of the divine knowledge is 'found out and attained but by a very few', what he calls 'the true Sons of Minerva' (p. 4). As a consequence, his preferred system of government appears to be one born of a mystical union of church and state, in which a divinely appointed monarch rules through his Magi:

> the Giver of Forms distributeth them by the Ministry of Intelligences, which he hath appointed over his works, Governors and Keepers, unto whom this ability is entrusted in things committed to them, That every vertue of Stones,

herbs, Minerals, and all the rest, might be from the Intelligences governing.   (p. 7)

There is however no sense of contract in this notion of sovereignty, or election of representatives. Instead Warren claims that the divine light that shines in man:

is manifest by the *disposition* of the *body*, as the Peripateticks will have it, or which I conceive is more true, according to the pleasure of the Cause giving, which distributes to every one according to his Will, from thence it passeth the *fancy*, and as yet it is above the *senses*, and being only imagineable, at length it attains to the *senses*, and especially to that of the *eyes*, in that it is made a *visible clearness*, and is stretched forth in each of these prospicious bodies, in which it becomes a *colour*, and a *shining fireness*.   (p. 12)

It is by this distinctly physiognomical means that Warren's magi become known, especially by the look in their eyes.   M. H. PORTER

Sources H. Warren, *Magick and astrology vindicated from those false aspersions and calumnies, which the ignorance of some hath cast upon them* (1651)

Warren, Sir (Thomas) Herbert (1853–1930), college head and classical scholar, was born at Cotham, a suburb of Bristol, on 21 October 1853, the second of three surviving sons and four daughters of Algernon William Warren, a wholesale druggist in Bristol, who held a leading position in the city as town councillor, alderman, and JP. His mother, Cecil, was the daughter of Thomas Thomas, of Llangadog, Carmarthenshire, and sister of Christopher Thomas, mayor of Bristol in 1878; to her family Warren owed his first forename. His father had literary and artistic interests, his mother both practical capacity and something of the Welsh imaginative temperament. Herbert— he was always known by his second name—was educated at Manilla Hall School, Clifton, Bristol, until he was fifteen, when he entered Clifton College, then recently founded with John Percival as its first headmaster. He quickly made his mark both in work and games, and left in 1872 as head of the school and scholar-elect of Balliol College, Oxford, captain of football and fives champion.

When Warren went up to Balliol, Benjamin Jowett had been two years master and the college was at the height of its reputation. Among the contemporaries whom Warren came to know well were H. H. Asquith and his brother, W. W. Asquith (afterwards a master at Clifton), Charles Lucas, Thomas Raleigh, and Alfred Milner; W. P. Ker and A. D. Godley were his juniors by two years. In this distinguished society Warren more than held his own; he obtained first classes in classical moderations (1873) and in *literae humaniores* (1876), and won the Hertford scholarship (1873), the Craven scholarship (1878), and the Gaisford prize for Greek verse (1875). He was occasionally chosen to represent the university at rugby football, maintained his supremacy at fives (a game which he continued to play with skill and vigour even after he became president of Magdalen College), and held the office of librarian at the union in 1875–6. Francis de Paravicini helped to put the finer edge on his scholarship, and Milner, his closest friend, introduced him to German learning and did much

Sir (Thomas) Herbert Warren (1853–1930), by Glyn Philpot, 1927–8

to form his mind and interests. But probably the main influence was that of Jowett himself, whose ideal of a college as not merely a home of learning but a training ground for public life, was destined to guide Warren's policy in his direction of Magdalen.

In October 1877, a year after he had taken his degree, Warren was elected to a prize fellowship at Magdalen and succeeded in the following term to a classical tutorship. The college, in the later years of the presidency of Frederic Bulley, had already ceased to be a close corporation and was coming to the front, but Warren himself made the greatest contribution to its remarkable development in the next twenty years. Not only was his brilliant scholarship a stimulus to his pupils' success, but he set himself to know and help them as a personal friend. He also cultivated close connections with the public schools, and made every effort to improve the quality of the scholars and commoners who entered the college. During the period of his fellowship, Warren, who was brought up a nonconformist, was confirmed in the Church of England, though he remained a layman.

On the death of Dr Bulley in 1885, Warren, at the unusually early age of thirty-two, was elected president, and held the office until 1928, a period of forty-three years. Shortly after his election, on 16 December 1886, he married Mary Isabel, youngest daughter of the chemist Sir Benjamin Collins *Brodie, bt; she assisted and advised him throughout his presidency, but they had no children. Warren now threw himself even more vigorously than before into the task of developing the college, gathering round him a distinguished staff of teachers including

H. W. Greene, C. R. L. Fletcher, C. C. J. Webb, and Christopher Cookson (A. D. Godley was already a classical tutor), and welcoming as a new strength to the college the professorial fellows added by the statutes of 1882. At the same time he increased the numbers of the undergraduates and raised the standard of the college, both intellectually and in other ways. It was sometimes said by outside critics that Warren was over-anxious about the social standing of his undergraduates; anecdotes on this theme were encouraged by the great satisfaction which he drew from the decision of George V in 1912 to choose Magdalen for the prince of Wales (the future Edward VIII). Warren was created KCVO by the king when the prince left Magdalen on the outbreak of war in 1914.

Meanwhile Warren was coming to hold a prominent position in university affairs. He was for many years a member of the hebdomadal council, a delegate of the University Museum, and a curator of the Taylor Institution. In these capacities he did much to promote the study of natural science and of modern languages in Oxford. His reputation for favouring the high born at Magdalen is balanced by his work within the university to promote adult education. In 1907 he was instrumental in establishing Oxford's connection with the Workers' Educational Association. A member of the council of Lady Margaret Hall, he supported the unsuccessful campaign to open Oxford degrees to women in 1896. He spoke often in congregation and, if he was sometimes prolix and over-conciliatory, he always gave the impression that he knew his subject thoroughly and carried weight accordingly. He was one of the founders in 1883 of the Oxford Magazine, an influential organ of academic opinion in the late-Victorian and Edwardian period. From 1906 to 1910 he was vice-chancellor. Lord Curzon, whose installation as chancellor Warren had arranged with great ceremony, was then engaged in drawing up his programme of university reform in response to external critics, notably Charles Gore, bishop of Birmingham. Warren supported Curzon wholeheartedly in his policy of averting the appointment of a royal commission in the unfavourable political climate following the Liberal landslide in 1906. When a royal commission was eventually set up in 1919, it proved sympathetic to limited reforms of the type which Warren and Curzon had promoted.

Outside the university Warren was a member of several government commissions and committees. He was a member, and later chairman, of the governing body of Clifton College, a councillor of the University of Bristol, and for a time a governor of St Paul's School. A member of the Oxford and Cambridge joint schools examination board from 1884 to 1915, he was a well-known figure in the educational world. Politically he was a Liberal in early life, but grew increasingly out of sympathy with Gladstone.

Warren's practical activities never swamped his devotion to literature. Although his only contribution to classical scholarship was a useful though unpretentious edition of the first five books of Plato's Republic (1888; seven times reprinted), his scholarship showed itself in other ways. The two great literary enthusiasms of his life were for Virgil and for Tennyson. Inspired while at Clifton by J. A. Symonds, with whom he remained on friendly terms, he published two volumes of poems, By Severn Sea (1897) and The Death of Virgil (1907). His wider literary interests found expression in his lectures as professor of poetry at Oxford (1911–16), which exhibit his range of reading, his taste, and his mature powers of criticism. The Creweian orations, which it fell to his lot to deliver at the Encaenia, proved also that his fine scholarship and 'Attic wit' remained unimpaired. The honorary degree of DCL was conferred upon him at Lord Curzon's first Encaenia in 1907, and he was also awarded the honorary degrees of LLD by Birmingham University and DLitt by Bristol University; he was made an honorary fellow of Balliol in 1924.

The long years of Warren's presidency were a time of almost unbroken prosperity for Magdalen College and of personal happiness to himself, but were marred by the First World War, when he received almost daily the news of the death of some Magdalen man, bringing him great distress. He steered the college through this time of anxiety and through the hardly less difficult period of reconstruction which followed, though not without some friction with the younger fellows on the governing body, impatient both with his habits of personal rule, and with his identification with outmoded Victorian ideals.

Warren was naturally a fine athletic figure, tall and broad, with very dark hair, a full beard, and slightly prominent teeth, but in the last twenty years of his life he became more and more crippled by arthritis. In 1928 age and increasing infirmity made him decide to resign; he received many tokens of affection and gratitude, and was elected an honorary fellow of the college. He continued to live in Oxford, at 74 Woodstock Road, and died there suddenly on 9 June 1930. He was buried in Holywell cemetery, Oxford, on 13 June. He was survived by his wife.

CYRIL BAILEY, rev. M. C. CURTHOYS

Sources The Times (10 June 1930) · The Times (11 June 1930) · L. Magnus, Herbert Warren of Magdalen (1932) · personal knowledge (1937) · Oxford Magazine (19 June 1930) · W. D. Macray, A register of the members of St Mary Magdalen College, Oxford, 8 vols. (1894–1915), vol. 6, pp. 189–91 · L. Goldman, Dons and workers: Oxford and adult education since 1850 (1995) · J. H. Howarth, 'The Edwardian reform movement', Hist. U. Oxf. 7: 19th-cent. Oxf. pt 2 · CGPLA Eng. & Wales (1930) · Men and women of the time (1899)

Archives Magd. Oxf., corresp. · priv. coll. | BL, letters to W. E. Gladstone, Add. MSS 44509–44526 · BL, corresp. with Macmillans, Add. MS 55127 · Bodl. Oxf., corresp. with Robert Bridges · Bodl. Oxf., corresp. with Geoffrey Dawson · Bodl. Oxf., letters to Gilbert Murray · Bodl. Oxf., letters to James Thompson · CUL, letters to Lord Acton · NL Scot., corresp. with Lord Rosebery · Richmond Local Studies Library, London, Douglas Sladen MSS · U. Birm. L., corresp. with Edward Arber · U. Hull, Brynmor Jones L., letters to John Ruskin

Likenesses W. B. Richmond, oils, 1899, Magd. Oxf. · G. Philpot, portrait, 1927–8, Magd. Oxf. [see illus.] · Hills & Saunders, photograph, repro. in Magnus, Herbert Warren, 40 · Lafayette, photograph, repro. in Magnus, Herbert Warren, 188 · Spy [L. Ward], caricature, chromolithograph, NPG; repro. in VF (8 April 1893) · photograph, repro. in Magnus, Herbert Warren, 146 · photograph, NPG

Wealth at death £8009 13s. 3d.: probate, 2 Aug 1930, CGPLA Eng. & Wales

Warren, James (1726–1808), revolutionary politician in America, was born at Plymouth, Massachusetts, on 28 September 1726, the eldest son of James Warren (b. 1695), who served as high sheriff of Plymouth county, and Penelope Winslow (b. 1704). He attended Harvard College from 1742, graduated AB in 1745, and then settled as a merchant and gentleman farmer in Plymouth. On 14 November 1754 he married the talented Mercy Otis (1728–1814) [see Warren, Mercy Otis], member of a prominent political family. Together they had five sons. They remained patriotic and prominent voices arguing for independence, active in Massachusetts and colonial government, and eventually ardent exponents of republicanism.

From 1766 until 1778 Warren held a seat in the lower house of the Massachusetts general court and provincial congress, and associated with the patriot leaders James Otis jun., John Adams, and Samuel Adams. He was selected as speaker of the house in 1769 and 1770, and helped to establish a local committee of correspondence in 1772. Talented and committed to the move towards revolutionary goals, he admitted humbly to John Adams in 1775: 'I am content to move in a small sphere. I expect no distinction but that of an honest man who has exerted every nerve' (*Warren–Adams Letters*, 1.78).

Warren was very active in the events of the mid-1770s that led up to the outbreak of the American War of Independence, assuming prominent roles in the patriot actions such as that at the Boston Tea Party, believing that 'the People should strike some bold stroke and try the Issue'. He was a delegate to the first Massachusetts provisional congress in October 1774, and after the death of Dr Joseph Warren at Bunker Hill he was a representative to the third Massachusetts provincial congress in 1775. He held that position until its dissolution, when he became the speaker of the house of representatives in the new general court. During the war he was appointed paymaster-general for the continental army by the continental congress and served with the army while it was at Cambridge and Boston. He also served on the navy board for the eastern department from 1776 to 1781. In 1776 also, Warren was appointed a major-general of the Massachusetts militia to lead a force into Rhode Island, but, unwilling to accept the command of an officer of a lesser rank, he resigned from the militia in August 1777.

A firm exponent of republicanism both during and after the period of government under the articles of confederation, Warren wanted a government founded on 'equal liberty and the happiness of mankind' and noted that 'I hate the monarchial part of our government' (*Warren–Adams Letters*, 72.183). In 1787 he was selected by the popular majority to occupy the speaker's chair in the house of representatives, though his popularity waned because of his stand on currency issues and criticism of the way that the government had handled the insurrection. But his republicanism was best reflected in his opposition to the ratification of the constitution from 1787 to 1788, because it lacked a bill of rights (Warren). He authored several key pamphlets that stirred up the debate, including a Boston pamphlet 'Disadvantages of federalism'; he also published as Helvidius Priscus in the *Independent Chronicle* and 'A republican federalist' in the *Massachusetts Centinel*.

In the 1790s Warren continued his advocacy of republicanism and sided with the Jeffersonian democrats, and his friendship with John Adams fell apart. He was selected to serve on the governor's council from 1792 to 1794, but was defeated as a candidate for lieutenant-governor, thereupon retiring more from active politics to pursue farming. Mercy especially responded bitterly to the fact that John Adams, as vice-president, overlooked the appointment of Warren to a government post. John Quincy Adams noted in this period that Warren 'was formerly a very popular man, but of late years he has thought himself neglected by the people. His mind has been soured, and he became discontented and querulous' (Adams, 150). Throughout the last years of his life Warren supported the ideals of Jeffersonian republicanism, and in 1804 was selected as one of the presidential electors for Massachusetts and voted for Jefferson. He died in Plymouth during the night of 27 November 1808.　　　　　　　　　MURNEY GERLACH

Sources W. E. A. Bernhard, 'Warren, James', *ANB* · *Collections of the Massachusetts Historical Society*, 72–3 (1917–25) [*The Warren–Adams letters: being chiefly a correspondence among John Adams, Samuel Adams, and James Warren … 1743–1814*] · C. H. Gardiner, ed., *A study in dissent: the Warren–Gerry correspondence, 1776–1792* (1968) · E. W. Roebling, *Richard Warren of the Mayflower and … his descendants* (1901) · C. K. Shipton, *Sibley's Harvard graduates: biographical sketches of those who attended Harvard College*, 11 (1960) · R. Zagarri, *A woman's dilemma: Mercy Otis Warren and the American revolution* (1995) · J. H. Richards, *Mercy Otis Warren* (1995) · C. Warren, 'Elbridge Gerry, James Warren, Mercy Warren, and the ratification of the federal constitution in Massachusetts', *Proceedings of the Massachusetts Historical Society*, 64 (1930–32), 143–64 · *Columbian Centinel* (30 Nov 1808) · J. Adams, *Life in a New England town, 1787, 1788* (1903)

Archives Mass. Hist. Soc., Elbridge Gerry papers · Mass. Hist. Soc., Ward family papers · Mass. Hist. Soc., Mercy Otis Warren papers · NYPL, Samuel Adams papers

Warren, John (1621–1696), clergyman and ejected minister, was born at Wolverley, Worcestershire, on 29 September 1621, the son of Thomas Warren, farmer. He attended school at Wolverley and (more importantly for his future) at Bridgnorth, Shropshire, before his admission to Sidney Sussex College, Cambridge, on 11 June 1641. He graduated BA in 1645 and proceeded MA in 1648.

By then Sir Thomas Barrington, leading patron of the godly in Essex, had dissuaded Warren from a merchant career and had offered him the lectureship at the Barrington home parish of Hatfield Broad Oak. Warren was lecturer by January 1646, later becoming vicar. While there he received offers of alternative posts but was often heard to say (according to Calamy) that 'he would not leave Hatfield Christians for any place in England' (Calamy, *Abridgement*, 2.298). Formally that is what Warren had to do in 1662, but his successor, the later nonjuring divine Francis Brokesby, made sure that informal links were maintained. The two became good friends, and Warren attended the parish church during Brokesby's ministry. In 1665 Warren formed a congregational church at Hatfield, where he was reported as preaching in 1669 and where he took out a licence under the declaration of indulgence in

1672. By 1690 he was preaching alternately at Hatfield Broad Oak and at Bishop's Stortford, where he had moved and where he was buried on 3 August 1696.

Warren was survived by his wife, Sarah (*née* Basnet), whom he made his executor and to whom he left land in Berkswell, Warwickshire. She came from a family of leading Coventry puritans: her father, Alderman Thomas Basnet, had been a leading activist for the parliamentary cause in the city, her brother Samuel was ejected from a lectureship there in 1662, and her nephew was another, the blind nonconformist minister John Troughton. The will mentions a son-in-law, Thomas Carpenter of London, haberdasher. Otherwise the kin recognized in the will are the midlands families of his brother Henry and of his wife. Warren remembered the Christians of Hatfield Broad Oak, leaving £3 to be distributed among the poor there. Sarah, who knew his mind in the matter, was to dispose of all his books and manuscripts.

Warren's importance is not to be measured by print (there is a funeral sermon for him by Henry Lukin in 1696 and a posthumous publication a year later called *The Method of Salvation*), but by the extraordinarily detailed manuscript exchanges between himself and Richard Baxter which are preserved in the fourteenth volume of the Baxter treatises in the Dr Williams's Library manuscripts. Warren had been a schoolboy when Richard Baxter had begun preaching at Bridgnorth; they shared the same house, and became friends for life. In 1649 Baxter published his first work, *Aphorisms of Justification*, which decisively detached English puritanism from its Calvinist roots. Warren was his first correspondent, and was frank and unsparing in his criticisms of Baxter's work. The exchanges between them reflect well on both men. Baxter, often so tetchy and thin-skinned in debate, warmed to the candour and scrupulousness of the younger man's response. For his part Warren showed that sweetness of nature that was to win over his supplanter, Francis Brokesby. But even so he did not mince his words. Baxter was too disputatious, made personalized attacks on those who disagreed with him, went over the heads of his Kidderminster readers and was overreacting to the perceived antinomian threat. Baxter was defensive on all these charges: 'the illiterate are more knowing than you are aware of'; he was constantly working for a mean between extremes; ten years previously, he had been very nearly an antinomian himself (Keeble and Nuttall, 1.50). But he still returned 'hearty thanks' for the 'most friendly' way that Warren had dealt with him; in 1651 would praise his 'extraordinary Apprehension' after another such series of exchanges (ibid., 1.71); would call on him in 1654 as a middleman for advice to a young pastor (ibid., 1.145); praised him in 1675 for being one of those who had put Baxter's 'crude and defective' (ibid., 2.177) first thoughts of 1649 into better order, and again in 1678 for avoiding the doctrinal misunderstandings of men like John Saltmarsh and John Bunyan (ibid., 2.201). The Essex minister Giles Firmin had written to Baxter in June 1656 of their mutual recognition of Warren as 'one of the ablest men wee have'

(ibid., 1.214), and writing again to Baxter in November 1660, at a critical time in the Church of England's fortunes, appealed to the judgement of their friend John Warren that 'wee shall quite undoe our ministry if wee shall yield to any thing which men now putt upon us, if we cannot convey it directly from the *Word*, which we tell our people is our *Rule*' (ibid., 2.10). Firmin, like Warren and Baxter, could live with bishops, but not with those who were professing for that office unscriptural *jure divino* claims. Warren, too self-effacing to publish much, and without Baxter's distinction or astringency, nevertheless stood for principles which were not too far apart from Baxter's, and for which the Restoration church, to its own great loss, could find no room.   WILLIAM LAMONT

Sources *Calendar of the correspondence of Richard Baxter*, ed. N. H. Keeble and G. F. Nuttall, 2 vols. (1991) • E. Calamy, ed., *An abridgement of Mr. Baxter's history of his life and times, with an account of the ministers, &c., who were ejected after the Restauration of King Charles II*, 2nd edn, 2 vols. (1713) • W. M. Lamont, *Richard Baxter and the millennium: protestant imperialism and the English revolution* (1979) • R. Baxter, *Aphorisms of justification* (1649) • *Reliquiae Baxterianae, or, Mr Richard Baxter's narrative of the most memorable passages of his life and times*, ed. M. Sylvester, 1 vol. in 3 pts (1696) • H. Lukin, *The good and faithfull saviour* (1696) • J. Warren, *The method of salvation* (1697) • DWL, Baxter treatises, vol. 14 • *Calamy rev.* • *Walker rev.* • Venn, *Alum. Cant.* • PRO, PROB 11/433, sig. 167, fols. 293v–294v • A. Gordon, ed., *Freedom after ejection: a review (1690–1692) of presbyterian and congregational nonconformity in England and Wales* (1917) • *An account of the ministers, lecturers … who were ejected or silenced*, 2 vols. (1713)
Archives DWL, *Baxter treatises*, 14
Wealth at death two messuages in Warwickshire; one was expected to cover legacies of at least £610: *Calamy rev.*; will, PRO, PROB 11/433, sig. 167

Warren, John (1730–1800), bishop of Bangor, was born on 12 May 1730 at Cavendish, Suffolk, the second son of Richard Warren (1681–1748), archdeacon of Suffolk, and Priscilla (d. 1774), daughter of John Fenner. His younger brother, Richard *Warren (1731–1797), was physician to George III. He was educated for seven years at Bury St Edmunds grammar school, and admitted a sizar of Gonville and Caius College, Cambridge, on 6 July 1747. On this foundation he was a scholar from 1747 to 1754, and from it he graduated BA as seventh wrangler in 1750; he proceeded MA in 1754 and gained the member's prize in 1753. He was ordained deacon on 17 June 1753, and took priest's orders on 26 May 1754. Warren was then presented to the rectory of Leverington in the Isle of Ely, and became chaplain to Edmund Keene, bishop of Ely, who collated him to the rectory of Teversham in Cambridgeshire. He was appointed to the seventh prebend of Ely on 23 January 1768, and the same day, upon his resigning Teversham, he was appointed to the rectory of Nailwell in Cambridgeshire. He acted for some time as chaplain to Lord Sondes, and later as chaplain and secretary to Matthias Mawson, bishop of Ely. In 1772 he proceeded to the degree of DD in the University of Cambridge. He married, on 12 April 1777, Elizabeth (d. 1816), daughter of Henry Southwell of Wisbech, Cambridgeshire, who brought him a considerable fortune.

John Warren (1730–1800), by Thomas Gainsborough

Nominated to the bishopric of St David's on 3 August 1779, on the translation of James Yorke to Gloucester, on 15 May 1783 Warren was elected to the see of Bangor on the advancement of John Moore to be archbishop of Canterbury. A strict high-churchman, he was a prelate of the greatest application to business. Warren was described by the historian of St David's diocese as a 'gifted and determined administrator' (Thomas, 66), and his undoubted talents, candour, and integrity clearly recommended themselves to Lord Chancellor Thurlow: indeed, it was said that no one was more in Thurlow's confidence than Warren (Mather, 129, n. 65).

As this implies, Warren was, in politics, a strong supporter of the government during the Napoleonic wars and he voted for its proposals to suspend habeas corpus in 1794. His support of the government, combined with his attention to detail and well-developed business sense lay behind the fact that he was chairman of committees on private bills in the House of Lords for most of the 1790s (Mather, 143). He was not shy of using his position to defend the interests of his family: he was chosen chairman of the committee when the House of Lords threw out the bill of the Company of Surgeons in 1797. His appointment was no doubt due to the high position his brother occupied in the medical profession. Warren died on 27 January 1800 at his house in George Street, Westminster, and was buried on 10 February in the north aisle of Westminster Abbey. He published, besides various sermons, *The Duties of the Parochial Clergy* (1785).

D'A. POWER, *rev.* MATTHEW CRAGOE

Sources S. R. Thomas, 'The diocese of St David's in the 18th century: the working of the diocese in a period of criticism', MA diss., U. Wales, Swansea, 1983 · F. C. Mather, *High church prophet: Bishop Samuel Horsley (1733–1806) and the Caroline tradition in the later Georgian church* (1992)
Archives U. Wales, Bangor, corresp. with Lord Uxbridge
Likenesses T. Gainsborough, oils, LPL [*see illus.*] · V. Green, mezzotint (after G. Romney), BM · oils, Gon. & Caius Cam.

Warren, John (1796–1852), mathematician, was born on 4 October 1796 at Bangor deanery, the son of John Warren (1766–1838), dean of Bangor, Caernarvonshire, and his wife, Elizabeth, daughter of Thomas Crooke MD, of Preston, Lancashire. Sir Charles *Warren (1798–1866), soldier, was his younger brother. Warren was educated at Westminster School and matriculated in 1814 at Jesus College, Cambridge, graduating BA in 1818 and MA in 1821. He held a fellowship at Jesus from 1818 to 1829, was a tutor there, and in 1825 and 1826 served the office of moderator and examiner. Ordained deacon in 1819 and priest in 1820, he was rector of Caldecott, Huntingdonshire, in 1822–52, and of Graveley, Cambridgeshire, in 1828–52.

In 1828 Warren published a short *Treatise on the Geometrical Representation of the Square Roots of Negative Quantities*, which was well received. The work displayed originality, though Warren was unaware that the topic had been investigated earlier in the century by French mathematicians. He countered objections in two papers delivered the following year at the Royal Society (*PTRS*, 119, 1829, 241–54 and 339–59), and concluded that any algebraic quantity may be geometrically represented, both in length and direction, by a line drawn in a given plane from a given point. He was convinced that geometry was superior to algebra when handling expressions involving the square roots of negative quantities, and that it might clarify certain obscure proofs of some of the fundamental rules of algebraic operations. His view was soon advocated, independently, by the great German mathematician C. F. Gauss. Faced with the objection that there is no necessary connection between algebra and geometry, Warren departed from tradition in recognizing that algebra need not have arithmetical numbers as its subject matter. He was elected FRS in 1830.

Warren was chancellor of the diocese of Bangor and owned the advowson of Caldecott, which as he lived at Gravely had no resident clergyman. He sold the advowson to the patron of the adjacent parish which also had no resident clergyman, and from the proceeds built a parsonage for the united parishes. He married in 1835 his cousin Caroline Elizabeth, daughter of Captain and Lieutenant-Colonel Richard Warren of the 3rd foot guards; there were no children. Warren died at Upper Bangor on 15 August 1852.   R. H. VETCH, *rev.* ANITA McCONNELL

Sources *Abstracts of the Papers Communicated to the Royal Society of London*, 6 (1850–54), 258–60 · Boase, *Mod. Eng. biog.* · *Old Westminsters*, vols. 1–2 · A. Gray, notes on members of Jesus College, Jesus College, Cambridge · E. Nagel, *Teleology revisited* (1979), 176–7

Warren, Sir John Borlase, baronet (1753–1822), naval officer, first son of John Borlase Warren (1699–1763) of Stapleford, Nottinghamshire, and his wife, Bridget, daughter of Gervase Rosell or Russell of Radcliffe-on-Trent, Nottinghamshire, was born on 2 September 1753 at Stapleford, Nottinghamshire, and baptized there on 5

October. Having been taught by the Revd John Prinsep at Bicester, he entered Winchester College in 1768 and matriculated at Emmanuel College, Cambridge, in 1769.

Entered on the books of the *Marlborough* guardship as an able seaman in 1771, Warren was discharged in 1772 to the sloop *Alderney*, which was then employed on the east coast. His naval service alternated with residence at Cambridge where he graduated BA in 1773 and proceeded MA in 1776. After discharge from the *Alderney* in 1774 he was elected on his own interest MP for Great Marlow in Buckinghamshire where his family had long owned property. He was created a baronet on 1 June 1775. Warren, known in his early years as a 'dandy' and 'young buck', was a heavy gambler and amused himself by the purchase of a yacht and Lundy island as a base for sailing in the Bristol Channel.

During the American War of Independence Warren resumed his naval career and went to America in the frigate *Venus* as a midshipman. After transferral to the frigate *Apollo* he was promoted fourth lieutenant of the *Nonsuch* (64 guns) in July 1778. He returned to England, was appointed first lieutenant of the *Victory* in March 1779, and in August was commanding the sloop *Helena*. In September 1781 he was posted to the frigate *Ariadne*, moved to the frigate *Winchester* in March 1782, and went on half pay at the peace in 1783. On 12 December 1780 he married Caroline (*d.* 1839), daughter of Sir John Clavering; they had three daughters, one of whom, Frances Maria, later married George Charles, fourth Lord Vernon, and two sons, one of whom entered the Coldstream Guards and was killed at Abu Qir in 1801.

Warren was forced to sell his property at Great Marlow in 1781 following a very expensive re-election contest in 1780, and he did not stand for parliament in 1784. At the beginning of his parliamentary service he voted with Lord North's administration, but his support became uncertain when he did not receive the naval preferment he sought. Although considered a supporter of William Pitt in 1783, he attended the St Alban's tavern meeting of coalitionists in 1784. While out of public life, he maintained his professional interest in naval affairs as vice-president of the Society for the Improvement of Naval Architecture. He was also the author in 1791 of *A View of the Naval Force of Great Britain*, which was dedicated to the duke of Clarence in whose household Warren had been a groom of the bedchamber since 1787. In this tract he attacked the excesses of press gangs and advocated the keeping of a register of seamen available for service in wartime which in peace would constitute a reserve force on half pay.

In the French Revolutionary War Warren was appointed to the frigate *Flora*, flagship of Rear-Admiral John Mac-Bride, in a squadron off Brest and the Channel Islands. Early in 1794 Warren himself commanded a squadron ordered to capture several French frigates off the coast of France that had damaged British trade. On 23 April his squadron captured three of the French frigates, and for this feat Warren was made a knight of the Bath on 30 May. In August his squadron drove on shore south of Brest a

French frigate and two corvettes. In addition to these warships Warren's squadron destroyed a large number of vessels engaged in the French coasting trade. In the spring of 1795 he was moved to the *Pomone* (44 guns), one of the frigates he had captured in April 1794, and was ordered to convoy an expedition of French royalist troops to Quiberon Bay. Although Warren landed the royalists safely and took three of the offshore islands as places of refuge after the royalists were decisively defeated by the republicans, the expedition was abandoned, and Warren returned the survivors to England. Warren's squadron, ordered in 1796 to attack the French coasting trade, destroyed or captured more than 220 vessels, thirty-six of which, including the frigate *Andromache* (36 guns), were armed. The patriotic fund for this service presented Warren with a sword worth 100 guineas. In 1797 he was appointed to the ship of the line *Canada* (74 guns) in the Channel Fleet. When a French squadron under Commodore Bompart with 5000 troops bound for Killala Bay in north-west Ireland escaped from Brest in September 1798, Warren was sent in pursuit with three ships of the line, five frigates, and several smaller vessels. Warren's squadron encountered the French squadron off Lough Swilly and engaged in a hard-fought action on 12 October; the flagship *Hoche* (74 guns) and three of the frigates were captured, five others being subsequently taken. Warren's conduct of this operation, for which he obtained a gold medal, was highly praised, and he received the thanks of both the English and Irish parliaments. After receiving promotion to rear-admiral on 14 February 1799 he hoisted his flag on the *Temeraire* (98 guns) in the Channel Fleet off Brest from where he was sent on detached service in the Bay of Biscay and off Ferrol. In 1800, while serving under Lord St Vincent off Brest and then under Lord Keith off Cadiz, he received more than £12,000 in prize money. When Keith in 1801 was co-operating with the army in Egypt, Warren was in charge of operations in the western Mediterranean.

Although Warren was actively engaged in naval service, he had been returned in 1797 as MP for Nottingham, a borough that had often been represented by a member of his family. Frequently absent from the Commons because of his duties at sea, he applied for leave in 1800 to look after affairs in his constituency. Lord St Vincent, his commander-in-chief, uncharitably held that Warren was unable to endure long periods at sea, which, 'looking back to the course of his services and manner of life when ashore, is easily accounted for'. St Vincent nevertheless testified that Warren was a 'good fellow in the presence of an enemy, but runs a little wild when detached' (Corbett and Richmond, 4.14). When re-elected to parliament in 1802, Warren declared when his return was challenged that 'having already supported the public cause to the utmost of my power', he would not spend another £1000 to represent 'that terrible place [Nottingham]' (HoP, *Commons, 1790–1820*, 5.492–3). Following the peace of Amiens in March 1802 Warren was appointed ambassador to Russia after the tsar had requested that a naval officer be named. He was sworn of the privy council on 8 September

1802, and his credentials as ambassador, dated 5 September, were presented in St Petersburg on 10 October. When war with France was renewed in 1803, Warren, hard pressed for money, sought to resume his naval career, but he remained in Russia until 1804. Recognizing the value of an Anglo-Russian alliance for protecting British interests in the Mediterranean, he promoted that goal, though he was careful to let the Russians know that Britain would never sacrifice Malta. Disappointed in his request for an increase in salary as well as in his quest for a peerage, he willingly left St Petersburg in November 1804 when recalled by Pitt. Although there was doubt about whether Warren was loyal to Pitt or Lord Addington, Lord Barham, first lord of the Admiralty, in 1805 offered him a seat on the Admiralty board; but the offer was withdrawn when Warren indicated that he did not want 'a place of confinement'. He did, however, support the Pitt government in the Commons where he presented the petition of the naval orphans' asylum for a parliamentary grant and spoke for the prize agency bill.

Warren was promoted vice-admiral on 5 November, and returned to naval duty in December 1805 when he was named commander-in-chief of one of the two squadrons sent to hunt down the squadrons of Leissègues and Willaumez that had escaped from Brest. He hoisted his flag on the *Foudroyant* (80 guns), and sailed from Spithead with six other ships of the line in January 1806. Sailing southwards towards Madeira, he missed the French squadrons from Brest, but south-west of Madeira captured the *Marengo* (80 guns), flagship of Rear-Admiral Linois, and the *Belle Poule* (40 guns), returning to France from the East Indies. On his return to Spithead, Warren was ordered in June to scour the western Atlantic for Willaumez's squadron, Leissègue's squadron having been destroyed by Sir John Duckworth off Santo Domingo in February. Warren touched at Barbados in July and reached the Chesapeake in September without encountering Willaumez's squadron, and returned to England in November. But before his return Lord St Vincent of the Channel Fleet once again castigated Warren's conduct, calling him 'a mere partisan, preferring prize money to the public good at all times' (*Selections from the Correspondence of … Markham*, 60). Thomas Grenville, first lord of the Admiralty, complained that Warren had 'played the devil' by leaving some of Willaumez's squadron unwatched in the Chesapeake. Holding that the admiral's conduct was 'indefensible' and that he was 'good for nothing but fine weather and easy sailing', Grenville declared that he was not entitled to any 'mark of approbation' (Grenville, 4.91–4, 103–4). But despite Grenville's poor opinion of him, Warren, who had not stood at Nottingham for re-election to parliament in 1806, was elected to fill a vacancy in March 1807 for Buckingham, which was controlled by Grenville's brother, the marquess of Buckingham. Warren's parliamentary career finally ended with the general election of May 1807 when the marquess chose his nephew to stand instead of Warren.

In October 1807 Warren succeeded Vice-Admiral George C. Berkeley as commander-in-chief of the North American

squadron based at Halifax. He sailed in December 1807 from Cawsand Bay in the flagship *Swiftsure* (74 guns), and reached Bermuda in January 1808 where he took command of the squadron from Berkeley in February. His chief task was to curb the aggressiveness unleashed by his predecessor that had led to a crisis with the United States when HMS *Leopard* attacked the USS *Chesapeake* off the Virginia Capes on 22 June 1807. Under Warren the squadron was largely concerned with routine matters, such as the protection of British trade and watching for stray French cruisers, three of which were captured in 1809. He was concerned with the establishment of more clearly defined limits for the North American station, the building of a permanent dockyard at Bermuda, and the protection of British and Spanish interests in East Florida from American filibusterers. As his three-year tour of duty neared an end in 1810 he requested to be relieved for reasons of health. Acceding to his request, the Admiralty promoted him in July 1810 to the rank of full admiral.

Warren relinquished the North American command in January 1811, returned to England, and was unemployed until the outbreak of the Anglo-American War in 1812. Sent out to America again in August 1812, he was made commander-in-chief of the consolidated North American, Jamaica, and Leeward Islands squadrons. Although Warren had had a good fighting record when younger, he was now less aggressive, and was sent to the American theatre because of his tact and diplomatic experience, which, it was thought, might be useful in negotiating terms of peace. Warren was soon criticized for his slowness in establishing a blockade of the American coast and not giving attention to the Great Lakes. He was not, however, lacking in strategic ideas, for he soon recognized that an offensive against New Orleans and the Gulf coast would relieve American pressure on Canada, and in 1813 he promoted a naval offensive in the Chesapeake region. He also advocated the breakup of the consolidated command, which he regarded as too unwieldy, and this was done in 1813 when he was ordered to return home and relinquish the command to Vice-Admiral Sir Alexander Cochran on the ground that the diminished command did not require the services of a full admiral.

With his recall, Warren's naval career came to an end, but he received ample recognition of his services. His final promotion to admiral of the white came in June 1814, and in the same month he was made a DCL of the University of Oxford. He became a knight grand cross of the Bath in 1815 and a knight grand cross of Hanover in 1819. Although he received the diplomatic pension he had long sought he never obtained the peerage that he wanted. He died suddenly on 27 February 1822 while visiting Greenwich Hospital, and was buried in the family vault at Stratton Audley in Oxfordshire on 5 March. A tablet to his memory is in Attenborough church in Nottinghamshire. He was survived by his wife, who died on 28 December 1839.

Fired with a zeal for naval service while still a schoolboy, Warren for nearly three decades was an active and faithful serving officer, though not of the first rank. Although noted as an aggressive and intrepid fighter he appears to have been lacking in practical seamanship; and although strongly motivated by true patriotism he was always eager for prize money to support his extravagant lifestyle. Yet even the demanding St Vincent recognized his abilities and courage as a fighter, and Barham once considered him for a seat on the Admiralty board. Until near the end of his career Warren had little opportunity to demonstrate any ability as an administrator or strategist. But as commander-in-chief of the North American station during the difficult period from 1807 to 1810, he was a capable and tactful administrator and an effective defender of British interests. As a wartime commander-in-chief in America from 1812 to 1814 his strategic insights were sound. Of the British admirals of his period, Warren, with his aristocratic and university background, was one of the most conspicuous, as a man of fashion and elegant manners.   MALCOLM LESTER

Sources W. V. Anson, *The life of Admiral Sir John Borlase Warren Bart.* (1914) • GEC, *Baronetage* • W. L. Clowes, *The Royal Navy: a history from the earliest times to the present*, 7 vols. (1897–1903) • W. James, *The naval history of Great Britain, from the declaration of war by France in 1793, to the accession of George IV*, [3rd edn], 6 vols. (1837) • P. A. Symonds, 'Warren, John Borlase', HoP, *Commons, 1790–1820* • J. A. Cannon, 'Warren, John Borlase', HoP, *Commons, 1754–90* • J. Ralfe, *The naval biography of Great Britain*, 4 vols. (1828) • P. Mackesy, *The war in the Mediterranean, 1803–1810* (1957) • A. T. Mahan, *Sea power in its relations to the war of 1812*, 2 vols. (1905) • J. K. Mahon, *The war of 1812* (1972) • *Private papers of George, second Earl Spencer*, ed. J. S. Corbett and H. W. Richmond, 4 vols., Navy RS, 46, 48, 58–9 (1913–24) • *Selections from the correspondence of Admiral John Markham*, ed. C. Markham, Navy RS, 28 (1904) • Duke of Buckingham and Chandos [R. Grenville], *Memoirs of the court and cabinets of George the Third*, 4 vols. (1853–5) • *Annual Register* (1822) • Venn, *Alum. Cant.* • will, PRO, PROB 11/656, fol. 287v

Archives NMM, corresp. and papers; journals; order book • Notts. Arch., household accounts • Sudbury Hall, Derbyshire | BL, letters to Lord Bridport, Add. MSS 35195–35199 • BL, corresp. with first and second earls of Liverpool, Add. MSS 38231–38328, 38570–38575 • BL, corresp. with Sir Arthur Paget, Add. MS 48400 • BL, corresp. with William Windham, Add. MSS 37875–37879 • Harrowby Manuscript Trust, Sandon Hall, Staffordshire, letters to earl of Harrowby • Hunt. L., letters to Grenville family • NL Scot., corresp. with Sir Alexander Cochrane • NL Scot., corresp. with Robert Liston • NMM, corresp. with Lord Melville • NMM, letters to Lord Sandwich • PRO, Admiralty MSS • PRO, corresp. with Francis Jackson, FO 353 • W. Sussex RO, letters to W. S. Badcock

Likenesses J. Opie, oils, 1794, Ulster Museum, Belfast • M. Oates, oils, c.1799, NMM • J. Opie, oils, c.1807, priv. coll.; copy, Royal Naval Museum, Portsmouth • F. P. Stephanoff, watercolour drawing (study for *The coronation of George IV*), V&A • J. Stow, stipple (after S. Drummond), BM • engraving, repro. in *Naval Chronicle*, 3 (1800), 333 • oils (after J. Opie), Sudbury Hall, Derbyshire

Warren, John Byrne Leicester, third Baron de Tabley

(1835–1895), poet, was born on 26 April 1835 at Tabley House, Knutsford, Cheshire, the eldest son of George Warren, second Baron de Tabley (1811–1887), and Catherina Barbara, daughter of Jerome, Count de Salis-Soglio, by his third wife, Henrietta, daughter of William Foster, bishop of Kilmore. The grandson of John Fleming *Leicester, first Baron de Tabley (1762–1827), Warren travelled widely with his mother in Italy and Germany during his childhood.

On his return to England, Warren received his education at Eton College and at Christ Church, Oxford (matriculating on 20 October 1852, and graduating BA in 1859 and MA the next year). While at Oxford he became good friends with a fellow collegian, George Fortescue, whose death by an accident in 1859 had a powerful effect on him. A short time before this event the friends had jointly published a small volume of *Poems* under the pseudonym George F. Preston. *Ballads and Metrical Sketches* (1860), *The Threshold of Atrides* (1861), and *Glimpses of Antiquity* (1862) followed under the same pseudonym, but met with no critical success. More power was evinced in *Praeterita* (1863), *Eclogues and Monodramas* (1864), and *Studies in Verse* (1865), all published under the pseudonym William Lancaster. The blank verse poems of which these volumes chiefly consist are Tennysonian in style and substance.

After leaving Oxford, where he gained a second class in classics and history, and a brief interlude of unpaid diplomatic work under Lord Stratford de Redcliffe at Constantinople, Warren was called to the bar from Lincoln's Inn in 1860, but probably never had any serious intention of following the law. In 1856 he became an officer of the Cheshire yeomanry, and in 1868 unsuccessfully contested Mid-Cheshire as a Liberal. On his father's second marriage in 1871, he took up his residence in London.

Warren's *Philoctetes*, a tragedy, published anonymously in 1866, was considered by contemporary critics to be the most powerful of his works. It departs from the Greek model in the introduction of a female character and in its pessimism, features which prevented it from being a mere copy of Sophocles. The principal character seems in not a few respects a portrait of the author himself. *Orestes*, published anonymously in 1868, attracted little attention. A volume of poems entitled *Rehearsals*, and also published under the pseudonym William Lancaster, indicates that the influence of Tennyson, though still strong, was yielding to that of Browning and Swinburne. *The Strange Parable*, however, and *Nimrod*, both written in blank verse, strike an original note. In another miscellaneous collection, *Searching the Net* (1873), the author for the first time placed his name on the title-page. The volume is mainly concerned with the description of nature and the expression of subjective feeling. Warren then unfortunately gave his time to the composition of a very long and entirely undramatic tragedy. Not one copy of *The Soldier's Fortune* (1876) was sold, and Warren's disappointment paralysed his activity as a poet for a long time. He began to retreat into an increasingly reclusive existence in London, although he retained his regard for many old friends, including Edmund Gosse, Theodore Watts-Dunton, and Sir Mountstuart Grant-Duff.

Warren's pursuits were many and interesting; he was a skilled numismatist, and by 1863 had written an essay on Greek coins as illustrative of Greek federal history. He was also an enthusiastic botanist, which accounts for much of the minute description observable in his poems, and was one of the earliest amateurs of the pursuit of collecting book-plates, on which he produced a standard work, *A Guide to the Study of Book Plates* (ex-libris) (1880). His *Flora of*

Cheshire was prepared from two posthumous manuscripts by Spencer Moore, and was published in 1899 with a prefatory memoir by Sir Mountstuart Grant-Duff. He was also a keen ice-skater.

In 1887 Warren succeeded to the title of Baron de Tabley by the death of his father, and at once found himself immersed in a multitude of business cares which made writing more difficult than ever. An impulse, however, was at hand from an unexpected quarter. In 1891 A. H. Miles published in his *Poets of the Century* a selection from de Tabley's poems, with an appreciative criticism. De Tabley was then persuaded by Watts-Dunton and John Lane to republish the best of his poems with additions. The volume, entitled *Poems Dramatic and Lyrical* (1893), obtained full public recognition for one who had seemed entirely forgotten. A succeeding volume, issued in 1895, demonstrated that much might still have been expected from the author if his physical powers had not begun to forsake him. His health undermined by an attack of influenza, he died somewhat suddenly on 22 November 1895 at Sandringham House, Ryde, on the Isle of Wight, where he had gone to recuperate. He was buried at St Oswald's churchyard, Little Peover, Cheshire. He was unmarried, and the peerage became extinct; his baronetcy devolved on a distant cousin.

RICHARD GARNETT, *rev.* MEGAN A. STEPHAN

Sources E. W. Gosse, *Critical Kit-Kats* (1896), 165–95 · T. Watts-Dunton, *The Athenaeum* (30 Nov 1895), 754–6 · Boase, *Mod. Eng. biog.*, 5.88–9 · J. Foster, *The peerage, baronetage, and knightage of the British empire for 1882*, 1 [1882] · M. G. Duff, 'Biographical notice', in J. B. L. Warren, *The flora of Cheshire* (1899), xi–liv · Allibone, *Dict.* · H. E. C. Stapylton, *The Eton school lists, from 1791 to 1850*, 2nd edn (1864), 231 · J. Foster, *Men-at-the-bar: a biographical hand-list of the members of the various inns of court*, 2nd edn (1885), 492 · W. D. Adams, *Dictionary of English literature*, rev. edn [1879–80], 675 · Foster, *Alum. Oxon.*, 1715–1886, 4.1504

Archives Ches. & Chester ALSS, corresp. and papers · JRL, corresp. and literary papers | BL OIOC, letters to Sir Mountstuart Grant Duff, MS Eur. F 234 · Bodl. Oxf., letters to Bertram Dobell · Bodl. Oxf., letters to John Lane and Elkin Matthews · British School at Athens, corresp. with George Finlay · JRL, letters to E. A. Freeman · LUL, letters to Austin Dobson · Trinity Cam., letters to Lord Houghton · U. Leeds, Brotherton L., letters to Sir Edmund Gosse · Yale U., Beinecke L., letters to Frederick Locker-Lampson

Wealth at death £87,461 17*s.* 1*d.*: probate, 4 May 1896, *CGPLA Eng. & Wales*

Warren, John Taylor (1770–1849), military surgeon, born on 10 November 1770, was the son of Thomas Warren of Dunstable, Bedfordshire. He entered Merchant Taylors' School, London, in 1780, and afterwards studied medicine at St George's Hospital, where he became a favourite pupil of John Hunter (1728–1793). In 1792 Warren was appointed assistant surgeon in the 20th dragoons, a regiment raised for service in Jamaica. After serving there for some time he was ordered to St Domingo. In June 1795 he was appointed surgeon to Colonel Keppel's regiment of foot but before joining, owing to the mortality among European officers, he was nominated surgeon to the 23rd infantry or Royal Welch Fusiliers; he was promoted to the post of staff surgeon to the forces in November 1795. In 1797 he returned to England with the wounded and, having distinguished

himself by his work, he was stationed at the recruiting depot in Chatham barracks. He subsequently moved to Gosport, and finally to the Isle of Wight, where he became a friend of Sir George Hewett, the commander of the forces stationed there. In 1800 Warren married Jane-Amelia, daughter of Chevalier Bartholomew *Ruspini; they had one daughter.

Warren was appointed deputy inspector of military hospitals in 1805 and was placed in charge of the home department. In 1808 he proceeded to Spain with a detachment of British troops, and, after being present at Vimiera, he accompanied Sir John Moore on his expedition, despite suffering from acute rheumatism which made it necessary for him to be assisted in mounting and dismounting his horse. When the troops embarked at Corunna he was placed in charge of the wounded, and he was the last British officer to leave the shore. In 1816 he was appointed inspector-general of hospitals, succeeding James Borland in the Mediterranean station. He retired from the regular service in 1820.

For many years Warren acted as vice-president of the Army Medical Benevolent Society for Orphans, and as trustee of the Society for the Widows of Medical Officers. In 1843, in recognition of his services, a silver vase was presented to him by his fellow officers and friends. He died on 6 October 1849 at his house in Marine Parade, Brighton, and he was buried in the family vault at South Warnborough, Hampshire, where his brother, Thomas Alston Warren, was rector. His wife and daughter survived him.

E. I. CARLYLE, *rev.* CLAIRE E. J. HERRICK

Sources A. Peterkin and W. Johnston, *Commissioned officers in the medical services of the British army, 1660–1960*, 1 (1968), 89 · N. Cantlie, *A history of the army medical department*, 1 (1974), 292, 304–5 · *GM*, 2nd ser., 32 (1849), 543 · C. J. Robinson, ed., *A register of the scholars admitted into Merchant Taylors' School, from AD 1562 to 1874*, 2 (1883), 149

Warren, Joseph (1741–1775), physician and revolutionary politician in America, was born on 30 May 1741 at Roxbury, Massachusetts, the eldest of four children of Joseph Warren (1695–1755), farmer, and his wife, Mary Stevens (*b.* 1712), daughter of Samuel Stevens of Roxbury and his wife, Mary. His father's untimely accidental death left his mother in financial difficulties, but she managed to educate all her sons and sent two to college. Warren attended Roxbury Latin school, then enrolled in Harvard College in 1755. After graduation he was appointed master of the Roxbury grammar school, where he taught for one year. In 1761 he joined the freemasons and in 1767 was made provincial grand master of his lodge. Determining to become a physician, he completed a master's degree at Harvard in 1762, writing a thesis on the cause of diseases. He served a one-year apprenticeship with Dr James Lloyd and in 1763 commenced his practice in Boston. He established his medical reputation by inoculating patients against smallpox during a terrible epidemic and within a decade was considered to be the foremost physician in Massachusetts. On 6 September 1764 he married Elizabeth Hooton (*b.* 1746). They had four children before she died on 26 April 1773.

As tensions grew between America and Britain during

Joseph Warren (1741–1775), by John Singleton Copley, *c*.1765

the decade leading to the revolution, Warren became increasingly involved in politics. Devoting himself to the patriot cause, he practically abandoned his medical practice and upon his death left debts of more than £2000. He was closely associated with John and Samuel Adams, John Hancock, and James Otis, and he became a great orator for the American cause. He emerged to prominence during the Stamp Act crisis in 1765 by making speeches in opposition to British taxation, and he also became a frequent contributor to the press. On 19 February 1768 he published an article in the *Boston Gazette* that caused Governor Francis Bernard to attempt a suppression of the printers. He was an active member of several political clubs, including the North End Caucus, and when British authorities seized Hancock's sloop *Liberty* in 1768, he argued forcefully against ministerial authority. After the Boston massacre of 5 March 1770, he was a member of a committee that published a report decrying the bloodletting and in 1772 he commemorated the massacre with an impassioned speech. He also became a member of the newly organized committee of correspondence and helped draft a report censuring British infringements of colonial rights. Two years later, as head of the Massachusetts committee of safety, he opposed the Regulating Act and wrote the 'Suffolk Resolves' to protest against the 'Intolerable Acts'.

In early 1775, despite fears that he might be arrested, Warren lingered in Boston to observe British military activities. On 6 March he delivered his famous second oration on the Boston massacre and on 18 April dispatched William Dawes and Paul Revere to warn patriots at Lexington that British soldiers were marching their way. After

the fighting began there on the 19th, he took charge of efforts in Massachusetts to organize military opposition. He was elected president *pro tempore* of the provincial congress on 23 April and permanent president in late May; in this role he began organizing a new civil government for Massachusetts. On 14 June he was appointed major-general of militia, refusing to accept the less hazardous position of physician-general. Three days later he hastened to join American forces in a redoubt on Breeds Hill as the British prepared to assault that place. He declined General Israel Putnam's offer to take command, and instead volunteered to serve alongside his fellow citizens. In the battle of Bunker Hill he fought gallantly, helping to repulse two enemy assaults before a third finally carried the American position. He was shot in the head and instantly killed as he attempted to rally retreating militiamen. Buried in an unmarked grave on the battlefield, he was thrice reinterred, the final time in 1855 in Forest Hills cemetery, Boston.   PAUL DAVID NELSON

Sources J. Cary, *Joseph Warren: physician, politician, patriot* (1961) · R. Frothingham, *Life and times of Joseph Warren* (1865) · R. Truax, *The doctors Warren of Boston: first family of surgery* (1968) · *Correspondence of General Joseph Warren*, in J. C. Warren, *Genealogy of Warren* (1854), 67–81 · *The Warren–Adams letters: being chiefly a correspondence among John Adams, Samuel Adams, and John Warren*, 1 (1917) · E. S. Rafuse, 'Warren, Joseph', *ANB* · L. Kinvin Wroth and others, eds., *Province in rebellion: a documentary history of the founding of the commonwealth of Massachusetts* (1975) · A. B. Tourstellot, *Lexington and Concord: the beginning of the War of the American Revolution* (1959) · E. Forbes, *Paul Revere and the world he lived in* (1942) · C. Amory, 'Funerals are fun', *State of mind: a Boston reader*, ed. R. N. Linscott (1948), 401
Archives Boston PL, MSS · Mass. Hist. Soc., MSS · NYPL, MSS | NYPL, Samuel Adams MSS
Likenesses J. S. Copley, oils, *c*.1765, Museum of Fine Arts, Boston [*see illus.*]
Wealth at death £475 3*s*. 3½*d*.; debts of £2200: Cary, *Joseph Warren*, 122

Warren, Joseph (1804–1881), composer and music editor, was born in London on 20 March 1804. He first studied the violin, and then the piano and organ under J. Stone. At an early age he conducted a society of amateurs, for whom he wrote two symphonies and many other vocal and instrumental pieces. In 1834 he was appointed organist of St Mary's Roman Catholic Chapel, Chelsea, and composed several masses and smaller works for the services there, which remained in manuscript. However, some piano pieces of Warren's were published, and in 1840 he entered into an arrangement with the firm of Cocks & Co., and edited or arranged a large quantity of music including collections of chants in 1840 (*A Selection of Cathedral Chants by the Old English Masters*), 1845, and *c*.1850, harmonizations of Bach's chorales (1842), a *Chorister's Handbook* (*c*.1850), and very many arrangements of works by prominent composers for the piano, harmonium, and concertina. He also wrote a number of useful short treatises on composition, orchestral writing, organ playing (2nd edn, *c*.1850), the harmonium (1855), and madrigal singing, and a method for the concertina (1855), which was very successful. Other works include *The Chanter's Hand-Guide* (1849) and *Warren's Psalmody* (1853, reissued *c*.1860).

Warren took an active part in the revival of early English

music, an objective of the Oxford Movement, and in November 1843 began work on a new edition of Boyce's *Cathedral Music*, for which he is chiefly remembered, which was published in 1849. To the original he added a complete organ accompaniment and inserted extra services by Creyghton and Tomkins, movements from services by Blow, Child, and Aldrich, Parsons's burial service from Edward Lowe's *A Short Direction for the Performance of Cathedrall Service* (1661), anthems by Gibbons, Byrd, Blow, Tallis, and Tomkins, with some chants, and the symphonies to the anthems by Pelham Humfrey and Blow. Biographies of Boyce and the other composers represented are given, along with lists of their works. As an editor, Warren was careful and thorough, and his works were warmly praised by critics. In conjunction with John Bishop of Cheltenham, he also began in 1848 to issue a similar selection of early Italian, German, and Flemish music for the Catholic church, under the title *Repertorium musicae antiquae*, but only two parts appeared. They were equally good models of editing, as was the collection of John Hilton's *Ayres or Fa Las* (1844–), which Warren edited for the Musical Antiquarian Society from the partbooks in his library.

Warren was an intimate friend of another pioneer of English musicology, Edward Francis Rimbault, although the two later appear to have become estranged and sneered in their prefaces at each other's publications. Warren fell into poverty late in life, and his valuable library, which included some of the most important early English manuscripts, sale catalogues, and autograph manuscripts of Haydn, Mozart, and Beethoven, among others (his editions of Beethoven's *Christ at the Mount of Olives* and Rossini's *Stabat mater* had appeared in 1844), was parted with piece by piece. Around 1872 he became paralysed, and was apparently saved from destitution by the musicologist W. H. Cummings. He died at Bexley, Kent, on 8 March 1881. HENRY DAVEY, *rev.* DAVID J. GOLBY

Sources *MT*, 22 (1881), 207 · W. H. Husk and B. Carr, 'Warren, Joseph', *New Grove* · F.-J. Fétis, *Biographie universelle des musiciens, et bibliographie générale de la musique*, 2nd edn, 8 (Paris, 1865), 417–18 **Archives** BL, musical papers, Add. MSS 28968–28969 · Bodl. Oxf., literary catalogue | FM Cam., letters to John Bishop

Warren, Lemuel (1770–1833), army officer, entered the army as an ensign in the 17th foot on 7 March 1787, obtained his lieutenancy in it on 27 October 1788, and was for some time on Lord Hood's fleet, in which the regiment served as marines. On 12 June 1793 he raised an independent company of foot, of which he was appointed captain; but on 2 January 1794 exchanged to the 27th (Inniskillings), then in Lord Moira's army camped at Southampton. He served with the 27th in Flanders from 1794 to 1796 under the duke of York; he was present at the siege of Nijmegen and at the sortie of 6 November, and commanded the advanced picquet of the garrison. He accompanied the force under Lord Cathcart sent to attack the French army at Bommel, and was present at the action of Geldermalsen in January 1796.

Warren embarked with the 27th for the West Indies in September 1796, and commanded their grenadiers at the storming of the advanced posts at Morne Fortuné, St Lucia; at the conclusion of the operations he was compelled by sickness to return to England. He served in the expedition to the Netherlands in 1799, including the actions of 27 August, 19 September, and 2 and 6 October. He served as a major of the 27th (from 31 December 1799) in the expedition to Ferrol in 1800; and in the Egyptian campaign of 1801, including the operations before Alexandria, receiving the Sultan's medal for the campaign. He was promoted lieutenant-colonel in the 27th on 16 August 1804. He served in the expedition to Sicily in 1809, and afterwards on the east coast of Spain. He commanded a brigade at the battle of Castalla, and the siege of Tarragona, and was present at the blockade of Barcelona.

On 4 June 1813 Warren was promoted colonel in the army. He accompanied the division of the British army across the Peninsula to Bayonne, and from there to Bordeaux, where the 27th immediately embarked for North America. He joined the 1st battalion of the Inniskillings before Paris in 1815, a few days before the entry of Louis XVIII. He was promoted major-general on 12 August 1819, and died suddenly in London on 29 October 1833.

ROBERT HOLDEN, *rev.* JAMES LUNT

Sources Regimental Committee, *The Royal Inniskilling Fusiliers, 1688 to July 1914* (1934) · *United Service Journal*, 1 (1834), 88 · *Army List* · *GM*, 2nd ser., 1 (1834), 226

Warren, Marjory Winsome (1897–1960), geriatrician, was born on 28 October 1897 at 15 Scarborough Road, Stroud Green, Hornsey, London, eldest of five daughters of Walter Richard Warren (*d.* 1930), barrister, and his wife, Annie *née* Dixon. Her younger sister Enid Charis *Warren later achieved prominence as a medical social worker. Marjory was educated at the North London Collegiate School and trained in medicine at the Royal Free Hospital, London; she qualified LRCP MRCS in 1923. After junior posts at the Queen's Children's Hospital, Hackney, and at the Royal Free and Elizabeth Garrett Anderson hospitals, she became assistant resident medical officer at the Isleworth Infirmary in 1926. She was promoted to be deputy medical director in 1931, and after the inception of the National Health Service in 1948 she became consultant physician.

Warren's early interest was in surgery but she later concentrated on medicine and medical administration. In 1935 the Isleworth Infirmary took over responsibility for the adjacent workhouse (Warkworth House) to form the West Middlesex County Hospital. During 1936 Warren systematically reviewed the several hundred inmates of the old workhouse wards. 'In the same ward were to be found senile dements, restless and noisy patients who required cot beds, incontinent patients, senile bed-ridden patients, elderly sick patients who were treatable, patients who were up and about all day, and unmarried mothers with infants' (*Lancet*, 656). Warren helped some of the unmarried mothers back into the community by finding them employment and was able to discharge other patients to their own homes or to residential care by providing active rehabilitation and appropriate equipment. Many of the patients were old and infirm and for these Warren's approach was to match care to needs by a system of classification. The success of her active approach to the rehabilitation of stroke victims had a particular and lasting impact on medical practice. She also initiated the upgrading of wards, thereby improving the morale of both patients and staff.

In two seminal papers, in the *British Medical Journal* (25 Dec 1943, 822–3) and the *Lancet* (8 June 1946, 841–3), Warren advocated the creation of a medical speciality of geriatrics, the provision of special geriatric units in general hospitals, and the teaching of medical students in the care of elderly people by senior doctors with specialist interest and experience in geriatrics. Her work aroused the interest of the Ministry of Health and during the 1950s geriatric medicine became a recognized medical specialism within the National Health Service. In 1947 she was one of eight doctors who founded the Medical Society for the Care of the Elderly (later renamed the British Geriatrics Society). She was founding chair of its committee under the presidency of Lord Amulree, the medical officer at the Ministry of Health who first appreciated the significance of her work. Many visitors from elsewhere in the UK and from overseas came to Isleworth to observe and learn from her methods. Warren was invited to lecture in Canada, Australia, and the USA, and she served as international secretary of the International Association of Gerontology. As chief of a busy medical team she expected high standards from those who worked with her, but her personal influence was enhanced by an energetic and engaging personality that earned her the affection as well as the respect of colleagues.

Warren was active in many professional and voluntary fields. She had a keen interest in nursing and nursing education and was an examiner for the General Nursing Council. She was an enthusiastic member of the London Association of the Medical Women's Federation and shortly before her death was elected its president. She was appointed CBE in 1959.

Warren was fatally injured in a road accident on her way to a conference in Germany, and she died in hospital in Maizières-lès-Metz, France, on 5 September 1960. Her body was cremated in Strasbourg, and a memorial service was held on 1 October 1960 at St Pancras Church, London. She never married.   JOHN GRIMLEY EVANS

Sources Central Middlesex Hospital · North London Collegiate College · private information (2004) · *The Lancet* (10 Sept 1960), 591 · *The Lancet* (17 Sept 1960), 656–7 · *The Lancet* (24 Sept 1960), 712 · *BMJ* (17 Sept 1960), 867–8 · *BMJ* (24 Sept 1960), 953–4 · T. Howell, 'Origins of the British Geriatrics Society', *Age and Ageing*, 3 (1974), 69–72 · archives, British Geriatrics Society · b. cert. · d. cert.
Likenesses photograph, repro. in *Gerontologia Clinica*, 3 (1960), 1 · photograph, repro. in M. Black, *West Middlesex University Hospital: a history* (1996), 71
Wealth at death £19,032 16s.: probate, 10 Nov 1960, CGPLA Eng. & Wales

Warren, Matthew (*bap.* 1642, *d.* 1706), nonconformist minister and tutor, was baptized on 4 December 1642 at Otterford, Somerset, a younger son of John Warren, 'a gentleman of good estate', and his wife, Anne (Calamy, 2.747). He was educated at Crewkerne grammar school and St John's College, Oxford, where he matriculated on 3 July 1658. At the Restoration he left Oxford and went to Reading for a year with his tutor but then returned to Otterford and began to preach. He held no benefice but was silenced by the Act of Uniformity in 1662.

Warren began a school which developed into an academy for training young men for the nonconformist ministry, one of the first to run such an academy (though such institutions had their antecedents in the training of godly ministers before the civil war). When he began to teach is uncertain but his earliest known pupil is John Shower, who joined him in 1671. About twenty of Warren's pupils are known, including Christopher Taylor (in whose ordination at Lyme Regis on 25 August 1687 Warren took part) and Henry Grove, who eventually succeeded Warren as tutor of the academy. After a year or two Warren moved his academy from Otterford to Taunton. In 1672 he was licensed under the declaration of indulgence as a presbyterian minister for the house of John Hill in Withypool, 24 miles away on Exmoor. The following year, on 14 April, he married Martha Rossiter in St Mary Magdalene Church, Taunton.

In 1687 Warren and Emmanuel Harford were called to be joint ministers of Pauls Meeting Presbyterian Church, built in Taunton in 1672 but closed in the disturbed times leading up to the Monmouth rebellion and opened again under James II's declaration of indulgence. Harford was linked to Warren by marriage. Warren continued to run the academy and the students, lay and ministerial, lived in his house as part of his family, the course normally lasting five years. Warren lectured in Latin, the usual language of converse in the academy. Warren, Harford, and the ministerial students preached in the village chapels in the vicinity, including Bishops Hull, Pitminster, and Hatch. Warren thought that the best system for ministerial training was Bible study but encouraged freedom of thought and the study of contemporary learning. Students seeking a church were issued with a certificate of proficiency signed by both Warren and Harford. Warren preached occasionally at meetings of the Exeter Assembly of presbyterian and congregationalist ministers, which gave bursaries to some of his students, but which in 1695 complained that some of them had Baptist beliefs.

Warren's son, another Matthew, is recorded in a Pauls Meeting document of 1699 as participating in a pastoral visitation. On 14 April 1692, after Martha's death, Warren married Elizabeth Baker at St Mary Magdalene; they had a son, also called Matthew, who was baptized at Pauls Meeting on 9 July 1704 when Warren was sixty-one, and who is recorded in the register of baptisms that Warren had started in 1699. Warren also took part in the town life of Taunton, acting as a conservator of the River Tone in 1698.

Warren died on 14 June 1706 at Taunton, and was buried in St Mary Magdalene, where there used to be a memorial to him. In his will he set aside £400 to be put out at interest for the education and maintenance of his son until he reached adulthood; the rest of his estate he left to his widow. John Sprint of Milborne Port preached his funeral sermon which was published with a memoir, thought to be by Christopher Taylor, who also wrote a Latin epitaph for Warren. Calamy, whose account drew heavily on the memoir, wrote that:

> Many young gentlemen that now behave worthily in civil stations, and others that are useful in the ministry, owe their education to him: and all that knew him, own him to have been well qualified for the service he did them, by a good share of useful learning joined with humility, modesty and good humour, which were his distinguishing characters. (Calamy, 2.747)

Harford died two months after Warren, and Sprint also preached his funeral sermon. Warren and Harford began their ministry with a small, fearful congregation but finished with a confident following of almost two thousand. Pauls Meeting in Paul Street became Taunton United Reformed Church in 1972.   BRIAN W. KIRK

Sources H. McLachlan, *English education under the Test Acts: being the history of the nonconformist academies, 1662–1820* (1931) · A. Brockett, ed., *The Exeter assembly: the minutes of the assemblies of the United Brethren of Devon and Cornwall, 1691–1717*, Devon and Cornwall RS, new ser., 6 (1963) · E. Calamy, *A continuation of the account of the ministers … who were ejected and silenced after the Restoration in 1660*, 2 vols. (1727), vol. 2, pp. 747–9 · J. Sprint, *Funeral sermon for the Reverend Mr Matthew Warren* (1707) · *The nonconformist's memorial … originally written by … Edmund Calamy*, ed. S. Palmer, [3rd edn], 3 (1803), 186–9 · *Calamy rev.* · A. Gordon, ed., *Freedom after ejection: a review (1690–1692) of presbyterian and congregational nonconformity in England and Wales* (1917) · J. Toulmin, *History of the town of Taunton* (1791) · J. Toulmin, *History of the protestant dissenters in England* (1814) · Foster, *Alum. Oxon.* · J. Toulmin, *The history of Taunton, in the county of Somerset*, ed. J. Savage, new edn (1822) · PRO, PROB 11/489, fols. 193r–194r · parish register, Otterford, Som. ARS, 4 Dec 1642 [baptism] · parish register, Taunton, St Mary Magdalene, 14 April 1673, Som. ARS [marriage] · parish register, Taunton, St Mary Magdalene, 14 April 1692, Som. ARS [marriage]
Wealth at death over £400; £400 to son; remainder to widow: *Calamy rev.*; will, PRO, PROB 11/489, fols. 193r–194r

Warren, Max Alexander Cunningham (1904–1977), Church of England clergyman and missionary society administrator, was born in Dún Laoghaire, Ireland, on 13 August 1904, the youngest of three sons and four children of the Revd John Alexander Faris Warren, a clergyman of the Church of Ireland, and his wife, Mary Kathleen East. After spending his first eight years in India, where his parents were missionaries of the Church Missionary Society (CMS), he was educated at Marlborough College and at Jesus College, Cambridge, where he was a scholar, gaining firsts in part one of the history tripos (1925) and part two of the theology tripos (1926). While still an undergraduate he showed remarkable gifts of intellect and leadership, organizing a group of friends, the Hausa Band, to serve as missionaries in Northern Nigeria. After studying for a year at Ridley Hall, Cambridge, he sailed to Nigeria in 1927 but was invalided home ten months later with tuberculosis. During three years of illness in bed he read widely and prodigiously, a practice he continued throughout his life. He also learned about darkness and the depths, but later he described it as one of his most worthwhile experiences.

In 1932 Warren married Mary, daughter of the Revd Thomas Collett, and was ordained to a curacy at St John's,

Boscombe, by C. F. Garbett, then bishop of Winchester, who also appointed him joint secretary to the Winchester diocesan council of youth. In 1936 he became vicar of Holy Trinity, Cambridge, which from the days of Charles Simeon, who died exactly a hundred years earlier, had been one of the most famous evangelical churches in the land and a place of great influence on successive generations of undergraduates. He soon established himself as a thoughtful preacher with marked gifts of leadership in public worship and pastoral counselling. As many fled from Nazi Germany, he welcomed to his church the Lutheran congregation of pastor Franz Hildebrandt, giving an early example of the ecumenical spirit which characterized his whole life. Despite the coming of war in 1939 and the responsibilities of a busy parish he continued his contacts with the CMS, and in 1942 was chosen to succeed W. Wilson Cash, who had become bishop of Worcester, as its general secretary.

For the next twenty-one years Warren was one of the most influential and best-known men in the Church of England and in the Anglican communion. Bishops and archbishops, scholars and students from all six continents read what he wrote and turned to him for advice and help. He covered a vast range of subjects in his monthly *CMS News-Letter* which gave a Christian interpretation to current affairs and particularly to the rapid changes occurring in Africa and Asia, which he visited frequently. More than anyone else he prepared the churches for the consequences of the rise of nationalism in these two continents and the resurgence of the old ethnic religions which followed the war. He was in great demand as a speaker at international conferences, particularly those of the International Missionary Council (Whitby, Canada, 1947; Willingen, Germany, 1952; Accra, Ghana, 1959), and gave one of the most notable and oft-quoted addresses at the Anglican congress at Toronto in 1963. Although a supporter of the World Council of Churches he was also one of its critics, being opposed always to mammoth organizations and therefore to the integration of the International Missionary Council with the World Council of Churches which took place at New Delhi in 1961. He was a staunch defender of the voluntary principle, disliking and distrusting centralization and bureaucracy in church as well as state.

For over thirty years Warren's was the leading evangelical voice in Britain but he was always liberal and forward looking, enjoying the friendship and confidence of many from whom he differed. His lifelong support of the Church of South India and of movements towards intercommunion in Britain was based on his insistence on a theology of difference. The revival of scholarship and theological research and writing among Anglican evangelicals owed much to his initiative in founding with others the Evangelical Fellowship of Theological Literature which had annual conferences from 1942 to 1971. He also encouraged the formation of religious communities outside the Catholic tradition, the most notable of these being St Julian's near Horsham. He himself wrote a large number of books, mainly on missionary subjects and related themes, always scholarly and often original. He made substantial contributions to the preparatory documents for the 1958 Lambeth conference, and he chaired the group which produced what was regarded as its most significant contribution, *The Family in Contemporary Society* (1958).

In 1963 Warren resigned from the CMS and became a canon of Westminster and later subdean. He took a leading part in the 900th anniversary of the abbey and was a prophetic preacher in its pulpit, bringing together his world vision and his devotion to the Bible. In 1973 he retired to Sussex where he died on 23 August 1977.

During these last years he pursued his long-standing concern with the relationship between Christianity and other world religions, particularly the implications of interfaith dialogue. He had refused more than one bishopric but he became an honorary fellow of Jesus College, Cambridge (1967), and was awarded five honorary doctorates. He had a winning smile, a keen sense of humour, and a well-stocked mind: he was an indefatigable letter writer. He and his wife extended hospitality almost daily to people of many races. They had two daughters.

DOUGLAS WEBSTER, *rev.*

Sources *The Times* (25 Aug 1977) • M. Warren, *Crowded canvas: some experiences of a lifetime* (1974) • F. W. Dillistone, *Into all the world: a biography of Max Warren* (1980) • personal knowledge (1986) • *CGPLA Eng. & Wales* (1977)
Archives Henry Martyn Library, book reviews and related corresp. • U. Birm. L., travel diaries | Bodl. RH, corresp. with Margery Pelham
Likenesses B. Bury, portrait; at Church Missionary Society, London in 1986
Wealth at death £11,258: probate, 5 Oct 1977, *CGPLA Eng. & Wales*

Warren, Mercy Otis (1728–1814), writer and historian in America, was born on 25 September 1728 in West Barnstable, Massachusetts, the third of the thirteen children of James *Otis (1702–1778), merchant and politician, and his wife, Mary Allyne (1702–1767) of Connecticut. Mercy did not receive any formal schooling, but when the Revd Jonathan Russell tutored her brothers James *Otis jun. and Joseph for entry to Harvard College, Mercy also attended the college preparatory classes. At these sessions we know that she read such authors as Pope, Dryden, and Raleigh. In obtaining some education along with her brothers, she was typical of other well-to-do early American women writers whose fathers, brothers, or husbands encouraged them to study and write within the confines of the home. But unlike such earlier colonial women intellectuals as Anne Bradstreet, for example, Mercy engaged very directly (and sometimes publicly) with current political events and used her writing talent for patriotic as well as aesthetic purposes. As Mercy herself states in the poem 'To Fidelio', which begins as a love letter to her husband but then moves to argue their joint revolutionary responsibilities, she accepts that 'A patriot zeal must warm the female mind'.

On 14 November 1754 Mercy married James *Warren (1726–1808), a farmer and politician who shared her family's whig beliefs, and moved to Plymouth, Massachusetts, where she spent the rest of her life (barring eight years just after the American War of Independence when she lived in nearby Milton, Massachusetts). There the couple raised five sons, who were born from 1757 to 1766. The marriage seems to have been a love match, and both partners fostered each other's private and public aspirations. In particular, James respected and supported his wife's intellectual pursuits and literary talents. By 1759, for example, she was already writing poems. But it was the heated political atmosphere of the 1770s in which her father, husband, and brother played such prominent roles that really propelled her into impassioned writing.

When her brother James was cruelly satirized in tory propaganda and then, in 1769, brutally beaten by one of his political enemies (an attack that left the patriot leader permanently impaired mentally and physically), Mercy Warren decided to use her writing skills for public and political ends. Her first works (which include some collaborative sections) were three propaganda pamphlet plays which appeared anonymously: *The Adulateur* (originally published in the *Massachusetts Spy* in 1772 and then separately in 1773), *The Defeat* (1773), and *The Group* (1775), which was her most famous satirical play. By using character names that exemplified a particular quality (for example, Governor Thomas Hutchinson was named Rapatio for his rapaciousness), Warren wrote in the tradition of eighteenth-century English political drama, but she added emotion and immediacy to heighten her strong convictions. Two socio-political plays traditionally attributed to Warren, *The Blockheads* (1776) and *The Motley Assembly* (1779), are not now believed to be by her.

During the American War of Independence, Mercy Warren maintained an active correspondence with several patriot leaders, including John Adams and Samuel Adams, and several influential women, including Abigail Adams, Hannah Winthrop, and the English historian Catharine Macauley. But as her eye problems increased, she cut back on her letter writing and might have curtailed her other literary activities too had it not been for the help of her son James, a wounded veteran who lived at home latterly and who acted as her amanuensis.

After the revolution, as Massachusetts became more federalist, the Warrens became more republican, and they spoke out against what they perceived to be tyrannical American behaviour. When they supported Shays's rebellion of 1786, which they interpreted as a justifiable reaction against a new despotism, they alienated themselves from such previously close friends and political allies as John Adams. But Mercy Warren decided once again to wield her pen for political and moral purposes, protesting against the diminution of rights so painfully won from the British and also reminding the lax younger generation of their parents' sacrifices. As she said in a note to her poem 'The genius of America', which appeared in her next publication, *Poems, Dramatic and Miscellaneous* (1790):

> This poem was written when a most remarkable depravity of manners pervaded the cities of the United States, in

consequence of a state of war; a relaxation of government; the sudden acquisition of fortune; a depreciating currency; and a new intercourse with foreign nations.

Poems, Dramatic and Miscellaneous contains two neo-classical verse tragedies, *The Sack of Rome* and *The Ladies of Castile*, as well as eighteen poems in the form of political satires, epistles, elegies, and lyrics. Mercy Warren dedicated the book to George Washington, who expressed his admiration of the volume, as did another prolific woman writer, Judith Sargent Murray. While *The Sack of Rome* and *The Ladies of Castile* are set in Rome and Spain respectively, the themes and situations are clearly American. According to Jean Fritz, Warren's message 'was as blatant as ever: liberty threatened, liberty lost, liberty married victoriously to virtue, liberty defeated by luxury—always liberty, and how could it be otherwise?' (Fritz, 235). One significant aspect of the plays is her interest in portraying strong women characters, particularly Donna Maria in *The Ladies of Castile*, who stands as Warren's depiction of the ideal woman.

Finally, at the turn of the century, Mercy Warren resumed work on her history of the revolution, a task she had laboured over for almost three decades. The three-volume *History of the Rise, Progress, and Termination of the American Revolution* was published in 1805 and 1806. It was her last publication and the one she most wished to be remembered by. Unfortunately, it appeared after other accounts by her contemporaries, so it did not have the same currency as theirs, and it received generally mixed reviews. With a moral patriotic eye, Warren had sought to memorialize the contributions of her brother James and to criticize those of her old friend John Adams. Her critique of Adams led to a series of angry letters between the two of them, then a breach in the friendship that was reconciled only in 1813.

On 27 November 1808 Mercy's husband, James, died. Over eighty at the time, Mercy herself became increasingly weak, and died in Plymouth on 19 October 1814. She was buried three days later at Old Burial Hill, Plymouth. Her sons James and Henry, the only two of her five children to outlive her, preserved her correspondence and other unpublished materials, most of which are deposited at the Massachusetts Historical Society, in Boston. A painting of Mercy Warren in her mid-thirties by the famous American artist John Singleton Copley shows a fashionably dressed, attractive woman with an intelligent, serious expression and an intent, level gaze. Her visual identity mirrors her verbal one. For the variety and complexity of her writings, her consistent production, and her position as one of the few early American women writers and intellectuals to be published in her own lifetime, Mercy Warren is now considered a major eighteenth-century author and commentator on her times.

KATHRYN ZABELLE DEROUNIAN-STODOLA

Sources J. H. Richards, *Mercy Otis Warren* (1995) · R. Zagarri, *A woman's dilemma: Mercy Otis Warren and the American revolution* (1995) · J. Fritz, *Cast for a revolution: some American friends and enemies, 1728–1814* (1972) · K. Anthony, *First lady of the revolution* (1958) · L. H. Cohen, 'Explaining the revolution: ideology and ethics in Mercy Otis Warren's historical theory', *William and Mary Quarterly*, 37 (1980), 200–18 · F. Shuffelton, 'Mercy Otis Warren', *American colonial writers, 1735–1781*, ed. E. Elliott, DLitB, 31 (1984) · W. J. Meserve, *An emerging entertainment: the drama of the American people to 1828* (1977) · T. F. Nicolay, *Gender roles, literary authority and three American women writers* (1995)
Archives Mass. Hist. Soc., papers
Likenesses J. S. Copley, oils, c.1763, Museum of Fine Arts, Boston

Warren, Pelham (1778–1835), physician, born in London on 7 October 1778, was the ninth son of Richard *Warren (1731–1797), physician to George III, and his wife, Elizabeth, only daughter of Peter *Shaw (1694–1763). Frederick *Warren (1775–1848) was his elder brother. He was educated at Dr Thompson's school at Kensington, at Westminster School, and from 1796 at Trinity College, Cambridge. He graduated MB in 1800 and MD in 1805.

Warren commenced practice in London immediately after he had taken his first degree in medicine, and on 6 April 1803 he was elected physician to St George's Hospital, an office which he resigned in April 1816, having established a large independent practice. He was admitted a candidate of the Royal College of Physicians in 1805, and a fellow in 1806. He was made censor in 1810, Harveian orator in 1826, and elect on 11 August 1829. He was elected fellow of the Royal Society on 8 April 1813. He married on 3 May 1814 Penelope, daughter of William Davies *Shipley (1745–1826), dean of St Asaph. On 24 July 1830 he was gazetted physician-extraordinary to the king, but he declined the honour.

Warren enjoyed one of the largest practices in the metropolis. According to his contemporaries he was an accurate and careful observer of disease, and a very sound practical physician. He was an accomplished classical scholar and a strong defender of the character and independence of the medical profession. 'His manners were peculiar and not always pleasing, being sometimes cold and abrupt. He took a prodigious quantity of snuff, and was plain and untidy in his dress, perhaps to affectation' (*Medical Gazette*, 405).

Warren died at his home, Worting House, near Basingstoke, of disease of the liver on 2 December 1835, survived by his wife and seven children. He was buried in Worting church, where there is a tablet with an inscription composed by his friend and schoolfellow Henry Vincent Bayley, canon of Westminster. In 1837 his widow presented his portrait painted and engraved by John Linnell to the Royal College of Physicians.

W. W. WEBB, *rev.* PATRICK WALLIS

Sources Munk, *Roll* · *London Medical Gazette*, 17 (1835), 405 · Venn, *Alum. Cant.* · G. F. R. Barker and A. H. Stenning, eds., *The Westminster School register from 1764 to 1883* (1892)
Likenesses J. Linnell, oils, 1835, RCP Lond.

Warren, Sir Peter (1703/4–1752), naval officer and politician, was the youngest son of Michael Warren of Warrenstown, co. Meath, an officer in the army of James II, and Catherine, only daughter of Sir Christopher Aylmer, baronet, brother of Admiral Matthew Aylmer. Born into a Roman Catholic family, Warren was brought up a protestant so as to enter naval service. He followed his eldest brother, Oliver (d. 1724), into the navy, entering at Dublin as an ordinary seaman on the *Rye* (30 guns) in 1716, under Aylmer's patronage and that of his son-in-law, Admiral Sir John Norris. After serving in Irish waters Warren spent most of his early years either on the coast of west Africa or in the West Indies, hunting pirates and warding off *guarda-costas*. He was made lieutenant in the *Guernsey* off the Liberian coast in January 1723, when natives killed one of his brother officers. Placed in command of the *Falkland* (50 guns) upon the death of his captain in 1726, he earned freight money by carrying bullion owned by the South Sea Company. In 1728 he took post as captain of the *Grafton* (70 guns) under Norris, then commanding the Baltic fleet. Later that year, in command of the *Solebay* (20 guns), he carried to Jamaica and Vera Cruz news of the peace treaty and called at South Carolina on his route home, where he met George Anson. In July 1731 Warren married Susannah, daughter of Stephen DeLancey of New York and sister of James DeLancey, later the colony's lieutenant-governor. The couple had six children.

Between 1730 and 1732 Warren commanded the *Solebay* on the New York and South Carolina stations. In 1734–5 he served in the *Leopard* (50 guns) as part of the western squadron commanded by Norris. In 1736–41 he was captain of the *Squirrel* (20 guns) at Boston, and in 1739 he submitted a report on the state of the Nova Scotia fisheries. Upon the outbreak of war with Spain, Warren served at the 1740 failed siege of St Augustine, under the senior captain, Vincent Pierce. From Florida he sailed for Jamaica to serve under Vernon, who thought him an 'active good officer' for his success in taking Spanish prizes. In January 1742 he was given command of the *Superbe* (60 guns) and was again appointed to the New York station. That August the Admiralty adopted Warren's suggestion that some of the ships stationed on the North American coast be formed into a squadron to serve in the West Indies during winter months. In this way he came to command the Leeward Islands squadron, which distinguished itself by taking prizes, especially in 1744 when war ensnared France.

Warren became well known as a result of the 1745 siege of Fortress Louisbourg on Cape Breton Island. In 1741 he had first discussed the idea with William Pepperell, appointed the military commander. In 1743 he told the Admiralty that its capture and that of Canada would prove of great consequence to Britain. In April 1745 he took his squadron (the *Superbe* and three frigates) north to Canso, where he found a dozen colonial armed vessels escorting the colonial expeditionary force. He effected a close blockade of the Louisbourg harbour, and was rewarded when the *Vigilant* (64 guns) was taken, and immediately commissioned by the commodore. Naval reinforcements thereafter joined him, so that by mid-June he commanded six ships of the line and five frigates mounting 558 guns with 3585 officers, seamen, and marines. In the face of this naval force and on the eve of a planned frontal assault by the New Englanders, the fortress capitulated on generous terms.

News of this success caused a great sensation in London. In celebration there were bonfires, the Tower guns were fired, poems and broadsheets were published, loyal greetings drafted, and public houses renamed. Warren's behaviour was contrasted with the unfortunate naval officers implicated in the inglorious affair off Toulon in February 1744, when a Franco-Spanish squadron had escaped the navy. For the first time American affairs commanded widespread attention at home. Warren was promoted rear-admiral. He declined a baronetcy as he had no son. Named first English governor of Cape Breton, he immediately begged to be relieved, pleading ill health with Anson and Sandwich, and his desire to serve at sea with Bedford and Newcastle. His real thoughts were probably on half pay and the governorship of New York, for which he had been negotiating with the governor, Vice-Admiral George Clinton, and where he had acquired important family and financial connections.

Warren's enthusiasm for Cape Breton was at first almost boundless. In letters home he wrote of Louisbourg as a mere stepping stone to the conquest of Canada, and thus Britain's domination of both fur and fish, while he pressed for an expeditionary force to be mounted in 1746. The politicians were divided. Henry Pelham thought Louisbourg's capture an obstacle to peace. By contrast, lords Newcastle and Hardwicke basked in the reflected glory while John Carteret, William Pitt, and George II spoke warmly of the action.

Relieved of his governorship in June 1746, Warren spent the summer in Boston concerting plans with Governor William Shirley to secure colonial support for a planned expedition to Canada. The plan, which was only formulated by the ministry in late March, called for a two-pronged attack: one centred on Albany via Lake Champlain and the Richelieu River to Montreal; the other based in Portsmouth involving 4000 regulars, an artillery train, and a large squadron under Warren's command to seize Quebec via the St Lawrence River. The campaign was a fiasco, as the force never left England, and the American troops accomplished nothing north of Saratoga. Without orders, Warren sailed home with a detailed plan for 1747 worked out with Governor Shirley. The Admiralty was now convinced that it had too few ships both to blockade the French in their home ports and also undertake the Canada expedition. At first Warren was given command of an eight-ship squadron planned to reinforce Louisbourg. Plans were altered when news arrived of a French armament, and Warren was named second-in-command to Anson to cruise in the Bay of Biscay. Off Cape Ortegal on May 1747 they caught the French force, under La Jonquière, and overwhelmed it. Anson was rewarded with a peerage and £62,991 in prize money, Warren with the Order of the Bath and £31,496. In July he was promoted vice-admiral. Yet France still retained formidable naval forces both in her Atlantic ports and in Toulon, while French trade to the Caribbean and Quebec was little hindered. Mastery of the western approaches was established only in October when Rear-Admiral Edward Hawke—illness having kept Warren ashore—crushed a French squadron off Cape Finisterre. Warren resumed command of this western squadron in 1748, but no French or Spanish fleet put to sea before peace preliminaries ended the war.

Warren never again went to sea. In 1747 he had been elected MP for the city of Westminster at the cost of £2200 and, as he then owned no land in England, the purchase of an annuity for £4800 on land from the duke of Bedford. In December 1748, despite Anson's support, he failed in a bid for a vacancy on the Admiralty board. He soon alienated his supporters by leading opposition to one clause of Anson's 1749 naval bill, by which half pay officers became subject to court martial on grounds identical to serving officers. Pamphlets were written and naval officers were summoned to meetings at which Warren and Norris presided. Warren and others addressed the Admiralty board, a most unusual circumstance. Warren's point carried the day, but it cost him his alliance with Bedford, Sandwich, and Anson. In parliament he was active in committees, chairing several and twice carrying bills to the Lords. He was one of the best informed members on American affairs, concerned especially with colonial trade, currency, boundary disputes, and the fisheries. Deeply suspicious of French ambitions, Warren advocated a strong navy and powerful European alliances. He also proposed in 1747 new designs for admirals' and captains' uniforms.

The war allowed him to garner £127,405 in prize money, the bulk of it in 1745 and 1747. Only Anson perhaps accumulated more. His wealth was invested in land and money-lending in England, Ireland, and the American colonies; he also bought heavily into the national debt. Much of Greenwich Village on Manhattan Island was later erected on his farm, which was sold by his heirs after 1787. He installed his nephew, William *Johnson, to superintend his Mohawk valley lands, launching the young man into a celebrated career on that frontier. His Hampshire estate in the Meon valley, conveniently close to Portsmouth, purchased in 1747, remained in the hands of his heirs until the 1860s. In 1747 he also purchased 15 Cavendish Square, in London. Of Warren's six children, two were born in Boston, two in New York, and two in London, to which he summoned his family in 1747. Two of his children, including his only son, died in a 1744 epidemic. His eldest daughter married Charles Fitzroy, later Baron Southampton, while his third daughter, Charlotte, married the earl of Abingdon. Warren died suddenly of a fever in Dublin on 29 July 1752 and was buried in Warrenstown, co. Meath. His widow commissioned Roubiliac to carve his monument, now in Westminster Abbey.

JULIAN GWYN

Sources J. Gwyn, *The enterprising admiral: the personal fortune of Admiral Sir Peter Warren* (Montreal, 1974) · *The Royal Navy and North America: the Warren papers, 1736–1752*, ed. J. Gwyn, Navy RS, 118 (1975) · J. Gwyn, 'Warren, Peter', *DCB*, vol. 3 · E. Cruickshanks, 'Warren, Peter', *HoP, Commons, 1715–54*, 2.522–3 · F. V. Recum, *The families of Warren and Johnson of Warrenstown, county Meath* (New York, 1950) · *Naval Chronicle*, 12 (1804), 257–75
Archives E. Sussex RO, papers · E. Sussex RO, papers relating to American estates · New York Historical Society, papers relating to legal and personal matters, incl. his estate · PRO, ADM 88 · PRO, admiral's dispatch, ADM 1/480 · PRO, captain's letters, ADM

1/2652–2655 · U. Mich., Clements L., naval papers · U. Mich., Clements L., papers | BL, Anson, Norris, Halifax papers, Add. MSS · Mass. Hist. Soc., Belknap, Hancock, Belcher, Louisbourg papers · Sussex Archaeological Society, Lewes, Gage papers · U. Mich., George Clinton papers
Likenesses J. Smybert, oils, 1746, Athenaeum, Portsmouth, New Hampshire · T. Hudson, oils, c.1747, NPG; version, NMM · T. Hudson, oils, 1752, National Gallery, Ottawa · T. Hudson, oils, 1752, NMM · J. Faber junior, mezzotint (after T. Hudson), BM, NPG · L. F. Roubiliac, marble bust, Hunt. L. · L. F. Roubiliac, marble monument, Westminster Abbey · brass medal, BM
Wealth at death £159,100: Sullivan, James, and others, *The papers of Sir William Johnson* (1965), 13.19–23; Gwyn, *Enterprising admiral*, 195

Warren, Sir Ralph (c.1483–1553), merchant and local politician, was apprenticed to William Botary, a prominent member of the London Mercers' Company, of which he became free in 1507. He was already exporting cloth to the Low Countries in 1506, and soon became a leading member of both the Company of Merchant Adventurers and the Staplers' Company. His cloth wholesaling brought him into contact with the royal household, of which he was a major creditor by 1532. His business acumen was often placed at the service of the crown, whose servants in Flanders and Italy he and the Greshams supplied with large sums through the 1540s. Closely associated with the court, he numbered among his friends royal servants such as Thomas Cromwell, for whom he helped secure the lease of the mansion place at Stepney from the Mercers' Company in 1534, and William Paulet, marquess of Winchester, lord treasurer from 1550, whom he described in his will as 'my very good lord' (PRO, PROB 11/36, fol. 114v).

By 1541 Warren's subsidy assessment of £4000 suggests that, after his fellow mercer Sir John Gresham, he was the wealthiest man in the City. He acquired several manors in Essex, Norfolk, Suffolk, Northamptonshire, and Cambridgeshire, as well as owning an extensive portfolio of property about the capital. At the beginning of his business career he resided in the parish of St Mary Magdalen, Milk Street, but by 1524 he was living in St Sythe's Lane in the parish of St Benet Sherehog, his London base for the rest of his life. By the time of his death he had acquired suburban residences at both Bethnal Green and Fulham.

Warren was a committed member of his livery company, serving as warden in 1521–2 and as master in 1530–31, 1542–3, and again briefly (on the death of Sir Richard Gresham in office) in 1549. After the surrender of the hospital of St Thomas Acre on the dissolution of the religious houses in 1538 he was instrumental, with Gresham and other leading mercers, in procuring the purchase by the Mercers' Company of the church and precincts for their hall. In 1542 the buildings were vested with Warren, who then surrendered his interest to the company. He was elected alderman for Aldersgate ward on 18 June 1528 and served the office of sheriff in 1528–9. On 26 October 1531 he moved to the ward of Candlewick, which he continued to serve until his death. His close connections with the court made him a more reliable agent in the troubled months surrounding the Pilgrimage of Grace than the conservative William Holles, whose turn it was to serve the office of lord mayor, and the king wrote to the City on the day of the election, 13 October 1536, to demand that Warren be elected. Although he was 'incontynent chosen', the City registered a formal protest with the crown. Another mark of royal favour was the elaborate procession on 22 December 1536 in which Warren accompanied the king, the queen, and the Lady Mary through the City on their way to Greenwich immediately after the mayor had been knighted in the Great Chamber of Presence. Warren, unusually, served a second term as lord mayor, being elected on 17 April 1544 to succeed Sir William Bowyer, who had died four days previously.

In spite of his close connections with Cromwell, Warren's religious sympathies seem to have been conservative. In his will, dated 4 July 1552, at the high water mark of the Reformation, he bequeathed his soul according to a conventional Catholic formula, and during his lifetime his gifts to the Mercers' Company included, in 1542, a hearse cloth embroidered with scripture and stained glass for the chapel windows, and, in 1544, a great bell to ring at mass there. He also acted as a commissioner against heretics in 1541. For a man of his wealth his charitable bequests were modest: in 1548 he had given his company a loan stock of £100 to be given to two young men, the interest from which was to pay for a dinner for the livery, but the bequests in his will (spread between St Bartholomew's Hospital, the lazar houses, the London prisons, highway repair, poor maidens' marriages, and poor scholars at the universities) amounted to only about £150.

Warren married twice. His first wife was Christiana, the daughter of Richard Warcup of Sinnington in Yorkshire, and the widow of Roger North (d. 1509), a London merchant. This first marriage appears to have been childless, but his stepchildren were a distinguished pair: Sir Edward *North, by the time of Warren's death, was a privy councillor, and Joanne Wilkinson was the Marian exile. Warren's second wife was Joan, probably the daughter of John Trelake, alias Davy, a Cornish gentleman; there were two surviving children at his death, Richard (d. 1598) and Joan (d. 1572). The latter married Warren's ward Sir Henry Williams (afterwards Cromwell) of Hinchinbrooke, Huntingdonshire, the grandfather of the Lord Protector. Warren himself died of the stone on 11 July 1553 at Bethnal Green, and was buried five days later in the chancel of the church of St Benet Sherehog near the tomb of his first wife, the funeral being followed by what the London undertaker Henry Machyn described as 'a gret dener as I have sene' (*Diary of Henry Machyn*, 36). His widow married, on 25 November 1558, alderman Sir Thomas *White, the founder of St John's College, Oxford, and died in 1572.

IAN W. ARCHER

Sources will, PRO, PROB 11/36, sig. 16 [see also customs accounts, subsidy assessments, inquisitions post mortem] • repertories of the court of aldermen and journals of common council, CLRO • Acts of Court, Mercers' Hall, London • *LP Henry VIII* • A. B. Beaven, ed., *The aldermen of the City of London, temp. Henry III*–[1912], 2 vols. (1908–13) • C. Wriothesley, *A chronicle of England during the reigns of the Tudors from AD 1485 to 1559*, ed. W. D. Hamilton, 2 vols., CS, new ser., 11, 20 (1875–7) • *The diary of Henry Machyn, citizen and merchant-taylor of London, from AD 1550 to AD 1563*, ed. J. G. Nichols, CS, 42 (1848) • GEC, *Peerage*, new edn • H. Ellis, ed., *The visitation of the county of Huntingdon … 1613*, CS, 43 (1849) • D. Keane and V. Harding, eds., *Historical gazetteer of London before the great fire*, rev. edn (1994) [microfiche] • will, PRO, PROB 11/36, sig. 16

Warren, Richard (1731–1797), physician, born at Cavendish, Suffolk, on 4 December 1731, was the third son of Dr Richard Warren (1681–1748), archdeacon of Suffolk and rector of Cavendish, and his wife, Priscilla (d. 1774), daughter of John Fenner. He was the younger brother of John *Warren (1730–1800), bishop of Bangor, and, like him, was educated at Cavendish School in Bury St Edmunds. He entered Jesus College, Cambridge, in 1748, shortly after the death of his father, and graduated BA as fourth wrangler in 1752, obtaining in succeeding years the prizes awarded to middle and senior bachelors for proficiency in Latin prose composition. He proceeded MA in 1755 and MD on 3 July 1762. He was a fellow between 1756 and 1759.

Warren was tutor at Jesus College to the only son of Peter *Shaw (1694–1763), physician-in-ordinary to George II and George III. He gained Shaw's esteem, married his daughter Elizabeth in 1759, and in 1763 succeeded to his father-in-law's practice. He was admitted a candidate of the Royal College of Physicians on 30 September 1762.

Shortly after Warren began to practise, Sir Edward Wilmot, physician to the court and son-in-law of Richard Mead, recommended him as a suitable assistant for his attendance on Princess Amelia. When Wilmot retired, Warren continued to act as physician to the princess, and by her influence was appointed physician to George III in 1762, after the resignation of his father-in-law. He was elected a fellow of the Royal College of Physicians on 3 March 1763, and delivered the Goulstonian lectures at the college in 1764 and the Harveian oration in 1768. He acted as censor in 1764, 1776, and 1782. On 9 August 1784 he was named an elect.

On 5 August 1756, having at that time a licence *ad practicandum* from the University of Cambridge, Warren was elected a physician to the Middlesex Hospital, and on 21 January 1760 he became physician to St George's Hospital. The former appointment he resigned in November 1758, the latter in May 1766. In 1787 he was appointed physician to the prince of Wales, and was the most sought-after society doctor of that time; a pre-eminence which he maintained to the last. Warren's annual income was in excess of anything previously accrued from the practice of medicine in Britain. He is said to have earned £9000 a year from the time of the onset of George III's insanity in 1788, and he bequeathed to his family upwards of £150,000. He had a reputation for exceptional powers of mind and solidity of judgement.

Warren published two papers in the *Transactions* of the Royal College of Physicians. His *Oratio ex Harveii instituto* was published in 1769.

Warren died at his house in Dover Street, London, on 23 June 1797, leaving a widow, eight sons, and two daughters. He was buried in Kensington church on 30 June 1797. Elizabeth Inchbald, who had a great admiration for him, produced some mourning verses to his memory, addressed to Mrs Warren. Of his sons, Frederick *Warren (1775–1848) became a rear-admiral and Pelham *Warren (1778–1835) became a physician.

D'A. POWER, *rev.* CATHERINE BERGIN

Sources Munk, *Roll* · Venn, *Alum. Cant.* · I. Macalpine and R. Hunter, *George III and the mad-business* (1969) · W. Macmichael, *The gold-headed cane*, 5th edn, ed. G. C. Peachey (1923) · *GM*, 1st ser., 67 (1797), 616 · *Memoirs of Mrs Inchbald*, ed. J. Boaden, 2 vols. (1833), 1.258, 269, 387; 2.13–14 · private information (1899) **Archives** BL, letters to the duke and duchess of Newcastle, Add. MSS 32919–33083 · BL, letters to Countess Spencer, MS Coll. ref: p5 **Likenesses** J. Jones, mezzotint, 1792 (after T. Gainsborough), Wellcome L. · G. Bartolozzi, stipple, 1810 (after W. Evans; after G. Stuart), BL, Wellcome L.; repro. in *The British gallery of contemporary portraits* (1810) · T. Gainsborough, oils, RCP Lond.; repro. in A. Aspinall, ed., *The correspondence of George, prince of Wales*, 3 vols. (1963), vol. 1 **Wealth at death** approx. £150,000: Munk, *Roll*

Warren, Richard Augustus [Jacobite Sir Richard Warren, baronet] (*c*.1705–1775), Jacobite army officer, was the son of John Warren of Corduff or Courtduffe, co. Dublin, and Mary, *née* Jones. The family were recusant gentry. One of three younger sons, two of whom, William and John, had joined Lally's Franco-Irish regiment in the French service, Richard Warren started in business as a merchant at Marseilles. On hearing of the preparations by Prince Charles, the Young Pretender, for an expedition to Scotland in 1744, he wound up his affairs and joined his brothers' regiment as a volunteer. On 10 August 1745 he was transferred as a captain without pay to Rothe's Franco-Irish infantry. In the middle of October he embarked for Scotland and landed at Stonehaven. He joined the prince at Edinburgh, became aide-de-camp to Lord George Murray, was made a colonel at Brampton on 12 November, and took part in the siege of Carlisle.

After the Young Pretender's retreat from Derby, Warren was sent to raise levies in Atholl, and he collected the fishing boats for the expedition by which Lord Loudoun's force of 1500 men, posted between the Moray and Dornoch firths, was surprised and dispersed. On 18 April 1746 he sailed from Findhorn with dispatches from the marquis d'Éguilles, the French envoy, urging reinforcements. He reached Versailles on the 30th, having been sent for the purpose of inflating the importance of the inconsequential Jacobite victory at the 'route of Moy', in March 1746. In gratitude for the news, and for the safe delivery of several prisoners captured at the battle, the French court awarded him the rank of colonel, and he was made a knight of the order of St Louis. Commissioned to rescue the prince, he embarked under great secrecy on 31 August at Cape Fréhel on the frigate *Heureux* with another ship, the *Prince de Conti*, and arrived at Lochmanuagh, Inverness-shire, on 6 September 1746. After three weeks' search he took the Young Pretender on board, on 30 September at Lochmanuagh, and landed him on 10 October at Roscoff, in Brittany.

Warren had desired the French title of baron if he succeeded in his task. Instead, James Francis Edward Stuart, the Old Pretender, made him a Jacobite baronet on 3 November 1746, but he was prohibited from publicly assuming that rank until 1751. He was aide-de-camp to Marshal Saxe until 1748, received the rank of brigadier-general from James Edward in 1750, and was advanced within the royal and military order of St Louis in 1755. He paid a visit to London in 1751 and was included on a list of proposed attainders for rebels in 1752. He had a French pension of 1200 livres, and in 1754 obtained a captaincy in Rothe's regiment. In 1762 he was made a *maréchal-de-camp*, was naturalized in 1764, and was appointed commandant of Belle Île, which post he held until his death on 21 June 1775. Unmarried, he left a will in favour of a young man named MacCarthy, but his debts exceeded the assets. His papers are preserved in the Morbihan archives at Vannes.

M. R. GLOZIER

Sources DNB · *Bulletin de la Société Polymathique du Morbihan* (1892–5) · lettres de noblesse, 1669–1790, Centre Accueil de la Recherche des Archives Nationales, Paris, O'54 · lettres d'anoblissement de confirmation ou de maintenu de noblesse, Centre Accueil de la Recherche des Archives Nationales, Paris, 1/bis · enregistrées à la chambre des comptes de Paris, de 1635 à 1787, Centre Accueil de la Recherche des Archives Nationales, Paris, 146/bis · lettres de naturalité et lettres de légitimation, 1635–1787, Centre Accueil de la Recherche des Archives Nationales, Paris, 151/bis · W. Chambers and R. Chambers, *History of the rebellion in Scotland in 1745*, 2 vols. (1828) [repr. 1869] · P. Cottin, *Protégé de Bachaumont; correspondance inédite du marquis d'Éguilles, 1745–1748* (1887) · *Inventaire des Archives du Morbihan*, Vannes, France · E. J. B. Rathery, ed., *Journal et mémoires du marquis d'Argenson*, 9 vols. (1859–67), 4.320 · L. Lallement, *Le maréchal de camp Baron de Warren* (1893) · M. H. Massue de Ruvigny, ed., *The Jacobite peerage* (1904); repr. (1974), 183 · F. J. McLynn, *France and the Jacobite rising of 1745* (1981) · J. O'Hart, *Irish pedigrees; or, the origin and stem of the Irish nation*, 2 vols. (1876–8) · *Revue rétrospective* (1885) · F. de Warren, *Notice sur famille Warren* (1860) · T. Warren, *A history and genealogy of the Warren family* (1902) **Archives** Archives du Morbihan, Vannes, France **Wealth at death** debts exceeded estate: DNB

Warren, Robert (1784/5–1849), blacking manufacturer, and his brother Jonathan (*fl. c*.1805–1824), were reticent about their origins. William Frederick Deacon's *Warreniana* (1824), comprising not very skilful parodies of well-known poets' work in praise of Warren's blacking, is a mine of biographical misinformation, claiming that Warren was of lowly origin, no cockney, but a Scot. An article in *The Town* (5 August 1837) states that he was 'suckled amid scenes repulsive to the growth of mind', hardly an apt description of the Scottish educational system.

More credibly, Warren and his brother appear to have been the sons of Thomas Warren (*d. c*.1810), who in the 1790s succeeded Samuel Warren—probably his father or brother—as boot- and shoemaker in St Martin's Lane, London. By 1805 Thomas Warren had diversified into liquid blacking manufacture, roughly at the same time that Charles Day helped to found the rival blacking firm of Day and Martin. The brothers then fell out over who owned the blacking recipe. After a spell of bootmaking, also in St Martin's Lane, Robert had by 1817 moved to 30 Strand, where his blacking warehouse remained for many years.

Meanwhile Jonathan Warren, proclaiming himself 'the original manufacturer of the real japan blacking', had his own works in Suffolk Street, Charing Cross, before removing in 1821 to 30 Hungerford Street, Strand, the words 'Hungerford Street' being written so small as to mislead the unwary. He soon gave up the struggle against his well-entrenched brother and sold out, for an annuity, to George and James Lamert. The latter was a cousin by marriage of Charles Dickens, who was then just twelve, and to whom he offered a job in the blacking warehouse at a time when the father, John Dickens, was in the Marshalsea. Young Charles was an employee for about three months in 1824, and a fragment of autobiography, given in the *Life of Charles Dickens* by John Forster depicts the 'crazy and tumbledown', rat-infested, dirty, and dingy premises at Hungerford Stairs, where Dickens wrapped and labelled pots. Soon afterwards, James Lamert in turn tired of the barely profitable business and sold his stake to a Mr Wood.

Robert Warren continued to prosper in the Strand, a tall, bright-eyed, and handsome but rather bowed figure. In the mid-1830s he was one of the largest customers of the firm (later known as Royal Doulton potteries) of Henry Doulton which made the blacking containers. Probably during that decade, Robert bought out Mr Wood, and by 1838 he took on some partners and the firm became Warren, Russell, and Wright, 'Premier Blacking Warehouse'. By then it also made ink and certain types of match.

Warren was one of the first to market a nationally advertised household product in Britain. His press publicity featured verses; one poet, Alexander Kemp, boasted of having written two hundred of these offerings. A popular theme, of a cat spitting at its reflection in a well-blacked Hessian boot, was illustrated by George Cruikshank. The *Gentleman's Magazine* reported the death of a Robert Warren, esquire, of Gloucester Place, London, on 13 February 1849, and a death certificate records the death of one of that name on that date at 87 Gloucester Place, but no will was proved. Jonathan Warren, not so commemorated, is reported to have died in a London street of heart failure on being informed that his premises were on fire. After several changes of ownership, in 1913 the firm became the Chiswick Polish Company Ltd, maker of Cherry Blossom and Nugget polishes, which went into voluntary liquidation in 1954.

T. A. B. CORLEY

Sources W. F. Deacon, *Warreniana* (1824) · 'Warren', *The Town* (5 Aug 1837), 50 · W. J. Carlton, 'In the blacking warehouse', *The Dickensian*, 60 (1964), 11–16 · W. Partington, 'The blacking laureate', *The Dickensian*, 34 (1938), 199 · J. Forster, *The life of Charles Dickens*, 3 vols. (1872–4) · D. Eyles, *Royal Doulton, 1815–1965* (1965), 26 · A. Davis, *Package and print* (1967), 30, 41–2 · E. S. Turner, *The shocking history of advertising!* [1952], 54, 56–7, 59 · T. R. Nevett, *Advertising in Britain: a history* (1982), 56, 111 · *London Directory* · d. cert. · J. Holden Macmichael, *The story of Charing Cross* (1906), 225

Warren, Sir Samuel (1769–1839), naval officer, was born at Sandwich, Kent, on 9 January 1769, entered the navy in January 1782 on board the *Sampson*, with his kinsman Captain John Harvey (1740–1794), and was present at the relief of Gibraltar and the encounter with the allied fleet off Cape Spartel. Promoted lieutenant on 3 November 1790, he was appointed to the *Ramillies* in 1793 with Captain

Henry Harvey, and was present at the battle of 1 June 1794. In 1795 he was in the *Royal George*, flagship of Lord Bridport, in the action off Lorient on 23 June. On 1 March 1797 he was promoted to command the sloop *Scourge* on the Leeward Islands station, where he made many rich prizes and captured several privateers. In August 1800 he brought the *Scourge* home. He married, on 27 October 1800, Sarah Moulden Burton, daughter of a clerk of the check at Chatham. They had seven children.

On 29 April 1802 Warren was advanced to post rank. In 1805 he commanded the *Glory* (98 guns) as flagship to Rear-Admiral Charles Stirling in the action off Cape Finisterre on 22 July. In 1806–7 he was again with Stirling in the *Sampson* (64 guns) and in the *Diadem* (64 guns) during the operations in the Plate River; in 1809 he commanded the *Bellerophon* (74 guns), one of the squadron in the Baltic, with Sir James Saumarez. In September 1810 he was appointed to the frigate *President* (44 guns), captured from the French in 1806, and in her took part in the operations resulting in the capture of Java. On 4 June 1815 he was made a CB. After the peace he successively commanded the *Blenheim* and the *Bulwark* third rates, and the *Seringapatam* (46 guns); in the last he took the British ambassador to Sweden in the summer of 1823. In January 1830 he was appointed agent for transports at Deptford. On 3 August 1835 he was made KCH and was knighted by the king; on 10 January 1837 he attained the rank of rear-admiral, and he was made a KCB on 18 April 1839. He died at Southampton (where he was then living) on 15 October 1839.

J. K. LAUGHTON, rev. ANDREW LAMBERT

Sources J. D. Grainger, ed., *The Royal Navy in the River Plate, 1806–1807*, Navy RS, 135 (1996) · C. N. Parkinson, *War in the eastern seas, 1793–1815* (1954) · *GM*, 2nd ser., 13 (1840), 92–3 · J. Marshall, *Royal naval biography*, 2/2 (1825), 570–72 · IGI

Warren, Samuel (1781–1862), Wesleyan Methodist minister, was born either in Great Yarmouth or Yarmouth, Isle of Wight, the son of Samuel Warren, a sea captain. In 1806 he married his first wife, Anne (1778–1823), daughter of Richard and Elizabeth Williams; they had a daughter and six sons, the eldest of whom, also Samuel *Warren, became a noted novelist. Anne died in 1823; Warren's second wife, Jane, survived him. Warren was an apprentice on his father's ship when it was captured by the French in May 1794. After some eighteen months as a prisoner of war he took up nautical studies in Liverpool. There he became a Wesleyan Methodist in 1800, entering the ministry two years later. He gained the degrees of MA (1818) and LLD (1825) from Glasgow University, produced a standard manual of Methodist law (1827), and commanded respect, if little influence, in the Wesleyan hierarchy.

In 1834 Warren unexpectedly emerged as the leading figure in a controversy that resulted in a major secession from Wesleyan Methodism and the formation of the Wesleyan Association (designated Wesleyan Methodist Association in 1839). The immediate cause of this division was the proposed establishment of the first Wesleyan Theological Institution. At the Wesleyan conference of 1834

Warren headed the unsuccessful opposition to this proposal and particularly objected to the further concentration of power in the hands of Jabez Bunting, the nominated president of the institution and the dominant Wesleyan figure of this period. Some connexional leaders alleged that Warren was motivated by his failure to secure a teaching post at the institution. The publication of Warren's conference speech (September 1834) and his refusal to defend it at the Manchester special district meeting led to his suspension from ministerial duties as superintendent of the Manchester Oldham Street circuit (22 October 1834).

These proceedings prompted a widespread protest movement that originated in south Lancashire, where the Grand Central Association, the forerunner of the Wesleyan Association, was formed in Manchester (6 November 1834). Originally known as Warrenites, the protesters also campaigned in defence of the local, lay-dominated Methodist institutions against the central powers of the exclusively ministerial Wesleyan conference. During the ensuing bitter contest, in which the Wesleyan authorities expelled all dissidents, Warren failed in his application to the court of chancery for restoration to the Oldham Street circuit pulpits (March 1835). He was formally expelled from the Wesleyan conference in August 1835.

The Wesleyan Association, the earliest reported membership of which was 21,275 (1837), elected Warren president at its first annual assembly (August 1836). It quickly became apparent, however, that Warren himself had serious reservations about the democratic character of this new body. He sought to check this tendency by promoting union with the Methodist New Connexion, but he was defeated at the annual assembly of 1837. Shortly afterwards he resigned from the Wesleyan Association (October 1837). The final twist in his public life occurred in the following year when he was ordained in the Church of England. He was inducted into the living of All Souls, Ancoats (December 1840), a languishing cause in a slum parish, where he remained until his death at Polygon Avenue, Ardwick, Manchester, on 23 May 1862.

D. A. GOWLAND

Sources S. Warren, *Remarks on the Wesleyan Theological Institution for the education of the junior preachers, together with the substance of a speech delivered at the London conference of 1834* (1834) · S. Warren, *Chronicles of Wesleyan Methodism*, 2 vols. (1827) · S. Warren, *Memoirs and select letters of Mrs A. Warren, with biographical sketches of her family* (1827) · 'Memoir of the Rev. Samuel Warren', *Imperial Magazine*, 8 (1826), 690–701 · *Memoir of … S. Warren … with a brief review of the … Manchester Special District Meeting*, 2nd edn [1834] · B. Gregory, *Side lights on the conflicts of Methodism during the second quarter of the nineteenth century, 1827–1852* (1898) · D. A. Gowland, *Methodist secessions: the origins of Free Methodism in three Lancashire towns* (1979) · W. R. Ward, *Religion and society in England, 1790–1850* (1972) · *Early Victorian Methodism: the correspondence of Jabez Bunting, 1830–1858*, ed. W. R. Ward (1976) · O. A. Beckerlegge, *A bibliography of the Wesleyan Methodist Association and other branches* (1988) · *CGPLA Eng. & Wales* (1862) · *Manchester Courier* (31 May 1862)
Archives JRL, Methodist Archives and Research Centre, letters
Likenesses J. Thompson, stipple, pubd 1834 (after R. W. Warren), BM · W. T. Fry, stipple (after J. Jackson), BM, NPG; repro. in *Methodist Magazine* (1824) · portrait, repro. in 'Memoir of the Rev. Samuel Warren', *Imperial Magazine*

Wealth at death under £450: administration, 15 July 1862, *CGPLA Eng. & Wales*

Warren, Samuel (1807–1877), lawyer and writer, was born on 23 May 1807 near Wrexham, Denbighshire, the elder son of Dr Samuel *Warren (1781–1862), clergyman, and his first wife, Anne (1778–1823), daughter of Richard and Elizabeth Williams. Little is known about Samuel Warren's early education except his statement in the preface to *Passages from the Diary of a Late Physician* that he was for six years before 1827 'actively engaged in the practical study of physic' ('Preface to fifth edition', edn of 1837 *Passages* in Warren, *Works*, 1854–5, vol. 1), perhaps as an apothecary's apprentice. From 1826 to 1828 Warren attended the University of Edinburgh where he studied various subjects and won prizes in comparative jurisprudence and poetry, but did not obtain a degree. His poetry prize led to introductions to Christopher North (John Wilson), and to Thomas De Quincey, two of the leading lights in *Blackwood's Magazine*.

Warren was admitted to the Inner Temple, London, in 1828; he studied law and worked as a special pleader there until 1837, when he was called to the bar. In 1831 he had married Eliza Ballinger (c.1802–1868); they had two sons and a daughter. This period also saw the serialization in *Blackwood's Magazine* of the work that made his literary reputation, *Passages from the Diary of a Late Physician* (1831–7). He later described his views and feelings in writing the book as 'those not of a Novelist, but of a Moralist' whose 'steady purpose … was to exhibit deathbeds' ('Preface', 1854 edn of *Passages* in Warren, *Works*, 1854–5, vol. 1). The success of the book depended on the sensational and melodramatic atmosphere of the stories which parade the horrors of debauchery, disease, madness, and death with an almost erotic fascination.

Warren had not restricted his writing to creative efforts during this time; he also published the first edition of *A Popular Introduction to Law Studies* (1835), a guide for those intending to become law students. In 1837 Warren, with John William Smith, published *Select Extracts from Blackstone's Commentaries*, and he was later to publish a much extended *Blackstone's* in 1855 and 1856.

Warren's second novel, published in *Blackwood's Magazine* from 1839 to 1841, was *Ten Thousand a-Year*. The novel, which was an immediate best-seller, concerns a firm of attorneys who discover that Tittlebat Titmouse, a poor draper's clerk, may have a claim to the large estate of Yatton. The attorneys commence an action which results in Titmouse displacing the unbelievably pious John Aubrey as the owner of the estate, and its annual income of £10,000. Titmouse revels in his new found wealth, until a new round of litigation is commenced which returns Aubrey to his place as squire of Yatton. Titmouse is disgraced, and ends his life in a lunatic asylum. The narrator repeatedly tells the reader that the English legal system is close to perfection, but the actual workings of the law in *Ten Thousand a-Year* paint a more negative picture.

Dickens seems to have read Warren's fiction and non-fiction, and to have borrowed images and ideas. Sir Leicester Dedlock and the solicitor Vholes in *Bleak House* (1852–3)

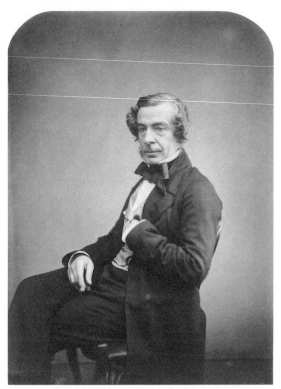

Samuel Warren (1807–1877), by Maull & Polyblank, 1850s

resemble the earl of Dreddlington and Gammon, Titmouse's principal lawyer, in *Ten Thousand a-Year*. The striking picture of barristers in court bobbing up and down like hammers in a pianoforte in the first chapter of *Bleak House* is similar to an image in chapter nine of the second edition of *A Popular Introduction to Law Studies* (1845). Wemmick's habit of collecting mementos from Jaggers's criminal clients in *Great Expectations* parallels Quirk's practice in *Ten Thousand a-Year*. Warren may have returned the favour by using elements of the Bardell v. Pickwick case in *Ten Thousand a-Year*.

Warren's third novel, *Now and then* (1847), tells the story of Adam Ayliffe who is convicted unjustly of murder, although his death sentence is commuted to transportation. The novel leaps forward twenty years to reveal that Adam was innocent of the murder, and we are told by the parish priest, a character apparently incapable of irony, that the wrongful conviction resulted from 'the unavoidably imperfect administration of justice' (ch. 18). Much of the novel is taken up with the struggle by the priest to convince the victim's father, the proud and vengeful earl of Milverstoke, that he should show Christian mercy and forgiveness to Ayliffe. The earl (and the reader) eventually gets the point. The broader religious goal of the novel is to justify God's ways to humanity, but Warren relies on assertion and sermonizing to urge the reader to faith.

In 1848 Warren published a series of four lectures, originally given to students and young attorneys at the Law Society, as *The Moral, Social, and Professional Duties of Attorneys and Solicitors* (1848). The book is a mixture of ethical advice, tips on practising law, and assurances that attorneys can, with effort, learn how to behave like gentlemen. Warren assures his audience that attorneys are not inferior to barristers, although he is less egalitarian elsewhere. Other legal publications included the second and third editions of *Law Studies* (1845, 1863) and two books on election law (1852, 1853). Warren continued to practise law until the mid-1850s and became a queen's counsel in 1851, but found it difficult to attract business. He achieved some success within the Inner Temple where he was elected as a bencher in 1851.

Warren continued to explore philosophical and religious issues in his creative work, especially in *The Lily and the Bee: an Apologue of the Crystal Palace of 1851* (1851), *The Intellectual and Moral Development of the Present Age* (1853), and 'Speculators among the stars' (1854). These texts are interesting as a catalogue of one religious Victorian's terrified vision of a world without Christianity: dark, amoral, determinist, animalistic, despairing, sinful, a charnel house of decayed and decaying opinions, a 'mental and moral shipwreck' (*Intellectual and Moral Development*).

William Blackwood & Sons published *Miscellanies: Critical, Imaginative, and Juridical* in 1854, and a collected *Works* in five volumes in 1854 and 1855. Warren's political fidelity, as well as his writing, were recognized when he was in 1853 made an honorary DCL of the University of Oxford, with Bulwer-Lytton and others, on the occasion of Lord Derby's installation as chancellor of the university. His Conservative political sentiments led him to support the policies of Peel and later Lord Derby in a series of books and articles. In 1856 Warren was elected to the House of Commons for the borough of Midhurst (Sussex). He held the seat until 1859 when he was appointed a master in lunacy 'at a munificent £2,000 a year stipend' (Sutherland, 660). The Lunatics Acts of the mid-nineteenth century empowered the masters in lunacy to make decisions about persons of unsound mind, including the management of their property. Most contemporary observers praised Warren's handling of the mastership. Warren became reader at the Inner Temple in 1865, and treasurer in 1866. He also held the judicial post of recorder of Hull from 1852 to 1874.

Warren's first marriage had been happy, and he was deeply affected by the loss of his wife on 29 August 1868. Some three years later, on 23 August 1871, he married Louisa Beaumont. Warren died on 29 July 1877 at his home at 16 Manchester Square, London. He was survived by his second wife, and was buried on 3 August 1877 at Christ Church, Esher, Surrey, where his son was rector.

C. R. B. DUNLOP

Sources S. A. Yorks, 'Samuel Warren: an early contributor to Victorian literature', PhD diss., University of Washington, 1956 · *DNB* · Mrs Oliphant, *William Blackwood and his sons* (1897), vols. 1–2 of *Annals of a publishing house* (1897–8) · Mrs G. Porter, *John Blackwood* (1898), vol. 3 of *Annals of a publishing house* (1897–8) · F. Watt, 'Samuel Warren', *Juridical Review*, 30 (1918), 85–98 · S. Warren, letters to W. R. Grove, Royal Institution of Great Britain, London, Grove correspondence · C. A. Cooper, *An editor's retrospect: fifty years of newspaper work* (1896) · *N&Q*, 9th ser., 4 (1899), 163 · J. Sutherland, *The Stanford companion to Victorian fiction* (1989) · M. Steig, 'Ten thousand *a-year* and the political content of *Barnaby Rudge'*, *Dickens Studies Newsletter*, 4 (1973), 67–8 • J. B. Atlay, 'The author of *Ten thousand a year'*, *Cornhill Magazine*, [3rd] ser., 23 (1907), 476–88 • W. L. Harle, *Law Times* (20 Oct 1877), 413–14 • *WWBMP*, vol. 1 • Allibone, *Dict.* • Boase, *Mod. Eng. biog.* • 'Samuel Warren', *Appleton's Journal of Popular Literature, Science, and Art*, 4 (1870), 492–4 • d. cert. • burial register, Christ Church, Esher, Surrey

Archives NL Scot., literary MSS and papers | BL, letters to Royal Literary Fund, loan 96 • Herts. ALS, letters to Sir Edward Bulwer-Lytton, D/EK C5/97 &100–101 • Lpool RO, MSS of fourteenth earl of Derby, letters to fourteenth earl of Derby, 920 DER (14), 158/8 & 8A • News Int. RO, *The Times* Archive, Delane corresp., letters to John Thaddeus Delane, 7/51 & 8/35 • NL Scot., corresp. with Blackwoods, MSS 4028–4937 • NL Scot., letters to John Lee • Princeton University, New Jersey, letters to Charles Kent • Royal Institution of Great Britain, London, Grove corresp., letters to W. R. Grove • Trinity Cam., letters to William Whewell, Add. MSS a. 214[35], c.66[67], a 216[105]–[112] • UCL, letters to Lord Brougham

Likenesses engraving, *c.*1826, JRL • attrib. J. Linnell, portrait, *c.*1835–1840, NPG • Maull & Polyblank, photograph, 1850–59, NPG [*see illus.*] • J. Watson-Gordon, oils, exh. RA 1856, Scot. NPG • engraving, *c.*1858, repro. in *Chambers's cyclopaedia of English literature*, vol. 2 • engraving, *c.*1870, repro. in 'Samuel Warren', *Appleton's Journal of Popular Literature, Science, and Art*, 4 • E. Edwards, photograph, NPG; repro. in L. Reeve, ed., *Portraits of men of eminence*, 2 (1864) • prints, NPG

Wealth at death under £12,000: probate, 25 Aug 1877, *CGPLA Eng. & Wales*

Warren, Thomas (*c.*1617–1694), Presbyterian minister, matriculated as a sizar from St Catharine's College, Cambridge, at Easter 1634, as of Suffolk, graduated BA in 1638 and proceeded MA in 1641. On 1 January 1647 he was admitted to the rectory of Houghton, Hampshire, though his formal presentation under the great seal took place on 6 February 1651 following its cession by the sequestered rector. From Houghton in April 1654 he issued *Unbeleevers No Subjects of Justification*, directed against the work of William Eyre (*d.* 1670), the curate of St Thomas's, Salisbury, and dedicated to the mayor, aldermen, and common councillors of Salisbury. Following the Restoration, Warren was on 19 July 1660 presented by the crown to the Houghton rectory, and on 22 December he was ordained deacon and priest in Scotland by the bishop of Galloway, Thomas Sydserff. Instituted on 1 February 1661 to his rectory by Bishop Brian Duppa, he was ejected under the Act of Uniformity of 1662 and a successor was collated soon after, on 23 September. According to his papers, Warren was offered a choice of the bishoprics of Salisbury and Winchester if he should conform.

At an unknown date Warren married Elizabeth, with whom he had three sons and four daughters. She was buried at Romsey, probably the couple's home during the early years of the Restoration. His second marriage, by licence of 10 July 1667, was to Mary Evans, aged forty-five, of St Mary Savoy, London. On 25 July 1672 he was licensed as a presbyterian preacher at the house of Clement Warren of Romsey, probably the mercer of that name later designated an executor. He is reported to have had doubts about taking advantage of James II's declaration of indulgence in 1687. In later years, he became almost blind, and the Common Fund of the Presbyterian and Independent ministers granted him £6 a year between 1690 and 1693. Warren was listed as one of the Hampshire preachers in

the winter of 1690–91, 'an ancient and learned man as any in ye county 70 years old' (*Calamy rev.*, 512). In his will dated from Romsey on 13 April 1693 and 25 January 1694 Warren mentioned a third wife, Hannah, and disposed of property at Andover. He died on 27 January 1694, aged seventy-seven or in his seventy-seventh year, and was buried at Romsey Abbey.   STEPHEN WRIGHT

Sources *Calamy rev.*, 511–12 • A. Gordon, ed., *Freedom after ejection: a review (1690–1692) of presbyterian and congregational nonconformity in England and Wales* (1917) • Venn, *Alum. Cant.* • T. Warren, *Unbeleevers no subjects of justification*, BL, E733/10 • will, PRO, PROB 11/421, fols. 381r–383r
Likenesses J. Caldwall, line engraving, NPG
Wealth at death property at Andover: will, PRO, PROB 11/421, fols. 381r–383r

Warren, William (*fl.* 1578–1581), poet, was the author of *A pithie and pleasaunt discourse dialoguewyse betwene a welthie citizen and a miserable souldiour briefelye touching the commodyties and discommodyties bothe of warre and peace* (1578). The work was entered in the Stationers' register, licensed to Richard Jones, on 7 November 1578, but no copies are known to have survived.

Warren is also the author of *A pleasant new fancie of a fondlings device, intitled and cald the nurcerie of names, wherein is presented (to the order of our alphabet) the brandishing brightnes of our English gentlewomen* (1581). The prefatory matter of the volume consists of some short Latin poems and a euphuistic 'Proaeme to the Gentleman Readers', signed 'W. Warren, Gent.', as well as an 'Address to the Gentlewomen of England'. In the latter Warren speaks of himself as 'your poor Poet and your olde friend'. The body of the work consists of extravagant poems, in fourteen-syllable verse, on women's names. The poem on Elizabeth is an excellent example of the contemporary style of compliment to the queen. Nothing is known of Warren's life. It is possible that he may have been one of the two William Warrens recorded as having matriculated at Oxford University in the 1570s, but this is purely speculative.

RONALD BAYNE, *rev.* ELIZABETH GOLDRING

Sources Arber, *Regs. Stationers*, 2.(153b), 179 • T. Corser, *Collectanea Anglo-poetica, or, A … catalogue of a … collection of early English poetry*, 5, Chetham Society, 91 (1873), 359 • Foster, *Alum. Oxon.* • W. C. Hazlitt, *Hand-book to the popular, poetical and dramatic literature of Great Britain* (1867)

Warren, Sir William (*bap.* 1627, *d.* 1695), naval contractor, baptized at Ilsington, Devon, on 7 January 1627, was the sixth son of Christopher Warren (*d.* 1626), vicar of Ilsington, and his wife, Alice Webb. William was admitted to the Drapers' Company in 1650. The first official record of him comes in March 1653, when he obtained a licence to import pitch and tar. On 27 September 1655 he married Mary Culling (*bap.* 1640, *d.* 1719) at St Alfege's, Greenwich; she was a fellow Devonian and a relation, as Warren's grandmother had married a Culling as her second husband. Warren was supplying substantial amounts of timber to the navy by 1656, though his future difficulties were presaged by the fact that he was already claiming arrears of payment. He was knighted on 12 April 1661. His comparative youth and relatively undistinguished career before this point make the honour hard to explain, but in 1663 Warren hinted that he had been involved in some of the secret dealings leading to the Restoration, especially those involving George Monck, duke of Albemarle (though Pepys found these claims unlikely). Warren became an alderman on 13 May 1662, and was sworn and discharged on 27 May for a fine of £420. He was master of the Drapers' Company in 1668–9, and served as auditor of the City in 1674–6.

During the early 1660s Warren became well known to the clerk of the acts to the Navy Board, Samuel Pepys, and often appears in Pepys's diary. They seem to have met first on 29 December 1660, when they discussed Warren's contract to provide deals for alterations at Hinchingbrooke, the home of Pepys's patron, the earl of Sandwich. By the end of 1661 they were socializing regularly, and Warren was soon advising Pepys on both the technicalities of the provision of timber for the navy, and on naval affairs and business practices in general. By the end of 1663 the alliance between the two was very close:

> he did give me most admirable advice, and such as doth speak him a most able and worthy man, and understanding seven times more then ever I thought to be in him … And did give me a common but a most excellent [saying] to observe in all my life: he did give it in rhyme, but the sense was this: that a man should treat every friend in his discourse and opening of his mind to him as of one that may hereafter be his foe. He did also advise me how I should take occasion to make known to the world my care and the pains that I take in my business; and above all, to be sure to get a thorough knowledge in my imployment, and to that add all the Interest at Court that I can—which I hope I shall do. (Pepys, *Diary*, 4.422–3)

A year later Pepys was looking on Warren as 'a good friend and help … the best friend I have had ever in this office' (ibid., 5.293, 337), and in February 1665 he 'concluded a firm league with him in all just ways to serve him and myself all I can' (ibid., 6.32). The question of whether their alliance was really founded on 'just ways' returned to haunt Pepys and Warren. Pepys himself recorded many payments and gifts to him from Warren: these ranged from the 'pair of plain white gloves for my hand a fair State-dish of Silver and cup with my arms ready-cut upon them, worth I believe about £18' that Warren gave him in February 1663 (ibid., 4.39–40) to the £100 that Warren paid him for arranging the 'great contract of masts' in 1664, handing the money over in a bag and 'expressly taking care that nobody might see this business done' (ibid., 5.229–30, 270, 271).

Regardless of the probity of Warren's relationship with Pepys, by the time the Second Anglo-Dutch War broke out in 1665 he was well established as the pre-eminent supplier of timber to the navy. In July 1663 he had agreed a contract for 40,000 deals, followed in September by one for £3000 of masts, 'the best bargain of masts [that] hath been bought these 27 years in this office' in Pepys's view, with at least a 5 per cent advantage over the alternative tender (Pepys, *Diary*, 4.303–4). On 21 July 1664 the 'great contract' was signed, 'the biggest that ever was made in the Navy' (ibid., 5.215–16), by which Warren undertook to

provide 997 Göteborg masts for the service. A succession of other major contracts followed throughout the war years. However, the perceived mismanagement of the war led to a detailed inquiry into Warren's contracts. He had made a number of enemies—notably the surveyor of the navy, Sir William Batten—and in 1668–9 his dealings were scrutinized closely by the Brooke House committee. Pepys and Warren had fallen out early in 1667 over Warren's attempt to build up an alliance with Lord Brouncker, and they never seem to have regained their earlier intimacy. Nevertheless, Warren perjured himself before the committee by denying that he had ever given presents to Pepys, and Pepys in turn defended Warren before the committee:

> [Warren] never received imprests where he was not indisbursed twice as much for his Majesty as the imprests comes to … £34,000 worth of imprests lies at this day out against him … there lie also before us pretences of his unadjusted to above £20,000 more. (Latham, 360)

Pepys argued that Warren's position effectively as sole supplier benefited the navy by guaranteeing economies of scale, and throughout his career Warren always seemed able to tender lower than his competitors, partly because he was prepared to take greater risks—as the committee heard from no less than Charles II and the duke of York, who praised 'the serviceableness of Sir W. Warren and readiness on all occasions to furnish the King with ships or goods at greater hazards and lower prices than others' (ibid., 423).

Warren continued to supply the navy before, during, and after the Third Anglo-Dutch War, for example signing four major contracts in May to July 1672 and another in October 1673, and in May 1672 he went on an extended visit to France to try to free one of his mast ships from New England that had been captured by a Dunkirker. A fire in Wapping on 29 June burned down his house and 'brought down my spirits and courage, so that for a while I was not fit for any business' (PRO, ADM. 106/314, fol. 212). However, his main concern became the settling of his accounts from the second war, the chaotic state of which both he and Pepys attributed to the malice of Batten and the neglect of Brouncker. In May 1669 he was 'requested to have a little patience' (*Calendar of Treasury Books*, 1669–72, 74), but by January 1675 Warren's patience had run out, and he set out his case as he saw it in a series of lengthy letters to the Navy Board. He recounted in detail his dealings with them from 1666, and claimed a total of £53,174 as the arrears due to him—much of it, he alleged, contained in bills of imprest that Brouncker had simply failed to settle, or else recorded in papers that had been lost in the fire that burned down the Navy Office on 29 January 1673, or else never even claimed until that time (primarily, Warren alleged, because of the intervening Third Anglo-Dutch War and the Wapping fire). Warren asserted that, as a result, 'I, who when I began trade with this board, had twenty thousand pound in cash of my own, am now reduced to as great straights, as he that is not worth one thousand pound' (PRO, ADM 106/314, fol. 211). The subsequent lengthy Treasury investigation in the summer of

1675 produced a quite different result, discounting many of his claims and concluding that in fact Warren owed the king £44,240, much of it in unpaid interest and freight charges: his response was said to be to 'offer your lordship [the earl of Danby, lord treasurer] a long canting story only to amuse your lordship were it possible' (*Supplementary Lindsey MSS*, 154). In 1679 Warren finally settled his account by paying the outstanding £6578 to the duke of Monmouth and Viscount Latimer, to whom the debt had been granted.

The ordering of thirty large new warships in 1677 revived Warren's career. In June 1677 he contracted for 4000 loads of oak, followed two months later by a contract for New England masts; when tendering for Norwegian timber in 1678, he claimed 'I will pitch so low a price that no man shall have them cheaper' (Warren to board, 22 April 1678, PRO, ADM 106/340, fol. 17). He made a further contract for New England masts in February 1679. The sums involved were substantial: between the middle of 1677 and the beginning of 1679 alone, Warren was paid well over £32,000. Despite his earlier experiences his success was due once again to his willingness to accept payment 'in course', in this case as and when the money voted by the last session of the Cavalier Parliament was received. However, Warren's career declined again in the 1680s. Naval business dried up as the Treasury commission of 1679–84 retrenched expenditure. Another disastrous fire in Wapping on 19 November 1682 devastated his yards and burned his house, though he was still able to agree a large contract with the Navy Board in 1686 for New England masts, yards, and bowsprits. In April 1687 the mayor, Sir John Peake, issued a plea for Londoners to show favour to Sir William, who was held 'in this very high esteem with the most eminent citizens of this City and of divers others of chiefest place and authority in this kingdom' (depositions of the mayor's court, 1687, CLRO, MCD 41). It was reported that Sir William had donated about £10,000 to the king in late 1659 and early 1660, but the 'severe frowns of privilege' had brought him to 'a very low and deplorable condition'. His losses were reportedly over £100,000.

In August 1688 Warren sounded Pepys unsuccessfully on the chances of his being a commissioner of the navy. Following the outbreak of war with France, he tendered in November 1689 to supply masts once more, and in 1690, jointly with Francis Riggs, he obtained several contracts for timber, deals, and Norwegian masts. Warren had to admit that he could no longer trade without partners: 'my stock is not what it was, when I did give the navy a credit of 40 or 50 thousand pounds at a time, yet I have friends will furnish me with money enough to perform any thing I shall undertake at the Navy Board' (Warren to board, 6 June 1690, PRO, ADM 106/402, fol. 60). Warren appears to have had no dealings with the navy from 1691 onwards. The date of his death is unknown, but he was buried at St Mary's, Rotherhithe, on 24 September 1695, leaving no will. From about 1665 he had kept houses at both Wapping and Rotherhithe, and after the 1682 fire he seems to have lived exclusively at the latter. He also had a property at Abridge, Essex. His widow, Mary, survived until 1719, when she was buried alongside him. Their son William married into the great trading family the Ingrams, but died in 1699; their daughter Mary married John Upton.

J. D. DAVIES

Sources PRO, admiralty MSS, ADM 20, 49 and 106 · Pepys, *Diary* · T. Warren, *A history and genealogy of the Warren family* (1902); repr. (1982) · J. R. Woodhead, *The rulers of London, 1660–1689* (1965) · C. G. O. Bridgeman and J. C. Walker, eds., *Supplementary report on the manuscripts of the late Montagu Bertie, twelfth earl of Lindsey*, HMC, 79 (1942) · *Samuel Pepys and the Second Dutch War: Pepys's navy white book and Brooke House papers*, ed. R. Latham, Navy RS, 133 (1995) [transcribed by W. Matthews and C. Knighton] · *CSP dom.*, 1652–90 · W. A. Shaw, ed., *Calendar of treasury books*, 2–9, PRO (1905–31), 1667–89 · B. Pool, *Navy board contracts, 1660–1832* (1966) · will, PRO, PROB 11/569 [Mary Warren], fols. 336–9 · J. B. Whitmore and A. W. Hughes Clarke, eds., *London visitation pedigrees, 1664*, Harleian Society, 92 (1940) · A. B. Beaven, ed., *The aldermen of the City of London, temp. Henry III–[1912]*, 2 vols. (1908–13) · A. H. Johnson, *The history of the Worshipful Company of the Drapers of London*, 5 vols. (1914–22) · F. T. Colby, ed., *The visitation of the county of Devon in the year 1620*, Harleian Society, 6 (1872) · parish register, Rotherhithe, St Mary, 24 Sept 1695 [burial] · N. Luttrell, *A brief historical relation of state affairs from September 1678 to April 1714*, 6 vols. (1857) · R. G. Albion, *Forests and sea power: the timber problem of the Royal Navy, 1652–1862* (1926) · IGI · parish register, Greenwich, St Alfege, 27 Sept 1655 [marriage] · *Le Neve's Pedigrees of the knights*, ed. G. W. Marshall, Harleian Society, 8 (1873)

Archives PRO, Admiralty MSS

Warrender, Sir George John Scott, of Lochend, seventh baronet (1860–1917), naval officer, was born at Bruntsfield House, Edinburgh, on 31 July 1860, the second son of Sir George Warrender of Lochend, sixth baronet (1825–1901), of Lochend, Haddingtonshire, and his wife, Helen (d. 1875), the only child of Sir Hugh Hume Campbell, seventh baronet, of Marchmont, Berwickshire. He entered the navy as a cadet at the Royal Naval College, Dartmouth, in 1873 and as a midshipman in the corvette *Boadicea* was part of the naval brigade landed during the Anglo-Zulu War in 1879. He was in the Eshowe relief column and was present at the battle of Gingindlovu, receiving the South Africa medal and clasp. He was promoted lieutenant in 1880 with three firsts in his examinations, specialized in gunnery, and was on the staff of the gunnery school HMS *Excellent* (1884–5). He was promoted commander in 1893 and after further service, including three years as commander in the royal yacht *Victoria and Albert*, was promoted captain in 1899.

On 6 February 1894 Warrender married Lady Ethel Maud Ashley-Cooper (1870–1945), daughter of the eighth earl of Shaftesbury. They had two sons and a daughter. Warrender's older brother, John, had died unmarried in 1894. Consequently Warrender succeeded to the baronetcy on the death of his father in June 1901. The family connections of both Warrender and his wife gave them the entrée into society and they were well known in the London social world. In addition his eldest son, Victor Alexander (later first Baron Bruntisfield), was a godson of Queen Victoria.

At the time of the Boxer uprising Warrender was flag captain (1899–1902) in the battleship *Barfleur* to Rear-

Admiral Sir James Bruce, second in command of the China station. He commanded the East India station (1907–9), first as a commodore and then as a rear-admiral after his promotion in July 1908. He then commanded the 2nd cruiser squadron (1910–12), and the 2nd battle squadron (1912–15). He was created a KCVO in 1911 and a KCB in 1913. He was promoted vice-admiral in June 1913 and is remembered for the visit of his battle squadron to Germany for Kiel week in June 1914 shortly before the outbreak of the First World War. His famous though not very prophetic signal on departure was: 'Friends in the past, friends forever' (Goldrick, 2). A few weeks later Warrender, in the absence of the commander-in-chief, commanded the movement of the Grand Fleet from the south coast to its point of concentration at Scapa Flow.

Warrender, flying his flag in the dreadnought *King George V*, had a squadron that enjoyed an excellent record in gunnery. He was an old friend of Admiral J. R. Jellicoe, visiting him so frequently in his flagship that Jellicoe later complained he delayed his work. Warrender enjoyed a high reputation in the navy but, as Jellicoe was slowly and reluctantly to realize, as an admiral during time of peace, not war.

Warrender played a leading and disappointing role in the events of 16 December 1914, generally known to the British as the Scarborough raid. The British by means of their ability to intercept and decode German wireless transmissions learned of a plan for Rear-Admiral Hipper's battle cruisers to raid the north-east coast. The Admiralty planned to trap them on their return with Admiral Beatty's battle cruisers and Rear-Admiral Goodenough's light cruiser squadron. Warrender, with the six dreadnoughts of the 2nd battle squadron, screened by eight destroyers, was ordered by Jellicoe to support them at a rendezvous off the south-east corner of the Dogger Bank. Warrender was in overall command of the interception force, something some historians in retrospect consider a bad choice for, whatever his skill in fleet work, initiative was not his strongest trait. Admiralty intelligence did not know that the high sea fleet would also be out to a position roughly halfway across the North Sea in support of the German raid. Consequently Warrender was standing into danger, and the Germans, who did not know the British would be at sea, might have had an opportunity to do what they had always dreamed of, that is trap and destroy a portion of the Grand Fleet with the entire high sea fleet. Warrender was saved on 16 December when in the poor visibility and squally weather the German commander Admiral Ingenohl, after his screening force of destroyers and light cruisers had clashed with Warrender's destroyers, decided he was facing the entire Grand Fleet and turned away because he did not have the Kaiser's permission for a general engagement. However, the German battle cruisers returning from their raid on the north-east coast also escaped. Goodenough made contact with a German light cruiser and destroyers screening the German battle cruisers but he failed to inform Beatty other German cruisers were in sight. This would have indicated Hipper's battle cruisers were probably behind them. Beatty therefore ordered two of Goodenough's four light cruisers to resume their position as lookouts in advance of his squadron. Unfortunately, a badly worded signal seemed to indicate that the entire squadron was to join Beatty, and Goodenough, not realizing that Beatty did not comprehend the complete situation, turned away and lost contact with the Germans. The German cruisers then passed Warrender's squadron and Rear-Admiral Arbuthnot commanding his 2nd division reported them but did not open fire, awaiting orders. Warrender, however, did not give the order to fire and merely reported the sighting and sent three armoured cruisers (which had joined from Beatty's force) in pursuit. Warrender's signal had the unfortunate effect of diverting Beatty from a course that probably would have permitted him to meet Hipper. In the end the Germans escaped.

The British made many mistakes that day and the most egregious probably were not made by Warrender. Nevertheless Warrender came in for his share of criticism and the redoubtable first sea lord Admiral Fisher called for his head, particularly for his perceived misuse of his cruiser and destroyer screen and failure to spread them properly. Jellicoe, whose retention of old friends and general kindliness was one of his faults, preserved Warrender for a year but lost confidence in him. He still regarded Warrender's experience in fleet work as 'unique' even though 'I am not always quite happy with him' (Patterson, 1.167). Nevertheless Warrender's increasing deafness and fits of absentmindedness indicating deteriorating health led eventually to his replacement in December 1915. Jellicoe still regretted his departure, considering him 'the soul of his squadron and the most loyal of commanders' (ibid., 1.189). Warrender became commander-in-chief, Plymouth, in 1916 and thereby missed a role in the Grand Fleet's major action of the war, the battle of Jutland. His health continued to deteriorate and in December 1916 he asked to be placed on the retired list. He died at his home in London, 23 Great Cumberland Place, on 8 January 1917. He was cremated at Golders Green on 12 January, and his ashes were interred at the church of the Annunciation, Bryanston Street, London. Warrender remains one of the prime examples of a naval leader who, whatever his personal qualities and distinguished record in time of peace, did not rise to the very different demands of war.

PAUL G. HALPERN

Sources *The Jellicoe papers*, ed. A. T. Patterson, 1, Navy RS, 108 (1966) · A. J. Marder, *From the Dreadnought to Scapa Flow: the Royal Navy in the Fisher era, 1904–1919*, 5 vols. (1961–70), vol. 2 · J. Goldrick, *The king's ships were at sea* (1984) · *The Royal Navy list, or, Who's who in the navy* (1915) · J. Winton, *Jellicoe* (1981) · *WW* (1916–28) · Burke, *Peerage* (1999) · *The Times* (9 Jan 1917) · *The Times* (13 Jan 1917) · Burke, *Gen. GB* (1903) · A. Gordon, *The rules of the game: Jutland and British naval command* (1996) · J. S. Corbett, *Naval operations*, 1–2 (1920–21) · b. cert.

Warriner, Doreen Agnes Rosemary Julia (1904–1972), rescuer of refugees and development economist, was born on 16 March 1904 at Weston Park, Long Compton, Warwickshire, the only daughter and eldest child of

Henry Arthur Warriner (1859–1927), land agent for Weston Park, and later a landowner, and his wife, Henrietta Beatrice (1876–1953), farm and estate manager, daughter of Thomas McNulty, a clergyman of a slum parish in the Staffordshire Black Country who had had to leave Ireland because of his Fenian sympathies. It was almost certainly that rebellious grandfather who had early influence in forming Doreen Warriner's radical politics. A brilliant student, she gained a place at St Hugh's College, Oxford, after her schooling at Malvern Girls' College and in 1926 she gained a first in philosophy, politics, and economics, followed by a research scholarship at the London School of Economics. In 1928 she became Mary Somerville research fellow at Somerville College, Oxford, and in 1931 she gained her PhD. In 1933 she became assistant lecturer in political economy at University College, London. From 1947 to 1966 she was on the staff of the School of Slavonic and East European Studies, University of London, where she was made a reader in 1960 and a professor in 1964.

Doreen Warriner's magisterial and hard-hitting books include *Economic Problems of Peasant Farming* (1939), *Food and Farming in Postwar Europe* (1943), *Land and Poverty in the Middle East* (1948), the first report on progress in land reform for the United Nations (1954), and *Land Reform in Principle and Practice* (1969). Whether she was doing research on eastern Europe, the Middle East, India, or South America, she always travelled indefatigably to collect materials on the real living conditions of the people about whom she wrote; her sympathies were always with the poorest and her intelligence and expertise devoted to their betterment—basically through the redistribution of land ownership and water rights.

But Doreen Warriner was not merely a world authority on under-development and land reform. She personally had taken the lead in some of the most audacious and successful efforts to rescue endangered political refugees in central Europe immediately before the outbreak of the Second World War: 'she must have been responsible for saving hundreds, probably thousands of Jewish and Social Democrat lives' (J. Rowntree, *The Times*, 30 Dec 1972). Her field of action was Prague in the winter of 1938–9. On 13 October 1938 she had intended to fly to the United States to finish work on her Rockefeller fellowship; instead, ashamed and incensed by Chamberlain's betrayal of Czechoslovakia, she felt compelled to fly to Prague. 'I had no idea at all of what to do, only a desperate wish to do something' (Warriner). At first she had thought vaguely of relief work for destitute refugee children, but she soon found something quite different was called for. She realized that the people most immediately in danger of concentration camp and death were the Sudeten German Social Democrat leaders who had resisted Hitler and who must now find political asylum abroad. By 9 November 1938, helped by the Labour MP David Grenfell and the international secretary of the Labour Party, William Gillies, as well as by the Swedish trade union movement, she had managed to raise both the necessary money and the

required Polish and British visas to enable nearly 250 leading Social Democrats, including MPs and trade union leaders, to flee—she herself having escorted one party of twenty 'wanted' men via Slovakia to Cracow. But then she realized the full extent of the problem remaining.

Of the 100,000 defeated anti-Nazi refugees from the Sudetenland roughly 10,000 were ethnic Germans and Jews who could not stay safely in Czechoslovakia. Doreen Warriner visited them in their camps and at the end of November 1938, having publicized their plight, she was given responsibility for administering the *News Chronicle* British committee refugee relief funds for the different stranded refugee groups in and around Prague. On 9 December 1938 she wrote to the *Daily Telegraph* explaining bluntly that it was not relief in the form of blankets or chocolate that these people needed but British visas. She felt she had to speak for the thousands of working-class families without money or connections abroad who could not 'push'. On 14 December she accompanied a group of 150 women and children across the German frontier on their way to rejoin their menfolk already allowed into Britain. But that left thousands still stranded.

On 4 January 1939 Robert Stopford of the Treasury announced that a British loan had been made to the Czech government of which £4 million was to aid emigration. Five thousand Sudeten families would have earmarked funds for their transport and resettlement in Canada to work on the railways or on farms. Doreen Warriner and her helpers worked from morning until late into the small hours collating lists of names, applying for the necessary individual Polish and British visas, administering relief funds, and organizing transport by train for the Reich German, Austrian, and Sudeten communists as well as for the Sudeten Social Democrats. (Eleanor Rathbone MP had phoned her assuring her that anyone she recommended for a visa would get one.) By the end of March, after Hitler had marched into Prague, Doreen Warriner was left responsible for nearly 300 women and children still waiting for their papers—she had to organize their secret feeding and shelter, trying to keep them from the Gestapo, while organizing false passports where necessary. She experienced the terror of Gestapo intimidation of communist and Jewish *Dreck* ('garbage') at the Wilson railway station in Prague as they hunted and seized 'wanted' women. Those whom she could not save were sent to perish in the camps.

Finally Doreen Warriner left with one of the last Czech refugee trains to cross Poland, at the beginning of April 1939. For all the desperate seriousness of her rescue work, she 'was never too solemn or too earnest' (*The Times*, 30 Dec 1972); a brilliant improviser, she would bribe a consul with rare postage stamps, or a train conductor to keep her compartment door locked, or steal a general's visiting card that might come in handy. She held the whole disparate volunteer rescue enterprise together by sheer force of personality, 'showing what one determined and courageous woman could achieve, without any large funds and faced by enormous difficulties' (*Slavonic and East European*

Review, April 1984, introduction). In 1941 she was appointed OBE.

Not surprisingly, Doreen Warriner did useful war work. She served the Ministry of Economic Warfare, first in Britain and then in Cairo, as well as working for the political intelligence department of the Foreign Office. From 1944 to 1946 she was chief of the food supply department in the United Nations Relief and Rehabilitation Administration mission to Yugoslavia. Later she worked for the International Labour Office in Geneva. For the rest of her life she dedicated herself to analysing the economic problems of worldwide under-development, specializing in the necessity for the redistribution of land. She virtually never talked about her experiences, but when she died suddenly of a stroke, on 17 December 1972 at Amersham General Hospital, Buckinghamshire, her friends knew they had lost an irreplaceable fount of optimism and force for good. She was buried later that month at Bloxham, Oxfordshire. SYBIL OLDFIELD

Sources *Slavonic and East European Review*, 51 (1973), 292–3 · *The Times* (21 Dec 1972) · *The Times* (30 Dec 1972) · *St Hugh's College Chronicle*, 45 (1972–3) · private information (2004) [family and friends] · D. Warriner, 'Winter in Prague', *Slavonic and East European Review*, 62 (1984), 209–40 · b. cert. · d. cert.
Likenesses photograph, *c*.1939, priv. coll.
Wealth at death £169,152: probate, 11 May 1973, *CGPLA Eng. & Wales*

Warrington. For this title name *see* individual entries under Warrington; *see also* Booth, Henry, first earl of Warrington (1652–1694); Booth, George, second earl of Warrington (1675–1758).

Warrington, Hanmer George (1776–1847), diplomatist and promoter of African exploration, was born on 5 September 1776 at Acton, near Wrexham, Denbighshire, the third son of the Revd George Warrington of Acton and his wife, Mary, *née* Strudwyck. The Warringtons were an old Welsh family. Hanmer Warrington's written accounts of his life and career start when he was eighteen in October 1794, when a cornetcy was bought for him in the 1st dragoon guards. On 27 November 1798 he married Jane Eliza Pryce (*d.* 1841) of Northwood, Isle of Wight, with whom he had six sons and four daughters. By December 1800 he was a major in the 4th dragoon guards, but he resigned his commission in May 1802. Nothing is known of his career up to 1810, when he raised and took command of a yeomanry corps of cavalry, became inspecting field officer with the rank of lieutenant-colonel, and served in Andalusia under General Lord Blayney. He returned home and left the army in 1812. He later claimed to have had the patronage of the commander-in-chief, the duke of York, but contemporary gossip linking Warrington and his wife to the prince regent remains unconfirmed. His occupation from 1812 to 1814 and reasons for his appointment as consul-general in Tripoli, Barbary, are obscure; however, he already had the severe money troubles that were to keep him in permanent exile.

Warrington and his large family arrived in Tripoli in December 1814. The regency of Tripoli (which approximated to modern Libya) was then ruled, practically independent of Ottoman Turkey, by Yusuf Pasha Karamanlı. Britain's naval ascendancy had already deprived this despot of revenues from Mediterranean corsairing, but expansion into and beyond the Sahara seemed to promise alternative income for him, particularly from more active black slave raiding and trading. Warrington believed Great Britain could exploit the pasha's ambitions as a means to further geographical knowledge (and especially the River Niger's course and outlet), as well as diplomatic, commercial, and abolitionist interests in inner Africa. In spite of their apparently contradictory interests, he soon established a close and even dominant relationship with the pasha. The French consul in Tripoli in the 1850s, Pellisier de Reynaud, recorded that Warrington 'était plus maître du pays que le Pacha lui-même, qu'un geste de sa part faisait trembler' ('was more the master of the country than the pasha himself, such that a gesture from him would make the pasha tremble'; Bovill, *Missions*, 1.154). A convinced, uncompromising, and not particularly intelligent patriot, Warrington often overlooked the practical, diplomatic, and wider implications of his expansive schemes for furthering British interests, 'civilization', and the 'legitimate' trade of inner Africa through Tripoli and the Sahara. Yet it was largely through his persistence with the Colonial Office and the Foreign Office that three important British expeditions penetrated Africa from Tripoli: the Ritchie–Lyon mission of 1819–20 reached the regency's southern province of Fezzan and shed much new light on the Sahara as a whole; the Bornu mission of 1822–5 was a strikingly successful exploration of Lake Chad and the western Sudan; while the fatal journey in 1825–6 of Major Alexander Gordon Laing ended beyond Timbuctu.

Although Warrington's relations with the pasha deteriorated in the mid-1820s, he had in the meantime started to cultivate another possible agent of British trans-Saharan interests, ʿAbd-al-Jallil Saif al-Nasser, sheikh of the rebellious Awlad Slaiman tribe that dominated the main southbound trade route of the central desert. This relationship survived the overthrow of the Karamanlı dynasty and the restoration of direct Ottoman rule from Constantinople in 1835; but Warrington's schemes collapsed in 1842 when Turkish forces captured and killed ʿAbd-al-Jallil and dispersed his tribe. Despite this setback, the Foreign Office in 1843 implemented Warrington's original plans for furthering British interests (first made in 1817) by opening a vice-consulate at the mid-Saharan oasis of Murzuq, a main entrepôt of the slave trade of the central desert. The opening of a vice-consulate at the important trading oasis of Ghadames in 1850 had also originally been suggested by Warrington. Owing to his enthusiasm and persistence, Britain had by then a dominant diplomatic influence on the trade and communications of the central Sahara and along the main roads to black Africa—a dominance that faded only with the opening up of the River Niger approach to the interior from the late 1850s.

Warrington's role as Tripoli agent for other powers,

including at various times Portugal, Austria, Russia, the papacy, and some Hanse towns, gave him further opportunities to promote British interests in the central Mediterranean.

A big man, both in stature and personality, Warrington enhanced his dignity by designing himself an arresting consular uniform in blue, red, and gold, while at his enchanting seaside estate outside Tripoli, the so-called English Garden, he was a generous, if bibulous, host. During most of his thirty-two years as a consul, discreet but superlative (possibly royal) patronage protected him from the consequences of his many diplomatic lapses. But in 1846 he was obliged to resign after quarrelling violently with his Neapolitan colleague. His wife had died in 1841, and retiring on a pension of £900 per annum he made his new home with his daughter Jane and son-in-law Thomas Wood, vice-consul at Patras, Greece. He died there on 17 August 1847, aged nearly seventy-one, and was buried in the town.

Because of Warrington's persistence, Tripoli was for decades one of Britain's main approaches to inner Africa. The real impetus for British exploratory, diplomatic, commercial, and abolitionist efforts in the central Sahara and the countries beyond was a result of his single-minded promotion of Tripoli as the natural gateway to Africa.

JOHN WRIGHT

Sources Warrington's consular correspondence, PRO, FO 76 and FO 101 · SOAS, E. W. Bovill MSS, boxes 1–3 (MS 282539/1–16) · J. Wright, '"Nothing else but slaves": Britain and the central Saharan slave trade in the nineteenth century', PhD diss., SOAS, 1998 · E. W. Bovill, ed., *Missions to the Niger*, 4 vols., Hakluyt Society, 2nd ser., 123, 128–30 (1964–6) · *ILN* (6 Nov 1847) · R. Grosvenor, *The Barbary regencies* (1830) · L. Feraud, *Annales tripolitaines* (1927) · S. Dearden, *A nest of corsairs: the fighting Karamanlis of the Barbary coast* (1976) · E. W. Bovill, 'Colonel Warrington', *GJ*, 131 (1965), 161–6 · parish register, Wrexham, 1 Oct 1776 [baptisms]
Archives PRO, consular corresp., FO 76 (Tripoli) series · PRO, FO 101 (Tripoli) series · PRO, FO 84 (slave trade) · PRO, CO 2 (exploration: original corresp.) · PRO, CO 392 (exploration: entry books)
Wealth at death £5000: administration, PRO, PROB 6/224, fol. 8v

Warrington, Percy Ewart (1889–1961), educationist and Church of England clergyman, was born at Newhall, Derbyshire, near Burton upon Trent, on 29 December 1889, the elder son of Thomas Warrington, farmer, and his wife, Mary Jane, daughter of William Wright, the registrar of South Derbyshire. Three generations had previously farmed Newhall Park farm. Warrington attended Stapenhill School, leaving to work on the farm, gaining a knowledge of estate management, and appreciation of antiques and works of art. He had guidance in reading through the help of local clergy. Accepted as an ordinand, he entered Hatfield College, Durham, obtained the licentiate in theology, and was ordained deacon (1914) and priest (1915) at Worcester Cathedral for St Matthew's Church, Rugby. He moved in 1917 to St Peter's, Congleton, in Cheshire where he covered an interregnum, and then accepted in 1918 the benefice of Monkton Combe, a small village with the well-known public school, in the Bath and Wells diocese. He remained there until his death in 1961, an incumbency of forty-three years.

Warrington was an enigma. Small of stature, of immense vitality, serious, sharp-witted, his marked ability was shown in his spare-time work as secretary of the Church Trust Society which focused evangelical influence in the field of education. First Wrekin College was acquired in 1921; then followed the founding of Stowe School and Canford in 1923; subsequently, Westonbirt (1928) and Felixstowe (1929) for girls. To further the objective a new trust was developed, incorporating the Church Trust Society, with the rallying title The Martyrs Memorial, extending its influence through advowsons. Other schools came under its aegis, until Warrington's vicarage was the administrative centre of some thirteen public schools. He also had a part in finding resources for a high school in Kenya, for St Peter's Hall, Oxford, and Clifton Theological College, and committed himself to the restoration of Pentonville church, London, derelict after the First World War and reconsecrated in 1933.

To mark appreciation of Warrington's work, the vice-chairman of the trust's governors, Sir Charles King-Harman, acclaimed him in the Mansion House, on 25 April 1923, to be the founder of Stowe: 'It was to Warrington's genius … and to his financial acumen that the acquisition of Stowe House and the converting of it into a public school was due' (private information, 1981). J. F. Roxburgh, the first headmaster, wrote to Warrington on 2 December 1923, praising his determination, and acknowledging that without him Stowe would not have existed.

At the speech day marking the tenth anniversary of Stowe in 1933, the photographs show Warrington in close association with the guest of honour, the prince of Wales. But disaster was imminent. Warrington had made enemies and questions were raised about his administrative style. The trust decided that Warrington must go; and the way was open through a technical error in the financing of Clifton Theological College.

There were unsuccessful attempts to make Warrington bankrupt. A cloud descended upon him; rumour unfairly questioned his dealings; he lived under a kind of judgment. When comments were made upon his isolation in church affairs, few realized the pressures to get him moved from Monkton Combe. Disillusioned, especially by what he described as the 'Protestant underworld', he was dangerous in defence; his tongue, always sharp, became vitriolic against hypocrisy, snobbery, place-seeking, and pious sentimentality. Within his parish, the Christian of wealth and opportunity was also his target, but the poor and underprivileged knew they could always rely upon him to be their champion, frequently making a difficult co-existence with the public school in the village, although in later years a happier relationship developed. After the war he concentrated on improving housing conditions and became fully involved in work for the aged. He founded two homes: Claremont House at Corsham in Wiltshire and later Waterhouse at Monkton Combe. These homes stand in his name.

To understand Warrington it must be realized that he

was a visionary with an intense sense of his call; as a prophet he was lopsided, but he got things done. In early days he had been influenced by evangelical clergy, especially Richard Weston, vicar of Burntwood in 1886–1923. From such men he sensed the kind of leadership which could meet what was then felt to be Roman Catholic encroachment on the one hand, and the new theological 'modernism' on the other. Warrington's movement was a child of its day, a contemporary reply to the challenge. With it, he saw that opportunities provided by the schools must have an outlet in practical, responsible service. Warrington never married. He died in Bath on 5 November 1961.   B. J. W. TURNOCK, *rev.*

Sources *The Times* (7 Nov 1961) · *The Observer* (19 Nov 1961) · *Bath Chronicle* (26 April 1923) · *Bath Chronicle* (29 July 1929) · *Bath Chronicle* (11 Aug 1961) · personal knowledge (1981) · private information (1981) · N. Annan, *Roxburgh of Stowe: the life of J. F. Roxburgh and his influence in the public schools* (1965)
Likenesses E. Swan, portrait, 1929, Trinity College, Bristol
Wealth at death bankrupt or in debt

Warrington, Thomas Rolls, Baron Warrington of Clyffe (1851–1937), judge, was born in London on 29 May 1851, the only son of Thomas Warrington, a partner in the firm of Garrard & Co., silversmiths and jewellers, of London, and his wife, Mary Jane, daughter of Henry George Radclyffe. He was educated at Rugby School from 1865, and was admitted in 1868 to Trinity College, Cambridge, where he was elected to a foundation scholarship and obtained a second class in the classical tripos of 1873. Called to the bar by Lincoln's Inn in 1875, he became a pupil of F. C. J. Millar QC. He soon gained a reputation as a junior and acquired a large Chancery practice. In his early years at the bar he was also an enthusiastic member of the Inns of Court rifle volunteer corps (known as 'the devil's own'). On 31 July 1883 Warrington married Emma Maud, eldest daughter of Decimus Sturges, a barrister of Lincoln's Inn; they had no children.

Warrington took silk in 1895, and following the system then in force, attached himself to the court of Mr Justice Kekewich, over whom he soon established a considerable influence. The possibility of such influence was one of the main objections to the 'tied silk' system, but Warrington never abused his influence, and thoroughly deserved the confidence of the judge. He set a fine example to other counsel: he knew his papers thoroughly, and treated his juniors and opponents with courtesy and respect.

Having been elected a bencher of his inn in 1897, Warrington was appointed a justice of the Chancery Division of the High Court on 25 April 1904, and was knighted on 7 June of the same year. His appointment to the bench was universally approved and he at once gained the respect and affection of those who practised before him. He was promoted to the Court of Appeal on 13 April 1915 and sworn of the privy council. On his retirement in October 1926 he was created Baron Warrington of Clyffe, of Market Lavington in Wiltshire, and continued for many years to render valuable judicial service both in the House of Lords and in the privy council.

Warrington's contribution to the development of equity was not comparable with that of Sir George Jessel, Lord Macnaghten, or the elder Lord Parker of Waddington, but he was a thoroughly sound equity lawyer and it was truly said that 'the higher he went the better he got'. He was not often involved in cases which attracted public attention, but three important cases in which he sat were *Hammerton v. Earl of Dysart* (1915), *Attorney-General v. De Keyser's Royal Hotel Ltd.* (1919), and *Banco de Portugal v. Waterlow & Sons Ltd.* (1932). *Hammerton's case* concerned disturbance to an ancient ferry on the Thames at Twickenham. Warrington's first-instance judgment, reversed in the Court of Appeal, was restored in the House of Lords. In *Attorney-General v. De Keyser's Royal Hotel Ltd.* the House of Lords, upholding Warrington's view in the Court of Appeal, held that the crown is not entitled as of right, either under the prerogative or by statute, to take possession of a subject's land or buildings for administrative purposes in connection with the defence of the realm without paying compensation. *Banco de Portugal v. Waterlow & Sons Ltd.* concerned the measure of damages for breach of contract where printers of banknotes had delivered some of the notes to an unauthorized person who had put them into circulation. In the House of Lords Warrington dissented, with Lord Russell of Killowen, holding that, on the facts, the bank had proved no loss beyond the cost of printing notes to replace those which it had had to withdraw.

Warrington's principal private interest was his house and garden at Clyffe Hall, near Market Lavington in Wiltshire, where he died on 26 October 1937. He was buried at Market Lavington church on 29 October.

L. L. COHEN, *rev.* N. G. JONES

Sources *The Times* (27 Oct 1937) · Venn, *Alum. Cant.* · R. F. V. Heuston, *Lives of the lord chancellors, 1885–1940* (1964), 61 · *VF* (27 Nov 1907), pl. 1094 · private information (1949) · *CGPLA Eng. & Wales* (1938) · J. Foster, *Men-at-the-bar: a biographical hand-list of the members of the various inns of court*, 2nd edn (1885)
Likenesses W. Stoneman, photograph, 1917, NPG · W. Rothenstein, chalk drawing, 1932, Athenaeum, London · Spy [L. Ward], caricature, mechanical repro, NPG; repro. in *VF* · photograph, repro. in *The Times*
Wealth at death £28,412 8s. 1d.: resworn probate, 6 Jan 1938, *CGPLA Eng. & Wales*

Warrington, William (1796–1869), stained-glass artist, was born at New Romney, Kent, the son of William and Sarah Warrington. He was baptized in St Nicholas's Church, New Romney, on 4 March 1796. Little is known of his family background. *The Journal of the British Society of Master Glass-Painters* (1961–2, 521) suggests that a William Warrington, described in the *Universal British Directory* of 1797 as a glazier, in business in Deptford Green, could be his father. The United Kingdom census returns for 1861 reveal that Warrington's wife was two years his junior, that her name was Elizabeth, and that she was born at Tottenham, Middlesex.

Footnotes in Warrington's *The history of stained glass from the earliest period of the art to the present time illustrated by coloured examples of entire windows in the various styles* (1848) record that at one time, Warrington worked for the heraldic artist Thomas Willement, and that in 1833 he restored a medieval window for Mr Pratt in Bond Street—perhaps Samuel Pratt of Samuel Pratt & Son, trunk makers and upholsterers, 47 New Bond Street (Warrington, 33, 37). The first reference to Warrington in the *Post Office London Directory* (1839), was as an 'Artist in Stained Glass, Heraldic and Decorative Painter, Plumber, Glazier and Paperhanger' (Harrison, 84). His first major work was, however, earlier. In 1837, he made the apse window for St Mary's College chapel, Oscott, near Birmingham, working under the direction of A. W. N. Pugin, who was then starting to revive the medieval principles of stained-glass design. The window exhibits these principles to a high degree, although, unusually for Pugin, it was in the sixteenth-century style, with pictorial elements. It was very well received. A contemporary noted that it was 'scarcely surpassed by any modern production of the kind' (*GM*, Aug 1838, 171), and another anticipated that it would establish, 'the little known Warrington', high in the public esteem (*Birmingham Journal*, 16 Jan 1838, cited in *London and Dublin Weekly Orthodox Journal*, 1838, 90–91). He was then working from premises at 42 Upper Berkeley Street, Marylebone, which he carried on using until 1856, when he moved to 35 Connaught Terrace, Hyde Park (from 1863 onwards his work address was given as Polygon Mews, west London). Warrington may have met Pugin through Willement, who had worked (possibly with Warrington) in the early 1830s, at Alton Towers in Staffordshire, for Pugin's later patron the earl of Shrewsbury. Warrington and Pugin continued to work together until about 1841, during which time windows were made for Pugin's first church, St Mary's, Derby, in 1839, and for his Roman Catholic cathedral—the first in Britain since the Reformation—St Chad's, Birmingham, *c*.1841. At this time it appears that Warrington became financially embarrassed: a letter from Pugin to Lord Shrewsbury mentioned Warrington being on the point of arrest, with Pugin, seemingly, alleviating the situation by paying on account for glass for St Chad's (cited in P. Stanton, 'Welby Pugin and the Gothic Revival', PhD diss., University of London, 1950, 202). Warrington's manner and his prices led to a break with Pugin, the latter writing to Lord Shrewsbury on 25 August 1841: 'The reason I did not give Warrington the window at the hospital [of St John, Alton] is that he has become lately so conceited, got nearly as expensive as Willement' (HLRO, historical collection no. 339, letter 71).

Warrington's combative nature was demonstrated publicly in his letters to *The Builder* over the window for St James, Piccadilly, for which, in 1845, he had been considered among others, but passed over in favour of William Wailes (1808–1881). On 25 August 1845 he lambasted the selection committee for acting 'ignorantly and unjustly' (*The Builder*, 3, 1845, 415), and on 15 July 1846 severely criticized the completed work, remarking: 'For I fearlessly state, that there is not a single artistic feeling in the whole window' (*The Builder*, 4, 1846, 353). The letters engendered strong rebuke from Charles Mayhew, the honorary secretary of the committee, on 26 July 1846, who

accused Warrington of behaving unprofessionally, while *The Ecclesiologist* expressed surprise at his advocacy of pictorial windows: 'in our ignorance we had fancied Mr Warrington a plodding and over-minutely careful copyist of the glass of Romanesque and First pointed days; he speaks for himself, and turns out a reformer, a Rubens-worshipper, an uncompromising developer' (*The Ecclesiologist*, 6, 1846, 104–5). Undaunted, Warrington replied in the January 1847 issue, accepting as a compliment the reference to being a careful copyist—overlooking the fact that it pointed to his tendency to 'antique' or exaggerate the contorted poses and features, drawn by some of the ancient artists—and claiming propriety as the basis for his choice of style.

In 1848 Warrington courted further controversy when he published his *The History of Stained Glass*. Curiously, and inadvisably, he had used illustrations of his own work, rather than those of ancient examples, to demonstrate the styles. The reviewer of *The Ecclesiologist*, was merciless:

> Our literary glazier proves what twelfth century glass is by depicting choice specimens from 'Bromley S. Leonard, Stepney S. Peter and Brompton Holy Trinity, designed and executed by W. Warrington Esq. in the year of grace 1841. And if we seek to know how Tudor artists painted glass, Mr Warrington courteously points to his own rejected 'design for some of the windows of the House of Lords [1844]' we ask for medieval facts; and we are put off with nineteenth century competition-sketches. We think this hardly fair. If Mr Warrington wished to put forth the largest and most expensive advertisement upon record, there is no need to dub it a 'History' of the past.　(*The Ecclesiologist*, 10, 1849–50, 81–2)

Warrington's text was also heavily criticized for inaccuracy in its literary references, interpretation of medieval arrangement of subject matter and use of sacred forms. The book, however, remains a useful indicator of the 1840s work of Warrington and is a source of information regarding some early nineteenth-century glass-painters.

Writers in *The Ecclesiologist* continued to criticize Warrington's work. His window in Ely Cathedral was regarded, in the October 1850 issue, as the worst of all the new windows there, while, later, one in St Mary's, Ottery St Mary, Devon, was described as being: 'deficient in beauty, refinement and dignity' (*The Ecclesiologist*, 13, 1852, 85). Again Warrington responded spiritedly, replying in the journal to the Ely criticisms in a letter dated 4 October 1850 that included a letter of defence by the dean of Ely, against the 'very unfair and offensive criticism' (*The Ecclesiologist*, 11, 1850, 266–7). Indeed, it is clear that however much Warrington inspired hostility from within stained-glass circles he could still attract country-wide patronage. Much of his work is recorded, by county, in his manuscript 'A list of some of the principal works in stained glass' (V&A). His importance resides in his being among the first of the English Gothic revival stained-glass artists. His early work with Pugin was perhaps his most notable and might be seen as potential unrealized, but he continued to make windows until 1866. He died on 4 June 1869 at Martello Cottages, Folkestone, Kent, aged seventy-three, and was buried six days later at SS Mary and Eanswythe Church in Folkestone. His son, James Perry Warrington, carried on the business for about another ten years.

STANLEY A. SHEPHERD

Sources M. Harrison, *Victorian stained glass* (1980) · W. Warrington, 'A list of some of the principal works in stained glass done at 42 Berkeley St West and 35 Connaught Terrace both in the parish of Paddington, London', V&A NAL, MS 86 BB 27 · S. A. Shepherd, 'The stained glass of A. W. N. Pugin c.1835–52', PhD diss., U. Birm., 1997 · *The Builder*, 3 (1845), 415 · *The Builder*, 4 (1846), 353, 363 · *The Ecclesiologist*, 6 (1846), 104–5 · *The Ecclesiologist*, 7 (1847), 38–9 · *The Ecclesiologist*, 10 (1849–50), 81–97 · *The Ecclesiologist*, 11 (1850), 160, 266–7 · *The Ecclesiologist*, 13 (1852), 85 · d. cert. · *Journal of the British Society of Master Glass-Painters* (1961–2), 521 · census returns, 1861, PRO, RG 9/8/52–9/8/54 · parish register, St Nicholas's Church, New Romney, Kent · burial register, SS Mary and Eanswythe Church, Folkestone, Canterbury Cathedral Archive, U3/88/1/32
Archives V&A, list of principal works

Warriss, Ben Holden Driver (1909–1993). *See under* Jewel, Jimmy (1909–1995).

Warriston, Lady. *See* Livingston, Jean (1579–1600).

Warter, John Wood (1806–1878), Church of England clergyman and antiquary, born on 21 January 1806 in Cruck Meole, Shropshire, was the eldest son of Henry de Grey Warter (1770–1853) of Cruck Meole, who married, on 19 March 1805, Emma Sarah Moore (d. 1863), daughter of William Wood of Marsh Hall and Hanwood, Shropshire. Upon leaving Shrewsbury School (under Samuel Butler) Warter matriculated from Christ Church, Oxford, in 1824, and graduated BA with third-class honours in classics in 1828, MA in 1834, and BD in 1841. In 1830 he published a translation of the *Acharnians*, *Knights*, *Wasps*, and *Birds* of Aristophanes.

Warter was a close friend of Robert *Southey, whose eldest daughter, Edith May Southey (1804–1871), he married at Keswick on 15 January 1834. Many letters from Southey to him, beginning on 18 March 1830, are in the sixth volume of *Southey's Life and Correspondence*. Ordained in 1830, Warter was from 1830 to 1833 chaplain to the British embassy at Copenhagen, and became an honorary member of the Scandinavian and Icelandic literary societies. During these years he travelled through Norway and Sweden, was closely acquainted with the leading scholars of northern Europe, including Professor Rasmus Rask, and was supplied with books from the royal library of Denmark. By this means he became an expert in 'Danish and Swedish lore, and in the exquisitely curious Icelandic sagas', and read 'German literature of all sorts, especially theological'. In 1834, just before his marriage, he had been appointed by the archbishop of Canterbury to the vicarage of West Tarring and Durrington, Sussex, a peculiar of the archbishopric, to which the chapelries of Heene and Patching were then annexed. He remained the vicar of West Tarring from 1834 until his death. For some years to 31 December 1851 he was the rural dean.

From the date of his appointment to this benefice he devoted his leisure 'to the pleasant task of rescuing from oblivion every fact that had the remotest bearing upon the history of Tarring' (D. G. C. Elwes and C. J. Robinson, *A History of the Castles, Mansions, and Manors of Western Sussex*, 1876, 231). The result was the publication of a valuable antiquarian work, *Appendicia et pertinentiæ: parochial fragments on the parish of West Tarring and the chapelries of Heene and Durrington* (1853), and *The Seaboard and the Down, or, My Parish in the South, by an Old Vicar* (2 vols., 1860), describing the social life of the parish's inhabitants. Selections from Warter's collections on the history of his native Shropshire appeared in *An Old Shropshire Oak*, edited by Richard Garnett (4 vols., 1886–91). These books displayed his wide reading.

Warter died at his vicarage on 21 February 1878, and was buried with his wife in West Tarring churchyard (the epitaphs are printed in *Notes and Queries* (6th ser., 7, 1883, 306, 517). Their second son, John Southey Warter (1840–1866), was a physician.

Warter was an old-fashioned churchman of the 'high and dry' school, and was frequently in dispute with the ecclesiastical commissioners. He published many tracts and sermons, which reflected his orthodox divinity. Although most of his works concerned religious and antiquarian topics, his greatest service to scholarship has been held to be his collection of material relating to Robert Southey (*Life and Correspondence of Robert Southey*, 505–6). Warter edited volumes 6 and 7 of Southey's *Doctor* and an edition in one volume of the whole work (1848). He also edited Southey's *Commonplace Book* in four volumes (1849–51), and four volumes of *Selections from Southey's Letters* (1856). A fierce review of the latter work by Whitwell Elwin appeared in the *Quarterly Review*, March 1856, 456–501. It was probably provoked by Warter's statement that he could draw up 'a most remarkable history' of that periodical, following a dispute over the use of Southey's letters to Lockhart and Murray. Edith Warter had begun in 1824 and continued for some time a collection of sayings. It was taken up by her husband and finally published in 1861 as *Wise Saws and Modern Instances: Pithy Sentences in Many Languages*. Warter also contributed to the *English Review*.

W. P. COURTNEY, rev. TRIONA ADAMS

Sources Boase, *Mod. Eng. biog.* · Burke, *Gen. GB* · *The life and correspondence of Robert Southey*, ed. C. C. Southey, 6 vols. (1849–50) · W. Knight, ed., *Memorials of Coleorton*, 2 vols. (1887) · A. Lang, *The life and letters of John Gibson Lockhart*, 2 vols. (1897) · *New letters of Robert Southey*, ed. K. Curry, 2 vols. (1965)
Archives Bodl. Oxf., John May MSS
Wealth at death under £9000: probate, 6 April 1878, CGPLA Eng. & Wales

Warton, Jane (*bap.* 1724, *d.* 1809), author, was the daughter of Thomas *Warton (1688–1745) and his wife, Elizabeth (1691–1762), daughter of Joseph Richardson, rector of Dunsfield, Surrey, and sister to the 'two learned brothers' Thomas *Warton (1728–1790) and Joseph *Warton (*bap.* 1722, *d.* 1800). She was baptized on 20 August 1724 at Basingstoke, Hampshire, where her father was vicar and master of the grammar school. She contributed a poem on her father's death, 'Ode on the Death of the Author, by a Lady', to the volume of *Poems on Several Occasions* which her brothers produced in 1748 in an effort to raise money to clear their father's debts. Her literary interests were marked and her critical abilities were respected within the family. In 1753 Joseph invited her to write an essay for Johnson's *Adventurer*, and *Adventurer*, no. 87, 'Politeness a necessary auxiliary to knowledge and virtue', may be by her. Also in 1753 she began working as a governess to the two daughters of William Thoyts of Whitechapel and Carshalton. She remained close to Joan (*b.* 1747) and Mary Anne (*b.* 1749) for the rest of her life. Her first major publication was the anonymous *Letters Addressed to Two Young Married Ladies, on the Most Interesting Subjects* (2 vols., 1782) which was addressed to them.

Though anonymous, Warton's writing was not secret: Joseph wrote to her in 1781: 'I am rejoiced to find you are becoming one of Us—Authors I mean. Depend on my doing my Utmost with Dodsley' (Bodl. Oxf., Don c 75, fol. 38). Like her friend Hester Mulso Chapone she found her way into becoming 'one of Us—Authors' by writing prescriptive literature aimed specifically at women. The *Letters* concern themselves with questions of morality and behaviour, with a particular emphasis on the role of the mother (or governess) in child-rearing. They advocate early learning; stress the duties of life and the necessity of religion, humility, and compassion; and pay particular attention to girls' education in a way which foreshadows Mary Wollstonecraft's later work. In 1783 James Dodsley published her novel *Peggy and Patty, or, The Sisters of Ashdale*, in four volumes. This novel both makes clear her identification with the Wollstonecraftian feminism of her own time and, in its sympathy for the fallen woman, anticipates the preoccupations of Victorian feminists. It develops the idea expressed in *Letters* that virtuous women should show charity to 'unfortunate women', the seduced and abandoned, because 'the villainy of men' knows no bounds. It is only 'particular circumstances' that protect fortunate women: 'these wretched women were once happy and innocent as yourselves' (Warton, *Letters*, 1.35). Peggy and Patty are happy, innocent country curate's daughters who go to London to find work and are lured into a brothel, drugged, raped, ruined, and turned into courtesans. The attractions of the courtesan's life are well shown: as the madam of the brothel says, 'who lives so grand as a kept lady? How infinitely is her situation to be preferred to a poor devil of a wife' (Warton, *Peggy and Patty*, 1.140). If the 'unbridled lust' of men is the initial danger, it is women's subsequent economic dependence on men in a society that offers so few employment opportunities that destroys them. Once turned off, Peggy and Patty have only the streets to go to and only their bodies to trade. In a number of affecting scenes they sicken, starve, and die in a garret. Though sentimental, the novel reveals a caustic impatience with the double standard. It is vividly written and outspoken.

Very little is known about Jane Warton's life, and the observations of others build a picture of an 'unfortunate girl', who had 'a Warton Genius, totally perverse in worldly affairs' (H. Reid, 'Jenny: the fourth Warton', *N&Q*, 231, 1986, 84). Warton died, unmarried, at Wickham, Hampshire, on 3 November 1809. In her obituary in the *Gentleman's Magazine* it was declared that she was disabled by rheumatism and could 'only move on her knees'. This, while metaphorically suggestive, seems most unlikely on the evidence available.   NORMA CLARKE

Sources H. Reid, 'Jenny: the fourth Warton', *N&Q*, 231 (1986), 84–92 • *The correspondence of Thomas Warton*, ed. D. Fairer (1995) • *GM*, 1st ser., 79 (1809), 1175 • *IGI*
Archives Bodl. Oxf., corresp. and papers

Warton, Joseph (*bap.* **1722**, *d.* **1800**), poet and literary critic, elder son of Thomas *Warton (1688–1745), clergyman and poet, and his wife, Elizabeth Richardson (1691–1762), was born at Dunsfold, Surrey, and baptized there on 22 April 1722, at the vicarage of his grandfather Joseph Richardson. His younger brother, Thomas *Warton, was also a poet and historian of English poetry, while his sister Jane *Warton contributed (at Joseph's request) to Samuel Johnson's *Adventurer* and wrote a novel and a two-volume book of advice for young ladies. His early education was at the grammar school in Basingstoke where his father was headmaster, and Gilbert White a fellow pupil. On 2 August 1736 he was elected a scholar of Winchester College (although he was probably there earlier) and began a near lifelong association with it; from there he published his first poem, 'Sappho's Advice', in the *Gentleman's Magazine* (1st ser., 9, October 1739, 545). Warton matriculated from Oriel College, Oxford, on 16 January 1740 but did not take up residence until the following September. While at Oxford Warton published his first major piece of poetry: *Fashion: an Epistolary Satire to a Friend* (1742).

Early career Warton graduated BA on 13 March 1744, the year when his most important piece of poetic work, *The Enthusiast, or, The Lover of Nature*, was published. Although Wooll claims that it was written four years earlier, it is in many ways just such a poem as a young recent graduate would write, full of love of nature and feeling, going against the prevailing taste for poetry epitomized by Alexander Pope. It was warmly received and Warton revised and enlarged it for inclusion in later editions of Robert Dodsley's *Miscellany*.

Upon leaving Oxford, Warton took holy orders and became his father's curate in Basingstoke until he received the charge of Chelsea in February 1746. But after a disagreement with some parishioners and a bout of smallpox he left Chelsea and took the curacies of Droxford and Chawton in Hampshire. During this time he published a number of poems in Dodsley's *Museum* and in 1746 contemplated a project with William Collins to publish their odes together. The project never materialized as Dodsley refused Collins's poems, but he published Warton's *Odes on Various Subjects* in 1746. The 'Ode to Fancy' became something of a contemporary favourite. In 1754 a writer in the *Gentleman's Magazine* (1st ser., 24, 592) felt that 'Fancy' was proof that Warton 'ought not to be confined to the drudgery of translation' and William Shenstone considered it the best of the odes inspired by Milton's 'Il penseroso'.

In the second edition of the *Odes* is a poem by Thomas Warton the younger. The process of borrowing from and revising each other's work, begun in the *Odes*, was carried on and enlarged while the brothers were editing their

Joseph Warton (*bap.* 1722, *d.* 1800), by John Raphael Smith, pubd 1777 (after Sir Joshua Reynolds, 1777)

father's poems. Thomas Warton the elder died on 10 September 1745, and to obtain money Joseph proposed putting together a number of his father's poems and selling them by subscription. The volume, *Poems on Several Occasions, by the Reverend Mr. Thomas Warton*, did not, however, include poems only by their father. Both Thomas and Joseph contributed to it in their father's name and in many cases they (particularly Joseph) heavily edited many of the remaining poems.

On 21 September 1747 Warton married Mary Daman (*d.* 1772), with whom he eventually had six children. In the next year Charles Paulet, third duke of Bolton, granted the living of Winslade to Warton and he continued his literary career with *Ranelagh House: a Satire in Prose: in the Manner of Monsieur Le Sage*. Three years later Warton made his only trip to the continent when he accompanied the duke, who was travelling with his mistress, Lavinia Fenton, universally known as Polly Peachum for the role she had made famous in Gay's *Beggar's Opera*. The duke needed a member of the clergy to marry him to Miss Fenton should the duchess's expected death occur while he was on the continent. However, Warton left the duke's party before the duchess's death and returned home without performing the ceremony. The experience did provide him with the subject for another poem, 'Verses Written at Montaubon' (*London Magazine*, 24, April 1755, 183–4).

Warton continued his literary endeavours as he worked on a translation of Virgil which was published (in both Latin and English) in four volumes in 1753. Although using Christopher Pitt's translation of the *Aeneid*, he himself translated the *Eclogues* and the *Georgics*. About this time he

made the friendship of Johnson who invited him to contribute to *The Adventurer*, Warton eventually writing nineteen or twenty of the papers signed 'Z', including five on Shakespeare.

Winchester years In 1754 Warton became rector of Tunworth, but despairing of further advancement in the church accepted the position of usher, or second master, at his old school, Winchester, on 3 December 1755. Here he remained until his retirement in 1793, becoming headmaster in 1766. On 23 June 1759 Oxford conferred upon him the degree of MA by diploma. On 15 January 1768 he proceeded at Oxford to the degrees of BD and DD.

Warton's major contribution to scholarship was *An Essay on the Writings and Genius of Pope* (1756; second volume, 1782; in subsequent editions the title was *Genius and Writings*). As Pope had died only twelve years earlier, it was anticipated that the work might arouse some controversy so it was published anonymously and Dodsley's name did not appear on the title-page until the second issue of the second edition (merely a reprinting of the title-page of the second edition) in 1762. The dedication to Edward Young acts somewhat as a manifesto for Warton's views. He writes in the dedication:

> No love of singularity, no affection of paradoxical opinions, gave rise to the following work. I revere the memory of Pope, I respect and honour his abilities; but I do not think him at the head of his profession. In other words, in that species of poetry wherein Pope excelled, he is superior to all mankind: and I only say, that this species of poetry is not the most excellent one of the art.   (pp. iii–iv)

Warton divided poets into four classes. Into the first, those who are 'sublime and pathetic', he placed Spenser, Shakespeare, and Milton (and curiously 'at proper intervals, Otway and Lee'). In the second class were poets who 'possessed the true poetical genius, in a more moderate degree, but had noble talents for moral and ethical poesy'. The third class were 'men of wit, of elegant taste and some fancy in describing familiar life'. The fourth class were 'mere versifiers, however smooth and mellifluous some of them may be thought' (pp. xi–xii). Warton, whose name did not appear on the title-page until the posthumous edition of 1806, placed Pope at the head of the second class of poets. The work was favourably reviewed by Johnson and went into several reprints. It also aroused some opposition—most notably from Owen Ruffhead (*The Life of Alexander Pope*, 1769), and Percival Stockdale (*An Enquiry into the Nature and Genuine Laws of Poetry*, 1778). But most critics seemed to agree with the review in the *Gentleman's Magazine* which described the *Essay* as 'a most interesting and useful miscellany of literary knowledge and candid criticism containing censure without acrimony, and praise without flattery'. Johnson, writing in the *Literary Magazine*, called it 'a just specimen of literary moderation'. Later, in the *Lives of the Poets* where Johnson criticized the *Essay* and defended Pope more explicitly than he had done earlier, he still said of the *Essay* that it is 'a book which teaches how the brow of Criticism may be smoothed, and how she may be enabled, with all her severity, to attract and to delight'.

Warton's personality and effusive nature were well known among his friends:

> But it was a particular Felicity to meet Jo: Warton at Oxford, we had a great Joy in the meeting; He is the same ardent Creature he always was, and when we parted it had like to have cost me the Bone-setting of my right Hand.   (R. Holt-White, *Life and Letters of Gilbert White*, 1901, 1 June 1757, I.121)

In June 1785 Hannah More found him 'as usual, very enthusiastic and very agreeable' and later labelled him 'that delightful enthusiast' (W. Roberts, *Memoirs of Hannah More*, 1835).

While Warton's 'enthusiasm' was popular with many, it was not with Johnson, who called Warton 'an enthusiast by rule', although there seems to have been a close friendship between them earlier. Wooll claims an incident at Sir Joshua Reynolds's house was the cause of the coolness between them. Apparently a dispute arose to which Wooll has recorded the conclusion:

> Johnson: 'Sir, I am not used to be[ing] contradicted.'
> Warton: 'Better for yourself and your friends, Sir, if you were; our admiration could not be increased, but our love might.'
> (Wooll, 98n.)

Wooll does not give a date to this incident but some change in the relationship had occurred by 22 January 1766 when Warton wrote to his brother:

> I only dined with Johnson, who seemed cold and indifferent, and scarce said any thing to me; perhaps he has heard what I said of his Shakespeare, or rather was offended at what I wrote to him—as he pleases.

It was probably a difference of personal style which caused the friendship to fade. Johnson, for all his reputation for gruffness, was, nevertheless, 'heard to lament, with tears in his eyes, that the Wartons had not called upon him for the last four years' (Boswell, *Life*, 1.270, n.1). And he wrote to Warton concerning Charles Burney's youngest son, Richard, and accompanied the boy and his father to Winchester.

Perhaps Warton's comments on Johnson in his edition of Dryden came closest to the truth about Warton's attitude:

> A love of paradox and contradiction, at the bottom of which was vanity, gave an unpleasant tincture to his manners, and made his conversation boisterous and offensive. I often used to tell the mild and sensible Sir Joshua Reynolds, that he and his friends had contributed to spoil Johnson, by constantly and cowardly assenting to all he advanced on any subject. Mr. Burke only kept him in order, as did Mr. Beauclerc, sometimes by his playful wit. It was a great pleasure for Beauclerc to lay traps for him to induce him to oppose and contradict one day what he had maintained on a former.   (p. 151n.)

While at Winchester, Warton corresponded with Walpole, Gibbon, Burney, Colman, Malone, Percy, Spence, and John Wilkes, as well as with numerous minor writers and booksellers. And he kept up his correspondence with his old friends Reynolds, Garrick, and Johnson. Walpole sent him the gift of *The Castle of Otranto*. Gerald Hamilton thanked him for recommending to him an unknown secretary named Edmund Burke. Reynolds proposed Warton's name for membership of the Literary Club on 10 January 1777 and he attended his first meeting one week later. He was used as an intermediary when John Oglander, warden of New College, Oxford, wanted Reynolds to design a window for the ante-chapel at the college. The king visited Winchester College and heard a speech written by Warton, who was given a new living (Thorley in Hertfordshire) and a prebend in St Paul's (1782). His literary work consisted of the second volume of his *Essay on Pope* (1782) and a combined edition of two famous works of literary criticism, *Sir Philip Sydney's defence of poetry and observations on poetry and eloquence, from the Discoveries of Ben Jonson* (1787).

The time was not without its sadder moments. Warton's mother died in April 1762 and his ten-year-old daughter, Ann, died after being inoculated against smallpox. The loss of his wife in October 1772 was a severe blow. She was universally liked and admired, and seems to have played no small part in Warton's success at Winchester. On 18 December 1773 he married Charlotte Nicholas (*c*.1742–1809), a descendant of a former warden of Winchester College. They had one child, Harriet Elizabeth. His daughter Molly married Colonel James Morgan in December 1774 and left with her husband soon after to spend ten years in India. Joseph's son Thomas, who was in holy orders, died in his father's study after college prayers in 1787, and his brother Thomas died at Trinity College, Oxford, in May 1790. Warton's other sons, Joseph (*b*. 1750) and John (*b*. 1756), also took holy orders.

Nevertheless the Winchester years were generally happy, as evinced by the letters. Poets and writers who attended the school wrote back to Warton and he took delight in receiving their works. He usually managed to spend Christmas in London visiting friends and attending the theatre. Bishop Lowth, a friend, appointed him prebendary of London in 1782, and presented to him the vicarage of Chorley, Hertfordshire, which he exchanged for that of Wickham, in Hampshire. And William Pitt, the prime minister, conferred on him a prebendal stall at Winchester in 1788. In 1790 Warton was presented with the rectory of Easton in Hampshire which he exchanged for Upham in the same county. The livings of Upham and Wickham he held for life and retired to Wickham after his resignation at Winchester in 1793.

Although Warton's letters indicate that he had been long contemplating retirement, it was the boys' rebellion in 1793 which occasioned it. Warton's role in this insurrection, and the minor one of 1774, has been misinterpreted. He has been accused of being a lax disciplinarian and his 'enthusiastic' character perhaps did not lend itself to the kind of authoritarian rule which the Victorians later expected from their schoolmasters. There is, however, another reason for the accusation and the understanding of it goes back to the insurrection of 1774. The incident for which it is mostly remembered concerns the boys' hissing of Warton and his retort: 'So, gentlemen; What? Are you metamorphosed into serpents!' Warton had stopped the boys from mimicking a hunchbacked servant. It was this imposition of discipline which brought forth the real demands of the boys, namely that the assistant master, George Isaac Huntingford, be dismissed.

The rebellion of 1793 was far more serious and it involved more than just the commoners. And again Huntingford played an important part. He had been appointed warden in 1789 and in 1793 had declared the Close out of bounds for the boys. When one boy was found there he punished the whole school, causing a general disturbance which was quieted only after he promised a general amnesty, which he broke once order was restored. The boys had agreed that if any were punished all would leave the college and this they did. Warton's role in the rebellion was minor. As headmaster he was nominally responsible. However, his only role in the affair seems to have been that of messenger between the boys and Huntingford as he was the only member of the governing body the boys trusted. No doubt Warton was not a strict disciplinarian in the mould of Huntingford, but it seems that his responsibility for the student rebellions in both 1774 and 1793 has been greatly exaggerated.

Retirement The years after Warton's resignation, spent in Wickham, were devoted to literary pursuits. An edition of Pope, originally proposed to him by John Wilkes in 1792, was finally published in 1797. In it he incorporated, as notes, much of his *Essay*, a move for which he was criticized. He also used the opportunity to 'give hard blows to the marvellous absurdities of Warburton' and to attack Johnson for his life of Pope—and perhaps also for Boswell's portrayal of Warton. Indeed, many of the comments in the notes are aimed directly at Warburton and Johnson. This caused another controversy involving Warton's former pupil, the poet William Lisle Bowles, who published a poorly edited version of Pope's works in which he acted, somewhat condescendingly, as a judge between Warton, Johnson, and Warburton. Warton did not live to see the edition, as it appeared in 1806. Towards the end of his life he began work on an edition of Dryden which was completed by his son John. Warton died on 23 February 1800 and was buried in Winchester Cathedral.

Warton's poetry, with a few exceptions, is undistinguished, and typical of the mid-century. He is best remembered, and rightly so, as a critic, the first to reassess Pope. He was also a friend of the great and near great and, as with many schoolteachers, had an influence far beyond his immediate circle.   HUGH REID

Sources *Biographical memoirs of the late Rev Joseph Warton*, ed. J. Wooll (1806) • *The correspondence of Thomas Warton*, ed. D. Fairer (1995) • J. Vance, *Joseph and Thomas Warton: an annotated bibliography* (1983) • J. Vance, *Joseph and Thomas Warton*, Twayne English Authors Series (1983) • H. Reid, '"The want of a closer union … ": the friendship of Samuel Johnson and Joseph Warton', *The age of Johnson*, ed. P. Korshin, 9 (1998), 133–41 • H. Reid, 'The printing of Joseph Warton's Odes', *Papers of the Bibliographical Society of America*, 84 (1990), 151–7 • D. Fairer, 'The poems of Thomas Warton the elder?', *Review of English Studies*, new ser., 26 (1975), 287–300, 395–406 • D. Fairer, 'The poems of Thomas Warton the elder? A postscript', *Review of English Studies*, new ser., 29 (1978), 61–5 • C. LePrevost, 'More unacknowledged verse by Joseph Warton', *Review of English Studies*, new ser., 37 (1986), 317–47 • BL, Murray Collection, Add. MS 42560 • Swann papers, Bodl. Oxf., Trinity College • Winchester College, Fellows' Library, Warton papers • H. Reid, 'A probable addition to the poetic works of Joseph Warton', *Review of English Studies*, new ser., 38 (1987), 526–9 • H. Reid, 'The letters of Joseph Warton', PhD diss., U. Lond., 1987 • IGI

Archives Bodl. Oxf., corresp., literary MSS, papers, and sermons • Winchester College, papers • Yale U., Beinecke L., papers | BL, corresp. with Thomas Warton, Add. MSS 42560–42561 • BL, letters to John Wilkes, Add. MS 30877 • Bodl. Oxf., Lee papers, MS Don c. 75 • Bodl. Oxf., Swann papers

Likenesses J. R. Smith, mezzotint, pubd 1777 (after J. Reynolds, 1777), BM, NPG [*see illus.*] • R. Cardon, engraving (after J. Reynolds), repro. in Wool, ed., *Biographical memoirs* • J. Fisher, watercolour drawing (after J. Reynolds), Trinity College, Oxford • J. Flaxman, effigy on monument, Winchester Cathedral • J. Reynolds, portrait, AM Oxf.

Wealth at death had number of livings and earnings from literature which he divided among children and wife

Warton [Perfey], **Robert** (*d.* 1557), bishop of Hereford, is of obscure origins. He composed his will as Robert Perfey and made bequests in it to a brother, a sister, and several kinsfolk with the same surname. But he is first recorded on 1 September 1525 as Robert Warton, a Cluniac monk who was chosen as his successor by the retiring prior of Bermondsey. In the same year Warton is said to have taken the degree of BTh at Cambridge, and he may also have studied at Gloucester College, Oxford. In the Canterbury convocations of 1533 and 1534 he supported the king against papal authority, which makes it less surprising that on 8 June 1536 he should have been elected bishop of St Asaph. The royal assent was given on 24 June, he was consecrated by Archbishop Cranmer eight days later, and the temporalities were restored on 21 July. The see was extremely poor, and Warton retained his abbacy *in commendam*. When Bermondsey was dissolved at the beginning of 1538, Warton received the substantial pension of £333 6s. 8d., no doubt to enable him to fulfil his episcopal duties.

Warton's predecessor as bishop had been the committed evangelical William Barlow, but Barlow was not at St Asaph for long enough to make much impact on the legacy of the conservative Henry Standish, who held the see from 1518 to 1535. Warton seems to have begun his episcopate by taking a reformist line, expelling a priest from the diocese 'for not rasing the bishop of Rome's name and other crimes' (*LP Henry VIII*, 10, no. 446), but his commitment to reform soon faltered. He appears to have been more interested in administration than doctrine, securing the support of a number of suffragans and recommending the removal of his see first to Wrexham and then to Denbigh, where he also showed a concern for education by proposing the establishment of a grammar school. Warton also had to contend with the rapacity of the locally powerful Salisbury family. Later allegations that he impoverished his see by making long leases of all its lands are probably exaggerated, but his recorded leases include one to Richard Salisbury for sixty years and one to the younger John Salisbury for eighty.

Although Warton certainly visited his diocese, staying at Denbigh or Wrexham rather than St Asaph, he was frequently employed outside it. He attended important court events like the baptism of Prince Edward and the funeral of Queen Jane Seymour in 1537, and the marriage of

Henry VIII to Anne of Cleves in 1540. In 1537 he was a signatory to the Bishops' Book, and two years later was consulted about the Act of Six Articles. He several times
attended parliament in the 1540s. Meanwhile he retained
an interest in Surrey, as a JP and property-owner—in 1542
he was licensed to acquire nine messuages in Bermondsey. By 1542 Warton was also coming to be employed in the
secular government of Wales and its marches. In that year
he was made a JP for Worcestershire and Gloucestershire,
and he was later named to the peace commissions for
Shropshire, Herefordshire, Chester, and Staffordshire,
while on 22 April 1543 he was appointed to the council of
the marches of Wales.

Following the death of Henry VIII, Warton accommodated himself without difficulty to the governments of
the dukes of Somerset and Northumberland. In 1547 he
voted in favour of holy communion being administered in
both kinds, and seems to have supported the Book of
Common Prayer of 1549. In April 1551 he was again named
to the council in the Welsh marches. But following the
death of Edward VI he found it equally easy to adapt to a
more conservative religious regime. Appointed on 13
March 1554 to the commission to deprive Archbishop Holgate and four other bishops, he was formally absolved of
error and schism by Cardinal Pole on the 17th, and nominated on the same day for translation to the see of Hereford; he was enthroned on 9 May. Little can be said of his
second episcopate, except that he acted as the government required to deprive married clergy.

In his will, which he drew up on 30 June 1555, Warton
showed his concern for his cathedral by leaving to it his
mitre, crozier, and a number of fine vestments, and making bequests to all the prebendaries, vicars-choral, choristers, and officers who should be present at his funeral
mass. He also remembered his chaplains, household servants, and numerous kinsmen, making individual cash
bequests totalling over £450. £20 were to be distributed to
the poor at his burial, another £20 at his month's mind.
His bequest of his soul, to the glorious Trinity, was surprisingly lacking in specifically Catholic commitment for a
Marian bishop, but it is probably significant that his
nephew John Perfey, whom he named as his executor,
later fled overseas to escape the Elizabethan settlement.
Warton died on 22 September 1557. Little remains of his
monumental effigy in the north-east transept of Hereford
Cathedral, and he may be more worthily commemorated
by an embroidered orphrey bearing his arms which survives at St Michael's Church, Abergavenny.

LUKE MACMAHON

Sources LP Henry VIII, vols. 4–21 · Venn, Alum. Cant., 1/3.304 ·
J. Strype, Ecclesiastical memorials, 3 vols. (1822) · G. Williams, Wales
and the Reformation (1997) · G. Aylmer and J. Tiller, eds., Hereford
Cathedral: a history (2000) · will, PRO, PROB 11/40, fols. 15–16 · G. M.
Griffiths, 'St Asaph episcopal acts, 1536–1558', Journal of the Histor-
ical Society of the Church in Wales, 9 (1959), 32–69 · E. B. Fryde and
others, eds., Handbook of British chronology, 3rd edn, Royal Historical
Society Guides and Handbooks, 2 (1986) · DNB
Wealth at death cash bequests of over £400: will, PRO, PROB
11/40, fols. 15–16

Warton, Thomas (1688–1745), Church of England clergyman and poet, was born in 1688 in Godalming, Surrey,
where he was baptized on 3 February 1688, the son of the
Revd Anthony Warton (1650–1715), and his wife, Mary. He
matriculated from Hart Hall, Oxford, on 9 April 1706, but
shortly after migrated to Magdalen College, Oxford,
where he was a demy from 1706 to 1717, and a fellow from
1717 to 1724. He proceeded BA (1710), MA (1712), BD (1725),
and was elected professor of poetry in succession to
Joseph Trapp on 17 July 1718, a post he held until 1728, having been re-elected in July 1723 for a second five-year term.
He is chiefly remembered at Oxford for his Jacobite sympathies, engendered initially when he circulated a number of his poems—most notably The Turnip Hoer, a satire on
George I's suggestion of turning St James's Park into a turnip patch. His boldest act, however, was delivering a Jacobite sermon on 29 May 1719 at the university church. In it
he spoke of the evil in dethroning a rightful king and setting up a usurper. Even though the sermon used Charles I
and Cromwell as reference points, George I and the Stuart
Pretender were clearly intended and taken as such by the
audience who waved their caps as Warton left the church
and 'his health was the toast of the night' (Remarks, 7.15).

On 2 February 1721 Warton married Elizabeth (1691–
1762), second daughter of the Revd Joseph Richardson,
rector of Dunsfold, Surrey, and Elizabeth Peebles. In 1723
when Magdalen College presented Warton with the living
of Basingstoke in Hampshire, he left Oxford for Basingstoke where he also became master of the grammar
school. Among his pupils was the naturalist Gilbert
White. He remained at Basingstoke until his death and
held successively with the living the vicarages of Fram-
field, Sussex (1726), Woking, Surrey (1727–30), and
Chobham, Surrey (1730–45). Two of Warton's children
were born in Basingstoke: Jane *Warton in 1724; and
Thomas *Warton in 1728, while Joseph *Warton was baptized at Dunsfold, Surrey in 1722. In 1738 Warton was
elected to a lectureship in Basingstoke that had been
established for the 'maintenance of a good and learned
preacher', who was to 'instruct the people in the principles of religion' (Baigent and Millard, 403). The honor-
arium was £50. Warton was a friend of Elijah Fenton,
Edward Young, and was introduced to Alexander Pope, to
whom he gave his copy of Gorboduc, by Pope's friend the
Hon. Robert Digby.

Warton died at Basingstoke on 10 September 1745 and
was buried in Basingstoke church. A memorial erected in
the church by his family was displaced during renovations
and a new memorial was subsequently erected by Victorian descendants of Joseph Warton. As a way of paying off
the debts owed by his father at his death, Joseph Warton
proposed publishing a volume of his father's poems by
subscription. This volume, Poems on Several Occasions,
appeared in March 1748 and increased Warton's reputation as a poet. It was subsequently praised as a transitional
volume containing poems typical of the early part of the
century and some which appeared to anticipate later
poets. However, modern scholarship has determined that

many of the poems previously thought to be somewhat forward reaching were, in fact, written by Warton's sons, Joseph and Thomas, or heavily edited by them.

HUGH REID

Sources D. Bishop, 'The father of the Wortons', *South Atlantic Quarterly*, 16 (1917), 357–68 · *Biographical memoirs of the late Rev Joseph Warton*, ed. J. Wooll (1806) · *The poetical works of Thomas Warton*, ed. R. Hart, 2 vols. (1802) · D. Fairer, 'The poems of Thomas Warton the elder?', *Review of English Studies*, new ser., 26 (1975), 287–300, 395–406 · D. Fairer, 'The poems of Thomas Warton the elder? A postscript', *Review of English Studies*, new ser., 29 (1978), 61–5 · *The correspondence of Thomas Warton*, ed. D. Fairer (1995) · Winchester College, Fellows' Library, Warton MSS · BL, Murray MSS, Add. MSS 42560–42561 · Swann papers, Bodl. Oxf., Trinity College · *Remarks and collections of Thomas Hearne*, ed. C. E. Doble and others, 11 vols., OHS, 2, 7, 13, 34, 42–3, 48, 50, 65, 67, 72 (1885–1921) · F. J. Baigent and J. E. Millard, *A history of the ancient town and manor of Basingstoke …: with a brief account of the siege of Basing house*, AD 1643–1645, 2 vols. (1889) · O. Manning and W. Bray, *The history and antiquities of the county of Surrey*, 1 (1804)

Archives Bodl. Oxf., literary MSS and papers · U. Leeds, Brotherton L., literary notebook | BL, Murray MSS, Add. MSS 42560–42561 · Bodl. Oxf., Lee MSS, MS Don c. 75 · Trinity College, Oxford, Swann MSS

Wealth at death left all to family: will

Warton, Thomas (1728–1790), poet and historian, was born in Basingstoke, Hampshire, on 9 January 1728, and baptized there on the 25th. He was the younger son of Thomas *Warton (1688–1745), vicar of Basingstoke, and Elizabeth (1691–1762), daughter of Joseph Richardson, rector of Dunsfold, Surrey, and younger brother of Joseph *Warton and Jane *Warton. Warton was educated at home by his father until 16 March 1744, when he entered Trinity College, Oxford, where he was to remain for the rest of his life. He graduated BA (1747) and MA (1750), and was elected a probationary fellow of Trinity on 25 May 1752 and perpetual fellow on 6 June 1753.

Early career Warton's poetic career began while he was an undergraduate at Trinity. *Five Pastoral Eclogues* was published anonymously by Dodsley in 1745. His first poem for Dodsley's *Museum*, 'Inscription in a Grotto', appeared on 11 October 1746. In April 1747 Dodsley published Warton's first major poem, 'The Pleasures of Melancholy' (although the poem had been written two years earlier). When Joseph Warton published his *Odes on Various Subjects* (1746) the volume contained two poems by Thomas, 'To a Fountain' and 'To a Gentleman upon his Travels thro' Italy'. This borrowing early illustrated the brothers' practice of helping each other with their work, a practice which culminated in 1748 when Thomas Warton the elder's *Poems on Several Occasions* was published. Thomas Warton the elder had died on 10 September 1745 and, in an attempt to raise money to cover debts which he had left, Joseph suggested putting together a volume of their father's poems and selling them by subscription. Both sons, however, contributed poems (anonymously) and both edited heavily (Joseph particularly) many of the remaining poems by Thomas Warton the elder. The volume, which many considered to be indicative of the nature and style of poetry to come, established a reputation for Thomas Warton the elder which was undeserved. All the forward-reaching

Thomas Warton (1728–1790), by Charles Howard Hodges, pubd 1784 (after Sir Joshua Reynolds, 1784)

poems were by the brothers. Thomas Warton changed style and adumbrated a different aspect of his later work when he published *Newmarket, a Satire* (1751), and contributed to (under the pseudonym of 'a Gentleman from Aberdeen') and edited *The Union, or, Select Scots and English Poems* (1753), a miscellany containing works by William Collins, Thomas Gray, Warton's brother Joseph, Mark Akenside, and Samuel Johnson.

As early as June 1753 Warton committed himself to writing a critical work on Spenser. *Observations on the 'Fairy Queen' of Spenser* was published by Dodsley in March 1754 and was well received. 'You have shown', Johnson wrote to Warton on 16 July 1754, 'to all who shall hereafter attempt the study of our ancient authours the way to success, by directing them to the perusal of the books which those authours had read' (Oxford, Trinity College, archives). The work was not universally admired. William Huggins took exception to what Warton said about Ariosto and published (anonymously) *The Observer Observ'd, or, Remarks on … Observations of the 'Faerie Queene' of Spenser* (1756). But this was the exception. In the second edition (2 vols., 1762) Warton added commentaries on Gothic architecture, medieval poets, and romances, and on the historical method of criticizing Spenser. The quality and influence of the work was such that a critic in 1911 called it 'the best book ever written about Spenser' (H. E. Cory, *The Critics of Spenser*, 1911).

Oxford poetry and prose As a response to William Mason's poem *Isis: an Elegy* (1749) Warton published *The Triumph of Isis* (1750), a poem praising Oxford's architecture, graduates, and history. The poem soon went into three editions and gained for the young author some early fame and status in the university. For the Encaenia of July 1751 Warton wrote an ode which William Hayes set to music.

While he was a serious scholar and poet, there was another side to Warton, that of the humorist and satirist. Early on in his time at Trinity he had been elected laureate of the bachelors' common room and in this role had written 'Verses on Miss C—s [Cotes] and Miss W—t [Wilmot]', published anonymously in July 1749 but written previously as separate poems. He further illustrated this aspect of his personality with 'A Panegyric on Oxford Ale' and 'The Pleasures of being out of Debt' which appeared on 31 March 1750 in *The Student*, an Oxford miscellany that appeared between 31 January 1750 and 3 July 1751. Both of these poems seem to have been inspired by personal experience. Warton published various other pieces of this ilk, including a number in *Jackson's Oxford Journal*, where he contributed 'The Oxford Newsman's Verses, 1760', and where he also wrote the annual verses for 1767, 1768, 1770, and 1771. In addition Warton wrote further items for *The Student*. His satire on Oxford guidebooks, *A companion to the guide and a guide to the companion, being a complete supplement to all the accounts of Oxford hitherto published*, appeared in 1760. Feeling a need to collect works by Oxford wits, Warton also contributed to and edited (anonymously) the amusing *The Oxford Sausage, or, Select Poetical Pieces Written by the Most Celebrated Wits of the University of Oxford* (1764).

Although much of Warton's writing about Oxford was satiric and humorous, he did write a number of more scholarly works on the subject, most notably biographies of men associated with Trinity College: Ralph Bathurst, a president of Trinity who was responsible for increasing the college's reputation and the building of the college chapel, and Sir Thomas Pope, the founder of the college, the latter piece originating in an article Warton wrote for *Biographia Britannica* (1760). In 1757 Warton was unanimously elected professor of poetry at Oxford, a post he held for two successive terms of five years each. Only one of his lectures, *De poesi Graecorum bucolica*, was printed and this was included in Warton's edition of Theocritus (1770). He did, though, publish other such works, including metrical inscriptions in Latin, 'Inscriptionum Romanarum metricarum delectus' (1758) and similar inscriptions in Greek (with a Latin preface), 'Anthologae Graecae' (1766).

Some time in the early 1750s Warton met Samuel Johnson, probably through his brother Joseph, and in 1754 Johnson stayed at Kettell Hall, Trinity College. He and Warton visited some local ruins and Warton introduced Johnson to a number of his friends, including Francis Wise, the Radclivian librarian. Altogether Warton and Johnson spent five weeks together and developed a lifelong friendship. Subsequently Warton helped in the campaign to get an MA degree for Johnson. The friendship stayed relatively strong until Johnson's death; there were however periods of coolness, perhaps resulting from Johnson's mockery of Warton's poetry, although hints of the coolness and its causes can be seen much earlier. Thomas wrote to Joseph in April 1755 about Johnson's dictionary: 'you may plainly perceive strokes of laxity and

indolence. They are two most unwieldy volumes … I fear his preface will disgust, by the expression of consciousness of superiority, and of his contempt of patronage' (Wooll, 230–31). Johnson was aware of Warton's feelings. 'Professors forget their friends', he wrote to Warton, partially as a tease in reference to Warton's new professorship, but partially it seems from a sense that it was true (21 June 1757, Oxford, Trinity College, archives). Johnson asked Warton to provide some notes for his Shakespeare and nineteen of these appeared in the appendix to the 1765 edition. Forty-nine appeared in the Oxford edition of 1770–71. Later editors, including Steevens and Malone, used these notes in their editions. However, Warton was unhappy with Johnson's *Lives* where Johnson criticized Milton and Gray and the tradition of historical criticism which Warton stood for.

On 7 December 1767 Warton took the degree of BD. In 1771 he was elected a fellow of the London Society of Antiquaries, and that year he was appointed to the small living of Kiddington, Oxfordshire; he later wrote a history of the parish. After his brother was appointed usher (assistant master) at Winchester College, and especially after Joseph became headmaster in 1766, Warton spent time there each year, studying the landscape and enjoying rambles to various local attractions. His sense of humour displayed itself often when he joined in pranks with the schoolboys (occasionally writing their exercises with just enough errors to avoid suspicion), behaviour which some thought rather below an Oxford don.

The History of English Poetry Warton probably started thinking in the early 1750s about what was to become his greatest project, but the serious writing of *The history of English poetry, from the close of the eleventh to the commencement of the eighteenth century* did not begin until 1769. Volume 1 appeared in 1774; volume 2 in 1778, and volume 3 in 1781. Warton decided on a chronological method in looking at the history of poetry. The work is, at times, obscure, and turgid. Warton's lists of manuscripts, his digressions, and his frequent quotations from long-lost poets often make the reading of the *History* heavy going. However, many of these quotations provided readers with the only accessible text of the poems and as such proved invaluable in creating an interest in the poetry of the past. Most contemporaries had great respect for the *History*, but not all. Joseph Ritson published a rather eccentric criticism of the work in 1782. His *Observations of the First Three Volumes of the 'History of English Poetry'* points out many errors of fact, misinterpretations, and other 'falsehoods'. But Ritson's views were in the minority. Most agreed with the writer in the *Gentleman's Magazine* who wrote, commenting on volume 3: 'This volume, like the former, does equal credit to Mr. Warton's taste, judgment, and erudition, and makes us impatiently desirous of more' (*GM*, 1st ser., 51, 1781, 230). The 'more' never appeared although Warton did begin work on volume 4. Why volume 4 never appeared has not been determined. It may be because at this time Warton became interested in producing an edition of Milton, but a comment by Samuel Deane in 1794 may provide a more accurate reason and also some insight into Warton's personality: 'Often have I regretted that the late Mr. Warton was too indolent to complete his proposed History … I have always understood that he wanted a spur to take pen in hand' (Nicholls, *Illustrations*, 6.633–4). Although by later standards of accuracy and inclusion the work would be considered unacceptable, it really is remarkable considering the time of its creation and the materials Warton had to work with. And the *History* has had far-reaching effects. Early in the next century Sir Walter Scott called it an 'immense commonplace book … from the perusal of which we rise, our fancy delighted with beautiful imagery, and with the happy analysis of ancient tale and song' (*Edinburgh Review*, 7 April 1804, 153). The *History*, despite its density and its digressions, cleared the way for later historians and gave legitimacy both to the study of early English poetry and to the historical method of doing so.

In 1777 Thomas Tyrwhitt's edition of the poems of Thomas Rowley began a controversy which, because of its concern with the authenticity of poems allegedly from the fifteenth century, naturally drew in the historian of English poetry. Initially Warton had felt that the poems were spurious and said so in a letter to Percy (25 January 1776) 'I owe, I lean to the side of the forgery' (BL, Add. MS 32329, fols. 83–4). In his *History* (2.139–64) Warton concluded, after examining internal evidence, spelling, and diction, that the poems were not from the fifteenth century. 'It is with regret that I find myself obligated to pronounce the Rowlie poems to be spurious' (2.164). He enlarged on this opinion later in *An Enquiry into the Authenticity of the Poems Attributed to Thomas Rowley* (1782). In this he admitted that he had made some errors in the *History*, but he concluded, firmly and convincingly, that the poems were forgeries; his opinion was taken as the final word and as accurate, and was corroborated by W. W. Skeat's edition of Chatterton which appeared in 1871.

In 1785 Warton issued an edition of Milton's shorter poems which received praises in the *Critical Review*, the *Monthly Review*, and the *Gentleman's Magazine*. Warton contemplated a second edition which was to include *Paradise Regained* and *Samson Agonistes* and by 1789 had revised the 1785 edition with hopes that volume 2 would be out by April 1790. All the notes for the second volume were lost after Warton's death, so that all that appeared was the revised edition of volume 1 in 1791. The edition is considered by many to be the best eighteenth-century edition of Milton and some of Warton's comments give an indication of his beliefs. He censured Milton for his politics and believed that Milton lost his sight and wasted his poetic genius working for the parliamentary cause. It is nevertheless clear that Warton admired Milton's work, even to the point of defending him against the strictures of his old friend Johnson. In a letter to Richard Hurd after Johnson's death, Warton says that Milton 'has been depreciated by Dr. Johnson, a specious and popular writer, without taste' (6 April 1785, Hartlebury Castle, Hurd Library, bound MSS V, Warton 9).

Poet laureate Although he had spent much of his time writing criticism, Warton continued to write poetry and his first volume of collected poems was published in 1777. The volume was quite popular and went into a number of editions. Warton's *Verses on Sir Joshua Reynolds's Painted Window at New College* (1782) was much admired by Reynolds and other contemporaries. Warton the poet reflected the many facets of Warton the man. Many of his poems, especially 'The Pleasures of Melancholy', show the influence of Milton, while many others demonstrate Warton's love of nature ('The First of April', 'On the Approach of Summer') and of the past ('The Grave of King Arthur'). His revival of the sonnet form was particularly important and had a lasting effect, while his satire and humorous pieces may still be read with pleasure. His poetry, written over many years, is some of the best of the period 1745–90. He had a particular influence over a number of old Wykehamists who studied at Trinity College. William Lisle Bowles, Henry Headley, and Thomas Russell all became poets after the Warton fashion. Bowles in particular was influenced by Warton and his 1789 volume of sonnets had in turn a great influence on Coleridge, Southey, and Wordsworth (S. T. Coleridge, *Biographia literaria*, 1817, chap. 1). Southey commented in 1825: 'If any man may be called the father of the present race, it is Thomas Warton' (*Quarterly Review*, 31, 1824–5, 289).

Largely through the influence and intercession of Reynolds, Warton was made poet laureate upon the death of William Whitehead in 1785. Warton's first official poem as laureate, an ode on the king's birthday, was somewhat hurried and perhaps his weakest work as laureate, and occasioned a satirical look at the laureateship, the *Probationary Odes*. This was a volume of poems written by a number of supposed candidates for the laureateship. As part of the satire, included in the volume were actual poems by Warton. He nevertheless took the incident in good part and did not feel any rancour towards the perpetrators, allegedly Richard Tickell and Joseph Richardson.

On 5 March 1782 Warton was admitted into the Literary Club, and although it is not certain how many meetings he was able to attend in London, he was a popular, and respected, member. He had, however, already known and corresponded with many of the members including Sir Joshua Reynolds, Thomas Percy, and Edmond Malone. In 1785 Warton was elected Camden professor of history at Oxford; his inaugural lecture was printed by his biographer, Richard Mant. During his lifetime Warton held a number of preferments after being ordained a priest on 10 March 1754. On 27 April 1755 he became curate of Woodstock, Oxfordshire, a post he held until 3 April 1774. He was appointed chaplain to the Royal Lancashire regiment, stationed in Winchester, on 24 July 1762. Lord Lichfield gave him the living of Kiddington, Oxfordshire, in October 1771, and Trinity College gave him the perpetual curacy of Hill Farrance, Somerset, in August 1782.

Warton generally enjoyed good health, but gout forced him to spend some time in Bath during 1788. In the winter of 1789–90 Warton and brother Joseph attended meetings of the Literary Club in London but at the beginning of May

Thomas suffered a small stroke which affected one of his hands and on 20 May he suffered a paralytic stroke in the senior common room at Trinity College, Oxford, and died the following day. He was unmarried. Warton was buried in the ante-chapel of Trinity on 27 May. The chair in which he is said to have been taken ill is preserved in the old library of the college. At his death all his effects, including his papers, were passed to his brother Joseph who kept them until his own death in 1800.

Jane Warton was to defend Thomas's character from some of what she perceived as criticism in Mant's memoir prefixed to his edition of Warton's poems.

> That Mr. Warton was totally free from pride, is certain; and that he might occasionally have drunk ale with inferior persons is possible; but, in my long acquaintance with him, I never knew that he was fond of, or kept low company.

She defends what others had criticized earlier: 'Mr. Warton was above the middle size, well made, stout, but never large, till latter in life, with a most pleasing countenance.' Concerning his manner of speaking she says: 'There was, indeed, sometimes a quickness in his manner, from the fulness of his mind; but I never heard it was thought a defect' (*GM*, 1st ser., 1803, 329–32, 396).

One modern critic has called the years from 1740 to 1790 more truly the 'Age of Warton than the Age of Johnson' (Fairer, *Correspondence*, xix). This is an accurate assessment. Warton's literary work really involved three kinds of literary history, beginning with his edition of Spenser, followed by his *History of English Poetry*, and culminating in his edition of Milton. All these, each in its own way, was a new examining of English poetry and provided a new validation for it. His indirect yet important contributions to Shakespearian scholarship changed that discipline for ever. His poetry, particularly the sonnets, influenced later generations. His antiquarianism, demonstrated in various digressions and other works, lent a credibility to that area of study. All of this makes Thomas Warton a difficult character to assess. He was more at ease with Oxford bargemen or drinking ale in a public tavern than he was as poet laureate or attending meetings of the Literary Club or in the palaces of the great, where he was often shy and retiring. He was a serious scholar whose critical methods and serious analysis of Spenser, Milton, and early English poetry were influential and admired, but at the same time he was a poet and writer of humour and satire. He enjoyed and revelled in the study and writing of history, yet he embarrassed his brother at Winchester by playing pranks with the boys. A multifaceted personality whose large amount of work and whose character were influential in his time and later, Warton was a writer whose importance was truly recognized only well after his death. An annual lecture on English poetry, given in tribute to Warton, has been organized by the British Academy since 1910.

HUGH REID

Sources *The correspondence of Thomas Warton*, ed. D. Fairer (1995) • J. Vance, *Joseph and Thomas Warton: an annotated bibliography* (1983) • J. Vance, *Joseph and Thomas Warton* (1983) • R. Mant, *The poetical works of Thomas Warton* (1802) • BL, Murray collection, Add. MSS 42560– 42561 • Swann papers, Bodl. Oxf., Trinity College • Winchester College, Fellows' Library, Warton papers • H. Reid, 'The printing of Joseph Warton's *Odes*', *Papers of the Bibliographical Society of America*, 84 (1990), 151–7 • H. Reid, 'The letters of Joseph Warton', PhD diss., U. Lond., 1987 • D. Fairer, 'The poems of Thomas Warton the elder?', *Review of English Studies*, new ser., 26 (1975), 287–300, 395– 406 • D. Fairer, 'The poems of Thomas Warton the elder? A postscript', *Review of English Studies*, new ser., 29 (1978), 61–5 • *Biographical memoirs of the late Rev Joseph Warton*, ed. J. Wooll (1806) • *DNB*
Archives BL, corresp., Add. MSS 42560–42561, Egerton MS 24000 • BL, memorandum book and diary, Add. MS 11139 • BL, heavily annotated copies of Spenser's *Faerie queene* and *Prosopopoeia* • Bodl. Oxf., corresp., literary MSS, and papers, deps. b 220–221, c 547–550, 635–643, d 483–487, 586–683, e 245, 276–295, 305, f 43 • JRL, notebook • Trinity College, Oxford, archives • Yale U., Beinecke L., papers | BL, letters to Edmond Malone, Add. MS 30375 • BL, letters to Thomas Percy, Add. MS 32329 • Bodl. Oxf., letters to Lord Guilford, MSS North d 14, 17 • Bodl. Oxf., Lee papers, MS Don. c. 75
Likenesses C. H. Hodges, engraving, pubd 1784 (after J. Reynolds, 1784), NPG [*see illus.*] • J. Reynolds, oils, *c.*1784, Trinity College, Oxford • W. Holl, engraving (after J. Reynolds), repro. in Mant, *Poetical works of Thomas Warton* • W. P. Sherlock, engraving (after J. Reynolds), repro. in Nichols, *Illustrations*, vol. 4
Wealth at death papers and effects to Joseph Warton: *Correspondence of Thomas Warton*, ed. Fairer

Warwick. For this title name *see* Beaumont, Henry de, first earl of Warwick (*d.* 1119); Roger, second earl of Warwick (*d.* 1153); Percy, Matilda de, countess of Warwick (*d.* 1204); Plessis, John de, seventh earl of Warwick (*d.* 1263); Basset, Philippa, countess of Warwick (*d.* 1265); Mauduit, William, eighth earl of Warwick (1221x3–1268); Beauchamp, William (IV) de, ninth earl of Warwick (*c.*1238–1298); Beauchamp, Guy de, tenth earl of Warwick (*c.*1272–1315); Beauchamp, Thomas, eleventh earl of Warwick (1313/14–1369); Beauchamp, Thomas, twelfth earl of Warwick (1337x9–1401); Beauchamp, Richard, thirteenth earl of Warwick (1382–1439); Berkeley, Elizabeth, countess of Warwick (*c.*1386–1422); Beauchamp, Henry, duke of Warwick (1425–1446); Neville, Richard, sixteenth earl of Warwick and sixth earl of Salisbury (1428–1471); Edward, styled earl of Warwick (1475–1499); Dudley, John, earl of Warwick (1527?–1554) [*see under* Dudley, John, duke of Northumberland (1504–1553)]; Dudley, Ambrose, earl of Warwick (*c.*1530–1590); Dudley, Anne, countess of Warwick (1538–1587) [*see under* Seymour, Lady Jane (1541–1561)]; Dudley, Anne, countess of Warwick (1548/9–1604); Rich, Robert, first earl of Warwick (1559?–1619); Rich, Robert, second earl of Warwick (1587–1658); Rich, Mary, countess of Warwick (1624–1678); Addison, Charlotte, countess of Warwick (*bap.* 1680, *d.* 1731) [*see under* Addison, Joseph (1672–1719)]; Greville, Frances Evelyn, countess of Warwick (1861–1938).

Warwick, Arthur (1604–1633), Church of England clergyman and writer, was born in February 1604, the son of Arthur Warwick, master of the grammar school in the close, Salisbury. The elder Warwick held the post from 1617 until his death in 1651 and it is to be presumed that both father and son resided for some of those years at Braybroke House, the master's official residence in the close. His father's neglect of professional duties and his consequent protracted quarrels with the Salisbury chapter may have made Warwick's adolescence unquiet; otherwise nothing is known of his early upbringing or schooling. At Oxford Warwick, matriculated from Magdalen Hall on 31 January 1623 and received his BA degree on 16 December 1624 (not 15 December, as given by both Foster and Clark); he appears not to have proceeded MA. In February 1627 he was made deacon by the bishop of Salisbury; where Warwick began his ministry is not known. He was admitted to priest's orders on 21 September 1628 and licensed to serve at Durley, a village about 10 miles south of Winchester. It was there that Warwick completed the first part of *Spare Minutes*, his only book. He dedicated it to Sir William Dodington, an important landowner of Breamore, 8 miles south of Salisbury. His son, Henry, was the same age as Warwick and had been his exact contemporary at Magdalen Hall. Although Warwick protested, in the dedication, that their acquaintance was 'short, and small' he gratefully acknowledged Dodington's former favours. As Dodington was both wealthy and influential such patronage could have been substantial.

Spare Minutes was entered in the registers of the Stationers' Company to Walter Hammond on 24 March 1632. Its title is given as *Resolved Meditations and Premeditated Resolutions*, and both the engraved title-pages that it eventually had carry variants of this form; neither bears the words 'Spare minutes' which are to be found only on the letterpress title-pages of all early editions.

Warwick's ministry at Durley lasted just five years. At a visitation on 23 September 1633 it was noted that he was ill, and within a few weeks he had died, at Durley. Warwick was buried there on 31 October 1633 but his grave has not been traced. He was twenty-nine years of age.

The earliest edition of *Spare Minutes* of which a copy is known is dated 1634 and described as the 'second Edition corrected and enlarged'. It is arranged in two parts. The first, containing sixty-one meditations, has an emblematic engraved title-page with accompanying verse in English by the 'Inventor' (apparently Richard Haydock, who designed the engraved title-pages), and also twenty lines of Latin by William Haydock, son of Richard. The second part is described in the dedication as a posthumous addition 'collected out of loose papers' after Warwick's death. This has a further thirty-seven similar meditations, together with three short passages of verse, one of which was the last thing that Warwick composed, a few days before his death. This latter part is dedicated by the author's father to a Mistress Anne Ashton. The 'meditations' of the second part, 'wanting filing, and polishing' (dedication), are the longer and the less concisely expressed. The meditations, or prose aphorisms, vary in length from 25 to 290 words. The whole is written in a witty, highly antithetical style, deploying familiar imagery to provide sound moral instruction. Its merit is considerable, and it enjoyed remarkable success. There were at least eight editions and reissues between 1634 and 1700, and the appearance of a further ten after 1800 is impressive evidence of its enduring vitality.

Before the next edition of *Spare Minutes* was published in 1635 its preliminaries were revised and rearranged. The book was embellished by the addition of a new engraved emblematic title-page (the earlier engraving then being prefixed to the second part) and a passage of verse by Francis Quarles with another by George Wither to accompany the two engravings respectively. Wither's contribution replaced the lines by the inventor, which were then omitted. With the 1635 third edition *Spare Minutes* assumed, in essentials, the form in which it has commonly been reprinted. The plates are signed by Thomas Clarke of Salisbury, as engraver, but their design is now attributed to Richard Haydocke, also of Salisbury. The theme that they symbolically express is of the pious soul overcoming the world and ascending to heaven, leaving behind his work and memory for the edification of those who remain. They are remarkable examples of their kind. Richard Haydock was an eminent physician, translator, and engraver. Since Haydock and Warwick senior, each a noted figure in Salisbury, both resided in the close, it is improbable that they were unacquainted. Possibly the contribution of the Haydocks to *Spare Minutes* was a token of esteem.

Warwick's life at Durley (known as 'dirty Durley' because of the bad state of its roads) was probably lonely and obscure. But he was not without influential connections. The Anne Ashton to whom his father dedicated the second part of *Spare Minutes* was the widow of Thomas Ashton of Bishop's Waltham, 3 miles from Durley. Thomas Ashton had been noted for his good works, and he left his wife a large estate and a considerable income. The elder Warwick acknowledges her 'favours' to himself and to his son, 'who in his life time studied to be thankfull to you' (dedication).   JOHN HORDEN

Sources K. J. Höltgen and J. Horden, 'Arthur Warwick, 1603/4–1633: the author of *Spare minutes*', *The Library*, 5th ser., 21 (1966), 223–30 • K. J. Höltgen, 'Richard Haydocke: translator, engraver, physician', *The Library*, 5th ser., 33 (1978), 15–32 • J. Horden, *Arthur Warwick's 'Spare minutes': an analytical bibliography* (1965) • *STC, 1475–1640* • Wing, *STC* • Foster, *Alum. Oxon.*, *1500–1714* [Arthur Warwicke] • *Reg. Oxf.*, 2/3.435

Warwick, Guy of. *See* Guy of Warwick (*supp. fl. c.*930).

Warwick, Sir Philip (1609–1683), politician and historian, was born in the parish of St Margaret, Westminster, on 24 December 1609, and baptized the same day. He was the only son of Thomas Warwick (*fl.* 1580–1620), organist of Westminster Abbey and the Chapel Royal, and Elizabeth Somerville of Aston Somerville, Warwickshire. He was educated at Eton College, which he entered about 1623, after which he may have attended Pembroke College, Cambridge, and he then spent time travelling in France and Switzerland. It seems that in 1634 he also had some practice with the pike in the Netherlands. While he was abroad, by a contract dated 2 April 1634, it was arranged that he would marry Dorothy (*d.* 1644), daughter of Matthew Hutton of Marske, Yorkshire. On his return Warwick became secretary to his distant relative Lord Goring, and it was through Goring's influence that he became secretary to William Juxon on the latter's appointment as lord treasurer in March 1636. Warwick was admitted to Gray's Inn on 12 February 1638, and on 11 April that year was created

Sir Philip Warwick (1609–1683), by Robert White, pubd 1701 (after Sir Peter Lely, c.1645)

LLB by Oxford University. A few months later, on 13 November, he became a clerk of the signet, an office he held until 1646.

Royalist support In 1640 Warwick was elected to sit for both Radnor borough and New Romney, Kent, in the Long Parliament, and chose to serve for the former. He was one of the fifty-nine 'Straffordians' who voted against Strafford's attainder, and the following year he rallied to Charles I. In his *Memoires of the Reign of King Charles I* (1701) Warwick blamed the outbreak of the civil war on 'an envy unto the regall prerogative', and 'the irreconcileable and never to be satisfied appetite unto a change in government in the Long Parliament' (pp. 8, 75). He fought as a volunteer at Edgehill, and in 1643 he acted as the king's emissary in two unsuccessful attempts to persuade the earl of Newcastle to bring his army southwards. In January 1644 he was among those who assembled at the Oxford parliament, whereupon he was deprived of his seat at Westminster on 5 February. At Oxford he lodged in rooms at University College, and he later helped to negotiate the terms of the city's surrender in June 1646. Warwick's first wife had died in August 1644, and in 1647 he married Joan,

née Fanshawe, widow of Sir William Boteler. She is not mentioned in his will, and probably predeceased him.

In the autumn of 1647 Warwick was allowed to attend Charles at Hampton Court as one of his secretaries, and he served the king in a similar capacity a year later at the treaty of Newport. In his *Memoires* Warwick subsequently left a firsthand account of the king's final months. Charles trusted him greatly, and in the evenings dictated to him dispatches on the progress of the treaty that were then sent to the prince of Wales. Warwick recorded that in private one day Charles warned, prophetically, that the parliamentarian commissioners 'will ask so much, and use it so ill, that the people of England will be one day glad to relodge the power they had taken from the Crown, where it is due' (Warwick, *Memoires*, 1701, 328). Warwick also described the only occasion when, late in the Newport talks, he saw the king shed tears and then compose himself with characteristic self-control: 'they were the biggest drops that ever I saw fall from an eye; but he recollected himselfe, and soon stifled them' (ibid., 326). In January 1649 Warwick was appalled when 'this good Prince was most barbarously and traiterously murdered by his owne subjects' (ibid., 8).

On 28 July 1644 the committee for the advance of money had imposed a fine of £1000 on Warwick, though it seems that no proceedings were taken on this. On 6 August 1646 Warwick begged to compound under the Oxford articles, and the following December he was fined at the rate of one-tenth of his estate (a sum of £477 18s.). However, in January 1649 he begged a review, having paid half his fine and compounded for a debt of £2500 which he was likely to lose. The following month, after review, the fine was reduced to £241, and later that year the Rump Parliament accepted his composition and granted him a pardon.

By compounding, Warwick was able to remain in England during the interregnum. Although he was imprisoned on suspicion in 1655 and detained for several weeks, he avoided any involvement in royalist conspiracy. Nevertheless, there is clear evidence that royalist leaders trusted his loyalty. In January 1660 Warwick was employed to negotiate with Lambert and to look after 'a very considerable sum of many thousand pounds' that had been collected 'for the advancement of the King's service' (Scrope and Monkhouse, 3.649). Hyde wrote that 'the King knows very well Mr Warwick's affection and zeal to his service and his abilities to promote it' (ibid.). It was reported that Warwick was sympathetic to the presbyterians, but at the Restoration he helped to thwart their attempts to exclude from the Lords those younger royalist peers who had gained their titles since 1642.

Secretary to the Treasury Charles II expressed his gratitude to Warwick by knighting him in 1660, reappointing him as clerk of the signet, and also making him secretary to the Treasury. The earl of Southampton became lord treasurer in September 1660, but according to Gilbert Burnet he 'left the business of the Treasury wholly in the hands' of Warwick (*Bishop Burnet's History*, 1.174). In 1661 Warwick was returned for Westminster and became an active member of the Cavalier Parliament: between then and 1678 he made a total of 49 recorded speeches and was appointed to 258 committees. Throughout he remained consistent in his loyalty to the crown and to the church. In the early 1660s he was appointed to all the committees that framed the Clarendon code, and chaired the committees that drafted the bills for the security of the king's person and against tumultuous petitioning.

Warwick's role as secretary to the Treasury ensured that he regularly acted as an official spokesman on financial matters in the Commons. In June 1661 he reported that the crown's revenue amounted to only £265,000 out of an expected £1,200,000, and he was promptly appointed to a committee to consider ways in which it could be augmented. In 1663 he announced that revenues had increased to £978,000, but the Commons rejected his request for additional supply to bridge the remaining gap, on the grounds that further economies and efficiency savings would solve the problem. However, in 1665 he succeeded in persuading the Commons to grant a new tax of £70,000 a month for the duration of the Second Anglo-Dutch War, and was appointed chairman of the committee to revise county tax assessments for this 'royal aid'. In September 1666 he presented a full statement of public accounts to the Commons.

When Southampton died in May 1667, the Treasury was put into commission. Warwick was not among the commissioners, and Sir George Downing took over his position as secretary. Gilbert Burnet thought Warwick 'an incorrupt man, and during seven years management of the Treasury made but an ordinary fortune out of it' (*Bishop Burnet's History*, 1.174). It is likely that he had gained about £2000 a year from the post. That and the permission in 1663 to build a house on the road between Charing Cross and St James's Palace, together with the reversion of the office of customer and collector of customs on woollen cloth in the port of London (worth £277 a year), appear to have been the only material benefits that he derived from his office. After 1667 he remained active in the Commons, where he was widely regarded as a court supporter and usually took a sympathetic line towards the crown's policies and advisers. This was evident, for example, in his denial that Clarendon had usurped the functions of the lord treasurer, and in his defence in 1669 of the former treasurer of the navy Sir George Carteret against charges of corruption.

Opinions on monarchy   Only very occasionally did Warwick deviate from the prevailing court line. His commitment to the established church led him to oppose greater toleration for either Catholics or protestant nonconformists. In 1670 he was among those appointed to consider the renewal of the Conventicles Act, and two years later he opposed Charles II's declaration of indulgence. However, he was soon won over by the king's conciliatory response in February 1673, even though it defended the royal suspending power and did not actually withdraw the declaration. He remained hostile to relief for protestant dissenters, and moved on 7 March that 'there may be a test upon persons to sit in this House, that the Church may not be destroyed' (Grey, 2.89). In April 1675 he was named to the committees for bills to suppress popery and to disable Catholics from sitting in either house. During the long prorogation of parliament from November 1675 to February 1677, Warwick wrote his *Memoires*, which was published posthumously in 1701.

Warwick was included on lists of government speakers, though Sir Richard Wiseman wrote to Danby: 'I wish your lordship would think of some way to make this gentleman industrious and hearty in the service' (HoP, *Commons, 1660–90*, 3.676). Shaftesbury had no doubt as to where Warwick's loyalties lay, and when parliament reconvened in February 1677 he marked Warwick as 'thrice vile' (ibid.). Nevertheless, Warwick's fear of popery was such that he spoke out against Charles II's policy of *rapprochement* with France. He told the Commons on 14 March 1678 that he had 'feared this greatness of the French King these forty years; and in my last Master's time, they had great correspondence in Court, and found casements to look in at' (Grey, 5.230). On 2 May he declared: 'I believe that if ever the nation was in danger, it is now … I believe all the powers in Christendom will stand by us, if we enter into a war with the King of France' (ibid., 5.300). In the autumn of 1678 he naturally believed the revelations of Titus Oates and Israel Tonge about the Popish Plot, and on 4 November he denounced popery as 'a confederacy against God, and against the kingdom' (ibid., 6.147). He was among those appointed to search the cellars of the Palace of Westminster amid fears of another Catholic plot to blow up parliament. Although he was listed as a court supporter, the logic of his horror of 'popery and arbitrary government' led him to vote for the impeachment of Danby.

During 1678 Warwick wrote *A Discourse on Government*, published posthumously in 1694. In this treatise he argued that the monarchs of England 'remain absolute though limited', and that the king was 'an absolute, though not an arbitrary monarch' (pp. 20, 41). He regarded England as 'a limited and mixt monarchy' (Warwick, *Discourse*, 185), but this did not imply that the crown, Lords, and Commons exercised co-ordinate powers. Indeed, Warwick denounced the doctrine of co-ordination as 'like to prove the mother of a civil war' (ibid., 19), and detested that 'destructive torrent of populacy' (ibid., 184) that had led the houses to take up arms against the king in 1642. His loyalty to the memory of Charles I remained beyond question, and in January 1678 he was appointed to chair a committee to consider the solemn reburial of the king's remains, though no legislation resulted from this.

After the Cavalier Parliament was dissolved in January 1679, Warwick did not stand for parliament again. He had sold his Westminster house in the mid-1670s, and henceforth lived quietly at his home at Chislehurst in Kent. He died on 15 January 1683, probably at Chislehurst, and was buried in Chislehurst church. His only son by his first wife, also named Philip *Warwick (*bap.* 1640, *d.* 1683), was appointed envoy to Sweden in 1680; he died shortly afterwards at Newmarket on 12 March 1683, after journeying home to take leave of his father.

Warwick's contemporaries varied widely in their assessment of him. Samuel Pepys regarded him as 'a very able and right honest man', whose exposition of the government's financial problems showed him to be 'a most exact and methodical man, and of great industry' (Pepys, 29 Feb 1664, 5.70; 24 Nov 1666, 7.382). By contrast, Andrew Marvell wrote that Warwick 'never lyes more than when he professes to speak the sincerity of his heart' (*A Seasonable Argument to Perswade All the Grand Juries in England to Petition for a New Parliament*, [1677], 12). There is, however, no evidence to support Marvell's further claim that Warwick 'got artificially from the Treasurer Southampton and the King £40,000'. A less vituperative but still fairly critical account was penned by Gilbert Burnet, who thought Warwick 'an honest but a weak man', who 'understood the common road of the Treasury; but, though he pretended to wit and politics, he was not cut out for that, and least of all for writing of history' (*Bishop Burnet's History*, 1.174). It is, however, worth noting that both Burnet and Marvell embraced whig principles that placed them out of sympathy with Warwick's consistent allegiance to crown and church.   DAVID L. SMITH

Sources E. Cruickshanks, 'Warwick, Sir Philip', HoP, *Commons, 1660–90*, 3.674–7 · Keeler, *Long Parliament*, 380 · *JHC*, 2–9 (1640–87) · PRO, state papers domestic, SP 16, Charles I · PRO, SP 23, committee for compounding MSS · A. Grey, ed., *Debates of the House of Commons, from the year 1667 to the year 1694*, 10 vols. (1763) · Cobbett, *Parl. hist.*, vols. 2–4 · *Bishop Burnet's History* · Pepys, *Diary*, vols. 2–8 · R. Scrope and T. Monkhouse, eds., *State papers collected by Edward, earl of Clarendon*, 3 vols. (1767–86) · parish register, St Margaret's, Westminster, 24 Dec 1609 [baptism] · 'Thomas Warwick', Grove, *Dict. mus.* · will, PRO, PROB 11/372, sig. 50
Archives Hunt. L., memoirs of reign of Charles I | Bodl. Oxf., letters to Thomas Pierce
Likenesses R. White, line engraving (after P. Lely, c.1645), BM, NPG; repro. in P. Warwick, *Memoires of the reign of King Charles I* (1701) [*see illus.*]
Wealth at death approx. £4770 p.a. from estates in 1646

Warwick, Philip (*bap.* 1640, *d.* 1683), diplomat, was baptized at St Margaret's, Westminster, on 7 December 1640, the only son of Sir Philip *Warwick (1609–1683), politician and historian, and his first wife, Dorothy (*d.* 1644), daughter of Matthew Hutton of Marske, Yorkshire. It may have been he, rather than his father (who had already been admitted to Gray's Inn), who in the year 1656 was admitted to the Inner Temple, London. Nothing else is known of his early life. In 1680 Warwick was appointed *envoyé extraordinaire* on a mission to the Swedish king, Karl XI, to renew the Anglo-Swedish alliance of 1664. This was to be both a commercial and a defensive alliance. Warwick took leave of Charles II in July 1680 and is noted to have arrived in Stockholm with his secretary, John Robinson, on 29 August. Although he did not obtain an audience with the Swedish king until a couple of months later, his time in Sweden was initially taken up by other commercial issues. Warwick's regular correspondence with the British secretary of state, Sir Leoline Jenkins, not only illuminates the mission but also confirms that Warwick's role extended beyond the commercial sphere. Indeed, Warwick's duties included interceding on behalf of British merchants who fell foul of Swedish and other foreign authorities in the

Baltic region. By the end of November 1680 at least five of Warwick's letters had been read out before Charles II and the committee of foreign affairs in London.

Early in this correspondence Jenkins warned Warwick of the malicious rumours he would encounter about Britain and its government, and instructed him to refute such allegations. Jenkins also kept Warwick up to date on negotiations between Sweden and France in Germany regarding troops in Pomerania. As Jenkins had himself served as an envoy to the Swedish court in 1679 he could suggest important Swedish contacts who might help Warwick to maintain a healthy relationship between Britain and Sweden. The Swedish chancellor in particular, Bengt Oxenstierna, proved an honest and sincere man who supported Warwick's mission, and Warwick finally obtained an audience with the Swedish king on 15 November. Although it is not known exactly what was discussed, a letter to Karl XI detailing Warwick's instructions reveals that Charles II was keen to maintain and cultivate friendly and commercial relations between the two kingdoms, and it invited a Swedish envoy at his court to discuss the renewal of the lapsed treaty of 1664.

Warwick seems to have handled effectively the affair of the Tobacco and Tar Company, closed at Jenkins's suggestion after difficulties over payment to London merchants. However, although Warwick's letters were replete with information on tolls and customs as well as shipping lists, Jenkins expressed dissatisfaction with the poor response he had received from some merchants to Warwick's work in Sweden. Their lack of interest was blamed on a preoccupation with domestic issues. This did not deter Warwick from supporting both English and Scottish merchants in Sweden, as when he sought compensation for Joseph Newcome, who had lost goods to the Swedes to the value of 400 riksdaler.

By January 1681, along with continued hopes of ratifying a new treaty, the main issue had re-emerged: obtaining the Swedish king's interest in reviving the 1664 commercial alliance between the two kingdoms. The conditions included granting reciprocal trade privileges: for Sweden in Portsmouth, and for Stuart subjects in Göteborg. Although the Swedes did not seem overly enthusiastic about these proposals, Jenkins twice reassured Warwick that his work in Sweden was highly valued in England. Warwick also appeared to have formed a trusted relationship with Swedish secretary of state Olivencrantz, using the latter as an intermediary in order to protect his correspondence.

As many of his letters to Karl XI show, Warwick continued his defence mostly of English merchants in their difficulties with local authorities over such issues as long overdue payment; in some cases these dated from the 1670s, unresolved in previous exchanges between Charles II and the Swedish king. This was the case with Richard Daniel, a merchant based at Riga (then a Swedish possession), who had complained in 1677 that he was being forced into becoming a burgess of the town—and therefore liable to local taxes—after marrying a Swedish woman there. However, Warwick was in Sweden to represent not only the English interest but that of all Stuart subjects, be it English, Irish, or Scottish. He therefore entered into correspondence over land disputes also in Livonia on behalf of Major James Bennet, a Scottish soldier who claimed the land by right of inheritance through marriage.

Warwick's ultimate aim was to re-create and strengthen the commercial ties between Britain and Sweden. He had already been informed in October 1681 of a defensive alliance being negotiated between the Netherlands and Sweden. British participation had also been sought, but only financially—to fund Swedish–Dutch relations. Warwick wanted to promote a purely British–Swedish connection, though Jenkins expressed the possibility of other European powers joining these negotiations. It was particularly feared that France would take any opportunity to destroy British trade. In a letter to Chancellor Oxenstierna in June 1682, Warwick clarified some of the British concerns when he passed on Charles II's desire totally to separate the issue of a friendly confederation between Sweden and Britain from that of a commercial alliance between the two kingdoms. Warwick's mission was bolstered by the arrival in July of an additional envoy who had been authorized specifically to discuss such an alliance.

By January 1683 Warwick had informed the Swedish court and government that he had obtained Charles's permission to return home to England in order to deal with a family matter; he fully intended to return to his duties in Sweden as soon as he could. In the meantime Warwick's secretary, John Robinson, continued to work towards the formation of a British–Swedish alliance. However, Warwick died at Newmarket, Suffolk, on 12 March 1683, and Robinson assumed his role as official Stuart envoy to Sweden.   A. N. L. GROSJEAN

Sources Riksarkivet, Stockholm, Anglica 527, Konferensprotokoll 24/1/1683 · Riksarkivet, Stockholm, Anglica 522, Engelska beskickningars memorial 1591–1692 · Svenske sändebud till utländske hof och dessas sändebud till Sverige, Riksarkivet, Stockholm · CSP dom., 1679–81 · IGI [St Margaret's, Westminster, parish register] · W. H. Cooke, ed., Students admitted to the Inner Temple, 1547–1660 [1878], 364 · E. Cruickshanks, 'Warwick, Sir Philip', HoP, Commons, 1660–90 · DNB

Warwick, Simon [Simeon] **of** (c.1225–1296), abbot of St Mary's, York, was of unknown origins. He had been a monk of St Mary's Abbey for fourteen years when he was elected the tenth abbot of his monastery on 24 June 1258. His many achievements during his extremely long abbacy are well documented in a St Mary's manuscript of the early fourteenth century (Bodl. Oxf., MS Bodley 39), which includes a unique copy of detailed annals for the history of the convent from 1258 to 1326. It seems likely that Abbot Simon was the compiler rather than the author (as has often been supposed) of the earlier sections of this manuscript, which nevertheless testifies to his exceptionally high reputation within and without his own cloister. He played an important role in trying to pacify jurisdictional disputes between the churches of York and Durham, and

frequently visited St Mary's five most important daughter houses. Although forced to leave his abbey for over a year in 1264 because of the violent onslaught of the citizens of York on his convent's economic franchises in the suburb of Bootham, in 1275 he brought that most difficult of his many legal disputes to a successful conclusion. Not surprisingly, it was during this period that Simon of Warwick supervised the building of a new stone wall (much of which survives) around the St Mary's Abbey precinct, as well as a strongly constructed abbot's house for himself. Remarkably, twenty-four years after he laid the first stone of its choir in 1271, St Mary's Abbey possessed a spectacular new church (110 metres long) constructed in the most fashionable decorated Gothic style. Abbot Simon died on 6 July 1296, and was buried before the high altar of this greatest of his many memorials.   R. B. DOBSON

Sources records relating to the Benedictine abbey of St Mary at York, c.1312–13, Bodl. Oxf., MS Bodley 39 · H. H. E. Craster and M. E. Thornton, eds., The chronicle of St Mary's Abbey, York, SurtS, 148 (1934) · W. A. Pantin, ed., Documents illustrating the activities of … the English black monks, 1215–1540, 3 vols., CS, 3rd ser., 45, 47, 54 (1931–7), vol. 1, pp. 247–8, 252–61; vol. 3, p. 276 · Yorkshire: York and the East Riding, Pevsner (1995), 181–94 · A. B. Whittingham, 'St Mary's Abbey, York: an interpretation of its plan', Archaeological Journal, 128 (1972), 118–46, esp. 121–3 · VCH Yorkshire, 3.108–12 · P. M. Tillott, ed., A history of Yorkshire: the city of York (1961), 51, 38–40, 358, 529 · An inventory of the historical monuments in the city of York, Royal Commission on Historical Monuments (England), 4 (1975), xxxix, 3–4, 11–12, 30

Archives Bodl. Oxf., MS Bodley 39

Wasbrough, Matthew (bap. 1753, d. 1781), engineer and inventor of steam engines, born at 3 Narrow Wine Street, Bristol, was baptized on 18 November 1753, the son of Mary and William Wasbrough. William Wasbrough was originally a barber–surgeon and peruke maker, who was in partnership with Roger Rice in a brass-founding and clockmaking business in Narrow Wine Street. Matthew Wasbrough had at least three older brothers. On 23 January 1776 he married Elizabeth Dowell at St Peter's, Bristol.

Taking an early interest in his father's work, Wasbrough constructed a steam engine with which to drive all the lathes and other machines; in order to do this, he had to convert the reciprocating movement of the Newcomen-type beam engine into rotary motion. He achieved this by using a ratchet and pawl mechanism to produce the rotary motion, combined with a flywheel which reduced the otherwise excessive variations in the speed of rotation.

On 10 March 1779 Wasbrough was granted patent no. 1213 for a machine which made use of this mechanism. It was, however, not robust or reliable enough in constant use: it seems that, after he completed an engine to drive a mill owned by James Pickard at Snow Hill in Birmingham, it was found to be unsatisfactory, and a crank was substituted—an idea probably taken from James Watt, and enterprisingly adopted by Wasbrough and Pickard. In the words of John Farey: 'The engine then answered so much better than anything which had been tried before that the same principle has been followed ever since'. This was probably the first successful application of the crank to a steam engine in order to produce rotary motion.

A patent granted to Pickard on 23 August 1780 for a 'new-invented method of applying steam engines to the turning of wheels, whereby a rotative motion is performed, and the power of the engine is more immediately and fully applied ... than by the intervention of water' was worded loosely and failed to define the method involved. There was apparently an agreement between Pickard and Wasbrough allowing the latter to use the crank, and the engine builder who was most incensed at the patenting of a device which he maintained had been known for centuries was James Watt. In any case, Wasbrough benefited little from either his invention or his arrangement with Pickard. He had entered into negotiations with the commissioners of his majesty's victualling office for the erection of an engine to drive a corn mill, and manufacture of the parts was well advanced, when for some reason they turned to John Smeaton for an opinion, and he recommended a pumping engine and water-wheel. This disappointment, coming at a time when he was already in a precarious state of health, is said to have accelerated Wasbrough's death from fever on 21 October 1781. He was survived by his wife.

A notice of Wasbrough's death in the *Bristol Journal* supports the view that had he lived he would have made an even greater mark as an engineer: 'The public have to deplore in him the loss of one of the first mechanics in the kingdom, whose early genius brought to perfection that long-wished-for desideratum, the applying the powers of the fire-engine to rotular movements' (*N&Q*, 293).

RONALD M. BIRSE, *rev.*

Sources *N&Q*, 3rd ser., 1 (1862), 292–3 · *The Engineer* (13 Feb 1920), 162–4 · H. W. Dickinson, *A short history of the steam engine* (1939); 2nd edn (1963) · H. W. Dickinson and R. Jenkins, *James Watt and the steam engine* (1927); facs. edn (1981) · L. Day and I. McNeil, eds., *Biographical dictionary of the history of technology* (1996)

Wase, Christopher (1627–1690), schoolmaster and classical scholar, was born in Hackney, Middlesex, and baptized on 6 January 1627, the son of John Wase of London (*d.* in or after 1670) and his wife, Susan, daughter of Richard Welby of London, merchant. He entered Eton College about 1639 and matriculated as a scholar from King's College, Cambridge, in Michaelmas 1645. A gifted polyglot and prolific scholar, while still an undergraduate he prepared a Greek translation of Hugo Grotius's *Baptizatorium puerorum institutio*, which was first published in 1647. He may have been the Christopher Wase, 'son of John Wase of Cambridge', admitted to Gray's Inn on 1 March that year. In 1648 he was elected to a fellowship at King's, from where he graduated BA in 1649. His translation of Sophocles' *Electra*, published the same year, was dedicated to Charles I's daughter Elizabeth, and in 1650 he was ejected from King's following his failure to take the engagement. He then travelled in France and the Low Countries. Captured at sea carrying letters to France for the royalists, he escaped and served as a soldier in Flanders. In 1652 he returned to England with financial assistance from John Evelyn the diarist and then became tutor to William Herbert (*b.* 1640), eldest son of the earl of Pembroke. Wase's translation of Faliscus Gratius's hunting poem *Cynegeticon* appeared in 1654. The following year he finally proceeded MA from Cambridge.

For the next thirteen years Wase gained his livelihood as a headmaster, from 1655 to 1662 at Dedham Royal Free School, Essex, and from 1662 to 1668 at Tonbridge School, Kent. By 1662, when his son Christopher was born, he had married Elizabeth, daughter of Gilbert Rayney, rector of St Mary-at-Stoke, Ipswich. In 1660 he published a celebration of the Restoration, *In mirabilem Caroli II*, and a dictionary, *Methodi practicae specimen; an Essay of a Practical Grammar*; another dictionary, *Dictionarium minus* (1662), followed. Convinced that Wase's talents were wasted and his salary of £40 a year was inadequate, Evelyn recommended him for the post of historiographer in the office of Joseph Williamson, secretary of state. Wase was 'of a most innocent, sincere, humble and sedulous mind', with a 'style nervous and material but quick', and in the diarist's opinion he lacked nothing 'to qualify him equal to the ablest writer of this age, but his Majesty's favour' (*CSP dom.*, 1668–9, 65). Wase was given his appointment in April 1669.

Office gave Wase the opportunity to help his relatives and advance his scholarly interests. In 1671 he published two translations into English—one of Cicero's orations against Cataline, the other *The History of France under the Ministry of Cardinal Mazarine*—and, in response to criticisms that the growth of free schools had threatened established social distinctions and (allegedly) contributed to the dissension that led to the civil wars, undertook a pioneer investigation of the nation's grammar schools. His work was interrupted, however, when, arriving in Oxford on Eton College business in October 1671, he found that he had been elected by the university as a supervisor of the press and bedell in civil law. Avowing to Williamson on 15 October that it was done in his absence and without his knowledge, he anticipated trouble, and, via 'Dr Wren', enlisted the support of Archbishop Sheldon. Dean John Fell of Christ Church, delegate of the press, had indeed written to Sir Leoline Jenkins expressing his disgust at the choice of 'a Cambridge man, who I hear is crazed in his head and void of all judgement' (*CSP dom.*, 1671, 523), but by 17 October Wase was able to write to Williamson that, 'the complete kindness of the university has defeated my fears and suspicions' (ibid., 529).

Wase's *Considerations Concerning Free Schools as Settled in England* was finally published in Oxford in 1678. 'Miserable is the face of any nation', he declared, 'where neither schools nor universities be frequented: no law, no safe commerce, a general ignorance and a neglect of duty both to God and man' (p. 34). He therefore proposed to increase rather than to limit the number of free schools in England and Wales, and concluded that adequate instruction should be provided for petty scholars in every parish in the land. This, he maintained, would be both socially and economically advantageous to the nation. The papers he had collected on the subject were consulted by Anthony Wood.

Wase's later publications included another dictionary, two further works on Cicero, *Aelfredi magni* (1678)—a Latin version of John Spelman's life of Alfred—and *Senarius, sive, De legibus et licentia veterum poetarum* (1687), a treatise on Greek and Latin metrics and rhythmics. Altogether his scholarship in the classical languages established him, according to John Loveday, as 'one of the most eminent Philologers which England could boast of in the last age' (Allibone, *Dict.*, 3.2595). Wase died in Oxford on 29 August 1690, and was buried in St Mary's, Oxford.

His son **Christopher Wase** (1662–1711), Church of England clergyman, matriculated from Magdalen College, Oxford, on 19 October 1677 aged fifteen, and then moved to Corpus Christi College, from which he graduated BA in 1681 and proceeded MA in 1685. From 1687 to 1690 he was vicar of Preston, near Cirencester, Gloucestershire. He returned in 1691 to Corpus Christi, serving as proctor in that year. He proceeded BD in 1694. He died, leaving his coin collection to the college, on 4 April 1711, aged forty-eight, and was buried in Corpus chapel.

RICHARD E. HODGES

Sources Venn, *Alum. Cant.* · Foster, *Alum. Oxon.* · W. Sterry, ed., *The Eton College register, 1441–1698* (1943), 352 · *CSP dom., 1668–71* · *DNB* · Allibone, *Dict.* · D. Cressy, *Education in Tudor and Stuart England* (1975)

Archives Bodl. Oxf., notebook, MS Add. b. 5 · CCC Oxf., MSS

Wase, Christopher (1662–1711). *See under* Wase, Christopher (1627–1690).

Wasey, William (1691–1757), physician, the son of William Wasey, attorney, and his wife, Bridget, was born at Brumstead, Norfolk, where he was baptized on 27 November 1691. He attended Norwich grammar school for five years, and was admitted as a pensioner at Gonville and Caius College, Cambridge, on 2 November 1708. He was a scholar of the college from 1708 to 1715, and graduated BA in 1713 and MA in 1716. He enrolled at Leiden University on 1 October 1716, but, returning to Cambridge, he graduated MD in 1723. He was admitted as a candidate of the Royal College of Physicians, London, on 23 December 1723, and as a fellow on 22 December 1724. He held the office of censor in 1731, 1736, 1739, and 1748; was named as an elect on 30 August 1746; and was consiliarius in 1749 and 1754. Following the death of James Jurin, he was elected president on 2 April 1750, and was reappointed in 1750, 1751, 1752, and 1753. He was chosen as the physician to the Westminster Hospital in 1719, but resigned in 1733, when he was one of the six physicians appointed to St George's Hospital at the first general board held on 19 October that year. He held this office until 1745. Wasey died on 1 April 1757. His library was sold by auction soon after his death by Davis, Lockyer, and Reymers.

W. W. WEBB, *rev.* CLAIRE L. NUTT

Sources Munk, *Roll* · J. Venn and others, eds., *Biographical history of Gonville and Caius College*, 1: 1349–1713 (1897) · *GM*, 1st ser., 27 (1757), 189 · records, St George's Hospital · S. C. Lawrence, *Charitable knowledge: hospital pupils and practitioners in eighteenth-century London* (1996) · *IGI*

Washbourn, John (1761–1829). *See under* Washbourn, John (1792–1847).

Washbourn, John (1792–1847), bookseller and antiquary, son of **John Washbourn** (1761–1829) and his wife, Mary Careless (*d.* 1833), was born in Gloucester on 2 May 1792. His father, a member of a family long connected with the Unitarian chapel in Gloucester, was a bookseller there in Westgate Street; born on 13 February 1761, he was mistakenly identified in the *Dictionary of National Biography* as the compiler of *Bibliotheca Glocestrensis: a collection of scarce and curious tracts relating to the county and city of Gloucester illustrative of and published during the Civil War*, published in Gloucester. The second part appeared first in 1823, but the first part, containing a historical introduction by John Webb, did not appear until 1825. This compilation was made, as the editorial preface stated, by 'John Washbourn, jun.'.

Soon after his father's death on 25 April 1829, the younger John Washbourn, who had joined his father's business as a young man, seems to have left Gloucester. He died on 12 April 1847 at 5 Stonefield Street, Islington, in his fifty-fourth year, leaving a widow and eight children.

BRIAN FRITH

Sources Unitarian chapel registers, Glos. RO · Gloucester freemen's roll, Glos. RO · *Gloucester Journal* (17 April 1847) · parish registers, Newent, Glos. RO · R. E. M. Peach, ed., *The Washbourne family* (1896) · *Bailey's British directory*, 4 vols. (1784) · R. Gell and T. Bradshaw, *The Gloucestershire directory* (1820) · *Gloucester new guide* (1802) · *Pigot & Co.'s national London and provincial new commercial directory for 1822–23* (1822) · *Pigot & Co.'s national commercial directory*, J. Pigot and Co. (1830) · d. cert.

Washbourn [Washbourne], **Thomas** (1607/8–1687), Church of England clergyman and poet, was the eldest son of John Washbourn esquire (1548/9–1634), local politician and magistrate of Wichenford, Worcestershire, and his second wife, Elenor, daughter of Richard Lygon (*d.* 1584) of Madresfield and Margaret (*née* Talbot) of Salwarpe, both in the same county. He had a younger brother and sister, five half-sisters, and five half-brothers. He entered Balliol College, Oxford, as a commoner in 1622, graduated BA in 1626, proceeded MA in 1628, was incorporated at Cambridge in 1631, and proceeded BD in 1636.

In 1639 Washbourn was presented by Charles I to the rectory of Loddington, Northamptonshire, probably through the influence either of Bishop John Towers of Peterborough, father of a close friend, William Towers, or of Dr Samuel *Fell, dean of Christ Church, Oxford, whose daughter Dorothy he married at Sunningwell, Berkshire, on 14 January that year. A son, Charles, was born to them at Loddington. In 1640 he resigned, and the following year was presented to Dumbleton rectory, Gloucestershire, probably by the lord of the manor. In 1643 he was nominated a prebendary of Gloucester Cathedral, and reportedly installed by night since the city was for parliament.

Washbourn escaped sequestration despite the fact that he was an ardent monarchist, describing Charles I's execution as 'a most inhuman unparallel'd Parricide, Regicide, I had almost said Deicide, for Kings are earths Deities, Gods pictures in a lesser form' (Washbourn, *Repairer*, 19). He deplored what he saw as the arbitrary regime and unelected legislature of the Commonwealth.

Thus in 1650 he agonized over taking the second engagement, especially as, he stated, he had five or six small children. He sent a messenger in midwinter to Dr Robert Sanderson in Lincolnshire to ask his advice about whether he was breaking his oath of allegiance if he signed, determined 'not to put the world in one scale, when my soul is in the other' (*Poems*, 38). He accepted Sanderson's argument that he might interpret it as demanding the least of him, for he remained at Dumbleton throughout the interregnum. He was deeply dismayed at the breakdown of the parochial system, but saw hardship as beneficial:

The Bush, the Church,
Affliction is the fire
Which serves not to destroy, but search
And try her gold, raising the value higher.
('The bush burning', *Poems*, 73)

He wrote many, mainly devotional, poems in the metaphysical style, circulated to his friends, which Mary, Lady Vere, persuaded him to publish as *Divine Poems* in 1654. The best show considerable merit. He did not hesitate to express his views on the current religious situation in some, with an outspokenness also evident in *A Sermon Preached at the Funerall of Charles Cocks* (1655), the lord of the manor, naïvely published to dispel talk that it attacked him.

Loyalty to crown and church was rewarded when, in 1660, Washbourn was formally installed in his prebend and also created a DD of Oxford University by chancellor's letters. He responded with *The Repairer of the Breach* (1661) preached at Gloucester Cathedral on 29 May that year to mark the king's birthday and the first anniversary of his return. From 1660 to 1668 he was vicar of St Mary de Lode, Gloucester. He died on 6 May 1687, in his eightieth year, and was buried in Gloucester Cathedral with an epitaph which, at his own insistence, described him as the greatest of sinners and the least of ministers of God.

ELIZABETH ALLEN

Sources *Poems of Thomas Washbourne*, ed. A. Grosart (1868) • T. Washbourn, *The repairer of the breach* (1661), 15–25 • R. Sanderson, *Works*, ed. W. Jacobson, 5 (1854), 21–36 • A. T. Butler, ed., *The visitation of Worcestershire, 1634*, Harleian Society, 90 (1938), 63, 100 • T. Nash, *Collections for the history of Worcestershire*, 2 (1782), 118, 459–60 • H. I. Longden, *Northamptonshire and Rutland clergy from 1500*, ed. P. I. King and others, 16 vols. in 6, Northamptonshire RS (1938–52), vol. 14, p. 187 • Peterborough institution book, Northants. RO, vol. 4, fol. 121 • *DNB* • R. Atkyns, *The ancient and present state of Glostershire*, 2 pts in 1 (1712), pt 1, pp. 406–7 • *Walker rev.*, 178 • IGI • memorial, Gloucester Cathedral

Washbrook, Cyril (1914–1999), cricketer, was born on 6 December 1914 at Barrow, near Clitheroe, Lancashire, the son of John William Washbrook, calico printer, and his wife, Sarah Everton. His father moved the family to Shropshire when Cyril was thirteen, and he attended Bridgnorth grammar school, where his cricketing skill attracted the interest of Warwickshire, Worcestershire, and Lancashire. He failed to gain a place at Birmingham University and on leaving school accepted a professional engagement with Lancashire. Although the county had many fine batsmen in the second eleven, Washbrook's class shone through, and following an unbeaten 202 against Yorkshire he won selection for the first team. In what was only his second match in 1933, when he was eighteen, he made a magnificent 152 against Surrey at Old Trafford. Five hours and twenty minutes at the crease brought him eighteen boundaries. A career was launched, and many good judges of a player predicted a long and successful career. Fifteen centuries flowed from Washbrook's bat before the Second World War, with 1000 runs in a season totalled every summer between 1935 and 1939. England's selectors recognized the 22-year-old's ability, and the first of thirty-seven caps came his way in 1937.

It was nine years before Washbrook again batted for England. He served during the war with the RAF, and on 8 February 1941 he married Marjorie Wileman (1924/5–2001), with whom he had a son. The war over, he linked up in 1946 with Yorkshire's Len Hutton, and their opening partnership was unchallenged at home and abroad for six years. They opened the England innings in thirty-one tests and eight times they achieved three-figure partnerships—twice in both innings of a match. They set a record opening partnership of 359 against South Africa at Johannesburg in 1948–9, with Washbrook's highest test score of 195. Washbrook was hugely popular with members and spectators. His approach to the game was always to give his best, whatever the situation. No bowler intimidated him, and with his cap at its usual jaunty angle he was always ready to hook, pull, and cut, usually with success. Speed over the ground, unerring pick up, and deadly throw to the top of the stumps made him a brilliant cover fielder. His anticipation of where the ball was going aided him enormously, and many run-out batsmen must have wondered how he had reached the ball so swiftly.

In 1954 the committee broke with tradition and appointed Washbrook as Lancashire's first professional captain. He said, 'I was very proud to be captain of Lancashire, but it was a position I never coveted. I enjoyed it but I'm not sure I wouldn't have been happier just to have continued opening and scoring more runs' (*The Guardian*, 1 May 1999). Two summers later and five seasons after his last appearance for England, Washbrook was recalled to the test team in unusual circumstances while he was a test selector. England's batting against the Australia eleven in 1956 had been fallible, and his fellow selectors persuaded him at forty-one to return to the international scene. When he joined Peter May, the England skipper, out on the Headingley pitch, England were 17 for three. At the close the total was 201 for four, with Washbrook 90 not out. On the following morning he was dismissed for 98. England went on to win by an innings, and then retained the Ashes in 'Laker's match' at Old Trafford. As a batsman he played the hook and square cut to perfection and excelled at driving the overpitched ball. He played exactly 500 matches for Lancashire, scoring over 34,000 runs with seventy-six centuries. He filled almost every role for the county in a sixty-year association with the club as captain, manager, committee member, and president.

Retirement beckoned at the end of summer 1959, but Washbrook was almost immediately elected to the committee. Except for a two-year break he remained on the committee until 1988, when he was elected president for the following two years. He was one of *Wisden*'s cricketers of the year in 1947, he was team manager for Lancashire in 1964, and was appointed CBE by the queen in 1991.

Washbrook's place in Lancashire history is guaranteed; he was arguably the county's finest opening batsman, and a man totally dedicated to Lancashire cricket. The opening partnerships of Washbrook and Hutton for England and with Winston Place for Lancashire have been woven into the fabric of cricket history. He died aged eighty-four on 27 April 1999 at the nursing home where he lived, Exeter House, Skaife Road, Sale, Cheshire, following a stroke, and was cremated at Bowdon the following day. There was a minute's silence at Old Trafford during the New Zealand test match to honour one of Lancashire's legends.

MALCOLM G. LORIMER

Sources *Wisden* (1933–65) · *Wisden* (2001) · Lancashire CCC yearbooks, 1933–65, 2001 · A. A. Thomson, *Hutton and Washbrook* (1967) · C. Washbrook, *Cricket: the silver lining* (1950) · *C. Washbrook testimonial brochure* (1959) · M. Lorimer and R. Cavanagh, *C. Washbrooke: his record* (1991) · *The Independent* (1 May 1999) · *The Guardian* (1 May 1999) · *Daily Telegraph* (30 April 1999) · b. cert. · m. cert. · d. cert.
Likenesses photographs, 1938–58, Hult. Arch. · photograph, repro. in *The Independent* · photograph, repro. in *The Guardian* · photograph, repro. in *Daily Telegraph*

Washingby, Joan (*d.* 1512). *See under* Lollard women (*act. c.*1390–*c.*1520).

Washington [*née* Waddell], **Catharine Marguerite Beauchamp** [Pat] (1892–1972), volunteer ambulance driver and member of the FANY, was born on 9 January 1892 at Howard Cottage, Warwick Bridge, near Wetheral, Cumberland, the only daughter and youngest of three children of Cranston Waddell (*d.* 1918), woollen manufacturer, and his wife, Catharine Beatrice Beauchamp Thompson (*d.* 1892).

Pat Waddell, as she was known, joined the First Aid Nursing Yeomanry (FANY) corps in 1912. Founded in 1907 as a uniformed female mounted ambulance unit, its members—'FANYs'—were trained in first aid, signalling, drill, camp cookery, and veterinary skills, and provided their own horses and uniform as well as paying a 10s. enrolment fee, plus 6s. monthly subscription. They went on weekend camp, appeared at the royal tournament, and were trained by the guards but their offer of service at the outbreak of the First World War was refused contemptuously by the War Office. The Belgians and French were not so dismissive and for the next four years the FANYs ran hospitals and casualty stations, and drove ambulances and supply cars for the two allies all along the western front.

On 1 January 1916 British military prejudice was finally overcome and members of the FANY became the first women to drive officially for the army. Pat Waddell went to France in 1915, where she served as a driver, transporting the dead and wounded from the casualty clearing stations, ambulance trains, and barges to hospitals or hospital ships. During the offensives the women frequently worked twenty-four-hour shifts. In May 1917, returning from convoy duty at Calais Dock, Pat Waddell's ambulance was hit by a train on an unguarded level crossing. The stretcher-bearer was killed and she herself was badly injured, losing a leg at the knee. She was evacuated to England but returned to France in 1918 after having an artificial limb fitted at her own expense—a man would have had artificial limbs (two were supplied in case of breakage) supplied free and kept in repair. Recalling the episode in her memoirs *Fanny Goes to War* (1918) she wrote that 'Despite the fact that I had done a man's job, I did not seem entitled to the care he would have had' (Waddell, 199). She received two gallantry awards: the Croix de Guerre from the French and the ordre de la reine Elizabeth from the Belgians.

After the war Pat Waddell became FANY adjutant but retired from active service to marry on 27 July 1922 Peter Washington (*b.* 1896/7), a British officer whom she had met while convalescing and who had also been badly wounded. They had two sons but the marriage did not last. At the outbreak of the Second World War, turned down for active service because of her disability, Pat was asked by the FANY to take a mobile canteen to France to serve the Free Polish Army. After the fall of France she escaped through St Malo, the canteen having been pushed over some cliffs. She was next sent to the Polish army headquarters in Edinburgh, where FANYs provided administrative support, for which they were granted permission by General Kukiel to wear Polish insignia. Pat Washington publicized the Polish struggle in *Eagles in Exile* (1943), and went to the United States to raise funds for the Poles. She was decorated by General Anders, the commander-in-chief of Polish forces, with the grand cross of merit (military class).

Pat Washington was a small, strikingly attractive woman—in old age as well as in youth. Augustus John wanted to paint her but she refused, saying that he had a bad reputation with his models (private information). In 1946 she returned to her beloved Cumberland and remained a staunch country member of the FANY until her death, from heart failure, on Christmas day 1972 at her home, Broadwath House, Heads Nook, near Wetheral. She was buried in Wetheral cemetery.

LYNETTE BEARDWOOD

Sources Duke of York's HQ, Mercury House, London, FANY archives · P. B. Waddell, *Fanny goes to war* (1918) · P. B. Washington, *Fanny went to war* (1940) · P. B. Washington, *Eagles in exile* (1943) · U. Leeds, Liddle collection · private information (2004) [Celia Washington, granddaughter] · *CGPLA Eng. & Wales* (1973) · m. cert. · d. cert.
Archives Duke of York's HQ, Mercury House, London, FANY archives · U. Leeds, Liddle collection | SOUND U. Leeds, Liddle collection [interview 1970]
Likenesses group portraits, photographs, 1913–72, Duke of York's HQ, Mercury House, London, FANY archives

Washington, George (1732–1799), revolutionary army officer and president of the United States of America, was born on 11 February 1732 at his family's plantation near Pope's Creek, Westmoreland county, Virginia, the first of six children of Augustine Washington (1694–1743), planter, and his second wife, Mary (1708/9–1789), daughter of Joseph Ball, an English emigrant and planter, and his

George Washington (1732–1799), by Gilbert Stuart, 1796
[unfinished; the 'Athenaeum portrait']

wife, Mary. His great-grandfather John Washington had moved from the family home, Sulgrave Manor, Northamptonshire, to Virginia in 1657 as a partner in a trading voyage and had settled on a plantation given to his new wife, Anne Pope, by her father, Nathaniel Pope. That region of Virginia, known as the Northern Neck, is a peninsula lying between the Potomac River and the Rappahannock River, which flow into Chesapeake Bay. Augustine Washington and his first wife, Jane Butler (1699–1729), had four children; the most important to George was the second son, Lawrence (1718–1752), who acted as a surrogate father after Augustine's death when George was eleven years old.

Early life In 1735 Augustine Washington moved his family to property he owned on Little Hunting Creek, overlooking the Potomac, later the site of the estate which Lawrence named Mount Vernon and which George subsequently acquired. Leaving Lawrence there, the rest of the family moved in 1738 to Ferry Farm on the Rappahannock near the town of Fredericksburg, where Augustine Washington's twenty slaves worked his tobacco. He had ample furnishings, china, and silverware for his six-room frame house. George received some education at home from private tutors, with an emphasis on geometry and trigonometry, later useful in surveying. One of his copybook exercises was *Rules of Civility and Decent Behavior in Company and Conversation*, maxims for correct gentlemanly bearing and conduct originally compiled in the sixteenth century.

After Augustine Washington's death in April 1743,

George divided his time, living with his mother but also visiting relatives in Westmoreland county and his half-brother Lawrence. Lawrence Washington had inherited Mount Vernon, which he named for Admiral Edward Vernon after taking part in the British expedition against Cartagena during the War of Jenkins's Ear. In 1743 Lawrence married Anne Fairfax, daughter of Colonel William Fairfax, a member of the family which had received from Charles II a vast proprietary grant of land in northern Virginia. Colonel Fairfax became another surrogate father to George, securing for him in 1744 an offer of a commission in the Royal Navy. Mary Washington, on the advice of her half-brother in England, declined to give her son permission to enter the navy.

The inheritor of the proprietary, Thomas Fairfax, sixth Lord Fairfax of Cameron, a cousin of Colonel William Fairfax, moved to Virginia in 1747. During the following year George Washington assisted a surveying party which marked lines within the grant in the Shenandoah valley. In July 1749 he received a commission as county surveyor for Culpeper county, and ran surveys in the Fairfax proprietary in Winchester county. Aged eighteen, he began to buy land as an investment, a practice he continued for many years.

Afflicted with tuberculosis, Lawrence Washington decided in September 1751 to consult a physician in Bridgetown, Barbados; George accompanied him. There George contracted smallpox, recovering after four weeks. The disease left him pockmarked, but he was thereafter immune. Lawrence sailed to Bermuda; George returned to Virginia, reaching Mount Vernon early in February 1752. Lawrence returned in June and died on 26 July. He bequeathed a life interest in Mount Vernon to his widow, Anne, who soon remarried and moved to Westmoreland county. On 17 December 1754 George Washington leased the Mount Vernon estate and house from her and her husband. The property became Washington's after her death.

Military career and the Seven Years' War Washington's military career began with his seeking one of the adjutancies of the Virginia militia with the rank of major. In 1753 he became the adjutant of the region south of the James River; in the following year he exchanged that position for the adjutancy of the Northern Neck. His first assignment came from the resident royal governor of Virginia, Lieutenant-Governor Robert Dinwiddie. The French claimed the region west of the Appalachian mountains, from Quebec to New Orleans. As British traders moved into the Ohio River valley and British colonists sought grants of land there, the governor of New France, Ange de Menneville, Marquis Du Quesne, ordered French troops to occupy the site where the Allegheny and Monongahela rivers flow together to form the Ohio (present-day Pittsburgh, Pennsylvania).

Dinwiddie, obeying orders from London, sent Washington on two missions to the French. In the first, at the end of 1753, Washington delivered to French officers a letter from Dinwiddie asserting Britain's claim to the transmontane west. With the aid of American Indian guides, Washington reached Fort Le Bœuf near Lake Erie and, after presenting the letter, endured a difficult return trek. In the second mission, during spring 1754, Washington commanded fewer than 300 militiamen, with orders to take Fort Duquesne at the confluence of the Allegheny and the Monongahela—a position already occupied by the French. He did not reach the site. After killing ten members of a detached French party in May, Washington and his men took refuge in a new fort, named Necessity, about six miles north of the Pennsylvania border. There they were surrounded by a superior force of French and allied American Indians; Washington surrendered on 4 July. By signing the capitulation, written in French, Washington acknowledged—unknowingly, he afterwards insisted—the 'Assassination' of the French officer killed earlier (*Papers*, Colonial ser., 1.165–7). These were the opening hostilities of the Seven Years' War.

In the following year the British government sent two regiments of infantry to Virginia, under the command of Major-General Edward Braddock, with orders to expel the French from Fort Duquesne. That summer Washington accompanied Braddock as an unpaid volunteer on the general's staff, anticipating that the general would reward him with, Washington wrote, 'preferment equal to my Wishes' (*Papers*, Colonial ser., 4.89). As the British column drew within an easy march of Fort Duquesne, Braddock detached 1200 men to move more rapidly. On 9 July 1755, along the Monongahela within 8 miles of the fort, this advance party walked into an ambush by 250 Frenchmen and Canadians with 640 American Indian allies. In the confused fighting, more than two-thirds of the British were killed or wounded. Washington, though on horseback and under fire, escaped injury; however, Braddock was mortally wounded, whereupon a general retreat began. Braddock died on 14 July and was buried in an unmarked grave in the road not far from the Maryland border. Others criticized Braddock for arrogance and inflexibility, but Washington blamed the defeat on the soldiers' lack of discipline, a concern which stayed with him throughout his military career.

After Braddock's defeat American Indians allied to the French attacked some of the westernmost British settlements in Virginia. Dinwiddie reconstituted Virginia's provincial regiment for the defence of the Shenandoah valley, and in autumn 1755 Washington accepted the command, with the rank of colonel. For the following three years he worked, with frequent setbacks, to recruit and retain soldiers, to secure adequate funds and supplies, to establish forts, and to claim the precedence of his rank in the British military establishment. Despite travelling to Massachusetts to meet William Shirley, commander of British forces in America, and despite his later approach to John Campbell, fourth earl of Loudoun, in Philadelphia, Washington failed in his efforts to obtain a royal commission and to have himself and his regiment incorporated into the British army. His official letters of the period were often querulous and fault-finding. He too was

criticized in Virginia both for exaggerating the danger posed by the French and the American Indians and for his inadequacies as a commander. The Virginia house of burgesses, however, twice voted him its thanks. He wished for a bold assault upon Fort Duquesne, but the position did not fall to the British until November 1758, after the French abandoned it, having lost their neighbouring American Indian allies. At the end of the year, Washington resigned.

Marriage and family life In spring 1758 Washington and Martha Custis, *née* Dandridge (1731–1802), a widow a few months his senior, agreed to marry. The ceremony took place on 6 January 1759. In July 1758 Washington won election to the house of burgesses, the colonial Virginian legislative, from Frederick county, having failed in two earlier candidacies in 1755 and 1757. The death of Martha's first husband, Daniel Parke Custis, in 1757 had provided her and her two children, John and Martha, with a sizeable inheritance of land, property, and slaves valued at £4853 14s. 1¼d. sterling, or £23,632 13s. 7½d. Virginia currency, the disposition of which George Washington directed. Marrying into this inheritance involved Washington in an already long-running suit in the court of chancery by which heirs of Daniel Parke Custis's late grandfather in Antigua, Governor Daniel Parke, tried to force Custis's estate to pay debts owed by the late governor's estate. Washington was still paying attorneys' fees fifty years after the inception of the suit.

In summer 1768 Washington's stepdaughter Martha first showed symptoms of epilepsy. She died during a seizure on 19 June 1773. Her estate, originally one-third of her late father's estate, was divided evenly between her brother and her mother. The latter half enabled George Washington to pay his debts to British merchants. John Parke Custis was often a trial to his stepfather. Frequently idle in his studies, Custis at the age of eighteen chose a wife without consulting the Washingtons. During the American War of Independence he visited the revolutionaries' headquarters at Yorktown, Virginia, where he contracted a disease which proved fatal. George Washington reached his stepson's bedside not long before he died, aged twenty-seven, on 5 November 1781.

When the Washingtons were in Virginia's colonial capital, Williamsburg, for sessions of the house of burgesses, they lived in Francis Street in a house that Martha Washington inherited from her first husband. At Mount Vernon, George Washington expanded and improved their home while their slaves and tenants cultivated tobacco on five farms, totalling about 4500 acres. Washington's land never produced tobacco of the best quality; between 1764 and 1766 he converted his crops primarily to wheat, abandoning tobacco. Though he later said that he thought slave auctions inhumane, in the 1760s he bought slaves. He owned eighty-seven in 1770. He purchased few after 1772, but the number of his slaves continued to grow by natural increase.

Washington wished to emulate successful Virginians of the early eighteenth century by enlarging his estate. In June 1767 he considered in writing:

how the greatest Estates we have in this Colony were made; Was it not by taking up & purchasing at very low rates the rich back Lands which were thought nothing of in those days, but are now the most valuable Lands we possess? Undoubtedly it was. (*Papers*, Colonial ser., 8.3)

He acquired acreage in the Shenandoah valley and along rivers flowing into the Ohio; in addition, he joined the Mississippi Company, which sought a royal grant of 2.5 million acres stretching eastwards from the Mississippi River. As an incentive to army recruits, Governor Dinwiddie in 1754 had promised to divide 200,000 acres in the Ohio valley among those who enlisted in the Virginia regiment. For twenty years Washington worked to have the promised grant surveyed and to have title to it confirmed by the British government. He induced veterans to sell their portions to him, and he secured appointment of his agent, William Crawford, as surveyor. Ultimately, Washington acquired 20,147 acres, 10 per cent of the grant.

Road to revolution Beginning in 1765, Washington represented Fairfax county in the house of burgesses. Virginia's politicians, with those of other seaboard colonies, quarrelled with governments in London—first George Grenville's and later Lord North's—about parliament's levy of new taxes on North American colonists. Washington called the stamp tax of 1765 'ill judgd' (*Papers*, Colonial ser., 7.395), and he was a leader of the burgesses' resistance to the Revenue Act of 1767. After the burgesses passed resolutions on 16 May 1769, declaring that only colonial legislatures could levy such taxes, the governor, Norborne Berkeley, fourth Baron Botetourt, dissolved the general assembly. The burgesses then met in a Williamsburg tavern, where Washington presented the text, prepared by George Mason, of an association to boycott many British goods. This stated that British taxes were designed to reduce colonists 'from a free and happy People to a wretched and miserable State of Slavery' (Van Schreeven, Scribner, and Tarter, 1.74). Agreements to curtail importation from Britain were intended to hurt British merchants and to induce them to bring about repeal of the taxes. This approach, combined with colonists' refusal to allow the law to be implemented, succeeded in the case of the stamp tax, and on 21 February 1766 a large majority in the House of Commons voted for its repeal. Washington welcomed this removal of an 'Act of Oppression' (*Papers*, Colonial ser., 8.15). The taxes in the Revenue Act of 1767, except the duty on tea, were repealed on 12 April 1770.

Events in 1774 brought Washington to prominence among those willing to defy the government in London. In the spring of that year parliament, responding to defiance of the Tea Act of 1773 (expressed most notably in Boston's Tea Party), enacted punitive laws to close that town's port, change the government of Massachusetts, revise operations of courts, and allow army officers to quarter soldiers on property owned by colonists. Such a direct attack on colonial self-government alarmed the political leaders of other colonies; they agreed to convene in Philadelphia what they called a continental congress. Virginia legislators met in an extra-legal session, identifying themselves as the Virginia convention, and elected seven delegates,

including Washington, to the congress. In August he wrote that parliament was 'trampling upon the Valuable Rights of Americans' and that 'we must assert our Rights, or Submit to every Imposition that can be heap'd upon us; till custom and use, will make us as tame, & abject Slaves, as the Blacks we Rule over with such arbitrary Sway' (*Papers*, Colonial ser., 10.155). He believed that the British government had formed 'a regular Systematick Plan' to break down American resistance and that only the colonies' unanimity and firmness could defeat the British intent to rule the 'Colonies with a high hand' (ibid., 10.156). The continental congress met during September and October 1774 and adopted a statement of the colonies' rights, with a list of grievances, attacking parliament's assertion of an authority to raise revenue in America and denouncing the recent coercive legislation. The delegates set dates for ending all trade with Britain as a means to force repeal of the objectionable measures. They discussed possible forms of political union among the colonies.

Before returning to Philadelphia in May 1775 for a second continental congress, Washington spent six months at Mount Vernon. During this period a campaign of preparation for forcible resistance spread through the thirteen colonies. Volunteer companies and militia units drilled, paraded, and armed themselves. Washington supervised the training of Fairfax county's volunteers and lent money to the county for the purchase of ammunition. At the same time Lord North's ministry augmented the army and Royal Navy, sending larger forces to North America. Fighting between a detachment of British troops and Massachusetts militiamen began on 19 April at Lexington. The militia soon surrounded British forces in Boston and began a siege. Word of the outbreak of combat reached Virginia before Washington left for Philadelphia.

In June the second continental congress, in response to a request from Massachusetts, adopted the troops around Boston as the continental army and summoned men from other colonies to strengthen it. On 15 June congress chose Washington as its general and commander-in-chief. Although his nomination encountered opposition and debate, his status as the chief military man from the most populous colony made his final, unanimous selection predictable. He wrote to his wife three days later: 'I was apprehensive I could not avoid this appointment' (*Papers*, Revolutionary War ser., 1.4). He took command of the army outside Boston on 3 July.

Commander-in-chief Throughout his eight years and six months as commander-in-chief, Washington strove to make his army resemble as much as possible a regular, professional, European army in administration, discipline, and combat. He argued that he and his men were serving in a 'glorious Cause' (*Papers*, Revolutionary War ser., 1.1), and he relied in large measure, especially after congress declared the independence of the United States in July 1776, on soldiers' patriotism for the cohesion and perseverance of the army during many hardships. All the while his military ideal was an army whose operations were as smooth and orderly as clockwork. From his first weeks near Boston, when he could not obtain accurate reports of how many men he had, until the disbandment of the army in November 1783, when he could not give soldiers the pay due them, Washington never fully attained in practice his vision of an efficiently functioning continental army. Keeping the army intact, rebuilding parts of it after defeat, and sustaining its ability to contest British occupation of sections of the seaboard were the chief military achievements of Washington and his soldiers.

Not until 1777 did congress authorize enlisting soldiers for a term of three years or the duration of the war. In the first two years Washington had to devote much attention to finding replacements for soldiers and militiamen whose short terms of service expired. In the camp outside Boston during the autumn and winter 1775–6 many who had rallied to besiege the British went home as new recruits arrived. Washington was forced to mobilize a new army, then rebuild it. At its peak, later in the war, the continental army in all its detachments numbered about 35,000. Washington never commanded in person more than about one-third of that number.

In March 1776 William Howe, commander of British forces in Boston since October 1775, evacuated the city. In the following month he was made commander-in-chief of the British army in the thirteen rebellious colonies. Howe and his army, eventually numbering 30,000, attacked New York city and its environs in the summer. During the last six months of 1776 Washington experienced a series of reverses and losses of men. Defeated on Long Island on 27 August, he withdrew to Manhattan Island, where he unwisely tried to hold a fortified position, in which he left 2600 men, captured by the British on 16 November. Washington retreated into New Jersey. He had operated under many difficulties in New York, including inferior numbers and poorly trained soldiers, but he had contributed to his defeats by dispersing his forces, by leaving his army open to flank attacks, and by trying to hold indefensible positions. Howe's critics at the time and later said that a more aggressive British campaign would have crushed Washington's army.

Washington's units in New Jersey were scattered. About 3000 men were with him as he retreated across the Delaware River into Pennsylvania on 7 December. Posting detachments at several points in New Jersey, including Trenton on the Delaware, Howe announced that his army would go into winter encampment. In a private letter Washington wrote that if recruitment of a new army in 1777 failed, 'I think the game will be pretty well up' (*Papers*, Revolutionary War ser., 7.291). Far from despondent, however, the commander-in-chief decided on a surprise counter-attack. On 25 and 26 December he recrossed the Delaware with more than 2000 men and attacked the garrison at Trenton—comprising 1200 Hessians from among the German auxiliaries hired by the crown. He captured the bulk of the garrison without losing any of his men. In the next week by a surprise march he expelled the British from Princeton. Howe withdrew from his most advanced positions in New Jersey, and the Americans went into winter encampment at Morristown. Though fought by small

units with few casualties, these engagements had great importance, restoring public confidence in the continental army, in Washington, and in the prospects for success.

During 1777 Washington began to build a more reliable, longer-serving army. In that year the British mounted two separate, unco-ordinated offensives. One, under Major-General John Burgoyne, advanced southwards from Canada towards New York city along the Lake Champlain–Hudson River route. In the other, Howe took 15,000 men by transport vessels to the head of Chesapeake Bay and marched against the American capital, Philadelphia. Burgoyne encountered Major-General Horatio Gates, commanding the continental army of the northern department and its militia auxiliaries. Washington confronted Howe with about 11,000 men, a number which fell to 6000 during autumn operations. As in the New York campaign of 1776, Howe outflanked Washington in the battle of Brandywine (11 September 1777) and outmanoeuvred Washington's efforts to cover Philadelphia. The city fell to the British on 26 September. An audacious American attack on a detachment of Howe's army at Germantown (4 October) relied upon Washington's overly complex, synchronized night-time advance from different directions; it ended in a rout of the Americans. By this date Burgoyne's invasion had reached Saratoga, New York, where his army was surrounded. He surrendered on 17 October.

Howe's army spent the winter of 1777–8 in Philadelphia. Having asked the ministry to relieve him of command, he awaited his successor. Washington's army camped in huts at Valley Forge, Pennsylvania, 20 miles from Philadelphia. In late autumn and early winter he received reports which led him to believe that criticisms in congress of his 1777 campaign were an attempt by certain members to remove him from command and replace him with, perhaps, Horatio Gates. However, few modern historians have concluded that the recriminations and private censure amounted to a concerted attack on Washington's position as commander-in-chief. Throughout his life Washington reacted angrily to criticism, and in this instance he sought to expose the supposed machinations. In effect he demanded from congress a statement of its confidence in him. He emerged from the episode strengthened in his role as the most important leader of the movement for American independence.

Although the winter was not severe, many soldiers at Valley Forge suffered from intermittent shortages of food and clothing, consequences not only of logistical and financial difficulties but also of misjudgement and maladministration in congress and the army, compounded by corruption among suppliers. Soldiers' willingness to stay with Washington under these conditions, while receiving little or no pay, became a story central to the army's pride, tradition, and future cohesion. In March 1778 Washington began a programme of drill, training, and discipline, led by a Prussian officer, Friedrich Wilhelm von Steuben. Since the continental soldiers were veterans of combat who had seen the consequences of inadequate co-operation on the battlefield, Steuben and his deputies were able to convince them of the advantages of conforming to conventional methods of march, manoeuvre, and engagement. The success of this training was first demonstrated in the battle of Monmouth, New Jersey, on 28 June 1778. Sir Henry Clinton, commander of British forces, marched from Philadelphia towards New York city. The engagement was inconclusive, but it demonstrated the continental army soldiers' improved ability to encounter British regulars. This was the last significant battle of the war to take place north of Virginia.

Later conflict and victory British forces launched no significant offensives for eighteen months after Clinton's withdrawal to New York. Even amid Washington's mistakes and reverses on the battlefield in 1776 and 1777, he had revealed a preference for audacity and for aggressive engagement of the enemy. The numbers and effectiveness of the British army, as well as the continental army's many difficulties, forced upon him a Fabian strategy: he kept his army intact, fought occasional skirmishes, and covered the countryside beyond British lines. Washington outlasted the British war effort. He was aided by other impediments to British success. The North ministry found the war expensive and, concerned about other theatres of conflict with France and Spain, was unable to send adequate numbers of soldiers to America as replacements for casualties and prisoners. Furthermore, the American militia and local governments usually suppressed Americans loyal to the crown by intimidation and violence. Thus the British, despite having occupied every important American city at some time in the war, never established effective control beyond the lines of their army.

This difficulty became more apparent when Sir Henry Clinton, urged on by the ministry, began a campaign in South Carolina, expecting to rally widespread loyalist support. He led it in person until the capture of Charles Town (12 May 1780), where the British took more than 2500 continental soldiers prisoner. Thereafter operations in the southern states were led by Lieutenant-General Charles Cornwallis, second Earl Cornwallis. Congress, rather than Washington, appointed Horatio Gates commander of the southern department. After Gates's defeat by the British at Camden (16 August 1780), the rebuilt continental force in the south was commanded by Washington's trusted and chosen subordinate, Major-General Nathanael Greene, beginning on 14 October 1780. Although unable to defeat Cornwallis in battle, Greene's army rendered British operations in South and North Carolina ineffective in holding the region. A civil war between loyalists and revolutionaries further thwarted Clinton's plan. In May 1781 Cornwallis abandoned the original strategy and marched northwards into Virginia.

As Washington inspected American fortifications along the Hudson River, he learned on 25 September 1780 that Major-General Benedict Arnold, commander of the most important post, West Point, was in the pay of the British and had agreed to British seizure of the fort. The plot was revealed with the capture behind American lines of Sir Henry Clinton's aide, Major John André, while carrying incriminating papers and dressed in civilian clothes.

Arnold fled to New York city, where Clinton commissioned him brigadier-general. André was condemned as a spy, then hanged on 2 October 1780. Washington declined to pardon him or to allow military execution by firing squad. In the didactic moral lessons drawn from the War of Independence by American writers, Arnold became the antithesis of Washington—Arnold the epitome of treason, Washington the paragon of patriotism.

From an early point in the war the French government, through intermediaries, had assisted the Americans. The defeat of Burgoyne at Saratoga and the resilience of Washington's army helped convince the French to recognize the independence of the United States in treaties signed on 6 February 1778 and to provide more financial assistance, as well as the overt aid of the French army and navy. Rejecting a British peace overture early in 1778, the continental congress ratified the French alliance on 4 May.

Co-operation between French and American forces near New York city in 1778 and 1779 achieved little. The arrival of 5500 French soldiers at Rhode Island in July 1780, under the command of Lieutenant-General Jean Baptiste Donatien de Vimeur, comte de Rochambeau, made possible combined infantry operations against the British. Washington and Rochambeau worked together but could not threaten the British position in New York without the aid of a large naval force. In August 1781 Washington learned that Rear-Admiral François Joseph Paul, comte de Grasse, would bring twenty-nine warships and 3000 soldiers to Chesapeake Bay to co-operate in capturing Cornwallis's army. Washington now abandoned his plan to take New York city, and with 4000 French and 2500 American soldiers marched for Virginia. They arrived at the northern end of Chesapeake Bay on 5 September, the day that de Grasse prevented Rear-Admiral Thomas Graves and the British fleet from entering Chesapeake Bay.

After Cornwallis moved his force of more than 9000 men into Virginia, he received conflicting orders from Sir Henry Clinton and from the ministry in London. In both cases, however, he was to occupy a defensible position accessible to the Royal Navy. He chose Yorktown on the York River and Gloucester on the opposite bank. His army was fortified there on 22 August 1781. Four days later de Grasse arrived off the Virginia coast. Washington and Rochambeau, joined by other continental army units, militia, and augmented French forces, began to encircle the defences of Yorktown on 28 September. Negotiations for Cornwallis's surrender began on 17 October. The North ministry fell in March 1782, and the king's speech at the opening of the December session of parliament acknowledged that the treaty of peace must recognize the independence of the United States.

Washington continued as commander-in-chief until after the withdrawal from New York of the last British forces, under the command of Lieutenant-General Guy Carleton, on 25 November 1783. In March of that year Washington single-handedly quelled a disturbance among some of his officers in the camp at Newburgh, New

York. Proposals were circulated, suggesting that the officers make threats to congress in order to secure arrears of pay and a promised pension. Washington's meeting with the officers on 15 March and his denunciation of the proposals ended the agitation. In December Washington travelled to Annapolis, Maryland, where congress was meeting, and returned his commission as commander-in-chief on 23 December. This ceremony loomed large in his subsequent reputation. Although his army had already disbanded, his voluntary surrender of his command nevertheless established him in the minds of Americans as a citizen general, respectful towards civilian authority, happy to return to his former life at war's end, unlike tyrants of the past who had used their victorious armies to impose dictatorships.

Washington had agreed on 19 June 1783 to serve as president-general of the newly created Society of the Cincinnati, a hereditary order of former continental army officers, officers of Rochambeau's army, and their eldest male descendants. Many Americans censured the organization as a group of crypto-aristocrats, who might subvert republican institutions by creating a nobility. At a general meeting on 5 May 1784 Washington agitatedly told the members in a long speech that the society must accommodate itself to public opinion or he would resign. The society survived by avoiding publicity. Washington remained its leader until his death.

Civilian life Upon his return to Mount Vernon at the end of 1783, Washington wrote: 'I am not only retired from all public employments, but I am retireing within myself; & shall be able to view the solitary walk, & tread the paths of private life with heartfelt satisfaction' (*Papers*, Confederation ser., 1.88). His house, which he continued to expand, needed work. He had decided during the war that he wished to 'get quit of Negroes' (*Writings*, 12.328); rather he now preferred that his land be farmed by tenants or contract labour. Yet he also became 'principled agt. selling negros, as you would do cattle in the market' (ibid., 34.47). He remained a slaveholder; had he ceased to be one, he still would have supervised his wife's slaves, and ties of marriage and children closely connected the two groups of blacks—ties that Washington did not wish to sunder. He was a demanding master; as did other slaveholders, he complained about the delinquencies of his white overseers and the malingering of his slaves, who would not work as hard as he wished. Other evidence of his assiduousness includes a 680 mile round trip which he made in September 1784 to inspect some of his land near the Ohio River. He began litigation, which he later won, to expel people who had settled on his property and had built houses and barns. He eventually owned about 45,000 acres in the present-day states of West Virginia, Pennsylvania, Ohio, and Kentucky.

Washington was especially preoccupied with the commercial and political future of the trans-Appalachian west. Migration to the region swelled after the war. He feared that, unless convenient channels of trade linked the Ohio valley with the eastern seaboard, people in the west would look to the Mississippi River, the mouth of which was in the hands of Spain, and contemplate political separatism. He thought that the Potomac could become the main channel of trade if a canal bypassed the falls 20 miles upriver from Mount Vernon and if improvements in the river bed brought the navigable extent of the upper Potomac within 20 or 30 miles of the tributaries of the Ohio. Virginians had begun such plans before the war, and Washington was among the most eager proponents of their renewed efforts. He was a director of the Potomac Company, which undertook the canal. A similar design was formed for the James River, with plans for another canal to connect Albemarle Sound in North Carolina with the Elizabeth River and the port of Norfolk, Virginia. 'The Mind can scarcely take in at one view all the benefits which will result therefrom', he wrote with regard to the proposal (*Papers*, Confederation ser., 3.420). None of these enterprises reached fruition during his lifetime.

Becoming president To American politicians of the era of the revolution, the union of the thirteen states and the survival of republican institutions had no assurance of permanence. George Washington was one of the prominent men in the 1780s who concluded that the continental congress, operating under the wartime articles of confederation, was inadequate. It lacked power to tax or coerce; state governments were able to ignore its mandates, a few delegates could forestall important legislation, and a single state could prevent congress from expanding its powers. Washington joined those who wished to adopt a new United States constitution. In May 1787 he travelled to Philadelphia for the convention to draft the constitution and he presided over its deliberations until it concluded its work on 17 September. The new government was to take effect as soon as special conventions ratified it in nine states. Virginia's did so on 25 June 1788. Washington often expressed his wish that all states would join the new union. Conversations at Mount Vernon touched on demagogues winning power in state elections, on the powerlessness of the old continental congress, and on the danger of anarchy and civil war in the absence of a stronger government.

One feature of the new federal institutions was an executive branch headed by a chief executive, the president of the United States, to be chosen by electors who were in turn chosen by the states. This office was an innovation, since state legislatures and, before the revolution, colonial legislatures had curtailed executive power, which they associated with the government in London and with threats to liberty. The constitution gave the president control of foreign relations, as well as the power to appoint diplomats, federal judges, and other federal officials; the office-holder was also to be commander-in-chief of the armed forces and to serve a four-year term with no restrictions on re-election.

Those who designed this office at the constitutional convention foresaw that Washington would be its first incumbent. He was elected unanimously on 4 February 1789, with John Adams as vice-president. The votes became official when the new congress convened in New York city in

April and counted them formally. Washington travelled to New York and took the oath of office on 30 April.

Washington had foreseen his election, and he had come to regard his acceptance of the presidency as a necessity for the successful establishment of the new government. His personal importance as a symbol of national unification appeared in his extensive travels in autumn and winter 1789–90 and spring 1791. He went as far north as Portsmouth, New Hampshire, and as far south as Savannah, Georgia. These movements, like his trip to New York in April 1789, were an almost constant series of public greetings by local officials and crowds of citizens, with ceremonial addresses, militia honour guards, parades, and music. Washington's eminence, popularity, and public services were supposed to reassure both supporters of the new constitution and critics of centralized power who had opposed ratification that the federal government was in safe hands.

In office Washington correctly anticipated that his serving as president was more likely to lessen than enhance his popularity. He would have to make decisions, especially in choosing office-holders, which would displease many people. Knowing that he would be criticized whatever his actions, he nevertheless did not meet opposition with equanimity; he interpreted it as an impugning of his motives. Early divisions were caused by the economic programme proposed by the secretary of the treasury, Washington's former aide-de-camp, Alexander Hamilton. In 1790 Hamilton submitted to congress reports with plans to fund both the national debt incurred by the late continental congress and the states' remaining wartime public debts. He further envisioned a national bank, modelled on the Bank of England, and, in December 1791, a programme of tariffs and incentives designed to encourage the growth of manufacturing in the United States. Washington took no part in drafting these proposals, but his approval was crucial to their enactment.

To Washington's secretary of state, Thomas Jefferson, and to many other Americans, Hamilton's measures looked sinister. They would enrich holders of the public debt, more than 80 per cent of whom lived in the northern states, at the disproportionate expense of people in the south. And Jefferson likened Hamilton's plans for America to the European, especially the British, polity which he thought the United States ought to eschew: urban concentrations of population, great disparities of wealth, masses of dependent wage workers, a powerful central bank making the executive less dependent upon elected representatives of the people, and discriminatory taxes by which government benefited the few at the expense of the many. Eventually critics asserted that Hamilton, Washington, and their supporters conspired to subvert republican institutions and to create a facsimile of monarchy. During his first term as president, Washington several times relied upon James Madison, a drafter and proponent of the constitution and a leader in the house of representatives, for advice and drafts of state papers. That connection ended as Washington turned more often to

Hamilton and as Madison allied with Jefferson. The opposition to Washington began to describe themselves as republicans, implying that federalists—the name originally attached to supporters of the constitution—were disloyal to republican principles. Notwithstanding their objections to the treasury programme, allies of Jefferson enabled Hamilton's provisions for the public debts to become law through an agreement that the new national capital—the District of Columbia, to replace Philadelphia in 1800—would be on the banks of the Potomac River.

Washington wished to leave the presidency at the end of his four-year term. In addition to his desire to return to Mount Vernon, he was concerned that serving a second term might suggest a sense of ambition and political careerism, in violation of the principle established by his resignation of his commission as commander-in-chief of the continental army in 1783. However, the intensifying political hostility, as well as concerns about the economy and relations with Britain and France, made Washington's continuance in office an imperative not only to Hamilton and Madison, but also to Jefferson and many others. Washington's acceptance often prompted him to look on his second administration with regret. Shortly after his re-election, reacting to newspaper criticism which portrayed him as a king who deserved the guillotine, he claimed to have 'never repented but once … having slipped the moment of resigning his office, & that was every moment since' (*Writings of Thomas Jefferson*, 1.254). While the imagery of the French Revolution offered a means to criticize Washington, actual events of 1789, followed by the European war from 1793, also provided an important stimulus to the development of political parties during Washington's presidency and to his own partisanship. The early phases of the revolution aroused sympathy in the United States. By 1793, however, the rise of the Jacobins and war on behalf of atheistic revolution alarmed many Americans, though the pro-France opinions of others remained unchanged. Washington's advisers were divided. Hamilton, for example, did not wish the United States to recognize the national assembly as the government of France. He urged Washington to proclaim neutrality in the war and to prevent Americans from aiding France. Jefferson, by contrast, recommended recognition, in the belief that the survival of republicanism in France would assure the security of republican government in the United States and the spread of liberty in Europe. Although Washington agreed to recognize the French regime, he took Hamilton's advice and asserted the president's right to proclaim the nation's neutrality, a power Jefferson wished to reserve to congress. After Washington's proclamation (22 April 1793), Jefferson's republicans denounced him for an unconstitutional aggrandizement of the executive and a betrayal of Americans' moral obligations to the French. Privately, Washington wrote of the French: 'those in whose hands the G[overnmen]t is entrusted are ready to tare each other to pieces, and will, more than probably prove the worst foes the Country has' (*Writings*, 32.450). Jefferson resigned as secretary of state at the end of the year. By August

1795 Washington's cabinet contained only federalists. Although Alexander Hamilton had stepped down as secretary of the treasury in January, he continued to wield influence with Washington and the cabinet.

One of George Washington's most controversial acts as president was to send Chief Justice John Jay to Britain to negotiate a treaty in 1794. Hamilton's plan for the public credit of the United States depended upon revenue from tariffs on imported goods, and therefore upon the continuation of trade between the United States and Britain. When Washington chose Jay as minister-plenipotentiary, Hamilton drafted Jay's instructions and privately assured the British minister in Philadelphia that the United States would not join neutral European nations in an armed threat to enforce the trading rights of neutrals. Jay's treaty secured little for the United States except continued peace with Britain, the withdrawal of British troops from posts in the far north-west of the United States, and minor trade concessions. Yet Jay acquiesced in British restrictions on neutrals' trade, gave Britain the status of most favoured nation in American ports, and closed American ports to the navies and privateers of Britain's enemies. The federalists' majority in the United States senate allowed them to ratify the treaty on 24 June 1795. Washington had hesitated to submit the document; but French diplomatic dispatches shown by the British minister convinced him that his secretary of state, Edmund Randolph, had solicited bribes from the French. Washington concluded that only the Jay treaty could forestall dangerous French influence in American politics. Republican denunciation of the treaty included abuse of the president, who was accused of usurpation and of having the aims of a tyrant. Even before this round of criticism, Jefferson had written of Washington: 'He is also extremely affected by the attacks made & kept up on him in the public papers. I think he feels those things more than any person I ever yet met with' (*Writings of Thomas Jefferson*, 6.293).

Further republican censure of Washington arose in summer 1794. Some residents of western Pennsylvania denounced the federal excise tax on privately distilled whisky, forcibly resisting its collection and stopping some federal judicial proceedings. Washington interpreted these activities not as an objection to the tax but as a product of republican attacks on his administration and of incitement by pro-France political clubs. He mobilized into federal service 13,000 militiamen from Pennsylvania, New Jersey, Maryland, and Virginia. This force marched into western Pennsylvania in November 1794, encountering no resistance. About twenty men were arrested; two were convicted of crimes and afterwards pardoned by Washington. To republicans this excessive show of force and the effort to link republican political activity with lawlessness marked Washington as a federalist partisan, a view confirmed in their minds by his support of the Jay treaty.

Early in 1796 Washington decided not to accept a third term as president. He brooded about republicans who had convinced many Americans that his administration threatened their liberties. He wrote privately: 'These things … fill my mind with much concern and with serious anxiety'. He believed that he had only a 'short time' to live, during which 'ease and retirement' were 'indispensably necessary' for both mind and body (*Writings*, 35.37). Washington published a farewell address in newspapers on 19 September 1796. He relied upon an outline written by Alexander Hamilton, incorporating elements of a draft written by James Madison in 1792, when Washington had contemplated leaving the presidency the first time. He left his readers with three admonitions: first, that the union of the states must be preserved by quelling sectional animosities; second, that political parties were dangerous, subordinating citizens to leaders of factions and thereby threatening liberty; and finally, that the interests of the United States would best be served by avoiding intense attachments or aversions to other nations. The subsequent presidential election—won by John Adams, with Thomas Jefferson, who received the second largest number of electoral votes, as vice-president—showed that Americans were not abandoning political parties. Nor did posterity follow Washington's advice on sectional antagonism or on foreign relations. This was the outcome he expected. His address, though wishing his country well, was pessimistic in tone. Of his own warnings he had little hope that 'they will make the strong and lasting impression, I could wish; that they will controul the usual current of the passions, or prevent our Nation from running the course which has hitherto marked the Destiny of Nations' (ibid., 35.236). To Washington and his contemporaries the course run by past nations had ended in decadence and dictatorship. Leaving the presidency, Washington put on record his assertion that if American history later led to that destiny, the fault was not his.

From 1791 through his years of retirement, Washington was active in establishing the new national capital, the District of Columbia, a distinct jurisdiction of 100 square miles, the site chosen by Washington and extracted from Maryland and Virginia. He owned almost 1200 acres within the district, but inclusion of this tract was not a source of profit to him. Surveys of the boundaries began in February 1791. In August the French engineer Pierre Charles L'Enfant submitted to the president a design for the city which would be named Washington—a bold scheme of radial avenues superimposed on a grid of streets. The capitol and the presidential mansion, on hills a mile apart, were to be the city's focal points and its first permanent buildings. President Washington appointed commissioners who superintended design, construction, and the sale of city lots, and on 18 September 1793 he laid the cornerstone of the capitol. The commissioners paid for the public buildings by selling real estate in the projected city to speculators who hoped to profit by resale. Fewer people bought lots than the commissioners and speculators had anticipated. Remittances were irregular, slowing construction. In his last annual message to congress, Washington repeated his recommendation that a national university be established in the capital. He saw such an institution as a force for union and as a school of republican principles. His plan was not fulfilled.

In his last year as president and in retirement Washington spent much time on repairing his home at Mount Vernon. He said that he planned to build a separate house 'for the security of my Papers of a public nature and to amuse myself in Agricultural and rural pursuits' (*Papers*, Retirement ser., 1.142). He doubted that he would ever again travel more than 20 miles from home. As he had begun to do while president, he tried to sell his western land, wishing to convert it to cash, then buy safe securities. But his prices attracted few buyers after the speculative bubble in western land collapsed in 1796.

Final years Retirement did not remove Washington from political life. After federalists passed the Alien and Sedition Acts in June and July 1798 to counteract supposed pro-France subversion, Washington censured the Virginia legislature's opposition to these laws and its challenge to the federal government's power expressed in the Virginia 'resolutions', written by James Madison and passed by the legislature in December 1798. Washington urged Patrick Henry to come out of political retirement to be a federalist candidate, and he supported the election of Virginia federalists John Marshall and Henry Lee to the United States house of representatives in 1798.

As the French government grew more openly hostile to the United States during the Adams administration, federalists allied with Alexander Hamilton anticipated war with France. Congress authorized an army of 10,000 men and a provisional force of 50,000 to be mobilized in the event of conflict. Adams invited Washington to become commander of the newly enlarged army. Washington chose its officers, and, much to Adams's displeasure, he made Alexander Hamilton senior major-general—in effect, the army's field commander. Washington took his last trip to Philadelphia at the end of 1798 to spend about a month dealing with routine military matters. Fortunately for Adams, who wished to avoid war with France, Washington did not share the eagerness of Hamilton and other federalists for war. In February 1799 Washington lent support to Adams's willingness to send a new emissary to France. Relations between the two countries turned to negotiations rather than to war.

After a sudden drop in temperature in northern Virginia on 12 and 13 December 1799, during which Washington spent several hours outdoors, he contracted a swelling of the throat and congestion of fluid in his lungs. His symptoms were consistent with a modern diagnosis of streptococcus infection. On 14 December he underwent a variety of unhelpful medical procedures, including four bleedings, a gargle, a purgative, and a laxative. From the onset of his illness he believed that it was fatal. He died in the evening, at Mount Vernon. His last words, after instructions about disposition of his body, were: "'Tis well' (*Papers*, Retirement ser., 4.551). His last action was to take his own pulse as it fell. His body was buried in the family vault at Mount Vernon on 18 December.

Washington had completed a new will on 9 July 1799. He bequeathed to his widow a life interest in all his estate. He directed that the 124 slaves belonging to him be freed upon Martha Washington's death, making provision for support of the old and infirm, with tenancy or apprenticeship for the others. The 153 slaves belonging to his wife would be inherited by her grandson, the heir-at-law of her first husband. Martha Washington died on 22 May 1802. George Washington's will ordered that his real estate other than Mount Vernon be sold, with a division of the proceeds among members of his and his wife's families. He drew up a list of his land holdings and set a value on each one. By this calculation his land was worth a little less than $500,000, or about £121,000. For tracts sold within three years of his death, his estimates proved sound. But the estate still held part of the land in the early decades of the nineteenth century, unable to find buyers at Washington's price. Washington's papers were purchased from the family by the United States government in 1834 and 1849. In 1860 the mansion and 202 acres of Mount Vernon were purchased by the Mount Vernon Ladies' Association of the Union, the organization which still owns the property.

Personality and legacy In late middle age George Washington stood 6 feet 3 inches tall; he weighed 209 pounds. He suffered from toothache and tooth decay, and experimented with a variety of false teeth. He began to use reading glasses in his forties. An able horseman, he rode to hounds and spent much of each day at Mount Vernon on horseback, visiting his farms and supervising work. He set a high value on system and method, reviewed his plans daily, and kept precise business and household accounts. He tried, not always successfully, to stay out of debt. He believed himself to be just and correct in his dealings with others. Any suggestion to the contrary made him angry and risked a harsh rebuke. Many of his letters complained about the conduct of others—subordinates, tenants, debtors, slaves, employees, business associates, public officials, merchants. He often felt aggrieved. Washington strove to maintain an even demeanour; observers described his gravity and dignity. However, he was also a man of strong feelings who sometimes lost his self-control, as in a cabinet meeting on 2 August 1793, during his second term as president of the United States: 'The Presidt was much inflamed, got into one of those passions when he cannot command himself' (*Writings of Thomas Jefferson*, 1.254). He had a dry wit—often directed at persons he deemed self-important—so subtle that people easily missed it. In a letter addressed to Nathaniel Sackett, one of his clandestine intelligence operatives during the war, he wrote in closing: 'It runs in my head that I was to corrispond with you by a fictitious name—if so I have forgot the name & must be reminded of it again' (*Papers*, Revolutionary War ser., 9.95).

Washington felt most comfortable in an active, outdoor life, concerned with tangible things such as soil, crops, horses, farm buildings, and machinery. Under the pressures of wartime command and peacetime public office, one of his chief diversions was to make detailed plans for improvements at Mount Vernon. He maintained a correspondence with Arthur Young, the British writer on agriculture. In the tradition of hospitality, Washington and his wife entertained at Mount Vernon not only invited guests but also strangers who appeared at the door in growing numbers after the war. In 1787 he likened his house to 'a well resorted tavern' (*Papers*, Confederation ser., 5.35). Washington found the volume of his correspondence burdensome, and in 1785 he recruited a secretary, Tobias Lear. At the same time he was well aware that his personal papers were important for the history of the United States and for his posthumous reputation. In addition to his plans for a new property to house his work, in later life he revised copies of letters in his letter-books from the 1750s to enhance their seriousness of tone and to improve his prose.

Washington was a communicant of the Church of England (and later of the American Episcopal church). As was customary for men of his social standing, he served as a vestryman, but he was not assiduous in attending church. He was also a freemason and an avid theatregoer. He received the honorary degree of doctor of laws from Harvard College in April 1776 and from Yale College in April 1781. From 16 January 1788 until his death he held the honorary post of chancellor of the College of William and Mary.

George Washington always paid close attention to his stature in the eyes of the public—first in Virginia, then in the whole of America. In his thirties he engaged in some sharp practices while acquiring land; in his sixties he became more partisan amid American political rivalries. Yet he saw himself and wished to be seen as a man of unquestioned probity and disinterested patriotism. Even American politicians who had a more complex view of Washington, such as Thomas Jefferson, understood the importance of Washington's public reputation in sustaining and validating the war for American independence and the new national government. 'He was', wrote Jefferson after Washington's death, 'in every sense of the words, a wise, a good, and a great man' (*Writings of Thomas Jefferson*, 9.448).

Many shared Jefferson's assessment. In late December 1799 and in January 1800 speeches, sermons, and public writings throughout the United States eulogized George Washington. The most often quoted words were spoken by Henry Lee in his oration before members of congress: 'First in war, first in peace, first in the hearts of his countrymen, he was second to none in the humble and endearing scenes of private life' (H. Lee, *A Funeral Oration on the Death of General Washington*, 1800, 19). Washington's enjoyment of private life, his readiness to return to it, his professed preference for it exalted him in the esteem of advocates of liberty. Robert Burns, William Blake, and Lord Byron wrote verses contrasting him with men of imperial ambition. In Francis Bailey's *Lancaster* [Pennsylvania] *Almanac for 1779* (1778) he was first hailed as the father of his country. Public celebration of his birthday began as early as 1779; for almost 200 years the day was a national holiday in the United States, a distinction shared by only one other president. For many years a portrait of Washington was a fixture in school classrooms. When the southern states attempted in 1861–5 to establish an independent Confederate States of America, they placed an image of George Washington on their new great seal as a symbolic assertion that they were the true heirs of the American revolution. Likenesses of Washington have been ubiquitous in American life—on postage stamps, coins, currency, and in many other forms. The capital city of the United States, one of the fifty states, thirty-one counties, and many towns, neighbourhoods, natural features, and institutions bear the name of Washington.

In the nineteenth century the life of Washington attracted such biographers as John Marshall (1804–7) and Washington Irving (1855–9), while Jared Sparks published a twelve-volume edition of Washington's papers (1834–7). However, the work which exerted the most widespread influence on Americans' conception of Washington was *A History, of the Life and Death, Virtues, and Exploits of General George Washington* (1800) by the Revd Mason Locke Weems which went through many printings and was regularly adapted for schoolbooks. Weems's depiction, which included fictitious episodes and imagined dialogue, presented Washington as an exemplar of private virtue and public patriotism, inviting emulation by subsequent generations, who inherited the duty to preserve the republic.

In the twentieth century scholarly historians, following the example of Charles A. Beard's *An Economic Interpretation of the Constitution of the United States* (1913), turned their attention to Washington as a man of his time and place rather than as a unique leader and patriot. His land speculation, political ambition, slaveholder's practices, conduct towards American Indians, and federalist politics received scrutiny. At the same time the most knowledgeable writers of the second half of the twentieth century continued to stress the distinctive importance of Washington's public service, as well as his uncommon gravity, courage, and sound judgement under many trying circumstances. Most books about him published during these years were narrative biographies, specialized topical monographs, or studies of Washington as an icon in American political or popular culture. Some popular writers tried to accommodate George Washington to the more egalitarian ethos of the twentieth century, as in Maxwell Anderson's play *Valley Forge* (1934). However, efforts to present Washington as a familiar, accessible figure largely failed. A story about Washington's 'reserved and aristocratic' demeanour—first published late in the nineteenth century, though surely as fictitious as Anderson's play—summarized the impression of Washington which has endured. At the constitutional convention in 1787 one of the delegates, Gouverneur Morris, to win a bet, supposedly shook Washington's hand while clapping him on the shoulder with the left hand and telling him that he looked well. 'Washington withdrew his hand, stepped suddenly back, fixed his eye on Morris for several minutes with an angry frown, until the latter retreated abashed, and sought refuge in the crowd' (J. Parton, *Life of Thomas Jefferson*, 1874, 369). Though praised for his domestic virtues, Washington, to posterity, was primarily a general, a president, and, in those capacities, the most important founder of his nation.   CHARLES ROYSTER

Sources D. S. Freeman, *George Washington*, completed by J. A. Carroll and M. W. Ashworth, 7 vols. (1948–57) · *The papers of George Washington*, ed. W. W. Abbot and others, [38 vols.] (1983–) [in 5 ser.: Colonial, Revolutionary War, Confederation, Presidential, and Retirement] · *The writings of George Washington*, ed. J. C. Fitzpatrick, 39 vols. (1931–44) · J. E. Ferling, *The first of men: a life of George Washington* (1988) · J. T. Flexner, *George Washington*, 4 vols. (1965–72) · G. Wills, *Cincinnatus: George Washington and the Enlightenment* (1984) · M. Cunliffe, *George Washington: man and monument*, rev. 2nd edn (1982) · D. Higginbotham, ed., *George Washington reconsidered* (2001) · C. Ward, *The war of the revolution*, ed. J. R. Alden, 2 vols. (1952) · P. Mackesy, *The war for America, 1775–1783* (1964) · C. Royster, *A revolutionary people at war* (1979) · C. Royster, *The fabulous history of the Dismal Swamp Company: a story of George Washington's times* (1999) · F. McDonald, *The presidency of George Washington* (1974) · D. R. McCoy, *The elusive republic: political economy in Jeffersonian America* (1980) · S. Elkins and E. McKitrick, *The age of federalism: the early American republic, 1788–1800* (1993) · R. F. Dalzell and L. B. Dalzell, *George Washington's Mount Vernon* (1998) · E. E. Prussing, *The estate of George Washington, deceased* (1927) · F. Hirschfeld, *George Washington and slavery: a documentary portrayal* (1997) · H. M. Scott, *British foreign policy in the age of the American revolution* (1990) · P. D. G. Thomas, *The Townshend duties crisis: the second phase of the American Revolution, 1767–1773* (1987) · W. J. Van Schreeven, R. L. Scribner, and B. Tarter, eds., *Revolutionary Virginia: the road to independence*, 7 vols. (1973–83) · S. E. Morison, 'The young man Washington', *By land and by sea* (1951), 161–80 · J. C. Fitzpatrick, 'Washington, George', *DAB* · F. McDonald, 'Washington, George', *ANB* · *The writings of Thomas Jefferson*, ed. P. L. Ford, 10 vols. (1892–9)
Archives BL, agricultural memoranda, Add. MS 11663B · Hunt. L. · L. Cong., papers · National Archives and Records Administration, Washington, DC · PRO, corresp. with British commanders-in-chief in America, PRO 30/55 · PRO, letters to various friends of the American cause, WO34 · U. Mich., Clements L. · Virginia Historical Society, Richmond · Wellcome L., papers | BL, letters to Henry Bouquet, Add. MS 21641 · BL, letters to Sir John Sinclair, Add. MS 5757 · NRA, priv. coll., corresp. with eighth Lord Fairfax · Westminster College, Cambridge, Cheshunt Foundation, letters to Selina, countess of Huntingdon
Likenesses C. W. Peale, oils, 1772, Washington and Lee University, Lexington, Virginia · C. W. Peale, oils, 1783, Princeton University, New Jersey · J.-A. Houdon, clay bust, 1785, Mount Vernon, Fairfax County, Virginia · J.-A. Houdon, marble statue, 1786, State Capitol, Richmond, Virginia · C. W. Peale, oils, 1787, Pennsylvania Academy of the Fine Arts, Philadelphia · T. Holloway, line engraving, pubd 1794, NPG · R. Peale, oils, 1796, Detroit Institute of Arts, Michigan · G. Stuart, oils, 1796, Smithsonian Institution, Washington, DC, National Portrait Gallery [*see illus.*] · line engraving, pubd 1799, NPG · stipple, pubd 1828 (after G. Stuart), NPG · A. H. Kernoff, three pencil drawings, 1939, NG Ire. · portraits, repro. in G. Eisen, *Portraits of Washington* (1932)
Wealth at death schedule of property (real estate, stocks, bonds) was $530,000; other property (incl. Mount Vernon, household possessions, but excl. slaves) was $250,000: Dalzell and Dalzell, *George Washington's Mount Vernon*, chap. 10; Prussing, *The estate*

Washington, John (1800–1863), naval officer and hydrographer, entered the navy in May 1812 on the frigate *Juno*, in which he served on the operations in the Chesapeake. In October 1813 he was moved into the *Sybille*, then in November 1814 he joined the Royal Naval College, Portsmouth, from which he passed out in May 1816 with the gold medal for mathematics. He then served for three years in the *Forth* on the North American station, and afterwards in the *Vengeur* and the *Superb* on the South American station, where he was promoted lieutenant on 1 January 1821. He was then at Valparaiso, and gained permission to return to England by an adventurous journey across the Andes and the pampas to Buenos Aires.

In February 1823 Washington was appointed to the sloop *Parthian* in the West Indies, after which he was for two years on half pay, and travelled in France, Spain, and Italy, improving his knowledge of their languages. In May 1827 he was appointed to the *Weazle* in the Mediterranean, and in December was moved to the frigate *Dartmouth*, returning to England in the following spring. During this time he obtained leave, and travelled in Morocco with John Drummond-Hay, and determined several positions by astronomical observations. From 1830 to 1833 he was flag lieutenant to Sir John Poo Beresford, commander-in-chief at the Nore, and on 14 August 1833 was promoted commander. On 3 September 1833 he married Eleonora, youngest daughter of the Revd H. Askew, rector of Greystoke, Cumberland. They had three sons.

From 1836 to 1841 Washington was secretary of the Royal Geographical Society, of which he was one of the original members. With one clerk, he did the whole work of the society, the early success of which was largely due to his energy. In March 1841 he was appointed to the steamer *Shearwater*, for surveying work on the east coast of England, and in January 1842 was temporarily lent to the yacht *Black Eagle*, appointed to bring the king of Prussia to England. In compliment to the king, Washington was made captain on 16 March. In January 1843 he was moved to the steamer *Blazer*, in which he continued the survey of the east coast until 1847. In January 1845 he was also appointed a commissioner for inquiring into the state of the rivers, shores, and harbours of the United Kingdom, and in February was elected FRS. Afterwards he was employed in the railway and harbour department of the Admiralty; in 1853, making a visit to Denmark, Sweden, and Russia to investigate a new type of lifeboat, he was directed by Sir James Graham, then first lord of the Admiralty, to obtain information on the Russian Baltic fleet and the defences of Kronstadt, Reval, and Sveaborg. Surprisingly, he was given full facilities by the Russians, including witnessing their fleet manoeuvres, and returned impressed by the strength of the Russian defences. He became assistant to Sir Francis Beaufort the hydrographer in 1854, and on Beaufort's resignation in 1855 Washington was appointed his successor. He held this office until his death, having been promoted to the rank of rear-admiral on 12 April 1862.

Under the pressure of the Crimean War, Washington managed to gain necessary increases in staff in the hydrographic office. He was less successful in moving the office from the unsalubrious attics of the Admiralty, and his recommendation to abolish the separate class of masters was unpopular ashore and afloat. Several ship casualties attributed, wrongly except in one case, to shortcomings in the hydrographer's department preyed on his sensitive nature. The last straw came when his second son, on return from the China station, was almost immediately sent abroad again despite Washington's pleas to the contrary. Washington became seriously ill and, on his way home from a short visit to Switzerland, died of 'nervous ailments' on 16 September 1863 at Le Havre; he was buried on 19 September in the protestant cemetery there. His wife survived him.   J. K. LAUGHTON, *rev.* R. O. MORRIS

Sources *The Times* (23 Sept 1863) · L. S. Dawson, *Memoirs of hydrography* (1885); repr. (1969) · A. Day, *The admiralty hydrographic service, 1795–1919* (1967) · G. S. Ritchie, *The Admiralty chart: British naval hydrography in the nineteenth century*, new edn (1995) · *Journal of the Royal Geographical Society*, 34 (1863), 112 · O'Byrne, *Naval biog. dict.* · *CGPLA Eng. & Wales* (1863)
Archives Hydrographic Office, Taunton · RGS, travel journals | Bodl. RH, corresp. with Sir T. F. Buxton · NRA, priv. coll., letters from David Livingstone · RGS, letters to James Brant · RGS, letters to RGS
Likenesses photograph, Hydrographic Office, Taunton
Wealth at death under £12,000: resworn probate, Jan 1865, *CGPLA Eng. & Wales* (1863)

Wasse, Joseph (*bap.* **1671**, *d.* **1738**), Church of England clergyman and classical scholar, was baptized on 19 March 1671 at Hawnby, Yorkshire, the son of Thomas Wasse. He entered Queens' College, Cambridge, as a sizar in 1691, and graduated BA in 1694. Thereafter he became a clerk, scholar, and fellow of the college, and graduated MA (1698) and BD (1707). He assisted Ludolph Küster in his edition of *Suidas* (1705), and in 1710 published a critical edition of Sallust, based on an examination of nearly eighty manuscripts. In 1711 he was presented to the rectory of Aynho, Northamptonshire, by Thomas Cartwright, with whom he was on intimate terms. He passed most of his time in his library at Aynho, and, according to William Whiston, Richard Bentley pronounced him the second scholar in England.

Wasse contributed extensively to Samuel Jebb's *Bibliotheca literaria*; according to the printer William Bowyer the elder, the length of Wasse's articles ruined that venture. He became a proselyte to Samuel Clarke's Arian opinions, and in 1719 published *Reformed Devotions*, dedicated to Thomas Cartwright and his wife. In 1731 there appeared at Amsterdam a fine edition of Thucydides by Wasse and Charles Andrew Duker; this was reprinted at Glasgow in 1759 with the Latin version by Robert and Andrew Foulis. The original notes contained in the book are not of great value, and compare unfavourably with the Sallust. In addition to his classical scholarship Wasse contributed scientific articles to the Royal Society's *Philosophical Transactions*.

Joseph Wasse died unmarried on 19 November 1738. In his will, proved on 6 June 1739, he left the majority of his possessions to his only brother, Matthew. Part of his library was acquired by his successor at Aynho, Francis Yarborough, afterwards principal of Brasenose College, Oxford. The books, which contain a great number of manuscript notes by Wasse, were given by Yarborough's heirs to the college. Wasse's copy of Thucydides, with many manuscript notes, is now in the Bodleian Library, Oxford.   E. C. MARCHANT, *rev.* PHILIP CARTER

Sources A. Chalmers, ed., *The general biographical dictionary*, new edn, 32 vols. (1812–17) · Nichols, *Lit. anecdotes*, 8.129, 367; 9.490 · W. Whiston, *Historical memoirs of the life of Dr Samuel Clarke* (1730) · PRO, PROB 6/114, fol. 183 [will] · IGI
Likenesses J. Richardson junior, pencil miniature, 1734–5, V&A

Wastell, John (*d. c.*1518), master mason, was probably born *c.*1460. He first appears in 1485 in Cambridge with **Simon Clerk** (*d.* 1489), then master mason of King's College chapel, in association with a contract for work on the church at Walden, Essex. Considering Clerk's great age, Wastell may have been guarantor for the completion of the contract. Wastell dined with the fellows at King's on several occasions from 1486, and by at least 1496 was master mason for King's Hall (now Trinity College), where contemporary work includes the lower facade of the present great gate. Concurrently, he probably designed the new nave for the college's town church, Great St Mary's. The elevations of St Mary's display common and unusual links with the nave of Walden church, built after Clerk's death. Between 1486 and 1490 Wastell settled in Bury St Edmunds, where Clerk had been master mason for the abbey since *c.*1445. Wastell's continued residence in Bury, and his documented role in its public life, might suggest that he succeeded Clerk as the abbey's master mason. Certainly, he received a corrody or pension from the abbey at some date after 1514.

In the early 1490s Wastell designed the central tower of Canterbury Cathedral for Archbishop John Morton (*d.* 1500), whose links with Wastell may have been established when bishop of Ely. The great tower, completed before 1509, underwent dramatic changes during construction, resulting in a doubling of its height after Easter 1494. Two years later Wastell was styled master mason for the cathedral when admitted to its monastic confraternity. By this time, essential work was required on the nave, including the strainer arches and the recasting of the eastern piers. Wastell's last contribution to the tower was the fan vault, a work of consummate beauty and strict control. It resembles closely the vaults of the eastern chapels, or New Buildings, at Peterborough Abbey, after 1496, and the tiny Redmount Chapel, Bishop's Lynn, *c.*1506 both probably attributable to Wastell on stylistic grounds.

While in Cambridge in 1506, Henry VII determined to complete the chapel of his uncle Henry VI's scheme at King's College. Before leaving the city, Henry gave a reward to John Wastell, who was presumably present. Work began in 1508 and over the next seven seasons, the antechapel was built almost from the foundations, the choir completed, the vaults made, and the exterior finished. The work is recorded in a series of fixed-term, fixed-price contracts that make clear Wastell's architectural authorship and supervisory responsibility. The elevational design for the antechapel was inherited from the work of the first master mason, **Reginald Ely** (*d.* 1471), with only minor amendments, but the awkward fit of the vault, plus alterations made to the upper sections of the choir bays completed by Clerk before 1485, make it clear that the fan vault is Wastell's alone. The close design links with Canterbury are obvious.

King's College chapel was completed in July 1515, by which time Wastell was perhaps fifty-five. His state of health may have been bad—references within several of the contracts make provision for his death or possible infirmity—and he seems to have undertaken no new major works after King's, though he designed a tomb for the duke of Norfolk in mid-1516, to be housed at Thetford Priory (lost). Other works attributable to Wastell on firm stylistic grounds include the south aisle of Great Barton church, Suffolk, c.1490, the nave of Lavenham church, after 1502 (perhaps a workshop product), St James's Church at Bury, from 1503, and the tomb of Archbishop William Warham (d. 1532), erected in Canterbury Cathedral in 1507.

Wastell had at least two sons and several daughters with his wife, who was probably called Margaret. One son, Thomas, is mentioned in the Cambridge contracts in connection with possible profit sharing in the event of his father's death. Another boy, John, apparently the architect's son, was a student of civil law at Cambridge from 1503/4—Henry VII paid his exhibition in 1506 by way of reward. Judging by his will, the younger John died in 1515, recently married but with no children. He owed money to London and Cambridge booksellers and made bequests to several known Cambridge academics plus a gift for the adornment of King's College chapel. As for his father, in 1518 a 'widow of John Wastell' was permitted to settle in Westgate (St Dunstan's), Canterbury. In the same year the architect was described in Bury records as recently dead; it is possible that he was buried at St Mary's Church, Bury. As his widow lived within the archbishop's manor, her new residence may have been arranged by Archbishop Warham.   FRANCIS WOODMAN

Sources F. Woodman, *King's College chapel* (1985) · J. Harvey and A. Oswald, *English mediaeval architects: a biographical dictionary down to 1550*, 2nd edn (1984) · F. Woodman, *The architectural history of Canterbury Cathedral* (1981) · R. Willis, *The architectural history of the University of Cambridge, and of the colleges of Cambridge and Eton*, ed. J. W. Clark, 4 vols. (1886) · R. M. Thomson, *The archives of the abbey of Bury St Edmunds*, Suffolk RS, 21 (1980) · will, May 1515, Bury wills, vii, 15v [John Wastell, presumed son] · will, Gon. & Caius Cam., muniments, box XXI, no. 18 [Reginald Ely] · will, 1 Feb 1459, records of Commissary Court of London, SHARPE, fol. 268 [John and Simon Clerk] · payments, muniments, mundum books, 1489/90, King's Cam. [Simon Clerk]
Archives King's Cam., muniments, mundum books, 1489/1490

Wastell, Simon (d. 1632), schoolmaster, was from a family originating from Wasdale, Cumberland. He entered Queen's College, Oxford, about 1580, and graduated BA on 15 March 1585. Before 18 June 1592, when his son John was baptized at All Saints' Church, Northampton, he was appointed headmaster of the free school in that town. There he acquired considerable reputation as a teacher.

In 1623 Wastell published a work based on John Shaw's *Biblii summula* (1621), entitled *A True Christians Daily Delight* (1623), dedicated to Robert Spencer, first Baron Spencer of Wormleighton (d. 1627). It was a short summary in verse of the contents of the Bible, intended for children to commit to memory. To make the task easier the stanzas began with the successive letters of the alphabet. The first edition was reprinted in 1683 under the title *The Divine Art of Memory*, with a preface by T. B., and Wastell himself issued a second enlarged edition in 1629 entitled *Microbiblion, or, The Bibles Epitome in Verse*, dedicated to Spencer's son, Sir William Spencer. The summary of the Old Testament was entirely recast, but the summary of the New Testament was merely reprinted.

On 1 July 1626 Wastell's first wife, Elizabeth, with whom he had eleven children between 1592 and 1611, was buried, and he subsequently married another Elizabeth (d. 1639). In 1631 Wastell, or more probably his son, also Simon Wastell (b. 1602), was vicar of Daventry in Northamptonshire, but resigned the living before 22 September of that year. In his will, drawn up on 19 August 1631, Wastell left a house in Gold Street, Northampton, to trustees who included the physician and author Dr James Hart, to be sold for the benefit of his surviving children, Samuel (b. 1599), Simon, Hannah (b. 1609), and Mary (b. 1611). He died at Northampton, and was buried at All Saints' Church there on 31 January 1632. Probate was granted to his widow and son Simon on 27 February.

E. I. CARLYLE, *rev.* S. E. MEALOR

Sources *Athenae Oxonienses … containing the life of Wood*, ed. P. Bliss, another edn, [1] (1848) · *STC, 1475–1640* · *Northamptonshire Notes and Queries*, 5 (1894), 116–17

Waterfield [*née* Duff Gordon], **Caroline Lucie** [Lina] (**1874–1964**), journalist and author, was born on 18 August 1874 at St Germain, France, the second and only surviving child of Sir Maurice Duff Gordon, fourth baronet (1849–1896), bon vivant, and his first wife, Frances (Fanny; c.1843–1890), widow of Seymour Ball Hughes and daughter of Henry Waterton of Woodlands, near Wakefield, Yorkshire. Lucie Duff Gordon, the author and translator, was her paternal grandmother. Baptized Caroline Lucie, but known as Lina, she spent her early years in London where her father, living well off various inheritances and involved with another woman, worked not very enthusiastically in the City. Her mother ensured that she had an intense Catholic education at the Sacred Heart Convent in Brighton and then at Sacré Cœur in Paris. Following her mother's death in 1890, she narrowly escaped becoming a nun by travelling to Florence to become the ward—as her dying mother had hoped—of her paternal aunt and uncle, Janet Ann *Ross and Henry James Ross. Coming under the influence of the remarkable Janet Ross was the turning point in Lina's life. Aunt Janet, as she was universally known, was a writer, journalist, and estate manager who in her medieval home, Poggio Gherardo, presided over one of the leading Anglo-Florentine salons. Lina thrived in this environment and co-wrote with Margaret Symonds *The Story of Perugia* (1898) and then, alone, *The Story of Assisi* (1900).

On 1 July 1902, despite the adamant and unending opposition of Aunt Janet, who feared permanent poverty for her niece, Lina married Aubrey William Waterfield (c.1872–1944), a graduate of New College, Oxford, the son of Ottiwell Charles Waterfield, the principal of Temple Grove School, East Sheen, London, and director of the Imperial Ottoman Bank. Aubrey was a painter and perfectionist who steadfastly refused to exhibit or sell his works. The early years of the marriage were a bohemian idyll as the young couple and their three children (who included (Ottiwell Henry) Gordon *Waterfield) moved between rented homes in Kent and in Italy at La Fortezza della Bru-nella, a medieval fortress above the Tuscan village of Aulla. Lina wrote *Rome and its Story* (1904) with the poet and travel writer Welbore St Clair Baddeley, *Home Life in Italy: Letters from the Apennines* (1908), both illustrated by Aubrey, and a *Concise and Practical Guide to Rome* (1905). She also began writing for the *Times Literary Supplement*.

In 1915, with Aubrey in the army, Lina Waterfield returned to Poggio Gherardo, where she worked for improved Anglo-Italian relations and helped to establish the British Institute in Florence for which she was appoin-ted OBE in 1920. After the war she and Aubrey moved per-manently back to Italy, dividing their time between La Fortezza (which they purchased), a summer camp in the Apennines, and Poggio Gherardo, in which Lina was given a life interest after the death of Aunt Janet in 1927.

Lina Waterfield began a new career in 1921 by accepting, without consulting Aubrey, an unsolicited offer to become *The Observer*'s Italian correspondent. Writing viv-idly and tellingly in *The Observer*, she also regularly sent J. L. Garvin, the paper's editor, blunt analyses of the fascist regime and of Mussolini, with whom she had consider-able contact. The more critical she was of the regime, the more strained became her relations with Garvin, who greatly admired Mussolini. Matters reached an inevitable climax over the Italo-Abyssinian war and in 1936, largely immobilized by a badly broken hip, she was dismissed from *The Observer*. Ten years later, aged seventy-one, she returned to a heavily damaged Poggio Gherardo and began filing stories for the Kemsley group, including *The Observer*'s arch-rival, the *Sunday Times*.

Waterfield's life interest in Poggio Gherardo was a mixed blessing. Its location made her *Observer* work easier but she also had to manage the 60 acre estate with its three rundown farms. Crushing succession duties and the costs of operating two medieval residences created growing financial difficulties, further exacerbated by the loss of her *Observer* income of £420 per year. By then she had turned part of the house into a boarding-school for Eng-lish girls. The Second World War meant an eventual return to England but links with Italy were retained as she worked for the political intelligence department prepar-ing a weekly newspaper for Italian prisoners of war.

Aubrey's death in 1944 intensified Lina Waterfield's desire to return to her beloved Italy. Re-established at Poggio Gherardo by early 1946, she set to work against impossible odds to rebuild her shattered estate but by 1950 had to admit defeat. The estate was sold and, after a sojourn at La Fortezza, she returned, lonely and badly dis-abled, to Eastry in east Kent. There she wrote her engaging autobiography, *Castle in Italy* (1961). She died at her home on 27 November 1964. She was cremated later that month, and the ashes were scattered.

Emotionally reserved, neglectful of her family, very hard-working but oblivious to life's mundane chores, the Edwardian Lina was an uncanny echo of that great Victor-ian, Aunt Janet. JOHN O. STUBBS

Sources L. Waterfield, *Castle in Italy: an autobiography* (1961) · K. Beevor, *A Tuscan childhood* (1995) · *The Times* (28 Nov 1964), 10e · Ransom HRC, J. L. Garvin MSS · British Institute, Florence, Lina Waterfield MSS · *Letters from Egypt (1862–1869) by Lady Duff Gordon*, ed. G. Waterfield (1969) · J. Stubbs, 'Appearance and reality: a case study of *The Observer* and J. L. Garvin, 1914–1942', *Newspaper history: from the seventeenth century to the present day*, ed. G. Boyce, J. Curran, and P. Wingate (1978), 320–38 · I. Origo, *Images and shadows: parts of a life* (1970) · C. Moorehead, *Iris Origo: marchesa di Val d'Orcia* (2000) · K. Clark, *Another part of the wood* (1974) · J. Ross, *The fourth generation: reminiscences* (1912) · E. Samuels, *Bernard Berenson*, 2 vols. (1979); (1987) · R. Dunn, *Geoffrey Scott and the Berenson circle: literary and aes-thetic life in the early 20th century* (1998) · O. Hamilton, *Paradise of exiles: Tuscany and the British* (1974) · J. O'Grady, 'The Egyptian corre-spondent of *The Times*', *Victorian Periodicals Review*, 27 (1994), 144–53 · E. Dyas, 'The mystery of the Egyptian correspondent of *The Times*', *Victorian Periodicals Review*, 28 (1995), 54–7 · J. O'Grady, 'More Egyptian correspondence', *Victorian Periodicals Review*, 29 (1996), 33–5 · Burke, *Peerage* (2000) [Duff Gordon] · private information (2004) [family]

Archives British Institute in Florence, MSS | U. Texas, J. L. Garvin MSS

Likenesses C. Furse, 1902 (*The return from the ride*), Tate collec-tion · photographs, repro. in Beevor, *Tuscan childhood*

Wealth at death £928: probate, 25 Aug 1965, CGPLA Eng. & Wales

Waterfield, (Ottiwell Henry) Gordon (1903–1987), jour-nalist and broadcaster, was born on 24 May 1903 at Nack-ington House near Canterbury, Kent, the home of his grandparents. He was the son of Aubrey William Water-field (*c*.1872–1944), painter, and his wife, Caroline (Lina) Lucie Isabella Jane Duff Gordon [see Waterfield, Caroline Lucie (1874–1964)]. They lived in Italy, she being the author of many books about Italy and for fourteen years Rome correspondent of *The Observer*. His younger brother, John, was killed in Malta during the Second World War and his sister Carinthia (Kinta) was married to John Grosvenor Beevor.

Waterfield was educated at Marlborough College and at New College, Oxford, where he took a fourth in politics, philosophy, and economics (1925), and went to Egypt with the aim of learning enough about cotton to join his uncle's firm in Manchester. But he fairly quickly found more congenial work as a journalist on the staff of the *Egyptian Gazette* and acting in 1928 as correspondent for *The Times*. This led him to Reuters, who sent him to Rome, but the fascist authorities expelled him after a year. On 10 August 1929, at Holy Trinity Church, Brompton, London, he married Margaret (Kitty; 1908–1989), daughter of Sir Bertram Hornsby, governor of the National Bank of Egypt. They had one son and one daughter.

Paris was the next posting, and Waterfield was there to witness the collapse of France, which he made the subject of a book, *What Happened to France* (1940). Back in England, he joined the army and was immediately sent for com-mando training in Scotland. With his fluent Italian and useful Arabic he was soon back in Cairo, the brief which he brought with him from London being to blow up the railway between Djibouti and Addis Ababa, in Italian hands since 1935, their east African empire consolidated that autumn by the overrunning of British Somaliland. General headquarters in Cairo thought sabotaging the railway not a good idea, so Waterfield moved to Aden and became involved in planning and then in executing the campaign which in 1941 put an end to that empire. He served as a platoon commander and intelligence officer in what he called 'a nice gentlemanly little war', and for some months found himself governor of Alula, the most easterly township on the Horn of Africa.

Though he was anxious to see more active service, Waterfield was first briefly diverted to be information officer in Addis Ababa and then returned to Reuters to act as their correspondent in Chungking (Chongqing), China. After only a few months he was in Delhi, now as a war correspondent, and actively involved in the war against the Japanese on the Arakan front in Burma, being wounded when a sampan in which he was travelling down the River Mayu was dive-bombed by Japanese fighter planes. While in Somaliland he had started a book about his war experiences (*Morning will Come*) which appeared in 1944. This was a vivid piece of writing, begun 'as a result of loneliness, immobility and prickly heat' (Waterfield, ix), and was reprinted after the war.

Waterfield's post-war career was with the BBC, first as head of the Eastern services, and then of the Arabic service alone. This was the first foreign-language service the BBC had put out, remaining arguably its most important. Waterfield had to face a serious challenge at the time of Suez. As the crisis mounted, following Nasser's nationalization of the Suez Canal Company in July 1956, pressure was put on the BBC to accept some form of censorship. This was resisted, but when the ill-fated Anglo-French assault began some Egyptian members of the Arabic service's staff resigned, and others threatened to do the same if they were expected to broadcast propaganda rather than objective news. Waterfield gave his personal assurance that this would not be asked of them. He was as good as his word, and they stayed.

Waterfield had already written a biography of his great-grandmother, Lucie Duff Gordon, in 1937. (His superiors at Reuters sent a telegram expressing horror that any member of the staff should find time to write a book; if there was any spare time it would be better spent playing tennis.) After his retirement in 1963 he followed this up with much literary activity. A biography, *Layard of Nineveh*, appeared in 1965, a new edition of Sir Richard Burton's *First Footsteps in East Africa* in 1966, an illustrated book on Egypt in 1967, *Sultans of Aden* in 1969, and *Professional Diplomat*, a life of Sir Percy Loraine, in 1973. These were all well researched and most readable.

Waterfield was a big man, over 6 feet, quiet, courteous, humorous, pipe-smoking, with considerable physical as well as moral courage. Shortly after recovering from his wounds in 1943 he was with the Indian navy when two Japanese launches were sunk, leaving a lot of their crews struggling in the water. Waterfield helped to pull four waterlogged Japanese aboard, and when a fifth shouted for help he jumped into the sea with a rope but without first ensuring that the other end was attached to anything. Both survived.

Waterfield died at his home, 23 Bartholomew Lane, Saltwood, Hythe, Kent, on 17 December 1987, and was buried in Nackington churchyard, near Canterbury.

E. C. HODGKIN

Sources personal knowledge (2004) · *The Times* (18 Dec 1987), 14 · private information (2004) [Harriett Leppam, daughter] · G. Waterfield, *Morning will come* (1944) · m. cert. · *CGPLA Eng. & Wales* (1988)

Wealth at death £81,642: probate, 10 Feb 1988, *CGPLA Eng. & Wales*

Waterfield, Sir (Alexander) Percival (1888–1965), civil servant, was born at 9 St Leonard Road, Exeter, Devon, on 16 May 1888, the younger son of William Waterfield JP (1832–1907), of the Bengal civil service, and his second wife, Matilda Rose Herschel. He was admitted to Westminster School as a King's scholar in 1901, was captain of the school in 1906, and proceeded to Christ Church, Oxford, in 1907, where he won the university Hertford scholarship (Latin) in 1909 and gained firsts in classical moderations (1909) and *literae humaniores* (1911). His ability as a classicist gained him second place in the open competition for appointments in the higher civil service, where he began his career in the Treasury in 1911. He married on 16 October 1920 Doris Mary (1895–1988), daughter of Otto *Siepmann, with whom he had two sons and two daughters.

Waterfield was Treasury remembrancer in Ireland (1920–22), principal assistant secretary in the Treasury (1934–9), was a member of the Palestine partition commission (1938), and part-time deputy secretary, Ministry of Information (1939–40). In 1939 he was appointed first civil service commissioner, a post he held until his retirement in 1951. He was made CB in 1923, knighted in 1944, and advanced to KBE in 1951. An honorary doctorate was conferred on him by the Ohio Wesleyan University, USA, in 1948.

Waterfield's greatest achievement was within the closed politics of Whitehall. During his period as first civil service commissioner a new method of assessment was introduced for the selection of applicants to what were later known as fast-stream posts in the civil service. Modelled on the procedure adopted by the War Office to select officers during the Second World War, it made use of new approaches to staff selection, including psychometric testing. It was the creation and management of the civil service selection board, responsible for the most rigorous part of the selection procedure, and especially the introduction of psychologists as active participants in it, which enabled Waterfield to demonstrate his meticulous attention to detail, his energy and enthusiasm for the task in hand, and his initiative, courage, and skill in dealing with the Treasury and other government departments and with a variety of outside bodies, including universities, which had special interests in the new development. This creation became the subject of public controversy, and Waterfield was willing to speak about it when invited. On 26 May 1948 there was a debate in the House of Lords on civil service recruitment during which Lord Cherwell was one of the selection board's severest critics.

Waterfield was a devout member of the Church of England and extremely loyal to his friends. Candidates who appeared before him at interview boards may have found him rather formal, but he was courteous and attentive to what others said and he inspired confidence. The selection methods which were developed under his leadership were among the most significant achievements of the civil service commission; they stood the test of time in civil service selection and influenced personnel selection methods elsewhere in the United Kingdom and abroad.

In retirement Waterfield was appointed a commissioner by the British and Maltese governments to resolve a dispute about dockyard wages and conditions of service in Malta (1958). Waterfield died of heart failure on 2 June 1965 at his home, The Paddock, Sotwell, Wallingford, Berkshire. His ashes were interred in the vault of the family grave at St Mary's Church, Cofton, near Starcross, Devon. RICHARD A. CHAPMAN

Sources R. A. Chapman, *Leadership in the British civil service* (1984) · PRO, CSC 11/260 · *WWW* · private information (2004) · *Old Westminsters*, vol. 3 · *CGPLA Eng. & Wales* (1965)
Archives PRO
Likenesses photograph, priv. coll.
Wealth at death £2515: probate, 2 Dec 1965, *CGPLA Eng. & Wales*

Waterford. For this title name *see* Talbot, John, first earl of Shrewsbury and first earl of Waterford (*c.*1387–1453); Talbot, John, second earl of Shrewsbury and second earl of Waterford (*c.*1413–1460); Talbot, George, fourth earl of Shrewsbury and fourth earl of Waterford (1468–1538); Talbot, John, sixteenth earl of Shrewsbury and sixteenth earl of Waterford (1791–1852); Beresford, Henry de la Poer, third marquess of Waterford (1811–1859); Beresford, Louisa Anne, marchioness of Waterford (1818–1891).

Waterford, Jofroi of (*fl.* late 13th cent.), translator and Dominican friar, perhaps born of English parentage, was associated with Waterford, Ireland. The order had a house there from 1226 and a number of Anglo-Norman writings, transcribed in England, were read in Waterford, together with a quantity of texts added by local scribes. The evidence is found in Cambridge, Corpus Christi College, MS 405, parts of which belonged to the brethren of St John of Jerusalem, the knights hospitaller, at Waterford. Jofroi is credited with three French prose translations which are all transmitted solely in Paris, Bibliothèque Nationale, MS Fr. 1822 (an insular manuscript of the late thirteenth century): the *De excidio Troiae* of Dares the Phrygian (Paris, Bibliothèque Nationale, MS Fr. 1822, fols. 46r–57r); the *Breviarium historiae Romanae* of Eutropius (ibid., fols. 58r–83v); the *Secretum secretorum* of Pseudo-Aristotle (ibid., fols. 84r–143v, and prologue, fol. 248v). A colophon following the *Secret des secrets* associates Jofroi of Waterford and Servais Copale, in their capacities, it is now believed, as translator and scribe respectively. The latter was a Walloon, probably from the region of Huy, and the texts combine syntactical and lexical features reflecting the Anglo-Norman habits of the translator with phonetic and graphical traits indicative of the Walloon origin of the scribe. Translator and scribe may have met at the University of Paris. Recently a fragment of the *Secretum* translation has been discovered at the Society of Antiquaries (S. Antiquaries, Lond., MS 101) by Tony Hunt. TONY HUNT

Sources F. Vielliard, 'La traduction du *De excidio Troiae* de Darès le Phrygien par Jofroi de Waterford', *Bien Dire et Bien Aprandre*, 10 (1992), 185–204 · K. V. Sinclair, 'Anglo-Norman at Waterford: the mute testimony of MS Cambridge, Corpus Christi College 405', *Medieval French textual studies in memory of T. B. W. Reid*, ed. I. Short, Anglo-Norman Text Society Occasional Publications Ser., 1 (1984), 219–38
Archives Bibliothèque Nationale, Paris, MS Fr. 1822 · S. Antiquaries, Lond., MS 101

Waterhouse, Agnes (1501/2–1566). *See under* Essex witches (*act.* 1566–1589).

Waterhouse, Alfred (1830–1905), architect, was born on 19 July 1830 in Aigburth, Liverpool, the eldest of seven children of Alfred Waterhouse (1798–1873), cotton broker of Liverpool (later of Whiteknights, Reading), and his wife, Mary Bevan (1805–1880).

Early years Both parents belonged to the Society of Friends and the young Alfred's upbringing was strictly Quaker. He was educated at Grove House School, Tottenham, where he mixed with the sons of influential Quaker families, many of whom were later to become clients. He showed an early aptitude for drawing, which he learned from the books of J. D. Harding and Samuel Prout. In 1848 he was articled to the staunchly Quaker P. B. Alley, then in partnership with Richard Lane, the leading neo-classical architect of Manchester. In 1853 his education was completed with a ten-month tour of France, Italy, and Germany, after which he set up in practice as an architect in Manchester. His first commissions came from relatives, from Quaker connections, and from the local body of nonconformist (mainly Congregationalist) businessmen; but he soon had quite a substantial practice, and was himself training a few pupils, among them G. T. Redmayne (1840–1912), who was later to become his brother-in-law, and Ernest Geldart (1848–1929). National acclaim came with his design for the Manchester assize courts, won in competition in 1859. In 1860 he married Elizabeth (1834–1918), daughter of John *Hodgkin of Tottenham, with whom he had three sons and two daughters, the eldest of whom married the poet Robert Bridges.

In 1865 Waterhouse opened a London office on the basis of several promising commissions and secure family connections. His brother Theodore (1838–1891) was already in practice there as a solicitor and developer, while another brother, Edwin *Waterhouse (1841–1917), was in practice as an accountant. From his office and home at 8 (later 20) New Cavendish Street he built up a large and highly successful practice that made him the most widely employed British architect in the years from *c.*1865 to *c.*1885. On 24 February 1877 he was baptized into the Church of England. In 1878 he purchased the manor of Yattendon in Berkshire, where he lived as the squire in a new house of his own design. He continued to work until 1901, taking his eldest son, Paul *Waterhouse (1861–1924), into partnership in 1891, and by the end of his career had been responsible for almost 650 separate works.

Professional practice Waterhouse's huge success as an architect (probate records reveal that he left a fortune of £215,036) was founded on a thoroughly professional approach rather than on brilliance or innovation as a stylist. His approach is characterized by a great ingenuity in

Alfred Waterhouse (1830–1905), by Sir Lawrence Alma-Tadema, 1891

both planning and designing; and he was always ready to offer alternative solutions to his clients' problems. He was meticulous in his attention to detail, and throughout his career did not scorn the smallest commissions, designing such things as prize book-plates for Girton College, Cambridge (while engaged on much larger commissions there), or letter-headings and an inn sign for the marquess of Westminster (for whom he later rebuilt Eaton Hall). However, like most young architects of the mid-century he was greatly influenced by A. W. N. Pugin, and espoused Gothic as the most exciting style for the times. Yet he was always ready to modify the style in order to produce workable buildings, claiming that he had 'not endeavoured slavishly to copy the Gothic of any particular period or country' (*Manchester Guardian*, 19 April 1859). It was this approach, coupled with his skill as a planner, that won him the competition for the new assize courts for Salford (dem.) with a design that was described as 'one of the remarkable experiences of our time' (*The Builder*, 30 April 1859) and second only to those for the government offices in Whitehall by Sir Giles Gilbert Scott, which had caused such controversy in the battle of the styles. His efficient planning set the standard for future court buildings, and its Gothic style, with sculpture by the O'Shea brothers, was described by Ruskin as 'much beyond anything yet done in England on [his] principles' ('On traffic', lecture delivered at Bradford, 21 April 1864).

Major works Once established in this way Waterhouse was able to win major public commissions such as that for Strangeways gaol (1861–9). His Manchester connections

were still strong enough in 1868 for him to win the competition to design the new town hall. This, which is probably his masterpiece, displays all his mastery of planning on an awkward triangular site. It is also, with its steep roofs, and three spires at different angles, a demonstration of the potential of picturesque composition in the Gothic style. However, it was also thoroughly modern in the adoption of fireproof construction and the lining of its interior walls with terracotta, the architect's first extensive use of the material. The building was fully fitted with furniture designed by the architect, and he remained engaged with this one structure until 1894. Waterhouse's ability to work amicably with committees and to modify his designs to suit the needs of large groups made him well suited to undertake such commissions, and allowed him to create another classic in the Natural History Museum (1866 and 1870–80). This is chiefly known as the first building completely faced in terracotta, with an array of moulded creatures, all designed by Waterhouse. Yet the building is important in other ways. It has an internal iron frame and the clear planning, the product of close collaboration with Richard Owen, the first director, is striking. That the building was achieved in spite of changes of government and perpetual parsimony is also a considerable tribute to Waterhouse's determination and tact.

The Natural History Museum was Waterhouse's first major work in the capital. He had initially been commissioned in 1866 to carry out the design by Captain Fowke, but had taken the opportunity to redesign that scheme, retaining only the two-light Italianate windows of the South Kensington style in his Romanesque revival design. The achievement of so important a building was some compensation for his failure in the competition for the law courts in 1867, which he had entered hoping his legal connections would give him a good understanding of what was needed. His design was preferred by the users, the bar committee, but rejected in favour of G. E. Street's design by the architects. Such a decision reflected the common view of his work that practicality rather than form was uppermost.

This was in fact precisely what Waterhouse advocated in his presidential address to RIBA students (presidential address, repr. in *Building News*, 1 Feb 1889), and was probably one of the reasons why he was given his third great commission of the 1870s—the rebuilding of Eaton Hall. This, the most expensive country house of the century, was essentially a flawed masterpiece, in that its design appears to have developed slowly round the client's desire to retain features of the old house, which had already been reworked by W. Porden (*c*.1803–1812) and by W. Burn (1845–54). As a result the house has been much reviled by later critics who blamed Waterhouse for its incoherence. Changes in taste in the twenty-five years it took to complete, as well as the death of the client's first wife, and his remarriage, led to considerable adjustments in the course of the work, even to the removal and replacement of substantial elements. The grounds contain one of Waterhouse's few classical designs in the shape of a circular

Ionic 'parrot house' in golden terracotta, complete with caryatids.

Waterhouse's Victorian clients seemed to like what he offered, and Eaton Hall was by no means his only domestic commission, merely the largest. Waterhouse built or substantially altered some ninety houses for clients of varying means. The earliest of these were for relatives, such as his cousin Sebastian Waterhouse in Liverpool; but these were soon followed by a range of mansions for industrialists on the urban fringes and several houses in the Lake District, among which was Fawe Park (1858), for James Bell MP. This last was the subject of the first watercolour Waterhouse exhibited at the Royal Academy. At the peak of his career he also designed a number of substantial country houses. Among these were: Blackmoor House, Hampshire (1865–73), for Roundell Palmer (Lord Selborne); Hutton Hall, Essex (1864–71), for Sir Joseph Whitwell Pease; Town Thorns, near Rugby (1871–6), for the American Washington Jackson; and Iwerne Minster, Dorset (1877–82), for Lord Wolverton.

Waterhouse's domestic work linked him to the successful establishment in a conventional way, as did the design and restoration of churches. However, he did comparatively little in this line, though he did produce convincing Gothic churches at Penmaen-mawr (St Seiriol's, 1865–9), where the Gladstone family were involved, at Blackmoor (St Matthew's, 1866–70), for Lord Selborne, and at Twyford, Hampshire (St Mary's, 1876–8), where Sir Thomas Fairbairn was the principal donor. His most successful church was probably the urban St Elisabeth's, Reddish, Lancashire (1883–5), for the local industrialist William Houldsworth. However, it is not surprising that Waterhouse was also involved in building for the nonconformists, such as the church at Besses o' th' Barn, Manchester (1863), for the Congregationalists, for whom he also enlarged the Lancashire Independent Theological College (1876–80). There was less scope for architectural employment by the Society of Friends, though his early commissions did include designing or enlarging meeting-houses. Among the later chapels the King's Weigh-house Chapel in Mayfair (1889–93) and the Lyndhurst Road Congregational Chapel, London (1883–7), are particularly striking.

Institutional designs However, Waterhouse is better known as a designer of large institutional buildings. Where some would say Eaton Hall should be classed as such, his skill as a planner was shown in a wide range of town halls, such as those at Darlington (1861–3), Hove (1880–83), and Reading (1871–6), institutions such as the Turner Memorial Home (1882–5) or the Seamen's Orphans' Institution in Liverpool (1870–75), or hospitals such as Liverpool Royal Infirmary (1886–92) or St Mary's Hospital, Manchester (1889–1901). This was a type of designing in which he excelled, from early beginnings with the Bingley Institute (1863) right up to University College Hospital, London (1894–1903), the first vertically planned hospital in Britain. Perhaps his most complex and effective planning exercise was in the National Liberal Club in London (1884–7), where he combined three floors of large public rooms with four of bedrooms and

service rooms on an awkward triangular site off Whitehall. Though distinctly conventional in its Italianate classical decoration, this building was extremely up to date in its steel and concrete fireproof structure, and in its servicing and electric lighting. It was one of the two designs (the other being the Natural History Museum) which Waterhouse selected to represent his work at the Chicago World Fair of 1893.

Partly for his fame and his planning skills, but partly also for his reputation as an economical designer, Waterhouse was extensively employed by the two universities of Oxford and Cambridge, having work in one or other city continuously from 1865 until his retirement. He began with the Cambridge Union Society, and continued with extensive work at Balliol College, Oxford (the college that his son Paul attended), but declined an invitation to design a block of rooms to replace William Wilkins's King's College screen in Cambridge. His buildings for Gonville and Caius College still provide a terminal feature for King's Parade; but his wish to provide a complete new set of buildings for Pembroke College was frustrated by an emerging respect for historic structures, and that college actually sacked him as their architect. At Girton, however, he was given the opportunity to design a new college from scratch, introducing the corridor plan instead of the traditional staircase system. He was chosen for Girton by Emily Davies for the beauty of his building, but it is also clear that a number of his friends and clients were involved in the movement for women's education. As an efficient and progressive architect, Waterhouse was also a natural choice as architect for the northern universities. His first work was for Owens College (later Manchester University), where he had a series of commissions from 1860 until his retirement. He also designed the first buildings for the Yorkshire College (later Leeds University) and for Liverpool University, using in the latter the red brick and terracotta for which he was famous, and which gave rise to the term 'red brick' universities. He was further involved in education with Leighton Park School in Reading (1890–95), the Quaker foundation that absorbed the trust of the Grove House School of Tottenham, and, among others, with Reading grammar school (1868–72 and 1873–4), Middlesbrough grammar school (1885–6 and 1888–90), St Paul's School, Hammersmith (1881–7), and the City and Guilds of London Institute (1881–6), the last two being closely connected with the Clothworkers' Company, who had also been involved with Leeds University.

Planning skills, practicality, and business efficiency also made Waterhouse an attractive proposition in industry. He designed structures as varied as the Binyon and Fryer warehouse in Manchester and Lime Street Hotel in Liverpool. The National Provincial Bank in Piccadilly and Foster's Bank in Cambridge are only two of several banks he designed, and later in his career he designed the Hotel Metropole in Brighton. However his best-known commercial work was in the form of offices and investment property. One of his first commercial works was the Royal Insurance office in Manchester (1861), in which for a while he had his own office. He and his brother were personally involved in the development of sets of chambers as a commercial venture in Carey Street (1872 and 1879–95). Later he built for the Pearl Insurance Company in Liverpool (1896–8) and the headquarters of the Refuge Insurance Company in Manchester (1891–6). But by far the most extensive set of such commissions came from the Prudential Assurance Company, for whom he designed some twenty-seven buildings in the years between 1877 and 1904, establishing what is probably the first example of an architectural house style.

In all these buildings great attention was paid, in addition to practical and structural matters, to the picturesque massing and the skyline, which were so important in the developing streetscape of late nineteenth-century cities. Waterhouse's eclectic approach to style allowed him to create degrees of richness that could accurately reflect status or meet a variety of cost constraints. His general preference for Gothic forms was combined with a structural logic that matched richly articulated façades with straightforward steel skeletons. Although he used a variety of stones, particularly early in his career, he was concerned at the problems of supplying large quantities of evenly coloured stone, and also at the problems of pollution. He was an early member of the Smoke Abatement Society, and this was a major factor in his adoption of the supposedly self-washing terracotta for which he is so famous. This moulded material also had the advantage of allowing rich ornament at an economical price, but required a good understanding and close co-operation between manufacturer and architect, something on which Waterhouse justifiably prided himself. From the 1880s his terracotta exteriors were matched by similar material inside in the form of moulded and glazed faience, mostly manufactured by the Leeds Fireclay Company. He also regularly designed furniture, including a grand piano for his own use, fittings, and even decorative items such as pen-rests. He produced designs for floor tiles, and evidently had close enough relations with suppliers of such things as door furniture and sanitary ware for the manufacturers to supply items of 'Mr Waterhouse's design'. His work therefore had a consistency that is thoroughly Victorian in its use of high-quality materials, attention to practical details, and its general solidity.

Death and reputation During his lifetime Waterhouse's work was only ever criticized with respect, and generally highly praised. However, it was seldom bold or formally avant-garde, and his preference for a safe conservative taste meant that by 1900 his work was little valued. In the first half of the twentieth century it was widely reviled; and his fondness for tiled interiors led one critic to rhyme his name with 'municipal slaughterhouse'. However, some historians took him seriously, and Kenneth Clark rated him superior to George Gilbert Scott (K. Clark, *The Gothic Revival*, 2nd edn, 1950, 262). For all the odium heaped on his designs by a modernist generation, it is significant that his obituary commented 'even those who did not like his architecture liked the man' (*Architectural Record*, 30 Aug 1905). This characteristic made him an excellent professional colleague. He was involved in adjudications on a number of occasions, but was also very widely in demand as a competition assessor. He assessed no fewer than sixty competitions between 1864 and 1899, and thus had a hand in the selection of the design of many of the major public buildings of the latter half of the nineteenth century. He also acted as a trustee of Sir John Soane's Museum and as treasurer of the Royal Academy and of the Artists' General Benevolent Institution. The respect of his colleagues was shown in his election as president of the RIBA from 1888 to 1891. He had already won a *grand prix* at the Paris Universal Exhibition in 1867, with a *rappel* in 1878, and the coveted RIBA gold medal (1878) for his Manchester town hall design. He was awarded diplomas from Vienna (1869), Brussels (1886), Antwerp (1887), Milan (1888), and Berlin (1889), as well as an honorary LLD from Manchester University in 1895, the year it became the Victoria University. To this professional success was added recognition as a watercolourist. He exhibited a total of eighty watercolours at the Royal Academy, exhibiting first in 1857 and regularly from 1868; and was praised in 1884 for producing 'beyond question the most brilliant' (*Building News*, 1884, 817) watercolour in the show. He was elected ARA in 1878 and RA in 1885. The majority of his paintings were architectural, but he produced a significant number of picturesque landscapes both for exhibition and for private pleasure. These were mostly given to family members or friends and remain in private hands; but the Victoria and Albert Museum and the RIBA have several of his fine architectural watercolours.

Waterhouse suffered a major stroke in 1901, and retired from business; but the practice was continued by his son Paul and subsequently by his grandson and great-grandson. He lived in retirement at Yattendon Court, Yattendon, until his death there on 22 August 1905; he was buried at Yattendon six days later, in the parish church of Sts Peter and Paul, which he had restored and improved. His productive capacity was enormous, but he trained few architects of note. However, he had a large artistic and literary circle of friends, which included Frederic Leighton, Frederic Shields, and Frank Dicksee, and the sculptor Hamo Thornycroft was a particular protégé. His portrait by William Quiller Orchardson hangs in the RIBA, while another, by Sir Lawrence Alma-Tadema, was until recently retained by the family. Corbels in the shape of portrait busts of himself and his wife, made for his first house at Barcombe Cottage in Manchester, survive in Manchester City Galleries.   Colin Cunningham

Sources C. Cunningham and P. Waterhouse, *Alfred Waterhouse, 1830–1905: biography of a practice* (1992) • S. Maltby, S. MacDonald, and C. Cunningham, *Alfred Waterhouse, 1830–1905* (1983) [exhibition catalogue, RIBA Heinz Gallery, 1983] • E. Waterhouse, *The descendants of Nicholas Waterhouse of Everton* (1910) • E. Waterhouse, *Extracts from the journal of Mary Waterhouse* (1907) • *Dir. Brit. archs.* • *Architectural Record* (30 Aug 1905) • M. Girouard, *The Victorian country house*, rev. edn (1979) • R. Dixon and S. Muthesius, *Victorian architecture* (1978) • J. H. G. Archer, 'A classic of its age', *Art and architecture in Victorian Manchester*, ed. J. H. G. Archer (1985), 127–61 • J. H. G. Archer, 'A civil achievement: the building of Manchester town hall, pt 1: the commissioning', *Transactions of the Lancashire and*

Cheshire Antiquarian Society, 81 (1982), 3–41 • J. Olley and C. Wilson, 'The Natural History Museum', *Timeless architecture*, ed. D. Cruikshank (1985) • C. Yanni, 'Divine display or secular science: defining nature at the Natural History Museum in London', *Journal of the Society of Architectural Historians*, 55 (1996), 276–99 • *CGPLA Eng. & Wales* (1905) • M. Parr, 'Waterhouse, Alfred', *DBB*

Archives Man. CL, Manchester Archives and Local Studies, corresp. and papers relating to Manchester town hall • NRA, priv. coll., Eaton Hall building accounts • Pembroke Cam., letters • priv. coll., office archives, office letter-book, and Yattendon archives • RIBA, family MSS; MSS relating to Eaton Hall; out-letter-books | U. Reading L., letters to Thomas Hodgkin

Likenesses A. S. Cope, oils, 1886, Aberdeen Art Gallery • L. Alma-Tadema, portrait, *c.*1890, priv. coll. • W. Q. Orchardson, oils, *c.*1890, RIBA • photograph, *c.*1890, priv. coll.; repro. in Cunningham and Waterhouse, *Alfred Waterhouse*, frontispiece • L. Alma-Tadema, oils, 1891, NPG [*see illus.*] • R. W. Robinson, print, NPG; repro. in *Members and associates of the Royal Academy of Arts, 1891* (1892)

Wealth at death £215,036 14*s.* 6*d.*: resworn probate, 26 Sept 1905, *CGPLA Eng. & Wales*

Waterhouse, Sir Edward (1535–1591), administrator, was born at Helmstedbury, Hertfordshire, the youngest son of John Waterhouse, administrator, of Whitechurch, Buckinghamshire, and his wife, Margaret, daughter of Henry Turner of Blunt's Hall, Suffolk. His father was auditor to Henry VIII, and according to family tradition the king, when visiting him one day, was particularly impressed with Edward, foretelling that he would be a man of great honour and wisdom, fit for the service of princes. Waterhouse went to Oxford University when he was twelve, 'where for some years he glistered in the oratorick and poetick sphere, until he addicted himself to conversation and observance of state affairs'.

Waterhouse spent several years at court under the patronage of Sir Henry Sidney. Sidney revived the practice of employing a personal secretary when appointed lord deputy of Ireland in 1565, and chose Waterhouse for the office. This proved an excellent decision and Waterhouse became a mainstay of the Dublin administration. He was devoted to Sidney, who sent him on missions to London, and corresponded regularly with Sir William Cecil and Sir Francis Walsingham. He was made clerk of the castle chamber on 1 February 1566, and about the same time received a grant of a lease of the manor of Evan, co. Kildare, together with the corn tithes of Dunboyne, co. Meath.

In 1568 Waterhouse accompanied Sidney on his tour of Ireland. The lord deputy left him in charge of Carrickfergus, co. Antrim, and he was instrumental in obtaining a charter for the town in 1570, as a result of which he was created a freeman and nominated to represent it in parliament, which he did in 1585. He surrendered his office of clerk in October 1569, and when Walter Devereux, first earl of Essex, embarked on a scheme for the plantation of co. Antrim in 1573 Waterhouse wrote seeking employment. His self-confident letter did not set out his qualifications for the post, but rather listed the many services he could perform for the earl. Essex employed him as his secretary, sending him on frequent missions to England in connection with the sale of his property and supplying his army with provisions. Waterhouse earned Essex's gratitude by his discretion and devotion. He was present during Essex's last illness, and the earl died in his arms on 22 September 1576.

The failure of Essex's enterprise left Waterhouse unemployed, but he obtained a grant on 25 April 1576 of an annual pension of £182 10*s.*, which was confirmed for life on 26 June 1579. Again, Sidney appointed him as his secretary, and he was sent to England with Philip Sidney to plead the lord deputy's case in 1576–9 over the matter of the cess, including government impositions such as purveyance, levied on the inhabitants of the pale. Waterhouse's first marriage, to Elizabeth, daughter of George Villiers, broke down during this time and the couple divorced in 1578. Waterhouse was appointed to the commission to inquire into concealed and forfeited lands in 1578. On 5 February 1579 he obtained a grant of the collectorship of customs on wine in Ireland, on 27 June he was appointed exchequer commissioner of the army, on 7 July receiver-general in the exchequer, and on 25 July receiver of all casual profits falling to the crown. He was present in Munster from August to November, while the army under Sir William Drury was there, and during the rebellion of James fitz Maurice Fitzgerald and Sir John Desmond, adding to his other duties that of overseeing victualling. At the end of October he was sworn of the Irish privy council. The outbreak of the rebellion of Gerald fitz James Fitzgerald, fourteenth earl of Desmond, in November saw Waterhouse recalled to his post with the army in Munster, and for the next two years his time was fully taken up as secretary, exchequer commissioner, and overseer of the commissariat. On 17 June 1580 he obtained a grant of the office of overseer and water bailiff of the River Shannon, with valuable perquisites. He was appointed a commissioner for ecclesiastical causes on 10 April 1581, and on 22 July was granted a lease for twenty-one years of the lands of Hilltown, co. Meath. Waterhouse served the lord deputies Arthur Grey, fourteenth Baron Grey of Wilton, and Sir John Perrot with the same faithfulness that he had shown towards Essex and Sidney, seemed to have no enemies, and everyone who came in contact with him had a good word to say of him. Despite his 'weak body', he fulfilled his numerous duties assiduously. He obtained a grant of the castle and lands of Doonass, co. Clare, on 26 August, to be held in fealty, by the service of providing the lord deputy with a pair of gloves whenever he visited the castle. He had by this time accumulated numerous perquisites, and while they may not have amounted to a large income, they aroused Elizabeth I's jealousy, especially over the positions of water bailiff and custodian of the boats at Athlone, co. Westmeath. He was ordered over to England in the autumn. Waterhouse's modest behaviour and the warm commendations he brought from Ireland won over Cecil (now Lord Burghley), and his offer to surrender his patent of water bailiff mollified the queen, although she insisted on having a list made out of all patents, fees, and other perquisites granted to him during the previous seven years.

Waterhouse returned to Ireland in April 1583. In March

1584 he was required, along with Sir Geoffrey Fenton, to carry out, according to Burghley's instructions, the unpleasant task of torturing Dermot O'Hurley, titular archbishop of Cashel, by toasting his feet before the fire. Waterhouse was knighted by Perrot in Christ Church, Dublin, on 20 June 1584, the lord deputy giving the reason for the promotion as the fact that Waterhouse spent more than 1000 marks a year in carrying out his duties. While Perrot's expedition against the Antrim Scots was greeted with general disapproval, Waterhouse spoke out in his favour. He had already given up his office of secretary to please Fenton; in November he surrendered his patent as water bailiff, and, shortly afterwards, in order to gratify Sir Henry Wallop, relinquished his receivership of casualties. He acted as peacemaker in the quarrel between Perrot and Adam Loftus, archbishop of Dublin, without forfeiting the respect of either. Perrot granted Waterhouse leave, 'having been long sick and in great danger', to go to England to plead his own case, and he urged Burghley to intercede for the restoration of his patent as water bailiff, as some reward for his long and faithful service. Waterhouse presented a detailed account of all his offices and rewards, and explained that, far from profiting by them, he had been obliged to sell land in England worth over £4000. He evidently persuaded Elizabeth, since on 19 October 1586 he was appointed chancellor of the exchequer and of the green wax in Ireland. The green wax was a legal process for recovering debts due to the crown for which the chancellor was responsible. He surrendered the office to George Clive in October 1589, having by that time received a grant (7 July 1588), in consideration 'of his sufficiency and painful good service', of the office of overseer, water bailiff, and keeper of the River Shannon for life (*Irish Fiants*, nos. 3641, 5231–2). He left Ireland in January 1591, retired to his estate of Woodchurch, Kent, and died there on 13 October. His second wife was Margaret Spilman of Kent. His last wife, who survived him, was Deborah, widow of a Master Harlackenden of Woodchurch. He had no children. Edward Waterhouse [*see below*] was probably his nephew. The heraldic writer Edward *Waterhouse (1619–1670) was his grandnephew.

Edward Waterhouse (*fl.* 1622), colonist in Virginia, was the son of Thomas Waterhouse of Berkhamsted, Hertfordshire. He was secretary of the Virginia Company and author of *A declaration of the state of the colony in Virginia. With a relation of the barbarous massacre … * (1622), with a preface dated 22 August 1622. Waterhouse was the principal spokesman for the colonists after the American Indian insurrection of spring 1622. It is clear that the colonists felt that this violent resistance by the native population liberated them from the constraints of their original moral justification for their occupation, that of 'civilizing' the indigenous population, a change of attitude that had its parallel in Ireland when Sir Edward Waterhouse served Essex in Ulster at the time of the massacre of the Clandeboye O'Neills.   ANDREW LYALL

Sources C. Brady, *The chief governors: the rise and fall of reform government in Tudor Ireland, 1536–1588* (1994), 152, 158, 202 • J. Morrin, ed., *Calendar of the patent and close rolls of chancery in Ireland for the reigns of Henry VIII, Edward VI, Mary, and Elizabeth*, 2 vols. (1861–2) • *CSP Ire., 1509–73*, 406–8 • N. P. Canny, *The Elizabethan conquest of Ireland: a pattern established, 1565–76* (1976) • J. G. Crawford, *Anglicizing the government of Ireland: the Irish privy council and the expansion of Tudor rule, 1556–1578* (Dublin, 1993) • G. E. Howard, *A treatise of the exchequer and revenue of Ireland*, 2 vols. (1776), vol. 1, p. 128 • *The Irish fiants of the Tudor sovereigns*, 4 vols. (1994) • *CSP Ire., 1571–5* • *DNB*
Archives NL Ire., corresp. | CKS, letters to Sir Henry Sidney

Waterhouse, Edward (*fl.* 1622). *See under* Waterhouse, Sir Edward (1535–1591).

Waterhouse, Edward (1619–1670), heraldic writer, was born in Greenford, Middlesex, the son of Francis Waterhouse, fishmonger, of Greenford and London, and Bridget, daughter of Morgan Powell; Edward was a greatnephew of Sir Edward Waterhouse, chancellor of the exchequer in Ireland (1535–91). Francis Waterhouse had at one time been chosen chamberlain of London, but his appointment had been stopped, according to his son, 'by one of those orders that then were in date, to exclude those whom that power termed disaffected' (Waterhouse, *A Short Narrative of the Late Dreadful Fire in London*, 1667, 186). The younger Waterhouse was admitted fellow commoner at Emmanuel College, Cambridge, on 30 June 1635 but appears not to have taken a degree (Venn, *Alum. Cant.*, 1.4, col. 344), though in 1668 he gained the degree of LLD *per literas regias*. During the interregnum he lived in Oxford, 'for the sake of the public library', according to Wood (Wood, *Ath. Oxon.: Fasti*, 2.163). By 1660, however, he had returned to London, where he resided at Sion College; he was still dwelling there for at least part of the year by 5 February 1665, the date on which he signed the dedication to his work *The Gentleman's Monitor*. He also had a house at Mile End Green and an estate at Greenford. Waterhouse married Mary, daughter and heir of Robert and Magdalen Smith, alias Carrington. After her death, he married Elizabeth, daughter of Richard and Christiana Bateman of Hartington, Derbyshire, and London. He outlived his second wife, with whom he had two daughters, Elizabeth and Bridget, and a son, Edward, who also predeceased him about 1659. In later life he was persuaded by Archbishop Sheldon to take holy orders, being ordained by faculty on 7 April 1668. He continued to reside at Greenford and London, where he became a 'fantastical preacher' (ibid.). He died in London on 30 May 1670 and was buried on 2 June at Greenford.

Although never a member of the College of Arms, Waterhouse had heraldic and historical interests, which are reflected in many of his works, such as *A Discours and Defense of Arms and Armory* (1660). His earliest work was *An Humble Apologie for Learning and Learned Men* (1653), in which he provided a historical survey of the contribution of learned men to human affairs, stressing the role of knowledge and reason in the workings of statecraft and the defence of true religion. These books reveal him as strongly influenced by Neoplatonic thought—God was a 'divine and architectonick artist' (*Humble Apologie*, 10)—as well as by neo-Stoicism. In the same year his *Two Brief Meditations* provide a sign of his future religiosity, as does *A Modest Discourse of the Piety, Charity and Policy of Elder Times*

Edward Waterhouse (1619–1670), by David Loggan, 1663

impermanence even of buildings, also placed the conflagration in the context of other fires through history. He dedicated it to his kinsman and friend Sir Edward Turnor (1617–1676), then speaker of the House of Commons.

Waterhouse was credited by Dugdale, who was almost certainly mistaken, with whole authorship of *The Sphere of Gentry* (1661) by the herald-painter Sylvanus Morgan, a peculiar work to which he doubtless contributed some parts, including the history of his family and its arms (Morgan, 2.67). He also wrote a life of his great-uncle and namesake, the Elizabethan official, for David Lloyd's *State Worthies* (1670, 537). But Waterhouse's two most significant works were without question *Fortescutus illustratus* (1663), a learned commentary on the fifteenth-century jurist Sir John Fortescue's *De laudibus legum Angliae* (a text most recently studied by the great Selden) and *The gentleman's monitor, or, A sober inspection into the virtues, vices and ordinary means of the rise and decay of men and families* (1665), on which his modern reputation as an acute social theorist largely rests. The former work was approved for publication by several leading jurists, including Sir Matthew Hale and Sir Orlando Bridgeman. The latter work, dedicated to Sheldon, offers an analysis of social mobility within the more conventional medium of a critique of vices such as prodigal spending and the irresponsibility of heirs in preserving their family's fortunes.

D. R. WOOLF

Sources A. Sharp, 'Edward Waterhouse's view of social change in seventeenth-century England', *Past and Present*, 62 (1974), 27–46 · M. Hunter, *The Royal Society and its fellows, 1660–1700: the morphology of an early scientific institution*, 2nd edn (1994) · D. Lloyd, *State worthies* (1670), 537 · *GM*, 1st ser., 62 (1792), 781, 988 · *GM*, 1st ser., 66 (1796), 366–7 · Fuller, *Worthies* · Wood, *Ath. Oxon.: Fasti* (1820), 163–4 · Venn, *Alum. Cant.* · S. Morgan, *The sphere of gentry* (1661) · *DNB*

Likenesses D. Loggan, line engraving, 1663, BM, NPG, V&A; repro. in E. Waterhouse, *Fortescutus illustratus* (1663) [see illus.] · A. Hertochs, line engraving, 1665, BM, NPG; repro. in E. Waterhouse, *The gentleman's monitor* (1665)

and Christians (1655). The majority of his writings, however, pertained to the history and fortunes of great families. A firm supporter of social distinction, Waterhouse was fascinated by distinguished ancestry, and in particular by the mutability of fortunes. His remarks on the vicissitudes of rank and prosperity have sometimes been seen as insightful sociological analysis in the tradition of the Tudor writer Sir Thomas Smith and of the Restoration political economists such as William Davenant, John Graunt, and Gregory King. More recent commentators have been less kind, seeing his work mainly as the pessimistic outpouring of a middle-aged man, beset by grief for his second wife and fixated on the impending extinction of his own direct line after the death of his son. On the other hand, Wood's contemporary assessment of Waterhouse as a 'cock-brain'd man' (Wood, *Ath. Oxon.: Fasti*, 2.164) of small ability seems unduly harsh. Contemporaries such as John Wilkins thought highly enough of Waterhouse to propose him in 1663 for fellowship of the Royal Society, in which body Waterhouse was mildly active until 1664, paying his subscription until 1666. In that year occurred the great fire, which occasioned his last outpouring on the subject of impermanence, *A Short Narrative of the Late Dreadful Fire in London* (1667). This work, which described the fire as a divine judgment on London, and a sign of the

Waterhouse, Edwin (1841–1917), accountant, was born on 4 June 1841 at Oakfield, Aigburth, Liverpool, the seventh and youngest child of Alfred Waterhouse senior (1798–1873), a partner in the firm of Nicholas Waterhouse & Sons, merchants and brokers of Liverpool, and his wife, Mary, née Bevan (1805–1880). He spent most of his childhood in the south of England at several family homes, including Sneyd Park, near Bristol, and various addresses in central London.

Having been taught by private tutors, and because his parents were committed members of the Society of Friends, in September 1855 Waterhouse entered University College School, a leading academy for dissenters. A diligent student, he won prizes in French and geometry, and two years later joined his elder brother Theodore (1838–1891) at University College, London, where he attended classes in mathematics, Greek, Latin, and English. He graduated in 1860 with second-class honours, but had made no decision about a future career. His elder brother Alfred *Waterhouse (1830–1905) was already established as an architect, Theodore was to take articles as a solicitor, and Edwin, as he later recalled,

Edwin Waterhouse (1841–1917), by unknown photographer, c.1907

had allowed this important matter to be in abeyance. I knew nothing of business, and felt a dislike of the 'city' and … the pale and anxious faces which I saw on my infrequent visits there. A doctor's career might have suited me, but I had no special bent in that way, and I feared a failure. (*Memoirs*, 68)

A chance introduction to William Turquand, a leading accountant, led to Waterhouse being articled to the City firm of Coleman, Turquand, Youngs & Co. in January 1861. There he learned the rudiments of bookkeeping and assisted with insolvencies and audits, but after three years of what he described as an 'apprenticeship' decided to set up on his own account. In February 1864 he took two rooms at 11 Old Jewry Chambers and wrote to business acquaintances of his father in order to seek employment. A major source of income during his first year in practice was the reorganization of the accounts of his brother, then a prominent architect in Manchester. While undertaking a cost-accounting assignment at John Fowler's steam plough works in Leeds, Waterhouse met William Holyland (1807–1882), a principal clerk of Turquand, who informed him that he was about to form a partnership with Samuel Lowell Price (1821–1887). Holyland suggested that he join them and, as Waterhouse wrote,

> I had been doing very well for myself during the last few months, but the offer seemed to open out chances of quickly attaining a wider experience, whilst ensuring a more steady practice and affording me the advantages of assistance should I need it. (*Memoirs*, 81)

Thus, the firm of Price, Holyland, and Waterhouse was formed on 1 May 1865; Edwin, the youngest and least experienced, took a quarter-share in the profits.

Having leased prestigious offices in the Queens Assurance Company building at the corner of Gresham Street (no. 13, later 44) and King Street, the firm flourished from the outset. Unlike the first generation of accountancy firms which prospered as insolvency specialists, Price, Holyland, and Waterhouse gained a reputation as auditors largely as a result of Waterhouse's work for railway companies, banks, and financial institutions. His probity and insistence upon prudent conventions won him important audits, including the London and North Western, South Eastern, Metropolitan, and London, Brighton and South Coast railways. Waterhouse was so busy with these tasks that in 1883 he declined to serve as the auditor of the Midland Railway. In addition, he was appointed joint auditor of the National Provincial Bank of England (from 1880) and of the London and Westminster Bank, while the firm audited Lloyds Bank, the Gresham Life Assurance Society, Atlas Assurance, the Equity and Law Life Assurance Company, and the Foreign and Colonial Government Trust Company from its foundation in 1868. The rising fee income of the partnership was a measure of its commercial success. In the first year of operation it earned £9138, increasing to an average of £14,450 between 1870 and 1885, with peaks in 1870 (£18,070), 1876 (£17,135), and 1877 (£17,749). Fees rose appreciably after 1889 and during the following decade were in excess of £40,000 per annum. In 1887, on the death of Price, Edwin Waterhouse became senior partner (Holyland having retired in 1874) and, as was customary, took a lion's share of the profits. In 1896–7, for example, when £35,897 was available for distribution among the four partners, he received £21,000 (59 per cent). This level of income enabled him to build a substantial home in the country, Feldemore, at Holmbury St Mary, Abinger, near Dorking, Surrey, which was designed by his brother-in-law George Redmayne, the Manchester architect; he occupied the house from 1880 and progressively extended it during the 1890s. At his death he left an estate worth £257,780 gross, and it appeared that the greater part of his fortune had been earned from professional fees rather than share dealing or other forms of financial speculation.

Waterhouse was also called upon to undertake a number of investigations by companies, institutions, and government bodies. In 1877 he devised a sliding scale for the Consett Iron Company, by which wages could be related to the sale price of iron; in 1889 he assisted Lancashire county council in allocating receipts and expenditure between boroughs and urban districts under the new Local Government Act; and in 1908 he reorganized the finances of the Underground Electric Railway of London. In 1887–8 Waterhouse, together with Frederick Whinney (1829–1916), produced a report on the accounting organization of the Woolwich arsenal for a parliamentary committee chaired by Lord Randolph Churchill. He was subsequently asked to conduct similar investigations into the Admiralty's dockyards (1888–9) and the Royal Ordnance factories (1901). A member of the 1894–5 Davey departmental committee on joint-stock companies, he was responsible for representing the profession's views, and the report which followed formed the basis for the Companies Act of 1900. When further change was considered, Waterhouse was invited to serve on the 1905–6 (Loreburn) committee, which, in turn, led to the Companies Act of 1907. However, despite these achievements, it would be wrong to view Waterhouse as one of the outstanding original thinkers of the profession. His talents lay not so much with the introduction of radical ideas as in the practical organization and running of a major City partnership. He had the social contacts to attract new clients, the ability to maintain established connections, and the judgement to select staff of youthful promise (he introduced a policy of recruiting prizewinners from the institute examinations).

Having been a founder member of the Institute of Chartered Accountants in England and Wales (ICAEW) on its foundation in 1880, Waterhouse became active in its organization. Although he failed at the first attempt to be elected to the council, in 1887 he took the place formerly occupied by Price. In 1892, without having held the customary post of vice-president, he was elected president and served for two years. Not all of his presidential initiatives were successful, and his campaign to establish a professional monopoly, as exercised by legal and medical practitioners, did not meet with government approval. His presidency corresponded with the opening in 1893 of the ICAEW's purpose-built hall in Moorgate. He retired from the council in July 1915 after twenty-eight years' service.

Ernest Cooper (1848–1926), another eminent City accountant, reported that Waterhouse 'always showed me rather more courtesy than I deserved' (Cooper, 49), while Nicholas Waterhouse, Waterhouse's youngest son by his first marriage, observed that 'he never suffered a fool gladly but had a wonderful insight into character, and those who really knew him held him in the highest respect and affection' (Waterhouse, Reminiscences, 3). An inability to tolerate any behaviour that might pass for slackness and his ingrained Quaker mores led to a prohibition of smoking. If Waterhouse 'found a pipe or pouch lying around in the office or in the audit room of a client, he thought nothing of throwing them on the fire but, then relenting, would compensate the offender with the price of a new outfit' (ibid., 102). He periodically suffered from the depression that had afflicted his mother in her later life, and a devotion to Christianity, together with a thorough commitment to his professional duties, may have served as defence against its onset.

In 1868 Waterhouse married Georgina, née Thöl (1848–1896); they had four daughters and two sons, William and Nicholas. Both boys joined Price Waterhouse as articled clerks, but William died suddenly of pneumonia in 1900 before taking his final examination; Nicholas qualified, was admitted to the partnership in 1906 on his father's retirement, and became the senior partner in 1945. In 1898, two years after the death of his first wife, Waterhouse married Helen Caroline, née Weber (1855–1941);

they had one son, Theodore (1907–1976), who also worked for Price Waterhouse. Edwin Waterhouse died, aged seventy-six, at Feldemore, on 17 September 1917 and was buried in the parish churchyard at Holmbury St Mary.

EDGAR JONES

Sources The memoirs of Edwin Waterhouse, ed. H. E. Jones (1988) • E. Jones, True and fair: a history of Price Waterhouse (1995) • J. R. Edwards, 'Waterhouse, Edwin', DBB • E. Cooper, 'Fifty-seven years in an accountant's office', Proceedings of the Autumnal Meeting [Institute of Chartered Accountants in England and Wales] (1921), 49 • N. Waterhouse, Reminiscences, 1899–1960 (1961), 3 • d. cert.
Archives Price Waterhouse archives, Southwark Towers, 32 London Bridge Street, London | Institute of Chartered Accountants in England and Wales archives, London
Likenesses J. Kopf, bronze relief, c.1898, Pricewaterhouse Coopers, Southwark Towers, 32 London Bridge Street, London; on loan from Institute of Chartered Accountants in England and Wales • photograph, c.1907, PricewaterhouseCoopers [see illus.]
Wealth at death £257,780 3s. 6d.: probate, 23 Jan 1918, CGPLA Eng. & Wales

Waterhouse, Sir Ellis Kirkham (1905–1985), art historian and administrator, was born in Lynwood Avenue, Epsom, Surrey, on 16 February 1905, the only child of (Percy) Leslie Waterhouse, architect, and his wife, Eleanor (d. 1905), daughter of William Margetson of Streatham. From Marlborough College he won a scholarship in classics to New College, Oxford; he took a first class in classical honour moderations (1925) and a second in literae humaniores (1927). Already his interests had focused irrevocably on art, and as Commonwealth Fund fellow at Princeton University (1927–9) he was rigorously trained as an art historian and, under the direction of Frank J. Mather Jr., made a special study of El Greco. As an assistant at the National Gallery, London, from 1929, he was shocked by the amateurish approach of his colleagues and, being now economically independent, he resigned in 1933. He became librarian at the British School in Rome (until 1936), where he sought out neglected baroque paintings; his Baroque Painting in Rome: the Seventeenth Century (1937; rev., 1976) and Italian Baroque Painting (1962; rev., 1969) were major pioneering achievements. In England, from 1936 to 1939, he worked on British art and for the Royal Academy on the exhibition held in 1938 of seventeenth-century art in Europe.

A research fellowship at Magdalen College, Oxford (1938–47), was interrupted by the Second World War, which stranded Waterhouse in Greece. After some cartographical work there for the British legation, he was commissioned in general headquarters Cairo as a member of the intelligence corps, and took part in the 1941 campaign from Macedonia to Crete. In 1943–4 he was seconded to the staff of the British ambassador in Cairo to the Greek government in exile. His intelligence, and his diplomatic and tactical skills, played a part in the arrangement of the Lebanon all-party conference of May 1944, and its agreement which, though fragile, frustrated the threatened communist take-over in Athens after the German withdrawal. In 1945, now a monuments and fine arts officer serving with the army and the Foreign Office, he was agreeably employed in the Netherlands and Germany,

Joshua Reynolds (1941), *Painting in Britain, 1530–1790* (1953 and subsequent revisions), and *Gainsborough* (1958)—and on his beloved Italian school constituted a lasting achievement. Among other writings there were numerous catalogues, articles, and reviews. His writing, apparently effortless in its classic economy and directness of expression, proceeded always from careful research and first-hand observation.

Waterhouse was of an independent temperament, equipped with formidable intellectual powers, supported by a remarkable certainty of principle and of purpose, and driven by inexhaustible energy. He dressed primarily for comfort (though owning a collection of startling neckties) and was no respecter of pretentiousness or pomposity. He could be wilful, and nurtured some idiosyncratic prejudices. His tongue was sharp, and the instrument of a nimble wit unmatched in his profession. He delighted in good company as in good music. Deeper than any critical acerbity, and the wit, were an affection for those whom he liked and respected (if not always for their scholarship), and an unstinting generosity with which he drew, in response to any serious enquiry, on his phenomenal memory supported by the superb resources in his own library and archive, which he shared liberally. His notebooks and papers are now in the collection of the Mellon Foundation in London, at the Getty Museum archives in Los Angeles, and at the Barber Institute in Birmingham. He did not personally collect works of art, judging that that might be inimical to a proper scholarly objectivity.

Waterhouse was made FBA in 1955, MBE in 1943, and CBE in 1956. He became an honorary fellow of New College in 1975 and was knighted the same year. Nottingham (1968), Leicester (1970), Birmingham (1973), and Oxford (1976) conferred honorary degrees upon him, and he was honoured by the Dutch and Italian governments. Through Waterhouse's last decade the distillation and dissemination of his knowledge continued. The companion (seventeenth-century) volume for his *Dictionary of British 18th Century Painters* (1981) was ready for press when he died, on 7 September 1985, at his home, Overshot, Badger Lane, on Hinksey Hill above Oxford.

Waterhouse's wife, **Helen Waterhouse** [*née* Thomas], Lady Waterhouse (1913–1999), classical scholar and archaeologist, was born on 5 March 1913 at Chaldon, near Caterham, Surrey, the only daughter of Frederick William Thomas (1867–1956), and his wife, Eleanor Grace, daughter of Walter John Hammond, engineer. She was educated at Roedean School, where she was a scholar and head of house, and at Girton College, Cambridge, where she gained a first in classics and a starred first in archaeology, and stayed on to win several college and university studentships and a bifellowship in 1938. From 1935 to 1938 she held a studentship at the British School at Athens. During the Second World War she joined the British legation at Athens, then the political intelligence centre in Cairo, before returning in 1941 to London, where she worked in the war office and then in the research department of the Foreign Office. From 1946 to 1947 she was librarian of the British School at Athens. She was a hard-

Sir Ellis Kirkham Waterhouse (1905–1985), by T. & R. Annan & Sons, *c.*1950

supervising the return of stolen works of art and defending buildings of merit from military vandalism. His activities also contributed to the exposure of the forger of Vermeer, Han van Meegeren.

In 1946 Waterhouse was briefly editor of the *Burlington Magazine* and in 1947–8 reader in art history at Manchester University, but in 1949 he accepted the important directorship of the National Galleries of Scotland. On 29 June of that year he married Helen Thomas [*see below*]; they had two daughters. In Edinburgh, although he made some memorable acquisitions, he endured with difficulty the bureaucracy of the Scottish Office, and in 1952 he resigned to become director of the Barber Institute of Fine Arts in the University of Birmingham. There, among congenial colleagues, Waterhouse blossomed unexpectedly in academic administration (he was dean of arts for three years). He deployed quite generous funds to maximum advantage in acquisitions especially of the British and seventeenth-century Italian schools. Another special care was the creation of the library, and the Birmingham School of Byzantine Studies also owed much to his fostering. From Birmingham he was able to lecture widely, notably as Slade professor of fine art at Oxford in 1953–5.

After retiring from Birmingham in 1970, Waterhouse became the London director of the Paul Mellon Centre for Studies in British Art at a critical period in the centre's evolution (1970–73). Throughout the post-war years he accepted various visiting professorships or consultancies in America. His work on British art—in particular his *Sir* working archaeologist and keen traveller, and contributed learned articles to the *Annals* of the school, chapters in collective works, and important surveys of the treasures of Mycenae, Ithaca, and early Minoan houses. She was assistant lecturer in classics at Manchester University (1948–9) and later honorary lecturer and research fellow at Birmingham University (1966–71). Her publications included *The British School at Athens: the First Hundred Years* (1986). She died of myelodysplasm and chronic wound infection on 9 September 1999 at St Luke's Nursing Home, 4 Latimer Road, Oxford, and was survived by her two daughters.   DAVID PIPER, *rev.* DAVID CAST

Sources C. Gould, 'Ellis Kirkham Waterhouse, 1905–1985', *PBA*, 72 (1986), 525–35 · G. Robertson, *Burlington Magazine*, 128 (1986), 111–13 · *The Times* (9 Sept 1985) · *The Times* (14 Sept 1985) · *The Times* (15 Sept 1985) · private information (1990) · b. cert. · m. cert. · d. cert. · *The Independent* (17 Sept 1999) · d. cert. [Helen Waterhouse]
Archives Barber Institute of Fine Arts, Birmingham, notebooks and MSS · John Paul Getty Museum, Los Angeles, notebooks and MSS · Paul Mellon Centre for Studies in British Art, London, notebooks and MSS | National Gallery, London, letters to Harold Isherwood Kay
Likenesses T. & R. Annan & Sons, photograph, *c.*1950, NPG [*see illus.*]
Wealth at death £618,691: probate, 8 June 1986, *CGPLA Eng. & Wales* · £878,963—gross; £869,535—net; Helen Waterhouse: probate, 13 March 2000, *CGPLA Eng. & Wales*

Waterhouse, George (*d.* 1602), musician, is of unknown parentage and education. The record of his admission as a gentleman of Elizabeth I's Chapel Royal in July 1588 noted that he was 'from Lincoln'. His erstwhile occupation there is unknown; he was not associated with the music or choir of the cathedral. On 7 July 1592 he supplicated the University of Oxford for admission to the degree of bachelor of music; there is no record of its having been conferred. His stated qualification for this award lay in his having spent many years in the study of theoretical and practical music.

The only surviving example of Waterhouse's composition is an extraordinary collection of canons upon the plainsong antiphon *Miserere mihi, domine*, occupying over 400 pages of closely written manuscript and numbered as 1163 individual pieces. Almost all are composed two parts in one above their subject, whose twenty-six-note theme is laid out at diverse pitches in notional semibreves. As well as plain canon they employ, in various permutations, the conventional techniques of inversion, augmentation, and equalization, and engage a robust diversity of intervals between the canonic voices; there are also quasi-mensuration canons and 'enigma' canons. The performance method envisaged was vocalization.

In moderation such exercises were a commonplace of musical education, and though Waterhouse's excess may seem 'a useless monument of patience and ingenuity' (*DNB*), it was regarded with admiration in its day. His Chapel Royal 'friend and fellow' Thomas Morley knew well 'those never enough praised travailes of master Waterhouse', wherein he 'for varietie surpassed all who ever laboured in that kinde of studie'. Waterhouse's industry and resourcefulness were indeed remarkable,

and there can be little dispute with Morley's judgement that the composer's efforts were 'sufficient to quench the thirst of the most insaciate scholler whatsoever' (Morley, 115, 183). In 1636 two manuscript copies of the canons were bequeathed by one Henry Bury to the universities; that destined for Cambridge, in a late sixteenth-century hand, was placed in the university library. Still a gentleman of the Chapel Royal, Waterhouse died on 18 February 1602.   ROGER BOWERS

Sources E. F. Rimbault, ed., *The old cheque-book, or book of remembrance, of the Chapel Royal, from 1561 to 1744*, CS, new ser., 3 (1872), 4, 6, 195 · T. Morley, *A plaine and easie introduction to practicall musicke* (1597); facs. edn with introduction by E. H. Fellowes (1937), 115, 183 · Wood, *Ath. Oxon.: Fasti* (1815), 257

Waterhouse, George Robert (1810–1888), zoologist, was born on 6 March 1810 at Somers Town, London, the son of James Edward Waterhouse, a solicitor's clerk and amateur lepidopterist, and his wife, Mary Newman. Waterhouse loathed his education at a school in Koekelberg, near Brussels (1821–4), and returned to England to be articled to an architect. He practised between 1831 and 1835, designing the Hampstead garden of the publisher Charles Knight. However, the capture of a pair of poplar hawkmoths while a schoolboy had fired him for a different career; the draughtsman turned to illustrating insect structure, and he became a gifted entomologist. Self-taught, like so many, he transformed an avocation into an occupation. He was among the founders (and was honorary curator) of the Entomological Society in 1833, an informal enthusiasts' club. Partly he financed his career move by writing on insects, fish, and mammals for Knight's *Penny Cyclopedia*. In 1834 he married Elizabeth Ann Griesbach, sister of fellow Entomological Society officer the Revd A. W. Griesbach. The couple had three sons and three daughters. Appointment to a museum curatorship at the Royal Institution at Liverpool in 1835 brought some security. However, Waterhouse returned to London the following year; when John Gould, the superintendent of the ornithological collections of the Zoological Society of London's museum, went on half pay, Waterhouse was appointed the museum's first curator in 1836 at £120 per annum. Newly located in John Hunter's Leicester Square house, the Zoological Society's museum was wealthy at first, with an annual budget of £1000 and bulging shelves. Within a year Waterhouse had completed his *Catalogue of the Mammalia* (1838), which listed all 665 mammals, though its publication was delayed because of his nomenclatural disagreements with the society's quinarians.

Waterhouse was a prolific describer of the world's Coleoptera (beetles), rodents, and marsupials, publishing 120 papers between 1833 and 1866. The species he enumerated told of Britain's imperial march: from scarab beetles to Australian butterflies, African giant rats to Indian squirrels. He first described the Australian numbat *Myrmecobius* in 1836. That year HMS *Beagle* returned, and Waterhouse examined Darwin's South American mice, recognizing nineteen new species and one new genus in February

1837. His findings—which came just as Gould was diagnosing Darwin's supposedly disparate Galápagos birds as representative species of finch—helped to convince Darwin that representative species were common, and that islands could evolve new races. Waterhouse contributed the volume *Mammalia* to Darwin's five-part *Zoology of the Voyage of HMS Beagle* in 1839. He also described Darwin's insects, again showing that the Galápagos species were largely unique to each island. Classification was then part of zoology's *raison d'être*, but Waterhouse's quinarian arrangement of mammals in 1843 had Darwin insisting (in a rare admission of his private views) that true classification should reflect 'descent from common stocks' (*Correspondence*, 2.376).

In 1843 the Zoological Society ended Waterhouse's appointment, evidently as an economy measure, and he became an assistant in the mineralogical branch of the department of natural history at the British Museum. His *Natural History of the Mammalia* (1846–8) stopped at two volumes (on marsupials and rodents) when the publisher Baillière was affected by the revolution in France. Waterhouse was president of the Entomological Society in 1849–50, and vice-president of the Zoological Society in 1862–3. His brother F. G. Waterhouse, who lived in South Australia from 1852, sent Waterhouse canisters of live Coleoptera, enabling him to become an expert on the Australian Curculionidae (weevils), and to monograph the family Amycterinae. His *Catalogue of British Coleoptera* (1858) cleared up the synonymy of many species.

In 1851 Waterhouse succeeded Charles König as keeper of the mineralogical branch, which was shortly renamed the mineralogical and geological branch. It became the department of geology and mineralogy in 1856, with Waterhouse its keeper; on its division into two departments in 1857, Waterhouse became keeper of geology. Richard Owen, the new superintendent of the natural history department, dispatched Waterhouse to Germany in 1862 to assess Karl Häberlein's Solenhofen fossils, especially the reptilian bird *Archaeopteryx* (or 'Gryphosaurus' as Owen was set to call it, and as it appears in the trustees' minutes). Waterhouse negotiated the British Museum's purchase of 107 fossils and 53 counterparts of Solenhofen reptiles and fish, including *Archaeopteryx*, for £450 in November 1862. He bought a further 1595 fossils from Häberlein in 1863. He added numerous collections from the mid-1860s, when he purchased J. S. Bowerbank's Mesozoic invertebrates, until 1880, when he acquired 50,000 non-British fossils from the Museum of Practical Geology. As a keeper and erstwhile architect, Waterhouse helped to design the galleries of the new Natural History Museum in South Kensington, but he blocked moves (suggested by T. H. Huxley) to build a lecture theatre and research galleries. Waterhouse retired in 1880, a year before the museum opened. He nevertheless saw his son Charles Owen Waterhouse (whose godfathers were Charles Darwin and Richard Owen) continue as an assistant in the zoology department. Waterhouse never entirely recovered from a stroke in 1885 and he died at his home, Curton Lodge, Werter Road, Putney, on 21 January 1888. ADRIAN DESMOND

Sources C. O. Waterhouse, 'Memoir of George Robert Waterhouse', *Transactions of the Entomological Society of London* (1888), proceedings, lxx–lxxvi · *Entomologist's Monthly Magazine*, 24 (1888), 233–4 · *Zoologist*, 12 (1888), 99–100 · minutes of council, Zoological Society of London · *Reports of the Council and Auditors of the Zoological Society of London*, Zoological Society of London (1828–) · trustees' minutes, NHM · archive file on the Häberlein purchase, NHM, DF105/54 · *The correspondence of Charles Darwin*, ed. F. Burkhardt and S. Smith, 2–5 (1986–9) · A. Desmond, 'The making of institutional zoology in London, 1822–1836', *History of Science*, 23 (1985), 153–85, 223–50 · W. T. Stearn, *The Natural History Museum at South Kensington: a history of the British Museum (Natural History), 1753–1980* (1981) · M. Girouard, *Alfred Waterhouse and the Natural History Museum* (1981) · S. A. Neave, *The centenary history of the Entomological Society of London, 1833–1933* (1933)
Archives NHM, archives, corresp., reports to trustees · NHM, letters to his father and other letters and notes on zoological topics · PRO, genealogical collection, PRO 30/27 | Museum of Scotland, Edinburgh, letters to Sir William Jardine · NHM, letters and corresp. with Sir Richard Owen and William Clift · Oxf. U. Mus. NH, letters to J. O. Westwood · U. Edin. L., letters to Sir Charles Lyell
Likenesses T. H. Maguire, lithograph, 1851, BM
Wealth at death £3296 7s. od.: probate, 14 Feb 1888, *CGPLA Eng. & Wales*

Waterhouse, Helen, Lady Waterhouse (1913–1999). *See under* Waterhouse, Sir Ellis Kirkham (1905–1985).

Waterhouse, Joan (b. 1547/8). *See under* Essex witches (*act.* 1566–1589).

Waterhouse, John William (1849–1917), figure painter, was born in January 1849 at Rome, Italy, and baptized there on 6 April, the first of the four children of William Waterhouse (*bap.* 1816, *d.* 1890), painter, from Heckmondwike, West Riding of Yorkshire, and his second wife, Isabella (*c.*1821–1857), painter and daughter of Union Club secretary John Mackenzie of Brompton. Waterhouse was nicknamed Nino for Giovannino. The family settled in 1854 in Kensington, where his mother and two brothers died of tuberculosis. His father remarried in 1860.

By 1861 Waterhouse was at school in Leeds, where he relished Roman history and contemplated pursuing engineering as a career. However, while assisting his father, he entered the Royal Academy Schools as a probationer in sculpture in July 1870. In January 1871 he became a student in sculpture recommended by the painter F. R. Pickersgill, but soon began to exhibit paintings at the Dudley Gallery, Society of British Artists (SBA), and elsewhere: these ranged from a pining *Undine* (exh. SBA winter 1872, ex Christies, 9 February 1990) to an exotic keepsake beauty *The Unwelcome Companion: a Street Scene in Cairo* (exh. SBA 1873; Towneley Hall).

In 1874 an allegory with Roman setting, *Sleep and his Half Brother Death* (ex Sothebys, 1 October 1979), became Waterhouse's first exhibit at the Royal Academy, where he showed regularly until 1917. In 1877 *A Sick Child Brought into the Temple of Aesculapius* (priv. coll.) appeared there. Such classicized pictures echo Alma-Tadema through their interior perspectives and illusion of archaeological accuracy, yet their scale is larger, colouring more muted, and mood more melancholy. A major patron of these classical scenes was the contractor John Aird. Waterhouse produced images of ancient and modern genre while visiting Italy in 1877. The foreshortening and asymmetry of *Dolce far niente* (1879; priv. coll.) suggest awareness of progressive French art.

Acquisitions by provincial museums began in 1883, when the Art Gallery of South Australia at Adelaide purchased *The Favourites of the Emperor Honorius*—which typically emphasizes physical and psychological distance between a single figure and group. Waterhouse married flower painter Esther Maria (1857–1944), daughter of James Lees Kenworthy, artist, and his wife, Elizabeth, a school-mistress, at St Mary's, Ealing, on 8 September 1883. Although he was married in the Church of England, Waterhouse's numerous depictions of magic suggest that he was fascinated with occultism. The childless couple rented rooms near 3 Primrose Hill Studios which Waterhouse had leased in 1878; neighbours in this studio complex included the painter William Logsdail who used the Waterhouses and their siblings as models in three of his urban scenes of 1887, 1888, and 1890.

In the 1880s Waterhouse's dramatic pictures of women in antiquity found prestigious buyers and critical praise at the Royal Academy. Three are now in the Tate collection: *Consulting the Oracle* (1884), *St. Eulalia* (1885), and *The Magic Circle* (1886). He sent smaller genre pictures, including some of Venetian life, to the Grosvenor Gallery, Institute of Painters in Oil Colours, and Royal Institute of Painters in Water Colours; he was a member of the latter two institutions as well as the Art Workers' Guild and the Arts Club. His widely commented upon depiction of St Eulalia's martyrdom ensured his election as associate of the Royal Academy on 4 June 1885. Waterhouse became a visitor in the academy's life and painting schools, serving frequently between 1887 and 1908.

As early as 1886, critics praised Waterhouse's capacity to compose without exhaustive preparations. His sketchbooks (V&A and priv. coll.) contain landscape studies and compositions tested from different angles, some of which led ultimately to fully executed canvases. In his studio with a model and occasionally a lay figure, he drew with charcoal and chalk and made lively oil studies in preparation for major canvases, many of which contain pentimenti, evidence that he revised compositions even at the easel. He altered several pictures after they were purchased, and for *Flora and the Zephyrs* (1897; priv. coll.) he extended the canvas with a lining to complete the composition. Although rarely short of funds, he sometimes used damaged canvases.

Acclaim grew after Waterhouse's enormous depiction of Flavius Josephus's martyr *Mariamne* (1887; priv. coll.) was loaned to exhibitions by the collector William Cuthbert Quilter, earning medals at Paris (1889), Chicago (1893), and Brussels (1897). In 1887 the Waterhouses moved their workplace to the larger 6 Primrose Hill Studios. Through contact with Logsdail and the Newlyn painter Frank Bramley, Waterhouse experimented with Jules Bastien-Lepage's Impressionist-influenced painting techniques, and it is ironic that one of the few works in this naturalistic style, *The Lady of Shalott* (1888), figured prominently in the collection that Henry Tate gave to the nation to form the National Gallery of British Art. Waterhouse's mature painting style retained Bastien's careful treatment of face and limbs and looser handling of costume and foliage.

From 1890 Waterhouse turned to mythological heroines and enchantresses from Homer and Ovid, leading to richly coloured academy successes such as *Ulysses and the Sirens* (1891; National Gallery of Victoria, Melbourne). This was acquired upon the advice of Hubert Herkomer, who—with Sir Frederic Leighton and E. J. Poynter—recommended *Circe invidiosa* to the Art Gallery of South Australia at Adelaide in 1892.

In addition to classical subjects such as Psyche and Ariadne, Waterhouse also painted characters from literature favoured by the Pre-Raphaelites: Keats's *La Belle Dame sans Merci* and *Lamia*, Tennyson's *Mariana* and *Lady Clare*, and Shakespeare's *Juliet*. He later turned to other Pre-Raphaelite favourites (Malory, Boccaccio) and revisited old ones (he devised three treatments each of *The Lady of Shalott* and *Ophelia*). He usually bypassed vigorous action for a decorative stillness conveying the stories' pivotal moments: 'pre-Raphaelite pictures in a more modern manner … a kind of academic Burne-Jones, like him in his types and his moods, but with less insistence on design and more on atmosphere' (*The Times*, 12 Feb 1917, 6).

Many critics supported Waterhouse, especially *The Studio*. Acclaim for *St. Cecilia* (priv. coll.) encouraged his election to full academician on 16 May 1895, after nominations since 1892. He served on the academy's council intermittently between 1896 and 1911. Delays with his diploma picture (*A Mermaid*, completed 1900) underscore chronic tardiness; in 1911 his patron the beef and tanning magnate James Murray wrote that 'W[aterhouse] & his wife have no sense of time' (annotation of a letter from Waterhouse to Murray, 25 Dec 1911). He rushed to complete works for sending-in day, and his not letting numerous paint layers dry may account for the cracking of many pictures' surfaces. Waterhouse knew of the problem: in 1899 he recommended filling cracks with watercolours to reduce this effect.

Waterhouse usually depicted women—alone, supplicating before or enchanting a man, in pairs and groups. The 1897 Royal Academy hit was *Hylas and the Nymphs* (Manchester City Galleries) in which wistful, mildly eroticized *jeunes filles fatales* seduce a typically powerless young man. Its languorous and melancholy mood, timeless setting, and interlocking gazes epitomize Waterhouse's mature style, reliant on a singular female beauty both natural and unattainable.

In 1900 the Waterhouses took 10 Hall Road, a large house with two studios in St John's Wood expanded by sculptor Harry Bates. Waterhouse served as a visitor in the St John's Wood Art School, King's College School of Art for Women, and Baker Street School of Animal Painting, and he joined the Athenaeum and St John's Wood Arts Clubs.

But although he was a member of artistic circles, contemporaries rarely mention Waterhouse in their correspondence; his scarce surviving letters suggest a man of few words. Portraits suggest he was of medium height with reddish-brown hair and blue eyes. Despite declining taste for narrative subjects after 1900, Waterhouse's recognizable style attracted patrons. In addition to the patronage of George McCulloch, Frederick Fry, and Ernest Moon, Waterhouse cultivated the financier Alexander Henderson, later first Baron Faringdon. Henderson's extended family socialized with Waterhouse from the 1890s—ultimately owning more than thirty pictures by him, including commissioned portraits.

Waterhouse made ten portraits after 1900, all of women who resemble his ideal type of beauty. He also turned to seemingly non-narrative images of women, seated by streams or picking flowers in bright landscapes: *Windflowers* (1902; priv. coll.), *Gather ye Rosebuds* (1909; priv. coll.), and *Song of Springtime* (1913; priv. coll.). Several canvases allude to passionate mythological themes such as the abductions of Oreithyia and Persephone. No longer considered progressive, Waterhouse still sold: in 1912 Aberdeen Art Gallery paid £1400 for *Penelope and the Suitors*, and *St. Cecilia* brought £2415 during the 1913 McCulloch auction at Christies. *The Annunciation* (priv. coll.), Waterhouse's only biblical scene, came in 1914, and marked a renewed emphasis on explicit narrative and women in medieval and Renaissance settings.

Several late pictures were acquired by Sir William Hesketh Lever; *The Enchanted Garden* (Lady Lever Art Gallery, Port Sunlight) was on Waterhouse's easel when he died at home, 10 Hall Road, St John's Wood, on 10 February 1917; he had long suffered from cancer of the liver. Appreciations appeared in *The Studio*, *Daily Telegraph*, *Birmingham Daily Post*, *Westminster Gazette*, and *The Times*. *The Studio* classed Waterhouse 'among the best of our romanticist painters' for 'the right atmosphere of poetic suggestion' (*The Studio*, 71/291, 1917, 10), yet *The Times* thought eclecticism limited Waterhouse's originality—a modernist perspective anticipating the rapid decline in his reputation.

Attending Waterhouse's funeral on 15 February at St Mark's, Hamilton Terrace, St John's Wood, were patrons such as Murray and H. W. Henderson, and artists led by E. J. Poynter, including Herbert Draper, A. C. Gow, Briton Riviere, William Strang, and Albert Toft. Waterhouse was interred the same day at Kensal Green cemetery, where his widow was also buried in 1944. Instead of receiving his own exhibition, as Alma-Tadema had in 1913, he was represented in 'Works by Recently Deceased Members of the Royal Academy', in 1922. His widow held a 100-lot studio sale at Christies on 23 July 1926, when Waterhouse was so unfashionable that canvases such as *Ophelia* (exh. RA, 1889) sold for comparatively little. Since the 1960s growing numbers of Waterhouse's pictures have been reproduced commercially. This revival of interest saw major paintings sell for millions of pounds by 2000, stimulating trade even of works not in Waterhouse's signature style.

PETER TRIPPI

Sources P. Trippi, *J. W. Waterhouse* (2002) · A. Hobson, *The art and life of J W Waterhouse RA, 1849–1917* (1980) · A. F. Hobson, 'The life and work of J. W. Waterhouse, R.A.', PhD diss., Leicester University, 1978 · R. E. D. Sketchley, 'The art of J. W. Waterhouse, RA', *Art Journal*, new ser., 29 (1909), 1–32 · J. A. Blaikie, 'J. W. Waterhouse', *Magazine of Art*, 9 (1885–6), 1–6 · A. L. Baldry, 'The late J. W. Waterhouse', *The Studio*, 71 (1917), 2–15 · baptism register of British chaplain at Rome, GL, MS 11208, p. 815, microfilm 0574492 · *The Times* (12 Feb 1917), 6 · *Daily Telegraph* (13 Feb 1917), A4 · *The Studio*, 70 (1917), 88 · A. L. Baldry, 'J. W. Waterhouse and his work', *The Studio*, 4 (1894–5), 101–15 · A. L. Baldry, 'Some recent work by Mr J. W. Waterhouse', *The Studio*, 53 (1911), 174–85 · 'Some drawings by J. W. Waterhouse', *The Studio*, 44 (1908), 246–55 · J. W. Waterhouse to Harry P. Gill, 24 Oct 1899, Adelaide, state records of South Australia, GRG 19/2 1899, box 1 · J. W. Waterhouse to James Murray, 25 Dec 1911, Aberdeen Art Gallery, curatorial file for J. W. Waterhouse · A. B. Marvick, 'The art of John William Waterhouse: eclecticism in late nineteenth-century British painting', PhD diss., Columbia University, 1994 · Kensal Green cemetery records · d. cert. · J. W. Waterhouse to George Birkett, 19 June 189[5?], Leeds City Art Gallery, curatorial file

Archives V&A, pressmarks, 86.GG Box 3, 86.PP.19, 86.PP.21 | Leeds City Art Gallery, curatorial file · RA, RAC/1/WA7–12

Likenesses E. Mackenzie, portrait, exh. RA 1857 · H. S. Mendelssohn, photograph, *c*.1886, NPG · W. Logsdail, portrait, *c*.1887, priv. coll. · R. W. Robinson, photograph, *c*.1889, NPG · Elliott & Fry, photograph, *c*.1908, repro. in Hobson, *Art and life*

Wealth at death £3389—gross; £2938 4*s*. 2*d*.—net: probate, 9 Oct 1924

Waterhouse, Nathaniel (*bap.* 1586, *d.* 1645), merchant and benefactor, was born at Woodhouse, Skircoat, Halifax, in the West Riding of Yorkshire, and baptized on 11 September 1586 at Halifax parish church, the only child of Michael Waterhouse (*d.* 1587), and his second wife, Cecilia, widow of William Rayner. His father, who had six sons and daughters by a previous marriage, died before Nathaniel was fifteen months old. He had, however, made careful provision for his large family, with each of the children from his two marriages, including Nathaniel, receiving a legacy of £40. The will also appointed his eldest son, Isaac, whose piety had impressed the influential puritan vicar of Halifax, Dr John Favour, as guardian to the infant Nathaniel. He evidently provided Nathaniel with both a sound religious upbringing and a rudimentary education, which enabled him to append his signature to legal documents later in life. Little other evidence, however, survives of his childhood, education, and youth, but he may have been apprenticed to a clothier at the age of fourteen since his own will stipulated this requirement for children at the Blue Coat Hospital, which he founded in the closing years of his life. He also developed sufficient knowledge of woollen manufacture to accumulate a substantial fortune from 'buying and selling … cloth and merchandizing in oil, indigo, dyeing stuff and other commodities', as the local textile industry expanded in the early seventeenth century (Hanson, 'Nathaniel Waterhouse', 79). On 16 November 1607 he married Dorothy (1589–1652), the daughter of Michael Wilson.

Waterhouse's surviving business correspondence, particularly with the Crispes of London, leading importers of dye wares, and the documentary evidence of his many local property transactions after 1615 reveal his sharp business acumen, propensity for hard bargaining, and his growing wealth, which he attributed, under the providence of God, to 'his own honest industry as a trader' (Walker, 7). By 1627, when he was appointed a governor of the local grammar school established in 1600 by Dr John Favour, he was becoming increasingly involved in the public life of the town. In 1627 he also signed a petition of protest against the payment of ship money. By 1635 he was among the four wealthiest men in Halifax fined for the distraint of knighthood, and his name appears increasingly as a witness to the wills of West Riding gentry such as John Savile of Morley Hall, near Bingley, who nominated him as co-tutor to his daughter, Anne, in 1629.

Waterhouse developed a particular concern for the problem of poverty, and in 1633 he attempted with others to regulate and administer an annuity which had been bequeathed in 1611 for the relief of the Halifax poor. His frequent business visits aroused his interest in the London bridewell, founded in 1552 to provide work for the poor within a disciplined environment, and he provided property in Halifax for use as a workhouse and house of correction. In 1635 he successfully petitioned with others for a royal charter, paid for out of charitable gifts and bequests. He then served initially as master of the workhouse and subsequently combined the roles of governor and justice of the peace for the remainder of his life, presiding over a strict regime at the workhouse, where no fewer than seventy men and women were whipped for idleness and other misdemeanours between 1635 and 1638. In 1638 he was also appointed a constable for the wapentake of Agbrigg and Morley. His commitment to the workhouse during his lifetime and his later charitable bequests helped shape a pattern of social welfare provision in Halifax which endured for 200 years.

After Waterhouse's support for the 1641 protestation, which criticized royal absolution and affirmed support for the protestant religion, he appears to have maintained a largely non-partisan role in the politics of the English civil war. However, most of those nominated as trustees in his will of 1642, apart from Dr Richard Marsh, the royalist vicar of Halifax, were men of puritan sympathies. He died on 3 June 1645. His widow presented plain-glazed windows to Halifax parish church in his memory in 1652. Their childless marriage resulted in a munificence to the Halifax poor which was unsurpassed until the heyday of Victorian philanthropy. The inscription on their tombstone in the north chapel of Halifax parish church, where Nathaniel had been buried on 6 June 1645, recorded that he left as his heirs 'the church and poor' (Watson, 638). A more conspicuous monument of classical design on the north wall of the church to 'the pious and charitable' local benefactor provided details of his numerous charitable foundations and bequests. They included twelve almshouses for the elderly or impotent poor, who were to receive a maintenance allowance of £2 each per annum; a hospital where twenty orphaned boys and girls were to be provided with training for work under the supervision of a master; accommodation and allowances to enable the lecturer at Halifax parish church 'to visit the aged' and catechize the young; £40 per annum to enable the curates of

the twelve chapels within the ancient parish of Halifax to preach midweek monthly sermons at Halifax parish church; and bequests for the repair of local highways, the free grammar school, and the poor of Huddersfield and Mirfield (Crossley, 51–2). The income derived from his estate increased from £130 17s. 0d. at its foundation to £1193 in 1827, when the first inquiry into the charity was held, and by 1894 the charity had investments totalling £20,061 17s. 10d., generating an income of £2352 19s. 6d. By 1996 this income had risen to £68,690 p.a.

JOHN A. HARGREAVES

Sources J. Watson, *The history and antiquities of the parish of Halifax, in Yorkshire* (1775) · T. W. Hanson, 'Nathaniel Waterhouse', *Transactions of the Halifax Antiquarian Society* (1919), 73–104 · Halifax Council of Social Welfare and the Rotary Club of Halifax, *Institutions and charitable agencies of Halifax* (1929), 110–14 · E. W. Crossley, ed., *The monumental and other inscriptions in Halifax parish church* (1909), 5, 51, 127 · R. Hardcastle, 'Charity pioneer's historic work goes on', *Evening Courier* [Halifax] (8 Dec 1989) · T. W. Hanson, *The story of old Halifax* (1920) · A. Betteridge, 'Halifax before the industrial revolution: a study of local administrative records, part 2', *Transactions of the Halifax Antiquarian Society* (1979), 81–103 · 'Reports on endowments of charity commissions', *Parl. papers* (1896), vol. 63/1, no. 192 [borough of Halifax] · J. Clayton, 'History of the Waterhouse charity, Halifax', MA diss., University of Leeds, c.1945, Calderdale Central Library · W. J. Walker, *Halifax Registers* (1885) · W. K. Jordan, *The charities of rural England, 1480–1660* (1961), 276, 290 · Charity Commission, Harmsworth House, 13–15 Bouverie Street, London

Archives BM, letters and MSS, pedigrees of Waterhouse family, Add. MSS 31007–31013 | W. Yorks. AS, Calderdale, Calderdale district archives, Waterhouse Charity Records

Wealth at death £130 17s. in charity derived from estate: charity commissioners' report, parish of Halifax, incl. county borough of Halifax

Waterhouse, Paul (1861–1924), architect, was the eldest son of the architect Alfred *Waterhouse (1830–1905) and his wife, Elizabeth (1834–1918), daughter of John *Hodgkin, conveyancer, and sister of Thomas Hodgkin (1831–1913), the historian. He was born on 29 October 1861 at Manchester, and he lived there until his father moved with his family to London in 1865. Paul Waterhouse was sent to St Michael's School, Aldin House, Slough, run by the Revd J. W. Hawtrey, and then to Eton College. He matriculated at Balliol College, Oxford, in 1880, and was awarded a second class in classical moderations (1882) and in *literae humaniores* (1884). Delicate in health, he did not participate much in games, but at Balliol he coxed the college eight, was captain of the college boat club in 1883, and coxed one of the trial eights, though he failed to get his blue. On 16 July 1887 he married Lucy Grace (b. 1861/2), daughter of Sir Reginald Francis Douce *Palgrave (1829–1904), clerk of the House of Commons; they had one son and two daughters. Monica Mary, the elder of his two sisters, married Robert Bridges (1844–1930), the poet laureate.

After leaving Oxford, Waterhouse went into his father's office. He became a partner in 1891, and, after the senior partner's death in 1905, carried on the practice alone, until joined by his own son, Michael, in 1919. His individual, and especially his more intimate, work has a quality of its own, contrasting in character with the specialized style of the large business and public buildings for which his father had become famous—a tradition which he carried on in the continuation of his father's practice. He inherited a facility for good planning, and completed many of his father's works, among them being buildings at Liverpool for the Royal Infirmary and for the university, laboratories at Manchester and Leeds universities, and St Mary's Hospital, Manchester.

Among the more important of Waterhouse's own works are the chemical laboratories at Oxford University (1913), and the university union (1921), the St Regulus Club (1922), and the Younger commemoration hall (1925) at St Andrews University. Hospital buildings designed by him include the medical school and the nurses' home, University College, London (1905), the offices of the Royal National Pension Fund for Nurses, Buckingham Street, Strand (1906), extensions to the Lister Institute of Preventive Medicine, Chelsea Bridge Road (1908), and new wards for the Bromley (Kent) and District Hospital (1910), the Yeovil and District Hospital (1921), and St Leonard's Hospital, Sudbury (1922). Alfred Waterhouse had been responsible for designing important office buildings for the Prudential Assurance and Refuge Assurance companies, and his son continued this connection, designing premises for the prudential in a variety of towns; the Atlas Assurance Company's office at Birmingham is also from his design. He extended the premises of the National Provincial Bank in Bishopsgate, London, and built branches for Lloyds Bank and for the National Provincial foreign bank in Paris, Brussels, and Antwerp.

Among examples of Waterhouse's domestic work, 73 South Audley Street, London, and Mount Melville, St Andrews, with its home farm and buildings, gardens, cottages, and bailiff's house, may be mentioned. His ecclesiastical work includes All Saints' Church, St Andrews (1918), St Francis's Church, Hammerfield, Hertfordshire, and the Convent of the Incarnation at Oxford.

In 1886 Waterhouse was awarded the essay medal of the Royal Institute of British Architects. He was elected an associate of that body in 1889 by examination, with the award of a special prize, and proceeded to the fellowship in 1895. During a lifelong association with the institute, he gave unstinted time to its committees, including the board of architectural education. He took particular interest in the education and training of students and in the development of schools of architecture in London and elsewhere in Britain. In 1921 and 1922 he occupied the president's chair, previously held by his father from 1888 to 1891, and during his years of office did much to promote the unification of the architectural profession. The institute was passing through a difficult period and Waterhouse's firm but tactful leadership was invaluable. By means of visits and addresses in all parts of the country he succeeded in strengthening the relations between the institute and its allied societies.

Town planning was a subject of which Waterhouse made a special study, and he was an authority on London bridges. He excelled as a draughtsman, and his line and wash drawings have much delicacy and charm. Examples of such work are his illustrations to William Sanday's *Sacred Sites of the Gospels* (1903). He was an accomplished speaker and writer; his literary work was confined mainly to professional subjects, which he treated in a style that was scholarly, humorous, and allusive. *Paul Waterhouse: a Collection of Certain of his Papers and Addresses* was published in 1930. Waterhouse died at his home at Yattendon Court, Berkshire, on 19 December 1924. His wife survived him. His son, Michael, succeeded him in his architectural practice.

P. S. WORTHINGTON, *rev.* CATHERINE GORDON

Sources *Dir. Brit. archs.* • A. S. Gray, *Edwardian architecture: a biographical dictionary* (1985), 371–2 • A. Webb, J. A. Gotch, and A. Keen, 'The late Paul Waterhouse', *RIBA Journal*, 32 (1924–5), 141–2, 192, 202, 321–2 [correspondence and tributes] • *The Times* (20 Dec 1924) • W. G. N., *ArchR*, 57 (1925), 45 • m. cert. • *CGPLA Eng. & Wales* (1925)
Archives RIBA BAL, papers
Likenesses W. Orpen, oils, 1923, RIBA • photographs, RIBA BAL
Wealth at death £54,253 8s. 6d.: probate, 10 Feb 1925, *CGPLA Eng. & Wales*

Waterland, Daniel (1683–1740), theologian, second son of Henry Waterland, rector of Walesby and Flixborough, Lincolnshire, and his second wife, was born at Walesby on 14 February 1683. He was educated at the free school in Lincoln and at Magdalene College, Cambridge, where he was admitted on 30 March 1699, elected scholar on 26 December 1702, and fellow on 13 February 1704. He graduated BA in 1703 and BD in 1714, and proceeded MA in 1706 and DD in 1717. On 8 May 1724 he was incorporated DD at Oxford University. He married in 1719 Theodosia (d. 1761), daughter of John Tregonwell of Anderton, Dorset.

Cambridge and the Arian controversy A dedicated teacher and an able administrator, Waterland devoted his considerable energies to his college and his university. In February 1714 he was appointed master of Magdalene by the visitor, Lord Suffolk and Bindon, whom he had tutored as an undergraduate, succeeding another Lincolnshire man, Gabriel Quadring, in the office; he was also presented to the living of Ellingham, Norfolk. He was a vigorous and very successful master of Magdalene, the college of his father and grandfather. This family connection was strengthened when he brought in his brother Theodore from Clare College as, successively, a foundation fellow, dean, and, by 1718, president of the college. On 14 November 1715 Waterland succeeded Thomas Sherlock as vice-chancellor of the university. On 7 June 1716 he preached a sermon on the occasion of the university's public thanksgiving for the suppression of the Jacobite rising, and on 22 October he presented to the prince of Wales, at Hampton Court, a congratulatory address that he had devised with Richard Bentley, the master of Trinity College; this entailed the beginning of an enmity with the not inconsiderable Jacobite elements in Cambridge. In 1717 Waterland became a chaplain-in-ordinary to the king; he received no further promotion at Cambridge and was especially disappointed never to have been offered either the Lady Margaret or the regius chair in divinity.

Waterland and Bentley were the leading moderate

Daniel Waterland (1683–1740), by John Faber junior (after Richard Philips)

whigs in early Hanoverian Cambridge and their acceptance of Bishop Moore's library, from George I, was symbolic of the good relations they successfully sought to have with whig politicians. Waterland was responsible for the arrangements in accepting and organizing this considerable gift of books. His relationship with Bentley cooled somewhat as a result of his involvement in the censure passed by heads of houses, in January 1721, on Bentley's libel on John Colbatch (1664–1748); Bentley had attacked Colbatch, a professorial fellow of Trinity, for writing a tract (in fact the work of Conyers Middleton) which was critical of Bentley's conduct during the 1717 ceremony for the presentation of DDs, at which Waterland had received his own degree. Waterland was a member of the syndicate appointed on 26 September 1723 to take such steps as might be advisable for the purpose of defeating or delaying Bentley's restoration to office in the university, which they eventually granted him in March 1724.

It was widely felt that Waterland studied too hard at great long-term cost to his health. He drew up a detailed programme of reading for undergraduates in the 1710s, which he first published as *Advice to a Young Student* in 1730; it reached a third edition in 1760. In this work he recommended much of the new learning, especially the mathematical works of Newton and his expositors; he also recommended a reading of Locke's *Essay*, though he alerted his readers to what he considered to be dangerous elements in that work. He advised that strictly theological study be left until after intensive study of the classics and philosophy for the BA degree. It was, however, in the study of theology that he was to make his own mark. He quickly took up the orthodox cause in the engagement over the doctrine of the Trinity, which began in earnest when Arianism began to be promoted by Samuel Clarke and his Cambridge followers. At the public commencement at Cambridge in 1714 Waterland held a much admired disputation with Sherlock on the question of Arian subscription to the Thirty-Nine Articles, which was then being discussed as a result of the Arian tendency of Clarke's controversial *Scripture Doctrine of the Trinity* (1712). John Jackson (1686–1763), an Arian-inclined disciple of Clarke, subsequently published the correspondence that he had had with Waterland on the matter, without Waterland's permission, leading Waterland to respond with a public attack on the Arianism of Clarke and of Daniel Whitby (an influential clerical critic of the doctrine of the Trinity) in a learned tract, *A Vindication of Christ's Divinity* (1719). In the course of this work Waterland attacked Clarke's motivation in pleading, as a human infirmity, the right of Arians to subscribe to Trinitarian formulas in the Thirty-Nine Articles; to Waterland this was pure dishonesty, an argument which he reaffirmed when he replied, in an *Answer* (1720), to Whitby's critique of the *Vindication*. In his own reply, *The Modest Plea, &c. Continued* (1720), Clarke indicted Waterland for relying on the testimony of the church fathers and tradition in making the Trinitarian case, stating that he himself preferred to argue about points of doctrine on purely scriptural grounds. The appeal to the fathers (principally as interpreters of scripture) to church history and to modern philosophy had become marked features of Waterland's style of thought very early in his publishing career, and in this he revealed his moderate high-churchmanship and his own preference for the considered results of theological learning over direct and simple appeal to scripture. He once again strongly condemned Clarke-inspired attempts at opening up the meaning of the articles away from orthodox interpretation, which he defined as the sense which the church intended, in a stinging rebuke, *The Case of Arian Subscription Consider'd* (1721). He continued on the orthodox offensive with the publication of *The Scriptures and the Arians, Compared in their Accounts of God the Father and God the Son* (1722), which tried to meet Clarke on his home ground of scriptural authority, and in two further supplemental works which also contained replies to his other critics, *A Second Vindication of Christ's Divinity* (1723) and *A Farther Vindication of Christ's Divinity* (1724). He had returned to the fray over subscriptions in *A Supplement to the Case of Arian Subscription Considered* (1722), in which he developed his strongly Arminian reading of the articles. His firmly liturgical sense of the Anglican tradition informed his final major engagement with Clarke's Arianism, *Remarks upon Dr. Clarke's Exposition of the Church Catechism* (1730). Waterland similarly replied to Arianizing tendencies among dissenters in *An Answer to some Queries Printed at Exon* (1721). He reaffirmed the importance of antiquity as a means of defending the orthodox doctrine of the Trinity in his last major work on the subject, *The Importance of the Doctrine of the Holy Trinity Asserted* (1734).

In defence of religious orthodoxy   Waterland's learning and acumen impressed Bishop Robinson of London, who consequently appointed him as the first lecturer on the Lady Moyer foundation (1719–20). The sermons that he preached on the foundation at St Paul's Cathedral restated, in a more polemical tone, his anti-Arian argument that the authority of antiquity and scripture vindicated the orthodox interpretation of Christ's divine nature. They were published as *Eight Sermons in Defence of the Divinity of our Lord Jesus Christ* (1720) and enjoyed a wide circulation; they were the most immediately influential of his works. Following the success of his Lady Moyer lectures Waterland was presented by the dean and chapter of St Paul's to the London rectory of St Augustine with St Faith. On 21 December 1722 he was appointed chancellor of the archdiocese of York by Archbishop Dawes. He was made a canon of Windsor on 27 September 1727 and he became archdeacon of Middlesex on 13 August 1730; he was also presented to the vicarage of Twickenham in October 1730, whereupon he resigned his London rectory. In 1723 he published another major defence of theological orthodoxy, his *Critical History of the Athanasian Creed*. This acted as a farther bulwark against Clarke's Arianism since the creed contained the most explicit formulation of the orthodox doctrine of the Trinity. In an exhaustive review of the evidence Waterland assigned composition of the Athanasian creed to the years 426–30 and attributed its authorship to St Hilary of Arles. He justified writing such a learned work in English by pointing to the obvious need to obviate the potentially dangerous effects of heterodox argument on this matter. Its importance was immediately recognized and a second edition was issued in 1728. He also actively engaged in the controversy about deism, producing *Scripture Vindicated* (1730–32), a reply to Matthew Tindal's *Christianity as Old as the Creation*, in three parts. This developed his method of interpreting the scriptures, which demonstrated that since their teaching was often parabolic and mystical in form then they could not be easily and simplistically condemned in the manner promoted by Tindal. Scripture was also, Waterland argued, a vital record of historical truth. He denied that natural religion was enough for humanity by emphasizing how only revealed religion contained the essential doctrines of the reward of eternal life and the status of Christ as mediator. A more sophisticated critique of Waterland's reading of scripture, a *Letter to Dr. Waterland Containing some Remarks on his Vindication of Scripture*, appeared in 1731. This was the work of Conyers Middleton, who had begun to enjoy something of a rivalrous relationship with Waterland at Cambridge. Middleton urged that many of the stories of the Old Testament could only make sense to rational people if they were understood allegorically, thus compromising Waterland's emphasis on other, more direct modes of exegesis; Waterland's vexed response to this work can be seen in his heavily annotated copy of the text, which is now in the Bodleian Library (8° Rawlinson, 437). These exchanges led, in the early 1730s, to something of a pamphlet war concerning deism. Waterland also rather conventionally attacked deism, as a morally corrupting

system of ideas, in a charge to the archdeaconry of Middlesex, which he published in 1732 as *Christianity Vindicated Against Infidelity*.

Waterland's continuing efforts at countering the influence of Clarke's metaphysics on religious orthodoxy led him to contribute *A Dissertation on the Argument a priori for Proving the Existence of a First Cause* as an anonymous appendix, 'the work of a learned hand', to Edmund Law's *Enquiry into the Ideas of Space, Time, Immensity, and Eternity* (1734). In this largely historical as well as philosophical work Waterland objected to Clarke's use of the ontological argument; he was supported in this endeavour not only by Law but also by Joseph Clarke, a young fellow of Magdalene, who would later edit Waterland's sermons for the press. This was a major element of a significant rearguard action against Clarke's version of Newton's physico-theology that occurred in Cambridge, hitherto the centre of such reasoning, in the 1720s and 1730s. Some of Waterland's correspondence in the British Library reveals his deep suspicion of Newton's Arianism, the influence of which at Cambridge he saw it as his duty to counteract (BL, Add. MS 5831, fols. 172–3, 173–5; BL, Add. MS 6396, fol. 14). Law dedicated his translation of Archbishop King's *The Origin of Evil* (1731) to Waterland, who had acted as his patron at the outset of his career.

Waterland also contributed to the debate on the eucharist that had been inaugurated by Bishop Hoadly's *Plain Account of the Nature and End of the Sacrament of the Lord's Supper* (1735) by producing a very detailed and scholarly *Review of the Doctrine of the Eucharist as Laid Down in Scripture and Antiquity* (1737). This work retained its status as a vigorous statement of Anglican doctrine until well into the nineteenth century. Waterland maintained that the sacraments were a major support of central elements of Christian teaching, not least because they emphasized Christ's divine nature. The eucharist was explained as a material and spiritual symbol of Christ's sacrifice; it could not then be merely the service of commemoration which the low-church Hoadly insisted it was. In the plethora of writings on the subject produced at this time Waterland's words were to prove the most influential. In making his argument he once again appealed to patristic authority and to the testimony of antiquity and tradition. He had been concerned with such matters some time before Hoadly went into print on the matter, having already produced a work entitled *The Nature, Obligation, and Efficacy of the Christian Sacraments Considered* in 1730. In common with so many of his fellow churchmen Waterland was also a critic of enthusiasm, as can be seen in his tract on the rite of baptism, *Regeneration Stated and Explained According to Scripture and Antiquity* (1740), which denounced the Methodists and the doctrine of the new birth. For Waterland baptism was a once-only event, the beginning of the Christian life, and any subsequent renewal was simply the maturing of that life, not some new salvific event. Regeneration was not, then, a distinct new birth but a continuing process of spiritual maturation. These considerations were extended in a posthumously published study, *An Inquiry Concerning the Antiquity and Practice of Infant Communion*, which discussed the history and doctrine that informed the proper time for the incorporation of young people into the church. The attack on Whitefield and Wesley was also continued in another posthumously published tract, *A Summary View of the Doctrine of Justification* (1742). Waterland was afraid that Methodist faith in justification would prove a stimulus to antinomianism and he wanted to emphasize the centrality of a moral life which is implied in the orthodox view of justification as the incorporation of the individual believer within the church. Waterland denounced any belief in the primacy of salvation by faith alone; he stressed instead the need for good works and a strenuous moral life in achieving salvation.

Later years, and reputation Although popular with his fellow clergy as a succinct defender of theological orthodoxy Waterland declined the office of prolocutor in the lower house of convocation in 1734; he also refused the see of Llandaff in 1738 and in 1740. Indeed his beliefs were closer to those of the lower clergy than they were to those of the latitudinarians, who tended to enjoy higher preferments in the church, which led his friend the antiquary William Cole to claim that 'Dr Waterland was long talked of for a Bishopric ... tho' his *Church notions* did not exactly square with the fashionable Opinions' (BL, Add. MS 5831, fol. 171). He was a deeply and unusually learned man and his researches encompassed a wide area of theological and historical enquiry. In common with a number of his clerical contemporaries he was a scholar of Old English; he also corresponded with the clerical historian John Lewis on the subject of Reginald Pecock, the controversial fifteenth-century theologian. Waterland died on 23 December 1740 and was buried in the south transept of St George's Chapel, Windsor. A fine funeral sermon was preached for him by his Middlesex colleague Jeremiah Seed, a fellow of the Queen's College, Oxford. His *Sermons* were published posthumously under the editorship of Joseph Clarke in 1742.

Waterland was one of the most able and influential theologians in the eighteenth-century Church of England. A firm opponent of the Arianism that had grown up in Cambridge as a legacy of Newton's and of Clarke's theologies, he helped to keep theological heterodoxy at bay in the first half of the eighteenth century. An able controversialist, he was suspicious of both mysticism and metaphysics, looking instead to history and external evidence, often of a textual kind, in making the orthodox case. He belonged to the Anglican patristic tradition championed by George Bull, to whom he became a natural successor in the theological debates of the first half of the eighteenth century. His theology remained influential into the early nineteenth century and he was championed both by Samuel Taylor Coleridge, who thought it the duty of all Anglican clergy to make themselves familiar with Waterland's writings, and by William van Mildert, who produced a major edition of Waterland's works, in ten volumes, at the Clarendon Press in 1823. Mark Pattison, in his important essay 'Tendencies of religious thought in England, 1688–1750', first published in *Essays and Reviews* in 1860, noted the continued importance of Waterland for high-

church thinking and saw in him the one figure in the eighteenth-century church to whom appeal could be made by 'the genuine Anglican', who, in 'constructing his *Catena patrum* ... closes his list with Waterland or Brett, and leaps at once to 1833, when the *Tracts for the Times* commenced—as Charles II dated his reign from his father's death' (M. Pattison, *Essays*, ed. H. Nettleship, 1889, 2.49). He was one of the most learned divines of his age and he used his considered erudition against such equally learned, but considerably less orthodox, Cambridge contemporaries as Clarke, Whitby, Whiston, and Middleton, as well as against deists such as Tindal, low-churchmen such as Hoadly, and Methodists such as Whitefield and Wesley. As a controversialist Waterland took on an unusually varied group of often extremely talented adversaries in engagements in which he invariably came out rather well. His writings are absolutely central to any appreciation of the religious life of eighteenth-century England, and they mark a degree of continuity in Anglican thinking from the close of the seventeenth century, in the tradition championed by George Bull, to the high-church revival that followed in the wake of the Oxford Movement.

The last volume of van Mildert's edition of the *Works* is largely taken up with letters, to which may be added *Fourteen Letters to Zachary Pearce* (ed. E. Churton, 1868), which covers a range of theological matters, and *Five Letters to William Staunton*, appended to Staunton's *Reason and Revelation Stated* (1722). There are also important letters in the British Library and the Bodleian Library.

B. W. YOUNG

Sources W. van Mildert, 'Life', in *The works of the Rev. Daniel Waterland*, ed. W. van Mildert, 10 vols. (1823), vol. 1 · R. T. Holtby, *Daniel Waterland, 1683–1740: a study in eighteenth century orthodoxy* (1966) · P. Cunich and others, *A history of Magdalene College, Cambridge, 1428–1988* (1994) · *GM*, 1st ser., 10 (1740), 623 · *GM*, 1st ser., 12 (1742), 280 · Foster, *Alum. Oxon.* · L. Stephen, *History of English thought in the eighteenth century*, 2 vols. (1876) · C. J. Abbey and J. H. Overton, *The English church in the eighteenth century*, 2 vols. (1878) · J. Gascoigne, *Cambridge in the age of the Enlightenment* (1989) · B. W. Young, *Religion and Enlightenment in eighteenth-century England: theological debate from Locke to Burke* (1998)

Archives BL, letters to John Anstis and others · Bodl. Oxf., letters to John Loveday · Lincs. Arch., letters to George Whichcote · LPL, letters to Edmund Gibson

Likenesses J. Faber junior, mezzotint (after R. Philips), NPG [see illus.] · J. Fittler, line engraving, BM, NPG · engraving, repro. in van Mildert, ed., *Works of Daniel Waterland*, vol. 1 · oils, Magd. Cam.

Waterlow, Sir Ernest Albert (1850–1919), landscape and animal painter, was born at 21 York Place, City Road, Islington, London, on 24 May 1850, the son of Albert Crakell Waterlow, stationer, and his wife, Maria Corfs. He was the nephew of Sir Sydney Hedley *Waterlow, first baronet, lord mayor of London in 1872–3. Waterlow was educated at Eltham College, London, before moving with his mother to Heidelberg, Germany, following his father's early death. The family later moved to Switzerland, the move prompted by the Austro-Prussian War of 1866, and Waterlow received lessons in painting from an artist at Ouchy, near Lausanne. He returned to London in the autumn of 1867, and became a student at Cary's Art School, where he drew from the antique for six months.

By 1868 his preferred subject was already landscape but, feeling that he would benefit from further tuition in drawing, he again entered Cary's Art School about 1870. He found the return to drawing from the antique to be uninspiring, and left to concentrate on landscape painting during the day while studying at St Martin's School of Art in the evenings.

In 1872 Waterlow entered the Royal Academy Schools, and he was awarded the Turner gold medal in the following year for his painting *A Land Storm*. He exhibited regularly at the Royal Academy from 1872. *Passing Showers; Glentanar*, shown in 1873, was purchased by his uncle. Waterlow rented a riverside studio at Hurley-on-Thames with his friend Tom Lloyd, and then in 1874 acquired a studio in Hayter House, Marylebone, London, from which time 'success … attended his every effort' (*Art Annual*, 1906, 5). Waterlow painted in Ireland, France, Germany, and Switzerland, as well as many parts of England, and was influenced in his style by George H. Mason and Frederick Walker. In 1876 Waterlow married Mary Margaret Sophia Hofman (*d.* 1899), daughter of Professor Carl Hofman of Heidelberg, with whom he had two sons and two daughters. In the same year they moved to the house and studio at 3 St Petersburgh Place, Bayswater, which had belonged to Frederick Walker at the time of his death in 1875.

In 1874 Waterlow illustrated a manuscript by David Ferrier, *The Localisation of Function in the Brain*; these diagrams were included in two further works by Ferrier, *Experiments on the Brains of Monkeys* and *Functions of the Brain* (1876). It is interesting to note that Waterlow, celebrated in his lifetime as a landscape painter and always described as such, produced these diagrams, especially when his 'illustrations of the monkey brain and/or their human analogies were reproduced in most leading anglophone texts of anatomy, physiology, or neurology by the 1880s' (Millett).

Waterlow exhibited regularly in London, at the Grosvenor Gallery, the New Gallery, Suffolk Street, the Royal Society of Painters in Water Colours (RWS), and elsewhere. In 1880 he was made an associate of the RWS, a member in 1894, and president in 1897 (holding this office until 1914). Waterlow painted *en plein air* to achieve an authentic depiction of light and atmosphere, for example *River Landscape with Cattle* (AM Oxf.) is a beautifully composed, quiet, and restful painting which shows the influence of Camille Corot and the Barbizon school, who advocated this technique. In general his landscapes are 'marked by harmony of colour and quiet refinement' (Hardie, 2.234), and while they are described as being 'idyllic' by both Martin Hardie and Adrian Vincent (Vincent, 317), Waterlow nevertheless managed to 'capture the essence of the English countryside without idealising it to the degree that Birket Foster often did' (ibid.). Waterlow was elected an associate of the Royal Academy in 1890, and an Academician in 1903. He was knighted in 1902. On 21 June 1907 he was among the 'Distinguished Company' (*New York Times*, 22 June 1907) invited by the American ambassador, Ambassador Reid, to meet Mark Twain at Dorchester House. Waterlow's fellow guests included Sir Lawrence Alma-Tadema, Sir Arthur Conan Doyle, Sidney Lee, and Bram Stoker. In 1909, following the death of his first wife in 1899, Waterlow married Eleanor Marion Sealy, widow of Dr George Sealy, of Weybridge, Surrey. He died at his home, 1 Maresfield Gardens, Hampstead, London, on 25 October 1919; his wife survived him. The contents of his studio were sold at Christies on 6 January 1920. Those paintings and drawings which were retained by his family were bequeathed to the Court Gallery, Somerset, in 2000. The Victoria and Albert Museum, London, and the Laing Art Gallery, Newcastle upon Tyne, also have examples of his work.   JESSICA KILBURN

Sources C. Collins Baker, *Art Annual* (1906) [issue devoted to Waterlow] · Wood, *Vic. painters*, 3rd edn · M. Hardie, *Water-colour painting in Britain*, ed. D. Snelgrove, J. Mayne, and B. Taylor, 3 vols. (1966–8) · Mallalieu, *Watercolour artists* · L. Lambourne and J. Hamilton, eds., *British watercolours in the Victoria and Albert Museum* (1980) · *The Times* (27 Oct 1919) · A. Vincent, *A companion to Victorian and Edwardian artists* (1991) · www.courtgallery.com/, June 2001 · D. Millett, abstracts, third annual meeting of the International Society for the History of the Neurosciences (ISHN) (1998), www.medsch.ucla.edu/som/bri/archives/ishn/abs1998.htm, July 2001 · *CGPLA Eng. & Wales* (1919)

Likenesses L. Alma-Tadema, oils, 1889, RA · E. A. Waterlow, self-portrait, oils, 1890, Aberdeen Art Gallery · drawing, 1893, NPG · R. W. Robinson, group portrait, photograph, NPG; repro. in *Members and associates of the Royal Academy of Arts, 1891* (1892) · R. W. Thomas, photograph, repro. in Collins Baker, *Art Annual*, p. 31 · photograph, NPG

Wealth at death £120,981 16s. 6d.: probate, 29 Dec 1919, *CGPLA Eng. & Wales*

Waterlow, Sir Sydney Hedley, first baronet (1822–1906), printer and philanthropist, born in Crown Street, Finsbury, London, on 1 November 1822, was fourth of the five sons of James Waterlow (1790–1876) of Huntington Lodge, Peckham Road, Surrey, and his wife, Mary (*d.* 1872), daughter of William Crakell. The family was of French Walloon descent, and the father, who was a member of the Stationers' Company and a common councilman for Cornhill ward, started in 1811 a small stationer's business in Birchin Lane, where in 1836 he was joined by his eldest son, Alfred James, and between 1840 and 1844 by other sons.

Brought up by his grandmother at Mile End until the age of seven, Sydney went first to a dame-school in Worship Street, then to a boarding-school at Brighton, and lastly to St Saviour's Grammar School in Southwark, living at that time with his father in Gloucester Terrace, Hoxton. His father was a member of the Unitarian congregation at South Place Chapel, Finsbury, under the ministry of William Johnson Fox; Fox's teaching greatly influenced young Waterlow, who was a Unitarian throughout his life. In November 1836 he was apprenticed through the Stationers' Company to his uncle Thomas Harrison, the government printer, with whom he lived at Pimlico and afterwards at Sloane Square. His hard work brought him in the fourth year of his apprenticeship the sole charge of the Foreign Office printing, with full responsibility for its secrecy. On finishing his apprenticeship in November

1843 he went to Paris, and was employed during the winter in printing for the publisher Galignani a catalogue of his library.

At Easter 1844 Waterlow joined his brothers Alfred, Walter, and Albert in adding a printing branch to the stationery business in Birchin Lane, the modest capital of £120 being provided by their father. They began by printing the *Bankers' Magazine*, of which the first number appeared in April. Success followed at once, largely through the great share which the firm secured in railway printing and stationery. Additional premises were taken at 49 Parliament Street (1846), London Wall (1851), Carpenters' Hall (1854), Great Winchester Street (1866), Castle Street, Finsbury (1872), Little Chart Mills, Ashford, Kent (1875), and Paris (1883). The firm became a limited company in February 1876, as Waterlow & Sons Ltd, and in February 1877 the company sold the Birchin Lane portion of their business to Waterlow Bros. and Layton. From this date until 1895, when he retired, Sydney Waterlow was managing director of the company. The company was reconstructed in 1879, and again in 1897.

Waterlow joined the city corporation in 1857, when he was elected a common councilman for the ward of Broad Street. He devised a system of telegraphic communication between the City police stations, for which he was publicly thanked (Minutes of the common council, 3 April 1862). He was elected alderman of Langbourn ward on 30 January 1863, and served as sheriff in 1866–7. Waterlow was knighted on 3 August 1867. On Michaelmas day 1872 he was elected lord mayor. Among the more important events of his mayoralty were the establishment of the Hospital Sunday Fund (21 November), the opening to the public of the newly built Guildhall Library (10 March 1873), and the entertainment of the shah of Persia at Guildhall (20 June). On 29 July 1873 he was made a baronet. He was for ten years (from 29 May 1873) governor of the Irish Society and visited Ireland annually on its behalf; in 1876–7 the society was the subject of controversy and a motion in the Commons, as more than a third of its receipts were spent on expenses. He was treasurer of St Bartholomew's Hospital from 1874 to 1892, and was chairman of the united Westminster schools from 1873 to 1893. He resigned as an alderman on 18 September 1883.

Waterlow was an active philanthropist, especially in the areas of the provision of clean water and good housing. In 1862 he built at his own expense in Mark Street, Finsbury, a block of working-class dwellings, with accommodation for eighty families; these tenements, although built for comfort and let at moderate rents, produced a good return for the outlay. In 1863 he started the Improved Industrial Dwellings Company Ltd, of which he was chairman until his death, by which time the company possessed 6000 tenements, which housed 30,000 persons. In 1865 he urged the passing of an act—eventually achieved—for state loans to the company, and he urged compulsory purchase of land for housing development.

In 1868 Waterlow won Dumfriesshire, standing as a Liberal against the Buccleuch interest, by forty-four votes. However, he was unseated in 1869, his firm having taken a

government contract of which he had no personal knowledge. After an unsuccessful contest for the same seat in 1869 and for Southwark in 1870, he was elected for Maidstone in 1874, and sat for that borough until 1880, when he was defeated. He was shortly afterwards elected for Gravesend, and held that seat until 1885, when he unsuccessfully fought the Medway division of Kent. A stalwart Liberal, he spoke in parliament in favour of a reform of the London corporation. He was a member of the royal commission on friendly and benefit societies of 1870 (report presented 1874), of the royal judicature commission of 1877 (which reported in 1881), and of the livery companies commission of 1880 (report presented 1884).

In 1872, a few months before his mayoralty, Waterlow presented Lauderdale House at Highgate, with its grounds, to St Bartholomew's Hospital, for use as a convalescent home. It was used as such from 1872 until 1880. In 1889 he presented the house with a surrounding estate of 29 acres to the London county council. The fine grounds were subsequently known as Waterlow Park, and a statue of Waterlow was erected there by public subscription in 1900.

Waterlow joined the livery of the Stationers' Company in 1847, serving as master in 1872–3, the year of his mayoralty. He also became by redemption a freeman and liveryman of the Clothworkers' Company on 30 July 1873, and the same day passed (by election and fine) through the offices of assistant, warden, and master. He was a juror for Great Britain at the international exhibitions of Paris (1867) and Philadelphia (1876), one of the royal commissioners of the Great Exhibition of 1851, chairman of the city of London income tax commissioners, and treasurer of the City and Guilds Institute from 1879 (the year after its inception) to 1891. He was also a director of the Union Bank of London, vice-chairman of the London, Chatham, and Dover railway, and vice-president and chairman of the distribution committee of the Hospital Sunday Fund. In 1902 he was made a KCVO.

Waterlow was twice married: first, on 7 May 1845 to Anna Maria (d. 1880), youngest daughter of William Hickson, merchant, of Fairseat, Wrotham, Kent, with whom he had five sons and three daughters, the eldest of whom was the educationist and women's welfare campaigner Ruth *Homan; second, in March 1882 in Paris to Margaret (d. 1931), daughter of William Hamilton of Napa, California, whom he met during an American visit. With her—a much younger person—he made several world tours but had no children. Waterlow retired to his villa, Monterey, near Cannes. In 1894 he suffered two strokes and was partially disabled. He died from dropsy on 3 August 1906, at his country residence, Trosley Towers, Trotterscliffe, Wrotham, Kent, and was buried at Stanstead, Kent. His eldest son, Philip Hickson Waterlow, succeeded to the baronetcy. CHARLES WELCH, rev. H. C. G. MATTHEW

Sources G. Smalley, *Life of Sir Sydney H. Waterlow* (1909) • *The house of Waterlows of Birchin Lane from 1811 to 1911* (1911) • A. T. C. Pratt, ed., *People of the period: being a collection of the biographies of upwards of six thousand living celebrities*, 2 vols. (1897) • *City Press* (11 Aug 1906) • *The Times* (4 Aug 1906) • *The Times* (29 Nov 1906) • *Men and women of the*

time (1899) · J. E. Ritchie, *Famous city men* (1884) · Burke, *Peerage* · *CGPLA Eng. & Wales* (1906)
Likenesses J. Durham, marble bust, 1873, St Bartholomew's Hospital, London · H. von Herkomer, oils, 1892, St Bartholomew's Hospital, London · F. M. Toubman, statue, *c*.1900, Waterlow Park, Highgate, London; replica, Westminster City School, London · W. & D. Downey, photograph, woodburytype, NPG; repro. in W. Downey and D. Downey, *The cabinet portrait gallery*, 3 (1892) · London Stereoscopic Co., photograph, woodburytype, NPG · Walery, photograph, NPG · caricature, chromolithograph, NPG; repro. in *VF* (9 Nov 1872) · oils, Stationer's Hall, London · photograph, repro. in Smalley, *Life*
Wealth at death £89,948 19*s.* 8*d.*: probate, 26 Nov 1906, *CGPLA Eng. & Wales*

Waters, Doris Ethel (1899–1978). *See under* Waters, (Florence) Elsie (1893–1990).

Waters, Edward (*d.* 1751), printer and bookseller, was the son of a John Waters (*d.* 1717?), a papermaker in Dublin. His name first appeared in 1707 as a printer, when he took over from John Brocas at School House Lane, near High Street, and used the metal-cast alphabet that had come originally from Amsterdam. In 1712 he and his father leased from Joseph Leeson a paper mill, printing press, and house at Milltown, near Milltown Bridge, co. Dublin. On 30 November 1717, presumably after his father's death, a new lease was made out in his name only. He married Sarah, daughter of Matthew Gunne, and they had a daughter, Annamaria, who was baptized on 13 June 1709.

Waters now owned a flourishing business. Between 1707 and 1740 he occupied at least five different printing premises in Dublin: in School House Lane, Smock Alley, Essex Street, Copper Alley, and then near Essex Street as well as at Milltown Bridge. In all he started or ran no fewer than seven newspapers, the most significant of which was the *Flying Post*, or, the *Post-Master* (1708–29), as well as occasional news sheets. He inherited three of the titles from Brocas.

A tory, Waters was often in trouble with the authorities for his Jacobite activities. Described as 'Protestant Printer to the late Pretender' (*Dublin Intelligence*, 3 May 1707), Waters and two other protestant printers, Cornelius Carter and Peter Lawrence, and a Catholic bookseller, James Malone, were taken into custody on 19 November 1708 on suspicion of 'printing and vending Popish Prayer-Book contrary to Law' (Pollard, 589). In February 1709 Malone and Carter were tried and found guilty, Waters and Lawrence having turned queen's evidence. Later that year Waters was indicted again for falsely reporting the burning of Wicklow by the French. On 10 June 1714 messengers were sent to arrest him for printing a scandalous ballad about Hanover called 'Tis time to come over &c' (*Portland MSS*, 5.460). But Waters had escaped and 'gone fishing', thereby foiling his prosecutors. When they came for him in June 1715 for printing *Polyphemus Farewell* he leapt out of the window, two storeys high, at the New Post Office printing house at the corner of Sycamore Alley, but was captured in a nearby cellar. He was again in difficulties in 1720 and was sent for trial by grand jury, and found not guilty, after a prolonged trial for printing Swift's 'Insolent and Seditious' *Proposal for the Universal Use of Irish Manufacture*

(Pollard, 590). It moved Swift to write to Sir Thomas Hanmer to persuade the lord lieutenant, the duke of Grafton, to drop the case, and when he arrived in Ireland in August 1721 a *nolle prosequi* was granted. But in 1735 Waters was committed to Newgate for reprinting Bishop Hort's *New Proposal for the Better Regulation of Quadrille*. He was soon released after a petition on his behalf was prepared and when the fines were paid. Within a few months, in 1736, he overstepped the mark again when he reprinted a pamphlet whose original publication a month earlier had led to George Faulkner's imprisonment in Newgate. Waters was sent to the same prison but was at work again in 1737.

Waters was the first Dublin printer to publish Jonathan Swift's works, printing in 1711 the *Conduct of the Allies*, a scathing exposé of the deficiencies of British allies in waging the War of the Spanish Succession, and *Proposals for the Universal Use of Irish Manufactures* (1720). Waters printed the manuscript work by Manoel Alvarez SJ, *A Jesuit Latin Grammar* (1716), as well as the *magnum opus* of Dr Cornelius Nary, *A New History of the World* (1720). One of the most intriguing pamphlets he printed was the eight-page *Letter to the author of the Catholic answer to the seeker showing who are the first foxes he ought to hunt* (1736). The pamphlet's theme was transubstantiation and one of the 'first foxes' to be hunted was the Jesuit controversialist Robert Bellarmine.

Waters died in Dublin of a lingering illness on 12 October 1751, after a full and troublesome life.

D. BEN REES

Sources M. Pollard, *A dictionary of members of the Dublin book trade 1550–1800* (2000), 589–91 · R. Hunter, *A dictionary of the print trade in Ireland, 1550–1775* (New York, 1988), 283–4 · H. Fenning, 'Dublin imprints of Catholic interest, 1701–1739', *Collectanea Hibernica*, 39–40 (1997–8), 106–54 · *The manuscripts of his grace the duke of Portland*, 10 vols., HMC, 29 (1891–1931), vol. 5, p. 460

Waters, (Florence) Elsie (1893–1990), comedian, was born on 19 August 1893 at 1 Rounton Road, Bromley by Bow, Poplar, London, the elder daughter of Edward William Waters, an undertaker's furnisher, and his wife, Maud Mary Best. Her younger sister, **Doris Ethel Waters** (1899–1978), also a comedian, was born at the same address on 20 December 1899. The sisters—neither of whom married—lived together throughout their lives, and were better known as Gert and Daisy, their cockney characters, whom they played in music halls, in concert parties, on radio, in films, and on television.

Edward Waters ran an amateur minstrel show made up of his entire family. There was his wife, Maud, sons Arthur (Art), who played the trumpet, John (Jack), who played violin, Bernard (Bill), who also played violin, and Leslie (Sam), who played percussion, then Elsie (Nan), who played violin, and Doris (Doll), who played piano. When not appearing as black-face minstrels the family was billed as E. W. Winter and his Bijou Orchestra. The Waters sisters occasionally, then permanently, formed a double act, singing current songs, plus a few they composed themselves, performing at temperance concerts, mothers' meetings, church bazaars, and the like, until in 1923 they made a

(Florence) Elsie Waters (1893–1990), by unknown photographer [left, with her sister, Doris Ethel Waters]

West lent a hand as their radio broadcasts became more frequent. Their semi-cockney accents made a refreshing change for listeners in those pre-war years of John Reith's BBC which was severely middle and upper class in tone.

On 17 March 1934 the Waters sisters made a most successful appearance on *Henry Hall's Guest Night*, the first in a long-running series of dance-band and variety shows. Two months later on 8 May they starred in their first royal variety performance, making a second royal appearance in 1938. They were special favourites of Queen Elizabeth (later the queen mother) and often were invited to royal functions and special appeals. In 1937 they formed their own touring show and travelled the nation's variety theatres, meanwhile continuing to make gramophone records such as the highly successful *Gert and Daisy's Christmas Party*, a double-sided special. In 1937 the women's magazine *Home Companion* published *Gert and Daisy's Song Book* as a 'grand free gift'. Apart from some of their own composed songs it included their signature tune, 'Daisy Bell'.

After war began in September 1939, the Waters sisters found themselves enlisted by the minister of food, Lord Woolton, to broadcast regularly from *The Kitchen Front*. Turning Gert and Daisy loose on official food economy recipes worked wonders, and their version of the vegetarian Woolton pie became famous. They also issued a wartime *Gert and Daisy Cookery Book*. In addition they joined the Entertainments National Service Association, and were soon entertaining the troops at home, then abroad. They made two overseas tours, to India and the Far East, and in between were regular top-of-the-bill turns in *Workers' Playtime*, the long-running radio show broadcast live from home-front factories during the war-workers' lunch break. Once they were even introduced by Ernest Bevin, the minister of labour.

After the war Elsie and Doris Waters were both made OBE in the 1946 king's birthday honours, and two elephants at London Zoo were promptly christened Gert and Daisy! They found time to star in three major cinema films: *Gert and Daisy's Weekend* (1941), an evacuee story; *Gert and Daisy Clean Up* (1942); and *It's in the Bag* (1943), all produced by Butcher's Films; their act was recorded for posterity in the 1933 variety film *Radio Parade*. Later radio series included *Gert and Daisy's Working Party* (1948) which travelled the country, and *Petticoat Lane* (1949), inspired by the famous London East-End market. In 1985 a play, *The Gert and Daisy Show*, was staged with Sylvia Syms as Elsie and Rosemary Leach as Doris. Their brother Jack *Warner, who changed his surname from Waters to avoid confusion, at first also became a radio comedian; but he later acquired an international reputation from his role, in film and later on television, as the eponymous policeman in *Dixon of Dock Green*.

Gert and Daisy continued to perform until the 1970s. Doris Waters died from cancer on 18 August 1978 at their home, Byfield, Goring Road, Steyning, Sussex. Elsie survived her until her own death from cancer and bronchopneumonia on 14 June 1990 at the Downlands Rest Home,

more professional début at a Sunday concert in St George's Hall, London. This led to their first full-time engagement with Will Pepper and his White Coons, a seaside concert party running through the summer season at Clacton-on-Sea. The pair were paid £8 a week between them. By 1927 they were stars of a touring concert party called the Enthusiasts, which led to their first BBC radio broadcast in 1929.

Oscar Preuse, the recording manager for Parlophone Records, chanced to hear the Waters sisters broadcasting from Birmingham, and gave them a contract to make three double-sided 78 r.p.m. records. The delighted pair had enough material for five musical sides, but were stuck for material for the last side. They decided to make a primarily talking record, and with a quickly improvised song called 'Wedding Bells' they chatted together for two minutes or so as a couple of cockney women watching a marriage from outside the church.

'What shall we call them, these two people?' recalled Elsie Waters in a radio interview. 'So Doris said, "Well, I'll call you Gert 'cause I like saying it." And I said, " I'll call you Daisy, cause there's always a Daisy among them." And so we called them Gert and Daisy' (personal knowledge). Ten days or so later the sisters arrived at the Savoy Hotel for one of their concerts, and the manager asked them to 'do the two old women'. Baffled, they asked which and why. 'I heard your funny new record on the wireless' he said. 'Christopher Stone played it' (ibid.). The sisters quickly improvised some suitable costumes and did their best to remember the 'Wedding Bells' routine. It was a hit with the audience, and so was immediately absorbed into their repertory.

Soon elaborations followed, with Gert having a sweetheart called Wally, Daisy having a somewhat simple husband called Bert, and a nosy neighbour called Old Mother Butler, and incidents such as visits to the local picture palaces gave their crosstalk a semblance of plot. Originally they wrote all their own material, including a closing song, but later experienced scriptwriters including Con

Laines Road, Steyning. As a cockney comic duo they were unique; and their collective name of Gert and Daisy has entered the national vocabulary.   DENIS GIFFORD

Sources R. Busby, *British music hall: an illustrated who's who from 1850 to the present day* (1976) • D. Gifford, *The golden age of radio* (1985) • M. Banks and A. Swift, *The joke's on us* (1987) • personal knowledge (2004) • b. certs. • d. certs. • *CGPLA Eng. & Wales* (1978) [Doris Ethel Waters]
Archives FILM BFI NFTVA, performance footage | SOUND BL NSA, performance recording • IWM SA, oral history interview • IWM SA, performance recordings
Likenesses double portrait, photograph, NPG [*see illus.*]
Wealth at death £35,138—Doris Waters: probate, 11 Dec 1978, *CGPLA Eng. & Wales*

Waters, Sir John (1773/4–1842), army officer, was born at Tŷ-fry, near Welsh St Donats, Glamorgan. His grandfather, Edward Waters of Pittcott, was high sheriff of Glamorgan in 1754. His father, name unknown, died young, leaving a large family. The marquess of Bute obtained a commission for the son in the 1st (Royal Scots) foot on 2 August 1797. He joined the 2nd battalion in Portugal, and served with it in the expeditions to The Helder in 1799, and to Egypt in 1801. He had become lieutenant on 15 February 1799, and in reward for his conduct during a mutiny at Gibraltar in 1802 the duke of Kent obtained a company for him in the York rangers on 24 September 1803. He remained, however, with the 1st, and went with them to the West Indies. On 28 February 1805 he was promoted captain in the 1st, to which two new battalions had been added, and soon afterwards returned to England.

In August 1808, owing to the duke of Kent's recommendation, he was made aide-de-camp to Brigadier Charles William Stewart (afterwards third marquess of Londonderry). He went with him to Portugal, and served in Moore's campaign. Sent out to obtain intelligence of the French movements in December, he bought from the Spaniards at Valdestillas an intercepted dispatch from Berthier to Soult, which gave Moore most important information, and at once altered his plans. He was promoted major on 16 February 1809, and was attached to the Portuguese army (with the local rank of lieutenant-colonel), but employed on intelligence duties, for which he was praised by Wellington, who wanted him definitely placed on his staff. The most conspicuous instance of Waters's usefulness was at the passage of the Douro on 12 May. The French had broken the bridge and removed the boats, and had 10,000 men on the opposite bank. Waters discovered a poor barber who had crossed the river with a small skiff the previous night; and they, joined by the prior of Aramante, crossed the river undetected, and returned with three large barges, in which the first troops crossed.

On 3 April 1811, before the action of Sabugal began, Waters was made prisoner, after he had crossed the Coa to reconnoitre. 'He had rendered very important services upon many occasions in the last two years, and his loss is sensibly felt' (Wellington to Lord Liverpool, 9 April 1911; *Selections from the Dispatches*, 7.433). He refused parole, and was sent to Salamanca with a guard of four gendarmes. Better mounted than they, he awaited his opportunity,

and put spurs to his horse. He was on a wide plain, with French troops before and behind him; as he rode along their flank some encouraged, others fired at him. Passing between two columns he reached a wooded hollow, and evaded his pursuers. Two days later he reached British headquarters, 'where Lord Wellington, knowing his resolute, subtle character, had caused his baggage to be brought, observing that he would not be long absent' (Napier, bk 12, chap. 5). On 15 April Wellington appointed him (subject to confirmation) an assistant adjutant-general, and on 30 May he was made brevet lieutenant-colonel.

Waters served throughout the war, being present at Talavera, Busaco, Ciudad Rodrigo, Badajoz, Salamanca, Vitoria, the battles of the Pyrenees (during which he was wounded while speaking to Wellington), the Nivelle and Nive, Orthez and Toulouse. At Badajoz and Salamanca he acted as adjutant-general. He received the gold cross with four clasps, and was made CB in 1815. He was at Waterloo, and again acted as adjutant-general after Sir Edward Barnes was wounded, and signed the returns of the battle, though he was himself wounded also. He received the Russian order of St Anne (2nd class). After a time on half pay, he became captain and lieutenant-colonel in the Coldstream Guards on 15 May 1817. He was promoted colonel on 19 July 1821, and was again placed on half pay on 15 February 1827. He became major-general on 22 July 1830, was made captain of Yarmouth Castle, Isle of Wight, on 22 April 1831, and KCB on 1 March 1832. He was made colonel of the 81st foot on 15 June 1840, and promoted lieutenant-general on 23 November 1841. He died at Park Place, St James's, London, on 21 November 1842, at the age of sixty-eight, and was buried at Kensal Green.

E. M. LLOYD, rev. JAMES LUNT

Sources *United Service Magazine*, 1 (1843), 95 • *GM*, 2nd ser., 19 (1843), 201 • T. Nicholas, *Annals and antiquities of the counties and county families of Wales*, 2 vols. (1872) • *Selections from the dispatches and general orders of Field Marshall the duke of Wellington*, ed. J. Gurwood, new edn (1851) • W. F. P. Napier, *History of the war in the Peninsula and in the south of France*, 3 vols. (1878)
Likenesses W. Salter, group portrait, oils (*Waterloo banquet at Apsley House*), NPG; oil study, c. 1834–40, NPG

Waters, William Alexander (1903–1985), organic chemist, was born at 23 Montgomery Street, Cardiff, on 8 May 1903, the only child of William Waters and his wife, Elizabeth Annie, daughter of William Roberts, bootmaker. His father (who envisaged a medical career for him) was a schoolteacher, and later headmaster of Gladstone council school, Cardiff. His mother and her sister were also teachers. Waters's educational progress was given every possible assistance, and he recalled that there were always many books at home that he was encouraged to read. He entered Gladstone council school in 1908, went on to Roath Park School in 1911, and then to Cardiff High School for Boys as the top city scholar in 1914. Persuaded by his father that, rather than follow the school's advice and go to the local Cardiff University College, he should try for Cambridge, he succeeded in winning one of the scholarships in mathematics and natural sciences recently endowed by Lord Rhondda at Gonville and Caius College. He went up in 1921, and obtained further scholarships and studentships, and first classes in both parts of the natural sciences tripos (1923 and 1924). He went on to a PhD in organic chemistry under the supervision of Hamilton McCombie.

Waters obtained his PhD in 1927 and the following year was appointed to a lectureship at the University of Durham. The department of chemistry there was then very small, with only three lecturers, and although half his time was free for research he felt isolated and without prospect of promotion. However, his applications elsewhere were unsuccessful. In 1932 he married his cousin Elizabeth (d. 1983), younger daughter of William Dougall, foreman steel smelter, of nearby Darlington; they had no children. His shyness was complemented by her gregariousness, and they were fond of entertaining, especially his pupils.

Waters had won a Leverhulme fellowship to study in the USA, at Chicago, in 1939–40, but at the start of the Second World War in 1939 was seconded as a wartime scientific officer to the Ministry of Supply's experimental station at Porton Camp in Wiltshire, where he found the work boring, but the company good. He returned to Durham in 1944, but the following year was elected to a tutorial fellowship at Balliol College, Oxford, linked to a university demonstratorship in the Dyson Perrins Laboratory. He remained in Oxford until the end of his life. He was appointed to a readership in 1960 and to an *ad hominem* professorship in 1967, when Balliol elected him to a professorial fellowship. He retired formally in 1970, but continued working in the laboratory until about 1977.

Waters's lifelong research interest was in the mechanisms of the reactions of organic compounds in solution, kindled during his PhD work on the mechanisms of chlorination and bromination of aromatic compounds. In 1927 he carried out a survey of the literature at the request of T. M. Lowry for a proposed joint publication, to check whether the theory of the ionic nature of organic reactions in solution that was then developing was fully consistent with all the facts. He soon concluded that it was not and that certain reactions took place by way of free-radical intermediates—uncharged species with one unpaired electron. In 1932 he published a speculative article along these lines. Two years later, independently, W. S. M. Grieve and D. H. Hey at Manchester University published experimental evidence that certain diazo-compounds yield free radicals in solution. Thereafter, Hey and Waters, in consultation, carried out independent research programmes that confirmed the free-radical character of a variety of reactions, and in 1937 they published a seminal article in *Chemical Reviews* that illustrated the considerable scope of this type of reaction and stimulated work worldwide. Waters's subsequent work focused mainly on radical reactions, including those involving oxidation by metal salts. He was elected FRS in 1954.

Waters was also devoted to teaching organic chemistry. His *Physical Aspects of Organic Chemistry* (1935) (the eventual result of Lowry's suggestion) was the first text on physical-

organic chemistry, and in his *The Chemistry of Free Radicals* (1946) the central theme was the unity of radical reactions in the gas phase and solution. He also played a prominent role in publicizing and reviewing the new electronic theories of Lapworth, Robinson, and Ingold. Although never a good lecturer, he was a kind and painstaking tutor with an impressive knowledge of his subject who stimulated in his pupils his own abiding interest. In Durham his research had been done on his own, but many of his Balliol pupils elected to do research degrees under his supervision and subsequently had distinguished careers in organic chemistry. He was also active in college life, having a spell as estates bursar of Balliol; his normally hesitant manner was put aside if he felt strongly, when he was firm and cogent about college business.

Waters always found time for gardening and for playing the piano, chess, and bridge. He was granted an honorary DSc by Warwick University (1977) and was awarded the Chemical Society medal (1973). In 1970 Waters and D. H. Hey were given a Festschrift for their contributions to free radical chemistry (Chemical Society Special Publication no. 24). He and his wife frequently travelled worldwide together, combining conferences and holidays. It was a most happy marriage, and Waters never fully recovered after his wife's death in 1983. He died at the John Radcliffe Hospital in Oxford on 28 January 1985.

R. O. C. NORMAN, rev. DAVID KNIGHT

Sources J. Jones, *Balliol College Annual Record* (1985), 20–24 · *The Caian* [magazine of Gonville and Caius College, Cambridge] (1985) · *The Times* (2 Feb 1985) · J. Venn and others, eds., *Biographical history of Gonville and Caius College*, 5–7 (1948–78) · R. O. C. Norman and J. H. Jones, *Memoirs FRS*, 32 (1986), 597–627 · personal knowledge (1990) · *CGPLA Eng. & Wales* (1985)
Archives Balliol Oxf.
Likenesses W. Stoneman, photograph, 1954?, RS · Ramsey and Muspratt, photograph, 1967?, RS · J. C. Edwards, chalk drawing, 1971, Balliol Oxf. · M. Powell, pencil drawing, 1976, Balliol Oxf. · photograph, repro. in Jones, *Balliol College Annual Record*, 20
Wealth at death £402,106: probate, 1985, *CGPLA Eng. & Wales*

Waterson, Elaine [Lal; *married name* Elaine Knight] (1943–1998), folk-singer and songwriter, was born on 15 February 1943 at 92 Park Street, Hull, the younger daughter and youngest of the three children of Charles Norman Waterson (c.1910–1948), ironmonger's clerk, and his wife, Florence Maude Ward (1908–1946). Her bloodlines were once described as a mixture of Irish, Gypsy, and Yorkshire farmer. Her elder sister, Norma, was born in 1939, and her brother, Michael, in 1941. After their mother's death, their father's health declined sharply; their maternal grandmother Eliza Ward, an extended family of relatives, and a family friend, Thurza (Tut) Hutty, stepped in and duly raised the three children. At the age of eleven Elaine won a scholarship to Hull's High School for Art and Crafts. She later left to join G. K. Beaulah & Co. Ltd, a market leader in heraldic shield manufacture, where she painted scholastic, military, and family coats of arms. She met her future husband, George Knight (b. 1944), through a snowball fight in the winter of 1961–2. They had two children,

Marry (b. 1964)—the name was spelt Marie on her birth certificate—and Oliver (b. 1969), and married on 16 March 1968.

Like many of her generation, Lal Waterson gravitated to folk music from skiffle and American-derived forms, becoming one of a group of like-minded people that went on to host Folk Union I, a folk club that ping-ponged around Hull before reaching Lowgate's Olde Blue Bell in the summer of 1961. The Mariners and the Folksons, in both of which she sang, evolved into the Watersons proper, which comprised the three Waterson siblings and their cousin John Harrison (b. 1945). When a fifth member, Pete Ogley, departed, their Anglo-American repertory departed too. Few acts shook up the British folk-song revival in the way the Watersons did. Although they initially used the guitar and the banjo, this hangover from their 'Anglo-American past' gave way to a stylishly dynamic unaccompanied singing style. Their official recording début—ignoring some earlier anthologized work—was in a cycle of pre-Christian ritual and calendrical songs, *Frost and Fire* (1965). It ignited the imagination of 'folkies', folklorists, bohemians, and hippies, and stands as one of the ten most important folk records of the twentieth century. The Watersons had far from purist musical tastes. Northern music-hall and Big Bill Broonzy's blues contributed to their musical palette. Other members of the extended family played the guitar, banjo, cornet, and piano. Norma taught Lal and Mike to play the guitar.

In 1968 the group broke up, weary of continual one-nighters, and Norma Waterson left for Monserrat. On her return in 1972 the Watersons re-formed, with Norma's husband, Martin Carthy, replacing Harrison. The group went on to make *For Pence and Spicy Ale*—voted *Melody Maker*'s folk album of 1975—and the exceptional *Sound, Sound your Instruments of Joy* (1977)—a counterblast to the pagan, as it were, with its 'lost' Victorian Christian hymns. In the hiatus before reuniting, however, Lal and Mike Waterson began fleshing out the songs that became *Bright Phoebus* (1972); it was 'remade' between 2001 and 2002 by musicians influenced by its songs. Acknowledging only Arthur Rimbaud as a conscious influence, Lal ensured that her own poetry and songwriting, of great originality, suffused with a kind of folk poeticism, lacked any literary posing. She would drive her brother to distraction with revisions, producing complete rewrites where he had suggested tweaking one phrase or note.

The Watersons effectively disbanded when, owing to poor health, Lal Waterson stepped off the touring treadmill. She continued to 'sing Yorkshire', however, with two collaborations with her son, Oliver Knight, *Once in a Blue Moon* (1996) and *A Bed of Roses* (1999). Her songs frequently flouted conventional melodic resolutions and rhyming. In 'Flight of the Pelican' from *Once in a Blue Moon* her imagery conjoined heraldry's vulning pelican and the stony-hearted 'old crow' of Thatcherism to deliver a political charge about the loss of 'your children's children's rights'. Songs such as 'The Scarecrow' or 'Altisidora' were touched by the numinous. To borrow Michael Hamburger's assessment of Rimbaud, listeners do not understand Lal Waterson's songs: they learn them by heart.

Lal Waterson died of cancer at her home, Normanhurst, Robin Hood's Bay, Whitby, Yorkshire, on 4 September 1998; she was cremated at Scarborough crematorium on 11 September. She was survived by her husband, George, her daughter, Marry, and her son, Oliver.   KEN HUNT

Sources K. Hunt, 'Water daughters', *Folk Roots* (May 1996), 24–5, 27, 29 • K. Hunt, 'All our yesterdays', *Folk Roots* (Nov 1997), 17, 19 • D. Knight, *Travelling for a living*, BBC, 1966 [television] • D. Knight, 'Travelling for a living', *Radio Times* (19 May 1966), 6 • K. Hunt, *Prince Heathen: Martin Carthy and the English folksong revival* [forthcoming] • H. K. Moss, 'Club review: Folk Union I, Hull—the Watersons', *Ballads & Songs*, 4 (1965), 2 • *The Independent* (8 Sept 1998) • *The Guardian* (8 Sept 1998) • *The Times* (9 Sept 1998) • *Daily Telegraph* (11 Sept 1998) • personal knowledge (2004) • private information (2004) • b. cert.

Elaine Waterson (1943–1998), by Brian Shuel [second from right, with the Watersons]

Waterston, George (1911–1980), ornithologist and conservationist, was born on 10 April 1911 in Edinburgh, the oldest of the seven children (four boys and three girls) of Robert Waterston (1878–1969), director of George Waterston & Sons, Edinburgh, stationers and printers (founded by Robert's great-great-grandfather), and his wife, Winifred, *née* Sandeman (1889–1978). He was educated at the Edinburgh Academy, where he gained colours for rugby football and cricket, later playing for the Academicals and captaining the second fifteen. On leaving school he joined his father's firm, remaining there until he became a full-time ornithologist in 1955. During the Second World War he served with the Royal Artillery and was captured in Crete.

Waterston's interest in birds was evident when he was a small child; while still at school he gave a lecture on bird-watching, during which he roundly denounced the hobby of egg collecting. He was a founder member of both the Inverleith Field Club and the Midlothian Ornithological Club, and in 1934 was the chief instigator of the Isle of May Bird Observatory, the first co-operative bird migration centre to be set up in Britain. In 1936 he became the primary force behind the formation of the Scottish Ornithologists' Club, and was elected its first honorary secretary in 1955.

Waterston had a deep interest in Fair Isle, an important resting site for migratory birds. He first visited the island in 1935; in 1943, having been repatriated from Germany because of kidney trouble, he was on board a hospital ship crossing the North Sea from Sweden when he sighted the Sheep Craig at Fair Isle—his first glimpse of his homeland. These experiences bound him fervently to the island: he was one of the instrumental forces behind the foundation of the Fair Isle Bird Observatory. In 1955 Waterston not only took on the secretaryship of the Scottish Ornithologists' Club, but became Scottish officer for the Royal Society for the Protection of Birds (RSPB). In time he so greatly developed this position that he was appointed full-time director (Scotland) of the RSPB, a post which he held for thirteen years. During his years in post he travelled all over Scotland and dealt with the full gamut of bird protection issues.

In 1947 Waterston married Nancy Ritchie (*b.* 1914). The couple had a son, William, who became a solicitor. However, the marriage was ultimately dissolved, and in 1958 he married Irene Kinnear (1914–1984), who shared his interests and activities to the full, and whose deep interest in Arctic botany led to the establishment of the couple as a formidable research team in Arctic wildlife; they undertook several expeditions to Greenland and Ellesmere Island. Irene jointly with George organized the first Scottish bird islands study cruise, part of the International Ornithological Congress of 1966, when over 900 ornithologists from thirty-two countries visited a number of Scottish islands.

In 1948 Waterston was elected a fellow of the Royal Society of Edinburgh, and in 1964 he was appointed OBE for his services to British ornithology: specifically for bird protection in Scotland. In 1974 he received an honorary degree (LLD) from the University of Dundee, and was elected president of the Arctic Club in 1978.

Waterston's active life in the field and as an organizer precluded the production of much published work, but he co-produced a long paper with James Fisher on the fulmar (*Journal of Animal Ecology*, 10, 1941, 204–72) and the chapter on the gannet in Bannerman's *The Birds of the British Isles* (1959). With Philip Brown he wrote *The Return of the Osprey* (1962), and with Roy Dennis, *The Osprey and Speyside Wildlife* (1969). His last book, *Fair Isle: a Photographic History* (1983), was completed after his death by Jean Jones.

On Waterston's retirement he and his wife moved to Keith Bridge, Humbie, East Lothian. In the early 1970s he began to suffer increasingly from kidney trouble; after a failed transplant attempt, he became dependent on a dialysis machine at home. Despite this logistic burden, he still managed to visit Fair Isle three times; the last time in June 1980. He died three months later, on 20 September 1980, at the Royal Infirmary, Edinburgh, and was buried on 24 September in the churchyard of the old parish church at Humbie.

Waterston arguably did more than anyone else to establish ornithology in Scotland, despite his lack of formal training. He was, additionally, a gregarious and kind man, with friends in all walks of life, who much enjoyed his great sense of humour. He was a determined and organized operator, who would ardently pursue an end product with keen verbal proddings, or (when this was impossible) a continual stream of 'George's memos'.

CLEMENCY THORNE FISHER

Sources J. Eggeling and C. G. Connell, *Year Book of the Royal Society of Edinburgh* (1979–80), 41–3 · B. Stenhouse, 'George Waterston: an appreciation', in G. Waterston and J. Jones, *Fair Isle: a photographic history* (1983), vi–vii · private information (2004)
Archives NRA Scotland priv. coll., diaries
Likenesses photograph, repro. in Waterston and Jones, *Fair Isle*, vi

Waterston, John James (1811–1883), physicist and physical chemist, was born in 1811 in Edinburgh, the sixth of nine children, at least five of them sons, of George Waterston, a manufacturer of sealing-wax and stationery requisites, of Edinburgh, and his wife, Jane Blair of Dunkeld. He was educated at Edinburgh high school, was a pupil in a firm of civil engineers, and attended lectures at the university in mathematics, physics, and other subjects.

At the age of twenty-one Waterston moved to London, working briefly as a civil engineer before joining the Admiralty hydrographer's department. From 1839 he worked as a naval instructor in Bombay, which left him time for his main interest, the study of science.

Waterston's ideas were advanced but, being outside the scientific establishment, he was not always taken seriously. His theory of the meteoric bombardment as the source of the sun's heat was, through its being taken up by William Thomson, quite influential for a short time. His most significant paper, in which he developed much of the kinetic theory of gases, was refused publication by the Royal Society in 1845. Some years later better-known physicists developed similar ideas, which gained acceptance rapidly. Waterston, never interested in personal glory, did not try to claim priority, but J. W. Strutt, third Baron Rayleigh, rediscovered the paper and had it published in the *Philosophical Transactions* in 1892, with an introduction which belatedly gave Waterston due credit. Between 1845 and 1868 Waterston published papers in various journals, on the nature of heat, the behaviour of gases and liquids, related chemical topics, and on astronomical matters. Other of his papers, however, were rejected.

In 1857 Waterston returned to Edinburgh to live an agreeable bachelor life among his family and friends. Through his family he was closely connected with the Sandemanian church but he does not seem to have been a member. On 18 June 1883 he left his lodgings and disappeared. It is surmised that he fell into the sea near Leith, perhaps overcome by the giddiness to which he was prone following an attack of sunstroke in India.

C. N. Brown, *rev.*

Sources J. S. Haldane, 'Memoir of J. J. Waterston', in *The collected scientific papers of John James Waterston* (1928), xiii–lxviii · *DSB*, 14.184–6 · F. A. J. L. James, 'Thermodynamics and sources of solar heat, 1846–1862', *British Journal for the History of Science*, 15 (1982), 155–81 · G. N. Cantor, *Michael Faraday: Sandemanian and scientist* (1991), 60–61, 303–4
Likenesses photograph, 1857, repro. in Haldane, 'Memoir of J. J. Waterston'

Waterton, Charles (1782–1865), naturalist, was born on 3 June 1782, at the family seat of Walton Hall, Sandal Magna, near Wakefield, the eldest son of the six children of Thomas Waterton (*d.* 1805), and his wife, Anne (*d.* 1819), a daughter of Edward Bedingfeld and his wife, Mary. Waterton's father, who had inherited Walton Hall in 1767, was a direct descendant of Sir Thomas More, chancellor to Henry VIII. The family had a long history in northern England: it was mentioned in Shakespeare (*Richard II*, II.1), distinguished at Agincourt, and a staunch royalist supporter at Marston Moor.

Waterton was educated as a Roman Catholic, and in 1792 was sent to a small preparatory school at Tudhoe, near Durham. Four years later he went to Stonyhurst College, Lancashire, where it was said he became a fanatical rat-catcher. In 1798 he made a promise (on the advice of his master, Father Clifford) never to drink wine or spirits—a promise he kept for the rest of his life. He remained at Stonyhurst until 1801 and spent the following year at home, hunting with Lord Darlington.

In November 1802 Waterton sailed for Spain with his younger brother Christopher on the brig *Industry*. They visited Cadiz, before travelling to Malaga to stay with two

maternal uncles, who were naturalized Spaniards. A year after Waterton's arrival, there was an outbreak of 'black vomit' (plague) in Malaga. He fell seriously ill and one of his uncles died. Nevertheless, both the Waterton brothers managed to escape from the quarantine city and returned to England in 1803. Waterton then enjoyed a season's hunting in Yorkshire, but his health was still not good, and he decided to sample the warmer climes of the family estates at Demerara.

Travels in South America On 29 November 1804 Waterton sailed from Portsmouth on board the *Fame*, and after a voyage of six weeks landed at Stabroek (later Georgetown). He managed the family plantations at Demerara and took the opportunity to pursue his natural history studies. On the death of his father in 1805, he inherited Walton Hall, and returned home. About 1806 or 1807 he returned to Demerara where he continued to manage the family estates, and travel extensively. In 1807 he received a commission as lieutenant in the 2nd regiment of the Demerara militia, a position which provided him with the opportunity to explore the Orinoco. On 2 August 1808 he departed from Demerara in the *Levina*, on behalf of the British government, to convey dispatches from Admiral Collingwood to the Spanish captain-general of the Orinoco, Don Felipe de Ynciarte. Furthermore, Waterton was granted permission to enter Dutch Guiana by Governor Carmichael.

Waterton relinquished responsibility for the family plantations in 1812 and in that April, at the beginning of the wet season, set out on an expedition into the Demerara forests. His primary aim for this expedition was to acquire samples of curare poison (or 'wourali'), thought at the time to be a possible remedy for rabies. He was also keen to visit Lake Parima, in search of the elusive golden city of El Dorado of the Amerindians. During the expedition he paddled up the Demerara River to the rock of Seba. Several weeks later, on reaching a settlement of Macusi Indians, he was successful in obtaining samples of curare. (His research into the anaesthetic properties of the drug brought curare to the attention of a wide audience and contributed to its later widespread use.) He journeyed on to the Essequibo and Burro Burro rivers, the savannahs on the Brazil frontier, and from the Pirara River he travelled by canoe on to the fort of São Joachim. However, four months after beginning his expedition, he fell ill and was forced to quit his journey. In 1813, probably sick with malaria, he sailed home to England on the *Fame*, docking at Liverpool in the spring of that year. Owing to his lingering illness, he was forced to decline an exploration of Madagascar, for which venture he had been personally recommended by Governor Carmichael to Lord Bathurst. He spent the next three years at Walton Hall, which stood on an island in a lake of about 30 acres, surrounded by a well-wooded park. In the autumn of 1814 Waterton was badly injured while loading a gun; he attended to the wound himself, and then bled himself using his lancet. He had been introduced to the practice of bloodletting by Dr John Marshall, in Guiana, and Waterton was a firm advocate of its beneficial use.

On 19 March 1816 Waterton sailed from Liverpool on

board the *Indian* to embark on his second 'wandering' in South America. He landed in April at Pernambuco (Recife), Brazil, where he collected a number of birds, before proceeding on a Portuguese brig to Cayenne, French Guiana, using a hen-coop on deck as his bed. He then sailed on a Yankee brig to Paramaribo, Surinam, New Amsterdam, and Georgetown. He spent six months in the forest collecting more than 200 specimens, and searching for the 'feathered tribe'. In 1817 he returned home, on board the *Dee*, with his numerous specimens. Waterton, a skilled taxidermist, had developed an alternative method for preserving specimens: skins were soaked in a solution of alcohol and bichloride of mercury (corrosive sublimate) for several hours, dried, and then modelled into shape from the interior—rendering internal stuffing unnecessary. A scarlet ibis was believed to be the earliest specimen preserved by this technique in 1810. His preserved specimens were often arranged on the staircase at Walton Hall. In later years John Edmonston, a freed slave Waterton had brought back from Guiana, taught Charles Darwin how to stuff birds, having been taught himself by Waterton.

In October 1817 Waterton visited Italy where he passed the winter of 1817–18. In Rome, accompanied by Captain Edwin Jones, his friend from Tudhoe School, he displayed his increasing eccentricity: placing a glove on top of the lightning conductor above the cross of St Peter's and standing on one leg on the head of the guardian angel which surmounted the castle of St Angelo. In 1818 he made another visit to Rome, this time accompanied by his old Stonyhurst friends, seeking an audience with a Vatican official. He returned to England on 19 February 1818.

In February 1820 Waterton set sail from the Clyde in the *Glenbervie* for his third 'wandering' in South America. He arrived back in Georgetown, where yellow fever had become epidemic, and by June that year he was himself ill with fever. He prepared his own cure, which consisted of cinchona bark, laudanum, calomel, and jalap, in addition to his routine bloodletting. During this trip to Demerara he ventured into the interior by way of the Essequibo River. He remained in the forest for eleven months, and collected 230 birds, 2 land tortoises, 5 armadillos, 2 large snakes, a sloth (his favourite subject), a giant anteater, and a cayman. On his return to Liverpool in the *Dee*, in 1821, he was met by excisemen who withheld his collection for several weeks until the duty was assessed.

After his return Waterton decided to surround the park at Walton Hall with a 9 foot wall which was completed in the summer of 1826. Within the enclosed park he banned the use of guns, and the area was transformed into what was probably the country's first nature reserve and bird sanctuary. Alexander Wilson's *Ornithology of the United States* inspired Waterton to visit America, and in the early summer of 1824, he sailed on board the *John Wells* to New York, and commenced his fourth 'wandering'. He travelled in Canada and the United States, where he was introduced to the ornithologist George Ord (1781–1866), with whom he regularly corresponded. In the autumn of 1824 Waterton sailed from New York to the West Indies, and passed on to Demerara. Here he proceeded to the forests of the interior, journeyed some 200 miles up-river, and studied jacamars, red grosbeaks, sunbirds, tinamous, and humming-birds, as well as 'vampires', sloths, and monkeys. In January 1825 he completed his final tour of Guiana, and sailed back to Southampton.

In August 1825 Waterton published his account of the four journeys in a quarto volume, *Wanderings in South America, the north-west of the United States, and the Antilles in the years 1812, 1816, 1820, and 1824*. The work was reprinted several times, and edited with illustrations and some alterations, by J. G. Wood, in 1879. Details of the 'Waterton method' for preserving natural history specimens were also appended to his travel observations—the frontispiece of his book represented a human face based on that of a red monkey, which had been modelled using his method.

In the chapel of the canonesses of St Augustine (an English convent), on the rue des Carmes, Bruges, at 5.30 a.m. on 18 May 1829, Waterton married Anne Mary (1812–1830), second of six children of Charles Edmonstone (*d*. 1827) of Cardross Park, Dumbarton, and his wife, Helen, daughter of William Reid, a timber cutter, and his wife, 'Princess Minda', an Arawak Indian. Waterton had often stayed at Charles Edmonstone's home, Warrows Place, Mibiri Creek, during his visits to Demerara. It was believed that Waterton had vowed, as he attended Anne Mary's baptism some seventeen years earlier, that he would some day marry the child. However, the marriage was short: Anne Mary died on 27 April 1830, the result of puerperal sepsis following the birth of their only child, Edmund. She was buried three days later, in the Waterton family vault at Sandal Magna church (St Helen's). Waterton placed a picture of St Catharine of Alexandria, which resembled his wife, over a mantelpiece at Walton Hall, and to the end of his life often fixed his eyes on it as he sat by the fire. His wife's sisters, Eliza Edmonstone (1807–1870) and Helen Edmonstone (1813–1879), took over the running of the house for him until he died. Eliza and Helen died at Ostend and Bruges, respectively; both were unmarried.

Later travels in Europe In 1830 Waterton travelled on the continent. During these travels he bought a collection of paintings from a Herr Berwind at Würzburg, and also revisited Bruges on his way home. In the summer of 1833 he paid another visit to Belgium, accompanied by his sisters-in-law, son, and two servants. In 1838 he published the first series of his *Essays in Natural History*, which were followed in 1844 by a second series, and in 1857 by a third series. Several of the essays first appeared in John Claudius Loudon's *Magazine of Natural History* and Waterton gave the proceeds from his second series to Mrs Loudon following her husband's sudden death in 1843. Each series of essays was preceded by a portion of autobiography, and while a few essays focused on tropical subjects, the majority examined English birds and wild animals. His *Essays*, including thirty-six of his letters, and a biography written by his close friend Sir Norman Moore (1847–1922) were published in 1870.

Waterton again travelled on the continent in 1840. However, on this occasion he was joined at Cologne by his friend Alexander Fletcher (1808–1888), with whom he journeyed to Rome. Waterton spent the winter of 1840–41 in Rome, where he attended mass at four o'clock every morning in the church of the Gesù, made many ornithological observations, and collected specimens of local birds. He started back to England on 10 June 1841, but was shipwrecked in the *Pollux* near Elba on the night of 17 June 1841, and returned to Italy. He departed for England from Rome for a second time, on 20 July 1841, visiting many places en route, including Aix-la-Chapelle. In later years he often visited Aix-la-Chapelle in addition to trips to Scarborough in the autumn and Stonyhurst College at Christmas.

In 1844 Waterton made another journey across continental Europe, in particular to Austria and Italy. The following year he was awarded the knighthood of the supreme order of Christ from Dom Miguel, exiled king of Portugal. He returned home in June 1845, and in November that year accompanied his sisters-in-law to Madeira, where he stayed until January the next year. During this period he made numerous improvements at Walton Hall, including a new garden and a pigeon-cot, and in 1855 he improved the drainage of the lake.

Penance and death Waterton lived on good terms with his neighbours, and at Walton Hall he exercised a continuous and genial hospitality. As penance, following the death of his wife, he slept on the bare floor of a small room at the top of the house, using a wooden block as a pillow, and a military cloak or blanket for a covering. He rose at three, lit his fire, and lay down for half an hour while it burned up. He then dressed, spending from four to five in the morning in his chapel. He then read a chapter on the life of St Francis Xavier, and one on Don Quixote, both in Spanish, and wrote letters or stuffed birds until eight, when he breakfasted. He dined at half-past one and had tea at six and spent a great part of the day in his park. He kept his hair very short, indoors he wore an old-fashioned swallow-tailed coat, refusing to adopt the formal fashion of his day, and also wore shoes several sizes too large. Until very late in life he continued to climb trees, and was said to impress friends by scratching the back of his head with his big toe.

On 25 May 1865 Waterton tripped and fell; the accident resulted in considerable internal injuries, from which he died at Walton Hall two days later. He was buried on 3 June 1865 (his birthday), between two old oaks, on the lakeshore in his park, under a stone cross which he had erected in the previous year, and which bore the epitaph 'Orate pro anima: Caroli Waterton: cujus fessa juxta hanc crucem sepeliuntur ossa' ('Pray for the soul of Charles Waterton, whose wearied bones lie beneath this cross'). A permanent display was dedicated to Waterton at the Wakefield Museum.

Waterton's only child, **Edmund Waterton** (1830–1887), antiquary, was born on 7 April 1830, at Walton Hall. In September 1841 he was sent to be educated, like his father, at Stonyhurst College, where he remained until 1850. Throughout his life he was a devout Roman Catholic. He married twice. His first wife, whom he married on 20

August 1862, while his father and aunts, Eliza and Helen, were abroad at Aix-la-Chapelle, was Josephine Margaret Alicia (d. 1879), second daughter of Sir John Ennis, of Ballinahown Court, co. Westmeath. The couple had two sons and four daughters.

Having run up large debts, Edmund Waterton sold Walton Hall (which later became Waterton Park Hotel) in 1876 (although his father's natural history collection was preserved at Alston Hall, near Preston). In 1879 he purchased Deeping Waterton Hall, Market Deeping, Lincolnshire, which later became the Old Manor House, and all except the chapel became the property of the Xaverian brothers. On 15 November 1881 he married his second wife, Ellen, only child of John Mercer of Alston Hall; they had two daughters.

Edmund Waterton wrote several essays on the devotion to the Blessed Virgin in England, formed a collection of rings, many of which went to the British Museum at South Kensington, and collected editions, printed and manuscript, of the *De imitatione Christi*. He also published a brief description of some of his rings. When abroad he would use the obsolete title of twenty-seventh lord of Walton on his visiting cards.

In 1858, like his father before him, Waterton was admitted as knight of the supreme order of Christ. He was also a knight of Malta, papal privy chamberlain, and a fellow of the Society of Antiquaries. He died after a long illness, on 22 July 1887, and was buried in the Waterton chapel, in Deeping Waterton, with his first wife. He was survived by his second wife, who died on 10 January 1909; she was buried in the Mercer family vault at Alston Lane.

YOLANDA FOOTE

Sources DNB · B. W. Edginton, *Charles Waterton: a biography* (1996) · G. Phelps, *Squire Waterton* (1976) · J. Blackburn, *Charles Waterton* (1989) · *Letters of Charles Waterton*, ed. R. A. Irwin (1955) · P. Gosse, *The squire of Walton Hall* (1940) · Burke, *Peerage* (1858) · Burke, *Peerage* (1879) · Walford, *County families* (1860) · IGI [Edmund Waterton]

Archives National Museums of Scotland Library, Edinburgh, corresp. · NHM, essay on the tropics · NRA, priv. coll., corresp. collected by his biographer · Wakefield Museum, journals and notebooks · Wakefield Reference and Information Library, local studies department, corresp. and papers · York City Archives, corresp. | York City Archives, letters to Thomas Allis

Likenesses C. W. Peale, oils, 1824, NPG · P. H. Fitzgerald, pen-and-ink drawing, 1860, NPG · W. Hawkins, bust, 1865, Linn. Soc. · illustrations, repro. in Phelps, *Squire Waterton*

Wealth at death under £14,000: probate, 11 Aug 1865, CGPLA Eng. & Wales

Waterton, Edmund (1830–1887). *See under* Waterton, Charles (1782–1865).

Waterton, Sir Hugh (d. 1409), administrator, was the second son of William Waterton of Waterton, Lincolnshire, and Elizabeth, daughter of Roger Newmarch of Womersley. His career was decisively shaped by his service to the duchy of Lancaster, as were those of his elder brother John and his cousin Robert, and all three rose to national prominence after the Lancastrian usurpation of 1399. His first association was with John of Gaunt, duke of Lancaster, with whom he served on campaign in France in 1373 and by whom he was retained from at least 1377. When Gaunt made his will in 1397, Waterton was among the executors. It was presumably through this connection that he took as his second wife Katherine, widow of another of Gaunt's retainers, Sir John Bromwich, by November 1394, a marriage that brought him estates in Herefordshire and Gloucestershire. His first wife is said to have been Ellen, daughter of the Lincolnshire esquire Robert Mowbray, though evidence is scarce.

Waterton rapidly developed a yet closer association with Gaunt's son Henry Bolingbroke, earl of Derby. He was in charge of Henry's household finances from the later 1370s, and had been appointed his chamberlain by 1386. In 1387 he was appointed constable of Henry's castles of Brecon and Hay, and in 1391 became chief steward of Brecon and of Henry's other lordships in Wales. He accompanied Henry on his expeditions to the Baltic and beyond in 1390–91 and 1392–3, and in 1398 was appointed one of his attorneys during his exile, a period during which Waterton also had custody of Henry's children Humphrey, Blanche, and Philippa.

Waterton had been knighted probably in 1394 and appointed a JP in Herefordshire three years later, but for him, as for other prominent Lancastrian retainers, Bolingbroke's accession to the throne in 1399 brought greater responsibilities and greater rewards. He became chamberlain of the duchy of Lancaster at the start of the new reign, a post he held until his death. He received many other appointments and grants, most of which reinforced the influence in Wales and the marches he already wielded by virtue of his office at Brecon and control of his wife's estates. In 1401, for example, he became steward and constable of Monmouth, Grosmont, Whitecastle, and Skenfrith, four of the Lancastrian castles in Wales, and steward of the duchy lands in Herefordshire and Gloucestershire. In 1399 he was granted custody of Chepstow and appointed steward of Swansea and the lordship of Gower during the minority of Thomas (II) Mowbray, heir to the duke of Norfolk; in the same year he was given the keeping of the castle of St Briavels in the Forest of Dean. He received a variety of other grants in the region, including custody of lands in Herefordshire and Wales belonging to the minor heirs of Sir Richard Talbot and the earl of Salisbury, and the duchy of Lancaster manors of Tibberton and More; his wife was granted the duchy manors of Ashperton and Stretton.

Waterton's increasing regional power was reflected and reinforced by his regular appointment as a JP, and to a variety of other commissions, in Gloucestershire and Herefordshire from 1399. Unsurprisingly, given the extent of his local responsibilities, he was active in the campaign against Owain Glyn Dŵr. However, it was not only in Wales and the marches that his influence was felt. He was regularly named as a member of the king's council, and in February 1405 became constable of Windsor Castle, an office that led to his appointment to the Berkshire peace commission. He also lent substantial sums of money to the king throughout the early years of the reign.

Waterton died on 2 July 1409. His heirs were his two daughters of his first marriage, Elizabeth, wife of the Herefordshire esquire John ap Harry, and Blanche, wife of Sir Robert Chalons. His widow, Katherine, married Sir Roger Leche, another prominent Lancastrian retainer; she died, having outlived her third husband, in 1420.

HELEN CASTOR

Sources Chancery records · PRO · R. Somerville, History of the duchy of Lancaster, 1265–1603 (1953) · J. W. Walker, 'The Burghs of Cambridgeshire and Yorkshire and the Watertons of Lincolnshire and Yorkshire', Yorkshire Archaeological Journal, 30 (1930–31), 311–419 · CIPM, 19, nos. 818, 819 · C. Rawcliffe, 'Waterton, John', HoP, Commons, 1386–1421, vol. 4 · N. H. Nicolas, ed., Proceedings and ordinances of the privy council of England, 7 vols., RC, 26 (1834–7), vol. 1 · S. Walker, The Lancastrian affinity, 1361–1399 (1990)

Waterton, Robert (d. 1425), administrator, was probably born in the 1360s, the son of William Waterton of Waterton Hall in the Isle of Axholme, Lincolnshire, and his wife, Elizabeth Newmarch. Apparently the cousin of Sir Hugh *Waterton, he followed him into Lancastrian service, but although prominent therein for over thirty years he was never knighted, and is usually described as an esquire. Retained from 1392 with an annual fee of £6 13s. 4d., he served Henry Bolingbroke as an esquire, accompanying him to the Baltic in 1392. Master forester of Pontefract from 1391, by 1399 he was steward and constable there, and also constable of Tickhill. In 1398 Bolingbroke granted him a second annuity, of 10 marks. Waterton remained in office following Richard II's confiscation of the Lancastrian estates, but was probably the first of Bolingbroke's retainers to meet Duke Henry at Ravenspur in June 1399, arriving at the head of 200 foresters.

Waterton was appointed master of the horse on 20 November 1399, and took part in embassies to Germany and Denmark in 1401–2. But it was primarily through seigneurial and regional administration that he exercised power and influence. His positions in the honours of Pontefract and Tickhill, in which he had been confirmed in 1399, made him a dominant figure in the West Riding of Yorkshire and in north Nottinghamshire. The grant to him on 28 November 1399 of the manor of Doubledyke in Gosberton, forfeited by Sir John Bussy, gave him a position in the parts of Holland as well.

In January 1400 Waterton was one of those responsible for the custody of Richard II in Pontefract Castle; four years later he forcefully denounced in parliament claims that the former king was still alive. When civil war broke out in 1403, Waterton helped to prevent the earl of Northumberland from joining forces with Henry Percy (Hotspur), and subsequently marched with the king against the earl, who had retreated to Newcastle upon Tyne. Sent to arrest Hotspur's widow and son, in August 1403 he received a life grant of the manor of Wallwickgrange in Northumberland, and lands at Fangfoss in Yorkshire; in 1409 this became a hereditary grant. In the spring of 1405 the king sent him with a message to the earl of Northumberland, who on 6 May seized and imprisoned Waterton at Warkworth; Northumberland's treason was subsequently dated from this event. Waterton himself was released in June, when his brother John took his place, and later received a life grant of the offices of steward and master forester of the Percy estates at Spofforth and Healaugh.

On 18 May 1407 Waterton was appointed chief steward of the north parts of the duchy of Lancaster during pleasure. In April 1408 he negotiated a prolongation of the truce in Guyenne and Picardy with French ambassadors, and in the same month was appointed to direct measures to restore order after the earl of Northumberland's final rebellion. He was sheriff of Lincolnshire in 1411–12. In 1409 Waterton witnessed Henry IV's will at Greenwich, and after 1413 acted as one of the king's executors. But although he remained in royal service under Henry V, he was probably less close to the new king, and lost his chief stewardship. Nevertheless he was an ambassador to France in 1414 and 1416, and from 1415 to 1423 had the custody of the young Duke Richard of York. From June 1417 he also had the keeping of the duke of Orléans at Pontefract; the two men appear to have become friends, and Waterton's wife and children received gifts of jewellery from Orléans. Henry V clearly felt that friendship was endangering security, and after a warning and an inquest had Orléans moved to Windsor, though Waterton was subsequently trusted with the keeping of other French prisoners. At the accession of Henry VI, Waterton was reappointed to his Pontefract and Tickhill offices, and in 1424 had temporary charge of the Scottish hostages for James I.

Throughout his career Waterton continued to acquire fees, and also accumulated considerable landed interests. In 1412 he and his wife received a hereditary grant of the former Percy manor of Healaugh from Queen Joan, but his principal estate was at Methley, where he rebuilt the manor house. He married three times. By 1398 he had married Joan (b. 1362), a coheir of the Everingham family and widow of the Yorkshire MP Sir William Elys, who brought Waterton manors in Yorkshire, north Nottinghamshire, and Lincolnshire. Between 1399 and 1403 he married Cicely Flemyng, from a knightly west Yorkshire family, with whom he had a son, Robert, who married Beatrice, daughter of John, Lord Clifford (d. 1422), and was MP for Yorkshire in 1435. It is not known if his daughter Joan (or Cecilia), who married Leo (or Lionel) *Welles, sixth Lord Welles, was born of Waterton's first or second marriage. In 1422, following his second wife's death, Waterton married Margaret Clarel, widow of John Fitzwilliam, who outlived Waterton and by 1426 contracted a clandestine marriage to William Gascoigne of Gawthorpe.

The evidence for Waterton's religious outlook is ambiguous. A story told by Walsingham of Waterton's squire, who in 1406 insulted a preacher maintaining the cause of orthodoxy against a Lollard, as a result of which Waterton was obliged to do penance, albeit in private, may only indicate a fashionable anti-clericalism—in 1408 Waterton and his wife received a papal indult licensing them to have a portable altar. His dependants included a number of clerics, whose careers he advanced through the patronage at his disposal. In particular he was an early and important patron of Richard *Flemming, later bishop of Lincoln, who may have been his second wife's brother.

As junior proctor of Oxford University in 1407–8, Flemming included Waterton's arms in the copy of the university's statutes which he commissioned and subsequently presented for the use of his successors.

Waterton made his will on 10 January 1425, and died at Methley on 17 January following. His tomb, with contemporary alabaster effigies of himself and his second wife, survives in Methley church, in a chantry chapel towards whose foundation he bequeathed £200. His effigy suggests that he either bore or cultivated a resemblance to Henry IV. He was also depicted with his second wife in the glass (now destroyed) in three windows in Castleford church.

J. R. WHITEHEAD

Sources *Chancery records* · R. Somerville, *History of the duchy of Lancaster, 1265–1603* (1953) · T. Walsingham, *The St Albans chronicle, 1406–1420*, ed. V. H. Galbraith (1937) · H. Ellis, ed., *Original letters illustrative of English history*, 1st ser., 3 vols. (1824); 2nd ser., 4 vols. (1827); 3rd ser., 4 vols. (1846) · GEC, *Peerage*, 5.191–2; 12/2.443–4 · RotP, vols. 3–4 · J. W. Walker, 'The Burghs of Cambridgeshire and Yorkshire and the Watertons of Lincolnshire and Yorkshire', *Yorkshire Archaeological Journal*, 30 (1930–31), 311–419 · E. McLeod, *Charles of Orléans, prince and poet* (1969)
Likenesses alabaster tomb effigy, Methley church, Yorkshire

Waterworth, William (1811–1882), Jesuit and historian, was born at St Helens, Lancashire, on 22 June 1811. He was educated at the Jesuit college at Stonyhurst in Lancashire, where he was admitted to the Society of Jesus on 26 March 1829. In 1833 he was appointed master of the grammar school opened by the society in London. After starting his theological training at Stonyhurst seminary, he was ordained priest there in 1836; he completed his studies at the Collegio Romano in Rome, where he passed his *examen ad gradum* in theology. From December 1838 to 5 January 1841 he was professor of dogmatic theology at Stonyhurst. He professed the four vows on 2 July 1850.

Waterworth served as a priest in Hereford until 1854, where he wrote a number of historical and apologetic works. In 1852 his *The Jesuits, or, An examination of the origin, progress, principles and practices of the Society of Jesus* was published in London, and in 1854 he brought out *England and Rome, or, The history of the religious connexion between England and the Holy See, from … 179 to the … Anglican Reformation in 1534, Origin and Developments of Anglicanism*, and *On the Gradual Absorption of Early Anglicanism by Popedom*. In 1854 he became rector of the church of the Immaculate Conception in Farm Street, London. Three years later he was sent to the mission at Worcester, and appointed superior of the College of St George, where he remained until 1878. During this period he published *The Church of St Patrick … a History of the … Ancient Church of Ireland* (1869) and *Queen Elizabeth versus the lord chancellor … a history of the prayer book of the Church of England* (1871). He was appointed spiritual father of the College of St Ignatius in London in September 1879, and in November 1880 he was appointed to the mission at Bournemouth, where he died on 17 March 1882. He was buried at Stapehill, near Wimborne, Dorset.

THOMPSON COOPER, rev. LEO GOOCH

Sources H. Foley, ed., *Records of the English province of the Society of Jesus*, 7 (1882–3), 821 · *The Tablet* (25 March 1882), 471

Wealth at death £548 2s. 6d.: probate, 22 May 1882, *CGPLA Eng. & Wales*

Wates, Neil Edward (1932–1985), builder and environmentalist, was born at 4 Sydenham Road, Croydon, on 4 February 1932, the eldest son and second child in the family of three boys and three girls of Norman Edward *Wates (1905–1969), builder, and his wife, Margot Irene Sidwell. Educated at Stowe School, Wates did national service in the Coldstream Guards. At Brasenose College, Oxford, he read law, was a keen sportsman, and learned to fly. He obtained a second-class degree in jurisprudence in 1954.

In the same year he began twenty-one years in Wates Ltd, for the last three as chairman and chief executive, succeeding his uncle, Sir Ronald Wallace Wates (1907–1986). By his working on the building sites, he and the men came to know and respect each other. Design, planning, and industrial relations absorbed him and he worked with W. John P. M. Garnett as treasurer of the Industrial Society. His widening interests were stimulated by his wife, (Ann) Jenifer, the daughter of William Guy Weston, of the Ministry of Transport. They married in 1953 after she had taken her degree at Oxford, and together they tackled social problems against a background of deep and common religious faith. Later, when Wates became a trustee of the Wates Foundation, set up to help the needy, he explored the facts of deprivation, meeting men such as Edward D. Berman who fired his imagination.

In 1970 a growing interest in the foreign scene took Wates to South Africa. He decided that business involvement would be immoral and was persuaded to allow his report to be published. He risked unpopularity, but gained a lasting reputation as a businessman prepared to subordinate expediency to morality.

In 1975, after disagreements, Wates resigned from the company. He and his wife set up a trust, Commonwork, and a centre where they and others could pursue their interests in a diverse farming community, at Bore Place, Kent. Wates's theme was responsible stewardship—harmonizing the claims and potential of people with the natural environment and resources. All products and residues were used—for methane, for bricks, and for a variety of crafts. The conference centre offered wide-ranging courses from ecology to peacemaking. Wates helped to launch the forum Rural (Responsible Use of Resources in Agriculture and on the Land).

By the early 1980s Wates saw the real seeds of conflict in global environmental deterioration, social injustice, and growing international instability. When an eminent American asked him what he was doing to avert a third world war, he was ready. A friend, Donald Reeves, was rector of St James's, Piccadilly; there they founded a forum—Dunamis—for the discussion of peace and security.

Wates was a peacemaker who sought common ground to resolve enmities by frank discussion. Dunamis considered conflict between east and west and, what Wates thought even more fundamental, between rich north and poor south, with pacifists and leaders of the defence establishment, the orthodox, and the revolutionary. Wates believed that problems were not so much technical—weapons or systems—as failures of human understanding. To fellow landowners he showed how respect for the land could be as successful as more ruthless methods. His pack of bloodhounds demonstrated how hunting, which he loved, could avoid the stigma of cruelty. When illness struck he was co-ordinating all these interests and a new one, holistic medicine.

Fit and dashing on a horse, skis, or hang-glider, Wates was a natural leader. A sense of drama made his ventures (South Africa or a pep talk at Wates) exciting and momentous; he had a capacity to inspire. In public he was fluent and confident; in private more abrupt and staccato, finding it hard to form close relationships outside the family. A man of paradox, he did not fit easily among his peers; a former part-time SAS officer who became a Quaker; very rich but truly abstemious; a bustling entrepreneur whose meetings started with a prayer. He often saw wealth and privilege as handicaps and this, with his admiration of his father, made him strangely anxious to justify himself. His father had made a national reputation for Wates Ltd and himself by his leadership in the building industry during the Second World War, and in the production of Mulberry harbours. Neil Wates was rich and impetuous enough to put ideas to immediate test. He pioneered projects for others to complete. Often demanding, even imperious, he could be impatient and lose interest if results were not rapid and important.

By 1982 his and his wife's interests diverged. They separated and were divorced in 1984, but remained close, and Jenifer continued with Commonwork. Their five children—four boys and a girl—in whose development Wates took delighted interest, were almost grown up. The last phase of his life was not spent alone. Susan Benn, long a supporter of Commonwork, shared his work and developed its artistic side. Wates died on 22 September 1985 in the Cromwell Hospital, London.   HENNIKER, *rev.*

Sources *The Times* (18 Oct 1985) · *The Times* (23 Oct 1985) · personal knowledge (1990) · private information (1990) · L. Weatherley, 'Wates, Norman Edward (1905–1969)', *DBB* · *CGPLA Eng. & Wales* (1986) · b. cert.

Wealth at death £7,311,069: probate, 21 Feb 1986, *CGPLA Eng. & Wales*

Wates, Norman Edward (1905–1969), builder and contractor, was born on 12 January 1905 in Streatham, London, the eldest of the three sons of Edward Wates, house furnisher and builder, and his wife, Sarah, *née* Holmes. His younger brother was Sir Ronald Wallace *Wates. He was educated at Emmanuel School, Wandsworth, leaving in 1922 to spend a year with a firm of chartered accountants before joining the building firm started by his father and three uncles. The firm had expanded rapidly after the First World War, building housing estates in south London, and in 1926 it embarked on an estate of 1000 houses in Streatham Vale, which took five years to complete. On 25 April 1929 Wates married Margot Irene (b. 1906/7), daughter of James Sidwell; they had three sons, the eldest of whom was the builder and environmentalist Neil Edward *Wates, and three daughters.

By 1930 Wates had been joined by his two younger brothers. This younger generation soon took charge of the firm and, in 1935, began to look beyond the building of houses to public works, including libraries, fire stations, and drill halls. Wates made several trips to the United States in the 1930s to study American building methods and business and management techniques, and he was one of the first builders to reduce the amount of casual labour, leading to the Wates staff-man scheme for qualified site workers, which provided security of employment.

As war approached Wates took on a number of government contracts, and by 1939 had over 100 contracts with the War Office, the Admiralty, and the London boroughs, including contracts for air raid shelters, lining units for trenches, and the construction of army camps and airfields. Wates advised the Admiralty on specialist concrete structures; during the war the firm made pre-cast concrete barges and the first pre-cast concrete floating dock. It was also involved in the construction of units for the Mulberry harbours used for the Normandy landings in 1944.

With the post-war housing shortage and the shortage of traditional building materials, including bricks, timber, and steel, as well as that of skilled site labour, the government subsidized the building of houses using non-traditional materials. The Wates firm was one of the leading builders of temporary, prefabricated bungalows for local authorities all over England, as part of the temporary housing programme from 1945 to 1948. Wates built on experience acquired during the war and, using the precasting works built for production of war materials, he developed a system of making large load-bearing concrete slabs, one storey high, for bungalows. This was especially useful in areas where there was a shortage of site labour. When the subsidies ended, and the prohibition on building for private ownership was lifted, Wates built permanent pre-cast concrete houses; between 1945 and 1955 the firm built nearly 20,000 of these, 9.6% of the total output in the country.

In the 1950s Wates set up a separate division in the midlands. The company built various styles of house, including over a thousand of the detached Dormy houses. In 1953 they were the first to import the tower crane from France, for use in high construction work. They were also one of the first contractors to move into urban redevelopment in the 1950s, working with the charitable foundation of Alleyn's College to redevelop Dulwich; with the Church Commissioners they embarked on the Parkhill development in Croydon, and the Hyde Park estate in Bayswater, where the firm built 763 flats and 112 houses. In the early 1960s the pre-cast concrete division made and put up many of the buildings at the new universities of Sussex and Essex. The Wates Group remained a private company, one of the largest family businesses in the construction industry, with Norman Wates as chairman.

Throughout his career Wates sat on many committees

concerned with housing standards. He was a founder member of the National Housebuilders Registration Committee in 1935. After the war he was one of a team sent to Germany by the government to study methods of prefabrication. He served for twelve years on the Central Housing Advisory Committee, set up by the minister of housing and local government in 1957; he was also on the Parker Morris committee, set up to establish minimum specifications for local authority housing, whose report, *Homes for Today and Tomorrow*, appeared in 1961.

Always interested in education Wates started an indentured student scheme in the company in 1947. He was a foundation governor of the United Westminster Schools foundation, a member of the council of King's College Hospital medical school, and on the court of governors of the London School of Economics. With his brothers he set up the Wates Foundation to encourage the arts and sciences. His main recreation was ocean racing. He died at King's College Hospital, Denmark Hill, Lambeth, London, on 21 July 1969.   ANNE PIMLOTT BAKER

Sources L. Weatherley, 'Wates, Norman Edward', *DBB* · M. Bowley, *The British building industry* (1966) · A. A. Jackson, *Semi-detached London*, 2nd edn (1991) · F. Shaw, *The houses and homeless of post war Britain* (1985) · O. Marriott, *The property boom* (1967) · *The Times* (22 July 1969) · *The Times* (26 July 1969) · *CGPLA Eng. & Wales* (1970) · m. cert. · d. cert.
Likenesses photograph, repro. in Weatherley, 'Wates, Norman Edward'
Wealth at death £703,279: probate, 17 Aug 1970, *CGPLA Eng. & Wales* · English probate resealed in the Bahamas, 31 Aug 1972, *CGPLA Eng. & Wales*

Wates, Sir Ronald Wallace (1907–1986), builder and benefactor, was born at 87 Mitcham Lane, Streatham, London, on 4 June 1907, the second child in the family of three sons and one daughter of Edward Wates, builder, and his wife, Sarah Holmes. He was educated at Emanuel School, Wandsworth, to which he remained affectionately loyal, becoming a governor and generous benefactor. Leaving school at sixteen, he worked in an estate agency while qualifying as a surveyor in 1928 (later FRICS) before joining the family building firm, of which he became a director in 1931. That year he married his childhood friend, Phyllis Mary, daughter of Harry Trace, innkeeper; they had four sons. Founded jointly by Wates's father, Edward, early in the twentieth century, by the 1920s the family firm was well placed to take advantage of the suburban growth in south London between the wars. A good range of well-built houses was offered, and output rose to 2000 a year.

Edward Wates's three sons were responsible for the business's expanding to become one of the largest family-owned firms in the country. The eldest, Norman Edward *Wates, was undoubtedly the dominant force, but Ronald's sound financial sense, feel for property, and organizing ability played an important part. The youngest, Allan, was largely responsible for a skilled and contented workforce. Tight family control and a united external front were maintained.

During the Second World War, Wates carried out much high-priority work and a significant development in the firm was the successful fulfilment of a major wartime contract for sections of Mulberry harbour, made for the 1944 Normandy landings. In the post-war years the firm's reputation grew as its activities widened, extending to contract housing, tower blocks, City redevelopment, and other large-scale construction projects. Wates's contribution lay in his keen eye for a valuable site and, increasingly, his City contacts. In 1969 Wates unexpectedly took over as chairman when his brother Norman died suddenly. It was not an easy time. In a family firm, there was little career structure; the next generation, with new ideas, was waiting in the wings, but not yet deemed ready. Subordinating his other interests, Wates held the fort solidly until 1973, when Norman's eldest son, Neil *Wates took over as chairman and he became president.

Wates's influence and interests had been growing steadily. A lifelong Conservative, he was a member of Wandsworth borough council (1937–46) and London county council (1949–52). He was made a freeman of the City of London in 1945 and a JP for inner London in 1947. He acquired the art of public speaking and was a good raconteur. He became master of the Worshipful Company of Innholders (1978–9), was a fellow of the Institute of Building, and a governor of the Brixton School of Building; he also gave his time to many other activities in support of the industry. He was for many years chairman of the Royal School for the Blind, Leatherhead (1971–82); a council member of King's College Hospital medical school; a trustee of the Historic Churches Preservation Trust; and a member of the church commissioners' committee on redundant churches. In 1966 he and his two brothers established from their personal resources the Wates Foundation, dedicated to improving the quality of life, especially for the disadvantaged young. By 1990 its annual income was £1.3 million.

Rubicund and dapper, with a twinkle in his eye, Wates was a congenial companion at ease with everyone. Careful of the pennies, he was shrewd and sound on large issues. He was, in every sense, a builder for both his firm and his family. He became a rich man but remained engagingly modest. Of strong Christian faith, he had a natural concern for others and a respect for traditional values, relishing all that was best in his country's heritage. His marriage was exceptionally happy—his equable temperament played its part in this. In 1947 Wates and his wife acquired the Manor House, Headley, where he put down roots. He became absorbed in the upbringing of his children, passing on to them his love of horses and field sports. He farmed with enjoyment, hunted until he was seventy, and became a popular member of the old-established Surrey Club. He was an involved and generous benefactor to his parish church, of which he was church warden and treasurer, to Guildford Cathedral (council member), and to Surrey University (foundation fellow, and DUniv 1975). In 1972 he was made an honorary fellow of University College, London. He was knighted in 1975 for his charitable and philanthropic services and was made deputy lieutenant for Surrey in 1981. Wates died of a cerebral thrombosis in Ashtead Hospital on 25 January 1986. Following cremation, his ashes were buried at Headley parish church. The value of his will, before inheritance tax, was £3,200,575.

JOHN MORETON, rev.

Sources *The Times* (21 Feb 1986) • personal knowledge (1996) • private information (1996) [colleagues; family; in-house company records]
Likenesses double portrait (with Lady Wates, *Conversation piece*), priv. coll.
Wealth at death £3,200,575: probate, 12 Aug 1986, *CGPLA Eng. & Wales*

Wath, Michael (d. 1350), administrator, probably belonged to a family that came originally from Wath upon Dearne in Yorkshire. He first appears in 1314 as an attorney and won his first ecclesiastical patronage from the crown in 1316. By 1323 he was described as 'constantly attendant on the king's service in chancery' (*CPR, 1321–4*, 337), and was clerk to Henry Cliffe, keeper of the rolls of chancery, by 5 May 1329. On 3 February 1330 he received, by papal provision, a canonry and prebend of Southwell in addition to his rectorship of Wath, and to them was added a canonry and prebend at St John's, Howden, in March 1331. He maintained close links with his home county, being appointed to assess a tallage in Yorkshire on 25 June 1332, and serving as supervisor of the taxes of a ninth and fifteenth there in 1340. Wath became keeper of the rolls on 20 January 1334, and on 17 April was presented to the living of Foston in Yorkshire. He surrendered the office of keeper of the rolls on 28 April 1337, and served as keeper of the great seal between 8 December 1339 and 16 February 1340. In December 1340 he was removed from his post in the chancery by Edward III, with other clerks and judges, and imprisoned on a charge of maladministration, but was afterwards released. Although not reappointed to the chancery, he continued to serve on various royal commissions in the 1340s. He died in 1350.

W. E. RHODES, rev. W. M. ORMROD

Sources B. Wilkinson, *The chancery under Edward III* (1929) • *Chancery records* • J. L. Grassi, 'Royal clerks from the archdiocese of York in the fourteenth century', *Northern History*, 5 (1970), 12–33 • *CEPR letters*, vol. 2

Wathen, James (bap. 1752, d. 1828), artist and pedestrian, was baptized on 1 July 1752 in the parish church of All Saints, Hereford, the son of Thomas Wathen (d. 1779), a glover of the city, and his wife, Dorothy Taylor (d. 1801) of Bristol. According to the Revd Richard Warner's *Literary Recollections*, Wathen's education was 'humble' but based upon 'considerable English reading' (1.383). Wathen worked in the trade of gloving until his middle years, but at an early age became 'an ardent admirer of Nature, and all her wild and picturesque scenery' (ibid.), making frequent excursions into the Herefordshire countryside with his sketchbook. With a pencil and simple washes it was said that he could produce up to twenty views a day. These sketches, which were often dated and were frequently framed in coloured paper, were presented to his friends, who knew him as Jemmy Sketch; certainly naïve, they have the freshness of the work of a self-taught primitivist. Wathen painted everyday scenes and took a particular delight in vernacular architecture, recording virtually all the timber-framed buildings of his native city. His earliest sketch in a public collection is dated 1779, but his most prolific period in Herefordshire was the 1790s.

Wathen appears to have offered his services as a guide to artists and tourists who wished to make expeditions down the River Wye, making a 'minute delineation of the course of the river, its picturesque points and the objects of curiosity in the neighbourhood' (R. Warner, *A Walk through Wales, August 1797*, 1799, 213). On these trips he frequently obtained paintings and sketches from notable artists and thus assembled his own collection of topographical art. His work became well known to the general public via the *Gentleman's Magazine*. Two sketches were published in June 1787 that depicted the collapsed west end of Hereford Cathedral and these were followed by four views of the cathedral, engraved by S. Middiman and F. Jukes, 'before, during and after the collapse' (*Hereford Journal*, 19 Sept 1787). These were highly regarded and were recommended to John Britton for his *History and Antiquities of the Cathedral Church of Hereford* (1831), although they were not used. During his lifetime Wathen provided many sketches for guidebooks to Wales and the marches, and his contributions to the *Gentleman's Magazine* included accounts and engravings of Aconbury chapel, Kilpeck church, Marden church, Burghope House, Longworth chapel, White Cross (Hereford), Dore Abbey, and Putley Cross.

In 1801 Wathen inherited Aconbury Court from his uncle and namesake, James Wathen, which enabled him to buy a fine property—Aylestone Hill House—in the suburbs of Hereford, where he lived until his death. Emancipated from gloving, he embarked upon a series of long-distance walking tours: sketchbooks survive for a northern tour to Scotland in 1808 and a south-western tour in 1825. His stamina on these tours became legendary. He could travel 32 miles a day and outpace the horses upon which his companions travelled. The horses required 'two hours to bait, whereas Mr. W wanted only an hour' (*GM*, 282). He was a vegetarian and never drank wine, beer, or spirits; tea was his principal refreshment.

In 1811 Wathen sailed with an old school friend, Captain James Prendergast, to India and China, and he published in 1814 *Journal of a Voyage to India and China* in two volumes, illustrated with twenty-four coloured prints from drawings by the author. It was well reviewed by the *Gentleman's Magazine* as 'a plain unvarnished tale' (Warner, 1.387). Wathen also intended to publish an account of his European tour on which he was cordially received by Byron but his numerous sketches for this remain, unpublished, in Hereford City Library. In 1821 he capitalized on Napoleon's exile to St Helena by publishing *A Series of Views Illustrative of the Island of St Helena*, which he had compiled on his return journey from the east in 1812. The book's frontispiece was a print of a portrait of Wathen painted by A. J. Oliver (1774–1842). Wathen made a trip to Heligoland in 1827 and in the following spring he completed his fortieth walk to London. He returned to Hereford and died at his home there on 20 August 1828 in his seventy-sixth year.

The *Gentleman's Magazine* ran a long obituary which began:

> The loss of this ingenious and worthy gentleman will be deeply regretted by a most numerous acquaintance in all parts of the United Kingdom; for in all parts of the country was he known by his talents as a Draftsman, and his pleasant and social manners as a friend. (*GM*, 281)

His will revealed the extent of his art collection and he made numerous bequests to his friends, including the artist David Cox, of works by artists including Thomas Gainsborough, Alfred Nicholson, John 'Warwick' Smith, Nicholas Pocock, and John Glover. His executors were requested to present sixty or seventy of Wathen's drawings to the Fitzwilliam Museum in Cambridge, where they can still be seen. The most substantial collection of his works is in Hereford City Library; Hereford Record Office and the bishop's library, Hereford, also have collections.

DAVID WHITEHEAD

Sources D. Whitehead and R. Shoesmith, *James Wathen's Herefordshire, 1770–1820* (1994) · R. Warner, *Literary recollections*, 2 vols. (1830), vol. 1 · *GM*, 1st ser., 98/2 (1828), 281–2 · *Hereford Journal* (27 Aug 1828) · will, Hereford City Library, Bird's Herefordshire collection [MS work in 2 vols., no callmark] · *Hereford Times* (24 Nov 1888) · *Hereford Times* (1 Dec 1888) · newscutting book, Hereford City Library, pc.2281 · C. J. Robinson, *A history of the mansions and manors of Herefordshire* (1872) · *Hereford Journal* (19 Sept 1787) · *Hereford Journal* (11 July 1801) · parish register, All Saints' Church, Hereford, 1 July 1752 [baptism]
Likenesses T. Bragg, line engraving (after A. J. Oliver), BM, NPG; repro. in *Journal of a voyage in India and China* (1814), vol. 1
Wealth at death substantial assets: will, 1827, Hereford City Library, Bird's Herefordshire collection, vol. 2, pp. 185–7

Watkin, Edward Ingram (1888–1981), writer and translator, was born on 27 September 1888 at Stand, Cheshire, the only child of Edgar Watkin (1860–1908) and his wife, Emmeline Paxton Ingram (1851–1937). His father was a cultivated dilettante and grandson of the Manchester Liberal reformer Absalom Watkin. His mother was the daughter of Herbert Ingram MP, founder of the *Illustrated London News*, whose fortune funded her husband's many interests which did not include his son. Watkin spent the first eight years of a lonely childhood with his widowed maternal grandmother in various family homes in Wales, Norfolk, Manchester, and Walton-on-Thames. Later he spent many of his holidays at his father's extensive property at Pantafon near Caernarfon, but isolation remained endemic and it was this, rather than his education, which led to an academic precocity which established his cultural, philosophical, and religious interests. His schooling was erratic but included four years at the marquess of Normanby's school at Malgrave Castle in Yorkshire—which retreated *en masse* each spring to Windsor where the marquess held a canonry—a grand tour in 1904, a year at Bletsoe rectory in Bedfordshire where a fellow pupil was his lifelong friend Christopher Dawson, and five terms at St Paul's School in London (1906–7) in preparation for Oxford. He matriculated at New College, Oxford, in 1907 and graduated with first-class honours in Greats in 1911.

Watkin lacked worldly ambition and despite his privileged background his needs were few. Sir Francis de Zulueta thought him too odd to be given an academic post even

Edward Ingram Watkin (1888–1981), by unknown photographer, 1960

in Oxford. Watkin was unfitted for a regular job. A permanent estrangement from his mother led to the withdrawal of her financial assistance and his life was a constant struggle to support his wife and children and to carry on the work he wished to do. He was a non-combatant in the First World War and was dedicated to a predominantly pacifist approach to conflict; he was among the founders, in 1936, of Pax, the Association for the Promotion of Peace, later Pax Christi. He had a wide European sympathy and among his translations, mainly from the French or German (he had spent a year in Germany after Oxford), was his *History of the English People in the Nineteenth Century* (1923–51), his version, in seven volumes, of Elie Halévy's classic work in French. His own writings were informed throughout by an abiding vision of Roman Catholicism to which he had been converted in 1908 while at Oxford; he was received into the church at Downside Abbey in Somerset. He saw Catholicism as a unifying force in society and culture, a dynamic, spiritual energy. He was a consistent and outspoken apologist for a Catholicism which appealed beyond the narrow confessional polemics of G. K. Chesterton and Hilaire Belloc to a broader and more open Catholicism, culturally inclusive, which put him under constant suspicion in orthodox circles and made ecclesiastical censors wary of him.

Watkin was twice married. In 1913 he married Helena Shepheard (1882–1972), from whom he became legally separated in 1937. She was the only daughter of Philip Candler Shepheard of Abbot's Hall, Aylsham, Norfolk. Her mother was Maria Pasqua, an Italian who as a small girl had once walked with her father from Rome to Paris and

found fame as a child model. They had five children, four girls and a boy; the eldest child, Christopher, became Dom Aelred Watkin of Downside Abbey. Watkin's second wife was Zoe Ella Bowen (*b*. 1902), a secretary, whom he married on 5 February 1973, after Helena's death: they had two daughters. After graduation Watkin lived for a time in Oxford, then moved to Sheringham in Norfolk; from 1937 he was mainly resident in Torquay, Devon.

Watkin was a prolific author, writing numerous books and contributing essays to symposia and periodicals. He wrote with clarity and enthusiasm from his first youthful effort, *Some Thoughts on Catholic Apologetics* (1913), whose title could serve as a summary of all his subsequent work until his later writings half a century later. He emphasized the overriding importance of contemplation in the Christian life and the decline and emptiness of so much in contemporary life and values, a society without a soul. Culture and religion, for him, were mutually supportive. His most substantial work was probably *A Philosophy of Form* (Oxford, 1938, 3rd edn, 1950) which combined the continuing classical and Christian tradition with a wide and sympathetic reading of modern philosophy. Like his friend Dom Iltyd Trethowan of Downside Abbey he was instrumental in introducing English Catholics to the thoughts of continental theologians who were preparing the way for the *aggiornamento* of the Second Vatican Council. In *The Catholic Centre* (1932) he argued that Catholic Christianity was the true *via media*, but as practised and understood, it too often failed to occupy this centre. Reform was needed, but it would fail unless prayer, the union of humanity with God and with each other, was placed at its very heart.

As a historian, hagiographer, or liturgist Watkin had no time for those iconoclasts who wished to eradicate the church's cultural and liturgical heritage. His books on aesthetics and his influential *Roman Catholicism in England from the Reformation to 1950* (1957) show a wide sympathy and an understanding of the difficulties of being the church in the world and the limits of history. 'For history cannot pierce the walls which enclose personal experience of God, His hidden action in souls. And it is personal experience alone which gives religious knowledge, knowledge therefore a religion' (*Roman Catholicism in England from the Reformation to 1950*, 234).

Watkin was of slight build and medium height with bright blue eyes and a fine head of hair. He suffered all his life from a form of dyspraxia, a lack of muscular co-ordination. He found it difficult to do up his shoelaces, knot his tie, shave, turn door handles, or lift a cup of tea. He detested all games despite robust good health and energy. He spoke quickly and his conversation was often interrupted by hoots of laughter. Always shabbily dressed, he was an absolutely unselfconscious eccentric who exuded a kindliness and childlike innocence. He sent his favoured publisher, Sheed and Ward, a page of a book typed without a ribbon in the machine with a covering note, 'I think you will be able to make this out if you hold the paper up to the light'. One of his children had a garden which bordered on to a field of buttercups. The farmer came with a tractor to spray the flowers and Watkin climbed over the fence and ran into the field towards the farmer shaking his fist and shouting 'Murderer! Murderer!' (private information).

Watkin died on 2 March 1981 at Torbay Hospital, Torbay, Devon, of respiratory failure, bronchial pneumonia, and dehydration. His funeral, at the church of the Assumption, Torquay, was celebrated by his son, Dom Aelred, and he was buried in Torquay cemetery where he has a gravestone. DOMINIC AIDAN BELLENGER

Sources private information (2004) · E. I. Watkin, 'Autobiographical note', typescript, [n.d.] [Mrs Magdalen Goffin] · I. Trethowan, 'E. I. Watkin at ninety', *The Tablet* (23 Sept 1978), 914–15 · M. Goffin, *Maria Pasqua* (1979) · C. Scott, *A historian and his world: a life of Christopher Dawson, 1889–1970* (1984) · J. Sullivan, 'E. I. Watkin: herald of the new spring', *Crisis* (May 1998), 32–5 · *CGPLA Eng. & Wales* (1981)
Archives priv. coll., papers
Likenesses photograph, 1960, priv. coll. [*see illus.*]
Wealth at death £10,049: probate, 27 May 1981, *CGPLA Eng. & Wales*

Watkin, Sir Edward William, first baronet (1819–1901), railway promoter, born in Ravald Street, Salford, on 26 September 1819, a son of Absalom Watkin (1787–1861), cotton merchant and prominent citizen of Manchester, and his wife, Elizabeth, daughter of William Makinson of Bolton. One brother, John (1821–1870), took holy orders and was vicar of Stixwold, Lincolnshire; another, Alfred (1825–1875), a merchant, was mayor of Manchester in 1873–4.

Watkin, after education at a private school, entered the office of his father. Interesting himself from youth in public movements, he became, when about twenty-one, a director of the Manchester Athenaeum, and with some other members he started the Saturday half-holiday movement in Manchester. He helped to organize a working class Anti-Corn Law Association to divert attention from Chartism. In 1845 he wrote *A Plea for Public Parks*, and acted as one of the secretaries of a committee which raised money for the opening of three public parks in Manchester and Salford.

Watkin soon became a partner in his father's business, but in 1845 he abandoned the cotton trade to take up the secretaryship of the Trent Valley Railway, which line was afterwards sold at a profit of £438,000 to the London and North Western Railway Company (LNWR). Watkin, who had ably negotiated the transfer, then entered the service of the latter company. In 1853 he was appointed general manager of the Manchester, Sheffield, and Lincolnshire Railway and entered on an intricate series of negotiations with the Great Northern, the London and North Western, and Midland railways, three lines whose hostile competition threatened disaster to his own company.

At the request of the duke of Newcastle, secretary of state for the colonies, he undertook, in 1861, a mission to Canada with a view to confederating the five British provinces into a dominion of Canada, transferring the Hudson Bay territory to the control of the government (accomplished in 1869), and planning railways designed to bring Quebec within easier reach of other parts of Canada and of the Atlantic. In 1868 he received a knighthood for his service in the British cause in Canada.

On returning home Watkin resigned his appointment as manager of the Manchester, Sheffield, and Lincolnshire Railway Company, through disagreement with his directors, who had come to terms in his absence with the Midland Railway, and he became president of the Grand Trunk Railway of Canada. Within two years, however, he resumed, in 1863, his connection with the Manchester company, first as director and from January 1864 as chairman. In that position, which he retained until May 1894, he did his chief work. With this office he combined the chairmanship of the South Eastern company from 1866 to 1894, and of the Metropolitan companies from 1872 to 1894. Other enterprises also occupied him. He carried out a scheme for a new railway between Manchester and Liverpool, which was opened in 1877.

Despite these varied calls on Watkin's attention, it was to the three railways of which he was chairman that he devoted his main energies. As chairman of the Manchester, Sheffield, and Lincolnshire Railway (later the Great Central), he met with great difficulties arising from the competition of both the Great Northern and Midland companies, but he greatly improved its affairs. In the 1880s he had two outstanding aims, the first being to establish a rail link between Manchester and Paris via a channel tunnel railway. To this end he created a new and independent line from Sheffield to Marylebone in London, opened on 8 March 1899.

A channel tunnel company had been formed in 1872, and under Watkin's direction excavations began in 1881 beneath the seashore between Folkestone and Dover. But the Board of Trade immediately sought an injunction forbidding Watkin to proceed, on the ground of his infringement of the crown's foreshore rights. Next session Watkin, who at that time was MP for Hythe, introduced a private bill authorizing his project; after consideration by a joint committee of the two houses, which pronounced against it by a majority of sixty-four, the bill was withdrawn. The plan was finally withdrawn in 1893. In 1886 Watkin, on receiving a report from Professor Boyd Dawkins, began boring for coal in the neighbourhood of Dover, and the work was continued until 1891, at the expense of the channel tunnel company. Sufficient evidence was obtained to justify the sinking of a trial shaft and the formation of companies for further exploration. Mining only began after his death.

His second great ambition was advanced when he became chairman of a company formed to erect at Wembley Park, Middlesex, a 'Watkin tower', modelled on the Eiffel Tower in Paris. After the first stage was completed, funds ran out. The tower was demolished in 1907.

Watkin was highly ambitious, flamboyant, and irascible, a railway imperialist, eager to extend his influence and control into new territories, at home and abroad. The legacy of his and his rivals' expansionism was sealed with the onset of motor transport competition in the 1920s and 1930s, when it proved impossible for the four main line companies, set up under the Railways Act, 1921, to provide acceptable dividends for their shareholders on an over-extended and ill-planned railway system.

Watkin was returned to parliament as Liberal member for Great Yarmouth in 1857, but was unseated on petition. He sat as member for Stockport from 1864 to 1868, when he was defeated. In 1869 he unsuccessfully contested East Cheshire, but was member for Hythe from 1874 to 1895. His political views remained Liberal until 1885, when he became a Unionist, but he often acted independently of any party. He was a friend of W. E. Gladstone, arranging his visit to Paris in 1889 and his speech on Snowdon in 1892. He was a member of the Manchester city council from 1859 to 1862 and high sheriff of Cheshire in 1874. He was created a baronet in 1880.

Watkin married in 1845 Mary Briggs (d. 1887), daughter of Jonathan Mellor of Oldham. Their son, Alfred Mellor Watkin, became MP for Grimsby (1877–80) and succeeded to the baronetcy; their daughter, Harriette, married H. W. Worsley-Taylor KC, of Moreton Hall, Whalley. His second wife, whom he married in 1893, when she was eighty-one years old, was Ann (d. 1896), daughter of William Little and widow of Herbert Ingram MP, founder of the *Illustrated London News*. Watkin died at Rose Hill, Northenden, Cheshire, on 13 April 1901, and was buried at Northenden parish church.   C. W. SUTTON, rev. PHILIP S. BAGWELL

Sources T. R. Gourvish, 'Watkin, Sir Edward William', *DBB* · G. Dow, *Dominion of Watkin, 1864–1899* (1962), vol. 2 of *Great Central* · A. W. Currie, 'Sir Edward Watkin: a Canadian view', *Journal of Transport History*, 3 (1957–8), 31–40 · C. H. Grinling, H. V. Borley, and C. H. Ellis, *History of the Great Northern Railway, 1845–1922*, new edn (1966) · Report of a meeting at Charing Cross Hotel, 20 Jan 1882, Submarine Continental Railway Co. · B. Dawkins [W. Boyd], 'The channel tunnel …', read before the Manchester Geological Society, 2 May 1882, 1882 · *Manchester Guardian* (15 April 1901) · Gladstone, *Diaries* · d. cert.
Archives Man. CL, Manchester Archives and Local Studies, political corresp. · NA Canada, corresp. and papers | BL, corresp. with W. E. Gladstone, Add. MS 44337 · W. Sussex RO, letters to duke of Richmond
Likenesses H. von Herkomer, portrait, exh. RA 1887 · A. H. Fox, oils, 1891, Museum of British Transport, York · Ape [C. Pellegrini], caricature, chromolithograph, NPG; repro. in *VF* (6 Nov 1875) · Barraud, photograph, NPG; repro. in *Men and Women of the Day*, 2 (1889) · PET, caricature, chromolithograph, NPG; repro. in *The Monetary Gazette* (17 Jan 1877) · wood-engraving (after photograph by J. & C. Watkins), NPG; repro. in *ILN* (23 July 1864)
Wealth at death £17,308 16s. 3d.: resworn probate, March 1902, *CGPLA Eng. & Wales* (1901)

Watkin, William Thompson (1836–1888),

Watkin, William Thompson (1836–1888), archaeologist, born at Salford on 15 October 1836, was the son of John Watkin of Salford. His mother, Mary Hamilton, daughter of Benjamin Brierley, was born at Portsmouth, USA. He received his education at private schools, and afterwards became a merchant in Liverpool, where his family had connections: he was the second cousin of Sir Edward William Watkin (1819–1901), the great railway promoter and entrepreneur. From early life, however, Watkin was very interested in archaeology and particularly in the Roman period in north-west England. From 1884 he was a council member and from 1885 honorary librarian of the Historic Society of Lancashire and Cheshire, and also an active council member of the Lancashire and Cheshire Antiquarian Society from its foundation in 1883.

Watkin was a very prolific writer on archaeological and antiquarian subjects, and published no fewer than 123 books and articles between 1871 and 1888. Most of these were concerned with the Roman occupation, his interests extending beyond the north-west to include Yorkshire and Northumbria, but his most important works were the twin volumes on *Roman Lancashire* (1883) and *Roman Cheshire* (1886), both of which are still widely used and cited. He was a most careful observer, not given to speculation or assumption, and for this reason his notes and writings are regarded as more reliable and trustworthy than those of most of his contemporaries. Valuable unpublished notes on Roman remains in north Wales and in various English counties and other manuscripts were purchased by subscription after Watkin's death and presented to Chetham's Library, Manchester.

On 6 July 1871 Watkin, who was already a widower, married Amelia Runcorn, a widow, daughter of William Broome, a brick merchant, and in 1872 they had a son, William, but Amelia died shortly afterwards and he then married, on 19 June 1876, Marion Smart, daughter of Henry Beeston, a stationer. With his third wife he had two sons and two daughters. He died on 23 March 1888 at his home, 55 Prescot Street, Liverpool, and was buried at Anfield cemetery. His third wife survived him.

ALAN G. CROSBY

Sources *Liverpool Courier* (24 March 1888) · *Journal of the Chester Archaeological and Historic Society*, new ser., 2 (1888), 199–200 · T. Formby and E. Axon, 'List of the writings of W. Thompson Watkin', *Transactions of the Lancashire and Cheshire Antiquarian Society*, 6 (1888), 173–8 · *DNB* · m. certs. · *CGPLA Eng. & Wales* (1888)
Archives Chetham's Library, Manchester, corresp. and papers
Wealth at death £85: probate, 31 Aug 1888, *CGPLA Eng. & Wales*

Watkins, Alfred (1855–1935), archaeologist and inventor of photographic equipment, was born on 27 January 1855 at the Imperial Hotel, Widemarsh Street, Hereford, the third of the ten children of Charles Watkins (1821–1888), a prosperous local farmer, miller, brewer, and hotel owner, and his wife, Ann, née Hill (d. 1899). Watkins was self-educated, having learnt very little at the small private school where he was sent. His career began as an 'outrider' for the Watkins Imperial Brewery and, later, the Imperial Flour Mills, a job which brought him into daily contact with country life. In his work for the family businesses he was an innovator from the outset, introducing the first dynamo and electric light to Herefordshire at the flour mills in 1876. In 1882 he installed the county's first roller mill and experimented with new flour recipes, notably the 'Vagos', a distinctive brown loaf.

On 28 April 1886 Watkins married Marion Mendam Cross (b. 1858/9). They had a son, Allen, and a daughter, Marion. He was known as a devoted family man who used to amuse his children with his conjuring tricks and slide shows. The death of his father, Charles, in 1888 was followed within a year by the premature death of his elder brother Henry. These events led Alfred and his brother Charles to assume control of the family businesses. They shrewdly appointed able managers and Alfred was able to devote time to his many interests.

Watkins's involvement with photography began with a

primitive pinhole camera which he made from a cigar box. He felt that the entire process of getting a good picture was simpler than was generally thought at that time and involved only one significant factor: the property of light. With that in mind, Watkins devised his 'exposure meter' after working out the mathematical relationship between light, the size of the camera lens, and the period of exposure. In April 1890 he published his findings in the *British Journal of Photography* and took out a patent for the exposure meter. The business community received the idea poorly but Watkins invested his own capital and set aside a room in his flour mill to make the meters. The Watkins Meter Company was active for over forty years and exported the meters to every corner of the globe. The device contributed greatly to photography's emergence as a mass-market art form. For the first time the photographer in the field could produce results as confidently as the professional in his studio. The company also developed the Watkins Time Tank, the Watkins Time Thermometer, and issued periodical plate-speed cards. Watkins published *Photography: the Watkins Manual of Exposure and Development* (1900), which become so popular that it ran to eleven editions.

In 1908 Watkins became president of the annual convention of the Royal Photographic Society, which was held in Hereford that year. Two years later he was made a fellow of the society and was awarded the eleventh of the progress medals awarded by the society for his scientific research in exposure and development. The then president, Lord Crawford, observed that 'The mere fact of the Society giving the highest honour at its command to Mr Watkins this year stamps his methods and inventions with a significance which no other Society in the world could give them' (Fellowes, 'Alfred Watkins'). In 1911 Watkins published *Photography: its Principles and Applications*, which, three times reprinted, became a valuable reference work. He did not believe in the need for expensive equipment and, having built his darkroom with suitable everyday materials, passed on his experience to his readers. His own collection of photographs is in the care of Herefordshire council, while specimens of his photographic equipment are in Hereford Museum.

Watkins was a staunch Liberal with a strong sense of public duty. In 1905 and 1906 he organized and spoke at several well-attended, slide show illustrated meetings held throughout the country against Joseph Chamberlain's proposals for protective tariffs. In 1919 he published *Must we Trade in Tenths?*, a broadside against decimalization. In 1902 he was appointed a trustee of the Hereford Municipal Charities, a duty he performed for over thirty years. In 1907 he became a county magistrate, and in 1914 county councillor for the Tupsley area of the city. He served on many of the council's committees and was a governor and patron to a large number of local institutions and charities.

Watkins was also a keen archaeologist and antiquary. He became a leading member of the Woolhope Naturalists' Field Club, founded in 1851 and based in Hereford. He undertook a survey of pigeon houses in the county and his report appeared in the *Royal Archaeological Journal* in 1889. He contributed to many topics but his longest and most comprehensive survey for the club was of church and market crosses. He photographed and measured some 120 extant crosses, all included in *The Standing Crosses of Herefordshire*, published by the Woolhope club in 1929.

Watkins is best remembered for his 'ley line' hypothesis, which is debated vigorously to this day. While studying a map in search of interesting archaeological features, he realized that many local landmarks of antiquity—standing stones, prehistoric tombs, stone circles, and crosses—could be linked by straight lines. He believed that these alignments could not be due to chance and that prehistoric man had deliberately made these tracks as a primitive road network, using various natural features as sighting points, and erecting monuments to mark the way. He published his first book about ley lines entitled *Early British Trackways* in 1922. His most famous work, *The Old Straight Track* followed in 1925, and has often been reprinted since. In 1927 *The Ley-Hunter's Manual* was published, and became a popular guide for field workers.

Following Watkins's death at 5 Harley Court, Hereford, on 7 April 1935, an obituarist paid tribute to:

> good citizen … the kind which keeps the public life of the countryside on the highest plane of any in the world. His name was Alfred Watkins. You can conjure with it in Herefordshire and in the counties of the Welsh border. (*Daily Express*, 9 April 1935)

His funeral service was held in the lady chapel of Hereford Cathedral, and his grave is to be found at the cemetery in Westfaling Street, Hereford.   R. G. FELLOWES

Sources A. Watkins, *Alfred Watkins: his life and pioneer work in the three fields of archaeology, photography, and flour milling* (1972) • P. K. Turner, *Photographic exposure* (1940) • *Daily Express* (9 April 1935) • R. G. Fellowes, 'Alfred Watkins 1855–1935', www.hereford webpages.co.uk/watkins.html
Wealth at death £24,749 6s. 5d.: probate, 30 Aug 1935, *CGPLA Eng. & Wales*

Watkins, Charles (d. 1808), lawyer and legal writer, was the youngest son of Revd William Watkins of Gelli in Llanwytherine parish, Monmouthshire. He was called to the bar at the Middle Temple on 10 June 1803. However, he practised from 1799 as a certificated conveyancer until his death.

During his lifetime Watkins was author of some able treatises on aspects of the law. These included an account of the powers of the king, as guardian of the duchy of Cornwall, as well as a study of the law of descents (1793). His *Reflections on Government in General* appeared in 1796. Watkins also edited the introduction (on the feudal system) for the fourth edition of Sir Geoffrey Gilbert's *Law of Tenures* (1796). Two further works no doubt arose from his professional practice. These were *A Treatise on Copyholds* (2 vols., 1797–9) and also *Principles of Conveyancing, Designed for the Use of Students* (1800). This work went into at least nine editions by 1845, and was regarded as 'a masterly and practical sketch' (Allibone, *Dict.*, 3.2602). Watkins died at Gloucester on 15 January 1808.

J. M. RIGG, *rev.* ROBERT BROWN

Sources J. Hutchinson, ed., *A catalogue of notable Middle Templars: with brief biographical notices* (1902) · J. G. Marvin, *Legal bibliography, or, A thesaurus of American, English, Irish and Scotch law books* (1847) · *GM*, 1st ser., 78 (1808), 172 · Allibone, *Dict.*

Watkins, Charles Frederick (1795–1873), writer and Church of England clergyman, was born on 16 January 1795 at Corsley, Wiltshire, the youngest son of the Revd William R. Watkins of Court Coleman and rector of Port Eynon, Glamorgan. He was educated at Christ's Hospital, London, and in 1810 he joined the frigate *Hotspur* as midshipman and was engaged in teaching the midshipmen mathematics and natural science, but left the service at the peace of 1815. He entered Christ's College, Cambridge, as a 'ten-year man' on 29 January 1818 and was ordained as a literate; although he was admitted for holy orders, he never took the BD degree. After serving curacies at Downton, Wiltshire (1818–19), and Windsor (1820–21), he was appointed in 1822 as warden of Farley Hospital, Salisbury, where he stayed until 1832. During this time (1822–32) he also held the post of curate at West Grimstead and Plaitford, Wiltshire.

Watkins was interested in geology and formed a collection of cretaceous fossils, some of which are in museums at Oxford and Cambridge and in the British Museum, London. In April 1832 he became vicar of Brixworth, Northamptonshire, and held this office until his death. While living there he communicated to the Royal Society an *Account of Aurora borealis of 17 Nov 1848* (*PRS*, 5 1843–50, 809). In keeping with his scientific interests he also wrote *A Treatise on the Leading Causes of Pleasure and Delight in the Human Mind* (1841) and *A Scientific and General Vindication of the Mosaic History of the Creation* (1867). He also demonstrated an attention to social issues and published various prose pamphlets, including *An address to the labouring population, on the folly and wickedness of burning agricultural property* (1831). His works of poetry include *Sacred Poems* (1829), *The Human Hand, and other Poems* (1852), and *The Twins of Fame, or, Wellington and Buonaparte: a National Poem* (1854). Watkins died at Brixworth on 15 July 1873 and was survived by his wife, Elizabeth, and at least one son, Justinian Charles Secundus Watkins (*b.* 1845).

T. G. BONNEY, *rev.* REBECCA MILLS

Sources *CGPLA Eng. & Wales* (1873) · Venn, *Alum. Cant.*, 2/6.365 · J. Peile, *Biographical register of Christ's College, 1505–1905, and of the earlier foundation, God's House*, ed. [J. A. Venn], 2 (1913), 388 · Ward, *Men of the reign*, 925 · Allibone, *Dict.* · private information (1899) [A. K. Pavey] · d. cert.
Likenesses H. L. Smith, watercolour drawing, 1862, Northants. RO
Wealth at death under £600: probate, 20 Aug 1873, *CGPLA Eng. & Wales*

Watkins, Dudley Dexter (1907–1969), comic artist, was born on 27 February 1907 at 40 Cedar Street, Cheetham, Manchester, and brought up in Nottingham. He was the eldest of the three children of James Willie Watkins, a lithographic artist, and his wife, Eva Charlotte, *née* Dexter. Watkins displayed his inherited skill at an early age: when he was six he received a commendation from the mayor of Nottingham for his drawing of a parade and, later, had his work included within an exhibition at Nottingham Castle.

In 1919 he attended evening classes at Nottingham School of Art and in the early 1920s took a job with Boots the chemist. His first published work appeared in March 1923 in Boots's staff magazine, *The Beacon*. Not long afterwards he was offered a position as a staff artist with D. C. Thomson, a publisher based in Dundee, and, after returning to art school for a year, moved to Dundee in 1925. The Scottish publisher had recently started a line of boys' story papers which were published weekly. The first was *Adventure* (1921), followed by *The Rover* and *The Wizard* (both 1922). Eventually there would be two more: *The Skipper* (1930) and *The Hotspur* (1933); collectively they became known as The Big Five. From his early employment with the firm and throughout the 1930s he contributed hundreds of drawings and paintings to these weeklies. Watkins's black and white illustrations to text stories also appeared in the Scottish publisher's *Topical Times*, an adult Thomson paper. On 8 March 1936 D. C. Thomson broke new ground in the UK with the inclusion of an American-style comic supplement entitled 'The fun section' with its newspaper the *Sunday Post*. Dudley Watkins drew two features: *Oor Wullie* (Our Willie) and *The Broons* (The Browns). Both are still running. Until the 1970s the artwork remained that of Watkins, his drawings being reprinted after his death. The success of 'The fun section' suggested to D. C. Thomson that a national comic was viable and the firm soon launched not just one but two weeklies: the *Dandy Comic* (4 December 1937) and the *Beano Comic* (30 July 1938). For the *Dandy* Watkins drew *Desperate Dan*; for the *Beano*, *Lord Snooty*. The former was a cowboy with a ten-gallon hat and permanent heavy stubble on his chin; he shaved with a blow-torch, swung bulls around his head by their tails, and carried his horse when it got too tired to carry him. Lord Snooty was a young aristocrat in a top hat and Eton suit who would rather fraternize with urchins than toffs. Both Dan and Snooty have become internationally well known and are national institutions in the UK. These classic comic characters and other lesser-known features Watkins continued to draw weekly until the 1960s.

Following the successful launch of the *Beano* and *Dandy* Dudley Watkins's status as the Dundee firm's principal artist was confirmed. He was not only one of the most prolific artists but also extremely versatile. Watkins also was able to turn out adventure stories in comic form. These included: *The Shipwrecked Circus* (*Beano*, 1943); *Jimmy and his Magic Patch* (*Beano*, 1944); *Danny Longlegs* (*Dandy*, 1945); and *Our Teacher's a Walrus* (*Dandy*, 1947). In the late 1940s he also drew classic adventure serials for Thomson's magazine the *People's Journal*. These included *Treasure Island*, *Kidnapped*, and *Oliver Twist* and were later reprinted in book form. In the 1950s Dudley Watkins became a principal contributor to D. C. Thomson's first post-war comic, *The Topper* (7 February 1953); he drew *Mickey the Monkey* on the front page and had several of his serials from *People's Friend* reprinted on the back in full colour. Similarly his work was to be found on the front page of *The Beezer* (21 January 1956) with *Ginger*, a slightly older version of *Oor Wullie* which he was still drawing for the *Sunday Post*. From

1946 he started to sign his work. His clear, distinct signature, 'Dudley D. Watkins' (or 'D. D. W.'), was noted by millions and led to him being the best-known of all British comic artists. Watkins was a member of the Church of Christ of Dundee and used his art to help the religious movement. From 1956 he produced a series called *William the Warrior* for the Worldwide Evangelization Crusade. These were comic strips published in small, paperback booklets. He lived at Broughty Ferry, near Dundee, and died of a heart attack there on 20 August 1969. Dudley Watkins was survived by his wife and son. If one man could be said to epitomize post-war British comics it would be Watkins; his influence is still apparent more than thirty years after his death.   ALAN CLARK

Sources D. Gifford, *The British comic catalogue, 1874–1974* (1975) · A. Clark, *The best of British comic art* (1989) · R. Moore, *The Beano diaries*, 1–2 (British Comic World, 1991) · R. Moore, *The Dandy monster index*, 1–2 (1990) · M. Horn, ed., *The world encyclopedia of cartoons* (1980) · b. cert.
Wealth at death £25,371: confirmation, 28 Nov 1969, *CCI*

Watkins, Francis (*bap.* 1723, *d.* 1791), optician, the fourth son of Jeremiah Watkins and his first wife, Mary (*née* Whitney), was baptized in the parish of Newchurch, Radnorshire, on 25 April 1723. At the age of fourteen he was taken to London and apprenticed to the instrument maker Nathaniel Adams at the Golden Spectacles, Charing Cross. Following his master's untimely death, Watkins completed his training under Edward Scarlett senior and Henry Walder at the Archimedes, Globe and Sun in Soho, where he remained until he was sworn free of the Spectaclemakers' Company in March 1746. In the following year he returned to his original master's premises at Charing Cross to trade on his own account under the sign of Sir Isaac Newton's Head.

Watkins developed his early trade among those wealthy gentlemen who, largely for reasons of 'polite learning', wished to partake in experimental philosophy. He began by arranging shilling demonstrations in electrical experiments to promote his own electrical machine, which he sold with an accompanying tract (*A Particular Account of the Electrical Experiments Hitherto Made Publick*, 1747). As time progressed, he became keen on optics, particularly the quality of images which, at this time, were not free of coloured effects. Following some experiments in late 1751, he criticized the teacher Richard Jacks who, together with another famous maker, George Adams senior, had designed an improved refracting telescope. Later Watkins designed and developed a microscope which he accompanied with a tract in French (*L'exercise du microscope*, 1754). He was assisted by two able apprentices: Addison Smith and Henry Pyefinch, who had joined him in 1750 and 1753 respectively.

Watkins's growing reputation caused John Dollond (1706–1761), holder of a patent for achromatic lenses, to approach him with a view to financial partnership in a venture to market refracting telescopes with these object glasses, and a binding agreement was made, dated 29 May 1758. However, this monopoly was not viewed kindly by those makers who already sold achromatic telescopes.

Realizing this, after John Dollond's death Watkins began to sell his own telescopes without declaring these sales to Dollond's son, Peter. The latter then paid Watkins £200 to cease manufacture, thereby becoming sole patentee. Watkins continued manufacturing, and was sued. Peter Dollond's case was upheld: this alleged injustice motivated the Spectaclemakers' Company to petition the king in June 1764 to have Dollond's patent annulled on the grounds that Chester Moor Hall was the true inventor of the achromatic lens. Watkins was master of the company at this time, and the first signatory on the petition was his former apprentice and current partner in business, Addison Smith. Much acrimony ensued but the court upheld Dollond's right to the patent, since the original inventor had not shown any financial interest in his invention. Later, when Dollond became master of the Spectaclemakers' Company, Watkins adamantly refused to pay his dues.

In 1748 or 1749, soon after setting up at Sir Isaac Newton's Head, Watkins married the widow Clarinda Walder; they had two daughters, Frances (*b.* 1749) and Clarinda (*b.* 1753), but no male heirs. To ensure the continuity of his business, he invited his nephews, Jeremiah and Walter, to join him. These were the sons of his elder brother's marriage to Elizabeth, *née* Mines, of Hereford. After some thirty-seven years of trading, Watkins retired to Richmond, though he retained an interest in both the business and his various properties at Charing Cross. He died in Richmond, Surrey, on 17 November 1791, and his nephews inherited the business. After Walter's death in 1798 the business was continued by Jeremiah until his death in 1810. It was then run on behalf of Jeremiah's widow, Charlotte, by William Hill, a reliable employee, until Jeremiah's son, another Francis, came of age in 1818. The partnership between Hill and the younger Francis Watkins lasted twenty-nine years until 1847, when both partners died. The Watkins business was exceptional in having traded for over a century, but in 1856 it was acquired from the family by the brothers C. A. and F. H. Elliott, the sons of William Elliott, a mathematical instrument maker.

                                                                                    BRIAN GEE

Sources G. Clifton, *Directory of British scientific instrument makers, 1550–1851*, ed. G. L'E. Turner (1995) · H. Barty-King, *Eyes right* (1986) · *Daily Advertiser* [London] (4 March 1747) · *Daily Advertiser* (22 April 1747) · *GM*, 1st ser., 61 (1791), 1070 · *GM*, 1st ser., 68 (1798), 907 · *GM*, 1st ser., 80 (1810), 186 · *PICE*, 7 (1848), 15 · parish register (baptism), 25 April 1723, Newchurch, Radnor · PRO, PROB 11/1211, sig. 548 · F. Watkins, *A particular account of the electrical experiments hitherto made publick; with a variety of new ones, and full illustrations for performing them* (1747) · F. Watkins, *L'exercise du microscope contenant un abregé de tout ce qui a été ecrit par les meilleurs autheurs touchant les objets le plus curieux, avec les precautions qu'on doit prendre pour faire les observations avec succes* (1754) · IGI

Watkins, Geoffrey Maurice (1896–1981), bookseller and publisher, was born on 7 June 1896 at 26 Trefoil Road, Wandsworth, London, the only child of John Maurice Watkins, founder of Watkins' Bookshop, and his wife, Bertha Maude, formerly Bullock. Watkins attended Emanuel School, Wandsworth, and completed his education at Heidelberg from 1909 to 1913. The emphasis of his schooling was so European that when he was invited to tea at Max Gate, while he was stationed at Dorchester during the First World War, he had no idea who Thomas Hardy was.

Watkins' Bookshop had been founded in 1893 as an adjunct of the publishing house of the Theosophical Society, but by 1896 it had become independent and was settled in Cecil Court, off Charing Cross Road. In 1919 Geoffrey Watkins left the army and officially joined the firm, which was now engaged in publishing as well as bookselling, in order to provide essential support for his father, who by 1922 was totally blind. Between the wars father and son catered for readers, with books, and for the writers of the books, with tea, at the almost daily sessions of 'tea, talk and theosophy' in the office at the back of the shop. Those who might be expected to appear included Yeats and AE (George Russell) to discuss fairies and Neoplatonism with G. R. S. Mead, A. E. Waite, and Stephen McKenna (the translator of Plotinus), and also the storytellers Algernon Blackwood, James Stephens, and Standish O'Grady, the oddities Edith Sitwell and Lady Ottoline Morrell, and the infamous Aleister Crowley; all were regular visitors.

Watkins was of necessity in charge of the day-to-day running of the business and oversaw both the shop and the publishing house, whose list ranged from Mead's remarkable journal *The Quest*, to Evelyn Underhill's editions of the English mystics and the first printing of C. G. Jung's *Septem sermones ad mortuos*. The shop survived the blitz and after the Second World War the breadth of vision in the firm's output was expanded to take in new works of the Gurdjieff–Ouspensky school, alchemy, and the tarot, and to issue reprints of classics within its specialist field. In 1947 John Watkins died and the business came completely into Watkins's hands. Under his sole direction it continued to be a haven for seekers after 'rejected knowledge', although the visitors were changing; now they included Aldous Huxley, Alan Watts, and Kathleen Raine. There were also innovations. In 1953 Geoffrey issued *The Hermetic Museum*, the first of a series of important reprints of alchemical texts and studies by A. E. Waite and others which have proved to be as valuable to historians of science as to would-be alchemists.

But for all his publishing genius Watkins wrote very little. He contributed anonymously to Christmas Humphreys's *Concentration and Meditation* (1935) and wrote a few other slight pieces. Beyond these and his enlightened publishing programme, his real contribution to scholarship came through the guidance, encouragement, and kindness he showed to all those who struggled to bring academic acceptance to 'rejected knowledge'. He always ensured that important books went to the right home—thus Yeats's copy of Mead's *Orpheus* came to rest in the National Library of Ireland via Kathleen Raine—and that students should avoid any book unsuited to their needs.

Watkins achieved all this without loss to his private life. Neither his wife, Flora Kate Phelps (1900–1975), whom he had married in 1933, nor their son Christopher, born in 1938, was sacrificed to the business. Nor did Watkins compromise his friendships. To avoid accusations of partisanship he never allied himself to any of the movements or personalities that came and went during his lifetime; the meetings of such societies as he did join (the Buddhist Society, and the Guild of Pastoral Psychology, for example), he attended discreetly, and he continued to observe the Anglican form of his Christian faith. He could not, however, continue the business indefinitely; his son did not wish to take it up and in 1974, shortly before his wife's death, he sold both shop and publishing house.

In his own words Geoffrey Watkins had 'put forward books to do with mysticism, meditation and self-training in its very best sense' (private information). However, to others the shop was something more than a stock, at once comprehensive and carefully selected, of books on 'Theosophy, Christian and Oriental mystical philosophy, astrology, alchemy, and other esoteric subjects' (Watkins, 'Yeats', 308). It was, in the eyes of the poet Kathleen Raine, a 'University of Lost Knowledge' (private information), a centre in which not only the books but also the people who read and wrote them were gathered, jointly aiding the gradual academic acceptance that the study of these subjects constitutes a legitimate facet of the history of ideas. During his retirement Watkins continued to offer his advice and support to all who sought it. When he died at Kings Ride Nursing Home, Richmond, Surrey, on 15 August 1981, Watkins' Bookshop died with him: it might exist in name, but without his presence it could not live.

R. A. GILBERT

Sources private information (2004) · G. M. Watkins, 'Foreword', in R. A. Gilbert, *A. E. Waite: a bibliography* (1983) · K. Raine, 'Geoffrey Watkins', *Light*, 101 (Oct 1981) · G. M. Watkins, 'Yeats and Mr. Watkins bookshop', *Yeats and the occult*, ed. G. M. Harper (1975), 308 · b. cert. · d. cert.
Wealth at death £96,923: probate, 24 Nov 1981, *CGPLA Eng. & Wales*

Watkins, Henry George (1907–1932), Arctic explorer, was born in London, probably in Eaton Square, on 29 January 1907, the eldest child and elder son among the three children of Colonel Henry George Watkins, Coldstream Guards (1880–1935), and his first wife, Jennie Helen (d. 1928), daughter of Colonel Bolton Monsell of Ireland and his English wife, Mary Ogle. Known from childhood as Gino, he was educated as a day boy in London until the age of nine, when he became a boarder at Elstree Lodge preparatory school in Bexhill, Sussex. In 1920 he went to Lancing College, where Quintin Riley, later a member of Watkins's expeditions, was also a pupil. Throughout the First World War his father was fighting in France. During holidays in the Lake District, the Swiss Alps, and the Austrian Tyrol, mainly with his father after the war, Watkins acquired a great love of climbing and the outdoor life, including skiing. He had already learned to shoot in the Officers' Training Corps at school.

In October 1925 Gino went up to Trinity College, Cambridge, and immediately applied to join the Cambridge air squadron, of which he became the first recruit. His studies at Cambridge were interrupted by his explorations, and

Henry George Watkins (1907–1932), by Lafayette, 1932

though he passed examinations in engineering (1926), geology (1927), and scientific aspects of polar exploration (1930), he never took a degree. While in Cambridge he attended a course of lectures, 'Man in the polar regions', by Raymond Edward Priestley. James Mann Wordie, who was then a tutor at St John's College, promised to take him in 1927 to Greenland. Watkins read widely about polar exploration and began to train for 1927.

It was the postponement of this venture which made Watkins an organizer and leader of Arctic expeditions. He chose to explore Edge Island (Edgøya), part of what is now Svalbard, during the summer vacation of 1927, with a party of eight—six contemporaries and two much older men—transported from Tromsø in the sealer *Heimen*, of 72 tons. Despite bad weather they mapped the island and studied its geology, botany, and wildlife. He showed his powers of leadership and an ability to organize, with the help of good advice and support from Wordie and from the Royal Geographical Society. Although just under age, he was made a fellow of the society and was awarded its Cuthbert Peek grant.

Labrador next claimed Watkins's attention, because of the boundary dispute between Canada and Newfoundland (not at that time part of the dominion). Having been asked to make a summary of the reasons for the dispute, he read widely and found that parts of Labrador had never been mapped. In the summer of 1928 Watkins led a small party by canoe up the Hamilton and Kenamu rivers. During the winter of 1928–9 the Snegamook Lake was

reached by dog sledge, Gino's being 'the first blue eyes to see it' (Scott, *Gino Watkins*, 123). Later in the winter the upper and lower falls on the Unknown River were located and the area mapped.

The British Arctic air route expedition of 1930–31 was Watkins's crowning achievement. Its aim was to monitor weather conditions on the east coast of Greenland and on the ice sheet, to make a number of traverses and flights over the ice sheet, as well as to survey part of the mountainous coast. These were meant as preliminaries to the establishment of an air route from England to Winnipeg via Iceland, Greenland, Baffin Island, and Hudson Bay. With this in mind, Watkins joined the Royal Air Force reserve, gaining a pilot's licence. He divided his time between London and Cambridge (where he was still an undergraduate) while organizing the expedition. This involved choosing its members, buying dogs and two aircraft, chartering a vessel, fund-raising, attending committees, and making up satisfying yet lightweight rations, plus much correspondence. He chose thirteen men with an average age of twenty-five to form the expedition. They sailed from the Thames in Shackleton's old ship, *Quest*, and established a base not far from Angmagssalik (now Ammassalik). The aims of the expedition were largely achieved. In addition, an open boat journey of 600 miles was made by Watkins and two companions round the south coast of Greenland to Julianehaab (now Qaqortoq), relying for food on hunting seals from kayaks, a new element in Arctic exploration. The expedition's success was acknowledged by the award to Watkins of the Hans Egede medal in Copenhagen and the founder's medal from the Royal Geographical Society in London. In addition, the polar medal was awarded to its members, the first for Arctic service for nearly sixty years. Few could believe, on first acquaintance, that this exquisitely dressed, rather slight and diffident young man, who always carried a rolled umbrella, and who wholeheartedly enjoyed the London season with his fiancée, Margaret Graham, family, and friends, could have been its leader.

At the age of twenty-four Watkins had become an international figure. He next endeavoured to raise funds for an expedition to cross the Antarctic. However, in the depths of a great economic depression, 'private finance was more surely frozen than the ice of the Antarctic' (Scott, *Gino Watkins*, 280). Watkins therefore returned in 1932 with three companions to east Greenland to continue the work of the British Arctic air route expedition. For this he had raised £800 (in contrast to the £13,000 for the previous venture), mainly contributed by Pan-American Airways. He planned to hunt seals from kayaks to feed the party, supplementing these with fish and birds. On 20 August 1932 he went hunting alone in his kayak to the dangerous north arm of Lake Fjord (now Tugtilik Fjord). Some hours later two of his companions found the boat upside-down in the water, its paddle floating nearby. They carried the empty kayak back to the base, scarcely believing that he could be dead.

Watkins's body was never found. In the words of his biographer:

Gino Watkins had gone from the world in the full pride of his youth and self-sufficiency; gone cleanly out leaving no relic of mortality; leaving only the memory of a vivid life and a bright inspiration … it was right that none should see him dead.   (Scott, *Gino Watkins*, 310)

Watkins's memory has been kept green since the establishment in 1933 of the Gino Watkins Memorial Fund, whose principal function is to award grants to small well-organized Arctic expeditions. His kayak came to the Royal Geographical Society. According to the *Arctic Pilot* (vol. 2), a monument to Watkins stands on the shores of Tugtilik Fjord.   ANN SAVOURS

Sources J. M. Scott, *Gino Watkins* (1935) • J. M. Scott, *The land that God gave Cain* (1933) • F. Spencer Chapman, *Northern lights* (1934) • F. Spencer Chapman, *Watkins' last expedition* (1934) • J. M. Scott and others, 'Henry George Watkins', *GJ*, 80 (1932), 273–80, pl. • M. Lindsay, *Those Greenland days* (1932) • J. Ridgway, *Gino Watkins* (1974) • F. Debenham, 'Men of the kayak', *In the Arctic* (1997), 24–43 • 'The Eskimo kayak', *Polar Record*, 7 (Jan 1934), 52–62 • J. M. Wordie, 'The Polar medal', *Polar Record*, 5 (Jan 1933), 57–61, plate • J. J. Thomson and others, 'The Watkins memorial fund', *Polar Record*, 5 (Jan 1933), 67 • F. Debenham, 'The Gino Watkins memorial fund', *Polar Record*, 6 (July 1933), 70 • Trinity Cam. • *CGPLA Eng. & Wales* (1933) • *Arctic pilot*, Ministry of Defence, UK Hydrographic Office, vol. 2, 6th edn (1961); 8th edn (1996), 457, 243

Archives priv. coll. • RGS, corresp. | Scott Polar RI, records of British Arctic air route expedition | FILM Scott Polar RI, 'Northern lights', 38 mins., 16 mm., sound, black and white. 1932 [British Arctic air route expedition, 1930–31]

Likenesses Lafayette, photograph, 1932, NPG [*see illus.*] • K. G., pencil drawing, repro. in *Polar Record* (1933), frontispiece • C. Thomas, bas-relief, Scott Polar RI • H. G. Watkins, oils (after photograph), repro. in Scott, *Gino Watkins*, frontispiece; priv. coll. • photograph (*Leaving for Angmagssalik in the Gertrude Rask, 14 July 1932*), repro. in Scott and others, 'Henry George Watkins', facing p. 273 • plaque, Dumbleton parish church, Worcestershire

Wealth at death £978 19s. 4d.: administration, 13 March 1933, *CGPLA Eng. & Wales*

Watkins, John (*fl. c.*1786–1831), writer, born in Devon, was educated at Bristol for the nonconformist ministry. Becoming dissatisfied, he joined the Church of England about 1786 with his friend Samuel Badcock (1747–1788) and for some years ran an academy in Devon. His first independent publication appeared in 1792, entitled *An Essay towards the History of Bideford*. The work was of great local interest, containing among other things an account of the depositions in a trial for witchcraft held at Exeter on 14 August 1682. In 1796 he published *The Peeper: a Collection of Essays, Moral, Biographical, and Literary*, which was dedicated to Hannah More. Watkins showed great interest in biography, even compiling a *Universal Biographical and Historical Dictionary*, which appeared in 1800. It went through several editions by 1827, and was translated into French, with additions, in 1803 by Jean Baptiste L'Ecuy of Paris. Among similar compilations are *Characteristic Anecdotes of Men of Learning and Genius* (1808) and *Boydell's heads of illustrious and celebrated persons, from the reign of Queen Elizabeth to William III, with biographical memoirs* (1812). Watkins's *Memoirs of Sheridan* (1816) was the first life of Richard Brinsley Sheridan to be published. Other memoirs published by him were *Memoirs of Queen Sophia Charlotte* (1819); *Memoirs of the Life and Writings of Lord Byron* (1822), translated into German in 1825; *A Biographical Memoir of … Frederick, Duke of York and Albany* (1827); and *The Life and Times of 'England's Patriot King', William IV* (1831). He also translated from the Latin George Buchanan's *History of Scotland*, adding a continuation (1827), and wrote a memoir of Hugh Latimer, prefixed to his *Sermons* (1824). On the title pages of his later publications, Watkins is described as LLD but from where he obtained the degree is unknown. So is the date of his death, the last that is known of him being a preface dated 30 May 1831. He moved to London soon after beginning his literary work, about 1794, and it is possible that he died there.   E. I. CARLYLE, *rev.* NILANJANA BANERJI

Sources [J. Watkins and F. Shoberl], *A biographical dictionary of the living authors of Great Britain and Ireland* (1816) • Allibone, *Dict.*

Watkins, John William Nevill (1924–1999), philosopher, was born on 31 July 1924 at Arden, Onslow Crescent, Woking, Surrey, the son of William Hugh Watkins and Winifred Ethel (*née* Jeffries). His father was director of an iron foundry in Shropshire and a keen and successful yachtsman—a passion that he passed on to his son. John, indeed, first planned a career at sea—training at the Royal Naval College, Dartmouth, before graduating as a junior officer in 1941. In April 1944 he was serving as navigator on HMS *Ashanti*—a tribal class destroyer—when it and a group of other destroyers were sent into action against a German fleet that had been blocking British convoys in the channel. Watkins was in charge of aiming the torpedoes that sank one German ship (the T 29) and forced another aground. He was awarded the Distinguished Service Cross for his gallantry in this action. (Watkins, who had a fine line in self-deprecating humour, used to joke that the navy's decision to award him the DSC was based largely on its surprise that one of its torpedoes had hit anything at all.)

Described by his colleagues as a 'brilliant navigator' and promoted to the rank of lieutenant in November 1944, Watkins saw further service on boats that he guided to China, Australia, and elsewhere. Some months after the war had finished, however, he began to feel that a peacetime naval career might be insufficiently challenging and he resigned his commission in order to study politics at the London School of Economics (LSE), with a possible parliamentary future now in mind.

Watkins later said that he would have voted Labour at the 1945 election had he been eligible to vote (the election came shortly before his twenty-first birthday). Reading Von Hayek's *Road to Serfdom*, however, convinced him of the 'dangers of socialism', and he became, and remained, a staunch Conservative and right-wing thinker. Despite this, he prospered as a student at LSE, where he attracted the attentions of, and came under the conflicting influences of, both Karl Popper and Harold Laski. He soon found the world of ideas more attractive than the world of practical politics and began to pursue a third and final choice of career. After graduating with a first in 1949, he won a Henry Fund scholarship to study for an MA at Yale; and he returned to LSE to take up a lectureship in the government department in 1950. Increasingly intrigued by philosophy and increasingly impressed by Popper's ideas, Watkins transferred to Popper's department (of philosophy, logic, and scientific method) in 1958 when he was appointed to a readership in the history of philosophy. He was promoted to a professorship in philosophy in 1966, a position he held with distinction until his retirement in 1989.

Watkins first became known to the academic world through his articulation and defence of the principle of 'methodological individualism'. Broadly stated, this principle holds that ultimately any explanations of social phenomena must be in terms of individuals (and relations between them) rather than in terms of social wholes such as economic classes, nations, or whatever. Always a man of wide interests, he also made significant contributions in the early part of his career to fields such as the interplay between metaphysics and science, ethics, confirmation theory, and rational decision theory. His first book, *Hobbes's System of Ideas*, was published in 1965 and is marked by the way in which it sees Hobbes's philosophical ideas as driving his political theory, and those philosophical ideas as set against the background of the ongoing scientific revolution. His second book, *Science and Scepticism*, published in 1984, is an attempt to 'succeed where Descartes failed: to submit our knowledge of the external world to an ordeal by scepticism and then, with the help of the little that survives, to explain how scientific rationality is still possible' (preface).

Watkins continued to work with impressive energy long after his retirement and a third book, *Human Freedom after Darwin*, completed shortly before his death, was published posthumously in 1999. This reflects another theme that runs through his academic career—the attempt to develop a view of human freedom that is compatible with what science tells us about the human constitution.

Watkins travelled widely, holding visiting positions in the USA and in New Zealand and speaking at a large number of international conferences around the world. Shortly before his retirement, his work was the focus of a conference held in Krakow, Poland (Polish being one of a number of languages into which his books and articles were translated).

John Watkins was a devoted family man as well as a successful and productive academic. As a student at LSE he met Millicent Joan (Micky) Roe (*b.* 1925), and they were married on 4 April 1952. Twins, Hugh and Susan, were born in 1953, and daughters Kate and Julie in 1956 and 1958. John's lifelong love of sailing boats meant that this very close family spent much time in their second home at Salcombe in Devon, where John for many years sailed his cherished Salcombe yawl. He died of a heart attack while happily preparing his boat for the regatta races at Salcombe on 26 July 1999, a few days' short of his seventy-fifth birthday. He was cremated at Golders Green crematorium.   JOHN WORRALL

Sources J. Worrall, 'John Watkins (1924–1999)', *British Journal for the Philosophy of Science*, 50 (1999), 787–9 · *The Independent* (5 Aug 1999) · *The Times* (7 Sept 1999) · *Who's who in the world* · *Dictionary of international biography* · *Debrett's People of today* · personal knowledge (2004) · private information (2004) · b. cert. · m. cert. · d. cert.

Likenesses photograph, repro. in *The Independent* · photograph, repro. in *The Times*

Watkins, Morgan (*d.* in or after 1672), Quaker preacher, was of Wigmore Grange, then Eyton, Herefordshire, though little else is known of his early life and background. On 7 May 1653 he was one of the signatories to a 'Letter from the People of Herefordshire to the Lord General Cromwell', expressing allegiance to the protector and pledging to 'attend' him with their 'persons, petitions, purses, lives and all that is dear to us' (Nickolls, 92).

Watkins was evidently a Quaker by 1657, for in that year George Fox met him at a meeting in Radnorshire and noted that he had become 'loving to Friends' (*Journal of George Fox*, 1.274). About 1658 he defended the Quaker notion of perfection at a disputation with the Baptist Vavasour Powell, details of which are given in *The Perfect Life of the Son of God Vindicated* (1658). In this Watkins protested that 'they that live in sin, and plead for it term of life, are all blind' (p. 4).

In 1660 Watkins was a prisoner in St Albans gaol, during which time he wrote *Swearing Denied in the New Covenant* [1660] which concerned the Quaker rejection of oaths. By July 1663 he was preaching in London at the Quaker meeting in Pall Mall and elsewhere. On 12 March 1665 he was sent to Newgate from the Bull and Mouth meeting, St Martin's-le-Grand. Two other imprisonments followed during the year, one at Westmorland, after a meeting at Elizabeth Strong's house, and another of about three months' duration at the Gatehouse prison, near Westminster Abbey, on a warrant of 9 August from the duke of Albemarle for attendance at a meeting with nine others. His letters to Mary Penington vividly describe the visitation of the plague both inside and outside prisons. On 18 September 1665 he wrote to her saying, 'the miseries that are upon many here are hardly to be uttered' (Barclay, 149). A later letter written on 5 December revealed that he had experienced 'several battles with death' while imprisoned in London (ibid., 156).

Afterwards Watkins preached and was imprisoned in Buckinghamshire, details of which are given in Thomas Ellwood's *Life* (1714). In 1666 he was accused by Justice Ambrose Bennet of being a Jesuit, for 'in his Preaching' the latter felt 'he trolled over his Latin as fluently as ever he heard anyone', though Ellwood states that Watkins was 'better Versed in Welch, than in Latin' (p. 249). Watkins and five others were committed to Aylesbury gaol, but owing to the plague were sent to the High Wycombe house of correction, where they were kept from 13 March to 7 June 1666. They refused to be bound over for their appearance at the next assizes and were sent back to the gaol until 25 June, when they were released by proclamation. Ellwood notes that while in prison he made 'Nets for Kitchin-Service, to boil Herbs, &c. in; which Trade I learned of Morgan Watkins' (ibid., 251). He also related that they 'kept a fair and Brotherly Correspondence, as became Friends, Prison-fellows and Bed-fellows' (ibid., 252). By 1670, some time after his incarceration, Watkins appears to have returned to Herefordshire when cattle and goods were distrained from his farm.

Watkins wrote a few more tracts in addition to those listed above, for example *The Children of Abraham's Faith*, written with Francis Gawler in 1663, of interest for its discussion of Quaker burials and in which Friends' practice was compared with that of the holy men of former ages. Other works include *A Lamentation over England* (1664), regarding persecution of Quakers, and *The Marks of the True Church* (1675).

Watkins died at some point after 20 June 1672, at which time he attended Somerset quarterly meeting at Ilchester.

CHARLOTTE FELL-SMITH, *rev.* CAROLINE L. LEACHMAN

Sources J. Besse, *A collection of the sufferings of the people called Quakers*, 2 vols. (1753), vols. 1, 2 • A. R. Barclay, ed., *Letters, &c. of early Friends* (1841) • *Original letters and papers of state addressed to Oliver Cromwell ... found among the political collections of Mr John Milton*, ed. J. Nickolls (1743) • *The journal of George Fox*, ed. N. Penney, 1 (1911) • J. Smith, ed., *A descriptive catalogue of Friends' books*, 2 (1867) • S. C. Morland, ed., *The Somersetshire quarterly meeting of the Society of Friends, 1668–1699*, Somerset RS, 75 (1978) • T. Ellwood, *The history of the life of Thomas Ellwood*, 2nd edn (1714)
Archives RS Friends, Lond., Ellwood MSS, letters, vol. 2, MS vol. 316 • Swarthmore MSS, letters, vol. 1/129, 132 (MS vol. 351), vol. 4/188 (MS vol. 356)

Watkins, Sir Percy Emerson (1871–1946), civil servant, was born on 3 December 1871 in the High Street, Llanfyllin, Montgomeryshire, the son of Evan Watkins (*d.* 1906), an auctioneer, valuer, and estate dealer, and his wife, Mary Mills. Watkins's father was a prominent figure in the county, having links with agriculture as well as with property; he was assistant overseer of the parish, town councillor, and (from 1889) Liberal county councillor on the new Montgomeryshire local authority. The Watkins family were characteristic products of the emerging Welsh ascendancy: middle-class, strongly Liberal in politics, nonconformist (Wesleyan Methodist) in religion, and attending a Welsh-speaking chapel, although using mainly English at home. In his memoirs Watkins noted the family's antipathy to the established church in Wales, and its deep devotion to Gladstone.

Watkins attended Oswestry high school and began his working life as a reporter on the *Oswestry Advertiser*. Then he served as clerk to the local Llanfyllin school board. In 1896 there came a major breakthrough, when he was appointed secretary of the Central Welsh Board (CWB). Two years later, on 23 December 1898, he married Mary Jane (1869/70–1939), daughter of Richard Jones, a Calvinistic Methodist minister, with whom he had a son.

The CWB was the new body set up to administer the 'county schools' set up in Wales after the passage of the Welsh Intermediate Education Act (1889). Here Watkins was much involved in making educational policy, including links with the university and the local authorities. At first he was enthusiastic about the CWB, dominated as it was by democratically elected authorities, but in time he became increasingly critical, especially of its prolonged conflicts with the Welsh department of the Board of Education created later in 1907. The latter, he came to feel, was the only body capable of looking at Welsh secondary education from a national standpoint, in contrast to the built-in parochialism of the county councillors on the CWB. In 1903 he was appointed clerk and director of the education department of the West Riding county council and found himself caught up in the conflict between that Liberal-dominated council and the Board of Education over the passage of the Balfour Education Act of 1902. In a famous case in 1906 the West Riding council's action in refusing to pay teachers in four non-provided schools that portion of their salary deemed to be remuneration for denominational instruction was found to be illegal in the House of Lords.

In 1911 Watkins became registrar of the University College of South Wales, Cardiff, but in 1913 his career as public administrator took an important step forward when his long-term friend Thomas Jones appointed him assistant secretary of the Welsh Insurance Commission, to administer Lloyd George's National Insurance Act (1911). This was a crucial body in the emergence of a new fabric of social welfare. Watkins, quiet and equable but shrewd and decisive, built up a powerful reputation for his liaison work with doctors, local authorities, the trade unions, the Welsh National Memorial Association, and many others. The new generation of public servants coming to the fore in Wales after Lloyd George's social insurance measure found its exemplar in Watkins. Less agreeable was the hostility he and Thomas Jones encountered from another commissioner, John Rowland, whom Lloyd George used as a personal fount of information on Welsh matters. When Watkins was appointed secretary of the new Welsh board of health in 1919, Rowland was beside himself with rage and held up Watkins's taking up of the appointment until 1920. However, Watkins soon found his feet at the board of health as well as in education, and was an effective administrator there until 1925. He remained closely associated with Thomas Jones in adult education and also served on the editorial board of his monthly journal, *Welsh Outlook*.

In 1925 Watkins moved to become permanent secretary of the Welsh department of the Board of Education. Here he was involved in critical negotiations during the depression years including those on grants for necessitous areas and the special needs of rural Wales. His proposal for creating comprehensive schools was a bold idea, but vetoed by the department, on the grounds that the implied devaluation of the secondary school would be 'a very serious setback'. He had to represent the department in tense discussions with the local authorities in south Wales, who were outraged by the severe cuts imposed in circulars 1421 and 170 in September 1932; his diplomatic talents were stretched to the full when he sought economies from what he later called 'the political bosses' of Labour-run councils. At the end of 1932 he became director of the Welsh School of Social Service, where he remained until 1938. Here he submitted countless schemes to create settlements and clubs for the unemployed in the coalfield; in all, he distributed £300,000 in grant aid. He also served on Thomas Jones's coalfield distress committee, and on the education committee of the Welsh League of Nations Union. He was president of the Workers' Educational Association in Wales and was much involved with Jones's adult education college, Coleg Harlech, serving as its vice-chairman until retiring in 1945.

Watkins was knighted in 1930. After the death in 1939 of his first wife he married in 1941 Lil, daughter of Augustus Lewis of Swansea and widow of F. F. Bush of Wakefield. He died in the Royal Infirmary in Cardiff on 5 May 1946.

Watkins's career is an unglamorous but important part of modern Welsh history. Along with his friend Thomas Jones, he symbolized the rise of the new bureaucracy: omnipresent committee men running public health, the social services, and especially education. A quiet but mentally strong administrator, with a strong social conscience, he embodied a major aspect of the political and social revolutions associated with Lloyd George. His delicately restrained memoirs, *A Welshman Remembers* (1944), convey many of his qualities as a constructive and pioneering public servant.   KENNETH O. MORGAN

Sources P. Watkins, *A Welshman remembers* (1944) · NL Wales, Thomas Jones papers, Class V · NL Wales, Ben Bowen Thomas papers · E. L. Ellis, *T. J.: a life of Dr Thomas Jones* (1992) · G. Elwyn Jones, *Controls and conflicts in Welsh secondary education, 1889–1944* (1982) · G. Elwyn Jones, *Which nation's schools?* (1990) · P. Stead, *Coleg Harlech: the first fifty years* (1977) · K. O. Morgan, *Rebirth of a nation: Wales, 1880–1980* (1981) · Coleg Harlech archives · *WW* · *WWW* · A. Mee, ed., *Who's who in Wales* (1921) · Burke, *Peerage* (1939) · b. cert. · m. cert. [Mary Jane Jones] · d. cert.

Archives NL Wales, letters to Sir Ben Bowen Thomas, mainly relating to Coleg Harlech · NL Wales, G. M. Lloyd Davies MSS · NL Wales, letters to Thomas Iorwerth Ellis · NL Wales, D. T. Guy MSS · NL Wales, corresp. with Thomas Jones, Class V · PRO, education files, ED 24, ED 110

Watkins, Vernon Phillips

Watkins, Vernon Phillips (1906–1967), poet, was born on 27 June 1906 at Lloyds Bank House, Talbot Street, in the mining town of Maesteg, in the Llynfi valley, Glamorgan, the second of the three children of William Watkins (1872–1949), bank manager, and his wife, Sarah (1876–1975), daughter of James Phillips of Sarnau, Carmarthenshire. His maternal grandfather, a devoted Congregationalist, came from a family which owned land in Carmarthenshire; towards the end of his life he lived at Goleufryn in Picton Terrace, Carmarthen, a house celebrated in his grandson's poem 'Returning to Goleufryn'. Both Watkins's parents were Welsh-speaking but, in the fashion of their time and class, they did not pass the language on to their children; of Welsh literary tradition Watkins, as a mature poet, was able to use only the legendary figure of Taliesin in the setting of his beloved Gower peninsula. Two years after their son's birth the family moved back to Bridgend, Glamorgan, where William Watkins had been based, and made their home at Quarella, a house (demolished during the 1970s) on the outskirts of the town. Watkins's father belonged to a Brecknockshire family which had settled in Gwaelod-y-Garth, a village just north of Cardiff. (On 31 December 1938 Watkins listened to a radio programme, broadcast from the village, about the Welsh folk-custom of the Mari Lwyd, a form of wassailing, which he

used as the basis for a long poem.) In 1912 the Watkins family left Bridgend for Llanelli, in Carmarthenshire, and, after about a year, moved to Swansea, where William Watkins took charge of the Wind Street branch of Lloyds Bank, a post in which he remained until his retirement twenty-three years later. For the first ten of these the family lived in Eaton Grove (later part of Eaton Crescent) in the Uplands area of the town.

In 1916, at the age of ten, Vernon Watkins entered Swansea grammar school but was not to meet its most famous pupil, Dylan Thomas, who was eight years younger, until 1935. At the age of eleven he was sent by his socially ambitious parents to Tyttenhanger Lodge, a preparatory school in Seaford, Sussex, and then in 1920 to Repton School in Derbyshire. At Repton, where the headmaster was Dr G. F. Fisher (later archbishop of Canterbury), he was confirmed into the Anglican church, which he never thereafter left. A dreamy, shy, and gentle lad already preoccupied with the inner life of the poet, and with aesthetic notions inspired by Rupert Brooke, he was regularly bullied by older boys, but as a sixth-former won a degree of popularity by excelling at tennis and cricket. In June 1924 he was awarded the Howe verse prize, the Lancelot Saye prizes for French and German, and the Schreiber prize for prowess in those languages. For Repton's quatercentenary in 1957 he wrote a sequence of poems entitled 'Revisited Waters' which, though almost totally lacking in autobiographical detail, recalled the idyllic nature of his last eighteen months at the school and made it clear that, for him, poetry was the only shield he had against impermanence, one of the major themes of his writing. In its terminal letter of May 1968, after Watkins's death, the school referred to him, somewhat cautiously, as 'perhaps the best poet Repton has had'.

Watkins entered Magdalene College, Cambridge, as a pensioner in October 1924, to read modern languages. But although his academic results at the end of his first year were satisfactory, he found the college a grave disappointment, particularly in its emphasis on language and criticism at the expense of literature. In a heated interview he told the master, A. C. Benson, that his only interest was in writing poetry; when Benson expressed scorn for this declaration, Watkins immediately left the college. This rash decision was to cause him great unhappiness. His father would not allow him to go for a year's stay in Italy, and, in the autumn of 1925, he became a junior clerk in the Butetown branch of Lloyds Bank in Cardiff, and took lodgings at 73 Connaught Road.

Two years later, deeply depressed by his daily routine, and yearning for the Arcadian life of Repton, Watkins suffered the first phase of a nervous breakdown after witnessing an accident in the street outside his lodgings for which he felt he was somehow to blame. He returned to Repton the next day, visited such boys as still remembered him, attended chapel, and then burst into Dr Fisher's study, accused him of 'destroying youth', tried ineffectually to assault him, and was taken to a nursing home in Derby. This crisis brought about what Watkins called 'a revolution of sensibility'. From that point on his life's work would be preoccupied with 'the conquest of Time', by which he meant the immortalization of his memories of Repton and the validation of all that he had known and loved there. After convalescence, he returned to his parents' home in Gower. In due course his father was able to arrange for his transfer to the St Helen's branch of Lloyds Bank in Swansea, so that he could live at home, and it was there that he was to spend the rest of his career as 'the oldest cashier at Lloyds'.

Watkins's first volume of poetry, *Ballad of the Mari Lwyd*, appeared in 1941 after he had left the bombed town of Swansea for service in the RAF police. When Philip Larkin heard him lecture in Oxford in 1943 Watkins wore a flight sergeant's stripes and was billeted at New Bradwell, Buckinghamshire. On 2 October 1944, at St Bartholomew-the-Great in London, he married Gwendoline Mary Davies (*b.* 1923) of Harborne, Birmingham, whom he had met at Bletchley where they both had been working in RAF Intelligence; Dylan Thomas was to have been the bridegroom's best man, but failed to turn up for the ceremony. The Watkinses made their home first on Glanmor Hill in the Uplands area of Swansea, then at The Garth, Pennard Cliffs; they had four sons and a daughter. In her memoir *Portrait of a Friend* (1983), Gwen Watkins gave an account of her husband's relationship with Dylan Thomas, whom he loved unreservedly (but not erotically), even after Thomas had died, and whom she described as 'the most important person in his life'; Thomas's letters to Watkins were published in 1957.

Among Watkins's books of poetry published during his lifetime were *The Lamp and the Veil* (1945), *The Lady with the Unicorn* (1948), *The North Sea* (translations from Heinrich Heine, 1951), *The Death Bell* (1954), *Cypress and Acacia* (1959), and *Affinities* (1962). His *Fidelities* (1968), *Uncollected Poems* (1969), *Selected Verse Translations* (1977), *The Breaking of the Wave* (1979), *The Ballad of the Outer Dark* (1979), and several selections, all appeared posthumously. His poetry is formal, highly crafted, metaphysical, and unorthodox in its Christianity, but relentless in its symbolism and its emphasis on the role of the poet and the immortal nature of his art. Watkins was intransigent in his opposition to any exegesis of his work and did not expect recognition during his lifetime. A memorial volume edited by Leslie Norris was published in 1970 and his *Collected Poems* appeared in 1986.

Shortly after his retirement from the bank in 1966 Watkins was awarded an honorary DLitt by the University of Wales and was a Gulbenkian scholar at the University College of Swansea. At the time of his death in Seattle, during a second visit as professor of poetry at the University of Washington, his name was being canvassed, with others, for the poet laureateship left vacant by the death of John Masefield. He died of a heart attack on the university's tennis court on 8 October 1967, after a two-hour game of doubles; his ashes were buried in the churchyard of St Mary, at Pennard, near Swansea, where a memorial was erected to him.   MEIC STEPHENS

Sources R. Mathias, *Vernon Watkins*, Writers of Wales (1974) · L. Norris, ed., *Vernon Watkins, 1906–67* (1970) · G. Watkins, *Portrait of*

a friend (1983) · 'Watkins, Vernon', *The Oxford companion to the literature of Wales*, ed. M. Stephens (1986) · J. P. Ward, ed., *Poetry Wales*, 4/12 (1977) [issue devoted to Vernon Watkins] · J. Harris and E. J. Davies, *A bibliographical guide to twenty-four modern Anglo-Welsh writers* (1994) · G. Watkins, *Vernon Watkins and the elegiac muse* (1973) · D. Polk, *Vernon Watkins and the spring of vision* (1977) · D. Watkins, *Vernon Phillips Watkins: the early years* [n.d.] · b. cert. · m. cert. · gravestone, St Mary's churchyard, Pennard, near Swansea, Glamorgan **Archives** Hunt. L., letters · NL Wales, drafts and other papers relating to 'Fidelities' · NL Wales, letters to his mother and sisters · NL Wales, literary MSS, notes, and corresp. · NL Wales, papers incl. drafts of published and unpublished poems · NRA, corresp. and literary papers · University of Washington Libraries, literary MSS and notebooks | NL Wales, letters to Eric V. Falk, a schoolfriend · NL Wales, letters to Meic Stephens · U. Wales, Swansea, letters to his wife and to Neville Masterman, papers | FILM BBC Wales, film by John Ormond | SOUND The Yale Springs of Recorded Poets (CMS 681), 1975, Vernon Watkins reads from his work **Likenesses** A. James, portrait · I. Lewis, bust **Wealth at death** £10,600: probate, 18 Feb 1968, *CGPLA Eng. & Wales*

Watkinson, Harold Arthur, Viscount Watkinson (1910–1995), businessman and politician, was born on 25 January 1910 at Manor Cottage, Walton-on-Thames, Surrey, the elder son in the family of two sons and one daughter of Arthur Gill Watkinson, master draper, and later the owner of a light engineering business, and his wife, Mary, *née* Casey. The family were of staunch Methodist persuasion, and Watkinson later recalled that the local minister 'would go down on his knees, quite naturally, to pray in our sitting room with a simple saintly dignity that touched the heart' (Watkinson, 3). The minister's son Wilberforce Allen was a Liberal member of parliament and gave the young Watkinson his first lessons in politics. Historically, the Methodist tradition has usually led those of a political bent to espouse the Liberal or the Labour Party, but Watkinson from an early stage was drawn to the Conservative Party. He did not, however, become seriously involved in politics until after the Second World War.

Watkinson was educated at Queen's College, Taunton, and at King's College, London, where he studied engineering. He left without taking a degree and entered the family business at the age of twenty. Outside work, his passion was for climbing. In his autobiography he wrote that at school 'I had been one of the instigators of scrambling at night over the high roofs and battlements (that were strictly out of bounds)' (Watkinson, 4). Later he was encouraged by one of Britain's first professional climbers, Jerry Wright, to take up the activity more seriously. In 1939 he met and became engaged to Vera (Peggy) Langmead, youngest daughter of John Langmead, of Ford, Sussex. When war broke out Watkinson joined the Royal Naval Volunteer Reserve: he had learned to sail on family holidays at Bournemouth and Poole, where he was taught by one of the local fishermen. Before he went on active service he and Peggy decided to get married; they did so on 18 November 1939. They had two daughters, Sarah Margaret (*b.* 1944) and Rosemary Jane (*b.* 1947). Watkinson served in the Royal Naval Volunteer Reserve throughout the Second World War. His engineering experience led him inevitably to the Royal Naval Gunnery School, where he was

Harold Arthur Watkinson, Viscount Watkinson (1910–1995), by Godfrey Argent, 1969

occupied for the whole of the war in the defence of merchant shipping. He ended the war with the rank of lieutenant-colonel.

In 1948 Watkinson became chairman of the Dorking Conservative Association. He was selected to stand for Woking in the February 1950 general election and was duly elected. With the return of a Conservative government in October 1951 he was given the junior, non-ministerial job of parliamentary private secretary to the minister of transport and civil aviation. In May 1952, owing to the personal intervention of Winston Churchill, who wanted to promote young men with a sound background in industry, he was appointed parliamentary under-secretary to the minister of labour and national service, Sir Walter Monckton, a post he held until December 1955, when he was appointed to the more senior post of minister of transport and civil aviation, not then a cabinet post. When in January 1957 Harold Macmillan succeeded Sir Anthony Eden as prime minister, he brought Watkinson into the cabinet (still as minister of transport and civil aviation) and in October 1959 promoted him to be minister of defence, where he succeeded Churchill's son-in-law Duncan Sandys. This appointment later led to his political downfall.

Initially, Macmillan thought of Watkinson in the same way as Churchill had: a thrusting young industrialist who could bring fresh life to a government of old men. However, it turned out that there were serious differences of

policy between the prime minister and his defence minister. Despite the demise of the British empire, Macmillan believed that a worldwide role for the British armed services could be sustained. Watkinson did not. He was determined that Britain's responsibilities should be reduced, and very sharply so. His view was influenced by his reading of the unhappy episode of Britain's intervention in the Suez War of 1956. In July 1962 Macmillan decided to reshuffle his cabinet. This resulted in the sacking of seven cabinet ministers and numerous junior ministers and came to be known as 'the night of the long knives'. In the press it was generally agreed that this was an act of panic in the face of falling Conservative popularity. The dismissal of Watkinson, however, was as much a result of the fundamental difference of opinion between Macmillan and Watkinson, as of the prime minister's desire to bring new blood into his government. In his autobiography Watkinson made it clear that he felt a deep sense of personal hurt at his peremptory—as he saw it—dismissal, and did not dwell on the important policy differences between himself and the prime minister. He was, after all, only fifty-two, and could justifiably have anticipated a long career in government. Most of the other ministers dismissed by Macmillan at that time were elderly, and happy to retire—though one of them, Selwyn Lloyd, made a somewhat spectacular return to politics as speaker of the House of Commons under the prime ministership of Sir Alec Douglas-Home. When in June 1964 Watkinson decided not to stand for re-election to the House of Commons in the general election of October that year, it was Douglas-Home who rewarded him with a viscountcy for his services to government and party.

Watkinson thereupon threw all his considerable energy into business affairs, concentrating on promoting Britain's economic interests abroad. From 1964 to 1970 he was a member of the British National Export Council and from 1964 to 1967 chairman of the Committee for Exports to the United States. For ten years he was a key figure in the British Institute of Management, serving as its chairman from 1968 to 1970, its vice-president from 1970 to 1973, and its president from 1973 to 1978. It was during this time that he published his *Blueprint for Industrial Survival* (1976), large parts of which were incorporated into his autobiography, *Turning Points* (1986). He was group managing director of Schweppes Ltd from 1963 to 1968, chairman of Cadbury's Schweppes Ltd from 1969 to 1974, a director of British Insulated Callender's Cables from 1968 to 1977 and of Midland Bank from 1970 to 1983, and president of the Confederation of British Industry from 1976 to 1977. He was also a member of the National Economic Development Council from 1976 to 1977. In all his business activities Watkinson followed the policies which he had so passionately espoused during his time in government, of building up Britain's economic potential abroad. While he had differed from Macmillan on the military potential of the United Kingdom overseas, he was convinced none the less that economic power was crucial to his country's future, and he made a worthy contribution to that future.

He was a member of the Falkland Islands review committee from 1982 to 1983. He died on 19 December 1995 at his home, Tyma House, Bosham, Chichester, Sussex, of cancer of the prostate. He was survived by his wife and two daughters. There was no heir to the viscountcy.

PATRICK COSGRAVE

Sources H. Watkinson, *Turning points* (1986) · *The Times* (21 Dec 1995) · *The Independent* (Dec 1995) · *WWW*, 1991–5 · Burke, *Peerage* · b. cert. · d. cert. · *WW*
Archives Ashridge Management College, Berkhamsted, Hertfordshire, papers · IWM, papers relating to his service in the Royal Naval Volunteer Reserve · U. Warwick Mod. RC, papers as president of the CBI | CAC Cam., corresp. with Sir E. L. Spears
Likenesses Folb, photograph, 1956, Hult. Arch. · G. Argent, photograph, 1969, NPG [*see illus.*] · N. Colvin, pen-and-ink caricature, NPG · photograph, repro. in *The Times* · photograph, repro. in *The Independent*

Watkyn ap Thomas ap Roger. *See* Vaughan, Watkyn (*d.* 1504), *under* Vaughan family (*per. c.*1400–*c.*1504).

Watkyns, Rowland (*c.*1614–1664), Church of England clergyman and poet, was born in Longtown, Herefordshire. His parentage has not been certainly established; however, a pedigree from the heraldic visitation of Hereford in 1634 refers to a Rowland Watkins who was the third son of Samuell Watkins (both spellings of the surname appear) and Sibell Parry. The 'most dear and pious Uncle, Mr. James Parry, Parson of Tedstone', to whom Watkyns dedicated a poem, was probably Sibell's brother. The Rowland of this pedigree had three brothers and four sisters; the eldest son, James, is described as having been aged twenty-six in 1634. The pedigree's format suggests that at least one sister as well as two brothers were born before Rowland. Watkyns's wife's name is unknown. Watkyns wrote 'an epitaph' on 'his beloved daughter, Susanna' (1655–1658), and a son matriculated at Jesus College, Oxford. His name, Samuel, was that of Rowland's father in the pedigree cited above, and strengthens the case that the pedigree refers to the poet. There is no record from either university, but Watkyns was probably an undergraduate at Jesus College, Oxford, which had a strong Welsh connection (the lists of entrants in that college's senior bursars' accounts give names only from 1633).

Watkyns became the vicar of Llanfrynach, 4 miles south-east of Brecon, in 1635. He was dispossessed of his living, probably in 1648, one of several clergy so treated by the Brecon sequestration committee before the Act for the Propagation of the Gospel in Wales came into effect in 1650. At the Restoration he was restored to his living, and held it until his death. In 1662 he published *Flamma sine fumo*, which consisted of three sections: a collection of verse mostly on religious and ethical themes; 'Proverbial Sentences' in seventy-three couplets; and 'A Looking-Glasse for the Sicke, or, Signs of Several Diseases, with their Cures and Remedies'. The poems reveal a Laudian Anglican contemptuous of Presbyterians, of 'the New Illiterate lay-Teachers', and of 'the common people'. Anti-democratic sentiment cut across party lines, being found in Milton, Vaughan, Dryden, and many other writers. Like his neighbour, the better-known poet Henry Vaughan,

Watkyns wrote on Christ's Nativity, the feast disliked by so many Puritans, and on the Virgin Mary. There is no known record of political activism, beyond poems apparently addressed in manuscript to royalist acquaintances. Watkyns did not publish his poems until 1662, when it had become not merely safe but possibly advantageous to do so.

'A Looking-Glasse for the Sicke' suggests that Watkyns may have practised as a physician while he was deprived of his living, and so have been in competition with Vaughan. In relation to contemporary medical controversy, they took opposing positions. Watkyns advocated herbal and questioned 'mineral' cures; the Vaughan brothers practised Paracelsian or 'chymical' medicine. Such differences may underlie an apparent antipathy between Watkyns and Henry Vaughan, suggested by the fact that no reference to Watkyns appears in Vaughan's work, while a poem prefaced to *Flamma sine fumo* contains thinly veiled, and certainly hostile, references to Vaughan. Watkyns's remedies are unappealing; his herbal remedies are laced with such additions as crow's dung applied directly for the toothache, goat's dung for the fistula, 'dog's toords' for the 'flux', and so on. His volume has no great aesthetic appeal, but is interesting in relation to contemporary doctrinal and social conflicts, and enhances knowledge of royalist society in Brecknockshire during the interregnum.

Watkyns's will was drawn up on 18 October 1664 and proved on 8 November 1664. His estate amounted to about £24, more than half of it in corn; his books were valued at £1.

ALAN RUDRUM

Sources *Flamma sine fumo*, ed. P. C. Davies (1962) · R. Mathias, 'In search of the Silurist', *Poetry Wales*, 11/2 (1975), 6–35 [repr. in *Essential articles for the study of Henry Vaughan*, ed. A. Rudrum (1987)] · A. Rudrum, 'Resistance, collaboration and silence: Henry Vaughan and Breconshire royalism', *The English civil wars in the literary imagination*, ed. C. J. Summers and T.-L. Pebworth (1999), 102–18 · private information (2004) [B. Allen, archivist of Jesus College, Oxford] · A. Rudrum, ed., *Complete poems of Henry Vaughan* (1983)
Wealth at death approx. £24: *Flamma sine fumo*, ed. Davies, 1968

Watson [*née* Craven; *other married name* Boles]**, Abigail** (1685–1752), Quaker minister, was born in Limerick on 30 January 1685, one among the sixteen children of Alderman James Craven (*d.* 1695), a Quaker merchant, and his wife, Dorothy Aldworth (*d.* 1722). Her father had been convinced of Quaker principles by Francis Howgill and Edward Burrough in Limerick in 1655, and suffered imprisonment for his faith in 1661 and 1669. Soon after his death, in 1695, Abigail came under the influence of Elizabeth Jacob, *née* Head (*d.* 1739), a Quaker minister in Limerick, when 'the Almighty mercifully reached to her … and preserved her all her life long' (*A Collection of Testimonies*, 276).

Abigail Craven began her ministry aged twenty-seven, and travelled frequently in Ireland for the next forty years, as well as visiting America once and Britain five times. She had a frank, courageous spirit and was not afraid to reprove those who deserved it, of whatever rank. On her first visit to Britain, in 1712 with Elizabeth Jacob, she condemned the rise of worldliness, pride, and covetousness among the Quakers of that time. She also had the gift of prophecy and became a popular speaker with people who 'liked to hear the Gospel well preached' (Tabitha Horner to Samuel and Abigail Watson, 23 Aug 1736, Watson papers). Her meetings were often very large, and her fame became such that an anonymous pamphlet of 1743, defending the 'right, authority and power of Women's ministry' and signed 'A. B.', mentions her on the title-page along with May Drummond and Elizabeth Smith.

Abigail Craven had a particular concern for youth and held meetings for the young of both sexes in Cork on her first visit there, in 1712, and on her many subsequent visits over the next three decades. In 1716 she travelled in the provinces of Leinster and Ulster with Margaret Hoare of Cork, visiting places where no Friends resided and holding meetings in court houses at Athlone, Sligo, Enniskillen, and elsewhere. In 1717 she revisited England with Elizabeth Jacob.

In May 1719 Abigail Craven married in Limerick, as his third wife, John Boles (1661–1731), a Quaker farmer of Woodhouse, near Cashel, co. Tipperary; she thus became stepmother to his nine children, one of whom, a daughter, accompanied her on her third visit to England, in 1722. She visited America between September 1725 and May 1727, having crossed the Atlantic, pursued by pirates, in the *Sizergh*, under Captain Cowman. She visited Maryland, Virginia, and Carolina accompanied by Grace Lloyd, the Cornish-born wife of David Lloyd, the chief justice of Pennsylvania. On a second journey she toured the Jerseys and New England with Jane Fenn (later Hoskens), travelling the Egg Harbours and Cape May by canoe, 'which some thought was impossible for women to go through in winter' (Sudbury). In Boston and Mendon crowds of Presbyterians and other non-Quakers flocked to hear her speak, 'which occasioned the Priests to rage exceedingly … and some said it would be well to whip me out of town' (ibid.). She was accompanied back to Britain by Jane Fenn and seen off by a large crowd, many of whom had been comforted and edified by her ministry.

Widowed in 1731, Abigail Boles married on 13 March 1735 a Quaker elder and landowner, Samuel Watson (1686–1762), of Kilconnor, co. Carlow. She became the affectionate stepmother of another seven children, from Watson's first marriage, who themselves were the progenitors of a famous fox-hunting dynasty. In 1735 she sailed with Elizabeth Jacob to England, where they travelled in Kent, Sussex, and Surrey with Mary Weston, and were later joined by Samuel Watson in the northern counties.

Abigail Watson's final visit to England, in 1748, was with Anne Barclay of Dublin, a kinswoman of the Quaker apologist Robert Barclay. By 1751 she had ceased travelling altogether, finding that 'her work was done and nothing in the way … and now I shall sing, sing, sing' (*A Collection of Testimonies*, 273). She died on 11 November 1752, after a long illness, at Kilconnor, near Fenagh, co. Carlow, where she had lived since 1735, and her body was interred at the nearby Friends' burial-ground at Ballybromhill (now Ballybrommel). The manuscript diary of her travels in America has been incorrectly attributed to Ketchtichia Sudbury, and as a result has been miscatalogued on the microfilm copy of the diary.   PETER LAMB

Sources Ketchtichia Sudbury [Abigail Watson], 'Diary of a journey … Dublin–Philadephia–Salem–Cork, 1725–1727', NL Ire. [microfilm] • *A collection of testimonies concerning several ministers of the gospel amongst the people called Quakers deceased* (1760), 272–7 • J. R. Gough, 'Annals of Limerick from the first commencement of Friends in 1655 with some anecdotes and notices of several of the early members, collected from records and traditionary accounts, 1830', Friends' Meeting House, Limerick • 'Record of Friends travelling in Ireland, 1656–1765 [pt 2]', *Journal of the Friends' Historical Society*, 10 (1913), 212–62 • A. Watson, correspondence, RS Friends, Lond., Watson papers • A. B., *The fair disputant, or, Woman's advocate: a familiar epistle from a Christian to a clergyman, in defence of Eliz. Smith, May Drummond, Abigail Watson, Rob. Barclay, W. Penn, G. Rooke and others of their most excellent and truly ancient religion, the* QUAKERS, *wherein is particularly and plainly shewn the right, authority, and power of* WOMEN'S MINISTRY, *and what idea we ought to have of* GOD, *as our sovereign and creator* (1743) • *Jane Hoskens: the life and spiritual sufferings of that faithful servant of Christ, a public preacher among the people called Quakers* (Philadelphia, 1771) • M. Weston, journal, RS Friends, Lond., vol. 312 • 'Elizabeth Jacob of Limerick, 1675–1739', *Journal of the Friends' Historical Society*, 11 (1914), 78–83 • J. O'Toole, 'The Carlow gentry' (Carlow, 1993) • registry of births and deaths of Limerick monthly meetings, Religious Society of Friends, Dublin • Webbs Irish Quaker pedigrees, Religious Society of Friends, Dublin
Archives NL Ire., 'Diary of a journey … Dublin–Philadelphia–Salem–Cork, 1725–1727' [microfilm] • RS Friends, Lond., papers

Watson, Albert (1828–1904), classical scholar and college head, was born at Astley, Worcestershire, on 4 December 1828, the fifth son of Richard Watson of Kidderminster. He was educated at Rugby School (1843–7), and entered Wadham College, Oxford, in 1847 as a commoner. In 1851 he obtained a first class in *literae humaniores* (BA 1851), proceeding MA in 1853, and for a few months in 1854 he was a master at Marlborough College. He had been elected fellow of Brasenose College, Oxford, in 1852 and took holy orders in 1853, becoming a priest in 1856, but he never held a benefice. Settling down to educational work in Oxford he was tutor of his college (1854–67) and lecturer (1868–73). He was also librarian (1868–77) and senior bursar (1870–81). He was elected principal of the college in 1886, but held the office for only three years, resigning in July 1889 for reasons that remain obscure. He was again fellow from 1890 until his death. His chief extra-collegiate positions were those of librarian of the Union Society (1852–3), examiner (1859, 1860, 1864, and 1866), and curator of the University Galleries. He died suddenly from heart failure at 20 Norham Gardens, Oxford, on 21 November 1904. He was unmarried.

Watson's only published work was an edition of Cicero's letters, with notes (*Select Letters of Cicero*, 1870; 4th edn, 1891), a task suggested to him, it is believed, by John Conington, and carried out with conspicuous acumen and industry. 'Watson's Letters' was for many years a household name at Oxford. He also translated part of Leopold von Ranke's history of England (1875). A wide reader in all branches of standard literature, but especially historical and political, and with a retentive memory, Watson combined a rare power of co-ordinating what he knew. The characteristics of decision and determination which his features suggested were quite overborne by his gentleness and benevolence. Reserved and retiring to an unusual degree, he yet in conversation drew on his stores of wit and learning for the edification of his guests. Throughout his life he was a convinced Liberal, and a considerable force in Oxford politics.

FALCONER MADAN, rev. M. C. CURTHOYS

Sources [C. B. Heberden], ed., *Brasenose College register, 1509–1909*, 2 vols., OHS, 55 (1909) · J. Foster, *Oxford men and their colleges* (1893) · *Oxford Magazine* (30 Nov 1904) · C. B. Heberden, *Address in Brasenose College chapel, 27 Nov 1904* (privately printed) · G. B. Grundy, *Fifty-five years at Oxford: an unconventional autobiography*, 2nd edn [1946], 76 · *CGPLA Eng. & Wales* (1904)

Likenesses A. McEvoy, oils, 1905 (after photographs), Brasenose College, Oxford

Wealth at death £61,031 17s. 7d.: probate, 31 Dec 1904, *CGPLA Eng. & Wales*

Watson, Alexander (1815/16–1865). *See under* Watson, Joseph (1764/5–1829).

Watson, Alexandra Mary Chalmers [Mona; *née* Alexandra Mary Geddes] (1872–1936), medical practitioner and head of the Women's Army Auxiliary Corps, was born in India on 31 May 1872, the eldest child of Acland (later Auckland) Campbell Geddes (1831–1908), civil engineer, and his wife, Christina Helen MacLeod Geddes, *née* Anderson (1850–1914). Mona Geddes was educated at St Leonard's School, St Andrews. Her first choice of career was teaching and she went to Aberdeen to study, but her mother fell ill and Mona returned home to Edinburgh. During this period she became attracted to medicine; this was not surprising because her mother and another relative, Elizabeth Garrett Anderson—the first woman to qualify as a doctor in England—were both pioneers in the cause of the medical education of women. Mona began the study of medicine in 1891 in the Medical College for Women, Edinburgh, of which her mother was one of the founders. Those were the days, according to the *Medical Women's Federation Quarterly Review* of October 1936, when to be a woman medical student in Edinburgh almost meant social ostracism: 'Certainly, although the era of rotten eggs and flour had passed, the throwing of contemptuous glances and sneering remarks was still in vogue.'

After graduating MB CM at Edinburgh University in 1896 Mona Geddes went to London, where she spent a year in Plaistow, working as medical officer in the Maternity District Association and for six months in Dr Barnardo's Homes, Kent. Her work at Plaistow formed the subject of her MD thesis, using a record of more than 1000 confinements with a mortality rate of just over 1 per 1000. She returned to Edinburgh and took her MD degree on 30 July 1898. The *Scots Pictorial* (8 Sept 1917), in commenting on her graduation, reported: 'The men took the innovation gallantly, and when the young lady, modest and charming, but wearing that air of immense capability that distinguishes all her family, appeared to be "capped", she was greeted with the very heartiest applause.' She had delayed her wedding until she could write MD after her name, and on the afternoon of her graduation day was married to Dr Douglas Chalmers Watson. The two then set up private practice together in 11 Walker Street, Edinburgh.

Chalmers Watson's years of private practice in Edinburgh were strenuous for she had her home and family responsibilities as well as many outside interests. One of her patients is on record as saying: 'She never left you without your realising that you had been given not merely professional skill and advice but a part of herself.' While her husband specialized in nutrition, Mona Chalmers Watson—inspired by Dame Millicent Garrett Fawcett, a relative by marriage—was drawn towards the suffrage movement, but she departed from Dame Millicent's constitutional organization and joined the ranks of the militant Women's Social and Political Union. Although she was not called upon to fight as a 'shock trooper' herself, her support was always active and not passive.

Although Chalmers Watson had two young sons, Irvine and Rupert, she still found time to take part in the development of the Queen Mary Nursing Home, and in the founding of the Elsie Inglis Hospital for Women, a pioneer institution of its kind, and to support actively the Patriotic Food League, the Women's Emergency Corps—of which she was honorary secretary—and the Scottish Women's Medical Association, of which she later became president. For a few years she was on the staff of the Edinburgh (Bruntsfield) Hospital for Women and Children and she assisted her husband in the editorship of the *Encyclopedia medica* (1899–1910), a work of fifteen volumes, in which she wrote the article on invalid feeding. She and Douglas also published *Food and Feeding in Health and Disease* (1910) and *The Book of Diet* (1913). She was for a time a manager of the Royal Infirmary, Edinburgh, and was also one of the two secretaries of the Queen's Institute of District Nursing. She also did much in securing the introduction of women medical students into Edinburgh University on an equal footing with the men. In addition to her professional activities she found time to become the first president of the Scottish Women's Hockey Association.

In December 1916, after two years of war and faced with the mounting toll of slaughter in the trenches, the War Office considered the formation of a women's corps to undertake some of the non-combatant duties in France. This scheme was supported by Sir Neville Macready, the adjutant-general, and the commander in the field, General Sir Douglas Haig. The urgency of the situation demanded swift action, and the director of recruiting at the War Office, Brigadier-General Sir Auckland *Geddes, Mona Chalmers Watson's brother, called his sister to London to attend a meeting of leaders of women's organizations on 26 January 1917. Lord Derby, who convened the meeting, opposed the full enlistment of women and, although discussion ranged over several topics, no firm decision was taken on the formation of a women's corps.

Sir Auckland urged his sister to seek a private interview with Macready. Their meeting lasted for ninety minutes, during which time Mona submitted her ideas in the form of rough notes that she had specially prepared. When she returned to London on Friday 9 February 1917 Sir Neville asked her to head the new corps, saying that although

Lord Derby favoured the appointment of 'a lady of title', he personally preferred a professional woman for the post (Terry, 40). She accepted on condition that she could appoint a deputy to command the women's forces in France; her choice fell on Helen Gwynne-Vaughan. It was an ideal partnership: Mona had a commanding and attractive presence, yet was charming, motherly, and good-humoured, with a record of superb organizational skills, while Helen was striking and statuesque with an hauteur born of her aristocratic background, yet impulsive and at times undiplomatic—they complemented each other perfectly. The combination of Mona's tact and Helen's forceful determination could hardly have been bettered and it contributed greatly to the success of the large organization which they were to head.

The Women's Army Auxiliary Corps (WAAC) was formally instituted by an Army Council instruction, dated 7 July 1917, and Mona Chalmers Watson described its formation as a step forward in two directions: 'It is an advance of the women's movement and it is a national advance', she wrote in the *B.E.U. Monthly Record* in November 1917. 'Women have now a direct and officially recognised share in the task of our armies both at home and overseas.' Mona was appointed chief controller of the WAAC, equivalent to the rank of brigadier-general, with an annual salary of £500. The official headquarters of the corps were established at Devonshire House in Piccadilly, London. Eighteen months of a life beyond their imaginings, doing a man's job in what had been strictly a man's world, lay ahead of Mona Chalmers Watson in London, Helen Gwynne-Vaughan in France, and the women they recruited. When it was all over they would return to a new Britain, and some of them would build on the feminist foundations that were even then being laid. During these early months of the WAAC Mona Chalmers Watson undertook the immense task of recruiting 40,000 women. In a recruiting pamphlet she wrote: 'This is the great opportunity for every strong, healthy and active woman not already employed on work of national importance to offer her services to her country' (Terry, 48). She devoted all of her energies to the task and, on 25 August 1917, she was among the first recipients of the newly instituted CBE. By February 1918 Mona realized that the strain of running the WAAC and also undertaking her domestic duties was proving too much: when one of her sons became seriously ill after an appendectomy she decided to resign so that she could return to her family in Edinburgh. There were many tributes to Mona Chalmers Watson's work. The *Ladies' Pictorial* on 20 February 1918 said she had 'nobly done her bit' and the *Daily Sketch* reported on the same day that she 'had organised and set going that most useful corps with conspicuous success'. There is no doubt that the cause of women's suffrage, for which she had worked more directly in the past, was advanced by her clear-sighted and capable direction of the WAAC.

In 1923 the Chalmers Watsons inherited a farm, Fenton Barns, near North Berwick, East Lothian, from Douglas's uncle, James Glendinning; there they began the task of breeding a herd of tuberculin-tested cattle. In the next few years the dairy farm became renowned across Europe as a pioneer in experiments directed towards improving the quality of milk and the production and distribution of certified milk for the safer feeding of children. The irradiation of milk, its use in the feeding of premature infants, the production of milk with a specially digestible curd, and other associated problems occupied Mona Chalmers Watson's thought and energies.

When women were given the vote in 1918 Mona Chalmers Watson became the first president of the Edinburgh Women Citizens' Association. She was also instrumental in securing funds for the development of the Women's United Services Club in Drumsheugh Gardens, Edinburgh, and she was a director of Time and Tide Publishing Company. When news of Mona Chalmers Watson's death on 7 August 1936—at the home of her brother Sir Auckland Geddes at Frensham, Rolvenden, Kent—reached Edinburgh, the first stunned reaction was the question of what all of the women's organizations would do without her. A contemporary wrote in *The Scotsman* (8 Aug 1936): 'Societies, hospitals, Queen's Nurses, Boards were upheld by her support and inspired by her practical energy.' She was notable for her clear thinking and her opinions had a weight beyond her own estimate of them. As a hostess she was charming, with a natural ease and grace.

'It has been an honour', she told a medical contemporary when reviewing her career, 'to have lived through such great times for women, and to know that the generation after us will not have the same fight for liberty'. Her contribution to feminist causes was considerable and her work as the first head of the WAAC, later the Queen Mary's Army Auxiliary Corps, laid the foundations for the Auxiliary Territorial Service in the Second World War, and for the Women's Royal Army Corps which it became in 1949.   ROY TERRY

Sources A. C. Geddes, *The forging of a family* (1952) · private information (2004) · M. Izzard, *A heroine in her time* (1969) · A. Marwick, *Women at war, 1914–18* (1977) · R. Terry, *Women in khaki* (1988) · *The Scotsman* (8 Aug 1936) · M. Macnicol, 'Alexandra Mary Chalmers Watson, C.B.E., M.D., C.M., an appreciation', *Medical Women's Federation Quarterly Review* (Oct 1936) · m. cert.

Archives CAC Cam., corresp. with her brother, first Baron Geddes

Likenesses E. A. Walton, portrait, IWM · photograph, repro. in Terry, *Women in khaki*, 43 · photographs, IWM · photographs, priv. coll.

Watson, Sir Alfred William (1870–1936), actuary and civil servant, was born at 11 James Street, Bristol, on 11 March 1870, son of Alfred Reuben Watson (*b.* 1845), violinist and composer, who became musical director of the Theatre Royal, Nottingham, and his wife, Emily Morris Hobro. He was grandson of Reuben Watson, a consulting actuary to several friendly societies, including the Manchester Unity of Oddfellows. After attending Nottingham high school Alfred Watson joined his grandfather's practice and studied for the fellowship of the Institute of Actuaries. In 1893, at the comparatively early age of twenty-three, he came top in the final examination for the fellowship, being the only candidate to be awarded a first class. He married, on 20 June 1895, Elizabeth Edith Moffrey (*b.* 1871/2), daughter of Robert William Moffrey JP, civil servant and a grand master of the Manchester Unity. They had one son (who died in childhood) and two daughters.

Watson's exceptional abilities as an authority on friendly society actuarial and financial matters were recognized in 1896 when—aged only twenty-six—he was invited to serve on the Treasury-controlled Rothschild committee which was set up by the government to investigate the viability of insurance-based old-age pension schemes. Despite his youth he played an important part in the committee's proceedings, subjecting several witnesses to rigorous cross-examination. Watson's strong support for the contributory insurance principle found favour with Treasury officials, who appreciated both his actuarial expertise and his views on the correct funding of any future state pension scheme. The most famous of his many publications was his pioneering study (published in 1903) of the sickness and mortality experience of Manchester Unity members during the five years 1893 to 1897 (contrasting this with data from earlier periods in the nineteenth century): though slightly flawed in methodology this work still stands as one of the few examinations of sickness and mortality by age, occupation, and region, and has been frequently cited by modern social historians.

Watson transferred his consulting practice to London in 1910, and was called upon to give expert advice to the framers of the 1911 National Insurance Bill. In 1912, after the bill had become law, he was invited to become chief actuary to the national health insurance joint committee (giving up his lucrative private practice in order to do so), and played a major part in steering the new scheme through its early years. During the First World War he gave statistical advice on innumerable issues to many government departments, most notably the Ministry of Shipping.

In 1917 Watson was appointed to the newly created post of government actuary. Ostensibly this position was necessitated by the development of national insurance, but its creation was also symptomatic of the Treasury's desire to impose greater control over public policy. (Watson's office was located in the Treasury, and in the inter-war years no policy proposal could proceed to legislation without the actuary's approval.) Watson was completely in accord with the Treasury's fiscal rectitude, and politicians found that their more exotic proposals were quickly squashed: as one official put it, Watson could be 'a little difficult, but more actuarial than awkward' (Dilks, 414). During his nineteen years as government actuary Watson served on numerous important official committees (including the 1924-6 royal commission on national health insurance), was a key figure in the planning behind the 1925 contributory pension scheme, and advised on many other social policies. He also played a part in the centralization of social security policy that took place in the inter-war years. Apart from one notable mistake in underpredicting the level of unemployment in the 1920s (with serious consequences for the solvency of the unemployment insurance scheme) Watson's judgement was

regarded as impeccable. He was knighted in 1915, created KCB in 1920, and was president of the Institute of Actuaries from 1920 to 1922.

On a personal level Watson was slightly unprepossessing in appearance. One associate affectionately portrayed him as 'a short, almost insignificant man, bald, a roundish face, sandy moustache, eyes that squinted so that it was hard to guess where they were looking or to whom he was speaking' (The Times, 12 May 1936). His undemonstrative and courteous manner was accompanied by a quiet voice; but this unassuming exterior concealed a firm resolve and powerful personality. He always impressed his colleagues by his acute intelligence, linguistic skills, and formidable ability to interpret the most complex of statistical tables at a glance. Watson never enjoyed robust health, and worked excessively hard at his official duties. He died unexpectedly on 7 May 1936 at his home, 16 Castello Avenue, Putney, London. His remains were cremated at Golders Green crematorium on 11 May. On his death many tributes were paid to his remarkable abilities as a senior civil servant and expert actuary. What is less well known is Watson's enormous influence on social policy making in the inter-war years, quietly exerted within the portals of Whitehall.

JOHN MACNICOL

Sources 'Memoir of Sir Alfred Watson', *Journal of the Institute of Actuaries*, 58/1, no. 320 (1936), 1–7 · *The Times* (9 May 1936) · *The Times* (12 May 1936) · *The Times* (13 May 1936) · *The Times* (14 May 1936) · *The Times* (26 June 1936) · J. Macnicol, *The politics of retirement in Britain, 1878–1948* (1998) · B. B. Gilbert, *British social policy, 1914–1939* (1970) · D. Dilks, *Neville Chamberlain: pioneering and reform, 1869–1929* (1984) · N. Whiteside, 'Private agencies to public purposes: some new perspectives on policy making in health insurance between the wars', *Journal of Social Policy*, 12/2 (April 1983), 165–93 · b. cert. · m. cert. · d. cert. · CGPLA Eng. & Wales (1936) · WWW

Wealth at death £22,334 1s. 10d.: resworn probate, 22 June 1936, CGPLA Eng. & Wales

Watson, Sir (James) Angus (1874–1961), food manufacturer and philanthropist, was born on 16 January 1874 at Ryton-on-Tyne, Northumberland, the eldest of three children and the only son of Alexander Watson, a sanitary pipe manufacturer, and his wife, Jane Anne, the daughter of the Revd Thomas Wilkinson, a Baptist minister in Tewkesbury, Gloucestershire. He was educated at schools in Ryton, and at the age of fifteen he started as a junior clerk with a Newcastle firm of grain and provision importers. After a year he went to a firm of wholesale grocers as a commercial traveller. In 1892 he made his first acquaintance with the product he was to pioneer in Britain when he contracted with a firm of Stavanger fish canners for exclusive British rights to sell Norwegian brisling. In 1898 he left his old employer to work for Lever Brothers Ltd at a salary of £250 per annum, and after nine months was made manager of their branch in Hull. After a year spent in the USA establishing a sales organization for Levers, he returned to Britain in 1903 to take up an offer from the Norwegian canners to take charge of their sales in Britain. In 1904 Watson married Ethel, daughter of James Reid, with whom he had two sons and two daughters.

In the same year Watson established in Newcastle, with a partner, Henry B. Saint, the firm of Angus Watson Ltd, the fish canners, who became chiefly known for the brand name Skippers Sardines. Watson employed pioneering techniques of marketing and brand advertising to promote product loyalty among consumers. He and Saint took great care in choosing the name Skipper, accompanied by a portrait of a fisherman in full oilskins, which appeared on tins of Norwegian brisling. His success eventually cost his company more than £50,000 in litigation, when the French canning trade took action in the British courts in 1910 to prevent the use of the word sardine to describe the Norwegian product, and, on appeal to the House of Lords, won their case. With typical advertising ingenuity, Watson turned the verdict to his advantage with a slogan saying: 'The word sardines guarantees nothing; the name "Skipper" everything'.

In the First World War Watson's firm purchased canned foods in North America and Scandinavia on behalf of the government. In 1918 shortage of capital forced him to approach his ex-employer, now Lord Leverhulme, for financial guarantees, which by 1923 had become a controlling interest. However, Leverhulme died in 1925, and Watson found the management approach of the new firm of United Canners, with which his firm had been amalgamated, had little in common with his own paternalistic style of management. So strongly did he feel about this that in 1930, shortly after becoming chairman of United Canners, he retired from business and devoted the rest of his life almost entirely to public service and charity work.

A man of strict puritan principles, Watson was an active Congregationalist and was elected chairman of the Congregational Union of England and Wales in 1935–6. A Liberal in politics, and a firm advocate of total abstinence, he was associated with Lloyd George in the First World War in seeking to promote prohibition. He gave time and energy to social and educational projects, and for many years he was a JP. After his retirement he became a member of Newcastle council and deputy lord mayor. He was made a knight of the order of St Olaf of Norway in 1912 for his services to the Norwegian fishing industry. In England the University of Durham made him an honorary DCL, and he was knighted in 1945. During the Second World War he was northern divisional food controller with the Ministry of Food. He was for some years a member of the staff of *The Spectator*, in which he had at one time a controlling interest, being a partner of Sir Evelyn Wrench; and he helped found the publishing firm of Ivor Nicholson and Watson, which issued Lloyd George's war memoirs and Philip Snowden's autobiography. He died at his home, Whitewell, Adderstone Crescent, Jesmond, Newcastle, on 31 January 1961.   RICHARD PERREN

Sources R. Perren, 'Watson, Sir James Angus', *DBB* · A. Watson, *My life: an autobiography* (1937) · A. Watson, *The faith of a business man* (1936) · C. Wilson, *The history of Unilever: a study in economic growth and social change*, 2 vols. (1954) · *The Times* (1 Feb 1961)
Likenesses two photographs, repro. in Watson, *My life*
Wealth at death £228,723 11s. 5d.: probate, 3 March 1961, *CGPLA Eng. & Wales*

Watson, Anthony (d. 1605), bishop of Chichester, was the son of Edward Watson of Thorpe Thewles in co. Durham.

He matriculated as a pensioner at Christ's College, Cambridge, in Michaelmas term 1567 and proceeded BA in 1571/2. A college fellowship followed in 1573, the year he was ordained; he commenced MA in 1575 and graduated BTh in 1582, the year in which he was licensed as a university preacher. A lifelong bachelor, Watson was by this time friendly with the Catholic peer, antiquary, and bibliophile John, sixth Baron Lumley, who in 1581 secured for him the rectory of Cheam in Surrey. Other preferments followed: the deanery of Bristol in April 1590, the prebend of Wedmore Secunda in Wells and the chancellorship of that cathedral, both in July 1592, and also in that year a second living from Lumley, the rectory of Storrington in Sussex. In 1596 Watson succeeded Richard Fletcher, bishop of London, as Queen Elizabeth's chief almoner. Meanwhile, Lumley pressed Watson's case for a bishopric and on 15 August 1596 he was duly consecrated bishop of Chichester, probably through the influence of Sir Robert Cecil with the queen.

As almoner and bishop Watson mainly resided in London or at Cheam; at his elevation the queen allowed him to spread payment of his first fruits over six years, the most generous terms offered to any of the late Elizabethan bishops who were not exonerated entirely. Watson attended Elizabeth in her last illness, his ministrations including an incongruous deathbed prayer against Irish rebels. In 1603 he was continued as almoner by James I and remained prominent in court affairs, distributing the royal Maundy at Westminster in April that year. He attended the execution of the conspirator George Brook in December and was nominated early in 1604 one of four bishops to a commission for the censorship of books. In the following April he was made a deputy chairman of convocation. In addition, Watson assisted at ten of the twelve consecrations of bishops that took place at Lambeth during his own episcopate.

In company with one or two contemporaries, Watson seems to have regarded episcopal elevation more as a reward for past services than as requiring commitment to strong diocesan government. In the main he controlled Chichester diocesan business from London, although he supervised personally the appointments and resignations of his clergy, probably returning to his see in the summer months of most years. He was absent for the diocesan visitation of 1597 but presided in 1600 and 1603. On the latter occasion Watson was confronted by the crisis of his episcopate. The suspension as bishop in 1578 of Richard Curteys (who had lived until 1582), the extreme old age of Curteys's successor, Thomas Bickley, and Watson's own prolonged absences from the diocese, coupled with his reluctance to deprive ill-educated lay readers or harry nonconformist ministers, had all combined to allow nonconformity to flourish among the clergy of Chichester. It was in Sussex that the national puritan campaign of 1603 to win the new king's support was inaugurated during the summer. In September Watson responded to the petitioners' complaints by putting in place a clergy training scheme, but in October the privy council ordered firmer measures: the puritan leaders were to be arrested and examined. Watson's investigation had scarcely begun, however, when news arrived that James had agreed to consider nonconformist objections to the Book of Common Prayer. Watson was one of the nine bishops to attend the Hampton Court conference in January 1604, his silence during proceedings probably arising from embarrassment that among all the county delegations sent to support and advise the four permitted puritan disputants, there was no larger contingent than that from Sussex. With Richard Bancroft in the ascendant by the year's end, one of Watson's last acts, in April 1605, was to give reluctant authorization for the deprivation of ten puritan clergy; that summer thirteen further presentments for nonconformity were made during Bancroft's metropolitical visitation of the diocese. Watson, who was 'somewhat corpulent' (Harington, 140), was by now losing his health, although he was able to officiate at the baptism of Princess Mary in May 1605, preach at the churching of Queen Anne a fortnight later, and accompany James on progress to Bedfordshire in July. Thereafter he was an invalid, and on 10 September he died at Cheam of a 'recidivation' (relapse). He was buried nine days later in the parish church.

According to Sir John Harington Watson was 'a verie good preacher' and 'well-beloved' at places where he resided, especially Bristol (Harington, 140). Watson took his Cambridge DTh in 1596 and in the same year acted for the university library in acquiring some of Lumley's books. In his will he made the substantial bequest of £100 to the Christ's College Library and gave the curate at Cheam all his books by Martin Bucer and Peter Martyr. He named more than twenty other legatees, and remembered students at Christ's, the poor of Cheam and of Aldingbourne, Storrington, and Chichester in Sussex, and prisoners in the White Lion at Southwark, Durham gaol, and Cambridge Castle. The letter writer John Chamberlain considered Watson as 'rich for so meane a living' (*Letters of John Chamberlain*, 1.209). He leased the bishop's residence at Aldingbourne Manor from 1600, and his income was augmented further by pluralities, his two rectories being held *in commendam* throughout his episcopate.

WILLIAM RICHARDSON

Sources K. Fincham, 'Ramifications of the Hampton Court conference in the dioceses, 1603–1609', *Journal of Ecclesiastical History*, 36 (1985), 208–27 · K. Fincham, *Prelate as pastor: the episcopate of James I* (1990) · Venn, *Alum. Cant.*, 1/4.347 · J. Nichols, *The progresses, processions, and magnificent festivities of King James I, his royal consort, family and court*, 4 vols. (1828) · Cooper, *Ath. Cantab.*, 2.410–11 · R. B. Manning, *Religion and society in Elizabethan Sussex* (1969) · J. Harington, *A briefe view of the state of the Church of England* (1653) · *The letters of John Chamberlain*, ed. N. E. McClure, 2 vols. (1939) · F. Heal, *Of prelates and princes: a study of the economic and social position of the Tudor episcopate* (1980) · *Calendar of the manuscripts of the most hon. the marquis of Salisbury*, 6, HMC, 9 (1895), 265

Archives BL, corresp., Add. MS 12507 · CUL, corresp., MS M.m.1.35 · LPL, corresp. in Carte miscellanee XIII

Wealth at death considered surprisingly rich by contemporaries: *Letters of John Chamberlain*, ed. McClure, 1.209; will described, Cooper and Cooper, *Athenae Cantabrigienses*

Watson, Arthur Ernest (1880–1969), journalist and newspaper editor, was born on 29 February 1880 in Newcastle upon Tyne, the second son of Aaron Watson, author and journalist, and his wife, Phebe, daughter of John Gibling of Norwich. He was educated at Rutherford College, Newcastle, Alleyn's School, Dulwich, and Armstrong College, Newcastle. The progression into journalism was a natural one. His father was editor of the *Newcastle Daily Leader*, which Arthur joined at the age of eighteen. His elder brother, Sir Alfred Watson (1874–1967), worked for more than twenty years for the *Westminster Gazette* before becoming editor (1925–33) of the Calcutta *Statesman*. In 1902 Watson joined the parliamentary staff of the *Daily Telegraph*. At twenty-two he was the youngest journalist on the paper. He was to stay with the *Telegraph* for forty-eight years, interrupted only by service in the First World War when he was commissioned as a field gunner and rose to acting major in command of a battery. In 1904 Watson married Lily (d. 1960), daughter of Edmund Waugh of Whitley Bay and Gateshead. There were no children.

After the war Watson rose rapidly, becoming in succession night editor, news editor, and in 1923 assistant editor. In 1924 he was appointed editor following the sudden death of his predecessor, Fred Miller. His early years in the post were difficult. The *Telegraph*, which had been selling 180,000 copies daily in 1920, lost sales steadily, falling by late 1927 to 84,000. Watson would later write that the paper had been 'too parsimonious', with 'too many advertisements, not enough news and features'. When the paper was taken over by Sir William Berry (later Lord Camrose) in late 1927, Watson initially felt apprehensive for himself and his staff, but Berry 'changed neither the chauffeur nor the route' (Koss, 464).

Retained as editor, Watson stayed in the post until 1950. The staff were also retained 'with no more changes than time will always bring'. The paper's fortunes were transformed by more extensive and diverse news and feature coverage, better equipment, and a judicious price cut from 2d. to 1d. in late 1929. Sales reached 200,000 in early 1930 and rose steadily throughout the decade. In 1937 the *Telegraph* took over the *Morning Post*, and by the time of Watson's retirement the daily sale was 980,000. Watson was always a low-profile editor. The takeover had changed his role—Sir William Berry appointed himself editor-in-chief and acted in keeping with the title, while a news editor took full control of that side of the paper, including the front page.

Watson described his relationship with Berry as 'good, if not always completely smooth' (Hart-Davis, 81). His skills were ideal for an editor working under a dominant proprietor. He wrote little himself—Berry was to write that 'more than one newspaper has been ruined by the writer in the editor's chair' (Hartwell, 88)—but was an 'expert technician' (Coote, 225), capable of cutting a leading article under extreme time pressure in the composing room. He spent almost all of his working time in the *Telegraph* office. 'A tall man, well-built, vigorous and upright in every sense of the word with a large dark moustache which turned white as he grew older' (Hart-Davis, 59), he rarely spoke above a whisper and was famously imperturbable. E. F. Lawson, fourth Lord Burnham, general manager of the *Telegraph* during his editorship, later wrote that 'in no crisis of any kind, technical or political, did anyone see him in the slightest rattled' (Burnham, 178).

While Watson was a Conservative loyalist, it has been written that he had 'practically no views about anything except gardening' (Hart-Davis, 60). Watson favoured a paper of 'moderate views' which he defined as:

> a paper that puts forward principles rather than causes. People are tired of newspapers which are constantly propagating causes one after another, and then working them to death. They dislike finding their morning paper full, day after day, of propaganda for the cause which is at the moment in the proprietor's mind. They want a real newspaper based on sound, steady, but progressive principles. (*World's Press News*)

There were controversies during Watson's editorship. In 1929 he was threatened with gaol by the director of public prosecutions for refusing to reveal the source of a leak about government plans to arrest Gandhi. While the paper was critical of appeasement—the foreign secretary, Lord Halifax, complained of 'provocative leaders' (Griffiths, 584)—Watson was also party to the decision to sack the *Telegraph*'s central European correspondent, Eric Gedye, in 1939. He argued that Gedye's publication of books of 'violently worded commentary' on Nazi expansionism destroyed his value as a regional correspondent expected to provide balanced coverage (Hart-Davis, 117).

Watson retired in April 1950 and is believed to have refused a knighthood. He was succeeded as editor by Colin Coote. He devoted much of his retirement to the care of his wife, who by 1950 was a permanent invalid. She died in 1960. Watson suffered a slight stroke in 1967, and died on 18 September 1969 in Merton Park, south London.

HUW RICHARDS

Sources D. Hart-Davis, *The house the Berrys built: inside the 'Telegraph', 1928–1986* (1990) • *World's Press News* (27 Nov 1930) • *Newspaper World* (27 Nov 1930) • *WWW* • *Daily Telegraph* (19 Sept 1969) • Lord Burnham [E. F. L. Burnham], *Peterborough Court: the story of the Daily Telegraph* (1955) • *DNB* • C. Coote, *Editorial* (1965) • Lord Hartwell, *William Camrose, giant of Fleet Street* (1992) • D. Griffiths, ed., *The encyclopedia of the British press, 1422–1992* (1992) • *Daily Telegraph* (4 April 1950) • S. E. Koss, *The rise and fall of the political press in Britain*, 2 (1984) • *CGPLA Eng. & Wales* (1969)
Wealth at death £161,474: probate, 27 Nov 1969, *CGPLA Eng. & Wales*

Watson, Sir Brook, first baronet (1735–1807), merchant and army official, born at Plymouth on 7 February 1735, was the only son of John Watson of Hull and his second wife, Sarah Schofield. He was left an orphan in 1741, was sent to Boston as an apprentice to a distant relative, and at the age of fourteen went to sea. While in the naval service he had his right leg taken off by a shark at Havana. This event became the controversial subject of a painting by the American colonial John Singleton Copley, commissioned by Watson in 1778. His Boston relative having become a bankrupt, he was, after his recovery, made a ward to a Captain Huston, who took him to Nova Scotia. The painting's significance arises from Copley's treatment of Watson in contemporary rather than in the expected neo-classical terms, thereby anticipating J. L. A. T. Géricault's *Raft of the Medusa* (1819), which ushered in the Romantic movement in art. Watson served as a commissary under Colonel Robert Monckton at the siege of Beauséjour in 1755, and under Wolfe at the siege of Louisbourg in 1758.

In 1759 Watson settled in London as a merchant. In the summer of 1773 he presented to Phillis Wheatley, the African-American colonial poet who was visiting the capital, a folio edition of Milton's *Paradise Lost* (now housed in Harvard University). He took a leading part in 1779 in the formation of the corps of light-horse volunteers which helped to suppress the riots in the following year. In 1782 he was appointed commissary-general to the army in Canada, under Sir Guy Carleton, and returned to England when peace was made in 1783. A pension of £500 per annum was granted to his wife, Helen, the daughter of Colin Campbell, a goldsmith of Edinburgh, whom he had married in 1760. Watson was elected MP for the City of London on 6 April 1784, and held the seat until 1793. He was also chosen as a director of the Bank of England. In 1786 he became alderman of Cordwainer ward and sheriff. He was chairman of the House of Commons select committee on the regency bill in 1788.

On 2 March 1793 Watson was appointed commissary-general to the duke of York's army in Flanders, and resigned his seat in parliament. He served with the army until it returned to England in 1795. Lord Liverpool spoke of him as 'one of the most honourable men ever known' (*Supplementary Dispatches*, 9.428).

Having been passed over in 1793 while in the service of the duke of York, Watson was finally elected lord mayor of London in November 1796. His year of office was a troubled one. At a common hall on 12 April 1797 a resolution was brought forward 'to investigate the real cause of the awful and alarming state of public affairs'. Watson ruled this out of order, and closed a heated discussion by having the mace taken up. At another hall, on 11 May, he was censured, and a resolution was passed denouncing the ministry for having plunged the country into an unnecessary and unjust war; but he had many supporters.

On 24 March 1798 Watson was appointed commissary-general to the forces in Great Britain, and on 26 November 1803 he was made a baronet, with remainder to his nephews. He died at East Sheen, Surrey, on 2 October 1807, and was buried at Mortlake. He had no children, and was succeeded in the baronetcy by his great-nephew, William Kay.   E. M. LLOYD, rev. JOHN C. SHIELDS

Sources C. Welch and P. Norman, *Modern history of the City of London* (1896) • *Supplementary dispatches … of Field Marshal Arthur, duke of Wellington, K.G.*, ed. A. R. Wellesley, second duke of Wellington, 9: *South of France, embassy to Paris, and Congress of Vienna, 1814–1815* (1862), 428 • W. Betham, *The baronetage of England*, 5 vols. (1801–5) • J. T. Flexner, *John Singleton Copley*, rev. edn (1948); repr. (1993) • R. B. Stein, 'Copley's *Watson and the shark* and aesthetics in the 1770s', *Discoveries and considerations: essays on early American literature and aesthetics, presented to Harold Jantz*, ed. C. Israel (Albany, NY, 1976), 85–130 • *The collected works of Phillis Wheatley*, ed. J. C. Shields (1988) • E. P. Richardson, 'Watson and the shark by John Singleton Copley', *Art Quarterly*, 10/3 (1947), 213–18 • will, PRO, PROB 11/1470, sig. 930

Archives BL, corresp. • NAM, letter-book and corresp. relating to public accounts • PRO, bill book, PRO T64/122 • PRO, corresp. relating to American war, PRO 30/55 | PRO, letters to William Pitt, PRO 30/8
Likenesses J. S. Copley, oils, 1778 (*Watson and the shark*), Museum of Fine Arts, Boston; version, National Gallery of Art, Washington, DC • J. Sayers, etching, 1788, BM, NPG • R. Dighton, caricature, coloured etching, 1803, BM, NPG • J. S. Copley, oils, John Herron Art Museum, Indianapolis • R. Dighton junior, coloured etching, BM, NPG
Wealth at death left baronetcy to great-nephew: Betham, *Baronetage of England*, 5.540

Watson, Caroline (1760/61–1814), printmaker, was born in London, the daughter of James *Watson (1739/40?–1790), an Irish mezzotint engraver, and his wife, Mary (*b. c.*1740, *d.* before 1790), the daughter of Reuben Judkins. She was trained by her father, but seems never to have worked in mezzotint; her work consists mostly of small-scale stipple engravings, many reproducing portraits, especially miniatures, for which the fineness of her technique was especially well suited. She engraved after the leading portrait painters of the day, including Joshua Reynolds, Thomas Gainsborough, George Romney, and John Hoppner. In 1785 she published a pair of portraits after Hoppner of princesses Mary and Sophia, the daughters of George III and Queen Charlotte (the British Museum owns a set of progress proofs for both prints); in the same year she was made engraver to the queen. She was also patronized by the Bute family, and engraved portraits of John Stuart, first marquess of Bute (after Gainsborough, 1791), and of his wife, Frances, whom she described in her will as 'my ever dear Patroness and kind friend'. Her engraving of a portrait after Sir Thomas Lawrence of *John Stuart, Marquess of Bute* was inscribed 'Frances Caroline Watson', the only known instance of this variant of her name.

Watson's only known aquatints were a series of twelve plates after Maria Cosway, *The Progress of Female Virtue and Female Dissipation*, illustrating a poem, *The Winter Day*, by Mrs Mary 'Perdita' Robinson and published by Ackermann in 1803. These were exhibited at the Scottish National Portrait Gallery Exhibition (Edinburgh and National Portrait Gallery, London, 1995, nos. 238–49). Some of her works were printed in colour, including the portraits of princesses Mary and Sophia, *Eliza Stanhope as 'Contemplation'* (1790), after Joshua Reynolds, and *Saint Matthew* (1788), after a painting in Reynolds's collection by Rubens; she produced a small number of prints after sixteenth- and seventeenth-century painters. The British Museum owns a fine proof printed on silk of her stipple after Reynolds's self-portrait, published in 1789. Watson published some of her own work between 1785 and 1788 from her address in Fitzroy Street, where she probably lived with her barrister brother, although she also worked for other publishers, including John Boydell, for whose *Shakspeare Gallery* she engraved plates, unusually large in her output, after Reynolds and Francis Wheatley. Among her later works are illustrations for William Hayley's *Life of George Romney* (1809).

Hayley described Watson as 'meek Caroline', and her obituarist in the *Gentleman's Magazine* thought 'her great modesty prevented her being so well known as her merit deserved'. Although she did not show her work at public exhibitions, Caroline Watson was one of few contemporary women who maintained an independent practice as an engraver, signing her own work (usually in the form 'Caroline Watson, Engraver to her Majesty') rather than working unacknowledged in a family business, and her wealth at her death suggests that her business was successful. She seems to have cultivated a female clientele: many prints, such as those after Samuel Shelley's miniatures, were dedicated to women, and the project with Cosway and Robinson seems to have been produced by women with a female audience in mind. She died, unmarried, in Pimlico, London, on 9 or 10 June 1814, and was buried in the 'old church', Marylebone.   SARAH HYDE

Sources *Engraved Brit. ports.* • *GM*, 1st ser., 84/1 (1814), 700 • G. Goodwin, *Thomas Watson, James Watson, Elizabeth Judkins* (1904) • J. C. Smith, *British mezzotinto portraits*, 4 (1882–4), 1487–8 • artist's file, archive material, Courtauld Inst., Witt Library • G. E. Bentley, *Blake records* (1969), 153–5, 160–61 • Bryan, *Painters* (1903–5) • M. Salamon, *The old engravers of England …, 1540–1800* (1906) • D. Gaze, ed., *Dictionary of women artists*, 2 vols. (1997) • S. Lloyd and others, *Richard and Maria Cosway: Regency artists of taste and fashion* (1995), 135 [exhibition catalogue, Scot. NPG, 11 Aug – 22 Oct 1995, and NPG, 17 Nov 1995 – 18 Feb 1996]
Archives FM Cam., letters to William Hayley
Wealth at death died rich; left £70 p.a. annuity, plus twenty-four books and a locket to aunt: Goodwin, *Thomas Watson*, 224 • will, PRO, PROB 11/1559/447

Watson, Charles (1714–1757), naval officer, was the son of John Watson, prebendary of Westminster (*d.* 1724); his mother was the daughter of Alexander *Parker. Watson entered the navy in 1728 as a volunteer per order on the *Romney* (Captain Charles Brown); at the end of 1730 he joined the *Bideford* (Captain Curtis Barnett), bound for the Mediterranean; he passed his examination on 31 January 1735, and was appointed lieutenant of the *Falkland*. As the nephew of Sir Charles Wager, first lord of the Admiralty, he was soon promoted captain (14 February 1738) and posted to the *Garland* (20 guns), attached to the fleet in the Mediterranean under the command of Rear-Admiral Nicholas Haddock. In 1741 he married Rebecca, eldest daughter of John Francis Buller of Morval, Cornwall; they had two daughters and a son, Charles. On 25 May of the same year Watson was moved by Haddock into the *Plymouth* (60 guns), and in November 1742, by Thomas Mathews, into the *Dragon*, which he commanded, though without particular distinction, in the action off Toulon on 11 February 1744.

On his return to England early in 1746 Watson was appointed to the *Princess Louisa*, which he commanded in the following year in the engagements off Cape Finisterre (3 May), and in the Bay of Biscay (14 October), acquitting himself well on both occasions. In January 1748 he was appointed to the *Lion*, in which in March he was sent out as commander-in-chief on the Newfoundland and North American station, with a broad pennant as an established commodore. On 12 May he was promoted rear-admiral of the blue, and in February 1754 appointed commander-in-chief in the East Indies, a post which had lapsed in 1752.

He sailed on 9 March in the *Kent*, with three other ships of the line, and for the first year observed the French on the Coromandel coast. In November 1755 he went round to Bombay, from where in February 1756, in company with the vessels of the Bombay marine under Commodore William James and a body of troops commanded by Lieutenant-Colonel Robert Clive, he launched a successful attack on Gheria, the stronghold of the pirate Angria.

After refitting his ships at Bombay Watson sailed for Fort St David's in late April, and at Madras had news of the loss of Calcutta. In consultation with Clive it was determined to restore the British position. By the middle of October the preparations were completed, and Watson, now vice-admiral, sailed for the Hooghly, carrying with him Clive and his small army. After many delays he arrived in the river on 15 December, and by 29 December the walls of Budge-Budge were breached and the place stormed. At Calcutta the fort was taken by a combined detachment of seamen and soldiers. On 9 February 1757 the nawab concluded a treaty with the British, but shortly afterwards he was bolstered by French offers of support. In the military operations which followed, Watson reinforced Clive's small force and had an important share in the victory of Plassey on 22 June, though Watson was not personally concerned. His health, severely tried by the climate, broke down, and he died at Calcutta on 16 August 1757. He was buried there on the following day.

Watson was a capable and straightforward officer who, despite a short temper, co-operated well with those he had to work with, in an era when disputes were only too common. 　　　J. K. LAUGHTON, *rev.* A. W. H. PEARSALL

Sources H. W. Richmond, *The navy in the war of 1739–48*, 3 vols. (1920) · *The Hawke papers: a selection, 1743–1771*, ed. R. F. Mackay, Navy RS, 129 (1990) · R. F. Mackay, *Admiral Hawke* (1965) · J. S. Corbett, *England in the Seven Years' War: a study in combined strategy*, 2 vols. (1907) · E. Ives, *A voyage from England to India in the year 1754* (1773) · P. Spear, *Master of Bengal: Clive and his India* (1975) · R. Beatson, *Naval and military memoirs of Great Britain*, 3 vols. (1790) · J. Charnock, ed., *Biographia navalis*, 4 (1796), 407 · logs, PRO, ADM 51/85, 145, 237, 4159, 392 · muster books, PRO, ADM 36/750, 1101 · letters, PRO, ADM 1/161
Archives BL, Egmont MSS, corresp. · BL OIOC, letter-book relating to India, MS Eur. D 1079 · NMM, logbooks · PRO | BL, corresp. with Lord Holdernesse, Egerton MS 3488 · NRA, priv. coll., letters to Anne Pole and Miss Buller
Likenesses school of G. Kneller, oils, 1725, NMM · P. Sheemakers, statue, 1757, Westminster Abbey · E. Fisher, mezzotint (after T. Hudson), NPG · T. Hudson, double portrait, oils (with his son), Victoria Memorial Hall, Calcutta
Wealth at death property in Abchurch Lane and Lamb Alley, City of London: will, 1748

Watson, Sir Charles Moore (1844–1916), army officer, was born in Dublin on 10 July 1844, the second son of William Watson JP, of Dublin and his wife, Sarah, daughter of the Revd Moore Morgan, rector of Dunlavin, co. Wicklow. He was educated at Trinity College, Dublin, and at the Royal Military Academy, Woolwich, joining as a lieutenant the Royal Engineers in 1866. In 1874–5 he served in the Sudan under General Gordon, and was engaged on the survey of the White Nile. He subsequently was at the War Office until 1878, when he was made a captain and aide-de-camp

to Sir John Lintorn Simmons. In 1880, the year of his marriage to Geneviève, daughter of the Revd Russell Cook, he began two years' duty in the India Office. In 1882 he was promoted brevet major and selected for special duty in the Egyptian campaign. At the head of a small force, he led the advance on Cairo after the battle of Tell al-Kebir, and received the surrender of the citadel (14 September 1882). He was awarded a brevet majority and the Mejidiye. He served in the Egyptian army 1882–6 with the rank of pasha, then became governor of the Red Sea littoral. In 1891 Watson was appointed assistant inspector-general of fortifications. In 1892 he was promoted lieutenant-colonel, and from 1896 he was deputy inspector-general of fortifications, with the rank of colonel, until he retired in 1902.

In 1904 Watson was appointed secretary to the royal commission for the organization of the British section of the St Louis Exhibition and commissioner-general. He acted as British delegate to the International Navigation Congresses at Düsseldorf in 1902, at Milan in 1905, and at St Petersburg in 1908. He was chairman of the Palestine Exploration Fund committee from 1905 until his death. CMG in 1887 and CB in 1902, in 1905 he was made KCMG. In his later years he published several books, including a *Life of Major-General Sir Charles William Wilson* (1909). Watson died at his London home, 16 Wilton Crescent, on 15 March 1916, his wife surviving him.

C. V. OWEN, *rev.* JAMES LUNT

Sources C. M. Watson, *Fifty years' work in the Holy Land* (1915) · *The Times* (16 March 1916) · E. M. Lloyd, 'Colonel Sir C. M. Watson', *Royal Engineers Journal*, new ser., 23 (1916), 265–70 · WWW · CGPLA Eng. & Wales (1916)
Archives RGS, field notebook, observations on Upper Nile
Wealth at death £4158 7s. 11d.: probate, 23 June 1916, CGPLA Eng. & Wales

Watson, Christopher (1545/6–1580/81), historian and translator, was born in Durham; the identity of his parents is unknown. In 1562 he matriculated as a pensioner from St John's College, Cambridge. He graduated BA from Corpus Christi College in 1566, and MA in 1569. It was at Cambridge that he produced his earliest published work, an English translation of the first book of the history of Polybius. This, the first printed English translation of any part of Polybius, was made from the Latin version of Niccolò Perotti. To this work he added a life of Henry V, which is dominated by the speech of the archbishop of Canterbury urging war with France, and the earl of Westmorland's reply. Watson's text follows Edward Hall's history, with some rhetorical expansions. Later, while a resident at Gawdy Hall in Norfolk, he dedicated both works to Thomas Gawdy. This patron was perhaps not, as is often assumed, the recorder of Norwich, but a less prominent relative, Thomas Gawdy of Weybread. Thomas Hackett acquired the licence to print Watson's translation of Polybius in 1565, but the only extant edition of the translation came from Hackett's press in 1568.

This Christopher Watson was very likely the same who

subscribed to a petition in favour of amending the new university statutes at Cambridge in May 1572. He was perhaps at Cambridge during 1573–4, for at this time he was compiling a history of Durham in which he recalled his twin loyalties by adopting the epithet Deiragrantus or Deiragranta. Watson had partly revised this work by 1574, and had received commendatory poems from Richard Cavendish and Gabriel Brandol, but it was apparently abandoned shortly afterwards. He may have decided to concentrate on an ecclesiastical career. A Christopher Watson became rector of Bircham Newton, Norfolk, in 1573; one of this name was ordained deacon at Norwich on 17 September 1574; and one became rector of Beachamwell in Norfolk, succeeding a Thomas Watson who had been appointed during Mary's reign. As a minister Watson composed a short catechism, *Briefe Principles of Religion for the Exercise of Youth*, which was printed in 1581. His will, dated 20 November 1580, appears to have been made during his final illness, and on 12 June 1581 Henry Carre paid for the licence to print 'a lamentac[i]on for the deathe of master Christofer Watsonne mynister' (Arber, *Regs. Stationers*, 1.302). He was survived by his wife, Joan, a son, and three daughters.   P. BOTLEY

Sources Venn, *Alum. Cant.* · will, PRO, PROB 11/62, fols. 393v–394r · BL, Cotton MS Vitellius C.ix 61, fols. 64–128 · C. Watson, *The hystories of the most famous and worthy cronographer Polybius …. Englished by C. W. whereunto is annexed an abstract, compendiously coarcted out of the life and worthy acts perpetrate by oure puissant prince king Henry the Fift* (1568) [modern facs., 1969] · Arber, *Regs. Stationers*, 1.302, 2.394 · F. Blomefield and C. Parkin, *An essay towards a topographical history of the county of Norfolk*, [2nd edn], 11 vols. (1805–10), vol. 7, p. 294; vol. 10, p. 291 · P. Millican, *The Gawdys of Norfolk and Suffolk* (1939), 12–14, 64 · J. Lamb, ed., *A collection of letters, statutes and other documents … illustrative of the history of the University of Cambridge during the Reformation* (1838), 359 · C. J. Wright, ed., *Sir Robert Cotton as collector: essays on an early Stuart courtier and his legacy* (1997), 369–70 · H. B. Lathrop, *Translations from the classics into English from Caxton to Chapman, 1477–1620* (1933); repr. (1967), 187–8

Archives BL, MSS for history of Durham, Cotton MS Vitellius C.ix 61, fols. 64–128

Wealth at death lands worth £8 p.a.; brother owed him £50: will, PRO, PROB 11/62, fols. 393v–394r

Watson, David (1710–1756), translator, is believed to have been born in Brechin, Forfarshire, though nothing is known of his parents, and to have studied at St Leonard's College, St Andrews. However, though he is described as an MA of that college on the title-pages of his works, the university records make no mention of his having studied or graduated there. Similarly, although some sources claim that Watson was professor of philosophy in St Andrews, losing his chair in 1747 when the colleges of St Leonard's and St Salvator's were united, university records fail to support this claim. Another tradition attributes to Watson a character for dissipation.

In 1741 Watson published the *Works of Horace Translated into English Prose, with the Original Latin* in two volumes octavo. Later editions appeared in 1747 and 1750. Included in the work was Douglas's catalogue of nearly 500 editions of Horace, as well as Bentley's various readings. Although

the work proved popular, scholars protested against Watson's decision to translate Horace into prose:

> What classic friend his altered Flaccus knows,
> Disguised in Oldisworth's verse, and Watson's prose?
> (Nichols, *Lit. anecdotes*, 1.151)

Watson himself had no illusions about the literary merit of his version; he explains in his preface that the translation is intended as a teaching aid rather than a literary translation: 'I don't pretend to transfuse the spirit of Horace into our language; I only design this as a help to younger persons to bring them more easily to understand the original.' Watson clearly took an active interest in pedagogical procedures:

> I have differed a little from the common way of printing books of this kind; for, instead of putting the version on the right hand page, as is usually done, I have printed the text on the right hand side, and the version on the left, that the reader may cast his eye upon that first which he understands best.

Watson's combination of historical and linguistic annotation with long explanatory notes on each poem anticipates later school editions. Revised editions of the translation were prepared by Samuel Patrick (1760) and William Cracklet (1792). Watson also published in 1752 *A Clear and Compendious History of the Gods and Goddesses and their Contemporaries*. A second edition was published in 1753. Watson spent the later part of his life near London; he died destitute in 1756, near the capital, and was buried at the expense of the parish.   SARAH ANNES BROWN

Sources Irving, *Scots.* · Allibone, *Dict.* · Anderson, *Scot. nat.* · Nichols, *Lit. anecdotes* · DNB

Watson, David (1713?–1761), military surveyor and engineer, was the son of Thomas Watson of Muirhouse, Scotland. He had a brother, John, and a sister, Margaret. Appointed ensign in Colonel Middleton's regiment, later the 25th foot, on 10 July 1725, he was at Gibraltar in 1731 and on 22 June 1733 was promoted lieutenant in the same regiment, with which he served in Flanders from 1742 to 1744. Skilled in fortifications, in field engineering, and as a draughtsman, he was attached to the ordnance train from 1742, and from 10 March 1744 was on the establishment of the engineers as a sub-engineer. He saw action in Flanders in 1745, but was recalled to Britain that autumn to fight against the Jacobite uprising.

After the battle of Culloden, Watson was commissioned to undertake engineering works for the better surveillance and control of the highlanders. Roads and bridges were built and military installations repaired or constructed. Numerous of his plans for such military works survive. While he was in Scotland, according to William Roy, Watson, 'himself an engineer, active and indefatigable, a zealous promoter of every useful undertaking … first conceived the idea of making a map of the Highlands' (O'Donoghue, 9–10). The idea that the complete survey and mapping of an area was a prerequisite to its effective governance was gathering support throughout Europe, and the argument had added force to an officer of an army

David Watson (1713?–1761), by Andrea Soldi, 1756

of occupation in a remote area whose topography presented strategic difficulties and whose population was hostile. Want of such a map had already been felt during the uprising. Watson's proposal, made in 1747, gained immediate approval, and he was appointed to superintend its execution, with the title of deputy quartermaster-general in Scotland. The highlands were mapped from 1747 to 1752, initially with only William Roy as surveyor and Paul Sandby as draughtsman. It was then decided to extend the survey to southern Scotland, where surveying and mapping were undertaken from 1752 to 1755 by a larger staff, including David Dundas (whose mother was Watson's sister), who had charge of the eastern area. Watson supervised the whole.

The survey produced maps in various forms: the original protractions compiled from the surveyors' measurements and field notes, a fair copy of the highland map, and a reduction of the northern and southern sections combined. Each year the surveyors worked in the field in the summer and at the Ordnance office in Edinburgh Castle in the winter, and each year the work was taken by Watson to London for the king's inspection and approval. It was the first time that the mainland of Scotland had been comprehensively surveyed and it set the pattern for other British military surveys in the latter half of the eighteenth century, such as the survey of Canada and the St Lawrence by George Murray, that of the east coast of North America by Samuel Holland, that of Bengal by James Rennell, and that of Ireland by Charles Vallancey.

The Scottish survey is seen by many historians as the direct forebear of the Ordnance Survey, whose initiator was William Roy, Watson's closest colleague on the Scottish survey, to whom Watson left his mathematical instruments. It was described by Hugh Debbieg, a surveyor and later a general, as 'the greatest work of this sort ever performed by British Subjects and perhaps for the Representations of the Country not to be equaled in the World' (O'Donoghue, 4). Watson was responsible not only for the conception and execution of the survey, but also for its standards. He was no scientist, and the survey which he superintended was not in the same scientific league as, for example, Roy's subsequent geodetic work. The surveyors used simple instruments (chains and circumferentors) and the emphasis was on speed and economy: but within these constraints standards were, for military surveys of the time, high. Roy wrote that Watson had taught him 'that in Military Maps nothing should ever be represented at Guess or Random' and that 'the space of one quarter of a mile truly laid down is more useful than an Imperfect and loose Representation of an entire Country' (O'Donoghue, 32).

Work on the southern survey was interrupted by the outbreak of the Seven Years' War, and, without making a fair copy of the southern section, Watson hurried south, accompanied by Roy and Dundas, to make reconnaissance maps of the southern counties in preparation for an expected attack on the channel coast by the French. His plans for defence works to Milford Haven were not executed.

On 23 May 1756 Watson was appointed quartermaster-general of the forces for Scotland with the rank of colonel of foot. On 14 May, when the engineers were reorganized, he became a captain of Royal Engineers. On 21 April 1758 he was made colonel of the 63rd foot and was appointed quartermaster-general to the expedition which sailed from Spithead on 1 June 1758. He helped destroy munitions and naval supplies at Cancale Bay, near St Malo. After returning to England he joined the allied army on the Rhine, and served with distinction in 1758 and 1759. He was promoted major-general on 25 June 1759 (gazetted 15 September). On 31 July 1759 he reconnoitred the land between the allied camp and Minden Heath. He distinguished himself at the battle of Minden on 1 August and the following day was thanked in general orders for his bravery and able service.

Watson died in London on 7 November 1761, while holding the appointment of quartermaster-general to the forces, after a long illness; he was tended throughout by his housekeeper, Sophia Wilson, whose devotion he mentioned in his will. He never married, but in his will provided for his natural son, David Watson, to be apprenticed when old enough. He died still waiting for reimbursement by the government for the many expenses he had incurred on the military survey, whose costs, like those of almost all other surveys, had exceeded estimates. His achievement in Scotland ranks as one of the most remarkable of its day by international standards.

ELIZABETH BAIGENT

Sources Y. O'Donoghue, *William Roy* (1977) · R. A. Skelton, *The military survey of Scotland* (1967) · G. Whittington and A. J. S. Gibson, *The*

military survey of Scotland, 1747–1755: a critique (1986) • *DNB* • *GM*, 1st ser., 31 (1761), 539 • 'Dundas, Sir David (1735–1820)', *DNB* • F. W. Steer and others, *Dictionary of land surveyors and local map-makers of Great Britain and Ireland, 1530–1850*, ed. P. Eden, 2nd edn, ed. S. Bendall, 2 vols. (1997) • W. A. Seymour, ed., *A history of the Ordnance Survey* (1980) • W. Porter, *History of the corps of royal engineers*, 2 vols. (1889) • PRO, PROB 11/873 • *Corrections and additions to the Dictionary of National Biography*, Institute of Historical Research (1966) • d. cert.
Likenesses A. Soldi, oils, 1756, priv. coll. [*see illus.*] • P. Sandby, chalk drawing, Windsor Castle; repro. in O'Donoghue, *William Roy* • A. Soldi, oils, priv. coll.

Watson, David Meredith Seares (1886–1973), palaeontologist, was born on 18 June 1886 at Higher Broughton, near Salford, Lancashire, the only son of David Watson (*d.* 1899) and his wife, Mary Louise, *née* Seares (*d.* 1900). Following the death of his mother Watson's uncle Henry Seares became his guardian. Watson was educated at Manchester grammar school and at the University of Manchester, from which he graduated in 1907 with a first in geology, becoming Beyer fellow in 1908 and demonstrator in 1909. While still an undergraduate he published, together with staff member Marie Stopes, a major paper on the anatomy of plants of the Upper Carboniferous.

Following graduation Watson became increasingly interested in palaeontology. His first palaeontological paper was on a fish from the Scottish Devonian, and he retained an interest in early fish for the rest of his life. In 1911 he published on *Diademodon*, the start of another of the major interests of his life: mammal-like reptiles and the origin of mammals. *Diademodon* had been collected from the Upper Triassic Karoo beds of South Africa; and in 1911 Watson visited South Africa himself, made a large collection, and established the biostratigraphical zones of the Beaufort series (Upper Karoo). In 1914 he visited Australia, collected material of the two monotremes (platypus and echidna), and later published the embryology of the skull of *Ornithorhynchus* (the duck-billed platypus). He returned to England via Texas, collecting in the Lower Triassic Texas red beds.

Watson's great strength was that he saw fossils as the remains of animals which had once lived, not simply as specimens in museum collections. This insight manifested itself in a joint paper with E. H. Hankin, entitled 'On the flight of pterodactyls' (*Aeronautical Journal*, 72, 1914, 1–20). The authors analysed the Pterosauria as flying machines. Watson discussed the work with G. T. R. Hill, who had earlier designed an innovative tailless Westland aircraft; its name, 'Pterodactyl', may have come from Hill's reading of the earlier paper.

In 1911 Watson began his long connection with University College, London, becoming honorary lecturer in vertebrate palaeontology. He spent the First World War commissioned first in the Royal Naval Volunteer Reserve, then in the newly formed Royal Air Force; he worked on balloon fabrics. In 1917 he married Katharine Margarite (*d.* 1969), daughter of the Revd I. Parker. She was an embryologist, and later taught in the zoology department of University College, London. The couple had two daughters, Katherine Mary and the geologist Janet Vida *Watson (1923–1985).

Following the war, Watson returned to University College in 1921 as Jodrell professor of zoology and comparative anatomy. He built up the department, creating two sub-departments in what were then new fields: cytogenetics and comparative physiology. Although J. B. S. Haldane (1892–1964) held the independent Weldon chair of biometry, Watson gave the biometry department space in the zoology building, and members of biometry contributed much to the life of the zoology department. Watson rescued and encouraged W. G. Kühne, who, having been forced to leave Germany, was interned in the Isle of Man at the outbreak of the Second World War. Watson arranged his release, and gave him a post in the zoology department—first as a technician, then as a lecturer. Kühne discovered the rich *Morganucodon* material from south Wales, the first Jurassic mammal known from more than jaws and teeth.

Watson was considered a superb teacher. He gave all the vertebrate lectures himself, illustrating them profusely with slides and never using notes. In alternate years he gave an intercollegiate course in vertebrate palaeontology. Among those who attended this course were O. M. B. Bulman and W. F. Whittard, both of whom subsequently became notable palaeontologists and fellows of the Royal Society. He was a magnificent lecturer, arguably without an equal.

Watson spent the first part of the Second World War as secretary of the scientific subcommittee of the war cabinet, rejoining his department in exile in Bangor in 1942. He returned to London in January 1945, with the task of re-equipping a run-down and war-damaged department. Here he failed: he had the obsession that, given time, prices would fall to levels equal to those of 1930, and he could wait until then before buying new equipment. He was wrong, and the department suffered. He became seriously ill and had a lung removed, an operation which was a success. Watson retired in 1951 and was Alexander Agassiz visiting professor at Harvard in 1952–3. He then returned to University College and occupied a room in the zoology department, working with his assistant, Joyce Townend, until his final retirement in 1965.

Watson's research into mammalian and reptile origins, which lasted over forty-five years, led to the publication of a considerable number of significant papers on fossil Amphibia and fish. However, his largest and best-known paper on the latter (*PTRS*, ser. B, 228, 1937, 49–146) was unfortunate. It was on the subject of the Acathodian fishes, a group of early, primitive fish, most difficult to interpret as fossils. Watson gave in his paper clear descriptions and figures, from which it was clear that one of the bones of the first gill arch supported the jaws, the usual condition in fish. Unfortunately, Watson failed to recognize this, and hailed these fish as the most primitive jawed vertebrates, creating a new class for them, the Aphetohyoidea. This left the taxonomy of fish in confusion for a considerable time.

Watson had a deep knowledge of Chinese archaeology and a fine collection of Chinese artefacts, which he enjoyed showing and expounding on to visitors to his house. He was awarded the following medals: Lyell (1935), Darwin (1942), Linnean (1949), and Wollaston (1965). He became a fellow of the Royal Society in 1922, and gave the Croonian lecture to the society in 1924. He gave the Romanes lecture at Oxford in 1928. Watson became an honorary fellow of University College, London, in 1948, and received honorary degrees from the universities of Cape Town (1929), Manchester (1943), Aberdeen (1943), Reading (1948), and Witwatersrand (1948). He died in the King Edward VII Hospital, Easebourne, near Midhurst, Sussex, on 23 July 1973.   K. A. KERMACK

Sources F. R. Parrington and T. S. Weston, *Memoirs FRS*, 20 (1974), 483–504 · personal knowledge (2004) · *DNB* · d. cert.
Archives U. Cam., Museum of Zoology, drawings and papers · UCL, corresp. and papers
Likenesses photograph, 1946–50, UCL · W. Stoneman, photograph, 1949, NPG · photograph, repro. in *Memoirs FRS*
Wealth at death £30,289: probate, 27 Dec 1973, *CGPLA Eng. & Wales*

Watson, Sir David Milne-, first baronet (1869–1945), gas industrialist, was born in Edinburgh on 10 March 1869, the only son and elder child of David Watson, a prosperous iron manufacturer, and his wife, Anne Carnegie Milne. His father, who died while his children were in infancy, was born in 1809; thus the lives of father and son covered the remarkable span of 136 years. David Watson (he assumed the additional surname of Milne- in 1927) was educated at Merchiston Castle School and Edinburgh University, where he graduated MA and LLB. From 1894 to 1896 he was at Balliol College, Oxford, and after contesting South Eastern Essex (Tilbury) as a Liberal in 1895, he went to Marburg University. The following year he was called to the bar by the Middle Temple, but in 1897 he made the decisive step in his career by joining the Gas Light and Coke Company as assistant to the general manager; he was to become general manager in 1903, managing director in 1916, and governor and managing director in 1918, holding this position until his retirement in April 1945. In 1899 he married Olga Cecily (d. 1952), daughter of the Revd George Herbert, vicar of St Peter's, Vauxhall; they had two sons and a daughter. Their younger son was Sir Michael Milne-*Watson.

In 1897 the gas industry consisted of some 1500 separate units, many of them parochial in outlook and traditional in practice. Watson foresaw that with the possible loss of the lighting load to electricity the future of the gas industry lay in the distribution of heat and in the better commercial use of coke and other by-products. In order to meet the growing competition, he decided to pursue both the reorganization of his own company and the co-operation and unity of the gas industry as a whole. Largely on his initiative the British Commercial Gas Association was formed in 1911 and in 1916 the National Gas Council of Great Britain and Ireland, of which he was president from 1919 to 1943, to represent the industry on a national basis.

By the time he became governor in 1918 Watson had an intimate knowledge of every aspect of his company's business. Since its original charter in 1812 the area it served had grown, as a result of a series of amalgamations, to 125 square miles. Watson followed the policy of his predecessors and by 1933 the company served an area of 546 square miles, stretching from Windsor to Southend. He then decided that it had reached its optimal size for the personal management at which he was so skilled, and further co-operation with neighbouring companies was secured by means of a holding company, the South Eastern Gas Corporation.

Reconstruction after the war gave Watson the opportunity to reorganize the works by introducing modern, mechanized plant and to concentrate gas making as far as possible at the most efficient stations. His foresight and courage, and his confidence in the future of the industry, were shown by his readiness to back his staff in new developments, such as the coke ovens at Beckton and the ring main connecting the works. Although he had no scientific training, he realized the need for scientific research in industry and he established three laboratories to deal with the manufacture and utilization of gas and its by-products. At the same time the commercial and service departments were reorganized, with a new emphasis on sales of domestic appliances through company showrooms and dealers.

A paternal if at times autocratic governor, Milne-Watson promoted the welfare of his employees, many of whom he knew personally. He was chairman of the co-partnership committee, at which the employees' representatives could raise any question of interest to the company. He refused to serve on any boards except those directly connected with the Gas Light and Coke Company, so that he could devote his undivided attention to the company; in talking to employees he could say that, like them, he had only one interest—the company. The value of these good relations was shown by the absence of any labour trouble for many years. Under Milne-Watson, Gas Light and Coke became the biggest gas company in the world, and his single-minded devotion to its interests and his shrewd wisdom contributed much to its success.

For twenty-five years Milne-Watson was also a most effective and fearless champion of the interests of the gas industry as a whole. As chairman of the joint industrial council for the gas industry from 1919 to 1944 he did much to maintain good feeling between employers and trade union leaders. He was a member of the employers' committee during the Mond–Turner conference of 1928 to consider industrial relations and industrial reorganization. He was president of the British Employers' Confederation and on three occasions he represented the employers at the International Labour Conference at Geneva.

Milne-Watson was knighted in 1927 and created a baronet in 1937. He died at his home, Ashley Chase, Abbotsbury, Dorset, on 3 October 1945, and was survived by his wife. He was succeeded in the baronetcy by his elder son, David Ronald (b. 1904); his second son, Michael, became governor of the Gas Light and Coke Company in 1947 and chairman of the North Thames Gas Board in 1949.

HAROLD HARTLEY, *rev.* ROBERT BROWN

Sources S. Everard, *The history of the Gas Light and Coke Company, 1812–1949* (1949) · M. Falkus, 'Milne-Watson, Sir David', *DBB* · *The Times* (4 Oct 1945) · T. F. Williams, *A history of the gas industry* (1981) · private information (1959)
Likenesses H. Knight, portrait, *c*.1937, Gas Industry House · E. Schilsky, bronze bust, *c*.1940, Watson House, Fulham, London · J. Gunn, oils; in possession of family in 1951 · W. Orpen, portrait, North Thames Gas Board, London · bronze bust, North Thames Gas Board, London · oils (after J. Gunn), North Thames Gas Board, London
Wealth at death £84,740 9*s*. 9*d*.: probate, 8 Feb 1946, *CGPLA Eng. & Wales*

Watson [*née* Wall], **Edith Mary** (1888–1966), suffragist and police officer, was born on 6 November 1888, in the infirmary, Hackney union workhouse, the illegitimate daughter of Martha Wall, a domestic servant. With her mother and step-family, Edith lived in Marylebone, helping with her mother's sweated labour, sewing buttons on shirts. She was educated at Bell Street board school and Hampden Gurney School. Leaving school at fourteen she travelled to South Africa as a children's nurse, later becoming a Salvation Army captain. At this time she was attacked and almost raped by a fellow officer, a decisive factor in her views on sexual violence. Chestnut-haired and tall, she married Ernest John Watson (1883–1969), a Post Office sorter, on 1 February 1912; they were divorced about 1926. Their only child, Bernard John Watson, was born on 29 July 1919.

Returning to England in 1909, Edith Watson abandoned her religious beliefs, became interested in socialist politics, and joined the Social Democratic Federation. She soon became involved in the Edwardian suffrage campaign and in 1911 enlisted in the Women's Freedom League, a militant, non-violent suffrage society. She was imprisoned for chaining herself to the doors of Marylebone magistrates' court and wrote a column for the *Daily Herald*, 'Sketches in green, gold and white' (the Women's Freedom League colours) for a time. She was particularly concerned about the treatment of women in the judicial system and outraged at the ways in which victims of domestic violence, sexual harassment, and abuse were treated in court. She felt very strongly that the legal system was weighted in favour of the perpetrators of violence, rape, and incest, that crimes against women were punished more leniently than crimes involving property, and that the experiences of women and girls were discounted. For three years from 1912, using the Women's Freedom League journal, *The Vote*, she recorded details about cases of domestic violence, sexual abuse, and harassment and compared their sentences with those handed down for other crimes. Patchy and inconsistent as the methods were, the work was an early attempt to quantify and analyse intractable social problems, hitherto withheld from the public domain. This all added to the demand for a judicial system fairer to women and for women to serve throughout police and judicial systems.

When the First World War began in 1914, Edith Watson and her colleague Nina Boyle (Constance Antonina Boyle, suffrage campaigner and writer, later a founder member of the Save the Children Fund) started a women's police service under Women's Freedom League auspices. Adapting late-Victorian morality campaigners' use of volunteer patrols to rid the streets of prostitutes, Watson and Boyle aimed to protect women's interests and guarantee their rights of access to public space. Edith Watson was the first woman to wear a police uniform, designed by Boyle—'a useful blue serge Norfolk jacket with pockets, straw Panama hat with blue ribbon and white armlet' (*The Vote*, 10, 252, 21 Aug 1914, 286). As the war progressed and military activity disrupted civilian life, other groups, similar to the volunteers though with rather more repressive attitudes, emerged and amalgamated with the women's volunteer police. Generally unpopular with regular police services, the volunteers patrolled the streets assisting women and children. Other tasks included supervising servicemen's wives and ensuring curfews were obeyed, which led to disagreement about whether women police should be used to preserve women's rights or to service the state. Ultimately, despite the original aims, women police were mainly used by the authorities to control the behaviour of working-class females. By 1915 Boyle and Watson acknowledged that their vision of a feminist framework to policing was untenable and relinquished their claims on the women police volunteers, most of whom became part of the renamed Women's Police Service, which continued in an uneasy relationship with official police bodies. It was not until 1923 that women police were officially sanctioned and given powers of arrest.

Active in the Independent Labour Party for many years, Edith Watson was a branch secretary in Marylebone and an election agent, standing unsuccessfully at local council elections. She helped union efforts to improve working conditions in mental hospitals, disguising herself as a nurse to obtain evidence. For many years she campaigned for the Divorce Law Reform Union—a small but vocal pressure group. In the early 1930s Nina Boyle had investigated the cruelties inherent in the practice of female genital mutilation, demanding its abolition in countries under British rule. One of Edith Watson's last campaigns was to publicize and criticize the practice in Kenya in the 1950s. She died in a nursing home at 3 St Botolph's Road, Worthing, Sussex, on 25 March 1966. Born illegitimate and poor, the victim of sexual harassment, a divorced lone parent, Edith Watson voiced the experiences of such women, campaigning on their behalf for over forty years.

HILARY FRANCES

Sources E. Watson, unpublished autobiography, priv. coll. · private information (2004) · *The Vote*, 1–10 (1909–15) [esp. 10, 252 (21 Aug 1914), 286] · b. cert. · m. cert. · d. cert.
Archives Women's Library, London, articles
Likenesses photographs, 1914, Women's Library, London · C.? M. Horsfall, oils, 1925, Women's Library, London
Wealth at death £1787: probate, 27 Sept 1966, *CGPLA Eng. & Wales*

Watson, Elizabeth Catherine (1870–1928). *See under* Carmichael, Alexander (1832–1912).

Watson, Foster (1860–1929), educationist, was born at 4 Sincil Banks, Lincoln, on 27 June 1860, the third in the family of five sons of Thomas Watson of Lincoln, who was in the agricultural machinery business, and his wife, Ann, daughter of Thomas Booth, worsted stuff manufacturer, of Little Horton, Bradford, Yorkshire. He was educated at Lincoln grammar school and at Owens College, Manchester, where he took first-class honours in English in 1879 and obtained the MA (London) degree in 1881. At Manchester he came under the influence of Adolphus William Ward and the school of historical research which Ward founded there.

After graduating, Watson taught in a preparatory school; then, from 1885 to 1891, he was second master at the Cowper Street Middle Class School (afterwards known as the Central Foundation School, Finsbury, London). During this period he became involved in the Teachers' Guild, which aimed to bring all the branches of the profession together to promote the systematic study of education as well as more narrowly professional objectives such as pensions and teachers' registration. In 1894 he was appointed head of the day training department and lecturer on education at the University College of Wales, Aberystwyth, and in 1895 was promoted to professor. He established courses leading to the Cambridge teachers' diploma, and established education as a degree-level subject in the University of Wales in 1905, with honours-level courses in 1911. In 1912 he was awarded a DLitt by the University of London, the first time that this degree was awarded for scholarship in the field of education.

Watson's interests ranged over education, philosophy, and literature. His main contributions were in the field of educational history, and especially the period 1500–1600 in England. His main work was *The English Grammar Schools to 1660: their Curriculum and Practice* (1908), a subject with contemporary application, as the 1902 Education Act established the grammar school pattern as the norm for secondary schools in England, though Watson did not promote this type of school uncritically. This was followed by *The Beginnings of the Teaching of Modern Subjects in England* (1909), again concerned with the early modern period, but with relevance to the development in the early twentieth century of new specialist subject areas in the school curriculum. For many years he collected material (much of which he published in journals and magazines between 1892 and 1909) for a projected work on the 'English educational renascence', a history of English education in the time of the Commonwealth.

Watson made a special study of the life and work of Juan Luis Vives, the friend and counsellor of Erasmus and More, presenting Vives as a pioneer of the inductive method. He published *Vives on Education: a Translation of the De tradendis disciplinis* (1912), *Vives and the Renascence Education of Women* (1912), and many articles on the subject in English, Spanish, Catalan, and Italian magazines; he also lectured at Barcelona and Valencia, and presented a tablet to Corpus Christi College, Oxford, in 1925 in memory of Vives's residence there from 1523 to 1525.

Watson's work on the history of education placed individual teachers and their ideas at the centre of the historical process. He wished to give the profession a sense of its historical perspective (as he argued in 'The study of the

history of education', *Contemporary Review*, 105, 1914, reprinted in P. Gordon and R. Szreter, *History of Education: the Making of a Discipline*, 1989), and his prolific contributions to dictionaries and encyclopaedias were intended to build up a body of precedent for teachers to draw upon. He wrote the chapter 'Scholars and scholarship' in volume seven of the *Cambridge History of English Literature* and a number of educational biographies in the *Dictionary of National Biography*; he contributed the article on Wales to F. E. Buisson's *Nouveau dictionnaire de pédagogie* and, as departmental editor, some 150 articles to the *Cyclopaedia of Education* (1911–13), edited by Paul Monroe of Teachers College, Columbia University.

Watson retired from his chair at Aberystwyth in 1913 to concentrate on research, though he was professor emeritus and special lecturer until his death, and professor of rhetoric at Gresham College, London, from 1915 to 1929. He first planned a study of eighteenth-century education in collaboration with Amy Kimpster, who had taken a first in English at Somerville College, Oxford, and after various teaching and lecturing posts was mistress of method at Aberystwyth from 1904 to 1914. They married on 4 April 1914; she was the daughter of Samuel Smith Kimpster of Masborough, Yorkshire. Her death in 1918 prevented the completion of the work. He also embarked on a more ambitious collaborative project, to which he recruited 900 contributors, *The Encyclopaedia and Dictionary of Education*, which appeared in four volumes (1921–2), covering biographies of teachers, and the history of educational practice and educational opinion. Had he lived long enough it is probable that he would have attempted to construct a theory of education based on the underlying reasons for the success of great teachers, as well as on the evidence, positive and negative, provided by the history of education. Those who heard him lecture recalled the vigour and conviction of his opinions and the dynamic enthusiasm of his delivery.

Watson married second on 17 December 1925 Nancy Agnes Lydia, eldest daughter of Llewelyn Wynne Roberts, of Buxton. There were no children from his marriages. He was a member of several learned societies at home and abroad, and in recognition of his work on the history of education received the honorary DLitt degree from the University of Wales (1922). He died at his home, the Red House, Green Street, Green, near Farnborough, Kent, on 13 February 1929, and was survived by his second wife.

C. R. CHAPPLE, rev. M. C. CURTHOYS

Sources W. H. G. Armytage, 'Foster Watson, 1860–1929', *British Journal of Educational Studies*, 10 (1961–2), 5–18 • personal knowledge (1937) • private information (1937) • F. Watson, *List of research and literary work in the subject of education* (1913) • *CGPLA Eng. & Wales* (1929) • b. cert. • m. certs.
Wealth at death £6257 14s. 1d.: probate, 23 May 1929, *CGPLA Eng. & Wales*

Watson, Sir Francis John Bagott (1907–1992), art historian and museum curator, was born on 24 August 1907 at St James Road, Dudley, Worcestershire, the son of Hugh Watson, headmaster of Dudley grammar school, and his wife, Ellen Marian Bagott. He was educated at his father's school, and from 1921 to 1926 at Shrewsbury School, before going on to St John's College, Cambridge, whence he graduated in 1929 with a second-class degree in mathematics (part one) and English (part two). His interests at Cambridge were literary rather than artistic, and at first he worked for various publishing firms, including Brentano's (1929–30)—where he published Anita Loos's *Gentlemen Prefer Blondes*—and Harold Shaylor (1930–33). In 1934 he joined the recently established Courtauld Institute of Art, as registrar, and there he attended lectures not as a student but as a technician operating the slide-projector. During this period his interest in art history grew, not least through his friendships with art historians, in particular with Charles Bell, keeper of fine art at the Ashmolean Museum, Oxford, until 1930. Bell taught him to value the skills of connoisseurship, learning about art objects through their close study and handling in museums and salerooms.

In 1937 James Mann brought Watson with him from the Courtauld to be his assistant at the Wallace Collection, in London, where he had been made director. Watson spent the next thirty-seven years at the Wallace. Within ten days of his appointment he was entrusted with writing the catalogue of furniture. His study of the artist Thomas Patch (*Walpole Society*, vol. 28) appeared in 1939–40 but his career was interrupted by the Second World War, during which he was seconded to the Admiralty. On 11 October 1941 he married Mary Rosalie Gray ('Jane') (1904–1969), daughter of George Strong, an architect, of Bognor. They had no children, and Mrs Watson channelled much energy towards the welfare of cats (of which at one time she had eighty-seven).

In 1945 Watson returned to the Wallace Collection, and published his furniture catalogue in 1956 to wide acclaim. It set new standards for the study and cataloguing of furniture and greatly enhanced the status of furniture studies. In 1947 he was appointed deputy surveyor of the king's (from 1952 the queen's) works of art. He continued to take a close interest in French and Venetian eighteenth-century painting, publishing monographs on Canaletto (1949; 2nd edn, 1954), Tiepolo (1966), and Fragonard (1967), and many articles and reviews. However, he became known principally for numerous publications on eighteenth-century decorative arts. His writing was distinguished by its elegant concision and breadth of vision, encompassing extensive knowledge of the literature and history of the period and his awareness of the importance of economic and social history to the study of the arts. He felt a profound connection with the period that he studied, commenting that through a complicated chain of acquaintance and descent he was 'seven kisses from Louis XIV' (private information). His principal publication after the Wallace Collection catalogue was the five-volume catalogue of the Wrightsman collection (1966–73), which he edited and mostly wrote.

In 1963 Watson succeeded Sir James Mann as director of the Wallace Collection and also as surveyor of the queen's works of art. He was knighted in 1973 and retired from both posts in 1974, continuing however to serve the Royal

Collection as adviser for works of art until his death. Among his many distinctions and offices he was created ufficiale del ordine al merito della republica Italiana in 1961 and elected fellow of the British Academy in 1969; he was Slade professor of fine art at Oxford in 1969–70, a trustee of the Whitechapel Art Gallery (1949–74), chairman of the Furniture History Society (1966–74), and chairman of the Walpole Society (1970–76).

Watson, who sought never to take himself too seriously and insisted that 'museums exist to give pleasure', treated his directorship of the Wallace Collection as an agreeable sinecure rather than as a heavy burden. He spent much of his time on activities outside the museum, sitting on exhibition committees, adding to his own collection, and advising private collectors, in particular Mr and Mrs Charles Wrightsman, whose great collection (now largely in the Metropolitan Museum of Art, New York) he was instrumental in forming. However, he also did much to improve the care of the works of art in his charge, initiating the introduction of air-conditioning throughout the Wallace Collection and establishing specialist workshops for the conservation of furniture and arms and armour in the Royal Collection.

Watson was an intensely sociable man who once commented that 'I am inclined to laugh a lot, I think' ('Sir Francis Watson'). He was 'of medium height and slender build, his most impressive feature is the bigness of his head ... In appearance he suggests a somewhat startled cherub, with a halo of frizzled, graying hair' (Walker). He retired to a manor house in Wiltshire, the attic of which was converted into a Buddhist shrine by Ch'eng Huan, whom he and his wife had befriended when he was a young Chinese student and whom Watson adopted as his son, following his wife's death in 1969. In his retirement Watson fully indulged his passions for social life, collecting, adventurous travel, and food, and was a frequent guest at the J. Paul Getty Museum in California, where he produced one of his final publications, the privately circulated 'Easy dinners for bachelors with Sir Francis Watson, Saturday May 21 1983'. He died on 27 September 1992 at Longbridge Deverill House, Wiltshire, and was survived by Ch'eng Huan.   JEREMY WARREN

Sources G. de Bellaigue, 'Francis John Bagott Watson', *PBA*, 84 (1994), 565–77 · Wallace Collection, Watson Archive · *Daily Telegraph* (29 Sept 1992) · *The Times* (29 Sept 1992) · *The Guardian* (2 Oct 1992) · *The Independent* (5 Oct 1992) · 'Sir Francis Watson, KCVO', *Giornale dell'Arte* (Nov 1987) [interview with Diana Scarisbrick] · J. Howard, 'Looking after the crockery ... Sir Francis Watson's last interview', *Apollo*, 137 (1993), 3–5 · J. Walker, *Self-portrait with donors: confessions of an art collector* (Boston, 1974), 270–77 · G. de Bellaigue, *Burlington Magazine*, 134 (1992), 811 · *WW* (1992) · private information (2004) [R. Savill] · b. cert. · m. cert. · d. cert.
Archives Wallace Collection, London, archive of art-historical writings, research materials and other biographical material
Likenesses L. Douglas-Menzies, bromide print, 1988, NPG · photographs, Wallace Collection
Wealth at death under £125,000: probate, 8 Dec 1992, *CGPLA Eng. & Wales*

Watson, George (*bap.* 1723, *d.* 1773), Church of England clergyman and classical scholar, was baptized at St Anne's, Soho, Westminster, on 15 March 1723, the son of

Humphrey Watson, a gentleman, and his wife, Anne. He matriculated from University College, Oxford, on 14 March 1740, graduating BA in 1743 and proceeding MA in 1746. He was elected to a scholarship on the Bennet foundation on 13 December 1744, and was chosen on 27 October 1747 for a fellowship on the same foundation. Although instinctively shy and retiring, Watson soon became an influential figure in University College. Not only was he an outstanding classical scholar, noted for his taste and judgement in poetry and oratory, but his appearance was elegant and striking, and his gentle nature commanded affection and respect. His acts of charity were proverbial, and it was said that all the beggars in Oxford knew the way to his rooms.

According to his most famous pupil, George Horne, afterwards bishop of Norwich, Watson was 'as complete a scholar in the whole circle of learning, as great a divine, as good a man, and as polite a gentleman, as the present age can boast of' (Jones, 1795, 28). He was a noted teacher, and it was widely believed that Horne's influential *A Commentary on the Book of Psalms* (1776) drew its inspiration from a sermon preached by Watson in 1749 on a text from Psalm 19 on 'Christ the Light of the World'. In this work and elsewhere Watson was clearly indebted to the theological opinions of John Hutchinson (1674–1737), whose ideas he transmitted to a small but important group of pupils. Watson was a high-churchman, who shared the concerns of that party. In a sermon, 'A seasonable admonition to the Church of England', preached at Oxford on 29 May 1751, he reaffirmed the lesson of the civil war, that 'Independency, … the devil's crime, … can never carry man to heaven', while in another sermon, 'Aaron's intercession and Korah's rebellion considered' (1756), he drew upon arguments from patristic writers and from the nonjuring bishop George Hickes to urge the dissenters to repent of their schism and return to regular episcopalian communion. Watson's concern about the danger of Arian influence within the Church of England, as manifested by the tendency of proposals for liturgical revision and the failure to take immediate disciplinary action against Robert Clayton, bishop of Clogher, for his heretical work *An Essay on Spirit* (1751), was revealed in a further sermon, 'The doctrine of the ever blessed Trinity proved' (1756). When this was attacked in the *Monthly Review*, Watson responded with a pamphlet urging the bishops again 'to preserve from sacrilegious invasion and transmit to posterity this sacred depositum which we have received of our fathers' (Watson, 1758, 20).

At about this time Watson resigned his fellowship, and thereafter lived in obscurity until his death (apparently unmarried) on 16 April 1773. In 1860 his four sermons were reprinted, with a preface by the writer John Matthew Gutch, under the title *Watson redivivus*; subscribers to this volume included W. E. Gladstone.   RICHARD SHARP

Sources J. M. Gutch, ed., *Watson redivivus* (1860) • G. Watson, *A letter from the author of a late discourse on the XVIIIth chapter of Genesis, to the Monthly Reviewers …* (1758) • *Memoirs of the life, studies and writings of … George Horne*, ed. W. Jones (1795), 25–30 • Foster, *Alum. Oxon.* • *GM*, 1st ser., 43 (1773), 203 • IGI

Watson, George (1767–1837), portrait painter, was the son of John Watson of Over Mains, a property in the parish of Eccles, Berwickshire, which lies between Duns and the River Tweed, and Frances Veitch of Elliock. In the early 1780s he trained as an artist in Edinburgh, with the obscure James Cumming and then with Alexander Nasmyth. He appears to have spent the years 1785 to 1788 in London, where he is said to have had training from Sir Joshua Reynolds. He established himself as a portrait painter in Edinburgh in 1788, when he lived in the Netherbow. This coincides roughly with the beginning of Raeburn's career, and Watson was to be one of his few viable rivals. Raeburn, however, seems to have taken his competition more seriously than was perhaps necessary. Subsequently Watson had addresses at the Royal Exchange (opposite the church of St Giles in the High Street), at St James's Square at the eastern end of the New Town of Edinburgh, and at 10 Forth Street, a modest but elegant street nearby, where he is recorded from 1809 until his death.

Shortly after returning from London, Watson married Rebecca, daughter of Jean Robertson and William *Smellie (1740–1795), printer of the first edition of the *Encyclopaedia Britannica* and of the Edinburgh edition of Burns's poems. Watson painted a rather dour portrait of Smellie in the early 1790s which does not reveal any of the wit and bawdry that Burns found in the man. About the same time he painted a characterful portrait of Smellie's business partner, the engraver Andrew Bell (both Scot. NPG). There is a portrait of Rebecca by Watson, unusually lit, painted quite late in life as a companion to a self-portrait (both NG Scot.).

Watson was instrumental in founding an exhibiting body, the Society of Artists of Edinburgh, of which he was made president and which held its first exhibition in 1808 in hired premises. Subsequently, from 1809 to 1813, annual exhibitions were held by the society in Raeburn's splendid premises in York Place. In the penultimate year of this series of exhibitions Raeburn took exception to the prominence Watson had given his own work and resigned from the society. He stated quite frankly that he could not afford to give precedence to anyone. Since the society had to retain Raeburn's support, Watson was forced to resign as president—to be succeeded the following year by Raeburn!

Still a force among the Edinburgh artists who were growing ever more aware of the need to organize, Watson was elected president of a new grouping, the Scottish Academy of Art, founded in 1826 on the same principles as the Royal Academy in London. This body was in essence a breakaway group from the government-sponsored Institution for the Encouragement of the Fine Arts, and precursor of the Royal Scottish Academy. Watson remained president until his death, the year before the academy received its royal charter.

Watson spent two further periods in London during the later part of his career. The first was in 1811 when he apologized to the committee of the Society of Artists for failing to exhibit with them: 'I have been wholly employed in painting Portraits since I came to London' (minutes of the committee of the Society of Artists of Edinburgh, 23 May 1811, Royal Scottish Academy library). In fact a painting was included in the 1811 exhibition, a very ambitious group portrait, *Captain William Johnstone Hope, his wife and two daughters in a jolly boat, the four sons as sailors* (priv. coll.). The second visit was in 1815 when he painted a rather impressive portrait of the president of the Royal Academy, Benjamin West (NG Scot.), which was exhibited at the academy the following year. Watson exhibited quite regularly in London, at both the British Institution and the Royal Academy. In 1819 he showed at the latter a history painting, *Columbus Encouraging his Desponding Followers*. His work was clearly not entirely portraiture: titles of other recorded subject pictures include *Last Will and Testament* and *The Woodcutter*.

Despite his training and his greater familiarity with the London scene, it was always of Raeburn's work that Watson was most conscious. His forms have simpler planes than Raeburn's and a more pronounced linearity, while his draughtsmanship with the brush is far inferior. Nevertheless, their works have quite often been confused. He was obviously deeply intrigued by Raeburn's *contre jour* experiments of the early 1790s, and he carried out similar experiments himself which produced interesting, and original, variations, though, curiously, this happened more than two decades later. A prime example is the picture called *A Young Female Artist* of 1813, which, interestingly, the marquess of Stafford bought for the Bridgewater House collection (priv. coll.). The source of light is so placed that the right half of the girl's face, tilted backwards, is brightly lit from her right side, while the left half is in half-shadow. Surprisingly, however, the darkest shadow forms a narrow central axis from the middle of the forehead, down through the bridge of the nose and the centre of the lips to the tip of the chin. This deep shadow appears to be formed by a second light source above the girl's head which is diverted by the brim of her hat. There are a number of portraits which are variations on this perceptual theme, including the portrait known as *Master Hay* (Auckland City Art Gallery, New Zealand), once regarded as a Raeburn, and a full-length, *Mary Clarke, Wife of Captain William Colin Clarke*, which contains an unusual mirrored reflection of the subject's head (priv. coll.). One of the most complex of this type of painting is a subject picture of a young couple playing chess (which is possibly a double portrait), called *A Chess Party* (ex Sothebys, 19 July 1978, lot 27). Paintings such as these give a distinctive artistic identity to Watson.

On his death in Edinburgh on 24 August 1837 Watson was survived by his wife, Rebecca, and five children, one of whom, William Smellie Watson, also became a portrait painter.   DUNCAN THOMSON

Sources *DNB* · Scottish artists' files, Scot. NPG, section 4 · W. D. McKay and F. Rinder, *The Royal Scottish Academy, 1826–1916* (1917) · D. Irwin and F. Irwin, *Scottish painters at home and abroad, 1700–1900* (1975) · L. R. Timperley, ed., *A directory of landownership in Scotland, c.1770*, Scottish RS, new ser., 5 (1976), 81 · G. Harvey, *Notes of the early history of the Royal Scottish Academy* (1873)

Archives Royal Scot. Acad., minutes of the committee of the Society of Artists of Edinburgh

Likenesses G. Watson, self-portrait, oils, *c*.1816, Scot. NPG · G. Watson, self-portrait, oils, *c*.1818, NG Scot.

Watson, George Lennox (1851–1904), naval architect, born at Glasgow on 30 October 1851, was the eldest son of Thomas Watson MD and his wife, Ellen, daughter of Timothy Burstall, an engineer. Educated at the high school and then at the collegiate school, Glasgow, he was apprenticed in 1867 to Robert Napier & Sons, shipbuilders and marine engineers, of Govan. In 1871 he found employment with A. and J. Inglis, shipbuilders, of Pointhouse, near Glasgow, making with a member of the firm experiments in yacht designing, and in 1872 he started business in Glasgow as a naval architect. Exact methods of yacht modelling were only then being introduced, and Watson was the first to apply to the designing of yachts the laws governing the resistance of bodies moving in water which William John Macquorn Rankine and William Froude had formulated. During a career of over thirty years he designed many of the most successful yachts that sailed in British waters.

Early successes were: the 5 ton cutter *Clotilde* (1873), which beat Fife's *Pearl*; the 10 ton cutter *Madge* (1875), which had great success in American waters; the *Vril* (1876); the 68 ton cutter *Marjorie* (1883); and the *Vanduara* (1880), which was the fastest vessel of her class, beating the prince of Wales's *Formosa* on several occasions. When Dixon Kemp's new rule of measurement for racing in 1887 required a broader and lighter vessel, Watson was equally successful. The *Yarana* (1888), the *Creole* (1890), and the *Queen Mab* (1892) were notable prizewinners, and a record success was achieved by the *Britannia*, which Watson built for the prince of Wales in 1893. Between 1893 and 1897 it won 147 prizes, 122 of them first prizes, out of 219 starts, the total value of the prizes amounting to £9973. The *Bona* (1900), the *Kariad* (1900, first named the *Distant Shore*), and the *Sybarita* (1901) were large vessels notable for their seaworthiness; a race between the two latter in the Clyde in 1901 during a storm, which compelled the accompanying steam yachts to put back, was one of the most remarkable yachting contests on record.

Between 1887 and 1901 Watson was prominently before the public as the designer of the British challenger's yacht in the contest in American waters between Great Britain and America. Watson designed J. Bell & Brothers' *Thistle* (1887), Lord Dunraven's *Valkyrie II* (1893) and *Valkyrie III* (1895), and Sir Thomas Lipton's *Shamrock II* (1901). Though they failed to regain the cup they were yachts of the highest class. The American yachts that defeated them had little success when they visited British waters.

Watson, in addition to racing craft, also designed passenger, cargo, and mail steamers, and many of the largest steam yachts of the day. Among the last were the *Lysistrata* (2089 tons), built for James Gordon Bennett; the *Atmah* (1746 tons), for Baron Edmond de Rothschild; the *Alberta* (1322 tons), for the king of the Belgians; the *Zarnitza* (1086 tons), for the tsar; and other yachts built for foreign owners. He designed a total of over 450 vessels.

Watson contributed to *Yachting* (2 vols., 1895, Badminton Library) and published in 1881 a series of lectures, *Progress in Yachting and Yacht Building*, delivered at the Glasgow Naval and Marine Engineering Exhibition (1880–81). In 1882 he was elected a member of the Institution of Naval Architects, before which he read a paper on a new form of steering gear. He was also for nearly twenty years consulting naval architect to the National Lifeboat Institution.

Watson married, in 1903, Marie (or Mary) Alice, the daughter of Edward Lovibond of Greenwich: they had no children. He died at his home at 9 High Burgh Terrace, Dowan Hill, Glasgow, on 12 November 1904; his wife survived him.   S. E. FRYER, *rev.* ANDREW LAMBERT

Sources K. C. Barnaby, *The Institution of Naval Architects* (1960) · *The Times* (14 Nov 1904) · *Transactions of the Institution of Naval Architects*, 47 (1905) · A. E. T. Watson, *King Edward VII as a sportsman* (1911) · *WWW, 1897–1915* · *CGPLA Eng. & Wales* (1905)
Wealth at death no value given: sealed in London, 8 Feb 1905, *CGPLA Eng. & Wales*

Watson, George Neville (1886–1965), mathematician, was born at Westward Ho!, Devon, on 31 January 1886, the elder child and only son of George Wentworth Watson, a schoolmaster and later an army coach, and his wife, Mary Justina, daughter of the Revd George Sandhorn Griffith, rector of Ardley, Oxfordshire. His father was an eminent genealogist who later took a large part in preparing both editions of Vicary Gibbs's *The Complete Peerage*. Watson was educated at St Paul's School, at that time a distinguished nursery of senior wranglers and Smith's prizemen. Among his contemporaries was the mathematician J. E. Littlewood. Watson went up to Trinity College, Cambridge, as an entrance scholar in 1904 and was senior wrangler in 1907. In 1908 he was placed in the second division of the first class of the mathematical tripos. The younger fellows of Trinity at this time included three very distinguished workers in complex variable theory, the field in which Watson was to specialize: Edmund T. Whittaker, E. W. Barnes, and G. H. Hardy. Although Whittaker left in 1906 and Barnes's interests were turning away from mathematics, their influence was very evident in Watson's early papers, which gained him a Smith's prize in 1909 and a Trinity fellowship in 1910. He left Cambridge in 1914 to become assistant lecturer at University College, London.

The four years which Watson spent in London were very fruitful. It is often the case in problems of mathematical physics that a solution can be obtained in the form of an infinite series or an integral but comparison with observation is frustrated because the solution does not lend itself to numerical computation. Watson's most valuable gift was his ability to bridge this gap. A striking example occurred in 1918, when he became involved in a discussion among applied mathematicians of the best way to explain the propagation of radio waves. The standard model, a Hertzian oscillator in an infinite dielectric surrounding a partially conducting sphere, yielded solutions, but not in a form which could be compared with observation. Although Watson was not much interested in problems of physics he was generous in helping those who

George Neville Watson (1886–1965), by James Russell & Sons

were, and when asked to bring his unique expertise to bear on the problem, he was able to show that the model was inadequate since it predicted an attenuation of the radio signal far more rapid than was observed. He was then asked to re-examine the question on the hypothesis that there was a conducting layer in the upper atmosphere as suggested by Oliver Heaviside. He showed that this did, indeed, account for the observations, provided that the layer was at a height of 100 km and of a certain conductivity.

Watson left London in 1918 to become Mason professor of pure mathematics in the University of Birmingham and continued in this post until his retirement in 1951. Though a man of enormous industry, he was a solitary worker and did not found a research school. Much of his time in the early years was devoted to writing an immense treatise on Bessel functions (1922), of unparalleled quality. He had already, while in London, collaborated with his old teacher, Whittaker, in publishing in 1915 a second, and greatly enlarged, edition of the latter's *A Course of Modern Analysis* (1902), the first English work on real- and complex-variable theory addressed to undergraduates. Further revised editions followed in 1920 and 1927; the fourth and standard edition was still being reprinted as late as 1980.

In 1925 Watson married Elfrida Gwenfil, daughter of Thomas Lane, a farmer of Holbeach, Lincolnshire. They had one son. For Watson the decade 1929–39 was largely devoted to elucidating the work of the remarkable, almost self-taught, mathematician Srinivasa Ramanujan, who had been in England in 1914 and died in his native

India in 1920. Ramanujan rarely gave proofs of his statements and some were not correct. Watson wrote some twenty-five papers connected with his work, and copied out the whole of his notebooks in beautiful handwriting. These are now in the Mathematical Institute, Oxford.

Watson was an untiring worker on behalf of the London Mathematical Society, above all as editor of its *Proceedings*. He was its president in 1932–3 and was awarded the De Morgan medal in 1947. He was elected FRS in 1919 and received the Sylvester medal in 1946. He was an honorary FRSE and received honorary degrees from Edinburgh and Dublin. Birmingham University chose the name Watson Building for a new building containing, among others, the mathematics departments. In appearance he was dark, and of spare build. Though mathematics was his absorbing interest he was also expert in his private hobbies of railway history and postage stamps. He was a devoted son of Trinity and prints of the college and its members covered his walls. He died at home, 46 Warwick New Road, Leamington Spa, on 2 February 1965, survived by his wife.   J. M. WHITTAKER, *rev.* IAN N. SNEDDON

Sources J. M. Whittaker, *Memoirs FRS*, 12 (1966), 521–30 · *Journal of the London Mathematical Society*, 1st ser., 41 (1966), 551–65 · personal knowledge (1981) · private information (2004) · *CGPLA Eng. & Wales* (1965)

Archives U. Birm. L., papers

Likenesses J. Russell & Sons, photograph, RS [*see illus.*]

Wealth at death £7525 0s. 0d.: probate, 1965, *CGPLA Eng. & Wales*

Watson, Henry (*bap.* 1738, *d.* 1786), army officer, was born in Holbeach, Lincolnshire, and baptized there on 18 January 1738, the second and last child, and only son, of John Watson (*d.* 1768), farmer and grazier, and his wife, Mary. He attended Birks's school at Gosberton, near Spalding, where he showed early promise in mathematics. This was brought to the notice of Thomas Whichcot of Harpeswell, one of the members of parliament for Lincolnshire, through whose good offices he was nominated to the Royal Military Academy, Woolwich. He was commissioned ensign in the 52nd foot, Abercromby's regiment, on 27 December 1755, and on 25 September 1757 was transferred as lieutenant to the 50th foot, Studholm Hodgson's regiment.

As early as 1753 Watson contributed mathematical papers to the *Ladies' Diary*, edited by Professor Thomas Simpson, who was both his instructor at the Royal Military Academy and an intimate friend. Simpson had such a high opinion of Watson's abilities that on his death in 1760 he left his unfinished mathematical treatises to him, with a request that he would revise them for publication, making any alterations or additions which he might consider desirable. Although Watson subsequently behaved generously to Simpson's widow, he failed to carry out the publication of his papers, and was consequently attacked by Charles Hutton in a biography of Simpson prefixed to a new edition of *Select Exercises* (1792).

Watson was commissioned sub-engineer and lieutenant on 17 March 1759. In 1761 he went in the expedition to Belle Île under Commodore Keppel and General Hodgson. He was present at the siege and the capitulation on 7 June.

On 23 February 1762 he was transferred to the 97th foot, James Forrester's regiment, and in March went as sub-engineer with the expedition under Admiral Sir George Pocock and the earl of Albemarle to Havana. He served in the siege with some distinction, and following the capitulation on 14 August 1762 Watson was thanked by the commander of the forces, and afterwards by the king. On 4 February 1763 he was promoted to a company in the 104th foot. In May 1764, on Lord Clive's recommendation, he was appointed field engineer with the rank of captain in the East India Company's military service and embarked for Bengal, arriving in Calcutta, after a prolonged passage, in 1765.

Watson was engaged on improving the fortifications of Fort William and in military construction work at Berhampore and Dinapore. But he had vision and drive which, combined with entrepreneurial and financial skills, carried him beyond the daily round. As early as 1768 he wrote to his father that he was 'in very Independent Circumstances' and that his remittance next season would be at least £10,000 (H. Watson to J. Watson, 26 Nov 1768, BL OIOC, MS Eur. D759). He was a moving spirit in a proposal to construct docks and shipbuilding facilities in Calcutta which were to be handed over to the East India Company on completion on the refund of their cost plus a gratuity. The Calcutta council provided the land, and the company approved the scheme in 1770. Refused leave of absence to return to England, Watson achieved his objective by resignation in March 1772. While in England he was reinstated in the company's military service, and in March 1776 was appointed chief engineer of Bengal, with the rank of lieutenant-colonel. He translated a work by the Swiss mathematician Leonhard Euler; his translation was published in 1776 as *A Compleat Theory of the Construction and Properties of Vessels*. Some time during his sojourn Watson fathered an illegitimate daughter, Susan, whom he placed in the care of a Mrs Richardson of Holbeach.

Watson was back in Calcutta by the end of October 1777. There, on 28 June 1780, he married Maria Theresa Kearnan (*d.* 1824), the daughter of Thomas Kearnan of the City of London. Although not close, Watson was well disposed towards Philip Francis, principal adversary of Hastings in the Bengal council after the death of General Clavering. He understood Francis's aspirations to be governor-general and his frustration at Hastings's tenacity of office. Watson asked Francis to secure him a building contract, and acted as second to Francis in his duel with Hastings on 17 August 1780. Progress on the docks was hampered by lawsuits over land grants and land ownership, although in 1783 the Bengal council reported that it was considering final proposals for their completion and a claim on the East India Company for losses of £200,000. Watson built two ships in Calcutta which were sailed to China with opium. He was an advocate of trade with the eastern and northern provinces of China as a way of avoiding the restrictions imposed by the *hong* merchants at Canton (Guangzhou). In 1784 he won the support of the governor-general for the establishment of a mathematical school in Fort William for engineer officers.

Deteriorating health obliged Watson to resign, and he sailed for England with his wife in 1786, only to die of 'flux and a bilious complaint' (*European Magazine and London Review*, 499) on 17 September after landing at Dover, where he was buried five days later at St Mary's Church. Having failed to amend a will made in April 1777 to take account of his marriage, Watson's fortune, reputedly some £300,000, went to his illegitimate daughter, who married the fourth Lord Carbery in 1792. His widow returned to India in straitened circumstances. In 1793 she married Alexander Nowell of the Bengal army, which he quitted to make a fortune in indigo.   R. H. VETCH, *rev.* T. H. BOWYER

Sources BL OIOC, MS Eur. D759 · *Bengal Past and Present*, 8–29 (1914–25) · K. K. Datta and others, eds., *Fort William–India House correspondence*, 4–10 (1962–72) · *GM*, 1st ser., 56 (1786), 996–8 · 'Sketch of the life and character of the late Colonel Henry Watson', *European Magazine and London Review*, 12 (1787), 497–9 · *N&Q*, 1 (1849–50), 133 · *Memoirs of William Hickey*, ed. A. Spencer, 2–3 (1918–23) · V. C. P. Hodson, *List of officers of the Bengal army, 1758–1834*, 4 (1947), 404 · GEC, *Peerage*, new edn, vol. 3 · H. E. Busteed, *Echoes from old Calcutta*, 4th edn (1908) · J. Parkes and H. Merivale, *Memoirs of Sir Philip Francis*, 2 vols. (1867), vol. 2 · parish register, Holbeach, 18 Jan 1738, Lincs. Arch. [baptism] · *Bengal Past and Present*, 26 (1923), 166
Archives BL OIOC, family coresp., MS Eur. D759
Likenesses T. Prattent, line engraving, BM; repro. in *European Magazine and London Review* (Dec 1787)
Wealth at death very wealthy; £300,000: *Memoirs of William Hickey*, ed. Spencer · £6000 p.a.: *Bengal Past and Present*, 26 (1923), 166; GEC, *Peerage*, 10

Watson, Henry William (1827–1903), mathematician and Church of England clergyman, was born in Marylebone, Middlesex, on 25 February 1827, the son of Thomas Watson RN and his wife, Eleanor Mary Kingston. Educated at King's College, London, he won the first mathematical scholarship instituted there and proceeded in 1846 to Trinity College, Cambridge, where he was a scholar. He graduated as second wrangler and Smith's prizeman in 1850 and became a fellow of the college in 1851, serving as assistant tutor in 1851–3. While at Cambridge he formed a close friendship with James Fitzjames Stephen, and other members of the exclusive and secretive undergraduate society known as the Apostles.

After a short stay in London studying law (with Stephen as a fellow student), Watson in 1854 became mathematics master in the City of London School and three years later was mathematical lecturer at King's College, London. In 1856 he married Emily, daughter of Henry Rowe of Cambridge. They had one son and two daughters. The mathematician Robert Baldwin Hayward later became his brother-in-law. In the year of his marriage Watson was ordained deacon, taking priest's orders in 1858. From 1857 to 1865 he was a mathematics master at Harrow School, which he left when he was offered the care of the parish of Berkswell, near Coventry. He delighted in mountaineering and was one of the founders of the Alpine Club in 1857; he left the club in 1862.

Watson served as an examiner for the mathematical tripos in Cambridge (1860–61, 1877), as well as for the University of London (1893–6). He was one of the founders of the Birmingham Philosophical Society and its president in

1880–81. He was elected FRS on 2 June 1881. Cambridge University conferred on him the ScD degree in 1884.

Watson published a textbook on two- and three-dimensional geometry in 1871 and his best-known work, *Treatise on the Kinetic Theory of Gases*, in 1876. This was both a summary of the work of his predecessors, in particular of Maxwell and Boltzmann, and a discussion and development of the issues. A second edition appeared in 1893, dealing with criticisms given in correspondence by Maxwell. In collaboration with Samuel Hawksley Burbury he wrote a monograph on the use of generalized coordinates in dynamics (1879) and *The Mathematical Theory of Electricity and Magnetism* (1885–9). The article on molecules in the *Encyclopaedia Britannica* (9th edn) was also written jointly with Burbury. In addition Watson contributed journal articles on partial differential equations and the kinetic theory of gases. He also collaborated with Sir Francis Galton to produce an article, 'On the probability of the extinction of families', for the *Journal of the Anthropological Institute*. He died at his home, 1 Chichester Place, Brighton, on 11 January 1903, five months after his retirement from Berkswell.   T. E. JAMES, *rev.* JULIA TOMPSON

Sources S. H. B., *PRS*, 75 (1905), 266–9 · *Nature*, 67 (1902–3), 274–5 · *Men and women of the time* (1899) · *The Times* (13 Jan 1903), 7 · Venn, *Alum. Cant.* · CGPLA Eng. & Wales (1903)
Likenesses T. C. Wageman, watercolour, Trinity Cam.
Wealth at death £8087 9s. 11d.: probate, 21 Feb 1903, CGPLA Eng. & Wales

Watson, Hewett Cottrell (1804–1881), botanist and phrenologist, was born on 9 May 1804 at Park Hill, Firbeck, Yorkshire. His parents, Holland Watson (1749/50–1829) and Harriett Powell (1768/9–1819), were both from Stockport families of clergy and gentry. Holland Watson was a zealous magistrate in Chester and Lancaster. The Watsons had seven daughters before the birth of their eldest son, Hewett, and thus he was probably raised with much indulgence until two younger sons were born in 1809 and 1811. His hostility toward his brothers seems tied to his notoriously argumentative personality. About 1809 the family moved to Congleton and Hewett attended its grammar school, transferring, after a few years, to a school in Alderley run by the Revd Isaac Bell. At the family home, perhaps to divert him from conflict with his brothers, he was sent out to the family gardener for companionship, and developed a love for plants. That love was steered toward botany by Edward Stanley (1779–1849), clergyman and later president of the Linnean Society.

The possibility of a military career ended with an accident in which Watson's right knee was permanently damaged, and when he was seventeen he was apprenticed to a firm of solicitors in Manchester, where a married sister lived. After two years he moved to Liverpool to help his widowed father raise the two younger sons, although he detested his father as much as his brothers.

Inheritances from his father and another relative left Watson with an independent income, and he entered the University of Edinburgh in 1828 to study medicine. He was primarily interested in phrenology. George Combe and his brother Andrew Combe (1797–1847), the leading

British phrenologists, welcomed him into the Edinburgh Phrenological Society. Watson was phrenology's rising star, and even though he left Edinburgh in 1832 without a medical degree he was entrusted with the ownership and editorship of the *Phrenological Journal* in October 1837. He was unhappy with the low scientific achievements of phrenologists and hoped to use his editorship to raise standards, but his caustic manner offended contributors and readers and by August 1840 he had acknowledged his failure and left the field.

During his time at Edinburgh University, Watson also studied botany, then part of the medical curriculum, under Professor Robert Graham. In 1831 he won the gold medal in Graham's contest for the best student essay on botanical geography, and preparation for the essay helped turn him into a phytogeographer.

In January 1833 Watson went to Barnstaple to live with his sister Louisa Judith, who had married their second cousin, Captain Gilbert Wakefield. That same September he purchased Fern Cottage in Thames Ditton, Surrey, where he lived for the rest of his life. By 1835 he had engaged his housekeeper, Grace Eastman, who remained until his death; probably she was also his mistress. Watson lived close enough to London to attend meetings there, and during the 1840s he was vice-president of the Botanical Society of London.

Watson, perhaps as a result of Alexander von Humboldt's writings, became interested in plant geography. By 1834 he was also a Lamarckian transmutationist, and he hoped that close attention to specimens collected in different parts of a species' range might provide evidence supporting transmutation. He published his transmutationist beliefs in a phrenological polemic, *An Examination of Mr Scott's Attack upon Mr Combe's 'Constitution of Man'* (1836). This may have encouraged Robert Chambers, a friend of the Combe brothers, to write *Vestiges of the Natural History of Creation* (1844). Watson published a review article that partly praised *Vestiges*, but mostly corrected its botanical speculations and offered his own evidence on 'the origin and transmutation of species' (*Phytologist*, 2, 1845, 108–13, 140–47, 161–8, 225–8).

Watson's major botanical endeavour was producing several versions of a work first entitled *Outlines of the Geographical Distribution of British Plants* (1832); it reached its most extensive form as *Cybele Britannica, or, British Plants, and their Geographical Relations* (4 vols., 1847–59). Volume four contains his most detailed phytogeographical conclusions. After publishing several supplements, he summarized his data in *Topographical Botany: being Local and Personal Records towards shewing the Distribution of British Plants* (2 vols., 1873–4). He was working on a second edition of it when he died; it was completed by John G. Baker and William W. Newbould (1883).

In 1829 Watson originated the idea of a national exchange club for botanists and explained how it could work, in Loudon's *Magazine of Natural History*. Since most botanists were amateurs, for them it would be merely a way to enlarge their herbaria, but for him, it would aid plant geography studies. Only in 1836 did the Botanical Society of Edinburgh found the first exchange club, and Watson made better use of it than anyone else. In 1841 he persuaded the Botanical Society of London to run its own exchange club under his management; he ran it so successfully that it survived the London society's demise in 1857 and, indeed, Watson's own death in 1881. (It was already in other hands long before then.) For more than a decade the London exchange club was facilitated not only by the London society but also by reports published in Newman and Luxford's *The Phytologist*. Watson rewarded its participants with accurately identified herbarium specimens and with the *London Catalogue of British Plants* (1844; further edns until 1881).

In 1842 William Hooker persuaded Watson to go on a naval mapping expedition to the Azores; Watson published his botanical findings in Hooker's *London Journal of Botany* (1843–7). In 1865 the zoologist Frederick Du Cane Godman led a small expedition to the Azores and later found experts on the different groups of plants and animals collected to write chapters for his *Natural History of the Azores* (1870). Watson's chapter on flowering plants synthesized all known data and constitutes half the book.

In December 1844 Joseph Hooker sent Watson's articles on the Azores to Charles Darwin, and in 1847 lent him the volume of *The Phytologist* containing Watson's review of *Vestiges*, along with the first volume of *Cybele Britannica*. Darwin would have contacted Watson, had Watson in 1846 not begun a verbal attack on Edward Forbes for having given a talk based partly upon Watson's *Remarks on the Geographical Distribution of British Plants* (1835) without acknowledging his debt. In the published version, Forbes was effusive in his acknowledgement to Watson but Watson would not be appeased. This situation dissuaded Darwin, a friend of Forbes, from writing to Watson, but Joseph Hooker, who had long known Watson, asked Darwin's questions for him without mentioning their source. Hooker sent Watson's lengthy reply to Darwin, who used it in *The Origin of Species*.

Forbes died on 18 November 1854, and nine months later Darwin wrote directly to Watson. Watson then wrote Darwin about eight letters in 1855 answering questions on the geographic distributions and variability of British species (the letters of 19 and 20 November are dated here to 1855). Darwin warmly acknowledged Watson's assistance, but since *On the Origin of Species* (1859) appeared with little documentation, few readers understood what Watson had contributed. Furthermore, when Darwin added a historical preface to the 1861 edition, he forgot to mention Watson. After reading the *Origin*, Watson wrote to Darwin that he was 'the greatest Revolutionist in natural history of this century, if not of all centuries' (Watson to Darwin, 21 Nov 1859). Later, however, he doubted the sufficiency of natural selection to account for all aspects of evolution.

Watson died at Fern Cottage on 27 July 1881 from gangrene, the end result of a minor gardening accident, and was buried a week later in the cemetery of St Nicholas's Church, Thames Ditton. His publications were widely read by British botanists, and he had one protégé, John

G. Baker (1834–1920). When the Botanical Society of the British Isles established its journal in 1949 it was named *Watsonia*. FRANK N. EGERTON

Sources F. N. Egerton, *Hewett Cottrell Watson: Victorian plant ecologist and evolutionist* (2003) · F. N. Egerton, 'Hewett C. Watson: Great Britain's first phytogeographer', *Huntia*, 3 (1979), 87–102 · 'The naturalist's literary portrait gallery, no. 3: Hewett Cottrell Watson, esq.', *The Naturalist*, 4 (1839), 264–9 · J. G. Baker, *Journal of Botany, British and Foreign*, 19 (1881), 257–65 · *The correspondence of Charles Darwin*, ed. F. Burkhardt and S. Smith, [13 vols.] (1985–) · U. Edin. L., Combe MSS · U. Cam., department of plant sciences, Babington MSS · U. Edin., Balfour MSS · RBG Kew, Hooker MSS [both N. and J. Hooker] · C. Gibbon, *The life of George Combe: author of 'The constitution of man'*, 2 vols. (1878) · A. Desmond and J. Moore, *Darwin* (1991) · D. E. Allen, *The botanists: a history of the Botanical Society of the British Isles through a hundred and fifty years*, St Paul's Bibliographies (1986) · D. E. Allen, *The naturalist in Britain: a social history* (1976) · F. N. Egerton, 'In quest of a science: Hewett Watson and early Victorian phrenology', *Essays in arts and sciences*, 24 (1995), 1–20 · P. F. Rehbock, *The philosophical naturalists: themes in early nineteenth-century British biology* (1983) · J. Browne, *The secular ark: studies in the history of biogeography* (1983)
Archives NHM, papers · RBG Kew, botanical papers | Elgin Museum, letters to George Gordon · NL Scot., corresp. with George Combe · NL Scot., letters to Sir William Jardine · RBG Kew, letters to Sir William Hooker and Joseph Hooker · U. Cam., department of plant sciences, Babington MSS · U. Edin., school of biology, Balfour MSS · U. Edin., Combe MSS · U. Newcastle, Robinson L., corresp. with Sir Walter Trevelyan
Likenesses M. Haghe, drawing, 1839, repro. in *The Naturalist*, facing p. 265 · M. S. Carpenter, oils, 1846, RBG Kew; repro. in 'The naturalist's literary portrait gallery, no. 3' · oils, RBG Kew · photograph (in later years), repro. in J. G. Baker, *Journal of Botany*, facing title page
Wealth at death £4851 14s. 0d.: probate, 20 Aug 1881, *CGPLA Eng. & Wales*

Watson, (George) Hugh Nicholas Seton- (1916–1984), historian and political scientist, was born in London on 15 February 1916, the eldest of three children (two sons and a daughter) of Robert William Seton-*Watson (1879–1951), historian, and his wife, Marion (May) Esther, daughter of Edward Stack, of the Bengal civil service. He was educated at Winchester College and at New College, Oxford, where he gained a second class in classical honour moderations in 1936 and a first in philosophy, politics, and economics in 1938.

Early in the war Seton-Watson served in the British legations in Belgrade and Bucharest. It was in Yugoslavia that he was recruited into the Special Operations Executive. The *coup d'état* which overthrew the regent Prince Paul on 27 March 1941 was followed by the German invasion and the flight of the British legation staff. Most of them, including Seton-Watson, were repatriated to Britain after internment by the Italians. In August 1941 he was flown out to Cairo, where he served at general headquarters, Middle East, special forces, until 1944. It was during this time that he wrote his first major work, *Eastern Europe between the Wars, 1918–1941*, most of it in Cape Town, to which he had been temporarily evacuated, and where his only source of reference was the public library. The book was finished at the time of the battle of El Alamein in 1942 but had to wait until 1945 for publication.

In 1947 Seton-Watson married Mary Hope, daughter of

(George) Hugh Nicholas Seton-Watson (1916–1984), by unknown photographer

Godfrey Denne Rokeling, of the Ministry of Education. They had three daughters.

After the war Seton-Watson's travels in eastern Europe for *The Times* and *The Economist* in 1947 and 1948 had a profound influence on him. His early sympathy with the Soviet Union was justified by his generation on the grounds that Stalin was Hitler's only opponent. These views were now rejected as he saw those who represented ideas of freedom and humanity similar to his own persecuted by the Soviets or by their east European communist allies. Thus what happened then enabled him to form a picture of communism as the ultimate antithesis to all the aspirations of his generation. His experience resulted in *The East European Revolution* (1950) which has provided scholars with a pattern of communist 'take-overs', and a model to think about those events in a systematic fashion.

In spite of an offer by R. M. Barrington-Ward of a job on *The Times*, there was never any doubt that Seton-Watson would follow an academic career. The war had prevented him from taking up a lectureship in international politics in Aberystwyth. In 1945 he was appointed praelector in politics at Oxford and elected a fellow of University College. He took up these positions after demobilization in 1946. In 1951 he was appointed to the chair of Russian history at the University of London in the School of Slavonic and East European Studies, and he remained there until his retirement in 1983. In 1952 appeared his first important work on Russian history, *The Decline of Imperial Russia, 1855–1914*. It was followed fifteen years later by his monumental study of Russian history in the century before the revolution, *The Russian Empire, 1801–1917* (1967). He wrote that he had come to Russian history for three reasons: it was a country which resembled and had always influenced eastern Europe; it was a country which under communism had produced the world communist movement; and thirdly it was the country within which Leninism had been born and which provided the first example of the impact of Western ideas and Western economy on a backward social and political structure. He stressed that it was the third of these factors which seemed to him to offer the most valuable lessons for our own time.

This set the theme for much of Seton-Watson's work. In 1953 came *The Pattern of Communist Revolution: a Historical Analysis* and in 1960 *Neither War nor Peace: the Struggle for Power in the Post-War World*. He had come to the conclusion that the historical analysis of his father's generation had been based on the belief that the destruction of Austria–Hungary had been the last stage of a process of liberal nationalist revolutions which had begun in 1848. His generation, on the other hand, had realized that that destruction had been the first stage of a process which had spread from Europe into Asia and Africa and which had destroyed all the colonial empires except the Soviet. He had always been interested in nationalism and in 1977 appeared his most important work on politics and international relations, *Nations and States: an Enquiry into the Origins of Nations and the Politics of Nationalism*, which analysed the problem of nation building and national movements in every region of the world.

The study of nationalism also brought Seton-Watson back to his father's activity and to the events in eastern Europe which created the Europe of 1918. *The Making of a New Europe: R. W. Seton-Watson and the Last Years of Austria–Hungary* was published in 1981; it was written together with his brother, Christopher (then a fellow of Oriel College, Oxford).

For more than thirty years Seton-Watson presided over the teaching of Russian and Soviet history in the University of London. His very name and reputation were a magnet for scholars and postgraduate students alike. He took an active part in the work of the *Slavonic and East European Review* and outside the university in the work of the British Academy, to which he had been elected a fellow in 1969. From 1952 to 1984 he also served on the council of the Royal Institute of International Affairs. He received a DLitt from Oxford in 1974 and an honorary doctorate from the University of Essex in 1983. In 1981 he was appointed CBE.

Seton-Watson was a scholar inspired by travel as much as by books, not merely for pleasure, but to learn and to understand. Eventually his travels took him to all the world's continents, to lecture and to study. Increasingly, contacts with the American academic world became an important element in his life and in his study. He died in Washington, DC, on 19 December 1984.

HARRY HANAK, *rev.*

Sources D. Obolensky, 'George Hugh Nicholas Seton-Watson, 1916–1984', *PBA*, 73 (1987), 631–42 • *WWW* • private information (1990) • personal knowledge (1990) • *CGPLA Eng. & Wales* (1985)

Archives UCL, school of Slavonic and east European studies, corresp. and papers | Bodl. Oxf., Zimmern MSS
Likenesses I. Mestrovic, bronze portrait on tablet, UCL, school of Slavonic and east European studies • photograph, British Academy [*see illus.*]
Wealth at death £149,478: probate, 10 May 1985, *CGPLA Eng. & Wales*

Watson, James (1664?–1722), printer and bookseller, was born, probably in 1664, the son of James Watson, a merchant in Aberdeen, and his wife, a Dutch woman. Some time prior to 1685 he had moved with his parents to Edinburgh where Watson's Catholic father established a press in the safety of Holyrood Palace under the protection of James II. Although James Watson senior died in 1687, there is no evidence that his son took over the family business until 1694, with the first surviving output from his press dated 1695. It has been suggested that he spent the period 1687–94 in Holland developing his understanding of printing, but there is no evidence to support this suggestion.

As a printer and bookseller, Watson spent almost his entire career in Edinburgh, operating first in Mary King's Close (1694), then in Warriston's Close, over against the Luckenbooths (1695–6), in Craig's Close, on the north side of the Cross (1697–1709), and finally next door to the Red Lion opposite the Luckenbooths (1709–22). A short period in exile from Edinburgh, a punishment for printing seditious literature in 1700, was spent in the Gorbals in Glasgow, from where he is known to have printed only one book.

As a printer Watson left a considerable legacy. He is known to have printed over 500 titles, with an annual output ranging from three in 1696, to a peak of forty-eight in 1710. Of these more than 400 are books and pamphlets, and over 100 broadsheets, or single-sheet folios. He also printed, from 1700, the *Edinburgh Gazette* and, from 1705, the *Edinburgh Courant*. His most famous publication was *A Choice Collection of Comic and Serious Scots Poems both Ancient and Modern* (1706–11), an important and influential anthology of vernacular Scottish poetry.

Watson's career as a printer began with the production of medical and school textbooks, theological works, and legal disputations, but soon reached out into the area of pamphleteering, resulting in the action against him and his fellow pamphleteer Hugh Paterson by the privy council. From 1701 onwards a prolonged series of legal actions began between Watson and Agnes Campbell, widow of the Edinburgh printer Andrew Anderson, who had inherited her husband's privilege as royal printer, a position which Watson sought to challenge. From 1701 until her death in 1716, Watson and Campbell were constantly at loggerheads, with Watson printing New testaments in direct opposition to her Bible printing privilege, arguing principally that his opponent's productions were riddled with errors. His publication of a type specimen in 1706 is an indication of Watson's intention to produce high-quality books, using the best modern typefaces (although in reality the quality of his presswork varies considerably).

Watson married second on 30 November 1709 Jean Smith (*d.* 1731), evidently a wealthy woman; no evidence survives concerning his first marriage. The backing of his second wife enabled Watson to renew his legal challenge to Agnes Campbell's printing privilege, which had come up for renewal in 1711. This time Watson chose to mount the challenge with the Edinburgh printer Robert Freebairn and the queen's printer in England, John Baskett. In this they were successful and planned to establish a joint business venture, but soon fell into dispute with one another; the business was never formally established.

Having secured the royal privilege for himself in 1713, Watson was on his way to becoming the most important printer in Scotland. He came under renewed attack from those who sought to undermine his new position as king's printer, particularly Baskett, who unsuccessfully contested Watson's Scottish privilege on several occasions. Watson responded to these challenges by attempting to import bibles into England, challenging Baskett's own monopoly south of the border, without success.

Watson was also an important bookseller in Edinburgh, selling his own books as well as new and secondhand books from all over Europe, principally English imports. His post-mortem inventory in 1722 listed a considerable stock of new books in sheets, and a large number of booksellers from Scotland, northern Ireland, and northern England were noted as debtors. He also acted as an auctioneer. In 1713 he published *The History of the Art of Printing*, one of the earliest accounts of the origins of printing in the English language, largely translated from the French of Jean de la Caille by John Spottiswoode, in the preface of which Watson outlined the recent history and present state of printing in Scotland. The work also included a specimen of types of Dutch origin. In his attempts to raise the quality of printing and presswork throughout Scotland Watson issued a set of *Rules & Directions to be Observed in Printing Houses* (1721), heavily influenced by Dutch printing-house practice, which seems to have been displayed in the main printing-house shops in Edinburgh.

Watson died in Edinburgh on 25 September 1722; his will, filed on 19 December, left his entire estate to his second wife.   RICHARD OVENDEN

Sources D. Wyn Evans, 'James Watson of Edinburgh: a bibliography of works from his press', *Edinburgh Bibliographical Society Transactions*, 5/2 (1971–87) [whole issue] · D. Wyn Evans, 'James Watson of Edinburgh: additions to the bibliography', *Edinburgh Bibliographical Society Transactions*, 5/5 (1971–87), 41–8 · W. J. Couper, 'James Watson, king's printer', *SHR*, 7 (1909–10), 244–62 · J. de la Caille, *The history of the art of printing* (1713) · J. Watson, *Rules and directions to be observed in printing-houses*, ed. D. Wyn Evans (1988)
Archives NL Scot., papers
Wealth at death £32,000 Scots: will, NA Scot., CC 8/8/88

Watson, James (1739/40?–1790), engraver, was born in Dublin of unknown parentage and received his early training in the schools of the Dublin Society. He went to London as a young man, probably as a pupil to his fellow Irishman James Macardell. He became a very fine engraver in mezzotint, his plates delicate and carefully finished. He exhibited with the Society of Artists from 1762 until 1775, and during those two decades was regarded as a leading master. He was a fellow of the society and a director in 1770. After 1765 he inherited Macardell's role as principal engraver to Joshua Reynolds, and interpreted fifty-six of his paintings in sixty plates. His work included notable portraits of friends of Reynolds such as Edmund Burke and Samuel Johnson, as well as expensive, full-length society portraits. He also scraped many excellent mezzotints from pictures by Gainsborough, Cotes, Catherine Read, Van Dyck, Metsu, Schalken, Rubens, and others. Most early plates were published by major printsellers such as Ryland and Bryer, Bowles, Sayer, and Parker and Bakewell, but Watson began to publish some of his own work about 1762, at first from the Golden Head, in Craven Buildings, off Drury Lane. By 1766 he was at 45 Little Queen Anne Street, from which he moved in 1775 to no. 64. He had done well enough by 1778 to be living in semi-retirement. Among his last work was six plates for Boydell's *Houghton Gallery*. In a working life of thirty years he scraped 200 plates, the vast majority being portraits. Goodwin writes: 'these are notable achievements, brilliant in their lights, luminous in their shadows, delicate in the modelling of the flesh, rich in the draperies' (Goodwin, 73).

Watson's marriage to Mary (*b. c.*1740), daughter of Reuben Judkins, produced a daughter, Caroline *Watson (1760/61–1814), who studied under her father and achieved fame in her own right, and a son, James Edmund Watson, who became a lawyer. Mary predeceased him; at the time of his death, probably in Fitzroy Street, London, on 20 or 22 May 1790, Watson was still paying interest on the sum of £200 that he had borrowed from his sister-in-law Elizabeth Judkins; this loan was transferred to Caroline, the remainder of his estate being divided between his children. He was buried in St Marylebone cemetery.

TIMOTHY CLAYTON and ANITA MCCONNELL

Sources G. Goodwin, *Thomas Watson, James Watson, Elizabeth Judkins* (1904) · will, PRO, PROB 11/1210, sig. 491 · *GM*, 1st ser., 60 (1790), 480; 84/1 (1814), 700 · W. G. Strickland, *A dictionary of Irish artists*, 2 (1913); repr. with introduction by T. J. Snoddy (1989), 507–9

Watson, James (1766–1838), radical, was born on 15 May 1766 at Kirton, near Boston, Lincolnshire. He claimed to be a surgeon by profession, but financial security seems to have eluded him in a succession of surgeon-apothecary shops in London and the provinces. He married Ann Milner on 4 February 1790 in London and had ten children, born in London, Yorkshire, Norfolk, and Staffordshire. Family circumstances deteriorated when the Watsons finally settled in London around 1808, having quit an ailing business in Cheadle, Staffordshire. In 1810 one of Watson's daughters died 'for want of nourishment … while ill, the bed that was under her was seized for rent … This was too much when the affluent were wallowing in riches' (PRO, TS11/200/869). Then his wife departed, taking the four youngest, and allegedly mistreated, children. Abandoning sobriety and political conservatism, Watson formed a 'connection' with his neighbour Thomas Evans, founder of the Society of Spencean Philanthropists. As expounded by Evans in the London taverns, Thomas

James Watson (1766–1838), by William Holl, pubd 1817 (after George Scharf) [*Spa Fields Rioters*: (left to right) Watson, Arthur Thistlewood, Thomas Preston, and John Hooper]

Spence's 'plan' for political equality and social welfare through parish ownership of land held out the promise of respectability and independent self-sufficiency for marginal middle-class professionals such as Watson. As war with Napoleonic France gave way to peace without plenty, Watson sought to carry the message beyond tavern debating clubs, to transform popular discontent into mass political insurgency. Through his efforts to mobilize what he called 'ragged radicals', Watson emerged as the leader of London ultra-radicalism.

Having joined Thomas Preston and Arthur Thistlewood in insurrectionary planning in autumn 1816, Watson combed alehouses to enlist navvies, demobilized soldiers, dock workers, gangs of roughs, the unemployed, and other physically intimidating groups, while his eldest son, also called James, put his recent seafaring experience to good use in recruiting discharged sailors. As a well-attended public meeting was regarded as the best springboard for action, all the leading reform celebrities were invited to a meeting of 'Distressed Manufacturers, Mariners, Artisans and others' at Spa Fields on 15 November 1816. Henry Hunt alone accepted, having satisfied himself that he was not being drawn into a revolutionary Spencean plot to abolish private property in land.

In a private interview with Watson, Hunt dictated terms: no reference to Spencean principles and no incitement to riot. The meeting would be strictly 'constitutional', enrolling the distressed masses in an extra-parliamentary campaign for universal suffrage, annual parliaments, and the ballot. In acceding, Watson formed a working agreement with Hunt which was to facilitate the remarkable expansion of political agitation in the postwar years. The establishment of this radical mass platform, however, revealed ideological, tactical, social, and cultural tensions in metropolitan ultra-radicalism. While Evans withdrew into refined and respectable circles to

uphold the ideological integrity of the Spencean formulary, other ultra-radicals, heirs to the traditional *putsch* strategy of Colonel Despard and the wartime underground, wanted immediate action. Denied this opportunity on 15 November, Thistlewood and the young Watson ensured that a second meeting was called so that they could go ahead with their original plan to inflame the assembled crowd and then storm the Bank of England and Tower of London. Unable to control his son, who had been treated in Bath for insanity, Watson was drawn into the scheme. To Thistlewood's fury, however, Watson was not to the fore in the actual attempt, on 2 December 1816. He took off in a separate direction as the small section of the crowd, detached by Thistlewood and the young Watson before Hunt had arrived at Spa Fields, looted its way across London until fleeing in the face of troops at the Tower. The ignominious failure of precipitate insurrectionism reinforced Watson's commitment to cumulative mass platform agitation to mobilize the people before decisive confrontation.

Watson's son escaped to the United States, leaving his father to face a charge of high treason. Aided by recent press revelations about Oliver the spy, Watson was acquitted in June 1817, when one of his own recruits, John Castle, was revealed as a government informer with a previous unsavoury record of brothel-keeping, bigamy, forgery, and blood money. Thereafter Watson's position was consolidated by close co-operation with Hunt in the Westminster election of 1818, and in the absence of Thistlewood, who was imprisoned for challenging Lord Sidmouth to a duel. As undisputed leader of the ultra-radicals, Watson channelled his energies into the Universal Union Fund of the Non-Represented People of Great Britain and Ireland, a penny-a-week subscription scheme to provide the necessary means—funds, organization, and rapid communication—to mobilize the labouring poor in readiness for confrontation and a national convention. Important links were forged with provincial radicals, trade unionists, and Irish immigrants, but the promotion of the scheme in pamphlets and in the short-lived *Shamrock, Thistle and Rose*, a twopenny monthly, overstretched Watson's limited resources, leading to his brief imprisonment for debt in December 1818.

On release, Watson worked closely with Hunt in the great platform campaign of 1819, an attempt to overawe the government by an overwhelming but orderly display of popular support. He organized mass meetings, introduced a new parish-based system of organization among the non-represented, strengthened links with the Irish immigrant community, drafted resolutions for meetings in the north, and even prevailed upon Thistlewood, on his release, to abandon armed conspiracy in favour of the forcible intimidation of the mass platform. The success of Hunt's August meeting in Manchester, planned as the climax of provincial support, was essential to the strategy. After Hunt set off for Lancashire, Watson kept him informed by post of traps and rumours, but most of his time was spent on plans for a monster 'final meeting' in London on Hunt's return. When news reached London of the Peterloo massacre, Watson was briefly drawn towards a broad reform alliance, joining 'respectable' radicals in planning a suitable reception for Hunt on his return to London. In a mixture of vanity and political calculation, however, Hunt used the dinner after his triumphal entry to dissociate himself from any suggestion of Spenceanism or levelling. Outraged by this deliberate snub, Watson engaged in an unseemly polemic with Hunt, a sorry end to their working alliance.

Beneath the obloquy there was a fundamental disagreement. Looking to the courts and public opinion, Hunt wanted to rest the radical case on Peterloo itself, eschewing any further platform agitation which might sully the moral victory gained at Manchester. Watson, by contrast, sought to exploit popular anger at the massacre through immediate escalation of platform agitation, combining the various tactics of ultra-radicalism, armed simultaneous meetings, tax refusal, and a national convention. Undermined by Hunt, these proposals were abandoned in favour of traditional conspiratorial ways and means. Soon after the introduction of the repressive Six Acts, Thistlewood was entrapped by an *agent provocateur* in the Cato Street conspiracy, a plot to assassinate the cabinet at dinner [see Cato Street conspirators (*act.* 1820)]. Watson was not involved, as he was again imprisoned for debt, this time for non-payment of Hunt's dinner bill! However, he drew up an address to soldiers and a proclamation to the people to be issued once the blow was struck.

Thereafter little is known of Watson's political career, although he briefly returned to prominence in the later stages of the Queen Caroline affair, by heading the funeral procession for the two workmen killed by troops escorting the queen's cortège. In the late 1820s he was a regular speaker at the 'Liberals', a debating-cum-literary group which attracted old Jacobins, Spenceans, and ultra-radicals. Some time afterwards he left for America, possibly to join his son. Watson died a pauper in New York on 12 February 1838.   JOHN BELCHEM

Sources I. McCalman, *Radical underworld: prophets, revolutionaries, and pornographers in London, 1795–1840* (1988) · T. M. Parssinen, 'The revolutionary party in London, 1816–20', *BIHR*, 45 (1972), 266–82 · I. J. Prothero, *Artisans and politics in early nineteenth-century London: John Gast and his times* (1979) · J. Belchem, *'Orator' Hunt: Henry Hunt and English working-class radicalism* (1985) · DNB
Archives PRO, Home Office MSS, HO 40/3–7, HO 42/155–97, HO 44/4–6 · PRO, treasury solicitor's MSS, TS 11/200/869, TS 11/201/870
Likenesses W. Holl, group portrait, stipple, pubd 1817 (*Spa Fields rioters*; after G. Scharf), BM, NPG [see illus.] · I. R. Cruickshank, etching, BM; repro. in *Fairburn's report of trial of Spa Field rioters* · portrait, repro. in W. B. Gurney, *A correct report of the trial of James Watson, senior, for high treason* (1817)
Wealth at death died in poverty: DNB

Watson, James (1799–1874), radical and publisher, was born at Malton, Yorkshire, on 21 September 1799. His father died when he was barely a year old. His mother, 'a Sunday school teacher', taught him to read and write. About 1811 she returned to domestic service in the family of a clergyman who had paid for James's schooling for a period. The boy became under-gardener, stable-help, and house servant, and acquired a strong taste for reading

over the kitchen fire in winter evenings. About 1817 the parson's household was broken up, and Watson accompanied his mother to Leeds, where he became a warehouseman. Two years later he was converted to free thought and radicalism by public readings from Cobbett and Richard Carlile. For the next few years he took an active part in disseminating advanced literature and in getting up a subscription on behalf of Carlile.

After Carlile was sentenced in 1821 to three years' imprisonment for blasphemy, Watson went to London in September 1822 to serve as a volunteer assistant in his Water Lane bookshop. In January 1823 Carlile's wife, having completed her term of imprisonment, took a new shop at 210 Strand. Watson moved there, still in the capacity of salesman. The occupation was a perilous one, and, despite all the precautions taken, salesman after salesman was arrested. This fate overtook Watson at the end of February 1823. He was charged with 'maliciously' selling a copy of Palmer's *Principles of Nature* to a police agent, and, having made an eloquent speech in his own defence, was sent to Coldbath Fields prison for a year. There he read Hume, Gibbon, and Mosheim's *Ecclesiastical History*, and was strongly confirmed in his anti-Christian and republican opinions. During 1825 he became a compositor, and was employed in printing Carlile's *Republican*, and for some time in conducting his business. In the intervals of work he suffered privation, and in 1826 was struck down by cholera. When he recovered, he became a convert to the co-operative schemes of Robert Owen, and in 1828 he was storekeeper of the First Co-operative Trading Association in London in Red Lion Square and was a member of the British Association for the Promotion of Co-operation (1829–35) and the National Union of the Working Classes (1831–8). He became a bookseller in 1830 and worked with Hetherington, Cleave, and Lovett in the production and the distribution of the *Poor Man's Guardian*. In December 1832 he launched the *Working Man's Friend and Political Magazine*, an influential journal advocating factory legislation, universal suffrage, and repeal of both the newspaper duty and the union with Ireland.

In 1831 Watson set up as a printer and publisher, and the following year he was arrested and narrowly escaped imprisonment for organizing a procession and a feast on the day the government had ordained 'a general fast' on account of the ravages of the cholera. In February 1833 he was summoned at Bow Street for selling Hetherington's *Poor Man's Guardian*, and was sentenced to six months' imprisonment at Clerkenwell. His championship of the right to free expression of opinion had won him admirers, and one of these, Julian Hibbert, on his death in January 1834, left Watson 450 guineas, with which sum he promptly enlarged his printing plant. He made a bold start by printing the life and works of Tom Paine, and these volumes were followed by Mirabaud's *System of Nature* and Volney's *Ruins of Empires*. Later he printed Byron's *Cain* and *Vision of Judgment*, Shelley's *Queen Mab* and *Masque of Anarchy*, and Clark on the miracles of Christ. All these were printed, corrected, folded, and sewn by Watson himself, and issued at 1s. or less per volume. His shop near Bunhill Fields (from where he removed first to the City Road, and in 1843 to 5 Paul's Alley) was well known to all the leading radicals of the day, and he had 'pleasant and informing words for all who sought his wares'.

Watson married Eleanor Byerley on 3 June 1834, and two months later was arrested and imprisoned for six months for having circulated Hetherington's unstamped paper, the ironically entitled *Conservative*. He had a little earlier come under government surveillance as a leader in the great April meeting of trade unions in support of the Tolpuddle Martyrs. He bore imprisonment with resignation: 'I love privacy', he wrote to his wife. This was his last imprisonment, though he continued without intermission to issue books upon the government 'index'.

In 1836 Watson helped to found the Working Men's Association, and in June 1837 he was on the committee appointed to draw up the People's Charter. He opposed both physical force and the overtures made to whig partisans, whom he consistently denounced for their selfishness. He remained constant in his demands for 'the charter, the whole charter, and nothing but the charter'. In 1848 he was one of the conveners of the first public meeting to celebrate the French revolution of that year. In 1847 he had given his adherence to the People's International League founded by his friend and correspondent Mazzini.

Frugal, severe, and self-denying in his habits, Watson was a thin, haggard, thoughtful man, with an intellectual face and a grave yet gentle manner. He was a publicist and organizer rather than an editor or leader. He lost money through his publishing, his object being profitable reading for uneducated people rather than personal gain. Yet he cared for the correctness and decent appearance of his books, even the cheapest. 'They were his children, he had none other.' An unstamped and absolutely free press became the practical object of his later years, and he led the Newspaper Stamp Abolition Committee in 1849.

About 1870 anxiety about the health of his wife induced a serious decline of Watson's own powers. He died at his home, Burns Cottage, Hamilton Road, Lower Norwood, London, on 29 November 1874, and was buried in Norwood cemetery, where a grey granite obelisk erected by friends commemorated his 'brave efforts to secure the rights of free speech'.

THOMAS SECCOMBE, *rev.* MATTHEW LEE

Sources W. J. Linton, *James Watson* (1880) · W. J. Linton, *Memories* (1895) · J. H. Wiener, 'Watson, James', *BDMBR*, vol. 2 · J. H. Wiener, *War of the unstamped* (1969) · R. Hackett, *XIX century British working class autobiographies* (1985) · J. Burnett, D. Vincent, and D. Mayall, eds., *The autobiography of the working class*, 2 (1984) · G. J. Holyoake, *Sixty years of an agitator's life*, 2 vols. (1905) · *CGPLA Eng. & Wales* (1875) · 'The reminiscences of James Watson', *Testaments of radicalism: memoirs of working class politicians, 1790–1855*, ed. D. Vincent (1977), 109–14

Archives BL, corresp., Add. MS 46345

Likenesses photograph, repro. in Linton, *Memories* · photograph, repro. in Vincent, ed., *Testaments of radicalism*, facing p. 109

Wealth at death under £100: probate, 8 March 1875, *CGPLA Eng. & Wales*

Watson [*married name* Sutton], **Janet Vida** (1923–1985), geologist, was born in Hampstead, London, on 1 September 1923, the younger daughter (there were no sons) of David Meredith Seares *Watson FRS (1886–1973), professor of zoology and comparative anatomy in the University of London, and his wife, Katherine Margarite, daughter of the Revd I. Parker, who was, until marriage, herself active in embryological research. Janet Watson grew up in a serious, nonconformist, but lively atmosphere; she played with the Huxley children on holiday and listened to her father's numerous intellectual visitors. From South Hampstead high school she went to Reading University, obtaining a first-class general honours degree (biology and geology) in 1943.

Following her degree Janet Watson worked on chicken growth and diet in a research institute, then taught in a girls' school. By the end of the Second World War she had decided to be a hard-rock geologist, and enrolled at Imperial College, emerging, inevitably, with a first-class honours degree. Professor H. H. Read then proposed that for her PhD project she should attempt, along with fellow student John Sutton, to understand the oldest rocks in the British Isles, the Lewisian gneisses. These, evolved deep in the earth's crust and riddled with dykes, could not be tackled by ordinary geological methods. Watson and Sutton had to forge their own techniques, in the mists and rock wastes of Sutherland. They were able to show that in the Lewisian gneiss, two components could be separated: the older, Scourian, mapped by Watson, evolved before, and the younger Laxfordian after, the injection of the dyke swarms. These results, presented to the Geological Society of London in 1951, represented a major breakthrough. They were later confirmed when radiometric dating showed that the Scourian was hundreds of millions of years older than the Laxfordian.

On 13 June 1949 she and John *Sutton (1919–1992), the son of Gerald John Sutton, consulting engineer, married. They had two daughters; sadly both died at birth.

After her PhD (1949) Janet Watson was awarded a senior 1851 studentship. She continued work on the Lewisian and similarly ancient rocks in western Tanzania. In 1952 she joined the staff of Imperial College, first as Read's research assistant, and later (1974–80) as professor. Always she was working on, and thinking about, geological problems, especially those of the earth's oldest rocks. The fascination with Scotland lasted: her first, still valuable, Scottish paper was published while an undergraduate, her last, a masterly presidential address to the Geological Society of London, in 1983. But her interests widened, to mineralization, heat flow through the crust, geochemistry, and much else. A visit to Italy in 1983 led her completely to reverse the accepted hypothesis for uranium deposits there. Her last paper, with John Sutton, 'Lineaments in the continental lithosphere', was read to the Royal Society the day before she died.

The whole of Janet Watson's work shows the same clear grasp of essentials, mastery of detail, skilled analysis, and lucid presentation. It adds up to a massive contribution to the understanding of the earth's oldest rocks. She wrote, with H. H. Read, a very successful *Introduction to Geology* (vol. 1, 1962; 2nd edn 1968; vol. 2, 1976); and also *Beginning Geology* (1966). The value of her work was recognized by awards, by the Geological Society of London of the Lyell fund, the Bigsby medal (both jointly with Sutton), and the Lyell medal, and by the Geological Society of Edinburgh of the Clough medal. She was elected FRS (1979), was president of the Geological Society of London (the first woman to be made president) from 1982 to 1984, and a vice-president and member of council of the Royal Society from 1983 until her death. Outside college she served effectively on the National Water Council (1973–6), the BBC science consultative group, and other bodies.

Janet Watson was, like her father, stocky, with a face full of character. She was reserved, quietly determined, generous, with integrity and warmth. These qualities showed in her teaching. Her lectures were lucid, carefully thought out, and penetrating, but it was in sitting down with research students, discussing and sorting out their problems and giving them ideas, that she excelled.

Watson and Sutton continued to work together from Imperial College (Sutton was appointed to the chair of geology in 1958) throughout her life. After a painful illness, but working and thinking to the end, she died at home at Sandy Drive, Oxshott, Surrey, on 29 March 1985.

ROBERT M. SHACKLETON

Sources D. J. Fettes and J. A. Plant, *Memoirs FRS*, 41 (1995), 501–14 · personal knowledge (2004) · *CGPLA Eng. & Wales* (1985)
Archives GS Lond., corresp. and papers
Likenesses photograph, repro. in *Memoirs FRS*
Wealth at death £96,949: probate, 12 June 1985, *CGPLA Eng. & Wales*

Watson, John (*d.* 1537), college head, was educated at Eton College from about 1479 until 1483, when he was admitted to King's College, Cambridge. He was elected a fellow of King's in 1486, was ordained priest in 1489, and became a fellow of Peterhouse at about the time that the humanist Henry Hornby was appointed master in 1501. He served as junior proctor of the university in 1504 and was made a Lady Margaret preacher in the following year. He was admitted BTh in 1511. He is remembered chiefly as a Cambridge friend and correspondent of Erasmus, who considered Watson a distinguished theologian and consulted him on his edition of the Greek Testament. Erasmus described Watson's character as being 'devout without bigotry, sociable without triviality and strict but not severe' (*Correspondence*, 4.181). In 1516 Watson travelled to Venice and the Holy Land in the company of John Reston, recording aspects of life on board ship with other friends of Erasmus. He was admitted rector of Elsworth, Cambridgeshire, on 30 March of the same year, resigning his fellowship at Peterhouse on 6 December.

In 1517 Watson graduated DTh and was instituted master of Christ's College. In that year he declared in a letter to Erasmus that he had formed 'a solemn resolution to devote the rest of my life exclusively to biblical and sacred studies' (*Correspondence*, 4.343). He served as vice-chancellor of Cambridge University in 1518–20 and 1530–32. On 30 April 1523 he was instituted rector of St Mary Woolnoth, London, and on 17 September 1523 became prebendary of Norwell-tertia-pars in the church of Southwell. In 1529 he was one of nearly 200 divines selected to answer, for Cambridge University, Henry VIII's questions about his divorce; he is not listed as one of those favourable to the king. In May 1530 he was one of twenty-four divines selected to examine certain English books feared to contain contentious material on the chief points and articles of religion. One of his fellow examiners was Hugh Latimer who had formerly been Watson's scholar. As master of Christ's, Watson was one of those who opposed Latimer at King's College in 1530. In May 1531, after censuring points made in a sermon by Nicholas Shaxton on Ash Wednesday, Watson, as vice-chancellor, attempted to ensure religious conformity in the university by issuing a decree which imposed an oath on scholars proceeding to degrees in divinity. The list of controversial issues covered by the oath included communion in both kinds, fasting, clerical celibacy, and the authority of the church. The decree was dropped by the next vice-chancellor, Simon Heynes.

Watson retired to King's College after ceasing to be master of Christ's in 1531 (he was replaced by Cromwell's client, Henry Lockwood). In 1536 he became rector of White Notley, Essex, where probably he died, unmarried, in March of the following year.

JUDITH FORD

Sources Emden, *Cam.*, 622 · Venn, *Alum. Cant.* · *The correspondence of Erasmus*, ed. and trans. R. A. B. Mynors and others, 22 vols. (1974–94), vol. 2, pp. 255–6, 283; vol. 4, pp. 34, 37n., 54, 131n., 181, 343 · Cooper, *Ath. Cantab.*, 1.39–40 · *LP Henry VIII*, 3/2, nos. 2052, 2390; 4/3, no. 6367 · *The acts and monuments of John Foxe*, ed. S. R. Cattley, 8 vols. (1837–41), vol. 7, p. 451 · H. C. Porter, *Reformation and reaction in Tudor Cambridge* (1958), 33, 37, 61 · *VCH Cambridgeshire and the Isle of Ely*, vol. 3 · *Sermons and remains of Hugh Latimer*, ed. G. E. Corrie, Parker Society, 20 (1845), xii · M. Dowling, *Humanism in the age of Henry VIII* (1986), 91 · L.-E. Halkin, *Erasmus: a critical biography* (1993), 122

Watson, John (*c.*1520–1584), bishop of Winchester, was born in Evesham, Worcestershire, son of Thomas Watson and his wife, Agnes, *née* Weekes. He had three surviving brothers, William, Thomas, and Robert, and six sisters. The family was of some means as he bequeathed silver plate left to him by his father and a house in Bengeworth, near Evesham. Watson was educated at Oxford, graduating BA in June 1539. Admitted a fellow of All Souls in 1540 he incepted MA in February 1545. On 9 December 1551 he received letters patent for the eleventh prebend in Winchester Cathedral. In April 1554 he was admitted to the rectories of Kelsall, Hertfordshire, and Winchfield, Hampshire, and may have been the man who matriculated at the University of Louvain in June that year. He did not take orders until 1557. On 12 June that year he was ordained to minor orders and as subdeacon, as of Worcester diocese, by Thomas Chetham, bishop of Sidon, suffragan of London, using his parish of Winchfield as his title. Following letters dimissory to take higher orders, issued on 28 August 1557 by Bishop Richard Pates of Worcester, he was ordained deacon in London on 24 September 1558 as of All Souls, although now stated to be of Gloucester diocese. Meanwhile, on 7 February 1558, he had been collated by Edmund Bonner, bishop of London, to the chancellorship of St Paul's, a post he retained until his consecration. Later that year he vacated his Winchester prebend.

Watson accommodated himself to the Elizabethan settlement and was granted letters patent for the hospital of St Cross, near Winchester, on 17 August 1559, and for the first prebend at Winchester at about the same time. That same month he was one of the few members of the St Paul's chapter to accept the oath of supremacy. Thereafter his rise was surprisingly rapid for one whose career had been actively promoted by Bonner. Becoming archdeacon of Surrey, also by letters patent, on 7 November 1559 he was, perhaps predictably, found on the conservative wing in the convocation of 1562–3. In 1568 he was admitted to the rectory of South Warnborough, Hampshire, and in February 1573 received letters patent for the deanery of Winchester, resigning his archdeaconry and his prebend. On 27 July 1575 he proceeded doctor of medicine at Oxford.

Watson was evidently on good terms with his bishop, Robert Horne, being named one of the four executors of Horne's will in June 1579. He was elected Horne's successor on 29 June 1580 and consecrated on 18 September, having discovered in the interim that he was expected to pay a substantially higher figure for his first fruits than Horne had negotiated in 1561. Perhaps as a form of compensation he was on 2 December 1580 granted the right to hold the hospital of St Cross for a further three years.

In November 1580 he began his primary visitation of the diocese but was interrupted by the parliamentary session that ended in March 1581. During this parliament and convocation Watson, along with bishops John Aylmer of London, John Whitgift of Worcester, John Piers of Salisbury, and Thomas Cooper of Lincoln, was ordered by the privy council to investigate the religious sect known as the Family of Love. The government was also much concerned to clamp down on recusancy at this time. In October 1580 Watson had been directed to hold the husbands of women recusants responsible for their wives' conformity, through fines if necessary. On 22 November he responded that it was surely unreasonable to punish men 'for their wives' faults' (PRO, SP 12/144/36).

It was perhaps for that reason, and because of his own Marian past, that he was suspected of leniency towards recusants. The charge would appear to be unjust since the evidence of his brief tenure of Winchester is largely concerned with the suppression of Catholicism. In 1580 he interrogated Elizabeth Sander, sister of Dr Nicholas Sander, and in August 1582 the seminary priest John Chapman. In 1583 two local schoolmasters, John Slade and John Body, were condemned at Winchester assizes and executed on 30 October and 2 November 1583 respectively. During the following month Watson and the mayor conducted a house-to-house search, which resulted in the discovery in Lady West's house of a trunk containing all the items necessary for conducting mass. Nothing else is known of his brief episcopate beyond the fact that he seems to have granted a lavish number of episcopal leases and, according to his successor, Thomas Cooper, left the episcopal manors poorly stocked and in a state of decay.

The unmarried incumbent of a still rich see, Watson was in a position to prove a generous benefactor. In 1582 he contributed £60, his dean and chapter adding £40, to endow the city of Winchester with a fund that would provide interest-free loans to needy freemen. His will, drawn up on 23 October 1583, contained a stream of impressive bequests. He left £40 to All Souls, £20 to Oxford University, 100 marks to the use of the university's poor scholars, and 'exhibitions' of £4 per annum payable over five years to five poor scholars appointed at the discretion of his executors. The poor of Winchester received £20; those of Evesham £10; and those of Bengeworth £5. A stock of £40 was to be set up for the poor of Evesham and of £10 for those of Bengeworth. He also remembered the thirteen poor brothers of St Cross, left £40 for the purchase of books to Winchester Cathedral Library, and bequeathed a horse to his principal overseer, Sir Francis Walsingham. Altogether his monetary legacies to his siblings and their numerous offspring, to protégés and to good causes amounted to about £1000. He left his medical books to a cousin, Simon Tripp.

Codicils to the will are dated 22 and 23 January 1584 and Watson died at Winchester on the latter day. On 17 February he was buried in his cathedral, as directed in his will, which was proved on 22 June 1584. Thereafter Bishop Cooper managed to extract £530 from his executors towards the repair of the episcopal manors.

JANE REEDY LADLEY

Sources will, PRO, PROB 11/67, fols. 2r–4r · BL, Harley MSS 1043, fol. 31; 1566, fol. 130 · chapter act book, 1553–1608, Winchester Cathedral Library, fols. 80–89 · J. Watson and T. Cooper, bishops' registers, Hants. RO, Winchester diocesan records, 21M65/A27 · J. Watson, visitation book, Hants. RO, Winchester diocesan records, 21M65/B1/15 · LPL, Grindal's register, vol. 1, fols. 58–9 · state papers domestic, Edward VI–James I, addenda, PRO, SP 15/144/96; 15/147/74; 15/152/4; 15/153/17; 15/155/8; 15/164/14 · T. Atkinson, *Elizabethan Winchester* (1963) · JHL, 2 (1578–1614), 21–35 · GL, MS 9535/1, fols. 64r–64v; 75r · *VCH Hampshire and the Isle of Wight*, 2.79 · F. Heal, *Of prelates and princes: a study of the economic and social position of the Tudor episcopate* (1980) · Emden, *Oxf.*, 4.610 · *Fasti Angl., 1541–1857*, [Canterbury] · B. Usher, 'Durham and Winchester episcopal estates and the Elizabethan settlement: a reappraisal', *Journal of Ecclesiastical History*, 49 (1998), 393–406 · state papers domestic, Elizabeth, PRO, SP 12/144/36
Wealth at death approx. £1000 excl. plate, horses, two feather beds, and a house: will, PRO, PROB 11/67, fols. 2r–4r

Watson, John (1725–1783), Church of England clergyman and antiquary, was born on 26 March 1725 at Lyme Handley in Prestbury, Cheshire, the son of Legh Watson and his wife, Hester, daughter of John Yates of Swinton, Lancashire. He was educated at the grammar schools in Eccles, Wigan, and Manchester before matriculating at Brasenose College, Oxford, on 8 April 1742. He graduated BA in 1745 and MA in 1748, having been elected to a Cheshire fellowship of the college in June 1746. He was ordained deacon in December 1746 and served the curacy of Runcorn for a few months before moving to Ardwick, Manchester, where he also acted as tutor to the family of Samuel Birch. Ordained priest in 1749, he was curate of Halifax from 1750 until September 1754, when he was presented to the

John Watson (1725–1783), by James Basire, 1780 (after Daniel Stringer)

perpetual curacy of Ripponden, a chapelry of Halifax parish, where he rebuilt the incumbent's residence at his own expense.

He married first on 1 June 1752 Susanna Allon (d. 1757), daughter of Samuel Allon, vicar of Sandbach, Cheshire, with whom he had a son. After her death he married on 11 July 1761 Ann Jacques, daughter of James Jacques of Leeds; they had a son, who also went to Brasenose, and a daughter.

Watson's antiquarian activities, particularly on Roman antiquities but also on the barrows of the Halifax area, which he referred to as druidical remains, led to his election as FSA in 1759. He continued these researches, but his time at Ripponden was chiefly occupied in writing a history of Halifax, published in 1775, which became a standard source. His determined whig principles made him unable to read the order of service set out for 30 January in memory of Charles I, though he preached on that anniversary publishing two of his sermons, in 1754 and 1755, in which he set out his views. He also wrote a pamphlet in 1756 critical of the Moravian hymnbook, detailing its non-scriptural elements and regretting what he saw as its emotional, or non-rational, emphasis; however, he ended his critique by wishing the congregation well. At Ripponden he embarked on research at the behest of Sir George Warren of Poynton Lodge, Cheshire, in order to prove that Sir George was the legitimate heir to the earldom of Warenne and Surrey. His *Memoirs of the Ancient Earls of Warren and Surrey and their Descendants* was published in a limited edition of six copies in 1776, with a second edition of fifteen copies following in 1779, and a third, larger, edition in 1782. Despite Watson's claim in the preface to the work, his researches were unable to establish Warren's right to

the title, but this did not deter Sir George from pursuing that claim vigorously, if unsuccessfully, over the next twenty years.

It was through his whig connections and the patronage of Warren that Watson secured further advancement, first to the rectory of Miningsby, Lincolnshire, in 1766 and then to the valuable living of Stockport, Cheshire, in 1769. There, he continued his antiquarian researches, which now focused on his native county. His extensive papers, deposited at the Bodleian Library, Oxford, John Rylands Library, Manchester, and York Minster Library, have been much used by subsequent writers. A fresh edition of his Halifax history was embarked upon by F. A. Leyland in 1869, but only the first part was published. His interests extended to the collection of literary remains, and he was a noted writer and collector of songs.

Watson died at Stockport on 14 March 1783, possibly as a consequence of injuries received from a kick by a horse. He was survived by his wife and all three children, and his will was proved in the prerogative court of Canterbury in May of that year.   WILLIAM JOSEPH SHEILS

Sources J. Watson, *History of Halifax* (1775), 523–5 · J. G. Nichols, review, *Herald and Genealogist*, 7 (1873), 193–219 · Foster, *Alum. Oxon.* · A. Porritt, 'The Society of Antiquaries and the Rev. John Watson MA, FSA', *Transactions of the Halifax Antiquarian Society* (1984), 36–9 · will, proved, May 1783, PRO, PROB 11/1104, sig. 272 · *DNB* · *IGI*
Archives Bodl. Oxf., antiquarian notes and papers relating to north of England incl. Yorkshire notes and collections · Chetham's Library, Manchester, political letters, verses, and commonplace books · York Minster Library, papers relating to Halifax | Bodl. Oxf., letters to John Charles Brooke · Bodl. Oxf., Cheshire collections; Lancashire collections · Bodl. Oxf., copy of *History of the ancient earls of Warren and Surrey* with his MS notes, additions, and corrections · Bodl. Oxf., letters to Samuel Pegge the elder · JRL, papers relating to Bradshaw family and Stockport · W. Yorks. AS, Leeds, Yorkshire Archaeological Society, corresp. and papers
Likenesses J. Basire, line engraving, 1780 (after portrait by D. Stringer), BM, NPG [*see illus.*] · W. William, etching, NPG

Watson, John (1847–1939), philosopher, was born on 25 February 1847 in the parish of Gorbals, Glasgow, Lanarkshire, the eldest of the four children of John Watson, a block printer, whose family were farmers in Lanarkshire, and his wife, Elizabeth Robertson, whose family came from Northumberland. He was educated at the Free Church school, Kilmarnock, Ayrshire, and worked briefly as a clerk in Dunbartonshire and Glasgow before entering Glasgow University in 1866 to train for the church, from which he was diverted by his mentor Edward Caird. He won numerous prizes including the rector's prize, and graduated MA with the highest honours in mental and moral philosophy on 1 May 1872. He was awarded the degree of LLD by Glasgow University in 1880; his first book, *Kant and his English Critics*, appeared in the following year. On 18 August 1874 he married, at Glasgow, Margaret Patterson (b. 1846/7), daughter of David Mitchell, a calenderer, and his wife, Jane. They had one son and three daughters.

Watson was appointed, on the recommendation of Caird, to the chair of logic, metaphysics, and ethics at Queen's University, Kingston, Ontario, Canada, a position he held from 1872 to 1889, when he became professor of moral philosophy. He retired in 1924. He was vice-principal of the university from 1901 to 1924. He delivered lay sermons to the students and through his 'rational religion' was influential in liberalizing the Presbyterian church in Canada. Candidates preparing for the ministry were among his pupils. He contributed to the general tendency in ideas which led to the creation of the United Church in Canada. A charter member of the Royal Society of Canada (1882), he was the first Canadian to deliver the Gifford lectures at Glasgow (1910–12), published as *The Interpretation of Religious Experience* (1912). He subsequently received honorary degrees from the University of Toronto, the University of Michigan, and Knox College, Toronto. He is widely acknowledged as one of the great influences on the development of Queen's University, and of university education in Canada.

Watson was an absolute idealist, one of a school that took its lead from Plato, Kant, and Hegel. He wrote extensively on German idealism and the positivist, empiricist, and evolutionist varieties of materialism to which he was opposed. Philosophical problems were understandable and resolvable only when their genesis and development were traced through classical thinkers. He described himself as a speculative idealist opposed to subjective idealism, which he associated with identifying reality with immediate awareness, or the ideas in one's head. For him reality was capable of being known as it actually was, absolutely rational. He did not deny the existence of a material world, only that it was separable from mind and spirit. In *An Outline of Philosophy* (1895; 4th edn, 1908) he argued that mind cannot be reduced to matter because matter is rationally intelligible and has within it the potentiality of mind. Watson endeavoured to supply religion with a rational foundation by arguing that absolute idealism and religious experience both affirm the unity of God, immortality, and freedom. Rationality finds its supreme expression in religion. He denies a transcendent God severed from individuals, or in which individuals are totally absorbed. The realization of one's deepest self is achieved only in the self-conscious identification of the individual with an immanent God.

Watson's political philosophy was communitarian and anti-contractarian. Wishing to preserve the self-identity of the individual as a social self and in relation to nature, he showed the necessity of conceiving both as rationally structured. The individual and the community are mutually dependent, the former an individuation of the latter, and neither is subordinate to the other. His book *The State in Peace and War* (1919) called for a world federation of states, and warned that both punitive measures against the central powers and the structure of the League of Nations would result in renewed hostilities, a prophecy whose fulfilment he did not live to witness.

Watson died at his home, 90 Bagot Street, Kingston, Ontario, on 27 January 1939 and was buried three days later in Cataraqui cemetery in Kingston.

DAVID BOUCHER

Sources *The Times* (28 Jan 1939) • *The Times* (3 Feb 1939) • W. E. McNeill, *Proceedings and Transactions of the Royal Society of Canada*, 3rd ser., 33 (1939), section 2, pp. 159–61 • L. Armour and E. Trott, *The faces of reason* (1981) • R. C. Wallace, *Some great men of Queen's* (1941) • *Philosophical essays presented to John Watson* (1922) • J. A. Irving, 'Development of philosophy in central Canada', *Canadian Historical Review*, 31 (1950), 251–85 • D. D. Calvin, *Queen's University at Kingston* (1941) • *Kingston Whig Standard* (27–8 Jan 1939) • 'Watson, John', *The Macmillan dictionary of Canadian biography*, ed. W. S. Wallace, 3rd edn (1963), 786 • *WWW* • parish register (birth), Gorbals, Lanarkshire, 25 Feb 1847 • m. cert. • *Montreal Daily Star* (28 Jan 1939)
Archives Balliol Oxf., Caird MSS, corresp. • Queen's University, Kingston, Ontario
Likenesses A. D. Patterson, oils, Queen's University, Kingston, Watson Hall

Watson, John [*pseud.* Ian Maclaren] (1850–1907), minister of the Presbyterian Church of England and author, was born in Manningtree, Essex, on 3 November 1850, the only child of John Watson (*d.* 1879), an Inland Revenue officer, and his wife, Isabella Maclaren (*d.* 1871/2). His ancestors were of highland stock and, on his mother's side, Roman Catholic. Some of his character traits, such as superstitiousness and a romantic Jacobitism, which were not normally associated with Presbyterian ministers, were later attributed to this background. His parents returned to Scotland when he was about four years old and he attended school in Perth before transferring to Stirling high school at the age of twelve, where he befriended Henry Drummond (1851–1897). In 1866 he entered Edinburgh University, where he displayed only average ability as a student, and graduated MA in 1870. Under pressure from his family, he entered New College, Edinburgh, to study for the ministry of the Free Church of Scotland, after which he spent a semester at the University of Tübingen in Germany. Watson later acknowledged that he would have been equally at home in the established church, but family loyalty prevailed. He did, however, remain aloof from the revivalism of Moody and Sankey, to which many of his New College contemporaries were drawn.

Watson endured a brief and unhappy assistantship at Barclay Free Church, Edinburgh, on account of his incompatibility with the minister, J. H. Wilson. However, his ordination to Logiealmond Free Church in Perthshire in 1875 initiated a short, but very happy, ministry there. In 1877 he was called to Free St Matthew's Church, Glasgow, as colleague and successor to Samuel Miller. Once again, however, he was out of sympathy with his colleague and the arrangement was not a success. Watson married, on 6 June 1878, Jane Burnie Ferguson, with whom he had four sons.

When, by chance, Watson happened to preach to the newly established Presbyterian congregation of Sefton Park, Liverpool, in 1880, he was offered the charge and thus began a ministry that lasted twenty-five years. The church itself was one of great architectural beauty, a 'Presbyterian cathedral' which reflected the congregation's influence and affluence. It proved the perfect environment in which Watson could achieve his potential as a preacher and a pastor. He also participated actively in civic affairs and he was deeply involved in the creation of the University of Liverpool.

Watson's health first gave cause for concern in October 1889 when problems with his lungs caused him to winter abroad, but this apparent vulnerability was at odds with the impression of vigour and robustness which he projected. His pastoral diligence, sociable personality, and restless habits all militated against the husbanding of physical resources. These were further taxed by another call on his abilities, that of the popular writer.

At the prompting of William Robertson Nicoll, Watson published, under the transparent pseudonym of Ian Maclaren, *Beside the Bonnie Brier Bush* (1894), the first chapter of which appeared in the *British Weekly* in November 1893. Watson, together with S. R. Crockett and J. M. Barrie, came to be known as the kailyard school, an unflattering coinage derived from Watson's own work. The popular success of the genre was as dramatic as the hostile critical reaction with which it was received, both at the time and thereafter. The combination of sentimentality, humour, and religion in a rural Scottish setting proved a successful formula both in Britain and North America and Watson achieved instant fame. If the work was suffused with nostalgia it was a natural consequence, the fictional Drumtochty being based on the Logiealmond of Watson's early ministry. *The Days of Auld Lang Syne* (1895) was essentially a continuation of the earlier work. Thereafter he maintained a steady output of fictional work, though none was as successful as his initial effort. Watson also wrote a number of theological works under his own name and he came briefly under suspicion of heterodoxy on account of views expressed in *The Mind of the Master* (1896).

Watson achieved recognition from St Andrews University in 1896 with the award of the degree of DD, a degree also bestowed by Yale University, where Watson was Lyman Beecher lecturer in 1896. The punishing schedule of the American lecture tour he undertook in that year, from October to December, quite agreed with him, to the astonishment of his manager, J. B. Pond, who had expected someone frailer. The tour was a resounding success, with the lecturer discovering a great affinity with America and its people; perhaps surprisingly so, given that in domestic politics he was a staunch Conservative and imperialist. Later he was vociferous in his support of the war in South Africa. Pond considered that he 'saw more happy faces while accompanying him than any other man was ever privileged to see in the same length of time' (Pond, 405). Watson's own view of his reception was his dry observation that the people were not unfriendly. An offer of $24,000 to extend his tour by ten weeks was declined, but he did return for a further tour in 1899.

Watson naturally promoted the broader objectives of his denomination and he played a large part in raising the finance for a new Presbyterian theological college, Westminster College, Cambridge, which opened in 1899. In the following year Watson served as moderator of the English Presbyterian synod. It was after this that some failing of his physical powers became noticeable. In September 1904 Watson informed his congregation of his intention

to quit in a year's time. He did not retire completely, and in 1907 he accepted the presidency of the National Free Church Council and allowed his name to go forward for the principalship of Westminster College, in succession to Oswald Dykes.

In January 1907 Watson departed for his third American lecture tour. On 23 April he arrived at Mount Pleasant, Iowa, to deliver a course of lectures in the Iowa Wesleyan University. However, tonsillitis gave rise to blood poisoning and he died in the Brazelton Hotel, Mount Pleasant, on 6 May, the same day that his principalship was to be confirmed. His body was returned to Liverpool, where he was given a public funeral at Smithdown cemetery on 27 May.

Pond described Watson as:

> a tall, straight, square-shouldered, deep-chested man of middle age, with a large, compact, round, and well-balanced head, thinly thatched with brown and grayish hair, well-moulded refined features that bear the impress of kindly shrewdness, intellectual sagacity, and spiritual clearness, tempered, too, with a mingled sense of keen humour and grave dignity.   (Pond, 405)

In addition to his commitments as a minister, a writer, and a public figure Watson gave generously of himself in any private gathering and it was often in such company that he was at his most brilliant. Yet he could not be described as a conversationalist, given that listening was not his forte and his capacity to entertain was overwhelming in its effect. He was also blessed with a sense of irony and a facility for sarcasm, though he used the latter sparingly. It is difficult not to conclude that Watson's intense personality, coupled with incessant demands on his time and energy which he was loath to refuse, wore out his physical frame prematurely.

LIONEL ALEXANDER RITCHIE

Sources W. R. Nicoll, 'Ian Maclaren': life of the Rev John Watson D.D. (1908) · J. B. Pond, *Eccentricities of genius* (1901), 405–51 · *The Scotsman* (7 May 1907) · *Glasgow Herald* (7 May 1907) · *The Times* (7 May 1907) · *Liverpool Daily Post and Liverpool Mercury* (7 May 1907) · *British Weekly* (9 May 1907) · *British Weekly* (16 May 1907) · *British Weekly* (23 May 1907) · *Scottish Review* (9 May 1907) · *Scottish Review* (16 May 1907) · G. Blake, *Barrie and the kailyard school* (1951) · W. Ewing, ed., *Annals of the Free Church of Scotland, 1843–1900*, 1 (1914), 352 · WWW · DNB
Likenesses R. Morrison, oils, Sefton Park Church, Liverpool · G. Reid, oils, Walker Art Gallery, Liverpool · photograph, repro. in Nicoll, 'Ian Maclaren', facing frontispiece · photograph, repro. in Pond, *Eccentricities of genius*, facing p. 404
Wealth at death £59,524 6s. 9d.: resworn probate, 13 July 1907, CGPLA Eng. & Wales

Watson, John Boles (1748–1813), theatre manager, was born on 9 November 1748 at Silver Fort, Cashel, co. Tipperary, Ireland, the second of the six children of Solomon Watson, possibly a farmer, and his wife, Susannah. The family belonged to the Society of Friends. After his twenty-first birthday Watson moved to England and became friendly with the actor John Philip Kemble. Forsaking earlier Quaker principles, he gained a footing in the company managed by Roger Kemble, John's father. Here he played under the assumed name of Carleton. However, ill health prevented him taking up the itinerant life of an actor; instead, in 1779 he opted for management, although he also appeared sporadically on the stage. At

Roger Kemble's retirement Watson purchased a number of his theatres, while others were assigned to Henry Masterman.

Cheltenham became the headquarters of Watson's activities, and his performers were nominated the 'Cheltenham Company of Comedians'. A converted malthouse off Pittville Street served as their theatre (the location is featured by Dinah Maria Muloch in chapter 6 of *John Halifax, Gentleman*, 1856). The second of Watson's Cheltenham theatres, opened in 1782, was situated in York Passage, near the High Street, a building visited by George III and the royal family when they took the waters in 1788. This was enough for Watson to dispense with the requirement of a patent in terming the playhouse the 'Theatre Royal'. The minor remains of the building are now marked by a blue plaque. On the king's birthday, 4 June 1805, Watson's last Cheltenham theatre—situated in Bath Street in the Cambray area of the town—was opened.

Watson created a circuit of more than forty theatres: from Bristol in the south-west it reached northwards to Holywell in Flintshire, and from Leicester it stretched across the midlands and Wales to Carmarthen. In addition to Cheltenham, the principal locations of activity were Gloucester, Cirencester, Stroud, Hereford, Leominster, Monmouth, Swansea, Oswestry, Evesham, Stourbridge, Wolverhampton, Coventry, Birmingham, Daventry, Walsall, and Tamworth.

Allowing for the difficulties under which a Georgian manager worked, Watson's company was proficient rather than distinguished. William Field, a contemporary Warwick historian, judged it to be averagely provincial. Visiting performers from London could take a harsher line: Dorothy Jordan wrote that at Worcester the supporting performers put her in a foul temper with their 'ignorance and stupidity' (Aspinall, 187). Nevertheless, Watson possessed the foresight to choose a band of players who would acquit themselves creditably for much of the time: Mrs Carleton, later to manage a company in Wales, was a leading lady praised for her tragic portraits, and was ably supported by her husband, an upstanding uniformed figure; William Buckle combined the heavy roles of tragedy and sentiment with the additional work of prompter and stage manager; Chamberlain, the company treasurer, specialized in comedy; Richards, a dancer, singer, and comedian, also engaged in ageing tragic nobles; Field was suited by youth and temperament to light romantic roles; George Shuter, the son of Edward Shuter of the London patent theatres, was a favourite over many years; and Samuel Seward gained more than a local name as a harlequin and also opened in Cheltenham his own theatre, the Sadler's Wells or English Fantoccini. The scenic artists were Samuel (?) Whitmore, later at Covent Garden, and Seward.

Some members of Watson's family worked in the theatre, and it is convenient to consider them and the non-theatricals together. According to the *Thespian Dictionary* Watson's first marriage was to a Miss Wilkinson. After her early death he married his second wife, Henrietta Withington, a widow, at Cheltenham by special licence on 18 October 1785. The couple had two children, Louisa and John Boles Watson II. Louisa married in 1802 John Richer, the rope-walker of Sadler's Wells Theatre. Having abandoned the Wells, Richer played a lively part in Watson's company, taking on such roles as Don Juan in the play of that name and the dumb Francesco in *The Tale of Mystery* (1802) by Thomas Holcroft, as well as continuing with his acrobatic feats. Louisa died 'of a decline' (*GM*, 696) in Cheltenham on 17 July 1804; she had played no part on the stage, possibly deterred by ill health. John Boles Watson II performed throughout his life on the stages of the Watson circuit. He eventually married Frances Margaret, but his children—two sons and three daughters—were the outcome of passing liaisons. In spite of an inability to cope with the finances, Watson II attempted to organize the circuit after his father's gradual relinquishing of responsibility around 1811. About 1826 the rapidly diminishing circuit passed to Watson II's eldest son, yet another actor, John Boles Watson III.

In addition to the regular company, visitors from the London and Bristol stages appeared for brief periods, and the calibre of the stars aids a just evaluation of the standard of the company. Sarah Siddons played at Cirencester and Cheltenham in the early days of Watson's management. Her brother John Philip Kemble played Hamlet at Cheltenham and Gloucester. Elizabeth Richards, a Gloucestershire woman who joined the prestigious Bath company, arrived both before and after her marriage to John Edwin, sometimes playing only for a night at proximate Cotswold theatres. William Henry West Betty, the 'Young Roscius', was a child actor whose appeal lasted longer in the provinces than on the London stage; he played on the circuit at the height of his popularity in 1804 and later in 1807. Alexander Pope, the Cork actor who progressed to the London patent houses, arrived with his powerful voice to assume the role of Macbeth in 1811. Thus, while Watson could afford to hire players of worth to act on the circuit for a few nights, these engagements were limited, and for the most part the locally known actors had to sustain the interest of the season's audiences.

On 19 September 1811 an ailing Watson made his will, bequeathing his circuit of theatres to his son, John Boles Watson II. During the former's working life elaborate mortgages, sharings, and leasings of the theatres make their value difficult to calculate. Watson died at his home in High Street, Cheltenham, 'affected with gout, which terminated his existence by an attack on the vitals' (*Gloucester Journal*, 22 March 1813), on 18 March 1813. He was buried in the graveyard of the parish church of St Mary, Cheltenham, on 22 March.   PAUL RANGER

Sources A. Denning, *Theatre in the Cotswolds*, ed. P. Ranger (1993) • A. Denning, 'Early theatricals in Cirencester', *Cirencester Archaeological and Historical Society Annual Report*, 14 (1971–2), 5–9 • T. Hannam-Clark, *Drama in Gloucestershire* [1928] • J. Osney, 'The theatre and related entertainments in Warwick, c.1800', Warwick Public Library • A. Aspinall, *Mrs Jordan and her family* (1951) • S. Ryley, *The itinerant, or, Memoirs of an actor* (1808) • W. Field, *A historical and descriptive account of the town of Warwick* (1815) • *The thespian dictionary, or, Dramatic biography of the present age*, 2nd edn (1805) •

GM, 1st ser., 74 (1804), 696 · *Gloucester Journal* (22 March 1813) · parish register (burial), 1813–24, St Mary's, Cheltenham, entry 27 · register of births, Tipperary meeting, Society of Friends, Dublin **Archives** Bingham Library, Cirencester, playbills · Birm. CL, Winston collection · Cheltenham Art Gallery and Museum, playbills · Gloucester Local Studies collection, playbills **Likenesses** A. Pope, miniature in ivory case, Cheltenham Art Gallery and Museum; repro. in Denning, *Theatre in the Cotswolds* **Wealth at death** see will, PRO, PROB 11/1544, 226, fols. 65–6

Watson [*formerly* Tanck], **John Christian** [Chris] (1867–1941), trade unionist and prime minister of Australia, was born on 9 April 1867 at Valparaiso, Chile, the only child of Johan Christian Tanck, and his wife, Martha, *née* Minchin (*d. c.*1890). Tanck was the chief officer of the brig *Julia*, which traded in the Pacific out of Chile, and arrived at Port Chalmers, New Zealand, on 24 December 1865. He married Martha there on 19 January 1866. They departed for Guam on 2 February. Martha Tanck subsequently returned to New Zealand with her son Chris. On 15 February 1869 at Waipori she married George Thomas Watson. Aged ten, Chris Watson left Cave Valley primary school and took up menial rural jobs. A precocious learner, in 1880 he became an apprenticed compositor. As a 'lanky alert-looking youth' and keen rugby player, he joined the *Oamaru Mail* in 1882 but, unemployed, he migrated to Sydney in 1886. After first working as a stable-hand at Government House, he became a compositor on the *Australian Star*; he supported the newspaper's policy of fiscal protectionism.

Watson joined the Typographical Association and became active in trade union affairs. In January 1890 he was a delegate to the New South Wales Trades and Labor Council (TLC), which tapped his organizing capacity as it consolidated its plans to found a new colonial political party. Watson was the first secretary of the West Sydney branch of the prototype Labor Party, and directed the local campaign that returned four members to parliament. Thirty-five out of 141 seats was an auspicious beginning for Labor, but the breakthrough raised difficulties for its control by the TLC.

Watson's enthusiasm combined gregariousness with sound judgement and strong will. After becoming, in 1892, president of the TLC and chairman of the executive committee of the Labor Party, he marshalled the momentum that sought solutions for the pioneering problems of the party. A series of protean disputes among the parliamentarians, and between them and the TLC, was stabilized in 1894. The foundational forms of sovereignty of conference, caucus solidarity with accepted pledge, and powerful extra-cameral executive became unique features of the party. After resigning his TLC and party positions, Watson won a country seat in the New South Wales legislative assembly in 1894. The temporary demise of the TLC required a restructuring of the party. Again Watson led the movement that resulted in harmonious settlement of city and country interests. By now he saw clearly that Labor had to participate in the mainstream of politics, while retaining its trade-union base: a dichotomy that strained even his exceptional powers of proportioned compromise.

John Christian Watson (1867–1941), by unknown photographer, *c.*1904

In parliament Watson honed his political skills, strengthened the leadership of J. S. T. McGowen, softened the spiky vigour of W. M. Hughes, and encouraged other Labor members. As the proposed federation of the Australian colonies gradually consumed provincial politics, he perceived that Labor had to foster the burgeoning of national aspiration. He was a great believer in the referendum as an essential part of democracy, and he thwarted the narrow plans of Hughes and W. A. Holman to prevent the premier, G. H. Reid, from putting the great question to the voters of New South Wales.

With federation accomplished in 1901, Watson won the country seat of Bland. His qualities of polite and determined persistence, perceptive and liberal awareness, and critical but humane fellowship complemented his unrivalled experience of Labor in politics. He was the natural leader of the party in the new commonwealth sphere. With members elected from five of the six widespread states of Australia, some of them with only embryonic organizations, the federal Labor Party needed the wise guidance that Watson could provide. He gradually moulded a united and effective team, which became accepted by 1903 as one of the 'three [cricket] elevens' in the parliament. The party became a potent force, helping to forge fundamental national principles: protectionism with imperial preference, an arbitration system to govern industrial relations, and a 'white Australia' policy that excluded coloured peoples and welcomed British immigrants.

As these objectives took legislative shape, Watson's friendship with, and respect for, Alfred Deakin conditioned co-operation with his Protectionist Party. But disagreement over details of a conciliation and arbitration bill precipitated withdrawal of Labor Party support, and on 27 April 1904 Watson formed the first Labor federal government. It lasted until 17 August, when a combination of Reid's Free Trade Party and conservative Protectionists prevailed. Watson became leader of the opposition, a symbol of the reduction of the three 'elevens' to two, a process consummated in 1909, when the conservatives formed the Liberal Party under Deakin. Meanwhile, the vital extra-cameral base of the Labor Party had ruled in 1905 that the parliamentarians should be an independent group and loosen its association with the Protectionist Party. Watson had been unhappy with the decision. He interpreted it as limiting his ability to manoeuvre and slighting the parliamentary party's achievements in gaining legislative concessions and their role in the maturing of the federal parliament.

These restrictions aggravated personal spurs. Watson's wife, English-born Ada, née Low, a dressmaker, whom he had married in the Unitarian church on 27 November 1889, resented his long absences in Melbourne, far away from their Sydney home. But the party pressures were uppermost, and when the final legislative stages of the complicated tariff were at last in sight, Watson decided that he had completed his arduous pioneering political work. He resigned as leader on 24 October 1907. He remained active in the Labor Party, attending conferences, sitting on the New South Wales executive, advising and encouraging prospective candidates, always emphasizing the need to extend and reinforce the national organization. He had had financial worries when in federal parliament: now he adjusted his aptitudes to include marginal entrepreneurial activity, with some minor success.

The First World War changed Watson's life. He was rejected for service in the Australian Imperial Force. He had always exulted in the British empire. When conscription became a seismic issue for the Labor Party, he refused to tolerate overwhelming opposition to it, soon translated into policy. The party expelled him in 1916. Thereafter Watson developed his business interests, by becoming a director of several companies, and helping Sir William Walkley to establish the Ampol oil company in 1936. He was also a founder of the National Roads Association in 1920, became its president, turned it into the National Roads and Motorists' Association in 1923, and remained in charge until 1941. His wife, Ada, died on 19 April 1921. They had no children. He married Antonia Mary Gladys Dowlan (1902–c.1960) in the Unitarian church on 30 October 1925. Watson died in Sydney on 18 November 1941, survived by his wife and daughter. His remains were cremated.

BEDE NAIRN

Sources B. Nairn, *Civilising capitalism* (1973); pbk edn (1989) • J. A. La Nauze, *Alfred Deakin: a biography*, 2 vols. (1965) • L. F. Fitzhardinge, *William Morris Hughes* (1964) • W. G. McMinn, *George Reid* (1989) • L. F. Crisp, *The Australian federal labour party* (1955) • G. Souter, *Acts of parliament: a narrative history of the senate and house of representatives, Commonwealth of Australia* (1988) • B. Nairn and J. C. Watson, 'A genealogical note', *Labour History*, 34 (May 1978), 102–3 • H. S. Broadhead, 'J. C. Watson and the caucus crisis of 1905', *Australian Journal of Politics and History*, 8/1 (1962), 93–7 • Births, deaths and marriages records, Wellington, New Zealand • Births, deaths and marriages records, Sydney, Australia • private information (2004)

Archives NL Aus., papers | Mitchell L., NSW, State Library of New South Wales, trades and labour records • NL Aus., Alfred Deakin papers

Likenesses photograph, c.1904, NL Aus. [see illus.] • J. Ashton, portrait, 1913, Australian Parliament House, Canberra

Wealth at death £3575: probate, 1941, Sydney

Watson, John Dawson (1832–1892), painter and illustrator, was born on 20 May 1832 in Sedbergh, Yorkshire, the eldest son of Dawson Watson, a wealthy solicitor, and his wife, Mary Bragg. Watson was educated at King Edward VI Grammar School, Sedbergh (1842–7), and at the Manchester School of Design between 1847 and 1851, later studying in the London studio of Alexander Davis Cooper and at the Royal Academy Schools. He returned to Manchester in 1852. His first exhibit was *The Wounded Cavalier* at the Manchester Institution in 1851, followed by *An Artist's Studio* (which contained portraits of himself, Cooper, and Cooper's family) at the Royal Academy in 1853.

Watson was predominantly a narrative figure painter, who worked in oils and watercolour and also produced very fluent line drawings. In 1856 he sold a number of works to the Liverpool merchant and art collector John Miller; these pictures attracted the attention of the Pre-Raphaelite painter Ford Madox Brown, who invited Watson to exhibit at his house in London. Watson was a member of the literary and artistic Letherbrow Club in Manchester from 1857, and over the next two years contributed twelve papers and numerous pen-and-ink drawings to the club's volumes. On 23 November 1858, at Giggleswick, Yorkshire, he married his cousin, Jane Dawson Edmondson (b. c.1831), the daughter of Christopher Edmondson, solicitor of Settle, Yorkshire, with whom he had two sons and three daughters. His elder son, Dawson Watson, was a pupil of the Royal Academician Mark Fisher.

In 1860 Watson settled in London where, a year later, he was commissioned by Routledge to execute 110 black and white drawings, engraved by the Dalziel brothers, for a new edition of *The Pilgrim's Progress*. These were pronounced by the *Art Journal* to be of 'uniform excellence' (1861, 46), and made Watson's name in the field of illustration. *Robinson Crusoe* followed in 1864 as a companion volume. Illustrations by Watson appeared regularly in *Good Words* (1861–3), *London Society* (1862–7), *The Graphic* (1870–77), and other similar periodicals. He was elected an associate of the Society of Painters in Water Colours in 1864, with full membership in 1869, when he exhibited *Carrying in the Peacock*, which the *Art Journal* considered 'brilliant as Veronese … Mr. Watson bids fair to become one of our first artists' (1869, 173). A version of this medieval theme was painted as a fresco for the Surrey home of Birket Foster, who had married Watson's sister, Frances, in 1864. *Raising the Maypole* for another room was never finished, although

Watson was living near by in the village of Milford from 1865.

Early success was said to have made Watson somewhat lazy, and critics were often disappointed with later work. Certainly he did not fully exploit his talent as a theatrical designer. In 1871 he organized an amateur performance of *Twelfth Night* at Newcastle in aid of victims of the Franco-Prussian War, for which he designed and cut out fifty costumes, and in 1872 he executed sixty-five costume designs in watercolour for a professional production of *Henry V* at the Princes Theatre, Manchester. Meticulous observation of historical dress was a feature of his work, as in the Elizabethan setting for *The Poisoned Cup* (exh. RA, 1866), which was awarded a medal at the Vienna International Exhibition in 1873. Watson also painted portraits and contemporary domestic genre scenes, many examples of which were set in and around Cullercoats, Northumberland, and depicted the local fishing community. *Saved*, a sea rescue scene (exh. RA, 1871), achieved exceptional popularity as a print. He was elected an honorary member of the Royal Watercolour Society of Belgium in 1876.

In 1877 Watson returned to London, from Milford, before settling in Conwy, Caernarvonshire, in 1884, where he was a founder member of the Royal Cambrian Academy. He maintained links with Manchester throughout his life, culminating in a retrospective exhibition at the Brazenose Club in 1877. Exhibits included a new oil painting, *The Yeoman's Wedding*, which was also shown at the Manchester Jubilee Exhibition that year. Works in public collections include *Sancho Panza* at the Victoria and Albert Museum and *Bubbles* (a characteristic study of children) at the Cecil Higgins Gallery, Bedford. There are examples in Manchester City Galleries and holdings at Conwy, Birmingham, Liverpool, Newcastle, Norwich, and Worcester. More than sixty of Watson's works remain, many on public view, at the Castle Hotel, Conwy, together with a bust of Watson by Edward E. Geflowski.

Watson was regarded as a kind, liberal-minded man and had many interests, including riding to hounds and amateur theatricals. He died at his home, Plas Uchaf, Lancaster Square, Conwy, on 3 January 1892 of a respiratory complaint and was buried on the 7th of that month at St Agnes cemetery, Conwy.   JAN REYNOLDS

Sources J. Reynolds, *Birket Foster* (1975) · J. Reynolds, *Collectors Guide*, 45/6 (Jan 1992), 24–7 · P. Bryant, *John Dawson Watson, RWS* (1979) · *Art Journal*, 23 (1861), 46 · *Art Journal*, new ser., 8 (1869), 173 · *Llandudno Advertiser* (16 Jan 1892) · *Llandudno Advertiser* (23 Jan 1892) · [G. Dalziel and E. Dalziel], *The brothers Dalziel: a record of fifty years' work … 1840–1890* (1901); repr. as *The brothers Dalziel: a record of work* (1978) · S. Houfe, *Dictionary of British illustrators and caricaturists* (1978) · F. Reid, *Illustrators of the eighteen sixties* (1928) [repr. 1975] · m. cert. · d. cert.

Archives Castle Hotel, Conwy, signed and annotated works
Likenesses D. W. Wynfield, photograph, *c.*1862–1864, NPG · group portrait, photograph, *c.*1864–1866, repro. in Reynolds, *Birket Foster* · Elliott & Fry, carte-de-visite, NPG · E. E. Geflowski, bust, Castle Hotel, Conwy · F. Walter, pencil and wash drawing, Man. City Gall. · portrait, repro. in catalogue for retrospective exhibition at Brazenose Club (1877) · portrait, repro. in *Magazine of Art* (1892), 179

Watson, John Forbes (1827–1892), physician and expert on India, was baptized on 20 June 1827, at Strathdon, Aberdeenshire, the son of George Watson, a farmer, and his wife, Jean McHardy. He was educated at the University of Aberdeen and graduated MA and MD in 1847. He continued his medical training at Guy's Hospital, London, and in Paris. In 1850 he was appointed assistant surgeon to the Bombay Army Medical Service. His Indian experience included medical service to the artillery at Ahmednagar; to the Sind horse at Kangur; to the Jamsetjee Hospital, where he was assistant surgeon; and to Grant Medical College, where he lectured on physiology and clinical medicine. After returning to England on sick leave in 1853, he studied the sanitary uses of charcoal for the Royal School of Mines in London, and published a pamphlet on the subject in 1855. He then returned to his interests in India, cataloguing and investigating its useful plants at the behest of the India Office's court of directors; he published his index in 1868. He was named director of the India Museum in London in 1858. From the mid-1850s his Indian interests largely supplanted his medical practice.

Watson selected the materials and wrote the catalogue for the Indian department of the London International Exhibition of 1862. This brought him into the circle, led by Henry Cole, that had been central to the shaping of London's South Kensington Museum; to international exhibitions on the site (as well as British contributions to foreign exhibitions); and to the reshaping of the Schools of Design according to principles of industrial art. In Cole's view the future of English industrialism depended on training manufacturers and workers as well as the consuming public on the proper principles of design.

The influence of such thinking was clear in Watson's next major project, *The Textile Manufactures and the Costumes of the People of India* (1866). The project, simultaneously an ethnographic catalogue and a brief for increased commerce with India, included a text by Watson detailing the cultural uses of specific costumes by Indians and twenty sets of an eighteen-volume collection of samples of Indian textiles, each including some 700 samples. Watson, terming the volumes 'industrial museums' (*Textile Manufactures*, 1), arranged for their distribution to twelve English cities and seven sites in India (with one copy retained by the India Museum). The distribution of these catalogues and samples to industrial cities in Great Britain and key craft centres in India was intended to acquaint British producers with the forms and styles of Indian costume, while preserving Indian craft traditions. The catalogue employed photographs to illustrate the proper wearing of Indian clothing.

Watson sought to encourage commerce between the countries, especially by training English manufacturers in the needs of the Indian people. 'India is in a position to become a magnificent customer', Watson wrote, but only if 'we endeavour to make the articles which we know will be liked and needed' (*Textile Manufactures*, 2). Watson insisted that the development of widened commerce between Britain and India would benefit both partners, especially as wider knowledge led to a demand for Indian handicrafts in Britain.

The same central principles of encouraging broader trade through education in the principles of Indian design shaped Watson's reorganization of the India Museum in 1870. Watson continued, too, to be actively engaged in selecting and cataloguing Indian works for international exhibitions, including those in Paris (1867), Vienna (1873), and Philadelphia (1876), as well as the annual international exhibitions in South Kensington from 1871 to 1874. Reviewing these, the *Art Journal* singled out Watson's 'power of organization, and clear method of imparting information' ('Indian court', 208).

Meanwhile, Watson's broader interests in promoting commerce between Britain and India led him to investigate a wide range of Indian products. He called for a comprehensive survey of Indian goods and products in a pamphlet of 1872. He published works on Indian tobacco (1871), tea cultivation (1872), rheea fibre (1875), and wheat (1879), as well as on the applicability of cotton gins to Indian cotton (1879). He expanded his 'industrial museums' of samples of Indian textiles with a new multi-volume set in 1872–4.

Watson continued to pioneer photography as a method of illustrating works, establishing a photographic department in the India Office in 1865. He collaborated with J. K. Kaye to produce an ethnographic survey of India (*Peoples of India*, 8 vols., 1868–75), and with James Fergusson he documented the Indian classical architecture (displayed at the Paris Universal Exhibition of 1867 and published in 1869). Watson also proposed the reorganization of the India Museum and its libraries in 1874, paving the way for its reconsolidation in South Kensington in 1879.

Watson retired from the India Office soon after the relocation of the museum, in 1880. He was elected a fellow of the Linnean Society in 1889. He died at his home, 56 Belvedere Road, Upper Norwood, Surrey, on 29 July 1892. He was survived by his widow, Amelia Mary Anne Watson.

E. I. CARLYLE, *rev.* THOMAS PRASCH

Sources M. Taylor, 'The textile fabrics of India', *Art Journal*, 29 (1867), 82–5 • F. R. Condor, 'Exhibition of Indian textile fabrics at the Indian Museum, Downing Street', *Art Journal*, 32 (1870), 106 • 'Indian court', *Art Journal*, 33 (1871), 208–9 • *The illustrated catalogue of the Universal Exhibition published with the Art Journal* (1867), 49 [exhibition catalogue, Paris, 1867] • C. Worswick and A. Embree, *The last empire: photography in British India, 1855–1911* (1976) • *Art Journal catalogue of the London International Exhibition* (1862) • *The Times* (1 Aug 1892), 4f • *CGPLA Eng. & Wales* (1892) • d. cert. • bap. reg. Scot.
Wealth at death £5582 2s. 11d.: resworn probate, Aug 1893, *CGPLA Eng. & Wales* (1892)

Watson, John Selby (*bap.* 1804, *d.* 1884), scholar and murderer, baptized at Crayford church on 30 December 1804, is stated to have been the son of humble parents in Scotland. He was educated at first by his grandfather, and then at Trinity College, Dublin, where he graduated BA in 1838, being one of the gold medallists in classics, and proceeded MA in 1844. On 30 March 1854 he was admitted *ad eundem* at Oxford. He was ordained deacon in 1839 by the bishop of Ely, and priest in 1840 by the bishop of Bath and Wells,

and from 1839 to 1841 he served the curacy of Langport in Somerset.

Watson continued his classical studies, and began a lifelong habit of writing. From 1844 he was headmaster of the Stockwell grammar school in the London suburbs. Watson continued to publish classical and other works. He translated many Latin authors for Bohn's Classical Library and wrote several biographies, including those of George Fox (1860), Richard Porson (1861), William Wallace (1861), and Bishop Warburton (1863), and Wilkes and Cobbett (1870). He wrote on the reasoning power of animals (1867) and prepared several other works, including a history of the papacy to 1530. He expected pupils to match his level of erudition. Not surprisingly, the number of pupils in his school declined and he was dismissed as headmaster in September 1870.

Watson lived from 1865 at 28 St Martin's Road, Stockwell, and there, in a fit of passion, he killed his wife on 8 October 1871. Her skull was fractured, probably by a horse-pistol in Watson's possession. She was an Irishwoman named Anne Armstrong, to whom he was married at St Mark's Church, Dublin, in January 1845. Three days after the murder he attempted to commit suicide by taking prussic acid, purchased a year earlier. He wrote a long suicide note, admitting his crime and giving instructions for the publication of his literary remnants. He claimed the loss of his post as 'the principal cause' of his melancholy. Watson was tried for murder at the Old Bailey and found guilty, but recommended to mercy, and the sentence was commuted to penal servitude for life. The 'Stockwell murder' and Watson's condition attracted much curiosity. *Watson, ein unglücklicher Ehemann. Psychologische Studien über die Ehe* was published at Berlin in 1875. Watson died at Parkhurst prison in the Isle of Wight on 6 July 1884 after a fall from his hammock, and was buried in Carisbrooke cemetery.

W. P. COURTNEY, *rev.* H. C. G. MATTHEW

Sources *The Times* (11 Jan 1872) • *The Times* (12 Jan 1872) • *The Times* (13 Jan 1872) • *The Times* (8 July 1884) • *Men of the time* (1868) • Boase, *Mod. Eng. biog.*

Watson, John Steven (1916–1986), historian and academic administrator, was born on 20 March 1916 at 20 Newton Terrace, Hebburn-on-Tyne, co. Durham, the only son of George Watson, naval architect, and his wife, Elizabeth Laybourn Gall. At the age of seven after his parents had moved to Finchley, Middlesex, he lost his right leg in a street accident, a handicap which even as a schoolboy he learned to overcome and exploit. Exhorted by a strong, ambitious mother, he proved a lively and talented pupil at Merchant Taylors' School, London (1929–35), from where he went as Andrews scholar to St John's College, Oxford. Despite missing a year through illness he took a first class in modern history at the age of twenty-three and in 1939 was elected Harmsworth senior scholar at Merton College. On 9 January 1942 he married Heba Sylvia de Cordoba (*b.* 1918), the daughter of Ernest Arthur Newberry, with whom he had two sons. In the same year he became temporary civil servant in the Ministry of Fuel and Power, acting as private secretary to successive ministers, including Emanuel Shinwell.

Watson returned to Oxford in 1945 as student and tutor at Christ Church. He was popular both with his colleagues, who valued his shrewd judgement (he was censor from 1955 to 1961), and with his pupils, who appreciated his stimulating teaching and personal interest. An ambitious man of tireless energy and mildly socialist views, he was active in Oxford Labour Party politics, even becoming an (unsuccessful) candidate for the city council. He was one of the first Oxford academics to enter broadcasting, writing scripts and speaking on radio and television. His growing reputation led to his inclusion by Lord Franks on the commission of inquiry (1964–6) into the university.

Though his postgraduate research on the speakership of the House of Commons never came to fruition, the two-volume work Watson edited in collaboration with his former St John's tutor, W. C. Costin, *The Law and Working of the Constitution, 1660–1914* (1952), was a fresh and imaginative collection of constitutional documents, lacking only the benefit of an editorial commentary. His main piece of historical writing was *The Reign of George III* (1960), an outstanding volume in the *Oxford History of England*, the product of wide reading and independent judgement. His 1968 Wiles lectures at the Queen's University, Belfast, 'The rise of party politics in England and America', did not prove satisfactory, however, and he always hoped to revise them before publication.

Watson's elevation as principal of St Andrews University in 1966 surprised his Christ Church colleagues, who assumed it owed much to his friendship with Harold Wilson and other members of the Labour government. There was a certain resentment at St Andrews, which had not been consulted or even forewarned; it was a tribute to his geniality and tact that he soon overcame that initial disadvantage. A politician by temperament rather than an administrator and unencumbered by previous St Andrews connections, he was admirably qualified to preside over the separation from Dundee, which was the first test of the new regime. Unsympathetic to the Scottish professorial tradition, he promoted a more egalitarian system which effectively detached the holders of established chairs from the leadership and administration of their departments. His other concerns were for the rapid expansion of the truncated university and a widening of its international links. An elaborate appeals campaign to strengthen the university's finances did not fulfil all his expectations but gave him the opportunity to travel extensively as a St Andrews ambassador, especially in the United States. Though slow to shed his ingrained Oxford and London predilections, he nevertheless became a loyal advocate of his adopted university. At St Andrews he was a well-liked and accessible figure, despite his difficulties in fixing on a congenial residence. His habitual unpunctuality and cavalier attitude to paperwork sometimes disconcerted colleagues and officials but he was always adroit in seizing the main points of an agenda and guiding committees to a conclusion. He was not without personal partialities and could be resentful of opposition; but his animosity seldom lasted. His wit was often mischievous, rarely malicious. To those who went to him for assistance he was invariably responsive and sometimes greatly helpful.

A large, untidy man of impressive appearance and much charm, Watson enjoyed being the centre of attention and relished the prestige and perquisites of his position. In his cheerful, worldly acceptance of what life offered him, he resembled the eighteenth-century aristocratic politicians about whom he wrote so perceptively. Essentially he was a frustrated man of action whom early circumstances had diverted into an academic life, and he was always ready to take on a wide range of public activities beyond the conventional duties of his office. Only in his later years, when his physical energy was sapped by disease and his absences from St Andrews became more frequent, did his popularity and effectiveness decline. Following a serious operation for cancer of the oesophagus in the spring of 1986 he died in the Royal Free Hospital, Hampstead, London, on 12 June 1986, a few months before he was due to retire. NORMAN GASH

Sources WW · WWW · private information (2004) · personal knowledge (2004) · register, Merchant Taylors' School · register, St John's College, Oxford, 1919–75 · *The Times* (16 June 1986) · *St John's College notes* (1986) · senate minutes 7, 1985–6, U. St Andr. · *Alumnus Chronicle* [U. St Andr.], 71 (June 1980) · *Alumnus Chronicle* [U. St Andr.], 78 (June 1987) · m. cert. · d. cert.
Archives U. St Andr., official archives | SOUND BBC
Likenesses D. Donaldson, oils, 1986, U. St Andr. · photographs, U. St Andr.
Wealth at death £221,105: probate, 25 Feb 1987, *CGPLA Eng. & Wales*

Watson, Jonas (1663–1741). *See under* Watson, Justly (c.1710–1757).

Watson, Joseph (1764/5–1829), teacher of deaf people, was educated at a school in Mare Street, Hackney, run by his uncle, Thomas *Braidwood, the pioneer teacher of deaf mute children. In 1784 he decided to follow his uncle's profession and was involved in the foundation in 1792, by public subscription, of the asylum for deaf and deaf mute children which opened in Grange Road, Bermondsey. He was principal of the new institution which, after further fund-raising, moved in 1809 to premises in Kent Road. His main object, shared by many of the asylum's promoters, who included the evangelicals Henry Cox Mason, Henry Thornton, and John Townsend, was religious instruction. The practical methods used by Braidwood were not publicized until after his death, when Watson published *Instruction of the deaf and dumb, or, A theoretical and practical view of the means by which they are taught to speak and understand a language* (2 vols., 1809). By then he held the degree of LLD but it was not specified from which university. He had a correspondence about the asylum with the French teacher the Abbé Sicard, who was interested in its work. While numbers of pupils in the asylum grew from 70 in 1810 to 200 in 1820, Watson took a decreasing part in the ordinary teaching, which he left to assistant teachers while he concentrated on his private pupils. Watson died at the deaf and dumb asylum, Kent Road, London, on 23 November 1829, and was buried at Bermondsey. One of his sons, Thomas James Watson (probably the individual of that name who matriculated at Clare College, Cambridge, in 1822), was director of the institution until 1857, when he was succeeded by his own son, Watson's grandson, James Harrison Watson (1827–1888). **Alexander Watson** (1815/16–1865), Church of England clergyman, a son of Joseph Watson, was educated at Corpus Christi College, Cambridge, graduating BA in 1837 and MA in 1840. After proceeding to Durham University, he passed as a licentiate in theology and was ordained as curate of St Andrew's, Ancoats, Manchester. In 1840 he took charge of St John's, Cheltenham, where he established schools. He published a number of devotional works of a high-Anglican type, including *The Devout Churchman, or, Daily Meditations* (2 vols., 1847). In 1851 he became vicar of St Mary Church-with-Coffinswell, Devon. He was married and had at least one son, born in 1853. On moving to the rectory of Bridestow and Sourton, near Oakhampton, Devon, in 1855, he borrowed money which led to the sequestration of the living and to his quitting it at the end of two years for the incumbency of Bedford Chapel, Bloomsbury, London. He was involved in a chancery suit concerning the chapel, became insolvent, and was declared bankrupt on 11 January 1862, but was discharged on 21 February 1862. During 1863–4 he assisted the ritualist clergyman John Charles Chambers at St Mary's, Soho, and in 1864 took charge of Middleton on the Wolds, near Beverley, Yorkshire. He died at Middleton on 1 February 1865.   M. C. CURTHOYS

Sources *GM*, 1st ser., 100/1 (1830), 183–4 · *GM*, 1st ser., 80 (1810), 635–7 · *GM*, 1st ser., 92/1 (1822), 305–7 · [J. Watkins and F. Shoberl], *A biographical dictionary of the living authors of Great Britain and Ireland* (1816) · M. G. McLoughlin, *A history of the education of the deaf in England* (1987) · Venn, *Alum. Cant.* · Boase, *Mod. Eng. biog.*

Watson, Joshua (1771–1855), wine merchant and Anglican philanthropist, was born on 9 May 1771 at Tower Hill, City of London, the second son of John Watson (*d.* 1821), a wine merchant of Tower Hill, and of Dorothy Robson, a cousin of the watercolour painter George Fennel Robson and sister of the Revd James Robson, master of Sherburn Hospital, co. Durham. He was educated, from the age of ten, under the private tuition of Mr Crawford at Newington Butts, and from thirteen to fifteen at a commercial school run by Mr Eaton in the City of London. He also attended schools at Bromfield and Maidstone. In 1786 he was taken into his father's counting-house, which at that time moved within the City of London from Tower Hill to Mincing Lane. In 1792, aged twenty-one, he was admitted as a partner in his father's business. In 1797 he married Mary Sikes (*d.* 1831), daughter of Thomas Sikes, a banker in Mansion House Street, City of London. Mary's uncle, Charles Daubeny (afterwards archdeacon of Sarum), and her brother, Thomas Sikes (1766–1834), rector of Guilsborough, Northamptonshire, who had been at Oxford with Joshua's elder brother, the Revd John James Watson (1767–1839), were among the most prominent churchmen of the day. Joshua and Mary Watson had two daughters; the first died unmarried, but the second, Mary (*d.* 1840), married Henry Michell Wagner (1792–1870), vicar of Brighton (from 1824), in 1838.

Joshua Watson (1771–1855), by William Overend Geller (after Sir William Charles Ross)

The Hackney Phalanx As a wine merchant Watson was part of the commercial world, but his heart was always in the church work to which as a young layman he dedicated his life. His early friends and advisers included notable high-churchmen of the preceding generation: William Stevens (1732–1807), hosier, treasurer of Queen Anne's Bounty and founder of the Club of Nobody's Friends (1800), of which Watson was an original member; William Jones (1726–1800), vicar of Nayland; Jonathan Boucher (1738–1804), vicar of Epsom (where John James Watson served his first curacy); and Sir John Richardson (afterwards a judge in the court of common pleas). Joshua Watson formed close friendships with numerous like-minded contemporaries who formed the nucleus of the high-church coterie known as the Hackney Phalanx, so called from the residence of some of its members in that locality. Apart from Watson himself, the most prominent members of the Hackney Phalanx included: Henry Handley Norris (1771–1850), perpetual curate (later rector) of South Hackney, with whom he maintained an unbroken friendship of nearly sixty years; William Van Mildert (1765–1836), rector of St Mary le Bow, City of London (afterwards bishop of Llandaff and Durham); and Christopher Wordsworth (1774–1846), master of Trinity College, Cambridge.

The two Watson brothers and Norris worked closely together in masterminding the various religious, educational, missionary, and philanthropic activities of the Hackney Phalanx. Watson and his friends responded to the need to provide elementary education on Christian principles in the industrial towns and to meet the challenge of the schools founded by Joseph Lancaster which rejected church control. In 1811 the National Society for Promoting the Education of the Poor in the Principles of the Established Church was founded at a meeting at Watson's house in Clapton. Watson became the National Society's first treasurer, holding this office until his resignation in 1842. He was largely responsible for the raising of £16,000 in subscriptions by May 1812. The appointment of the archbishop of Canterbury as president, and the other bishops as vice-presidents, ensured that the National Society conformed to Watson's model of the church acting in its corporate capacity and was not a mere private pressure group. The society encouraged parishes to open their own schools, but Watson insisted on instruction in the liturgy and catechism, attendance at church, and the use of no books except those published by SPCK before authorizing the payment of grants.

Watson supported various literary ventures on behalf of the church. Along with Norris and Van Mildert he published a literary series called The Churchman's Remembrancer, which appeared in three instalments between 1807 and 1810. At the end of 1811 Watson and Norris purchased the *British Critic*, originally founded as an organ of Anglican orthodoxy in 1793 by Jones of Nayland, but which in subsequent years had somewhat diverged from its original character; after 1814 the *British Critic* once more became an effective mouthpiece of high-church principles. In 1818 Watson and Norris induced the Revd Frederick Iremonger to start another high-church periodical, the *Christian Remembrancer*; there is evidence to suggest that they had a financial concern in the *Remembrancer* and were influential in appointing its editors.

Administrative work for Anglican causes In 1814 Watson retired from business in order to devote himself exclusively to charitable activities and to the service of the Church of England. His voluntary efforts were not deflected by the ridicule heaped upon him by his former friend William Cobbett, in a vitriolic attack in his *History of the Protestant Reformation* (1822). He was treasurer of the Clergy Orphan Society, a governor of the London Fever Hospital, and subscribed in all to fourteen societies, including the Philanthropic Society, founded with the aim of reforming juvenile criminals. He became secretary of the relief fund set up in 1814 for German refugees from the Napoleonic wars. On account of this charitable work he received presents from the kings of Prussia and Saxony, was granted a diploma of honour at the University of Hamburg, and was elected a member of the Hamburg Patriotic Society for the Encouragement of the Liberal and Useful Arts. Although he never personally crossed the English Channel, Watson assumed that the Anglican church throughout the world was his concern. For many years he held leading positions in both of the oldest church societies connected with missionary work, the SPCK and the Society for the Propagation of the Gospel in Foreign Parts (SPG). In 1814 he was appointed joint treasurer of the SPCK and helped link the society more closely

to the SPG. His financial ability and integrity were legendary. He transformed the SPG into an effective missionary society; its total annual income increased from just over £8100 in 1814 to more than £82,000 by the time of his death in 1855.

Watson also encouraged the bishops to take a more active interest in missionary work. His deep interest in the colonial churches and beginnings of what later became known as the Anglican communion was reflected in his role in the creation of new colonial bishoprics. It was at Watson's house in Westminster that 'was first fostered the good design of sending bishops to the British colonies' (Churton, 18–19). Several of his intimate friends were appointed to these bishoprics: T. F. Middleton (Calcutta, 1822), John Inglis (Nova Scotia, 1832), William George Broughton (Australia, 1829), and George Selwyn (New Zealand, 1838). These bishops remained in regular correspondence with Watson, who offered practical advice and support. In 1841 he supported the foundation of the Colonial Bishoprics Fund, and in 1848 he became one of the founders and a member of the council of the new Missionary College of St Augustine, Canterbury. Watson's work for the overseas church was animated by his staunch high-church principles—he was determined to support the building up of churches linked organically to the Church of England.

Watson was no less attentive to the practical concerns of the church at home. He was largely instrumental in the foundation and drawing up of the original resolutions of the Church Building Society in 1817. He became a member of the royal commission for church building set up under Lord Liverpool's government, managed expenditure of the £1,500,000 parliamentary grant, and raised further large sums from voluntary sources over the next twenty years. In 1823 he took a house at 6 Park Street, Westminster, where he lived for the next sixteen years in order to be near the commission's headquarters. To aid the commission's revival of the church in industrial areas, the Church Pastoral Aid Society was founded in 1836. High-churchmen like Watson, however, objected to its evangelical ethos and use of lay assistants. In 1837, along with his friends Benjamin Harrison (1808–1887), later archdeacon of Canterbury, and Sir Robert Inglis, MP for Oxford University, Watson founded the Additional Curates Society, pledged to work through the bishops and to respect ministerial order. Watson himself donated money and also acted as joint honorary treasurer.

In 1828 Watson played a prominent part in the Anglican foundation of King's College, London. This brought him into contact with a leading figure in the incipient Anglo-Catholic revival, Hugh James Rose (1795–1838), with whom he became close friends. Watson opposed Roman Catholic emancipation on both religious and political grounds, and deplored the passing of the Reform Bill. In 1833 he was instrumental in the drawing up of a lay declaration and in supporting a clerical address to the archbishop of Canterbury in defence of the embattled Church of England; an involvement which, through his link with Rose, first brought him to contact with the leading figures in the emergent Oxford Movement, Newman, Keble, Froude, and, later, Pusey. Watson's withdrawal from the ruling committee of the SPCK in 1833, however, marked the end of an era of Hackney ascendancy in the counsels of church and state, with the initiative in galvanizing opposition to the forces of liberalism and dissent passing to the younger Tractarians.

Orthodox divinity and the Tractarian movement Although nicknamed the Archtreasurer, Watson was no mere ecclesiastical and financial bureaucrat: through his exhaustive reading and study he could claim to be an accomplished lay theologian. His favourite divine was the eighteenth-century orthodox churchman Daniel Waterland (1683–1740), and he was steeped in the high-church principles of the Caroline divines and later eighteenth-century high-churchmen. As a high-churchman Watson disapproved of both evangelicalism and the sort of latitudinarianism espoused by Thomas Arnold, as different but equally false manifestations of a 'Christianity of men above ordinances'. He was implacable in opposition to protestant dissent and objected to the SPCK's sale of books written by nonconformists such as Isaac Watts and Philip Doddridge, and even Bunyan's *Pilgrim's Progress*. However, unlike some tory high-churchmen, he supported several evangelical-dominated moral and philanthropic ventures, such as William Wilberforce's Society for the Suppression of Vice. Watson came to be widely consulted on doctrinal as well as practical matters, and his learning as well as practical attainments were recognized by the University of Oxford when he was awarded an honorary DCL on 14 June 1820. When the Oxford Movement emerged after 1833, the eagerness with which individual Tractarians sought Watson's benediction for their efforts is testimony to the value which they placed upon his judgement.

Watson's relationship with the Oxford Movement was ambivalent. Like other members of the Hackney Phalanx he initially welcomed the Tractarians as allies in the cause of Anglican orthodoxy. Keble's *Christian Year* (1827) was one of his favourite works, and he delighted Newman by his 'munificent subscription' to his new chapel at Littlemore in 1836. Watson warmly praised Newman's work advocating suffragan bishops in 1835, and had the highest regard for Newman's sermons. The evidence of Newman's published letters and diaries contradicts the assertion of Watson's biographer, Edward Churton, that Newman and Watson were never in the same room and that no correspondence passed between them.

Watson was happy to enlist Tractarian contributors to the ailing *British Critic* in 1836, and sympathized with Newman's objections to the liberal line being pursued by the then editor, J. S. Boone. He developed a sincere regard for some of the younger disciples of Newman in London, notably John William Bowden, James Robert Hope-Scott, and Samuel Francis Wood. In 1840 Watson handed over much of the business of the various church societies, which he had managed for over three decades, to Samuel Wood. He welcomed the energetic activities of Wood and other Tractarians on the council of the National Society who organized strong resistance to the government's proposals concerning lay state inspection of church schools in 1839. He was more committed than the Tractarians to establishment and the union of church and state, but was no less opposed than they were to state encroachment on the church's educational prerogatives.

Watson always hoped that Tractarian individualism might be curbed and harnessed by deference to the counsels of his own generation of high-churchmen, and at an early stage supported attempts to have the Tracts for the Times submitted to the editorial supervision of a committee. In this he failed; Newman and Froude resisted such moves and jettisoned Hackney caution. Whereas the ideal of ecclesiastical action preferred by Watson was later derided by Newman as being that of 'a board of safe, sound, sensible men' (*Apologia pro vita sua*), the Oxford Movement represented a voyage of discovery for many of its followers. The publication of Hurrell Froude's iconoclastic *Remains* (1838), with its strictures on the English reformers and Reformation, was a source of private dismay for Watson. Newman's Tract 90 (1841) and the increasingly 'romanizing' character of the *British Critic* heightened his private alarm over the apparent direction of the Oxford Movement. Watson deprecated the party spirit of the Tractarians, and compared Newman with the evangelical Charles Simeon as partisan leaders who equally strayed from the orthodox mainstream. He sympathized with most of the official academical and episcopal attempts to curb the Tractarians in the 1840s, such as the suspension of Pusey from preaching by the Oxford University authorities in 1843.

There were strict limits, however, to Watson's negative appraisal of Tractarianism: he was more reluctant than many of his Hackney friends, such as Norris, to make his profound misgivings public, and more ready than they to make allowances for what he regarded essentially as misplaced zeal and youthful excess. He assumed that Newman was being carried along unwillingly by his younger disciples, and restricted himself to private expressions of unease. He also supported the restatement of classical high Anglican principles enshrined in Christopher Wordsworth junior's (1807–1885) *Theophilus Anglicanus* (1843), the proofs of which he helped to correct. Newman's conversion to Rome in 1845 came as a shock, but Watson remained convinced that the Oxford Movement represented gain as well as loss for the Church of England. His own generation of high-churchmen had concentrated on church policy and parliamentary manoeuvrings, but with the collapse of the old constitutional order in church and state Watson rightly sensed that the old high-church party needed the rejuvenating intellectual and religious force provided by Tractarian Oxford in order to respond to new challenges. He regretted the need to caution his younger Oxford friends and referred to himself as 'the wet blanket'. Although his own sacramental views fell short of those propagated by the Tractarians, he welcomed Newman's attempt to recreate an Anglican form of semireligious life at Littlemore based on retirement and self-denial.

The Tractarian leaders for long remained anxious to shelter under Watson's mantle. In September 1839 Watson and Pusey had an amicable interview at Brighton, after which Pusey told Newman that Watson's teaching was the same as their own, and that the older man linked them with past generations of high-churchmen. Most old high-churchmen of Watson's generation were more conscious of the discontinuities between the Tractarians and themselves, and Pusey may have exaggerated the extent of Watson's approval of Tractarian endeavours in order to gain credibility. Watson was clearly embarrassed by Tractarian attempts to link his name with the movement, and deprecated attempts to attach too much importance to 'the movement of 1833' (Webster, 29). He dealt, however, with the problem of Tractarian use of his name with characteristic delicacy and courtesy. In 1840 he gracefully declined Newman's offer to dedicate the fifth volume of his *Plain and Parochial Sermons* to himself. After much agonizing and apparent reluctance Newman went ahead anyway, making an unsanctioned and somewhat stilted dedication. Newman remained devoted to Watson's memory, being 'greatly struck with him' (W. Copeland to E. B. Pusey, 16 March 1855, Oxford, Pusey House, LBV).

Later years and character In his last years Watson acted as a calming influence on more extreme high-churchmen, who were more troubled than himself by contemporary events. He counselled against a high-church overreaction to the Gorham judgment (1850), arguing that the verdict involved no new heresy, and did not touch or undermine the church's teaching on baptism as enshrined in her formularies. He deprecated the party spirit manifested by the formation of church unions. He was no less opposed to Arnoldian liberalism than were the Tractarians, but unlike the Tractarians pleaded for the toleration of differing opinions within the church so long as credal fundamentals were not endangered.

Although a city man and Londoner, Watson was an ardent Wordsworthian, with an intense love of nature. His piety was deep but unobtrusive; his favourite spiritual writer was Jeremy Taylor, in whose work he found a welcome scope for the imaginative faculty in devotion. Watson was too diffident to publish anything on his own account, but in 1825 he edited Hele's *Sacred Offices*, an eighteenth-century book of devotions based on the Bible and Book of Common Prayer, which he regularly used. He also printed several selections from Jeremy Taylor's shorter devotional manuals. He was instrumental, in the pre-Tractarian era, in helping restore the print of the communion office in the Book of Common Prayer to large, bold type.

Watson's later years were beset by domestic sorrows. His wife, Mary, died in 1831, and brother, Archdeacon Watson, in 1839. These losses, along with that of his daughter, Mary, in 1840, led him to sell his Westminster house in 1840 and to live during his remaining years with his late wife's sister and family at Clapton, and with his sister-in-law, Mrs J. J. Watson, *née* Caroline Powell (1775–1865), and her two daughters at Daventry. He also made regular visits to his friend the Revd Edward Churton (1800–1874), his later biographer, at Crayke, near York.

A shy, reserved, and self-effacing man, Watson yet had a great gift for gaining and retaining friendships. His friends found him a conversationalist of wit and charm, never short of amusing stories and anecdotes, especially relating to his favourite author, Dr Samuel Johnson. He remained active until the end of his life. He died at Clapton on 30 January 1855 and was buried on 7 February in the family vault at Hackney.   PETER B. NOCKLES

Sources E. Churton, ed., *Memoir of Joshua Watson*, 2 vols. (1861) • *GM*, 2nd ser., 44 (1855), 648–52 • E. Churton, *The gifts of God to the good. A sermon preached … the Sunday after the funeral of Joshua Watson Esq.* (1855) • *Christian Remembrancer*, new ser., 42 (1861) • LPL, Watson MS, 1562 • E. Powell, *Pedigree of the family of Powell* (1891) • A. Webster, *Joshua Watson: the story of a layman* (1954) • Foster, *Alum. Oxon.* • M. Watson, 'Book of reminiscences', Additional Curates Society Archives, Spitfire Road, Birmingham • Bodl. Oxf., MSS Eng. lett. c. 789–90 • Pusey Oxf., British Critic MSS, 1836–1843 • Pusey Oxf., Ollard papers, VI, XXIV • J. Keble, letters to J. Watson, 1836–7, Bodl. Oxf., MS Eng. lett. c. 469 • E. Churton, letter to W. Gresley, May 1846, Pusey Oxf., Gres 3/7/66 • C. le Bas, *The life of the Rt. Rev. Thomas Fanshaw Middleton, late bishop of Calcutta*, 2 vols. (1831) • J. A. Park, *Memoirs of William Stevens* (1812) • W. Cobbett, *A history of the protestant Reformation* (1824), letter 1 • W. R. W. Stephens, *The life and letters of Walter Farquhar Hook*, 7th edn (1885), 102 • H. P. Liddon, *Life of Edward Bouverie Pusey*, ed. J. O. Johnston and others, 4th edn, 4 vols. (1894–8), vol. 1, p. 259 • M. H. Port, *Six hundred new churches: a study of the church building commission, 1818–1856, and its church building activities* (1961) • F. K. Brown, *Fathers of the Victorians: the age of Wilberforce* (1961), 91, 353 • P. Corsi, *Science and religion: Baden Powell and the Anglican debate, 1800–1860* (1988), 10–11, 15–17 • E. A. Varley, *The last of the prince bishops: William Van Mildert and the high church movement of the early nineteenth century* (1992) • C. Dewing, *The passing of Barchester: a real life version of Trollope* (1991) • P. B. Nockles, *The Oxford Movement in context: Anglican high churchmanship, 1760–1857* (1994) • *The letters and diaries of John Henry Newman*, ed. C. S. Dessain and others, [31 vols.] (1961–), vol. 6, pp. 121–2; vol. 7, pp. 125–6, 143, 147, 253, 406, 410–11 • [W. Copeland], 'Narrative of the Oxford Movement', ed. P. Borlase, 1881, Pusey Oxf.

Archives LPL, corresp. and papers • LPL, papers relating to Westminster Association | Additional Curates Society, Birmingham, Mary Watson's 'Book of reminiscences' • Bodl. Oxf., Norris MSS • Church of England Record Centre, London, records of the National Society • LPL, corresp. with Christopher Wordsworth • Spiceland Road, Birmingham, Curates Society MSS

Likenesses W. O. Geller, stipple (after W. C. Ross), NPG [*see illus.*] • W. Ross, miniature

Wealth at death gave away half his fortune by time of his death

Watson, Justly (*c.*1710–1757), military engineer, was the son of Colonel **Jonas Watson** (1663–1741) and his wife, Miriam (*bap.* 1686, *d.* 1754), daughter of John and Anne West. Jonas Watson served for over fifty years in the artillery, and after distinguishing himself, first in the campaigns of William III in Ireland and Flanders, and then in those of Marlborough, succeeded to the command of the artillery train. He was promoted lieutenant-colonel on 17 March 1727, and commanded the artillery at the siege of Gibraltar in that year. He was killed at the siege of Cartagena on 30 March 1741. His widow was granted a pension of £40 p.a. in acknowledgement of her husband's services.

Justly Watson entered the ordnance train as a cadet gunner about 1726 and served under his father at the siege of

Gibraltar. He was appointed practitioner-engineer on 13 June 1732, and promoted sub-engineer on 1 November 1734. By then he had married, on 15 November 1733, Susan Curtis, at Pagham, Sussex. He received a commission as ensign in Harrison's foot on 3 February 1740 and in June was appointed to the ordnance train of the expedition to the West Indies. He sailed on 26 October and arrived at Jamaica on 9 January 1741. His father was killed at the subsequent siege of Cartagena, but he had made his will before he left England, and bequeathed Justly his books, maps, and 'instruments relating to the affairs of artillery'. Justly Watson took part in the assault on Fort St Louis on 25 March and the assault on Fort Lazar on 9 April, and following this he was promoted lieutenant in Harrison's regiment of foot.

Watson returned to Jamaica on 19 May 1741, and was appointed engineer-extraordinary on 11 August, when he was serving in the expedition to Cuba. He returned again to Jamaica in November, and in March 1742 he joined in the abortive expedition to attack Panama. In September he was back in Jamaica as chief engineer. In 1743 he visited Darien and Florida to make surveys and reports. He returned to Jamaica and was promoted engineer in ordinary on 8 March 1744. He returned to England in the autumn of 1744, and was promoted captain-lieutenant in Harrison's regiment on 24 December 1745. On 30 April he joined the expedition under Admiral Richard Lestock and Lieutenant-General James St Clair originally intended for North America, but which attacked the coast of Brittany. He took part in the siege of Lorient (20–27 September), the attack on Quiberon, and the capture of forts Houat and Heydie. Back in England again, he was promoted sub-director of engineers on 2 January 1748, and was appointed chief engineer in the Medway division which included Gravesend, Tilbury, Sheerness, Harwich, and Landguard.

Watson was promoted director of engineers on 17 December 1754, and was sent to Annapolis Royal as chief engineer of Nova Scotia and of settlements in Newfoundland. However, he was soon moved to serve on the west coast of Africa, arriving before December 1755. He returned to England in summer 1756, his reports on the military stations in Africa resulting in the House of Commons granting money to carry out his proposals for improved fortifications. After examining Rye harbour in October and November 1756 he was sent at the end of the year to Annapolis Royal to resume his duties in Nova Scotia and Newfoundland. On 14 May 1757 he was commissioned lieutenant-colonel of Royal Engineers. He died at St John's, Newfoundland in the summer of 1757 from the effects of poison administered in his coffee, probably by a female servant. His will was proved by his widow on 4 August 1757, and she was granted a pension of £40 p.a. from 1 January 1758. His daughter Miriam (d. 1782) married Watson's sometime assistant Sir William *Green (1725–1811). Several of his plans and surveys are in the British Library.   R. H. VETCH, rev. STUART HANDLEY

Sources T. W. J. Connolly and R. F. Edwards, eds., *Roll of officers of the corps of royal engineers from 1660 to 1898* (1898), 3, 6 · J. Kane, *List of officers of the royal regiment of artillery from the year 1716 to the year 1899*, rev. W. H. Askwith, 4th edn (1900), 1, 1a · W. Porter, *History of the corps of royal engineers*, 1 (1889), 73 · *IGI* · will, PRO, PROB 11/832, sig. 263 · will of Jonas Watson, PRO, PROB 11/709, fol. 368 · will of Miriam Watson, PRO, PROB 11/810, fol. 327
Archives Royal Artillery Institution, Woolwich, London, papers [Jonas Watson]

Watson, Lewis, first Baron Rockingham (*bap.* 1584, *d.* 1653), landowner, eldest son of Sir Edward Watson (*d.* 1617) and his wife, Anne (*d.* 1612), daughter of Kenelm Digby of Stoke Dry, Rutland, was born at Rockingham, Northamptonshire, and baptized there on 14 July 1584. He matriculated at Magdalen College, Oxford, on 24 May 1599, but did not graduate. He was admitted to the Middle Temple as a student in 1601. He was constantly at the court of James VI and I over the following years and was knighted on 19 August 1608. He was associated with George Villiers, later earl and then duke of Buckingham. He had succeeded his father on 1 March 1617; on 21 July 1619 he received by patent the fee simple of Rockingham Castle which he had previously held by knight service. On 23 June 1621 he was created a baronet. He married twice. His first wife was Catherine (*d.* 1611), daughter of Peregrine *Bertie, Lord Willoughby de Eresby. They married in 1609 but she died in childbirth. His second wife, whom he married on 3 October 1620, was Eleanor Manners (*d.* 1679), daughter of Sir George Manners of Haddon Hall, Derbyshire. They had six children, a son and five daughters.

Watson sat for Lincoln in the Addled Parliament of 1614 and in the parliaments of 1621 and 1624. In his own county he was a commissioner for martial law and oyer and terminer in 1628, and in 1632–3 served as high sheriff. He was master of the royal buckhounds from 1634 and verderer of Rockingham Forest from 1638. He failed to provide a horse for a muster at Huntingdon during the second bishops' war, for which he was summoned by the privy council.

Watson was a nominal royalist who at the outset of the civil war was appointed commissioner of array for Northamptonshire, on 4 July 1642. He was also ordered to garrison Rockingham Castle. Before he did so, the parliamentarian commander of the east midlands association, Lord Grey of Groby, seized the castle on 19 March 1643 and installed a garrison himself. The role of Watson in this is unclear. There were claims in the royalist press that he had facilitated the surrender of the castle and that he was living under parliamentarian protection at Stoke Park in Northampton after Rockingham had been garrisoned. Some time in early June 1643 the royalist regional commander Henry Hastings had Watson arrested and imprisoned at the garrison at Belvoir Castle and for this he was thanked in an anonymous letter by 'certain inhabitants of the counties of Northampton, Rutland and Leicester' (*Hastings MSS*, 2.102). The garrison at Rockingham served as a base for part of the Northamptonshire county committee and the garrison was able to infiltrate royalist territory in the east midlands throughout the war. The castle was used to imprison some royalist captives after the battle of Naseby (14 June 1645).

Watson petitioned the king for his freedom in June 1643 and Hastings was asked to send 'whatsoever shall be objected against him' by Secretary Edward Nicholas on 13 June (*Hastings MSS*, 2.103). By the beginning of 1645 Watson had not only cleared his name, but on 29 January Charles I ennobled him as Baron Rockingham of Rockingham. He was resident at Oxford until the garrison surrendered in June 1646. The defeat of the royalists left Watson facing a composition levy of £5000 for his delinquency. He died on 5 January 1653 and was buried in Rockingham church a week later. His widow died in London on 23 October 1679 and was buried with her husband at Rockingham on 8 November. MARTYN BENNETT

Sources *CSP dom.*, 1611–18; 1627–8; 1640–41 · M. A. E. Green, ed., *Calendar of the proceedings of the committee for advance of money, 1642–1656*, 2, PRO (1888) · M. Bennett, 'The royalist war effort in the north midlands, 1642–1646', PhD diss., Loughborough University, 1986 · *Report on the manuscripts of the late Reginald Rawdon Hastings*, 4 vols., HMC, 78 (1928–47), vol. 2 · C. H. Harts Horne, *Rockingham Castle* (1852) · GEC, *Peerage* · parish register, Rockingham, 14 July 1584, Northants. RO [baptism]

Likenesses W. Dobson, oils, *c.*1644–1645, Rockingham Castle, Northamptonshire · oils, Rockingham Castle, Northamptonshire

Watson, Sir Malcolm (1873–1955), malariologist, was born in Cathcart, Renfrewshire, Scotland, on 24 August 1873, the second son of George Watson, commercial traveller and clothier, of Bridge of Allan, and his wife, Mary McFarlane, and a kinsman of Sir David Bruce, who was famed for his work on the tsetse fly. Educated in Glasgow at the high school and later at the university he read medicine and arts and graduated with commendation in 1895. He graduated MD with commendation in 1903. Watson held resident posts at Glasgow Royal Infirmary and the Smithson Asylum, Greenock. In 1900, after studying at University College, London, taking the Cambridge diploma in public health, and travelling as a ship's surgeon, he entered the Malayan medical service.

At the turn of the century the Federated Malay states were then in a phase of rapid development. Devastating epidemics of malaria were an inevitable sequel, including around the town of Klang where in January 1901 Watson took up his duties as district surgeon. Inspired by Ronald Ross, who had proved that malaria was carried by mosquitoes, Watson embarked on a vigorous programme of mosquito control. His success was a landmark in preventive medicine. Henceforth malaria and its prevention were Watson's lifelong interests. In 1900 Watson had married Jean Alice (*d.* 1935), eldest daughter of David Gray, engineer, of Coatbridge, Lanarkshire; being a nurse she was able to assist Watson in his hospital work. They had three sons.

Working in a field where little was known, Watson studied the carrier mosquitoes and the terrain in which they bred. He found that the vector mosquitoes differed in habitat: one species bred in sunlit streams, another in shade, and a third in the brackish water of the coastal plains. From these and other differences he realized that anti-mosquito measures must be adapted to each of the vector species. He therefore introduced into malaria prevention the new and important concept of species sanitation. Adapting his technique to the species and terrain, he developed various methods of mosquito control: subsoil and other types of drainage, larvicidal oiling, the clearing of jungle, or the promotion of shade, and other methods which, tested and proved in the Malay States, were woven into the pattern of malaria prevention throughout the world. Watson wrote the first accounts of the early sexual development in the blood of the malignant malaria parasites and of the renal complications of quartan malaria. In the field of industrial technology he also contributed a patent process for tapping rubber trees.

In 1907 Watson left government service for general and consultant practice. Rubber planters and others saw the promise of his practical approach to malaria control—a factor in the early development of the great Malayan rubber industry—and Watson's guidance was eagerly sought in Malaya and elsewhere. A founder member of the Malayan malaria advisory board Watson was at various times an adviser on the prevention of malaria to governments or industries in the Malay States, Singapore, India, Nepal, Africa, the Balkans, and South America. Watson was knighted in 1924 for his work on malaria prevention. In 1928 he left Malaya at Ross's request, to become director of the malaria department at the newly created Ross Institute of Tropical Hygiene. From 1933 until he was persuaded to retire in 1942 he was the director of the institute and of branches he established in India and west Africa. There, and in the Rhodesian copperbelt, where he was medical adviser to a group of mining companies, he continued to promote the spread of preventive medicine with a special regard to the health problems of the industry and the training of laymen. Watson's first wife died in 1935 and in 1938 he married one of his research assistants, Constance Evelyn Loring (1899–1990), daughter of Lieutenant-Colonel Walter L. Loring of the Royal Warwickshire regiment; they had one daughter. In 1948, with the second Lady Watson, he patented a device for controlling dust in mines.

Watson received the honorary degree of LLD from the University of Glasgow in 1924. He was an honorary fellow of the Incorporated Society of Planters, Malaya (1925), and of the Royal Faculty of Physicians and Surgeons of Glasgow (1933), and a fellow of the Geological Society of London (1943). Among his awards were the gold medal of the Rubber Growers' Association (1914), the Stewart prize of the British Medical Association (1927), the Sir William Jones gold medal of the Asiatic Society of Bengal (1928), the Mary Kingsley medal of the Liverpool School of Tropical Medicine (1934), and the Albert medal of the Royal Society of Arts (1939). In 1948, while honorary president of the fourth International Congresses of Tropical Medicine and Malaria, he delivered the Ronald Ross oration in Washington, DC. His writings included *The Prevention of Malaria in the Federated Malay States* (1911), *Rural Sanitation in the Tropics* (1915), and *African Highway* (1953), the last discussing sanitation and prevention of disease in mining settlements in the Rhodesian copperbelt.

Watson died as a result of a cerebral thrombosis on 28 December 1955 at his home, Hillside, Peaslake, Guildford, Surrey, where he had spent an active and rewarding retirement. He was cremated at St Mark's, Peaslake, on 31

December. In his obituary in *The Lancet* George Macdonald described Watson as having been surrounded by controversy, probably because he pioneered Sir Ronald Ross's unpopular ideas of malaria control, and because he advocated a more general approach to malaria epidemiology than the narrowly focused attitude of many of his colleagues. His funeral was held at St Mark's, Peaslake, Surrey.   JOHN FIELD, *rev.* MARY E. GIBSON

Sources BMJ (7 Jan 1956), 52–3 · *The Lancet* (7 Jan 1956), 57 · *The Times* (29 Dec 1955) · J. W. Field and J. A. Reid, 'Malaria control in Malaya', *Journal of Tropical Medicine and Hygiene*, 59 (1956), 24–7 · *WWW*, 1951–60 · d. cert. · personal knowledge (1971) · private information (1971) · *The Times* (2 Jan 1956)
Archives Wellcome L., notebook | London School of Hygiene and Tropical Medicine, corresp. with Sir Ronald Ross | FILM BFI, Sir Ronald Ross, c.1930 · BFI, 'Nepal—the unknown', 1928
Likenesses photographs, London School of Hygiene and Tropical Medicine
Wealth at death £7577 8s. 3d.: probate, 4 May 1956, CGPLA Eng. & Wales

Watson, Margaret Alexandra Hannan (1873–1959), headmistress, was born on 20 July 1873 at 219 St Vincent Street, Glasgow, one of six or more children of William Brown Watson, a cotton manufacturer, and his wife, Rebecca Arthur Hannan. Both her parents came from the families of Glaswegian burgesses. Her mother's father, James Hannan, was chairman of the Glasgow Savings Bank. Watson was educated from the age of nine at a private Glasgow girls' school, Woodside Crescent. She matriculated at St Andrews University in 1892, one of the first eleven female students; she was active in the 1896 student rectorial election and graduated MA in 1897, having taken Greek, Latin, education, philosophy, and English literature.

Between 1897 and 1900 Margaret Watson gained teaching experience, first at a private school in the south of England, then at Blackburn Girls' High School, visiting Paris during the vacations and so beginning her lifelong affection for travel and France and her passion for the French language. In 1900 she returned to teach in Woodside Crescent School, intending to purchase the school. This fell through, but as the owner was also a Miss Watson from then on she was always known as Miss M. A. Hannan Watson.

Miss Hannan Watson and Janet Spens, a Glasgow graduate, established their own school, Laurel Bank School, Glasgow, which opened in 1903 with thirty pupils. In 1908 'Watty' became the sole proprietor, when Spens left to become a university lecturer. In 1920 she turned Laurel Bank into an incorporated school to obtain the grant available under the 1918 Education Act, but remained as headmistress. Art, music, and drama were much encouraged, and performers and speakers visiting Glasgow were often invited to the school. Specialist teachers were employed for some unusual subjects such as ju-jitsu and eurhythmics.

Hannan Watson was remembered by contemporaries for her Glasgow burr—'gurls'—her love of children, and her sense of humour. An able administrator who gave her staff and pupils freedom to develop in their own way, she was always accessible to them. Though the school she founded was rigidly upper-middle class (references were required from everyone and no 'trade' was admitted for the first ten years) she had great personal warmth and a genuine concern for all people. She believed strongly in personal public service, and was co-founder with Mrs Hope Gordon of the Phoenix Park Kindergarten in 1913 and began the crèche in 1917. The school pupils, as well as old girls, were partners in the schemes, both fund-raising and assisting at the kindergarten. When that was taken over as a model institution by the city authorities, she founded the Hillside Holiday Home, Clynder, for convalescing working-class Glasgow children.

Miss Hannan Watson's wide-ranging educational, cultural, and social welfare interests involved her in many activities in the city. In 1909 she became secretary of the Teachers' Guild and later president of the Women's Educational Union. In 1909 she was also asked to act as secretary of the geographical section of the Royal Philosophical Society of Glasgow, although women were not then admitted as members. In 1928, when women were admitted, she became a member of council and, in 1936–8, vice-president. Although she was reticent on the subject of women's suffrage, she was a practical if not a public feminist, employing as staff and inviting as speakers women specialists or professionals whenever possible. She was a member of the Glasgow branch of the Women Citizens' Association, and vice-president in 1938. She was also vice-president of the Glasgow branch of the Federation of University Women. She supported causes such as the Scottish Council for Women's Trades and Union for the Abolition of Sweating, the Queen Margaret College Settlement Association, and the Scottish Fund for the Children of Greece.

In 1937 Miss Hannan Watson was vice-president of the Scoto-Italian Society formed in 1918 to promote friendship between Scotland and Italy. She was also vice-chair of the Franco-Scottish Society and was awarded the diplôme d'officier d'Académie by the French government in 1927, followed by the médaille de la reconnaissance française, and was made officier de l'instruction publique in recognition of her work with the society. She considered world citizenship the ultimate loyalty.

In 1938 Hannan Watson retired as headmistress, remaining a governor and director of Laurel Bank, president of the Old Girl's Club, and president of Hillside Holiday Home. In 1939 the school was evacuated to country locations, but some girls remained in Glasgow and she was reappointed as co-headmistress, in charge of the Glasgow contingent, retiring for the second time in 1944.

Family ties remained strong throughout Miss Hannan Watson's life: a brother acted as business adviser and was the official secretary of the school when it became a company, 'Jinty' helped with gardening and sewing, while Rebecca lived with her at St John's Terrace. Margaret Hannan Watson died on 2 September 1959 in a nursing home, 63 Southpark Avenue, Glasgow. The funeral was on 5 September at Belmont and Hillhead Church followed by cremation at Maryhill crematorium.   LINDY MOORE

Sources M. A. H. Watson, 'History, 1903–1938', *Laurel Bank School, 1903–1953*, ed. [M. G. Andrew and others] (1953), 1–32 · M. Cameron, *The Laurel Bank story, 1903–1978* (1978) · *Laurel Bank School Magazine* (June 1938), 1–5 · *Glasgow Herald* (4 Sept 1959) · 'Founder of Laurel Bank School: Miss M. Hannan Watson's retirement', *Glasgow Herald* (25 Oct 1938) · 'Kindergarten school opened', *Glasgow Herald* (8 Dec 1913) · *Scottish biographies* (1938) · 'Holiday home opened by Princess Louise', *Glasgow Herald* (22 Sept 1919) · *Annual Report 1920–21* [Glasgow Women Citizens' Association], 3 (1921) · *College Echoes* [U. St Andr.], 4 (1892–3) · H. Tombazio, letter, *Glasgow Herald* (7 Sept 1959) · b. cert.
Archives Laurel Bank School, Glasgow
Likenesses T. & C. Annan, photograph, Laurel Bank School, Glasgow · photograph, repro. in Cameron, *The Laurel Bank story* · photographs, repro. in *Laurel Bank School*

Watson, Sir Michael Milne-, third baronet (1910–1999), industrialist and public servant, was born Michael Milne Watson on 16 February 1910 at 39 Eccleston Square, Belgravia, London, the younger son and youngest of the three children of Sir David Milne Watson, later Milne-*Watson, first baronet (1869–1945), industrialist, and his wife, Olga Cicely (d. 1952), daughter of the Revd George Herbert. His father was a leading figure in the gas industry and vice-president of the Federation of British Industries; he was knighted in 1927 and created baronet in 1937. Michael Milne-Watson was educated at Eton and, following his father and elder brother (David) Ronald, at Balliol College, Oxford, graduated with a second-class degree in politics, philosophy, and economics in 1932. He then worked for a short time for a firm of City accountants, before joining the Gas Light and Coke Company (GLCC) as a probationer trainee; this was apparently without any prompting from his father, governor (chairman of the board) of the GLCC from 1919 until 1945.

Milne-Watson worked closely with the accountant (Arthur) Edgar Sylvester, who in 1930 had been brought in to modernize the procedures and organization of the company; Sylvester later became governor of the GLCC (1945–6) and first chairman of the nationalized Gas Council (1949–51). Milne-Watson rose rapidly, becoming commercial manager of the GLCC and also, from 1940, manager of the London regional gas centre, which co-ordinated mutual assistance between gas companies in wartime emergency conditions. On 27 March 1940 he married Mary Lisette Bagnall (d. 1993), younger daughter of Harold Carleton Bagnall, of Auckland, New Zealand. They had one son, Andrew Michael (b. 1944). In 1943 Milne-Watson volunteered for the Royal Navy as an ordinary seaman. He was commissioned as a sub-lieutenant (navigation officer) in the Royal Naval Volunteer Reserve in 1944, and served on escort duty off the west coast of Africa.

Milne-Watson returned to the GLCC in 1945 as managing director and, despite his relative inexperience, was elected governor in 1946 on the retirement through ill health of Sylvester. The tasks he faced were manifold: wartime damage and neglect to rectify, competition becoming progressively more intense, and the prospect of nationalization. Milne-Watson and the GLCC gave a lead to the industry, not welcoming but certainly not obstructing state ownership. This took effect in 1949, Milne-Watson being appointed first chairman of the North

Thames Gas Board, effectively the former GLCC. Over the next decade competition from electricity and oil intensified and the industry was trapped between rising fuel costs, imposed by the National Coal Board, and falling sales. Milne-Watson, with W. K. Hutchison, a former GLCC colleague, played a leading role in the events that reversed this trend.

The industry needed alternatives to coal for gas-making to prevent its being priced out of its markets. These were found first in oil refinery waste products for which there was no ready market, and later in natural gas. Milne-Watson, though no engineer, was one of the first to recognize the potential of these non-traditional feedstocks. Under his leadership the North Thames Gas Board negotiated a ten-year contract with Shell to supply refinery tail gas which could be processed into a coal gas equivalent, halving the cost of gas-making. Even more important in the longer term was his strong support for a project to transport liquefied natural gas by sea from the Gulf of Mexico to a terminal at Canvey Island, Essex. As soon as the practicability of the method was fully established, further contracts were negotiated to ship Algerian natural gas to Canvey. In 1964, a couple of years later, exploration for natural gas and oil in the North Sea began; its success led to the conversion of homes throughout Britain from coal gas to natural gas, once again halving the cost of gas.

Milne-Watson did not stay to see the outcome of the process to which he had been midwife. In 1964 he moved on to become chairman of the state-owned steel company Richard Thomas and Baldwins. He was passed over for the post of chairman of the new British Steel Corporation in 1967; after a period as deputy chairman (1967–9) he resigned. He became chairman of William Press (1969–74), a civil engineering company which did much work for the gas industry. In 1974 it was he who signed the contract with the North Thames Gas Board when Press won the work for converting central London. He had several other business interests: he was a director of the Industrial and Commercial Finance Corporation (1963–80) and of Commercial Union Assurance (1968–81), and from 1976 to 1981 he was chairman of the private health care company BUPA. He was president of the council of Reading University (1975–80) and a governor of the National Hospital for Nervous Diseases.

Milne-Watson was a successful gas board chairman but lacked the attributes to progress further. 'By temperament he was autocratic … somewhat inward-looking … a little disdainful both of the Gas Council and of ministerial involvement' (Falkus, *Always under Pressure*, 134). He was, however, charming and courteous; he warmly supported the paternalistic tradition of the GLCC and was genuinely involved in the social, welfare, and sporting aspects of North Thames Gas Board activities, regularly attending functions such as joint consultative meetings and long-service awards to staff. His support for engineering innovation was recognized in 1961 when he was elected a companion of the Institution of Gas Engineers. He was appointed CBE in 1953, was knighted in 1969, and succeeded to the baronetcy on the death of his elder brother in 1982. He died of pneumonia at Battle Hospital, Reading, on 27 April 1999. He was survived by his son Andrew, who succeeded him as fourth baronet.   FRANCIS GOODALL

Sources S. Everard, *The history of the Gas Light & Coke Company, 1812–1949* (1949) • M. Falkus, *Always under pressure: a history of North Thames Gas since 1949* (1988) • K. Hutchison, *High speed gas: an autobiography* (1987) • *Daily Telegraph* (5 May 1999) • *The Times* (1 June 1999) • *Thames Gas Magazine* (April 1964) • *Gas Journal* (19 Feb 1964) • M. Falkus, 'Milne-Watson, David', *DBB* • *WWW* • Burke, *Peerage* • b. cert. • d. cert.
Likenesses photograph, 1964, repro. in *Daily Telegraph* • R. Moynihan, oils, repro. in Everard, *History of the Gas Light & Coke Company*
Wealth at death £2,015,265—gross: probate, 2 Nov 1999, *CGPLA Eng. & Wales* • £2,002,466—net: probate, 2 Nov 1999, *CGPLA Eng. & Wales*

Watson, Musgrave Lewthwaite (1804–1847), sculptor, was born at Hawksdale Hall, near Carlisle, on 24 January 1804. He was one of six children of Thomas Watson (1754–1823), a farmer and ironmonger, and his wife, Mary Lewthwaite (*c.*1770–1829). Although he showed early artistic promise, at his parents' insistence Watson spent two reluctant years (1821–3) training as a solicitor in Carlisle following his attendance at Raughton Head School, Cumberland. Immediately after his father's death in 1823 he abandoned his legal career and went to London, where he visited John Flaxman. Following Flaxman's advice, Watson briefly studied at the Royal Academy Schools which he entered on 31 March 1825 when his age was given in the register as nineteen and also worked in the studio of the sculptor Robert Sievier. Watson then spent almost three years in Italy (1825–8) where he worked as a cameo engraver, etcher, and watercolourist as well as a sculptor. On his return he showed six works at the Carlisle Exhibition (1828) and carved two significant church monuments in the locality. The relief commemorating his father (St Mary's, Sebergham) was regarded by Nikolaus Pevsner as 'one of the most effective monuments of the 1820s in all England' (Pevsner, *Cumberland*, 36). It reflects the strong influence of the romantic classicism of Henry Fuseli's painting *The Three Witches* (1783; Royal Shakespeare Museum, Stratford upon Avon). A more pensive note is struck by Watson's monument to his schoolmaster and mentor, the Revd Robert Monkhouse (Raughton Head parish church).

Watson returned to London in 1829. With characteristic pride, he initially refused to work for anyone, but by 1833 poverty had forced him to approach the leading portrait sculptor of the period, Sir Francis Chantrey. Shortly afterwards he received an offer from Chantrey's main rival, Sir Richard Westmacott, and for a while evidently put in sixteen-hour working days assisting them both. Although Chantrey admired Watson's abilities as a modeller, he refused to raise his wages. Watson angrily handed in his notice, but in the process he earned the respect of Allan Cunningham, Chantrey's chief assistant. Watson subsequently assisted the sculptors William Behnes and Edward Hodges Baily, and for two years worked as a modeller in terracotta at the Lambeth factory of William Croggan.

Although Watson first exhibited at the Royal Academy in 1829, it was several years before his work became known to a wide public. Lack of encouragement—and of private means—often meant that his sculpture did not progress beyond the plaster model stage. Two such examples are a wittily realistic statuette of the inebriated *Jolly* (or *Crutched*) *Friars* and the more lyrical and elegant relief *Sleep Bearing off the Body of Sarpedon* (1844) (both Carlisle Museum and Art Gallery). Watson's belated breakthrough came in 1842 with his frieze for the Royal Exchange building, Threadneedle Street, City of London (later relocated to Napier Street, Islington). This work successfully fused classical traditionalism with contemporary references to commerce and was admired by the architect C. R. Cockerell.

Following Chantrey's sudden death in 1841, Cunningham helped to secure Watson the commission for the colossal seated marble group of the brothers Lord Eldon and Lord Stowell (1842–54; University College, Oxford). Unfinished at the time of Watson's death, the statue was completed by George Nelson and this perhaps explains Pevsner's terse verdict: 'very cold' (Pevsner, *Oxfordshire*, 212). Watson's most prominently located work was also posthumously completed, the bronze *Battle of St Vincent*, for the Nelson memorial in Trafalgar Square, London (1850). One of four reliefs, it reveals Watson's emergence from dependence on Flaxman's neo-classicism into a more robust realism. In this respect it anticipates the work of the leading mid-Victorian sculptor John Henry Foley. At the time of his death, Watson had almost finished a seated marble sculpture of Flaxman (1843–7; University College, London), foregoing proper payment for the work, generosity that he could ill afford.

Watson died of tuberculosis and heart failure at his home, 13 Upper Gloucester Place, Marylebone, Middlesex, on 28 October 1847 and was buried in Highgate cemetery. He was unmarried, but there is some evidence that he lived with a woman possibly called Helen, a publican's daughter, as his common-law wife, and that they had a child (Lonsdale, 38, 51–2, 89–90). Physically he was slightly built and his delicate constitution was strained by overwork in the damp and draughty conditions of a sculptor's studio. He also suffered from what may today be diagnosed as bulimia nervosa and depression. In a mood of self-criticism shortly before his death, he destroyed many of his studio models despite the protests of friends. As with many artists, critical recognition and major commissions came too late for Watson to appreciate them. Echoing Watson's contemporaries, Rupert Gunnis believed that 'had he lived he would assuredly have been one of the greater sculptors of the nineteenth century' (Gunnis, 415). The sensitively written and well-documented biography by Watson's fellow Cumbrian, Henry Lonsdale, *The Life and Works of Musgrave Lewthwaite Watson, Sculptor* (1866), rescued him from obscurity and helped to establish his art-historical status.   MARK STOCKER

Sources H. Lonsdale, *The life and works of Musgrave Lewthwaite Watson, sculptor* (1866) • B. Read, *Victorian sculpture* (1982) • R. Gunnis,

Dictionary of British sculptors, 1660–1851 (1953); new edn (1968) · *Cumberland and Westmorland*, Pevsner (1967) · M. Stocker, 'Watson, Musgrave Lewthwaite', *The dictionary of art*, ed. J. Turner (1996) · *DNB* · J. Darke, *The monument guide to England and Wales* (1991) · *Art Union*, 10 (1848), 27 · *Oxfordshire*, Pevsner (1974) · S. C. Hutchison, 'The Royal Academy Schools, 1768–1830', *Walpole Society*, 38 (1960–62), 123–91, esp. 177–8
Likenesses G. Nelson, marble relief effigy on monument, *c*.1850–1855, Carlisle Cathedral; repro. in Lonsdale, *The life and works of Musgrave Lewthwaite Watson*, frontispiece

Watson, Sir Patrick Heron (1832–1907), surgeon, born at Edinburgh on 5 January 1832, was the third of four surviving sons of Charles Watson DD, minister of Burntisland, Fife, and Isabella Boog, his wife. His three brothers all attained distinction, two (Charles and Robert Boog) in the church, and the third (David Matthew) in business.

Patrick Watson was educated at Edinburgh Academy and Edinburgh University, graduating MD in 1853. Admitted LRCS (Edinburgh) in 1853, he was elected FRCS in 1855. After a year's residence at the Royal Infirmary, Edinburgh, Watson volunteered for service at the start of the Crimean War. He was appointed a staff assistant surgeon, but his operative skill and his teaching powers were so obvious that he was retained at Woolwich to instruct other volunteer surgeons. He went to the Crimea some months later, and was attached to the Royal Artillery; but an attack of dysentery caused him to be invalided home in 1856. He received the Crimean, Turkish, and Sardinian medals. As soon as his health was restored, Watson returned to Edinburgh to teach surgery at the High School Yards, and to become lecturer on systematic and clinical surgery at the Royal College of Surgeons. Watson afterwards acted as private assistant to Professor James *Miller, whose eldest daughter, Elizabeth Gordon (*d*. 1900), he married in 1861; they had two sons and two daughters. Watson declined the offer of a post under Professor James Syme, and in 1860 he was chosen as assistant surgeon to the Edinburgh Royal Infirmary, and in 1863 full surgeon. At the end of his term of office in 1878 the managers appointed him an extra-surgeon for five years.

Watson, who endeared himself to his patients, was as an operator unrivalled in Edinburgh for his speed and skill. He devised and carried out many of the operations which only later became more widely accepted. Before the introduction of Listerian methods he had removed the whole larynx, extirpated the spleen, performed ovariotomy with success, and popularized excision of the joints. As a lecturer he was eloquent, clear, and impressive; as a hospital surgeon and clinical teacher he was effective and popular. His published works included *The Modern Pathology and Treatment of Venereal Disease* (1861), *Excision of the Knee Joint* (1867), and *Excision of the Thyroid Gland* (1873).

In 1878 Watson accompanied the third earl of Rosslyn on the special embassy sent to Spain on King Alfonso XII's marriage, and he was decorated caballero of the order of Carlos III of Spain.

At the Royal College of Surgeons in Edinburgh, Watson was president in 1878 and again in 1905. From 1882 to 1906 he represented the college on the General Medical Council. He was one of the honorary surgeons in Scotland to Queen Victoria and to Edward VII. He was made honorary LLD of Edinburgh in 1884 and honorary FRCS (Ireland) in 1887. He was knighted in 1903. Throughout life he was a keen volunteer. He joined the Queen's Edinburgh brigade as a surgeon and retired with the rank of brigade surgeon lieutenant-colonel, VD. He died at his home, 16 Charlotte Square, Edinburgh, on 21 December 1907.

D'A. POWER, rev. B. A. BRYAN

Sources *BMJ* (4 Jan 1908), 62 · *The Lancet* (4 Jan 1908), 69 · *Scottish Medical and Surgical Journal*, 22 (1908), 66 · *WWW* · private information (1912)
Archives Royal College of Surgeons, Edinburgh, letters to relatives, mainly from the Crimea
Likenesses photograph, Wellcome L.
Wealth at death see confirmation, sealed, 24 Jan 1908, *CGPLA Eng. & Wales*

Watson, Peter William (*bap.* 1761, *d.* 1830), botanist, was born at Hull and baptized at Holy Trinity Church there on 26 August 1761. He was educated at the grammar school under Joseph Milner (1744–1797), and occupied in early life in trade; he was an enthusiastic student of botany, entomology, chemistry, and mineralogy, and a skilful landscape painter. In 1812 he took an active part in the establishment of the Hull Botanic Garden. In his *Dendrologia Britannica, or, Trees and shrubs that will live in the open air of Britain throughout the year*, published in twenty-four parts in 1824–5, he alludes (pt 1, p. xii) to his

> own endeavours to furnish the institution with many indigenous plants, which I collected at considerable expense and labour, by traversing the whole East Riding … in my gig, with proper apparatus for cutting up roots, collecting seeds, &c. of the rarer sorts, whose habitats had been rendered familiar to me from numerous previous herborisations.

Dendrologia Britannica was described by John Claudius Loudon in his *Arboretum Britannicum* of 1833 (p. 188) as 'the most scientific work devoted exclusively to trees which has hitherto been published in England'. It contained an introduction to descriptive botany, occupying seventy-two pages, and 172 coloured plates of exotic trees and shrubs, each accompanied by a page of technical description.

Watson was elected a fellow of the Linnean Society in 1824. He died at Cottingham, near Hull, on 1 September 1830. G. S. BOULGER, rev. GILES HUDSON

Sources Desmond, *Botanists*, rev. edn · R. W. Corlass and W. Andrews, eds., *Sketches of Hull authors* (1879)

Watson, Richard (1611/12–1685), Church of England clergyman, was born in the parish of St Katharine Cree, London, and was probably the son of William Watson, citizen and mercer (*d*. *c*.1634), and his wife, Ursula Pearce. Although there were other London merchants of the same name this parentage is suggested by Richard Watson's attendance for five years at Mercers' School, under Mr Auger, prior to his admission, aged sixteen, to Gonville and Caius College, Cambridge, on 22 December 1628. Watson graduated BA in 1633, and MA in 1636, and from 1636 to 1644 was fellow of the college, acting as Greek lecturer (1642) and Hebrew lecturer (1643), as well as being master of the Perse School, Cambridge (1636–41). He was almost certainly aligned with the Arminians in the university, and joined Richard Crashaw, Bishop William Juxon, and Bishop Matthew Wren in penning verses which prefaced Robert Shelford's *Five Pious and Learned Discourses* (1635).

Upon the outbreak of civil war Watson demonstrated his allegiance to the royalist cause with a provocative lecture at the university church of Great St Mary's, published as *A Sermon Touching Schisme*. He was inevitably ejected from the college by the parliamentarian visitation in April 1644, but by then he had already joined the royalist army as chaplain to Lord Hopton, with whom he probably remained in the field during the remainder of the first civil war. After the defeat of the royalist army at Truro in March 1646 Watson went with Hopton into exile, attending Prince Charles in Jersey in 1646 before joining the exiled court at St Germain by December 1647. By 1649 he was in The Hague, where he preached a sermon after the execution of Charles I which was published as *Regicidium judaicum*, with a dedication to Hopton. During the months that followed, Watson, like Hopton, formed part of the constitutional royalist faction at court which opposed negotiations with the Scots. In April 1649 Watson described the Scots as 'brazen-fac'd rebels and barbarous brutes' (*Clarendon State Papers*, 2.53). This stance led to both men being alienated from the prevailing mood at court, and they subsequently moved to Wesel, where Watson continued to rail against the Scottish presbyterians, whom he described as the 'veriest villains the king hath for his enemies' (Scrope and Monkhouse, 2.491). During 1650 and 1651 he corresponded with other exiles such as Robert Creighton and William Edgeman about a response to Robert Baillie's reply to John Bramhall's attack upon presbyterianism; Watson's intervention appeared as *Akolouthos, or, A Second Faire Warning*, dedicated to Hopton against 'these bloody Presbyters'. Watson spent most of 1652 with Hopton at Bruges, insistent that he would not return to England under the Act of Oblivion, but alienated from those royalists, such as the duke of Buckingham, who sought to work with John Lilburne, whom Watson refused to consider as anything other than an *agent provocateur*.

After Hopton's death in September 1652 Watson remained in exile, in Wesel and Brussels, adamant that the royalists could expect little assistance from the Dutch, and trenchant in his opposition to the presbyterians, against whom he continued to favour a model of the Church of England closer to Laudians such as Richard Montague and John Cosin than strict Calvinists such as Thomas Morton or Ralph Brownrigge. In 1656 Watson published Isaac Basire's *De antiqua ecclesiae Britannicae libertate*, which he had found in Hopton's papers, and which he later translated into English. He later moved to Caen, from where he dedicated his *Historicall Collections of Ecclesiastick Affairs in Scotland* to John Warner, bishop of Rochester, by whom he had been ordained. Watson's aim was to 'confirm all pious and humble hearts in the preferring the ancient and universal successive government of the Christian church before the new Genevatising bloody discipline of some heady Scots' (Watson, sig. A5). He also

entered into print against the poet Edmund Waller, whom he described as a 'vassall' for writing a panegyric on the protector's death, and wrote a preface for Eleazor Duncon's *De adoratione Dei* (1660). His greatest friend and ally during these years appears to have been Richard Browne, the royalist diplomat in Paris.

Watson remained in Caen until after the Restoration, and returned to England only in 1661 to reclaim his college fellowship, although he felt compelled to issue a petition for confirmation of a grant made by Charles I for an annuity of £30 from his college, and for his restoration as a senior rather than a junior fellow. Watson displayed his allegiance in 1661 with a flurry of publications including *Epistolaris diatribe*, *Effata regalia*, *The Prudential Advice and Observations*, and *Icon animae basilicae*, the last three containing ideas and observations culled from the writings of Charles I. Watson was rewarded in 1662 with a doctorate in divinity at Oxford, a chaplaincy to the duke of York, and the rectory of Pewsey in Wiltshire. He subsequently became prebendary at Salisbury Cathedral of Warminster (1666), which he exchanged for that of Bitton in 1671, and master of Heytesbury Hospital (1671). He remained active as a scholar and author, publishing *Aquilae cruso* (1665), and writing *An Answer to Elymas the Sorcerer* (1682), and *A Fuller Answer to Elimas the Sorcerer* (1683), in which he replied to allegations regarding the Popish Plot. He also published some of his own correspondence with John Cosin from 1646, as *The Right Reverend Doctor John Cosin … his Opinion* (1684). Nevertheless, Watson's last years appear to have been far from happy. He was repeatedly troubled by serious allegations over tithe payments at Pewsey, and on at least one occasion, in 1665, was taken into custody. He also felt that he had received insufficient reward for his loyalty, and that he had been passed over for preferment in favour of younger less capable men. It was such attitudes which led Anthony Wood to conclude that Watson was 'a good scholar but vain and conceited' (Wood, *Ath. Oxon.: Fasti*, 2.264). Watson died on 13 January 1685 and was buried at Pewsey.　　　　J. T. PEACEY

Sources R. Watson, *Historicall collections of ecclesiastick affairs in Scotland* (1657) · *Calendar of the Clarendon state papers preserved in the Bodleian Library*, ed. O. Ogle and others, 5 vols. (1869–1970) · R. Scrope and T. Monkhouse, eds., *State papers collected by Edward, earl of Clarendon*, 3 vols. (1767–86) · Wood, *Ath. Oxon.: Fasti* (1820) · *CSP dom.*, *1661–80* · *Report on manuscripts in various collections*, 8 vols., HMC, 55 (1901–14), vol. 1 · T. Phillipps, *Monumental inscriptions in the county of Wilton*, 2 vols. (1822) · will, PRO, PROB 11/382, fol. 69v · W. Kennett, *A register or chronicle* (1728) · *Fasti Angl.*, *1541–1857*, [Salisbury] · J. Venn and others, eds., *Biographical history of Gonville and Caius College*, 1: *1349–1713* (1897), 286–7 · will, PRO, PROB 11/167, fol. 66v [William Watson, father]

Watson, Richard (1737–1816), bishop of Llandaff, was born at Heversham, Westmorland, in August 1737, the third surviving child of Thomas Watson (1672–1753), Church of England clergyman and schoolmaster at Heversham, and his wife, Agnes Newton. He was educated at his father's grammar school but never became fully proficient in either Latin or Greek—a severe handicap at Cambridge University, where he referred to his 'barbarous Latin' (*Anecdotes*, 8).

Richard Watson (1737–1816), by Sir Joshua Reynolds, 1769

Academic career at Cambridge Watson was admitted sizar at Trinity College, Cambridge, on 2 November 1754; there his tutor was William Backhouse. Cambridge offered him both an escape from rural-provincial life and an opportunity for self-advancement. He avoided the idle rich sons of the gentry, retained his north-country accent and plain clothes, and worked hard. He took his BA in January 1759 as second wrangler, was elected fellow of his college in October 1760, and became assistant tutor in November 1760. He proceeded MA in 1762 and was moderator for Trinity in 1762, 1763, and 1765, and for Christ's College in 1764. He was senior tutor at Trinity from 1764 to 1771 and junior dean from 1769 to 1771.

Watson was appointed professor of chemistry in 1764 and held the post until 1773. Hitherto the chair had not been valued, since it carried neither a stipend nor a requirement to read lectures, but Watson perceived it as a way to advance his career and offered to deliver a course of chemistry lectures, though he admitted 'I knew nothing at all of Chemistry, had never read a syllable on the subject; nor seen a single experiment in it; but I was tired with mathematics and natural philosophy' (*Anecdotes*, 28–9). He acquired an operator from Paris, studied the topic fully, and in fourteen months gave the first of five courses of lectures. In 1767 an unsuccessful experiment led to an explosion that caused considerable damage to his house. He contributed short articles to the transactions of the Royal Society, of which he was elected a fellow in 1769, and later he published his *Chemical Essays* in five volumes (1781–7). These are intelligent and lucid but derivative, revealing Watson as an intelligent layman not a research scientist. They show a particular interest in applying science to

manufacturing processes and a belief that chemistry could help to realize Britain's industrial potential. Watson worked on the efficiency of gunpowder and discovered that a thermometer in which the bulb was painted with black ink gave a higher reading than an ordinary thermometer. His account of the lime processes used in tar and lead smelting and his work on pit coal shows a particular interest in metallurgy. He saw a need to bridge the gap between academic chemists and the artisans of industry: 'a man must blacken his own hands with charcoal, he must sweat over the furnace, and inhale many a noxious vapour, before he can become a chemist' (R. Watson, *Chemical Essays*, 1, 1781, 40). Watson saw of course no conflict between science and religion: 'the books of Nature and Revelation … are both written by the finger of the one incomprehensible God' (ibid., 1.vii).

In October 1771 Watson was elected regius professor of divinity at Cambridge, which he admitted 'had long been the secret object of my ambition' (*Anecdotes*, 35). Lacking the necessary qualification of a doctorate in divinity he rushed to London to obtain one by royal mandate. He admitted to knowing as little about the subject as he had about chemistry and gave no lectures in divinity, suggesting that the obligatory Latin would deter the students. He held a number of university offices, sat on senate committees (the syndicates), and preached and published university sermons. He supported reform of the university examination system and refused bribes while moderator; on one occasion he rejected £1000 and insisted that William Paley should be senior wrangler. In 1787 ill health and a newly acquired fortune led to retire from academic life, although he retained the regius chair of divinity until his death, paying Thomas Kipling an annual stipend of £200 to act as his deputy.

Ecclesiastical career: politics, patrons, and preferment Watson was ordained priest on 28 February 1768. The duke of Grafton, chancellor of Cambridge University, used his influence to get him a sinecure rectory in north Wales, which he exchanged for the second prebendal stall at Ely in 1774; he became archdeacon of Ely in 1779. He was rector of Northwold from 1779 to 1781 and of Knaptoft from 1781. He entered the national political arena on 29 May 1776, when he preached the Restoration day sermon at Cambridge, entitled *The Principles of the Revolution Vindicated*. In other years this would have been seen as an unexceptionable restatement of Locke's whig doctrine, but with the Americans on the brink of declaring independence it was perceived by many as a bold support of the rebels. Five months later he restated those whig principles in the university accession sermon on 25 October 1776. He had already corresponded on scientific topics with the marquess of Rockingham, and in November 1775 he assured Rockingham that he had 'ever considered [him] as the head of the Whig Interest in this kingdom' (*Anecdotes*, 57). In a fast sermon of February 1780 he supported economic reform and condemned the American War of Independence; his support for his old pupil Charles Manners, duke of Rutland, was evident. The fall of the North administration in the wake of defeat in America brought Watson's friends Grafton, Rutland, and Rockingham, to the edge of power. Shelburne, seeking to draw Rutland closer to his administration, offered Watson the see of Llandaff. Watson accepted but understood the reason, observing that he had:

> no great reason to be proud of the promotion; for I think I owed it not to any regard which he who gave it to me had to the zeal and industry with which I had for many years discharged the functions and fulfilled the duties of an academic life. (ibid., 94)

Llandaff was not a great prize in itself but was the first rung on the ladder of episcopal preferment. Worth only £500 a year it was normally occupied for an extremely brief period but Watson languished there from 1782 until his death thirty-four years later. His friends were no longer men of influence; Shelburne left office in 1783, Rutland died in 1787, and Rockingham was dead even before Watson's elevation. The new men, Pitt and Dundas, had no reason to trust or advance this 'ageing radical whose vote could not be relied on' (Brain, 29–30). As bishop of Llandaff, Watson was mostly non-resident but he did not neglect the diocese entirely, making an annual ordination visit and extensive triennial visitations, which he combined with confirmations of the laity. Time and again he was overlooked in episcopal reshuffles, despite considerable efforts on his part to be translated to a better see. His desire for advancement was undermined by a streak of independence that made it difficult for him constantly to please his patrons or to commit himself entirely to one man; if, as his critics alleged, he was a cynical time-server, his thirty-four years at Llandaff show him to have been a remarkably ineffective one.

Political views and controversy Watson's contemporaries regarded his politics as inconstant and ascribed their changes to his ambition and hopes of advancement; historians see a greater degree of consistency. In the 1770s conservatives perceived him as a dangerous radical; in the 1790s radicals denounced him as an apostate. His views in both decades were those of a thorough-going whig who hardly deviated from the classic principles of John Locke. In 1782 he defended Locke against the theoretical criticisms of Soame Jenyns but normally he was more interested in political practice than abstract theory. Ignoring the work of David Hume he defended Locke's concept of an original compact as well as his views on the strictly limited possibilities of revolution. The application of those principles to the dispute with the American colonies in the 1770s, in the Restoration day and accession day sermons of 1776, earned Watson a reputation as a radical, though he was doing little more than restating Locke's views at a time when others were abandoning them. He stopped short of outright support of the colonists; he argued that men had an abstract right to rebel against unjust government, not that the Americans were justified in doing so at that juncture. He was less concerned with America than with what he perceived to be the increasing power of the crown in Britain. In the 1780s he interested himself more in the question of economic reform than in the final settlement of American independence. He supported the Cambridgeshire petition but did not argue as strongly for the reform of parliament as he had earlier. After his elevation to the House of Lords in 1782 he spoke and voted as an independent whig and abstained on the crucial vote that brought down the Fox–North coalition. At first he welcomed the younger Pitt but in 1787–9 he opposed him on three issues: the commercial treaty with France, the repeal of the Test and Corporation Acts, and the regency crises.

Having retired from Cambridge to the Lake District in 1787 Watson remained politically active. He kept his London house in Great George Street until 1803 and appeared regularly in the House of Lords, speaking in the debates on the regency in 1789 and the union with Ireland; he made one of his final appearances in March 1807 to support the abolition of the slave trade. The French Revolution dominated political controversy in these years and, like many Englishmen, Watson first welcomed and later denounced it. Its early stages appeared consistent with Lockean principles, and in October 1791 Watson insisted that the rights of man 'are founded in nature; they exist antecedent to and independent of civil society; and the French constitution is the only one in the world which has deliberately asserted these rights and supported them in their full extent' (Anecdotes, 256). But the French Revolution changed significantly in 1792, and after the execution of Louis XVI in January 1793 Watson could no longer support it. In 1793 he lamented the king's death and the abandonment of a balanced constitution; he denounced republican government as 'the most oppressive to the bulk of the people: they are deceived in it, with the show of liberty; but they live in it, under the most odious of all tyrannies, the tyranny of their equals' (R. Watson, Miscellaneous Tracts on Religious, Political, and Agricultural Subjects, 2 vols., 1815, 1.475). Watson's immutable Lockean principles at this time look distinctly old-fashioned, left behind both by Burke's conservative idea of the gradual organic growth of society and by the English Jacobins' radicalism. Wordsworth wrote 'A Letter to the Bishop of Llandaff by a Republican', in which he indicted Watson as 'an enemy lurking in our ranks' (W. Wordsworth, Poetry and Prose, 1955, 81). In summer 1795 Watson argued in two sermons and a charge that it was French atheism, not military might, that posed the real threat to British stability. His support for the government's conduct of the war in An Address to the People of Great Britain (1798) was the subject of bitter attacks by the Unitarians and radicals Gilbert Wakefield and Benjamin Flower. These led to their trial and imprisonment, which Watson regretted but did nothing to prevent. In 1798 he reiterated his belief that the political principles 'on which the Revolution [of 1688–9] was founded … are in my judgement, principles best calculated to protect the liberty and property of the subject, and to secure the honour and happiness of the sovereign' (R. Watson, A Charge … to the Clergy of the Diocese of Llandaff, 1798, 2). Far from changing his principles Watson could be criticized for persisting in rigid Lockean concepts that were outdated both philosophically and politically.

Religious opinions and church politics A student of mathematics before he turned his hand to chemistry, Watson came fresh to the study of religion on his appointment as regius professor of divinity in 1771. He then applied himself not to theology or patristics but to biblical study of the New Testament. Like his mentor Edmund Law he soon established his latitudinarian credentials and was critical of the unreformed constitution in the church. He refused to support the Society for the Propagation of the Gospel, arguing that it aimed to convert dissenters to Anglicanism not heathens to Christianity. In 1772 he gave some support to the Feathers tavern petition to relieve clergy and graduates of the universities of the need to subscribe to more than a statement of belief in the scriptures but he did so under the pseudonym of 'a Christian Whig' and his own trinitarian beliefs were never in doubt. He was more orthodox in his theology than many imagined. He steered 'an epistemological *via media*' (Searby, 293) and had 'a becoming modesty about the possibility of theological knowledge' (Waterman, 'Via media', 427), which led him to tolerate all varieties of protestantism. In his six volumes of *Theological Tracts* (1785), which reprinted twenty-four extracts from nineteen writers for 'young persons of every denomination' (1.v), he included works by a number of dissenters, even some Unitarians, insisting that he 'did not at all consider the quarter from whence the matter was taken, but whether it was good, and suited to my purpose' (1.xix). His aim was to establish the truth of Christianity and defend his young readers 'from that contagion of Infidelity which is the disgrace of the age' (1.ix); his target was deists not dissenters. He insisted:

> I do not conceive it to be any man's duty to anathematize those who cannot subscribe to *his* catalogue of fundamental Christian verities. That man is not to be esteemed an *Atheist*, who acknowledges the existence of God the Creator of the universe … nor is he to be esteemed a *Deist*, who acknowledges that Jesus of Nazareth *is indeed the Christ, the Saviour of the world*, though he cannot assent to all the *truths* of revealed religion which *other* men may think themselves warranted in deducing from thence. (1.xv)

Watson was careful however to use only those arguments of these writers that were consonant with the beliefs of the Church of England; the extracts relate mainly to the Bible and never discuss the doctrine of the Trinity. The views expressed, if not their authors, were orthodox.

Watson recognized the need for an established church and was anxious not to undermine the constitution in church and state but he believed that the religious establishment needed reformation. After his elevation to the bench of bishops he proposed to Shelburne reforms in the church involving an equalization of episcopal revenues and increased provision for the lower clergy. Shelburne ignored the advice and Watson published the proposal in a letter to the archbishop of Canterbury in 1783. In 1790 he suggested a revision of the liturgy and articles, which included the abolition of the Athanasian creed. Like many of his fellow bishops he recognized the need for the provision of new church buildings to accommodate the rapidly increasing population, and in April 1800 he suggested to Wilberforce a scheme for twenty new churches in London. As a disciple of Locke he was an advocate of religious toleration, supporting the attempt to repeal the Test and Corporation Acts in 1787 and praising the religious toleration of the French national assembly in 1791. Originally hostile to the measure, in 1804 he supported Catholic emancipation. Twice in his career he came forward as a defender of the Christian faith: in 1776 his *Apology for Christianity* addressed Gibbon's sceptical account of the growth of Christianity in *Decline and Fall of the Roman Empire*; twenty years later his *Apology for the Bible* (1796) responded to the second part of Thomas Paine's deist *Age of Reason*, published in 1795. While his rejoinder to Gibbon was relaxed and courteous that to Paine was urgent and anxious; the debate was no longer an intellectual exercise but a crucial defence of the political and social order.

Family, retirement, and death At Lancaster on 21 December 1773 Watson married Dorothy (1750–1831), daughter of Edward Wilson of Dallam Tower, Milnthorpe, Westmorland. The Wilsons were one of the most important families in Watson's home county and benefactors of the grammar school at Heversham. Although the Watsons had six children and appeared conventionally happy Dorothy is hardly mentioned in her husband's *Anecdotes* and, as his biographer acutely observes, 'women do not appear to have played a very significant part in Watson's life' (Brain, 15). His thirty-year-long close friendship with his fellow student John Luther appears to have been of much greater emotional importance to Watson. When in 1764 Luther left his wife Watson borrowed the money to rush to Paris to support and rescue his friend: 'I crossed the channel four times, and travelled twelve hundred miles in very bad weather in a fortnight, I brought my friend back to this country' (*Anecdotes*, 28). Watson, who had named his eldest son Charles Luther Watson, was at his friend's bedside when he died on 13 January 1786. The childless Luther left him his large Sussex estate, which Watson sold for the huge sum of £23,500. This gave him the financial independence that hitherto he had lacked and enabled him to retire from Cambridge and, in 1788, buy Calgarth, a large estate on the shores of Windermere, between Ambleside and Bowness. In the early 1790s he built a new house, Calgarth Park, where house-guests included Wilberforce, Coleridge, Walter Scott, and the duke of Orléans, later Louis XVIII of France. Watson became 'the leading person about the Lakes … a joyous, jovial and cordial host … pleasant and kind in his manners … overbearing and arrogant in argument' (De Quincey, 83–6). Watson claimed that he had not wasted his time at Calgarth but had spent it 'principally in building farm-houses, blasting rocks, enclosing wastes, in making bad land good, in planting larches' (*Anecdotes*, 240). A friend of Arthur Young, he was soon a keen and knowledgeable landowner and an improving farmer; in 1793 he became one of the first members of the newly founded board of agriculture.

Watson was no genius but an able man whose relatively humble origins required him to make his own fortune. He successfully turned his hand to chemistry and divinity and ecclesiastical politics when his career demanded it and happily abandoned them when that need disappeared. His friend's generosity permitted him to become a landowner and improving farmer and it was as such that he found contentment. But he was perhaps less important than his reputation suggested. The legend of the radical bishop who supported revolution and later turned apostate concealed the duller reality of a consistent, independent-minded but rather old-fashioned whig. Watson had a habit of destroying his papers when he had no more use for them: in 1786 he announced that he had destroyed all his chemical manuscripts; in 1811 his papers on divinity went the same way. It is probable that about 1814, having constructed his own version of his life in the *Anecdotes* (a version that frankly exposed his ambition, disappointment, and bitterness), he destroyed all the personal and political papers in his possession; none appears to have survived. In July 1781 he fell gravely ill with a 'paralysis of the stomach' (*Anecdotes*, 87) from which he never fully recovered; in 1804 he complained that 'the original disorder, which seized me twenty-four years ago, is not removed' (ibid., 395). He suffered paralytic strokes in October 1809 and April 1811 and endured increasing ill health until his death at Calgarth Park on 4 July 1816. He was buried on 13 July in the graveyard of his local parish church at Bowness.   ROBERT HOLE

Sources *Anecdotes of the life of Richard Watson*, ed. R. Watson (1817) · T. J. Brain, 'Some aspects of the life and work of Richard Watson, bishop of Llandaff, 1737–1816', PhD diss., U. Wales, 1982 · P. Searby, *A history of the University of Cambridge*, 3: *1750–1870*, ed. C. N. L. Brooke and others (1997) · A. M. C. Waterman, 'A Cambridge "via media" in late Georgian Anglicanism', *Journal of Ecclesiastical History*, 42 (1991), 419–36 · J. Gascoigne, 'Anglican latitudinarianism and political radicalism in the late eighteenth century', *History*, new ser., 71 (1986), 22–38 · A. M. C. Waterman, *Revolution, economics and religion: Christian political economy, 1798–1833* (1991) · R. Hole, *Pulpits, politics and public order, 1760–1832* (1989) · J. Walsh and others, eds., *The Church of England, c.1689–c.1833* (1993) · J. Gascoigne, *Cambridge in the age of the Enlightenment* (1989) · *Fasti Angl., 1541–1857*, [Ely] · *GM*, 1st ser., 86/2 (1816), 93, 274–8 · Venn, *Alum. Cant.* · T. De Quincey, *Recollections of the Lakes and the Lake poets*, ed. D. Wright (1986) · G. Wakefield, *A reply to some parts of the bishop of Llandaff's address to the people of Great Britain* (1798) · H. Gunning, *Reminiscences of the university, town, and county of Cambridge, from the year 1780*, 1 (1854) · *DNB*
Archives Herts. ALS, corresp. | Cumbria AS, Carlisle, executorship papers · Cumbria AS, Carlisle, letters to earl of Lonsdale · N. Yorks. CRO, corresp. with Christopher Wyvill · NL Scot., corresp. with Lord Muncaster · NRA, priv. coll., letters to Lord Shelburne · Suffolk RO, Bury St Edmunds, letters to duke of Grafton
Likenesses J. Reynolds, portrait, 1769, National Museum, Havana [*see illus.*] · J. Sayers, caricature, etching, pubd 1787, NPG · J. Sayers, caricature, etching, pubd 1789, NPG · H. H. Meyer, stipple, pubd 1809 (after G. Romney), BM, NPG · W. T. Fry, print (after G. Romney), NPG · G. Romney, oils, Trinity Cam. · W. Walker and G. Zobel, group portrait, engraving (after drawing by J. F. Skill, J. Gilbert, and W. and E. Walker; *Men of science living in 1807–8*), NPG
Wealth at death over £30,000

Watson, Richard (1781–1833), Wesleyan Methodist minister and theologian, was born on 22 February 1781 at Barton-on-Humber, Lincolnshire, the seventh of the eighteen children of Thomas Watson (1741/2–1812), a saddler, and his wife, Ann Watson. Though early connected with Methodism, Thomas became a Calvinistic dissenter and gave Richard a religious upbringing among dissenters and the Countess of Huntingdon's Connexion. He had a good classical education, beginning Latin at the age of six, entering Lincoln grammar school in 1791, and eagerly acquiring literary and general knowledge. In 1795 he was apprenticed to a joiner in Lincoln. After being somewhat careless about religion, attendance at a Wesleyan chapel to learn arguments against Calvinism led to his conversion in 1794. Speaking in public prayer meetings led to his first sermon on 23 February 1796 aged fifteen, then to preaching in villages, sometimes in the open air. His master having released him from apprenticeship, he assisted the Wesleyan preacher at Newark, and was received as an itinerant preacher on trial in 1796 and into full connection in 1801. In 1800 he published *An Apology for the Methodists* in answer to a local Anglican attack.

In 1801, however, Watson's theological and philosophical reading and love of argument led to suspicions that he had denied the full divinity of Christ. Though the charge was apparently unjust and not formally presented, Watson took offence and left the Wesleyan ministry. After a failure in business, he married in 1801 Mary Henslow of Castle Donington, Leicestershire, the daughter of a Methodist New Connexion local preacher. This led him to join that denomination as a local, then as an itinerant, preacher on probation (1803) and in full connection (1807). His abilities were recognized by his appointment as assistant secretary of conference in 1805 and secretary in 1807. Meanwhile, during stationing in Liverpool (1806–8) with time for study and literary work, he published a popular guide to Liverpool and expounded conservative politics as editor of the *Liverpool Courier* (1808). Poor health forced him to become a supernumerary in 1809, but he resumed his active ministry and secretaryship of conference in 1810. Meanwhile he became dissatisfied with the Methodist New Connexion's subordination of the ministry to the laity, became friendly with the leading Wesleyan Jabez Bunting, and wrote against the 1811 attempt to restrict the Toleration Act. He then resigned from the Methodist New Connexion, was soon accepted as a local preacher by the Wesleyans, and in 1812 was reinstated as a Wesleyan itinerant.

Wesleyans had worked overseas for many years without a formal missionary society. Stimulated by competition from existing societies, in 1813 they began forming local missionary societies and Watson became deeply involved. In 1816 he was made a connectional missionary secretary responsible for home correspondence, reports, and publications. In 1817 he drew up a plan for a national Wesleyan missionary society, accepted by the conference in 1818. He became the leading advocate and most successful speaker and fund-raiser for Wesleyan missions. His annual

Richard Watson (1781–1833), by Samuel William Reynolds junior, pubd 1842 (after John Jackson)

reports, with their persistently optimistic and triumphalist tone, did much to shape policy. From 1821 to 1827 and again in 1832 he became a full-time missionary secretary in London. His missionary concerns led him to write his *Defence of the Wesleyan Methodist Missions in the West Indies* (1817) and to support the anti-slavery campaign. He drafted the resolution in favour of emancipation adopted by the missionary committee in 1825 and by the conference in 1830. He claimed that 'Christianity will not snap the chains of the slave but it will melt them' (Stevenson, 566). In 1826 he was elected president of conference for that year.

Watson, along with Jabez Bunting and Robert Newton, was credited with introducing more style and refinement into Wesleyan pulpit oratory, his sermons being characterized by measured eloquence and a poetic use of language. A keen naturalist, he liked to descant on the beauty and harmony to be found between the natural and moral worlds.

Watson's theological ability was first shown in his *Remarks on the Eternal Sonship and the Use of Reason in Matters of Religion* (1818), in which (perhaps sensitive to the old charge of Arianism) he defended the traditional doctrine of the eternal sonship of Christ against Adam Clarke's denial of it. He also firmly subordinated reason to revelation, and his attack on Clarke probably helped to antagonize Clarke's admirers in later disputes. His *Theological Institutes* (1823–8) was the first systematic theology by a Wesleyan, covering the evidence, doctrines, morals, and institutions of Christianity 'adapted to the use of young

ministers and students in divinity', 'neither Calvinistic on the one hand nor Pelagian on the other' (*Theological Institutes*, preface). As an exposition of evangelical Arminianism it was certainly 'Wesleyan', yet it contained few references to Wesley's writings despite defending Wesley's doctrines of assurance and perfection as scriptural. These findings were, however, absorbed into an evangelical version of scholastic protestant theology, upheld by the stock 'evidences' of miracle and prophecy. He rejected any compromise between Genesis and geology. He defended Wesley's teaching that perfection can be both a process and an instantaneous experience; but, unlike Adam Clarke, he preferred to see it as a gradual development.

In his *Observations on Southey's Life of Wesley* (1820) Watson, while recognizing Southey's literary qualities and superiority to most of Wesley's critics, attacked him severely for charging Wesley with ambition and credulity. He saw Southey as undermining Christianity as well as Methodism by his failure to understand salvation doctrine and his naturalistic explanations of religious phenomena. Though some thought his strictures overdone, the prince regent is said to have remarked that 'Mr Watson has the advantage of my laureate' (Jackson, 326). In his own *Life of Wesley* (1831) Watson aimed to produce a biography for general readers, though with some original material. He saw Wesley's theology as being permanently settled in terms of justification by faith after his 1738 conversion, thereby failing to recognize Wesley's later emphasis on sanctification and perfection. He offered some cautious criticisms of the Wesley brothers, but his claim that Wesley had effectively ordained all his lay preachers (and not simply those on whom he formally laid hands) reflected later Wesleyan disputes and Anglican criticisms.

Though Watson was not hostile to the Church of England and liked the Anglican liturgy, he was convinced that Wesleyan Methodism was now an independent church and he upheld Wesleyan ministerial authority. Adumbrated in his *Institutes*, this authority was hammered home in his *Affectionate Address* (1829) to the protestant Methodists who favoured greater lay control. While arguing that Wesleyan rules offered safeguards against abuse of ministerial power, Watson asserted that the duties given by God to 'the office of a Christian pastor' for oversight and discipline of the people meant that 'the powers needed to fulfil these [duties] are therefore of right, inalienable right, belonging to his office' (*Affectionate Address*, 7).

Watson's comprehensive *Theological and Biblical Dictionary* (1831) was largely a compilation from conservative authorities. The supplement to the Wesleyan hymnbook (1831) was mainly selected by him. (He favoured congregational singing rather than choirs though he cautiously allowed for organs.) He also contributed solid reviews to the *Wesleyan Methodist Magazine*. Despite some criticisms by the admirers of Adam Clarke, the conference bought his surviving manuscripts for £2000.

Watson had stood 6 feet 2 inches since the age of fourteen. He was extremely slender, with a lofty forehead, dark brown hair, piercing eyes, and a dignified bearing.

Though lively when young, in later years his emaciated appearance and reputation for coldness and reserve, especially in mixed company, were probably aggravated if not actually caused by ill health. A clear and mellow voice added force to his preaching. His biographer Thomas Jackson complained that much could not be known about Watson's inner life because he destroyed his private papers.

With Jabez Bunting and Robert Newton, Watson stood among the dominant figures of his generation in Wesleyan Methodism. Though prominent as a preacher and as an upholder of the high-Wesleyan view of the ministry, he was especially significant for his theology and culture. His only intellectual rival was Adam Clarke, who was more of a polymath but theologically less focused and more eccentric. Clarke was a hero to revivalist and reforming Wesleyans, and he and Watson were often seen as leaders of rival parties, apparently to Watson's regret.

Watson died in London on 8 January 1833 from a long-standing gall bladder and liver condition, and was buried behind City Road Chapel, London, on 15 January. His marriage to Mary, who survived him, produced two children, Thomas and Mary (who married James Dixon).

HENRY D. RACK

Sources T. Jackson, *Memoirs of the life and writings of Rev. Richard Watson*, 3rd edn (1840) · JRL, Methodist Archives and Research Centre, Watson MSS, MAM PLP 111.7.1–56 [including letters, speeches, sermons, and *Manchester Times* biographical sketch by J. Bromley] · E. J. Brailsford, *Richard Watson, theologian and missionary advocate* (1906) · [J. Beaumont and J. Everett], *Wesleyan takings*, 2nd edn, 2 vols. (1840), 119–51 · J. Kent, *Holding the fort* (1978), 315–16 · R. E. Davies, A. R. George, and G. Rupp, eds., *History of Methodism in Great Britain*, 2 (1978), 215–16, 228–9, 233 · I. Sellers, *Adam Clarke, controversialist* (privately printed, St Columb Major, [1976]), 9–10 · B. Gregory, *Side lights on the conflicts of Methodism during the second quarter of the nineteenth century, 1827–1852*, popular edn (1899), 138–9 · R. Maddox, ed., *Rethinking Wesley's theology for contemporary Methodism* (1998), 216–18 · J. Stoughton, *Religion in England, 1800–50* (1884), 324–7 · G. J. Stevenson, *City Road Chapel* (1872), 119, 301, 564–6, 583

Archives John Wesley's Chapel, Bristol, letters · JRL, Methodist Archives and Research Centre, letters, speeches, sermons, MAM PLP 111.7.1–56

Likenesses T. Blood, stipple, 1824 (after J. Renton), BM; repro. in *Methodist Magazine* (1824) · S. W. Reynolds junior, mezzotint, pubd 1842 (after J. Jackson), BM, NPG [*see illus.*] · J. Cochran, stipple and line engraving (after J. Jackson), NPG · J. Jackson, oils, Wesley's house, City Road, London · attrib. Lovett, oils, Wesley's house, City Road, London · charcoal and pastels, Wesley's house, City Road, London · oils, Methodist Publishing House, London

Wealth at death manuscripts sold to conference for £2000: Gregory, *Side lights*, 139

Watson, Robert (*d.* 1559), lawyer and evangelical preacher, was born in the city of Norwich. He was admitted BCL at Oxford on 1 July 1528. Nothing else is known about Watson before 1539. On 23 February that year, Bishop William Rugge preached a sermon at Norwich arguing that good works played a qualified role in the attainment of salvation. Watson called on the bishop the next day and vigorously criticized the sermon, denying that humans had free will. Rumours about the encounter circulated, the matter escalated, and Rugge, intimidated by the number

of Watson's supporters, denounced his critic to the authorities. This manoeuvre backfired. Thomas Cromwell summoned Watson to London and interrogated him about the incident. Cromwell was so impressed with Watson that he wrote to the mayor and aldermen of Norwich, recommending that Watson be given a municipal office. The Norwich civic leaders wrote back to Cromwell declaring that, because they knew Watson to be learned in both scripture and law, they would make him town clerk. Watson, however, never took the post, probably because even greater opportunities were available elsewhere.

It is likely that Cromwell had recommended Watson to Archbishop Thomas Cranmer, as well as to the city fathers of Norwich. John Bale claimed that Watson became Cranmer's steward. There is no corroboration for this and Watson seems to have spent a considerable amount of time away from Cranmer's household. But Bale's statement cannot be lightly dismissed. He and Watson shared a close friend in John Barrett, a former Carmelite and popular evangelical preacher in Norwich, so Bale would have been well informed about Watson. Furthermore, Watson was described in a document of 1550 as a priest in Cranmer's household. In any case, Watson had unmistakable official support in building a career in the church, despite having never been ordained. Early in Edward VI's reign he was granted a national preaching licence, in which he was inaccurately styled 'Professor of Divinity' (PRO, SP 10/2/34, fol. 116r). Then on 26 May 1549 he received a prebend in Norwich Cathedral despite his not being a priest and despite (as the letters patent for the living noted) his having been married twice. This benefice suggests that, whatever his connection to Cranmer's household, Watson remained active in his native Norwich. In 1548 a member of the confraternity of St George in Norwich was stripped of his civic privileges for refusing, on religious grounds, to provide the annual feast for the members of the confraternity. Watson not only used his legal skills to defend the man, he also had the case brought before the privy council. Protector Somerset ordered that Watson's client have his privileges restored.

Watson was also prominent in the early stages of the most momentous event in the history of Tudor Norwich: Kett's rebellion. He preached to the rebels and was one of a trio of leading Norwich residents (including the mayor) elected as nominal leaders of the rising. As protest escalated into overt rebellion and events spun out of control, the trio fell out with Kett and were imprisoned by the rebels. None of this harmed Watson's relationship with Cranmer; in the following year, 1550, he received one of the plum livings in the archbishop's gift, the rectory of Saltwood, in Kent.

Mary's accession to the throne deprived Watson of his patron and his livings, but worse was to follow. Early in 1554 Henry Crook, the mayor of Norwich, questioned Watson about his failure to attend mass; Watson answered that attending mass was against his conscience and refused ever to be present when it was celebrated. He was arrested and formally examined by the civic authorities, and then imprisoned while they wrote to the privy council for instructions. The council ordered that Watson be sent to London. This time, instead of meeting an appreciative Cromwell, Watson faced a blistering interrogation by Stephen Gardiner. He refused to submit, and in February 1554 was returned to Norwich, where on the council's order he was placed in the custody of Miles Spencer, the chancellor of the diocese. Watson was confined in the episcopal palace, and by his own account was well treated, although he was denied visitors.

In spring 1555 John Barrett, now a loyal Catholic, wrote to Watson urging him to recant and trying to persuade him of the truth of the real presence in the sacrament. More ominously, John Christopherson, the dean of Norwich, visited Watson and debated eucharistic theology with him. Eventually Watson was given a statement to sign, declaring his unqualified belief in transubstantiation. Watson signed the document but not before adding the crucial proviso: 'I assent to all these [doctrines] in so far as they are based on the Word of God and in the sense in which they are understood by the catholic Church and by the holy fathers' (Watson, *Aetiologia*, sig. G3r–3v). The document was witnessed by Christopherson, Spencer, Barrett, Thomas Pecock (a prebendary of Norwich Cathedral), and Alexander Mather, a Norwich alderman who had been active in persecuting Watson. The document was seized upon by the authorities; it was read aloud in St Peter Mancroft, one of Norwich's leading churches, during services.

Yet subscribing to the document did not end Watson's troubles. He was detained in prison for another five weeks before being released in late spring 1555. John Young, the vice-chancellor of Cambridge University, objected that Watson's signed statement was not sufficient and demanded that Watson sign an unqualified declaration of belief in transubstantiation. Orders were given that Watson be rearrested but he went into hiding. Although two Norwich aldermen, Thomas Codde and Thomas Marsham, zealously pursued the fugitive, Watson's friends successfully threw them off his trail and concealed him. He soon fled overseas to Emden.

From this haven Watson wrote an account of his Marian ordeals, the *Aetiologia*, which was designed to demonstrate that he had emerged from them 'unharmed in body and undiminished in conscience' (Watson, *Aetiologia*, title-page). The book was finished by November 1555 and published (only in Latin) in Emden in 1556. Beyond this little is known of Watson's activities in exile, although he and John Scory apparently debated the subject of free will with Wouter Delenus, a leading member of the Emden reformed community. The wheel had come full circle: Watson sprang into prominence championing predestination and his last known public activity was to defend the doctrine in disputation. Having returned to England, Watson died in 1559, when his will was proved.

THOMAS S. FREEMAN

Sources R. Watson, *Aetiologia* (Emden, 1556) [STC 25111] · Bale, *Cat.*, 729–30 · B. L. Beer, ed., '"The Commoyson in Norfolk, 1549": a narrative of popular rebellion in 16th century England', *Journal of Medieval and Renaissance Studies*, 6 (1976), 73–99, at 82 and 88 ·

A. Pettegree, *Marian protestantism: six studies* (1996), 26, 98, 186–7, 198 · G. R. Elton, *Policy and police: the enforcement of the Reformation in the age of Thomas Cromwell* (1972), 138–41 · D. MacCulloch, *Thomas Cranmer: a life* (1996), 433–4 · M. C. McClendon, *The quiet reformation: magistrates and the emergence of protestantism in Tudor Norwich* (Stanford, CA, 1999), 125–9 · J. Foxe, *Actes and monuments* (1563), 1679 · Emden, *Oxf.*, 4.610 · will, PRO, PROB 11/428/31

Watson, Robert (*fl.* 1581–1611), almanac maker, matriculated as a sizar of Queens' College, Cambridge, on 22 November 1581 and graduated BA from Clare College in 1585. He had returned to Queens' College by 1589, in which year he was licensed by the university to practise physic. He lived at Braintree, Essex, where he combined the study of medicine with that of astrology. He published for several years an almanac containing a forecast for the year. The earliest surviving example is for the year 1594, the latest for 1611.

John Mott of Braintree, who had been with the earl of Essex on the expedition to Cadiz in 1596, has recently been identified as the author of a 30,000 line Jacobean poem by J.M. (now BL, Add. MSS 14824–14826) of which book 8, composed about 1621–5, consists of a series of Chaucerian tales told by the ship's crew on the return voyage. The ship's cook recounts the story of Mott's Braintree neighbour 'Nostaw', (the name disguised by inversion of its letters). The poem begins

> Nostaw sometimes skild in Astronomie'
> mongst th' Country Medices held he soveraigntie
> for both those Arts he certainly profest…
> Quod gratis grate was his motto still
> w[ch] wth his practice suited very ill
> his Lying-bookes at highest rate he sold
> he could not give his physicke though he would
> Eger & Indiges evermore did knock
> (BL, Add. MS 14825, fol. 171r–171v)

The poem runs on with the increasingly scurrilous tale of Watson's seduction of one of his patients, of his being afflicted with the pox, trying to keep this fact from his wife, and ultimately dying of this disease.

Nothing is known of Watson's later years nor of his date of death.   E. I. CARLYLE, *rev.* ANITA McCONNELL

Sources Cooper, *Ath. Cantab.*, 3.310 · B. S. Capp, *Astrology and the popular press: English almanacs, 1500–1800* (1979), 388 · W. H. Keliher, 'John Mott and *The newe metamorphosis*', *English Manuscript Studies, 1100–1700*, 11 (2002)

Watson, Robert (1730?–1781), historian and rhetorician, was born in St Andrews, the son of Andrew Watson, an apothecary and brewer. Nothing is known of his early years, though records show he studied at St Andrews University from 1744 to 1748, receiving his MA degree on 6 May 1748. He subsequently spent time in Glasgow and Edinburgh, perhaps taking some classes at their respective universities. While in Edinburgh he probably attended the rhetoric lectures given by Adam Smith in 1748–9, and at the same time he is said to have 'secured the countenance, approbation, and friendship of Lord Kames, Mr Hume, and other eminent men of that day' (Anderson, 740). When Smith left Edinburgh in 1751 to assume the chair of logic at Glasgow, Kames recruited Watson to continue the series of rhetoric lectures. Watson's exact dates of lecturing are not known, but they must have been some time between 1751 and 1756, when, having been licensed by the presbytery of St Andrews, he applied for a vacancy in a St Andrews parish. Although denied that position, he then sought to replace the retiring Henry Rymer as professor of logic, rhetoric, and metaphysics at St Andrews. Watson received the appointment on 18 June 1756.

After a year in his academic appointment Watson married Margaret Shaw, the daughter of the professor of divinity in St Mary's College, on 29 June 1757; they subsequently had five daughters. He taught courses in rhetoric and *belles-lettres* and in logic; various sets of student notes survive for both courses as they were delivered between 1756 and 1778. He does not appear to have taught a separate course in metaphysics. His lectures clearly reflect the new trends in rhetoric and logic developed by the Scottish Enlightenment. In logic he gave a prominent place to Locke, as did Thomas Reid at Aberdeen, John Stevenson at Edinburgh, and James Clow at Glasgow. In rhetoric he joined figures such as Adam Smith, Hugh Blair, and George Campbell in rethinking rhetoric in terms of human nature, thus linking rhetoric, through psychology, to ethics, aesthetics, and criticism. In neither logic nor rhetoric, however, was Watson a strongly original thinker; instead, his work is valuable in offering 'a general contribution to our understanding of the scope, method, and role of rhetoric in the Scottish university curriculum in the eighteenth century' (Bator, 104).

Watson was also active in university business outside the classroom. He was instrumental in having honorary degrees conferred on Hugh Blair (1757) and Benjamin Franklin (1759), but perhaps his most important assignment was the expansion of the university library, which included both gathering library materials and overseeing the construction of improved facilities. These concerns for the university helped prepare him for more important administrative assignments. From the time of his rhetoric lectures in Edinburgh he had maintained close ties with the moderate party leadership in the church. Thus, on 9 January 1778—following a plan formed several years earlier by the earl of Kinnoul and moderate colleagues such as William Robertson—Watson was named principal of St Andrews University, and, later that year, rector of the United College of Saint Salvator and Saint Leonard in the University of St Andrews, succeeding Thomas Tullidelph, who had died after years of failing health in November 1777. Watson was a genial, scholarly representative of the university. When James Boswell and Samuel Johnson visited St Andrews in 1773 they found him to be 'a well-informed man, of very amiable manners', and they spent some time discussing Watson's 'favourite topick' of composition (Boswell, 66–8). The United College—the main buildings of which Watson had actually purchased in 1772 to house his family—'seemed quite academical; and we found in his house very comfortable and genteel accommodation' (ibid., 58). Johnson, who later edited Watson's two histories, observed that Watson's 'easy civility quickly made us forget that we were strangers; and in the whole time of our stay we were gratified by every mode of

kindness, and entertained with all the elegance of lettered hospitality' (Johnson, *Journey*, 5).

Despite Watson's work in rhetoric and education, he remains best known for his two histories. *The History of the Reign of Philip the Second, King of Spain* was published in two volumes in London by Strahan and Cadell in 1777, with six further editions appearing between 1778 and 1812. *The History of the Reign of Philip the Third, King of Spain* was left incomplete at his death. The first four books of this were transcribed directly from Watson's manuscripts, the last two were added by William Thomson, and the whole published in 1783 by Robinson. Both histories form a sequel to William Robertson's *History of the Reign of Charles V* (1769), being generally modelled on that earlier work in terms of structure and style as well as their broad conception of Philip II's character. Like Robertson, Watson faced the problem of unifying his subject around the life and career of his central figure, with the result that there is a constant tension between the great dispersion of events in the Habsburg empire and the biography of the ruler. As a rhetorician, however, Watson was very sensitive to the importance of unity in history, and his ability to create smooth transitions among events was praised by reviewers. Watson also wore his learning very lightly, having none of the heavier annotation or learned appendices of Hume or Robertson. He did not often cite manuscript or archival sources in his histories, though at the time of his death he was in possession of some of the earl of Hardwicke's manuscripts that he was consulting in his research for *Philip the Third*. Instead Watson seems even more insistent than his fellow historians in aiming for a polite audience, one more interested in moral education than in the details of historical interpretation. Both histories may, in fact, be read as illustrations of the dangers of narrow education and 'illiberal superstition' (*History of … Philip the Second*, 1.2). Watson attributed the bloody struggles of Philip II's reign to Philip's narrow Catholic education in which he 'had imbibed, in all its virulence, that spirit of bigotry and persecution, which gave birth to the inquisition' (ibid., 1.93). Watson thought Philip III an even greater failure, combining his father's 'bigotted [*sic*] attachment to the superstition of the church of Rome' with a strong aversion 'to almost every species of manly exertion and activity' (*History of … Philip the Third*, 3rd edn, 1808, 1.1–2). In contrast Watson describes Philip II's arch-rival, the prince of Orange, as the embodiment of moderate-party educational ideals: flexible, adaptable, polite, and possessed of 'a peculiar dexterity in governing the inclinations of men, and in conciliating and preserving their affections' (*History of … Philip the Second*, 2.166).

Watson died unexpectedly on 31 March 1781 in St Andrews. Almost immediately the wheels were set in motion through Robertson for another well-established moderate, Joseph MacCormick, to succeed as principal. Watson's cousin Hugh Blair was asked by John Davidson, the executor of the estate, to be responsible for handling Watson's papers dealing with history and literary–financial affairs. In a sermon of 1793 Alexander Carlyle included Watson in his retrospective list of moderate party clergymen who he felt had brought particular lustre to the Scottish church through their accomplishments in polite learning. Watson thus takes his place as a fine example of a liberally educated Presbyterian clergyman, the unique creation of the Scottish Enlightenment.   JEFFREY R. SMITTEN

Sources P. G. Bator, 'The unpublished rhetoric lectures of Robert Watson, professor of logic, rhetoric, and metaphysics at the University of St Andrews, 1756–1778', *Rhetorica*, 12 (1994), 67–113 · R. B. Sher, *Church and university in the Scottish Enlightenment: the moderate literati of Edinburgh* (1985) · I. S. Ross, *Lord Kames and the Scotland of his day* (1972) · *Fasti Scot.*, new edn · Chambers, *Scots.* (1870) · W. Anderson, *The Scottish biographical dictionary* (1845) · Boswell, *Life* · S. Johnson, *Journey to the western islands of Scotland*, ed. M. Lascelles (1971) · *The letters of Samuel Johnson*, ed. R. W. Chapman, 3 vols. (1952) · W. Robertson, letter to J. MacCormick, 9 April 1781, U. Edin. L., MS La. II. 241 · W. Robertson, 8 March 1774, U. Edin., New Coll. L., MS box I · W. Robertson to earl of Hardwicke, 10 May 1781, BL, Add. MS 35350, fol. 68 · A. Carlyle, *The usefulness and necessity of a liberal education for clergymen* (1793) · R. M. Schmitz, *Hugh Blair* (1948) · *DNB*

Archives NL Scot., manuscript work · U. Edin. L., manuscript works · U. St Andr. L., manuscript works

Watson, Robert (1746?–1838), revolutionary and adventurer, was born in Elgin. A Robert Watson, son of a horse hirer, Robert Watson, and his wife, Catherine Demster, was baptized there on 29 June 1746, but at his death in 1838 Watson was described as eighty-eight years old. Throughout his life Watson confused and embroidered details of his career. The credence hitherto given to 1746 as his birth date rests mainly on accepting unverified claims that he had fought with the American army during the American War of Independence (and had achieved the rank of colonel, been wounded, and in recompense been granted land). These claims, made to the artist who painted his portrait in 1817, seem not to have been made elsewhere. Moreover by 1780 Watson was living in London and working as the private secretary to Lord George Gordon. Shortly before his death Watson claimed to have been deeply implicated in the riots of 1780. This is more plausible but, like the medical degree from a Scottish university of which he boasted, cannot be verified.

However, in August 1794 Watson did help foment a riot in London against coercive recruiting and was sentenced to two years in Newgate for circulating a handbill attacking the Militia Act and magistracy. While in prison he wrote a *Life of Lord George Gordon* which *inter alia* welcomed the fall of the Bastille as 'a step to universal emancipation' (p. 91). Watson also attacked continental Catholic clergy for their opposition to the French Revolution in the *Moral and Political Magazine* (March 1796) of the London Corresponding Society, which he had joined in 1792. Once released from Newgate, Watson was soon predicting the people would swiftly have 'recourse to steel' (*Moral and Political Magazine*, March 1797). A member of the society's executive, he was one of two delegates it sent to consult with the leaders of the Spithead naval mutiny in 1797. They were accompanied, perhaps without the executive's sanction, by a representative of the United Irishmen. How far the society's subsequent repudiation of Watson reflected a loss of nerve or was meant to obscure its complicity in revolutionary conspiracy is debatable. Watson was now communicating with the French agent at Hamburg about

Robert Watson (1746?–1838), by Carl Christian Vogel von Vogelstein, 1817

Britain's readiness for revolution, claiming that 50,000 Scots and 200,000 English were waiting on a French invasion as their cue for rising. In April 1798, on hearing a warrant had been issued for his arrest, Watson fled abroad. After travelling through Scandinavia and Germany he arrived in Paris in September.

For a brief period Watson was the principal English republican envoy in France. He issued a grandiloquent 'Address to the people of Great Britain' (*Moniteur*, 4 frimaire, an VII [24 Nov 1798]). In July 1799, in a memorial to the governing directory, he claimed (falsely) to be president of the London Corresponding Society and disclosed plans for provincial British radicals to greet a French invasion with a series of uprisings to force the dispersal of troops away from London and the south coast. Watson claimed briefly to have been English tutor to Napoleon, who appointed him to the presidency (1800–06) of the Scottish College in Paris, a secular revival of the medieval foundation dispossessed at the revolution. He also travelled to Italy where (in an effort to support the beleaguered Napoleonic economy) he tried unsuccessfully to cultivate cotton on the Pontine marshes. In 1817 he became involved in a dispute with the Vatican over the ownership of papers that had belonged to Cardinal York, the Jacobite pretender Henry IX. Watson was instrumental in their acquisition by the British government, for which he was financially rewarded (inadequately he vehemently claimed) and the arrest warrant of 1798 annulled. Watson was also connected, possibly through marriage, to the aide-de-camp to the Young Pretender (Charles Edward

Stuart), James Johnstone, the manuscript of whose history of the 1745 rising he sold to Longmans on returning to Britain in 1820.

Details of the later years of Watson's life are as opaque as the earliest. He spent some time in Greece but seems to have lived mainly in France. In 1825 he was writing from Paris begging for money needed, he said, to recover various possessions including the missal of Mary, queen of Scots, and the Constantinople Bible. By early 1838 he was living once again in London, at the Blue Anchor tavern, Thames Street, St Mary-at-Hill. There, on 19 November, he strangled himself by twisting his silk cravat with a poker as tourniquet. A 'little lame man', his body was found to bear the scars of nineteen previous wounds. The *Gentleman's Magazine* reported that 'the body of the wretched old man was conveyed to the grave as that of a pauper, at the expense of the parish' (*GM*, 2nd ser., 11/1, 1839, 328).

Watson's Jacobitism represents a significant strand in British radicalism. His continued attachment to Jacobinism may be reasonably inferred from the identity of the friend who arranged his affairs after his death: Colonel Francis Macerone, sometime Italian revolutionary and aide-de-camp to Murat, whose writings on street fighting had been circulating among English ultra-radicals since the reform crisis. MALCOLM CHASE

Sources A. P. Forbes, 'Some account of Robert Watson', *Proceedings of the Society of Antiquaries of Scotland*, 7 (1866–8), 324–34 · A. Tayler and H. Tayler, eds., *The Stuart papers at Windsor* (1939) · R. Watson, *The life of Lord George Gordon, with a philosophical review of his life and conduct* (1795) · M. Elliott, *Partners in revolution: the United Irishmen and France* (1982) · *Moral and Political Magazine of the London Corresponding Society* · BL, Add. MSS 27812, fols. 20–23; 27815, fol. 151; 36653(1) fols. 69–72 · PRO, PC 1/41/A138; 1/43/A152; HO 42/42, 15 April 1798; TS 11/956/3501 · *DNB* · *The Times* (22–3 Nov 1838) · *GM*, 2nd ser., 11/1 (1839), 327–8 · A. Goodwin, *The friends of liberty: the English democratic movement in the age of the French Revolution* (1979) · R. Wells, *Insurrection: the British experience, 1795–1803* (1983) · G. Bain, *The thunderbolt of reason* (1996)

Archives Archives du Ministère des Affaires Étrangères, Paris, 'Memoirs et documents', vol. 53, fols. 263–4; 361 · Archives Nationales, Paris, AF III 57 doss. 225, p. 113 1–2; GG I 72, fols. 114–15

Likenesses C. C. V. von Vogelstein, oils, 1817, Scot. NPG; permanent loan from National Museum of Scotland [*see illus.*]

Wealth at death none; owed his landlord £30–£40: *GM*, 327

Watson, Robert Irving

Watson, Robert Irving (1878–1948), oil industrialist, was born at Nith Bank, Dumfries, on 22 November 1878, the younger son of Thomas Watson, editor and proprietor of the *Dumfries and Galloway Standard*, and his wife, Nancy Hamilton. At Dumfries Academy, he became classical *dux*, or star pupil of his year.

Having determined on a career in the East, Watson obtained some legal training and in 1900 joined the Burmah Oil Company. At the company's agency in Rangoon, his talent for hard work and a capacity for unravelling the most complex issues marked him out for future promotion. In 1909 he married Caroline, daughter of Alexander Walker Mouat, a dentist from Edinburgh; they had a daughter and two sons. In 1912 Watson returned to become deputy manager in Burmah Oil's London office. Among his many tasks was that of maintaining regular

contact with Robert Waley Cohen of Royal Dutch Shell over the workings of their eastern marketing agreements.

Soon after the outbreak of the First World War, Watson took charge of Burmah Oil's London office, later becoming a member of the petroleum pool board, which was responsible for allocating oil products throughout Britain. As his company's *de facto* managing director, although not appointed as such until 1920, he had the agreement of the chairman in Glasgow, Sir John *Cargill, to overhaul systematically every part of the company's operations: for example, he introduced electrification of the drilling process in the Burmese oilfields and up-to-date refining and prospecting techniques. In 1921 he oversaw the company's acquisition of the languishing Assam Oil Company, and the expenditure of millions on making it efficient and profitable.

However, Watson failed in an ambitious attempt, together with Cohen, to form a major all-British oil group comprising Burmah Oil, Shell, and Anglo-Persian. Although Conservative ministers favoured selling the government-held shares in Anglo-Persian in order to help forward the merger, that company's top management was broadly hostile to the scheme, as were the Admiralty, the government of India, motorists' organizations, and the trade unions. It was finally rejected by the first Labour government in 1924, a decision upheld by the incoming Conservative cabinet later that year. Watson had very adroitly played a mediocre hand in promoting the scheme in Whitehall and Delhi; he was greatly disappointed at its collapse. As a second best, therefore, he helped to create a joint marketing organization, the Burmah–Shell Oil Storage and Distributing Company of India; in 1928 Burmah Oil bought a large shareholding stake in Shell, after which Watson was elected to that company's board.

Almost single-handedly, Watson turned the Burmah Oil Company from a collection of loose-knit managing agencies into a modern and centralized multinational company; this survived the depression years with reduced profits but a robust corporate structure. By the 1930s his reputation among oil magnates on both sides of the Atlantic was such that scarcely any important international petroleum conference would have been complete without this unassuming but resourceful man, who was always ready with a fresh idea or a relevant fact. Slight and dapper, he nevertheless had a personal authority that was out of all proportion to the relative smallness of his own company.

In 1938 Watson was offered the chairmanship of the Petroleum Board, designed to control oil distribution in Britain in the event of war. He declined the post, but when war came he arranged for the oilfields in Burma and Assam to increase production to meet the needs of the forces and civilian markets in the Far East. Then, after the entry of Japan into the war, Burma itself was invaded by the Japanese. Watson therefore had to agree to the destruction of the refineries in Rangoon and the oilfield installations, to deny them to the invaders. However, continued output from Assam, together with investment income from the shareholdings in Anglo-Persian and in Shell, kept Burmah Oil's profits at a reasonable level.

By 1943, when Watson became company chairman on Cargill's retirement, he was thinking ahead to the end of the war. He collected evidence for a future compensation claim from the British government for the assets destroyed in Burma, and attempted to cajole uninterested Whitehall civil servants into making plans for immediately resuming operations once Burma was recaptured. The company was not allowed to restart until 1946, by which time he was greatly concerned with the likely consequences for oil of the proposals, which became reality in 1948, for giving independence to Burma. However, Watson retired at the end of 1947, after a serious illness that year. He died of a heart attack on 26 January 1948 at his home, Lower Bowden, in Pangbourne, Berkshire. He was cremated at Reading, but his ashes were later buried at Dumfries.   T. A. B. CORLEY

Sources T. A. B. Corley, *A history of the Burmah Oil Company*, 2 vols. (1983–8) • R. W. Ferrier, *The history of the British Petroleum Company*, 1: *The developing years, 1901–1932* (1982) • T. A. B. Corley, 'Watson, Robert Irving', *DBB* • T. A. B. Corley, 'Watson, Robert Irving', *DSBB* • *Dumfries and Galloway Standard and Advertiser* (31 Jan 1948) • *Glasgow Herald* (27 Jan 1948) • *Institute of Petroleum Review* (Feb 1948) • *The Times* (27 Jan 1948) • *The Times* (5 Feb 1948) • *The Times* (18 Feb 1948) • J. Reid, 'Mr. Robert I. Watson', *Some Dumfries and Galloway Men* (1922) • *Directory of Directors* (1944–7) • General Register Office for Scotland, Edinburgh • d. cert. • private information (2004)
Archives Burmah Castrol plc, Swindon, archives • U. Warwick Mod. RC, BP archive
Likenesses photographs, U. Warwick Mod. RC; also BP Archive, Burmah Castrol archives
Wealth at death £429,796 19s. 11d.: will, PRO

Watson, Robert Spence (1837–1911), politician and educationist, born at 8 Claremont Place, Gateshead, on 6 June 1837, was the eldest son in a family of five sons and seven daughters of Joseph Watson of Bensham Grove, Gateshead, and his wife, Sarah, daughter of Robert Spence of North Shields. His father was a solicitor of literary attainments, who was northern secretary of the Anti-Corn Law League; he and his wife were Quakers. In 1846 Spence Watson became a pupil of Dr Collingwood Bruce, proceeding to York School, the Friends' school in that city, in October 1848. He entered University College, London, in 1853 and tied for the English literature prize that year. He was articled to his father on leaving college, and after admission as a solicitor in 1860, entered into partnership with him; he remained active in the profession throughout his working life. On 9 June 1863 he married Elizabeth, daughter of Edward and Jane Richardson of Newcastle upon Tyne. She became a strong women's suffragist. They had one son and five daughters, only two of the children surviving their father.

From youth Spence Watson played an energetic part in public life, interesting himself in political, social, philanthropic, and educational movements. For nearly half a century he held a position of influence in his native city and the north of England. He gave close attention to means of improving and disseminating popular culture, and published, in 1909, a biography of his friend Joseph Skipsey, the pitman poet. In 1862 he became honorary secretary of the Literary and Philosophical Institution, Newcastle upon Tyne, and served for thirty-one years before becoming its vice-president; he succeeded Lord Armstrong as president in 1900. Between 1868 and 1883 he delivered seventy-five lectures to the society, mainly on the history and development of the English language.

In 1871 Spence Watson helped to found the Durham College of Science, later known as Armstrong College, first a part of the University of Durham, then of the University of Newcastle upon Tyne. For forty years he took a leading part in its government, becoming its first president in 1910, and one of its representatives on the senate of Durham University, which conferred on him an honorary DCL in 1906. He was also elected a member of the first Newcastle school board in 1871, and he continued to sit on the board for twenty-three years. He was a pioneer of university extension in the north of England and of the Newcastle Free Public Library. From 1885 to 1911 he was president of the Tyneside Sunday Lecture Society, and he became chairman of the Newcastle upon Tyne grammar school in 1911.

From an early age Spence Watson was an ardent traveller and mountaineer, and he joined the Alpine Club in 1862; his recreations included angling as well as mountaineering. In 1870, at the invitation of the Society of Friends, he went to Alsace-Lorraine as one of the commissioners of the War Victims Fund for the distribution of relief to the non-combatants in the Franco-Prussian War. In January 1871 he revisited France to superintend similar work in the *département* of the Seine. The French government, through the duc de Broglie, offered him the Légion d'honneur in 1873, but he declined it; he was, however, presented with a gold medal specially struck in acknowledgement of his services. In 1879 he visited Wazzan, the sacred city of Morocco, which no Christian European had entered before. With the assistance of Sir John Drummond Hay, British minister at Tangier, he obtained an introduction to the great sharif of Wazzan and his English wife. He published an account of his journey, *A Visit to Wazan, the Sacred City of Morocco*, in 1880.

Spence Watson was an enthusiastic politician and a lifelong adherent of the Liberal Party. He was Joseph Cowen's election agent in Newcastle, and in 1874 he founded the Newcastle Liberal Association on a representative basis of ward elections, and was its president from 1874 to 1897. He was one of the original convenors of the National Liberal Federation in 1877, and was its president from 1890 until 1902. During that period he was probably the chief Liberal leader outside parliament, influencing the policy of the party by force of character. His political friends included Cowen, John Morley, John Bright, Lord Ripon, and Earl Grey, and he was well acquainted with Gladstone, from the latter's tour of Newcastle, from 1862 onwards. Personally he had no desire to enter the House of Commons, and refused all invitations to become a parliamentary candidate. He was, however, a prominent public speaker and a pronounced defender of home rule. As president of the National Liberal Federation he encouraged 'the widest and freest discussion', and opposed attempts to make it into more of a party organization. He wrote its history to 1906 (1907). On 27 February 1893 the federation presented him with his portrait by Sir George Reid, which he gave to the National Liberal Club; a replica by the artist was presented to Mrs Spence Watson. In 1907 Campbell-Bannerman made him a privy councillor.

Spence Watson's political principles embraced the cause of international peace, and the welfare of indigenous peoples under British rule, especially in India. He was president of the Peace Society for several years, and took an active part in the Indian National Congress movement. The development of free institutions in Russia was another of his aspirations. He co-operated with S. M. Kravchinsky (known as Stepniak), and other Russian political exiles in England, in the attempt to spread information among the English of existing methods of governing Russia. He was president of the Society of Friends of Russian Freedom from 1890 to 1911. Spence Watson was a pioneer in the settlement of trade disputes by arbitration. He first acted as an arbitrator in 1864, and he was sole arbitrator on forty-seven occasions between 1884 and 1894 in disputes in leading industries in the north of England. Such services, which ultimately numbered nearly a hundred, were always rendered voluntarily.

Spence Watson was ill from 1905 and died at his home, Bensham Grove, Gateshead, on 2 March 1911; he was buried in Jesmond old cemetery, Newcastle upon Tyne. He published ten books, including some poetry, and sixty pamphlets and articles, notably *The History of English Rule and Policy in South Africa* (1897), which sold over 250,000 copies. He represented the Quaker tradition of public action at its sturdiest.

PERCY CORDER, *rev.* H. C. G. MATTHEW

Sources P. Corder, *Robert Spence Watson* (1914) · J. W. Steel and others, *A historical sketch of the Society of Friends … in Newcastle and Gateshead, 1653–1898* (1899)
Archives HLRO, corresp. and journal letters · Newcastle Central Library · U. Newcastle, Robinson L., corresp. and papers | BL, corresp. with Sir Henry Campbell–Bannerman, Add. MSS 41234–41242 · BL, Gladstone MSS, Add. MS 44518 · BL, corresp. with Lord Ripon, Add. MSS 43638, 43640 · Bodl. Oxf., corresp. with Sir William Harcourt · Harvard U., Houghton L., letters to F. V. Volkhovsky · HLRO, letters to David Soskice · Tyne and Wear Archives Service, Newcastle upon Tyne, letters to Mabel Spence Watson
Likenesses L. Etherington, oils, 1890, National Liberal Club, London · G. Reid, oils, 1893, National Liberal Club, London · R. Hedley, oils, 1898; at Bensham Grove, Gateshead, in 1912 · P. Bigland, oils, U. Newcastle · L. Etherington, oils, U. Newcastle · C. Neuper, bust; known to be in Newcastle upon Tyne Free Library, in 1912 (*DNB*) · G. Reid, oils, Laing Art Gallery, Newcastle upon Tyne
Wealth at death £35,850 5*s.* 10*d.*: probate, 6 May 1911, *CGPLA Eng. & Wales*

Watson, Robert William Seton- (1879–1951), historian and political commentator, was born in London on 20 August 1879, the only child of William Livingstone Watson (*d.* 1903), a well-to-do Scottish merchant in Calcutta and London and a small landowner in Scotland, and his wife, Elizabeth Lindsay (*d.* 1899), daughter of the Scottish genealogist George *Seton. His mother was an invalid and his upbringing was entrusted to a female relative whose

Robert William Seton-Watson (1879–1951), by Vandyk

strict discipline may have accounted in part for an apparent diffidence of manner which he never quite overcame. Behind this manner lay a passionate devotion to what he felt to be right and true, and a temperament in which his father's cautious shrewdness and his mother's idealism were curiously blended. Winchester College, which he attended from 1892 to 1897, and New College, Oxford, where H. A. L. Fisher was his tutor, set their stamp on him and encouraged him to follow his bent for exact historical research. Before taking his degree with a first class in modern history in 1902 he revealed his talent by winning the Stanhope historical essay prize in 1901 with a work on Emperor Maximilian I, which was subsequently published. He next spent a winter at Berlin University and a year at the Sorbonne, then roamed through the cities of Italy, half-disposed to undertake a history of Bologna. For most of his career he financed himself from private means.

In 1905 Seton-Watson (he added his maternal family name in 1897) arrived in Vienna with the intention of writing a history of the Habsburg monarchy since Maria Theresa. The constitutional conflict between the emperor–king, Franz Josef, and a majority of the Hungarian parliament, especially over the right of the crown not to permit the substitution of Magyar for German as the language of command in the Hungarian regiments of the joint regular army, was at its height and rekindled Seton-Watson's Scottish liberal sympathies for Hungary as 'a nation rightly struggling to be free'. He had already written occasionally to *The Spectator* over the signature Scotus Viator and now resolved to use this channel to correct what he thought the unfairness to Hungary of British newspaper reports from Vienna. With characteristic thoroughness he went to Hungary in the spring of 1906 to spend three months studying the situation before writing upon it. His appetite for facts was keen, and he felt sure they would give him full proof that his cherished convictions were well founded. Within six weeks he returned to Vienna, filled with wrath. The Magyars, he explained, had 'lied' to him. Exactly how they had disillusioned him was not quite clear. His apparent timidity, abundant good faith, and eager simplicity may have tempted them to overload his mind with assurances which would not bear investigation. The trouble was that he did investigate them, making it his business—despite official obstacles—to meet many representatives of other nationalities, especially Slovaks and Romanians, whose grievances about political and cultural discrimination he found increasingly persuasive. His faith in Hungarian parliamentary democracy was shattered by the discovery that the non-Magyar half of the population held fewer than 40 seats in a lower chamber of 415 (fewer still in the upper), and that electoral malpractice was deployed against it at every turn.

Seton-Watson's conscientious diligence was exemplary. To his proficiency in German, French, and Italian he added a working knowledge of Magyar, Serbo-Croatian, and Czech/Slovak. On this basis he issued a series of carefully documented indictments of government policy, especially in the Transleithanian half of the dual monarchy: *Racial Problems in Hungary* (1908), *Political Persecution in Hungary* (1908), *Corruption and Reform in Hungary* (1911), and especially *The Southern Slav Question and the Habsburg Monarchy* (1911), with an enlarged, German, edition (1913) and its supplement, *Absolutism in Croatia* (1912), were painstaking records of facts and documents almost unknown to British readers. They attracted much attention both in Britain and abroad, embroiling him in controversies which he handled with both tenacity and adroitness. His work on the southern Slav (or Yugoslav) question was remarkable for its scope and erudition. It remains an indispensable record of the movement for Yugoslav unity and of the inner history of Austro-Hungarian failure to deal constructively with an issue decisive for the survival of the Habsburg monarchy itself. So impressed was Seton-Watson by the importance of the problem that he dedicated his book to 'that Austrian statesman who shall possess the genius and the courage necessary' to solve it; but he also expressed his forebodings. He was deeply distressed by the administrative and judicial unmorality, not to say the downright wickedness, he had seen in the notorious 'high treason' trial of Habsburg Serbs at Zagreb in the summer of 1909 and by the proof that forgeries had been officially used against the Yugoslav leaders in the Croatian diet which was furnished by the still more notorious Friedjung trial in the following December.

In these years Seton-Watson's attitude towards the dual monarchy as a whole was nevertheless by no means hostile. His first contacts with central Europe had been guided by enthusiasm for German culture. Growing worries about Germany's political threat to the European balance at first disposed him to see an added need for a strong Austria, in as close association as possible with the Western powers: hence, in part, his animosity over what he took as Hungarian attempts to rock the boat. These are the themes of his first full publication on the subject, *The Future of Austria–Hungary* (1907). As a progressive liberal, with Scottish and puritan sensibilities, Seton-Watson

argued the case for urgent reform to federalize the monarchy and effectively democratize its public life. In this he co-operated closely with the *Times* correspondent in Vienna, Henry Wickham Steed, and also came increasingly into contact with the Czech politician and scholar Tomáš G. Masaryk, who had played a prominent part in criticizing the authorities at the Zagreb trials.

The events of mid-1914 transformed Seton-Watson's life. The assassination at Sarajevo of the Habsburg heir, Franz Ferdinand, removed the one man who he had still believed might save the monarchy: he later devoted a book (1926) to refuting any direct official Serb complicity in the outrage. Then the outbreak of war, as a consequence of what he deemed to be the aggression of an Austria–Hungary in its death throes, suddenly meant that dismemberment of the latter chimed in for Seton-Watson with British patriotic duty. He promptly began a co-operation to that end with the now fugitive Masaryk. His little work *Masaryk in England* (1943) tells too modestly the story of their relations at that time, and of the part Seton-Watson played in obtaining for Masaryk in 1915 a lectureship in the new School of Slavonic Studies at King's College, London, which he was largely instrumental in setting up.

During the war years Seton-Watson's activities were many and varied. He was honorary secretary of the Serbian relief fund (1914–21). He published a range of works from articles and short pamphlets to a substantial study of *The Rise of Nationality in the Balkans*. In 1916 he and Masaryk founded and, for a while, edited jointly a weekly review, the *New Europe*, which Seton-Watson financed, and which gained noteworthy influence upon serious opinion, though it always ran at a loss and had to be terminated in 1920. In quarters where its message was resented an attempt was made to silence it, and him, by calling him up for military service; and, since he was physically unfit for active soldiering, he was drafted in 1917 into the Royal Army Medical Corps, and employed in scrubbing hospital floors. Only after the war cabinet had twice ordered his release was he seconded for work in the cabinet's intelligence bureau until, early in 1918, he was entrusted with the Austro-Hungarian section of the Crewe House enemy propaganda department. As a member of that department's mission to Italy, he helped to prepare a basis for the successful Rome congress of subject Habsburg nationalities in April 1918. At the Paris peace conference, as a private observer, his advice was sought upon many aspects of the delimitation of new frontiers in eastern Europe, particularly those between Italy and Yugoslavia, but he grew increasingly indignant about the inadequacies of 'the pygmies at Paris', notably what he perceived as a sell-out of south Slav rights along the Adriatic. He found compensation in the many honours bestowed on him by those for whose independence and national statehood he had worked so unflaggingly. The universities of Prague (1919), Zagreb (1920), Bratislava (1928), Belgrade (1928), and Cluj (1930) gave him honorary degrees, and he was an honorary citizen of Cluj (Transylvania) and Turčiansky Sv. Martin (Slovakia). In Romania in 1920 the chamber of deputies suspended its sitting to acclaim him when he appeared in the gallery. In Czechoslovakia he remained a close confidant of President Masaryk and his foreign minister, Eduard Beneš.

From 1922 Seton-Watson held the new post (financed by the young Czechoslovak government) of Masaryk professor of central European history at King's College, London. His inaugural lecture on 'The historian as a political force in central Europe' amounted to a profession of faith. With Sir Bernard Pares he founded and edited the *Slavonic Review* (later *Slavonic and East European Review*) and helped the eventual establishment of the School of Slavonic Studies (later of Slavonic and East European Studies) as a 'central activity' of the university. He continued to write on topical themes in his area of expertise, particularly as editor of a pair of volumes on *The New Slovakia* (1924) and *Slovakia then and now* (1931), and with the important study of Sarajevo already mentioned. Now, however, he had time to revert to more scholarly endeavours. On the one hand he began to engage in extended historical treatment of the nations of east central Europe with which he had become particularly associated. The main fruit of this appeared in his *History of the Roumanians* (1934), a pioneering and valuable book in its day. On the other hand, again as a natural outgrowth from his recent commitments, he pursued the history of British policy on the continent, especially towards Slavonic Europe. A British Academy Raleigh lecture, 'The role of Bosnia in international politics' (1931)—soon followed by his election to the academy the following year—led to a major and still authoritative investigation of *Disraeli, Gladstone and the Eastern Question* in the 1870s (1935). In 1937 he published *Britain in Europe, 1789–1914*, a thorough and sober survey, mainly of the Palmerston era, with a shrewd portrayal of the chief characters involved.

Seton-Watson took seriously his teaching commitments, especially after 1931, when personal losses on the stock market forced him to draw his professorial salary. If, as a lecturer, he never quite shook off the semi-apologetic shyness which usually marked his bearing on public occasions, the depth and range of his learning, and his personal kindliness, won him the admiration and often the affection of students, who found him untiring in his efforts to lead them, as an elder comrade, in search of knowledge and truth. Yet for university business he found no time; he was unpunctual, untidy, and too preoccupied with other matters. Pupils were advised not to hand over their work to him, for it would probably be mislaid; but when they read out their essays in his study, or contributed to his seminar at the Slavonic school, he was the most unassuming and supportive of critics. The atmosphere of genteel erudition at the Seton-Watson home was enhanced by his wife, May (Marion) Esther (1883–1963), daughter of Edward Stack, of the Bengal civil service, whom he married on 25 July 1911 and to whose companionship and devotion Seton-Watson owed much. Their two sons, George Hugh Nicholas Seton-*Watson and Christopher Ivan William, and daughter, Mary Rose, all achieved academic distinction in fields intimately related to their father's interests.

By the late 1930s current affairs resumed their primacy for Seton-Watson. At no period of his life was he more clear-sighted or more insistent in a conscientious endeavour to enlighten public opinion than during the years immediately before and after the sacrifice of Czechoslovakia to Hitler at Munich in September 1938. In closer touch, it seemed, with the realities of the European situation than any member of the government, he published in May 1938 *Britain and the Dictators* as a massive warning against a foreign policy neglectful of moral values. An equally outspoken though smaller work, *Munich and the Dictators* (March 1939), dealt perspicaciously with 'the crisis that culminated, or at least seemed to culminate, in the settlement of Munich'. It closed with the prediction 'Nondum est finis'. On the outbreak of war he joined the foreign research and press service and in 1940 the political intelligence department of the Foreign Office, serving as a personal link with Beneš, then head of the provisional Czechoslovak government in London.

As in 1917–19, however, Seton-Watson found his direct influence on policy through official channels to be frustratingly slight. This stimulated the last of his major works, *A History of the Czechs and Slovaks*, which appeared late in 1943, avowedly with the aim of depriving future politicians of any pretext for saying that the Czechs and Slovaks were 'people of whom we know nothing'. It was an exhaustive and somewhat exhausting account of its subject which, despite an excessive emphasis upon ethnic criteria in the history of Bohemia and a certain dryness of style (for Seton-Watson set no great store by literary artistry), became a standard work for many years. Like the parallel volume on the Romanians, it remains valuable especially for its comments on more recent events.

1945 should have brought the climax of Seton-Watson's career. The post-war reconstitution of the political map in east central Europe coincided with his appointment as professor of Czechoslovak studies at Oxford (a post again sponsored by the restored government in Prague) and his presidency of the Royal Historical Society. Yet the situation in Romania and Yugoslavia was unpromising from the outset; while the satisfaction he had felt in 1945 at the restoration of Czechoslovak independence, within the pre-Munich frontiers, waned as the ascendancy of communist Russia became more evident there too. His decline was undoubtedly hastened by grief at the tragic death of his intimate friend Jan Masaryk in March, and that of Beneš, the former president, in September 1948. If his faith in 'the indwelling righteousness of things' was too deeply rooted for despair to prevail over his conviction that his life's work had been done to the best of his ability and with total honesty of purpose, his sorrow told upon a physique that had never been robust. Yet it was in keeping with his undeniable greatness of spirit that no word of complaint should have escaped him. On relinquishing his chair at Oxford in 1949 he was elected an honorary fellow of both New College and Brasenose and retired to his country home, Kyle House, Kyleakin, in the Isle of Skye—

where in happier days he could indulge a modest taste for yachting and sea fishing—until he died there, of Parkinson's disease, on 25 July 1951. He was buried at Abernethy churchyard, Perthshire.

During the half-century after his death Seton-Watson remained a controverted figure. A vigorous historiography of broadly revisionist tendency has argued that the Habsburg monarchy, or some variant upon it, would have better served the security and prosperity of the people of the area than the new structures with which Seton-Watson so closely identified himself. He had his blind spots, among them a degree of lasting vindictiveness towards Hungary which probably fed on his early disenchantment with it. But on the whole this most important of all British commentators on east central Europe displayed a fair-mindedness consistent with his lifelong liberal ideals and firm religious principles. His policy prescriptions always rested ultimately on the need for a just international order, which would guarantee the rule of law and democracy in the region.

Though Seton-Watson himself never exaggerated the role of Western experts such as himself in the dismemberment of Austria–Hungary and the early history of the successor states, his voluminous surviving papers provide rich testimony to extensive links with influential contemporaries. Relating to all aspects of his career, and including correspondence with over 200 significant individuals, they are held at the library of the School of Slavonic and East European Studies, where they have been expertly catalogued. He also assembled a remarkable collection of books and pamphlets pertaining to east central Europe. Those in east European languages passed mostly to the same destination; but the rest, together with files of valuable press cuttings which relate to the First World War and the years immediately before and after, were left to the library of New College, Oxford.

WICKHAM STEED, rev. R. J. W. EVANS

Sources H. Seton-Watson and C. Seton-Watson, *The making of a new Europe: R. W. Seton-Watson and the last years of Austria-Hungary* (1981) • G. H. Bolsover, 'Robert William Seton-Watson, 1879–1951', *PBA*, 37 (1951), 345–58 • H. Seton-Watson and others, eds., *R. W. Seton-Watson and the Yugoslavs: correspondence 1906–41*, 2 vols. (1976) • C. Bodea, H. Seton-Watson, and others, eds., *R. W. Seton-Watson and the Rumanians, 1906–20*, 2 vols. (1988) • J. Rychlík and others, eds., *R. W. Seton-Watson and his relations with the Czechs and Slovaks: documents, 1906–51*, 2 vols. (1995) • I. W. Roberts, *History of the School of Slavonic and East European Studies* (1991) • H. Hanak, *Great Britain and Austria-Hungary during the First World War: a study in the formation of public opinion* (1962) • K. J. Calder, *Britain and the origins of the new Europe, 1914–18* (1976) • G. Jeszenszky, *Az elveszett presztízs: Magyarország megítélésének megváltozása Nagy-Britanniában, 1894–1918* (1986) • L. Péter, *Az Elbától keletre: tanulmáryok a magyar és kelet-európai történelemből* (1998), 290–338 • personal knowledge (1971) • private information (1971, 2004)
Archives UCL, school of Slavonic and east European studies, corresp. and papers | Bodl. Oxf., letters to Sir Alfred Zimmern
Likenesses I. Meštrović, bronze, 1919, priv. coll. • I. Meštrović, bronze tablet, 1945, UCL, school of Slavonic and east European studies • Vandyk, photograph, British Academy [*see illus.*]
Wealth at death £39,561 5s. 8d.: confirmation, 9 Oct 1951, *CCI* • £1503: additional estate, 16 Oct 1951, *CCI*

Watson, Rosamund Marriott [*née* Rosamund Ball; *pseuds.* Graham R. Tomson, R. Armytage] (**1860–1911**), poet and journalist, was born on 6 October 1860 at Homerton Row, Homerton, Hackney, London, youngest of the five children of Benjamin Williams Ball (1818–1883), bank clerk and bibliophile, and his wife, Sylvia Good (1818–1874). Educated at home, and prevented by family opposition from attending art school (Marriott Watson to Chesson, 2 March 1905), she produced six volumes of poems, including *The Bird-Bride: a Volume of Ballads and Sonnets* (1889), *A Summer Night, and other Poems* (1891), *Vespertilia, and other Verses* (1895), and a volume of posthumous collected poems (1912). She was the author of books on interior decoration (1897) and gardening (1906), edited border ballads (1888) and *Selections from the Greek Anthology* (1889), headed a woman's magazine (*Sylvia's Journal*, 1893–4), and contributed articles on fashion, art, interiors, gardens, and literature (as well as signed poems) to prominent journals such as the *Yellow Book*, W. E. Henley's *Scots Observer*, the *Pall Mall Gazette* and *The Athenaeum*. Her contemporaries praised her for impeccable poetic technique and refined diction; equally notable are her female perspective on aestheticism and her anticipation of twentieth-century themes such as troubled (or serial) marriage and divorce.

On 9 September 1879 Rosamund married George Francis Armytage (1853–1921), an affluent colonial from Australia who attended Jesus College, Cambridge; their daughters Eulalie and Daphne were born in 1882 and 1884. In 1884 she also published anonymously her first volume of poems, *Tares*. At this time marital discord surfaced, allegedly because of Rosamund's flirtations with other men (*News of the World*, 1)—a charge not unrelated to her remarkable beauty. 'Tall, willowy', with expressive brown eyes crowned by masses of black hair (Pennell, 157–8), she captivated others through her physical grace, beautiful attire, and exceptional intelligence and wit. Several contemporaries testified to the effect, from Elizabeth Pennell to Richard Le Gallienne, Oscar Wilde—who inscribed a portrait, 'For a Poet and a Poem' (*Oscar Wilde*, 2.302)—and Thomas Hardy. Years after her death Hardy wrote 'An Old Likeness (Recalling R. T.)', and Mrs Pine-Avon in *The Well-Beloved* may be a partial portrait (Millgate, 'Thomas Hardy and Rosamund Tomson', 254–5).

Following her separation from Armytage (and adoption of the publishing name 'R. Armytage') Rosamund eloped in 1886 with the painter Arthur Graham *Tomson (1859–1905), a member of the New English Art Club. Her divorce from Armytage was finalized on 9 August 1887, and he took custody of their daughters; Arthur Tomson and Rosamund married on 21 September 1887, a month before their son Graham was born. As 'Graham R. Tomson' she was 'discovered' by Andrew Lang; became friends with William Sharp, Austin Dobson, and Alice Meynell; and entertained other notables such as G. B. Shaw; and quickly rose in prominence as one of the era's finest women poets. In 1892 she was elected president of the 'Literary Ladies', a group formed in 1889 to promote women writers.

As the *Scots Observer* contributor and 'patroness' to J. M.

Barrie's Allahakbarries (Pennell, 214), Rosamund met Australian-born Henry Brereton (H. B.) Marriott Watson (1863–1921), the atheist son of an Anglican clergyman, co-author with Barrie of *Richard Savage* (1889), and a handsome member of Henley's 'regatta'. By 1894 they were lovers, leading Tomson to divorce her on 17 February 1896. Although she adopted H. B.'s two surnames, they never married, but expressed devotion to each other and to their son Richard, born in 1895 on his mother's birthday. Rosamund's decision to change her publishing name a third time compromised her visibility as well as reputation, and she gradually lapsed into obscurity despite William Archer's inclusion of her among genuine (if minor) poets in 1902. In 1903 she suffered a nervous breakdown (Marriott Watson to Paine, 31 March 1903) and moved with H. B. and their son to Shere, Surrey; she died of uterine cancer on 29 December 1911 at Vachery, her home in Shere. She was buried on 2 January 1912 in the churchyard of St James's in Shere; the grave marker of Eulalie Armytage Brown-Hovelt, four years old when her mother eloped with Tomson, was later placed upon that of her mother. LINDA K. HUGHES

Sources L. K. Hughes, '"Fair Hymen holdeth hid a world of woes": myth and marriage in poems by Graham R. Tomson', *Victorian Poetry*, 32 (1994), 97–120 • E. R. Pennell, *Nights: Rome and Venice in the aesthetic eighties, London and Paris in the fighting nineties*, 2nd edn (1916) • M. Millgate, 'Thomas Hardy and Rosamund Tomson', *N&Q*, 218 (1973), 253–5 • L. K. Hughes, 'A fin-de-siècle beauty and the beast: configuring the body in works by Graham R. Tomson (Rosamund Marriott Watson)', *Tulsa Studies in Women's Literature*, 14 (1995), 95–121 • L. K. Hughes, 'A female aesthete at the helm: *Sylvia's Journal* and "Graham R. Tomson", 1893–1894', *Victorian Periodicals Review*, 29 (1996), 173–92 • M. Millgate, *Thomas Hardy: a biography* (1982) • Rosamund Marriott Watson to Albert Bigelow Paine, 31 March 1903, Hunt. L., AP 1974–82 • D. A. P. Atkinson, 'Rosamund Marriott Watson', *The Cambridge bibliography of English literature*, ed. J. Shattock, 3rd edn, 4 (1999) • W. Archer, 'Mrs Marriott-Watson', *Poets of the younger generation* (1902), 469–80 • *Oscar Wilde: interview and recollections*, ed. E. H. Mikhail, 2 vols. (1979) • '*Armytage v. Armytage and Tomson*', *News of the World* (6 Feb 1887), 1 • R. Le Gallienne, *The romantic '90s*, new edn (1951) • b. cert. • m. certs. • d. cert. • divorce certs. • parish register (baptism), 19 April 1861, Hackney, St John's • R. M. Watson, letter to Maria Chesson, 2 March 1905, Morgan L., Gordon Ray MS • rate books, St Marylebone • b. certs. [Eulalie Armytage; Daphne Armytage, Graham Tomson] • *Surrey Advertiser* (6 Jan 1912)
Archives Dorset County Museum, Dorchester, Thomas Hardy collection • Hunt. L., Albert Bigelow Paine MSS • L. Cong., Louise Chandler Moulton MSS • L. Cong., Pennell MSS • Morgan L., Gordon Ray collection • NYPL, Berg collection • Ransom HRC, Garnett MSS • Ransom HRC, John Lane MSS • Ransom HRC, T. F. Unwin MSS • University of Illinois, Urbana-Champaign, H. G. Wells collection
Likenesses R. Bryden, woodcut, repro. in Archer, *Poets* • F. F. Hollyer, photograph, repro. in *English illustrated magazine* (April 1894) • photograph, repro. in R. M. Watson, *The poems of Rosamund Marriott Watson* (1912)

Watson, Rundle Burges (1809–1860), naval officer, was the eldest son of Captain Joshua Rowley Watson (1772–1810). He entered the navy in November 1821, and was promoted lieutenant on 7 October 1829. He served on the coast of Portugal and on the North American station, until in November 1837 he was appointed to the frigate *Calliope* (26 guns), with Captain Thomas Herbert (1793–1861). After two years on the coast of Brazil the *Calliope* was sent to China, where she was actively employed during the First Opium War. On 6 May 1841 Watson was promoted commander, and was moved with Herbert to the *Blenheim* (72 guns), and while in her was repeatedly engaged with the enemy, in command of either boats or landing parties. On 23 December 1842 he was advanced to post rank, and on 24 December was made a CB.

On 1 February 1845 Watson married Helen, second daughter of John Bettington of Pittville; and they had a large family. From February 1846 to October 1849 he commanded the small frigate *Brilliant* (20 guns) on the Cape of Good Hope station; and in December 1852 was appointed to the new steam frigate *Impérieuse* (50 guns), then, and for some years later, considered one of the finest ships in the navy. In 1854 she was sent into the Baltic in advance of the fleet, Watson being senior officer of the squadron of small vessels appointed to watch the breaking up of the ice, and to see that no Russian warships got to sea. It was an arduous service well performed. The *Impérieuse* continued with the flying squadron in the Baltic during the campaigns of 1854 and 1855, and until the signing of peace in March 1856. As the senior officer of the frigate squadron, and generally on detached service, Watson demonstrated the highest standards of seamanship, judgement, and leadership. After the peace the *Impérieuse* was sent to the North American station; she returned to England and was paid off early in 1857. From May 1856 until his death Watson was naval aide-de-camp to the queen. In June 1859 he was appointed captain-superintendent of Sheerness Dockyard, where he died on 5 July 1860. An officer of great ability, Watson was one of the last great sailing-ship captains, and the first frigate captain of the steam era.

J. K. LAUGHTON, rev. ANDREW LAMBERT

Sources A. D. Lambert, *The Crimean War: British grand strategy, 1853–56* (1990) • Boase, *Mod. Eng. biog.* • *GM*, 3rd ser., 9 (1860), 217 • O'Byrne, *Naval biog. dict.* • *CGPLA Eng. & Wales* (1860)
Wealth at death £4000: probate, 26 Dec 1860, *CGPLA Eng. & Wales*

Watson, Samuel (*bap.* 1662, *d.* 1715), sculptor, was born at Heanor in Derbyshire, the son of Ralph Watson (*d.* 1713), husbandman of Heanor, and his wife, Bridget Townsend (*d.* 1718); he was baptized there on 2 December 1662. Little is known of his early life until he was apprenticed to Charles Oakey, a carver of St Martin-in-the-Fields, London. He probably worked under Oakey about 1683 as a woodcarver on the first duke of Beaufort's house at Badminton and is known to have worked under another London carver, Thomas Young, for the earl of Exeter at Burghley House, and briefly for George Vernan at Sudbury Hall. Grinling Gibbons, who also worked at Badminton, Burghley, and Sudbury, had a great influence on Watson's subsequent work.

The earl of Exeter passed on Young and Watson to his brother-in-law the fourth earl (first duke in 1694) of Devonshire, and they arrived at Chatsworth in 1690–91. In

1692 Watson became the principal carver there when, following a dispute over their wages, the earl dismissed his architect, John Talman, and most of the London and foreign craftsmen. He retained Watson until 1711, and the carver became an assistant to Sir Christopher Wren in his independent valuation of the work done by Talman's team. His outstanding carvings at Chatsworth, especially in the chapel, are in limewood, stone, alabaster, and marble and his skill was praised by his contemporary George Vertue who described him as 'a most engenious artist' (*Walpole Society*, 20, 1931–2). Watson also executed commissions for other clients, including vases for the gardens at Melbourne Hall and an unidentified monument for the duke of Newcastle.

Watson's work at Chatsworth has traditionally been attributed to Grinling Gibbons; this theory, first advanced by the earl of Egmont in 1744 and by Horace Walpole in 1760, is still current among contemporary commentators. The myth has prevailed despite the fact that many payments to Watson are recorded in the accounts at Chatsworth and his various preparatory drawings survive there. Among the latter are drawings by Watson of work by Gibbons, which have confused scholars; Gibbons himself was certainly never at Chatsworth.

Most prominent among Watson's works at Chatsworth are the famous limewood cravat and the portrait medallion in a glass case, first claimed as Gibbons's work by Horace Walpole. The medallion is of special interest, as it may well bear the only surviving likeness of the carver. Watson was married to Katherine Greensmith (*c*.1679–1739) of Pilsley, a Chatsworth estate village, and they retired to Heanor, where he died of a stroke; he was buried at Heanor on 31 March 1715. He left two sons, Henry (1714–1786), and the posthumous Samuel the younger (1715–1778). Both were trained as carvers, as too was Samuel the younger's son White Watson (1760–1835), who designed his grandfather's monument in Heanor church. Drawings by Watson are held in the Bodleian Library, Oxford, and at Alnwick Castle, Northumberland, but the main collections of his designs are at Chatsworth, and the Derbyshire Record Office at Matlock.   TREVOR BRIGHTON

Sources S. Glover, *The history and gazetteer of the county of Derby*, ed. T. Noble, 2 (1833) · Chatsworth building accounts, Chatsworth House, Derbyshire, Chatsworth MSS · Samuel Watson's accounts and drawings, Chatsworth House, Derbyshire, Chatsworth MSS · Samuel Watson's drawings, Derbys. RO · parish registers, Heanor, Derbys. RO · Samuel Watson's will and inventory, Lichfield diocesan RO · D. Green, *Grinling Gibbons* (1964) · G. Beard, *The work of Grinling Gibbons* (1989) · Vertue, *Note books*, vol. 2 · G. Jackson-Stops, 'Duke of creation', *Country Life*, 188/14 (7 April 1994), 52–7 · R. Gunnis, *Dictionary of British sculptors, 1660–1851* (1953); new edn (1968) · F. Thompson, *Chatsworth* (1949) · D. Esterly, *Grinling Gibbons and the art of carving* (1998) · T. Brighton, 'Samuel Watson not Grinling Gibbons at Chatsworth', *Burlington Magazine*, 140 (1998), 811–18 · T. Brighton, 'A monument to Samuel Watson', *Journal of Bakewell and District Historical Society* (Jan 1999)
Archives Bodl. Oxf., account and sketch book (with Henry Watson) · Chatsworth House, Derbyshire, Chatsworth MSS, accounts and drawings | Chatsworth House, Derbyshire, Chatsworth MSS, Chatsworth building accounts

Likenesses medallion (S. Watson?), Chatsworth House, Derbyshire
Wealth at death £159, excl. his house and some lead on the docks at Bawtry: inventory, Lichfield Diocesan RO

Watson, Samuel (1898–1967), trade unionist and politician, was born on 11 March 1898 at 52 Heckels Row, Boldon Colliery, co. Durham, the son of Duncan Watson and his wife, Elizabeth, *née* Hammill. His father was a fourth-generation coalminer, from a family located in Durham since the eighteenth century. Watson's great-grandfather was an itinerant Chartist preacher. Boldon pit, employing 2000 men, was one of the large modern collieries opened in the late nineteenth century to exploit the deep seams of coal stretching out under the North Sea. Watson attended the local elementary school, where he showed great promise. However, having worked half-time in the pit since the age of twelve, he left school at fourteen in 1912 to begin full-time work as a boy on the screens.

Watson continued his education at the reading class established by the local vicar, and when the Boldon lodge of the Durham Miners' Association (DMA) established a Miners' Institute Library, he became its secretary. His interest in trade unionism may have been awakened by the assistance provided by the Boldon lodge when his father broke his back in a pit accident, and became a permanent invalid. He was elected on to the lodge committee in 1917, and in 1926, at the comparatively young age of twenty-eight, was elected lodge secretary. In addition to the routine union business, he was preoccupied with preserving unity between left and right within the lodge, and in dealing with cases for public assistance from his many unemployed members.

Sam Watson's interest in politics began early. In 1919 he became secretary of the Boldon branch of the Independent Labour Party, in which Jack Lawson had been active before the war. Watson was regarded as very left-wing, and worked closely with members of the Communist Party in Durham and in the left-wing caucus inside the Miners' Federation of Great Britain (MFGB). He visited the USSR in 1931, probably as a member of a trade-union delegation organized by the Friends of the Soviet Union. Despite an onerous schedule of union and political work, he continued to find time to pursue his own studies, and in 1934 he won a national essay competition organized by the TUC to mark the centenary of the Tolpuddle Martyrs' pardon with an essay on their political and economic significance.

In 1934–5 the deaths of two DMA leaders created vacancies for two full-time agents, which were filled by ballot vote of the entire membership. Both contests were hard fought, with large fields of ambitious candidates. The second position was eventually won by Watson after an unprecedented third ballot in which he beat two more senior challengers, becoming the youngest ever DMA agent and also the first agent to take office without having served on the DMA executive. His leading role in a six months' strike over working practices at Boldon from July 1934 to January 1935 had enhanced his reputation. The Boldon lodge chairman, a member of the DMA executive committee, strongly supported him, as did Will Lawther, a DMA agent as well as MFGB vice-president. Watson started work as an agent on 1 July 1936, assuming the post of general treasurer. He and his wife, Margaret Jane O'Connor, whom he had married on 4 February 1935, moved to Durham city. Jenny Watson, as she was known, was born into a mining family (her father, Francis Joseph O'Connor, was a hewer) on 9 February 1911 in Boldon Colliery. Before her marriage she had been a state registered nurse. Their son, David, was born soon after their move to Durham, and their daughter, Christine, some six years later.

Watson's established expertise in unemployment matters was utilized when he was immediately appointed DMA unemployment officer. He wrote a union booklet explaining changes in the public benefits system, which he updated regularly; in 1939 a new edition sold over 14,000 copies. In 1940 the DMA published his *Local Officials' Manual*, described by the general secretary, John Edmund Swan, as a 'rather voluminous book (like the Author) … packed with valuable information' (DMA, *General Secretary's Report*, 1940, 7–8).

From 1935 Watson played a notable part in formulating and directing MFGB policy. He served on the MFGB executive committee between 1935 and 1937 and from 1939 until 1944, when the MFGB was transformed into a unified industrial union: the National Union of Mineworkers (NUM). He worked in concert with left-wing leaders from other coalfields, including Arthur Horner, the communist president of the south Wales miners. The MFGB conference of 1937 appointed Horner and Watson to work out a scheme for reorganization upon national lines. In April 1938 Horner moved and Watson seconded the executive's resolution at the MFGB special conference in support of arms for the Spanish republican government. At the end of January 1939 Watson was among the first to sign the national petition organized by Stafford Cripps in support of his campaign for a popular front against fascism.

In 1939 Lawther's election as president of the MFGB created a gap in the DMA hierarchy, enabling Watson to become the dominant figure in the union. When Swan retired as Durham area general secretary of the NUM in 1946, Watson easily won the ballot against five other challengers to become his successor. During the war he had quickly grasped the new problems which the total war economy posed for miners and the nation. From the formation of the coalition government in May 1940 Watson worked with Horner and Jim Bowman of Northumberland to provide government ministers, including Dalton and Gaitskell, with viable solutions. In 1940 he replaced Swan as the MFGB's nominee on the Labour Party national executive committee (NEC) and used his position to ensure that representatives from the Labour Party, the TUC general council, and the MFGB executive met regularly to agree the outlines along which a future Labour government would nationalize the coal industry.

At the same time Watson's politics were undergoing a decisive change. When Hugh Dalton first observed him in September 1941, he noted that Watson 'used to have the reputation of being near-Communist' (Pimlott, 287). At the MFGB conference in July 1942 Watson seconded the south Wales resolution demanding that the government open a second front without delay. By 1943 he was a committed social democrat, a transition which may have been facilitated by his acquaintance with the American industrial relations expert, Sam Berger, W. Averell Harriman's special assistant in Britain for trade-union affairs and a protégé of the American anti-communist theorist Sidney Hook. After the war Berger remained in London as labour attaché. He and Watson became firm political allies as well as friends. Berger's successor, Joe Godson, inherited and strengthened both bonds. A closer connection was formed when Watson's daughter, Christine, married Godson's son, Roy.

From 1945 Watson assumed a prominent place in the first rank of national trade union leaders. The incoming Labour government awarded him a CBE in 1946, and the Labour Party NEC made him its chairman for 1949–50, the party's fiftieth anniversary year. He had been appointed to serve on the revamped, expanded international subcommittee of the NEC in 1943. The subcommittee played an increasingly important role in formulating Labour policy, and Watson succeeded Hugh Dalton as its chairman in 1952, a post which he held until his retirement. In this capacity he made regular visits to western Europe, the United States, and Canada, and cultivated an abiding interest in the socialist experiments taking place in Scandinavia, Israel, and Yugoslavia. He was an acute, highly critical observer on visits to the Soviet Union and China. Nevertheless, he persisted in treating Marxism and the international communist movement as serious political entities. Thus, he noted after visiting the Soviet Union in 1954 that there had been real improvements in the Russian workers' standard of living since 1930–36, and

> the fact that they are a long way behind the West by no means presupposes that they are fundamentally dissatisfied. The Russian Trade Unions are instruments of Government … but within this limitation they have succeeded in improving the lot of the Russian worker … Changes are still possible in the leadership at the top [of the Soviet communist party and state]. (script for BBC talk, c.January 1955, Sam Watson papers, Box 36, Durham County RO)

Watson refused to be associated with the diabolism of many anti-communist campaigns, instead rebutting communism with forceful appeals to the post-war revisionism being developed by western European social democrats. His continuing intellectual and emotional commitment to socialism, his warm humanity, and humour enabled long-standing friendships with left-wingers like Aneurin Bevan and Jennie Lee to endure. While George Brown judged Watson to be 'sometimes … too uncritically pro-American', he observed that Watson had 'great intellect' and 'a rare integrity' (*In my Way*, 1972, 218).

Richard Crossman and Hugh Gaitskell both recorded their great admiration for Watson in the 1950s, and both relied heavily on his advice to enable them to deal expeditiously with the intensifying left–right division inside the Labour Party. As chairman of the international committee and Gaitskell's trusted confidant, Watson was one of the chief arbiters in the ongoing conflicts over unilateral nuclear disarmament, nationalization, and the EEC. His physical distance from Westminster, his apparent lack of personal political ambition, his informed intelligence, and his experience in negotiation made him indispensable to Gaitskell in keeping the party together. Watson's role at the party conference of 1957 in persuading Aneurin Bevan to abandon, without rancour or regret, his unilateralist stance was legendary. At the party conference of 1960, Watson moved the NEC's policy statement on foreign policy and defence, combining sympathy and understanding for the unilateralists' sincerity with a reasoned defence of party policy. In 1962 he worked closely with George Brown to mitigate the growing anti-Common Market sentiments inside the NEC. He used his best endeavours, equally unsuccessfully, to persuade Gaitskell to dilute his stand against British membership of the EEC.

Watson could easily have embarked on a successful parliamentary career after the war. He chose instead to remain Durham area NUM secretary. Nevertheless, if Labour had won the general election of 1959, Watson might have allowed himself to be persuaded to become foreign secretary, an appointment which Gaitskell was widely rumoured to be desirous of making. Watson clearly enjoyed the immense local power which went with his Durham miners' office, using it not for himself, but on behalf of 'his people'. He exercised the Durham miners' customary patronage inside the Labour Party with rigour and discrimination, if not discretion, taking a close interest in candidates for parliamentary seats as well as local government.

During his tenure as Durham area secretary, Watson served as a justice of the peace, deputy lieutenant of the county, chairman of the National Health Service executive committee for co. Durham, and a member of the Durham University court. Durham University made him an honorary doctor of civil law in 1955, an apt reward for this talented union leader who fulfilled the traditional roles of English benevolent paternalism with such conspicuous success. Despite these time-consuming duties of office, he continued to nurture his appetite for reading. In 1954 his library numbered 2000 volumes, with an emphasis on nineteenth-century Russian literature.

Watson's sense of personal responsibility to reproduce his own kind prompted him to convene a Sunday afternoon school at the miners' offices in Durham. The writer Sid Chaplin described him as 'a man of very great intellectual ability with a wonderful gift for exposition—a born teacher, and a teacher in fact to "Sammy's class", the tutorial he ran for more than 100 … right to the end' (*The Guardian*, 8 May 1967). Known by some of its pupils as 'Sam's Bible classes', the sessions were conscientiously attended by young men and women in the Labour Party, not only from the NUM but from all trades and professions, who enjoyed and matured under the regime of penetrating discussions over which Watson presided.

Until the late 1950s the Durham coalfield continued to employ large numbers of miners. In 1947 the Durham area NUM had 114,667 members, declining to 111,184 in 1956. Durham, together with the small Northumberland area, still contained 20.5 per cent of the National Coal Board's labour force in 1957. It is not surprising that Watson wielded a decisive influence over the policy and conduct of NUM business. While occupying the leading centre-right role on the NUM executive, he nevertheless maintained good working relationships with Horner and his successor as NUM secretary, Will Paynter, evidently appreciating their intellects and formidable negotiating capacities, in addition to their abilities to persuade left-wing militants to accept compromise solutions.

Watson retained an abiding concern with advancing the conditions of his members, never allowing his interest in national and international politics to predominate over his union responsibilities. From the early 1950s he recognized the new problems encountered by the NUM and the trade-union movement and responded without illusions to the dramatic contraction in the demand for coal which began in 1957. Together with Horner and Paynter, he formulated plans for an orderly and humane contraction of the industry, in which redundant miners, including large numbers from the Durham area, would be able to find alternative employment either through re-training or transferring to more productive collieries in other areas.

Watson retired as an NUM official and also from the Labour Party NEC in March 1963. He was appointed a part-time member of the National Coal Board and the Electricity Council. He died on 7 May 1967 at his home since 1946, Bede Rest, Beech Crest, in the city of Durham, the house built by the earlier Durham miners' leader, Peter Lee.

NINA FISHMAN

Sources CVs for Sam Watson and Jenny Watson, Durham RO, Sam Watson papers, Box 6 and other boxes · *The Observer* (19 Sept 1954) · *The Guardian* (8 May 1967) · *The Times* (8 May 1967) · b. cert. · m. cert. · d. cert. · *Daily Worker* (11 July 1934) · *Daily Worker* (24 Nov 1934) · *Daily Worker* (1 Dec 1934) · *Daily Worker* (20 Dec 1934) · *Daily Worker* (31 Dec 1934) · *Daily Worker* (2–5 Jan 1935) · W. R. Garside, *The Durham miners, 1919–1960* (1971), 79, 281, 374, 459 · H. Beynon and T. Austrin, *Masters and servants: the Durham miners and the English political tradition* (1994), 357–62 · J. Lawson, *A man's life* (1944), 27–43 · wartime diary, BLPES, Dalton MSS · *The Second World War diary of Hugh Dalton, 1940–1945*, ed. B. Pimlott (1986) · diaries, 1945–63, U. Warwick Mod. RC, Richard Crossman papers · R. P. Arnot, *The miners: a history of the Miners' Federation of Great Britain*, 3: … *from 1930 onwards* (1961), 265–7, 274, 357–60 · M. Foot, *Aneurin Bevan*, 1 (1962), 289

Archives Durham RO, papers | Durham RO, Durham Area National Union of Mineworkers papers

Likenesses group portrait, photograph, Trades Union Congress, London

Wealth at death £2743: probate, 5 Sept 1967, *CGPLA Eng. & Wales*

Watson, Thomas (1513–1584), bishop of Lincoln, was born in 1513 in the diocese of Durham, probably at Nun Stinton near Sedgefield. He was educated at St John's College, Cambridge, where he graduated BA in 1533. The humanist training he received there was to permeate all his later thought. Roger Ascham, his contemporary at St John's, refers to Watson in his *Scholemaster* as one of the best scholars ever bred by that college, and writes admiringly of his tragedy *Absolom*. Watson is also recorded as producing a translation of the *Odyssey*, now lost, and a version of a sermon of St Cyprian. In his time he was known for his good humour as well as for his scholarship and other merits; it would appear that his posthumous reputation for being morose and sullen, as propounded by writers like Burnet and Strype, is unfounded in fact.

Catholic activist Watson became a fellow of St John's in 1533, and proceeded MA in 1536. He received his degree in theology in 1543, the year in which he became domestic chaplain to Stephen Gardiner, bishop of Winchester, who collated him to two benefices in his patronage. In 1547 he added the vicarage of Buckminster, Leicestershire. He assisted Gardiner in opposing many of the changes of religion taking place in the early part of Edward VI's reign. On one occasion in that reign he preached a sermon in the north of England that almost led to his arrest and prosecution for treason. He was saved by the intervention of John Rough, formerly a Dominican and now a noted protestant preacher in Hull. When in December 1557 Rough was brought before the bishop of London charged with heresy, Watson did not return the favour. Rough appealed to Watson for clemency on the basis of their encounter in the previous reign, only to be stigmatized by him as a pestilent heretic who had done much hurt in the north; Rough was burnt at Smithfield. As chaplain to Gardiner, Watson was confined with him in the Fleet during 1550 and 1551, and was called as a witness at the bishop's trial, though in December 1551 he is found taking part in private discussions on the sacraments at the house of Sir Richard Morison.

After the accession of Mary, Watson continued to be an active promoter of the old faith. Throughout the reign he was a noted preacher and controversialist. On 20 August 1553, he gave a sermon at Paul's Cross in London before the mayor and aldermen, with the guilds in their livery, as well as several members of the council who had been sent by the queen to keep order. It was feared that the serious disorder that had accompanied the previous Sunday's sermon would be repeated, so Sir John Jerningham was dispatched with a guard of 200 men with bills and halberds, who stood around the pulpit and in the churchyard. Mary's bishop of London, Edmund Bonner, watched the proceedings from a window.

On 25 September 1553 Watson was sent by Gardiner, then chancellor of the University of Cambridge, to the vice-chancellor and senate of the university to act on his behalf in restoring the old religion, and to report back to him on the state of the colleges. On arrival Watson was admitted as master of St John's, and soon afterwards received his doctorate in theology. By 18 October, he was back in London, where he was a proctor at the meeting of convocation at St Paul's, as a firm advocate of the Catholic cause. Further ecclesiastical preferment followed, when on 18 November he became dean of Durham. His note as a preacher led to his being called in the following year to give two of the Lenten sermons before the queen on the third and fourth Fridays, in support of the traditional teaching about the real presence of Christ in the eucharist and the sacrificial nature of the mass (these were published as *Twoo notable sermons … concerninge the reall presence of Christes body and bloude in the blessed sacrament; also the masse, which is the sacrifice of the Newe Testament*, London, 1554; STC 25115).

Bishop of Lincoln Watson resigned the mastership of St John's in May 1554. He became actively involved in the prosecution of heresy, and took part in proceedings against John Hooper and others. In December 1556 he was appointed to the bishopric of Lincoln; his election by the cathedral chapter took place on 7 January 1557. Between his election and consecration he received a commission from Cardinal Pole to carry out a visitation of the University of Cambridge. Arriving there on 9 January 1557, he preached a sermon on Sunday 31 January in King's College against the doctrines of Martin Bucer, and promoting the restoration of certain ceremonies, referring particularly to the traditional usage of candles in procession on Candlemas (2 February). On the following Saturday (6 February), he preached at some length in Great St Mary's Church against the 'wyckedness and heretycall doctryn' (Cooper, *Ath. Cantab.*, 1.492) of Martin Bucer (whose remains were interred there) and his fellow Cambridge reformer Paul Fagius, who was buried in St Michael's Church. Later that day the remains of Bucer and Fagius were disinterred and burnt publicly in the market place.

Over the next few months Watson is noted by the diarist Henry Machyn as preaching in London on a number of occasions: on 27 March before the queen, on 4 April at All Hallows-the-Great, 'wher was grett audyens of pepull', and on 22 April 'a godly sermon' at St Mary Spital (*Diary of Henry Machyn*, 131). The papal bull providing him to Lincoln was issued on 24 or 25 March, and in May he was given licence by Cardinal Pole to hold the deanery of Durham *in commendam* with his bishopric. He was consecrated bishop at Chiswick on 15 August by Archbishop Nicholas Heath of York (acting under commission from Pole), assisted by Thomas Thirlby, bishop of Ely, and William Glynn, bishop of Bangor. Watson's enthronement in his cathedral took place by proxy on 10 October, and in person on 15–16 October. After his appointment he was active in restoring property to his cathedral church, including vestments, plate, and other furniture, and on 9 November obtained by letters patent a grant of some estates alienated ten years previously along with the patronage of a number of benefices in his diocese which had belonged to religious houses before the Henrician dissolutions. As bishop he continued his active preaching, and is recorded as giving 'a godly sermon' at Paul's Cross in London on 20 February 1558 before the lord mayor, aldermen, ten bishops, judges and lawyers, and a great audience. He also produced a book of sermons, *Holsome and catholyke doctryne concerninge the seven sacramentes … set forth in maner of shorte sermons* (1558; STC 25112 ff.), for use in parish churches where the parish priest was not able or qualified to preach; this was one of a number of responses to the drive by Cardinal Pole to reform and revive the English church in the Catholic faith by the provision of educational material for the laity.

Watson's career was curtailed by the death of Queen Mary on 17 November of that year, and the accession of Elizabeth. He was one of the bishops appointed to dispute with a number of reformers at Westminster Abbey on 3 April 1559. The proceedings broke down when the bishops failed to produce the questions for their opponents that had been required of them. That night Watson, along with John White, bishop of Winchester, was sent by water to the Tower. The bishops were each allowed one of their own servants, and their own bedding and furniture. It is at this point that the sickness, which was to plague Watson for the rest of his life, first became apparent. The council instructed the lieutenant of the Tower to treat the bishops well, 'specially the Bysshopp of Lyncolne, for that he is syck' (*APC, 1558–70*, 78). Watson was permitted to join the lieutenant at his table 'for the better relief of his quartayne ague' (ibid., 93–4).

Prisoner in the Tower On 25 July Watson was deprived of his bishopric, and the next day released from confinement. A year later, on 26 June 1560, he was again sent to the Tower, whence he was discharged into the custody of Edmund Grindal, bishop of London, then to Edmund Guest (or Gheast) of Rochester, and finally to Richard Cox of Ely. According to Brady there is a paper in the Vatican archives that appears from internal evidence to have been written in 1560 with a view to making changes in the English hierarchy and filling vacant sees, on the basis that (as far as the Holy See was concerned) the remaining Catholic bishops were still in legal possession of their sees. The document suggests that the archbishop of York, Nicholas Heath, should be translated to Canterbury, and that Watson (who, it was noted, was at the time in prison) should become archbishop of York. This document, which reflects the ultimately unfounded hopes felt in some quarters in Rome and elsewhere at the time that Elizabeth might eventually settle on a restoration of Catholicism, also gives an indication of the esteem felt in the upper echelons of the church in Rome for the bishop of Lincoln.

Watson appears to have remained in the custody of Cox until January 1565, when he was once again sent to the Tower. After the publication in 1570 of the papal bull excommunicating Elizabeth, Watson and other leading Catholic prisoners were examined. His answers appear to have been moderate, showing due allegiance to the sovereign. None the less, he is noted as being in the Tower in March 1571; there he remained until 5 July 1574, when he was released by the privy council into the custody of his brother John. His health at this time was very poor, and he seems to have been half blind and disabled. A condition of his release was that he should place sureties with the archbishop of Canterbury that he would not act contrary to the laws of the established religion, nor seek to induce others to any such contrary act or opinion. He was not to leave his brother's house without licence of the council, and was to see only those visitors who had legitimate business with his brother. It appears that he failed to meet these conditions of his bail. On 24 June 1577 the council complained to the bishop of London that Watson, John Feckenham, the former abbot of Westminster, and others, had abused their bail and consorted with 'certen of her Majesties evill disposed subjectes … whom they have

perverted in Religion' (*APC, 1558–70*, 371). Evidence corroborating Watson's part in such illegal activity is found in documents relating to the imprisonment in 1577 of Francis Tregian and his indictment for recusancy. Among the papers is a letter from William Wigges to Cuthbert Mayne, stating that he had sent to Mayne 'all his stuff' (his portable mass set and vestments) which had been hallowed by the bishop of Lincoln (Watson), indicating that he continued to exercise episcopal functions even after his deprivation and confinement (Morris, 85).

Final captivity and death The council responded to such activity by requiring new bonds of their keepers that they would not allow their charges to have any further contact with anyone on matters of religion. In Watson's case the council found this to be insufficient and on 28 July 1577 committed him to the custody of Robert Horne, bishop of Winchester. A letter of the council to Horne dated 11 August permitted Watson to have the use of one of his own servants; while reluctant to allow him to be served by one of his own religion, the council considered this less dangerous than providing him with a 'sound person' whom he might corrupt. By the beginning of 1578 Horne was in poor health, and requested that he be allowed to be discharged of Watson's custody so that he might go to London to recover his health; the council replied on 16 January that he should come to London and bring his prisoner with him, as Watson too was in poor health and wished to go to London. Shortly afterwards, however, Horne was granted his request and on 19 February his charge was transferred to John Young, the newly appointed bishop of Rochester. Young was to attempt to bring Watson to conform, and to ensure that he was unable to corrupt anyone further in matters of religion.

The attempts of the council to prevent Watson, Feckenham, and others from influencing others in matters of religion was proving difficult to enforce. The beginning of the Jesuit mission to England, as well as the continuing influx of secular priests, was further complicating the situation. In 1580 a solution was offered by Richard Cox, namely that the recalcitrant clergy should be sent to a former palace of the bishops of Ely, which was suitable for use as a prison. Wisbech Castle had been rebuilt in brick between 1478 and 1483 by John Morton, then bishop of Ely, to be an episcopal residence. It stood on a high terrace surrounded by a moat. Possibly because of its location in the fens of East Anglia, later bishops allowed it to fall into disrepair, and by 1580 it was in a ruinous and dilapidated condition, as well as in what the Jesuit Robert Persons described as 'a most unhealthy spot' (Hicks, 79). Preparations were soon under way, undertaken on behalf of the bishop of Ely by two engineers and merchant adventurers, George Carleton and Humfrey Michell, who had been undertaking the draining of the fens. The two men notified the council of the completion of their preparations, and of the arrival of Feckenham and Watson, in a letter of 11 August. By October six more prisoners had joined them, and Carleton and Michell were seeking advice from the council as to whether the prisoners were to be allowed their own servants, and to take meals in common as had become their practice, despite the council's original insistence that Feckenham, at least, should be kept in solitary confinement. It seems that the prisoners were allowed no books other than a Bible, and were not permitted any writing instruments. The bishop of Ely had appointed a preacher to them, but they refused to listen to him or to attend Anglican services. Watson died in prison in Wisbech Castle in September 1584. He was buried in the church of St Peter and St Paul, just outside the castle, on 27 September. KENNETH CARLETON

Sources W. M. Brady, *The episcopal succession in England, Scotland, and Ireland, AD 1400 to 1875*, 2 (1876) · W. Stubbs, *Registrum sacrum Anglicanum*, 2nd edn (1897) · *Fasti Angl., 1541–1857*, [Lincoln] · Venn, *Alum. Cant.*, 1/4.350 · Cooper, *Ath. Cantab.*, 1.491–4 · J. G. Nichols, ed., *The chronicle of Queen Jane, and of two years of Queen Mary*, CS, old ser., 48 (1850) · *The diary of Henry Machyn, citizen and merchant-taylor of London, from AD 1550 to AD 1563*, ed. J. G. Nichols, CS, 42 (1848) · C. Wriothesley, *A chronicle of England during the reigns of the Tudors from AD 1485 to 1559*, ed. W. D. Hamilton, 2, CS, new ser., 20 (1877) · J. H. Pollen, *The English Catholics in the reign of Queen Elizabeth* (1920) · *APC, 1558–81* · L. Hicks, ed., *Letters and memorials of Father Robert Persons*, Catholic RS, 39 (1942) · *CSP dom., 1547–80; 1553–8* · J. Morris, ed., *The troubles of our Catholic forefathers related by themselves*, 1 (1872) · J. K. McConica, *English humanists and Reformation politics under Henry VIII and Edward VI* (1965) · *VCH Cambridgeshire and the Isle of Ely*, vol. 4

Archives Lincs. Arch., episcopal register XXVIII

Watson, Thomas (1555/6–1592), poet and translator, has been identified as the boy who entered Winchester College in 1567, aged eleven (Eccles, *Brief Lives*, 130). This Thomas Watson was born in the city of London parish of St Helen, Bishopsgate, according to the school admissions register. It is not known who his parents were; several Watson families lived in London at the time.

Youth and travel After acquiring a reliable facility in classical languages and literature, Watson seems to have attended Oxford University briefly (without obtaining a degree) in the early 1570s. His friends at Oxford included the poets John Lyly and George Peele, the antiquarian William Camden, William Beale, a preacher of Westminster, and others who were about the university at that time. Wood says that he neglected his proper studies for 'poetry and romance' (Wood, *Ath. Oxon.*, 3rd edn, 3.601), a habit continued during the next seven years while travelling in France and Italy; there, Watson says, although he was supposed to be studying law, he visited the camps of Apollo and the Muses whenever he could. He absorbed the culture and language of both countries thoroughly, making contact with poets, and writing and translating poetry; but neither this nor the French religious wars in which he was sometimes caught up prevented him achieving proficiency in civil and canon law, as he was pleased to advertise. Opportunities for travel were no doubt helped by his acquaintance with Sir Francis Walsingham, from whose Paris embassy he would have embarked on his long tour, and from where he seems finally to have left for England in August 1581, carrying official letters from the secretary to William Cecil. Four entries in the diary of the English College at Douai, and witness statements made in 1587 (Eccles, *Christopher Marlowe in London*, 128–44, 151) may possibly indicate earlier journeys home. After Walsingham's

death he expressed his gratitude to him for offering comfort in some unspecified sadness which affected him at this time.

Although still in his early twenties, Watson had translated Petrarch's *Canzoniere* into Latin and written two Latin poems (all these only surviving as excerpts in other of his works), and fashioned what was probably the first Latin translation available to the Tudor reader of Sophocles's *Antigone*, printed in London in the summer of 1581 by John Wolfe, who became his regular printer. The dedication (to Philip Howard, first earl of Arundel) provides information on Watson's travels, and the preparatory material includes support in verse from his Oxford friends, and encouragement from the German jurist Stefan Broellmann. The work itself establishes what became Watson's lifelong intention—to inform and instruct as well as enlighten. A prologue presents the moral arguments, and added after Sophocles's text are original dramatic sections called 'pompae' and 'themata' which examine the issues further. This is an edition appropriate for acting in the university or the inns of court, and Camden's line 'tu pompis Latiis nostra theatra quatis' ('your Latin pomps make our audience tremble') suggests a previous staging. The work was much approved by Gabriel Harvey.

Settled in London Back in London in 1581 Watson took up lodgings again in St Helen's. At this time English lyric poetry writing was quite impoverished, a fact emphasized by several later writers, and strong puritan factions attacked the activity; little was being published except anthologies. The two poets who had made genuine attempts to incorporate in their verse the lessons of the long traditions of Italian and French literature, Thomas Wyatt and Henry Howard, were dead long since, and the only significant lyric poet of recent times, George Gascoigne, was of a decidedly English inspiration.

Watson, however, was keen to present the fruits of his foreign experiences in concentrated form, and to the general reader (rather than to a limited group of élite admirers). As a Latinist marching into the field of English lyric verse he was being bold and showed some apprehension, but he received much encouragement, this time from a literary coterie based around John Lyly in Holborne. *The Hekatompathia, or, Passionate Century of Love* was printed in the spring of 1582, and in dedicating it to Edward de Vere, seventeenth earl of Oxford, who had already seen a manuscript (BL, Harley MS 3277), the author modestly apologizes for his temerity in offering English verse, for the 'trifling' nature of its subject, and for his own lack of skill. It became his best-known and most quoted English work and Watson was hailed as a Petrarch who had brought the Muses to live in England, enriching his native tongue (as Harvey noted) and giving intellectual respectability to love poetry. Each 'sonnet' (of eighteen lines) is provided with a heading which explains the nature of the poem, points out rhetorical devices, narrates mythological references (mainly from Homer, Ovid, and Propertius), and acknowledges, or quotes, literary sources (altogether some thirty-two classical authors and twenty-five from Renaissance Italy and France). Each poem confronts an aspect of a lover's suffering, and although Watson says it is merely imagined on his part, he shows considerable insight and humour, and some depth, and deals efficiently with metrical and structural aspects. In the opening protrepticon he imagines the volume's reception at the court, and several of the poems appear to be addressed to Elizabeth herself. The later poems examine feelings once 'love is past'.

Early Latin works Watson thought of himself primarily as a Latin writer, and his next three works were in this language. The first, a prose treatise, called in manuscript 'Artificiosæ memoriæ libellus' (1583; BL, Sloane MS 3731) and in print *Compendium memoriae localis* (1585), is a simple exposition of the theory and practice of the classical art of memory training. Interest in the subject was current due to the presence in London of Giordano Bruno, a champion of the magical element in memory systems, and a contender in the controversy raging in the universities over the replacement of Aristotelian methods with those of the French philosopher Pierre Ramus (*d.* 1572). Watson intended his manuscript for Albert Lasko, a visiting prince of Poland and another hermeticist, who was specially invited to the reader's banquet in the Middle Temple hall, but it seems that he did not turn up for the event. So two years later the published *Compendium* was dedicated to Henry Noel, one of Elizabeth's gentleman pensioners and a close friend.

Watson's next work (and eventually his most famous) was a set of eleven Latin verse lamentations called *Amyntas* (1585), dedicated again to Noel, in which an Arcadian shepherd mourns the death of his companion, Phillis, on the banks of the Thames. There is much rustic sentiment and earthy nostalgia, but the laments become more intense as the eleven days progress, the final day culminating in the shepherd's suicide, the only way in which he can rejoin his lover. His corpse is metamorphosed into an amaranthus plant, and Amor (Cupid) gives it the property of staunching bleeding, an ironic twist since it was Cupid's arrow which first injured his heart. But fame did not come for this work until Abraham Fraunce's unacknowledged translation of it into 'high-witted' English hexameters (1587), made for his patron, Mary Herbert, countess of Pembroke, as an offering of consolation on the death of her brother (Sir Philip Sidney). Later Fraunce published a different edition in which the translation (now acknowledged) was joined on to another, Tasso's *Aminta*, his 'Sylvia' changing her name to Watson's 'Phillis' to preserve continuity.

Last in this group is a translation (1586) of the fifth century Greek poem of Paris and Helen by Colluthus, which Watson made for Henry Percy, ninth earl of Northumberland. That he may have been an intimate of the earl's group is suggested by the fact that he also dedicated to him a treatise on the collection and preservation of fresh water for domestic purposes (formerly a Petworth MS, now Harvard, Houghton English 707), translated from the French of Bernard Palissy, the Huguenot potter. Much work was being done on the gardens of Petworth House at this time.

Theatre and musical lyrics About 1587 Watson moved lodgings to Norton Folegate, in which year he is described as 'a man very well learned' being 'late of St Helen's' (BL, Lansdowne MS 53/79, 162–3). The thrust of new theatrical activity was happening in these 'liberties' outside Bishopsgate, and among the playwrights were Watson's friends Lyly and Peele, as well as the youngsters Christopher Marlowe, Thomas Kyd, and Robert Greene. Watson addressed a commendatory hexasticon to Greene in 1589, and in September of that year he intervened in a brawl in Hog Lane (now Curtain Road), Finsbury, between Marlowe and William Bradley, who was attacking Marlowe with sword and dagger, apparently over a money problem. Earlier Bradley had petitioned for an injunction against Watson and John Alleyn, an actor, to keep the peace. Watson suffered serious injury to his thigh before killing Bradley in self-defence; the trial gave a verdict of manslaughter and Watson was kept in Newgate prison until pardon the following February. Although no plays by Watson are extant, his employer William Cornwallis wrote later that devising 'twenty fictions and knaveryes in a play' was his 'daily practyse and his living' (Hall, 256), and in *A Knight's Conjuring* (1607) Thomas Dekker imagines the actor John Bentley in heaven near Watson and Kyd, because 'he had bene a Player molded out of their pennes'. There is also textual evidence to suggest that Watson may have written some speeches for the entertainment given to Elizabeth by Sir Edward Seymour in 1591.

Before his imprisonment Watson made the acquaintance of both William Byrd, the composer, and Thomas Este, his music printer, in 1589 writing a lyric for a vocal piece by Byrd, published on broadsides. This extolled the virtues of the Oxford divine John Case, who had recently been railing in print against the ill effects of the puritan ethic on music, church music particularly; Byrd had often suffered from such restricting invasions. Watson's introduction to Este had far-reaching consequences, for following on from the success of Este's production in 1588 of an anthology of (mostly) Italian madrigals with lyrics translated into English, the idea was conceived of Watson writing English lyrics to some newer Italian madrigals, so as to demonstrate more effectively that the madrigal form relied on the very instant interdependence of words and music. Watson had shown his sensitivity to music in earlier poems, and he perceived (with his eye set again on instruction) that as yet neither England's composers nor her poets had applied themselves to understanding the Italian method completely.

The result was *The first sett of Italian madrigalls Englished, not to the sense of the originall dittie, but after the affection of the noate* (1590), in which was printed the music of twenty-six madrigals in four, five, and six parts, mostly by Luca Marenzio, whose music was already a favourite with English singing-groups through illegally imported foreign prints and home-made copies (often without words), and the earlier anthology. Watson's lyrics show hardly any translations, the new content being determined by the flow of the melodies and harmonies, and by the overall spirit of the original. Byrd himself illustrated the method with two examples of his own.

The way in which the book for the 'medius' part is collated suggests that at first there were to be only twenty-four madrigals, all in five parts, but that the death of Watson's mentor Sir Francis Walsingham in April 1590 necessitated a rearrangement to include several lyrics praising his life and regretting his death, set to the greater sonority of six vocal parts; included in these is also an account of his imagined astral meeting with his son-in-law, Sidney. This anthology and its predecessor soon involved native composers in active participation in madrigal writing, the first of the eventual large school being Thomas Morley in 1593.

Last works and the Cornwallis affair Watson further marked the secretary of state's death with a pastoral eclogue in Latin, dedicated to Thomas Walsingham, Sir Francis's first cousin, of Scadbury Manor in Kent, whom (as he notes in the poem) Watson had known since their youthful days together in the Paris embassy (*Meliboeus Thomae Watsoni*, 1590). An English version soon followed (*An Eglogue upon the Death of … Sir Francis Walsingham*, 1590), dedicated to Lady Frances Sidney, the secretary of state's daughter, which Watson translated himself in order to avoid what happened to his earlier epic. The poem is in the form of a conversation (Latin, 445 lines; English, 426) between the poet and Thomas Walsingham in which they rehearse the virtues and achievements of Sir Francis (called Meliboeus, the title of the Latin version), invoke angry responses from the universe around (which here is still Ptolemy's), pity his abandoned country, and console the family. Watson seems to present himself as a sort of national laureate in this, for Elizabeth's sadness is also imagined, and her favourite poet, Spenser, is invoked to remind her of all those devoted state servants who are still in office.

From time to time Watson may have been used by Sir Francis Walsingham as a political agent; perhaps even his position with William Cornwallis, as tutor to the son, was organized so that he could be Walsingham's ears during the official inquiries into the recusancy of the father, Sir Thomas Cornwallis of Brome in Suffolk, who was under surveillance from 1587. It was about this time that Watson took up his duties at Fisher's Folly opposite St Botolph without Bishopsgate, which the Cornwallises had just taken over from the earl of Oxford; John, aged fifteen, was soon to enter the then openly Catholic Gonville and Caius College, Cambridge.

One of Watson's colleagues in the household was Thomas Swift, a Norwich-born musician, sheltered in the family since boyhood. Watson had married his older sister, Anne (b. 1564), at St Antholin, Budge Row, London, on 6 September 1585. About 1589 Swift conceived the notion that William Cornwallis had been 'miserable towards him', and, 'by the advice of the said Watson, whom he … confessed the plot-layer of this matter' (Bodl. Oxf., MS Tanner 97, fol. 29), he began a blackmail worthy of presentation at a nearby playhouse. The scheme was to lend ten gold angels to Cornwallis's fourteen-year-old daughter,

Frances (not an unusual event, for Swift was 'in love' with her, and it was a miser's house), in return for her signature to a document which promised repayment with interest on her wedding day. The signing was hurriedly effected before morning lessons in front of witnesses, but the document (drawn up by Swift's brother, the attorney Hugh Swift) actually concealed a contract to marry the musician. Watson doubtless thought that he would never dare use it, and attempted later to get it away from him; but use it he did on Frances's betrothal, setting a blackmail price. Cornwallis's fury at this calumny and his daughter's besmirchment knew no bounds, and as a relative of Burghley through his wife, he managed to get a hearing in the Star Chamber in 1593, at which (the late) Watson's involvement was exposed by John, Frances's honour restored, and Swift very severely punished.

Watson wrote two other significant works, both published posthumously. In the ambitious (and speedily written) 2000-line Latin pastoral *Amintae gaudia* (which Marlowe saw through the press in November 1592) he narrates the earlier relationship of his lovers, Phillis now alive and so virtuously addressed that it seems almost that she is the dedicatee, Mary Herbert. The epistolary form is derived from Propertius, there are several well-crafted erotic incidents of an Ovidian nature, and a long epyllion narrates the installation by the immortal gods of Sidney on his star. Also included is a description, based on Virgil, of the defeat of the Armada, and several episodes of an apparently autobiographical nature.

The second work, a sixty-sonnet sequence printed in 1593, was no doubt intended by its publisher to take advantage of the current fashion of sonnet sequences, many of which, though stimulated by the publication of *Astrophil and Stella* (1591), reflected Watson's direct style more than Sidney's subtleties. The author of *The Tears of Fancie* is shown only by the initials T. W., but Watson is a strong candidate, for the poems exhibit characteristics of his style (but less Petrarchan) and cover similar amatory concerns, and there is a final line to sonnet 59 which balances the final couplet of *Hekatompathia*; sonnet 60 has been shown to be by the earl of Oxford. The sonnets are frequently based on Gascoigne and seem to be tentative experiments in the English quatorzain form (14 lines, resembling a sonnet), perhaps not for publication; only one badly printed and mutilated copy is extant (Hunt. 32085).

Throughout his poetry Watson creates a sort of imaginary universe, and many repeated references to subjects, characters, and events, fictional and autobiographical and national, lead to an appreciation of his sense of the unity of things, and a clearer understanding of his pioneering efforts in improving the language, and of his intellectual control of form and content, tempered often by a humorous detachment, even self-parody. 'One can only wonder what he would have achieved, had his life not been cut short at a relatively young age' (*Complete Works*, 2.192).

Watson's burial, during the plague year of 1592, is registered at St Bartholomew-the-Less inside the purlieus of the hospital, under 26 September, ten days before that of Hugh Swift in the same place. Through references to him by many authors (usually by the name Amyntas or to the amaranthus plant), through the praises of critics, and through reprintings of his poems in anthologies (some of which, however, are mere bogus copies of his style), his considerable reputation remained for a decade after his death. ALBERT CHATTERLEY

Sources Thomas Watson, poems, ed. E. Arber (1870) · The complete works of Thomas Watson, 1556–92, ed. D. Sutton, 2 vols. (1996) · P. Brett, ed., The Byrd edition, 16 (1976) · A. Chatterley, Thomas Watson: Italian madrigals Englished (1999) · M. Eccles, Christopher Marlowe in London (1934) · M. Eccles, Brief lives: Tudor and Stuart authors (1982) · H. Barnett, 'John Case—an Elizabethan music scholar', Music and Letters, 50 (1969), 252–66 · Venn, Alum. Cant. · Foster, Alum. Oxon. · parish register, St Simon and St Jude, Norwich, 13 Aug 1564 [baptism: Anne Swift, wife] · parish register, St Antholin, Budge Row, London, 6/9/1585 [marriage] · parish register, St Bartholomew-the-Less, London, 26/9/1592 [burial] · PRO, STAC 5/A36/5; STAC 5/C33/38; STAC 7/1/6 · 'A collection of letters relating to the Hobart family', Bodl. Oxf., MS Tanner 97, fols. 27r–44v, 55 · PRO, C 260/174/5 and 27 · BL, Lansdowne MS 53, no. 79 · V. Stern, Gabriel Harvey: a study of his life, marginalia and library (1979) · H. Hall, 'An Elizabethan poet and his relations', The Athenaeum, 3278 (1890), 256 · J. Scott, 'The sources of Watson's Tears of fancie', Modern Language Review, 21 (1926), 303–6, 435 · W. Murphy, 'Thomas Watson's Hecatompathia and the Elizabethan sonnet-sequence', Journal of English and German Philology, 56 (1957), 418–28 · W. Staton, 'The influence of Thomas Watson on Elizabethan Ovidian poetry', Studies in the Renaissance, 6 (1959), 243–50 · A. Chatterley, 'Thomas Watson and the Elvetham entertainment', N&Q, 245 (2000), 37–40 · R. E. G. Kirk and E. F. Kirk, eds., Returns of aliens dwelling in the city and suburbs of London, from the reign of Henry VIII to that of James I, Huguenot Society of London, 10/2 (1902) · T. F. Kirby, Winchester scholars: a list of the wardens, fellows, and scholars of … Winchester College (1888), 141

Watson, Thomas (d. 1686), ejected minister, was recorded as 'of Yorkshire' when he matriculated at Emmanuel College, Cambridge, in 1635; no more can be said of his background and early years. At Cambridge he was noted for being a 'hard student' (Nonconformist's Memorial, 1.188). He graduated BA in 1639 and MA in 1642, acting after this as a chaplain to the puritan Lady Vere. In 1646 he was at the City church of St Stephen Walbrook, probably as a lecturer. In 1649 he signed the Vindication, disclaiming implication in the king's execution. In 1651 he was involved with several others in Love's plot to recall Charles II; he was imprisoned but returned to St Stephen's in 1652. Watson married Abigail Beadle (b. 1627), daughter of the Essex puritan minister John *Beadle. Between 1648 and 1660 the baptisms of five sons and two daughters are recorded at St Stephen's, to be followed by the melancholy toll of four burials. After his ejection a further daughter was buried at St Stephen's in 1672 (and also a son at Enfield), and at St Stephen's, it seems, his wife was buried in 1692.

At the beginning of Watson's time at St Stephen's, Ralph Robinson was the rector, and represented the classis in the London provincial assembly in 1652 and 1653, becoming moderator in November 1654. Watson was meanwhile an assessor of the provincial assembly and scribe of the third classis. On 3 November 1656, however, Watson was returned to the provincial assembly representing the third London classis. He attended sporadically and on 1 August 1660 was present at the penultimate meeting. The likelihood, therefore, is that Watson became rector of St Stephen Walbrook in the place of Robinson in 1655 or 1656. In 1662 he was ejected from the rectory of St Stephen. In 1665 he was reported by an informer as holding a conventicle at his house in the Minories. Nevertheless, he continued his ministry in London at various conventicles, including a well-equipped meeting-house in Bishopsgate. In 1671 and 1677 Mary, countess of Warwick, heard him preach in Essex. Under the declaration of indulgence he was licensed to preach at his house in Dowgate; his congregation later moved to Crosby Hall, Bishopsgate. In November 1681 Watson was one of several London ministers prosecuted and fined for holding conventicles, and he was presented again in April 1683. Another aspect of his ministry was that he kept a school at Bethnal Green, whose students wrote to Baxter of their reverence for him.

Watson died in 1686 and was buried on 28 July at Barnston, Essex, in the same grave as his father-in-law, John Beadle, the ejected minister there. According to Henry Newcome he 'died poor' (Autobiography, 2.276). This is borne out by the fact that in 1684 Baxter paid him £2 out of the £50 fund he had been given by the earl of Bedford to distribute to poor ministers (Keeble and Nuttall, letter 1128).

Watson was a prolific writer whose work went into many editions in his own century and later. His early literary output was exhortatory and devotional rather than didactic; even when the occasion arose for a topical sermon, as at the Restoration, he rejected it. His Discourses was addressed to the godly and does not, for the most part, concern itself with doubts or threats. It is primarily meditational, at times even mystical, and often expressed in ecstatic language. The Christian's Charter (1652) is a paean on the privileges and delights of the Christian; inter alia it describes the Christian's resurrection body as 'enamelled with glory' (Watson, Discourses, 1.79). This leads logically to A Christian on the Mount, or, A Treatise on Meditation described as 'the chamber of delight … the soul's retiring on itself … the wing of the soul' (ibid., 1.199). Christ's Loveliness of 1657 was Watson's own meditation on the Canticles: 'the whole book is bespangled with the praises of Christ' (ibid., 1.295). The same year saw a long treatise, The Character of a Godly Man, which included sections on 'helps to perseverance', and 'an answer to those that doubt their salvation'. Lastly, the longest discourse was on Christ's sermon on the mount, seen as an exemplar of the minister's preaching: 'when ministers are upon the mount, let them not be on the rocks' (ibid., 2.35).

Watson's magnum opus was published posthumously in 1692. This was A Body of Practical Divinity, sermons on the shorter catechism of the Westminster assembly, a massive work of some 880 quarto pages. Unlike many puritan writings which started as a sermon and expanded into a book, these bear the marks of being sermons. They are short, oratorical in style, and exhibit a happy turn of phrase. Each starts with a tabulated exposition, amply supported from scripture, of the passage from the catechism, followed by a number of 'uses'—the application of the doctrine. These are interspersed with 'objections' to clarify difficult points or move the argument forward. There are recurring passages which show Watson's priorities and the typical emphases and problems of Calvinist belief. There is a forthright statement of God's election to salvation: 'they were not elected because they believed, but believed because they were elected … The book of God's decree hath no errata in it, no blottings out, once justified never unjustified' (Watson, *Body of Practical Divinity*, 42). This position is often repeated, but equally often Watson addresses the problem of assurance and answers the questions of those who doubt their salvation: 'I fear the kingdom of grace is not yet come into my heart … I fear the plough of the law hath not yet gone deep enough, therefore I have not grace'. Watson's recurring counter to these doubts is that 'a weak faith is not to be despised'; a weak faith is still true faith and may be growing. He is wont to offer advice strange in the context of election: 'let us above all things labour for forgiveness of sins'; 'let them labour to find grace … take pains for it' (ibid., 128, 152, 387). In practice this meant the formula of frequent prayer, meditation, and reading of scripture, coupled with attendance at the 'ordinances' of the church. Here one can see the pastor in Watson seeking to square the circle of a fixed belief in double predestination and the doubts and troubles of his flock. A recurring concern is the sufferings of the elect. These are to 'expectorate and purge our sins' (ibid., 445ff.); as such they are 'love tokens' (ibid., 529) from God. In general Watson has an apocalyptic view of his world: 'we live in the dregs of time … England has a kachexy; it is all over disease' (ibid., 371). The picture which emerges is that of a godly man, devoted to his pastoral ministry. Calamy has a story which partly encapsulates this summary:

> once on a lecture day Bishop Richardson came to hear him, who was much pleased with his sermon, but especially with the prayer after it, so that he followed him home to give him thanks, and earnestly desired a copy of it. 'Alas (said Mr Watson) that is what I cannot give, for I do not use to pen my prayers; it was no studied thing, but uttered *pro re nata*, as God enabled me, from the abundance of my heart and affections'. Upon which the good bishop went away wondering that any man could pray in that manner extempore. (*Nonconformist's Memorial*, 1.189)

BARRY TILL

Sources Calamy rev. · DNB · T. Watson, *A body of practical divinity in a series of sermons on the shorter catechism of the Westminster Assembly* (1862) · T. Watson, *Discourses on important and interesting subjects* (1829) · records of the provincial assembly of London, LPL, MS 40.2. E17 · CSP dom., 1651; 1670; 1678 · W. Wilson, *The history and antiquities of the dissenting churches and meeting houses in London, Westminster and Southwark*, 4 vols. (1808–14) · A. Gordon, ed., *Freedom after ejection: a review (1690–1692) of presbyterian and congregational nonconformity in England and Wales* (1917) · *Calendar of the correspondence of Richard Baxter*, ed. N. H. Keeble and G. F. Nuttall, 2 vols. (1991) · *The nonconformist's memorial … originally written by … Edmund Calamy*, ed. S. Palmer, [3rd edn], 1 (1802) · *The autobiography of Henry Newcome*, ed. R. Parkinson, 2, Chetham Society, 27 (1852), 276 · W. B. Bannerman and W. B. Bannerman, jun., eds., *The registers of St Stephen's, Walbrook, and of St Benet Sherehog, London*, 2 vols., Harleian Society, register section, 49–50 (1919–20) · IGI

Likenesses H. Schaten, line engraving, BM, NPG; repro. in German translation of *Works* (1662) · J. Sturt, line engraving, NPG · F. H. Van Hove, line engraving, BM, NPG; repro. in T. Watson, *Art of divine contentment* (1662) · oils, DWL

Wealth at death died poor owing to exigencies of family: Newcome, *Autobiography*, vol. 2, p. 276

Watson, Thomas (1637–1717), bishop of St David's, was born on 1 March 1637 at North Ferriby, near Hull, the son of John Watson, a seaman. He was educated at Hull grammar school and entered St John's College, Cambridge, on 25 May 1655, graduating BA in 1659 and proceeding MA in 1662. He was ordained a deacon and priest in the diocese of Ely on 22 December 1667 and proceeded BD and became a fellow of St John's in 1669. He was presented to the rectory of Burrough Green, Cambridgeshire, in 1672 and made a DD in 1675. In 1678–9 he supported the tory candidates at the county election in Cambridgeshire.

Watson continued to hold Burrough Green *in commendam* with the bishopric of St David's, to which he was consecrated on 26 June 1687, apparently upon the recommendation of Henry Jermyn, Lord Dover, a Roman Catholic with Cambridgeshire connections. Watson was a committed supporter of James II and in November 1687 he was expected to support repeal of the Test Acts should James II call a new parliament. Unlike the seven bishops he was an advocate of the Anglican clergy reading the second declaration of indulgence from their pulpits, and made efforts to ensure that they complied in his diocese. In December 1688 such was his unpopularity that 'the rabble in Cambridge' attacked St John's and imprisoned Watson 'with a halter around his neck' (*Le Fleming MSS*, 230), but he was rescued by the college fellows. This may account for his absence from London during the revolution. He attended the Convention and opposed the motion declaring that James II had abdicated, and supported the proposal for a regency in January and February 1689. After initially refusing to take the oaths of allegiance and supremacy to William and Mary he took them on 31 March 1690. However, he was still omitted from the Act of Grace, which pardoned all but a handful for their actions committed in the previous reigns, in May. Watson's survival as bishop is to be explained by the king's desire not to drive even more of the episcopal bench into nonjuring. Thereafter Watson opposed the government of the day, most notably in supporting the place bill in January 1693, refusing the oath of Association in February 1696 (which in threatening action against his enemies in the wake of the assassination plot declared William king *de jure* as well as *de facto*) and opposing the bill of attainder against the Jacobite Sir John Fenwick in November 1696.

Watson seems to have been in conflict with some of his clergy from the very onset of his episcopate. He blamed the tenure of Bishop Robert Lucy for much bad practice among the clergy, and in his visitation of 1691 set about remedying their faults. He may have targeted whig clergy, and certainly was at odds with his chancellor, Robert Lucy, the son of Bishop Lucy. However, his clergy fought back, accusing Watson of simony and extortion, and one Jeremiah Griffith brought a case to the assizes at Brecon in 1693 which found the bishop guilty of taking excessive fees. In 1694 Watson announced that his chancellor, residentiary canons, and beneficed clergy should be resident, a further salvo in his battle with his whig clergy. Lucy responded with a petition to Archbishop Tillotson to inquire into the charges against the bishop. Thus, on 24 July 1694 commissioners were appointed to visit the diocese and on 21 August Watson was suspended.

The death of Archbishop Tillotson saw Watson petition his successor, Thomas Tenison, for the suspension to be lifted, which it duly was in February 1695. However, Watson continued to pursue Lucy, who responded by issuing a series of charges against Watson. These included simony, the taking of excessive fees at ordinations, institutions, and visitations, and of conferring orders without administering the oaths, yet certifying that he had done so. Watson was called before Archbishop Tenison on 24 October but after the charges were read he claimed parliamentary privilege. Lucy petitioned the House of Lords on 7 March 1696, praying that the case be allowed to go forward, and Watson waived his privilege on 20 March after the petition was dropped. Various hearings were held during 1696–9, and on 3 August 1699 judgment was given by Tenison, assisted by five bishops, and Watson was found guilty and sentenced to deprivation, although Thomas Sprat, bishop of Rochester, dissented from the sentence and did not attend the final hearing. Watson appealed against the sentence to the court of delegates, arguing that the archbishop did not have that power, and then resumed his privilege, taking his seat again in the Lords on 18 November 1699. However, after hearing counsel the Lords decided on 6 December that Watson should not be allowed to resume his privilege. He last sat in the Lords on 22 December 1699. An attempt to use the court of king's bench to force the court of delegates to admit more evidence also failed, and on 22 February 1700 the delegates confirmed the sentence of deprivation. On 3 March 1700 Watson failed in an attempt to get the king's bench to reverse its earlier decision. Problems then arose on how to eject Watson from the temporalities of his see, and on 8 March the Lords petitioned the crown not to fill the vacancy 'for some convenient time'.

Watson refused to accept the sentence as confirmed by the delegates and refused to pay the costs of the suit, now over £600. For the second offence he was excommunicated, and in June 1702 he was imprisoned in Newgate for not paying his fees, remaining in custody until October. On 9 October he petitioned the queen for 'a commission of review' (Carpenter, 226) nominated by the crown. In reply the crown merely claimed the bishop's lands as he was suspended, but Watson continued to maintain that he was still bishop. The crown proceeded against Watson in the court of exchequer on 15 June 1703, and having lost his case Watson appealed to the exchequer chamber, which ruled against him on 24 November 1704. Finally Watson brought a writ of error before the Lords, but lost by forty-nine votes to twenty. George Bull was consecrated as Watson's successor on 5 March 1705.

Henceforth Watson retired to Great Wilbraham in Cambridgeshire, where he died 'very rich' (*Remarks*, 6.65) on 3 June 1717. As an excommunicant he was buried privately the following evening at Great Wilbraham. Although at least one document appears to refer to his wife, Joanna, that was also the name of the wife of his brother, William, who proved his will.   STUART HANDLEY

Sources Venn, *Alum. Cant.* · *Report on the manuscripts of the late Reginald Rawdon Hastings*, 4 vols., HMC, 78 (1928–47) · *The manuscripts of the House of Lords*, new ser., 12 vols. (1900–77), vol. 2, pp. 206, 221; vol. 3, pp. 235–7; vol. 4, pp. 115–17; vol. 6, pp. 228–9 · E. Carpenter, *Thomas Tenison, archbishop of Canterbury* (1948), 205–37 · *State trials*, 14.447–71 · *Bishop Burnet's History*, 4.415–17, 460–61; 5.188–9 · N. Luttrell, *A brief historical relation of state affairs from September 1678 to April 1714*, 3–5 (1857) · *The London diaries of William Nicolson, bishop of Carlisle, 1702–1718*, ed. C. Jones and G. Holmes (1985), 247, 253, 258–60, 263–6, 275 · *Letters illustrative of the reign of William III from 1696 to 1708 addressed to the duke of Shrewsbury by James Vernon*, ed. G. P. R. James, 3 vols. (1841), vol. 2, pp. 334, 338, 376–7 · *The correspondence of Henry Hyde, earl of Clarendon, and of his brother Lawrence Hyde, earl of Rochester*, ed. S. W. Singer, 2 (1828), 171, 255–60, 312–13 · H. Horwitz, *Parliament, policy and politics in the reign of William III* (1977), 108, 110, 337 · *The manuscripts of S. H. Le Fleming*, HMC, 25 (1890), 210, 230 · *Remarks and collections of Thomas Hearne*, ed. C. E. Doble and others, 6, OHS, 43 (1902), 65

Archives BL, corresp., etc. | Hunt. L., letters to seventh earl of Huntingdon, HA 13083–13151

Likenesses oils (of Watson?), St John Cam.

Wealth at death approx. £20,000: *State Trials*, 14.471

Watson, Thomas (*d.* **1744**), naval officer, may have served as a midshipman with Edward Vernon, though it is also possible that he entered the navy from the merchant service. In any event he became first lieutenant of the *Antelope* in 1733, and rose to become her captain on 7 October 1737.

On 10 July 1739 Watson was appointed to the *Burford* as Vernon's flag-captain, and he acted in that capacity at the reduction of Porto Bello. He moved with Vernon to the *Princess Caroline* in January 1741, was flag-captain during the abortive attack on Cartagena, and in June 1741 moved again with Vernon to the *Boyne*, in which he returned to England in December 1742. In September 1743 he was appointed to the *Northumberland* (70 guns), which in the following spring was one of the fleet sent to Lisbon under the command of Sir Charles Hardy the elder. On the homeward voyage at daybreak on 8 May the *Northumberland*, looking out ahead, was ordered by signal to chase a strange sail seen to the northward. She did not come up with it, and did not obey her recall, which was made about two o'clock. The weather deteriorated and she lost sight of the fleet, then of the chase; but about four o'clock she sighted three ships to the leeward, the wind being westerly. The *Northumberland* ran down towards these strangers. They lay-to to wait for her; it was seen that they were French, two of 64 guns and the third a frigate of 26 guns. One of the 64-gun ships, the *Content*, was about a mile to windward of her consort, the *Mars*. Had Watson engaged her, he might possibly have disabled her before the *Mars* could come to her support. It was probably Watson's best option, if he refused to accept the advice offered by the master and endeavour to lead the Frenchmen back to Hardy's fleet.

But Watson was in no mood to follow advice which smacked of caution. It was said that his skull had been fractured in a fall, 'and a small matter of liquor rendered him quite out of order—which was his unhappy fate that day' (*A True and Authentick Narrative of the Action between the Northumberland and Three French Men of War*, 7). According to the anonymous author of the account,

> We bore down on them so precipitately that our small sails were not stowed nor top-gallant sails furled before the enemy began to fire on us, and at the same time had the cabins to clear away; the hammocks were not stowed as they should be; in short, we had nothing in order as we should before action. (ibid., 3)

About five o'clock the *Northumberland* closed with the *Content* and received her fire, but, without replying to it, ran down to the *Mars*. The *Content* followed, as did the frigate. The *Northumberland* was a target for the three of them. The men at the wheel were killed, and nobody thought of sending others to take their place. Watson was wounded, and before the first lieutenant could get on deck, the master struck the colours, and the ship was captured. Watson died in France on 4 June 1744. By his will, dated 8 May 1744—the day of the *Northumberland*'s fateful battle—Watson left all his possessions to his uncle Captain John Roberts, of Reading, who himself died early in the following year. The master, tried by court martial on 1 February 1745, was sentenced to imprisonment in the Marshalsea for life; he was spared capital punishment on the ground that he had given good advice to his captain before the action. J. K. LAUGHTON, *rev.* J. D. DAVIES

Sources *A true and authentick narrative of the action between the Northumberland and three French men of war. By an eye-witness* (1745) · PRO, ADM MSS 1/5284, fols. 263–87; 6/424; 107/1–3; 33/277; 33/300; 7/77 · PRO, PROB 11/735, fols. 50–51 [Watson's will] · PRO, PROB 11/739, fols. 181–2 [will of Captain John Roberts] · J. Charnock, ed., *Biographia navalis*, 4 (1796), 370 · *GM*, 1st ser., 15 (1745), 106

Archives PRO, ADM MSS

Wealth at death see will, PRO, PROB 11/735, fols. 50–51

Watson, Thomas (1750–1781), engraver, was born in London, the son of Thomas Watson (*d.* 1791), printseller, and his wife, Esther. Nothing is known of his training but he rapidly matured as a fine engraver in mezzotint and in stipple. He exhibited with the Society of Artists between 1773 and 1776, showing a series of fine mezzotints. Most of his early prints were published by himself (or more probably by his father) from Broad Street, London, in alliance with the book and printsellers Samuel Hooper and Walter Shropshire. He took Francis Haward apprentice in 1774 for a £75 premium. He engraved portraits and fancy subjects with equal dexterity and interpreted a number of artists, notably Sir Joshua Reynolds and Daniel Gardner. In January 1779 Watson and Shropshire published a fine set of six 'Windsor Beauties', portraits of ladies of the court of Charles II after paintings by Sir Peter Lely now at Hampton Court. About that time Watson went into partnership with William Dickinson, a fellow engraver in stipple and mezzotint and another favourite engraver of Reynolds.

Thomas Watson senior and Dickinson insured the contents of a brick dwelling at 158 New Bond Street on 2 February 1779, with over £2000 cover allowed for the joint stock of prints. From then until 1781 Watson junior engraved or supervised the making of some twenty-eight plates that went under his own name and contributed to the establishment of a thriving business. Early in the summer of 1781 Thomas Watson junior died suddenly at Westminster, and he was buried probably at St George's, Hanover Square. The insurance policies show that his father moved from Bond Street to Carnaby Street in 1781 and the next year to 33 Strand. He continued to sell his son's prints and, apparently, to support Dickinson, who managed the Bond Street business until the elder Watson's death in 1791. A sale of 'Mr Watson's plates and prints' took place in January 1792.

TIMOTHY CLAYTON and ANITA MCCONNELL

Sources G. Goodwin, *Thomas Watson, James Watson, Elizabeth Judkins* (1904) · Royal Exchange fire insurance policies, GL, MS 7253, nos. 74949, 81798, 83341, 83342

Watson, Sir Thomas, first baronet (1792–1882), physician, eldest son of Joseph Watson (*d.* 1813) of Thorpe-le-Soken, Essex, and his wife, Mary, daughter of Thomas Catton, was born at Montrath House, Broadhembury, Cullompton, Devon, on 7 March 1792. He was educated at the grammar school, Bury St Edmunds, Suffolk, where Charles James Blomfield, afterwards bishop of London, was his contemporary; they continued friends throughout life. Watson entered St John's College, Cambridge, in 1811, and graduated BA as tenth wrangler in 1815. He was elected a fellow in 1816, retiring in 1826, and in 1818 graduated MA. He studied medicine at St Bartholomew's Hospital under John Abernethy in 1819. After spending the session of 1820–21 at Edinburgh, he returned to Cambridge, obtained the university licence in medicine in 1822, was junior proctor in 1823–4, and graduated MD in 1825.

On 15 September 1825 he married Sarah (*d.* 1830), daughter of Edward Jones of Brackley, Northamptonshire, and took a house in Henrietta Street, London, establishing a practice in a nearby house. He was elected a fellow of the Royal College of Physicians in 1826, and in May 1827 physician to the Middlesex Hospital, which was then connected with London University. He was professor of clinical medicine, and lectured from 1828 to 1831. In 1831 he became lecturer on forensic medicine at King's College, London, and in 1835 professor of forensic medicine, an office which he held until 1840. He continued to be physician to the Middlesex Hospital until 1843. In that year he published his famous *Lectures on the Principles and Practice of Physic* (2 vols.), which had first been printed week by week in the *Medical Times and Gazette* between 1840 and 1842. It was for thirty years the chief English textbook of medicine; based upon sound clinical observations, it gave a complete view of English medicine of its period, and was remarkable for its good literary style.

At the Royal College of Physicians Watson gave the Goulstonian lectures in 1827, the Lumleian lectures on haemorrhage in 1831, and was a censor in 1828, 1837, and 1838. In 1862 he was elected president, and was re-elected for five successive years. He was elected FRS in 1859, and in 1864 was made an honorary LLD at Cambridge. In 1857 he became president of the Pathological Society, and in 1868 of the Clinical Society. Watson's practice as a physician was large, and in 1859 he was appointed physician-extraordinary to the queen, and in 1870 physician-in-ordinary. He was one of the physicians who attended Albert, prince consort, in his last illness. He was created a baronet on 27 June 1866. He retired from practice soon after 1870. At the last meeting he attended at the Royal College of Physicians in March 1882 all the fellows present rose when he entered the room, a rare mark of respect, and the highest honour which the college can bestow on one of its fellows who has ceased to hold office.

Watson died on 11 December 1882 at Reigate Lodge, Reigate, Surrey, the house of his son, Sir Arthur Townley Watson QC (1830–1907). A daughter, Margaret Catherine Watson, also survived him. Watson died 'full of years and honours … and, withal, he was modest and unassuming, as becomes a truly great and wise man' (*The Lancet*, 1040). He was buried at Reigate on 16 December.

NORMAN MOORE, *rev.* ANITA MCCONNELL

Sources *The Times* (13 Dec 1882), 6f • *The Times* (15 Dec 1882), 7f • *The Times* (16 Dec 1882), 7e • *The Lancet* (16 Dec 1882), 1040 • Venn, *Alum. Cant.* • *BMJ* (23 Dec 1882), 1282–5 • *CGPLA Eng. & Wales* (1883) **Archives** Wellcome L., casebook **Likenesses** H. Weeks, bust, 1839, Sheffield Royal Infirmary • G. Richmond, oils, RCP Lond. **Wealth at death** £164,407 2s. 7d.: probate, 15 Feb 1883, *CGPLA Eng. & Wales*

Watson, Walter (1780–1854), poet, was born at Chryston, in the parish of Calder, Lanarkshire, on 29 March 1780, one of the three sons and four daughters of William Watson, hand-loom weaver. At the age of eight he became a herd, and attended the village school during winter. From eleven he worked as a weaver, and after a couple of years worked as a farmhand at home and as a sawyer in Glasgow. He enlisted in the Scots Greys in May 1799 but saw nothing more serious than drills and parades. He was discharged at the peace of Amiens, 1802. In March 1803 he married Margaret, daughter of Alexander Wilson of Hill Farm, near Chryston. They were to have eight sons and two daughters; however, only four children survived Watson.

From 1803 to 1820 Watson worked as a weaver in Chryston. He began writing poetry but was reprimanded by the village teacher for his lack of grammar. In 1808 he published a small volume of his poems. This was a troubled period in the weaving industry and Watson was periodically obliged to find employment as sawyer, stonecutter, and printer as the family moved around Stirlingshire, Lanarkshire, and Dunbartonshire. Another volume of poems was published in 1823 and yet another in 1843. In 1849 he settled at Duntiblae, near Kirkintilloch, Dunbartonshire, where he worked as a weaver. His *Poems and Songs, Chiefly in the Scottish Dialect* was published in 1853. He died on 12 September 1854 at Duntiblae and was buried in Calder churchyard where a granite monument was erected in 1875.

T. W. BAYNE, *rev.* SAYONI BASU

Sources H. Macdonald, 'Memoir', in W. Watson, *Poems and songs, chiefly in the Scottish dialect* (1853) • C. Rogers, *The modern Scottish minstrel, or, The songs of Scotland of the past half-century*, 2 (1856) • J. G. Wilson, ed., *The poets and poetry of Scotland*, 2 vols. (1876–7) **Likenesses** A. D. Robertson, chalk drawing, 1849, Scot. NPG

Watson, William (1559?–1603), Roman Catholic priest and conspirator, was born, by his own calculation, on 23 April 1559. Apart from the fact that he hailed from co. Durham nothing is known of his family. According to his never entirely trustworthy autobiographical note, apparently written for Sir Edward Coke while Watson was a prisoner in the Gatehouse in April 1599, he was 'brought up in learning', and 'sent to Oxforde at 10 years of age', but his name does not appear among the surviving records. By his own account he cannot be the 'William Watson of Durham' who matriculated aged twenty-six from All Souls on 28 November 1581, and who graduated BA the following February. According to the hostile testimony of Robert Persons, Watson attended the university merely as servant to John Boste. There can be no doubt, however, that he was well read. In his own words Watson's studies up to the age of eighteen 'were in the 7 liberall sciences intermixte withe the tongues, phisicke, common lawe & especially histories all my life time for recreacon', while in the following three years he absorbed 'the lawes canon & civil withe positive divinitie & perfecting of my metaphisicke and philosophie' (Law, 1.212–13).

Independent sources record that Watson was confirmed at Rheims on 25 March 1581, and that he received minor orders on 23 September 1583, and was ordained deacon on 22 March and priest at Laon on 5 April 1586. He was sent into England on 16 June in the same year, 'broughte of the sea in mariners apparell' (Law, 1.211–12). Like so many of his colleagues on the English mission Watson was soon arrested. He was in the Marshalsea by October 1586. By his own account he was released on the understanding that he would leave the realm, was rearrested before the time allowed expired, and was subsequently ill treated by Richard Topcliffe in the Bridewell prison: 'all the plagues & torments of that place', he writes, were 'inflicted upon me (whereof fewe I think were lefte oute, & some I dare say unknowen to her majestie or councell that ever I suffered, as whipping, grinding in the milne, withe the like)' (ibid.; PRO, SP 12/202/61). Watson, however, managed to escape, in March 1588, thanks to the good offices of Margaret Ward, who smuggled a rope to him past lax security. Ward was put to death for this offence later in the year.

Again relying on Watson's own account he spent the next couple of years at Liège, returning to England in the autumn of 1590. One spy report suggests that he visited Ireland with Simon Fennel in 1593. There followed further imprisonments in Bridewell and the Gatehouse, and further escapes, first on 18 May 1597, and then on 24 June 1599. It was during the latter incarceration that he wrote his autobiographical memoir. This long-winded self-justification includes an interesting summary of the contents of his library:

> lawe bookes Machiavels werkes, tragedies, cronicles, coleccions of Doleman, Philopater, Leycesters

commonwealthe (all 3 one man as is said) the bishop of Londons Genevian platforme, the discovery of the originall cause & begining of our dislike of the Jesuites & their procedings: and many other notes colleccions & breifes of prophecies, genealogies, discents of hunting, hawking & the like. (Law, 1.213)

Once again Watson was arrested. He was in Wisbech Castle in 1600 and was later moved to the Clink, but upon being surprised when about to say mass for forty poor Catholics he was transferred to the much stricter confines of the King's Bench prison in April 1602. He was, though, soon released. Watson had, by then, emerged as one of the most vociferous of the so-called appellant Catholic priests, a grouping of those opposed to the introduction of an archpriest to administer the English church. While at Wisbech in November 1600 he signed the appeal made by the secular priests against Blackwell's appointment, and about this time he set out thirty reasons why he and his colleagues could not 'in conscience, policie, nor equitie admitt of Mr Blackwell archepresbiterie' (Law, 90–98). The secular priests all shared a distrust of the Jesuits, who enthusiastically supported government by archpriest; but Watson's hatred and, indeed, fear of the society, sharpened by worries that the Jesuits favoured a Habsburg over a Stuart succession after Elizabeth I's death, verged on paranoia. His single solo published contribution to the archpriest controversy, the so-called *Quodlibets, or, Decacordon of Ten Quodlibeticall Questions Concerning Religion and State* (1602), is characterized by the extremity of its opinions and the eccentric intemperance with which these are expressed. The *Decacordon*, and other works in a similar vein, were countered by Robert Persons in his *A Manifestation of the Great Folly*, also published in 1602. Persons set on record his contempt for Watson, heaping personal abuse upon his opponent. He recalled that Watson had come to Rheims 'a poor little begging boy', had made his way through taking on menial tasks, and had entertained fellow students by tumbling and other demeaning tricks, 'for which his body was fitly made' (fols. 83–4). So the unedifying debate rumbled on.

Elizabeth's government was prepared to be lenient towards the secular priests, realizing that in so doing they helped divide English Catholics and isolate the extremists bent on foreign intervention to reinstate the old religion. Following negotiations with Richard Bancroft, bishop of London, Watson and other seculars took an oath of allegiance in November 1602, specially fashioned to draw moderate Catholics apart from the intransigent recusant community. Those taking the oath were subsequently set at liberty. These contacts seem to have turned Watson's head, sharpening at the same time a taste for diplomacy and negotiation. Determined to forestall supposed Jesuit plots in favour of a Spanish successor to Elizabeth, he travelled to Edinburgh in the months prior to the queen's death. There, in return for pledging his loyalty to the Stuart cause, he received from James VI and his ministers vague but encouraging assurances of future toleration for Catholics in England. Such assurances were readily given—to the earl of Northumberland and to the future gunpowder plotter Thomas Percy, among others—but Watson, characteristically, built up this predictable molehill of platitudes into a mountain of promises guaranteeing an improvement in the lot of Catholic Englishmen. Like Thomas Percy he undoubtedly felt betrayed when no immediate toleration was forthcoming after March 1603. This consideration, combined with fears based on little evidence that the Jesuits were planning some form of coup before James's coronation, prompted Watson to participate in an enterprise which would oblige the new king to honour his supposed obligations.

The so-called Bye plot which followed proved a ludicrous fiasco. The principal conspirators hoped to recruit a band of Catholic gentlemen who would surprise the court at Greenwich on midsummer night in 1603, kidnap the king, seize the Tower of London, and hold James there as a hostage for toleration of Catholic religion—to be guaranteed by secure strongholds and important prisoners—and the removal from office and incarceration of ministers identified with the old, repressive, Elizabethan ways. Officially, no blood was to have been shed, but even the optimistic Watson accepted that Robert Cecil and other leading privy councillors might be prosecuted on the highest charges. When Watson and his chief confederate, the Catholic gentleman Sir Griffin Markham, discussed these matters Sir Griffin 'answered that, for his part, he carried no bloody mind; but he feared, when it came to it, they should be constrained, for safety of their own lives, to take away some of theirs' (Tierney, 4, appx, xli).

Markham's and Watson's colleagues—another secular priest named William Clark, George Brooke (the discontented protestant younger brother of Henry Brooke, Lord Cobham), and the Catholic gentleman poet Anthony Copley—eagerly discussed all the changes that they would like to see. Watson himself earmarked the office of lord chancellor, albeit ostensibly on a caretaker basis. Still more absurd, he undertook to convert James to Catholicism by working upon the king's known inclination for theological debate. Here, as elsewhere in this conspiracy, optimistic expectation far outran good sense. Copley confessed that on another occasion he, Watson, and another fellow conspirator, Nicholas Kendall, discussed the project over a meal. 'What our discourse was', he declared, 'and how vain and variable all that supper time, I blush to remember: being wholly of tumult, without head or foot' (Tierney, 4, appx, iv). The principal plotters failed entirely to secure any show of support from their supposed backers. While Watson talked airily of supporters numbered in the thousands, he and his colleagues never seem to have discussed their plans with more than fifty or so possible recruits. Brooke and Markham tried to enlist support from the protestant peer Lord Grey of Wilton—an experienced military commander thoroughly disenchanted with the new regime and, in particular, with the favour shown his enemy the earl of Southampton. But Grey, flatly opposed to Catholic toleration, distrusted Watson and Markham just as, when the test was made, they distrusted him. Midsummer day came and went. Watson lost heart and fled into the west country. Their hopes now dashed, the plotters who remained in London busily engaged in a round of recriminations.

Then their world began to fall apart. Copley was betrayed to Bancroft by the archpriest, George Blackwell, and by Henry Garnett, the Jesuit superior. Upon interrogation the unfortunate prisoner disclosed everything, or, at least, everything he knew. There were limits to Copley's knowledge, for he had been recruited by Watson and Markham at a fairly late stage. But it is Copley who, recalling Watson's discourses, puts the famous words into King James's mouth: 'Na Na, gud fayth, wee's not need the papists now!' (PRO, SP 14/2/51). A proclamation was issued for the arrest of the fugitive conspirators, Watson being described as 'a man of the lowest sort', about the age of thirty-six, 'his hair betwixt abram and flaxen, he looketh asquint, and is very purblind' (*Stuart Royal Proclamations*, 1.43).

Watson remained at large until early in August. According to John Aubrey he was captured 'in a field by the Hay in Herefordshire (or Brecknockshire)' by the magistrate Henry Vaughan. Aubrey, inevitably, could not resist an old tale in which the captor suffered alongside his quarry: ''Twas observed', he wrote, 'that Mr Vaughan did never prosper afterwards' (*Brief Lives*, 161). Watson was imprisoned in the Tower on 10 August 1603. In a series of highly detailed confessions, readily given, he provided the council with a colourful picture of his treason, professing penitence and regret for his actions. Unfortunately he added further insinuations that the king had gone back on promises to the English Catholics. At his trial at Winchester on 15 November he pleaded not guilty and persisted in this fatal line. Equally futile was his argument that a king uncrowned did not exercise full royal authority, and that in the interim between accession and coronation men might seek redress for particular grievances. Naturally, no observer had a good word to write about his stubbornness. We are told that Watson's 'absurd' speeches, 'without grace, or utterance, or good deliverance', left spectators embarrassed and contemptuous rather than sympathetic (*State trials*, 2.61–5).

Sentenced to death, Watson and Clark were hanged, drawn, and quartered in the market place at Winchester on 29 November. Brooke was beheaded within a week, but both Copley and Markham were reprieved. Watson died well, asking forgiveness of the king, the Jesuits, and any others whom he might have offended. The executions were clumsily handled, Clark in particular being cut down from the gallows when still conscious. Robert Hobart, without advancing any evidence to support his theory, argued that the sentences were carried out on his own initiative by the lord chief justice, Sir John Popham, a fierce opponent of priests who is supposed to have feared that both men might be pardoned. It is, however, extremely unlikely that either priest would have been spared.

MARK NICHOLLS

Sources PRO, SP 12/202/61; SP 12/208/102; SP 14/2/51; SP 14/3/16; SP 14/3/18; SP 14/3/28 · Hatfield House, Salisbury (Cecil) MSS, MSS 51/6; 71/13 · Bodl. Oxf., MS Carte 80 · Inner Temple Library, London, Petyt MSS · T. G. Law, ed., *The archpriest controversy: documents relating to the dissensions of the Roman Catholic clergy, 1597–1602*, 2 vols., CS, new ser., 56, 58 (1896–8) · G. Anstruther, *The seminary priests*, 1 (1969), 372–4 · M. Nicholls, 'Treason's reward: the punishment of conspirators in the Bye plot of 1603', *HJ*, 38 (1995), 821–42 · M. Nicholls, 'Two Winchester trials: the prosecution of Henry, Lord Cobham, and Thomas, Lord Grey of Wilton, 1603', *Historical Research*, 68 (1995), 26–48 · *State trials*, 2.61–5 · T. F. Knox and others, eds., *The first and second diaries of the English College, Douay* (1878) · A. F. Allison and D. M. Rogers, eds., *The contemporary printed literature of the English Counter-Reformation between 1558 and 1640*, 2 vols. (1989–94) · P. Milward, *Religious controversies of the Elizabethan age* (1977) · *Dodd's Church history of England*, ed. M. A. Tierney, 5 vols. (1839–43) · *John Aubrey: 'Brief lives' and other selected writings*, ed. A. Powell (1949)

Watson, Sir William (1715–1787), physician and natural philosopher, was born in St John's Street, Smithfield, London, on 3 April 1715, the son of William Watson, a corn chandler. He entered the Merchant Taylors' School in 1726 and on 6 April 1731 was apprenticed to an apothecary, Thomas Richardson. A keen student of pharmacy and botany during the eight years of his apprenticeship, Watson won a prize that included a copy of John Ray's *Synopsis methodica stirpium Britannicarum*, awarded annually by the Society of Apothecaries for identifying plants during country excursions from the Chelsea Physic Garden. During the summer of 1738 Watson married, purchased his freedom from the society ten months before completing his apprenticeship, and set up as an apothecary in Aldersgate, London.

Watson began attending the Royal Society in March 1738, first as a guest of the Cambridge botany professor John Martyn, then under the patronage of the president, Hans Sloane. Watson was elected a fellow on 9 April 1741 and regularly joined both the society's public meetings and its private club, founded in 1743, at The Mitre in Fleet Street, and later at the Crown and Anchor in the Strand. He sat on many of the society's committees, and after 1772 served as its vice-president. He also belonged to the Monday Club, which met at the George and Vulture Coffee House, Cornhill, from at least the 1760s; and he was an ally both of the whig magnate Philip Yorke, Lord Hardwicke, for whom he acted as physician, and of John Pringle, the society's president in the 1770s. He was a sociable and energetic member of London's learned world, hardworking, an early riser, and endowed with a remarkable memory. His initial publications concerned the means and importance of correct plant identification. In December 1744 he wrote on the previously undescribed star puffball, attracting interest from European botanists. He produced several accounts of accidental poisoning by hemlock and henbane, and in 1754 argued for the polygamous character of holly. Much of his work as a naturalist involved reviews of foreign studies, such as a 1742 paper on Albrecht von Haller's list of Swiss plants and a paper of May 1752 on the hitherto neglected French report that corals were animal, not vegetable. In the spring of 1748 Per Kalm, a pupil of the great Swedish naturalist Linnaeus, stayed with Watson before a botanical survey in America. The history and the reform of English botany were among Watson's concerns. In 1749 he re-examined

Sir William Watson (1715-1787), by Lemuel Francis Abbott

the ruins of the Tradescants' garden at Lambeth, and in 1752 accompanied the Swiss naturalist Abraham Trembley to investigate the vegetable origin of coal deposits in Sussex. The first English account of Linnaeus's *Species plantarum* (1753) was a laudatory and detailed review Watson published, with Linnaeus's approval, at the end of 1754 in the *Gentleman's Magazine*. When the British Museum was founded in 1756 Watson, named a trustee by Sloane, arranged its gardens at Montague House. Unimpressed by the staffing arrangements, Watson strongly backed the appointment of specialist naturalists to maintain the museum's natural history collections. In 1760 he made a pilgrimage to the Essex house and grave of John Ray, whom he viewed as English natural history's patriarch. Richard Pulteney, chief English campaigner for Linnaean taxonomy, and Watson's eulogist, judged Watson himself 'the living lexicon of botany' (Pulteney, 337).

From late 1744 Watson initiated experimental work on electricity, based first on reports from the Leipzig professor Johann Winkler that warm alcohol in a spoon could be ignited by an electric spark. As yet unfamiliar with electrical lore, the apothecary Watson saw chemical significance in the effect. In March and April 1745 he reported that many volatile liquids could also be fired electrically, and distinguished between firing into an earthed spoon and what he called 'repulsive' firing when the spark was passed over the surface of an electrified one. During 1745 Watson developed his electrical expertise, showing the weakening of successive electrical shocks between insulated experimenters and the varying behaviours of glass, metal, and cork when held by an electrified man standing on an insulating wax cake. These trials, which took place

with the assistance of the society's new president, Martin Folkes, were witnessed by the prince of Wales and the duke of Cumberland. On Sloane's nomination the trials won Watson the Royal Society's Copley medal in 1745 and were described in a pamphlet first published that year, *Experiments and Observations Tending to Illustrate the Nature and Properties of Electricity*, which in a new version had four reprints during 1746.

In February 1746 Watson matched this success with experiments linking electrical effluvia with the active fire described by the Dutch medical chemist Hermann Boerhaave. Watson considered electricity a particulate, elastic, and subtle fluid which moved objects by impact and would naturally seek to restore any temporary imbalance in its distribution. It flowed in straight lines away from a rubbed tube, was refracted through conductors, but must reach a certain strength as it soaked into a conductor before then being able to penetrate glass. He showed that sparks could be drawn from a metal conductor attached to a frictional electrical machine only if the operator of the machine, or else the conductor itself, were grounded. During the rest of 1746 he established that such machines would work better if their operators were not insulated but earthed, and reckoned these devices should be understood as pumps, drawing the fluid up from the ground. Watson's theory of pumping, which he compared with the prestigious fluid theory of the French natural philosopher Jean Nollet, became significant when in early 1746 the Royal Society learned of the invention of the Leyden jar, a glass bottle which gave huge shocks if a grounded experimenter simultaneously touched its outer surface and a metal conductor linked to the inside surface of the bottle. On the suggestion of the London physician John Bevis, Watson increased the jar's effect by covering both sides of the glass with lead and making the glass thin. He designed tricks to convey the jar's shock unawares to his victims, then argued at the society in late October 1746 that his fluid theory perfectly explained its effects. The electric fire flowed out from the experimenter's body to the jar and to the conductor, and was resupplied to the experimenter from the ground. Watson's work was again released as a pamphlet before the end of the year.

Early in 1747 Watson revised this initial electrical theory. Bevis reported that if an insulated man touched a rotating globe worked by an insulated operator, both became electrified though cut off from the ground. Watson explained the phenomenon as a redistribution of electrical fluid across zones of different fluid density, preserving aspects of his model of equilibrium and pumping. Later in 1747, in collaboration with Folkes, Bevis, James Bradley, and Charles Cavendish, Watson spent several weeks trying to measure electricity's speed by laying a wire from a Leyden jar across Westminster Bridge, then passing the fluid back through the Thames and their own bodies. Similar trials were conducted at Highbury and Shooter's Hill. They judged the fluid's speed was too fast to measure. Just as he acted as reviewer of natural history, so Watson made himself the expositor of electrical doctrines of colleagues such as the clockmaker John Ellicott and the painter Benjamin Wilson, who also designed competing theories of the electrical fluid. Charles Cavendish forwarded to Watson a letter from Benjamin Franklin, written in June 1747 in Philadelphia, which also proffered a theory of the jar's action. On 21 January 1748 Watson read to the society extracts from Franklin's letter and claimed that his own density theory and Franklin's apparently novel doctrine of electrical atmospheres and positive and negative charges were to all intents identical. Watson's role as the Royal Society's reviewer, in such fields as thermometry, industry, or chemistry, also brought him news about electricity. In 1749 he criticized claims by Venetian experimenters and Winkler that medically active fluids could allegedly be transmitted from the interior of sealed electrified glass tubes, and he revealed the recipe for various German tricks involving the electrical discharge from metal hidden beneath a performer's clothes. In 1752 he reported on trials done with Charles Cavendish of electric discharge in vacua, which he compared with the phenomena of the northern lights. Cavendish provided Watson with a remarkable mercurial tube which made a vacuum and electrical flow simultaneously. When the Quaker physician John Fothergill, a friend of Watson, arranged the publication of Franklin's letters on electricity in 1751, Watson reviewed them for the Royal Society rather favourably, though he denied that the electrification of the jar took place entirely within the glass; in 1752 he failed to draw electricity during a thunderstorm. By the later 1750s Watson had become an ally of Franklin in natural philosophy and in politics. They both joined the reformist Society of Honest Whigs; in December 1762 Watson petitioned the first lord of the Admiralty, Lord Anson, for the installation of Franklin's designs for lightning rods at Purfleet arsenal, and published a pamphlet on the rods in 1764. In 1772 Watson joined Franklin on a Royal Society committee which decisively recommended such a strategy for the defence of Purfleet.

Watson's pharmaceutical skills and interest in aerial activity helped to prompt his subsequent medical work. As early as 1742 he published in the *Philosophical Transactions* on ways of extracting foul air from ships, and from the 1750s set out to establish himself in medical practice. He wrote on public welfare, including advice in 1757 on preventing the freezing of lead water pipes by means of pairs of taps rather than by covering the pipes with horse manure. On 6 September 1757 Watson was created a doctor of physic at Halle, and may also have got similar degrees from Wittenberg and Edinburgh. At the end of that year he was disfranchised from the Apothecaries' Society for a fee of £50. Watson had employed several apprentice apothecaries, including William Jordan (from 1740) and Rudolph Hobbes (from 1745): one of them, Timothy Lane, took over Watson's apothecary's business and continued his electrical studies into the 1760s. Watson was eventually admitted a licentiate of the Royal College of Physicians on 22 December 1759.

After moving to Lincoln's Inn Fields, Watson became physician for the Foundling Hospital, a central institution of whig philanthropy, in October 1762. He published in the *Philosophical Transactions* on the influenza and dysentery epidemics of that year and in 1763 used his electrical expertise to describe cures of muscular rigidity in tetanus by the application of shocks. In 1768 Watson published an influential pamphlet on smallpox inoculation, arguing on the basis of his major work at the Foundling Hospital against treating children less than three years old, and recommending abstinence from meat and heating liquors. After violent attacks by licentiates on the Royal College establishment in 1767–8, Watson joined the Society of Collegiate Physicians' campaign, backed by allies such as Fothergill and William Heberden, to force the college to admit fellows from outside the English universities. Watson contributed papers on putrid measles to Fothergill's reformist *Medical Observations*, and in 1771 Heberden tried unsuccessfully to get both Fothergill and Watson elected fellows of the Royal College, a status Watson gained only on 30 September 1784. He was made censor in 1785–6 and was knighted on 6 October 1786. Many of Watson's circle, such as the Cavendish clan, Heberden, and Pringle, shared his engagement in enlightened reform and some of his sympathy for dissent. In his last years Watson rose to a central place in the genteel world of metropolitan philosophical society. He died at Lincoln's Inn Fields on 10 May 1787, leaving a son, and a daughter who was married to Edward Beadon, rector of North Stoneham, Hampshire, brother of Richard Beadon (1737–1824), bishop of Bath and Wells.

Watson's son, **Sir William Watson** (1744–1824), was, like his father, a physician and naturalist. He was born in London in early September 1744 and educated at Charterhouse before entering Queens' College, Cambridge, as pensioner on 17 February 1761, whence he migrated to Gonville and Caius College on 26 April 1762. Watson obtained his MB in 1766 and was elected fellow of the Royal Society on 10 December 1767. A resident of Bedford Square in London, he graduated MD in 1771, then practised medicine in Bath. About 1772 Watson married Christiana Freame, *née* Barclay (*c*.1739–1796); she was the mother of Priscilla Hannah *Gurney. In 1778 he published on the blue shark in the *Philosophical Transactions*, and maintained considerable interest in botany and mineralogy. In December 1779 he joined the new Bath Philosophical Society, and was instrumental in introducing William Herschel, then a Bath musician, to the society's membership. Watson became Herschel's close friend and correspondent. They discussed problems in natural history and astronomy and collaborated on measures of the heights of the hills round Bath, the results being published in 1810 in Joseph Wilson's *History of Mountains*. Watson supplied Herschel with a valuable nebular catalogue in late 1781, successfully lobbied for Herschel's royal pension in 1782, produced important drawings of Herschel's 7 foot telescope in 1783, and in 1784 advised on the proper depiction of Uranus on Josiah Wedgwood's portrait medallion of Herschel. In January 1785 Watson suggested to Herschel that the regular distribution of stars in space might resemble the patterns of mutually repulsive particles of powdered resin on the surface of an electrically charged wax and tur-pentine cake. The same year Watson published *A Treatise on Time*, a philosophical essay dedicated to Herschel and heavily indebted to Joseph Priestley, another member of the Bath Society. Watson was linked by marriage with some members of the Lunar Society of Birmingham, including Samuel Galton. He was knighted on 6 March 1796, joined a revived Philosophical Society in Bath in 1799, and became the city's mayor in 1801. Watson died in Bath on 15 November 1824. SIMON SCHAFFER

William Watson, Baron Watson (1827–1899), by John Singer Sargent, 1897

Sources R. Pulteney, *Historical and biographical sketches of the progress of botany in England*, 2 (1790), 295–340 · J. L. Heilbron, *Electricity in the 17th and 18th centuries: a study of early modern physics* (1979) · Venn, *Alum. Cant.* · A. J. Turner and others, *Science and music in eighteenth-century Bath* (1977) [exhibition catalogue, the Holburne of Menstrie Museum, Bath, 22 Sept – 29 Dec 1977] · R. H. Fox, *Dr John Fothergill and his friends* (1919) · P. J. Wallis and R. V. Wallis, *Eighteenth century medics*, 2nd edn (1988), 633 · *GM*, 1st ser., 57 (1787), 454
Archives RAS · RS | BL, letters to second Lord Hardwicke · Linn. Soc., corresp. with Richard Pulteney
Likenesses J. Thornwaite, line engraving, 1784 (after L. F. Abbott), Wellcome L. · L. F. Abbott, oils, RS [*see illus.*]

Watson, Sir William (1744–1824). *See under* Watson, Sir William (1715–1787).

Watson, William, Baron Watson (1827–1899), judge, the elder son and second of the six children of Thomas Watson (1794–1864), minister of the Church of Scotland, and his wife, Eleonora (*d.* 1887), daughter of David McHaffie of Eastwood and Overton, was born on 25 August 1827, at the manse, Covington, Lanarkshire. His parents were both Scottish and, like them, he became a member of the Church of Scotland. He was educated at the universities of Glasgow (1842–3) and Edinburgh (1843–7). Both later conferred on him the degree of LLD, the latter in 1875 and the former in 1879. He was admitted advocate on 8 March 1851, but had almost no practice until the 1860s. On 6 August 1868, then residing at 6 St Colme Street, Edinburgh, Watson married Margaret Bannatyne (1846–3 March 1898), youngest daughter of Dugald John Bannatyne (1805–1863), writer and solicitor, and his wife, Janet Bogle. They set up house in Dublin Street. Before moving to London on his promotion in 1880, they were living at 34 Moray Place. They had seven children—six sons and one daughter. Their second son predeceased them in 1891. All their surviving sons became lawyers. The second and most distinguished of these, William *Watson, became a lord of appeal in ordinary, in 1929, as Lord Thankerton of Thankerton.

In July 1865 Watson appeared for the defence in the *cause célèbre* of Dr Edward Pritchard, the poisoner. Thereafter his practice grew steadily. In July 1874, when he was well established, Disraeli rewarded his Conservatism, then exceptional at the Scottish bar, with the office of solicitor-general for Scotland. On 6 November 1875 he was elected dean of the Faculty of Advocates. In 1876 he succeeded Edward Strathearn Gordon as lord advocate and as member of parliament for the universities of Glasgow and Aberdeen. On 26 March 1878 he was sworn of the privy council, and on 2 April he was placed on the committee of

the council for education in Scotland. In 1879 as lord advocate he successfully conducted the prosecution of the fraudulent directors of the City of Glasgow Bank, and he appeared in several civil actions which followed the bank's failure. On 28 April 1880 he was appointed a lord of appeal in ordinary, in place of Lord Gordon, who had died in August 1879. He was created a life peer by the title of Baron Watson of Thankerton, Lanarkshire, taking his seat on 7 May 1880.

With his limited experience Watson might well have occupied himself mainly with Scottish cases but he was, it seems, determined to make his mark as neither of his Scottish predecessors, the lords Colonsay and Gordon, had done. Almost from the outset he grappled with the multifarious, intricate, and frequently recondite legal problems then facing the House of Lords and the privy council, which exercised a much wider territorial jurisdiction than subsequently. Watson's natural acumen and assiduity gave soundness and solidity to his decisions. In later life he was reputed the most profound lawyer in the three kingdoms, and his influence was commensurate. His familiarity with the civil law, which he owed to his Scottish training, stood him in good stead in dealing with appeals from civil law systems (see *Gera v. Ciantar*, 1887), but where such aid failed him, as in vexed questions of domicile (see *Le Mesurier v. Le Mesurier*, 1895) or French or Indian custom, his judgments were no less able. The part he took in determining the policy and practice of the privy council in Canadian appeals was of capital constitutional importance, and his mastery of English law, if less conspicuous, was hardly less consummate; the English bench and bar came to look on him as one of their own.

Watson's authority in Scots law was immense and he showed himself sedulous to preserve its purity where he saw no cause to follow English precedent (see *Royal Bank of Scotland* v. *Commercial Bank of Scotland*, 1882). Both on the bench and in the legislature, however, Watson was ready to work for its assimilation to English law where he thought it was justified. At times he carried this policy too far, as in *Mayor of Bradford* v. *Pickles* (1895), when he denied the existence in Scots law of an action in respect of malicious exercise of a right in order to prejudice a neighbour.

Watson was homely in appearance and unassuming in manner, though a merciless dissector of bad argument and famous for interrupting counsel in the course of argument in his anxiety to examine every aspect of the case before him. He never lost his broad Scottish accent or acquired niceties of English style. His judgments are distinguished by methodical arrangement rather than elegance. His 'Address on the repression of crime', delivered by him in 1877 before the National Association for the Promotion of Social Science, is printed in the association's *Transactions*. Watson was a keen sportsman—an angler, an excellent shot, and a curler—but was otherwise somewhat indolent. He would probably have been happier living a quiet country life than dispensing justice in the most august tribunals of the British empire.

In London Watson lived at 20 Queen's Gate, but he kept up a Scottish residence. At the time of his death it was Sunlaws House, Kelso, Roxburghshire, where he died on 14 September 1899 from an enlarged prostate and cystitis. His funeral took place in Edinburgh on 19 September 1899. J. M. RIGG, *rev.* W. M. GORDON

Sources E. Macnaghten and others, 'Lord Watson', *Juridical Review*, 11 (1899), 269–81 · 'Lord Watson', *Scottish Law Review*, 15 (1899), 229–43 · 'Notes from London', *Scottish Law Review*, 15 (1899), 254–7 · *The Times* (15 Sept 1899) · *The Scotsman* (15 Sept 1899) · *Scots Law Times: News* (14 Oct 1899), 83–4 · G. W. T. Omond, *The lord advocates of Scotland, second series, 1834–1880* (1914), 308–15 · *Annual Register* (1899), pt 2, p. 165 · 'Obiter dicta', *Law Journal* (16 Sept 1899), 483 · *Law Times* (23 Sept 1899), 449–50 · GEC, *Peerage* · Burke, *Peerage* · parish register (birth), Erskine · Scottish registers of marriage · Scottish registers of deaths · d. cert.

Archives U. Glas.

Likenesses J. S. Sargent, oils, 1897, Parliament House, Edinburgh [*see illus.*] · C. E. Fry & Son, photograph, repro. in 'Lord Watson', *Scottish Law Review*, facing p. 229 · photograph (after J. S. Sargent), repro. in *Scots Law Times: News*, 6 (1898), 109 · photograph, repro. in Macnaghten and others, 'Lord Watson', following p. 268

Wealth at death £116,436 14*s.* 3*d.*: confirmation, 1 Dec 1899, CCI

Watson, Sir (John) William (1858–1935), poet and literary critic, was born on 2 August 1858 at Peel Place, Burley in Wharfedale, Yorkshire, the youngest son of three sons of John Watson (*d.* 1887), master grocer, and his wife, Dorothy, *née* Robinson.

From a young age Watson, who grew up in Liverpool, showed an unusual susceptibility to literary and musical influences. His first volume, *The Prince's Quest and other Poems*, was published in April 1880. Possessed of an extraordinarily retentive memory, Watson laced his poems—as he did so much of his later verse—with echoes, motifs,

rhythms, and diction of his favoured Romantic and Victorian poets. Although Dante Gabriel Rossetti praised the title poem, reviews of Watson's first book were few and none shared Rossetti's enthusiasm.

The failure of his early poetry to attract attention brought about a new Watson, a poet who turned away from the highly subjective, Romantic verse of his early years and embraced, instead, a disciplined, more objective craft. Moreover, his subject matter in future would deal, primarily, with two themes: the decline of traditional modes and values in literature and the political and social shortcomings of his own times. *Epigrams of Art, Life, and Nature*, which appeared in January 1884, exhibited this major shift in direction.

Having disciplined himself by achieving perfection of form within the narrow compass of the epigram, Watson completed his transformation by turning outward to the sphere of politics in June 1885 when he published a series of sonnets, *Ver tenebrosum*, in the *National Review*. Following in the tradition of Milton and Wordsworth, Watson chose the sonnet as a means of upbraiding Britain for its unjust actions in the Sudan and for its weak, indecisive response to Russia's hostile moves in Afghanistan.

The full impact of Watson's reorientation is evident in his finest poem, 'Wordsworth's Grave', completed in 1887. This elegy serves as both a lament for the poetry of the past and an attack on the 'misbegotten strange new gods of song'—the young poets and artists of an aesthetic and / or decadent persuasion. It was his growing reputation as a defender against 'the tendency of English verse … all towards obscurities, affectations, eccentricities' (G. Allen, 'Note on a new poet', *Fortnightly Review*, Aug 1891) that placed Watson in strong contention for the poet laureateship after the death of Alfred Tennyson in 1892. His series of essays *Excursions in Criticism* (1893) further consolidated his artistic beliefs.

In 1895, with the arrest of Oscar Wilde on suspicion of sodomy, Watson led the fight to remove Aubrey Beardsley from the art editorship of the Bodley Head's new magazine, the *Yellow Book*. His power and influence now at its height, Watson published *The Father of the Forest and other Poems* in November.

Increasingly bedevilled by bouts of creative inactivity, Watson nevertheless managed to produce several books of poetry during the later 1890s: *The Purple East* (1896), *The Year of Shame* (1897), and *The Hope of the World* (1898), which included his most famous lyric, 'April, April'. His premier work of the new century appeared in 1902, the celebrated *Ode on the Day of the Coronation of King Edward VII*.

On 16 December 1904 John Lane published *The Poems of William Watson* in two volumes with an introduction by John Alfred Spender, the editor of the *Westminster Gazette*, in which Watson's august position as a man of letters was clearly indicated in the opening lines by Spender's cautiously worded apology for standing between 'the public and a poet of Mr. Watson's eminence'. Yet the poet already was in a decline even more astonishing than his rise to fame. Inextricably tied to the poetic tradition of the old century, Watson, unable or unwilling to change his stance, rapidly found himself adrift from the poetic main-stream of the twentieth century. Increasingly pessimistic and disheartened by his loss of popularity, Watson thought of himself as an exile, the theme of his prose work *The Muse in Exile* (1913).

Despite the fact that his views as well as his poetry were out of step with the modernist trends in literature, Watson continued to bring out books of poetry. *New Poems* (1909) included the viciously satirical poem 'The Woman with the Serpent's Tongue' (a scarcely disguised attack on Prime Minister Asquith's wife, Margot, and his daughter, Violet). On 11 August 1909, after a two-week courtship, Watson married Adeline Maureen, *née* Pring (1885–1972). They had two daughters. Various other volumes followed including *Sable and Purple* (1910), his drama *Heralds of the Dawn* (1912), his prose essay *Pencraft* (1917), and *Retrogression and other Poems* (1917).

Also in 1917 Watson published *The Man who Saw and other Poems Arising out of the War*. The title poem, a tribute to the wartime prime minister, David Lloyd George, earned Watson a knighthood, bestowed on 4 June 1917. His final poetic efforts were the long poem *The Superhuman Antagonists* (1919), which espoused a guarded meliorism, two short volumes of verse (1919) in support of the Irish rising: *Ireland Unfreed* and *Ireland Arisen*, and *Poems Brief and New* (1925).

When Sir William Watson died on 12 August 1935 in a nursing home, Limes Convalescent Home, at Ditchling Common, Sussex, he was almost totally forgotten and many were surprised that he had survived so long into the century. He was buried on 16 August in the family tomb in Childwall churchyard, Childwall Abbey, Liverpool.

JAMES G. NELSON

Sources J. G. Nelson, *Sir William Watson* (1966) • W. E. Swayze, 'The early career of Sir William Watson, 1858–1905', PhD Diss., Yale U., 1951 • J. M. Wilson, *I was an English poet: a biography of Sir William Watson* (1981) • M. Watson, 'England are you proud', Yale U., Beinecke L., Watson Collection [biography of W. Watson]

Archives Bodl. Oxf., corresp. and papers incl. literary MSS • Hunt. L., letters and literary MSS • Yale U., Beinecke L., papers | BL, corresp. with William Archer, Add. MS 54297 • BL, corresp. with Sir Sydney Cockerell, Add. MS 52758 • BL, letters to G. L. Craik, Add. MS 61895 • BL, letters to Macmillans, Add. MS 61895 • BL, corresp. of him and his executors with the Society of Authors, Add. MS 56841 • BLPES, letters to A. G. Gardiner • Bodl. Oxf., letters to A. C. Benson • Bodl. Oxf., corresp. with John Lane • Bodl. Oxf., Walpole 'Nineties' Collection • CAC Cam., corresp. with Lord Fisher • CUL, letters to E. H. Blakeney • L. Cong., Watson material • NL Scot., letters to Sir Herbert Grierson • Ransom HRC, corresp. with John Lane • TCD, corresp. with Edward Dowden • U. Leeds, corresp. with Sir Edmund Gosse • U. Leeds, Brotherton L., collection • U. Lpool L., letters to W. B. Nichols • U. Newcastle, Robinson L., letters to Frederic Whyte • U. Reading, letters to Charles Elkin Mathews

Likenesses R. G. Eves, oils, 1929?, NPG • S. W. Andrews, drawing (aged thirty-five), Yale U. • M. Beerbohm, caricature, drawing, Princeton University Library, New Jersey • Elliott & Fry, cabinet photograph, NPG • London Stereoscopic Co., cabinet photograph, NPG • J. Russell & Sons, photograph, NPG • photograph (aged fifty), Yale U.

Watson, William, Baron Thankerton (1873–1948), judge, was born in Edinburgh on 8 December 1873, the third son of William *Watson, Baron Watson of Thankerton (1827–1899), and his wife, Margaret Bannatyne (1846–1898). He was educated at Winchester College and at Jesus College, Cambridge, where he was placed in the third class in both parts of the law tripos in 1894 and 1895. In 1899 he was admitted to the Faculty of Advocates and achieved considerable success, for he was a man of tireless industry. He married in 1902 Sophia Marjorie, daughter of John James Cowan, of Bavelaw Castle, Balerno; there were two sons and one daughter of the marriage.

Watson became a KC in 1914, procurator of the Church of Scotland in 1918, and an advocate depute in 1919. He also entered politics, and was Unionist member for South Lanarkshire from 1913 until 1918. In 1922, not being then in the house, he was appointed solicitor-general for Scotland, and, later in the year, lord advocate, and was sworn of the privy council. In October 1924 he was elected Conservative member for Carlisle, defeating the Labour candidate by more than 2000 votes and gaining the first Conservative success in the constituency for some fifty years. In 1929 Watson became a lord of appeal in ordinary, in succession to Lord Shaw, and took the title of Baron Thankerton, of Thankerton, in the county of Lanark; his grandfather had been minister of the parish of Covington and Thankerton. He explained, in all good humour, that he refrained from taking the title assumed by his father 'lest haply he should besmirch it'. Like his father, and Lord Macnaghten, he went straight from the bar to the House of Lords. There were those who thought that his lack of experience might stand in his way; but they were soon to be undeceived. In what Theobald Mathew once described as the 'most eminent and least taciturn of tribunals' Thankerton soon made his mark. His industry was such that he would generally get up a case beforehand, and come into the chamber much better prepared than most of his colleagues. He was always kind and considerate to youthful counsel, going out of his way to help them in their difficulties. At the sitting of the appellate committee of the House of Lords, 14 June 1948, Lord Porter said:

> Perhaps his most characteristic quality was the devotion which he gave to his work, and the eagerness with which he sought a true solution of the problems presented to him. He always took a broad and comprehensive view of the matters which came up for consideration, and never spared himself.

Thankerton's opinions were masterpieces of concise and lucid statement. Every now and then he would coin a phrase, or sum up his view of the matter in a pithy sentence, well calculated to abide in the memory of those whose task it is to discover the law in the annals of the past. In the case of *Fender v. Mildmay* (1938), Thankerton said: 'There can be little question as to the proper function of the Courts in questions of public policy. Their duty is to expound, and not to expand, such policy'. Again, in *Franklin and others v. Minister of Town & Country Planning* (1948), the question was whether the decision of a minister could be impugned on the ground of 'bias'. The proper significance of the word, said Thankerton, 'is to denote a departure from the standard of even-handed justice which the law requires from those who occupy judicial office, … such as an arbitrator'. And here is a rule for the guidance of those who have to interpret a statute: 'The intention of Parliament', said he, 'is not to be judged of by what is in its mind, but by its expression of that mind in the statute itself' (*Wicks* v. *Director of Public Prosecutions*, 1947). Towards the end of his life it fell to Thankerton to preside in two of the heaviest appeals to come before the House of Lords in recent years. One, in July 1946, was the case of an Indian who had been seen apparently to be burnt on a funeral pyre in 1909 and who in 1930 'returned' to life and successfully claimed his wife and property. The other was the series of 'whisky appeals' (*Ross and Coulter* v. *Inland Revenue*, 1948).

Thankerton was tall and in later years developed a slight stoop, but he never looked an old man; his black hair became just tinged with grey, and he was very active to the last, walking long distances, even in town. He had a ready smile, enjoyed a good story, and had a considerable fund of after-dinner anecdotes with which he would delight the lawyers of Gray's Inn, of which he became an honorary bencher in 1928. In 1929 he was made an honorary fellow of his college, and received the honorary degree of LLD from Edinburgh University. In 1936 he and Lady Thankerton visited Canada and the United States as guests of the American and Canadian bar associations. In Canada he received an honorary degree from Acadia University. Thankerton was a member of the Royal Company of Archers, took a keen interest in golf and shooting, and spent many an hour at the cinema. Indoors, his hobby was knitting, at which he was very skilful. He died in London on 13 June 1948. His wife survived him.

W. V. BALL, *rev.*

Sources *The Times* (14 June 1948) · *The Scotsman* (14 June 1948) · private information (1959) · *WWW*
Likenesses W. Stoneman, photograph, 1935, NPG
Wealth at death £5781 19s. 5d.: confirmation, 22 Oct 1948, *CCI*

Watson, Sir William Henry (1796–1860), judge and legal writer, was born at Nottingham on 1 July 1796, son of John Watson, captain in the 76th foot, and his wife, Elizabeth, daughter of Henry Grey of Bamburgh, Northumberland. He was educated at the Royal Military College, Marlow, commissioned as cornet in the 1st (Royal) Dragoons by the duke of York on 14 November 1811, and promoted lieutenant on 7 May 1812 while serving in the Spanish peninsula. The 1st dragoons were reduced in 1814, and in April 1815 Watson exchanged into the 6th (Inniskilling) dragoons. He served with the regiment in Belgium and France, sharing in the Waterloo prize money in the process, and being present at the entry of the allied armies into Paris.

Placed on half pay on 25 March 1816, Watson entered Lincoln's Inn as a student on 19 June 1817. By hard work he soon became competent to practise as a special pleader, and continued to do so until 1832, when he was called to the bar by Lincoln's Inn. He joined the northern circuit, where he found work and became popular, taking silk and becoming a bencher of his inn in 1843. His advocacy was honest and earnest rather than eloquent, but he was a

sound lawyer and author of two (for a time) standard professional works, one on arbitration and award (1825; 3rd edn, 1846), and the other on the office of sheriff (1827; 2nd edn, 1848, by William Newland Welsby).

On 17 August 1826 Watson married Anne (d. 1828), only daughter of William Armstrong of Newcastle upon Tyne, and sister of Lord Armstrong. After Anne's death he married Mary, daughter of Anthony Capron (later Hollist) of Midhurst, Sussex, in August 1831. Each marriage produced one son.

Watson entered the House of Commons in 1841 as Liberal member for Kinsale, retaining his seat until 1847. His Liberal candidacy for Newcastle upon Tyne in July 1852 was unsuccessful, but in 1854 he was elected member for Hull, and sat as such until his appointment to the exchequer bench on 5 November 1856 in succession to Sir Thomas Platt. Watson was knighted on 28 November 1856. He had a clear head and a strong mind, but his judicial career was cut short when at the conclusion of his charge to the grand jury at Welshpool on 12 March 1860 he was seized with apoplexy. He died the next day, and was buried at the new church in Welshpool.

WILLIAM CARR, *rev.* N. G. JONES

Sources E. Foss, *Biographia juridica: a biographical dictionary of the judges of England … 1066–1870* (1870) · *Law Magazine*, new ser., 9 (1860), 189 · *GM*, 3rd ser., 8 (1860), 422 · *Morning Post* (14 March 1860) · R. Welford, *Men of mark 'twixt Tyne and Tweed*, 3 vols. (1895) · *Army List* (1813–17) · *CGPLA Eng. & Wales* (1860)
Wealth at death under £50,000: administration, 7 April 1860, *CGPLA Eng. & Wales*

Watson, William John Ross (1865–1948), Gaelic scholar, was born in the parish of Kilmuir-Easter, in Ross-shire, on 17 February 1865, the son of Hugh Watson, blacksmith, and his wife, Maria Ross; he was a native speaker of the Gaelic of that area. He graduated in classics at Aberdeen University in 1886, and repeated the first class he had achieved there at Merton College, Oxford, in 1889 and 1891. He was rector of Inverness Royal Academy from 1894 to 1909, and head of the Royal High School in Edinburgh from 1909 to 1914, when he was appointed to the chair of Celtic in the University of Edinburgh. At Oxford he had attended the classes of Sir John Rhys, and during his Inverness years he was friendly with Alexander MacBain. These influences helped to focus his scholarly gifts on Celtic, and especially Scottish Gaelic, studies. In 1904 he published *The Place-Names of Ross and Cromarty*, and place-name study remained an abiding preoccupation. In 1916 he delivered the Rhind lectures on archaeology, and from these there ultimately came his most extensive and ambitious book, *The History of the Celtic Place-Names of Scotland* (1926). The study of place names in Scotland had never been organized under the detailed county-by-county system used in England, and Watson had to break new ground in many different ways: as collector, organizer, and philologist. He was well aware of the tentative nature of some of his conclusions, especially on names of Welsh, Pictish, and Norse origin, and he may have relied overmuch at first on

MacBain's etymological findings. Some of the detail in his explanations of names has been challenged, but his book is still widely consulted, and Watson deserves great credit and lasting recognition for this monumental achievement.

In the course of his own schooling, and especially during his rectorship at Inverness, Watson must have been acutely aware of the inadequate range of textbooks for Gaelic students, and he made two important contributions in this area, publishing an anthology of Gaelic prose from the twelfth century to the twentieth in *Rosg Gàidhlig* (1915) and of Gaelic verse from the sixteenth century to *c.*1900 in *Bàrdachd Ghàidhlig* (1918). These anthologies were long used in school and university teaching, and helped to create more rigorous editorial procedures.

Watson now expanded his literary studies very purposefully, studying the surviving body of classical Gaelic verse dating from medieval and early modern times. He published editions of individual poems and discussions of this genre as practised in Scotland, in 1917, 1922, and 1931, and in 1937 there appeared his major contribution to such researches, *Scottish Verse from the Book of the Dean of Lismore.* Here he presented the first scrupulously edited text of many poems from this sixteenth-century manuscript, which includes a large range of classical verse and heroic balladry. It was a daunting task, and one which could not be definitively completed by any one individual, but there were few advances on his work in the succeeding half-century. Appropriately, this was the first volume in the series published by the Scottish Gaelic Texts Society, a society which owed its establishment largely to Watson. He had published regularly in the *Celtic Review* and also in the *Transactions of the Gaelic Society of Inverness*, and he edited the *Transactions* for many years. In 1913 and 1915 he published articles in the *Proceedings of the Society of Antiquaries of Scotland* on circular forts in Lorn and Perthshire. Hugh Watson, a son of his first marriage and a prominent lawyer in Edinburgh, continued the family connection with the Scottish Gaelic Texts Society, acting as secretary into the 1960s.

Watson retired from the chair of Celtic in 1938 after a distinguished career which established new parameters in several fields of Celtic study. After the death of his first wife, he married, in 1906, Elizabeth Catherine (Ella) Carmichael, daughter of Alexander *Carmichael. Their only son, James Carmichael Watson, succeeded his father in the chair of Celtic in 1938, and edited two volumes of Alexander Carmichael's *Carmina Gadelica* before losing his life in 1942 during World War Two. Watson died in Edinburgh on 9 March 1948, and was still a positive influence on Gaelic scholarship at the end of the twentieth century.

DERICK S. THOMSON

Sources *Scottish Gaelic Studies*, 6/2 (1949) · b. cert. (Scotland) **Archives** U. Edin.

Watson, (James) Wreford (1915–1990), geographer and poet, was born on 8 February 1915 in Sanyuan, Shensi (Shanxi), China, the third of five children of the Revd James Watson (1878–1952), and Evelyn Russell (*d.* 1926). His parents were Scottish Baptist missionaries in the Far East and the young Wreford travelled much, a fact he regarded as influential in his geographical writing.

Wreford Watson was educated at George Watson's College, Edinburgh, between 1927 and 1931 and at the University of Edinburgh from where he graduated with first-class honours in geography in 1936 and where he met fellow geographer Jessie Wilson Black (1915–1989), with whom he founded the university's Geographical Society (he was first president, she first secretary). They married in 1939. Watson received part of his training from Alan Ogilvie and Arthur Geddes, son of Sir Patrick, both of whom emphasized the importance of regions and regional differentiation. These issues, central to Watson's own work, were reinforced following his meeting, in 1937, the Australian geographer Griffith Taylor, professor of geography at Toronto. In 1939, after two years as an assistant lecturer in geography at the University of Sheffield, Watson moved to Canada as a PhD student under Taylor, and became an instructor at McMaster University. He spent the war years in Canada.

In 1949 Watson moved to Ottawa to take up an appointment as chief geographer and director of mines and technical surveys. From this time Watson developed interests in applied and social geography, initially evident in a key paper, 'The sociological aspects of geography' (1951). In 1952 he took up the chair in geography at Carleton in Ottawa, a position held concurrently with that of chief geographer.

From 1954 until retirement in 1982, Watson held a chair in geography at the University of Edinburgh. Watson's inaugural lecture at Edinburgh—'Geography: a discipline in distance'—was ahead of its time in its attention to mental perceptions of distance and landscape. It has been undeservedly neglected. While in Edinburgh, he was prominently involved in international geographical congress meetings, was president of the geography section of the British Association for the Advancement of Science (1970), vice-president and president of the Royal Scottish Geographical Society (1968–76, 1977–83 respectively), and, for 1982–3, was president of the Institute of British Geographers. He was elected a fellow of the Royal Society of Edinburgh in 1978. In Edinburgh he established the Centre for Canadian Studies in 1972, a largely humanities-based research centre which provided both a home for visiting scholars and courses on Canada's history and geography. In Edinburgh, with his wife and their son and daughter, Watson created a happy home and a welcoming environment for students, colleagues, and visiting scholars. His retirement was spent quietly in south-west Scotland.

Watson's contribution to geography is most evident in his regional and social geography texts, notably *General Geography* (1953), *Canada: its Growth and Prospects* (1968), *Social Geography of the United States* (1979), and *The United States: Habitation of Hope* (1983), although he took greatest pleasure from co-writing with his wife *The Canadians: how they Live and Work* (1978). For his geographical work, Watson received honorary degrees from five Canadian universities, awards from the Association of American Geographers, the Canadian Association of Geographers, and the Murchison medal (in 1960) and the research medal (1964) from the Royal Geographical Society. For contributions to Canadian studies, he was awarded the gold medal of the International Council for Canadian Studies in 1984. His poetry volume, *Of Time and the Lover*—published under the *nom de plume* James Wreford—was awarded the governor-general of Canada's poetry medal in 1954.

Both for his writings and for his immense organizational abilities, Watson may be considered one of the great British and North American geographers of the post-1945 era. His written work and fluent lecturing style owed much to his literary skills. His textbooks stressed the regional differentiation of social characteristics, and, in his papers on social geography, he extended geography's conceptual boundaries by emphasizing the place of the imagination in geography. In such ways, he helped develop what would now be understood in geography as 'behaviouralism' and stressed the importance of perception and belief in understanding the social world.

Watson died on 18 September 1990 at Castle Douglas, Kirkcudbrightshire, where he was buried on 22 September.   CHARLES W. J. WITHERS

Sources L. Collins, 'James Wreford Watson', *Transactions of the Institute of British Geographers*, new ser., 16 (1991), 227–32 · G. M. Robinson, 'James Wreford Watson: an appreciation with a bibliography of his work', *A social geography of Canada: essays in honour of J. Wreford Watson*, ed. G. M. Robinson (1988), 374–84 · private information (2004) [daughter] · U. Edin., department of geography, Watson MSS, MSS DG 3/1–30 · Watson's matriculation certificate and correspondence, U. Edin. L., special collections division, MS E94.36 · personal knowledge (2004)
Archives U. Edin., department of geography, archives; MSS
Likenesses photograph, 1954, U. Edin., department of geography archives, MS DG 3/23 · photograph, 1989, U. Edin., department of geography
Wealth at death £204,791.10: confirmation, 1991, NA Scot., SC/CO 528/195

Watt (*fl.* 692). *See under* South Saxons, kings of the (*act.* 477–772).

Watt, Alexander Pollock (1838–1914), literary agent, was born on 28 October 1838 at Bridgeton, Lanarkshire, Scotland, the eldest child of James Watt, bookbinder and bookseller, and his wife, Elizabeth Pollock. Watt spent several childhood years in Edinburgh, where his father had a bookselling business at 9 Brighton Street. According to his close friend W. Robertson Nicoll, Watt 'was not accustomed to say much of his early days'. He 'educated himself by incessant reading' and as a young man 'had addicted himself to books' (*British Weekly*, 12 Nov 1914). On 10 May 1866 Watt married Roberta (Bertha) Ferrier Strachan, or Strahan (1844/5–1908), daughter of the late John Strachan, messenger-at-arms, and sister of the publisher Alexander *Strahan (1833–1918). Watt was at this time a drapery warehouseman in Glasgow, and he was still employed as such at the birth of his first child, James, on

12 March 1867. By October 1869 Watt was living in The Cottage, Dartmouth Grove, Blackheath, London, and was occupied once again as a warehouseman. Shortly thereafter he joined Alexander Strahan as clerk, reader of manuscripts, and head of advertising. In 1876 he became a partner in Strahan & Co. Ltd.

The exact dates when Watt began to function as a professional advertising agent and professional literary agent are uncertain. The London Post Office directory first cites Watt as an advertising agent in 1880, and as a literary agent in 1881. Watt's first business address appears to have been 34 Paternoster Row (also the address of Strahan & Co.). In 1886 he moved to 2 Paternoster Square, and in 1891 to Hastings House, Norfolk Street, Strand. Nicoll records Watt's success as an advertising agent (he served as agent for *Blackwood's Magazine*, the *Contemporary Review*, the *Art Journal*, and other periodicals), noting that his 'sound sense, his unfailing tact, and his businesslike habits, secured for him a very solid success' (*British Weekly*, 12 Nov 1914). Watt's work as an authors' agent began casually, perhaps as early as 1875, when George MacDonald, a leading Strahan author, asked for assistance in negotiating contracts (*The Bookman*, London, Oct 1892). Watt defined the role of the literary agent as:

> to conduct all business arrangements of every kind for Authors; that is to say, to place MSS. to the best advantage; to watch for openings; to sell Copyrights, either absolutely or for a limited period; to collect Royalties, and to receive other moneys due; to conduct Arbitrations; to transfer Literary Property; to value Literary Property; to obtain opinions on MSS., etc.   (foreword, *Collection of Letters*)

By the 1890s A. P. Watt was a recognized power in the world of literature—a literary broker not only for authors, but also for publishers, periodicals, and newspapers, and the first successful British literary agent. William Ingram of the *Illustrated London News* testified in 1887 that Watt had supplied 'nearly all our Serial Novels and Special Number Stories' (*Collection of Letters*). Watt also supplied fiction to the leading syndicators, including Tillotson & Son, John Leng & Co., and the Northern Newspaper Syndicate; and in America to Irving Bachellor and S. S. McClure. McClure acknowledged in 1895 that 'most of my [UK] purchases are made through Mr. Watt' (*The Bookman*, London, May 1895). Watt's agency also arranged for translations, and significantly increased advances and royalties given to authors. Thus Rudyard Kipling acknowledged that Watt 'doubled my income' (*Collection of Letters*). Watt's power created anxiety among publishers, William Heinemann's apprehension being perhaps the most intemperate. However, even Heinemann conceded that the literary agent is 'useful for such offices as the serializing of fiction, the registration and securing of copyrights, &c' (*The Athenaeum*, 11 Nov 1893).

In 1892 the A. P. Watt literary agency became A. P. Watt & Son (for Alexander Strahan Watt). By the turn of the century other British literary agencies were competing with Watt (notably James Brand Pinker and Curtis Brown). But Watt's success continued, and notable authors on his list included Arnold Bennett, G. K. Chesterton, Wilkie Collins,

Marie Corelli, Arthur Conan Doyle, Ellen Glasgow, Sarah Grand, Rider Haggard, Bret Harte, Rudyard Kipling, W. Somerset Maugham, Elizabeth Robins, Olive Schreiner, Edgar Wallace, H. G. Wells, and W. B. Yeats. Watt served as literary executor for many of his writers, including Walter Besant, Wilkie Collins, and George Mac-Donald.

Watt claimed never to advertise, asserting that his success was due to personal recommendation. This was partly true, the recommendation of Kipling, for example, attracting several Australian writers. But Watt was also an 'enthusiastic self-publicist' (Rubinstein), publishing his changes of address in the trade journals, and circulating his testimonial letters. He had literary gifts of his own—his obituary article on his close friend John Pettie RA (*British Weekly*, 9 March 1893) demonstrates literary craft, as well as revealing Watt's generous and affectionate heart.

A. P. Watt & Son had occasional dissatisfied clients, but published testimonial letters (which were almost wholly unedited) as well as private correspondence reveal genuine and heartfelt gratitude for Watt's 'great experience, wide connection, and high standing both with authors and publishers' (Chatto and Windus); 'promptitude, zeal and energy' (Kegan, Paul, Trench & Co.); 'extraordinary business acumen' (Gilbert Parker); 'unvarying kindness and courtesy' (Guy Boothby); 'great tact, delicacy and patience' (Bret Harte). W. B. Yeats testified: 'You have saved me a great deal of worry and I thank you'.

Watt printed *The Author* for the Society of Authors and published many works for the esteemed Palestine Exploration Fund as well as W. F. Smith's translation of Rabelais (1893). He undertook international visits, including to America, where he served, at least twice, in 1899 and 1903, as witness in support of Kipling's actions against piracy by American publishers. He was a member of the Reform Club (from 1896, proposed by Arthur Conan Doyle and seconded by Anthony Hope Hawkins); the Pen and Pencil Club, Edinburgh (honorary), and the Grolier Club, New York (from 1893). He enjoyed golf, and he worked devotedly for his United Presbyterian congregation, in which he was ordained as an elder in 1881.

Watt died on 3 November 1914 at his home, Abinger House, 29 Abbey Road, St John's Wood, London. His funeral, on 6 November, was at Hampstead cemetery. He was survived by four sons, three of whom joined the agency, and two daughters. His estate was proved at approximately £60,000, and included several portraits of family members painted by John Pettie, including a handsome portrait of Watt 'as a scholar of the time of Titian' (first exhibited at the Royal Academy, 1879), as well as manuscripts of Rudyard Kipling and Robert Burns, and a 'despatch box of Wilkie Collins and its contents'.

Nicoll's glowing obituary article in the *British Weekly* pays eloquent tribute to Watt's gentle dignity, deep family affection, and 'profound religious feeling', and cites Watt as 'the foremost literary agent': 'No one was better known among authors than he. No one was so intimately in the heart of the whole mystery of the art and craft of publishing'. The agency (cable address 'Longevity') remained a family concern until 1953, ceasing to be so only in 1965, upon the death of Peter Watt. The office removed from Hastings House to 26/28 Bedford Row, Holborn, in 1968 and A. P. Watt Ltd continues to flourish at 20 John Street, Holborn, London.   ELAINE J. ZINKHAN

Sources University of North Carolina, Chapel Hill, Wilson Library, A. P. Watt & Son archives · testimonial letters, Col. U., Butler Library, A. P. Watt & Son papers · A. P. Watt, letter-books, 16 vols., Oct 1879 – June 1891; author files; royalty statements, NYPL, Humanities and Social Sciences Library, Berg collection · general corresp. (A. P. Watt), BL, Macmillan papers · bap. reg. Scot. · b. certs. [sons and daughters] · m. cert. · d. certs. · F. W., 'An interview with Mr. A. P. Watt', *The Bookman* [London], 3/13 (Oct 1892), 20–22 · 'English authors and American royalties: a chat with Mr. A. P. Watt', *The Bookman* [New York], 1/2 (March 1895), 132–3 · W. R. Nicoll, 'The literary agent', *The Bookman* [New York], 1/4 (May 1895), 249–51 · A. S. [A. Strahan] and A. P. W. [A. P. Watt], 'John Pettie, R.A., by two old friends', *British Weekly* (9 March 1893), 313–14 · *Collection of letters addressed to A. P. Watt by various writers* (1893) [and later edns] · *Publishers' Circular* (15 April 1876), 296 · *Publishers' Circular* (18 Jan 1881), 6 · *Publishers' Circular* (31 Dec 1886), 1699 · *Publishers' Circular* (20 May 1899), 559–60 · *Publishers' Circular* (2 Dec 1899), 596 · *Publishers' Circular* (7 Nov 1914), 465 · W. Heinemann, 'The middleman as viewed by a publisher', *The Athenaeum*, 3446 (11 Nov 1893), 663 · 'A talk with Mr. S. S. McClure', *The Bookman* [London], 4/8 (May 1895), 43–5 · private information (2004) [S. Blundell, C. Israel, E. Khorishko, G. Law, P. Milito, P. Nascimento, M. Pomeroy, A. Potter, J. Rawlings, L. Roundtree, L. Shaughnessy, R. Shrader, C. Stewart, J. White] · Claudius Clear [W. R. Nicoll], 'A. P. Watt: the great Napoleon of the realms of print', *British Weekly* (12 Nov 1914), 127 · *The Times* (4–5 Nov 1914) · *The Times* (10 Feb 1915) · Glasgow Post Office directory · Edinburgh Post Office directory · London Post Office directory · M. A. Gillies, 'A. P. Watt, literary agent', *Publishing Research Quarterly*, 9 (1993), 20–33 · M. Hardie, *John Pettie, R.A.*, *H.R.S.A.* (1908) · J. Hepburn, *The author's empty purse and the rise of the literary agent* (1968) · H. Rubinstein, 'A. P. Watt: the first hundred years', *The Bookseller*, 3619 (3 May 1975), 2354–8 · P. T. Srebrnik, *Alexander Strahan: Victorian publisher* (1986) · *WWW*, 1897–1915 · E. J. Zinkhan, 'Early British publication of *While the billy boils*: the A. P. Watt connection', *Bibliographical Society of Australia and New Zealand Bulletin*, 21/3 (1997), 165–82 · G. Law, *Serialising fiction in the Victorian press* (2000)

Archives Col. U., Butler Library, A. P. Watt & Son corresp., testimonial letters · NYPL, Berg collection, A. P. Watt letter-books; author files; royalty statements · University of North Carolina, Chapel Hill, Wilson Library, A. P. Watt & Son archives | BL, corresp. with Macmillans · Bodl. Oxf., Tillotson's Fiction Bureau agreement books · Pembroke Cam., corresp. with Wilkie Collins

Likenesses J. Pettie, exh. RA 1879, repro. in Hardie, *John Pettie*

Wealth at death £59,608 2s. 6d.: resworn probate, CGPLA Eng. & Wales (1915)

Watt, Alexander Stuart (1892–1985), plant ecologist, was born at Monquhitter, near Turriff, Aberdeenshire, on 21 June 1892, the third son and third of four children of George Watt (*d.* 1895), a farmer, and his wife, Margaret Jean Stuart. His father and sister died when Watt was less than three years old. His mother purchased a farm closer to Turriff, and farming continued to support the family. Watt was educated at Turriff School and (for six months) at Robert Gordon's College, Aberdeen. From there he entered Aberdeen University in 1910 with a bursary to read for an arts degree but when he found that it was permissible to work for a BSc (agriculture) simultaneously he did this and qualified for both in the minimum time of three years and one month, graduating in 1913. As part of his degree work he had taken a course in forestry which aroused a special interest that was to stay with him all his life. In 1914 he was awarded a Carnegie scholarship and was intending to spend a year in Germany studying forestry. The outbreak of war prevented this and he used the award to work under A. G. Tansley (1871–1955) at Cambridge on the regeneration of oak woods.

In 1915 Watt returned to Aberdeen University as lecturer in forest botany and forest zoology but after a brief spell of teaching he was called up for service in the Royal Engineers. He survived the battle of the Somme but was badly gassed in 1918, an experience which shattered his nerves and left him with only one functional lung. However, he made such a good recovery that few people who saw him working in the woods or on the mountains were ever aware of any disability.

Watt returned to Cambridge in 1919 and completed the requirements for his BA. He then resumed his lectureship at Aberdeen, in vacations travelling by motorcycle to the South Downs to continue work on English beechwoods for a Cambridge PhD awarded in 1923. Following his PhD Watt conducted research into the beechwoods of his native Aberdeenshire. However, the work was never finished; in 1928 the university told him that financial constraints meant his post would be abolished from 1929. Fortunately, in the latter year he gained a position at the Imperial Bureau of Entomology at Farnham Royal, Buckinghamshire, whence, a few months later, he obtained the Gurney lectureship in forestry at the University of Cambridge. It was in July 1929 that Watt married Annie Constable, daughter of William Kennaway, who had established a baker's and confectioner's in Aberdeen. They had two sons and a daughter.

Watt's early work, published in 1919, on the failure of regeneration in oak woods attracted immediate attention but it was his studies of the Chiltern beechwoods which clearly marked him out as one of the leaders of plant ecology in Britain. His careful descriptions of the major types of beechwoods and their correlation with distinct soil types set new standards in ecology and played a major role in the integration of the rapidly developing soil sciences into plant ecology.

In 1933, following a review of forestry schools, the Cambridge school was closed. Watt was transferred to the botany school but his research in ecology continued and he turned his attention to the vegetation of the breckland in East Anglia. He established a series of permanent observation sites and began careful measurement and recording which continued for almost fifty years even though hindered during the war by tank training in his experimental areas. His elucidation of the way in which the original chalky boulder clay with its grassland cover became progressively leached to form an acid sandy soil dominated by heath and bracken, and how local erosion often down to the unchanged clay restarted the process, thus giving rise to the mosaic of various developmental stages, ranks as one of the classic ecological studies.

Watt was not a particularly good lecturer. The student clerihew, much quoted in the thirties:

Doctor Watt
knows a lot
but confines his speeches
to native beeches

illustrates that when he did speak it was from a basis of deep understanding. He was at his best with a small group in the field, whether it was made up of students or well-established ecologists, half reclining on the ground as he dissected a small tuft to point out essential features overlooked by less penetrating observers. The value of his guidance in the conduct of fieldwork is well shown in the important studies of the oak woods of Killarney and of the vegetation of the Cairngorms undertaken by groups from Cambridge.

Watt's most important contribution to ecology is contained in his presidential address to the British Ecological Society, 'Pattern and process in the plant community', in 1947. His convincing description of the cyclical processes which occur in what appear to be fixed and stable entities threw new light on many features of plant communities not previously recognized or understood.

Watt was elected FRS in 1957 and awarded the gold medal of the Linnean Society in 1975. He was visiting professor in the University of Colorado in 1963 and the University of Khartoum in 1965. He died in Cambridge on 2 March 1985.   ALAN BURGES, *rev.*

Sources C. H. Gimingham, *Journal of Ecology*, 74 (1986), 297–300 · J. Sheail, *Seventy-five years in ecology: the British Ecological Society* (1987) · *Memoirs FRS*, 35 (1990), 402–23 · personal knowledge (1990) · *CGPLA Eng. & Wales* (1985)

Archives CUL, notebooks, corresp., papers, Add. MS 8851

Likenesses photograph, repro. in *Memoirs FRS*

Wealth at death £75,422: probate, 10 April 1985, *CGPLA Eng. & Wales*

Watt, Christian (1833–1923), fisherwoman and memoirist, was born on 24 February 1833 at 72 Broadsea, Fraserburgh, Aberdeenshire, the seventh of the eight children of James Watt (1787–1868), fisherman, and his wife, Helen Noble (1788–1860). Her family was distantly related to the Saltouns, clan chiefs of the Frasers.

Christian Watt grew up in a tradition of nationalism, Jacobitism, and anti-Presbyterianism, and was greatly influenced by her maternal grandmother, Helen. Her family were poor and lived in a small house at Broadsea. She attended Broadsea School, and from the age of eight also helped the family with the work of the fishing. At the age of eight and a half, Christian worked as a domestic servant. In 1843 she became a maid to Lady Saltoun, and her diligence was rewarded with a dictionary. From 1844 onwards she accompanied the Broadsea fishermen on their summer expedition to the west coast to gut and cook herring. She recounts that subsequently she personally confronted Lord MacDonald of Sleat about his part in the clearances. She also described seeing Queen Victoria and Prince Albert in royal Deeside.

In 1849 the duchess of Leeds arranged for Watt to work as a domestic servant in London, where she stayed for several months. In 1856 she travelled to America in order to receive money from the legacy of her recently deceased brother. She obtained a post as a tablemaid with a wealthy American family and spent time exploring New York. Eight months later she returned home and, on 2 December 1858 at Broadsea, she married James Sim (1831–1877), a fisherman. They had ten children. In 1874 her son Peter was drowned at sea, and Watt dated the onset of her mental breakdown from this point. Another son, Joseph, died of tetanus in 1876, and in the following year her husband was also drowned. Shortly afterwards, she lost another son and a daughter.

In 1877 Watt was admitted to the Royal Aberdeen Asylum. On returning home the following month, she was shunned by the local population and it proved impossible to maintain a livelihood. She applied to emigrate to America but was turned down because of her history of insanity. She was readmitted to the asylum twice again. The last occasion, in 1879, proved permanent and she spent her remaining forty-four years there. The case-notes state that she suffered from 'mania' with 'religious delusions'. A tall, attractive woman of forthright opinions, in later years she was also said to have had an eccentric dress-sense.

During her stay in the asylum, she was encouraged to write down her memoirs by two fellow patients. The asylum authorities ruled that all inmate writing was done in pencil, as there was a concern that patients might drink the ink or use the quills to injure themselves. Her manuscript is written in a confident, legible hand and the tone is forthright and opinionated. Watt often quotes from the Bible but her prose is also enlivened by the use of local dialect. In addition to relating her own experiences as a long-term mental patient and giving a positive account of her care, the memoir gives a vivid insight into the social history of Watt's time, encompassing as it did the plight of the fishing industry and the effects of the highland clearances.

Christian Watt died on 20 June 1923 in the Aberdeen asylum. The cause of death was chronic myocarditis and arteriosclerosis. She was buried at Kirkton cemetery, Fraserburgh. Watt's story was made known to the wider world by the publication of *The Christian Watt Papers* in 1983, which represented an edited version of her handwritten autobiography, which is now the property of her family. The difficulty for any appraisal of the life of Christian Watt is that surviving knowledge of her is almost entirely based on her own account. Further, this appears to have been composed in her last years, making it susceptible to distortion and inaccuracy. Nevertheless, the published version aroused some interest and inspired a play, *Precarious Living* (1985), and a drama documentary, both of which somewhat romanticized her plight.

ALLAN BEVERIDGE

Sources original Christian Watt papers, priv. coll. [James Marshall, Fraserburgh] · *The Christian Watt papers*, ed. D. Fraser (1983) · asylum records, Royal Aberdeen Asylum, Northern Health Services archives, Aberdeen · *A stranger on the bars: the memoirs of Christian Watt Marshall of Broadlea*, ed. G. Sutherland (1994) · S. Lobban, 'Healing for the body as well as for the soul: treatment in the Aberdeen Royal Lunatic Asylum during the nineteenth century', *The city and its worlds: aspects of Aberdeen's history since 1794*, ed. T. Brotherstone and D. Withrington (1996) · A. Hardie, *Precarious living* (1985) · b. cert. · m. cert. · d. cert.
Archives priv. coll., papers · Royal Aberdeen Asylum, Aberdeen, Northern Health Services Archives, asylum records | FILM Lochran Media Ltd, Christian Watt papers, 1994
Likenesses A. Cowan, oils, 1920, repro. in *Christian Watt papers*, ed. Fraser; priv. coll. · group portrait, photograph, repro. in *Christian Watt papers*, ed. Fraser

Watt, (John) David Henry (1932–1987), journalist, was born on 9 January 1932 in Edinburgh, the only son and second of three children of the Revd John Hunter Watt and his wife, Helen Garioch, daughter of Reuben Bryce, accountant. His childhood years were spent principally in Kent, where his father was vicar of Boxley, near Maidstone. He was educated at Marlborough College and did two years' national service with the Royal Artillery (partly in the canal zone and after that on secondment to the Mauritian guard). He then went up to Hertford College, Oxford, with a classics scholarship in 1951. He obtained second-class honours in both classical honour moderations and *literae humaniores* (1953 and 1956). He had only just taken moderations when his university career was interrupted by his falling victim to poliomyelitis. The effects were to stay with him all his life, bringing a slightly lopsided look to his previously tall, erect figure, with his left arm hanging limply by his side. He was seldom without pain, which he bore with remarkable stoicism. He continued to experience breathing difficulties, which involved in later years the regular use of a portable respirator. Nevertheless, the illness forged and shaped his whole character, transforming a conventional, public school, games-playing product into the acerbic possessor of one of the shrewdest minds and sharpest pens in British political journalism.

Polio also gave Watt his start as a writer. His first published article was called simply 'Last gasp' and appeared in *The Spectator* of 14 October 1955, when he had just ceased undergoing treatment in an iron lung. It was a detached description of what it felt like to live, as he put it, in 'a long box, monstrous and coffin-like, with bellows attached'. As a piece of spare, cool prose, it sufficiently impressed *The Spectator*'s editor, Ian Gilmour, for Watt to be offered a job when, a year later, he left Oxford. He spent two years (1956–7) with *The Spectator*, ostensibly as the paper's drama critic, but in reality as the office dogsbody. In 1958 he moved to *The Scotsman* as its London-based diplomatic correspondent, and from there was tempted in 1960 to join a revamped *Daily Herald* as its Common Market correspondent. A year later the *Herald* passed into the ownership of the International Publishing Corporation, and Watt did not, under the new proprietorship, linger long. Instead he went back to *The Spectator*, this time in the rather grander capacity of political correspondent (1962–3).

It was his second coming at *The Spectator* that marked Watt's real arrival as an influential journalist. After a brief flowering with Henry Fairlie—and a rather longer one with Bernard Levin—*The Spectator*'s political commentary had become spasmodic and patchy. In less than a year and a half Watt provided it with consistency, coherence, wit, and intelligence. It was no surprise when, towards the end of 1963, the *Financial Times* snapped him up to be its correspondent in Washington.

Although without any economic training, Watt soon vindicated his selection and became, in the words of the *Financial Times*'s own official history, 'the pick of the [paper's] foreign correspondents'. Starting from scratch, he rapidly built up an impressive network of sources, prompting the International Monetary Fund once to complain that it had to read a London newspaper to discover what was going into its own minutes. But Watt was equally penetrating in covering American politics and by 1967 had returned to London—and to the important appointment as political editor of the paper. The next ten years, in which his Friday column came to be recognized as the best-informed example of 'insider' journalism in Britain, probably represented the high point of Watt's influence over public affairs.

In 1968 Watt married Susanne, daughter of Frank (Fritz) Adolf *Burchardt, statistician and fellow of Magdalen College, Oxford; they had four sons. By 1977, having been disappointed in his bids for two editorships (for *The Economist* in 1974 and *The Observer* in 1975), Watt had become bored. He had grown tired, as he characteristically phrased it, of 'turning the prayer wheel'. So, when the offer came in 1978 to take over from Andrew Shonfield as director of the Royal Institute of International Affairs (Chatham House), he accepted it. He was afterwards to regret doing so. Cut off from its Foreign Office subvention, Chatham House was going through a difficult phase and its new director had little appetite for fund-raising. It was with some relief that he laid down his burden at the end of his five-year term.

While at Chatham House, Watt had already put a toe back into journalism, writing a weekly column in *The Times* from 1981 until his death. He was a visiting fellow of All Souls, Oxford, in 1972–3 and was a research fellow there in 1981–3, appointments which gave him great pleasure, as did his joint editorship of the *Political Quarterly* from 1979 to 1985. He was once described as having 'a clergy-boned face', and it was typical of this aspect of his personality that he should have served on the board of visitors of Wandsworth prison for five years (1977–81). In the last period of his life he also became a highly valued political consultant to the multinational company Rio Tinto Zinc, which, a year after his death, established in his memory a prize for journalism. Watt died on 27 March 1987 at his country cottage in Lewknor, near Oxford, after, on a stormy night, picking up an electric cable that turned out to be live. He was instantly electrocuted.

ANTHONY HOWARD, rev.

Sources D. Kynaston, *The Financial Times: a centenary history* (1988) · F. Mount, ed., *The inquiring eye: the writings of David Watt* (1988) · *The Times* (30 March 1987) · *The Independent* (30 March 1987) · personal knowledge (1996) · private information (1996)
Wealth at death £37,967: probate, 6 July 1988, *CGPLA Eng. & Wales*

Watt, (George) Fiddes (1873–1960), portrait painter, was born in Aberdeen on 15 February 1873, the only son and the eldest of the five children of George Watt, joiner and shipwright, and his wife, Jean Frost, daughter of a north of England weaver working at an Aberdeen linen factory. His mother, a handsome woman of musical tastes, was the active force in bringing up the family and looking after their welfare. As a boy Fiddes Watt was handicapped by a stammer which he overcame later in life. On leaving school at fourteen, he was apprenticed, like so many artists, to a firm of lithographic printers, in Aberdeen. During these seven years he attended evening classes at Gray's School of Art in Aberdeen, where among his fellow students were Robert Brough and Douglas Strachan.

At the age of twenty-one Watt went to Edinburgh to study in the life class of the Royal Scottish Academy. For a time he found life hard, and a struggle to make ends meet, but through exhibiting his paintings at the academy from 1897 he soon obtained small commissions, particularly for portraits of local dignitaries such as Provost Smith of Peterhead (1901) and Provost Wallace of Tain (1908). When commissions continued to come in steadily, he felt justified in taking premises in London about 1910, eventually renting a large studio at 178 Cromwell Road (by 1921) and exhibiting at the Royal Academy and the Royal Society of Portrait Painters.

In 1903 Watt had married Jean Willox (*d.* 1956), art teacher at Peterhead Academy, and youngest daughter of William Willox of Park, a farmer in the Buchan area of Aberdeenshire. They had three sons and a daughter. At about the same time, he began to attract attention with a number of portraits of women, including one of his wife which was his first exhibit at the Royal Academy in 1906. A portrait of his mother painted in 1910 was later bought out of the Chantrey bequest for the Tate Gallery in 1930.

Watt's later reputation, however, rests on his portraits of men. He was interested in strong character, expressed with vigour and freedom of handling. Watt believed 'that good portraits happen when the minds of sitters and artists "click", when some spark of sympathy temporarily unites them'. His most vital works probably date from before the First World War and he is seen at his best, for example, in the series of senior legal figures at the Faculty of Advocates in Edinburgh: Lord Salvesen (1911), Lord Kingsburgh (1912), and Lord Dundas (1916).

Watt's work may be regarded as that of a sound practitioner in the Scottish tradition stemming from Henry Raeburn, with its unaffected simplicity and robust directness of handling. Among early influences were those of the more overtly 'impressionist' Robert Brough, but also that of Sir George Reid, a fellow Aberdonian, whose work had a refinement of draughtsmanship and a largeness of design which attracted him. He was much in demand in both Scotland and England for official portraits and painted, among others, Herbert Henry Asquith and Lord Loreburn (both 1912) for Balliol College, Oxford; Cosmo Gordon Lang (1914) for All Souls, Oxford; Arthur James Balfour (1919) for Eton College; Lord Ullswater (1922) for the House of Commons; and Sir Joseph Thomson (1923) for Trinity College, Cambridge. None of these portraits could be described as more than efficient, and a tendency towards superficiality, always present in his work, became gradually more marked during his career. Some of this may have been due to failing eyesight, and after 1930 he ceased exhibiting at the Royal Academy and painted less and less. He had been elected an associate (1910) and a full member (1924) of the Royal Scottish Academy and his last exhibit there was in 1941.

In 1940, when the bombing of London became severe, Watt retired to Cults, near his native Aberdeen. In 1955 the University of Aberdeen awarded him the honorary degree of LLD and late in life he was granted a civil-list pension. His wife died in 1956; all through their long married life she had been a steadying influence and her death was a severe blow to him. The writer of Watt's obituary in *The Times* (23 November 1960) described him as 'a typical Scotsman … with his solid head, heavy-lidded observant eyes and rather dour expression'. In his later years, a well-known figure in Aberdeen, with his Vandyke beard, wearing a deer stalking cap, and carrying a long shepherd's crook, he attracted attention wherever he went. Fiddes Watt died at his home, 73 Cranford Road, Aberdeen, on 22 November 1960. His work is represented in most Scottish collections, including the Scottish National Portrait Gallery, Edinburgh, which has four paintings.

D. M. SUTHERLAND, *rev.* ROBIN GIBSON

Sources *The Scotsman* (23 Nov 1960) · C. B. de Laperriere, ed., *The Royal Scottish Academy exhibitors, 1826–1990*, 4 vols. (1991), vol. 4 · Graves, *RA exhibitors* · *The Times* (23 Nov 1960) · M. Chamot, D. Farr, and M. Butlin, *The modern British paintings, drawings and sculpture*, 2 (1964), 762 [Tate Gallery, London, catalogue] · *CCI* (1961) · personal knowledge (1971) · private information (1971)
Likenesses T. Huxley Jones, bronze head, 1943, Aberdeen Art Gallery · H. A. Crawford, oils, Scot. NPG · C. W. Norton, portrait, oils; Christies 10 Nov 1987 · G. F. Watt, self-portrait, oils, Aberdeen Art Gallery · photograph, repro. in *The Times* · photograph, repro. in *The Scotsman*
Wealth at death £1908 18s. 10d.: confirmation, 4 April 1961, *CCI*

Watt, Harry Raymond Egerton (1906–1987), film director, was born on 18 October 1906 in Edinburgh, the son of Henry Anderson Watt (1863–1929), Liberal MP for the College division of Glasgow, and his wife, Caroline Frackelton. His mother was of Irish origin. He was educated at Dollar Academy in Clackmannanshire, the Edinburgh Academy, and Edinburgh University, but left before completing his BA in commerce. He suffered from asthma as a child but became an accomplished middleweight boxer and captain of the rugby second fifteen while at university. Watt stood as the socialist candidate in a mock election at the Edinburgh Academy and was a stalwart of the Edinburgh University Labour Party but he showed no inclination to follow his father into politics. He worked briefly as a commercial traveller before signing as a deckhand on a schooner bound for Newfoundland. After the six-week journey he made his way down the coast, working for General Motors at Oshawa, on a funfair in Toronto, and as a wine waiter in Montreal. On returning to Britain he used his £3000 patrimony to set up the Hercules Rubber Company to make beach balls from rubber recycled from the inner tubes of car and aeroplane wheels. Unfortunately, the balls developed a leakage problem and

Harry Raymond Egerton Watt (1906–1987), by unknown photographer, 1951

Watt's attempts to raise further capital from the music-hall star Sir Harry Lauder failed, and the company was declared bankrupt. Watt attempted various other jobs, including storeman at the Kilburn base of British Home Stores, before joining John Grierson's documentary film unit at the Empire Marketing Board in 1932.

In 1933 Grierson sent Watt to help Robert Flaherty, who was making *Man of Aran* off the coast of Ireland. The film was being financed by a commercial company, Gaumont-British, and Watt was shocked at the extravagant use of time and film stock. He also disagreed with Flaherty's tendency to heighten the isolation and romanticism of the islanders' lives. But he learned from Flaherty the advantage of building a story into the documentary form and he shared his enthusiasm for making films about the lives of ordinary people. On returning to London he took over the direction of *Six-Thirty Collection* and *BBC-Droitwich* from Edgar Anstey. Watt was then loaned out to the American March of Time series to contribute items on football pools and the controversy around church tithes. In 1936, by which time the documentary unit had been transferred to the Post Office, Watt began collaborating on a film about the mail train that ran nightly from London to Scotland. It was Basil Wright who brought in W. H. Auden to write the poetic commentary and Benjamin Britten to compose the music, but Watt was primarily responsible for directing *Night Mail* (1936).

Over the following five years Watt, with the backing of Alberto Cavalcanti, who succeeded Grierson as head of the unit in 1937, developed a unique form of story documentary. In *The Saving of Bill Blewett* (1937) and *North Sea* (1938) he used a simple, realistic story to string together the events of his documentary rather than relying on a commentary. This proved tremendously successful during the Second World War, when his documentary drama *Target for Tonight* (1941) reached a wide audience in commercial cinemas. In 1942 Watt left the documentary unit and followed Cavalcanti to Ealing Studios, where he made the grimly realistic *Nine Men* (1943). After the war Watt carved a very individual furrow making films for Ealing Studios in Australia and Africa. *The Overlanders* (1945) and *Where No Vultures Fly* (1951) were two of the most profitable films made for the studio and are interesting manifestations of that post-war enthusiasm for the new life that countries such as Australia and Kenya appeared to offer. His fortunes seemed to decline with those of the British empire, however. After a brief spell presenting a wildlife programme for Granada Television, he returned to Ealing to make his—and the studio's—last film, *The Siege of Pinchgut* (1959), about an escaped convict set in Australia.

Harry Watt's most famous documentaries, *Night Mail* and *London Can Take It*, tend to be attributed to his more prestigious colleagues Basil Wright and Humphrey Jennings. *Target for Tonight*, his pioneering wartime documentary drama, has been overshadowed by Jennings's *Fires were Started* and Pat Jackson's *Western Approaches*. His contribution to Ealing Studios—a considerable one in making films which continued to uphold a realist ethos—tends to be overlooked among an output of films defined by comedies and domestic dramas. In 1974 he wrote in his autobiography: 'I had been given a small, instinctive talent for dramatic journalism. I was able to see and select the events in ordinary people's lives that made them exciting and moving and dramatise this into a film document' (*Don't Look at the Camera*, 57). Watt's modesty about his own achievements no doubt contributed to an underestimation of one of the most interesting directors in British cinema. He died on 2 April 1987 in the General Hospital, Amersham, aged eighty. Married twice, Watt was survived by Stella Ann, his second wife.

ROBERT MURPHY

Sources H. Watt, *Don't look at the camera* (1974) · E. Sussex, *The rise and fall of British documentary* (1975) · H. Watt, 'Down under', *Picturegoer* (22 June 1948), 8 · H. Watt, 'On the work of the director', *Film Forum* (Feb 1949), 4 · *Screen* (summer 1972), 47–8 [filmography] · National Film Theatre programmes, April–May 1974 · *The Times* (7 April 1987) · E. Anstey, *The Independent* (14 April 1987) · *Daily Telegraph* (13 April 1987) · *The Scotsman* (13 April 1987) · *Variety* (8 April 1987) · P. Jackson, *Film and television technician* (May 1987) · d. cert. · WWBMP, vol. 2
Archives FILM BFI NFTVA, *Great directors*, 20 Sept 1974
Likenesses photograph, 1951, Hult. Arch. [*see illus.*] · photograph, 1951 (with Leslie Norman), Hult. Arch. · photographs, repro. in Watt, *Don't look at the camera*
Wealth at death £83,126: probate, 21 Jan 1988, *CGPLA Eng. & Wales*

Watt, James (1698–1782). *See under* Watt, James (1736–1819).

Watt, James (1736–1819), engineer and scientist, was born on 19 January 1736 in Greenock, Renfrewshire, the eldest surviving child of the eight children, five of whom died in infancy, of **James Watt** (1698–1782), merchant, and his wife, Agnes Muirhead (1703–1755), whom he married about 1728. His family were prominent citizens of Greenock, and his grandfather, Thomas Watt (1642–1734), was a well-known teacher there of mathematics, surveying, and navigation. The elder James Watt was also described at various times as a shipwright, chandler, carpenter and joiner, and shipowner; and he served as chief magistrate (or bailie) of Greenock in 1751. His wife was said to be a woman of forceful character and intellect. James and Agnes were buried in the churchyard of Greenock's West Church, and in 1808 their son had a tombstone erected in memory of his 'revered parents'. The inscription on it, written by the younger James, praised his father as: 'A benevolent and ingenious man and a zealous promoter of the improvements of the town' (Williamson, 188).

Childhood, education, and training James Watt was a delicate child and suffered from frequent headaches during his childhood and adult life. He was taught at home by his mother at first, then was sent to M'Adam's school in Greenock. He later went to Greenock grammar school where he learned Latin and some Greek but was considered to be slow. However, on being introduced to mathematics, he showed both interest and ability. He helped in his father's workshops and began work there on leaving school. He made models at the bench and it is likely that his father intended James to follow him in his business. However, some of the elder Watt's commercial speculations having failed, both James and his brother had to find employment as soon as possible and it was decided that James should go to Glasgow to learn the trade of mathematical instrument maker.

On his arrival in Glasgow in June 1754 Watt stayed with his mother's family. He had brought some carpentry tools and a quadrant with him to Glasgow, which were presumably intended for his first workshop. Through his mother's relative George Muirhead he came into contact in this university city with a number of men who profoundly influenced him. Muirhead had recently moved from the chair of oriental languages to the chair of humanity at Glasgow University. He, John Anderson, and Robert Dick, as well as Joseph Black and Gilbert Hamilton, were all members of the Literary Society of Glasgow. Dr Robert Dick, who became one of Watt's closest friends, had succeeded his father as professor of natural philosophy. It was he who advised Watt to go to London to obtain better tuition in instrument making than could be obtained in Scotland, and he gave him an introduction to James Short, a mathematician and well-known telescope maker of Scottish origin. Watt was now in his twentieth year and, never having served an apprenticeship, could not rank as journeyman; moreover, in order to lessen any financial burden on his father, he needed to learn the greatest amount in the shortest time possible. He arrived in London in June 1755 and had some difficulty in finding a

James Watt (1736–1819), by Carl Fredrik von Breda, 1792

made various instruments for Black's experimental work, including an organ (built in 1761) and a perspective machine which became the prototype for some fifty to eighty made subsequently. Black described Watt as: 'a young man possessing most uncommon talents for mechanical knowledge and practice' (*Origin and Progress*, 1.xxxv). Black later wrote that Watt was as 'remarkable for the goodness of his heart and the candour and simplicity of his mind, as for the acuteness of his genius and understanding' (ibid., 1.xxxvi). In 1758 Watt met John Robison, who succeeded Black as lecturer on chemistry in Glasgow and later became professor of natural philosophy at Edinburgh. Both Robison and Black became lifelong friends, testifying, forty years later, on behalf of Watt and his partner Matthew *Boulton during the lawsuits against engine patent infringers in 1796–7.

Robison described a visit to Watt's workshop in the university: 'I saw a workman … but was surprised to find a philosopher as young as myself and always ready to instruct me' (*Origin and Progress*, 1.xliii). Robison relates how Watt thrived on solving problems and was consulted by many of the young men with scientific interests in and around Glasgow: 'everything became to him a subject of new and serious study. Everything became science in his hands' (ibid., 1.xlvi). Watt learned German in order to read J. Leupold's *Theatrum machinarum* (1727), and he also learned Italian, sharing his enthusiasm for knowledge with his friends.

As Watt had made little money in his first year he decided that the best opportunity lay in making Hadley's quadrants. He believed that he would need to travel to Liverpool and London to sell them (he did go to London), though he also found some demand in Glasgow. In order to expand his business he required capital, and this was achieved by entering into partnership with John Craig, said to have been an architect. Watt was to receive £35 p.a. in wages and an equal share of the profits. The partners took premises in Saltmarket in Glasgow in 1759. An inventory drawn up at the time shows Watt to have been selling quadrants, compasses, burning-glasses, and microscopes, among other goods. By 1763 the business was prospering, and Watt employed several journeymen and took on apprentices. He moved to Trongate, one of the main streets in Glasgow, and announced in a newspaper advertisement that besides mathematical and musical instruments he offered a variety of 'toys and other goods' for sale (Dickinson, 28). These were the steel ornaments made in Birmingham by a number of manufacturers, including Watt's future business partner, Matthew Boulton. In 1763 Watt acquired a financial interest in the Delftfield Pottery Company in Glasgow. Porcelain manufacture had not long been introduced to Britain and manufacturers were keen to improve the quality. Watt took an active scientific interest in the Delftfield concern, advising on clays, flint-grinding mills, and furnace construction, and eventually he came to have a considerable financial share in the concern. During his canal work he improved the surveying level and produced a new micrometer and a dividing

tutor. He spent a short time with a Mr Neale, a watchmaker, but Short introduced Watt to John Morgan, a mathematical instrument maker of Cornhill, and Morgan undertook to instruct Watt for one year in return for 20 guineas and Watt's labour. Watt told his father that Morgan 'can teach me most branches of the business such as rules, scales, quadrants etc.' (*Origin and Progress*, 1.xxv) and within a month he was making the brass part of Hadley's quadrants. He described his master as: 'as good a character, both for accuracy in his business and good morals, as any in his way in London' (ibid., 1.xxiv).

Watt lived in considerable poverty in London. Anxious to cost his father as little as possible, it is believed he lodged with his master, though not receiving board. But the draughty workshop, poor food, long hours, and painstaking work made him ill. By the year's end he noted: 'I am now able to work as well as most journeymen' (*Origin and Progress*, 1.xxvi), and, purchasing the bare necessities of materials and tools, he returned to Scotland in August 1756. After a few months' recuperation he went back to Glasgow, where he was given quarters in the university; he apparently found difficulty in establishing himself in the city, as he was neither the son of a burgess nor had served a full apprenticeship. Watt assisted Robert Dick to unpack and to renovate a valuable collection of astronomical instruments, formerly the property of Alexander Macfarlane, which had arrived from Jamaica. He was permitted to open a workshop in the university and to call himself mathematical instrument maker to the university.

Instrument making Through his interest in natural philosophy Watt came to the attention of Dr Joseph Black, who by 1757 was professor of the practice of medicine. He engine. He also devised a drawing machine, though this did not meet his expectations.

Early work on the steam engine Watt's interest in steam engines dates from about 1759, when John Robison suggested that he consider the application of steam power to road carriages and mining. But the idea was not developed further and, on Robison's departure from Glasgow, the project was abandoned. In the early 1760s Watt began some experiments on the force of steam in a Papin's digester and 'formed [a model of] a species of steam engine' (*Origin and Progress*, 1.lxvii); but he abandoned the idea due to pressure of other work and in the belief that an engine on the principle employed might suffer the same drawbacks as Thomas Savery's engine—namely, the danger that the boiler might burst, the difficulty of making the joints sufficiently tight, and the loss of much of the power of the steam on the downward stroke of the piston. Nevertheless, he was to describe this mechanism in his 1769 and 1784 patents.

In the winter of 1763–4 Watt was asked to repair the model of a Newcomen engine which belonged to the natural philosophy class at Glasgow University. At this time his knowledge of steam engines was largely derived from J. T. Desaguliers's *A Course of Mechanical and Experimental Philosophy* (1734) and B. F. De Belidor's *Architecture hydraulique* (1753). He set about repairing the model engine 'as a mere mechanician' (*Origin and Progress*, 1.lxix) but found that the boiler could not supply it with steam. Watt identified several problems, of which the wastage of steam during the ascent of the engine piston and the method of vacuum formation in which the system was cooled were two of the most fundamental. He therefore made a new model, slightly larger than the original, and conducted many experiments on it. This led him to his well-known tea kettle experiment in which he discovered the latent heat of steam while not understanding the scientific principle, though he subsequently learned the explanation from Joseph Black.

The theory of latent heat underpinned Watt's experiments on the separate condenser, in which the steam cylinder remained hot while a separate condensing vessel was cold. He is said to have had the inspiration for this device while walking in the environs of Glasgow one spring afternoon in 1765. Writing more than forty years later, he stated that, once the separate condenser was conceived, 'all … improvements followed as corollaries in quick succession, so that in the course of one or two days the invention was thus far complete in my mind, and I immediately set about an experiment to verify it practically' (*Origin and Progress*, 1.lxxvi). While in a general sense this was probably true, many practical problems remained to be solved—not all of them by Watt.

In 1765 and 1766 Watt erected several atmospheric engines in Scotland, probably incorporating parts made to his own designs. Work on steam engines was displaced for over a year by civil engineering engagements, but in 1768 he recommended trials on model engines and in the autumn of 1768 began designing a colliery engine, incorporating a separate condenser and air-pump, for Dr John

*Roebuck at Kinneil. Roebuck, having studied medicine at Edinburgh and Leiden, had initially settled in Birmingham to practise as a doctor. His interest in chemistry led to a number of discoveries in the refining of precious metals and, together with Samuel Garbett, a member of the Lunar Society in Birmingham, he developed the lead chamber process of sulphuric acid manufacture which permitted large-scale production for the first time. Factories for the production of sulphuric acid were established in Birmingham as well as at Prestonpans in Scotland and, both being highly profitable, Roebuck, who was now settled in Scotland, turned his attention to the large-scale manufacture of iron at Carron. The partners in Carron ironworks were advised on a number of issues by the engineer John Smeaton. The coke-smelting process of cast-iron manufacture was employed and it was this that led Roebuck to take leases of extensive mines on the estate of the duke of Hamilton. It was in the exploitation of these coalmines that Roebuck was to overstretch himself financially.

Roebuck was probably introduced to Watt by Dr Black. It is likely that he quickly recognized the potential that Watt's engine improvements might have for his own industrial interests, but neither he nor Watt anticipated the time that would elapse before the Watt engine was sufficiently developed for manufacture. Watt's first patent for 'A new method of lessening the consumption of steam and fuel in fire-engines' (no. 913) was obtained in January 1769. Roebuck was assigned two-thirds of the invention by Watt in consideration of meeting Watt's debts of almost £1000 (which comprised those incurred during the development of the engine plus the costs of obtaining the patent). Roebuck's financial situation was, however, precarious. Improvements to the Kinneil engine were undertaken *in situ* under Watt's direction, but in June 1770 Roebuck was declared bankrupt and further development was postponed.

Watt as civil engineer Watt married his cousin Margaret Miller (*d.* 1773) of Glasgow on 16 July 1764. Probably in anticipation of this, he left his rooms in the university and took up residence in the city. Needing to provide for his wife and himself, he took an office in King Street and began to undertake surveying work in the summer of 1766, while retaining the instrument-making business. In October 1766 he began a survey for a projected canal between the Firth of Forth and the Firth of Clyde, together with another surveyor, Robert Mackell. He attended parliament in connection with the Canal Bill, remarking: 'I think I shall not long to have anything to do with the House of Commons again—I never saw so many wrongheaded people on all sides gathered together' (Watt to Margaret Watt, 5 April 1767, Boulton and Watt MSS). On the journey to London, in connection with the promotion of the parliamentary bill, he visited Birmingham but did not see Matthew Boulton.

In 1769 Watt was involved in a survey of the River Clyde. He also acted as engineer for a projected canal between Monkland and Glasgow, for which he received a salary of £200 per year, as engineer to the canal, until 1772 when the undertaking faltered through lack of capital. While engaged in these projects he was concerned to improve levelling instruments. But in 1770 he was beginning to experience the tension of conflicting demands—surveying, which was bringing in an income on the one hand, and the urging of Roebuck, his partner, to develop the engine on the other. He told the physician and natural philosopher William Small that the remainder of his time was 'taken up partly by headaches & other bad health & partly by consultation on various subjects of which I can have more than I am able to answer & people pay me pretty well' (Dickinson, 72). He was involved in 1770 in the Strathmore canal survey and in the following year he reported on improvements to the harbour of Ayr and surveyed routes for canals through the isthmuses of Crinan and Tarbet. In 1772 he undertook to survey for a water supply to his native town of Greenock. Surveys for several canals and navigations were undertaken in 1773, including a canal for coal in the Mull of Kintyre, a canal from Hurtet to Paisley, the Forth Navigation, and the Water of Leven. He also undertook a survey of Glasgow docks and harbours.

The last and most significant civil engineering project of Watt's was a survey and estimate for a canal between Fort William and Inverness. He carried this out in 1773 and the canal—later named the Caledonian Canal—was to be successfully constructed in the early nineteenth century. Towards the end of 1784 Watt was approached by James McGrigor, father of his second wife, Anne, to become engineer to the project, but the proposal came to nothing and the canal was finally constructed under Thomas Telford from 1802. Telford acknowledged the quality of Watt's work: 'If I can accomplish this [drawing the utility of the scheme to public attention] I shall have done my duty: and if the project is not executed now, some future period will see it done, and I shall have the satisfaction of having followed you in promoting its success' (*Origin and Progress*, 1.cxxvi). Having completed his part of the Inverness Canal project by April 1774 Watt was able to turn his mind to Birmingham.

Family and home In 1767 Watt and his wife had a daughter, Margaret; she married James Miller and died in 1791. A son, James *Watt, was born in 1769; he died, unmarried, in 1848. It was on 26 September 1773, when Watt was surveying for a projected canal in the highlands, that he heard that his wife, who was expecting their third child, was dangerously ill. He started immediately for home, only to hear that the child had been stillborn and that his wife had died on 24 September. He was left a widower with two children, the elder of whom was six. In Margaret, he wrote: 'I lost the comfort of my life, a dear friend and a faithful wife' (Dickinson, 82). In 1776 he married for a second time. His new wife was Anne McGrigor (*d.* 1832), daughter of James McGrigor, a dyer of Glasgow. Anne's father agreed to the marriage but requested that Watt show him the partnership contract between Watt and Boulton. However, no document existed and Watt feared that if he admitted this his prudence would be doubted. He therefore asked Boulton to draw one up: 'I have been

obliged to allow him to suppose such a deed did exist but was simple, so what you send must pass for a duplicate'. Watt continued: 'whether a man of the world such as you look upon my present love as the folly of youth or the dotage of age—I find myself in no humour to lay it aside'. Fearing Boulton's ability to be discreet, he chided 'you are a very bad confidant in love affairs, you look upon them as too good things to be kept to yourself' (Watt to Boulton, 3 July 1776, Boulton and Watt MSS). Five days later Watt asked Boulton to come to Glasgow for, though agreements on the marriage had been reached, 'I am afraid I shall otherwise make a very bad bargain in money matters' (Watt to Boulton, 8 July 1776, Boulton and Watt MSS). Watt and his second wife had two children: Gregory (1777–1804) and Janet (Jessy; 1779–1794); both died, unmarried, of consumption.

Partnership with Boulton On his journey to London in 1767 to attend the House of Commons committee on the Forth and Clyde Canal Bill, Watt had passed through Birmingham, intending to see Samuel Garbett, Roebuck's partner. On his return journey he called at Lichfield to see Dr Erasmus Darwin, to whom he revealed his invention of the separate condenser, which, with the air-pump, was the unique element of his fuel-saving improvements to the steam engine. Roebuck was sufficiently sanguine of the potential of Watt's engine to agree to become a partner and, in return for a two-thirds interest in the project, took over Watt's indebtedness to Black, undertaking to pay the cost of a patent.

In 1768 Watt visited Boulton's Soho Manufactory in Birmingham after going to London on business in connection with his intended patent. This time he met Boulton and afterwards wrote: 'I explained to him my invention of the steam engine, and several other schemes of which my head was then full, in the success of which he expressed a friendly interest' (*Origin and Progress*, 1.cxlvii). Watt would have been impressed by the scale and organization of the factory and in Boulton he met not only an able entrepreneur but also an innovator. Boulton was the first to mechanize the laps for polishing steel, he developed a shaking box for scouring button blanks (a version of which continued to be used into the twentieth century), and later he developed the first flow-production system (key elements of which were mechanized) for the manufacture of coinage and medals. Watt stayed with Boulton for two weeks and on his return to Glasgow in October 1768 suggested that Boulton be offered a one-third share in the patent, possibly with Dr Small. Watt wrote to Boulton, referring to Boulton's wish to be concerned in an engine partnership (a point made clear during Watt's recent visit to him) and setting out the situation with regard to Roebuck.

Roebuck initially responded positively to Boulton's proposed involvement, but then recognizing the potential value of the patent proposed offering Boulton a licence to manufacture Watt's engine in the midlands only. Boulton declined, drawing attention to the need for capital, accurate workmanship, and effective control 'to keep the executive part out of the hands of the multitude of empirical engineers, who from ignorance, want of experience and want of necessary convenience, would be very liable to produce bad and inaccurate workmanship'. He added, 'It would not be worth my while to make for three counties only, but I find it very worth my while to make for all the world' (Dickinson, 54). Roebuck travelled south in September 1769 and Watt expected that a 'proper offer' would be made (Watt to Small, 20 Sept 1769, Boulton and Watt MSS), adding: 'As to the Doctor, he has been to me a most sincere generous friend and is a truly worthy man' (ibid.). Watt experienced a tension between a desire to satisfy Roebuck and himself in the successful completion of the Kinneil engine and the need to earn a living in civil engineering. 'Nothing', he wrote, 'is more contrary to my disposition than hustling and bargaining with mankind, yet that is the life I now constantly lead' (Dickinson, 72).

The period of indecision concerning the steam engine was exacerbated by a number of bank and business failures in 1772–3. Watt reported that Roebuck was now willing to part with his share of the engine on terms which, under better trading conditions, he believed Boulton would have had no difficulty in accepting. By March 1773 Roebuck could no longer meet his financial obligations and had not paid the costs additional to the original £1000 as agreed. Watt discharged these in return for the Kinneil engine, which was dismantled and dispatched to Birmingham.

Yet Roebuck still owned two-thirds of the patent. Boulton, however, was one of Roebuck's creditors. Rather than press for settlement, Boulton postponed negotiating for the patent until he could acquire it from the trustees of Roebuck's estate. This was achieved in August 1773. The death of Watt's first wife in September 1773, occurring in a year of small profit for Watt, and Small's subsequent urging that he go to Birmingham led Watt to decide to leave Scotland and join Boulton at Soho. He arrived in Birmingham in May 1774.

Boulton proposed seeking a parliamentary bill to extend the term of Watt's patent and in May 1775 the act was passed, extending the patent for a further twenty-five years (15 Geo. III c.61). The partnership between Boulton and Watt commenced a month later.

Watt recorded the terms of his partnership with Boulton at the time of his second marriage, in 1776. From this it is clear that Boulton was to bear the financial risk for the expense of the 1775 act and the costs of future experiments, and be responsible for the stock-in-trade as well as the keeping of the accounts, all in return for two-thirds of the property of the invention. Watt was to make drawings, give directions, and make surveys.

On his arrival in Birmingham, Watt lived in Boulton's former house in New Hall Walk but in 1777 he and his family moved to Regents Place, Harpers Hill, a substantial but plain house conveniently near Soho. The Watts maintained an establishment of two maids and a manservant at Regents Place, where Watt did his drawings, correspondence, and calculations, and where his assistants also worked. However, in 1790 he commenced the building in Handsworth of Heathfield, a larger, attractive two-storey house, to the designs of Samuel Wyatt, the architect who had remodelled Boulton's Soho House. He had a garret built over the kitchen to be used as a workshop, while in the yard below there was a forge. As land became available on the heath after enclosure, Watt acquired some and continued to add to it until he owned about 40 acres. He laid out the grounds, built a walled kitchen garden, and erected hothouses and lodges. The house was demolished in the 1920s.

Organization of the engine business At the beginning of their partnership Boulton and Watt made few engine parts. The engine workshop at Boulton's Soho Manufactory was small and there was no very clear demarcation between those people employed in Boulton's various enterprises and those employed by Boulton and Watt. Materials and parts for engines were obtained from the best rather than the nearest suppliers. Swedish iron was obtained from Birmingham merchants, tubes from Izons of West Bromwich, and piston rods, sometimes, from Jukes Coulson of Rotherhithe. But, above all, the partners depended heavily on the ironmaster John Wilkinson, for it was he who was capable of boring engine cylinders with greater accuracy than any other iron-founder. Even after other iron-founders had installed boring machines similar to those of Wilkinson, they seemed unable to produce goods of such consistent quality as his. In the early years of the Boulton and Watt partnership Wilkinson's advice was sought as well as sometimes given unsolicited. His interests were both as a manufacturer in the supply-chain and also as a customer for Boulton and Watt engines. Indeed, he was one of the largest single customers, installing eleven engines at his Bradley ironworks by the 1790s and at least seven elsewhere. The Coalbrookdale Company, too, was both an important customer and supplier of engine parts. It had been to Coalbrookdale that William Small had looked when seeking parts for the Kinneil engine before Watt had moved to Birmingham, and this company and its associates became Wilkinson's chief rival in the supply of engine parts. Even when the customer for a particular engine was as eminent an iron-founding company as the Walkers of Rotherham, Watt was cautious about permitting them to cast all their own engine parts. In general, Boulton and Watt subcontracted the manufacture of parts to firms of their own choice, most of them in the midlands region. Only piston rods seem to have been forged as far afield as Whitehaven, Workington, and Rotherhithe.

During the 1780s and early 1790s, while continuing to depend on subcontractors for many engine parts, Boulton and Watt increased both the range of operations and the capacity of their engine workshop at Soho Manufactory and by 1793 were making over 50 per cent by value of their engine parts. The reasons for this move towards the production of complete engines may have been partly financial, the partners wishing to secure to themselves the profits of forger and founder as well as those of consulting engineer. They claimed to make no profit on the parts made by other founders and, while they probably did not add a percentage to Wilkinson's castings, Boulton was certainly of the view that the partners should receive commission on all parts made by subcontractors. The main reason, however, for extending the production of engine parts at Soho Manufactory was probably an acceptance of the considerable organizational problems with subcontracting in the late eighteenth century. The unpredictability of completion time for an engine was a major difficulty, as were problems of transporting large castings by canal. Moreover, quality control was a prime concern. While standardization was only slowly introduced by Watt to engine production during the 1780s, and while a lack of it constrained output and increased costs, this drawback was at least partly offset by ensuring that all parts were made to the tolerances demanded by Boulton and Watt. There were often advantages in subcontracting, notably the smaller capital base from which the partners were able to operate. Moreover, Watt could continue experimental work while subcontractors bore a larger proportion of manufacturing risks. For the first few years each engine manufactured was largely custom-built. Sizes were relatively standardized but improvements were incorporated as developments were made by Watt and suggestions made by employees as well as some friends and customers.

Watt's role was largely that of development, design, and drawing, as well as working on patent specifications. He also visited customers, notably in Cornwall. The partners employed a small group of itinerant mechanics who were responsible for the erection of engines for their British customers. Skilled mechanics were in short supply and were not above exploiting their scarcity value. It was partly in order to protect the reputation of the firm that Boulton and Watt initiated a protocol of customer visits: when either of the partners or a senior employee visited an area in which they had several customers, attempts were made to inspect each engine and to offer maintenance guidance.

For the term of the extended patent a significant contribution to Boulton and Watt profits was derived from the royalty imposed on users of the Watt engine. For reciprocating engines this was computed at one-third of the savings in fuel effected by Watt's engine in comparison with a Newcomen engine capable of performing an equivalent amount of work. Premiums on rotative engines were charged at £5 per horse power per year in the provinces and £6 in London. Towards the end of the term of their patent the partners usually commuted the annual royalty to a lump sum payable upon purchase of the engine.

A shortage of capital inhibited Boulton in his desire to establish a separate engine factory, which had been his stated intention on first meeting Watt and conducting negotiations with him. But the discovery that Wilkinson had been pirating Watt's patent, together with the knowledge that the patent had only five and a half more years to run, and coupled with the fact that the partners had already extended their own repertory of engine parts, led to their making a quick decision in 1795 to establish a separate engine foundry. Watt seems to have played little part in the design of the foundry, which was built adjoining the Birmingham Canal near to adequate supplies of coal. It was intended that cylinders, pumps, and all other engine parts would be made there. It was also acknowledged that the partners would aim to make improvements to the engines, a task which had been more difficult while they depended on subcontracting much of the foundry work. They perceived further advantages in being able to make engines more cheaply and in a shorter time, as well as in keeping engines in stock. Thus, Soho Foundry was opened in 1796. Watt gradually withdrew from active participation in the business, and it was managed by his son, James Watt, and Matthew Robinson Boulton. The elder Watt retired in 1800.

Further patents The engine manufacturer who could solve the problem of rotary power generation other than by means of a water-wheel in the early years of the industrial revolution was likely to reap considerable financial reward. As early as 1765–9 Watt had devised a steam wheel to generate rotary motion. Both he and, later, Boulton had in mind a hollow annular chamber mounted on a shaft, and in 1774–5 Watt laid drawings of one before a committee of the House of Commons.

It is clear that a steam wheel was made and set to work at Soho in 1774, and a year later Boulton reported that another one was being developed. But in the early years of the partnership Watt was kept busy with reciprocating engines, and plans for rotary power were laid aside. Yet Boulton continued to draw attention to the opportunities, pointing out in 1776 that he could dispose of a hundred wheel engines, were they available.

The opportunities were also perceived by others. Robert Cameron, an employee who later became an independent engineer, approached Boulton with an idea. Watt discouraged Boulton, and Cameron's ideas were not proceeded with. But as early as 1779 a Newcomen engine had been fitted with rotary motion at a Birmingham flour mill owned by James Pickard, who in 1780 replaced the ratchet-and-pawl mechanism with a crank patented in the same year (no. 1263).

It has been alleged that the idea of the crank had been stolen from Watt and there is evidence to substantiate this, though Watt's stated reason for not patenting or developing rotary power at this time—pressure of work—was weak. It is more likely that he still needed to be persuaded of the usefulness of rotative power. However, under increasing pressure from Boulton he was persuaded to do so and, probably not wishing to contest the crank patent, developed, instead, 'sun and planet motion', which was patented in 1781 (no. 1306). The firm used this mechanism on all its rotative engines until 1794, when Pickard's patent expired, and in some cases for several years afterwards, after which time it also employed the crank, which was a far more effective way of generating rotative power.

In 1782 Watt was granted a patent for several major improvements to his engine (no. 1321). Of greatest significance was rotative motion. Other improvements included the use of the expansive principle and the double-acting engine, as well as a means of connecting the piston rod and beam for use in double-acting engines. Of these improvements it was the double-acting engine that had potential application, fuel savings in the expansive engine being found, in practice, to be too small to warrant development. The rack-and-sector connection for the double-acting engine was superseded by parallel motion, which was patented by Watt in 1784 (no. 1432) together with various other improvements, including the application of steam engines to wheel carriages. Of all his inventions it was parallel motion that appears most to have pleased James Watt.

Boulton and Watt were a natural target for industrial espionage. Employees talked or were bribed, and over-curious visitors would make drawings when possible. In turn the partners were vigilant in tracking down patent infringers. Friends described new engine installations around the country, while faithful employees such as William *Murdock reported on anything suspicious, particularly in Cornwall. The partners sought patent protection and privileges overseas, some form of privilege being obtained in France, Spain, and the Netherlands. Discussions were also initiated regarding patents in the United States and the Austrian empire but none was granted.

The market for engines Estimates for the number of engines manufactured by Boulton and Watt for the British market during the term of their patent have varied considerably, ranging from 318 to 512. While the smaller figure is a considerable underestimate, the latter includes a number of double counts; the most likely figure is 449 engines. Demand for the Watt engine was low at first but so too was the company's capacity to produce the requisite drawings and patterns for the subcontracting of parts. Until 1783 all the engines built were reciprocating ones, but thereafter rotative engines appear in the orderbooks. These were smaller engines and up to eighteen rotative engines per year were produced before the opening of Soho Foundry. From the opening of the foundry in 1796 the number of rotative engines manufactured increased markedly, fulfilling Boulton's expectations of a rapidly increased rate of engine production.

While some writers have alleged that no steam engine manufacturer was capable of supplying workable engines with a nominal rating of over 100 hp until the nineteenth century, when reciprocating engines are converted to a horsepower equivalent it is clear that some of the largest double-acting pumping and blowing engines were generating over 100 hp equivalent. By the end of 1800 Boulton and Watt engines totalling approximately 11,205 hp had been erected in Britain at an average size of just under 25 hp per engine.

A large proportion of the pumping engines sold by Boulton and Watt during the first ten years or so of their partnership was supplied to the Cornish copper and tin mines. The Cornish activities of the partners are significant for several reasons: first, for the sheer scale of their operations, both in the number and size of engines supplied to the region as well as the proportion of the partners' total profit contributed by Cornish engines; and second,

because Boulton and Watt became large investors in Cornish mines to enhance demand for its engines at a period when the Cornish copper industry was subject to considerable fluctuation. The demand for the Boulton and Watt engine in Cornwall was enhanced by the fact that the mines had reached a depth from which neither water engines nor the Newcomen engine could extract water adequately and consequently the mines were in danger of being flooded out. Moreover, Newcomen engines consumed greater quantities of coal than the Watt engine. Thus Cornwall provided an ideal setting for a demonstration of the considerable savings in coal that Watt's engine would effect over a Newcomen engine of comparable power. Between 1777 and 1801 forty-nine Boulton and Watt engines were erected in Cornwall. During the early 1780s the proportion of Boulton and Watt's engine business accounted for by Cornwall ranged from as low as 5 per cent to as much as 80 per cent in any one year.

Until 1784 all the Watt engines erected on the Cornish mines were single-acting, but in that year both the double-acting pumping engine and the rotative engine were introduced to Cornwall. In all cases rotative engines were of a lower horsepower equivalent than the pumping engines. A distinguishing feature of the partners' Cornish business was the extent to which engines were moved. While engine moving was not unique to the Boulton and Watt engine (for it had been a regular occurrence with its Newcomen predecessors), in no other region were nearly as many of these engines moved. Out of the total of forty-nine recorded Boulton and Watt engines in Cornwall, only thirteen appear not to have been moved. Some engines were moved three times or more.

A significant aspect of Boulton and Watt's marketing strategy was the identification of key innovating entrepreneurs in different industries. Some, such as Richard Arkwright, were approached by a partner intent on selling an engine. Other manufacturers approached Boulton and Watt. The result was that in a number of key industries prospective customers could be encouraged to follow a precedent already set by the larger innovators.

The great market for rotative power was, as Boulton had anticipated, the textile industry—in particular, cotton. While Arkwright, patentee of the water frame, was not among the first customers for Watt engines in cotton spinning (though in time he was), other leading entrepreneurs in water frame spinning provided the impetus, and with the introduction of mule spinning the number of orders escalated. The application of steam power to the wool textile industry was slower. Steam power was applied to worsted spinning relatively soon after the invention of the water frame, since a modified form of the frame could be applied to the longer filaments employed in this sector of wool textile manufacture. In woollen manufacture steam power was applied to carding and roving first, the diffusion of steam power in this sector of the wool textile industry being assisted by the early adoption of a Boulton and Watt steam engine by a leading Yorkshire innovating entrepreneur, Benjamin Gott. In both the cotton and wool textile industries a by-process of the use of steam engines was the employment of steam from the boilers to heat dying and bleaching vats.

The application of the Watt engine to manufacturing industry was assisted in two sectors by the direct financial interest the partners took in these sectors severally or together. Among the various business enterprises run by Boulton at Soho Manufactory was the Soho Mint. Besides supplying British and overseas customers with coin, he used the mint as a laboratory for the design of a flow-production system for minting, employing steam power in several of the processes. Within a few years he was accepting orders for complete mints to be supplied to various overseas customers as well as to the Royal Mint, and the steam engines would be supplied by Boulton and Watt. An experimental corn mill, driven by steam power, was set up at Soho Manufactory and this formed the proto-type for the Albion steam corn mill at Blackfriars in London, in which both Boulton and Watt, besides others, were shareholders. This, driven by two Boulton and Watt engines, was the largest steam-driven corn mill in the world at that time. It was seen by a number of British visitors and those from overseas, some of whom ordered engines for steam corn mills; on several occasions they ordered a total package—the milling machinery to be supplied by John Rennie, the London-based engineer who had been, for a while, a Boulton and Watt employee.

In addition to the home market, Boulton and Watt supplied engines to a number of overseas customers. The first foreign order was received as early as 1778, only three years after the partnership had commenced. Two further engines were ordered in 1779 and then there was a six-year interval before any further orders were obtained. Between 1785 and 1799 twenty-one engines were ordered, which made a total of twenty-four, comprising approximately 773 hp, at the expiry of Watt's patent, of which six engines were countermanded. The majority of the orders were from countries in western Europe: France, Germany, Italy, Spain, the Netherlands, Austria, and Sweden. Two engines were ordered for Russia and one (later countermanded) for India. The applications ranged from sawmilling, flour milling, coalmining, land drainage, and minting to town water supply.

Impact of the patents One of the consequences of the extension of Watt's 1769 patent for a term of twenty-five years from 1775 was that it hindered, at least in principle, developments in steam power technology for a total of thirty-one years during a period of accelerated economic growth and technological change. While Watt was granted other patents subsequently, they all concerned refinements and additions to his basic engine principle patented in 1769. So all-embracing were the terms of his 1769 patent that almost any modification, patented or not, which was incorporated in an engine of another make and which had any contrivance that operated in lieu of a separate condenser and air-pump, could be deemed an infringement. There was an increase in the number of patents taken out for steam engines in the period covered by Watt's patent. Some may have been taken out with the intention of bypassing Watt's. Others were for improvements and modifications which, had they been made widely available, might have made significant advances to steam engine technology. For the first few years of the Boulton and Watt partnership the partners took little notice of other engine patentees, but by 1790 piracy had increased to the extent that Boulton directed a legal friend to obtain copies of drawings and specifications of all the patents for steam engines taken out since the beginning of that year. It was only after considerable deliberation that the partners decided to contest significant pirates, being prepared ultimately to pursue them to the highest British courts. While their anti-piracy campaign did not commence in earnest until the early 1790s, earlier reports of the activities of two competitors had prompted investigation and discussion of possible legal action in the 1780s. The largest single pirate was John Wilkinson, the iron-master responsible for casting the early Watt engine cylinders. The extent of his piracy was divulged by his brother William after a quarrel. The other pirate of whom Boulton and Watt had most to fear was Jonathan Hornblower jun., who had designed a double-cylinder engine and was directing his efforts particularly towards the Cornish mine adventurers. In the face of overwhelming evidence of his piracy John Wilkinson capitulated, as did most of the other pirates. One partnership, J. C. Hornblower (elder brother of Jonathan Hornblower jun.) and J. A. Mabberley, then manufacturing engines in London, was pursued relentlessly through the courts, and it was not until 1799 that the court of king's bench upheld Watt's patent and the partners were able to collect the unpaid premiums owed to them.

Watt the scientist While Watt was undoubtedly a craftsman of the highest order he was also a philosopher and scientist. As an instrument maker he had a remarkable diversity of scientific interests, from building an organ and mastering the theory of harmonics from a book, to investigating new methods for the manufacture of alkali from common salt; and he nearly anticipated Henry Cavendish and Antoine Lavoisier in identifying the composition of water. He earned honours in international circles in Russia, the Netherlands, and France, and was elected to the Royal Societies of London and Edinburgh. He conducted a voluminous scientific correspondence. Dr Joseph Black of Glasgow and Edinburgh universities was one of the most outstanding scientists of his day—someone who believed that chemistry was not an art but a science which had both philosophical and utilitarian objects. Black did not inhabit an intellectual ivory tower but recognized the usefulness of his work to practical ends, acting as adviser to a number of industrial concerns. Watt corresponded extensively with him on the subject of the latent heat of steam, as well as on the development of synthetic soda manufacture, ceramics firing, mineralogy, and scientific instruments—all intermixed with domestic details.

Watt's relationship with Dr John Robison was, perhaps, partly influenced by the fact that both men were of similar ages. Robison had intended to have a naval career, but after having been present at the capture of Quebec, he returned to academic life. Like Black, he was close to industrialists and gave them advice on chemical or engineering matters. He was described as 'one of the greatest mathematical philosophers of his age' (Dickinson and Jenkins, 16), and he suggested to Watt that a textbook should be written for mechanics to enable them to advance in their careers: 'the running text should be intirely [sic] practical, containing no science, but only the results of scientific investigation' (Musson and Robinson, 183). Robison, like Black, was indefatigable in his support for Watt, searching in libraries for materials on steam engines when Watt was based in Glasgow. On Robison's death in 1805 Watt wrote: 'He was a man of the clearest head and the most science of anybody I have ever known' (Dickinson and Jenkins, 75).

Someone else who influenced Watt was Dr James Hutton, the Scottish geologist, who had studied medicine at Edinburgh, Paris, and Leiden. In 1756 he established a sal ammoniac factory in Edinburgh and published various works on geology. In their partnership Boulton and Watt shared interests in chemistry and mineralogy as well as steam engines. To depict the engine partnership as one in which Watt provided the science and Boulton the finance and business acumen would be to stereotype both partners inappropriately. Boulton did much work on the engine in Watt's absence and conversely Watt could be decisive in financial matters.

Besides the attraction of partnership with Boulton in Birmingham, Watt was attracted by the circle of scientifically minded friends that Boulton had gathered around him at Soho. The Lunar Society, probably the most important (though informal) provincial philosophical society, was established in 1766. Boulton, Erasmus Darwin, James Keir, and William Small met for dinner on the Monday nearest to the full moon. Watt became a member on his arrival in Birmingham and the membership eventually increased to fourteen, a number of whom were to become fellows of the Royal Society.

While there were many literary and philosophical societies in the provinces during the early years of the industrial revolution, its informality set the Lunar Society of Birmingham apart. The conviction that conversation was a fertile source of self-improvement drew men together in clubs. The scientific interests of the members ranged broadly across the natural and physical sciences as well as engineering. In addition, many of the members shared interests in education and some had interests in the arts. Three members of the Lunar Society, including Watt, were Scotsmen and three others had been educated at Scottish universities. Watt maintained particularly close links with science in Scotland through both kinship and friendship. He began to prosper in the engine partnership with Boulton, and as his fame grew it was to his Scottish friends that he turned for help in the defence of his patents-at-law.

Of all the interests of the Lunar Society members it was perhaps instrumentation for measurement that drew the largest number of members together. Watt, with his interest in the theory of latent heat and its practical application in steam engines, was interested in the measurement of heat and the expansive properties of steam. Linear measurement was also a subject of interest to Watt through his previous career in surveying. It was their discussions on advances in instrumentation that led to a particularly close relationship between Watt and Dr William Small.

One of the most significant examples of the Lunar Society members' activities in support of applied research was in the field of medicine. The driving force was that of consumption. Watt's daughter Janet (Jessy) died of consumption in 1794 at the age of fifteen and his son Gregory died of the same disease in 1804. William Withering, one of the members of the Lunar Society, suffered from it, as did the wife and daughter of Richard Lovell Edgeworth, another member. Members of the society supported the proposal of Dr Thomas Beddoes for a pneumatic medical institute in 1793. It was proposed to establish a laboratory and hospital where newly discovered gases could be clinically tested to assess their curative properties, particularly in relation to consumption. But by the time the institute was opened in 1799 belief in the curative powers of gases had begun to decline and, though the plans continued, Humphry Davy being recommended by Gregory Watt as assistant for the laboratory, the direction of the focus of the institute's activities became one of preventative medicine rather than curative. James Watt had other interests in health, notably in the relief of atmospheric pollution in industrial towns. He patented a smoke-consuming furnace in 1785 which attracted the attention of leading members of the community in rapidly industrializing towns such as Liverpool.

The large amount of correspondence occasioned by Watt's business and scientific interests and the laborious method of making handwritten copies of all important letters prompted him to invent a mechanical method of letter-copying which was patented in 1781. A gelatinous ink was used for writing, and, on completion of a letter, a sheet of damp, unsized paper was placed on the original and even pressure was applied until the ink came through. The press was employed extensively by Boulton and Watt, not only for letters but also for drawings. J. Watt & Co. was established to manufacture and sell the copying press. Watt held a 50 per cent share in the business and Boulton and James Keir 25 per cent each. A number of Lunar Society members were interested in the mechanism, including Erasmus Darwin and Joseph Priestley. The copying-press business was directed by Keir for a year or so before he left to establish an alkali manufacturing plant. J. H. Magellan was agent for continental sales of copying presses as well as steam engines.

Retirement In 1798 Watt had purchased a property with a farmhouse at Doldowlod, near Rhayader in Radnorshire. The farmhouse was converted into a comfortable country house where he quite frequently spent the summer months. His retirement was clouded by the loss of his son Gregory in 1804, a young man who seemed 'to have all the genius of his father with a great deal of animation and ardour, which is all his own' (Dickinson and Jenkins, 73). Watt wrote 'We ... cannot help feeling a terrible blank in our family' (*Origin and Progress*, 2.247).

In retirement Watt and his wife travelled a good deal. In 1802 they journeyed up the Rhine to Frankfurt and on to Strasbourg, returning to England via Paris. He visited Scotland frequently, and was particularly fond of Edinburgh. His dry humour, and the Scots accent that he never lost, made him welcome north of the border.

A number of Watt's friends died at the turn of the century. Josiah Wedgwood had died in 1795, Black in 1799, Erasmus Darwin in 1802, and Joseph Priestley in 1804. John Robison died in 1805. But a greater loss was that of his partner, Matthew Boulton, who died in 1809 at the age of eighty-one. Watt well knew the debt he owed to Boulton: 'few men have had his abilities and still fewer have extended them as he has done' (Watt to M. R. Boulton, 23 Aug 1809, Boulton and Watt MSS).

Watt deeply felt the loss of some of his friends from the Lunar Society. And he is said to have been haunted by the fear that his mental faculties were failing. There is much evidence to the contrary: he was consulted by the Glasgow Waterworks Company in 1811 and took pleasure in inventing as a hobby rather than a business. The problem which concerned the directors of Glasgow Waterworks was how to convey the filtered water across the River Clyde to the company's pumping station at Dalmarnock. Watt supplied a drawing for a flexible water main on the analogy of a lobster's tail. The installation was successful, and when Watt declined to accept any payment for his services the directors of the waterworks presented him with a service of silver plate. Further evidence of his continued inventive powers in his old age is the sculpturing machine copying irregularly shaped three-dimensional objects such as busts. He spent a great deal of his spare time in the garret workshop at Heathfield. By April 1809 he had made considerable progress and claimed that he could do two or more copies at once. He appears to have received much friendly assistance from William Murdock of the Soho works. Experiments continued and in 1814 he considered taking out a patent for the invention. He drafted a concise specification but does not appear to have taken the matter any further. At his death in 1819 he was still continuing to develop two machines—a proportional sculpturing machine and an equal sculpturing machine. A baronetcy was offered to him but he declined the honour. He was also asked to be high sheriff of Staffordshire and later Radnor but declined these as well.

Personality and death In appearance Watt was somewhat above medium height, with a spare figure and a pronounced stoop of the shoulders. His eyes were grey and his hair turned white early in life. It is known that he was not an early riser and required ten hours' sleep each night. For much of his life he suffered from severe headaches; and he took snuff and smoked tobacco. In his portraits he is shown as a serious man deep in thought; he was also cautious and modest, with a tendency to be self-deprecatory.

Watt's correspondence shows him to have been a man assailed by self-doubt, whose strengths lay in radical and elegant solutions to specific scientific and engineering problems. He was far less focused on business opportunities or wider issues. His reluctance to develop the rotative engine, for instance, cost the partners the opportunity to use the crank before the 1790s. Watt was greatly supported by his Scottish friends, though the support appeared to be one-way on occasion. He was, however, always generous in sharing scientific ideas while being an emphatic protector of his patented intellectual property. Nevertheless, his partner, Boulton, bore the financial risks of the business. As a father, he was less liberal than Boulton, though he was clearly devoted to his children, and was devastated by the deaths of Jessy and Gregory.

Watt died at Heathfield in Handsworth, Birmingham, on 25 August 1819 and was buried beside Matthew Boulton in St Mary's Church, Handsworth, on 2 September. His wife, Anne, and son James were appointed executors of his estate. In his will he requested that he might 'be interred in the most private manner without show or parade as soon after my decease as may be proper' (Dickinson and Jenkins, 79). He left his wife £1400 p.a. and Heathfield for life, and to his son the residue of the estate which included all documents, drawings, and tools. The will was proved on 13 October for a sum in excess of £60,000. In 1824 Lord Liverpool initiated a public subscription for a memorial sculpture by Francis Chantrey in Westminster Abbey. It additionally had an inscription, written by Henry Brougham, which read: 'James Watt ... enlarged the resources of his country, increased the power of man and rose to an eminent place amongst the most illustrious followers of science and the real benefactors of the world.' The coat of arms with the motto *Ingenio et labore*, borne by the Watt family and shown on many of the monuments erected to Watt's memory, was granted in 1826.

Significance Between 1775 and 1825 the Watt engine was adopted by many of the most eminent leaders of the manufacturing industry and canal transport. To Victorian and later writers the steam engine was almost synonymous with industrial growth and progress. Watt's near contemporary, the engineer John Farey, thus argued that the engine was the most important invention 'in the history of the arts' (Farey, 473). In his seminal essay, *The Industrial Revolution, 1760–1830*, T. S. Ashton in 1948 accorded a similar role to the engines produced by Boulton and Watt: 'The new forms of power, and no less, the new transmitting mechanisms by which this was made to do work previously done by hand and muscle, were the pivot on which industry swung into the modern age' (Ashton, 58).

Although the exclusive nature of the 1769 patent and its extension for twenty-five years undoubtedly hindered other developments, steam power was not the most widely employed prime mover until well into the nineteenth century. The cultural impact of the Watt engine far exceeded its economic impact. Indeed, it has been estimated that the saving effected by the Watt engine by 1880 was no more than 0.11 per cent of current national income, or, to put it another way, without the engine the industrial revolution would have been held up by no more than one month.

Watt, a modest man, would not have approved of the role in which he was cast by his son James and others from the late 1820s onwards—namely, the inventor as hero. He was included in the hall of Scottish heroes in the Wallace monument erected near Stirling in the 1860s, and his name became a byword for Scottish ingenuity and assiduity. The Watt Institution and School of Arts in Edinburgh was in 1852 named after him; this was later amalgamated with the George Heriot Trust and subsequently became Heriot-Watt University. His life, as depicted by Samuel Smiles and later writers, became a paradigm of mechanical genius.

Although his steam engine may not have triggered off industrialization in the manner traditionally stated, it was still of profound cultural and economic significance and has to be viewed against the backdrop of the Scottish Enlightenment. And of Watt's humanity and of his genius as an engineer there can be little doubt.

JENNIFER TANN

Sources *The origin and progress of the mechanical inventions of James Watt*, ed. J. P. Muirhead, 3 vols. (1894) · J. P. Muirhead, *The life of Watt, with selections from his correspondence*, 2nd edn (1859) · G. Williamson, *Memorials of the lineage, early life, education and development of the genius of James Watt*, ed. J. Williamson (1856) · H. W. Dickinson and R. Jenkins, *James Watt and the steam engine* (1927) · E. Roll, *An early experiment in industrial organisation, being a history of the firm of Boulton & Watt, 1775–1805* (1930) · J. Tann, ed., *The selected papers of Boulton and Watt*, 1 (1981) · J. Tann and M. J. Breckin, 'The international diffusion of the Watt engine, 1775–1825', *Economic History Review*, 2nd ser., 31 (1978) · J. Tann, 'Fixed capital formation in steam power, 1775–1825', *Studies in capital formation in the United Kingdom, 1750–1920*, ed. C. H. Feinstein and S. Pollar (1988) · R. E. Schofield, *The Lunar Society of Birmingham* (1963) · E. Robinson and A. E. Musson, *James Watt and the steam revolution* (1969) · J. Tann, 'Mr. Hornblower and his crew: steam engine pirates at the end of the 18th century', *Transactions* [Newcomen Society], 51 (1979–80), 95–109 · *Partners in science: letters of James Watt and Joseph Black*, ed. E. Robinson and D. McKie (1970) · E. Robinson, 'Training captains of industry: the education of Matthew Robinson Boulton [1770–1842] and the younger James Watt [1769–1848]', *Annals of Science*, 10 (1954), 301–13 · A. E. Musson and E. Robinson, *Science and technology in the industrial revolution* (1969) · G. N. von Tunzelmann, *Steam power and British industrialization to 1860* (1978) · J. Farey, *A treatise on the steam engine* (1827) · T. S. Ashton, *The industrial revolution, 1760–1830* (1948) · H. W. Dickinson, *James Watt, craftsman and engineer* (1936) · S. Smiles, *Lives of Boulton and Watt* (1865) · S. Smiles, *Lives of the engineers*, 3 vols. (1861–2) · D. J. Bryden, *Scottish scientific instrument-makers, 1600–1900* (1972) · Birm. CL, Boulton and Watt collection · *DNB*
Archives Birm. CA, corresp. and papers | Birm. CA, corresp. with Boulton family · Birm. CA, Muirhead MSS · Hergest Trust Archives, Kingston, Herefordshire, letters to Mr and Mrs James Crummer, Joseph Davies, and Richard Banks · U. Edin. L., letters to Joseph Black
Likenesses C. F. von Breda, oils, 1792, NPG [*see illus.*] · W. Beechey, oils, 1801, Birmingham Museums and Art Gallery · P. Rouw, wax sculpture, 1802, NPG · T. Lawrence, portrait, 1813 · C. Turner, mezzotint, pubd 1815 (after T. Lawrence), BM · F. L. Chantrey, marble statue, 1825, St Mary's Church, Handsworth, Birmingham · F. L. Chantrey, marble bust, Scot. NPG · F. L. Chantrey, marble statue, U. Glas. · F. L. Chantrey, statue, Westminster Abbey · F. L. Chantrey, statue, Scot. NPG · G. Dawe, pencil and wash drawing, Scot. NPG · J. Graham Gilbert, oils, U. Glas. · Henning, portrait,

Scot. NPG · H. Howard, oils, NPG · H. Raeburn, oils, Hunt. L. · oils, Scot. NPG
Wealth at death over £60,000: will, H. W. Dickinson, *James Watt, craftsman and engineer*

Watt, James (1769–1848), engineer and manufacturer, was born on 5 February 1769 at Glasgow, the son of the engineer James *Watt (1736–1819) and his first wife and cousin, Margaret Miller, who died in 1773. The younger James had difficulties with his father and his father's second wife, Anne McGrigor (*d.* 1832), almost from the age of six.

Like Matthew Robinson Boulton, with whom he later took over the direction of Boulton and Watt, James Watt first went to the Revd Henry Pickering's school at Winson Green, Birmingham. In 1780 his father wrote to a schoolmaster, perhaps the Revd Deane of Shifnal, Shropshire, saying that he had received complaints about young James's 'insolence, sauciness and disobedience' (J. Watt, 5 Aug 1780, Doldowlod MSS). His father wanted him disciplined for this and for his slovenliness. Yet, at twelve years of age, Watt was reading Caesar and Virgil as well as extracting cube roots. His father wanted him to continue in writing, drawing, Latin, arithmetic, and Euclidean geometry, and to begin French and dancing. At fifteen he was then steered towards a practical education at John Wilkinson's ironworks at Bersham, near Wrexham. There, for a year, he studied bookkeeping, geometry, and algebra in his leisure-hours and spent three hours every day in the carpenter's shop. His father asked about his progress in carpentry and requested a drawing of a furnace from him. He was then sent off to France *en route* to Geneva.

James Watt senior insisted upon a 'punctual and regular correspondence' from his son, constantly complaining about his handwriting and telling him that 'he succeeds best who writes like a correct Speaker in common conversation' (J. Watt, letter, 13 July 1784, Doldowlod MSS). The great engineer's own letters can be compared only to *Lord Chesterfield's Letters to his Son*. In Geneva young Watt was to study the classics, history, science, mathematics, drawing, and French. His father watched his morals and manners. He was not to curse, gossip, drink, or gamble but he was to show respect, pay his share of the reckoning, and not to read novels or frequent the theatre. He was to learn to fence. In Switzerland he was under the roof of the chemist Nicolas-Théodore de Saussure and was introduced to a number of other Swiss natural scientists, including J. A. de Luc and M. A. Pictet.

By July 1785 Watt's father was thinking of sending him to a merchant's counting-house in Germany or to Göttingen University 'to pursue the study of usefull science' (J. Watt, letter, 17 July 1785, Doldowlod MSS). In August, at the home of one Reinhard, at Eisenach in Saxony, Watt settled down to study German, after which he might go to the miners' school at Freiburg to study 'Mechanicks mathematicks & metallurgy' (ibid.). If this plan failed, he could go on to a counting-house in Leipzig.

Watt returned to England in 1788 and joined the firm of Taylor and Maxwell, fustian manufacturers, in Manchester. (Charles Taylor was later to become the secretary of the Society for the Encouragement of Arts, Commerce, and Manufactures.) His father had at last realized that the future of the steam engine lay with Lancashire rather than Cornwall. Besides learning his business and acting as an agent for steam engines, Watt quickly entered into the intellectual life of Manchester, consorting with Dr Thomas Percival, Thomas Henry and his sons, Thomas Cooper MD, Joseph Baker, Dr John Ferriar, Joseph Priestley junior, Thomas and Richard Walker, and others. With Ferriar, he became co-secretary of the Manchester Literary and Philosophical Society (known as the Lit. and Phil.) and submitted two papers, one on 'a Mine in which the Aerated Barytes is found' (*Memoirs*, 598) and the other on the effects of *terra ponderosa* given to animals. These were published in the *Memoirs* of the society in 1790. He also attended lectures by Thomas Henry and Charles White at the College of Arts and Sciences. He read extracts from his translation of a work by Jacob Joseph Winterl to the Lit. and Phil. and was encouraged by James Keir to translate a work by Christoph Meiners. He assisted Keir with the article on bleaching in Keir's *Dictionary of Chemistry* (1789), a book to which Charles Taylor contributed articles on dyeing and calico printing. Watt secured Lorenz Crell as a corresponding member of the Lit. and Phil. and gained subscribers to Crell's *Annalen*. In these years he was close to the 'young Turks' at Boulton and Watt—Peter Ewart, John Southern, and James Lawson—who favoured the French Revolution.

Through Thomas Cooper, Watt joined the Manchester Constitutional Society, which met at Thomas Walker's house. He tried to drum up a message of sympathy to Joseph Priestley after the riots in 1791. Joining the firm of Richard and Thomas Walker, he planned a sales trip to France, intending also to sell Watt copying machines. On 4 March 1792 he arrived in St Omer with Cooper, proceeded to Paris, and met Antoine-Laurent Lavoisier and other leading scientific figures; but the talk was of politics not chemistry. On 22 March 1792 he wrote to his father that Cooper and he had presented an address from the Manchester Constitutional Society to the Club des Jacobins. Thomas Walker, Cooper, and he were immediately denounced in the Commons by Edmund Burke as traitors. His father wrote to Dr Joseph Black:

My son James's conduct has given me much uneasiness, though I have nothing to accuse him of except being a violent Jacobin, that is bad enough in my eyes, who abhor democracy, as much as I do Tyranny, being in fact another sort of it.   (J. Watt to Dr J. Black, 17 July 1798, Doldowlod MSS)

Watt witnessed the massacres of 10 August in France, still a revolutionary. In 1792 or 1793 he met William Wordsworth in Paris and long remained a friend. Watt may have been denounced as an English spy and forced to flee to Italy. Despite the Traitorous Correspondence Act of 1793 he returned safely to England in 1794.

From that time forward Watt became increasingly useful to Boulton and Watt. With M. R. Boulton, he investigated and prosecuted pirates of his father's patents, he

promoted the copying machine, he introduced the principle of 'rationalization' into the construction of Soho foundry in 1796, he recruited founders from Wilkinson's works, and he took over the main direction of the steam-engine company. In assessing the contribution of the second generation of Boulton and Watt, a useful distinction describes the parents as 'builders' and the sons as 'organisers' (Roll, 270). Nevertheless, it is clear that Watt earned his father's respect, and was able to carve out an independent career.

In 1817 Watt purchased Bell's steamship *Caledonia* and, refitting her with two 14 hp Boulton and Watt engines, took her to the Netherlands and ascended the Rhine as far as Koblenz. It is claimed that this was the first steam crossing of the channel. On the way home the ship visited Antwerp and Rotterdam, returning to the Thames in the spring of 1818. As a result of this and other experiments, the manufacture of marine engines increased in his firm, culminating perhaps in HMS *James Watt* (1853), fitted with Soho engines. Watt finished his days in grand style at Aston Hall, having become a pillar of society as well as something of a dandy. Unmarried, he died at Aston Hall, Birmingham, on 2 June 1848.   ERIC H. ROBINSON

Sources J. P. Muirhead, *The life of James Watt, with selections from his correspondence* (1858) · H. W. Dickinson and R. Jenkins, *James Watt and the steam engine* (1927); facs. edn (1981) · A. E. Musson and E. Robinson, *Science and technology in the industrial revolution* (1969) · E. Roll, *An early experiment in industrial organization: being a history of the firm of Boulton & Watt, 1775–1805* (1930) · E. Robinson, 'An English Jacobin: James Watt, junior, 1769–1848', *Cambridge Historical Journal*, 11 (1953–5), 349–55 · V. Glenn, 'George Bullock, Richard Bridgens and James Watt's Regency furnishing schemes', *Furniture History*, 15 (1979), 54–67 [with 16 pp. of illustrations] · R. E. Schofield, *The Lunar Society of Birmingham* (1963) · *Memoirs of the Literary and Philosophical Society of Manchester*, 3 (1790), 598–618 · Birm. CA, Doldowlod MSS · *DNB*

Archives Birm. CA, corresp. and papers; personal and business corresp. and papers · BL, letters and papers of Watt and his father · Watt Library, Greenock, letters · Birm. CA, corresp. with Boulton family · Birm. CA, corresp. with Count von Bulow [photocopies] · Birm. CA, Doldowlod MSS · Hergest Trust Archives, letters of Watt and his parents to Mr and Mrs James Crommer, James Davies, and Richard Banks · NL Wales, letters to William Mylne and Robert Mylne

Likenesses De Longastre, pastels, priv. coll.

Watt, James Henry (1799–1867), line engraver, born in London, was probably the elder brother of the portrait engraver William Henry Watt (*b.* 1804). He was educated at Mensall's academy, Kentish Town, and at the age of eighteen became a pupil of the engraver Charles Heath (1785–1848). Watt engraved many beautiful vignettes for *The Amulet*, the *Literary Souvenir*, and similar productions from designs by Robert Smirke, Richard Westall, and others, as well as several plates for the official publication *Ancient Marbles in the British Museum*. His larger works were mostly executed in pure line on copper, and include *The Flitch of Bacon*, after T. Stothard (1832), *May Day in the Time of Queen Elizabeth*, after C. R. Leslie (1836), *Highland Drovers' Departure* and *Courtyard in the Olden Time*, both after E. Landseer, and *Christ Blessing Little Children*, after C. L. Eastlake (1859). The last named was exhibited at the Royal Academy in

1859. Watt suffered ill health for a number of years, and as a consequence of that and domestic problems he was said to have been something of a recluse. He died in London on 18 May 1867.

F. M. O'DONOGHUE, rev. DENNIS HARRINGTON

Sources *Art Journal*, 29 (1867) • *GM*, 4th ser., 4 (1867), 116 • R. K. Engen, *Dictionary of Victorian engravers, print publishers and their works* (1979) • B. Hunnisett, *A dictionary of British steel engravers* (1980) • A. M. Hind, *A history of engraving and etching*, 3rd edn (1923) • Bryan, *Painters* (1903–5) • Bénézit, *Dict.*, 4th edn • Thieme & Becker, *Allgemeines Lexikon*

Watt, John Ernest (1901–1960), radio broadcaster and producer, was born on 27 October 1901 at 4 Hidbrooke Park Road, Blackheath, London, the only son of Richard Ernest Watt, a solicitor, and his wife, Minnie Louisa Sophia Dale. Following his education at Cranleigh Institute of Technology and at University College, London, John Watt tried his hand at many different occupations, including painting a frieze at the first Wembley exhibition, managing a bookshop, and much freelance writing. However, it was while working on the *Daily Express* that he applied for a position at the BBC and in 1927 he was offered the post of assistant at the station in Belfast. On 10 October 1927 he married Violet Esmé (b. 1899/1900), daughter of Francis William Holl, a tea agent; his wife wrote under the name Angela Jeans. The couple had two sons.

With just a small staff and limited resources, the Belfast station proved an excellent base for Watt to learn about all aspects of broadcasting. On children's programmes he became the station's Uncle Pierre; he also announced and commentated as well as put on dramas, revues, and musical shows. His work quickly impressed, with an early BBC staff report noting that he had 'great potentialities' and that his variety programmes and revues were 'brilliant'.

In April 1930 Watt was promoted back to London and given charge of the new revue section, which later became part of the variety department. In his new role he established himself as one of the most creative and productive figures in radio variety and was responsible for some of the more popular programmes of the time. This included producing *Music Hall* and adapting *Show Boat* and Walt Disney's *Mickey Mouse* as features for the radio as well as writing some musical plays which were considered to have made significant advances in that genre. He was also keen to experiment: he presented a 'first night' from a theatre and in April 1933 wrote *Looking in*, the first revue specially written for television.

However, one of Watt's greatest successes began in November 1931 when he started *Songs from the Shows*, a series which was to run intermittently until 1958. The show consisted of a selection of musical comedy numbers with Watt providing a brief commentary between the songs. His style and informed knowledge drew much praise and the popularity of the programme quickly made him into a household name. This in turn led to much freelance work, and in addition to journalism and writing film scripts he commentated on official films and made a noteworthy appearance as the compère in the Pathé film *Saturday Night Review* (1937).

In July 1937 Watt was appointed acting director of variety and confirmed as director in January 1938. In this role he had overall charge of the BBC's considerable variety output and, in addition to the administration this entailed (something he did not particularly like), he continued to initiate, produce, present, and oversee many of the variety successes of the time, including *Workers' Playtime*, *Monday Night at Eight*, *Happidrome*, *Garrison Theatre*, *Band Waggon*, and *ITMA*.

Watt's job was made no easier by his department's being evacuated at the outbreak of the Second World War, first to Bristol and then to Bangor, and by having to persuade artists to travel long distances to studios. Similarly, quality material was in short supply, something he tried to remedy by encouraging listener feedback and a script-writing competition. There were also rigid guidelines to be adhered to and, as he declared, 'It is said that there are only six jokes in the world, and I assure you that we can only broadcast three of them' (Cain, 29).

The pressures, some differences of opinion with colleagues, together with some accidents, which included being hit by a taxi during a blackout, took an undoubted toll upon Watt's health and he resigned as director of variety in July 1945, stating to the press that having reached the top position in the radio variety business he considered it time for a change. Although he received many lucrative offers, Watt decided to form his own production company and mount a stage show at Butlins in Skegness. With a large theatre to fill and free entertainment elsewhere on the holiday camp, the show proved a financial disaster.

To help recoup his losses, Watt and his wife threw their energies into renovating a property in Essex. He continued writing, broadcasting, and adapting but it was not until 1948 that he broadcast again with any regularity. In addition to further series of *Songs from the Shows*, he made a successful adaptation of Warwick Deeping's *Sorrell and Son* (1950) and in 1950 established himself as a well-liked compère of *Housewives' Choice*.

In appearance Watt was of medium build, possessed a wide Cheshire Cat grin, and was a witty conversationalist. Although he rarely enjoyed the best of health and suffered from a bad curvature of the spine, he remained forever active. In addition to his creative work, he took much delight in model railways, making 'a madcap assembly of miniature gardens' (*Saffron Walden Weekly News*), and enjoyed 'fake cookery', making almost any article of haute cuisine from local sources of supply. Watt died at his home in Brighton, 18 Montpelier Street, on 23 February 1960; he was survived by his wife.

NEIL SOMERVILLE

Sources A. Jeans [V. E. Watt], *The man who was my husband: a biography of John Watt* (1964) • BBC WAC, John Watt special collection, S 193/1–29 • J. Cain, *The BBC: 70 years of broadcasting* (1992) • *The Times* (25 Feb 1960) • private information (2004) • staff files, BBC WAC, L 2/233 • contributor files, BBC WAC, RCONT 1946–62 • b. cert. • m. cert. • d. cert. • *Saffron Walden Weekly News* (26 Feb 1960)

Archives BBC WAC, John Watt special collection, S 193/1–29 | FILM BFI NFTVA, documentary footage | SOUND BL NSA, oral history interview · BL NSA, performance recordings
Wealth at death £4642 15s. 6d.: probate, 7 Nov 1960, CGPLA Eng. & Wales

Watt, Dame Katherine Christie (1886–1963), nurse and civil servant, was born at 40 Victoria Road, Govanhill, Glasgow, on 31 August 1886, the second daughter of James Christie Watt, a master butcher, and his wife, Margaret Leper Semple. Little is known of her life until she began to train as a nurse at the Western Infirmary, Glasgow, at the relatively late age of twenty-four. Having undertaken her general nurse training in Glasgow (1911–16), she took her midwifery training at the Middlesex Hospital, London. During the latter training she joined the Queen Alexandra's Imperial Military Nursing Service reserve and spent some time working in a field hospital in Flanders during the First World War. She joined the Princess Mary's Royal Air Force Nursing Service (PMRAFNS) in 1919 and remained in that service until 1938. While there she had various postings in Britain and abroad, and in 1930 she was appointed to the Air Ministry as matron-in-chief. That post, which she held until 1938, brought her into contact with the civil service, beginning an association that she maintained for the rest of her working life.

In 1939 Katherine Watt was seconded to the Ministry of Health as principal matron of the civil nursing reserve. Initially she had two specific responsibilities: to advise on the nursing services that would be required to support the evacuation of mothers and children from the major cities, and to set up the civil nursing reserve for the emergency hospital service. Having fulfilled these two responsibilities, in 1941, when the problems of identifying an adequate supply of people with nursing qualifications and experience reached extreme proportions, the minister of health appointed her chief nursing officer of the newly created division to advise on nursing matters. She was then actively involved in discussions on the plans for the National Health Service (NHS), specifically in setting up inquiries that attempted to establish the size and composition of the workforce that would be required. She was also a key source of advice to the ministry as it attempted to resolve some of the problems associated with the recruitment and training of nurses, and of assistant nurses in particular. In addition she was the first nurse appointed to represent the minister of health on the General Nursing Council for England and Wales.

Watt held the post of chief nursing officer until 1948. She then held the title of chief nursing adviser for another two years and travelled to India, Australia, and New Zealand as the government's representative, advising these Commonwealth countries on Britain's new NHS and on the position of nursing within the service. After retiring in 1950, she continued to travel widely as an adviser on nursing services. She was a governor of St George's Hospital, London, and a member of the grants committee of the RAF Benevolent Fund and of the Nations Fund for Nurses. She was also involved with a number of voluntary organizations, the St John Ambulance Brigade, the British Red Cross, and the Women's Voluntary Service. She received a number of honours for her nursing work: she was awarded the Royal Red Cross in 1930, was appointed CBE in 1935, was created a dame of the British empire in 1945, and was awarded the Florence Nightingale medal of the International Red Cross in 1949.

Katherine Watt was the first nurse to be appointed to a permanent post within the British civil service to advise on nursing matters. In the post of chief nursing officer she had a unique opportunity to contribute a nursing perspective to policy debates on the health-care services in time of war and to plans for the new services of the NHS, both of which were dependent on a trained nursing service. Although the major part of her career was with the PMRAFNS, it is the records of the Ministry of Health that provide the most helpful insights into the person of Katherine Watt. The records of the Cabinet Office pre-war discussions on the organization of nursing services suggest that, as the senior matron for the armed services, she may have been intimidated by the position in which she found herself; that hesitancy was not a feature of her career in the Ministry of Health. A small, quiet, but quite determined woman, Katherine Watt never married. She died in St George's Hospital, London, on 1 November 1963.

E. J. C. SCOTT

Sources PRO, ministry of health files, 1939–1948, MH71 and MH55 series · PRO, cabinet office files, CAB 57 NS (N) and CAB 117 series · RAF Innsworth, Gloucestershire, Royal Air Force personnel management agency · Mitchell L., Glas., Greater Glasgow health board archives · St George's Hospital archives, London · Royal College of Nursing Archives, Edinburgh · The Times (4 Nov 1963) · Nursing Times (7 Nov 1963) · Nursing Mirror (7 Nov 1963) · New Zealand Nursing Journal (April–May 1950) · E. J. C. Scott, 'The influence of the staff of the ministry of health on policies for nursing, 1919–1968', PhD diss., London School of Economics, 1994 · RAF Museum, Hendon, London, Royal Air Force Museum Archives · British Red Cross, London, British Red Cross Archives · b. cert. · WWW · d. cert. · CGPLA Eng. & Wales (1964)

Watt [née Robertson], **Margaret Rose** (1868–1948), promoter of women's institutes, was born at Collingwood, Ontario, Canada, on 4 June 1868, the eldest of the two daughters of Henry Robertson QC and his wife, Margaret Rose. Both her parents were of Scottish descent. Her father was prominent in the municipal life of Collingwood, serving on the public school board. After being educated privately she read modern languages and history at the University of Toronto and graduated BA with first-class honours in 1889 and MA in 1890. Pursuing a career as a journalist in New York, she wrote literary criticism for American and Canadian newspapers. She continued to work as a journalist after her marriage in 1893 to Alfred Tennyson Watt (d. 1913), medical officer of health for British Columbia. They had two sons.

Margaret Watt's lifelong interest in women's institutes began when she became a founder member of the Metchosin Women's Institute, Vancouver Island, in 1909. She helped to develop the movement in British Columbia as secretary, from 1911, to the British Columbia government's women's advisory board. After the death of her husband in 1913, she brought their sons to England for their education. Soon after her arrival she threw herself into promoting women's institutes at public meetings and private gatherings. Her efforts were ineffective until she wrote a pamphlet which promoted women's institutes as part of the war effort, by encouraging country women to increase and safeguard the food supply. This idea convinced Nugent Harris of the Agricultural Organisation Society that his organization should foster women's institutes, and Mrs Watt was appointed to organize them on behalf of the society. Under the society's sponsorship the first institute was started at Llanfair, Anglesey, Wales, in September 1915 as a non-party political, non-denominational body. Some months afterwards the first English institute, at Singleton, Sussex, came into being. Following her experience in Canada, Mrs Watt favoured government support, and financial backing was provided by the women's branch of the Board of Agriculture and Fisheries food production department. This paid for a small staff of organizers, of which Mrs Watt was at the head. A National Federation of Women's Institutes was founded, chaired by Lady Denman, and by the end of 1918 there were 760 institutes in operation. Ill health forced her to give up the post of chief organizer and in July 1919 she returned to Canada. In 1919 she was made an MBE for her contribution to the war effort; in 1923 she received the Belgian médaille de mérite agricole, and in 1935, a rare honour for a woman, the French médaille d'agriculture.

One of the 'impassioned apostles of the movement' (Scott, 86), Mrs Watt, through the force of her personality and strength of her convictions, played a significant role in recruiting members and equipping future leaders. As well as lecturing and writing she served on the executive committee of the National Federation of Women's Institutes from 1925 to 1939. By the late 1920s she was on the brink of an even greater achievement. For a long time she had sought to create a worldwide association of rural women, whose interchange of knowledge and experience would be of mutual advantage and would increase international understanding. She was instrumental in the foundation in 1930 of the Associated Country Women of the World, first as an offshoot of the International Council of Women, then as an independent organization. Under her leadership the association brought together country women from the Americas, Europe, Australasia, South Africa, and Ceylon.

At the outbreak of the Second World War Margaret Watt was in Canada, where she continued to serve as president of the Associated Country Women of the World until her retirement in September 1947. She died in Montreal on 29 November 1948 after a heart attack, and was buried there. Her death was publicly marked by memorial services in Victoria, British Columbia, and at St Martin-in-the-Fields, London. Shortly after her death membership of the women's institutes in England and Wales numbered 450,000 and that of the Associated Country Women of the World exceeded 5 million.   CORDELIA MOYSE

Sources *DNB* · Mrs Watt file, Denman College, Abingdon, National Federation of Women's Institutes Archives · *The Gazette* [Montreal] (30 Nov 1948) · M. Andrews, *The acceptable face of feminism: the Women's Institute as a social movement* (1997) · J. W. R. Scott, *The story of the Women's Institute Movement* (1925) · I. Jenkins, *The history of the Women's Institute movement of England and Wales* (1953) · S. Watt, ed., *What the countrywomen are doing* (1932) · *The Times* (1 Dec 1948) · G. M. Rose, *A cyclopedia of Canadian biography* (1888)

Archives Denman College, Abingdon, National Federation of Women's Institutes archives

Likenesses R. Watt, portrait, Denman College, Abingdon · photographs, Denman College, Abingdon, National Federation of Women's Institutes archives · portraits, priv. coll.

Watt, Robert (1761x8–1794), wine merchant and conspirator, was the illegitimate son of a 'respectable gentleman', and was brought up by a succession of guardians. He was educated at the Perth Academy, and moved about 1785 to Edinburgh to seek his fortune. Following a period as a clerk, and a failed attempt to forge a literary career, Watt settled on the wine trade as his source of income. It was probably the failure of his hopes for this business which led him to offer his services as a political informer in April 1792 to the lord advocate, Robert Dundas. July 1792 saw the establishment in Edinburgh of the first society of the Friends of the People in Scotland.

Watt's motives for informing appear to have been principally financial. His reports concerned radical activities not just in the capital but in Perth, Dundee, and Glasgow. Written in a small, spidery hand, they tended to the alarmism typical of opportunist informers of this period. In the spring of 1793 Watt offered Dundas information from two unnamed individuals who supposedly wanted payment of at least £100. Watt was reimbursed the sum of £30, which he claimed he had given to his sources. No helpful information was forthcoming, and from the late summer of 1793 contact between Watt and the authorities in Edinburgh lapsed.

Watt resurfaced in the following year as one of two men—the other was David Downie, an Edinburgh goldsmith—prosecuted for high treason for involvement in a murky plot to seize Edinburgh Castle, the post office, and banks, raise the manufacturing districts in Scotland, and establish a provisional government in Edinburgh. Watt appears to have been the main architect of the plan; in fact, it probably fully existed only in his imagination. He was one of seven individuals who comprised the permanent secret Committee of Ways and Means, formed in March 1794, following the suppression of the famous convention of British radicals in Edinburgh in the previous December and the subsequent crackdown on radical activities, from delegates of the remaining radical societies in Edinburgh and the neighbourhood. The plot had come to light only because of an unconnected search of Watt's house on 15 May for property belonging to a bankrupt. This unearthed a small number of pikes and the type for a handbill which was designed to suborn the loyalties of the soldiery. A subsequent search of a blacksmith's, a certain Orrock, produced further pikes.

The extent of support for the plot, as well as Watt's motivation—and indeed the motivations and degree of understanding of others involved—remain unclear. The period from late 1793 to early 1794 was one of ambiguity and confusion with respect to radical intentions as they struggled to formulate a response to government repression and the imposition of restraints on 'liberty'. Watt's counsel at his trial claimed that he was acting as an unofficial *agent provocateur*, although Watt also declared in a confession composed when his execution was certain that he had become a convert to the radical cause through attendance at their meetings. At the trial, at which he pleaded not guilty, his fellow conspirators turned king's evidence, with the exception of Downie. Although Lord Braxfield, whose extreme hostility to the radicals had been manifest in earlier political trials, did not preside—Watt was tried under a special commission of oyer and terminer under the terms of the 1709 Treason Act—a guilty verdict was a foregone conclusion. The jury did, nevertheless, recommend mercy.

Downie was to receive a pardon; Watt was not so fortunate. His execution, on 15 October 1794, was used by the authorities to demonstrate the supposedly bloody and revolutionary intent of popular radicals and the heavy penalty to be paid for such activity. Watt was drawn, backwards, from the castle in Edinburgh to the Tolbooth, his place of execution, in a procession composed of the sheriff depute and his substitutes attired in black and wearing white gloves, constables, and 200 Argyllshire fencibles, all walking at a dead pace. At Watt's feet were placed several of the pikes found in his house. After being hanged for fifteen minutes, his body was cut down and beheaded, and the severed head presented to the reportedly silent crowd who witnessed his grisly end. One account of his life, published shortly after his execution, claimed that the roots of his misfortune and villainy were a secretive, unstable, and corrupt personality, which for much of his life he had struggled against, to no avail, through excessive religious devotion.

The trials of Watt and Downie have wider significance in that they foreshadowed the treason trials of leading English radicals in the same year in the emphasis which was placed by the authorities on the supposedly sinister intent of the plans for an emergency convention under discussion among British radicals in late 1793 and early 1794. The 'Watt plot' also furnished a crucial element in the Pitt ministry's efforts, by means of two reports by a Commons committee of secrecy appointed in 1794, to demonstrate the supposed revolutionary goals of the radicals, goals which it was claimed had been deliberately disguised by the radicals' continual professions of a preference for parliamentary reform achieved through peaceful, constitutional means.   BOB HARRIS

Sources R. Watt, *The declaration and confession of Robert Watt, written, subscribed, & delivered by himself, the evening before his execution, for high treason, at Edinburgh, October 15, 1794* (1794) · *The life and character of Robert Watt, who was executed for high treason, at Edinburgh, the 15th October 1794* (1795) · *Trials of Robert Watt and David Downie for high treason, before the court of oyer and terminer, held at Edinburgh August 14, 15, 22, 27–September 3, 5, 6 1794* (1794) · H. W. Meikle, *Scotland and the French Revolution* (1912) · A. Goodwin, *The friends of liberty: the English democratic movement in the age of the French Revolution* (1979) · 'Committee of secrecy: first and second reports', *JHC*, 49 (1793–4), 600–

10, 656–734 · correspondence from Watt to Dundas, 1792, NA Scot., RH 2/4/64, fols. 302–4
Likenesses engraving, repro. in *Life and character of Robert Watt*

Watt, Robert (*bap.* **1774**, *d.* **1819**), physician and bibliographer, was baptized on 1 May 1774 in Stewarton parish church, Stewarton, Ayrshire, the youngest of the three sons of John Watt, farmer, of Bonnyton, Ayrshire, and his wife, Jean Calderwood. Watt's early years were spent on his father's small farm. At the age of six he was sent to the local parish school, where he was an able pupil whose intellectual abilities aroused the jealousy of his contemporaries. He remained at this school until he was twelve, when he became a jobbing ploughman around the neighbourhood of his father's farm. While still in his teens he travelled to Dumfriesshire as a member of a road mending gang. While there he spent some time at Ellisland, the farm of the Scottish poet Robert Burns. Burns allowed Watt to borrow from his library, and this intellectual contact and encouragement appear to have whetted Watt's appetite for learning.

In 1791, at the age of seventeen, Watt was apprenticed to his brother as a cabinet-maker. During his apprenticeship Watt had a chance meeting with a Glasgow University student and from him 'I received marvellous accounts of what mighty things were to be learned, what wonders to be seen, about a University; and I imbibed an unquenchable desire to follow his course' (Finlayson, 8). The following year he began to receive tuition in Latin and Greek from Duncan MacFarlane, schoolmaster in Stewarton. In 1793 Watt matriculated at Glasgow University, and in that session won a prize for Greek. In session 1794–5 he studied Greek and logic. The following session his subjects were moral and natural philosophy. In the summer of 1795 he taught in a private school in Kilmaurs, Ayrshire, following which he enrolled at Edinburgh University as a student of anatomy and divinity. He was again a prizewinner at Edinburgh, earning £10 for his essay 'Regeneration', of which Professor Andrew Hunter, professor of divinity at Edinburgh University from 1779 to 1809, remarked 'that it was not only the best essay, but the first time, under him, that a student of the first year's standing attempted so well and so deservedly' (Finlayson, 10). Watt returned to Ayrshire in 1797 and was the master of the parochial school at Symington until 1798. During that session he was enrolled again as a divinity student at Edinburgh University, winning a prize of £8 for an essay on prayer. He subsequently withdrew from his divinity studies and completed his education with a course in medicine at Glasgow University in 1798–9.

Having acquired the licence of the Faculty of Physicians and Surgeons of Glasgow in 1799 Watt set up practice as a general practitioner in Paisley. On 14 September 1800 he married Marion Burns (*d.* 1856); they had nine children. In 1802 he entered partnership with John Muir, who had been a fellow student in Edinburgh. Watt published a number of articles on medical subjects during his time in Paisley. His main contribution to the medical profession during this period, however, was as one of the founder members of the Paisley Medical Society, which held its first meeting on 19 September 1806. On 5 January 1807 he was elected a member of the Faculty of Physicians and Surgeons of Glasgow, thereby entering the local medical élite. His medical status was raised further when he gained the MD of King's College, Aberdeen, in 1810. Thereafter he set himself up in practice as a physician in Glasgow, and he also lectured on medicine. As an adjunct to his medical lectures he established a library of some thousand books which he made available to his students. He published a catalogue of the library in 1812, which was prefaced by 'An address to medical students on the best means of prosecuting their studies'. The catalogue also notes that the library contained about a thousand theses not listed there.

Watt was active in medical and intellectual circles in the period 1810–17. His enhanced status as a member of the Faculty of Physicians and Surgeons of Glasgow enabled him to hold office in that body, and he was president from 1814 to 1816. In 1814 he was a founder member of the Glasgow Medical Society and its first president. That same year he was elected physician to Glasgow Royal Infirmary, holding the post until 1817. In 1816 he became president of the Glasgow Philosophical Society.

In 1813 Watt published a treatise on whooping cough, in which he included an epidemiological study comparing the number of deaths among children under ten in Glasgow before and after the introduction of smallpox vaccination. This was an important early study which concluded that deaths from smallpox had fallen steeply since the introduction of vaccination, but that the total number of deaths of children remained the same, measles and other diseases accounting for the deaths of vaccinated children who had not contracted smallpox.

Watt gave up practice in 1817 through a combination of ill health and a desire to see published a work he had been undertaking since about 1799. This work was his massive bibliography, *Bibliotheca Britannica*, the aim of which was to list by author and subject the works of all authors from Britain, or the British dominions at the time. He also included what he termed 'a copious selection from the writings of the most distinguished authors of all ages and nations' (Goodall and Gibson, 45). He retired to Campvale, then a village to the south of Glasgow, later part of the city, where, assisted by his sons, the poet William Motherwell, and Alexander Whitelaw, he began to bring the work to fruition. *Bibliotheca Britannica* was initially published in nine parts, parts 1–4 appearing from 1819 to 1820 in Glasgow, and parts 5–9 appearing between 1821 and 1824 in Edinburgh. A four volume printing of the work by Constable appeared in Edinburgh in 1824. The first two volumes consist of an alphabetical author index, in which each author's work is arranged chronologically. Volumes 3 and 4 are a subject index, again with each work arranged chronologically. Each author entry has an alphanumeric mark, which is used in the subject index, to refer the reader from the subject entry for the book to the bibliographically more complete author entry. Watt also indexed a number of leading periodicals, increasing the value of the work as a bibliographical tool. Its value is further enhanced by biographical notes on many of the authors.

Watt saw only the first few sheets of his *magnum opus* off the press. He died on 12 March 1819, and was buried in Glasgow Cathedral churchyard. The burial register states the cause of his death as consumption. Watt's widow received no money for the *Bibliotheca*, as the publisher went bankrupt shortly after the work was published.

JAMES BEATON

Sources A. Goodall and T. Gibson, 'Robert Watt: physician and bibliographer', *Journal of the History of Medicine and Allied Sciences*, 18 (1963), 36–50 · J. Finlayson, *An account of the life and works of Dr Robert Watt* (1897) · F. Cordasco, *A bibliography of Robert Watt MD author of the Bibliotheca Britannica* (1950) · 'Robert E. Watt, 1774–1819: bibliographer Britannica', *Journal of the American Medical Association*, 195 (1966), 172–3 · J. Symons, 'Medical bibliographers and bibliographies', *Thorntons medical books, libraries and collectors*, ed. A. Besson (1987) · A. Grant, *The story of the University of Edinburgh during its first three hundred years*, 2 vols. (1884) · W. I. Addison, ed., *The matriculation albums of the University of Glasgow from 1728 to 1858* (1913)
Archives Paisley Central Library, Bibliotheca Britannica MS · Royal College of Physicians and Surgeons of Glasgow, student lecture notes
Likenesses oils, *c*.1815, Royal College of Physicians and Surgeons of Glasgow

Watt, Sir Robert Alexander Watson- (1892–1973), developer of radar, was born in Brechin, Forfarshire, on 13 April 1892, the fifth son and youngest of seven children of Patrick Watson Watt, a carpenter and joiner, and his wife, Mary Small Matthew. Both the Watsons and the Watts were Aberdeenshire families, the most illustrious scion of the latter being James Watt, the inventor of the condensing steam engine. Watson Watt first attended Damacre School in Brechin. After winning a local bursary, he attended Brechin high school, and then, with a further bursary, University College, Dundee, then part of the University of St Andrews. He graduated BSc (engineering) in 1912, having won medals in applied mathematics and electrical engineering as well as the class prize in natural philosophy. The last led the professor of natural philosophy, William Peddie, to offer him an assistantship after graduation, and it was Peddie who excited his interest in radio waves.

On the outbreak of war in 1914 Watson Watt volunteered his services in any capacity that would make use of his training, and in September 1915 started as a meteorologist at the Royal Aircraft Factory at Farnborough, where he proposed to apply his knowledge of radio to locate thunderstorms by the atmospherics which they emit, so as to provide warnings to airmen. Experiences with the newly created Admiralty network of radio direction-finding stations convinced him that some extremely rapid method of recording and display would be essential, and in 1916 he proposed the use of cathode ray oscilloscopes for this purpose. These, however, did not become available until 1923, when he quickly showed that the method was feasible; by 1927 cathode ray direction finders (CRDF) were installed at Slough and Cupar. The system could be used to locate the sources of other radio signals besides atmospherics and became one of Watson Watt's 'three steps to victory' in the Second World War; he described this phase of his work in *Applications of the Cathode Ray Oscillograph in Radio Research* (1933). Also to this phase belongs his proposal (1926) of the term 'ionosphere' for the ionized upper layers of the earth's atmosphere (Gardiner, 1096).

In 1924 Watson Watt's work had been moved from the Aldershot area to Slough, where the Radio Research Station had been formed under the auspices of the Meteorological Office and the Department of Scientific and Industrial Research; in December 1927 the work at Slough was amalgamated with that of the radio section of the National Physical Laboratory (NPL) into an expanded Radio Research Station, with Watson Watt as superintendent at Slough, an outstation of the NPL. In 1933, with a further reorganization, he became superintendent of a new radio department at the NPL in Teddington.

With the growing menace to Britain from the German air force after 1933, the Air Ministry began to seek scientific help to counter the doctrine that 'the bomber will always get through'. One of the wildest proposals was to direct beams of high frequency radio energy at the bomber so that its metal components would be heated, if not to destruction, at least so as to set off explosions in its bombs, or make conditions intolerable for the crew by heating their body tissue. H. E. Wimperis, then director of scientific research at the Air Ministry, asked Watson Watt to investigate this proposal, a task which Watson Watt handed on to his assistant, A. F. Wilkins, presenting it as a request to calculate the amount of radio energy that would have to be radiated to raise the temperature of 8 pints of water 5 kilometres distant from 98 °F to 105 °F. Wilkins's calculations quickly showed that the idea was quite impracticable, but in reply to Watson Watt's question of whether anything could be done for air defence, he recalled some earlier work on VHF communications by the General Post Office, whose engineers had noticed that the signals fluttered when an aircraft flew near by. Wilkins then calculated the amount of energy that could be reflected by an aircraft from a transmitter of feasible strength, and showed that there should be enough for detection at useful distances.

Watson Watt reported this conclusion qualitatively to Wimperis, and his report was laid before the first meeting of the newly formed committee for the scientific survey of air defence under Henry Tizard. On 12 February 1935 Watson Watt submitted a draft giving detailed proposals and estimates; this draft was finalized by 27 February 1935 under the title, *The Detection of Aircraft by Radio Methods*. A trial took place on 26 February 1935, using the BBC's short-wave (about 50 metres wavelength) transmitter at Daventry against a Heyford bomber with a mobile receiver a few miles away. The trial was immediately successful and on 1 September 1936 Watson Watt became superintendent of a new establishment, Bawdsey Research Station, under the Air Ministry and based at Bawdsey Manor near Felixstowe. Its objective was to exploit for air defence the principles of radar under the cover of RDF (radio direction finding, to

camouflage its *modus operandi* which involved range finding in addition to direction finding).

Despite many difficulties, and sometimes failures, the achievements of Watson Watt's team of physicists and engineers were such that by 1938 the first chain of CH (chain, home) radar stations was working on the east coast, using wavelengths between 7 and 14 metres. A second chain (CHL) to provide low cover on 1.5 metres wavelength for aircraft flying below the detection zones of the CH stations was planned, and trials had shown it feasible to provide airborne radar sets (also on 1.5 metre wavelength) which would enable a fighter to close with a bomber at night (AI) and a maritime reconnaissance aircraft to locate ships at sea (ASV). A 1.5 metre radar set for controlling anti-aircraft fire (GL) was also being made, an identification device (IFF) which would enable friendly targets to identify themselves was being developed, and a method of radio-navigation for aircraft using pulses (GEE) had been proposed. Co-operation between scientists and serving officers was exemplary: Tizard described it as 'the great lesson of the last war'. The transition from the flickering and truant radio echoes of 1936 into the reliable defence system of 1940 was one of the greatest combined feats of science, engineering, and organization in the annals of human achievement.

Watson Watt's part in all this had been that of the leader who had recruited the original team, who foresaw both the possibilities and the problems, and who fought the team's administrative battles with overwhelming enthusiasm and energy. By the time he left Bawdsey in the summer of 1938, the organization that fought the battle of Britain two years later was safely in being.

Watson Watt moved from Bawdsey to the Air Ministry as director of communications development, with general responsibilities for radar, radio, and other aspects of detection and communication. By 1940 he had become scientific adviser on telecommunications, with footings both in the Air Ministry and (from May 1940) in the newly formed Ministry of Aircraft Production. This work in the administrative centre of the war effort probably called for a greater aptitude in personal relations than his qualities would allow, and his proposal, for example, that he should become responsible for all scientific activities in the Air Ministry and the RAF came to nothing, despite his great contributions in the nascent stages of radar and of operational research.

In 1941 Watson Watt was appointed CB and elected FRS; in 1942 he was knighted, and at this stage he hyphenated his surname to Watson-Watt. At the end of the war he set up the private firm of Sir Robert Watson-Watt & Partners, as consultants to a range of industrial enterprises, including the Rank Organization, which sought advice as to the most suitable material from which to construct God's throne for a film, and received the answer 'Perspex'. The Royal Commission on Awards to Inventors gave a tax-free sum of £87,950 to the Bawdsey team, Watson-Watt's share being £52,000. He moved for some years to Canada, but later returned to Britain.

In the meantime he had led the UK delegations in 1946

and 1947 to the international meetings on radio aids to marine navigation and to a meeting of the International Civil Aviation Organization in Montreal. He had been president of the Royal Meteorological Society, of the Institute of Navigation, and of the Institute of Professional Civil Servants (in which he had been very active in the 1920s), and a vice-president of the Institute of Radio Engineers in New York. His civil honours included the US medal for merit in 1946 (a direct award from the president), the Hughes medal of the Royal Society (1948), and the Elliott Cresson medal of the Franklin Institute (1957), as well as honorary degrees from St Andrews, Toronto, and Laval universities. From 1958 to 1960 he took part in the Pugwash conferences, writing up his ideas elaborately in *Man's Means to his End* (1961). Previously he had written his autobiography up to the mid-1950s in *Three Steps to Victory* (1957).

In 1916 Watson Watt married Margaret, daughter of David Robertson, of Perth. They divorced in 1952, and in the same year he married Jean Wilkinson, a Canadian, the widow of a historian, Professor George M. Smith. She died in 1964. Watson-Watt's third wife, Jane [see Forbes, Dame (Katherine) Jane Trefusis (1899–1971)], the daughter of Edmund Batten Forbes, MICE, was the wartime head of the WAAF. They married in 1966. There were no children of any of the marriages.

Watson-Watt described himself in a broadcast talk of 1948:

> Now I am fifty-six, five foot six, an unlucky thirteen stone, tubby if you want to be unkind, chubby if you want to be a little kind, fresh complexioned, organically sound and functionally fortunate, if fat, after a thirty-years' war of resistance to taking exercise … I smile a lot … Thirty years a civil servant, now a socialist in private enterprise.

Both in speech and in writing his style was usually elaborate, sometimes to the point of ornateness, which led one colleague to comment, 'He never said in one word what could be said in a thousand'; but by contrast the most vital thing he ever wrote, his report to the Tizard committee on the feasibility of radar in February 1935, was a model of brevity and clarity. Without the crucial step that it represented, and without the drive that he put into its realization, the battle of Britain would have been much more difficult to win, and could have been lost. Watson-Watt died at Craig Dunain Hospital, Inverness, on 5 December 1973.

R. V. Jones, rev.

Sources B. Collier, *The defence of the United Kingdom* (1957) · R. A. Watson-Watt, 'The evolution of radio location', *Journal of the Institution of Electrical Engineers*, 93 (1946), 11–19 · A. F. Wilkins, 'The early days of radar in Britain', CAC Cam. · G. W. Gardiner, 'Origin of the term Ionosphere', *Nature*, 224 (1060), 1096 · J. A. Ratcliffe, *Memoirs FRS*, 21 (1975), 549–68
Archives NL Scot. · Queen's University, Kingston, Ontario | IWM, Tizard MSS · Nuffield Oxf., Cherwell MSS | SOUND BBC talk, 1948
Likenesses photographs, 1931–51, Hult. Arch. · W. Stoneman, photograph, 1943, NPG · Y. Karsh, bromide print, 1960, NPG · L. Applebee, oils, IWM
Wealth at death £6382.29: confirmation, 14 May 1974, *CCI* · £104.17—estate outside UK · £11,251.40—estate held in trust

Watton, Nun of. *See* Nun of Watton (*b.* 1146x9).

Watts, Alaric Alexander (1797–1864), journalist and poet, was born in London on 16 March 1797, the youngest son of John Mosley Watts, of an old Leicestershire and Northamptonshire family, and his wife, Sarah, the daughter of Samuel Bolton, of Fair Mile, near Henley-on-Thames, Oxfordshire. His parents separated, apparently in his infancy, owing to his father's disreputable conduct, and were consequently involved in a lengthy chancery suit. His mother, an able and cultivated woman, did all that she could to bring up her children and to see that they were properly educated. In 1808 Watts went to Wye College Grammar School, Kent, where his eldest brother was an assistant master and where he spent a happy year or two. When he and his brother moved in 1810 to an academy at Ashford, Kent, kept by the Revd Alexander Power, he had a more miserable time, but acquired a good knowledge of French from an émigré teacher, which stood him in good stead in later years. At the same time, a new imaginative world was opened to him when he read John Bell's 109-volume collection of *The Poets of Great Britain* (1782), on Shakespeare, Fielding, Smollett, and Goldsmith.

After leaving the academy in 1812, Watts held a variety of posts. He was an usher in a school in Fulham, Middlesex, kept by the Revd George Crabb and then a private tutor in the family of Bartholomew Ruspini, the prince regent's dentist. In the latter employment he met George Cruikshank and Byron, among others. In 1816 he became a clerk in the office of the controller of army accounts but very soon afterwards moved to Runcorn, Cheshire, as an assistant teacher in a boys' boarding-school. When the school changed ownership he was employed as a tutor to the son of a Manchester manufacturer. With his heart set on a literary career, he was beginning to have poems published in periodicals. From January to June 1819, when he was only twenty-two years old, he edited the *New Monthly Magazine*. At about this time he met the Revd Charles Maturin (author of *Melmoth the Wanderer*), who asked him to superintend the production at Covent Garden in May 1819 of his tragedy, *Fredolfo*. Although the actors included Charles Kemble and William Macready, the performance was a failure.

On 16 September 1821, at Woburn, Bedfordshire, Watts married Priscilla Maden Wiffen (1799–1873), always known as Zillah, who belonged to a prominent Quaker family. The Society of Friends disowned her, however, upon her marriage. A son, who died in infancy, was born to them on 23 August 1822. Another son, Alaric Alfred, was born on 18 February 1825 and a daughter, Zillah, on Christmas day 1831. Alaric Alfred married Anna Maria Howitt, the elder daughter of William and Mary Howitt, in 1859. Watts had expressive and mobile features, thick, silky hair, and a sallow complexion. His occasional irritability and hot temper were liable to lead him into quarrels and litigation which sometimes had unfortunate consequences, but he found comfort in a secure domestic life. An extravagant man, he filled his places of residence with books, pictures, and *objets d'art*, many of which he had not fully paid for.

Alaric Alexander Watts (1797–1864), by John & Charles Watkins

Thanks to his association with William Jerdan, Watts regularly contributed to the *Literary Gazette* in the early 1820s, including a series of papers (24 February – 17 March 1821), 'Lord Byron's plagiarisms', in which he juxtaposed passages from Byron with passages from other poets. 'An Austrian army awfully arrayed', a piece popular with anthologists of light verse, appeared in the *Literary Gazette* on 23 December 1820 (826–7) in an article on alliteration and is sometimes attributed to Watts. He contributed to other periodicals, including the *Gentleman's Magazine* and possibly *Blackwood's Edinburgh Magazine*, and brought out a volume, *Poetical Sketches*, in 1822 (with further editions in 1823 and 1824). These poems, conventionally Romantic in content and form, have long been forgotten, but Lamb and Wordsworth, among others, seem to have admired them. At the end of 1822 he became the editor of the *Leeds Intelligencer* at a salary of £300 a year. After a controversial beginning, in which he attacked the factory owners' treatment of their workers and hence lost subscribers, he eventually made the paper successful. But in 1825 he moved to Manchester, where he established the *Manchester Courier*, remaining its editor for about a year.

Watts claimed that between 1827 and 1847 he established or assisted in establishing upwards of twenty conservative periodicals. With Charles Baldwin and Stanley Lees Giffard he founded *The Standard*, a right-wing newspaper, in 1827. From 1833 to 1841 he published and edited

the *United Services Gazette*. Although he aimed in the *Gazette* to criticize patronage and other abuses in the armed forces, he broadly supported the status quo because of his tory sympathies.

For literary historians Watts's main achievement is his editorship and later proprietorship of two annuals, the *Literary Souvenir* (1824–35) and its successor, the *Cabinet of Modern Art* (1836–7). Annuals, elegantly produced volumes of selected prose, verse, and engravings on sale at Christmas, were fashionable at the time, with over sixty appearing in 1832, for example. Among the most popular were *Forget-me-not*, *Friendship's Offering*, and *The Keepsake*. Zillah Watts, who often associated herself with her husband's work, also edited an annual, the *New Year's Gift* (1829–36). Among the contributors to Watts's early numbers were Scott, Coleridge, Southey, Campbell, and Felicia Hemans. The engravings were mostly of pictures by minor artists, though Turner was represented, and, as a result of yearly excursions he made to Paris from 1828 to 1831, Watts was also able to include engravings of French pictures. He used work by contributors to the *Literary Souvenir* in the *Literary Magnet*, which he owned between 1825 and 1828. In addition to his involvement in journalism he published a collection of contemporary verse, *Fugitive Poetry* (2 vols., 1828–9).

A feud which had developed between Watts and William Maginn and others on *Fraser's Magazine* culminated in Watts's depiction as Alaric Attila Watts in the 'Gallery of illustrious literary characters' (*Fraser's Magazine* 11, June 1835, 652; repr. in W. Bates's edition of the *Gallery* 1873, 161–3). Watts thought that Daniel Maclise's drawing and Maginn's accompanying description made some scurrilous imputations concerning his honour and honesty. He therefore brought an action for libel on 5 December 1835, winning damages of £150 but later claiming that the attacks helped to bring about the decline of the *Literary Souvenir*.

In the 1840s Watts, who had seldom been free from debt, increasingly found himself in financial difficulties, which were exacerbated by lawsuits which absorbed much of his energy over seven years. He severed all connection with the press in 1847 and was made a bankrupt in 1849 (but was discharged on 13 August 1850). In 1851, however, his *Lyrics of the Heart* appeared, and in 1853 his biographical sketch of Turner was prefixed to *Liber fluviorum*, a volume of engravings of some of the painter's work.

The days of Watts's multifarious literary and journalistic activities were over. In 1853 he became a clerk in the Inland Revenue office at Somerset House in London, where his son was employed in a senior position. On 7 January 1854 he was awarded a civil-list pension of £100 a year in consideration of services rendered by him to literature and art. He edited the 1857 edition of *Men of the Time*, the biographical compendium, and included a lengthy autobiographical entry. His life became comfortable and uneventful and he delighted in re-reading and annotating at leisure the poetry of Chaucer, Spenser, Milton, and Dryden. After suffering a stroke Watts died on 5 April 1864 at his home in Blenheim Crescent, Notting Hill, London, and was buried in Highgate cemetery in London. He was survived by his wife. DONALD HAWES

Sources A. A. Watts, *Alaric Watts: a narrative of his life*, 2 vols. (1884) · *Men of the time* (1857), 737–40 · *DNB* · *GM*, 3rd ser., 16 (1864), 676–7 · *ILN* (23 April 1864), 403 · W. Maginn and D. Maclise, *A gallery of illustrious literary characters, 1830–1838*, ed. W. Bates (1873), pp. 161–3, no. 60 · *The letters of Alaric Alexander Watts from the Blackwood papers in the National Library of Scotland*, ed. E. C. Polk (1952) · J. Don Vann and R. T. VanArsdel, eds., *Victorian periodicals and Victorian society* (1994) · F. W. Faxon, *Literary annuals and gift-books* (1912) · *Literary Gazette* (1820–22) · *Wellesley index*, vols. 2–3 · A. Sullivan, ed., *British literary magazines*, [2]: *The Romantic age, 1789–1836* (1984)
Archives University of Iowa Libraries, Iowa City, papers | BL, letters to J. Clare, Egerton MSS 2247–2250 · BL, corresp. with Sir Robert Peel, Add. MSS 40387, 40524, 40601 · BL, letters to Royal Literary Fund, loan 96 · Herts. ALS, corresp. with Lord Lytton · NL Scot., corresp. with Blackwoods · NL Scot., letters to D. M. Moir · Wordsworth Trust, Dove Cottage, Grasmere, letters to William Wordsworth
Likenesses W. Brockedon, chalk drawing, 1825, NPG · H. Howard, oils?, exh. RA 1835 · C. Bacon, bust, 1847, NPG · D. Maclise, lithograph, BM; repro. in *Fraser's Magazine*, 11 (June 1835), facing p. 652 · J. & C. Watkins, photograph, NPG [*see illus.*] · wood-engraving, repro. in *ILN*

Watts, Charles (1836–1906), secularist and journalist, was born in Bristol on 27 February 1836, the son of George Watts, a bootmaker. His parents were strict Wesleyan Methodists, his father being a local preacher. Having made his lecturing début on the temperance platform when he was fourteen, Watts was converted to freethought by the lectures of G. J. Holyoake. At the age of sixteen he left home for London, where he associated with the freethinkers in south London. He was joined by his older brother John (1834–1866), a printer who worked for the Holyoake brothers at 147 Fleet Street and then set up his own business in 1858. When John became editor of Charles Bradlaugh's *National Reformer* in 1864, Charles was appointed sub-editor. At the same time he became a full-time lecturer in the secularist movement, and in 1866 was made first secretary of the National Secular Society, a post he held until 1871 and again from 1873 to 1875.

When Austin Holyoake died in 1874, his printing and publishing business at 17 Johnson's Court was purchased by the freethought movement from the widow and presented to Watts. He was at this date second only to Bradlaugh in the secularist movement, but in 1877 the two quarrelled bitterly over Watts's refusal to defend an action brought against him as nominal publisher of Charles Knowlton's birth-control work *The Fruits of Philosophy*. He resigned from the National Secular Society and, with other secularists opposed to Bradlaugh, founded the British Secular Union as a short-lived rival to the National Secular Society, and acquired G. J. Holyoake's weekly periodical the *Secular Review* as its organ. He edited this until 1882, when he made the first of three visits to North America, leaving his son Charles Albert *Watts (1858–1946) in charge of his printing and publishing business, and W. S. Ross as editor of the *Secular Review*. On his third visit, in 1884, he settled in Toronto, where in 1887 he published a

weekly periodical, *Secular Thought*. Having resettled in England after Bradlaugh's death in 1891, he resumed lecturing for the National Secular Society until 1902, when he again resigned following accusations by G. W. Foote that he had diverted donations from the National Secular Society to the Rationalist Press Association, which had been founded by his son Charles Albert in 1899. He devoted the rest of his life to supporting this latter organization.

Charles Watts was an amiable man, and a popular lecturer and debater. Through the misfortune of falling foul of both Charles Bradlaugh and G. W. Foote his contribution to the National Secular Society and radical freethought in over forty years of public life has been underestimated. He published nearly fifty books and pamphlets on controversial political and religious topics, some of which were gathered together in *The Meaning of Rationalism and other Essays* (1905), but his writings lacked style and originality and are now seldom read. All his entries in the *British Library Catalogue of Printed Books* are mistakenly attributed to his son Charles Albert Watts.

Watts was married twice. His first wife, Mary Ann Tomkins, whom he had married on 12 June 1856, died of consumption in 1870, aged thirty-three. His children by this first marriage were Clara Agnes (1857–1921), Charles Albert, Frank (1862/3–1913), William (1863/4–1872), Annie (1866/7–1913), and Wallace George (1867/8–1870). His second marriage (on 19 November 1870) was to Eunice Kate Nowlan (1847/8–1924), the daughter of William Nowlan, a bootmaker and fellow freethinker; he had met her while staying at her father's house in Nottingham on a provincial lecture tour. She was an active secularist who also acted on the London stage under the name of Kate Carlyon. They had one daughter, Kate Eunice, born on 20 May 1875. Watts died on 16 February 1906 at 13 Carminia Road, Balham, and was cremated at Golders Green on 21 February; his ashes were buried in Highgate cemetery the following day. EDWARD ROYLE

Sources *Agnostic Journal* (24 Feb 1906) · *Literary Guide* (March 1906), 43–4 · *The Freethinker* (25 Feb 1906) · A. B. Moss, 'Famous freethinkers I have known. IV: Charles Watts', *The Freethinker* (23 May 1915) · 'Watts, Charles', *Labour Annual* (1899), 166 · *The Freethinker* (22 July 1894) · H. T. Law, 'Charles Watts', *Secular Chronicle* (21 April 1878) · E. Royle, *Radicals, secularists and republicans: popular freethought in Britain, 1866–1915* (1980) · m. cert. · d. cert.
Likenesses engraving, repro. in Law, 'Charles Watts' · engraving, repro. in *Secular Review* (26 Aug 1882) · oils, Rationalist Press Association, London · photograph, repro. in *Freethinker* (22 July 1894) · photograph, repro. in *Literary Guide* · photograph, repro. in F. J. Gould, *The pioneers of Johnson's Court* (1929), 5
Wealth at death £269 15s. 7d.: probate, 14 May 1906, CGPLA Eng. & Wales

Watts, Charles Albert (1858–1946), freethought editor and publisher, was born at 72 Hill Street, Walworth, London, on 27 May 1858, the eldest son of Charles *Watts (1836–1906), secularist and journalist, and his first wife, Mary Ann Tomkins (1836–1870). He was educated at national schools and night school, and at the age of twelve followed his father into the freethought movement. In 1870 he was apprenticed to Austin Holyoake (1826–1874), who ran a printing and publishing business in Johnson's

Court, Fleet Street. He continued there when his father took over the business on Holyoake's death, and took it over himself when his father went to North America in 1882; the arrangement was made permanent when his father settled in Canada in 1884. He established Watts & Co. as the leading freethought publisher in Britain, and also initiated new departures in periodicals and organizations. At first he preferred the rubric of agnosticism, under the influence of Herbert Spencer and T. H. Huxley, but he later adopted that of rationalism, on the advice of F. J. Gould (1855–1938).

In 1884 Watts launched the *Agnostic Annual*, which continued as the *RPA Annual* and later as the *Rationalist Annual*, and edited it until 1943. At the beginning of 1885 he launched a monthly paper, *The Agnostic*, which lasted only until the end of the year; but in November 1885 he launched another monthly paper, *Watts's Literary Guide*, which continued as the plain *Literary Guide*, and edited it until 1946 (possibly a record).

Watts took his father's part in the quarrel with Charles Bradlaugh in the National Secular Society in 1877, and joined him in the rival British Secular Union in 1878. When this collapsed on his father's departure, he worked to form a new freethought organization. In 1885 he called for an agnostic press fund and in 1889 for a propagandist press fund. In 1890 he founded the Propagandist Press Committee, which in 1893 was renamed the Rationalist Press Committee and in 1899 incorporated as the Rationalist Press Association Limited (RPA), with the veteran G. J. Holyoake as chairman. He served as managing director until 1930 and as vice-chairman until his death, and was largely responsible for making it the main sponsor of freethought publications in English.

Unlike his father and most other freethought leaders Watts was a poor speaker and writer (all the publications listed under his name in the British Library catalogue were written by his father). He concentrated instead on editing and publishing, and on laying personal and financial foundations for such work. He secured the endorsement of the RPA by distinguished sympathizers as honorary associates and the involvement of wealthy supporters as financial benefactors. The main benefactors were George Anderson, Henry Cooke, Lady Florence Dixie, Sydney Gimson, Clair Grece, Lord Hobhouse, Herbert Leon, T. Pepperell, marquess of Queensberry, and Horace Seal. The honorary associates included William Archer, A. W. Benn, Arnold Bennett, Georg Brandes, J. B. Bury, Georges Clemenceau, Patrick Geddes, J. B. S. Haldane, J. A. Hobson, Julian Huxley, Leonard Huxley, Ray Lankester, H. J. Laski, Cesare Lombroso, Bronislaw Malinowski, Hiram Maxim, John Morley, Bertrand Russell, Leslie Stephen, G. M. Trevelyan, Graham Wallas, H. G. Wells, and Emile Zola. The membership of the RPA rose steadily during the rest of his life, and he launched several successful series of cheap publications which sold millions of copies. He was also a strong though silent supporter of the ethical movement.

In 1930 Watts was forced by ill health to retire from full-time work, though he remained editor of his periodicals and maintained daily contact with the office until his death, when a third generation of the family took over from him. On 14 September 1885 he married Sarah Chater (1862–1915), the daughter of a Nottingham druggist. They had three children: a son, Frederick Charles Chater Watts (1896–1953), who succeeded his father as managing director, and twin daughters Gladys, later Dixon (1886–1971), and Sallie (1886–1915), who also worked for the organization, as later did their granddaughter Marion Watts. On 14 October 1916 Watts made a second marriage, to Bessie Maud Wright (1880–1960), the daughter of a London mariner. In 1938 they left London and settled in the Oxfordshire village of Sibford Gower, where he died on 15 May 1946, having served the freethought movement without pause for seventy-six years, done what he could to make it respectable and reliable, and established some of its most stable periodicals and organizations. A secular cremation was held at Oxford and a memorial service was held at Conway Hall in London on 10 October 1946, after which his ashes were interred at Highgate cemetery.

Watts contributed editorial material to most issues of his magazines and occasional autobiographical articles to the *Literary Guide*, including 'About personal matters' (June 1918), 'Some reminiscences of no. 17 Johnson's Court' (January 1924), and 'Twilight thoughts' (April 1924). Obituaries appeared in the freethought press, including the *Literary Guide*, 61/7 (1946) and 61/11 (1946). But, as he said himself, his true biography appeared in his publications and his organization. Although he soon shed the vestiges of his family's Calvinism, he always remained a puritan in his personal and professional character. He worked long hours for most of the days of his extensive career, inspired many colleagues to follow his lead, earned a formidable reputation not only among freethinkers but in the wider world of publishing and the press, and enjoyed a happy private life with his family and friends.

NICOLAS WALTER

Sources C. A. Watts, 'About personal matters', *Literary Guide* (June 1918), 89–90 • C. A. Watts, 'Some reminiscences of no. 17 Johnson's Court', *Literary Guide* (Jan 1924), 19–20 • C. A. Watts, 'Twilight thoughts', *Literary Guide* (April 1924), 69–70 • *Literary Guide*, 61/7 (1946), 101–6 • *Literary Guide*, 61/11 (1946), 167–70, 172, 476 • *Literary Guide* (Jan 1936) [jubilee issue] • *Literary Guide* (Feb 1936) [jubilee issue] • *Secular Review* (1878–85) • *The Agnostic* (1885) • *Watts's Literary Guide* (1885–94) • *Literary Guide* (1894–1946) • *Agnostic Annual* (1884–1907) • *R. P. A. Annual* (1908–43) • Rationalist Press Committee/Association, annual reports, 1893–1946, Rationalist Press Association archives • F. J. Gould, *The pioneers of Johnson's Court: a history of the Rationalist Press Association from 1899 onwards* (1929); rev. edn (1935) • A. G. Whyte, *The story of the RPA* (1949) • J. McCabe, *A biographical dictionary of modern rationalists* (1920) • Rationalist Press Association, membership register, Rationalist Press Association archives • *Memoria mori*, 1946, Rationalist Press Association archives [programme of memorial service] • Rationalist Press Association, minute books, Rationalist Press Association archives • *Rationalist Review*, 8 (spring 1996), 1–3 • b. cert. • m. certs. • d. cert.

Archives Bishopsgate Institute, London, corresp. with Hypatia Bradlaugh Bonner • Bodl. Oxf., corresp. with Gilbert Murray

Likenesses J. Collier, oils, 1920–29, Rationalist Press Association, London • Elliott & Fry, photograph, 1920–29, repro. in *Literary Guide* (July 1946)

Watts, Frederick Waters (1800–1870), landscape painter, has often been mistakenly called (Frederick) William

Watts. According to his second wife, Julia Watts, he was born in Bath, Somerset, on 7 October 1800, his father had been in the navy, and his mother was Mary Eyre, daughter of Ambrose Eyre, rector of Leverington, Isle of Ely, Cambridgeshire; he may also be the Frederic Waters Watts, son of William and Mary Watts, who was baptized on 9 July 1801 at St Albans Abbey, St Albans, Hertfordshire. Watts was probably the William Watts who entered the Royal Academy Schools in London in 1817, aged seventeen, and won its silver medals in 1819, 1820, and 1821. He was certainly the Frederick W. Watts who exhibited at the Royal Academy from 1821 to 1860, the British Institution from 1823 to 1862, and elsewhere.

Watts lived all his working life in the Hampstead area of London but painted landscapes throughout much of Britain; he appears also to have visited France in 1826. (Two pictures with Rouen as subject matter were shown at the British Institution in 1827.) His exhibited pictures of the 1820s and 1830s usually bore specific topographic titles and were closely handled; later canvases were more broadly painted and often imitated the mature work of John Constable. Many carried generalized titles such as *River Scene with Barges*, enabling others subsequently to identify them as scenes in 'Constable country' and to misattribute them to Constable himself. Watts was regarded as a follower of Constable even in his earlier work: in 1833 one critic saw him as 'trying to outrun the Constable' but concluded that: 'He never will, ... daub away as he may' (Ivy, 180). That same year, however, Constable suffered the indignity of being mistaken for his follower: one of his paintings of Helmingham Dell in Suffolk was put up for sale at Christies but arrived too late for inclusion in the catalogue. It was bought in at 50s. because, Constable told a friend, 'it was considered Watt's, and at least not certain, if mine' (Beckett, 164). Like Constable, Watts was a prolific outdoor oil sketcher. (Two examples are in the Tate collection.) Although possessing their own distinctive character, such sketches have also been misattributed to Constable in the past.

No details of Watts's first marriage are known except that two sons and three daughters were born of it, and that one, Alice J. Watts, became a painter. Most details of his second marriage also remain to be discovered. According to the second Mrs Watts, Julia Joanna Louisa, her husband 'had an humble opinion of his works & talents' and 'ceased to paint for 10 years before his death' (J. Watts to E. E. Leggatt, 13 Feb 1911). Watts died at his home, 11 Lawn Road, Hampstead, London, on 4 July 1870 of lung disease compounded by diabetes.   LESLIE PARRIS

Sources I. Fleming-Williams and L. Parris, *The discovery of Constable* (1984), 205–11 · J. Watts, letter to E. E. Leggatt, 13 Feb 1911, priv. coll. · J. Watts, letter to E. E. Leggatt, 21 Feb 1911, priv. coll. · *John Constable's correspondence*, ed. R. B. Beckett, 5, Suffolk RS, 11 (1967), 164 · J. C. Ivy, *Constable and the critics, 1802–1837* (1991), 180 · S. C. Hutchison, 'The Royal Academy Schools, 1768–1830', *Walpole Society*, 38 (1960–62), 123–91, esp. 170 · d. cert. · *IGI* · registers, RA, Royal Academy Schools · Graves, *RA exhibitors* · Graves, *Brit. Inst.*
Wealth at death under £8000: probate, 18 July 1870, *CGPLA Eng. & Wales*

Watts, George Frederic (1817–1904), painter and sculptor, was born on 23 February 1817 at 52 Queen Street, Bryanston Square, Marylebone, Middlesex, the eldest child of the second marriage of George Watts (1775–1845), pianoforte maker and tuner, and his wife, Harriet Ann (1786/7–1826), daughter of Frederic Smith.

Watts became, by the last two decades of his long life, one of the most famous painters in the world. The progress of this extended career resulted in an enormous output of some 800 paintings, as well as countless drawings and some sculpture. At the time of his death in 1904 he held a clutch of honours, most notably the newly instituted Order of Merit. He is still widely recognized as one of the greatest English portrait painters, but his critical fortunes have fluctuated widely since his death, and many of his major 'symbolical' subject paintings still provoke questions.

Family history and early life Watts's grandfather, also George (b. 1746), a cabinet-maker, left Hereford, the family's home, to settle in London in the mid-1790s. His eldest son, Watts's father, was first married in St Mary-le-Bone Church in 1799 to Mary Ann Williams, who died in 1813 after four children were born. Among the three children who survived to adulthood were Watts's half-brother, Thomas (b. 1799), who carried on the family pianoforte business and had his own large family, and two half-sisters, Maria (1801–1884) and Harriet (1803–1893). These two women took charge of their father's home after the death of his second wife, whom he had married in 1816. Watts repaid this attention by accepting responsibility for them once he had some success, continuing to do so until their deaths, even though his own wife did her best to expunge references to Watts's family in her memoirs of the artist.

Despite social aspirations, Watts's father struggled to maintain his family in difficult circumstances. His sickly infant was baptized privately at home. The name George Frederic seems to have been an allusion to his father's musical interests by invoking Handel, the anniversary of whose birth fell on the same day as that of the new baby. Life in the strict sabbatarian and evangelical household had its constraints, with a severe routine on Sundays, later recalled by the artist, and this narrow religious routine seems to have prompted his own turn away from organized religion. Family deaths dominated Watts's early life, as the three brothers born after him died, two in a measles epidemic in 1823 when Watts, aged six, was old enough to feel the impact of this double tragedy. Still worse was the death of his mother, probably from consumption, in 1826 when he was only nine, an event that made the reality of death painfully immediate. Declining family fortunes led to a move to Star Street, Paddington, Middlesex. Poor health prevented Watts from attending school regularly, but his talent for drawing emerged in numerous sketches and copies, and in these efforts his father encouraged him. Many early drawings are still preserved in his earliest sketchbook (priv. coll.). A keen reader, Watts knew the Bible, the *Iliad*, and the works of Sir Walter Scott from an early age and their content inspired his first drawings.

George Frederic Watts (1817–1904), self-portrait, 1864

In 1827 Watts entered the studio of the sculptor William Behnes, a family friend of Hanoverian descent whose father was also a pianoforte maker. In the busy open studio on Dean Street, in Soho, London, Watts worked on an informal basis, learning in the accepted academic method of copying: studies in physiognomy (1828, after *Fright*, one of Charles Le Brun's *têtes d'expression*); engravings after the old masters (1828, heads after Raphael); and modern artists, such as Richard Westall (1830, *Archangel Uriel and Satan*) and John Hamilton Mortimer. Watts's father brought some drawings to the attention of the president of the Royal Academy, Sir Martin Archer Shee, who pronounced: 'I can see no reason why your son should take up the profession of art' (Watts, *Annals*, 1.22). This comment did not deter the young artist in his independent studies, but it may well have encouraged his lifelong scepticism about the powers of the Royal Academy. Behnes provided Watts with access to plaster casts of the Elgin marbles and these led him to seek out the originals, newly installed in the British Museum in 1832. Watts's own assessment of his early training focused exclusively on the impact of these works: 'The Elgin Marbles were my teachers. It was from them alone that I learned' (Watts MSS, Strachey 1895). Benjamin Robert Haydon, the great propagandist for these masterpieces, visited Behnes's studio in the mid-1830s and, according to Emilie Barrington, encouraged Watts to continue studying the marbles, inviting the young artist to visit his own studio.

Behnes's example as an accomplished draughtsman turned sculptor presaged Watts's own willingness to work in different media. He admired Behnes's portrait drawings, soon developing a facility for such works himself,

enabling him to earn his own money from 1833, with portraits in coloured chalks and pencils. Based by this time in the new studio at Osnaburgh Street, Watts befriended Behnes's younger brother, Charles, a miniature painter whose steady temperament offset that of his wilder, more successful brother. Charles introduced Watts to wider literary horizons and on a practical level arranged for a friend to provide some tuition in oils. The success of his copies, including one after Van Dyck (formerly Watts Gallery) smoked to appear old, started Watts towards more formal training as a painter.

Early career Watts entered the Royal Academy Schools on 30 April 1835 and, as was the norm, he studied first in the antique school. In 1863 he evaluated the experience, stating that he entered the schools 'when very young, I do not remember the year, but finding that there was no teaching, I very soon ceased to attend' (RA Commission). His handling of oils had already advanced to a degree of fluency, as exemplified by the *Self-Portrait* of about 1834 and a portrait of his father (1836; both Watts Gallery, Compton, Surrey), both sensitive character studies. By this time, aged eighteen, he already earned his own way, in small-scale portraiture, a further disincentive to pursuing his studies in the schools. Even so, Watts matured as an artist in the 1830s when the ideal of history painting was still very much alive and he inherited a belief in 'high art'. At this time William Hilton was the leading representative of history painting in the academy and some of Watts's early paintings show this influence, as, for example, *Ruth and Boaz* (c.1835–6; Tate collection). As keeper of the Royal Academy during Watts's time there, Hilton praised the young man's drawings but discouraged him from painting 'anything original in the way of composition' (Watts, *Annals*, 1.26–7) when the young artist already felt able to do so. Recorded on the schools' books for two years, Watts attended only intermittently; he first exhibited at the Royal Academy in 1837 with *The Wounded Heron* (Watts Gallery, Compton, Surrey) and two portraits, from 33 Upper Norton Street, Marylebone. By 1838 he had taken his own studio at nearby Clipstone Street where, according to family tradition, the Watts pianoforte business traded.

During the 1830s Watts's leisure pursuits included studying languages, choral singing, and cricket. These interests combined in his friendship with Nicholas Wanostrocht the younger (1804–1876), of the Alfred House school in Blackheath, who became better known as the cricket authority Nicholas Felix, author of *Felix on the Bat* (1845). For Felix, Watts drew a series of accomplished drawings of cricket positions (he presented five of the seven to the Marylebone Cricket Club in 1895; now in the museum at Lord's cricket ground) that served as the basis for a set of lithographs published in 1837.

Patronage provided the key for Watts's continuing success as a portraitist of small, neat oils. Commissions from London's middle classes along with the occasional aristocratic portrait, such as *The Children of the Earl of Gainsborough* (c.1840–42), helped the young painter establish his practice. He painted John Roebuck MP (engraved 1840) which led to a curious commission to paint a portrait of

Jeremy Bentham (ex Christies, 14 July 1994) from a wax effigy (now at University College, London). The most important source of work came from the family of émigré Greek shipping merchant Constantine Ionides (1775–1852) whose business was located in the City of London. In 1837 Watts received a commission from his son Alexander Constantine Ionides (1810–1890) to copy Samuel Lane's portrait of Constantine (exh. RA, 1837) for the sum of £10. The family preferred Watts's copy, which they kept, to the original, which they sent back to Greece. Watts also painted the young family of Alexander Constantine Ionides, who was close in age to the artist and an eventual friend, in a vivid portrait (now destroyed; oil study, V&A) of the transplanted Greeks in their traditional dress. Watts's association with the Ionides family carried on through several generations and indirectly fuelled his own appreciation of ancient Greek sculpture.

Although Watts's portrait practice flourished, the ideals of high art impelled him to succeed as a history painter. His earliest efforts at subject painting derived from romantic literature; he soon tackled the traditional subjects for history painting, from classical literature and history, as in *The Fount* (*c*.1839; exh. British Institution, 1840) from the *Iliad*. His history paintings became increasingly ambitious, as *Cincinnatus* (*c*.1840; priv. coll.) suggests; the subject had a clear stoical message and obvious moral, thus looking back to neo-classical history paintings. In this work, for the first time, Watts's style with massively conceived, over life-sized figures reflected the inspiration of the Elgin marbles.

In April 1842 the Fine Arts Commission announced an important competition to promote large-scale historical painting to decorate Charles Barry and A. W. N. Pugin's new Palace of Westminster. Artists submitted cartoons (large drawings) with life-sized figures, illustrating scenes from British history or from the native poets, Shakespeare, Milton, and Spenser. By now with his own larger studio in Robert Street off Hampstead Road, Watts prepared an entry to fit the requirements, selecting a work he already had in hand, *Caractacus Led in Triumph through the Streets of Rome* (original in three fragments, V&A), from Tacitus's *Annals of Imperial Rome* (12.31–5). The exhibition of 140 entries opened in June 1843 in Westminster Hall. Watts's work impressed the judges, who included Samuel Rogers, Henry Petty-FitzMaurice, third marquess of Lansdowne, Sir Robert Peel, and three Royal Academicians. *Caractacus* bore the hallmarks of good draughtsmanship and a textbook composition based on the example of Raphael, with many figures amassed into clearly readable groups. Watts, along with Edward Armitage and Charles West Cope, won the highest premium of £300, enabling him to travel abroad to study the techniques of fresco painting in Italy. His poverty had prevented him from making an artistic 'grand tour' earlier but clearly he saw it as a way to improve his prospects, and embarked early in July 1843.

Travel and life in Italy, 1843–1847 After crossing the channel Watts initially spent six weeks in Paris, staying with his friend and fellow premium winner, Armitage, who trained in the studio of Paul Delaroche. At the Louvre, Watts studied the old masters but there is little evidence of his other activities. In early September he travelled by diligence from Paris to Chalon-sur-Saône, an uncomfortable journey of several days. He carried on by river steamboat via the Saône and Rhône to Avignon and thence to Marseilles. *En route* for the next port of call, Livorno, Watts met English travellers, General Robert and Mrs Ellice, friends of the British minister at the court of Tuscany, Henry Fox, fourth Lord Holland. They suggested Watts seek out Lord Holland in Florence. He meanwhile travelled onward in an open country cart during the Tuscan vintage season, stopping in Pisa for a few days, then going on to Florence, where he planned to stay for a month or two.

In Florence Watts initially studied art and culture, but on prompting from General Ellice he finally made several visits to Lord Holland's house, Casa Feroni, a vast eighteenth-century villa on the via dei Serragli. He accepted the offer to stay there for a few days until he found suitable lodgings to extend his stay in Florence, eventually staying for several years.

The Fox/Holland papers document Watts's life at the heart of a cosmopolitan circle of rich aristocrats and expatriates (Holland House MSS). In the Casa Feroni and the Villa Careggi, the former Medici villa in the hills outside Florence, to which the Hollands retreated, the young artist enjoyed many comforts, befriending Lord Holland's childless wife, Lady Augusta, in particular. Her informal portrait in a 'Riviera' (or 'Nice') straw hat (1843; Royal Collection) documents the spirit of their new friendship with a lighter palette reflecting the artist's newly lightened mood. Watts made many personal friends from among the Holland circle and, by way of thanks to his hosts, he made a series of sensitive portrait drawings in the manner of Ingres, indicating his assimilation of a continental mode in his own work. He also executed lively caricatures and more seriously conceived oil portraits, such as *Lady Augusta Fitzpatrick* (Tate collection), a full-length, grand-manner portrait. Social occasions provided opportunities, such as the costume ball in February 1845 when Watts donned a discarded suit of armour for a *Self-Portrait* (priv. coll.). He displayed his new self-image as a young man imbued with the Italian Renaissance past, reinventing himself as a romantic, far from London. Italian literature and history inspired the series of grand subject paintings that the artist executed in his spacious garden studio at Careggi, including *The Origin of the Quarrel between the Guelph and Ghibelline Families* (Watts Gallery, Compton, Surrey).

Watts expanded his artistic repertory with landscape paintings and scenes of Italian life, such as *Peasants of the Roman Campagna* (1844; priv. coll.). Small-scale experiments in fresco painting, ostensibly his reason for travelling, exist in the Victoria and Albert Museum, including *Paolo and Francesca*, a subject which became almost an obsession in many later versions. Watts executed one large-scale fresco at Careggi, still *in situ*, showing a scene from Medici family history inspired by the villa itself, *The*

Drowning of Lorenzo de Medici's Doctor, a scene of animated energy and Romantic brio (1844–5). Sculpture first entered his repertory while in Italy as well. Essentially Watts absorbed the culture of Italy, both its past and present. He mixed with an international community at coffee houses such as the Caffè Doney, where he socialized with artists and expatriates; one, Count Cottrell, who acted as chamberlain to the duke of Lucca (and who can now be properly identified as the amateur artist Henry Cottrell), became custodian of many of Watts's works of art when he left in 1847. His contacts with English aristocrats, great connoisseurs, and continental artistic society expanded his horizons immeasurably. Watts travelled with Lord Holland back to London for a few days in autumn 1844, but on returning to Italy went to Rome, Naples (where the Hollands had another residence), Pompeii, Milan, and Perugia. In 1845 he visited Lucca with Cottrell.

The latter portion of Watts's stay in Italy revolved around work on two history paintings in the large studio at Careggi, where he carried on even after Lord Holland resigned his diplomatic post and left Florence with his wife in 1846. Withdrawing from social life in town, Watts mixed mainly with the Duff Gordon sisters (whose mother, Lady Duff Gordon, had rented the Villa Careggi). He corresponded with Alexander Ionides in London, and a plan evolved for a commission to paint a large historical work destined for the university in Athens, with Watts explaining in a letter of June 1846 his aim 'to tread in the steps of the Old Masters' (Watts, *Annals*, 1.76). The plan foundered, yet the episode marked an important moment in the artist's career as his philhellenistic instincts and adoration of Phidias combined, albeit at this stage in the genre of history painting. Instead, in 1847, Watts prepared to enter the most recent of the series of competitions announced for the new houses of parliament with *Alfred Inciting the Saxons to Prevent the Landing of the Danes by Encountering them at Sea* (houses of parliament). Choosing a subject from English history with obvious nationalistic sentiments for one of his entries, Watts nevertheless proclaimed Phidias as his inspiration for a heroic style. Watts left Florence in mid-April 1847 to bring this painting and others back, fully intending to return to Italy; instead he remained based in London.

Watts at mid-career: changing direction in the late 1840s and 1850s Winning another first premium of £500 confirmed Watts's status as a history painter. In addition, the Fine Arts Commission purchased *Alfred Inciting the Saxons* for a further £200. Despite winning a premium, Watts received no immediate commission to paint fresco decorations in the new Palace of Westminster. It is likely that he was seen as an outsider, who had not stayed within the academy and its circle. Some sections of the art world expected Watts to take the lead as a history painter, but in the wake of B. R. Haydon's suicide in 1846 this genre was undergoing a re-evaluation. Thackeray, writing as Michelangelo Titmarsh, caricatured misguided artistic aspirations in 'Our Street' with the character of George Rumbold, a thinly disguised spoof of his friend Watts.

Watts assumed some responsibility for the support of his half-sisters on returning to London, eventually obtaining a house for them in Long Ditton, Surrey. He lodged at 48 Cambridge Street until 1849. The eminent collector and connoisseur Robert Holford lent him studio space in Dorchester House on Park Lane while it was under construction. Here Watts painted ambitious large works, including *Time and Oblivion* (c.1848–9, exh. RA, 1864; priv. coll.), one of his most difficult subjects, part allegory, part Watts's own invention. The massive canvas did not go to public exhibition at this point, but was well enough known for another of Watts's new friends, John Ruskin, to borrow it. Although occupied with the young Pre-Raphaelites, Ruskin tried to guide Watts as well, with no success, yet they did discuss the aims of art. Watts wrote to him (c.1850): 'my own views are too visionary and the qualities I aim at are too abstract to be attained, or perhaps to produce any effect if attained' (Watts, *Annals*, 1.91).

To further his career, Watts relied on annual exhibitions and on his influential friends. Over the next few years he unveiled several large paintings in a poetic spirit, including *Life's Illusions* (exh. RA, 1849; Tate collection), with only varying success. His falling spirits and ill health fed into a series of social realist canvases depicting problems of Victorian society at the time (*The Irish Famine* and *Found Drowned*, c.1848–50; both Watts Gallery, Compton, Surrey) but also reflecting his own depressed state of mind. These works did not appear at public exhibitions and were instead on view in his studio for his own circle to see. They relate closely to the modern life paintings by the Pre-Raphaelites, who admired Watts's originality. His sympathy with younger artists led him in 1850 to act as teacher to a young Oxford student, John Roddam Spencer-Stanhope, a grandson of the earl of Leicester.

By now living and working in Mayfair near Berkeley Square, London, Watts shared his studio at 30 Charles Street with his friend Charles Couzens, a miniature painter whose portrait of the artist (c.1848; Watts Gallery, Compton, Surrey) depicts Watts alongside casts of the Parthenon frieze. There he met Sara Prinsep and her husband, Thoby, a retired East India Company official, who were neighbours. Outside the public arena, Watts moved freely in their bohemian circle. In 1849 he became infatuated with Sara's beautiful sister, Virginia, another of the eight extraordinary Pattle sisters, many of whom featured in Watts's paintings at this time. In October 1850 Virginia married Charles, Viscount Eastnor (third Earl Somers from 1853); a trip to Ireland late in 1850 with the poet Aubrey de Vere provided distraction for Watts in the wake of the marriage and allowed him to see the country he had so movingly depicted in *The Irish Famine*. Yet it should be noted that he stayed in the upper echelons of Irish society at the de Vere seat, Curragh Chase in co. Limerick.

It was a major turning point in Watts's career when, in 1850, he sent *The Good Samaritan* (Manchester City Galleries) to the Royal Academy with the explanation that it was 'painted as an expression of the artist's admiration and respect for the noble philanthropy of Thomas Wright of Manchester' (Watts, *Annals*, 1.130). When the academy's hanging committee positioned the painting poorly, Watts took it as an insult and for some eight years he ceased sending important subject paintings to the Royal Academy, using it initially for his lesser productions, chiefly portrait drawings; he did not exhibit anything at all there from 1853 to 1857. He stage-managed his return in 1858 with the ruse of sending his contributions under an assumed name, F. W. George. With so many colleagues and friends in art circles, Watts could not disguise his paintings, yet the event reflects his uneasy relationship with the Royal Academy as an institution.

Watts helped his new friends the Prinseps by persuading his erstwhile benefactors, the Hollands—now back in London—to grant them a 21-year lease on the dower house, Little Holland House, from 25 December 1850. Mirroring his experiences in Florence, Watts soon moved in with the Prinseps as guest and resident artistic luminary, becoming the central attraction in Sara's salon, prompting her famous remark: 'He came to stay three days; he stayed thirty years' (Watts, *Annals*, 1.128). He had private studio space, but the relaxed atmosphere of family life lifted his depression and provided him with a comfortable, even cosseted lifestyle. At about this time, Sara dubbed Watts Signor, a nickname that reflected his courteous manner and alluded to his years in Italy. Thereafter most intimate friends addressed him this way; he even grew into the image by adopting a skullcap, seen in many of his self-portraits. Suffering from frequent headaches, he seems to have decided ill health was to be a way of life. Serious-minded about more than his art, Watts did not encourage 'anything savouring of the free and easy', according to William Michael Rossetti (Rossetti, 1.204), yet he relaxed completely in the company of strong women and little children.

Watts's Charles Street studio remained a meeting-place, even when he left and his friend the painter Henry Wyndham Phillips took it over. Late in 1852 it became the home of the newly formed Cosmopolitan Club. Here Watts mixed with a wide range of intellectuals, writers, artists, and politicians with his own large paintings on permanent exhibition, including *Echo* (exh. houses of parliament competition, 1847; Tate collection) as a backdrop to the literary evenings there. The group included close friends of Watts such as Ruskin, the architect Philip Charles Hardwick, Tom Taylor, and Henry Layard. Mixing with this group encouraged Watts to formulate a plan to paint portraits of eminent men of the day for his own collection eventually destined to be presented to the nation (a gesture perhaps inspired by Turner, who died in 1851). Watts painted these portraits for his own collection over the next fifty years. His intention to bestow them on the nation became a regular talking point in the press during his life. Watts never named this collection but it came to be called the Hall of Fame.

Mural projects, travel, and public statements on art in the 1850s Watts's allegiance to Italy prompted a short trip there in 1853 when he finally travelled to Venice in company with young Stanhope. Here for the first time he saw the glories of Venetian colour in painting. Further travels included several months in the winter of 1855–6 in Paris, where he took studio space on the rue des Saints Pères near the Seine on the Left Bank. For Lord Holland, then posted in France, Watts painted Adolphe Thiers, Prince Jérôme Bonaparte, and Princess Lieven (all priv. coll.), unexpected exercises in a style of sophisticated continental portraiture rarely attained by his English contemporaries.

Watts's talent for friendship testifies to his own natural behaviour and belief in himself and his work. His great friend Tom Taylor invited Watts to contribute to his life of Haydon in progress during 1852 thanks to Watts's already recognized position as an 'eloquent advocate of the claims of High Art' (Taylor, 3.361). He contributed to the first and second editions of *The Life of Benjamin Robert Haydon, Historical Painter* (1853). This text was the first of his many public pronouncements on art. Though ostensibly writing about Haydon, Watts extended the discussion to the idea of 'awakening a national sense of Art' (ibid., 3.372). For this he advocated large-scale wall paintings in fresco to adorn public buildings, with the sponsorship of the government. As an advocate for the public role of art, Watts attracted the attention and friendship of eminent individuals, such as Ruskin, Henry Acland of Oxford, and Layard, as well as younger up-and-coming men, including Charles Newton of the British Museum, who helped with various projects.

With Newton, Watts indulged his passion for the classical Greek sculptor Phidias, eventually travelling to Greece with Newton in October 1856. Watts accompanied his friend's expedition (sponsored by the government and the British Museum) to locate and excavate the site of the ancient mausoleum at Halicarnassus, one of the seven wonders of the ancient world (concluding in spring 1857). Travelling via Constantinople and the Greek islands, the artist witnessed antique sculptures, as they were unearthed, complete with original colouring which, once exposed to the air, rapidly faded. Such transitory effects fuelled Watts's later reinterpretation of classical subjects.

Through the contacts he made at Little Holland House, meeting the Tennysons, the Pre-Raphaelites, and others, Watts found much work as a portrait painter, but he also pursued his other ambitions. By November 1852 he finally received a commission to paint a mural in the new Palace of Westminster. In the Upper Waiting Hall (the 'Poets' Hall') Watts and five other artists were allocated authors from whose work they chose a subject to fill six upright spaces of about 10 feet in height. Watts painted a scene from Spenser's *Fairie Queene*, *The Triumph of the Red Cross Knight*, also known as *St George Overcoming the Dragon* (restored).

Mural decoration amounted to an obsession with Watts. He painted some strictly decorative additions to a scheme at old Holland House (*c.*1849) in the Gilt Room and Inner Hall. At Little Holland House (*c.*1851–3) he had more freedom and painted a series in the dining-room prefiguring his later 'symbolical' works. One commission led to another: Lord and Lady Somers invited him to decorate their London town house, 7 Carlton House Terrace (*c.*1854–5). Not an exact scheme, but described by a contemporary writer as 'the Gods of Parnassus and Olympus' (Stephens, 47), these vigorous wall paintings evoke the baroque decorations of Italian palazzi. The scheme is also an important landmark in a more imaginative use of classical subject matter in English art. Further private commissions followed, including the two murals *Achilles Watching Briseis Led Away from his Tents* (1858; Watts Gallery, Compton, Surrey) and *Coriolanus* (1860, ex Christies, 25 June 1998) painted for Bowood, Wiltshire, for the third marquess of Lansdowne.

Watts advocated mural painting for public buildings in the 1850s as 'a means of developing these qualities which would place British artists by the side of British poets, and form a great national school' (Watts, *Annals*, 1.135). His most ambitious plan, conceived in late 1852, to paint a massive mural, 'The Progress of Cosmos', in the great booking hall at Euston Station, never progressed beyond a proposition he made, with the backing of P. C. Hardwick, his good friend and the architect involved. The directors of the London and North Western Railway Company rejected his plan, despite the fact that he wanted payment only for materials. More successfully, in 1852, Watts offered to paint a mural at the Great Hall of Lincoln's Inn, proposing his plan to the benchers, again with Hardwick's support. Completed in October 1859, *Justice: a Hemicycle of Lawgivers* won him praise in the press. His own programme depicting legal innovators throughout history must have required considerable reading and planning. It was not a true fresco and suffered some deterioration and restoration over the years. However, *Justice* remains Watts's most successful and most public mural, and a grand dinner in April 1860 along with a gift of £500 for his efforts sealed the triumph. One further public project in London, his last mural, was painted for the church of St James-the-Less, Pimlico (1861), depicting *The Saviour in Glory* (later replaced with a mosaic).

The 1860s During this extremely productive decade, Watts's social life intersected with his art. For several years running he spent a few winter months at Sandown House, Esher, Surrey, with Thoby Prinsep's sister, at gatherings that included Tom Taylor and the Duff Gordons. The émigré Orléans family at nearby Claremont added to the social mix. A keen rider, Watts hunted with the Old Surrey foxhounds and the duc d'Aumale's harriers. Like his friend Frederic Leighton, he found continental society congenial. Little Holland House still formed the centre of his world, with Tennyson becoming a firm friend and the subject of a series of masterly portraits, including the 'Moonlight' portrait (priv. coll.), which exemplifies Watts's new, more 'poetic' interpretation of his sitters in a richer style inspired by Venetian art.

Tom Taylor introduced two young actresses, Kate and Ellen Alice *Terry (1847–1928), to the Little Holland House circle in Kensington. For Watts personally, the meeting with Ellen Terry changed his life. Taken with her youthful spirit and fresh looks, he apparently first thought of adopting the sixteen-year-old girl; then, with the encouragement of Taylor and Sara Prinsep, Watts and Ellen

became engaged. They married at St Barnabas Church, Kensington, on 20 February 1864, three days before Watts's forty-seventh birthday and a week before Ellen's seventeenth. However she did not fit easily into the Little Holland House circle, though her image inspired Watts in several paintings, including *Choosing* (RA, 1864; NPG). The marriage (if it was ever consummated) did not last; they separated in 1865, with Watts agreeing to pay her £300 a year 'so long as she shall lead a chaste life' (Loshak, 'Watts and Ellen Terry', 480). Ellen returned to her family and to the stage (somewhat embarrassingly for the artist, she appeared on playbills as Mrs G. F. Watts). In 1868 she left London to live with the architect E. W. Godwin, temporarily retiring from the stage to have a family.

Watts moved more emphatically into the public realm with successes such as the Lincoln's Inn mural to his credit. He returned to the forum of the Royal Academy, even though not yet a member of this institution. This exclusion gave rise to public comment at a time of growing dissatisfaction with the academy, culminating in a government inquiry led by a select committee in 1863. Watts testified himself, offering another cogent public statement on art, focusing on improvements to life drawing in the schools, showing models in action. He objected to the idea of an artist putting himself up for election to the academy. Four years later, under newly revised rules, Watts's name went forward without any intervention by him. Elected associate of the Royal Academy on 31 January 1867, he was quickly elevated to full membership on 18 December of the same year—a unique event in the academy's history and an indication of the esteem in which fellow artists held him. In a position to take on academy duties, such as hanging exhibitions (which he did in 1869), he came into even closer contact with Leighton, his close friend (and Kensington neighbour since 1866).

Portraiture occupied much of Watts's time, not only commissioned works such as grand-manner portraits, *Hon. Mrs. Percy Wyndham* (late 1860s; priv. coll.) and *Lady Bath* (begun *c.*1862; priv. coll.), but also portraits of sitters of his own choosing, for example, *William Gladstone* (1859, exh. 1865), *Dean Henry Milman* (*c.*1863), *Robert Browning* (1866), and *Algernon Swinburne* (1867, NPG), retained for his own gallery of worthies. He ventured into new types of subject matter with poetically inspired paintings finally appearing at public exhibitions, encouraging younger artists. Designs under way by the late 1860s included early versions of *The Court of Death*, *Time, Death and Judgement*, and Old Testament subjects, such as *The Creation of Eve* and *The Denunciation of Cain*. Supportive patrons such as Sir William Bowman, the London oculist, and Charles Rickards, a well-to-do philanthropist from Manchester, sought out Watts and his work, providing avenues for his more experimental subjects. Indeed, the upturn in Watts's increased sales encouraged him at one point, about 1869–70, to engage the dubious entrepreneur Charles Augustus Howell as an unofficial agent.

Eminent men crossed Watts's path and became supporters. Gladstone, in sympathy with Watts's modern 'classical' works, requested paintings from him and gave tangible support to his ideas for bequeathing his work to the nation. Dean Milman interceded for commissions to participate in the scheme to decorate St Paul's Cathedral, but although Watts produced designs (c.1861–2, *St John*; *St Matthew*), along with Alfred Stevens, the scheme dragged on until mosaics after his two designs went into position much later. Watts devoted more time to sculpture both as an aid to composing and in its own right. His first tomb monument was to Thomas Cholmondely Owen (1867; Condover church, Shropshire). The marble bust *Clytie* (exh. RA, 1868; London, Guildhall) stands as a testament of his own reinterpretation of the spirit of Phidian art, revealing a new freedom of movement to younger sculptors. Its appearance at the Royal Academy led to further commissions for sculpture. The long illness of his friend William Kerr, eighth marquess of Lothian, had already inspired early versions of *Love and Death*; after Lothian's death in 1870 Watts executed a recumbent memorial figure (Blickling church, Norfolk) characterized by deep cutting and expressive carving, also seen in the monument to the bishop of Lichfield (commission 1869, Lichfield Cathedral). He also collaborated with J. E. Boehm on the full-length seated statue of the first Lord Holland (Holland Park) at about this time. He transformed the equestrian figure of Hugh Lupus for the marquess of Westminster (1870–84; priv. coll.) into *Physical Energy*, which became his best-known sculpture. The first version later formed part of the memorial to Cecil Rhodes in South Africa.

The 1870s With Lady Holland selling off sections of the Holland estate, Watts foresaw a departure from Little Holland House within the next few years. In late 1871, he bought property on the Isle of Wight, where Julia Margaret Cameron and Tennyson already had homes. Near Freshwater, Watts had The Briary built for the Prinseps by the autumn of 1873. His connections with them led him to adopt their young relation Blanche Clogstoun (later Somers-Cocks), who featured in several of his paintings in the 1870s. This gesture seemed to be his way of creating a family, as the Prinsep children grew up and left. Before 1875, when Little Holland House was knocked down, he bought a parcel of land, number 6 on the new Melbury Road, backing on to Leighton's property, and commissioned C. R. Cockerell to build a home and studio, complete with a top-lit gallery to display his collection. He moved into New Little Holland House in February 1876. His neighbour, Emilie Barrington, an amateur painter, writer on art, and friend of artists, made herself indispensable to Watts, along with her husband, Russell, who for a while acted as a financial agent for the artist. At about this time, Watts discovered that his wife had some years earlier set up home with Godwin. He petitioned for divorce (perhaps at her instigation); the case appeared before the Probate, Divorce, and Admiralty Division on 13 March 1877 and a decree nisi was awarded. Soon after, Ellen remarried.

Watts embarked on a wide range of commissions to pay for building projects, stepping up his portrait work with reluctance. However, ongoing patronage meant he could also paint large subject paintings and find purchasers. His

professional stature as a full academician also helped considerably. For his diploma piece, he painted on life scale a multi-figure composition, *The Denunciation of Cain* (exh. RA, 1872; RA). He saw it as part of a cycle of paintings which (much later in the 1890s) eventually came to be called *The House of Life* (not Watts's own title). This grand scheme never materialized, but he continued to paint oils derived from it, presenting them as independent works. He insisted that 'these I always destined to be public property' (Watts, *Annals*, 1.261). He exhibited early versions of *The Titans* (later called *Chaos*), his own personal reworking of earth's origins, combining a post-Darwinian perspective with a partly invented variation on classical myth. Smaller exhibition venues, such as the Dudley Gallery, provided convenient places to show experimental works, such as early versions of *Love and Death*, as well as works in progress. To the Royal Academy Watts generally sent portraits, considering that venue as 'no place for a grave, deliberate work of art' (Bryant, 'Watts at the Grosvenor Gallery', 109). He worked through several compositions, such as *Time, Death and Judgement* and *The Court of Death*, from the 1860s onward, increasing the scale of these works and refining the imagery during the 1870s. His method involved reworking compositions on a more and more monumental scale and with varying qualities of mood and changes in colour. With the volume of work increasing, Watts took on assistants, including Matthew Ridley Corbet and, in the 1880s, Cecil Schott, who carried out preliminary work on his larger canvases.

With the opening of the Grosvenor Gallery in May 1877, Watts found his ideal venue where he showed his work for the next ten years. His friend Coutts Lindsay, owner of the gallery, included him as one of the featured artists who sent in several paintings. The triumphant appearance of the prime version of *Love and Death* (Whitworth Art Gallery, Manchester) marked the first time Watts's 'symbolical' paintings were revealed to the public as he intended. This turning point in his reputation saw critical and public favour—particularly that of the artistic élite—heaped upon him. The prime version of *Time, Death and Judgement* (National Gallery of Canada, Ottawa) followed in 1878 to equal acclaim. His art travelled abroad to international exhibitions, particularly the Universal Exhibition in Paris in 1878, where *Love and Death* among his other works earned a first-class medal. In 1879, along with a handful of internationally celebrated British artists, Watts was asked by the Uffizi Gallery to paint a *Self-Portrait* (exh. RA, 1880) for their gallery of artists' portraits, a request to which he acceded with enthusiasm. His stature increased not only with such international recognition, but also with further writings and statements on art at conferences and in periodicals.

The 1880s In 1880, with his reputation secure, Watts published 'The present conditions of art' in a literary journal, the *Nineteenth Century*. In this article he complained about the Royal Academy, its commercial spaces being unsuited to his 'poems painted on canvas' (Bryant, 'Watts at the Grosvenor Gallery', 109). Even more tellingly, he spoke of art as a way to 'lift the veil that shrouds the enigma of being' (Bryant, 'Watts and the symbolist vision', 73), fore-casting symbolist concerns of the 1880s. His imaginative subject paintings dominated the Grosvenor Gallery: taking classical culture as the point of departure in *Orpheus and Eurydice* (exh. Grosvenor Gallery, 1879; Salar Jung Museum, Hyderabad, India) and *Endymion* (c.1869, exh. Grosvenor Gallery, 1881; priv. coll.), the artist explored other levels of meaning, introducing ideas of death, mysticism, and spiritualism, that fuelled symbolism in contemporary art both at home and abroad, providing an example for a younger generation of artists.

A key indication of Watts's ascending position was the exhibition of Rickards's collection of works by Watts staged at the Royal Manchester Institution in 1880. This event, in turn, led to Coutts Lindsay's decision to stage an even more ambitious event in the winter of 1881–2. Containing more than 200 works, the *Collection of the Works of G. F. Watts, R.A.* has the distinction of being the first full retrospective of any living British artist. By now into his sixties, Watts had a full career behind him, well worth examining. His introduction to the catalogue defined a type of painting he dubbed 'symbolical'—non-narrative works with a poetic spirit. His status as an inspiration to a younger generation and as a British artist seen in an international context (thanks to the ties between the Grosvenor Gallery and the Paris art world), contributed to the cult of the artist as a personality, a relatively new idea in the late nineteenth-century art world. His work became well known abroad, on exhibition in the Paris Salon of 1880.

After 1880 Watts's art was continually on view as he took the presentation of his art into his own hands, further enhancing his reputation. His own picture gallery opened at New Little Holland House, free to the public on Saturday and Sunday afternoons. He lent or gave his works to London institutions (*Time, Death and Judgement* to St Paul's Cathedral; a selection of works lent to the South Kensington Museum in the 1880s). An exhibition entitled the 'Watts collection' travelled to various cities throughout Britain during the mid-1880s. He presented paintings to institutions abroad, for example *Time, Death and Judgement* to Canada in 1886; versions of *Love and Life* to the USA in 1893 (sold from the national collections in 1987), and to France (now Musée d'Orsay, Paris). In 1884, with the encouragement and help of a young American, Mary Gertrude Mead, who later married Edwin Austin Abbey, Watts showed a group of some thirty works at New York's newly opened Metropolitan Museum of Art. Although he did not travel himself to New York, Watts took a unique step in promoting his work abroad through a one-man exhibition. The event placed contemporary British art on the map in America with the first 'blockbuster', open for six months.

In the wake of the Grosvenor Gallery retrospective of 1882–3, Watts received a range of honours: Oxford made him a DCL and Cambridge awarded an honorary degree of LLD in 1882 'in recognition of his distinguished services to art'. In 1885, when Gladstone, as prime minister, offered baronetcies to Watts and J. E. Millais, Watts declined on the grounds that he felt his financial means insufficient for the role; Gladstone persisted but his offer was rejected again in 1894. Further recognition came in 1886 with the government indicating that it would accept his bequest of paintings in due course.

During the 1880s Watts exhibited paintings now considered as a distinctly British contribution to international symbolism, such as his own invented subjects, *Hope* (exh. Grosvenor Gallery, 1886; first version, priv. coll.) and the enigmatic *Dweller in the Innermost* (exh. Grosvenor Gallery, 1886; Tate collection), a personification of the idea of conscience. Such paintings reflect Watts's own thinking on a variety of ideas never before considered subject matter for painters. He grappled with these notions, as did like-minded men such as his friend Frederic Myers, founder of the Society for Psychical Research, a group Watts joined as an honorary member in 1884.

Watts remarried on 20 November 1886 in Epsom, Surrey. Mary Seton Fraser-Tytler (1849–1938), aged nearly thirty-seven, the third daughter of a Scottish gentleman from Inverness-shire, Charles Edward Fraser-Tytler of Balnain and Aldourie, had studied art in London since the 1860s and worshipped Watts; she moved into his circle through the Freshwater community, especially J. M. Cameron. According to Holman Hunt, Watts had several ladies pursuing him at this time. His decision to wed Mary, surprising to many friends, seems to have been dictated by his age (sixty-nine), increasingly poor health (rheumatism had set in by 1883), and the need for a sympathetic person to take charge of the household. Honeymooning in the winter of 1886–7, they travelled to Egypt, including the Nile, as well as to Constantinople, Athens, and Messina. The Greek portion of the journey enabled him for the first time to see the monuments of the Acropolis in their own surroundings. Mr and Mrs Watts returned via Paris, and eventually home to Kensington in June 1887. Further international travel followed the next winter, as the ageing Watts sought to escape damp London winters for warmer climes. November 1887 found them in Sliema, Malta: Mediterranean light and colour fed into Watts's art in a series of evanescent seascapes such as *Fog off Corsica* (exh. New Gallery, 1889; priv. coll.). On the return journey in February 1888 they visited the alpine regions of Haute-Savoie; the scenery of the high Alps inspired several visionary landscapes including *Sunset on the Alps* (1888–94; Watts Gallery, Compton, Surrey).

Social concerns continued to preoccupy Watts. In September 1887 he wrote to the national press proposing a record of heroic deeds of common people as a fitting jubilee memorial. He also formed a close friendship with Canon Samuel Barnett and his wife Henrietta, who were active in helping the poor in the East End of London at their church, St Jude's, Whitechapel; when art exhibitions became part of their programme from 1885, Watts readily lent his paintings. Works such as *Mammon* (1884–5; Tate collection), a statement on the horrors of worshipping money, revealed the artist's social impulse in symbolist visual imagery.

Watts valued his artistic friendships, often seeking the opinions of his colleagues in connection with progress on individual paintings. In addition to his friends Burne-Jones and Leighton, he particularly (and rather unexpectedly) sought out Briton Riviere, Henry Holiday, Walter Crane, and William Blake Richmond. Support for worthy causes led to writing, including the preface to A. H. Mackmurdo's *Plain Handicrafts* in 1892, and to financial contributions to the Home Arts movement beloved by his wife, by now a craftswoman in her own right.

In the late 1880s Watts's art assumed an even higher position in public and critical estimation. In 1887 M. H. Spielmann wrote a substantial article in the *Pall Mall Gazette* based on conversations with the artist, including a catalogue of his work. Watts's powers were at their height. He worked on the large version of *The Court of Death* (c.1868–1903; Tate collection). Portraits such as the masterly *Cardinal Manning* (exh. Grosvenor Gallery, 1882; NPG) reveal an ability to penetrate the character of his sitters. In 1888 he switched allegiance from the Grosvenor Gallery to the newly formed New Gallery, along with Burne-Jones. Here his major works appeared until his death; yet he contributed to a wide range of exhibiting venues, including the Royal Society of British Artists, the Society of Portrait Painters, and the Grafton Gallery. Internationally, Watts and Burne-Jones triumphed at the Universal Exhibition in Paris in 1889. Watts showed eight works, including *Hope* and *Mammon*, recognized by the French critics as 'allégories poétiques' (Bryant, 'Watts and the symbolist vision', 76).

From the 1890s to 1904 In 1890, encouraged by his friend Andrew Hichens, Watts agreed to the purchase of land in Compton, near Guildford, in Surrey, for a house to be built by Ernest George. Watts and his wife named it Limnerslease, a combination of the word 'limner', meaning artist with 'leasen' or glean. Watts bought it by 1891, obtaining the freehold from Hichens in 1899. Still based in Kensington, he continued to work on a massive sculpture, *Physical Energy*, as well as a large statue of Tennyson (1898–1903) for the city of Lincoln. Ill health punctuated the decade but he still produced an enormous amount for a man approaching eighty. Travel to Scotland in 1898 inspired landscape paintings. By 1890 he and Mary were introduced to a young orphan, Lilian (also known as Lily) Mackintosh (later Mrs Michael Chapman), who later came to live with them. She eventually became heir to the entire estate left by Mrs Watts.

Watts's international profile meant visits from admirers from abroad. In autumn 1890 his conversations with the queen of Romania inspired his thinking about the painting *Sic transit* (1890–92; Tate collection), a symbolist *memento mori* produced at a time when Watts himself suffered a severe illness. In 1893 a visit from Léonce Benedite, the director of the Luxembourg (a collection of modern paintings) in Paris, led to his choice of a version of *Love and Life*, which Watts presented to the French nation. In the same year twenty-four paintings and one sculpture travelled to an exhibition in Munich, with the Bavarian government purchasing *The Happy Warrior* (exh. Grosvenor Gallery, 1884; Bayerische Staatsgemäldegalerie, Munich).

Watts's celebrity status resulted in numerous articles in the British press, including interviews filled with photographs of the artist at work and at rest. His personal regime, always rather abstemious, became even more regulated as he followed the 'Salisbury diet', consisting of small amounts of nearly raw meat, toast, and milk, with no fruit or vegetables. A hearing aid improved his increasing deafness. In December 1891 the caricature by Spy in *Vanity Fair* showed the snowy-haired Watts in frock coat and Titian-like skullcap, along with the quotation 'He paints portraits and ideas', summing up his popular image. His pamphlet *What Should a Picture Say* in 1894 indicated his continuing concern that his paintings should be widely understood. He drove a hard bargain with the many new clients seeking his paintings for their collections, asking upwards of £2000 for large subject paintings and £500 for landscapes in 1895.

To control the publication of his work, Watts retained copyright of his paintings. His working relations with the art photographer Frederick Hollyer also ensured that most of his paintings existed in black and white photographs advertised regularly for easy ordering. This steady supply also enabled the press to produce well-illustrated articles. By 1900 more than a dozen of these articles had appeared, embedding Watts's work in the popular imagination. With the death of many of his closest friends by this time, he became by default the most famous living British painter. Although officially retiring from the Royal Academy, taking on the title of honorary retired academician from November 1896, Watts still sent paintings to a whole range of exhibition venues until his death.

Watts's long-planned bequests to the nation finally came to fruition in the late 1890s. In 1895 the National Portrait Gallery received a group of portraits; in 1896 Watts became a trustee. In 1897 the new National Gallery of British Art, popularly known as the Tate Gallery, after its benefactor, opened with seventeen paintings forming the first instalment of the Watts Gift. Specially displayed in two rooms (later one), this bequest formed a significant portion of the new gallery. By the late 1890s Watts's paintings were more widely available in London than those by any other living artist. Another retrospective exhibition was held at the New Gallery in 1896–7, with Watts writing a preface to the catalogue. Friends marked his eightieth birthday in February 1897 with a congratulatory address signed by several hundred distinguished men and women of the day, and including a specially composed tribute from Swinburne—'High Thought and Hallowed Love'. In 1900 the memorial to heroes in everyday life, funded by Watts, took the form of a canopied area decorated with Doulton tiles in part of the old churchyard of St Botolph, Aldersgate (in the Postman's Park) in the City of London. The crowning moment of his career came in 1902, when Edward VII instituted the Order of Merit with Watts among the inaugural twelve.

Watts's intellectual vigour produced more original compositions about 1900, including the startlingly visionary *Sower of the Systems* (exh. New Gallery, 1903; Art Gallery of Ontario, Toronto) along with *Progress* and *Destiny* (c.1903/1904, both Watts Gallery, Compton, Surrey). Such works embraced the new century, as Watts, ever conscious of his impact on posterity, initiated his own dialogue with future generations. The *Court of Death* was completed in 1903 when, after decades of work, it finally went to join the Watts Gift at the Tate Gallery. His bronze version of *Physical Energy* went on view at the Royal Academy in May 1904, prior to being sent to South Africa as a memorial to Cecil Rhodes.

In 1902 Watts bought a further 3 acres in Compton, across the road from his house, with the intention of building a separate picture gallery. Opening in April 1904, this building is the home of the Watts Gallery, where Mrs Watts presided as 'keeper of the flame' until her death in 1938. Overall, she was far from a benign influence, distancing him from certain friends. Her plan for a mortuary chapel for the village, designed and decorated by herself, complete with nearby memorial to Watts, served as a constant reminder of his approaching death. After 1904 she nurtured the Watts legend, sometimes distorting evidence, which she published in the long-gestating *Annals of an Artist's Life* in 1912. Her lack of information about his career before 1886 has also caused problems of dating and of chronology; her compendious manuscript catalogue of his works (Watts Gallery) is often unreliable.

The illness that finally caused his death started in early June 1904 while Watts worked on the gesso model of *Physical Energy* in Kensington. He died at 6 Melbury Road on Friday 1 July with the cause recorded on his death certificate (dated 2 July) as 'cystitis with high fever, from old septic absorption', along with bronchitis and a weakened heart. The obituary in *The Times* opened with the declaration, 'the most honoured and beloved of English artists is dead' (2 July, p. 5). Such was the importance of the event that the sermon in St Paul's Cathedral two days after his death focused on the artist. The next week, on 4 July, a train to Brookwood conveyed his body for cremation 'at Mr. Watts's express wish'. The ashes went to Compton for eventual interment in the cemetery adjacent to the mortuary chapel. A memorial service took place in London at St Paul's Cathedral with dignitaries, as well as friends; the funeral was held at Compton on Friday 8 July. Watts's will named some specific bequests of individual portraits to friends, and a group of drawings to the Royal Academy, but left virtually everything else in the hands of his executors headed by his wife. She cannily queried some unclear wording in the will which enabled her and the other executors to bestow most of his works on the Watts Gallery, rather than to public museums throughout Britain, as the artist intended. The gallery, somewhat depleted by sales over the years, remains an important collection of the artist's work.

Watts's posthumous reputation flowered for a decade, with a series of memorial exhibitions in 1905–6 and a flood of publications. In 1905 Charles Stanford, who had composed some accompanying music for the funeral, wrote his symphony no. 6 in E♭ major 'in honour of the life-work of a great artist: George Frederic Watts'. With the era of modernism, the artist's reputation plummeted as the Tate Gallery closed the room devoted to his work by the late 1930s. Yet Watts lived on in the collective memory of Bloomsbury thanks to his friendships with the Prinseps and Stephenses, even if this survival became the subject of humour rather than respect, as in Virginia Woolf's short play, *Freshwater* (1923) which mercilessly lampooned Watts, Tennyson, and Mrs Cameron. His appeal to the literary world continued: Watts's memorial to unsung heroes in the Postman's Park took an integral role in the play *Closer* (1997) by Patrick Marber.

Watts's portraits have always sustained his position as one of the major figures of the nineteenth century. His role as an innovator in international symbolism is now acknowledged. Watts is essentially important as an artist who, in the course of the century, transformed the ideals of 'high art' which he inherited in the 1830s into an original visual language of universals for a range of genres. Equally important is the way Watts's life and career epitomized the modern notion of the artist as celebrity and hero.   BARBARA COFFEY BRYANT

Sources B. Bryant, *Portraits by George Frederic Watts* (2004) [exhibition catalogue, NPG] • M. H. Spielmann, *The works of Mr George F. Watts* [1886] • 'Catalogue of the works of G. F. Watts, compiled by his widow', 3 MS vols., c.1910, Watts Gallery, Compton, Surrey • J. Cartwright, 'George Frederic Watts', *Easter Art Annual* (1896), 1–32 • E. Barrington, *G. F. Watts: reminiscences* (1905), 1 • M. S. Watts, *George Frederic Watts: the annals of an artist's life*, 3 vols. (1912) • NPG, Heinz Archive and Library, Watts papers • *The Times* (2 July 1904), 5 • Earl of Ilchester [G. S. Holland Fox-Strangways], *Chronicles of Holland House, 1820–1900* (1937) • D. Loshak, *George Frederic Watts, O.M., R.A., 1817–1904* (1954) [exhibition catalogue, Tate Gallery, London, 1954–5] • *Collection of the works of G. F. Watts* (1881–2) [exhibition catalogue, Grosvenor Gallery, London] • *Paintings by G. F. Watts R.A.* (1884–5) [exhibition catalogue, Metropolitan Museum of Art, New York] • *The works of G. F. Watts* (1896–7) [exhibition catalogue, New Gallery, London] • *Exhibition of works by the late George Frederick Watts* (1905) [exhibition catalogue, RA, winter 1905] • J. Gage and C. Mullen, *G. F. Watts: a nineteenth-century phenomenon* (1974) [exhibition catalogue, Whitechapel Art Gallery, London] • 'Royal commission to inquire into … the Royal Academy', *Parl. papers* (1863), 27.329, no. 3205 [minutes of evidence] • D. Loshak, 'G. F. Watts and Ellen Terry', *Burlington Magazine*, 110 (1968), 476–85 • A. Staley, 'Watts', in *Victorian high renaissance*, Minneapolis Institute of Arts (1978) [exhibition catalogue, Man. City Gall., 1 Sept – 15 Oct 1978] • B. Bryant, 'G. F. Watts at the Grosvenor Gallery: "Poems painted on canvas" and the New Internationalism', *The Grosvenor Gallery: a palace of art in Victorian England*, ed. S. Casteras and C. Denney (1996), 109–28 • B. Bryant, 'G. F. Watts and the symbolist vision', *The age of Rossetti, Burne-Jones and Watts: Symbolism in Britain, 1860–1910* (1997), 65–81 and *passim*. [exhibition catalogue, Tate Gallery, London, 1997–8] • R. Chapman, *The laurel and the thorn* (1945) • W. Blunt, *England's Michelangelo: a biography of George Frederic Watts* (1975) • R. Ormond, *G. F. Watts: the hall of fame* (1975) • private information (2004) • W. M. Rossetti, *Some reminiscences*, 2 vols. (1906) • D. Johnson, *The true history of the first Mrs Meredith and other lesser lives* (1973) • F. G. Stephens, *Artists at home* (1884), 45–8 • E. Kilmurray, *Dictionary of British portraiture*, 3 (1981), 218 • *Life of Benjamin Robert Haydon, historical painter*, ed. T. Taylor, 3 vols. (1853) • C. Dakers, *The Holland Park circle* (1999) • m. certs. • d. cert. • *The Times* (14 March 1877), 11

Archives Bodl. Oxf., corresp. • Hunt. L., letters • NPG, corresp. • Watts Gallery, Compton, Surrey, corresp., notebooks, and sketch books | BL, corresp. with W. E. Gladstone, Add. MSS 44391–44525 · BL, Holland House MSS · Bodl. Oxf., letters, mainly to Edward and Georgiana Burne-Jones · Bodl. Oxf., corresp. with Ida and Una Taylor · FM Cam., letters mainly to Edward and Georgiana Burne-Jones · Herefs. RO, letters to Brian Hatton and his parents · JRL, letters mainly to Manchester City Art Gallery · JRL, letters to M. H. Spielmann · NRA, priv. coll., letters to earl of Wemyss · Trinity Cam., letters to F. H. W. Myers and Eveleen Myers · U. Leeds, Brotherton L., letters to Edmund Gosse · U. Newcastle, letters to Lady Paulina Trevelyan

Likenesses G. F. Watts, self-portrait, oils, c.1830–1904, Watts Gallery, Compton, Surrey · G. F. Watts, self-portrait, oils, c.1834 (as a young man), Watts Gallery, Compton, Surrey; unfinished · G. F. Watts, self-portrait, drawing, c.1840, Watts Gallery, Compton, Surrey · G. F. Watts, self-portrait, oils, c.1844–1845, V&A · G. F. Watts, self-portrait, oils, 1845, priv. coll. · C. Couzens, watercolour, c.1848, Watts Gallery, Compton, Surrey · H. W. Phillips, oils, c.1850, NPG · J. Soame, photograph, 1858, NPG · G. F. Watts, self-portrait, oils, c.1860, NPG · D. W. Wynfield, photograph, 1860–69, NPG · G. F. Watts, self-portrait, oils, 1862–4, Tate Collection; related oil sketch, Municipal Gallery of Modern Art, Dublin · G. F. Watts, self-portrait, oils, 1863? (Eve of peace), Dunedin Public Art Gallery, New Zealand · J. M. Cameron, photographs, c.1863–1868, NPG · J. M. Cameron, albumen print, 1864, NPG · G. F. Watts, self-portrait, oils, 1864, Tate collection [see illus.] · R. Lehmann, crayon drawing, 1868, BM · G. F. Watts, self-portrait, oils, 1879–80, Uffizi Gallery, Florence, Italy · A. Legros, etching, c.1880, NG Scot., NPG · G. F. Watts, self-portrait, oils, 1882, Aberdeen Art Gallery · G. F. Watts, self-portrait, oils, c.1882, Compton, Surrey · P. Burne-Jones, oils, c.1888–1889, Johannesburg Art Gallery · A. Gilbert, bronze bust, 1888–9, Tate Collection; reduced bronze cast, Watts Gallery, Compton, Surrey · Mrs Watts, watercolour, 1894, Watts Gallery, Compton, Surrey · C. Holroyd, bronze medallion, c.1897, NPG · C. Holroyd, oils, 1897, Tate Collection · bronze medallion, 1897, Watts Gallery, Compton, Surrey · E. Webling, miniature, 1899 (after photograph), Watts Gallery, Compton, Surrey · E. Steichern, photogravure, 1903, NPG; repro. in A. Strasser, Immortal portraits (1941) · G. Frampton, marble bust, 1905, South London Art Gallery · T. Spicer-Simson, cast of bronze medallion, c.1905, Watts Gallery, Compton, Surrey · T. H. Wren, plaster effigy, c.1905, Watts Gallery, Compton, Surrey · R. Goulden, statue, 1909, V&A · L. Deuchars, oils (after photograph, 1897), NPG · J. V. Gibson, oils (after photograph), Watts Gallery, Compton, Surrey · H. Jamyn Brooks, group portrait, oils (Private view of the Old Masters exhibition, Royal Academy, 1888), NPG · Lock & Whitfield, woodburytype photograph, NPG; repro. in T. Cooper, Men of mark: a gallery of contemporary portraits (1882) · M. Menpes, etching, NPG · H. Poole, bronze statuette, NPG · R. W. Robinson, photograph, NPG; repro. in Members and associates of the Royal Academy of Arts (1891) · Spy [L. Ward], caricature, watercolour, NPG; repro. in VF (26 Dec 1891) · G. F. Watts, self-portrait, drawing, Watts Gallery, Compton, Surrey · bronze statuette, Watts Gallery, Compton, Surrey · photographs, NPG · photographs, Watts Gallery · statuette, Postman's Park, Aldersgate Street, London

Wealth at death £84,179 6s. 5d.: resworn probate, 2 June 1905, CGPLA Eng. & Wales

Watts, Gilbert (d. 1657), Church of England clergyman and translator, was born, reportedly, at Rotherham, Yorkshire, the second son of Richard Watts and his wife, Isabel, daughter of Arthur Alcock of St Martin Vintry, London, and widow of Richard's cousin Thomas Scott of Barnes Hall, Ecclesfield, Yorkshire. From about 1607 Watts kept some terms at Cambridge and after moving to Lincoln College, Oxford, was allowed, on 10 October 1610, to count them towards his BA, taken on 28 January 1611. As founder's kin to Thomas Rotherham he was elected a fellow of Lincoln on 9 November 1611, proceeding MA on 7 July 1614

and BD on 10 July 1623. Watts was put out of commons for six months on 6 May 1625 for 'being sixe severall nights in the towne'; on 19 December 1629 part of a book he wrote 'redounding to the scandal and discredit of the College' was ordered to be burnt; he was 'divers times distempered in drink' and in chapel told the rector he 'spake like a mouse in a cheese' (Green, 184).

Watts was, however, a notable scholar and 'a Master of so smooth a Pen, whether in Lat. or English, that no Man of his time exceeded him' (Wood, Ath. Oxon., 2.212). His English version, published in 1640, of Bacon's De augmentis scientiarum had several printings. Unfortunately a rival translation of Davila's history of the French civil wars prevented his being published. He catalogued Charles I's works (including proclamations), as groundwork for a projected book called 'Imperiale politiques' (Oxford, Corpus Christi College, MS 326).

When Charles was visiting Oxford, on 1 November 1642, Watts was created DD. His rectory of Willingdale Doe, Essex, held since 1621, was sequestered some time before 9 October 1646. He petitioned the committee for plundered ministers, which on 11 August 1647 asked the county committee to certify the cause of sequestration. Watts lost his suit against the next incumbent but, having pleaded great poverty, was recommended on 26 September 1649 to be discharged without paying fees. In 1653 Lincoln gave him leave of absence because of his 'age and poverty' (Green, 185). Watts died at Eynsham, Oxfordshire, on 9 September 1657, while returning from Bath, 'where he had overcome his antient Body by too much sweating' (Wood, Ath. Oxon., 2.213); he was buried in Lincoln's chancel of All Saints' Church, Oxford. His will, dated 5 September that year, left Lincoln 'soe many Bookes as cost mee Threescore pounds', each fellow one book, and his brother Abraham the residue of his estate (PRO, PROB 11/270, fols. 81r–81v).   HUGH DE QUEHEN

Sources V. Green, The commonwealth of Lincoln College, 1427–1977 (1979) · Walker rev. · Wood, Ath. Oxon., 2nd edn · Foster, Alum. Oxon. · J. Hunter, Hallamshire: the history and topography of the parish of Sheffield in the county of York, new edn, ed. A. Gatty (1869) · Reg. Oxf., 2/1 · R. W. Gibson, Francis Bacon: a bibliography (1950)

Watts, Henry (1815–1884), chemist, was born in London on 20 January 1815, the son of William Watts. He went to a private school, and was articled at the age of fifteen as an architect and surveyor but, finding himself unsuited for this profession, supported himself by teaching, chiefly mathematics. He attended lectures at University College, London, and in 1841 graduated BA (London). He was a competent mathematician and a good classical scholar and also had a sound knowledge of French and German (and later of Italian and Swedish). He was also interested in botany and in the fine arts, becoming skilled in sketching plants in watercolours.

As assistant to University College's professor of practical chemistry, George Fownes, from 1846, Watts directed students' laboratory work in the college's new Birkbeck Chemical Laboratory. After Fownes's death in 1849 he continued these duties (until 1857) under Professor Alexander William Williamson. Owing to an incurable impediment in speech he was unable to obtain a professorship, and instead devoted himself to the literature of chemistry. In 1847 he was elected fellow of the Chemical Society. The following year he was engaged by the Cavendish Society to translate and enlarge Leopold Gmelin's classical *Handbuch der Chemie*, a work which occupied much of his time until 1872, when the last of its eighteen volumes appeared.

On 17 December 1849 Watts was elected editor of the *Journal of the Chemical Society* and in 1860 he also became librarian to the society, holding both posts until his death. On 1 August 1854 he married Sophie, second daughter of Henri Hanhart, a grocer of Mulhouse, Alsace; the couple had eight sons and two daughters.

In 1858 Watts brought out a revised and enlarged second edition of Thomas Graham's *Chemistry* and he was also engaged by Longmans to prepare a new edition of Andrew Ure's *Dictionary of Chemistry and Mineralogy*. However, he soon decided that Ure's work was so far out of date that he could not revise it satisfactorily and instead began to compile a new *Dictionary of Chemistry and the Allied Branches of other Sciences*, assisted by a team of distinguished contributors. This work in five volumes was completed in 1868, but additions were required to keep up with the rapid advances in chemistry, and three supplementary volumes were issued, in 1872, 1875, and 1879–81. Watts's *Dictionary* contained sound summaries of the facts and theories of chemistry, and was highly commended by his contemporaries.

With H. Bence Jones Watts brought out two editions of Fownes's *Manual of Chemistry* between 1868 and 1872; he completed the twelfth edition in 1877. By his revisions Watts almost entirely rewrote the book. He was engaged on the thirteenth edition with W. A. Tilden at the time of his death.

Early in 1871 the Chemical Society decided to print abstracts in its *Journal* of all papers on chemistry appearing in full elsewhere. A committee was appointed to superintend the publication of the *Journal* and these summaries, but when the scheme proved unworkable, the revision of the abstracts was left entirely to Watts. The abstracts in the *Journal* may be regarded as models, and the success of this scheme must be attributed to Watts alone.

In 1866 Watts was elected FRS; on 19 June 1876 he was granted a civil-list pension of £100 a year and in 1879 he was elected fellow of the Physical Society. He was also an honorary member of the Pharmaceutical Society and a life governor of University College, London. He died of heart failure on 30 June 1884 at his home, 151 King Henry's Road, Primrose Hill, South Hampstead, London, after a short illness. P. J. HARTOG, rev. N. G. COLEY

Sources Allibone, *Dict.* · *Nature*, 30 (1884), 217 · *JCS*, 47 (1885), 342–4 · *The jubilee of the Chemical Society of London: record of the proceedings, with an account of the society, 1841–1891*, Chemical Society of London (1896) · Boase, *Mod. Eng. biog.* · m. cert.

Wealth at death £2249 3s. 2d.: probate, 18 July 1884, *CGPLA Eng. & Wales*

Watts, Henry Edward (1826–1904), biographer and translator, was born in Calcutta on 15 October 1826, the son of

Henry Cecil Watts, head clerk in the police office at Calcutta, and his wife, Emily, *née* Weldon. He was educated at a private school in Greenwich, and later at Exeter grammar school, where he became head boy. He hoped to proceed to Exeter College, Oxford, or to train for military service in the East India Company, but these plans came to nothing. Aged twenty, Watts returned to Calcutta, where he worked as a journalist for some years. He then went to Australia in search of an elder brother, who had gone to prospect for gold but was never heard of again. After an unsuccessful venture in mining, Watts joined the staff of the *Melbourne Argus*, and became its editor in 1859. On his return to England he worked for *The Yorkshireman*, a short-lived Liberal newspaper. In York he contracted smallpox, which scarred him for life. Later he moved to London, and about 1868 joined the *Standard* as a leader writer and subeditor in the colonial and literary departments. At this period he was also the London correspondent for the *Melbourne Argus*. He contributed to the *Encyclopaedia Britannica*, the *Westminster Review*, *Blackwood's*, *Fraser's*, the *Saturday Review*, and the *St James's Gazette*. He started to collaborate with Alexander James Duffield on a new translation of *Don Quixote*, but the two men had so many differences that they decided to publish separate versions. The first edition of Watts's translation appeared in 1888. It contained 'a new life of Cervantes', which was corrected, enlarged, and issued separately in 1895. Watts also wrote a biographical sketch of Cervantes for the Great Writers series in 1891.

Watts was not a gifted Spanish speaker, and only once travelled in Spain, when he went with his friend Carlisle Macartney to visit places associated with Cervantes or with *Don Quixote*. But his workmanlike knowledge of Spanish, his literary taste, and fluent English style enabled him to produce a well-annotated translation that was a marked advance on the eighteenth-century versions which he condemned. His life of Cervantes was considered less satisfactory, as he seemed unaware of recent scholarship and indulged in too much hero-worship. Watts also wrote an essay on Quevedo for an English edition of *Pablo de Segovia* (1892) and 'Spain' (1893) for the Story of the Nations series. A man of violent prejudices, Watts is said to have allowed his personal likings and antipathies to disturb his literary judgements. Though harsh in speech and brusque in manner, he was not unpopular at the Savile Club, London, of which he was an original member. After living for a time in rooms in Pall Mall, Watts settled at 52 Bedford Gardens, Campden Hill, London, where he died, unmarried, of cancer on 7 November 1904. JAMES FITZMAURICE-KELLY, rev. DONALD HAWES

Sources *The Times* (8 Nov 1904) · *The Athenaeum* (12 Nov 1904) · *Wellesley index*, vols. 1–3 · *BL cat.* · R. S. Rudder, *The literature of Spain in English translation: a bibliography* (1975) · R. U. Paine, *English translations from the Spanish, 1488–1943* (1944) · d. cert.

Wealth at death £318 1s.: probate, 3 Dec 1904, *CGPLA Eng. & Wales*

Watts, Hugh (1582/3–1643), bell-founder, was born at Leicester, the second son of Francis Watts (d. 1600), bell-founder, and his wife, Mary. His grandfather may have

been the Hew Wat who in 1563 cast a bell for South Luffenham, Rutland. In 1600 Watts cast for Evington in Leicestershire a bell bearing for the first time his own name as
founder, with the device of three bells that his father had
employed. The same device had been borne by Northamptonshire and Bedfordshire bells made by a William Watts,
and in 1450 by Richard Brayser of Norwich, to whom the
first member of the Watts family to enter the trade may
have been apprenticed.

In 1611 Watts was admitted to the chapmans' or merchants' guild; and he probably married soon afterwards. His
wife, Mary, sons Hugh (1611–1656) and Francis, and daughters Frances and Ellen survived him. In 1620–21 Watts was
elected chamberlain of the borough, and in 1633–4 he
became mayor of Leicester, for which he received the customary allowance of £3 6s. 8d. During his mayoralty
Charles I and his queen passed through Leicester, their
reception costing the city over £200. Watts accumulated
considerable wealth and he lent generously to the corporation of Leicester in times of difficulty, £400 being repaid
to him in the period 1637–9. He contributed again when
Prince Rupert called on Leicester for money in 1641–2.

Watts's younger son, Francis, was made free in the chapmans' guild in 1636. The Revd Philip Hackett recounted
how Francis had asked his father to go to London to hear
the best tenor bell, and while Hugh was there Francis
wrote instructing him to return at a given hour on a set
day. Francis meanwhile succeeded in casting, at the second attempt, a very fine bell, which was then hung. As his
father drew within earshot of Leicester the sound of the
purity and tone of this bell gladdened his heart (Nichols,
358).

In 1876, when T. North was writing, nearly 200 of
Watts's bells remained in Leicestershire, including several complete rings that were admired for the beauty of
their tone—the peal of ten bells for St Margaret's, Leicester, was said to be the finest in England (North). Many of
the bells bore inscriptions—Watts's favourite being
'J.H.S.: Nazareus: rex: Iudeorum: Fili: Dei: miserere: Mei'—
these came to be known as Watts's Nazarenes. He worked
his foundry until his death in Leicester, aged sixty, in February or March 1643; he was buried in St Mary's Church,
Leicester. His son Hugh inherited his bell-metal and tools,
and he married Jane, daughter of Sir Thomas Burton, bt of
Stockerston, Leicestershire. However, soon after 1643 the
business was wound up and partly taken over by Nottingham founders.

L. M. Middleton, rev. Anita McConnell

Sources J. Nichols, *The history and antiquities of the county of Leicester*, 1/2 (1815), 316, 350, 427, 558 • T. North, *The church bells of Leicestershire* (1876) • *VCH Leicestershire*, 3.47–9

Watts, Isaac (1674–1748), Independent minister and
writer, was born on 17 July 1674 in Southampton, the eldest of the eight children of Isaac Watts (1650–1737), clothier, and his wife, Sarah, daughter of Richard Tanton
(Taunton), who was of Huguenot descent. In a note to an
elegy on his paternal grandmother (*d*. 1693) in *Horae
lyricae*, Watts said that his grandfather Thomas Watts,
commander of a ship in 1656, was drowned when the ship

Isaac Watts (1674–1748), by George White, 1727

was blown up in the Dutch war (*Works*, 7.288). Isaac Watts
senior was imprisoned for nonconformity in 1674, 1678,
and 1683; his son noted of the last experience, 'my father
Persecuted & imprisond for Nonconformity 6 months.
after that forced to leave his family & live privately in London for 2 years' ('Coincidents', appended to Hood). During
this absence he sent his children at the request of the eldest a long letter of religious advice (21 May 1685, Milner,
36–44). The Independent meeting to which he belonged
was organized in 1688 into the Above Bar Congregational
Church; he was its secretary and deacon, and according to
Thomas Gibbons, Watts's friend and first biographer, he
became master of a successful boarding school (Gibbons,
1). He had begun to teach his son Latin in 1678. He wrote
some religious poetry, identified as his by Gibbons and
included in Milner (pp. 47–53). He lived to see the son who
had imbibed his religious and educational principles in
the period of persecution become the leading figure
among English protestant dissenters.

Education From 1680 to 1690 Watts was educated at the
free grammar school in Southampton by a Church of England cleric, John Pinhorne, rector of All Saints', Southampton, and holder of other benefices. In addition to
Latin Pinhorne taught the boy Greek, French, and Hebrew
('Memorable affairs in my life', appended to Hood); Watts
expressed his gratitude in a Latin Pindaric ode written in
1694 and included in *Horae lyricae* (English translation in
Gibbons, 11–18). Because of his evident precocity a local
doctor, John Speed, offered to send him to university;
acceptance would have obliged him to conform to the
Church of England, but Watts chose to remain a dissenter.

From 1690 to 1694 he was a student at the dissenting academy run by Thomas Rowe in succession to Theophilus Gale. Gale's academy was based at Stoke Newington, then a village north-east of London with an established and prosperous dissenting community. Rowe moved the academy to Little Britain in the City of London a few years before Watts's arrival; it is unlikely that Watts's education was at Newington, though this is often stated. The influence of Rowe on Watts's intellectual and religious development was considerable. Watts later wrote an ode to 'the Director of my youthful Studies' subtitled 'Free philosophy': Rowe is thanked for his 'gentle influence' which

> bids our thoughts like rivers flow,
> And choose the channels where they run.
> (*Horae*, *Works*, 7.259)

Under his direction Watts read widely in a range of subjects including classical and modern philosophy as well as divinity, wrote Latin and English theses (some are in Gibbons, 21–58), and made abridgements of standard works such as Burgersdicius's *Institutiones logicae* (Watts's brother Enoch gave Gibbons his manuscript volumes). He told Philip Doddridge approvingly in 1725 that 'plain easy books of Divinity [were] recommended to the pupills to be read in their own Closets on Saturdays, from the very beginning of their Studies' (DWL, MS 24.180). He also acquired the habit of interleaving books and adding comments. His interleaved and annotated copy of John Wilkins's *Ecclesiastes* (7th edn, 1693, in DWL) provides a very useful guide to Rowe's teaching and Watts's reading in the 1690s and early 1700s. His annotations to Martin Clifford's *Treatise of Humane Reason* were printed by Palmer (*Life … by … Johnson*, appx 1). Student friends at the academy included the poet John Hughes, Samuel Say, who became a dissenting minister and successor to Edmund Calamy, and Josiah Hort, who conformed to the Church of England and became archbishop of Tuam. In December 1693, towards the end of his time with Rowe, Watts was admitted a member of the Independent church at Girdlers' Hall of which his tutor was minister (Gibbons later held the post for many years after the church had moved to Haberdashers' Hall).

Ministerial career In June 1694, according to his 'Memorable affairs', Watts returned to his father's house in Southampton for two and a quarter years; here he continued reading intensively and writing regularly, both in verse and prose. This seclusion was unusual—young dissenters trained for the ministry frequently began work straight after leaving their academies. On 9 March 1696 the minutes of the Congregational Fund Board recorded that an endeavour should be made 'that Mr. Watts do go out to the Ministry' (*Congregational Historical Society Transactions*, 5, 1911–12, 139). On 15 October 1696 he went to live in Newington as tutor to Sir John Hartopp's son, also named John, to whom he later dedicated his *Logick* (1725). He remained for six years with the Hartopps, who had inherited the house of Elisabeth Hartopp's father, the Cromwellian general Charles Fleetwood. In 'Memorable affairs' Watts noted that he began to preach on 17 July 1698 (his twenty-fourth birthday), after eight years of university studies

(presumably including the period in Southampton and at the Hartopps). By February 1699 he was appointed assistant to Isaac Chauncy, minister of the Independent church which met at Mark Lane, London; his association with this church, despite his own initial reluctance, was to last for the rest of his life. The church had a famous history and membership. It was begun by Joseph Caryl following the Act of Uniformity of 1662; after Caryl's death in 1673 the congregation united with that of the Independent leader John Owen. Owen was succeeded in turn by David Clarkson, Isaac Loeffs, and in 1687 by Chauncy. Many of Oliver Cromwell's wealthy descendants and connections such as the Fleetwoods and the Hartopps were members of the congregation (a full list is provided in the church book; see Crippen, 27–30).

Chauncy proved a very unpopular minister; the church which had flourished under his predecessors was losing members, and on 15 April 1701 Chauncy resigned. The church was much exercised for several months by the problem of replacing him. Watts was considered, but his poor health was a serious obstacle. As he recorded in 'Memorable affairs', he became ill immediately after becoming Chauncy's assistant, and for long periods of time from 1699 to 1701 he was away recuperating at Southampton, Bath, and Tunbridge. On 23 November 1701 he resumed preaching; on 14 January 1702 the church members agreed to call him to the office of minister. On 8 February Watts wrote them an important letter, preserved in the church book, giving as requested an account of his principles of church discipline, in which he set out his view of the respective roles of pastor and people; on 15 February he gave them a letter of dismission from Rowe's church and recommendation to Mark Lane; on 8 March, the day of William III's death, he accepted the call, and on 18 March he was ordained. The ordination sermon was preached by his former tutor Rowe (Crippen, 31–6).

Despite his recurrent ill health, the previously declining Mark Lane Church flourished under Watts (numbers are recorded in the church book; see Crippen, 29–30). 'Though his Stature was low, and *his bodily Presence but weak*, yet *his Preaching was Weighty and Powerful*' (Jennings, 32). In 1704 the church moved its meeting place temporarily to Pinners' Hall, and then in 1708 to a new purpose-built meeting-house in Duke's Place, Bury Street, St Mary Axe. Details of the building plans, the funding, and the disposing of pews and places survive (*Congregational Historical Society Transactions*, 3, 1907–8, 117–25). The Bury Street Church under Watts's guidance was to become an important centre of the evangelical wing of dissent in the first half of the eighteenth century; the best guide to its theological and pastoral concerns is the collection of lectures known as the Bury Street sermons, *Faith and Practice Represented in Fifty-Four Sermons … Preached at Berry-Street 1733*, by Watts, Daniel Neal, John Guyse, Samuel Price, David Jennings, and John Hubbard, which was supported by the Independent philanthropist William Coward.

Watts was unable to manage the duties of pastor singlehanded; Samuel Price (uncle of the philosopher Richard Price) became his assistant in 1703 and his co-pastor in

1713, when a complete breakdown, lasting from September 1712 to October 1716, prevented Watts from performing his public duties. He described the experience in a series of blank verse poems, 'Sickness and recovery' (*Reliquiae juveniles*, no. 47). In the course of his ministerial and authorial career he was very much indebted to the services of others to enable him to work. In December 1703 he noted in 'Memorable affairs', 'after having intermitted in a great measure a method of study and pursuit of Learning, 4 years, by reason of my great indispositions … (except w: was of absolute necessity for my Constant preaching) … I took a boy to read to me and write for me, whereby my studies are much assisted'. This was his practice for the rest of his life; his last amanuensis, Joseph Parker, who used Watts's system of shorthand, remained with him for over twenty-one years.

A succession of generous friends took Watts into their houses. In late 1702 he moved from the Hartopps at Newington to Thomas Hollis senior, the philanthropist, in the Minories, City of London; at the end of 1710 he moved to a Mr Bowes; and then about 1712 the prominent dissenting whig Sir Thomas Abney invited him for what was initially a week's stay. Watts was to spend the rest of his life in considerable comfort with the Abneys, at Lime Street in the City and at Theobalds in Hertfordshire, and then, after Sir Thomas's death (1722), at Abney Park, Stoke Newington, where he moved *c*.1733 with Lady Abney and her two surviving daughters. They represented for him the ideal dissenting household. Watts thanked Lady Abney in the dedication to *Divine Songs* (1715): 'It is to her unwearied Tenderness, and many kind Offices by Night and Day, in the more violent Seasons of my Indisposition, that (under God) I own my Life, and Power to write or think.' Jennings urged that 'wheresoever Dr. WATTS's Works are read, or his Name remembered, that of Abney ought not to be forgotton' (Jennings, 26). Watts acted as tutor to the children—*Divine Songs* and *The Art of Reading and Writing English* (1721) were dedicated to them—and continued whenever possible his pastoral duties, but the greater part of his time was spent on his prolific and increasingly successful literary work.

Poet and hymn writer   In the first half of his literary career Watts published four verse collections: *Horae lyricae* (in two books, 1706; much enlarged and reorganized in three books, 1709); *Hymns and Spiritual Songs* (1707, enlarged 1709); *Divine Songs Attempted in Easy Language, for the Use of Children* (1715); and *The Psalms of David Imitated in the Language of the New Testament* (1719). He also included some hymns in his *Sermons on Various Subjects* (1721) and some early poems in *Reliquiae juveniles: Miscellaneous Thoughts in Prose and Verse* (1734); a handful of poems appeared at the beginning of the posthumously published *Remnants of Time* (1753). As part of these collections he published some very important manifestos: the enlarged preface to *Horae* (1709); 'A short essay toward the improvement of psalmody', which followed the text of *Hymns* (1707), but which was not republished in his lifetime; and the prefaces to *Hymns* and *Psalms* (the last incorporating some material from the 'Essay').

Watts had begun writing poetry as a child; in 1691, at seventeen, he wrote a Latin poem to his brother Enoch (*Horae*, book 2) and Pindaric elegies for the deaths of his infant sisters (*Divine Songs*, appx 3). A few of the poems in *Horae* were dated 1694 and 1695, the year after he left Rowe's academy, and it was also during this period that he composed most of his hymns. Watts told Gibbons that he thought it better to send his lyric poems into the world before his hymns—if the former were accepted then the hymns would be more likely to be so, and if not then it would be prudent to withhold the latter, 'in which, in condescension to the plainest capacities, he had purposely reduced his poetry to a lower strain' (Gibbons, 255). In the preface of 1706 to *Horae lyricae* (that is, 'Lyric hours', so called to show that 'Poesy is not the Business of my Life') he said that the devotional poems in that collection were a small part of 200 hymns ready for public use (*Divine Songs*, appx 1, 103–4). The topics of the three-book version of *Horae*, in which there is much experimentation with verse form, were 'Devotion and Piety', 'Virtue, Honour and Friendship', and 'The Memory of the Dead'; most of the poems in the last two books are addressed to friends in his dissenting circle, several of them Cromwell connections, but they also include poems in praise of John Locke, William III, and Queen Anne (in 1721 Watts added a note retracting his optimistic picture of her reign: Watts, *Works*, 7.253).

Watts essentially regarded poetry as a divine gift which should be dedicated to God but which had been profaned. In the revised preface to *Horae* he invoked the example of the Old Testament poets and associated himself with the principles and practice of John Dennis, Abraham Cowley, Richard Blackmore, John Norris, and John Milton, arguing that the Christian preacher could find abundant aid from the poet. His hymns and psalms clearly illustrated this principle. According to Gibbons (the story originated with Watts's co-pastor Price), Watts complained about the quality of the hymns sung at the meeting at Southampton (perhaps by William Barton), and his father told him to mend the matter, which he did with great success (Gibbons, 254). His brother Enoch in a letter of March 1700 criticizing existing hymns and versions of the psalms urged him to publish his own (Milner, 176–9); the success of *Horae* evidently encouraged him to do so.

Watts divided his *Hymns* into three books, the first paraphrases of biblical texts, the second on general divine subjects, and the third designed for the Lord's supper. In the preface he said that he had sunk the metaphors 'to the level of vulgar capacities', though he hoped 'not to give disgust to persons of richer sense, and nicer education' (*Works*, 7.122). His work on the hymns and psalms was closely related: the 1706 edition of *Horae* and the early editions of the *Hymns* contained several psalms, which he moved to the collected *Psalms* in 1719. Psalm 114 appeared in *The Spectator* (no. 461, 19 August 1712). In a note to 'Sickness and recovery' (Watts, *Works*, 7.364) he explained that he had written only half by 1712–13 and after his recovery applied himself to finishing them. His version of the Psalms was not intended as a translation: as the title made clear, they were 'Imitated in the Language of the New Testament and applied to the Christian State and Worship'. This meant bringing David up to date, and substituting Jesus for Jehovah and Britain for Israel. One of Watts's best-known hymns, 'Jesus shall reign where'er the sun', is an imitation of Psalm 72, part 2; another, 'Our God our help in ages past', is based on Psalm 90: 1–5 (it was later altered by John Wesley to 'O God our help'). From *Hymns* the best-known are 'Come let us join our cheerful songs' (1.62, based on Revelation 5: 11–13) and 'When I survey the wondrous cross' (3.7). Watts was unequivocal about the value of his religious poetry and the revolution he had brought about in congregational worship: in a note dated 3 March 1720 in the seventh edition of *Hymns* he said of his two books of hymns and psalms: 'if an Author's own Opinion may be taken, he esteems it the greatest Work that ever he has publish'd, or ever hopes to do for the Use of the Churches' (Escott, 136).

Educator and philosopher As an educational writer Watts had an extraordinary capacity to address a very wide range of audiences, from infants and schoolchildren to students in academies and universities, while as a philosopher he engaged in a number of pressing contemporary debates. 'Every man', observed Samuel Johnson, 'acquainted with the common principles of human action will look with veneration on the writer who is at one time combating Locke, and at another making a catechism for children in their fourth year' (*Lives of the English Poets*, ed. G. B. Hill, 1905, 3.308). Watts's works for children were both secular and religious. The first category included *The Art of Reading and Writing English* (1721), cast in what was to become a favourite question-and-answer form. Religious works included the *Catechisms* (1730), written in response to 'a multitude of requests' (letter to Samuel Say, 11 April 1728, Milner, 458) and dedicated to the parents belonging to the Bury Street congregation; this was prefaced by 'A discourse on the way of instruction by catechisms', and included a catechism for a three- or four-year-old as well as an explication of the Westminster assembly's shorter catechism for twelve- or thirteen-year-olds. Several of the short texts which composed *Catechisms* were sold separately (Green, 738–9). A work designed for a wider audience was the substantial *Short View of the Whole Scripture History* (1732), also cast in question-and-answer form, which was written for 'persons of younger years, and the common rank of mankind' (*Works*, 4.345).

Watts gave a great deal of thought to the principles and methods of education; his most important works on the subject for students and teachers are *Logick: or the Right Use of Reason in the Enquiry after Truth* (1725) and its sequel, *The Improvement of the Mind* (1741, with a second part published posthumously in 1751). These works provide helpful advice, from an evangelical perspective, on reading, writing, and interpretation, and are designed to combat dogmatism and foster the rational testing of ideas. The long-lasting success of *Logick* as a textbook is attested by the increasing number of editions in the later eighteenth century and the first decade of the nineteenth. *A Discourse on the Education of Children and Youth* (published posthumously

in 1753) is an interesting attempt to reconcile the traditional values of the dissenting community with liberty of thought. In philosophy Watts described as 'a favourite employment of my thoughts' the relation between soul and body and the function of the sensations, appetites, and passions (preface to *Philosophical Essays on Various Subjects*, 1733; *Works*, 6.481). His most important works on these topics, in addition to the *Philosophical Essays*, are *The Doctrine of the Passions* and *Discourses of the Love of God, and the Use and Abuse of the Passions in Religion* (1729), and *Self-Love and Virtue Reconciled Only by Religion* (1739). Watts objected to Locke's attack on innate ideas and supported the existence of the moral sense, provided it was regarded as 'reason exercising itself' (*Works*, 6.526), but for religious reasons he strongly disapproved of Shaftesbury. His interest in the passions was closely related to his concern with the ways in which the preacher might work on them for religious ends.

Pastor and theologian Watts's religious writings were aimed at a range of audiences, from his Bury Street congregation and other dissenting churches to protestants in general and doubting and heterodox Christians; they included sermons and other exhortatory works, defences of the political status of dissent, and explorations of Christianity's most difficult doctrines. His standing was recognized by the award of the DD in 1728 by the universities of Edinburgh and Aberdeen. As a dissenting minister he was concerned with the growing breach between the evangelical and rational wings of dissent, epitomized in the Salters' Hall debates of 1719 over the principle of demanding subscription to orthodox trinitarian doctrine; Watts voted against subscription not because his views about the Trinity were doubtfully orthodox but because he espoused the Lockian principle of freedom of religious worship (set out fully in the last work he published, *The Rational Foundation of a Christian Church, and the Terms of Christian Communion*, 1747). He was also exercised by the problem of the decay of the dissenting interest, addressed in 1730 in a provocative essay by Strickland Gough; Watts's reply, *An Humble Attempt towards the Revival of Practical Religion among Christians* (1731), emphasized that the essence of religion as the dissenters' puritan fathers had known it lay in the proper relationship between minister and congregation. He recommended to preachers John Jennings's *Two Discourses* (1723, for which he wrote a preface), in which the puritans are held up as models for their skill in moving the passions. Watts's ideal minister Ergates in *The Improvement of the Mind* 'makes the nature of his subject, and the necessity of his hearers, the great rule to direct him what method he shall choose in every sermon, that he may the better enlighten, convince and persuade' (*Works*, 6.336). Whereas in his view the preachers of the established church and the rational wing of dissent delivered moral essays in their pulpits, Watts in his *Sermons on Various Subjects* (1721, 1723, 1729), *The World to Come* (1739, 1745), and *Evangelical Discourses* (1747) preached an experimental and affectionate religion but with a rational framework that would defend him against the charge of enthusiasm.

In his letter to the Mark Lane Church of 8 February 1702, Watts reminded them that 'When You first called me to minister the Word of God among you, I took the freedom to acquaint you That, in the chief Doctrines of Christianity, I was of the same mind wth your former Revd Pastor Dr Jno. Owen' (Crippen, 32). In the course of his preaching career of over forty-eight years, Watts modified his position of Calvinist orthodoxy. In *Orthodoxy and Charity United* (1745, but written twenty or thirty years earlier) he identified orthodoxy as consisting of the doctrines of the fall, sanctifying grace, the atonement, repentance of sins, justifying faith, obedience, and the resurrection, and he addressed himself to the differences between men of moderation, distancing himself from the high-flyers on either side (*Works*, 2.403, 433). He knew that such a stance provoked hostility: 'a moderator must expect to be boxed on both ears' (Gibbons, 146). In a number of works, from *The Christian Doctrine of the Trinity* (1722) to the late *The Glory of Christ as God-Man Displayed* (1746) and the posthumously published 'The author's solemn address to the great and ever-blessed God', the last work in *Remnants of Time* (1753), he struggled to find a way of explicating the doctrine of the Trinity that would keep him within the bounds of orthodoxy, but these attempts aroused the suspicions of the rigidly orthodox, including William Coward, and long after his death encouraged Unitarians to think erroneously that he had joined them.

Religious and literary relationships Despite his sheltered and sickly life, Watts had a wide range of friends and visitors and a large and important correspondence, among members of the established church as well as dissenters, and in New England and Germany as well as at home. He was a close friend of Elizabeth Rowe (*née* Singer), whom he is thought to have courted unsuccessfully; she married instead the nephew of his tutor Thomas Rowe. He included an ode in *Horae* in praise of the poems of Philomela; in turn, she wrote a commendatory poem for the 1709 edition under that name, and she left him the manuscript of her *Devout Exercises of the Heart*, which he published in 1737 with a preface treating her religious transports with some caution. He dedicated *Reliquiae juveniles* (1734) to her Anglican friend the countess of Hertford (who refused the dedication of *Devout Exercises*), and included some of the countess's poems under the name Eusebia (no. 63, 'Piety in a court.—To Philomela').

Watts's most important dissenting friend and correspondent was Philip Doddridge, in whose Northampton academy he took great interest from its inception at Harborough onwards, and whose immensely popular *The Rise and Progress of Religion in the Soul* (1745) was written at Watts's request. He was known to or corresponded with most of the principal Anglican figures in the evangelical revival, including John Wesley, George Whitefield, James Hervey, and the countess of Huntingdon, though he had doubts about aspects of Methodism. His mainstream Church of England correspondents included Thomas Secker, who had started out a dissenter, and for whom he found a place at Samuel Jones's academy at Gloucester (Milner, 232–7); Watts regularly sent him his books in later

years, and as bishop of Oxford Secker thanked him for *The Improvement of the Mind*, 'which is peculiarly well adapted for the direction and improvement of students in the university, where your Logic is by no means the only piece of yours that is read with high esteem' (19 June 1741, Milner, 664–5). Watts similarly sent books to Edmund Gibson, bishop of London: his anti-deist *The Strength and Weakness of Human Reason* (1731) chimed with Gibson's *Second Pastoral Letter* of 1730 (*Works*, 2.7–8; Milner, 490–91), and at the other end of the religious spectrum he shared Gibson's doubts about Whitefield (Milner, 638).

Watts also played an important role in religious developments in New England. He corresponded with a number of American ministers and educators, including Cotton Mather (who disapproved of his views on the Trinity), Elisha Williams, Thomas Prince, and especially Benjamin Colman. He made gifts of forty-nine of his books to Yale, where many still survive; an appreciative reader of his *Philosophical Essays* wrote in it, 'the man that Liketh not this Book is a Whippleswick' (Pratt, 25). In turn Mather, Colman, Prince, and others sent him copies of their sermons, many of which survive in Dr Williams's Library. Through Colman, Watts followed Whitefield's transatlantic evangelizing with some misgivings. A significant outcome of this correspondence was that Watts and John Guyse published a cautiously edited version of Jonathan Edwards's account of the beginning of the revival in New England, *A Faithful Narrative of the Surprising Work of God* (1737), after receiving the manuscript from Colman. A similar pattern of reciprocal influence in Germany resulted from Watts's friendship with Anton Wilhelm Boehm (characterized as Bohemus in *Reliquiae juveniles*, no. 52), translator of works by the pietist A. H. Francke. Francke arranged for Watts's *Death and Heaven* (his funeral discourses for the Hartopps) to be translated into German with a preface by J. J. Rambach; in 1736 a new English edition included this preface (*Works*, 2.139). A collection that brought together the writing and interests of English, German, and New England pietists and evangelicals was *Instructions to Ministers* (1744), which contained John Jennings's *Discourses*, with Watts's preface, Francke on preaching, translated by David Jennings, and the life of Cotton Mather, abridged by David Jennings with a recommendation by Watts.

Death and afterlife Though he was widely loved, Watts's later years were at times difficult: he was on bad terms with some members of his family, quarrelled with his former ministerial friend Thomas Bradbury, and became increasingly ill. He died at Abney Park on 25 November 1748 'without a struggle or a groan', as his amanuensis Joseph Parker told his brother Enoch (Gibbons, 318). He was buried on 5 December in Bunhill Fields in the City of London, attended at his request by two ministers from each of the three dissenting denominations, Independent, Presbyterian, and Baptist. He wrote his own inscription for his grave, defining himself as pastor and successor to Caryl, Owen, Clarkson, and Chauncy (Gibbons, 345). Nathaniel Neal, one of his executors, sold the copyright of his works in 1749 for £600 (Nuttall, *Calendar*, no. 1549);

Watts sold that of the *Hymns* for £10 in 1709 (Wilson, 1.300–01). He left his manuscripts to David Jennings and Doddridge; in due course they published the second part of *The Improvement of the Mind* (1751) and included some new material in his *Works* in six volumes (1753, following Doddridge's own death in 1751). Among subscribers to the *Works*, in addition to prominent dissenters, were Archbishop Secker, the countess of Huntingdon, and the president of New Jersey College.

In his funeral sermon David Jennings said that 'there is no Man now living of whose Works so many have been dispersed, both at Home and Abroad, that are in such constant Use, and translated into such a Variety of Languages' (Jennings, 28). In the later eighteenth and early nineteenth centuries there was considerable interest in Watts's theology, with recurring disputes over his views on the Trinity and attempts to capture him for rival camps. On the evangelical side, William Cowper wrote in 1766, 'I know no greater names in Divinity than Watts and Doddridge' (*Letters and Prose Writings*, ed. J. King and C. Ryskamp, 1979, 1.143). John Wesley, who in *The Doctrine of Original Sin* (1757) defended Watts's *The Ruin and Recovery of Mankind* (1740) against the Arian John Taylor, warned in 1788 against Watts's dangerous speculations on the glorified humanity of Christ (*Letters*, ed. J. Telford, 1931, 89–90). The Unitarian Joseph Priestley published Watts's *Historical Catechisms* (1783) with the Calvinist principles altered. The Independent Samuel Palmer was the first to attempt to clarify his views on the Trinity and the nature of his surviving manuscripts (*Life … by … Johnson*, appx 3), and in *Dr Watts No Socinian* (1813) he defended Watts from appropriation by the Unitarian Thomas Belsham.

It was as poet and hymn-writer that Watts made his most lasting impact. In 1779, on Samuel Johnson's recommendation, *Horae lyricae* and *Divine Songs … for Children* appeared as volume 46 of *Works of the English Poets*, followed by the life in volume 8 of Johnson's *Prefaces* (1781). In Watts's lifetime the success of his hymns and psalms was partly owing to the Methodists. John Wesley included a large number (with modifications) in his first hymnbook, *A Collection of Psalms and Hymns* (1737), and Watts's hymns kept their central place in several later collections by Independents, Methodists, and Anglicans, often described as supplements to Watts. James Montgomery in the introductory essay to *The Christian Psalmist* (1825) explained why Christians found Watts's combined collection, *Psalms and Hymns*, so powerful: they 'include and illustrate every truth of revelation, throw light upon every secret movement of the human heart' (1828 edn, xix). The sales of *Psalms and Hymns* in the English-speaking world in the late eighteenth century and nineteenth century were phenomenal, and in the same period the *Divine Songs*, imitated and parodied in very different ways by William Blake in *Songs of Innocence* (1789) and Lewis Carroll in *Alice in Wonderland* (1865), reached the height of their fame. Watts's extraordinary success is in some ways paradoxical. As an early eighteenth-century Independent he belonged to an exclusive minority:

We are a garden wall'd around,
Chosen and made peculiar ground,

he wrote in Hymn 1.74 (based on the Song of Solomon, 4 and 5; *Works*, 7.137), and in his cool, rational approach to the psychology of religion he distrusted emotional indiscipline, yet his warm, affectionate, practical writings were a powerful impetus to the evangelical revival of the eighteenth century and continued to shape the growing evangelicalism of the nineteenth. ISABEL RIVERS

Sources A. P. Davis, *Isaac Watts: his life and works* (1948) [appx A lists Watts's letters] · T. Milner, *The life, times, and correspondence of the Rev. Isaac Watts D.D.* (1834); new edn (1845) · T. Gibbons, *Memoirs of the Revd. Isaac Watts D.D.* (1780) · *The works of the Revd. Isaac Watts D.D.*, ed. E. Parsons, 7 vols. (1800) · I. Rivers, *Reason, grace, and sentiment: a study of the language of religion and ethics in England, 1660–1780*, 1 (1991), chap. 4 · H. Escott, *Isaac Watts, hymnographer: a study of the beginnings, development, and philosophy of the English hymn* (1962) · *The life of the Revd Isaac Watts, D.D., by the late Dr Samuel Johnson, with notes*, ed. S. Palmer, 2nd edn (1791) [esp. appxs] · A. S. Pratt, *Isaac Watts and his gifts of books to Yale College* (1938) · C. C. Goen, introduction, in J. Edwards, *The Great Awakening*, ed. C. C. Goen (1972) [gives details of Watts's American correspondence and pubn of *A faithful narrative*] · I. Watts, *Divine songs attempted in easy language for the use of children*, facsimile of the first edn (1715); and an illustrated edn (c.1840), with introduction and bibliography by J. H. P. Pafford (1971) [appx 3 incl. a hitherto unpubd early poem] · *Calendar of the correspondence of Philip Doddridge*, ed. G. F. Nuttall, HMC, JP 26 (1979) [incl. several letters to and from Watts, and many about him] · E. P. Hood, *Isaac Watts; his life and writings, his homes and friends* (1875) [Watts's table of 'Coincidents' and 'Memorable affairs in my life' following p. 341] · T. G. Crippen, 'Dr Watts's church-book', *Congregational Historical Society Transactions*, 1 (1901–4), 26–38 · W. E. Stephenson, 'Isaac Watts's education for the dissenting ministry: a new document', *Harvard Theological Review*, 61 (1968), 263–81 · W. Wilson, *The history and antiquities of the dissenting churches and meeting houses in London, Westminster and Southwark*, 4 vols. (1808–14), vol. 1, pp. 251–328; vol. 3, pp. 168–72, 526–7 · G. F. Nuttall, 'Continental pietism and the evangelical movement in Britain', *Pietismus und Réveil*, ed. J. van den Berg and J. P. van Dooren (1978), 209–33 · S. L. Bishop, *Isaac Watts's 'Hymns and spiritual songs' (1707): a publishing history and a bibliography* (1974) · I. Green, *The Christian's ABC: catechisms and catechising in England c.1530–1740* (1996) [esp. appx 1] · 'Catalogue and sale of Dr Watts's manuscripts', *Congregational Magazine*, new ser., 11 (1835), 189–93 · 'Isaac Watts's family Bible', *Congregational Historical Society Transactions*, 1 (1901–4), 275–7 · D. Jennings, *A sermon occasioned by the death of … Watts* (1749)

Archives BL, sermons, etc., RP1360 [copies] · Bodl. Oxf., sermons [copies] · Boston PL, papers · DWL, books and pamphlets in his library, presentation copies and annotated copies of his works · DWL, handlist of MSS · Hunt. L., notebook, HM 4955 | DWL, letters to Samuel Say

Likenesses G. Vertue, line engraving, 1710? (after I. Whood), BM, NPG · G. Vertue, line engraving, pubd 1722, BM, NPG · G. White, mezzotint, 1727, BM, NPG [see illus.] · G. Vertue, line engraving, 1742, BM, NPG; repro. in I. Watts, *Horae Lyricae*, 8th edn (1743) · engraving, repro. in Gibbons, *Memoirs* · mezzotint (after G. White), BM, NPG · oils, DWL; version, NPG · statue, Southampton

Wealth at death approx. £2700 plus books, paintings, prints, maps, mathematical instruments: will, 23 July 1746 and 3 codicils, 2 April, 3 April, and 17 November 1747

Watts, Isaac (1797–1876), naval architect, was born in Plymouth. Details are uncertain but it is likely that he was baptized on 31 July 1797, the only son of William and Elizabeth Watts, and had two younger sisters, Ester and Marie.

He was apprenticed to a shipwright and passed the competitive entry examination for the School of Naval Architecture at Portsmouth, which he entered in 1814. The seven-year course was divided between theory and practice and was both advanced—it was among the first schools of higher education to teach calculus—and demanding. He graduated in 1821 but, owing partly to post-war reductions in staff and partly to resentment of the new graduates by the older dockyard officers, promotion was slow. He was eventually promoted foreman at Portsmouth, a fairly senior post, in 1833 and remained there for some years. During this time he married Emmeline Anne (maiden name unknown; d. 1861); they had three daughters and two sons. In May 1847 he became master shipwright (or general manager) of Sheerness Dockyard at the age of fifty.

Only a year later Watts became an assistant surveyor, responsible jointly with John Edye until the latter's retirement, for the design of all ships. In 1851 he visited French naval establishments with the surveyor, Baldwin Walker, and the chief engineer, Thomas Lloyd. Their report on progress with the screw battleship *Napoléon* led to work being hastened on Edye's *Agamemnon*, the first British screw battleship to be designed as such. It was an exciting time: the screw propeller had been proved and there was a big programme of wooden screw battleships and frigates, both new construction and conversions.

During the war with Russia, Watts was responsible for the building of numerous novel ships, some with armour. After the war the building race with France resumed. In this period he designed some of the biggest wooden ships ever constructed, though with an increasing use of iron stiffeners and brackets, amounting to some 130 tons in a 120 gun ship. His big screw frigates were among the longest wooden ships ever built, for example *Orlando*, of 5416 tons, had a length of 366 feet overall. There were signs of weakness in these frigates, showing that wooden construction had reached its limit.

In 1859 news was received of the French ship *Gloire*, which was armoured but still with a wooden hull, and Watts was asked to design the counter. The board had asked for a wooden ship but Watts decided that a ship which would be long enough to carry the specified armament would only be satisfactory with an iron hull. There were many problems to be solved, particularly in the support and fastenings of the 4½ inch armour, and a large full-scale section was built and fired on by heavy guns. Watts's design was sent to the Board of Admiralty in January 1859 and, by their direction, was passed to the royal dockyards and to experienced commercial builders of iron ships to see if they could offer a better design. Fifteen submissions were received and, in his report, Watts gave detailed explanations of why they were all inferior to his own design.

A reorganization in 1860 gave Watts the title of chief constructor with much the same duties and with a salary of £900. When *Warrior* was completed in 1861 she was second in size only to the enormous *Great Eastern* and was much faster and more heavily armed than *Gloire*, while

her iron hull made her more durable; she may still be seen at Portsmouth. Watts designed some variants on *Warrior* and was then involved in the conversion of the prototype turret ship *Trusty* before designing the first operational turret ships *Royal Sovereign* and *Prince Albert*, all before the better-known USS *Monitor*.

Like many great designers, Watts was an autocrat who had little use for discussion except with the surveyor, the chief engineer (Lloyd), and his own deputy, Joseph Large, who played an important part in the design of *Warrior*. *Warrior* initiated a revolution in warship design even though she was evolutionary in most technical aspects, such as iron hull, machinery, guns, and even armour. It was the combination of all these features which made her novel. Watts, Large, and Lloyd were all graduates of the School of Naval Architecture. Watts saw the navy through two technical revolutions—screw propellers and armour—and was created CB for his services. He retired in 1863 and died at 32 Albion Street, Broadstairs, Kent, on 11 August 1876.   DAVID K. BROWN

Sources private information · Boase, *Mod. Eng. biog.* · O. Parkes, *British battleships, 'Warrior' 1860 to 'Vanguard' 1950: a history of design, construction, and armament* [1957] · D. K. Brown, *Warrior to Dreadnought: warship development, 1860–1905* (1997) · *CGPLA Eng. & Wales* (1876)

Wealth at death under £6000: probate, 12 Oct 1876, *CGPLA Eng. & Wales*

Watts, Jane (1793–1826). *See under* Eaton, Charlotte Anne (1788–1859).

Watts, Sir John (c.1550–1616), merchant and privateer, was the son of Thomas Watts of Buntingford in Hertfordshire, where he was born. He married Margaret Hawes, daughter of Sir James Hawes, who was lord mayor of London from 1574 to 1575. They had eight children, four sons and four daughters.

During his early career Watts developed extensive trading interests with Spain, the Canary Islands, and the Azores. He was a founder member of the ill-fated Spanish Company of 1577, in which he served as an assistant and chief councillor. The development of these interests was cut short by the outbreak of the war with Spain in 1585; thereafter Watts turned his attention to privateering. He had ships at sea on voyages of reprisal throughout the war years, becoming the most important merchant-promoter of privateering in England. He sent squadrons of privateers to the Caribbean in 1588, 1590, 1591, 1592, 1594, and 1597. Four of his vessels were employed on Sir Francis Drake's voyage to the West Indies in 1595. In addition he contributed six vessels to the earl of Cumberland's Caribbean venture of 1598. He was an investor in several other important expeditions, including Drake's voyages to Spain and Portugal in 1587 and 1589, James Lancaster's voyage to Pernambuco in 1595, and John Chidley's abortive voyage to the South Seas in 1589. During the armada campaign of 1588 he served as a volunteer aboard his own ship, the *Margaret and John* of 200 tons, and was involved in some of the fiercest fighting off Calais. In 1597 he was also one of the promoters of an ambitious, but abortive, attempt to take over the Magdalen Islands at the mouth of the St Lawrence and establish English control over the walrus fishery.

Although Watts's Caribbean venture of 1590 was linked with the relief of the English colony at Roanoke, his main interests throughout the 1580s and 1590s were focused on privateering. The renown he earned in the business is confirmed by the Spanish ambassador's description of him, in 1607, as 'the greatest Pirate that has ever been in this Kingdom' (Brown, 1.99). Though unfair, there is no doubt that Watts, and the captains he employed on his ships, were often prepared to resort to unscrupulous methods in the search for plunder. Indeed, the seizure of neutral ships or cargoes involved him in several long-running and potentially expensive suits. Nevertheless, Watts reaped a rich reward from privateering. The 1591 expedition returned with prize goods that Watts estimated to be worth £31,380, although their real value was probably nearer £40,000. Not all of his ventures were as successful as this, but Watts was one of the few promoters to make a profit from privateering. By 1603 he was a wealthy man, with capital to spare for other commercial or colonial interests.

Despite his privateering interests, Watts never abandoned trade entirely. He became a member of the Levant Company in 1592. He was a member of the East India Company in 1600, and served as its second governor from 1601 to 1602. He also played a prominent role in the re-establishment of the Spanish Company in 1604. He became an active member of the Virginia Company of London, serving as a member of its council in 1609. In 1615 he was a founder member of the Somers Island Company.

Commercial success enabled Watts to become a prominent figure in the City corporation of London. A freeman of the Clothworkers' Company, he was an alderman from 1594 to 1616: representing Aldersgate ward from 1594 to 1601, Tower ward from 1601 to 1605, Aldersgate from 1605 to 1606, and Langbourn from 1606 to 1616. He served as sheriff from 1596 to 1597. In the later 1590s he was involved in the collection of money in the City for the redemption of English captives in Algiers. Although caught up in the earl of Essex's attempted uprising in the City in 1601 and removed to the Tower, there is no evidence to suggest that he was a party to the conspiracy. He was knighted on 26 July 1603, shortly after the coronation of James I. He was mayor of London from 1606 to 1607, and in that capacity entertained the king to dinner on 12 June 1607. In the last year of his life he was appointed colonel of the north regiment of trained bands, following their division into four regiments.

Watts died early in September 1616 and was buried at Ware, in Hertfordshire, on the 7th. He left the manor of Mardocks in Hertfordshire to his eldest son, John, and various bequests for the relief of the poor in his native village of Buntingford, as well as £10 to Christ's and £20 to St Thomas's hospitals in London. His son John followed him

into the East India Company, becoming a 'seaman of great note' (CSP col., 1.97), who served in the naval expeditions to Cadiz in 1625 and the Île de Ré in 1627.

JOHN C. APPLEBY

Sources K. R. Andrews, ed., *English privateering voyages to the West Indies, 1588–1595*, Hakluyt Society, 2nd ser., 111 (1959) · D. B. Quinn, ed., *The Roanoke voyages, 1584–1590: documents to illustrate the English voyages to North America under the patent granted to Walter Raleigh in 1584*, 2, Hakluyt Society, 2nd ser., 105 (1955), chap. 10 · A. B. Beaven, ed., *The aldermen of the City of London, temp. Henry III–[1912]*, 2 (1913), 5, 12, 45, 169, 173, 201, 240, 349 · *APC*, 1586–7, 22, 329–30; 1587–8, 113, 156, 160; 1588, 248; 1588–9, 52–3, 271; 1589–90, 166–7; 1590, 126–7; 1590–91, 40–41, 164; 1591, 237–8; 1591–2, 141–2, 186–7; 1592, 248–9; 1595–6, 117–18, 436–7, 486–7, 519–20; 1596–7, 260, 514–15; 1597, 186–7, 201–2; 1597–8, 41, 247–8; 1598–9, 213, 223, 312; 1599–1600, 283, 404, 422–3; 1600–01, 436–7; 1601–4, 479; 1615–16, 48–9, 72, 253–4 · *CSP dom.*, 1581–90, 171, 311, 314–15, 358, 505, 655; 1591–4, 382, 390, 397; 1595–7, 75–6, 411; 1598–1601, 588; 1601–3, 77; 1611–18, 398 · *CSP col.*, 2.110–11, 115, 124, 126–7, 130, 138–9, 154, 163, 187, 197, 203–4, 302, 385 · *CSP for.*, 1585–6, 354–5, 412, 666; 1586–8, 413; 1586–7, 296; 1588, 530–31; 1589–90, 195, 197, 214–15; 1591–2, 413, 425 · J. K. Laughton, ed., *State papers relating to the defeat of the Spanish Armada, anno 1588*, 1, Navy RS, 1 (1894), 350; 2, Navy RS, 2 (1894), 327, 337, 340 · *The naval tracts of Sir William Monson*, ed. M. Oppenheim, 1, Navy RS, 22 (1902), 259, 268; 2, Navy RS, 23 (1902), 229 · J. S. Corbett, ed., *Papers relating to the navy during the Spanish war, 1585–1587*, Navy RS, 11 (1898), 99, 105–6 · A. Brown, ed., *The genesis of the United States*, 1 (1890), 99, 198, 212; 2 (1890), 1043–4 · P. Croft, *The Spanish Company*, London RS, 9 (1973), xiv–xv, xxix, xxx, 2–6, 10–11, 18, 23, 96–7, 101 · K. R. Andrews, *Trade, plunder and settlement: maritime enterprise and the genesis of the British empire, 1480–1630* (1984), 219–20, 232, 245, 250–51, 252, 306 · R. Clutterbuck, ed., *The history and antiquities of the county of Hertford*, 3 (1827), 305, 437 · will, PRO, PROB 11/128, sig. 129

Archives BL, Lansdowne MSS 69, 144, 158 · BL, Harley MS 1546, fol. 108 · Hatfield House, Hertfordshire, Salisbury MSS · PRO, Admiralty examinations, HCA 13

Wealth at death land in Hertfordshire, Norfolk, and Kent: will, PRO, PROB 11/128, sig. 129

Watts, John (1818–1887), educationist and social reformer, was born at Coventry, on 24 March 1818, one of twelve children of James Watts, ribbon weaver. When five years old, scarlet fever left him partially paralysed. He was educated largely at Holy Trinity church school in Coventry, where he came under the influence of the Revd W. F. Hook, and despite strongly non-denominational religious beliefs, subsequently retained his connection with the Church of England.

Watts began his working life as general assistant, librarian, and assistant secretary of the Coventry Mechanics' Institute. From early 1840 he served as an Owenite social missionary in the east midlands, the Manchester district, and Glasgow. After the curtailment of the Owenite lecturing organization in the spring of 1841, he was eventually, in October 1841, appointed lecturer and teacher at the Manchester Hall of Science. Until abandoning this post in June 1844 and setting up as a tailor, he lectured and debated regularly in Manchester and the surrounding area. In October 1844 he married Catherine Shaw, of Coventry; they had three sons and four daughters.

In July 1844 Watts obtained a PhD from the University of Giessen for a revision of his lectures on political economy, *The Facts and Fictions of Political Economists* (1842), which influenced the early economic ideas of Friedrich Engels.

Watts flirted briefly with trade unionism in 1850, editing the *Trades Advocate* for the engineering unions. Subsequently, his lectures (including a paper to the British Association in 1861 which was widely discussed), numerous pamphlets, and extensive newspaper correspondence, concentrated almost exclusively on rigid Cobdenite attacks on trade unionism and strikes.

In the periods 1844–51 and 1857–62, Watts was involved in a range of social reforms, including the public parks movement and the Manchester Free Public Library scheme (begun on his initiative), which, alongside his championing of an amalgam of Cobdenite economics and Chartist politics, enabled him to become a pivotal figure in the realignment of working-class radicalism in Manchester. He remained a committed Liberal and democrat, and served on the committee of the Manchester National Association for Women's Suffrage. Otherwise, after 1864, despite serving as secretary of the Manchester Reform Club from 1867, he largely stood aloof from politics and committed himself to furthering the two enduring legacies of his Owenism: the amelioration of the conditions of the working classes, and a universal system of national education.

In February 1851 Watts was appointed the full-time agent of the National Public Schools Association (NPSA), for which he lectured extensively in 1851, before spending considerable time in London in 1852 and 1853 assisting the association's witnesses (of which he himself was one) before the select committee on education in Manchester and Salford. Although thereafter the NPSA campaign quickly faded, Watts remained active in several local efforts to demonstrate the inadequacy of the voluntary system, including the Manchester Education Aid Society. After the 1866 social science congress he took a leading role, especially in drafting the vital twenty-fifth ('Cowper–Temple') clause, in a committee which framed H. A. Bruce's 1868 Education Bill, the basis for the Elementary Education Act of 1870. From its inception in 1870 until his death Watts was one of the non-sectarian party members of the Manchester school board, being instrumental in the early adoption of the compulsory education clauses and remaining at the forefront of the struggle to extend the board's activities. He fought hard to preserve and extend free educational provision at the Manchester grammar school. As 'Earnest' he led the campaign of 1862–3 to reform the Union of Lancashire and Cheshire Mechanics' Institutes, serving as its chairman from 1872 to 1886. He became a campaigner for scientific and technical education, and was chairman of the Manchester Technical School (which he helped to create out of the Manchester Mechanics' Institute) and secretary of the extension committee of Owens College.

In 1853 Watts accepted the position as promoter of the People's Provident Assurance Society (later the European), travelling extensively in 1853–4 selling shares and appointing agents. From 1854 to 1857 his directorship required residency in London, after which he returned to Manchester as district agent. The traumatic failure of the European at the end of the 1860s caused a breakdown in Watts's health, and during a period of recuperation in Torquay in the winter of 1866–7, he drafted what became the 1870 Life Assurance Act. The failure of the European did not prevent Watts continuing as an insurance broker and commercial arbitrator.

While living in London, Watts gave vigorous support to the Association for the Repeal of the Taxes on Knowledge, deploying his logical mind to help frame the parliamentary questions with which Thomas Milner-Gibson MP fronted the campaign. He served as sub-treasurer from 1856 and treasurer from 1870. From 1878 until his death he was also treasurer of the travelling tax abolition committee.

Although he eschewed direct organizational involvement, Watts was an enthusiastic advocate of the co-operative movement. The influential articles entitled 'What is co-operation?', which appeared in the early issues of the *Co-operative News* (1872–3) and established Watts's position as the leading advocate of the 'federalist position', demonstrate that he never lost his belief in the transformative power of co-operation. Nevertheless, tension remained between the visionary remnants of his Owenism and a more prosaic preoccupation with thrift, and his later newspaper controversies with E. V. Neale (as J. W.) suggest an increasing emphasis on co-operation as a provident mechanism for the accumulation of savings. His concern for this aspect of the movement underpinned his activity on the central relief committee during the Lancashire cotton famine, which provided the impetus for his most substantial work, *The Facts of the Cotton Famine* (1866). It was also manifested in his tireless support for the Provident Dispensaries movement, which he launched in Manchester in the early 1870s, serving as president from 1878.

Watts never entirely overcame suspicion of his 'socialist' past, but by dint of what George Jacob Holyoake called his 'Manchester mind, clear, sagacious, persistent, progressive, with a passion for facts' (*Co-operative News*, 19 Feb 1887), his calm, reasoned, metallic, platform style, and his capacity for administrative work, he imposed himself on the development of mid-Victorian Manchester, and of universal national education. He died at his home, The Sycamores, Seymour Grove, Old Trafford, Manchester, on 7 February 1887 after an extended illness, and was buried in the parish church of Bowdon.   M. HEWITT

Sources G. Entwhistle, 'Dr John Watts, 1818–1887, and his work for the education and welfare of the working classes in Manchester', MEd diss., University of Manchester, 1981 · *Manchester Guardian* (8 Feb 1887) · *Manchester Courier* (8 Feb 1887) · *DLB* · P. N. Backstrom, *Christian socialism and co-operation in Victorian England: Edward Vansittart Neale and the co-operative movement* (1974) · C. D. Collet, *History of the taxes on knowledge: their origin and repeal*, 2 vols. (1899) · CGPLA Eng. & Wales (1887)

Likenesses sketch, repro. in *Bee-Hive* (14 Aug 1875)

Wealth at death £12,133 13s. 10d.: resworn probate, Oct 1887, CGPLA Eng. & Wales

Watts, John [Jack] **(1861–1902)**, jockey, was born at Stockbridge, Hampshire, on 9 May 1861, one of the family of ten children of Thomas Watts. In due course Jack, as he was usually known, was apprenticed to Tom Cannon, then training at Houghton, near Stockbridge. At the age of thirteen he weighed less than 4 stone, though this had risen to 6 stone by May 1876 when he rode his first winner, Aristocrat, at Salisbury.

In 1879 Watts began an association with Richard Marsh, then training at Lordship Farm, Newmarket, who obtained for him a retainer from the duke of Hamilton and later a position as first jockey for the prince of Wales. Despite his ability, Watts's weight problems restricted the number of mounts which he could take and thus he never became champion jockey, though he was runner-up in 1891 with 114 winners. In the winter of 1895 he contemplated retirement because of the difficulty in controlling his weight, but was persuaded to continue by Marsh; this led to his riding the prince of Wales's Persimmon to victory in the 1896 Derby, his third success in that race. In all he rode nineteen classic winners.

Watts was a quiet and unspectacular rider who relied on timing and 'hands', and getting the best out of a horse when apparently doing very little. He was undemonstrative and, according to George Lambton, would enter the winner's circle 'looking as solemn as a judge who had just passed a death sentence' (Lambton, 221). His health undermined by excessive wasting, Watts retired from the saddle in 1900 and began to train racehorses at Newmarket. That season he only saddled one winner of a £100 plate, but in 1901 he turned out seven winners of fifteen races. He was twice married: first, in 1885, to Annie, daughter of Mrs Lancaster of the Black Bear Hotel, Newmarket; and second, in 1901, to Lutetia Annie, daughter of Francis Hammond of Portland House, Newmarket. On 19 July 1902 Watts had a seizure at Sandown Park, and on 29 July he died in the hospital at Esher. He was buried in Newmarket cemetery. His widow in 1911 married Kempton, son of

Tom Cannon, formerly a successful jockey. Two of Watts's sons adopted their father's profession, and Jack, the eldest, afterwards became a trainer at Newmarket.

WRAY VAMPLEW

Sources R. Mortimer, R. Onslow, and P. Willett, *Biographical encyclopedia of British flat racing* (1978) · M. Tanner and G. Cranham, *Great jockeys of the flat* (1992) · G. Lambton, *Men and horses I have known* (1924) · A. E. T. Watson, *King Edward VII as a sportsman* (1911) · *The Sportsman* (30 July 1902) · *CGPLA Eng. & Wales* (1902) · *DNB*
Likenesses J. A. Wheeler senior, portrait, *c.*1886; Phillips, 12 July 1982, lot 12 [*see illus.*] · D. M. Hardy, oils, repro. in Watson, *King Edward VII*, 160 · Lib [L. Prosperi], caricature, lithograph, NPG; repro. in *VF* (25 June 1887) · photograph, repro. in Lambton, *Men and horses*, facing p. 226
Wealth at death £27,070 2s. 6d.: administration, 27 Sept 1902, *CGPLA Eng. & Wales*

Watts, Sir Philip (1846–1926), naval architect, born at Deptford, Kent, on 30 May 1846, was the son of John Watts, of Havelock Park, Southsea, then chief assistant to John Fincham, shipwright at Portsmouth Dockyard, a famous builder of warships, and author of *The History of Naval Architecture* (1851), in the preparation of which John Watts assisted. His mother was Mary Ann Featherstone. Watts's father, grandfather, and great-grandfather were all master shipwrights, and his great-grandfather took part in the building of Nelson's flagship, *Victory*. Philip Watts was educated at the principal school at Portsmouth, and in 1860 was apprenticed as a shipwright in the royal dockyard, where he was taught mathematics and physical science in the dockyard school. He was selected to receive a 'superior course' in naval construction, and in 1866 was one of the three Admiralty students promoted to the Royal School of Naval Architecture and Marine Engineering at South Kensington. In April 1870 he left the Royal School with the title of fellow, and was appointed to the

John Watts (1861–1902), by John Alfred Wheeler senior, *c.*1886 [Miss Jummy with John Watts up]

chief constructor's staff at the Admiralty (which in 1883 became the Royal Corps of Naval Constructors), where he made calculations with regard to the design of new ships and acted as Admiralty overseer on several ships then building by contract. In this capacity Watts made a practice of calculating on scientific principles the proper size of various parts of a ship's structure, and did much to break down the old 'rule of thumb' methods. On completing this work he spent over two years at Torquay in assisting William Froude, who was the first to develop an accurate theory of the behaviour of ships under way. This association was the beginning of a lifelong friendship with Froude and his son and assistant, Robert Edward Froude (1856–1924).

In 1872 Watts became a draughtsman on the constructor's staff. On completion of his service with Froude he was appointed assistant constructor at Pembroke Dockyard during the building of the battleship *Shannon*, launched in 1875, gaining a reputation as an ingenious designer of mechanical appliances and details of all sorts. On returning to the Admiralty he was entrusted with the organization and supervision of a 'calculating section' to serve the growing complexity of naval designs. He was also made responsible for the calculations relating to the torpedo-ram *Polyphemus*, laid down in 1878, a vessel of novel construction with a very small reserve of buoyancy, which made extreme accuracy necessary in calculating her range of stability and buoyancy. He was also concerned in the controversy over the battleship *Inflexible*, launched in 1876, and in connection with it conducted some steering experiments on the battleship *Thunderer* in Portland harbour, the results of which were afterwards issued for the instruction of the fleet. In connection with the *Inflexible*, Watts experimented with water chambers for the purpose of moderating the rolling of ships whose bulk was considerably higher than their centres of gravity. In 1883 he was promoted to the grade of constructor, and in November 1884 appointed to the staff of Chatham Dockyard; but in October 1885 he resigned from the Admiralty in order to succeed Sir William Henry White as naval designer and general manager to Armstrong & Co. at their warship yard at Elswick.

During his seventeen years at Elswick, Watts was placed in a position of great responsibility, both as a naval designer and as a captain of labour on a large scale; he brought the Elswick shipyard to the foremost position by designing and constructing foreign warships, and also by building several British warships designed by the Admiralty and secured for the Elswick yard in open competition. The ships designed for foreign powers were remarkable for their firepower and speed, which later were the outstanding features of Watts's additions to the British fighting fleet. He had signal success in obtaining high speed and heavy armament on abnormally small displacements. The cruisers he designed for Japan, Argentina, Brazil, Chile, Norway, Portugal, Romania, and Turkey established his reputation as a constructor and gave him experience for his later achievements. Nearly all the warship fighting done by the Japanese fleet in 1904 and 1905

was carried out by Watts's ships, the battleships *Yashima* and *Hatsuse*, and the cruisers *Idzumo*, *Iwate*, *Asama*, and *Tokiwa*. For his services he was awarded the Japanese order of the Rising Sun. Among Watts's Elswick ships may be mentioned especially the Italian cruiser *Piemonte*, built in 1888, then for her size the most heavily armed war vessel in the world, and the Japanese *Yashima*, launched in 1896, a battleship with the speed of a cruiser, and in many respects the forerunner of his battle cruisers of later times. From 1894 to 1910 Watts was lieutenant-colonel and honorary colonel of the 1st brigade of the Royal Garrison Artillery volunteers, and while at Elswick he equipped and sent out to the Second South African War the Elswick battery.

In February 1902 Watts returned to the Admiralty as director of naval construction. At that time two of the King Edward VII class of eight battleships had been begun, and three more were to be laid down before the end of the year. In this class the main armament was much the same as that of the Collingwood class of battleships designed in 1880, though the secondary armament was heavier. Watts considered the class not powerful enough, though he was not able immediately to carry out his ideas to the full. In 1903 he produced designs for battleships of much greater gun power. The Admiralty, however, while approving what afterwards was named the Lord Nelson type, resolved to build first the three remaining vessels of the King Edward VII class, which were accordingly laid down in 1903, and were followed by the *Lord Nelson* and *Agamemnon*, of the new and more powerful type, in 1904 and 1905. The appointment on 21 October 1904 of Sir John Arbuthnot Fisher as first sea lord gave Watts the opportunity of realizing more completely his desire for powerful ships. As far back as 1881 he had accompanied the *Inflexible* in the Mediterranean when Fisher was in command, had had the opportunity of discussing with him matters of naval construction, and had brought away an outline design, evolved during the cruise, for a battleship with an 'all big gun' armament of four pairs of 16 inch 80 ton guns mounted in turrets. This design, however, had been rejected on account of the large displacement involved. Fisher, on becoming first lord, introduced a design for an 'all big gun' battleship having six pairs of 12 inch guns all mounted on the middle line, three pairs at each end of the ship in steps. A vessel so armed could fire six guns directly ahead and six directly astern, and all twelve guns on either broadside.

Fisher got a powerful committee of design appointed by Lord Selborne, including Prince Louis of Battenberg, naval officers such as John Jellicoe, Henry Bradwardine Jackson, Reginald Bacon, Charles Madden, Sir Albert John Durston, and Alfred Winsloe, and men of expert knowledge such as Lord Kelvin, Sir John Isaac Thornycroft, R. E. Froude, John Harvard Biles, Alexander Gracie, and Watts. Fisher's proposal of a twelve-gun battleship was generally approved, but on consideration it was found too large and costly. The dreadnought was as near an approach as was possible, taking into account dockyard capacity and naval estimates.

The final result of the committee's aspirations, as interpreted by Watts, was the recommendation of the remarkable series of ship types of which the *Dreadnought* battleship and *Indomitable* battle cruiser were the chief. The principles underlying these new designs were a much more powerful armament on a given displacement, higher speed through the use of steam turbines and the water-tube boiler, unification of gun-calibre to secure gun control, greater manoeuvring power, the internal subdivision of the vessel into separate watertight compartments, each self-contained as regards access, drainage, and ventilation, and greater protection against guns and torpedoes in the arrangement of the armoured decks and the underwater protection of the sides. In the dreadnought battleship class the main armament was raised from the four 12 inch and four 9.2 inch guns of the King Edward VII class to ten 12 inch guns, mounted in pairs *en barbette*, three pairs on the centre line, and a pair on each broadside opposite each other amidships. The secondary armament disappeared and was replaced by quickfirers to deal with torpedo craft. But in later classes of dreadnoughts the secondary armament was restored, to meet the increased menace from air and torpedo attack.

The first *Dreadnought* was laid down at Plymouth on 2 October 1905, and began her sea trials on 3 October 1906. She had a speed of over 21.6 knots, and owing to her rectangular construction amidships was comparatively free from rolling. During his ten years of office Watts improved and developed the dreadnought type. He was the designer of the Bellerophon, St Vincent, Neptune, Orion, King George V, Iron Duke, and Queen Elizabeth classes, each containing several battleships, and each marking an increase in armament, displacement, and speed. He himself considered that the Orion class, laid down in 1909–10, practically realized Fisher's first design. In the Queen Elizabeth class, 1912–13, eight 15 inch guns were substituted for ten 13.5 inch guns. The main armament of the dreadnought type set the fashion to the whole world. 'If Sir Philip's fame rested on no other basis than that of the armament of the *Dreadnought*, his name would be handed down as one of the world's great naval designers' (*Transactions of the Institution of Naval Architects*, 68, 1926, 289). Lord Fisher wrote: 'The *Dreadnought* could not have been born but for Sir Philip Watts' (Fisher, 258).

Hardly less remarkable was the creation of the battle cruiser. At the outbreak of the First World War in 1914 all the effective battle cruisers in the Royal Navy were of Watts's design. The battle cruisers *Indomitable*, *Inflexible*, and *Invincible* were launched in 1907. They were armed with eight 12 inch guns, and had a speed of 24 knots. On account of their heavy armament and substantial armour protection they might have been classed as battleships. They were followed by the Indefatigable class, launched in 1909, which included besides the *Indefatigable* the Australian cruisers *Australia* and *New Zealand*. In 1910 were launched the *Lion*, *Princess Royal*, and *Queen Mary*, of greater size and a speed of 28 knots, and in 1912 the *Tiger*, with a speed of 30 knots. It was the speedy arrival and intervention of the *Inflexible* and *Invincible*—wholly unexpected by the enemy—which proved the decisive factor in the action with Admiral von Spee off the Falkland Islands on 8 December 1914. Considerable improvements were also made by Watts in the designs of light cruisers and destroyers.

All these changes in design were fundamental and not merely developments of pre-existing types. As they were made in time of peace it was not easy to explain their desirability to the public and they met with considerable opposition. In parliament in July 1906 Mr Balfour criticized the designing and building of dreadnoughts, and Sir William White, Watts's predecessor as constructor, suggested in the *Nineteenth Century* in April 1908 that Britain had started an unnecessary naval armament race. There were strong reasons, however, for thinking that the improvements in naval construction were making the race inevitable. It has been asserted that Germany designed more powerful ships as early as 1904. If an advance was certain, it was important to have the initiative. Subsequent events showed this. Watts's work designed in time of peace stood the vital test of war. Naval developments in Britain caused the continental powers to change their whole outlook on naval affairs. The Kiel Canal had to be widened and harbours reconstructed, and when war broke out in 1914 the German navy, with a greatly inferior firepower, was not in a position to meet the demands made on it by the military chiefs in Berlin. The fact that Britain from the beginning was greatly superior at sea was of primary importance. At the battle of Jutland (31 May 1916) twenty-nine of the thirty-four British battleships and battle cruisers engaged were of Watts's design.

In August 1912 Watts resigned his post as director of naval construction, but his services were retained in an advisory capacity until January 1916, when he returned to Elswick and became a director of Armstrong, Whitworth & Co. He was created KCB in 1905, and in 1900 was elected a fellow of the Royal Society, of which he was afterwards a member of council and a vice-president. He received the honorary degree of LLD from Glasgow University and that of ScD from Trinity College, Dublin. He became a member of the Institution of Naval Architects in 1873, and contributed to its *Transactions*, a member of the Institution of Civil Engineers in 1901, and of the Institution of Mechanical Engineers in 1902. He wrote on 'Ships' and 'Shipbuilding' for *Encyclopaedia Britannica*. On the formation of the Society of Nautical Research in 1910 he was made a vice-president. In June 1921, at the annual meeting of that society, he called attention to the dangerous state of Nelson's *Victory* in Portsmouth harbour, and as a result of his efforts and those of Sir F. C. Doveton Sturdee the famous ship was refitted and preserved. In restoring her to her Trafalgar conditions Watts was assisted by old plans of the ship which had come down to him from his great-grandfather. He contributed an article on this subject in 1923 to the *Transactions of the Institution of Naval Architects*. Like all great organizers, he attached a high value to education. He assisted in the creation of the professorial chairs and the schools of naval architecture in the universities of Glasgow, Durham, and Liverpool. Watts married in 1875 Elise Isabelle, daughter of Chevalier Gustave Simoneau de St Omer, of Brussels. His wife and his two daughters survived him. He died of pneumonia at his residence, 4 Hans Crescent, Chelsea, London, on 15 March 1926 and was buried in Brompton cemetery.

E. I. CARLYLE, *rev.* ANITA MCCONNELL

Sources *Transactions of the Institution of Naval Architects*, 68 (1926), 285ff. • *The Times* (16 March 1926) • J. A. Fisher, *Memories* (1919), 257–9 • *Engineering* (19 March 1926) • *Nature*, 117 (1926), 457–8 • F. Manning, *Life of Sir William White* (1923), 464–80 • E. L. Woodward, *Great Britain and the German navy* (1935), 104–16
Archives CAC Cam., letters to Lord Fisher • Durham RO, letters to Lord Rendel • Sci. Mus., corresp. with Oswald John Silberrad
Likenesses Spy [L. Ward], caricature, Hentschel-colourtype, repro. in *VF* (7 April 1910)
Wealth at death £5525 6s. 3d.: probate, 24 April 1926, *CGPLA Eng. & Wales*

Watts, Richard (*c*.1529–1579), naval administrator and benefactor, was born at West Peckham, Kent, and migrated to Rochester in or about 1552. In 1547 he was appointed joint purveyor of naval victualling with Edward Baeshe, an appointment which foreshadowed the latter's appointment in June 1550 as general surveyor of victuals for the navy. As surveyor of victuals for Ireland, Watts acted as Baeshe's deputy, and was paid to supply English forces sent to Ireland in 1550 and 1551. His work may explain his move to Rochester, whence supplies were sent to the fleet which was increasingly using the Medway as a safe winter and peacetime anchorage. By a patent dated 26 March 1560 he was appointed paymaster and surveyor of the works at Upnor Castle to erect a blockhouse 'for the savegarde of our Navye'. Saunders attributes the plan and initial design to Sir Richard Lee and the practical supervision to Humfrey Locke, described as surveyor and chief carpenter, with Richard Watts acting as the accounting officer and administrator. His accounts cover the period 1559–64, with a second set covering the period to 1567, when the final payment was made to the 'paynters for paynting the Lyon with the vane and handle of yeon, set upon the toppe of the steis with 16d. for one gallon of Oyle and with 9s. for haulfe a hundrethe of fyne gold' (Saunders, 271). Work on Upnor Castle then ceased until it was decided to improve the fortifications in the vicinity of Chatham in 1599.

Watts sat in Elizabeth's second parliament, 1563–7, as MP for Rochester and received a visit from the queen during her progress through Surrey and Kent in 1573. The story goes that when at leave-taking the host apologized for the insufficiency of his house, the queen remarked 'satis'. Watts took this as a compliment and named his house on Rochester's Bully Hill 'Satis'. He died on 10 September 1579 and was buried in Rochester Cathedral. In his will, made on 21 or 22 August 1579 and proved at Rochester a month later, he left Satis House to his wife, Marian, for life; afterwards it was to be sold to build and maintain almshouses. However, he failed to make it clear whether the widow and sole executor was to keep Satis if she remarried. In 1586 the corporation claimed the property

from her and her second husband, but agreed to a settlement by which they retained possession. According to his will, Watts's charity also provided for the provision of:

> six matrices or flock beds and other good and sufficient furniture … to harbour or lodge in poor travellers or wayfaring men, being no common rogues … the said wayfaring men to harbour therein no longer than one night unless sickness be the farther cause thereof; and those poor folks there dwelling should keep the same sweet and courteously intreat the said poor travellers; and every of the said poor travellers at their first coming in to have fourpence. (*DNB*)

The revenue of the charity, originally 20 marks, had risen to £500 a year in 1771 and to £7000 a year in 1859. At this date the charity was remodelled and twenty almsfolk lodged in a new building on the Maidstone road, with an allowance of £30 a year each. The unusual character of the charity attracted the interest of nineteenth-century antiquarians, including Charles Dickens, who urged its reform in the Christmas number of *Household Words* for 1854. A bust of Watts, copied from one that is said to have been executed during his lifetime, surmounts a monument erected to his memory in 1736 by the corporation at the instance of the then mayor, also named Richard Watts.

SARAH BARTER BAILEY

Sources *DNB* • *HoP, Commons, 1558–1603* • A. D. Saunders, 'The building of Upnor Castle, 1559–1601', *Ancient monuments and their interpretation: essays presented to A. J. Taylor*, ed. M. R. Apted, R. Gilyard-Beer, and A. D. Saunders (1977), 263–83 • *APC, 1550–52* • D. M. Loades, *The Tudor navy* (1992) • N. A. M. Rodger, *The safeguard of the sea: a naval history of Britain*, 1: *660–1649* (1997) • F. F. Smith, *A history of Rochester* (1928) • *Kent: west and the weald*, Pevsner (1976), 484 • PRO, E 351/2204; E 351/2352; E 351/2353 • PRO, A01 2513/535 • BL, Add. MS 5752, fols. 370–88
Likenesses C. Easton, bust on monument, 1730 (after contemporary bust), Rochester Cathedral • F. E. Adams, mezzotint, BM, NPG

Watts, Robert (1820–1895), minister of the Presbyterian Church in Ireland and theological writer, was born at Moneylane, near Castlewellan, co. Down, on 10 July 1820, the youngest of fourteen children of a Presbyterian farmer. He was educated at the parish school of Kilmegan, co. Down, and at the Royal Academical Institution, Belfast. In 1848 he went to America, where he graduated at Washington College (now Washington and Lee University), Lexington, Virginia, in 1849 and studied theology at Princeton Theological Seminary under Charles Hodge DD (1797–1878). He organized a Presbyterian mission at Philadelphia in 1852, gathered a congregation in Franklin House Hall, was ordained its pastor in 1853, and obtained the erection in 1856 of Westminster Church for its use. He got into a controversy over Arminianism with Albert Barnes (1798–1870), a Philadelphia Presbyterian of liberal views. On a visit to Ireland he accepted a call to Lower Gloucester Street congregation, Dublin, and was installed there in August 1863. During a previous visit to Ireland in 1853 he had married Margaret, daughter of William Newell of Summerhill, Downpatrick, co. Down. They had two sons and two daughters. The eldest son, Robert Watts, was Presbyterian minister of Kilmacrenan, co. Donegal, and died on 4 December 1889. The two daughters married Presbyterian ministers.

On the death of John Edgar in 1866, Watts was elected to the chair of systematic theology in the Assembly's College, Belfast. He was a keen theologian, of very conservative views, opposed to the tendencies of the late nineteenth century's so-called higher criticism, and especially to the influence of German exegesis. He studied the then current speculations with some care and in a spirit of uncompromising antagonism. His writings were acceptable to the older minds in his denomination, and were in some measure successful in combating the new theological views. He helped to give the college a reputation for vigorous Calvinism. However, in matters where he considered that no theological interest was involved he was not so conservative; he advocated the use of instrumental music in public worship, though this was against the general sentiment of Irish presbyterians.

Watts held the chair of moderator of the general assembly from 1879 to 1880 and was a representative at the pan-Presbyterian councils in the 1870s and 1880s. His literary output was extensive. His works often addressed the new forms of criticism and other theological and doctrinal issues. These include: *The New Apologetic* (1879), *The Rule of Faith and the Doctrine of Inspiration* (1885), and *The Sovereignty of God* (1894). He was also a regular contributor to periodicals. After the close of the college session in April 1895, his health completely broke down. He died at College Park, Belfast, on 26 July 1895, and was buried on 29 July in the city cemetery.

ALEXANDER GORDON, *rev.* DAVID HUDDLESTON

Sources *Belfast News-Letter* (27 July 1895) · *Northern Whig* (27 July 1895) · R. Allen, *The Presbyterian College, Belfast, 1853–1953* (1954), 177–80, 304 · C. H. Irwin, *A history of presbyterianism in Dublin and the south and west of Ireland* (1890), 233 · W. T. Latimer, *A history of the Irish Presbyterians*, 2nd edn (1902), 510, 516 · P. Schaff and S. M. Jackson, *Encyclopedia of living divines: being a supplement to Schaff-Herzog encyclopedia of religious knowledge* (Toronto, 1894), 231
Likenesses E. Taylor, oils, 1895, Union Theological College, Belfast
Wealth at death £2423 4s. 8d.: probate, 23 Aug 1895, CGPLA Eng. & Wales

Watts, Susanna (*bap.* 1768, *d.* 1842), writer and translator, was born in Danett's Hall near Leicester, and baptized on 5 July 1768, the youngest of three daughters (the two elder of whom died young from tuberculosis) of John Watts, the last of an impoverished genteel family (related to Alaric A. Watts), and his wife, Mary Halley (*d. c.*1807), an 'uneducated country girl' whom he had married for her beauty. Susanna's father died when she was a baby. To support her mother, she learned French and Italian in order to teach and translate. Her remarkable landscapes composed of feathers won a medal from the Society for the Encouragement of Arts, Manufactures, and Commerce.

Susanna Watts's first book was *Chinese maxims, translated from* [Robert Dodsley's] *The oeconomy of human life, into heroic verse* (1784). Specimens of her verse translations of Tasso, *Jerusalem Delivered*, and Verri, *Roman Nights*, circulated to

warm critical praise; but 'unforeseen circumstance' prevented their publication. She wrote a scholarly life to preface the Tasso, and clearly identified with his confinement and melancholy. She wrote for public occasions and for magazines, 'fagging and scribling whole summers & winters' (Watts, scrapbook, 2.166). Her *Original Poems, and Translations, Particularly Ambra, from Lorenzo de'Medici* (1802) includes some items by others. Her pioneer guidebook, *A Walk through Leicester* (1804), remained anonymous until her death. Maria Edgeworth mentions, in 1802, that Watts had sold a four-volume novel (untraced) to William Lane for 10 guineas and that Richard Lovell Edgeworth doubted her talent too much to recommend her to the publisher Joseph Johnson; Watts seems to have kept a copy of Maria Edgeworth's condescending letter.

About 1806 Susanna Watts's mother became insane; next year a relative of her friend Elizabeth Heyrick secured her £20 from the Royal Literary Fund. Her mother died soon afterwards. She supported herself by teaching little girls, and, with Heyrick, won local fame for philanthropy: when slaves were emancipated in 1834, she was fêted. She published in many forms (often with wit and playfulness) against slavery and cruelty to animals, and founded (*c.*1828) and held office in a Society for the Relief of Indigent Old Age. Her anthology of poems for children, *The Selector* (1823), ranges eclectically from Alexander Pope to Lord Byron and Jane Taylor. A well-kept secret until recently has been Watts's *The Wonderful Travels of Prince Fan-Feredin, in the Country of Arcadia* (1799), well reviewed in the *Gentleman's Magazine*. She translated this from the French of 1735 (reprinted 1788) of G. H. Bougeant. The book is a spirited and intricate blend of romance and mock romance. Watts's anti-slavery periodical, the *Humming Bird* (twelve numbers, 1824–5), shows equal panache. The professed editors are the three sisters Truth, Common Sense, and Philanthropy; when the magazine passes comment on pro-slavery views, Philanthropy is represented as so angry that Common Sense has to censor her.

On Watts's death an anonymous memoir appeared in a volume of her *Hymns and Poems* (1842). A better picture of her lively intellectual life emerges from her scrapbook. This begins with her Tasso and diverges into immense variety—from poems (manuscript and printed, by herself and many others), mementoes, statistics, portraits (many of women writers), and data on Hindu and Arabic languages, to diagrams of the hold of a slave ship. She died in Leicester on 11 February 1842 and was buried at St Mary de Castro Church on 15 February. She was unmarried.

ISOBEL GRUNDY, *rev.*

Sources Royal Literary Fund MSS · J. Heydrick, *First flights* (1797) · M. Pilkington, *Memoirs of celebrated female characters* (1811) · *Maria Edgeworth: chosen letters*, ed. F. V. Barry (1931) [Maria Edgeworth to Mary Sneyd] · J. Simmons, 'Introduction', in S. Watts, *A walk through Leicester*, facsimile of 1st edn of 1804 (1967) · S. Watts, scrapbook, dated London Road 11 Feb 1834, 2 vols., Leicester Public Library [prefaced by MS biographical sketch by Clara Parkes, 1865]
Archives Leicester Central Library, scrapbook

Watts, Thomas (1523/4–1577), Church of England clergyman, was born in the diocese of Chester, evidently into a wealthy family. He did not attend university until he was in his twenties, matriculating as a pensioner from Christ's College, Cambridge, in 1549 and graduating BA early in 1553. Following Queen Mary's accession he departed for Frankfurt am Main, where in October 1556 the property which the authorities had allowed him to acquire was assessed at an impressive 380 florins. By June 1557 several other exiles, including Alexander Nowell and John Mullins, were living in his house. He signed Frankfurt's 'new discipline' that year, thus proclaiming his allegiance to a democratic form of church government whereby a show of hands could outvote the wishes of the presiding pastor.

Upon his return to England after Elizabeth's accession Watts apparently resumed his studies at Cambridge but in early 1560, still a layman, he was collated by Edmund Grindal, bishop of London, to the valuable prebend of Tottenham Court (Totenhall) in St Paul's Cathedral. He compounded for his first fruits on 3 February, Nowell acting as one of his sureties. He was ordained deacon at Lambeth by Nicholas Bullingham, bishop of Lincoln, on behalf of Matthew Parker, archbishop of Canterbury, on 10 March 1560 and priest by Grindal on 24 March following, when he stated that he was BA, born in Chester diocese, and aged thirty-six. Later in 1560 he proceeded MA from Christ's. Thereafter he married Grace, daughter of John Cocke of Colchester: their only recorded child, Susan, was still a minor at his death.

In June 1560 Watts leased his prebend, for £46 per annum, to a syndicate of officers of the royal household for ninety-nine years—a transaction apparently designed to secure the timber of Highgate Wood for the court's use. In return he received, on 24 July, a royal warrant exonerating him from first fruits (also set at £46) and other sums.

On 31 January 1561 Watts was collated Nowell's successor as archdeacon of Middlesex and on 13 August received letters patent for the twelfth stall at Westminster. In December he and Mullins were among the married candidates proposed for the provostship of Eton by Grindal, who described them both as his chaplains and as 'sober, honest and learned' (Strype, 1.208–9).

In the convocation of 1563 Watts was among those who voted in favour of liturgical reforms which, if implemented, might effectively have prevented the vestiarian controversy of 1564–6. A member of the ecclesiastical commission from 1562 (and perhaps acting by 1570 as its secretary), Watts appears thereafter to have abandoned the radical views first generated in Frankfurt and sided with Archbishop Parker on the question of ritual conformity. Unlike Nowell and Mullins (now archdeacon of London) he was not one of those who on 20 March 1565 requested Parker's forbearance over the use of the canonical vestments. In October 1568 he was admitted a freeman of the Mercers' Company, 'the Court understanding that … Mr Watts mindeth to establish some monument and good thing within the City for some godly purpose' (Mercers' Company, acts of court 1560–95, fol. 142r).

Watts retained strong links with Cambridge: he was university preacher in 1569 and received the degree of DTh

early in 1570. At this time he also endowed seven Greek scholarships at Pembroke College, a college with which he is not known to have had any previous connection beyond his enduring friendship with Grindal, its former master. He drew up a highly elaborate code of regulations for his scholars, awarding preference to Londoners—this was perhaps the 'good thing' of 'godly purpose' which had gained him the freedom of the Mercers—and thereafter to candidates from Yorkshire and Lancashire. Two early Watts scholars were Thomas Dove, future bishop of Peterborough, and Lancelot Andrewes, who afterwards established a fellowship in Watts's memory.

Watts was appointed by Parker to exercise spiritual jurisdiction during the brief vacancy of the diocese of London between March and July 1570. The archbishop also collated him rector of Bocking, Essex, on 20 August 1570, and from 5 April 1571 he and John Still, archdeacon of Sudbury, held Parker's joint commission for the deanery of Bocking, with responsibility for Canterbury's peculiars in Essex and Suffolk respectively.

Despite his evident learning Watts published nothing. No records except those of probate survive for his tenure as archdeacon, but a valuable report on the clergy of the archdeaconry, drawn up in December 1576 for submission to Grindal as archbishop of Canterbury, is preserved at Lambeth Palace.

Watts made his will on 23 May 1577, bequeathing his soul merely 'unto the hands of Almighty God'. An estate in Little Abington, Cambridgeshire, and lands in Gestingthorpe and Belchamp Walter, Essex, went to Grace and then to Susan at her majority. Several provisions involved Nowell and Mullins, who were appointed overseers. There were bequests to no fewer than fourteen servants as well as to Grindal, his 'special good lord and trusty friend', who was appointed joint executor with Grace. In a codicil added the next day he left an impressive collection of books, in Latin, Greek, and Hebrew, to the library of Pembroke. They included works by Luther, Erasmus, Zwingli, Bullinger, Bucer, Gualter, and Calvin, as well as classical authors (Herodotus, Plutarch, and Josephus), Grafton's *Chronicle* and Polydore Vergil's *History of England*.

Watts died before 12 June 1577, when his successor was collated as archdeacon. Probate was granted on 3 August. One of the will's five witnesses was John Young, doubtless the incumbent master of Pembroke. When he resigned the mastership following his consecration as bishop of Rochester in March 1578 Young married Grace Watts.

BRETT USHER

Sources J. Peile, *Biographical register of Christ's College, 1505–1905, and of the earlier foundation, God's House, 1448–1505*, ed. [J. A. Venn], 2 vols. (1910–13) · P. Collinson, *Archbishop Grindal, 1519–1583: the struggle for a reformed church* (1979) · A. L. Attwater, *Pembroke College, Cambridge: a short history*, ed. S. C. Roberts (1936) · J. Strype, *The life and acts of Matthew Parker*, new edn, 3 vols. (1821) · Cooper, *Ath. Cantab.*, 1.364–5 · C. H. Garrett, *The Marian exiles: a study in the origins of Elizabethan puritanism* (1938) · *Correspondence of Matthew Parker*, ed. J. Bruce and T. T. Perowne, Parker Society, 42 (1853) · G. Hennessy, *Novum repertorium ecclesiasticum parochiale Londinense, or, London diocesan clergy succession from the earliest time to the year 1898* (1898) · LPL, carte antique et miscellanee XII/1 [survey of archdeaconry of

Middlesex] · W. P. Haugaard, *Elizabeth and the English Reformation: the struggle for a stable settlement of religion* (1968) · *Registrum Matthei Parker, diocesis Cantuariensis*, AD 1559–1575, ed. W. H. Frere and E. M. Thompson, 3 vols., CYS, 35–6, 39 (1928–33), 292–6, 342, 593, 604, 863 · register of Edmund Grindal, bishop of London, GL, MS 9531/13 · London ordination book, 1550–77, GL, MS 9535/1 · exchequer, office of first fruits and tenths, composition books, PRO, E334/7, fol. 45v [composition record for Tottenham] · exchequer, office of first fruits and tenths, plea rolls, PRO, E334/7, no. 370 [warrant of exoneration for first fruits] · will, PRO, PROB 11/59, sig. 31 · Mercers' Company, acts of court, 1560–95, Mercers' Hall, London

Archives Pembroke Cam., regulations for his seven Greek scholarships | LPL, carte antique and miscellanee XII/1

Wealth at death substantial property; plate, jewels, and large number of books bequeathed to Pembroke College, Cambridge; c.£300 in monetary bequests; also bequests to fourteen servants: will, PRO, PROB 11/59, sig. 31

Watts, Thomas (d. 1742), mathematician and entrepreneurial agent, was the son of William Watts of Shanks House, near Wincanton, Somerset. He was probably born before 1695 and his education must have been good, although he did not attend either English university. He first appears as author of *An Essay on the Proper Method of Forming the Man of Business* (1716), setting out the curriculum of the school he was about to found in Abchurch Lane, in the City of London, called the Accomptant's Office. The accompanying advertisement offered writing, bookkeeping, computation, and many branches of mathematics. The anonymous addressee could have been James Brydges, later duke of Chandos, who became Watts's lifelong patron. In the same year Watts published *A Treatise of Mechanicks* by Jacques Rohault, having revised the English translation, a project originated by Humphry Ditton.

Watts seems to have had substantial funds, as about 1719, in partnership with Benjamin Worster (1685–c.1725), he moved the school to purpose-built premises in Little Tower Street, with an existing large house for boarders. Watts taught bookkeeping; both men lectured on natural philosophy, which they also did in the evenings at Richard Steele's 'Censorium' in York Buildings, and by 1722 in booksellers' premises. The course was described in Worster's *Compendious … Account … of Natural Philosophy* (1722). The academy, as it became known, flourished, employing more staff, among whom were James Stirling, James Thomson, and Watts's brother William, who had taken over the school by 1730.

Thomas Watts, contrary to some assumptions, had not died, but was otherwise occupied. He had used the decade from perhaps 1712 to build a network of connections—to the Newtonian scientific lecturers, including Ditton, William Whiston, J. T. Desaguliers (chaplain to Brydges), and Stirling; to the burgeoning world of insurance; to the freemasons, in the Royal Exchange lodge, of which Brydges became grand master in 1737; to the entrepreneurs, most importantly Brydges; and through family relationships.

A John Watts, in particular, was from 1707 involved in the group that became the Sun Fire Office, and perhaps through him Thomas came to undertake the calculations for an annuity scheme proposed, about 1716, by another group member, the goldsmith Sir James Hallett. In September 1720 Watts joined the Sun Fire committee in a complete change of personnel following the acquisition of a large proportion of the shares by members of Royal Exchange Assurance. He had probably had a hand in the take-over, and became the 'ruling genius' (Relton, 286), secretary (1727–34), then cashier, until his retirement in 1741. Besides himself, his brother William, a manager (that is, on the board) from 1726 and a successor as secretary (1734–42), acquired shares, as did Worster. Brydges operated in the background, his transactions in this and other companies conducted by Thomas as his agent.

The family influence was further strengthened by Watts's marriage, perhaps in the mid-1720s, to Susannah, the daughter of Benjamin and Anne Gascoyne of Chiswick and the sister of John Gascoyne (d. 1750), a manager of Sun Fire from 1725, and secretary following William Watts. Another brother, Crisp Gascoyne, a manager from 1749 to 1761, was lord mayor in 1752.

Watts was 'one of the great entrepreneurs of eighteenth-century natural philosophy' (Stewart, 376) who contributed to the construction of an interlocking set of directorships between commercial enterprises, particularly in mining and water supply, and financial organizations. The scientific lecturers advised on the practicality or otherwise of the many money-making schemes that came forward. Brydges was largely concerned in the York Buildings Company, and Scotch Mines (of which Watts was a director and Stirling chief agent), but the ramifications were many and various.

About 1728 Watts became the (sinecure) deputy ranger of Enfield Chase, where he leased the New Lodge from Brydges; he was also designated clerk in the signet office. In 1734 he was elected opposition whig MP for Mitchell, and in 1741 for Tregony. In 1740 he was living in Threadneedle Street, strategically placed at the heart of the financial world. He died on 18 January 1742, leaving his whole estate to his wife Susannah, his sole executor. She further inherited the £200 pension that had been voted to her husband by Sun Fire for his 'contrivances and good services' (Relton, 286).

Susannah could have been considerably his junior, as there were two under-age sons, Thomas and Hugh, on whom she was empowered to spend as she thought fit. The younger Thomas (d. 1799) became a manager of Sun Fire in 1753 and served as secretary from 1764 to 1786, while Hugh followed him as secretary until 1806; the latter's son, Thomas, was a manager from 1799 to 1808.

RUTH WALLIS

Sources L. R. Stewart, *The rise of public science: rhetoric, technology, and natural philosophy in Newtonian Britain, 1660–1750* (1992) · P. J. Wallis, 'Thomas Watts, academy master', *History of Education Society Bulletin*, 32 (1983), 51–3 · N. A. Hans, *New trends in education in the eighteenth century* (1951), 82–7, 142 · P. G. M. Dickson, *The Sun Insurance office, 1710–1860* (1960), 52–3, 268–75, 306 · F. B. Relton, *Account of the fire insurance companies* (1893), 286 · E. Cruickshanks, 'Watts, Thomas', HoP, *Commons* · R. V. Wallis and P. J. Wallis, eds., *Biobibliography of British mathematics and its applications*, 2 (1986), 18, 87, 120 · Sun Insurance, general committee minutes, 1720–39, GL, MS 11931 · *GM*, 1st ser., 12 (1742), 51

Wealth at death whole estate to wife; £200 annuity from Sun Fire Office passed to wife in 1743 and later to sons: Relton, *Account*; will, PRO, PROB 11/707, sig. 38

Watts, Thomas (1811–1869), librarian, was born in London, in the parish of St Luke's, Old Street, Finsbury, on 28 April 1811. He was one of the three children of Joseph Watts (*c*.1770–*c*.1835), a bricklayer, originally from Northamptonshire, and his second wife, Sarah Phillips (1773–1857), born in Hemel Hempstead, Hertfordshire. Thomas was always close to his brother Joshua (1808–1875) and his sister Ann Elizabeth (1815–1880). His father bought the Peerless Pool baths in the City Road, London, about 1805, and built over part of the grounds. As owner of the baths and of houses in the area, he was in comfortable circumstances. Thomas Watts received his education at Linnington's academy, Fountain Place, City Road, where he distinguished himself by his facility in composing essays and verses.

After leaving school, Watts initially devoted himself to literature. A retentive memory and a natural linguistic aptitude enabled him to learn all the languages of western Europe (including the Celtic ones), as well as the Slavonic languages and Hungarian, and to make some progress with oriental languages. In 1837 he wrote an article on the British Museum (*Mechanics' Magazine*, 26, 454–60), which to some extent anticipated Panizzi's subsequent design for the new reading-room surrounded by bookstacks within the interior quadrangle. After being a frequent user of the reading-room for some years, he was engaged as a volunteer to catalogue a small collection of Russian desiderata, purchased by H. H. Baber, the keeper of printed books, at his recommendation. At the invitation of Panizzi, Baber's successor as keeper, Watts became a temporary assistant on 17 January 1838, and was mainly responsible for the removal of the books from Montagu House to the new museum building, designed by Sir Robert Smirke. On 27 November he became a permanent assistant, and in 1839 he was one of the four assistants who helped Panizzi draft the new rules for the catalogue of printed books. His duties until 1857 were twofold: he was the principal agent in the selection of current foreign literature for the museum, although he also gave attention to the acquisition of older books; and he arranged all newly acquired books on the shelves according to his own system of classification when the books were moved from Montagu House. In 1847 he introduced his 'elastic system' of placing books on the shelves, which prevented the interruption of the numerical series when the growth of the collections required the transfer of books within the library. He estimated that between 1838 and 1857 he arranged on the shelves at least 400,000 volumes. 'He appeared', wrote Cowtan, 'never to have forgotten a single book that passed through his hands, and always remembered its exact locality in the library' (Cowtan, 118). With John Winter Jones, he gave great assistance to Panizzi in producing the memorable report of 1845 which showed the inadequacy of the library's stock and the need for an increased grant for purchases, which the Treasury accepted. Of his achievements as a selector of books, especially in the lesser-known European languages, he himself wrote in 1861:

> In Russian, Polish, Hungarian, Danish, and Swedish, with the exception of perhaps fifty volumes, every book that has been purchased by the museum within the last three-and-twenty years has been purchased at my suggestion … every future student of the less-known literatures of Europe will find riches where I found poverty. (British Museum, central archives, CE 4/69, 176)

In 1855, again in advance of his time, he advocated the printing of the catalogue despite the fact that Panizzi was opposed to such a course of action until the revision of the catalogue in manuscript had been completed. The royal commission on the British Museum of 1847–9 had recommended that Watts's services should be rewarded; as a result his salary was increased in 1851 from £215 to £300 per annum, and he was promoted assistant keeper on 17 April 1856.

When the new reading-room was opened in 1857, Watts was appointed its first superintendent. This led to his relinquishment of his favourite duty of shelving books, but he continued to direct acquisitions: he estimated that between 1851 and 1860 he had ordered 80 thousand Greek, Latin, French, Italian, Spanish, Portuguese, German, Dutch, Scandinavian, Slavonic, and Hungarian books and examined 600,000 titles. He had also prepared lists of desiderata in Welsh, Icelandic, and Chinese, as well as a long list of American orders. On 19 August 1866 he succeeded John Winter Jones as keeper of printed books. His short term of office was marked by his determination to unite

> with the best English library in England or the world the best Russian library out of Russia, the best German out of Germany, the best Spanish out of Spain; and for every language from Italian to Icelandic, from Polish to Portuguese. (British Museum, central archives, CE 4/69, 176)

Among other important acquisitions during his tenure of office were large sections of the Mexican libraries collected by Father Fischer (secretary to the emperor Maximilian) and the bookseller Andrade, and the Japanese library of Philipp von Siebold.

Watts was a warm-hearted and occasionally a warm-tempered man. In spite of some brusquerie and angularity he was popular with his colleagues: in 1867 W. B. Rye referred to his 'usual ursine amiability of temper' (Miller, *That Noble Cabinet*, 155). His inexpressive face and an ungainly figure were alleviated for contemporaries by the charm of his conversation. Watts wrote little. His *Letter to Antonio Panizzi, Esq.* (1839) exposed the fabrication of the alleged first English newspaper, the *English Mercurie*. His fine *Sketch of the History of the Welsh Language and Literature* was privately reprinted in 1861 from Charles Knight's *English Cyclopaedia*, to which he also contributed a very good article upon the British Museum. He also wrote many biographical articles for the same publication, mainly on foreign men of letters, and he was (with his brother Joshua) a leading contributor to the unfinished *Biographical Diction-ary of the Society for the Diffusion of Useful Knowledge* (1842–4). He frequently contributed articles to a number of period-icals, including the *Gentleman's Magazine* and *The Athen-aeum*. A valued member of the Philological Society, in January 1852 he read to the society his paper on Cardinal Joseph Mezzofanti, whom he described as 'the greatest linguist the world has ever seen' (*Proceedings of the Philologi-cal Society*, 5, 1854, 111–25). A subsequent paper 'On the recent history of the Hungarian language' (*Transactions of the Philological Society*, 1855, 285–310) won him election to the Hungarian Academy.

In August 1869, while on holiday with his brother and sister, Watts suffered a slight accident at Bridgnorth, Shropshire, which caused phlebitis of the leg; this led to his death from heart disease at his residence in the British Museum on 9 September 1869. He was interred at High-gate cemetery on 15 September. He never married.

RICHARD GARNETT, *rev.* P. R. HARRIS

Sources F. J. Hill, 'Thomas Watts, 1811–1869', *British Museum Quar-terly*, 18 (1953), 32–9 · E. Miller, *That noble cabinet: a history of the British Museum* (1973) · E. Miller, *Prince of librarians: the life and times of Antonio Panizzi of the British Museum* (1967) · R. Cowtan, *Memories of the British Museum* (1872) · P. R. Harris, ed., *The library of the British Museum* (1991) · BM · BL, archives · parish register, London, Old Street, St Luke, 1811, LMA · personal knowledge (1899) · d. cert. · Highgate cemetery records, Camden Public Library
Archives BL · BM | UCL, letters to Society for the Diffusion of Useful Knowledge
Likenesses W. Carpenter, drawing, 1851, BM
Wealth at death under £10,000: administration, 27 Oct 1869, CGPLA Eng. & Wales

Watts, Walter Henry (1776–1842), journalist and artist, was born in the East Indies, the son of a captain in the Royal Navy. He was sent to England at an early age and placed in a school in Cheshire. A talented artist, he ini-tially devoted himself to the study of drawing and paint-ing. In 1808 he was a member of the Society of Associated Artists in Watercolours. He was primarily known as a miniature painter, and from 1808 to 1830 exhibited at the Royal Academy. In 1816 he was appointed miniature painter to Princess Charlotte.

Watts was unable to earn his living from painting alone, and in 1803 became a parliamentary reporter on the staff of the *Morning Post*, joining the *Morning Chronicle* in the same capacity about 1813. In 1826 he managed the report-ing department of the *Representative*, but returned to the *Morning Chronicle* in the following year. In 1837 he was co-founder and first chairman of the Newspaper Press Benevolent Association (1837–47), an ultimately unsuc-cessful organization which aimed at providing pensions for journalists and small grants to assist them in emergen-cies. Watts also continued to act as a parliamentary reporter for the *Morning Chronicle* until ill health forced him to retire in 1840.

Throughout this time Watts wrote and edited fifteen volumes of the *Annual Biography and Obituary* (1817–31). He also contributed fine art criticism to the *Literary Gazette*,

and is credited with the authorship of a rejoinder to Mar-tin Shee's *Rhymes on Art* (1805). Watts, who never married, died at his lodgings at Earl's Court Terrace, Old Brompton, London, on 4 January 1842.

E. I. CARLYLE, *rev.* VICTORIA MILLAR

Sources GM, 2nd ser., 17 (1842), 223 · *Morning Chronicle* (8 Jan 1842) · W. Jerdan, *The autobiography of William Jerdan: with his literary, political, and social reminiscences and correspondence during the last fifty years*, 4 vols. (1852–3), vol. 4, pp. 118–27 · N. Cross, *The common writer: life in nineteenth-century Grub Street* (1985) · [J. Watkins and F. Shoberl], *A biographical dictionary of the living authors of Great Brit-ain and Ireland* (1816) · Redgrave, *Artists*
Archives Bodl. Oxf., letters to Isaac D'Israeli

Watts, William (*c.*1590–1649), Church of England clergy-man and author, the son of William Watts, was born in Tibbenham, Norfolk. He attended school at Moulton and was admitted as a sizar to Gonville and Caius College, Cambridge, in 1606. He graduated BA in 1611 and pro-ceeded MA three years later. He was appointed chaplain of St Sepulchre's, Cambridge, in 1615, was vicar of St Peter's between 1615 and 1617, became chaplain and a fellow of his college in 1616, and was incorporated at Oxford in July 1618. In December 1620 he acted as chaplain to Sir Alber-tus Morton on his mission to deliver £30,000 to the prot-estant princes of Germany. In 1624 Watts became vicar of Barwick, Norfolk, and the following year was also appoin-ted rector of St Alban, Wood Street, London, apparently as a result of the patronage he enjoyed from the provost of Eton. In 1626 he resigned his fellowship and married, on 21 February in Canterbury Cathedral, Dorothy Vaughan, the daughter of a Surrey clergyman.

Watts's first published work, a translation, *St Augustines Confessions* (1631), was dedicated to Lord Keeper Thomas Coventry's daughter Elizabeth, Lady Hare of Stow, Nor-folk. It was, he claimed, 'the hardest taske that ever I yet undertooke' (A5r); uncontroversial marginal notes included classical, biblical, and historical references. Between 1632 and 1634 he produced nearly twenty issues of a serial publication, *The Swedish Intelligencer*, which eulo-gized 'that Caesar and Alexander of our times', King Gus-tavus Adolphus of Sweden. According to Anthony Wood, Watts's *Mortification Apostolicall* (1637), dedicated to Sir Henry Wotton, provost of Eton and to a number of its fel-lows, 'his ever honored patrones', gave great offence to puritans. The continental scholar Gerard Vossius praised Watts's edition of Matthew Paris's *Accesserunt duorum offarum* (1638).

Watts was made a prebendary of Wells in 1633 and awarded a DD degree in 1639. In February that year he was appointed a chaplain-extraordinary and in August a chaplain-in-ordinary to the king. He was also serving as chaplain to Lord Arundel, the commander of the invasion of Scotland. On his return to England in 1642 Charles I made Watts chaplain to Prince Rupert, whom he subse-quently accompanied in 'all the battles which he fought with the parliamenteers' (Wood, *Ath. Oxon.*, 1.383). As a result of his presence in the royalist army, in March 1643 he was removed from the parish of St Alban and his wife and family were temporarily homeless. On 19 May the committee for sequestrations ordered the seizure of his goods, worth about £129; an allowance to his family from their sale was ordered by the House of Commons on 29 June. In 1645 Watts was appointed archdeacon of Wells, but he never took possession of the post. He seems to have held the vicarage of Barwick until 1648.

Watts wrote a treatise on the surplice, 'The church's linen garment' (Bodl. Oxf., MS Tanner 262), and he may also have written two manuscript accounts of Prince Rupert's exploits during the 1640s, subsequently reproduced in B. E. G. Warburton, *Memoirs of Prince Rupert and the Cavaliers* (1849). In 1649 he travelled with Rupert's navy to Kinsale in Ireland, where he became ill and died about December that year. He was buried in Kinsale. His wife survived him.   JASON MᶜELLIGOTT

Sources Venn, *Alum. Cant.* • Wood, *Ath. Oxon.*, new edn • *Walker rev.*, 62 • *CSP dom.*, 1628–9, 511 • *STC, 1475–1640*
Archives BL, Lansdowne MS 985, fol. 154 • Bodl. Oxf., MS Tanner 262

Watts, William (*bap.* 1753, *d.* 1851), line-engraver, was baptized on 25 March 1753 at St Leonard, Shoreditch, London, the son of William Watts, master silk weaver in Moorfields, and his wife, Hannah. In 1767, aged fourteen, he was apprenticed to the engraver Edward Rooker. He is said also to have been taught by Paul Sandby: certainly he, like Rooker, became a principal engraver of Sandby's landscapes. Watts took over Rooker's *Copper Plate Magazine* when Rooker died in 1774 and contributed largely to the series of 150 landscapes that was eventually repackaged and republished by Boydell as *Sandby's Views*. Watts's own *Seats of the Nobility and Gentry*, which he drew as well as engraved, was published in twenty-one parts between 1779 and 1786.

In spring 1786—owing, as he told subscribers, to poor and declining health—Watts curtailed the publication, sold the furniture and prints at his house at Kemp's Row, Chelsea, in July, and went to Italy, reaching Naples in September 1786. He returned about a year later to live at Sunbury, Middlesex. Health as well as work may have inspired his journeys to Carmarthen in 1789; to the Hotwells, Bristol in 1790; and in 1791 to Bath, where he spent two years. At Bath he produced a set of twelve views of the principal buildings in Bath and Bristol. *Thirty-Six Views in Scotland* appeared in two parts, 1791 and 1794.

A great enthusiast for the French Revolution, Watts went to Paris; there in 1793 copies of some of his views of English country seats were aquatinted and published in colour by Laurent Guyot. He invested much of his money in the French public funds, only to find his property confiscated with that of other British subjects when war broke out. Much dispirited, he returned to work, engraving three of the plates in *Select Views in London and Westminster* (1800) and sixty-five coloured plates, from drawings by Luigi Mayer, for Sir Robert Ainstie's *Views in Turkey in Europe and Asia* (1801). This was his last major publication and he retired from business to live at Mill Hill, Middlesex. He was well read, fluent in French and Italian, and his health recovered well from the exertions of the 1780s.

Watts was unmarried—his companion 'Mrs Watts' being, as Joseph Farington remarked from time to time, 'a spinster'. A natural son, William Watts, and a natural daughter, Mary, later Mrs Turner, survived him. He recovered some of his French investment at the peace in 1815. In 1814 he purchased a small property at Cobham, Surrey, and had been blind for some years when he died there on 7 December 1851.   TIMOTHY CLAYTON

Sources Redgrave, *Artists* • *GM*, 2nd ser., 37 (1852), 420–21 • J. Ingamells, ed., *A dictionary of British and Irish travellers in Italy, 1701–1800* (1997), 983 • Farington, *Diary* • will, PRO, PROB 11/2146, sig. 83 • parish register, Shoreditch, St Leonard, LMA • d. cert.

Watts, William Whitehead (1860–1947), geologist and educationist, was born on 7 June 1860 at Broseley, Shropshire, the eldest son of Isaac Watts, music teacher, and his wife, Maria, *née* Whitehead. After early education at a dame-school he attended Bitterley grammar school (1869–70), where he developed an interest in chemistry and ventured into firework making, Shifnal grammar school (1871–3), and Denstone College, near Uttoxeter, Staffordshire (1873–8). In 1878 he won an exhibition (converted to a scholarship) to Sidney Sussex College, Cambridge. He gained first-class honours in the natural science tripos in 1881, and graduated BA in 1882. His MA was awarded in 1885 and his ScD in 1909.

From 1882 to 1891 Watts was a university extension lecturer for Cambridge; in 1888 he was deputy professor of geology at Oxford. In 1891 he became petrographer to the British Geological Survey, working in Ireland and in London, characteristically undertaking much more fieldwork than was necessary in order to ascertain geological facts to his own satisfaction and high standards. He also had responsibility for the survey's geological specimen collections in Dublin Museum and with A. McHenry wrote *Guide to the Collection of Rocks … Belonging to the Geological Survey of Ireland* (1895).

Watts returned to teaching in 1897 and was appointed deputy professor under Charles Lapworth at Mason College, Birmingham. The following year, Watts published his very successful *Geology for Beginners*, which ran to six editions, the last in 1937. In 1906 he became professor and head of the geology department of the Royal School of Mines (RSM) in London. Watts enlivened the department and developed a new postgraduate and research programme, encouraging both staff and students to attend Geological Society meetings and to read the latest literature. He built up the departmental library (later named the Watts Library) and developed the specimen collections. He always insisted on teaching the part one students, believing that it was both his job and his right to make and mould young geologists. Students and staff revered him for his intellectual abilities, his warmth, humour, and witty remarks, dubbed 'Watticisms' (Williams, 16; Boswell, 'Presentation', 6). Indeed, Watts believed teaching was paramount, saying in response to a critic of his relatively small research output: 'I felt it was more profitable to produce tools than goods, and thus by producing researchers, one was putting one's talent out at compound interest' (Williams, 48).

Watts introduced courses in engineering geology in

1910 and qualifications in oil technology (1913) and mining geology (1918), to the RSM, by then a constituent college of Imperial College. These subjects were innovative, timely, and important additions to geological training in Britain. Watts was a far-sighted man with an interest in geology as a fieldworker and as a teacher. Though most of his career was spent as a lecturer, his fieldwork—particularly on Charnwood Forest, Leicestershire—is recognized as an outstanding contribution to the geological understanding of Britain. His *Studies of the Ancient Forests of Charnwood* was published in 1947. Watts retired from the RSM in 1930 and in appreciation of his work the geology department founded the Watts medal, for the best postgraduate student annually, and arranged for his portrait to be painted by Sir William Rothenstein. He was made emeritus professor of Imperial College and then of London University.

Married twice, coincidentally into the same old family, Watts had two daughters. First he married Louisa Adelaide Atchison (*d.* 1891) in 1889. She was descended by the female line through the Turnour (Winterton) and Richardson families from Robert the Bruce. There was one daughter from this marriage, Beatrix Mary Adelaide, who married the geologist William George Fearnsides. Second, in 1894 Watts married Rachel Atchison, widow of Arthur Turnour Atchison (secretary of the British Association and a civil engineer), daughter of Ebenezer Rogers, a mining engineer and geologist in Monmouthshire. The couple later had one daughter.

Watts was a gregarious man, enjoying learned society meetings and dinners; this and his interest in progress led him to be an active member of various organizations and committees related to geology and to university teaching, working tirelessly as a committee member, secretary, or president. Among these was the chairmanship of Sutton Coldfield higher education sub-committee (1904-6) during which he succeeded in building and opening a technical school. Elected FRS in 1904, he held a record for periods as a councillor (1913-14, 1917-19, 1929-31). He was president of the Geological Society of London between 1910 and 1912, and was awarded their Wollaston fund in 1895, the Murchison medal in 1915, and the Wollaston medal in 1927. Watts was twice president of section C of the British Association, in 1903 and 1924, and president of the British Academy in 1935. His 1924 address summed up his attitude to the science of geology; it was entitled 'Geology in the service of man'. He received many awards throughout his distinguished career in public service as a civil servant and lecturer, including honorary LLDs from St Andrews and Edinburgh universities; fellowship of Sidney Sussex College, Cambridge, in 1888 and honorary fellowship in 1910; and fellowship of Imperial College, London, in 1945. Watts died on 30 July 1947 at the Kingslea Nursing Home, Mulgrave Road, Sutton, Surrey. After cremation at Church Stretton, Shropshire, his ashes were buried in Cambridge. It was said of him that 'No man … has exercised more influence on the development of British Geology during his lifetime than Professor W. W. Watts' (Williams, 8). ANNE BARRETT

Sources W. W. Watts, curriculum vitae, ICL, archives · D. Williams, 'History of the department of geology, Imperial College', ICL, archives · P. G. H. Boswell, *Obits. FRS*, 6 (1948-9), 263-79 · J. Stubblefield, correspondence with William George and Beatrix Fearnsides, 1937-45, ICL, archives, Watts collection · P. G. H. Boswell, 'Presentation by past and present members of the geological department of his portrait to W. W. Watts and of the first copy of the Watts medal to Mrs Watts', 1932, ICL, archives, Watts collection · *Geological Magazine*, new ser., 6th decade, 2 (1915), 481-7 · L. J. Spencer, *Mineralogical Magazine*, 28 (1947-9), 175-229

Archives BGS, drawings and papers · ICL, archives, corresp., notebooks, and papers

Likenesses photograph, 1915 · W. Rothenstein, oils, 1931, ICL · P. Metcalf, medal, 1932, ICL · photograph, repro. in Boswell, *Obits. FRS*

Wealth at death £30,196 19s. 2d.: probate, 17 Dec 1947, CGPLA Eng. & Wales

Wauchope, Andrew Gilbert (1846-1899), army officer, born at Niddrie Marischal, Midlothian, on 5 July 1846, was the second son of Andrew Wauchope (1818-1874) of Niddrie and his wife, Frances Maria (*d.* 26 June 1858), daughter of Henry Lloyd of Lloydsburg, co. Tipperary. Sir John Wauchope, the covenanter, was his ancestor. At the age of eleven he was sent to Dr Ellenberger's Pestalozzian school at Worksop, Nottinghamshire, and in June 1858 to Foster's school, Stubbington House, Gosport, to prepare for the navy; there he formed a lasting friendship with Lord Charles Beresford. In 1859 he entered the *Britannia* as a naval cadet, and on 5 October 1860 was entered as midshipman on the *St George*, where he formed a friendship with Prince Alfred. The *St George* was not a happy ship, and Wauchope was disgusted by the conduct of some of the officers. He decided to change to the army and obtained his discharge on 3 July 1862, then studied with tutors.

Wauchope obtained a commission, by purchase, in the 42nd regiment (the Black Watch) on 21 November 1865, was promoted lieutenant on 23 June 1867, and served as adjutant from 1870 to 1873 at Aldershot and Devonport. He served in the Second Anglo-Asante War from 30 November 1873, obtaining special employment with Russell's regiment of Hausa during its advance from the River Pra to Kumasi. He took part in several engagements, was twice wounded, the second time severely, and was mentioned in the dispatches.

In July 1878, on the annexation of Cyprus, Wauchope was appointed commissioner of the Papho district, where he improved local government and suppressed crime. On his return to England in August 1880 he was made CMG. On 14 September 1878 he was promoted captain. In 1881 he served in the First South African War, in a staff appointment on the line of communication. In 1882 he served with his regiment in the Egyptian campaign, and was one of the first to enter the trenches at Tell al-Kebir. On 14 March 1884 he was promoted major, and in the eastern Sudan that year served under Sir Gerald Graham as deputy assistant adjutant and quartermaster-general. At the battle of al-Teb he was again severely wounded. He was mentioned in dispatches, and was rewarded on 21 May with a brevet lieutenant-colonelcy. In 1884-5 he

Andrew Gilbert Wauchope (1846–1899), by J. A. Horsburgh

'as if they had been ladies' (Douglas, 166). A Wolseleyite, and effectively one of the younger members of the 'ring', he wrote that Wolseley was 'the biggest man in our service' (ibid., 301). On 21 May 1888 he became colonel, and CB in 1889, and in 1894 he was appointed to command the 2nd battalion, the Black Watch. In October 1893 he married Jean, a daughter of Sir William Muir. They had no children and she survived him.

Wauchope combined his military duties with civilian activities. He was a benevolent and popular landlord and employer. He denounced the 1894 coal strike but helped the strikers' families. He was a master of foxhounds, a member of the local school board and parish council, an elder of his parish church, and a member of the general assembly of the Church of Scotland. He enjoyed reading Scott and Marryat and disliked Kipling's portrayal of soldiers. He was tall, lean, blue-eyed, red-haired, and clean-shaven, with a 'strangely ascetic face' (Doyle, 154).

In 1898 Wauchope commanded a brigade in Kitchener's reconquest of the Sudan. He took part in the battles of the Atbara and Omdurman, and on 16 November 1898 was promoted major-general for his services. In April 1899 he received an honorary LLD from Edinburgh, and in June he unsuccessfully contested the South Edinburgh by-election against Arthur Dewar.

On the outbreak of the Second South African War in October 1899 Wauchope was appointed to command the 3rd (or Highland) brigade. It formed part of the force under General Lord Methuen for the relief of Kimberley, and Wauchope took part in the engagements of Belmont and Modder River. Methuen ordered the Highland brigade to attack the Boer position at Magersfontein by a night march and dawn attack. He failed to secure adequate reconnaissance or use his observation balloon, so the attackers did not know where the Boer defences were. In the early morning of 11 December Wauchope delayed deployment from quarter-column, and they met intense rifle fire from the concealed Boer trenches. Leading them, Wauchope was shot in the groin and temple and killed. Reportedly, his dying words were, 'Don't blame me for this, lads' (Douglas, 412). He was buried on 13 December 1899 at the township of Modder River, and on 18 December was reinterred at Matjesfontein.

served on the Nile expedition, in the river column under Major-General William Earle. At Kirbekan on 11 February 1885 he was again severely wounded.

After the return of the expedition Wauchope went back to Scotland to recover, and for a time devoted himself to his estates. On the death of his elder brother, Major John Wauchope, on 28 November 1882, he had become laird of the family estates of Niddrie Marischal, Midlothian, and Yetholm, Roxburghshire. Scottish agriculture was depressed, and his wealth came from his Niddrie collieries. He was reportedly one of the richest men in Scotland. On 9 December 1882 Wauchope married at Cambo, Elythea Ruth, daughter of Sir Thomas Erskine, baronet, of Cambo: she 'united great personal beauty with an equal charm of character' (Douglas, 173). Following childbirth, she died on 3 February 1884. They had twin sons. One died in 1887, and the other was mentally handicapped.

A staunch tory, Wauchope was Unionist candidate for Midlothian, opposing Gladstone in the 1892 general election and reducing Gladstone's majority from 4631 to 690, despite his refusal to support the Eight Hours Bill for miners, of whom there were many in the constituency. Gladstone, however, attributed the result not to Wauchope but to 'the "Church"'.

Wauchope was a brave, keen professional soldier, devoted to his regiment, and was considerate and paternalist. He paid the fares of his soldiers' wives not on the 'strength', and used to raise his hat to his soldiers' wives

E. I. CARLYLE, rev. ROGER T. STEARN

Sources W. Baird, *Major-General Wauchope* (1900) · *Hart's Army List* (1882) · A. C. Doyle, *The great Boer War: a two years' record, 1899–1901*, 15th edn (1901) · C. N. Robinson, *Celebrities of the army*, 18 pts (1900) · G. Douglas, *The life of Major-General Wauchope* (1904) · T. Pakenham, *The Boer War* (1979) · B. Farwell, *The great Anglo-Boer war* (New York, 1976); repr. as *The great Boer War* (1977) · *Annual Register* (1899) · R. Kruger, *Good-bye Dolly Gray* (1959) · Gladstone, *Diaries* · H. C. G. Matthew, *Gladstone, 1875–1898* (1995)
Archives Hove Central Library, Sussex, letters to Lord Wolseley · NL Scot., letters to Sir Charles Dalrymple
Likenesses photograph, c.1886, repro. in Douglas, *Life*, facing p. 196 · J. A. Horsburgh, cabinet photograph, NPG [*see illus.*] · J. A. Horsburgh, photograph, repro. in Robinson, *Celebrities of the army* · Horsburgh (Edinburgh), photograph, repro. in L. S. Amery, ed., *The Times history of the war in South Africa*, 2 (1902), facing p. 414 · G. Reid, engraving, repro. in Douglas, *Life*, frontispiece · photograph,

repro. in Baird, *Major-General Wauchope* · photograph, repro. in Douglas, *Life*, facing p. 310
Wealth at death £82,742 6s. 9d.: confirmation, 21 Feb 1900, *CCI*

Wauchope, Sir Arthur Grenfell (1874–1947), colonial governor and army officer, was born on 1 March 1874 in Edinburgh, the second son of David Baird Wauchope, wine merchant in Leith and cadet of the old family of Wauchope of Niddrie Marischal, and his wife, Helen Anne Mure, of Caldwell. Wauchope was educated at Repton School and in 1893 was commissioned into the Renfrew militia battalion of the Argyll and Sutherland Highlanders. In January 1896 he was gazetted a regular second lieutenant in the 2nd battalion of the Black Watch, of which the commanding officer was his second cousin Andrew Gilbert Wauchope. The 2nd Black Watch was one of the first units to embark for South Africa on the outbreak of war and the elder Wauchope, now major-general commanding the Highland brigade, made his young kinsman his galloper. At Magersfontein (11 December 1899), where General Wauchope and most of his commanding officers were killed, young Wauchope was severely wounded in the legs. From these injuries Wauchope never fully recovered. He was appointed DSO in 1900 and served as an extra aide-de-camp to the governor of Cape Colony in 1902–3 until fit to return to his battalion stationed at Ambala in India. Serving in it was A. P. Wavell who, although nine years his junior, became his lifelong friend.

When war broke out in 1914 Wauchope, now a major, sailed immediately with his battalion for France. He was wounded in December but returned to the trenches near Neuve Chapelle and was present at the Aubers Ridge fighting in May 1915 and commanded his battalion on 25 September at Loos, when it overran four lines of enemy trenches. In November the battalion left for Mesopotamia. In January 1916 at Shaykh Sa'd, during the first attempt to relieve Charles Townshend at Kut, he was severely wounded in the chest, but he continued to command until the battalion was digging in on its objective. While recovering in India he exerted his influence toward an improvement of rations for the troops in Mesopotamia. Wauchope returned to take command at Sannaiyat in February 1917, at the fall of Baghdad in March, and at Mashahida later in the same month. He subsequently commanded the 8th and 34th Indian brigades, continuing with the latter until after the Turkish armistice.

In 1920 Wauchope resumed command of his old battalion, now in Upper Silesia. In September 1922 he took command of the Londonderry brigade, and was promoted major-general in January 1923. In that rank he held four appointments: military member of the overseas settlement delegation to Australia and New Zealand in 1923; chief of the British section of the military inter-allied commission of control in Berlin in 1924–7; general officer commanding the 44th Home Counties division in 1927–9; and general officer commanding the Northern Ireland district in 1929.

In 1931 Wauchope was appointed high commissioner and commander-in-chief for Palestine and high commissioner for Transjordan, in succession to Sir John Chancellor. Ramsay MacDonald, no doubt recalling the relatively peaceful days that characterized the rule of Lord Plumer, had said that he wanted to appoint a general, 'but one who does it with his head, not his feet' (Weizmann, 335). The years in which Wauchope ruled, however, were more politicized than those of Plumer: the significant increase in Jewish immigration in the mid-1930s greatly alarmed the majority Arab population who feared the transformation of Palestine into a Jewish state.

Wauchope was a man of high ideals, cultivated tastes, tireless energy, and considerable personal fortune. He entered upon his tasks in Palestine with enthusiasm, spending the greater part of his personal fortune on cultural, educational, and agricultural projects, Jewish and Arab, and he travelled continuously to watch their growth. He encouraged the arts of both the indigenous Arabs and those imported by European Jews, and encouraged such ventures as the Jewish kibbutzim movement, the Palestine Symphony Orchestra, and the town planning of Jerusalem. The early years of Wauchope's administration were generally adjudged successful and there was little criticism when, for the first time in the history of mandate Palestine, his term of office was renewed. However, as the flood of Jewish immigration gained momentum, so too did the Arab campaign for its restriction and for the prohibition of the sale of land to the immigrants, whose funds were great enough to tempt impoverished Arab landowners. To these protests Wauchope was reluctant to yield, but the tension seriously hampered his efforts to create a legislative council for Palestine. He aimed for constitutional change but, despite the success of a new municipal government ordinance in 1934 and a limited amount of co-operation among government officials, plans for a truly representative legislative institution could not overcome the Arab demand that the high commissioner's powers be reduced to a minimum and the Jewish fear that the Arabs would use their majority to prohibit Jewish immigration and land purchase.

In April 1936 further constitutional initiatives were blocked by the outbreak of Arab demonstrations and a national strike. Frustration with the slow pace of self-government, fear of imminent Jewish domination, and awareness of successful demonstrations in Egypt and Syria combined to bring about a major Arab revolt against British rule. The six-month old general strike was called off in October 1936 on the understanding that neighbouring Arab rulers would mediate new solutions in Palestine. Britain agreed to an inquiry under Lord Peel which published its recommendations in August 1937 in favour of partition into Arab and Jewish states. Arab rejection of partition was followed by the great Arab uprising of 1937–9. Wauchope has been widely criticized for not showing more strictness in the early stages of the uprising when a firmer handling might have prevented it from acquiring any momentum. Yet to suppress so widespread a movement would have meant a brutal campaign against the mass of the Palestinian peasantry, an action which may well have proved counter-productive and for which support in Britain and abroad was far from assured. Reasons of strategy and prestige ensured in 1937 that the hand of the military be strengthened at the expense of the high commissioner. Hundreds of activists were arrested or deported. Wauchope, whose health, already frail, had been greatly worn down, relinquished his office in February 1938. He took no further part in public life, beyond serving as colonel of the Black Watch from 1940 until succeeded by Wavell in 1946, but lived quietly in London and Hampshire until his death in London on 14 September 1947. He was unmarried and was buried among his forebears at Niddrie Marischal.

Wauchope was small in stature and most unmilitary in appearance. He was, nevertheless, a stalwart soldier, who had spent the whole of the First World War commanding troops in the line, except when recovering from his wounds. Until these restricted him in later life, he was a keen shot, shikaree, and games player, and travelled widely in India and Burma in pursuit of game. There was almost no limit to his interests or to his inquisitive mind; his searching catechisms, with the answers to which he usually provided himself, were all too familiar to his subordinates. Although widely read, he published little himself except a short history of his regiment, an edited three-volume account of its activities in the First World War, and an article entitled 'Palestine and Transjordan' published about 1941. He was appointed CIE (1919), CB (1923), KCB (1931), GCMG (1933), and GCB (1938). He was made a general in 1936.   MARTIN BUNTON

Sources *The Times* (15 Sept 1947) · *DNB* · C. Sykes, *Crossroads to Israel* (1965) · J. Sherman, *Mandate days: British lives in Palestine, 1918–1948* (1997) · C. Weizmann, *Trial and error: the autobiography of Chaim Weizmann* (1949) · P. Jones, *Britain and Palestine, 1914–1948* (1979) · *CGPLA Eng. & Wales* (1948) · N. Shepherd, *Ploughing sand: British rule in Palestine, 1917–1948* (1999)
Archives Black Watch Regimental Museum, Balhousie Castle, Perth, albums · PRO, corresp. relating to Palestine, CO 967/92–93 · PRO, observations on future development of German industry, WO 32/5798 | BL OIOC, letters to Lord Reading, MSS Eur. E 238, F 118 · Bodl. Oxf., corresp. with Sir Aurel Stein · King's Lond., Liddell Hart C., corresp. with Sir B. H. Liddell Hart · St Ant. Oxf., Middle East Centre, corresp. with Bishop Rennie MacInnes · Rehovot, Israel, Weizmann Archives, corresp. with Chaim Weizmann
Likenesses crayon drawing, Black Watch Regimental Museum, Balhousie Castle, Perth · photograph, repro. in Sherman, *Mandate days*
Wealth at death £172,780 6s. 3d.: confirmation, 13 Feb 1948, *CCI*

Wauchope, Sir John, of Niddrie (1592/3–1682), politician, was the son and heir of Sir Francis Wauchope of Niddrie (d. in or before 1632) and his wife, Margaret, daughter of Sir James Sandilands of Slamannan. Wauchope was said to have been fourteen in July 1607 (*Reg. PCS*, 1st ser., 14.50). The Wauchope family originated in the borders and had settled at Niddrie Marischal in Edinburghshire by 1404, when Gilbert Wauchope was granted a charter. The estate was forfeited in 1592 after Archibald Wauchope joined Bothwell's rebellion. In 1609 the royal favourite Sir James Sandilands effected its transfer to Sir Francis Wauchope, who was both Archibald's son and his own son-in-law. The

debts incurred in the transaction were such that Sir Francis was obliged to leave his family and join the Scots brigade in the Netherlands.

John Wauchope, 'by his frugal way of living, pay'd the 200,000 merks of cautionry' (Paterson, 29) which had been the price of regaining the family estate, and rebuilt Niddrie House. He succeeded to the family estate at Niddrie in 1632, in August of which year he married Anna, daughter of Sir Andrew Hamilton of Redhouse. They had two sons and two daughters who reached adulthood.

Wauchope was knighted by Charles I on his visit to Edinburgh in 1633. He was a commissioner to parliament in 1639–41 and in 1643 sat on the committee of war. He was appointed a colonel in June 1644 and in July a commissioner to enforce the provisions of the Coal Act. In furtherance of these appointments he raised a regiment and served under Lord Leven in the siege and storming of Newcastle on 19 October 1644. Within a month he was back in Edinburghshire where he became involved in a dispute over possession of a coal pit from which he was accused of chasing his rival 'with a drawin sword and had killed him therewith if he had not hardlie escaped' (*Reg. PCS*, 2nd ser., 8.38). The privy council found the accusation of riot not proven by seven votes to three.

Wauchope was a commissioner to parliament and sheriff of Edinburghshire in 1649 and in that year again raised a regiment for service against the English. He advanced money for Charles II's expedition to Scotland and, when Cromwell marched to Scotland in 1650, the English army garrisoned Niddrie from where they stripped the copper from the roof. He sat in Charles II's parliaments at Perth and Stirling between June 1651 and June 1652. He was expelled from his lands by the English and obliged to accept for Edinburghshire the English parliament's 'Tender of Union' at Dalkeith.

Wauchope's first wife having died, on 16 June 1652 he married Jean (d. in or after 1692), widow of Sir John Ker of Lochtour and daughter of Sir Thomas Ker of Redden, with whom he had one son. He was fined £2000 under the Act of Pardon and Grace published by General Monck in Edinburgh on 5 May 1654, but the fine was remitted in 1655 after he acted as a commissioner for the cess.

Wauchope was in London for the coronation of Charles II and in July 1661, at the age of sixty-eight, he joined the privy council of Scotland on which he sat for the following twenty years. He lived to be one of the longest serving members of Charles's government in Scotland, attending meetings into his eighty-ninth year when he was barely able to scratch his signature on the orders in council. He last sat on 20 September 1681, and died at Niddrie the following January. He was buried in Niddrie Chapel. He was succeeded by his son Andrew Wauchope (1633–1711), who converted to Catholicism and sat on the privy council of James VII and II, in consequence of which the chapel at Niddrie was burnt by the Edinburgh mob in 1688. Sir John's second son, John Wauchope, Lord Edmonstone (1633–1709), sat as a lord of session until he was deprived by William III for not taking the test in 1689.

PIERS WAUCHOPE

Sources J. Paterson, *History and genealogy of the family of Wauchope of Niddrie-Merschell* (1858) · C. T. Terry, ed., *Papers relating to the army of the solemn league and covenant, 1643–1647*, 2 vols., Scottish History Society, 2nd ser., 16–17 (1917) · M. D. Young, ed., *The parliaments of Scotland: burgh and shire commissioners*, 2 (1993) · *APS*, 1643–69 · *Reg. PCS*, 2nd ser., vol. 8 · *Reg. PCS*, 3rd ser., vols. 1–7 · J. M. Thomson and others, eds., *Registrum magni sigilli regum Scotorum / The register of the great seal of Scotland*, 11 vols. (1882–1914), vols. 1, 11 · *Reg. PCS*, 1st ser., vol. 14
Archives BL, letters to duke of Lauderdale and Charles II, Add. MSS 23116–23137, 23242–23247 · Buckminster Park, Grantham, corresp. with duke of Lauderdale
Likenesses oils, *c.*1670, Scot. NPG
Wealth at death wealthy; large estate and coal works at Niddrie, Edinburghshire; estate at Yetholm, Berwickshire: Paterson, *History and genealogy*

Waugh, Alexander (1754–1827), United Secession minister, was born at East Gordon, Berwickshire, on 16 August 1754, the youngest of three children of Thomas Waugh (*d.* 1783), farmer, and his wife, Margaret Johnstone. From his earliest years he was destined for the ministry. After attending the parish school at Gordon he entered the grammar school at Earlston in 1766, from which he progressed to Edinburgh University in 1770, where he showed a particular aptitude for moral philosophy. In the same year Waugh joined a congregation of the Burgher branch of the Secession church at Stichill, and in 1774 he began to study divinity under John Brown (1722–1787) at Haddington. In 1777 he attended, for a session, the classes of Beattie and Campbell at Marischal College, Aberdeen, where he graduated MA the following year.

Having been licensed at Duns by the presbytery of Edinburgh on 28 June 1779 Waugh briefly supplied for the Wells Street congregation in London, vacant since the death of Archibald Hall (1736–1778). He returned to Scotland and was called by the small congregation of Newtown, Roxburghshire, which had not previously enjoyed a stated ministry, and was ordained there on 30 August 1780. The charge was inconvenient, in that there was no manse and Waugh had to travel some miles to attend to his congregation. Moreover a call from Wells Street was soon received and twice repeated. Waugh transferred there in 1782 and began his ministry in London on 16 June. He married, on 10 August 1786 at Edincrow, Berwickshire, Mary Neill (*d.* 1840), daughter of William Neill and Margaret Henderson of that parish; they had four daughters and six sons.

Waugh's forty-five-year ministry at Wells Street was characterized by his virtues as a preacher and a pastor. The congregation prospered and the church itself was rebuilt during that time. Waugh worked readily with clergymen of other denominations and was a friend of national establishments. Nowhere was his non-denominational approach more evident than in his support for the London Missionary Society, his most cherished cause and one with which he was involved from its inception in 1795; for twenty-eight years he served as chairman of its examination committee. He supported a host of other religious and philanthropic bodies, including the British and Foreign Bible Society, the Society in Scotland for Propagating Christian Knowledge, the Scottish Hospital, and Mill Hill

Academy. He contributed to the *Evangelical Magazine* and made missionary tours in England, Ireland, Scotland, and France. He was also instrumental, in 1812, in securing the adoption by his church of an enlarged psalmody. He was honoured with the degree of DD from Marischal College in 1815.

By nature Waugh was a cheerful, amiable, and kindly man, mild-mannered and free of any contentious tendencies: 'there was not an atom of fixed animosity in his whole composition' (Hay and Belfrage, 66). Though he presented a tall, striking, and apparently robust figure he was dogged by a dropsy-like ailment which at one point became so acute that in 1806 he retired to Scotland for a year. In May 1823 he sustained injuries from a fall when scaffolding gave way during the laying of the foundation stone of the Orphan Asylum, Clapton. The death of his son Alexander (1795–1824), who had followed his father into the ministry of the Secession church, was another blow to him; Alexander had taken the opportunity to pursue his ministry in close proximity to his father as minister of the Scots Church in Mile Lane, London, and it was his *Sermons, Addresses and Expositions at the Holy Communion* that was published by his father, with a memoir, in 1825. Waugh died at his home in Salisbury Place, London, after a short illness, on 14 December 1827. A large crowd attended his funeral at Bunhill Fields on 22 December.

ARTHUR WAUGH, *rev.* LIONEL ALEXANDER RITCHIE

Sources J. Hay and H. Belfrage, *A memoir of the Revd Alexander Waugh DD* (1830) · *Evangelical Magazine and Missionary Chronicle*, new ser., 6 (1828), 27–8, 45–53 · R. Small, *History of the congregations of the United Presbyterian church from 1733 to 1900*, 1 (1904), 197; 2 (1904), 464 · Chambers, *Scots.* (1855) · D. M. Lewis, ed., *The Blackwell dictionary of evangelical biography, 1730–1860*, 2 vols. (1995), vol. 2, p. 1163 · private information (1899)
Archives SOAS, Council for World Mission Archives
Likenesses J. & W. Tassie, paste medallions, Scot. NPG · engraving (after T. Wageman [*sic*]), repro. in *Evangelical Magazine and Missionary Chronicle*, facing p. 289

Waugh, Alexander Raban [Alec] (1898–1981), novelist, was born in Hampstead, London, on 8 July 1898, the elder son and elder child of Arthur *Waugh (1866–1943) and his wife, Catherine Charlotte (1870–1954), daughter of Henry Charles Biddulph Colton Raban, of the Bengal civil service. Alec Waugh's younger brother was the writer Evelyn *Waugh (1903–1966). Arthur Waugh, who became a publisher and literary critic, was among contributors to the first *Yellow Book*, of April 1894, and a cousin, among others, of Sir Edmund Gosse and the sculptor Thomas Woolner and, through Hunt's marriage to two Misses Waugh in succession, a connection of W. Holman Hunt. Waugh was educated at Sherborne School and the Royal Military College, Sandhurst, leaving Sherborne under a cloud at the age of seventeen. This episode was later to feature in his first novel, *The Loom of Youth* (1917), which caused a sensation by what then seemed to be its frank treatment of homosexuality in public schools. This was the first time the subject had been mentioned, and Waugh's name was removed from the roll of old boys, much to the distress of his father, another Old Shirburnian, who nevertheless defended his son loyally.

By the time it became apparent that *The Loom of Youth* was a best-seller, Waugh was a prisoner of war near Mainz, having fought at Passchendaele with the Dorset regiment and been captured as a machine-gunner near Arras. Shortly after his release, on 29 July 1919 he married Barbara Annis Jacobs (*b.* 1900/01), the eldest daughter of William Wymark Jacobs, the short story writer, but the marriage was not successful. As he wrote in *The Early Years of Alec Waugh* (1962): 'I had been nicknamed Tank at Sandhurst, yet I could not make my wife a woman' (p. 156). They separated in January 1922, and the marriage was annulled in 1923.

Despite this set-back, despite his small size, and despite emerging from his prisoner of war camp, at the age of twenty, rather bald, Waugh enjoyed a considerable success with women. Some of these successes are recounted in his various autobiographies, starting with *Myself when Young* (1923). The chief source for this aspect of his life remains *The Early Years of Alec Waugh*, where, at the age of sixty-four, he is able to record in a memorable sentence, that 'Venus has been kind to me.' He joined his father's publishing firm of Chapman and Hall in September 1919, but left after eight years to be a freelance writer. He wrote short stories and newspaper essays and embarked upon a world tour.

On 25 October 1932 Waugh married as his second wife Joan (1901/2–1969), the adopted daughter of Andrew Chirnside, estate owner, of Victoria, Australia. They had two sons and a daughter, and, when Joan's father died, she was able to provide him with a handsome eighteenth-century home, set in its own park, at Silchester, near Reading. Despite this, Waugh lived a nomadic existence between the wars, as, indeed, he did throughout his entire life, travelling in the Far East, America, and the Caribbean most particularly. His wife returned to Australia with the children. In the Second World War he rejoined the Dorset regiment and retired with the rank of major in 1945. His travels inspired him to write about forty books, none particularly successful nor deserving of more than moderate success until, in 1956, he hit the jackpot with a torrid romance, set in the West Indies, called *Island in the Sun*. This touched upon the sensitive subject of another 'forbidden love'—sexual relations across the colour bar—and in 1957 was made into a successful film starring James Mason, Joan Fontaine, and Harry Belafonte.

After this success, in the opinion of his brother Evelyn, Alec Waugh never drew another sober breath, but this was an exaggeration. He lived for much of the year in Tangier, Morocco, where an old age pension from the state of New York enabled him to equip a house with cook, butler, and houseboy; at other times, he lived austerely as writer-in-residence at a midwestern university, eating his meals from divided, plastic plates in a room above the students' canteen, and emerging from time to time to entertain his friends in London at elegant dinner parties, where he wore immaculately tailored but increasingly eccentric suits.

Within the writing fraternity, Waugh will be remembered as a great survivor, rather than as the author of any particular work of talent. In his later years he turned his hand to what he called an 'erotic comedy': *A Spy in the Family* (1970) raised a few eyebrows, but by then he was following a fashion set by others rather than breaking new ground as he had with *The Loom of Youth* and, to a lesser extent, with *Island in the Sun*.

Of mild and modest nature, Waugh had few enemies and many friends. He belonged to innumerable clubs and societies in London and New York, and was generally revered in them. He never grudged his younger brother's greater success as a writer, and the two remained on cordial terms until Evelyn's death in April 1966. A year later he published *My Brother Evelyn and other Profiles*.

Waugh died on 3 September 1981 in Tampa, Florida, where he had gone to live with his third wife, Virginia Sorensen (*b.* 1912), a writer and the daughter of Claude Eggertsen, of Springfield, Utah, USA; he had married Virginia in 1969.   AUBERON WAUGH, *rev.*

Sources Alec Waugh, *The early years of Alec Waugh* (1962) · Alec Waugh, *The best wine last* (1978) · E. Waugh, *A little learning* (1964) · personal knowledge (1990) · m. certs. · *The Times* (5 Sept 1981) · *CGPLA Eng. & Wales* (1982)
Archives Boston University, corresp., literary MSS, and papers · Ransom HRC, corresp. and literary papers · Sherborne School, corresp. and papers incl. MS of 'Loom of youth' | CAC Cam., letters to Cecil Roberts · Col. U., Rare Book and Manuscript Library, letters to literary agent with MSS of two essays · Georgetown University, Washington DC, corresp. with Sir Arnold Lunn · Lords, London, corresp. Marylebone Cricket Club
Wealth at death £4935—in England and Wales: administration with will, 28 Sept 1982, *CGPLA Eng. & Wales*

Waugh, Sir Andrew Scott (1810–1878), army officer and surveyor, eldest son of General Gilbert Waugh, military auditor-general at Madras, grandson of Colonel Gilbert Waugh of Gracemount, Midlothian (descended from Waugh of Shaw, standard-bearer at Flodden Field), and nephew of Sir Murray Maxwell of the Royal Navy, was born in India on 3 February 1810. He was educated at Edinburgh high school, and, after passing through Addiscombe in 1827 in half the usual time, came out first of his term and was commissioned lieutenant in the Bengal Engineers on 13 December 1827. After training at Chatham he went to India, arriving there on 25 May 1829.

Waugh was appointed in 1830 to help build a new foundry at Kashipur. On 13 April 1831 he was appointed adjutant of the Bengal Sappers and Miners, and on 17 July 1832 to the great trigonometrical survey of India under the immediate direction of George Everest, the surveyor-general. Waugh and his friend Lieutenant Thomas Renny (afterwards Major Thomas Renny-Tailyour) were the first engineers on the Indian establishment to join the department as subalterns and to make their careers in it. In 1833 they were sent to Sironj, to carry a series of triangles up one of the meridians fixed by the longitudinal series. They explored the jungle country between Chunar and the sources of the Son and Narbada up to Jubbulpore, and submitted a topographical and geological report to the geographical department of the India Office.

In November 1834 Waugh joined the headquarters of the surveyor-general at Dehra Dun, to help measure the

Sir Andrew Scott Waugh (1810–1878), by unknown photographer, c.1860

baseline. In April 1835 he was appointed astronomical assistant for the celestial observations connected with the measurement of the great arc, and at the end of that year he was at Fatehgarh, conducting the rougher series of the great trigonometrical survey. In January 1836 he joined Everest at Saini, to help measure the arc of the meridian extending from Cape Comorin to Dehra Dun, starting with the northern baseline in the Dehra Dun valley, and connecting it with the baseline near Sironj, some 450 miles to the south; and remeasuring the latter in 1837 with the new compensation bars which had been used at Dehra Dun. The operation was so accurate that the difference of length of the Dehra Dun baseline as measured and as deduced by triangulations from Sironj was only 7·2 inches.

In November 1837 Waugh was appointed to work southwards on the base Pagaro to Jaktipura. The work was completed by March 1838, when he was sent to test the accuracy of the triangulation between Bedar and Takalkhard and to lay out the site of an observatory at Damargidda. In October he began fieldwork with azimuth observations at Damargidda, and, working north with the triangulation, completed the work by April 1839. He shared with Everest the arduous observatory work carried on simultaneously at the stations of Kaliana, Kalianpur, and Damargidda from November 1839 to March 1840, by which the arc of amplitude was determined. In 1841 Waugh was engaged in the remeasurement of the Bedar base. Between 1834 and 1840 he had conducted the Ranghir series of triangles in the North-Western Provinces, and in 1842 he rapidly but accurately carried the triangulation through the malarious Rohilkhand *terai*.

At the end of 1843 Everest retired, recommending that Waugh, whose abilities in both the theoretical and practical aspects of survey work he had consistently praised, succeed him as surveyor-general. Although only a subaltern of Royal Engineers, and although he had only eleven years' experience of surveying, Waugh was accordingly

appointed from 16 December 1843. In 1844 he married Josephine (d. 1866), daughter of Dr William Graham of Edinburgh, and was promoted captain on 14 February of that year. He began his tenure as surveyor-general by carrying out the remaining seven series projected by Everest. These covered some 28,000 square miles and originated from the Calcutta longitudinal series on the 'gridiron system'. The eastern side was formed by the Calcutta meridional series (1844–8), which terminated in another baseline near the foot of the Darjeeling hills.

Waugh took a leading role in the north-east Himalaya series, connecting the northern end of the meridional series. The line of the country was along the base of the Himalaya *terai*, a malarial submontane tract in which many of his staff died. These operations fixed the positions and heights of seventy-nine of the highest Himalayan peaks in Nepal and Sikkim, including Peak XV, named Mont Everest in 1856 by Waugh. The series was then the longest ever carried between measured bases, being 1690 miles long from Sonakoda to Dehra Dun.

On 3 December 1847 Waugh was given the local rank of lieutenant-colonel. After completing the South Konkan, the Madras coast series, the South Parisnath, and South Maluncha series, he was free to undertake a system of triangulation to the west of the great arc series over the vast territory, much of it recently acquired, that lay in Sind, the North-Western Provinces, and the Punjab. The Chach base, near Attock, was measured in 1851–2, and the northwest Himalayan series, emanating from the Dehra Dun base, extended to it; and from Sironj the Calcutta great longitudinal series was carried westward to Karachi, closing on another baseline at Karachi, measured in 1854–5 under the surveyor-general's immediate supervision. Waugh was promoted major in the Bengal Engineers on 3 August 1855, and in 1856 the great Indus series was begun, forming the western side of the survey on its completion in 1860. In 1856 Waugh instituted a series of spirit-levelling operations to determine more accurately the heights of the baselines in the interior, beginning in the Indus valley. He was promoted regimental lieutenant-colonel on 20 September 1857, and the same year was awarded the patron's gold medal of the Royal Geographical Society. In 1858 he was elected fellow of the Royal Society. In 1859 the survey of Kashmir under T. G. Montgomerie was completed, earning Waugh, who had supervised it, many congratulations.

During Waugh's tenure of office he advanced the triangulation of India by 316,000 square miles, and of this 94,000 were topographically surveyed. He was promoted colonel on 18 February 1861, and retired from the service on 12 March following. He received the honorary rank of major-general on 6 August 1861, and in the same year he was knighted. He retired to London where he was a deputy lieutenant of the city for many years, a prominent member of the council of the Royal Geographical Society (and its vice-president from 1867 to 1870), honorary associate of the geographical societies of Berlin and Italy, a fellow of Calcutta University, and an active committee-man of the

London Athenaeum. In 1870 he married Cecilia Eliza Adelaide, daughter of Lieutenant-General Thomas Whitehead KCB, of Uplands Hall, Lancashire. He died at his home, 7 Petersham Terrace, Gloucester Road, London, on 21 February 1878, leaving his wife and at least one son from his first marriage.

The results of Waugh's work while surveyor-general are given in some thirteen volumes and reports deposited in the India Office and in 1861 he published *Instructions for Topographical Surveying*. He was energetic and enthusiastic, as well as meticulously accurate. He was a distinguished surveyor-general even by comparison with such predecessors as Lambton and Everest.

R. H. VETCH, *rev.* ELIZABETH BAIGENT

Sources C. R. Markham, *A memoir on the Indian surveys*, 2nd edn (1878) · *The Times* (28 Feb 1878) · *Geographical Magazine*, 5 (1878) · *Nature*, 17 (1877–8), 350–51 · H. M. Vibart, *Addiscombe: its heroes and men of note* (1894) · *Nature*, 18 (1878), 145 · *Reports of the great trigonometrical survey of India* (1834–61) · E. W. C. Sandes, *The military engineer in India*, 2 vols. (1933–5) · *CGPLA Eng. & Wales* (1878) · J. R. Smith, *Everest: the man and the mountain* (1999) · M. H. Edney, *Mapping an empire: the geographical construction of British India, 1765–1843* (1997)
Archives BL OIOC, corresp. and papers, MS Eur. F 181 | RGS, letters to Royal Geographical Society
Likenesses photograph, *c.*1860, BL OIOC [*see illus.*]
Wealth at death under £60,000: probate, 1 April 1878, *CGPLA Eng. & Wales*

Waugh, Arthur (1866–1943), publisher and writer, was born on 24 August 1866 at Midsomer Norton, Somerset, the eldest of the five children of Alexander Waugh (1838–1906), a general practitioner, and his wife, Anne Gosse (1837–1908), daughter of John Morgan, senior surgeon at Guy's Hospital, London, and Anne Gosse. Waugh's great-grandfather on his mother's side was the actuary William *Morgan FRS (1750–1833) and his paternal great-grandfather was the Scottish divine Alexander *Waugh DD (1754–1827). From 1875 Arthur Waugh attended a Victorian dame-school at Lansdown Crescent, Bath, but, suffering from asthma and bronchitis (complaints which were to dog him for the rest of his life), was removed for a year in order to build up his health in the countryside. His father, who lived for shooting and fishing, was a cruel man. Waugh and his young siblings were locked into dark cupboards or propped onto mantlepieces, where they were left for hours, and woken at dead of night to kiss their father's guncase (A. R. Waugh, *The Early Years*, 8). In 1879 Waugh was sent to Sherborne School in Dorset where, under the influence of an inspiring schoolmaster, James Rhoades, he resolved to pursue a career in literature. At Sherborne he co-founded the *Fifth Form Magazine* and later edited the official school publication, *The Shirburnian*. In 1885 he went to New College, Oxford, where he cultivated passions for poetry, drama, and cricket (in preference to academic work), graduating with a third class in classics in 1889. In 1888 he was awarded, in succession to John Ruskin, Oscar Wilde, Matthew Arnold, and others, the coveted Newdigate prize for poetry for a flowery submission on the subject of General Gordon of Khartoum. The prize poem, *Gordon in Africa*, was published in 1888. A year later he acted, directed, and wrote the libretto for a burlesque, *Julius Seesawcer* (with music by Claud Nugent), which was presented at the Holywell Music Room.

After Oxford, Waugh lived in London, where initially he struggled to set himself up as a literary journalist. His first published article, entitled 'The decline of comedy', was printed in *Lippincott's Magazine* in 1890. In the same year he had published *Schoolroom and Home Theatricals*, which consisted of six short plays with notes on how to perform them. With the help of his senior cousin and mentor, Edmund Gosse, Waugh found his first job, as a reader at the English office of an American publishing firm, John W. Lovell & Co. It was at regular Sunday reunions in Gosse's London home that Waugh became acquainted with Henry James, Rudyard Kipling, Thomas Hardy, Bram Stoker, J. M. Barrie, Arnold Bennett, and others. While working for Lovells, Waugh supplied articles and reviews to the *Illustrated London News* and the *National Observer* and when, in 1892, Gosse declined an offer from William Heinemann to write the first full-length life of Tennyson, the commission passed to Waugh. Tennyson was known to oppose any intrusion into his privacy and, consequently, Waugh conducted much of his research in secret. The book, *Alfred Lord Tennyson*, which went to print two days after the poet's death on 6 October 1892, was a commercial success which helped to launch Waugh on a journalistic career as a columnist for *The Sun* and regular correspondent to the New York *Critic*.

On 6 February 1893 Waugh married Catherine Charlotte Raban (1870–1954), daughter of Henry Biddulph Colton Raban of the Bengal civil service and his wife, Elizabeth Cockburn, grand-daughter of the Scottish judge Henry, Lord Cockburn. They had two sons, Alexander Raban (Alec) *Waugh (1898–1981) and Evelyn Arthur St John *Waugh (1903–1966). Arthur Waugh continued to write and edit books; a six-volume edition of *Johnson's Lives of Poets* which appeared in 1896 was followed by quaint anthologies of poems, *Legends of the Wheel* (1898), and *Rhymes to Nicholson's Square Book of Animals* (1899), with a popular biography of the poet Robert Browning appearing in 1900.

In 1894 Waugh contributed an article to the first issue of the infamous *Yellow Book*, the success of which ultimately led to his reviewing over 6000 books in a long career as literary critic for the *Daily Telegraph* which began in December 1906 and lasted nearly twenty-five years. He was offered the job of drama critic on the *Telegraph* and the editorship of the *Morning Post* but turned them down. After a period as adviser to the publishing house Kegan, Paul, Trench, Trubner & Co., he was appointed in 1902 to be managing director of Chapman and Hall, the famous publishers of Dickens. From 1926 to 1936 he was chairman of the same company, and in 1930 was elected first chairman of the Publishers' Circle. In the same year he published a detailed history of Chapman and Hall, *A Hundred Years in Publishing*, since regarded as an important source of information, and in 1931 he wrote a seductively sentimental autobiography, *One Man's Road, being a Picture of Life in a*

Passing Generation. The best of his literary criticism was collected into two volumes: *Reticence in Literature* (1915) and *Tradition and Change* (1919). In 1907 he built Underhill, a plain, commodious villa in Hampstead where he lived until 1933 when he moved to Highgate.

Waugh was short in stature and handsome, but as a young man was thin, whey-faced, and timid of appearance. Later he was corpulent. The actress Ellen Terry called him 'dear little Mr. Pickwick', a sobriquet which stuck. He was inclined to smother Alec, his elder son, with excessive affection while making little secret of his inability to understand Evelyn. None the less, his astute appreciation of literary form and style, his passion for books, his love of acting and poetry, and the generosity he showed as a critic towards other writers were among the finer qualities which Waugh succeeded in passing on to both his sons. He died after a short illness on 26 June 1943 at his home, 14A Hampstead Lane, Highgate, London, and was buried in Hampstead. *The Times* recorded that he managed to 'combine a real feeling for art with an aptitude for business and a shrewd judgement of his colleagues and assistants'.

ALEXANDER WAUGH

Sources A. Waugh, *One man's road, being a picture of life in a passing generation* (1931) · A. Waugh, *A hundred years of publishing* (1930) · A. Waugh, diaries (14 vols.), Boston University Library · A. R. Waugh, 'My father: Arthur Waugh', *The early years of Alec Waugh* (1962), 3–11 · A. R. Waugh, 'Arthur Waugh's last years', *My brother Evelyn and other profiles* (1967), 201–20 · E. Waugh, 'My father', *A little learning* (1964), 63–79 · *The Times* (28 June 1943) · b. cert. · d. cert. · CGPLA Eng. & Wales (1943)

Archives LUL, letters to Austin Dobson

Likenesses photographs, repro. in Waugh, *One man's road*

Wealth at death £5474 8s. 8d.: probate, 30 Sept 1943, CGPLA Eng. & Wales

Waugh, Benjamin (1839–1908), social reformer, was born on 20 February 1839 at Settle, Yorkshire, the eldest son of James Waugh, a saddler, and his wife, Mary, the daughter of John Harrison of Skipton. After five years of education in a private school in Stretton under Fosse (1848–53), he was apprenticed at the age of fourteen to a Southport linen draper, Samuel Boothroyd. But in 1862 he entered Airedale College, Bradford, to prepare for the Congregational ministry. Soon after completing his theological studies he married, on 26 September 1865, Sarah Elizabeth Boothroyd, the eldest daughter of his former master. The tenth of their twelve children was the painter Edna Clarke *Hall. Waugh then served as a Congregational minister at Newbury (1865–6), Greenwich (1866–85), and New Southgate (1885–7), after which he devoted himself largely to child protection work.

Waugh began his crusade on behalf of neglected and ill-treated children while at Greenwich. In conjunction with John Macgregor ('Rob Roy') he established a day institution for the care of vagrant boys known as the Wastepaper and Blacking Brigade. They also arranged with local magistrates to employ young first offenders on fishing boats rather than sending them to prison. Public appreciation of Waugh's work was shown by his election in 1870 for Greenwich to the first London school board, a position he

held until 1876, when poor health forced him to retire. Listening to the excuses of parents for the truancy of their children, Waugh soon came to believe that English law must address itself to the care and control of children in their own homes. An early expression of his thinking on this subject was *The Gaol Cradle, Who Rocks it?*, a far-sighted book published in 1873 that argued for the creation of a juvenile court system.

From 1874 to 1896 Waugh served as editor of the *Sunday Magazine*. He became an author as well as an editor of didactic tales, and eventually published four collections of religious stories for children. But by 1884, in good health once more, he was keen to perform on a wider stage. He therefore welcomed the suggestion of Sarah Smith ('Hesba Stretton') that a society for the prevention of cruelty to children, modelled on the body founded in Liverpool one year earlier, be established in London. The London SPCC at first faced a public sceptical of its claim that child abuse was both widespread and classless. To puncture what he saw as dangerous complacency, Waugh collaborated with Cardinal Manning in 1886 to write an important article, published in the *Contemporary Review*, entitled 'The child of the English savage', which described the evils that festered under cover of domestic privacy. The London SPCC gradually gained public support, and in 1889 was established through Waugh's efforts on a national, non-sectarian footing, with a constitution approved by Manning, the bishop of Bedford, and the chief rabbi. It was incorporated by royal charter in 1895 as the National Society for the Prevention of Cruelty to Children. Up to this date Waugh, the father of three sons and five daughters, received no remuneration save a small salary for editing the society's organ, the *Child's Guardian*. From 1895 until 1905, however, he served as paid director.

Waugh's organizing skill and flair for the dramatic made him a figure to be reckoned with in the crowded world of Victorian philanthropy. Short, bearded, with piercing blue eyes and an excess of nervous energy, he was an impassioned platform advocate, although his enthusiasm occasionally outran his evidence, as, for example, when he assured a House of Lords select committee in 1888 that a thousand children were murdered every winter for the insurance policies on their lives. Yet as an architect of legislative reform on behalf of the young he was highly influential. He supported the agitation of W. T. Stead against 'white slavery' in 1885, and caused to be inserted in the Criminal Law Amendment Act of that year a provision allowing courts of law to accept as evidence the testimony of children who were too young to understand the meaning of an oath. Waugh was also instrumental in promoting the landmark Anti-Cruelty Act of 1889, legislation which allowed a child to be taken from abusive parents. This act recognized a child's civil right to be fed, clothed, and properly treated. In accordance with Waugh's views, more stringent legislation followed in 1894, 1904, and 1908, all of which greatly improved the legal position of abused and neglected children.

Waugh's organization worked in co-operation with the

police through a system of local aid committees directed from the headquarters. Eager to avoid breaking up families if at all possible, Waugh saw to it that parents usually received a warning from one of the society's inspectors (popularly known as 'cruelty men') before being prosecuted. Until 1891 mixed success with fund-raising limited the scope of operations, but later the finances of the society improved. When in 1897 the press attacked its administration as an example of philanthropic extravagance, a formal inquiry, headed by Lord Herschell, vindicated Waugh and his fellow workers. Thereafter the society's progress was unimpeded. Waugh resigned the active direction of the society in 1905 on account of failing health. He died at 4 Runwell Terrace, Westcliffe-on-Sea, Essex, on 11 March 1908, and was buried in the Southend borough cemetery on 17 March. His widow was granted a civil service pension of £70 in 1909.   GEORGE K. BEHLMER

Sources R. Waugh, *The life of Benjamin Waugh* (1913) • R. J. Parr, *Benjamin Waugh: an appreciation* (1908) • H. Higgins, 'The Revd Benjamin Waugh: the apostle of childhood', *The Quiver* (May 1907), 591–5 • G. K. Behlmer, *Child abuse and moral reform in England, 1870–1908* (1982) • *The Times* (13 March 1908) • *The Times* (14 March 1908) • *The Times* (17 March 1908) • *Truth* (18 March 1908) • B. Waugh, *William T. Stead: a life for the people* (1885) • m. cert.
Archives National Society for The Prevention of Cruelty to Children, London • priv. coll., family MSS
Likenesses photograph, *c.*1890, National Society for the Prevention of Cruelty to Children, London • E. Clark, oils, NPG • A. Montiville, photograph, NPG • medallion portrait (on memorial affixed to the wall), NSPCC offices, Leicester Square, London • oils, NPG • photograph, NPG • portrait, repro. in *The Review of Reviews Annual* (1891) • portrait, repro. in Parr, *Benjamin Waugh* • portrait, repro. in H. Higgins, 'The champion of the child', *Sunday Magazine*, 34, 661–5
Wealth at death £1871 3*s.*: probate, 16 April 1908, *CGPLA Eng. & Wales*

Waugh [*married name* Lotherington], **Dorothy** (*c.*1636–1666?), Quaker preacher, was probably born in Hutton, Westmorland; though further details of her parentage are unknown, her sister, Jane Waugh (later Whitehead), was also a Friend.

Dorothy Waugh converted to Quakerism in the early 1650s, and she was one of the 'valiant sixty' whose efforts ensured that the movement quickly achieved a national and international profile. For Waugh, whose exposure to the Quaker message probably came when she was a maid at the house of another Friend, John Camm, the call to service involved ministering campaigns both at home and abroad, and not infrequently resulted in spells of imprisonment. A term in Kendal prison in 1653 was followed later by another four months' detention in Norwich in 1654—but neither sentence deterred Waugh. She subsequently published the Quaker message in Buckinghamshire (1655), Cornwall (1655), Carlisle (1655), Reading (1656), and, on two separate occasions, on ministering journeys to New England (1656, 1657). In Carlisle during Michaelmas 1655 Waugh preached against the citizenry's 'deceit & ungodly practices' to the consternation of the town's mayor who, believing that Waugh's incendiary presence might 'spoile a whole Cittie', imprisoned Waugh

and, furthermore, placed her head in a scold's bridle (Waugh, 29–30).

The penalties for preaching in New England were equally harsh: Waugh first suffered imprisonment and expulsion from the colony, sharing the common fate of seven other Quakers who had ventured into Boston in July 1656. Several of the party, among them Waugh, defied the rules of transportation, returning once more to the colony in the summer of 1657; this time, the courageous Quaker travelled from Boston to Salem with another woman, Sarah Gibbons, defying the harsh New England weather as much as the authorities. She and her female companion were commended in contemporary accounts for enduring 'storms and tempests … frost and snow' in order to 'accomplish the will and work of God' (Norton, 69). On returning once more to Boston in February 1659, however, the two women were imprisoned and later whipped for preaching. According to accounts, the women praised God even while the lashes were laid on.

Waugh's marriage to the Quaker William Lotherington (*d.* 1674?) of Whitby probably occurred around the time of her return from New England, where she had become a vocal advocate of marital celibacy. She probably rescinded her public testimony in favour of the domestic life from this point onwards; at least, she appears no longer to figure in the compendium of Quaker sufferings compiled by the eighteenth-century martyrologist William Besse. If she and William settled in Whitby, Yorkshire, to become members of the Pickering meeting, as seems likely, then it was two of their children, Hannah and Benjamin, who died there in 1664. Dorothy herself probably died on 9 December 1666, in Whitby, though both the cause of death and her place of burial are unknown. Her husband probably died in their home town on 1 March 1674.

Dorothy Waugh's place in Quaker history is as a preacher and a writer, whose courage spreading the Quaker message secured her significance as one of the first 'publishers of truth'. Though she was a literate woman, Waugh's only published account of her travels relates to her treatment in Carlisle, while her testimony is one of the few records surviving from the seventeenth century describing firsthand the constraints of a scold's bridle.   CATIE GILL

Sources 'Dictionary of Quaker biography', RS Friends, Lond. [card index] • Quaker register of births, marriages, and burials, RS Friends, Lond. [Yorkshire] • C. Atkinson, *The standard of the Lord* (1653) • J. Besse, *A collection of the sufferings of the people called Quakers*, 2 vols. (1753) • J. Bowden, *The history of the Society of Friends in America*, 2 vols. (1850) • W. C. Braithwaite, *The beginnings of Quakerism*, ed. H. J. Cadbury, 2nd edn (1955); repr. (1981) • H. Norton, *New Englands ensigne* (1659) • N. Penney, ed., *'The first publishers of truth': being early records, now first printed, of the introduction of Quakerism into the counties of England and Wales* (1907) • C. G. Pestana, *Quakers and Baptists in colonial Massachusetts* (1991) • R. T. Vann, *The social development of English Quakerism, 1655–1755* (Cambridge, MA, 1969) • A. J. Worrall, *Quakers in the colonial northeast* (1980) • D. Waugh, 'A relation concerning Dorothy Waughs cruell usage by the mayor of Carlile', in J. Parnell, *The lambs defence against lyes* (1656), 29–30
Archives RS Friends, Lond., Swarthmore collection

Waugh, Edwin (1817–1890), poet, was born on 29 January 1817 in a house adjoining the Clock Face inn, Toad Lane,

Edwin Waugh (1817–1890), by William Percy, 1882

Rochdale, Lancashire, the second son of Edward Waugh (1789–1826), shoemaker, and his wife, Elizabeth, daughter of William Howarth, stonemason, and previously the wife of a man named Hawkward. His paternal forebears hailed from prosperous Northumbrian farming stock and his maternal ancestors were zealous Wesleyans and talented musicians. Waugh was taught to read Foxe's book of martyrs, Wesley's *Hymns*, and a compendium of English history by his mother. He attended school in Drake Street, Rochdale, from 1824, subsequently transferring to the national free school, and finally Davenport's Commercial School from 1828.

The death of his father in 1826, when Waugh was only nine years of age, reduced the family to a subsistence diet of milk and porridge in a Rochdale cellar dwelling. After assisting his mother selling boots in Rochdale market he earned his first wages running errands for a local Wesleyan printer. In 1831 he became an apprentice to Thomas Holden, another Rochdale printer and bookseller. This employment enabled him to develop his love of reading and introduced him to the folklorist John Roby and the antiquary Canon F. R. Raines, who became Waugh's mentor. After serving his apprenticeship he became a journeyman printer, chiefly in the provinces but also for six or seven years in London. He returned to Rochdale in 1844 and re-entered the service of Thomas Holden and played a prominent role in the establishment of a literary institute, editing for three months a manuscript magazine, *The Incentive*.

In 1847 Waugh was appointed assistant secretary to the Lancashire Public School Association, which had been recently founded in Manchester to campaign for a national system of unsectarian education. He remained with the association until 1852, during its period of most rapid growth. His new employment allowed him time to develop his literary skills, and he submitted prose accounts of rural rambles to the *Manchester Examiner and Times*. In 1855 a Manchester bookseller published his *Lancashire Sketches*, which included early examples of his dialect humour. During this period he was introduced by his colleague Frances Espinasse to a literary circle known as the Shandeans and subsequently became one of the founders of the Manchester Literary Club. Meanwhile, having failed to secure appointment as sub-librarian of the Manchester free libraries, he became a commercial traveller for a Manchester printing firm.

His new literary pursuits and his work in Manchester, however, imposed a considerable strain on Waugh's marriage. He had married Mary Ann Hill on 11 May 1847, shortly before commencing work in Manchester, and she had borne three children. However, they had little in common, and some of the difficulties within the relationship are revealed in an unpublished diary which Waugh kept after his marriage. He was intolerant of her illiteracy, her lack of interest in self-improvement, and 'that repulsive coarseness of deportment which she puts on so frequently to the utter damnation of all that is attractive in her appearance and disposition' and they often brawled in public (Vicinus, 15). Waugh was impetuous by nature, with a reputation as a womanizer. He had fathered a son, for whom he continued to pay maintenance, before their marriage, and about 1850, after Mary Ann had returned to Rochdale, he appears to have taken up with a female barber, variously described as 'a female whiskerando' and 'a mad shaver' (ibid., 14). By 1856 he had separated from Mary Ann and moved in with a well-to-do Irish widow, Mrs Moorhouse, in Strangeways.

Ironically, during this period of marital upheaval Waugh became known to a wider public for his celebration of family relationships in his dialect poetry and songs. His best known song, 'Come whoam to the childer an' me', initially published in a Manchester newspaper in 1856, ultimately sold more copies than any previously published song. Its commendation of marital faithfulness and its sentimentality appealed to contemporary Victorian society. The *Saturday Review* pronounced it 'one of the most delicious idylls in the world' (quoted in *Manchester Examiner and Times*) and the song, reprinted as a penny card, was soon being 'hummed all over Lancashire' (Hollingworth, 139). It was also actively promoted by the philanthropist and social reformer Angela Burdett-Coutts, who arranged for the free distribution of some 20,000 copies among the London poor, and in subsequent years was reprinted on calendars, in church bulletins, temperance pamphlets, anthologies, and other newspapers. One modern critic has concluded that 'in a very real sense this poem, with all its faults, put Lancashire dialect poetry on the map' (ibid., 138). Its astonishing success led to the publication of Waugh's *Poems and Songs* in 1859 and enabled him to become a full-time professional writer in 1860.

Waugh subsequently published a wide range of dialect songs, tales, and character sketches illustrative of Lancashire life, and also produced accounts of his travels in the Lake District, Scotland, Ireland, and even the Rhineland. His most impressive commissioned work comprised a series of newspaper articles on the impact of the Lancashire cotton famine of 1862. He demonstrated an acute empathetic understanding of poverty and hardship, but has been criticized for his failure to probe complex issues such as unemployment and working conditions in factories and for his lack of sympathy for Chartism and the political aspirations of the working classes. His writing appeared at a time of transition, when the survival of dialect was threatened by the impact of the 1870 Education Act. His inspiration was drawn from the smaller Lancashire manufacturing towns and villages on the Yorkshire border, where dialect speech was more pronounced than in the big cities. 'The past, and still more the disappearing present, of this important district', he wrote, 'teem with significant features, which, if caught up and truthfully represented, might perhaps, be useful to the next generation' (Vicinus, 22). Between 1881 and 1883 he published a collective illustrated edition of his works in ten volumes, to which an eleventh volume, containing a second series of poems and songs, was added in 1889. He was often referred to as the Lancashire Burns or the Laureate of Lancashire and praised for his 'wonderful command of native vigorous idiom', his insights into character, and his representation of 'the pathos of human life' (*Manchester Guardian*). His most popular character was Besom Ben, a broom maker living in contentment on the moors of north Lancashire, 'whose wants were simple and his cares were few' (Vicinus, 39).

To supplement his income Waugh also gave public readings from his works and gained a reputation as a jovial raconteur. He also enjoyed singing traditional and patriotic songs in his distinctive tenor voice; indeed, his friend Ben Brierley maintained that he 'could sing a song as sweetly as any man I have listened to' (Brierley, 9). Photographs and sketches reveal an extrovert personality. He possessed a full head of wavy hair and neatly trimmed beard into old age, and usually sported a bow-tie, jacket, and waistcoat, and one of the many walking sticks from his vast collection. Athletic in his youth, when he had enjoyed racing and wrestling, he remained a keen rambler until his health began to fail in the 1870s. In 1881 Gladstone conferred upon Waugh a civil-list pension of £90 per annum, and in 1887 he was presented with a silver-mounted walking stick, gold pen, and silver pencil case by his friends on the occasion of his seventieth birthday. After undergoing two operations for cancer of the tongue he retired to the coast to convalesce at New Brighton, near Liverpool. He died on 30 April 1890 at his home, The Hollies, Percy Street, Liscard, Cheshire. His body was brought back to Manchester for burial, and thousands followed the cortège through the city, where flags flew at half mast, to St Paul's Church, near his former home on Kersal Moor, where he was buried on 3 May. A contemporary obituary writer in the *Manchester Guardian* observed that Lancashire

had demonstrated 'a peculiar affection for the poet and story-teller who spoke its language and expressed its mind with such fidelity'. Professor Martha Vicinus, writing almost a century after his death, pronounced him the 'leading literary spokesman for the working class of mid-nineteenth-century Lancashire' (Vicinus, 44).

JOHN A. HARGREAVES

Sources M. Vicinus, *The Lancashire dialect writer, Edwin Waugh* (1984) • *Manchester Examiner and Times* (1 May 1890) • *Manchester City News* (3 May 1890) [Manchester CL, Manchester Archives and Local Studies] • *Manchester Guardian* (1 May 1890) • G. Milner, 'Edwin Waugh: an estimate and biographical sketch', *Manchester Quarterly*, 12 (1893) [Manchester CL, Manchester Archives and Local Studies] • B. Brierley, *Personal recollections of the late Edwin Waugh* (1891) • P. Joyce, *Visions of the people: industrial England and the question of class, 1848–1914* (1991) • B. Hollingworth, ed., *Songs of the people: Lancashire dialect literature of the industrial revolution* (1977) • E. Waugh, *Collective works*, 10 vols. (1881–3) • E. Waugh, *Poems and songs: second series* (1889) • *E. Waugh: selected writings*, ed. G. Milner (1892–3) • F. Espasse, 'Manchester memories: Edwin Waugh', *Literary recollections and sketches* (1893) • *Todmorden and Hebden Bridge Historical Almanack* (1888) • *Todmorden and Hebden Bridge Historical Almanack* (1891) • *DNB* • d. cert. • *CGPLA Eng. & Wales* (1890)

Archives BL, list of songs in music catalogue • Edwin Waugh Dialect Society, Rochdale, collection • Man. CL, Manchester Archives and Local Studies, diary, notebooks, commonplace book, scrapbook, MSS, personalia, corresp. • NRA, priv. coll., corresp., papers, notebooks • Rochdale Local Studies Library, corresp., literary MSS, and papers • Rowenstall District Library, corresp. | JRL, letters to J. H. Nodal • Man. CL, Manchester Archives and Local Studies, letters to Dr Samuel Buckley

Likenesses E. E. Geflowski, marble bust, 1878, Gawsworth Hall, Cheshire • W. Percy, oils, 1882, Man. City Gall. [*see illus.*] • photograph, c.1885, Rochdale Local Studies Library • photographs, 1885, Rochdale Local Studies Library • P. Lange, photograph, 1890, repro. in *Manchester Quarterly* (July 1890) • W. Percy, portrait, Manchester Corporation • Swan Electric Engraving Co., portrait (after photograph by W. Brooks), repro. in E. Waugh, *Lancashire sketches* [n.d.], frontispiece • photograph (as a young man), repro. in Hollingworth, ed., *Songs of the people*, 155 • sketch (after photograph by P. Lange), repro. in *Manchester City News* • sketch (after photograph), Man. CL • two photographs, Man. CL

Wealth at death £465 7s. 10d.: resworn probate, Dec 1892, *CGPLA Eng. & Wales* (1890)

Waugh, Evelyn Arthur St John (1903–1966), writer, was born on 28 October 1903 at 11 Hillfield Road, West Hampstead, London, the younger son of Arthur *Waugh (1866–1943), publisher and editor, and his wife, Catherine Charlotte, *née* Raban (1870–1954). His father had become managing director of Chapman and Hall in 1902 and his mother was a quiet, meticulous woman devoted to her family and to her garden; his brother, Alexander Raban (Alec) *Waugh (1898–1981), five and a half years his senior, was vigorously athletic. Evelyn, at first timid, never felt close to his brother or to his father, preferring his mother's company. In September 1907 the family moved to a new, larger house—Underhill, on North End Road, Golders Green, Hampstead—and Alec left to board at Fernden School. For the next sixteen years (Alec went on to Sherborne School), the brothers saw little of each other and the age gap represented a barrier until Evelyn was at Oxford.

Schooling and adolescence, 1907–1921 Between 1907 and 1910 Evelyn was taught the three Rs by Catherine in the

Evelyn Arthur St John Waugh (1903–1966), by Felix H. Man, c.1943

corps, establishing societies—the Dilettanti (for art lovers) and the Corpse Club ('for those who were weary of life'). His autobiography cites two 'mentors': Francis Crease and J. F. Roxburgh. Crease, delicate and effeminate, taught Evelyn calligraphy and decorative design. Roxburgh—brilliant, elegant, and droll—had more social polish. The conflict of interests represented by these mentors—the aesthetic life of the reclusive artist–craftsman versus the panache of the man of the world—Evelyn never resolved but, as he once said, he was essentially an aesthete. At fourteen he had published an essay on cubism; he won school art prizes for illuminated prayers in fine script; he was chairman of the Dilettanti's art group and designed modernist book jackets for Chapman and Hall. Settling for 'limited Bolshevism', however, he also sought conventional success: became house-captain, editor of *Lancing College Magazine*, and president of the debating society; he also won the Scarlyn essay prize, the English verse prize, and, ultimately, the senior history scholarship to Hertford College, Oxford.

Oxford, schoolmastering, apprentice craftsman, 1922–1928
Waugh went up to Oxford in January 1922 in the middle of the academic year, and the neurotic, rather ferocious schoolboy, who had found disciples at Lancing rather than friends, relaxed. He learned to smoke a pipe, bought a bicycle, gave his maiden speech at the Oxford Union, and for two terms led a blameless existence rather like Paul Pennyfeather in *Decline and Fall*. He even passed his preliminary examination in history. All this changed when Harold Acton came up in the autumn. Through the union, Waugh had met Christopher Hollis, an old Etonian. Hollis had been at school with Acton, Henry Yorke (Henry Green, the novelist), Anthony Powell, Eric Blair (George Orwell), Brian Howard, Cyril Connolly, John Lehmann, Robert Byron, and Ian Fleming. Introduced to Acton, Waugh immediately discovered an artistic, social, and sexual ethos which contextualized his discontents with Lancing and with his father and brother. Acton and Howard were extravagantly 'gay', rich, cosmopolitan, and avant-garde. From this point, Waugh devoted himself to a life of pleasure: became actively homosexual, took seriously to drink, and baited his tutor, C. R. M. F. Cruttwell. (Cruttwell's name was used for a series of foolish characters in Waugh's early novels.) Waugh's ambition was to 'draw, decorate, design and illustrate' (*A Little Learning*, 190), and although he contributed various stories and articles to undergraduate magazines, he was principally known as a skilful graphic artist. He passed his final examinations in 1924 with a third, saw no point in returning for the required ninth term to claim his degree, and went down with huge debts and with no choice but to return home.

Arthur paid the debts and Waugh attended a London art school, Heatherley's, after his lover, Alastair Graham, had left for Greece. This marked the end of Waugh's homosexual phase. Abandoning Heatherley's, he became a schoolmaster at Arnold House in north Wales, a purgatorial experience. Part of his purgatory was separation from Olivia Plunket Greene, a Roman Catholic with whom he was in love and who later claimed to have brought him to

company of Stella Rhys, daughter of Ernest Rhys (founder of Everyman's Library and a close family friend), and then attended a local preparatory school, Heath Mount, until 1917. In that year Alec published his *roman à clef*, *The Loom of Youth*. Although not actually expelled from Sherborne (his father's school), he had been 'asked to leave' in 1915, and had begun officer training at Sandhurst. The novel, acknowledging the public-school homosexuality with which he had been associated, caused such a scandal that it was impossible for Evelyn to follow his brother to Sherborne. His mother wanted him to continue as a day boy at a London school. His father, impatient with debate, insisted that the boy must board and, as Evelyn recalled, 'with a minimum of deliberation his choice fell on Lancing, which he had never seen and with which he had no associations' (*A Little Learning*, 96). This comment aptly suggests his bitterness and sense of abandonment.

Lancing College was high-church. A Gothic structure incorporating much flint, it stands isolated on the South Downs, near Shoreham in Sussex. The regime was harsh, with a confusing set of rules aping grander schools. Most of the younger teachers had left for the First World War. Rationing rendered the meals unpalatable. At first pious and shy, Evelyn felt desolate amid the scrum of boisterous youth. He never forgot his first Ascension day 'holiday', wandering alone in the rain. But he soon settled down, fear of failure driving him to bury his sensitivities beneath a sceptical persona. He appeared to be both a boy determined to succeed within the school, ambitious and abrasive, and a subversive, ragging the army training the faith. Waugh was infatuated with the whole Plunket Greene family. But his glamorous friends seemed now to move in a remote world. He worked in two more schools at Aston Clinton in Buckinghamshire and a state school in Notting Hill, London, investigated training as a printer, and eventually began a course in carpentry. Fascinated by the Pre-Raphaelite Brotherhood and by the idea of the artist–craftsman, he had written an essay, 'P.R.B.' (1926), soon privately printed by Graham. Powell, who was then working for Duckworths, used the essay to secure Waugh a contract for a biography of Rossetti. Much to Arthur's surprise, his son settled down and wrote it, while making stabs at what became a first novel: *Decline and Fall*. Waugh's objection to becoming a writer was based on his rejection of the family trade. But he had made various attempts at fiction: an aborted novel at Lancing, Websterian short stories at Oxford. 'The Temple at Thatch' (1924) was destroyed after Acton's dismissive assessment. One remarkable piece, however, was published by Chapmans in Alec's anthology *Georgian Stories: 1926*. 'The Balance', a study of depression and alienation, written in fractured modernist prose, was reprinted only after Waugh's death in Everyman's *Complete Short Stories* (1998). Perhaps it gave too much of himself away. It clearly draws on his own sense of sexual and social rejection, the futility of secular hedonism, and an attempted suicide revealed to the public only in *A Little Learning*. There, Waugh's swimming out to sea, only to be stung back to reality by a shoal of jellyfish, is presented as the dividing line between feckless youth and 'the steep path leading to the years ahead'. By 1927 he was in love again with the woman he was to marry: Evelyn Florence Margaret Winifred Gardner (1903–1994).

Early success and marriage, 1928–1930 *Rossetti: his Life and Works* appeared in April 1928 to good reviews from all except Peter Quennell, an Oxford friend whom Waugh never forgave for this disloyalty. Critics admired the soundness of Waugh's aesthetic judgement: the knowledge of the practical techniques of painting, the terse humour, and the scholarly correction of Marillier's authoritative catalogue. A front-page spread in the *Times Literary Supplement* ensured good publicity, but there was little money to be made from such a book. Waugh had already failed as a cub reporter on the *Daily Express* and had abandoned cabinet-making. There seemed no alternative but to try to make his living as a writer, so he had set himself to complete his novel. *Decline and Fall*, originally entitled 'Untoward Incidents', is a hilarious satire in which a naïve undergraduate is (wrongly) sent down for indecent behaviour and becomes, in turn, a schoolmaster, socialite, and convict, finally returning to Oxford to study theology as though nothing had happened to him.

With this finished in late April, Waugh proposed to Evelyn Gardner. To their friends, He-Evelyn and She-Evelyn, as they became known, appeared to complement each other perfectly. She was pretty, vivacious, a thoroughly bright young thing with an Eton crop and literary aspirations of her own. She had set up house with Pansy Pakenham in a London flat, itself an act of defiant independence. Pansy's lover, later her husband, the painter Henry

Lamb, formed part of their inner circle and produced the now famous portrait of Waugh holding a glass of beer. She-Evelyn's mother, however, Lady Burghclere, daughter of the fourth earl of Carnarvon, was distinctly displeased by the prospect of having a penniless former schoolmaster as a son-in-law. The marriage was held 'secretly' at St Paul's, Portman Square, London, on 27 June 1928. No parents were present—just Acton, Robert Byron, Alec, and Pansy. After a shoestring honeymoon in a country pub, the Evelyns made their home at 17A Canonbury Square, a small flat in the then unfashionable London district of Islington. Lady Burghclere was furious when she learned of the wedding and was a regular, disapproving visitor to the flat when her daughter fell seriously ill.

Duckworth refused *Decline and Fall* on the grounds of obscenity, and Chapman agreed to publish only after censorship. When it appeared in September 1928, however, its reviews were glorious. Arnold Bennett, king of the London critics, hailed 'a genuinely new humorist'. Connolly lauded it while condemning Acton's first novel, *Humdrum* (1928). Although there was, again, small financial return, Evelyn Waugh had 'arrived'. Duckworths commissioned a travel book, a shipping company paid for a free cruise, and the Waughs set off round the Mediterranean for a proper honeymoon. This is recorded in *Labels: a Mediterranean Journal* (1930), published in America as *A Bachelor Abroad*, in which a honeymoon couple are coolly observed as childlike and sentimental. By the time he came to write it She-Evelyn had already deserted Waugh for John Heygate, an old Etonian news editor for the BBC and a friend of Powell. The honeymoon had been a disaster. She-Evelyn had been stretchered ashore with double pneumonia, spitting blood. On their return He-Evelyn had retired to a country pub to write *Vile Bodies* (1930). He was half way through it when she admitted adultery, a wound from which he never entirely recovered. 'Evelyn's defection', he wrote to Acton, 'was preceded by no kind of quarrel or estrangement. So far as I knew we were both serenely happy' (*Letters*, 38). After a brief attempt at reconciliation, Waugh filed for divorce on 3 September 1929 while, with great difficulty, trying to finish his novel.

Divorce, conversion, and travels, 1930–1936 *Vile Bodies* appeared in January 1930 and was an instant best-seller, ironically establishing Waugh at the forefront of 'youth politics' when he had already deserted the cause. At Lancing he had lampooned the 'grotesque, decaying old men, with the supreme arrogance of the impotent' who had made the war and left the young to fight it. He had also written an editorial for the *Lancing College Magazine*, 'The youngest generation' (December 1921), stating that they 'are going to be very hard and analytical and unsympathetic' but possessed of 'a very full sense of humour'. At Oxford Acton's set were ostentatiously childish in reaction against the machismo of the war generation which Waugh had mocked in an article, 'The claim of youth' (1929). Since his divorce, though, his defence of the bright young things had collapsed. Now they were the object of savage satire and his attention turned instead to defending Christian civilization. On 29 September 1930 he was received into the Roman Catholic church.

In the early 1930s Waugh produced two novels: *Black Mischief* (1932), a satire on European notions of 'progress' imitated by an imaginary African nation, and *A Handful of Dust* (1934), now widely regarded as his masterpiece, a satire on the collapse of civilized values, concentrating on the barbarism of contemporary sexual mores and divorce. He also published numerous book reviews and articles; a biography, *Edmund Campion* (1935), winner of the Hawthornden prize; collected his short stories in *Mr. Loveday's Little Outing and other Sad Stories* (1936); and published three travel books: *Remote People* (1931), *Ninety-Two Days* (1934), and *Waugh in Abyssinia* (1936). Two of his visits to Ethiopia (Abyssinia) were as a journalist when he produced daily reports: in 1930 covering Haile Selassie's coronation for *The Times*, and in 1935 for the *Daily Mail*, covering the Italian invasion. *Ninety-Two Days* described his journey to British Guiana in South America. The only time he did not travel alone to remote places was in 1934 when he joined Alexander (Sandy) Glen's expedition to Spitzbergen, and nearly lost his life when the party was endangered by freezing torrents. No book emerged from this, merely a brief article, 'The first time I went north: fiasco in the Arctic', perhaps because the island was barren and almost uninhabited. All Waugh's books involve the comic confrontation of civilization and barbarism, the observation of 'alien' social practices (including white colonial ones) in which there is nothing to choose between the degraded secularism of contemporary Western culture and the rites of 'primitive' peoples. The 'scheme' of *A Handful of Dust*, he explained to Henry Yorke, was that of 'a Gothic man in the hands of savages' (*Letters*, 88).

Waugh's pre-war fiction is not obviously the work of an ardent Catholic. Nevertheless, taking Catholic Christendom as his cultural gold standard, he was effectively writing hilarious 'Catholic novels' by negative suggestion: damning a world ignoring the truths of his church. He was enraged when Ernest Oldmeadow, editor of *The Tablet*, condemned *Black Mischief* as 'a disgrace to anybody professing the Catholic name' (*The Tablet*, 7 Jan 1933, 10), and Waugh's suppressed, vitriolic, reply (first published in 1980 in the *Letters*) insists that loyal Catholicism did not involve the artist in proselytizing. As a convert, however, he was particularly sensitive to charges like Oldmeadow's, and *Edmund Campion*, a passionate defence of the faith, was his best riposte. All the proceeds were donated to Campion Hall, Oxford, the master of which, Father Martin D'Arcy, had received him into the church.

Thanks partly to a superlative agent, A. D. Peters, Waugh became the best-paid author of his generation. Always a dandy and a sybarite, at a time when goods and services were cheap he was able to spend liberally on his own and others' pleasures, and to move without embarrassment in the company of his rich friends. But he never owned property during this period, and a string of futile infatuations—with Lady Diana Guinness, Lady Diana Cooper, and Teresa Jungman—depressed him. As a Catholic he

had committed himself to celibacy until She-Evelyn's death, but he could not live like that. There were various brief affairs, and he was reduced to the use of prostitutes. It was all profoundly unsatisfactory for a man who craved a home, a family, and life as a scrupulous Catholic. The resolution of this state of exile emerged when, in 1934, he fell in love with Laura Letitia Gwendolen Evelyn Herbert (1916–1973) and initiated the annulment of his first marriage.

Remarriage and life as a country gentleman, 1937–1939
Waugh's annulment proceedings dragged on until July 1936. By an unfortunate coincidence, Laura was a first cousin of Evelyn Gardner, being the youngest of the three daughters of the late Henry Molyneux Herbert, half-brother of the fifth earl of Carnarvon. Laura's family, staunch Catholic aristocrats, were not easily impressed by literary reputations and were cautious of Waugh's social credentials. Once the annulment was confirmed, and the couple engaged, Mary Herbert, her mother, infuriated him by trying to delay the wedding. During this hiatus he had returned to Ethiopia for a third visit at his own expense to examine the country under occupation, returned, wrote the last chapters of *Waugh in Abyssinia* lauding Italian fascism, and began *Scoop* (1938). When Laura and he married on 17 April 1937, the novel was put aside. Her grandmother, Lady de Vesci, had bought them Piers Court, an elegant country house in Gloucestershire.

Setting up house, being polite to county neighbours, and adjusting to cohabitation tested Waugh's patience but never his devotion to Laura. It was an odd but successful union. She was twenty, shy, a virgin, aristocratic, and astute. He was thirty-three, pugnacious, worldly, middle-class, and rash. It was a particular sadness to Laura that he could never like Auberon, her brother, for the Herberts were a close family. At first it seems that they saw Waugh as something of a *parvenu*. It did not help that he lampooned their Pixton Park household as Boot Magna Hall in *Scoop*. But they were eccentric, intelligent people who appreciated his eccentricities and, for his part, he grew to love Mary, and to like Gabriel and Bridget (Laura's sisters), while preferring to keep his distance. During these years his first two children, Auberon and Teresa, were born.

Waugh's financial position was more perilous than it appeared to outsiders. Laura had a small private income but the considerable expenses of their life together had mostly to be met from his writing. *Waugh in Abyssinia* had not sold well, thanks to those pro-fascist chapters, and his emergence as an apologist for right-wing Catholicism was endangering his broad public appeal. In order to raise money he took whatever reviewing work he could, including a weekly book column in Graham Greene's *Night and Day* from January to July 1938. Chapmans issued a collected works in late 1937 but it was only when Penguin Books began to publish Waugh in 1937 that any substantial revenue derived from earlier titles. Waugh used A. D. Peters as banker and accountant, setting his income at about £2000 a year. It was difficult to keep this up without journalistic work, and this delayed the production of his novel.

Scoop (1938) was favourably reviewed and sold well. Shortly after its publication Waugh went to Hungary for the Eucharistic Congress in Budapest as special correspondent for the *Catholic Herald*, witnessing Nazi oppression at first hand in Austria. Just before Waugh left, Clive Pearson had offered a lucrative visit to Mexico to write a book defending his family's interests there (the socialist government had expropriated the Pearson oilfields and was also persecuting the priesthood). Waugh's trip, from August to October 1938, was much tamer than Greene's earlier in the year. He took Laura, stayed in expensive hotels, and wrote of the country from a distance. *Robbery under Law: the Mexican Object Lesson* (1939) is his weakest pre-war book, and he knew it. None of it appears in his edited travel writings *When the Going was Good* (1946).

In July 1939 Waugh began what he hoped would be his finest work in a more conventional and highly wrought prose style than that of the five previous novels. It was abandoned when war was declared. The first chapter was published in Connolly's *Horizon* as 'My Father's House' (1941), then the entire fragment (two chapters) by Chapmans in 1942 as *Work Suspended*. It was never completed. After various refusals, Waugh secured a commission in the Royal Marines, and by November 1939 was at Chatham barracks undergoing officer training.

War service, 1939–1945 At thirty-six Waugh was the oldest recruit in the marine infantry brigade (RM1), a crack battalion skilled in the techniques of amphibious landing and sabotage. In January 1940 his group moved to Kingsdown Camp near Deal in Kent for a tactical course. He already felt alienated from RM1's raucous mess life, and later parodied the place in *Men at Arms* (1952) as Kut-al-Imara House. Here he encountered the eccentric Brigadier Albert Clarence St Clair Morford who appears in that novel as the crackpot crusader Ben Ritchie-Hook. At Bisley, just before Easter, the company lists came out and Waugh's hopes for a captaincy were dashed. He was given charge of only a platoon in B company. Laura was pregnant with their third child; the Germans had invaded Calais by 25 May. Waugh, however, seemed no closer to the fighting he craved than in September 1939. Through the agency of Brendan Bracken (pilloried as Rex Mottram in *Brideshead Revisited*), he was able to transfer in November 1940 to the newly formed, and socially smarter, commandos, but was first involved in August in a futile attempt to land General de Gaulle at Dakar, west Africa. This experience of military disorganization seriously damaged the crusading spirit with which Waugh had entered the war.

With no. 8 commando in Largs, Scotland, Waugh was with Randolph Churchill (the prime minister's son), Peter Milton (later Lord Fitzwilliam), and Henry Stavordale (Lord Stavordale, later earl of Ilchester). Hundreds of pounds changed hands across the gambling table but Waugh strove to restrict expenditure for Laura's sake. He was liaison officer, a lieutenant, when they sailed for Egypt aboard the *Glenroy*, part of Layforce, under the command of Brigadier Robert Laycock. Their initial objective was the invasion of Rhodes. With the German occupation of Cyrenaica, however, and the allies falling back on all fronts, Waugh's B company was drafted from Cairo to Sidi Bish, near Alexandria, where they sat for another idle month. The first real action he saw, a raid on Bardia on the Libyan coast in mid-April 1941, was another fiasco. When in May 1941 the Germans overran Crete, B company was called to assist in the evacuation. The breakdown in discipline amid the fleeing troops, above all the 'cowardice' of the shell-shocked Lieutenant-Colonel Felix Colvin (mocked as Major Hound in *Officers and Gentlemen*), made a lasting impression. 'I have been in a serious battle', he wrote to Laura in June, 'and have decided I abominate military life' (*Letters*, 153). A man of indomitable physical courage, Waugh despised any shrinking in the face of the enemy. He returned to England by troopship in July and during the voyage wrote *Put out More Flags* (1942).

Posted to 12RM land defence force at Hayling Island, Waugh was bitter and frustrated when moved on again to 5RM at Hawick, Scotland, for further training. No one seemed willing to find him a 'real' job, and when in November 1941 he published an article on the Bardia raid in *Life Magazine* the War Office was furious, despite the fact that clearance had been authorized by Bracken. *Put out More Flags* appeared in April 1942. Most reviewers found it brilliant and, correctly, detected a new seriousness in his tone but this did little to raise him in the estimation of his commanding officers. He was therefore delighted with his next transfer, in May 1942, to the 'Blues' (Royal Horse Guards), thanks to Laycock's recommendation.

On his thirty-ninth birthday Waugh, now a captain, was based in Sherborne, Dorset, after spending six more futile months at Ardrossan, Scotland. Laycock had moved Special Service brigade headquarters to Sherborne in early October 1942, making Brigadier 'Shimi' Lovat (Lord Lovat) second-in-command. Waugh was happy to be back with his glamorous commando chums, but Lovat and he loathed each other; Waugh, increasingly depressed, was shifted to London as Laycock's representative at combined operation headquarters, Richmond Terrace, in spring 1943. With his new commanding officer, General Haydon, it was also hate at first sight. Waugh hoped to be included in Operation Husky (the invasion of Italy) but on the very day of headquarters departure, 26 June 1943, his father died and he had to stay behind and settle the estate. Lovat then blocked his attempts to rejoin his unit, Haydon sacked him for impertinence, and Waugh was returned to the Blues' Household Cavalry training unit at Windsor and, being largely redundant, spent most of his time in London.

Visiting the deathbed of Hubert Duggan, an old Oxford friend, provided Waugh with the seed of *Brideshead Revisited* (the famous scene in which Lord Marchmain, after years of apostasy, finally crosses himself). Shortly afterwards, in December 1943, Waugh broke his leg in parachute training, and was granted leave without pay to write the novel. It was written, between various recalls to service, from January to June, 1944. In July, Randolph Churchill invited Waugh to join him on Fitzroy Maclean's military mission to Croatia, assisting the partisans against the retreating Germans. Waugh flew out with him to Bari, then Vis, an island off the Dalmatian coast, where they met Marshal Tito. In July they flew into Yugoslavia, their plane crashed, and Waugh was burned. After a further month's recuperation in Bari, they returned to Topusko, a blitzed spa in Croatia. Waugh's sympathies lay with the Catholics, not with the communist partisans, and he wrote an extensive report, 'Church and state in liberated Croatia', denigrated by the Foreign Office. Proofs of *Brideshead* were returned via Downing Street and he arrived in London on 15 March 1944 to find himself in funds, Peters having secured serial rights with *Town and Country*.

Celebrity in the USA, 1945–1950 British reviews of *Brideshead Revisited* (1945) were generally good but the turning point came when the Book of the Month Club selected it, a deal worth some £20,000, enabling Waugh to fix his income at about £5000 a year, and one which made him a best-seller in America for the first time. Financial security, however, did not produce equanimity. Piers Court had been let to a convent school for the duration and Laura had seen out the war at Pixton Park. They now had four children. They could not repossess Piers Court before September, and until then Waugh stayed largely apart from his wife. When they did return, his love for the house had died and he made plans (without consulting her) to buy a castle in Ireland. She resisted. It was a difficult moment. Waugh had to learn that the frail, rather dependent creature he had married had been transformed by the war into a resilient woman.

Waugh relished the rout of the Conservatives in the 1945 general election. They had received, he felt, their just deserts, not only for failing to resist an enemy (socialism) against which he had persistently warned them, but also for Winston Churchill's betrayal of eastern Europe and the Balkans. From this point, Waugh became something of a recluse, a Catholic Conservative defending liberty, diversity, and privacy, walled up in Gloucestershire, pondering the sack of Christendom but still hungry for the gossip of Metroland. Most weeks he would travel to London, ostensibly to get his hair cut but really to find someone to talk to. At work on what he always considered his best novel, *Helena* (1950), he often put it aside for jaunts abroad, journalism, and shorter fiction. In 1945 he visited the Nuremberg trials, then Lady Diana Cooper in Paris. Douglas Woodruff, as editor of *The Tablet*, had been invited to Spain to attend the fourth centenary of the birth of Francisco de Vittoria, founder of international law. In July 1946 Woodruff took Waugh along. This journey, with its discomforts and what Waugh took to be its exploitation of the guests, became the germ of *Scott-King's Modern Europe* (1947). 'Why is it', he asked in his diary, 'I smell all the time … the reek of the Displaced Person's Camp?' (10 Nov 1946).

In February 1947 Waugh travelled with Laura to Hollywood via New York to discuss the possibility of filming *Brideshead*. Peters had arranged this free trip and America began to release in Waugh a curiosity about human behaviour he had thought long dead. He also came to view American Catholicism as the main hope for the faith.

When the Johnston-Hays office condemned the film script as likely to undermine the conception of Christian marriage, Waugh grasped the excuse, refused changes, and the deal collapsed. He instructed his driver to take him not to the studio but to the pets' cemetery and to its elaborate counterpart for the defunct plutocracy, Forest Lawn. The latter became an obsession which focused in *The Loved One* (1948), a satire on American attitudes to death, first published as a single issue of *Horizon*. He paid three other visits to America: one to New York in November 1948, another to do a lecture tour from January to March 1950, and a third with Laura in November 1950. Waugh admired and edited the British edition of Thomas Merton's *The Seven Storey Mountain*. The tour enabled Waugh to collect material for an article in *Life Magazine*, 'The American epoch in the Catholic church' (1949). Merton, a Cistercian monk in Kentucky, represented to Waugh a nascent revival of the monastic tradition in America. Although asceticism never came easily to him, Waugh saw his own life as increasingly cenobitic. The article, penitential in its austerity, reveals a man of sincere faith honestly examining the conflict between Christian teaching and his defence of social hierarchy.

Withdrawal and 'Pinfold' delusions, 1950–1955 Christopher Sykes, Waugh's friend and first biographer, stressed that the indifferent reception of *Helena* (1950) 'was the greatest disappointment of [Waugh's] whole literary life'. This novel imagined the life of St Helena, the discoverer of the true cross and mother of Constantine. Waugh had been at work on it since D-day. Gentler in tone than *Brideshead*— mellow, distant, and resigned—it marked a change in his fiction. Between 1951 and 1953 Sykes and he were closer than they had ever been (they had known each other in the thirties and had served together in the army). In 1951 Sykes arranged a trip for them to the Holy Land which resulted in Waugh's *The Holy Places* (1953), and on his return Waugh began *Men at Arms* (1952), the first volume of his trilogy. He tried and failed to be elected rector of Edinburgh University. Sykes dramatized *Helena* for the radio. The Inland Revenue presented a huge bill for unpaid tax; persecution mania began to set in, not unconnected with his feeling of being terrorized by punitive socialist taxation.

From 1952 there was a steady contraction of the grand style at Piers Court. Peters advised caution. Waugh reduced his household but not his expenses. In 1950 he had established a trust, what he termed his 'Save the Children Fund', a tax-avoidance scheme, on receiving a large advance from Penguin Books reprinting ten titles. Waugh had committed the advance and all his copyrights to the trust, which became his children's property. None of the capital could be touched until the last child came of age. Laura was pregnant with their seventh and last child, Septimus (a daughter was stillborn during the war) in summer 1950, tying the money up until 1971. Waugh resolved this difficulty by buying whatever he wanted for the house (silver, paintings, fireplaces) and charging it to the trust. Later he devised a subtler refinement. Anything that remained his property he could sell to the trust. Most of Piers Court's art objects and some of his manuscripts were thus 'bought' to release tax-free capital.

Waugh's sense of living in an alien culture bent on his extermination was integral to his frame of mind while writing *Men at Arms*, and was reflected in a novella, *Love among the Ruins* (1953). Waugh was the first to admit the weakness of the latter and thought *Men at Arms* imperfect, but his powers, far from declining, were maturing in the trilogy in a new direction. Its Catholic hero, Guy Crouchback, was deliberately dull but nevertheless a man of honour. The subject was 'the humanizing of Guy', the exact opposite of an acceptance of humanism.

As a public figure Waugh took every opportunity to abuse communism because of its godlessness, and consistently mocked and vilified Tito as a tyrant. When the British Conservative government welcomed Tito as an honoured guest in 1953, Waugh embarked on a campaign of abuse in the national press, amid which he visited Goa, India, for the final exposition of the body of St Francis Xavier. Articles critical of Waugh appeared and he became convinced of a Beaverbrook conspiracy to malign him. Anxious about money, he allowed himself to be interviewed on the radio by Stephen Black, and detected in the questions a desire to humiliate. Waugh, fast approaching fifty, was prematurely aged: selectively deaf, rheumatic, irascible. Manic depressive boredom had always dogged him but now it increasingly spoiled his life. Attempts to write the third volume of his trilogy collapsed and he determined to finish it during a sea voyage to Ceylon in February 1954.

This was a disaster. Waugh went mad. Always an insomniac, he had for years been dosing himself with bromide and chloral, washed down with crème de menthe, and, as he discovered later, was suffering from bromide poisoning. This produced aural hallucinations in which he believed himself to be mocked by Stephen Black, the BBC, psychologists, a beautiful woman, and various other (usually youthful) tormentors. Everything he said was repeated in his ear. On Waugh's return, Father Caraman (a friend, and editor of *The Month*), called in Dr Strauss, a Catholic psychologist who had treated Greene. Waugh was delighted by the diagnosis: poisoning rather than demonic possession. He changed his sleeping draught, recovered, regaled neighbours with the story, and later wrote it up, almost unchanged, as a novel, *The Ordeal of Gilbert Pinfold* (1957).

Last years, Catholic conservative, and the Second Vatican Council, 1955–1966 Waugh began *Pinfold* during January 1955. He was in Jamaica, taking a winter holiday after completing the second volume of his trilogy with *Officers and Gentlemen* (1955). On 6 December 1954 his mother had died. The funeral and finishing the book marked another watershed in his life. *Officers and Gentlemen*, he thought, was better than *Men at Arms*, but he was prevented from continuing the trilogy by the urgent need to get *Pinfold* written while it was still fresh in his mind, and by the death of his friend, Monsignor Ronald Knox. When dying from cancer in 1957, Knox had asked Waugh to be his literary executor and biographer. As an act of *pietas*, Waugh

accepted, spent thousands of hours on research, travelled to Rhodesia to interview Daphne Acton, and published *The Life of the Right Reverend Ronald Knox* (1959).

The Pinfold experience, it seems, had stirred rather than shaken Waugh. He was thankful to have been presented with a new subject, and it became a form of dry run for his autobiography. One is struck by his courage, both in the way he coped with the breakdown and in the ruthlessly honest self-portrait of the novel. Here we see the alienated artist–craftsman disguised as don or colonel; the family man pretending distaste for his children; the writer who creates books not as a form of confession or as though he were a branch of the social services, but as 'things quite external to himself to be used and judged by others' (p. 2). The cold intimacy of these revelations often shocked reviewers. Waugh was delighted. Embarrassment was his stock-in-trade.

Pinfold, though, was a valedictory book. In Jamaica Waugh heard of more attacks in the Beaverbrook press, Nancy Spain's among them. In June 1955, seeking an interview, she had called at Piers Court, uninvited, with Lord Noël Buxton. Waugh had sent them packing. She wrote a libellous piece. Waugh sued and was awarded £2000 (tax-free). He also won another action (£3000) against Beaverbrook Newspapers for endorsing defamatory extracts from Rebecca West's *The Meaning of Treason* (1949, revised 1956). Much of the money was spent on a carpet, copied from one displayed at the Great Exhibition of 1851. But such successes were rare fragments of pleasure in the general bleakness which now characterized Waugh's outlook. Even the good reviews and sales of his books could not cheer him.

The invasion of his privacy made Waugh determined to move, and by Christmas 1956 he and his family were installed in Combe Florey House, Somerset. No sooner had he arrived and finished *Pinfold* than Knox fell ill. While Waugh was writing *Knox*, his son Auberon accidentally shot himself in Cyprus and nearly died. When *Knox* was published, Catholic reviews were stiff and guarded, notable more for their embarrassed reticence than for the welcome he had expected. This hurt him deeply. *A Tourist in Africa* (1960), the account of his trip to Rhodesia, was a thin piece of book making of which he was ashamed. Desperately trying to raise money to support his family, he even accepted another invitation from the BBC to be interviewed. John Freeman's encounter with Waugh on *Face to Face* (26 June, 1960) is now legendary. Freeman was noted for his relentless probing of sensitive memories. Waugh, soberly dressed, a carnation in his buttonhole, puffing at his cigar with a quizzical glare of amused condescension, answered all questions designed to reveal psychological instability with devastating brevity. At last, somewhat desperate, Freeman pinned him to a definite statement. Waugh agreed that he hoped people would ignore him. 'You like that when it happens, do you?' 'Yes.' 'Why are you appearing in this programme?' 'Poverty', came the reply. 'We've both been hired to talk in this deliriously happy way.'

After completing his trilogy with *Unconditional Surrender*

(1961), Waugh felt exhausted, arranged a lucrative contract for his autobiography, and in November of that year took his favourite child, Margaret, on a holiday to the West Indies and British Guiana. They returned refreshed but when Ann Fleming told him that he had bored his hosts, this plunged him into a depression from which he never recovered. His social life was reduced to intimate gatherings, preferably with Diana Cooper. Then, when Margaret announced that she wished to marry, he lost his dearest companion and, again with startling honesty, he fictionalized his jealousy in a novella, *Basil Seal Rides Again, or The Rake's Regress* (1963). His dejection was compounded by the news emerging from Rome in November 1962 about the Second Vatican Council, Pope John XXIII's revolutionary council of bishops. Until his death, Waugh battled in articles and speeches against these changes, but to no avail. The replacement of Latin, the lingua franca of the universal church, by the vernacular was a particular distress which brought him close to apostasy. He rarely attended church. When Father Caraman stayed, he would say mass at Combe Florey. On Easter day, 10 April 1966, Waugh had attended Caraman's mass according to the old rite at a nearby village. Several of the family were present. It was a joyous occasion with Waugh radiating good humour. They returned to Combe Florey House for luncheon and Waugh pottered off alone. He was never seen alive again. Laura discovered the body in the downstairs toilet where he had collapsed from a massive coronary thrombosis. He was buried in St Peter and Paul's churchyard in Combe Florey.

Reputation Waugh's reputation is now secure as one of the finest novelists of the twentieth century. At his death, however, he left a time bomb in the form of his diaries. For some months they lay untouched. None of the family read them. Then Laura, anxious about money, sold them, along with all the other contents of his library, to the University of Texas at Austin. David Astor bought the rights shortly before Laura's death. When they were published, first as lengthy serialized extracts in *The Observer* (1973), then as a book (*The Diaries of Evelyn Waugh*, ed. Michael Davie, 1976), they generated considerable controversy and sales. Waugh had mutilated the documents, excising his homosexual period at Oxford and most of the entries concerning his first marriage. Otherwise, this record was largely intact. Reviewers were, by turns, perplexed, outraged, and amused. There was much talk of warts. Frederic Raphael saw in these jottings a 'portrait of the artist as a bad man' (*Sunday Times*, 5 Sept 1976, 27). The book met with a critical reception which, although frequently inane, was entirely in keeping with the sort of press to which Waugh had become inured throughout his life. Sykes's loyal, 'official' biography (*Evelyn Waugh: a biography*, 1975) did little to rectify this impression. Waugh's enemies detected what they had always suspected: that he was pompous, sadistic, and snobbish, with something of the fascist and the philistine about him. Mark Amory's collection *The Letters of Evelyn Waugh* (1980) offered more ammunition. Philip Larkin wrote:

It is impossible to imagine getting a letter from Evelyn Waugh, unless it were of the 'Mr Waugh deeply regrets that he is unable to do what is so kindly proposed' sort. In the first place, one would have to have a nursery nickname and be a member of White's, a Roman Catholic, a high-born lady or an old Etonian novelist. (*The Guardian*, 4 Sept 1980)

In an egalitarian age Waugh has seemed to some a redundant élitist but to most others, a genius. The list of his admirers included Graham Greene, Muriel Spark, Rebecca West (at first), Arnold Bennett, Cyril Connolly, L. P. Hartley, Nigel Dennis, Sir Frank Kermode, David Lodge, Sir Angus Wilson, William Plomer, and Kingsley Amis. His detractors included: James Agate, Ernest Oldmeadow, Edmund Wilson, David Garnett, Donat O'Donnell, Delmore Schwartz, J. B. Priestley, Joseph Heller, Kingsley Amis (at first), Rebecca West (after his libel suit caused *The Name of Treason* to be withdrawn). Amis's changing sides is not unusual.

Donat Gallagher's *The Essays, Articles and Reviews of Evelyn Waugh* (1983) presented most of Waugh's journalism and revealed the full extent and complexity of Waugh's aesthetic ideas, too often ignored in a rancorous (political) taking of sides. Martin Stannard's *Evelyn Waugh: the Critical Heritage* (1984) offered a range of contemporary reviews of Waugh's books and papers. The debate between these reviewers, frequently muddled by reductive assumptions about Waugh's character, has continued. Two full-scale biographies followed Sykes's—Stannard's two-volume *Evelyn Waugh: the Early Years, 1903–1939* (1986) and *Evelyn Waugh: No Abiding City, 1939–1966* (1992); and Selina Hastings's *Evelyn Waugh* (1996). Two further biographical studies, catalogues, and critical works have appeared. Ann Pasternak Slater's *The Complete Short Stories of Evelyn Waugh* (1998) has republished 'The Balance', all his juvenilia, ten stories out of print since 1949, and a good selection of his drawings and woodcuts. All Waugh's novels remain in print and the estate still makes a healthy income. Film and television adaptations have included Terry Southern's *The Loved One* (1965), a version of *Decline and Fall* (*Decline and Fall of a Birdwatcher*, 1968), *A Handful of Dust* (1988), and, most famously, *Brideshead Revisited* (1982).

Diverse views among literary critics first emerged strongly with the publication of *Brideshead*. Up to this point, most (with the exception of Oldmeadow) had praised the early comic novels as hilarious black comedy, although few had detected, and fewer still had analysed, the darker strains of these novels or their experimental form. Thanks to critics like David Lodge, Kermode, and Malcolm Bradbury, Waugh's early work is now happily considered alongside the more obviously 'serious' work of modernists like Joyce and Woolf. His non-fiction after 1930 was another matter. Here his right-wing Catholicism was overt and *Campion*, *Waugh in Abyssinia*, and *Robbery under Law* all had their opponents. With *Brideshead* Waugh's 'political' and religious views entered undisguised into his fiction. Edmund Wilson, Donat O'Donnell, Kingsley Amis, and Rose Macaulay fiercely attacked its romantic snobbery. The book seemed to present an élitist Catholic vision, fundamentally uncharitable, aligning

Waugh's faith with the aristocracy against the partially educated, unkillable children of the lower orders epitomized by the ranker officer, Hooper. Waugh later regretted the novel's sensual luxuriance and completely revised it in 1959. He did not, however, regret the introduction of the mystical element. In a *Life Magazine* article, 'Fan-fare' (1946) he explained that in future his work would have two things to make it unpopular: 'a preoccupation with style and the attempt to represent man more fully which, to me, means only one thing, man in his relation to God.'

Waugh was never, of course, 'unpopular' in terms of book sales. The bad reviews of *Brideshead* set the tone of antagonism for much of the left-wing or liberal humanist criticism of later work, interpreting Waugh's implicit political position as facile or pernicious. But he had many right-wing supporters and, in between, critics like Bernard Bergonzi and Frank Kermode offering the notion of Waugh's concern with aristocratic values as a structural myth which it is largely irrelevant to oppose or support. In the drab, immediately post-war world, and particularly after the soft-focus TV adaptation, *Brideshead* became institutionalized as part of the nostalgia industry, echoing a mythical Englishness which remains mysteriously appealing to the American mass market. But both the sentimental and the political approaches do the book a disservice. Ultimately, as the various biographies have revealed, Waugh loathed politics and politicians of whatever colour and owed no loyalty to anything opposing his faith. *Brideshead* is a religious book, a contemplation of the meaninglessness of human existence without God. Beneath that public mask of arrogance there lay a dedicated artist and a man of earnest faith, struggling against the dryness of his soul. As *Pinfold* reveals, no one could level an accusation against him which he had not already used to torment himself. Looking back over his schoolboy journal, he was appalled by its lack of charity. Auberon Waugh wrote of the *Diaries* as a whole,

Certainly one receives few impressions of any spontaneous gaiety or sweetness of nature, for which his friends remember him best, and which obviously made him such an agreeable companion. Similarly there have been few glimpses of the kindliness, or the sudden disarming gentleness, which members of his family most particularly remember. (*New Statesman*, 13 April 1973)

MARTIN STANNARD

Sources *The letters of Evelyn Waugh*, ed. M. Amory (1980) · *The diaries of Evelyn Waugh*, ed. M. Davie (1976) · *The essays, articles and reviews of Evelyn Waugh*, ed. D. Gallagher (1983) · C. Sykes, *Evelyn Waugh: a biography* (1975) · M. Stannard, *Evelyn Waugh: the critical heritage* (1984) · M. Stannard, *Evelyn Waugh: the early years, 1903–1939* (1986) · M. Stannard, *Evelyn Waugh: no abiding city, 1939–1966* (1992) · E. Waugh, *A little learning* (1964)
Archives BBC WAC · BL, corresp. · Col. U., Rare Book and Manuscript Library, letters and literary MSS · NRA, corresp. and literary papers · Ransom HRC, papers | BL, letters to Lady Diana Cooper, Add. MSS 69796–69798 · BL, corresp. with Edward Sackville-West, Add. MS 68905 · CUL, letters and postcards to F. J. Stopp · Georgetown University, Washington, DC, Lauinger Library, letters to Handasyde Buchanan · Georgetown University, Washington, DC, Lauinger Library, letters to Graham Greene · Georgetown University, Washington, DC, Lauinger Library, corresp. with Bruce Marshall · Georgetown University, Washington, DC, Lauinger Library, letters to Leonard Russell · Georgetown University, Washington, DC, Lauinger Library, letters to Christopher Sykes, letters to A. D. Peters [copies], diaries [copies] | FILM BBC | SOUND BBC
Likenesses H. Lamb, oils, 1930, priv. coll. · H. Coster, photographs, 1930–40, NPG · F. H. Man, bromide print, *c*.1943, NPG [*see illus.*] · I. Penn, bromide print, 1950, NPG · F. Topolski, pencil, *c*.1960, NPG · Y. Karsh, bromide print, 1964, NPG · M. Gerson, photographs, NPG
Wealth at death £20,068: probate, 14 July 1966, *CGPLA Eng. & Wales*

Waugh, James (1831–1905), racehorse trainer, born at Jedburgh, Roxburghshire, on 13 December 1831, was the son of Richard Waugh, a farmer there. Brought up on his father's farm, he first rode as a steeplechase jockey, being too heavy for the flat. In 1851 he became private trainer of steeplechasers at Cessford Moor for a Scottish banker named Grainger. He married in 1854 Isabella (*d.* 1881), daughter of William Scott of Tomshielhaugh, Southdean. In 1855 he went to Jedburgh to train for Sir David Baird and Sir J. Boswell, and four years later he succeeded Matthew Dawson in the training establishment at Gullane in East Lothian. From there he soon moved to Ilsley, in Berkshire, where he became private trainer to Mr Robinson, an Australasian for whom he won the Royal Hunt Cup at Ascot with Gratitude. In 1866, on Robinson's retirement from the turf, Waugh succeeded Matthew Dawson at Russley Park, near Lambourn, where he was a successful private trainer for the Scottish ironmaster James Merry, and saddled Macgregor for his Two Thousand Guineas victory in 1870.

At the close of the 1870 season Waugh left Russley for Kentford, Newmarket, but soon afterwards he went to Nakło, on the Polish frontier, to train for Count Henckel. After two years at Nakło he spent seven years at Karlburg, in Hungary, where he trained winners of every big race in Austria–Hungary. His horses also won many important prizes in Germany. Following a deterioration in his wife's health he returned to Newmarket in 1880, and settled first at Middleton Cottage and from 1893 at Meynell House. Several continental owners sent horses to be trained by him, among them Prince Tassilo Festetics, for whom he won the Grand Prize at Baden Baden, the German Derby, and other important races. Although further classic success eluded him, he won the Cambridgeshire with Laureate in 1889.

A skilful and conscientious trainer, Waugh achieved some success as a breeder of racehorses, and when at Newmarket bought and sold thoroughbreds for continental patrons and foreign governments, who respected his judgement. After some years of failing health, he died at his home, Meynell House, Exning, near Newmarket, on 23 October 1905, and was buried in Newmarket cemetery. Of his eleven children, six sons also became trainers.

EDWARD MOORHOUSE, *rev.* WRAY VAMPLEW

Sources R. Mortimer, R. Onslow, and P. Willett, *Biographical encyclopedia of British flat racing* (1978) · T. McConnell, *The tartan turf* (1988) · J. Fairfax-Blakeborough, *Northern turf history* (1973) · *The Sportsman* (24 Oct 1905)
Wealth at death £17,810 5*s.* 5*d.*: probate, 18 May 1906, *CGPLA Eng. & Wales*

Waurin [Wavrin], **Jean de** (*b.* **1399/1400**, *d.* in or after 1473/4), compiler and collector of histories, was the illegitimate son of Robert de Waurin, hereditary seneschal of Flanders, and Michielle de Croix. He was related to many influential members of the court of Philip the Good, duke of Burgundy (*d.* 1467). Legitimated in 1437, knighted and lord of Fontaines and Forestel by 1442, he married Marguerite Hangouart, a wealthy *bourgeoise* and the widow of Guillaume de Tenremonde, and became part of the urban patriciate of Lille. As a boy of fifteen he witnessed the battle of Agincourt from the French camp; he fought on the Anglo-Burgundian side at Cravant and Verneuil in 1423, and served under Sir John Fastolf during the controversial English defeat at Patay in 1429. He participated in the campaign against the Hussites in 1426 and followed Duke Philip on the expedition of 1427–8 into Holland. As a member of the pro-English party at the Burgundian court he did not welcome the French–Burgundian alliance which resulted from the treaty of Arras (1435) and after the disaster of the siege of Calais in 1436 he brought his military career to an end. He continued to serve Duke Philip as ambassador and counsellor, being sent to the pope to discuss the matter of the crusade in 1463, and joining the retinue of Antoine, count of La Roche (the Great Bastard of Burgundy), for the famous Smithfield tournament of 1467.

In the mid-1440s his nephew, Waleran de Waurin, suggested that Waurin write a full-length history of England, because no such work existed. The *Recueil des croniques et anchiennes istoires de la Grant Bretaigne, a present nomme Engleterre* ('Collection of the chronicles and ancient histories of Great Britain, now called England') is indeed a 'collection': it used every existing work available to Waurin in French, such as Geoffrey of Monmouth's *History of the Kings of Britain*, Jean Froissart's historical work, a chronicle of Normandy, and perhaps the memoirs of Jean Lefevre, Toison d'Or king of arms, Jean Duclercq, and Enguerrand de Monstrelet, as well as a number of contemporary newsletters. Originally Waurin planned to divide the work into four books, from the arrival of Albina, legendary founder of Albion, to the accession of Henry V in 1413, but eventually he needed six volumes and ended with Edward IV's newsletter describing his return to power in 1471. The *Recueil* makes no attempt at originality and it is difficult to gauge Waurin's own contribution: he was prepared to copy other authors almost verbatim even when describing events he witnessed himself; he used fictional material indiscriminately and included irrelevant sections of his originals without comment. In spite of its shortcomings the *Recueil*, which runs to almost 4000 large manuscript pages when complete, is important and useful, containing some unique records and providing an insight into the interests and method of a fifteenth-century historian. Separate illuminated volumes from seven or eight sets of the *Recueil* survive in collections in Europe and the United States; one set belonged to Edward IV; the only series that is still complete was owned by the famous Flemish book collector Louis de Gruuthuse. The work was not printed until 1858 and it was never edited in full.

Waurin is also remarkable for the books he owned and for his patronage of an unusual illuminator. At least a dozen of his books survive, many of them romances that show a preoccupation with the semi-legendary ancestry and family history of noble families of Hainault, Flanders, and Artois, and with the crusades and the wonders of the Orient; titles include *Paris et Vienne*, *Le roman du comte d'Artois*, and *La chronique du bon chevalier Gilles de Chin*. Some of these texts appear to have been actually rewritten to please a particular Burgundian aristocratic audience, including Duke Philip, and in some cases there is evidence that Waurin himself was the editor, in a way comparable to his editorial activity for the *Recueil*. The manuscripts that Waurin owned are marked with his coat of arms or his name—'Jean, bastard de Wavrin, seigneur du Forestel'—or both, and many are illustrated with innumerable elegant and very lively line drawings by a single artist, who has been called the Waurin Master after his principal patron. Waurin was alive in 1473 or 1474, but is not recorded thereafter. LIVIA VISSER-FUCHS

Sources J. de Wavrin [J. de Waurin], *Anchiennes cronicques d'Engleterre*, ed. E. Dupont, 3 vols. (1858–63) · *Recueil des croniques … par Jehan de Waurin*, ed. W. Hardy and E. L. C. P. Hardy, 5 vols., Rolls Series, 39 (1864–91) · G. Doutrepont, *La littérature française à la cour des ducs de Bourgogne* (1909) · A. Naber, 'Jean de Wavrin, un bibliophile du quinzième siècle', *Revue du Nord*, 69 (1987), 281–93 · A. Naber, 'Jean de Wavrin, un bibliophile du quinzième siècle', *Revue du Nord*, 72 (1990), 23–48 · G. Dogaer, 'The Master of Wavrin (school)', *Flemish miniature painting in the 15th and 16th centuries* (1987), 91–3 · F. M. Horgan, 'A critical edition of the *Romance of Gillion de Trazegnies* from Brussels Bibliothèque Royale MS 9629', PhD diss., U. Cam., 1985

Wauton, Simon de. *See* Walton, Simon of (*d.* 1265/6).

Wavell, Archibald Percival, **first Earl Wavell** (1883–1950), army officer and viceroy of India, was born on 5 May 1883 at Colchester, the only son and second of the three children of Major, afterwards Major-General, Archibald Graham Wavell (1843–1935) and his wife, Lillie (*d.* 1926), daughter of Richard N. Percival, of Springfields, Bradwall, Cheshire. The family (of whom traces have been found for four or more centuries in and around the city of Winchester) had for some generations been soldiers (A. J. B. Wavell was his cousin).

The young officer Wavell received his education at Winchester College, and passed fourth into the Royal Military College, Sandhurst, in 1900. After a six-month course he was gazetted to the Black Watch in time to see service in South Africa. In 1903 he went to India, where his early childhood (1888–91) had been spent, and he took part in the Bazar valley campaign of 1908. At his first attempt he headed the list of entrants to the Staff College and in 1911, having graduated with an 'A' pass, one of two awarded, he was sent for a year to the Russian army. When the First World War broke out in 1914 he was in the War Office, but managed to join the British expeditionary force in September. Wavell married on 22 April 1915 Eugénie Marie (Queenie), daughter of Colonel John Owen Quirk, with whom he was to have three daughters and one son. At

Archibald Percival Wavell, first Earl Wavell (1883–1950), by
Bassano, 1936

Ypres on 16 June 1915 he lost his left eye in an artillery barrage and was awarded the MC. In October 1916 Major Wavell was sent as liaison officer to the army of the Grand Duke Nicholas, which was fighting in Turkey before Erzurum. On returning to London in June 1917, he became the chief of the Imperial General Staff's personal liaison officer to General Sir Edmund Allenby, who became his mentor and model in later years when Wavell held the equivalent post. After three months with the Supreme Allied War Council in Versailles, he returned to Palestine in March 1918 as a brigadier-general, and joined the staff of Sir Philip Chetwode, commanding the 20 corps. He played a major role in the final offensive which shattered the Turks, and was appointed CMG in 1919.

The next ten years were divided between the War Office and the staff. During this period Wavell, already well known within the army, became known outside it as an officer untrammelled by convention; and the general public came to associate him with a phrase he used in a lecture: that his ideal infantryman was 'a successful poacher, cat-burglar and gunman'. In 1930 he received command of the 6th brigade at Blackdown which had been chosen for experimental purposes. This was his first significant experience of command in thirty years of service, and he excelled at it. In 1935, after fifteen months on half pay (which he spent on reconnaissance between Haifa and Baghdad and in rewriting field service regulations), he was appointed to the coveted command of the 2nd division at Aldershot, confirming the very high regard in

which the army held him. He was recognized as an exceptional trainer of troops and a highly creative thinker. Among the younger generals there was a feeling that the older ones had grown lethargic; public interest in the army was at a low ebb. Wavell's views were sought with respect by both old guard and new. Before he had completed his term with the 2nd division, he was appointed in July 1937 to command in Palestine and Transjordan. Soon after his arrival Arab troubles, which had died down since the outbreak of 1936, broke out with fresh ferocity, and were at their height when he was brought home in April 1938 and promoted over many senior to him to take over the southern command, one of the two most important commands in the country.

In 1939 he gave the Lees Knowles lectures at Cambridge, 'Generals and generalship', one of the best statements on military command ever written: Rommel carried a copy with him in the north African campaign.

The Middle East, 1939–1941 In late July 1939 Wavell was sent to Cairo to form the new command of the Middle East. When war broke out in September the forces at his disposal were small; when Italy came into the war in June 1940 his command had been reinforced by Australian, New Zealand, and Indian troops, but was menaced by superior forces on several fronts. Bold patrolling by light covering troops in the western desert imposed upon Graziani's Italians a caution quite out of proportion to the relative strengths of the two armies. Wavell was able also to delay the Italian advances into Sudan from Ethiopia; but upon the Somaliland front, where the defection of the French in Djibouti prejudiced the defence, the local commander was forced to give ground. During Wavell's temporary absence in London the decision was taken to evacuate the protectorate rather than lose its small but valuable garrison. The prime minister disapproved of this decision, Wavell defended it, and relations between Winston Churchill and Wavell were never very happy thereafter. But Wavell's stock never sank either with his troops or with the public, and it rose with the authorities during and after his remarkable run of success in the winter of 1940–41. He had been keeping a careful eye on the gingerly advance of the Italians in the west, and he detected unsoundness in their dispositions. Containing the threat to Sudan with an elaborate bluff, he switched the 4th Indian division from that front for use in the western desert, and caught the Italians napping at Sidi Barrani on 9 and 10 December. The 4th Indian division returned to Sudan, while the remainder of the western desert army swept up Bardia and Tobruk. By mid-February the whole of Cyrenaica was in British hands, with 125,000 prisoners, more than 800 field guns, and 400 tanks. This advance of 400 miles did much to raise British spirits after the losses of 1940.

Meanwhile Alan Gordon Cunningham's army from Kenya and William Platt's in Sudan were forcing the Italians from Ethiopia back into their remotest mountains; they capitulated in the north in May and in the south some weeks later. Elsewhere, however, the odds against Wavell had mounted. He had been urged to send help on a larger scale to Greece, which since the end of October 1940 had been fighting stoutly and successfully against greatly superior Italian forces in Epirus. Hitherto Britain had contributed only air support with ground defence, anti-aircraft, and medical units; but on 9 January 1941 he was told that the support of Greece must now take precedence of all operations in the Middle East. His first reaction was sharply adverse; but throughout January and February mounting pressure was brought to bear on him to reinforce the Greeks with fighting formations and units. After conversations with the Greeks, in which both the cabinet and the chiefs of staff were represented by Anthony Eden and Sir John Dill, and during which various stipulations which he made were accepted by the Greeks, Wavell agreed to intervention at a moment when the enthusiasm of the cabinet and chiefs of staff was cooling.

In two respects he had been misled: the Greeks had accepted in the conversations that they would withdraw from their exposed positions to a line on the River Aliakmon more in keeping with the weakness of the joint armies; and Wavell's intelligence had assured him that the German ground forces in north Africa, whose arrival was known to be imminent, would not be able to take the field until mid-April at the earliest. But the Greeks did not shorten their line; and the Germans appeared in strength on the frontiers of Cyrenaica before the end of March. By that time a high proportion of Wavell's army, and much of the best of it, was irrevocably committed in Greece; by the middle of April both Greece and Cyrenaica had been lost, Tobruk was invested, and vast quantities of fighting troops, military technicians, tanks, and material were in enemy hands.

Stout efforts were made to defend Crete, but it was invaded from the air on 20 May and lost after desperate fighting before the month ended. The Royal Navy and the Royal Air Force in the Middle East had both crippled themselves in these operations. New anxieties had developed; Rashid Ali in Iraq had thrown in his lot with the axis powers, and Syria, occupied by Vichy forces, was harbouring Germans and seemed likely to follow the example of Iraq. Wavell was urged to undertake three almost simultaneous operations: against Iraq, against Syria, and against Rommel in the desert. He protested that he had not the resources for all three, but was overruled. Although the operation against Iraq was successful by early June, operation Battleaxe against Rommel proved a costly failure by 17 June; in Syria, however, the French asked for an armistice early in July. Churchill had lost confidence in Wavell, particularly after learning that plans had been prepared for evacuation of the Middle East. After the failure of the offensive against Rommel, Churchill replaced Wavell with Sir Claude Auchinleck, whose place he took as commander-in-chief in India.

Commander-in-chief and viceroy of India, 1941–1947 At first India was by comparison almost a sinecure; but when, in December 1941, Japan came into the war, Wavell, whose reputation stood high in the United States, was nominated supreme commander of the ill-fated American, British, Dutch, and Australian (ABDA) command of south-

east Asia and the south-west Pacific. The speed, preparedness, and overwhelming strength of the Japanese were in inverse ratio to those of the defence. Wavell was criticized for the loss of the British 18th division in Singapore, which was landed only two days before the capitulation; but he still enjoyed the confidence of his troops, and his resilience as a commander was exemplified by the fact that he gave orders for the eventual recapture of Burma to be studied by his planning staff before its evacuation was complete. The ABDA command was dissolved in February 1942. Policy dictated that the German war should be won before the Japanese, and Wavell had to fight the war in Burma with the minimum of help from home. He had little success, and in June 1943 he was appointed viceroy of India in succession to the marquess of Linlithgow and in July was raised to the peerage as Viscount Wavell of Cyrenaica and of Winchester. He had been promoted field marshal in January of that year.

Wavell shouldered a profoundly difficult task in this his last public service, for which he had little of the diplomatic or political training customary for the viceregal appointment. He faced enormous political and administrative problems, presiding over an imperial government committed since the Cripps offer of 1942 to permitting Indians self-determination after the war, yet meantime having to maintain imperial authority and to extract from India all possible human and material resources for the war effort. Wavell's first challenge was the Bengal famine of 1943, which occurred when wartime shortages of rice were compounded by a devastating failure of administration. He went to Bengal within six days of taking office, offered the help of the army to move food grains, and prevailed on the provincial government to adopt a more interventionist role, including rationing. He continued thereafter to urge on an insensitive London government which had other priorities the vital need of more food imports into India.

Although Wavell was thought of by his London masters as a 'stop-gap viceroy' to hold India steady until political change occurred after the war, he saw that the political situation was not static, and that as viceroy he could not avoid politics but must do what he could to encourage Indians to co-operate not only in the war effort but in preparations for a new peacetime political order. In this he displayed considerable political acumen, sensitivity, and courage, but was severely hampered, indeed debilitated, by the lack of understanding from London, either from Churchill or from Attlee's Labour government after 1945. In 1943 he prevailed on London to permit the release of Gandhi from gaol, having been assured that the aged nationalist leader would never be strong enough to become politically active again. When Gandhi proved resilient, Churchill was greatly angered. Two years later, in the summer of 1945, the cabinet permitted the release of the remaining leadership of the Indian National Congress, who had been imprisoned since the autumn of 1942 and the Quit India campaign. Even this conciliatory move to enable the resumption of political negotiations with authoritative Indian voices had cost Wavell frustrating weeks of valuable time in London as he tried to persuade Churchill of the urgency of political movement in the face of growing administrative weakness, Indian expectations of post-war change, and the erosion of the raj's legitimacy in the eyes of many Indians. Immediately Wavell began the process of political discussion and negotiation with various groups of Indian politicians, in the hope of securing their agreement in a new form of executive council which, by providing opportunities for co-operation among them, would ease the way to a new constitution for a united post-war India. But the war years had served to harden divisions between the predominantly Hindu Congress, which claimed to speak for all Indians, and the Muslim League, led by the astute and intransigent M. A. Jinnah, which claimed to represent all Muslims as a separate political 'nation'. Moreover, the Cripps offer, confirming that no minority would be coerced into a post-war settlement, had given Jinnah an enormously strengthened bargaining position and a virtual veto in any negotiations. The issue of whether the League alone could nominate Muslim members of any new government became the rock on which were wrecked Wavell's attempt at political advance through the Simla conference of 1945, and, subsequently, the plans of the three-man cabinet mission in 1946, dispatched by Attlee's government to achieve agreement on the future of India and an interim representative government.

Dismissal and retirement, 1947–1950 Meanwhile, Wavell was acutely aware of the ebbing strength of the raj, and the inability of the British to control a continent increasingly wracked by vicious communal conflict, such as the 'Great Calcutta Killing' of 16 August 1946. In September 1946 he argued that on administrative grounds alone the raj could not last more than eighteen months, and urged the cabinet to accept a 'breakdown plan' for orderly British withdrawal at a time of their own choosing, if agreement with Indians could not be reached. London judged Wavell, unfairly, to be politically incompetent and alarmist: and in February 1947 he was sacked, to make way for the flamboyant Viscount Mountbatten. Wavell noted laconically in his journal on 4 February that he had received a letter from Attlee 'dismissing me from my post at a month's notice. Not very courteously done'. (Mountbatten rapidly concurred with Wavell's diagnosis of the Indian situation, and, given co-operation and considerable freedom by London, presided over the end of the raj within six months.)

Wavell's journal testifies to his vivid appreciation of a complex political situation; to the tireless political efforts he made to achieve political co-operation and advance, despite his distaste for some of the Indian leaders, particularly Gandhi; and to his intense frustration at the attitude of successive London governments, and at the intransigence of the three elderly politicians who seemed to thwart political advance, Gandhi, Jinnah, and Churchill (entry of 11 June 1944). He was created Earl Wavell with the additional title of Viscount Keren of Eritrea and Winchester, and returned to London, free at last from the burden of high office.

The last three years of his life were spent in London and in travel. He was able to indulge at leisure the taste in literature which had long been among his most precious relaxations. He became president of the Royal Society of Literature, and of the Kipling, Browning, Poetry, and Virgil societies; he had been chancellor of Aberdeen University since 1945. He was colonel of the Black Watch; and he steeped himself in regimental matters, visiting its allied regiments in Canada and South Africa. He received honorary degrees from the universities of Aberdeen, St Andrews, Cambridge, London, Oxford, and McGill. He was a commander of the Légion d'honneur and received decorations from many countries including Greece, Ethiopia, Poland, Czechoslovakia, Holland, China, Russia, and the United States. He was appointed CMG (1919), CB (1935), KCB (1939), GCB (1941), and GCSI and GCIE in 1943, in which year he was sworn of the privy council.

In 1950 Wavell showed signs of illness, culminating in jaundice; in May he underwent a severe operation, from which he seemed to be recovering, when he relapsed and died at Beaumont House, Beaumont Street, London, on 24 May. His body lay in the chapel of St John at the Tower, of which he had been constable since 1948; on 7 June it was carried upriver in a barge to Westminster, where a service was held; and he was buried that evening by the men of his regiment in the chantry close of his old school at Winchester. His wife survived him.

Character and reputation In appearance Wavell was broad and thickset, sturdy and physically tough, with a deep ridge on either side of his mouth. His silences were proverbial, but among intimates he was the most congenial and jovial of company. He delighted in horses and horsemanship, in golf, and shooting. He had a prodigious memory and would quote poetry with gusto and at length. His widely popular anthology, *Other Men's Flowers* (1944), consisted entirely of pieces which he had by heart, and showed how catholic was his taste: it remained in print until the end of the century. His *The Palestine Campaigns* (1928) and his biography of his former chief Allenby (produced during years of high pressure and published in two volumes, 1940 and 1943, and in one volume in 1946) were masterly and easy to read. He also published essays and lectures on military subjects, which were collected during his lifetime under the title *The Good Soldier* (1948).

As a soldier, for all his misfortunes in the Second World War, his reputation at its end stood as high as those of any of his contemporaries. In none of the eleven campaigns which he fought did he have preponderance in men or in weapons. He left the Middle East and he was relieved of command in south-east Asia before the arrival of the material and reinforcements with which his successors were to win their country's battles and their own renown. Yet at no time, in public or in private, in print or by the spoken word, did he ever complain or repine. His son,

Archibald John Arthur (1916–1953), succeeded to his titles, which became extinct when he was killed in Kenya on 24 December 1953, in an attack on Mau-Mau terrorists.

BERNARD FERGUSSON, *rev.* ROBERT O'NEILL and
JUDITH M. BROWN

Sources J. Connell, *Wavell, soldier and scholar* (1964) · H. E. Raugh, *Wavell in the Middle East, 1939–1941* (1993) · R. J. Collins, *Lord Wavell, 1883–1941: a military biography* (1947) · C. N. Barclay, *On their shoulders* (1964) · D. Fraser, *Knight's cross: a life of Field Marshal Erwin Rommel* (1993) · W. S. Churchill, *The Second World War*, 6 vols. (1948–54) · J. R. M. Butler, *Grand strategy, 2: September 1939–June 1941* (1957) · M. Howard, *The Mediterranean strategy in the Second World War* (1968) · B. H. Liddell Hart, *The memoirs of Captain Liddell Hart*, 2 vols. (1965) · J. Kennedy, *The business of war* (1957) · R. Lewin, *The chief: Field Marshal Lord Wavell, commander-in-chief and viceroy* (1980) · B. Fergusson, *Wavell: portrait of a soldier* (1961) · *Wavell: the viceroy's journal*, ed. P. Moon (1973)

Archives BL OIOC, papers relating to India, MS Eur. D 977 [copies] · Black Watch Regimental Museum, Balhousie Castle, Perth, personal and regimental corresp. · IWM, letters relating to his poetry anthology *Other Men's Flowers* · King's Lond., Liddell Hart C., corresp. and papers relating to his biography of Allenby · King's Lond., Liddell Hart C., Staff College papers · NRA, priv. coll., corresp., diaries, and papers · priv. coll. | BL, corresp. with Sir Sydney Cockerell, Add. MS 52759 · BL OIOC, corresp. with R. H. Dorman-Smith, MS Eur. E 215 · BL OIOC, corresp. with Sir Hugh Dow, MS Eur. E 372 · BL OIOC, corresp. with Sir Francis Mudie, MS Eur. F 164 · Bodl. Oxf., corresp. with Lord Monckton · JRL, corresp. with Sir Claude Auchinleck · King's Lond., Liddell Hart C., corresp. with Lord Alanbrooke; corresp. with Sir B. H. Liddell Hart; corresp. with G. M. Lindsay · NAM, corresp. with Alan Cunningham · NL Scot., corresp. with Lord Ballantrae · NL Scot., corresp. with John Dover Wilson | FILM BFI, news footage · BFI NFTVA, 'Wavell's 30,000', 1942 · BFI NFTVA, *The world at war*, Thames Television, 1974 · IWM FVA, 'War pictorial news no. 40', *War pictorial news*, 2 Feb 1942, WPN 40 · IWM FVA, 'Mind behind war', MGH 469 · IWM FVA, documentary footage · IWM FVA, news footage | SOUND IWM SA

Likenesses W. Stoneman, photographs, 1920–33, NPG · Bassano, photograph, 1936, NPG [*see illus.*] · E. E. Spencer Churchill, photographs, 1940–49, NPG · Y. Karsh, bromide print, 1943, NPG · H. L. Oakley, silhouette, 1949, NPG · C. Beaton, photograph, NPG · S. Elwes, portrait, repro. in Connell, *Wavell*, frontispiece · J. Epstein, bronze bust, IWM · J. Gunn, portrait, Black Watch, regimental collection · A. John, portrait, repro. in Connell, *Wavell*, jacket · J. Rosciwewski, pen-and-ink caricature, IWM · photographs, Hult. Arch. · statue, probably Whitehall, London

Wealth at death £49,579 18s. 11d.: probate, 8 Nov 1950, CGPLA Eng. & Wales

Wavell, Arthur John Byng (1882–1916), army officer and explorer, was born on 27 May 1882 at 6 Neville Street, South Kensington, London, the first of four children (three sons and a daughter) of Colonel Arthur Henry Wavell (1836–1891) of the Welsh regiment, and Beatrice Matilda (1848–1918), daughter of the Revd John Byng, a collateral descendant of the unfortunate admiral of that name. Field Marshal Lord *Wavell, greatest of all the Wavells, was a cousin. Arthur Wavell spent three years at Winchester College before going to the Royal Military College, Sandhurst. He was commissioned in the Welsh regiment in 1900, and saw service in the Second South African War before he was nineteen, being awarded the queen's medal, with three clasps. Afterwards he was specially employed by the War Office to travel and make maps and

Arthur John Byng Wavell (1882–1916), by unknown photographer, 1908

report on practically the whole of Swaziland, Tongaland, and northern Zululand. In 1905 he was again employed by the War Office to cross the Kalahari Desert and report on the protectorate of Bechuanaland.

In 1906 Wavell resigned his commission and went to British East Africa to indulge in big-game shooting. Later, with others, he acquired a vast tract of land from the Nyali (a sept of one of the twelve Swahili tribes of Mombasa); in due course this was registered as Nyali Sisal Estate Ltd and, in 1911, as the Nyali Plantation Ltd. In Mombasa he learned Arabic and Swahili, and interested himself in Islam. From this study grew a desire to explore Arabia, and in 1908 he proceeded to realize his ambition by setting out from London disguised as a Zanzibari with a Turkish passport, using the name Ali bin Muhammad, in the company of a Swahili from Mombasa called Masaudi; at Marseilles Wavell invited ʿAbd al-Wahid, an Arab from Aleppo who had been long resident in Berlin, to join them. The trio reached Damascus and ultimately Medina and Mecca without serious difficulty. In Mecca, Wavell hired rooms in the house of a brass-worker, paying £7 for the month; these things were recorded by Wavell in the first part of his book *A Modern Pilgrim in Mecca and a Siege in Sanaa* (1912). Though he had awkward moments, and appears to have been suspected in both Medina and Mecca, he was not unmasked.

In 1910 Wavell made a second Arabian journey, travelling from the Yemeni port of al-Hudaydah to San'a', then under Ottoman rule. Going without disguise, he rented an unfurnished house in the Yemeni capital for about £1 a month. The chief interest of his experience arises from the fact that he was in the city during the three months that it was under siege by the imam Yahya. While in San'a' he tried to buy a sabikah, a dagger almost as large as a sword-bayonet, but was told it was unsuitable for small men like himself, and that he should content himself with a janbiyyah. His own account of this journey appeared in the latter part of *A Modern Pilgrim* (1912 impression only). Neither of Wavell's Arabian adventures did much to increase scientific knowledge. Nevertheless, he had the gift of narrating his tale vividly and with humour.

Wavell then returned to his sisal estate at Nyali, and was still there at the outbreak of the First World War in August 1914. Although he had already joined the special reserve of his old regiment, the Welsh, he was retained in British East Africa because he was regarded as necessary to its defence. At this time there were no coastal forces in Mombasa, but two so-called reserve companies were soon formed, one from former askaris (native soldiers) in the King's African rifles, and one from Haramis and other Arabic speakers. This latter unit, created and inspired by Wavell's unique personality, was widely known as 'Wavell's own'. Promoted major and put in charge of Mwele, near the border with German East Africa, he received the MC and proved conspicuously successful in handling the men under his command until, on 8 January 1916, he marched out against a German column reported in his neighbourhood, and fell into an ambush. In spite of wounds he kept on firing, dying on 9 January; he was buried with Lieutenant John Lachlan Mackintosh at Mkonjane (also known as Mwele Ndogo), the place where they fell. A little to the east were buried three NCOs and some thirty askaris of the Arab rifles who died in the same operation. There can be little doubt that for a brief period, from August 1914 to January 1916, it was principally on account of Wavell and Wavell's Arabs that Mombasa, with its port and railway terminus, remained unoccupied by German forces. On 15 March 1922 the governor of the protectorate, Sir Edward Northey, unveiled a monument in honour of Wavell and the Arab rifles outside Mombasa's Portuguese-built fort. Wavell never married.

P. J. L. FRANKL

Sources A. J. B. Wavell, *A modern pilgrim in Mecca and a siege in Sanaa* (1912); repr. as *A modern pilgrim in Mecca* (1918) [1912 edn includes pt II, *A siege in Sanaa*; 1918 edn excludes pt II, but includes Darwin's biographical note] · *The Times* (18 Jan 1916) · C. Hordern, ed., *Military operations: East Africa*, History of the Great War (1941) · *The Times* (16 June 1911) · *The Times* (4 July 1911) · archival material from Commonwealth War Graves Commission, PRO, CO/533/166, fol. 677 · b. cert. · *CGPLA Eng. & Wales* (1918) · *DNB*
Archives GL, MS relating to Nyali Sisal estate | FILM IWM FVA, actuality footage
Likenesses photograph, 1908, NPG [*see illus.*] · photograph (of tombstone), Mkonjane, near Mombasa, Kenya · portrait, repro. in Wavell, *A modern pilgrim* (1912–18), frontispiece

Wealth at death £2542 15s. 4d.: resworn administration with will, 1918, *CGPLA Eng. & Wales*

Waverley. For this title name *see* Anderson, John, first Viscount Waverley (1882–1958).

Waweton [Walton], **Sir Thomas** (*d.* in or after **1450**), landowner and speaker of the House of Commons, was the son of John Waweton of Great Staughton, Huntingdonshire, who was ten times knight of the shire for Huntingdonshire, and whose influence probably lay behind Thomas's being first elected to the Commons for Huntingdonshire in 1397, and becoming a JP in that county in 1402. During the next thirty years Thomas Waweton regularly returned to the Commons, representing Bedfordshire in 1413, 1414, 1419, 1425, and 1432, and Huntingdonshire in 1397, 1401, 1402, 1414, 1420, and 1422. By 1419 he had been knighted. That he was elected speaker in 1425 was a reflection both of his long experience in the lower house, and also of his growing social eminence, in both Huntingdonshire and Bedfordshire. A retainer of Edmund (V) Mortimer, earl of March, until the latter's death in 1425, he was a friend and associate of Sir John (later Lord) Tiptoft (*d.* 1443) and Reynold Grey, Lord Grey of Ruthin (*d.* 1440), and perhaps of Archbishop Henry Chichele (*d.* 1443). Waweton's fortunes changed in 1429, however, when he twice attempted illegally to influence the outcome of parliamentary elections. In Huntingdonshire he forced the sheriff to return candidates of his choice, while as sheriff of Buckinghamshire he abused his position by substituting the names of two individuals selected by himself for those returned by the electors. The ensuing scandal turned local opinion permanently against him, and effectively ended his career in the Commons—he was never elected again for Huntingdonshire, and only once more for Bedfordshire, in 1432. A gap between 1429 and 1435 in his appointments as JP in Bedfordshire may also have resulted from this *faux pas*.

Despite this setback Waweton remained a figure of considerable standing, and was still influential in Bedfordshire, where he was sheriff again between 1432 and 1435. This may have been in part due to his marriage (his third) *c.*1431 to Alana, daughter and coheir of the wealthy Sir Simon Felbrigg, formerly standard-bearer to Richard II. (Few details are known of his first two wives, Elizabeth, who had died by 1422, and Maud, who had died by 1431.) In the late 1430s Waweton became involved in the contest between Lord Grey and John Cornwall, Lord Fanhope (*d.* 1443), for supremacy in Bedfordshire. Ostensibly a supporter of Grey, Waweton played an important part in the struggle, above all in 1439, when a quarrel over precedence between him and Fanhope at the peace sessions held at Bedford on 12 January led to a crush in which eighteen people died. Waweton was closely questioned before the king's council in the following month, and though he received a pardon on 30 May, he once more lost his place on the Bedfordshire peace commission, and did not regain it until 1443. After Lord Grey's death in 1440 the rest of Waweton's life was uneventful. In 1450 he was appointed a collector of taxes for Bedfordshire, and although the date of his death is unknown, it probably occurred soon afterwards. He was survived by his third wife, Alana (*d.* 1458), his son and heir, Thomas, and three other children.

MAX SATCHELL

Sources HoP, *Commons* • J. S. Roskell, *The Commons and their speakers in English parliaments, 1376–1523* (1965) • P. Maddern, *Violence and the social order: East Anglia, 1422–1442* (1992), 206–25

Way, Albert (1805–1874), antiquary, born on 23 June 1805, in Bath, and baptized on 23 June 1807 at St Martin-in-the-Fields, Westminster, was the son of Lewis *Way (1772–1840), barrister, and Mary Drewe (1780–1848). He was their third child of three sons and six daughters, but his two brothers and one sister died in infancy. Albert suffered from poor health throughout his life. He was privately educated at home in Stansted Park, Sussex, and at the age of seventeen travelled through Europe to Syria with his father. An accurate draughtsman, a good classical scholar, and a linguist with a knowledge of most European languages, Hebrew, and Old English, he matriculated at Trinity College, Cambridge in 1824, where he encouraged his contemporary Charles Darwin in insect collecting. He graduated BA in 1829 and proceeded MA in 1834. Like his father, he trained as a barrister and was admitted to the Inner Temple in 1833. However, by 1837 his interest had turned to the study of medieval antiquities; he contributed notes to the Norfolk volume of J. S. Cotman's *Engravings of Sepulchral Brasses in Norfolk and Suffolk* (1838), and he was elected fellow of the Society of Antiquaries of London in 1839.

In 1840 Way's father died and he inherited sufficient wealth, later augmented by legacies from other relatives, to be able to live off his private income. His first sole publication was based on a paper read to the Society of Antiquaries in 1841 'On an effigy of King Richard Coeur de Lion in the cathedral of Rouen' (*Archaeologia*, 29, 1842); his next communication introduced the term palimpsest brasses to the English language ('On palimpsest sepulchral brasses', *Archaeologia*, 30, 1844). In 1842 he was elected the society's director, responsible for its publications and possessions. The publishing of proceedings of meetings was started at his suggestion in 1844. The first volume of his principal work was issued in 1843, his edition of the English–Latin dictionary *Promptorium parvulorum sive clericorum* (c.1440) by Geoffrey the grammarian (Camden Society, 25, 1843; 54, 1853; 89, 1865). Way donated many books to the society's library in his lifetime, and his collection of early dictionaries was later presented to the society by his widow. He helped Sir Samuel Meyrick revise his *A Critical Inquiry into Antient Armour* for the second enlarged edition of 1844 and contributed many drawings and notes to Henry Shaw's *Dress and Decoration of the Middle Ages* (1858). Way was meticulous in recording archaeological finds and historical sources but his interpretation of the evidence for the existence of the Pilgrims' Way in medieval times has been disputed.

As a moderately wealthy gentleman and learned amateur, Way appeared a traditional antiquary, but his interest in the collection, classification, and publication of antiquities made him an important figure in the movement towards a more scientific approach to archaeology. While director, he compiled a classified catalogue to the Society of Antiquaries' museum collections (published 1847) and his interest in medieval seals was aroused by the Prattinton seal casts bequeathed in 1841. He published many articles on the subject and assembled several thousand impressions, which his widow gave to the society to provide the foundation of the largest classified collection of British seal impressions.

Way purchased a country seat, Wonham Manor, Betchworth, Surrey, in 1840, and was appointed a JP in 1850 and deputy lieutenant for Surrey. On 30 April 1844 he married his cousin Emmeline Stanley (1809–1906), youngest surviving daughter of John Thomas, first Lord Stanley of Alderley. Their only child, Mary Alithea, was born in 1850. He resigned the directorship of the Society of Antiquaries in 1846 because of the difficulty of attending evening meetings after he had given up his London residence; but by then he had become more involved in the (Royal) Archaeological Institute. This was established as a body distinct from the British Archaeological Association largely through his efforts and because of his disagreements with Thomas Wright and Charles Roach Smith. In his memoirs the latter paid tribute to Way's insufficiently acknowledged services to archaeology, but characterized him as extremely cautious.

Way and Smith were joint honorary secretaries to the original British Archaeological Association between 1843 and 1845, and Way was one of the honorary secretaries to the Archaeological Institute from 1845 to 1868; he organized many of the annual meetings and temporary exhibitions in different parts of the country. He saw the role of the institute as one of promoting the preservation of historic monuments throughout England and providing a forum for the exchange of new ideas. *The Athenaeum* claimed he did a great deal to encourage local archaeological societies whose formation had been prompted by the two national associations. He edited the *Archaeological Journal* for many of the first twenty-five years of its publication and contributed seventy-two articles to the first thirty volumes, mostly on medieval costume, jewellery, seals, and documents. With an up-to-date and extensive knowledge of most periods of British archaeology, Way enjoyed the friendship of and corresponded with many leading antiquaries throughout Europe. He was known for privately giving enthusiastic help to others engaged in research. His letters to Sir A. W. Franks and Sir F. Madden are in the British Museum and British Library respectively, and many others have survived. He was a strong advocate for developing the British collections and was a generous donor to the British Museum.

A man of strong religious principle but of moderate opinions within the Church of England, Way rebuilt the Marboeuf Chapel, founded in Paris by his father for English protestants. He travelled to France and Italy on several occasions for the sake of his health, and withdrew from active involvement with the Archaeological Institute in 1863, although he continued to help with the *Journal* until

1868. His health deteriorated before he could complete his major catalogue of the duke of Northumberland's antiquities at Alnwick Castle. He died after a lingering illness at Le Trouville, Cannes, on 23 March 1874 and was buried at Betchworth. His collections of prints and drawings were sold at Sothebys on 16 June 1875 and 3 April 1876 and his *objets d'art* in their sale of 27–9 July 1908; books from his library were sold by Thomas Thorp in March 1907.   BERNARD NURSE

Sources *Archaeological Journal*, 30 (1873), 389–94 · *Proceedings of the Society of Antiquaries of London*, 2nd ser., 6 (1873–6), 198–200 · *The Athenaeum* (28 March 1874), 427 · A. M. W. Stirling, *The Ways of yesterday: being the chronicles of the Way family from 1307 to 1885* (1930) · C. R. Smith, *Retrospections, social and archaeological*, 3 vols. (1883–91) · Venn, *Alum. Cant.* · B. Vyner, ed., *Building on the past* (1994) · *The correspondence of Charles Darwin*, ed. F. Burkhardt and S. Smith, 1–2 (1985–6) · M. Caygill and J. Cherry, eds., *A. W. Franks: nineteenth-century collecting and the British Museum* (1997) · A. Way, *A descriptive catalogue of antiquities, mainly British, at Alnwick Castle*, ed. J. C. Bruce (1880) · d. cert. · C. G. Crump, 'The Pilgrims' Way', *History*, new ser., 21 (1936–7), 22–33 · parish register, St Martin-in-the-Fields, City Westm. AC
Archives BL, corresp. and papers, Add. MSS 39325, 41749, 42571, 42727–42728 · BM, department of medieval and modern Europe · S. Antiquaries, Lond., notes and papers | BL, letters to Philip Bliss, Add. MSS 34575–34580, *passim* · BL, corresp. with Sir Frederick Madden, Egerton MSS 2842–2848, *passim* · Bodl. Oxf., letters to John Gough Nichols · Bodl. Oxf., corresp. with Sir Thomas Phillipps · Bodl. Oxf., corresp. with Sir J. G. Wilkinson · Essex RO, Chelmsford, papers relating to ring collections of fourth Baron Braybrooke · JRL, letters to Edward Freeman · NL NZ, Turnbull L., letters to Gideon Algernon Mantell · S. Antiquaries, Lond., letters to C. R. Smith · U. Edin. L., letters to David Laing · W. Sussex RO, letters to duke of Richmond
Likenesses J. Downman, portrait, 1817, BM · R. C. Lucas, wax medallion, 1850, S. Antiquaries, Lond. · R. & E. Taylor, wood-engraving (after photograph by G. Evans), NPG; repro. in *ILN* (25 April 1874) · photograph, repro. in *Journal of British Archaeological Association*, new ser., 38 (1933), p. 228 [for 1932]
Wealth at death under £60,000: probate, 2 May 1874, *CGPLA Eng. & Wales*

Way, Sir Gregory Holman Bromley (1776–1844), army officer, born at London on 28 December 1776, was fifth son of Benjamin Way (1740–1808) FRS of Denham Place, Buckinghamshire, MP for Bridport in 1765, and of his wife, Elizabeth Anne (1746–1825), eldest daughter of William *Cooke (1711–1797), provost of King's College, Cambridge. Lewis *Way (1772–1840) was his elder brother. His grandfather, Lewis Way (*d.* 1771), director of the South Sea Company, the descendant of an old west-country family, first settled in Buckinghamshire. His aunt Abigail was the wife of John Baker Holroyd, first earl of Sheffield.

Way entered the army as ensign in the 26th (Cameronian) regiment of foot in 1797, was captured by French privateers on his way to his regiment in Canada, and was a prisoner in France for a year before he was exchanged. He was promoted lieutenant in the 35th foot on 3 November 1799, and sailed with it in the expedition under General Pigot on 28 March 1800 for the Mediterranean. Arriving at Malta in June, he took part in the successful siege of Valletta. He returned to England in 1802, was promoted captain in the 35th foot on 13 August 1802, and shortly after was placed on half pay on reduction of that regiment.

Way was brought in as captain of the 5th foot on 20 January 1803, and, after serving in the Channel Islands, embarked with the 5th in the expedition under Lord Cathcart for the liberation of Hanover in 1805; but he was wrecked off the Texel, and he was taken prisoner by the Dutch. After his exchange he sailed at the end of October 1806 in the expedition, under Major-General Robert Craufurd, which arrived at Monte Video in the beginning of June 1807, joining the force under General John Whitelocke, of which Way was appointed assistant quartermaster-general. At the storming of Buenos Aires, Way led the right wing of the infantry brigade. He returned to England after the disastrous surrender.

Way was promoted major in the 29th foot on 25 February 1808. He served under Sir Brent Spencer off Cadiz, and with him joined Sir Arthur Wellesley's army, landing in Mondego Bay, Portugal, on 3 August. He took part in the battle of Roliça on 17 August, when, on gaining the plateau with a few men and officers of the 29th, he, when charged by the enemy, was rescued from the bayonet of a French grenadier by General Brenier, and made a prisoner. He was exchanged in time to take part in the operations in Portugal when Sir Arthur Wellesley returned in April 1809. He commanded the light infantry of Brigadier-General R. Stewart's brigade, which led the advance of the British army, and was present in the actions of the passage of the Vouga on 10 May and the heights of Grijon the following day, at the passage of the Douro and capture of Oporto on the 12th, and in the subsequent pursuit of Soult's army.

At the battle of Talavera on the night of 27 July, Way took part with his regiment, under Major-General Hill, in the repulse of the French attack on the heights on the left of the British position. He was at the battle of Busaco on 27 September 1810, and at the battle of Albuera on 16 May 1811, when, on the fall of his lieutenant-colonel, he succeeded to command of the 29th foot during the action. He was himself, in charging with his regiment, shot through the body and his left arm fractured at the shoulder joint by a musket shot. He was promoted brevet lieutenant-colonel on 30 May 1811, and on 4 July was gazetted to command the 29th foot.

On his return to England in 1812 with the remnants of the 29th, about a hundred effective men, Way by considerable exertion reformed the corps, and embarked for the Peninsula in 1813. In 1814, however, the effect of climate and wounds compelled him to return to England, when he was placed on the half pay list of the 22nd foot. He was knighted the same year, was awarded a £200 wound annuity, and received permission to become knight commander of the Portuguese order of the Tower and Sword. On relinquishing the command of the 29th he was presented by his officers with a valuable piece of plate.

Way married, on 19 May 1815, Marianne, daughter of John Weyland, of Woodeaton, Oxfordshire, and Woodrising, Norfolk; they had no children. In 1815 Way was made a CB, military division, and was appointed to the staff as deputy adjutant-general in north Britain. He was promoted colonel in the army on 19 July 1821. On the abolition of his staff appointment he was nominated, on 7 November 1822, colonel of the 3rd Royal Veteran battalion, which was disbanded in 1826, when he was placed on half pay. He was promoted major-general on 22 July 1830, and lieutenant-general on 23 November 1841, and was made colonel of the 1st West India regiment on 21 November 1843. He died at Brighton on 19 February 1844, and was buried in the family vault at Denham church, Buckinghamshire.   R. H. VETCH, rev. JAMES LUNT

Sources GM, 2nd ser., 21 (1844), 537 · PRO, War Office Records · J. Philippart, ed., The royal military calendar, 3rd edn, 5 vols. (1820) · W. F. P. Napier, History of the war in the Peninsula and in the south of France, 3 vols. (1878) · Colburn's United Service Magazine, 1 (1844), 480 · Burke, Gen. GB · C. W. C. Oman, Wellington's army, 1809–1814 (1912); repr. (1968)
Likenesses portrait, NPG

Way, Lewis (1772–1840), religious activist, born on 11 February 1772, was the second son of Benjamin Way (1740–1808) of Denham and his wife, Elizabeth Anne Cooke (1746–1825). He was the elder brother of Sir Gregory Holman Bromley *Way (1776–1844). Educated at Eton College, he graduated BA in 1795 and MA in 1798 from Merton College, Oxford, and in 1797 was called to the bar by the Inner Temple. Way married Mary (1780–1848), daughter of Herman Drewe, rector of Comb Raleigh in Devon, on 31 December 1801. They had three sons and six daughters. From 1805 his home was Stanstead Park, near Racton, Sussex.

From an early age Way was influenced by such evangelical clergymen as Charles Simeon of King's College, Cambridge, and also by members of the Clapham Sect, including William Wilberforce. Following the inheritance of a large legacy from John Way (who was not related, despite bearing the same surname) Lewis Way devoted his fortune, and also his home, to religious works. He was especially active in the London Society for the Promotion of Christianity among the Jews. At one point he allowed a number of young Jewish men, supposedly Christian converts, to lodge at his house, with a view to training them as missionaries. They responded to his kindness by running away with his valuables. It was this incident which lay behind the youthful verse by T. B. Macaulay:

> Each, says the proverb, has his taste.
> 'Tis true Marsh loves a controversy, Coates a play, Bennet a
>   felon, Lewis Way a Jew,
> The Jew the silver spoons of Lewis Way.
> (Trevelyan, 1.54)

Lewis Way was made a deacon in 1816 and a Church of England priest the following year. In 1817–18 he made a long journey through the Netherlands, Germany, Poland, and Russia, investigating Jewish communities and worship. On reaching Moscow he had four fascinating audiences with Tsar Alexander I. In 1823 Way made a further trip, to the Holy Land, where he met Lady Hester Stanhope. On his return he established the Marboeuf (English protestant) Chapel in Paris, and devoted his latter years to the idea of establishing a Hebrew college (to train missionaries to the Jews) at Stanstead. This never came to fruition,

and Lewis Way died on 23 January 1840 at Barford, Warwickshire. He was the father of the antiquary Albert *Way (1805–1874).   ROBERT BROWN

Sources Foster, Alum. Oxon. · 'Way, Sir Gregory Holman Bromley', DNB · G. Trevelyan, The life and works of Macaulay, 2 vols. (1876) · A. W. M. Stirling, The Ways of yesterday: being the chronicles of the Way family from 1307 to 1885 (1930) · GM, 2nd ser., 13 (1840), 663 · R. A. Austen-Leigh, ed., The Eton College register, 1753–1790 (1921)
Archives U. Southampton L., corresp. and papers
Likenesses L. Vaslet, pastel drawing, 1796, Merton Oxf.

Way, Sir Richard George Kitchener [Sam] (1914–1998), civil servant and university administrator, was born on 15 September 1914 at 21 Margaret Street, St Marylebone, London, the son of Frederick Way, apartment housekeeper, and his wife, Clara, née Willetts. He was educated at the Polytechnic secondary school, London. On leaving school at eighteen he joined the War Office as an executive officer, serving in finance and audit in London and later in Hong Kong. From this time he was always known as Sam Way. He was recalled to London on promotion, fortunately for him and the public service, before the Japanese invasion. He was promoted rapidly—to principal in 1942 and assistant secretary in 1946. On 29 March 1947 he married Ursula Joan Starr (b. 1924/5), secretary and daughter of Hubert Francis Starr. They had a son and two daughters.

From 1949 to 1952 Way was command secretary, British army of the Rhine, where he was responsible for the large British and German civilian labour force supporting the army. He was made CBE in 1952. He was promoted to deputy secretary in 1955 and was recommended to succeed as permanent under-secretary one year later, but the prime minister, Anthony Eden, thought him too young, and he was moved sideways—first to the Ministry of Defence (1957–8) and then to the Ministry of Supply (1958–9). The permanent under-secretaryship of the War Office came his way in 1960. In 1963 Way became permanent secretary of the Ministry of Aviation, working first with Julian Amery and then, from 1964, with Roy Jenkins, with whom he forged a close partnership. This was a difficult period for the ministry, with the cancellation of several military aircraft projects and the attempt to cancel the Anglo-French supersonic airliner Concorde. Way was appointed CB in 1957 and advanced to KCB in 1961.

Way left the civil service in 1966 to join the fork-lift truck manufacturers Lansing Bagnall as deputy chairman, becoming chairman a year later. He found this an activity less challenging than Whitehall, but was soon back in the thick of public affairs when in 1970 he was appointed chairman of the London Transport executive. His five years at London Transport were exacting. Government pay restraint led to serious staff shortages and consequent disruption to bus and underground services. The election of a Labour Greater London council administration led by the radical Ken Livingstone in 1972 brought a commitment not to increase fares for two years; this damaged London Transport's finances. When Way finally obtained authority from the government to raise fares, he ensured that public odium fell on the Greater London council rather than London Transport, which endeared him to his staff. During this time he served on the board of the British Overseas Airways Corporation and chaired the National Economic Development Committee for the machine tool industry.

When the Greater London council failed to renew his contract, Way was appointed to succeed his old friend from his days with the British army of the Rhine, General Sir John Hackett, as principal of King's College, London. From 1975 until his final retirement in 1980 he piloted King's successfully through financial difficulties; he also initiated important constitutional and administrative reforms which enabled the college later to expand five-fold. He served twice as vice-president of the London Zoo at the urging of another old friend and colleague, Lord Zuckerman. He had chaired the council of Roedean School from 1969 to 1974, and was also a governor of Cranleigh School. From 1978 to 1987 he chaired the Royal Commission for the Exhibition of 1851. He was made an honorary doctor of science by Loughborough University in 1986. He died of heart failure at his holiday home in Menton in the south of France on 2 October 1998 and was buried on 17 October in Shalden churchyard, Alton, Hampshire. He was survived by his wife Ursula and their three children.

Sam Way was an outstanding public service administrator. Although he had never been to university and had started his civil service career in a humble grade, he was 'a cut, rather than a rough, diamond'. Politicians, civil servants, and university professors alike had the greatest respect for his incisive mind and the quality of his judgement. His working style could seem relaxed, but this was deceptive, more characteristic of the mask of the professional civil servant of his day than of the real man beneath. He inspired affection from his subordinates, not least because he was unstuffy and approachable. The chairmanship of London Transport was at the time ideally suited to his particular combination of managerial and political skills. Way's career was significant in a wider social context as an example that even before the post-1945 reforms in education the opportunity existed for talented boys from an unprivileged background to rise to the top of the public service.   ROGER FACER

Sources *The Times* (7 Oct 1998) · *Daily Telegraph* (7 Oct 1998) · *The Independent* (10 Oct 1998) · WWW · Burke, *Peerage* · personal knowledge (2004) · private information (2004) [Ursula Way] · b. cert. · m. cert.
Likenesses photograph, 1970, repro. in *Daily Telegraph* · photograph, 1970–79, repro. in *The Times* · photograph, 1974, repro. in *The Independent*
Wealth at death £525,359—gross; £522,859—net: probate, 23 April 1999, *CGPLA Eng. & Wales*

Way, Thomas (1837–1915), printer, was born at Carpenter's Coffee House, Covent Garden, London, on 1 May 1837, the eighth and youngest child of George Way (*bap.* 1794), a market victualler, and his wife, Ann, *née* Clewett (*bap.* 1796). He was baptized in St Paul's Church, Covent Garden, on 24 May 1837, not far from Carpenter's Coffee House, where his father was the licensee. He married Louisa Mary (1834–1911), the daughter of John Chapman, an auctioneer, on 16 June 1859, and the couple had seven

Thomas Way (1837–1915), by James Abbott McNeill Whistler, 1896

children, one of whom died in infancy. Thomas Way first appears in trade directories in 1859 as a 'lithographer, engraver and general printer' at 32 Brydges Street, Covent Garden, but not long afterwards he acquired the well-established lithographic business of George Edward Madeley (*d.* 1858) at 3 Wellington Street. Madeley (initially in partnership with Ingrey) was one of the most important early lithographers in London and one of the very few to survive in business into the second half of the century. Way worked as a commercial lithographer for over fifty years, for most of this time from Wellington Street, though the building he shared with Sothebys at this address was destroyed by a disastrous fire in 1865, which led to the loss of his equipment, stock, and records. He continued to print much the same kind of commercial jobbing work as his predecessor, specializing in lithographed plans and views for the sale particulars of property auctioneers. Other surviving commercial work of his includes art gallery catalogues, fashion plates for the monthly *West End Gazette*, and illustrations for other publications.

Way's principal contribution to lithography was his encouragement of artists—the most important being James McNeill Whistler—to turn to what was then a rather unfashionable method of making prints. Though his background was in the printing trade, he took a lively interest in the arts and had several artist friends. His tireless efforts to encourage British artists to take up lithography led to a revival of the process in Britain as a means of making prints, which began with a portfolio of twelve lithographs drawn by fellow members of the Hogarth Club on 15 December 1874. Three years later he was introduced to Whistler and printed a pamphlet describing the Peacock Room decorations that Whistler had painted for Frederick Leyland. Over the following twenty years Way printed nearly 200 of Whistler's lithographs, including lithotints, and many lithographs that were drawn on transfer paper in Paris and printed in London. Way was responsible for reviving both these branches of lithography, the second of which was widely used by artists because of its convenience. Fulsome praise from Whistler resulted in Way becoming the chosen printer of most artists in the country who practised lithography on a regular basis, including William Rothenstein, Joseph Pennell, Charles Shannon, and Theodore Roussel. At Whistler's bankruptcy in 1879 he was one of the main creditors and consequently suffered directly from the artist's deliberate destruction of saleable works of art. None the less, he remained one of Whistler's staunchest supporters and provided him with financial and material assistance. According to Rothenstein, Way 'was a cross-grained old man, with an uncertain temper, but where Whistler was concerned, a willing slave' (Rothenstein, 131). By 1902 financial pressures forced him to start selling his outstanding collection of Whistler's prints, drawings, and paintings, most of which were bought by the American collector Charles Lang Freer, though Way gave several of the finest proofs to the British Museum. About the same time the firm moved to 6/7 Gough Square.

In 1914, following the death of his son, Way sold his business to Estates Gazette, the publisher of a journal that undertook lithographic printing for property auctioneers. He died of bronchitis on 6 April 1915 at his home, 14 Eton Villas, Hampstead, London.

Thomas Way's son, **Thomas Robert Way** (1861–1913), artist and printmaker, was born at 13 Wellington Street, Strand, London, on 13 August 1861. He was educated at St John's College, Hurstpierpoint, Hassocks, Sussex, Archbishop Tenison's Grammar School, London, and King's College School, London. Later he studied at the Government Art School in South Kensington and, briefly, at the Académie Julian in Paris. On 10 July 1888 he married Amy Ellen (b. 1865), the daughter of Cornelius Cox, a stockbroker and collector; they had eight children, two of whom died in infancy.

The younger Way is usually distinguished from his father by being called T. R. Way. In 1880 he worked as an assistant to Whistler, helping to print the latter's etchings of Venice. In his early twenties he regularly exhibited oil paintings and watercolours at the Royal Academy and other leading galleries, but by 1895 had turned his attention almost exclusively to lithography. Later he produced many pastel drawings, some of which were shown at solo exhibitions at the Baillie Gallery. He was not financially successful as an artist and was dependent on an income from employment in his father's business, where he worked until his death. Rothenstein wrote that his father kept him 'in rigid subservience' (Rothenstein, 131),

though he was vital for the survival of the firm and shouldered the burden of dealing with the outside world.

Way carried on his father's crusade to encourage the best artists of the day to use lithography: he was a member of the Art Workers' Guild, serving on its committee from 1902 to 1904, lectured on lithography, and gave demonstrations of it to guild members and to others, including the Royal Society of Arts. He was also a member of the Senefelder Club, which was dedicated to the advancement of lithography. In 1896 he published the first catalogue of Whistler's lithographs, which is still used to identify and number the works. Later he wrote one of the best biographies of Whistler, *Memories of James McNeill Whistler the Artist* (1912), was co-author of another, and contributed numerous articles on lithography. He was an accomplished lithographic draughtsman and tried to supplement his income by publishing his own lithographs, many of which were drawn on transfer paper. He is best-known for a series of eight limited-edition books on London, illustrated with his lithographs and with text by several different authors, culminating in the one (with text by W. G. Bell) that includes some of his finest work, *The Thames from Chelsea to the Nore* (1907). He illustrated other books, produced many individual prints, drew about forty lithographic posters for the London Underground, and published some 200 lithographic postcards of London under the imprint of the Pastel Publishing Company. His usual signature was 'T. R. Way' or 'T. R. W.'. He died from heart failure, following bronchitis, on 28 February 1913 at his home, 110 Regent's Park Road, and was buried in Highgate cemetery on 4 March. He and his family were active members of the church, and the rood beam in St Mary's, Primrose Hill, was commissioned by his family as a memorial to him.   MICHAEL TWYMAN

Sources P. Frazer, 'Thomas Way and T. R. Way: commercial and artistic lithographers', PhD diss., U. Reading, 1999 · N. Smale, 'Whistler, Way, and Wellington Street', *The lithographs of James McNeill Whistler*, 2 (1998) · N. Smale, 'Whistler–Way correspondence', *The lithographs of James McNeill Whistler*, ed. H. K. Stratis and M. Tedeschi, 2 (1998) · K. S. Moore, 'The revival of lithography in England, 1890–1913', PhD diss., University of Washington, 1990 · T. R. Way, *Mr Whistler's lithographs*, 2nd rev. edn 1905 (1896) · T. R. Way and G. R. Dennis, *The art of James McNeill Whistler* (1903) · T. R. Way, *Memories of James McNeill Whistler the artist* (1912) · J. Pennell and E. Robins Pennell, *Lithography and lithographers*, [new edn] (1915) · A. S. Hartrick, *Lithography as a fine art* (1932) · W. Rothenstein, *Men and memories: recollections of William Rothenstein*, new edn, 2 vols. (1934) · N. Smale, 'Thomas R. Way: his life and work', *Tamarind Papers*, 10/1 (1987), 16–27 · parish register (baptism), St Paul's, Covent Garden · d. cert. · b. cert. [T. R. Way] · parish magazine of St Mary the Virgin, Primrose Hill · d. cert. [T. R. Way]
Archives Smithsonian Institution, Washington, DC, Freer Gallery of Art, letters · U. Glas., letters
Likenesses T. R. Way, self-portrait, lithograph, 1890 (T. R. Way), Art Workers' Guild, London · W. Rothenstein, lithograph, 1893 (T. R. Way), FM Cam. · J. A. M. Whistler, two portraits, 1896, BM [*see illus.*] · drawing (T. R. Way), repro. in Smale, 'Whistler, Way, and Wellington Street' · photographs, repro. in Smale, 'Whistler, Way, and Wellington Street'
Wealth at death £3212 15s. 10d. · £536 13s. 11d.—T. R. Way

Way, Thomas Robert (1861–1913). *See under* Way, Thomas (1837–1915).

Wayland, Edward James [Jim] (1888–1966), geologist and prehistorian, was born on 23 January 1888 at 18 White Lion Street, Clerkenwell, London, the son of Edward Wayland, a builder, and his wife, Emily Street. Jim, as he was widely known, was educated at the Central Foundation School and at the City of London College. He first considered a career in architecture, having completed a five-year apprenticeship, but 'his attention was attracted to geology' (Davies, 'Edward James Wayland, 1888–1966', 231) and he spent the next three years (1907–10) studying the subject at the Royal College of Science. He received numerous awards there, including a national science studentship, the Lubbock prize, an Imperial College national scholarship, and a Royal College of Science Marshall (biological/palaeontological) research scholarship. While still at the Royal College, in 1909 he travelled to Egypt, making a geological study of an area near Aswan. In 1911 he conducted geographical reconnaissance in Portuguese East Africa for Memba Minerals Limited and in the following year went to Ceylon, where he became assistant mineral surveyor in the Ceylon government service. He returned to Europe for war service in 1916 and, on 17 March 1917, married Ellen Morrison in the parish church in Kentish Town, London.

Toward the end of the First World War the British government turned to its colonies for economic mineral resources, creating in the process numerous geological surveys. Wayland was sent to Uganda as geological expert; he soon became government geologist (a position later renamed director of the geological survey). It has been said that one of the first things he did after arrival was 'to walk right round Uganda, a journey of several months' (Davies, 'Edward James Wayland, 1888–1966', 231).

Wayland produced a broad outline of Ugandan geology, stressing his interest in rift valley structure, volcanics, and equatorial lake and river systems. He hypothesized the presence of erosional levels (peneplains I, II, III) and proposed the compression theory of rift valley formation in contrast to Gregory's crustal tensional theory. In 1929 he published on a new mineral from Uganda—bismutotantalite. In 1923 he founded the Uganda Literary and Scientific Society (later reconstituted as the Uganda Society), and he was an active contributor to the society's periodical—the *Uganda Journal*. He was president of the society in 1934–5, having served as vice-president, honorary vice-president, and honorary secretary.

During his twenty years' dedicated service with the geological survey Wayland cultivated broad research interests, participating in Kenyan reconnaissance surveys, and developing a climatic pluvial sequence. He also collaborated with van Riet Lowe on classification of Stone Age cultures. His wide interests resulted in more than 200 publications covering geology, natural philosophy, palaeontology, anthropology, and prehistory. His articles often included his own hand-drawn sketches and photographs. His archaeological work concentrated along the Kagera River and in the Sango hills. Although he never completed the first part (geology) of a proposed Uganda monograph, the second, on prehistory, was finished and published by van Riet Lowe (1952).

In 1939, aged fifty, Wayland retired and returned to England to join up as a royal engineer. Commissioned in 1940, he told colleagues that he was the oldest second lieutenant in the British army. Wayland's son, a Royal Air Force pilot, was killed on a sortie over the Adriatic Sea. Following a 'one man secret mission to a neutral country' (*WWW*), in 1943 Wayland travelled to Bechuanaland where he was responsible for water conservation projects (and for creating the geological survey of Bechuanaland, of which he was director from 1948/9 until 1952).

Wayland was considered a great asset to the surveys in which he took part. 'Imaginative in thought, robust in constitution and prepared to contend even with Governors if he thought the Survey was being unfairly treated, he earned the deep respect of all sections of the community for himself and his department' (Davies, 'Edward James Wayland, 1888–1966', 232). He received many honours, including appointment as CBE (1938), the Bigsby medal (1933) of the Geological Society of London, and the Victoria medal (1935) of the Royal Geographical Society. He was a fellow of the Geological Society of London, an associate of the Royal College of Science, a corresponding member of the Académie Royale des Sciences d'Outre-Mer, and an honorary member of the Geological Society of Belgium. He died on 11 July 1966 at Brenan House Nursing Home, 21 Vale Square, Ramsgate. In recognition of his palaeontological exploits near Kaiso, Cooke and Coryndon (1970) honoured Wayland with a species name of an east African Suidae (*'Sus' waylandi*), which has been revised to *Nyanzachoerus waylandi* (Pickford).

JULIE L. CORMACK

Sources K. A. Davies, 'Edward James Wayland, 1888–1966', *Proceedings of the Geological Society of London*, 1642 (1967), 231–2 · K. A. Davies, 'E. J. Wayland CBE—a tribute', *Uganda Journal*, 31 (1967), 1–8 · private information (2004) [colleagues] · *WWW* · J. Le Personne, 'Edward James Wayland, 23 Janvier 1888–11 Juillet 1966', *Académie Royale des Sciences d'Outre-Mer; Bulletin des Séances*, 14 (1967), 133–42 · B. W. Langlands, 'The published works of E. J. Wayland', *Uganda Journal*, 31 (1967), 33–42 · M. Posnansky, 'Wayland as an archaeologist', *Uganda Journal*, 31 (1967), 9–12 · H. B. S. Cooke and S. C. Coryndon, 'Pleistocene mammals from the Kaiso formation and other related deposits in Uganda', *Fossil vertebrates of Africa*, ed. L. S. B. Leakey and R. J. G. Savage, 2 (1970), 107–224 · M. Pickford, 'New specimens of *Nyanzachoerus- waylandi*', *Geobios*, 22 (1989), 641–51 · C. van Riet Lowe, *The Pleistocene geology and prehistory of Uganda: prehistory* (1952), part 2 of *The Pleistocene geology and prehistory of Uganda* · E. J. Wayland and L. J. Spencer, 'Bismutotantalite, a new mineral from Uganda', *Mineralogical Magazine*, 22 (1929–31), 185–92 · b. cert. · m. cert. · d. cert.

Archives BGS, notebooks and papers · BM, African artefacts · Geological Survey of Uganda, African artefacts · Ipswich Museum, African artefacts · NHM, African artefacts · Royal Anthropological Institute, London, report on the Oldoway skeleton · U. Cam., Museum of Archaeology and Anthropology, African artefacts · U. Oxf., Donald Baden-Powell Quaternary Research Centre, African artefacts | Bodl. Oxf., corresp. with J. L. Myres

Wealth at death £4842: probate, 24 Aug 1966, *CGPLA Eng. & Wales*

Wayland, John (*c.*1508–1571×3), printer and scrivener, was probably born at Cranford, Middlesex, as his grandfather and father were yeomen there. His father died at some point before 1520, when his mother married John Pilkington, an affluent London baker, who became Wayland's guardian. He may have moved to London at this time and is first mentioned as a printer there in 1537.

Wayland lived at the sign of the Blue Garter in Fleet Street from at least 1537, and printed works by Richard Whitford and Erasmus in his first year as a printer. In 1539 several editions of Bishop Hilsey's *Primer* were printed with Wayland's imprint, but they were in fact printed by John Mayler, to whom Wayland sold his stock-in-trade in September of that year. Wayland continued to work as a bookseller, but his chief trade during the years 1540–53 was that of a scrivener. He entered, and accepted the ordinances of, the Scriveners' Company on 10 December 1540. He is mentioned as living in the parish of St Dunstan-in-the-West in the London subsidy rolls in 1541, where he was assessed as having goods to the value of £40. In 1555 he contributed towards a benevolence for the Scriveners' Company. There is no record of his serving an apprenticeship as a scrivener, but it is likely that he was a man of some education who nevertheless served his due time of apprenticeship. He was probably the brother of Edward Wayland, another London scrivener, whose will of 1551 leaves a bequest 'to my brother John Wailand' (Byrom, 314n.).

Wayland was involved in a series of lawsuits from 1541 onwards. He took action against his stepfather, John Pilkington, for defrauding him by 'subtyll and untrue practyse' out of his legacy, the manor of Cranford; the suit was eventually pronounced void in 1568. Wayland unsuccessfully attempted to remove the occupants, Richard Alcester and later Alcester's son, from the manor. It is from a deposition taken during this unsuccessful suit that we know Wayland was born about 1508, for he is described on 12 November 1550 as being 'of the age of xlii yeres or theraboute' (PRO, Town Dep., C 24/24, Cupper v. Alcester). Wayland also challenged John Whitpaine, a wealthy merchant tailor with connections to other London printers, over an unpaid debt of £500. In fact, debts were to become a constant burden upon Wayland throughout his life, and he increasingly borrowed more than he ever lent or repaid. Such debts resulted in his imprisonment in 1547, 1558, and again during 1561–5.

In 1553 Wayland returned to his former trade as a printer. It is not known why he switched trades, or what influence he exacted, but in October 1553 he successfully procured the royal patent to print primers and all books of private devotion. John Day and William Seres had printed primers under Edward VI before they were both deprived and imprisoned by Mary, and the patent passed to Wayland. After Edward Whitchurch was deprived of his patents, Wayland took over his shop at the sign of the Sun in Fleet Street in 1554, whence he issued his Sarum primers. Approximately thirty-five editions of the Sarum primer survive from Mary's reign; more than half of these were printed by Wayland or his assigns. Jackson and Gillespie note a unique title-page for what they believe to be an unfinished or cancelled edition of *The Fall of Princes* (1554) in the Dyce collection of the Victoria and Albert

Museum, which conflates two editorial projects: the work by John Lydgate and the continuation by contemporary poets in *The Mirror for Magistrates*, as gathered by John Bochus. Bochus's *Tragedies* was printed with Wayland's imprint, but with Day's title-page compartment, during 1558.

From 1556 onwards the additional phrase 'by the assigns of' occurs throughout Wayland's publications. Duff erroneously dates Wayland's will to that year, while McKerrow assumes that Wayland either was taken ill or died in 1556, as a result of which his work was assigned to others. William Seres worked for Wayland as a named assign as late as 1559; John Day as an unnamed assign in 1558 for a Sarum primer, but possibly as early as 1556. In 1551 Wayland had been bound with John Redshaw, a mariner, for the sum of £20 to deliver haberdashery to Boston in Lincolnshire. The deed was never undertaken and so the £20 became forfeit to the crown. Action was taken against Wayland for this only in 1558, when he was imprisoned for being unable to pay the sum owed. Thus works bearing Wayland's imprint during this period must have been printed by his assigns.

Wayland is mentioned twice in John Foxe's *Actes and Monumentes*: Wayland's servant, Thomas Greene, was imprisoned and whipped at Grey Friars in 1557 for his involvement in the printing of a book called *Antichrist*; and in his second edition Foxe attacks the content of the Sarum primers printed by Wayland. It is unlikely that any of the later Wayland primers were in fact printed by Wayland. He probably did none of his own printing after 1556, probably owing to ill health and the constant problems caused by his attempts to evade imprisonment for bad debts. In 1561 he faced imprisonment again, this time for keeping back £20 from the estate of Roger Hote, a goldsmith. He was freed in June 1565 only because of his poor health. A year or so before he died he was back in court yet again due to bad debts.

Wayland died at some point between 22 May 1571, when he drew up his will, and 16 March 1573, when it was proved. The will, made about the time of the final suit against Wayland, states that he left his 'lands, chattels and debts' in the hands of his executor Thomas Hartoppe, a London goldsmith, with the residue after payment of debts going to his wife, of whom nothing else is known (PRO, PROB 11/55, sig. 9, fol. 65v).

ELIZABETH EVENDEN

Sources will, PRO, PROB 11/55, sig. 9 · J. Foxe, *Actes and monumentes* (1570), 1773–6 · J. Foxe, *Actes and monumentes*, 3rd edn, 2 vols. (1576), 1953 · E. G. Duff, *A century of the English book trade* (1948), 167–8 · R. B. McKerrow, *Printers' and publishers' devices in England and Scotland, 1485–1640* (1949) · E. Evenden, 'John Day, Tudor printer', PhD diss., University of York [in preparation] · E. Duffy, *The stripping of the altars: traditional religion in England, 1400–1580* (Yale, 1992), 526–7 · W. C. Ferguson, *Pica roman type in Elizabethan England* (Oaknoll, 1990), 24 · J. P. Collier, ed., *The Egerton papers* (1840), 140 · H. J. Byrom, 'John Wayland: printer, scrivener and litigant', *The Library*, 4th ser., 11 (1931), 312–42 · chancery proceedings, PRO, ser. II, bundle 199, nos. 24, 104 · PRO, Town Dep. C24/24, Cupper v. Alcester · STC, 1475–1640 · F. W. Steer, *Scriveners' Company common papers, 1357–1628* (1968), 26, 27, 73 · A. J. Gillespie, 'Chaucer and Lydgate in print: the medieval author and the history of the book, 1476–1569', DPhil diss., U. Oxf., 2001 • W. A. Jackson, 'Wayland's edition of the *Mirror for magistrates*', *The Library*, 4th ser., 13 (1933), 155–7

Waylett [*née* Cooke; *other married name* Lee], **Harriet** (1800–1851), actress and singer, was born on 7 February 1800, the daughter of an upholsterer in Bath named Cooke. Her uncle was a member of the Drury Lane company and the actress Sarah West was her cousin. After receiving some instruction in music from the violinist John Loder, she appeared on the Bath stage as Elvina in W. R. Hewetson's *The Blind Boy*, in which she earned praise from both press and public. In the next season she appeared as Leonora in *The Paddock* and as Madge in *Love in a Village*. She then went to Bristol and Brighton. In 1818 it was reported that a severe indisposition caused her disappearance from the theatre for about eight months. She returned to the stage at Coventry, where she met and married on 17 June 1819 an actor named Waylett (*d.* 1840), who was described as 'insignificance personified'. The marriage was discordant. It was said that the couple were paired but not matched. In October 1820 they were engaged by the proprietors of the Adelphi, where Harriet was the original Amy Robsart in J. R. Planché's adaptation of *Kenilworth* and the first Sue to her husband's Primefit in W. T. Moncrieff's *Tom and Jerry*. In the latter part she was said to have displayed liveliness and mischief. However, husband and wife soon separated, in 1821 or 1822.

By 1823, during a recess at the Adelphi, Waylett was acting in Birmingham under Alfred Bunn, where she played a multitude of parts. She accompanied Bunn to Drury Lane, where she again appeared as Madge in *Love in a Village* (4 December 1824). Around this time 'foul insinuations' were made against her and Bunn, and he threatened to prosecute for libel. Mrs Waylett promptly and spiritedly refuted all innuendoes, and the maligning party apologized and bought an expensive ticket for her benefit. At this time too, her husband made a claim for her salary to help him keep his mistress and their child, and she went to Newmarket to confront him. In order to economize she left her London apartment in Tavistock Street for cheaper lodgings and visited her family in Bath. On 14 January 1825 she was Mrs Page in *The Merry Wives of Windsor* and at the end of the season she went to the Olympic and then to King's Lynn in Norfolk. On 12 May 1825 she made, as Zephyrina in *The Lady and the Devil*, her first appearance at the Haymarket, under D. E. Morris. It was a successful début, but she was not encouraged by the managers, and after playing many different parts, some original, she went to Dublin. Here she took, at the Hawkins Street Theatre, the part of Phoebe, written especially for her by John Poole in his *Paul Pry*. She also stood in high favour in Dublin and Cork as a singer.

After her return from Dublin, Waylett went again to King's Lynn, where local families bestowed gifts upon her. She was then seen at the Haymarket, Drury Lane, the Queen's, the Olympic, Covent Garden, and elsewhere. She sang from the gallery at Drury Lane on 18 April 1831, on the occasion of the dinner of the Friends of the Drury Lane Theatrical Fund, at which the duke of Sussex presided. In the same year she appeared there with success in

The Ice Witch, or, The Frozen Hand. In 1832 she was at Vauxhall Gardens for a short period, and appeared in *Professionals Puzzled* and *Mystification* at Rayner's New Subscription Room. She became the sole manager at the Strand in 1834. Admission to this theatre was nominally free but actually by payment of 4 *s*. an ounce for sweets at a neighbouring shop or by purchasing tickets for the Victoria Theatre, which admitted also to the Strand. It was closed by the lord chamberlain in March 1835. By October 1835 Waylett was again in Hawkins Street, Dublin, where she received £800 and half the proceeds of a benefit for twenty-one nights' performances. Diamonds were given her by a lady at the court. In 1838 she was again back at the Haymarket. Waylett's husband died in 1840 and she soon married George Alexander *Lee (1802–1851), a musician and singer, who composed many of her favourite songs. She was known as the Queen of Ballad Singers. She sang at the Marylebone Theatre and at the English Opera House in February 1843. In May she was at the Lyceum. Soon afterwards she was involved in a speculative venture at management in Chester, which failed. Her appearances became infrequent through ill health, and by 1849 she was spoken of as retired. She died in April 1851 after a long illness and was buried in Norwood cemetery.

JOSEPH KNIGHT, *rev.* J. GILLILAND

Sources Mrs C. Baron-Wilson, *Our actresses*, 2 vols. (1844) • Boase, *Mod. Eng. biog.* • *Ladies' Monthly Museum* (May 1823) • *Ladies' Magazine*, 3 (1831) • [J. Roach], *Authentic memoirs of the green-room* [1814] • *The life and reminiscences of E. L. Blanchard, with notes from the diary of Wm. Blanchard*, ed. C. W. Scott and C. Howard, 2 vols. (1891) • *The biography of the British stage, being correct narratives of the lives of all the principal actors and actresses* (1824) • 'Memoir of Mrs Waylett', *Oxberry's Dramatic Biography*, new ser., 1 (1827), 56–64 • Genest, *Eng. stage* • *A new biographical dictionary of 3000 cotemporary* [sic] *public characters, British and foreign, of all ranks and professions*, 2nd edn, 3 vols. in 6 pts (1825) • W. C. Lane and N. E. Browne, eds., *A. L. A. portrait index* (1906) • Hall, *Dramatic ports.*

Archives Theatre Museum, London, letters

Likenesses T. Hodgetts, mezzotint, pubd 1830 (after F. Meyer), NPG • T. G. Wageman, portrait (after engraving by Woolnoth), repro. in *Ladies Monthly Museum*, p. 241 • portrait, repro. in *Actors by Daylight* (8 Sept 1838) • portrait, repro. in *Life and amours of Mrs Waylett* (1830) • portrait, repro. in *Illustrated London Life* (23 April 1843) • portrait, repro. in *Apollo* (1830) • portrait, repro. in *Drama Magazine* (May 1830) • portrait, repro. in *Biography of the British stage* • portrait, repro. in 'Memoir of Mrs Waylett', *Oxberry's Dramatic Biography* • portrait, repro. in *London Magazine* (1820) • prints, Harvard TC

Waymouth [Weymouth], **George** (*fl.* 1587–1611), navigator, was the younger son of William Waymouth of Cockington, Devon. In 1587 George's grandfather, also William Waymouth, made his will: to his son he left a half-share of the ship *Lyon*, and to George the eventual possession of his chattels. The younger William Waymouth probably took part in the Newfoundland fishery in the 1570s, and from the 1580s was building ships, for which he received royal subsidies. From his father George Waymouth almost certainly learned the shipbuilder's trade and gained a knowledge of the north Atlantic. Then on 24 July 1601 he proposed to the East India Company a voyage to discover a north-west passage to the East. His proposal was accepted and on 2 May 1602, provisioned for eighteen months, bearing a letter from the queen to the emperor of China, and with the Revd John Cartwright, recently returned from Persia, as his mentor, he left London with the *Discovery* of 70 tons and the *Godspeed* of 60.

On 28 June Waymouth was off the American coast, in all likelihood Resolution Island. Coasting along the eastern shore of Baffin Island, he reckoned that he was almost in latitude 69 degrees north when during the night of 19–20 July, their morale destroyed by days of fog and ice, the crews mutinied and, encouraged by Cartwright, persuaded Waymouth to turn back. On his way south he sailed 100 leagues into the Hudson Strait before bad weather drove him out again (26 July–5 August). By mid-September London knew of his return to Dartmouth; a month later (13 October) the ships were in the Thames. He was examined by the privy council, his examination being relayed to the company on 25 October. His optimism regarding the likelihood of finding a passage led the company to sanction a second voyage, but the project was soon allowed to lapse, and by 1609 his log book of the voyage was in Amsterdam, where Hudson saw it before sailing on his last voyage.

In 1604 Waymouth twice presented the king with versions of his treatise *The Jewell of Artes*. In five sections of unequal length, he emphasized the explorer–colonizer's need for a knowledge of navigational instruments, shipbuilding, machinery, gunnery, and fortification. This last incidentally assumed that colonists would live together in towns rather than scattered over the countryside. Doubtless the treatise was intended to justify Waymouth's employment on other voyages of exploration, and this goal it achieved. In 1605 he found sponsors from the worlds of commerce and colonization: Plymouth merchants interested in the cod fishery; Sir Thomas Arundell, who wished to establish an American colony for Roman Catholics; and possibly Arundell's brother-in-law the earl of Southampton. Waymouth's true destination was perhaps the region between Chesapeake Bay and Cape Cod, but, sailing from London in the *Archangell*, he took two months to reach the New England coast (5 March–14 May). Pushed further north by bad weather, he was off Monhegan Island four days later. For a month he reconnoitred the Maine coast, and traded with the Abenaki Indians, five of whom he brought back with him. The return to Dartmouth took only a month (16 June–18 July).

Once again Waymouth intended a sequel that was not to occur. On 30 October 1605 Sir John Zouche appointed him his second-in-command on a (possibly crypto-Catholic) colonizing venture that was to sail within six months, but during 1606 the voyage was superseded by the much larger expedition to the Chesapeake commanded by Christopher Newport. Nevertheless, Waymouth was not entirely passed over: he was probably the Captain Waiman said in August 1607 to have been 'taken … shipping himself to Spaine with intent as is thought to have betrayed his friends and shewed the Spaniards a meanes how to defeat this Virginian attempt' (Quinn and Quinn, 61). If Waiman was indeed Waymouth, he is more likely to

have been a double agent helping to expose Spanish espionage, for on 27 October 1607, pending his further advancement, he received a royal pension of 3s. 4d. a day, and in March 1609 he joined a commission inquiring into Phineas Pett's building of the *Prince Royal*.

Alone among the commissioners Waymouth was the object of Pett's animosity, Pett terming him, *inter alia*, 'a great braggadocio, a vain and idle fellow', and alleging on one occasion that Waymouth was 'between drunk and sober'. According to Pett, Waymouth had said that the *Prince Royal* 'was unfit for any use but a dung boat, with many other such false opprobrious defamations, wherein he was better practised than in any other profession' (*Autobiography of Phineas Pett*, 38, 40). Pett's unsupported allegations of incompetence are unlikely to be true. Waymouth had studied mathematics 'these twenty years' and 'during this time applied myself to know the several ways of building and the secrets of the best shipwrights in England and Christendom, and have likewise observed the several workings of ships in the sea in all the voyages I have been' (BL, Harleian MS 309, fol. 68). He has been considered the author of an anonymous manuscript entitled 'A most excellent briefe and easie treatize' (Perrin, 'Introduction', in *Autobiography of Phineas Pett*, lxxiv), but recent scholarship regards this identification as questionable (Lavery, 9).

Those who respected Waymouth included court figures such as Sir Walter Cope, the earl of Northampton, Sir Edward Cecil, and even Prince Henry. In 1610 Waymouth accompanied Cecil to the siege of Julich, later that year writing for the prince 'A Journall relation … of the taking … of Gulicke … with a platt of the town and castle as it is againe to be fortified' (BL, Royal MS 13. B. xxxiii). In 1611 Sir James Bond, a London merchant, commissioned from him a vessel of 40 tons in which he was to make a year-long voyage with twenty men. Whether or not she was built is unclear, but she may be the vessel that Pett alleged Waymouth had built and sailed to Antwerp in such circumstances that orders for his arrest as a pirate were given.

Waymouth's career is thus a mystery at its beginning and its end. There seems no reason to doubt that he was a knowledgeable mathematician, a skilled navigator, and a competent designer of ships and fortifications, but the stop–start nature of his career at sea suggests that he lacked necessary qualities of leadership.

DAVID R. RANSOME

Sources D. B. Quinn and A. M. Quinn, *The English New England voyages, 1602–1608*, Hakluyt Society, 2nd ser., 161 (1983) · *CSP col.*, vol. 2 · G. Birdwood, ed., *The register of letters … of the governour and company of merchants of London trading into the East Indies, 1600–1619* (1893); repr. (1965) · H. Stevens, ed., *The dawn of British trade to the East Indies as recorded in the court minutes of the East India Company, 1599–1603* (1886) · *CSP dom., 1603–10* · M. Christy, ed., *The voyages of Captain Luke Fox of Hull, and Captain Thomas James of Bristol, in search of a north-west passage, in 1631–32*, 2 vols., Hakluyt Society, 88–9 (1894) · *The letters of John Chamberlain*, ed. N. E. McClure, 2 vols. (1939) · *The autobiography of Phineas Pett*, ed. W. G. Perrin, Navy RS, 51 (1918) · B. Lavery, *The colonial merchantman Susan Constant, 1605* (1988), 9

Wayne, Anthony (1745–1796), revolutionary army officer in America, was born on 1 January 1745 at his family's

Anthony Wayne
(1745–1796), by
John Trumbull,
c.1791

estate, Waynesborough, in Chester county, Pennsylvania, the second of three children of Isaac Wayne (d. 1776), farmer, and his wife, Elizabeth (d. 1793), daughter of Richard and Margaret Iddings of Chester county. At an early age Wayne manifested a spirit of independence, challenging his father's authority to regulate his life. He was enrolled in a school run by his uncle, Gilbert Wayne, and excelled in mathematics. At the age of sixteen he entered the Philadelphia Academy, where he studied for two years without taking a degree. He became a surveyor, and in 1765 was hired to survey and settle 100,000 acres of land in Nova Scotia. On 25 March 1766 he married Mary Penrose (d. 1793); they had two children. Later Wayne became enamoured of Mary Vining, a socialite in Wilmington, Delaware, and he and his wife drifted apart. Wayne ran a tannery and supervised a farm. Upon the death of his father, he inherited Waynesborough.

As American opposition to British policies grew during the early 1770s, Wayne assumed a leadership role in Pennsylvania. A handsome, well-proportioned man, he was admired and respected by his fellow citizens. On 13 July 1774 he became chairman of a Chester county committee appointed to draft resolutions of protest against the Coercive Acts. In the same year he was elected to the provincial assembly. On 3 January 1776 congress appointed him colonel of the 4th battalion of the Pennsylvania line. He joined General George Washington in mid-May at New York, and immediately was sent to reinforce an American army retreating from Canada. In the battle of Trois Rivières on 8 June he and his battalion were in the hottest part of the fighting. Having retired to New York, he commanded at Fort Ticonderoga during the following winter and contended with near mutiny among his troops because of harsh conditions. On 21 February he was promoted brigadier-general and shortly received orders from Washington to rejoin the main army in New Jersey.

Wayne reached Morristown on 20 May 1777 and was given command of the Pennsylvania line, which consisted of two brigades. In the battle of the Brandywine on 11 September 1777 he was in charge of the American left wing and was assaulted by the British in the first hours of fighting. When Washington's right wing collapsed and the American army was compelled to retreat, Wayne masterfully covered the withdrawal. A few days later Wayne was detached by Washington from the main army to harass the British army's left flank as it advanced on Philadelphia. On 20 September at Paoli he was attacked in camp by Charles Grey, and barely managed to extricate himself from a débâcle. Charged with negligence for his handling of troops at Paoli, he was exonerated by a court of inquiry. In the battle of Germantown on 4 October he led a spirited and almost victorious attack upon enemy lines, but was compelled to retreat when gunfire erupted to his rear. In disgust Wayne concluded that Washington was responsible for this reversal. For a time he considered resigning his commission but remained with the American army at Valley Forge during the winter. He was in the thick of the fight at the battle of Monmouth on 28 June 1778, and later almost fought a duel with Charles Lee when the latter made offensive remarks about Wayne's performance on the field.

In the late summer of 1778 Washington reorganized his army, giving Wayne command of an élite continental light infantry corps. On the evening of 15 July Wayne led these troops in a successful assault on a British garrison at Stony Point. As a reward for this triumph, he received a gold medal from congress and much praise from Washington and his fellow continental officers. Shortly thereafter the light infantry corps was disbanded. In 1780 Wayne led an ineffective attack against a British blockhouse at Bull's Ferry, near Bergen, New Jersey, and in other ways attempted to disrupt the enemy's collection of supplies in the lower Hudson valley. He acted promptly on 25 September to frustrate Benedict Arnold's attempt to deliver West Point to the British by rapidly marching his men to that post. When the Pennsylvania line mutinied in early 1781, he kept control of affairs while presenting to congress the soldiers' demands for pay and provisions. Four months later, when the Pennsylvanians mutinied again, he ruthlessly suppressed the malcontents and hanged four of the ringleaders. He thereupon marched to Virginia and joined the marquis de Lafayette in fighting British troops under Charles, Lord Cornwallis. At the battle of Green Spring Farm on 6 July he almost came to disaster when he ordered an army of 800 men to attack Cornwallis's 5000 veterans. Although he extricated his soldiers from this dangerous situation, a newspaperman called his action 'Madness'. When Cornwallis capitulated at Yorktown on 19 October 1781, Wayne was recuperating from a leg wound inflicted by one of his own sentries and took no part in the ceremonies.

In the last two years of the war Wayne served under General Nathanael Greene in the south. From January to July 1782 he commanded American forces in Georgia, fighting Native Americans and suppressing warfare between patriots and loyalists. After the British evacuated Savannah on 11 July, he joined Greene in South Carolina.

He almost died of a fever but was well enough on 14 December to march with Greene into Charles Town after enemy forces departed the town. In October 1783, just before the American army was disbanded, congress promoted him major-general. He entered Pennsylvanian politics in late 1783 and was elected to the council of censors and the assembly. He was an ardent proponent of the constitution of 1787 and served in the Pennsylvania ratifying convention late that year. Having moved to Georgia in 1785 to operate a rice plantation that the state had given him for his role in the war, he was elected to congress in 1791 but was compelled to give up his seat when the election proved fraudulent. His attempts to make the rice plantation a financial success failed miserably, for he could not repay huge loans to Dutch bankers. Finally he had to sell the plantation and seek employment in the new federal government. As luck would have it, Arthur St Clair, commander of American troops in the Northwest Territory, had been defeated by a Native American army in 1791, and President Washington was seeking a replacement. He appointed Wayne, with the rank of major-general, to lead a recently organized legion army.

In June 1792 Wayne joined the army at Pittsburgh. Over the next two years he prosecuted a rigorous training regimen while opposing attempts by his second in command, James Wilkinson, to undermine his position. On 20 August 1794 he defeated the Native Americans in the battle of Fallen Timbers and imposed his will upon them by constructing forts in the newly conquered territory. Although tempted to attack British soldiers that were aiding the Native Americans, he curbed his ardour, knowing that Washington was negotiating the Jay treaty with London at the time and did not want a diplomatic disarrangement. In 1795 he compelled the Native Americans to sign the treaty of Greenville and then returned to Philadelphia, where he was fêted as a hero. Having rejoined his army in 1796, he died of gout at Presque Isle, Pennsylvania, on 15 December that year, and was buried the following day on the parade ground of a local blockhouse. He was reburied on 3 October 1809 at St David's Church, near Waynesborough.   PAUL DAVID NELSON

Sources P. D. Nelson, *Anthony Wayne: soldier of the early republic* (1985) · R. C. Knopf, ed., *Anthony Wayne, a name in arms* (1960) · C. J. Stillé, *Major-General Anthony Wayne and the Pennsylvania line of the continental army* (1893) · H. F. Rankin, 'Anthony Wayne: military romanticist', *George Washington's generals*, ed. G. A. Billias (1964) · H. E. Wildes, *Anthony Wayne: troubleshooter of the revolution* (1941) · H. N. Moore, *Life and services of General Anthony Wayne* (1845) · R. H. Kohn, *Eagle and sword: the federalists and the creation of the military establishment in America, 1783–1802* (1975) · J. R. Jacobs, *Tarnished warrior: Major-General James Wilkinson* (1938)
Archives Hist. Soc. Penn., MSS · National Archives and Records Administration, Washington DC, MSS · U. Mich., Clements L., MSS | L. Cong., Washington MSS · U. Mich., Clements L., Greene MSS
Likenesses J. Trumbull, drawing, *c.*1791, Fordham University Library, New York [*see illus.*] · J. Sharples, oils, *c.*1792, Independence National Historical Park, Philadelphia, Pennsylvania · E. Savage, oils, 1795, New York Historical Society, New York · H. Elouis?, oils, 1796, Hist. Soc. Penn.

Wayne, Sir Edward Johnson (1902–1990), physician, was born on 3 June 1902 in Leeds, the elder child and only son of William Wayne, chief surveyor to a building society, of Roundhay, Leeds, and his wife, Ellen Rawding, of Leadenham, Lincolnshire. He attended Leeds central high school and then entered Leeds University as Akroyd scholar, graduating with first-class honours in chemistry in 1923. At Manchester University he worked on the intermediary metabolism of the fatty acids with H. S. Raper, obtaining a PhD degree in 1925. It was at this point that his instincts led him to medicine, and he returned to Leeds in 1926 to complete a medical course. He graduated MB ChB in 1929 with first-class honours and was awarded the Hey gold medal, as the most distinguished graduate of the year. In 1932 he married Honora Nancy (*d.* 1992), a teacher of classics and daughter of David Halloran, schoolteacher; they had a son, who became a consultant physician, and a daughter.

In 1931 Wayne had become an assistant in the department of clinical research in University College Hospital, London, under the directorship of Sir Thomas Lewis, and he carried out some of the earliest trials with digoxin and an investigation into angina. In 1934 he was appointed to the chair of pharmacology and therapeutics in the University of Sheffield. He became FRCP in 1937 and MD in 1938. In this pre-war period he coped with his university teaching commitment as well as his clinical duties. He had one lectureship, to which he appointed Hans Krebs, a refugee from Nazi Germany. Krebs completed his work on the citric acid cycle, for which he obtained the Nobel prize.

During the Second World War Wayne's clinical duties were expanded by his appointment as physician to the Children's Hospital, Sheffield, and to the Emergency Medical Service. He also had his private practice. After the war he became once again a full-time professor of therapeutics. He was appointed chairman of the joint formulary committee of the British Medical Association and the Pharmaceutical Society, and later chairman of the British Pharmacopoeia Commission (1958–63), which gave him unrivalled experience in the assessment of drugs. He recruited able young men returning from the armed forces to his department. At last his flair for directing clinical research was able to reach its full potential. His collaboration with his team led to advances in the use of radioiodine in the diagnosis and treatment of thyroid disease, as well as the use of angiography and cardiac catheterization for cardiac disease.

In 1954 Wayne was appointed regius professor of the practice of medicine at Glasgow University, which had a purpose-built clinical research building (the Gardiner Institute) attached to the professorial wards of the Western Infirmary. He was determined to continue his successful run in Sheffield and the Gardiner Institute was the ideal vehicle for his ambitions. From 1953 until his retirement in 1967 he sparked off and encouraged research in a number of areas—in his own field of thyroid disease, cardiovascular disease, osteoporosis, and blood disorders. He developed and encouraged the use of tapes and slide-tapes as ancillaries for clinical teaching. Coming from Sheffield he gradually, but successfully, integrated himself into the life and work of Scottish medicine.

From 1954 to 1967 Wayne was honorary physician to the queen in Scotland and in 1958 he was recruited to the Medical Research Council, becoming chairman of the clinical research board (1960–64). In 1959 he was elected Sims Commonwealth travelling fellow and with his wife visited most of the medical schools in Canada. He was knighted in 1964 and became an honorary DSc of Sheffield in 1967, the year he retired to Chipping Campden in the Cotswolds. After fourteen years he and his wife went to live with their son's family at Lingwood Lodge, Lingwood, near Great Yarmouth.

Wayne was one of the new breed of full-time clinical scientific professors which evolved in the mid-twentieth century. His training as a young man in chemistry, biochemistry, and clinical science, and his appointment to various drug committees, gave him a unique opportunity to perceive and contribute to the therapeutic revolution. His drive and ability to attract younger men of merit allowed him to promote and superintend important advances. He was chairman of the British Medical Association committee on alcohol and road accidents from 1948 and his work on this topic for two decades was responsible for the government's introduction of the blood alcohol limit of 80 mg per 100 ml of blood (Road Safety Act, 1967).

Of medium height, Wayne had a sturdy frame with slender limbs. He had iron grey hair brushed back to show a good forehead, and was strong-jawed and clean shaven until late in life, when he sported a grey beard which finally completed the mellow, venerable image. He was dynamic and his movements were mercurial, matching his quick enquiring mind. He kept those round him on their toes, but he was usually sensitive to their feelings, employing his Yorkshire wit in the most effective way. A man of wide reading, he enjoyed short poems and had a great love of music. Wayne died on 19 August 1990 in the James Paget Hospital, Gorleston, near Great Yarmouth, from heart failure. His ashes were buried in Norwich.

ABRAHAM GOLDBERG, *rev.*

Sources Munk, *Roll* · *BMJ* (22 Sept 1990), 604 · *The Lancet* (13 Oct 1990), 932 · *The Guardian* (22 Aug 1990) · *The Times* (23 Aug 1990) · personal knowledge (1996) · private information (1996) [David J. Wayne, son]
Archives Wellcome L., corresp. and papers | University of Sheffield, corresp. with Hans Krebs | FILM CIBA Foundation Archives
Likenesses portrait, 1966–7, U. Glas. · photograph, repro. in *The Times*
Wealth at death £195,884: probate, 24 April 1991, *CGPLA Eng. & Wales*

Waynflete [Wainfleet, Patten]**, William** (*c.*1400–1486), bishop of Winchester and founder of Magdalen College, Oxford, was the elder son of Richard Patten (also known as Barbour) of Wainfleet, Lincolnshire, and Margery, daughter of William Brereton of Cheshire and Lincolnshire. Little is known of the Patten family, who were of gentry

William Waynflete (*c.*1400–1486), tomb effigy

stock. Richard Patten's younger son, John Waynflete, also entered the church, rising to become dean of Chichester.

Schoolmaster at Winchester and Eton William Waynflete's early career, already obscure, has been further complicated by confusion with a number of near contemporaries of the same name. Nothing is known of his early career before his ordination as acolyte, and then subdeacon, at Holbeck in Lincolnshire in 1425. Clear and unequivocal documentation of his career only begins in June 1430, when he became headmaster of Winchester College. It is likely that Waynflete was educated at Oxford, probably attached to one of the ephemeral halls of the university—none of the attempts to link him with any of the colleges can be substantiated. There is no record of either his arts degree or subsequent theology degree; the first reference to him as a bachelor of theology dates from September 1443, after he had become provost of Eton College.

Throughout the 1430s Waynflete taught at Winchester College, where he attracted the attention of Henry Beaufort (d. 1447), bishop of Winchester, who presented him to the mastership of the small hospital of St Mary Magdalen near Winchester. Then in 1441, after a visit of Henry VI to

Winchester College, Waynflete entered royal service, initially in some undefined role connected with the development of the embryonic royal foundation of Eton College. This move to Eton College marked a vital turning point in his career, bringing him into regular communication with the king and other members of the court circle. In March 1442 he replaced Henry Sever (d. 1471) as provost of Eton. In this role he was highly influential in guiding the development of Eton College and King's College, Cambridge, along the lines of William Wykeham's dual foundation of Winchester College and New College, Oxford, and was a prime mover in the making of the *Amicabilis concordia* (1444) between the four institutions. He also oversaw the school's physical development, an interest he retained after leaving Eton, and from 1467 until his death was a generous patron and benefactor to the college, concentrating his resources on the building and decoration of its chapel.

Bishop of Winchester In 1447 Waynflete was promoted to the see of Winchester, in succession to his one-time patron, Henry Beaufort. Closely directed by the king, whose letter recommended him as 'a notable clerc and a substantial personne' (Chandler, 299), the cathedral chapter elected Waynflete on 15 April. In a letter from the prior to the pope, advancing the reasons for the convent's choice of prelate, he is described as:

> a man whose discretion, knowledge and blameless way of life are to be commended … in addition his prudence, both in spiritual and secular affairs and his remarkable virtues and abilities will enable him to defend the rights of their church. (*Register of St Swithun*, 101)

Consecrated bishop in the incomplete chapel of Eton College on 30 July 1447, his installation in Winchester Cathedral did not take place until January 1449. Waynflete was an unexpected choice to succeed Beaufort at Winchester, the richest see in England, and the fact that he succeeded Beaufort with apparent ease is proof of his considerable skills as a political manoeuvrer. Nevertheless, he was unusual in that his background was that of a schoolmaster, who lacked either experience in government service or previous church preferments (saving the mastership of St Mary Magdalen Hospital).

Waynflete proved a conscientious bishop. Well supported by his circle of administrators, direction of affairs came clearly from the top. Policies and actions were the result of his personal initiative. His patronage within the diocese shows him favouring particularly Wykehamists and boys he had known at Eton. His protégés were highly educated, a number with theological training; men who were primarily administrators in either the diocesan or educational sphere. Commonly resident in his diocese Waynflete attacked non-residence by others. But in neither parochial affairs nor those of religious houses was he an innovator or reformer. In 1476 the relics of St Swithun were translated to a new shrine in the cathedral, in Waynflete's presence. He gave much attention to the administration of his extensive episcopal estates, thereby sometimes stirring up his tenants against him. In August 1461 his tenants at East Meon seized and imprisoned him, and

then petitioned the king for relief from episcopal exactions. Waynflete was responsible for a number of innovations in estate management, in particular the appointment of a professional auditor from 1448, followed in 1454 by a major change in the physical form of the ministers' accounts, from pipe rolls into book form, which greatly facilitated consultation of the accounts. His annual income from his estates was over £4000.

The foundation of Magdalen College, Oxford In 1448 Waynflete set in motion the foundation of Magdalen Hall in Oxford. On 20 August a foundation charter was issued, which established a hall with a president, John Hornley, and fifty graduate scholars. His reasons for establishing Magdalen Hall were set out as the not uncommon ones of wishing to stamp out heresy and provide well-educated and suitable clergy to serve in parishes. Magdalen Hall was refounded as Magdalen College in 1458, and a new charter reserved to the bishop of Winchester complete authority over his foundation—an authority that Waynflete himself exercised actively until the end of his life. The dedication was a reflection of Waynflete's devotion to St Mary Magdalen, dating from his early promotion to the Winchester hospital dedicated to that saint. Between 1455 and 1486 he purchased or acquired property worth about £600 a year for the endowment of Magdalen College, in addition to the property of the hospital of St John the Baptist, Oxford, which formed the nucleus of the collegiate endowment and which was itself worth about £75 yearly. Waynflete retained control of the purse strings and funded the college directly from several of his temporal estates. His interest extended to the details and progress of collegiate buildings which from 1467 were being constructed on the site, using masons and artisans he employed elsewhere. Nor did Waynflete restrict himself to his own resources. Sir John Fastolf (d. 1459) nominated Waynflete as executor of his will, a trust that both involved him in prolonged controversies on behalf of the Paston family and enabled him to enhance the endowment for Magdalen College. Fastolf had intended a collegiate foundation at Caister in Norfolk, but in 1474 Waynflete, disregarding Fastolf's own stipulations for alternative provision, and aided by a dispensation from Pope Sixtus IV (r. 1471–84), diverted the endowment to his own college of Magdalen, where Fastolf was to be commemorated by the establishment of Fastolf fellows.

In the early 1480s Waynflete appointed a new president, Richard Mayew, and promulgated statutes for his college, enshrining his ideas for the college's development. Administratively the statutes drew on those of William Wykeham (d. 1404) for New College, Oxford; innovation came with their educational provisions, in particular with the division of members of the foundation into demys and fellows, and the arrangements for lectureships. The bishop's personal concern with the teaching of grammar was also reflected in his foundation of two grammar schools, one at his birthplace in the mid-1460s, the other attached to the Oxford college—Magdalen College School, which was flourishing by 1479. In the last years of his life Waynflete was twice successful in bringing his college to the attention of the reigning sovereign; both Edward IV and Richard III visited the college in the company of the bishop, and were lavishly entertained.

Involvement in politics Waynflete was essentially a public rather than a political figure, a man loyal to the person of Henry VI but whose ties with the political interests within the court circle were loose. There is no record that he was ever a royal chaplain, but he had a close personal relationship with the king while at Eton College and afterwards. In the 'King's Will', the document containing the arrangements made by Henry VI for his foundations of Eton College and King's College, Cambridge, Waynflete was given overall responsibility for their implementation, the king referring to 'his high trough and fervent zele whiche at all tymes he hath hadde and hath unto my weel and which I have founde and proved in hym' (muniments, Eton College, 39/78).

Political activities were not Waynflete's principal concern, but as bishop of Winchester between 1447 and 1486 he held an important see throughout a period of considerable strife, and in such circumstances he could hardly avoid being caught up in national affairs. Although he was not seen by contemporaries as an undesirable influence on Henry VI, he was closely identified with the Lancastrian monarchy. His most active involvement in politics came during the 1450s. During Cade's revolt in 1450 he was one of the emissaries sent to persuade the rebels to seek pardons, and he later negotiated with them in St Margaret's Church in Southwark, in his own diocese. At Dartford in March 1452, in an atmosphere of growing political tension, Waynflete went with Lord Stourton and Henry, Lord Bourchier (d. 1483), in an attempt to dissuade Richard, duke of York (d. 1460), from hasty action. In October 1453, following the lapse of Henry VI into insanity, Waynflete baptized the new-born Edward, prince of Wales (d. 1471), and on 23 March following he led a delegation to the king seeking advice (without success) as to who should be promoted to the archbishopric of Canterbury and the chancellorship, both vacant since the death of John Kemp on 22 March. As one of the proposed members of the protectorate council headed by the duke of York during Henry's illness, Waynflete expressed a preference for a rota of the bishops nominated as councillors, since, he said, while he was prepared to serve for a period, 'his consyence [concerning his diocesan interests and involvements elsewhere] … wold not suffer hym contynuyaly to serve' (Griffiths, 80). However, council records show he attended frequently, and after Henry VI's recovery, in January 1455, Waynflete was one of the first lords to visit him, according to the Paston letters.

Waynflete came to the forefront of the royal administration with his appointment as chancellor on 11 October 1456. He remained loyal to Henry VI, so that in 1459 Friar John Brackley wrote to the Pastons concerning him, 'The chauncelere is not good to these lordys [Yorkists] for he feryth the Erle of Marche wil clayme the inheritauns'

(*Paston Letters*, no. 582). But he tried to counteract the growing enmity between Lancastrians and Yorkists, in particular by organizing a 'love day' in March 1458, and his sermon preached at the opening of the Coventry parliament, on 20 November 1459, only weeks after the battle of Bloreheath (23 September) and the rout of the duke of York and his allies at Ludford Bridge (13 October), on the text, 'Let peace and unity be given unto you', reflects what he saw as the aim of his endeavours whether as bishop or chancellor. Waynflete resigned the chancellorship on 7 July 1460, the day before the battle of Northampton, and then came to an accord with the Yorkists, who now had possession of the king. In November he appointed Humphrey Stafford (d. 1469), a supporter of the earl of March, to be constable of the strategically important castle of Taunton, which was owned by the bishops of Winchester. This obtained for him a letter addressed by the new Yorkist administration to Pope Pius II (1458–64), probably intended to protect Waynflete's position against the activities of Francesco Coppini, the papal legate in England. In the politically crucial early months of 1461 he remained detached (or perhaps excluded) from political affairs, residing at his manor in Taunton, but he returned to his Southwark residence in time to attend the coronation of Edward IV on 28 June 1461, at which, according to Jean Waurin, he accepted the new king on behalf of all the prelates, barons, nobles, and commoners.

Other Lancastrian sympathizers were to be politically active under Edward IV, and his earlier loyalties would have been of little disadvantage to him had Waynflete wished to follow suit. Instead he largely withdrew from politics, although he did attend parliaments and fulfil such necessary public duties as commissioner of the peace and *ex officio* prelate of the Order of the Garter. At Henry VI's readeption in 1470 Waynflete's role was restricted to escorting the king from his place of imprisonment in the Tower and conducting him to the bishop of London's residence by St Paul's. After Edward IV's return Waynflete was granted a general pardon on 30 May 1471. He was not one of the bishops who suffered a brief imprisonment, and his relationship with Edward IV was subsequently cordial; he acted as godfather to Edward's youngest daughter, Bridget, when she was baptized at Eltham Palace on 11 November 1480. The following year, in September 1481, the king visited Magdalen College.

Patron of learning and architecture Waynflete remained interested in the teaching of grammar throughout his career. In the early 1480s a revolution in grammar teaching began in England, spread by means of the printing press, and partly based on books by contemporary Italian grammarians. Waynflete was the patron of John Anwykyll (d. 1487), headmaster of Magdalen College School, and author of the most important of the early grammatical works emanating from Magdalen, *Compendium totius grammaticae*, printed at Oxford in 1483. In a dedicatory preface by Pietro Carmeliano, Waynflete is praised as patron of the work:

> Fame will sing such great praises of you, William, most celebrated father who is now bishop of the church of

Winchester, and will celebrate for you as long as the steady pole-star is in its stable axis, for the author John wrote this book at your persuasion, whence your fame will be for ever. (Anwykyll, 1)

Among the several men in Waynflete's household who were interested in humanist studies, Thomas Chaundler (d. 1490) stands out as one of the leading English scholars of his day, and Waynflete himself was recognized by his contemporaries as an important figure in English humanistic circles. In the early 1480s Lorenzo da Savona, the leading Italian rhetorician in England at this time, dedicated his *Triumphus amoris Jesus Christi* (1485) to Waynflete and prefaced it with a eulogy of him. Waynflete was also an active patron of bookbinding. Support for printing can also be seen in his association with the earliest known printed indulgence to be issued by members of the English episcopate (c.1479–1483).

Waynflete was an active patron of building, on an impressive range and scale. He extended the Winchester episcopal palaces at Farnham and Esher, and built a substantial brick grammar school at Wainfleet. In his cathedral church at Winchester he constructed a lavish chantry and may also have been the patron of the magnificent great screen of the cathedral. The nucleus of Magdalen College, Oxford, was designed and completed in his lifetime under his watchful eye. In addition he oversaw the completion of two projects begun by other patrons—Eton College chapel (including the grisaille frescos) and Tattershall College in Lincolnshire, the latter founded by Ralph, Lord Cromwell (d. 1456). Of particular importance was his role in the dissemination of the use of brick in southern England, and he also set an influential example for the later use of brick for domestic purposes.

Waynflete retained links with his native Lincolnshire throughout his life, although from the late 1420s he never lived there. His kin were still there, and Waynflete's association with the county can be seen in a number of ways throughout his career: as a benefactor to the town of Wainfleet and its inhabitants; as executor to Ralph, Lord Cromwell, and thus the overseer of the completion of Tattershall College; as co-founder of a chantry in Coningsby; and by the promotion of Lincolnshire men within his circle after he became a bishop.

Waynflete possessed an extensive library, but the titles of few of his books are known. His will does not mention any books, or, indeed, any personal possessions. In 1483 Waynflete had transferred books in cartloads to Magdalen College, Oxford, reputedly 800 volumes in all. Among the few that can be identified in the college library today are two works of Albertus Magnus, a collection of sermons designed to be read in Lent, and a copy written in a humanist hand of Jacobus de Cessolis, *Liber de ludo scacchorum*. He also possessed a Bible, said to have belonged to St Louis of France, which had been bequeathed to him by John Stanbury, bishop of Hereford (d. 1474). He had also received a book as a bequest from Sir John Fastolf, and Fastolf's secretary presented him with several books in an unsuccessful attempt to win his patronage, including a copy of Boccaccio's *De casibus virorum*

illustrium and a copy of an English translation of Cicero's *De senectute*. A member of Waynflete's household may have been responsible for the initial compilation of BL, Add. MS 60577, which includes a poem presented to Waynflete as bishop of Winchester, as well as some Middle English verse and prose, sermons, verse alphabets, medical recipes, and a lapidary.

William Waynflete measures up well against his contemporaries on the episcopal bench, not least for the range of his interests—diocesan, educational, architectural, scholarly. His experiences as a schoolmaster dominated his life, for his success at Eton made possible his promotion to the episcopate, and afterwards the resources—financial, political, and administrative—placed at his disposal by his position as bishop of Winchester were ploughed back into education. Waynflete's last months were a period of physical decline. In December 1485 he returned from Southwark to Bishops Waltham, Hampshire, and on 26 April 1486 drew up his will, which was conventional in form. He bequeathed his goods for the cost of his funeral and to members of his household, the residue for pious purposes and to relieve the necessities of his college. He died at Bishops Waltham on 11 August 1486. He had already constructed a majestic chantry chapel in Winchester Cathedral, dedicated to his spiritual patron, Mary Magdalen, with a tomb therein waiting to receive his body. The tomb contains an effigy of the bishop and his arms, which included lilies drawn from the arms of Eton College. There is also a representation of the bishop, as a small kneeling figure in episcopal dress, on the tomb of his father, originally in Wainfleet church, now in Magdalen College chapel.   VIRGINIA DAVIS

Sources V. Davis, *William Waynflete: bishop and educationalist* (1993) • R. Chandler, *The life of William Waynflete, bishop of Winchester* (1911) • Emden, *Oxf.* • J. Greatrex, ed., *The register of the common seal of the priory of St Swithun, Winchester* (1979) • N. Davis, ed., *Paston letters and papers of the fifteenth century*, 2 vols. (1971–6) • muniments, Eton • Winchester College muniments • H. Anstey, ed., *Epistolae academicae Oxon.*, 2 vols., OHS, 35–6 (1898) • *Memorials of the reign of Henry VI: official correspondence of Thomas Bekynton, secretary to King Henry VI and bishop of Bath and Wells*, ed. G. Williams, 2 vols., Rolls Series, 56 (1872) • *CPR* • *CClR* • N. H. Nicolas, ed., *Proceedings and ordinances of the privy council of England*, 7 vols., RC, 26 (1834–7) • *CEPR letters* • I. Fenlon and E. Wilson, eds., *The Winchester anthology* (1981) [BL MS Add. 60577] • *Statutes of the colleges of Oxford*, 3 vols. (1853), vol. 2 • V. Davis, 'William Waynflete and the Wars of the Roses', *Southern History*, 11 (1989), 1–22 • W. D. Simpson, ed., *The building accounts of Tattershall Castle, 1434–1472*, Lincoln RS, 55 (1960) • W. H. St J. Hope, *Report on Bishop Waynflete's chapel in Winchester Cathedral* (privately printed, Burlington House, 1898) • C. Richmond, 'A letter of 19 April 1483 from John Gigur to William Wainfleet', *Historical Research*, 65 (1992), 112–16 • R. Brown, H. M. Colvin, and A. J. Taylor, eds., *The history of the king's works*, 1–2 (1963) • H. C. Maxwell Lyte, *A history of Eton College, 1440–1898*, 3rd edn (1899) • J. de Wavrin [J. de Waurin], *Anchiennes croniques d'Engleterre*, ed. E. Dupont, 3 vols. (1858–63) • R. A. Griffiths, 'The king's council and the first protectorate of the duke of York, 1453–1454', *EngHR*, 99 (1984), 67–82 • J. Anwykyll, *Compendium totius grammaticae* (1483)

Archives Hants. RO, episcopal register • Magd. Oxf., estate papers, college muniments | BL, Add. MS 60577

Likenesses R. Greenbury, oils, 1638, Magd. Oxf.; version, New College, Oxford • effigy (on his father's tomb), Magd. Oxf. • oils, Magd. Oxf.; version, New College, Oxford • stained-glass window,

Magd. Oxf. · tomb effigy, Winchester Cathedral, Hampshire [*see illus.*]
Wealth at death see will, Chandler, *Life*, 379–88

Weale, Charlotte Julia (1829–1918), religious philanthropist, was born in 1829, probably on 9 December, the daughter of James Weale and his wife, Susan (*née* Vesien). She had a sister, Henrietta, and a brother, William Henry (1832–1917), a convert to Roman Catholicism, two of whose daughters became Roman Catholic nuns. One of her godparents was Hugh James Rose, the leading orthodox high-churchman. Confirmed by Bishop Blomfield in 1846 at St Marylebone, where her early years were spent, Charlotte Weale was a lifelong Anglican. She developed strong Tractarian leanings; Pusey, whom she revered, was among her friends. At the age of nineteen she went to live at Whitchurch Canonicorum, Dorset, to be under the guidance of the high-church priest William Palmer (1803–1885), an old family friend. Whitchurch remained her home until her death.

On 6 February 1850 Weale went to Clewer to spend six months assisting Mariquita Tennant in the 'rescue' work she had begun among women and girls in the nearby garrison town of Windsor. During that time she made her mark. Thanks to her eye for detail a very full picture of the Clewer House of Mercy has been preserved, including verbatim case histories of the women to whom Tennant ministered. She recorded the daily routine, diet, and spiritual teaching, the relations with benefactors including Gladstone, and Tennant's attempts, subsequently carried out by her successor, Harriet Monsell, to found a religious sisterhood. Weale was the ideal assistant for Tennant (who called her Sister Dorotea), a rather eccentric Spanish widow whose command of English was as poor as Weale's was accomplished.

At Whitchurch, to which she returned in September 1850, Weale is known to have employed women as servants after they left the Clewer House of Mercy. She was a generous benefactor within the parish, donating in 1856 more than £200 towards the restoration and extension of the church at Stanton St Gabriel. She founded a House of Mercy for girls and women in Birmingham, and recommended and paid for inmates at the House of Charity in Soho, founded to assist the 'needy poor'. Her work at Clewer had brought her into contact with Elizabeth Herbert (wife of Sir Sidney Herbert), whose interest in emigration may have inspired her visit to New Zealand in 1860–61, where she made some friendships among the Maori. Travelling in the steerage class so as to gain an insight into the conditions experienced by emigrants, she was reported to have survived a shipwreck.

Weale's last years were spent as an invalid, almost totally blind and deaf, nursed by her companion of thirty-five years, Miss K. Sutton. She received holy communion three hours before her death at Church House, Whitchurch Canonicorum, on 27 December 1918. She was buried in the churchyard at Stanton St Gabriel. Her will (dated 16 December 1914) included legacies to Maori missions, Maori clergy, and the Anglican poor of the parish of Whitchurch. Sharing the aversion to Catholic converts held by

Charlotte Julia Weale (1829–1918), by John Deane Hilton, 1882

some Tractarians, she requested that no Roman Catholics, including her relatives, be permitted to set foot in her home after her death.   VALERIE BONHAM

Sources *Whitechurch Canonicorum with Marshwood and Stanton St. Gabriel* [parish magazine] (Jan 1919) · *Bridport News* (3 Jan 1919) · V. Bonham, *A place in life: the Clewer House of Mercy, 1849–83* (1992) · will, Principal Registry of the Family Division, London
Archives Community of St John Baptist, Clewer, Berkshire, archives relating to foundation, daily routine, and lives of the penitents at Clewer House of Mercy
Likenesses J. D. Hilton, photograph, 1882 (in old age), Convent of St John the Baptist, Clewer, Hatch Lane, Windsor, Berkshire [*see illus.*]
Wealth at death £1521 8s. 2d.: probate, 14 March 1919, *CGPLA Eng. & Wales*

Weale, John (1791–1862), publisher and writer on architecture, began work as an errand-boy to Thomas King, a bookseller of Tavistock Street, Covent Garden, London. Nothing is known of his parentage or life prior to this, but, suffering mistreatment at the hands of King, he subsequently moved to the nearby establishment of George Priestley, a bookseller and publisher at 5 High Street, St Giles-in-the-Fields, and he continued to work for Priestley's widow, Mary, after the former's death about 1812. He was taken into partnership about 1819; while neither of the Priestleys had published extensively, Weale's interest in architecture soon led to a rapid expansion of the firm's activity in this area. Priestley and Weale became one of the leading architectural publishers of the period, although it was not particularly financially successful.

Moreover, Weale's evident ability attracted the attention of the pre-eminent architectural bookseller and publisher Isaac Taylor, who instructed his executors to assist Weale in purchasing his business at 59 High Holborn, London, on his death, which occurred in 1834. Weale accepted the offer, and rapidly expanded his business, publishing extensively on all aspects of architecture and engineering. According to his *Statistical Notices of Works on the Fine and the Constructive Arts* (1859; 2nd edn, 1861), he expended over £200,000 on the production of books during his forty years as a publisher, although not with great profit to himself.

Weale had a hand in suggesting and improving many of the books he published, and he displayed considerable ability as the author or editor of numerous works on a wide range of architectural and technical subjects. Most noteworthy of his works was the elaborately illustrated and widely praised *Divers Works of Early Masters in Christian Decoration* (1846), which earned him a gold medal from the king of Belgium in 1847. In addition, his *Rudimentary Dictionary of Terms used in Architecture, Building, and Engineering* (1849–50) elicited favourable reviews, and reached a fifth edition in 1876. This volume became part of what was arguably Weale's greatest publishing success, namely his Rudimentary Series, begun in 1848, which comprised more than 130 scientific and technical works, generally written by eminent men, and usually published at 1s. per volume. Weale invested over £48,000 in the series during the thirteen years before he sold it to James Sprent Virtue, and the venture was a considerable financial success, with sales of some volumes reaching 40,000 copies by 1854. Weale subsequently published an educational and a classical series in a similar format, these works together constituting an important innovation in cheap educational literature.

Weale died of bronchitis at his home at 19 Canterbury Villas, Maida Vale, London, on 18 December 1862. The business was continued by his wife, Sarah Isabella Hollis Jackson Weale, for the benefit of their still young family of four daughters and four sons, until 1864, when it was taken over by their second son, James Watt Weale (*b.* 1843).   JONATHAN R. TOPHAM

Sources *The Bookseller* (28 Feb 1863) · *The Bookseller* (30 April 1863) · P. A. H. Brown, *London publishers and printers, c.1800–1870* (1982) · J. Weale, *Statistical notices of works on the fine and the constructive arts*, 2nd edn (1861) · J. Archer, *The literature of British domestic architecture, 1715–1842* (1985) · J. Weale, will, proved, 17 April 1863, PRO · 'Literature for the people', *The Times* (9 Feb 1854) · *BL cat.* · *GM*, 3rd ser., 14 (1863), 246 · 'Weale's rudimentary series', *The Bookseller* (26 June 1861) · *The Times* (5 June 1847) · E. Harris and N. Savage, *British architectural books and writers, 1556–1785* (1990) · Boase, *Mod. Eng. biog.* · d. cert.

Wealth at death under £6000: probate, 17 April 1863, *CGPLA Eng. & Wales*

Weale, William Henry James (1832–1917), art historian, was born on 8 March 1832 at 19 York Buildings, Marylebone, Middlesex, the second of the four children of James Weale (*d.* 1838), librarian, and his wife, Susan Caroline de Vezian (*d.* 1855). His father was not the London bookseller John Weale (*d.* 1862), as the *Dictionary of National Biography*

assumed, but James Weale, secretary and librarian to John Holroyd, later first earl of Sheffield. Weale's father amassed a fine collection of books, and was acquainted with Edward Gibbon and Voltaire; although he died when Weale was only six years old, his antiquarianism made a lasting impression on his son.

The young James Weale attended King's College School, London from 1843 to 1848, intending to continue his education at Christ Church, Oxford. This plan had to be abandoned when, in 1849, he was converted to Roman Catholicism, under the influence of the writings of A. W. N. Pugin and John Henry Newman. Weale took up residence with other young converts in Islington, London, while working as a clerk in the Office of Woods and Forests (1848–51). Formative experiences followed in 1851 when he became master at the Catholic poor-school in Islington, and within weeks was arrested for flogging a boy named John Farrell. Weale was imprisoned for three months at Cold Bath Fields following an unfair trial, prejudiced by press coverage and anti-Catholic debate. A petition to the home secretary for his release was refused in a printed circular. Happily this affair urged Weale's career in new directions: he left London for two years and travelled through Belgium, beginning his lifelong study of early Flemish arts and crafts.

On 30 August 1854, Weale married Helena Amelia Walton (1838–1921) at the Catholic church of St John the Evangelist, Islington: it proved to be a happy union, which produced six sons and five daughters. An inheritance in 1855, on the death of his mother, gave Weale financial independence, and in the same year he and his wife settled in Bruges, where a lively community of British Catholics was united in the promotion of neo-Gothic architecture and Christian art. Weale continued to gather evidence on early Flemish painting; his *Catalogue du musée de l'académie de Bruges* (1861) and *Notes sur Jean Van Eyck* (1861) established his expertise. They were followed by the organization of two major exhibitions—a highly innovative practice—at Malines (1864) and Bruges (1867), with Weale even sleeping on the premises to protect the art works entrusted to his care. He provided scholarly catalogues for each exhibition, drawing attention in Belgium and elsewhere to a largely neglected artistic heritage. He also petitioned fiercely for the conservation of buildings and monuments in Bruges in the face of brutal modernization. His efforts were initially met with hostility, but recognition came with election to the Commission royale d'art et d'archéologie in 1860 and to the Commission royale des monuments et des sites in 1861. Weale's residence in Bruges was characterized by prodigious activity, including the foundation of two antiquarian societies—the Gilde de Saint-Thomas et de Saint-Luc in 1863 and the Société Archéologique in 1865—and three periodicals. Of these, *Le Beffroi* (1863) is noteworthy as the first art historical periodical concerning Flanders, combining archival evidence with critical commentary. Weale also published widely in the *Journal des Beaux Arts*, the *Gazette des Beaux Arts*, the *Messager des Sciences et des Arts*, and *The Athenaeum*. Yet he was never fully accepted into the official life of Bruges, partly because of his combative nature, evident in disputes with many of his contemporaries. When his application to become archivist of Bruges was rejected in 1878 Weale returned to London with his family, to a large house at 29 Crescent Grove, Clapham Common, where he spent the following decade cataloguing various collections of printed manuscripts.

In 1890 Weale became keeper of the National Art Library, South Kensington. The post was doubtless intended by the library to fund a relaxation of Weale's labours, pending his retirement. Weale evidently thought otherwise; his impact on the institution merited his dismissal in 1897, following a meeting with the select committee on the museums of the Department of Science and Art. The official report concluded, 'the Late Keeper of the Art Library has been too active a reformer, has been too frank to the Committee, and has done too much for the benefit of his readers and the public' (Brockwell, 204). This proved fortuitous, for Weale was finally able to collate his many notebooks on early Flemish painting. His painstaking reconstructions of artists' lives bore fruit in *Hans Memlinc* (1901), *Gerard David* (1905), and, most importantly, *Hubert and John Van Eyck* (1908), later revised as *The Van Eycks and their Art* (1912). He also catalogued a further exhibition at Bruges (1902).

Weale was a formidable personality, 'skilled neither in the art of concealing his opinions nor in paying deference to official superiors with whom he disagreed' (Mitchell, 243). His physical appearance was perhaps at odds with his temperament; his long beard, shuffling stance, and bespectacled peering belied a fiery temper. This manifested itself memorably during Weale's keepership at South Kensington, when he chased a purveyor of obscene prints from the reading rooms, shouting in rage. His works remain invaluable: his rediscovery of early Flemish painting was achieved through archival research and first-hand observation, informed by a lively mistrust of received opinion and resulting in the correction of many previous errors. Other than a modest civil-list pension in 1913, arranged by loyal friends, he received little recognition in Britain for his work. Far greater was that awarded him in later life by Belgium, where he was appointed an honourable member of the Royal Flemish Academy in 1887, an associate of the Royal Academy of Belgium in 1896, an honourable member of the Royal Academy of Fine Arts, Antwerp in 1901, and an officer of the order of Leopold. A plaque now commemorates his former home in the rue St Georges in Bruges. Weale died at his home at 29 Crescent Grove, Clapham Common, on 26 April 1917, and was buried at St Mary Magdalene, Mortlake, near Richmond.   JENNY GRAHAM

Sources L. van Biervliet, *Leven en werk van W. H. James Weale, een engels kunsthistoricus in Vlaanderen in de 19de eeuw* (1991) · M. W. Brockwell, 'W. H. James Weale, the pioneer', *The Library*, 5th ser., 6 (1951–2), 200–11 · H. P. Mitchell, *Burlington Magazine*, 30 (1917), 241–3 · *The Times* (28 April 1917), 3 · F. Oakeley, *Statement of facts relative to the case of Mr. William Weale, master of the poor-school at Islington* (1851) · [J. M. Capes], 'Protestant justice and royal clemency', *The Rambler*, 9 (1852), 79–84 · J. J. Delaney and J. E. Tobin, *Dictionary of Catholic biography* (Garden City, NY, 1961) · F. R. Miles, ed., *King's College School: a register of pupils in the school … 1831–1866* (1974), 338 · *The letters and diaries of John Henry Newman*, ed. C. S. Dessain and others, [31 vols.] (1961–), vol. 14, p. 436 · *DNB* · F. Haskell, *History and its images* (1993), 452–65

Archives Downside Abbey, near Bath, archive · Provinciale Bibliotheek en Cultuurarchief and Stadsbibliotheek, Bruges, archive · V&A, MSS | V&A, MS 3461-1948 · V&A, MS L 2524-1951

Likenesses photograph, 1904, repro. in van Biervliet, *Leven en werk van W. H. James Weale* · portrait, repro. in van Biervliet, *Leven en werk van W. H. James Weale*

Wealth at death £1803 2s. 4d.: probate, 21 June 1917, *CGPLA Eng. & Wales*

Weamys, Anna (*fl.* 1650–1651), author, was probably born in the 1630s and was possibly the child of Dr Ludowick Weames (*d.* 1659), a Church of England clergyman whose living of Lambourne, Essex, was sequestered and given to a puritan minister in the 1640s. Little is known about the life and family connections of Anna Weamys; even her name is derived from secondary sources.

Weamys has been identified as the author of the prose romance *A Continuation of Sir Philip Sydney's Arcadia* (1651). Although the title-page of this volume distinguishes the author only as 'Mrs A. W.', a letter from James Howell, in his *Epistolae Ho-elianae* (1650), supports the ascription of the work to Weamys. In a letter 'To Dr Weames', Howell offers his thanks for a gift of a 'continuance of Sir Philip Sidney's *Arcadia*' written by Weames's daughter. Howell saw Weamys's *Arcadia* in manuscript, and offered the father a commendatory poem for the daughter's publication. His poem, included in the published text, praised 'Mistress A. W.', claiming that 'some sparks of Sidney's soul' had inspired the young female author. Weamys's dedication of the work to members of the Pierrepont family and her father's relationship with James Howell suggests a connection to royalist literary and political circles. During the interregnum, many authors used the prose romance genre to express royalist sympathies. Weamys picks up several story lines left unfinished in Sidney's work, primarily love stories which were left unresolved, and brings them to the traditional romance ending: marriage. There is no information about Weamys's life after the publication of her *Arcadia*.   JANE COLLINS

Sources P. Cullen, 'Introduction', in A. Weamys, *A continuation of Sir Philip Sidney's Arcadia*, ed. P. Cullen (1994) · J. Howell, *Epistolae Ho-elianae*, 2nd edn (1650) · E. Arber, ed., *The term catalogues, 1668–1709*, 3 vols. (privately printed, London, 1903–6), vol. 2 · *Fasti Angl.* (Hardy) · P. Cullen, 'Anna Weamys', *Encyclopedia of British women writers* (1998) · Venn, *Alum. Cant.*

Weare, Meshech (1713–1786), revolutionary politician and judge in America, was born on 16 January 1713 in Hampton (after 1726 Hampton Falls), New Hampshire, America, the eleventh child and youngest son of Nathaniel Weare, judge and politician, and his wife, Mary Wait. Growing up in one of the leading families of New Hampshire, Weare enjoyed the greatest privileges of colonial American life. In 1731 he entered Harvard College, where, after an initial phase of laziness and suffering the faculty's admonishments for playing at cards and dice, he excelled in his studies. After completing his AB in 1735, he taught at the Exeter School and continued his study of divinity, taking the MA course in 1738. He returned to Hampton Falls and on 20 July 1738 married Elizabeth (*d.* 1745), daughter of Samuel Shaw and his wife, Esther Bahelder, prominent figures in Hampton Falls. They had two children before Elizabeth's death in 1745. On 11 December the following year, Weare married Mehitable, daughter of Captain John Wainwright and his wife, Hanna Redford. With her, Weare had a further eight children. Two successful marriages and an inheritance from his father made Weare one of the wealthiest men in New Hampshire.

Although he abandoned any aspirations for ordination, Weare was a staunch Congregationalist and member of the First Congregational Society of Hampton Falls. He was known to give the occasional sermon, and served as a lay delegate at ordinations and ecclesiastical councils and regularly represented the parish in its lawsuits. Weare led the effort to block Presbyterians' attempts for legal exemption from the town's taxes that supported the Congregationalist church—a situation that became so contentious that the Presbyterians split from Hampton Falls to create their own town, Seabrook, in 1768.

Weare's career in public office began soon after his return to Hampton Falls in 1738. In 1739 he was elected the town's moderator. The following year he was elected a selectman—a position he held until the outbreak of the American War of Independence. He filled the seat positions left vacant by his father's death in the New Hampshire general court, as a judge and a colonel in the militia. In the general court, Weare excelled as an option on which the warring Wentworth and Waldron political factions could compromise. He held a series of lesser offices before being elected speaker in 1752, a position he held until he left the general court three years later. He resumed his seat in 1762 and assumed the position of house clerk. Weare has been described as moderate, but he nevertheless joined the extra-legal New Hampshire provincial congress in the summer of 1774, serving on virtually every major committee and presiding over a number of sessions. He led New Hampshire's government throughout the War of Independence, organizing the fragile, fledgeling revolutionary government and facing the crises brought on by nine years of war. He chaired the all-important committee of safety, which controlled the militia, trade, and tax collection, and could even appoint delegates to the continental congress. He was a member of the council, the legislature's upper house, and served as its president for the entire war, which, in the absence of an executive, made him the highest office-holder. From 1776 to 1782 he was also the chief justice. Weare clearly had the people's trust. As one observer remarked in 1779, he had 'acquired so much popularity his countrymen expected salvation from his wisdom or arm alone' (Daniell, *Experiment in Republicanism*, 127–8).

After seeing his state through the war, Weare's final act was to secure the future of its government, pushing for a new constitution. The second attempt succeeded, and he was elected the state's first president under it in 1784. He retired the following year, and died shortly afterwards at his home in Hampton Falls on 14 January 1786. He was survived by his wife, Mehitable. TROY O. BICKHAM

Sources J. R. Daniell, *Experiment in republicanism: New Hampshire politics and the American Revolution, 1741–1794* (1970) · J. R. Daniell, 'Weare, Meshech', *ANB* · J. R. Daniell, *Colonial New Hampshire: a history* (1981) · C. K. Shipton, *Sibley's Harvard graduates: biographical sketches of those who attended Harvard College*, 9 (1956) · R. F. Upton, *Revolutionary New Hampshire* (1936) · N. Bouton and others, eds., *Provincial and state papers: documents and records relating to the province of New Hampshire*, 40 vols. (1867–1943), vols. 6–10, 17–21

Wearg, Sir Clement (1686?–1726), lawyer and politician, was born in Kensington, London, the eldest son of Thomas Wearg of the Inner Temple and his wife, Mary Fletcher of Ely. He was baptized at the church of St Botolph, Aldersgate, the parish where his grandfather, Thomas Wearg, a wealthy merchant, lived. He was admitted to Peterhouse, Cambridge, in 1705, and became a student at the Inner Temple on 25 November 1706. In 1711 he was called to the bar; he became a bencher in 1723, a reader in 1724, and treasurer in 1725.

Wearg was a zealous whig and protestant. In 1722 he contested, without success, the borough of Shaftesbury in Dorset. He acted as the counsel for the crown in the prosecutions of the Jacobites Christopher Layer and Bishop Francis Atterbury, and his replies, made with Thomas Reeve, to Atterbury's defence in court were published in 1723. On 1 October of the same year he married Elizabeth (*d.* 1746), the daughter of Sir James *Montagu, chief baron of the exchequer. Following the resignation of Sir Robert Raymond as attorney-general, he was appointed solicitor-general on 3 February 1724. He was knighted three days later, and was returned for the Godolphin parliamentary borough of Helston on 10 March. While solicitor-general, Wearg managed the impeachment of Lord Chancellor Macclesfield (the attorney-general, Sir Philip Yorke, declined to undertake the impeachment, as a friend of Macclesfield), and also gave legal support to Lord Bolingbroke's petition for the restoration of his estates. He died of a violent fever on 6 April 1726 and was buried, in accordance with the request in his will, in the Temple churchyard, under a plain raised tomb, on 12 April. His oratory has been described as that of 'a master of terse and forcible reasoning; and if his life had not been cut short by a premature death he would probably have attained a high judicial position' (Holdsworth, *Eng. law*, 12.460).

Following Wearg's death, Edmund Curll advertised late in 1726 the publication of six volumes of *Cases of Impotence and Divorce, by Sir Clement Wearg, Late Solicitor-General*. Curll was attacked for this by 'A. P.', perhaps Alexander Pope, in the *London Journal* on 12 November 1726, but two days later swore an affidavit that a book published by him in 1715 entitled *The case of impotency as debated in England, anno 1613, in trial between Robert, earl of Essex, and the Lady Frances Howard* was by Wearg. It was dated from the Inner Temple, 30 October 1714. As Wearg then had chambers in the new court, there might have been some grounds for the controversy. Lady Wearg died on 9 March 1746, and was buried with her husband on 14 March. There were no children from the marriage.

W. P. COURTNEY, rev. MATTHEW KILBURN

Sources G. Duke, *A brief memoir of Sir Clement Wearg* (1843) · E. Cruickshanks, 'Wearg, Sir Clement', HoP, *Commons, 1715–54* · *State trials*, 16.94–694, 767–1402 · Holdsworth, *Eng. law*, 11.236; 12.460 · *N&Q*, 2nd ser., 3 (1857), 501 · Venn, *Alum. Cant.* · Sainty, *King's counsel*

Wearmouth, Robert Featherstone (1882–1963), Methodist minister and historian, was born at 62 Joicey Terrace, Oxhill, co. Durham, on 10 June 1882, the son of William Wearmouth, a miner, and his wife, Sarah Walker. His mother came from Etherley, connected with the Featherstones of Weardale. She died in his infancy. The youngest of six children, he grew up in poverty. After Oxhill board school he became a pit boy at the age of twelve. He joined the Northumberland Fusiliers aged nineteen, and served in the West Indies and South Africa. Returning to mining he became a Primitive Methodist, trained as a local preacher, and then at Hartley College, Manchester, as a candidate for the ministry. After ordination in 1912 he married Mary Hannah Gibson (*b.* 1880/81), a teacher, daughter of Mr and Mrs Septimus Gibson, on 2 July 1913. They had one son.

Wearmouth served in the Grimsby and Oakham circuits, and was then a chaplain to the forces from 1915 to 1920. He later published a vivid account of his military service in *Pages from a Padre's Diary* (1958). After leaving the army he served in a number of circuits: Birmingham, Penzance, West Ham, Willesden Green, Leighton Buzzard, Berkhamsted, South Bank, and Eston. Wearmouth had a certificate of education from Manchester, read (part-time) for a BA and MA in history at Birmingham University, and in London obtained a BSc in economics. Supervised by G. D. H. Cole and H. L. Beales at the London School of Economics, he later obtained a PhD for a thesis which was published as *Methodism and the Working Class Movement in England, 1800–1850* (1937). His most notable book, it explored the relationship between Methodism and such movements as Chartism. Its strength lay in its pioneering use of primary documents, especially Home Office material, hardly used before. J. L. and Barbara Hammond acknowledged that the book led them to modify their rather harsh view of Methodism. Wearmouth demonstrated, according to H. J. Laski, that:

> the psychological influence of Methodism was to teach its votaries self-respect, self-confidence, the ability to organize and the ability to formulate their ideas and his book is an illuminating explanation of the foundations upon which some of the more characteristic of the features of the British Socialist Movement have been built. (Hempton, 11)

Wearmouth then turned to the eighteenth-century working class and early Methodism, again making massive use of primary sources, a feature continued in his third book on the late nineteenth century. He explored the role of Methodism in the north-east but with an emphasis on local history and personalities. However, this method was not so successful when Wearmouth attempted contemporary history in his last major work, *The Social and Political Influence of Methodism in the Twentieth Century* (1958). His *Some Working Class Movements of the Nineteenth Century* (1948), though somewhat dated now, was a notable account of the Luddites, radical societies, Chartists, and early trade unions with stress on religious influence.

While ministering at Berkhamsted from 1940 to 1946, Wearmouth also taught at Berkhamsted School and was a part-time forces chaplain. When he retired he became an extramural lecturer for the University of Durham from 1948 to 1958. By then a widower, he married Olive Summerbell, a teacher from East Stanley. They lived at Cullercoats, where Wearmouth died at 313 Broadway on 28 March 1963. He was survived by his second wife.

A man of enormous energy, R. F. Wearmouth was a fine product of the Primitive Methodism of the north-east. His life, as well as his books, illustrated its ability to make 'nobodies' into 'somebodies' with a spirituality of discipline and freedom.

JOHN MUNSEY TURNER

Sources R. Lowery, *Robert F. Wearmouth of Oxhill, social historian* (1982), 26 · J. M. Turner, 'Robert Featherstone Wearmouth, 1882–1963, Methodist historian', *Proceedings of the Wesley Historical Society*, 43 (1981–2), 111–16 · *Minutes of the Methodist Conference 1963*, 202 · R. F. Wearmouth, *Pages from a padre's diary* (1958) · d. cert. · m. cert. · D. Hempton, *The religion of the people* (1996) · CGPLA Eng. & Wales (1963)

Likenesses photographs, *c.*1901–*c.*1940, repro. in Wearmouth, *Pages from a padre's diary*

Wealth at death £9905 1s. 0d.: probate, 18 Nov 1963, CGPLA Eng. & Wales

Weatherhead, George Hume (1790?–1853), physician, born in Berwickshire, graduated MD at Edinburgh University on 1 August 1816 with a thesis entitled 'De diagnosit inter erysipelas, phlegmonim et erythema'. He was admitted a licentiate of the Royal College of Physicians on 27 March 1820. He was a prolific writer on a range of medical and other subjects; in particular he published several works on spas and waters, and on the treatment of fevers. He also wrote *A Pedestrian Tour through France and Italy* (1834). Weatherhead died from kidney disease at The Cottage, Foots Cray Park, near Bromley, Kent, on 22 June 1853.

E. I. CARLYLE, rev. PATRICK WALLIS

Sources Munk, *Roll* · *Nomina eorum, qui gradum medicinae doctoris in academia Jacobi sexti Scotorum regis, quae Edinburgi est, adepti sunt, ab anno 1705 ad annum 1845*, University of Edinburgh (1846) · d. cert.

Weatherhead, Leslie Dixon (1893–1976), Methodist minister, was born on 14 October 1893 at Harlesden, London, the youngest of the three children and only son of Andrew Weatherhead, a factory manager from Moffat, and his wife, Elizabeth Mary Dixon of London. Both his parents were Methodists. He was educated at Alderman Newton's secondary school, Leicester, and Richmond Theological College, and obtained an MA in English literature from Manchester University (1926).

Weatherhead's ministry began in 1915 at Farnham, but in 1917 he joined the Indian army as second-lieutenant, and later served as chaplain to the Devonshire regiment in Mesopotamia. In 1919 he became minister of the English

Methodist church in Madras. In 1920 he married Evelyn (*d.* 1970), daughter of Arthur Triggs, a Wesleyan minister from the Isle of Wight. She was at the time vice-principal of a girls' boarding-school in Madras. They had two sons and one daughter.

On his return to England in 1922 Weatherhead joined the Manchester (Oxford Road) circuit until 1925, when he became minister of Brunswick Church, Leeds. In 1936 he was called to the City Temple, London, where he remained until his retirement in 1960. Although more than half his career was spent in a Congregational church, he remained a Methodist throughout, and in 1955–6 and 1966–7 was elected president of the Methodist conference.

In every church he served Weatherhead's preaching drew large congregations. His eloquence was not achieved without careful preparation. He took delight in the apt use of words, and he preached with a passionate simplicity, ample illustration, sympathy with the needs of ordinary people, and a conviction of the day-to-day relevance of the gospel. The centre of his own faith was expressed in the title of his best-known book, *The Transforming Friendship* (1928), and he had a lifelong impatience with any orthodoxy which robbed the humanity of Jesus of its power by converting it into a dogma in a creed.

Weatherhead's desire to help people in their daily problems and frustrations led him early in his ministry to the study of psychology, and he became a pioneer in establishing a partnership between religion and psychiatry. His experience in counselling, both in clinics and by correspondence, convinced him that much physical and mental illness was caused by the loss of true religion. He was particularly outspoken on matters of sex, even at a time when the subject was still taboo, particularly in religious circles. His book *Psychology, Religion and Healing* (1951) was an original contribution to the subject, for which he received the degree of PhD from London University. He believed in working in close co-operation with medical specialists, and in 1966–7 became president of the Institute of Religion and Medicine.

Weatherhead was a prolific writer of books on popular and pastoral theology, and the worldwide reputation he earned by preaching, counselling, and writing led to many invitations to lecture. When on 16 April 1941 the City Temple was destroyed by a bomb, he not only kept his congregation together in a variety of temporary homes but never wavered in his confidence that the church would be rebuilt; and it was largely his fame in the United States that made the appeal for funds successful.

Weatherhead had his critics, who could point to his concentration on personal problems and piety to the neglect of matters of public concern, his disregard for traditional forms of theology and churchmanship, his appeal more to the emotions than to the intellect, and particularly his emphasis on sex, and to the personality cult which he never intended or courted but could not prevent. But no criticism could detract from the gratitude of the thousands he had helped to live a fuller life, or from the public recognition which came in the award of the honorary degree of DD by the universities of Edinburgh and California and an honorary DLitt from Puget Sound, and in his appointment as CBE in 1959. He was also a freeman of the City of London.

Weatherhead liked people, especially the young, and even in old age he never lost his faith in the idealism of youth. But his love of people was balanced by a love of solitude, and he was never happier or more relaxed than when he could return to the hills of his boyhood round his grandfather's home. He had a boyish sense of humour, often mischievous, sometimes macabre, regularly evoked by false solemnity, never held in restraint for fear of causing embarrassment.

In spite of his devotion to the cause of healing, Weatherhead himself never enjoyed robust health. One reason why he was able to help others was that he himself was sensitive and vulnerable, and his immense labours took their toll of his strength. After retirement he lived at Bexhill, his public activity increasingly restricted by ill health; and there he died on 3 January 1976.

G. B. CAIRD, rev.

Sources K. Weatherhead, *Leslie Weatherhead, a personal portrait* (1975) · *The Times* (5 Jan 1976) · private information (1986) · *WWW* · *CGPLA Eng. & Wales* (1976)

Archives U. Birm. L., additional corresp. and papers; diary, corresp., scrapbooks, papers; papers relating to the City Temple, London | NL Scot., corresp. with T. and T. Clark, publishers | FILM BFI NFTVA, news footage | SOUND BL NSA, Bow dialogues, 28 June 1966, C812/13 C8 · BL NSA, Bow dialogues, 19 June 1968, C812/19 C20

Wealth at death £83,879: probate, 13 April 1976, *CGPLA Eng. & Wales*

Weatherly, Frederic Edward (1848–1929), songwriter and barrister, was born on 4 October 1848 at 7 Woodhill, Portishead, near Bristol, the eldest son in the large family of Frederick Weatherly (1820–1910), a country doctor, and his wife, Julia Maria, *née* Ford (1823–1898). He was educated at Hereford Cathedral School (1859–67) and admitted with a scholarship at Brasenose College, Oxford, in 1867. Walter Pater was his tutor. Being small and slight he made a useful cox for the college boat. Despite poor examination results he secured a college exhibition, took his BA degree in 1871 (MA 1874), and remained in Oxford, briefly as a schoolmaster, and then as a drudging university 'coach' and author of textbooks on logic. On 31 December 1871 he married Anna Maria Hardwick (*d.* 1920), and they had a son and two daughters. They later lived apart. Weatherly left teaching to qualify as a barrister at the Inner Temple in 1887 and moved to London. In 1893 he joined the western circuit, living first at Clifton and from 1900 at Bath, busy in his profession until the end of his life. With Edward Cutler he published *The Law of Musical and Dramatic Copyright* (1890). On 2 August 1923 he married a widow, Mrs Miriam Bryan, *née* Davies (*d.* 1941). He was appointed king's counsel in 1925.

Although he competed unsuccessfully for the Newdigate prize three times, as an undergraduate Weatherly published poems and his first song lyrics, and they were followed during his years at Oxford by two novels, many children's books, and librettos for cantatas and oratorios.

In devising texts for music he found a talent in which he was fluent and lucky from the start, and came to have no rival. Weatherly wrote the words of many of the most popular songs in the English-speaking world for half a century, in association with composers such as Molloy, Cowen, Tosti, Michael Maybrick (Stephen Adams), and Coates. His songs were performed by the leading singers of three generations. Although he seldom wrote for existing music, he took pains in translating Italian and French opera, and his versions of *Cavalleria rusticana* (1892) and *I pagliacci* (1893) have lasted. He did not claim that his lyrics were fine poetry, nor pretend to musical ability beyond a good ear, but he felt strongly that the words of a ballad were as important as its setting, as their author was the equal of the composer. He was alert to changing tastes and versatile in several styles from the patriotic and naval to the humorous, religious, rustic, and sentimental. Inevitably he attracted parodists who reflected his success; this itself depended on the popularity of ballad concerts promoted by music publishers that created a vast lucrative market for sheet music for home entertainment. William Boosey, the music publisher, remembered him as 'certainly the most prolific lyric writer and the happiest in his ideas' (Boosey, 84). He was described as 'always a cheery, happy, good-humoured little man' (R. W. J., 13).

For many years Weatherly gave lively, anecdotal lectures on his craft, illustrating, for example, the need to 'get a point at the end of each verse, and the best point in the last' (Weatherly, 166). The advent of recording and later of radio kept his songs alive, and in the 1920s he broadcast for the BBC. Unashamed of popularity and prosperity, he had no patience with musical snobbery that equated popular songs with want of artistry or scorned a good melody. A jubilee dinner was held in his honour in London in December 1919. Weatherly lost count of his songs, but claimed to have published more than 1500. Dozens of them were extremely popular in his lifetime, and a number, including *Nancy Lee* (1876), *The Holy City* (1892), *Danny Boy* (1912) to the 'Londonderry Air', and *Roses of Picardy* (1916) set by Haydn Wood, survived him. Weatherly's autobiography, *Piano and Gown*, in which he glossed over unhappy parts of his life, appeared in 1926. He died at his home, Bathwick Lodge, Bath, after a short illness on 7 September 1929 and was buried four days later in Bathwick cemetery. A memorial tablet was unveiled in Bath by Clara Butt in 1931.   JOHN D. PICKLES

Sources F. E. Weatherly, *Piano and gown* (1926) • H. Simpson, *A century of ballads, 1810–1910* (1910) • R. Blathwayt, 'The songs of the people: a talk with Mr. F. E. Weatherly', *Great Thoughts and Christian Graphic* (7 May 1898), 88–9 • 'Mr. Fred. E. Weatherly', *Strand Musical Magazine*, 5 (1897), 263 • E. Coates, *Suite in four movements* (1953), 117–20 • W. Boosey, *Fifty years of music* (1931), 16, 17, 72, 84 • R. W. J., 'Frederic Edward Weatherly', *Brazen Nose*, 5/1 (1929), 12–13 • *N&Q*, 7th ser., 3 (1887), 47 • *N&Q*, 10th ser., 8 (1907), 410, 513 • *The Times* (9 Sept 1929), 7 • 'Literary intelligence', *London Mercury*, 20 (1929), 552 • O. Seaman, 'Yet', *Owen Seaman: a selection* (1937), 104–5 • grave monument, Bath • *Bath Chronicle* (14 Sept 1929), 10
Archives Bath Central Library • BL, papers, incl. songs, MSS Mus 105–115

Likenesses Barrauds, photograph, *c.*1897, repro. in 'Mr Fred E. Weatherly' • Elliott & Fry, photograph, *c.*1910, repro. in Simpson, *Century of ballads* • H. Lambert of Bath, photograph, 1926?, repro. in Weatherly, *Piano and gown* • woodcut (after photograph by Elliott & Fry), repro. in Blathwayt, 'The songs of the people'
Wealth at death £41,932 5*s.* 8*d.*: probate, 24 Oct 1929, *CGPLA Eng. & Wales*

Weaver [*née* Farley], **Elizabeth** (*fl.* **1661–1678**), actress, joined the King's Company in 1661 under her maiden name, Farley. Little is known about her family. Pepys heard from Elizabeth Knipp that 'the King first spoiled Mrs. Weaver' (Pepys, 9.19). Subsequently she became the companion of James Weaver, assuming his name during the 1660s. A daughter, also Elizabeth, was baptized on 20 May 1661. The following year James Weaver asked permission to sue Elizabeth Farloe on a bond of £30 for using his name to defraud creditors. Lawsuits over debt dogged Mrs Weaver throughout the 1660s, as did personal problems. In 1664 the dramatist Sir Robert Howard wrote to Henry Bennet, Lord Arlington, explaining why Mrs Weaver 'of her own accord brought in all her parts and … wou'd act noe more'. 'Big with child' and clearly unmarried, her appearance offended 'women of quality'; and the actress, indignant her parts had been reassigned, 'continued her resolution to goe' (PRO, SP 29/109, no. 16). Despite this vow, by April 1665 she was acting again.

Never a prominent actress, Mrs Weaver mainly performed minor roles although early on she did play several leading parts: Richard Flecknoe intended her for the title role in *Erminia* (1661), but the play was probably never staged. In a revival during 1663–4 of John Ford's play *Love's Sacrifice* she played Biancha, a proudly unrepentant adulteress. Roles assigned after her notorious pregnancy were far more slight: Alibech in Dryden's *The Indian Emperour* (1665); Mrs Martha in Wycherley's *Love in a Wood* (1671); Eudoria in Leanerd's *The Rambling Justice* (1678); and the whore in D'Urfey's *Trick for Trick* (1678). In 1671 Mrs Weaver resumed performing under her family name of Farley. She disappeared from the stage after 1678. An obscene poem, 'Dreaming Last Night on Mrs Farley', incorrectly attributed to the earl of Rochester (*Rochester's Poems*, 77), suggests that she subsequently became a prostitute, unfortunately a likely conjecture given the downward spiral of her life.   DEBORAH PAYNE FISK

Sources Highfill, Burnim & Langhans, *BDA*, vol. 15 • W. Van Lennep and others, eds., *The London stage, 1660–1800*, pt 1: *1660–1700* (1965) • J. H. Wilson, *All the king's ladies: actresses of the Restoration* (1958) • J. Downes, *Roscius Anglicanus*, ed. J. Milhous and R. D. Hume, new edn (1987) • Pepys, *Diary*, vol. 9 • A. Nicoll, *Restoration drama, 1660–1700*, 4th edn (1952), vol. 1 of *A history of English drama, 1660–1900* (1952–9) • PRO, SP 29/109, no. 16 [*CSP domestic, 1664–5*] • *CSP dom., 1664–5* • *Rochester's poems on several occasions*, ed. J. Thorpe (1950) • *The works of John Wilmot, earl of Rochester*, ed. H. Love (1999) • E. Howe, *The first English actresses: women and drama, 1660–1700* (1992)

Weaver, Gertrude Baillie- [*née* Gertrude Renton; *pseud.* Gertrude Colmore] (**1855–1926**), writer and feminist, was born on 8 June 1855 at 5 Upper Lansdowne Terrace, Kensington, the sixth daughter of John Thomson Renton, stockbroker, and his wife, Elizabeth, *née* Leishman. Having been privately educated in Germany, Paris, and London she married, on 18 July 1882, Henry Arthur Colmore Dunn, barrister; he died in the 1890s and on 2 January 1901 Gertrude married another barrister, **Harold Baillie-Weaver** (1860–1926), who was the son of Henry Edward Weaver, superintendent of the Telegraph Company, and his wife, Annie, *née* Alcock. He was a supporter of feminism and, like his wife, a humanitarian, theosophist, and campaigner for animals.

Having adopted the name Gertrude Colmore, Gertrude's reputation as a writer has rested upon two suffrage works reissued in the 1980s. Her novel *Suffragette Sally* (1908) was reissued in 1984 under the title *The Suffragettes: a Story of Three Women* and her hagiographic account *The Life of Emily Davison*, originally written as an extended obituary after Emily Wilding Davison died in 1913, attempting to gain publicity for the suffrage cause by grabbing the reins of the king's horse at the Derby, was reissued in 1988 as *The Life and Death of Emily Wilding Davison*. However, Gertrude's output was much broader, including poetry, short stories, pamphlets, and a number of melodramatic novels dealing with social, political, and animal questions. Her early novels had covered social themes from a feminist perspective; *Conspiracy of Silence*, for example, tackles the hypocritical hiding of hereditary madness.

Gertrude's use of melodramatic narratives and devices is most strikingly found in three of her novels that deal directly with the suffering of animals: *The Angel and the Outcast* (1907), *Priests of Progress* (1908), and *A Brother of the Shadow* (1926). These are melodramatic narratives based on contests of moral authority. In *The Angel and the Outcast* Gertrude explores the nature/nurture debate in the context of the morally contaminating Deptford slaughterhouses. So forceful was her anti-vivisection message in *Priests of Progress* (1908) that it was condemned by physiologists, who discussed how to mount a 'counter-attack' (Research Defence Society, minutes, 8 Feb 1908, Wellcome L., SA/RDS C1). Her last book, *A Brother of the Shadow* (1926), developed such themes. The villain, a professor of physiology, exercises power over men, women, and animals, using hypnotic and devilish powers to coerce them to self-destruction. Gertrude's suffrage and animal campaigning fiction drew on her contemporary political activity and the humanitarian milieu in which she lived. From 1910 she sat on the management committee of the pioneering Battersea Hospital, an anti-vivisection establishment for the local poor, which forbade experiments on animals and patients alike.

Following Gertrude's marriage to Baillie-Weaver, a member of the Humanitarian League that was founded in 1891 by Henry Salt and campaigned for human and animal rights, they worked together on political, social, and animal questions. Baillie-Weaver was also a member of the Men's League for Women's Suffrage; he spoke regularly on their behalf and participated in the men's league contingent in the suffrage procession in June 1910. Gertrude supported the militant suffrage organization the Women's Freedom League, which published a collection of her campaigning suffrage stories entitled *Mr Jones and the Governess* [1913]. In 1914 she probably joined the United Suffragists, a new suffrage society for men and women that campaigned throughout the war on women's suffrage.

Harold and Gertrude shared common interests in the welfare of animals and in theosophy, which attracted many with progressive views. They joined the fashionable central London branch of the Theosophical Society in 1906. Harold was general secretary of the society in England from 1916 to 1921; he was active in their anti-vivisection group, the Starry Cross, and, as chairman of the European Theosophical Federation, was described by theosophist colleagues as 'a tower of calm and peaceful strength' (*International Theosophical Year Book*, 187).

Gertrude wrote pamphlets for the Theosophical Society on progressive ideals in education and against cruelty to animals. Harold also took a keen interest in educational matters, chairing the Theosophical Educational Trust, which ran the theosophist school St Christopher's, in Letchworth. Subsequently he was active in the New Education Fellowship, an international organization of educators interested in the new ideals of progressive education, and he chaired and organized European conferences in Calais and Montreux in the 1920s. Gertrude and Harold's empathy with, and practical help for, animals was exemplified by their membership of the National Canine Defence League. Harold chaired the 1910 annual general meeting and, to loud and prolonged cheers, he supported the sentiments of the guest speaker, Women's Freedom League president Charlotte Despard, declaring 'the sooner you get women's suffrage, the sooner will you succeed in emancipating dogs from cruelty' (National Canine Defence League, *Annual Report*, 1910, 27). With Ernest Bell of the Humanitarian League he wrote a pamphlet, *Horses in Warfare* (1912), exposing the plight of horses in the Second South African War and calling for the extension of the Geneva convention to include them.

After their marriage Gertrude and Harold moved to Newport, near Saffron Walden, Essex, where Gertrude was local secretary both of the National Canine Defence League branch and of the animal welfare group Our Dumb Friends' League (later Blue Cross). As supporters of the Animal Defence and Anti-Vivisection Society they also campaigned for the humane slaughter of animals. In the 1920s they moved to Wimbledon, Surrey, with the intention of acting as guardians to Krishnamurti, hailed by the theosophists as a new messiah. After a long struggle with stomach cancer Harold died at their Wimbledon home, Eastward Ho, North View, The Common, on 18 March 1926. Gertrude survived him by only eight months, dying of heart failure at 6 Hunter Road, Wimbledon, on 26 November. She was cremated at Golders Green.

The Baillie-Weavers were typical of many humanitarians of their time—active in a range of progressive political causes underpinned by theosophical principles affecting both animals and people. Hartwell's statue *Protecting the Defenceless*, dedicated to them for their pioneering work in founding the National Council for Animals' Welfare Work, stands in the St John's Lodge public gardens of Regent's Park in London as a reminder of their important activity.   HILDA KEAN

Sources H. Kean, *Animal rights: political and social change in Britain since 1800* (1998); pbk edn (2000) • *International Theosophical Year Book*, Theosophical Society (1937) • A. Morley and L. Stanley, *The life and death of Emily Wilding Davison* (1988) • E. Lutyens, *Candles in the sun* (1957) • Theosophical Society register, European members, Theosophical Society Archives, London, vol. 7 • attendance book, 20th annual report, 1917, annual general meeting, 1924, Blue Cross, Burford, Oxfordshire, Our Dumb Friends' League Archive • National Canine Defence League, annual report, 1910, National Canine Defence League Archive, London • minute book of management committee of the Anti-Vivisection Hospital, Battersea, LMA • K. J. Brehony, '"A dedicated spiritual movement": theosophists and progressive education in England, 1875–1935', unpublished paper • K. J. Brehony, 'Among women: the participation of men in the Froebel and Montessori societies', unpublished paper presented to the History of Education Society's annual conference, December 1999 • H. Kean, 'The moment of the *Shambles of science* and the *Priests of progress*', unpublished paper given to Womens' History Network conference, September 1998 • A. V. John and C. Eustance, eds., *The men's share? Masculinities, male support and women's suffrage in Britain, 1890–1920* (1997) • b. cert. • m. cert. (1882) • d. cert. • b. cert. [Harold Baillie-Weaver] • d. cert. [Harold Baillie-Weaver] • WWW

Wealth at death £8930 0s. 11d.: probate, 13 Jan 1927, *CGPLA Eng. & Wales*

Weaver, Harold Baillie- (1860–1926). *See under* Weaver, Gertrude Baillie- (1855–1926).

Weaver, Harriet Shaw (1876–1961), political activist and journal editor, was born in Frodsham, Cheshire, on 1 September 1876, the sixth of eight children of Frederic Poynton Weaver (*d.* 1913), a medical doctor, and his wife, Mary Wright (*d.* 1909). The family was wealthy, her mother having inherited a fortune from her father, made in the cotton industry. She was educated at home, by a governess, first in Cheshire and later in Hampstead, north London. Her parents were strict and pious and though, as an adult, she rejected their evangelical beliefs, she took with her their idealism and austerity. Virginia Woolf described her as 'modest judicious & decorous' (*Diary*, 13 April 1918); slim, with clear blue eyes, she usually wore her brown hair tied up in a bun. When her parents denied her wish to go to university, she dedicated herself to social work. She attended a course on the economic basis of social relations at the London School of Economics and, increasingly interested in the women's suffrage movement, joined the Women's Social and Political Union.

In 1911 Weaver began subscribing to *The Freewoman*, a radical periodical, founded and edited by Dora Marsden. When, in 1912, it was condemned as immoral and lost the support of its proprietors, Weaver stepped in. Over the following years she gave regular donations of money, usually anonymously, and became involved in all the details of its organization and finance, finally taking on the role of editor. Though lacking confidence in her own writing, she contributed a number of reviews (signing herself Josephine Wright) and, as editor, wrote the occasional leader article.

In 1913 *The Freewoman* was renamed *The Egoist* at the suggestion of Ezra Pound, who was involved in finding contributors, among them James Joyce. Overwhelmingly convinced of Joyce's genius, Weaver committed herself to supporting him. In 1914 *The Egoist* began serializing *A Portrait of the Artist as a Young Man* and, when Joyce was unable to find anyone willing to publish it in book form, Weaver determinedly converted *The Egoist* into a press. She not only guaranteed the new Egoist Press against loss, but also covered the production costs of the book, as well as paying Joyce serial rights and 'royalties', at her own expense and far in excess of what his books had actually earned. Joyce's *Ulysses* also made its first appearance as a serial in *The Egoist* before being published by the Egoist Press. It proved even more troublesome than *A Portrait*: it was rejected by all the printers Weaver approached, and she was advised that prosecution was certain to follow publication. When it was finally printed abroad, Weaver lessened the risk of police seizure by hiding copies of the book in a wardrobe in her flat.

From 1916 Joyce and Weaver corresponded almost daily: she commented on his manuscripts, corrected his proofs, discussed his frustrations and aspirations, and gradually became involved in every aspect of his own and his family's well-being. Though she was aware that he spent money recklessly and sometimes drank to excess, she endeavoured to provide him with an assured family income by transferring him substantial sums of her capital. Joyce greatly valued the sincerity of Weaver's opinions, and became dependent on her sympathy and encouragement. Thus he found it difficult to accept her initial reservations over 'Work in progress' (published as *Finnegans Wake*), and began to interpret anything she did as a sign of betrayal. The final breach in their relationship followed Weaver's involvement in the care of Joyce's daughter Lucia, who was suffering from a severe mental breakdown. After 1935, Joyce wrote to her only sporadically and without his former frankness, but Weaver never withdrew her support. On his death she paid for his funeral, and also acted as administrator and executor of his personal and literary estates.

In 1931, Weaver joined the Labour Party, convinced that social justice, at home and abroad, could be achieved only through political action. Profoundly affected by reading Marx's *Das Kapital*, she was increasingly critical of the reformist Labour Party line and, in 1938, she openly declared her allegiance to the Communist Party. Over the following years Weaver (Comrade Josephine) worked on the committee of her local party, sold copies of the *Daily Worker*, and took part in demonstrations, first in London and later in Oxford. The last decades of Weaver's life were largely dedicated to her role as Joyce's literary executor. She meticulously researched any proposals for translation and publication, responded to enquiries from Joyce scholars from all over the world, and helped to compile *The Letters of James Joyce*. In 1932, T. S. Eliot dedicated his *Selected Essays* to her, 'in recognition of her services to English letters'. Weaver died at her home, Castle End, near

Saffron Walden, Essex, on 14 October 1961 and was cremated at Oxford. She bequeathed her extensive collection of literary material to the British Library and the National Book League.

Those who knew Weaver were often struck by the contrast between her gentle and modest personality and her avant-garde convictions. At an early age she determined that living on an unearned income amounted to usury; though she lived frugally, she was unstintingly generous and loyal to both family and friends. For many years she supported not only Joyce but also Dora Marsden, and assisted her in her philosophic and scientific research. Until recently, the importance of the publishing and editorial activities of Weaver (and other women of the period) to the modernist enterprise was underestimated. Yet, as Rebecca West wrote, had it not been for Weaver's dedication, it is 'doubtful whether Stephen Dedalus and Leopold Bloom would have found their way into the world's mind' (*Sunday Telegraph*, 11 Nov 1970).

RACHEL COTTAM

Sources J. Lidderdale and M. Nicholson, *Dear Miss Weaver: Harriet Shaw Weaver, 1876–1961* (1970) · S. Benstock, *Women of the left bank, Paris, 1900–1940* (1987) · N. R. Fitch, *Sylvia Beach and the lost generation* (1985) · B. Maddox, *Nora: a biography of Nora Joyce* (1988) · *The diary of Virginia Woolf*, ed. A. O. Bell and A. McNeillie, 5 vols. (1977–84) · R. West, 'Spinster to the rescue', *Sunday Telegraph* (11 Nov 1970); repr. in *The gender of modernism: a critical anthology*, ed. B. K. Scott (1990), 577–80 · R. Ellmann, *James Joyce* (1959) · *Letters of James Joyce*, ed. S. Gilbert and R. Ellmann, 3 vols. (1957–66) · B. K. Scott, *Joyce and feminism* (1984) · *The Times* (17 Oct 1961) · *The Times* (19 Oct 1961) **Archives** BL, corresp. and papers, Add. MSS 57345–57365 · UCL, corresp. and papers | Cornell University, Ithaca, New York, letters to James Joyce · Princeton University, New Jersey, letters to Sylvia Beach · TCD, corresp. with Patricia Hutchins relating to James Joyce **Likenesses** W. Lewis, oils, c.1921, State University of New York, Buffalo · M. Ray, photograph, 1924, priv. coll. **Wealth at death** £17,618 19s. 4d.: probate, 27 Nov 1961, *CGPLA Eng. & Wales*

Weaver, John (*d.* 1685), politician and government official, is thought to have been born of a family in the north of England. One suggestion is that his father kept an inn; another that his parents, whose names are unknown, were in financial difficulties. Nothing is known of his early years and he first emerged into public life in 1631 when he became a freeman of the borough of Stamford. Subsequently he sat for the town in parliament. It is possible, but not certain, that he had a legal education, since during the 1640s he was appointed judge advocate in the parliamentarian army. He next appeared as a supporter of parliament in the civil war, rising in the eastern association to be its treasurer. In 1645 he took the side of Oliver Cromwell when he attacked the commander of the association, the earl of Manchester. He was said to share Cromwell's religious preferences, being recorded as a zealous supporter of the Independents. Later, however, he was supposed to incline more towards the presbyterians. In 1645 he was elected as a recruiter MP for Stamford. In the ensuing controversies he took the side of the army and opposed those who sued for peace with Charles I. Towards the end of 1648 he was calling for the trial of the king, but

when he found himself named to the high court he refused to sit. Nevertheless, he quickly rallied to the new republican regime, returning to the purged House of Commons early in 1649. In parliament he energetically promoted measures designed to achieve religious and moral reform.

The administrative abilities which Weaver had revealed during the 1640s, together with political alliances with the important, notably Cromwell, brought his appointment as one of the parliamentary commissioners to whom the government of a reconquered Ireland was entrusted in 1649. Among his other services he attracted his brother-in-law, the minister, Samuel Winter, to Dublin, where he was soon installed as provost of Trinity College. Later Weaver wrote a posthumous life of Winter. In the Rump Parliament he also forwarded measures to spread protestantism in Ireland. He acquired permanent Irish links through a marriage into the family of one of the leading merchants of Dublin, Daniel Hutchinson, who also favoured the religious Independents. Weaver was among those MPs who successfully opposed the appointment of John Lambert to be lord deputy in Ireland. This position was in line with his staunch championing of civilian government. But he incurred the hostility of the army in Ireland, and early in 1653 resigned from his Irish office.

Thereafter Weaver gravitated towards the commonwealthsmen, such as Sir Henry Vane. Returned to parliament in 1654 and 1656, again for Stamford, he was secluded on the second occasion on account of his supposed estrangement from the Cromwellian protectorate. He was suspected of using his residual contacts in Ireland to encourage the opponents there of Cromwell's regime. In 1659, once more member for Stamford, he joined the republicans opposed to Richard Cromwell's government. When the commonwealthsmen briefly returned to power he was included in the council of state in December 1659, and was named to the new commission to govern Ireland. He neither acted as a councillor nor travelled to Dublin to assume the appointment. However, his earlier services had been rewarded with lands in Ireland, some of which he retained after the restoration of Charles II. These gave him an interest in the town of Maryborough, Queen's county, where he—or his son—was identified with the sectarian and political opponents of the returned Stuart monarchy. Despite these sympathies he escaped any serious punishment after 1660, and seems to have lived in relative obscurity, mainly in the environs of Stamford. He died in March 1685 probably at North Luffenham, Rutland, where he was buried on the 25th.

TOBY BARNARD

Sources De Vesci MSS, NL Ire. · *The memoirs of Edmund Ludlow*, ed. C. H. Firth, 2 vols. (1894) · J. W. [J. Weaver], *The life and death of Samuel Winter* (1671) · B. Worden, *The Rump Parliament, 1648–1653* (1974) · C. Holmes, *The eastern association in the English civil war* (1974) · Greaves & Zaller, *BDBR*, 296–7 · T. C. Barnard, *Cromwellian Ireland* (1975) · *DNB*

Weaver, John (1673–1760), dancer and choreographer, the son of John Weaver (*d.* 1701) and his wife, Anne (*d.* 1721), was baptized at the abbey church of Holy Cross, Shrewsbury, Shropshire, on 21 July 1673. His father, who taught dancing to pupils at Shrewsbury School, took his family to Oxford after his son's birth and ran a dancing school and boarding-house in Holywell, under the jurisdiction of the vice-chancellor of the University of Oxford. Weaver spent his early years at Oxford but was educated at Shrewsbury School, presumably as a boarder. He trained as a dancing-master either under his father in Oxford or under Edward Dyer in Shrewsbury. He is recorded as a dancing-master in Milk Street, Shrewsbury, in 1695–6 but appears to have left for London by 1697. From then, until his return to Shrewsbury in 1708, he established a reputation both as a theatrical dancer and as an authority on dance notation. His translations from Feuillet—*Orchesography* (1706) and *A Small Treatise of Time and Cadence in Dancing* (1706)—and his notation of Isaac's dances—*A Collection of Ball-Dances Performed at Court* (1706) and *The Union* (1707)—had a significant influence on the development and status of dance in England. During this first period in London he also began his experiments as a choreographer, which have led many dance historians in the twentieth century to see Weaver as 'one of the most far-sighted and important early exponents of *ballet d'action*' (Ralph, 84).

By 1702 Weaver had married his first wife, Catherine. They had seven children. The first three were baptized at St Andrew's, Holborn, London. John, who died in infancy, was baptized on 27 December 1702; Elizabeth on 12 August 1704; and Katherine on 19 August 1705 (buried 4 May 1706). The last four were baptized in Shrewsbury, where Weaver had returned to set up a dancing school and to write his influential *An Essay towards an History of Dancing* (1712). Anne Elizabeth was baptized on 12 March 1708 at St Julian's Church. John, on 11 July 1709; Richard, on 3 November 1710; and Catherine, on 13 September 1712, all at St Chad's Church. Weaver's wife died giving birth and was buried on the same day as their last child was baptized and in the same month as Weaver's *Essay* was published. The stir caused by its publication, particularly in the pages of *The Spectator* and *The Lover*, obscures what little is known about Weaver's personal life during these critical years. In 1716 his second wife, Susanna, who was twenty-eight years younger than he, gave birth to the first of their five children. Prisilla was baptized on 31 May 1716 at St Chad's; Dorothy on 20 January 1721 at St Mary's; Anne on 3 May 1722 at St Alkmund's; Susannah on 10 September 1723 at St Alkmund's; and William on 21 June 1728 at St Alkmund's.

The years that followed Prisilla's birth saw Weaver's second and most creative period as a dancer and choreographer in London. Between March 1717 and April 1721 he composed and directed at Drury Lane three serious dance pantomimes (records of one of these no longer survive) and two grotesque dance pantomimes 'after the manner of the Modern Italians, such as Harlequin, Scaramouch, etc' (J. Weaver, *The History of the Mimes and Pantomimes*, 1728, 45). He danced one of the major roles in all these entertainments, as well as a variety of ordinary stage dances throughout this period. He also gave a series of

anatomical lectures to an audience of distinguished dancing-masters, who subscribed to a printed version of them which was published in 1721. These lectures 'are the first attempt to base dancing and dance instruction on the knowledge of the body' (Sachs, 395). Between 27 April 1721 and 16 March 1728 Weaver turned his back on the London stage and re-established his dancing school in Shrewsbury. He lived and taught in Shrewsbury for the rest of his life, and returned to Drury Lane only on three brief occasions. In 1728 and in 1729 he both danced in and directed pantomimes in collaboration with Monsieur Roger, a French Pierrot dancer, while in 1733 he choreographed his last serious entertainment, *The Judgment of Paris*. This was the only experiment of his in which he did not perform.

It was Weaver, rather than John Rich, who introduced into England entertainments called pantomimes. In 1703 he staged at Drury Lane, probably in late February or early March, *The Tavern Bilkers*, which he describes as 'the first entertainment that appeared on the English Stage, where the Representation and Story was carried on by Dancing Action and Motion only'. The text does not survive, but it is clear that this was a pantomime that involved 'commedia' characters such as Harlequin and what Weaver terms 'grotesque dancing'. *The Shipwreck* (1717), *Harlequin Turned Judge* (1717), and the two comic interludes Weaver composed for *Perseus and Andromeda* (1728) were also this type of pantomime. Apart from their emphasis on dancing, all of them must have been similar to the rival burlesques that Rich produced at Lincoln's Inn Fields from 1717 to 1726, and that were based on themes and plots associated with Weaver's work. Weaver's serious compositions, however, were of a different type. They were 'attempted in imitation of the pantomimes of the Ancient Greeks and Romans'. *The Loves of Mars and Venus* (1717) was the most successful with contemporary audiences of these experiments. The published text of its danced action, together with the text of *Orpheus and Eurydice* (1718) and his publications on dance, establish Weaver as 'the major figure in British dance before the present [twentieth] century' (Ralph, ix). As an innovator he was closer to Fokine than Noverre in his belief that 'there is no dividing line between pantomime and dance' (Cohen, 47).

In Shrewsbury, Weaver was a respected and respectable figure, 'a little, dapper, cheerful man' (Owen and Blakeway, 2.152, n. 1). His activities and longevity as a dancing-master in the town are remembered with warmth and respect by Dr Burney. In London, however, his reputation was more complex:

> Happy if not a Tavern cou'd be found,
> Or Bawdy-house in fifty Miles around.
> …
> Tho' always getting, he is always poor.
> (*The Dancing-Master*, 16–17)

How far such satires reflected his character or revealed antipathy to the stage and, in particular, to dance, it is difficult to discern. As a dancer Weaver 'shewed the Passions to great Advantage' (Essex, preface, p. ix). For Richard Steele, he was:

... corruptor of this present age,
Who first taught silent sins upon the stage.
(BL, Add. MS 25391, fol. 3*v*)

Weaver died at his home, at the Market Place, Shrewsbury, on 24 September 1760, and was buried in the south aisle of Old St Chad's Church on 28 September. The inscription on his grave, now destroyed, is preserved in BL, Add. MS 21236, fol. 65*b*., and gave his age as ninety. He was in fact eighty-seven.   LESLIE DU S. READ

Sources R. Ralph, *The life and works of John Weaver* (1985) · S. J. Cohen, 'Theory and practice of theatrical dancing', *Famed for dance*, ed. I. K. Fletcher (1960), 21–58 · W. J. Lawrence, 'The father of the English pantomime', *Pall Mall Gazette* (27 Dec 1897) · W. J. Lawrence, 'The genesis of English pantomime', *The Theatre*, 4th ser., 25 (1895), 28–34 · C. Sachs, *World history of the dance*, trans. B. Schönberg (1937) · C. Cibber, *An apology for the life of Mr. Colley Cibber* (1740) · G. Davies, 'Music for the ballets of John Weaver', *Dance Chronicle*, 3 (1979), 46–60 · *The dancing-master: a satyr* (1722) · C. Crisp and P. Brunson, *Ballet for all* (1970) · H. Owen and J. B. Blakeway, *A history of Shrewsbury*, 2 vols. (1825) · W. A. Leighton, 'Notes relating to the abbey parish church estate, Shrewsbury', *Transactions of the Shropshire Archaeological and Natural History Society*, 1 (1878), 15–98, esp. 78–93 · parish register, Shrewsbury, St Chad, 24 Sept 1760 [death] · [P. Rameau], *The dancing master*, trans. J. Essex (1728) · *DNB* · Highfill, Burnim & Langhans, *BDA*
Wealth at death 1 guinea to each child; remainder to wife: will, 2 Jan 1759, Lichfield Joint Public Library, Lichfield; Ralph, *Life and works*

Weaver, Sir Lawrence Walter William (1876–1930), civil servant and architectural writer, was born at Clifton, Bristol, on 2 July 1876, the only child of Walter Weaver and his wife, Frances Mary Taylor. Brought up at Clifton by his mother, he was educated at Clifton College. He left school at the age of seventeen with the intention of becoming a dentist, but he found better scope for his abilities as a commercial traveller, selling builders' ironmongery. Study of old leadwork in his spare time led Weaver to write for *Country Life* a series of articles which were later published in 1909 as *English Leadwork: its Art and History*. As a result, he was taken on to the staff of *Country Life* in 1910 as architectural editor, a position which he held until 1916. Here his enthusiasm for good craftsmanship and good building, especially as applied to the small country house, found an outlet. His writings on this subject were collected in *Small Country Houses of To-Day* (2 vols., 1910; rev. edn, 1922–5) and *Houses and Gardens of Edwin Lutyens* (1913; rev. edn, 1925). The latter book contributed much to the recognition of Lutyens as one of the leading domestic architects of the time.

After the outbreak of war in 1914 Weaver volunteered as an able-bodied seaman in the Royal Naval Volunteer Reserve (anti-aircraft corps). The attention of the director-general of food production, Sir Arthur Lee, was called to this waste of Weaver's ability, and he was consequently appointed in April 1917 unpaid controller of the supplies division of the newly formed food production department. In this post Weaver was responsible for organizing the supply of fertilizers, feeding-stuffs, seeds, and other requirements of the agricultural industry; his department was very effective in extending wartime allotments.

Sir Lawrence Walter William Weaver (1876–1930), by Walter Stoneman, 1920

On the reorganization of the Ministry of Agriculture in 1919, Lee, now the minister, appointed Weaver commercial secretary, and in 1920 director-general, of the land department. He was made responsible for all questions relating to agricultural supplies, and, when director-general, for the development of smallholdings and the settlement of suitable ex-servicemen on the land. Here he was again in a position to insist on sound building design and the employment of competent architects (there were no architects at all on the staff of the ministry until Weaver's appointment). The land settlement scheme was initiated under difficult conditions: the extravagant cost of building materials led Weaver to undertake experiments in the revival of traditional materials, such as cob and weather-boarding. Some of the results are published in *The 'Country Life' Book of Cottages* (1913; rev. edns, 1919 and 1926) and *A manual for the guidance of county councils and their architects in equipment of small holdings* (1919; 3rd edn, 1920), dealing with the planning and construction of cottages and farms, issued by the Ministry of Agriculture under Weaver's direction. His wartime experiences suggested to him the need of a single institution to co-ordinate and direct experiments in crop improvement. To this end he founded the National Institute of Agricultural Botany at Cambridge in January 1919, with the help of funds contributed by firms interested and supplemented by a government grant; he was chairman of its council from 1919 to 1924. Weaver and his first wife, Kathleen (1874/5–1927), daughter of Major-General Edward Tobias Willoughby Purcell, whom he had married on 30 April 1908, were instrumental in founding the Ashtead potteries for the employment of disabled ex-servicemen. He was also honorary treasurer of the housing association for officers' families, and of the Douglas Haig memorial homes. After the closing of his department in 1922 as the result of the economy scheme inaugurated by Sir Eric Geddes, Weaver became director-general of the United Kingdom exhibits section of the British Empire Exhibition held at Wembley in 1924. A visit to the Göteborg Exhibition in that year had impressed upon him the then unfamiliar ideals of industrial art, which he sought to realize in his section of the Wembley exhibition. Subsequently he was an active speaker and writer on the subject of aesthetic ideals in industry.

Weaver's character was a combination of strong religious, puritanical, and philanthropic convictions—he was a deacon of the Catholic Apostolic, or Irvingite, church—with hard-headed shrewdness and steadfast loyalty to friends and employers. He was an excellent debater and after-dinner speaker—enthusiastic, confident, and witty. He was created CBE in 1918 and advanced to KBE in 1920, and he was a fellow of the Society of Antiquaries and an honorary associate of the Royal Institute of British Architects. After his first wife died in 1927, leaving him with two sons, he married on 23 June 1928 Elizabeth Margaret Orr (b. 1887/8), younger daughter of William de Caux, of Norwich, a minister in the Catholic Aspostolic church.

In his later years, Weaver returned to a business career, accepting various directorships. In 1925–6 he served under Lord Lee of Fareham on the royal commission on cross-river traffic in London, the expeditious and practical report of which owed much to his collaboration. In 1927 he succeeded J. C. Squire, the founder, as president of the Architecture Club. It was shortly before a meeting of the club at his office that he had a fatal seizure of angina pectoris and died at 15 Welbeck Street, Marylebone, on 9 January 1930. The changes in design and taste shown in industrial and commercial art in the subsequent decade owed much to Weaver's energetic advocacy. His second wife survived him.

CHRISTOPHER HUSSEY, rev. CATHERINE GORDON

Sources C. Williams-Ellis, *Lawrence Weaver: a memoir* (1933) · *ArchR*, 67 (1930), 110–11 · *The Times* (11 Jan 1930) · L. Weaver, 'The land settlement building work of the ministry of agriculture and fisheries', *RIBA Journal*, 28 (1920–21), 309–25 · private information (1937) · m. cert. · d. cert. · *CGPLA Eng. & Wales* (1930)
Archives RIBA BAL, grangerized copy of his English leadwork and notes concerning an interleaved copy of Wren's *Parentalis*
Likenesses W. Stoneman, photograph, 1920, NPG [*see illus.*]
Wealth at death £28,911 7s. 7d.: resworn probate, 29 March 1930, *CGPLA Eng. & Wales*

Weaver, Robert (1773–1852), Congregational minister and antiquary, born at Trowbridge, in Wiltshire, on 23 January 1773, was the son of Richard Weaver, clothier, and his wife, Mary. Aiming at the Congregational ministry, he chose study over the tailoring apprenticeship offered by his father, and entered Rotherham Independent college

early in 1794, where he resided with the president, Edward Williams (1750–1813). On 15 February 1802 he became pastor at Mansfield in Nottinghamshire, where he remained until his death; he reconstituted the dispersed congregation in 1805, and twice enlarged the place of worship, in 1812 and in 1829.

Weaver was a keen student of the Greek Testament, and taught the subject to residential students. The educational theme was pursued in his publications, particularly *Education Based on Scriptural Principles, the True Source of Individual and Social Happiness* (1838). Other theological writings included *A Complete View of Puseyism* (1843), *Dissent: its Character* (1844), and, in the year of the Ecclesiastical Titles Act, *Popery, Calmly, Closely, and Comprehensively Considered* (1851). He also took an interest in antiquities, and in 1840 published *Monumenta antiqua, or, The Stone Monuments of Antiquity yet Remaining in the British Isles*, in which he ascribed the remains of pre-Roman times to Phoenician influence and supported his theory by the particulars of similar Canaanite and Jewish monuments given in the Bible. Weaver died at Mansfield on 12 October 1852, and was buried in the ground attached to Mansfield Independent Chapel.   E. I. CARLYLE, *rev.* J. M. V. QUINN

Sources *Congregational Year Book* (1853), 233–5 · *GM*, 2nd ser., 39 (1853), 671
Likenesses stipple and line engraving (after J. Cochran), NPG

Weaver, Thomas (1616–1662), poet, was born in Worcester, the son of Thomas Weaver. He matriculated from Christ Church, Oxford, on 21 March 1634, graduating BA in 1637 and MA in 1640. He became a chaplain or petty canon at Christ Church Cathedral in 1641, and stayed in Oxford following the outbreak of the civil war.

As a member of Christ Church in the late 1630s and early 1640s, Weaver was heir to a vibrant and expansive poetic tradition. During the early years of the civil war he wrote most of the lyric poems which appear in the extensive collection now in the Bodleian (MS Rawlinson poet. 211). Weaver's poetry was typical of royalist verse of the early 1640s—politically engaged, satirical, and witty. He had a modest reputation, and several of his early poems were circulated in Oxford manuscripts. Furthermore, 'Zeal Over-heated', which deals with the comic consequences of a fire in an Oxford puritan merchant's shop, was published as part of John Taylor's *A Three-Fold Discourse betweene Three Neighbours* (1642). The poem particularly attacks the avaricious and hypocritical character of the puritan and his brother.

Weaver was ejected from his position at Christ Church Cathedral by the parliamentary visitation in 1648. He may have been imprisoned also at this time: a poem entitled 'A Song in Prison' appears in his manuscript of poetry from the 1640s. This verse asserts:

> no foule offence,
> But Loyaltie unto my King
> Caus'd my Restraint.

He fled Oxford, and Anthony Wood says that he 'shifted from place to place and lived upon his wits' (Wood, *Ath. Oxon.*, 3.622). His whereabouts until the Restoration are unclear. A verse letter in the Bodleian manuscript 'From

Hangiby Castle in Monmouthshire to Sir Evan Lloyd in London' seems to indicate that he was in Wales for a period. He evidently spent much time wandering between loyalist country houses, as there is a poem in the 1640s manuscript written from Lengiby Castle and also a lyric in his *Songs and Poems* (1654) 'To the Three Incomparable Ladies at K. Castle'.

Songs and Poems of Love and Drollery, by T. W. was dedicated 'To my most obliging friend E. M. Esquire' and the 'Epistle Dedicatory' asserts that

> It was not by my endeavor, but permittance only, that these trifles were preferred to the Press; nor had the perswasions used procured so much from me, but that upon strict Examination, I conceived them to be good for nothing, but to be printed.

The collection includes lyrics, ballads, carols, and pastoral dialogues; the majority of the poems appear in the 1640s manuscript. The poems, which are very political, include 'To Sylvia Going to an Enemies Quarters', 'An Epitaph on Major Owen and Captain Edward Wynne', and 'On Mauricia's Wound which she Received from a Round-Head'. The poem 'Rotundos' mocks the 'pretty tricks' of the roundheads. However, as printed in 1654, the volume betrays a royalist sense of loss: 'For since the late Deluge of Ignorance overflowed this Land, it fares with Books, as with Men; the light and frothy float and flourish, whilst the Grave and Solid sink and perish.' The updated version of 'Zeal Overheated' changes the ending of the ballad as printed in 1642, adopting a more defiant tone:

> God blesse this Land, and keep it Aye
> Against all that oppose:
> And let the Supream head bear sway
> In stead o'th Supream nose.

The volume concludes with 'An Epitaph on the Right Honorable the Lord Byron, Buried in France' and the sarcastic 'An Epithalamium, upon the Late Nuptial Act' which attacks the puritan attempts to unify religion and the law:

> Justice and Priesthood by Supreme Decree,
> For mutual helps sake must remarried be.

The printing of these poems led to Weaver's being arrested and tried for treason; he was only saved by the judge who, according to Wood, advised the jury to acquit this 'scholar and a man of wit'.

After the Restoration, Weaver was appointed by Charles II as the excise collector for Liverpool. A petition for the retrieval of moneys paid to '[the late] Thos. Weaver, late collector of customs at Liverpool', probably refers to an old case (*CSP dom.*, 1670, 346). Weaver has sometimes been credited with the writing of *Plantagenets True Story* which is in fact by Thomas Wincoll (Wing, *STC*, 672). Weaver died in Liverpool on 3 January 1662. JEROME DE GROOT

Sources Foster, *Alum. Oxon.* • M. Burrows, ed., *The register of the visitors of the University of Oxford, from AD 1647 to AD 1658*, CS, new ser., 29 (1881) • Wood, *Ath. Oxon.*, new edn, 3.622 • *DNB* • *CSP dom.*, 1670, 346
Archives Bodl. Oxf., Rawlinson Poet. MS 211

Weaver, Thomas (1773–1855), geologist and mining consultant, was born in King Street, Gloucester, the son of Thomas Weaver (d. 1805) and his wife, Mary. His father was an important pin manufacturer and, from 1772, a partner in Roe & Co.'s copper company of Macclesfield and Neath Abbey. From 1779 he was also an alderman of Gloucester.

In 1790 the younger Thomas Weaver entered the Bergakademie at Freiberg, Saxony, where he studied mining and geognosy under Abraham Werner. His contemporaries there included Alexander von Humboldt (1769–1859) and Leopold von Buch (1774–1853). He returned to Gloucester in 1792, and it is likely he attended Thomas Beddoes's geological lectures at Oxford before taking up the management of the Cronbane and Tigrony copper mines in the Wicklow Mountains in 1793.

The mines were an important source of copper for the elder Thomas Weaver's pin-making—he had been a proprietor of them since 1787. In September 1795 the discovery of alluvial gold at the foot of Croghan Mountain (south of the mines), caused a gold rush. From 1796 to 1803 Weaver was one of the superintendents of government operations there. (During interruption to mining caused by the uprising of 1798, he acted as a yeomanry officer.) While still manager of the Cronbane mine, in 1805 Weaver published the first English translation of Werner's *A Treatise on the External Characters of Fossils*. For this work, in 1811, he was elected a member of the Edinburgh-based Wernerian Society.

In 1812 Weaver's involvement at Cronbane ceased, and that year and in 1813 he applied unsuccessfully for positions in mining and mineralogy at the Royal Dublin Society. In 1817 the Gloucester pin-making firm (now run by his two younger brothers) went bankrupt but by then Weaver's work on the geology of Ireland had begun. In January 1816 he was reportedly 'engaged in a Geognostical map of a great part of Ireland'. In May 1818 he read a paper to the Geological Society in London on the geology of the east of Ireland, which was accompanied by a geological map of the south-east of Ireland, and discussed his involvement in Irish metal mining.

Weaver moved to Tortworth, Gloucestershire, about 1819, the year in which his second paper, on the geology of part of Gloucestershire and Somerset, was read. It was one of the first studies of what were later recognized as Lower Palaeozoic rocks. Weaver was elected a member of the Geological Society in 1820, having earlier been elected a member of the Royal Irish Academy. Throughout the 1820s he acted as a consultant mining geologist, particularly in Ireland, preparing reports for mining companies on the metalliferous prospects of the Waterford coast (1824) and the Kenmare district (1825).

In 1825 Weaver read a paper recording the comparatively modern age of the Irish elk, for which he was elected FRS in 1826. This was followed in 1830 by the first of many papers which recorded his part in the controversy over the age of rocks in Devon (which ultimately led to the naming of the Devonian system). Publication of his main contribution to the debate, a paper on geological relations of the south of Ireland, was, however, twice suppressed because many other geologists did not believe his report of fossil plants found in the greywacke, and it appeared only in 1838. In 1831 Weaver went to Mexico where he was a mining consultant for three years, and in 1834 he went on to New York. On his return to Britain he remained active as an author, writing on American rocks in 1836 and 1837, and also on Irish gold workings. In 1836 he made a tour of Scotland.

By 1841 Weaver was in retirement in London. He died at Stafford Place, Pimlico, on 2 July 1855. Prior to his death he had given many fossils and minerals to the Geological Society and the Yorkshire Philosophical Society. What remained of his large collection was sold at auction that month; the unsold residue is reported to have formed the hard core for a urinal at Bewdley, Worcestershire.

H. S. TORRENS

Sources W. J. Hamilton, *Quarterly Journal of the Geological Society*, 12 (1856), xxxviii–xxxix · G. L. Herries Davies, *Sheets of many colours* (1983), 51–2 · T. Weaver, 'Mines of Ireland', *Mining Journal* (1–22 Aug 1840), 245–70 · 'Verzeichniss', *Festschrift zum 100 jährigen Jubiläum der Konigl. Bergakademie zu Freiberg*, 2 (1867), 234 · A. Mills, 'Native gold lately discovered in Ireland', *PTRS*, 86 (1796), 38–45 · M. J. S. Rudwick, *The great Devonian controversy* (1985) · letters, A. Mills to W. Watson, 1792, Sheffield City Museum · A. Raistrick, *The Hatchett diary* (1967), 11 · A. E. Musson and E. Robinson, *Science and technology in the industrial revolution* (1969) · H. F. Berry, *A history of the Royal Dublin Society* (1915), 157, 163 · letters, A. Mills to J. Banks, 1795–6, Sutro Library, San Francisco · C. Coquebert, 'Notice sur les mines de cuivre', *Journal des Mines*, 3/16 (1796), 77–87 · C. D. Sherborn, *Where is the — collection* (1940), 141

Archives Bristol RO, Bristol Philosophical Institution archive · NMG Wales, De La Beche archive, letters

Webb. *See also* Webbe.

Webb, Alfred John (1834–1908), Irish nationalist and printer, was born in Dublin on 10 June 1834 into a prosperous Quaker family. He was the eldest son of Richard Davis Webb, a printer in Abbey Street, and Hannah, *née* Warring, of Waterford. He attended a Quaker school in Dublin and then Dr Hodgson's High School, Manchester, before being apprenticed to his father's business. In 1854 he was sent to Australia for health and commercial reasons but returned to Dublin the following year. He then rejoined the family business and became its manager when his father died.

In his youth Webb supported a number of social causes. During the famine of the 1840s he toured Ireland with another Quaker, the future chief secretary for Ireland, W. E. Forster. In 1861 he married Elizabeth (d. 1906), daughter of George Shackleton of Ballytore, co. Kildare. They had no children.

An early supporter of self-government principles, Webb was among those who attended the meeting at the Bilton Hotel in May 1870 which founded the modern home-rule movement. Unlike many of his fellow protestants, he remained an active member of the movement, being present at the national conference in November 1873 that converted the private group the Home Government Association into the public organization the Home Rule League. He wrote pamphlets and newspaper articles on its behalf and served as honorary treasurer of the league. During the 1870s he published his best-known work, *A Compendium of Irish Biography* (1877). Though remaining loyal to the nationalist leader Isaac Butt during the dispute over parliamentary 'obstruction', Webb gradually came to support Charles Stewart Parnell after he assumed the leadership in 1880, and became treasurer of the Irish National League on its foundation in 1882. Webb took no direct part in the Land League agitation though he helped Anna Parnell with underground printing for the Ladies' Land League. In 1886 he was a founder of the Protestant Home Rule League and was one of its vice-presidents. Webb's pamphlet *The Opinions of some Protestants Regarding their Irish Catholic Fellow-Countrymen*, published in 1886, was meant to show that protestants in Ireland had no fear of Catholic intolerance. This theme was developed the following year in another pamphlet, *The Alleged Massacre of 1641*, which argued that Catholics had not committed the atrocities against protestants ascribed to them.

Webb's firm was a major publisher of Irish National League literature. Sensitive to being seen as primarily a Catholic organization, the Irish party induced several protestant home-rulers to accept safe parliamentary seats. Webb heeded this plea and was returned unopposed for Waterford West on 24 February 1890. Not long afterwards, when he was confronted by the tribulations of the O'Shea–Parnell divorce scandal, he chose to support the majority who followed Justin McCarthy and spoke out against Parnell's continued leadership on the first day (2 December 1890) of the Irish party meeting in committee room 15 of the House of Commons. Dismayed by the party's failure to take decisive action against T. M. Healy's attack upon its conduct of the general election in July, he retired from the Commons in August 1895.

After leaving parliament, Webb remained involved in national political organizations but also travelled widely. During a visit to India he was elected president of the Indian National Congress for 1898. In semi-retirement he continued to be an enthusiastic traveller, and wrote frequent sketches of his journeys for Irish and American periodicals. In 1902 he published a critique of how law and order were administered in Ireland. In 1906 he wrote an unpublished autobiography that, among other things, gave attention to the traumatic events of December 1890. He died on 31 July 1908, when on holiday in the Shetland Islands.

D. J. O'DONOGHUE, rev. ALAN O'DAY

Sources *Freeman's Journal* [Dublin] (1 Aug 1908) · *The Times* (1 Aug 1908) · H. Boylan, *A dictionary of Irish biography*, 2nd edn (1988) · *WWBMP*, vol. 2 · *Dod's Parliamentary Companion* · J. Loughlin, *Gladstone, home rule and the Ulster question, 1882–1893* (1986) · J. Loughlin, 'The Irish protestant Home Rule Association and nationalist politics, 1886–1893', *Irish Historical Studies*, 24 (1984–5), 341–60 · D. Thornley, *Isaac Butt and home rule* (1964) · R. F. Foster, *Charles Stewart Parnell: the man and his family* (1976) · F. S. L. Lyons, *The Irish parliamentary party, 1890–1910* (1951) · C. C. O'Brien, *Parnell and his party, 1880–1890* (1957) · F. S. L. Lyons, *John Dillon* (1968) · F. S. L. Lyons, *The fall of Parnell, 1890–1891* (1961) · F. Callanan, *The Parnell split* (1992)

Archives NL Ire. · Religious Society of Friends, Dublin · TCD, corresp. of him and his father, R. D. Webb | NL Ire., O'Neill Daunt, Isaac Butt, John Redmond MSS · TCD, corresp. with John Dillon

Wealth at death £1985 4s. 8d.—in England: Irish probate sealed in England, 28 Oct 1908, CGPLA Eng. & Wales · £8191 4s. 1d.: resworn probate, 1 Oct 1908, CGPLA Ire.

Webb, Allan Becher (1839–1907), bishop of Grahamstown, was born in Calcutta on 6 October 1839. He was the eldest son of Allan Webb (surgeon to the governor-general of Bengal and professor of anatomy at the Calcutta Medical College) and Emma, daughter of John Aubrey Danby.

Webb was educated at Rugby School from October 1855, and won a scholarship to Corpus Christi College, Oxford, in 1858. He graduated BA in 1862 with a second-class degree in *literae humaniores* (having gained a first in moderations), and proceeded MA in 1864 and DD in 1871. In 1863 he was elected a fellow of University College, Oxford, was ordained deacon, and became curate of St Peter-in-the-East, Oxford. From 1864 to 1865 he was vice-principal of Cuddesdon College under Edward King. He resigned his fellowship on his marriage in 1867 to Eliza, daughter of Robert Barr Bourne, rector and patron of Donhead, St Andrew; he accepted the rectory of Avon Dasset, near Leamington Spa.

In 1870 Webb was nominated bishop of Bloemfontein in the Orange Free State, and he soon showed which side he was on in the controversy that had been sparked in the church by the Colenso affair. Supported by Robert Gray, bishop of Cape Town, Webb declined to take the oath of allegiance to the English primate on the grounds that it was opposed to the canons of the South African synod. Instead he offered to take the oath of obedience to his metropolitan, the bishop of Cape Town. Archibald Campbell Tait, archbishop of Canterbury, however, held that this procedure infringed the Jerusalem Act of 1841 (5 Vict. c. 6), which regulated the appointment to bishoprics within the British dominions (*Guardian*, 23 Nov 1870). Since the act was not in force in Scotland, the primate finally allowed Webb to take the oath of canonical obedience to Bishop Gray and his successors in Inverness Cathedral on 30 November 1870.

Webb, like most churchmen in the South African province, was firmly high-church in his views. He was accordingly active in promoting the work of sisterhoods, whether missionary, educational, or medical. His diocese extended over the Orange Free State, Basutoland, and Bechuanaland, and his youth and vigour stood him in good stead. In 1883 he succeeded Nathaniel James Merriman as bishop of Grahamstown. Here, too, he actively engaged in developing mission and educational work for both local people and Europeans, and fostered diocesan institutions like the College of St Andrew and the Sisterhood of the Resurrection. He also worked hard to heal the schism which had divided the South African province since the Colenso affair, despite his own clear views on the question. The chancel of the cathedral at Grahamstown, which was consecrated in 1893, stands as a permanent memorial of his episcopate.

In 1898, after twenty-eight years, Webb left South Africa. He was subsequently appointed provost of Inverness Cathedral, and also acted as assistant bishop in the diocese of Moray and Brechin. In 1901 he became dean of Salisbury in succession to George David Boyle. Webb favoured stately worship, and though never a fluent speaker was an impressive preacher at missions and retreats. In addition to sermons, he published several devotional works, including *The Priesthood of the Laity in the Body of Christ* (1889), *The Life of Service before the Throne* (1895), *The Unveiling of the Eternal Word* (1897), and *With Christ in Paradise* (2nd edn, 1898).

Webb died on 12 June 1907 at the deanery, Salisbury, survived by his wife and two sons. He was buried in the cloisters of Salisbury Cathedral where a stained-glass window and screen were erected to his memory.

G. S. WOODS, *rev.* LYNN MILNE

Sources *The Times* (13 June 1907) · *The Times* (18 June 1907) · *Church Times* (14 July 1907) · *The Guardian* (19 June 1907) · H. L. Farrar, *Life of Robert Gray*, 2 (1876), 509 · S. C. Gayford, *Cuddesdon College, 1854–1904: a record and a memorial* (1904) · *Pelican Record*, 8 (1905–7), 172–3 · *DSAB*
Likenesses F. Miles, crayon drawing, 1878; in possession of A. C. B. Webb in 1912 · A. Walker, oils, 1902; in possession of A. C. B. Webb in 1912 · photograph, NPG · portrait, Grahamstown Cathedral, South Africa, chapterhouse
Wealth at death £6950 6s. 11d.: probate, 20 July 1907, CGPLA Eng. & Wales

Webb, Arthur (1868–1952), building society manager, was born on 8 July 1868 at Battersea, London, the son of Thomas Burgess Webb and his wife, Christine, *née* Young. Thomas Webb had worked at Price's candle factory, Battersea, and was a founder of the Battersea Co-operative Society, a director of the Co-operative Wholesale Society, and president from its foundation in 1884 of the Southern Co-operative Building Society. When Arthur Webb left the local Sir Walter St John School, he became a clerk with the Battersea Co-operative Society and a collector for the Southern Co-operative Building Society. In 1892 he was appointed secretary of the building society, which then had assets of £24,000, at a salary of £120 per year. He married Mabel Elizabeth, daughter of George Benjamin Edwards, an auctioneer, in 1898. She was a journalist, broadcaster, and author of works on domestic economy. They had two sons and two daughters.

Webb proved to be an able and vigorous leader who took full advantage of the building society's co-operative connections to give it wide publicity. His insistence, in 1894, that 'Southern' be eliminated from the title showed his ambitions. He tirelessly addressed co-operative gatherings, especially meetings of local retail societies. Innovation and awareness of members' needs characterized Webb's administration. A triplicate slip was devised so that mortgage instalments or investments could be made at the branches of many retail societies. 'Home safes' in a variety of styles were soon made available. Mortgages backed by endowment assurance policies were introduced. Retail societies could borrow to finance new shops. An insurance policy was negotiated covering all the properties mortgaged to the society, giving savings both to the members and to the society. The need for appropriate office space both for mechanization and the expansion of business was promptly dealt with. Webb encouraged his staff with an independent superannuation scheme, professional education and sports facilities. He supported attempts to create a professional staff organization and, when the Building Societies Institute was formed in 1934, Webb was a foundation council member, president (1939–41), and one of its first fellows. He was also a fellow of the Chartered Institute of Secretaries. The assets of the Co-operative Building Society grew steadily until 1914, and spectacularly after 1918. Webb joined the board in 1927, and in 1928 became the society's first managing director. He resigned that post in 1939 to serve as president (1939–41) and continued as a director until 1951. When he resigned in 1939 the society had a network of thirty-five branches and 576 agencies; it was the country's sixth largest society.

Webb was elected to the executive committee of the National Association of Building Societies in 1903, holding office continuously until increasing deafness led him to resign in 1945; he then became a vice-president. He served as chairman both of the parliamentary and of the finance committees. In 1916 he sought direct involvement for societies in the post-war design of houses and the development of estates, but gained little support. In the 1930s he correctly judged that collective voluntary action by societies could not successfully restrain their cut-throat competition to lend, which threatened their financial stability. For Webb the solution lay in legislation, and he welcomed the 1939 Building Societies Act. In 1943 he published *Signposts of Building Finance*, where he questioned the long-run viability of the large number of small societies, and they were offered a merger with the Cooperative Society. His view met general resistance and the offer was withdrawn, although there were fifteen such mergers between 1943 and 1947. However, subsequent events confirmed his judgement.

Webb lived in Wimbledon, and was elected to the local urban district council, and later to the Surrey county council. Education was his strong interest, particularly the establishment of secondary schools under the 1902 Education Act. He served as chairman of the Wimbledon Higher Education Committee, of the School of Art, and of the Technical College, and was a governor of Wimbledon Girls' High School. Appointed a magistrate in 1915, he was vice-chairman of the Wimbledon bench and chairman of the juvenile court; he retired in 1941. Webb died at his home, 6 Blenheim Road, Grand Drive, Wimbledon, on 16 October 1952, and was cremated five days later at the South London crematorium, Streatham Vale. He was survived by his wife and four children.

ESMOND J. CLEARY

Sources A. Mansbridge, *Brick upon brick* (1934) · H. Ashworth, *The building society story* (1980) · M. Cassell, *Inside Nationwide* (1984) · *Wimbledon Borough News* (24 Oct 1952) · *The Times* (18 Oct 1952) · *The Times* (31 Oct 1952) · b. cert. · m. cert.
Likenesses H. Knight, oils, 1928, Nationwide Building Society, London · R. Haines, photograph, 1930–34, repro. in Mansbridge, *Brick upon brick*, facing p. 72
Wealth at death £16,431 6s. 7d.: probate, 29 Dec 1952, *CGPLA Eng. & Wales*

Webb, Arthur Marmaduke (*fl.* 1760–1792). *See under* Webb, Peter (*d.* 1775).

Webb, Sir Aston (1849–1930), architect, was born on 22 May 1849 at Park Hill, Clapham, Surrey, the second of the three children of Edward Webb (1805–1854), watercolourist and steel-engraver, and his wife, Anna (1823–1850), daughter of John Evans (1787–1865) of Worcester and London, and his second wife, Anna. He was educated at a small private school in Brighton, and in September 1866 was articled for five years to the architects Robert Richardson Banks and Charles Barry junior. He set up in independent practice in 1873.

On 12 September 1876 Webb married Marian (1850–1930), the second daughter of David Everett FRCS, a surgeon at Worcester Ophthalmic Hospital, with whom he had two sons and one daughter. The elder son, Maurice Everett Webb (1880–1939), continued his father's practice under the title Sir Aston Webb & Son; the younger, Philip Edward Webb (1886–1916), was killed in action during the First World War.

Apart from the early patronage of his extended family, much of Webb's work came through success in architectural competitions. His entry for the Admiralty and War Office in 1884 received the most favourable comment in the press, though an inferior design was selected. It was the first of many designs Webb produced over the next twenty-five years in collaboration with Edward Ingress Bell [*see below*]. Their winning entry in the competition for the Victoria law courts, Birmingham (1886–91), improved on the plan suggested by the assessor, Alfred Waterhouse, and their choice of the pseudonym Terracotta cannot have failed to catch his eye. The same material was proposed in their unsuccessful entry for the Imperial Institute in 1887, when again Waterhouse was the assessor. Their winning design for the new Christ's Hospital, near Horsham, Sussex (1897–1904), sensibly adapted the latest ideas on the sanitary arrangement of hospitals to the requirements of a boys' boarding-school, and at the University of Birmingham (1902–9) an unusual formal semi-circular arrangement with radiating pavilions was built.

Webb's common-sense approach made him a favourite for government work. Though the job of completing the Victoria and Albert Museum (1899–1909) came via competition in 1891, other buildings were directly commissioned. The Royal College of Science (1900–06) at South Kensington—originally to have shared the new building for the Victoria and Albert Museum—gave him the expertise that made him the natural choice as architect for the institution of the same name in Dublin (1904–11); the joint appointment of Sir Thomas Manley Deane was a concession to the Irish architectural profession. This project also brought him the commission for the Britannia Royal Naval College, Dartmouth (1898–1907). Had the president of the Royal Institute of British Architects, William Emerson, not insisted on a limited competition in 1901 for the design of the architectural surroundings of Sir Thomas Brock's memorial to Queen Victoria in front of Buckingham Palace, Lord Esher would have been happy to see Webb handed that job too. Webb won anyway, and with it came other related work: the Admiralty Arch (1905–11)

Sir Aston Webb (1849–1930), by Solomon Joseph Solomon, c.1906

and the refacing of the entrance front of Buckingham Palace (1913).

As a designer, Webb was known for the clarity of his planning; his success was considered by many to be more practical than artistic. He paid close attention to the requirements of his clients and was careful not to exceed his estimates. The eclectic style of his earlier buildings, many of which had a François Premier flavour, better accommodated his taste for repetitive small-scale detail than his later, more severe works. He is said to have felt 'especial satisfaction' (*DNB*) with the French protestant church in Soho Square (1891–3), where red and buff terracotta was used in the same richly plastic way as at the Birmingham law courts, and the façade of the Metropolitan Life Assurance Company's offices in Moorgate (1890–93) was praised by his contemporaries for its originality. An important work which occupied him from 1885 onwards was the restoration of the Norman church of St Bartholomew-the-Great in the City of London.

Webb's calm demeanour and diplomatic personality suited him for an active role in the various institutions concerned with architecture. The architect H. V. Lanchester remembered him as a 'born leader of men' who 'possessed the happy gift of seeing not only the right course to pursue but also the best method of convincing others of the soundness of his opinions' (*The Builder*, 139, 1930, 333). He was president in turn of the Architectural Association (1881–2), the Royal Institute of British Architects (1902–4), and the Royal Academy (1919–24), the only previous architect to have filled that office being James Wyatt in 1805. He was honoured with the royal gold medal

of the Royal Institute of British Architects (1905) and the inaugural gold medal of the American Institute of Architects (1907) and was knighted in 1904.

Webb was known by his professional colleagues for his charm and courtesy, even if the large gingery-brown moustache which completely obscured his mouth gave some the impression of secretiveness. His description of the work of the Royal Institute of British Architects—'wisely steering a middle course with justice and foresight' (*RIBA Journal*, 3rd ser., 14, 1906–7, 122)—might be applied equally well to the conduct of his architectural practice.

In 1924 Webb was injured in a traffic accident while returning home from the Royal Academy annual dinner and never completely recovered his health. He died in his sleep at his house at 1 Hanover Terrace, Kensington, on 21 August 1930, and though his funeral was held in St Paul's on 25 August 1930, he was not buried in the crypt as arrangements had already been made for his interment in the family plot at Gunnersbury cemetery, Middlesex. A memorial tablet carved by William McMillan was unveiled in St Paul's in 1932. His wife survived him by only two months.

Edward Ingress Bell (1837–1914), architect, was born on 7 February 1837 at Greenhithe, Kent, the son of Edward Bell (*fl.* 1837–1860), a surveyor, landscape gardener, and architect, and his wife, Anna. He was trained by his father. He joined the War Office in 1859 as a draughtsman and worked there until his retirement as first-class surveyor in 1898. On 14 June 1860 he married Elizabeth Larcomb (*b.* 1837). From 1890 Bell was responsible for barrack design. His appointment about 1882 as a consulting architect to the crown agents for the colonies led to a collaboration with Aston Webb which lasted until 1909. They worked well together: Bell was a skilful planner and a rapid draughtsman, but had a retiring disposition, in contrast to Webb's taste for public life. He died at his home, St Stephen's, Winchester Road, Worthing, on 30 August 1914 and was buried at Broadwater cemetery, Worthing.

IAN DUNGAVELL

Sources I. Dungavell, 'The architectural career of Sir Aston Webb (1849–1930)', 2 vols., PhD diss., U. Lond., 1999 · *The Builder*, 139 (1930), 333–4 · *Architects' Journal* (27 Aug 1930) · E. G. Dawber, 'Sir Aston Webb', *RIBA Journal*, 37 (1929–30), 710–11 · H. B. Creswell, 'Sir Aston Webb and his office', *Edwardian architecture and its origins*, ed. A. Service (1975), 328–37 · *CGPLA Eng. & Wales* (1930) · *DNB*
Archives Commonwealth War Graves Commission, corresp. and MSS relating to work for Imperial War Graves Commission · ICL, corresp. relating to Imperial College · RIBA | RIBA, biography file; nomination MSS · U. Birm. L., letters to M. H. Spielmann
Likenesses S. J. Solomon, oils, *c.*1906, NPG [*see illus.*] · S. J. Solomon, oils, *c.*1906, RIBA · W. Llewellyn, oils, exh. RA 1921, RA
Wealth at death £96,421 16*s.* 6*d.*: probate, 8 Nov 1930, *CGPLA Eng. & Wales*

Webb [*née* Potter], **(Martha) Beatrice** (1858–1943), social reformer and diarist, and **Sidney James Webb**, Baron Passfield (1859–1947), social reformer and politician, were among the most prominent and productive pioneers of social science in Britain. Beatrice, as she was always known, was born on 22 January 1858 at Standish House in

(Martha) Beatrice Webb (1858–1943), by George Bernard Shaw, *c.*1900

Gloucestershire, the eighth of the ten children (nine of them daughters) of Richard Potter (1817–1892), business-man and railway director, and his wife, Lawrencina Hey-worth (1821–1882). Catherine *Courtney (1847–1929) was an elder sister. Sidney was born on 13 July 1859 at 45 Cran-bourn Street, near Leicester Square in London, the second of the three children (two of them sons) of Charles Webb (1828/9–1891), variously described as an accountant, a per-fumer, and a hairdresser, and his wife, Elizabeth Mary Sta-cey (1820/21–1895), hairdresser and dealer in toiletries. Each made a substantial independent contribution to the infant 'science of society' in Britain, but it was the work of the Webb 'partnership', after they met in 1890, that estab-lished their significance.

Beatrice Potter's early life Beatrice was born into wealth. Her father, Richard Potter, had inherited a fortune in French stocks which he had lost in the commercial crisis of 1847 and had largely rebuilt through his partnership in a timber firm during the Crimean War. Knowledge of Beatrice's early life comes largely from her first volume of autobiography, *My Apprenticeship* (1926), written in the early 1920s when her rejection of the capitalist system was crystallizing. It is impossible to tell how far her depic-tion of a father rigorously honourable in business but with 'no clear vision of the public good' and a mother 'brought up in the strictest set of Utilitarian economists' was heightened for effect (*My Apprenticeship*, 1938 edn, 23, 31), but it is clear that Beatrice was brought up in comfort

and that she sought, from an early age, to question her cir-cumstances. Her upbringing encouraged this. Richard Potter was 'the only man I ever knew who genuinely believed that women were superior to men' (ibid., 27), and all his daughters were endowed with an intellectual train-ing far beyond the conventional needs of a Victorian wife. 'If only I had been brought up to know how to cook and clean', she lamented during the Second World War, when servants were hard to find (diary, 24 Feb 1942; *Diaries*, ed. Mackenzie and Mackenzie, 4.479). Instead a succession of resident governesses had trained her in music and paint-ing, languages and literature, mathematics, and philo-sophy, and the young Beatrice acquired a precocious knowledge of the French encyclopaedists, English polit-ical economy, Buckle and Lecky, Mill and Comte, and above all Herbert Spencer, a family friend. Intellectual debate flourished in a household in which neither reading nor discussion was censored.

The surviving correspondence between Beatrice and her father suggests a relationship which was not only affectionate but also less deferential than was usual between Victorian fathers and daughters. Her relation-ship with her mother was more complex. Lawrencina Heyworth had been 'reared by and with men, and she dis-liked women' (*My Apprenticeship*, 29), but she was cursed with nine daughters and only one son, who died in infancy. She dismissed Beatrice as the only one of her children to display below-average intelligence. There was, though, much of her in Beatrice: she anticipated in her-self Beatrice's central conflict between the search for a rational guide to life and the search for spiritual comfort.

Emotional upheaval Beatrice grew to adulthood in the years of the 'Victorian crisis of faith', and the tensions inherent in this post-Darwinian mood are evident in the diary account of her early life. Though brought up as a Unitarian, she followed her father into the Anglican faith, being confirmed in March 1875, during her only spell of formal education, a few months spent at Miss Tapp's establishment, Stirling House, in Bournemouth. Signifi-cantly, this step was taken during one of the depressions that afflicted her throughout her life, and her commit-ment to conventional Christianity was even then quali-fied: she found the doctrine of atonement 'repugnant' and expected Christ to save the world 'not so particularly by His death, as by His Word' (diary, 27 March 1875; *Diaries*, ed. Mackenzie and Mackenzie, 1.20). In the years after 1876, during which she toyed with scientific explanations of the meaning of life, she also experimented with 'an alternative form of religious emotion', as the Eastern scholar Brian Hodgson introduced her to Hinduism and Buddhism (*My Apprenticeship*, 105 ff.). But she did not con-vert: 'all that happened was my detachment from Chris-tianity' (ibid., 110). In 1915, under the clouds of war, she explicitly rejected Christianity and tried instead to con-ceptualize 'the Ideal that moves me … an Abstract Being divested of all human appetite but combining the quality of an always working intellect with an impersonal love' (diary, 14 Nov 1915; *Diaries*, ed. Mackenzie and Mackenzie, 3.242). Her younger sister maintained correctly that for most of her life 'she was what one might call a religious minded agnostic & did believe in some sort of spiritual force at work in the universe' (R. H. Dobbs to R. H. Tawney, 3 June 1947?, Tawney papers, BLPES, 24/2). Whatever she considered this force to be, she prayed to it throughout her life.

During the formative but stressful decade of the 1880s, Beatrice's wish to reconcile her religious outlook with her faith in scientific method led her first to the doctrines of Herbert Spencer and later to those of Auguste Comte. Spencer had been an associate of Beatrice's maternal grandfather, and nurtured her as an intellectual protégée in his old age. Coming to his work at the time when she was dabbling in Eastern religions, Beatrice was initially fascinated by Spencer's mystical side. In time, though, she became convinced that Spencer's interest in God the unknowable was pursued at the expense of a concern for humanity that Beatrice herself could not disavow. His attempt to impose biological laws upon social conduct was not only bogus but also inhumane, leading him to an extreme individualism which she could not accept. She continued to value his method—in particular the collection of facts and the concern to establish patterns of evolutionary development—but his philosophy only 'sealed my conviction in the bankruptcy of science when it attempts to realise the aim or the cause of human existence' (diary, 8/9 Dec 1903; My Apprenticeship, 57).

Comte's positivism offered a more pleasing synthesis of humanism and scientific method. An encounter with his catechism induced Beatrice to begin a new diary volume with the sentence 'our harmony as moral beings is impossible on any other foundation but altruism' (diary, 8 Sept 1884; Diaries, ed. Mackenzie and Mackenzie, 1.119). She resisted conversion to the 'Religion of Humanity', but Comte's philosophy remained an enduring influence. His inadequate understanding of that 'superhuman force' towards which Beatrice strove did not deter her from 'the transference of the emotion of self-sacrificing service from God to man' (My Apprenticeship, 153). With hindsight she identified her mother's death in 1882 as the point at which she made this change: 'believing that I could alter the conditions of human life for the better I began to love humanity' (diary, 1 Jan 1901; Diaries, ed. Mackenzie and Mackenzie, 2.190). The immediate outcome was a devotion to philanthropy, and in 1883 she began an unrewarding spell of work for the Charity Organisation Society (COS) among the poor of Soho, in central London.

Beatrice was conjuring with notions of service to humanity and of the meaning of faith at an age when many women of her class were more concerned with the London marriage market. Exposure to London 'society' convinced her that convention was more numbing upon female intellect at this than at any other social level. The 'marriage question' imposed itself more disturbingly upon her in 1883, when she became drawn into a corrosive infatuation with the radical politician Joseph Chamberlain. Elegant and forceful, Chamberlain was also more than twenty years older than Beatrice, and it appears likely that her obsession was the kind of 'crush' suffered by a young woman emotionally close to her father. It is unlikely that Chamberlain became seriously committed. Twice widowed, he was a man 'in want of a wife' (Nord, 98), and his visit to the Potter household in January 1884 was probably a routine enquiry, stifled immediately by Beatrice's unwillingness to play the submissive spouse. This unwillingness was final. Beatrice recognized that Chamberlain was 'an enthusiast and a despot' who denied his sisters and daughter freedom of expression and would be certain to curb her own heterodoxies. But this rational understanding left uncurbed the emotional force behind the attraction. Beatrice was unsettled by the 'deadly fight between the intellectual and the sensual' that her encounter with Chamberlain had provoked in her (diary, 10 Dec 1886; Diaries, ed. Mackenzie and Mackenzie, 1.189). His eventual third marriage in 1888 and, more painfully, rumours of a separation in 1901, when Beatrice was herself married, threw her into spells of profound depression. Meeting Chamberlain had been, she wrote in a self-scrutinizing diary entry heralding the new century, 'the catastrophe of my life' (diary, 1 Jan 1901; Diaries, ed. Mackenzie and Mackenzie, 2.190).

Beatrice and feminism With an irony that Beatrice noted in her autobiography, her father's open-mindedness towards women had turned all the Potter sisters into anti-feminists. The most contentious manifestation of this in Beatrice's case was her decision to add her name to a petition of women opposing female suffrage, published in the Nineteenth Century in 1889. Beatrice had inherited her father's hostility to democracy (Richard Potter had moved from radicalism to toryism over the second Reform Act in 1867). It did not oblige her to oppose female suffrage, but the underlying sentiments governing her view of the vote—her objection to 'that false metaphysical idea of rights' (diary, 1 Feb 1885, 29 June 1889; Diaries, ed. Mackenzie and Mackenzie, 1.131, 288)—ran deep. Having seen the conditions of sweated female workers in the London tailoring trades in the 1880s, she became hostile to the then dominant strain of feminism that placed civic equality before economic emancipation. As female suffrage rose up the political agenda, it became more difficult for Beatrice to maintain her opposition. She recanted in 1906, and in 1913 the Webbs wrote that 'the Socialist takes for granted not only an extension of the suffrage to all adults but also the entire removal of artificial disabilities for duty or office' (New Statesman, 5 July 1913). Beatrice's conversion was none the less inhibited by the fact that the female suffrage campaign intensified while the Webbs were developing their own thesis that representative democracy was an inadequate expression of man's complex role as producer, consumer, and citizen. Even after her recantation, Beatrice continued to reject narrowly constitutional conceptions of women's rights. 'We shall never understand the Awakening of Women until we realise that it is not mere feminism', she wrote in 1913 (New Statesman, 1 Nov 1913).

Beatrice did not take up the women's issue in earnest until 1912–14, when the constitutional suffragists moved, like herself, closer to the Labour Party. She interpreted this realignment as part of a growing revolt against 'an essentially masculine capitalism'. The suffrage movement was democratizing itself: it no longer reflected 'the vested interests and personal prejudices of the existing order', but comprised 'nearly all that is mentally active and personally energetic in the whole female population' (*New Statesman*, 14 Feb 1914). Her new stance implied support for constitutional suffragism rather than militancy. Just as the Webbs counselled the labour movement against syndicalism, so Beatrice criticized the militant suffragists. When most women were enfranchised, in 1918, she noted that the vote held no glamour for her; there is no indication in her diary that she ever used the vote once she had gained it. She found her solution to the 'women question' in the Soviet Union in the 1930s, where 'emancipation was never thought of as merely the removal of legal disabilities … the economic and even the household subjection of women had equally to be abolished' (S. Webb and B. Webb, *Soviet Communism: a New Civilisation?*, 1935, 814–15). In the meantime her feminism remained cautious and selective.

Social observation and socialism In the wake of the Chamberlain episode Beatrice recorded her admiration for those independent women prominent in the world of philanthropy such as Octavia Hill and Emma Cons— 'these "governing and guiding" women … who give up their lives to the management of men' (diary, 12 Aug 1885; *Diaries*, ed. Mackenzie and Mackenzie, 1.136). Yet she was aware from her Soho experience that the field of philanthropy—and particularly the casework approach of the COS—was already being characterized as ladies' work. Beatrice wanted, as Professor Nord puts it, 'to do the kind of work that she did not see other women doing' (Nord, 136). This view reinforced the awareness instilled by her spell with the COS that most social workers understood little of poverty. The result was a move away from philanthropy towards 'social diagnosis' (diary, 5 Nov 1883; *Diaries*, ed. Mackenzie and Mackenzie, 1.96), in the hope that by applying Spencer's methods of observation and classification she could develop a more scientific understanding of poverty.

Beatrice's first such exercise was a visit in November 1883 to Bacup, in east Lancashire (where she had maternal relatives), disguised as 'Miss Jones', the daughter of a Welsh farmer. The decision to visit a small manufacturing town had been motivated by the belief that London's slums did not provide a representative cross-section of the English working class, and her attention in Bacup was accordingly directed towards the institutions of working-class association and self-help in the town. Most prominent were the dissenting chapels and the co-operatives. The chapel impressed her as 'a self-governing community, regulating not only chapel matters but overlooking the private life of its members', and in the process 'educating this class for self-government' (Beatrice Webb to Richard Potter, November 1883; *Letters*, 1.19). Still more impressive, because largely unfamiliar, were the co-operative stores. She described to her father the operation of one of these stores, which over twenty years had never paid less than

12.5 per cent to its working-class shareholders, noting at the same time the failure of co-operative mills. This part of Lancashire was the cradle of consumer co-operation in England, and Beatrice noted that co-operation was far stronger than trade unionism in Bacup. Her encounter with co-operation left a lifelong impression: the belief that co-operation was superior to trade unionism as an associational force, and the lesson that consumer co-operatives succeeded where producer co-operatives failed, influenced her life's work. Immediately, though, she stressed the moral benefits of the conjunction of the ethos of the chapel and the practice of co-operation in Bacup.

Beatrice made a second trip to Bacup in 1886, but before then she had joined the ranks of middle-class missionaries to the East End of London, then emerging as Britain's poverty capital. During 1885 she worked as a rent collector in a new block of working-class dwellings, Katherine Buildings, in Whitechapel, which provided the material for her first publication, a letter in the *Pall Mall Gazette* in February 1886 entitled 'A lady's view of unemployment at the east'. She saw East Enders in modish Darwinist terms, as 'a constantly decomposing mass of human beings, few rising out of it but many dropping down dead, pressed out of existence in the struggle' (diary, 8 March 1885; *Diaries*, ed. Mackenzie and Mackenzie, 1.132). The contrast with Bacup's respectability clearly guided her thoughts, so that broad moral conclusions were drawn from what were essentially the differences between a small industrial town and an inner-city district. By east London standards the residents of Katherine Buildings, though hardly affluent, were relatively comfortable, and they took exception to Beatrice's description of them as 'the lowest class of working poor' (Lewis, 114).

However misconceived, though, Beatrice's work in Katherine Buildings cast as long a shadow as her Bacup trips. She developed observational techniques in her case studies of tenants, particularly through the device of the questionnaire, which became a permanent part of the Webbs' investigative armoury. She gained an understanding of the structural nature of poverty: the main point of her *Pall Mall Gazette* letter was to emphasize the effects on employment of the de-industrialization of the London waterside. Above all, she learned that private philanthropy was largely ineffective in the face of poverty on an East End scale. It was at this point that Beatrice understood the limitations of the COS's policy of targeting help at the deserving poor. Many of the poor of Katherine Buildings owed their poverty to invalidity, industrial accident, or similar acts of God. They might well be deserving, but no amount of personal attention could repair their infirmity. The COS could not dissipate its limited funds on the long-term sick, however deserving, and consequently consigned them to the poor law. Beatrice did not lose—would never lose—her belief that 'something-for-nothing' charity merely exacerbated poverty, but she formed in these years her enduring belief that much poverty was caused by factors beyond the control of the poor, and could be tackled only by public agencies.

Beatrice's Whitechapel work was curtailed by the paralysing stroke suffered by her father in November 1885, which forced her, as the eldest unmarried daughter, to become his nurse and household manager for eight months in the year. For the remaining four months her sisters deputized, allowing her sabbaticals in which to continue her studies of the East End. She was one of the original members of the team gathered by Charles Booth—her cousin by marriage—to carry out his pioneering study of east London poverty from 1886, and was detailed to investigate dock labour and the tailoring trade. In April 1888 she offered her services as a jobbing tailoress in the Mile End Road to gain knowledge of London's principal sweated trade. This was one of the more implausible deceits perpetrated by Victorian social observers, but she gathered a comprehensive understanding of the operation of the trade and the material for two articles published in the journal *Nineteenth Century* in autumn 1888. Her study of dock labour had appeared in the same journal in the previous year, and it, along with one of the tailoring articles and a new essay on the East End Jewish community, appeared under Beatrice's name in the first volume of Booth's survey, published in 1889.

The articles varied in quality. Beatrice herself later dismissed the docks essay as 'an inferior piece of work' (*My Apprenticeship*, 356). It actually provides a valuable anatomy of the casual labour system, but contrasts in its sententiousness and occasionally lurid style with the rest of Booth's survey. The piece on tailoring was weightier, destroying by careful analysis of the trade's structure the myth of the exploitative middleman. The essay on the Jewish community was an odd production, marked both by a pervasive sympathy with individual Jews—Beatrice believed herself to have Jewish blood—and by the racial stereotyping typical of middle-class English opinion in this period. In each of the three pieces, though, there are signs of the directions that Beatrice's social thought was taking. The essay on London's Jews contained a eulogy of the Chevras, religious associations with secular benefit functions, combining the moral and material roles which Beatrice feared would be separated in English co-operatives. In the docks essay she predicted that the East End's 'leisure class' of demoralized unemployed was a pointer to the future of 'our great cities'. She warned that 'the extensive charitable assistance doled out in the metropolis' was the principal cause of this malaise, but her principal remedy was not the traditional COS prescription of charitable continence but 'a kind of municipal socialism', the creation of a public trust to regulate dock labour (*Life and Labour of the People*, 1: *East London*, ed. C. Booth, 1889, 204, 206, 207). Still more pointedly, the essay on tailoring attributed sweating not to the elusive middleman but to the system which sustained him: 'the real "sweater"' had 'a threefold personality—an ignorant consumer, a grinding and fraudulent wholesaler or retail slop trader, a rack-renting landlord', but the sweater's true soul was 'the evil spirit of the age, unrestrained competition' (ibid., 238).

Though much of Booth's survey might be read as an indictment of individualism, Beatrice was the most outspoken contributor in this vein. The triumphant diary declaration—'at last I am a socialist!' (1 Feb 1890; *Diaries*, ed. Mackenzie and Mackenzie, 1.322)—was predicted by her intellectual development over the previous decade: by her rejection of Spencer's individualism, her adoption of Comtean humanism, her enthusiasm for the moralized collectivism of the Bacup co-operatives, and her revulsion at the social debasement produced by individualism in the East End.

This was, as many of Beatrice's twentieth-century admirers failed to understand, a socialism with a substantial moral freight. It followed that she rejected—indeed scarcely considered—the hedonistic prescriptions of class warfare and revolutionary socialism. Gradualism was inherent in the developmental framework which she had derived from Spencer and Comte, and the journal version of the docks essay had concluded with the Comtean sentiment that 'all things are in the process of becoming, and the yesterday vies with today as a foreteller of tomorrow' (quoted in Nord, 162). Booth had omitted the sentence—his project was a snapshot rather than a history, let alone a prediction—but it reflected Beatrice's wish to place observation in an evolutionary setting. For that reason, on reading the collection of *Fabian Essays in Socialism* edited by George Bernard Shaw for the Fabian Society in 1889, she was most impressed by the essay by Sidney Webb, as 'he has the historic sense' (*My Apprenticeship*, 453). A few months later she met him. She had resolved to write a study of co-operation, placing it in its historical context. Seeking an expert on the history of the British labour movement, she was put in contact by her second cousin Margaret Harkness with a young man already possessing an encyclopaedic knowledge of British labour history. On 8 January 1890 she met Sidney Webb at Harkness's house in Great Russell Street.

Sidney Webb's early life Sidney Webb's background, though nowhere near as opulent as Beatrice's, was comfortable. His father was a man of local substance—a rate collector, a guardian and a sergeant in the volunteers—and the family employed a live-in servant. Sidney attended what his brother described as a 'first class middle class Day school in St Martin's Lane' (C. Webb to R. H. Tawney, n.d., Tawney papers, BLPES, 24/2), run by Mr Pincher, and his parents were later able to send him abroad to extend his education, first at Herveville, Switzerland, from 1871 to 1873, and from 1873 to 1875 near Wismar in Mecklenburg-Schwerin. These ventures gave him a lifelong competence in French and German. Ten days after returning to England, Sidney gained a position in a colonial broker's office. Such was his ability there that he was offered an interest in the business, which he declined in order to seek entry to the civil service. He gained a post in the War Office in 1878, then moved to the Inland Revenue in 1879 and to the Colonial Office, as a first-division clerk, in 1881. Meanwhile he continued his education through extension classes at the City of London College and enrolment at no fewer than four other continuing education institutions in London, membership of the London Library, and prodigious reading at the British Museum. A story of extraordinary success in competition for academic prizes culminated in the award of one of the Whewell scholarships at Trinity College, Cambridge, in 1883. Prevented by his Colonial Office work from living in college as required, he was unable to take up the scholarship, a disappointment which perhaps explained his 'complex, but basically antipathetic' attitude towards Oxbridge in his subsequent educational work (Harrison, 12).

Sidney's intellectual evolution This episode ended Sidney's academic ambitions and confined him to what he called the 'Impasse du bureau des Colonies' (Sidney Webb to G. Wallas, 2 July 1885; *Letters*, 1.87). Creative life continued outside the Colonial Office, though, in the numerous debating societies of late Victorian London, most prominently the Zetetical ('truth-seeking') Society of Conduit Street. This club was a venue for political and philosophical discussion. Its members included several who later became prominent in the Fabian Society, and it was at a Zetetical meeting in 1879 that Sidney first encountered George Bernard Shaw. Participation in the life of the Zetetical, the 'Lambeth Parliament', and other discussion groups fostered Sidney's continuing intellectual evolution. His background was a familiar mid-Victorian mixture of evangelicalism on his mother's side and utilitarian radicalism on the side of his father, who had worked for John Stuart Mill's election to parliament as MP for Westminster in 1865. There was much utilitarianism in Sidney himself. Beatrice famously claimed that Bentham was 'certainly Sidney's intellectual godfather' (diary, 25 Jan 1901; *Diaries*, ed. Mackenzie and Mackenzie, 1.200), and early references by Sidney to the 'beneficial influence' of Bentham and James Mill support this. Throughout his life Sidney displayed Edwin Chadwick's habit of arguing by means of a fusillade of statistics, and his first significant publication, the Fabian tract *Facts for Socialists* (1887), made its case by mining blue books and statistical dictionaries for official measurements of rent, national income, pauperism, and other economic indicators. Throughout his life he invoked J. S. Mill as an authority, though almost invariably the later Mill, the convert to 'socialism' of the 1860s.

Mill's most substantial intellectual bequest to Sidney Webb was the 'law of rent', the idea of a differential profit or advantage enjoyed by the monopoly possessor of a commodity, normally land. Mill had not invented this law, which had an eighteenth-century pedigree, but he had, towards the end of his life, given it a sharp radical edge by attacking parasitical urban landlords, whose incomes 'are rising while they are sleeping' by their possession of land made valuable by the exertions of the community (A. Offer, *Property and Politics, 1870–1914*, 1981, 183). This doctrine, most obviously pertinent to London, influenced Sidney as a young metropolitan radical. It remained central to his thought for the remainder of his life, making him resistant to Marxian economics. Critically, though, Sidney distanced himself from mainstream radicalism in the

1880s by refusing to see the law of rent merely as an indictment of landlordism. He argued that monopoly ownership of industrial enterprises excluded the 'mere worker' from economic benefit just as effectively as monopoly ownership of land: 'the proprietor of this so-called "capital" seems to me but the old landlord writ large' (*Church Reformer*, 1, Jan 1889; 2, March 1889). Sidney remained lukewarm towards land nationalization, which he saw as a partial panacea being offered as a comprehensive solution. He further broadened the concept of rent to include what he termed 'rent of ability'—the return to educated brain-workers like himself and to others privileged by their expertise. The concept of rent was thus turned from a radical weapon against aristocratic landlordism into something broader—the justification for the view that those privileged by fortune should acknowledge and make good their obligations to the community.

This demonstrated the lasting, if less obvious, presence in Sidney of the evangelical conscience. Although the adult Sidney became a convinced freethinker and remained so throughout his life, he retained an evangelical ethical sense. This manifested itself in some of his early works, in his habit of invoking examples of social inequity to shame his readership, and even in occasional use of biblical language. Passages in some of his early unpublished lectures strike an unfamiliar note to those used to the colourless style of his later work (see, for example, his lecture 'The way out', 1884/5, Passfield papers, BLPES, 6/19, fol. 8). Like many lapsed evangelicals in the 1880s, Sidney found his way through free thought to Comtean positivism. Like Beatrice Potter he took what he wanted from positivism, stressing its scientific approach and its emphasis upon social altruism. Comte's view that social solidarity grew as society became more complex underpinned Sidney's essentially optimistic approach to society's problems. He rejected Marx's materialism for failing to take into account the non-economic motives driving men and thus retarding the growth of public spirit. The Comtean Sidney saw a moralized civic spirit as the only means of securing social justice in an economic system that was inescapably inequitable.

The gradualism which characterized Sidney's thought for the rest of his life had its foundations in Comte's model of phased progress towards social improvement. Sidney argued for a slow but steady evolution of sentiment. He stressed in particular that rent of ability accounted for as great a share of the national product as the other two monopoly rents, and that the middle class had therefore to accept its share of social responsibility. This explains his belief that simple expropriation of private property was pointless without an attendant moralization of the propertied, and that by the time such moralization had been achieved, socialism would be redundant. He was avowedly not a socialist when he first spoke to the Fabian Society in March 1885, or even when he joined the society two months later (the Fabians did not make socialism a condition of membership until 1887). At a time when 'socialism' most frequently implied revolutionary

Marxism or anarchism, he was indeed caustic about its impracticability.

None the less, Sidney's collectivism, his asceticism, and his stress on public morality were self-evidently compatible with strains of non-revolutionary socialism, and his acceptance of the label 'socialist'—by January 1886 at the latest—was achieved with little *éclat*. This move was apparently prompted by a growing pessimism about the possibility of moralizing the monopolist without the sort of compulsion that could be applied only by public agencies. An increasing emphasis upon the citizen's public obligations became evident in the late 1880s. A lecture on ancient Rome, delivered in two instalments at Hampstead in July and August 1888, described an ascetic ideal of civic duty which remained a Webbian constant. In late nineteenth-century Britain natural selection ensured that at the highest levels of civilization social organization had superseded physical strength and even mental culture as society's prime requirement. 'We must abandon', therefore, 'the self-conceit of imagining that we are independent units, and bend our proud minds ... to this subjection to the higher end, the Common weal' ('Rome: a sermon in sociology', pt 2, 88, BLPES, Passfield papers, 6/34).

This was a pointed rejection of individualism even by the standards of the 1880s. Sidney was able to maintain his gradualist faith, and to avoid coercive state socialism, by arguing that society was already evolving spontaneously in a socialist direction. In his contribution to the *Fabian Essays in Socialism* in 1889 and still more markedly in *Socialism in England* (1890), he outlined the extent to which English society had already socialized itself through the regulation of industry and the municipal acquisition of public services. In his evidence (17 November 1892) to the royal commission on labour he depicted the process not as a humanitarian brake upon enterprise, but as the very root of industrial prosperity. Industrial growth thus brought the silent spread of collectivism, endorsed by tories as well as Liberals. The speculative Comtean faith in moralizing the monopolist yielded in Sidney's mind to a confidence that society was unconsciously moralizing itself. The Sidney Webb whom Beatrice Potter met in January 1890 was already a man of assured convictions.

The early partnership The pair were not obviously well matched. Sidney's shortcomings included not only his unattractiveness, which Beatrice depicted with little restraint in her diary, but also his lower-middle-class origins: 'his tiny tadpole body, unhealthy skin, cockney pronunciation, poverty, are all against him' (diary, 26 April 1890; *Diaries*, ed. Mackenzie and Mackenzie, 1.329–30). His socialism deterred some of Beatrice's sisters and the Booths. Bruised by the Chamberlain episode, Beatrice originally envisaged little more than intellectual contact with him. Temperamentally and spiritually they appeared to have little in common, and only the development of the 'partnership' over half a century would demonstrate the compatibility of opposites. Beatrice suffered the mental restlessness of one anxious for spiritual assurance but lacking a settled faith and a supportive church; Sidney's spiritual outlook was simpler: Canon Samuel Barnett

believed that if Sidney had a soul, he had 'buried it deep in his pocket' (Hobhouse to Tawney, Tawney papers, BLPES, 24/2). Beatrice was psychologically frail and occasionally depressive; Sidney's rationalism produced in him a faith in human nature and human progress. This helped him to sustain his wife in her weaker moments, when she could be steadied by Sidney's cockney injunction to 'keep your hair on, missus' (*Our Partnership*, 344).

Beatrice's determination to give a candid account of her own inner turmoil in her diaries may have led her to simplify Sidney's nature—to depict her husband as a man of uncomplicated serenity. There is anger and self-doubt in some of Sidney's early letters; he suffered a severe nervous breakdown and was forced to abandon work for three months in 1922, and it is likely that occasional overheating was the price of his general placidity. Yet the Webbs' secretary F. W. Galton could remember only two or three occasions in fifty years when he saw Sidney annoyed or flustered, and he does seem to have been impressively capable of self-control. The stability of the Webbs' marriage suggests that their emotional characteristics were complementary, allowing the partnership to succeed above the level of mere intellectual collaboration that Beatrice had once envisaged.

Intellectually Beatrice and Sidney had much in common. Both were intrigued by the prospect of constructing a science of society, and from the start of their relationship this shared aim neutralized latent party political differences—his radical Liberal background, her family's anti-democratic toryism. Leonard Woolf later noted that they had 'drawn for themselves a circle which enclosed certain subjects and departments of human life. Those subjects were *their* subjects; they studied them closely and continually' ('Political thought and the Webbs', in M. Cole, ed., *The Webbs and their Work*, 259–60). These subjects—co-operation, trade unionism, collectivism, social policy, public administration—formed the basis of a doctrine of social evolution which altered very little over their lifetime. Founded upon analysis of underlying structures and systems and consequently deterministic in tone, this doctrine proved resistant to the ebb and flow of political events.

Beatrice joined the Fabian Society at Sidney's prompting in January 1891, and the pair dominated the organization for the next half-century, but—at least until they committed themselves to the Labour Party, shortly before the First World War—they distanced themselves from party politics. The corollary was an often surprising indifference to political issues with no place in their scheme. They were largely unmoved by questions of foreign affairs and observed an odd reticence on many contentious issues of economic policy. 'My wife and I have never felt able to deal properly with economic theory', Sidney admitted to Karl Kautsky in 1933 (Sidney Webb to Karl Kautsky, 17 Oct 1933, Karl Kautsky papers, D xxiii, 75, Internationaal Instituut voor Sociale Geschiedenis, Amsterdam), but they were manifestly better versed in economic questions than many who were less hesitant, and their limited contribution to the public debates over, for example, tariffs and monetary policy remains striking. A conviction that the advance of collectivism was a silent but irresistible trend absolved them from analysis of what they considered transient political details, though it made their rejection of the Westminster system all the more fundamental when British collectivism failed them.

The Webbs' differing ideological ancestries made each of them sympathetic to the reassessment of *laissez faire* in the late Victorian period. Both had been touched by Comtean positivism, in its English form. Both had been influenced by Herbert Spencer—Beatrice the more directly—but had rejected the extreme individualism that Spencer had reached in the 1880s. Their anti-individualism led each of them to emphasize the need for individual devotion to the common good—a doctrine that germinated in their joint work and culminated in their encomia to the Soviet system in the 1930s. The emphasis in British idealist thought in the late Victorian period upon the organic nature of community touched both. Though neither appears to have devoted much time to studying T. H. Green, let alone Hegel, their writings display 'an Idealist residue' beneath their positivist methodology (S. Den Otter, *British Idealism and Social Explanation*, 1996, 71), reflected particularly in Sidney's stress upon the interdependence of society's members. This emphasis upon the need to look to the well-being of the community as a whole was the most distinctive feature of Webbian socialism, distancing the Webbs not only from the advocates of revolutionary violence but also from those socialists who sought to privilege the industrial working class.

Beatrice initially repelled the advances of the sexually unappetizing Sidney. But the Chamberlain episode had left her, as she admitted, 'susceptible to real deep devotion' (diary, 6 Nov 1890; *Diaries*, ed. Mackenzie and Mackenzie, 1.343). She yielded slowly to Sidney's unrelenting enthusiasm for her, persuading herself that 'it is only the head that I am marrying' (Harrison, 194). Their engagement in May 1891 remained secret, for fear that the ailing Richard Potter would be hastened to his grave by learning that Beatrice intended to marry into the lower middle class. When Potter died in January 1892 and the engagement was duly publicized, many of Beatrice's intimates did indeed see the connection as socially eccentric. Today it is perhaps the self-parodic asceticism of the courtship that appears unusual—Beatrice's warning that 'the permanence and worth of a relationship depends on the consciousness in both partners that moral and intellectual growth arises out of it' (Beatrice to Sidney, 16 June 1890; *Letters*, 1.149) or Sidney's seductive claim that together they could transform economic theory (diary, 27 July 1890; *Diaries*, ed. Mackenzie and Mackenzie, 1.337). Fittingly, the marriage, which took place at St Pancras vestry hall on 23 July 1892, was delayed by the collection of material for their trade union history, and the couple spent part of their honeymoon working on Irish trade union records.

Sidney and London politics The resolution of Sidney's youthful emotional turmoil coincided with the onset of the most fruitful period of his public life. The couple had resolved after Richard Potter's death to keep themselves

on the private income of about £1000 per annum that Beatrice had inherited, freeing Sidney for writing and public work. Believing that he could learn more about public administration by gaining election to a public body, he stood successfully for the London county council (LCC) in 1892. He represented Deptford, a working-class area of south-east London, and joined the ruling Progressive Party—a Liberal–radical group with a labour wing, which had pioneered municipal social policy in the capital since the council's creation in 1889. He proved well suited to council work, based as it was upon toil in committee, where his civil service experience and innate manipulative skills proved invaluable. He graduated rapidly to the party committee, effectively constructing the policies which the dominant Progressive group pushed through the council. He also found his own niche as chairman of the LCC's new technical education board (TEB). The board, enjoying considerable autonomy, became Sidney's vehicle, allowing him to reshape London education. In pressing upon the council the conclusions of a report commissioned from Hubert Llewellyn Smith in 1892, Webb argued that London, with the largest artisan population in Britain, had fallen behind not only foreign centres but also British provincial cities in the quality of its industrial training. The intended implication was that London's industrial economy depended upon technical education, but Sidney always saw the board's role as promoting something closer to a broader secondary curriculum. Helped by an understanding Liberal minister in A. H. D. Acland, Sidney defined technical education extremely broadly—including all sciences, the arts, foreign languages, modern history, economics, geography, commercial education, domestic economy 'and what not' (*Our Partnership*, 80)—with the result that the technical education board became a *de facto* secondary education authority for London. Webb hoped to have constructed 'the greatest capacity-catching machine that the world has ever yet seen' (speech of 1897, quoted in Brennan, 29).

Sidney used the scholarship system as a ladder to raise able London children from elementary school to intermediate or even university education. London's tertiary provision was providentially boosted by a windfall in the form of a legacy to the Fabian Society from a wealthy member, H. H. Hutchinson, in 1894, earmarked for the promotion of socialist propaganda. Another piece of free translation by Sidney—subsequently vehemently criticized by Shaw—induced the society to devote the cash to the formation of the London School of Economics (LSE) in 1895. Sidney had visited the Massachusetts Institute of Technology on his visit to the United States in 1888, and was familiar with the École Libre des Sciences Politiques in Paris: he hoped to develop in London a comparable example of modern university education in a major commercial centre. He believed that the ancient universities had been enervated by the divorce of thought from action and considered that London conditions were highly favourable to the promotion of research-based disciplines to produce both social scientists and public administrators. Lectures and classes at the LSE commenced in October 1895; vocational courses, alien to Oxbridge, in such subjects as railway economics, were always prominent in its curriculum. The school's first director, W. A. S. Hewins, enticed from an Oxford fellowship by the Webbs, sketched the school's principal disciplines as economics, statistics, commerce, banking and finance, commercial law, political science and public administration, and after the formation of the University of London in 1900, the LSE dominated its faculty of economics and political science.

The intellectual partnership Sidney's single-minded commitment to the municipal tasks at hand allowed him to bear a council workload as great as that of a cabinet minister, though at the cost of playing only a supportive role in the intellectual work of the partnership. The letters he wrote to Beatrice in the first years of their marriage contain repeated apologies for his limited contribution to the projected trade union history. That it appeared at all was due to Beatrice's own enthusiasm, which Sidney never fully shared, for the processes of archival research and interviewing, the lonely pursuits to which she devoted herself in the mid-1890s. There was a degree of displacement here. In choosing what was in effect a professional career as a researcher and writer, she had to come to terms with a childless future. The couple had decided against children soon after marriage. Beatrice, 'dried up at thirty-five after ten years' stress and strain' (diary, 25 July 1894; *Diaries*, ed. Mackenzie and Mackenzie, 2.52), felt physically unable to bear children, and she remembered that her mother had produced ten children 'at the cost of her own career as an intellectual' (diary, 28 April 1932; *Diaries, 1924–1932*, 306). More conscious than most of the duty owed by the individual to society, Beatrice remained uncomfortable with her failure to undertake the duty of motherhood.

'Are the books we have written together worth (to the community) the babies we might have had?', Beatrice wondered in 1901 (diary, 24 April 1901; *Diaries*, ed. Mackenzie and Mackenzie, 2.207). If they were, the Webbs were very good citizens. The British Library catalogue lists thirty-eight jointly authored works, including eighteen full-length books, and almost all the works published under a single Webb name after 1890 involved some degree of collaboration. Beatrice had essentially compiled her study of co-operation before the intellectual partnership with Sidney took root, but even that work shows Sidney's influence upon the finished product, in particular the passage in which municipal government was depicted as a Spencerian 'functional adaptation' of co-operation: obligatory rather than voluntary association to supply public services as the co-operatives provided consumer goods.

Much of Beatrice's 'little book on co-operation' laid the foundations for the life work of the Webbs: the conjunction of consumer and municipal co-operation formed the basis of their conception of civic socialism, and it is impossible to understand their progressive rejection of profit-making capitalism without acknowledging the centrality of the consumer co-operative movement to their thought. Beatrice's underlying message was that co-operation rested on a profoundly different foundation from capitalism: the book's early sections emphasized Robert Owen's belief that 'the one legitimate object of society is the improvement of the physical, moral and intellectual character of man' (B. Potter, *The Co-Operative Movement in Great Britain*, 1899 edn, 20), an anti-individualist argument that anticipated the Webbs' later doctrine of the national minimum. The rejection of producer co-operatives also cast a long shadow. Lacking capital, custom, and administrative expertise, they came to act like small masters, who were the worst employers in industry. Years later she modestly described her differentiation of the two types of co-operative as 'perhaps the most pregnant and important piece of classification in the whole range of sociology' (*The Discovery of the Consumer*, 1928, 5). It underpinned the Webbs' subsequent treatment of co-operation, and lay behind their consistent hostility to doctrines of worker control, in the form of syndicalism, guild socialism, or early Bolshevism. Consumer co-operatives could embrace the whole community, including its women; worker co-operatives served only the workers.

The co-operation study also pointed the Webbs towards their first shared undertaking, their study of trade unionism. In co-operative-dominated Bacup, Beatrice had found trade unionism relatively weak, but in the nation as a whole, unions were already the strongest arm of the labour movement, inviting study. Beatrice envisaged a more extensive, empirically founded, historical study of trade unions than she had produced for co-operatives. Mindful of her frailty, Sidney asserted that 'you are not *fit* to write this big book alone: you will never get through it' (Sidney to Beatrice, 14 Sept 1891; *Letters*, 1.299), and the production of the trade union history, which appeared in 1894, demonstrated what became the usual Webbian division of labour. With Sidney tied to London and the LCC, Beatrice toured the country to unearth 'minute-books, in which generations of diligent, if unlettered, secretaries, the true historians of a great movement, have struggled to record the doings of their committees' (S. Webb and B. Webb, *The History of Trade Unionism*, 1894, preface, xi); Sidney's capacity for sustained writing was deployed to produce the final text. The work embodies the virtues of the Webbs' historical writing. Elaborate archival detective work enabled them to trace the origins of trade unionism to a period—the late seventeenth century—far earlier than contemporaries would have expected, and to carry the development forward to the late Victorian era. Their reliance upon unions' own records gave the *History* an institutional emphasis which modern labour historians have criticized, but their chronology of union evolution from the late eighteenth century—the clandestine years of the early nineteenth century, the emergence of 'new model' unionism in the mid-Victorian period, the battle between exclusive 'old' unionism and inclusive 'new' unionism in the 1880s—remains central to historical study of the movement.

At the time and subsequently, the Webbs contrasted their own rigorous, demythologizing approach with the weaknesses of the forensic method adopted by the contemporaneous royal commission on labour, whose unfocused questioning of trade union witnesses failed to establish with any reliability the most fundamental facts about unionism. Beatrice attributed her empiricism to Herbert Spencer: 'he taught me to look on all social institutions exactly as if they were plants or animals, things that could be observed, classified and explained' (diary, 9 Dec 1903; *Diaries*, ed. Mackenzie and Mackenzie, 2.307). Sidney was an empiricist by temperament—one reason why he was bored by religious discussion was, supposedly, that 'there were so few established facts on which to form a hypothesis' (K. Martin, in M. Cole, ed., *The Webbs and their Work*, 300). A characteristic rhetorical tactic in his early writings was to attack the advocates of revolutionary socialism by aggregating the number of enterprises collectivized as if by stealth, stunning the reader with an inventory of gasworks, waterworks, and so on already in public hands. Their empiricism led the Webbs towards inductive techniques familiar to present-day historians: the search for archival evidence either in person or through research assistants, the isolation of evidence from potentially misleading context, and the attempt to extrapolate a pattern of development from the evidence thus accumulated.

This 'scientific' history contrasted starkly with the literary approach familiar to the Victorian reader. The Webbs made few concessions to their public, and whatever appeal their empirical rigour carried was offset by an unalluring prose style. If this was a stylistic fault, though, it was more Sidney's than Beatrice's. Her two volumes of autobiography, *My Apprenticeship* (1926) and the posthumously published *Our Partnership* (1948), read fluently, as does her diary. But Sidney was the scribe of the partnership. This made sense, given his formidable productivity, but it meant that much of the Webbs' work displayed Sidney's unwelcome mannerisms, notably an addiction to subordinate clauses and a tendency to repetition. Some of his sentences read like parliamentary statutes—unambiguous, no doubt, but unwieldy and indigestible. H. H. Asquith noted that the Webbs had 'jointly produced some twenty solid, though for the most part unreadable books' (R. Jenkins, *Asquith*, 1964, 518). H. G. Wells, parodying the pair as Oscar and Altiora Bailey in *The New Machiavelli* (1911), made the point with barbed irony:

> Their first book, *The Permanent Official*, fills three plump volumes, and took them and their two secretaries upwards of four years to write. It is an amazingly good book, an enduring achievement. In a hundred directions the history and the administrative treatment of the public service was clarified for all time. (Everyman edn, 1994, 151)

The Webbs were not, though, writing to entertain a salon readership. They underwrote the sale of 19,000 copies of the 1920 reissue of the *History of Trade Unionism* to the trade union movement in a cheap edition so that it should be 'read by the right people' (diary, 25 Dec 1919; *Diaries*, ed.

Mackenzie and Mackenzie, 3.354). Inter-war surveys found Sidney Webb among the authors most familiar to working-class readers.

Nor did Beatrice and Sidney *wish* to write Macaulayan history; Beatrice noted that in his seven volumes Macaulay included only one chapter on the condition of the people. All their historical writing was intended to illustrate their distinctive view of social and political evolution, and the most wounding criticism of their work was that they jeopardized scientific objectivity in promoting their political message. Bernard Bosanquet, husband of Beatrice's adversary on the poor law commission of 1905–9, felt that the forensic isolation of facts central to the Webbian method allowed them to select evidence to suit their argument: index cards bearing inconvenient information might fall from their office table. The relationship between the Webbs' facts and their hypotheses was often more complex than that which they presented. Neither Webb was above presenting monstrous claims in the form of hard fact.

Such creative thinking was more frequent, though, in the Webbs' polemical speeches and pamphlets than in their full-scale histories. The latter usually rested upon solid scholarship: footnotes in the Webbs' history *English Local Government* serve even today as primary sources for students of eighteenth-century administration. But the Webbs were evolutionary socialists who believed the study of the past vindicated their analysis of the present: they could not comfortably 'neutralize' their history by divorcing it from their political aims. What might now appear their most 'objective' writing, their study of the eighteenth-century local state, seems to have satisfied them least: Beatrice dismissed *The Parish and the County*, from the local government series, as 'a ponderous volume' (*Our Partnership*, 152). When their work was forged in the heat of controversy, however, as with their studies of poor-law history and policy for the royal commission, the autonomy of fact and hypothesis came under threat. What most worried the Webbs about their writing, however, was that the wood might be concealed by the trees—that voluminous factual research might obscure underlying arguments of principle. Only after the publication of their trade union study, with its patient excavation of a hidden history, did they realize 'to our surprise' that 'we had no systematic and definite vision of how trade unionism actually operated' (*Methods of Social Study*, 1932, 94).

In response Beatrice and Sidney embarked upon another volume, shuffling trade union facts until a theory of unionism emerged. *Industrial Democracy* (1897) displayed not only that 'definite vision' but also a didactic prescription for the Webbian state. The lengthy final section of this work amounted to a response to a modern capitalism which, they argued, was becoming as monopolistic as landlordism had long been. Arguing that free competition in these circumstances 'tends to the creation and persistence in certain occupations of conditions of employment injurious to the nation as a whole' (*Industrial Democracy*, 1897, 767), they called for the extension of the trade union

'Common Rule', that is the concept of a union rate within an individual trade, to the nation as a whole.

This was the first full exposition of one of the Webbs' central doctrines, that of the national minimum—a minimum level of wages and of quality of life to which the worker was entitled as citizen and below which he could not, as a citizen, be allowed to fall. The idea embodied both the insistence that a living wage was conducive to productivity and the belief in the individual's obligation to society—the unproductive individual lowered the efficiency of society as a whole. 'In the democratic state', they argued, 'no man minds his own business': Robinson Crusoe had been the last to enjoy such autonomy (*Industrial Democracy*, 1897, 845–6). Any trade unionist battling to the end of the work would have realized that the role envisaged for unionism was somewhat residual: unions would police the national minimum and seek by collective bargaining to raise particular groups above it, but there must be no more Luddism, and unions' benefit role would dwindle. Perhaps all industrial unionism would dwindle: strikes injurious to the community were proscribed, and the model union of the future was taken to be the white-collar National Union of Teachers, concerned with professional standards and operating in the public service. The Webbs' guarded view of trade unionism could hardly have been clearer: *Industrial Democracy* was a collectivist statement by socialists who considered traditional collective bargaining a random and partial way of promoting social progress.

Having completed their trade union studies, the Webbs embarked almost immediately upon research into local government. This was predetermined. Beatrice's study of co-operation had pointed to municipal government as the extension of co-operation into the civic sphere just as it had obviously steered her towards trade unionism. The Webbs' conception of the triple identity of man as producer, consumer, and citizen dominated their work. Local government had a longer history than trade unionism and had kept fuller records; in consequence the Webbs suffered drastic 'research creep', as the scope of the study continued to expand. The result was to push their focus ever backwards. Intending to examine Victorian local government from the 'revolution' of 1834–5 (the new poor law and the Municipal Corporations Act), they were driven to investigate first the early nineteenth century and then the eighteenth century in order to understand later developments. As their material proliferated, the survey exploded. It ran eventually to nine volumes, the last of which was not published until 1929 (a tenth was intended but unwritten), and it became essentially an eighteenth-century study. Material compiled by Beatrice for the royal commission of 1905–9 carried poor-law history into the twentieth century, and there is a brief, suggestive section on Victorian municipal evolution in the unappealingly titled *Statutory Authorities for Special Purposes* (1922), but, the Webbs regretfully acknowledged, the evolution of parish and borough and county into twentieth-century local government had to be left for younger authors to describe.

Believing, like many late Victorians, that local government was overtaking central government in importance, the Webbs set out to study 'a new form of state ... the "housekeeping state" as distinguished from the "police state"' (*Our Partnership*, 149–50). Sidney had seen the Municipal Corporations Act of 1835 as the critical moment at which government by guilds—or, using Beatrice's terminology, municipal associations of producers—had been superseded by modern corporations—municipal associations of consumers—'for the purpose of satisfying their common needs' (*The Cambridge Modern History*, 12: *The Latest Age*, 1910, 733). He had seen municipal ownership of public services as the means by which collectivism would spread painlessly in Britain. But study of the provincial authorities provided little evidence of this silent revolution. Finding some jobbery and much inefficiency, Beatrice acknowledged by 1902 that 'our work in local government will be a big indictment, not only of the eighteenth century, but also of the present-day' (diary, July 1902; *Our Partnership*, 173). Still more seriously, their investigations gradually revealed a very different model of local government from that which they had envisaged. The burden of local taxation had engendered a ratepayer democracy, while the non-payment of members imposed a *de facto* property qualification. Authorities were consequently dominated by 'shopkeepers, builders and publicans in the towns, and farmers in the country', ensuring that the municipal revolution of the 1830s 'failed to make the Ratepayers' Democracy co-extensive with the consumers of the public services which it had collectively to provide' (*Statutory Authorities for Special Purposes*, 1922, 477, 480).

Not all authorities, in other words, resembled the LCC, where a high proportion of the electorate did not pay rates directly, and the extension of municipal services had proved electorally popular. The discovery raised awkward questions. If municipalities could not be depended upon as vehicles for collectivism, the question of how man could achieve civic collectivism became more pressing. 'Socialists have contributed so far very little to the theory or practice of Democracy', Sidney wrote in 1919 (*New Statesman*, 28 Nov 1919, 2); the claim was certainly true of him. The Webbs eventually produced their answer to current constitutional questions in *Constitution for the Socialist Commonwealth of Great Britain* (1920), but in the 1900s their attitude to the state remained *ad hoc* and untheoretical. The lack of any clear thinking about questions of democracy and accountability accentuated élitist impulses always present in their thought.

Expertise and efficiency This became evident as the Webbs plunged into national politics in the 1900s, first in their veneration of the bureaucratic expert and second in their attempts to influence policy by manipulating the possessors of power. They will always be identified with the ideal of government by enlightened expert. Their preference for order over chaos was rooted in their rejection of utopian socialism: as Douglas Cole remembered, 'the world, they would say, was made up of "A's" and "B's"—anarchists and bureaucrats; and they were all on the side of the "B's"' (G. D. H. Cole, 7). Their more specific reverence for expertise reflected an aversion to the casual ways of Britain's *ancien régime*; problematically, Britain's political leaders tended to be expert in issues—such as diplomacy and denominational matters—which left the Webbs cold, but unversed in those social policy areas which did concern them. Their conviction was really forged as Britain's statesmen made heavy weather of education reform in the 1890s, and was understandable in that context, but it left the Webbs open to the allegation that they preferred unaccountable bureaucrats to elected politicians.

This charge was levelled at Sidney and Beatrice in the Fabian Society's internal disputes of the 1900s, when the society's young turks accused its old guard of centralizing and anti-democratic tendencies. The core of the criticism, voiced by H. G. Wells and others, that the Webbs wished the nation to be run by a samurai class consisting of themselves and those who thought like them, was plausible. The Webbs had promoted efficiency in government in their writings of the 1890s, and became the leading exponents on the left of the 'national efficiency' drive generated by Britain's Second South African War embarrassments in the early 1900s. They did cultivate a gaggle of approved administrators—Sir Robert Morant at the Board of Education, William Garnett at the technical education board, the public health expert George Newman, and later the Indian administrator John Hope Simpson—and they did tend to assume the existence of administrative solutions to essentially political problems.

The charge, though, that the Webbs sought to create a British 'boffinocracy' misrepresents their administrative thinking, which was rooted in their Spencerian understanding of social development. Society's evolution towards greater organizational efficiency did not entail, as they explained in 1913, the subordination of 'a whole class of laymen to a separate expert class', but the 'subordination of the person who does not know to the person who knows', whoever that might be. The prime minister in his automobile would thus be directed through the Piccadilly maelstrom by the police constable earning 25*s.* per week (*New Statesman*, 3 May 1913). In fact the Webbs cannot adequately be described as statists. 'Their bureaucracy was never *étatisme*', suggested Douglas Cole, 'it claimed much for the State but much for the group also. Only the individual seemed somehow to get left out' (G. D. H. Cole, 7). They generally advocated municipal rather than national control of industry, and early Fabian programmes limited nationalization proper to the railways, canals, and mines. The insight that municipal enterprises could be equated with co-operatives, as a compulsory rather than a voluntary association of consumers, was of catalytic significance. It mattered because associations of consumers 'constitute an automatic democracy' (*New Statesman*, 24 May 1913), evolving from below. In essence the Webbs remained faithful to Mill's classic prescription that 'power may be localized, but knowledge, to be most useful, must be centralized' (J. S. Mill, 'Considerations on representative government', 1861, in *Three Essays*, 1975, 377), though they never stated their position so clearly. They took a fitful interest in forms of direct democracy on

their tour of India in 1911–12 before finding their solution in the participatory democracy of the Russian soviet. In short, enthusiasm for the enlightened expert was only one side of the Webbian coin, but the charge of élitism was reinforced by their attempts to short-circuit the democratic process by suborning men of power.

The Grosvenor Road salon 'Personally I see no objection to what is called "wire-pulling",' Beatrice protested in 1929 (diary, 27 Oct 1929; *Diaries*, ed. Mackenzie and Mackenzie, 4.199). Since most citizens were uninterested in most political issues, it was more profitable to work on the knowledgeable and the influential. In 1902 the Webbs formed a small but high-powered dining club known as the Coefficients, whose name reflected contemporary concern with national efficiency following Second South African War embarrassments, and whose glittering membership list included Bertrand Russell, H. G. Wells, Edward Grey, Leopold Amery, and Halford Mackinder. Sidney remained a member for the five years or so for which the club survived, but the somewhat formal procedure of this association, which met at the neutral venue of the Ship tavern in Whitehall, did not provide the opportunity for intellectual permeation of the élite that the Webbs gained from their own dinner parties. During the 1900s many of that élite were drawn into the political salon that the Webbs established in their Grosvenor Road home. The dinner party, which became the partnership's principal weapon in these years, was deployed with Webbian efficiency: a typical week in 1906 saw thirty persons pass through Grosvenor Road for lunch or dinner, with a further six coming to tea, 'nearly all of the lot being on business of some sort' (diary, 2 July 1906; *Our Partnership*, 346).

One consequence of this dining offensive—and a reason why the Webbs played most of their social games at home—was Beatrice's increasing dietary fastidiousness. She began to impose a frugal food regime upon herself in October 1901, and during 1903 she became a vegetarian, declaring herself against flesh, fish, eggs, alcohol, coffee, and sugar. She was unable to abandon smoking, though, suggesting that her concerns about food were another symptom of her nervous disposition. She remembered as a girl being 'detestably aware of my body' (diary, 1 Jan 1901; *Diaries*, ed. Mackenzie and Mackenzie, 2.189–90); there are hints of eating disorders in her memory of 'over-exhaustion and over-eating followed by exhaustion and under-nourishment' (ibid.), in such assertions as 'the less I eat the better I am' (diary, 12 Nov 1904; *Diaries*, ed. Mackenzie and Mackenzie, 2.333), and in the cessation of her periods for six months in 1902. Her dietary asceticism became a lifelong commitment, and she lost weight steadily. As the pair aged, the tall but willowy Beatrice formed an ever starker contrast to her tubby husband. Though she attempted sporadically to regulate Sidney's diet, she did not force her philosophy of food on her guests: the meals appear to have been simple but wholesome rather than actively repellent. Gastronomy was not Beatrice's concern; her guests 'were all there with a purpose', as she admitted to Herbert Samuel forty years later (Viscount

Samuel, *Memoirs*, 1945, 293), acknowledging that that purpose was generally political manipulation.

Educational reform A frequent guest was Arthur Balfour, Conservative prime minister from 1902. With education high on his agenda, he became a treasured contact as the Webbs sought to mould legislation on one of 'their' subjects. They could not greatly influence the shape of the Education Act of 1902, the outlines of which had been clear since the mid-1890s, though they doubtless encouraged Balfour to resist nonconformist protests over the funding of Anglican schools from local taxation. Nor could they do much to shape the extension of the 1902 measure to London in the following year: Sidney was prominent in opposing Conservative back-bench suggestions that the second-tier metropolitan boroughs be made education authorities, but the small scale of some of these authorities made devolution of education to them a fantasy. The Webbs controversially promoted the bill of 1903 which extended the 1902 measure to London. Sidney was conscious of the low standard of denominational education in London, and did not believe that the schooling of 218,000 of the capital's children should effectively depend upon private charity. His Progressive Party colleagues in the LCC included, though, a sizeable nonconformist contingent bitterly unhappy with the measure, but unable in practice either to amend the bill or to abjure the responsibilities of a local education authority once it had passed. Aware that the Webbs had been coquetting with Balfour, the nonconformists vented their frustration on Sidney, who relished the image of a conspirator.

Sidney's view of the inevitable spread of collectivism had long convinced him that reform was as likely from Conservatives as from Liberals, while Beatrice, with her tory background, maintained that 'it is only Conservatives who can make revolutions nowadays' (diary, 26 July 1897; *Diaries*, ed. Mackenzie and Mackenzie, 2.120). Sidney's Progressive colleagues, most of whom were conventional Liberal–radicals, did not take this flouting of party allegiance so lightly. His standing in the party never really recovered from the education controversy, particularly as the cost of education, and in particular the council's growing responsibilities for secondary education, left the Progressives open to ratepayer attack. He was thrown off the party committee in 1905, and although he remained a councillor until 1910, his municipal career really ended at that point. It had encompassed his most successful public work, though, and even after the furore of 1903 he was able to take advantage of the LCC's unified control of education to construct a new London scholarship ladder that lasted in essence until comprehensivization in the 1970s. Approved by the council in February 1905, the scholarship scheme was Sidney's last substantial piece of municipal work.

The poor-law commission and the minority report Beatrice, though, was about to venture more deeply into public life. Her friendship with Balfour brought her nomination to the royal commission on the poor laws, the appointment

of which in 1905 was one of the last acts of the Conservative ministry. This was the first time she had been called upon to serve upon a public body, but she displayed none of the deference of a novice. Fearing that as a woman she would be ignored by the male majority, and that the commission as a whole would be steered by the permanent officials of the Local Government Board (whom she considered part of the poor-law problem), she resolved from the start that she would '*have* to make myself disagreeable in order to reach my ends' (diary, 15 Dec 1905; *Diaries*, ed. Mackenzie and Mackenzie, 3.18). This made her slow to understand that the majority of the commission (whose leading thinker was also a woman, Helen Bosanquet) included many with experience of poor-law practice or theory, who were neither slavish advocates of the principles of 1834 nor tools of the Local Government Board. She consequently succeeded in making herself disagreeable but failed to win over many of her colleagues. Halfway into the four-year investigation, she resolved to write a separate minority report, which would be 'a thoroughly Webbian document' (diary, 9 Dec 1907; *Diaries*, ed. Mackenzie and Mackenzie, 3.82).

The poor-law 'problem' was really two problems. The legislation of 1834 had intended to isolate the genuinely destitute by making conditions in the workhouse so deterrent as to drive all who could work into employment. In practice at most times the poor law's clientele included both those actually unable to work—the elderly, the chronically sick, the disabled, young mothers, and orphans—and the able-bodied unemployed who could not find work. It was difficult to assess both groups equally, and the commission's fractious atmosphere left most members reluctant to try.

Bosanquet and the majority of the commissioners tended to emphasize the problem of the unemployed: Bosanquet's modernized Hegelianism stressed the need to reclaim the destitute for the community and warned of the danger that indiscriminate doles would produce a demoralized underclass. She was prominent in the Charity Organisation Society, which had for more than thirty years sought to save the poor from unfocused philanthropy by restricting charity to those with the character and strength to respond to measured assistance. So far as the COS succeeded in controlling the flow of private charity, the danger—as the society believed—increased that poor-law guardians would become an alternative source of indiscriminate relief. The COS was therefore determined to keep the able-bodied poor at the heart of the question of poor-law reform.

The Webbs, conversely, had always approached the reform issue from the angle of the 'deserving' categories. They believed that the principle of deterrence upon which the act of 1834 had been based had failed because it made no distinction between voluntary and involuntary destitution; their emphasis was always upon the involuntarily destitute. Sidney, who claimed that a fifth of the London population died in the workhouse or a poor-law hospital, had argued since the early 1890s for the separation of the sick from the poor-law system, a pension scheme for the aged, and a more humane treatment of pauper children. This was the basis for the 'break-up of the Poor Law' for which the Webbs campaigned for the next twenty years, and which Beatrice developed on the commission. Her east London experience twenty years earlier had left her convinced of the particular contribution of sickness to poverty, and the sick became the focus of her own attack upon the principles of 1834. Medical relief under the poor law had been steadily stripped of its stigma, and had not been punished by disfranchisement since 1885. By the 1900s the poor-law medical service had become an embryonic public health service for much of the working class—not merely paupers—but it was patchy in its coverage and neglected preventative medicine.

The COS commissioners wished, however, to prevent medical relief clouding the question of the able-bodied poor, and argued for poor-law medical relief to be restricted to the genuinely destitute. This *revanchiste* proposal goaded Beatrice into a Pauline moment, convincing her that the object should rather be the extension of medical inspection and treatment to all sick persons, paupers or not, than its restriction to the pauper sick. In a phrase which conjured up the earlier case for the national minimum, she argued that illness should be considered 'a public nuisance to be suppressed in the interests of the community' (diary, 17 June 1906; *Our Partnership*, 348). The insight that sickness—including pauper sickness—could be better handled outside the poor law pointed naturally to the conclusion that other deserving groups—the aged, the disabled, and the children—should also be taken out of the hands of the guardians and treated by specialist departments of local authorities.

The idea of breaking up the poor law was, to Beatrice, exhilarating in its radicalism. The Webbs believed that the guardian boards, concerned with 'a purely deterrent and repressive treatment of destitution and vagrancy' (S. Webb and B. Webb, *Statutory Authorities for Special Purposes*, 1922, 484), had failed to attract creative administrative talent, and that their accumulation of power had consequently been damaging. The prospect of breaking them up therefore appealed, but it raised problems the significance of which Beatrice was reluctant to acknowledge, namely those of the widow with young children and the able-bodied unemployed. Both groups now dogged the Webbs' attempt to sweep away the guardians. Proposals to consign pauper children to specialist children's agencies of local authorities suggested that the breakup of the poor law could be achieved only by the breakup of the pauper family. The Webbs responded that this was already the case with the treatment of truants, fever patients, and lunatic children, but their hard-nosed approach to family solidarity was a liability.

The unemployed proved even more intractable. If the COS exaggerated their centrality, the Webbs were inclined to minimize them: Sidney dismissed the able-bodied in 1907 as only 'a few tens of thousands' among the mass of paupers (*United Parish Magazine*, Nov 1907, 2). The minority report countered the emphasis of the COS upon moral elevation by stressing the need for physical improvement of the 'emaciated and flabby' unemployed (*Report of the Royal Commission on the Poor Laws and Relief of Distress*, 1909, 3.669). 'Which of us, indeed, is *not* capable of improvement by careful testing and training?', wrote the unathletic Sidney (ibid., 3.670). But greater understanding of the problems of structural unemployment had, by the 1900s, demonstrated the inadequacy of this solution. In the event the minority report developed a solution as radical as that of the breakup of the poor law, arguing that public authorities, national and local, should schedule their major capital projects so as to offset the ebb and flow of the trade cycle. The involuntarily unemployed would be absorbed by these means, leaving only a core of work-shy people to be dealt with by coercive methods.

As the commission approached its conclusion, Beatrice was unworried by the prospect of competing reports, 'as mine would be the best' (Beatrice to Sidney, 2 May 1908; *Letters*, 2.313). The majority report was far better received than the Webbs had expected, but they still set about lobbying for their own proposals. A national committee for the prevention of destitution was formed to campaign for the minority report. Beatrice took voice production lessons and practised 'orating to the Waves' (Beatrice Webb to Georgina Meinertzhagen, 8 Aug 1909, *Letters*, 2.332) at Harlech. The campaign was impressive by the standards of such exercises, and Beatrice found an unexpected talent for public speaking, but the voice of poor-law reform was drowned by the protracted furore over the people's budget and the future of the House of Lords in 1909–11.

The Webbs' greatest problem, though, lay in the determination of the Liberal government to tackle poverty by other means. Old-age pensions had been enacted in 1908, before the commission had reported. Low pay was attacked by the Trade Boards Act in 1909, and 1911 saw the key measure of Liberal social reform, a scheme for insurance against unemployment and sickness, based upon contributions from workers, employers, and the state. The Webbs considered national insurance an illegitimate short cut, giving the state nothing in return for its contribution. National insurance offended Beatrice's 'rooted prejudice to relief instead of treatment' (diary, 13 May 1911; *Our Partnership*, 474); it did nothing to prevent sickness, covered only a fraction of the unemployed, and left both sick and unemployed at the mercy of the poor law when their entitlement expired. But it thwarted the minority report.

The whole episode demonstrated the failure of the Webbs' attempts to influence the powerful. Churchill and Lloyd George, along with other leading Liberals, had been regular visitors to the Grosvenor Road salon, but in the three years in which these men reshaped British social policy, the Webbs were hardly consulted. Their attempts to lobby ministers for poor-law reform merely proved how irksome they could be: Churchill declined the Local Government Board in 1908 for fear of being 'shut up in a soup kitchen with Mrs Sidney Webb' (R. S. Churchill, *Young Statesman: Winston S. Churchill, 1901–1914*, 1967, 243);

Lloyd George resolved that 'he *did not* feel inclined to consult Sidney Webb much more' after a harangue on the evils of compulsory insurance in 1911 (*Lloyd George's Ambulance Wagon: being the Memoirs of William J. Braithwaite, 1911–12*, ed. H. N. Bunbury, 1957, 117). In fact the comprehensiveness which Beatrice so valued in the minority report impeded its acceptance. The breakup of the poor law might have been feasible if accompanied by more conventional provision for the able-bodied, but the contracyclical works proposals were unrealistic, as Beatrice privately acknowledged in 1910.

The Webbs' departure on a tour of India and the Far East in June 1911 marked their implicit abandonment of the poor-law campaign. They made few more attempts to prescribe detailed social policy. Beatrice served with limited enthusiasm and to little effect on a committee investigating women's wages during the First World War, and to greater effect with the new Ministry of Reconstruction, planning post-war Britain, from 1917. The failure of the minority report diminished, though, her faith in the tactic of permeating the governing élite: Beatrice later described the report as 'the high-water mark of Reformist Socialism', and the book *The Prevention of Destitution*, written to publicize it, as the Webbs' 'final statement of this policy of "Compensation" for the capitalist system' (Beatrice to W. A. Robson, 26 Oct 1934; *Letters*, 3.404).

At least two substantial pieces of policy innovation were stillborn as a result. The minority report had sketched out a theory of partnership between state and voluntary agencies in the field of philanthropy, by which the latter would be used as testing grounds for experiments in social-work practice. It also sketched out a solution to the problem of central–local relations in the targeted use of central grants-in-aid to local authorities, weighted in favour of poor districts. Such initiatives went unheard as the minority report failed to take root, and detailed policy making of this sort tended, in the Webbs' future works, to give way to more ambitious criticism of the capitalist system.

The Far Eastern tour, 1911–1912 When the Webbs had toured the Anglo-Saxon world in 1898 'it never occurred to us that we were engaged in scientific research' (S. Webb and B. Webb, *Methods of Social Study*, 1932, 199). Their tour of India and the Far East in 1911–12, however, 'acted as a powerful ferment, altering and enlarging our conception of the human race, its past, its present and its future' (*The Webbs in Asia*, 2). Their jointly written diary provides occasional echoes of the Victorian travel journals, but in general the Webbs were less absorbed by the conventional tourist sites than by their inspections of schools, factories, municipal tramways, and even the famine relief works at Godhra, where they noted that 'none who were adult and ablebodied were given ... doles' (*Indian Diary*, 169).

In unfamiliar societies the Webbs could adopt a more detached 'observer status' than was open to them in Britain. The result was a schematic treatment of social organization that contrasted with their empirical studies of British trade unionism and local government. Occasionally their broad-brush accounts of civilizations only

briefly visited could be disappointingly crude. The Chinese incurred the full force of their social Darwinism—'a striking example of arrested development', evocative of the sophisticated insect, which 'has gone very far, but ... along a line in which further progress seems to be impossible' (*Crusade*, March 1912, reprinted in *The Webbs in Asia*, 371)—while Korea showed 'how a whole nation may take a long turn and steadily decline in civilisation' (*The Webbs in Asia*, 106–7).

Japan and India received, though, more mature consideration. Japan fascinated the Webbs as 'reproducing, with minute accuracy, all the features of the industrial England of 1790–1840' (*Crusade*, January 1912, reprinted in *The Webbs in Asia*, 362); they deplored the exploitation of women silk workers in Nagano and the slums of Osaka. Japan needed a national minimum, but the Webbs were heartened by the efficiency of its centralized government and the 'extraordinary idealism or mysticism' in the Japanese character (*The Webbs in Asia*, 61, 153).

India was less strikingly dynamic, but two features of Indian society struck the Webbs especially forcibly. The first was the example of local democracy evident in village government, presented to them as a pure, pre-raj form of Indian self-rule, and contrasting with the restricted ratepayer democracy that they had observed in England. Primitive democracy was attractive in itself, counteracting, as they believed, the divisive force of caste. Moreover, it reinforced the view which the Webbs had formed from their local government research that any government, 'however mechanically perfect, will fail to take root in the minds of the mass of the people ... unless it is in some way grafted on the spontaneous groupings of the people themselves' (S. Webb, introduction to J. Matthai, *Village Government in India*, 1916, xii). True Indian self-government, they concluded, would result not from a nationalist capture of the central imperial institutions or even provincial government, but through the development of 'the Village Council, the District Board and the Municipality' (ibid., xviii).

The second striking feature of Indian life was the Arya Samaj, a sect of Hindu modernizers whom the Webbs depicted as Vedic protestants, seeking to combat superstition and such anti-social rites as childhood marriage, and active in the relief of destitution. The Asian tour provoked the Webbs into speculations upon national spirituality of a kind that they would never have attempted in Britain, but which reflected Beatrice's enduring concern with the moral purpose of social organization. Much Indian popular religion was, in the Webbs' terms, superstitious and superficial, but the followers of the Arya Samaj displayed 'self-effacement in the service of Hindu society and self-reliance towards the outer world' (S. Webb, introduction to L. Rai, *The Arya Samaj*, 1915, xiii). Here was the epitome of the life of selfless social commitment for which Sidney had called in his essay on Rome in the 1880s and which Beatrice had drawn from Comte. The Webbs would find it again in soviet Russia.

Few, if any, of the Webbs' social opinions had been changed by their Far Eastern trip, but they were drawn to a broader view of British social development by the opportunity to compare Britain with other societies. From that point they thought less of detailed social-policy prescriptions and more of the problems intrinsic to capitalism as a system. They also committed themselves to Labour Party politics.

The Webbs embrace Labour The Webbs' attitude towards independent labour representation had previously been ambivalent. At heart they feared that a separate party founded purely as a vehicle for the working class would be sectional, and would conflict with their social collectivism. Sidney had, though, co-written with Shaw the article 'To your tents, oh Israel!', published in the *Fortnightly Review* of November 1893, which called upon the trade unions to give their financial and organizational support only to independent labour and socialist candidates. The article reflected Sidney's disenchantment with the last Gladstone government, which had just wasted a parliamentary session on the lost cause of Irish home rule. It was also, though, informed by the Webbs' trade union researches, which had demonstrated the political efficacy of the 'junta' of new model union leaders in the 1870s and the continued political role of the larger unions. The reluctance of the Trades Union Congress in 1894 to support separate Labour candidates caused the Webbs to pause, while the formation of the Independent Labour Party (ILP) in 1893 had aroused more interest in provincial than in London Fabians. The Webbs, unimpressed by the utopian programme adopted by the ILP in the general election of 1895, regarded them as amateurs. It is therefore unsurprising that the Webbs barely noticed the effective creation of the Labour Party in 1900, with the formation of the Labour Representation Committee, embracing unions, ILP, and socialist societies.

The *Fortnightly Review* article of 1893 therefore proved, in the short term, a blind alley. The Webbs' disenchantment with the Liberal Party steered them not towards independent labour politics but rather towards their *ad hoc* lobbying of the influential. Indeed, during the debates over the Fabian Society's future in the mid-1900s, it was the old guard's opponents, explicitly critical of the Webbs' élitism and obsession with administrative solutions, who called for the society to turn itself into a middle-class affiliate of the ILP. It was the failure to convince either major party of the merits of the minority report that persuaded the Webbs to look to third-party politics, and thus to Labour: 'the Labour Party exists and we have to work with it', Beatrice wrote unenthusiastically, '"A poor thing but our own"' (diary, Christmas 1912; *Diaries*, ed. Mackenzie and Mackenzie, 3.184).

What was most conspicuously poor about Labour was the quality of its trade unionist MPs. Beatrice feared that the party's middle-class membership, hopelessly outnumbered, had settled for the self-deceit that 'respectable but reactionary Trade Union officials are the leaders of the Social Revolution' (diary, 12 Feb 1914; *Diaries, 1912–1924*, 19). Her conclusion that there was 'a clear call to leadership in the labour and socialist movement to which we feel that we must respond' (diary, 11 Oct 1912; *Diaries*, ed.

Mackenzie and Mackenzie, 3.179) appears bumptious, but the intellectual leadership that Beatrice surely meant was indeed needed by a Labour Party in the process of reassessing its relationship to Liberalism.

Two initiatives embodied the attempt to provide this intellectual guidance. The first was the creation of a Fabian Society committee, which Beatrice chaired, to report upon the public control of industry. With a three-figure membership comprising Fabians, co-operators, and trade unionists, it evolved into the Fabian research department and, in 1917, into the Labour research department. The second initiative was the founding of a political weekly journal, the *New Statesman*. The *New Statesman* was launched in April 1913 under the editorship of Clifford Sharp, formerly editor of the anti-poor law campaign journal *The Crusade*. Beatrice saw it as 'primarily an organ of research and secondarily a general weekly paper' (diary, 8 March 1914; *Diaries*, ed. Mackenzie and Mackenzie, 3.198). It could, accordingly, be dauntingly cerebral— H. G. Wells thought it 'as dull as a privet hedge in Leeds' (Smith, 44)—particularly in what the Webbs considered its most important feature, the special supplements analysing current political issues and surveying recent official publications. Its first twenty-two issues carried the Webbs' series 'What is socialism?', the first comprehensive expression of the partnership's social thought since their horizons had been broadened in the Far East. This series rested upon familiar foundations. The three pillars of the Webbs' collective democracy were reinforced— consumer co-operation as the successor to individualism, municipalities as agents of the housekeeping state, trade unions as the expression of man's identity as producer— but the Webbs now avoided detailed policy prescriptions in favour of a broader analysis of social and economic structure. With it came a doctrinal fundamentalism, immanent in their earlier works but now expressed with full force.

The 'What is socialism?' articles formed a more explicit criticism of capitalism than the Webbs had produced before, invoking the moral decay that Beatrice had feared since the 1880s. They stressed the social rights of women and children, whose lot in poverty had become clearer to Beatrice from her poor-law investigations. They ventured a Fabian view of empire, which promised 'a higher stage of administrative organisation than any "local particularism" can achieve', and charged the great powers with the protection of the 'non-adult races', some of which they had studied in the Far East, from 'the private trader, the unchartered adventurer, or even the missionary' (*New Statesman*, 26 July, 2 Aug 1913). One of the Webbs' motives in founding the journal had been to counter propaganda from Fabian guild socialists, and they duly took the opportunity for another attack on syndicalism and anarchism. Anarchism had simply refused to recognize that developed societies required more elaborate government; syndicalism failed to cater for those groups outside the factory (women, children, the sick, and the elderly), whose needs had been made evident to the Webbs during the poor-law inquiry. In a subtle dilution of their former bureaucratic élitism, the Webbs concluded by arguing that the emergence of a 'vast army of … head workers rather than hand workers' had been the most telling social feature of the last hundred years, and that it was this anonymous body of 'minor professionals'—'an extraordinarily honest, habitually unbribable, continuously devoted, and increasingly efficient class of subordinate officials'—who were fostering the growth of collectivism (*New Statesman*, 6 Sept 1913). The intention to publish the series in book form was thwarted by the outbreak of the First World War.

War and the Webbs In a rare aside upon foreign affairs in the *New Statesman* series, the Webbs had warned that the intensification of global capitalism threatened 'to develop in the international relations of all the Great Powers a "Bismarckian Imperialism" naked and unashamed', leading to 'constantly increasing armaments and to periodical wars of a destructiveness that the world has never witnessed' (*New Statesman*, 30 Aug 1913). They were none the less taken aback by the outbreak of war in 1914. Beatrice was in fact devastated by the conflict, lapsing into depression and hypochondria. Sidney, who thought Britain to be in the right in declaring war in 1914, also regarded the conflict as a setback to hopes of social reconstruction, but the realization that the war was encouraging a form of *ad hoc* collectivism in Britain soon revived his optimism. It also allowed him to regain the national political role that appeared to have been lost with the collapse of the poor-law campaign, and to help direct the emergent Labour Party.

War effectively released Labour from its pre-war dependence upon the Liberal party and allowed it to go beyond the limits of Liberal social policy. With Westminster politics dominated by war issues, the focus of labour politics shifted from parliament to the shop floor and the working-class home, where the effects of the war economy were felt most keenly. The War Emergency Workers' National Committee, a federal group of representatives of the Labour Party and the wider labour movement, was formed in August 1914 to shield the working class from wartime economic disruption. For the first two years or so of the war, it was—far more than the parliamentary Labour Party—the principal outlet for working-class grievances induced by wartime privations. It allowed Sidney—one of six members elected to the committee at its inaugural conference—to become Labour's intellectual leader. He formulated much of the policy of the committee, which lobbied the wartime governments directly for measures against mass unemployment, for curbs on profiteering employers and landlords, for public control of key industries and of food supplies, and for support for trade unions in the face of industrial dislocation.

The war brought rent control, food rationing, and the nationalization of strategically important industries, all avowedly temporary, all adopted in a somewhat expedient manner, but all representing striking departures from pre-war habits. Sidney was characteristically disposed to see these developments as harbingers of a new collectivist

Britain, which he sketched in a *New Statesman* series, 'The rebuilding of the state', in the spring of 1917. In Webb's post-war Britain the trade unions would accept the permanent loss of pre-war restrictive practices in return for government pledges to prevent unemployment ('which is quite practicable') and to protect standard rates of pay. A ministry of health would give the nation 'at last … an organised service of health and healing'. A national scholarship system would help revitalize the education system. Successful education authorities would receive enhanced grants, knighthoods for their officials, and 'a visit by the King to present a shield of honour', while failing ones would be mulcted of aid and 'held up to public opprobrium'. Exchequer grants would also be used, on a massive scale, to replenish the nation's housing stock. Such had been the drift of public opinion since 1914 that few of Sidney's sentiments appeared unrealistic in the reconstructionist climate that prevailed towards the end of the war.

Beatrice, initially floored by the onset of war, took on worthy public work, becoming one of the Labour nominees to the statutory pensions committee, charged with compensating disabled servicemen. She also chaired a war cabinet committee on male and female pay, for which she produced a minority report which Margaret Cole considered 'one of the best statements of the case for equal pay' (*Diaries, 1912–1924*, 148 n. 3). Invited in 1917 to serve on the reconstruction committee, planning post-war reform, Beatrice found her niche on two subcommittees—on local government and the machinery of central government—which enjoyed substantial autonomy and survived the replacement of the committee by a full-scale ministry in July 1917. She succeeded in persuading the local government committee to produce a report in January 1918 advocating most of the proposals of the 1909 minority report. No legislation had appeared before the committee was wound up, but another minority report proposal, the call for a ministry of health, was clearly an idea whose time had come. Beatrice had no difficulty pressing it upon the machinery of government committee, under Haldane, though it was actually accepted by the Lloyd George government before the committee reported, following the recommendation of a separate parliamentary inquiry.

The Labour Party constitution and programme During 1917 the need to refashion the Labour Party became evident. The Liberals' split in 1916 had diminished their plausibility as a party of government, while the end to the war, whenever it came, would also end the party electoral truce. The war emergency committee accordingly dwindled in significance as the task of building a unified national Labour Party out of the federal creation of 1900 became more urgent. Sidney worked closely and harmoniously on this task with Arthur Henderson, evicted from Lloyd George's coalition government in 1917. Webb provided the basis for the intellectual refurbishment of Labour in 1917–18, drafting virtually all the party's policy statements as it prepared for peace and reconstruction. The most important of them was the briefest: the socialist commitment which became clause 4 of Labour's constitution of 1918. This pledged the party 'to secure for the producers by hand or brain the full fruits of their industry, and the most equitable distribution thereof that may be possible, upon the basis of the Common Ownership of the Means of Production'. Webb was working in the knowledge that one outcome of Labour's overhaul would be the tightening of trade union control over the party, in return for greater financial help: his clause aimed to guard against what he considered the conservatism and narrow horizons of the union leadership by seeking to broaden the party's electoral base. He stressed that clause 4 was designed only to injure 'the "so-called" idle rich' and that Labour hoped to attract 'many men and women of the shopkeeping, manufacturing and professional classes who are dissatisfied with the old political parties' (*The New Constitution of the Labour Party*, 1918, 2, 3). In the interests of inclusiveness the old feud with syndicalism was suspended: the wording of clause 4 echoes, in fact, the definition of the aims of 'the more "class-conscious" of its members' in the Webbs' pre-war pamphlet criticizing the movement (*What Syndicalism Means*, 138). Sidney stressed that all forms of common ownership and control of industry were feasible.

Uninhibited in his criticism of Russian Bolshevism, which he interpreted as a gigantic adventure in the futility of worker control, Sidney was radical in his own policy proposals. The Labour Party manifesto *Labour and the New Social Order*, which he drafted in 1918, was described by him as an 'essentially anti-Bolshevist programme' (*New Statesman*, 7 Dec 1918). It sought to combat Lenin's British emulators by combining radical policies with a commitment to parliamentary methods. The bulk of the programme echoed the Webbs' *New Statesman* articles of 1913. Onto a familiar Webbian core—the national minimum, a public works programme on minority report lines—was grafted common ownership of land and a call for 'the progressive elimination from the control of industry of the private capitalist' by means of the nationalization of railways, mines, and power. The most innovative feature was a fiscal programme more explicit than anything the Webbs had produced before 1914. Previously fiscal policy had been oddly marginal to the Webbs' thinking, but the war had revealed the constricting nature of pre-war finance. It was now no longer true to say that the nation could not afford social reform, Webb argued: an increase in public expenditure to attain the national minimum would be an investment resulting in increased productivity. The introduction of military conscription in 1916 had fuelled demands within the labour movement for the 'conscription of riches'; in that year a Fabian inquiry under Sidney's chairmanship called for a 10 per cent levy on the capital value of all property to pay off war debt and an 80 per cent tax on incomes above £100,000. During 1917 Sidney pressed on the war emergency committee a sweeping fiscal programme entailing a doubling of income tax on the very rich, the capital levy, and the sequestration of unearned incomes. The capital levy resurfaced in *Labour and the New Social Order*, along with 'the direct taxation of the incomes above the necessary cost of family maintenance', a 95 per cent tax on millionaires' incomes, and the steeper graduation of death duties (*Labour and the New Social Order*, 1918, 11, 12, 17).

These proposals lay at the root of middle-class fear of labour after 1918. So far as Sidney's own thought was concerned, when combined with the national minimum they made explicit an egalitarian tendency implicit in his work from the 1880s onwards. The Webbs' mischievously straight-faced suggestion in 1920 that the 'pleasant but expensive country houses of the wealthy' could be converted into 'the holiday homes and recreation grounds of the urban toilers by hand or brain' (*A Constitution for the Socialist Commonwealth of Great Britain*, 1920, 265–6) reflected this shift. They believed the war to have emphasized 'the sharp division of our community into a party of the "haves" and a party of the "have nots"' (ibid., 274–5), and their response was an overt disavowal of the capitalist order, well before they committed themselves to soviet communism.

Post-war writings A belief that war had fatally undermined capitalism suffused most of the works produced by the partnership after 1918. Assuming that the post-war order would bring the confiscation of Beatrice's unearned income and thus jeopardize their writing, the Webbs produced a remarkable creative burst in the years after the armistice. In 1920 they brought their trade union history up to date. They also experimented ambitiously with constitutional prescription in their *Constitution for the Socialist Commonwealth of Great Britain*, which argued for two separate parliaments—a 'social' parliament to deal with welfare issues, and a 'political' parliament handling judicial and diplomatic affairs. In 1921 they revisited co-operation in *The Consumers' Co-Operative Movement*. In 1922 appeared *Special Authorities for Statutory Purposes*, the volume which the Webbs themselves considered the most important of the local government series, and in 1923 they published a lively essay entitled *The Decay of Capitalist Civilisation*, which, like the *Constitution*, borrowed some material from the 'What is socialism?' articles of 1913. Except for the detached *Special Authorities*, these works reflected the Webbs' heightened conviction of the evil of capitalism; the revisions to the trade union history, for example, contrasted with the relatively dispassionate tone of the original.

The Webbs now doubted whether the pre-war 'consent that the social order had to be gradually changed, in the direction of a greater equality in material income and personal freedom' could any longer be relied upon (*The Decay of Capitalist Civilisation*, 1923, 175–6). Unashamedly cartelistic, capitalism possessed a power that threatened social progress; it brutalized the poor and vulgarized the rich. Mental degradation (through the capitalist press), prostitution and vice, food adulteration and environmental damage—a new Webbian concern—were laid at its door.

Yet the Webbs also believed that capitalism was in decline, 'dissolving before our eyes' as feudalism had dissolved before it (*The Decay of Capitalist Civilisation*, 1923, 1), and counselled patience in the context of the fevered labour politics of the post-war years. Both the revised trade union history and the new co-operation study rehearsed familiar arguments against syndicalism and worker control: the Labour Party remained the appropriate vehicle for worker aspirations. So did parliament: 'to protect ourselves from Bolshevism we must, at all costs, maintain the popular faith and confidence in the House of Commons' (*New Statesman*, 7 Dec 1918). As if to emphasize the point, Sidney sought a parliamentary career himself. Having contested the London University seat unsuccessfully in 1918, he gained in 1920 the Labour nomination for the mining seat of Seaham in co. Durham.

Sidney's return to public life Until the previous year, Sidney would have appeared an unlikely nominee for a mining constituency, but in February 1919 he had been induced by Lloyd George to serve on the royal commission appointed under Sir John Sankey to investigate the troubled coal industry. There he worked with R. H. Tawney, Chiozza Money, and the nominees of the Miners' Federation to torment the slow-footed and under-prepared representatives of the industry. This resulted in, first, unanimous recommendations for higher wages and shorter hours, and subsequently, proposals from the chairman and from the miners' representatives for nationalization of the industry. The aftermath proved anticlimactic. The miners' material gains diminished their appetite for nationalization, which the government was able to reject in August 1919, and the material gains largely disappeared with the collapse of the industry's profitability after 1921, but Sidney had gained popularity with rank-and-file miners. It led to an invitation to contest Seaham, which was eventually confirmed in the face of the misgivings of the Durham Miners' Association, which had hoped to place a union man in the seat. Characteristically, Sidney sought to propitiate the union by writing a popular history of it, *The Story of the Durham Miners, 1662–1921* (1921). Liberalism's collapse in industrial England made Seaham a safe Labour seat, and Sidney was returned comfortably in 1922, 1923, and 1924 before retiring from the Commons.

Shaw described Sidney's parliamentary years as 'the only years he ever wasted' ('The Webbs', in S. Webb and B. Webb, *The Truth about Soviet Russia*, 1942, 13). The committee skills that he had brought to the LCC could not easily be deployed in parliament, and Sidney proved a poor chamber speaker, easily wounded by barracking from 'the more vulgar of the [Tory] young bloods' (diary, 20 Feb 1925; *Diaries*, ed. Mackenzie and Mackenzie, 4.48). Beatrice played the constituency wife with more diligence than enthusiasm, helping Sidney campaign and producing a series of newsletters, initially distinctly patronizing, for the women of Seaham. She regretted the demands on Sidney's time and the disruption of the partnership's work, but she spent her own time profitably, compiling her first volume of autobiography. Covering life before Sidney, it was published as *My Apprenticeship* in 1926. A classic of female autobiography, it drew extensively upon the diary which Beatrice had kept since 1873. The modern image of Beatrice owes much to the publication of diary extracts,

first in the 1950s and then in a four-volume selection emerging between 1982 and 1985. The later edition revealed her spiritual uncertainties, her obsession with Chamberlain, and her insecurity under pressure, as on the poor-law commission. It displayed the frustrated novelist in Beatrice, particularly in a demanding appraisal of personalities ('"Wasted gifts" is writ large over Bertrand Russell's life' (diary, 20 July 1936; *Diaries*, ed. Mackenzie and Mackenzie, 4.373)) that was virtually absent from the Webbs' joint works. The Chamberlain fixation and the more uninhibited personal judgements were omitted from *My Apprenticeship*, but the work still displayed a sensitive, vulnerable woman—a woman unfamiliar to those who, as she acknowledged, respected her without liking her.

Sidney's ministerial career The unpredictable three-party electoral system of the 1920s ensured that Labour was twice thrust into minority office. In a party short of administrative expertise, Sidney twice became a cabinet minister. By an irony which did not escape Beatrice, he occupied the first and last cabinet posts held by Joseph Chamberlain, becoming president of the Board of Trade from January to November 1924 and colonial secretary from June 1929 to August 1931.

The life of the first Labour government was so brief that few of its ministers made much of a mark in office. Sidney had originally been earmarked for the relatively new Ministry of Labour—appropriately, as that ministry was a partial answer to the minority report's call for an agency to tackle able-bodied unemployment. He was switched at the last minute to the Board of Trade, but still chaired a cabinet committee on unemployment. There, as the deputy cabinet secretary complained, 'all Sidney Webb ... has been able to prescribe as a remedy, after 30 or 40 years of reflection on the problem, is "a revival of trade"'. He concluded that 'Webb's mountainous brain always succeeded in producing an infinitesimal mouse' (T. Jones, *Whitehall Diary*, 1, 1969, 274). The board's own tally of its achievements in 1924 boasted only mice, including a bill to regulate petrol pumps and a measure to compel the sale of bread by weight.

Sidney's spell at the Colonial Office, in Ramsay MacDonald's second Labour government of 1929–31, was longer and less relaxed. His public career had been prolonged by accident. Having retired from the Commons in May 1929 he was summoned suddenly to the Lords in June 1929, after the formation of MacDonald's administration, because convention required two secretaries of state in the upper house. He adopted the title Baron Passfield, after Passfield Corner, the Hampshire house which the partnership had bought in 1923, but he refused a coat of arms, and Beatrice declined to call herself Lady Passfield. Aged almost seventy, Sidney had to master an area of policy that had scarcely previously concerned him. Widely assumed, even by Beatrice, to be a tool of his civil servants, he contrived to apply a watered-down version of the broadly humanitarian colonial policy elaborated by a Labour Party which had itself thought little about colonial affairs. In the two territories which proved most contentious during his spell of office, this meant protecting African interests in British east Africa and protecting the interests of the Arab community in Palestine.

In each case the fear, at least as expressed by Beatrice, was that the settler community was set upon expropriating the indigenous one to produce a landless proletariat and a cheap labour force. With this in mind, the Webbs found attractive the colonial variant of Tory paternalism expressed by the great imperial administrator Sir Frederick Lugard, whom they had met and admired on their pre-war Eastern tour, when he was governor of Hong Kong. They accepted Lugard's view that self-government, the traditional staple of the nineteenth-century Colonial Office, was inappropriate to areas where 'the inhabitants are broken up into communities whose economic interests, religious faith or manners and customs are irreconcilable' (diary, 13 Aug 1929; *Diaries, 1924–1932*, 215).

Sidney inherited a complex situation in Kenya, where tension existed not only between the British and Indian settler communities, but between the settlers and the Kikuyu natives. The British settlers sought to maintain their constitutional ascendancy over the more numerous Indians, who called for a common electoral roll for the Kenyan legislative council, and their economic ascendancy over the Kikuyu, who wanted both equitable representation and the protection of tribal lands. Whitehall's policy was unsettled in 1929. The previous secretary of state, Leopold Amery, had promoted a closer union of Britain's east African possessions for reasons of imperial strategy, but the white settler community in Kenya had sought to make assent to this conditional upon the reinforcement of their ascendancy in the legislative council, with the ultimate aim of white-dominated self-government. This threatened Whitehall's power to implement its policy of trusteeship, defined in 1923 as 'the protection and advancement of the native races' (Gregory, 5).

Sidney, in line with the paternalistic attitude towards 'non-adult races' expressed in the 'What is socialism?' series before the war, assumed that democracy was a hundred years away in Kenya, and made no attempt to encourage black enfranchisement. Trusteeship was rather promoted through attempts to protect black economic interests, crystallized in the *Memorandum on Native Policy in East Africa*, published in June 1930. This provided that, when the interests of Africans and those of the immigrant races (British and Indian) conflicted, 'the former should prevail' (P. S. Gupta, *Imperialism and the British Labour Movement, 1914–1964*, 1975, 186–7). A second white paper, published in the same month, sought to promote closer union in east Africa by establishing a single high commissioner with full power over native policy and substantial control over the colonial legislatures in other respects.

The result of these two statements was the comprehensive alienation of the British settlers in Kenya, whose lobbying in London ensured not only that the closer union policy was referred to a joint committee of both houses of parliament, as had always been intended, but that the *Native Policy* memorandum was as well. Webb ineptly

allowed the committee to be tory-chaired and tory-dominated. It recommended maintaining the *status quo*, effectively undermining Sidney's attempts to protect black interests and sowing the seeds of Mau-Mau rebellion in 1948.

The situation in Palestine was still more difficult. However valid Beatrice's materialistic analysis of settler motives, the rise of political Zionism had given the Jewish cause an idealism and articulacy scarcely evident among the Kenyan white population. Beatrice, for all her professed affinity to the Jews, thought talk of a return to a 2000-year-old inheritance 'sheer nonsense', and believed that the promise of a Palestinian Jewish home in the Balfour declaration of 1917 implied the gradual marginalization of the Palestinian Arabs. She considered that 'the case for the Arab has not yet been heard; whilst the case for the Jew has been vehemently and powerfully pressed on the Government' (diary, 2 Sept 1929; *Diaries, 1924–1932*, 218)— on only his second day in office Sidney received visits from the British Zionist sympathizers Leopold Amery and W. G. Ormsby-Gore. The change of government also, though, stimulated the Palestinian executive to send a delegation to London, which opened negotiations with the colonial secretary in March 1930. These did little to settle Palestinian concerns over Jewish immigration, but did lead to a promise of an official investigation into the sale of Palestinian land to Jews. Sir John Hope Simpson, the 'model' Indian administrator discovered by the Webbs in 1912 and a land expert, was appointed to conduct the investigation. Simpson's report of October 1930 stressed the paucity of cultivable land in Palestine and the extent of Arab unemployment, arguing against further settlement until agricultural productivity had been improved. As Sidney put it to the principal Zionist leader, 'Dr Weizmann, do you not realise there is not room to swing a cat in Palestine?' (*The Letters and Papers of Chaim Weizmann*, ed. B. Litvinoff, 1984, 2, B, 116). When Simpson's conclusions were embodied in the 'Passfield white paper' of 1930, however, the intensity of Zionist protest in Britain produced a retreat, in the form of an open letter from MacDonald to Weizmann in February 1931, reasserting the government's commitment to establish a Jewish national home. The letter heralded a change in attitude which, in Weizmann's words, 'enabled us to make the magnificent gains of the ensuing years' (quoted in R. John and S. Hadawi, *The Palestine Diary*, 1: *1914–1945*, 1970, 233). Sir John Chancellor was replaced as high commissioner by Sir Arthur Wauchope, who 'opened the doors to mass Jewish immigration', while the Palestinians learned the need for pan-Arab support (B. M. Nafi, *Arabism, Islamism and the Palestine Question, 1908–41*, 1998, 106).

In both areas Sidney had made policy broadly consistent with Labour's objectives, only to see the results overturned by external lobbying. In both cases he had received little support from MacDonald. When later he accused MacDonald of 'the gross error' of listening to outsiders' complaints about ministers, 'which he took up and made himself unpleasant about' (memoranda on the crisis of August 1931, BLPES, Passfield papers, IV/26/1), Sidney surely had his own experience in mind. In May 1931, weighed down by the pressures of office, he sought to retire as soon as some means could be found of maintaining the requisite government presence in the House of Lords.

No solution had been found before the government was overwhelmed by the financial crisis of August 1931. Sidney's entrapment in colonial affairs left him a marginal figure in the economic debates in the cabinet and the wider labour movement. In the party's internal battles he remained broadly loyal to MacDonald: 'his instinct is to obey the orders of his chief', as Beatrice put it (diary, 28 Nov 1929; *Diaries, 1924–1932*, 230). He felt frustrated by the 'most irritating self-righteous superiority' displayed by the Labour left and by the TUC's demands for prior consultation on industrial matters (memoranda on the crisis of August 1931, BLPES, Passfield papers, IV/26/1). Escalation of the financial crisis during the summer of 1931 brought an uncharacteristic display of impatience with the refusal of the TUC's general council to agree to cuts. In fact Sidney led a successful protest in cabinet against a proposal to transfer half a million transitional benefit recipients to the poor law, but in the critical cabinet vote which destroyed the government he supported MacDonald's proposal for reductions in unemployment benefit (though Beatrice appears to have believed that he voted with Henderson against them (diary, 25 Aug 1931; *Diaries, 1924–1932*, 284 n. 1). He was undaunted by the prospect of the government's collapse, which he had long foreseen, but he had expected its replacement by the Conservative opposition in the conventional way. It was MacDonald's decision to go into an emergency coalition with leading Conservatives and Liberals which really irked him, causing Sidney to conclude that such coups as the capture of MacDonald represented 'the last ditch in the defensive position of the British *rentier* class' (*Political Quarterly*, 3, 1932, 16). Sidney retired from public life, to join his wife in the promotion of soviet communism.

A new civilization? Away from the pressures of government, Beatrice assessed the developing crisis in strategic terms, in the context of the apparent collapse of capitalism after 1929. The period of the second Labour government and the months after its fall saw her conversion to the 'new civilisation' of soviet communism.

For most of the 1920s soviet communism had embodied what the Webbs most feared in the totalitarian state. During their post-war battles with the revolutionary left they had argued that the Bolsheviks' 'dictatorship of the proletariat' meant that 'the proletariat was dictated to, and the government prisons were as full, and its rifles as active, as those of the Tsardom' (*The Decay of Capitalist Civilisation*, 1923, 161). In 1927 Beatrice warned that soviet communism might delay economic democracy in Britain by half a century. She later maintained to John Parker that she had warmed to the USSR once Lenin abandoned worker control, but in reality she remained hostile to the soviet system after Lenin's death, and her conversion owed more to her despair over the British system than to any substantial change in the Soviet Union.

'Great Britain for the ten years since the War', Beatrice wrote in 1931, 'has been governed *exclusively* in the interest of the *rentier*' (diary, 2 Feb 1931; *Diaries, 1924–1932*, 265). The 1920s had seen a steady retreat from the high point of collectivism reached during the war. Sidney had, in his youth, been fond of pointing out that no collectivist measure had ever been reversed, but as the decade wore on, it became clear that de-control was a lasting feature of post-war Britain, and that the Conservative—or Conservative-dominated—governments which presided over the explosion of unemployment after 1920 would suffer little political penalty. Moreover, the post-war deflation questioned the power of other engines of democracy. The Webbs' 1921 study of co-operation celebrated the rapid numerical growth of the movement, but the evidence of the co-operatives' 'arrested development' was inescapable. They had made little headway in larger cities or among the middle class. Co-operative retailing had been slow to move beyond the basic staples of groceries and clothes, and as a result the average co-operator was spending a lower proportion of his income in the co-operative store in 1921 than in 1913. Worse was the moral and intellectual atrophy of the movement. Co-operative libraries stocked 'the cheapest, often the trashiest … novels' (*The Consumers' Co-Operative Movement*, 85), the central organs of the movement underpaid their brainworkers, and, as the membership succumbed to complacency, the internal democracy of the movement had decayed.

The co-operative movement had been slow to adopt a political role, and by the 1920s there could be no doubt that trade unionism rather than co-operation formed the leading sector of the labour movement. The Webbs' recurrent doubts about unionism were reinforced by the drift of many unions into militancy in the early 1920s, culminating in what Beatrice considered the 'monstrous irrelevance' of the general strike in 1926 (diary, 4 May 1926; *Diaries*, ed. Mackenzie and Mackenzie, 4.77). These doubts were reinforced in the 1920s as collectivism faltered in the face of deflation and mass unemployment. Although Sidney, chairing the Labour Party conference in 1923, had invoked 'the inevitability of gradualness' in holding the party to the parliamentary road, over the next few years first Beatrice, then Sidney, lost faith in the coming of the socialist state in Britain.

Mass unemployment weighed heavily on Beatrice. She saw 'whole sections of fellow countrymen … slowly becoming a harmless but worthless mass of low-grade humanity' (diary, 9 Sept 1930; *Diaries, 1924–1932*, 252). She understood that their existence made the national minimum unattainable but also acknowledged, in 1927, that the remedies for unemployment proposed in the minority report had been inadequate. She sought 'some treatment of the unemployed which will be "less eligible" than wage labour without being blatantly inequitable to the men and their families who are out of work through no fault of their own' and resented their 'semi-starvation', but she still considered the maintenance of the able-bodied in idleness 'ultra-dangerous' to society (diary, 5

March 1927, 30 May 1928; *Diaries*, ed. Mackenzie and Mackenzie, 4.117–8, 146). When the collapse of world trade after 1929 intensified an unemployment problem already chronic in Britain, Beatrice anticipated 'a far deeper cleavage between the *Haves* and the *Have Nots* throughout the world than we have as yet experienced' (Beatrice to Sidney, 9 Feb 1931; *Letters*, 3.344).

This situation accentuated the clear choice between capitalism and its alternative. Beatrice compared the position to that in the medieval period, when Christianity and Islam had competed for the soul of Europe. The contemporary choice was unappetizing: the USA offered a strident capitalism which had always repelled her, but the Soviet Union, enduring the five-year plan, offered grim austerity. Beyond this judgement, though, lay a growing interest in the soviet ethos of self-denial and a growing enthusiasm for the soviet transformation of society.

In the summer of 1930 Beatrice had been impressed by two studies of Russia written by American fellow travellers, M. G. Hindus's *Humanity Uprooted* (1929) and W. H. Chamberlin's *Soviet Russia: a Living Record and a History* (1930). They convinced her that the USSR exemplified 'the Mendelian view of sudden jumps in biological evolution as against the Spencerian vision of slow adjustment' (diary, 22 June 1930; *Diaries, 1924–1932*, 245). The significance of this challenge to assumptions to which she had subscribed since girlhood cannot be exaggerated. Spencer's model of social evolution lay at the root of the philosophy of 'the inevitability of gradualness'. The rapid soviet transformation of 'one of the most dishonest and dishonourable of peoples' (diary, 30 June 1931; *Diaries, 1924–1932*, 274) into a nation prepared to endure indefinite austerity for the common good challenged Webbian gradualism. It did not turn the pair into revolutionaries— repelled by violence, they expected the soviet model to be adopted through willing emulation rather than by force— but it demonstrated the scope for political leadership, moved by faith in the perfectibility of man, to change social mores. Soviet citizens had, Beatrice believed, been induced to spurn the 'medieval sin of covetousness ... a sin which was turned into a virtue by the economists of the Industrial Revolution. It is *greed*, pecuniary self-interest, which is the Soviet Devil—the source of all wickedness' (diary, 30 June 1931; *Diaries, 1924–1932*, 274).

It was this collective altruism which engaged Beatrice, as the economic crisis occasioned further assaults upon the condition of the poor in Britain. The proposals of the 1931 May report for cuts in social expenditure showed the strength of the British *rentier*, depriving the poor of necessities while the consumption of luxuries by the rich went unchecked. Meanwhile the Soviet Union propagated 'consumers' economics: production for a known demand' (diary, 17 Jan 1932; *Diaries, 1924–1932*, 299) of the sort that the Webbs had expected the co-operative movement to generalize in Britain. It was gratifying to learn from Shaw, who visited Russia in the summer of 1931, that the soviets had 'given up "workers' control" for the Webbs' conception of the threefold state—citizens', consumers' and producers' organisations' (diary, 8 Aug 1931; *Diaries, 1924–1932*,

278), but Beatrice was now more interested in the soul of soviet Russia than in its constitution.

Beatrice inferred that the strain imposed by soviet economic planning—upon both the leaders required to devise it and the workers obliged to suffer its stringency— was sustainable only through the cultivation of a collective faith providing almost a religious motive and discipline. The Communist Party had accordingly become a secular priesthood, playing a guiding role lost to capitalist society but one which she had previously ascribed to the Arya Samaj in India. When in 1934 Arthur Henderson suggested, with some acuity, that the Webbs had foreshadowed the soviet constitution in the last chapter of Beatrice's book on the co-operative movement, she replied 'Ah! But we forgot the Communist Party ... We discovered the body but left out the soul' (diary, 22 Aug 1934; *Diaries*, ed. Mackenzie and Mackenzie, 4.338). This moral direction was paramount.

Like many whose views had formed in the 1880s, Beatrice had spent much of her life seeking a social system ethically equipped to counter acquisitive individualism. She readily identified the communist creed with the positivist 'religion of humanity' that had fascinated her since girlhood, though she remained disturbed by the fear that the quasi-religious enthusiasm of soviet communism carried the seeds of intellectual intolerance. Less of an enthusiast by nature, Sidney was slower to devote himself to communism. His immediate reaction to the events of 1931 was, given the scale of Labour's catastrophe, relatively optimistic; he believed the party to have been purified and made more definitely socialist in its policy. He appeared less defeatist than Beatrice at this point, and it is likely that his final conversion to soviet communism awaited his experience of the system in action. It is unlikely, though, that that conversion was painful: the man who in 1888 had praised the Roman republic, in which 'in every age the individual is ruthlessly sacrificed to the mass, and the whole generation to the common weal' (BLPES, Passfield papers, 6/34), found nothing alien in Beatrice's stringent conception of soviet communism.

The Russian trips In May 1932 the Webbs joined the queue of Western tourists inspecting soviet Russia. They toured the country together in 1932, and Sidney made a follow-up visit, accompanied by Beatrice's niece Barbara Drake, in 1934, gathering material for their last major work. It appeared as *Soviet Communism: a New Civilisation?* in 1935, a second edition appearing, without the question mark in the title, two years later. They found, as Beatrice recorded in 1934, that 'the problem we have been seeking to solve for the last fifty years—poverty in the midst of plenty—is today being solved, and very much as we should have solved it, if we had had our way' (diary, 7 Jan 1934; *Diaries*, ed. Mackenzie and Mackenzie, 4.322). What they saw in soviet Russia was a 'multiform democracy', which recognized not only man's civic function but his function as a producer and as a consumer. They rejoiced that 'the Soviet Trade Union Movement is, in fact, first and foremost, not machinery for collective bargaining about hours and wages, but a huge social welfare organisation' (text of article for *The Listener*, 28 Sept 1932, BLPES, Passfield papers, 6/86). Soviet trade unions, 'not formed to fight anybody', and embracing managers as well as workers now that class distinctions had been abolished, worked to enhance productivity and welcomed labour-saving machinery. Better still, the co-operative movement was flourishing, with a magnificent new store in Leningrad offering 25,000 different commodities. Citizen, producer, consumer—the three aspects of Webbian man appeared undisguised in soviet Russia. The party proved more elusive. It proved 'extraordinarily difficult to get any descriptive detail of how this organisation actually works', as soviet officials were 'very cautious about giving information about the Communist Party' (Beatrice to Harold Laski, 12 March 1935, Laski papers, 27.2, Internationaal Instituut voor Sociale Geschiedenis, Amsterdam), though this information vacuum did nothing to still Beatrice's enthusiasm for the party as she conceived it.

The Webbs looked at the Soviet Union on two levels. First they saw it as a settled and successful system. During the trip of 1934 Barbara Drake noted Sidney observing the country 'with the relish of a scientist whose theoretical proposition has stood the test of practical experiment: "See, see, it works, it works"' ('The Webbs and Soviet communism', in M. Cole, ed., *The Webbs and their Work*, 227). It worked, he believed, by abolishing involuntary unemployment: centralized planning had succeeded in smoothing the cycle of boom and slump as the Webbs had sought to do in the minority report. 'The Soviet Union has quite obviously grown richer in the very years in which most, if not all, other countries have grown poorer' (*Soviet Communism*, 651). Throughout their lives the Webbs had seen material comfort as the essential precondition of moral improvement. Now they were convinced that Stalin's government worked 'not merely to benefit the people whom it served but actually to transform them' (ibid., 805), through the educative agency of the Communist Party.

This moral purpose was what made the Soviet Union a new civilization. Party members observed higher standards than the rest of the population, and were subjected to harsher penalties if they strayed. The Webbs clearly valued the participatory democracy of the soviets and considered it superior to Western parliamentarianism; the party was creating an earnest community, schooled in asceticism and social duty. They noted approvingly that 'the soviet newspaper contains no "society news" and no gossip' (*Soviet Communism*, 1028), while '"spooning" in public is "not done" in the USSR' (ibid., 1061). What they most valued in the soviet constitution of 1936 (which appears to have prompted the removal of the question mark from their second edition) was the provision in article 12 that all should be required to work. Thus resurfaced a theme running throughout their own writings, from Beatrice's early emphasis upon obligations over rights and Sidney's attacks upon *rentiers* to the strictures of the minority report.

A month before their joint trip, in March 1932, the Webbs had finished the manuscript of their *Methods of Social Study*, a manual for social researchers. There they recognized that bias was inescapable in humans observing human actions, but urged the investigator to 'choose methods of approaching the subject … that will, for the time being, throw [his] bias out of gear' (*Methods of Social Study*, 1932, 44–7). In their soviet studies, the Webbs' bias was stronger than in any of their previous academic work and the scholarly apparatus to curb that bias was, by their standards, unusually weak. They could not read Russian and did not, in their seventies, attempt to learn the language. They had no way of verifying official statistics and other soviet material likely to have been less reliable than the British official publications with which they were familiar. In Russia they found themselves honoured guests, on the grounds that Lenin himself had translated their trade union history, but their movements were still controlled by their hosts, and the country was too vast for septuagenarians to cover much ground in two months. These constraints left obvious marks on the book: the frequent borrowing of large chunks of text from fellow travellers' accounts of the USSR, for instance, and an occasional un-Webbian lack of evidential rigour.

The Webbs' visit in 1932 was made at a relatively placid moment in Stalinist history, before that year's disastrous harvest. The class warfare in the early years of the 1929 plan had waned, making Russia safer for the previously persecuted technocrats whom the Webbs so valued. Sidney's return came after the healthy harvest of 1933, so that neither Webb witnessed directly the catastrophic famine of 1932–3. This perhaps enabled them to accept and repeat official explanations for the causes of the famine. A deadening of the senses is evident in their blithe discussion of the treatment of local officials held culpable for the famine and in their response to the culling of the old Bolshevik élite in the show trials from 1936. The Webbs oscillated between accepting the official version—that Kamenev and Zinoviev had indulged in a 'crazy conspiracy', that the military leadership had been intriguing with the Germans, and, in 1940, that Trotsky was murdered by one of his followers—and deploying a more sophisticated argument that such blood-letting was the inevitable consequence of a protracted revolutionary struggle, comparable to Judge Jeffreys's 'bloody assizes' in England in the 1680s. Had they known the scale of the terror, the Webbs could hardly so readily have depicted the Soviet Union as a successfully functioning society, or avoided a more searching appraisal of Stalinist power. As it was, the eventual disclosure of the regime's horrors damaged their posthumous reputation. Their defenders were forced to treat their soviet infatuation as a senile aberration, but it was never that. They saw what they wanted to see, no doubt, but the soviet Russia they saw was the closest approximation in practice to their exemplary socialist society—the Webbian design that they had sketched, with little deviation, over a period of fifty years.

Final years The Webbs' enthusiasm for soviet communism relieved a gloomy old age. Sidney suffered a stroke in January 1938 which left him able to read but not write, condemned, as he saw it, to 'a "do-nothing life"' (diary, 25 Jan 1939; *Diaries*, ed. Mackenzie and Mackenzie, 4.427). The Nazi-soviet pact of August 1939 appeared incomprehensible, 'a great disaster to all that the Webbs have stood for' (diary, 25 Aug 1939; *Diaries*, ed. Mackenzie and Mackenzie, 4.438–9). Beatrice longed for 'a German to bomb the aged Webbs out of existence' (Beatrice to H. G. Wells, 7 July 1942; *Letters*, 3.459), but the Nazis left Passfield Corner unscathed, and she clung to life for fear of leaving Sidney alone. They derived consolation, though, from the turning of the tide of war at Stalingrad, concluding that it validated the soviet system. Beatrice's inner turmoil subsided:

> we have lived the life we liked and done the work we intended to do; and we have been proved to be right about Soviet Communism: a new civilisation. What more can we want than a peaceful and painless ending of personal consciousness? (diary, 25 March 1943; *Diaries*, ed. Mackenzie and Mackenzie, 4.495)

Beatrice, who had had a kidney removed in 1934, died of renal failure at Passfield Corner on 30 April 1943. Sidney survived for four more years, still reading voraciously, though his memory became increasingly 'sporadic' (Viscount Samuel, *Memoirs*, 1945, 293). He lived long enough to see, and to resent, the divergence between Britain and the USSR in the early cold war, dying of heart disease at Passfield Corner on 13 October 1947. He was, like Beatrice, cremated, and the ashes of both were buried initially at Passfield Corner until, at Shaw's suggestion, they were re-interred together, somewhat incongruously, in Westminster Abbey on 12 December 1947.

Conclusion 'What moves me is a desire to *get things done*. I want to diminish the sum of human suffering', Sidney wrote to H. G. Wells on 15 June 1907 (*Letters*, 2.264). Establishing what the Webbs got done is straightforward. The foundation of the LSE, the relaunching of the Labour Party, the remodelling of London education, the invigoration of the Fabian Society, even the creation of the *New Statesman* were substantial and durable achievements. Assessing how far the Webbs succeeded in their wider aim of diminishing human suffering is, however, more difficult. In the years after their deaths, when Fabian stock stood at its highest, they were hailed as the intellectual founders of the post-war welfare state: 'so much of the policy for home affairs which the Webbs worked out over fifty years is now accomplished fact', wrote Margaret Cole in 1956 (introduction, *Diaries, 1924–1932*, xvii). Her husband, writing Sidney's obituary, claimed that 'in Great Britain, Webb's influence has been as pervasive as Bentham's, and as deep' (G. D. H. Cole, 8). 'Millions are living fuller and freer lives today', Clement Attlee asserted at the re-interment ceremony, 'because of the work of Sidney and Beatrice Webb' (Muggeridge and Adam, 258).

The claim was plausible enough as Attlee's Britain took shape: the nationalization programme, the health service, and the welfare state could all be said to have Webbian roots. In detail, though, it requires qualification. The public corporations running the nationalized industries might have appeared superficially Webbian, and they certainly avoided worker control, but 'commanding heights' nationalization fell far short of the conception of the socialized economy envisaged in clause 4 of the Labour Party's constitution of 1918. The Webbs' influence was apparent in the foundation of the National Health Service: indeed the official historian of the service states that the minority report was the 'effective blueprint' for virtually all steps taken towards socialized medicine between the wars (C. Webster, *The Health Services since the War*, 1, 1988, 17–18). But the wider welfare state, based upon the Beveridge report of 1942 and its proposals for social insurance from cradle to grave, was not Webbian. The Webbs remained, from 1911, steadfast opponents of compulsory social insurance. Beatrice expected a Beveridgean welfare system merely to increase the number of unemployed while diminishing the nation's capacity to support them: 'hence it is destined to fail' (diary, 6 Dec 1942; *Diaries*, ed. Mackenzie and Mackenzie, 4.489–90). 'The sad fact is that the better you treat the unemployed, the worse the unemployment will become', she wrote (*Co-operative News*, 19 Dec 1942).

This was hardly the language of the welfare consensus, but by 1942 the Webbs had put the minority report far behind them, and rejected the concept of welfare capitalism. The Webbs' intellectual progress had led them to a faith in a soviet system whose other admirers were on the marginalized left of Attlee's Labour Party. Consequently they had few, if any, political heirs. They had once fêted Herbert Morrison as 'a direct disciple of the Sidney Webbs', but by 1940 he was dismissed as 'able and incisive but reactionary' (diary, 14 March 1934, 29 Feb 1940; *Diaries*, ed. Mackenzie and Mackenzie, 4.330, 448). Webbian technocrats of that sort were usually to be found on the Labour right and generally had little affection for the Soviet Union. Labour distanced itself from the USSR as cold war tensions worsened, and in the 1950s, punished electorally for its association with bureaucracy and post-war austerity, it removed the Webbs from its pantheon. Anthony Crosland's *The Future of Socialism*, bible of the 1950s revisionists, brought an attack upon the 'priggish puritanism' and administrative preoccupations of the Webbs: 'total abstinence and a filing system are not now the right signposts to the socialist utopia' (A. Crosland, *The Future of Socialism*, 1956, 523). The first battle for the modernization of Labour was fought in 1959 over the retention of clause 4. It was lost by the modernizers, but the clause survived for thirty-five more years as little more than a symbol.

The deepening of the cold war, the discovery of the murderous extent of Stalin's tyranny, and the eventual collapse of the soviet experiment served to discredit Russia's inter-war admirers, including the Webbs. There is rough justice in this: the Webbs' determination to believe in the eventual success of the Soviet Union left them vulnerable when the USSR failed to display either the efficiency or the social justice that they had predicted. Their infatuation with the Soviet Union was not simply a matter of backing the wrong horse, but reflected deeper methodological tensions. It was, of course, impossible for them to operate as they urged others to operate, as disinterested processors of observed facts. Like anybody, they needed a structure to their thought. Perhaps they needed one more than others, as the scale of their empirical research threatened to overwhelm them. In the event they avoided the sin of eclecticism by enclosing their material in a tight framework formed by their own impulses and insights.

The principal impulse was the search, from the 1880s on, for an alternative to what they considered the amorality and inefficiency of Victorian individualism. The guiding insight was the realization in their early works on co-operation and trade unionism that citizenship in a modern democracy should embrace man's role as consumer and producer as much as his role as voter—a genuine insight at a time when much of Britain was struggling even to comprehend the implications of franchise extension. In constructing a model reflecting the three facets of citizenship, the Webbs created a structure which was coherent and thus defensible, but over time it also became a mental prison, a habit of thought from which it became ever harder to escape, even as British society moved in other directions. Rather than adapt their prescriptions, the Webbs became over-receptive to an emergent society elsewhere which could plausibly be taken to exemplify their multiform democracy, which effected a 'scientific' approach to government, which implemented a national minimum, and which claimed to be animated by the spirit of self-sacrifice for the community.

However dogmatic the Webbs became in their own work, they never lost their intellectual curiosity. This ensured that, whatever tension there might have been between observation and prescription, their commitment to investigation for its own sake remained wholehearted. Part of the Webbs' achievement lay not only in establishing agencies for social investigation but also in letting them follow their own independent course: the Fabian research department, the *New Statesman*, and the London School of Economics all drifted from their Webbian moorings during the Webbs' lifetimes. Indeed, the LSE's first two directors, chosen by the Webbs, were both tories. Many of its luminaries—Beveridge, Tawney, Laski, W. A. Robson—might be seen as the Webbs' intellectual protégés, but they could hardly be described as their acolytes. The Webbs enjoyed gathering 'clever men from the universities' around them (Muggeridge and Adam, 203), but they made no attempt to establish a Webbian 'school'. The Millite Sidney remained committed to Mill's central doctrine of the free play of ideas: 'he could listen as well as talk', Douglas Cole recalled, 'and pursue your thought as well as his own' (G. D. H. Cole, 3). Beatrice was 'a good deal more dogmatic' (ibid.), but she was no less committed to intellectual debate: her one recurrent concern about the soviet system was that its quasi-religious enthusiasm would bring the suppression of free thought, 'without which science—that supreme manifestation of the curiosity of man—would wither and decay' (diary, 4 Jan 1932; *Diaries, 1924–1932*, 299).

In that respect the Webbs may best be seen as the originators of an ethos of social research that has proved more pervasive than most of their doctrines. Beatrice maintained in the 1890s, 'the collectivists alone have the faith to grind out a Science of Politics' (diary, 18 Jan 1897; *Diaries*, ed. Mackenzie and Mackenzie, 2.106), but a century later the Conservative minister Sir Keith Joseph—no Fabian—invoked the Webbs as the influence behind his establishment of the Centre for Policy Studies in the 1970s (private information). The practice of empirical investigation has become central to British political science and sociology in the twentieth century. It is arguably the Webbs' most enduring legacy.   JOHN DAVIS

Sources BLPES, Passfield MSS · BLPES, Tawney MSS · Harold Laski papers, Internationaal Instituut voor Sociale Geschiedenis, Amsterdam · Karl Kautsky papers, Internationaal Instituut voor Sociale Geschiedenis, Amsterdam · *The diaries of Beatrice Webb*, ed. N. Mackenzie and J. Mackenzie, 4 vols. (1982–5) · *Beatrice Webb's diaries, 1912–1924*, ed. M. I. Cole (1952) · *Beatrice Webb's diaries, 1924–1932*, ed. M. Cole (1956) · *The Webbs in Asia: the 1911–12 travel diary*, ed. G. Feaver (1992) · *Sidney and Beatrice Webb: Indian diary*, ed. N. G. Jayal (1987) · *The letters of Sidney and Beatrice Webb*, ed. N. Mackenzie, 3 vols. (1978) · B. Webb, *My apprenticeship* (1926) · B. Webb, *Our partnership* (1948); new edn, ed. G. Feaver (1975) · S. Webb and B. Webb, 'Reminiscences', pts 1–6, *St Martin's Review* (1928–9) · R. Harrison, *The life and times of Sidney and Beatrice Webb, 1858–1905: the formative years* (2000) · M. Cole, ed., *The Webbs and their work* (1949) · G. D. H. Cole, 'Sidney Webb', *Fabian Quarterly*, 56 (winter 1947) · M. Cole, *Beatrice Webb* (1945) · M. Muggeridge and R. Adam, *Beatrice Webb: a life, 1858–1943* (1967) · A. M. McBriar, *Fabian socialism and English politics, 1884–1918* (1962) · D. E. Nord, *The apprenticeship of Beatrice Webb* (1985) · J. Lewis, *Women and social action in Victorian and Edwardian England* (1991) · H. G. Wells, *The new Machiavelli* (1911) · W. Wolfe, *From radicalism to socialism: men and ideas in the formation of Fabian socialist doctrines, 1881–1889* (New Haven, 1975) · R. Dahrendorf, *LSE: a history of the London School of Economics and Political Science, 1895–1995* (1995) · E. J. T. Brennan, *Education for national efficiency: the contribution of Sidney and Beatrice Webb* (1975) · A. Saint, 'Technical education and the early LCC', *Politics and the people of London: the London county council, 1889–1965*, ed. A. Saint (1989) · N. Mackenzie and J. Mackenzie, *The first Fabians* (1977) · A. M. McBriar, *An Edwardian mixed doubles* (1987) · J. Winter, *Socialism and the challenge of war* (1974) · A. Smith, *The 'New Statesman': portrait of a political weekly, 1913–1931* (1996) · R. G. Gregory, *Sidney Webb and east Africa: Labour's experiment in the doctrine of native paramountcy* (Berkeley, CA, 1962) · H. J. Laski, *The Webbs and soviet communism* (1947) [Beatrice Webb memorial lecture] · private information (2004) [B. H. Harrison]

Archives BLPES, Passfield papers, corresp., diaries, and papers · BLPES, corresp. and papers [Sidney Webb] · BLPES, further corresp. and papers [Sidney Webb] · BLPES, letters · BLPES, papers · BLPES, working papers on English local government · Bodl. RH, corresp. and dispatches written as colonial secretary [Sidney Webb] · Labour History Archive and Study Centre, Manchester, papers [Sidney Webb] · U. St Andr. L., papers relating to a summer holiday in Scotland | BL, letters to John Burns, Add. MS 46287 · BL, letters to George Bernard Shaw, Add. MS 50553 · BL, corresp. with the Society of Authors, Add. MS 56842 [Sidney Webb] · BLPES, corresp. with Lord Beveridge · BLPES, letters to Joseph Fels [Sidney Webb] · BLPES, corresp. with the independent labour party · BLPES, corresp. with Dr McLeary · BLPES, letters, mainly to Edward Pease [Sidney Webb] · BLPES, R. H. Tawney papers · BLPES, letters to Graham Wallas [Sidney Webb] · Bodl. Oxf., corresp. with Viscount Addison together with some notes relating to Home Marketing Board [Sidney Webb] · Bodl. Oxf., corresp. with H. H. Asquith · Bodl. Oxf., letters to James Bryce [Sidney Webb] · Bodl. RH, corresp. with Lord Lugard [Sidney Webb] ·

CAC Cam., corresp. with A. V. Alexander [Sidney Webb] · CKS, letters to Hubert Hall [Sidney Webb] · Col. U., Rare Book and Manuscript Library, letters to *Political Science Quarterly* [Sidney Webb] · Col. U., Rare Book and Manuscript Library, letters to Paul Reynolds [Sidney Webb] · Col. U., Rare Book and Manuscript Library, letters to Edwin Seligman [Sidney Webb] · HLRO, letters to Herbert Samuel and other papers · HLRO, corresp. with Herbert Samuel [Sidney Webb] · Internationaal Instituut voor Sociale Geschiedenis, Amsterdam, letters to Harold Laski · Internationaal Instituut voor Sociale Geschiedenis, Amsterdam, letters to Harold Laski [Sidney Webb] · Internationaal Instituut voor Sociale Geschiedenis, Amsterdam, corresp. with Dora Russell · King's AC Cam., letters to Oscar Browning [Sidney Webb] · King's AC Cam., letters to John Maynard Keynes · Labour History Archive and Study Centre, Manchester, corresp. with war emergency workers national committee · LMA, records of London county council and technical education board · Man. CL, Manchester Archives and Local Studies, letters to Lord Simon [Sidney Webb] · McMaster University, Hamilton, Ontario, William Ready division of archives and research collections, corresp. with Bertrand Russell · NL Scot., letters to Lord Haldane · NL Wales, corresp. with Thomas Jones · NRA, priv. coll., letters to Miss Rendel · Plunkett Foundation, Long Hanborough, Oxfordshire, corresp. with Sir Horace Plunkett · PRO, records of cabinet, board of trade, and colonial office · PRO, records of cabinet, Board of Trade, Colonial Office · PRO, corresp. with J. Ramsay MacDonald, PRO 30/69/1/210 [Sidney Webb] · U. Sussex, letters to W. W. Bartlett [Sidney Webb] · U. Sussex, corresp. with Leonard Woolf [Sidney Webb] · U. Sussex, letters to Leonard Woolf · U. Sussex, corresp. with Leonard Woolf [Sidney Webb] · University of Sheffield, letters to William Hewins [Sidney Webb] · University of Sheffield Library, corresp. with W. A. S. Hewins · University of Wisconsin, Madison, letters to Richard Theodore Ely [Sidney Webb] | SOUND BL NSA, recorded talk

Likenesses photograph, 1890–99, repro. in Drake and Cole, eds., *Our partnership*, facing p. 202 · photographs, c.1890–1941, Hult. Arch. · G. B. Shaw, photograph, c.1900, NPG [*see illus.*] · J. Holliday, chalk drawing, c.1909, Beatrice Webb House, Dorking, Surrey · G. Coates, oils, exh. 1924, London School of Economics · W. Nicholson, double portrait, oils, 1928 (with her husband), London School of Economics · E. S. Swinson, oils, 1934, NPG · A. G. Chappelow, two photographs, 1942, NPG · photograph, 1942, repro. in Cole, *Beatrice Webb*, facing p. 178 · G. B. Shaw, photograph, NPG · cartoon (Sidney Webb; *The inevitability of gradualness*), repro. in *Punch* (4 Aug 1923) · double portrait, photograph (with her husband), NPG · photograph, repro. in Cole, *Beatrice Webb*, facing p. 62 · photograph, repro. in Muggeridge and Adams, *Beatrice Webb: a life*

Wealth at death £59,419 11s. 4d.—Sidney James Webb: probate, 1948, *CGPLA Eng. & Wales*

Webb, Benedict (*b.* 1563, *d.* after 1626), clothier, was the third generation in the trade, following his grandfather, a small clothier (who died in Kingswood, Wiltshire, in 1558), and a father and uncles who were more substantial men, collecting aulnage in Gloucestershire, Wiltshire, and Bristol, exporting undressed cloth, and importing logwood. Benedict worked under his father until he was sixteen; he was then apprenticed to a London linen-draper and merchant in the French trade, and went abroad. For four to five years he was in Paris and Rouen, with occasional visits to Italy. He admired the quality of foreign workmanship and noted all new techniques. He had two foreign looms copied, and returned to England, setting up business in Taunton, where in 1589 he experimented with a multicoloured Spanish cloth, called medley, or 'Webb's' cloth. In or before 1595, following his father's death, Webb moved to Kingswood to take over the business, married Alice Trobridge, and had many daughters, and one

son, Benedict. He traded with France in salt and cloth, and had landed and farming interests in the Vale of Berkeley and the Forest of Dean. His cloth trade encompassed a large annual contract with George Mynne, the London draper, for which he hired 500 additional workers. Webb expected in normal years a clear trading profit of £400, though his contracts with Mynne were the subject of lengthy dispute and actions at law which cost him dearly. He successfully negotiated the repeal of a clause in the statute of 4 & 5 Philip and Mary, c. 5, which seriously prejudiced west-country clothiers' interests (43 Eliz., c. 10), and was one of three who visited France to persuade the French to repeal, in February 1606, a decree prohibiting the import of English tentered cloth.

This French visit gave Webb the idea of growing rapeseed for oil to dress cloth. He brought the model of a French oil mill to England, and set up a copy at Kingswood in 1605. In 1611 he was consulted by Londoners setting up the Londonderry plantation in Ireland, and showed positive interest in joining an oil-milling venture there. Milling at Kingswood expanded about 1618, and in December 1624 Webb received a fourteen-year patent of monopoly, claiming that he was the first inventor. His design of mill may have been original, but others had long been growing rapeseed in East Anglia and milling rapeseed around London. A lawsuit in 1625 disclosed that Richard Warner, a soap-boiler of Bristol, had a mill in Caerleon, Monmouthshire, and by offering double wages, had secured some of Webb's workers to build it. Webb was then growing at least 550 acres of rapeseed, and milling 20 gallons of oil a day. In 1626 senior west-country clothiers strongly commended Webb's oil, for cheapness, economy, and effectiveness, even on their best quality cloth. Webb, and others, stressed the amount of work he gave to the poor.

Webb was an immodest publicist of his achievements, and amassed wealth but also large debts. Local creditors included his nephew, John Smith or Smyth of Nibley, who preserved Webb's autobiography among his papers. He was still alive in 1626.   JOAN THIRSK, *rev.*

Sources E. Moir, 'Benedict Webb, clothier', *Economic History Review*, 2nd ser., 10 (1957–8), 256–64 · lawsuits in Court of Exchequer: state papers Ireland, PRO
Archives Glos. RO, autobiography

Webb, Benjamin (1819–1885), ecclesiologist and Church of England clergyman, was born on 28 November 1819, at Addle Hill, Doctors' Commons, London, the eldest son of Benjamin Webb (*d.* 1870), of the firm of Webb & Sons, wheelwrights, of London. On 2 October 1828 he was admitted to St Paul's School under Dr John Sleath, and he went on as an exhibitioner to Trinity College, Cambridge, in October 1838. He graduated BA in 1842 and proceeded MA in 1845. While still a freshman, in May 1839, he was instrumental with J. M. Neale in founding the Cambridge Camden Society. Beresford Hope joined their committee the following year. In 1845 the society moved to London and became the Ecclesiological Society. As secretary, and editor of *The Ecclesiologist* from 1839 to 1868, Webb played a pivotal role in what came to be known as the Cambridge Movement, an aesthetic equivalent to the theology of the

Benjamin Webb (1819–1885), by Eden Upton Eddis, 1881

Oxford Movement. The Oxford Tractarians had aimed to revive the theological basis of the authority of the Church of England; the Cambridge ecclesiologists set out to recreate its architectural and liturgical expression. By 1854 a quarter of all Anglican parish churches in England had been 'restored' according to Camdenian rules, by 1873 a third; and the influence of Cambridge ecclesiology was eventually felt in Anglican churches throughout the English-speaking world.

Webb was ordained deacon in 1842 and priest in 1843, and served as curate first at Kemerton in Gloucestershire (1843–4) under his college tutor, Archdeacon Thorp (first president of the Cambridge Camden Society), and afterwards at Brasted in Kent (1849–51) under William Hodge Mill, who, as regius professor of Hebrew, had encouraged his ecclesiological work at Cambridge, and whose daughter, Maria Elphinstone Mill (d. 1904), he married in 1847. Immediately after his marriage, Webb also became (1847–9) curate to William Dodsworth at Christ Church, Albany Street, London. He did not, however, follow Dodsworth to Rome. In 1851 he was presented by Hope to the perpetual curacy of Sheen in Staffordshire, and in 1862 by Lord Palmerston—again at Hope's instigation—to the crown living of St Andrew's, Wells Street, London, which he retained to his death. Under his care St Andrew's became celebrated for the musical excellence of its services; it was also distinguished by the efficiency of its parochial schools, confraternities, catechetical classes, and day nursery, the last of these being perhaps the first of its kind in London.

Webb was appointed by Bishop Jackson of London in 1882 to a prebend in St Paul's Cathedral. From that date until his death he was also editor of the *Church Quarterly Review*. He had been elected FSA on 26 May 1870. He died at his house, 3 Chandos Street, Cavendish Square, London, on 27 November 1885, and was buried in the churchyard at Aldenham, Hertfordshire. There is a monument by Armstead in the crypt of St Paul's. Webb left £21,529. His youngest son, Clement *Webb (1865–1954), became professor of the philosophy of the Christian religion at Oxford University.

As a tory high-churchman, Webb was known for his moderation. Although an enthusiastic ritualist, often accused of Romanism, he never strayed far from Anglican conventions. 'Rubrics were made for the Church', he used to say, 'not the Church for the Rubrics' (*Saturday Review*, 53, 1877, 66–7). In this he differed from J. M. Neale. In Hope's words, Webb 'never wasted himself by the superfluous indulgence of creating otiose change … Neale, with all his genius, was not judicious' (*Saturday Review*, 40, 1885, 772).

In 1841, while still at Cambridge, and working closely with J. M. Neale, Webb was involved in the production of two highly influential pamphlets: *A Few Words to Church Wardens, Suited to Town and Manufacturing Parishes* and *A Few Words to Church Builders*. Together Webb and Neale also published a translation of Durandus entitled *The Symbolism of Churches and Church Ornaments* (1843). Webb's first solo publication, *Sketches of Continental Ecclesiology, or, Church Notes in Belgium, Germany and Italy* (1848), struck out in a new direction: henceforward models for Camdenian churches, at least in towns, were more likely to be continental than East Anglian. And it was perhaps in this area— in the prolonged debates about an architectural style suitable for the Victorian age—that Webb did his most original work. From the 1840s to the 1870s, notably in *The Ecclesiologist* and the *Saturday Review*, he argued forcibly for modern Gothic: brick-built, polychrome, eclectic; the style in fact of his favourite architect, William Butterfield. He was elected ARIBA in 1878.

As a Cambridge undergraduate, Webb seems to have been more than a little precious. 'His dress was very peculiar', wrote one contemporary, 'and intended to designate ultra-highchurchmanship'; so much so that he was known as the 'Blessed Benjamin' (*Romilly's Cambridge Diary, 1842–47*, ed. M. E. Bury and J. D. Pickles, Cambridgeshire RS, 10, 1994, 208–9). Nevertheless, despite a retiring manner and frequent ill health, he proved himself an able propagandist as well as a learned liturgiologist.

CLEMENT C. J. WEBB, rev. J. MORDAUNT CROOK

Sources J. M. Crook, 'Benjamin Webb and Victorian ecclesiology', *The church retrospective*, ed. R. N. Swanson, SCH, 33 (1997) · B. Webb, diary, Bodl. Oxf., MSS Sc. 44750–88
Archives Bodl. Oxf., diaries and papers · LPL, corresp. | Bodl. Oxf., letters to E. B. Pusey · JRL, letters to E. A. Freeman · LPL, letters to William Hodge Mill · LPL, reports on churches for Cambridge Camden Society
Likenesses E. U. Eddis, oils, 1881, Westminster School, London [see illus.] · H. H. Armstead, marble relief, exh. RA 1889, St Paul's Cathedral, London
Wealth at death £21,529 0s. 10d.: probate, 11 Feb 1886, *CGPLA Eng. & Wales*

Webb, Catherine (1859–1947), co-operative movement activist and writer, was born on 4 May 1859 at 4 Wilson Street, Battersea, London, the daughter of Thomas Edward Burgess Webb, a journeyman coppersmith, and his wife, Catherine (*née* Young). Her father was a founder of Battersea and Wandsworth Co-operative Society, and an early director of the Co-operative Wholesale Society. In addition to believing in consumers' co-operation as a progressive industrial system in embryo, and holding strong views about the rights and responsibilities of women, Catherine gained from her parents a view of education as a lifelong process (her mother's interests included astronomy and polar exploration), convictions which shaped the six decades of her public service.

Miss Webb, as she was invariably known, became a prominent co-operator at a time when very few women sat on committees, appeared on public platforms, or even travelled alone. She was elected on to the co-operative southern sectional board in 1895, and from 1895 to 1902 sat on the central board of the Co-operative Union. In 1897 she described how on a late train back to London after a board meeting, she gratefully agreed to the guard's offer to lock her into her carriage to safeguard her privacy and comfort, as she was the only woman passenger. She was also a member of the co-operative education committee, and edited *Industrial Co-operation* (1904), for many years the standard text for students of consumers' co-operation.

Catherine Webb was best known through her work in the Women's Co-operative Guild, formed in 1883 to develop the role of women in the movement. She was a close friend and colleague of Margaret Llewelyn Davies. In 1885 she was a founder member and the first secretary of the Battersea Guild, a member of the central committee in 1885–8 and 1892–4, and national vice-president in 1893. Catherine Webb was an early advocate of the need for women to undertake public speaking for the guild (despite the opposition of Alice Acland). At the 1892 Manchester festival, she spoke on 'The guild and store life', encouraging women to play an active part in the business of their co-op shop, and at the 1894 guild annual meeting in Leicester gave a paper entitled 'Co-operation as applied to domestic work', in which she outlined the ways in which co-operative enterprises—wash-houses, laundries, bakeries, restaurants—could ease 'toilsome drudgeries', and free the housewife to play a more public role as a citizen.

In 1894 Catherine Webb represented the guild at the Women's Trade Union Association conference which set up the Women's Industrial Council, a central body which investigated the condition of women in different trades, and pressed for reforms. As one of the councils' lecturers, and as its secretary from 1895 to 1902, in succession to Amelia Hicks, she publicized such issues as the need for women factory inspectors, and the exploitation of home workers and women in the 'sweated' trades.

As a writer and lecturer Catherine Webb continued to make an important contribution to the guild's education and propaganda work. She regularly contributed to, and for a time edited, the 'Women's corner' in *Co-operative News*, and in 1927 published a guild history, *The Woman with the Basket*. From 1905 to 1930 she was the secretary of the Guild Convalescent Fund, established in 1895 in memory of a guild pioneer, Mrs Ben Jones (1848–1894), for guildswomen in need of rest and recuperation.

Alongside her career as a co-operator, Catherine Webb was involved in adult education through Morley College which was founded in 1889. She attended university extension courses at Morley in the 1890s, and was closely associated with Graham Wallas. He encouraged her to undertake lecturing for Morley College, and she subsequently carried out lecture tours in the midlands and the north of England. She sat on the college council from 1915 until her death, and for many years acted as its vice-chairman. In 1946 she was vice-president of the college, and in 1947 produced her *History of Morley College for Working Men and Women in Lambeth, London*. In this history she wrote that, following her election to the council, 'Morley College became a part of my life's greater interests' (*DLB*, 347).

Catherine Webb remained single; she was known as an intelligent and enlightened woman with a charming personality. Despite failing health she went on working until the last weeks of her life, and retained a lively interest in the various progressive causes with which she was associated. She died at 162 Coombe Lane, Wimbledon on 29 July 1947. She was cremated at Streatham Vale crematorium on 1 August 1947.   GILLIAN SCOTT

Sources *DLB* · *Co-op News* (9 Aug 1947) · *Co-op News* (5 June 1897) · T. Webb · b. cert. · d. cert.
Likenesses photograph, 1904?, repro. in M. L. Davies, *The Women's Co-operative Guild, 1883–1904* (1904) · photograph, 1947?, repro. in *Co-operative News* (9 Aug 1947)
Wealth at death £783 4s. 3d.: probate, 6 Dec 1947, *CGPLA Eng. & Wales*

Webb, Clement Charles Julian (1865–1954), theologian and philosopher of religion, was born in London on 25 June 1865, the youngest child of Benjamin *Webb (1819–1885), incumbent of St Andrew's, Well's Street, and prebendary of St Paul's, and his wife, Maria Elphinstone, daughter of the Sanskrit and Arabic scholar William Hodge Mill, regius professor of Hebrew at Cambridge, and his half-Indian wife. Webb's father was a pioneer of the ecclesiological revival in the Church of England, and initially Webb was much influenced by his ritualism. However, after a spiritual crisis in his first year at Oxford, which he later called his 'conversion' or the 'turning point in my spiritual history' (Webb, 'Outline', 336), he moved away from Anglo-Catholicism. He told Baron von Hügel on 30 November 1908 that he was not prepared to call himself a high-churchman 'tho' I was brought up as one, and am accustomed to some of their ways: for I have hardly ever, since I grew up, found myself in sympathy with the High Church *party*.' (von Hügel MSS, St Andrews University Library, MS 3179). Much later in his career he wrote a book on the history of the Oxford Movement (*Religious Thought in the Oxford Movement*, 1928).

Education and early career Webb was admitted as a halfboarder to Westminster School on 22 September 1876, and there he gained what he claimed was a 'habit of reflection which was to turn me at last into a professional philosopher' (Ross, 339). He was an exhibitioner (1879), queen's scholar (1880–84), Mure scholar (1882), and captain of the school (1883). He exerted 'immense influence' (Grensted, 16) on the life of the school and was the last 'liberty boy', which meant that he was exempt from fagging. He maintained close contact with the school throughout his life, serving as a governor from 1905 until his death and as a Busby trustee from May 1914. He was also a governor of Aylesbury grammar school from 1938.

Webb matriculated at Christ Church, Oxford, as a Westminster scholar on 10 October 1884. He displayed no special aptitude for classical literature, achieving only a second class in classical moderations in 1886, but began to mature as a philosopher reading for Greats under the influence of his tutors J. A. Stewart and, later, James Cook Wilson, from whom he learned the importance of scepticism and the critical method and with whom he remained in close contact until Wilson's death. He also read the English translation of Kant's *Grundlegung der Metaphysik der Sitten* in 1887, a book which he claimed made 'a greater impression upon me than any other single work that fell in my way' (Webb, *Religious Thought*, 15) and on which he later gave lectures (published as *Kant's Philosophy of Religion*, 1926). His undergraduate experiences left him with the conviction, which he held throughout his career, that it was the

> first of religious duties to keep one's ears to any voice, from whatever quarter, which might convey a message from God; a delightful sense of expectation of strange and wonderful things, though it might be stern and severe things, that any such voice might have to tell me. (Webb, 'Outline', 336–7)

His natural sense of enquiry gave him broad academic interests and an inquisitive mind, as well as the enjoyment of foreign travel: during long vacations he visited the continent whenever possible from 1887 onwards.

Fellowship and lectureship After being placed in the first class in Greats, Webb was elected to a fellowship at Magdalen College, Oxford, on 6 November 1889. There being no tutorship available immediately, he taught initially for New College, where one of his pupils was the future philosopher Horace Joseph, son of Alexander Joseph, rector of St John's, Chatham, and honorary canon of Rochester. Joseph later became one of his closest friends, and Webb married his sister, Eleanor Theodora Joseph (1869–1942), headmistress of Leeds high school, on 15 August 1905. Although childless, their marriage was happy, and they shared many interests. Webb's diaries reveal his wife's lively interest in questions of theology and philosophy, and a depth of theological insight. She was a respected and entertaining hostess to their many friends, and there are many letters written to her in her own right. On 12 March 1890 Webb was appointed to a tutorship at Magdalen, where he was responsible for half of the teaching of philosophy. From 1907 to 1920 he also taught philosophy for non-collegiate students. At the same time he was a leading light in the Oxford Aristotelian Society and the Synthetic Society. Throughout his time in Oxford he was involved in administration, serving as senior dean of

his college from 1894 to 1897, vice-president from 1898 to 1899, pro-proctor of the university from 1894 to 1895, and senior proctor from 1905 to 1906. He also served on the hebdomadal council and the general board of the faculties. These commitments meant that his literary output was relatively small, although he managed to produce an edition of the *Devotions of St Anselm* in 1903 and a two-volume critical edition of John of Salisbury's *Policraticus* in 1909. He followed this up with an edition of the *Metalogicon* (1929) and a popular book, *John of Salisbury* (1932). In 1911 he published his first original book, *Problems in the Relations of God and Man*. Throughout his life he also wrote a large number of fair-minded and judicious reviews.

Webb's literary output increased dramatically after his election as Wilde lecturer on natural and comparative religion (1911–14). Despite a high-pitched voice 'in which authority and modesty were curiously blended' (*The Times*, 12 Oct 1954), his lectures were popular, and were noted for their precision and clarity. As Wilde lecturer he gave an influential inaugural lecture entitled 'Natural and comparative religion' (1911) and produced a detailed history of natural theology (*Studies in the History of Natural Theology*, 1915) which confirmed the abilities as a medievalist that he had already demonstrated in his critical editions. The breadth of his interests was shown in his book *Group Theories of Religion and the Individual* (1916), which is a thoroughgoing account of the religious theories of E. Durkheim and L. Lévy-Bruhl, as well as his popular *History of Philosophy* for the Home University Library (1915) and a set of popular addresses, *In Time of War* (1918).

Nolloth professorship Webb was Gifford lecturer at Aberdeen from 1918 to 1919, publishing two sets of lectures, *God and Personality* (1918) and *Divine Personality and Human Life* (1920), his most accomplished works. Influenced by J. Royce, H. A. E. Driesch, and B. Bosanquet, Webb offered a cautious and judicious summary of contemporary theories of personality both human and divine. Webb maintained a devotion to the human personality of Christ, which he saw as the chief grounds for asserting divine personality against the pantheistic tendencies of Hegelian idealism (*God and Personality*, 82). It was on the basis of these lectures that C. F. Nolloth chose to establish a new chair at Oriel College for the philosophy of the Christian religion, to which Webb was elected on 6 February 1920. In 1922 he was elected fellow of Oriel and moved out of Magdalen accommodation at Holywell Ford to Walnut Tree Cottage, Old Marston, where he also served as churchwarden. His published works during his period as professor were chiefly reworked lectures, which display a breadth of interest and popular appeal, but which made little impact on the academic community (they included *Religion and the Thought of To-day*, 1929, and Pascal's *Philosophy of Religion*, 1929). During his time as professor he was awarded many academic distinctions, including an LLD from St Andrews in 1921, and in 1927 he was elected fellow of the British Academy, an institution he actively supported until his death. He was appointed to the archbishops' commission on doctrine set up in 1922, his 'great critical power, coupled with his desire to do justice to all our varied points of view, [making] him an invaluable member of our counsels' (Grensted, 20). He received his Oxford DLitt in 1930.

Webb retired in 1930, receiving an honorary fellowship from Oriel and commencing a period of intense intellectual activity which continued almost until his death. Shortly before his eightieth birthday he was able to fill Oriel dining hall with a lively lecture entitled 'Religious experience' (1945). After retirement he travelled extensively, delivering the Stephanos Nirmalendu Ghosh lectures in Calcutta in 1930–31 (published as *The Contribution of Christianity to Ethics*, 1932) and the Olaus Petri lectures at Uppsala University in 1932 (*Religious Thought in England from 1850*, 1933); the latter university awarded him a DTheol in the same year. He also gave the Forwood lectures in the philosophy of religion at Liverpool in 1933 (published as *Religion and Theism*, 1933, and also containing his thoughts on Freud) and the Lewis Fry lectures at Bristol in 1934 (*The Historical Element in Religion*, 1935). He was awarded a Glasgow DD in 1937 and was made an honorary fellow of Magdalen in 1938. Christ Church eventually elected him to an honorary studentship in 1953. Before the outbreak of the Second World War he moved to Pitchcott, near Aylesbury, continuing to write until 1945. He died on 5 October 1954 at the Royal Buckinghamshire Hospital, Aylesbury, as a result of complications following a major operation, and was buried in Pitchcott churchyard on 9 October.

Personal influence Throughout his life Webb displayed a 'genius for friendship' (Ross, 340) and a modesty and 'simplicity of character which never made his junior and less learned colleagues feel for one moment ill at ease' (Grensted, 20). He was a lively conversationalist, had a keen sense of humour, and was endearingly absent-minded, becoming a close and trusted friend to a large number of people, both inside and outside Oxford. His closest friend and confidant was C. B. Shebbeare, whom he had known since his Westminster days. He later became close friends with his colleagues at Magdalen, H. A. Wilson, Paul Benecke, R. L. Poole, and C. H. Turner, as well as with the modernist theologian Hastings Rashdall and the leading Roman Catholic layman Baron Friedrich von Hügel; with both he maintained an extensive correspondence. The extent and variety of his circle of friends, who ranged across the whole theological spectrum, are noted in the long list of subscribers to the 'wartime substitute for the *Festschrift*' (Grensted, 13) which was presented to him on his eightieth birthday in 1945 and which also contains an exhaustive bibliography of his writings. Not surprisingly, as his circle of friends was gradually reduced through death, he became a favourite obituarist.

Webb worked hard, often behind the scenes, to help spread the international reputation of Oxford, inviting a number of overseas scholars to lecture for him and promoting their cause through honorary degrees. Among those who were invited was the great German scholar Ernst Troeltsch, in one of the first attempts at theological reconciliation after the First World War. Since Troeltsch died before he could visit Oxford, Webb delivered the intended lecture. Throughout his life he kept extremely full diaries, which provide a unique commentary on theological and philosophical life for well over half a century, as well as many astute reflections on human character. Although Webb's approach to religion was characterized by an undogmatic and critical orthodoxy, displaying the 'open-mindedness and honesty' he had discovered as an undergraduate (Webb, 'Outline', 336), he nevertheless retained a deep sense of the mysterious, feeling what he called a 'Real sense of Real presence' at high mass at the Cowley Fathers' church in Oxford (diaries, Bodl. Oxf., 13 Aug 1922). Overall, Webb's influence on philosophy and theology was as much personal as academic, his works attracting 'as much by the charm of the personality that lies behind them as by the force of the argument' (Ross, 344). Although the popular books which originated as lectures were straightforward and clear, in his more academic work 'he was a master of a Henry-James-like sentence' (ibid., 346). Apart from his editions of John of Salisbury—'remarkable for the sureness with which the text is established', according to R. W. Hunt (*Oxford Magazine*, 18 Nov 1954, 102), 'and for the sobriety and elegance of the annotation'—his works made little lasting impression and were dominated by an already outmoded idealism. He left no disciples but many friends and students who continued to exert influence on the Oxford theology faculty for much of the twentieth century.

MARK D. CHAPMAN

Sources C. C. J. Webb, diaries and letters, Bodl. Oxf. • W. D. Ross, *PBA*, 41 (1955), 339–47 • L. W. Grensted, 'Foreword', in C. C. J. Webb, *Religious experience* (1945), 13–24 • C. C. J. Webb, 'Outline of a philosophy of religion', *Contemporary British philosophy: personal statements*, ed. J. H. Muirhead, 2nd ser. (1925), 335–59 • C. C. J. Webb, *Religious thought in the Oxford Movement* (1928) • *The Times* (7 Oct 1954) • P. H. Nowell-Smith, memoir, *The Times* (12 Oct 1954) • *Old Westminsters*, vols. 1–2 • *WWW* • U. St Andr. L., von Hügel MSS, MS.3179, esp. letter of 30 Nov 1908 • *CGPLA Eng. & Wales* (1954) • *Hist. U. Oxf. 7: 19th-cent. Oxf. pt 2* • J. Patrick, *The Magdalen metaphysicals: idealism and orthodoxy at Oxford, 1901–1945* (1985)
Archives Bodl. Oxf., corresp. and papers, MSS Eng. misc. c 726–727, d 475–478, 1104–1132, e 406–447, e 1135–1196, f 97–100, 644–650, g 214–230; MS Eng. Lett. d. 474, e 175–194 | Bodl. Oxf., corresp. with Hastings Rashdall • RIBA BAL, corresp. with W. Begley • U. St Andr., corresp. with von Hügel
Likenesses D. H. Banner, oils, 1929, Oriel College, Oxford • W. Stoneman, photograph, 1930, NPG • W. Rothenstein, chalk drawing, 1933, Magd. Oxf.
Wealth at death £39,748 3s. 10d.: probate, 6 Dec 1954, *CGPLA Eng. & Wales*

Webb [Webbe], **Cornelius Francis** (*b.* 1789, *d.* in or after 1852), poet and essayist, the son of William and Charlotte Webb, was born in London and baptized on 1 November 1789 at St George's Church, Bloomsbury. His place in literary history is due chiefly to an unfortunate association with Keats. A quotation from a poem by Webb, now lost, referring to 'Keats, / The Muses's son of promise' and placing Keats, with Hunt, alongside 'Chaucer, Spenser, Shakspeare, Milton', headed the first of John Gibson Lockhart's savage articles entitled 'The cockney school of poetry' (October 1817) in *Blackwood's Edinburgh Magazine*. In a letter to Benjamin Bailey (3 November 1817), Keats alludes with some bitterness to the 'Motto from one Cornelius Webb Poetaster', whose effusion provided so convenient a starting point for Lockhart's ridicule. Thenceforward, 'Corny' Webb was frequently linked with 'Johnny' Keats as belonging to a new urban breed of writers, marked by the absurdity of their pretensions, the vulgarity of their productions, and the effeminacy of their style.

Keats's remark and the 'cockney' label notwithstanding, Webb had an established, if modest, literary reputation in his time. He was prolific as a poet between 1813 and 1821, publishing in many major contemporary periodicals, and contributing to the *New Monthly Magazine* in its first four years (1814–17) the largest proportion of its new poetry. About 1820 he turned from poetry to prose writing, and his essays and sketches were published in periodicals such as the *Literary Gazette*, the *New Monthly Magazine*, the *New European Magazine*, and the *London Magazine*. Of Webb's published collections of poetry, *Sonnets, Amatory, Incidental, and Descriptive, with other Poems* (1820) and *Lyric Leaves* (1832) found great, indeed disproportionate, critical favour. If his poetry is less than remarkable, his prose pieces are more successful, his two main essay collections *Glances at Life in City and Suburb* (1836) and *The Man about Town* (1838) evincing the talent for 'original description and gentle humour' that Leigh Hunt described (*Leigh Hunt's Literary Criticism*, ed. L. H. Houtchens and C. W. Houtchens, 1956, 487). Webb was a proof-reader for some years in the printing office of Messrs Clowes, in charge especially of the *Quarterly Review* proofs. His last years were passed in the Charterhouse, a charitable institution which offered refuge to indigent writers; he died there probably in or after 1852. U. NATARAJAN

Sources G. L. Marsh, 'A forgotten cockney poet—Cornelius Webb', *Philological Quarterly*, 21 (1942), 323–33 · R. M. Healey, 'Webb, Cornelius', *Encyclopedia of Romanticism*, ed. L. Dabundo (1992), 607–9 · D. H. Reiman, 'Introduction', in C. Webb, *Sonnets: summer* (1978) · IGI · N. Goss, *The common writer* (1985) · J. N. Cox, *Poetry and politics in the cockney school* (1998)
Archives BL, letters to Royal Literary Fund, loan 96 · NL Scot., Blackwood MSS, MS 4002
Wealth at death in indigent circumstances: Goss, *The common writer*

Webb, Daniel (*c*.1719–1798), art critic, born at Maidstown, co. Limerick, was the eldest son of Captain Daniel Webb and his wife, Dorothea Leake of Maidstown Castle. His brother Thomas was dean of Kilmere. Webb matriculated at New College, Oxford, on 13 June 1735. In his first work, *An Inquiry into the Beauties of Painting* (1760), Webb proposed that taste was a natural sense that recognized the beauty of moral ideas within the constraints of art. His thesis is similar to that of the theorist and painter Anton Raphael Mengs, whom Webb met while in Rome in 1755–6, and whose ideas the antiquarian Winckelmann claimed Webb subsequently plagiarized. Webb's *Inquiry* was reviewed widely and translated into French (1765) and German (1766). Webb also wrote *Observations on the Correspondence between Music and Poetry* (1769), which expanded on Samuel Say's theory of music and poetic prosody. Other works include conjectures on the origins of Greek from Chinese.

Webb was married twice, first to Jane Lloyd and second to Elizabeth Creed, and lived in Maidstown and Bath, where he died on 2 August 1798. He left lands in Ireland and over £12,000 to two friends, property and an annual income to his second wife, his pictures and books to his nephew Daniel James Webb, and £300 to his housekeeper's daughter. NICHOLAS GRINDLE

Sources GM, 1st ser., 68 (1798), 725, 807 · will, Family Record Centre, London, Prob.11/1314.688 · Burke, *Gen. Ire.* (1899) · S. Roettgen, *Anton Raphael Mengs, 1728–1779, and his British patrons* (1993) · J. Ingamells, ed., *A dictionary of British and Irish travellers in Italy, 1701–1800* (1997) · New Grove · 'Reflections upon beauty and taste in painting', *The works of Anthony Raphael Mengs*, trans. J. N. d'Azara, 2 (1796) · Foster, *Alum. Oxon.* · DNB
Likenesses A. R. Mengs, portrait; now lost?
Wealth at death over £13,800—incl. £12,000 to two friends; pictures and books to nephew; lands to friends; property and annual income to wife: will, PRO, PROB 11/1314/688

Webb, Francis (1735–1815), General Baptist minister and writer, was born at Taunton on 18 September 1735, the third son of John Webb and his wife, Mary, daughter and coheir of William Sweet, also of Taunton. Educated privately at Abingdon and at Mr Foot's in Bristol, he entered the dissenting academy at Daventry under Caleb Ashworth in 1753; he finished his theological training under Thomas Amory at Taunton Academy. He became pastor of the General Baptist congregation at Honiton, and was so successful that in September 1758 he moved to the General Baptist chapel in Paul's Alley, London, as assistant to Joseph Burroughs, whom he succeeded as sole pastor in 1761.

On 31 March 1764, at Wareham, Dorset, Webb married Hannah (1730/31–1822), daughter of William Milner of Poole. In 1766 he resigned his pulpit, publishing two volumes of his sermons (later augmented to four) in the same year. He became deputy searcher at Gravesend at £500 a year, a move an admirer plausibly explained by Webb's having taken a house at a rent greater than his income (*Monthly Repository*, 1816, 71). In 1777 he retired to Dorset to pursue a literary career. Above middle height, handsome, and an excellent conversationalist, he entered the circle around Lord Carmarthen, later fifth duke of Leeds, and formed a lifelong friendship with Sir Isaac Heard, Garter king of arms.

'I love to go to the bottom of things', he wrote to Heard (F. Webb to I. Heard, 10 Oct 1793, Library of Congress), '& write on *fundamental principles*'. His steadfast radical whiggism is displayed in an anonymous pamphlet of 1772, *Thoughts on the constitutional power and right of the crown in the bestowal of places and pensions*, with an appendix containing lists of placemen and pensioners in the House of Commons and of members who had voted for the expulsion of John Wilkes, the seating of Colonel Luttrell, and the commitment of the lord mayor to the Tower. A firm supporter of the American colonists, in 1775 he republished Samuel Johnson's *Marmor Norfolciense*, with a satirical preface contrasting the early, unconcealed Jacobitism of its author with Johnson's support of the crown in the 1770s. The whig/tory overtones in the much-canvassed case of the forged Shakespeare manuscripts put forward by W. H. Ireland may have persuaded Webb to publish, under the pseudonym Philalethes, a pamphlet attesting to the authenticity of the documents in 1796. It may have been his friendship with Heard, who had apparently introduced him to Ireland, that led him to overcome his initial reluctance and support Ireland in print. His support of the French Revolution and an early sympathy with Napoleon (later revised) made him an effective negotiator when he served as secretary to Francis James Jackson in the preliminaries to the treaty of Amiens of 1802; he disagreed, however, with some of his fellow diplomats, and left for home, on the pretext of ill health, before the conclusion of the peace.

In 1770 the General Baptists had fallen into schism, the larger New Connexion turning to evangelicalism, while the Old Connexion remained loyal to the rational religion of mid-century, moving steadily towards the Unitarian end of that spectrum, as did Webb, although he inclined more towards the Arian position on the divinity of Christ than to the fully humanitarian view of the Unitarians. He despised mystery, that 'reproach to human intellect' on which faith too often anchored (F. Webb to I. Heard, 28 Sept 1796, Library of Congress). The foundations of his rational beliefs are clearly set out in the second of his *Poems on Wisdom, on the Deity, on Genius* (1790), and he eloquently defended religious liberty in *An Epistle to the Rev. Mr. Kell, with an Ode on Fortitude* (1789): Robert Kell (1761–1843), an Arian, was embroiled with the Trinitarian congregation at Wareham, to which he had gone a year earlier as assistant minister.

For a time after 1802 Webb lived in Crewkerne, where he attended the Unitarian chapel presided over by William Blake (1773–1821), son and successor of the William Blake (1730–1791) who had been a fellow student at Daventry; later, living near Yeovil, he joined the Unitarian congregation under Samuel Fawcett (1754–1835). He became a member of the Western Unitarian Society, taking the chair at its meeting in Yeovil in 1814. Forced from his Yeovil house, a parsonage, by the Church of England clergyman, he spent his last years in Barrington, Somerset, where he died on 2 August 1815, and was buried in the parish church.

Delighting in the wit and ingenuity of other poets, Webb displays those qualities in some of his occasional verses, notably in a poem on his first tasting char (F. Webb to I. Heard, 16 Feb 1800, Library of Congress), but his odes, marked by evocations of the sublime, the heightened rhetoric typical of the form, and a parade of classical learning that even his admiring obituarist found at times obscure—notably in *Hymn to the Dryads* (1796) and *Somerset* (1811)—reveal the limitations of his poetic gift. In Somerset, Webb had early formed a friendship with the painter Giles Hussey, whose theories of proportion and their equivalence to musical harmony found in Webb a willing convert. He published a sketch of Hussey in volume 8 (1814) of John Nichols's *Literary Anecdotes of the Eighteenth Century*, and his last publication, *Panharmonicon* (1815),

restates and expands Hussey's views to incorporate Webb's explication through an all-embracing harmony of the divine intelligence manifested in creation.

R. K. WEBB

Sources T. Howe, 'Sketch of the life, character and writings of the late Francis Webb', *Monthly Repository*, 11 (1816), 189–93 · *Monthly Repository*, 10 (1815), 687–8 · *Monthly Repository*, 11 (1816), 331 · *Monthly Repository*, 11 (1816), 71 · *Monthly Repository*, 17 (1822), 163 · 'Sermons on various occasions, by the late Francis Webb', *Monthly Repository*, 15 (1820), 112–14 · *GM*, 1st ser., 85/2 (1815), 562–5 · 'Memoir of the late Francis Webb, esq.', F. Webb, *Sermons on various occasions* (1818) [preface] · B. Grebanier, *The great Shakespeare forgery* (1966), chaps. 5–7 · letters to I. Heard, L. Cong., manuscript division, Isaac Heard MS box 1, 10 Oct 1793, 28 Sept 1796, 16 Feb 1800 · E. Kell, 'Memoir of the late Rev. Robert Kell', *Christian Reformer, or, Unitarian Magazine and Review*, 10 (1843), 205–11 · W. T. Whitley, 'Loughwood and Honiton, 1650–1800', *Transactions of the Baptist Historical Society*, 4 (1914–15), 129–44 · *DNB*
Archives BL, Warren Hastings corresp., Add. MSS 19174, fols. 122, 419; 17176, fol. 171 · L. Cong., letters to Sir Isaac Heard and G. F. Beltz, box 1
Likenesses C. Townley, mezzotint, pubd 1793 (after L. F. Abbott), NPG
Wealth at death under £2000: PRO, death duty register, IR 26/662, no. 500 (will, PRO, PROB 11/1523, sig. 520)

Webb, Francis Cornelius (1826–1873), physician and medical writer, born in Hoxton Square, London, on 9 April 1826, was the eldest son of William Webb (1780–1831), a cadet of the family of Webb of Odstock Manor, Hampshire, and his second wife, Elizabeth Priscilla (*d.* 1850), daughter of Thomas Massett and widow of Ambrose Holloway. He was educated at King's College School, London, and at Devonport grammar school, where he became a sound classical scholar. On 25 September 1841 he was apprenticed to James Sheppard, a surgeon at Stonehouse, Plymouth, and in 1843 he joined the medical school of University College, London. He was awarded five gold or silver medals for proficiency in different classes. In 1847 he became a member of the Royal College of Surgeons, and in 1849 he proceeded to Edinburgh, graduating MD there in 1850. In 1851 he returned to London and became a licentiate of the Society of Apothecaries. On 10 February 1852 he married Sarah Schröder (*b.* 1828), daughter of Joseph Croucher, of Great James's Street, Buckingham Gate, London; they had twelve children, ten of whom survived their father.

In 1859 Webb was admitted a member of the Royal College of Physicians, and he was elected a fellow on 31 July 1873. In 1857 he was nominated to the chair of medical jurisprudence in the Grosvenor Place school of medicine, and subsequently he was lecturer on natural history at the Metropolitan School of Dental Science. In 1861 at the Grosvenor Place school Webb delivered the introductory lecture, 'The study of medicine: its dignity and rewards', which was published by request. His first important literary effort was his article 'The sweating sickness in England'; first published in the *Sanitary Review and Journal of Public Health* for July 1857, it was afterwards republished separately. Webb next wrote 'An historical account of gaol fever', read before the Epidemiological Society on 6 July 1857 and printed in its *Transactions*. In 1858 his essay

'Metropolitan hygiene of the past' appeared in *Sanitary Review*; it was published in the January issue and was reprinted separately in the same year; it comprised a brief survey of the sanitary conditions of London from the time of the Norman conquest until the nineteenth century. When Hunter's work on teeth was published in the *Dental Review*, Webb contributed notes to the text, embodying results of contemporary research on the subject which were designed to bring Hunter's work up to date. *Hunter's Natural History of the Human Teeth*, with notes by Webb and R. T. Hulme, appeared in 1865.

A few years later Webb became one of the editors of the *Medical Times and Gazette*, and for the last years of his life he was editor-in-chief. He was elected a fellow of the Society of Antiquaries on 22 May 1856, of the Linnean Society on 21 January 1858, and of other learned bodies. He was an accomplished musician, and took an interest in literature, art, and philosophy.

On 23 December 1873, having spent a busy day correcting proofs and preparing the *Medical Times and Gazette* for press, Webb had a hurried dinner before returning home to 22 Woburn Place, Russell Square, to help arrange a party planned for that evening. He had suffered from heart trouble for some time, and early the following morning he began to complain of chest pains; he died the same day, 24 December 1873, at home; he was buried in Highgate cemetery. A fund was started to help support his widow and ten children, who were aged between four and twenty-one, as most of the money from his life insurance had to be used to pay debts incurred in bringing up his children. The appeal raised over £2000 for the family.

W. W. WEBB, rev. MICHAEL BEVAN

Sources *The Lancet* (3 Jan 1874), 30 • *The Lancet* (17 Jan 1874), 100, 104 • *BMJ* (3 Jan 1874), 23 • *BMJ* (10 Jan 1874), 63 • *The Times* (Dec 1873) • *The Times* (Jan 1874) • B. W. R., *Medical Times and Gazette* (3 Jan 1874), 22–3 • private information (1899) • Burke, *Gen. GB* (1914) • *London and Provincial Medical Directory* (1860) • *London and Provincial Medical Directory* (1867) • CGPLA *Eng. & Wales* (1874)

Likenesses C. Bell Burch, bust, exh. RA 1874; in possession of his widow, 1899 • C. Bell Birch, oils; at Netley Abbey, Hampshire, 1899

Wealth at death under £3000: administration, 29 Jan 1874, CGPLA *Eng. & Wales*

Webb, Francis William (1836–1906), civil engineer and local politician, was born at Tixall rectory, Staffordshire, on 21 May 1836, the second son of William Webb, rector of Tixall. Showing a liking for mechanical pursuits from an early age, he became at fifteen a pupil of Francis Trevithick, then locomotive superintendent of the London and North Western Railway (LNWR). Save for an interval of five years, he was associated with that railway throughout his life. When his pupillage ended he was engaged in the drawing office; in February 1859 he became chief draughtsman, and from 1861 to 1866 he was works manager.

After a spell as manager for the Bolton Iron and Steel Company from 1866 to 1871, Webb returned to Crewe and the LNWR, taking up the post of chief mechanical engineer and locomotive superintendent on 1 October 1871. The post carried heavy responsibility. Not only was the company's system extensive, but the locomotive superintendent also had charge of departments dealing with signals, permanent way, cranes, water supply, and electrical work. For more than thirty years, during which the Crewe works underwent considerable expansion, Webb was its autocratic ruler.

Webb was a prolific inventor, and patented many improvements in the design and construction of locomotives and other machinery, but his name is chiefly associated with the compound (multi-cylinder) locomotive, the more widespread use of steel for locomotive boilers, sleepers, the electric train staff for working single-line railways, and the electrical operation of points and signals.

Webb began work on the compound locomotive in 1878, converting an old locomotive to the compound principle, and working it experimentally for several years on the Ashby and Nuneaton branch. Deeming this a success, he put into service a three-cylinder compound engine of an entirely new type, named *Experiment*, in which he used two outside high-pressure cylinders, the high-pressure and low-pressure cylinders driving on separate axles. This was followed by further modification of engine size, driving wheels, and valve gear in successive classes of locomotives: the Dreadnought in 1884, Teutonic in 1889, and Great Britain in 1891. Finally, in 1897, Webb brought out the Black Prince or Jubilee class of compounds, which had two high-pressure and two low-pressure cylinders, all driving on one axle. He was a strong advocate of compounding, believing that it was an economical way of providing the greater power called for by the steady increase in the weight of trains. His own designs for three-cylinder locomotives appear with hindsight, however, to have been wrongly conceived, and the majority were scrapped by his successor. His four-cylinder design was rather more successful. The relative merits of simple versus compound engines excited controversy among engineers for many years, but Webb's practice was not generally followed.

The town of Crewe owed much to Webb's public spirit. He took a keen interest in the Mechanics' Institution, of which he was president for many years. The cottage hospital was founded on his initiative and with his generous support. In 1887, the year of Queen Victoria's jubilee, he persuaded the directors of the railway company to grant land to the town to create Queen's Park. He served on the town council as an independent (conservative), and was elected mayor in November 1886, serving for two terms. During his first term the 4000th locomotive was completed at Crewe, an event marked by the presentation to him of the freedom of the borough. In 1886 he was created an alderman of the borough; and he was for some time magistrate for the county and an alderman of Cheshire county council. To him was due the formation of the engineer volunteer corps at Crewe, a reserve of the Royal Engineers, which rendered valuable service in South Africa. Webb's political activities aroused considerable controversy, as it was felt by his opponents that the LNWR was exercising undue political influence over its work-force.

Webb joined the Institution of Civil Engineers in May 1865, and regularly contributed to its *Proceedings*. He was elected to its council in May 1889, and at the time of his retirement from the council in 1905 he was the senior vice-president. He bequeathed to the institution money for a prize for papers on railway machinery, and a gener-ous legacy to its benevolent fund. He was also a member of council of the Iron and Steel Institute and the Institution of Mechanical Engineers. He was a life member of the Société des Ingénieurs Civils de France.

Webb retired in December 1902, the LNWR directors recording their appreciation of his 'devoted and excep-tional services'. After retirement his health failed; he died at his home, Red Lodge, Parsonage Road, Bournemouth, on 4 June 1906, and was buried in Bournemouth. Webb, who never married, bequeathed £10,000 to found a nurs-ing institution at Crewe and £50,000 to establish an orphanage for children of deceased employees of the Lon-don and North Western Railway Company, which was opened in 1911.   W. F. SPEAR, *rev.* MIKE CHRIMES

Sources *PICE*, 167 (1906–7), 373–5 • *The Times* (6 June 1906) • *Crewe Chronicle* (29 Dec 1906) • *Railway Magazine* (Feb 1900) • *WWW*, 1897–1915 • private information (1912) • J. T. van Riemsdijk, 'The com-pound locomotive, pt 1, 1876–1901', *Transactions* [Newcomen Soci-ety], 43 (1970–71), 1–17 • J. T. van Riemsdijk, 'The compound loco-motive, pt 2, 1901–1921', *Transactions* [Newcomen Society], 44 (1971–2), 79–98 • W. H. Chaloner, *The social and economic development of Crewe, 1780–1923* (1950) • *CGPLA Eng. & Wales* (1906)
Likenesses G. H. Neale, oils, 1903, Museum of British Transport, York • C. H. Charnock, oils; at Cottage Hospital, Crewe, in 1912 • H. B. Robertson, bust; at Cottage Hospital, Crewe, in 1912
Wealth at death £211,543 4s. 2d.: probate, 30 June 1906, *CGPLA Eng. & Wales*

Webb, Geoffrey Fairbank (1898–1970), art historian, was born at 35 Grange Mount, Birkenhead, on 9 May 1898, the only child of John Racker Webb and his second wife, Eliza-beth Hodgson Fairbank. His father, who held a good pos-ition at Booth's Steamship Company, had a number of considerably older children from his first marriage. Webb was educated at Birkenhead School, and then served as an able seaman in the royal naval volunteer service from 1917 to 1919. After the war he went in 1919 to Magdalene Col-lege, Cambridge, where he read English and graduated in 1921 with a third-class degree.

After leaving university Webb lived for a time in Lon-don, where he came to know a number of the members of the Bloomsbury circle, including, in particular, Roger Fry. Although he was later to specialize in architecture, at this time Webb was not concerned exclusively with this field. Among his first published works were articles on architec-ture and sculpture in the *Burlington Magazine*, and mono-graphs on Spanish and Georgian art. His chief work dur-ing these early years, however, was editing, with Bonamy Dobrée, *The Complete Works of Sir John Vanbrugh* in four vol-umes (1927; the Nonesuch edition).

In 1929 Webb returned to Cambridge as a lecturer in the extramural department. In 1933 he was appointed a uni-versity demonstrator, and in 1938 lecturer, in the faculty

of fine arts. He also taught in the department of architec-ture. It was during this period that he was drawn particu-larly to the study of the architecture of the late seven-teenth and early eighteenth centuries, and to the emer-gence of what Webb himself termed the baroque period in English architecture. In 1931 he published some letters and drawings of Nicholas Hawksmoor in the journal of the Walpole Society (1931), and in 1937 he wrote a most dis-tinguished short life of Sir Christopher Wren. His inter-ests, however, were by no means confined to this period, and he became deeply concerned with English Gothic architecture in its Perpendicular phase.

On 18 December 1934 Webb married Marjorie Isabel (1902/3–1962), the daughter of John Holgate Batten, com-pany director. She was herself an architectural historian, though later she became particularly interested in Eng-lish sculpture of the eighteenth century, and in 1954 pub-lished an important book on John Michael Rysbrack. The similarity of their interests gave scope for much shared enjoyment. There were no children of the marriage.

For a man of such scholarship and creativity of mind, his published works were comparatively few, and it was perhaps as a lecturer that Webb left the most indelible impression. His technique was unorthodox and unforget-table. Delivered at high speed, usually while pacing rest-lessly about the platform, and with a wealth of gesture and vivid imagery, his lectures provided a torrent of infor-mation and comment which fired the imagination and implanted the desire for further knowledge in the minds of his listeners. From 1934 to 1937 he was lecturer at the Courtauld Institute of Fine Art, and his work at Cam-bridge was crowned by his appointment in 1938 as Slade professor of fine art, a post that he held, with the interrup-tion of the Second World War, until 1949. He served on the committee that originally formulated the recommenda-tions that led to the establishment of the tripos in archi-tecture and fine arts.

On the outbreak of war in 1939 Webb returned to the navy, serving on the intelligence staff of the Admiralty until 1943. He then joined the historical section of the War Cabinet Office, and in 1944 he became adviser on monu-ments, fine arts, and archives at Supreme Headquarters Allied Expeditionary Force (SHAEF), with the rank of lieutenant-colonel. He ended the war as director, monu-ments, fine arts, and archives, Control Commission for Germany, British element, with the rank of colonel. He was mentioned in dispatches and was awarded the croix de guerre in 1945, became an officer of the Légion d'hon-neur in 1946, and achieved the bronze medal of freedom (USA) in 1947.

At the end of the war Webb returned to Cambridge to resume his Slade professorship, but, to his disappoint-ment, no permanent teaching post was available to him in the university. Instead in 1948 he went to London, where he became secretary to the Royal Commission on Histor-ical Monuments (England), a post that he held until 1962. From 1943 to 1962 he was a member of the Royal Fine Arts Commission. In 1953 he was appointed CBE, and in 1957 he was elected a fellow of the British Academy. He was also FSA (1945) and honorary ARIBA (1934). In 1948 his wife's long and depressing illness started, and the consequent demands on his time had a most deleterious effect on his intellectual life. She died in 1962. Shortly after her death, he retired to live in the village of Solva on the Pembrokeshire coast in a cottage which he and his wife had acquired some years earlier.

Inevitably during this time Webb had less opportunity for his own writing, and there were only two post-war publications of major importance. In 1947 he delivered the Hertz lecture on baroque art, which appeared in the *Proceedings of the British Academy* (vol. 33), and he wrote the volume *Architecture in Britain: the Middle Ages* in the Pelican History of Art published in 1956. In this book his specialized knowledge of the evolution of the late medieval style in England was of particular value.

Webb was a striking personality. Tall and spare of build, his beard became a war casualty, with only the moustache surviving. An almost permanently raised left eyebrow gave to his face an enquiring, half-humorous expression, which accurately suggested some of the salient characteristics of the man. He had an infectious sense of humour, and was a great raconteur. He loved the country and looking at architecture, and the sea and sailing upon it. He enjoyed conversation, and had the rare gift of being able, from the depths of his knowledge and the vivid and enthusiastic way in which he expressed his ideas, of kindling in the minds of his listeners a heightened comprehension and a desire for increased knowledge of the subject he was discussing. His final home was at Prospect House, Tower Hill, Fishguard, but it was at the Sancta Maria Nursing Home, Ffynone, Swansea, that Webb died on 17 July 1970.   JOHN CRITTALL, *rev.*

Sources M. D. Whinney, *PBA*, 57 (1971) · *The Times* (21 July 1970) · personal knowledge (1981) · private information (1981) · *CGPLA Eng. & Wales* (1971) · b. cert. · m. cert. · d. cert.

Wealth at death £13,237: probate, 20 July 1971, *CGPLA Eng. & Wales*

Webb, George. *See* Webbe, George (b. 1581, d. in or before 1642).

Webb, Harri (1920–1994), poet, was born on 7 September 1920 at 45 Tŷ Coch Road, Sketty, Swansea, the only child of William John Webb (1890–1956), coal trimmer and later stoker at the Tir John North power station, and Lucy Irene (1890–1939), the youngest child of John Gibbs of Oxwich, a worker on the Kilvrough estate in Gower. He was baptized Harry but, from about 1950, used the Welsh form of his name for all purposes. He was brought up in a happy, working-class home. The Webbs' origins in the farming communities of Pennard and Ilston in Gower meant a great deal to the poet in later life, especially the family's connection with Cyril Gwynne, 'the Bard of Gower'. Harri attended the national school in nearby Oxford Street and, in 1931, entered Glanmor Secondary Boys' School. In 1938 he won a college exhibition to Magdalen College, Oxford, where he read French, Spanish, and Portuguese. He made few friends at Oxford and never wrote about his time

there; his mother died during the long vacation of his first year and this bereavement affected his studies; he graduated with a third in 1941.

A few weeks later Webb volunteered to serve in the Royal Navy and saw action in the battle of Crete, an experience which left a permanent mark on his nervous complexion; towards the end of the war he was posted to combined operations headquarters with the rank of petty officer. Demobilized at Largs in Ayrshire in August 1946, and feeling demoralized and aimless, he spent the rest of the year wandering in Scotland, during which he discovered the writings of Hugh MacDiarmid (Christopher Murray Grieve), particularly his autobiography, *Lucky Poet* (1943). Under the Scot's influence, he grew more conscious of his Welsh identity and resolved to return to Wales as a political activist. Back in Swansea in 1947, he learned Welsh in a few months but drifted from job to job in various parts of south Wales. He worked for a while in Carmarthen with Keidrych Rhys, editor and publisher of the magazine *Wales*, and was active with the Unity Theatre in Cardiff. He joined Plaid Cymru on 23 April (St George's day) 1948, but was soon disenchanted with the party's pacifism and 'milk-and-water' policies, yearning for 'the hard stuff' he had learned from MacDiarmid. He then threw in his lot with the newly founded Welsh Republican Movement, a left-wing, nationalist group which greatly enlivened the political scene in Wales over the next decade.

Webb worked for a while at the movement's bookshop at Bargoed but the venture failed and he took a job as assistant librarian at Cheltenham Public Library. It was in Cheltenham, a Conservative stronghold, that he joined the Labour Party. In 1954, without any formal professional qualifications, he was appointed librarian in charge of the Dowlais branch Library in Merthyr Tudful. He became active with the local branch of the Labour Party, developed an interest in the town's radical history, learned to speak its distinctive form of Welsh with some panache, played a prominent part in founding the local eisteddfod, and edited the newspaper the *Welsh Republican*. His lecture *Dic Penderyn and the Merthyr Rising of 1831* was published in 1956, shortly before the Welsh Republican Movement was wound up. Two years later, disillusioned with the Labour Party's lack of policy on the question of self-government for Wales and the brutishly anti-Welsh attitudes of some of its local representatives, he left the party and rejoined Plaid Cymru, editing its newspaper *Welsh Nation*.

A collaborative book of poems, *Triad*, appeared in 1963 and in 1964, the year in which his essay *Our National Anthem* was published, Webb took up the post of librarian at Mountain Ash in the Cynon valley. His first collection of poems, *The Green Desert*, was published in 1969 and he stood as Plaid Cymru candidate in Pontypool in the general election of 1970. On the reorganization of local government in 1974 Webb took early retirement from the library service.

During the 1970s Harri Webb became one of the best-known poets in Wales. His second collection, *A Crown for*

Branwen, appeared in 1974. His work was given a wider currency by frequent reading on radio and television, particularly in the popular BBC programme *Poems and Pints*. Although he wrote almost exclusively in English, his most famous poem, hauntingly sung by Heather Jones, is 'Colli Iaith', a threnody for the loss of the Welsh language which nevertheless ends on a defiant note of hope for the future. He also at about this time began writing scripts for broadcasting, notably *How Green was my Father*, a typically satirical look at contemporary Wales in which all the parts were brilliantly played by the actor Ryan Davies. A collection of his lighter verse, *Rampage and Revel*, appeared in 1977 and another, *Poems and Points*, in 1983.

Harri Webb once remarked that he had 'only one theme, one preoccupation' and that his work was 'unrepentantly nationalistic'. Yet his poems demonstrate a remarkable variety of form and a wide field of allusion including translations from Romance and Celtic languages, tender love poems, rollicking ballads, and longer verse passages on both historical and contemporary themes. A gregarious man, with a prodigious appetite for food and drink, he had a reputation in political and literary circles for wit and erudition, especially as a public speaker who could use hyberbole and an impish sense of humour to excellent effect. For two decades he enjoyed his status as people's poet of English-speaking Wales.

Webb's last years were sad and lonely: unmarried and dogged by poor health, he lived alone in sheltered accommodation. He saw few of his old friends and showed little interest in current literary or political affairs. In April 1985 he announced, as provocatively as ever, that he had given up writing in English—'a dying language'—and suffered a stroke in October of the same year. Yet he remained militant to the last. 'I've had my say', he would tell his former comrades. 'My stuff will be there when the Welsh need it'.

At his own request, and insisting to the last that he was a 'Swansea Jack', Webb was moved from hospital in Aberdâr to St David's Nursing Home in his home town, and it was there that he died in his sleep in the early hours of the morning of 31 December 1994. His funeral service was held on 6 January 1995 at St Mary's Church in Pennard, the Gower village where his family had its roots, after which his remains were buried in the same grave as those of his parents. A celebration of his life and work was held under the auspices of the Welsh Academy and the Welsh Union of Writers at the Royal Hotel, Cardiff, on 23 March 1995, and shortly afterwards a prize fund was opened in his memory. His *Collected Poems* was published in 1995, followed by a selection of his political journalism, *No Half-Way House*, and his literary writings, *A Militant Muse*, in 1997, all three under the editorship of Meic Stephens, his literary executor.   MEIC STEPHENS

Sources *The collected poems of Harri Webb*, ed. M. Stephens (1995) · *No half-way house: selected political journalism*, ed. M. Stephens (1997) [ed. with an introduction by M. Stephens] · *A militant muse: selected literary journalism*, ed. M. Stephens (1997) [ed. with an introduction by M. Stephens] · b. cert. · d. cert.
Archives NL Wales, corresp. and papers | NL Wales, letters to John Legonna | FILM HTV Wales

Likenesses F. Topolski, caricature · photographs, priv. coll.

Webb, John (1611–1672), architect, was born in Little Britain, Smithfield, London, the son of a gentleman of a Somerset family who had, according to Webb's own son James, 'had some Crosses in the World' (Pritchard, 139). The relative lateness and short duration of his formal education, at Merchant Taylors' School (1625–8), where he 'attained a competent perfection in all schole learning' (Pritchard, 140), suggest that the family fortunes could not have been great.

The pupil of Inigo Jones According to his own statement, made in 1660, Webb was 'brought up by his unckle Mr Inigo Jones [the surveyor of the king's works, with whom he went to live in 1628] upon his late Majestyes comand in the study of Architecture, as well that wch relates to building as for Masques, Tryumphs and the like' (Bold, *John Webb: Architectural Theory*, 181). As Jones's pupil, Webb received the thorough training in classical architecture which equipped him to embark upon his own successful career, although following the interregnum he was denied the achievement of the highest office in the royal works which had been intended for him by Jones and King Charles I. On Jones's death in 1652, Webb inherited his books and drawings, while his wife, Anne, Jones's first cousin once removed and his principal legatee, received an inheritance which enabled the Webbs to purchase property in Butleigh, Somerset, and thus allowed them to re-establish the family in that county. Webb was not only Jones's executor and the chronicler of his career, but also displayed a more than filial sense of obligation and gratitude, and seems to have cast himself as the promoter of Jones's reputation, to the extent that he was still regarded, nine years after his master's death, as 'Inigo Jone's man' (*Diary of John Evelyn*, 430).

Webb's own absence of self-promotion, coupled with the misattribution of his works to Inigo Jones in Colen Campbell's *Vitruvius Britannicus* (1715–25) and William Kent's *Designs of Inigo Jones* (1727), has in the past contributed to the underestimation of the extent and value of a body of work of considerable significance. He was the author of about 500 surviving drawings, with almost thirty architectural commissions to his name, numerous theatre designs, and three books. When he unsuccessfully petitioned King Charles II in 1660 for the surveyorship of the royal works, 'whereunto yor Royall father designed him & to that end only ordered his education', he recalled his '30 yeares study' and that there were 'scarce any of the greate Nobility or eminent gentry of England but he hath done service for' (Bold, *John Webb: Architectural Theory*, 181–2). Frustrated by the absence of royal works in the 1640s and 1650s, he took the new architectural language of the Caroline court to the country in a series of notable domestic projects, in which he bridged the gap between the school of Inigo Jones and that of Wren.

Webb had made strenuous efforts in the royalist cause during the civil war: he was imprisoned after taking £500 to the king at Beverley in 1642, lent to him by Jones, 'sewed up in his waistcoat'; he sent to the king at Oxford the designs of all the fortifications around London and how they might be overcome; and he attended the king again in 1647–8, when he received his optimistic command to design a palace at Whitehall (Bold, *John Webb: Architectural Theory*, 181–2). But it was probably disadvantageous to his future preferment that he worked in the later 1640s and 1650s for parliamentary soldiers and for figures active in support of the Commonwealth, as well as for royalists. Having received a practical and theoretical training in architecture and in stage design from Inigo Jones—he had worked alongside Jones as clerk and draughtsman on the rebuilding of old St Paul's Cathedral in the 1630s, as well as on the court masques during the same period—Webb embarked on his first significant independent designs at Hale Lodge, Hampshire (1638), for John Penruddock, and Maiden Bradley, Wiltshire (c.1644–50) for the parliamentary colonel Edmund Ludlow. It is possible that neither of these was built, but they are known through Webb's drawings and are significant in demonstrating an approach to design which was to be characteristic of his practice. The designs show him drawing on the precedents of work by Inigo Jones and Palladio, using them as a basis for further experimentation with alternative room shapes, the placement of stairs, and circulation. The choice of direction offered by the interconnecting rooms in the Maiden Bradley design, a feature typical of the Palladian villa, would have offered a freedom of circulation unusual in the English house of the mid-seventeenth century.

Domestic designs In being published in the eighteenth century as the works of Jones, many of Webb's major house designs provided, along with the actual works of the master, exemplars for eighteenth-century English neo-Palladianism. The engravings tended to be based on Webb's own surviving drawings, which included his own designs and his presentation drawings of designs by Jones, which perhaps he had made with publication in mind. Later authors had difficulty in distinguishing between them, a problem compounded by the fact that the houses themselves often did not exist in the planned form. For example, at Belvoir Castle belonging to the earl and countess of Rutland, for which he produced designs in the 1650s for what might have become the first great neo-Palladian mansion in England sixty years before Colen Campbell's Wanstead, Webb had to confine himself to rebuilding the house to its existing ground-plan (1655–68). He retained some of the Tudor building in his remodelling, but succeeded in incorporating a grand Imperial staircase (of three parallel flights within an open well) which provided a triumphal approach to the great dining-room on the first floor. For the fourth duke of Lennox and Richmond at Cobham Hall, Kent, and for the fourth earl of Pembroke at Durham House, London, Webb had also supplied grand schemes for palatial rebuildings in the 1640s. Neither of these was carried out, and both remained unpublished, but aspects of the designs were to resurface first at Belvoir, then in his unbuilt schemes for Whitehall Palace. All of these designs confirm Webb's use of precedent—not only the designs of Jones and Palladio, but also those of the latter's follower Scamozzi—and his putting

into practice of his training in theory: at Belvoir he drew on his earlier studies of the form of the ancient Roman house, as reconstructed by Palladio. He did not follow his sources slavishly, but drew lessons from them, arriving through the process of drawing—which was habitual to him—at his own distinct formulation. The results may be best appreciated by considering the only two houses which remarkably, in view of the extent of his practice, he was able to design and build from start to finish: Gunnersbury House, Middlesex (c.1658–63, for Sir John Maynard; dem. 1800–01), and Amesbury Abbey, Wiltshire (c.1659–64, for the marquess of Hertford; rebuilt after 1834).

Gunnersbury, which appeared in Campbell's *Vitruvius Britannicus* and was owned from 1762 until 1786 by Princess Amelia, the third daughter of King George II, was the fashionable suburban villa *par excellence*, recognized in the eighteenth century as a house of archetypal importance. In its planning Webb contrived to combine a central sequence of public spaces with groups of interconnecting private rooms, indicative of a new impetus in English architecture towards spatial separation and the provision of privacy. A processional route led from a columned entrance hall via an Imperial staircase to a coved first-floor saloon of double-cube form, and a loggia which afforded views south towards Surrey and the River Thames. Such a sequence, of unprecedented classical grandeur in English architecture, had not met with unqualified approval in the seventeenth century: Webb's reliance on classical and Renaissance precedents had been criticized by both Sir Roger Pratt and Roger North, both of whom found the poor lighting of the hall and saloon a drawback in the design.

At Amesbury, which appeared in both Campbell's and Kent's publications, Webb achieved a more sophisticated synthesis in a composition whose 'uncommon grandeur [*sic*]', according to the architect C. R. Cockerell, who visited in 1823, 'fills & occupies the mind' (Harris, 'Cockerell', 7). By positioning the hall and first-floor saloon across the front of the house, rather than transversely, as they had been placed at Gunnersbury, and providing short corridors through the centre of the house between the suites of private rooms, Webb was able to achieve an economical balance between well-lit public spaces and discrete but accessible private ones. The staircase, an extraordinary contrivance, rose through two storeys, with the ingenious oval service stair rising in the central newel. This feature, particularly admired by Cockerell, and copied in designs by both Sir William Chambers (at Roehampton, Surrey, 1760–68) and James Paine (at Belford Hall, Northumberland, 1754–6) was perhaps more of an architectural conceit than a practical solution to problems of circulation. Although appearing elegant in planning terms, it perhaps did not achieve the same significant division between householders and servants at Amesbury as Webb had achieved between public and private spaces in his layout of the rooms.

Webb's most substantial surviving domestic works are the sequence of staterooms at Wilton House, Wiltshire, and a wing at Lamport Hall, Northamptonshire. The dating and authorship of the work at Wilton has been the subject of some debate, but the evidence of both documentation and drawings suggests that Webb was at work here for the fourth and fifth earls of Pembroke on two occasions. In the late 1630s, as a young man, he appears to have assisted Inigo Jones in designing ceilings and doors for a new south range, the building of which was overseen by Isaac de Caus; following a major fire in 1647, a dated drawing of 1649 indicates his responsibility for the remodelling of the distinctive towers and for the lavish, francophile redecoration of the Single Cube and Double Cube rooms. Here his innovative substitution of deeply coved ceilings for the flat ceilings destroyed in the fire provided rich fields for painted decoration. The naturalistic carving of the overmantels throughout the sequence of staterooms, and the liberal deployment of exuberant swags and garlands in the panelling of the walls make Wilton, despite some later alterations, the supreme surviving example of the Caroline grand style.

At Lamport Hall, built for Sir Justinian Isham in 1654–7, Webb provided a new wing, attached to an older house, which had the appearance of a free-standing small villa. The house has since been remodelled and extended, but Webb's wing survives in all its essentials. In a compact amalgamation of one- and two-storey spaces he supplied the newly married Isham with a handsome 'High Roome', now known as the Music Hall, and two further ground-floor rooms with bedchambers above. The most distinctive interior feature, the powerfully modelled chimneypiece and overmantel, is comparable with Webb's surviving work at nearby Drayton House, Northamptonshire (1653), for the second earl of Peterborough, and at Wilton. Lamport's significance rests not only on its being a rare survival but also on its unusually rich documentation. A substantial number of Webb's letters to Isham survive, with a large body of drawings, together with a further group of letters from the contractor and the mason which chronicle the progress of the building work for the benefit of the royalist client who in 1655 was detained in St James's Palace. At this early period in the development of the architectural profession the letters offer insights into architectural practice and the design process. Webb stands revealed, here as elsewhere, as a man with clear ideas on what he wants to achieve but is fundamentally pragmatic: 'smale things must give way to great' (Bold, 'John Webb and the Lamport Recinct', 55). He was not able to convince Isham in 1654 of the desirability of building a portico: although, being a critical user of his sources, he was aware that Palladio was indulging in special pleading in arguing that porticoes were used on the houses of the ancients after the model of temples, he had nevertheless recommended one to Isham as 'a great ornament & much usefull', engaging in some special pleading himself by seeking to reassure his patron that 'it shall not appear temple like' (Gotch, 568). He succeeded the following year in building the first projecting temple front on an English country house at The Vyne, Hampshire, for the parliamentarian Chaloner Chute MP.

Royal works Notwithstanding his success in domestic practice, Webb's chief professional hopes lay in the royal works. He had worked with Inigo Jones in the 1630s on designs for Somerset House, producing drawings of Jones's two grand, unbuilt designs for a new Strand front, and in 1661–4 he built the handsome arcaded river-front building for the dowager Queen Henrietta Maria which survived until Sir William Chambers's rebuilding of 1776–96. Again following Jones, Webb worked for twenty-five years on a succession of unrealized designs for a new Whitehall Palace and, after the Restoration, was employed on the designing of a new royal palace at Greenwich. At the request of the council of state he had prepared Whitehall against the king's return in 1660, spending over £8000. His petitions to King Charles II for the surveyorship in 1660 and 1669 made clear both his experience and his expectation of preferment, but he was disadvantaged through having no official post to reclaim, having been employed as deputy by Inigo Jones himself, rather than by King Charles I. He was passed over on both occasions, first in favour of Sir John Denham, described by John Evelyn as 'a better Poet than Architect' (*Diary of John Evelyn*, 430), then, more justifiably in favour of Christopher Wren. He received some consolation in 1666 in being appointed 'Surveyor Assistant unto Sir John Denham' (*CSP dom.*, 1666–7, 286) at Greenwich at a fee of £200 per year, payable from the commencement of work in January 1664.

The experience gained by Webb in producing a succession of designs for Whitehall Palace was fundamental to the success of his design for Greenwich. Although only one block, the King Charles building, of a projected three-range palace was built, it illustrates how far Webb's architecture had developed from its Jonesian beginnings. The early Whitehall drawings by Jones, in common with his schemes for Somerset House, were composed of an accumulation of small units, so although the overall size of the proposed buildings was considerable, the scale was not. Webb, first in his Whitehall schemes, then emphatically at Greenwich, demonstrated a command of the large units as well as the mastery of detail which characterize the baroque palace. The King Charles building, given vertical emphasis by the giant order at the centre and ends which balances the strong horizontals of string course and rustication, represented the culmination of Webb's prolonged investigation of the possibilities of the classical language of architecture. He was again drawing on the work of Palladio and Scamozzi but now, in his full maturity as an architect, fully assimilating his sources and deploying them to new and more dramatic ends. Regrettably, the King Charles building was left uncompleted and boarded up in 1670, and it stood empty for over twenty years until it was converted by Christopher Wren to become the first block of the Royal Hospital for Seamen. Webb's drawings for the interior, which show details of the decoration proposed for all of the main staterooms, give an idea of what might have been if the royal finances had permitted completion. The coved ceilings, with inset rectangular panels, and the francophile swags and gar-lands, recall Wilton, although at Greenwich the degree of naturalism in the carving appears still more advanced for its date.

Publications At Greenwich, as he had done in his country house designs and in his one institutional building, the short-lived Physicians' College, London (1651–3; destroyed in the great fire, 1666), Webb employed his characteristic composite capitals, combining the lion and unicorn from the royal arms with the acanthus leaves of the Corinthian order. He appears to have intended to publish a 'Book of Capitols', for which he prepared a number of finished drawings of heraldic and mythological capitals, 'in tender and worke for sundry Noblemen and persons of Quality in England' (RIBA BAL, and Chatsworth Album 26, no. 125). There were Italian and Jonesian precedents for such emblematic designs, but those by Webb were of particular significance since many of them were carried out. They might appear to have been fanciful, but in view of what can be gleaned of Webb's seriousness of purpose in architecture, it is more likely that they were designed to carry a significant message. In 1669, towards the end of his architectural career, Webb entered the debate on the identification of the language spoken by Adam by publishing *An historical essay endeavouring a probability that the language of the empire of China is the primitive language*. An expanded essay, written in response to criticism of the first, survives in manuscript. Just as he had sought in architecture to draw on the example of antiquity, mediated by Palladio and Jones, so in the consideration of language he looked for evidence of unsullied antiquity and purity. For Webb Chinese characters, uncorrupted by the effects of foreign contact and understood by 200 million people, expressed concepts in a language of antiquity, simplicity, and generality. It is probable that he regarded his composite capitals in the same way, as vehicles for the communication of ideal conceptions.

Webb's enthusiasm for the investigation and explanation of origins was demonstrated throughout his career. Writing as if in the person of Inigo Jones, Webb published in 1655 *The most Notable Antiquity of Great Britain, Vulgarly called Stone-Heng*, based on Jones's theory that the monument was built as a Roman temple of the Tuscan order, open to the sky, dedicated to the god Coelus, the heaven. Following the publication in 1663 of *Chorea gigantum*, in which Dr Walter Charleton attributed Stonehenge to the Danes, Webb sought to defend Jones's unprecedented explanation in *A Vindication of Stone Heng Restored* (1665), in which he presented a vindication of Jones's argument and provided an invaluable account of the character, life, and work of 'the Vitruvius of his age': 'What was truly meant by the Art of Design was scarcely known in this Kingdom, until he … brought it in use and esteem among us here' (*Vindication*, 125). The seal would have been set on this revolution wrought by Jones and built upon by Webb if he had succeeded in publishing the large corpus of theoretical drawings, embracing the classical orders, temples and churches, the ancient and modern house, and miscellaneous urban buildings which he made, probably, between about 1635 and about 1650. Although he failed to publish, Webb was fully aware of the significance of his own and Jones's legacy of drawings and books, and bequeathed them to his son William with the instruction to 'keepe them intire together without selling or imbezzling any of them' (PRO, PROB 11/340/145), but the Webb family fortunes did not long survive his death in 1672 and dispersal of his collections was under way within three years. The large part of the collection which is now divided between Chatsworth House and the British Architectural Library was in the possession of Lord Burlington in the 1720s, augmented in 1740 by the acquisition of Webb's Greenwich drawings. The collection was to play a fundamental part in Burlington's promotion of the neo-Palladian style. The remainder of the principal corpus of Jones/Webb drawings and Jones's library was acquired by Dr George Clarke, who bequeathed it to Worcester College, Oxford, in 1736.

Legacy Webb died at Butleigh on 30 October 1672 and was buried there in the parish church on 4 November. Although at the time of his death he was regarded as a wealthy man, his wife, Anne, and their eight children (James, William, Henry, Katherine, Elizabeth, Martha, Rebecca, and Anne) received a complicated inheritance, with mortgages on the property at Butleigh and financial obligations to the family of the previous owner. A great deal of time, money, and effort was spent on the ensuing litigation; the property finally passed from the family upon the death of Webb's great-granddaughter Catherine in 1738.

John Webb saw himself as heir to a great tradition: he analysed and interpreted the historical reconstructions of Palladio and Scamozzi and he learned directly from the instruction and example of Inigo Jones; by the 1650s he had become an architect of considerable consequence in his own right. At a time when the practice of architecture in England was in its early stages as a profession, he was the consummate professional, providing an architecture which was rooted in the classical tradition but wholly applicable to contemporary requirements. His success was clearly demonstrated by the number of commissions which he received, from both sides of the political divide of his uncertain times, and the skill with which he fulfilled them. Amesbury Abbey, Gunnersbury House, the monumental King Charles building, and the interiors of Wilton House were among the outstanding pieces of architecture of seventeenth-century England. After his death, Webb's designs stood as an example not only to Wren at Greenwich but also to the neo-Palladian architects of the eighteenth century, and still later to the architects of the Edwardian baroque. The continuing relevance of his work for these later generations confirms the high importance of his place in English architectural history.

JOHN BOLD

Sources J. Bold, *John Webb: architectural theory and practice in the seventeenth century* (1989) · J. Harris, trans., *Catalogue of the drawings collection of the Royal Institute of British Architects: Inigo Jones and John Webb* (1972) · J. Harris and A. A. Tait, eds., *Catalogue of the drawings by Inigo Jones, John Webb and Isaac de Caus at Worcester College, Oxford* (1979) · Colvin, *Archs.* · H. M. Colvin and others, eds., *The history of* *the king's works*, 6 vols. (1963–82), vols. 3–5 · A. Pritchard, 'A source for the lives of Inigo Jones and John Webb', *Architectural History*, 23 (1980), 138–40 · J. Harris, 'C. R. Cockerell's *Ichnographica domestica*', *Architectural History*, 14 (1971), 5–29 · M. Whinney, 'John Webb's drawings for Whitehall Palace', *Walpole Society*, 31 (1942–3), 45–107 · J. Gotch, 'Some newly found drawings and letters of John Webb', *RIBA Journal*, 28 (1920–21), 565–82 · J. Bold, 'John Webb and the Lamport Recinct', *N&Q*, 226 (1981), 55–6 · J. Bold and J. Reeves, *Wilton House and English Palladianism* (1988) · J. Heward, 'The restoration of the south front of Wilton House: the development of the house reconsidered', *Architectural History*, 35 (1992), 78–117 · *The diary of John Evelyn*, ed. E. S. De Beer (1959) · *Of building: Roger North's writings on architecture*, ed. H. Colvin and J. Newman (1981) · R. T. Gunther, ed., *The architecture of Sir Roger Pratt* (1928) · *CSP dom.*, 1666–7 · J. Summerson, *Architecture in Britain, 1530–1830*, 7th edn (1983) · E. Eisenthal, 'John Webb's reconstruction of the ancient house', *Architectural History*, 28 (1985), 7–31 · Ch'en Shou-yi, 'John Webb: a forgotten page in the early history of sinology in Europe', *Chinese Social and Political Science Review*, 19/3 (1935), 295–330 · O. Hill and J. Cornforth, *English country houses: Caroline, 1625–1685* (1966) · J. Orrell, *The theatres of Inigo Jones and John Webb* (1985) · J. Bold, *Greenwich: an architectural history of the Royal Hospital for Seamen and the Queen's House* (2000)

Archives Chatsworth House, Derbyshire, incl. the 'Book of capitols' · PRO, petitions · Worcester College, Oxford | Northants. RO, letters and drawings of, relating to building of, Lamport Hall, Northampton

Wealth at death 'att the tyme of his death he was allwayes esteemed to be a very rich and wealthy man as well in real and personal estate'; left mansion house and land at Butleigh to first son, parsonage to second son; cash (*c*.£3000) and goods to his other children: PRO, C7/386/66; will, PRO, PROB 11/340, sig. 145

Webb, Sir John (1772–1852), surgeon and medical administrator, was born at Cork on 25 October 1772, the son of John Webb of Woodland Hill, Staffordshire, afterwards of Dublin, and his wife, Ann, daughter of Thomas Heath. He graduated at Trinity College, Dublin, in 1793, and it was stated that he had the MD, but of what university is not known. He entered the Army Medical Service in the 53rd regiment in March 1794 and rose through the ranks to become director-general of the ordnance medical department at Woolwich on 1 August 1813. During these years he travelled widely and saw active service in Flanders, the West Indies, The Helder, in the Mediterranean and Egypt, in the Baltic, where he was at the siege of Copenhagen, and at Walcheren. Webb received the silver war medal with one clasp, and the sultan's gold medal for Egypt; he was knighted in 1821, principally for having volunteered to stay with the troops at Alexandria when plague broke out among them. This circumstance led him to collect materials for his *Narrative of facts relative to the repeated appearance, propagation, and extinction of the plague among the troops employed in the conquest and occupation of Egypt* (1801–3). He was appointed a knight commander of the Royal Guelphic Order of Hanover in 1832, and made CB in 1850, when he retired on full pay.

Webb married, in 1814, Jane Theodosia, eldest daughter of Samuel Brandram of Lee Grove, Kent; she and their sons, the Revd John Moss Webb (*b*. 1815), the Revd Theodosius Webb (*b*. 1817), and their daughter, Sophia Barnes Webb (Mrs Parratt; *b*. 1819), survived him. Webb became a member of the Royal College of Surgeons of London in 1817 and was made a fellow of the Royal College of Surgeons of England on 11 December 1843, one of the first batch of 300 fellows created at that date. He was for many years a magistrate and deputy lieutenant for the county of Kent. He died on 16 September 1852 at his home, Chatham Lodge, Woolwich, and was buried on 22 September in St Thomas's Church, Woolwich.

W. W. WEBB, rev. ANITA MCCONNELL

Sources *N&Q*, 8th ser., 1 (1892), 482 · *GM*, 2nd ser., 38 (1852), 528–9 · Burtchaell & Sadleir, *Alum. Dubl.*, 865 · PRO, PROB 11/2160, sig. 799 · *ILN* (2 Oct 1852), 282

Archives Morgan L., letters to Sir James Murray-Pulteney

Likenesses Hunter, mezzotint (after Escazana), NPG · mixed-method engraving (after unknown artist), NPG

Webb, John (1776–1869), Church of England clergyman and antiquary, was the eldest son of William Webb (1738–1791) of Castle Street, London, a member of the family of Webb of Odstock, Wiltshire, and his wife, Ann (1747/8–1849), the daughter and coheir of James Sise, medical officer to the Aldgate dispensary, was born on 28 March 1776. His father, who was of independent means, was an able linguist, mathematician, and political writer. John Webb was admitted to St Paul's School, London, on 28 July 1785, and was captain of the school in 1794–5. In 1795 he proceeded to Wadham College, Oxford, as Pauline exhibitioner; he graduated BA on 21 March 1798 and proceeded MA on 3 November 1802. He married Sarah Harding (1776–1849), niece of Judd Harding of Solihull, Warwickshire; they had two children, Thomas William *Webb and Sarah, who died in infancy.

In 1800 Webb was ordained to the curacy of Ravenstone in Leicestershire. He was subsequently curate of Ripple, Worcestershire, and of Ross, Herefordshire, and lecturer of St Martin's, with the chapelry of St Bartholomew, Birmingham. He became perpetual curate of Waterfall in Staffordshire in September 1801; he was a minor canon of the cathedral of Worcester, with the rectory of St Clement's in that city, from February 1811. In January 1812 he became rector of Tretire with Michaelchurch, Herefordshire (in the gift of Guy's Hospital); in 1857 he rebuilt the church of Tretire at his own cost. From January 1822 he was a minor canon of the cathedral of Gloucester, and vicar of St John's, Cardiff (in the gift of the dean and chapter of Gloucester), which he held with Tretire until Christmas of 1863.

Webb was a keen antiquary; he was elected a fellow of the Society of Antiquaries in 1819. Learned in Latin and Norman-French, he was a talented palaeographer. He contributed several papers to *Archaeologia*, and also published works on Gloucester Abbey and Cathedral. He edited *A Roll of the Household Expenses of Richard de Swinfield* (2 parts, 1853–4), which was probably his most significant work. At his death he left unfinished an edition of the *Military Memoir of Colonel John Birch* for the Camden Society; it was completed by his son and published in 1873. *Memorials of the Civil War … as it Affected Herefordshire*, which he also left unfinished, was published in 1879 by his son.

Webb also wrote poetry; some verses by him in the manner of Henry Howard, earl of Surrey, imitated the Tudor poet's style so convincingly that G. F. Nott included them in his seminal edition of Surrey's poetry. Also interested in music, Webb adapted Étienne-Nicholas Méhul's oratorio *Joseph* and part of Haydn's *Seasons* for the Birmingham musical festival. He wrote the words for the oratorio *David*, composed by his friend Chevalier Newkomm and first performed in 1834 at the Birmingham musical festival. He prepared a similar foundation for a libretto of Mendelssohn's projected but unaccomplished oratorio *The Hebrew Mother*. Webb died at Hardwick vicarage near Hay, Herefordshire, his son's residence, on 18 February 1869. W. W. WEBB, *rev.* BRIAN FRITH

Sources *The Athenaeum* (6 March 1869), 344–5 · Boase, *Mod. Eng. biog.* · Foster, *Alum. Oxon.* · Herefs. RO, Webb MSS · Burke, *Gen. GB* (1914)
Archives Herefs. RO, corresp. and papers | Herefs. RO, letters to Hopton family
Likenesses miniature (in early life); formerly at Odstock, Wiltshire, 1899 · watercolour (in old age); formerly priv. coll., in 1899
Wealth at death under £9000: probate, 20 March 1869, *CGPLA Eng. & Wales*

Webb, John Richmond (1667–1724), army officer, was born at Rodbourne Cheney, Wiltshire, on 26 December 1667, the third, but second surviving, son of Colonel Edmund Richmond alias Webb (*c*.1639–1705) and his first wife, Jane (1649–1669), daughter of John Smith of Tidworth, Hampshire, and previously of St Mary Aldermanbury, London. His family had acquired the name 'Richmond alias Webb' from the marriage of William Richmond to Alice Webb about 1430 and this form was typically used in family legal documents including Webb's own will. The family had owned the manor of Rodbourne Cheney since the reign of Edward VI.

Webb's father had served as a colonel of a Wiltshire militia regiment from 1680 to 1688 and was elected eight times, between 1679 and 1695, as MP for Cricklade, Wiltshire, and then three times in 1701–2 for the nearby borough of Ludgershall. In 1683 Edmund became gentleman usher to Prince George of Denmark on his marriage to the future Queen Anne. In 1684 Charles II pardoned Edmund and his cousin Henry St John, father of the first Viscount Bolingbroke, following the death of Sir William Estcourt in a duel. Edmund Richmond alias Webb commanded his militia regiment during Monmouth's rising in June and July 1685, but later that year lost his local and militia offices and was temporarily unseated in parliament. His court and political connections served as the basis for his two surviving sons' careers. The elder son, Thomas Richmond alias Webb (1662/3–1731), was educated at the Middle Temple and called to the bar in 1689, served as recorder at Devizes (1697–1707), clerk of alienations, solicitor to Prince George (*c*.1692–1708), and serjeant-at-law of the Middle Temple (1705–31). He was elected MP for Calne in 1685, for Cricklade in 1702, and for Devizes in 1710.

Early military career Webb commented that he had served in the army since the age of sixteen. This would place his entry into military service during the last few days of 1683 or in 1684 and clearly differentiates him from a John Webb

who had served in Virginia before being promoted to lieutenant in the first guards under Marlborough in the Low Countries in 1691. On 2 August 1685 he received a commission as cornet in the Queen's regiment of dragoon guards (later, the 3rd hussars). On 20 November 1688 at Wincanton he was one of the 120 horsemen under Patrick Sarsfield who encountered a party of 25 soldiers from the prince of Orange's Anglo-Dutch brigade. Webb was seriously wounded in the engagement. On 29 November he was promoted to captain, replacing Captain Thomas Pownall in the Queen's regiment of dragoons. He remained in the army following the revolution, and on 1 April 1689 was posted as captain of the 1st foot guards. On 3 February 1690 he married Henrietta (*d*. 1711), daughter and coheir of Sir John Borlase and widow of Sir Richard Ashley (*d*. 1687) of Everley, Wiltshire. The couple had seven children. In 1692 he purchased the land and building that would become the nucleus for his future Wiltshire estate at Ludgershall.

In June 1693 Webb was promoted to lieutenant-colonel of foot and, two and a half years later, undoubtedly assisted by his father's connections, he became colonel of Princess Anne's (8th) regiment of foot, a post he retained until 1715. In January 1695 he entered parliament as MP for Ludgershall, for which he was returned successively in twelve elections until 1713. Although duelling was banned, army officers were continually involved in such incidents during the reign of William III. Like his father, John Webb was not immune to the impulse and, in 1697, both he and his opponent, Captain Mardike, seriously wounded one another in a duel. After serving in England for the entire period of the Nine Years' War, Webb's regiment was ordered to Ireland in February 1698. Webb arrived in Dublin in early March and remained in Ireland for more than three years, until he and his regiment moved to the Netherlands in June 1701.

War of the Spanish Succession During the first campaign in the War of the Spanish Succession, Webb served under Marlborough in the combined Anglo-Dutch field army during the offensive against the towns along the River Meuse, distinguishing himself at the storming of Venlo in September 1702. On his return to England following the frustrating campaign of 1703, he was promoted to brigadier (1 January 1704). While sitting in parliament in this period Webb, it became clear, had joined his kinsman Henry St John (later Viscount Bolingbroke) in the political camp of Robert Harley. The following summer, after a long wait for favourable weather at Harwich to get back to the Low Countries for the 1704 campaigning season, Webb with two other general officers, John, Baron Cutts, and Richard Ingoldsby, carried money for the army, travelled to Frankfurt, and then joined Marlborough in the camp at Burgheim on 15 July. On 13 August Webb was with the troops that encircled the Bavarian village of Blindheim (Blenheim) and prevented the French force in the village from escaping across the Danube. In the following year he distinguished himself in battle when Marlborough forced the lines of Brabant near Heylissem and Elixhem on 17–18 July 1705. During the next campaign Webb commanded in the left centre of the English lines at the battle of Ramillies on 23 May 1706. In September, when the Dutch promoted several of their brigadiers for the action at Ramillies, Marlborough successfully persuaded Queen Anne to promote both Webb, as the army's senior brigadier, and John Campbell, second duke of Argyll, to the rank of major-general, and to backdate their commissions to 1 June.

In March 1708, on the news of James Stuart's attempt to invade Scotland, Webb's regiment was one of those embarked at Ostend and sent to Tynemouth. Not landed, they lay off the coast for several weeks and then returned to Ostend. On 11 July Webb participated in the battle of Oudenarde and in the weeks after the battle was one of the commanders in the force of twelve battalions that raided Picardy. Near Lens, Webb's detachment encountered a French force of eight hundred cavalry and pursued them into the town. An anonymous poet described the events in 322 lines of couplet verse that included a single reference to Webb, 'like Paris handsome, and like Hector brave' (*The Battel of Audenard: a Poem*, l. 257).

Early in September Webb was recalled to take part in the siege of Lille. The French were bringing in reinforcements to threaten the allied communication lines, and supplies for the besieging forces were running low. The only available route for allied supplies was the road from Ostend. A convoy of some 700 or 800 wagons, filled with two weeks of supplies, including substantial quantities of powder and shot, left Ostend on 28 September 1708, escorted by 2500 men. Webb was assigned, with a force of some 4000 men drawn from the British, Dutch, Prussian, Hanoverian, and Danish armies and three squadrons of dragoons, to cover the convoy as it passed through Brabant. As the wagons reached Koekelare, Webb learned that French forces under the comte de Lamothe, based at Bruges with some 22,000 men, had been sighted a mile and a half to the east at Ichtegem. Webb advanced towards the convoy and, accompanied by Count Nassau-Woudenberg and 150 cavalry, he personally reconnoitred and selected an advantageous position where he could intercept Lamothe's force, at least twice the size of his own. Close to the castle of Wijnendale, 15 miles from Ostend, Webb positioned ten battalions in three lines across an opening on a wooded slope, with one regiment posted in the coppice to the left, two additional platoons nearby facing the plain, and seven platoons placed in the wood to the right. He had barely finished this placement when Lamothe approached and opened fire. The French had marched to within fifteen paces of the allied right flank when the battalions that Webb had hidden in the wood opened fire and forced the French left wing into its centre. Despite hostile fire from Prussian forces the French continued onwards, driving two allied regiments into confusion, but, with support from Albemarle's regiment of Swiss, Webb and Count Nassau were able to gain enough time to bring three more regiments to bear. With such deep support, the French tried again to penetrate the allied line, but the allied troops were able to advance and force the two French wings into their centre; the confusion thus created

forced the French to retire, but the allies continued to fire at long range. Major-General William Cadogan arrived on the scene shortly after the engagement began, but Webb declined his offer to charge the enemy with his two squadrons of horse, thinking they would be too much at risk when the enemy was protecting its retreat with its own horse. Corporal Matthew Bishop, who had fought with Webb in his own regiment, later recalled that Webb

> was an old and experienced general and a man that knew every part of the country, without which he could not have known how to dispose of his men. And this plainly appears from his beautiful disposition of his troops. (*Life and Adventures*, 189)

When the two-hour battle of Wijnendale was over, the allies had lost 912 killed and wounded to an estimated 3000 or 4000 French. The allied army maintained its position on the field until two the following morning, and so the convoy was able to pass.

Breach with Marlborough Having witnessed the victory Cadogan returned to Marlborough with the news and Marlborough immediately sent his congratulations to Webb, writing on 29 September 1708 that this success 'must be attributed chiefly to your good conduct and resolution' (*The Letters and Dispatches of John Churchill, First Duke of Marlborough, from 1702 to 1712*, ed. G. Murray, 1845, 4.424). In reporting the victory to Godolphin, Marlborough wrote:

> Webb and Cadogan have on this occasion as they always do, behaved themselves extremely well. The success of this vigorous action is in a good measure owing to them. If they had not succeeded, and our convoy had been lost, the consequence must have been the raising the siege the next day. (*Marlborough–Godolphin Correspondence*, 2.1106)

Marlborough's choice of words, while well intentioned, seemed to give equal credit to Cadogan, and appeared in the *London Gazette*. Outraged, Webb immediately protested and requested that Marlborough send him to London to report in person on his victory to Anne. Agreeable, Marlborough privately advised Godolphin 'that when she has a position this winter, he [Webb] may be sure of being a lieutenant-general, which really this action makes his due' (ibid., 2.1117). On 18 October Anne received Webb with warm approval at Kensington and the following day he reported to Godolphin at Newmarket. During his visit to London, Webb provided his own detailed account of the battle to the *London Gazette* (23 September 1708). In conversation with Godolphin he made it clear that he would not return to the Low Countries without his commission as lieutenant-general in hand. Dismayed that the country would lose Webb's military talent for the remainder of the campaign, and also that the incident might fuel the rising political criticism of Marlborough, Godolphin suggested that he be promised the first available governorship. Captain Robert Parker reflected:

> Webb very deservedly acquired great honour and reputation by the gallant action; but then he spoiled it all by making it the subject of his conversation on all occasions. This should have been left to fame, which seldom fails to give the hero his due praise, and does him infinitely greater honour than his own vain boasting. (Chandler, 80)

The tory politicians and writers seized upon Webb's situation. In December 1708 Sir Thomas Hanmer moved the thanks of the Commons for Webb and was amply seconded by William Bromley. This honour for Webb, as Godolphin clearly saw, was 'not so much out of any real kindness to him, but that one of their [party political] leaders might take the handle to show as much malice as he could to [Marlborough]' (*Marlborough–Godolphin Correspondence*, 2.1175). Malicious gossip mongers and political hacks even went so far as to suggest that a jealous Marlborough had offered a bribe payable if the enemy had captured the allied convoy.

Promoted to lieutenant-general on 1 January 1709, Webb became the only tory general MP among the twenty-one officers who became major-general or lieutenant-general in the period May 1707 to January 1709; in contrast, six generals, who were sitting whig MPs, were promoted. Webb returned to the Low Countries and, in March, the queen granted him a pension of £1000 per year for ninety-nine years from Post Office funds during her own lifetime, until such time as the government could provide him a governorship or other appointment. At the battle of Malpalquet in September 1709 Webb was initially reported killed but was, in fact, very seriously wounded, and disabled for the remainder of his life.

Webb continued to believe that Marlborough had tried to deny him credit for the victory at Wijnendale and strongly supported the duke's tory critics. During the summer of 1710 it was reported that he contemplated standing for parliament in Westminster, against the whig general James Stanhope. In August 1710, however, the new government under Robert Harley offered him the post of captain and governor of the Isle of Wight, a position that he held until 1715.

In parliament during January 1711 Webb carried on the whig proposal, echoed in parliament since December 1707, that British forces in Spain should be strengthened by sending the best and most experienced regiments from the Netherlands. His views on this occasion, however, were not seconded. One of Jonathan Swift's *Letters to Stella*, dated 11 April 1711, reports that Webb had come to call. 'He goes with a crutch and a stick, yet was forced to come up two pair of stairs' (*Prose Works*, 2.160). On 27 June 1711 Webb's wife, Henrietta, died; she was buried at Ludgershall, where he had just begun to enlarge the original Biddesden House, including a heraldic carving on its curved pediment and classic trophies of arms over the pediments. He also installed a church bell that had been taken at Lille and laid out the trees and bushes as they had been at Wijnendale. Concerned about his future, Webb proposed several alternatives to Harley, now earl of Oxford, to regularize his financial position, including the governorship of Chelsea College or the colonelcy of the Coldstream Guards. Webb's career survived Marlborough's dismissal, and on 11 June 1712, six months after James Butler, second duke of Ormond, was appointed Marlborough's successor, he was commissioned lieutenant-general and commander-in-chief of all land forces in England. The meaning of this appointment raises questions, since Richard Savage, fourth Earl Rivers, was appointed in the following week as commander-in-chief in Britain during Ormond's absence abroad, and Webb's appointment is recorded only in the non-regimental commissions and not, as would be expected, among general officers' commissions. It appears to be a subordinate appointment under Rivers, restricted to England.

Later career and legacy In the parliamentary election of 1713 Webb was returned for both Ludgershall in Wiltshire and Newport, Isle of Wight, and he chose the governor's prerogative to sit for the Isle of Wight until the election of 1715. At about this point Webb shifted his political allegiance from Oxford back to his cousin, Bolingbroke, as those two political leaders fought for political supremacy. With the fall in tory fortunes that followed the death of Queen Anne in 1714, Webb was removed as governor of the Isle of Wight and colonel of the 8th foot. However, he was returned to sit for Ludgershall between 1715 and 1724. In November 1718 Webb made his most memorable statement in parliament—one that is sometimes referenced as the basis for providing parliament with documents written only in English. When the secretary of state, James Craggs, laid the texts of newly concluded treaties before the house, some of which were in Latin, an objection was heard. Defending himself, Craggs replied that Latin should not be a language strange to any member of the Commons, whereupon Webb stood up. He declared that:

> he was not ashamed of his ignorance; that he was never brought up in a University but in the Army ever since he was 16 and had never looked in a grammar since and that he did not understand one word that was read and therefore insisted that they should be turned into English and not be forced to vote for what they did not know. (Hugh Thomas to the duke of Mar, 13 Nov 1718, *Stuart Papers*, 7.568)

On 20 May 1720 Webb married Anne Skeates, *née* Borlase, a widow and the sister of his first wife, with whom he had been living for some time. They had three children together, in addition to his previous seven. The first two, Catherine (1716–1730) and Frances (1717–1777), had been born before the marriage; their son, John Richmond Webb (1721–1766), was later of Lincoln's Inn and MP for Bossiney and justice for Glamorgan, Brecon, and Radnor. During the trial of Christopher Layer in November 1722 Webb's name came up in connection with a Jacobite association called 'Burford's'. Not long afterwards Webb retired from political life. He died on 5 September 1724 at Biddesden House and was buried, at his direction, in the nearby parish church of Ludgershall, next to his first wife. His widow later married Henry Fowke or Fookes. She died a widow in April 1737 and was buried next to Webb.

Webb's image in literature and history owes much to a collateral family connection. A distant cousin, Colonel Richmond Webb (1715–1785), has a monument in the east transept of Westminster Abbey. In 1776 Colonel Richmond Webb's daughter, Amelia (1758–1810), married William Makepeace Thackeray (1749–1813), the grandfather of the author of the same name. Thackeray was very proud of his Webb family connections and used family information in at least two of his novels. His grandmother

Amelia Webb provided the model for Emmy's godmother in *Vanity Fair*, and the *History of Henry Esmond* is the fictional account of an officer who was gazetted to Webb's regiment as a lieutenant in 1704 and served under him in several campaigns. The picture that Thackeray penned of Webb in part 2, chapter 15 of *Henry Esmond* was the principal reminder of Webb's military career in the late nineteenth and twentieth centuries. Drawing on a variety of sources, Thackeray dramatically coloured the image of Marlborough's calculated personal animosity in his description of Webb's resentment at Marlborough's official report on Wijnendale published in the *Gazette*.

JOHN B. HATTENDORF

Sources H. I. Richmond, *Richmond family records*, 3 vols. (1933–8), 2 · E. Cruickshanks, 'Webb, John Richmond', HoP, *Commons, 1715–54* · L. Naylor, 'Webb, Edmund', HoP, *Commons, 1690–1715* [draft] · L. Naylor, 'Webb *alias* Richmond, Thomas', HoP, *Commons, 1690–1715* [draft] · C. Dalton, ed., *English army lists and commission registers, 1661–1714*, 6 vols. (1892–1904) · C. Dalton, *George the First's army, 1714–1727*, 2 vols. (1910–12) · *CSP dom.*, 1687–9; 1690–91; 1695–1704 · C. T. Atkinson, 'Wynendael', *Journal of the Society for Army Historical Research*, 34 (1956), 26–31 · *The manuscripts of his grace the duke of Portland*, 10 vols., HMC, 29 (1891–1931), vol. 10, pp. 86, 89, 90, 92 · *Calendar of the Stuart papers belonging to his majesty the king, preserved at Windsor Castle*, 7 vols., HMC, 56 (1902–23), vol. 7, p. 568 · *Manuscripts of the earl of Egmont: diary of Viscount Percival, afterwards first earl of Egmont*, 3 vols., HMC, 63 (1920–23), vol. 1, p. 74 · T. Lediard, *The life of John, duke of Marlborough*, 3 vols. (1736), 2 · F. Taylor, *The wars of Marlborough, 1702–1709*, 2 vols. (1921) · *The Marlborough–Godolphin correspondence*, ed. H. L. Snyder, 3 vols. (1975) · *The life and adventures of Matthew Bishop, written by himself* (1744) · *The letters and private papers of William Makepeace Thackeray*, ed. G. N. Ray, 3 (1946), 3.446–8 · *The prose works of Jonathan Swift*, ed. T. Scott, 12 vols. (1897–1908), vol. 2, p. 160 · F. J. G. ten Raa, ed., *Het staatsche leger, 1568–1795*, 8, ed. J. W. Wijn (Breda, 1956) · *De briefwisseling van Anthonie Heinsius, 1702–1720*, ed. A. J. Veenendaal and others, [17 vols.] (The Hague, 1976–) · *Robert Parker and Comte de Mérode-Westerloo: the Marlborough wars*, ed. D. Chandler (1968) · A. Wace, *The Marlborough tapestries at Blenheim Palace and their relation to other military tapestries of the War of the Spanish Succession* (1968) · G. S. Holmes, *British politics in the age of Anne* (1967) · A. Boyer, *The history of Queen Anne* (1735) · *The battel of Audenard: a poem, occasion'd by the glorious victory obtain'd over the French near that place, the 11th of July, 1708. N.S. by the confederate army under the command of his grace the duke of Marlborough, Monsieur d'Auverquerque, and Prince Eugene of Savoy, with the characters of the general officers, who were present in the engagement* (1708) · H. A. Tipping, 'Country homes, gardens old and new: Biddesden House, Wiltshire, the seat of Hon. Mrs Guy Baring', *Country Life*, 45 (1919), 782–90
Archives BL, Blenheim papers, corresp. of Marlborough and Cardomell, Add. MSS 61283, fol. 138b; 61296, fols. 88–9; 61302, fols. 128–31; 61312, fols. 106, 132; 61285, fols. 31–2, 110; 61297, fols. 60–61; 61298, fols. 56–7
Likenesses J. Wotton, oils, 1712, Biddesden House, Ludgershall, Wiltshire · J. Faber senior, mezzotint (after M. Dahl), BM, NPG · portrait, repro. in Richmond, *Richmond family records* (1935), vol. 2
Wealth at death manor and farm at Biddesden, Ludgershall, Wiltshire; lands at Kympton, Hampshire, and Chute or Wakeswood, Hampshire; £4000 to daughters and £2000 to each of his ten children: will, PRO, PROB 11/599, fols. 234–40

Webb, Jonas (1796–1862), stock breeder, was born on 10 November 1796 at Great Thurlow in Suffolk, the second son in the family of nine children of Samuel Webb, who later moved to Streetly Hall, West Wickham, in Cambridgeshire. Webb began farming on a 1000 acre farm at Babraham, near Cambridge, in 1822. Following experiments he carried out with his father, he decided against the native Norfolk breed of sheep and devoted himself to the breeding of Southdowns, which were then relatively rare in the area. He bought sheep from John Ellman of Glynde, in Sussex, and worked to produce his own improved strain, with a better fleece quality and earlier maturity. This had a permanent influence on the breed, which was sometimes called the Cambridge Down. After the death of Ellman in 1832, Webb became the leading Southdown breeder. At full strength, his flock numbered 2400. The Babraham Southdown was exported to Spain, France, and Germany, and also to Australia and America.

Webb first exhibited at the second country meeting of the Royal Agricultural Society of England, held at Cambridge in 1840, where he won two prizes for his Southdown ewes. This success was followed up at nearly every subsequent annual meeting at which he exhibited, until at Canterbury in 1860 he took all of the six prizes offered by the society for rams, and he sold the first prize ram, 'Canterbury', for 250 guineas. He had great success with the Shearling rams that he exhibited at the Paris Universal Exhibition in 1855, for which he received a gold medal of the first class. Webb presented a ram to Emperor Napoleon III after the latter had admired his exhibits, and he received a present of a large silver candelabra in return.

During the last two years of Webb's life the Babraham flocks were sold, with 1406 sheep fetching £16,646 at auction in 1861, but Webb continued to breed cattle successfully. His herd of shorthorns, begun in 1838 when he bought animals from Lord Spencer and Lord Ducie, was mentioned by M. Tréhonnais in 1859 as the most important shorthorn herd then existing, and one which few other breeders had surpassed in beauty and perfection. At the Royal Agricultural Society's show held at Battersea in 1862, after the dispersion of his flock of Southdowns, Webb's shorthorn bull calf 'First Fruit' gained the gold medal as the best male animal in the shorthorn class.

Webb died at 7 Peas Hill, Cambridge on 10 November 1862, five days after the death of his wife. He was buried at Babraham on the 14th. He left four sons and five daughters. A statue of Webb was put up in the corn exchange in Cambridge.

ERNEST CLARKE, *rev.* ANNE PIMLOTT BAKER

Sources J. Thirsk, ed., *The agrarian history of England and Wales*, 6, ed. G. E. Mingay (1989) · *Farmer's Magazine*, 3rd ser., 22 (1862), 464–6 · R. Trow-Smith, *A history of British livestock husbandry, 1700–1900*, 2 vols. (1957–9) · *ILN* (22 Nov 1862), 551–3 · *Annual Register* (1862), 411–12 · R. M. Hartwell, 'A revolution in the character and destiny of British wool', *Textile history and economic history: essays in honour of Miss Julia de Lacy Mann*, ed. N. B. Harte and K. G. Ponting (1973) · d. cert.
Likenesses portrait, repro. in *ILN*, 553 · statue, Corn Exchange, Cambridge
Wealth at death under £45,000: probate, 27 Jan 1862, *CGPLA Eng. & Wales*

Webb [married names Brierley, Hunter, Searle], (**Kathleen**) **Kaye** (1914–1996), children's publisher and journalist,

(**Kathleen**) **Kaye Webb** (1914–1996), by Michael Dyer, 1986 [with a group of children at the Puffin Bookshop, Covent Garden, London]

was born on 26 January 1914 at Flanders Road, Chiswick, London, only daughter and second child of Arthur Webb (d. c.1971) and his wife, Kathleen Stevens (d. c.1962), both journalists.

Webb's family had a strong journalistic and theatrical tradition. One grandfather was William Webb, whose 'penny plain, twopence coloured' toy theatres were eventually taken over by the publishing firm of Pollocks. Her father, Arthur Webb, was foreign correspondent of the *Daily Herald* and news editor of the *Irish Times*, and her mother, Kathleen Stevens, was the drama critic of the *Irish Times*. Webb's brother Bill worked on the *Sporting Life*.

When she was nine, Webb was kept in bed for a year by rheumatic fever. During this time she read voraciously, encouraged by her mother. Formal education was at Hornsey high school and Ashburton School in Devon, where she and her brother boarded. She detested Ashburton, but was fortunate in her English teacher, Ben R. Gibbs, who sent poems written for the school magazine by some of his pupils to Walter de la Mare. These were returned with the comment 'There is one exceptional poem here': it was Webb's. Years later, she met and became friends with de la Mare.

At the age of fifteen Webb wrote replies to children's letters for *Mickey Mouse Weekly*, receiving 2d. for each answer. She also wrote film reviews for her mother and in 1931 she joined *Picturegoer* as George the Answerman, moving later to *Caravan World* and *Sports Car*. She later admitted, 'I didn't know a thing about it—I read it all up in books' (interview, *Mother*, December 1979).

In 1938 Webb moved to Sir Edward Hulton's new publication, *Picture Post*, as a secretary. When war broke out and many of the staff joined up Webb became assistant editor of another Hulton publication, the magazine *Lilliput*, in 1941. Tom Hopkinson, who edited both magazines, left her to produce *Lilliput* practically single-handed: 'Without the war, it could have taken years to bring me to the point when I was asking Dylan Thomas to write captions, and ringing up H. G. Wells and Bernard Shaw to get articles out of them' (quoted in L. Birch, 41–4). At this time Webb was also an ambulance driver, an air raid warden, a canteen worker, and a member of the Fleet Street women's rifle brigade. She married Christopher Brierley and then Andrew Hunter but both marriages ended in divorce. On 12 March 1948 Webb married Ronald Searle (b. 1920), the artist who had illustrated some of *Lilliput*'s most successful cartoons about the dreadful girls' school St Trinian's. Webb and Searle had twins, a boy and a girl.

Webb left *Lilliput* and worked as a freelance from her home at 32 Newton Road, London W2. She became theatre correspondent to *The Leader*, wrote weekly features for the *News Chronicle*, broadcast regularly on *Woman's Hour*, and had her own television programme. With Searle she started the Perpetua Press, and she worked with him on a number of books, for which she provided the text and he the illustrations.

In 1955 John Grigg asked Webb to edit the children's magazine *Young Elizabethan*, which he had bought from Collins. Webb worked on this magazine, soon renamed *Elizabethan*, until 1961, publishing work by many of the foremost children's authors and illustrators of the day. She also developed her special genius for communicating with children, especially through the magazine's club, which encouraged young readers to submit their own work.

In 1961 Webb's marriage to Searle collapsed and divorce followed in 1967. Also in 1961 Allen Lane, founder of Penguin Books, asked Webb to become editor of Puffin Books, replacing Eleanor Graham, editor for twenty years, who was retiring. Webb tackled her new job with characteristic verve and enthusiasm. Publishing children's books was new to her, so she set about investigating just what children enjoyed and wanted to read. Discovering that a child could read about 600 books during the period of childhood, she determined that 'every single book must count'. Lane allowed her to publish more than Eleanor Graham's twenty titles a year, agreeing also to keep the prices low.

There were 124 Puffins on the list when Webb arrived. Her first Puffin was J. R. R. Tolkien's *The Hobbit*. It was on her list for only one year due to a fixed-term contract from Allen and Unwin, Tolkien's publisher. Webb widened and diversified the list, adding Young Puffins, Picture Puffins, and Peacocks. Many titles came from the explosion of new and exciting writers that appeared in the 1960s and 1970s. She published books by authors whom Graham had been unable to buy, and introduced authors from overseas. She also published Puffin Originals—some were stories rejected elsewhere but in which she saw merit; work was also specially commissioned and there were film and television tie-ins. Some books supported charities.

Webb became director of the children's division of Penguin Books in 1966. Like Graham before her, she believed that children deserved the highest quality of writing and artwork, whatever their age. With her instinct for promotion, Puffin sales soared, and authors longed to be 'Puffined'. But Puffin's success encouraged other publishers to start their own paperback publishing and some of the titles Puffin had made famous reverted to appear on the new lists. Each loss was a personal blow.

Perhaps Webb's most extraordinary achievement was the creation of the Puffin Club in 1967. This was designed to cut out layers of adults, and to tell children directly about books and the authors and artists who wrote and illustrated them. Club members could also submit their own work for publication in the quarterly journal, *Puffin Post*, and competition winners' work was shown at the annual Puffin exhibition. Members enjoyed badges and books, a secret code, a song, and passwords. There were parties, activities, and holidays. Club members raised money to buy a mile of cliff for a seabird sanctuary and buried a time capsule containing Puffin books and memorabilia. Webb won the Eleanor Farjeon award for distinguished services to children's literature in 1969, and became one of the first women members of the Society of Bookmen in 1972. In 1973 she became a director of the Unicorn Children's Theatre, and chairman of the Independent Broadcasting Authority's local advisory committee. She was made an MBE in 1974.

Webb ran Puffin Books and the Puffin Club with a small staff. Dedicated to her work, she demanded—and almost got—the same twenty-four-hour devotion to children and their books that she herself displayed. She commanded great affection and great exasperation, often both at the same time.

Kaye Webb was about 5 feet 6 inches tall and had a mass of grey wavy hair. Her nickname of 'Fat Puffin' was not to do with her appearance, but originated with the Puffin Club. Via its magazine, *Puffin Post*, it developed characters such as Odway the dog, TOMCAT (Totally Obedient Machine, Can't Actually Think), the unreliable computer, and Fat Puffin, who was the leader of many of the cartoon puffins, illustrated by Jill McDonald. He was fat because he ate too many doughnuts, but Webb became identified as Fat Puffin because she was the chief Puffin.

During the 1970s Webb left Newton Road, living for a while in Chiswick before moving to a mansion flat by the canal in Little Venice. She suffered for many years from osteo- and rheumatoid arthritis, ill-health finally forcing her to retire in 1979. That same year, Puffin 1295 was *I Like this Poem*, her own compilation of children's favourite poetry. She continued to work from her wheelchair, editing *Puffin Post* until 1981, acting as children's adviser to Goldcrest Television until 1984, broadcasting, reviewing, and editing books. Kaye Webb died on 16 January 1996 and was cremated at Kensal Green cemetery.

When Webb arrived at Puffin Books, she had already enjoyed a career in journalism which many might have envied. Yet it was her later career as a children's publisher which brought her the greatest fame, and perhaps more importantly, the friendship and gratitude of many thousands of children around the world who discovered because of her that books are fun.

FELICITY TROTMAN

Sources J. Grigg, address at memorial service, 21 May 1996 · S. Gritten, *The story of Puffin Books* (1989) · *WW* · L. Birch, 'Den mother to the world', *Daily Telegraph Magazine*, no. 576 (12 Dec 1975) · 'Queen Puffin retires', *The Bookseller* (20 Oct 1979) · interview, *Mother* (Dec 1979) · personal knowledge (2004) · private information (2004)

Archives Centre for the Children's Book, Newcastle, corresp. and literary MSS | Bristol University, Puffin author files · Penguin Books, London, Puffin archive

Likenesses M. Dyer, photograph, 1986, NPG [*see illus.*] · J. Wildgoose, photograph, repro. in *The Guardian* (17 Jan 1996) · photograph, repro. in *The Times* (18 Jan 1996)

Wealth at death £301,496: 31 May 1996, *CGPLA Eng. & Wales*

Webb [*née* Child], **Lydia** (1736/7–1793), actress and singer, became one of the most popular actors of comic roles at the Haymarket and Covent Garden theatres. Nothing is known of her parents, nor has her forename been definitively established.

A Miss Child first appeared at the Norwich theatre on 17 March 1760. She went on to perform in many companies as far apart as Ipswich and Dublin, but, of the early part of her career, most is known about her work at the Theatre Royal, Edinburgh. Here she first appeared in 1772 using the name Mrs Day, but by 1774 she had taken the name of the company member 'Dicky' Webb, and the couple acted there until 1779. Although as Mrs Day she had performed several serious roles at Edinburgh, ageing from Cordelia in *King Lear* to Gertrude in *Hamlet*, as Mrs Webb she specialized in comedy roles, the most familiar now being Mrs Malaprop in Sheridan's *The Rivals*, Mrs Peachum in John Gay's *The Beggar's Opera* (1777), Lucy in George Farquhar's *The Recruiting Officer*, Mrs Frail in William Congreve's *Love for Love*, Mrs Hardcastle in Goldsmith's *She Stoops to Conquer* (1778), and Mrs Candour in Sheridan's *The School for Scandal* (1779).

It seems she and her second husband, Richard (Dicky) Webb, adopted a foundling daughter, whom Mrs Webb introduced to the public at the Haymarket Theatre in 1788. This daughter went on to become the second most popular actress of her time in America, after Anne Merry; her reputation there was made initially (from 1793) as Mrs (Thomas) Marshall, and then (from 1800) as Mrs Wilmot. The Webbs may also have had a son, if this was the Master Webb who danced at Covent Garden in 1791 and at the Haymarket in 1792. Mrs Webb first appeared at the Haymarket under the management of the elder George Colman in 1778 and at Covent Garden in 1779, and she worked the summer season at the Haymarket and the winter at Covent Garden until shortly before her death. Her background in playing musical roles and comic eccentricities made her useful to the management, and her skills helped to originate forty-three characters in new plays during these fifteen years. The jollity and generosity of character she shared with her husband must have endeared her to her audience. By 1778 she was already corporeally as large as her reputation was soon to become, for, like her husband, she apparently weighed at least 16 stone. Not only did her size support her stage presence, but also the power and resonance of her voice and clarity of enunciation, and these facts no doubt influenced the choice of Falstaff in *I Henry IV* as her benefit role in 1786. She was equally adept as a cheesemonger or a queen, and most of her London roles were in now long-since forgotten comedies, comic operas, farces, and musical farces, with the occasional prelude, interlude, and pastoral afterpiece.

This industrious woman was paid £2 a week in 1779, which rose incrementally to £5 in 1790. Her husband, however, died a debtor in the king's bench prison in July 1784, although they had apparently been living as a family at 15 Bedford Street, Covent Garden, from 1779 until 1782. Never more than a stone's throw from her place of employment, Mrs Webb was selling benefit tickets in 1787 from 22 Broad Court, Bow Street, Covent Garden, and in 1791 she was living at 19 Catherine Street, Strand. She apparently suffered a paralytic stroke, and died 'of a worn out constitution' (*GM*, 1147) on 24 November 1793, aged fifty-six. According to the *Gentleman's Magazine*, despite her considerable income from the theatre, 'she was genteelly buried by the Theatrical Fund, and attended respectfully by those gentlemen to the church of St. Paul, Covent-garden' (ibid.); there is no record of her burial there.

LESLEY WADE SOULE

Sources [J. Haslewood], *The secret history of the green rooms: containing authentic and entertaining memoirs of the actors and actresses in the three theatres royal*, 2 vols. (1790) · Highfill, Burnim & Langhans, *BDA* · *GM*, 1st ser., 63 (1793), 1061, 1147 · C. B. Hogan, ed., *The London stage, 1660–1800*, pt 5: 1776–1800 (1968)
Likenesses T. Sayers, caricature, pubd 1786, repro. in Highfill, Burnim & Langhans, *BDA*, vol. 5 · J. Gillray, caricature, 1797, repro. in Highfill, Burnim & Langhans, *BDA*, vol. 15 · P. Audinet, line engraving (after S. De Wilde), BM, NPG; repro. in T. Bell, *Bell's British theatre* (1792) · S. De Wilde, oils (as Lady Dove in *The Brothers*), Garr. Club

Webb [*née* Lamb], **Maria** (1804–1873), writer and philanthropist, was born on 6 August 1804 at Peartree Hill, near Lisburn, co. Armagh, the only daughter and third child of Thomas Lamb and his wife, Dorothy Wright. The family were Quaker, and Maria Lamb appears to have been educated at home. On 21 August 1828 she married William Webb at Lisburn. The couple lived in Belfast and had eleven children, six daughters and five sons (five of the children died in early childhood), who appear to have been educated at home by Maria Webb. While living in Belfast she became an active philanthropist and helped to form the Servants' Friend Society, which was established to encourage servants to remain in their place of employment, and offered rewards for long service. Webb also acted as secretary to the Belfast Ladies' Anti-Slavery Society and in that capacity corresponded with abolitionists in America. She was active in providing relief during the years of the great famine and helped to found the Belfast Ladies' Industrial National School for Girls in 1847. This school was intended to help directly girls afflicted by the famine, and trained them for domestic service and factory work.

In 1848 the Webb family moved to Dublin and took up residence in Rathmines. In 1857 Maria Webb published her *Annotations on Dr D'Aubigné's Sketch of the Early British Church* in London. This examined the Swiss historian Merle D'Aubigné's contention that the church missionaries of the sixth and later centuries were from the north of England and Scotland. Webb disagreed with this thesis and argued that Ireland produced many of these missionaries, emphasizing the role which the Irish church and Irish clerics had played in extending Christianity throughout Europe.

From 1860 Webb suffered much ill health and was generally confined to her home. It was during this period that she wrote her most popular works. She completed *The Fells of Swarthmoor Hall and their friends, with an account of their ancestor Anna Askew, the martyr: a portraiture of religious and family life in the 17th century compiled chiefly from original letters and other documents*, published in London and Dublin in 1865, and *The Penns and the Peningtons of the seventeenth century in their domestic and religious life, illustrated by original family letters, also incidental notices of their friend Thomas Ellwood, with some of his unpublished verse*, published in London and Dublin in 1867. Both works were concerned with the early history of the Religious Society of Friends. *The Fells* was particularly concerned with the role played by Margaret Fell (1614–1702) in Quakerism. In *The Penns and Peningtons* Webb depicted the lives of Isaac Penington (1616–1679), William Penn (1644–1718), and Thomas Ellwood (1639–1713). Her aim was to 'show the trials and tribulations arising from the open advocacy and inflexible maintenance of religious truth and the affectionate interest displayed for each other's welfare' (*The Fells*, Introduction). In both works Webb used the original correspondence of her subjects, sought letters from descendants of these families, and published much material which had not previously been printed. Webb researched the subjects of her books by corresponding widely with other Quakers in England and America. The books, which were well received and reviewed widely in the press, showed the common tendency among mid-Victorian women historians to explore social, religious, and political history through the biography of an individual or a family history. Maria Webb died on 8 January 1873 at 7 Palmerston Road, Rathmines, Dublin, and was buried in the Quaker burial-ground at Temple Hill, Blackrock, co. Dublin, on 11 January.

MARIA LUDDY

Sources Archives of the Religious Society of Friends in Ireland, Swanbrook House, Morehampton Road, Dublin · *Annual Monitor* (1874), 220–33 · CGPLA Eng. & Wales (1873)
Archives priv. coll. | Religious Society of Friends, Dublin
Likenesses photograph, Religious Society of Friends, Dublin

Webb [*née* Meredith], **Mary Gladys** (1881–1927), novelist and poet, was born on 25 March 1881 at Leighton Lodge, Leighton, Shropshire, the first of the six children of George Edward Meredith (1841–1909), Oxford MA, tutor, and country gentleman of Welsh descent, and his wife, Sarah Alice, *née* Scott (1852–1924), only daughter of a wealthy Edinburgh physician, reputedly of kinship with Sir Walter Scott. Celtic in temperament, Mary felt a strong

Mary Gladys
Webb (1881–1927),
by Emil Otto
Hoppé, 1923

affinity with Wales and lived most of her life in Shropshire's border country. She was first educated at home in her father's school, and by governesses, until at fourteen she went to Mrs Walmsley's Finishing School, Southport, for two years. Later she attended Cambridge University Extension Society literature courses in Shrewsbury.

Mary spent an idyllic childhood at The Grange, Much Wenlock (1882–96). The two deepest influences on her development were her father and the Shropshire countryside. George Meredith nurtured her love of nature in its minutiae, and introduced her to the traditions and folklore of Shropshire. Her bond with the countryside, quickening her acute senses, was intimate, spiritual, a lifelong passion. She was writing creatively from the age of six: poems, stories, and plays. Primarily a poet, devoted to the craft, she was adept in the sonnet, always drawing her imagery from nature.

Intuitive, intense, humorous, tender-hearted, firm, Mary was complex, a mixture of antithetical qualities, reflected in her mystical yet precise novels. Strong characteristics were her compassion and inordinate generosity. Keenly affected by cruelty and suffering, she loathed blood sports, especially fox-hunting, and was vegetarian from childhood, revolted by the slaughter of animals. She was small, dark-haired, aquiline; early photographs show her expression of mingled kindness and sensitivity. Unfortunately, at twenty, when living at Stanton upon Hine Heath (1896–1902), she developed Graves' disease (thyrotoxicosis), an incurable endocrine disorder which marred her features. She was seriously ill, yet began in convalescence the philosophical nature essays later published as *The Spring of Joy* (1917), a key to an understanding of her.

During the next ten years, at Meole Brace, near Shrewsbury (1902–12), painfully conscious of her altered appearance, Mary found solace in pantheistic nature mysticism, the impulse behind much of her writing. She was also studying literature, reading voraciously, but was again ill after the death of her adored father (January 1909).

On 12 June 1912 Mary married Henry Bertram Law Webb (1885–1939), schoolmaster and writer. Their unconventional wedding was typical of Mary, whose guests were mainly old people from the workhouse. Afterwards they spent two years at Weston-super-Mare, where Henry Webb was teaching. Sadly for Mary, their marriage was childless. Missing her native hills and valleys, she began her first novel, *The Golden Arrow*, creating a fictional Shropshire world and a portrait of her father in the character John Arden.

The Webbs returned to Shropshire in 1914, spending two years at Pontesbury in the south-west border countryside, the source of Mary's inspiration and setting of her six novels, written within twelve years. Rich in sense of place, folklore, and humour, they are imbued with her individual vision, ideas, and beliefs ahead of her time. The first two, *The Golden Arrow* (1916) and *Gone to Earth* (1917), favourably reviewed, were admired by Rebecca West, John Buchan, and other writers.

In 1916, after a short period in Chester, Mary Webb moved to Lyth Hill, south of Shrewsbury, building Spring Cottage, which became her haven (1917–27). There she wrote many of her poems, a third novel, *The House in Dormer Forest* (1920), and part of her fourth, *Seven for a Secret* (1922). Her reputation growing, her novels were published in America. However, in 1921, a move to London, when her husband joined the King Alfred School, proved a fatal mistake, bringing sorrows and stresses precipitating her early death. Undoubtedly her literary career benefited, as she mixed with critics and writers, reviewed for *The Spectator* (1922–5) and *The Bookman* (1925–7), and was placing her short stories and poems (*Mary Webb: Collected Prose and Poems*, 1977). Her fifth, and best-known novel, *Precious Bane* (1924), won the coveted Femina Vie Heureuse prize. Mary Webb achieved a mature artistic command in this first-person narrative, eliminating earlier weaknesses, such as didacticism.

In January 1927 Mary received a letter from the prime minister, Stanley Baldwin, praising *Precious Bane*. But by then personal problems were overwhelming her, including financial difficulties exacerbated by her generosity to London destitutes. With her marriage and her health failing, she was unable to finish her sixth novel, *Armour Wherein he Trusted* (1929). On 8 October 1927, at the age of forty-six, she died of pernicious anaemia and Graves' disease at Quarry Hill Nursing Home, St Leonards, Sussex, and was buried at Shrewsbury cemetery on 12 October.

Mary Webb did not win popular success in her lifetime, although her work was appreciated by a growing circle in the literary world. St John Adcock assessed her as 'a novelist of great and growing ability … with more than a touch of genius' (*The Bookman*, December 1927). She became famous posthumously when Baldwin, addressing the Royal

Literary Fund dinner (25 April 1928), acclaimed her work. A belated *Times* obituary declared 'she was probably at her death on the verge of making a great reputation' (27 April 1928). This followed with the *Collected Works* (1928–9), introduced by eminent writers. Mary Webb's books were best-sellers throughout the thirties and forties, after which interest waned. A revival of her reputation was generated by *The Flower of Light*, a critical biography (1978), the relevance of her writing increasing in the late twentieth century, particularly her perception of the natural environment and man's relationship with it. While her novels are classics of the rural and regional genre, they also transcend categories. These, her poems, and her nature essays can be read as spiritual autobiography.

There are stage, radio, and television adaptations of Mary Webb's novels, and a Powell and Pressburger film of *Gone to Earth* (1950), shot in Shropshire locations. Commemorative plaques in the Mary Webb Library, Shrewsbury, and on her home in 1912–14, Penrose, Weston-super-Mare, were arranged by the Mary Webb Society (founded 1972). However, her most fitting memorial is the landscape now designated the Mary Webb Country.

GLADYS MARY COLES

Sources G. M. Coles, *The flower of light: a biography of Mary Webb* (1978) • G. M. Coles, *Mary Webb* (1990) • *Mary Webb: collected prose and poems: the ungathered writings*, ed. G. M. Coles (1977) • private information (2004) • C. Sanders, 'An annotated bibliography', *English Literature in Transition, 1880–1920*, 9 (1966), 119–36 • *DNB* • H. Addison, *Mary Webb: a short study* (1931) • T. Moult, *Mary Webb: her life and work* (1932) • bap. cert. • m. cert. • d. cert.

Archives NRA, priv. coll.

Likenesses E. O. Hoppé, photographs, 1923, Mansell Collection, London [*see illus.*] • photographs, priv. coll.; repro. in Coles, *Mary Webb* • photographs, Shrops. RRC

Wealth at death £1645 17s. 0d.: administration, 7 Feb 1928, *CGPLA Eng. & Wales*

Webb, Matilda Maria. *See* Evans, Matilda Maria (1843/4–1909).

Webb, Matthew [*known as* Captain Webb] (1848–1883), swimmer, was born on 18 January 1848 at Dawley, Shropshire, one of a family of twelve children of Matthew Webb (1813–1876), a country doctor, and his wife, Sarah. By the age of eight he had learned to swim in the River Severn below Ironbridge, and shortly afterwards he saved the life of his younger brother, who almost drowned when attempting to swim across the river. At the age of twelve, inspired by W. H. G. Kingston's sea tale *Old Jack*, he joined the mercantile training ship *Conway* in the Mersey. Another cadet there remarked of Webb: 'We thought very little of him as a swimmer, but admired his staying powers. He could swim for an hour without putting his foot to the floor, though in a race he was nowhere' (Elderwick, 8). His first opponent was a Newfoundland dog, whose master boasted of its extraordinary stamina in the water. Webb backed himself against it. He continued floating happily in a choppy sea for over an hour until the dog swam exhausted back to its master's boat.

Webb then entered the merchant navy, where he made his mark and displayed his contempt for danger with some resolute and lone swims in various parts of the

Matthew Webb [Captain Webb] (1848–1883), by Elliott & Fry, *c*.1875

world. He submerged into the Suez Canal to release some hawsers, recovered off Natal some wrecked cargo in heavy surf, and dived through huge waves in the Atlantic in a forlorn attempt to rescue a passenger, for which he was awarded the first Stanhope gold medal in 1874. By this time he had grown into a man of herculean build, with a wrestler's body that was particularly strong 'in the loins and legs'.

Early in 1875 Webb was briefly captain of the *Emerald of Liverpool*. A newspaper report of an unsuccessful attempt to swim the English Channel prompted him to abandon the navy and concentrate on swimming it himself. No one had ever succeeded and it was generally considered impossible at the time. Webb trained solidly along the south coast while the journalist Robert Patrick Watson, who accompanied him in a small boat, grew tired of watching his 'slow, methodical, but perfect, breaststroke, and the magnificent sweep of his ponderous legs' (*Memoirs of Robert Patrick Watson*, 1899, 113). On 12 August 1875 he made his first attempt, but rough seas forced him to give up at midnight when over half-way there, in consideration not for himself but for those in the boat, as the waves were pouring over the sides.

Twelve days later Webb tried again. At 1 p.m. he dived off the Admiralty pier, Dover, wearing a red silk costume. He kept up a slow and steady pace. The crew of a French steamer came up on deck and gazed in astonishment. When the *Maid of Kent* passed by at night, the passengers cheered as a red light was held over the stern to enable them to watch the swimmer. They roared him on with some verses of 'Rule Britannia'. Seven miles from the French coast the tide changed and he seemed to be driven backwards, but eventually he landed after twenty-two hours in the water. The varying currents had forced him to swim over 40 miles. He quickly recovered, however, and merely felt a peculiar sensation in his limbs 'similar to that after the first day of the cricket season'.

Webb's triumphant return to London brought business to a close at the stock exchange, and bonfires illuminated the valleys of his native Shropshire. He then embarked on a lecture tour round the country, but he never made much money, and had the reputation of being generous to a fault. Poverty forced him to return to swimming. He took part in endurance races, and sailed to America to challenge Boynton, a coastguard who had 'swum' the channel before him, albeit equipped with a rubber suit and paddle. Although Boynton retained this equipment for the race, Webb still won. On his return to England Webb floated for up to sixty hours in various tanks in front of queuing spectators, but a race with a Dr Jennings at Hollingsworth Lake, Lancashire, on 1 October 1881, marked the turning point of his career. After it, Webb was so exhausted that he could hardly be pulled from the water. 'His career from now on had a downward tendency', wrote Watson. 'He had almost played his last card' (Elderwick, 97).

Once again Webb was almost destitute, and he now had a young family to provide for, having married Madeleine Kate Chaddock on 27 April 1880. As a final gesture he resolved to swim downriver below the Niagara Falls, perhaps the most dangerous stretch of water in the world. Three miles below the falls the river rushes violently down a narrow gorge into a deep depression in the cliff-side. On emerging from the depression it forms a whirlpool a quarter of a mile wide, surrounded by jagged rocks. Webb was warned by his friends and doctors that he was no longer in his prime, but it was evidently a topic he chose to avoid. Above all, he dreaded a quiet life.

Webb sailed to America in 1883 with his wife, son, and daughter of seven months. He spent some days training off Nantucket beach, while his family remained ignorant of his intentions, then travelled alone to Niagara. He reckoned $10,000 was at stake. The date was fixed for 21 July, but was postponed to enable railway companies to expand their travel arrangements: over ten thousand spectators were expected. At 4 p.m. on 24 July Webb was rowed out into midstream. He dived into the river and was instantly gripped by the force of the current. He was seen heading for the whirlpool, then abruptly he threw up his arms and was drawn under. His last words to the boatman had been: 'If I die, they will do something for my wife' (Williams, 8). Some days later his body was found by fishermen. His skull had been cracked by the submarine rocks around the whirlpool, and the red silk costume that he had worn for his channel swim was torn to shreds. He was buried in the Oakwood cemetery at the edge of the falls, in a heart-shaped plot of ground known as the Stranger's Rest.

CHARLES SPRAWSON

Sources *The Times* (26 July 1883) • *The Times* (27 July 1883) • *ILN* (28 July 1883) • A. Sinclair and W. Henry, *Swimming* (1894), 161–6 • *Land and Water* (28 July 1883) • Boase, *Mod. Eng. biog.* • J. Randall, *Captain Webb, the intrepid champion channel swimmer* (1875) • H. L. Williams, *The adventurous life and daring exploits in England and America of Capt. Matthew Webb* (1883) • D. Elderwick, *Captain Webb: channel swimmer* (1987) • C. Sprawson, *Haunts of the black masseur: the swimmer as hero* (1992) • K. Watson, *The crossing: the curious story of the first man to swim the English channel* (2000)

Likenesses Elliott & Fry, photograph, c.1875, NPG [*see illus.*] • Studio Bassano, photograph, c.1877, repro. in Elderwick, *Captain Webb* • effigy on monument, 1909, Dawley, Shropshire • Ape [C. Pellegrini], caricature, NPG; repro. in *VF* (9 Oct 1875) • bronze effigy on tablet, Holy Trinity Church, Coalbrookdale • photograph, repro. in Randall, *Captain Webb* • portrait, repro. in *Illustrated Sporting News*, 3 (1875), 375, 517 • portrait, repro. in *Illustrated Sporting News*, 17 (1880), 17 • portrait, repro. in *ILN*

Webb, Peter (d. 1775), jeweller, was the youngest son of Arthur Webb of Kilkenny, Ireland, and Deborah, his wife. He married Catherine Le Court (d. 1776), daughter of David Le Court, a London jeweller, and Mary Anne, his wife, on 27 April 1717; she brought with her a marriage portion of £1000. They lived in London and had three children: a daughter, Frances, and two sons—William, who died in 1768, and **Arthur Marmaduke Webb** (fl. 1760–1792), who took over the family business.

Owing to the existence of a rare cache of business records which survived as a result of chancery proceedings, it is possible to reconstruct what Webb's fashionable jewellery business must have been like. The first client ledger to survive dates from 1735 and reveals that Peter Webb worked from 28 Throgmorton Street until 1771. Daybooks dating from 1766 to 1771 show that his customers came largely from the ranks of the nobility and included Lady Cornwall, Lady Kinnaird, Lord Lanesborough, the earl of Rockingham, and the countess of Tyrone, as well as the banker Henry Drummond, who bought oriental pearl bracelets and other jewellery amounting to £941 in one order alone. The list of clients shows that the business maintained close links with Ireland. Accounts with other jewellers and associated craftsmen reveal a network of shared skills, operated through a group of specialist sub-contractors, including Bercher Barel, Peter Trisquet, and the well-known pearl and diamond merchant Mr Saloman. By 1740 Peter Webb was also sending diamond rings and other stock to India and China in partnership with Frederick Pigou.

Webb's first journal to survive (dated 1735 to 1750) shows that he was in the unusual position of being paid nearly always in cash for his product, only two of his twenty-nine sales between September 1735 and September 1737 being on credit. He acquired his working materials either from his customers themselves or on credit from other jewellers and goldsmiths. In this two-year period he made over £250 a year with very little capital outlay save his tools. This astute start was followed by a period of expansion, during which many of his aristocratic customers failed to honour their bills.

In 1771 Webb fell 'under a dolefull paralytic infirmity', and his son organized his parents' move to Hammersmith (Arthur Webb to G. E. Hurst, 27 April 1771, PRO, Chancery Masters Exhibits). By September 1771 he was 'composed tho' in a state of childhood', and the family had 'entirely quitted the old house in Throgmorton Street' (Arthur Webb, letter, 27 Sept 1771, PRO, Chancery Masters Exhibits). As well as taking over the business, Arthur Webb also took over many debts which were revealed when he analysed the accounts. In the next five years he had to sell the family house in Throgmorton Street and much of the furniture. He managed to save the business, then based in Great Portland Street, by pawning a large pair of diamond earrings to raise £700, and by securing a commission to make jewellery worth £2000. Peter Webb died on 1 September 1775, after being 'seized at tea in the afternoon' (Arthur Webb, letter, 19 Sept 1775, PRO, Chancery Masters Exhibits). In his will he left all his household plate, pictures, books, and furniture to his wife and over £18,000, of which £10,000 was to be invested in public funds or government securities on behalf of his son. However, most of the money had been lost in unpaid debts, and Arthur only managed to salvage the small £100 legacies left to close relatives. By careful balancing of the books he restored the business, and a ledger of 1785 includes over £8000 in stock.

Arthur Webb's letter-book kept from 1771 to 1781 reveals the impact both of the collapse of James Cox's jewellery and automata business and of political and economic events on the London jewellery trade in the second half of the eighteenth century. The letters also confirm that the business, in Arthur's words, was 'employed by some of the first Familys in England' (Arthur Webb, letter, 19 Sept 1775, PRO, Chancery Masters Exhibits). Arthur Webb died unmarried, at Great Portland Street in February 1792. His executor, Richard Dugdale, a jeweller who appears in the Webb daybooks from 1761, organized the four-day sale by auction of the house contents in March 1792. The contents reveal that Arthur was a keen collector of natural history, and that he had an impressive collection of prints and paintings. The sale fetched £476 18s. 9d. His jewels and stock, sold in May, raised a further £4533.

Although not the most important jewellers in London, Peter Webb and his son Arthur made a major contribution to the London jewellery trade, and their surviving accounts provide a valuable window onto the world of one of the major eighteenth-century luxury trades.

HELEN CLIFFORD

Sources P. Earle, *The making of the English middle class*, 2nd edn (1991) · A. Heal, ed., *The London goldsmiths, 1200–1800: a record of the names and addresses of the craftsmen, their shop-signs and trade-cards* (1935); facs. edn (1972) · letter book of Arthur Webb, PRO, Chancery Masters Exhibits, C.108.284 · sale of house and business, PRO, Chancery Masters Exhibits, C.108.285 · will, proved, 12 Sept 1775, 12/145, microfilm P.11/1011, p. 312 · probate will, proved, 6 Feb 1792, 11/1215/219 [Arthur Marmaduke Webb]

Archives PRO, Chancery Masters Exhibits | Northumbd RO, Delaval MSS

Wealth at death £20,000: will, 12 Sept 1775, proved · £5009 18s. 9d.—sale of household goods; Arthur Marmaduke Webb: will; annotated inventories and printed sale catalogue, 1792, PRO, Chancery masters exhibit C 108.285

Webb, Philip Barker (1793–1854), traveller and natural historian, was born on 10 July 1793 at Milford House, near Godalming, Surrey, the eldest son in a family of three sons

Philip Barker Webb (1793–1854), by Lalogero di Bernardis, 1820

and three daughters of Captain Philip Smith Webb (1764–1799) and his wife, Hannah (d. 1853) daughter of Sir Robert Barker bt. He was a great-grandson of the lawyer and politician Philip Carteret Webb. He was educated firstly at a private boys' school, then at Harrow School and at Christ Church, Oxford, matriculating on 17 October 1811. At Christ Church, William Buckland inspired him with a taste for geology. In 1812 he entered Lincoln's Inn and in 1815 he graduated as BA, but after the death of his father put him in command of a handsome fortune he at once began to satisfy his desire to travel, for which he had equipped himself by a study of Italian and Spanish while at Oxford.

Webb visited Vienna, where he made the acquaintance of the Italian Chevalier Alberto Parolini of Bassano (1788–1867), who was of the same age, class, wealth, and tastes as himself, and had studied botany and geology under Giovanni Battista Brocchi (1772–1826). Webb stayed with Parolini at Bassano, and Parolini returned his visit at Milford in 1817, when they planned a joint expedition to the East. In the meantime Webb paid a short visit to Sweden, visiting Göteborg, Uppsala, and Stockholm, and going as far as lat. 61° N.

The winter of 1817–18 Webb spent at Naples with his mother and two of his sisters. From Naples he and Parolini started their tour in April 1819 by way of Otranto, Corfu, Patras, and Athens, to the Cyclades, Constantinople, and the Troad (the plain of Troy), returning by Smyrna and Malta to Sicily. Webb, who was well versed in Homer and Strabo, carefully studied the topography of the Troad and came to conclusions very different from those propounded by Le Chevalier in his *Voyage de la Troade dans 1785 et 1789*. He published his views in 1821 as *Osservazioni intorno allo stato antico e presente dell'agro Trojano*, which was expanded in 1844 into *Topographie de la Troade ancienne et moderne*. This work showed much antiquarian and geological erudition. He rediscovered the River Scamander and Simois, and settled some other important points in Homeric geography.

In 1821 Webb returned to England and spent some time at Milford, managing his estate and collecting many interesting plants in his garden. In July 1825 he visited the entomologist Léon Dufour at St Sever, and after wintering in the south of France, made a year's tour of the eastern and southern coasts of Spain, collecting birds, fish, shells, and especially plants, a tour afterwards described in his *Iter Hispaniense* (1838) and *Otia Hispanica* (1839, enlarged ed. 1853). In April 1827 he went from Gibraltar to Tangier, and, though he found it impossible to get far into the interior, made a short exploration of Jebel Beni-Hosmar and Jebel Darsa, mountains near Tetuan, the flora of which was then entirely unknown. In June 1827 he left Gibraltar for Lisbon and devoted the remainder of the year to a journey on horseback through Portugal, the botanical results of which were included in his *Iter Hispaniense*, though his many geological and mineralogical notes, including a geological map of the Lisbon basin, made in conjunction with Louis da Silva Mouzinho d'Albuquerque, remain unpublished.

In May 1828 Webb left Lisbon for Madeira, where he spent some months botanizing, and in the following September went on to Tenerife, intending to proceed to Brazil. At Tenerife his Spanish assistant resigned and his place was taken by Sabin Berthelot (1794–1880), a young Frenchman who had already spent eight years in the island and who had formed a herbarium. Webb remained nearly two years in the Canary Islands, visiting with him Lanzarote, Fuerteventura, Gran Canaria, and Palma. They studied and collected the plants, birds, fish, shells, and insects, examined the rocks, analysed the waters, made climatological observations, and neglected nothing which could help towards a complete natural history and geography of the archipelago. In August 1830 Webb and Berthelot embarked at Santa Cruz, and, being kept out of France by cholera and revolution, went by way of the coast of Algeria to Nice, and thence to Geneva and Montpellier. In June 1833 they established themselves in Paris, at a house on the Champs Elysées, where Webb assembled a good library and a herbarium finer than any private collection in France save that of Delessert. In preparing their great work *Histoire naturelle des îles Canaries* (3 vols., 1836–50, plus folio atlas), Webb reserved to himself most of the geology and botany and the description of the mammals, while Berthelot contributed the ethnography, the history of the conquest and of the relations of the islanders with the Moors and with America, and the geography. The services

of A. Valenciennes were secured for the description of the fish; of Alcide d'Orbigny for the molluscs; of C. G. A. Brullé, P. H. Lucas, and P. J. M. Macquart for the insects; of F. L. P. Gervais for the reptiles; and of A. Moquin-Tandon for the birds. Articles were also contributed by J. D. Hooker, Alphonse de Candolle, Jacques Gay, Parlatore, and others. The atlas included 441 plates by the best artists obtainable.

After having spent fourteen years over the preparation of this work, travelling only between Milford and Paris, Webb wished to visit Tunis and Egypt to solve some botanical problems left unsettled by Vahl and Desfontaines, but was twice prevented by indifferent health and the news of unsatisfactory political and sanitary conditions of those countries. In January 1848 he travelled to Florence and Rome and devoted two years to collecting Italian plants. He had a pleasant time in Italy: at Rome he made the acquaintance of the Countess Elizabeth Mazzanti-Fiorini, the cryptogamist, the only woman, he said, whom he had ever met who loved botany passionately; and at Florence he was specially attracted by the botanical gallery of the museum, then under the care of his friend Parlatore, to which he planned to bequeath his library and herbaria. It was there that, in the winter of 1848–9, he prepared his *Fragmenta florulæ Aethiopico-Aegyptiacæ*, which, however, was not published until 1854 owing to the Tuscan revolution of 1849.

After six weeks at Bagnères-de-Luchon, where he had been ordered to take the waters, in the summer of 1850 Webb revisited Spain to put some finishing touches to *Otia Hispanica* and to visit his friend Graëlls, director of the museum and garden at Madrid. He had recently been given the order of Charles III by Queen Isabella, and on the occasion of this visit was elected corresponding member of the Academy of Sciences at Madrid.

In 1851 he returned to England, and in August, with his nephew, Godfrey Webb, visited Ireland, and, having received suggestions from his friend the botanist John Ball, explored the west coast from Cork to Killarney, Dingle, Tralee, Limerick, Galway, Roundstone, and the Aranmore Islands, the home of an interesting offshoot of the Iberian flora which he so well knew. After a year devoted to a synopsis of the flora of the Canaries, which he did not live to finish, and a second futile attempt to start for Tunis in the autumn of 1852, Webb again visited Italy and his friend Parolini, but was recalled to England by the death of his mother in 1853. In May 1854 he started for Geneva to visit his younger brother, Admiral Webb, but at Paris was seized with gout; although he recovered sufficiently to be able to superintend on crutches the classification of his library by Moquin-Tandon, he died on 31 August 1854. He was buried in a mausoleum which he had built in the churchyard of Milford. The whole of his fine botanical library, collections, and herbarium, which by this time included the herbaria of Philippe Mercier, Desfontaines, La Billardière, Pavon, and Gustave de Montbret, together with complete sets of the plants collected by N. Wallich, R. Wight, G. Gardner, and Schimper, he bequeathed, with an endowment for their maintenance, to the Grand Duke

Leopold II of Tuscany. Webb's executors lost a law suit to declare his will invalid, and the collections finally arrived in Florence in 1855, where they are housed at the Institute of Botany.

Webb was elected a fellow of the Royal Society on 25 March 1824. He was also a fellow of the Linnean Society (1818), Society of Arts, and Geological Society. Besides the works already mentioned he was the author of seventeen papers, mainly on botany, published between 1833 and 1852. Nine of these appeared in the *Annales des Sciences Naturelles*. His most important paper was perhaps his 'Spicilegia Gorgonea', a determination of the plants of the Cape Verde Islands, prefixed to W. J. Hooker's *Niger Flora* (1849).					G. S. BOULGER, *rev.* ANDREW GROUT

Sources J. Gay, 'Notice sur la vie et les travaux de Philippe Barker Webb', *Bulletin de la Société Botanique de France*, 3 (1856), 51–2 · W. T. Stearn, 'Philip Barker Webb and Canarian botany', *Monographiae Biologicae Canarienses*, 4 (1973), 15–29 · F. A. Stafleu and R. S. Cowan, *Taxonomic literature: a selective guide*, 2nd edn, 7, Regnum Vegetabile, 116 (1988), 118–22 · W. T. Stearn, 'On the dates of publication of Webb and Berthelot's "Histoire naturelle des îles Canaries"', *Journal of the Society of the Bibliography of Natural History*, 1 (1936–43), 49–64 · C. H. Steinberg, 'The collectors and collections in the herbarium Webb', *Webbia*, 32 (1977), 1–49 · *Catalogue of scientific papers*, Royal Society, 6 (1872) · d. cert.
Archives BL, corresp., Egerton MS 2851 · RS, letters · University of Florence, institute of botany, herbarium | RBG Kew, corresp. with Jacques Gay
Likenesses L. di Bernardis, oils, 1820, NPG [*see illus.*] · S. Berthelot, drawing, 1830, repro. in Stearn, 'Philip Barker Webb and Canarian botany' · oils, *c.*1837, repro. in Stearn, 'Philip Barker Webb and Canarian botany' · G. Lusini, marble bust, 1874, Botanical Institute, Florence · Martini, oils (after Roemer, 1847), Botanical Institute, Florence · J. J. Williams, drawing, repro. in Stearn, 'Philip Barker Webb and Canarian botany' · portrait, Hunt Institute for Botanical Documentation, Pittsburgh, Hunt Botanical Library

Webb, Philip Carteret (1702–1770), barrister and antiquary, was born at Devizes in Wiltshire on 14 August 1702. His father was Daniel Webb. His mother is unknown; nor is there any record of his schooling. From such obscure beginnings he surfaces in London, being admitted attorney-at-law on 20 June 1724. He practised in Old Jewry, then Budge Row, before settling in Great Queen Street, Lincoln's Inn Fields. On 18 December 1727 he was admitted at the Middle Temple, and on 8 April 1741 at Lincoln's Inn. On 22 November 1730 he married Susanna Lodington (*d.* 1756), the daughter of Benjamin Lodington, consul at Tripoli. They had three children, two of whom died in infancy; the surviving child was also called Philip Carteret Webb (*d.* 1793).

Webb was a legal beaver, and early gained the reputation for knowledge of records and constitutional precedents which would make him such a valued servant of government. It was enhanced by such publications as *Observations on the Course of Proceedings in the Admiralty Courts* (1747) and *Short but True State of Facts Relative to the Jew Bill* (1753). In this period the law, soon to be defined by Blackstone in his magisterial *Commentaries* (1765–9), was held in highest respect and permeated the business of parliament. An expert with the ambition and stamina to take on political cases would not lack for employment. After the

defeat of the Jacobite rising of 1745 Webb was influential as solicitor in the trials of the prisoners. He was the author of *Remarks on the Pretender's Declaration and Commission* (1745), and the subsequent *Remarks on the Pretender's Eldest Son's Second Declaration* (1745). His patron, Lord Chancellor Hardwicke, made him secretary of bankrupts in the court of chancery; he retained the post until 1766.

In 1748 Webb purchased the estate of Busbridge, which gave him influence in the nearby burgage borough of Haslemere. 'That sink-hole of a borough' (W. Cobbett, *Rural Rides*, ed. J. P. Cobbett, 2 vols., 1853, 1.97) was Cobbett's later verdict on Haslemere, whose venal electors Webb represented in parliament from 1754 to 1768. His first election inspired Dr King's ballad of *The Cow of Haslemere* which had eight calves, for each of which a vote for Webb was claimed. Webb may seem more of a civil servant than a politician but the distinction was not then so readily recognized: most senior civil servants sat in the Commons and there were numerous legal placemen. In December 1756 he was made joint solicitor to the Treasury and he held that office until June 1765. When he caused a row by toasting the unpopular Lord Bute—'my master'— at a public dinner, his whig friend Lord Hardwicke defended him: it was 'natural for the Sollicitor of the Treasury to toast the head of it' (Namier, 38). With his reputation as a government workhorse, and the 'Old Bailey' manner that went down badly in the Commons, he might still have escaped political historians' notice had it not been for his involvement in the Wilkes affair, when he was a prime agent in the ministry's proceedings. He then earned the scorn of Horace Walpole, who described him as 'a most villainous tool and agent in any iniquity' (*Letters of Horace Walpole*, 1.277).

It was required of Webb to counsel ministers and devise tactics in a situation where the law was uncertain and the political implications, especially regarding a possibly improper use of the royal prerogative, were sinister. After the publication of the crudely xenophobic number 45 of the *North Briton*, he, along with Robert Wood, the undersecretary of state, attended the seizure of Wilkes's papers on 30 April 1763, on the instruction of lords Halifax and Egremont and was armed with a general warrant which ordered the arrest of all concerned with the publication of the *North Briton*. The papers included the salacious *Essay on Woman* which had been privately printed for Wilkes and which ministers would use to discredit him. When the legality of general warrants was challenged, Webb had printed, privately and anonymously, a volume of *Copies taken from the records of the court of king's bench, the office-books of the secretaries of state, of warrants issued by secretaries of state*. He followed it up with some *Observations* on the discharge of Wilkes from the Tower.

When an action was brought against Wood for seizing Wilkes's papers, Webb, as a witness, swore that, while in the house, 'he had no key in his hand'. For this, on 22 May 1764, he was tried for perjury before Lord Mansfield, with a special jury, and was acquitted. The general warrants issue was used by opposition politicians to identify parliamentary lawyers as agents of a new absolutism. In the resulting furore Webb found himself in the front line, the object of a political vendetta. A parliamentary motion was proposed in November 1768 for the return of all moneys paid to him for prosecutions but was refused. When he was charged, on 31 January 1769, with having bribed an informer against Wilkes, his counsel pleaded that he was now blind and of impaired mind: the motion was defeated, but in a way that left an impression of past chicanery and offered Webb little comfort.

Antiquarian friends who met regularly at the Young Devil tavern in Fleet Street, later in the courtyard of Burlington House, knowing Webb to be a cultivated man, would not have recognized the 'dirty wretch' and 'sorry knave' described by Horace Walpole (*Letters of Horace Walpole*, 2.332, 38.316). Webb was elected FSA on 26 November 1747 and FRS on 9 November 1749. In 1751 he assisted in obtaining the charter of incorporation for the Society of Antiquaries. He was a scholarly investigator of the past and read several papers to the society, including 'A short account of Danegeld' (April 1756) and 'A short account of Domesday Book, with a view to its publication' (December 1755). He surely enjoyed exposing as forgery a record of an oath allegedly taken by Henry II before the pope after the murder of Becket (April 1756). After having written *An account of a copper table with two inscriptions, Greek and Latin, discovered in 1732 near Heraclea* (April 1755), he presented the table to the king of Spain and received in return a valuable diamond ring. He was also a serious collector and was rich enough to buy ambitiously. He purchased a third of the great collection of manuscripts of Sir Julius Caesar, now among the Lansdowne manuscripts in the British Museum. He sold to the House of Lords thirty manuscript volumes of the rolls of parliament. Susanna Webb died at Bath on 12 March 1756, aged forty-five, and, following her wishes, she was buried with their two children in a cave at Busbridge. They were afterwards disinterred and placed in a vault in Godalming church. On 21 August 1758 Webb married Rhoda Cotes (*bap.* 1731), from Dodington in Cheshire. They had no children. He died at Busbridge Hall on 22 June 1770 and was buried in Godalming church, where a monument to him and to his first wife was erected. His great library was sold over the course of sixteen days in February and March 1771. His most valuable coins and medals were acquired by Matthew Duane; the rest of his collection, together with his ancient marbles and bronzes, were sold in 1771. His widow married, on 5 September 1771, Edward Bever of Farnham. In 1775 she sold Busbridge. Webb's memorial there was the forest of oak trees, for planting which, in 1758, he had received the silver medal of the Society of Arts. In this way he had conformed to what society expected of a gentleman.

GEOFFREY TREASURE

Sources L. B. Namier, *The structure of politics at the accession of George III*, 2nd edn (1957) • J. C. D. Clark, *English society, 1688–1832: ideology, social structure and political practice during the ancien régime* (1985) • J. Evans, *A history of the Society of Antiquaries* (1956) • H. Walpole, *Memoirs of the reign of King George the Third*, ed. D. Le Marchant, 1 (1845) • *Annual Register* (1763) • Nichols, *Lit. anecdotes*, vol. 2 • Walpole, *Corr.* • HoP, *Commons* • DNB • parish register, Devizes, St Golus, 1702 • monumental inscription, Godalming parish church

Archives BL, collection of Armenian and Persian mercantile MSS, Lansdowne MSS 1046–1048 • BL, legal papers and list of Sir J. Caesar's MSS purchased by Webb • BL, Lansdowne MSS, notes, collections, and papers relating to Domesday and danegeld | BL, corresp. with Lord Hardwicke and C. Yorke; corresp. with Lord Liverpool, Add. MSS 35587–35597, 35634–35637, MSS 38198–38204, 38304 • BL, letters to duke of Newcastle, Add. MSS 32880–32938, 33055 • Bodl. Oxf., grangerized copy of account of Domesday • HLRO, MSS of roll of parliament
Wealth at death considerable

Webb, Philip Speakman (1831–1915), architect, was born on 12 January 1831 at 1 Beaumont Street, Oxford, the second among the eleven children of Charles Webb (*c.*1795–1848), physician, and his wife, M. Elizabeth Speakman. His parents moved *c.*1834 to 15 St Giles', the former Oxford home of the dukes of Marlborough.

Education Webb was a boarding pupil from the age of eight at Aynho Free Grammar School, Northamptonshire, where he gained a good education and developed a broad and independent outlook. Accompanying his father on his rounds, he grew to love the English countryside and the ancient buildings of Oxford. His father, the son of Thomas Webb (*fl.* 1804–1827), a renowned medallist of Birmingham, taught him to understand and sketch animals, and a Mrs Richardson, a skilled flower painter of Oxford, instructed him in drawing.

The death of his father when Webb was seventeen led him to abandon painting for architecture, which offered greater financial security. He became an articled pupil in 1849 of John Billing, who had a varied practice in Reading, Berkshire. He trained Webb in the Gothic and classical styles, and provided ample practical experience in and around the then unspoilt old market town. After his apprenticeship was completed, Webb worked as Billing's assistant for two years until 17 March 1854, when he joined Bidlake and Lovatt in Wolverhampton, and encountered the appalling effects on the area of heavy industries, which influenced his subsequent thinking about architecture. He returned to Oxford on 15 May 1854 to work at half the salary for the diocesan architect, George Edmund Street, who soon appointed him chief assistant. In January 1856 Webb met and became a close friend of the new pupil William Morris, whose training Street had put into Webb's charge.

Red House In August 1856 Street moved his office to London, where Webb became a member of the circle surrounding the Pre-Raphaelite Brotherhood, of which Morris was an associate. According to another member of the brotherhood, D. G. Rossetti, Webb was very active within this circle. In August 1858 Morris, having changed his career to painting and being about to marry, asked Webb to design him a home, Red House (1859–70), which was built at Upton near Bexleyheath, Kent, and named after the colour of its bricks and tiles. Long considered revolutionary in plan and appearance, in fact it was a masterpiece in the so-called 'parsonage' style developed by Pugin, Street, and Butterfield for their small vicarages, cottages, and schools. What Webb was aiming at was a development of vernacular tradition, free of academic

Philip Speakman Webb (1831–1915), by Charles Fairfax Murray, 1873

convention and based on good building and simplicity. Although he was influenced by Ruskin, comments in Webb's letters to close friends show that the influence was not nearly so wide as has been believed by some architectural historians. He endorsed Ruskin's view of art as the expression of man's pleasure in work, but regarded his contention that a building without ornament could not be architecture as a 'fallacy' (Lethaby, 132). There is not even a moulding on the exterior of Red House. Its L-shaped room-and-a-passage plan was adopted for many houses of the arts and crafts movement, of which it may even be regarded as the first example. The fittings and pieces of furniture by Webb, like his later ones for the Morris firm and for his own houses, became an inspiration for arts and craft designers. The prototype arts and crafts garden, designed jointly by Webb and Morris, was inspired by those depicted in medieval manuscripts. The future of the Red House was secured in 2003 when it was acquired by the National Trust.

Red House was an early studio-house, designed to accommodate Morris's artist friends during working weekends and holidays. Morris's designs for the interior included painted murals, embroidered hangings, stained glass, and furniture, though the last was chiefly by Webb. This informal co-operation between friends led to the founding on 11 April 1861 of Morris, Marshall, Faulkner & Co., through which Morris and his circle subsequently made well-designed artefacts to commission and for the market, and thereby greatly influenced the development of the arts and crafts movement. Webb, a founding partner, played a major role in the firm's success, being the architectural adviser, voluntary part-time business manager, and the designer of all the architectural fittings, most of the furniture, and many other products. In 1861,

for example, for the stained-glass windows of two churches by G. F. Bodley (All Saints, Selsley, Gloucestershire, and St Martin-on-the-Hill, Scarborough), he arranged the general layout and designed several small lights and all the quarries. Webb was almost solely responsible for the decoration in 1866 of two prestigious interiors: the Armoury and the Tapestry Room of St James's Palace, London, and the Green Dining Room in the South Kensington Museum (now the Victoria and Albert Museum). His furniture designs for the firm and its successor Morris & Co. influenced many later arts and crafts pieces.

Independent practice After designing Red House, Webb had left Street on 27 May 1859 to set up his own practice at 7 Great Ormond Street, London. He never had to seek work. Studio-houses were commissioned by his painter friends, including J. R. Spencer Stanhope (Sandroyd, Surrey, 1860–64), V. C. Prinsep (1 Holland Park Road, 1865), G. P. Boyce (West House, Glebe Place, 1869), and George Howard (1 Palace Green, 1868–74), the last three built in London. Through his membership of the Hogarth Club from January 1859 until its dissolution in December 1861 Webb received several commissions from non-painter members, including a terrace of combined dwellings, workshops, and shops, for craftsmen (91–101 Worship Street, London, 1861–3). He enjoyed a relationship of equality and mutual respect with his chiefly upper middle-class clients because, although he insisted on autonomy of design, he fulfilled all their practical needs. In the spring of 1864, he took chambers at 1 Raymond Buildings, Gray's Inn, where he spent the rest of his working life. He declined election to the Royal Institute of British Architects or the Royal Academy, believing them to be too much concerned with the professional and social status of members, but he joined the Sanitary Institute in order to become an expert on drainage.

Truthful and honourable, tall, slim, and handsome, Webb had a gentlemanly manner leavened by a ready wit that made him popular as a dinner guest; a man of simple tastes, he preferred a plain supper with close friends. He enjoyed concerts and the opera, but otherwise disliked grand social occasions or receiving praise or being in the limelight. He dressed appropriately for the occasion but, detesting greed, aimed 'to consume the least possible, yet without impoverishment' (Lethaby, 252). What little he bought was of the best, including cigars for friends and snuff for himself. He relished companionship from friends of both sexes, to whom he was loyal and supportive. By c.1870 he had become an agnostic who followed Christian ethics.

Webb was enamoured of an unidentified girl in the 1860s but he never married because, as he told his friend S. C. Cockerell late in life, he never could afford to keep a wife. Had he chosen to conduct a large commercial practice, this might not have been the case. As he explained to D. G. Rossetti, however, Webb believed that anyone who wished 'to follow art with advantage to the world and with hope of competing with art gone before' had to be 'very severe in the liability of disturbance from collateral causes, such as payment, popularity—position &c'

because while these were not 'of necessity ruinous to art' they did 'often ruin the workman' (Webb to Rossetti, 21 May 1866, in the G. W. Taylor to Webb letters, V&A). Architecture itself was of overriding importance to Webb.

Apart from minor cottages, only thirty-six complete buildings, all influential, were executed to Webb's designs. The larger ones show that, as well as from the local vernacular, Webb took inspiration for his designs from some of the more significant buildings of national character constructed before *c*.1714, including some early Tudor courtyard houses, Elizabethan prodigy-houses, and mansions by Wren and Vanbrugh. His studio-houses in London, which reflected local seventeenth-century buildings, made him an unintentional pioneer of the so-called 'Queen Anne' style—an eclectic system of design—that, paradoxically, ignored local custom. Webb's most important country houses were Joldwynds, Surrey (1872–5; dem. 1930); Rounton Grange (1873–6; dem. 1951–4), and Smeaton Manor, Yorkshire (1877–9); Clouds, Wiltshire (1881–6; designed 1877–81; partly dem. 1938), the largest, with influential interior ornament; and Standen, Sussex (1892–4; National Trust). His smaller houses, notably Coneyhurst (later Coneyhurst-on-the-Hill), Ewhurst, Surrey (1884–5), influenced the new category of middle-class small houses in the country. Webb, who disliked working for a committee, designed few non-domestic buildings. The significant ones are the solicitors' offices at 19 Lincoln's Inn Fields, London (1868–70), St Martin's Church, Brampton, Cumberland (1877–8), and Bell Brothers' main offices at 7 Zetland Road, Middlesbrough (1889–91; designed 1881–3).

The Society for the Protection of Ancient Buildings, and active socialism In 1877, following an earlier suggestion by Ruskin, Morris and Webb founded the Society for the Protection of Ancient Buildings (SPAB) which turned public opinion against current methods of restoring ancient churches. In this way and through the unobtrusive methods of repair he introduced, Webb became an important figure in building conservation history. He never had an articled pupil or published his designs or ideas; and yet, largely through the SPAB and his direct contact with its young architect members, Webb's approach to architectural design and his own executed buildings came to exercise the greatest of all influences on British arts and crafts architecture. His significance was well understood at the time, but in the mid-twentieth century his rejection of academic styles caused Webb to be seen chiefly as a modern movement pioneer. That movement's international style, however, ignored his basic pursuit of good building growing out of local and national architectural character.

Webb became a socialist in 1883, and worked actively until the late 1890s towards the violent social revolution he believed to be necessary if art were to become again a part of everyday life. He chose not to become a public figure like Morris, but worked loyally as treasurer of the Socialist League. In the long run he at least helped Morris to ensure that late nineteenth-century British socialist theory encompassed Ruskin's belief that spiritually rewarding work, art, and fellowship are essential to a full life. By 1910, however, he had abandoned revolution: he

found that he preferred the 'rule by Parliament of tongues, and seeming waste of words, to the rule of blood and thunder' (Webb to W. H. White, 22 Jan 1910, MR10, Bedfordshire county council, Bedford).

Later years By 1899 Webb was in poor health and losing money. His meagre savings were insufficient to build a cottage, so he accepted Caxtons, a four-bedroom sixteenth-century yeoman's house at Worth, near Crawley, Sussex, offered at a selflessly low rental by his friend William Scawen Blunt. After handing over his practice to his chief assistant George Jack, Webb moved on 4 January 1901 into Caxtons, where he spent a comfortable retirement, looked after by a housekeeper, Margaret Dickinson, whose two children also lived in the house. Rheumatism stopped him from earning by designing artefacts as he had intended, but his general health improved with physical work in the house and garden. He enjoyed walking in the nearby forest, friends' visits, reading, and trips to London to attend SPAB committee meetings. After suffering intermittent memory failure in his last years, Webb died peacefully at home at Caxtons on 17 April 1915. After his cremation at Golders Green on 20 April, his ashes were scattered on White Horse Hill, Berkshire. At his request, he has no memorial. Webb's estate was worth only £1643, but he left greater legacies in the foundation of the SPAB and in his approach to architectural design: an approach applicable at any time in any country with a heritage of traditional architecture. Examples of furniture designed by Webb are in the Victoria and Albert Museum, London, and at Kelmscott Manor. Standen, together with much of its Morris & Co. furniture, is now owned by the National Trust.   SHEILA KIRK

Sources W. R. Lethaby, *Philip Webb and his work*, new edn (1979) · G. W. Taylor, letters to Philip Webb, V&A NAL, 86.SS.57 · Philip Webb to William Hale White, Central Library, Bedfordshire County Council, Bedford, Mark Rutherford Papers, MR 10/34 · S. Kirk, 'Philip Webb (1831–1915): domestic architecture', PhD diss., U. Newcastle, 1990 [incl. full lists of primary and secondary sources] · S. Kirk, *Philip Webb* [forthcoming] [a full life and work with lists of primary and secondary sources] · private information (2004) · Webb papers and drawings, priv. coll. · d. cert. · *CGPLA Eng. & Wales* (1915) · will, probate department of the principal registry of the family divison, London · J. Brandon-Jones, 'Philip Webb', *Victorian architecture*, ed. P. Ferriday (1963), 249–65 · E. Hollamby, *Red House: Philip Webb* (1991)

Archives BL, letters, Add. MS 46354 · Courtauld Inst., corresp. · RIBA BAL, architectural drawings and notes relating to provenance of materials in the drawings collection · V&A NAL, letters, 86.SS.57, 86. TT.13, 86.TT.16 | Bedford Central Library, corresp. with W. H. White · BL, letters to George Price Boyce, Add. MS 45354 · BL, corresp. with Sir Sydney Cockerell, Add. MSS 52760–52767 · BL, letters to Elizabeth Weston Wickham Flower, Add. MS 45355 · BL, letters to William Morris and Jane Morris and family, Add. MSS 45342–45343, 45346–45347 · Castle Howard, North Yorkshire, letters to ninth earl of Carlisle · FM Cam., letters to Charles Fairfax Murray · RIBA BAL, corresp. and papers relating to the Village Room, Arisaig, Inverness · U. Durham L., papers relating to Brampton church and other Howard properties · V&A NAL, corresp. with Sir Sydney Cockerell · V&A NAL, corresp., mainly with William Morris · W. Sussex RO, letters to J. S. Beale

Likenesses C. F. Murray, sepia, *c*.1869, repro. in Lethaby, *Philip Webb and his work*, frontispiece · C. F. Murray, wash drawing, 1873, NPG [*see illus.*] · E. Walker, photographs, NPG

Wealth at death £1643 2s. 2d.: probate, 7 July 1915, *CGPLA Eng. & Wales*

Webb, Sidney James, Baron Passfield (1859–1947). *See under* Webb, (Martha) Beatrice (1858–1943).

Webb, Thomas Ebenezer (1821–1903), university professor and lawyer, was born in Portscatho, Cornwall, on or about 8 May 1821. He was eldest of the twelve children of the Revd Thomas Webb, a Methodist minister who owned a small estate in Cornwall, and his wife, Amelia, daughter of James Ryall, of an Irish family. After education at Kingswood College, Sheffield, where he was afterwards for a time an assistant master, he won a classical scholarship at Trinity College, Dublin, in 1845. He was moderator in metaphysics there in 1848, obtained vice-chancellor's prizes for English, Greek, and Latin verse composition, and distinguished himself at the college historical society. He gained a poor degree in philosophy, graduating BA in 1848, and proceeded MA in 1857 and LLB and LLD in 1859. Webb was always a brilliant talker and an eloquent speaker. Well read in English literature, from an early age he contributed verse and prose to the press and to *Kottabos* and other magazines. In 1849 he married Susan Gilbert, daughter of Robert Gilbert of Barringlen, co. Wicklow. They had three sons and a daughter. His wife outlived him.

In 1857 Webb was elected professor of moral philosophy at Dublin University, and published *The Intellectualism of Locke*, an attempt to show that Locke anticipated Kant's recognition of synthetic *a priori* propositions. His literary gifts were greater than his philosophical powers. But he was re-elected to his professorship in 1862, and held the position until 1867. In 1863 he was chosen fellow of Trinity College, a post which he held for the next eight years.

Webb was called to the Irish bar in 1861, and took silk in 1874. He was regarded as a talented barrister and remembered for a brilliant cross-examination of the informers in connection with the Phoenix Park murders. He was regius professor of laws at Trinity College from 1867 to 1887. He petitioned the college unsuccessfully to be allowed to hold a tutorship while practising at the bar and in 1871 he agreed to resign his fellowship, retaining his chair with a salary of £500. He was also public orator at Trinity College from 1879 to 1887. In 1888 he withdrew from academic office to become county court judge for Donegal. He filled that position until five weeks before his death. He was elected bencher of the King's Inns in 1899.

Apart from his professional duties Webb was keenly interested in politics and literature. In 1868 he stood for parliament without success as a whig candidate for the University of Dublin. But in 1880 he abandoned his old party, and was thenceforth a rigorous critic of Liberal policy in Ireland. In a pamphlet on the Irish land question (1880) he denounced proposed concessions to the tenants as ruinous to freedom of contract, although he approved legislation enabling tenants to purchase their holdings. He was hostile to Gladstone's home-rule scheme of 1886 and attacked it in two pamphlets that year.

In 1880 Webb produced a verse translation of Goethe's *Faust*, which is more faithful and poetical than the versions of many of his contemporary rivals. In 1885 there followed *The Veil of Isis*, essays on idealism which failed to establish his position as a philosopher. His later years were largely devoted to formulating doubts about the received Shakespearian tradition. With characteristic love of paradox he claimed in *The Mystery of William Shakespeare: a Summary of Evidence* (1902) to deprive Shakespeare of the authorship of his plays and poems. He was well acquainted with Shakespeare's text, but had small knowledge of Elizabethan literature and history.

Webb's favourite recreation was hunting, and he long followed the Ward and Kildare hounds. He died at his home in Dublin, 5 Mount Street Crescent, on or about 10 November 1903, and was buried in Mount Jerome cemetery.   R. Y. TYRRELL, *rev.* C. A. CREFFIELD

Sources *Irish Times* (11 Nov 1903) · *The Times* (12 Nov 1903) · *The Athenaeum* (21 Nov 1903), 685 · *WW* · R. B. McDowell and D. A. Webb, *Trinity College, Dublin, 1592–1952: an academic history* (1982) · private information (1912) · personal knowledge (1912)

Wealth at death £4405 10s. 6d. (in Ireland): probate, 14 Dec 1903, *CGPLA Ire.* · £452 15s. 10d. (in England): Irish probate sealed in England, 29 June 1904, *CGPLA Eng. & Wales*

Webb, Thomas William (1806–1885), astronomer, was born on 14 December 1806 at Ross-on-Wye, Herefordshire, the second child of John *Webb (1776–1869), a clergyman and antiquarian, and his wife, Sarah, *née* Harding (1776–1849). His sister Anne Frances died, aged seven, in May 1807. Webb's childhood was spent mainly in Ross and Gloucester, where his father served at the cathedral. He was educated by his father, and lived with his parents in Tretire, Herefordshire, from 1812 until his marriage.

Webb was a competent draftsman and a precise and detailed observer. In his first notebook he recorded careful observations of spiders, but his interest soon moved to astronomy. He went to Magdalen Hall, Oxford, where he matriculated on 8 March 1826 and received his BA degree with honours in mathematics on 2 June 1830. He took his MA and was elected a member of the British Association in Oxford in 1832. After being ordained deacon at Hereford Cathedral on 1 August 1830 he was appointed curate at Pencoyd, Herefordshire; he was ordained priest on 6 August 1831. For twenty-five years he served conscientiously in several parishes north of Ross-on-Wye, and as curate to his father. He was musical, played the organ, and installed the first instrument at St Weonard's in 1840. Webb was a minor canon and librarian of Gloucester Cathedral from 1844 to 1849 and a prebendary of Hereford Cathedral from 1882. In December 1856 he was invited to be vicar of Hardwick, a new parish near Hay-on-Wye, which he served attentively until his death.

Webb was a gentle man who possessed a wry sense of humour. He was shy, and when young used shorthand in his diary to disguise his unremarkable encounters with young ladies. At Troy House, Monmouth, he met Henrietta Montagu Wyatt (d. 1884), the daughter of the duke of Beaufort's agent; they were married at Mitcheltroy on 16 May 1843. Though the couple remained childless, they enjoyed long visits from nephews and nieces. Henrietta painted in watercolours and oils, and occasionally supplemented her husband's astronomical work.

As a young man Webb spent many hours making specula for his home-made telescopes. He became an expert in optics. From 1852 to 1866 he mainly used a Tully 3¾ inch refractor. Later he borrowed or purchased an Alvan Clark refractor (1859) and reflectors by With. He was elected to the Royal Astronomical Society in 1852. His observational work was concerned principally with the moon, double stars and nebula, meteors, and comets, as meticulously recorded in a series of surviving notebooks, covering various periods from 1825 to 1874, and including a number on natural phenomena. He served on the British Association's moon committee, and was active in the Selenographical Society.

The Webbs entertained a wide circle of friends, including the diarist Francis Kilvert and the astronomers Espin, Ranyard, and Sadler. Young astronomers enjoyed Webb's generous and prolific correspondence. Webb edited and completed his father's books on the civil war in Herefordshire and the military memoirs of Colonel John Birch. He also collected many details of local and oral history. He wrote articles in several popular periodicals, including *Nature*, *Knowledge*, and the *English Mechanic*; in the last he contributed a regular column answering readers' astronomical queries. He also lectured at both the Ladies' College and working men's club in Cheltenham. He privately published *The Earth a Globe* (1865), a rebuttal of the flat earth theory of Samuel Burley.

Webb's charming and inexpensive *Celestial Objects for Common Telescopes* (1859) brought him enduring fame among the growing number of amateur astronomers. It ran to three editions during his lifetime, and the sixth edition of 1917 was reprinted in 1962. Whereas Admiral W. H. Smyth's expensive two-volume *Bedford Catalogue* (1844) was aimed at gentlemen able to obtain and house 5 inch refractors, Webb described all Smyth's double stars and nebulae within reach of a portable 3½ inch telescope.

Webb died from a disease of the bladder at Hardwick vicarage on 19 May 1885 and was buried at Mitcheltroy. His obituary in the *Hereford Times* stated that he had 'probably induced more amateurs to interest themselves in the study of astronomy than any other man of his generation' (11 June 1885).   MARK G. ROBINSON

Sources T. W. Webb, *Celestial objects for common telescopes*, ed. M. W. Mayell, new edn, 2 vols (1962) · T. E. Espin, 'T. W. Webb — a reminiscence', in T. W. Webb, *Celestial objects for common telescopes*, rev. T. E. Espin, 6th edn, 1 (1917), xvii–xx · Foster, *Alum. Oxon.* · RAS, A. C. Ranyard MSS · T. W. Webb, diaries, 1826–40, Hereford City Library · T. W. Webb, notebooks, Hereford City Library · T. W. Webb, astronomical notebooks, RAS · T. W. Webb, letters, RAS · *Kilvert's diary: selections from the diary of the Rev. Francis Kilvert*, ed. W. Plomer, new edn, 3 vols. (1960) · *The diary of Francis Kilvert, June–July 1870*, ed. D. Ifans (1989) · *Hereford Times* (11 June 1885) · *Monthly Notices of the Royal Astronomical Society*, 46 (1885–6), 198–201 · *Nature*, 34 (1886) · bishop's transcripts, parish register (baptisms), Ross-on-Wye
Archives Cathedral Library, Hereford, scrapbooks · Hereford Library, journals and notebooks · RAS, notebooks of observations | RAS, letters to Arthur Ranyard · RAS, letters to Royal Astronomical Society

Likenesses A. K., photograph, repro. in Webb, *Celestial objects for common telescopes* · A. K., photograph, RAS · C. W. Smartt, carte de visite, F. W. H. Bedford collection
Wealth at death £16,986 5s. 1d.; contents of vicarage auctioned: probate, 17 June 1885, *CGPLA Eng. & Wales*

Webb, William (*d.* 1657), composer and musician, is first heard of as a singing-master employed between April 1627 and October 1628 at £3 a quarter to teach 'division' to the daughter of Judith Edwards and the late Thomas Edwards (*d.* 1625), a London mercer who had a country house near Wadhurst in Sussex. Some years later, on 3 and 13 February 1634, Webb was listed among the performers in James Shirley's masque *The Triumph of Peace*. He became one of the waits of the City of London in 1637 and was still serving in 1645; in the meantime he had acquired a probationer's place in the Chapel Royal (17 June 1640). According to Anthony Wood he had a house in Charterhouse Yard soon after the outbreak of the civil war where he taught singing to maintain himself. John Playford listed him among teachers 'For the Voyce or Viole' in 1651, and he was one of the band in the first English opera, William Davenant's *The Siege of Rhodes* (1656).

Webb is known principally as a songwriter, though not a very prolific one. About fifteen songs are extant, some in early sources dating from the 1620s, such as Christ Church, Oxford, MS 87, and New York Public Library, Drexel MS 4175. Generally they are simpler and more tuneful than those of his most famous contemporary, Henry Lawes. Several were either written or arranged as partsongs and later published by Playford in *Select [Musical] Ayres and Dialogues* (1652–9). There are a few catches by him in *Catch that Catch Can* (1653–67). Webb was buried on 16 March 1657 at St Margaret's, Westminster.

IAN SPINK

Sources A. Ashbee and D. Lasocki, eds., *A biographical dictionary of English court musicians, 1485–1714*, 2 (1998), 1135–6 · I. Spink, *English song: Dowland to Purcell* (1974) · C. E. McGee, 'Music for marriage: the education of Susanna Edwards', *The Early Drama, Art and Music Review*, 13/1 (1990), 7–12

Webbe, Edward (*b.* 1553/4), soldier and adventurer, son of Richard Webbe, 'master gunner of England' (Webbe, *Travailes*, 17), was born at St Katharine by the Tower, London. Nothing is known of his mother. 'A simple man voide of learning' (ibid., 29), at the age of twelve Webbe was placed by his father in the service of Captain Anthony Jenkinson, ambassador to Russia, who sailed from England on his third voyage to that region on 4 May 1566. As Jenkinson's personal attendant, Webbe served in and about Moscow, eventually returning with him to England in 1568.

In 1570 Webbe sailed in the *Hart*, under Captain William Borough, for Narva, in the Gulf of Finland and was in Moscow on 24 May 1571, when it was burnt by the Crimean Tartars. Though he escaped, he was subsequently captured by the Tartars and enslaved. With seven other Englishmen Webbe was transported to Caffa in the Crimea. According to his *Rare and most wonderful thinges which Edward Webbe an Englishman borne, hath seene and passed in his troublesome travailes*, he was held there for five years before being ransomed for the sum of 300 crowns. However, this seems to have been something of an exaggeration, for he also claims to have been at Tunis in October 1572, when it was taken from the Turks. He was then serving under Don John of Austria, and it is while in the forces of the Christian commander that he is first described as being of the rank of master gunner.

Some months later Webbe, on board the *Henry*, was captured by the Turks off the coast of Leghorn. Transported to Constantinople, Webbe became a galley slave, in which capacity he says he served for six years. Eventually, 'constrained for want of victualles' (Webbe, *Travailes*, 20), he fought for the Turks as a gunner and accompanied the Turkish army on their campaign to Persia. Though the balance of Webbe's travels during his period as a slave cannot be independently confirmed, he states that he was in Calabria, Damascus, Cairo, Goa, Bethlehem, Jerusalem, and in a place which he identifies as 'the land of Prester John' (ibid., 24). According to Webbe, this was a place located within 18° (1080 miles) of the equator. Given the rest of his itinerary, it is not likely that this was Ethiopia, the site more usually associated with this semi-legendary potentate in the sixteenth century. Finally, though, Webbe returned to Constantinople, where in 1588 he was one of twenty captives ransomed through the intercession of William Harborne, the English ambassador.

On his way back to England, Webbe was arrested and tried as a heretic through the machinations of an unidentified English friar resident in Padua. But, he records, the charge was not substantiated and he was freed. For reasons which are unclear, Webbe turned south from Padua to Rome, where he fell foul of the English cardinal William Allen. Though he was examined many times and abused by the English college of the city, Webbe records that the pope intervened directly and set him at liberty.

Continuing to Naples, Webbe was denounced as an English spy by a Genoese. Confined to a dark dungeon, enduring periodic torture for twenty-five days, he refused to implicate himself. As a result, he languished in gaol for another seven months before the viceroy, upon instruction from the king of Spain, recommended that Webbe be made a gunner and given an allowance of 35 crowns a month. A short time after this, he was able to escape in the *Grace* with the collusion of its captain, Nicholas Nottingham. However, while Webbe notes that in May 1589 he set foot in England for the first time in thirteen years, this again may be something of an exaggeration, for on 8 April 1587 one Mr Webbe was consulted by John Popham, the attorney-general, about the market for English cloth in Muscovy and the possibility of expanding English trade in that region.

In November 1589 Webbe journeyed to France and was made chief master gunner by Henri IV, in whose service he fought at the battle of Ivry on 14 March 1590. However, Webbe records that some French gunners, jealous of his skill, tried to poison him. He was pulled back from the brink of death only by the intervention of the king's physician, who cured him with a potion made from unicorn's horn. After his return to England a short time later, he

took lodgings at Blackwall, where on 19 May 1590 he completed his account of his travails. On 14 January 1592 Webbe was made a cannonier for life, receiving a fee of 10s. per diem. Nothing further is known of his life.

RICHARD RAISWELL

Sources E. Webbe, *The rare and most wonderful thinges which Edward Webbe … hath seene* (1590) • E. Webbe, *His travailes*, ed. E. Arber (1868) • *CSP dom.*, 1581–90, 403; 1591–4, 172

Webbe, Egerton (1810?–1840). *See under* Webbe, Samuel, the younger (1768–1843).

Webbe, George (*b.* 1581, *d.* in or before 1642), Church of Ireland bishop of Limerick, was born in 1581, the third son of Hugh Webbe, rector of Bromham, Wiltshire. He entered University College, Oxford, in April 1598, and migrated to Corpus Christi College as a scholar. He was admitted BA in February 1602 and MA in June 1605. Soon after he was inducted as vicar of Steeple Ashton, Wiltshire, on 15 May 1605, seemingly on the presentation of the earl of Pembroke. He married some time before the birth of his son Theophilus in 1607. Webbe kept a grammar school at Steeple Ashton and also at Bath, where he was rector of St Peter and St Paul from 1621 to 1634, when his son succeeded him. Appointed a chaplain to James VI and I before 1621, he was made DD in 1623.

Webbe was a man of strict life and conversation, and a distinguished preacher, both in his parish, at Paul's Cross, and at court; the portrait of him by Thomas Slater catches him unawares 'As he in Pulpit did discharge his place' (AH, frontispiece and sonnet, in G. Webbe, *The Practice of Quietness*, 1705). *God's Controversie with England* (1609), his first sermon at Paul's Cross, 'the chiefest Watchtower in the land' (sig. A3v), has been seen as within the Jacobean tradition of exposition of Hosea, as established by John Downame in his 1608 lectures, using that prophet to explore God's relations with England. It also reflected Webbe's close association with the likes of Richard Rogers, William Perkins, and Richard Greenham, with whom he later published one of the most successful early Stuart handbooks of devotion, *A Garden of Spirituall Flowers*, in 1616; some thirty imprints and editions appeared by 1630. Webbe's own popularity as a preacher can be gauged from the 1613 epithalamion homily he dedicated to Princess Elizabeth, *The Bride Royall, or, The Spirituall Marriage between Christ and his Church* (1613) and in six other Steeple Ashton sermons, gathered in 1610 as *A Poesie of Spirituall Flowers*. Convinced that 'experience sheweth how little preaching profiteth where catechising is neglected', he published *A Brief Exposition of the Principles of the Christian Religion* (1612), a catechism for the primary use of his parishioners (sig. A2v). His *Catalogus protestantium, or, The Protestants Kalendar* (1624) surveyed 'the protestants religion long before Luthers daies' in the light of the Spanish match. He enjoyed the friendship of the lord chief justice, Sir Henry Hobart, to whom he dedicated his most popular series of sermons, *The Practice of Quietness*, in June 1615. It ran to six editions before Webbe expanded it in 1638.

Charles I, with Archbishop Laud's approval, selected Webbe for promotion to the bench at the age of fifty-

MINOR MINIMIS DEI MISERATIONIBVS.

Effigies Reverendi in Christo Patris, Georgii Webbe, Limericensis apud Hibernos Episcopi.

George Webbe (*b.* 1581, *d.* in or before 1642), by Thomas Cross

three. On the death of his fellow Wiltshireman Francis Gough he was nominated bishop of Limerick, despite the support of the archbishop of Armagh and the lords justices for the dean, George Andrews (later bishop of Ferns and Leighlin). William Prynne later used Webbe's appointment as part of his attack on Laud for allegedly usurping the royal prerogative. He was consecrated in St Patrick's Cathedral, Dublin, on 18 December 1634. Eight days earlier Lord Deputy Wentworth had put pressure on the convocation of the Church of Ireland to accept the Thirty-Nine Articles and the 1604 canons of the Church of England (proceedings challenged by George Andrews). With the outbreak of the 1641 rising Webbe was imprisoned by insurgent sympathizers within the city and had died of prison fever at Limerick Castle, by 22 June 1642. He was buried in St Munchin's churchyard, but apparently his remains were dug up twenty-four hours later by persons hoping to find jewels, then re-interred in the same place. He was succeeded, on 7 April 1643, by another Englishman, Robert Sibthorp, bishop of Kilfenora, whom the Irish bishops had unsuccessfully petitioned Charles to make bishop of Ossory in 1640.

RICHARD BAGWELL, rev. NICHOLAS W. S. CRANFIELD

Sources M. MacLure, *Paul's Cross sermons, 1534–1642* (1958) · G. Radcliffe, *The earl of Strafforde's letters and dispatches, with an essay towards his life*, ed. W. Knowler, 2 vols. (1739) · M. McGiffert, 'God's controversy with Jacobean England', *American Historical Review*, 88 (1983), 1151–74 · Foster, *Alum. Oxon.* · H. Cotton, *Fasti ecclesiae Hibernicae*, 1–5 (1845–60); 2nd edn, 1 (1851) · T. W. Moody and others, eds., *A new history of Ireland*, 9: *Maps, genealogies, lists* (1984)
Likenesses T. Cross, line engraving, BM, V&A [*see illus.*] · T. Slater, line engraving (after T. Cross), BM, NPG; repro. in G. Webbe, *The practice of quietness* (1705), frontispiece

Webbe, Joseph (*d. c.*1630), linguist and physician, was said to be from Dorset when, as a Roman Catholic, he visited the English College at Rome in 1600. Details of his parentage and of the date and place of his birth are unknown but he was perhaps related to the old Catholic family of Webb in Canford Magna, Dorset, who sent their children abroad to Catholic seminaries and convents for their education. Webbe, having obtained a foreign doctorate, returned to the English College at Rome on 12 November 1603 and, since no date of departure is recorded, he may have stayed there for some time. By 1612 he had obtained two doctorates, both noted on the title-page of his *Minae coelestes* (1612) as 'Phi.' and 'Me.D.'. This text consists largely of a set of tables which list, according to astrological predictions, the most unlucky days in 1612 for dealing with various diseases. The second degree was obtained at Padua and Webbe probably studied at Bologna as well, since one of the dedicatees of *Minae* is G. Antonio Magino, a distinguished mathematician whom Webbe describes as a most celebrated teacher at Bologna.

Webbe's association with Italy continued at least until 1614, when he published in Florence what he describes, in *Usus et authoritas* (1626, preface), as his 'universal tables' (now lost but probably similar to those in *Minae coelestes*). Thereafter his name occurs in English contexts, first in 1616, when he was a candidate for a licence to practise medicine, which the Royal College of Physicians agreed to award subject to his obtaining incorporation at either Oxford or Cambridge University. In 1626 the college noted that he had failed to do so, though he may have practised illegally since an anti-Catholic contemporary includes him in a list of 'popish Physicians'. However, he made a living teaching languages by his own unique method at his house in Black and White Court in the Old Bailey. His system interested Samuel Hartlib, who instigated a debate on its merits between Webbe and another schoolmaster, William Brookes; the relevant correspondence is preserved in British Library, Sloane MS 1466. Having published a translation of Cicero's *Familiar Epistles* in 1620 Webbe set out on his major project of language teaching, using his new methods in works published between 1626 and 1629. But eventually he admitted that his 'gaping Grave' was 'calling' him (J. Webbe, *Andria*, 1629, sig. ¶ 4r) and he died soon afterwards, possibly in financial difficulties, without achieving his goal of publishing in his new format all of Terence's comedies.

Webbe contributed to the development of language teaching and of linguistic thought generally in three respects. The first of these was in his strong support of, and reasoned arguments for, the teaching of any language by the 'direct' method, in which students learned Latin, for example, by imitating phrases from classical authors; he strongly opposed the alternative method of first learning paradigms on which students constructed their own sentences. Such a debate was not uncommon in the sixteenth century, one participant being Georgius Haloinus Cominius (c.1473–1536), a Belgian scholar whose *De restauratione linguae latinae* (1533) Webbe frequently cites. Webbe's most important contribution to this discussion was to design and publish relevant textbooks, for the production of which he solicited financial support from subscribers. He explained his ideas in *An Appeale to Truth, in the Controversie, betweene Art, & Use* (1622), where 'art' refers to grammar and 'use' to the usage of the learned; he also pleaded for parliament's support in *A Petition* (1623), which led to the grant in 1626 of a patent giving him the monopoly of teaching languages by his method for thirty-one years. His textbooks, which gave both the original Latin and Webbe's translation, were designed with the use of various typographical devices to enable students to see at a glance the links between the Latin phrases and their English equivalents. His system became progressively more complicated, beginning with *Lessons and Exercises out of Cicero* (1627) and ending with two comedies by Terence, *Eunuchus* and *Andria* (1629). Webbe also published a dictionary of phrases from Ovid, with which students could form new sentences and verses in imitation of the Latin original.

Webbe's second contribution to linguistic thought was to draw attention to the difficulties involved in translation, such as those that related to word order and idiomatic usage. His third contribution was an analysis, preserved in Sloane MS 1466, of the nature of language acquisition. In this work he sees the child's acquisition of language as an automatic reaction in an appropriate context, where the child learns the meaning of the word drink, for example, when he is given a pot to drink from, and he compares this situation to a dog's reaction to the sound of a bell. The dog, 'once hearinge the bell and presently feeling the lash, will never after heare the bell, but will runne away barking or crying, out of a memory of the former punishment' (Salmon, 'Problems', 9).

Webbe's work was highly valued by younger contemporaries, such as the eminent schoolmaster Thomas Hayne (d. 1645), and later by John Webster (1611–1682), who argued that if only Webbe's method had been followed it would have been an 'incredible advantage to the whole nation' (J. Webster, *Examination of Academies*, 1654, 3). He has also been praised by more recent scholars, such as Foster Watson, who describes the *Petition* as an 'outstanding educational document' (F. Watson, *The English Grammar Schools to 1660*, 1908, 285–6); but his method ultimately failed because it was superseded, from about 1630, by the internationally known and admired language teaching system of J. A. Comenius. VIVIAN SALMON

Sources V. Salmon, 'Joseph Webbe: some seventeenth-century views on language-teaching and the nature of meaning', *The study of language in 17th-century England*, 2nd edn (1988), 15–31 · V. Salmon, 'Problems of language-teaching: a discussion among Hartlib's friends', *The study of language in 17th-century England*, 2nd edn (1988), 3–14 · V. Salmon, 'An ambitious printing project of the early seventeenth century', *The Library*, 5th ser., 16 (1961), 190–96 · A. P. R. Howatt, 'Joseph Webbe', *Lexicon grammaticorum*, ed. H. Stammerjohann (1996), 998–9 · Munk, *Roll* · *DNB* · *VCH Dorset*, 2.34 · BL, Sloane MS 1466

Archives BL, corresp. and papers, Sloane MS 1466

Wealth at death probably nil: letters to Hartlib mentioning financial problems, BL, Sloane MS 1466, fols. 377r, 327v

Webbe, Samuel, the elder (1740–1816), church musician and composer, was born in London on 7 October 1740, the son of well-to-do parents. Before he was a year old his father took up a government appointment in Minorca, but he died before his wife and family could join him there. Thereafter the family's financial situation was straitened, and Webbe's mother was obliged to curtail his education and apprentice him at the age of eleven to a cabinet-maker for a period of seven years. Within a year of the expiry of his articles Webbe turned his attention to music, at the same time also embarking on a vigorous programme of self-education. He successively applied himself to Latin, French, and Italian, and later also acquired a competent knowledge of German, Greek, and Hebrew; he is said also to have excelled in fencing and dancing. When later asked by Charles Butler how he managed to acquire so much additional knowledge in an already busy life, he replied that it was by 'a rigid observance of two rules: never to let a bit or scrap of time, pass unemployed, and, whatever, he did, to fix his whole mind upon it' (Butler, 2.356). Through the music publisher Peter Welcker, for whom he undertook work as a copyist, he met Charles Barbandt, the organist of the Bavarian embassy chapel, and became his pupil, and it may have been at this time that he converted to Roman Catholicism. By the time he was twenty-five he had become a teacher of music. On 30 May 1763 he married Anne Plumb; of the eight children of the marriage, born between 1764 and 1775, his eldest son Samuel *Webbe also became a musician. He became a member of the Royal Society of Musicians in 1770.

In addition to teaching Webbe was also becoming established as a bass singer in London's pleasure gardens and theatres. By the summer of 1767 he was appearing at Marylebone Gardens, and later in the same year also sang in the chorus at Covent Garden. He is included as a chorus member in the account books for Drury Lane in 1776 and 1778, and can probably be identified as the 'Webb' who was director of the chorus at the King's Theatre in 1785. He also composed for and sang at Vauxhall Gardens.

Early in his career Webbe established a reputation as a composer of glees, and rapidly became the leading exponent of his age in this genre. His first collection of vocal part music appeared about 1764. In 1776 he won his first prize medal from the Catch Club for his canon 'O that I had wings', and won a further twenty-six medals between then and 1793. He became a member of the Catch Club in 1771, and became its secretary in 1794 on the death of Edmund Thomas Warren, resigning in 1812. On the foundation of the Glee Club in 1787 he was appointed its librarian; his most celebrated glee, 'Glorious Apollo', was performed at the beginning of every meeting during the

Samuel Webbe the elder (1740–1816), by William Skelton, pubd 1820 (after William Behnes)

club's history. He was also a member of the Anacreontic Society and the Concentores Sodales, two other glee clubs. Seventy-three of his glees appeared in nine volumes he published himself, a further twenty-five were included in Warren's collection, and many more were published in his lifetime and afterwards in other collections.

Webbe was also the most important and influential English Roman Catholic church composer of his generation. At one time or another he was involved with the music of all the principal foreign embassy chapels, which were at this time the main centres for Roman Catholic worship in London. In the late 1760s he was at the Bavarian embassy chapel, probably initially as Barbandt's assistant and later as his successor. In October 1775, following the death of George Paxton, he became organist of the Sardinian embassy chapel, and from 1776 was simultaneously organist of the Portuguese embassy chapel. At the Sardinian chapel he offered free instruction on Friday evenings 'to such young gentlemen as present themselves to learn church music' (*Laity's Directory*, 1793), and numbered among his pupils John Danby, Charles Knyvett the younger, Vincent Novello, and probably Samuel Wesley. His masses and other church music compositions, written in a predominantly simple and straightforward style, were an important part of the repertory of the embassy chapels from the early 1770s. Many of them were subsequently published in *A Collection of Sacred Music, as used in the Chapel of the King of Sardinia* (*c*.1785), *A Collection of Masses* (1792), and *A Collection of Motets and Antiphons* (1792), and continued in widespread use in Roman Catholic churches until well into the nineteenth century. He is best-known to present-day congregations for his hymn tune 'Melcombe', originally composed as a setting of *O salutaris*

hostia, but now usually sung to the words of John Keble's hymn 'New every morning is the love'.

Little is known of Webbe's activities in the last years of his life. By 1808 he appears to have been in reduced circumstances, probably as a result of declining health. In March of that year R. J. S. Stevens recorded that he had organized a subscription among Webbe's friends and had collected £115. A benefit concert consisting entirely of his own music was organized for him on 30 May of that year under the patronage of the prince of Wales, the dukes of Cumberland and Cambridge, and the other members of the Catch Club, and raised £450. Two further benefits were held on 13 April 1809 and 18 April 1814.

During his last years Webbe was confined to his apartments in 1 Great Square, Gray's Inn; by this time he had given up composition and chiefly amused himself by playing chess with a friend. He died at home on 25 May 1816 and was buried in the churchyard of St Pancras Old Church. His extensive library of books and music was sold at White's on 4 July 1816 and on two successive days.

Webbe was widely respected by his friends and professional colleagues. His obituary notice stressed the affection in which he was held, the wide range of his learning and accomplishments, and his unaffected manner. Although little is known of his life outside music, it is clear that he had an extensive range of interests, including an involvement in radical politics and membership of the London Corresponding Society.   PHILIP OLLESON

Sources *GM*, 1st ser., 86/1 (1816), 569 • *GM*, 1st ser., 86/2 (1816), 643–4 • Highfill, Burnim & Langhans, *BDA* • *The Mawhood diary: selections from the diary note-books of William Mawhood, woollen-draper of London, for the years 1764–1770*, ed. E. E. Reynolds, Catholic RS, 50 (1956) • *Recollections of R. J. S. Stevens: an organist in Georgian London*, ed. M. Argent (1992) • C. Butler, *Historical memoirs respecting the English, Irish and Scottish Catholics, from the Reformation to the present time*, 2nd edn, 2 (1819), 335–6 • 'The late Mr. Samuel Webbe', *Quarterly Musical Magazine and Review*, 4 (1822), 362–9 [incl. list of Webbe's glees] • 'Introduction', *A requiem to the memory of the late Mr. Samuel Webbe, the words by Mr. Linley, and set to music, severally by Lord Burghersh, Messrs. Linley, W. Knyett, Hawes, Elliott, Beale & Evans* (1820?) • *The autobiography of Francis Place, 1771–1854*, ed. M. Thale (1972), 176 • A. Beedell, *The decline of the English musician, 1788–1888* (1992), 61 and n. 90 • *The Times* (30 May 1808) • *The Times* (12 April 1809) • *The Times* (18 April 1814) • Grove, *Dict. mus.* (1927) [incl. list of prize glees] • B. Matthews, ed., *The Royal Society of Musicians of Great Britain: list of members, 1738–1984* (1985) • D. Rohr, 'A profession of artisans: the careers and social status of British musicians, 1750–1850', PhD diss., University of Pennsylvania, 1983 • will, PRO, PROB 11/1581, sig. 343

Likenesses W. Skelton, engraving, pubd 1820 (after W. Behnes), NPG [*see illus.*]

Wealth at death see will, PRO, PROB 11/1581, sig. 343

Webbe, Samuel, the younger (1768–1843), musician and composer, was born on 15 October 1768 in London, the fourth child and the eldest of the three sons of the seven children of the musician Samuel *Webbe the elder (1740–1816) and his wife, Anne Plumb. His first musical education was from his father, who as the leading figure in Roman Catholic church music in London introduced him at an early age to the music of the embassy chapels and to other Catholic musicians. He may also have studied with Muzio Clementi. His early professional career was as a singer and a performer on the violin, oboe, and trumpet. He took part as a tenor in the Handel commemoration concerts in 1784, and sang in the chorus in the Academy of Ancient Music concerts in the 1787–8 season.

Webbe followed in his father's footsteps as a Roman Catholic church musician, and by the time of his election to membership of the Royal Society of Musicians in 1791 he was already organist of the Bavarian Chapel. Like his father he was also a successful composer of glees and catches; his numerous published compositions also include piano and organ music, and church music for both the Roman Catholic and Anglican rites. Either he or his father was the composer of the operatic farce *The Speechless Wife*, performed at Covent Garden on 22 May 1794. It is probable that he and his father were also active in radical politics in the 1790s as members of the London Corresponding Society.

About 1798 Webbe moved to Liverpool, where he became organist of the Unitarian chapel, Paradise Street. On 7 October 1803 he married Diana Smith (*d.* 1843) at St John's Church, Old Haymarket, Liverpool; they had at least three children. One of their daughters, Louisa, married the writer on music Edward *Holmes in 1857. Their son **Egerton Webbe** (1810?–1840), named after his uncle the Liverpool publisher Egerton Smith, was a composer, a man of letters, and a friend of Charles Cowden Clarke, Leigh Hunt, and Holmes. He wrote on music, literature, and ballet for the *London Journal*, *Bentley's Miscellany*, *Atlas*, *The Spectator*, and *Musical World*, which he also co-edited with Holmes between October 1838 and April 1839. Egerton Webbe died of tuberculosis at Park Terrace, Wellington Road, Toxteth Park, Liverpool, on 24 June 1840.

Little is known of Samuel Webbe's activities in Liverpool. In 1810 or 1811, for reasons perhaps connected with the advancing years and failing health of his father, he returned to London and resumed his musical career there. He was active in the earliest years of the Philharmonic Society: he was one of its thirty original members at its foundation in February 1813, was a director for the 1815–16 and 1817–18 seasons, and played an active part in the autumn of 1815 in the negotiations with the Professional Concert about a possible merger of the two bodies. In 1817 he visited Dublin to observe the controversial system of piano teaching practised by Johann Bernhard Logier (1777–1846), in which pupils were taught in groups using Logier's patent chiroplast, a device for holding the hands in the correct position while playing. On his return to London he set up his own academy according to Logier's principles. A demonstration of the system to members of the Philharmonic Society led to a lengthy and acrimonious public dispute: Logier was accused of charlatanry and Webbe's own integrity was called into question. He eventually resigned from the society in December 1817.

While in London, Webbe continued his career as a Roman Catholic church musician in the position of organist to the Spanish embassy chapel. In the late 1820s he

returned to Liverpool, where he was successively organist of St Andrew's, Renshaw Street, St Nicholas's, and St Patrick's Chapel, Toxteth. He moved back to London in 1840 and died at Park Cottage, Hammersmith, on 25 November 1843. His wife had died a few weeks earlier.

PHILIP OLLESON

Sources [J. S. Sainsbury], ed., *A dictionary of musicians*, 2 vols. (1824) · general minute book, 1813–54, BL, Royal Philharmonic Society MSS, Loan 48/3/1 · J. C. Kassler, *The science of music in Britain, 1714–1830: a catalogue of writings, lectures, and inventions*, 2 vols. (1979), 711–14, 1157–9 · *The Times* (18 Nov 1817) · *The Times* (24 Nov 1817) · *The Times* (25 Nov 1817) · *The Times* (1 Dec 1817) · *The Times* (6 Dec 1817) · *The Times* (12 Dec 1817) · J. B. Logier, H. De Monti, and others, 'Mr Logier's system of musical instruction', *Quarterly Musical Magazine and Review*, 1 (1818), 111–39 · L. Hunt, *The autobiography of Leigh Hunt, with reminiscences of friends and contemporaries*, 3 vols. (1850) · *The correspondence of Leigh Hunt*, ed. T. L. Hunt, 2 vols. (1862) · L. Langley, 'The English musical journal in the early nineteenth century', PhD diss., University of North Carolina at Chapel Hill, 1983 · *GM*, 2nd ser., 14 (1840), 329 · *Musical World* (14 Dec 1843), 416 · Webbe's personal file, Royal Society of Musicians · d. cert. · d. cert. [Egerton Webbe]
Archives BL, letters to W. Hedgley, Add. MS 40856 · BL, letters to Leigh Hunt, Add. MSS 38108, 38110 · BL, letters to Vincent Novello, Add. MS 11730 · BL, letters to Philharmonic Society, loan 48 13/35
Likenesses W. Skelton, line engraving (after W. Behnes or his father?), NPG; repro. in *European Magazine* (1820)
Wealth at death bankrupt on 3 July 1840: Highfill, Burnim & Langhans, *BDA* · existed on aid of £5 5s. 0d. per week from Royal Society of Musicians for last four years of life: *Musical world*

Webbe, Thomas (*b.* 1624×6?), Ranter, first achieved notoriety in 1644 when he was arrested by order of the House of Lords for blasphemous preaching in London. At this point, he was a feltmaker and hatmaker living in Southwark. He was charged with the more advanced heresies of his day, asserting the primacy of immediate, divine inspiration by rejecting the historical Christ, the literal truth of scripture, and the immortality of the soul. Some of his alleged opinions were couched in the crude and provocative terms later attributed to the libertine antinomians known as Ranters, such as that a drunkard did the will of God and that God knew no difference between the flesh of the best saint and the flesh of a toad. Under examination by divines from the Westminster assembly he denied the more extreme heresies and grosser statements attributed to him but stood by his commitment to the primacy of personal spiritual inspiration. Thomas Edwards, the London Presbyterian minister who publicized Webbe's errors in his heresiography *Gangraena* (1646), alleged that he had recanted to secure his liberty; Webbe answered in print that he had been cleared of all charges. According to Edwards, Webbe was twenty or twenty-one years old.

Webbe embarked on a career of itinerant preaching during the last years of the civil war and by 1647 had acquired the living of Langley Burrell, in Wiltshire, allegedly by promising not to collect his tithe. A colourful account of Webbe's pastoral care was published in 1652 by Edward Stokes, a Wiltshire magistrate, based on the extensive documentation he had collected for the parliamentary committee for plundered ministers, which ejected Webbe in 1651. In the winter of 1649–50 Webbe lost his wife, married a woman called Mary (who, according to Stokes, was Webbe's third wife), but also took as his mistress the patron's wife, Mary White. He attempted to resolve the resulting friction between wife and mistress by setting up a commune in the manor house which became the centre of a libertine sect. He procured the seduction of his wife by a young rustic and took for himself a 'man-wife' named John Organ of Castle Combe. Thoroughly debauched, Organ abandoned his wife and children, acquired a mistress, and took to the life of itinerant preaching with Webbe's blessing. Stokes sought to discredit Webbe as a libertine antinomian and published evidence of his connections with the notorious group of Ranters led by Abiezer Coppe. Webbe was accused of Ranter-like opinions, including that Moses was a conjuror and Christ a deceiver. Preaching and lying were alike to him; he could sleep with any woman except his mother. In Ranter style, Webbe's sect were said to 'curse and swear, sing lewd songs, and drink prophane and blasphemous healths' (Stokes, 31). However, Webbe was never charged under the Blasphemy Act of August 1650 which proscribed his sect's doctrines. Rather the move against him came from his own followers. In September 1650 his mistress accused him of various sexual offences; Webbe publicly repented and the case went no further. The next month two disciples accused parson and mistress of adultery, a capital offence under an act of May 1650, both with each other and various members of their group. However they were acquitted by the assize jury.

By August 1651 Webbe was under investigation by the committee for plundered ministers. His enthusiastic opinions were duly catalogued, along with the immoral behaviour they were assumed to promote. He was also accused of rejecting all political authority and supporting the radical Levellers. Other charges were more specifically designed to secure his ejection, notably that he had excluded the lawful incumbent and wasted the glebe. Webbe lost his living in September 1651 and, after a brief pamphlet skirmish with Stokes in 1652, returned to the obscurity whence he came. Webbe's last known appearance may have been in 1654, when a Thomas Webbe was tried at the Old Bailey for an adultery committed in London the year before: the prosecution referred to his dangerous principles and opinions of four or five years earlier. During his brief period of notoriety Webbe furnished the opponents of religious radicalism with damning evidence of the moral anarchy produced by the collapse of civil and ecclesiastical authority during the English revolution.

J. F. McGregor

Sources E. Stokes, *The Wiltshire rant* (1652) · T. Edwards, *Gangraena, or, A catalogue and discovery of many of the errours, heresies, blasphemies and pernicious practices of the sectaries of this time*, 2nd edn, 1 (1646) · *JHL*, 7 (1644–5), 70, 80–81 · T. Webbe, *Mr. Edwards pen no slander* (1646) · K. Lindley, *Popular politics and religion in civil war London* (1997), 280, 290, 300 · *The juries right, asserted … by the ancient … law of England … occasioned by the late unjust … triall of Mr. Tho. Webbe, at the Old Bayly. By A. Lawmind, ear-witness of the said triall* (1654)

Webbe, William (*fl.* 1566?–1591), author, is known chiefly for his *A discourse of English poetrie, together with the authors judgment, touching the reformation of our English verse*, published in 1586; little is known of his life. A letter by Webbe addressed to Robert Wilmott, prefacing the latter's 1591 printed edition of an Inner Temple play, *Tancred and Gismund*, implies that Webbe was present at its performance before the queen, probably in 1566. He is probably the William Webbe who graduated BA from St John's College, Cambridge, in 1572/3, in the same year as Edmund Spenser, although from a different college. In *A Discourse*, Webbe draws extensively and admiringly upon *The Shepheardes Calender* (published anonymously in 1579) and demonstrates that he knows the identity of its author. He refers admiringly to the discussion of quantitative metres in the correspondence between Spenser and Gabriel Harvey which appeared as *Three Proper and Wittie Familiar Letters* and *Two other Very Commendable Letters* in 1580. However, *A Discourse* does not suggest any intimate acquaintance between Webbe and Spenser or Harvey.

Webbe's *Discourse* yields some clues about his career. It is dedicated to 'my verie good Master, Ma. Edward Suliard, Esquire' who resided at Flemyngs, a large house in the parish of Runwell, in the hundred of Chelmsford, Essex. Webbe indicates that he was employed as tutor to Sulyard's two sons, Edward and Thomas, and refers on a number of occasions to his manuscript translation into quantitative verse of the *Georgics* which he presented to Sulyard. By 1591, the date of his letter to Wilmott, Webbe was living, possibly also as a tutor, at Pirgo, in the parish of Havering atte Bower, Essex, a house owned by Henry Grey, a relative by marriage of the Sulyards. *Tancred and Gismund* was partly dedicated by Wilmott to Lady Anne Grey, wife of Henry Grey. Nothing further is known of Webbe's life.

In his dedication to Edward Sulyard, Webbe describes himself as a scholar 'never acquainted with the learned Muses' (*Discourse*, 15). While this should be understood as a modest disclaimer, it does convey the limitations of Webbe's treatise. His enthusiasm for applying the rules of classical quantitative metres to the writing of a 'reformed' English verse should be understood in the context of contemporary scholarly attitudes. In *The Scholemaster* (1570), Roger Ascham scorned 'barbarous and rude Ryming' and advocated 'trew versifying' in English, that is, unrhymed verse written to classical metrical rules (Smith, 1.29–30). Ascham's view was shared by many for whom classical models formed the sole standard and rhyming verse was the product of mere ignorance and laziness. Webbe shared these views, but was more discriminating about contemporary verse. He parodied the technique of popular ballads: 'an Alehouse song of five or six score verses, hobbling upon some tune of a Northern Jigge, or Robyn hoode … and there withal an A to make a jerke in the ende' (Smith, 1.246; see also *Handefull*, 100–01). On the other hand, in a survey of English verse, he cited with approval any contemporary rhyming verse that demonstrated learnedness or laid claim to moral seriousness, above all, Edmund Spenser whose *Shepheardes Calender* would, were it not for the imperfectness of English, rival Virgil and Theocritus in skill (Smith, 1.263).

A small black-lettered tract entitled *The Touchstone of Wittes*, chiefly compiled, with some slender additions, from William Webbe's *Discourse of English Poetry*, and written by Edward Hake, was reported by Thomas Warton in the eighteenth century, but no copy is known to be extant.   ELIZABETH HEALE

Sources *A discourse of English poetrie, 1586, by William Webbe*, ed. E. Arber (1895) · G. G. Smith, ed., *Elizabethan critical essays*, 2 vols. (1904) · E. Spenser, *Poetical works*, ed. E. de Selincourt (1910) · D. Attridge, *Well-weighed syllables: Elizabethan verse in classical metres* (1974) · J. W. H. Atkins, *English literary criticism: the Renascence* (1968) · C. Robinson and others, *A handefull of pleasant delites* (1584); new edn, ed. H. E. Rollins (1924); repr. (New York, 1965) · E. K. Chambers, *The Elizabethan stage*, 4 vols. (1923) · *DNB*

Webber, Charles Edmund (1838–1904), army officer and electrical engineer, born in Dublin on 5 September 1838, was the son of the Revd T. Webber of Leekfield, co. Sligo, and his wife, of Kellavil, Athy. After education at private schools and at the Royal Military Academy, Woolwich, he was commissioned lieutenant in the Royal Engineers on 20 April 1855. The demands of the Crimean War cut short his professional instruction at Chatham, and he was sent to the Belfast military district, being employed principally on the defences of Lough Swilly.

In September 1857 Webber was posted to the 21st company of Royal Engineers at Chatham, which was ordered to India, to join the Central India field force, commanded by Major-General Sir Hugh Rose. Brigadier C. S. Stuart's 1st brigade, to which Webber's company was attached, marched on Jhansi, which Sir Hugh Rose's column reached by another route. Webber was mentioned in dispatches for his services on this arduous march. He took part in the battle of the Betwa River on 1 April and in the assault of Jhansi on the 3rd, for which he was promoted. Webber took part in the operations attending the capture of Kunch (7 May), of Kalpi (23 May), and of Gwalior (19–20 June). He commanded a detachment of engineers which joined a flying column under Captain McMahon, 14th light dragoons, in Central India against Tantia Topi, Man Singh, and Firuz Shah, and was mentioned in dispatches. He continued in the field until April 1859, after which he was employed in the public works department, first at Gwalior and afterwards at Allahabad, until he returned to England in May 1860.

After service in the Brighton sub-district until October 1861, Webber was until 1866 assistant instructor in military surveying at Woolwich. He was promoted captain on 1 April 1862. During the latter part of the Austro-Prussian War in 1866 he was attached to the Prussian army to report on the engineering operations and military telegraphs. Various services on special missions abroad followed, with duty at the Curragh camp (1867–9). The 22nd company of Royal Engineers, of which he was in command at Chatham, was as a temporary expedient lent to the Post Office from 1869 to 1871 to assist in constructing and organizing the telegraph service. In May 1870 Webber took his headquarters to London, the rest of the company being distributed about the country. In 1871 the 34th company was added to Webber's command and stationed at Inverness. The total strength of the Royal Engineers at that time employed under the Post Office was six officers and 153 non-commissioned officers and men. The mileage both over and under ground constructed and rebuilt in 1871 was more than 1000 line miles and more than 3200 wire miles.

Webber, who was promoted major on 5 July 1872, was director of telegraphs with the southern army in the autumn manoeuvres of that year. In 1874, at his suggestion, the south of England was permanently assigned for the training and exercise of military telegraphists, five officers and 160 non-commissioned officers and men being employed by the Post Office there. The scheme proved of value both to the army and the Post Office. While employed under the Post Office he, with Colonel Sir Francis Bolton, founded in 1871 the Society of Telegraph Engineers (subsequently the Institution of Telegraph Engineers); he was treasurer and a member of council, and in 1882 was president.

Webber's reputation as an expert on military telegraphy was well established when in May 1879 he resumed active military service in the field. Accompanying Sir Garnet Wolseley to South Africa for the Anglo-Zulu War, he became assistant adjutant and quartermaster-general on the staff of the inspector-general of the lines of communication. He was stationed at Landmann's Drift. He afterwards took part in the operations against Sekukuni in the Transvaal, and was mentioned in dispatches.

Promoted regimental lieutenant-colonel on 24 January 1880, Webber on his return home was successively commanding Royal Engineers of the Cork district (July 1880 to February 1881), of the Gosport sub-district of the Portsmouth command (February 1881 to July 1883), and of the home district (July 1883 to September 1884). He was at Paris in 1881 as British commissioner at the electrical exhibition, and as member of the International Electrical Congress.

In 1882 Webber accompanied Sir Garnet Wolseley as assistant adjutant and quartermaster-general in the Egyptian campaign, and was in charge of telegraphs. He was present at the battle of Tell al-Kebir, and was mentioned in dispatches, being created a CB, and receiving the Mejidiye (third class). He was promoted brevet colonel on 24 January 1884, went again to Egypt in September, and served throughout the Nile expedition under Wolseley as assistant adjutant and quartermaster-general for telegraphs. On returning to Britain in 1885 he retired with the honorary rank of major-general. From that time he engaged in electrical pursuits in London. He was at first managing director, and later consulting electric adviser of the Anglo-American Brush Electric Light Corporation, and was thus associated with the early application of electric lighting in London and elsewhere. He was also consulting electric engineer of the City of London Pioneer Company and of the Chelsea Electric Supply Company. Webber married firstly, at Brighton on 28 May 1861, Alice Augusta Gertrude Hanbury Tracy (d. 25 Feb 1877), daughter of Thomas

Charles, second Lord Sudeley; second, he married at Neuchâtel, Switzerland, on 23 August 1877, Mrs Sarah Elizabeth Stainbank, *née* Gunn (*d.* 1907), widow of R. Stainbank. With his first wife he had three sons, and a daughter who died young. The eldest son, Major Raymond Sudeley Webber, served in the Royal Welch Fusiliers. Webber died suddenly at Cliftonville Hydropathic Hotel, Margate, of angina pectoris on 23 September 1904, and was buried at St Margaret's, Lee, Kent. Webber was a member of the Royal United Service Institution, of the Institution of Civil Engineers, an original member of the Société Internationale des Electriciens, and a fellow of the Society of Arts. Among many papers, chiefly on military and electrical subjects, were those on 'The organisation of the nation for defence' (United Service Institution, 1903); 'Telegraph tariffs' (Society of Arts, May 1884); and 'Telegraphs in the Nile expedition' (Society of Telegraph Engineers).

R. H. VETCH, *rev.* JAMES FALKNER

Sources Army List · The Times (24 Sept 1904) · Hart's Army List · W. Porter, *History of the corps of royal engineers*, 2 vols. (1889) · *Royal Engineers Journal* (1904) · E. W. C. Sandes, *The royal engineers in Egypt and the Sudan* (1937) · WWW · CGPLA Eng. & Wales (1904)
Archives UCL, letters to Edwin Chadwick
Wealth at death £6693 1s. 7d.: resworn probate, 13 Dec 1904, CGPLA Eng. & Wales

Webber, John (1751–1793), landscape and portrait painter, was born in London on 6 October 1751, the second and probably oldest surviving of six children of Abraham Wäber (1715–1780), a Swiss sculptor from Bern, Switzerland, who moved to London in the early 1740s, Anglicized his name, and married Mary Quant, a London girl, in 1744. In 1757 straitened circumstances led to Webber's dispatch to Bern, where he was raised by his unmarried aunt Rosina with the family of a celebrated *ébéniste*, Mathäus Funk, whose household she ran after the death in 1750 of Funk's wife Maria, another Wäber sister. Rosina recognized his talent and his artistic education was also financially supported by the Bern merchants' corporation, of which the Wäbers had been members from 1544. In 1767 Webber was apprenticed to Johann Ludwig Aberli (1723–1786), a leading Swiss topographical artist, who trained him in landscape watercolour drawing and may have introduced him to oils. In 1770 he left to study painting at the Académie Royale in Paris and with an introduction to the engraver, teacher, and art scholar Jean-Georges Wille (1715–1808), from whom he gained additional skills in recording scenes of rural life. In 1775 Webber returned to London and on 8 April enrolled as a student in the Royal Academy Schools. He also painted portraits and mythological subjects, the latter as house decorations for an unnamed architect who encouraged him to submit works for the Royal Academy exhibition in 1776. Two were views near Paris: one was entitled *Portrait of an Artist*, possibly a drawing of his sculptor brother, Henry. These impressed Daniel Solander, botanist on Captain Cook's first Pacific voyage (1768–71), who sought him out and recommended him to the Admiralty as draughtsman for Cook's impending third voyage in the *Resolution* and *Discovery*.

Webber was appointed at 100 guineas a year on 24 June 1776 and on 12 July he sailed from Plymouth in Cook's *Resolution*. His fame largely rests on his fine topographical and ethnographic work from the voyage, planned with Cook and with publication in view. Guided by the surgeon, William Anderson, he also drew natural history subjects (as did William Ellis, surgeon's mate and the other active draughtsman). He returned in October 1780, after Cook's and Anderson's deaths, with over 200 drawings and some twenty portraits in oils, showed a large selection to George III, and was reappointed by the Admiralty at £250 a year to redraw and direct the engraving of sixty-one plates, plus unsigned coastal views, in the official account. It appeared in June 1784 as *A Voyage to the Pacific Ocean …* (3 vols, ed. J. Douglas). Webber also painted other views for the Admiralty, his last payment being in July 1785. He also published two sets of voyage prints; four aquatints made by Marie Catherina Prestel (1787–88: one repeating his own etching of 1786), and sixteen soft-ground etchings by himself (1788–92) of which more were probably intended. The latter were pioneering, both in the medium used and as an artist's rather than publisher's selection. Reissued in aquatint from about 1808 as *Views in the South Seas*, they continued to sell into the 1820s.

In 1785 Webber also assisted his older friend P.-J. de Loutherbourg in designing scenery and costumes for the celebrated pantomime *Omai, or, A Trip Round the World* at the Theatre Royal, Covent Garden. Webber resumed exhibiting at the Royal Academy in 1784, with two China Sea views and *A party from … 'Resolution' … shooting sea-horses* [walrus] … 1778. In 1785 his first South Seas exhibit was a portrait of the Society Islands beauty Poetua, together with views of Macao and Krakatoa. These, except the China Sea pictures of 1784, are all in the National Maritime Museum (Admiralty House collection). All twenty-two exhibits from 1784 to 1787 were subjects from Cook's voyages, with seven more voyage subjects (to 1791) among the twenty-five pictures he exhibited from 1788 to 1792. A portrait excepted (1789), the rest were landscapes in Britain, France, the French and Swiss Alps and around Lake Como, resulting from tours probably encouraged by his artist friends Joseph Farington, Thomas Hearne, and the engraver William Byrne, another Wille pupil who made plates for all three official Cook voyage accounts. In 1786 Webber went to south Wales. In 1787 he visited Wille in Paris, then Lyons, Geneva, northern Italy, and the Alps, and his relations in Bern. In 1788 he returned to south Wales, possibly with the natural historian William Day, who accompanied him to Derbyshire in 1789. In 1790 and 1791 he revisited south and north Wales. He also sketched in the Lake District, possibly in Scotland, in the Isle of Wight and southern England (1792), and continued to paint portraits. Webber was lively, well-liked and professionally successful. He gained the approval and recommendation of Reynolds as a draughtsman (*c.*1781–1785), and was elected an associate of the Royal Academy in 1785 and Royal Academician in 1791. He died unmarried at his home, 312 Oxford Street, London—where he had moved in 1784 from 3 Bolsover Street—on 29 April 1793, of kidney disease, and left an estate of nearly £5000, with bequests to Swiss family members, servants, and friends, including Farington (one of his executors), Hearne, and Day. Webber had earlier presented his own South Seas ethnographic collection (101 items) to the Library of Bern, where it arrived in 1791. Much of his estate passed to his sculptor brother Henry (1754–1826), a pupil of John Bacon the elder. He also attended the Royal Academy Schools, was a Royal Academy silver and gold medallist in 1774 and 1779 (exh. 1775–6 and 1779), worked extensively for Josiah Wedgwood, and carved Garrick's monument in Westminster Abbey (1795–7).

All John Webber's known voyage work was catalogued by R. Joppien and B. Smith (1988), including his portraits of Cook. The half-length portrait of 1782, then privately owned, is now in the National Portrait Gallery of Australia, Canberra; the original bust length, painted at Cape Town in 1776, is in the National Portrait Gallery, London, and a small undated full length in the National Art Gallery, Wellington, New Zealand. A fourth no longer survives. A portrait of Webber by Johann Daniel Mottet (1812), from a contemporary miniature, is in the Historisches Museum, Bern, which also now holds his ethnographic collection (Joppien and Smith, pl. 202).

PIETER VAN DER MERWE

Sources R. Joppien and B. Smith, *The voyage of the 'Resolution' and 'Discovery', 1776–1780* (1988), vol. 3 of *The art of Captain Cook's voyages* (1985–8) • W. Hauptman and others, *John Webber, 1751–1793: Landschaftsmaler und Südseefahrer mit Captain Cook / Captain Cook's painter … Pacific voyager and landscape artist* (Bern, 1996) [exhibition catalogue, Kunstmuseum, Bern, and Whitworth Art Gallery, Manchester, 27 March – 15 Sept 1996] • R. Gunnis, *Dictionary of British sculptors, 1660–1851*, new edn (1968), 417–18 • Graves, *RA exhibitors*
Archives Historisches Museum, Bern, John Webber Ethnographic Collection (Die ethnographische Sammlung John Webbers)
Likenesses P.-J. de Loutherbourg, group portrait, 1776 (*A Winter Morning, with a Party Skating*), priv. coll.; engraved V. M. Picot as *Hyde Park* (London, 1784); republished as *Winter* (1794) • J. D. Mottet, portrait, 1812 (after contemporary miniature), Historisches Museum, Bern, Switzerland • H. Meyer, line engraving, 1820 (after J. Webber), NPG
Wealth at death approx. £5000

Webber, William Southcombe Lloyd (1914–1982), composer and organist, was born at 274 King's Road, Chelsea, London, on 11 March 1914, the son of William Charles Henry Webber, a self-employed plumber, and his wife, Mary Winifred Gittins. His father was a considerable authority on pipe-organ building, and from an early age the younger William was taken to see famous organs all over the country, developing an almost obsessional interest in the instrument. Aged thirteen he broadcast a recital from St Mary-le-Bow in London, and by the age of fourteen he was well known throughout the country as a recitalist. Webber won an organ scholarship to Mercer's School in 1925 and the Sir John Goss scholarship to the Royal College of Music in 1931. It was at this time that he changed his surname to Lloyd Webber, as there was another organist at the Royal College with a similar name. He studied composition with Ralph Vaughan Williams and the organ

with Dr Henry Ley. In 1933 he obtained the fellowship diploma of the Royal College of Organists, becoming the youngest person ever to do so.

Throughout his life Lloyd Webber maintained an interest in the organ, becoming successively organist at Christchurch, Newgate Street (1929–32), St Cyprian's, Clarence Gate (1933–9), All Saints, Margaret Street (1939–48), and Westminster Central Hall (1958–82). As a performer, he was much admired. A former curate of All Saints remarked that he was 'an organist of rare distinction. His playing had about it a vitality and colour and crispness which were unequalled' (Williams, 117). At the Royal College of Music he played Max Reger's fiendishly complicated *Phantasie und Fuge über B-A-C-H* from memory, only a week after purchasing a copy of the score. This raw talent never left him; as a reviewer in the *Musical Times* noted on one performance, 'Dr Lloyd Webber really must not give up the instrument that was his first enthusiasm … we cannot afford to spare native ability such as that' (Farmer). He gained his BMus in 1933 and his DMus from the London College of Music in 1938. In 1942 he married Jean Hermione Johnstone, a violinist and pianist who too was a pupil of Vaughan Williams. They met at All Saints, Margaret Street, where Jean was one of several sopranos who had been drafted in to sing in the choir in the wartime absence of the boys. They had two sons, Andrew (*b.* 1948), a popular composer, and Julian (*b.* 1951), a cellist. Life as a professional musician during the Second World War and in its immediate aftermath was difficult. Lloyd Webber was forced to supplement the meagre income he made from composing with various academic posts. From 1942 he taught as professor and examiner in theory and composition at the Royal College of Music, and he became the director of the London College of Music in 1964. He was appointed CBE for his services to music education in 1980.

Lloyd Webber wanted to make his living as a composer, but as he noted in an interview in the *Daily Mail* shortly before his death, 'it became basically a matter of finance. It's very difficult to make a living out of composition unless you succeed in the kind of work that Andrew does' (Gillard). As a composer, Lloyd Webber can be seen very much as a man in another age. His style is post-Romantic, echoing Rachmaninoff, Sibelius, and Franck, but never mere pastiche. Ironically, his own harmonic language is, in places, almost as daring as that of composers who were experimenting with the serialist and avante-garde techniques that he deplored, and yet he felt his style to be at odds with what was expected of composers at the time. His unwillingness to promote himself as a composer, in an era that heralded musicians such as Benjamin Britten, Michael Tippett, and William Walton, meant that most of his music did not receive the attention that it deserved until after his death. There were too many exceptional British composers active at the time for the music of the rather reserved Lloyd Webber to make any real impact. The reviewer and critic Felix Aprahamian noted, 'It was the same in France. We've all heard of Debussy and Ravel, but contemporary with these were at least twenty marvellous French composers … too many of them to find room at the top' (Campbell, 4). Lloyd Webber took each rejection as a profound and bitter blow. He all but ceased composing between 1960 and 1980, but, as the small number of works that date from this period demonstrate, the criticism of his music that he so painfully endured did not diminish his ability to compose, but rather his desire to do so.

At heart, Lloyd Webber was a miniaturist. He had a great capacity for expressing himself in a short space of time, and often much emotion is distilled in brief, intense statements. This leads some way towards an understanding of the brevity of much of his output, which consists largely of chamber music, songs, and works for solo instruments. Among his orchestral music, the tone poem *Aurora* (1951), depicting the arrival of the Roman goddess of the dawn, is his only real symphonic statement. Lloyd Webber seems to have been proud of this piece, given that he would talk about it with family and friends—something that he rarely did in the case of any of his other works. There are a large number of sacred works, comprising short anthems, motets, and canticles and two settings of the ordinary of the mass—the *Missa princeps pacis* (1962), written for the choir of Westminster Cathedral, and the *Missa sanctae Mariae Magdelenae* (1979). In addition to this, there are three larger-scale oratorios, of which *St Francis of Assisi* (1951) is of note.

Lloyd Webber died at Beaumont House, Beaumont Street, Westminster, London on 29 October 1982, having suffered a heart attack; his wife, Jean, survived him. With him died virtually all knowledge of his ability as a musician and composer, save for that of his family and a few close friends. By the beginning of the twenty-first century his music had begun to undergo something of a renaissance, and it was only posthumously that he came to be regarded by some as 'One of the finest all-round musicians this country has produced this century. A fine and refined composer whose contribution … was of considerable significance' (Hesford).   PETER PARSHALL

Sources L. Wolz, 'The music of William Lloyd Webber', *American Organist*, 25/2 (1991), 58–60 · M. Campbell, *Married to music* (2001) · Gillard, *Daily Mail* (29 Jan 1980) · B. Hesford, *Musical Opinion*, 106 (1982), 65 · A. Farmer, *MT*, 98 (1957), 147 · H. A. Williams, *Someday I'll find you* (1982) · b. cert. · d. cert.
Archives SOUND BL NSA, oral history interview
Wealth at death under £25,000: probate, 31 Jan 1983, *CGPLA Eng. & Wales*

Webb-Johnson. For this title name *see* Johnson, Alfred Edward Webb-, Baron Webb-Johnson (1880–1958).

Weber, Carl Maria Friedrich Ernst von (1786–1826), composer and conductor, was born probably on 18 November (baptized 20 November) 1786 in Eutin, Holstein, the ninth of the ten children of the composer Franz Anton von Weber (1734?–1812), and the first with his second wife, Genovefa Brenner (1764–1798), an actress and singer. The baronial 'von' seems to have been misappropriated by his father, and was used in good faith by the composer. He was a sickly child who retained all his life a

Carl Maria Friedrich Ernst von Weber (1786–1826), by unknown artist, 1826

frail form and a pronounced limp. In 1817 he married the singer Caroline Brandt; they had three children, the second of whom, Max Maria, became his father's first major biographer.

Weber's European fame dated from the triumphant première of *Der Freischütz* in Berlin in 1821. By 1824 five different versions were playing in London, though these were travesties, burlesques, or other distortions. Nevertheless, the work's popularity led Charles Kemble, the manager of Covent Garden (where one of the versions was staged), to offer him a commission for an opera. Now mortally ill with tuberculosis, Weber accepted in the hope of making some money to keep his family after his death. He was further persuaded to accept and to go to England to conduct by his doctor's advice that he had only months to live, and hoped to supplement Kemble's niggardly offer of £500 plus expenses with concerts in wealthy London homes. He was in ignorance of the conditions of the London stage that made impossible the production of a continuously composed German opera such as he was pioneering. He realized his mistake only when he received the first drafts from his librettist, the pantomime writer James Robinson Planché, who persuaded him that an entertainment with lavish scenery and stage machinery, star singing, copious dialogue, and only an incidental role for music was what the English understood by opera. To help his task, he took 153 English lessons, and was not only able to express himself clearly ('my little bit of English is incredibly useful to me', he later wrote to his wife, Caroline) but made very few errors in setting the text of *Oberon*. He was also commissioned by George Thomson of

Edinburgh to contribute to the publishing venture of setting British folk-songs, and he wrote *Ten Scottish Folksongs* in 1825.

Weber arrived in England on 3 March 1826, and was made comfortable in Sir George Smart's house in Great Portland Street. On the 6th he visited Covent Garden, where the audience recognized him and cheered him repeatedly ('Are these the *cold* English welcoming me?', he wrote to Caroline). Kemble further commissioned him to conduct some concerts, one of them of selections from *Der Freischütz* (a lithograph by J. Hayter shows him in three positions and using a roll of paper, as was the custom).

The first of sixteen *Oberon* rehearsals was on the 9th, and after various difficulties, caused chiefly by the singers, the first of twelve sold-out performances took place on 12 April. It was a triumph, but the effort brought Weber's health even lower. Despite all Smart's solicitude, and the attentions of Londoners who had observed his weakness with sympathy and admiration, he continued to sink. The late, cold spring and thick fogs hastened his decline. He gave many piano recitals in aristocratic houses, though often barely able to stand or get his breath, and managed to write some small pieces for which he was asked, including, as his last composition, an English setting of Thomas Moore's 'From Chindara's warbling fount'. His letters home are cheerful, but his diary betrays his weakness and fright. His last concert was at a benefit for one of his *Oberon* singers, Mary Anne Paton, on 30 May. He insisted on planning to set off for home on 6 June, but was found dead on the morning of the 5th at 91 Great Portland Street, London.

The death certificate gave as the cause of death tuberculosis of the lungs and many secondary conditions. The body was embalmed and taken in a solemn procession on 21 June to Moorfields Chapel, where it rested until it was returned, largely at the insistence of Richard Wagner, to Dresden in 1844. JOHN WARRACK

Sources M. M. von Weber, *Carl Maria von Weber* (1864–6) • J. Warrack, *Carl Maria von Weber* (1968) • C. von Weber, ed., *Reise-Briefe von Carl Maria von Weber an seine Gattin Carolina* (1886) • C. M. von Weber, diary, Deutsche Staatsbibliothek, Berlin • D. Reynolds, ed., *Weber in London, 1826* (1976) • J. R. Planché, *The recollections and reflections of J. R. Planché*, 2 vols. (1872) • F. A. Kemble, *Record of a girlhood*, 3 vols. (1878) • *Leaves from the journals of Sir George Smart*, ed. H. B. Cox and C. L. E. Cox (1907) • *Quarterly Musical Magazine and Review*, 8 (1826), 121 • review of *Oberon*, *Literary Gazette* (15 April 1826), 236–8 • review of *Oberon*, *The Harmonicon*, 4 (1826), 107–8 • materials, BL, Dept of MSS

Archives BL | BL, Smart MSS

Likenesses J. Cawse, portrait, 1826, Royal College of Music, London • pencil sketch, 1826, Royal Society of Musicians, London [*see illus.*] • J. Hayter, engraving, Royal College of Music, London • J. Kendrick, bust, Royal College of Music, London • sketch, Royal College of Music, London

Weber, Henry William (1783–1818), literary scholar and secretary, was born on 22 September 1783 at St Petersburg, the second of three children of H. W. Weber (*d.* 1786), merchant and commissioner for trade, and Dorothy Foster (*d.* 1816), relative of Henry Lord Holland and niece of Joseph Foster-Barham MP. Weber's father was a native of Neustadt, Westphalia, and a member of the Moravian Brethren community in St Petersburg. Most of Weber's German and English relatives belonged to the Moravian communities at Herrnhut in Saxony and at Bedford and Fulneck near Leeds in England.

In 1795 Weber was briefly enrolled at an élite Moravian boarding-school at Uhyst in Saxony, before the family left Germany for England in 1797. In 1803–4 he enrolled in medicine at the University of Edinburgh, continuing his studies at the University of Halle in 1805 and the University of Jena in 1806. After the university at Jena was temporarily closed in 1806 following the defeat of the Prussian army by Napoleonic forces, he returned to Edinburgh to study. From 1807 to 1814 he worked as an amanuensis and secretary, primarily for Sir Walter Scott, and it was during this period that Weber's literary and scholarly career flourished, with all his published works dating from these years.

Scott described Weber as 'a man of very superior attainments, an excellent linguist and geographer, and a remarkable antiquary' (*DNB*). He was widely read in medieval romance literature, both British and European, and had personally studied more than three-quarters of the fifty-six Middle English romances known about 1800 (Gamerschlag, 212). In 1808 he published an edition of *The Battle of Floddon Field: a Poem of the Sixteenth Century*, celebrating a historical event that Scott recounted in the sixth canto of *Marmion* (1808). This was followed by his *Metrical Romances of the Thirteenth, Fourteenth, and Fifteenth Centuries*, with introduction, notes, and glossary (3 vols., 1810), described by Southey as 'admirably edited' (*Selections from the Letters*, 2.308) and considered by modern scholars as Weber's major work (Mitchell, 8–10).

Weber's next publication, *Dramatic Works of John Ford*, with introduction and explanatory notes (2 vols., 1811), was not of such high quality and aroused a storm of angry comment, including pamphlets by Octavius Gilchrist, G. D. Whittington, and the Revd John Mitford. The criticism stemmed from the fact that Weber was not skilled in early modern English literature and had not collated the early editions of the plays. Similar problems beset his *Works of Beaumont and Fletcher*, with introduction and explanatory notes (14 vols., 1812), which Scott, whose own annotated edition had supplied the most valuable notes, acknowledged to have been 'carelessly done'. However, Dyce, in his *Works of Beaumont and Fletcher* (1843, 1.iii) considered it as 'on the whole the best edition of the dramatists which had yet appeared'.

Weber's next publication was *Tales of the East; comprising the most popular romances of oriental origin and the best imitations by European authors* (3 vols., 1812). He also edited *A Genealogical History of the Earldom of Sutherland* in 1813. In 1814, in collaboration with Robert Jamieson, Weber produced another significant work of scholarship in *Illustrations of Northern Antiquities from the Earlier Teutonic and Scandinavian Romances*. At one time the two scholars had intended to establish a new periodical devoted to 'ancient Romance and Antiquities in general' (H. Weber to

F. Douce, 31 Jan 1810), but lack of support forced them to compromise on this one-volume collection of medieval European romances, illuminated by interpretative essays. Scott contributed an abstract of the Old Icelandic *Eyrbyggja saga*, taken from Thorkelin's Latin edition and translation of 1787. Weber's contribution to the volume included a historical sketch of medieval Germanic poetry and romance and English summary translations of *Das Nibelungenlied* and *Das Heldenbuch*. His essay on medieval romance in Germany and Scandinavia was one of the sources of Scott's later 'Essay on romance' (1824).

Scott's attitude to Weber seems to have been ambivalent; he described him as 'an excellent and affectionate creature' but 'a violent Jacobin', and Scott admitted he used to taunt him about his political views. He also wrote that Weber was 'afflicted with partial insanity especially if he used strong liquors' (*Journal*, 110). The Scott family, with whom Weber often dined, liked his appearance and manners, and enjoyed his conversation. In early 1814, however, Weber apparently suffered a breakdown while resident in Scott's household, which brought his career as the latter's secretary to an abrupt end. At the close of a day's work in the same room as his employer, he suddenly appeared to become mentally disturbed, produced a pair of loaded pistols, and challenged Scott to a duel. Scott managed to calm Weber down, even to the point of inviting him to dine with the family that evening. Surreptitiously, however, he had made arrangements for Weber to be restrained and straitjacketed. After this the two men never again met, although they corresponded, but Scott apparently made a substantial contribution to Weber's support in the mental asylums in which he spent a good part of the rest of his life. This breakdown was apparently in part a consequence of what Weber called a 'fever', which may have come on after a strenuous walking tour of the highlands, for which he had been hired to act as a guide for a rich Jamaican named Johnstone. The two men had become very drunk at the duke of Sutherland's Dunrobin Castle, an incident that is likely to have embarrassed Scott and caused him to restrict Weber's drinking in what was probably a humiliating way, further contributing to his eventual breakdown.

In March 1814 Weber returned with his mother to the Moravian community at Fulneck. He later accompanied his sister and her children to London, doubtless with the intention of working in libraries there, but, despite his family connections, Weber was unable to secure any regular employment, and he eventually returned to Fulneck and then to York. The loss of his mother in 1816 compounded his mental and physical deterioration, and on 17 October 1816 he was admitted to the York Lunatic Asylum. There he died on 25 March 1818 of an epileptic attack after suffering prolonged atrophy and dementia.

MARGARET CLUNIES ROSS and AMANDA J. COLLINS

Sources K. Gamerschlag, 'Henry Weber: medieval scholar, poet, and secretary to Walter Scott', *Studies in Scottish Literature*, 25 (1990), 202–17 • *The letters of Sir Walter Scott*, ed. H. J. C. Grierson and others, centenary edn, 12 vols. (1932–79), vols. 2–4, 12–13 • *The journal of Sir Walter Scott*, ed. W. E. K. Anderson (1972), 109–10 • J. G. Lockhart, *The life of Sir Walter Scott*, [new edn] (1893), 251–2 • W. M. Parker, 'A Scott amanuensis: Henry Weber and his highland tour', *The Scotsman* (29 Nov 1937) • A. Chalmers, ed., *Appendix to the general biographical dictionary* (1820) • J. Mitchell, *Scott, Chaucer and medieval romance: a study in Sir Walter Scott's indebtedness to the literature of the middle ages* (1987) • H. Weber, letter to Francis Douce, 31 Jan 1810, Bodl. Oxf., MS Douce d. 22 • *Selections from the letters of Robert Southey*, ed. J. W. Warter, 2 (1856)

Weber, (Carl Emil) Otto (1832–1888), painter and engraver, was born on 17 October 1832 in Berlin, son of Wilhelm Weber, a merchant of that city, and his wife, Henrietta. He studied under the animal painter Carl Steffeck and was much influenced by Eugen Krüger, another animal painter, from Düsseldorf. He settled in Paris where he worked under the neo-classicist Thomas Couture. His reputation was made by his skilful paintings in oil and watercolour of landscapes and animals; these were much admired and fetched high prices. In 1864 he exhibited at the Paris Salon for the first time, winning a medal in that year and again in 1869.

On the outbreak of the Franco-Prussian War in 1870 Weber left France for Milan and Rome, where he lived for two years. In 1872 he moved to London where, in a studio at Brignall House, Greville Road, St John's Wood, he had stables and could work from live animals as models. He exhibited regularly at the Royal Academy between 1874 and his death, and in 1876 he was elected an associate of the Society of Painters in Water Colours. He also became a member of the Institute of Painters in Oil Colours. For Queen Victoria, Weber painted a portrait of Prince Christian Victor (exh. RA, 1874) and two of her Skye terriers (exh. RA, 1876; Royal Collection). Probably his best picture was *The First Snow on the Alp*, now in the Melbourne Gallery, New South Wales. Weber travelled in the south and west of England, in the Scottish highlands (1876–7), in north-west France and Italy (1877–8). He died at 32 Great Ormond Street, Queen Square, Holborn, London, after a long illness, on 23 December 1888. On 20 May 1889 more than sixty of his remaining finished pictures and studies were sold at Christies.   DELIA MILLAR

Sources J. L. Roget, *A history of the 'Old Water-Colour' Society*, 2 vols. (1891) • *DNB* • Bénézit, *Dict.*, 3rd edn • d. cert. • *CGPLA Eng. & Wales* (1889)

Wealth at death £1028 10s. 0d.: administration, 27 April 1889, *CGPLA Eng. & Wales*

Webster. For this title name *see* Fox, Elizabeth Vassall, Lady Holland [Elizabeth Vassall Webster, Lady Webster] (1771?–1845).

Webster family (*per. c.*1650–1836), gentry, of Battle Abbey, originated in Derbyshire. Its first notable member, **Sir Godfrey Webster** (*c.*1648–1720), was born in Chesterfield but moved to London about 1663 as apprentice to his uncle Peter Webster, a prominent member of the Clothworkers' Company. Godfrey was admitted to the company in 1670 and was to become its elected master in 1695. In 1672 he married Abigail (*bap.* 1651, *d.* 1704?), daughter and coheir of the merchant adventurer Thomas Jordan of

Stratford-at-Bow and The Mere in Staffordshire, and established himself in Fenchurch Street and at Nelmes in Hornchurch, Essex. Webster was often described as a packer, and acquired many of his interests in shipping and property as the assignee of bankrupt estates; his holdings included the Bear Quay Coffee House in Thames Street. His loans to William III were rewarded with a lucrative contract to supply clothing to the army, probably the foundation of his great wealth. He was knighted in 1708, and by 1710 held sufficient stock in the Bank of England to qualify as a governor. At his death on 16 January 1720, in addition to his landed estate in London, Essex, and Kent, he left £23,000 in stock and displayed his wealth in charitable bequests, including £700 for twenty poor clothworkers of London, £500 for dissenting teachers, and £1100 for the poor of Chesterfield, where his sister Ann Phipps still lived, married to a shoemaker.

Sir Godfrey's son **Sir Thomas Webster**, first baronet (1676–1751), who entered the Middle Temple in 1697, made the greater part of his own fortune before he was thirty. He pursued an active mercantile trade, investing in shipping, property, a distillery in Ratcliffe, east of London, and a share in the waterworks at Toledo on the Tagus. In 1700 he purchased a country estate—Copthall in Waltham, Essex—from Charles Sackville, sixth earl of Dorset, for £13,500, and successfully assumed the aspects of gentility. On 21 May 1703 he secured a baronetcy in return for a contribution of £1095 to the garrison of Ulster; he became sheriff of Essex in the same year. Thomas's frequent absences in the country required his father to serve as deputy to his son when the latter was elected master of the Clothworkers, at the age of twenty-seven, in 1704. He and his father speculated in the supply of hemp for the navy, but seem to have had the confidence of the Treasury: in 1711 Sir Thomas acted as the spokesman of the navy creditors, and in 1713 cooperated with the commissioners to break a rival syndicate which was exacting much higher prices. He was appointed verderer of Waltham Forest for life in 1718 and on his father's death a deputy lieutenant. From this base Sir Thomas began the Websters' long participation in national politics: a whig, he sat in three parliaments between 1705 and 1727 as MP for Colchester, a constituency where his background in the cloth trade and strong sympathy with nonconformity counted as considerable assets.

In 1701 Sir Thomas married Jane (*bap.* 1682, *d.* 1760), daughter of Edward Cheeke, citizen and soap maker of London, and of Sandford Orcas in Somerset. In 1719 Jane inherited her father's property and the vast estates of her maternal grandfather, Henry Whistler (1634–1719) of Abchurch Lane and Epsom, including a lease of the manor of Combe in Hampshire, property in Londonderry, a share of the waterworks at York, and coal wharves near the Tower among extensive London property; the sale of his bank stock alone had realized over £30,000. A year later Thomas inherited his own father's estate and began to invest heavily in the West End; he bought a house in St James's Street (later the site of Boodle's) for £6000 from Charles Seymour, sixth duke of Somerset, and in 1722 a

house on the north side of Jermyn Street, which he proceeded to demolish and rebuild at a cost of over £2000.

Sir Thomas's decision to turn his attention to investment in the weald of east Sussex cannot yet be explained. He began his campaign of purchase in 1721 with the Battle Abbey estate, which included four advowsons and 8000 acres, and moved on to the Bodiam Castle and Robertsbridge Abbey estates; in the course of twelve years he spent over £96,000 in the county. Within three years of his arrival he joined with its established landowners in an attempt to revive the iron industry of the weald, going into partnership with Lord Ashburnham at Beech Furnace in Battle; in 1727 he began to exploit the works at Robertsbridge, and in 1733 took a lease of Etchingham Forge. Sir Thomas's new estates were particularly rich in timber—sales of underwood alone could make £1000 a year—a resource which was to cushion his descendants from the consequences of their profligacy.

The 1720s represent the high water mark of Sir Thomas's career. As well as his Sussex purchases, the Webster and Whistler estates remained largely intact; in 1721 he was able to bestow a dowry of £20,000 on the marriage of his fifteen-year-old daughter, Abigail, to Edward Northey of Compton Bassett near Calne. By an astute series of financial dealings, in the 1730s Webster began to convert the family's scattered inherited estates into a consolidated holding in the weald, and to redeem, by transfers of land, the generous legacies that his father had charged on the estate. In 1733 arrangements were made to sell off the Whistler estate to reduce the running debt of £54,000. In 1739 Sir Thomas acquired a parliamentary seat for his heir **Sir Whistler Webster**, second baronet (1709–1779) by exchanging Copthall for the East Grinstead property of Edward Conyers, the sitting member, and at the end of his life was so sure of his position that he flatly refused to yield the seat to the influence of the prince of Wales.

With the sale of Copthall the family had unequivocally settled in Sussex, where Sir Thomas indulged his antiquarian interests by making his country home within the dilapidated grandeur of Battle Abbey; in 1743 Jeremiah Milles found that he had made 'a habitable, though not a handsome, house out of some of the apartments' (Farrant, 93). A year after Sir Thomas's death Horace Walpole observed 'the grounds and what has been the park lie in a vile condition' (Cleveland, 207), and his companion mused on the opportunities lost for gothick improvement. As late as 1744, when the Sussex estate alone produced an annual income of over £4000, Sir Thomas drew up a scheme to deal with the difficulties of managing what was still a large and dispersed estate 'which my age makes uneasy to me, and the necessary attendance upon it impossible' (E. Sussex RO, Lewes, RAF 16/16). He proposed the further sale of outlying branches 'that give trouble and don't add to the figure and weight of a family' to reduce the mortgage on the home estate. His intentions had been substantially fulfilled at his death on 30 or 31 May 1751.

After contesting Hastings unsuccessfully in 1734, Whistler Webster was returned in 1741 unopposed at East Grinstead. Voting consistently against the government, he was classed as an opposition whig in 1747. He did not stand at the general election of 1761, and began the disposal of the East Grinstead property, a process completed by his nephew. In 1766 he married Martha Nairn (1730–1810), daughter of the dean of Battle, some twenty-one years his junior; two years later, he pleaded ill health to decline an invitation from Lord Pelham and the duke of Richmond to represent Sussex. He died childless on 22 September 1779, and the survival of his widow for over thirty years was to blight the family and the estate. The baronetcy passed to his brother Godfrey Webster of Nelmes, who enjoyed his inheritance for less than six months; on Godfrey's death the title passed to the eldest son (also Godfrey) of his marriage to Elizabeth Gilbert.

Sir Godfrey Webster, fourth baronet (*bap.* 1749, *d.* 1800) brought a 'gloomy and at times sullen' (*Journal of Lady Holland*, 1.xiii) eccentricity to the baronetcy, to which he succeeded on 6 May 1780. The estates he inherited remained ample but heavily encumbered by three generations of portions and bequests. He continued to liquidate property in East Grinstead and Worth, sought additional profit from the gunpowder mills in the town of Battle, and on 27 June 1786 made a strategic marriage to Elizabeth Vassall [*see* Fox, Elizabeth Vassall (1771?–1845)], over twenty years his junior and the sole heir to her family's rich holdings in the West Indies. Webster would be required to assume his wife's surname on her father's death as a condition of inheriting his plantations. The marriage temporarily mended his finances, but was tempestuously repented by both parties. Elizabeth was soon to write that she longed to be free from the 'oftimes frantic temper of the man to whom I had the calamity to be united' (ibid., 1.6). Unable to evict Sir Godfrey's aunt Martha, life tenant of Battle Abbey, the couple were obliged to live in relative obscurity at Rose Green nearby; touring the abbey in 1788, John Byng was told that 'Sir Godfrey longs to succeed the old lady, that he may entirely pull it all down' (Andrews, 121). Expensive tours of the continent, undertaken as a sop to Elizabeth's pursuit of style, brought an affair (and perhaps her second child) with Lord Henry Spencer, a daughter with Sir Godfrey's political patron Thomas Pelham, and ultimately her scandalous elopement with Henry Richard Fox, third Lord Holland. Sir Godfrey instituted a divorce and on 4 July 1797 Elizabeth recorded that 'My wretched marriage was annulled by Parliament. On the fifth I signed a deed by which I made over my whole fortune to Sir G W for our joint lives' (*Journal of Lady Holland*, 1.147). Reverting to his original name Webster might have made a new start while sinking her wealth in his estates; instead he took to the tables and, as depression gathered over him, twice tried to end his life with laudanum. On 3 June 1800 he had success with a pistol.

In politics Webster was a client of the Pelhams, who secured him four undistinguished parliamentary years as the member for Seaford; in 1790 he lost the seat in a disputed election. When the Pelham interest promised him the next vacancy, he repaid their patronage with the European travels that kept him out of the running for six years. On his return to England he was found a seat at Wareham. His conduct in parliament showed 'an indecision of purpose, almost verging at times upon insanity' (*Journal of Lady Holland*, 1.xvi). He is not known to have voted more than twice in the four years before his death, and then, erratic to the last, he joined the minority who intended to promote Charles James Fox, the uncle of his wife's seducer, to the committees for public accounts and the abolition of sinecures.

Sir Godfrey Vassall Webster, fifth baronet (1789–1836) succeeded to the baronetcy at the age of ten, when his mother found him 'clever but … not handsome …, cold in his disposition, and taught by his father to be a boaster' (HoP, *Commons, 1790–1820*, 5.500). His great-aunt Martha had allowed the abbey to fall in ruins about her, and his income from land had not recovered from the extravagances of his parents. Her death coincided with his majority and Sir Godfrey, already known as 'one of the greatest blackguards in London' (ibid.) and the model for the arrogant and selfish Buchanan in Lady Caroline Lamb's *Glenarvon*, placed financial recovery in the hands of his stewards. Their efforts—£130,000 was raised from the sale of timber, advowsons, and property at Fairlight, Ewhurst, and Robertsbridge—were more than matched by Sir Godfrey's capacity to spend. He began a major programme of restoration at Battle Abbey, to which he brought his bride, Charlotte Adamson (1791–1867), whom he had married by special licence at her father's house at 25 Hill Street, Berkeley Square, on 22 August 1814. He gained no significant resources from the match, which, if it had begun in love, ended in recrimination; formal provisions for separation and the maintenance of their four children were concluded in 1828. Meantime Webster's precarious financial position was marked by the appointment of trustees and a flight from creditors in 1819, the construction and precipitate sale of his luxury yacht *Scorpion*, part share in a string of racehorses, ferocious gambling, and too close association with the extravagances of the prince regent. In 1835 he resorted to selling the Battle Abbey muniments (subsequently acquired by the Huntington Library, San Marino) to raise £300, and at his death a year later was found to have disposed of all his own property and to have exchanged his life interest in the estate for an annuity which died with him.

The final strain on Webster's finances was his persistent attempt to build a political career. In 1812 his election for the county was in the tory interest, in which he 'most stupidly squandered between £2,000 and £3,000 on the precious mobbility of Brighton and Lewes' (HoP, *Commons, 1790–1820*, 5.500). He immediately upset his supporters by voting with their opponents. Six years later he was re-elected on the same platform and promptly resumed erratic support for liberal measures. In 1820 leading men in both east and west Sussex, exasperated by his unreliability and deranged personality, forced him to withdraw, unable, as he said, to find the money to defeat a coalition determined 'that Sir Godfrey Webster should never sit again for Sussex' (*An Account of the Sussex Election*, 86). Having established himself as a parliamentarian who respected neither party loyalty nor consistent personal principle, he none the less attempted to regain his county seat in 1826 and 1831, and on three occasions unsuccessfully contested Chichester borough as a radical. He maintained his seat on the county bench, and his position was to put him in danger during the agricultural disturbances of the 1830s. He was manhandled by the Swing rioters at Herstmonceaux when attempting to calm a meeting at the Woolpack Inn, and was regarded as a marked man. 'How are you armed? Barkers?' asked a fellow magistrate. 'Pooh,' he replied, pulling from his pockets a couple of hog-knives, 'these are the tools—they never misfire' (Hills, 223–4).

Unable to sustain his ruinous rate of expenditure, Webster retired from county life and his last years saw him cruising impecuniously between the ports of southern England and the Channel Islands. In November 1835 and in failing health he took up residence at the York Hotel in Albemarle Street, where he died on 17 July 1836, his personal estate insufficient to pay the bill, which was settled by his family to obtain the release of his body.

The naval career of Sir Godfrey's eldest son, Sir Godfrey Vassall Webster, sixth baronet (1815–1853), was not disturbed by his inheritance of the estate; his service on the Mediterranean station included action aboard HMS *Thunderer* at the siege of Acre in 1840. His four brothers' demands for their portions as they came of age were met by further mortgages, which marriage in 1851 to a Jamaican heiress enabled him to discharge before his death. His brother Sir Augustus (1819–1886) inherited Battle, which he sold four years later to Lord Harry Vane for £114,000, and moved to East Tytherley in Hampshire. His son Sir Augustus (1864–1923), brought up in the nursery with the maxim 'when Gussy buys back Battle' (Behrens, 117) and whose means had been transformed by marriage to Mabel Crossley, the daughter of a Halifax carpet millionaire, fulfilled the prophecy in 1901 when, on the death of the duchess of Cleveland, he gave £200,000 for the estate, consisting of 6000 acres with a rent roll of £5500 and timber valued at over £42,000; the abbey was let and the family eventually settled at Powdermill House in Battle. Most of the outlying portions of the estate were sold between 1902 and 1912. Sir Augustus's son Godfrey, a lieutenant in the Grenadier Guards, was killed at Ypres on 4 August 1917 and on his father's death in 1923 the estate passed to his sister Lucy Webster (1900–1989), who remained in the jurisdiction of the court of protection for much of her adult life. Since 1922 the abbey has been let to a private school for girls. Gutted by a fire in 1931, the house and ruins were restored by Sir Harold Breakspear. The abbey and the site of the battle of Hastings were sold to the Department of the Environment in 1976.

Sir Thomas Webster had brought to the weald of Sussex a scale of wealth that could never have been made in it. His son made no effort to match his spectacular purchases, and their successors pillaged the natural resources of their inheritance to finance their political aspirations

and unremitting profligacy. Yet the estate was sufficient to withstand the assaults of its owners, and to keep alive hopes of the renewal of the house of Webster. As his widowed and childless sister-in-law wrote to Sir Augustus (*d.* 1886) in 1858, after the storm of extravagance had forced the sale of the abbey itself, marriage would enable him 'to found a family on different principles—refresh and regenerate our name—in short dear Augustus—to do as your ancestors have *not* done!' (E. Sussex RO, Lewes, Battle Abbey archives, BAT 4825). But their brief realization perished on the western front with his grandson, the last Godfrey Webster. CHRISTOPHER WHITTICK

Sources J. A. Brent, *A catalogue of the Battle Abbey estate archives* (1973) · Battle Abbey archives, Hunt. L. · HoP, *Commons, 1690–1715* · HoP, *Commons, 1715–54* · HoP, *Commons, 1754–90* · HoP, *Commons, 1790–1820* · Clothworkers' Company archives · F. W. Ticehurst, *Gleanings respecting Battel and its abbey by a native* (1841) · Duchess of Cleveland, *History of Battle Abbey* (1877) · L. Boys Behrens, *Battle Abbey under thirty-nine kings* (1937) · *The journal of Elizabeth, Lady Holland, 1791–1811*, ed. earl of Ilchester [G. S. Holland Fox-Strangways], 2 vols. (1908) · S. R. Keppel, *The sovereign lady: a life of Elizabeth Vassall* (1974) · B. Dolan, *Ladies of the grand tour* (2001) · J. Gross, ed., *Byron's 'corbeau blanc': the life and letters of Lady Melbourne* (1997) · W. H. Hills, *History of East Grinstead* (1906) · J. W. Ward, ed., *Letters to 'Ivy'* (1905), 162 · C. Bruyn Andrews, ed., *The Torrington diaries* (1934) · J. H. Farrant, *Sussex depicted: views and descriptions, 1600–1800*, Sussex RS, 85 (2001) · *An account of the Sussex election, held at Chichester, March 13, 1820* (1820) · *GM*, 2nd ser., 6 (1836), 426–7 · E. Sussex RO, RAF 16/16 [Webster papers among the archive of Raper & Fovargue of Battle, solicitors] · T. Thorpe, *Descriptive catalogue of the … muniments of Battle Abbey* (1835) · C. Whittick, 'Wealden iron in California', *Wealden Iron*, 2nd ser., 12 (1992), 29–62 · *The Times* (22 Nov 1830); (24–5 Nov 1830); (30 Dec 1830) · T. Geering, *Our Sussex parish* (1884), 74–5 · will, PRO, PROB 11/584 [Sir Godfrey Webster, *d.* 1720]

Archives BL, corresp. with duke of Newcastle; corresp. with second earl of Chichester, Add. MSS 32724–33126, *passim* [Whistler Webster (*d.* 1779)] · E. Sussex RO, manorial records and estate papers · E. Sussex RO, title deeds, manorial records, estate management papers, genealogical, personal and public office papers, household accounts · Hunt. L., deeds, manorial records, family and estate papers, incl. records of Battle Abbey before its dissolution

Likenesses English school, portrait, *c.*1725 (Whistler Webster), English Heritage · English school, portrait, *c.*1730 (Thomas Webster), English Heritage · English school, portrait, *c.*1760 (Whistler Webster), English Heritage · L. Gauffier, portrait, 1791 (Sir Godfrey Webster), English Heritage · P. Lely, portrait (Godfrey Webster), English Heritage · follower of G. Stuart, portrait (Sir Godfrey Webster), English Heritage · follower of J. M. Wright, portrait (Thomas Webster), English Heritage · nineteen family portraits, English Heritage

Wealth at death Sir Godfrey Webster: bequests of personal estate alone over £53,000: will, PRO, PROB 11/584 · Sir Thomas Webster: in scheme for its resettlement 1744, valued Sussex estate (at twenty-six years' purchase) at £126,000, remaining estate at £35,000, and plate, jewels, and furniture at £4000: E. Sussex RO, RAF 16 · Sir Godfrey Webster: considerable; allegedly £7000 p.a. income from former wife Elizabeth Vassall: E. Sussex RO, BAT 4880 · Sir Godfrey Webster: insolvent · Sir Whistler Webster: sister Abigail Thomas suggested assets value £68,000 deriving from will of grandfather Henry Whistler had been vested in Sir Whistler between 1733 and 1751: Hunt. L., HEH BA 75/8

Webster, Alexander (1707–1784), Church of Scotland minister, was born in Edinburgh, the son of **James Webster**

Alexander Webster (1707–1784), by David Martin

(1658/9–1720), Church of Scotland minister, and his third wife, Agnes, daughter of Alexander Menzies of Culter in Lanarkshire. Alexander's father studied at St Andrews University but left the university without taking his MA degree. He joined the covenanters and was twice imprisoned for his religious opinions. In 1688 he was appointed Presbyterian minister of Liberton (near Edinburgh), and was translated first to Whitekirk in 1691 and then in 1693 to the collegiate church, Edinburgh, where he remained for the rest of his life. He gained some notoriety by opposing the union with England and by attempting to preserve orthodoxy in the Church of Scotland. James Webster was three times married, first to Margaret Keir (d. 1698), second to Mary Stewart, and finally, in September 1703, to Agnes Menzies. He died on 18 May 1720.

Alexander Webster attended the high school in Edinburgh. In 1733 he was licensed as a preacher by the presbytery of Haddington and was appointed assistant and successor to Allan Logan, minister of Culross, who died that September. In June 1737 he was translated to the Tolbooth Church, Edinburgh, where he became a popular preacher. In 1737 he married Mary Erskine (1715–1766), the daughter of Lieutenant-Colonel John Erskine and his third wife, Euphemia Cochrane. They had six sons and one daughter, Ann, who married Captain Eyre Robert Mingay in 1777. Webster's wife's elder sister, Euphemia, was the mother

of James Boswell and Webster his uncle; he and his children formed an important part of Boswell's social circle and are frequently mentioned in Boswell's journals.

In the early 1740s Webster played a leading role in supporting the Cambuslang revival, a spiritual awakening which began in the parish of Cambuslang, near Glasgow, and spread through much of western and central Scotland. In 1742 he published an important pamphlet, *Divine influence the true spring of the extraordinary work of Cambuslang and other places in the west of Scotland*, in which he argued that the conversions were a result of the influence of the Holy Spirit. In the same year Webster prepared a scheme for a provision for the widows and children of the ministers of the Church of Scotland, which he presented to the general assembly. In 1743 an act of parliament enabled the general assembly to raise money and establish the fund. Although he was largely responsible for initiating the fund which provided annuities, the actuarial basis of the scheme was largely the work of a colleague who shared Webster's interest in mathematics and demography, the Revd Robert Wallace.

Webster is remembered as the author of an early and respected private census of Scotland. In 1755 Lord President Robert Dundas, upon the instigation of the government, commissioned Webster to obtain figures on the population of Scotland providing information in three main areas: an alphabetical list of parishes showing the extent, patrons, stipends, and population in each case; a list of shires in Scotland detailing parishes, ministers, population, and numbers of Roman Catholics and men able to fight; and an estimate of the age structure of Scottish subjects in yearly age groups. Because of Webster's position within the church, his initiation of the fund for widows, and the fact that he was acting on behalf of the government, parish ministers throughout Scotland complied with his requests for specific information. He published the results of his study in *An account of the number of people in Scotland in the year one thousand seven hundred and fifty-five* (1755).

Webster was a leader of the popular party within the Church of Scotland in opposition to the more liberal faction, the moderates. He showed his conservative and evangelical stance in his sermon *Supernatural Religion the Only Sure Hope of Sinners*, preached on 12 January 1741 and published later that year in which he argued for divine revelation against the arguments raised by rationalists and deists. He was also a devoted Hanoverian. After the Jacobite defeat at the battle of Culloden he preached two sermons in the Tolbooth Church on the occasion of Thanksgiving, 23 June 1746, published later that year as *Heathens Professing Judaism, when the Fear of the Jews Fell upon them*, dedicated 'To all those whose concern for the Welfare of our Jerusalem, and Zeal for the British Israel, commenced Before the Battle of Culloden'. Using Esther as his text, he compared the Jews' deliverance with Mordecai and Esther's rescue of the Jews from Hamon to the revolution of 1688 and the Hanoverian succession. By adopting the language of British liberty and by de-emphasizing the rhetoric of the covenant, Webster signalled a break with the orthodox Presbyterian past and 'set a pattern for the next generation of evangelical political preaching' (Landsman, 203). In 1748 Webster was appointed to serve as chaplain to Frederick, prince of Wales, and on 24 May 1753 he was elected moderator of the general assembly. On 24 November 1760, he obtained the degree of DD from Edinburgh University. In the following month he was a member of a deputation sent by the general assembly to present an address to George III on his succession to the throne. He retired from the Tolbooth Church and became administer of the widows' fund in 1771, when he was also made one of his majesty's chaplains in ordinary for Scotland.

Webster was a convivial companion who loved his claret, a fondness for which earned him the nickname Dr Bonum Magnum. In 1773, when Samuel Johnson visited Scotland, Boswell noted in his journal:

> At supper we had Dr. Alexander Webster, who, though not learned, had such a knowledge of mankind, such a fund of information and entertainment, so clear a head and such accommodating manners, that Dr. Johnson found him a very agreeable companion. (*Boswell's Tour*, 32)

Webster died on 25 January 1784 in his home at the foot of Webster's Close on the south side of Castle Hill, Edinburgh, leaving his property to his daughter Ann and her children, even though two of his sons were still living. He was buried in the city's Greyfriars churchyard.

MARY MARGARET STEWART

Sources *DNB* • 'Biographical sketch of the late Alexander Webster', *Scots Magazine*, 64 (1802), 277–85 • J. G. Kyd, ed., *Scottish population statistics including Webster's analysis of population, 1755*, Scottish History Society, 3rd ser., vol. 43 (1952) • M. Flinn, ed., *Scottish population history from the 17th century to the 1930s* (1977) • E. C. Landsman, 'Presbyterians and provincial society: the evangelical enlightenment in the west of Scotland', *Sociability and society in eighteenth-century Scotland*, ed. J. Dwyer and R. B. Sher (1993), 194–207 • R. B. Sher, 'Witherspoon's *Dominion of providence* and the Scottish Jeremiah tradition', *Scotland and America in the age of the Enlightenment*, ed. R. B. Sher and J. R. Smitten (1990), 46–64 • *Boswell's journal of a tour to the Hebrides with Samuel Johnson*, ed. F. A. Pottle and C. H. Bennett (1963), vol. 9 of *The Yale editions of the private papers of James Boswell*, trade edn (1950–89) • *Boswell: the applause of the jury, 1782–1785*, ed. I. S. Lustig and F. A. Pottle (1981), vol. 12 of *The Yale editions of the private papers of James Boswell*, trade edn (1950–89) • *Boswell: the ominous years, 1774–1776*, ed. C. Ryskamp and F. A. Pottle (1963), vol. 8 of *The Yale editions of the private papers of James Boswell*, trade edn (1950–89) • *Boswell in search of a wife, 1766–1769*, ed. F. Brady and F. A. Pottle (1956), vol. 6 of *The Yale editions of the private papers of James Boswell*, trade edn (1950–89) • F. Brady, *James Boswell: the later years, 1769–1795* (1984)
Archives NL Scot., MSS of census of 1755
Likenesses D. Lizars, cartoon, line engraving, pubd 1784, NPG • J. Kay, etching, 1785, BM, NPG • D. Martin, oils, Scot. NPG • D. Martin, oils, priv. coll. [*see illus.*] • engraving, Scot. NPG; repro. in 'Biographical sketch of the late Alexander Webster', frontispiece

Webster [*née* Davies], (**Julia**) **Augusta** [*pseud.* Cecil Home] (1837–1894), poet, was born on 30 January 1837 at Poole, Dorset, one of the six children of Vice-Admiral George Davies RN (1800–1876) and his wife, Julia Hume (1803–1897), fourth daughter of Joseph *Hume (1767–1844), clerk at Somerset House, London, who was of mixed English, Scottish, and French extraction and claimed descent from the Humes of Polwarth, Berwickshire. Augusta's literary interests may well have stemmed from her mother's family; Lamb, Hazlitt, and Godwin were intimate friends of her grandfather Joseph and regular guests at his London home in Bayswater. He was the author of two publications, one a blank-verse translation (1812) of Dante's *Inferno* and the other *A Search into the Old Testament* (1841).

Augusta's father was born in the parish of Cuthbert, Wells, Somerset, and joined the Royal Navy at the age of thirteen. He was distinguished for his bravery at sea, having performed many dramatic rescues involving feats such as jumping overboard to save drowning comrades. Described as 'a perfect and noble specimen of the British sailor' and 'in his unpretending way, a hero' (Watts-Dunton, 355), his honest and generous character may have shaped the strong humanitarian side in Augusta's work. From her father she also inherited a passionate love of the sea, apparent in her poetry, having spent her childhood years living by the water.

Until 1851 the family moved up and down the coast of England, for some time living on the brigantine HMS *Griper* in Chichester harbour, Sussex. They resided from 1844 to 1848 in Banff Castle in Scotland, Augusta attending school in the town, and then moved to Penzance on the Cornish coast. In 1851 they finally moved inland to Cambridge when George Davies accepted the post of chief constable for Cambridgeshire, to which Huntingdonshire was added in 1857.

In Cambridge, Augusta became known as 'one of the brilliant daughters of Admiral Davies' (Watts-Dunton, 355). She read widely, learned Italian and Spanish, and travelled to Paris and Geneva where she became proficient in French. She liked painting and was a pupil at the new Cambridge School of Art, which opened its doors in 1858 to an inaugural speech given by Ruskin. She enrolled at the South Kensington Art School in London, but here ran into terrible trouble for a spirited attempt at whistling. This resulted in her being expelled from the school, which 'almost dashed the prospects of women art students for ever' (Strachey, 96), so controversial was institutionalized education for women at the time.

Augusta learned Latin and Greek, apparently to help a younger brother with his schoolwork. She later published two skilled literal translations from the Greek, Aeschylus' *Prometheus Bound* (1866) and Euripides' *Medea* (1868), which achieved critical recognition when women were still largely excluded from the classics. At least two of her siblings shared her academic disposition. In 1864 her elder sister Louisa married the Cambridge mathematician Isaac Todhunter. Her younger brother Gerald Stanley Davies (1845–1927), was for many years master of Charterhouse, his own school since the age of ten. He wrote and published widely on art and sports and is remembered at Charterhouse today for his learned and authoritative history of the institution, *Charterhouse in London* (1921).

Augusta's early publications, which include two volumes of verse (*Blanche Lisle*, 1860; *Lilian Gray*, 1864), the novel *Lesley's Guardians* (1864), and the prose article 'The Brissons' (*Macmillan's Magazine*, 1860), were published under the male pseudonym Cecil Home. It was only after her marriage to Thomas Webster (1832–1913), fellow of Trinity College, Cambridge, on 10 December 1863 that she gained the confidence to use her own name. During the next seven years she enjoyed the greatest popularity she would ever achieve as a poet with *Dramatic Studies* (1866), *A Woman Sold* (1867), and *Portraits* (1870), of which the last volume ran into three editions that same year. These works contain a series of dramatic monologues, in part inspired by Robert Browning. Several of the characters who speak out are women, and their concerns reflect the feminist interests which Augusta was developing by now.

On 14 November 1864 Augusta gave birth to her only child, Margaret (1864–1936). She lived in Cambridge with her husband and daughter until 1870, when she persuaded her husband to give up his law practice and move to London. Here she was introduced to literary circles by the critic Theodore Watts-Dunton, who constantly supported and reviewed her work. She worked as reviewer for *The Athenaeum* and during the 1870s wrote articles on a wide variety of subjects for *The Examiner*, later collected in the self-deprecatingly entitled *A Housewife's Opinions* (1878). Her poetry at this period includes a Chinese tale in verse, *Yu-Pe-Ya's Lute* (1872), and *A Book of Rhyme* (1884), which contains an innovative attempt to adapt Italian *rispetti* to English verse. She began a sonnet sequence, *Mother and Daughter* (1895), left uncompleted, and wrote a novel for children, *Daffodil and the Croaxaxicans* (1884). She also wrote four plays, notably *In a Day* (1882) and *The Sentence* (1887). The former was performed as a matinee at Terry's Theatre in London in May 1890, with her daughter—as 'Davies' Webster —playing the female lead.

During the 1870s and 1880s Augusta participated in a number of conferences on feminist causes and proved herself a talented public speaker. She was twice elected head of the Chelsea division of the London school board and worked hard for the improvement of women's education. She suffered from ill health for most of her adult life, struck by frequent attacks of pleurisy and on occasion obliged to winter in Italy. She died on 5 September 1894 at her home, Springfield, Kew Gardens Road, Kew, London, and was buried on 8 September in the west cemetery of Highgate cemetery, Middlesex. She was survived by her husband.

Webster's poetry, with its strong social concerns, was largely put aside by the aesthetes of the *fin de siècle* and entirely forgotten by the modernists. Late twentieth-century criticism led to a revival of interest in her verse, and her place in the history of poetry now seems secured. She deserves recognition as one of the foremost Victorian women poets.　　　　　　　　　　　　　PETRA BIANCHI

Sources DNB · T. Watts-Dunton, *The Athenaeum* (15 Sept 1894), 355 · O'Byrne, *Naval biog. dict.* · T. St E. Hake and A. Compton-Rickett, *The life and letters of Theodore Watts-Dunton*, 2 (1916), 2.17 · *The Carthusian* (March 1927), 202–4 [magazine of Charterhouse School] · H. Blackburn, *Women's suffrage: a record of the women's suffrage movement in the British Isles* (1902), 116–17, 153–4 · R. Strachey, *The cause: a short history of the women's movement in Great Britain* (1928); facs. edn (1978), 96 · CGPLA Eng. & Wales (1894) · private information (2004)

Likenesses wood-engraving (after photograph by Ferrando), NPG; repro. in *The Queen* (5 Dec 1891), 896
Wealth at death £1540 8s. 1d.: administration, 18 Oct 1894, CGPLA Eng. & Wales

Webster, Benjamin (1798–1882), actor and theatre manager, was born in Bath on 3 September 1798. His father, Benjamin Nottingham Webster (*c*.1760–1836), whose middle name the younger Webster also sometimes used, came from Sheffield. The father, through whom Webster claimed descent from Sir George Buc or Buck, was at one time a musical 'composer' and pantomimist; he married Elizabeth Moon of Leeds, joined the army, served in the West Indies, was engaged in Bath in organizing volunteer forces, and settled there as a dancing and fencing master. Benjamin Webster senior married three times and had twelve offspring. Apart from 'Ben' and Frederick Vestris (1802–1878), who became stage-manager of the Haymarket Theatre, Clara Webster, a ballerina, was the most theatrically distinguished. She died in 1843 at Drury Lane after her dress caught fire on stage.

Early acting career After receiving some education at Dr Barber's naval academy in Bath, Webster had to abandon the chances of a promised commission as a midshipman from the duchess of York on his mother's death. He made his first appearance on the stage as a dancer in 1809 and assisted his father in his occupations. In 1815, however, he ran away from home, and obtained from the younger Watson at Cheltenham an engagement at 25 shillings a week to play Harlequin, small speaking parts, and second violin in the orchestra. He began his career as an actor as Thessalus in *Alexander the Great* at Warwick in 1818, and also played at Lichfield and Walsall races. He then joined in a sharing scheme with a manager called 'Irish' Wilson, who fitted up a barn at Bromsgrove, where Webster (announced, with no apparent claim, as from the Theatre Royal, Dublin) doubled the parts of Sir Charles Cropland and Stephen Harrowby in Colman's *The Poor Gentleman*, danced a hornpipe, and played in his own dress, and with a head chalked to look like grey hair, Plainway in James Kenney's *Raising the Wind*. He then went as Harlequin to the Theatre Royal, Belfast, under Montague Talbot, acted in Londonderry and Limerick, and joined the Dublin company to play with it in Cork as Harlequin.

After appearing in Manchester and Liverpool Webster went to London, and played on 11 May 1818 a smuggler in *Trial by Battle*, the opening entertainment of the Coburg Theatre, later the Old Vic. According to a speech he made at a complimentary dinner given to him at the Freemasons' Tavern on 24 February 1864, he had at this time (in fact, in 1821) married a widow, Sophie West (1794–1835), with a family of children. Webster became ballet master and walking gentleman at Richmond, then leader of the band at Croydon, which led to his engagement as dancer and walking gentleman under Beverley at the Tottenham Street Theatre, called many names before it became the Prince of Wales's. After a period at the English Opera House (the Lyceum), he accepted from Elliston an engagement at Drury Lane, where he appeared on 28 November

Benjamin Webster (1798–1882), by unknown photographer

1820 as Almagro in *Pizarro*, and at Christmas played Pantaloon. At the end of the 1821–2 season he joined Alfred Bunn's company at Birmingham, where he was seen in low-comedy parts, then acted at Sheffield, Newcastle, and Chester. He was re-engaged by Elliston for three seasons at Drury Lane in 1823 at more favourable rates than previously, but he also sought to consolidate his financial position by opening a newspaper and bookshop near the theatre. This was to become the base for a later play-publishing venture, the series Webster's Acting National Drama.

Growing reputation During a revival of *Measure for Measure* on 1 May 1824, John Harley, who played Pompey, was taken ill, and Webster took the part, and was promoted to the first green room, a significant rise in status. In this year he was the first Tuditanus in Sheridan Knowles's *Caius Gracchus*, and in 1825 the first Erni in *William Tell* by the same author. Although he gained some recognition, he was kept back by Elliston. The *Theatrical Inquisitor* of 1826 'blamed the Drury Lane management for stifling a valuable talent'.

It was about this time that Webster began writing plays, mostly short comic pieces and farces. Some thirty-eight of these are listed in *English Drama of the Nineteenth Century* (1985). Throughout the 1820s and 1830s Webster played regularly at Drury Lane and at the Haymarket, where he

made his first appearance in 1829. At the same time he worked for other theatres as a playwright and stage-manager. In 1832 he was with Madame Vestris at the fashionable Olympic, where he played in Dance's *Kill or Cure* and in an adaptation by himself of *L'homme de soixante ans*. In the same year he managed the City Theatre in Cripplegate for a short season in association with Harriet Waylett. This experience gave him a taste for management, sharpened by the fact that conditions for actors at the patent houses had deteriorated under the tyranny of Alfred Bunn, who was by 1833 in charge of both Covent Garden and Drury Lane. Webster resorted to the Haymarket, where, in 1835, he and J. B. Buckstone were greatly praised for their performances as Dogberry and Verges in an otherwise disappointing production of *Much Ado About Nothing*, with Charles Kemble as Benedick.

In 1835 Sophie West Webster gave birth to a son, Benjamin, but she died several months later. Shortly afterwards Webster married Harriet Ireland (1816–1862), who bore him a son, William, in 1836 and a daughter, Harriette, in 1838. In 1836 his father died.

Management at the Haymarket In the following year Webster undertook the management of the Haymarket Theatre, which had a 'summer licence' for the presentation of legitimate drama. He was proud that he began the venture supported solely by his own earnings and was not beholden to any financial backers. The advantage of the Haymarket in comparison with the patent houses of Drury Lane and Covent Garden was that it was small enough to allow the audience both to hear the actors and to see subtle changes in facial expression, so that the management did not have to rely on lavish and costly spectacle to attract the crowds. In an age when visual extravagances were *de rigueur*, Webster was criticized for his lack of interest in decoration, but it is to his credit that during his management he chose to present the highest standards of acting and writing that were available at the time.

From the first season, when Webster, with considerable bravado, successfully persuaded 'the eminent tragedian' W. C. Macready to appear in his company, the Haymarket became known as the actors' theatre, which unashamedly operated a 'star' system. Macready and his stage partner, Helen Faucit, appeared regularly, as did Mr and Mrs Charles Kean, the Keeleys, Louisa Nisbett, Julia Glover, Mary Warner, J. L. Toole, and Webster's friend and fellow comedian Buckstone. Madame Vestris and Charles Matthews found there a refuge from bankruptcy and the insults of the patent holders, and another welcome visitor was the American actress Charlotte Cushman. Three distinguished performers of the later nineteenth century were given their London débuts by Webster: Tyrone Power, Samuel Phelps (later a rival manager at Sadler's Wells), and G. B. Shaw's favourite actor, Barry Sullivan. Acting standards were extremely high and Webster never fell into the managerial pitfall of casting himself in roles more suited to members of a brilliant company. He paid high salaries and, perhaps most importantly, seemed to have the knack of keeping his temperamental geniuses in order, if not always in good humour.

A further notable feature of Webster's Haymarket which encouraged the best of contemporary acting talent to join him was his serious commitment to the presentation of good new plays. At a time when the guardians of the 'national drama' were frequently reduced to presenting animal and freak shows, crude melodrama, and adaptations by hack writers from the trivia of the Parisian stage, Webster actively encouraged contemporary playwrights and men of letters to submit work to him. Sadly, his great playwriting competition in 1843, when a prize of £500 was offered for the best comedy, was a disaster, in that the winning piece, *Quid pro quo* by Catherine Gore, selected by a panel of distinguished judges including Charles Kemble, was booed from the stage, but there were a number of notable successes.

The Bridal, Sheridan Knowles's adaptation of Beaumont and Fletcher's *The Maid's Tragedy*, an excellent vehicle for Macready, consolidated the first season. Webster's faith in Bulwer-Lytton was vindicated by the success of *Money* in 1840, which had Macready in the leading role of Evelyn, Helen Faucit as Clara Douglas, and Webster in the comic part of Graves. Another nineteenth-century classic, *Masks and Faces* (1852), by Charles Reade and Tom Taylor, had Mary Ann Stirling in the leading part of Peg Woffington and Webster as the impoverished author Triplet, regarded by many as his finest performance.

At a time when playwrights were frequently exploited by actors and managers, Webster was highly respected for his fair dealings, particularly his willingness to offer advances on scripts (or even 'treatments') rather than delay payment until the piece's success was assured. The young Dion Boucicault was one such beneficiary. His *Love by Proxy*, *Alma Mater*, and *Curiosities of Literature* were all premièred under Webster's management. By the time Webster left the Haymarket he claimed, no doubt with justification, to have spent over £30,000 in encouraging dramatic writing.

The repertory of the Haymarket was distinguished largely by contemporary comedy, supplemented from time to time by farces by Buckstone and by Webster himself, but an innovatory excursion into the presentation of Shakespeare was made with the production of *The Taming of the Shrew* in 1844. Under the guidance of the antiquary J. R. Planché, the play was presented in full, including the prologue, and the main action took place in the Lord's bedroom incorporating the basic features of an Elizabethan stage. The actors wore Elizabethan costume. On closer inspection this presentation owed more to the decorative aesthetic of Victorian *mise-en-scène* than to the Shakespearian architectural and emblematic stage, but it may be seen as an interesting precursor to the reforms of William Poel some forty years later.

Webster's improvements to the Haymarket were not restricted to raising the standards of the repertory and the performances. As he remarked in his farewell speech in 1853, he had spent some £12,000 in redesigning and refurbishing the auditorium: the angular balcony was replaced by an elegantly curved circle, the seats in the pit were backed, orchestra stalls were introduced, the proscenium arch was widened by 11 feet and remodelled, gas lighting was installed and a centre chandelier given to the proprietors, 'and behind the curtain money has not been spared to render the stage as perfect for dramatic representation as its limited means will furnish'.

The Adelphi theatre In 1844 Webster had acquired the lease of the Adelphi, which he passed over to his long-term companion, the dancer Céline *Céleste (Madame Céleste), who had appeared in the 1838–9 season at the Haymarket. In 1853 he joined her at the Adelphi and handed over the Haymarket lease to his old friend Buckstone. Webster gave Buckstone a valuable legacy. Even before the passing in 1843 of the Theatre Regulation Act, which broke the monopoly of Covent Garden and Drury Lane, he had played his part in the growing respectability of the stage, presenting a series of dramatic entertainments before the queen at Windsor in 1848–9. He provided regular employment for both established actors and those at the beginning of their careers in good working conditions and in plays which exploited their talents. He had initiated touring with the entire company during the short time when the Haymarket was 'dark', another means of keeping the company together. A presentation by members of the company marked the extent of their appreciation of his achievement.

The new joint management of the Adelphi began in 1853 with Mack Lemon's farce *Mr Webster at Home*. Webster played Falstaff in a revival of *The Merry Wives of Windsor* in the same year. Early successes included *Two Loves and a Life* by Taylor and Reade (1854), Boucicault's *Janet Pride* (1855), and Taylor's *Helping Hand* (1855). Céleste won acclaim for her performance as a Watteauesque Harlequin. She was the first woman to attempt the part.

In 1859, in the new Royal Adelphi Theatre, erected on the site of the old house, Webster played Penn Holder, one of his greatest parts, in his own adaptation *One Touch of Nature*, and in the same year he was the original Robert Landry in Watts Phillips's *The Dead Heart*. This was a period of considerable controversy for Webster. Relations with Céleste became strained, leading to the severance of the partnership. *The Dead Heart* was thought by some to be plagiarized from Dickens's *A Tale of Two Cities*, or vice versa, and the old friends Webster and Dickens were (thankfully temporarily) estranged. Webster's financial problems were exploited, somewhat opportunistically, by his former protégé Boucicault, who, after his brilliant successes in America, returned to England with his three masterpieces, *The Colleen Bawn*, *Arragh-na-Pogue*, and *The Octoroon*. These were presented at the Royal Adelphi, but only on condition that their author had control of the theatre's artistic policy, leaving Webster as little more than a front-of-house manager. *The Colleen Bawn* (1860) was one of Queen Victoria's favourite plays; it ran for more than 230 performances in London and won acclaim in the provinces. But Webster, although he remained active in the Royal Adelphi management until 1872, never again exerted the managerial control he had previously enjoyed. A subsequent partnership with Chatterton failed on the grounds of his associate's extravagance.

Late career On 1 November 1869 Webster opened as lessee of the Princess's Theatre, which he had long owned, playing in Byron's *The Prompter's Box*, and in April 1873 he played his last new role, Rodin the Jesuit in *The Wandering Jew*, adapted by Leopold Lewis.

In the 1860s Webster was closely associated with a philanthropic venture, the establishment of a royal dramatic college to provide funds and accommodation for elderly and infirm members of the profession. There was also talk of building a training school for actors, necessitated by the demise of the provincial stock companies. Both schemes were attempts to raise the social respectability of the theatrical profession. Webster promised stone for the building from his quarries in Wales, but neither scheme was implemented and his ownership of the Welsh quarries has never been proved.

In 1874 Webster was given his farewell benefit at Drury Lane. The piece was *The School for Scandal*, and all the principal living actors took part. Helen Faucit came out of retirement to play Lady Teazle, there was a recitation by the new star Henry Irving, and Mary Ann Keeley, a stalwart of the Haymarket comedy team, presented the cheque for £2000, reputedly the largest sum ever to be raised by a Drury Lane benefit. Webster's last performance was for the benefit of his friend Buckstone, in 1877. The part was Graves in the production of *Masks and Faces* by the Bancroft management at the Prince of Wales's Theatre.

On his seventy-ninth birthday Webster remarried. The bride was 26-year-old Eleanor Phillips, who some months later bore him a son. Neither was mentioned in contemporary obituaries and biographies. Webster, nicknamed the Nestor of the Stage, died at his home, 3 Church Side, Kennington, Lambeth, on 8 July 1882.

Legacy and reputation Webster left two sons connected with the stage. Ben Webster the younger wrote the one-act farce *Behind Time* for the Adelphi in 1865; seven other farces or adaptations from the French came from his pen between that date and 1873. John Webster, his stepson, a juvenile star whose success did not last, played about 1837 and 1838 at Covent Garden, the Haymarket, the St James's, and the Adelphi. Webster's daughter Harriette married Sir Edward Lawson, bt, proprietor and editor of the *Daily Telegraph*. Benjamin Webster, his grandson, was a well-known actor in the late nineteenth and early twentieth century. Together with his wife, Dame May Whitty, he acted in many of the plays of the 'new drama' movement in London and in the repertory movement in the provinces. Their daughter, Margaret (Peggy) Webster, born in 1905, was an actress and director who found much success in the United States. Her book about the Webster dynasty, *The Same Only Different* (1969), is the most authoritative source on this distinguished theatrical family.

In his line as a character actor Webster stood foremost in his day. His greatest characters were Richard Pride, Robert Landry, Penn Holder, Triplet, Graves, Tartuffe, and Rodin in *The Wandering Jew*. He was happiest in characters in which serious purpose, puritanical fervour, and grim resolution were shown, and had not indeed more comedy than would serve like light points in a picture to indicate

the gloom. He was a spirited manager so far as the engagement of good actors and the encouragement of playwrights was concerned, but was out of tune with the times in respect of stage mounting and the employment of supernumeraries. Any assessment of his career must nevertheless acknowledge that, however ephemeral his performances and however trivial his own dramatic writings, he was a theatre manager of vision and integrity keeping alive the English dramatic tradition at a time when it was sorely pressed.

JOSEPH KNIGHT, rev. JAN McDONALD

Sources M. Webster, *The same only different* (1969) · H. J. Nichols, 'Ben Webster's management of the Haymarket Theatre', PhD thesis, University of Indiana, 1971 · W. Macqueen-Pope, *Haymarket: theatre of perfection* (1948) · C. Maude, *The Haymarket Theatre: some records and reminiscences* (1903) · J. W. Marston, *Our recent actors*, new edn (1890) · C. E. Pascoe, ed., *The dramatic list* (1879) · D. Mullin, ed., *Victorian actors and actresses in review: a dictionary of contemporary views of representative British and American actors and actresses, 1837–1901* (1983) · E. B. Watson, *Sheridan to Robertson* (1926) · J. Ellis, J. Donohue, and L. A. Zak, eds., *English drama of the nineteenth century: an index and finding guide* (1985) · J. McDonald, 'The Taming of the Shrew at the Haymarket Theatre, 1844 and 1847', *Essays on nineteenth century British theatre* [Manchester 1970], ed. K. Richards and P. Thomson (1971), 157–170 · m. cert. · d. cert.

Archives City Westm. AC, corresp. · Harvard U., Houghton L., family papers · NRA, priv. coll., papers · Theatre Museum, London, corresp. · U. Birm., corresp. and papers | BL, Lord Chamberlain's collection of plays · BL, letters to J. M. Kemble, Add. MSS 42957–43037 · BL, letters to Royal Literary Fund, loan 96 · Herts. ALS, letters to Lord Lytton · U. Birm., letters to B. W. Webster and J. Webster

Likenesses T. H. Wilson, two watercolours, 1840, Garr. Club; repro. in *A catalogue of pictures in the Garrick Club* (1936) · T. Hollis, stipple and line engraving (after daguerreotype by Mayall), BM, NPG · P. Hoyoll, oils, Garr. Club; repro. in *A catalogue of pictures in the Garrick Club* (1936) · D. J. Pound, print (after photograph by Mayall), BM, NPG · carte-de-visite, NPG · engraving, Garr. Club; repro. in *ILN* (22 July 1882) · engraving (as Tartuffe, Haymarket, 23 March 1851), Garr. Club · oils, Garr. Club; repro. in *A catalogue of pictures in the Garrick Club* · photograph, NPG [see illus.] · photographs, Garr. Club · photographs, Harvard U., Houghton L. · portrait (as John in *The minister and the mercer*), Garr. Club · portrait, Garr. Club · portraits, Harvard U., Houghton L. · print, Garr. Club · theatrical prints, NPG

Webster, Benjamin (1864–1947), actor, was born in London on 2 June 1864, the son of William Shakespeare Webster and his wife, Anne Sarah Johnson. He was a grandson of the famous theatre manager Benjamin *Webster. Ben's father was a solicitor, and after leaving King's College School, London, Ben was trained for the law and was called to the bar by the Inner Temple in 1885. But soon afterwards, through his sister, he met May Whitty [see below], then a junior member of the company of John Hare and W. H. and Madge Kendal; he joined the company in 1887 to be near to her, and so became an actor. Then a golden-haired youth with classical features and immense charm, he soon won his way as an accomplished juvenile lead. In 1888 he joined Henry Irving to play Malcolm in *Macbeth*; then with George Alexander from 1890 he was in the original casts of A. W. Pinero's *The Second Mrs Tanqueray*, R. C. Carton's *Liberty Hall*, and Oscar Wilde's

Lady Windermere's Fan. In 1892, after a seven years' courtship, he married May, and with her he went to Irving at the Lyceum Theatre in 1895. They remained with Irving there and in America until Irving's last season at the Lyceum in 1898. At the age of forty, in 1904, Webster was still youthful and he played Hippolytus brilliantly for Harley Granville Barker. In the Royal Court Theatre season that followed he played a number of parts, including the original Ridgeon of *The Doctor's Dilemma* by G. B. Shaw. In 1905 and 1907 he was in America again, playing leads for Mrs Patrick Campbell and others. In later years his skill and distinction of style always earned him a position in London, but he was too well balanced to excel as a tragedian and perhaps too grave to reach the heights as a comedian. In 1936 he shared in his wife's great success in Emlyn Williams's *Night Must Fall* in New York, and when the play was filmed in 1937 he went to Hollywood and remained there with her until his death on 26 February 1947.

Dame May Whitty [*real name* Mary Louise Whitty] (1865–1948), actress, was born in Liverpool, on 19 June 1865, the daughter of Alfred Whitty, journalist, and his wife, Mary Ashton. Her grandfather was Michael James *Whitty, founder and editor of the *Liverpool Daily Post* and chief constable of Liverpool. She made her début in Liverpool in 1881 and, after an appearance in London in 1882 at the Comedy Theatre, she joined the company of Hare and the Kendals; her work always bore the impress of Madge Kendal's training. As a charming *ingénue* she appeared with all the leading actor–managers of the day, including the Bancrofts, Forbes-Robertson, and Wyndham, and she made her first big personal success in Mrs Musgrave's *Our Flat* in 1889. With her husband she joined Irving's company (1895–8), but was still cast for rather colourless parts that somewhat belied her own character. Her Susan Throssell in the original run of J. M. Barrie's *Quality Street* in 1903 was the climax of this part of her career, but she played Countess Cathleen in Dublin in 1899 in the play of that name by W. B. Yeats and in America in 1905–7 she was given stronger work. Her daughter, Margaret *Webster, who became an eminent producer, was born in New York at this time.

Back in London in 1910 May gave a series of clever character studies in Charles Frohman's repertory season in plays by Meredith, Barker, and Pinero, as well as in other engagements, until the outbreak of war in 1914 changed the current of her life. She had always been a public-spirited woman and about 1900 she had taken up the cause of women's suffrage, becoming chair of the Actresses' Franchise League. Although a convinced pacifist, she now switched the whole organization over to beneficent war work. A Women's Emergency Corps was formed, pioneering in such causes as women's land work, camp shows for the troops, and workrooms for out-of-work actresses. She chaired the Three Arts Women's Employment Fund and the British Women's Hospitals Committee, which eventually created the Star and Garter Home for disabled servicemen at Richmond, Surrey; for the great organizing ability that she showed in this and other similar causes she was appointed DBE in 1918. Practical charity, based on self-help, and a keen eye for humbug were characteristic of all her work.

After the war May Whitty returned to the theatre with a much more assured and dominant style. In her youth she was a tiny delicate figure with a small round face, dark hair, blue-grey eyes, and an air of impudent innocence; in mature age her face and figure expressed a downright common-sense motherliness. She played in Pinero's *The Enchanted Cottage*, Frederick Lonsdale's *The Last of Mrs Cheyney*, made a hit in both London and New York as the old Nanny in John Van Druten's *There's Always Juliet*, and was with John Gielgud in Ronald Mackenzie's *The Maitlands*. In 1935, at the age of seventy, she made the greatest success of her life in Emlyn Williams's *Night Must Fall*, a terrifying performance of a terrified woman. She repeated the success in New York in 1936 and again when the play was filmed in Hollywood in 1937, for which she received an Oscar nomination. From this followed a completely new and successful career as a series of indomitable old ladies in films, of which *The Thirteenth Chair* (1937), *The Lady Vanishes* (1938), and *Mrs Miniver* (1942; for which she was again nominated for an Oscar) will be the best remembered. She made one or two notable appearances again on the stage in New York, including those as Madame Raquin and as the nurse in Laurence Olivier's production of *Romeo and Juliet*.

May and Ben never returned to England but made their home in Hollywood, drawing round them there a circle of friends that was almost as close as that in England. Their home in Covent Garden from the 1890s onwards had always been both a meeting-place of the famous English and American actors and a refuge for all in trouble. They were both deeply interested in actors' organizations. British Actors' Equity, the actors' trade union, was founded at their home and they did active work for all of the theatrical charities. Retaining throughout the affection and respect of the whole profession, Ben and May Webster served the theatre with integrity and distinction, almost continuously through the changing period from Hare and the Kendals, through Irving, Pinero, Wilde, Barrie, Barker, and Van Druten, and from the first silent English film to modern Hollywood. Perhaps Ben missed London more than May did, especially his beloved Garrick, of which he had once been the youngest member the club had ever had. But Ben and May were inseparable from their marriage in 1892 to their golden wedding in 1942; Ben was proud of May's late success, and he continued, they say, almost to his death the loving nightly custom of brushing his wife's hair. She did not long survive him, dying in Hollywood on 29 May 1948. Margaret Webster was their only child, except for a son who died at birth.

LEWIS CASSON, *rev.*

Sources J. Parker, ed., *Who's who in the theatre*, 6th edn (1930) • private information (1959) • personal knowledge (1959)
Likenesses A. Ellis, photographs, 1893–5, NPG • Spy [L. Ward], pencil caricature, NPG
Wealth at death £5697 2*s.* 5*d.*—in England: administration with will, 24 March 1948, *CGPLA Eng. & Wales* • £26,581 17*s.* 1*d.*—effects in

England; May Whitty: administration with will, 26 Feb 1949, *CGPLA Eng. & Wales*

Webster, Sir Charles Kingsley (1886–1961), historian, was born at Rye Ground Lane, Formby, Lancashire, on 25 April 1886, the sixth of the seven children of Daniel Webster, shipping agent, and his wife, Annie Willey. He was educated at Merchant Taylors' School, Crosby, Liverpool, and at King's College, Cambridge, where he was a history scholar. After gaining a first class in part two of the historical tripos in 1907, he was awarded the university Whewell scholarship in international law. In 1910 he won a fellowship at King's College on the strength of a dissertation on foreign policy between 1814 and 1818. The diplomatic history of the nineteenth century continued to be the focus of his academic interest for the next forty years. His first article, 'Castlereagh and the Spanish colonies', appeared in the *English Historical Review* in 1912 (27.78–95), and he took part in organizing the International Congress of Historical Sciences, which met in London in 1913. Although he worked for long periods in foreign archives, King's College, Cambridge, continued to be his base until he accepted the chair of modern history at the University of Liverpool in March 1914.

The outbreak of the First World War in 1914 led Webster to volunteer for military service in 1915, but poor eyesight precluded a combatant role and he took a commission in the Army Service Corps. In 1917 he was transferred to an intelligence section of the general staff at the War Office, of which his former tutor, H. W. V. Temperley, was the head. He prepared papers on the Balkans and the possible creation of 'Jugoslavia' after the war, on the circumstances in which an armistice might be concluded, and, more especially, on the military and political future of Palestine. He became interested in Zionism and came to admire Chaim Weizmann. His pre-war research had concerned the settlement at the end of the Napoleonic wars, and, on the strength of it, in the summer of 1918 he was seconded to the Foreign Office to advise on how earlier mistakes might be avoided. He prepared a Foreign Office handbook, published by Oxford University Press in 1919 (revised, 1934), entitled *The Congress of Vienna*, which became a classic. At the peace conference Webster acted as secretary to the military section of the British delegation. During the war, on 7 July 1915, Webster married Nora Violet, daughter of Richard Perry Harvey, who had been brought up in Italy. It was a happy marriage in which Nora supported him in his many public activities. There were no children.

In 1919 Webster returned to Liverpool, but his academic life was now combined with a passionate interest in current affairs and a fervent hope that the new international organizations would succeed. He worked energetically for the League of Nations Union. In 1922 he was invited to take the chair of international relations in Aberystwyth (University of Wales), founded by his friend David Davies (later first Baron Davies) and his two sisters, in memory of the fallen of the First World War, and with a remit to promote peace between nations. Nothing could have been more congenial to Webster, and the terms of the appointment were also generous. He was obliged to spend only one term a year in Aberystwyth and was free to travel and accept appointments at other universities for the rest of the time. He travelled worldwide, and in 1927 agreed to spend one term every year at Harvard. The failure of the United States to join the League of Nations deeply disappointed him, and in 1925 he helped to organize a lobby of the churches of Wales to the churches of America in an attempt to sway American opinion.

While at Aberystwyth Webster wrote his two major books on the foreign policy of Lord Castlereagh, the first (published in 1925) covering the period 1815–22, the second (1931) that from 1812 to 1815. Both were massive works of scholarship, based on the archives which were now becoming open to scholars. In the course of examining the attempts then made to establish international peace, he rehabilitated Lord Castlereagh as one of the major (and often progressive) figures of British foreign policy.

In 1932 Webster moved to the newly established Stevenson chair of international relations at the London School of Economics (LSE). In 1934 he gained access to the Palmerston papers at Broadlands and began his work on Palmerston's foreign policy. An early fruit of this was his Raleigh lecture 'Palmerston, Metternich and the European system, 1830–1841' (*PBA*, 20, 1934, 125–58). He had hoped to complete the first part of his study, covering the period up to 1841, in 1940, but the Second World War intervened and the two-volume work was not published until 1951.

In London in the 1930s Webster was active in public speaking and journalism, and an outspoken opponent of appeasing Hitler. He had been a member of the Royal Institute of International Affairs since its foundation in 1919, and when, on the outbreak of the Second World War, the institute set up its foreign research and press service, based at Balliol College, Oxford, to furnish information and advice to government departments, Webster became head of its American section.

Webster undertook a successful lecture tour in the United States in the spring of 1941 and must have seemed the ideal choice when asked to take charge of the British Library of Information in Washington, DC. This was a government organization entrusted with influencing American opinion in Britain's favour. Unfortunately it proved the most frustrating year of his life. From the beginning he complained of being overworked, underresourced, and denied the support promised in advance by the government. It turned into a clash of personalities, and in February 1942 Webster offered his resignation at almost the same time as Brendan Bracken, the minister of information, informed him that he was amalgamating the library with the British Press Service, and that Webster's post had consequently become redundant.

Webster expected to return to the LSE, but was asked instead to go back to the foreign research and press service. In April 1943 this gained official status as the Foreign Office research department. In September 1942 Gladwyn Jebb brought Webster into the economic and reconstruction department of the Foreign Office. There was a general belief that there would have to be 'a period of convalescence' after the war. Webster's papers in the LSE library show that he received and commented on a wide variety of drafts concerning domestic as well as international affairs. The latter ranged over future relations with Europe, the Commonwealth, the United States, the Soviet Union, and the Arab states. But the subject with which Webster was most closely concerned was replacing the now discredited League of Nations with a new organization: the United Nations. He was an expert adviser at both the Dumbarton Oaks conference in the summer of 1944 and the San Francisco conference in April 1945. He kept detailed diaries in which he sometimes gave vent to his own feelings, including his exasperation with Winston Churchill. Extensive extracts were later published (see Reynolds and Hughes). Immediately after the war he became adviser to his old friend Philip Noel-Baker, then minister of state at the Foreign Office, and was alternate at the second preparatory commission of the United Nations, which met in London. He attended the first meetings of both the general assembly and the Security Council in January 1946 and the final meeting of the League of Nations in April. He was made KCMG in the new year's honours list in 1946.

Webster returned to academic life, but continued to be active in UNESCO. He was particularly interested in international co-operation between scholars. He worked for it when he became president of the British Academy (of which he had been a fellow since 1930) in 1950. As president (1950–54) he represented the British Academy in the Union Académique Internationale from 1948 to 1959. He was also energetic in the International Congress of Historical Sciences, with which he had been associated since 1913, presiding at the Stockholm meeting in 1960. He tried in particular to re-establish relations with scholars from behind the iron curtain, which had cut off Russia and eastern Europe from the west. He was showered with honours and invitations, among them honorary degrees from Oxford, Wales, Rome, and Williams College, as well as an honorary fellowship at King's, Cambridge. He retired from his chair at the LSE in 1953.

In 1947 Webster gave the Ford lectures in the University of Oxford, speaking on the history of the European state system, but after the publication of *Palmerston* in 1951 he turned to an entirely new field, the official history of the Anglo-American bombing offensive during the Second World War, which he wrote with Noble Frankland. He saw the proofs but did not live to see the publication of the four volumes. After a short illness he died of cancer at University College Hospital, Gower Street, London, on 21 August 1961; his wife survived him.

As Reynolds remarks (Reynolds and Hughes, 1), Webster was a figure more familiar in American than in British history, an academic specialist from outside the civil service who played an important advisory role in forming his country's policy—although Webster himself sometimes wondered how far his warnings had been heeded. He did believe in the ultimate efficacy of international organization, remarking that although he 'had no illusions' about

the United Nations charter he did believe that it registered an advance in relations between states (ibid., 73). His meticulous and ultra-detailed scholarship, written straight from the archives, was in many ways out of fashion even when his *Palmerston* was published in 1951, but his academic work should be seen as part of his labours for peace and progress. Webster believed, as did others of his generation, that if they could understand the workings of the international system better, catastrophes like that of 1914 might be avoided, although as he ruefully observed in his Ford lectures, 'I underestimated both the pace at which history would be made and the pace at which it could be written' (*PBA*, 430). His physical frame was large and loosely assembled, and his dress untidy. Sometimes impatient or tactless, he was not sensitive to the impression made by his outspoken opinions; but he was so transparently a man of goodwill that he had no enemies.

G. N. CLARK, rev. MURIEL E. CHAMBERLAIN

Sources BLPES, Webster MSS · S. Bindoff, *PBA*, 48 (1962), 427 · P. A. Reynolds and E. J. Hughes, *The historian as diplomat: Charles Kingsley Webster and the United Nations, 1939–1946* (1976) [incl. extensive extracts from Webster's diaries] · *The Times* (23 Aug 1961) · *WW* · *WWW* · Webster's letters, NL Wales · C. Weizmann, *Trial and error: the autobiography of Chaim Weizmann* (1949) · Burke, *Peerage* (1959) · b. cert. · *CGPLA Eng. & Wales* (1961) · personal knowledge (1981) · private information (1981)

Archives BLPES, corresp. and papers · London School of Economics, papers · NL Wales, letters | IWM, Chatham House corresp. · King's Cam., letters to Oscar Browning · King's Lond., Liddell Hart C., corresp. with Sir B. H. Liddell Hart

Likenesses W. Stoneman, photograph, 1937, NPG · W. Stoneman, photograph, 1953, NPG · photograph, repro. in Bindoff, *PBA* · photographs, London School of Economics

Wealth at death £44,838 4s. 7d.: probate, 30 Oct 1961, *CGPLA Eng. & Wales*

Webster, Sir David Lumsden (1903–1971), theatre and opera house administrator, was born in Dundee on 3 July 1903, the only child of Robert Lumsden Webster, advertising agent, and his wife, Mary Ann Alice, *née* Webster. In 1913 the family moved to Liverpool where he was educated at the Holt School. In 1921 he won a scholarship to Liverpool University where he read economics and became deeply involved in university life as secretary of the university guild and chairman of the dramatic society. Such was his interest in the theatre that many believed that it was there that he would find a career.

Following postgraduate studies in education at Oxford and Liverpool, Webster joined the retail store organization run by F. J. Marquis. He quickly made his mark and in 1932 was appointed general manager of the Bon Marché in Liverpool. On the outbreak of the Second World War he became general manager of Lewis's. Meanwhile he maintained his interest in music, opera, and the theatre, becoming in 1940 chairman of the Liverpool Philharmonic Society. During his tenure of office (which lasted until 1945) he made the Liverpool Philharmonic Orchestra into a permanent body.

In 1942, on the recommendation of Lord Woolton, Webster was seconded from Lewis's to the Ministry of Supply with the brief to improve productivity and quality at ordnance factories. This mission was successfully completed and at its conclusion in 1944 Webster was offered and accepted a post with Metal Box.

Boosey and Hawkes, the music publishers, who had acquired a lease on the Royal Opera House, Covent Garden, intended (contrary to the practice of the inter-war years) to present opera and ballet throughout the year and began to search for a person to organize this inspired venture. Their choice fell upon David Webster, who was released from his Metal Box commitment and took up his Covent Garden post, as administrator of its preliminary committee, in August 1944. In 1946 he was appointed general administrator of the Royal Opera House. For many it was an unlikely choice and for years Webster was the subject of harsh criticism which he bore silently, but not painlessly. Few understood the formidable task of setting up permanent opera and ballet companies at Covent Garden and this hostility and lack of understanding drove Webster, a shy man, into an obsessive secretiveness and a tendency to procrastinate, which was not always to his advantage but which he could use to good effect on occasions.

For ballet there was a relatively simple solution to Covent Garden's needs. The Sadler's Wells Ballet, founded by Ninette de Valois in 1931, was again at its theatre in Rosebery Avenue and was ready for bigger challenges. Covent Garden offered these and eventually the Sadler's Wells governors agreed to release the company to the Covent Garden Trust, which had been created in February 1946, under the chairmanship of Lord Keynes, to supervise the running of the opera house. Sadler's Wells Ballet later became known as the Royal Ballet.

For opera there was no simple answer, for nothing of permanence had been created in the inter-war years. It was thus a matter of starting from scratch and after the appointment of Karl Rankl as music director, work on the formation of a company (known as the Covent Garden Opera Company, later to be named the Royal Opera) began with the selection of soloists, choristers, and orchestral musicians.

A lesser man than Webster would not have survived these early and chequered years, but such was his faith in the concept of permanent opera and ballet companies at Covent Garden and in those who performed and worked there, and such were his patience and skill, that the enterprise prospered through many financial crises, through various changes of artistic policy, and through several changes of music director (Karl Rankl in 1946–51, Rafael Kubelik in 1955–8, and Sir Georg Solti from 1961 to 1971). In many ways the years of interregnum between music directors were the happiest for Webster. He enjoyed the freedom of choice of repertory and of artists just as he sometimes felt that he would like to run Covent Garden without a board of directors, although inwardly he knew the value of that and the depth of support which he could expect from it. Webster also had a flair for discovering singers and furthering their careers at home and abroad—for example, Joan Sutherland, Jon Vickers, and Geraint Evans.

Webster developed his interests in other directions.

From 1948 he was chairman of the Orchestral Employers' Association. In 1957 he became a director of Southern Television Ltd, and in 1965 chairman of the London Concerts Board. He held visiting lectureships at the universities of Bristol (1955–6) and Liverpool (1958). He became president of the Wagner Society in 1957 and worked hard to arouse wider interest in Wagner's operas in Britain.

The strain of the vast tasks which Webster had undertaken since the mid-1940s and the burden of maintaining and improving standards of performance at Covent Garden in the face of general under-finance and, in the early days, of fierce criticism, eventually took their toll. The last few years at Covent Garden were not happy for him. He was unwell and he became prey to doubts and fears about himself and his ability to carry on. In July 1970 he retired and was appointed KCVO (he had been knighted in 1960). He was also an honorary FRCM and RAM. He was an officer of the Légion d'honneur and was awarded Swedish, Portuguese, and Italian honours.

Webster enjoyed food and wine and giving parties, which he frequently did with great style at his house, 39 Weymouth Street, London. From 1931 his companion was James Cleveland Belle. Webster died at his home on 11 May 1971.   JOHN TOOLEY

Sources M. Haltrecht, *The quiet showman: Sir David Webster and the Royal Opera House* (1975) · *The Times* (12 May 1971) · personal knowledge (2004) · **Archives** SOUND BL NSA, *Time of my life*, P304W BD1 · BL NSA, current affairs recording · BL NSA, documentary recording · **Likenesses** D. Hackney, acrylic on canvas, 1971, NPG · **Wealth at death** £12,278: probate, 29 Oct 1971, *CGPLA Eng. & Wales*

Webster, Elizabeth Vassall. *See* Fox, Elizabeth Vassall, Lady Holland (1771?–1845).

Webster, George (1797–1864), architect, was born in Kendal, Westmorland, on 3 May 1797, the second of the three sons and third of the seven children of Francis Webster (1767–1827), mason, builder, and architect of Kendal, and his first wife, Janet (1771–1805), daughter of George Slater, yeoman of Kirkby Lonsdale, Westmorland. Where he received his training is not known—an apprenticeship in a professional architect's office away from Kendal seems likely—but as he did not attend the Royal Academy Schools it was probably elsewhere in the north rather than in London. On returning to become a partner in his father's business, he designed his first recorded work, Read Hall, near Whalley, Lancashire, in 1818 at the age of twenty-one and quickly appears to have become the principal architect member of the firm. He evidently then left his father to concentrate on the production of marble chimney-pieces and funerary monuments, which were his speciality. Thereafter during the 1820s and 1830s he greatly expanded the firm's architectural side—following his father's death in 1827 he devoted his time entirely to architecture, leaving the management of the marble works to his younger brother, Francis—and established a substantial practice in the north-west and the adjacent parts of Yorkshire. In 1827 he married Eleanor (1804–

1867), daughter of George Lowrey of Ulverston, Lancashire: they had one son and four daughters, of whom one died young.

Many of Webster's earliest works, including Read Hall and Rigmaden (1825), near Kirkby Lonsdale, are in an orthodox neo-classical manner which was also used by his father, but his principal contribution was as a pioneer in the scholarly revival of the Jacobean style. Two of his country houses, Eshton Hall, Yorkshire (1825–7), and Underley Hall, near Kirkby Lonsdale (1825–8), are among the very earliest examples of this idiom, as well as being notably accomplished productions which were singled out for praise in the preface to Henry Shaw's *Specimens of the Details of Elizabethan Architecture* (1839). Subsequent examples included Moreton Hall, Whalley (1829; dem.), while a further dimension of his work was the occasional introduction of details of a localized vernacular derivation—as in his unexecuted designs for a house in Rydal, Westmorland, for William Wordsworth (1826), which incorporated the cylindrical chimneys characteristic of traditional building in the Lake District. From the early 1820s onwards he also designed a number of churches in a conventional Gothic style, but in some of his later works, such as his alterations to Broughton Hall, Yorkshire (1838–41), and Flasby Hall, Yorkshire (1840), he experimented with the picturesque Italianate manner.

In 1845 Webster took into partnership his assistant Miles Thompson, who had been with the firm since the 1820s, and shortly after that he virtually retired from active business. From 1836 he visited Italy on more than one occasion, but these travels appear to have been prompted more by recreational than professional pursuits—he made a collection of Roman coins, medals, and other antiquities—and perhaps also by the state of his health. In 1829–30, like his father before him, he served as mayor of Kendal, and in addition to the house he had built for himself in the town (*c*.1823) he had a country property at Lindale, Lancashire, which he inherited from his father, and he later built an occasional residence in nearby Grange-over-Sands. Webster died at his home, Ellerhow, Lindale, on 16 April 1864, leaving an estate of under £25,000, and a collection of his architectural drawings. He was buried in Lindale churchyard.　　　　　　　PETER LEACH, *rev.*

Sources Colvin, *Archs.* [incl. work list] · N. Cooper, 'Growth of a Lakeland town', *Country Life*, 154 (1973), 762–4 · A. K. Placzek, ed., *Macmillan encyclopedia of architects*, 4 vols. (1982) [incl. list of works] · C. Hussey, 'Broughton Hall, Yorkshire, I', *Country Life*, 107 (1950), 876–9 · C. Hussey, 'Broughton Hall, Yorkshire, III', *Country Life*, 107 (1950), 1034–7 · A. Taylor, 'The lowly dwelling of William Wordsworth esq^re', *Georgian Group Journal*, 7 (1997), 43–55 · R. Gunnis, *Dictionary of British sculptors, 1660–1851* (1953); new edn (1968) · J. P. Haworth and A. C. Taylor, *The Websters of Kendal* (1973) · *CGPLA Eng. & Wales* (1864) · private information (2004) [A. Taylor]
Archives Cumbria AS, Kendal, letter-books and sketchbooks
Wealth at death under £25,000: probate, 21 May 1864, *CGPLA Eng. & Wales*

Webster, Sir Godfrey (*c*.1648–1720). *See under* Webster family (*per. c*.1650–1836).

Webster, Sir Godfrey, fourth baronet (*bap.* **1749**, *d.* **1800**). *See under* Webster family (*per. c*.1650–1836).

Webster, Sir Godfrey Vassall, fifth baronet (**1789–1836**). *See under* Webster family (*per. c*.1650–1836).

Webster, Hannah Maria. *See* Mitchell, Hannah Maria (1872–1956).

Webster, James (**1658/9–1720**). *See under* Webster, Alexander (1707–1784).

Webster, John (**1578×80–1638?**), poet and playwright, was born in London, the son of John Webster (*c*.1550–1614/15) and Elizabeth, daughter of Thomas Coates, blacksmith, of St Giles Cripplegate. The parish records of St Sepulchre, Newgate, where the family lived, were destroyed in the great fire of London, but surviving documentary sources indicate that there were at least five children of the marriage, which took place on 4 November 1577. That John Webster the younger, as he is referred to in documents of the time, was the first son is suggested by the fact that he was given his father's name, but since this cannot be proved his birth cannot be dated more precisely than 1578–80.

John Webster the elder, probably a Londoner, spent his entire working life in the parish of St Sepulchre, where in Cow Lane, Smithfield, he both lived and ran a thriving business, building and hiring out coaches and wagons. He also became a prominent member of the Guild of Merchant Taylors, to which coach makers, with no guild of their own, were admitted on the grounds of community of interest, there being 'a close and obvious connection between tailors, who made trappings for funerals, plays and pageants, and the men who provided hearses for coffins' (Edmond, 'In search of John Webster', 1621).

Though the school's records for the period are incomplete, John Webster the younger presumably attended Merchant Taylors' School, where he would have remained until the age of sixteen or seventeen—between 1594 and 1598—after which it seems likely that he spent one or perhaps two years at the New Inn, one of the inns of chancery, in preparation for admission to the inns of court, since an entry in the records of the Middle Temple, dated 1 August 1598, notes the admission to the society of 'Magister Johannes Webster nuper de Novo Hospitio generosus, filius et heres apparens Johannis Webster de London generosi' ('Master John Webster, formerly of the New Inn, gentleman, son and heir apparent of John Webster of London, gentleman'). Webster may have intended practising law, but young men of means often lived and studied at one of the inns with no intention of doing so, and it is even possible that he was sent to the Middle Temple 'to qualify him for helping with large mercantile ventures, and for dealing with distinguished customers' (Bradbrook, 4). If so, then it may be assumed that subsequently John Webster the younger ran the office, while his father and brother Edward, also a qualified coach builder, ran the works.

Such involvement in the family business would explain how Webster made a living, given his slowness of composition. It may also help to explain that slowness, if office duties occupied a good deal of his time. Henry

Fitzgeffrey's famous jibe about 'Crabbed (*Websterio*) | The *Play-wright*, *Cart-wright*' (Fitzgeffrey, sig. F6v–F7r) is generally assumed to be a cut at Webster's family connections, but may allude more precisely to the fact that the dramatist was himself actively engaged in the running of the business in Cow Lane. Also germane, perhaps, is Webster's decision (in June 1615) to claim membership of the Merchant Taylors by patrimony. This is generally assumed to be associated with the death of his father, at some time between April 1614 and February 1615. But there would be added point to the dramatist's application for membership of the Merchant Taylors were he actively involved in the coach building business.

But whether or not Webster intended taking up the law, it seems, from the knowledge that he displays in his plays and the frequency with which they include trial scenes, that some time, at least, was spent in legal study. Acrid portraits of the lawyer in *The White Devil*, Contilupo and Sanitonella in *The Devil's Law-Case*, and the Orator in *Appius and Virginia* make it at least possible that, like the dramatist John Marston, who was living (but not, it seems, studying) at the Middle Temple at the same period, the young Webster grew disenchanted with the law and turned to a less lucrative but more appealing profession.

Early career The first evidence of Webster's writing for the stage is an entry in Philip Henslowe's diary for 22 May 1602, noting a payment of £5 'unto antoney monday & mihell drayton webester & the Rest mydelton in earneste of A Boocke called sesers ffalle' (*Henslowe Papers*, 201). A week later a further £3 was paid to 'Thomas dickers drayton myddellton & Webester & mondaye in fulle paymente for ther playe called too shapes' (ibid., 202). The entries are taken to refer to the same play, now lost. Written for the Admiral's Men, it presumably dealt with the life and death of Julius Caesar.

Further evidence of Webster's dramatic activity comes from a series of entries in Henslowe's diary made later in the same year. In October a team comprising Henry Chettle, Thomas Dekker, Thomas Heywood, Webster, and 'mr smythe' were paid a total of £5 16s. for two parts of 'A playe called Ladey Jane' (*Henslowe Papers*, 218), while in November Henslowe paid the same group (minus 'smythe') £7 for 'A playe called cryssmas comes but once A yeare' (ibid., 219). Webster, it seems, was serving an apprenticeship as part of a team in which professionals like Dekker and Heywood took the lead. *Caesar's Fall* and *Christmas Comes but Once a Year* were presumably potboilers, but like the two parts of *Lady Jane*, which it is generally agreed survive in corrupted form as *Sir Thomas Wyatt*, served to initiate Webster into writing for the theatre.

Regular entries in Henslowe's diary cease in March 1603, and there is no surviving evidence of Webster's dramatic activity until 1604, when his name is linked with that of Marston on the title-page of the third edition of the latter's *The Malcontent*. What is meant by the words 'Augmented by Marston. With the additions played by the Kings Maiesties servants. Written by Ihon Webster' has long been debated, but it is now generally agreed, as by

Hunter and by Lake (1981), that Webster wrote not only the induction but also additional material involving the clown, Passarello. Providing a comic scenario both for the delicate task of justifying the 'theft' of *The Malcontent* from the boys' company, the Children of the Chapel Royal, by whom it was first played, and for explaining the reasons for the 'additions', Webster displays considerable skill.

Later in 1604 there appeared *Westward Ho*, the first of two city comedies written by Dekker and Webster for the Children of Paul's. A racy account of London middle-class culture, it gave rise within months to a kindred piece by Marston, George Chapman, and Ben Jonson—*Eastward Ho*—in the prologue to which the dramatists refer to 'that which is opposed to ours in title' as 'good, and better cannot be'. Both *Westward Ho* and the more strongly satirical *Northward Ho*, written by Dekker and Webster in 1605, were highly popular and frequently performed.

A gap of five years separates the publication in 1607 of the *Ho* plays and *Sir Thomas Wyatt* and the appearance of Webster's first tragedy, *The White Devil*. Such a hiatus invites speculation, even though Webster admitted, in 'To the reader', that he 'was a long time in finishing this tragedy'. It is possible, of course, that Webster was working on his tragedy over the entire five years, but two other explanations for the silence are possible. One is domestic and financial, relating to his marriage, which may have forced him to put most of his time and energy into earning a living, perhaps in his father's business. The second, particularly intriguing, derives from the discovery in 1985 of the Melbourne manuscript, a 144-line fragment of a play on the subject of Alessandro de' Medici, duke of Florence—a fragment of which Antony Hammond and Doreen del Vecchio consider Webster more likely to be the author than any other known Jacobean dramatist, and which they date, tentatively, early in the period 1605–30. It is thus possible that in the five years between *Northward Ho* and *The White Devil* Webster did some work, at least, on a tragedy which he either abandoned or never felt happy to acknowledge or offer for performance.

Marriage and family While the details of Webster's literary activity between 1605 and 1612 are uncertain, significant moments in his personal life during those years can be established. His marriage, on 18 March 1606, took place not at St Sepulchre's, nor in the parish of his bride, Sara Peniall (*bap.* 1589), but at St Mary's in Islington, then a village outside London (M. Edmond, 'Webster's wife', *TLS*, 24 Oct 1980). The reason for this, and for marrying, by special licence, during Lent, is to be found in the fact that fewer than two months later Sara Webster gave birth to their first child, John, baptized on 8 May 1606 at St Dunstan-in-the-West, Fleet Street, 'out of Simon Penials sadler' (M. Eccles, 'John Webster', *TLS*, 21 Jan 1977; M. Edmond, 'John Webster', *TLS*, 11 March 1977). That other children were born to John and Sara Webster is clear from the will of Margery Pate, who in 1617 left 20s. each to their son John and his sisters, Elizabeth and Sara, and 40s. to 'the rest of Websters Children' (Edmond, 'In search of John Webster', 1622).

The years of greatness *The White Devil* was first performed by Queen Anne's Men at the Red Bull in Clerkenwell, probably early in 1612. In an address 'To my loving, and Loved Friends and Fellowes, the Queenes Maiesties Servants', prefacing his *If this be not a Good Play, the Devil is in it*, Webster's friend and collaborator Dekker had wished the company a '*Faire* and *Fortunate Day* to your *Next New-Play* (for the *Makers-sake* and your *Owne*)'. That the '*Next New-Play*' was *The White Devil* is clear from Webster's echoing, in his address 'To the reader', Dekker's wish for a '*Full, Free,* and *Knowing Auditor*'. The audience, however, was unappreciative, as is clear from Webster's acerbic comment that 'most of the people that come to that Play-house, resemble those ignorant asses (who visiting Stationers shoppes their use is not to inquire for good bookes, but new bookes)' (*The White Devil*, 'To the reader'). Yet such a reception should not have been surprising, given the unsophisticated fare generally staged at the Red Bull (Gurr, 218). To an audience perhaps anticipating a more direct and literal handling of the diabolic, as by Dekker in *If this be not a Good Play*, the complexity and sophistication of *The White Devil* would have come as a shock (A. Leggatt, 'The failure of *The White Devil*', *Jacobean Public Theatre*, 1992, 123–9).

As Hammond notes, Vittoria Corombona, Webster's 'white devil', 'marks a new departure in Jacobean drama, a heroine … thoroughly corrupt, but with whom it is impossible not to sympathize' (Hammond, 292). In a male-dominated world, she manipulates those around her (and particularly the infatuated Duke Brachiano) in order to attain, at least for a time, freedom of action. Her dominance, dramatically, is demonstrated in three great scenes, 'the Arraignment of Vittoria', in which she defends herself against charges of immorality (but manages to convince an audience, and many critics, that she is actually on trial for her life), the quarrel with Brachiano in the House of Convertites, to which she has been confined, and the last scene, where she faces death with immense and memorable courage.

Sharing that death scene, equally memorably, is Vittoria's brother Flamineo, whose courage, wit, and resourcefulness match his sister's. The classic Jacobean malcontent, as Brachiano's secretary he promotes the liaison with Vittoria with an eye to his own advancement, murdering his brother-in-law to clear the way for Brachiano and Vittoria to marry. In doing so he displays a moral insouciance which, as his hopes of advancement fade after he murders his brother, is seen to mask uncertainty and a vestigial remorse.

Webster probably began work on his second tragedy, *The Duchess of Malfi*, soon after the completion of *The White Devil*, but in November 1612 set the new play aside to compose *A Monumental Column*, commemorating the death, on the 6th of that month, of Henry, prince of Wales. Webster's elegy, published with those of Heywood and Cyril Tourneur, was entered in the Stationers' register on Christmas day 1612, and in it the poet excuses his 'worthlesse lines' on the grounds that 'I hasted, till I had this tribute paid / Unto his grave' (lines 310–11). Haste may also explain Webster's extensive reuse of material in his half-finished tragedy, but parallels—as between the experiences of Bosola and Webster's account, in the elegy of:

> *Sorrow* that long had liv'd in banishment,
> Tug'd at the oare in *Gallies*
> (lines 162–3)

—suggest that *A Monumental Column* embodies views important to Webster and given utterance also in *The Duchess of Malfi*. Webster evidently felt deeply the death of a prince of whom much was hoped, but his elegy remains, as Hammond remarks, 'obstinately earthbound: the brilliance and originality of Webster's imagery seemingly deserts him in the formal couplets of this poem' (Hammond, 293).

By general consent Webster's masterpiece, *The Duchess of Malfi* was first performed before 16 December 1614, when William Ostler, the first Antonio, died. Mindful, presumably, of the poor reception of *The White Devil* at the Red Bull, Webster had offered his second tragedy to the King's Men. The outcome seems to have been a happy one, with *The Duchess of Malfi* well received by the more sophisticated audience at the Blackfriars (Gurr, 220) and, later, at the second Globe.

The Duchess herself is one of the greatest of tragic heroines, and her struggle, in the face of opposition from her brothers, Ferdinand and the Cardinal, to live a life true to her feelings is given memorable expression in verse as brilliant as that of *The White Devil*, but within a dramatic structure clearer and less convoluted than that of the earlier tragedy. Her brothers are also brilliantly portrayed, Ferdinand volatile, obsessive, and perhaps driven by an incestuous passion for his sister, and the Cardinal cold, ruthless, and concerned above all with family honour, while Bosola, their spy in the Duchess's household, is a compelling portrait of a man divided within himself, serving evil, yet drawn to admire and sympathize with the Duchess, whom he is employed to torment and finally to kill.

The Duchess's death scene is the most celebrated in Webster, and one of the greatest in Jacobean drama. Separated from her husband, Antonio, and her children, tormented by madmen introduced by Ferdinand, and then tested to the limits of endurance by the disguised Bosola, the Duchess passes from pride of rank ('I am Duchesse of *Malfy* still'; IV.ii, line 131) through stoic endurance to Christian humility, kneeling in acceptance of death, since

> heaven gates are not so highly arch'd
> As Princes pallaces, they that enter there
> Must go upon their knees
> (IV.ii, lines 219–21)

Such transcendence is followed by retribution as Ferdinand sinks into madness and the Cardinal into cowardice, while Bosola, who kills both, dies 'In a mist' (V.v, line 93), still a divided soul, unaware of how much he has done, wittingly or unwittingly, to assist the Duchess to reach spiritual peace.

Webster's next surviving play, *The Devil's Law-Case*, was probably completed about 1618, but it seems that in the interval there appeared another, now lost, entitled

'Guise'. Lists of printed plays dating from 1656–71 disagree as to its genre, but Samuel Sheppard, writing *c*.1650, speaks of Webster's 'three noble tragedies' (Forker, 460), and it seems safe to assume that the lost work was a tragedy. Since in his dedication of *The Devil's Law-Case* to Sir Thomas Finch Webster himself linked 'Guise' with *The White Devil* and *The Duchess of Malfi*, a work of considerable importance has presumably been lost.

Early in 1614, a few months after the author's death in the Tower of London, there appeared one of Jacobean England's bestsellers, Sir Thomas Overbury's *The Wife*. A second edition of the poem later that year was accompanied by twenty-two 'Characters' written '*by* [Overbury] *himselfe and other* learned gentlemen his friends'. By the eleventh edition, in 1622, the twenty-two characters (brief generalized sketches of personality and occupational types) had become eighty-three, of which thirty-two, added in the sixth edition (1615), were by Webster. It is generally accepted, also, that Webster edited the sixth edition, as he may have edited the four which preceded it, and the suggestion (Forker, 122) that Webster perhaps acted as Overbury's literary executor and gathered together the original collection of characters, then circulating in manuscript, is plausible, since it is highly likely that Webster had known Overbury since their days at the Middle Temple, which the latter also entered in 1598.

Some of Webster's characters, such as 'An Excellent Actor' and 'A Franklin', describe idealized figures, but the majority are, like 'An Ordinary Widow', satiric in tone. A similar tone pervades *The Devil's Law-Case*, written probably for performance by the Queen's Men at their new private theatre, the Cockpit in Drury Lane. A tragicomedy, in which theatricality and contrivance co-exist with near tragic elements, *The Devil's Law-Case* has the characteristic Websterian bite, particularly in the figure of the merchant, Romelio, a bourgeois reworking of the malcontents of the two great tragedies, Flamineo and Bosola. The leading women in the play, Romelio's sister, Jolenta, and their mother, Leonora, lack the stature or magnetism of Vittoria and the Duchess, but there is power none the less in Leonora's admission to her waiting woman that:

we have growne old together,
As many Ladies and their women doe,
With talking nothing, and with doing lesse:
We have spent our life in that which least concernes life,
Only in putting on our clothes
(III.iii, lines 419–22)

Later career The last of Webster's major plays, *The Devil's Law-Case* is also the last, it seems, that he wrote unaided. Why he wrote only in collaboration in his later years is unclear, though in general the plays suggest fitful artistic inspiration. The first of the collaborative works, *Anything for a Quiet Life*, was written *c*.1621. The title-page of the only edition (1662) of this city comedy attributes it to Thomas Middleton, but all the evidence, including computer-aided linguistic testing, points to collaboration and to Webster's authorship of perhaps 45 per cent of the play (D. J. Lake, *The Canon of Thomas Middleton's Plays*, 1975, 175–

84; M. P. Jackson, *Studies in Attribution: Middleton and Shakespeare*, 1979, 142–4). Paid little attention by Middleton or Webster scholars, *Anything for a Quiet Life* is an uneven work, with several strong scenes, but overall the weakest of Webster's late collaborations.

1624 was a busy year for Webster. In the spring and early summer he was at work on *A Cure for a Cuckold*, which the master of the revels, Sir Henry Herbert, licensed on 26 July (*Control and Censorship*, 153). Herbert gives Webster as sole author, but the only edition (1661) also credits William Rowley, while it may be that Heywood too had a hand in the tragicomedy (Gray; Jackson, 'Late Webster'). Webster wrote, it seems, the major scenes in the main plot, involving the couples, Lessingham and Clare and Annabel and Bonvile, and Rowley was responsible for the fine comic subplot, featuring the seaman, Compass, of what is generally agreed to be the best of Webster's late collaborative work.

Later in 1624 Webster and Rowley joined Dekker and Ford in writing the now lost 'A Late Murther of the Son upon the Mother, or, Keep the Widow Waking'. The play dramatized two recent scandals: Nathaniel Tindall's murder of his mother and the tricking into matrimony of an elderly widow, Anne Elsdon, by an unscrupulous fortune-hunter. Mistress Elsdon was resident in the parish of St Sepulchre, and her son-in-law, Benjamin Garfield, the son of a friend and fellow councilman of John Webster the elder, instigated legal proceedings to prevent further performances of 'Keep the Widow Waking'. It is through legal records that the available knowledge of the play has been established (C. J. Sisson, *Lost Plays of Shakespeare's Age*, 1936, 80–124).

Webster's other project in 1624 was the lord mayor's pageant, *Monuments of Honour*. Written at the behest of the Merchant Taylors' Company to celebrate the election of one of its own, Sir John Gore, it is one of the most elaborate civic pageants of which records survive. The Merchant Taylors spent over £1000 on it, of which £270 was paid to 'Iohn Webster the Poet' and three others, John Terry, William Patten, and George Lovett, who built 'all the land & water shewes' (Forker, 9). A major feature of *Monuments of Honour* is a 'show' called 'The Monument of Gratitude', which features and eulogizes the dead Henry, prince of Wales.

The following year, 1625, brought yet another collaboration, with Webster joining (linguistic evidence suggests) with Ford and Philip Massinger to complete *The Fair Maid of the Inn*, a tragicomedy on which John Fletcher (perhaps with Massinger) was working before Fletcher's death of the plague in August, Webster writing nearly half of the play (C. Hoy, 'The shares of Fletcher and his collaborators in the Beaumont and Fletcher canon', *Studies in Bibliography*, 13, 1960, 100–08). And Webster seems again to have collaborated (here with Heywood) on what is generally agreed to be his last play, the tragedy *Appius and Virginia*, although the title-page of 1654 credits him alone; Webster was, however, responsible for well over half of the play (Jackson, 'John Webster and Thomas Heywood'). Treating the story of Virginius, the Roman general who killed his daughter Virginia to prevent her dishonour at the hands of the corrupt decemvir Appius, *Appius and Virginia* exhibits a classical austerity, emphasizing the Roman virtues of duty and honour and the priority of public over private claims upon the individual. It also seems to provide a vehicle for criticism of the duke of Buckingham, the deeply unpopular favourite of King Charles I (*Works*, 2).

The dating of *Appius and Virginia* is in doubt, despite general agreement that it is probably Webster's last work. Apparently topical references have been adduced in support of a date of about 1624–6. A plausible chronology of Webster's last plays is thus 1624 for *A Cure for a Cuckold*, 'Keep the Widow Waking', and *Monuments of Honour*, 1625 for *The Fair Maid of the Inn*, and 1626–7 for *Appius and Virginia*.

After the characters, Webster published no further non-dramatic prose, unless, as has been suggested (Forker, ix), he was the '*I. W. Gent.*' who wrote *A Speedie Post* (1625), a collection of specimen letters 'for the helpe of such as are desirous to learne to write letters'. Nor, after *A Monumental Column*, did he produce significant non-dramatic verse, the most intriguing being verses in Latin and English accompanying an engraving of King James I and his family. In its original form this must predate the king's death in March 1625, but the only surviving copy is a version altered after October 1633 to take account of the birth of the first four of Charles I's children, as well as the death of James himself. Whatever their historical interest, however, the verses are undistinguished. Throughout his writing career, it is by his plays that John Webster must be judged.

Last years and death It is not known when Webster died. Heywood's reference to him in the past tense in *Hierarchie of the Blessed Angels* (licensed 7 November 1634) suggests that he was by then dead. But since Dekker and Middleton, both dead, are referred to in the present tense, little weight can be attached to this. Nor is it clear what significance is to be attached to William Hemminges's facetious allusion, in 1632, to the refusal of 'webster's brother' to 'lend a Coach' for the funeral of Thomas Randolph's finger because:

> he swore thay all weare hired to Convey
> the Malfy dutches sadly on her way
> (*William Hemminge's Elegy on Randolph's Finger*, ed. C. G. Moore-Smith, 1923, 12)

Forker (p. 58) believes that such a jest would be inappropriate were the dramatist dead, and particularly if recently so, whereas Bradbrook (p. 194) takes it to imply that the dramatist was now dead and his brother Edward head of the family.

Where John Webster died and where he was buried are also unknown. If he still lived in Nag's Head Lane, by St Sepulchre's Church, as he did shortly after his marriage, then he was presumably buried there, with his parents, brother, and sister-in-law. But an entry in the parish register of St James, Clerkenwell, stating that 'John Webster was buried' on 3 March 1638 may quite plausibly refer to the dramatist. For the parish of St James adjoined that of

St Sepulchre, and it was there that both Dekker and Rowley were buried. There would be nothing surprising in Webster, in his last years, living close to old friends and colleagues.

Personality and critical assessment Of Webster's personality we know little, yet can infer a good deal, particularly from the dedications and addresses prefacing *The White Devil*, *A Monumental Column*, *The Devil's Law-Case*, and *Monuments of Honour*. The impression they create is of a man assertive of his own worth yet thin-skinned and sensitive to criticism. It is a personality recognizable, travestied, in Fitzgeffrey's malicious portrait of 'Crabbed (*Websterio*) | The *Play-wright*, *Cart-wright*', a portrait which lampoons Webster's slowness in composition:

> Was ever man so mangl'd with a Poem?
> See how he drawes his mouth awry of late,
> How he scrubs: wrings his wrests: scratches his Pate

and as a critic:

> Heer's not a word *cursively* I have *Writ*,
> But hee'l *Industriously* examine it.
> And in some 12. monthes hence (or there *about*)
> Set in a shamefull sheete, my errors *out*.
> But what care I it *will* be so obscure,
> That none shall understand him (I am sure.)
> (Fitzgeffrey, sig. F6v–F7r)

Other aspects of his personality, however, belie the epithet 'crabbed'. There is evidence, for instance, of his good relationship with the companies which performed his plays in his praise of the cast of *The White Devil*, and particularly Richard Perkins, almost certainly the first Flamineo, and in his inclusion of a cast list in the 1623 quarto of *The Duchess of Malfi* (both 'firsts' by an English dramatist). Equally, he is generous, in the prefatory address to *The White Devil*, in his praise of his fellows Chapman, Jonson, Francis Beaumont, Fletcher, Shakespeare, Heywood, and Dekker, and he worked harmoniously, so far as can be established, with a range of dramatists from the first rate, such as Middleton and Ford, to the mediocre, like Munday and Chettle. Moreover, as the dedicatory poems to *The Duchess of Malfi* attest, he enjoyed the friendship and esteem of such men as Middleton, Ford, and Rowley.

Of the social circles in which Webster moved next to nothing is known, though some details can be inferred. Through his family he would have had a wide range of acquaintance, at least, among the wealthier citizens of London, while his sojourn at the inns of court would have brought him into contact with lawyers and writers such as Marston and Overbury. Among fellow dramatists, he seems to have maintained the longest and closest relationships with Heywood and with Dekker, to whom in 1613 John Webster the elder lent £40, a sum which the chronically insolvent Dekker had difficulty in repaying. With Shakespeare, however, as with Chapman, Jonson, Beaumont, and Fletcher, Webster seems, despite his approbation, to have had little contact, this perhaps because, *The Duchess of Malfi* apart, he worked almost exclusively with Queen Anne's Men rather than the King's Men.

Critically, Webster has been the centre of disagreement

more profound than that over any of his fellow dramatists, with his status as a great poet conceded but his dramaturgy and his vision of life fiercely criticized (T. S. Eliot, *Collected Essays*, 1951, 117, describing him as 'an interesting example of a very great literary and dramatic genius directed towards chaos') and equally fiercely defended. After the 1960s, however, the nature of the debate changed, the issue no longer being whether Webster had a coherent world vision but what that vision might be, and equally, acknowledging their existence, what the structural principles underlying Webster's two great tragedies are. In the 1960s there was a tendency to see Webster as a proto-existentialist, but since then he has been viewed in more strictly Jacobean terms, debate about his world vision centring on whether he is a providentialist, albeit with doubts and anxieties (P. B. Murray, *A Study of John Webster*, 1969; T. McAlindon, *English Renaissance Tragedy*, 1986), or a Renaissance sceptic, interrogating the traditional providential view of the world (J. Dollimore, *Radical Tragedy*, 1984). Likewise, analysis of a range of features in *The White Devil* and *The Duchess of Malfi* from imagery to emblems and from symbolism to staging has revealed that structures earlier decried as 'a gothic aggregation' (J. R. Brown, in Hunter and Hunter, 241) or 'broken-backed' (W. Archer, in Hunter and Hunter, 95) are organized according to principles just as rigorous as those governing the well-made play, but involving circularity, parallelism, and repetition rather than a strictly linear and narrative-based development (*Works*, ed. Gunby and others, 1.57–81, 381–407; C. Luckyj, *A Winter's Snake*, 1989). Seminal in respect of this revised understanding is I.-S. Ekeblad's article 'The "impure art" of John Webster' (*Review of English Studies*, 9, 1958, 253–67).

The greatly increased critical attention devoted to Webster has been matched (indeed stimulated) by a greatly increased number of productions of his two great tragedies. Highly acclaimed London productions of *The Duchess of Malfi* (1945) and *The White Devil* (1947) marked the beginning of regular commercial exposure. Great actors such as Robert Helpman, John Gielgud, Eric Porter, Bob Hoskins, and Ian McKellen have brought distinction to the roles of Ferdinand, Bosola, and Flamineo, but the most memorable performances have on the whole been by the great women actors, including Peggy Ashcroft, Margaret Rawlings, Glenda Jackson, Helen Mirren, Judi Dench, Eileen Atkins, Juliet Stevenson, and Harriet Walter, who have played the Duchess and Vittoria. In general, indeed, productions have been measured by the success of the female leads, reinforcing on the stage the impression which *The White Devil* and *The Duchess of Malfi* create in the study: that the tragedies revolve around the two female figures after whom they are named.

'Webster was much possessed by death'; so, famously, wrote T. S. Eliot in 'Whispers of Immortality' (*Collected Poems, 1909–62*, 1963, 55). So indeed he was, and the death scenes of Vittoria and her brother Flamineo and of the Duchess are intensely moving. But Webster was much possessed also by life, and by what Catherine Belsey has described as 'the problem of how to survive in a corrupt

world' ('Emblem and antithesis in *The Duchess of Malfi*', *Renaissance Drama*, 11, 1980, 133). His vision of that world and the struggle to live a life of integrity within it matures and mellows as he moves from the almost unrelieved darkness of *The White Devil*, where Vittoria, Flamineo, and her lover, Brachiano, perish without ever emerging from the mist which is Webster's standard metaphor for moral and spiritual disorientation, through *The Duchess of Malfi*, where the darkness which envelops Bosola and the Duchess's brothers is relieved by her progression from pride to humility and from despair to faith, to *The Devil's Law-Case*, where the plots of Romelio and his mother Leonora are foiled and they are rescued from evil by the efforts of the law (in the person of Ariosto) and the church (the Capuchin), to share in the play's (just) comic outcome.

Compared with those of contemporaries such as Shakespeare, Middleton, Fletcher, and Massinger, Webster's dramatic output is small. Of the fifteen or so plays in which he had a hand, four are lost, and a fifth—the Melbourne manuscript, if his—is a fragment, while a further seven are collaborative. And though of these four (the two *Ho* plays, *A Cure for a Cuckold*, and *Appius and Virginia*) deserve better than their long-standing stage neglect, it is by the two great tragedies and *The Devil's Law-Case* that Webster must ultimately be judged. The last of these has gained critical attention but lacks stage exposure, there having been only three commercial productions since the seventeenth century. But with *The White Devil* and *The Duchess of Malfi* firmly established in the commercial repertory, Webster's reputation as the greatest English tragic writer for the stage after Shakespeare seems assured. The famous lines in these tragedies—'I am Duchesse of *Malfy* still', 'Cover her face: Mine eyes dazell: she di'd yong' (*The Duchess of Malfi*, IV.ii, line 251), and

> My soule, like to a ship in a blacke storme,
> Is driven I know not whither
> (*The White Devil*, v.vi, lines 243–4)

—which so caught the imagination of nineteenth-century critics like Lamb and Swinburne, resonate still, but not in isolation. Rather, they are to be seen as moments of transcendence in highly subtle and coherent works of art, in which all the resources of poetic drama are directed towards the embodiment of a complex and powerful vision of human existence.   DAVID GUNBY

Sources *The works of John Webster*, ed. D. Gunby and others, 2 vols. (1995–) [*The white devil*, *The duchess of Malfi*, and *The devil's law-case* are cited from this edn] · *The complete works of John Webster*, ed. F. L. Lucas, 4 vols. (1927) [all other Webster texts are cited from this edn] · *The dramatic works of Thomas Dekker*, ed. F. T. Bowers (1953–61) · C. R. Forker, *Skull beneath the skin: the achievement of John Webster* (1986) · M. C. Bradbrook, *John Webster: citizen and dramatist* (1980) · A. Hammond, 'John Webster', *Jacobean and Caroline dramatists*, ed. F. Bowers, DLitB, 58 (1987) · *The Henslowe papers*, ed. R. A. Foakes (1977) · M. Edmond, 'In search of John Webster', *TLS* (24 Dec 1976), 1622 · H. Fitzgeffrey, *Satyres: and satyricall epigrams* (1617) · G. K. Hunter and S. K. Hunter, eds., *John Webster* (1969) · A. Gurr, *The Shakespearean stage, 1574–1642*, 3rd edn (1992) · *The control and censorship of Caroline drama: the records of Sir Henry Herbert, master of the revels, 1623–73*, ed. N. W. Bawcutt (1996) · M. P. Jackson, 'John Webster and Thomas Heywood in *Appius and Virginia*: a bibliographical approach to the problem of authorship', *Studies in Bibliography*, 38 (1985), 217–35 • H. D. Gray, 'A *cure for a cuckold* by Heywood, Rowley and Webster', *Modern Language Review*, 22 (1927), 389–97 • M. P. Jackson, 'Late Webster and his collaborators: how many playwrights wrote *A cure for a cuckold*?', *Papers of the Bibliographical Society of America*, 95/3 (2001), 295–313 • D. J. Lake, 'Webster's additions to *The malcontent*', *N&Q*, 226 (1981), 158 • *John Marston, The malcontent*, ed. G. K. Hunter (1975) • *George Chapman, Ben Jonson, John Marston: Eastward Ho*, ed. R. W. Van Fossen (1979) • parish register, London, St Giles Cripplegate, 4 Nov 1577, GL [marriage: John Webster and Elizabeth Coates, parents] • C. H. Hopwood, ed., *Middle Temple records*, 4 vols. (1904–5) • parish register, Islington, St Mary, 18 March 1606 [marriage] • parish register, London, St James, Clerkenwell, 3 March 1638 [burial]

Webster, John (1611–1682), schoolmaster and polemicist, was born on 3 February 1611 at Thornton on the Hill in the parish of Coxwold, Yorkshire, the son of Edward Webster. Claims that he was a student at Cambridge appear to be without foundation. In the early 1630s he studied chemistry under the Hungarian Johannes Banfi Hunyades (1576–1646), chemist to the earl of Pembroke, living in Whitechapel. Chemistry and medicine, together with teaching, were to be his lifelong occupations. In 1632 he was ordained as a minister by Thomas Morton, bishop of Durham, and was appointed curate to the parish of Kildwick, near Skipton, in Yorkshire. In 1637 Webster was deprived of his living, possibly for his sympathies with the Grindletonians, a radical sect which originated in his part of the Yorkshire dales. As curate of Kildwick, he detected a case of imposture connected with accusations of witchcraft.

In 1643 Webster was appointed master of the grammar school of Clitheroe and from 1660 to 1662 served as governor in the same school. He left his post for two periods: in 1647, when he was intruded as minister in the village of Mitton, apparently with no income from the parish, and in 1648, when he served as surgeon in the parliamentary regiment of Colonel Shuttleworth. In 1649 he was admitted as a Clitheroe burgess and, with the exception of a short stay in London in 1653, he spent the rest of his life at Clitheroe.

Activities during the Commonwealth Webster's importance rests on his participation in the debates concerning the reconstruction of religious and social life during the Commonwealth. In sermons delivered in London at All Hallows, Lombard Street, and at Whitehall, in June 1653, he attacked the idea of a professional clergy, claiming that ministers were not created by the university or by the civil magistrate, whose powers in spiritual affairs he firmly opposed. A member of no sect, he advocated the right of free interpretation of the scriptures and unambiguously denied that human learning could have any role in ensuring grace and redemption. In his sermons he dealt with two themes which were to be developed in his subsequent works, the criticism of traditional learning and the view that the Devil is no physical agent. He maintained that the biblical references to the Devil are to be interpreted as a synonym of the depraved condition of the human soul.

In October 1653, together with William Erbery (whose works he edited in 1658), and John Cardell, who acted as moderator, Webster took part in a dispute at All Hallows on the question of who ordered ministers. The opposite side comprised a Presbyterian, an Independent, and a Baptist. According to the report published by the *Mercurius Politicus* of 13–20 October 1653, the dispute was particularly lively, but Webster found this report false and somewhat offensive. The anonymous author of the report had stated that Webster and his associates wanted to 'knock down Learning and the Ministry'. Webster replied that he was not 'an enemy to humane, or acquired learning, as it is considered in natural, civil, artificial, or moral respect, but as it is considered in a theological respect' (*The Picture of Mercurius Politicus*, 1653, 6). Religious toleration and opposition to an established state-supported church are reasserted in *The Saints Guide* and in *The Judgement Set, and the Bookes Opened* (1654), the latter being a collection of his sermons. His views were attacked in G. W[ither]., *The Modern States-Man* (1654), a work advocating the benefits of human learning for the understanding of the sacred text.

The reform of learning is the topic of Webster's controversial *Academiarum examen* (1654), which was dedicated to Major-General John Lambert, to whom he had sent a draft of the work a few years before its publication. In the dedicatory epistle (dated 21 October 1653) he attacked Episcopalians, Presbyterians, and Independents alike, and declared that he was no recipient of tithes or state payment. He went on to launch a fierce attack on the English universities, both for their claim to provide the training for the clergy and for their scholastic curricula. He put forward his own plan, which was generally Baconian in its inspiration and aims, but also relied on a wide spectrum of more recent philosophical writings.

The reformed universities, according to Webster, had to promote experimental and utilitarian learning, which should include alchemy and natural magic, which he vindicated against the impostors' misuse. His philosophical views, as expressed in his project of reform, are eclectic: besides Baconianism and Helmontian iatrochemistry, he also supported the theosophy of Fludd and Boehme, and the atomism of Digby and Gassendi. Along with Van Helmont, he attacked the Aristotelians' overestimate of human reason and stressed the role of divine illumination as the foundation of true learning. Although he himself knew and taught Hebrew and Greek, he dismissed the study of languages as useless to the understanding of the scriptures, which, he claimed, could only be achieved by the aid of the Spirit of God. On the other hand, he maintained that the search for natural languages and the study of the Paracelsian doctrine of signatures were to be included in the reformed curricula.

Academiarum examen aroused vehement reaction from the Oxford academics John Wilkins and Seth Ward, and from the Presbyterian writer Thomas Hall. Ward published his reply to Webster, *Vindiciae academiarum* (1654), anonymously, but the introduction was written by Wilkins. According to Wilkins and Ward, Webster was ignorant both of the sciences he wanted to promote, and of the actual state of the universities he wanted to reform. The universities, they maintained, were no longer dominated by Aristotelianism, but had already adopted the new experimental philosophy. In addition, they criticized Webster for having contaminated the 'sound' experimental philosophy with alchemy, astrology, cabbala, Rosicrucianism, and magic. Wilkins also engaged himself in a defence of academic teaching for the training of ministers. Hall, in his *Histrio-Mastix: a Whip for Webster* (1654), denounced Webster (whom he mistook for the homonymous dramatist) as a leveller, a familist, and a magician.

Although he was licensed as a medical practitioner by the archbishop of York in 1661, Webster was already successfully practising medicine in the early 1650s. In 1654 he was paid the considerable sum of £42 by a Henry Waite for a three-year medical apprenticeship to him. Webster's life at Clitheroe was rather prosperous. He had acquired substantial property, much of it land sequestered from royalists. He was able to purchase apparatus for his chemical investigations, and a substantial number of books, which, at the time of his death, reached approximately 1660 volumes. A somewhat litigious man, he was engaged in disputes and conflicts for many years. In 1654 he had a dispute with Thomas Jolly, an Independent minister. On 2 November 1657 Webster appealed to John Lambert for assistance in a suit brought against him by one Robert Inman, who was claiming compensation for the loss of an animal requisitioned by Webster during the second civil war. In 1658, as a result of a judicial inquiry, he was arrested and had his books and papers confiscated.

In 1657 Webster became in-bailiff of Clitheroe, a post he held from October 1657 to October 1659, then in 1665 and again in 1675. It is apparent that his appointment as a bailiff was opposed by, among others, Roger Keynon, Thomas Alston, and Edmund Robinson, on the grounds that Webster was guilty of political and legal abuses, heretic opinions, and lax morals.

Webster's attacks on the state church and its clergy, on ceremonies, and on the universities which trained the clergy, had much in common with the Quakers' views. An undated letter in Friends' House in London shows that Thomas Lowson tried to persuade Webster to join the Quakers. However, in the late 1650s disillusionment and disappointment over the fate of the English revolution seemed to prevail in Webster's mind. In his introduction to the *Testimony of William Erbery* (1658) he expressed his pessimistic view along these lines: 'the restitution of all things is yet afarr off; the Saints running from Mountain to Hill, is rather an exchange of one bondage for another then any reall redemption from the Ancient yoke'.

Life after the Restoration After the Restoration, Webster's behaviour seems to have been inspired by loyalty to the new regime. In 1661 he voted for Ambrose Pudsay, the royalist candidate to the Cavalier Parliament. His appointment as magistrate for Clitheroe in 1665 was possible because he conformed to the restored church. In the dedicatory epistle of his *Metallographia* (addressed to Prince Rupert) he referred to the Royal Society as 'one of the happy fruits of His Majesties blessed and miraculous Restoration' (*Metallographia*, 1671). In the *Displaying of Supposed Witchcraft* (1677) he styled the Quakers as fanatics and

rebuked those who pretended to be guided by the Spirit in their own interpretations of the scriptures. It is apparent that in the 1670s his religious views underwent a substantial change and his previous radicalism was abandoned. None the less, he restated his opposition to the notion that human reason could be of some help in interpreting the scriptures.

Webster married, on 6 November 1667, Elizabeth (*b.* 1627), daughter of Roger Aspinall of Clitheroe. They had no children. His wife survived him and was married to the Revd William Bankes of Mitton for twenty years. Webster's life at Clitheroe was isolated, though not entirely separated from the world of learning. He was able to pursue his chemical and mineralogical studies and was aware of the latest news in science and philosophy both in England and on the continent. He corresponded with a number of natural philosophers and is very likely to have been responsible for *The Last Will and Testament of Basil Valentine*, an English translation which was published in 1670.

The Metallographia, or, An History of Metals is Webster's major scientific achievement. (The book was dated 1671, though it may have been published during the previous two years.) As attested by internal evidence, the work, containing references to a huge volume of alchemical, chemical, and mineralogical literature, was completed after 1666. Webster's professed end was that of stimulating metallurgical knowledge and the exploitation of mines in England. The work, however, deals with a wide range of topics, including a vindication of the ancient origins of alchemical knowledge, the generation of metals, their use in medicine and their transmutation. Helmontian chemical views are strictly linked with the corpuscular theory of matter, which is mainly based on the works of Robert Boyle. The *Metallographia* had a noticeable impact on the world of learning. It was reviewed in the *Philosophical Transactions of the Royal Society* of 1670 and in the *Journal des Sçavans* of 1678. John Beale praised it in a letter to Henry Oldenburg of January 1671, while D. G. Morhof (*De metallorum transmutatione*, 1673) dismissed it as scarcely original . Webster's proficiency in chemistry was extolled by a Durham schoolmaster, Peter Nelson, in a letter to Oldenburg of 25 March 1671, where he spoke of him as 'a man of more than ordinary acuteness and very fit for your Correspondence' (*Correspondence of Henry Oldenburg*, 7.535). With a few exceptions, historians now recognize Webster's *Metallographia* as a valuable contribution to seventeenth-century science of metals.

Webster's last work was *The Displaying of Supposed Witchcraft* (1677), a criticism of the traditional demonology. It is apparent that material for it had been collected for several decades and the work was completed by 1674, but initially it failed to gain an imprimatur, apparently because of opposition from the ecclesiastical authorities. Webster had asked for the support of his friend and correspondent Martin Lister, to whom he sent a draft of the work in 1674. He also sent a copy to the Royal Society, which was forwarded by Oldenburg to Hooke, who read it on 19 March 1675. In the event, *The Displaying of Supposed Witchcraft* was published in 1677 with the imprimatur of the society's vice-president, Sir Jonas Moore, dated 29 June 1676, and was dedicated to the justices of the peace in the West Riding of Yorkshire. The work, which opens with a vindication of freedom in philosophical matters, is aimed at answering the arguments in favour of the existence of witchcraft held by Meric Casaubon and by Joseph Glanvill. Although he denied that demons have a pure spiritual nature, Webster stated that men can only have mental, not physical, contact with the Devil. He maintains that what is commonly taken as a sign of possession is to be imputed to melancholy, imposture, or ignorance. Having denied the Devil's capacity to intervene in the natural world, Webster engages in a vindication of natural magic, which is largely indebted to Van Helmont's arguments. *The Displaying of Supposed Witchcraft* was attacked by Glanvill and by Henry More (*Sadducismus triumphatus … with a Letter of Dr. H. More*, 1681), who asserted the real existence of witches. Webster's demonological views were also attacked by Benjamin Camfield, a Leicester cleric, who accused him of denying the existence of spiritual substances (*A Theological Discourse … also an Appendix Containing some Reflexions upon Mr. Websters Displaying …*, 1678).

Webster died at Clitheroe on 18 June 1682 and was buried there on 21 June 1682. In his will, which he made in January 1680, he left his goods to his wife, Elizabeth, and after her death to his nephews Edward Webster, John Webster, and Richard Webster, and 40s. to the poor of Grindleton. His will mentions chirurgical and chemical instruments, as well as his library. An epitaph written by himself is in the parish church of Clitheroe.

ANTONIO CLERICUZIO

Sources W. S. Weeks, 'John Webster, author of *The displaying of supposed witchcraft*', *Transactions of the Lancashire and Cheshire Antiquarian Society*, 39 (1921), 55–107 • P. Elmer, *The library of Dr John Webster: the making of a seventeenth-century radical* (1986) • D. Harley, *From seeker to cavalier: chemistry and anti-Calvinism in the chequered career of John Webster of Clitheroe* [forthcoming] • W. S. Weeks, 'Further information about Dr John Webster', *Transactions of the Lancashire and Cheshire Antiquarian Society*, 48 (1932), 30–59 • A. G. Debus, *Science and education in the seventeenth century: the Webster–Ward debate* (1970) • C. Webster, *The great instauration: science, medicine and reform, 1626–1660* (1975) • C. Hill, *The world turned upside down: radical ideas during the English revolution* (1972) • *The correspondence of Henry Oldenburg*, ed. and trans. A. R. Hall and M. B. Hall, 5 (1968); 7 (1970) • *Mercurius Politicus* (13–20 Oct 1653), 2795–6 • J. R. Partington, *A history of chemistry*, 2 (1961)
Archives BL, Add. MS 4255, fol. 39r–v • Bodl. Oxf., Lister MSS, MS 34, fols. 145, 147–8, 157r–158v, 173r–v • RS Friends, Lond., Swarthmore MSS, MS 7/23Br–v
Wealth at death £507: will and inventory, Elmer, *Library of Dr John Webster*, 235–7

Webster, Margaret (1905–1972), actress and theatre director, was born on 15 March 1905 in New York, the only child of Benjamin (Ben) *Webster (1864–1947), actor and member of a well-known theatrical family, and his wife, Mary Louise (May) *Whitty (1865–1948) [see under Webster, Benjamin], actress and campaigner for good causes. When Ben's American tour ended the Websters returned with their baby daughter to 31 Bedford Street, off the Strand, their London home for forty-seven years.

Peggy, as she was then known, was educated at Queen Anne's School, Caversham, where she played Puck in a school production of *A Midsummer Night's Dream*. She studied for the stage at the Etlinger Theatre School. Realizing that her chosen profession was going to be a struggle and that the slight cast she had in one eye would be a handicap, she underwent two successful operations. Her first job was in 1924 as a member of the chorus in *The Trojan Women* at the New Theatre, with Sybil Thorndike and Lewis Casson (at 1 guinea a performance). In 1925 she played the Gentlewoman in *Hamlet* with John Barrymore at the Theatre Royal, Haymarket, and then returned to the Cassons to lead the chorus in *Hippolytus* followed by her first experience of touring when she understudied Sybil Thorndike in *Saint Joan*. Small parts in unmemorable plays were interspersed with appearances with Sunday societies.

On the suggestion of the critic St John Ervine she changed her name to Margaret, but solid success still evaded her until she was spotted in a makeshift production by Lilian Baylis, who offered her a place in the Old Vic company of 1929–30, in which John Gielgud had his first shot at *Richard II* and *Hamlet* (in which she appeared as the Player Queen). She was in two other plays with Gielgud. The first, *Musical Chairs* by Ronald Mackenzie, directed by Komisarjevsky, had a long run which prevented Margaret from joining the Vic at the start of the next season, although she was released to play Lady Macbeth in a production that lived up to the play's reputation for ill luck. She commented that she was probably the only Lady Macbeth to have had four husbands in three weeks. She grew restless during the run of *Richard of Bordeaux* (1933), her second engagement with Gielgud in a new play, so in 1935 she turned to directing. In 1937 Maurice Evans, whom she had known when he was an ambitious amateur in London, invited her to direct his *Richard II* on Broadway. This was the first of her Shakespearian productions in New York. Although critical of the high costs and a lack of good speaking in the American theatre, she relished the opportunities. Her production of *Othello* with Paul Robeson (in which she played Emilia) ran throughout the 1943 Broadway season, which no other Shakespeare play had previously done, and her percentage was the largest she ever received.

With Eva Le Gallienne Margaret Webster hoped to establish the American Repertory Theatre, but this proved to be a short-lived and expensive failure. Having decided that New York was not the right place for the kind of serious theatre they had in mind, she embarked on gruelling bus and truck tours, often visiting towns that had not had a professional theatre for thirty-five years. The long distances, union troubles, and unhappy actors would have broken the spirit of a less determined and idealistic management. The venture was a financial disaster and was dissolved in 1948. To her surprise Rudolf Bing invited her to direct *Don Carlos* at the Metropolitan Opera House in 1950. There was a chorus of ninety-eight people, whereas on tour there were eight. She found the production schedules difficult to put into practice but on the whole enjoyed her operatic interlude.

Margaret Webster inherited from her mother a devotion to good causes and fought hard on behalf of Actors' Equity on both sides of the Atlantic. This, and directing Paul Robeson in *Othello*, made her suspect in the eyes of Senator McCarthy, and in 1953 she received a summons to appear before the Senate Sub-Committee on Investigations. Her case was dismissed but the experience damaged her confidence for some time. When she returned to Britain in 1955 she was impressed with the state of the theatre and was delighted with an invitation to direct *Measure for Measure*, a play which had always interested her, although the 1957 Old Vic production was disappointing. In 1960 she was back with the Cassons when she directed Noël Coward's *Waiting in the Wings*. Set in a home for retired actresses, the play had a cast which, as well as Sybil and Lewis, contained several other old friends. She took to lecturing chiefly on Shakespeare, and travelled all over the United States and to South Africa, where she directed Eugene O'Neill's *A Touch of the Poet* in 1961. She made good use of her experiences for her book *Shakespeare without Tears* (1942). She disliked intensely the idea that Shakespeare wrote for scholars. She wrote and acted in a one-woman programme on the Brontës which she performed in America and at the Arts Theatre, London, in 1963–4.

In her last years Margaret Webster divided her time between her house on Martha's Vineyard and one in Hampstead, London, which she shared with the novelist Pamela Sydney *Frankau (1908–1967). She died of cancer in St Christopher's Hospice, Sydenham, London, on 13 November 1972. WENDY TREWIN

Sources M. Webster, *The same only different* (1969) • M. Webster, *Don't put your daughter on the stage* (1972) • I. Herbert, ed., *Who's who in the theatre*, 16th edn (1977) • *The Times* (14 Nov 1972) • M. Vickery-Bareford, 'Webster, Margaret', *ANB* • *CGPLA Eng. & Wales* (1973) • private information (2004) [friend]
Archives SOUND BL NSA, performance recordings
Wealth at death £5,118 in England and Wales: administration with will, 11 Dec 1973, *CGPLA Eng. & Wales*

Webster, Maurice (d. 1635), lutenist and composer, was probably the son of George Webster, lutenist at the Bückeburg court near Hanover, perhaps taking his unusual first name from Landgrave Moritz of Hesse-Cassel. A George Webster was among Robert Browne's company of English actors and musicians at Kassel between at least 1596 and 1603. Maurice in turn worked at the Holstein-Schaumburg court of Count Ernst III in Bückeburg until the count's death in 1622. He contributed four dances to Thomas Simpson's *Taffel Consort* (published in Hamburg in 1621; most of the composers featured in the collection were working at Bückeburg).

Following Count Ernst's death Webster travelled to England and was appointed as 'musician for the Consort' to James I, serving among the lutes from 25 March 1623. He was allowed regular supplies of strings for the bass lute, but may also have played the bass viol since all his extant compositions are for string consort; two bass viol 'divisions on a ground' also survive. His importance as a composer was in apparently introducing to England a consort style already prevalent in Germany, in which the two

upper parts engage in dialogue through short phrases, freely exchanging places within the texture. The inner parts were simplified or even omitted as the textures were reduced to three or four parts only. Five sets of music and papers belonging to the composer were listed on 9 November 1636 among 'Severall … Setts of bookes' in the possession of William Cavendish, duke of Newcastle (1593–1676), suggesting he had been employed by the duke. He was a member of the Corporation of Musick of Westminster, reconstituted by charter of 15 July 1635, but Maurice Webster, described as gentleman, was buried at St Peter's, Nottingham, on 22 December that year, presumably while in service with Cavendish.

ANDREW ASHBEE

Sources G. Dodd, *Thematic index of music for viols* (1980–) • A. Ashbee, ed., *Records of English court music*, 3 (1988) • A. Ashbee, ed., *Records of English court music*, 4 (1991) • A. Ashbee, ed., *Records of English court music*, 5 (1991) • A. Ashbee, ed., *Records of English court music*, 8 (1995) • P. Holman, *Four and twenty fiddlers: the violin at the English court, 1540–1690*, new edn (1993) • L. Hulse, 'Apollo's Whirligig: William Cavendish, duke of Newcastle and his music collection', *Seventeenth Century*, 9 (1994), 213–46 • P. Walls, *Music in the English courtly masque, 1604–1640* (1996) • A. Ashbee and D. Lasocki, eds., *A biographical dictionary of English court musicians, 1485–1714*, 2 vols. (1998) • administration, PRO, PROB 6/15, fol. 145v
Wealth at death £76: administration, PRO, PROB 6/15, fol. 145v

Webster [*née* Bevan], **Nesta Helen** (1875–1960), conspiracy theorist, was born on 14 August 1875 at Trent Park, Enfield, Middlesex, the ninth daughter and last of sixteen children of Robert Cooper Lee *Bevan (1809–1890), banker, by whose second wife, Emma Frances (1827–1909), she was the sixth daughter and ninth child. Her maternal grandfather was Philip Shuttleworth, who had been successively warden of New College, Oxford, and bishop of Chichester. Robert Bevan was for most of his active life a director of the family bank, Barclay, Bevan & Co. (later Barclay's Bank). The family lived at Trent Park, Middlesex, at Fosbury Manor, Wiltshire, and at 25 Princes Gate, London (and, because of Robert Bevan's health, at a villa in Cannes in the winter months).

Shortly before Nesta's birth her mother had joined the Plymouth Brethren, and the atmosphere at home tended to be somewhat stifling, despite Nesta's deep affection for her ageing father. He died in 1890; Trent Park and Fosbury Manor passed to Nesta's half-brother Frank, and she and her mother went to live abroad, in Cannes and Switzerland.

Nesta's brothers Anthony Ashley *Bevan and Edwyn Robert *Bevan both became distinguished scholars, in Cambridge and Oxford respectively. The Websters did not believe in formal schooling for girls and Nesta was educated privately by a succession of governesses, apart from one disastrous year at a school called Brownshill Court, near Stroud. In 1894, however, she enrolled at Westfield College, London, where she found the work for matriculation too demanding but stayed on as a general student. Dogged by ill health, she left in 1896.

Owing to an inheritance from her father Nesta now had considerable independent means. Between 1899 and 1902 she undertook two round-the-world trips, on the second of which, in India, she met Arthur Templer Webster (1865–1942), district officer of the United Provinces region, who was the son of Henry Benny Webster, of the Bengal civil service. They married in London on 14 May 1904. They had two daughters and for most of their married life they lived at 84 Cadogan Place, Chelsea, London.

On a visit to Switzerland in 1910 Nesta Webster had an experience that strongly affected her future activities. Reading the letters of the comtesse de Sabran, written at the time of the French Revolution, she became convinced that she herself was a reincarnation of someone who had lived in that period; previous premonitions when passing through Paris (where she had seen the rue St Honoré 'running with blood') now became clear. She set about writing on the French Revolution, and in 1916 produced *The Chevalier de Boufflers*. This was followed, in 1919, by *The French Revolution: a Study in Democracy*, in which she developed a wide-ranging conspiracy theory of history, based on the abiding influence of 'Illuminated Freemasonry' behind all revolutionary activities. The lack of serious reviews of this book proved to her that the conspiracy was still alive.

Amid the post-war furore caused by the 'discovery' of *Protocols of the Elders of Zion* Webster became convinced that Jews were the main force behind this international conspiracy. Even after *Protocols* was shown to be a forgery she asserted that it had nevertheless shown of what the Jews were capable. With her book *World Revolution: the Plot Against Civilization* (1921) she developed the theory of a perennial 'Judaeo-Masonic' plot based on international finance, of which the latest manifestation had been the Bolshevik revolution. She was soon taken up by the anti-semitic eighth duke of Northumberland (Alan Ian Percy), to whose newspaper, *The Patriot*, she contributed for the next quarter of a century and whose Boswell publishing house published most of her subsequent books, the best-known being *Secret Societies and Subversive Movements* (1924) and *The Socialist Network* (1926). In the mid-1920s she joined Rotha Lintorn-Orman's 'British Fascisti', eventually serving on their grand council.

By the 1930s Webster's publications had brought her to the attention of many like-minded people in Britain, including members of the antisemitic 'patriotic societies', such as Captain Ramsay and Admiral Sir Barry Domvile. Her attitudes were, like Ramsay's, intimately bound up with her Christian beliefs, with 'Judaeo-Bolshevism' being seen as plotting the undermining of Christianity. Her former, resolute anti-Germanism was dispelled by the advent of Hitler, whose mission she saw as being 'to cleanse Germany of the Jewish influence'. In 1938 Domvile recruited her to his pro-Nazi movement, The Link. A series of articles in *The Patriot* in 1938–9, entitled 'Germany and England', outlined her admiration for the new German state. Interestingly in this same period her brother Edwyn Bevan was a vocal proponent of academic sanctions against Nazi Germany because of its attitude to the Jews. It took the Nazi-Soviet pact of August 1939 to turn her against Hitler, whom she now saw as a dupe of the very forces against which he had appeared to be a bulwark. In 1939–40 she wrote a further 'Germany and England' series of articles for *The Patriot*, modifying her earlier views.

Nesta Webster's husband, Arthur, died in 1942. In 1949 she published the first volume of her autobiography, *Spacious Days*, which covered merely the period to 1919. (The manuscript of the second volume, *Crowded Hours*, was stolen—leading of course to further conspiracy theories on the part of her admirers.) In her final years, she spent much time preparing, with Anthony Gittens, a revised edition of *World Revolution*, which dealt with the post-war spread of communism. This appeared in 1971, after her death. She died of a heart condition on 7 May 1960, in her flat at 66 Cadogan Place, Chelsea, London.

Since Webster's death a great industry relating to her works has developed. Her message has been taken up by assorted conspiracy theorists and antisemites all over the world; this has been much facilitated by the internet, where she features in hundreds of entries, including the book lists of a wide variety of extremist organizations in the United States. This entirely unremarkable woman has proved to be a lasting example of the fact that the most extreme and unreal views, even when naïvely expressed, can find a ready response in those political areas that thrive on the myth of a world plot.

RICHARD GRIFFITHS

Sources R. M. Gilman, *Behind world revolution: the strange career of Nesta H. Webster*, 1 (1982) • N. Webster, *Spacious days: an autobiography* (1949) • R. Griffiths, *Fellow travellers of the right: British enthusiasts for Nazi Germany, 1933–9* (1980) • *The Times* (18 May 1960) • R. Thurlow, 'Powers of darkness: conspiracy belief and political strategy', *Patterns of Prejudice* (Nov–Dec 1978) • Burke, *Gen. GB* (1937) ['Bevan formerly of Trent Park'] • b. cert. • m. cert. • d. cert.
Likenesses portrait (aged twenty-five), repro. in Webster, *Spacious days*, frontispiece • portrait (aged twenty-two), repro. in Webster, *Spacious days*, facing p. 128 • portrait (in middle age), repro. in Gilman, *Behind world revolution*, cover
Wealth at death £2023 16s. 1d.: probate, 29 Dec 1960, *CGPLA Eng. & Wales*

Webster, Noah (1758–1843), lexicographer, was born on 16 October 1758 in West Hartford, Connecticut, the fourth of the five children of Noah Webster (1722–1813), farmer, a descendant of John Webster, one of the earliest migrants to Connecticut, and Mercy Steele (*bap.* 1727, *d.* 1794), great-great-granddaughter of William Bradford of Plymouth Colony fame. Prepared for college by his local pastor, the bookish Webster gained admission to Yale College in 1774. Although the War of Independence 'occasioned various interruptions', including, Webster later recalled, his having to endure the 'hardships of a soldier' (*Autobiographies*, 133) as a volunteer with the militia in 1777, he completed his studies in a timely fashion and received the BA degree in 1778. Knowing that his father had been forced to mortgage the family farm in order to pay for his years at Yale and, therefore, that he should expect no further assistance, Webster accepted a teaching assignment in Glastonbury. Within a year he moved to Hartford to teach while studying the law under Oliver Ellsworth, an eminent jurist who went on to become chief justice of the United

Noah Webster (1758–1843), by James Herring, 1833

States. Webster completed his legal training by assisting Jedidiah Strong in Litchfield and gained admission to the bar in 1781. With few clients to sustain his legal practice, Webster returned to teaching, first in Sharon, Connecticut, in 1781, then in Goshen, New York, in 1782.

About this time Webster conceived of a spelling book better suited to American schoolchildren than Thomas Dilworth's *A New Guide to the English Tongue*, the English speller that had served as the standard in America since the 1760s. The result—after, according to Webster, he had sacrificed 'ease, pleasure, and health in the execution of it' (Unger, 59)—was a spelling book published in 1783 as the first part of Webster's *A Grammatical Institute of the English Language* (the second part was a grammar published in 1784; the third, a reader published in 1785). The speller, which he retitled *The American Spelling Book* in 1787, was intended, Webster declared, not only to correct Dilworth's errors but 'to promote virtue and patriotism' (*Autobiographies*, 79) in the new nation. It constituted his first substantial contribution to the 'common treasure of patriotic exertions' (ibid., 78), and its success must have been gratifying to him. By 1829, when he composed an entirely new edition under the title *The Elementary Spelling Book*, Webster estimated that ten million copies of his speller had been printed. Only sales of the Bible equalled those of *The American Spelling Book* for many of these years. Webster's other publications did not approach the financial or popular success realized by the spelling book, but their underlying assumption was essentially the same: political independence must be coupled with cultural nationalism. His reader, for example, included the Declaration of Independence, the poetry of Philip Freneau and Joel Barlow, the speeches of George Washington and John Hancock, and other 'American pieces ... in order to call

the minds of our youth from ancient fables ... & fix them upon objects immediately interesting in this country' (Malone). The want of 'proper books' to accomplish this was a principal defect which, 'since the Revolution, is become inexcusable' (F. Rudolph, ed., *Essays on Education in the Early Republic*, 1965, 64).

The difficulties Webster encountered in seeking copyright protection for his spelling book confirmed his sense of the inadequacies of the union under the articles of confederation. Not surprisingly, especially in view of his patriotic programme of education, Webster was an ardent supporter of the proposed constitution in 1787–8. Cultural nationalism and constitutional unionism were two sides of the same coin for Webster. With the American character still unformed, the new republic could ill afford factional contests that were 'liable to all the evils of jealous dispute ... nay, liable to a civil war', he wrote in *Sketches of American Policy* (1785). A more perfect union bolstered by a common American language was the surest basis for national greatness.

Webster married Rebecca (1766–1847), daughter of Boston merchant William Greenleaf, on 26 October 1789, and they had two sons, one of whom died shortly after birth, and six daughters. For much of the 1790s Webster was the editor of the *American Minerva* (renamed the *Commercial Advertiser* in 1797), a daily newspaper he founded in New York in 1793 with federalist backing. By 1798, however, he had grown weary of the factional infighting among the federalists after Washington's retirement and decided to move to New Haven to resume his linguistic work in earnest. Convinced now more than ever that the bonds of national affection were contingent upon a 'uniformity of language' (N. Webster, *Dissertations on the English Language*, 1789), he redoubled his efforts at eliminating regional variations of spelling and pronunciation. He commenced working on a dictionary he envisioned as the pinnacle of the American plan of education he had launched in 1783 with the first edition of his speller.

That most American schoolchildren continued to rely on dictionaries compiled in Britain was unacceptable. 'New circumstances, new modes of life, new laws, new ideas ... give rise to new words', Webster announced in an advance advertisement of his work; hence it was essential that 'we should have *Dictionaries* of the *American Language*' (Unger, 247, 248). His first compilation, *A Compendious Dictionary of the American Language* (1806), contained over 40,000 entries, of which some 5000 were of American or Native American derivation. Even before its completion, however, Webster began compiling what he hoped would be the most comprehensive English-language dictionary ever produced. The final product did not disappoint. *An American Dictionary of the English Language*, published in two volumes in 1828, was an instant success. Containing 70,000 words, it was almost universally acclaimed to be the best English dictionary extant. By differentiating between American and English usages, including colloquial and idiomatic expressions that were peculiarly American, and incorporating lessons on morality and patriotism into its definitions, the dictionary also advanced

Webster's idea of weaning Americans away from British authorities. Adopted by congress, state legislatures, the courts, and classrooms throughout the nation as the new standard for spelling and pronunciation, it went a long way towards making Webster's name synonymous with dictionary in the United States. Webster died in New Haven of pleurisy on 28 May 1843, and was buried in the local Grove Street cemetery.   MELVIN YAZAWA

Sources H. G. Unger, *Noah Webster: life and times of an American patriot* (1998) · R. M. Rollins, *The long journey of Noah Webster* (1980) · H. R. Warfel, *Noah Webster: schoolmaster to America* (1936) · K. A. Snyder, *Defining Noah Webster: mind and morals in the early republic* (1990) · E. J. Monaghan, *A common heritage: Noah Webster's blue-back speller* (1983) · *The autobiographies of Noah Webster: from the letters and essays, memoir, and diary*, ed. R. M. Rollins (1989) · W. F. Vantorella, 'Noah Webster', *American writers before 1800: a biographical and critical dictionary*, ed. J. A. Levernier and D. R. Wilmes (1983), 1530–41 · N. K. Risjord, 'Webster, Noah', *ANB* · K. Malone, 'Webster, Noah', *DAB*
Archives Connecticut Historical Society, Hartford · Morgan L. · NYPL · Yale U. | American Philosophical Society, Philadelphia, Mathew Carey MSS · Dickinson College, Pennsylvania, Poulson family MSS
Likenesses W. Verstille, miniature, 1788, Litchfield Historical Society, Connecticut · S. F. B. Morse, portrait, 1823, Henry Ford Museum and Greenfield Village, Dearborn, Michigan · J. Herring, portrait, 1833, Smithsonian Institution, Washington, DC, National Portrait Gallery [*see illus.*]

Webster, Richard Everard, **Viscount Alverstone** (1842–1915), judge, was born in London on 22 December 1842, the second son of Thomas *Webster QC (1810–1875) and his wife, Elizabeth (*d.* 1848), eldest daughter of Richard Calthrop of Swineshead Abbey, Lincolnshire. He was educated at King's College School (1852–8) and at Charterhouse (1859–61), before matriculating in 1861 at Trinity College, Cambridge, where he graduated as thirty-sixth wrangler in 1865. He was called to the bar by Lincoln's Inn on 28 April 1868, and took chambers in the Temple at 2 Pump Court, where he remained throughout his career. In 1872 he married Mary Louisa, daughter of Charles William Calthrop MD, of Withern, Lincolnshire. She died in 1877, leaving a son, who died in August 1902, and a daughter.

Webster quickly developed a large practice, and after a remarkably short period as a junior took silk on 26 April 1878. The swiftness of his rise reflected his particular strength as a barrister, which lay not so much in his advocacy or in his knowledge of law, as in his industry and mastery of the facts. Webster was appointed attorney-general by Lord Salisbury on 26 June 1885, refusing to become home secretary because he wished to continue his profession. He sat initially for Launceston, and then for the rest of his parliamentary career for the Isle of Wight.

He served as attorney-general from June 1885 to February 1886, from August 1886 to August 1892, and from July 1895 to May 1900. Until 1895, when he agreed to forgo the right to do so, he continued in private practice, and in 1888–9 appeared before the Parnell commission as leading counsel for *The Times*. In 1893 he appeared for Great Britain in the Bering Sea arbitration, and was appointed GCMG. In 1899 he was leading counsel in the Venezuela

arbitration and was created a baronet early in the following year.

On 10 May 1900, having previously refused it, Webster reluctantly accepted appointment as master of the rolls in succession to Sir Nathaniel Lindley, and was sworn of the privy council. On 18 July 1900 he was created Baron Alverstone, of Alverstone in the Isle of Wight. Following the death of Lord Russell of Killowen, Webster was appointed lord chief justice of England on 22 October 1900. He was not a profound lawyer, and as a judge disliked making statements of principle, although he played an important part in the success of the court of criminal appeal, established in 1907. In 1903, with two Canadians and three Americans, he was an arbitrator on the Alaska boundary question. The decision, which was that of Webster and the three Americans, made him, and for a time Great Britain, very unpopular in Canada.

Webster resigned as lord chief justice on 20 October 1913 on account of ill health, and was created a viscount. In retirement he published his *Recollections of Bar and Bench* (1914), the literary quality of which was, as he admitted, impaired by his failing health. Outside the legal sphere he had a lifelong interest in athletics, having won the mile and 2 mile races for Cambridge against Oxford in 1865, and subsequently serving as president of the Amateur Athletic Association. Interested in music, he sang for forty years in the choir of Kensington parish church. He was generous with his money, and a keen billiards player, though some regarded his boisterous geniality as artificial. Webster died at Winterfold, the house which he had built at Cranleigh, in Surrey, on 15 December 1915, and was buried in Norwood cemetery on 18 December 1915.

F. D. MACKINNON, *rev.* N. G. JONES

Sources *The Times* (16 Dec 1915) · *Law Journal* (18 Dec 1915) · Viscount Alverstone [R. E. Webster], *Recollections of bar and bench* (1914) · R. F. V. Heuston, *Lives of the lord chancellors, 1885–1940* (1964)
Archives BL, family corresp. and papers, Add. MSS 61737–61740 | Bodl. Oxf., corresp. with Lord Kimberley · CKS, letters to Aretas Akers-Douglas · LPL, corresp. with Archbishop Benson · U. Birm. L., corresp. with Joseph Chamberlain
Likenesses F. Verheyden, caricature, watercolour, 1883, NPG; repro. in *VF* (26 May 1883) · S. P. Hall, pencil drawing, 1888–9, NPG · S. P. Hall, group drawing, 1889, NPG · S. P. Hall, pencil drawing, 1889, NPG · F. Pegram, drawings, 1889, V&A · Russell & Sons, photograph, *c.*1895, NPG · J. S. Lucas, chalk drawing, 1902, NPG · J. S. Lucas, colour photogravure, 1902, NPG · A. S. Cope, oils, 1903, Lincoln's Inn, London · J. Collier, oils, 1911, Royal Institution of Chartered Surveyors, London · J. Brown, engraving (after H. T. Wells), NPG · F. Dodd, etching, BM · F. Lockwood, caricatures, repro. in Alverstone, *Recollections* · London Stereoscopic Co., cabinet photograph, NPG · Spy [L. Ward], caricature, chromolithograph, NPG; repro. in *VF* (1 Nov 1900) · G. J. Stodart, stipple (after H. T. Wells), BM, NPG · W. H., caricature, chromolithograph, NPG; repro. in *VF* (15 Jan 1913) · oils, Harvard U., law school · photograph, repro. in Alverstone, *Recollections*, frontispiece
Wealth at death £311,373 4*s.* 11*d.*: probate, 14 March 1916, *CGPLA Eng. & Wales*

Webster, Sir Thomas, **first baronet** (1676–1751). *See under* Webster family (*per. c.*1650–1836).

Webster, Thomas (1772–1844), geologist, was born on 11 February 1772, probably in Kirkwall, Orkney, the only son of Alexander Webster (d. c.1780) and his wife, Mary (b. 1733), daughter of Thomas Baikie, chief Presbyterian minister in Kirkwall, and his third wife, Elizabeth Traill. A natural artist, he was educated at Kirkwall grammar school and by private tutors, and then, from 1785 to about 1789, attended lectures at Aberdeen University. There he assisted Professor Patrick Copland (1749–1822), a popularizer of science. After two years as a tutor in Dublin, he received private architectural training in London and from October 1793 studied architecture, art, and draughtsmanship at the Royal Academy.

While working as an architect Webster taught building workers scientific principles relevant to their trade. Count Rumford, hearing of this, asked him to establish an artisans' school in the newly founded Royal Institution, to which Webster agreed, hoping to further his career. From 14 September 1799 until 26 April 1802, as the poorly paid clerk of works and clerk, he supervised the building work, designed and built the lecture theatre and chemistry laboratory, assisted the lecturers, and developed Rumford's theories concerning the heating, ventilation, and lighting of buildings. However, for political reasons, his widely praised technical school, begun in 1801, was soon closed. Rather than returning to architecture, Webster chose the more independent and then lucrative occupation of landscape painting in watercolours. Additionally he resumed teaching and compiled introductory textbooks. His revised and enlarged edition of J. Imison's Elements of Science and Art (1804) ran to further revised editions (1808, 1822). Also during this period, he assisted with geological field sketches and illustrations, and realized that geology offered scope for his accomplishments.

During 1811–13, on a geological commission in the Isle of Wight and Dorset for Henry Charles Englefield (1752–1822), Webster made the first geological map of the region and elucidated the Mesozoic–Tertiary stratigraphy and structural geology of the Hampshire and London basins. His major paper on the Freshwater formations in the Isle of Wight (1814), published in the Transactions of the Geological Society, and his earlier-written illustrated descriptive letters in Englefield's Picturesque Beauties of the Isle of Wight (1816) were highly regarded and established his geological career. Seven further papers followed (1821–9), including four on the Mesozoic stratigraphy of southern England.

Webster was an early member (1809), later fellow, of the Geological Society. From 1812 until 1827 he was its part-time (in reality, full-time) curator, librarian, and draughtsman; he was later also house secretary. Additionally he was draughtsman for the society's 'Geological map of England and Wales' (1820). From July 1827, after failing to gain improved remuneration and terms of employment, he lived by public lecturing on geology, consultancy work, geological illustration, and commissioned writing, including compilation of An Encyclopaedia of Domestic Economy (1844).

From 1841 Webster was professor of geology at University College, London. The income from his post was minimal and, by then in poor health, he existed mainly on the

charity of geological colleagues and an annual state pension of £50 for services to geology. He died of bronchitis, 'apparently in straitened circumstances' (GM), on 26 December 1844 at his lodgings at 41 Middlesex Street (now Maple Street), St Marylebone; he was buried at Highgate cemetery on 2 January 1845. Although at his death Webster was still highly regarded as a geologist, his reputation was based largely on his earliest research. Significantly this was funded by a patron; thereafter lack of the means and time to pursue further major research prevented him from building on his early achievement and denied him a continuing role in the elucidation of British geology.

NICHOLAS EDWARDS

Sources T. Webster, 'Autobiography', 1837, Royal Institution of Great Britain, London, 121A–121B · N. Edwards, 'Thomas Webster, (circa 1772–1844)', Journal of the Society of the Bibliography of Natural History, 5 (1968–71), 468–73 · J. Challinor, 'Some correspondence of Thomas Webster, geologist, 1773–1844', Annals of Science, 17 (1961), 175–95; 18 (1962), 147–75; 19 (1963), 49–79, 285–97 · N. Edwards, 'Some correspondence of Thomas Webster, circa 1772–1844, concerning the Royal Institution', Annals of Science, 28 (1972), 43–60 · GM, 2nd ser., 23 (1845), 211–12 · H. B. Jones, The Royal Institution: its founders and its first professors (1871) · W. J. Sparrow, Knight of the white eagle: a biography of Sir Benjamin Thompson, Count Rumford (1964) · A. D. R. Caroe, The house of the Royal Institution (1963) · H. B. Woodward, The history of the Geological Society of London (1907) · Redgrave, Artists · H. H. Bellot, University College, London, 1826–1926 (1929) · J. M. Bulloch, A history of the University of Aberdeen (1895) · [B. F. Duppa], A manual for mechanics' institutions (1839) · G. B. Greenough, Memoir of a geological map of England (1820) · R. I. Murchison, The Silurian system, 1 (1839), 256 · F. T. Cansick, A collection of curious and interesting epitaphs, 2 (1872) · H. Torrens, 'Arthur Aikin's mineralogical survey of Shropshire, 1796–1816, and the contemporary audience for geological publications', British Journal for the History of Science, 16 (1983), 111–53 · d. cert.

Archives Bodl. Oxf., draft copy of Sir Henry Englefield's 'Description of the Isle of Wight', annotated by Webster · FM Cam., corresp. · GS Lond., drawings and papers · Royal Institution of Great Britain, London, autobiography, corresp., and papers · U. Wales, Aberystwyth, corresp. · UCL, corresp. and papers | BL, letters to G. Cumberland, Add. MSS 3656, 36510, 36512 · NL NZ, Turnbull L. · U. Southampton L., corresp. with Sir H. C. Englefield; geological notes

Wealth at death apparently in near-poverty: GM

Webster, Thomas (1800–1886), genre painter, was born on 20 March 1800 in Ranelagh Street, Pimlico, London, the son of a member of George III's household. In his youth he was trained as a chorister at St George's Chapel, Windsor, and at the Chapel Royal, St James's, London, but he preferred art to music and entered the Royal Academy Schools in 1821, where he won a gold medal in 1825. In the course of a long and successful career he exhibited eighty-three works at the Royal Academy (1823–79), thirty-nine at the British Institution (1824–44), and eight at the Society of British Artists (1825–34). He was elected an ARA in 1840 and an RA in 1846. He also contributed illustrations to the Etching Club's Deserted Village (1841), Songs of Shakespeare (1843), and Etch'd Thoughts (1844). His genre paintings were very popular and reached a wide general public in the form of steel-engravings.

Although his earliest exhibited paintings were portraits, such as Mr Robinson and Family (exh. RA, 1823), Webster soon received acclaim for a scene of playful children,

Rebels Shooting a Prisoner (exh. Society of British Artists, 1827). The following year he continued the amusing narrative with *Rebels Defeated* (exh. Society of British Artists, 1828). Such pendants became an especially popular feature of his career, as seen, for example, in *Going into School* and *Coming out of School* (both exh. RA, 1836), *Going to the Fair* and *Returning from the Fair* (both exh. British Institution, 1838; Victoria and Albert Museum, London), and *The Frown* and *The Joke, or, 'The Smile'* (both exh. RA, 1841; Guildhall Art Gallery, London). The latter were especially popular 'before and after' scenes which depicted a row of rustic schoolboys exchanging miserable expressions for giggling demeanours in companion paintings. Webster's production was characterized by such anecdotal childhood scenes, which were skilfully composed, highly detailed, and informed with a keen observation of human nature. Popular literature was often the inspiration. Lines from Oliver Goldsmith's *Deserted Village* accompanied *The Frown* and *The Joke*; other works made reference to Charles Dickens, Charles Lamb, Shakespeare, William Shenstone, or Wordsworth. Indeed, a small painting for Dickens illustrating a school scene in his *Nicholas Nickleby*, entitled *The Interior Economy of Dotheboys Hall* (exh. 1848; Fogg Art Museum, Harvard University, Cambridge, Massachusetts), earned Webster the nickname 'Do-the-Boys' Webster. One of his most famous paintings, *A Village Choir* (exh. RA, 1847; Victoria and Albert Museum, London), was exhibited with a lengthy quotation from Washington Irving's *The Sketch Book* (1820): it depicted an array of rustic villagers of different classes, genders, and ages gathered together in a church choir, singing and playing assorted musical instruments with great gusto and earnestness. It was just this kind of reassuring image of tranquil and contented country life, unruffled by class or economic divisions, which pleased the Victorian public by ignoring the real transformations overtaking the newly industrialized and increasingly urban society. Even contemporaries recognized the fictive nature of Webster's idyllic scenes: a writer in the *Art Journal* in 1855 described *Good Night* (exh. RA, 1846; City of Bristol Museum and Art Gallery) as:

> a subject representing the interior of a rural cottage, occupied by the family of an honest yeoman, one of the class … among the extinct races, a victim to the Moloch of wealth; but we cannot stop to lament his decay,—besides, we should get political, and perhaps angry, which would be out of place and unseemly here. (*Art Journal*, 295)

Webster's works were not 'unseemly', as Richard Muther explained:

> Webster's rustics, children, and schoolmasters are the citizens of an ideal planet … [where] all of the agricultural labourers were quite content with their lot. No one ever quarreled with his landlord, or sat in a public-house and let his family starve. (Muther, 2.88)

Although the children were occasionally unruly, they displayed only true British pluck, the vital spirit necessary for building the British empire. As the *Art Union* declared in 1839 with regard to the boys in Webster's *Football* (exh. RA, 1839), their 'spirit of rivalry' would later be brought to bear on 'more important purposes in after life' (*Art Union*, 69–70).

William Mulready's earlier paintings of pugnacious boys had garnered similar comments and served as models for Webster's works. For years (1833–56) the two artists lived near each other in London in the suburban area of Kensington and Bayswater: Webster on The Mall, Kensington Gravel Pits, and Mulready just a short distance away. This semi-rural neighbourhood provided a suitable setting for their paintings. Both looked back to Dutch and Flemish seventeenth-century examples by David Teniers, Jan Steen, and Adriaen van Ostade—though their work was cleansed of what was perceived as the earlier artists' often vulgar foreign tone. Indeed, it was the sense that Webster's subjects were 'indigenous to the English soil' (*Art Journal*, 1855, 293) which ensured their immense popularity. His paintings were purchased by a new breed of middle-class collector (Elhanan Bicknell, John Chapman, Joseph Gillott, John Sheepshanks, Robert Vernon, and William Wells, among others) who brought a nationalistic fervour to their patronage of contemporary British art.

In 1857 Webster moved to the village of Cranbrook, Kent, and became the informal leader of the Cranbrook colony, a group of younger artists who shared his interest in scenes of rural life and childhood. Although he sent fewer paintings to the London exhibitions in later years (he became an honorary retired RA in 1876), their subjects and style remained virtually unchanged. His long and satisfactory life was nicely summed up in the lines attached to his late self-portrait (exh. RA, 1878): 'As the sweet afterglow lights up the western skies, so is my evening bright with fond memories'. His first wife, Betsy, died on 27 January 1859 at the age of fifty-nine; another spouse, Ellen, survived him. Thomas Webster died on 23 September 1886 at Cranbrook; a memorial to him by the sculptor Hamo Thornycroft was erected in St Dunstan's Church in Cranbrook. The largest collection of his works is in the Victoria and Albert Museum, London.

KATHRYN MOORE HELENIAK

Sources 'British artists, their style and character: no. X, Thomas Webster', *Art Journal*, 17 (1855), 293–6 • F. G. Stephens, *Artists at home* (1884), 9–11 • A. Greg, *The Cranbrook colony: F. D. Hardy, G. Hardy, J. C. Horsley, A. E. Mulready, G. B. O'Neil, T. Webster* (1977) [exhibition catalogue, Central Art Gallery, Wolverhampton, 22 Jan – 12 March 1977; Laing Art Gallery, Newcastle upon Tyne, 26 March – 17 April 1977] • R. Parkinson, ed., *Catalogue of British oil paintings, 1820–1860* (1990), 297–302 [catalogue of V&A] • Graves, *Brit. Inst.* • Graves, *RA exhibitors* • J. Johnson, ed., *Works exhibited at the Royal Society of British Artists, 1824–1893, and the New English Art Club, 1888–1917*, 2 vols. (1975) • Thieme & Becker, *Allgemeines Lexikon* • D. S. Macleod, *Art and the Victorian middle class: money and the making of cultural identity* (1996) • 'The Royal Academy: the seventy-first exhibition, 1839', *Art Union*, 1 (1839), 69–70 • R. Muther, *A history of modern painting*, 4 vols. (1907), 2.88 • L. Lambourne, *An introduction to 'Victorian' genre painting from Wilkie to Frith* (1982), 23–7 • *Remaining works of the late Thomas Webster* (1887) [sale catalogue, Christies, 21 May 1887] • *Art Journal*, new ser., 6 (1886), 351–2 • *The Times* (24 Sept 1886) • d. cert. [Betsy Webster] • CGPLA Eng. & Wales (1886) • DNB

Likenesses E. M. Ward, pencil drawing, 1862, NPG • J. Durham, marble bust, 1877, Cranbrook School, Kent • Lock & Whitfield, photograph, woodburytype, 1878, NPG; repro. in T. Cooper, *Men of mark: a gallery of contemporary portraits*, 7 vols. (1876–83) • J. P. Mayall, photograph, c.1884, repro. in Stephens, *Artists at home* • J. C. Horsley, oils, 1886, Aberdeen Art Gallery • London Stereoscopic

Co., cartes-de-visite, NPG · Maull & Polyblank, cartes-de-visite, NPG · J. & C. Watkins, cartes-de-visite, NPG · woodcuts (after photographs), BM, NPG

Wealth at death £18,705 9s. 2d.: probate, 10 Nov 1886, *CGPLA Eng. & Wales*

Webster, Thomas (1810–1875), barrister, was born in Oakington, Cambridgeshire, on 16 October 1810, the eldest son of Thomas Webster, vicar of Oakington. From Charterhouse he proceeded to Trinity College, Cambridge, where he graduated BA as fourteenth wrangler in 1832 and MA in 1835. He was secretary to the Institution of Civil Engineers from 1837 to 1839 and honorary secretary until 1841. In that year he was called to the bar at Lincoln's Inn, and joined the northern circuit.

Webster soon acquired a large practice in connection with scientific cases, and for many years was recognized as a leading authority on patent law. His *Reports and Notes of Cases on Letters Patent for Inventions* (1844) was for many years the chief textbook on the subject. It was largely due to his efforts that the Patent Law Amendment Act of 1852 was passed, an act by which numerous abuses that had grown up round the ancient system of granting patents were swept away and the cost of a patent was greatly reduced.

Webster had also a considerable parliamentary practice. He was one of the counsel engaged for Birkenhead in contests respecting the Liverpool and Mersey docks and published two texts which became standard works of reference concerning the Mersey. He was for long an active member of the governing body of the Society of Arts. He was in the chair at the meeting of the society in 1845 when the first proposal was made for holding the Great Exhibition of 1851, and formed one of the first committee appointed to organize it. He was elected a fellow of the Royal Society in 1847, and in 1865 he was appointed one of her majesty's counsel.

Webster was twice married: first in 1839 to Elizabeth (*d.* 1848), eldest daughter of Richard Calthrop of Swineshead Abbey, Lincolnshire; and second to Mary Frances, daughter of Joseph Cookworthy MD of Plymouth. With his first wife he had three sons and two daughters; with his second wife he had one son and one daughter. His second son was Richard Everard *Webster, first Viscount Alverstone, Conservative attorney-general and lord chief justice.

Webster died at his London home, 97 Ladbroke Road, Notting Hill, on 3 June 1875.

H. T. WOOD, rev. ERIC METCALFE

Sources Venn, *Alum. Cant.* · *Law Times* (12 June 1875) · *Journal of the Society of Arts*, 23 (1874–5), 665–6 · personal knowledge (1899) · private information (1899) · *CGPLA Eng. & Wales* (1875)

Archives Birkenhead Central Library, minutes of evidence and report relating to Birkenhead Dock Bills | UCL, letters to Society for the Diffusion of Useful Knowledge

Wealth at death under £450: administration, 9 Sept 1875, *CGPLA Eng. & Wales*

Webster, (Gilbert) Tom (1886–1962), sporting cartoonist and caricaturist, was born on 17 July 1886 in Church Street, Bilston, Staffordshire, the son of Daniel Webster, ironmonger, and his wife, Sarah Ann, *née* Bostock. He was educated at the Royal Wolverhampton School, where he

received his first drawing lessons from Louis Frederick Stiles, the art-master. At the age of fourteen he entered the employment of the Great Western railway as a clerk in the ticket-office at Handsworth, Staffordshire. While earning 12s. 6d. a week in that capacity he increased his knowledge of all aspects of sport by daily study of the *Athletic News*. Before he was twenty he had won a 5s. prize offered by the Birmingham *Weekly Post* for a humorous drawing, and other prizes in competitions run by the Manchester *Evening Chronicle* and the *Athletic News*. Soon afterwards he joined the staff of the Birmingham *Sports Argus*, being paid £2 10s. for twelve cartoons a week in the third and final year of his contract.

On the outbreak of the First World War Webster enlisted in the Royal Fusiliers but was so badly disabled by rheumatic fever in 1916 that he nearly died. Following the end of the war in 1918 he was out of work for a long period and, at one time, so low in funds that he was obliged to sleep on London's Thames Embankment.

When invited to submit a specimen of his work to the London *Evening News*, he bluffed his way into the National Sporting Club to see the fight between Tommy Noble and Joe Symonds and produced the first running commentary on a sporting event in cartoon form. In 1919 his work in the *Evening News* came to the notice of the paper's proprietor Lord Northcliffe, who told the editor of his principal publication, the *Daily Mail*, to give Webster a staff appointment. The editor offered Webster £1500 a year. Seeing, on the desk between them, a *Daily Mail* headline offering £10,000 for the first flight of the Atlantic, Webster concluded the paper could afford to pay him more and successfully demanded a starting salary of £2000 a year. In 1924 he was the highest-paid cartoonist in the world.

Webster was a round-faced man with a broad forehead under a receding hair-line with the parting a little to the left. He had a slightly upturned nose set between large eyes, and a wide, generous mouth. As well as in boxing, he found the material for his cartoons in racing, football, cricket, golf, and billiards. He also contributed to the *Daily Mail* humorous articles illustrated by himself.

A highly developed sense of humour gave Webster a quick eye for the quirks and eccentricities of character and the ridiculous, and enabled him to follow in the best tradition of cartoonists by bringing out personality and recording absurdity. Flamboyant and extravagant in his use of lines, many of them characteristically sharply serrated, he was relatively economic with shading. As well as captions, he made frequent use of 'balloons' to put words into the mouths of his subjects. He depicted horses in human postures, usually with disproportionately bulbous muzzles, and large teeth in contrast to small pricked ears. He worked very rapidly, often laughing aloud as he did so, and had a cartoon across three columns on the presses of the *Daily Mail* within a little more than an hour after the fight between Jimmy Wilde and Moore at Olympia.

One of Webster's best-known cartoons was of Tishy, a racehorse with its forelegs twisted round each other. This exemplified how exaggeration of the factual, or allegedly factual, inspired his work. The only excuse offered to the public for the failure of Tishy to justify favouritism in the Cesarewitch of 1921 had been that she had crossed her legs in running. As a result of his cartoon the expression 'doing a Tishy' passed into everyday racing parlance.

In 1920, the year after he had joined the *Daily Mail*, Webster visited the United States and sent back a number of cartoons, including one of Chick Evans beating Francis Ouimet in the American amateur golf championship. Four years later he played a prominent part in arranging the revue *Cartoons* at the Criterion Theatre, London, and in 1929 his popularity was recognized by a selection of his cartoons being projected onto a screen in Trafalgar Square for the amusement of Londoners on the night of the general election. That year he married Mae Flynn in New York. The couple divorced in 1933. His second marriage was to Ida (*b*. 1911/12), daughter of John Rupert Michael, master mariner, at St James's Church, Spanish Place, London, on 4 December 1935. With his second wife, who was twenty-five years his junior, he had one son and two daughters.

Webster made his first venture into colour when he was one of the artists commissioned to decorate the *Queen Mary* in 1936. He was responsible for the sporting panorama lightly laid on in oils on fourteen panels in the gymnasium.

Having retired from the *Daily Mail* in 1940, Webster resumed work on joining Kemsley Newspapers in 1944. In 1953 he joined the *News Chronicle* before finally retiring in 1956. Each year he had published the best of his work in *Tom Webster's Annual*. Webster died at his home, 22 Bishopswood Road, Highgate, Middlesex, on 21 June 1962. There is a large collection of his work at the Centre for the Study of Cartoons and Caricature, University of Kent at Canterbury. To mark the centenary of his birth in 1986 the centre mounted an exhibition, designed by Liz Ottaway, of a wide variety of his sporting drawings.

RICHARD ONSLOW, *rev.*

Sources *Daily Mail* cuttings library, London · *The Times* (22 June 1962) · b. cert. · *CGPLA Eng. & Wales* (1962) · C. Seymour-Ure, 'Tom Webster (1886–1962)—"The best cartoonist now writing"', unpubd MS, Templeman Library, University of Kent, Centre for Cartoons and Caricature
Archives *Daily Mail* cuttings library
Likenesses H. Coster, photographs, 1930–39, NPG · two photographs, 1934–7, NPG
Wealth at death £51,532 14*s*.: probate, 9 Aug 1962, *CGPLA Eng. & Wales*

Webster, Wentworth (1829–1907), Basque scholar and folklorist, was born at Uxbridge, Middlesex, the eldest son of Charles Webster. Owing to delicate health he had no regular schooling, but he was a hard-working boy with a retentive memory, and was a well-informed student when he was admitted commoner of Lincoln College, Oxford, on 15 March 1849. He graduated BA in 1852, was at Wells College from 1853 to 1854, proceeded MA in 1855, and was ordained deacon in 1854 and priest in 1861. After serving as curate at Cloford, Somerset (1854–8), he was ordered by his medical advisers to settle in the south of France. He lived for some time at Bagnères-de-Bigorre, Hautes-Pyrénées, and at Biarritz, Basses-Pyrénées, taking pupils,

among them Henry Butler Clarke. An indefatigable walker, he became familiar with the Basque provinces on both sides of the Pyrenees, and with the Basques themselves, their language, traditions, and poetry. At the same time he grew well versed in French and Spanish, and in all the Pyrenean dialects. He married on 17 October 1866, at Camberwell, London, Laura Thekla Knipping, a native of Cleve in Germany. They had four daughters and one son, Erwin Wentworth, later fellow of Wadham College, Oxford.

From 1869 to 1882 Webster was Anglican chaplain at St Jean-de-Luz, Basses-Pyrénées. In 1881 he settled at Sare, in a house which overlooked the valley of La Rhune. There he mainly devoted himself to study, writing on the Basques and also on church history. He contributed much on Basque and Spanish philology and antiquities to *Bulletin de la Société des Sciences et des Arts de Bayonne*, *Bulletin de la Société Ramond de Bagnères-de-Bigorre*, *Revue de Linguistique*, and *Bulletin de la Real Academia de la Historia de Madrid*. He was a corresponding member of the Real Academia de la Historia, Madrid. With all serious students of Basque, whether French, Spanish, English, or German, he corresponded and was generous in sharing information. He wrote many papers on church history and theology in the *Anglican Church Magazine*. Gladstone visited him in January 1893 and found a 'family & home most cheering, most edifying' (Gladstone, *Diaries*, 13.175). He awarded him a pension of £150 from the civil list on 16 January 1894, having benefited from Webster's knowledge of the Basques.

Basque Legends, Collected Chiefly in the Labourd (1877; repr. 1879) was probably Webster's best and most characteristic work; many of the legends were taken down in Basque from the recitation of people who knew no other language. He also published *Spain* (1882), a survey of the geography, ethnology, literature, and commerce of the country, founded mainly on information supplied by Spanish friends of high position, and several foreign-language works, including *De quelques travaux sur le basque faits par des étrangers pendant les années 1892–4* (Bayonne, 1894) and *Le dictionnaire latin-basque de Pierre d'Urte* (Bayonne, 1895). *Gleanings in Church History, Chiefly in Spain and France* (1903) was his final publication. Webster died at Maison Crespo, Sare, on 2 April 1907, and was buried at St Jean-de-Luz.

ANDREW CLARK, *rev.* JOHN D. HAIGH

Sources Crockford (1906) · private information (1912) · *The Times* (9 April 1907), 10 · Gladstone, *Diaries* · *Guardian* (10 April 1907) · W. Webster, *Basque legends, collected chiefly in the Labourd* (1877) · Foster, *Alum. Oxon.* · *CGPLA Eng. & Wales* (1907)
Archives Bodl. Oxf., essays, notes, and reviews | BL, corresp. with W. E. Gladstone, Add. MSS 44514–44526, *passim*
Wealth at death £9736 9*s.* 4*d.*: probate, 13 July 1907, *CGPLA Eng. & Wales*

Webster, Sir Whistler, second baronet (1709–1779). *See under* Webster family (*per. c.*1650–1836).

Webster, William (1689–1758), Church of England clergyman and theological writer, was born at Cove in Suffolk in December 1689, the son of Richard Webster (*bur.* 1722) and his wife, Jane, daughter of Anthony *Sparrow (1612–1685), bishop of Norwich. His father was a nonjuring clergyman, who afterwards submitted and became vicar of Posling-ford in Suffolk. Webster was educated at school in Beccles under Mr Leeds, and was admitted to Gonville and Caius College, Cambridge, on 2 March 1708. He graduated BA in 1712, MA in 1716, and DD in 1732. He was ordained deacon on 24 June 1713 as curate of Depden in Suffolk, and priest on 26 February 1716 as curate of St Dunstan-in-the-West, London. He edited the manuscript life of General Monck written by Thomas Skinner (1629/30–1679) and published it in 1723 with his own preface vindicating Monck's char-acter. He followed this with *The Clergy's Right of Maintenance Vindicated from Scripture and Reason* (1726; 2nd edn, 1727), and two translations of French works: Louis Maimbourg's history of Arianism, and Richard Simon's edition of the New Testament.

After leaving St Dunstan's in 1731, Webster was appoin-ted in August 1732 to the curacy of St Clement Eastcheap, and in February 1732 was presented to the rectory of Depden. On 16 December 1732, under the pseudonym of 'Richard Hooker of the Inner Temple', he began to edit a periodical entitled the *Weekly Miscellany*, which continued until 27 June 1741. Nicknamed 'Old Mother Hooker's Jour-nal', the *Miscellany* was 'a lively mouthpiece' for high-churchmen and nonjurors and it 'poured out defiant Jere-miads against the spirit of the age' (Walsh and Taylor, 33). It attracted most attention for the attacks made in its col-umns on William Warburton's *Divine Legation of Moses*. Webster's contributions to the controversy were repub-lished under the title of *Remarks on the Divine Legation* [1739]. They earned him a place in Alexander Pope's *Dun-ciad*, in a passage (bk 2, l. 258) in which Webster was coupled with George Whitefield, who had also criticized Warburton.

In 1740 Webster published a pamphlet on the woollen manufactory based on information supplied by a mer-chant in the trade, and entitled *The Consequences of Trade to the Wealth and Strength of any Nation, by a Draper of London*. It sold well and went into a fifth edition in 1741, the same year as Webster wrote a refutation of his own arguments, published under the pseudonym Andrew Freeport as *The Draper Confuted*.

In July 1740 Webster was instituted to the vicarages of Ware and Thundridge and South Mimms in Hertford-shire, which he retained until his death, resigning his rec-tory and curacy. In later life he fell into considerable pov-erty, and after vainly petitioning the archbishops and bishops for charity and publishing a treatise on church preferment, he appealed to the public in *A Plain Narrative of Facts, or, The Author's Case Fairly and Candidly Stated* (1758).

Webster was a voluminous writer, chiefly on theological subjects, and published a volume of tracts, sermons, and addresses in 1745. His *Casuistical Essay on Anger and Forgive-ness* (1750) won compliments from Christopher Smart in his seventh ode. Unmarried, Webster died at Ware on 4 December 1758.   E. I. Carlyle, *rev.* S. J. Skedd

Sources Venn, *Alum. Cant.* · J. Nichols, *Biographical and literary anecdotes of William Bowyer, printer, FSA, and of many of his learned friends* (privately printed, London, 1782), 83, 539–42 · R. Clutter-buck, *The history and antiquities of Hertfordshire*, 3 vols. (1815–27), 3.280, 308 · J. Walsh and S. Taylor, Introduction, in J. Walsh, C. Hayden, and S. Taylor, *The Church of England, c.1689–c.1833* (1993), 33 · *The works of Alexander Pope*, ed. J. Warburton, 9 vols. (1751)

Weck, Richard (1913–1986), civil engineer, was born on 5 March 1913 in Franzenbad, Bohemia, the elder son and eldest of three children of Francis Weck, manager of a small restaurant, and his wife, Katie Dauber. His early life was frugal, for his mother and younger sister died early, and he had to care for his younger brother and become accustomed to casual teaching work. Despite these set-backs he entered the Technical University of Prague to study civil and structural engineering in 1931, and gradu-ated in 1936. After he had gained some practical experi-ence from 1937 to 1938, he was engaged with Professor J. Fritzsche in research on plastic theories of structural analysis and design. In 1933 he married Katie, daughter of Karl Bartl, master tailor and cutter. They were a mutually devoted couple; although without children, they treas-ured those of others.

Weck's life at this stage was dominated by the problems of his native country (which had become Czechoslovakia in 1918), and the adjacent Nazi rise to power, so that it is not surprising that he should have become a student activ-ist, founding a democratic liberal society and engaging with the anti-fascist student movement. When Czechoslo-vakia was annexed by Germany in 1938, he and fifteen similar activists, with the help of leading members of the British Liberal Party, were secretly evacuated to Britain, where Weck was joined by his wife.

At the age of twenty-six, already with worldly experi-ence, and having a sparkling, seductively iconoclastic temperament, Weck was soon deeply involved in the war effort. He gave technical assistance to foundries, and then edited a handbook for welded structural steelwork on behalf of the Institute of Welding, thereby both improv-ing his English and meeting the institute's originator J. F. *Baker. When Baker became professor of mechanical sci-ences at Cambridge in 1943, Weck joined him, as his research assistant, in teaching, research, and later in expanding the British Welding Research Association (BWRA). Their most pressing wartime research task was to understand and correct the mysterious blight of brittle fractures in welded steel ship hulls, which threatened the transatlantic supply lifeline to an extent only masked by submarine torpedo losses. His seminal research on weld-ing residual stresses was rewarded with a Cambridge PhD degree in 1948, and matched by metallurgical research conducted by Dr Constance Tipper at the same laboratory. Both co-operated in this work for more than a decade, but Weck increasingly turned his attention to fatigue testing of welded structures; both saw the culmination of their efforts even later, in the successful placement and service of welded steel oil platforms in the hostile environment of the North Sea.

Meanwhile, driven by the excessive bulk and noisy oper-ation of his testing machines, Weck sought an outstation site, and discovered the derelict Abington Hall estate nearby, which then offered the desired space and remote-ness. It soon became the home of BWRA, of whose fatigue laboratory he had been head since 1946, and a purpose-built fatigue testing laboratory was added in 1952, the first of several buildings there to employ the new plastic methods of Baker. Weck served BWRA at this juncture, but returned to Cambridge as a lecturer in 1951, and stayed there until 1957, creating a postgraduate course, which was both well supported and influential. He did, however, continue to live at Abington until his death.

Weck was appointed in 1957 as director of research at BWRA, and as director-general of the Institute of Welding and BWRA when they were merged as the Welding Institute in 1968. At the time of his retirement in 1977 the latter body had expanded greatly, and acquired a reputation for quality of service, confirmed by the substantial proportion of its revenue drawn from overseas, and in particular from the USA, Japan, and Europe. Weck was also for six years a visiting industrial professor at Imperial College, London (1968–74), and from 1976 he added a complementary post in the department of civil engineering.

The international outlook of Richard Weck gained respect and recognition in the International Institute of Welding, where for more than a decade he was chairman of the commission devoted to the study and control of welding residual stresses. He was a competent linguist, embracing German, Spanish, Russian, and later Japanese, and his many publications (he wrote over sixty articles) reflect this. His style as a leader was fearless and outspoken, but always both courteous and generous. He was naturalized in 1946, appointed CBE in 1969, FRS in 1975, and FEng in 1976. He also held honorary fellowships of the Welding Institute, the Institution of Mechanical Engineers, and the Institution of Civil Engineers. An array of medals for distinguished services included the Bessemer gold medal of the Metals Society (1975).

Weck had a serious heart attack in March 1971. He was an expert grower of exotic plants. He had been typically in search of gifts on 9 January 1986 when he collapsed and died of a second heart attack on the train returning to Cambridge from London. His wife survived him. His ashes were scattered in Cambridge.   A. A. WELLS, rev.

Sources A. A. Wells and E. G. West, *Memoirs FRS*, 32 (1986), 631–47 · personal knowledge (1996)
Likenesses photograph, repro. in Wells and West, *Memoirs FRS*, 630
Wealth at death £55,718: probate, 3 March 1986, *CGPLA Eng. & Wales*

Weckherlin, Georg Rudolph (1584–1653), government official and poet, was born in Stuttgart on 15 September 1584, the fifth of eleven children, and one of ten sons of Johannes Weckherlin the younger (d. 1610), a bureaucrat in the service of Baden-Württemberg, and his wife, Ursula Sadeler. The family were deeply pious Lutherans. Weckherlin was counted as a gentleman in a Westminster census of 1635 and in April 1639 was granted English arms on the basis of his family's armigerous status in Stuttgart. Educated at the Pädagogium zu Stuttgart, in 1599 he matriculated in the faculty of law at the University of

Tübingen. He studied languages at both school and university, where his studies were inclined more toward politics than the finer points of the law.

By 1606 Weckherlin was employed in a Württemberg embassy to France, and between 1607 and 1615 spent about three years in diplomatic missions to England. During these trips he met Elizabeth (d. 1645), daughter of Francis Raworth, town clerk of Dover. They were married in England on 13 September 1616 and then travelled to Württemberg, where Elizabeth soon gave birth to their two children, Ralph and Elizabeth. Weckherlin and both children were naturalized English citizens in 1630 by letters patent.

In 1616 Weckherlin was appointed secretary interpreter and court historiographer to the duke of Württemberg. In the same year he participated in arranging the festivities associated with the baptism of the duke's eldest son, and published a description of the events, in German, blending verse with prose. He followed this with an English version, *Triumphall Shews Set Forth Lately in Stutgart* (1616). A similar work followed in 1618 associated with the ducal baptism and wedding. Then in 1618–19 he published two volumes of 'Oden und Gesänge' ('Odes and Songs') embracing a considerable range of verse forms. In 1619 he was back in England apparently on a mission from the princes of the union, and the following year joined the Bohemian court-in-exile at Heidelberg. He seems to have worked in England on behalf of the Palatines in the early 1620s, although by his own account he was employed by Sir Edward Conway, secretary of state, from November 1625. On Conway's personal staff as opposed to holding an official crown appointment, he continued in the employ of each of Conway's successors until 1640. He was appointed secretary interpreter for the German tongue in 1631 and deputy secretary interpreter for the French tongue not long afterwards. His duties involved acting as a cryptographer as well as dealing with diplomatic correspondence and translation work. The secretary of state, Sir John Coke, old and infirm toward the end of his tenure, allowed Weckherlin to perform a large part of his duties, including application of the signet and privy seals, to the envy of fellow bureaucrats, who complained of Weckherlin's 'dexterity' at cutting them out, with the loss of their fees. Many of these duties brought Weckherlin into close, informal contact with Charles I, and he became attached to the king's entourage, travelling with him at almost all times and assisting the king with personal tasks, such as writing poetry.

In 1627 Weckherlin was given oversight of the pre-publication licensing of news for the press, soon expanded to include history and 'matters of state'. The only item he is known to have prohibited was Sir Robert Filmer's *Patriarcha*, presented for a licence in 1632. Weckherlin had personal ties to the publishing business through his brother-in-law, Robert Raworth, a London printer, and his patent to print Latin school books, obtained in 1631 to reward him in part for his service, for which he had been badly paid. His role as licenser, and his support of his brother-in-law in the face of official censure, brought him into conflict with Archbishop Laud, who vigorously exercised the church's authority in oversight of the press and apparently tried to have Weckherlin removed from his post in the 1630s. Weckherlin, who had a long memory of all slights dealt to him, later testified at Laud's trial as a witness for the prosecution.

Though Weckherlin had performed the duties of secretary for the Latin tongue since 1625 he was never formally appointed to the position, nor paid its wages. When Sir Henry Vane became secretary in 1640, Weckherlin hoped he would receive 'some small fruit of the great toil & labours I have undergone in all foreign affairs, which afford no benefit nor comfort at all', but the king asked only that Weckherlin continue in the same capacity in Vane's service (PRO, SP 16/444/53). Weckherlin continued to write government letters after Vane's dismissal late in 1641. Despite his personal relationship with the king, which apparently endured to some degree, and with Sir Edward Nicholas, Weckherlin did not join the royalist cause. His creation as MA of Cambridge University in 1642 may have been intended to serve as reward or as an enticement. He later wrote that he had served the Long Parliament since 1642, and in February 1644 was employed by its committee of both kingdoms. Designated secretary for foreign affairs he performed the same sorts of duties he had in service to successive secretaries of state. He continued to work with codes and ciphers and helped decipher and prepare for publication Charles I's sensitive private correspondence and papers of the king's secretary of state, George, Lord Digby, captured at the battle of Naseby. In 1647 he was appointed secretary for foreign languages to the committee.

In these years Weckherlin rejoiced in his eleven grandchildren, the children of his daughter Elizabeth and her husband, William Trumbull, of Easthampstead Park, Berkshire, where Weckherlin taught French and Latin to one of his grandsons, William, a future secretary of state. But his beloved wife died in 1645, while his son, Ralph, went to fight in the king's army and subsequently into exile with the royal court, not to return to England until after the Restoration. Weckherlin continued to complain of small reward for a large amount of work and made repeated attempts to collect wages and arrears over the course of the 1640s. All of these blows, added to his own ill health due to gout and circulatory problems, the execution of the king, and the reorganization of the government, caused him to leave his post by March 1649 when he was replaced by another poet and Latin scholar, John Milton. But by March 1652 Milton had substantially lost his sight and the council of state recalled Weckherlin to assist with foreign affairs. This reappointment was short-lived, however, as Weckherlin died in office, some time between 27 January and 21 February 1653.

Weckherlin worked long and hard in the service of his adopted country, sacrificing his health and his greatest source of happiness—spending time with his family—in the process. At the same time he attained the standing of a considerable poet, well recognized by his contemporaries, especially the German-speaking émigré community in London, as well as by modern scholars. He is credited with pioneering the vernacular form of German verse in the seventeenth century and has been considered one of the most notable German poets of the period, prior to Martin Opitz. He wrote sonnets in Italian and English, but despite living for many years in England continued to write most of his poetry in German and published his works in German-speaking areas, for example the volume of poems shepherded through the Elsevier press in Leiden by his friend Theodore Haak in 1641. Expanded in 1648, it contained a notable lament for Gustavus Adolphus, a rallying call to protestant Germany, and spiritual poems. He also wrote masques, at least one in English. Weckherlin's papers passed to his daughter's family and are to be found in the Trumbull papers in the British Library.

S. A. BARON

Sources *CSP dom.*, 1639–53 • PRO, state papers domestic, Charles I, SP16 • F. M. G. Evans, *The principal secretary of state: a survey of the office from 1558 to 1680* (1923) • BL, Trumbull papers • BL, Coke papers • L. Forster, 'The Weckherlin papers', *British Library Journal*, 19 (1993), 133–41 • *The Trumbull papers: the property of the most honourable the marquess of Downshire* (1989) [auction catalogue, Sothebys, London, 1989] • L. W. Forster, *Georg Rudolph Weckherlin: zur Kenntnis seines Lebens in England* (Basel, 1944) • R. E. Schade, 'Weckherlin, Georg Rodolf', *German Baroque writers, 1580–1660*, ed. J. Hardin, DLitB, 164 (1996), 353–6 • W. B. Rye, *England as seen by foreigners in the days of Elizabeth and James the First* (1865) • L. Forster, 'Sources for G. R. Weckherlin's life in England: the correspondence', *Modern Language Review*, 41 (1946), 186–95 • L. Forster, 'G. R. Weckherlin in England', *German Life and Letters*, 3 (1938–9), 107–16 • Venn, *Alum. Cant.* • G. J. Armytage, ed., *A visitation of the county of Kent, begun … 1663, finished … 1668*, Harleian Society, 54 (1906)

Archives BL, papers, Dep 8826 | BL, Trumbull MSS, Weckherlin MSS • CKS, letters to second earl of Leicester

Likenesses W. Faithorne, line engraving, 1653? (after D. Mytens), NPG; repro. in G. Könnecke, *Bilderatlas* (1887), p. 114.1765.b.26 • D. Mytens, portrait (aged fifty?)

Weddell, James (1787–1834), navigator, was the younger son of an upholsterer of Dalserf, near Lanark, who had settled in London and there married Sarah Pease, a Quaker. James is said to have been born on 24 August 1787 in Ostend, where the family had removed because of the father's poor health, but his birth there has proved untraceable and he himself gave his place of birth as Massachusetts when he entered the navy in 1810. His father died soon after James's birth, leaving his family with little money. In 1796 James joined his elder brother Charles who was in the Royal Navy in the *Swan* at Yarmouth; and after this he was at sea, first on a coasting vessel (probably a collier), and later on a frigate, to which he was sent in irons after having struck his captain. Suggestions that this frigate was the *Rainbow* are probably wrong. In 1810 he entered the navy again on the *Rainbow*, and was rated first a seaman and then a midshipman, before his discharge in December 1810 on his promotion by warrant to acting master in the *Firefly*. He eagerly grasped opportunities for study and taught himself navigation. In December 1811 he was moved to the *Thalia*, and, on her return to England and being paid off, he was on 21 October

James Weddell (1787–1834), by P. G. Dodd, 1828

1812 promoted master of the *Hope*. A few months later he was moved to the brig *Avon* with Commander, later Admiral of the Fleet, Sir George Sartorius, who in 1839 described Weddell as 'one of the most efficient and trustworthy officers I have met'. The *Avon* was paid off in March 1814, and after this he served on the sloop *Espoir*, the frigate *Cydnus*, and then the *Pactolus*.

The peace left Weddell on half pay for three years before he accepted command of the *Jane*, a brig of 160 tons belonging to Messrs Strachan and Gavin of Leith, for a sealing voyage to the Antarctic. No record is extant of the voyage, which lasted from 1819 until 1821, but Weddell seems to have visited the South Shetland Islands and is credited with having discovered the South Orkneys. The voyage was not profitable, but Weddell persuaded James Strachan to fit out the *Jane* again and to purchase the cutter *Beaufoy* for a further voyage which set off on 17 September 1822, searching for fur seals. Weddell reached the Falklands, the South Shetlands, South Georgia, and the South Orkneys, and reached latitude 74° 15″, the southernmost latitude then achieved. He returned home in July 1824 and in 1825 published *A Voyage towards the South Pole*, which was recognized as of considerable importance for its account of the voyage and its survey of the South Shetlands where names such as Boyd's Strait, Duff's Strait, and Sartorius Island recalled the captains with whom Weddell had served. An enlarged edition and a German translation appeared in 1827, in which year Weddell was elected fellow of the Royal Society of Edinburgh.

Weddell's later life was marked with misfortune. In 1829 he was trading in Buenos Aires in the *Jane*, but was forced to abandon her in the Azores on the return journey as she was taking in water. He and his crew embarked as passengers on a ship bound for England, but narrowly escaped death when she was shipwrecked. In 1830 he sailed as master of the *Eliza*, reaching Hobart, Tasmania, in May 1831, where he met and helped fellow Antarctic explorer John Biscoe. Weddell had transported an alleged escaped convict, Richard Brown, to Hobart, but when Brown cleared his name, he sued Weddell for having transported him against his will. In poor health and penniless since his shipwreck, Weddell died, unmarried, on 9 September 1834, at 16 Norfolk Street, Strand, London, and was buried at St Clement Danes churchyard.

P. G. Dodd described Weddell in earlier life as tall and strongly built, energetic in company, but melancholy when alone (Savours, 156). William Jerdan suggested that his heart lay in exploration, not commerce, and he seems to have taken hard the misfortunes which lack of means put in his path. Weddell Island and the Weddell Sea in the Antarctic are lasting memorials to his achievements.

ELIZABETH BAIGENT

Sources A. Savours, 'Biographical note on James Weddell', *Polar Record*, 11 (1962–3), 155–7 · private information (2004) · A. G. E. Jones, 'New light on James Weddell, master of the brig *Jane* of Leith', *Scottish Geographical Magazine*, 81 (1965), 182–7 · W. Jerdan, *The autobiography of William Jerdan: with his literary, political, and social reminiscences and correspondence during the last fifty years*, 4 vols. (1852–3) · *DNB* · Allibone, *Dict.*
Archives Scott Polar RI, papers
Likenesses P. G. Dodd, miniature, 1828; Christies, 27 Sept 1996, lot 151 [*see illus.*] · F. Peake, oils, 1839 (after P. G. Dodd), RGS · P. G. Dodd, miniature, Royal Scottish Geographical Society, Edinburgh; repro. in Savours, 'Biographical note on James Weddell', facing p. 155
Wealth at death 'penniless': Savours, 'Biographical note'; Jones, 'New light'

Weddell, John (c.1583–1639/40), sea captain, first came to notice in 1617 when the directors of the East India Company appointed him to a position of responsibility as master's mate aboard the *Dragon*. He achieved prominence five years later at the age of thirty-eight, when English naval forces helped the Persians to take Hormoz. The directors appointed him to be the joint commander, with Robert Blythe, of a squadron of nine ships which sailed for Jask in Persia, and onwards to Surat. His arrival coincided with negotiations between Edward Moxon, chief merchant in Persia, and Shah Abbas (1587–1629) for a joint attack on Hormoz. In June 1621 they finalized an agreement in principle which they put into effect in January 1622, when Weddell and Blythe arrived in the Persian Gulf.

The agreement was a product of long-standing tensions between the Portuguese and Persians in the Persian Gulf as well as the desire of the English to supplant the Portuguese in Asian trade. Hormoz was an island city of 40,000 inhabitants at the mouth of the Persian Gulf. Together with Goa, Malacca, and Macao, it was one of the most important Portuguese possessions. Abbas had already laid siege to the city in 1602, 1608, and 1616, and recaptured nearby Gombroon in 1615. Beginning in 1616, the East India Company, with the encouragement of Sir Thomas Roe as well as the endeavours of Robert and Anthony Sherley, had begun to trade with Persia. Co-operation with Abbas in the attack was to result in additional trading privileges and receipts from the customs revenues at Gombroon.

With the assistance of the English, the attack on Hormoz proceeded swiftly and with success. The Persians provided 10,000 troops under Imam Quli Bey, the shah of Shiraz, and the English provided four ships under the command of Weddell and Blythe. The immediate pretence for war was the fortifications the new Portuguese commander Ruy Freire had constructed on the neighbouring island of Qishm. His five galleons were unable to retain control of the sea around the two islands, however, and in January 1622 Weddell laid siege to Qishm and took it. Two weeks later, with support from Weddell's ships, troops under Imam Quli Bey stormed the city. Only the fortress held out for two months longer, falling in April. Trade had been destroyed and the city depopulated; or, as one English observer pithily put it a year later, 'Hormuz is become a ruined heap' (Steensgaard, 346).

The war between the English, often in alliance with the Dutch, and the Portuguese resumed two years later. Weddell returned in 1624 to England with a squadron and departed later that year again for Surat. On his return to the Indian Ocean he found that a new Portuguese commander, Nun Alvarez Botelho, had arrived with a squadron of eight galleons and threatened trade in the Persian Gulf. With the encouragement of Abbas, Weddell sailed to the gulf in command of eight ships and four pinnaces, half of them Dutch. Over the first three days of February 1625, off Gombroon, the two squadrons joined in a fierce battle, and the Portuguese withdrew with heavier losses. On the last day alone Weddell's crew fired around a thousand shot: 'at sunset we were so faint and weary', he wrote, 'that our men began to drop down for very faintness' (Foster, 3.81). Thereafter the intensity of the war diminished, although rancour and acts of brutality continued. Weddell organized and led another Anglo-Dutch expedition when Ruy Freire captured an English vessel, the *Lion*, and killed all those aboard except one. Searching for the Portuguese in the Persian Gulf did not lead to battle, and the murders went unrevenged.

When, in 1627, Weddell returned to England, he joined the navy and participated in the war against France. He began as the captain of the *Rainbow* and, within a year, became a vice-admiral. The duke of Buckingham first commended his skill in command when the *Rainbow* ran aground and Weddell successfully refloated the ship. Weddell then commanded a small squadron sent to gain intelligence of French preparations at Le Havre and fought at the battle off the Île de Ré. In January 1628, during a royal visit to Southampton, Buckingham presented him to Charles I. As of February 1628, however, Weddell had yet to receive his full wages, and it may have been monetary considerations which led him to return to the service of the East India Company.

In April 1629 Weddell commanded a squadron of five ships, bearing capital worth £208,000 provided by a special subscription for trade to Surat and Persia. He had been given the title of captain-general of the company ships, but the war against the Portuguese had quieted substantially. On two occasions Weddell skirmished with Portuguese galleons, but the viceroy had committed most of his resources to relieving Malacca from an attack by the king of Achin. He returned in April 1631 to England, and in 1632 departed again in command of five ships, with capital of £146,000 raised by subscriptions to the third joint stock.

On his return to England in 1634, however, longstanding tensions between Weddell and the directors of the company resulted in an open impasse. His dissatisfaction with the terms and conditions of company service had in 1627 already been apparent. In February of that year he admitted to having conducted a private trade in commodities, acknowledged the public censure of the directors, but remained convinced that 'upon consideration of his services they would think he deserved better'. In April 1631, nevertheless, he had again been publicly censured for conducting a private trade. And these tensions came to a head when, in January 1633, a freak accident led to the loss of two ships and, as captain-general, he was held partly responsible. When leaving Surat the captain of the *Swallow* had fired a salute in contravention of standing orders; the ship had caught fire and sailed into the flagship, *Charles*, while Weddell was ashore. Despite support from the president of Surat, William Methwold, and others that he could not be held culpable, the directors ordered Weddell home for questioning. He later explained his indignation in a letter to Methwold: 'If fines and undeserved reproaches, instead of remuneration for honest services be the East India Company's favours and honours (as nowadays they are) we pray God keep both you and us from such indulgences' (Foster, 5.317).

Two developments enabled Weddell to act on his disaffection and to help found a trading organization, the Courteen Association, to compete with the East India Company. First, Methwold had negotiated a truce in January 1634 with the viceroy of Goa, which offered the possibility that trade might be expanded to the Malabar coast and Macao, areas controlled by the Portuguese. Second, a group of adventurers led by Endymion Porter who were well connected at court had, in 1633 and 1634, obtained royal commissions for privateering ventures in the Indian Ocean, and now wanted to exploit the new possibilities for trade. They were able to win the considerable financial backing of Sir William Courteen; and the new Courteen Association received a royal commission to trade in areas under Portuguese authority.

Between 1636 and his death in 1639 or 1640 at the age of fifty-six, Weddell directed negotiations for the association and commanded their first squadron to Asia. With four ships—the *Dragon*, *Sun*, *Planter*, and *Catherine*—two pinnaces, and capital valued at £120,000, he left England in April 1636 for Goa. Sailing with Weddell were many others, including the diarist Peter Mundy, who shared his disaffection. Noted the directors of the existing company, 'there is not one of them but have had his bringing up, maintenance and preferment by us and our service' (Foster, 5.260). After arriving in October, Weddell negotiated over three months an agreement with the viceroy to trade in Portuguese Asia, although details of it were not published, and ambiguity about the specific terms was later to cause difficulties. He established a first factory in February 1637 on the Malabar coast at Bhatkal and a second at Achin. From there he sent back the *Planter* bearing 150,000 lb of pepper as well as benzoin, cinnamon, gum lac, cassia fistula (the fruit of the pudding pipe tree), and calicoes. In May he sailed for Malacca and Macao, where he arrived at the end of June.

After initial difficulties, by a mixture of force and negotiation Weddell traded for a valuable cargo. The ostensible reason for the governor of Macao refusing him permission to trade was that confirmation of the commercial agreement had yet to be received from the viceroy; but Weddell came to believe, as Mundy recorded, that 'they kept the main cause to themselves which was that our coming would quickly eat them out of all trade' (Temple, 175). Weddell then sought to establish contact with Chinese merchants directly at Canton (Guangzhou). He encountered conflicting interests and actions among Chinese officials as he sailed cautiously up the Canton River. Local officials and militias who controlled forts along the river, perhaps with the encouragement of the Portuguese, intermittently resisted the advance of the ships, particularly at Anunghoy (Yaniangxie), and Weddell fought a number of skirmishes with them. Cantonese officials welcomed the trade, however, and invited his three chief merchants to the city. In August and September 1637 these merchants bought a rich cargo, including at least 500 to 600 tons of sugar, gold, raw silk, green ginger, China roots, musk, porcelain, and silk stuffs such as damasks, satins, grograms, and tafiettas. Even the provisions they bought, which were inexpensive according to Mundy, suggested exotic wealth, and included crabs, porpoises, geese, duck, pears, chestnuts, dried 'leeches' (probably lychees), oranges, and grapefruit. Weddell departed in November and four months later he arrived on the Malabar coast, where he found the factory at Bhatkal abandoned and re-established it. He sailed with the *Dragon* and *Catherine* for Masulipatam (where the East India Company had a factory) to buy fine cloth, and returned to Bhatkal before going to Cannanore in late November 1638, just before the homeward voyage. 'We conceive', wrote factors in Masulipatam, 'never Englishmen were ever richlier laden than they are now with goods' (Foster, 6.74).

On the return journey in 1639 Weddell and the two ships disappeared in uncertain circumstances. Rumours circulated afterwards that a Dutch fleet had captured and sunk them, putting the scene of the action, according to different accounts, off Malacca, Ceylon, or Mauritius. According to a Scot who claimed to have been aboard one of the ships, after being entertained by a Dutch captain Weddell had been thrown overboard and the ships seized. A more likely cause of his disappearance, however, was shipwreck in severe storms off the Cape of Good Hope, which

other English captains reported experiencing in December 1639 and January 1640.

Most judgements of Weddell, written by colleagues in India to the directors of the company, were unequivocal in their respect for his abilities and attributes. Chief among them, according to Methwold, were valour and resolution. 'The care of his charge, especially at sea, submits to no man you ever employed' (Foster, 5.67). Thomas Russell, a predecessor as president of Surat, wrote that he possessed 'discretion joined with valour, among your sea [captains] hath not his fellow' (Foster, 4.48). In public life this discretion gave way to pugnacious and often impetuous actions, whether in protesting or circumventing the strictures of company directors, or overcoming by violence the intransigence of Portuguese or Chinese officials. Weddell was at pains, however, to dispel the image that he acted chiefly for his own gain, particularly at the time of his break with the company: 'blame us not', he wrote to Methwold, 'nor brand us with the title of mercenaries, if, being commanded upon a lawful and honest design, we have embraced a better master's better pay' (Foster, 5.317).

In May 1643 William Courteen, the son of the original financier of the association, received letters of administration in which officials declared Weddell dead 'in partibus transmarinis' and intestate. A son, Jeremy, and a daughter, Elizabeth, the wife of Edward Wye, survived Weddell's wife, Frances, *née* Churry (d. 1656), whom he had married in 1614; another son, John, died young. Frances bequeathed to Elizabeth a portrait of Weddell which, for lack of any further evidence, must be presumed lost.

J. K. Laughton, *rev.* Trevor Dickie

Sources W. Foster, ed., *The English factories in India*, 1–6 (1906–12) · *The travels of Peter Mundy in Europe and Asia, 1608–1667*, ed. R. C. Temple and L. M. Anstey, 3, Hakluyt Society, 2nd ser., 45–6 (1919) · N. Steensgaard, *The Asian trade revolution of the seventeenth century: the East India companies and the decline of the caravan trade* (1974) · *Commentaries of Ruy Freyre de Andrada*, ed. C. R. Boxer (1930) · parish register (marriage), 1614, St Katharine by the Tower, London · admons, PRO, PROB 6/19, fol. 26r; PROB 6/32, fol. 203r
Likenesses portrait; now lost

Wedderburn, Alexander (*bap.* 1581). *See under* Wedderburn, David (*bap.* 1580, *d.* 1646).

Wedderburn, Sir Alexander, of Blackness (1610–1676), politician, was born on 22 March 1610, the eldest son of James Wedderburn (1589–1627), town clerk of Dundee, and Margaret, daughter of James Goldman, a Dundee merchant. Sir Peter *Wedderburn, a future lord of session, was his younger brother. In 1628 Alexander Wedderburn married Matilda, daughter of James Fletcher, provost of Dundee; they had five sons and six daughters. Their second son, James (1649–1696), was the grandfather of the Jacobite Sir John Wedderburn.

Wedderburn was educated for the law and was admitted advocate; but upon the death of his uncle Alexander of Kingennie, whose son was then a minor, he was appointed town clerk of Dundee in 1633, and held the office until 1675. He received a tack of the customs of Dundee from

Charles I in 1639, and in 1640 was granted an annual pension of £100 out of the customs, ratified in 1664. In September 1640 he was appointed one of the eight Scots commissioners to arrange the treaty of Ripon. He was knighted in 1642 and received a grant of the lands of Blackness in Forfarshire, which were later incorporated into a free barony.

Wedderburn represented Dundee in the Scottish parliament from 1644 to 1647 and from 1648 to 1651, and served in the protectorate parliaments of 1654 and 1656. He served on numerous committees of the estates, including the committees of war for 1645–7 and 1651. At the Restoration in 1661 he was appointed one of the commissioners for regulating weights and measures. He died on 18 November 1676.

T. F. HENDERSON, rev. SHARON ADAMS

Sources A. D. O. Wedderburn, *The Wedderburn book*, 2 vols. (privately printed, 1898) · M. D. Young, ed., *The parliaments of Scotland: burgh and shire commissioners*, 2 (1993) · *APS*, 1643–60

Wedderburn, Alexander, first earl of Rosslyn (1733–1805), lord chancellor, was born on 13 February 1733, probably in Edinburgh, the eldest of three children of Peter Wedderburn (*d.* 1756), advocate, and latterly judge, and his wife, Janet, daughter of David Ogilvie, an officer in a regiment of dragoons. Although his family owned a small estate outside Haddington called Chesterhall, it had long been associated with the legal profession in Scotland; his great-grandfather was Sir Peter Wedderburn (1616–1679), a lord of the court of session under the title of Lord Gosford. His father had difficulty building a legal practice, and became secretary to the board of excise in Scotland. It was only a year before his death that he was elevated to the court of session as Lord Chesterhall. According to John Ramsay of Ochtertyre, Wedderburn's father derived most of his ideas 'upon most subjects' from England, 'where, it is believed, he either received part of his education or spent part of his youth' (*Scotland and Scotsmen*, 1.139). Ramsay suspected that Peter Wedderburn had spent some time at the inns of court in London as preparation for possible practice before the court of exchequer in Scotland, which had been created in 1707 to deal with revenue cases. Ramsay also remarked that Wedderburn's father spoke 'proper English' at a time when the literati of Scotland were more concerned with the written language than its pronunciation, and that 'his manner of breeding [educating] his eldest son, the Lord Chancellor, was exceeding admired at the time' (ibid., 1.148). Ramsay also stated that Wedderburn's father was not only episcopalian but a member of the Church of England, attending the chapel in Edinburgh endowed by one of the English judges of the court of exchequer to provide public worship for Anglicans.

Wedderburn was educated at the famous burgh school kept at Dalkeith, Edinburghshire, by James Barclay, whose alumni included the historian and Church of Scotland minister William Robertson as a predecessor and the politician Henry Dundas at a later date. He matriculated at the University of Edinburgh at the age of thirteen early in 1746, before the last Jacobite rising in Scotland had come

Alexander Wedderburn, first earl of Rosslyn (1733–1805), by Sir Joshua Reynolds, 1785

to an end. He did not take a degree, but at this time made the acquaintance of many of the leading figures of what is now called the Scottish Enlightenment. He attended the lectures Adam Smith presented on language and rhetoric in Edinburgh in 1748 and became a lifelong friend of Smith. He was known to David Hume who at that time was keeper of the Advocates' Library, and made the acquaintance of William Robertson, who with Hume was embarking on a career as a historian. He read law with those teaching it at Edinburgh, particularly John Erskine, author of *The Institutes of the Law of Scotland*. He also began to consider the possibility of practising in England, and with his father's approval was admitted to the Inner Temple in London on 8 May 1753 and began to visit that metropolis annually. He was admitted to the Faculty of Advocates in Edinburgh in 1754 and began to practise in Edinburgh.

It was at this time that Edinburgh experienced a remarkable resurgence of club life supported by its professional middle class of lawyers, doctors, ministers, and professors, with the support of the Scottish gentry who still treated Edinburgh as a national centre of social life and culture. Of these clubs perhaps the most famous was the Select Society founded in 1754, whose members included Hume, Robertson, Smith, and many other prominent members of Edinburgh civic society. Wedderburn was called to the chair of the first meeting at the age of twenty-one. The following year he took a leading role in the publication of the 'first' *Edinburgh Review*, a short-lived periodical which preceded its more famous successor by more than half a century. The intention was to review every publication originating in Scotland, and the preface to the first of the two issues which did appear is one of Wedderburn's few known publications. It was in effect a manifesto for a programme of social, economic, and cultural improvement in Scotland. Wedderburn stated that the journal's purpose was to establish 'the progressive state of learning in the country' (*Edinburgh Review*, 1755, i–iv).

Through the Select Society Wedderburn met a number of Robertson's fellow ministers in the Church of Scotland, including John Home, who were just beginning to operate self-consciously as a 'moderate party' within the church, and in particular in its general assembly, where Wedderburn was selected as a lay elder for the parish of Inverkeithing and later Dunfermline. As such he took the lead in general assembly debates over whether David Hume could be called before the general assembly as a heretic. Wedderburn, Robertson, and the moderate party were successful in persuading the assembly that as Hume was no longer a member of the Church of Scotland, its general assembly had no authority over him. Later that year Wedderburn was part of the group which encouraged John Home to allow the public performance in Edinburgh of his play *Douglas*, and in 1757 Wedderburn argued unsuccessfully against attempts in the general assembly to forbid ministers of the Church of Scotland to attend theatrical productions.

This period of intense activity in Edinburgh by Wedderburn famously came to an end in August 1757 when he clashed before the bar of the court of session with the notoriously Jacobite, Scots-speaking dean of the Faculty of Advocates, Alexander Lockhart. The younger man allowed all his impatience at the weight of tradition at the bar and in Scotland generally to express itself in language directed at Lockhart and eventually at the bench itself. On being required to retract and apologize, Wedderburn took off his gown, laid it before the astonished judges, bowed, and left the court. That night he departed for London and the Inner Temple.

Wedderburn's struggle to establish himself in English practice was a difficult one, and at a time of pervasive English mistrust of Scots on the make, the transition from representing Anglicization as cultural improvement in Scotland to making professional progress as a Scottish lawyer and politician in England marked Wedderburn for life. Through his friendship with John Home, however, Wedderburn was introduced to the third earl of Bute and with his patronage was successful eventually in obtaining a Scottish seat, Ayr burghs, in parliament after the election of 1761. By 1763, with Bute's help, he was made king's counsel. He shocked lawyers on the northern circuit by appearing there in search of business in 1764. It was as a result of this foray that he met and subsequently married his first wife, on 31 December 1767, Betty Anne (*d.* 1781), only child and heir of John Dawson and Elizabeth Taylor of Morley, Yorkshire, 'with whom he Got £10,000' according to his friend Alexander Carlyle (*Autobiography*, ed. Burton, 230). By this time he had become principal legal

adviser to Robert Clive on his return from India. This connection enabled him to defy the government of the day and speak in the Commons in support of Wilkes in 1769, and led to his move to a Shropshire seat, Bishop's Castle, in parliament under Clive's patronage. A year later he made his peace with the North ministry and became solicitor-general. He became a valued government speaker in the House of Commons during the difficult years of the American War of Independence and used his position to put pressure on Lord North to advance his legal career. He was made attorney-general in 1778 and in 1780 became chief justice of the court of common pleas and a peer as Baron Loughborough. His first wife died on 15 February 1781, and on 12 September 1782 he married Charlotte Courtenay (1751–1825/6), fourth and youngest daughter of William Courtenay, first Viscount Courtenay (1710–1762), of Powderham Castle and Frances Frich (1721–1761). He had remarked in a letter of 5 September 1782 to a friend regarding his future wife that 'She is not a beauty, nor a wit, nor a fortune, neither does she profess any talents; but she has a good figure, a great deal of countenance, a very right understanding, and an exceedingly pleasant temper' (GEC, *Peerage*, 11.174 n.). Their only child, William, died in infancy.

Throughout the 1780s Wedderburn was associated with the opposition whigs, having entered their camp via the Fox–North coalition, during which he held office as first commissioner of the great seal from April to December 1783. His hopes of becoming lord chancellor were dashed by the failure of the coalition and the political success of the younger Pitt. His great rival legally and politically at this time was Edward Thurlow, who held the chancellorship as a member of Pitt's government. The outbreak of the French Revolution led to a chain of events in which Wedderburn once again revolved politically and came to join Pitt's wartime cabinet, eventually bringing William Bentinck, third duke of Portland, and other moderate opposition whigs in his wake. The initiator of negotiations was Wedderburn's fellow Scot Henry Dundas, who was anxious to identify a candidate to replace Thurlow as the latter became increasingly unreliable in his support of government measures in the House of Lords. When Thurlow was dismissed as chancellor in 1792 the great seal again went into commission. The imminence of war between France and Britain made it easier for Wedderburn to justify his latest political conversion and the gratification of his ambition. He became lord chancellor at the end of January 1793.

Wedderburn as lord chancellor followed Thurlow in identifying himself as the king's representative in the cabinet. Consequently he was not an ideal colleague in that he was capable of discussing cabinet business with the monarch without consulting fellow members of the ministry. For many years this was not a major problem but at the time when union with Ireland was undertaken and Catholic emancipation was proposed by Pitt as its corollary, Wedderburn, a past advocate of Roman Catholic relief as a member of North's ministry in 1779 and 1780, appears to have encouraged the king in the belief that by approving Catholic emancipation he would be violating the terms of his coronation oath. Wedderburn did not foresee that the issue would lead to the end of Pitt's ministry and his replacement by Henry Addington as a known opponent of emancipation. Neither had he realized that it would lead to his own removal as lord chancellor. This he found hard to accept or even believe, apparently continuing to attend cabinet after he had given up the seals until he was told not to do so. As a consolation for his loss he was created earl of Rosslyn on 21 April 1801, with his nephew, James St Clair Erskine, the son of his sister Janet Wedderburn and Sir Henry Erskine, named as heir to the title. He died less than four years later on 2 January 1805 at Baylis, Stoke Poges, Buckinghamshire, and was buried in St Paul's Cathedral on 12 January.

Wedderburn's place in British political history has not been viewed by many as a positive one. Early in his career he was referred to in *The Letters of Junius* as having 'something about him which even treachery cannot trust' (GEC, *Peerage*, 11.174 n.) and biographers of Pitt have been stern in their disapproval. His friend Alexander Carlyle, who had met him in his early days as a young lawyer in Edinburgh, referred to Wedderburn ambiguously in several asides in his memoirs, recalling that when he first met Wedderburn in 1757 with a friend he 'open'd himself to us, as much as he was capable of Doing to any body' (*Autobiography*, ed. Burton, 166). At another point, referring to a visit from Wedderburn, he stated that 'my friend Wedderburn Seldom Did any thing without a Reason' (ibid., 207). In an entry for 1764, Carlyle recalled Wedderburn's conversation as 'stiff and pompous', and his general demeanour while on circuit at Newcastle one of 'Self-conceit' (ibid., 230).

Wedderburn was a man of great application who attained considerable credit as a public speaker in the law courts and in parliament. No one ever described him as a great lawyer in the abstract sense, but he served as a judge in England for more than twenty years without discredit, and it could be argued that his Scottish training in civil law gave him a useful perspective in equity cases that was not available to those schooled exclusively in the English common law tradition. His early break with his Edinburgh education and upbringing and the need to pursue his career in what was in effect a foreign country, clearly influenced his political conduct in England and encouraged him in the development of a cold, detached public manner that contrasted with a private personality that could be warm, kindly, and charming. His insistence on securing the reversion of his peerage to the son of his beloved sister Janet indicated that he saw his essential loyalties as belonging to family just as in his political career he saw himself as personally loyal to George III as king rather than to a political party or an individual politician.

ALEXANDER MURDOCH

Sources J. Campbell, *Lives of the lord chancellors*, 7 vols. (1845–7) · J. Ehrman, *The younger Pitt*, 2–3 (1983–96) · GEC, *Peerage* · R. B. Sher, *Church and university in the Scottish Enlightenment: the moderate literati of Edinburgh* (1985) · *Scotland and Scotsmen in the eighteenth century: from the MSS of John Ramsay, esq., of Ochtertyre*, ed. A. Allardyce, 1 (1888), 138–44 · *Autobiography of the Rev. Dr. Alexander Carlyle … containing memorials of the men and events of his time*, ed. J. H. Burton (1860); repr. as *Anecdotes and characters of the times*, ed. J. Kinsley (1973) · 'Wedderburn, Alexander', HoP, *Commons* · *Edinburgh Review* (1755–6) · A. Murdoch, '*The people above': politics and administration in mid-eighteenth-century Scotland* (1980) · F. O'Gorman, *The whig party and the French Revolution* (1967) · M. Fry, *The Dundas despotism* (1992) · D. Duman, 'The English bar in the Georgian era', *Lawyers in early modern Europe and America*, ed. W. Prest (1981), 86–107 · DNB

Archives Lincoln's Inn, London, legal papers · NA Scot., corresp. and papers · priv. coll., corresp. and papers · U. Mich., Clements L., corresp. and papers relating to America | BL, corresp. with Lord Auckland, Add. MSS 34412–34461, 46490–46491, *passim* · BL, corresp. with Lord Grenville, Add. MS 58938 · BL, corresp. with Lord Liverpool, Add. MSS 38212–38217, 38306–38310, 38403, *passim* · BL OIOC, corresp. with Philip Francis, MSS Eur. C 8, D 18, E 12–22, F 5–6 · Castle Howard, Yorkshire, letters to fifth earl of Carlisle · CKS, letters to William Pitt · NA Scot., corresp. with Lord Melville · NL Scot., corresp. with Andrew Stuart · PRO, letters to William Pitt, PRO 30/8 · Sheff. Arch., corresp. with Edmund Burke · U. Nott. L., corresp. with duke of Portland

Likenesses J. Reynolds, oils, 1785, Lincoln's Inn, London [*see illus.*] · M. Brown, oils, *c.*1791, Scot. NPG · H. Edridge, pencil drawing, 1795, BM · R. Dighton, caricature, coloured etching, pubd 1797 (*A chance seller, with a capital prize in the state lottery*), NPG · F. Bartolozzi, engraving (after J. Northcote), Scot. NPG · M. Brown, oils, Schweitzer Gallery, New York · M. Brown, oils, Walker Art Gallery, Liverpool · J. S. Copley, group portrait, oils (*The collapse of the earl of Chatham in the House of Lords*), Tate collection; on loan to NPG · P. Doghton, oils, priv. coll. · J. Grozer, engraving (after J. Reynolds), Scot. NPG · H. Meyer, stipple (after J. Northcote), BM, NPG; repro. in *Contemporary portraits* (1812) · G. Murray, engraving (after R. K. Porter), Scot. NPG · W. Owen, oils, NPG; on loan to the Law Courts · C. Warren, engraving (after C. Courbould), Scot. NPG · etchings, BM, NPG · print, repro. in A. F. Steuart, *The Douglas cause* (1909)

Wedderburn, David (*bap.* 1580, *d.* 1646), poet and Latin grammarian, was baptized in the parish church of Aberdeen on 2 January 1580, the eldest son of William Wedderburn (1550?–1620), a burgess of the town, and Marjorie Annand. There is some confusion as to where Wedderburn completed his education. Although Marischal College, Aberdeen, appears to be the strongest contender, it is possible that he matriculated at the University of St Andrews during the period 1598–1600. He was appointed as a master in the grammar school of Aberdeen in April 1602 but resigned his post the following year with the intention of pursuing a clerical vocation. For reasons unknown he appears to have abandoned this aim and returned in 1603 to his teaching post in the grammar school, where he remained until failing health compelled him to resign the rectorship in 1640. He married twice. On 30 April 1611 he married Janet Johnstone, with whom he had a son who was baptized on 25 March 1612 but whose name went unrecorded in the parish register of Aberdeen. Janet died on 29 October 1613 and was buried in the church of St Nicholas, Aberdeen, where Wedderburn had a monument erected in her memory. On 25 October the next year he married Bathia Mowat, with whom he had two sons and five daughters.

Wedderburn was granted a professorship and taught humanities in Marischal College after the death of Gilbert Gray in 1614. A complaint from the civic authorities, however, forced him to resign this charge ten years later in order that he might focus solely on raising standards in the grammar school. In February 1628 he successfully petitioned the town council to have Andrew Howat appointed to teach arithmetic in the grammar school. In July of that same year and 'for the godlie and vertuous educatioun and teaching of the youth in pietie, gude letters, and gude maneres' (*Extracts from the Records of the Burgh of Aberdeen, 1625–1642*), Alexander Fraser was added to the teaching staff after an anonymous benefactor bequeathed 500 merks for that purpose. Wedderburn's own annual salary was boosted by 80 merks in September 1629. On resigning his post in 1640 he received a pension of 200 merks in recognition of his service to education in the burgh.

Wedderburn was a Latin poet and scholar of notable distinction. In 1612, after the premature death of Prince Henry, he composed *In obitum summae spei principis Henrici, Jacobi VI*, which was printed by Andrew Hart the following year. In 1617 the town council of Aberdeen paid him 500 merks for the compilation of *Invictissimo et potentissimo monarchae Jacobi VI, Britanniae magnae* and *Propempticon charitum Abredonionsium*, which were read to King James at Falkland Palace on 19 May 1617. On 6 February 1620 Wedderburn was made poet laureate of Aberdeen, for which he received an annual sum of 80 merks from the city magistrates. On 14 August that same year he was awarded the freedom of the city. It was probably at the prompting of the town council that he produced a Latin poem on the death of the king in 1625, entitled *Abredonia atrata sub obitum serenissimi et potentissimi monarchae Jacobi VI*, which was printed by Edward Raban.

In 1633 Wedderburn composed *Vivat rex* on the visit of Charles I to Scotland. In 1635 he also contributed to the Funerals, a series of verses produced in memory of Patrick Forbes, the late bishop of Aberdeen. In 1641 he composed six Latin elegies on the death of his old schoolfriend and fellow classicist Arthur Johnstone. These were later reprinted in 1731 in the *Poetarum Scotorum musae sacrae*. He produced a similar obituary in celebration of the life of George Jameson in 1644. Between 1643 and 1644 Wedderburn further compiled two volumes containing 300 moral epigrams and several elegies. Eight of his Latin poems are to be found in the *Delitiae poetarum Scotorum* compiled by Sir John Scot of Scotstarvit in 1637.

In spite of his prodigious output and reputation as a poet, Wedderburn was probably best known for his *Short Introduction to Grammar*, for which he received payment of £100 Scots from the town council of Aberdeen. This work, which was to become a standard text on Latin in grammar schools throughout Scotland, was first published in 1632 and later reprinted several times; it was on its account that he was given the freedom of Dundee on 20 May 1632 *in erudiendo juventutem*. His *Institutiones grammaticae* and *Vocabula*, first published in 1633 and 1636 respectively, were similarly reprinted for the benefit of future generations of young Scots. Wedderburn died in Aberdeen, probably on 23 October 1646. He was buried in St Nicholas's Church there.

Wedderburn's younger brother, **Alexander Wedderburn** (*bap.* 1581), was also a Latin scholar of some renown. He was baptized at Aberdeen on 3 September 1581; he appears to have received part of his education in England before matriculating as a bursar of Marischal College on 29 January 1623, after a successful petition by his brothers David and William secured his place. He was responsible for the preparation of *Persius enucleatus, sive, Commentarius exactissimus et maxime perspicuus in Persium, poetarum omnium difficillimum*, which was subsequently published in Amsterdam in 1664. He was probably the author of *Radii Augustiniani sive praecupuae S. P. Augustin in s. scripture locus annotationes*, published in 1652. It is not known when he died or whether he married and raised a family.

More is known of the chequered career of **William Wedderburn** (*c.*1582–1659/60), Church of Scotland minister. He taught alongside his eldest brother, David, in the grammar school at Aberdeen in 1616/17 before his appointment as a regent in Marischal College shortly afterwards. He had burgess status conferred on him by the town of Aberdeen on 25 October 1623. On 10 June the following year he married Margaret Tullidelph, with whom he had a son, William.

In 1633 Wedderburn was inducted minister of Bethelnie (also named Old Meldrum) parish church in Aberdeenshire, and was officially presented to this charge by Charles I on 22 June 1636. He was a member of the famous general assemblies of 1638 and 1639 which abrogated Erastian episcopacy and re-established presbyterianism in the Church of Scotland. He was deposed for fornication in 1642 but was fully restored to the ministry by the general assembly of August the following year. Nevertheless he had to be censured and suspended yet again since on 2 November 1648 the presbytery of Aberdeen reinstated him to the pastorate. At an unknown date his first wife died, and on 22 November 1649 he married Agnes Howisone. He was subsequently, on 21 October 1651, called to the charge of Strathdon or Innernochtie, where he remained until his death at Strathdon at some date between 19 April 1659 and 19 April 1660.

A. S. WAYNE PEARCE

Sources A. D. O. Wedderburn, *The Wedderburn book*, 2 vols. (privately printed, 1898) • J. Nichols, *The progresses, processions, and magnificent festivities of King James I, his royal consort, family and court*, 2–3 (1828) • D. Wedderburn, *A short introduction to grammar* (1632); repr. (1970) • J. F. Kellas Johnstone and A. W. Robertson, *Bibliographia Aberdonensis*, ed. W. D. Simpson, Third Spalding Club, 1 (1929) • *Extracts from the records of the burgh of Aberdeen, 1625–1642* (1871) • L. B. Taylor, ed., *Aberdeen council letters*, 6 vols. (1942–61), vol. 2 • *Fasti Scot.*, new edn, vols. 3, 6 • *APS*, 1625–41

Wedderburn, James (*c.*1495–1553), reformer and poet, was born in Dundee, the eldest son of James Wedderburn (*d.* 1514?), merchant 'at the West Kirk stile' in Dundee, and Janet Barrie. He matriculated at St Andrews University in 1514 and studied under Gavin Logie, a leading reformer of the time. He left the university without taking his bachelor's degree and travelled to France, where he worked as a merchant in Rouen and Dieppe. It is possible that he was the same James Wedderburn who some time before 1528 married Janet Forrester of Nevay, daughter of David Forrester, and had three children with her.

On his return to Dundee, Wedderburn took religious

instruction from James Hewat, a Dominican friar who strengthened James's reforming convictions. James had two plays performed in the burgh in 1539–40, though there are no extant texts of these. *The Beheading of Johne the Baptist*, a tragedy, was staged at the West Port in Dundee, and *The Historie of Dyonisius the Tyrant*, a comedy, was staged at the burgh playfield. Both plays strongly attacked Roman Catholicism.

It was probably around this time that Wedderburn began composing poems that promoted protestant doctrine and denounced Roman Catholic corruption. These, along with works by his brothers John [*see below*] and Robert [*see below*], were to form a substantial part of the collection now generally known as *The Gude and Godlie Ballatis* but titled, in the 1578 edition, *Ane Compendious Buik of Godlie and Spirituall Songs*. The collection is made up of translations of scripture into Scots, satirical pieces, and adaptations of popular song which turn them to the service of the reformers in promoting protestant doctrine and attacking Roman Catholic corruption. The title-page of the 1578 edition announces that it contains 'an augmentation of sundrie gude and godlie Ballates not contenit in the first edition'. The only known previous edition is from 1567, but this contains only five pieces fewer than the 1578 edition. It is thus probable that an earlier edition existed, but no trace of it has been found. Topical allusions in some of the songs indicate that they were composed about 1540, and they may have been circulated in pamphlet form in the 1540s. The collection undoubtedly includes pieces not by the Wedderburn brothers, and exactly which poems were composed by which brother is unclear.

There are only five extant copies of the four known early editions of the Wedderburns' collection. These were published in 1567, 1578, 1600, and 1621, an indication of the influence and continuing popularity of the *Ballatis* in post-Reformation Scotland. As Helena Shire has noted, while the collection's adaptations of popular song aim at displacing these secular pieces, they have in fact helped to preserve many from oblivion (Shire, 33). In 1540 James Wedderburn was delated to James V for having counterfeited the conjuring of a ghost. This alluded to a similar summoning enacted at Kinghorn by one Friar Walter Laing, who had been confessor to the king. James Wedderburn fled to France to avoid arrest and once more took up commerce in Rouen and Dieppe. Other Scottish merchants at Dieppe informed the bishop at Rouen that Wedderburn had been declared a heretic in Scotland, but no action was taken. He remained at Rouen and Dieppe until his death, which appears to have been in 1553, since in this year his son, John (*d.* November 1569), was declared his heir. On his deathbed James is reported to have said to his son 'We have beene acting our part in the theater: you are to succeed; see that you act your part faithfullie!' (Calderwood, 1.142).

His brother **John Wedderburn** (*c.*1505–1556), the second son of James Wedderburn and Janet Barrie, was born in Dundee. He was incorporated in 1525 into the pedagogium (later St Mary's College) at St Andrews University when Patrick Hamilton and George Buchanan were residing there and John Major was lecturing in theology. He may have studied earlier at St Leonard's College under Gavin Logie. Wedderburn graduated BA in 1526 and MA in 1528. He returned to Dundee to join the priesthood, and he too received religious instruction from the Dominican James Hewat. In 1532 he is mentioned as chaplain of St Matthew's Chapel in Dundee.

In 1538–9 John Wedderburn fled to the continent after being accused and convicted of heresy, though it is unclear whether or not he actually stood trial. A king's messenger was sent to Dundee in 1538–9 to search his goods, suggesting that the trial and flight took place in early 1539. His possessions were seized by the crown and passed on to his youngest brother, Henry, for a small payment. Wedderburn took shelter in Wittenberg, an important protestant centre, where he encountered both Martin Luther and Philip Melanchthon. It is possible that the name Joannes Scotus entered in Wittenberg University's register in 1539 refers to John Wedderburn. The time he spent in Wittenberg suggests that he is responsible for the many poems in *The Gude and Godlie Ballatis* that are based on German sources and on Luther's verses.

John Wedderburn returned to Dundee in early 1543, after the death of James V, when the appointment of the supposedly pro-Reformation James Hamilton, earl of Arran, as regent gave the reformers hope that the authorities were now prepared to show greater tolerance towards protestantism. Wedderburn joined with a Dundee printer, John Scot, in publishing pro-Reformation works, these probably being the earliest editions of the works contained in *The Gude and Godlie Ballatis*. Later in 1543 an act of privy council was issued declaring that printers should destroy any slanderous ballads and works of condemned heretics. John Scot was ordered to be arrested, no doubt largely because of his role in disseminating the *Ballatis*, but the order was not carried out. In 1546, presumably as a result of the state's renewed attempts to suppress pro-Reformation writings, Wedderburn was forced to flee to England for his own safety, and he remained there until his death in 1556.

Another brother, **Robert Wedderburn** (*c.*1510–1555x60), the third son of James Wedderburn and Janet Barrie, was born in Dundee, and also attended St Andrews University. Having entered St Leonard's College in 1526 he graduated BA in 1529 and MA in 1530, with his name listed at the head of the roll of graduates. In 1528 he was granted the reversion of St Katherine's Chapel in Dundee, despite being under age. In the mid-1530s he came under suspicion of heresy and fled to Paris, where he attended the university. He may also have spent some time with his brother John at Wittenberg in the 1540s, a suggestion given credence by the fact that on his return journey to Scotland in 1546 he embarked at Frankfurt an der Oder. Crawford relates that when Robert was journeying back to Scotland and his ship had put in on the coast of Norway, a dispute arose between the Roman Catholic and protestant passengers, which led Robert and his fellow reformers to burn Cardinal David Beaton in effigy. Beaton was assassinated in St Andrews that same day. Robert succeeded his uncle, John Barry, as vicar of Dundee in 1546. He remained in this post until his death, in Dundee, some time between 1555 and 1560. With Isobel Lovell he had two illegitimate sons, David and Robert, who were declared legitimate in 1552–3. Isobel Lovell married David Cant in 1560 and had died by 1587. It has been suggested that Robert Wedderburn was the author of *The Complaynt of Scotland* (1548), but that work's positive attitudes towards the established church make it unlikely that the ascription is accurate.

J. K. M^cGINLEY

Sources D. Calderwood, *The history of the Kirk of Scotland*, ed. T. Thomson and D. Laing, 8 vols., Wodrow Society, 7 (1842–9), vol. 1, pp. 141–3 · A. F. Mitchell, ed., *A compendious book of godly and spiritual songs, commonly known as 'The gude and godlie ballatis'*, STS, 39 (1897) · A. H. Millar, *Roll of eminent burgesses of Dundee, 1513–1886* (1887), 21 · T. McCrie, *The life of John Knox*, 6th edn (1839), 389–90 · A. Maxwell, *Old Dundee prior to the Reformation* (1891), 139, 145 · G. Burnett and others, eds., *The exchequer rolls of Scotland*, 14 (1893) · H. M. Shire, *Song, dance and poetry at the court of Scotland under King James VI*, ed. K. Elliott (1969) · [J. Robertson], ed., *Concilia Scotiae*, 2 (1866), 294

Wedderburn, James (1585–1639), bishop of Dunblane, was born in Dundee, the second son of John Wedderburn, a Dundee mariner and shipowner, and his wife, Margaret Lindsay, and grandson of James Wedderburn (1495?–1553), the protestant sympathizer and dramatist. Although the extant records reveal nothing of his early education, he was sufficiently qualified to matriculate at the University of St Andrews in 1604. He graduated MA four years later. Like many of his contemporaries Wedderburn chose to further his studies outside Scotland, most probably at Cambridge University. While in England he was tutor to the children of the French classical scholar Isaac Casaubon. Wedderburn was instituted minister of Harston parish church in Cambridgeshire in 1615, but his incumbency was of a relatively short duration. He returned to Scotland in 1617 to take up the prestigious post of professor of divinity at St Mary's College, St Andrews. At some point prior to January 1623 the degree of doctor was duly conferred upon him. While Wedderburn was evidently an extremely able and learned divine, his appointment at St Andrews had more to do with his Anglican sympathies than his academic qualifications and suitability for the post. It was no coincidence that his elevation to the professorship coincided with the crown's attempt to reform the university on an Anglican template. Nevertheless, animosity towards Wedderburn's Arminian theology and his strong advocacy of Anglican practice in Scotland probably accounted for his decision to quit his post after nine years.

In February 1626 Wedderburn took up a new charge at Compton parish church within the diocese of Winchester. Later that same year he was also made a canon of Ely Cathedral. Further preferment followed when, on 12 September 1628, Charles I presented him to the vicarage of Mildenhall in the diocese of Norwich, and on 26 May 1631 he was made a prebendary of Whitchurch in the bishopric of Bath and Wells.

After returning to Scotland, under the auspices of William Laud, archbishop of Canterbury, Wedderburn was appointed dean of the Chapel Royal, Stirling, in October 1635. On 11 February 1636 he was finally elevated to the episcopate when he succeeded Adam Bellenden as bishop of Dunblane. Wedderburn is best remembered for his contribution to and involvement in the introduction of the highly controversial Scottish prayer book of 1637. Although Wedderburn rejected many of the central tenets of Tridentine Roman Catholicism, he believed that the reformers had been too hasty in leaving the Roman fold. His advocacy of the re-unification of Western Christendom, encapsulated in his 'Notes' and 'A treaty on reconciliation', some of which were published in Robert Baillie's *A Large Supplement of the Canterburian Self-Conviction* (1641), gained him few admirers in Scotland. He fled Scotland in the wake of the covenanting revolution and was deposed along with his fellow bishops by the Glasgow assembly in December 1638. He died, unmarried, at Canterbury on 23 September 1639 and was buried in the chapel of the Virgin Mary in the cathedral there.

A. S. WAYNE PEARCE

Sources *Fasti Scot.*, new edn, 7.338 · *DSCHT* · G. Donaldson, 'Leighton's predecessors', *Society of Friends of Dunblane Cathedral*, 12/2 (1975), 14–15 · G. Donaldson, *The making of the Scottish Prayer Book of 1637* (1954), 49–55, 81–2 · D. G. Mullan, *Episcopacy in Scotland: the history of an idea, 1560–1608* (1986), 169–72, 175–6, 189–90, 192 · *The letters and journals of Robert Baillie*, ed. D. Laing, 1 (1841) · D. Calderwood, *The history of the Kirk of Scotland*, ed. T. Thomson and D. Laing, 8 vols., Wodrow Society, 7 (1842–9), vol. 7, p. 569
Archives BL, Burnley MSS
Likenesses G. Jamesone, portrait, Birkhall, Fife; repro. in A. D. O. Wedderburn, *The Wedderburn book*, 1 (1898)

Wedderburn, John (*c*.1505–1556). *See under* Wedderburn, James (*c*.1495–1553).

Wedderburn, Sir John (1599–1679), physician, was the fifth son of Alexander Wedderburn (1561–1626) of Kingennie, and Helen, daughter of Alexander Ramsay of Brachmont in Fife, and was born at Dundee. Alexander was the second town clerk of Dundee, representative in the Scottish parliament, and one of the commissioners for union between England and Scotland. John Wedderburn matriculated at St Andrews University in 1615, graduated in 1618, and was professor of philosophy there in 1620–30. Having chosen the medical profession and become 'a gentleman of known learning and vast experience' (Wood, 93), he was appointed physician to the king and obtained a pension of £2000 Scots from Charles I, which was confirmed to him by Charles II. Following family example, Wedderburn studied medicine on the continent, and was with Prince Charles in the Netherlands. On 9 April 1646 he was incorporated DM of Oxford University upon the recommendation of the chancellor. On 14 December 1649 he was admitted a licentiate of the College of Physicians. He acquired a large fortune, and was so generous to his two nephews that one, Sir Alexander Wedderburn, acquired the estate of Blackness, while the other, Sir Peter Wedderburn, bought Gosford in Haddingtonshire in

1659. Wedderburn was knighted between January 1661 and April 1663. Infirmity and old age compelled his partial retirement to Gosford in 1662. There he was still sought for his hospitality, advice, and conversation. He died there in July 1679 and was probably buried in the churchyard of Aberlady, Haddingtonshire. He was unmarried. By his will he bequeathed his extensive and valuable library to St Leonard's College, St Andrews University, of which he was regent. A. H. MILLAR, rev. ROGER HUTCHINS

Sources A. H. Miller, ed., *The compt buik of David Wedderburne merchant of Dundee, 1587–1630, together with the shipping lists of Dundee, 1580–1618* (1898) · Munk, *Roll*, 1.251 · Wood, *Ath. Oxon.: Fasti* (1820), 93 · G. Bate, *Elenchi motuum nuperorum in Anglia*, 2 vols. (1661–3)
Archives NL Scot., commonplace book, corresp., and papers
Likenesses portrait, repro. in Miller, ed., *Compt buik*

Wedderburn, Sir John, fifth baronet (1704–1746), Jacobite army officer, son of Sir Alexander Wedderburn, fourth baronet (1675–1741), and Katherine, daughter of John Scott, was born on 4 August 1704. After his father was deprived of the clerkship of Dundee in 1717, the family fell on hard times and began selling off parts of the estate, although Wedderburn worked as a factor on the Forfar estates of the duke of Douglas. In 1724 he married Jean, daughter of John Fullerton of that ilk, and they had seven surviving children. He succeeded to the baronetcy on his father's death in September 1741, but had to sell part of his estate that year for debts. In 1745 he collected excise for the rebels in Perth and Forfar, as well as joining as a volunteer in Lord Ogilvy's regiment, serving at Falkirk, Stirling, and Culloden, where he was captured on 16 April 1746. His eldest son, John, who served as a standard-bearer, escaped to France with the help of relatives.

Held at Inverness, Wedderburn was transported on the *Exeter* to London's new gaol at Southwark, where he was tried for treason on 4 November 1746. Although he claimed that he had been forced out and his property stolen by the rebels—and presented witnesses to that effect—the justices ruled that his collection of the excise tax for rebel use, attested by receipts signed by him, sufficed as the overt action needed to prove treason. When he was found guilty, his estate of Blackness, Forfarshire, and his title were forfeited, and he was sentenced to death. Before his execution he wrote to his wife, instructing her to raise their children in the Church of England and in loyalty to the Jacobite cause, and to Charles Edward Stuart, entrusting his family to the Pretender's care. He was executed by hanging on Kennington Common on 28 November 1746. MARGARET D. SANKEY

Sources *DNB* · Burke, *Peerage* (1980) · B. G. Seton and J. G. Arnot, eds., *The prisoners of the '45*, Scottish History Society, 3rd ser., 13–15 (1928–9) · J. Allardyce, ed., *Historical papers relating to the Jacobite period, 1699–1750*, 1, New Spalding Club, 14 (1895) · W. M'Leod, *List of persons concerned in the rebellion* (1890) · A. MacKenzie, *Muster roll of the Forfarshire or Lord Ogilvy's regiment* (1914) · J. Wedderburn, *A general account of the honorable and equestrian surname of Wedderburn* (1824)
Archives NA Scot., Hope of Craighall MSS
Wealth at death estate confiscated: Wedderburn, *General account*

Wedderburn, Sir Peter, Lord Gosford (c.1616–1679), judge and politician, was the third and youngest son of James Wedderburn (1589–1627), town clerk of Dundee, and Margaret, daughter of James Goldman, merchant of Dundee, and a younger brother of Sir Alexander *Wedderburn. He was educated at St Andrews University, graduating MA in 1636. He was admitted advocate on 19 January 1642, beginning a successful legal career. He represented Dundee, becoming 'town's agent' in 1648 and a burgess in February 1657. The covenanting revolution and the Cromwellian period acted as a temporary brake on his career, his royalist sympathies leading to a brief imprisonment in 1645 and fines under Cromwell's Act of Grace of 1654.

The Restoration, however, led to preferment and public service. On 28 August 1660 Wedderburn was appointed clerk to the privy council and keeper to the signet. In January 1661 he was knighted and the same month began a long parliamentary career as commissioner for Haddingtonshire, representing the shire in parliaments and conventions of estates until 1674, and sitting on various important committees. On 17 June 1668 he became an ordinary lord of session, taking the title Lord Gosford after his estates at Haddington. At the same time he resigned as clerk of the privy council to concentrate on his legal duties. While in the early 1660s he was allied to secretary of state Lauderdale against the earl of Middleton, Wedderburn was largely removed from the subsequent political tension that dogged the Lauderdale administration.

Wedderburn's collection of the decisions of the court of session from 1 June 1668 until July 1677 was considered authoritative. No ordinary judge, Mackenzie of Rosehaugh described him as a judge 'whose deeds were prompted by truthfulness, and whose law was directed by justice and sympathy' (Wedderburn, 1.364), and his surviving portrait reflects a mood of integrity. He married three times: first, on 1 February 1649, Christian Gibson, with whom he had a son who died young; second, on 20 October 1653, Agnes, daughter of John Dickson of Heartrie, with whom he had five sons and four daughters; and third, on 15 June 1677, Elizabeth Goldman, with whom he had no children. He was succeeded by his sons John (d. 1688) and Peter (d. 1746), who took the name of Halkett. His will and testament has not survived but he was a wealthy man. Though his estates at Gosford, Haddingtonshire, were purchased in 1659 with the help of his uncle Sir John Wedderburn, physician to Charles I, from 1660 he went on to acquire numerous properties in the counties of Haddingtonshire, Renfrewshire, Forfarshire, and Edinburghshire. He died at Gosford on 11 November 1679. A. H. MILLAR, rev. A. J. MANN

Sources A. D. O. Wedderburn, *The Wedderburn book*, 1 (privately printed, 1898), 363–70; 2 (1898), passim · *APS*, 1670–86 · G. Brunton and D. Haig, *An historical account of the senators of the college of justice, from its institution in MDXXXII* (1832), 394 · F. J. Grant, ed., *The Faculty of Advocates in Scotland, 1532–1943*, Scottish RS, 145 (1944), 217 · M. D. Young, ed., *The parliaments of Scotland: burgh and shire commissioners*, 2 (1993), 723 · *Reg. PCS*, 3rd ser., 2.469 · register, U. St Andr. · *The historical works of Sir James Balfour*, ed. J. Haig, 4 vols. (1824–5) · Register of testaments, Brechin, NA Scot., SRO.CC.3/3/5 · H. Paton, ed.,

Sir Peter Wedderburn, Lord Gosford (*c.*1616–1679), by unknown artist

The register of marriages for the parish of Edinburgh, 1595–1700, Scottish RS, old ser., 27 (1905) · NA Scot., Biel MSS, SRO.GD.6 · NA Scot., Scrymgeour-Wedderburn MSS, SRO.GD.137 · Dundee council minute books, 1613–1707, Dundee District Archives, vols. 4, 5, 6
Archives NL Scot., family corresp. and financial papers | BL, letters to duke of Lauderdale and Charles II, Add. MSS 23117–23138, 23244 · Buckminster Park, Grantham, corresp. with duke of Lauderdale · U. Edin. L., letters to duke of Lauderdale
Likenesses D. Scougall, oils, Scot. NPG · portrait, repro. in Wedderburn, *Wedderburn book*, vol. 1, facing p. 369 · portrait, priv. coll. [*see illus.*]
Wealth at death wealthy; extensive property in southern (esp. south-eastern) Scotland

Wedderburn, Robert (*c.*1510–1555×60). *See under* Wedderburn, James (*c.*1495–1553).

Wedderburn, Robert (1762–1835/6?), radical, was born in Kingston, Jamaica, the illegitimate son of an African-born slave, Rosanna, and a sugar planter, James Wedderburn of Inveresk, near Edinburgh. The latter sold Rosanna when she was five months pregnant but Robert was deemed free from birth by her new owners, baptized an Anglican, and given a modicum of education. After service as a rating in the Royal Navy, Wedderburn arrived in Britain in 1778. He eked out a precarious living—he was occasionally involved in petty thieving but also acquired the skills of a tailor—until some time between 1802 and 1813, when he was licensed as a Unitarian preacher. Now firmly part of London's plebeian culture of millenarianism and tavern radicalism, he met the agrarian Thomas Spence shortly before the latter's death in 1814. He then became a close

associate of Thomas Evans, the Spenceans' leader, and was instrumental in holding the group together during the difficult months of 1817, while Evans was in prison. Early in 1818 he and Evans were jointly licensed to operate a 'Church of Christian Philanthropists', where his sermons soon acquired a reputation for truculent libertarianism in theology and politics.

After quarrelling with Evans, Wedderburn moved into the political orbit of Thistlewood and the revolutionary Spenceans. In 1819 he opened a new chapel in Soho, which immediately became a centre for insurrectionary activity. Wedderburn likened slave masters to cotton masters, and enslaved black people to oppressed Britons: 'Before Six Months were over there would be Slaughter in England for their Liberty' (spy's report [Robert Baker] to H. M. Dyer, 18 Sept 1819, PRO, HO 42/195). Thistlewood depended 'more on Wedderburns division for being armed than all the Rest' (spy's report [by B. C.] to Home Office, PRO, HO 42/197), but Wedderburn was saved from being embroiled in Cato Street by the fact that he had been arrested for blasphemous libel the month before. He was sentenced in May 1820, to two years' imprisonment, and served the sentence at Dorchester along with Richard Carlile. His chief associates at this time, however, were a radical lawyer, George Cannon, who wrote most of the materialist-theist writings that appeared over Wedderburn's name, and William Dugdale, a publisher of infidel and obscene literature. Wedderburn's autobiographical *The Horrors of Slavery* was published from Dugdale's shop in 1824.

Wedderburn was largely responsible for the awareness of slavery among London artisans, and his reception undermines the notion that working-class radicals were hostile to the slave cause. *Horrors of Slavery* was both spirited and thoughtful. It shows Wedderburn's political convictions to have been undimmed by prison despite the best efforts of Wilberforce, who visited him there. However, Wedderburn had always interwoven politics with his peculiar brand of 'Pure Christian Diabolism': this met with dwindling support in the late 1820s. Popular radicalism was also becoming more self-consciously 'respectable', and Wedderburn's continued association with Cannon and Dugdale, both now pornographers of some notoriety, particularly drew Carlile's wrath. In 1831 he received two years' imprisonment for brothel-keeping. Thereafter his involvement in popular deism and radicalism was peripheral. His last recorded public appearance, in March 1834, was among the 'congregation' of the infidel preacher Robert Taylor at the Theobalds Road Institute, run by Benbow. Wedderburn does not appear in the registers of deaths, which commenced in 1837.

MALCOLM CHASE

Sources *'The horrors of slavery' and other writings by Robert Wedderburn*, ed. I. McCalman (1991) · I. McCalman, 'Wedderburn, Robert', *DLB*, vol. 8 · I. McCalman, *Radical underworld: prophets, revolutionaries, and pornographers in London, 1795–1840* (1988) · M. Chase, *The people's farm: English radical agrarianism, 1775–1840* (1988) · PRO, HO 42/195, 197
Archives BL, Place MSS, Add. MS 27808, fol. 322

Likenesses G. Cruikshank, cartoon, 1817, BL · portrait, repro. in I. McCalman, ed., 'The horrors of slavery', 42

Wedderburn, William (c.1582–1659/60). *See under* Wedderburn, David (*bap.* 1580, *d.* 1646).

Wedderburn, Sir William, fourth baronet (1838–1918), administrator in India and politician, was born in Edinburgh on 25 March 1838, the youngest son of seven children born to Sir John Wedderburn, second baronet (1789–1862), of the East India Company service, and his wife, Henrietta Louise Milburn (*d.* 1881). He was educated at progressive private schools in Europe and Scotland and then at Edinburgh University, where he prepared himself for the Indian Civil Service public examinations. In choosing a career in India he was following in the footsteps of both his father and his eldest brother, John, who was killed in the uprising of 1857. William ranked third among some 160 candidates in the public examinations of 1859 and in the following year began his career in the Bombay presidency. During a British furlough, on 12 September 1878, he married Mary Blanche (*d.* 1933), daughter of Henry William Hoskyns of North Perrott Manor, Crewkerne, Somerset. They had two daughters: Dorothy, born at Poona in 1879, and Margaret Griselda, born in London in 1884. He succeeded as fourth baronet on 18 September 1882.

Wedderburn filled increasingly responsible revenue and judicial positions in Bombay district administration. Coming from a liberal background, he was greatly influenced by peasant disturbances in 1875 against the increasingly powerful village moneylenders. Between 1878 and 1883 he publicly criticized the government's high rates of land assessments and the destruction of traditional village institutions, and formulated a model project of co-operative agricultural banks to provide credit to cultivators at reasonable interest rates. This innovative proposal won official endorsement in India, but was blocked by the India Office in London, and another twenty years passed before the government experimented with agricultural credit. Wedderburn also supported the reform initiatives of the viceroy, Lord Ripon, designed to remove racial barriers against Indian judges and to develop local self-government throughout India. He was involved with Indian leaders in establishing the Bombay Presidency Association in 1885, and attended that year's inaugural session of the Indian National Congress as an observer. His open identification with Indian political aspirations was disapproved of by senior officials and in 1885 he was denied a prestigious judgeship of the Bombay high court. Feeling unfairly treated he took early retirement in 1887.

Freed from bureaucratic office, Wedderburn committed the rest of his life to promoting political reform for India. A close connection with Bombay's influential Congress leaders and with the general secretary, Allan O. Hume, resulted in his election as president of the 1889 session in Bombay. That session, at which Liberal MP Charles Bradlaugh was a special visitor, endorsed a forward-looking scheme of representative government. In 1890 Wedderburn became chairman of the newly created British committee of the Indian National Congress, which attempted

Sir William Wedderburn, fourth baronet (1838–1918), by Bassano, 1899

by various means, including the publication of the journal *India*, to mobilize support in the metropolis for that country's political advancement. His disinterested commitment to India influenced his decision to run for parliament in 1892, an enterprise in which he succeeded through a Banffshire by-election in 1893. Along with fellow Liberal Dadabhai Naoroji, a Bombay Congressman and MP for Finsbury Park (1892–5), Wedderburn organized an Indian parliamentary committee, a loose collection of India sympathizers which at its peak had a nominal membership of over 150. It played a hand in influencing the government to establish the Welby commission to inquire into the apportionment of costs between the British and Indian governments for military and civil expenditure incurred by the secretary of state for India. The commission, on which Wedderburn and Naoroji constituted a pro-India minority, resulted in some readjustments in India's favour. Indian committee activists also caught the Liberal government off guard by winning a parliamentary vote to introduce simultaneous public service examinations in India, and won a last-minute pledge from the same ministry not to retain the north-west frontier outpost of Chitral: but neither of these decisions was implemented. As an activist against the Second South African War, Wedderburn anticipated defeat in the 1900 election and did not stand.

Wedderburn was disheartened by this era of imperialist ascendancy, but the Liberal re-election of 1905 and the retirement of Curzon as viceroy filled him with renewed hope for India. He pressured Lord Morley, the Indian secretary of state, to be more genuinely reformist, and developed a close relationship with G. K. Gokhale, the most dedicated leader of the constitutionalist wing of Congress. In 1910 he risked his health to return to India, as Congress president, and appealed for Hindu–Muslim co-operation and for reconciliation between Congress constitutionalists and militants. He was saddened by the death in 1912 of his more outspoken Indian co-worker Hume, and the following year published his biography, *Allan Octavian Hume, C. B., 'Father of the Indian National Congress'*. Later he utilized India's heavy commitment in the First World War to reinforce the case for a substantial measure of self-government. Wedderburn died at his home, Meredith, Gloucestershire, on 25 January 1918, active to the end in supporting India's political aspirations and in trying to transform an empire into a commonwealth.   EDWARD C. MOULTON

Sources E. C. Moulton, 'Wedderburn, William', *BDMBR*, vol. 3, pt 2 · E. C. Moulton, 'William Wedderburn and early Indian nationalism', *Changing South Asia: politics and administration*, ed. K. A. Ballhatchet and D. Taylor (1984), 37–66 · S. K. Ratcliffe, *Sir William Wedderburn and the Indian reform movement* (1923) · *CGPLA Eng. & Wales* (1918) · Burke, *Peerage* (1939)
Archives NA Scot., estate and family papers | BL, corresp. with Lord Ripon, Add. MS 43618 · Bodl. Oxf., corresp. with Lord Kimberley · CUL, corresp. with Lord Hardinge · National Archives of India, New Delhi, G. K. Gokhale MSS
Likenesses Bassano, photograph, 1899, NPG [*see illus.*] · photograph, 1910, repro. in Ratcliffe, *Sir William Wedderburn*, frontispiece
Wealth at death £39,481 6s. 3d.: probate, 8 March 1918, *CGPLA Eng. & Wales*

Weddington, John (b. c.1525, d. in or after 1593), writer on bookkeeping, was born in London. He was a citizen of London, a grocer, and member of the Merchant Adventurers of the English Nation in Antwerp. He spent many years in Antwerp as a merchant and, for a period, as factor of Sir Thomas Gresham. He also worked as a professional bookkeeper. He brought an action against one Baptist van Achelen for payment for more than a hundred days' work on his account books. He probably taught bookkeeping as well, Antwerp being the commercial centre which served as training ground for many youths, including young Englishmen bent on a mercantile career.

In 1567 Pieter van Keerberghen published in Antwerp Weddington's *A breffe instruction, and manner, howe to kepe, marchantes bokes, of accomptes after the order of debitor and creditor*. This rare work, of which only one copy is known (St Mary's College, Blairs, deposited in the National Library of Scotland), has several distinctive features. The major feature is the arrangement of account books in the double-entry system. In the standard procedure described in most of the early accounting manuals, all transactions were entered in a journal in which the entries in each case identified the ledger accounts to be debited and credited. From the journal, entries were then made in the relevant accounts in the ledger, Weddington's 'great boke or lidger'. Weddington, in effect, dispensed with the journal

and broke it up into several separate books, one for each of several categories of transaction. Entries in the ledger were to be made directly from the entries in those various books of first entry. Weddington explained that dismemberment of the journal as the ledger-posting medium was desirable 'because marchantis of great dowingis ought to have many servantes to helpe them to write'.

Weddington also introduced the use of a secret ledger in the literature on accounting. In this ledger the merchant segregated those accounts, such as the capital account, that he wanted to keep secret from his employees who would, of course, need access in the ordinary course of business to the other non-secret ledger. In this way 'no man shall understande or knowe his estate, but hym selff only, or suche as he shall apoint to kepe' the secret ledger. Weddington, 'for breviation', did not give an example of a secret ledger. James Peele, in his *Pathe Waye to Perfectnes* published two years later, provided a worked-out illustration.

It is not known how far Weddington was describing practices and procedures that he had encountered or had himself implemented in practice. However, his innovations in the literature, and indeed his book itself, had little influence on subsequent books on the double-entry system, though John Mellis did use some of Weddington's examples in his *A Briefe Instruction* of 1588. In 1564 Willem Silvius, an Antwerp printer, was granted a licence to publish a book, apparently in Dutch, on bookkeeping, by 'Jan Wadington ende Noel N'. No book corresponding to this description has been recorded. Weddington was, however, certainly responsible for a short book on arithmetic for merchants. It was a translation into English by Weddington of a book by François Flory in French, first published in Antwerp in 1577. *The Practize of Cifering Made by Fraunces Flory of Lyle* was published in London in 1593. This work, like his book on bookkeeping, Weddington dedicated to the governor of the Merchant Adventurers of the English Nation. In the preface Weddington described himself as a poor member who was receiving support from the company. The publication of the book is the last known date in Weddington's life.   BASIL S. YAMEY

Sources O. De Smedt, *De Engelse Natie te Antwerpen in de 16ᵉ eeuw (1496–1582)*, 2 (Antwerp, 1954) · B. S. Yamey, 'John Weddington's *A breffe instruction*, 1567', *Accounting Research*, 9 (1958), 124–33 · H. L. V. De Groote, 'Drukte Willem Silvius te Antwerpen?', *De Gulden Passer*, 48 (1970), 107–11

Wedge, John Helder (1793–1872), surveyor and politician in Tasmania, was born at Shudy Camps, near Linton, Cambridgeshire, on 27 February 1793, the second son of Charles Wedge (1747?–1842), a surveyor, and his wife, Elizabeth. John worked with his older brother, Edward, on a Lincolnshire farm, but agricultural depression induced them to think of emigrating. His father had trained him as a surveyor and in 1823 obtained for him an appointment in Van Diemen's Land, where he arrived the following April with Edward and his family. He helped Edward in saw-milling and farming ventures and trained his nephews, Charles Wedge and John Darke, as surveyors, while investigating former frauds in the survey department and, as an energetic and resourceful bushman, undertaking exploring expeditions in difficult parts of the colony. His report on the land grant to the Van Diemen's Land Company led to its increase from 250,000 to 350,000 acres, but his recommendation to reserve land at Emu Bay for a township was disregarded, though it was the only site suitable for a port not already in the company's possession.

On his arrival Wedge had been granted 1500 acres (Leighlands) near Perth and soon became friendly with John Batman; like him he wanted more land for his sheep and in 1835 was glad to join the Port Phillip Association, formed to 'buy' grazing land from the Port Phillip Aborigines. When Batman reported in June a successful 'purchase', Wedge drew the maps needed to support its claims, resigned from the survey department, and in August crossed to Port Phillip, the first of the partners to do so, landing near its entrance at the association's base at Indented Head on the Bellarine peninsula. He explored the area to the south-west (he later published his *Narrative* in the proceedings of the Royal Geographical Society), and then went to the River Yarra, where on 2 September he found the party financed by J. P. Fawkner encamped on land which he claimed (mistakenly) that Batman had 'bought'. He reached agreement with this group, and moved the association's 'headquarters' to the site, but before the imperial government's decision on its claims was known he sold his interest in it to his partners. For two years he frequently visited Port Phillip: he bought two city blocks in 1837 and shared a 'run' with his relatives at Werribee, selling out (for £18,000) only in 1854 after floods destroyed the homestead and drowned Edward, his wife, and unmarried daughter.

In December 1837 Wedge had returned to England, when he presented a collection of birds, animals, and ethnological specimens to the museum at Saffron Walden. He farmed in Suffolk, and protested to the Colonial Office about the treatment of both the Port Phillip Association and the Aborigines at Port Phillip. After his father died in 1842, he returned to Van Diemen's Land, becoming engaged aboard ship to Maria Medland Wills, of Dartmouth, Devon, the governess to Bishop Francis Russell Nixon's six children. They were married in St David's Cathedral, Hobart, on 28 December 1843; tragically Maria died in childbirth the following November.

A devout Anglican, Wedge remained a friend and adviser to the bishop, who asked him to manage the church lands at Bishopsbourne. He was elected to the legislative council in 1855, where he led protests against maladministration in the convict department and helped to settle the question of state aid to religion.

Described in the *Hobart Mercury* by one of his successors, the surveyor J. E. Calder, as 'a high-minded gentleman who never thought a mean thought and was incapable of doing a dirty action', Wedge resided for many years at Leighlands, but in 1865 he moved to property at Medlands, on the River Forth, where he died on 22 November 1872. He was buried in Perth cemetery.   A. G. L. SHAW

Sources G. H. Stancombe, G. H. Crawford, and W. F. Ellis, eds., *The diaries of John Helder Wedge, 1824–1835* (1962) · G. H. Stancombe, 'Wedge, John Helder', *AusDB*, 2.575–6 · J. Bonwick, *The Port Phillip settlement* (1883) · J. M. Uhl, 'The men from East Anglia—the Wedge family', *Victorian Historical Magazine*, 37 (1966), 22–49 · P. Billot, *John Batman and the founding of Melbourne* (1979) · W. A. Townsley, *The struggle for self-government in Tasmania, 1841–46* (1951) · *The pioneer bishop in Van Diemen's Land, 1843–1863: letters and memories of Francis Russell Nixon*, ed. N. Nixon [1953] · M. Cannon, ed., *Historical records of Victoria* (1981–91), vols. 1–6 · T. F. Bride, ed., *Letters from Victorian pioneers*, [new edn], ed. C. E. Sayers (1969) · [F. Watson], ed., *Historical records of Australia*, 1st ser., 20–21 (1924); 3rd ser., 5 (1922) · *Hobart Mercury* (26 Nov 1872)
Archives Mitchell L., NSW · State Library of Tasmania, Hobart · State Library of Victoria, Melbourne, La Trobe manuscript collection | Mitchell L., NSW, Port Phillip Association MSS · State Library of Victoria, Melbourne, La Trobe manuscript collection, Port Phillip MSS
Likenesses photograph, Mitchell L., NSW · photograph, State Library of Victoria, Melbourne, La Trobe picture collection, T. F. Chuck
Wealth at death under £3000: probate, 2 Dec 1873, *CGPLA Eng. & Wales*

Wedgwood, Camilla Hildegarde (1901–1955), anthropologist and lecturer, was born on 25 March 1901 at Harracles, Westgate Road, Newcastle upon Tyne, the fifth of seven children of Josiah Clement *Wedgwood, later first Baron Wedgwood (1872–1943), politician, and his first wife, Ethel Kate Bowen (d. 1952). She was educated at Orme Girls' School, Newcastle, Staffordshire, at Bedales School, Petersfield, at Bedford College, London, and at Newnham College, Cambridge, which she entered in 1920. There she read for the English and anthropological triposes. She was trained in anthropology by A. C. Haddon at Cambridge and Bronislaw Malinowski in London. After holding temporary teaching and research posts in Australia, South Africa, and England, she was appointed principal of the Women's College at Sydney University in 1935. In 1943 she joined the Australian army's directorate of research and civil affairs as a lieutenant-colonel helping to plan post-war reconstruction in New Guinea. In 1946 she joined the Australian School of Pacific Administration (ASOPA) in Sydney, where for the rest of her life she lectured to young men from the government service in New Guinea.

Students at Sydney University and ASOPA benefited from her clarity, honesty, and humour as a lecturer and administrator. They also took pleasure in her foibles—habitually mispronouncing 'r' as 'w' she caused hilarity at an introductory lecture on 'physical anthwopology' by stressing, to young men fresh from the war, the importance of 'mowal fibre' in dealing with 'pwimitive people' (Wetherell and Carr-Gregg, 186).

Although Wedgwood failed to make a career in anthropology proper her knowledge of the ethnographic literature of Melanesia and her field research (Manam Island off the New Guinea coast in 1933, Nauru Island in 1935) resulted in substantial publications (including sixteen articles in *Oceania*, 1930–59), many of them coloured by the then new functionalist approach. In the field she concentrated on women and children and on culture contact, but never completed the Manam monograph for which Malinowski hoped. Although warmly recalled a generation later by Manam islanders as one who knew how to plant and cook taro and 'was just like us black-skinned folk' (Hogbin and Rowley, 112), her own opinion was that she understood neither their psychology nor the minutiae of their social life. Perhaps Manam lacked the dramatic features around which an anthropologist who is not quite of the first rank can effectively organize material. Also her work from 1943 solving practical problems and training officials militated against concentration on pure anthropology. That she had the capacity for major work is proven, however, by *Malekula*, the monumental book she prepared from A. B. Deacon's disordered field notes.

Like her parents Camilla Wedgwood was independently minded and willing to take public stands. Between 1937 and 1940 she threw herself into bringing European refugees to Australia. She abandoned unbelief for Quakerism in 1925 and in 1944 was received into the Church of England. At about the same time she forsook pacifism and embraced the war effort. A keen smoker who enjoyed rolling her own cigarettes, she died of lung cancer in the Royal North Shore Hospital, Sydney, on 17 May 1955; she was buried in Sydney. KENNETH MADDOCK

Sources D. Wetherell and C. Carr-Gregg, *Camilla: a life of C. H. Wedgwood* (1990) · I. Hogbin and C. D. Rowley, 'Camilla Hildegarde Wedgwood', *South Pacific*, 8 (1955), 110–13 · A. P. Elkin, 'Camilla Hildegarde Wedgwood: 1901–1955', *Oceania*, 26 (1955–6), 174–80 · N. Lutkehaus, '"She was very Cambridge": Camilla Wedgwood and the history of women in British social anthropology', *American Ethnologist*, 13 (1986), 776–98 · WWW · b. cert.
Archives NL Aus. | Royal Anthropological Institute, London, notes and papers relating to Maleku
Likenesses photographs, 1916–44, repro. in Wetherell and Carr-Gregg, *Camilla* · cartoon, 1929, repro. in Wetherell and Carr-Gregg, *Camilla* · C. Wedgwood, oils, 1930–34, repro. in Wetherell and Carr-Gregg, *Camilla*
Wealth at death bequests and legacies to relatives and institutions, incl. house at Day Street, Cheltenham, Sydney, to her goddaughter: Wetherell and Carr-Gregg, *Camilla*

Wedgwood, Hensleigh (1803–1891), philologist, was born on 22 January 1803 at Gunville, Dorset, the fourth and youngest son of Josiah Wedgwood of Maer Hall, Staffordshire, and Elizabeth Allen of Cresselly, Pembrokeshire. He was also the grandson of Josiah *Wedgwood (1730–1795), master potter. Hensleigh Wedgwood was educated at Rugby School. He matriculated from St John's College, Cambridge, and graduated from Christ's College BA in 1824 and MA in 1828. He took a high mathematical degree (1824), and in the classical tripos, initiated the same year, he came last, giving rise to the title 'the wooden wedge' by which the classical equivalent of the mathematical wooden spoon continued to be known for sixty years. After leaving Cambridge he read for the chancery bar, and qualified as a barrister in 1828, but never practised. He was a fellow of Christ's College from 1829 to 1830. On 10 January 1832 he married Frances Emma, the daughter of Sir James Mackintosh; they had six children, the eldest of whom was the writer (Frances) Julia *Wedgwood.

In 1831 Wedgwood was appointed police magistrate at Union Hall, Southwark. This led to the most characteristic action of his life. In 1837, having become convinced that the administration of oaths was inconsistent with the commands of the New Testament, he resigned his office, in spite of the protests of his friends. He stated his decision to his father in the memorable words:

> I think it very possible that it may be lawful for a man to take a judicial oath, but I feel that it is not lawful for me, and there is no use in letting £800 a year persuade one's conscience.

In 1838 the loss of income was partially recovered by his appointment to the post of registrar of metropolitan carriages, which he held until its abolition in 1849.

Wedgwood's career as a scholar began with two small, interesting treatises, *The Principles of Geometrical Demonstration* (1844) and *On the Development of the Understanding* (1848); the keen interest in psychology that inspired them was the decisive factor in his pursuit of the philological studies by which he first became well known. One of the original members of the Philological Society (founded 18 May 1842), in 1857 he published his *Dictionary of English Etymology*, a work far in advance of all its predecessors, displaying an extraordinary command of linguistic material and considerable insight, but marred by imperfect acquaintance with recent discoveries in philology. Much attention, and initial criticism, was excited by the elaborate introduction, in which he energetically combated the theory, then recently advanced by Professor Max Müller, that language originated in a series of ultimate and irresoluble roots, spontaneously created by primitive man as expressions for his ultimate and irresoluble ideas. Wedgwood himself regarded language as the elaborated imitation of natural sounds, but onomatopoeia proved to be too limited and subjective a notion to provide the complete explanation he sought, despite his ingenious arguments and illustrations. Two years later his theory was placed in a new context by the publication of *The Origin of Species* by his cousin Charles Darwin. When in 1881 Professor Skeat completed his *Etymological Dictionary*, Wedgwood was among its ablest critics; his *Contested Etymologies* (1882) deservedly exercised a considerable and mainly beneficial effect upon the dictionary's second edition.

In his last years Wedgwood became a confirmed spiritualist and contributed to the periodical *Light*. Personally he was a man of extreme modesty. His reputation came unsought, and he lived to welcome the final triumph of the movement for the remission of the compulsory oath, a movement in which his own early efforts were forgotten. He died on 2 June 1891 at his house at 94 Gower Street, London. C. H. HERFORD, rev. JOHN D. HAIGH

Sources private information (1899) [family] · Boase, *Mod. Eng. biog.*, 3.1254 · Venn, *Alum. Cant.*, 2/6 · Allibone, *Dict.* · *The Academy* (27 June 1891), 610 · *CGPLA Eng. & Wales* (1891)
Wealth at death £123,694 3s. 1d.: resworn probate, June 1892, *CGPLA Eng. & Wales* (1891)

Wedgwood, Josiah (1730–1795), master potter, was born in Burslem, Staffordshire, probably on 12 July 1730, the date on which his baptism was registered at St John's Church in that parish. He was the thirteenth and youngest

Josiah Wedgwood (1730–1795), by George Stubbs, 1780

child of Thomas Wedgwood (1687–1739) and his wife, Mary, *née* Stringer (*d.* 1766), of Churchyard Pottery. The Wedgwood family had a long connection with Staffordshire pottery, starting with Josiah's great-great-grandfather, Gilbert Wedgwood, who is recorded as working a small pottery in Burslem towards the end of the seventeenth century. No trace has been found of any wares made by Thomas Wedgwood and it is probable that, like other potters, he supplemented his small income from it by farming a smallholding on the same land.

Early years Scarcely anything is known of Josiah's childhood. He was brought up in the thatched Churchyard house and pottery, which Thomas Wedgwood had inherited from his father, and began his education at about the age of six, walking the 7 miles round trip to attend a small school in Newcastle under Lyme. His mother was the daughter of the Unitarian minister at Newcastle under Lyme, and she brought up her children in the same faith. Josiah's father died in 1739, bequeathing the small family business to his eldest son, Thomas, and on 11 November 1744 Josiah was apprenticed for five years to his brother at the Churchyard works to learn the 'Art of Throwing and Handleing' (Reilly, *Wedgwood*, 1.26–7). The terms of the contract are significant because the difficult art of throwing was the most highly rated of all the potter's skills and only those expected to become master potters served such an apprenticeship.

At an early stage of his indenture, probably about 1745 or 1746, Josiah suffered a severe attack of smallpox which left his right knee permanently weakened, and he was unable without assistance to work the 'kick-wheel' that provided the motive power of the thrower's wheel.

Wedgwood's business partners and marriage Josiah nevertheless acquired considerable skill as a thrower and completed his apprenticeship. He continued to work for his brother until 1752, when he formed a partnership with John Harrison and Thomas Alders of Cliff Bank, Stoke-on-Trent. Two years later he was taken into partnership by Thomas Whieldon, one of the most respected potters in England, at his factory at Fenton Vivian, near Stoke. According to his experiment book, Wedgwood's work with Whieldon was largely concerned with the improvement of ceramic bodies, glazes, colours, and shapes, and it is clear that his efforts were directed principally towards the development of lead-glazed, cream-coloured earthenware ('creamware') and the creation and improvement of coloured glazes. He wrote later of this period: 'I saw the field was spacious, and the soil so good, as to promise an ample recompence to any one who should labour diligently in its cultivation' (Wedgwood MS 29–19121).

In 1759 Wedgwood left Whieldon to become an independent potter, renting the Ivy House works for £15 a year and hiring his cousin, Thomas Wedgwood, as journeyman. By 1765 Thomas was Josiah's principal assistant and a year later he was taken into partnership with a one-eighth share of the profits. This partnership, which was limited to the production of 'useful' wares (generally, tablewares), lasted until 1788.

Little evidence exists of the wares produced at the Ivy House works, but they almost certainly included typical Staffordshire pottery of the period for which there was an established market: salt-glazed stoneware, redware, and earthenware decorated with glazes in imitation of agate, marbling, and tortoiseshell. To these Wedgwood would have been anxious to add ware decorated with his fine green and yellow glazes, perfected in March 1759 and 1760, and his first cauliflower and pineapple shapes probably date from this period. His most important development, however, was the further improvement of his creamware body and in September 1761 a small quantity of this was bought from him by John Sadler of Liverpool, probably for experiments in transfer-printed decoration. The first delivery of Sadler's printed decoration on Wedgwood's creamware was made in March 1762. From 1762 Sadler and his partner Guy Green decorated increasingly large quantities of Wedgwood's creamware, which was sent to Liverpool for the purpose, and this valuable business, which grew rapidly in worth from £30 a month in 1763 to £650 a month in 1771, continued at least until 1795.

Wedgwood's success with these early wares enabled him, by the beginning of 1763, to move to the larger Brick House ('Bell') works. The change coincided with his decision to commission supplies of salt-glazed wares (which he ceased to produce in his own factory), moulded shapes, and large quantities of biscuit (unglazed) wares from William Greatbatch, a former employee of Whieldon's, who had set up his own pottery.

In the spring of 1762, while on a visit to Liverpool, Wedgwood fell and damaged his vulnerable right knee. Confined to his bed he was attended by Dr Matthew Turner, who introduced his patient to Thomas *Bentley, a cultivated man, already experienced in commerce, who had acquired both classical learning and a knowledge of French and Italian. The two men found that their personalities were both compatible and complementary, and they began a friendship which was the foundation of one of the foremost manufacturing partnerships in industrial history. In Wedgwood's letters to Bentley, more than 1000 of which have been preserved, there has survived a remarkably full and lively account of their intimate association, which was to last for more than eighteen years. Bentley's replies, all but a few of them now lost, were described by Wedgwood as 'my Magazines, Reviews, Chronicles, & I had allmost said my Bible' (Wedgwood MS 25–18256, September 1769).

From the start Wedgwood demonstrated an initiative unique among potters of his time, and he was usually the first to adopt or adapt innovative aids and techniques. An important example was the engine-turning lathe, primarily a metalworking tool, the use of which he introduced to pottery in 1763.

On 25 January 1764 Wedgwood married Sarah (1734–1815), the daughter of his kinsman Richard Wedgwood, a prosperous merchant and the eldest brother of Thomas and John Wedgwood of the Big House, Burslem, from whom Josiah had rented the Ivy House works five years earlier. Sarah was a substantial heiress and brought with her a considerable dowry, said to have been £4000, which came under Wedgwood's control. It was a love match, successfully negotiated in spite of initial opposition from her father, and there is ample evidence that the marriage was a happy one. Sarah was intelligent, shrewd, and well educated—better, in fact, than her husband—and they shared a broad sense of humour and a strong sense of family duty. In the first years of their marriage, she helped Josiah with his work, learning the codes and formulae in which he recorded his experiments, keeping accounts, and giving practical advice on shapes and decoration.

In 1765 Wedgwood opened his first London showrooms in Charles Street, off Grosvenor Square, and in June he received a commission to make an elaborate tea service in green and gold creamware for Queen Charlotte. In the following year he was officially appointed potter to her majesty and his creamware was renamed 'Queen's ware'.

The Etruria factory In 1766 Wedgwood bought for £3000 the Ridgehouse estate of some 350 acres, situated between Burslem, Hanley, and Newcastle under Lyme, and built there a factory which he named Etruria. A crucial advantage of the location of the factory was its position in the path of the projected Trent and Mersey Canal, in the promotion of which Wedgwood played an active part. He was also a leader in the fight for turnpike roads to improve communications between the Staffordshire potteries, London, and Liverpool.

Bentley, meanwhile, had formed a partnership in Liverpool with Samuel Boardman and, starting in 1764, had built up a solid and expanding trade in Wedgwood wares, much of which he shipped to America and the West Indies. In February 1767, after fourteen months of persuasion and discussion, Bentley agreed to become Wedgwood's partner in the manufacture of ornamental wares, for which the Etruria factory was to be designed. This project was threatened when, in April 1768, Wedgwood 'over walk'd & over work'd' his right knee (Wedgwood MS 17760, 30 April 1768); four weeks later, his leg was amputated, without anaesthetic, in his own house, by a local surgeon. By the third week of June, Wedgwood was sufficiently recovered to visit his Burslem factory and the Etruria site, and shortly afterwards he was fitted with the first of the wooden legs which he wore for the rest of his life.

The Wedgwood and Bentley partnership books were opened in November 1768, and the Etruria factory was officially inaugurated on 13 June 1769, a date commemorated by the production of six 'First Day's Vases' thrown by Wedgwood on a wheel turned by Bentley. Products of the new partnership included cameos, medallions, tablets for chimney pieces, and library busts in Wedgwood's refined black stoneware which he called black basaltes. Far more important were the ornamental vases, an innovation in English pottery, formerly thought fine enough only for tableware. By the end of 1768 Wedgwood had three types of vases in production: creamware, often enriched with gilding; 'variegated', in imitation of natural stones such as agate, marble, porphyry, and lapis lazuli; and black basaltes, ornamented in bas-relief or, from 1769, painted in imitation of Greek and Roman red-figure vases. He told Bentley that it was his modest intention to become 'Vase Maker General to the Universe' (Wedgwood MS 25–18240, 1 May 1769). By August 1772 he already had 'upwards of 100 Good Forms of Vases' (Wedgwood MS 25–18392, 23 Aug 1772), most of them copied or adapted from shapes illustrated in books of engravings but disguised by altered ornament or added decoration.

The display of Wedgwood's vases in the Wedgwood and Bentley London showrooms, which moved in 1768 to larger premises in Great Newport Street, created a new fashion—a 'violent Vase Madness' (Wedgwood MS 25–18314, 2 Aug 1770), which, by its sudden success, revealed serious flaws in the management of the partnership. Wedgwood was heavily in debt. Although profits for both partnerships were satisfactory, failure to regulate production had led to a vast accumulation of stock and a serious lack of ready cash, classic symptoms of uncontrolled expansion with insufficient capital resources. The pricing of ornamental wares was haphazard, production runs were often too short to be economical, and the lack of a costing system had allowed the wasteful use of labour and materials to go unnoticed. Wedgwood responded to the threat to the business by planning production and creating a 'price book of workmanship', one of the first essays in cost accounting in the history of manufacturing (Reilly, *Josiah Wedgwood*, 112–14).

It was not only the products of the Etruria factory that were innovative: the layout of the factory and the management techniques employed there were exceptionally advanced, and the finished estate included an elegant house, Etruria Hall, for the Wedgwood family, and housing for many of the workers. Wedgwood insisted on strict factory discipline but he subsidized an early form of sick-benefit scheme, and conditions for work at Etruria compared favourably with those to be found anywhere in Europe. Originally intended for the production of ornamental wares only, the plan of the factory was extended in 1767 to embrace the Queen's ware 'useful' wares, the production of which was moved from the Brick House works in 1772.

The Queen's ware revolution Queen Charlotte's patronage of Wedgwood's creamware was followed by orders for tableware from the king and many of the nobility. In 1770 Wedgwood received his first order from Empress Catherine II of Russia. Three years later she commissioned a large Queen's ware dinner and dessert service of nearly 1000 pieces for the Chesmensky Palace, familiarly known as La Grenouillière (the frog marsh). The 'Frog' service, then the largest ever ordered from a British potter, was decorated with hand-painted landscapes and a frog emblem at Wedgwood's Chelsea decorating studio, supervised by Bentley. Its completion in 1774 marked the removal of the firm's London showrooms from Great Newport Street to even larger premises in Greek Street, where the service was displayed, by invitation, to the public. This great service is now permanently exhibited at the Hermitage Museum, St Petersburg.

Wedgwood's Queen's ware, the most influential development in the history of British pottery, achieved almost a monopoly of the high-quality earthenware tableware market in Europe. It was widely imitated, notably in France (*faïence-fine*, *faïence anglaise*), Germany (*Steingut*), and Italy (*terraglia*), and by the end of the century the manufacture of the traditional European tin-glazed earthenware had virtually ceased.

Marketing From 1772 it was Wedgwood's policy to mark everything made at Etruria. He was the first earthenware potter consistently to mark his goods and the first ever to use his own name, which was impressed in the clay. He and Bentley undertook market research, cultivating influential patrons (several of whom permitted him to copy objects in their private collections), enlisting the help of ambassadors, and taking pains to produce wares suited to specific markets. In 1771–2, in a daring and ultimately successful experiment in inertia selling, unsolicited parcels of ware were sent to many of the noble houses of Germany in the hope of attracting orders and advertising the quality of the goods. Between 1773 and 1787 Wedgwood issued illustrated catalogues of his Queen's ware and ornamental wares, the later editions being published in French, German, and Dutch translations.

Design played an important part in Wedgwood's success and he owed to Bentley his conversion to the neo-classical style, which he applied to his Queen's ware tablewares as he did to his ornamental wares at a time when all other pottery and porcelain manufacturers were dedicated to the rococo.

Porcelain and jasper Wedgwood became a master potter at a time when it was the ambition of almost every potter in Europe to make porcelain. His commonplace book shows that he was well informed about porcelain manufacture, but he was also aware of the crippling losses associated with it and the failure of many of the English factories which had made it. In 1775 he led the potters when they successfully contested the renewal of Richard Champion's patent for the exclusive use of Cornish clay and china stone, but he failed in his attempt to establish a 'Public Experimental Work' in co-operation with other leading Staffordshire potters for the manufacture of 'an useful white porcelain body' (Reilly, *Josiah Wedgwood*, 311–12).

By that time Wedgwood was well advanced with his long and arduous series of more than 5000 recorded experiments which culminated in his invention of jasper, but it was not until November 1777 that he was able to assure Bentley that he could make it 'with as much facility & certainty' as the black basaltes (Wedgwood MS 25-18790, 3 Nov 1777). The most significant ceramic invention since that of porcelain by the Chinese nearly a thousand years earlier, jasper was an original white stoneware body which was capable of being stained by metallic oxides and ornamented in bas-relief to produce the two-colour appearance of cameos. It was perfectly suited to neo-classical decoration, and the colours that Wedgwood chose for his new medallions, plaques, and tablets for chimney pieces were intended to complement those most fashionable in interior decoration. It was no coincidence that they closely matched some of those used by Robert Adam. Wedgwood developed advanced ornamenting techniques to produce in jasper an enormous variety of ornamental wares from buttons to vases, and his cameos were mounted in metal as jewellery or as ornament for boxes, cabinets, and clocks.

The smaller designs for Wedgwood's bas-relief ornaments were cast or copied from antique gems, often borrowed from the collections of such patrons as the duke of Marlborough and Sir Watkin Williams Wynn. Portraits of 'Illustrious Moderns', of which Wedgwood produced more than 300 as jasper medallions, and larger reliefs, were modelled for him by professional sculptors and modellers, including the younger John Flaxman and Joachim Smith in London, or by William Hackwood, employed at Etruria for sixty-three years. After Bentley's death in 1780 Wedgwood extended his range of commissioned models, setting up a studio in Rome. There Italian sculptors, supervised by Flaxman and Henry Webber, were employed to adapt subjects from the antique, buying work from London modellers and using designs in the Romantic style from three gifted amateur artists, Lady Diana Beauclerk, Lady Templetown, and Emma Crewe.

From 1781 Wedgwood was able to make jasper vases, for several of which Flaxman also provided bas-relief ornaments, and it was Flaxman who in February 1785 drew Wedgwood's attention to the Portland vase. In 1786 Wedgwood obtained permission to copy it in jasper. Work on the vase continued for more than three years before he was able to send the first perfect copy to his friend, Dr Erasmus Darwin, who later included a description of it in *The Botanic Garden* (1791), with an illustration engraved by William Blake. Wedgwood's jasper Portland vase was exhibited in London in May 1790 and copies were sold by subscription. Fine 'first edition' vases rank among the greatest technical achievements of European pottery and they provided a triumphant finale to Wedgwood's career.

Arts and sciences In 1782 Wedgwood had worked on a method for improving the accuracy of firing pottery. His new instrument for measuring heat in the kilns, a form of thermoscope, was called a 'pyrometer', and he read the first of four papers describing his invention to the Royal Society in May of that year. He was elected fellow of the Royal Society in 1783. In March 1786 he was elected fellow of the Society of Antiquaries and in October of the same year fellow of the Society for the Encouragement of Arts, Manufactures, and Commerce.

Wedgwood's interest in the arts was undoubtedly stimulated by his long friendship with Bentley and by his association with patrons whose collections he was invited to visit. In 1780 George Stubbs, at whose request Wedgwood had made some large earthenware tablets for the artist to paint on, was his guest at Etruria. Stubbs stayed for several months, making sketches for a large painting on panel of the Wedgwood family, painting portraits on Wedgwood's ceramic plaques of Josiah and Sarah and on panel of her father, Richard, and modelling two large bas-reliefs for reproduction in jasper and black basaltes. Portraits of both Josiah and Sarah Wedgwood were painted by Sir Joshua Reynolds in 1784, and in 1785 Wedgwood bought three paintings from Joseph Wright of Derby. As the Reynolds portrait shows, Wedgwood's features were undistinguished and his dress unostentatious; but the jaw is firm and the grey-blue eyes show humour as well as resolution. The subject's high colour may be evidence of his fondness for red meat, porter, and fortified wines. Profile portraits of Wedgwood, modelled by Joachim Smith and William Hackwood, were reproduced in jasper.

Wedgwood's geological explorations in search of raw materials, and his chemical experiments in their use, often required the superior scientific knowledge and experience of his friends. After Bentley his closest friend was Dr Erasmus Darwin, Sarah Wedgwood's 'favourite Esculapius' (Wedgwood MS 25–18430, 26 Dec 1772), who attended the family whenever serious illness threatened and who inoculated the Wedgwood children against smallpox. Darwin was a member of the Lunar Society of Birmingham. Wedgwood's membership is disputed but it is certain that he attended meetings of the society, where he met Joseph Priestley, James Watt, William Withering, and other members, as well as distinguished visiting speakers. From about 1779 Wedgwood freely supplied Priestley and other scientists with chemical wares for their experiments, and in 1791 he offered Priestley a home at Etruria after the Birmingham riots in which his house and laboratory were destroyed. Matthew Boulton, also a member of the society and famous for his manufacture of metalwork of the highest quality, was for many years a

friendly rival whom Wedgwood described as 'very ingenious, philosophical & agreeable' (Wedgwood MS 25–18147, 23 May 1767).

Wedgwood's family Of the seven children of Josiah and Sarah Wedgwood born between 1765 and 1778, two died young: their second son, Richard, who lived less than a year, and their youngest daughter, Mary Ann, who was retarded and suffered from fits and died at the age of eight. The eldest child, Susannah, Josiah's favourite, was to marry Erasmus Darwin's son, Robert; their fifth child was the naturalist Charles Darwin. The three surviving sons, John, Josiah, and Tom [*see* Wedgwood, Thomas], were educated privately before going on to Edinburgh University. All received training in the pottery business but in 1779 Wedgwood confided to Bentley that he expected his eldest son to be 'settled as a gentleman farmer' while Josiah (II) and Tom were to be 'potters & partners in trade' (Wedgwood MS 26–18946, 19 Dec 1779). Despite Bentley's warnings Wedgwood indulged his children and was especially patient with his sons. Although privately he hoped that all three might follow him in the firm, he told them that they should 'judge for themselves before they engaged in it' (Wedgwood MS W/M 32, 17 June 1793). Wedgwood's cousin Thomas, his partner in the manufacture of 'useful' wares, left the firm in 1788 and died shortly afterwards, leaving Wedgwood in sole control. Only Wedgwood's nephew, Tom Byerley, to whom he had entrusted the London showrooms after Bentley's death, combined sufficient experience in the business with a genuine desire to share the burden.

In 1790 Wedgwood nevertheless took his three sons and his nephew into partnership and began progressively to retire from active control; but his plan 'to ease myself of increasing care in the decline of life' (Wedgwood MS W/M 32, 17 June 1793) was frustrated by the resignation of both his eldest and his youngest sons from their partnerships in 1793. Tom, the cleverest of the brothers, was later to be known as one of the pioneers of photography.

Last years Wedgwood's political sympathies were generally whig and towards the end of his life he found more time for activity in this area. He founded the General Chamber of Manufacturers of Great Britain, acting as spokesman for the pottery industry in opposition to Pitt's proposed commercial treaty with Ireland, and as adviser to William Eden in negotiations for the French commercial treaty of 1786. His enthusiasm for the French Revolution was less public and less sustained than his belief in the American cause in 1776; but he was unequivocal in his championship of the campaign for abolition of the slave trade, becoming a committee member of an anti-slavery society, distributing pamphlets, and issuing a jasper cameo depicting a kneeling slave in chains.

In November 1794 Wedgwood's health began to fail and he took several weeks away from the potteries, leaving the management of Etruria in the hands of his second son. Erasmus Darwin was consulted and Wedgwood appeared to recover, but a few weeks later his face swelled and he suffered acute pain in the jaw, attributed to a decayed tooth. The surgeon summoned to extract it discovered 'signs of mortification' and Darwin decided that nothing could be done. Wedgwood's condition deteriorated rapidly and he became unconscious. He died, probably from cancer of the jaw, on 3 January 1795, at Etruria Hall. He was buried on the 6th in the parish church of Stoke-on-Trent. Seven years later a marble memorial tablet commissioned by his sons was installed there. The portrait, carved in high relief by John Flaxman, was considered a good likeness and the inscription bore a suitable tribute, but the tablet is remarkable for the date, 'August 1730', given for Wedgwood's birth, suggesting that the present-day ignorance of his early life was shared by his family. Wedgwood's will was proved on 2 July 1795. He had made substantial gifts to his children during his lifetime but the total value of his estate nevertheless approached £500,000.

Wedgwood's legacy Josiah Wedgwood belonged to the fourth generation of a family of potters whose traditional occupation continued through another five generations. No other family business is recorded as surviving in unbroken succession for so long. The reason for its survival is plain: the strength of its foundations. Wedgwood was the most innovative of English potters and, in his time, the most enlightened. As he told his young cousin, Ralph Wedgwood, 'Everything gives way to experiment' (Reilly, *Josiah Wedgwood*, 311). Gladstone paid tribute to him in 1863 as 'the greatest man who ever, in any age or country, applied himself to the important work of uniting art with industry' (Reilly, *Wedgwood*, 1.16). Wedgwood himself might have preferred the less fulsome appreciation inscribed on his monument: 'He converted a rude and inconsiderable Manufactory into an elegant Art and An important part of the National Commerce'.

ROBIN REILLY

Sources Keele University, Etruria Collection, Wedgwood MSS · Keele University, Liverpool collection, Wedgwood MSS · Keele University, Mosley collection, Wedgwood MSS · R. Reilly, *Josiah Wedgwood, 1730–1795* (1992) · R. Reilly, *Wedgwood*, 2 vols. (1989) [incl. full bibliography] · J. C. Wedgwood, *A history of the Wedgwood family* (1908) · J. C. Wedgwood and J. G. Wedgwood, *Wedgwood pedigrees* (1925) · E. Meteyard, *The life of Josiah Wedgwood, from his private correspondence and family papers*, 2 vols. (1865–6) · parish register (baptism), 12 July 1730, Burslem, St John's Church

Archives BL, extracts from transactions of scientific societies, Add. MSS 28309–28318 · JRL, corresp., English MSS 1101–1110 · Keele University, Etruria collection · Keele University, Liverpool collection · Keele University, Leith Hill Place collection · Keele University, Mosley collection · Keele University Library, corresp. and papers · RS, papers · Wedgwood Museum, Stoke-on-Trent, corresp.; Wedgwood ware | Birm. CA, corresp. with Boulton family; corresp. with James Watt · Birmingham Museums and Art Gallery, Wedgwood ware · BL, papers among those of Samuel Smiles, Add. MSS 71070–71093 · BM, Wedgwood ware · City Museum and Art Gallery, Stoke-on-Trent, Wedgwood ware · Lady Lever Art Gallery, Port Sunlight, Wedgwood ware · National Museums and Galleries on Merseyside, Wedgwood ware · Nottingham Castle Museum, Wedgwood ware · V&A, Wedgwood ware · Wilts. & Swindon RO, voucher and accounts for pottery made for earl of Pembroke

Likenesses J. Smith, Wedgwood medallion, *c*.1773, Man. City Gall. · W. Mackwood, Wedgwood medallion, 1779, NPG · G. Stubbs, ceramic colours on ceramic, 1780, Wedgwood Museum, Barlaston [*see illus.*] · G. Stubbs, group portrait, oils, 1780 (*The Wedgwood family*), Wedgwood Museum, Barlaston · W. Hackwood, ceramic relief medallion, 1782, Wedgwood Museum, Barlaston · J. Reynolds, oils, 1784, Wedgwood Museum, Barlaston · E. Davis, bronze statue, 1860, Stoke-on-Trent railway station; copy, Wedgwood factory, Barlaston · Chitqua, miniature · J. Flaxman, marble relief on memorial tablet, St Peter ad Vincula, Stoke-on-Trent; copy, Wedgwood Museum, Barlaston · attrib. J. Reynolds, oils, Down House, London · S. W. Reynolds, engraving (after J. Reynolds, 1784) · J. Smith, ceramic relief medallion, Wedgwood Museum, Barlaston · R. Unwin, miniature · J. T. Wedgwood, engraving (after J. Reynolds, 1784)

Wealth at death approx. £500,000: will, Wedgwood, *History of the Wedgwood family*, 173–5

Wedgwood, Josiah (1899–1968), master potter, was born on 20 October 1899 at Newcastle upon Tyne, the second son of Josiah Clement *Wedgwood (1872–1943), later first Baron Wedgwood of Barlaston, politician, and Ethel Kate (1869–1952), daughter of Lord Chief Justice Bowen [*see* Bowen, Charles Synge Christopher]. During his childhood Josiah saw little of his father, who was elected in 1906 MP for Newcastle under Lyme, and the principal influence in his life was his mother, an early Fabian whose interests were, however, more intellectual than domestic. At the age of eleven Josiah was sent to Bedales School, where he was happy and developed into an outstanding scholar. In 1913 his parents separated (they were divorced in 1919) and some twelve months later war with Germany was declared. Josiah's father and elder brother, Charles, joined the army and served together at Gallipoli. In 1916 Josiah volunteered, and he became an officer cadet in the Royal Field Artillery and attended courses at University College, London. In February 1919 he married Dorothy Mary (1893–1974), daughter of Percy J. Winser, of Biddulph, Staffordshire. In the following year Wedgwood's wife contracted poliomyelitis, which left her permanently disabled.

Josiah considered a career in politics but soon decided instead to study at the London School of Economics, where he took a BSc in economic history in 1922. In 1928 he was awarded a PhD for his thesis, published as *The Economics of Inheritance*, in which he attacked the principle of inherited wealth; but by 1939, when the paperback edition appeared, he saw the 'social aspects of inherited wealth … in a new light' and looked back with nostalgia to 'those statesmen … who inherited, along with their material fortunes, traditions of beneficence and a scorn of tyranny' (Wedgwood, *Economics*, 9).

The great pottery firm founded by the first Josiah Wedgwood (1730–1795), Josiah's great-great-great-grandfather, was then still under the active direction of the Wedgwoods, and in 1927 Josiah's uncle Frank invited him to join the firm as company secretary. Three years later, when Frank died suddenly, Josiah succeeded him as managing director, a position he retained for thirty-one years.

For much of the previous thirty-five years the Wedgwood firm had operated at a loss. Josiah's appointment as chief executive coincided with one of the worst periods of depression ever experienced in Britain, and many potteries failed. His resolution in this crisis undoubtedly saved the company from collapse, but Josiah was not content with survival. In a confidential memorandum he identified 'the present chaotic condition of the trade' as due to the existence of too many small potteries making similar products, leading to 'the crudest form of price competition at the expense of the wage-earner', 'a poor standard of management', and 'a conspicuous absence of research into new methods and materials'. He also reported low standards of design, presided over by 'entirely unqualified' directors and managers and too often initiated by 'equally unqualified' retailers and salesmen; out-of-date plant; lack of standardization and uneconomic duplication of patterns; and 'the complete lack of coordination between producer and retail distributor' (Reilly, *Wedgwood*, 2.195–7, 240).

With the energetic support of his cousins, Tom and John Wedgwood, and with the brilliantly inventive production director, Norman Wilson, Josiah rationalized production, modernized plant and machinery, and reinvigorated Wedgwood design by the employment of independent artists such as John Skeaping, Keith Murray, Arnold Machin, and Eric Ravilious. An even more fundamental problem was the dangerous subsidence of the old Etruria factory. Josiah chose the most radical of solutions: he obtained financial backing to buy the 380 acre Barlaston Hall estate and commissioned the building of the most modern pottery in Europe, with 100 houses for employees. The move to the new factory, interrupted by the Second World War, was finally completed in 1950.

Josiah had succeeded his cousin Kennard Wedgwood as chairman in 1946, but he continued as managing director until 1961. During the post-war years he concentrated on improving production and distribution. Designers were selected from the Royal College of Art and more work was commissioned from independent artists. The first Wedgwood rooms (specialist concession shops in department stores, staffed, stocked, and administered by Wedgwood), were opened in 1953. Their success helped to transform the business of china retailing. Between 1938 and 1967, when Josiah retired, ex-factory sales rose from about £200,000 to £3.25 million. His *Times* obituary described him as 'one of the outstanding master potters of the twentieth century' (*The Times*).

Josiah Wedgwood possessed exceptional qualities of leadership, foresight, and courage, combined with business acumen and a total devotion to his family firm. His was a complex character: his charm and humour failed to hide an inherited and sometimes daunting reserve; his humanity and sense of justice were sometimes overlaid by ruthless pursuit of the company's interests; he was by nature retiring, the least ostentatious of men, but he could appear autocratic and unreasonably demanding. His strength of purpose was accompanied by a highly strung temperament, which was the cause of frequent minor disturbance to his health. His marriage to Dorothy

Winser, which produced three children, brought lasting happiness to neither of them and they lived apart for many years.

Josiah Wedgwood was a director of the Bank of England from 1942 to 1946; a part-time member of the Monopolies and Restrictive Practices Commission from 1949 to 1953; chairman of the advisory council of the Royal College of Art; and a founder member of the Council of Industrial Design. He died suddenly on 5 May 1968 at his home, 7 Holland Park Road, London; his ashes were buried on 18 May in Barlaston churchyard, which overlooked the Wedgwood factory that he had built.   ROBIN REILLY

Sources J. Wedgwood, *A personal life of the fifth Josiah Wedgwood, 1899–1968* (1979) · R. Reilly, *Wedgwood*, 2 vols. (1989), vol. 2 · R. Reilly, 'Wedgwood, Josiah', *DBB* · J. Wedgwood, *The economics of inheritance* (1939) · R. Reilly, *Wedgwood: the new illustrated dictionary* (1995), 470–74, 479–80 · private information (2004) · *The Times* (6 May 1968) · *CGPLA Eng. & Wales* (1968)
Archives Wedgwood Museum, Stoke-on-Trent
Likenesses photograph, *c*.1952, Wedgwood Museum, Stoke-on-Trent · T. Hustler, photograph, *c*.1960, Wedgwood Museum, Stoke-on-Trent · D. McFall, bronze bust, 1975, Wedgwood Museum, Stoke-on-Trent · H. Coster, photographs, NPG · J. Wilbraham, medallion, Wedgwood jasper, Wedgwood Museum, Stoke-on-Trent · photographs, Josiah Wedgwood & Sons Ltd, Barlaston, Stoke-on-Trent
Wealth at death £300,351: probate, 4 June 1968, *CGPLA Eng. & Wales*

Wedgwood, Josiah Clement, first Baron Wedgwood (1872–1943), politician, was born at Barlaston, north Staffordshire, on 16 March 1872. He was the second surviving son of Clement Francis Wedgwood (1840–1889), pottery manufacturer, and his wife, Emily Catherine (d. 1921), daughter of James Meadows *Rendel, and on his father's side a direct descendant of Josiah Wedgwood, founder of the famous pottery manufacture. Educated at Clifton College, he at first hoped for a military career, but could not pass the necessary medical tests. He was sent to Germany to 'finish', as was the custom of the family, and returned to England to learn the shipbuilding trade. He began as a 'premium pupil' at Armstrong's Elswick shipyard on Tyneside in September 1890, but in 1892 won a scholarship at the Royal Naval College, Greenwich. On 3 July 1894 he married his first cousin, Ethel Kate (d. 1952), daughter of Charles Synge Christopher *Bowen, Baron Bowen.

After passing out of Greenwich Wedgwood worked for a year in the drawing offices at Portsmouth Dockyard before returning to Elswick in 1896 to work as a naval architect. During the Second South African War Wedgwood served as a captain in a field-gun battery, manned mostly with Elswick workers, attached to the 2nd cavalry brigade. This gave him his first military experience. After a short time back in England he joined Milner's 'kindergarten', and in 1902 was made resident magistrate at Ermelo, Transvaal, an area the size of Wales with a population of 7000 Boers and 30,000 indigenous inhabitants. On informing Milner that he knew no law, Wedgwood was told: 'That does not matter: keep them happy' (J. C. Wedgwood, 48). The life suited Wedgwood, but in 1904 he was reluctantly obliged to resign his post and return to England because of his wife's ill health. He now immersed himself in local and national politics, becoming an ardent advocate of the taxation of land values as preached by Henry George. He was returned in the election of 1906 as Liberal member for Newcastle under Lyme, a borough which he represented without a break until 1942.

Despite a maiden speech that Wedgwood himself described as 'lamentable' (J. C. Wedgwood, 63), he gained a reputation as a vigorous speaker in the House of Commons and a vehement defender of the liberties of the individual. He attracted considerable attention with a speech on 25 March 1912 in which he condemned the government over its decision to prosecute five writers of the left-wing press, including Tom Mann, for their part in a campaign, publicized in *The Syndicalist*, to urge troops not to fire on striking workers. Two days later he was one of a dozen signatories of a letter to *The Times* (28 March 1912) which contrasted the government's severity in this case with its leniency towards the protestant Ulstermen then preparing for armed rebellion against home rule. Among the others who signed the letter were Bertrand Russell, Joseph Rowntree, and G. M. Trevelyan, and from this time forward Wedgwood was 'more often against the government than on its side' (C. V. Wedgwood, 94).

In September 1914 Wedgwood was made a lieutenant-commander in the Royal Naval Volunteer Reserve. He served first in Belgium in command of a squadron of armoured cars, and in April 1915 was in the Gallipoli expedition, where he played a prominent part in the famous landing from the *River Clyde* on V Beach, for which he was afterwards awarded the DSO. Badly wounded on 6 May after being shot while leading a counter-attack in the open, Wedgwood was invalided home and was for a short time in the Ministry of Munitions. He later served under General Smuts in east Africa, and in August 1916 was appointed to the royal commission on Mesopotamia. He subsequently submitted a somewhat controversial minority report emphasizing the need to gratify Indian aspirations towards independence. Late in 1916 he visited the United States on a mission of goodwill, and after the October revolution of 1917 he was sent to investigate the situation in Russia, with the British army rank of colonel. Wedgwood was later recalled by the War Office after cabling a report advising against the financing or supplying of the counter-revolutionary forces.

Immediately after the war Wedgwood's divorce received considerable publicity. His marriage to Ethel Bowen had at first been happy, and there were two sons, the younger of whom was the master potter Josiah *Wedgwood (1899–1968), and five daughters, but in 1913 she left him. Described as a 'clever, passionate woman' (C. V. Wedgwood, 97), she had ceased to love him, and when it was clear that there would be no change of heart, Wedgwood sought a divorce. In order that he might obtain one, as the law then stood, he was obliged to give his wife the statutory causes of 'desertion and adultery'. He therefore went through the sordid ritual of signing a

hotel visitors' book for himself and another woman as man and wife, and a few days after the 1918 general election his wife was granted decree nisi. The following Sunday a parish priest in Wedgwood's constituency denounced him as an adulterer and urged his parishioners to petition against him. Opinion was by no means all against Wedgwood, but he was unable to defend himself until the decree had been made absolute, in June 1919. He then revealed the true facts of the matter in an open letter to the *Staffordshire Evening Sentinel*. Though there had been many hundreds of such cases in 1918, this was the first open revelation of the state of the divorce laws by a public man. It caused a considerable stir at the time and was partly responsible for the gradual alteration of the law which afterwards took place. On 25 June, shortly after the divorce was made absolute, Wedgwood married Florence Ethel (d. 1969), daughter of Edward Guy Willett of London; her quiet and congenial help and companionship were to be of great value to him.

In April 1919 Wedgwood abandoned the Liberal Party for the Independent Labour Party, and in August joined the Labour Party, being for a time a member of the executive and vice-chairman of the Parliamentary Labour Party (1921–4). In the first Labour cabinet he was chancellor of the duchy of Lancaster, and was sworn of the privy council, but owing to disagreement with his colleagues about the rigidity of party discipline he became, during the later 1920s and the 1930s, steadily more independent of the party, although he never wholly severed his connection with it.

During the last twenty years of his life Wedgwood devoted himself to various causes, of which the taxation of land values, the independence of India, and the Jewish question were the most important. He elaborated his views on the British empire as a free association of democratic peoples in such books as *The Future of the Indo-British Commonwealth* (1921) and *The Seventh Dominion* (1928), which dealt respectively with the future of India as a dominion and with the possibility of giving dominion status to the Jewish national home in Palestine. In 1920–21 he toured India and attended a meeting of the Indian National Congress. Later he toured America, the Balkans, and South Africa speaking on Zionism. With the advent of Hitler in 1933 he threw himself wholeheartedly into the work of helping refugees from Nazism. He strongly condemned appeasement, and early on advocated rearmament to meet the menace of the dictators. His interest in foreign questions did not, however, interfere with his attachment to his native potteries, and his constituents found him well informed and consistently helpful in local affairs. He was twice (1930–32) mayor of Newcastle under Lyme.

After the outbreak of war Wedgwood became the first member of parliament to join the Local Defence Volunteers (later the Home Guard). Having foreseen the danger of the dictators he was eager to see the active prosecution of the war, but this led to an ill-judged intervention in the first day of the famous debate on Norway in the House of Commons on 7–8 May 1940, during which he appeared to question the fighting spirit of the British navy. Harold Nicolson thought that Wedgwood's speech contained 'everything that he ought not to have said', and Admiral Sir Roger Keyes, who followed in the debate, described his remarks on the navy as 'a damned insult' (Nicolson, 76–7; *Hansard 5C*, 360, 1940, 1125). In the summer of 1941 Wedgwood sailed to the United States, chiefly to speak on Zionism, but also hoping, as in 1916, to mobilize American support for the war. The trip, however, was interrupted by illness and darkened by attacks from the isolationist press. He was raised to the peerage as Baron Wedgwood of Barlaston in January 1942. During his year in the House of Lords he suffered increasingly from heart trouble but intervened none the less vigorously in debate, especially on the Palestine question. He died in London on 26 July 1943 and was buried at Barlaston. His son Francis Charles Bowen (1898–1959), succeeded him as second baron.

Outside politics Wedgwood's chief interests were local and family history. He was for many years treasurer of the English Place-Name Society, and it was largely as a result of his endeavours, as chairman of the committee on House of Commons records from 1929 to 1942, that the scheme for compiling the *History of Parliament* was set in motion. Disagreements on methods of work, and the demands of war, caused the work to be interrupted shortly before his death, but it was resumed in 1951.

Wedgwood's vigorous opinions and combative temperament did not always make him an easy colleague, but his sincerity, generosity, and wit won him friends in all parties and in every walk of life. He summarized his guiding ideas in his last book, *Testament to Democracy* (1942); many of them ran against the general current of progressive thought in his time. He adhered strongly to an ethic of individual responsibility and personal courage, and was widely believed to have challenged General Dyer to a duel after the Amritsar massacre. A love of justice and contempt for caution were the strongest forces in his character, and he feared neither indiscretion nor irresponsibility, believing 'that these things might be, often were, the duty of the good man' (C. V. Wedgwood, 244). When in the Second World War a colleague in the Home Guard asked him to autograph a book, he inscribed in it: 'To a firewatcher, from an incendiary' (ibid.).

C. V. WEDGWOOD, *rev.* MARK POTTLE

Sources C. V. Wedgwood, *The last of the radicals* (1951) · J. C. Wedgwood, *Memoirs of a fighting life* (1940) · private information (1959) · personal knowledge (1959) · H. Nicolson, *Diaries and letters*, ed. N. Nicolson, 2 (1967) · Burke, *Peerage* (1999)
Archives Keele University Library, corresp. and papers | BLPES, letters to Fabian Society · Bodl. Oxf., corresp. with Lewis Harcourt and notes on British East Africa · CAC Cam., corresp. with Sir E. L. Spears · HLRO, letters to David Lloyd George · Mitchell L., Glas., letters, incl. family letters to J. L. Kinloch · NA Scot., corresp. with Lord Lothian · People's History Museum, Manchester, letters to labour party · U. Edin. L., corresp. with Charles Sarolea · U. Newcastle, corresp. with C. P. Trevelyan · U. Newcastle, Robinson L., corresp. with Walter Runciman · W. Sussex RO, corresp. with Oswald Barron | SOUND BL NSA, recorded talk
Likenesses B. Stone, two photographs, 1911, NPG · W. Stoneman, photograph, 1920, NPG · H. Coster, photographs, 1930–39, NPG · T. Cottrell, cigarette card, NPG · London Stereoscopic Co., photograph, NPG · attrib. J. Reynolds, oils, Down House, London
Wealth at death £56,734 1s. 4d.: probate, 21 Feb 1944, *CGPLA Eng. & Wales*

Wedgwood, (Frances) Julia (1833–1913), novelist and writer, was born in Langham Place, London, on 6 February 1833 in the middle of a violent snowstorm (hence the pet name Snow, used by her family throughout her life). She was the first of five children of the barrister and philologist Hensleigh *Wedgwood (1803–1891), who was the grandson of Josiah Wedgwood, founder of the Etruria pottery works. Her mother, Frances Emma, was her father's first cousin and daughter of Sir James *Mackintosh MP, the celebrated lawyer and historian. Her father's sister Emma was the wife of another first cousin, Charles *Darwin. As a child Julia moved frequently among four different households, each of which shaped her future interests and outlook in different ways. At her parents' London home in Cumberland Place her mother kept a regular salon patronized by Macaulay, Thackeray, F. D. Maurice, Ruskin, and Carlyle. Much time was spent in the house of her maternal grandfather, presided over by her mother's fervently spiritual and pietistic widowed sister, Mary Rich. Frequent visits were also paid to her paternal grandfather's home at Maer Hall, in Staffordshire, and to the Darwins at Down House, Kent, where Julia heard the conversation of many great Victorian scientists, such as Huxley, Playfair, and Tyndall. Members of her family were deeply engaged in the great debates of the 1840s and 1850s about science, history, and religion, her own father's *Dictionary of Etymology* (1859) being widely seen as a counterpart in linguistic studies to the work of Darwin on the evolution of species.

Early associations and influences: her novels Despite this intensely intellectual family background Julia appears to have received almost no formal education apart from a few months at Harriet Martineau's school in Leeds at the age of thirteen. The reasons for this educational neglect seem to have been partly the indifference of her father (who underrated the talents of all his children, both male and female) and partly the early onset of deafness, from which she suffered throughout her life. (Moved by her plight, one of her cousins, Godfrey Wedgwood, later became a major patron of schools for deaf children.) Nevertheless from an early age she showed a strong intellectual bent, and as a young girl resolved to resist her parents' view that the only career open to a woman was to make a good marriage. She taught herself Latin, Greek, French, and German; studied drawing, with encouragement from Ruskin; and acted as research assistant to Mrs Gaskell in the latter's preparation of her *Life of Charlotte Brontë*. Despite her deafness she became renowned, while still a very young woman, as a brilliant conversationalist with a passion for scientific and theological debate. In her mid-twenties she wrote two multi-volume novels, published under the pseudonym Frances Dawson, both dealing with intellectual conflict, confused gender roles, and ill-starred sexual passion, which met with some degree of literary success. When her father read them, however, he poured scorn on her attempt to portray male characters, declared that they gave him a 'pain in the stomach', and demanded that she rewrite them: 'Pray write something more chearful [sic] the next time'. The resulting 'damage to her confidence was irreparable'. Despite strong encouragement from Mrs Gaskell she abandoned her third novel, concluding that 'she had no imaginative powers' and that her 'mind was "merely analytical"' (Wedgwood and Wedgwood, 261–2). Thereafter she devoted herself for some years to the care of her invalid brother, writing only occasional book reviews for periodical magazines. Her first more weighty work, an article on the theological significance of *Origin of Species*, won favourable comment from Darwin himself, who wrote: 'I think that you understand my book perfectly, and that I find a very rare event' (Curle, 7).

Redrawing the boundaries between scientific knowledge and religious belief became the pre-occupation of a lifetime. Contemporaries noted that, although intensely rational in intellect, Julia Wedgwood was profoundly anti-rationalist in temperament—'at once a powerful reasoner and an inexorable critic of reason' (J. Wedgwood, *Personal Life*, xx). She described herself as 'glaringly modern' in her determination to carry rational inquiry into religion to its furthest limits (Curle, 157). At the same time, however, she had a strongly spiritual and mystical streak, and became the fervent, though not uncritical, disciple of powerful and unorthodox religious teachers: the Unitarian philosopher James Martineau, the Irvingite preacher Alexander John Scott, the mystic recluse Thomas Erskine of Linlathen, and the incarnationalist theologian F. D. Maurice. Of these the greatest influence was Thomas Erskine, who held the view that formal theological doctrine was redundant except in so far as it fused with subjective moral and spiritual experience. Until his death in 1870 Julia spent many summers staying in the religious community that Erskine had established in his Forfarshire family home.

Friendship with Robert Browning The turning-point in Julia Wedgwood's life, however, proved to be her relationship with Robert Browning, twenty years her senior, whom she met in 1863, when he was still mourning the death of his wife, two years earlier. At a dinner party at Julia's parents' house Browning was taken ill with a severe migraine. Julia brought ice packs for his head, and 'an intimate moment' occurred, 'recognised as such by them both' (Wedgwood and Wedgwood, 277). Their surviving correspondence, covering the period 1863 to 1870, seems to indicate that Browning fell at least temporarily in love with Julia. Certainly he was enchanted with her tremendous powers of one-to-one intellectual conversation, and it was he who pursued their friendship most warmly in its early days, ascribing to her many of the attributes of his dead wife. Julia—awkward, uncertain, and convinced of her own unattractiveness—insisted from the start that their friendship should be entirely 'spiritual', with 'the clear understanding that the "man-woman" feelings … would not enter into it' (ibid.). For two years they corresponded on a wide variety of intellectual topics, until Julia abruptly put an end to the relationship, giving as a reason that 'people' were beginning to put a wrong construction on it. Browning protested but Julia was immovable. Their correspondence was briefly and intensely resumed during the winter of 1868–9, when Browning sent Julia an advance copy of *The Ring and the Book*, which Julia criticized caustically and at length for its sympathetic portrayal of wickedness and immorality. When she wrote a year later in a rather more placatory tone Browning replied, 'Goodbye, dear friend, it was very pleasant to hear your voice in the dark'—which she took as a sign that on both sides their relationship was finally over (Curle, 209).

Non-fictional works: later years This odd, fraught episode has invited a variety of speculative interpretations. There can be no doubt that, despite her dismissal of Browning, it caused Julia Wedgwood intense suffering and depression. The experience seems eventually to have transformed her, however, from the dutiful household bluestocking of her early years into a woman determined to assert some degree of domestic and intellectual independence. Her first major work of non-fiction, a study of the life and historical significance of John Wesley, was published to much acclaim in 1870. In the early 1870s she was helping Darwin with his translations of Linnaeus, and she began to contribute numerous heavyweight articles to periodical magazines on science, religion, philosophy, literature, and social reform. She set up a home of her own in Notting Hill and embarked upon what she came to see as her major life's work: a history of the evolution of ethics in the great world civilizations, from earliest antiquity down to the scientific positivism and theological modernism of the mid-nineteenth century. This appeared in 1888 as *The Moral Ideal: a Historic Study* (dedicated to 'a friend', whom she privately admitted to be Browning); it met with great critical acclaim, led to the reissue of her early novels, and marked the apogee of her literary success. Six years later, however, a further work in the same genre— *The Message of Israel*, which aimed to re-interpret the Judaeic tradition in the light of critical 'modernism'—fell flat. Her family, always her severest critics, told her that she was out of step with changing times and that the book was 'tiresome and old-fashioned' (Wedgwood and Wedgwood, 340). Thereafter she wrote much less but was persuaded to start work on a biography of her great-grandfather Josiah Wedgwood of Etruria—a commission that she reluctantly accepted, in order to correct the 'wretched twaddle' written on the subject by Samuel Smiles (ibid., 342). A collection of her major articles, covering intellectual debates over more than half a century, was published in 1909.

At the height of her reputation, in the 1870s and 1880s, Julia Wedgwood was seen as one of the great female intellects of Victorian England, second only to George Eliot in her ability to handle difficult, 'masculine' subjects and 'modern' themes. Her intellectual powers were greatly admired, not just by Browning but by such men as Darwin and F. D. Maurice. She wrote with great precision and clarity about many of the religious, ethical, and scientific issues that vexed the leading minds of her age. She viewed her own writing not as original but as accurately reflecting the great intellectual revolutions of her time: the eclipse of traditional fundamentalist belief, followed by the zenith of militant scientific materialism, culminating in the slow, end-of-the-century emergence of what she hoped was a new *modus vivendi*, in which science and religion would be seen as addressing two wholly different but equally legitimate sets of questions. Her originality was perhaps greater than she herself imagined. Though she never wrote as a 'feminist' writer much of her literary and theological writing addressed issues whose resonance is perhaps greater in the early twenty-first century than it was in her own time. Her novels, essays, and private letters constantly explored themes of male and female identity and gender role reversal (one of the many points on which her ideas reminded Browning of his late wife). Both sexes, she suggested, ought to practise 'manly endurance', for 'womanly endurance is common and so is manly action' (Curle, 150). In particular she wrote at length about the gendered character of traditional constructions of the deity, and about what she perceived as the unhealthy repression of matriarchal thought in orthodox Christian theology. The reconciliation of both male and female ideas within conceptions of the godhead she saw as an even more pressing task for intellectual Christianity than that of coming to terms with Darwinism. She wrote in rather similar terms about morality, deploring the fact that the word 'virtue' had come to be almost exclusively synonymous with female sexual propriety and had lost all connection with civic and public life. Like J. S. Mill she saw women's suffrage less as a right than a duty—a duty that women needed to exercise if they were ever to be more than mindless drudges or household pets.

A family history of the Wedgwoods characterized Julia as 'that most Victorian of Victorian women' (Wedgwood and Wedgwood, 355), a judgement that glosses over the strong vein of underlying tension and tragedy in her now largely forgotten life. Widely acknowledged as the cleverest of her generation among the Wedgwood–Darwin–Mackintosh connection, her opportunities for making an intellectual mark comparable with that of her male relatives were almost fatally limited by the conventions of her day and were further hampered by her chronic deafness. Throughout her youth and middle age much of her life as a spinster daughter was absorbed in caring for sick and aged relatives and their children (both male and female Wedgwoods and Darwins were notorious hypochondriacs and valetudinarians, only too anxious to hand over their offspring to a dutiful childless aunt). Her reading and writing were done between five and seven in the morning, before the onset of daily domestic tasks. In 1889 she gave up her own house to care for her widowed father, who had spent the previous fifty-six years ignoring or disparaging her talents. Throughout her life she suffered from 'feelings of inferiority and self-disgust' (her friendship with Browning was shot through with morbid fear that his interest in her stemmed merely from patronizing pity). And, despite her lifelong search for religious truth, she

enjoyed only in fleeting moments the consolations of religion. 'I consider her essentially Christian', wrote her closest friend, Emilia Gurney, 'but her mind is too much alive to intellectual difficulties to admit of the Hope and Joy of faith' (ibid., 324). Towards the end of her life she wrote in an article for an American women's magazine that 'my life ought to have been so much more than it has been' (*Woman's Herald*, 23 May 1891), and, surveying the opening up of university education for women in the latter part of the century, she was deeply conscious that she had achieved far less than her mental powers might have warranted. She described herself as having 'all the faults of the intellectual nature, though with so few of its advantages' (ibid., 301).

In her old age Julia Wedgwood was increasingly devoted to the Church of England and she donated generously to new church buildings and church extension. In the 1900s she withdrew her earlier support for women's suffrage and objected that the Conciliation Bill of 1910–11 was merely a Trojan horse for indiscriminate mass democracy. Her last years were troubled by cancer, for which she underwent a successful operation, and by increasing blindness. Nevertheless she continued to work on her monumental history of the life of her great-grandfather, which remained unfinished at the time of her death. She died at her London home, 16 Lansdowne Road, Notting Hill, on 26 November 1913 and was buried in the churchyard of Idlerocks, Staffordshire, close to the Wedgwood family home. Her biography of Josiah Wedgwood was completed after her death by her friend Professor C. H. Herford, a prominent Browning scholar; he prefaced the book with a sympathetic and illuminating memoir of Julia's own life. The bulk of her quite substantial fortune was left to the anti-vivisection movement, in which she had been active since the 1860s. A pencil drawing of her in 1888, by Edward Clifford, was reproduced in Barbara and Hensleigh Wedgwood's *The Wedgwood Circle, 1730–1897* (1980).　　　　　JOSE HARRIS

Sources R. Curle, ed., *Robert Browning and Julia Wedgwood: a broken friendship as revealed in their letters* (1937) • B. Wedgwood and H. Wedgwood, *The Wedgwood circle, 1730–1897* (1980) • F. J. Wedgwood, *The moral ideal: a historic study* (1888) • F. J. Wedgwood, *Nineteenth-century teachers and other essays* (1909) • J. Wedgwood, *The personal life of Josiah Wedgwood, the potter*, ed. C. H. Herford (1915) [with a personal memoir of Julia by Herford] • *Letters of Emma Darwin*, ed. H. Litchfield, 2 vols. • *Letters of Emilia Russell Gurney*, ed. Mrs Nisbet (1902) • J. Wedgwood, *A history of the Wedgwood family* (1909) • d. cert.
Archives Keele University, letters
Likenesses E. Clifford, pencil drawing, 1888, repro. in Wedgwood and Wedgwood, *Wedgwood circle*
Wealth at death £63,887 7s. 2d.: probate, 24 Dec 1913, CGPLA Eng. & Wales

Wedgwood, Sir Ralph Lewis, first baronet (1874–1956), railway manager, was born at Barlaston, north Staffordshire, on 2 March 1874, the third son of Clement Francis Wedgwood, master potter, and his wife, Emily Catherine, daughter of James Meadows Rendel (1799–1856), civil and hydraulics engineer. Josiah *Wedgwood (1872–1943) was an elder brother. His interest in railways began at an early age, when on family holidays he collected engine numbers, and coloured a Bradshaw map with the locomotive livery of each company. He received his education at Clifton, and Trinity College, Cambridge, where he obtained first class in both parts of the moral sciences tripos (1895–6).

In September 1896 Wedgwood joined the North Eastern Railway (NER), gaining experience in docks and traffic operations before becoming secretary of the company in 1904. He soon returned to traffic management, and after successive promotions, in 1912 became chief goods manager, succeeding Eric Geddes, on the latter's appointment as deputy general manager. In February 1914 Wedgwood took charge of all traffic matters, when he assumed the additional responsibility of running the passenger department.

On the outbreak of the First World War in August 1914, Wedgwood volunteered for service abroad, and as a major, Royal Engineers, acted as deputy assistant director of railway transportation in France, before being promoted to lieutenant-colonel in July 1915, and transferred to the Ministry of Munitions. In October 1916 Geddes, who was now director-general of transportation, appointed Wedgwood to his staff as director of docks, with the rank of brigadier-general. Wedgwood was appointed CMG in 1917, and CB in 1918, as well as being five times mentioned in dispatches. He was also made an officer of the Légion d'honneur and a commander of the Belgian Order of the Crown. He returned to his pre-war position in June 1919, and two months later assumed the additional responsibility of deputy general manager.

The Railways Act, 1921, amalgamated the railways in Great Britain into four groups, the North Eastern Railway (NER) forming the largest constituent of the east coast group. The NER directors were intent on obtaining a leading position among the six companies concerned, and on 1 January 1922 appointed Wedgwood as general manager, with the expectation that the other constituents would agree to his taking up the similar position in the group. This was accepted, and Wedgwood became chief general manager of the new London and North Eastern Railway (LNER), under William Whitelaw as chairman, from 1 January 1923. The company then employed over 200,000 staff, possessed some 6000 route miles of line, and was the largest dock-owning railway company in the world.

The LNER devolved its traffic operations to three areas, over which Wedgwood exercised a gentle, but firm, control. A small head office was retained for overall administrative functions, together with a mechanical engineering department under H. N. Gresley, with whom Wedgwood worked closely. However, the LNER suffered increasing difficulties from falling revenue, as a result of industrial depression and loss of traffic to the roads. Under Wedgwood's guidance, the company made strenuous efforts to hold on to business and reduce costs, at the same time introducing innovations which kept the LNER in the forefront of transport developments. These included the introduction of fast, streamlined trains, and a company-wide publicity image, based on a design of lettering devised by the sculptor Eric Gill. Further, the LNER's system of training staff apprentices was regarded as a model of its kind.

In addition to his activities with the LNER, Wedgwood acted as spokesman for the four railway groups, giving evidence at parliamentary inquiries and rates and wages tribunals. He led the 1938 campaign for a 'square deal' for the railways in the face of unfettered road competition. He was a recognized expert on the intricate subject of rail and road freight rates, although, in common with the thinking of the time, his instincts were to regulate traffic, rather than leave it to free competition. He also served on bodies such as the Weir committee on main line electrification (1930–31), the Central Electricity Board (1931–46), the Indian railways committee of inquiry (of which he acted as chairman, 1936–7), and also the Chinese government purchasing commission. He served as president of the National Confederation of Employers Organizations during 1929–30. He retained his interest in military matters as a member of the engineer and railway staff corps RE (TA), in which he again rose to the rank of brigadier-general. Wedgwood retired in March 1939, but continued for the next two years as chairman of the railway executive committee, the body co-ordinating the railways during the years of the Second World War.

'RLW', as Wedgwood was known in railway circles, was remembered for his tall, distinguished appearance. He retained an innate modesty, and was widely respected for his clarity of mind, not least by those nearer the day-to-day stresses of railway operations. Yet with all his accomplishments, he never lost a childhood love of maps and the complexity of a railway timetable. He received a knighthood in 1924, and was created a baronet in 1942 simultaneously with the elevation of his brother to the peerage. They were proud of their origins in the potteries, and while Josiah assumed 'of Barlaston' as his territorial designation, Sir Ralph took 'of Etruria', in remembrance of the original pottery works of Josiah Wedgwood (1730–1795).

In 1906 Wedgwood married Iris Veronica, daughter of Albert Pawson of Leeds. They had a son, John Hamilton (1907–1989), who succeeded to the baronetcy, and a daughter, the historian Dame (Cicely) Veronica *Wedgwood. Wedgwood died at his home, Leith Hill Place, Wotton, near Dorking, Surrey, on 5 September 1956, and was buried at Barlaston. He was survived by his wife.

GEOFFREY HUGHES

Sources WWW · *Railway Gazette* (3 March 1939) [biographical article] · C. V. Wedgwood, *The last of the radicals* (1951) · Class Rail 527, various pieces, PRO, North Eastern Railway records · Class Rail 390, various pieces, PRO, London and North Eastern Railway records · private information (1995) · R. J. Irving, 'Wedgwood, Sir Ralph Lewis', *DBB* · b. cert. · d. cert. · *CGPLA Eng. & Wales* (1956)
Archives CUL, letters to G. E. Moore
Likenesses photograph, *c.*1916, priv. coll. · W. Stoneman, photograph, 1940, NPG · W. Stoneman, photograph, 1948, NPG · A. Machin, bust; in possession of Wedgwood family in 1971 · nameplate, National Railway Museum, York · photograph, repro. in *Railway Gazette* (July 1923), p. 24 · photograph, repro. in *Railway Gazette* (3 March 1939), p. 362

Wealth at death £52,171 5s.: probate, 8 Nov 1956, *CGPLA Eng. & Wales*

Wedgwood, Thomas (1771–1805), chemist, was born at Etruria Hall, Staffordshire, on 14 May 1771, the third and youngest surviving son of the potter Josiah *Wedgwood (1730–1795) and his wife and cousin, Sarah Wedgwood (1734–1815). Together with his brother Jos, Tom was sent to school in Bolton when six years old. He was a precocious child, but also a frail one. He was educated almost entirely at home. He spent a few terms at Edinburgh University between 1787 and 1789, and while there met the mathematician and natural philosopher John Leslie, whom he subsequently invited to Etruria to help in the laboratory and to teach him and his brother Josiah mathematics and natural philosophy.

Wedgwood's father had determined that 'Jos and Tom [would] be potters, and partners in trade. Tom to be the traveller and negotiator, and Jos the manufacturer' (Wedgwood, 74). For a very short while Tom worked energetically at the potteries. In April 1792, when almost twenty-one, he had a nervous breakdown, experiencing exhaustion, depression, severe headaches, and trouble with his eyesight. He gave up his philosophical (scientific) pursuits, and, on the advice of Erasmus Darwin, sought a change of scene. His father sent him to Paris to celebrate the third anniversary of the fall of the Bastille, from which he returned even more depressed. His health worsened, and in April 1793 he resigned his partnership in the firm. Subsequently a new partnership agreement was drawn up in which he and his brother Jos took more of the profits. He expected to take on responsibilities again when his health allowed. Meanwhile he took an interest in medical science, and helped to spread information about vaccination against smallpox.

On his father's death in 1795 Wedgwood inherited a considerable fortune which enabled him to travel extensively in vain search of a cure, and also enabled him to contribute funds personally to literary, medical, and scientific men of genius. He went on a five-month walking tour in Germany, after which he awarded an annuity of £150 to Leslie. He then consulted Erasmus Darwin's son Robert, who advised him to seek other medical opinion. As a result he moved to Bristol, where he consulted the radical physician Thomas Beddoes. In 1798 Beddoes opened his Pneumatic Institution, to which Wedgwood donated £1000, writing that 'the attempt must be successful in part if it only goes to show that airs are not efficacious in medicine' (Litchfield, 35). He met the tanner Thomas Poole and, through him, Samuel Taylor Coleridge, to whom he gave a pension of £75 a year. In 1797 Wedgwood went to Penzance for its mild climate and there renewed a friendship with Gregory Watt, son of James Watt. Through Watt he met Humphry Davy, who was soon to work in Beddoes's institution; Wedgwood took part in the trials and breathed nitrous oxide there.

Still vainly travelling in search of health Wedgwood went to the West Indies in 1800. Back in England he attended Davy's lectures at the Royal Institution, experienced a brief bout of health, and in Davy's laboratory resumed his experiments on 'silver pictures', which he published in 1802 as 'An account of a method of copying paintings upon glass, and of making profiles by the agency of light upon nitrate of silver, invented by T. Wedgwood, esq., with observations by H. Davy' (*Journal of the Royal Institution*, 170–74). He showed that a copy or a silhouette of any object could be obtained when its shadow was thrown on a piece of white paper or leather which had been moistened with a solution of silver nitrate. In a similar manner a silhouette of a picture painted on glass could be obtained by placing the glass in the light of the sun upon the sensitized surface. His goal was to obtain silver pictures of the image produced in a camera obscura, but he failed, since no effect could be obtained in any moderate time. Davy, however, found that he was successful in obtaining images of small objects projected by a solar microscope. But he could not fix the image. As Davy noted, 'nothing but a method of preventing the unshaded parts of the delineation from being coloured by exposure to the day, is wanting to render the process as useful as it is elegant' (Litchfield, 194). Thus Wedgwood had tackled the project of using the chemical action of light for making pictures—that is, of photography—but did not discover a practical photographic process.

Wedgwood's illness returned with severe depressions. He left London for a continental tour in May 1802 and returned to England in September in worse health. During the alarm of invasion by the French in 1803 and 1804 he equipped at his own expense a corps of volunteers raised in the country round Ullswater. He visited Coleridge and Wordsworth in the Lake District. Restless and ever moving, he died at Eastbury Park, Dorset, which he owned, on 10 July 1805.

Wordsworth said that Wedgwood produced in him 'an expression of sublimity beyond what I ever experienced from the appearance of any other human being' (Litchfield, 127). Coleridge noted in him a fine and ever watchful sense of beauty, united with the most patient accuracy in experimental research. Humphry Davy found his opinions 'a secret treasure' (Treneer, 48). Sydney Smith said that he knew 'no man who appears to have made such an impression on his friends' (*DNB*), and his friends included many of the leading literary and scientific figures of his day.

Wedgwood's only writings are two papers on the 'Production of light from different bodies, by heat and by attrition' (*PTRS*, 82, 1792, 28–47; 270–82), read before the Royal Society of London in 1791 and 1792, in which we find the earliest suggestion of the general law that all bodies become red hot at the same temperature.

TREVOR H. LEVERE

Sources R. B. Litchfield, *Tom Wedgwood: the first photographer* (1903); facs. edn (1973) · B. Wedgwood and H. Wedgwood, *The Wedgwood circle, 1730–1897* (1980) · *Journal of the Royal Institution*, 1 (1802), 170–74 · A. Treneer, *The mercurial chemist: a life of Sir Humphry Davy* (1963) · D. A. Stansfield, *Thomas Beddoes, MD, 1760–1808: chemist, physician, democrat* (1984) · T. Wedgwood, 'Experiments and observations on the production of light from different bodies, by heat and by attrition [pts 1–2]', *PTRS*, 82 (1792), 28–47, 270–82 • E. Meteyard, *A group of Englishmen* (1871) • *DNB*

Archives Keele University

Likenesses chalk drawing, repro. in Wedgwood and Wedgwood, *Wedgwood circle* • chalk drawing, Wedgwood Museum, Stoke-on-Trent

Wedgwood, Dame (Cicely) Veronica (1910–1997), historian, was born on 20 July 1910 at Hindley House, Broomley, Stocksfield, Northumberland, the only daughter of Sir Ralph Lewis *Wedgwood, first baronet (1874–1956), chief general manager of the London and North Eastern Railway (1923–39) and chairman of the railway executive committee (1939–42), and his wife, Iris Veronica, *née* Pawson (1912/13–1985), novelist and travel writer. The Wedgwoods were direct descendants of Josiah *Wedgwood (1730–1795) the potter, and cousins to Ralph Vaughan Williams (1872–1958) the composer. Veronica Wedgwood was educated from the age of five at Norland Place preparatory school, Holland Park Avenue, London, to which she later attributed almost all her formal education, for at thirteen she was brought home to be taught by governesses. Her father and maternal grandfather, Albert Henry Pawson, of whom she was especially fond, took her on visits to the continent. She developed an exceptional visual memory for art and became fluent in French and German; she could also read Dutch, Italian, Spanish, and Swedish. Additionally, she educated herself by reading some of the many history books in her father's library. She was later to translate from the German Elias Canetti's novel *Die Blendung* (as *Auto da Fé*, 1946) and Karl Brandi's *The Emperor Charles V* (1939). She went up to Lady Margaret Hall, Oxford, as senior scholar in 1928, graduating in the first class in classical moderations and in modern history finals.

A. L. Rowse declared Veronica Wedgwood his first outstanding pupil, but she decided against an academic career. By the time she was twelve she had written a play, three novels, and a history of England, all of which were thrown away, and after graduation she began to write professionally. She was to command an exceptionally wide readership, rejecting what she called 'the theory that in the interest of scholarship it is wrong to write history comprehensible to the ordinary reader' (*History and Hope*, 1987, 16). She worked for a time as literary adviser at Jonathan Cape (1940–44), acted as literary editor and deputy editor to Lady Rhondda on the feminist weekly paper *Time and Tide* (1944–52), reviewed for the *Daily Telegraph*, and tutored occasionally for Somerville College, Oxford. Her first book, *Strafford, 1593–1641*, was published by Cape in 1935 after being read and criticized constructively by Professor John Neale. The book gained immediate recognition; when the Strafford family papers were opened to research twenty-five years later, Veronica Wedgwood revised it substantially and expanded it as *Thomas Wentworth, First Earl of Strafford, 1593–1641: a Revaluation* (1961), judging her subject not to be a benevolent authoritarian as she had originally thought, but unscrupulous and self-seeking. She consolidated her reputation as a historian with her study *The Thirty Years' War* (1938), which she called

Dame (Cicely) Veronica Wedgwood (1910–1997), by Sir Lawrence Gowing, 1944

'the outstanding example in European history of meaningless conflict' (p. 526). She was very conscious of the background of depression at home and tension abroad against which she wrote. As she commented in 1956 when the book was reprinted, 'Preoccupation with contemporary distress made the plight of the hungry and homeless, the discouraged and desolate in the Thirty Years' War exceptionally vivid to me' (preface).

Wedgwood's *William the Silent* (1944) was awarded the James Tait Black prize. But undoubtedly her most important work was the planned trilogy on the English civil war. *The King's Peace, 1637–41* (1955) was followed by *The King's War, 1641–49* (1959), but the third volume, *The English Republic*, never appeared. Instead, *The Trial of Charles I* (published in America as *A Coffin for King Charles I*) came in 1964 and was revised in 1980. Always a hard worker, Veronica Wedgwood researched for the trilogy for twelve years, making a special study of the Thomason tracts, the collection of 20,000 contemporary newssheets and pamphlets in the British Library, and also personally inspecting the battlefields of the civil war. None the less she offered no startling insight into the events of the period, recording history rather than illuminating it, and writing in the manner of G. M. Trevelyan, to whom she dedicated *The King's Peace*. Narrative was her special gift and, as she wrote in *The King's War*, 'A narrative history, a description of what happened and how it happened often answers the question of why it happened' (p. 11). She also published *Charles I, 1649–1949* (1949), *The Common Man in the Great Civil War* (1957), and *Civil War Battlefields, 1642–6* (1966). She was the author of many other studies of the seventeenth century: *Oliver Cromwell* (1939), *Richelieu and the French Monarchy* (1948), *A Life of Montrose* (1952), *The World of Rubens* (1967), *Milton and his World* (1969), and *The Political Career of Peter Paul Rubens* (1975). She wrote a biography of her uncle Josiah C. *Wedgwood, first Baron Wedgwood (1872–1943), who was MP for Newcastle under Lyme (1906–42), entitled with his approval *The Last of the Radicals* and published in 1951. In 1955 she produced a biography of Edward Gibbon. There are two short books, *Seventeenth Century English Literature* (1950) and *Poetry and Politics under the Stuarts* (1960). Her collected essays appeared as *Velvet Studies* (1946), as *Truth and Opinion* (1960), and as *History and Hope* (1987). Her projected world history was rather unsatisfactory: only the first volume, *The Spoils of Time: a Short History of the World* (1984), which covered from earliest times to the death of Charles V in 1550, appeared. J. M. Roberts anticipated her book and market with his *Hutchinson History of the World* and she never completed her own.

As a lecturer, Veronica Wedgwood appealed to her audiences by the warmth of her manner as well as by the depth of her knowledge. She lectured widely in Britain and America and gave as careful a preparation to her voluntary lectures to student societies and to branches of the Historical Association as to her 1957 Leslie Stephen lecture, 'The sense of the past', at Cambridge (a first for a woman); or her Neale lecture at University College, London, 'Oliver Cromwell and the Elizabethan inheritance' (1970); or her Trevelyan Centenary lecture, 'History as a branch of literature' (1976).

Wedgwood was also a dedicated public servant. She made major contributions as a member of the Royal Commission on Historical Manuscripts (1953–78), as the first woman trustee of the National Gallery (1962–76), as a member of the advisory committee of the Victoria and Albert Museum (1960–69), as president of the English Association (1955–6), and as president of the Society of Authors (1972–7). She was involved in judging many literary prizes and she identified herself with the campaign to establish public lending right. Honours were showered upon her. She was the third woman (after Florence Nightingale and Dorothy Hodgkin) to be made a member of the Order of Merit, in 1969. Appointed CBE in 1956, DBE in 1968, she was given the Dutch order of Orange Nassau in 1946 and the German Goethe medal for her translation of Brandi's huge work on Charles V (1939). She was a fellow of the British Academy from 1975, honorary fellow of Lady Margaret Hall, Oxford, and University College, London, a member of the Academy of Arts and Science in America, and held many honorary degrees. None of this affected Veronica Wedgwood's modest and generous personality, her deep concern for people, and her delight in simple pleasures, whether intellectual as in poetry, painting, and opera or practical as in cooking and gardening at the house in Sussex which she shared with her great and lifelong friend, Jacqueline Hope-Wallace. She aroused much affection as a person and admiration as a historical writer.

Dame Veronica Wedgwood died in St Thomas's Hospital, London, on 9 March 1997 from bronchopneumonia, after suffering from Alzheimer's disease for some years.

G. R. BATHO

Sources *The Times* (11 March 1997) · *Daily Telegraph* (15 March 1997) · *The author's and writer's who's who* (1963) · *PBA*, 97 (1998), 521–34 · b. cert. · d. cert. · personal knowledge (2004) · Burke, *Peerage* (1963) · Burke, *Peerage* (1999)
Archives Bodl. Oxf., working papers · University of Bristol Library, corresp. and statements relating to trial of *Lady Chatterley's lover* | Georgetown University, Washington, DC, letters to E. Jennings · King's Lond., Liddell Hart C., corresp. with Sir B. H. Liddell Hart
Likenesses L. Gowing, oils, 1944, NPG [*see illus.*] · photograph, repro. in *The Times* · photograph, repro. in *Daily Telegraph* · photograph, repro. in *PBA* (1998), 520
Wealth at death £1,037,545: probate, 8 May 1997, *CGPLA Eng. & Wales*

Weedall, Henry (1788–1859), Roman Catholic priest and college head, was born in London on 6 September 1788, the son of a doctor. He was educated at Sedgley Park School in Staffordshire (1794–1804) and chosen by Bishop John Milner, vicar apostolic of the midland district, to transfer to Oscott College in 1804. He was one of only six students for the priesthood in residence when Milner took direct control in 1808. Ordained on 6 April 1814 he became the first Oscott student to join the staff of the college, where he taught classics and theology; he was made vice-president and succeeded Thomas Walsh as president in 1826. Diminutive in stature, he was never robust in health and suffered from poor eyesight and severe headaches (possibly migraine). Even in his portrait as college president he is shown wearing spectacles. Despite his physical weakness he worked closely with Bishop Walsh to enhance the intellectual and spiritual stature of Oscott. Two years abroad renewed his strength and he returned in 1832 full of plans to rebuild the college. He bought a new site in 1833 and masterminded an ambitious project modelled on an Oxford college; it was finally completed by A. W. Pugin. The buildings were finished in 1838, and in 1839 Weedall achieved affiliation for the college to London University. Oscott was one of the first Catholic colleges to be affiliated, and Weedall regarded this as the climax of his work of consolidation and expansion.

By 1840 Nicholas Wiseman was the rising star in English Catholicism and Walsh wanted him as coadjutor in the midland district, using Oscott as a platform. In a curiously callous move, Weedall was removed from Oscott after thirty-six years as student, professor, and president to make room for Wiseman. Weedall was nominated as vicar apostolic of the northern district, despite being weak in health and, as Walsh wrote, of 'so anxious a mind' that he was most unsuitable for the episcopal role. Weedall was desperate to escape the appointment and vocal opposition from a section of the northern clergy gave him the opportunity. He actually encouraged them to make clear their dislike of his nomination, and they gladly helped him to renounce it. The pope's direct intervention freed Weedall, and he returned triumphantly from Rome only to find Wiseman safely installed in Oscott. For a time

Weedall was head of the preparatory school at Old Oscott but in 1843 left for the mission at Leamington Spa.

At the restoration of the hierarchy in 1850 Weedall was appointed provost of the chapter of the new diocese of Birmingham. William Ullathorne, Walsh's successor, had turned to Weedall in frustration at the poor government of Oscott in the late 1840s. As early as 1848 Ullathorne was convinced that Weedall's influence would restore the confidence of the midland clergy in Oscott. In Weedall's own view, there had been 'too much of splash and dash', to the detriment of the college's reputation. Ullathorne pressed Weedall to return in the role of general overseer, to which finally he agreed in 1853, the year in which he also hosted the first Westminster synod. The last six years of his life were spent as president of Oscott; under Ullathorne's influence he gradually steered the college in the direction of a Tridentine seminary, separating lay and clerical education, and restoring its 'sober ecclesiastical character'. Weedall died at Oscott on 7 November 1859 and was buried in the chantry. He had been the admired orator on many similar occasions, including the funerals of Bishop Walsh and the earl of Shrewsbury; his own eulogy was preached by John Henry Newman.   JUDITH F. CHAMP

Sources F. C. Husenbeth, *The life of … Monsignor Weedall* (1860) • F. C. Husenbeth, *The life of … John Milner* (1862) • V. A. McClelland, *English Roman Catholics and higher education, 1830–1903* (1973) • D. Milburn, *A history of Ushaw College* (1964) • J. F. Champ, 'The crown of the diocesan structure', *Oscott College, 1838–1988: a volume of commemorative essays*, ed. J. F. Champ (1988), 93–105 • M. Pawley, *Faith and family: the life and circle of Ambrose Phillipps de Lisle* (1993) • *The Oscotian*, new ser., 15 (1885), 275–9 • *GM*, 3rd ser., 7 (1859), 653

Archives Birmingham Roman Catholic Archdiocesan Archives, official corresp. • Oscott College, Birmingham, papers relating to Oscott

Likenesses J. R. Herbert, oils, Oscott College, Birmingham

Wealth at death under £450: probate, 4 Jan 1860, *CGPLA Eng. & Wales*

Weekes, Henry (1807–1877), sculptor, was born on 14 January 1807 in the parish of St Andrew, Canterbury, the son of Capon Weekes (*b.* 1778/9, *d.* after 1851), a banker's clerk, and his wife, Mary Pearson (*b.* 1778/9). After attending the King's School at Canterbury he was apprenticed in 1822 to William Behnes, a talented but chaotic London sculptor. A year later he entered the Royal Academy Schools, and won a silver medal in 1826 for the best model from the antique. Having completed his apprenticeship in 1827, he became a studio assistant to the fashionable sculptor Francis Chantrey, who provided him with a house and studio. Chantrey encouraged Weekes to work on his own account and passed clients on to him. At Chantrey's request, on his death Weekes took over his studio and completed his unfinished sculptures, notably the equestrian bronze statue of the duke of Wellington (1841–4; Royal Exchange) for the City of London. Working for a famous sculptor identified him—reassuringly for many potential patrons—as an approved disciple, but this closeness did not advance his standing with contemporary critics.

From his home county, Kent, came Weekes's early commissions: a sundial base for the Dane John Garden at Canterbury (exh. RA, 1829) and busts of Lord Harris of Seringapatam and Harris's son-in-law Stephen Lushington, MP for Canterbury and governor of Madras from 1827 to 1835 (exh. RA, 1834), for the Canterbury Philosophical Society. These connections led to a series of impressive Indian commissions, notably—in St George's Cathedral, Madras—a statue of Stephen Lushington's son James (exh. RA, 1836) and a monument to John Dent (*d.* 1845), who is shown with his Indian secretary under a palm-leaf cresting.

Weekes's reputation for portraiture—his forte—was established with the first bust made of Queen Victoria following her accession (exh. RA, 1838; priv. coll.), which she commissioned as a birthday present for her mother, the duchess of Kent. It combines typical Chantrey touches—parted lips, as if speaking, and meticulously modelled hair—with Behnes's sensitivity to the innocence of youth. Weekes held that the primary objective of portraiture is 'to give the eye permanently that which no history or biography will be able hereafter thoroughly to convey to the imagination' (Weekes, *Prize Treatise*, 58). He often hit this target. Of the 124 works he exhibited at the Royal Academy between 1828 and 1877 over 100 were portrait busts or statues, the later ones being larger, more imposing, and more broadly modelled. His diploma work following his election as a Royal Academician in 1863 was a bust of Joseph Henry Green (RA), president of the Royal College of Surgeons and professor of anatomy at the academy—a tactful choice, as between 1853 and 1867 the college ordered six busts of members costing around £110 each. Such commissions enabled Weekes to leave the substantial sum of nearly £30,000 at his death.

Understatement, humanity, and technical excellence—all outstanding Chantrey qualities—also characterize Weekes's church monuments, well illustrated by his acknowledged masterpiece, the monument to Samuel Whitbread and Lady Elizabeth Whitbread at Cardington, Bedfordshire (exh. RA, 1849). The couple, modelled in high relief, devoutly kneel, she leaning affectionately on his shoulder. Weekes met the fashion for historic figures in period dress with skill and intelligence. His output in this genre is impressive and includes Cranmer, Latimer, and Ridley for George Gilbert Scott's Martyrs' Memorial (1841) in Oxford; a monumental seated Francis Bacon (1845), for Trinity College, Cambridge; a pensive John Hunter (exh. RA, 1864), based on the portrait by Sir Joshua Reynolds, for the Royal College of Surgeons, London; *William Harvey* (model exh. RA, 1864), for the new University Museum, Oxford; and a swagger Charles II, complete with spaniel (model exh. RA, 1869), for the Palace of Westminster, now in the central criminal court, Old Bailey.

In the 1850s Weekes developed a more personal style, leaving Chantrey's shadow. He tackled ideal figures and attempted to revive the classical style by introducing naturalistic detail and taking a more pictorial approach. *The Suppliant* (exh. RA, 1850), his first publicly exhibited work in this vein, secured his election as an associate of the Royal Academy in 1851. *Resting after a Run*, a marble statue depicting the daughter of Frederick J. Reed with a hoop (exh. Great Exhibition, 1851; ex Sothebys, New York, 26 May 1994), portrays childhood itself as much as the individual girl. His ideal figures had some success with patrons: a *Sardanapalus* (exh. RA, 1861; Mansion House) was ordered by the corporation of London. The monument, commissioned by their son, to Percy Bysshe Shelley and Mary Wollstonecraft Shelley (exh. RA, 1853; priory church, Christchurch, Hampshire) is Weekes's outstanding work in his new manner and earned plaudits from the *Art Journal*. Touches of naturalistic detail, such as the seaweed wrapped around the poet's arm and the broken rocks, evoke the beach where his drowned body was washed ashore.

Weekes's most ambitious later commission (after John Gibson's refusal to participate) was to carve *Manufactures*, one of four marble groups representing the industrial arts, in 1864 for Scott's Albert Memorial (finished by April 1870). The genius of *Manufactures* holds an hourglass, symbolizing the importance of time to industry, and is offered cloth by a young weaver; alongside, an ironworker (modelled on the Farnese *Hercules*) stands by his anvil and a potter exhibits his wares. This group, though well received, highlights the dilemmas facing a sculptor schooled in the neo-classical tradition who attempted a modern subject.

In 1852 Weekes published the essay that had won him a gold medal from the Royal Society of Arts: *The Prize Treatise on the Fine Arts Section of the Great Exhibition of 1851*. As well as reviewing the sculpture in the exhibition he gives a rare account of the practicalities of bronze-casting and marble-carving. To some themes—the issue of modern dress, Roubiliac's genius, the differing roles of portrait sculptors and those of ideal works, and the importance of education to sculptors—he returns in the eighteen lectures that he delivered following his election as professor of sculpture at the Royal Academy in 1869 (published posthumously in 1880). Besides the usual theoretical issues—beauty, style, taste, and composition—he discusses in three lectures the importance of Sir Joshua Reynolds's teaching and, in one masterly lecture, the characters of Chantrey, Behnes, and Gibson. His intelligence, technical skill, and moderate stylistic innovation kept him in steady demand. John Ernest Weekes, his son and the author of a brief memoir prefacing the lectures, describes him as an earnest and thoughtful man with a simple, kindly manner. Weekes died of heart disease, at his home, 96 Buckingham Palace Road, London, on 28 May 1877.

TIMOTHY STEVENS

Sources H. Weekes, *Lectures on art, delivered at the Royal Academy, London with portrait, a short sketch of the author's life, and eight selected photographs of his works* (1880) · H. Weekes, *The prize treatise on the fine arts section of the Great Exhibition of 1851: submitted to the Society of Arts in competition for their medal* (1852) · B. Read, *Victorian sculpture* (1982) · F. Chantrey, letter to John Lewis, 28 Nov 1838, FM Cam., MS 23–1949 · *Art Journal*, 39 (1877), 234 · *ILN* (25 July 1863), 94 [biography of Weekes on his being elected RA] · N. Penny, *Church monuments in Romantic England* (1977) · S. Bayley, *The Albert Memorial: the monument in its social and architectural context* (1981) · W. LeFanu, *A catalogue of the portraits and other paintings, drawings, and sculpture in the Royal College of Surgeons of England* (1960) · F. Palgrave, *Essays on art* (1866) · F. Chantrey, letter to Allan Cunningham, FM Cam., MS 24–1949 · *CGPLA Eng. & Wales* (1877) · d. cert. · will, 1877, Probate Department, London, principal registry of the family division
Likenesses Elliott & Fry, photograph, NPG · group portrait, wood-engraving (*Members of the Royal Academy in 1863*), BM, NPG; repro. in *ILN* (25 July 1863) · group portrait, wood-engraving (*Members of the Royal Academy in 1857*), BM, NPG; repro. in *ILN* (2 May 1857) · photograph, repro. in Weekes, *Lectures on art*, frontispiece
Wealth at death under £30,000: resworn probate, Jan 1878, *CGPLA Eng. & Wales* (1877)

Weekley, Ernest (1865–1954), linguist and writer, was born on 27 April 1865 at New End, Hampstead, London, the second of the nine children of Charles Weekley (*b.* 1834), a relieving officer for the Hampstead board of guardians, and Agnes (*b.* 1840), daughter of George McCowen, a schoolmaster and parish clerk of Uxbridge.

Weekley began his education at Dane Hill House, Margate, Kent, a private boarding-school run by the Revd Alfred Boulden, a cousin of his father. He achieved a number of spectacular results in the local examinations conducted by the universities of Oxford and Cambridge, and left at seventeen to take up schoolmastering at Colchester. This apprenticeship was brief, however, and he soon returned to become a member of Dane Hill's teaching staff, using his scanty leisure and school holidays for intensive study. His true bent was always towards languages and philology, but he also did well at mathematics, and was able to offer it among the group of subjects in which he passed the examination for the ordinary bachelor of arts degree of University College, London.

In 1892, following a year at the University of Bern, where he learned to speak German fluently, Weekley obtained a London master of arts degree in French and German, and so created the prospect of a Cambridge career. This began when William Briggs, founder of the University Tutorial Correspondence College, based at Cambridge, offered him a part-time post on his staff. The arrangement enabled Weekley to combine his work for Briggs with reading for the medieval and modern languages tripos as a student of Trinity College from the autumn of 1893. In 1896 he secured a major scholarship at this college and obtained a brilliant first-class degree, with special distinctions in French and German, and a notation indicating proficiency in the pronunciation of modern German.

Weekley spent the next year in Paris, and the one following in Germany, at Freiburg-im-Breisgau. He attended the lectures of Gaston Paris (1839–1903) at the Sorbonne, narrowly supporting himself by writing one of his series of French textbooks for Briggs and by private tutoring. At Freiburg he held the university post of *Lektor* in English, devoting his free time to studying under Friedrich Kluge (1856–1926), author of the monumental *Etymologisches Wörterbuch der deutschen Sprache*.

In 1898 Weekley was appointed professor of French and head of the modern languages department at University College, Nottingham. When in Freiburg he had met and fallen in love with Emma Maria Frieda Johanna, Baroness von Richthofen (1879–1956), second daughter of Baron Friedrich von Richthofen (1846–1915), a Silesian-born engineer, and they were married in that city on 29 August 1899. They would have three children: Montague Karl

Richthofen (Monty), born on 12 June 1900; Elsa Agnes Frieda, born on 13 September 1902; and Barbara Joy (Barby), born on 20 October 1904. The Weekleys made their home at 9 Goldswong Terrace, Nottingham, where Ernest's university lecturing frequently kept him away from his wife and growing family. The latter necessitated a move in 1904 to a larger house, at 8 Vickers Street, and in 1910 to an even bigger one, Cowley, in Victoria Crescent.

It was at Cowley on 3 March 1912, at a time when Weekley was preoccupied with the publication of his first popular book on etymology, *The Romance of Words* (1912), that Frieda first met the budding novelist D. H. *Lawrence (1885–1930), a former French student of Weekley's, who had come to discuss a possible job as a lecturer in Germany. The acquaintanceship rapidly developed into a passionate affair, and a mere eight weeks later the two eloped to Frieda's parents' home in Metz, eastern France. Frieda took her two daughters with her as far as London and left them with Weekley's parents at their house in Hampstead. Montague remained with his father at Cowley.

Weekley was devastated, but despite writing incessantly to Frieda, and even hiring detectives to trace her movements when she and Lawrence moved on to Mayrhofen, near Innsbruck in Austria, he was unable to persuade her to return. His parents insisted that he and Montague come to live with them as well. Their arrival meant that the Hampstead house was now home to nine: Ernest's parents, Ernest himself, his three children, his two sisters, Kit and Maude, and his bachelor brother, George. The number was too great for comfort, and in September 1912 the combined families moved to a larger house at 49 Harvard Road, Chiswick, Middlesex, conveniently close to St Paul's School, which Montague would soon attend. (The girls went to a local dame-school before entering St Paul's Girls' School.) Having initially denied Frieda the right to visit her children, on 11 February 1913 Weekley filed a petition for divorce on the grounds of adultery. That summer Frieda and Lawrence were back in England and managed a secret meeting with the children on 1 July in London. The divorce became absolute on 27 April 1914, and on 13 July that year Frieda and Lawrence were married at Kensington register office, London.

Having sold Cowley to a surgeon, Weekley now commuted every week between London and Nottingham, spending his nights in the latter city at 30 Clarendon Street, a bedsit near the college. Frieda visited him there in November 1914 with the aim of obtaining access to the children, but was met with a refusal and verbal abuse. He relented, however, after consulting his London solicitor, and Frieda and her offspring were officially reunited for half an hour at the solicitor's office on 11 August 1915. She was soon allowed to see them more regularly, subject to Ernest's approval. His sole provision was that Lawrence should not be with her.

Weekley continued to write and research, and he is best remembered for his popular books on words and names, almost all published by John Murray. *The Romance of Words* was the most successful, running into four editions. A further edition, with an introduction by Ivor Brown, appeared posthumously in 1961. The more substantial *An Etymological Dictionary of Modern English* (1921), with its succinct origins, wide-ranging citations, and diverting discursions, also did well. An American edition in two volumes, published in 1967, was still in print thirty years later. *A Concise Etymological Dictionary of Modern English*, also published in 1921, was issued in a revised edition in 1953. Other titles, no less interesting and informative, included *The Romance of Names* (1914), *Words Ancient and Modern* (1926), *The English Language* (1928), *Adjectives and other Words* (1930, a selection of past articles and lectures), and *Jack and Jill: a Study in our Christian Names* (1939). A curiosity is *Saxo Grammaticus, or, First Aid for the Best-Seller* (1930), published by Kegan Paul Trench Trubner in their To-day and To-morrow series, in which each author assumed the name of an appropriate mythological or historical character. (Saxo Grammaticus was a twelfth-century Danish historian.) This slim volume is devoted to 'the linguistic absurdities perpetrated by contemporary authors', and is essentially a critique, with many examples, of the various errors and infelicities rife in contemporary English writing, in the spirit of Fowler's *Modern English Usage* (1926). The tone is sometimes tetchy, but sensible guidance is offered to the would-be writer in the contentious matter of split infinitives and other solecisms.

Weekley's regular home remained that of his parents in Chiswick until 1938, when the house was compulsorily demolished to make way for a new road to the airport. Weekley was thus obliged to make another move, although this time without the children, who were now grown up and with families of their own. He rented a house in Richmond, Surrey, but it was bombed in the autumn of 1940, and he spent the rest of the war years at Cricieth, Caernarvonshire, renting a flat near old friends who had a holiday residence there. After the war, Weekley finally settled at 446 Upper Richmond Road, Putney, London, the home of his elder daughter, Elsa, her naval officer husband, Bernal Edward (Teddy) de Martelly Seaman, and their two boys, Geoffrey and Richard.

In 1952 Frieda paid a last visit to England to see her children and their families, but could not be invited to Elsa's home because of Ernest's presence there. She wished to see the garden, however, and Elsa deputed Teddy to show her the flowers from a distance. As they drove past, Frieda spotted the back of Ernest's head through the window of his study. Now nearly blind, he sat at his desk, apparently peering at a book. She was moved enough to propose a meeting, if the children approved, but Elsa and Montague rejected the offer, without mentioning it to Barbara, who later recalled her disappointment on learning of the incident.

Within three days of taking to his bed at his home in Putney, Weekley died of lung cancer in his ninetieth year on 7 May 1954. The character of the Revd Arthur Saywell, a country parson in Lawrence's *The Virgin and the Gypsy* (1930), is based on Weekley, as in part at least is John Beavis, a sarcastic sociologist in Aldous Huxley's *Eyeless in Gaza* (1936). ADRIAN ROOM

Sources J. Byrne, *A genius for living: a biography of Frieda Lawrence* (1995) · M. Weekley, 'Biographical memoir of Ernest Weekley', in E. Weekley, *An etymological dictionary of modern English* (1967), i–v · *The Times* (8 May 1954) · A. C. Wood, *Manchester Guardian* (10 May 1954) · *Frieda Lawrence: the memoirs and correspondence*, ed. E. W. Tedlock (1964) · *University of Nottingham Gazette*, 15 (1954), 209 · b. cert. · d. cert.

Archives U. Nott., annotated books, business corresp., and research notes | U. Nott., D. H. Lawrence collection

Likenesses Killick and Abbot Rosslyn Hill Studios, Hampstead, photograph, 1899, Nottingham County Library · Elliott & Fry Studios, London, photograph, 1935, U. Nott. · group photographs, repro. in Byrne, *A genius for living* · group photographs, repro. in Tedlock, ed., *Frieda Lawrence*

Wealth at death £6807 0s. 5d.: probate, 16 Aug 1954, *CGPLA Eng. & Wales*

Weeks, Ronald Morce, Baron Weeks (1890–1960), industrialist and army officer, was born on 13 November 1890 at Helmington Row, co. Durham, the second son in the family of five children of Richard Llewellyn Weeks, a mining engineer, and his wife, Susan Helen Walker McIntyre. He was educated at Charterhouse School and Caius College, Cambridge, where he obtained third-class honours in part one of the natural sciences tripos in 1911 and captained the university association football team, before joining Pilkington Brothers Ltd, in 1912, as a technical trainee.

Commissioned into the Prince of Wales's volunteer training force in 1913, Weeks experienced active service from February 1915 until the end of the First World War. He displayed notable aptitude for soldiering and in recommending him in 1917 for a regular commission as captain in the rifle brigade, the general commanding, Fourth Army, described him as a first-rate staff officer with an exceptionally quick brain embodied in an effective, rounded personality. Attaining his brevet majority, Weeks was mentioned in dispatches three times, awarded the MC (1917) with bar (1918), and the Croix de Guerre (1918), and was appointed to the DSO (1918).

On returning to Pilkington's in 1919, Weeks's maturing capacities steadily established themselves on the basis of a far-seeing view of the wider commercial and financial implications of contemporary technical change in the glass industry. Appointed in 1920 manager of the plate-glass works, he was made a director in 1928 and eventually chairman of the executive directors in 1939 while still under fifty. Such advance demonstrated the catalytic contribution which Weeks's persistently persuasive energies made in leading a family firm towards diversifying, modernizing, and extending its scope internationally as well as at home. On 20 April 1922 he married Evelyn Elsie (1899–1932), daughter of Henry Haynes, of Clifton, Nottinghamshire. They were later divorced and on 3 February 1931 he married Cynthia Mary Cumming, daughter of John Wood Irvine, a Liverpool stockbroker; she and their two daughters survived him.

Notwithstanding his business commitments, in 1934–8 Weeks made time to command the 5th battalion of the South Lancashire regiment of the Territorial Army. On the outbreak of the Second World War in 1939 he was appointed GSO 1 of the 66th division; then a combination of personal capacity and circumstances took him to the top of a ladder of appointments responsible for equipping the army in war. He was first posted as brigadier general staff, home forces headquarters, in July 1940, concerned with home forces equipment; then in March 1941 he was given the comprehensive responsibilities of director-general of army equipment. In June 1942 he was made deputy chief of the Imperial General Staff, with the rank of lieutenant-general and a seat on the army council, a unique position for a citizen soldier. This was a newly created post, acknowledging on the one hand that both chief and vice-chief of the Imperial General Staff must become more exclusively preoccupied with allied operations, and on the other, the need to concentrate responsibility for equipment and organization under an authority qualified to appraise industry's ability to provide what would be required. In clarity of mind, tireless industry, decisiveness, and balanced approach, Weeks was strikingly equipped to assess the changing needs of a fighting army, and to negotiate through the Ministry of Supply the priorities for meeting them. This work completed in June 1945, Weeks spent two months as deputy military governor and chief of staff in the Allied Control Commission for Germany before returning to civil life.

While retaining his seat on the Pilkington board, Weeks was invited to join Vickers in 1945 and was made deputy chairman a year later, with the chairmanship ultimately in prospect. Attaining this post in 1949, Weeks saw as his task the detailed co-ordination of changes which were needed if this diverse industrial group, which embraced engineering, steel shipbuilding, aviation, and nuclear power, was to adapt to the new economic climate. His varied experience, vitality, and familiarity with the working of the government machine were effective in successfully putting this major industrial organization on a sound footing.

Having retired from the chairmanship of Vickers in 1956, at which time he was created baron, Weeks found his experience and energies in pressing demand, despite his indifferent health, for a wide range of activities bearing mainly on industrial affairs and development. He became treasurer of the Industrial Fund for the Development of Scientific Education in Schools which raised £3.5 million for a purpose in which he felt close personal interest; he had been chairman (1948–56) of the National Advisory Council on Education for Industry and Commerce. He also became chairman of the Finance Corporation for Industry, vice-chairman of the King George's Jubilee Trust, a trustee of Churchill College, Cambridge, and a governor of Charterhouse. He was appointed government director of British Petroleum Ltd, and served on the boards of various companies including Associated Electrical Industries, Royal Exchange Assurance, and the Hudson's Bay Company.

The contribution which Weeks made in three interrelated environments, industry, the army, and public service, reflected his personal qualities. In particular, he was prompt to recognize the revolutionary character of economic change. His mind was inquisitive, questioning of established practice, and attuned to progress, hence his preoccupation with technical education in school and industry. He was gifted with an acute capacity for penetrating detail to reach an objective, and then delegating responsibility. Sociable, of handsome presence, and resolute personality, he identified himself with his assignments and expected his associates to be equally unsparing. Fair-minded, tempering criticism with kindness, he remained accessible at all levels, with a retentive interest in people's personal affairs from shop floor to boardroom. Informing these qualities was a catholic and imaginative acquaintance with the world at large and how it could be made to function.

Weeks was appointed CBE in 1939 and KCB in 1943, and made commander of the US Legion of Merit. He was elected honorary fellow of Caius College (1945); was awarded honorary doctorates by the universities of Liverpool (1946), Sheffield (1951), and Leeds (1957); and was accorded honorary recognition by the colleges of technology of Manchester and Birmingham.

Weeks died at the Middlesex Hospital, London, on 19 August 1960. The title became extinct. His body was cremated at Golders Green crematorium on 23 August.

H. O. HOOPER, rev.

Sources private information (1971) • *The Times* (20 Aug 1960), 8e • *The Times* (24 Aug 1960), 10b • *The Times* (25 Aug 1960), 10d • *The Times* (29 Aug 1960), 15g • P. W. Brooks, 'Weeks, Ronald Morce Lord Weeks of Ryton in the County of Durham', *DBB*, 5.715–18 • T. C. Banker, *The glassmakers, Pilkington: the rise of an international company 1826–1976* (1977) • J. D. Scott, *Vickers: a history* (1962) • m. certs. • d. cert.

Likenesses H. Holt, oils, 1959, ICL • G. Kelly, portrait; in family possession, 1971 • photograph, repro. in *The Times* (20 Aug 1960), 8e

Wealth at death £84,110 5s. 11d.: probate, 25 Oct 1960, *CGPLA Eng. & Wales*

Weelkes, Thomas (*bap.* 1576?, *d.* 1623), composer and organist, was probably the son of John Weeke, rector of Elsted in Sussex, and his wife, Johanne, who was baptized at Elsted on 25 October 1576. Weeke held this living in plurality with that of Twyford and Owslebury, near Winchester, and his case for paternity is strengthened by the fact that the dedicatee of Weelkes's first publication, *Madrigals to 3, 4, 5, & 6 Voices* (1597) was George Phillpot, who lived in Compton Place, only 1 mile from Twyford, and that Winchester College, barely 2 miles away, was where Weelkes received his first confirmed appointment—as organist, evidently in 1598. Certainly at this date Weelkes was still very young for he wrote in the preface to his *Ballets and Madrigals to Five Voices* (1598) of 'my yeeres yet unripened', also noting that he had earlier been in the service of 'his Maister Edward Darcye Esquire, Groome of hir Majesties privie Chamber'.

Little is known of Weelkes's life during the three or four years that he passed at Winchester College. There is some suspicion that he felt out of place in what was one of the leading schools in the country, being proficient only in music: 'this small facultie of mine, because it is alone in mee, and without the asistance of other more confident sciences, is the more to bee favored' he pleaded in the preface to his *Madrigals of 5 and 6 Parts, Apt for the Viols and Voices* (1600). Certainly it is difficult to believe that the sometimes extraordinary music that he wrote during this phase would have found ready approval from the staff of the college, for what he published between 1597 and 1600 contained some of the boldest music yet conceived in England, and the best of the twenty works in his 1600 volume are among the greatest of all English madrigals. In the three-voice 'Cease sorrows now', from his 1597 volume, Weelkes had already opened up a vein of musical pathos that was by now commonplace in the madrigal as composed in its native Italy but that was quite unprecedented in English music; at the opposite expressive extreme, in the ballets of 1598 he had revelled in a degree of rhythmic vitality as yet unmatched in the music of his own country. In the volume of 1600, however, Weelkes's radicalism was consummated, above all perhaps in two compositions: the five-voice 'O care, thou wilt despatch me' and the six-voice 'Thule, the period of cosmography'. In the former, using the structure of the normally vivacious ballet with its 'fa-la' refrains, Weelkes set a grief-ridden text to grave music filled with dissonance and, at the opening of its second half, startling chromatic harmony against which the intervening fa-la refrains seem like nostalgic reflections of that joy of which the lyric itself despairs. It was a brilliant conception, brilliantly worked. But 'Thule', a setting of a text which listed some of the wonders of the world that travellers had begun to report upon during the preceding century, was even bolder. It was the text's imaginative suggestions, especially the volcanic ones, that set Weelkes's inventiveness ablaze: Hekla's 'sulphureous fire', 'Trinacrean Etna's flames', and above all 'how strangely Fogo burns', an image which drew from Weelkes perhaps the weirdest chromatic passage in all English music of the period. Also vastly impressive is 'As Vesta was from Latmos Hill descending', which Weelkes contributed to *The Triumphs of Oriana* (1601), the collection of madrigals assembled in praise of the aged Queen Elizabeth; especially striking is his treatment of the final line, 'Long live fair Oriana', where the melodic idea setting these words is repeated to saturation point in the upper five voice parts, while this same idea, in twelve-fold augmentation, also provides the bass, thus directing the music's harmonic course. It was a unique procedure—monolithic, sonorous, and pulsating with concentrated energy—that Weelkes also used in other madrigals. In fact Weelkes's Winchester phase was, for all his youth, creatively the most brilliant, perhaps even the supreme peak, of his composing career. His one remaining madrigalian publication, *Ayres or Fantastic Spirits for Three Voices* (1608), containing some attractive, tuneful pieces, is relatively unimportant, as is his handful of compositions for keyboard and viol consort.

At some time between October 1601 and October 1602 Weelkes moved to Chichester Cathedral as organist and *informator choristarum*. By 1605 he had been appointed a Sherborne clerk, one of four such lay singers' positions. His career was advancing well; on 13 July 1602 he had been admitted BMus of Oxford University and now, with a yearly income of £15 2s. 4d. plus accommodation and other gratuities, he was well provided for. On 20 February 1603 he married Elizabeth Sandham, daughter of a wealthy Chichester merchant. There were at least three children of the marriage: Thomas, baptized on 9 June, less than four months after the marriage, and two daughters—Alice, baptized on 17 September 1606, and Katherine, of whose baptism there is no record, but who is mentioned in her father's will. During Weelkes's early years at Chichester there is nothing to suggest that he did not give good and efficient service to the cathedral, and on the title-page of his final madrigalian publication (1608) he is styled 'Gentleman of his Majesty's Chapel', though the chapel's own records never mention him and at most he must have been only a gentleman-extraordinary.

However, in the following year, 1609, Weelkes was declared contumacious for not attending the bishop's visitation; his personal decline had begun. True he was not the only disorderly member of the cathedral establishment, though in due course he would become its most celebrated. In December 1613 he was accused of a 'fama publica ebrietatis' (Chichester Diocesan RO, Ep.1/18/31). No further action was taken against him, nor were there any personal consequences when, two years later, the archbishop's visitation exposed a deplorable state of affairs, Weelkes and ten other choirmen being sternly upbraided for failure to attend cathedral services. In May 1616 he was for the first time singled out for negligence, and the cathedral chapter prescribed for him a very precise schedule for training the choirboys. This was reaffirmed at the bishop's visitation in September, which also discovered that Weelkes had not been properly performing his duties during divine service itself. Matters came to a head in October, when he was brought before the chapter to answer the charge that he had become notorious both for drunkenness and for outrageous blaspheming. Because he was unable to produce witnesses who would testify for him, on 16 January 1617 he was dismissed as organist and *informator choristarum*, though he retained his Sherborne clerkship.

Nevertheless, Weelkes remained unreformed, and in 1619 William Lawes, the sub-chanter, reported that, while most of the choir behaved in a seemly manner during prayers, Weelkes frequently turned up so 'disguised' from the tavern or alehouse that he would utter curses and oaths that both profaned the service and outraged those who were present. Moreover, Lawes added, despite numerous admonitions from the bishop, Weelkes not only continued to behave thus every day but was even tending to get worse. Yet this still had no adverse consequences for him, nor was there any reaction even to the report made to the bishop during his visitation of 1622 by two of the four Sherborne clerks that, while three of them were performing their duties as required by the statutes, Weelkes was not. Most surprising of all, in the accounts for the financial year to Michaelmas 1622 Weelkes reappears as organist. On 7 September, however, he buried his wife and his own end came a year later. By then he had clearly been living for some time in the parish of St Bride's in London, for his will, made on 30 November 1623,

acknowledges a 50s. debt for board and lodging. His death followed swiftly, and the next day, 1 December, he was buried in the church of St Bride's, Fleet Street. His possessions proved insufficient to cover his debts, and the site of his grave is unknown. The close friend at whose house he died was called, ironically, Henry Drinkwater.

None of Weelkes's church music can be dated precisely but presumably most of it was composed during his Chichester years. While single madrigals of his were sporadically printed in the late eighteenth century and three of his complete collections (1597, 1598, and 1608) were issued in the nineteenth, not one of his verse anthems saw print until 1966, and until recently his church music had been badly underestimated. In fact Weelkes was one of the most important church composers of his time. He wrote both services (music for the standard texts in the morning and evening rituals, and in the eucharist) and anthems, in both forms using the two established types: the full type, written for voices only, and the verse type, where choruses for the full choir alternated with verses for soloist(s), the organ accompanying throughout. As a composer of services Weelkes was by far the most prolific of all major Elizabethan and Jacobean composers, producing ten in all (seven verse, and three full), though sadly most survive incomplete.

Some of Weelkes's verse services and verse anthems are studiedly restrained in manner, with relatively simple choruses, and these, one suspects, were designed for Chichester, where they would not have overstretched the limited musical resources of that establishment. But others are far grander—the spacious *In medio chori* service employs an additional semi-chorus placed between the choirstalls and the service for trebles exploits the brilliance of the boys' voices at the top of their range, while the grand verse anthems 'Give the king thy judgements' and 'Christ rising' were surely envisaged for performance in the Chapel Royal; the latter is a particularly impressive piece. The prevailing (though not exclusive) musical demand in the Church of England was for dignified and sober compositions, and Weelkes's full anthems fall into two categories, the style of some clearly designed to be acceptable for general church use as allowed for in the morning and evening liturgies, and others, almost certainly secular anthems, intended for extra-liturgical use, including private domestic devotions (as, explicitly, were Weelkes's two contributions to Sir William Leighton's *The Tears or Lamentations of a Sorrowful Soul*, 1614, his only sacred pieces printed in his lifetime). There is, nevertheless, clear evidence that some at least of Weelkes's full anthems served in both contexts. In secular anthems he was free to employ a more rhetorical, or affective, style; here he was something of a pioneer—and often at his best, as in the splendid six-voice 'Hosanna to the Son of David' and 'Gloria in excelsis Deo. Sing, my soul'. Of his full services, that for seven voices is especially impressive; set this noble, monolithic creation alongside the trails of dazzling imagery and heightened expressive states from which the greatest of the early madrigals were assembled, and the breadth of Weelkes's expressive range is impressively displayed, confirming him as one of the most prodigiously gifted of all English Renaissance composers, whose personal decline was one of the great tragedies of English music.   DAVID BROWN

Sources D. Brown, *Thomas Weelkes: a biographical and critical study* (1969) • W. D. Peckham, ed., *The acts of the dean and chapter of the cathedral church of Chichester, 1545–1642*, Sussex RS, 58 (1959) • D. Brown, 'Weelkes, Thomas', *New Grove*, 2nd edn • Chichester Diocesan RO, Ep.1/18/31, fol. 7v; Ep.1/18/32; Ep.1/18/33; Ep.1/20/9; Ep.1/20/10; Par. 80/1/1/1, fol. 2; Par. 36/1/1/1, fol. 77 • will, Chichester Diocesan RO, STD II/Box 3/130 • U. Oxf. congregation register, 1595–1606, Bodl. Oxf., (M.11), fol. 128 • W. Sussex RO, Ep.1/29, Chichester no. 58
Wealth at death died in debt; 2s. to daughter: W. Sussex RO, Ep.1/29, Chichester no. 58

Weemes [Wemyss], **John** (*c*.1579–1636), Church of Scotland minister and exegetist, was the only son of John Weemes of Lathockar, in Fife. He was educated at the University of St Andrews, graduating MA in 1600, and—probably soon afterward—married Margaret Cockburn. The couple had a son, David. Weemes was appointed minister of Hutton, Berwickshire, in 1608. In the same year he was one of several commissioners appointed by the general assembly to consult 'upon all maters standing presentlie in controversie … anent [the] discipline of the kirk' (Calderwood, 7.27–8), and took the side of those who opposed the imposition of episcopacy. Subsequently his proposed transfer to a vacant charge at Edinburgh was refused and he was admitted to the parish of Duns, Berwickshire, in 1613. At an unknown date Weemes lost both his wife and son. He married Janet Murray, and they had a son, John, and a daughter.

Weemes remained steadfast in his opposition to royal policy. In 1617 he signed a petition condemning the king's attempts to curtail the 'power of … Generall Assemblies', and he was one of the 'cheefe reasoners' against the five articles—both 'in conference', and in 'open assemblie'—during the following year (Calderwood, 7.253, 332). In March 1620 Weemes appeared before the court of high commission for 'not ministering the Communion according to the order prescrived at Perth'. In answer to the charge he claimed that 'all the brethrein of the shire where he was minister agried with [his] judgement', that to administer the sacrament to kneeling communicants was 'evill … [and] directlie against the institution'. 'Therfor', he concluded, 'we will never doe it'. He was dismissed on his assurance that he would return to his parish, 'be quyet, and not hinder others' (ibid., 412–13, 425–6).

True to his word Weemes retired from active opposition. He was considered 'one of the best learned' of ministers (*DNB*), and devoted the remaining years of his life to a study of the scriptures. His most famous work, *The Christian Synagogue, Wherein is Contayned the Diverse Reading, Poynting, Translation, and Collation of Scripture with Scripture* (1623), was reprinted on five occasions during his lifetime. He wrote several other highly regarded books, including *The Pourtraiture of the Image of God in Man* (1626), *The Right Understanding of the Scriptures* (1632), *The Right Understanding of the First Table of the Morall Law* (1632), *An Explanation of the*

Ceremoniall Laws of Moses [1632], *An Explication of the Judiciall Lawes of Moses* [1632], and *Observations, Naturall and Morall* (1633). At the latter date a three-volume set of the *Workes of Mr John Weemse* was published at London. In 1634 his contribution to theological debate was recognized by no less an authority than Charles I, who recommended the minister to the second prebend of Durham Cathedral. Weemes accepted, and was installed honorary canon in the same year. His final work, *A Treatise of the Foure Degenerate Sonnes, viz. the Atheist, the Magician, the Idolater, and the Jew*, was published as 'the fourth volume of the Workes' in 1636. Weemes died, aged about fifty-seven, in November of that year; his wife apparently survived him.

VAUGHAN T. WELLS

Sources D. Calderwood, *The history of the Kirk of Scotland*, ed. T. Thomson and D. Laing, 8 vols., Wodrow Society, 7 (1842–9) • *Reg. PCS*, 1st ser., vol. 11 • *Fasti Scot.*, new edn • M. Wood, ed., *Extracts from the records of the burgh of Edinburgh, 1604–1626*, [7] (1931) • *STC, 1475–1640* • *DNB*

Weeton [*married name* Stock], **Ellen** [Nelly] (1776–1844?), letter writer and governess, was born on 25 December 1776 in Lancaster, possibly in Church Street, the second of the four children of Thomas Weeton (1744–1782), privateersman and slave-ship captain, and Mary (1746?–1797), daughter of Richard Rawlinson, a Preston butcher.

Weeton's writings consisted mainly of seven letter-books (three of these have never been found) into which between 1804 and 1825 she meticulously copied the long letters which she sent to friends and relatives. One of these letter-books contains a short memoir, 'The retrospect', which gives information about her early life. A separate manuscript volume includes 'Occasional reflexions', written in 1818, and 'The history of the life of N. Stock', composed in 1824. The letter-books remained unpublished during Weeton's lifetime and came to light only accidentally in 1925, when their first editor, Edward Hall, discovered one of them in a Wigan bookshop. *Miss Weeton: a Journal of a Governess* was published in two volumes in 1936, the first covering the years 1807 to 1811, and the second 1822 to 1825. A reprint, *Miss Weeton's Journal of a Governess*, in two volumes with an introduction by J. J. Bagley, was published in 1969.

In 1784, after losing her father aboard ship during the American War of Independence, Weeton, her mother, and her only surviving sibling, a younger brother, Thomas (Tom), moved from Lancaster to the small village of Upholland, near Wigan. Weeton's childhood was spent in adoration of Tom, whose educational needs were always taken more seriously than her own: 'I revered and loved my mother, but I loved my brother a great deal better' (*Miss Weeton's Journal*, ed. Bagley, 1.19). Weeton gained a modicum of education mainly from her mother, who opened a local school in 1788. From an early age she felt the disadvantages of her inadequate schooling very keenly: 'From the peculiarly recluse manner in which I had been educated, I was averse to society' (ibid., 1.20). Weeton assisted in her mother's school and, after her mother's death in

1797, ran the establishment alone in an effort to pay off her mother's debts and to support her brother through his legal education in Preston.

Tom Weeton's marriage in 1803 and his unfeeling financial manipulation of his sister obliged Weeton to find other ways of supporting herself. In later years her idealization of Tom was poignantly tempered by a hatred of the many injustices he had perpetrated against her: 'What have I done to you, hard-hearted selfish brother, to merit such strange cruelty of conduct?' (*Miss Weeton's Journal*, ed. Bagley, 2.87). As a result of her precarious pecuniary situation, Weeton spent the years 1808–9 lodging in Liverpool. In 1809 she was obliged to take up work as a governess to the Pedder family at Ambleside in the Lake District. Here she witnessed with horror the death of ten-year-old Mary Pedder, who fell into the fire. Between 1811 and 1814 Weeton was governess to the Armstrong family at Milnsbridge, near Huddersfield, where she had the task of bringing to order children whom she found 'as unruly, noisy, insolent, quarrelsome a set, as I ever met' (ibid., 2.59).

In September 1814, at her brother's instigation, Weeton returned to Wigan to marry a local widower and cotton manufacturer, Aaron Stock (b. 1776). The marriage was an unmitigated failure: Weeton suffered the excesses of domestic abuse, 'extreme want and houseless at one time; imprisonments and bruises at another; my life daily in danger' (*Miss Weeton's Journal*, ed. Bagley, 2.140). She was herself charged with assault and threatened with detention in a lunatic asylum. Her only daughter, Mary (b. 1815), was removed from her care and sent to a local boarding-school. Weeton and Stock were separated by deed of separation in 1822, Weeton being thereby banned from the vicinity of Wigan.

Weeton returned to Upholland and was later reunited with her daughter. Described by Hall as a 'freethinker' (*Miss Weeton's Journal*, ed. Bagley, l.xxix), she attended both established and nonconformist churches regularly. She became a member of Hope Independent Chapel, Wigan, in 1827. She probably died in 1844, but the exact date, and her place of death and burial, are not known.

Lanky, sickly, and beset by acne, Weeton was, by her own admission, physically unprepossessing: 'I never was a beauty and sure enough I grow uglier every day' (*Miss Weeton's Journal*, ed. Bagley, 1.226). But the letters reveal a woman of impressive mental accomplishments whose many sufferings seem only to lend a clarity to her quick humour, quiet dignity, and powers of observation. She could, however, be caustic, arrogant, and ferociously self-centred: 'Any ridicule I may thoughtlessly scatter, is not meant to wound, but only to amuse—perhaps tinged with a latent desire to excite a little admiration at my talents' (ibid., 1.306).

The letters and journal entries have enormous interest as social history, providing vivid first-hand accounts of the life of the governess and of the developing industrial landscape of north-west England, with its packet steamers and emergent railways. Weeton travelled alone to places as far afield as Yorkshire, London, the Lake District, and the Isle of Man, an itinerary that makes her a fascinating resource for information on the practice of contemporary travel. Since the mid-1980s Weeton's musings on the legal, educational, literary, and professional difficulties faced by women in the early nineteenth century have also attracted the attention of feminist historians.

RUTH A. SYMES

Sources papers, Wigan Archives Service, Leigh, EHC A–D · *Miss Weeton's journal of a governess*, ed. E. Hall, 2 vols. (1936–9); repr. with an introduction by J. J. Bagley (1969) · J. Swindells, *Victorian writing and working women* (1985) · R. A. Symes, 'Educating women, 1780–1820: the preceptress and her pen', PhD diss., University of York, 1995
Archives Wigan Archives Service, Leigh, MSS

Weever, John (1575/6–1632), poet and antiquary, was born in Preston, Lancashire, to 'poor but religious parents', and received an excellent education 'by the care of his uncle Thomas' (Whittle, 198). This may have been Thomas Langton, from whom Weever later wrote that he had 'received many favours' (Honigmann, *Weever*, 7), and Weever's father may have been 'Johne Weyver', one of thirteen followers of Langton who were tried for murder in 1590 after a riot at Lea Hall, Lancashire. Weever also addressed Henry Butler of Rawcliffe, Lancashire, as his uncle, but the precise blood relationship of the two men is uncertain.

On 30 April 1594 Weever was admitted as a sizar to Queens' College, Cambridge. His first tutor there was the Lancashireman William Covell, whose *Polimanteia* (1595) contains one of the first printed notices of Shakespeare, along with praise for several other poets. Later Weever studied under Robert Pearson, whom he referred to more than thirty years later as a 'reverend, learned divine', to whom he was 'bound to acknowledge all thankfulness' (Weever, 864). Weever's BA supplicat was submitted on 16 April 1598, and the grace was conceded on the same day. While he had apparently considered taking holy orders, instead he went to London after graduation and immersed himself in the city's literary scene.

In late 1599 Weever's *Epigrammes in the Oldest Cut, and Newest Fashion* was published in London. The front matter contains commendatory verses by Cambridge friends and an address 'To the Generous Readers' in which the author apologizes for the epigrams being out of date by a year. He dedicated the volume to Richard Hoghton, high sheriff of Lancashire, and also included six other dedications to prominent Lancashire residents, one before each of the seven 'weeks' into which the book is divided.

Many of the epigrams appear to have been written while Weever was at Cambridge, since they are addressed to fellow students or professors, in many cases invoking puns on the subject's name. However, he also addressed several epigrams to contemporary literary figures. 'Ad Gulielmum Shakespear' is the earliest known complete poem addressed to Shakespeare, and is also the only poem in the volume to take the form of a Shakespearian sonnet. He also addressed poems to Michael Drayton, Edward

Lanchaſhire gaue him breath,
And Cambridge education.
His ſtudies are of Death.
Of Heauen his meditation.

John Weever (1575/6–1632), by Thomas Cecill, 1631

Alleyn, Samuel Daniel, John Marston and Ben Jonson, William Warner, and Edmund Spenser (then recently dead). In the same year, Weever also wrote commendatory verses for his Cambridge friend Henry Buttes's *Dyet's Dry Dinner*.

In 1600 Weever published a curious volume called *Faunus and Melliflora*, dedicated to Sir Edward Stanley of Lancashire. The first part consists of an Ovidian erotic poem influenced by Shakespeare's *Venus and Adonis*, but after a thousand lines this changes abruptly to a mythological account of the origin of satires, followed by translations of satires by Horace, Persius, and Juvenall. The volume concludes with a reference to the burning of satirical books ordered by the archbishop of Canterbury and bishop of London in London on 4 June 1599 and an ironic 'Prophecie' in which Weever alludes to the satires of Joseph Hall and John Marston, pretending to rebuke those men for making fun of the current age.

In 1601 an anonymous satirical pamphlet called *The Whipping of the Satyre* was published, which Davenport persuasively argued was written by Weever. The book attacks three people called the Satirist, the Epigrammatist, and the Humorist, probably representing John Marston, Everard Guilpin, and Ben Jonson. Weever's authorship seems to have been widely guessed, and he came in for some counter-attacks. Honigmann argued that Weever is lampooned as Simplicius Faber in Marston's *What You Will*,

Shift in Jonson's *Every Man out of his Humour*, and Asinius Bubo in Thomas Dekker's *Satiromastix*. These works portray Weever as a small man and a lover of tobacco (both characteristics admitted by Weever in his own writings), a hanger-on of Jonson, and possibly a homosexual. Weever may also have been lampooned as Ingenioso, a former Cambridge student searching for a patron, in the three Cambridge-produced plays of 1598–1601 known as the Parnassus plays.

Weever appears to have been tiring of these wars of words by 1601, for in that year he also published two works which suggest that he was hoping for a career in the church after all. *The Mirror of Martyrs* is a 1464-line narrative poem about the life and death of proto-protestant martyr Sir John Oldcastle, written as part of the backlash against Shakespeare's Falstaff (originally named Oldcastle). It is heavily influenced by Christopher Middleton's *The Legend of Humphrey Duke of Glocester* (1600), for which Weever had written commendatory verses, and John Bale's 1544 life of Oldcastle. Weever's other religious work of 1601 was *An Agnus Dei*, a pedestrian verse history of Jesus Christ published as a tiny book less than 2 inches square. Later editions came out in 1603, 1606, and 1610, probably published for the book's novelty value rather than for any literary merit.

After this burst of publication, Weever appears to have left London for a few years. In April 1603 he was in York for King James's procession from Scotland to London, and early in the reign of James he was at Kendal in Lancashire to witness a Corpus Christi play. He may have settled in Lancashire for a time, since in 1609 he signed depositions in a chancery suit there. However, at some undetermined point he returned to London, married a woman named Anne, and bought a house in the parish of St James's, Clerkenwell. He may be the John 'Weaver' who married Anne Edwards at St James's, Clerkenwell, on 25 July 1614, or the man of the same name who married Anne Panting in the same parish on 21 October 1617, or he may be neither of these.

During the first three decades of the seventeenth century, Weever travelled 'at painful expense' throughout England and the continent collecting inscriptions from funeral monuments, an interest he had exhibited as early as the *Epigrammes*. He claimed to have travelled through most of England and parts of Scotland, as well as to Italy, France, and Germany. About 1620 he befriended the herald Augustine Vincent, who gave him access to the records of the heralds' office and introduced him to Sir Robert Cotton and many other antiquaries.

In 1631 Weever published a portion of his findings in a 900-page folio volume entitled *Ancient Funerall Monuments*. This contains inscriptions from Canterbury, Rochester, London, and Norwich, interlarded with Weever's commentary and poetical extracts ranging from the ancients to works of the late 1620s. The frontispiece has a portrait of Weever, giving his age as fifty-five. Two notebooks in Weever's hand, containing an early draft of this work along with much unpublished material, survive as Society of Antiquaries manuscripts 127 and 128. The folio and notebooks preserve many inscriptions which have since been lost, and are thus invaluable to present-day historians and biographers.

Weever did not live long after the publication of his *magnum opus*. He made his will on 16 February 1632, and probate was granted on 29 March to his widow, Anne, who received the bulk of his estate. The will mentions houses in Gray's Inn Lane and Clerkenwell, and makes bequests to a brother, William, and to sisters Alice Cawthorne, Anne Caton, and Isabel Holt. A monument was erected to Weever in his parish church, where he was buried, but this does not survive; however, the verses from it were preserved by Anthony Munday in his 1633 edition of John Stow's *Survey of London*.   DAVID KATHMAN

Sources E. Honigmann, *John Weever* (1987) · J. Weever, *Ancient funerall monuments* (1631) · A. Davenport, introduction, in J. Weever, *Faunus and Melliflora*, ed. A. Davenport (1948), v–vii · A. Davenport, introduction, in [J. Weever, N. Breton, and E. Guilpin], *The whipper pamphlets: (1601)*, ed. A. Davenport (1951) · P. Whittle, *History of the borough of Preston* (1837) · Venn, *Alum. Cant.*, 1/1 · E. Honigmann, *Shakespeare: the lost years* (1985)
Archives S. Antiquaries, Lond., notebooks for *Ancient funerall monuments*, MSS 127–128
Likenesses T. Cecill, line engraving, 1631, BM, NPG [*see illus.*]

Weguelin, Thomas Matthias (1763/4–1828), army officer, born at Moorfields, London, was the eldest son of John Christopher Weguelin and his second wife, Elizabeth. He was appointed an East India Company cadet in March 1781 in the Bengal presidency. He arrived in Calcutta in April 1782, having been promoted ensign on 16 June 1781. He joined the 3rd European regiment at Burhanpur, and became a lieutenant on 22 September 1782. In November he was transferred to the 1st battalion, 22nd native infantry, at the frontier station of Fatehgarh in the dominions of the nawab of Oudh. In March 1783 he went to the Farrukhabad district, where he took part in some minor operations, and in 1796, when his regiment was incorporated with the 2nd native infantry, he received the brevet rank of captain.

Weguelin served against Tipu Sahib from 1790 to 1792 with Lieutenant-Colonel John Cockrell's detachment. He fought at the battle and siege of Seringapatam in 1791–2. In December 1797 he was transferred to the 1st battalion, 13th native infantry, which he commanded in 1799 during the deposition of the nawab of Oudh, and shortly after joined the 1st European regiment at Cawnpore, removing with it to Dinapore at the close of the year. On 10 August 1801 he received the regimental rank of captain, and in September 1803 he went in command of the flank companies of his regiment to join the army under Lord Lake, then engaged with the Marathas in the north-west, where he took part in the siege of Gwalior. In September 1804 he accompanied Lake's army as judge-advocate-general in the field provinces north and west of Allahabad, and took part in the siege of Bharatpur. He held the post until his appointment to major on 3 March 1808.

In June Weguelin commanded an expedition to defend Macao against the French, with the local rank of colonel: he returned to Bengal in February 1809. On the establishment of the commissariat in Bengal on 1 February 1810 he

was appointed deputy commissary-general. He accompanied Major-General Sir John Abercromby in the expedition against Mauritius in 1810 as head of the commissariat department, and after the capture of the island was appointed by the governor, Sir Robert Townsend Farquhar, commissary-general of Mauritius, Bourbon, and their dependencies. He returned to Bengal in March 1812. On 1 July 1812 he was nominated commissary-general of Bengal with the rank of lieutenant-colonel, attaining the regimental rank on 16 March 1814.

Weguelin was commissary-general through the two Nepal wars between 1814 and 1816, and that with the Pindaris from 1816 to 1818, so ably conducting his office that the extra expenses of the wars did not exceed the comparatively small sum of £600,000. Obliged by private affairs to return to England, he resigned his office at the close of 1820, embarking in January 1822. He received the rank of colonel commandant on 20 July 1823.

Weguelin was twice married. He married at Calcutta on 26 January 1814 Miss Mary Cooper: they had a son and a daughter. He and his second wife, Mary (d. 15 Sept 1856), had three sons. He also had, with Elizabeth Shaw, an illegitimate daughter. He died aged sixty-four at 25 Montagu Square, London, on 23 May 1828: a monument was placed in Marylebone church.

E. I. CARLYLE, *rev.* JAMES LUNT

Sources *GM*, 1st ser., 96/2 (1828), 180 · Dodwell [E. Dodwell] and Miles [J. S. Miles], eds., *Alphabetical list of the officers of the Indian army: with the dates of their respective promotion, retirement, resignation, or death … from the year 1760 to the year … 1837* (1838) · private information (c.1899) [Mr A. W. Greene] · V. C. P. Hodson, *List of officers of the Bengal army, 1758–1834*, 4 (1947), 422 · S. R. Pandey, *From sepoy to subedar*, trans. J. T. Norgate, new edn, ed. J. Lunt (1970)

Wehnert, Edward Henry (1813–1868), watercolour painter, was baptized on 14 February 1813 at St Anne's Church, Soho, London, the son of Henry Wehnert, a German tailor, and his wife, Susanna; he had at least two brothers. In 1825 he was sent to Germany to study in Göttingen, and in 1829 he returned to England, where he studied drawing from classical sculptures in the British Museum, London, and did a large oil painting, *The Death of Hippolytus*, which was exhibited at the Society of British Artists in Suffolk Street in 1832. From 1832 to 1834 he studied art in Paris, and then lived and worked in Jersey for three years before returning permanently to London in 1837, when he became a member of the New Society of Painters in Water Colours. From then on he mainly painted historical genre scenes, including *Luther Reading his Sermon to some Friends*, *The Death of Wycliffe*, *Caxton Examining the First Proof Sheet from his Press*, and *The Prisoner of Gisors*. He exhibited three pictures at the Royal Academy between 1839 and 1863, including *The Elopement—Eve of St Agnes* (exh. 1852) and *The Death of Jean Goujon* (exh. 1863). He took part in the Westminster Hall cartoon competition in 1845, and the chalk cartoon of *The Triumph of Justice*, submitted by him, is in the Victoria and Albert Museum in London, which also has his *George Fox Preaching in a Tavern* (1865).

Wehnert's large works, Germanic in style, did not sell

well, and he was more successful as a book illustrator, doing the drawings for editions of Keats's *Eve of St Agnes* (1856), Coleridge's *Ancient Mariner* (1857), Hans Christian Andersen's *Eventyr* (as *Fairy Tales*, 1861), and Edgar Allan Poe's *Poetical Works* (1865). He died, unmarried, at his home, 9 Fortress Terrace, Kentish Town, London, on 15 September 1868, aged fifty-five. A memorial exhibition was held at the Institute of Painters in Water Colours (the former New Watercolour Society) in 1869.

F. M. O'DONOGHUE, rev. ANNE PIMLOTT BAKER

Sources *Art Journal*, 30 (1868), 245 • Wood, *Vic. painters*, 3rd edn • Mallalieu, *Watercolour artists*, vols. 1–2 • Boase, *Mod. Eng. biog.* • L. Lambourne and J. Hamilton, eds., *British watercolours in the Victoria and Albert Museum* (1980) • J. Johnson, ed., *Works exhibited at the Royal Society of British Artists, 1824–1893, and the New English Art Club, 1888–1917*, 2 vols. (1975) • Bryan, *Painters* (1903–5) • IGI • d. cert. • CGPLA Eng. & Wales (1868)
Wealth at death under £200: administration, 2 Dec 1868, CGPLA Eng. & Wales

Weigall [*née* Fane], **Lady Rose Sophia Mary** (1834–1921), literary editor and social worker, was born on 5 September 1834 at Hyde Park Terrace, London. She was the youngest of the nine children of John *Fane, Lord Burghersh (1784–1859), soldier and diplomat, later the eleventh earl of Westmorland, and his wife, Priscilla Anne *Fane, *née* Wellesley-Pole (1793–1879), political hostess, youngest daughter of William Wellesley-*Pole, third earl of Mornington (1763–1845), and niece of Arthur Wellesley, first duke of Wellington (1769–1852). In 1841 her father was appointed minister in Berlin, where he and his family remained for ten years. He was subsequently, between 1851 and 1855, ambassador in Vienna. Lady Rose's education was entrusted to Swiss and German tutors. In Berlin she witnessed the revolution of 1848 and established a lifelong friendship with Princess Luise of Prussia, later grand duchess of Baden (1838–1923), with whom she corresponded until the end of her life. She was in Vienna at the time of the Crimean War, and in both capitals came to meet a number of the leading figures of the day.

After her father's death Lady Rose and her mother lived in London and had a large circle of prominent acquaintances and friends, including Gladstone and Palmerston. In 1866 Lady Rose met, sat for, and married (15 August) the society painter Henry Weigall (1829–1925), whose subjects had included the duke of Wellington. They had six sons, one of whom, Sir Archibald Weigall (1874–1952), was subsequently governor of South Australia, and one daughter.

Lady Rose's diary reveals a widely read and serious-minded woman, watchful for any signs of personal 'intellectual deterioration'. She combined literary and historical interests with active social and educational concerns. An article, 'Our friends in the village', published in *Macmillan's Magazine* in October 1869, describes her experiences of the rural poor in the neighbourhood of Apethorpe, Northamptonshire, the Westmorlands' country seat, the 'decline of the old feudal feeling', and the duties of the advantaged towards the poor. A great admirer of Agnes Strickland's *Queens of England*, Lady Rose published her *A Brief Memoir of the Princess Charlotte of Wales*

in 1874: the princess's husband, Prince Leopold of Saxe-Coburg (1790–1865), had been a close friend of her father. The book was dedicated to Queen Victoria (1819–1901), who had originally encouraged her to write it.

After the death of her mother in 1879 Lady Rose and her family moved to Southwood, an eighteenth-century mansion on the outskirts of Ramsgate, Thanet. She and her husband became prominently involved in social and educational work. She was a member of the board of guardians and a frequent workhouse visitor, and the Weigalls arranged the construction in their garden of a holiday home for London children.

There is a sharp contrast between the court social life of Lady Rose's youth and the essentially local involvement of her later years. The very different circumstances of her youth were kept before her as she published three volumes of her mother's correspondence: *The Letters of Lady Burghersh … from Germany and France during the Campaign of 1813–14* (1893), *Correspondence of Lady Burghersh with the Duke of Wellington* (1903) (with her husband's portrait of the duke), and *The Correspondence of Priscilla, Countess of Westmorland, 1813–1870* (1909). Lady Rose never travelled abroad again after her marriage. She frequently corresponded with her continental friends, however, working hard for improved Anglo-German relations before the First World War. During the war she conducted a considerable correspondence over the treatment of prisoners of war in the two countries. Southwood was severely damaged by bombardment from a Zeppelin in 1917 and her family were forced to evacuate to Wimbledon until the following year. Lady Rose died at Southwood after a stroke on 14 February 1921, and was buried three days later in Ramsgate.

DAVID WEIGALL

Sources R. Weigall, letters, CKS, Weigall papers, U1371 • R. Weigall, *Lady Rose Weigall* (1923) • R. Weigall, *A brief memoir of the Princess Charlotte of Wales, with selections from her correspondence and other unpublished papers* (1874), 1–29, 134 • *The correspondence of Priscilla, countess of Westmorland*, ed. R. Weigall (1909) • R. Weigall, 'Our friends in the village', *Macmillan's Magazine*, 20 (1869), 519–27 • *The Times* (15 Feb 1921) • m. cert.
Archives CKS, personal and family papers, U1371
Likenesses L. Fischer, watercolour, 1853, priv. coll. • H. Weigall, portrait, 1866, priv. coll. • portrait, 1892, priv. coll.

Weight, Carel Victor Morlais (1908–1997), painter and art teacher, was born on 10 September 1908 in Paddington, London, the only son of Sidney L. Weight, a bank cashier, and Blanche Harriet Caroline (*b.* 1882), daughter of Julius William Süssenbach, a first generation immigrant from the Hamburg area who changed his name to Williams after settling in London, where he established himself as a chiropodist and attended to the feet of Edward VII, among others. Like her brother, Blanche trained under her father as a chiropodist, and also became a fashionable manicurist. The combination of her work and her social commitments made it necessary for her son to be farmed out during the week, an arrangement that began when Carel Weight was only a few months old. A widowed acquaintance, Rose Matkin, became his unofficial foster mother. She lived with her elderly mother at World's End, then a slum area within Chelsea, and some four years later moved to a flat above a shoe shop at 184 Dawes Road, Fulham, where Carel shared a boxroom with her son, Henry. As a child Weight shuttled between this down-at-heel, rough area and the relative comfort and security of his parents' flat. They lived first in Paddington and later in a flat over a bank at Shepherd's Bush. Carel returned to his parents at weekends but, unlike the live-in maid, did not have a room of his own. 'It was all rather uncomfortable', Weight recalled (Weight, 9). His loyalties became split: such was his devotion to Rose, who stimulated his interest in books by reading aloud Dickens, popular fiction, and by recounting many of Shakespeare's plots, that when his father suggested the arrangement might end, Carel insisted things should stay as they were. The fact that his parents always addressed him by his second name, Victor, a name he loathed, may have further reinforced the division inside himself. Certainly the business of moving, throughout his childhood and youth, between two sets of parents left him anxious, an emotion that lay always beneath the surface of his life.

A lonely child, Weight made his playgrounds the shabby, derelict streets and alleys and parks of south-west London. Bishop's Park in Fulham and Battersea Park were two of the places that fed into the imaginative terrain in his work, which, as he admitted, had its roots in his early childhood. 'The products of memory, mood and imagination rise upon the foundation of fact. My art is concerned with such things as anger, love, hate, fear and loneliness emphasized by the setting in which the drama is played' (C. Weight, 'The way I work', *Painter and Sculptor*, 4/4, spring 1962). He himself experienced difficult feelings in relation to his brutal grandfather, Louis Petit Weight, who commanded the young boy, during his visits, to remain silent, and who lingered in his mind as an emblem of sheer fear. Likewise, he suffered from the headmaster of Sherbrooke Road School, the board school to which he was sent. Once when he was reading aloud, his hesitant performance caused the headmaster to strike him across the face, an incident that is thought to have begun the slight stutter which became a characteristic of his speech.

Weight progressed to Sloane secondary school and in 1926, at the age of eighteen, entered Hammersmith School of Art. There he met Ruskin Spear, who remained a lifelong friend, and under the tutelage of Clive Gardiner and James Bateman, a former pupil of Henry Tonks, he began to explore his interest in narrative content. Three years later he was offered a scholarship by the Royal College of Art, but as it came with no grant he had to turn it down as his parents refused to continue funding his artistic training. His mother hoped that, with his fine baritone voice, he would gain a musical career. He was given singing lessons which, like much of Weight's life, were mildly bizarre, his teacher, a large prima donna, placing volumes of the *Encyclopaedia Britannica* on his chest in order to develop his lungs, while he sang lying on the floor. An alternative story has it that she sat on him in order to achieve the same end.

Unable to enter the Royal College of Art, Weight took his future into his own hands. He borrowed £25 from a friend and mounted an exhibition of his work in an upstairs room in a Bond Street gallery. A notice in the *Observer*, written by a former art school friend, helped make it a success, and on the proceeds Weight followed his teacher James Bateman to Goldsmiths' College. There he studied two days a week and met the painter and writer Helen Grace Roeder (1909–1999), who attributed their immediate sympathy to the fact that they were both in part of German origin. Their intimate relationship, aside from one brief hiatus, lasted until the end of his life, though they did not marry until 1990. There were no offspring: 'We were both too childish', Helen Roeder explained, commenting also of Weight's many girlfriends, 'I didn't have a jealous temperament' (private information, H. Roeder). With Helen, Weight set up home in Portinscale Road, Putney, later buying a house, 33 Spencer Road, in Wandsworth, and keeping a studio in Putney after his Shepherd's Bush studio was bombed during the war.

Weight first showed in the Royal Academy summer exhibition in 1931. Two years later another academy exhibit, *An Episode in the Childhood of a Genius*, caught the attention of Henry Carr, then head of Beckenham School of Art. He offered Weight a two-day-a-week teaching job,

Carel Victor Morlais Weight (1908–1997), self-portrait, 1974

in which post he remained until 1942 when he was called up for war service. At Beckenham, as later at the Royal College of Art, Weight was competent, friendly, and always ready to rescue anyone who was, as Helen Roeder observed, 'in a bit of a stew'. With his kindliness, mild manner, large shambling frame, quizzical expression, solemn utterance, and habit of standing, like Pooh Bear, with his feet slightly apart, he emitted a benign presence, betraying little of the tension and pain that he put into his work. Yet in the final year of his life he said of his art: 'It's myself. I'm trying to solve all sorts of things inside me. And I do it in the form of painting' (*Financial Times*, 8 June 1996). Both vulnerable and independent, sensitive yet self-contained, he was by nature a survivor, taking only what he wanted from life and leaving the rest. He never cultivated animosities, not having sufficient interest in people to dislike them, despite his sweet and lovable nature.

As an artist Weight employed a painterly style that brought a refreshing immediacy to narrative scenes. Christopher Wood was an early influence, as can be seen in *Allegro strepitoso* (1932; Tate collection). His mother posed for the central figure who is about to give the escaping lion, as he lunges ravenously towards her, an almighty whack with her raised umbrella. This teasing mix of the humorous with the sinister was to recur, as was the theme of attack and escape. Weight's narratives became more poignant as he gradually learnt from Stanley Spencer's example how to deploy the drama across the entire scene. In *The Moment* (1958; Castle Museum, Nottingham) the sense of terror expressed by the momentarily stilled, open-mouthed foreground figure echoes down the empty, derelict street and is imbued in every part of the landscape.

Owing to his friendship with Kenneth Clark, chairman of the War Artists' Advisory Committee during the Second World War, Weight was assured of commissions during this difficult period. His first painting for the committee showed people abandoning a bus during a bombardment, the driver crawling for safety underneath. It was rejected on the grounds that, unpatriotically, it depicted the British public in a state of panic. Far more successful was *The Escape of the Zebra from the Zoo during an Air Raid* (1941; Manchester City Galleries). The subject had been suggested by Clark after a bomb hit the zebra house at London Zoo, killing some animals, leaving others in a state of frenzy, and causing one to gallop off in the direction of Camden Town, with the keepers running after it. Weight treated the story in four episodes which were housed in one frame. The following year he entered the army and moved from tanks to the Royal Engineers field survey, owing to a superior's misguided belief that being an artist he would be good at drawing maps. In 1944 he transferred to the army education corps with the rank of sergeant and took over the art department of the command college in Queen's Gate. Between 1945 and 1946 he acted as an official war artist and, having never visited the continent before, found himself in Italy, Greece, and Vienna, eating good food, drinking wine, and revelling in all he saw. In one letter to Helen Roeder he apologized that his letters

were becoming just 'a catalogue of operas and picture galleries' (*The Curious Captain*). He later looked back on this period as equivalent to a travelling scholarship from the army.

There is evidence in these letters that on Christmas day 1945 Weight attended mass in Florence. As Helen Roeder commented, 'he had a strong sense of God in a way, but it was very much his own affair' (private information, H. Roeder). Outwardly he was not religious, and would simply explain his occasional use of religious subjects by pointing to their dramatic potential. But in 1963 he painted murals to fill the fifteenth-century stone tracery over the door of the chapter house in Manchester Cathedral; the following year he gave to St Aidan's Roman Catholic Church in East Acton his painting *Christ Preaching to the People*, possibly with the encouragement of the priest Father Etherington, who had also obtained for the church a painting by Graham Sutherland; and in October 1970 Weight agreed that his *Transfiguration* should be presented to the pope by Father Etherington, during a high mass in St Peter's, in a service for the canonization of forty English and Welsh martyrs. 'I never do more than wonder because it's beyond me', Weight told a journalist during the last year of his life, adding: 'One is always slightly careful what one says to God in case he really is there' (*Financial Times*, 8 June 1996).

Weight had resumed his teaching career in 1947 with a job at the Royal College of Art. When Robin Darwin arrived as the new rector, Weight, like others in the painting school, was promptly sacked. But he was immediately reinstated and quickly emerged as a key figure within the department, taking over in 1957 as professor of painting after Rodrigo Moynihan left. In this role he presided over one of the most lively periods in the history of the Royal College, as one avant-garde style succeeded another. Weight did not always like or approve these new developments, and himself went on painting in a style untouched by changes in artistic fashion. Though he gave the impression of professorial vagueness, he was a good administrator and as a result managed to produce little work in the magnificent studio set aside for him at the college. He retired in 1973, on reaching the age of sixty-five, and was first made professor emeritus, then senior fellow in 1983. Among other awards, he was appointed CBE in 1962 and received an honorary doctorate from Edinburgh University in 1982. In 1995 he was made a Companion of Honour.

All his life Weight remained loyal to the Royal Academy, exhibiting in the summer exhibition each year, and asking modest prices for his work, so that people who enjoyed his paintings could afford them. He had been elected an associate in 1955 and a Royal Academician in 1965. The following year he was thought to be the favourite in the elections for the presidency, but internal factions defeated him and bolstered the election of Tom Monnington. Weight showed no disappointment and did much to help Monnington in his successful attempts to modernize the Royal Academy. He also got on well with the queen, on her visits to the academy or the college, enjoying what he called 'nice chats'. His most successful years were the late 1980s when, largely owing to the collecting instincts of Charles Saatchi and the drive of the dealer Bernard Jacobson, his art greatly increased in value and he was suddenly regarded as a precursor for the revival of interest in expressionist painting.

Weight produced some outstanding portraits, among them two of his friend Orovida Pissarro (Ashmolean Museum, Oxford, and Tate collection), and excelled at relating the sitter to her or his setting. But the characteristic tenor of his art is best found in those scenes where the figures are pulled, twisted, or swept along by the violence of their emotions, generated by fear, conscience, the weight of memories, or loneliness. In 1959 a *Times* critic, noting Weight's eye for piquant anecdote, for street furniture, and his ability to set in motion echoes, associations, and moods, called him 'the John Betjeman of painting'. But his empathy with unhappiness often brought him closer to Samuel Beckett. With his dignified gait and large tolerance, he emitted a mature stability but knew otherwise, for in his art the world is always on edge and the anxiety portrayed was also his own. No other artist has caught so well the poetry of certain aspects of south-west London, particularly its humdrum Victorian suburbs, barely pretending to gentility, and its back streets, often scavenged and forlorn. He died of a stroke at his home, 33 Spencer Road, London, on 13 August 1997, and was cremated at Battersea crematorium.

FRANCES SPALDING

Sources M. Levy, *Carel Weight* (1986) · R. V. Weight, *Carel Weight: a haunted imagination* (1993) · *The curious captain: Carel Weight war artist, 1939–45: letters to Helen Roeder* (1989) · *Carel Weight RA: a retrospective* (1982) [exhibition catalogue, RA] · press cuttings, Tate collection · private information (2004) [H. Roeder, N. Williams, C. Williams, J. Horwood] · *CGPLA Eng. & Wales* (1998)
Archives Tate collection, personal papers, incl. corresp., draft articles, photographs
Likenesses C. Weight, self-portrait, oils, *c.*1930, NPG · C. Weight, self-portrait, 1974, priv. coll. [*see illus.*]
Wealth at death £870,222: probate, 1 April 1998, *CGPLA Eng. & Wales*

Weiner, Joseph Sidney (1915–1982), human biologist and environmental physiologist, was born on 29 June 1915 at Nourse Mines in Johannesburg, Transvaal, South Africa, the second of the seven children of Robert Weiner (1885–1966), general dealer, and his wife Fanny (Chana), *née* Simon (1896–1978), Jewish immigrants from Lithuania. After attending the East Central School and the boys' high school (1927–31) at Pretoria he went to the University of Witwatersrand medical school, Johannesburg (1932–6), being awarded an MSc in physiology in 1937, in which year he moved to Great Britain. He married Marjorie Winifred Daw (1912–2003) in 1943; they had a daughter and a son.

Weiner obtained the degree of PhD from the University of London in 1946, and was admitted LRCP and MRCS from St George's Hospital, London, in 1947; he was made DSc of Oxford University in 1971. He was successively demonstrator in the department of applied physiology in the London School of Hygiene and Tropical Medicine (1940–41); scientific member of the Medical Research Council (MRC) unit

Joseph Sidney Weiner (1915–1982), by unknown photographer, early 1970s

at Queen Square (1942–6); reader in physical anthropology at Oxford University (1945–63) and honorary deputy director of the MRC climate and working efficiency unit (1955–63); director of the MRC environmental physiology unit at the London School of Hygiene and Tropical Medicine (1963–80); and professor of environmental physiology at London University (1965–80).

Weiner came to public attention in November 1953 when he, K. P. Oakley, and W. E. Le Gros Clark announced the exposure of the Piltdown forgery [*see* Piltdown Man]. Oakley's 1949 fluorine tests had suggested that the mandible and skull cap of the enigmatic Piltdown Man (*Eoanthropus dawsoni*), the English 'missing link' discovered in 1912, were of late Pleistocene age, and that all the fragments might belong to one individual. Weiner found it extraordinary that a composite 'man-ape' could have existed in England at this date, and was puzzled by the circumstances of the discovery. He began to investigate seriously the possibility that the so-called fossil was a fraud. Using modern chimpanzee teeth, he showed Le Gros Clark and Oakley how the molar teeth might have been deliberately filed and all the materials superficially stained. Oakley then confirmed that the Piltdown materials in the British Museum had indeed been artificially abraded and stained, and on repeating the fluorine test, found that the skull and jaw were of different dates (the jaw being that of a modern orang-utan). A battery of further tests, including X-ray crystallography, clinched the case. The story of the exposure and Weiner's investigation of the forger (whom he believed to be the discoverer, Charles *Dawson) is told in his book *The Piltdown Forgery* (1955; republished 1980). His removal of Piltdown Man from the palaeontological record decisively clarified the sequence of human evolution, largely in accord with the Darwinian hypotheses.

Weiner was first and foremost an experimental physiologist; starting from his MSc thesis on the effects of heat on workers in the Rand mines in 1935-6, he specialized in the mechanism of sweating and human adaptation to environmental temperature variation. Approximately 100 of his 290-odd publications deal with aspects of human physiology, culminating in the authoritative *Principles and Practices of Human Physiology* (with O. G. Edholm, 1981). He contributed extensively to applied physiology, carrying out defence research during the Second World War, assisting in the establishment of the science of ergonomics (he was a founder of the Ergonomics Research Society), and advising the coal and steel industries in Britain and the EEC.

The post-war development of physical anthropology was transformed by Weiner's appointment to the Oxford readership in 1945. He soon assumed a leading role in the movement to establish human biology as a discipline studying human beings at the population level, integrating genetics, demography, ecology, physiology, experimental anatomy, and evolutionary theory. He was a founder, in 1958, of the Society for the Study of Human Biology, and later of the International Association of Human Biologists. Weiner and his colleagues G. A. Harrison, J. M. Tanner, and N. A. Barnicot co-authored the landmark textbook *Human Biology: an Introduction to Human Evolution, Variation, and Growth* (1964). He served as president of the Royal Anthropological Institute (1963-4) and published about 120 anthropological papers, including studies of both fossil hominids and living populations. He summarized his understanding of human evolution and variation in *Man's Natural History* (1971; also published in French, Spanish, German, and Italian). He led field expeditions in South and South-West Africa in 1958 and 1961 to investigate the affinities of the Khoi and San peoples; his work on the region is encapsulated in the last book to which he contributed, *Peoples of Southern Africa and their Affinities* (with G. T. Nurse and T. Jenkins; 1985). He was largely responsible for the establishment and administration (as world convenor, 1962-74) of the human adaptability section of the International Biological Programme, on the basis of which thousands of research projects were undertaken worldwide; these were reported in his *Human adaptability: a history and compendium of research in the international biological programme* (with K. J. Collins, 1977). It was said of him:

> Professor J. S. Weiner has pioneered the modern holistic approach to the study of man; more than anyone else he is responsible for the transformation of physical anthropology from a dry and dusty academic byway … to its present focal position in the human sciences.   (Harrison, review, 504)

Weiner was noted for his tireless scientific activity, his power of distinguishing significant from trivial research, his ability to bring out the full potential of groups of researchers, and his generosity, especially to younger colleagues. A sympathy for scientific humanism took the place of religious belief for most of his life. Between 1941 and 1944 he was active in the Association of Scientific Workers, which aimed to improve the condition of scientific workers, and also with increasing the scientific input to the war effort. Like many intellectuals, he believed that only the Left could defeat Nazism and bring in a new era of science-based democracy. Constantly travelling, he particularly enjoyed literature, theatre, history, music, and gardening. Weiner died from lung cancer on 13 June 1982 at his home, 20 Harbord Road, Oxford. He was cremated at Oxford four days later.   EDMUND WEINER

Sources G. A. Harrison and K. Collins, 'In memoriam Joseph Sidney Weiner (1915-1982)', *Annals of Human Biology*, 9 (1982), 583-92 [incl. bibliography] · P. T. Baker, 'Joseph Sidney Weiner, 1915-1982', *American Journal of Physical Anthropology*, 60 (1983), 421-3 · private information (2004) · G. A. Harrison, review of J. S. Weiner's *Man's natural history*, *Nature*, 232 (1971), 504 · G. A. Harrison, 'J. S. Weiner and the exposure of the Piltdown forgery', *Antiquity*, 57 (1983), 46-8 · personal knowledge (2004) · WWW · b. cert.
Archives Wellcome L., letters to A. E. Mourant
Likenesses photograph, 1970-74, priv. coll. [*see illus.*]
Wealth at death £12,587: probate, 19 Aug 1982, *CGPLA Eng. & Wales*

Weir, Andrew, first Baron Inverforth (1865-1955), shipowner, was born at Kirkcaldy, Fife, on 24 April 1865, the eldest son of William Weir and his wife, Janet, daughter of Thomas Laing of the same place. Both his father and his maternal grandfather were cork merchants, and none of his immediate ancestors was connected with shipping.

After attending the high school at Kirkcaldy, Weir at an early age entered the Commercial Bank of Scotland, but this routine work gave little scope for his ambitions and interests and after a few years he forsook his cashier's desk and moved to Glasgow, where he served for a short time in a shipping office. On 5 May 1885, shortly after his twentieth birthday, he began his life as a merchant shipowner, buying a sailing ship, the barque *Willowbank*, which he employed in the coasting trade, renting a small room in Hope Street, Glasgow, as an office. His inborn optimism and opportunism were the seed from which grew the great shipping business of Andrew Weir & Co., which became managing owners of the Bank Line, Invertanker, Inver Transport and Trading Company, and several other shipping companies. The next year Weir began building sailing ships of modern design and within a few years had built up a fleet of fifty-two, the largest sailing ship fleet flying the red ensign under one owner.

In 1896, on moving to London, Weir turned from sail to steam. At a later period he recognized the advantages of the marine internal combustion engine and converted the majority of his ships to diesel power. In all these developments he showed an innate skill and efficiency in management and ensured that the foundations of his company were on sound business lines.

During the First World War, when Lloyd George formed his government in 1916, Weir was mentioned as a possible minister of shipping, but this appointment went to Sir J. P. Maclay and Weir directed his talents into other wartime channels. In March 1917 Lord Derby, then secretary of state for war, asked Weir to report on the commercial organization of the supply branches of the army. Weir recommended the appointment of a surveyor-general of supply, with a seat on the army council, to take over from the various War Office departments the work of supplying the army with all its stores and equipment other than munitions. His recommendations were accepted and he himself appointed to the post. At first that caused some resentment and opposition among certain senior civil servants, but his directness and sincerity of purpose, his natural friendly manner and approachability soon won their co-operation. Shortly after his appointment he made a tour of the battlefields on the continent, accompanied by Sir John Cowans and Crofton Atkins. As a consequence he drew up far-reaching schemes, which resulted in salvage of materials in the various war zones and the elimination of much previous wastage.

Weir's success in this field led to his appointment in January 1919 as minister of munitions, with the gigantic task of liquidating the enormous commitments of the war, entailing the examination of some hundreds of thousands of accounts and contracts and their subsequent disposal. He remained in this office until March 1921, when he took over the chairmanship of the disposals and liquidation commission, which was responsible for selling the vast quantities of army stores throughout the various theatres of war and in the British Isles. Again his genius for organization and great business acumen converted what might have been worthless goods or liabilities into considerable assets. It was not without reason that he was termed 'the man who saved Britain millions'. For his services in the war Weir was in 1919 sworn of the privy council, created Baron Inverforth, and received the American DSM.

On returning to the world of commerce and business, Lord Inverforth devoted his energies particularly to communications. He interested himself in the Marconi group of companies, becoming president of the Radio Communication Company, the Marconi International Marine Communication Company, and Cable and Wireless (Holding). In other spheres he was chairman of the Anglo-Burma Burma Rice Company and of the Wilmer Grain Company, and was also on the board of Lloyds Bank. In 1945 he was elected president of all the associated enterprises of the group of communications companies.

Inverforth was also founder and first chairman of the United Baltic Corporation, which came into existence in 1919 largely through King George V's desire, after the war, that British shipping and trading should replace that of Germany in the Baltic and with Denmark. To this end the king consulted Inverforth and H. N. Anderson, founder and chairman of the East Asiatic Company of Denmark. The corporation was unique in that its shares were to be divided equally between British and Danish shareholders, the chairman having the casting vote. In recognition of this work Inverforth received in 1937 the grand cross of the order of Dannebrog of Denmark and in the following year the grand cross of the Grand Duke Gedinimas of Lithuania.

Inverforth possessed great energy and enthusiasm, and also that almost essential quality of leadership: the ability to select suitable subordinates and leave them to carry on without interference. His integrity, great driving force, and brilliant organizing ability made him a man of power and influence in the commercial world although he shunned the limelight of publicity. His friends and employees, terms frequently synonymous, knew his unobtrusive generosity and kindness. He was particularly approachable: even the most junior employee who had some suggestion towards the improvement or well-being of the firm would be sure of a patient and appreciative hearing and would carry away the remembrance of a kindly twinkle in Inverforth's eye and a good-humoured quiet voice. In many ways he was a model employer, taking interest in the welfare of his staff and their families both during and after their service with him. For many years, until he was eighty, he was treasurer of the Royal Merchant Navy School and, even after he had handed over this office to his friend, Sir Leighton Seager, he continued to take a deep interest in the children.

Inverforth married in 1889 Tomania Anne, younger daughter of Thomas Kay Dowie, coach-builder, of Kirkcaldy. The celebration of their golden wedding in 1939 was a particularly happy occasion and Lady Inverforth's death in 1941 was keenly felt by her husband. They had one son and five daughters. The son, Andrew Alexander Morton (*b.* 1897), besides succeeding his father in the title and as chairman of the United Baltic Corporation, did so also as chairman of Andrew Weir & Co.

Inverforth continued his active life, attending his office in Bury Street four days a week, into his ninety-first year. On his ninetieth birthday he received many tributes of affection from his friends and staff. He died at his home in Hampstead on 17 September 1955.

G. K. S. HAMILTON-EDWARDS, *rev.*

Sources *The Times* (19 Sept 1955) · *The Times* (24 Sept 1955) · *Manchester Guardian* (19 Sept 1955) · J. K. Weir, *Institute of Marine Engineers: Transactions*, 67 (Nov 1955), 454 [contribution to discussion on passenger liner with engines aft] · G. Hamilton-Edwards, 'Andrew Weir (1865–1955), genius of the shipping world', *The Navy*, 70/4 (April 1965), 107–11 · private information (1971) · W. J. Reader, *The Weir group: a centenary history* (1971) · *DSBB* · *The Scotsman* (19 Sept 1955)

Archives NRA, papers · PRO, papers as surveyor-general of the army | HLRO, corresp. with Andrew Bonar Law · HLRO, letters to David Lloyd George, etc.

Likenesses W. Stoneman, photograph, 1919, NPG · R. G. Eves, portrait, priv. coll. · F. O. Salisbury, four portraits, priv. coll. · F. O. Salisbury, oils, Art Gallery and Museum, Glasgow

Wealth at death £548,214 1s. 8d.: probate, 3 Oct 1955, *CGPLA Eng. & Wales*

Weir, Sir Cecil McAlpine (1890–1960), industrialist and civic administrator, was born at Bridge of Weir, Renfrewshire, on 5 July 1890, the youngest of four sons of Alexander Cunningham Weir and his wife, Isabella McLeish. He was educated at Morrison's academy, Crieff, and in Switzerland and Germany. On his return, he spent two years in business training before joining the family firm, Schrader, Mitchell, and Weir, leather and hide merchants in Glasgow, of which he was a partner from 1910 until 1956. On his frequent business visits to the continent his fluency in French and German was invaluable. In 1915 Weir married Jenny Paton, daughter of William Paton Maclay, and a niece of the first Lord Maclay; her death in an air crash in Italy in 1958 was a tragic loss. They had a son and a daughter.

In the First World War, Weir served in the Cameronians, was wounded, and awarded the MC. Settling afterwards in Helensburgh, he took a keen interest in church work and other local activities, including tennis and golf, and was chairman of the company which administered St Bride's School. A concern with politics led him to become secretary of the Scottish Liberal Federation. He became increasingly interested in public affairs and it was he who formulated the idea of holding an Empire Exhibition in Glasgow, for which he obtained wide support. He was chairman of the administrative committee, and it was largely through his remarkable leadership that the exhibition of 1938 achieved a large measure of success despite the menacing international situation. He was appointed KBE in 1938; was president of the Glasgow chamber of commerce in 1939–40; and a director of the Union Bank of Scotland from 1939 until 1947.

From August 1939 until March 1940 Weir was civil defence commissioner for the western district of Scotland and responsible for the operation of the civil defence organization serving 60 per cent of the population of Scotland. Early in 1940, however, he was called to London by Sir Andrew Duncan to become an executive member of the Industrial and Export Council of the Board of Trade, on which he remained until 1946. In 1941–2 he was controller-general of factory and storage premises; and in 1942–6 director-general of equipment and stores, Ministry of Supply. In 1946 he became economic adviser, Allied Control Commission for Germany, and, on his return to the United Kingdom in 1949, full-time chairman of the Dollar Exports Board until 1951. In 1952 he became head of the United Kingdom delegation to the High Authority of the European Coal and Steel Community and served in that capacity for three years. He was appointed KCMG in 1952. In his latter years he was executive chairman of International Computers and Tabulators, and a part-time member of the British Transport Commission.

Weir's capacity for organization was accompanied by great personal charm. He had a remarkable memory, seldom forgetting a face or a name, a good sense of humour, and a gift for getting the best out of those associated with him in any project.

Weir died at his home, 19 Thorney Court, Kensington, London, on 30 October 1960.   BILSLAND, *rev.*

Sources C. M. Weir, *Civilian assignment* (1953) · *The Times* (31 Oct 1960), 20f · d. cert.
Likenesses W. Stoneman, photograph, 1938, NPG · W. Stoneman, photograph, 1952, NPG
Wealth at death £36,687 12*s*. 3*d*.: probate, 12 Dec 1960, *CGPLA Eng. & Wales*

Weir, Harrison William (1824–1906), artist and author, was born at Lewes, Sussex, on 5 May 1824, the second son of John Weir and his wife, Elizabeth Jenner. John was successively manager of a bank in Lewes and an administration clerk in the legacy duty office, Somerset House, London. A brother, John Jenner Weir, an ornithologist and entomologist, became controller-general of customs. Harrison Weir was sent to be educated at Albany Academy, Camberwell. However, as he showed an aptitude for drawing, he was withdrawn in 1837 and articled for seven years to the printer George Baxter (1807–1867), a native of Lewes who had moved to London. In 1835 Baxter had obtained a patent for reproducing paintings in colour using oil inks on a succession of wood or metal relief blocks laid down on a key from an intaglio or lithographic source. Baxter prints enjoyed great popularity, and for a time the business prospered.

Weir was employed in all branches of the enterprise, but mainly in printing off the plates, as a result of which he became restless. Nevertheless, he learned how to draw on the woodblock for the engraver and became proficient himself with the wood-engraving tools. His spare time was devoted to drawing and painting, with particular emphasis on birds and animals; although self-taught, he showed great promise. In 1842 the *Illustrated London News* was founded by Herbert Ingram. Weir broke his indentures with Baxter in order to join Ingram, where, from the first issue of the journal, he was employed both as a draughtsman on the block and as an engraver. Ingram recognized Weir's artistic merit and purchased, reputedly for £150, his painting of a robin, *The Christmas Carol Singer*, which he issued in the *Illustrated London News* as a colour plate and which is believed to have led to the elaborate Christmas numbers for which the magazine later became noted.

About this time Weir became acquainted with the family of the animal painter John Frederick *Herring, whose eldest daughter, Anne, he married on 29 October 1845. He was married a further two times: to Alice (*d*. 1898), the youngest daughter of T. Upjohn MRCS, of Norfolk, and to Eva Emma, the daughter of George Goble of Worthing, Sussex, who survived him. Weir had two sons, Arthur Herring Weir (1847–1902) and John Gilbert Weir, and two daughters.

In 1845 Weir exhibited *The Dead Shot*, an oil painting of a wild duck, at the Royal Institution, and from that time he was an occasional exhibitor at the Royal Academy and other London venues. In 1849 he was elected to the New Watercolour Society. More than a hundred of his pictures were shown in its exhibitions, but his main activity was the provision of illustrations for books and periodicals. By the end of the 1850s he had contributed to most of the significant titles in the continually expanding area of serial publication.

Few contemporary artists were more prolific or more popular. George and Edward Dalziel, in *The Brothers Dalziel* (1901), a chronicle of one of the most highly competent and successful wood-engraving firms of the nineteenth century, described Weir as a man of many parts, a gifted and brilliant conversationalist, a genial companion, and an old friend. Weir was welcomed into literary society, and his intimate friends included the publisher Douglas Jerrold, the author and social reformer Henry Mayhew, the author Albert Smith, and the humorist and editor Tom Hood the younger; he was also well acquainted with Thackeray and other important men of letters.

Weir's drawings of landscape have the finish and smoothness common to contemporary wood-engravings, but his animals and birds show a distinctive treatment. Many of his finest illustrations were drawn for the Revd J. G. Wood's *Illustrated Natural History*, and his work generally was of a high standard. He was rarely guilty of facile or slipshod work. In some cases Weir compiled the books which he illustrated, and *The Poetry of Nature* (1867) was an anthology of his own choosing. He sought to improve the quality of books for children and of those intended for less affluent members of society, and his carefully prepared drawing copybooks gained wide acceptance.

Weir was steadfast in his devotion to animal welfare. He originated the first cat show, in 1872, and later became a judge, and he wrote and illustrated *Our Cats and All about them* (1869). More importantly, he was an experienced poultry breeder and judge, and he designed colour plates for publication in *The Poultry Book* (1856), by W. Wingfield and G. W. Johnson. His own book *Our Poultry and All about them* was worked on for many years prior to its publication in 1903, when his colour plates and black and white drawings excited great admiration. Although technical aspects of the text were rapidly superseded, the section on old English game fowl proved enduring. Weir's other interests included horticulture, and he contributed articles and drawings to the gardening press over a long period. He was employed by the goldsmiths and silversmiths Garrard & Co. for more than thirty years, designing trophies for Goodwood, Ascot, and other race meetings.

In 1891 Weir was granted a civil-list pension of £100 per year. His busy life left him little time for travel, and his leisure time was divided between his garden and his clubs. After a long residence at Lyndhurst Road, Peckham, London, he built himself a house at Sevenoaks, Kent. His last years were spent at Poplar Hall, Appledore, Kent. He died there on 3 January 1906 and was buried at Sevenoaks.

ROGER INGPEN, rev. IAN ROGERSON

Sources *The Times* (5 Jan 1906) · *The Field* (5 Jan 1906) · *WW* (1906) · E. Bond, 'Bird-man extraordinary', *Country Life*, 158 (1975), 1578, 1580 · S. Houfe, *The dictionary of 19th century British book illustrators and caricaturists*, rev. edn (1996) · *BL cat.* · C. T. C. Lewis, *George Baxter, colour printer: his life and work* (1908) · R. McLean, *Victorian book design and colour printing* (1963) · *Men and women of the time* (1899) · *Royal Kalendar* · [G. Dalziel and E. Dalziel], *The brothers Dalziel: a record of fifty years' work … 1840–1890* (1901) · *Daily Chronicle* [London] (6 May 1904) · *Daily Chronicle* [London] (5 Jan 1906) · R. K. Engen, *Dictionary of Victorian wood engravers* (1985) · m. cert. [Anne Herring] · m. cert. [Eva Emma Goble]

Likenesses Elliott & Fry, carte-de-visite, NPG · group portrait, wood-engraving ('Our artists—past and present'), BM, NPG; repro. in *ILN* (14 May 1892) · portrait, repro. in H. Weir, *Our poultry and all about them* (1902) · portrait, repro. in Bond, 'Bird-man extraordinary'

Wealth at death £6031 13*s*. 10*d*.: resworn probate, 12 Feb 1906, *CGPLA Eng. & Wales*

Weir, Sir John (1879–1971), homoeopathic physician, was born in Glasgow on 19 October 1879, the second of three sons (there were no daughters) of James Weir, joiner, of East Kilbride, and his wife, Agnes Baird. He was educated at the Allan Glen School and worked as an engineer before entering Glasgow University medical school. His interest in homoeopathy began before his decision to embark on a medical career. As a teenager he suffered severely from boils, and, after traditional medicine had failed, was cured by a homoeopathic doctor in Glasgow, T.M. Dishington.

Weir graduated MB BCh in 1906, and held several resident appointments at the Glasgow Western Infirmary. He was then awarded a Tyler scholarship to study homoeopathy at the clinic of Dr James Tyler Kent in Chicago. Weir returned with the firm conviction that Kent was the greatest exponent in the world of Samuel Hahneman's homoeopathic philosophy and determined to put his materia medica into practice, in spite of criticism from some of his senior colleagues in England. He set up in practice at 47B Welbeck Street in London, and soon acquired a reputation that led to his appointment in 1910 to the staff of the London Homoeopathic Hospital. In later years he acted as a consultant to homoeopathic hospitals in Bristol, Birmingham, Bromley, and Eastbourne. However, he never allowed his success in private practice to interfere with his academic responsibilities for teaching, lecturing, and initiating clinical research at his hospitals.

In 1911 Weir acted as assistant secretary to the eighth international homoeopathic congress in London and in the same year he was appointed Compton Burnett professor of materia medica by the Homoeopathic Society. In 1916 he was appointed secretary of the society. In the following years he devoted much time and energy to promoting the society's growth and influence, and when in 1943 it became a faculty with responsibilities for teaching, training, and examining candidates for its fellowship (FFHom) he served two terms as its first president. Five years later the royal charter was granted to the Homoeopathic Hospital. During the important post-war changes that led to the establishment of the National Health Service Weir fought hard to ensure that, although the hospital was transferred to the Ministry of Health, the practice of homoeopathy and postgraduate courses in that subject should continue as before. His long association with the Royal Homoeopathic Hospital was recognized when one of its wards was named after him. When the Homoeopathic Research and Educational Trust was founded, Weir became a trustee and played a leading part in the drafting of the Faculty of Homoeopathy Act (1950).

Weir's connection with the royal family, whose interest in homoeopathy was well known, began in 1923, when he was appointed physician-in-ordinary to the prince of Wales. The royal connection continued until his retirement in 1968. From 1929 to 1938 he was physician to Queen Maud of Norway and from 1936 onwards to Queen

Mary, the duke and duchess of York (later George VI and Queen Elizabeth), and to Princess Elizabeth (later Elizabeth II). Many royal honours were conferred upon him: CVO (1926), KCVO (1932), knight grand cross of the order of St Olaf of Norway (1938), and GCVO (1939). In 1949 he was awarded a unique accolade by the king, the Royal Victorian Chain, a 'pre-eminent mark by the Sovereign of esteem and affection towards such persons as His Majesty especially desired to honour'.

Weir was a bachelor, and a traditionalist with firm religious convictions. His conservatism spilled over into his personal lifestyle. His annual golfing holiday at Gullane in Scotland took him to the same bedroom in the same hotel year after year. For all that he was a superb mixer, joining in the many activities of the medical societies and clubs to which he belonged in Glasgow, Ayrshire, and London. He was a great raconteur and delighted in accosting his friends with the question 'Have you heard this one?' He always carried a little notebook as an aide-mémoire for his stories. His patients were very fond of him, for though he was strict about the details of any treatment he prescribed he always showed a great understanding and kindness. He is reported to have told the prince of Wales on one occasion, 'No cigars, four cigarettes a day, and not more than two small slices of beef for lunch.' He was punctilious to a degree and enjoyed spending time making sure that any bulletins issued by his colleagues and himself concerning any of his royal patients were absolutely correct in wording and allowed for no misunderstanding.

Weir contributed many papers to academic journals and was in great demand as a lecturer. His publications included 'Samuel Hahnemann and his influence on medical thought' (*Proceedings of the Royal Society of Medicine*, 26, 1932–33). Weir occupied a pre-eminent place in the history of homoeopathic medicine in Britain. For those who knew him personally he was the epitome of the traditional compassionate physician. Weir died on 17 April 1971 at St George's Nursing Home, St George's Square, London.   JOHN PEEL, rev.

Sources *BMJ* (1 May 1971), 282–3 · *The Times* (19 April 1971) · private information (1986) · personal knowledge (1986) · *WWW*
Likenesses W. Stoneman, photograph, 1949, NPG · J. Gunn, portrait, Royal London Homoeopathic Hospital · photograph, repro. in *The Times*
Wealth at death £349,367: probate, 17 May 1971, *CGPLA Eng. & Wales*

Weir, Thomas (d. 1670), criminal and reputed sorcerer, was the son of Thomas Weir of Kirkton, near Carluke in Lanarkshire. At the time of his trial in 1670 he was described as 'past the age of 70' and 'of great age' (Scott-Moncrieff, 2.10–11). The family land was sold in 1636, and in February 1642 Weir married Isobel Mein, the widow of John Bourdoun, an Edinburgh merchant, entitling himself to become a merchant burgess. He served in the Scottish army in Ireland in 1642–3, and in 1644 was a major in the Scots army in England.

When the radical covenanting kirk party regime seized power in 1648 it was decided to raise a guard to protect Edinburgh, and on 25 October Weir was given command of this burgh guard. His duties included guarding parliament from January to March 1649, but on 9 May orders were given for paying off Weir and his men. It was later to be asserted that he had had charge of the royalist marquess of Montrose during his imprisonment before his execution in May 1650, and had treated him harshly. Certainly Weir remained closely associated with security in the burgh, and when in 1650 levies were ordered to counter the anticipated English invasion he was appointed major (third in command) of the burgh's forces (7 August).

In 1650–51 the Church of Scotland split into two conflicting factions and Weir gave his allegiance to the uncompromising remonstrant minority. His zeal survived the restoration of the monarchy in 1660, and he was by then living in the West Bow of Edinburgh, an area favoured by the 'saints'—those who retained allegiance to the later generally discredited covenants. James Fraser (minister of Wardlaw) recalled seeing him in 1660: 'His garb was still a clock [cloak], and somewhat dark, and [he] never went without his staffe. He was a tall black [dark] man, and ordinarily looked down to the ground: a grim countenance and a big nose.' His prowess in prayer led some to call him 'Angelicall Thomas' (Fraser, fols. 156r–158r; Wilson, 2.158).

In 1670 Weir suddenly began to exhibit terror at the word 'burn', presumably in fear of the fires of hell, and began to confess to many sexual crimes. At first the authorities regarded him as mad, but after he had been examined by physicians he was judged to be sane. On 9 April 1670 he was tried before the justiciary court for 'Incests, Adulteries, Fornications, and Bestialitys'. Charges included attempted incest with his sister Jean when she was aged about ten, and actual between 1620 (when she was sixteen) and 1624, at the family 'House of Wicketshaw', the relationship continuing intermittently for many years; incest with his stepdaughter Margaret Bourdoun; habitual adulteries, persisted in even when 'he was of great age'; bestiality with a mare in 1651 at Newmylns in Ayrshire, and lying with 'Cows and other beasts'. His outward piety and professions of purity beyond other men were denounced as aggravating such offences (Scott-Moncrieff, 2.10–11).

Weir, by now sunk in despair, failed to plead directly to the charges, although he said that 'he thinks himself guilty of the forsaid Crimes and cannot deny them' (Scott-Moncrieff, 2.12), but his confessions had been detailed, specific and consistent, and some aspects of them were corroborated by confessions by his sister Jean, who had lived with him. She also related how they had once, back in the 1620s, been discovered committing incest by their sister Margaret. Margaret confirmed catching her brother and sister in the act. Otherwise no independent witnesses were called, but there was evidence that the 1651 bestiality incident had been observed and reported by a witness at the time, but that no charges had been brought through lack of supporting evidence.

Thomas Weir was found guilty on all charges, and 'not being able to travell for age, was dragg'd on a sled' on 11

April to the Gallowlee, between Edinburgh and Leith, where he was strangled at the stake and then burnt, dying in 'despair' (Scott-Moncrieff, 2.14). Jean was convicted of incest and sorcery, to which she had confessed, and was hanged in the Grassmarket on 12 April, trying to tear her clothes off so 'she might die with all the shame she could' (Scott-Moncrieff, 2.14).

The confessions of Thomas and Jean Weir may have exaggerated their misdeeds, but they may be accepted as basically truthful. Their confessions in old age may simply have been the expression of long suppressed guilt which became intolerable, but it seems possible that the Weirs had fallen into the antinomian heresy, and believed that, as the elect of God predestined for salvation, they could do no wrong—but then lost conviction in their own election and collapsed into wild despair.

The story of Major Weir's crimes was exploited for propaganda purposes as sensational evidence that the supposedly godly presbyterian dissidents in Scotland were immoral hypocrites. In time the propaganda value of his case vanished, but his name survived in popular tales of outstanding wickedness, their crimes being usually bowdlerized as unsuitable subject matter for oral or literary treatment. Weir was transformed into a sorcerer, though he had never been charged with any offences relating to the supernatural, the surviving tales drawing on his sister Jean's confessions rather than his own. Her confessions to witchcraft, including dealings with 'the Queen of the Fairie, meaning the Devil' (Scott-Moncrieff, 2.11), alleged that Thomas too had had dealings with the devil, owning a magical staff that gave him power. As a result, even contemporary reports attributed 'horrible witchcraft' as well as sexual offences to 'that monster of men and reproach of mankind' (J. Lauder, *Journals*, 1900, 232).

A number of literary figures took an interest in the Weir legend in this form, including Sir Walter Scott, who refers to Weir in *Redgauntlet* (1824). His friend Charles Kirkpatrick Sharpe, however, made it clear in correspondence with Scott that those who exploited stories of Weir as a warlock were well aware of his real crimes: Sharpe refers to Byron's *Manfred*, with its themes of the supernatural and incest combined, and suggests that, as with Weir so with Byron, incest would lead on to bestiality. Lady Scott, however, was evidently spared such knowledge of Weir's sexual offences, for she called her husband's walking stick 'Major Weir' (*Journal of Sir Walter Scott*, 270), oblivious to the phallic resonances of the staff which had given Weir his power.   DAVID STEVENSON

Sources D. Stevenson, 'Major Weir: a justified sinner?', *Scottish Studies*, 16 (1972), 161–73 • W. G. Scott-Moncrieff, ed., *The records of the proceedings of the justiciary court, Edinburgh, 1661–1678*, 2 vols., Scottish History Society, 48–9 (1905) • J. Fraser, 'A collection of providential passages', 1678, NL Scot., Adv. MS 32.4.7 • M. Wood, ed., *Extracts from the records of the burgh of Edinburgh, 1642–1655*, [9] (1938) • G. Hickes, *Ravillac redivivus* (1678) • W. Roughead, *Twelve Scottish trials* (1913) • G. Sinclair, *Satan's invisible world discovered* (1685); repr. with supplements by T. Stevenson (1871) • H. Arnot, *A collection of celebrated criminal trials in Scotland* (1785) • H. Paton, ed., *The register of marriages for the parish of Edinburgh, 1595–1700*, Scottish RS, old ser., 27 (1905) • D. Wilson, *Memorials of Edinburgh*, 2 vols. (1878), vol. 2, p. 158 • *The journal of Sir Walter Scott*, ed. W. E. K. Anderson (1972), 270

Weir, William (1802–1858), journalist, was born on 9 February 1802 at Mount Hamilton, St Quivox parish, Ayrshire, the only child of Oswald Weir, factor to the Oswalds of Auchencruive, pre-eminent local landowners, and of May Denholm (b. 1775) of Holywell, Dumfriesshire. He was orphaned by the age of thirteen, and the Oswalds became his guardians. After leaving Ayr Academy in 1817 with the reputation of being 'talented, honourable, kind-hearted, somewhat eccentric, and a most rapacious reader' (*DNB*) Weir studied arts and law at the universities of St Andrews (1817–20), Edinburgh (1820–22; 1825–6), and Göttingen (1824–5). Although admitted to the Faculty of Advocates in Edinburgh on 31 January 1827, he soon plunged into literary work and journalism. Reminiscences of student life in Germany provided material in 1829–30 for serialized articles in the *Edinburgh Literary Journal*. This introduced him into the publishing stable of the radical bookseller William Tait, whose *Edinburgh Magazine*, launched appropriately in 1832, accepted articles by Weir promoting liberalism at home and abroad.

Political credentials established, Weir was engaged in February 1833 as editor of the *Glasgow Argus*, a new organ published by Glasgow's dominant whig clique. During six years Weir brought journalistic flair and rising circulation figures, but also propagated a radical gospel of further constitutional change (including the ballot and suffrage extension), religious dissent, national education, and, above all, total repeal of the corn laws.

Weir's energies were not monopolized: he married Ellen Reid, daughter of John Reid, advocate, on 18 December 1837, lectured at Glasgow Mechanics' Institute, and in the same decade engaged to duel, with the proprietor of the tory *Glasgow Chronicle*, John Douglas of Barloch, but was fortunately interrupted. More significantly, from 1833 he laid the Scottish foundations of the anti-cornlaw agitation, which combined with Cobden and Manchester free-traders to create the Anti-Corn Law League in 1838–9. Initially Weir was one of its foremost strategists. However, his advocacy in 1839, through the *Argus*, of schismatic tactics by radicals against whigs in support of an uncompromising free trade programme provoked dismissal by his exasperated whig employers.

Weir fulfilled a long-standing ambition by moving to London. He was admitted as a barrister to the Middle Temple on 4 March 1840, but literary and journalistic commissions soon took precedence. Through Charles Knight, he contributed in 1841–4 to Knight's *London* and *The Pictorial History of England during the Reign of George the Third*. Contemporaneously, the Society for the Diffusion of Useful Knowledge employed him on the *Penny Cyclopaedia* and the *Biographical Dictionary*. He also wrote for *The Spectator* and was employed for one year in 1841 to edit the *Journal of the Royal Geographical Society*. Biographical and geographical assignments suited his wide education, encyclopaedic interests, and magpie approach.

Weir re-entered full-time political journalism appropriately on the eve of corn law repeal in 1846, when he was recruited by Charles Dickens to be railway and colonial editor on the launching of the *Daily News*. In 1854 he became one of Dickens's successors as general editor of the paper. He had 'at last obtained a position in which [he hoped] to be of some use', but felt that had he attained it when he was 'a little younger and stronger', he 'would have spoken with more confidence' (W. Weir to Lord Brougham, 1856, Brougham MS 29,792). His tenure coincided nevertheless with several major developments abroad, including the Crimean War, the Indian mutiny, and crises in Europe. Weir's endorsement of liberal causes in Italy and Hungary, and of the dissenting cause of national education at home marked his period as editor. He was equally lauded, however, by political friend and foe alike for the high moral tone, professional standards, and gentlemanly conduct which he brought to the journal.

Although suffering indifferent health for years, Weir died as the result of an accident that precipitated a strangulated hernia, on 15 September 1858, at his home, 4 Hunter Street, Brunswick Square, London. He was buried on 21 September at Kensal Green cemetery. Weir's career as a whole reflected the attraction of journalism as a source of political influence through the expanding Victorian fourth estate. KENNETH J. CAMERON

Sources K. J. Cameron, 'Weir of the *News*: yesterday's mediaman', *Library Review*, 26 (1977), 29–38 · K. J. Cameron, 'William Weir and the origins of the "Manchester league" in Scotland, 1833–1839', *SHR*, 58 (1979), 70–91 · K. J. Cameron, 'Finance, politics and editorial independence in the early Victorian provincial press: the case of the *Glasgow Argus*, 1833–1847', *Publishing History*, 5 (1979), 79–103 · R. M. W. Cowan, *The newspaper in Scotland: a study of its first expansion, 1815–1860* (1946) · J. Hedderwick, *Backward glances, or, Some personal recollections* (1891) · parish register (birth), General Register Office for Scotland, Edinburgh, St Quivox, 612/1/1, 16 Feb 1801 · parish register (marriage), General Register Office for Scotland, Edinburgh, St Quivox, 685.1/65, 18 Dec 1837 · register of deaths, General Register House, London, St Giles and St George, 17 Sept 1858 · minute book of Glasgow Mechanics' Institute, 1834–52, University of Strathclyde, C.1.2 · *DNB* · LMA, DL/T/41/26 · UCL, Brougham MSS

Archives NL Scot., John Hill Burton MSS · RGS, archives · U. Birm. L., letters to Harriet Martineau · UCL, Brougham MSS · UCL, letters to Society for the Diffusion of Useful Knowledge · W. Sussex RO, Cobden MSS

Weir, William Douglas, first Viscount Weir (1877–1959), industrialist and public servant, was born on 12 May 1877, in a top flat at Albert Crescent, Crosshill, Glasgow, the eldest of three children of James Weir (1843–1920), and his wife, Mary, formerly Richmond (1848–1931), daughter of William Douglas, blacksmith. His paternal grandmother was the child of Robert *Burns's illegitimate daughter Elizabeth Paton. James Weir and his brother George had in 1873 launched a marine engineering and maintenance company; James patented several inventions (including the Weir feed-pump), which in 1886 the brothers began to manufacture in a machine shop and smithy at Cathcart near Glasgow. These premises were developed into the Holm Foundry, and the business of G. and J. Weir was formed into a limited liability company in 1895.

Weir was educated at Allan Glen's school in Glasgow

William Douglas Weir, first Viscount Weir (1877–1959), by unknown photographer

and at Glasgow high school. At the age of sixteen he entered an apprenticeship in his family's business. He was successively director (1898), managing director (1902–15), and chairman (1910–53) of G. and J. Weir. Its success during his managing directorship owed much to standardization and was based on a controversial system of payments by results for the workforce. William Weir was never a friend of collective bargaining. He was an energetic, masterful, tenacious, and self-sufficient man who drove himself hard. His organizing powers were exceptional. By 1914 the company's annual sales of main and auxiliary condensers, air-pumps, feed-pumps, oil-fuel pumps, fire and bilge pumps, evaporators, and distilling machinery were worth £750,000. Although he discarded daily managerial responsibility after 1915, he superintended the company's survival during the poor trading years of the 1920s and oversaw its resurgence after 1937.

Weir's strengths as an industrialist are indicated in a memorandum on nationalization prepared by him for the coal industry commission under John, Viscount Sankey. Weir believed that 'most successful enterprises in the history of industry' were 'directed by individual instinct, an instinct almost of adventure', and he deprecated the civil-service mentality:

> Responsibility is avoided on account of the fear of criticism, thus spoiling initiative. The sporting and emulative instinct does not exist on account of the delay in taking action. Decisions are frequently made of a half-hearted character dependent on approval of others. Everything must be judged from every point of view.

This was not Weir's way (Weir MSS, 4/3, 12 May 1919).

By 1913 work on warships accounted for two-thirds of Weir's work and consequently he had strong views about the organization of munitions production after the outbreak of war in 1914. David Lloyd George invited him to join his central advisory committee on munitions, and he was appointed (unpaid) director of munitions in Scotland in July 1915. Weir relished the challenge, and in one day incurred £3 million of expenditure without authority. The greatest obstacle to increased output was in the labour field. As a way of obtaining 'dilution' (the use of unskilled labour, including women) Weir suggested the appointment of dilution commissioners to arbitrate between employers and employees on government contracts. This earned him the lifelong suspicion of some Scottish trade unionists.

In May 1916 Weir urged Lloyd George to create a single Air Board under the Ministry of Munitions to supersede the Royal Flying Corps and the Royal Naval Air Service. After his nomination as controller of aeronautical supplies and as a member of the Air Board (December 1916), he was knighted (February 1917). Christopher Addison, a prominent member of Lloyd George's cabinet, liked Weir's 'cheery and vigorous personality', and later wrote of this appointment that Weir 'rejoiced in a task that involved workshop organisation and technical knowledge' (Addison, 2.92). As a sequel to the German bombing of London in July 1917, legislation was passed leading to the creation of the Air Ministry in January 1918 and the Royal Air Force in April 1918. Weir was director-general of aircraft production and a member of the Air Council from November 1917; he succeeded Harold Harmsworth, Viscount Rothermere, as president of the Air Council in April 1918. This appointment, which Alfred, Viscount Milner, had urged months earlier, was widely welcomed: 'Weir was a right good man at his job' (Repington, 2.282). He was sworn of the privy council (27 April 1918) and created Baron Weir, of Eastwood, Renfrewshire (26 June 1918).

Weir was an early advocate of strategic bombing and of an air force independent of military or naval control. He planned to create a huge force of bombers by 1919, but the armistice made this unnecessary, and he resigned as minister in December 1918. John Salmond in August 1918 had judged 'that Weir is doing well and has plenty of imagination' (Repington, 2.362). Similarly Addison praised 'that charming and efficient, if sometimes volcanic, Secretary of State for Air' as 'alert, nimble, friendly, capable … one of the real successes of the war among businessmen in government' (Addison, 2.174). Weir never desired political advancement. As he told Winston Churchill in 1936, 'I have avoided political power and have confined myself to helping by advice in particular directions. My reason is simply this. Official responsibility covering political exposition would kill me' (Gilbert, 156).

Weir continued, however, to be a valued governmental adjunct. He chaired an advisory committee on civil aviation which recommended a government subsidy for two years to companies operating regular air services (1919–20). Next he chaired an advisory committee on amalgamating the common services of the navy, army, and air force

(1922–3) and a departmental committee on economies in the fighting services (1923). He was a member of the committee chaired by the marquess of Salisbury on co-ordination between the navy, army, and air force and on the desirability of a Ministry of Defence (1923); and he was the most influential member of its sub-committee, under the first earl of Balfour, which preserved the independence of the Fleet Air Arm from Admiralty control. Weir was a pragmatist who did not shrink from state intervention where private capitalism had failed. Thus the committee on electricity supply which he chaired (1924–5) recommended the institution of a government-appointed central electricity board to build a national grid and standardize frequencies. The resultant Electricity (Supply) Act of 1926 seemed almost socialistic. Similarly, state subsidies were adopted on the advice of Weir's confidential report to the government on British north Atlantic shipping (1932). Weir was industrial adviser to the British delegation at the Imperial Conference at Ottawa (1932), served on the government committee on trade and employment (1932–4), and on a committee on Scottish hydro-electric development (1941–2).

In the rearmament crisis of the 1930s Weir was critically placed. He was adviser to the principal supply officers' committee from 1933 and insisted upon membership of the defence policy and requirements committee from 1935. On this committee he was an articulate disciple of Sir Hugh Trenchard's gospel of strategic bombing, and of Basil Liddell Hart's theories on the pre-eminence of tanks over infantry in the coming war. Sir Philip Cunliffe-Lister, later Viscount Swinton, and John Baird, Viscount Stonehaven, were Weir's closest confidants. When Cunliffe-Lister became secretary of state for air in 1935 (shortly before he was made a viscount), Weir was appointed as his adviser. Without staff, an office, formal authority, or official responsibility, Weir now reached the acme of his career. Lord Rothermere wrote of his work in co-ordinating the service ministries in February 1936, 'It looks as if Weir is going to be the big figure of the Government. The fact that he holds no political office should give him great power' (Gilbert, 56).

Weir's standing in public affairs depended on his personal influence within a small set of highly placed men. He was neither easily impressed nor jealous. On the few occasions when he involved himself in departmental intrigues, it was in the cause of policies and not personalities. Although objective in his approach to procurement matters he was less cool and lucid during the Admiralty's resumed attempt to take control of the Fleet Air Arm (1937). Weir and Swinton constituted a powerful partnership with the former concentrating on the industrial side of rearmament. The system of 'shadow aircraft factories' was created by the energetic Weir, with Swinton's shrewd political backing. Weir was additionally an adviser to the government on measures necessary for national defence (1937), but he resigned in May 1938 when Neville Chamberlain dismissed Swinton. In 1939 Weir became director-general of explosives at the Ministry of Supply, but again resigned, on the appointment in June

1941 of Lord Beaverbrook, whom he disliked, as minister. For some months of 1942 he was chairman of the Tank Board.

Weir was chairman of the Anglo-Scottish Sugar Beet Corporation (1924), and a director of Lloyds Bank (1928–38), Imperial Chemical Industries (1928–53), International Nickel (1928–59), and Shell Transport and Trading (1939). In 1923 Weir determined to provide standardized, mass-produced, steel houses to alleviate housing shortages and unemployment. Some 3000 houses were built at his Cardonald factory, but his scheme was opposed by vested interests and abandoned in 1927–8. Weir was created GCB in 1934 and elevated to a viscountcy in June 1938. He was a founder and later president of the Royal Scottish Automobile Club and was elected to the Other Club (1932). He received an honorary doctorate from Glasgow University (1919), the freedom of the City of London (1957), and high foreign decorations. Among other benefactions he gave £15,000 to the National Playing Fields Association (1953).

In 1904 Weir married Alice Blanche (1882–1959), daughter of Jessie and John MacConnachie, a Glaswegian solicitor. They had two sons and one daughter. He died on 2 July 1959, at Eastwood Park, Giffnock, Renfrewshire; his wife died just four months later, on 9 November.

RICHARD DAVENPORT-HINES

Sources Churchill College, Cambridge, Weir MSS · W. J. Reader, *Architect of air power: the life of the first Viscount Weir of Eastwood* (1968) · C. Addison, *Politics from within*, 2 vols. (1924) · C. À Court Repington, *The First World War*, 2 vols. (1920) · M. Gilbert, ed., *Winston S. Churchill*, companion vol. 5/3 (1982) · *The Times* (3 July 1959) · *Glasgow Herald* (3 July 1959) · Lord Gorell, *One man, many parts* (1956) · Lord Swinton, *I remember* (1948) · F. Sykes, *From many angles* (1942) · A. Boyle, *Trenchard* (1962) · GEC, *Peerage* · *CGPLA Eng. & Wales* (1959) · *DNB* · *DSBB* · d. cert.
Archives CAC Cam., corresp. and papers · U. Glas. L., corresp. and papers | Bodl. Oxf., corresp. with Viscount Addison · HLRO, letters to David Lloyd George · PRO, Ministry of Supply and Air Ministry MSS
Likenesses W. Stoneman, photograph, 1919, NPG · photograph, 1928, repro. in Reader, *Architect of air power*, facing p. 129 · T. Dugdale, oils, c.1939, Weir Group plc, Glasgow · L. Knight, oils, priv. coll. · C. Orde, oils, Royal Aeronautical Society, London · photograph, NPG [*see illus.*] · photographs, repro. in Reader, *Architect of air power*
Wealth at death £3,304,392 17s. 6d.: confirmation, 17 July 1959, *CCI*

Weiss, Roberto (1906–1969), Italian scholar and author, was born in Milan on 22 January 1906, the only son of Eugenio Natale Weiss and of Rita Fattori; his family was of Austrian origin and had settled in Italy. He received a classical education in Rome at the *Liceo* E. Q. Visconti and the *Liceo* Umberto I. After his final school examinations, he went, on the advice of his father, to England to read law and prepare himself for a diplomatic career; in 1928 he matriculated at Oxford as a non-collegiate student (later St Catherine's Society) and was awarded an honours degree in jurisprudence in 1932. But the study of law had not appealed to him, and, having worked as temporary assistant in the department of Western manuscripts of the Bodleian Library in 1932–3, he began in 1934 postgraduate

studies in the faculty of modern history. His DPhil thesis, submitted in 1938, was published in 1941 (*Humanism in England during the Fifteenth Century*; rev. edns, 1955, 1967). Sometimes styled count (probably of the Holy Roman empire), he was naturalized a British subject on 30 May 1934; on 18 July 1936 he married at St Aloysius Roman Catholic Church, Oxford, Eve (*b.* 1907), daughter of William Raymond Cecil, with whom he had four children.

In 1938, Weiss joined the Italian department of University College, London, as assistant lecturer, and apart from his military service in the Royal Artillery from 1942 to 1945 he taught at University College until his death. From 1946 he was professor of Italian and head of department. Through his teaching and his many contacts with British and Italian scholars, he made his department a leading centre of Italian studies. In 1969 the British Academy awarded him the Serena medal for Italian studies.

When Weiss wrote his book on humanism in England, aspects of the subject had been dealt with by historians of fifteenth-century England, and a comprehensive survey based on printed sources had recently been published. Weiss, however, not only used a wealth of manuscript material, but also broke new ground by studying early English humanism in the context of the classical revival in Italy and by examining both the influence of Italian humanists on English intellectual life, and the careers of English students at Italian universities, who thus participated in the humanist movement in Italy.

It was this movement which after Weiss's return to London in 1945 came to occupy the centre of his scholarly work, but with a shift back to the early fourteenth century. His pioneering inaugural lecture, *The Dawn of Humanism in Italy*, mapped out in 1947 a new direction of his studies, which was again to prove innovating. Only scant attention had hitherto been paid to what came to be called Italian prehumanism, and his studies on Lovato Lovati, Geremia da Montagnone, Geri d'Arezzo, and Albertino Mussato opened new perspectives; but he also published in 1950 an unknown version of a chapter of Petrarch's *Trionfo della fama* which he had discovered in the British Museum. It was the most spectacular of his innumerable discoveries in the manuscript collections of British and Italian libraries, the former in the footsteps of his mentor Cesare Foligno. He told the author of this biography that many of his discoveries went back to his systematic reading, on the train journeys between Henley-on-Thames, where he lived, and London, of Mazzatinti's massive inventories of manuscripts in Italian libraries. But it was only his vast and profound knowledge of the contemporary literature which made these discoveries possible. At the same time, Weiss became increasingly interested in a hitherto little explored field, the knowledge of Greek and the translations from Greek in fourteenth-century Italy, as well as in France and England; his essays on this subject, mainly from the years 1951 to 1953, were republished in 1977 under the title *Medieval and Humanist Greek*, which also included a bibliography of his publications.

Ever since his schooldays, Weiss had collected ancient

coins and medals; by the time of his death, his Renaissance medals formed a scholarly private collection unrivalled in Britain, which he used for his pioneering studies of Renaissance collectors and collections. While studying the life and writings of humanists, he had taken notes on the humanists' interest in classical antiquities and their survival in Renaissance Italy; during the last years of his life, he drew on the vast amount of material he had gathered for yet another groundbreaking work. Completed in 1968, *The Renaissance Discovery of Classical Antiquity* (1969; 2nd edn 1988) constitutes a unique synthesis. While earlier studies of this subject, many of them by Weiss, had concentrated on a few towns, foremost among them Rome, and on single humanists, the book embraces the whole of Italy within a span of time which stretches from the early fourteenth to the sixteenth century. Combining consummate scholarship with economy of exposition, it discusses the rise of classical archaeology and epigraphy, the development of the topography of ancient Rome, the collections of Roman and later also of Greek antiquities, and other aspects of the new and enthusiastic interest in the surviving remains of classical antiquity.

Like his other writings, this book testifies to one of the pervasive traits of Weiss's scholarship, his insistence on the absolute priority of contemporary sources. Another was his reluctance to attack other scholars. This absence of polemic in his writings, together with his endless generosity in sharing his knowledge, were among Weiss's most striking and endearing characteristics. He writes of Pope Pius II, the humanist Enea Silvio Piccolomini, that 'he bore lightly his massive erudition'. The same judgement could also be applied to him.

Notwithstanding his complete integration into English ways of life and his absorption of the cultural traditions of his adopted country, Weiss remained mindful of his intellectual roots in Italy, cemented by his many friendships with Italian scholars—a dual bond which he chose to indicate, in his lapidary style, by alternatively signing, in his publications in England, his name as Roberto, in those in Italy, as Robert. He died on 10 August 1969 at his home, 44 St Andrews Road, Henley-on-Thames, Oxfordshire, of a heart attack. He left his papers and offprints to the Warburg Institute, University of London; his collection of Renaissance medals is on long loan to the Fitzwilliam Museum, Cambridge. NICOLAI RUBINSTEIN

Sources C. Fahy, 'Roberto Weiss (1906–1969)', *Lettere Italiane*, 22 (1970), 252–6 · O. Skutsch, 'Roberto Weiss: a memorial address given at the university church of Christ the King, London, on Wednesday, 22 October 1969', *Italian Studies*, 25 (1970), 1–5 · *WW* (1968) · *The Times* (16 Aug 1969) · personal knowledge (2004) · private information (2004) · Oxf. UA · m. cert. · certificate of naturalization, PRO, HO 334/56
Archives Bodl. Oxf., letters
Likenesses photograph, repro. in Skutsch, 'Roberto Weiss', 25, facing p. 1
Wealth at death £11,340: probate, 26 Nov 1969, *CGPLA Eng. & Wales*

Weiss, Willoughby Hunter (1820–1867), singer and composer, the son of Willoughby Gaspard Weiss, a flute

Willoughby Hunter Weiss (1820–1867), by Southwell Brothers [in *Desert Flower*]

teacher and music publisher in Liverpool, was born there on 2 April 1820. He was a pupil of George Smart and Michael Balfe, and made his first public appearance at a concert of his own at Liverpool on 5 May 1842. His opera début was as Oroveso in Bellini's *Norma* at Dublin on 2 July 1842, and he subsequently became a member of the Pyne-Harrison and other opera companies, singing bass. His first London appearance was as Count Rodolfo in Bellini's *La sonnambula* on 26 December 1842 at the Princess's Theatre. He had a distinguished reputation as a singer of opera, and he excelled in oratorio, which he first performed at the Gloucester festival in 1844. On 15 September 1845 he married Georgina Ansell Barrett (1826–1880), a soprano and the daughter of a music teacher in Gloucester. They had one daughter, Georgina Angelique.

Weiss's chief claim to distinction was, however, as the composer of 'The Village Blacksmith', a setting of Longfellow's words which he wrote about 1854. It was extraordinarily popular and remains well known. After a firm of music publishers refused to buy the copyright for £5, he published the song himself, thus earning a considerable income for himself and his family for the next forty years. He composed many other songs and ballads, and arranged a piano edition of Weber's mass in G, but none enjoyed the success of 'The Village Blacksmith'. Weiss died at his home, St George's Villa, Gloucester Road, Regent's Park, London, on 24 October 1867, and was buried in Highgate cemetery. His widow remarried in 1872.

F. G. EDWARDS, *rev.* ANNE PIMLOTT BAKER

Sources *New Grove* · Brown & Stratton, *Brit. mus.* · *GM*, 4th ser., 4 (1867), 828 · *Musical World* (26 Oct 1867), 732 · *Musical World* (2 Nov 1867), 749 · Grove, *Dict. mus.*
Archives U. Cam., Pendlebury Library of Music, diaries, programmes, and scrapbooks
Likenesses Southwell Brothers, photograph (in *Desert flower*), NPG [*see illus.*] · wood-engraving, NPG; repro. in *ILN*, 51 (1867)
Wealth at death under £2000: administration, 20 Jan 1868, *CGPLA Eng. & Wales*

Weisz, Victor [*pseud.* Vicky] (**1913–1966**), caricaturist and cartoonist, was born in Berlin on 25 April 1913, the son of Desider Weisz and his wife, Isabella. His parents were Hungarian Jews and he was registered as Hungarian. As a child he showed aptitude as an artist and attended the Berlin Art School before his father died in 1928, which ended his schooling and compelled him to become the family breadwinner. He found work on the Berliners' *12 Uhr Blatt*, and he published his first anti-Hitler cartoon as a precocious fifteen-year-old. He was a successful caricaturist of theatrical and sporting personalities but his political drawings attracted public attention and the resentment of the Nazis. After the Reichstag fire he lost his job and was hounded by the Gestapo; only his Hungarian passport saved him and his family from deportation to a concentration camp. Friends arranged an escape to England. In 1938 the *Daily Herald*, the paper of the Labour Party with which his political sympathies lay, was looking for a successor to Will Dyson as staff cartoonist. He was given a brief trial but was unsuccessful, as he could barely speak English and his humour was alien to the British. He became a freelance, relying on the indulgence and instruction of professional friends, of whom, with his engaging personality, he had many.

In 1939 Weisz was introduced to Gerald Barry, editor of the *News Chronicle*, who recognized the verve and peculiar talent of his drawings but also their limitations. The drawings were boisterously funny but lacked insights into the whimsicality of British humour, the eccentricities of British manners and thought, and the contradictions of British politics. Barry, however, gave him a retainer to do conventional illustrations and pocket sketches. With a patient editor and much friendly advice, he was given a crash course in British humour. He was an earnest student, setting himself to read the works of Shakespeare to discover the tragicomic characteristics of the Elizabethan 'clown'. Barry set him his homework—*Alice in Wonderland*, Dickens, Edward Lear, A. A. Milne, back numbers of *Punch*, and *Wisden*. (For the rest of his life he was to ask plaintively, 'What's funny about cricket?') He listened avidly to the BBC, not only to improve his English and to follow the news but also to dissect the weekly wireless broadcast *ITMA* (or *It's That Man Again!*) of Tommy Handley. He frequented the gallery of the House of Commons and read *Hansard*, and also applied himself to the study of political

history, the party system, and the uncontinental character of the trade unions. With Richard Winnington, the film critic and fellow cartoonist, he engrossed himself in films, watching the throwaway lines of British understatement and self-ridicule. He discovered pantomime, Gilbert and Sullivan, the football terrace, the dog track, the public bar and the legal bar, and cockneys with their rhyming slang. After two years, word-perfect in English, he could have lectured (as he did later) on the nature of humour itself—wit, wisecrack, satire, music-hall burlesque, pun, spoonerisms, slapstick, drollery, and situation comedy. All of them he had been rehearsing on the drawing-board.

In 1941 Weisz graduated as staff cartoonist on the *News Chronicle*. Still an enemy alien (he was not granted British nationality until 1946) he was now a British humorist. In wartime circumstances in which sensitive ministers had fairly drastic powers to deal with such people, he was as critical, satirical, funny, or pungent about personalities and policies as his emotional ebullience prompted and his protective editor allowed. He was frequently denounced as an enemy alien, subject to drafting into the Pioneer Corps. He was not easy to handle then or after the war. Barry was to write a preface to *The Editor Regrets* (1947), a book of his cartoons rejected for good, or sometimes timid, reasons. When Barry left the editorial chair, Weisz became more and more dissatisfied. After fourteen years in which he had established himself as an outstanding cartoonist, he resigned from the *News Chronicle* when it did not publish a bitter cartoon on Kenya.

While he deferred to David Low as a finer draughtsman, Weisz had been vying with him in popularity and, upon Low's semi-retirement, succeeded him as the best cartoonist in Britain. He later joined the *Daily Mirror*, which then had one of the largest daily newspaper sales in the world and which gave him unlimited scope for his left-wing sympathies. In 1958 he moved to the *Evening Standard*. Lord Beaverbrook, whom he had regularly drawn as a diminutive gnome in crusader's armour, had pursued him as he had once pursued Low. As in Low's case, he gave him a contract guaranteeing him complete freedom of expression. Weisz, who was quite incorruptible in terms of money or of flattery, could not resist the opportunity of preaching to the unconverted, the Conservative readers of the *Evening Standard*. The incongruity exaggerated his effects: the Trojan horse stampeded the sacred cows.

From 1954 Weisz drew a regular weekly cartoon for the *New Statesman*. It was a labour of love for which his original fees barely covered his taxi fares. Every Monday morning he would shyly join the editorial board with an assortment of yard-square drawings, variants of his chosen commentary. He was never conceited about his drawings. He would pass them round one by one and wait for reactions—laughs, rather than comments, which, however, he never resented. He would modestly concede on details but never on his theme, for that was his 'editorial'. If he were challenged on a likeness he would produce his original from-the-life sketch and patiently explain how and why he had exaggerated the characteristics. He once said:

'I don't make fun of a face. I make fun of what is behind that face.'

According to Michael Foot (*Evening Standard*, 21 Feb 1956), Vicky (Weisz) became the fifth estate of the realm. No public personality, particularly his political friends when they faltered, escaped the ridicule of his pen. His caricatures were impudent rather than malicious: the totem pole Charles de Gaulle, the Micawberish Churchill, the zither-playing Attlee, the White Rabbit Eden, the street urchin Bevan, the Supermac (or, on occasion, Mac the Knife) Macmillan. Indignant supporters protested more often than did the victims, many of whom collected the originals. When he met President Truman, Vicky congratulated him on being more like his own cartoons than he had imagined.

Weisz's energy and output were prodigious. He had no gag men or caption writers, and he always found his own subjects. He loved good company, good music, and good theatre. He slept badly, relying on the sleeping-pills with which he eventually took his life. He rose at 5.45 every morning, breakfasted, listened to the news bulletin, read all the national dailies, and arrived at his newspaper office at 7.30. He would decide upon his topic, do a series of large-scale roughs, and by 3 p.m. deliver the finished drawing. When events were moving fast he would frequently substitute a fresh cartoon for later editions. He produced six cartoons a week for his newspaper as well as his weekly subject for the *New Statesman*. In addition he produced painstaking pen-and-ink portraits in the Spy/Beerbohm tradition for the *New Statesman* 'profiles'. These disproved his modesty about his draughtsmanship; they had the strength of line, incisiveness, and character penetration of Low at his best.

Weisz was small in height and build, with a large head, bald on top and shaggy on its back and sides. His lively, twinkling eyes were magnified by large, thick glasses. He was exactly like the miniature of himself which frequently figured in his cartoons as the puzzled little man bewildered by events. He was a boon companion, amusing in conversation and abundantly compassionate. Except when he was fighting editors or defending causes, mainly those of the poor and persecuted, he was mild-mannered and endearing. Even at the height of his career, however, he felt insecure. He was thoroughly worried about the way the world was going and was depressed by the political expediency of his friends in power. He drew a cartoon on the Labour government's acquiescence in the Vietnam War, took an overdose of sleeping-pills, and died at his home, 22 Upper Wimpole Street, London, in the early morning of 23 February 1966 at the age of fifty-two. His mother, who was eighty-six, died six weeks after from the shock of his death. Weisz had been married four times and had no children. Ingelore, his fourth wife, whom he had married in 1965, committed suicide on the ninth anniversary of his death. During his lifetime he had been sketched by his fellow cartoonists, and on that done by Abu, which was reproduced in *The Observer* (27 February 1966), he wrote 'too flattering'.   RITCHIE-CALDER, *rev.*

Sources *The Times* (24 Feb 1966) · G. Barry and Abu, 'One of the rare great ones', *The Observer* (27 Feb 1966) · M. Shulman, *Evening Standard* (31 Oct 1958) · Cassandra [W. Connor], *Daily Mirror* (1 Feb 1954) · C. H. Rolph, *Kingsley* (1973) · personal knowledge (1981) · private information (1981) · *CGPLA Eng. & Wales* (1966) · 'Vicky took overdose of drugs', *Daily Telegraph* (1 March 1966)
Archives U. Hull, Brynmor Jones L., illustrated letters to his second and fourth wives
Likenesses two photographs, 1950–51, Hult. Arch. · V. Weisz, self-portrait, pen, ink, and wash drawing, 1958, NPG · W. Suschitzky, bromide print, 1962, NPG · Abu, sketch, repro. in Barry and Abu, 'One of the rare great ones'
Wealth at death £22,322: probate, 20 June 1966, *CGPLA Eng. & Wales*

Weizmann, Chaim (1874–1952), Zionist leader and president of Israel, was born at Motol, near Pinsk, Belorussia, in the Jewish pale of settlement, the third child of Ozer Weizmann (1850?–1911) and his wife, Rachel-Leah Tchemerinsky (1852?–1939). He was one of fifteen children, twelve of whom (seven boys and five girls) survived to adulthood. Although the exact date of his birth is not known, it most probably took place on 27 November 1874. Ozer, a relatively prosperous timber transporter, was also a local personage of some note. A follower of the Enlightenment, he was elected *starosta* (headman) of Motol and at times served as its *chazan* (prayer leader) at the local synagogue. Although Chaim was brought up in a traditional Jewish environment, his father's bookshelves stocked works by Gorky and Tolstoy, scientific textbooks, even radical journals, as well as Zionist literature and modern Hebrew authors. A deeply observant man, Ozer abhorred the exploitation of religion for personal or political gain. In later life, detestation of clericalism was to become a pronounced feature of Weizmann's political outlook.

According to his own account Weizmann knew hardly a word of Russian before he was eleven (*Trial and Error*, 20); Yiddish was his mother tongue, the language that always allowed him most freedom of expression. Nor was it possible for Weizmann to escape from rudimentary Zionist beliefs. The idea of the Return and the centrality of Palestine were drummed into generation upon generation of Jewish children in *cheder* (primary school), values that were strengthened by the activities of the Hibbath Zion ('Love of Zion') movement, an amalgamation of loosely organized societies that promoted settlement in Palestine.

Scientist On completing his elementary school education Weizmann continued his studies at the *Gymnasium* at Pinsk. By all accounts a precocious student, he developed a special talent for chemistry. At the same time he pursued his Zionist interests. Here, in embryo form, were the two callings that were to absorb him until the end of his life. Blocked by the *numerus clausus* imposed on Jews by Russian universities, Weizmann, like many of his contemporaries, turned westwards to complete his higher education, first at the polytechnics at Darmstadt and Charlottenberg, Berlin, specializing in organic chemistry, and finally at the University of Fribourg, Switzerland, where he was awarded his doctorate, *magna cum laude*. In August 1899 he

Chaim Weizmann (1874–1952), by Sir Oswald Birley, exh. Royal Society of Portrait Painters 1935

obtained a modest position as a *Privatdocent* at the University of Geneva, launching his academic career.

By now Weizmann was heavily involved in Zionist politics. In Berlin he had been a leading member of the Russian-Jewish Academic Society, a glittering circle of intellectuals that he described in his memoirs as 'the cradle of the modern Zionist movement' (*Trial and Error*, 52). Later some of them regrouped as the kernel of the first effective oppositionist group in the Zionist movement. Known as the Democratic Fraction, they openly criticized the seemingly obsessive preoccupation with purely political activities of Theodor Herzl (the movement's founder). Weizmann argued for a more balanced programme: practical work in Palestine augmented by greater educational and cultural work among the Jewish masses to stimulate national consciousness. Weizmann was among the first to put the case for a Jewish university.

By the autumn of 1904 Weizmann, acting upon an invitation from William Perkin, had taken up a junior position at Manchester University. Perkin was a specialist in fermentation processes and synthetic dyes, fields that also interested Weizmann. Painstakingly Weizmann climbed the academic ladder. In 1913, with thirty-one articles to his name, he was appointed to a readership in biochemistry. However, he saw this as poor compensation for his failure to realize two cherished ambitions: a full professorship and admission to the Royal Society, set-backs that he put down to squalid antisemitic sentiments. He found redress elsewhere. In 1910 Weizmann became a naturalized British subject. A profound admiration for England, its traditions and political style, marked him for life. Weizmann's Anglophilia never blunted his criticism of Britain's Palestine policy, when necessary. On the whole his English connection served him (and Zionism) well, even though, eventually, it also contributed to his political downfall.

In 1906 Weizmann married a doctor, Vera (1881–1966), daughter of Isaiah Khatzman, from Rostov-on-Don. They had first met during Weizmann's student days in Geneva. Vera came from a moderately assimilated background: unversed in Yiddish, she was also ill-informed about Zionism. A genuine love-match, their marriage survived until Weizmann's death. However, it was not free of tension: on one occasion they even separated for a brief period. But Vera nursed and protected him. Acting as his sheet anchor, she provided the stability and order essential for his well-being. Two sons were born: Michael, who was killed in 1942 while on an air force mission over the Bay of Biscay, and Benjie, who ended his days farming in Ireland.

Zionist Weizmann never tired of pointing out that he served two gods, 'the laboratory and Jews' street' (*Letters and Papers*, series A, 5.165). While he at no time neglected his scientific work, Weizmann's Zionist activities never slackened. In August 1907, at the eighth Zionist Congress, he scored a great triumph. 'Synthetic Zionism', as defined by him, carried the day (ibid., series B, 1.65–71). For Weizmann practical work in Palestine would be the lever to pry a political charter out of reluctant foreign governments. He never deviated from this outlook. The acknowledged leader of a circle of young Zionist activists, which included Simon Marks and Israel Sieff, Weizmann in 1911 was elected to a vice-presidency of the English Zionist Federation. Much of his energy during these years was spent on laying the groundwork for a Hebrew university in Jerusalem, then a visionary concept. Guiding the motion through congress, Weizmann envisaged it as a kind of 'spiritual dreadnought', as the kernel of the Jewish national renaissance (ibid., series B, 1.101–10). By any reckoning, this was an extraordinary performance. At the outbreak of the First World War Weizmann, now approaching forty years of age, was widely recognized as a coming man, a prominent figure but one not holding any representative position empowering him to speak for the Zionist movement as a whole.

The outbreak of war recast outmoded political calculations. The Zionist movement was split between various— at times, competing—centres: Berlin, Copenhagen, St Petersburg, New York, London. Unlike many of his associates Weizmann believed in a British victory. Once Turkey had joined the central powers, and it became clear that an allied victory would lead to the dismemberment of the Ottoman empire, Weizmann elected to link Zionism's fortunes with those of Britain's, calculating that a British victory—at the time, by no means certain—would enable him to put in a claim for Palestine. To most leaders of Zionism this looked like a dangerous gamble. Weizmann disagreed. Profiting from his friendship with C. P. Scott, editor of the *Manchester Guardian*, Weizmann embarked upon his 'reconnoitring' expeditions (*Letters and Papers*, series A, 7.119), courting Britain's social-political élite, the Rothschilds or the Astors, as well as leading figures in public life, such as Sir Herbert Samuel, Lloyd George, and A. J. Balfour (whom he had first met in 1906), all warmly sympathetic to Zionism. So began the campaign that led eventually to the Balfour declaration.

This first flurry of political work soon died down as Weizmann became absorbed in his wartime scientific duties. By the spring of 1915 the need to provide a cheap and plentiful supply of acetone, an essential ingredient in the manufacture of explosives, had become a matter of extreme national urgency. Weizmann had perfected a fermentation process that met these requirements. He placed his findings at the disposal of the government. Appointed official adviser to the Admiralty on acetone supplies, Weizmann, within a year, was supervising an acetone-producing empire from King's Lynn to Belfast to Toronto. Weizmann's vital contribution to Britain's war effort realized significant side-effects. Not only did it bring him into closer and more cordial relations with leading politicians and senior civil servants, it also confirmed for them his unconditional loyalty to Britain's cause at a moment of national crisis.

With Lloyd George's appointment as prime minister in December 1916 the tide began to flow more strongly in favour of the Zionists. Together with Lloyd George himself, J. P. Smuts and Lord Milner, co-members of his five-man war cabinet, were self-avowed gentile Zionists, as was his foreign secretary, Balfour. In Palestine, General Allenby's armies were set to conquer Palestine. When asked about the future of Palestine, Lloyd George replied, 'Oh! We must grab that' (*Political Diaries of C. P. Scott*, 255). Weizmann exploited these favourable circumstances with consummate skill. Sir Isaiah Berlin called him 'an irresistible political seducer' (Berlin, 53). Weizmann put it differently. Politics, he once explained, 'is a matter of *Fingerspitzengefühl* (instinct, intuition, flair)' (*Letters and Papers*, series A, 23.196). By all accounts he possessed extraordinary powers of elucidation. By convincing the sceptical with a bewitching mixture of paradox and ironic wit, he succeeded in kindling the imagination of his audience, imparting to them his faith in the destiny of the Jewish people and the significance of its survival. He employed these skills in his negotiations with the British government during 1917, neutralizing opposition both within the Anglo-Jewish establishment and in the cabinet. Taking advantage of a presumed community of interests between Zionist goals and British imperial interests, his persistence and debating artistry finally paid off. The Balfour declaration of 2 November 1917, however ambiguously phrased, led to international recognition for Zionism's claims on Palestine, or at least part of it. It constituted the first crucial stage on the road to eventual Jewish statehood.

Zionist leader Weizmann's feat catapulted him into the leadership of the Zionist movement. Elected president of the World Zionist Organization in 1920, he rapidly assumed a complete ascendancy over his constituency, not seriously challenged until the late 1930s. Termed the 'benevolent despot' (Rose, 223), Weizmann led the movement, in effect, for almost a generation. His policy, however, based on co-operation with Britain, the mandatory power, soon ran into pitfalls. Arab opposition to the Balfour declaration and the mandate was absolute. Britain's attempts to bridge the gap between Zionist expectations

and Arab hostility inaugurated an ill-fated episode in Britain's imperial history. And so there began for Weizmann a period full of promise but also of intense frustration. One cynic noted that the process of whittling down the Balfour declaration began on 3 November 1917. Weizmann would have concurred.

By the 1920s Weizmann was a man of considerable means. Royalties from his scientific patents, together with prudent investments, afforded him an income estimated in the hundreds of thousands of pounds. Financially secure, he devoted himself to full-time Zionist work. Based in London, the principal political centre, Weizmann's main aim was to secure the well-being of the *Yishuv* (the Jewish community in Palestine). Only increased immigration and land purchases would guarantee its future, goals threatened by the impecunious state of the Zionist treasury. To remedy this situation Weizmann raided the coffers of American Jewry, 'eating my way from coast to coast', as he put it (Rose, 224). He called himself, with some truth, 'the greatest tax collector in the history of the Jewish people' (ibid.). But fund-raising was not his only concern. In April 1925 the Hebrew University was officially inaugurated in an impressive ceremony at its site on Mount Scopus. At last he had launched his 'spiritual dreadnought'. Forging the unity of the Jewish people was another concern. Weizmann would enrol world Judaism to the cause of Zionism, and in particular redeem the 'Yankee Doodle Judaism' of American Jewry (ibid.). By August 1929 he had cobbled together an enlarged Jewish Agency, mobilizing Zionist and non-Zionist Jews to work together for a common cause.

This singular achievement was overshadowed by events in Palestine. Violent anti-Jewish riots, unprecedented in their scope and ferocity, broke out in Palestine. In response the government issued the Passfield white paper of October 1930 that imposed harsh restrictions on the development of the Jewish National Home. Weizmann reacted swiftly to this challenge, skilfully orchestrating a public campaign to nullify the damaging effects of Passfield's paper. He succeeded. Four months later Ramsay MacDonald reinterpreted Passfield's paper to the Zionists' advantage, his letter to Weizmann being duly registered in *Hansard* as an official document and laid before the council of the League of Nations. But this striking success did not restore Weizmann's shaken prestige. Accused of sitting for 'too long at English feasts', he quit his position as president following a vote of no confidence in his leadership at the Zionist Congress in 1931. His successor, Nahum Sokolow, was seen as little more than a stand-in. One wit compared him to an empty clothes-stand waiting for Weizmann to return to hang his coat on.

Ending of the mandate Weizmann's enforced retirement witnessed no let-up in his Zionist activities. The rise of Nazism in Germany and the spread of antisemitism in Europe gave rise to a flood of Jewish refugees, many of them seeking sanctuary in Palestine, and lent an added urgency to the need to create a viable National Home as expeditiously as possible. At the same time Weizmann returned to his scientific work. He opened a laboratory in

London and sought a position at the Hebrew University. But here academic politics frustrated him. The university that owed so much to his drive and initiative refused him a professorship. Rebuffed by Jerusalem, Weizmann (funded initially by his close friends Israel Sieff, Simon Marks, and Harry Sacher), founded the Sieff (later Weizmann) Institute of Science in Rehovot, adjacent to which he built his home in Palestine. In this way Weizmann established, virtually single-handed, two institutions of higher learning and research of international repute.

In 1935 Weizmann was recalled to the presidency of the movement. With the international situation steadily deteriorating, Weizmann's prestige and diplomatic talents were never more needed. Now, however, heavily dependent upon support from Mapai (the Palestinian labour party) and its assertive leader, David Ben Gurion, he discovered limits to his freedom of manoeuvre. In the spring of 1936 the so-called Arab revolt broke out, to last, intermittently, until the outbreak of the Second World War. These 'troubles' spawned the 1936 Peel royal commission on Palestine. Its report, revolutionary in concept, concluded that the mandate was unworkable and recommended the partition of Palestine into Jewish and Arab states, with certain strategic areas reserved for the mandatory power. So began the great debate on partition, the decisive political issue of Zionism for the coming decade. Weizmann's attitude was clear-cut from the outset. A firm advocate of partition, he persuaded the elective Zionist bodies to accept the idea in principle. He never deviated from this view. But against a background of impending war, fierce opposition from the Arabs, and above all the necessity to secure British imperial interests, the government retreated from partition. Early in 1939 a conference convened at St James's Palace. Its efforts to seek an agreed settlement of the Palestine question proved abortive. As a result the government imposed its own solution. The draconian May 1939 white paper virtually crippled the development of the National Home, condemning the *Yishuv* to the status of a permanent minority. Forever damned by the Zionists, it held, in effect, until the establishment of the state of Israel in 1948.

On the outbreak of war Weizmann committed the Jewish Agency's support for Britain's war effort against Nazi Germany, a pledge frequently undermined by bureaucratic red tape and hostile voices in government service. Attempts to raise an independent Jewish fighting force did not achieve their aim until late in the war. Immigration became the touchstone of Anglo-Zionist relations, particularly when authenticated news of the Holocaust began to reach the West. But with few exceptions the British would not be moved: the gates of Palestine remained closed. In May 1942 the Zionist leadership met at the Biltmore Hotel, New York. Inspired by Weizmann, the convention called for unrestricted immigration into Palestine and the establishment there of a Jewish commonwealth. Towards the end of the war Churchill's cabinet revived partition. Welcomed by Weizmann, it was put on hold following the killing of Lord Moyne at the hands of Jewish assassins in November 1944. Appalled by the phenomenon of Jewish terrorism, Weizmann thought it not only morally reprehensible, but also politically counter-productive. Anglo-Zionist relations worsened, Weizmann being one of its chief casualties.

These controversies were carried over into the post-war period, and even intensified as a result of the newly elected Labour government's refusal to rescind the May white paper. Weizmann found himself under intolerable pressure from the so-called Jewish 'activists', that now included Ben Gurion, who were bent on armed confrontation with the British. All this was totally foreign to Weizmann's political philosophy. Half-blind from glaucoma and in poor health, Weizmann was eased out of office at the Zionist Congress of December 1946. His last address to congress was a stirring peroration. Inveighing against Jewish terrorism—'a cancer in the body politic of Palestine'—he quoted from his favourite prophet, Isaiah, telling the delegates that 'Zion will be redeemed through righteousness—and not by any other means' (*Letters and Papers*, series B, 2.642–51). After the vote went against him, he told the delegates: 'The Jewish people, especially those waiting in the camps, look to you to open the gates' (ibid.). Weizmann left the rostrum, never again to return to congress politics.

Final years Although Weizmann had been retired, 'Weizmannism' lived on. The Jewish Agency readopted partition and broke with the Jewish terrorist groups, while 'unofficial' negotiations were resumed with the British government. Although holding no official position, Weizmann continued to argue the Zionist case before international bodies. In November 1947 his vigorous lobbying was vital in securing the crucial vote in favour of partition at the United Nations. Some months later he intervened with President Truman, persuading him to recognize a viable Jewish state, to include the Negev area, and later to extend to Israel its first life-giving loan. In 1948, to general acclaim, he was elected Israel's first president, for as the leaders of the *Yishuv* agreed, 'Of all those living, no one contributed as much as you to its creation' (*Letters and Papers*, series A, 23.117).

As president, Weizmann was denied an active political role. Frustrated, he once complained caustically that '[my] handkerchief is the only thing I am allowed to poke my nose into' (Rose, 445). He consoled himself with the achievements of the Weizmann Institute and the company of his family. On 9 November 1952 he died at his home, Weizmann House in Rehovot where he was also buried. Tributes poured in from world figures; 250,000 Israelis came to pay him personal homage. The feeling was general that one of the great, formative personalities of the twentieth century had passed away. What was the secret of the spell he cast? For Richard Crossman, and other gentiles, it was '*because* he was utterly proud to be a Russian Jew from the Pale, *because* he had no feeling of double loyalty, *because* he knew only one patriotism, the love of a country that did not yet exist' (Crossman, 41). For his part Ben Gurion hailed him as 'the greatest Jewish emissary to the Gentile world … the most gifted and fascinating envoy the Jewish people ever produced' (Weisgal and Carmichael, 2).   NORMAN ROSE

Sources *The letters and papers of Chaim Weizmann, series A: letters*, ed. M. W. Weisgal and B. Litvinoff, 23 vols. (London, Jerusalem, and New Brunswick, NJ, 1968–80) · *The letters and papers of Chaim Weizmann, series B: papers*, ed. B. Litvinoff, 2 vols. (New Brunswick, NJ, 1983–4) · C. Weizmann, *Trial and error: the autobiography of Chaim Weizmann*, ed. B. Horowitz, illustr. edn (1950) · V. Weizmann, *The impossible takes longer* (1967) · C. Weizmann, 'Palestine's role in the solution of the Jewish problem', *Foreign Affairs* (Jan 1942) · M. Weisgal and J. Carmichael, eds., *A biography by several hands* (1963) · N. Rose, *Chaim Weizmann: a biography* (1986) · M. Verete, 'The Balfour Declaration and its makers', *Middle Eastern Studies* (Jan 1970) · *The political diaries of C. P. Scott, 1911–1928*, ed. T. Wilson (1970) · private information (2004) · I. Berlin, *Personal impressions* (1981) · DNB · R. Crossman, *A nation reborn* (1960) · d. cert. · Weizmann Institute, Rehovot, Israel, Weizmann MSS

Archives Weizmann Institute, Rehovot, Israel, corresp. and papers | Bodl. RH, corresp. with Lord Lugard · Central Zionist Archives, Jerusalem, S24, S25, and A312 series · HLRO, letters to David Lloyd George · JRL, letters to the *Manchester Guardian* · Marks and Spencer plc, London, archive, corresp. with I. M. Sieff · NA Scot., corresp. with Lord Lothian · Nuffield Oxf., corresp. with Lord Cherwell · PRO, FU 371, CO 733, CAB.PREM., and WP(G) series · UCL, corresp. with Moses Gaster | FILM BFI NFTVA, documentary footage · Weizmann Institute, Rehovot, Israel, videotaped interviews | SOUND BL NSA, 'Portrait of Dr Weizmann', NP 475W, NP 476W CI

Likenesses O. Birley, oils, exh. Royal Society of Portrait Painters 1935, Weizmann House, Rehovot, Israel [*see illus.*] · B. Elkan, bronze bust, Weizmann House, Rehovot, Israel · J. Epstein, bronze bust, Hebrew University, Jerusalem

Welby, Henry (*d.* 1636), recluse, was the eldest son of Adlard Welby (*c.*1506–1570), gentleman, of Gedney, Lincolnshire, and his first wife, Ellen Hall of Hull. Henry's age at death was given on his monument and in a memorial biography as eighty-four. This is inconsistent with the information that he matriculated as a pensioner of St John's College, Cambridge, on 24 May 1558, and was a student of the Inner Temple in November 1562. He was probably born in the 1540s.

Welby bought the country estate of Goxhill in Lincolnshire from Lord Wentworth and, wishing to enlarge his mind, spent some years travelling in the Low Countries, Germany, France, and Italy. He was married to Alice White, daughter of Thomas White of Yorkshire and Nottinghamshire and his wife, Anne *née* Cecil, sister of William Cecil, Lord Burghley. They had one daughter, Elizabeth, who was to be his sole heir.

Welby continued his life of gentlemanly ease until 1592, when his younger half-brother John, angered by Henry's efforts to reform his dissolute habits, attempted to shoot him with a pistol. Profoundly shocked, Henry went into total seclusion for the rest of his life. He took a house on Grub Street, near Cripplegate in London. He lived abstemiously there for forty-four years, reading and praying, eating gruel porridge or salad, and drinking only small beer.

Welby was generous to his neighbours, especially at Christmas, and to any pauper he noticed passing below. The parish of St Giles Cripplegate in which he lived was experiencing rapid growth in population, in economic activity, especially in the tailoring and carrying trades, and in poverty. Welby had cousins and other family members in London. His daughter married Sir Christopher Hildyard of Winestead, Yorkshire, in the church of St Giles Cripplegate on 13 July 1598. She was buried at Routh, East Riding of Yorkshire, on 28 November 1638; the Hildyard family of Flintham Hall, Newark, Nottinghamshire, descended from her.

Henry Welby was buried in St Giles Cripplegate on 20 October 1636, only nine days after his long-faithful servant, Elizabeth Villier. Welby's life was eccentric and he achieved some notoriety in his lifetime, and lasting attention from the biography of 1637, *The Phoenix of these Late Times, or, The Life of Mr Henry Welby Esq.*—'He died living that he might live dying'. Some details are incorrect (including his exact date of death), but the quarto volume rehearsed the main features of its subject's life and contained a sequence of commemorative verses by, among others, Shackerley Marmion, John Taylor the Water Poet, Thomas Nabbes, and Thomas Heywood, who gave the funeral elegy. The frontispiece portrait shows Welby in old age, when he was described as being like a wild hermit, his hair being so overgrown. Two further editions appeared the same year, and a century later in 1741 a new edition was published under the title *The City-Hermit*.

DAVID SOUDEN

Sources *The phoenix of these late times, or, The life of Mr Henry Welby esq.* (1637) · pedigree, 1634, Coll. Arms, MS C.23, fol. 22 · visitation of Lincolnshire, 1564, Coll. Arms, MS D.8, fol. 37 · parish register, St Giles Cripplegate, 20 Oct 1636, GL, MS 6419/3 [burial] · Venn, *Alum. Cant.* · *N&Q*, 3rd ser., 3 (7 March 1863) · monuments in city churches, GL, MS 2480/2 · Burke, *Gen. GB* (1969) [under Hildyard] · A. Gibbons, *Notes on the visitation of Lincolnshire, 1634* (1898), 193–207

Likenesses pen-and-ink drawing, 1636, NPG · W. Marshall, line engraving, 1637, BM; repro. in *Phoenix* (1637) · portrait, repro. in *Phoenix*

Welby, Reginald Earle, Baron Welby (1832–1915), civil servant, was born on 3 August 1832, at Harston, Leicestershire, the fifth son of John Earle Welby (1786–1867), rector of Harston. His father was the younger son of Sir William Earle Welby, first baronet (*d.* 1815), of Denton Moor, Lincolnshire; his mother, Felicia Eliza, was the daughter of the Revd George Hole of Chumleigh and North Tawton, Devon. After attending Eton College from 1845 Welby was admitted a pensioner at Trinity College, Cambridge, in October 1851. As was common among his contemporaries he did not read for honours. He performed creditably at first in college examinations in mathematics and classics, but did little subsequently to justify the reputation claimed for him by an obituarist as a 'fairly good classical scholar' (*The Times*, 12), and was awarded an ordinary pass degree in 1856. He had no very clear ideas about a career, but, prompted by a friend, the son of a Treasury minister, he obtained a nomination to the Treasury on the impulse of a moment. A candidate in one of the first of the new limited competitive examinations, he joined the Treasury as a third-class clerk with an initial salary of £100. Within fifteen years he was principal clerk in charge of the finance division, having spent less than four years in the divisions. He served instead as private secretary successively to six financial secretaries, acquiring a reputation as a financial expert. At first promotion came with seniority: to second-class clerk in 1860 and first-class clerk in February 1871, with a salary of £700 rising to £900. Within nine months he was promoted over the heads of seven more senior colleagues to the post of principal clerk of the finance division, which carried with it the status and duties of Treasury auditor and a seat on the public accounts committee of the House of Commons. His internal appointment marked the end of twenty years' weakness, during which the Treasury had to look outside the department for its principal financial adviser. In 1880 he became financial assistant secretary, a new post which put him third in line to the head of department. The following year he added to it the duties of the auditor of the civil list, the holder of which was traditionally recognized as second in command. His salary was now £1500. Shortly after he was created GCB. Five years later, at the age of fifty-three, he was promoted permanent secretary in succession to Ralph Lingen, becoming the only Old Etonian to head the Treasury in the nineteenth century, and the first of a long line of home-bred appointments.

A man of formidable intellect, Welby's 'penetrating and analytical mind was an unfailing resource to governments' both whig and tory, albeit while holding strongly to the principles of Cobdenite free trade and of Gladstonian economy (Roseveare, 217). 'The embodiment of the late-Victorian "Treasury-mind"', he had an unrivalled knowledge of public finance (*The Times*, 12), in which he was the Treasury's leading expert for more than a quarter of a century. He made his own distinctive contribution, most notably the implementation in 1877 of Bagehot's suggestion of Treasury bills as a short-term means to raise money. His correspondence with Gladstone reveals the developing maturity of his knowledge and skill as a financial adviser, from 'some rather amateurish calculations on price fluctuations in the 1860s' while still a junior clerk in the finance division to 'the masterful memoranda on the Naval Defence Acts of the 1880s and on the financial implications of Irish Home Rule' which he drafted with Edward Hamilton (Roseveare, 217). Welby made no secret of his admiration of Gladstone and his political sympathy for the Liberal Party, although his family were old tory. In the 1880–85 administration he failed to persuade Gladstone to seize the political opportunities offered by the reform of local government. While Gladstone held the combined posts of prime minister and chancellor, Welby was regularly consulted about senior appointments in the civil service and the distribution of honours. While these and some other duties were consistent with the description of his post as head of the civil service, the title was not formally recognized and conferred upon the Treasury's permanent secretary until 1919.

Welby believed in a strong Treasury as a necessary brake upon the growth of expenditure and the civil service. Throughout the second half of the nineteenth century the subject of the efficacy of the Treasury's control was the cause of a long-running and inconclusive debate conducted through the inquiries of several select committees and royal commissions. Welby was the Treasury's star witness at them all, repeatedly emphasizing the inadequacy of the Treasury's control as a financial check, and arguing that while it could and did demand *prima facie* good grounds for additional spending, it was powerless to say whether the policy which led to it was right or not. That judgement was a political one: the preserve of the departmental minister alone. No remedy was found to resolve that dilemma or to provide the 'independent authority' which Welby publicly urged in order to strengthen the Treasury. Within the department he wrote perceptively about the nature of Treasury control and tried without much success to interest ministers in proposals for general rules to guide officials in its exercise, but they preferred to deal with each case *ad hoc*, on its merits.

Welby had immense energy and worked hard, but lacked the gift of delegation. He preferred to get deeply involved in the details of the day-to-day business. As a result he did not dispatch business as briskly as the increasing workload of an understaffed department demanded. He was dilatory, slow to come to the point and to make up his mind, expansive and reflective, and easily deflected from the matter in hand.

> His room became a kind of gigantic 'In-Tray' and it was a Treasury joke, upon the occasion of a celebrated murder, that if the criminal had had the sense to conceal the body on Welby's desk he would have certainly escaped detection. (Roseveare, 212)

Colleagues with business requiring urgent decisions tended to bypass him, going instead directly to ministers. He was responsible for the recruitment of the first woman to the Treasury in November 1889, but his motive characteristically was more a concern for greater economy than enthusiasm for the cause of emancipation. The introduction of typewriters, and of female secretarial staff to operate them and to take shorthand, helped reduce the rising costs of the Treasury's copying bill. Prudently, he arranged for a room where the women could be made comfortable 'without interference of the clerks', under the watchful eye of the superintendent to 'prevent the chance of mischief' (Treasury departmental arrangement book). Such was the authority he commanded and the influence he wielded at the very heart of government that he was described by his contemporaries, with some understandable exaggeration, as 'easily the most powerful man in the British Empire' (Roseveare, 212).

On retirement in 1894 Welby was ennobled as Baron Welby of Allington (16 April) and embarked upon a second career as a politician, espousing his favourite causes of free trade and sound, economical finance. He contributed his financial expertise to debates in the House of Lords and took an active part in the work of the London county council, becoming its chairman in 1900. From the Cobden Club, which he also chaired from 1899, he campaigned against protectionism and rearmament, and with the outbreak of war watched with mounting alarm the accumulation of the national debt. A sociable and popular 'bachelor-dilettante' (Roseveare, 217), he was an excellent host, organizing Old Etonian boating parties at Datchet and keeping a superb table at his London home. He enjoyed London society and the intimate, closed world of the clubs. 'Though quite free from vanity, conceit and pomposity, he was quick to resent any breach of manners or intrusiveness' (*DNB*). He died on 29 October 1915 at his home at Malwood, Lyndhurst, Hampshire, and was buried at Allington, Lincolnshire, on 4 November. The executors of his estate, valued at £111,392, were his nephew, the earl of Lindsey of Uffington House, Stamford, Montague Peregrine Albemarle, Sir George Earle Welby, and Sir George Edward Dallas.　　　　　　　　　　MAURICE WRIGHT

Sources H. Roseveare, *The treasury: the evolution of a British institution* (1969) · *The Times* (1 Nov 1915), 12 · *DNB* · M. Wright, 'Treasury control, 1854–1914', *Studies in the growth of nineteenth-century government*, ed. G. Sutherland (1972), chap. 8 · 'Royal commission to inquire into civil establishments', *Parl. papers* (1887), vol. 19, C. 5226; (1888), vol. 27, C. 5545; (1889), 21.1, C. 5748; 21.17, C. 5748-I; (1890), 27.1, C. 6172; 27.17, C. 6172-I [reports 1–4] · 'Royal commission on the civil service and revenue departments', *Parl. papers* (1912–13), vol. 15, Cd 6209–10, 6534–5 [first and second reports]; (1913), vol. 18, Cd 6739–40 [third report]; (1914), vol. 16, Cd 7338–40 [fourth report] · treasury departmental arrangement book 6, Nov 1888, PRO · M. Wright, *Treasury control of the civil service, 1854–1874* (1969) · Burke, *Peerage* (1867) · Gladstone, *Diaries* · d. cert. · GEC, *Peerage*

Archives BLPES, papers · Lincs. Arch., corresp. and papers | BL, letters to Lord Gladstone, Add. MSS 46050–46068, *passim* · BL, corresp. with W. E. Gladstone, Add. MS 44338 · BL, letters to Sir Edward Hamilton, Add. MSS 48623–48628 · BL, papers relating to imperial defence, Egerton MS 3291 · BL OIOC, letters to Arthur Godley, MS Eur. F 102 · BLPES, letters to Lord Farrer · Bodl. Oxf., corresp. with Sir William Harcourt and Lewis Harcourt · NL Scot., corresp., incl. with Lord Rosebery · NL Wales, letters to Lord Rendel · Trinity Cam., corresp. with Sir Henry Babington Smith | FILM BFI NFTVA, news footage

Likenesses J. Collier, oils, 1913, Society of Dilettanti, Brooks's Club, London

Wealth at death £111,392 13s. 8d.: probate, 18 Dec 1915, *CGPLA Eng. & Wales*

Welby [later Welby-Gregory; *née* Stuart-Wortley], **Victoria Alexandrina Maria Louisa**, Lady Welby (1837–1912), philosopher, was born in England on 27 April 1837, the last of three children of Charles James Stuart-Wortley (1802–1844), and his wife, Lady Emmeline Charlotte Elizabeth Stuart-*Wortley, *née* Manners (1806–1855), poet and traveller. James Archibald Stuart-*Wortley (1776–1845) was her grandfather. She had little formal education aside from some private tuition, and from 1848 to 1855 she travelled widely with her mother in the United States, Canada, Mexico, Spain, Morocco, Turkey, Palestine, Syria and many other countries. In 1852 she published her travel diary. After her mother's death she lived with a succession of relatives before being taken in by her godmother, the duchess of Kent, mother of Queen Victoria. In 1861 she was appointed maid of honour to Queen Victoria; she spent almost two years at the royal court before her marriage at St George's Church, Hanover Square, London, on 4 July 1863, to William Earle Welby (1829–1898), military official, MP, and high sheriff, who with his father's death

in 1875 became fourth baronet and assumed the additional surname Gregory. Consequently Victoria Welby's surname became Welby-Gregory. Alternatively to a series of pseudonyms or recourse to anonymity, she mainly published under her full name until the end of the 1880s, under the name of Hon. Lady Welby from 1890 to 1892, and as Victoria Welby from 1893 onwards, although she continued signing all official and business documents with her full name.

Welby's children were Victor Albert William (1864–1876), Charles Glynne Earle Welby (1865–1938), assistant under-secretary of state at the War Office and MP, and Emmeline Mary Elizabeth (Nina; 1867–1955), painter, sculptor, and writer, who wrote Welby's biography and edited her correspondence in two volumes, under her married name, Mrs H. Cust. During the first years of her marriage, Victoria Welby founded the Royal School of Art Needlework.

Not at all attracted to life at court, after her marriage Welby retreated to Denton Manor, Grantham, where she soon began her research, with her husband's full support. Initially her interest was directed towards theological questions and in 1881 she published *Links and Clues*, which expressed her sympathy at that time with evangelical movements. It was unorthodox and unsuccessful and its poor reception caused her to reflect on the inadequacies of religious discourse, which was, she came to believe, cast in outmoded linguistic forms. She was drawn into an examination of language and meaning, and found a pervasive linguistic confusion which stemmed from a misconception of language as a system of fixed meanings, and which could be resolved only by the recognition that language must grow and change as human experience changes. She also made a serious study of science, believing that important scientific discoveries supplied the new experiences by which religious discourse could be transformed into something more meaningful.

Central to Welby's philosophy was her analysis of meaning into three components: sense—'the organic response to environment' (Hardwick, xxii); meaning—the specific sense which a word is intended to convey; and significance—which encompasses 'the far-reaching consequence, implication, ultimate result or outcome of some event or experience' (ibid.). This triadic relationship relates closely to that established by Charles Sanders Peirce between immediate interpretant, dynamical interpretant, and final interpretant (ibid., pp. 109–11). Peirce read her 1903 book *What is Meaning?* and reviewed it for *The Nation* alongside Bertrand Russell's *Principles of Mathematics*, to which he compared it in importance. A flourishing correspondence developed between Welby and Peirce, which was crucial to the development of his thought. She has been regarded as the 'founding mother' of semiotics and her continuing importance is illustrated by the publication in the 1980s and 1990s of editions of her work and volumes of commentary on her thought. She contributed significantly to modern theories of signs, meaning, and interpretation, and introduced, in 1894, the neologism 'significs' to denote the science of meaning.

Significs examined the interrelationship between signs, sense—in all its signifying implications—and values.

Besides numerous articles in newspapers, magazines, and scientific journals (notably *The Spectator*, *The Expositor*, the *Fortnightly Review*, the *Open Court*, *Nature*, *Mind*, *The Monist*, the *Hibbert Journal*, and the *Journal of Philosophy, Psychology and Scientific Methods*) Welby published a long list of privately printed essays, parables, aphorisms, and pamphlets on a large range of subjects in numerous spheres: science, mathematics, anthropology, philosophy, education, and social issues.

As her research progressed, Welby increasingly promoted the study of significs, channelling the great breadth and variety of her interests into a significal perspective. Shortly after the publication of two fundamental essays—'Meaning and metaphor' in 1893 and 'Sense, meaning and interpretation' in 1896—the Welby prize for the best essay on significs was announced in the journal *Mind* in 1896 and awarded to Ferdinand Tönnies in 1898 for his essay 'Philosophical terminology' (1899–1900). Important moments of official recognition for significs are represented by the publication of the entries 'Translation' (Welby, 1902), 'Significs' (co-authored with J. M. Baldwin and G. F. Stout, 1902), and 'Sensal' (with G. F. Stout, 1902) in the *Dictionary of Philosophy and Psychology in Three Volumes* (1901–5). However, the official recognition Welby had so tenaciously hoped for came only after approximately thirty years of 'hard labour', with the publication of the entry 'Significs' in the *Encyclopaedia Britannica* in 1911. The signific movement in the Netherlands, which developed in two phases from 1917 to 1926 and from 1937 to 1956, originated from Welby's significs through the mediation of the Dutch psychiatrist, poet, and social reformer Frederik van Eeden (1860–1932).

From 1863 until her death in 1912 Welby was a friend and source of inspiration to leading personalities from the world of science and literature. She wrote regularly to over 450 correspondents from diverse countries including Great Britain, the United States of America, France, Italy, Germany, and the Netherlands. It was largely through such correspondence that she developed her theories. She began writing to politicians, representatives of the church, aristocrats, and intellectuals as early as 1870 and created an epistolary network which expanded rapidly from 1880 onwards, both locally and internationally. She used this network for her own enlightenment, as a sounding board for her own ideas, and as a means of circulating her own ideas and those of others. Thanks also to her social position and court appointment as maid of honour to Queen Victoria, she counted friends and acquaintances among the aristocracy and government officials. Because of her interest in religious and theological questions she corresponded with leading churchmen of her day and subsequently with eminent scientists, philosophers, and educationists, whom she welcomed into her home where they met to discuss their ideas. Her correspondents included Michel Bréal, Bertrand Russell, C. K. Ogden, Herbert Spencer, Thomas Huxley Benjamin Jowett, F. H. Bradley, Henry Sidgwick, H. G. Wells, and William James. None

the less, in spite of general awareness of the importance and originality of Welby's work, she did not for many years receive the recognition she hoped for, at least not publicly. In an attempt to avoid flattery, she either published anonymously or signed her work with pseudonyms, various combinations of initials, or simply as Victoria Welby. The only honour she valued was 'that of being treated by workers as a serious worker' (Hardwick, 13). Though she had no institutional affiliations, she was a member of the Aristotelian and Anthropological societies and was one of the original promoters of the Sociological Society between 1903 and 1904.

Welby was an open-minded female intellectual in the Victorian era despite—or, perhaps, thanks to—her complete lack of a formal education, which led her to search for the conditions which made her theoretical work possible. She highlighted the importance of her extensive travels as a child with her mother, which often took place in dramatic circumstances and ended with her mother's tragic death in the Syrian desert, leaving Victoria all alone until help came from Beirut. In a letter of 22 December 1903 to Peirce, who fully recognized her genius (as testified by their correspondence), Welby suggested that her unconventional childhood

accounts in some degree for my seeing things in a somewhat independent way. But the absence of any systematic mental training must be allowed for of course in any estimate of work done. I only allude to the unusual conditions of my childhood in order partly to account for my way of looking at and putting things: and my very point is that any value in it is impersonal. It suggests an ignored heritage, an unexplored mine. This I have tried to indicate in 'What is meaning?'. (Hardwick, 13–14)

Welby's scientific remains are now mainly deposited in two archives: the Welby collection in the York University archives (Downsview, Ontario, Canada) and the Lady Welby Library in the University of London Library. The latter includes approximately 1000 volumes from Victoria Welby's personal library and twenty-five pamphlet boxes containing pamphlets, reprints and newspaper cuttings, religious tracts, sermons, and published lectures by various authors. Four boxes without numbers contain duplicates of most of Welby's own publications. The main part of her scientific and literary production is to be found at the York archives. Half of the collection consists of Welby's as yet mostly unpublished correspondence covering the years 1861–1912. A large part of the remainder comprises notes, extracts, and commentaries on a variety of subjects—biology, education, ethics, eugenics, imagery, language and significance, logic and significance, matter and motion, numbers theory, philosophy and significance, significs, and time. There are also speeches, lessons, sermons by other authors, numerous unpublished essays and a collection of poems by Welby, diagrams and photographs, translations, proofs, copies of some of her publications, and newspaper cuttings.

Suffering from partial aphasia and paralysis of the right hand owing to bad blood circulation caused by flu caught at the end of January 1912, Welby died on 29 March 1912 at Duneaves, Mount Park, Harrow, and was buried in Grantham, Lincolnshire.   SUSAN PETRILLI

Sources 'Representative women', *Now & Then*, 34 (1929), 30–31 • J. M. Baldwin, *Dictionary of philosophy and psychology in three volumes* (1901–5) • W. K. Clifford, 'Victoria Lady Welby: an ethical mystic', *Hibbert Journal*, 23 (1924), 101–6 • Mrs H. Cust, ed., *Wanderers: episodes from the travels of Lady Emmeline Stuart-Wortley and her daughter Victoria, 1849–1855* (1928) • Mrs H. Cust, ed., *Echoes of larger life: a selection from the early correspondence of Victoria Lady Welby* (1929) • Mrs H. Cust, ed., *Other dimensions: a selection from the later correspondence of Victoria Lady Welby* (1931) • C. S. Hardwick, introduction, *Semiotic and significs: the correspondence between Charles S. Peirce and Victoria Lady Welby*, ed. C. S. Hardwick (1977) • S. Petrilli, 'Victoria Lady Welby and significs: an interview with H. W. Schmitz', *The semiotic web* 1987, ed. T. A. Sebeok and J. Umiker-Sebeok (1988), 79–92 • S. Petrilli, *Su Victoria Welby: significs e filosofia del linguaggio* (1998) [incl. bibliography of Victoria Welby's works and a critical bibliography on Welby and on the signific movement in the Netherlands] • W. H. Schmitz, 'Victoria Lady Welby's significs: the origin of the signific movement', in V. Welby, *Significs and language* (1985) • W. H. Schmitz, ed., *Essays on significs: papers presented on the occasion of the 150th anniversary of the birth of Victoria Lady Welby* (1990) • V. Welby, *A young traveller's journal of a tour in North and South America during the year 1850* (1852) • W. Macdonald, *Sociological Review*, 5 (1912), 152–6 • *Westminster Gazette*, 34 (1912) • *Blackwood*, 191 (1912), 706–10 • E. Winton, *The Spectator* (6 April 1912), 543–4 • m. cert. • d. cert.

Archives York University, Toronto, archives, corresp., and literary MSS | LUL, Lady Welby Library • Milan University, Giovanni Vailati archives • Schleswig-Holsteinische Landesbibliothek, Kiel, Germany, Ferdinand Tönnies archives • UCL, letters to Sir Francis Galton • UCL, Pearson MSS • University of Amsterdam, Frederik van Eeden Museum • University of Amsterdam, Significs archives

Likenesses F. Dicksee, double portrait, 1880 (with Sir William Earle Welby-Gregory), priv. coll.; repro. in Schmitz, ed., *Essays on significs* • E. Taylor, watercolour miniature, repro. in V. Welby, *Significs and language* (1911) • portrait, repro. in Cust, ed., *Echoes of larger life* • portrait, repro. in Cust, ed., *Other dimensions*

Wealth at death £1192 9s.: probate, 15 May 1912, *CGPLA Eng. & Wales*

Welch, Adam Cleghorn (1864–1943), Church of Scotland minister, was born on 14 May 1864 at Goshen, Jamaica, the sixth child of the Revd John Welch (d. 1870/71), a missionary, and his wife, Flora (d. 1870/71), the daughter of Robert Hogg, a member of a well-known Scottish border farming family. On the death of both parents when he was six years old, he was brought to Scotland by his mother's family. Educated at Galashiels Academy, George Watson's College, and Edinburgh University, he graduated MA in 1883 and entered the ministry of the United Presbyterian church. In 1903 he married Grace Marion (d. in or after 1943), daughter of Thomas Steven, of Helensburgh; they had one son and two daughters. The loss of his three brothers in early manhood, and later of his only son in childhood, gave his ministry the unusual sensitiveness to the sorrows of men and women that characterized it to the end.

Welch exercised ministries at Waterbeck in Dumfriesshire, Helensburgh, and Glasgow from 1887 to 1913, and was recognized as one of the most powerful expository preachers of his time. His published work dates from early in his ministry, his first scholarly interests being in systematic theology and church history. His first book was *Anselm and his Work* (1901), which was his only published work when, in 1909, on the occasion of the Calvin quatercentenary, the University of Halle conferred on him the honorary degree of doctor of theology. Old Testament studies had, however, already claimed his interest. His second main work, in 1912, was *The Religion of Israel under the Kingdom* (the Kerr lectures). Edinburgh University enrolled him as an honorary DD in 1913, and in the same year he was appointed professor of Hebrew and Old Testament exegesis at New College, Edinburgh.

A teaching career of twenty-one years made Welch one of the greatest Old Testament scholars and theologians Scotland has produced. His biblical and historical studies made him very uneasy about the accepted dating of the Pentateuch (as elaborated by Julius Wellhausen), and for many years he was convinced of the need for a radical recasting of it. In October 1921 he gave a lecture, 'On the present position of Old Testament criticism', published in *The Exposition* in 1923, which presented a threefold challenge to the dominant critical theories of the Pentateuch. Subsequent books were to develop the positions adumbrated in this lecture: *The Code of Deuteronomy* (1924), *Deuteronomy: the Framework to the Code* (1932), *Post-Exilic Judaism* (1935), and *Prophet and Priest in Old Israel* (1936). Notable among many other publications, widely ranging over the Old Testament, are *Jeremiah: his Time and his Work* (1928; repr. 1951) and, on a more popular level, a Bible class handbook, *The Preparation for Christ in the Old Testament*.

Welch retired in 1934, in which year he was elected president of the Society for Old Testament Study, of which he was a founder member. He delivered the Schweich lectures in 1938, which were published as *The Work of the Chronicler* (1939), and a memorial volume of his lectures, *Kings and Prophets of Israel*, edited by N. W. Porteous, with a memoir by G. S. Gunn, was published in 1952. Warmly appreciated by generations of students for his academic integrity and communication skills, Welch was an able and trusted churchman, who brought incisive wisdom and pungent candour to every discussion. He played a leading part in the reunion of the Scottish church in 1929. He died at Helensburgh on 19 February 1943; his wife survived him.   G. S. GUNN, rev. ROBERT DAVIDSON

Sources G. S. Gunn, 'Memoir', in *Kings and prophets of Israel*, ed. N. W. Porteous (1952), 13–44 • D. F. Wright and G. D. Badcock, eds., *Disruption to diversity: Edinburgh divinity, 1846–1996* (1996), 60–61 • personal knowledge (2004) • *CGPLA Eng. & Wales* (1943) • G. W. Anderson, 'Welch, Adam Cleghorn', *DSCHT*

Archives NL Scot., corresp. with publishers

Likenesses D. Alison, oils, 1934, New College, Edinburgh

Wealth at death £19,754 1s. 8d.: confirmation, 27 April 1943, *CCI*

Welch, (James) Colin Ross (1924–1997), journalist, was born at Ickleton Abbey, Ickleton, Cambridgeshire, on 23 April 1924 or, as he put it, 'St George's Day, Shakespeare's birthday and the very day in 1924 when the Empire Exhibition opened at Wembley with the statue of the then Prince of Wales carved in New Zealand butter'. He was the only son of James William Welch, gentleman farmer, and his wife, Irene Margherita Paton; he had one sister. After one horrible and one tolerable prep school (the change followed the death of his father when he was eight) Welch was educated as a scholar of Stowe School. There he met Peregrine Worsthorne, whose path paralleled his for nearly half a century. They were coached for university entrance by the literary journalist John Davenport, working for the time as a schoolmaster, and Welch won a major scholarship to Peterhouse, Cambridge, where Worsthorne also went. After a brief spell as wartime undergraduates they were called up for military service. Both hoped but failed to join the Coldstream Guards; Welch was commissioned into the Royal Warwickshire regiment in 1942 and was posted on active service to the Lincolnshire regiment.

Welch fought gallantly as an infantry subaltern from Normandy to the Reichswald, was twice wounded, and was marked by the war more profoundly. He ever after remembered the half-trained adolescent soldiers whom he—aged only twenty himself—had commanded in action, the large young German corporal he had shot in a moment of fright, the loving kindness of the Dutch family on which he was billeted at Christmas 1944, the 'Caliban-like revolt of greed, lust, hatred, envy, cruelty and destructive rage' which was national socialism, the grandeur of Europe even at that moment of horror, the heartless stupidity of senior officers and military bureaucrats, and the sheer comedy of army life. He used to say that whoever first used the phrase 'with military efficiency' could never have worn uniform, and the war left him with a scepticism about the organizational capacity of the state, although also with a deep if unavailing longing for stability.

On demobilization Welch returned to Cambridge, where his tutors included D. W. Brogan, Peter Laslett, and Desmond Williams. The last was his undoing: as a silly prank, they telephoned the college bursar from London with a bomb threat. Welch took the blame and was sent down. He found his first job in 1948 on the *Glasgow Herald*, where Worsthorne had preceded him, to learn something about newspaper editing and production. In Scotland he met the striking and intelligent Sybil Russell, whom he married on 3 June 1950. They had a son and a daughter. After an improbable interlude working in the Colonial Office in 1949–50 Welch joined the *Daily Telegraph* in 1950 and, for better and for worse, found his destiny.

It was an unlikely combination. Sober, sombre, and almost wilfully dull, the *Telegraph* was the voice of commercial conservatism and of the lumpenbourgeoisie. The sparkling bohemian Welch, well read and intellectually sophisticated, nevertheless claimed without affectation to admire the stolid City clerks and bank managers who were the paper's staple readership. He wrote leaders at the *Telegraph* before he demonstrated his real flair at parliamentary sketch-writing—the first of what proved a scintillating line at the paper that reviewed the House of Commons as theatre—and then, in 1955, began 'The Way of the World' (in fact a revival: a column of that name had existed in the old *Morning Post* before it was folded into the *Daily Telegraph* before the war). The column became a little island of style and wit in the grey pages of the *Telegraph*,

where bylined columnists of any kind, let alone idiosyncratic or 'viewy' ones, were frowned on by Michael Berry (created Lord Hartwell in 1968), whose family owned the paper and who was its chairman and editor-in-chief from 1954 to 1987. Before long Welch handed over the column to his friend Michael Wharton, who embellished it over more than forty years.

By a twist of fate the two men's private lives were entwined as well, when Welch and Wharton's wife, Kate, *née* Catherine Mary Derrington (1931–1992), became lovers. They eventually established a home together and had a son and a daughter; he divided his time between that menage and his marital residence until Kate's death in 1992. The story is memorably told in Wharton's memoir *A Dubious Codicil*, where Welch appears as Kenneth. That book also describes the incongruously dissolute life led by the staff of the staid tory *Telegraph*, with their nightly drunken revels in the King and Keys. Like his friend Perry Worsthorne, who had also joined the *Telegraph*, Welch was consciously *déclassé* and still more at home in the pub, even if wasted there. He was a handsome man, with attractive wavy hair, fine teeth, a beguiling smile, and a voice that just held back from the donnish or drawling. Courteous and courtly despite the squalid surroundings, gravely bespectacled, sometimes clad in the leathers in which he would later alarmingly ride his motor bike home, he would converse with sardonic verve on topics learned and worldly, perform long stretches from Wagner unaccompanied, and consume many an aperitif as he took the familiar path from conviviality to inebriety. His admiration for the *Telegraph*'s professed principles of order and restraint, and for its very ordinary readers, was surely connected with his horror of personal chaos.

When Sir Colin Coote retired as editor of the *Daily Telegraph* in 1964, he appointed Maurice Green his successor as a parting shot, and Welch deputy editor. Berry regretted the latter appointment, but did not feel that he could rescind it. There was no personal animosity between the two men, but Berry thought Welch too frivolous, and simply too funny, for high executive office (his mildly radical-chic wife, Lady Pamela, disapproved rather of Welch's form of toryism). And yet, although Berry's misgivings were doubtless amplified by the deputy editor's taste for wine, women, and song, Welch always edited the paper industriously and conscientiously when he was in the chair, doing his best to stop levity breaking in. His legacies to the *Telegraph* were indeed numerous, from an infusion of hard-headed economic liberalism which made the paper 'prematurely Thatcherite', to the nurturing of younger journalists who were devoted to him. Some recognition of his achievement came with the award of Granada journalist of the year in 1974. In 1972 he had been appointed knight grand cross of the order of Polonia Restituta.

When Green retired in 1974 he was succeeded by Sir William Deedes, and Welch realized that he would never become editor. He stayed at the *Telegraph* until 1980, when he left to take on a couple of frankly unsuitable jobs, editing a short-lived American magazine called *Chief Executive* in 1980–82 and returning, without his former zest, to parliamentary sketch-writing in 1984–92, this time for the *Daily Mail*. He wrote columns for *The Independent* for a time, and more happily, for *The Spectator* over many years, as well as book reviews for *The Times*. Although his resentment about his treatment at the *Telegraph* was subjectively understandable, a more serious cause for regret might have been that he did not write more. Welch's exiguous publications in book form included a new edition of Sir Frederick Ponsonby's *Recollections of Three Reigns* (1951), and a translation for the BBC, with his wife, of Nestroy's *Liberty Comes to Krähwinkel* (1954).

Welch was an excellent reporter, whether in the Commons press gallery or covering the trial of Adolf Eichmann for the *Telegraph* in articles less celebrated than, though at least as penetrating as, those of Hannah Arendt. He wrote charming causeries, in a style sometimes ornate, sometimes whimsical. But his best writing took the form of longer essays in magazines such as *The Spectator* and *Encounter*, as could be seen in the posthumous collection *The Odd Thing about the Colonel* (1997), edited by his daughter Frances Welch and son-in-law Craig Brown. Very amusing when he wanted to be—on the Fabians, or Nkrumah's tragi-farcical regime in Ghana, or eccentric wartime officers—he belied any reputation as a dandyish *flâneur* when he wrote with acute insight about music, or national socialism, or the Indian revolt (in a piece that refuted any idea that he was a reactionary imperialist). Nothing better was written about the *Lady Chatterley's Lover* case than the long essay in which Welch demolished the complacent evidence for the defence, especially from clerical witnesses, and pointed out that, so far from being a 'religious' book, the novel's only supernatural flavour 'is the tradition of witchcraft'.

While waiting on a station platform in 1995, Welch suffered a severe cerebral haemorrhage. He survived without regaining consciousness for more than two years and in three hospitals before he was moved to the Brendon Care Foundation Nursing Home in Froxfield, where he died on 28 January 1997, aged seventy-two. Despite his yearnings, and partly perhaps because of his irregular life, Welch had never been able to channel a strong religious instinct into institutional form, but he would have wanted the Christian funeral he received at Aldbourne, Marlborough, Wiltshire, where he had settled with Sybil. Together with his memorial service at St Bride's, Fleet Street, it seemed an elegy for a more dashing way of newspaper life, which had been replaced before his death by the rule of sophists, economists, and calculators.

GEOFFREY WHEATCROFT

Sources C. Welch, *The odd thing about the colonel and other pieces* (1997) · M. Wharton, *A dubious codicil* (1991) · *Daily Telegraph* (28 Jan 1997) · *The Times* (29 Jan 1997) · *The Independent* (29 Jan 1997) · *WWW* · personal knowledge (2004) · private information (2004) · b. cert. · m. cert. · d. cert. · d. cert. [Catherine Wharton]
Likenesses photograph, 1962, repro. in *Daily Telegraph* · photograph, repro. in *The Independent* · photograph, repro. in *The Times*
Wealth at death under £180,000: probate, 9 Dec 1997, CGPLA Eng. & Wales

Welch, (Maurice) Denton (1915–1948), writer and painter, was born in Shanghai on 29 March 1915, the youngest of the four sons (there were no daughters) of Arthur Joseph Welch, a wealthy English rubber merchant, and his American wife, Rosalind Bassett. After spending an itinerant early childhood he was educated first at an eccentric preparatory school intended for the sons of Christian Scientists, St Michael's in Uckfield, Sussex, and later at Repton School, from where, at the age of sixteen, he ran away. When he was seventeen he returned to China for several months.

Welch's original ambition was to be a painter, and in 1933 he enrolled at Goldsmiths' College School of Art. Welch's spell as an art student came to an abrupt end, however, in 1935, at the age of twenty, when he was knocked off his bicycle by a motorist. He sustained appalling injuries, including a fracture of the spine. Long periods of enforced solitude as a semi-invalid threw him back on the resources of his own imagination, and after reading *Hindoo Holiday* by J. R. Ackerley, he resolved to write a semi-autobiographical novel, based on Repton and China. The result, *Maiden Voyage* (1943), was acclaimed by Edith Sitwell, who contributed a foreword in which she wrote: 'This is a very moving and remarkable first book and the author appears to be that rare being, a born writer.' Welch's second novel, *In Youth is Pleasure*, recalling a summer holiday at the age of fifteen, was published two years later, and was dedicated to the memory of his mother, who had died when he was eleven. A number of Welch's short stories, all in effect autobiographical, were published during his lifetime, by Cyril Connolly in *Horizon*, John Lehmann in Penguin *New Writing*, and Peter Quennell in the *Cornhill Magazine*. Within the space of only eight years, although desperately ill, and while painting and illustrating as well, he completed some sixty short stories, all published posthumously, three novels, and a quarter of a million words of journals.

Because Welch was so isolated physically, and knew only a handful of fellow artists—his friends did include John Minton, with whom he collaborated over the line drawings for *Vogue's Contemporary Cooking*, by Doris Lytton Toye, Keith Vaughan, and Graham Sutherland, a near neighbour in Kent—Welch never attached himself formally to any school of painting, yet he became an almost unconscious and very prolific exponent of the neo-Romantic movement. He provided quixotic endpapers for his own first editions, which later became collectors' items, and his paintings, in oils, watercolours, and pencil, crayon, and gouache, were exhibited in the 1940s at the Leicester Galleries. After his death many were given away or sold for a few pounds, and he was largely ignored as a painter until in 1987 six examples of his work were loaned to an exhibition entitled 'A paradise lost' at the Barbican Art Gallery, devoted to the neo-Romantic movement. There are self-portraits in the National Portrait Gallery in London and at the University of Texas in Austin.

The quality, quantity, and character of Welch's output as a writer were inevitably circumscribed by his relative immobility, and the restrictions this placed on the acquisition of new material and experience. But he was in any event fascinated by his childhood and adolescence, and by the time he died this juvenile field had been fruitfully tilled and probably exhausted. It is his interest in the minutiae of life and his shrewd and perceptive descriptions of people, places, and events that have left the most indelible impression on his admirers. His journals in particular constitute a moving memorial to a young man of integrity and moral courage, whose determination not to succumb to pain and humiliation was at times heroic. It took him four years to write his third, and posthumously published, novel, *A Voice through a Cloud* (1950), an account of the accident itself and his struggle to convalesce. The manuscript was found beside his bed, complete except for about half a dozen pages, when he died, on 30 December 1948, at his home, Middle Orchard, Crouch, near Sevenoaks, Kent. During the last four years of his life he had been nursed by Eric Oliver, his partner for those years.

MICHAEL DE-LA-NOY, rev.

Sources M. De-la-Noy, *Denton Welch: the making of a writer* (1984) · **Archives** Ransom HRC, corresp. and literary MSS · University of Exeter Library, notebooks and photographs · **Likenesses** D. Welch, self-portrait, NPG · D. Welch, self-portrait, U. Texas · **Wealth at death** £5575 6s. 6d.: probate, 21 April 1949, *CGPLA Eng. & Wales*

Welch, (Grace) Eileen [*name in religion* Werburg] (1894–1990), Benedictine nun and artist, was born on 17 May 1894 at Beaumont, Sherdington Road, Cheltenham, the eldest of the four children (one brother died aged seven) of John Grindon Welch (1854–1939), gentleman, and his wife, Grace Mary (1868–1949), daughter of John Edward Crosby of Dublin and his wife, Rose. The future nun, baptized Grace Eileen, was known as Eileen until her entry into religious life. On the Crosby side she was related to St Oliver Plunket (*d.* 1681) and the earls of Fingall. Her father's family was protestant. He himself, influenced by Cardinal Newman's writings, had been received into the Roman Catholic church at the Birmingham Oratory in 1889. Soon after Eileen's birth he moved his family to his home town of Kidderminster. Her education began at the high school (1901–4) and continued at Elderslie, a convent school opened by Trinitarian nuns exiled from France by the anti-clerical regime. In 1906 the family moved to Boscombe, near Bournemouth, where Eileen and her sister were sent to school at the Convent of the Cross. Delicate, sharp featured, and intellectually precocious, Eileen's main interest was art. She studied at the Southampton School of Art and, after the family settled in Albert Road, Clifton, Bristol, at the Bristol Art School. Her mother's friendship with the mother of Desmond Chute, later a member of Eric Gill's Ditchling community, led to influential contacts.

On 19 May 1913 Eileen entered the Convent of the Religious of the Cross at Boscombe as a postulant. Realizing that life in a teaching order did not suit her she left the following February. On 23 March 1915, wearing a fashionable skirt so tight she could scarcely kneel, she entered the noviciate of Stanbrook Abbey, near Worcester, and was given the religious name of Werburg. After solemn vows on 30 November 1919 she became Dame Werburg—the title traditionally accorded to Benedictine nuns. Due to her hypersensitivity and independent mind the early years were stormy. Inner discipline was acquired through an attraction to the spirituality of the desert fathers.

Initially prepared to give up art, she was encouraged to continue; she came under pressure from the future abbess, Dame Laurentia McLachlan, and Dame Laurentia's friend Sydney Cockerell to abandon the angular style derived from Eric Gill to which she was to adhere throughout her life. The only other influences she would claim were William Blake in her youth, and Ernst Barlach in maturity. Werburg was thrilled to meet Gill when he visited Stanbrook with Chute on 23 July 1921. She described him as 'a small hairy man with thoughtful blue eyes and a bunch of red silk for a tie' (Stanbrook Abbey Archives). Chute, in consultation with Gill, had been tutoring her in wood-engraving by correspondence. 'How did you do anything so good using tools the wrong way round?' was his first criticism (ibid.). Between diagrams came passages of Ditchling aesthetic theory. Gill detected art school influence and advised against 'anatomy business'.

Commissions for vestment designs, paintings, and wood carvings followed an enthusiastic response to Werburg's contributions to the *Catholic Times* Arts and Crafts Exhibition of September 1929. In the 1930s and 1940s she frequently exhibited with the Guild of Catholic Artists and Craftsmen under the pseudonym of a Benedictine of Stanbrook. Reproductions of her work appeared in periodicals devoted to contemporary Catholic art such as *Art Notes* and *L'Artisan Liturgique*. Her most widely distributed wood-engraving, *The Praying Christ*, was commissioned by Abbé Paul Couturier at the suggestion of Evelyn Underhill for the 1940 Octave of Prayer for Christian Unity. In the 1950s she designed or painted stations of the cross for several churches, including those for St Edmund's, Isle of Dogs, which were restored for the new church in 1998.

Werburg's artistic and ecumenical interests were pursued in the context of faithful attention to the divine office and community duties. Over the years she assisted chantresses, portresses, printers, and sacristans, and served as sub-prioress from 1956 to 1968. During the Second World War she volunteered to take charge of the orchards, becoming an expert on fruit trees. She continued pruning into her eighties. High-spirited and affectionate, she remained close to her sister, Mollie Moriarty, who learned to weave her designs, and to her historian brother, Oliver.

Her monastic vocation both nurtured and narrowed Werburg's artistic vision. Her austere adaptation of Gill's style is masculine, emphasizing lines and angles. She had little use for femininity in art or life. Working exclusively on scriptural themes, her originality of design is at its finest in her wood-engravings and carved reliefs. These reveal and convey her deep spirituality. In November 1989

Werburg suffered a severe stroke. She died at Stanbrook Abbey aged ninety-five on 1 February 1990 and was buried in the monastery cemetery five days later.

JOANNA JAMIESON

Sources personal knowledge (2004) · private information (2004) [family] · Stanbrook Abbey Archives, Worcester · J. Jamieson, 'Letters to a Ditchling disciple', *Matrix: a review for printers and bibliophiles*, 14 (1994), 51–65 · confirmation certificate, Corpus Christi Church, Boscombe, 22/7/1907
Archives V&A NAL | Bodl. Oxf., John Johnson collection
Likenesses G. E. Welch, three self-portraits, pencil sketches, *c.*1913, Stanbrook Abbey, Worcestershire · photograph, *c.*1950–1959, Stanbrook Abbey, Worcestershire · S. Harrison, photographs, 1980, Stanbrook Abbey, Worcestershire

Welch, John. *See* Welsh, John (1568/9–1622).

Welch, Joseph (*c.*1750–1805), compiler of biographical reference works, was for forty years assistant to William Ginger, bookseller to Westminster School. He prepared a list of scholars, which for many years he sold in manuscript. In 1788, encouraged by the success of Pote's *Registrum regale* of Eton College (1774), he printed it under the title *A List of Scholars of St Peter's College, Westminster, as they were elected to Christ Church College, Oxford, and Trinity College, Cambridge, from … 1561 to the Present Time*. To it he prefixed lists of the deans of Westminster, the deans of Christ Church, Oxford, the masters of Trinity College, Cambridge, and the masters of Westminster School. The work, which was the first printed register of the school, was republished in 1852, under the editorship of Charles Bagot Phillimore, with the addition of the queen's scholars from 1663, and of copious biographical notes. The work is generally known as *Alumni Westmonasterienses*.

At the time of his death, in April 1805, Welch was living in Bowling Street, Westminster. He died 'not in affluence' (Nichols, *Lit. anecdotes*) and was buried at St John the Evangelist, Westminster, on 16 April 1805.

E. I. CARLYLE, rev. TONY TROWLES

Sources GM, 1st ser., 75 (1805), 389 · Nichols, *Lit. anecdotes*, 9.38 · parish register, St John the Evangelist, Westminster, 16 April 1805 [burial]
Wealth at death not in affluence: Nichols, *Lit. anecdotes*

Welch, Robert Radford (1929–2000), designer and silversmith, was born on 21 May 1929 in Hereford, the only son of Leonard Welch (*d.* 1971) and his wife, Dorothy Perkins (1897–1982), who trained as an artist. He grew up in Malvern, Worcestershire, and was trained at Malvern School of Art from 1946 to 1950, with interruptions for national service. From 1950 to 1952 he studied silversmithing at Birmingham College of Art, and from 1952 to 1955 he was at the Royal College of Art in London.

At another time Welch might have left the Royal College and followed a distinguished career as a silversmith. But in the 1950s the larger notion of 'design' was current at the college, thanks to the policies of the new principal, Robin Darwin, and the modernism of the decade. Robert Welch particularly admired the new, austerely beautiful cutlery and tableware designed by Scandinavians such as Folke Arstrom and Sigurd Persson in stainless steel; this became the subject of his diploma thesis. He began to think of himself as a designer and a silversmith, and this double identity remained with him for the rest of his life.

In 1955 Welch set up as a freelance designer–craftsman. He had a one-day-a-week job as consultant designer to Old Hall Tableware, the only British firm of any consequence producing stainless steel cutlery and tableware; it was at Bloxwich, just north of Birmingham. With the help of Gordon Russell, an early champion of his work at the Council of Industrial Design, he found a workshop on the top floor of an old silk mill in the beautiful Cotswold town of Chipping Campden, within reach of Bloxwich. In the early 1900s the silk mill had housed C. R. Ashbee and his Guild of Handicraft, one of the best-known workshops of the arts and crafts movement. In 1955 Welch was unaware of this, but later he was intrigued to find that such a figure had been there before him, and he formed a fine collection of Ashbee's silverwork. For his own part, he was soon successful, his work answering to the new modernism of British taste and 1960s inventiveness in domestic design. Some of his early designs—Alveston cutlery (1961), the Westclox alarm clock (1962), and the Chantry knife sharpener (1963)—were classics of their time.

The shape of all Welch's later life and work was settled in these early years. From now on he worked on the top floor of the silk mill in Chipping Campden; a shop in the High Street, selling his own designs, was opened in 1969, and another in Warwick in 1991. In 1959 he married Patricia Marguerite Hinksman, whom he had first met at Malvern, and they lived just outside Stratford upon Avon. He worked as a silversmith, producing church and presentation silver, and domestic tableware of moving simplicity; from 1958 he was helped by the silversmith John Limbrey, who also made models for his industrial designs. He worked as a designer of stainless steel cutlery and tableware, for Old Hall until 1970 and later for Prestige, the Japanese company Yamazaki, and others. And he worked as a designer of all kinds of domestic products, door furniture, pottery, light fittings, and kitchen tools. The distinction of all this work, whether it was made by hand or by machine, consists in a mixture of English modernist restraint, playfulness, and a sense of shapeliness and weight. Some of his designs are like small sculptures.

Welch was a big man, kindly, widely read, keen on sport. He designed by drawing—that was his basic visual language. But towards the end of his life he started to produce big, vibrant oil paintings, of which there were about 250 at the time of his death. He did not worry too much about professional success or changing trends, and his life was grounded in regular hours, the rhythm of work, and the cycle of the seasons. The recipient of many honours, he was appointed a royal designer for industry (1965) and was made an MBE (1980), and his work is represented in many collections, including those of the Worshipful Company of Goldsmiths and the Victoria and Albert Museum in London, and the Museum of Modern Art in New York. But professional critics made Robert Welch uneasy; so, to some extent, did London. Something deep in him belonged to the country, and he remained rooted in his chosen part of the south midlands.

Robert Welch died in Warwick on 15 March 2000, at the age of seventy, and was buried on 24 March in Chipping Campden. His company, Robert Welch Designs, was carried on by his children, Rupert, Alice, and William.

ALAN CRAWFORD

Sources C. Forbes, ed., *Robert Welch: design in a Cotswold workshop* (1973) · R. Welch, *Hand and machine: Robert Welch, designer silversmith* (1986) · *Robert Welch, designer silversmith: a retrospective exhibition, 1955–1995* (1995) [exhibition catalogue, Cheltenham Art Gallery and Museum] · *The Guardian* (23 March 2000) · F. MacCarthy, *British design since 1880: a visual history* (1982) · T. Harrod, *The crafts in Britain in the 20th century* (1999) · private information (2004) [Welch family] · *CGPLA Eng. & Wales* (2000)
Archives Guild of Handicraft Trust, Chipping Campden, designs, sketchbooks, working drawings, models, finished works, business MSS, catalogues, corresp., and photographs
Likenesses R. R. Welch, self-portraits, priv. coll. · photographs, Guild of Handicraft Trust, Chipping Campden, Robert Welch Archive
Wealth at death £604,949—gross; £603,479—net: probate, 17 Oct 2000, *CGPLA Eng. & Wales*

Welchman, Edward (1665–1739), Church of England clergyman and religious writer, was the son of John Welchman, gentleman, of Banbury, Oxfordshire. He matriculated as a commoner from Magdalen Hall, Oxford, on 7 July 1679 and was one of the choristers of Magdalen College from 1679 until 1682. He graduated BA on 24 April 1683 and was admitted a probationer fellow of Merton College in 1684; he graduated MA on 19 June 1688.

In 1690 Merton presented Welchman to the rectory of Lapworth, Warwickshire, in which county he was also rector of Berkeswell. At Lapworth eleven children born to him and his wife, Mary, were baptized between 1696 and 1719, the first being John, on 7 July 1696. Welchman was made archdeacon of Cardigan and a prebendary of St David's on 7 August 1727. He was later appointed chaplain to the bishop of Lichfield, who made him a prebendary of Wolvey in that cathedral on 28 September 1732; Welchman remembered the bishop in his will and left him a thirteen-volume Hebrew Bible. Welchman went on to gain the rectory of Solihull, Warwickshire, in 1736, which he held until his death.

Welchman published widely on religious subjects; his works include a piece against the nonjuring bishops in 1691, a sermon on charity in 1707, a popular anti-Roman Catholic tract in 1719, and a contribution to the Arian debate in 1721. His main work is his edition of the Thirty-Nine Articles. It was first published in Latin as *XXXIX articuli ecclesiae Anglicanae* (1713); an English translation from the sixth edition appeared in 1740 as *The Thirty-Nine Articles of the Church of England, Illustrated with Notes*. The English version proved particularly successful; it was reprinted regularly throughout the eighteenth century and well into the next.

Welchman's *Husbandman's Manual* (1695) was also very popular. In it he gives a prayer for every countryside activity, from sowing and ploughing to the singing of the birds. The manual went through eighteen editions in the eighteenth century and, like the edition of the Thirty-Nine Articles, was reprinted in the nineteenth century; it was translated into Welsh in 1711 and was one of the works distributed by the SPCK.

Welchman died on 19 May 1739 and was survived by his wife, who inherited most of his estate, in the manors of Balsall and Knowle, and in the parish of Tamworth. Of their large family only five—Samuel, Richard, Mary, Anne, and Constance—are mentioned in Welchman's will of 30 April 1739.

THOMPSON COOPER, *rev.* EMMA MAJOR

Sources Foster, *Alum. Oxon.* · *ESTC* · will, PRO, PROB 11/696, sig. 143 · *Fasti Angl.* (Hardy), 1.315, 320, 642 · *GM*, 1st ser., 9 (1739), 327 · L. W. Brüggemann, *A view of the English editions, translations and illustrations of the ancient Greek and Latin authors* (1797), 724, 747 · R. Graves, *The spiritual Quixote* (1773) · Wood, *Ath. Oxon.*, new edn, 4.481 · J. Cooke, *The preacher's assistant*, 2 vols. (1783) · [M. de la Roche], *New memoirs of literature*, 6 vols. (1725–7), 2.122
Wealth at death left over £2200 in money bequests; also property of unspecified value in the manors of Balsall and Knowle, and in the parish of Tamworth: will, PRO, PROB 11/696, fol. 405

Welchman, (William) Gordon (1906–1985), codebreaker, was born at Fishponds, near Bristol, on 15 June 1906, the younger son (the elder was killed in 1914) and youngest of three children of William Welchman (1866–1954), a missionary who became a country parson and archdeacon of Bristol, and his wife, Elizabeth Marshall, daughter of the Revd Edward Moule Griffith. He went to Marlborough College in 1920 and to Trinity College, Cambridge, in 1925. In the mathematical tripos he obtained a first class in part one (1926) and part two (1928). He then went on to teach at Cheltenham for one year before returning to Cambridge where he became a fellow of Sidney Sussex College in 1929 and wrote *Introduction to Algebraic Geometry* (1950). He was recruited for service at the government communications headquarters at Bletchley Park in 1938 or 1939 and worked there until 1945.

It was during the early years of the Second World War that Welchman made a significant contribution to the solving of the Enigma machine cipher which was used extensively by the Germans. He worked with Alan Turing and C. H. O'D. Alexander. Some of his key technical solutions had already been devised by the Poles and by others at Bletchley, but he instinctively grasped a whole range of problems, possibilities, and solutions which included two vital mathematical constructs as well as a concept of the total process required, from the intercepted German ciphered traffic to passing on significant intelligence implications to the commanders in the field—a highly complex logistical operation for which total secrecy was an added condition.

Welchman, assigned by Dillwyn Knox on arrival at Bletchley Park to comparatively low-level research on call signs, quickly realized that he and his few colleagues were dealing with an entire communication system that would serve the needs of the German ground and air forces. It was the development of traffic analysis which was his greatest contribution, but in these early months he made two startling breakthroughs in enabling Enigma-coded signals to be read. The first had to do with the indicator setting and indicator of an Enigma message. A long and intricate series of mathematical thought processes resulted in Welchman reinvestigating a system of perforated sheets, ignorant of the fact that the Poles had done this before, and that a colleague elsewhere in Bletchley Park already had production in hand. Early in 1940 Alan Turing had the idea of making a machine which would test all possible rotor positions of the Enigma to find those at which a given cipher text could be transformed into a plain text. Welchman greatly improved on Turing's design by his invention of a device known as a diagonal board, which Turing himself immediately recognized to be invaluable.

These two relevant and vital achievements took place within months of his arrival, and it was not long before Welchman was applying his mind in a wider context. He had practical gifts and a strong personality. Once it was clear that Bletchley Park would be able to read enemy traffic on a massive scale he established the need for increased facilities and close co-operation between the intercepting stations, the cryptographers, the intelligence processors, and the ultimate users. An informed view is clear that the task of converting the original breakthrough into an efficient user of the material was one for which Welchman should receive much of the credit. He himself wrote about his work long after the war in a book for which he was wrongly attacked by the authorities for divulging secrets which might still be of use to a hostile power. His motives however were transparently honourable and the sustained powers of thought and memory evinced in the early chapters of *The Hut Six Story* (1982), somewhat amended in a subsequent article in *Intelligence and National Security*, are characteristic not only of his considerable mental powers but also of his deep conviction that there were important lessons to be learned from the breaking of the Enigma secrets, and that governmental refusal to disclose such matters in order to learn from them was a matter of overriding public concern. After the publication of his book his accreditation to the Mitre Corporation, which he had joined in America in 1962 and where he concentrated on the development of secure communications systems for the US forces, was withdrawn and the last months of his life, as he was dying of cancer, were marred by the authorities trying to stop him from publishing. He had moved permanently to America in 1948 and became an American citizen in 1962.

Welchman's great achievement took place in 1940–43. At Bletchley Park he became assistant director for mechanization. He was appointed OBE in 1946. After the war he became director of research for the John Lewis Partnership but settled in America in 1948. His wartime experience led him to the computer field and he pioneered developments in digital compiling.

Welchman had an acute analytical mind, boundless drive and enthusiasm, but rather limited imagination. At a crucial moment in the Second World War he brought together discrete ideas and divergent pieces of evidence to produce a total policy framework. As a man, though not always easy for his colleagues to communicate with, he was admired, trusted, and liked, for his great charm as well as intelligence and kindness.

Welchman married in 1937 a professional musician, Katharine, the daughter of Francis Faith Hodgson, a captain in the 84th Punjabis, Indian army. They had one son and two daughters. After divorce in 1959 he married Fannie Hillsmith, an artist, the daughter of Clarence Hillsmith, consulting engineer, of New Hampshire. This marriage also ended in divorce (1971) and in 1972 he married Elisabeth, daughter of his second cousin, Myrtle Octavia Hussey, and her husband, Anton Wilhelm Huber, owner of a sawmill and a carpentry contractor, in Aschau in Chiemgau, Bavaria, Germany; she was a physiotherapist. He loved mountains, for climbing and skiing. He was an avid gardener and a keen amateur musician. He died on 8 October 1985 at Newburyport, Massachusetts. He was survived by his third wife. ROBIN DENNISTON, *rev.*

Sources G. Welchman, *The hut six story* (1982) · private information (1990) · personal knowledge (1990)

Weld, Charles Richard (1813–1869), author, was born at Windsor in August 1813, eldest son and only surviving child of Isaac Weld (d. 1824) and his second wife, Lucy (d. 1834), daughter of Eyre Powell of Great Connell, Kildare. The Welds claimed descent from an ancient Catholic family of Dorset, through the protestant convert and American pioneer Thomas Weld (1595–1661). This branch of the family possessed considerable estates in Ireland, where Charles's father held a lucrative government appointment, agreeably surrounded by educated and influential men. Charles was named for his father's friendship with Charles James Fox. Isaac *Weld (1774–1856), son of Isaac's first marriage, to Elizabeth Kerr, was already well known in literary and scientific circles and had written of his travels in North America before Charles was born.

From 1820 Charles Weld and his parents resided in a château near Dijon for several years and on their return they settled in north Wales. After his father died, Charles lodged with Isaac at Ravenswell, near Dublin, sharing his circle of associates and attending classes at Trinity College, without taking a degree. He also stayed on the Isle of Wight with a married half-sister; on one such occasion, running on the pier at Ryde, he fell and damaged his spine, to which accident he attributed his later stoop. In 1836 he went on the grand tour of the continent with John Potter, and thereafter he generally spent two months each year touring in Britain or abroad. His positions in later life admitted him to all manner of libraries and institutions on the continent.

Weld moved to London and in 1839 took employment as secretary to the Statistical Society. He contributed several papers to the society's journal and with C. T. Banfield compiled the statistical *Companion to the Pocket Book* (1843), which went through many editions. In 1842 he married Anne, daughter of Henry Selwood, of an old Berkshire family; they had one daughter, Agnes Grace (b. 1849). This marriage bonded him into other influential circles. His wife was a niece of Sir John Franklin, the Arctic explorer;

her elder sister Emily was married to Alfred Tennyson and her younger sister Louisa to Charles Tennyson. Weld studied law at the Middle Temple and was called to the bar in 1844, but he had succumbed to the attractions of science and, with the help of Sir John Barrow, in December 1843 he was appointed assistant secretary and librarian to the Royal Society, where he drew a salary of £200, with accommodation on the society's premises. Despite his lowly status, he was invited to dine with the Royal Society Club in the 1844/5 session as the guest of Sir John Franklin.

The Royal Society at this time was in a fever for reform and Weld was frequently asked for details concerning its past organization. Encouraged by Dr Peter Mark Roget, its then secretary, Weld decided to compile an administrative history, a task which, as he pursued his researches well beyond the society's archives, absorbed four years of his spare time. The two volumes, published in 1848, with illustrations by his wife, combined accuracy with style and were well received. Weld had demolished the myth surrounding the society's mace, erroneously said to be that which Cromwell had ordered to be removed from the House of Commons, although *The Athenaeum's* reviewer took exception to Weld's version of the gossip surrounding Newton's patrons.

Weld proved a diligent servant, bringing order to the society's library and compiling a list of its portraits. His annual tours, unaccompanied by his wife and daughter, generated a series of travel books, beginning in 1850 with Auvergne, Piedmont, and Savoy, extending to North America in 1854, and eventually including Scotland, Ireland, and other parts of western Europe. His relationship with Sir John and Jane Franklin led him to lecture and write on Arctic travel and, after Franklin's disappearance, on the search for Franklin's expedition.

In March 1861 Weld left the Royal Society, as a consequence of having introduced a lady to his rooms at Burlington House. His explanation, that 'she was of independent fortune', cut no ice. The affair was disguised by Sir Edward Sabine and Sir George Stokes, who compelled Weld to tender his resignation to the Society's council 'for family reasons'. Wishing him to depart immediately, Sabine and Stokes reluctantly decided to pay his salary to the end of the year.

In his later years Weld became a partner in a publishing business with Lovell Reeve (*d.* 1865). He enjoyed poetry, especially that of his brother-in-law Alfred Tennyson, and himself wrote verse. He liked dogs, and almost always had one by him, even in town. He was happiest when fishing in some rural stream. In 1862 he was appointed a district superintendent of the international exhibition held in London, responsible for the organization of the philosophical instruments section, which he reported on for the *Illustrated London News*. He represented Great Britain at the Paris Exhibition of 1867 and, while there, made the acquaintance of a friend who invited him to Burgundy the following year. This provided material for his last book, which his wife edited after his death. From 1865 he had lived near Bath, Somerset, and had been active in the Bath

Literary and Philosophical Association. Weld died suddenly at his home, Belle Vue House, Newbridge Hill, Bath, on 15 January 1869. ANITA MCCONNELL

Sources M. B. Hall, *The library and archives of the Royal Society, 1630–1990* (1992), 29–31 · *The Athenaeum* (23 Jan 1869), 130 · 'Report of the commissioners for the exhibition of 1862', *Parl. papers* (1863), 14.1–12, 25–39, no. 001 · *Reports on the Paris Universal Exhibition, 1867* (1868), 2.237–62, 2.543–61 · J. Hutchinson, ed., *A catalogue of notable Middle Templars: with brief biographical notices* (1902), 256 · A. Weld, 'Preface', in C. R. Weld, *Notes on Burgundy* (1869) · CGPLA Eng. & Wales (1869) · DNB
Archives CUL, corresp. with Sir George Stokes, etc.
Likenesses photograph, repro. in Weld, *Notes on Burgundy*, frontispiece
Wealth at death under £7000: resworn probate, June 1870, CGPLA Eng. & Wales (1869)

Weld, Sir Frederick Aloysius (1823–1891), premier of New Zealand and colonial governor, was born on 9 May 1823 at Chideock Manor, Bridport, Dorset. He came from a well-known Roman Catholic family, being the third son of Humphrey Weld of Chideock Manor, and his wife, Christina Maria, the second daughter of Charles Clifford, sixth Baron Clifford of Chudleigh. Following his education at Stonyhurst College and at the University of Fribourg, Switzerland, he sailed in November 1843 to join relatives already in the New Zealand Company settlement of Port Nicholson. In partnership with his cousin Charles Clifford, he established sheep stations in the Wairarapa (Wharekaka), Marlborough (Flaxbourne), and Canterbury (Stonyhurst) districts, and he drew on this practical experience to produce an informative pamphlet, *Hints to Intending Sheepfarmers in New Zealand*, which was published in London in 1851. Pastoralism and exploration were major preoccupations at this time of his life, and early in 1855 Weld succeeded in finding a shorter stock route between Nelson and Christchurch. His competence as an artist is revealed in the sketches and paintings that resulted from his explorations within the North and South Islands of New Zealand and his ascent of the active Hawaiian volcano Mauna Loa in November 1855.

Weld was elected member for Wairau, and attended the first session of the New Zealand house of representatives, which opened in Auckland in May 1854. He was one of the three members chosen to serve in a ministry which sought, unsuccessfully, to expedite the transition from crown colony to responsible government status. Political involvement over the next five years was erratic, but in November 1860 Weld's fundamental belief in the need to assert the supremacy of British rule in New Zealand led him to accept the native affairs portfolio in the ministry of Edward Stafford. On 3 March 1859 he married Filumena (Mena) Mary Anne Lisle Phillipps (*d.* 1903) of Garendon Park, Leicester; the couple had six sons and seven daughters, all but one of whom survived to adulthood.

Following political defeat in July 1861, Weld concentrated on developing a 300-acre family estate at Brackenfield, north of Christchurch. He continued to deplore official handling of the armed conflict in Taranaki, advocating instead a policy of military self-reliance whereby the colonists would dispense with the imperial regiments and would conduct colonial campaigns using colonial resources. In November 1864, believing, unwisely, that he had secured Governor Sir George Grey's support for such a policy, the 41-year-old was sworn in as premier.

The prospects for success were inauspicious. Weld's personal reputation as a man of integrity was no match for Grey's duplicity. Prolonged wrangling between the governor and Lieutenant-General Duncan Cameron undermined all prospect of the colonists' military success against Maori, while the removal of the seat of government from Auckland to Wellington fuelled provincial hostilities. Confiscation of 1.2 million acres of Waikato land in December 1864 caused widespread bitterness and resentment among those tribes most affected. Financial difficulties, petty political wrangling, and lack of co-operation from the governor contributed to the strain of holding office. Utterly exhausted, Weld announced his resignation on 13 October 1865 and retreated to Brackenfield to recover his health. Later ministries were to build on the financial and military initiatives of the self-reliance advocates, but the destructive legacy of confiscation persists to the present, a legacy which Weld did not acknowledge when reviewing political developments in his pamphlet *Notes on New Zealand Affairs* published in London in 1869.

The Welds returned to England in 1867. In December 1868, his health restored, Weld approached the Colonial Office seeking employment, a request favourably received and promptly actioned, for in May 1869, with his wife and their family of six children, he departed England for Western Australia and the start of an eighteen-year career as a colonial governor.

Once in the colony, Weld moved quickly to establish the style of energetic and active administration that was to be his hallmark. He promoted such public works as the inauguration of a coastal shipping service and the extension of telegraph lines; he facilitated the expansion of the timber industry; and fostered the farming sector through his introduction in 1873 of the Torrens system of land registration. He presided over the introduction of an elective element into the legislative council in December 1870; and he encouraged settler participation in local self-government through membership of school and roads boards and other municipal institutions. Eventually in 1871, but only after heated debate, he achieved his goal of an elementary education act, which included the principle of state aid to denominational schools. Although Weld displayed significant errors of judgement both in his handling of the controversial Landor–Burges affair of 1872–3, which involved a white settler facing criminal charges for the shooting of an Aborigine, and with his precipitate advocacy of responsible government in 1874, his achievements in Western Australia were substantial. He was created CMG for services rendered and promoted to the self-governing colony of Tasmania at the end of 1874.

Political factionalism and personal financial difficulties marred Weld's enjoyment of an otherwise pleasant and successful term of office in Tasmania. The intense personal antipathy between the chief justice and the premier affected Weld most directly when he acted on ministerial advice to pardon a convicted arsonist in November 1876. His conduct throughout the subsequent two-year controversy was upheld by the Colonial Office, but Weld was constantly irritated by the Tasmanians' reluctance to address more substantial issues—provision for meeting imperial self-defence requirements especially. In personal terms the Welds paid a high price for the Tasmania interlude, for official economies in 1872 had significantly reduced the level of the governor's salary and abolished all allowances. Weld's difficulties in meeting official expenses while maintaining a household of twelve children were exacerbated when his aide-de-camp incurred substantial debts by misusing the governor's household account. Weld had therefore to sell Brackenfield and to draw heavily on personal income in an effort to cover the costs of his Tasmanian term of office.

Weld was promoted to the Straits Settlements, in March 1880, at a time when the possible extension of British influence in the Malay peninsula was under review, and he relished the return to a more active style of governorship. He made sustained efforts to resolve land-tenure problems, fostered improved communications and public services, supported the construction of a new museum and library at Singapore, and promoted effective management of the country's timber resources. His primary interest, though, was the consolidation of relations with the princely states, and by the end of his term of office he was able to record progress in Perak, Selangor, Sungei Ujong, and the states of the Negri Sembilan and Rembau, while new accords with the rulers of Johore and Pahang led to closer administrative links between Malay and British authorities. Weld had nevertheless annoyed the Foreign Office by his persistent suggestions for undermining Siamese influence in the northern part of the peninsula and by his independent actions when sent, in 1887, on a mission to Borneo to resolve the rival claims of Sarawak and the North Borneo Company.

Weld was made KCMG in 1880 and GCMG in 1885. He retired on a first-class pension in October 1887, and he returned with his family to England, to Chideock Manor, where on 20 July 1891 he died of illnesses contracted during a visit to the Straits Settlements in his capacity as a director of the Pahang Exploration and Development Company. A man of ability, culture, and deep faith, straightforward and chivalrous but occasionally lacking in judgement, Weld had a lifelong devotion to the cause of empire.

JEANINE GRAHAM

Sources J. Graham, *Frederick Weld* (1983) · A. Lovat, *The life of Sir Frederick Weld, GCMG, a pioneer of empire* (1914) · J. Graham, 'Weld, Frederick Aloysius', *DNZB*, vol. 1

Archives Archives New Zealand, Wellington, corresp., journals, and papers · Catholic Archives, Perth · Dorset RO, corresp., pedigrees, etc.; diary · NL NZ, Turnbull L., corresp. and papers relating to New Zealand | Auckland Public Library, letters to Sir George Grey · Bodl. Oxf., corresp. with Lord Kimberley · Canterbury Museum, Christchurch, corresp. with J. R. Godley · PRO, CO 18/158–80; CO 280/383–8; CO 273/102–48

Likenesses A. R. Venables, oils, priv. coll.

Wealth at death £4784 1s. 1d.: probate, 17 Aug 1891, *CGPLA Eng. & Wales*

Weld, Humphrey (1612–1685), property developer and administrator, was born on 22 January 1612, the second but first surviving son of Sir John Weld (1582–1622) of Arnold's Court, Edmonton, Middlesex, and his wife, Frances (*d.* 1656), daughter of Sir William Whitmore of Apley Park, Shropshire. Both Sir John's father and Lady Frances's grandfather had been lord mayors of London. Weld matriculated at Trinity College, Cambridge, in 1629 but migrated to the Inner Temple in November 1630. Touring the continent during 1633–6 he met the mysterious Catholic known as Peter Fitton and developed complex financial ties with him that endured twenty years at least. Though the Welds were staunch protestants, Humphrey Weld became a devout Catholic, as did his younger brother John. By December 1638 Humphrey Weld had married Clare (*d.* 1691), the eminently Catholic daughter of Thomas, second Baron Arundell of Wardour. In January 1639 Weld was appointed cupbearer to the queen, and he appears to have served the king in Scotland. The Welds' only child, Mary (*d.* 1688), was born in 1640. The following year (1641) Weld sold his grandfather's London house and acquired two properties of considerably greater value. The Lulworth Castle estate in Dorset cost £42,860 and necessitated significant borrowing, yet about this time Weld also bought part of Aldwych Close, west of Lincoln's Inn Fields in London.

Weld spent much of the civil war at Oxford and he surrendered with the garrison at Worcester in 1646. Armed with certificates of communion, he petitioned to compound on the Oxford articles and was fined £1981 in 1647, of which he paid £996. By now Weld's life was full of the paradoxes it would manifest until the Popish Plot: though a royalist, he had supplied four canon to parliament; while buying expensive art from abroad, he pleaded poverty at home, and while some of those pieces were devotional and his servants all Catholics, he managed to evade the oath of abjuration. Indeed, his recusancy was so suppressed that he was able to buy in various forfeited estates on behalf of their Catholic owners, including his nephew, the third Lord Arundell. Weld acquired the rest of Aldwych Close in 1649 and embarked on redeveloping the whole property. The family spent time abroad in the 1650s, but by 1658 the Weld House complex was complete. It became a centre for Catholicism, with the Welds living in one part, various, mainly Catholic, tenants residing in another, and a succession of diplomats from Catholic crowns (Portugal, France, and Spain) occupying the main house, which included a Catholic chapel.

At the Restoration, Weld petitioned for several offices and was made governor of Portland Castle and keeper of Sandsbrook Castle. In 1661, he was returned as member of parliament for Christchurch, Hampshire, where his wife and her sisters owned the manor. He became also a justice of the peace for the counties of Dorset (1660–79), Middlesex (1660–79), and, later, Cambridgeshire (1677–9). On 17 March 1661 Weld was granted a secret service pension of £1000 per annum, perhaps for local intelligence, but possibly in connection with his foreign diplomatic tenants. Whatever service he provided, it was clearly valued enough for the grant to be renewed in 1668, in which year he became a gentleman of the privy chamber.

Some believed that Weld used his offices to protect Catholics. When he arrested a man sent by Sir Richard Everard to seize Catholic property, Everard wrote that 'to revenge the seisure of Popish trinketts upon a poore man whose warrant … enforced him to his duty, argues more affection to Babilon then to the Crowne of England' (Dorset RO, D/WLC C2, no. 6, Everard to Weld, 11 April 1663). A mob attacked Weld House in 1671, shouting 'this is the grand justice that hangs and quarters us all' (*CSP dom.*, 1671, 241), but Weld's recusancy, rather than his executive diligence, may have been its instigator. In 1674, when Sir Thomas Preston inherited lands that he wanted to put to the use of Jesuits, Weld was among those who helped to find suitable priests and administer the estate.

Considering Weld's record, his connection with Fitton, and his Catholic household and tenants, it was unlikely that even such a brilliantly evasive man could live through the Popish Plot untarnished, even though as late as 1675, he served, albeit briefly, on the first Hampshire recusancy commission. In his only recorded speech in parliament he denied ever hearing mass in his house, and he secured a certificate of conformity from the church of St Martin-in-the-Fields. But Weld House was searched and he had to mortgage his estates. In 1679 he was removed from his magistracies and, with Christchurch Manor now sold, he did not seek re-election to parliament. That year offered some consolation when his daughter Mary married Nicholas Taafe, second earl of Carlingford.

Litigation and financial straits darkened Weld's last years: various creditors brought an action for recovery in 1676; the attorney-general named him in a suit against Preston in 1682; he was sued in 1683 for receiving rents on mortgaged lands, and some tenants also brought him to court. In 1680 Weld himself sued Spanish ambassador Pedro Ronquillo for rent overdue. Only the first of these cases was even near settlement when Weld died in London in November 1685. By this time he had been outlawed for debt, but the bulk of his property had already been settled in 1672 on his nephew and successor, William Weld (1649–1698). Family tradition suggests a clandestine Roman Catholic burial at Westminster Abbey, but no record appears. In 1688 Weld House was badly burnt, but Wild Street marks its location. RODERICK CLAYTON

Sources J. P. Ferris, 'Weld, Humphrey', HoP, *Commons, 1660–90* · J. Berkeley, *Lulworth and the Welds* (1971) · Dorset RO, Weld MSS D/WLC, esp. F9–10, C1–4, L13–27, X16–17, E187 · W. E. Riley, *The parish of St Giles-in-the-Fields*, ed. L. Gomme, 2, Survey of London, 5 (1914) · Bodl. Oxf., MS Top. Lancs. d. 4 · BL, Add. MS 46457 · *CSP dom.*, 1656; 1660–62; 1667–8; 1671 · Venn, *Alum. Cant.* · W. H. Cooke, ed., *Students admitted to the Inner Temple, 1547–1660* [1878] · W. A. Shaw, ed., *Calendar of treasury books*, 1–7, PRO (1904–16) · R. E. Clayton, 'Diplomats and diplomacy in London, 1667–1672', DPhil diss., U. Oxf., 1995

Archives Dorset RO, letters and papers

Likenesses C. Janssen, oils, *c*.1638, Lulworth Castle, Dorset; repro. in Berkeley, *Lulworth and the Welds*
Wealth at death bankrupt; most property (especially Lulworth) already settled on nephew in 1672

Weld, Isaac (1774–1856), topographical writer, born in Fleet Street, Dublin, on 15 March 1774, was the eldest son of Isaac Weld (*d.* 1824) and his first wife, Elizabeth Kerr, and the half-brother of Charles Richard *Weld. His great-great-grandfather, the Revd Edmund Weld (*c.*1631–1668), chaplain of Blarney Castle, co. Cork, was the descendant of Sir Richard Weld of Eaton. His grandfather was named Isaac after Newton, the friend of his great-grandfather, Dr Nathaniel Weld (1660–1730). Both Nathaniel and his son Isaac (1710–1778) were nonconformist ministers at New Row, Dublin. Isaac's edition of John Leland's *Discourses* (4 vols., 1769) has an autobiographical preface.

Young Isaac, the third of the name, was sent to the school of Samuel Whyte at 75 Grafton Street, Dublin, and thence to that of Rochemont Barbauld at Palgrave, near Diss, Norfolk. From Diss he went to Norwich as a private pupil of Dr William Enfield, a well-known dissenting minister; he left Norwich in 1793. He gained the degree BA from Trinity College, Dublin. In 1795, having decided to explore the United States and Canada, he set sail from Dublin for Philadelphia. He spent a little over two years in America. Often guided by Indians, he explored the vast forests and great rivers. While in the towns he mixed in the best society, and he met George Washington. He returned home at the close of 1797 'without entertaining the slightest wish to revisit [North America]', and published in 1799 his *Travels through … North America and … Canada*. The work was well received and it went to several English editions and was translated into French, German, and Dutch. It was, however, described as 'a silly book by one Weld', one of a number of European 'birds of passage' whose books had done 'much mischief' and whose enquiries often bothered George Washington (letter of Richard Peters, American patriot and jurist, to James Madison). None the less, his descriptions were influential because they were relatively early and were long included in compilations of travellers' reports on the United States in this period, despite his general lack of sympathy with the American patriots. Weld was introduced at the Institut at Paris as an American traveller, and was elected a member of the Historical and Literary Society of Quebec, and, on 27 November 1800, of the Royal Dublin Society, of which he in 1849 became vice-president.

In 1801, at the request of the lord lieutenant of Ireland, Lord Hardwicke, Weld drew up a paper based on data in his book, in the hope of diverting Irish emigrants away from the United States to Canada. Lord Hardwicke in return procured for him a post in the Irish customs, which had been held by Weld's father, but which brought Weld himself very little money. He married at Edinburgh, in 1802, Alexandrina Home; they had no children.

Shortly afterwards Weld published *Illustrations of … Killarney* (1807 and 1812), which, like his American work, he illustrated himself, and which included a description of his journeys made in a boat which he manufactured out of compressed brown paper. His taste for unusual craft continued when, in May 1815, he sailed in the pioneer 14 horsepower steamboat *Thames*, from Dún Laoghaire to London, a voyage which he described in an appendix to George Dodd's *Dissertation on Steam Engines* (1818). In 1838 he drew up for the Royal Dublin Society a *Statistical Survey … of Roscommon*. He took a keen interest in Irish industries, and suggested the triennial exhibitions which the Royal Dublin Society later inaugurated.

In his later years Weld travelled extensively in Italy and spent much time in Rome, where he became a close friend of Canova. He died on 4 August 1856 at Ravenswell, near Bray, where most of his later life (when he was not travelling) had been spent. The Royal Dublin Society raised a monument to his memory in Mount Jerome cemetery in 1857. He apparently regretted the ill humour and anti-American tone of his first book (letter of Joseph Dulles cited in Allibone, *Dict.*) but it is none the less the work for which he is best remembered.

THOMAS SECCOMBE, *rev.* ELIZABETH BAIGENT

Sources *Dublin University Magazine*, 49 (1857), 70–80 • *The Athenaeum* (3 Jan 1857), 19 • R. Peters, letter to James Madison, 1801, University of Virginia, Virginia, USA • *GM*, 2nd ser., 43 (1855), 610 • Allibone, *Dict.* • W. B. S. Taylor, *History of the University of Dublin* (1845) • Boase, *Mod. Eng. biog.*

Weld, Joseph (1777–1863). *See under* Weld, Thomas (1773–1837).

Weld, Maria Anne. *See* Fitzherbert, Maria Anne (1756–1837).

Weld, Thomas (*bap.* 1595, *d.* 1661), Independent minister and religious controversialist, was baptized on 13 July 1595 in Sudbury, Suffolk, the son of Edmund Weld. He graduated BA from Trinity College, Cambridge, in 1613 and MA in 1618. He was soon active in Essex puritan networks, may have served as a lecturer at Haverhill in the early 1620s, and became vicar of Terling in 1625. By then he had married his first wife, Margaret; they had four children. He worked hard and contentiously to suppress moral disorder in Terling, boarded divinity students, including the future New England divine Thomas Shepard, in his house, and occasionally hosted the regular meetings of the informal Essex ministerial conference led by Thomas Hooker; Weld signed a petition dated 10 November 1629 to William Laud, then bishop of London, in support of Hooker.

Weld's activism caught the attention of the church authorities, who were unhappy with the extent of puritan agitation in Essex. They already had their eye on him for his nonconformity in 1628, and in 1629 his churchwardens had to explain to diocesan officials why Hugh Peters, a silenced minister, had been allowed to preach in their church. Weld was called before the archdeacon's court in May 1630 to explain why he lectured on weekdays. He cleared himself but investigation continued. A paper drawn up by Laud, dated 25 November 1630, lists Weld as one of Essex's nonconformable ministers and he was asked to subscribe. Fined £20 by the ecclesiastical commission in 1631 for an unspecified offence, Weld was deprived by Laud on 2 September for his nonconformity, a process completed by the high commission in January 1632. After his excommunication, at the instigation of a number of Essex ministers, he personally confronted Laud following a church service. Weld left behind him in Terling a core of nonconformist lay puritan militancy which his puritan successor, John Stalham, had to manage discretely to avoid more conflict with the authorities.

Later in 1632 Weld went briefly to the Netherlands but he was already in touch with the leaders of the Massachusetts Bay Colony and he arrived at Boston, Massachusetts, on 5 June. In July he became pastor of the newly founded church at Roxbury, serving along with its teacher, John Eliot, the future 'Apostle to the Indians'. A glowing letter from Weld to Terling that summer, describing Massachusetts as a model puritan polity, induced some of his former parishioners to join him in Roxbury, where he took the freeman's oath on 6 November 1632. In 1636 he married his second wife, Judith.

Roxbury was heavily affected by the antinomian controversy, a religious dispute over how one could know one was saved, that shook the colony in the mid-1630s. Perhaps because Roxbury bordered Boston, source of the dissident opinions, more of its laity actively sided with the dissidents than in any town outside Boston. Weld worked vigorously to re-establish orthodoxy. He was a member of the synod that met at the end of the summer of 1637 and condemned a variety of the teachings of Boston's teacher, John Cotton, the minister, John Wheelwright, and the leading Boston lay person, Anne Hutchinson. In January 1638 Roxbury excommunicated three members, the only church besides Boston to resort to this extreme measure. Weld's brother boarded Anne Hutchinson in Roxbury in her period of house arrest between her trial in November 1637 and the execution of her sentence of banishment the following March. Weld's other major contribution to New England religious life was to serve on a committee with John Eliot and Richard Mather that devised a new metrical version of the psalms, *The Whole Book of Psalmes, Faithfully Translated into English Metre*. Printed in Cambridge, Massachusetts, in 1640, it was the first book published in the English colonies. Its versification has won little praise.

On 2 June 1641 the Massachusetts general court appointed Weld, along with the minister Hugh Peters and Boston merchant William Hibbins, to serve as agents in England. The agents were to seek for financial relief for the hard-pressed colony, to raise funds for Harvard College and evangelizing the Native Americans, and to support further church reform in England. Weld helped to secure customs relief for New England trade and had some success in fund-raising, but his efforts became mired at the New England end in mismanagement and corruption.

Weld threw himself into the religious controversies of England, with mixed results. Once again he confronted William Laud, by now imprisoned, for his harrowing of Essex puritans, and may have been involved in an abortive scheme to exile Laud and Matthew Wren to Massachusetts. As Independents and presbyterians began to dispute over church government, Weld wrote tracts defending New England Congregationalism, and, with Peters, edited and published the works of his New England brethren. As disputes over the nature of salvation similar to the antinomian controversy surfaced in England, a collection of related documents compiled by John Winthrop was published in London as *A Catalogue of Erroneous Opinions Condemned in New England* (1644). The compilation had little narrative thread, and Weld, at the urging of others, he claimed, remedied that deficiency with a preface and conclusion added to a second edition, *A short story of the rise, reign, and ruin of the antinomians, familists, & libertines, that infected the churches of New-England* (1644). *Short Story* was intended to show that Congregationalism was capable of defending religious orthodoxy; presbyterians seized upon the example to show that Congregationalism fostered religious anarchy, and that the toleration that Independents were claiming for themselves in England was belied by the intolerance of their Massachusetts brethren. Some in New England suspected that presbyterians had manoeuvred Weld into publishing it. Presbyterians also stirred up rumours that Weld and Peters had embezzled funds destined for Massachusetts. The Massachusetts authorities recalled the two men in October 1645, but both elected to remain in England. Weld served briefly in 1646 as rector at Wanlip, Leicestershire, and on 1 February 1649 was installed at St Mary's, Gateshead.

In Newcastle, Weld became embroiled in more religious controversy. He worked with other Newcastle ministers, Independent and presbyterian, to attack the sects. He helped expose the 'False Jew', Thomas Ramsey, whom the Hexham Baptists had assumed they had converted—an exposure Weld was able to turn into an effective attack on the Baptists. He joined forces with other local ministers for a number of attacks on Quakers, but those opponents, including James Nayler, were not easily cowed and a nasty pamphlet war ensued. Weld also had to deal with difficulties in his own congregation. He employed Independent standards of eligibility for the Lord's supper which were notably stricter than presbyterian and always a bone of contention between the two groups. By 1657 dissatisfied parishioners claimed that Weld had excluded over a thousand people from the sacrament, and only administered it to ten marginal members of the congregation (Weld claimed the figure was twenty). His renegation on a compromise to admit a presbyterian lecturer resulted in his parishioners bringing an unsuccessful complaint against him to the northern commissioners on 3 March 1658.

There is no evidence that Weld attempted to retain his post at the Restoration, and Charles II appointed John Landler to the position on 16 March 1660. Weld signed the declaration of London Independent ministers denouncing Venner's Fifth Monarchy insurrection of January 1661, and died in the city on 23 March that year. His second wife had died (she was buried at Gateshead in 1656) and he had married again; his third wife, Margaret, died after him, in 1671.

MICHAEL P. WINSHIP

Sources R. C. Anderson, ed., *The great migration begins: immigrants to New England, 1620–1633*, 3 vols. (Boston, MA, 1995) • T. Webster, *Godly clergy in early Stuart England: the Caroline puritan movement,* *c.1620–1643* (1997), 37, 189–90, 195–6 • R. Howell, 'Thomas Weld of Gateshead: the return of a New England puritan', *Archaeologia Aeliana*, 4th ser., 48 (1970), 303–32 • E. Emerson, ed., *Letters from New England: the Massachusetts Bay Colony, 1629–1638* (1976), 94–8 • *Memoirs of the life of Mr Ambrose Barnes*, ed. [W. H. D. Longstaffe], SurtS, 50 (1867), 375–82 • P. Sterns, 'The Weld–Peters mission to England', *Publications of the Colonial Society of Massachusetts*, 32 (1937), 188–246 • K. Wrightson and D. Levine, *Poverty and piety in an English village: Terling, 1525–1700*, 2nd edn (1995), 137–8, 160–61, 222 • *The history of the troubles and tryal of William Laud to which is prefixed the diary of his own life* (1695), 201, 213–14 • T. Weld and J. Winthrop, *A short story of the rise, reign, and ruin of the antinomians, familists, & libertines, that infected the churches of New-England* (1644) • T. Weld, *A vindication of Mr Weld* (1658) • *Records relating to the early history of Boston* (1884), 78, 79, 91 • letter, T. Hooker to D. Shepard, 17 Sept 1646, Massachusetts Archives, Thomas Hutchinson MSS, 100, vol. 1 • *The journal of John Winthrop, 1630–1649*, ed. R. S. Dunn, J. Savage, and L. Yeandle (1996), 69, 72, 354, 402–4, 428–9 • J. Snow, 'The life of Master John Shaw', *Yorkshire diaries and autobiographies*, ed. C. Jackson, [1], 121–62, SurtS, 65 (1877), esp. 124

Weld, Thomas (1750–1810), landowner and benefactor, was born on 24 August 1750 at Lulworth Castle, Dorset, the fourth son of Edward Weld (1705–1761) and Mary, *née* Vaughan (1713–1754). The Weld family originally came from Cheshire and bought the Lulworth estate, including the castle (built in 1610) from the third earl of Suffolk in 1641. Thomas was educated at the English colleges on the continent run by the Jesuit fathers, first at St Omer (1759–62) and then for the next three years at Bruges. On 27 February 1772 he married Mary (1753–1830), daughter of John Massey Stanley of Hooton Hall, Cheshire. They had fourteen children of whom the eldest son, Thomas *Weld (1773–1837), became a cardinal in the Roman Catholic church.

In 1775 Thomas succeeded his brother Edward (1741–1775) to the family estates. His inheritance made Thomas a wealthy man with five estates including Stonyhurst and Shireburn (both in Lancashire), the latter bequeathed by Elizabeth, heiress of Sir Nicholas Shireburn and wife of William Weld, Thomas's great-grandfather. At Lulworth, Thomas continued the building work started by Edward. He constructed the first free-standing Roman Catholic chapel built since the Reformation. In this chapel in 1790 were consecrated on separate days John Carroll, founder of the Roman Catholic hierarchy in the United States, and bishops John Douglass and William Gibson. In 1789 George III visited Lulworth while staying at Weymouth. He was handsomely entertained and revisited the Weld family five times before 1792.

Thomas Weld's wealth and position made him an important figure in the Roman Catholic struggle for relief of the penal laws. However, despite his earnest support for the campaign, he was also determined to remain aloof from movements of which he disapproved and which he believed undermined the position of the vicars apostolic. So he refused to become a member either of the Catholic committee which preceded the second Relief Act of 1791 or of the Cisalpine Club which followed it. During the 1790s Weld offered support for continental Roman Catholics who had been displaced by the French Revolution.

Particularly close relations were forged between the Franciscan nuns and the Trappists who he helped to establish a monastery in the grounds of Lulworth. A keen sportsman, fond of shooting and hunting, Weld himself followed a strict lifestyle similar to those who benefited from his philanthropy.

In 1794 Weld offered his house and grounds at Stonyhurst, Lancashire, to a group of twelve exiled Jesuits who had been driven from the English college, then based at Liège. Stonyhurst College quickly developed from this new foundation, and Weld had his younger sons educated at the school. In 1802 he gave a former mill owner's house on the estate to the college, first as a noviciate, and soon after as a preparatory school. Weld died on 1 August 1810 at Stonyhurst, one day after suffering a stroke while attending the school's feast day. He was buried at Lulworth Chapel.   F. J. TURNER

Sources archives of the diocese of Clifton, Bristol • Dorset RO, Weld papers • Burke, *Gen. GB* • J. Berkeley, *Lulworth and the Welds* (1971) • J. Gerard, *Stonyhurst College centenary record* (1894) • G. Holt, *St Omers and Bruges colleges, 1593–1773: a biographical dictionary*, Catholic RS, 69 (1979) • M. Whitehead, '"In the sincerest intentions of studying": the educational legacy of Thomas Weld (1750–1810), founder of Stonyhurst College', *Recusant History*, 26 (2002), 169–93
Archives archives of diocese of Clifton, Bristol • Bodl. Oxf. • Dorset RO, corresp. and papers
Likenesses oils, *c.*1765 (aged fifteen; after portrait at Lulworth), Stonyhurst College, Lancashire • G. Hussey, pencil drawing, *c.*1780, repro. in Whitehead, '"In the sincerest intentions of studying"', 183 • oils, *c.*1805 (in middle age; after B. West), Stonyhurst College, Lancashire • B. West, portrait, Lulworth Castle, Dorset
Wealth at death substantial, especially land

Weld, Thomas (1773–1837), cardinal, was born in London on 22 January 1773, the eldest son of Thomas *Weld (1750–1810) of Lulworth Castle, Dorset, and his wife, Mary Massey Stanley (1753–1830), eldest daughter of Sir John Massey Stanley of Hooton Hall, Cheshire. Weld was educated at home by Father Charles Plowden SJ, and may also have spent a year at the Jesuit academy at Liège. He was a keen amateur artist and musician; a French horn and a flageolet were found in his possession at his death. In the 1790s he served as a sergeant in the Dorset yeomanry. During these years he was also associated with his father in offering hospitality to French clerics and religious communities in exile. On 14 June 1796 he married, at Ugbrooke, Lucy Bridget (d. 1815), second daughter of Thomas Clifford of Tixall. He and his wife spent their early married life at Westbrook House, at Upwey, near Weymouth, where their only child, a daughter named Mary Lucy, was born in 1799.

In 1810, after the death of his father, who had provided liberally for his younger sons and his widow, Weld, as heir, was probably left with a straitened income. He decided to economize by closing Lulworth Castle and living in Clifton, near Bath, for six years. His next years were troubled ones. His financial situation worsened as the agricultural slump of the second decade of the century affected his income. In addition, Weld was drawn into the arguments between Bishop John Milner, an old family friend and political ally of his father, and the other vicars apostolic over the question of concessions to the British government in order to secure Catholic emancipation. Weld had joined the Catholic board organizing the campaign against the remaining disabilities in 1812, but resigned when Milner was expelled from it in 1814. Then, on 1 June 1815, his wife died.

Soon after her death Weld decided to become a priest, but before he could begin his studies several matters needed to be settled. The first was a crisis in the Cistercian monastery of St Susan, which Weld's father had established at Lulworth for emigré French monks: a renegade monk had made several serious allegations against the monastery before local magistrates. Secretary of state Lord Sidmouth demanded that Weld close the monastery, but Weld managed to persuade him against any active measures and to induce the monks to return to France voluntarily in 1817. In addition, Weld wished to see his daughter married and his estate settled before following his vocation. Mary's marriage in September 1818 to her second cousin, Hugh Charles Clifford, later seventh Baron Clifford, removed one anxiety, but the settlement of his estate proved complicated: Lulworth was not transferred to his brother Joseph until 1828.

Weld began his studies for the priesthood under Abbé Carron, taking minor orders in 1820; he was ordained on 7 April 1821. In June 1822 he became assistant priest at the Chelsea mission and at St Mary's, Cadogan Street. He subsequently moved to Hammersmith, where he was spiritual director to a community of Benedictine nuns. In 1826 he was appointed coadjutor to Alexander Macdonell, bishop in Upper Canada, and was consecrated as bishop of Amycla on 6 August. However, legal business, his own frail health, and the sickness of his daughter meant that he never left for Canada. Accompanying his daughter and her family on a trip to Italy, Weld visited Rome; shortly after his arrival there he was made a cardinal by Pius VIII, being admitted to the College of Cardinals on 15 March 1830. Weld's unexpected elevation, which made him the first English cardinal since Philip Thomas Howard (1629–1694), was seen as a gesture of papal goodwill towards England in the wake of the Catholic Emancipation Act. A Weld family legend less credibly interpreted it as a compliment to George IV: Mrs Fitzherbert, the king's mistress (or wife), was the widow of Weld's uncle. Weld is said to have received assurances from leading figures in England that his elevation was viewed favourably.

Weld's daughter died on 15 May 1831, but her widower and children continued to live with the cardinal, who occupied splendid apartments in the Odescalchi Palace. He was well-known for his hospitality, entertaining Roman society as well as his fellow countrymen. Unable to learn Italian, he probably participated little in the management of Vatican business, appointing secretaries and advisers to assist him. But he was held to be influential in English affairs with the pope, and he acted as cardinal protector of the English College in Rome. Weld died on 19 April 1837 in Rome, and, like his daughter, was buried at the church of St Marcellus. His contemporaries were effusive in their praise of his character; Nicholas Wiseman (389) commented that if he had a fault, it was 'the excessiveness of his kindness'.

Joseph Weld (1777–1863), younger brother of Cardinal Weld, was born on 27 January 1777 at Lulworth Castle. Educated at home, he was sent to Stonyhurst College in November 1794. In November 1802 he married Elizabeth Charlotte Stourton (1782–1864), daughter of Charles Philip, sixteenth Lord Stourton; his father settled the estate of Pylewell, near the Solent, on the couple. Pylewell was situated very conveniently for the pursuit of Weld's yachting interests, and he spent over £3000 on improvements to the property. In 1830 Weld received the family of Charles X, the exiled French king, at Lulworth, when the castle became their temporary refuge.

Yachting was Weld's main occupation: in 1815 he was a founder member of the club which later became the Royal Yacht Club, and he dominated yacht races from 1825 until 1861, winning—according to his own estimate—£3000 in prize money. He was extremely interested in boat design: on one occasion he wrote to the Admiralty offering to build a naval brig to his own design on their approval. The successes of his yachts, particularly the *Arrow* and the *Alarm*, witnessed to his considerable expertise. He died at Lulworth Castle on 19 October 1863, survived by three sons and a daughter.   ROSEMARY MITCHELL

Sources J. Berkeley, *Lulworth and the Welds* (1971), 209–54 · G. Oliver, *Collections illustrating the history of the Catholic religion in the counties of Cornwall, Devon, Dorset, Somerset, Wilts, and Gloucester* (1857), 52, 434 · N. Wiseman, *Recollections of the four last popes* (1858), 383–90 · *GM*, 3rd ser., 16 (1864), 120 · J. H. Pollen, 'Weld', *The Catholic encyclopedia*, ed. C. G. Herbermann and others, 15 (1912) · B. N. Ward, *The eve of Catholic emancipation*, 3 vols. (1911–12), vol. 3, pp. 184–6 · B. Ward, *The sequel to Catholic emancipation*, 1 (1915), 43, 126–7 · Gillow, *Lit. biog. hist.*

Archives Dorset RO, devotional papers, etc. · NRA, priv. coll., accounts and corresp. | Devon RO, Clifford MSS · Westm. DA, corresp. with Bishop Bransdon

Likenesses portrait, 1820–29, repro. in Ward, *Eve of Catholic emancipation*, facing p. 186; at archbishop's house, Westminster, in 1912 · portrait, 1830–39, repro. in Ward, *The sequel to Catholic emancipation*, facing p. 43; at English College, Rome, in 1915 · portrait, 1830–39, priv. coll. · W. Furze, pencil drawing, 1837, NPG · J. Ramsay, oils, Ugbrooke Park, Devon · oils, English College, Rome

Wealth at death under £30,000—Joseph Weld: will, 1863

Weldon, Sir Anthony (*bap.* 1583, *d.* 1648), local politician and reputed satirist, was baptized at East Peckham, Kent, on 29 January 1583, the eldest son of Ralph Weldon (1545/6–1609) of Swanscombe, Kent, and his wife, Elizabeth (*d.* 1616), the daughter of Leven Buskin. Anthony's father, knighted by James I on 24 July 1603, was clerk of the green cloth to both Elizabeth I and her successor, while his uncle, also Anthony, was clerk of the kitchen. Weldon succeeded to both these places in the royal household: acquiring his uncle's office in 1604 when the latter resigned, and in 1609 inheriting that of his father. On 5 June 1604 Weldon married Elinor, or Ellen (*bap.* 1588, *d.* 1622), daughter of George Wilmer. They had four daughters and eight sons (of whom six survived to adulthood). Two of his sons, Ralph *Weldon, the eldest, and Anthony *Weldon, held commissions as officers in the parliamentarian armies of the civil war period.

In the tenth year of the reign of James I, Weldon was granted the ownership of Rochester Castle. Firmly ensconced in a place of influence within the royal household, Weldon accompanied the king on his progress to Scotland in 1617 and on the way north was knighted at Berwick on 11 May. However, something went wrong to disrupt the long career at court that Weldon might have anticipated. After his death it was claimed that he was the author, long shrouded in mystery, of a letter which had been written from Leith, near Edinburgh, ostensibly directed to an English correspondent, on 20 June 1617, describing the poverty, bigotry, and foolish traditions of the Scots in exaggerated terms. It is said that, discovering the depths of his official's distaste for the land of his birth, the king dismissed Weldon from his post. However, attribution of the letter to Weldon is very insecure. The many surviving manuscript versions are signed by different names, including John E. and John R. The first surviving printed edition, *A Discription of Scotland*, apparently published in the Netherlands in 1626, was credited to one Doctor Corbett. More printed versions were published in the 1640s and 1650s, none of which is ascribed to Weldon. James Howell's name appears on the title-page of the 1649 edition. Claims for Weldon's authorship of the *Perfect Description of the People and Country of Scotland* are further undermined by the fact that the clerk of the green cloth and the kitchen does not appear to have relinquished his position in the king's household until October 1623, six years after supposedly falling into disgrace. While it may be possible to see euphemism in the formal instrument by which he laid down his patent, where the reason given for his resignation was his retirement into the country on health grounds, he was nevertheless granted compensation for the loss of office to the tune of £1000, a show of munificence which does not bespeak disfavour. There are hints that he may have fallen victim to Lionel Cranfield's reform of the household. On 11 February the secretary, Conway, had written to Cranfield about taking in hand the articles against Weldon and another household official, Sir Robert Bannister, while in a letter apparently written around that time Weldon sought the assistance of a colleague in moving the case against him from the exchequer chamber to king's bench. It seems entirely likely that Weldon's name became associated with the *Perfect Description* only when the violently anti-Jacobean tract of 1650, *The Court and Character of King James*, was attributed to him, apologists for the house of Stuart seeking to depict its author as an embittered former courtier. Weldon was imaginatively portrayed as the victim of James I's ire in order that he might be further smeared with the vices of ingratitude, hypocrisy, and tale bearing. After the Restoration Anthony Wood further undermined the former courtier's reputation by offering additional evidence for Weldon's authorship of *The Court and Character*. Wood stated that Weldon had shown the work to fellow courtiers before the civil war, but that their horrified reactions convinced him not to publish. But there would appear to be no contemporary evidence whatever to suggest that Weldon even moved into a position of hostility towards the court after he left service there. Certainly, he promoted a scheme for improving assessment of ship money in 1638 by ending the 'abuse' of employing sheriffs and high constables as collectors (*CSP dom.*, 1637–8, p. 233). In 1641 he complained against the administration of the gunpowder monopoly. But such actions do not clearly mark him out as an opponent of royal policies, much less of the king himself.

However, after 1642 Weldon's loyalties were not in question for a moment. As the head of the county committee he held Kent for parliament, remorselessly engrossing every jurisdiction and applying 'dictatorial methods' which rendered him 'personally detestable' to the historian of the great rebellion in that shire (Everitt, 15). He has been portrayed as an autocrat and tyrant, needlessly oppressive in his treatment of the county's numerous royalists, increasingly dependent on an ever narrowing clique of lesser parliamentarian gentry, and most of the blame for the Kentish revolt of 1648 has been laid at Weldon's door. But although much has been made of his reputedly violent and embittered temperament, construed almost entirely on the basis of his supposed sufferings at the hands of James I, it seems likely that Weldon was as much a victim of the 'functional radicalisation' which the harsh and terrifying experiences of civil war inflicted on Englishmen in the 1640s, as any malevolence of spirit. His fellow Kentishman, sworn foe, and passionate royalist, Sir Roger Twysden, was gracious enough to acknowledge the 'noble principles' which jostled with the 'many vanities, if not vices' in Weldon's breast (Everitt, 134–5). Twysden also believed that it was not Weldon's support for the two houses which motivated him so much as a 'desire of rule' inspired by feuds with his neighbours which 'brought hym to run with the forwardest' (ibid.).

Weldon did what he could to protect Kent from the exactions of a parliament too easily prey to the many temptations of the rich and populous county on its doorstep, and he himself was quick to blame the 1648 revolt on the disproportionate burden of parliamentary taxation placed on his countrymen. It is probably equally true that Weldon and his cohort too often found their interests betrayed at Westminster, where parliament was prepared to extend a lenient hand to the royalists of the county who rebelled with alarming frequency. For instance, a failure of resolve at Westminster in the prosecution of the Christmas 1647 Canterbury rioters probably also contributed to the rebellion the following summer. Faced with the uncertainty of support at Westminster, Weldon and his clique owed the security of their position in Kent almost entirely to their own efforts, a fact which doubtless helps to explain their vigour in the government of the county.

It is equally clear that the full story of Weldonian 'tyranny' cannot be told independently of the factional struggles within the county committee, and their correlation with the conflicts at Westminster between presbyterians and Independents. From 1646 the maintenance of Weldon's supremacy in Kent in the face of the challenges posed by his fellow committee man Sir John Sedley of St Clere depended very largely on the closeness of his ties with the Independent leadership in the House of Commons, and their ability to bear down Sedley's supporters, among them Denzil Holles and Sir William Waller. On 24 October 1648 Weldon was awarded £500 for his service in suppressing the royalist rebellion in Kent. However, he may already have been dead when the award was made. He was buried at Swanscombe on 27 October.

In 1650 *The Court and Character* was published. The following year William Sanderson first made the allegation that Weldon was its author, and set in train the tradition of the embittered former courtier. In 1653 a brief history of the English monarchy was published entitled *A Cat may Look upon a King*. This book has also been attributed to Weldon, evidently incorrectly, as the author refers to the execution of Charles I, and it is considered far more likely to have been the work of Marchamont Nedham. Despite the somewhat perilous uncertainty of evidence for Weldon's role as a satirist, the publications with which he is commonly associated have enjoyed enormous popularity and influence on later historians. Sir Walter Scott's republication of *The Court and Character* in *The Secret History of the Court of James I* (1811) revived them, and modern historians have frequently had cause to lament the way in which 'Weldon' succeeded in distorting history. He may have been unfair, and his satire was certainly just one example drawn from a rich contemporary vein of courtly criticism, but his version of James VI and I as a perverted, hypocritical, slobbering villain remains compelling.

Michael Weldon (d. in or before 1654), army officer, was a kinsman of Sir Anthony, a member of the Northumberland branch of the family. He was employed by parliament as an agent to the Scottish committee of estates in May 1643 and commanded a regiment of horse in the Scottish army which entered England the following year, continuing to serve in that capacity until 1646. Letters of administration were granted to his widow, Mary, on 12 July 1654. JOSEPH MARSHALL and SEAN KELSEY

Sources DNB · A. Everitt, *The community of Kent and the great rebellion, 1640–60* (1966) · Wood, *Ath. Oxon.*, new edn, 2.867–9 · G. J. Armytage, ed., *A visitation of the county of Kent, begun … 1663, finished … 1668*, Harleian Society, 54 (1906) · E. Hasted, *The history and topographical survey of the county of Kent*, 12 vols. (1797–1801), vol. 1, p. 261; vol. 8, p. 106 · W. A. Shaw, *Knights of England*, 3 vols. (1906) · warrants for the resignation of Sir Anthony Weldon from the clerkship of the green cloth, PRO, LS 13/168, fol. 253r and 253v · CSP dom., 1619–23, 428; 1623–5, 550; 1633–5, 220, 244; 1637–8, 233, 598 · L. B. Larking, ed., *Proceedings principally in the county of Kent in connection with the parliaments called in 1640, and especially with the committee of religion appointed in that year*, CS, old ser., 80 (1862) · W. A. McNeill and P. E. B. McNeill, 'The Scottish progress of James VI, 1617', SHR, 75 (1996), 38–51 · nineteenth-century Kentish genealogies, BL, Add. MS 16279 · administration, PRO, PROB 6/29, fol. 207r [Michael Weldon] · list of royal servants, BL, Lansdowne MS 273, fol. 31v · chancery lawsuit, 14 Jan 1617, PRO, C 78/216/6 · www.ihrinfo.ac.uk/office/greencloth-clerk.html, 19 Sept 2002 · 'Sir Roger Twysden's journal', *Archaeologia Cantiana*, 1 (1858), 184–216; 2 (1859), 175–220; 3 (1860), 145–76; 4 (1861), 131–202 · [W. Sanderson], *Aulicus Coquinariae* (1650 [i.e. 1651]) · W. Scott, *Secret history of the court of James I* (1811) · G. Goodman, *Court of King James the First* (1839) · J. Wormald, 'James VI and I: two kings or one?', *History*, 68 (1983), 187–209 · J. Rushworth, *Historical collections*, 5 pts in 8 vols. (1659–1701) · STC, 1475–1640 · *Antiquarian Repertory*, 2 (1808), 326–7 · *Miscellany of the Abbotsford Club, volume first* (1837) · J. Nichols, *The progresses, processions, and magnificent festivities of King James I, his royal consort, family and court*, 3 (1828), 338–43 · IGI
Likenesses line engraving, pubd 1779 (after Bullfinch), NPG · portrait, repro. in *Antiquarian Repertory*

Weldon, Anthony (*bap.* 1610), parliamentarian army officer, was baptized at East Peckham, Kent, on 29 June 1610, the fourth son, of eight sons and four daughters, of Sir Anthony *Weldon (*bap.* 1583, *d.* 1648) of Swanscombe, Kent, and his wife, Helen (or Elinor) Wilmer (*bap.* 1588, *d.* 1622). His father, knighted in 1617, lost his place at court in 1623, emerging in the 1640s as the county boss who controlled Kent for parliament. Anthony's eldest brother, Ralph *Weldon, was also a parliamentarian army officer.

By his own account Weldon was a professional soldier from 1622 or 1623 onwards. In 1639 he met at Lyons the returning ambassador to Venice, Basil Feilding, earl of Denbigh, who persuaded him to come back to England and march in the king's army against the Scots. Weldon was colonel of a Northumberland regiment during the first bishops' war, but chose not to serve when the army reformed the following year 'as not being at all satisfied with the lawfulness of that Engagement, and for some other reasons which I expressed in a Letter to the earl of Northumberland the General of that Army' (Weldon, *To the Parliament*, 3). He went abroad and returned in time, he later claimed, to refuse to accompany the king in demanding the five members from parliament in January 1642. He went to fight in Ireland where, he later recalled with characteristic self-righteousness, while other less worthy men were given senior posts, he 'was forced (if I would go at all), to go with a single Company (which my zeal prompted me cheerfully to accept)' (ibid., 4).

Weldon was sent to the relief of Duncannon, co. Wexford, where he served as captain of the garrison until 1643. However, he quarrelled with the garrison commander, Laurence Esmonde, Lord Esmonde, whom he regarded as too much the friend of the king rather than of parliament and too easy-going in his relations with his Catholic neighbours whom he was holding the fort against. He returned to England and took a commission as major in the horse regiment of Theophilus Clinton, earl of Lincoln, part of the army of the eastern association. This posting proved no more congenial than the former, and Weldon was soon presenting parliament with charges against the Lincolnshire county committee. In 1644 he transferred as major to a Kentish horse regiment in Sir William Waller's army, commanded by Sir Michael Livesey. Livesey was not a success as a soldier. In May 1644 Weldon preferred articles against his commander, accusing him of dishonouring his regiment, exposing his major to grave personal danger for no better reason than his own timidity, then trying to rid himself of the embarrassment by putting Weldon and his troop under another command. He also referred to Livesey's desertion of his post at Cheriton Down in March. A committee was set up by the Commons to investigate. Sir William Waller accused Livesey of running away from the battle at Cropredy Bridge in June, and at the same time

Weldon 'posted him [Livesey] for a mutineer and a coward' in Westminster Hall (Weldon, *True Declaration*, 14).

The Commons regarded Weldon's accusation as an act of disrespect to their authority, and referred the matter to the committee of examinations, who ruled Weldon's claims 'a false and scandalous Libell' and sent him to Newgate until he should give Livesey satisfaction (Weldon, *True Declaration*, 18). They no doubt meant an apology and possibly financial recompense; an unrepentant Weldon interpreted the word rather differently and compounded the offence: 'I challenged him [Livesey], told him I would Cudgell him, and publisht it, which satisfied me, for my private affronts I received by him' (ibid., 19). After ten months' imprisonment in Newgate, and several petitions for his release, he published his defiant *The True Declaration of Colonell Anthony Welden*. Gaoled without a hearing, and denied a trial, he charged parliament with arbitrary actions every bit as bad as those of Star Chamber or high commission:

> And since I suffer for accusing, and my accusation not heard, nor my witnesses accepted, I leave to the world to judge the measure I have received. And I hope this will satisfie all men I am not the least sufferer for the Publike but the greatest for this particular. (ibid.)

Weldon was released in 1646, after the Lords pressed his case on the Commons in March. He left England and took service in the Spanish army in the Netherlands. However, he lost his command, and was imprisoned on account of yet another quarrel with a commanding officer, this time George Goring, Lord Goring. In 1648 Weldon returned to England and attempted to raise a regiment from royalist prisoners for service in the pay of the Venetian state. On 19 March 1649, having alerted the Rump Parliament to the recent publication of the Koran, Weldon was sent with a party of soldiers and a sergeant-at-arms to search out and seize the press responsible, and to bring the printer before the council of state, who seem to have regarded Weldon as an officious nuisance for his efforts. Obstructed in his Venetian scheme by his enemies in parliament, owed eight years' arrears, and denied the opportunity of service in England or Ireland, Weldon vented his frustrations in another pamphlet, *To the Parliament of England and Army*. He repeated his charge of parliamentary tyranny:

> It goes much against my heart and conscience, to see that arbitrary power continue in them, for which they plucked others down, and see so many poor oppressed cry at their doors daily for justice, without dispatch, hearing, redress or hope thereof. (Weldon, *To the Parliament*, 45)

He now added the bitterness of the old soldier overtaken by younger men, of the gentleman displaced by the social upstarts of the New Model Army:

> 'Tis high time for me to learn some mechanick Trade after twenty six yeers Service; and so come to be admitted a Colonel in the Army, as others are, who are not known by their birth, garb or merit. I am sorry to see Gentry so trodden down, as if they were lesse meritorious, or less faithfull than these new upstarts. (ibid., 41)

On 20 April 1649 Weldon had a pass for himself, his wife (of whom nothing is yet known), and three servants to take ship overseas, to an unspecified destination. On 11 December 1650 a warrant went out from the council of state for his arrest, for reasons unstated. On 30 November 1654 the lord protector granted Weldon's personal request to go abroad once more. Nothing more is heard of him.

SEAN KELSEY

Sources A. Weldon, *The true declaration of Colonell Anthony Welden* (1645) [probably 1646 ns] • A. Weldon, *To the parliament of England and army* (1649) • nineteenth-century genealogy of Weldon family, BL, Add. MS 33895, fol. 133*r* • *CSP dom.*, 1644–54 • *JHC*, 3–6 (1642–51) • C. H. Firth and G. Davies, *The regimental history of Cromwell's army*, 2 vols. (1940) • *IGI*

Weldon, George Anthony Thomas (1908–1963), conductor, was born on 5 June 1908 at Herondean, Newfishbourne, Sussex, the second of the two children of Francis Harry Weldon (1869–1920), army officer, and his wife, Eveleen (*d.* 1955), amateur artist and daughter of Thomas Fielden Campbell of Devonshire Place, London. Weldon entered Sherborne School in 1921. Exclusion from physical activities through a lower leg withered from birth allowed him to concentrate on his established instrument, the piano. He won the school's Halliday music prize in 1925 and, the following year, left for the Royal College of Music to study piano under Arthur Benjamin. Conducting, an extra with Billy Reed and Aylmer Buesst, became Weldon's main subject under Malcolm Sargent.

From 1930 until 1943 Weldon conducted the Tunbridge Wells Symphony Orchestra. The Choral Society elected to join the orchestra under his leadership in 1942, and under his baton the orchestra grew in numbers and reputation. Between 1931 and 1943 Weldon also conducted the Newbury Amateur Orchestral Union. In 1937 he was appointed deputy conductor of Hastings Municipal Orchestra. Rejected for military service after the outbreak of war, he subsequently worked for ENSA, the Entertainments National Service Association. From 1942 Weldon conducted the London Symphony Orchestra on tour and in London theatres and, after the war, abroad and in the Albert Hall. He was one of the five fiftieth jubilee concert conductors (1954) and made at least twenty-eight recordings with the orchestra.

One of eight selected candidates for the conductorship of the City of Birmingham Orchestra, Weldon gave his trial concert in 1943. In spite of appreciation from audiences and also from music critics, he was not offered a full contract until the following year. By then he had formed the city's first salaried orchestra, which gave its initial concert in September. Through ENSA contacts he obtained recording work for it and introduced a wide range of concerts. In addition, the orchestra undertook educational work and toured extensively, using Weldon's wartime venues. In 1947, following his conductorship of the BBC Symphony Orchestra, the City of Birmingham Orchestra gave at least twenty-one BBC broadcasts. In 1948, prior to the orchestra's Albert Hall début, he initiated its name change to the City of Birmingham Symphony Orchestra. However, its financial problems were aggravated when its committee responded to critics' demand for more modern and unfamiliar music. Weldon,

George Anthony Thomas Weldon (1908–1963), by unknown photographer

believing programmes should be balanced, did not renew his contract after 1951, although he returned to conduct Birmingham's 1951 music festival and, as guest conductor, fill the town hall.

His busy schedule encouraged Weldon to freelance, but classical music was a shrinking market. In 1952, therefore, he accepted an invitation from his friend Sir John Barbirolli to become associate conductor of the Hallé, which was still expanding its audiences with Promenade and industrial concerts. During Barbirolli's illness in 1955 Weldon successfully conducted performances, including the Hallé's first television appearance, at short notice. According to Barbirolli, Weldon had two great loves, music and very fast cars. The latter included two revolutionary Atalantas (in one of which, as 'Gat' Weldon, he had won the 1937 Lewes speed trials).

A financially conscious music director, Weldon was an ingenious improviser, producing remarkable music under difficult conditions. He promoted the work of English musicians, including Elgar, Bliss, Bax, Vaughan Williams, Walton, and Sullivan (whose music he introduced to the concert platform). His recordings were mainly of popular classics, which offered an outlet for his flair and professionalism but failed to reveal his full potential. However, his arrangement of 'Suo gan', for a long time concluded every Hallé promenade season. Another work, 'Mice', composed for performance at Newbury (1937), also played in Birmingham, Manchester, and broadcast, now is lost. A popular figure abroad, Weldon notably conducted in Turkey, Yugoslavia, Germany, and Africa.

In 1963, suffering from asthma, and against medical advice, Weldon toured through Athens, Istanbul, Ankara, and on to Cape Town, for his third winter concert series there. He died of heart failure in the West County Hotel, Cape Town, during the night of 16/17 August. Following private Cape Town and London church ceremonies, his body was cremated and his ashes were scattered in his garden at 37 St John's Wood Road, London. Unmarried, he was survived by his sister, Sybil. JEAN POWRIE

Sources private information (2004) [friends and colleagues] · wills [George Weldon; Eveleen Weldon; Dame Harty] · Burke, *Peerage* (1975) · b. cert. · *WWW* · R. Hardcastle, *Royal Tunbridge Wells Symphony Orchestra* (1997) · J. W. Eykyn, *1879–1979: The story of the Newbury Symphony Orchestra in its centenary year* (1979) · *CGPLA Eng. & Wales* (1963) · Sherborne School register · Royal College of Music register
Archives BBC WAC
Likenesses I. Clegg, portrait, in or after 1958 (conducting the proms), Manchester · D. Allen, photographs · A. McBean, photographs · L. Wood, portrait (*Weldon tour de force*) · photograph, John Whybrow Collection, Birmingham [*see illus.*]
Wealth at death £33,922 11s. 7d.: probate, 30 Dec 1963, *CGPLA Eng. & Wales*

Weldon [*née* Thomas], **Georgina** (1837–1914), campaigner against the lunacy laws and celebrated litigant, was born at Tooting Lodge, Clapham Common, on 24 May 1837, the eldest of three daughters and two sons of Morgan Thomas (1803–1867), a member of the Welsh landed gentry, and his wife, Louisa Frances, daughter of John Apsley Dalrymple of Gate House, Mayfield, Sussex. Her father was a non-practising barrister, having inherited a considerable sum of money from his father and uncle, and concentrated on becoming Conservative MP for Coventry. In 1856 the family at the behest of her father changed its name to Treherne, the surname of his more illustrious ancestors up to the mid-eighteenth century. She spent most of her girlhood in Florence and her fine soprano voice was trained by her mother, with the exception of a few lessons in 1855 from Jules de Glimes in Brussels. On 21 April 1860 she married (William) Henry Weldon, a lieutenant in the eighteenth hussars; this went against her father's wishes, prompting him to disinherit her. She had ambitions for a career on the stage but her husband, like her father before him, refused to allow her to appear as a professional and she was restricted to performing in amateur theatricals and charity concerts.

In 1869 Mrs Weldon, whose childless marriage was breaking down, devised a scheme for a National Training School of Music to teach music to poor children. Establishing herself at Tavistock House, Bloomsbury, she filled her house with orphans, pursuing a highly progressive plan of education. Attendance at the opera, vegetarianism, and indiscipline were among the least controversial of her methods. Most educational establishments sought to mould their pupils into acceptance of their class status, but not Mrs Weldon's. She became an advocate of rational dress and took up an interest in spiritualism. She also joined Henry Leslie's famous choir and through that met the French composer Charles Gounod in March 1871. That year she sang the solo in Mendelssohn's *Hear my Prayer* at various venues in London, and took the solo soprano part in Gounod's patriotic cantata *Gallia* at the Conservatoire and the Opéra Comique in Paris. By November Gounod, who was in poor health, had moved into Tavistock House. During this period Mrs Weldon's career benefited from her association with Gounod. However, in June 1874, Gounod, dismayed by growing gossip about what was portrayed as the 'Weldon affair', returned to his wife in Paris. Casting herself in the role of a martyr, Mrs Weldon declined to forward his personal belongings, including the draft of his opera *Polyeucte*. When he asked her to return them to him, she insisted that he claim them from her in person. It was not until he had virtually reconstructed the music, a task that took nearly a year, that she returned the original draft to him with her name scrawled diagonally across each page in crayon. She went on to launch a number of lawsuits against him for libel, none of which was successful. Indeed, in 1880 and again in 1885, she was herself imprisoned for libels connected with her musical career.

In 1875 Harry Weldon, unhappy with his wife's philanthropic orphanage scheme and her increasing interest in spiritualism, separated from Georgina and gave her the lease of Tavistock House and £1000 a year in settlement. Three years later, wishing to retrench financially, Weldon sought to use Georgina's spiritualist activities as grounds for establishing her insanity and to have her confined in a lunatic asylum kept by L. Forbes Winslow. His unsuspecting wife was seen by the necessary two doctors, who gained an interview with her under false pretences, and the lunacy order was signed. Georgina, however, sensed that something was amiss and, when the asylum-keeper's people came to take her away forcibly, she evaded capture for the seven days that the order remained valid. She then went to the Bow Street police court to press charges for assault. The magistrate expressed his sympathy for her plight and his conviction of her sanity, but because she was a married woman it was impossible for her to instigate a civil suit against her husband and the medical men who had sought to confine her. The moral victory was hers, however, and she capitalized on it by publicizing her story widely, giving interviews to the daily newspapers and the spiritualist press, and telling her tale of male and medical villainy and female victimization in articles, pamphlets, speeches in favour of reform of the lunacy laws, and in attempts to provoke the participants into pressing libel charges against her.

Georgina Weldon became a skilled self-publicist and kept her case in the public eye, successfully suing Harry Weldon in 1882 for the restoration of her conjugal rights (although he continued to refuse to return to the marital home). The passage of the Married Women's Property Act later that year enabled her to take the action she had been denied in 1878, for the act granted married women the right to pursue civil suits in the courts. Between 1883 and 1888 she successfully sued all the participants in the plot against her, at one point in 1884 having seventeen cases in

progress at once. Significantly, she chose to represent herself and to conduct all her cases without legal counsel, discovering that her skill as a storyteller translated well into the legal sphere. The 'Portia of the Law Courts', as she was dubbed, provided ample copy for the newspapers, and her image became ubiquitous, sometimes portrayed positively as a champion of oppressed womanhood, sometimes shown as an unfeminine man-hater, but sufficiently familiar to all to be awarded the commercial accolade of an image in a Pears Soap advertisement. To finance her legal activities she sang two songs nightly at the London Pavilion music-hall in 1884, and in 1886 appeared in a brief run of a melodrama, *Not Alone*, but the public preferred her performances in the law courts to those on the stage.

In the late 1880s Georgina Weldon's popularity waned as public attention moved on to the next big sensation, the Jack the Ripper murders. In her latter years she was a paying guest at Gisors, France, where she became an avid gardener. Her notoriety resumed following her association with the descendants of Karl Wilheim Naundorff, who was one of the many pretenders to the names and titles of Louis XVII of France. An increasingly discerning public ignored her book *Louis XVII, or, The Arab Jew*, and her legal memoirs, published in eight volumes, did little to alleviate her continuing impoverishment. She participated in a series of séances where she claimed to have contacted the recently deceased Gounod. In 1905 she moved back to London, where she instigated a libel suit in a vain attempt to clear her name with Gounod's biographers. The remaining years of her life were spent living in London and Brighton, where she died at 6 Sillwood Street on 11 January 1914.   JOHN MARTIN

Sources E. Grierson, *Storm bird: the strange life of Georgina Weldon* (1959) · J. R. Walkowitz, *City of dreadful delight: narratives of sexual danger in late-Victorian London* (1992) · S. Huebner, *The operas of Charles Gounod* (1990) [pb edn 1992] · *New Grove* · 'Le procès Gounod–Weldon', *Le Figaro* (11 May 1885) · G. Weldon, *The history of my orphanage, or, The outpourings of an alleged lunatic* (privately printed by Mrs Weldon, 1878) · G. Weldon, *How I escaped the mad doctors* (privately printed by Mrs Weldon, 1882) · 'Mrs Weldon's orphanage', *The Spiritualist* (21 Sept 1877)
Archives priv. coll., books and MSS
Likenesses photographs, 1857–84, repro. in Grierson, *Storm bird*
Wealth at death £2571 18s. 5d.: probate, 22 Aug 1914, *CGPLA Eng. & Wales*

Weldon, John (1676/7–1736), musician, was born at Chichester on 19 January 1676 or 1677 of unknown parentage. He was a chorister at Eton College under the organist, John Walter, and the college paid for him to receive lessons from Henry Purcell for a year from about March 1693 to March 1694. Later in 1694 he became organist of New College, Oxford. Three years later he wrote an ode, *A Song on the Peace of Ryswick* (Fitzwilliam Museum, Cambridge, MU MS 120, pp. 60–75). In March 1700 four prizes were offered for the best settings of Congreve's masque *The Judgment of Paris*. Weldon's setting, first performed on 6 May 1701, was awarded the first prize of £100. Although John Eccles and Daniel Purcell, the second and third prize-winners, published their settings, Weldon did not, and the complete score survives in only one manuscript

(Folger Shakespeare Library, Washington, MS W. b. 526). On 6 January 1701 Weldon was sworn in as a gentleman-extraordinary of the Chapel Royal and at the end of that year resigned his post in Oxford.

Weldon was appointed organist at St Bride's, Fleet Street, on 18 June 1702, and on 11 November 1703 he married Susanna Betton (*bap.* 15 July 1682) at Lavant, near Chichester. They had seven children. During this period he wrote a number of songs for plays and concerts, including vocal music for Motteux's interlude *Britain's Happiness* (1704), of which only one duet survives. On the death of John Blow on 1 October 1708 Weldon succeeded him as one of the two organists at the Chapel Royal. His appointment as second composer to the Chapel Royal also dates from this time, although the establishment of this post was not acknowledged in the Chapel Royal chequebook until 8 August 1715. He became organist of St Martin-in-the-Fields on 2 February 1714 without relinquishing his other posts. Two years later he published *Divine Harmony*, containing six solo anthems written for the countertenor Richard Elford, and at about the same time he composed a service in D (Royal College of Music, MS 2043) and a communion service in E♭. Most of his extant anthems, however, seem to be earlier than this. A revival of *The Tempest* with music by Weldon was advertised in the *Daily Courant* for 30 July 1716. No setting ascribed to him is known but it has been suggested that the setting usually attributed to Purcell may actually be Weldon's (Laurie, 'Did Purcell set *The Tempest?*'). He died at his home in Downing Street on 7 May 1736 after a long illness and was buried on 11 May in the churchyard of St Paul's, Covent Garden; he was survived by his wife. At the Chapel Royal he was succeeded as composer by William Boyce and as organist by Jonathan Martin, and at St Martin's by Joseph Kelway.

In addition to the works mentioned above, Weldon wrote about thirty anthems, two odes, some fifty songs, and a few instrumental pieces, although not all have survived. He was a composer of considerable talent but uneven achievement. At its best his music is by turns elegantly tuneful and deeply expressive, showing a keen sensitivity to the text and imaginative handling of harmony, key, and structure. He did not, however, always have the skill to sustain his ideas and tended to over-decorate his melodic lines and rely too heavily on repetitive patterns. Two of his anthems were printed in Boyce's *Cathedral Music*, volume 2 (1768), and others in Arnold's *Cathedral Music* (1790) and Page's *Harmonia sacra* (1800). Several of his songs, especially 'Let Ambition Fire thy Mind' from *The Judgment of Paris*, 'From Grave Lessons', and 'The Wakeful Nightingale', remained popular throughout the eighteenth century. A few of his works were available in print at the end of the twentieth century.

MARGARET LAURIE

Sources H. W. Shaw, *The succession of organists of the Chapel Royal and the cathedrals of England and Wales from c.1538* (1991), 10–11, 390 • M. Laurie, 'Weldon, John', *New Grove* • E. F. Rimbault, ed., *The old cheque-book, or book of remembrance, of the Chapel Royal, from 1561 to 1744*, CS, new ser., 3 (1872) • M. Laurie, 'Did Purcell set *The Tempest?*', *Proceedings of the Royal Musical Association*, 90 (1963–4), 43–57 • J. Hawkins, *A general history of the science and practice of music*, new edn, 2 (1875), 759, 784–5 • D. Dawe, *Organists of the City of London, 1666–1850* (1983), 153 • Burney, *Hist. mus.*, new edn, 2.487–8, 984 • H. Davey, *History of English music* (1895), 345 • W. Congreve, *Letters and documents*, ed. J. C. Hodges (1924), 20–22 • M. Tilmouth, 'A calendar of references to music in newspapers published in London and the provinces (1660–1719)', *Royal Musical Association Research Chronicle*, 1 (1961), esp. 37 • A. Ashbee, ed., *Records of English court music*, 5 (1991) • *Calendar of Sussex marriage licences … January 1582–3 to December 1730*, Sussex RS, 12 (1911), 232 • *IGI* • St Martin-in-the-Fields, vestry minutes, 1683–1739, City Westm. AC, MSS F2005–2006 • *Daily Courant* (30 July 1716) • W. H. Hunt, ed., *The registers of St Paul's Church, Covent Garden, London*, 4, Harleian Society, register section, 36 (1908), 350 • will, PRO, PROB 11/677

Likenesses oils, U. Oxf., faculty of music; repro. in *New Grove*

Wealth at death whole estate to wife: will, PRO, PROB 11/677

Weldon, Michael (*d.* in or before **1654**). *See under* Weldon, Sir Anthony (*bap.* 1583, *d.* 1648).

Weldon, Ralph (*bap.* **1606**, *d.* **1676**), parliamentarian army officer, was baptized at Swanscombe, Kent, on 12 January 1606, the eldest son of Sir Anthony *Weldon (*bap.* 1583, *d.* 1648) of Swanscombe, and his wife, Elinor (1588–1622), daughter of George Wilmer. His father held the office of clerk of the green cloth under James I and became the leading parliamentarian committeeman in Kent during the civil war. Anthony *Weldon, another parliamentarian army officer of note, was one of Ralph's seven younger brothers. Ralph Weldon was admitted to Jesus College, Cambridge, on 24 November 1620 and matriculated in 1621. Some time before 1639 he subsequently married the widow of Thomas Francklyn, probably the Mary who later appears as his wife; when Weldon was called upon to pay Francklyn's debts the accounts committee of Essex did 'much marvel he took no notice' (Everitt, 183).

Ralph Weldon was serving as a parliamentarian captain by September 1643, but quarrelled with his superior officer, Sir Michael Livesey. He was offered a commission under the earl of Essex, but according to his father, in a statement which may perhaps reflect his own attitudes more than those of his son, Ralph refused it on the ground that Kent should maintain control over its own forces. He served as colonel under Sir William Waller in 1644 in command of a regiment of foot raised in Kent, and his regiment was selected for the New Model Army the following year. On 10 March 1645 the House of Lords approved his officers' commissions, and Fairfax subsequently appointed Weldon 'as eldest Colonel' (Sprigge, 17), to command the brigade of 2000 horse and 4000–5000 foot sent to relieve Taunton, a task they accomplished on 11 May. Consequently Weldon was absent from Naseby, but he was active in engagements at Bridgwater and Bristol. On 10 September Weldon's brigade, storming the well-fortified south side of Bristol, lost 100 men 'by reason of the height of the Works … and the shortness of the Ladders' (Sprigge, 116). On 16 October Weldon's forces overran Tiverton and on 25 October parliament commissioned him governor of Plymouth. His regiment saw further action in 1646 at the siege of Exeter and captured Charles Fort and Inchmere House for parliament.

In April 1647 Weldon's regiment mustered 124 officers and 1060 men. When his soldiers' arrears of pay grew extreme Weldon raised money for them on his personal bond. He wrote to Speaker Lenthall on 30 July: 'I have now no way left, but in most humble manner to lay down the command of this garrison of Plymouth to the honourable houses of parliament, who were pleased to bestow it on me without my knowledge' (Cary, 1.324–5). On 2 August, with his soldiers enduring famine, and in fear for his life, he requisitioned £500 out of the customs house to buy them bread. On 27 August he wrote to Lenthall complaining that he was reduced to forced billeting and that parliament had ignored his letter of resignation. He spent a staggering £6000 on settling his soldiers' debts to Plymouth's inhabitants, a sum apparently never fully repaid. Robert Lilburne succeeded to command his regiment upon his retirement.

On 12 February 1653 Weldon's wife, Mary, was buried. In or before 1656 he married Ellen or Eleanor; their son George was buried on 17 April 1662, aged five; their daughter Elinor (*bap.* 1660) was buried on 15 February 1662; and their daughter Elizabeth was baptized on 22 August 1662. Weldon was MP for Kent in the protectorate parliaments of 1654 and 1656. On 23 December 1656 the £3300 still owed to Weldon was ordered to be paid out of the arrear assessments of the City of London, but on 6 June 1657 the House of Commons had to reiterate orders for him to receive £4000. In 1663 the Restoration government received information against Weldon that:

> He was a hater of monarchy, a seeker for popularity, rather an Anabaptist than a presbyterian, as he pretends to be. Before the Restoration he declared himself a Commonwealth man; he has called the punishment of the horrid regicides martyrdom; he is suspected of being implicated in the last two attempts against the King, and makes his house a resort for discontented persons. (*CSP dom.*, 1663–4, 406)

On 12 May 1676 'not likely to continue long in this world' (will, PRO, PROB 11/373, fol. 107v) Weldon made his will. His wife had died in 1669, and he made his son Anthony (*d.* 1698) his executor, who proved the will on 4 May 1683.

ANDREW J. HOPPER

Sources I. Gentles, *The New Model Army in England, Ireland, and Scotland, 1645–1653* (1992) · A. Everitt, *The community of Kent and the great rebellion, 1640–60* (1966) · Venn, *Alum. Cant.*, 1/4 · H. Cary, ed., *Memorials of the great civil war in England from 1646 to 1652*, 1 (1842) · J. Sprigge, *Anglia rediviva, or, England's recovery* (1647) · will, PRO, PROB 11/373, sig. 65 · *JHC*, 6–7 (1648–59) · *CSP dom.*, 1656–7; 1663–4 · 'Weldon, Sir Anthony', *DNB* · G. J. Armytage, ed., *A visitation of the county of Kent, begun … 1663, finished … 1668*, Harleian Society, 54 (1906) · nineteenth-century pedigree of Weldon family of Kent, BL, Add. MS 33895, fols. 33r, 34b · *Diary of Thomas Burton*, ed. J. T. Rutt, 4 vols. (1828)
Wealth at death £527; bond of £600 due from Merchant Adventurers of England; appointed feoffees in trust to raise further £1500 portion for daughter; plus lands at Milbank House in parish of Newchurch, Kent, totalling 43 acres with all barns and outbuildings: will, PRO, PROB 11/373, sig. 65

Weldon, Ralph [*name in religion* Benet a Sancto Raphaelo Archangelo] (**1674–1713**), Benedictine monk and chronicler, was born on 12 April 1674 in London, the seventeenth child of Colonel George Weldon (*d.* 1679), youngest son of Sir Anthony *Weldon, historical writer, and of his wife, Lucy Necton (*d.* 1702). He belonged to an ancient but impoverished family from Swanscombe, Kent. Converted to Roman Catholicism by Father Joseph Johnston, he made his abjuration at St James's Chapel on 12 October 1687. After schooling with the Maurists at Pontlevoy, he was clothed as a Benedictine monk in the priory of St Edmund the King at Paris on 17 December 1690, taking the name Benet a Sancto Raphaelo Archangelo. He made his profession on 13 January 1692, but lameness prevented his ordination.

Weldon was of a scrupulous and nervous disposition, prone to following advice given him in dreams, which led to a degree of instability throughout his monastic life. He was for a brief period in 1694 a novice at La Trappe. At St Edmund's, Paris, he was librarian, and in 1702 compiled the catalogue (Paris, Bibliothèque Mazarine, MS 4057). He also drew up for this library in 1706 his draft of a life of King James II (BL, Add. MS 10118) to celebrate the deposition of the king's remains at St Edmund's in 1701. In an attempt to draw him away from his personal difficulties his superiors recommended he collect material to illustrate the history of the post-Reformation English Benedictines. This large collection, written between 1707 and 1711, he called 'Memorials' (Douai Abbey, Woolhampton, Reading, deposit IA), and incorporated much autobiographical detail in it. Summaries of it, entitled 'Chronological notes', were drafted by him in 1709 and 1711. Weldon lived within his community as a recluse, spending much of the day in study and writing, and was found dead in his locked cell on 23 November 1713, having been accidentally asphyxiated; he was buried at St Edmund's. His compilations contain the most comprehensive survey of early modern English Benedictine history.

GEOFFREY SCOTT

Sources B. Weldon, 'Memorials', Douai Abbey, Woolhampton, Berkshire, English Benedictine Congregation Archives [deposit IA] · B. Weldon, *Chronological notes … of the English congregation of the order of St Benedict* (1881) · G. Scott, 'The collector: a look at Benedictine archives, through the eyes of Bro. Benet Weldon', *Catholic Archives*, 6 (1986), 25–42 · S. Marron, 'Weldon and his critics', *Douai Magazine*, 2/2 (1922), 7–19 · E. Bishop, 'The beginning of Douay convent', *Downside Review*, 16 (1897), 21–35 · V. Marron, 'Some sources for English Benedictine history', *Downside Review*, 81 (1963), 50–60 · D. Lunn, *The English Benedictines, 1540–1688* (1980) · G. Scott, *Gothic rage undone: English monks in the age of Enlightenment* (1992) · Y. Chaussy, *Les bénédictins anglais réfugiés en France au XVIIᵉ siècle (1611–1669)* (Paris, 1967) · P. A. Allanson, *Biographies of English Benedictines*, ed. A. Cramer, Catholic RS, Occasional Publications, 3 [forthcoming]
Archives Bibliothèque Mazarine, Paris, catalogue, MS 4057 · Douai Abbey, Woolhampton, Berkshire, memorials · Douai Abbey, Woolhampton, Berkshire, second MS draft of chronological notes · Downside Abbey, near Bath, chronological notes from memorials

Weldon, Thomas Dewar [Harry] (**1896–1958**), philosopher, was born at 3 Bryanston Mansions, York Street, Marylebone, London, on 5 December 1896, the son of Thomas Weldon, formerly a leather factor, and his wife, Amelia Ellen, *née* Dewar. He was educated at Tonbridge School and won a scholarship to read *literae humaniores* at Magdalen College, Oxford. His arrival at Magdalen was delayed, however, when, in September 1915, he was commissioned in the Royal Field Artillery and spent the war in France, reaching the rank of acting captain. Having been wounded and decorated (with the Military Cross and bar), Weldon went up to Magdalen in 1919 and took a first-class degree in 1921. He began tutoring at Magdalen the year after, was elected a fellow and tutor in philosophy in 1923, and spent the rest of his academic life—with the exception of a year as a Rhodes travelling fellow in 1930—at the college.

Weldon's early academic reputation rested largely on the quality and results of his undergraduate teaching, to which he devoted considerable time and energy. He was committed to his students' success rather than striving for academic preferment. He always lived in college and was not only accessible but also hospitable to his students, rewarding their efforts with a glass of sherry or a tankard of beer. Although he inspired affection among his pupils, his friendliness did not extend to intimacy.

Weldon was determined that Magdalen should be a place from which any bright applicant might benefit. Under the long presidency of Sir Herbert Warren, who retired in 1928, the college had become something of a playground for the well-born; intelligence often came a poor third to wealth and family as a criterion of selection. It was largely due to Weldon's efforts that entry to both the junior and senior common rooms became more meritocratic.

As a tutor for modern Greats (philosophy, politics, and economics) Weldon recognized the important connections between philosophy and practical affairs. In his crusade to modernize the college he did not shy away from disputes with his more traditional and intransigent colleagues. C. S. Lewis portrayed Weldon as cynical and quick to anger, concluding that 'Contempt is his ruling passion: courage his chief virtue' (*All My Road*, 483). Certainly Weldon did not suffer fools gladly and he was intolerant of lazy thinking; yet he could also be a loyal friend. This combination of qualities helped win the respect of his peers. The reforms which Weldon desired could not have occurred without the support of other influential members of the senior common room.

Between 1939 and 1942 Weldon worked as a civil servant in London and Washington. In 1942 he was posted to Bomber Command in High Wycombe, where he became the personal assistant of Arthur (Bomber) Harris. As such he was required to justify Harris's strategy of bombing German cities to sceptical politicians such as Stafford Cripps. Weldon argued that strategic bombing would make it possible for the allied forces to re-enter Europe by diverting German resources towards repair and away from new offensives. Replying to the accusation of terrorism, Weldon justified the air attacks on German cities by arguing that they aimed to shorten the war and thus reduce, in total, the loss of human life.

Only after the war did Weldon publish. In 1945 his *Introduction to Kant's 'Critique of Pure Reason'* attempted both to analyse and to contextualize this major philosophical work. It was a short and technical study, yet alive to the context of German thought from which Kant's *Critique* emerged. It was soon followed by *States and Morals* (1946), which sketched 'a method of approach' to political conflicts. Written in a typically clear and terse style, Weldon's book was concerned to understand 'the moral sentiments which political theories formulate' (p. xiv) rather than attempt to construct a whole new theory. He regarded moral and political values as incommensurable and concluded that theoretical dogmatism was 'dangerous and should be avoided' (p. 300).

Weldon's last published book, *The Vocabulary of Politics* (1953), was an attempt to communicate with a broader public. In it Weldon analysed the logic of political language. This approach—influenced by Wittgenstein and J. L. Austin—was typical of the period and viewed philosophy as having a limited, yet vital, role to play in clarifying the conceptual muddles of other disciplines. Weldon denied that this led to a cynical or sceptical position with regard to political evaluations, but rather demonstrated that the concerns of political philosophy were largely the 'confused formulations of purely empirical difficulties' (p. 193). Despite his somewhat cloistered life at Magdalen, Weldon had first-hand experience of human antagonisms.

Weldon died suddenly on 13 May 1958. In an obituary published in the *Oxford Magazine* Gilbert Ryle remembered Weldon as 'a jovial rather than a happy man' (*Oxford Magazine*, 528). Many years earlier C. S. Lewis had remarked on Weldon's melancholy appearance, adding, 'He believes that he has seen through everything and lives at rock bottom' (*All My Road*, 483). Weldon's experiences of the trenches in the First World War, before he arrived at Magdalen, had left a deep mark. None the less, his adult life revolved around the college which had offered him not only a career but also a fraternity. He never married and there were rumours around the college after his death that he had committed suicide. In fact he died of a cerebral haemorrhage, having retired for the night from a college dinner party, alone in his rooms. He was cremated on 16 May. MARK J. SCHOFIELD

Sources *The Times* (14 May 1958), 15a; (16 May 1958), 13c · *Oxford Magazine* (19 June 1958), 527–8 · D. I. Hall, '"Black, white and grey": wartime arguments for and against the strategic bomber offensive', www.blvl.igs.net/~jlynch/bharris2b.htm [winning essay of the Bomber Harris Trust essay competition, 1997] · K. Burk, *Troublemaker: the life and history of A. J. P. Taylor* (2000) · *All my road before me: the diary of C. S. Lewis, 1922–27*, ed. W. Hooper (1991), 482–3 · M. Moynihan, 'C. S. Lewis and T. D. Weldon', *Seven*, 5 (1984), 101–5 · *Magdalen College record* (1955) · A. King, 'How many lives was it worth?', *Times Higher Education Supplement* (25 Nov 1994) · b. cert. · d. cert. · E. S. Craig, ed., *Oxford University roll of service* (1920)
Archives Magd. Oxf., papers
Wealth at death £16,585 16s. 11d.: probate, 28 Aug 1958, CGPLA Eng. & Wales

Weldon, Walter (1832–1885), chemist, was born on 31 October 1832 at Loughborough, the eldest son of Reuben Weldon, manufacturer, and his wife, Esther Fowke. He was employed for some years in his father's business, and on 14 March 1854 married Anne Cotton (c.1832–1881) at Belper; they had three children.

Shortly after his marriage Weldon went to London as a journalist. He contributed to the *Dial*, afterwards incorporated with the *Morning Star*, an influential Liberal daily newspaper of the time. On 1 August 1860 he issued the first number of a sixpenny monthly magazine called *Weldon's Register of Facts and Occurrences Relating to Literature, the Sciences, and the Arts*, by which he hoped primarily to record scientific facts and discoveries in a popular form. Although ably conducted, it proved a failure, and was abandoned in 1864. Among the contributors were George Augustus Sala, Edmund Yates, William Michael Rossetti, James Hain Friswell, and Percy Greg.

About this time, probably through the influence of a friend and fellow-Swedenborgian, Charles Townsend Hook, a paper manufacturer of Snodland, near Rochester, Weldon became interested in technological chemistry. Without any formal or practical training, he began to consider certain industrial problems, particularly chlorine and alkali manufacture, mainly by reading at the British Museum. He took out his first patents for the 'manganese-regeneration process', which eventually made his name famous, before he had ever seen a chemical experiment.

By September 1865 Weldon had devised two new processes for the cheaper manufacture of magnesium and aluminium, but was advised that they were impracticable. In the latter part of 1866 he met the chemical manufacturer David Gamble, and explained, in the chemical language of the day, that he thought he had obtained a 'peroxide' of manganese from the 'protoxide' by suspending it in water and blowing air through. He was then totally unacquainted with quantitative chemical analysis and the results to be obtained thereby, and did not realize that his process had already been worked on a large scale and found unsatisfactory. The object of Weldon (and of various unsuccessful predecessors) was to regenerate the manganese peroxide used in enormous quantities in the manufacture of chlorine, and converted into a valueless by-product which was discarded.

From this time onwards Weldon carried out experiments on a large scale, first in 1866 at the demolished works of the Walker Chemical Company on the Tyne, and later at those of J. C. Gamble & Co. at St Helens. These led to the 'magnesia–manganese' process patented in 1867, and the 'lime–manganese' process patented a little later, which was finally adopted, but not worked commercially until 1869. By this latter process ninety to ninety-five per cent of the manganese peroxide formerly lost was recovered, the price of bleaching powder was reduced by £6 per ton, and its production was quadrupled. The essential detail of the process which distinguished it from earlier attempts was the use of an excess of lime over and above that required for the precipitation of the manganese. Jean-Baptiste Dumas, in presenting to Weldon the gold medal of the Société d'Encouragement pour l'Industrie Nationale in Paris, said: 'By this invention every sheet of paper and every yard of calico throughout the world was cheapened'. In addition, his proposers for membership of the Royal Society cited the invention's 'great importance in preventing the pollution of streams and of

the atmosphere' (RS, election certificate, 1882). For his discovery Weldon was also awarded a grand prix at the Paris Exhibition of 1878.

In 1870 the invention of a new chlorine process, 'the Deacon process', by Henry Deacon (d. 1876) and Ferdinand Hurter (1844–1898) led Weldon to fear that his work might be superseded, and he invented another process, known as the 'magnesia–chlorine' process, which was developed later at the works at Salindres by Messrs Péchiney and M. Boulouvard, and was then called the Péchiney–Weldon process. This process did not prove ultimately successful, while the lime–manganese process was widely employed. In 1880 Weldon read at the Swansea meeting of the British Association an important paper, in which he showed that the heat of formation of compounds increases in nearly all cases with the atomic volume, the heat of formation of equal volumes of different compounds being approximately equal. On 11 July 1883 he was elected president of the Society of Chemical Industry, of which he had been one of the founders in 1881. During the first half of 1884 he voluntarily undertook the laborious duty of abstracting large numbers of patents for the society's journal. On 9 July 1884 he delivered his presidential address at Newcastle upon Tyne on the soda and chlorine industries. A paper on the numerical relations between the atomic weights, read at the Montreal meeting of the British Association, was not published, but in 1885 Weldon printed, for private circulation, the first chapter dealing with the glucinum family, of a memoir 'On the ratios ... of the atomic weights.' In it, he attempted to show that the ratios of the atomic weights of the members of a series of elements (Mendeleyev's periodic table) could be expressed by a simple constant. Like his scientific contemporaries Alfred Russel Wallace and Sir William Crookes, Weldon was a believer in spiritualism.

Weldon went, despite illness, to the Aberdeen meeting of the British Association in 1885, but was obliged to return, and died at his house, Rede Hall, Burstow, Surrey, of heart disease on 20 September. He was survived by his son Walter Frank Raphael *Weldon FRS (1860–1906), professor of comparative anatomy at Oxford. A second son, Walter Alfred Dante (b. 1862), died suddenly at Cambridge in 1881 shortly before his mother's death. The manganese recovery process has been remembered not only for its intrinsic importance to chemical industry, but as a marvellous achievement by a man without previous training.

P. J. HARTOG, rev. K. D. WATSON

Sources *Journal of the Society of Chemical Industry*, 4 (1885), 577–81 · *PRS*, 46 (1889), xix–xxiv · Boase, *Mod. Eng. biog.* · *CGPLA Eng. & Wales* (1885)
Likenesses photograph (after F. Holl), RS
Wealth at death £25,495 11s. 10d.: administration, 31 Oct 1885, *CGPLA Eng. & Wales*

Weldon, Walter Frank Raphael (1860–1906), zoologist and biometrician, was born on 15 March 1860, at Highgate, Middlesex, the second child of the journalist and industrial chemist Walter *Weldon (1832–1885) and his

Walter Frank Raphael Weldon (1860–1906), by unknown photographer

wife, Anne Cotton (d. 1881). His father's wealth came from his patents of the manganese regeneration process and the magnesia chlorine process. The family moved so frequently that Weldon's early education was desultory until he was sent to a boarding-school at Caversham, near Reading, in 1873. He spent some months in private study before matriculating at University College, London in the autumn of 1876 with the intention of pursuing a medical career. During his time at University College he acquired a respectable knowledge of mathematics from the Danish mathematician Olaus Henrici, and attended the lectures of the zoologist E. Ray Lankester as well as those of the botanist Daniel Oliver. In the following year he transferred to King's College, London, and stayed for two terms. He was admitted to St John's College, Cambridge, as a bye-term student on 6 April 1878.

Once at Cambridge, Weldon met the zoologist Francis Maitland Balfour and subsequently gave up his medical studies for zoology. Weldon became an exhibitioner in 1879 and a scholar in 1881 (when he also gained a first-class degree in the natural sciences tripos). In the autumn of the latter year he left for the Zoologica Stazione in Naples to begin the first of his studies in marine biological organisms. On returning to Cambridge in September 1882 he became a demonstrator for Adam Sedgwick. Six months later, on 14 March 1883, Weldon married Florence Joy Tebb (d. 1936). In April 1884 he was elected to a fellowship at St John's College and appointed university lecturer in invertebrate morphology. Weldon was one of the founding members of the Marine Biological Station in Plymouth in 1884 along with Lankester, Sedgwick, William Turner Thistleton-Dyer, Michael Foster, and J. Burdon Sanderson. From 1887 until 1891 Weldon lived in Plymouth during

June to December, and he stayed in Cambridge in the Lent and May terms.

From 1887 Weldon's work was centred around the development of a fuller understanding of marine biological phenomena and, in particular, the examination of the relationship between various organs of crabs and shrimps to determine selective death rates in relation to the laws of growth. Some of his early work at the Marine Biological Station involved the breeding of the common lobster and the rock lobster or craw fish (*Palinurus*). In 1887 he started a notebook to study the classification, morphology, and the development of various species of *Decapod crustacea* (including the Plymouth shore crab, lobsters, shrimp, and prawns). His only work on invertebrate morphology contained an account of the early stage of segmentation and the building of the layers of shrimp. Weldon was both a master of histological techniques and a powerful and accurate draughtsman.

Some time in 1889 Weldon read Francis Galton's *Natural Inheritance*. In this book Galton had shown that the frequency distributions of the average size of certain organs in man, plants, and moths were normally distributed. Similar investigations had been pursued by the Belgian statistician Adolphe Quetelet whose work was confined to 'civilised man'. Weldon was interested in investigating the variations in organs in a species living in a wild state which were acted upon by natural selection and other influences. His first attempts to find a working hypothesis for variation within Darwin's theories were morphological and embryological. Neither approach enabled him to examine the variation that Darwin emphasized. Galton's *Natural Inheritance* had, however, suggested to Weldon the possibility of a statistical approach for the analysis of biological variation.

When Galton was writing on heredity in 1889 he predicted that selection would not change the shape of the normal distribution; he expected that the frequency distributions of any given characteristic would remain normally distributed in all cases, whether or not animals were under the action of natural selection. Weldon then began to study the variation of four organs in the common shrimp (*Crangon vulgaris*) and he collected five samples from waters fairly distant from Plymouth. His statistical analysis published in 1890 confirmed Galton's prediction. Shortly after the paper was published Weldon was elected a fellow of the Royal Society.

In the summer of 1890 Weldon was appointed to succeed E. Ray Lankester in the Jodrell chair of zoology at University College, London. Soon after he took up the post, in 1891, he joined the association for promoting a professorial university of London. It was at this time when he met the biometrician and statistician Karl Pearson (who had been appointed professor of applied mathematics and mechanics at University College in 1884). Weldon, Pearson, and George Carey Foster drafted the scheme of the proposed Association for Promoting a Professorial University for London. The main idea was to unite all the London lecturers so that the separate colleges would then become absorbed. Weldon was a tireless campaigner and his commitment to Pearson marked the beginning of a lifelong friendship. Their relationship could be characterized by an emotional and intellectual intimacy that engendered a symbiotic alliance. It is thus not surprising that one of the most extensive sets of letters in Pearson's archives are those of Weldon and his wife, Florence—consisting of nearly 1000 pieces of correspondence.

During the Easter vacation of 1892 Weldon and his wife went to Malta and the Bay of Naples to collect 23 measurements from 1000 adult female shore crabs (*Carcinus moenas*). Over the course of the summer they calculated crab measurements at the biological station in Naples. Weldon discovered that all but one of the 23 characters he measured in the Naples group were normally distributed: he found that the frontal breadth of the carapace was instead a double humped (bi-modal) curve. His first attempt to interpret the data involved breaking up the curve into two normal distributions as Galton had advocated. Weldon then approached Pearson for assistance with interpreting his data. At that time, Pearson was teaching applied mathematics to engineering students at University College and was also giving geometry lectures at Gresham College.

By the end of 1892 Pearson began to devise a probability system of curve fitting for Weldon's data, and he used this material in his Gresham lectures in the following year. Weldon's attempt to break up his double humped curve into two normal components seems to have been derived from Galton's belief that all biological characteristics should be normally distributed. Weldon also seems to have been exploring Galton's claims that a new species could be established only by a 'hopeful monster' or saltation (sudden evolutionary change) producing a new type (that is, instantaneous speciation). Up until the middle of the nineteenth century species were defined in terms of types or essences by a consistent majority of naturalists. Weldon and Pearson developed a more gradualistic approach to understanding the process of species divergence than that of Galton and a number of other biologists. When they first examined the double humped curve, they were trying to detect two curves produced by the intermingling of populations corresponding to parent and saltated form. Weldon's finding of the double humped curve in the distribution of the forehead of the carapace of the Plymouth shore crab led to his first project for the evolution committee of the Royal Society in 1894 when he hoped to have found dimorphism in herring as well. After Weldon discovered that his measurement from his herring data did not indicate that all the characters of the herring were dimorphic, neither he nor Pearson pursued any further work on speciation.

Charles Darwin's recognition that species comprised different sets of statistical populations, rather than types or essences, prompted a reconceptualization of statistical populations by Pearson and Weldon. Moreover, this required the use of new statistical methods, and, largely owing to Weldon's influence, Pearson founded biometrics

(though some of the statistical work of John Venn and Francis Ysidro Edgeworth played a role in Pearson's early work on probability). Weldon's influence in the emergence and development of Pearsonian statistics was paramount; he also offered continual moral support and promulgated the Pearsonian corpus of statistics throughout the 1890s and until his death in 1906. From the joint biometrical projects they undertook Pearson went on to develop the modern theory of mathematical statistics.

Weldon's most fruitful venture with Pearson came about when he demonstrated empirical evidence of natural selection in the forehead of the carapace of the shore crab at Plymouth Sound. In 1894 the primary source of evidence of natural selection acting upon biological variation had been established by Henry Bates with his work on mimicry. In the same year Weldon was drawn to looking at changes in the shore crab because Plymouth Sound had undergone environmental changes after a breakwater had been built in the middle of the nineteenth century. When the fine china clay which came down from Dartmoor in rainy weather was carried into the sea, the breakwater increased the amount of clay that settled into the sound. Moreover, the great dockyard in Devonport was expanded, which led to an increase in the size of the population; subsequently, the sound became polluted from the sewage that spilled into the sea. In the summer of 1895 Weldon collected 600 female shore crabs and measured the frontal breadth of these crabs and he found that the fine china clay was a selective agent. The mortality rate was greatest for crabs whose frontal breadth was narrower. The process by which natural selection was affected was thought to be largely associated with the way in which crabs filtered the waters entering their gill chambers. A narrow frontal breadth seems to have made one part of the process of filtration of water more efficient than in crabs with larger frontal breadths. Five years later Weldon undertook further research on the structure of the whorls in snails *Clausilia laminata* (Montagu) which has been considered to be some of his most convincing work in pointing to empirical evidence of natural selection.

In his presidential address to the zoological section of the British Association in 1898, Weldon introduced the corpus of Pearsonian statistics to a group of zoologists. He demonstrated two statistical innovations: the first involved using the standard deviation as a statistical method to express the full range of organic variation for a variety of biological characteristics. Second, he emphasized the necessity for using the relative frequency approach to probability by showing how probability could be used for curve fitting. Weldon then urged all zoologists who professed to have a genuine interest in animal evolution to use the statistical machinery devised by Pearson. Weldon also introduced the idea of a negative correlation when Pearson was working out the mathematical properties of simple correlation and regression in 1896. (Galton had used positive correlations only.)

When Weldon moved to Oxford in 1899 to take up the Linacre chair of comparative anatomy he carried on the biometric tradition by gathering a number of students who began to look for empirical evidence of natural selection acting upon various animals and plants. Despite Weldon's move he made arrangements to be with Pearson every year during the Easter and Christmas vacations and throughout the summer months. During the summer, they spent most weekends in Oxfordshire or in London near Pearson's home in Hampstead. They continued their collaborative work investigating biometrical problems such as natural selection, inheritance and, in particular, Mendelian inheritance. Following a much heated debate initiated by William Bateson on one of Pearson's papers on inheritance at the Royal Society on 15 November 1900, Weldon suggested to Pearson that they start their own journal for papers dealing with matters of statistical biology. Galton acted in consultation and Pearson named the new journal *Biometrika*.

In October 1900 Weldon began to analyse Gregor Mendel's results of three of the seven sets of discrete characters of the common sweet pea (*Pissum sativum*) on the assumption of phenotypic dominance and independent assortment. He did not challenge Mendel's integrity or the results, but only the interpretation and universality of the findings. He also regarded Galton's ancestry as an essential component to Mendelism. Weldon's statistical interpretation of Mendel's data led Bateson to publish his fiercely polemical 100-page chapter to 'defend Mendel from Professor Weldon' (W. Bateson, *Mendel's Principles of Heredity. A Defence*, 1902, viii). Bateson's criticisms seem actively to have discouraged Weldon from adopting virtually any aspect of Bateson's work. Nevertheless Weldon continued to work on determining the relationship between Mendel and Galton's ancestral theory of inheritance for the rest of his life.

Weldon's last project was on the inheritance of coat colour in horses. By November 1905 he was spending nine hours a day on this project and he continued this work throughout the winter of 1905 and into the early spring of 1906. During the Easter vacation of 1906 the Pearsons were in Berkshire, where they took a cottage at Longcott House, a mile from the Weldons, who were staying at the little inn at Woolstone, at the foot of the White Horse Hill. On Sunday 8 April Weldon and Pearson cycled into Oxford. When Pearson saw Weldon on the Tuesday afternoon, he found him in bed suffering from what appeared to be an attack of influenza. By evening his health had worsened and he was taken to a nursing home. He died of double pneumonia on Easter Monday, 13 April 1906, at 3 Nottingham Place, Marylebone, London. A service was held in the chapel at Merton College, Oxford, on 18 April and he was buried at Holywell cemetery, Oxford.

Shortly after the funeral Pearson approached Henry Richard Hope-Pinker to sculpt a marble bust of Weldon. The bust remained in Pearson's office until his retirement in 1933 when it was moved to the University Museum at Oxford. Pearson also established the Weldon memorial prize in 1907 in Oxford to be awarded once every three years to contributions to biometry. Weldon's widow left the residue of her estate to found the Weldon chair of biometry in October 1936 and J. B. S. Haldane became the first holder. 　　　　M. EILEEN MAGNELLO

Sources DNB · R. S. Cowan, 'Weldon, Walter Frank Raphael', *DSB*, 14.251–2 · M. E. Magnello, 'Karl Pearson: evolutionary biology and the emergence of a modern theory of statistics', DPhil diss., U. Oxf., 1993 · M. E. Magnello, 'Karl Pearson's Gresham lectures: W. F. R. Weldon, speciation and the origins of Pearsonian statistics', *British Journal for the History of Science*, 29 (1996), 43–63 · M. E. Magnello, 'Karl Pearson's mathematization of inheritance: from ancestral heredity to Mendelian genetics (1895–1909)', *Annals of Science*, 55 (1998), 35–94 · K. Pearson, 'Walter Frank Raphael Weldon, 1860–1906', *Biometrika*, 5 (1906), 1–52; repr. in E. S. Pearson and M. G. Kendall, eds., *Studies in the history of statistics and probability*, 1 (1970) · K. Pearson, *The life, letters and labours of Francis Galton*, 3 vols. in 4 (1914–30), vol. 3a · LUL, Karl Pearson MSS · *CGPLA Eng. & Wales* (1906) · *DNB*
Archives Marine Biological Association of the United Kingdom, Plymouth, notebook relating to decapod crustacea of Plymouth area · RS · U. Oxf., department of zoology, papers · UCL, corresp. and papers · UCL, papers
Likenesses R. H. Hope-Pinker, marble bust, 1908, Oxf. U. Mus. NH · photograph, UCL [see illus.]
Wealth at death £28,988 0s. 11d.: administration with will, 12 May 1906, *CGPLA Eng. & Wales*

Welensky, Sir Roland [Roy] (1907–1991), prime minister of the federation of Rhodesia and Nyasaland, was born Raphael Welensky in Pioneer Street, Salisbury, Southern Rhodesia, on 20 January 1907, the thirteenth of fourteen children of Michael Welensky (*b. c.*1843), boarding-house keeper, and his wife, Leah, *née* Ferreira (*c.*1865–1918), an Afrikaner from Willowmore, Cape Colony, who was originally named Aletta, but had taken the name Leah on her marriage and conversion to Judaism.

Early life Welensky's father had led a colourful if profligate life. Originally from Vilna, Lithuania, he had been an itinerant trader in Russia and a horse smuggler to both sides during the Franco-Prussian War, before roaming as a saloon keeper to the American mid-west. In 1881 he emigrated to the Cape Colony. After losing another fortune in the ostrich feather trade, he and his family drifted to Southern Rhodesia, where he served in the Ndebele uprising. By 1907 he was running a hotel, effectively a doss house, in the poorest district of Salisbury, a world of white destitutes, drunkards, and prostitutes who lived cheek by jowl with Indians, 'coloureds', and Africans.

It was into such a world that Welensky was born, and this experience profoundly conditioned his character and political outlook. He frequently had to share beds with inebriated and poverty-stricken lodgers who often failed to pay the rent. This, together with his father's fondness for alcohol, made him a lifelong if not intolerant teetotaller. He mixed with all races from an early age, and boasted that he had not slept between sheets before he was sixteen. As he later famously stated in a BBC television interview, he swam 'bare-arsed in the Makabusi with many picannins' (Freeman, 12). He soon became aware of his Jewish ancestry, for at the lower end of white society Jews were often as disliked as Indians. 'I suffered the stigma of being a Jew', he later recalled, 'which one doesn't shed lightly in this world' (Freeman, 4). He attended the Salisbury primary school barefoot, where, because of his love of history and English, he was forced to defend himself against his peers' charge of being a swot. Fortunately he was a larger-than-average child with big fists, which stood him in good stead among Salisbury's roughest urchins.

In 1918 Welensky suffered a major blow with the death of his mother, who had been a crucial stabilizing figure. In 1921, having adopted the name Roland (though in fact he was known throughout his life as Roy), he left school to become a storeman in the farming and mining areas, in order to look after his elderly father, and also worked as a butcher, a baker, and a secondhand dealer's clerk. He was unable, however, to prevent his father's departure for an old people's home in Johannesburg, where he died alone. At seventeen Welensky moved to Bulawayo, becoming a locomotive fireman with Rhodesia Railways. He was two years under age, but the examining doctor was taken in by his 6 feet, 20 stone frame. He augmented his income by becoming a professional boxer and heavyweight champion of the Rhodesias by 1927. On 28 April 1928 he married Elizabeth Henderson (c.1911–1969), a Bulawayo waitress, with whom he had two children, Joan and Michael. Soon after his marriage he was transferred to the Wankie coalfields, where, after a few successful bouts, he decided to retire from the ring.

Trade unionist Soon after Welensky's arrival in Wankie the railway workers' union called a strike. Impressed by serious disunity in worker ranks, he became a popular and vocal critic of the railway bosses, who came to regard him as a troublemaker. He managed to keep his job, however, in spite of the world depression that hit the Rhodesian economy in 1931, unlike his brother Dave, prominent in the miners' union in Wankie, who had once been arrested for syndicalist activity in Johannesburg. Welensky helped his brother as well as keeping his wife and two

children on a meagre shunter's wage, although he soon went into debt. In 1933, by then an engine driver, he was transferred to Broken Hill in Northern Rhodesia, where he was forced to use his fists against a virulently anti-semitic combination of neo-Nazi Afrikaner and Mosleyite English-speaking white workers. He became convinced that only trade unionism on the British model would counter the fear and demoralization on which fascism bred. He faced down the fascist element and reorganized the railway workers' union in the town, becoming its branch chairman.

Acutely aware of his lack of formal education, Welensky embarked on an urgent programme of self-education, drawing eclectically on the writings of such figures as Marx, Mill, Bentham, Shakespeare, Disraeli, Conan Doyle, and Robert Service. He once described himself as 'a socialist conservative', preferring negotiations to strikes (Taylor, 178). He nevertheless came to regard himself as 'the champion of the under-dog' and organizer of the white working class against 'the boss class', at a time when the impact of the world depression was creating a growing class of poor whites in Northern Rhodesia. White worker insecurity was sharpened still further by the growing organization of African miners, who organized a significant strike on the copperbelt in 1935. Northern Rhodesia's racially divided labour practices resembled those of Southern Rhodesia and the Union of South Africa, but its white settlers lacked the self-governing institutions of their southern counterparts, resenting the vulnerability of the territory's government to Colonial Office directives and metropolitan humanitarian opinion.

Politician Welensky's ambitions now turned to the political sphere. In 1938 he was elected unopposed as member of the legislative council for Broken Hill. He developed an unlikely but intimate political alliance with Lieutenant-

Sir Roland Welensky (1907–1991), by Granville Davies, 1989

Colonel Stewart Gore-Browne, patrician leader of the unofficial members, based on their common faith in the colony's economic future and opposition to what they regarded as Colonial Office high-handedness. Gore-Browne, moreover, was aware of Welensky's great sway with the white miners and railwaymen, an influence Welensky strengthened by forming the Northern Rhodesian Labour Party in 1941. He also co-founded a newspaper, the *Northern News*, which became highly successful. The outbreak of the Second World War in 1939, moreover, further enhanced his stature. Avowedly anti-fascist, he tried to join the army but was regarded as too vital to the Northern Rhodesian war effort. He became a member of the executive council (1940–53) and in 1941 was appointed director of manpower, a pivotal position at a time when the copperbelt, crucial to the war effort, was vulnerable to strikes organized by a bizarre alliance of communist and neo-fascist white workers. He was also appointed a member of Sir John Foster's commission of inquiry into the riots on the copperbelt. He served on various railway arbitration tribunals. In these positions he did much to moderate white worker opinion during wartime.

In 1946 Welensky succeeded Gore-Browne to the powerful position of leader of the unofficial members. He had two chief political objectives: to force the British South Africa Company to relinquish its mineral rights to the Northern Rhodesia government, and the amalgamation of the colony with self-governing Southern Rhodesia, building on close wartime inter-territorial co-operation. After years of tough negotiations, he succeeded in the first cause, resulting in huge revenues for the Northern Rhodesia government. This success strengthened his determination to gain amalgamation. At the end of the war, however, aware of the growing international mood against racism and colonialism, neither main political party at Westminster could countenance a wholesale transfer of the African population of a protectorate to the white-dominated and self-governing Southern Rhodesia, with its segregationist racial policies. The British government made clear that it would only permit a federation of the Rhodesias provided Nyasaland was added, and that the existing forms of government would continue in all three territories. Thus, ministers hoped, a pro-British dominion would eventually evolve as a counterbalance to the increasingly segregationist and republican-leaning Union of South Africa, as well as forestall any advance of communism in the region.

Welensky played a leading part in the negotiations leading to federation, including the Victoria Falls conference of 1951, where he developed close links with the Southern Rhodesian prime minister Sir Godfrey Huggins (who had attended his mother in her last illness), becoming a leading member of his United Federal Party. In London, Labour ministers warmed to his Bevin-like working-class bluntness. The federation that came into existence in 1953 was amazingly complicated, involving five different governments. Britain dealt with the federation and Southern Rhodesia through the Commonwealth Relations Office,

while the two northern territories came under the Colonial Office, which enjoyed mutually antagonistic relations with the Commonwealth Relations Office. Welensky's role in the creation of the federation was rewarded with a knighthood (1953), and cabinet rank, as minister of transport, communications, and posts (1953–6), and concurrently leader of the house and deputy prime minister (1955–6). Despite their different backgrounds, Huggins rated Welensky highly as a 'first-rate colleague [with] … a first-class brain and lots of commonsense' (Taylor, 175).

Federal prime minister On 1 November 1956, ominously coinciding with the Suez operation, Welensky succeeded Huggins (now Lord Malvern) as prime minister, minister of external affairs, and (until 1959) minister of defence. One of his first actions was to express the federation's support for the Anglo-French action. He declared:

> [W]hatever the course of events may prove to be, our loyalty to the Crown is unquestioned. As a people whether white or black, we are British, and we are determined that this will not change, whatever our status within the Commonwealth may become. (Leys, 247)

His Britishness, in spite of his lack of British blood, was a sincere boast that he returned to again and again. 'I'm probably old fashioned', he once told the speaker of the Northern Ireland House of Commons, 'but I am not ashamed of the word Empire' (Welensky to Sir Norman Strong, 8 Feb 1955, Bodl. RH, Welensky papers 674/3). He distinguished, however, between 'the imperial mission' and the actions of British governments, likening the determination of the Rhodesians to that of the American colonists of 1776. 'I, of course, have no loyalty to your Government whatsoever', he reminded Malcolm Muggeridge. 'But I have a loyalty to the Crown. We look upon the Queen as the Queen of the Federation' (Muggeridge, 3). Welensky belonged to the old Commonwealth of white dominions, led by familiar figures such as Sir Robert Menzies, to whom Welensky seemed 'addicted to plain speech' (R. Menzies, *Afternoon Light*, 1967, 215).

Welensky anticipated that his country would achieve dominion status following the federal review conference due in 1960, but the federation had been fatally flawed from the outset, having been driven through in the face of African opposition, particularly in the two northern territories. Northern Rhodesian Africans in particular felt, with good reason, that Southern Rhodesia was being built up with northern copper revenues. Nyasaland Africans, regarding their territory as the Cinderella of the federation, shared the belief that federation represented the northward extension of Southern Rhodesian segregationism. Both regarded federal reforms such as the removal of petty discrimination and the admission of Africans to senior positions in parliament and the civil and diplomatic services as mere tokenism, particularly as Southern Rhodesia remained a bastion of white supremacy. External factors did not favour Welensky's imperial vision. The Suez crisis was followed by the independence of Ghana, whose leader, Kwame Nkrumah, made clear that African nationalism would soon triumph throughout the continent. The rapid decolonization of much of French Africa was followed by the crisis in the former Belgian Congo, in which Welensky backed the secessionist state of Katanga. He was suspected, absurdly, of arranging the death of the UN secretary-general Dag Hammarskjöld in an air crash in Northern Rhodesia in 1960.

In 1958 Welensky won significant concessions, including greater devolution in external affairs and an undertaking not to intervene legislatively except at the request of the federal government, from the British government, which shared his fear of the right-wing Dominion Party opposition. For him the attraction of foreign investment and immigration were priorities, along with re-equipping the army and air force with sophisticated weaponry. Within the federation itself, however, he was swimming against the tide of African opinion. By 1958–9 it became clear that in all three territories this was hardening. The replacement of Garfield Todd by Sir Edgar Whitehead as Southern Rhodesian prime minister seemed to portend a rightward and anti-federation tendency in an electorate on which Welensky crucially depended. He responded to manifestations of African nationalism largely by believing that African unrest could be contained by economic rather than political progress. In Nyasaland a state of emergency, which he supported with federal troops, failed to curtail the strength of Dr Hastings Banda. The report of the Devlin commission into the disturbances, with its damning conclusion that the territory was a 'police state', combined with revelations about the Kenyan Hola camp 'massacre' of Mau Mau detainees, alienated still further metropolitan opinion. Welensky none the less enjoyed strong support within the right of the Conservative Party, led by the vociferous if declining marquess of Salisbury.

In the closing years of the federation Welensky was diplomatically outclassed by British ministers. He was encouraged to present complicated British reforms of the Northern Rhodesian and Nyasaland electoral systems as final, only to find that these positions were soon abandoned in favour of accelerated progress towards majority rule and secession. He felt particularly deceived by the Monckton report which, though favourable to the economic aspects of federation, made major recommendations about alterations in the territorial and federal franchises and suggested that the British government clarify the territorial right to secession. He would have been reluctant to see Nyasaland withdraw, because of the precedent it set, but on the retention of Northern Rhodesia he seemed resolute. He made preparations for a federal unilateral declaration of independence, including, it was said, a plan to kidnap the Northern Rhodesian governor, but the absence of direct British military provocation, together with the difficulty of effecting a *coup d'état* over so vast an area, undermined his threat. First Nyasaland and then Northern Rhodesia, under Banda and Kenneth Kaunda respectively, were given the right to secede. By then the future of Welensky's federal ideal had been fatally compromised in any case by the election in Southern Rhodesia in 1962 of the white supremacist and anti-federalist Rhodesian Front. Welensky blamed Macmillan and Iain Macleod for this betrayal, when in fact Rab Butler, the minister for central Africa whom he admired, was a reluctant if resolute architect of this policy. Welensky's last-minute proposal to detach the copperbelt and 'line of rail' and amalgamate them with Southern Rhodesia, as well as British promises to maintain some sort of economic association, came to nothing. Nevertheless, he co-operated fully in the orderly winding up of the federation in 1963, transferring the bulk of the powerful federal armed forces to Southern Rhodesia, a crucial factor in the unilateral declaration of independence crisis that followed after November 1965.

Final years In 1964 Welensky decided to stand for the Southern Rhodesian assembly, as leader of the Rhodesia National Party (successor to the United Federal Party), but Clifford Dupont of the Rhodesian Front in a heated by-election defeated him. During the campaign extreme Rhodesian Front supporters branded him 'a bloody Jew', a 'communist', and a 'traitor' (Blake, 388). When the unilateral declaration of independence came in November 1965 he opposed it as unjustified, believing that Ian Smith made a fatal error in consulting the unenfranchised majority on the issue (by means of an indaba), thus making this a principle in any future Anglo-Rhodesian negotiations. Nevertheless he advised Rhodesians to prevent chaos by obeying their 'revolutionary government' (Joyce, 285). In 1969 he opposed Smith's moves towards a republic, but supported acceptance of the Anglo-Rhodesian settlement in the Pearce commission of 1971.

Following the death of his first wife in 1969, Welensky married, in 1972, (Miriam) Valerie Scott, a British Conservative Party worker thirty years his junior, with whom he had two daughters. He declined offers of safe Conservative seats in Britain, just as he had refused a peerage on the dissolution of the federation. He enjoyed an extensive correspondence with such figures as Desmond Donnelly, maverick Labour MP for Pembroke, sharing Donnelly's disillusionment with post-imperial Britain. Personally incorruptible, the only public pension he drew was £9 a year as a former railwayman. In 1981, his health failing, he retired to Blandford Forum in Dorset. He died at Blandford Hospital, Blandford Forum, on 5 December 1991 following a heart attack, and was survived by his second wife, their two daughters, and the two children of his first marriage.

Assessment Born into the direst poverty, Welensky experienced acutely the insecurities of the white minorities of central and southern Africa. Yet he enjoyed warm personal relations with individual Africans, including Kenneth Kaunda. Among his most treasured possessions was an African bust presented to him by a fellow freemason, Sir Abubakar Tafawa Balewa. According to Margaret West, a British diplomat stationed in the federation, Welensky was 'so nearly a great man'. To have risen from grinding privation to such political influence was an achievement in itself. It is not surprising that he failed to preserve the federation, a cause that would have defeated statesmen born into far more fortunate circumstances.

DONAL LOWRY

Sources G. Allingham, *The Welensky story* (1962) · Lord Alport, *Sudden assignment* (1965) · J. Barber, *Rhodesia: the road to rebellion* (1967) · R. Blake, *A history of Rhodesia* (1978) · T. Bull, ed., *Rhodesian perspective* (1967) · L. J. Butler, 'Britain, the United States and the demise of the Central African Federation', *Journal of Imperial and Commonwealth History*, 28/3 (2000), 132–51 · R. Butler, *The art of the possible* (1971) · F. Clements, *Rhodesia: the course to collision* (1969) · T. Creighton, *Southern Rhodesia and the Central African Federation: the anatomy of partnership* (1960) · J. Darwin, 'The central African emergency, 1959', *Journal of Imperial and Commonwealth History*, 21 (1993), 217–34 [special issue] · C. Dunn, *Central African witness* (1959) · H. Franklin, *Unholy wedlock: the failure of the Central African Federation* (1963) · J. Freeman, *Face to face: Sir Roy Welensky* (1960) · L. H. Gann, *A history of Northern Rhodesia: early times to 1953* (1963) · L. H. Gann and M. Gelfand, *Huggins of Rhodesia: the man and his country* (1964) · P. Gifford, 'Misconceived dominion: the creation and disintegration of federation in British central Africa', *The transfer of power in Africa: decolonization 1940–1960* (1982) · J. Greenfield, *Testimony of a Rhodesian federal* (1977) · R. Gray, *The two nations: aspects of the development of race relations in the federation of the Rhodesias and Nyasaland* (1960) · I. Hancock, *White liberals, moderates and radicals in Rhodesia, 1953–1980* (1984) · P. Hemming, 'Macmillan and the end of the British empire in Africa', *Harold Macmillan and Briatin's world role*, ed. R. Aldous and S. Lee (1996) · H. Holderness, *Lost chance: Southern Rhodesia, 1945–58* (1985) · P. Joyce, *Anatomy of a rebel: Smith of Rhodesia, a biography* (1974) · P. Keatley, *The politics of partnership: the Federation of Rhodesia and Nyasaland* (1963) · C. Lamb, *The Africa house* (1999) · R. Lamb, *The Macmillan years, 1957–1963* (1995) · C. Leys, *European politics in Southern Rhodesia* (1959) · D. Lowry, '"Shame upon 'Little England' while 'Greater England' stands!": Southern Rhodesia and the imperial idea', *The round table, the empire/commonwealth and British foreign policy*, ed. A. Bosco and A. May (1997) · H. Macmillan, *Riding the storm, 1956–1959* (1971) [vol. 4 of autobiography] · H. Macmillan, *Pointing the way, 1959–1961* (1972) [vol. 5 of autobiography] · H. Macmillan, *At the end of the day, 1961–1963* (1973) [vol. 6 of autobiography] · H. Macmillan and F. Shapiro, *Zion in Africa: the Jews of Zambia* (1999) · R. Maudling, *Memoirs* (1978) · M. Muggeridge, *Appointment with Sir Roy Welensky* (1961) · P. Murphy, *Party politics and decolonization: the Conservative Party and British colonial policy in tropical Africa, 1951–1964* (1995) · P. Murphy, *Alan Lennox-Boyd: a biography* (1999) · R. Ovendale, 'Macmillan and the wind of change in Africa, 1957–1960', *HJ*, 38 (1995), 455–77 · R. Palmer, *Land and racial domination in Rhodesia* (1977) · C. Palley, *The constitutional history and law of Southern Rhodesia, 1888–1965 with special reference to imperial control* (1966) · A. H. Richmond, *The colour problem: a study of race relations* (1961) · R. Shepherd, *Iain Macleod* (1994) · A. R. W. Stumbles, *Some recollections of a Rhodesian speaker* (1980) · D. Taylor, *The Rhodesian: the life of Sir Roy Welensky* (1955) · R. Tredgold, *The Rhodesia that was my life* (1968) · L. Vambe, *From Rhodesia to Zimbabwe* (1976) · R. Welensky, *A case for amalgamation* (1944) · R. Welensky, 'Trade unions in Northern Rhodesia', *United Empire*, 27 (1946), 236–40 · R. Welensky, 'The development of central Africa through federation', *Optima*, 2/4 (Dec 1952) · R. Welensky, *Welensky's 4000 days: the life and death of the federation of Rhodesia and Nyasaland* (1964) · R. Welensky, 'Federation of Rhodesia and Nyasaland', *Rhodesia and East Africa*, ed. F. S. Joelson (1958) · R. Welensky, *The federation and the commonwealth* (1961) · M. West, *Catching the bag: who'd be a woman diplomat?* (2000) · H. I. Wetherell, 'N. H. Wilson: populism in Rhodesian politics', *Rhodesian History*, 6 (1975), 53–76 · J. R. T. Wood, *The Welensky papers: a history of the Federation of Rhodesia and Nyasaland* (1983) · WWW · Burke, *Peerage* · *The Independent* (7 Dec 1991) · *The Times* (6 Dec 1991) · *Daily Telegraph* (6 Dec 1991) · *The Guardian* (6 Dec 1991) · *Rhodesia Herald*, *passim* · *Bulawayo Chronicle*, *passim* · *Africa Daily News*, *passim* · *Central African Examiner*, *passim* · *Northern News*, *passim* · *Livingstone Mail*, *passim* · Northern Rhodesia government, legislative council debates, 1938–53 · Federation of Rhodesia and Nyasaland, federal assembly debates, 1953–63

Archives Bodl. RH, corresp. and papers · National Archives of Zimbabwe, Harare, corresp. and papers | Afrika Instituut, Pretoria, papers of J. M. Greenfield · BL, corresp. with P. V. Emrys-Evans, Add. MS 58251 · BL, letters to O'Donovan, deposit 9437 · Bodl. Oxf., papers of Harold Macmillan · Bodl. RH, letters to R. T. Hungerford; corresp. with Sir Albert Robinson; papers of Sir Robert Tredgold; papers of Sir Edgar Whitehead · Borth. Inst., corresp. with Sir Ian Wilson · National Archives of Zimbabwe, Harare, papers of Sir Malcolm Barrow · NL Wales, corresp. with Desmond Donnelly · U. Birm. L., corresp. with Lord Avon and Lady Avon · University of Essex, Colchester, Albert Sloman Library, papers of Lord Alport | FILM Granada Television, 'Appointment with Sir Roy Welensky: interview with Sir Roy Welensky, KCMG, MP', Malcolm Muggeridge, 7 April 1961

Likenesses G. Davies, photograph, 1989, NPG [*see illus.*]

Wealth at death £1007—in England and Wales: probate, 22 April 1992, *CGPLA Eng. & Wales*

Welin [*née* Hedenström], **Agnes Carolina Albertina** (1844–1928), missionary to seafarers, was born on 15 March 1844 in Härad, Södermanland, south-west of Stockholm, Sweden. Her strong, Slavic features reflected her partly Russian paternal ancestry. Her father, Claes August Hedenström, a gamekeeper, died when she was seven. Her mother, Carin, *née* Nilsdotter (*b.* 1805), died only three years later. In the custody of a singularly gifted aunt in nearby Nyköping, Augusta Mörth, herself a doctor's widow, young Agnes imbibed her warm spirit and acquired many of her practical (including medical) skills.

Agnes Hedenström was in her twenties when, as the trusted housekeeper on a large estate (also in Södermanland), she experienced a life-transforming event. Delegated by the owners of the estate to report back on disquieting news of religious revival resulting from a roving lay preacher's meetings in the area, she was herself confronted by the claims of 'familiar truths which had hitherto lain dormant' (Lindskog, 13). Initial rancour was replaced by 'indescribable joy'. Soon she found herself sharing those same truths first at Sunday school gatherings for the children of the estate, later also among growing numbers of adults.

As word spread of proliferating popular response, overt hostility erupted too among men who rejected the right of women to preach and teach the scriptures. Meanwhile, a powerful sense of call began building in 'Mamsell Agnes' to bring the gospel to India or China. True to that call, she left for London in 1876, hoping soon to be sent out by one of England's major mission societies. However, ill health forced her to postpone her plans and instead, on her doctor's insistence, seek recuperation in the coastal climate of south-west England. It was in 1877, on her return to London, that Agnes Hedenström, now thirty-three, was to realize precisely her future place of mission, and that she would not, after all, have to cross half the globe to reach it.

On learning of a recently opened Strangers' Rest, a mission and reading-room for seafarers of different nationalities in London's East End, Agnes determined to see this for herself. Undeterred by her friends' warnings that the mission's location, on Ratcliffe Highway, was the very hub of London's most notorious Sailortown slums, swarming with crimps and pimps and other so-called 'land-sharks', Agnes Hedenström set forth from fashionable Kensington, soon to find herself in an entirely different world. Finally forced to submit to police escort, in the midst of drunken brawls and a hail of insults, she was welcomed at the mission by the superintendent, Miss McPherson, as 'a direct answer to prayer' (Lindskog, 17). Among the masses of abused and exploited mariners were many from Scandinavia, and it was quite beyond the mission's capacity to cope with these men. Moving into a humble room in the nearby Home of Industry, Agnes continued as associate missionary at the Strangers' Rest for the next two years, preaching, counselling, and caring for her seafaring fellow ethnics, as well as those from other parts of the world.

By then, word of the woman at the Strangers' Rest, who went alone where police only dared go well armed and in pairs, had reached forecastles on the farthest seas. However, Agnes's keen mind and practical sense soon discerned the need for a radically new strategy. The average sailor ashore had little choice beyond a seamy, bordello-like boarding-house, run by those bent on exploiting him, and the street. With her natural intuition and extraordinary networking skills, coupled with her 'glowing faith and contagious enthusiasm' (Lindskog, 22), she won over a growing group of highly influential friends, foremost among them T. A. Denny. With their help she managed to form a committee, rent a property at 88–90 Leman Street, near Princes Square, and in 1880 open the first Scandinavian Sailors' Temperance Home in the port of London. Here, by offering famished seafarers a quality of care and cuisine clearly superior to that provided by her competitors, she managed to overcome the counter-attraction of alcohol and instil a sense of self-worth in many a marginalized mariner.

In their frustration, the fraternity of local land-sharks launched a smear campaign against their lone adversary. There were even attempts against her life. Beaten, kicked, and spat upon, Agnes Hedenström nevertheless refused to be intimidated. Instead, she simply redoubled her efforts, even adding a highly valued referral service for seafarers in search of a ship. As a result, the eighty-bed facility was frequently overfilled, as seafarers continued to come in droves. In Agnes Hedenström's mind there was now only one way to go—build and build boldly. This, she well knew, would depend on the most strategic site and enormous funds. Therefore, she made both the subject of sustained prayer.

An ideal site was soon found—close to the West India Dock's main gate. As to funding, the costs appeared at first prohibitive. But again, Agnes Hedenström was able to enlist the aid of powerful patrons, notably David Carnegie and Lord Blantyre. Finally, on 13 February 1888, a massive new five-storey Scandinavian Sailors' Temperance Home could be officially dedicated by Prince Oscar Bernadotte of Sweden. Here, that 'remarkable girl', as Carnegie called her, continued to monitor the myriad concerns of this no less remarkable institution to the end of her life. From 21 January 1889, when she married Axel Welin, an engineer and prominent member of the Swedish community in London, she would have the companionship and invaluable support of a devoted husband.

Proprietors of disreputable boarding-houses, bars, and bordellos in the neighbourhood eventually found it futile to harass the home and its indefatigable executive director. The seafarers simply kept coming, literally in their thousands. Here was holistic maritime ministry at its best, and they knew it. Even though the seafarers might put up a vigorous resistance, they consistently surrendered every time she disarmed them with her forthright humour, resolutely removed their hard-earned wages, and sent these off to family back home rather than risk their being squandered in some Sailortown spree. Non-Scandinavian seafarers (including many torpedoed crews during the First World War) would also be fed in the 600-seat dining hall and accommodated as needs arose and space allowed. The home's policy was perhaps best reflected in its founder's maxim: no sailor to be turned away as long as there is one foot of floor space.

Herself never a narrow sectarian, Agnes Welin was warmly endorsed by not only the established (Lutheran) church but also the free churches of her native Sweden (notably the Mission Covenant Church of Sweden). She maintained as firm a hand on the helm after more than fifty years in the work as when she first began. Then, in her eighty-fifth year, after a stroke a few days previously, she died at her post on 23 June 1928. The ceremonies surrounding the return of her remains from London's docklands to her native soil, via Göteborg and on to Stockholm, were fit for royalty, with innumerable seafarers taking part on either side of the North Sea. While every vessel in port hoisted its flag at half mast, her body was buried at Solna churchyard on 4 July 1928.

'Agnes Welin, the Seafarers' Incomparable Friend': those were the words, engraved in granite, which were chosen to mark her grave. What was it about her which motivated such a level of love—bordering on infatuation—among the many she served? All available evidence indicates that she was on the one hand utterly fearless, on the other unconditionally compassionate, thereby confirming a calibre of love which could, indeed, 'cast out fear'. Agnes Welin had no children of her own, yet she insisted on treating all seafarers as if they were hers by birth. This they felt, regardless of how they might individually respond to the faith she professed with such unflinching persistence. Perhaps that was why they commonly called her not only their friend, but pre-eminently their mother. At all events, 'Mother' Agnes Welin achieved among Scandinavian seafarers—and beyond—a renown no less than that of her namesake 'Mother' Agnes Weston among the British. Meanwhile, the sailors' home that Agnes Welin raised and ran for forty years, later known as Riverside House, at 20 Garford Street, Poplar, and operated by the Salvation Army as a hostel for the homeless, still stands as a monument to a heroic enterprise. ROALD KVERNDAL

Sources J. Lindskog, *Agnes Welin och hennes livsverk* [Agnes Welin and her lifework] (Stockholm, 1929) · *Svenska Morgonbladet* (25 June 1928) · *Svenska Morgonbladet* (5 July 1928) · S. Walder, 'Fru Agnes Welin: "Sjömännens moder"', *Ur svenska kvinnors kamp för Guds rike* (1930), 39–45 [Mrs Agnes Welin: 'The Seafarers' Mother'] · E. J. Ekman, *Illustrerad missionshistoria*, 2 (Stockholm, 1891), 560–63 [illustr. mission history] · parish register, Kärad, National Archives, Uppsala, Sweden, C:3, Al:14, and Al:15 · R. Kverndal, *Seamen's missions: their origin and early growth* (1986), 606, 608 · private information (2004) [M. Malmgren, Archivist, National Archives, Uppsala, Sweden] · C. J. Engvall, *Vaar sjömansmission: naagot om Svenska Missionsförbundets arbete bland sjöfolk* (Stockholm, 1914), 32–5
Archives Mission Covenant Church of Sweden, Stockholm, Sweden · Riksarkivet, Stockholm · Stadsbiblioteket, Stockholm, Sweden
Likenesses line engraving, repro. in Ekman, *Illustrerad missionshistoria*, 561 · photographs, repro. in Lindskog, *Agnes Welin och hennes livsverk*

Wellbeloved, Charles (1769–1858), Unitarian minister and tutor, was born on 6 April 1769 in Denmark Street, St Giles, London, the only child of John Wellbeloved (1742–1787) and his wife, Elizabeth (*b.* 1747), daughter of Thomas Plaw. Owing to his parents' unhappy marriage he was brought up from the age of four by his grandfather Charles Wellbeloved (1713–1782), friend of John Wesley, who had an estate at Mortlake, Surrey. He was educated principally by the Revd Robert Delafosse of Richmond. Placed with a firm of drapers on Holborn Hill, Wellbeloved found the experience 'utterly uncongenial', claiming he only learned 'how to tie up a parcel' (Kenrick, 5). In 1785 he entered the orthodox Homerton Academy, but, influenced by two of the students, David Jones (1765–1816) and David Jardine (*d.* 1797), his opinions became heterodox. In September 1787 he entered New College, Hackney, recently established by rational dissenters. In January 1792 he accepted an invitation from Newcome Cappe to become his assistant at St Saviourgate Chapel, York, though the salary was only £60. All the duties were undertaken by Wellbeloved as Cappe had suffered a paralytic stroke. On Cappe's death in 1800 he became sole minister, continuing until his death, though with the help of assistants from 1845. Because of ill health he did not officiate after 1853. Wellbeloved married Ann (*d.* 1823), eldest daughter of John Kinder, a linen draper in Cheapside, London, on 1 July 1793, at St Mary's, Stoke Newington. They had four sons and five daughters, including three sets of mixed twins. Two daughters married Unitarian ministers, John *Kenrick (1788–1877) and J. R. Wreford; the youngest, Emma (*d.* 1842), married Sir James Carter, later chief justice of New Brunswick (1815–65).

Because of his small salary, his growing family, and some initial discouragement as a minister, Wellbeloved for some years remained unsettled at York. About 1795 he began his own school; in 1796 it was reported that he had thirteen day pupils at £15 p.a. each. In November 1797 he was invited to succeed Thomas Barnes (1747–1810) as divinity tutor at the dissenters' academy in Manchester, but he declined, discouraged by the financial state of the institution and the coldness of Barnes, an Arian, who was unwilling to see a Unitarian successor. When in 1803 the invitation was renewed Wellbeloved accepted, and Manchester College moved to York. He received much valuable support from Cappe's widow, Catherine (1744–1821), and William Wood (1745–1808), minister at Mill Hill, Leeds. During the early years the chronic financial difficulties persisted, and, assisted only by a classics tutor, Wellbeloved was grossly overworked. He was noted for his methodical allocation of time and habit of rising early. Nevertheless, a former student, Joseph Hunter, privately believed that 'There was always something too much of a procrastinating spirit in Mr Wellbeloved, & of the representing himself as having too much business on his hands' (BL, Add. MS 36527, fol. 50r). He was seriously ill through stress and exhaustion in 1807 and 1809. Gradually there were sufficient benefactions and subscriptions for a third tutor. William Turner (1788–1853) was appointed mathematics tutor in 1809, and was succeeded in 1827 by William Hincks. From 1810 Wellbeloved had the invaluable co-operation of John Kenrick as classics tutor.

Wellbeloved substituted biblical exegesis for systematic theology. By carefully reading the whole of the Old and New testaments with his students, Wellbeloved sought to encourage them to develop their own views. He scrupulously avoided teaching any particular system of doctrine, or indeed openly expressing his own theological opinions, though it did leave some students 'in a painful state of doubt ... without definite conceptions of the system of Christian truth' (Kenrick, 102). He also rarely introduced controversial subjects into his pulpit. His approach angered those who wanted a clearer identification of the college with Unitarianism. Doubts concerning his commitment were not finally resolved until his brilliant defence of Unitarianism against Archdeacon Francis Wrangham in 1823 and 1824. Sydney Smith wrote: 'If I had a cause to gain I would fee Mr Wellbeloved to plead for me, and double fee Mr Wrangham to plead against me' (ibid., 152). He closely followed the theological system of Newcome Cappe, particularly in his treatment of prophecy. James Martineau, a student at York, recalled the depth of Wellbeloved's scholarship: 'a Lightfoot, a Jeremiah Jones and an Eichhorn all in one, yet no mere theologian after all, but scarcely less a naturalist and an archaeologist as well' (J. Martineau, *Essays, Reviews and Addresses*, 1890–91, 4.54). Wellbeloved was fluent in Greek and Latin, proficient in Hebrew, Syriac, and Chaldee, and read Arabic; he could also read French and Italian, and understand German. He was responsible for the theological and metaphysical section of the short-lived *Annual Review* (1802–8). His principal work was a revised translation of the Bible for families: the undertaking proved too great for Wellbeloved and only nine parts of the Old Testament were published during his life, the first in 1819 and the last at his own expense in 1838. After his death the text was revised by John Kenrick and republished in three volumes in *Holy Scriptures of the Old Covenant* (1859–62), with translations of the remaining books of the Old Testament. Wellbeloved's most popular work was his *Devotional Exercises for Young Persons* (1801), which reached an eighth edition in 1838. He retired as theology tutor in 1840, when the college returned to Manchester.

For nearly seventy years Wellbeloved was actively concerned in all the major reform and social movements in York. In 1813 he helped expose the shameful abuses of the York Lunatic Asylum. He was one of the founders of the York Book Society (1794), subsequently the Subscription Library, the York Mechanics' Institute (1827), the York Whig Club (1827), and the School of Art (1842), and although not among the original promoters of the Yorkshire Philosophical Society (1822), he was curator of antiquities from 1823 until his death. He was largely responsible for the interpretation and preservation of York's historic past. In 1981 his *Eburacum* was described as 'a valuable scholarly summary epitomising the breadth of learning, systematic method and practical approach of Victorian antiquarianism at its best' (Addyman, 58). In 1829 he headed the subscription list for the restoration of York Minster following the devastating fire, and led the opposition to the proposals to alter the position of the undamaged choir screen. He also supported the preservation of the city walls. He died on 29 August 1858 at Monkgate, York. He was buried in the graveyard behind the St Saviourgate Chapel on 3 September. His reputation rested on his work as principal of Manchester College, but as a reformer and scholar he also made an important contribution to nineteenth-century York.   DAVID L. WYKES

Sources J. Kenrick, *A biographical memoir of the late Charles Wellbeloved* (1860) • D. L. Wykes, 'Manchester College at York (1803–1840): its intellectual and cultural contribution', *Yorkshire Archaeological Journal*, 63 (1991), 207–18 • A. J. Peacock, 'Charles Wellbeloved', *Annual Report of the Yorkshire Philosophical Society* (1971), 52–9 • J. Hunter, 'Biographical notices of some of my contemporaries who have gained some celebrity', BL, Add. MS 36527, fols. 48r–50v • J. Hunter, 'Collectanea Hunteriana volume VIII: being memoirs to serve for a history of protestant dissenters', BL, Add. MS 24442, fols. 3r–5r • P. Addyman, 'Archaeology in York, 1831–1981', *York, 1831–1981: 150 years of scientific endeavour and social change*, ed. C. Feinstein (1981), 53–87 • minutes of proceedings of the committee of the Manchester Academy, 1786–1810, Harris Man. Oxf., MSS M.N.C. Misc. 65 • minutes of the proceedings of the committee of the Manchester New College removed to York, 1810–16, Harris Man. Oxf. • B. Smith, ed., *Truth, liberty, religion: essays celebrating two hundred years of Manchester College* (1986) • Burke, *Gen. GB*, vol. 3, p. 667 • J. Hunter, *Familiae minorum gentium*, ed. J. W. Clay, 1, Harleian Society, 37 (1894), 182

Archives Harris Man. Oxf., corresp. • York Minster Archives, papers relating to Yorkshire Philosophical Society and Yorkshire Antiquarian Club | Harris Man. Oxf., Wood MSS

Likenesses H. Cousins, engraving, after 1826 (after Lonsdale), Harris Man. Oxf. • J. Lonsdale, oils, 1826, Harris Man. Oxf. • attrib. C. Earles, oils, 1859 (after J. Lonsdale), City Art Gallery, York • H. Cousins, mezzotint (after J. Lonsdale), BM, NPG

Wealth at death under £4000: resworn probate, Nov 1859, CGPLA Eng. & Wales

Wellcome, Sir Henry Solomon (1853–1936), pharmacist and benefactor, was born on 21 August 1853 in his grandfather's log cabin at Almond in northern Wisconsin, USA. He was the younger son of Solomon Cummings Wellcome (*d.* 1876), an unsuccessful farmer and subsequently

Sir Henry Solomon Wellcome (1853–1936), by Hugh Goldwin Riviere, 1906

an itinerant Adventist minister, and his wife, Mary Curtis. The land was poor, and the failure of the potato crop in 1861 resulted in the Wellcome family abandoning their plot and making the long, arduous, and dangerous trek by covered waggons to the ill-named small township of Garden City, in the new state of Minnesota, where Wellcome's uncle Jacob was a popular and successful doctor. Their anticipated idyll was swiftly and abruptly ended by the bloody Sioux uprising of 1862, during which young Henry moulded bullets and assisted his uncle in tending the wounded. It was then that he met the English physician, William Worrell Mayo, who later persuaded Henry to join him in Rochester, Minnesota. Curiously, the experience of the war made Wellcome a lifelong admirer, advocate, and benefactor of the Native Americans.

Wellcome's childhood and adolescence were dominated by deep and genuine poverty. If his father and brother totally lacked ambition, the young Henry did not. He left school at fourteen with a fair grounding which he improved with his own self-education and determination to succeed. His purpose was to escape from the suffocating combination of ill-paid drudgery in his uncle's drugstore, the limitations of Garden City, and the severity of his parents' Adventist faith. From Rochester he went briefly to the Chicago College of Pharmacy, then to the Philadelphia College of Pharmacy. After qualifying, having submitted a characteristically ingenious paper on a new type of mass-produced suppository, he became a successful traveller for two of the top American drug companies, at the same time contributing to professional journals. In

1878 he set out for the forests of Peru and Ecuador, to search for the increasingly rare native cinchona trees, whose bark was a source of quinine. His subsequent account of this exploration received acclaim in Britain and the USA. His love of travelling and adventure was stimulated once more when a fellow American, Silas Mainville Burroughs, who had started in business in London in 1878 with a franchise to sell the products of John Wyeth of Philadelphia, invited Wellcome to join him in partnership; in 1880 Wellcome arrived in London.

Burroughs was a rich young man of great charm, a salesman of near genius, but highly erratic in temperament and judgement. While Burroughs travelled the world in search of markets for the partners' American drugs and other products between 1881 and 1884, Wellcome effectively created the firm of Burroughs, Wellcome & Co. He decided that they must manufacture their own products in Britain and make their own equipment to mass produce the compressed pills that revolutionized Western pharmacy; he invented, and patented, the word 'tabloid' (an admixture of tablet and ovoid) for these products, and established the company's first factory in Wandsworth.

Strains and tensions developed in the partnership. These became acute after Burroughs returned to Britain and as a result of Wellcome's serious illness in 1885 (an undiagnosed ulcer) and his long absence in the USA in 1886, when he wrote *The Story of Metlakahtla*, an impassioned defence of a dispossessed Native American people. Wellcome returned to London in 1887 to find Burroughs intending to terminate the partnership and take full control.

A bitter dispute ensued, lasting into the early 1890s. Wellcome was triumphant in the law courts, but Burroughs was plotting his revenge when he died of pneumonia in Monte Carlo in February 1895. After further unpleasant legal controversies with Burroughs's widow, Wellcome took full control of what was by then a significant, reasonably prosperous, and certainly very well-known and respected company.

If Burroughs had been a superb salesman, Wellcome proved himself a brilliant publicist. The Burroughs and Wellcome exhibitions had astounded the pharmaceutical and medical professions with their skill and showmanship; their travelling medical chests were made famous by H. M. Stanley and no expedition was complete without them, clients including Theodore Roosevelt, Robert Peary, and Captain Robert Falcon Scott. But what marked Wellcome out was his passion for research. Unlike Burroughs, he wanted to be an initiator of drugs, not simply a purveyor. He brought his oldest friend, the distinguished chemist Frederick Belding Power, from the United States to Britain, and used his contacts in the British medical profession to find and employ the most talented young men. With Burroughs gone he could shape his own future.

In 1894 Wellcome had founded the Wellcome Physiological Research Laboratories and this was followed, in 1896, by the Chemical Research Laboratories, headed by Power; in 1901 Wellcome launched a plan, which came to fruition

in 1903 under the direction of Andrew Balfour, for a tropical research laboratory in the Sudan associated with the Gordon Memorial College at Khartoum. In 1913 he founded in London the Wellcome Historical Medical Museum for which he had been collecting since he was a young man. In the same year the Wellcome Bureau of Scientific Research was established in London for the investigation in England of tropical diseases, and with this in 1914 was associated a museum which later became the Wellcome Museum of Medical Science (1923). All these were subsequently incorporated in the Wellcome Research Institution as part of the Wellcome Foundation, established in 1924 to unite the business of Burroughs, Wellcome & Co. with the various laboratories and museums. To crown his many benefactions Wellcome left practically the whole of his wealth to scientific research and education.

Wellcome's formidable energies were not confined to the establishment of medical research laboratories and museums: he encouraged and financed archaeological research in Africa and Palestine. At Jebel Moya, in the Sudan, he selected a late neolithic site where extensive excavations, which he himself directed for three years up to the outbreak of war in 1914, were carried out, though with disappointing results. He took an active interest in medical missionary work and was an important adviser to General W. C. Gorgas, resolving the malaria crisis during the construction of the Panama Canal.

The reputation of the Burroughs and Wellcome laboratories became so high that it became the first commercial company to receive a licence for animal research, and attracted young men of outstanding calibre, including Henry Dale. The exceptional feature of Wellcome's character was that he was genuinely more interested in pure research than the commercial benefits that might accrue. The long, and ultimately successful, attempt to find an effective anti-diphtheria vaccine was a classic example; but there were many others, including the first mass production of insulin. Many of Wellcome's young researchers went on to positions of great eminence and achievement in medicine.

After Wellcome's marriage in 1901 to Syrie Barnardo [*see* Maugham, (Gwendoline Maud) Syrie (1879–1955)], daughter of Thomas Barnardo, which produced a son, (Henry) Mounteney (*b.* 1903), his other interests, and especially his vast collections and archaeology, became paramount. He became an obsessive collector, now with the wealth to fulfil his grandiose ambitions. His numerous agents were virtually given permission to buy anything of historical interest, and the results ranged from the invaluable to the meretricious; warehouses in London were filled with a bizarre accumulation of artefacts, pictures, statuary, books, armour, weaponry, and plain junk, nestling among items of real value. After his death his appalled trustees realized that Wellcome's collection amounted to over 1 million items, and far exceeded, in volume and in the expense incurred in their acquisition, those of the British Museum and the Louvre. Its disposal was to be one of their most severe difficulties. Some items were sold, or donated to other museums, but the priceless medical history library was retained in the Wellcome Building in Euston Road, London, which Wellcome commissioned in 1931.

Wellcome's personal life was shadowed by the disaster of his marriage, which ended effectively in 1910, with much bitterness on Wellcome's part, and formally in 1916 when he divorced Syrie on the grounds of her adultery with Somerset *Maugham, with whom she had had a daughter, afterwards Lady Glendevon. The Wellcomes' son, Mounteney, lacked the ability and inclination to emulate his father, and became a contented farmer.

Wellcome, so gregarious and hospitable in his prime in the 1880s and 1890s, became almost a recluse after 1919. The fortunes of his company declined; he himself made inadequate provision for his great bequest to his adoptive country, with the result that his trustees found that they had inherited not a large fortune but heavy death duties. In the first twenty years of the Wellcome Trust it disposed of only £1 million for the medical research for which Wellcome had endowed it. But, as the fortunes of the company dramatically revived in the 1960s and 1970s, the scale of Henry Wellcome's benefactions and visions spectacularly changed, and the funds available rapidly increased. The Wellcome Trust became not only the largest independent investor in British medical research by the early 1990s, but, by 1995—nearly sixty years after Henry Wellcome's death—almost equalled the investment of the British government, the resources of the trust then approaching £7000 billion.

Wellcome became a British citizen in 1910, but, despite his unique contributions, honours came late, and somewhat grudgingly. In 1932 he was elected a fellow of the Royal College of Surgeons and—on Dale's initiative—of the Royal Society, and was, rather belatedly, knighted.

In 1935 Wellcome was operated on for cancer of the prostate at the Mayo Clinic. In May 1936 he went back to Almond, Wisconsin, to buy back the family 14 acre farm where he had spent the first eight years of his life. It still stands, adorned with a historical marker donated by the Wellcome Trust. He died of pneumonia in the London Clinic on 25 July 1936. His body was cremated, and in February 1987 the ashes were buried in the churchyard of St Paul's Cathedral, London.   ROBERT RHODES JAMES

Sources R. R. James, *Henry Wellcome* (1994) · A. R. Hall and R. A. Bembridge, *Physics and philanthropy: a history of the Wellcome Trust, 1936–86* (1986) · J. Symons, *Wellcome Institute for the History of Medicine: a short history* (1993) · H. H. Dale, *Adventures in physiology* (1953) **Archives** AM Oxf. · Wellcome L., corresp., financial accounts, personal papers, photographs | RGS, corresp. with Sir Henry Stanley, William Hoffman, etc. · U. Oxf., Griffith Institute, excavation records (Abu Geili, Jebel Moya, Saqadi, Dar el-Mek, etc.), journals, indexes, maps, plans, and photographs **Likenesses** H. G. Riviere, portrait, 1906, Wellcome L. [*see illus.*] **Wealth at death** £2,138,959 11s. 6d.: probate, 19 Sept 1936, CGPLA Eng. & Wales

Welldon, James Edward Cowell (1854–1937), headmaster and dean of Durham, was born at Tonbridge on 25 April 1854, the eldest son of the Revd Edward Ind Welldon (*d.* 1879), second master of Tonbridge School, and his wife,

James Edward Cowell Welldon (1854–1937), by Sir Benjamin Stone, 1902

Ellen Laura, second daughter of Samuel Byles Cowell, head of a printing firm in Ipswich. Welldon was a scholar at Eton College, where he won the Newcastle scholarship in 1873. He went as a scholar to King's College, Cambridge, where he won the Bell and Craven university scholarships (1874 and 1876) and was Browne medallist (Greek ode, 1875 and 1876) and senior classic and senior chancellor's medallist (1877). He was president of the Cambridge Union in 1876. In 1878 he was elected to a fellowship at his college, which he held until 1889. In 1882 he travelled to Greece with two Eton friends, G. N. Curzon and Edward Lyttelton, and in 1887 accompanied Curzon to North America.

Welldon was appointed master of Dulwich College in 1883. In that year he was ordained deacon, and in 1885 priest. A strict disciplinarian, he raised Dulwich from a low ebb; the school song, 'Pueri Alleynienses', was his composition. From 1885 to 1898 he was headmaster of Harrow School. Some complained that he owed his appointment to the fact of his being a clergyman; it was at Harrow, however, that he established his fame as a great schoolmaster. His lifelong love for Harrow and his undying interest in the careers of his pupils, who included Winston Churchill, revealed the depth of his affection for the school, which he ruled with the masterly force of an infectious personality and an imposing physique (he was 6 feet 5 inches tall). Disliked by many of the masters as an autocratic administrator, he was more popular with the boys, by whom he was known as 'the Porker' (Tyerman, 364). He was a freemason and a keen imperial patriot. He contributed to the then fashionable genre of school fiction, *Gerald Eversley's Friendship: a Study in Real Life* (1895), which depicted an intense relationship between two schoolfellows. He never married, but for nearly fifty years enjoyed the close companionship of a manservant, Edward Hudson Perkins, from whose death in 1932 he never recovered.

Welldon left the educational world on his appointment in 1898 as bishop of Calcutta. His episcopate was not a happy one. Although he tried to master Indian problems and travelled to every part of the country in order to get in touch with Indian Christians, ill health and his missionary zeal, which brought him into conflict with the viceroy, his old friend Lord Curzon, led to his resignation in 1902. This setback probably prevented him from gaining that position in the church which had been widely predicted. Welldon's health was re-established by an operation and by four and a half years of quiet work as canon of Westminster (1902–6). The coronation of Edward VII, in which he took an important part, was the leading event at the abbey in his time.

As dean of Manchester (1906–18) Welldon devoted himself zealously to the cathedral, which became a centre of spiritual and civic influence. When he went to the deanery of Durham in 1918 he was past the age for initiating new undertakings. His relations with the bishop of Durham, Hensley Henson, were cool and were not improved when Welldon, a leader of the temperance movement in the Church of England, criticized Henson's opposition to prohibition in a speech at the Durham Miners' Gala in July 1924. At the miners' gala in the following year Welldon was himself severely jostled by a crowd of miners and very nearly rolled into the river following reports of a speech he had made that was critical of trade unions. A serious fall, which left him permanently disabled, led to his resignation in 1933. He retired to Sevenoaks, where he died at his home, The Dell, on 17 June 1937.

Welldon's brilliant scholarship was exemplified in his translations of Aristotle—*Politics* (1883), *Rhetoric* (1886), and *Ethics* (1892). Aristotle coloured both his style and his manner of reasoning. He had a wide knowledge of English, French, German, and Italian literature. His historical sense was keen: his theological outlook both orthodox and human (*The Hope of Immortality*, incorporating his Hulsean lectures delivered at Cambridge in 1897 and 1898, 1898; *The Revelation of the Holy Spirit*, 1902; an edition of St Augustine's *De civitate Dei*, 2 vols., 1924). As an ecclesiastic it is impossible to give him a party label. Brought up a strict evangelical, he shook himself free of all narrow conceptions, retaining that sense of individual relationship to the person of Jesus which was the keynote of his thinking. He was a frank but friendly critic of all parties and denominations, measuring them by a robust common sense and untarnished sincerity. He was a believer in the national character of the Church of England (*The Religious Aspects of Disestablishment and Disendowment*, 1911; *The English Church*, 1926) but nourished the hope of reunion, first with the British nonconformists and ultimately with all Christian churches. He was an impressive preacher and several volumes of sermons mark the stages of his ministry. His autobiographical writings, *Recollections and Reflections* (1915) and *Forty Years On* (1935), are a storehouse of his sometimes trenchant views on various topics.

J. W. S. TOMLIN, rev. M. C. CURTHOYS

Sources *The Times* (19 June 1937) · J. E. C. Welldon, *Recollections and reflections* (1915) · J. E. C. Welldon, *Forty years on* (1935) · Venn, *Alum. Cant.* · R. S. Churchill, *Winston S. Churchill*, 1: *Youth, 1874–1900* (1966) · O. Chadwick, *Hensley Henson: a study in the friction between church and state* (1983) · M. Hennell, *The deans and canons of Manchester Cathedral, 1840–1948* [1988] · *CGPLA Eng. & Wales* (1937) · C. Tyerman, *A history of Harrow School, 1324–1991* (2000)
Archives Harrow School, Middlesex, papers as headmaster of Harrow School | BL OIOC, letters to Sir Harcourt Butler, MS Eur. F 116 · King's AC Cam., letters to Oscar Browning
Likenesses J. Collier, oils, 1898, Harrow School, Middlesex · B. Stone, photograph, 1902, Birm. CL [*see illus.*] · G. Kelly, oils, 1921, Man. City Gall. · A. Albemarle, caricature, pencil and watercolour, FM Cam. · Barraud, photograph, NPG; repro. in *Men and women of the day*, 2 (1889) · Elliott & Fry, photograph, NPG · S. P. Hall, pencil sketch, NPG · J. Russell & Sons, photograph, NPG · Spy [L. Ward], caricature, chromolithograph, NPG; repro. in *VF* (17 Nov 1898)
Wealth at death £70,765 12s. 4d.: probate, 31 Aug 1937, *CGPLA Eng. & Wales*

Welles. For this title name *see* individual entries under Welles; *see also* Cecily, Viscountess Welles (1469–1507).

Welles [Welle], **Adam de**, first Lord Welles (*d.* 1311), baron and soldier, was the son of a Lincolnshire landowner, William de Welle (*d.* 1264), and his wife, Isabel Periton (*d.* 1315). The family derived its name from Well, near Alford in Lincolnshire. Adam succeeded his elder brother, William, in or after 1286. He went abroad with Hugh Despenser on a royal embassy to Germany in 1294. The date of his entry into the royal household is not known, but he was listed as a banneret of the king's household from 1297 to 1306. In 1297 he was among those appointed to receive fines from those clergy who wished to re-enter the king's protection during Edward I's dispute with Archbishop Winchelsey. It seems certain that he continued to support the king during the developing political crisis in that year; he participated in the fruitless royal expedition in Flanders in the autumn with a retinue of one knight and twelve squires. Two of the latter were knighted in the course of the campaign. Welles fought with Edward at the battle of Falkirk in 1298. In 1299 he was given custody of Rockingham Castle and was made keeper of the royal forests between Oxford and Stamford, a clear sign of royal favour. In the same year he was summoned to parliament as a baron. In 1300 he was present on the Caerlaverock campaign in Scotland, serving with a contingent of three knights and nine squires. He served in Scotland again in 1301 and in 1303–4. His involvement in the Scottish wars continued under Edward II, with service in the campaign of 1309–10. He was also summoned regularly to parliament.

Adam de Welles died on 1 September 1311, and was buried in Greenfield Priory, Lincolnshire. He was survived by his wife Joan (*d.* 1315), daughter of Sir John Engaine and widow of Walter Fitzrobert, whom he had married by 1296. Virtually all his estates were in Lincolnshire. In 1297 he acquired lands in that county from William (II) of Wyleby, and he later bought the manor of Wyberton from John Holland. Edward II granted him lands there worth £42. The inquisition taken on his death showed that he held the whole or parts of seventeen manors, and five advowsons. He left two sons, Robert and Adam.

MICHAEL PRESTWICH

Sources GEC, *Peerage*, new edn, 12/2.439–41 · *Chancery records* · J. Topham, *Liber quotidianus contrarotulatoris garderobae: anno regni regis Edwardi primi vicesimo octavo* (1787) · BL, Additional MS 7965

Welles, John, Viscount Welles (*d.* 1499). *See under* Welles, Leo, sixth Baron Welles (*c.*1406–1461).

Welles, Leo [Lionel], **sixth Baron Welles** (*c.*1406–1461), soldier, was the eldest son of Eudo Welles and Maud, daughter of Ralph, Lord Greystoke. Eudo predeceased his father, the Lincolnshire baron John, Lord Welles, on whose death in 1421 Leo succeeded while still a minor. He had been married on 15 August 1417 at Methley, Yorkshire, to Joan (or Cecilia), daughter of Robert Waterton of Methley, trusted retainer both of John of Gaunt and of the Lancastrian kings, who was granted his custody on his grandfather's death in 1421. How much this marriage and the Waterton connection mattered to him is suggested by his choice, long after Joan's death, of the Waterton chapel in Methley church for his burial. Knighted in 1426, Leo Welles was granted seisin of his inheritance in 1427, summoned to parliament from 1432, and was a royal councillor from 1434. He went to France with the king in 1430 and with Humphrey, duke of Gloucester, to relieve Calais, in 1436. Essentially a Lincolnshire landowner Welles served as commissioner principally of sewers and of the peace for the three parts of Lincolnshire and Northamptonshire. Appointed as lieutenant of Ireland for seven years from 1437, perhaps reluctantly, and actually resident there from 1438, he failed to control the contending factions and resigned prematurely in 1442. Welles was quite well endowed for a baron, with an income of £604 in 1436, but he had only £322 net, the balance supporting his mother, aunts, brother, son, and repayments of his grandfather's debts. Following Joan's death, which had occurred by 1447, his wedding in that year as third husband to Margaret Beauchamp, duchess of Somerset (*d.* 1482), gave him an interest in her two dowers and her Beauchamp of Bletsoe inheritance. It also married him into the royal family, and placed him on the fringes of the dominant court faction. From 1451 to 1455 he was at Calais as a lieutenant of his brother-in-law Edmund Beaufort, duke of Somerset, apparently continuing until possession was secured by Richard Neville, earl of Warwick (*d.* 1471), on 20 April 1456. Elected a Garter knight before 13 May 1457, he was allegedly captured by the Yorkists at Bloreheath and took the Lancastrian oath of allegiance in 1459. Having joined Margaret of Anjou in the north in 1461, he was with her at the battles of St Albans (17 February) and

Towton (29 March), where he was killed, and was subsequently attainted.

Richard Welles, seventh Baron Willoughby and seventh Baron Welles (*c.*1428–1470), magnate, was Leo Welles's son with Joan Waterton and his heir. Richard Welles married by 9 January 1449 Joan, sole daughter and heir of the Lincolnshire baron Robert, Lord Willoughby, whom he succeeded in 1452. The Willoughby barony was worth £1002 in 1436. Welles was knighted and first attended parliament in 1453, and was a royal councillor in 1454. With the expectation of the Welles and ultimately the Waterton of Methley inheritances he was destined to be the principal magnate in the Lincolnshire area. Like his father Richard Welles was with Queen Margaret in the north, and at St Albans and Towton in 1461, but he was allowed to make his peace with Edward IV, escaped attainder and was pardoned on 5 February 1462, and continued to attend parliament. Richard's first wife, Joan, was the daughter of Elizabeth Montagu, sister of Thomas, earl of Salisbury (*d.* 1428), and Richard and Joan Welles were therefore included in the Salisbury roll of arms, which was probably prepared for the funeral of Richard Neville, earl of Salisbury (*d.* 1460), at Bisham Priory (Berkshire) in 1463. He associated himself with the dominant Nevilles in the destruction of the northern Lancastrians in 1464, at the enthronement of Archbishop Neville, and through his second marriage in 1468 to the widowed Margery Ingelby, *née* Strangways, a family of important Neville retainers. He was rewarded by the grant of his father's chattels on 9 October 1464, of his Welles estates on 11 July 1465, and by the reversal of Leo Welles's attainder in 1467. However, he had to overturn previous grants to his stepmother, the duchess of Somerset, who had been admitted both to her dower and to a life estate in the principal Welles lands with remainder to her own son, his half-brother John Welles, which was cancelled only in 1468 on the king's command. Welles had thus painfully reunited his inheritances, but not his local pre-eminence, which was shared instead by the king's kinsman Humphrey Bourchier, Lord Cromwell, and his household knight Sir Thomas Burgh— hence, perhaps, the marriage of Richard Welles's heir Sir Robert Welles to Elizabeth Bourchier (*d.* 1470), heir of Lord Berners and niece of Lord Cromwell, and his feud with Burgh, which resulted after 2 February 1470 in the destruction of Burgh's house at Gainsborough. Although Welles was summoned to London by Edward IV to account, and pardoned, he was already in alliance with the earl of Warwick and duke of Clarence, on whose behalf the Lincolnshire rebellion was organized as part of a much larger uprising. Edward IV advanced in person to suppress it, discovered the Welles family's role, arrested and executed Richard at Stamford on 12 March 1470, the date of Robert's defeat at Losecote Field (Empingham), and executed Robert also on 19 March at Doncaster. Although both were attainted and Robert died childless, their lands were diverted to the loyal Richard Hastings, Lord Welles, husband of Richard Welles's daughter Joan (*d. c.*1474).

John Welles, Viscount Welles (*d.* 1499), soldier and administrator, was the son of Leo, sixth Baron Welles and his second wife, Margaret Beauchamp, duchess of Somerset. As the younger son of both parents, he had no hereditary expectations. During the 1460s his mother sought to divert the Welles inheritance to him, and, but for the attainders, he would have succeeded c.1474 to the Welles barony. His pardon in 1478 as of Bletsoe, Bedfordshire, and Maxey, Lincolnshire, both properties of the duchess, suggests that he depended on his mother until her death in 1482. Apparently in the royal household at Edward IV's death, he was commissioned to victual the fleet sent against Sir Edward Woodville, but was already in rebellion against Richard III by 13 August 1483, when his property was seized. Knighted and recognized as Lord Welles by Henry Tudor on his landing at Milford Haven on 7 August 1485, he fought at Bosworth, and by February 1486 had been restored to his inheritance, created Viscount Welles, and elected knight of the Garter. Such favours recognized his special status as the king's uncle, half-brother to the king's mother, Margaret Beaufort, a connection which was reinforced by his marriage as 'a safe man' to the queen's eldest surviving sister, *Cecily (1469–1507). Hence he was appointed in 1485 constable of Bolingbroke, Lincolnshire, constable, steward, and master forester of Rockingham, and JP in six counties. In 1488 he was granted several forfeitures and in 1490 the castles of Caerleon and Usk for life. He served in France in 1492 and in 1496 treated with Burgundy. Such limited activity and moderate rewards indicate that he was never politically of the front rank. He had two daughters by 1493, Anne and Elizabeth, whom he planned to marry to the Stanley heir, but both predeceased him. At his death in London on 9 February 1499 the Welles inheritance devolved on the children of his four half-sisters.   MICHAEL HICKS

Sources P. S. Routh, 'Lionel, Lord Welles and his Methley monument', *Yorkshire Archaeological Journal*, 63 (1991), 77–83 • *Chancery records* • T. B. Pugh, 'The magnates, knights and gentry', *Fifteenth-century England, 1399–1509*, ed. S. B. Chrimes, C. D. Ross, and R. A. Griffiths (1972), 86–128 • GEC, *Peerage* • *RotP* • M. K. Jones and M. G. Underwood, *The king's mother: Lady Margaret Beaufort, countess of Richmond and Derby* (1992) • J. G. Nicholls, ed., 'Chronicle of the rebellion in Lincolnshire, 1470', *Camden miscellany, I*, CS, 39 (1847) • 'Confession of Sir Robert Welles', *Excerpta Historica*, ed. S. Bentley (1840) • A. Payne, 'The Salisbury Roll of Arms', *England in the fifteenth century* [Harlaxton 1986], ed. D. Williams (1987), 187–98
Likenesses alabaster tomb effigy, after 1457, St Oswald's Church, Methley, Yorkshire • MS illumination (Richard Welles), BL, The Salisbury Roll, Loan MS 90

Welles, Richard, seventh Baron Willoughby and seventh Baron Welles (c.1428–1470). *See under* Welles, Leo, sixth Baron Welles (c.1406–1461).

Welles, Thomas (c.1590–1660), colonial governor, was born in Whichford, Warwickshire, the second of the three children of Robert Welles (1540–1617), yeoman, and his wife, Alice. Several nineteenth- and early twentieth-century sketches of Welles's life provide conflicting details of his English origins, but recent work shows that these earlier biographers had confused him with two other men named Thomas Welles, one of whom lived in

Northamptonshire and did not migrate to New England, while the other was of unknown English background and arrived in Massachusetts in 1636, the same year as Thomas Welles of Whichford. As far as can be determined, the family of Welles had lived in Warwickshire for four generations and owned a substantial amount of property there but were not members of the gentry. Welles's parents had sufficient funds to educate him in Latin, however, and his reception in New England suggests that he had the bearing of a gentleman.

Several accounts of Welles's life state that he emigrated to New England as secretary to William Fiennes, first Viscount Saye and Sele, and settled briefly at a fort named Saybrook, the nucleus of a settlement Saye and Sele was trying to create under the terms of a royal land grant called the Warwick patent. Both Welles's official relationship with Saye and Sele and his residence at Saybrook appear fanciful, an invention intended to elevate his status. Members of the Welles and Fiennes families certainly knew each other in Warwickshire, but no evidence exists to link them in the New World. Inasmuch as Welles arrived in New England with his wife, Alice Tomes (c.1592–1640), whom he married about 1615, and six children, Fort Saybrook, with its all-male garrison, seems unlikely to have been his early residence.

Instead, when Welles arrived in June 1636, he probably disembarked in Boston. Before the year was over he and his family had moved twice, first to Newtown (later Cambridge) and then to Hartford as part of an overland expedition led by Thomas Hooker into the Connecticut river valley. Chosen a magistrate in Connecticut in 1637, Welles was one of the seven magistrates who in 1639 drafted and signed the famous fundamental orders of Connecticut, often called the first English constitution written in the New World. Under it he served as treasurer of Connecticut (1639–51), secretary (1640–48), deputy governor (1654–5, 1656–8), and governor (1655–6, 1658–9). His terms as governor were not consecutive because the fundamental orders specified that no one could serve two years in a row. He also frequently served as Connecticut's delegate to the meetings of the United Colonies of New England, a loose confederation of puritan settlements that was created to maintain a common defence against military threats. His greatest talents seemed to lie in his ability as a diplomat to inspire trust in people and to bring disputants together in compromise. He represented Connecticut in thorny negotiations with all of its neighbours, Massachusetts, the Dutch in New Netherland, and the Mohican Indians in the Narragansett country of south-east New England. In each case Welles exercised a restraining hand and quelled apprehended disturbances.

One of Connecticut's wealthiest residents, Welles acquired much of his estate from his second marriage in 1646, to Elizabeth (*née* Deming) Foote (c.1595–1683), the widow of Nathaniel Foote (1593–1644) from the neighbouring town of Wethersfield, Connecticut. Welles moved to his wife's Wethersfield home shortly after their marriage and died there unexpectedly in his sleep on 14

January 1660. Buried in the First Society cemetery in Wethersfield, Welles also has his name inscribed on the founders' monument in the ancient burial-ground in Hartford.   BRUCE C. DANIELS

Sources D. H. Siemiatkoski, *The descendants of Governor Thomas Welles of Connecticut, 1590–1658 and his wife, Alice Tomes* (1990) · J. H. Trumbull, ed., *The public records of the colony of Connecticut*, 1 (1850) · H. Stiles, *The history of ancient Wethersfield*, vol. 2 (1904) · A. E. van Dusen, *Connecticut* (1961) · L. A. Welles, *The English ancestry of Governor Thomas Welles of Connecticut* (1926)
Archives Connecticut State Library, Hartford, letters · Connecticut State Library, Hartford, Archives of Connecticut, reports
Wealth at death £1069 8s. 2d.: probate, 11 April 1660, particular court of Hartford, Hartford district, probate file 5860, Connecticut State Library, Hartford

PICTURE CREDITS

Wallingford, Richard (c.1292-1336)—The British Library

Wallis, Sir Barnes Neville (1887-1979)—© Estate of Sir Barnes Wallis / National Portrait Gallery, London

Wallis, John (1616-1703)—© Bodleian Library, University of Oxford

Wallis, Samuel (1728-1795)—© National Portrait Gallery, London

Wallis, Tryphosa Jane (1774-1848)—© National Portrait Gallery, London

Wallmoden, Amalie Sophie Marianne von, suo jure countess of Yarmouth (1704-1765)—© National Portrait Gallery, London

Walmesley, Charles (1722-1797)—Downside Abbey, Stratton-on-the-Fosse

Walpole, Horatio, first Baron Walpole of Wolterton (1678-1757)—private collection; photograph: The Paul Mellon Centre for Studies in British Art

Walpole, Horatio, fourth earl of Orford (1717-1797)—© National Portrait Gallery, London

Walpole, Robert, first earl of Orford (1676-1745)—courtesy of the Hanbury-Williams Family Collection / Lyme Hall, Disley; photograph National Portrait Gallery, London

Walpole, Sir Spencer (1839-1907)—© reserved; collection National Portrait Gallery, London

Walpole, Spencer Horatio (1806-1898)—© National Portrait Gallery, London

Walsh, Adela Constantia Mary Pankhurst (1885-1961)—Mary Evans / The Women's Library

Walsh, William Joseph (1841-1921)—© National Portrait Gallery, London

Walsingham, Sir Francis (c.1532-1590)—© National Portrait Gallery, London

Walter, (William) Grey (1910-1977)—by permission of the Burden Neurological Institute; photograph Science & Society Picture Library

Walter, Hubert (d. 1205)—The British Library

Walter, John (1739?-1812)—© News International Newspapers Ltd

Walter, John (1776-1847)—© News International Newspapers Ltd

Walter, John (1818-1894)—© News International Newspapers Ltd

Walters, Catherine [Skittles] (1839-1920)—© National Portrait Gallery, London

Waltham, John (d. 1395)—© Dean and Chapter of Westminster

Walton, Brian (1600-1661)—© National Portrait Gallery, London

Walton, Cecile (1891-1956)—Scottish National Portrait Gallery

Walton, George Henry (1867-1933)—Scottish National Portrait Gallery

Walton, Izaak (1593-1683)—© National Portrait Gallery, London

Walton, Sir William Turner (1902-1983)—© Estate of Michael Ayrton;

collection National Portrait Gallery, London

Walwyn, Fulke Thomas Tyndall (1910-1991)—© Empics

Walwyn, William (bap. 1600, d. 1681)—© National Portrait Gallery, London

Wanamaker, Samuel (1919-1993)—© News International Newspapers Ltd

Wanley, Humfrey (1672-1726)—© Copyright The British Museum

Warburg, Sir Siegmund George (1902-1982)—Getty Images - Hulton Archive

Warburton, George Drought (1816-1857)—© National Portrait Gallery, London

Warburton, John (1682-1759)—© National Portrait Gallery, London

Warburton, Sir Robert (1842-1899)—© National Portrait Gallery, London

Warburton, William (1698-1779)—courtesy the Church of England; photograph: The Paul Mellon Centre for Studies in British Art

Ward, Sir Adolphus William (1837-1924)—Master and Fellows of Peterhouse, Cambridge

Ward, Barbara Mary, Baroness Jackson of Lodsworth (1914-1981)—© Foundation Rodrigo Moynihan / private collection; photograph National Portrait Gallery, London

Ward, Edward [Ned] (1667-1731)—© National Portrait Gallery, London

Ward, Edward Matthew (1816-1879)—© National Portrait Gallery, London

Ward, Francis Kingdon- (1885-1958)—The Royal Geographical Society, London

Ward, Dame (Lucy) Genevieve Teresa (1837-1922)—from the RSC Collection with the permission of the Governors of the Royal Shakespeare Company / University of Warwick Photograph Collection

Ward, Irene Mary Bewick, Baroness Ward of North Tyneside (1895-1980)—© National Portrait Gallery, London

Ward, John, second Viscount Dudley and Ward (1725-1788)—photograph by courtesy Sotheby's Picture Library, London

Ward, John William, earl of Dudley (1781-1833)—© National Portrait Gallery, London

Ward, Joshua (1684/5-1761)—© Copyright The British Museum

Ward, Sir Leslie [Spy] (1851-1922)—© National Portrait Gallery, London

Ward, Mary (1585-1645)—English Institute of the Blessed Virgin Mary, Augsburg; photograph © National Portrait Gallery, London

Ward, Mary Augusta [Mrs Humphry Ward] (1851-1920)—© National Portrait Gallery, London

Ward, Samuel (1577-1640)—Ipswich Borough Council Museums and Galleries

Ward, Seth (1617-1689)—photograph: The Paul Mellon Centre for Studies in British Art

Ward, Wilfrid Philip (1856-1916)—© reserved

Ward, William (1769-1823)—in a private collection; photograph courtesy the Scottish National Portrait Gallery

Ward, William George (1812-1882)—© National Portrait Gallery, London

Ware, Sir Fabian Arthur Goulstone (1869-1949)—© National Portrait Gallery, London

Warham, William (1450?-1532)—© National Portrait Gallery, London

Waring, Edward (c.1735-1798)—unknown collection / Christie's; photograph National Portrait Gallery, London

Waring, Edward Marsden [Eddie] (1910-1986)—Getty Images - Green

Warne, Frederick (1825-1901)—Frederick Warne & Co. / Penguin Books; photograph National Portrait Gallery, London

Warneford, Samuel Wilson (1763-1855)—© National Portrait Gallery, London

Warner, Charles (1846-1909)—© National Portrait Gallery, London

Warner, Sir Frank (1862-1930)—© National Portrait Gallery, London

Warner, Jack (1895-1981)—© National Portrait Gallery, London

Warner, Joseph (1717-1801)—reproduced by kind permission of the President and Council of the Royal College of Surgeons of London

Warner, Mary Amelia (1804-1854)—© National Portrait Gallery, London

Warner, Sir Pelham Francis (1873-1963)—© National Portrait Gallery, London

Warner, (Nora) Sylvia Townsend (1893-1978)—© Cecil Beaton Archive, Sotheby's; collection National Portrait Gallery, London

Warnock, Sir Geoffrey James (1923-1995)—© David Hockney

Warrack, Harriet (bap. 1825, d. 1910)—private collection

Warre, Edmond (1837-1920)—by permission of the Provost and Fellows of Eton College. Photograph: Photographic Survey, Courtauld Institute of Art, London

Warren, Sir Charles (1840-1927)—© National Portrait Gallery, London

Warren, George John, fifth Baron Vernon (1803-1866)—© National Portrait Gallery, London

Warren, Sir (Thomas) Herbert (1853-1930)—© Estate of Glyn Philpot

Warren, John (1730-1800)—reproduced by kind permission of His Grace the Archbishop of Canterbury and the Church Commissioners. Photograph: Photographic Survey, Courtauld Institute of Art, London

Warren, Joseph (1741-1775)—Copyright 2004 Museum of Fine Arts, Boston; gift of Buckminster Brown, M. D., through Carolyn M. Matthews, M. D., Trustee

Warren, Samuel (1807-1877)—© National Portrait Gallery, London

Warton, Joseph (bap. 1722, d. 1800)—© National Portrait Gallery, London

Warton, Thomas (1728-1790)—© National Portrait Gallery, London

Warwick, Sir Philip (1609-1683)—© National Portrait Gallery, London

Washington, George (1732-1799)—Copyright 2004 Museum of Fine Arts, Boston; William Francis Warden Fund, John H. and Ernestine A. Payne Fund, Commonwealth Cultural Preservation Trust. Jointly owned by the Museum of Fine Arts, Boston and the National Portrait Gallery, Washington DC

Waterhouse, Alfred (1830-1905)—© National Portrait Gallery, London

Waterhouse, Edward (1619-1670)—© National Portrait Gallery, London

Waterhouse, Edwin (1841-1917)—courtesy of PricewaterhouseCoopers

Waterhouse, Sir Ellis Kirkham (1905-1985)—© National Portrait Gallery, London

Waterland, Daniel (1683-1740)—© National Portrait Gallery, London

Waters, (Florence) Elsie (1893-1990)—© National Portrait Gallery, London

Waterson, Elaine (1943-1998)—photograph Brian Shuel / Redferns

Watkin, Edward Ingram (1888-1981)—private collection

Watkins, Henry George (1907-1932)—© National Portrait Gallery, London

Watkinson, Harold Arthur, Viscount Watkinson (1910-1995)—© Godfrey Argent Studios; collection National Portrait Gallery, London

Watson, David (1713?-1761)—in the collection of the Dundas-Bekker Family; photograph courtesy the Scottish National Portrait Gallery

Watson, George Neville (1886-1965)—Godfrey Argent Studios / Royal Society

Watson, (George) Hugh Nicholas Seton- (1916-1984)—photograph reproduced by courtesy of The British Academy

Watson, James (1766-1838)—© National Portrait Gallery, London

Watson, John (1725-1783)—© National Portrait Gallery, London

Watson, John Christian (1867-1941)—by permission of the National Library of Australia

Watson, Joshua (1771-1855)—© National Portrait Gallery, London

Watson, Richard (1737-1816)—courtesy of the National Museum, Havana

Watson, Richard (1781-1833)—© National Portrait Gallery, London

Watson, Robert (1746?-1838)—in the collection of the Trustees of the National Museums of Scotland

Watson, Robert William Seton- (1879-1951)—photograph reproduced by courtesy of The British Academy

Watson, Sir William (1715-1787)—© The Royal Society

Watson, William, Baron Watson (1827–1899)—in the collection of the Faculty of Advocates

Watt, Harry Raymond Egerton (1906–1987)—Getty Images - Hulton Archive

Watt, James (1736–1819)—© National Portrait Gallery, London

Watts, Alaric Alexander (1797–1864)—© National Portrait Gallery, London

Watts, George Frederic (1817–1904)—© Tate, London, 2004

Watts, Isaac (1674–1748)—© National Portrait Gallery, London

Watts, John (1861–1902)—Phillips Picture Library

Wauchope, Andrew Gilbert (1846–1899)—© National Portrait Gallery, London

Waugh, Sir Andrew Scott (1810–1878)—The British Library

Waugh, Edwin (1817–1890)—© Manchester City Art Galleries

Waugh, Evelyn Arthur St John (1903–1966)—© Estate of Felix H. Man / National Portrait Gallery, London

Wavell, Archibald Percival, first Earl Wavell (1883–1950)—© National Portrait Gallery, London

Wavell, Arthur John Byng (1882–1916)—© National Portrait Gallery, London

Way, Thomas (1837–1915)—© Copyright The British Museum

Wayne, Anthony (1745–1796)—Charles Allen Munn Collection, Fordham University Library, Bronx, NY

Waynflete, William (c.1400–1486)—by courtesy of the Dean and Chapter of Winchester

Weale, Charlotte Julia (1829–1918)—private collection

Weaver, Sir Lawrence Walter William (1876–1930)—© National Portrait Gallery, London

Webb, Sir Aston (1849–1930)—© National Portrait Gallery, London

Webb, (Martha) Beatrice (1858–1943)—The Society of Authors, on behalf of the Bernard Shaw Estate; photograph National Portrait Gallery, London

Webb, Benjamin (1819–1885)—© reserved

Webb, (Kathleen) Kaye (1914–1996)—© Michael Dyer; collection National Portrait Gallery, London

Webb, Mary Gladys (1881–1927)—by permission of the E. O. Hoppé Trust, Curatorial Assistance, Inc., Los Angeles

Webb, Matthew [Captain Webb] (1848–1883)—© National Portrait Gallery, London

Webb, Philip Barker (1793–1854)—© National Portrait Gallery, London

Webb, Philip Speakman (1831–1915)—© National Portrait Gallery, London

Webbe, George (b. 1581, d. in or before 1642)—© Copyright The British Museum

Webbe, Samuel, the elder (1740–1816)—© National Portrait Gallery, London

Weber, Carl Maria Friedrich Ernst von (1786–1826)—The Royal Society of Musicians of Great Britain. Photograph: Photographic Survey, Courtauld Institute of Art, London

Webster, Alexander (1707–1784)—Phillips Picture Library

Webster, Benjamin (1798–1882)—© National Portrait Gallery, London

Webster, Noah (1758–1843)—National Portrait Gallery, Smithsonian Institution

Weddell, James (1787–1834)—Christie's Images Ltd. (2004)

Wedderburn, Alexander, first earl of Rosslyn (1733–1805)—The Honourable Society of Lincoln's Inn. Photograph: Photographic Survey, Courtauld Institute of Art, London

Wedderburn, Sir Peter, Lord Gosford (c.1616–1679)—© reserved; private collection

Wedderburn, Sir William, fourth baronet (1838–1918)—© National Portrait Gallery, London

Wedgwood, Josiah (1730–1795)—Wedgwood Museum, Barlaston

Wedgwood, Dame (Cicely) Veronica (1910–1997)—© National Portrait Gallery, London

Weever, John (1575/6–1632)—© National Portrait Gallery, London

Weight, Carel Victor Morlais (1908–1997)—private collection. Photograph: Photographic Survey, Courtauld Institute of Art, London

Weiner, Joseph Sidney (1915–1982)—Institute of Biological Anthropology

Weir, William Douglas, first Viscount Weir (1877–1959)—© National Portrait Gallery, London

Weiss, Willoughby Hunter (1820–1867)—© National Portrait Gallery, London

Weizmann, Chaim (1874–1952)—Estate of the Artist; courtesy of the Weizmann Institute of Science, Israel

Weldon, George Anthony Thomas (1908–1963)—reproduced from the John Whybrow Collection

Weldon, Walter Frank Raphael (1860–1906)—The College Art Collections, University of London; photograph National Portrait Gallery, London

Welensky, Sir Roland (1907–1991)—Granville Davies

Wellcome, Sir Henry Solomon (1853–1936)—Wellcome Library, London

Welldon, James Edward Cowell (1854–1937)—reproduced by permission of Birmingham Library Services

Oxford dictionary of
national biography